INTERNATIONAL TRADE LAW: INTERDISCIPLINARY THEORY AND PRACTICE

THIRD EDITION

INTERNATIONAL TRADE LAW: INTERDISCIPLINARY THEORY AND PRACTICE

THIRD EDITION

Raj Bhala

Rice Distinguished Professor
The University of Kansas School of Law

Member, Royal Society for Asian Affairs,
Council on Foreign Relations,
and American Law Institute

Library of Congress Cataloging-in-Publication Data

Bhala, Raj.
    International trade law: interdisciplinary theory and practice / Raj Bhala. — 3rd ed.
      p. cm.
    Includes index.
    ISBN 978-1-4224-1940-3 (hard cover)
    1. Foreign trade regulation—Cases. I. Title.
K3943.B49 2007
343'.087—dc22

2007041528

NOTE TO USERS
To ensure that you are using the latest materials available in this area, please be sure to periodically check the LexisNexis Law School web site for downloadable updates and supplements at www.lexisnexis.com/ lawschool

Editorial Offices
744 Broad Street, Newark, NJ 07102 (973) 820-2000
201 Mission St., San Francisco, CA 94105-1831 (415) 908-3200
701 East Water Street, Charlottesville, VA 22902-7587 (434) 972-7600
www.lexis.com

(Pub.03069)

There are seven sins in the world: Wealth without work, Pleasure without conscience, Knowledge without character, Commerce without morality, Science without humanity, Worship without sacrifice, and Politics without principle.
—Mahatma Gandhi (1869-1948)

To Our Little Gift, Shera—

As the Psalmist teaches,
fear of God is the beginning of Wisdom.
Love for God, and all His creation, is the end of Wisdom.
In between are journeys to faraway places,
Hard contemplation with true friends of the big questions,
Easy choices between the excellent and the expedient, and
Wondrous invitations to examine your heart.

Preface to the Third Edition: Five Propositions About International Trade Law

There are ineluctable features to the study of international trade law in the post-9/11 world. First, the technicalities of rules must be mastered. What do the rules say? How did they evolve? What justifies them? Where do the uncertainties lie? Second, country-specific and sector-specific contexts in which rules are formulated, interpreted, applied, and violated must be understood. Which countries have a keen export or import interest in a particular rule? What economic, political, cultural, and religious forces motivate and constrain countries? How does the market for trade in a particular good or service operate? What are the trends in that market?

These features — technicalities and contexts — intimate a single fact about the field: it is interdisciplinary. As a corollary, interdisciplinary means importantly, but not only, law and economics. To study international trade law is to study how and why people and their governments interact, or do not interact. It is a study of human behavior in a global framework of law that itself changes, sometimes radically. As a second corollary, international trade law is not an easy field. There are no masters, only students (including this author) of varying degrees of accomplishment.

Thus, for the reader looking for the proverbial "Law and Ice Cream" course, it is best now to put this textbook aside and continue the search. But, for the adventurous, this textbook might just play a sweet, albeit modest, role in understanding issues that fall under the hackneyed term "globalization," broadening and sharpening critical legal analysis of those issues, and even shaping choices about profession and lifestyle. At least, that role is an aspiration for the textbook.

There is, and indeed ought to be, a dramatic tension in any textbook. At one extreme, a textbook by an author with strong views risks being idiosyncratic, even a tract. No textbook should be a vehicle for articulating and defending the views of the author. The appropriate venues for such argumentation are articles and monographs. At the other extreme, no author who earnestly responds to the vocational calling of a teacher writes in an entirely selfless manner. As C.S. Lewis long ago pointed out in *The Abolition of Man* (1943), value-free scholarship is a chimera, and to pursue it endangers students. (Textbooks can rise to works of scholarship, but that is another matter.) Put simply, inherent in the drafting of any teaching materials is the dramatic tension between argumentation and neutrality.

To manage this tension, it is useful to invoke the distinction between imposition and proposition. Never is the object of *International Trade Law* to impose a view, least of all my own — assuming it were possible to do so, which it is not. Always, the goal is to propose — that is, to be provocative by setting out ideas for students to ponder and debate. The reader quickly would put down this textbook with a thump if it did no more than regurgitate the views of the author from other venues. Rightly so. The reader seeks not indoctrination but enlightenment on theoretical and practical dimensions of a topic. At the same time, even the least experienced of reader surely appreciates the subject is not algorithmic. Even seemingly slight details sometimes illuminate weighty matters of war and peace, poverty and wealth, injustice and fairness, and chaos and order. The reader needs and deserves guidance, at least to help chalk out an independent course of study and practice.

The specific overture, then, to mitigate the dramatic tension between argumentation and neutrality is to provide cogency to the textbook through Five Propositions. These Propositions are on what international trade law is, or ought to be, all about. They are woven throughout the textbook. They relate to one another, as complements, antagonists, and sometimes both.

Proposition One: Growth

International trade law ought to promote economic growth and poverty alleviation.

Proposition Two: Schisms

International trade law is inherently divisive, both among countries and within countries, resulting in no long-term alliances.

Proposition Three: Tests

International trade law is tested not only by hegemonic powers like the U.S. and EU, but also by emerging leaders like China, Islamic countries like the Kingdom of Saudi Arabia, and tiny ones like Antigua.

Proposition Four: Sectors

International trade law is shaped, at any given juncture, by a few key economic sectors, such as agriculture, services, and intellectual property.

Proposition Five: Security

International trade law ought to advance the cause of "peace through trade," reduce fear and anxiety, and thereby enhance national security.

Manifestly, these Propositions go beyond the conventional neoclassical economic analysis of international trade. That analysis is plentiful in the textbook. But, so too are perspectives from other disciplines, notably history, philosophy, politics, and religion. Most importantly, these Propositions are just that, and lest there be doubt, as a student of the field, my own views of them hardly remain static.

The Preface to the First and Second Editions of *International Trade Law* concluded with an invitation premised on what Friedrich Nietzsche (1844-1900) wrote in 1888 in his last book, *Ecce Homo* (published in 1908): "that which does not kill you makes you stronger." The Fourth Edition of *International Trade Law* can be better than the Third Edition with the help of the most important target audience: students. Scarcely is there a finer moment in teaching than when the teacher learns from the student. Please do communicate your comments and criticisms to me.

Or, call just to chat about trade for fun. After all, lawyers who have the most fun usually provide the best service — to their faith, health, families, and clients.

With all good wishes,

Raj Bhala
Rice Distinguished Professor
The University of Kansas
School of Law
Green Hall, 1535 West 15th Street
Lawrence, Kansas
U.S.A. 66045

Tel: +1-785-864-9224
Fax: +1-785-864-5054

Website: www.law.ku.edu
E-mail: bhala@ku.edu

Acknowledgments

A publication of this breadth and depth is the product of many good and energetic minds. That is all the more true because it is not one publication but four — the present volume, which is accompanied by a *Documents Supplement*, *Dictionary of International Trade Law*, and *Teacher's Manual*. I am blessed by such minds around me that not only contribute to a better product than possibly could be achieved alone, but also make the research and writing process every bit as fun as quiet contemplation (an equally indispensable process).

Deep thanks go to my Research Assistants at the University of Kansas School of Law: Owen Andrew Grieb (from Kansas), J.D. Class of 2007; David Roy Jackson (from Virginia), J.D. Class of 2007; and Dan Spencer IV, J.D. Class of 2006 (also from Kansas). They worked diligently on hundreds of draft pages. Mr. Jackson's work on Free Trade Agreements (FTAs), including Tables in the accompanying *Dictionary of International Trade Law*, as well as on Customs Law, was at the level of a seasoned trade lawyer. He did all that while passing, on first attempt, the U.S. Customs Brokers Examination, and keeping up his expertise in Chinese (Mandarin). Mr. Grieb labored over parts of the manuscript, and edited and updated many *Dictionary* items, while keeping up his expertise in Japanese language. Similarly, Mr. Spencer labored with enthusiasm on early drafts. Outstanding papers by my Research Assistant, Devin S. Sikes, J.D. Class of 2008, and my former student David Dean, J.D. Class of 2006, were indispensable in helping prepare material on causation.

Deep thanks also go to my editor at LexisNexis, Ms. Pali Chheda, Esq. In every respect, and at every step, she has been an efficient, supportive, and responsive professional — and, importantly in a major endeavor like this one — a fun person with whom to work.

A publication of this nature is the product of a family. At least that is so for me, my wife and best friend Kara, and our little Gift, our daughter, Shera. I would not wish it any other way. Besides, in our family, Kara and Shera are endowed with the truly splendid talent.

Note on Sources

To prepare this textbook, I rely on a monstrously large number of news stories from the *Financial Times*, *The Economist*, and *International Trade Reporter* (BNA). In my humble estimation, these publications include the finest journalists on international trade in the English language. Their stories, which fill three stuffed file cabinets in my garage in Kansas, stories help keep my students and me current. It is impossible to cite every story I have used. Special mention deservedly should be made for the many pieces by Alan Beattie, Guy de Jonquières, Frances Williams, and Martin Wolf of the *Financial Times*, and Rossella Brevetti, Daniel Pruzin, and Toshio Aritake of the *International Trade Reporter*. (*The Economist* does not identify author bylines.) With apologies to them and their colleagues, this new Edition would be nothing but a multi-volume citation list, were I not to adopt a simple policy: a footnote appears only to accompany a direct quote, or extensive use of key data. In brief, then, may I express my deepest thanks and professional respect for these three publications and their staff? May I also express gratitude to the *Khaleej Times*, *Gulf News*, and *The Gulf Today*, for their superb coverage, to which I look, of developments concerning trade and the Middle East?

What I have learned from legal sources referenced in earlier *International Trade Law* editions resonates in the present edition. Space does not permit a full list of the hundreds of law books, book chapters, and articles I have examined, in varying degrees of intensity, over the years, and to which I remain indebted. That list grows daily. The same policy applies to legal sources: a footnote accompanies a direct quote or great dependence. Yet, there are a few core economics books on international and development topics on which I draw to prepare material (including graphs). It is only right to acknowledge them explicitly:[1]

1. P.T. BAUER, DISSENT ON DEVELOPMENT (1976).

2. THE ECONOMICS OF PREFERENTIAL TRADE AGREEMENTS (Jagdish Bhagwati & Arvind Panagariya eds., 1996).

3. ROBERT J. CARBAUGH, INTERNATIONAL ECONOMICS (7th ed. 1999).

4. RICHARD E. CAVES, JEFFREY A. FRANKEL & RONALD W. JONES, WORLD TRADE AND PAYMENTS: AN INTRODUCTION (6th ed. 1993)

5. ROBERT M. DUNN, JR. & JOHN H. MUTTI, INTERNATIONAL ECONOMICS (5th ed. 2000).

6. MALCOLM GILLIS ET AL., ECONOMICS OF DEVELOPMENT (4th ed. 1996).

7. ROBERT GILPIN, THE POLITICAL ECONOMY OF INTERNATIONAL RELATIONS (1987).

8. STEVEN HUSTED & MICHAEL MELVIN, INTERNATIONAL ECONOMICS (4th ed. 1998).

9. MELVYN KRAUSS, THE NEW PROTECTIONISM (1978).

10. MELVYN KRAUSS, HOW NATIONS GROW RICH (1997).

11. PAUL KRUGMAN, THE AGE OF DIMINISHED EXPECTATIONS (1990).

---

[1] The *Teacher's Manual* for this textbook sets out a longer list of consulted works, particularly in the fields of international and development economics. I trust instructors will share the list with interested students.

12. PAUL R. KRUGMAN & MAURICE OBSTFELD, INTERNATIONAL ECONOMICS: THEORY AND POLICY (4th ed. 1997).

13. V.I. LENIN, IMPERIALISM: THE HIGHEST STATE OF CAPITALISM (1916, Junius Publications Ltd. ed., 1996).

14. STUART R. LYNN, ECONOMIC DEVELOPMENT: THEORY AND PRACTICE FOR A DIVIDED WORLD (2003).

15. W. CHARLES SAWYER & RICHARD L. SPRINKLE, INTERNATIONAL ECONOMICS (2003).

16. AMARTYA SEN, DEVELOPMENT AS FREEDOM (1999).

17. DEPENDENCY THEORY — A CRITICAL REASSESSMENT (Dudley Seers ed., 1981).

18. T.N. SRINIVASAN, EIGHT LECTURES ON INDIA'S ECONOMIC REFORMS (2000).

19. THE MARX-ENGELS READER (Robert C. Tucker Ed., 2d ed. 1978).

20. IMMANUEL WALLERSTEIN, THE ESSENTIAL WALLERSTEIN (2000).

In addition, the Carnegie Endowment for International Peace generously granted reprint permission for its publication, *Reflections on Regionalism: Report of the Study Group on International Trade* (Washington D.C.: Carnegie Endowment for International Peace, 1997). An excerpt (from pages 11-18) appears in a Chapter on free trade agreements (FTAs). Likewise, the Organization for Economic Co-operation and Development (OECD) kindly granted reprint permission for its work, *Trade and Labor Standards* (1995). An excerpt (from pages 9-17, 19, and 21) appears in a Chapter on trade and labor.

Certain parts of the textbook draw on my other books. On GATT topics, it is only natural to peek at my treatise, *Modern GATT Law*, published in 2005 by Sweet & Maxwell in London. Eleanor Norton, the Publishing Editor there, understands fully my desire to avoid "re-inventing the wheel," as it were. To a lesser degree, I draw on *Trade, Development, and Social Justice* (Carolina Academic Press 2003), and a treatise with Professor Kevin Kennedy of Michigan State, *World Trade Law* (Lexis Publishing 1998, with 1999 *Supplement*). Dr. Keith Sipe, President of Carolina Academic Press, and Ms. Adriana Sciortino, Lexis Publishing, indulge my efforts to economize on my efforts.

Similarly, I rely on previous articles, some of which are not cited in, or subsequent to, the *Modern GATT Law* treatise. Material on trade preferences for Africa uses *The Limits of American Generosity*, 29 FORDHAM INTERNATIONAL LAW JOURNAL 299-385 (2006), and some discussion of FTAs is based on *Competitive Liberalization, Competitive Imperialism, and Intellectual Property*, 28 LIVERPOOL LAW REVIEW (2007). The trade sanctions analysis is informed by *MRS. WATU and International Trade Sanctions*, 33 THE INTER-NATIONAL LAWYER 1-26 (1999). The review of the European Union (EU) Common Agricultural Policy (CAP) draws on *Empathizing with France and Pakistan on Agricultural Subsidy Issues in the Doha Round*, 40 *Vanderbilt Journal of Transnational Law* (2007). The annual *WTO Case Review*, published by the *Arizona Journal of International and Comparative Law*, and co-authored with David Gantz, the Samuel M. Fegtly Professor and Director of the International Trade Law Program at Arizona, assists in many spots. It is not easy to set aside views expressed in the trilogy *The Myth About Stare Decisis and International Trade Law (Part One of a Trilogy)*, 14 AMERICAN UNIVERSITY INTERNATIONAL LAW REVIEW 845-956 (1999), *The Precedent Setters: De Facto Stare Decisis in WTO Adjudication (Part Two of a Trilogy)*, 9 FLORIDA STATE UNIVERSITY JOURNAL OF TRANSNATIONAL LAW & POLICY 1-151 (1999), and *The Power of the Past: Towards De Jure Stare Decisis in WTO Adjudication (Part Three of a Trilogy)*, 33 GEORGE WASHINGTON INTERNATIONAL LAW REVIEW 873-978 (2001). To all these journals, I am most grateful.

SUMMARY TABLE OF CONTENTS

—————

Page

TABLE OF CONTENTS

Part One

HISTORICAL FOUNDATIONS OF FREE TRADE

Chapter 1

MULTILATERAL TRADE NEGOTIATIONS THROUGH THE 1970s

When goods do not cross borders, soldiers will.

> —Frédéric Bastiat, French classical liberal political economist, 1801-50

DOCUMENTS SUPPLEMENT ASSIGNMENT

1. July 1941 *Atlantic Charter*

2. *Havana Charter* Articles 1, 71-106

3. GATT Articles XXV-XXVI, XXVIII *bis*, XXIX-XXXV

4. Tokyo Round *Enabling Clause*

I. ANCIENT AND MEDIEVAL PHILOSOPHICAL AND THEOLOGICAL VIEWS OF TRADE AND TRADERS

International trade law did not start on 30 October 1947 with the General Agreement on Tariffs and Trade (GATT). Trade economics did not begin with Adam Smith (1723-1790) and David Ricardo (1772-1823), and their respective Laws of Absolute and Comparative Advantage. Trade itself did not commence after the Second World War (1939-45). The roots of the study and praxis of trade are ancient and interdisciplinary. The presumption trade ought to be free remains highly controversial.

Embedded in these roots, but buried by much modern legal and economic scholarship, is an integral link between trade and morality. In the first Chapter of his splendid account, *Against the Tide* (1996), Douglas A. Irwin explores the dichotomous views in Ancient and Medieval times of foreign commerce. Plutarch of Delphi (46-127 A.D.) and the Roman lyric poet Horace (65-8 B.C.) embody the extremes. In *Moralia* (specifically, the essay *On Whether Water or Fire is More Useful*). Plutarch argues:

> God created the sea to promote interaction and to facilitate commerce between the various peoples of the earth. . . . Without the exchanges made possible by the sea, . . . man would be "savage and destitute."[1]

Horace, instead, in *Odes*, proffers:

> [t]he sea brought contact with strangers who could disrupt domestic life by exposing citizens to the bad manners and corrupt morals of barbarians.[2]

---

[1] DOUGLAS A. IRWIN, AGAINST THE TIDE 11, 11-21 (1996).

[2] *Id.* at 12.

3

Is trade an opportunity for peaceful intercourse to advance prosperity? Or, is it a threat to moral fiber and civic security? The dichotomy remains to the present, resonating in contemporary debates about globalization.

For Ancient thinkers, traders themselves were part of the problem. In Plato's (428/427-348/347 B.C.) division of labor, retail trade was an occupation beneath the dignity of a Greek citizen. It was best left to an inferior person — preferably a segregated foreign resident in a Greek city-state — incompetent at other activities. In the *Republic*, Plato acknowledged the need to import a good only if a city-state cannot supply itself, and to do so only if the good is a necessity, paying for it by shipping abroad an exportable surplus. Aristotle (384-322 B.C.) in *Politics*, looked askance at traders and dependency on foreign trade. A port facility is necessary only to import necessities that cannot be obtained elsewhere, and that facility should be physically separate from a city, and closely monitored by authorities, to ensure no vices are brought in with merchandise. Surely merchants and their loyalties cannot be trusted, added Xenophon (431-355 B.C.). In *Oeconomicus*, he urged "all men naturally love whatever they think will bring them profit." How vulgar it is, added Ancient Romans like Cicero (106-43 B.C.) in *De Officiis*, to buy merchandise at one price, and sell it at a higher price, unless the exchange brings great benefit or enhances the intelligence of Romans.

Early Christian Fathers, too, viewed commerce as ethically unseemly, an occasion for many of the Seven Deadly Sins — anger, covetousness, envy, greed, lust, pride, and sloth. They recalled the Gospel account of Christ throwing merchants from the Temple. Saint Augustine (354-430 A.D.) intoned in *Exposition on the Book of Psalms*, "Let Christians amend themselves, let them not trade." Given the risks of foreign commerce, coupled with an ethnocentric sense of superiority, the trade policy — if it be called that — of many Ancient philosophers and theologians was to ban imports of non-necessities and forbid exports of necessities. Self-sufficiency was preferred, and so much the better if it could be achieved through autarky.

However, the tide began to turn in favor of free, or freer, trade with the Doctrine of the Universal Economy. This Doctrine was espoused by philosophers and theologians, notably Seneca the Younger (4 B.C.-65 A.D.) in *Naturale Quaestiones*, Philo of Alexandria (20 B.C.-50 A.D.), in *On the Cherubim*, Origen (185-254 A.D.) in *Contra Celsum*, Libanius (314-394 A.D.) in *Orations (III)*, Saint Basil the Great (329-379) in *Exegetic Homilies* (specifically, *On Hexameron, Homily 4*), Saint John Chrysostom (349-407 A.D.) in *Discours Sur La Componction (2)*, and Saint Theoderet of Cyrrhus (393-457 A.D.) in *On Divine Providence*. This Doctrine states:

> . . . trade between regions should be accepted as beneficial and even be permitted to run its course free from interference. . . . Providence deliberately scattered resources and goods around the world unequally to promote commerce between different regions. According to [noted economist] Jacob Viner [who identifies the Doctrine as the oldest, longest lived economic precept, and a forerunner of the factor endowments theory of trade, such as the Hecksher-Ohlin Theorem], [there are] four distinct elements [in the Doctrine]. First, it embraces the stoic-cosmopolitan belief in the universal brotherhood of man. Second,

it describes the benefits to mankind arising from the trade and exchange of goods. Third, it embodies the notion that economic resources are disturbed unequally around the world. Finally, it attributes this entire arrangement to the divine intervention of a God who acted with the deliberate intention of promoting commerce and peaceful cooperation among men.[3]

The Doctrine entered into Natural Law theory, and by Medieval Scholastic era (1100-1500 A.D.), the paradigm moved further — albeit slowly and with opposition — in favor of trade and traders. Trade routes were paths for evangelization, and small, impoverished traders were worthy of sympathy. Merchandise itself is not merely an object of arbitrage, but a chance to express human creativity by enhancing the value of that object.

St. Thomas Aquinas (1225-1274) had much to do with this shift. In *Summa Theologica*, he delineates three kinds of useful economic activity (*i.e.*, engagements with a value added to society): storing goods, importing necessity goods, and transporting goods to regions of scarcity. Pecuniary gain from these activities, says Saint Thomas, is not inherently sinful. To be sure, domestic production is more dignified than trade. But, conducted in moderation — and, critically, with the proper motives — trade could be a morally virtuous activity. Later, Martin Luther (1483-1546) later would not take such a positive view in *To the Christian Nobility of the German Nation* (1520). Still, subsequent theologians — including John Calvin (1509-1564) in *Commentary on the Book of the Prophet Isaiah* — generally continued the tradition of synthesizing the Doctrine of the Universal Economy with moral precepts. That tradition is ecumenical. For example, various *ayat* (verses) in the *Qur'an* address interaction among peoples and upright conduct among merchants.

In sum, scholarship about trade is neither new nor the province of one discipline. Contemplation about trade and morality, not just calculations about trade and economics, has long roots. Those roots spread into international law through jurists like Francisco de Vitoria (1480/83-1546) in *De Indis De Jure Belli*, Francisco Suarez (1548-1617) in *De Legibus, Ac Deo Legislatore* (1612), Alberico Gentili (1552-1608) in *The Three Books on the Law of War* (1612), and Hugo Grotius (1583-1645) in *The Law of War and Peace* (1625). They urged the right of countries to trade, and presumption of free trade, exists in the Law of Nations (*jus gentium*), not just Natural Law. Today, is the paradigm in which international trade law operates reverting from free trade to protectionism? How is a paradigmatic shift gauged? What factors cause a shift? Is the dichotomy between "free trade" and "protectionism" false, *i.e.*, is there such a thing as "free" trade? As a matter of law, is trade invariably restricted by encumbrances and contingencies? Does the *de jure* scheme created by lawyers result, to one degree or another, in *de facto* managed trade?

II. THE BIRTH OF GATT AND STILLBIRTH OF THE ITO

The General Agreement on Tariffs and Trade (GATT) was supposed to be a provisional accord, a bridge between the immediate post-Second World War period and the subsequent years in which the *Charter for the International*

---

[3] IRWIN, *supra* note 1, at 15.

Trade Organization (ITO) would govern. It was the *Charter*, not GATT, which was to be the Constitution for the world trading system. When the *Charter* failed, largely because President Harry S. Truman elected not to submit it to the Senate for advice and consent, GATT was left to govern that system.

President Truman appreciated the Senate would look askance at the *Charter*. Politicians had many reasons to oppose the *Charter*. One reason was the plethora of exceptions to trade-liberalizing rules in the *Charter*. In examining the *Charter* in relation to GATT and contemporary World Trade Organization (WTO) texts, is this a fair criticism? Another basis for opposition was ideological. Since President George Washington's *Farewell Address* (17 September 1796), in which he advised against unnecessary entanglements with foreign powers (declaring "[i]t is our true policy to steer clear of permanent alliances with any portion of the foreign world. . ."), there has been an isolationist tendency among prominent national leaders. Senator Henry Cabot Lodge (1850-1924, Republican-Massachusetts) championed isolationism following the First World War, and led the successful fight against U.S. participation in the League of Nations. Senator Robert Taft (1889-1953, Republican-Ohio) picked up that mantle following the Second World War. Followers of the Lodge-Taft tradition had little interest in, and considerable suspicion of, committing America to yet another international organization (in addition to the Bretton Woods institutions, the International Monetary Fund, and the World Bank).[4]

To be sure, GATT was neither an accident nor an afterthought. The U.S. Department of State had conceived a design for a post-Second World War international economic order that included a multilateral trade body. An early version of an American blue print was published as *U.S. Proposals* in DEPARTMENT OF STATE PUBLICATION NUMBER 2411 (1945). A subsequent version came out as *U.S. Suggested Charter* in DEPARTMENT OF STATE PUBLICATION NUMBER 2598 (1946).[5] In drawing up such plans, the U.S. worked closely with its steadfast ally, the United Kingdom.

In August 1941, President Franklin Delano Roosevelt and Prime Minister Winston S. Churchill approved the *Atlantic Charter*, in which more seeds for GATT were planted. In the *Atlantic Charter*, the U.S. and Great Britain sought

> the fullest collaboration between all nations in the economic field with the object of securing, for all, improved labour standards, economic development and social security" and, "with due respect for their existing obligations," aim "to further the enjoyment by all states, great or small, victor or vanquished, of access, on equal terms, to the trade in the raw materials of the world which are needed for . . . economic prosperity.[6]

That the two wartime leaders could focus on a post-War economic order, and plan for it, at a time when victory over the Axis Powers hardly was assured, is a testament to their great vision.

---

[4] The *Bretton Woods Agreement* was negotiated in July 1944 and took effect on 27 Dec. 1945.

[5] *See Suggested Charter for an International Trade Organization*, 93 COMMERCIAL POLICY SERIES (U.S. Dep't of State 1946).

[6] *See Atlantic Charter*, 14 Aug. 1941, 55 Stat. 1600, E.A.S. No. 236.

As for the text of GATT, it was drafted in two sets of pivotal meetings of delegates from many countries that took place in 1946-47:

- First Session of the Preparatory Committee of the United Nations Conference on Trade and Employment, held in London from 15 October to 20 November 1946, and known as the "London Preparatory Conference."

- Second Session of the Preparatory Committee of the United Nations Conference on Trade and Employment, held in Geneva from 10 April to 30 October 1947, and known as the "Geneva Preparatory Conference."

On 30 October 1947, delegates from 23 countries signed the GATT. The official citation to the original publication of GATT is *Final Act*, Geneva, 55 U.N.T.S. 194 (1947). The 23 signatories to GATT are the original "contracting parties" to GATT. But for the withdrawal by Josef Stalin, the Union of Soviet Socialist Republics (USSR), which participated in early negotiations, would have been the 24th original contracting party.

If GATT — by default — became the Constitution of the post-Second World War trade order, then these contracting parties, and in particular the London and Geneva Preparatory Conference delegates who drafted GATT, are the Founding Fathers of that system. In retrospect, the spring, summer, and fall in which they worked would define many contours of the political economy in which we still live: the Partition of British India (and soon thereafter, of Palestine), the Marshall Plan for reconstructing Europe, the Communist-Nationalist civil war in China, and the strengthening movement for independence in less developed regions. On 1 January 1948, GATT entered into force, and the modern multilateral trading system was born.[7]

For almost the next half century, GATT as a document and an institution would go about making the world safe for free trade. It would get little attention or credit outside of trade *aficionados*, as the attention of international diplomats and lawyers focused on the weighty matters of the Cold War, and decolonization. And yet, the theory of world peace through world trade — a theory articulated by Cordell Hull, the Secretary of State to President Roosevelt, and manifest in the *Reciprocal Trade Agreements Act of 1934* — was never lost.

The drafting history of the *ITO Charter* is largely parallel to that of the GATT. For the *Charter*, the key drafting conferences, which occurred between 1946-48, were:

- The 1946 London Preparatory Conference (as above).

- The 1947 New York Preparatory Conference, held from 20 January to 25 February 1947.

---

[7] Almost immediately after its entry into force, the U.S. published two studies:

- *Analysis of GATT*, DEP'T OF STATE PUBLICATION NUMBER 2983 (1947).

- *The Geneva Charter for an International Trade Organization*, DEP'T OF STATE PUBLICATION NUMBER 2950 (1947).

These documents provide helpful explanations into certain textual provisions, and also lend insight into the thinking of drafters, and the positions of the U.S.

- The 1947 Geneva Preparatory Conference (as above).
- The Havana Conference, held from 21 November 1947 to 24 March 1948.

Because the text of the *ITO Charter* was finalized in Havana, the document also is referred to as the *"Havana Charter."* All of these sessions took place under the auspices of the United Nations Conference on Trade and Employment. The *Charter* remains important as a legal document in no small part because of express references to it in various Interpretative Notes (the *Ad Articles*) of GATT. It also provides a window to what would come — on 1 January 1995, when the World Trade Organization (WTO) was born, and the *Agreement Establishing the World Trade Organization (WTO Agreement)* entered into force.

That *Agreement* has four Annexes — the core texts that form the legal foundation of modern international trade law. Technically, "GATT 1947" — now known as "GATT 1994" — is item (1) in Annex 1A to the *WTO Agreement*. Article XVI, entitled "Miscellaneous Provisions," of the *WTO Agreement* contains two Paragraphs that emphasize continuity. Paragraph 1 ensures a continuing role for GATT decisions, procedures, and customary practices, and Paragraph 2 essentially continues the position of the GATT Director-General of the GATT Secretariat through to the WTO Director-General. In brief, the first accord, in the first Annex, is none other than GATT, and notwithstanding the proliferation of multilateral trade law, especially during and after the 1986-94 Uruguay Round of trade negotiations, GATT remains the true Constitution.

To be sure, no longer is the GATT the pre-eminent document, in terms of priority. Article XVI:3 of this Article XVI explains the hierarchy between the *WTO Agreement*, on the one hand, and all other annexed accords, on the other hand:

> In the event of a conflict between a provision of this Agreement and a provision of any of the Multilateral Trade Agreements, *the provision of this Agreement shall prevail to the extent of the conflict.* (emphasis added).

Of course, as Article XVI:4 of the *WTO Agreement* sets out, WTO Members are obligated to make their trade measures consistent with the *Agreement* and all annexed accords, including GATT. But, to say GATT is an "annexed" agreement and thereby incorporated by reference into the *WTO Agreement* is to understate its contemporary importance.

Certainly, no longer is GATT the constitutive document in the sense of setting up the institutional infrastructure for the WTO and its dispute settlement mechanism, nor in the sense of containing trade-liberalizing principles for new frontiers like services, foreign direct investment, and intellectual property. However, even these features of the WTO draw on, or are inspired by, GATT provisions — for example, Article XXIII on dispute settlement, Article XXV on joint action, and Articles I, II, III, and XI on trade liberalization obligations. In the sense of laying out trade-liberalizing principles the WTO oversees, and that have been extended to new frontiers precisely because they are so valuable, GATT is the Constitution.

This point is evident not only in the indirect influence of GATT on the development of *GATS*, but also in a number of specialty areas. For instance, in antidumping (AD) law, GATT Article VI is the font of many AD rules found in the WTO *Antidumping Agreement*. As another example, in customs law, Article VII, which deals with valuation, is the foundation for the WTO *Customs Valuation Agreement*. Indeed, it is difficult to find an end point to the influence of GATT. For example, Article XIX, which establishes a general safeguard action, is the conceptual basis for special safeguard actions, such as the remedy in Article 5 of the WTO *Agreement on Agriculture*. It is hard to conceive of disciplines on agricultural support (or, for that matter, non-agricultural support) without the GATT Articles VI and XVI rules.

The extensions from GATT into specialty areas of international trade law adduce there is no adamantine distinction between many of Articles in GATT, on the one hand, and one or more of the large number of agreements and understandings reached in multilateral trade rounds, on the other hand. However, whether the thematic influence of GATT, of heralding peace through trade, continues in the Post-9/11World perhaps is more in doubt than at any time since President Roosevelt and Prime Minister Churchill drew up the *Atlantic Charter*.

III. TRENDS IN THE ROUNDS

In the modern international trade history, *i.e.*, since the birth of GATT on 30 October 1947, there have been a total of nine sets, known as "rounds," of multilateral trade negotiations (MTNs) aimed at reducing trade barriers.

1. The *original GATT negotiations* in Geneva in 1947, known as the *Geneva Tariff Conference*:

The 23 original contracting parties participated. The 24th country involved (to a limited degree) in preparing the *ITO Charter*, the former Soviet Union, declined to join. Negotiations covered roughly 45,000 tariff concessions and $10 billion of trade (measured in 1938 prices).

2. The *Annecy Tariff Conference*, known as the *Annecy Round*, 1948-1949:

The Round, involved 33 countries and roughly 5,000 tariff concessions.

3. The *Torquay Tariff Conference, known as the Torquay Round*, 1950-1951:

This Round involved 34 countries. About 8,700 concessions were negotiated, resulting in tariff reductions of 25 percent compared to the 1948 level.

4. The *Geneva Tariff Conference*, known as the *Geneva Round*, 1955-1956:

This Round involved 22 countries and $2.5 billion of trade.

5. Another *Geneva Tariff Conference*, known as the *Dillon Round*, 1960-1962:

This Round involved 37 contracting parties, 23 of which offered concessions. There were 4,400 tariff concessions covering $4.9 billion of trade.

6. The *Kennedy Round*, 1964-1967:

The Round, which also transpired in Geneva, involved 76 contracting parties, though only 31 of them, including the 6-member EEC, granted tariff concessions. The negotiations covered $40 billion of trade, or roughly 75 percent of world trade at the time.

7. The *Tokyo Round*, 1973-1979:

The Round involved 85 contracting parties. Yet, just 36 of them, including the 10-member EC, granted tariff concessions. The talks, which happened in Geneva, covered $300 billion of trade, and was the most ambitious to date.

8. The *Uruguay Round*, 1986-1994:

This Round involved 118 contracting parties and covered $3.7 trillion of trade. Launched in September 1986, the last day of substantive negotiations was 15 December 1993 (though bargaining, in fact, continued well beyond then). This Round easily eclipsed the Tokyo Round as the most far-reaching and complex. Most negotiations occurred in Geneva. However, a Mid-Term Review was held in Montreal in 1990. In addition, an accord on farm support (particularly export subsidies) was hammered out between the U.S. and European Union (EU) at Blair House in Washington, D.C. (the *"Blair House I Accord"*) in November 1992, a deal on industrial tariffs was reached in July 1993 in Tokyo among the "Quad" countries (Canada, EC, Japan, and EU), and another accord between the U.S. and EU at Blair House focusing on oilseeds subsidies (the *"Blair House II Accord"*) was reached in November 1993.

9. The *Doha Development Agenda*, 2001-2007:

This Round involved approximately 150 WTO Members and roughly $3 trillion of trade. Known colloquially as the *"Doha Round,"* it was launched in Doha, Qatar, at the Fourth WTO Ministerial Conference, held from 9-13 November 2001. Agreeing to an agenda, in the dark shadow of the terrorist attacks of 11th September, and the reality of many competing interests among not only Members, but also non-governmental organizations (NGOs), was a major achievement.

How did each Round obtain its appellation? The name of the first four Rounds is based on the place in which all or most negotiations transpired, such as Annecy, France, and Torquay, England. The name of the next two Rounds is named after individuals who inspired the Rounds. Most poignantly, the Kennedy Round is named after the late President John Fitzgerald Kennedy (who was assassinated on 22 November 1963). The recent practice is to name a Round after the location in which trade ministers adopt a *Declaration* to launch it, such as Tokyo for the Tokyo Round.

Observe also the historical record, in terms of the number of Rounds in a reasonably short span of modern economic history, is remarkable. It should not, however, be inferred from this record that commencing a round is easy. It is not. A mix of political and economic factors must come together.

In particular, trade policy makers, heads of government, and domestic constituencies must agree on a common agenda. The mix of factors world leaders must marshal to trigger a round is ever-more complex. That is because the membership of the multilateral trading community grows in number and diversity, hence the range of topics that members seek to discuss, and their perspectives and interests on the topics, expand. To some degree, leadership from the GATT Secretariat, and now the WTO — in the person of the Director-General, affects the launch and course of a round. However, as Dr. Supachai

Panitchpakdi of Thailand, who served as Director-General in 2002-05, was fond of saying, the WTO is a "member-driven organization." Strong and charismatic leadership can compel Members to compromise on an agenda to some degree, but pushing the Members too far when the political and economic environment is not ripe for a round may marginalize the Director-General.

What general trends emerge from the many Rounds of multilateral trade negotiations? The question is asked during a time of living history, as multilateral trade negotiations continue. The following six broad observations, however, might be offered:

- The successive Rounds involve an increasing number of countries, reflecting new accessions to GATT and the WTO. Consequently, the WTO Membership is far more diverse, in terms of levels of economic development and nature of political systems, than the original GATT contracting parties of 1947.

- The successive Rounds cover a greater dollar value of world trade. This coverage is partly a mark of success. It reflects growth in world trade made possible in part by liberalization from preceding Rounds. It also is owed to the ambition of trade negotiators to cover a larger number of product categories.

- The successive Rounds, particularly since the Kennedy and Tokyo Rounds, expand well beyond the traditional topic of tariffs. Trade negotiations no longer are just about tariff reductions (if, in reality, they ever were). Depending on the Member and its perspective, they relate to matters from agriculture to national security, and from dispute settlement to sanitary standards.

- Especially since the Uruguay Round, a large number of NGOs have "participated" in trade talks, in one way or the other. Sometimes, the "participation" is observation and reporting. Other times, it is advocacy of a position. Still other times, it is through protest, which is not always respectful or peaceful.

- Much of the "optionality" of participation that characterized Rounds up to the Uruguay Round has disappeared. In the Geneva, Annecy, Torquay, Geneva, and Dillon Rounds, technically, it was necessary for a contracting party to participate if it sought a concession, and a contracting party could seek a concession only if it held an initial negotiating right (INR) or had a principal supplying interest. As a practical matter, if trade flows were small, then contracting parties tended not to exchange concessions. And, less developed countries (abbreviated "LDCs," though during and after thee Uruguay Round the acronym can connote the narrower category of "least developed countries") sometimes observed from the sidelines. However, in the Uruguay Round, every contracting party had to schedule concessions on goods. In effect, no free riding was permitted.

- Reciprocity is perhaps the most fundamental operating principle in multilateral trade negotiations. In searching for an overall balance of rights and obligations in any proposed trade liberalization plan, representatives of different countries always ask a bottom line question — what are they receiving in exchange for what they are conceding? To what extent is reciprocity a legal obligation, expressly or implicitly, in GATT, such as Article XXVIII *bis*?

The obvious inference from these trends is multilateral trade rounds have become increasingly comprehensive, time consuming, and difficult.

IV. THE EARLY GATT ROUNDS (1948-1961)

The framework for a round of multilateral trade negotiations is set forth in Article XXVIII bis, coupled with the provisions of Article XXV on joint action. In addition, brief mention is made in Article III:2 of the *WTO Agreement* of the supporting role played by the WTO. Still the framework is skeletal. It provides no details regarding the mechanics or procedures for conducting negotiations. Moreover, Article XXVIII *bis* was not added to GATT until 7 October 1957, following its preparation through a 1954-55 Review Session.

Not surprisingly, then, during the first three Rounds, the contracting parties followed procedures laid out in the *ITO Charter*, particularly Article 17, even though it was clearly dead letter law by the time of the second Round. The essential features of these procedures were as follows:

- Negotiations to cut tariffs were conducted on products selected by one or more contracting parties, and the offers and counter-offers were made on a product-by-product basis.

- A contracting party could ask for a reduction in a tariff on a product only if that party was a principal supplier of the product to the country from which it sought a concession.

- Every contracting party had full autonomy to grant, or not grant, a concession on any particular product.

- If a contracting party already maintained duty free treatment with respect to a product, or a low rate of duty on that product, and if it agreed to bind the tariff on that product against increase from the zero or low rate, then the other contracting parties accepted this concession as, in principle, equal to either the substantial reduction of a tariff from a high level, or the elimination of a preference.

- Bargaining was based on reciprocity. Thus, no contracting party was obliged to offer or grant unilateral concessions.

After three Rounds of using these procedures, the contracting parties gained a level of comfort that comes only from experience. Not surprisingly, then, they crafted Article XXVIII *bis* of GATT by incorporating these features from the *ITO Charter*. The brief Interpretative Note to this Article makes no reference to the *Charter*, nor need it, precisely because of this incorporation.

The Geneva Tariff Conference of 1947 occurred in the context of finalizing the GATT document itself and preparing the *ITO Charter*. In 1946, the U.S. invited all 24 countries represented on the "Preparatory Committee for the Charter for the International Trade Organisation" to enter into negotiations to reduce tariff and other trade barriers. The United Nations Economic and

Social Council appointed them to the Committee. When the Americans circulated a *Suggested Charter* for the ITO in 1946, this draft

> included two articles that would have facilitated Soviet participation. Article 28 included a variant of the quantitative import commitment inserted into many bilateral agreements with the Soviet Union in the interwar years. The clause specified that a country with a complete or substantially complete monopoly of its import trade should under- take a global import commitment, of an amount to be agreed upon, in reciprocation of the tariff concessions granted by market countries. A commercial considerations clause, designed to ensure that the increased trade arising from the import commitment be conducted in a nondiscriminatory manner, was simultaneously inserted in the *Suggested Charter* as article 26.[8] [These two articles were not carried through to the *ITO Charter*, given the Soviet decision not to participate in the final two drafting conferences for the *Charter*.]

This U.S. encouragement extended to the preparation of charters for the World Bank and IMF. The Soviet Union participated in these exercises, as well as in the Bretton Woods Conference of 1944 (at which the articles of agreement for the Bank and Fund were finalized), and signed the Bretton Woods Agreement. Nevertheless, the political relationship between the allies of the Second World War deteriorated. The Soviet Union abstained from joining the World Bank and IMF, and elected not to participate in the last two conferences at which the draft *ITO Charter* was debated and completed, and never joined GATT.

Accordingly, of the 24 countries on the United Nations Committee, 23 of them accepted the American invitation — the notable exception being the former Soviet Union. The acceptance by 23 countries led to what became known as the first Geneva Round, which was completed in August 1947. Why they accepted the American invitation is evident from a *Report* emerging from the Geneva Preparatory Conference:

> *Considering that the objectives underlying the endeavour to set up the I.T.O. would be promoted if concrete action were taken* . . . to enter into reciprocal negotiations directed to the substantial reduction of tariffs and other barriers to trade . . . the governments represented on the Preparatory Committee adopted a resolution . . . regarding the carrying out of such negotiations. . . . [These governments currently are] in the final stages of negotiations [*i.e.*, of the first Geneva Round]. . . . It is expected that the concessions resulting from these negotiations . . . will shortly be incorporated in a General Agreement on Tariffs and Trade.[9]

In brief, the 23 countries thought they would advance their shared interest in establishing an ITO, with its central mission of liberalising trade, if they commenced expeditiously to cut tariff barriers even before they finished

---

[8] Leah A. Haus, Globalizing the GATT — The Soviet Union's Successor States, Eastern Europe, and the International Trading System 89 (1992).

[9] *Report of the Second Session of the Preparatory Committee of the United Nations Conference on Trade and Employment*, United Nations Document EPCT/186, at 6 (1947).

drafting the *Charter*. (In all likelihood, some of them may have appreciated the possibility the *Charter* never would take effect.)

In the Geneva Round, the 23 countries achieved tariff reductions using a selective, product-by-product methodology, on which they had agreed at the 1946 London Preparatory Conference, and in 1947 in New York. In turn, this methodology, coupled with the principal supplier rule, was drawn in large part from American practice, namely, the way in which the U.S. had conducted negotiations under its reciprocal trade agreements program up to 1945. After all:

> The General Agreement was conceived as a *product* of the negotiations, not as a framework for conducting them. The *ITO Charter* contained the framework for future negotiations.[10]

Thus, having negotiated successfully, the 23 countries logically sought to implement their trade liberalizing deals, even before they finalized the *ITO Charter*. Consequently, the countries not only drafted GATT, completing it on 30 October 1947, but also agreed to its effective date as of 1 January 1948. These countries became the original GATT contracting parties. The results of the bargains on lowering tariff and other trade barriers they reached during the first Geneva Round also took effect at that time.

Following the initial GATT talks, the "Early Rounds" of multilateral trade negotiations — specifically, Annecy, Torquay, Geneva, and Dillon — focused on the reduction of tariffs. There appears to be no standard definition of "Early Rounds." One convention, followed here, is to consider the Rounds completed during the first 15 years following the entry into force of GATT on 1 January 1948, as "Early." That would mean the first five Rounds (up through the Dillon Round, which ended in 1962) are "Early."

During the first three Rounds, *i.e.*, until the Dillon Round, the contracting parties exchanged offers and counter-offers on a bilateral basis. (In the Annecy and Torquay Rounds, the contracting parties used the rules of Article 17(c) of the *ITO Charter*. Essentially, these rules stated that reduction of an MFN tariff rate on a product automatically operates as a reduction in the margin of preference on the same product, and *vice versa*, and no margin of preference could be increased.) Moreover, high priority in the first three of these Rounds was placed on the gradual elimination of colonial-era trade preferences. The reason for commencing the 1948-49 Annecy Round was to create an opportunity for tariff negotiations between the 23 original contracting parties and 11 countries seeking accession to GATT. That is, the Annecy Round dealt with the possible accession of 11 more countries as GATT contracting parties under the auspices of Article XXXIII. Of the 11 applicant countries, nine joined GATT — Denmark, the Dominican Republic, Finland, Greece, Haiti, Italy, Nicaragua, Sweden, and Uruguay.

It was in 1950, at the start of the Torquay Round, when the U.S. publicly declared — through a press release of the Department of State — that it would not submit the *ITO Charter* to the Senate as a treaty for its advice and consent (nor to both Houses of Congress as a Congressional — Executive agreement).

---

[10] JOHN H. JACKSON, WORLD TRADE AND THE LAW OF GATT § 10.4, at 220-21 (1969) (emphasis in original).

The small but growing body of contracting parties then clearly understood the GATT "was to become an *institution considerably different* from that originally contemplated."[11] During the 1950-51 Torquay Round, the contracting parties negotiated tariff reductions among themselves and with six other countries that had applied for accession pursuant to Article XXXIII — Austria, Germany, Korea, Peru, the Philippines, and Turkey. Four of the six became contracting parties at the end of the Round. Korea and the Philippines did not join until after further negotiations years later.

A noteworthy feature of the Torquay Round was the challenge posed by countries (whether existing or potential new contracting parties) that had relatively low tariffs. This challenge sometimes is called "tariff dispersion," or "tariff disparities," across countries (as distinct from the phenomenon of widely varying tariff rates maintained by one country). As observed in a 1952 study on the operation of GATT, several European countries felt themselves to be disadvantaged from the outset of the Round. They had bound their tariffs in the 1947 Geneva Round and 1948-49 Annecy Round, so by the start of the Torquay Round, they had low tariffs in comparison with other countries. This earlier trade liberalization meant they had less to offer, to induce reciprocal concessions, than higher tariff countries. The latter group refused to grant concessions they perceived as unilateral and unrequited. So, for example, high tariff countries generally avoided making major tariff cuts in exchange for prolongation by low tariff countries of bindings of duties at low rates.

Unfortunately, the Torquay Round ended without a solution to the problem of negotiations involving a mix of low and high tariff countries. The tariff cuts were neither as broad or deep as had been hoped when the talks began. France responded with a plan that, after some modifications, the contracting parties adopted on 13 October 1953. (The original French Plan called for an automatic, across-the-board cut of tariffs by 10 percent (phased in over a three-year period), with a ceiling rate on each of four broad categories of products, and with exceptions to give credit to contracting parties that already had low tariffs.) This "GATT Plan," as it was dubbed, set forth the modalities to deal with tariff dispersion.

In brief, the GATT Plan contained the following features:

- Classification of traded products into ten categories; calculation of a "demarcation line" (in effect, a target for the average incidence of the weighted average of duties in ten European and North American countries).

- Use of an across-the-board (not a selective, product-by-product) method to cut tariffs by a fixed rate of 30 percent.

- A phased reduction of tariffs to the demarcation line or below (with lower reductions, and even exemptions, for countries that already had tariffs below the line).

- Ceiling rates on individual product categories; measurement of reciprocity on an overall basis (not in a product-by-product way).

- Special and differential treatment for poor countries.

---

[11] *Id.* § 10.4, at 222 (emphasis added).

Before ever trying it, the contracting parties shelved the Plan. They failed to achieve a consensus to use their 1953 Plan as the modalities for the 1955-56 Geneva Round.

In the Geneva Round, only 25 of the then 39 contracting parties agreed to engage in negotiations, and only 22 of the participating countries made concessions. Many LDCs declined to participate, and the ones that did elected not to make concession offers. Not surprisingly, contracting parties fell back on a selective, product-by-product approach, and followed the modalities laid out in the predecessor to Article XXVIII *bis* (*i.e.*, the former Article XXIX). Worse still, because the contracting parties adopted procedures whereby any two or more of them could begin talks at any time, and because several countries did not participate at all, it is more accurate to eschew the label "Round" for what really was a Tariff Conference. However, the label is applied because participants included the major trading powers, all of which exchanged concession lists.

The Geneva Round was disappointing in terms of the scope of coverage of tariff reductions. It affected only $2.5 billion in trade. The reason was the delegation from the Congress gave the American trade negotiating team a limited mandate (which it made nearly full use of). But, in two other respects, the Geneva Round was a success. For the first time, the contracting parties recognised the importance of trade liberalisation in the agricultural sector, which (in practice) remained at the margins of the disciplines of GATT. Agricultural protectionism among developed countries was having adverse trade effects, and something had to be done.

Moreover, the contracting parties acknowledged the need to tackle the trade and development needs of LDCs. They memorialized their plan by publishing a report, *Trends in International Trade* — informally known as the *Haberler Report* (in honor of the chair of the panel of experts who wrote it, Gottfried Haberler, Professor of Economics at Harvard). The *Report* set forth the first-ever GATT guidelines for how the contracting parties could help LDCs. In turn, it led to a "Program for the Expansion of Trade," which was adopted by the contracting parties in October-November 1958. Pursuant to the Program, the contracting parties established three committees: Committee I, which focused on the agenda for the next Round; Committee II, which reviewed the domestic agricultural policies of each contracting party; and Committee III, which addressed the concerns of LDCs in the world trading system.

As for the 1960-62 Geneva Tariff Conference, or Dillon Round, the American Under-Secretary of State, Douglas Dillon, is said to have proposed it because of two threats from the European Economic Communities (EEC), which formed in 1957 with 6 member states. The Round was the first one in which the EEC negotiated as a single bloc. The first threat was the common external tariff (CET) of the EEC. Under Article XXIV:6, large-scale tariff negotiations were required of the EEC to compensate individual contracting parties for any imbalance that would result when the EEC replaced the variegated tariffs of each EEC member with a single external tariff. Thus, the first part of the Round was dedicated to renegotiating tariff with the EEC under Article XXIV:6. The balance of the Round was spent on new tariff concessions among the contracting parties. During the second phase, countries applying to join GATT carried out tariff negotiations in connection with their accession.

The second threat concerned agricultural subsidies pursuant to the CAP. The Geneva Round and Committee III had drawn attention to trade-distorting agricultural policies. The new Dillon Round provided an opportunity to discuss these distortions. However, the problem proved too difficult. Agricultural and other politically sensitive products were, for the most part, left out of the final deal.

For three additional reasons, the Dillon Round results disappointed expectations of the contracting parties. First, effective participation was limited. Of the 37 contracting parties at the time, just 23 of them offered concessions. Second, nothing was done to combat non-tariff barriers, even though the rules for the Dillon Round expressly mentioned barriers under Article XI:2(c) (which has exceptions to the Article XI:1 rule against quantitative restrictions). Third, tariff cuts could have been deeper. The EEC offered to slash tariffs on a linear basis. The fixed rate would be 20 percent, though there would be some exceptions to the across-the-board cut. The EEC had legal authority for this ambitious offer. The Dillon Round was the first set of multilateral trade talks conducted with Article XXVIII bis in force, and the contracting parties adhered to its terms. The EEC suggested they follow the first sentence of Paragraph 2(a) of this Article, which empowers them to agree on the application of procedures other than a product-by-product approach. The United Kingdom matched the EEC offer. But, because of limited negotiating authority, the U.S. could not meet this offer. Consequently, the contracting parties stuck by the language in this sentence empowering them to use the old-fashioned selective, product-by-product method.

In the Early Rounds, negotiations to cut tariffs were conducted on a product-by-product basis. The product-by-product method was implemented according to the principal supplier rule. The principal supplier of a particular product is expected to entertain the possibility of offering concessions only on a product for which another country that also is a major supplier of that product has requested a concession. In this way, negotiations on tariff reductions for a particular product are held between pairs of principal suppliers. Other countries are kept appraised of the talks, and from time to time are brought into the negotiations. That way, all countries periodically can assess the value of concessions on the table and how those concessions would affect them.

In brief, the theory of the principal supplier rule is only countries that are significant exporters of a product ought to have a right to request tariff cuts in that product. That way, tariff cut requests remain reasonable, and free riding problems avoided. Once principal suppliers agree on concessions on a product on a reciprocal, mutually advantageous basis, the deal is multilateralized, by operation of the Article I:1 MFN obligation. The new, lower tariff is bound under Article II:1(b). Yet, there are obvious problems with this theory as it was practiced in early decades of GATT history.

First, as the number of contracting parties grew, and the range of product categories expanded, the product-by-product approach and principal supplier rule became more cumbersome to implement. The method was not efficient for the organization GATT had become. Conversely, with a large number of countries acceding to GATT, there was less fear of free riding, in the sense of benefits from tariff cuts redounding to non-members that had made no trade reforms of their own. Second, the approach gradually fell victim to its own success. Having provoked significant cuts by developed countries in industrial tariffs in the late 1940s through early 1960s, there was little more headway to be made using the approach. That is, many of the important industrial product categories had been the subject of a cut. Third (and following the second point), the product-by-product approach is inherently selective, as it relies largely on the desires and efforts of principal suppliers. If no single negotiating partner is the principal supplier of a particular product, then the result may be no offer on that product is made. The result is a gap in coverage of tariff cuts. A gap also can result because a product is deemed too sensitive to permit an aggressive tariff cut. Fourth, the approach does not systematically address tariff dispersion and peak problems (either within or among countries).

These shortcomings suggested a new approach would be needed. Yet, overall, what might be said of the actual results of tariff cuts in the Early Rounds? On the one hand, "[n]o reliable evaluation of the tariff reductions and other commitments made during the first five rounds of negotiations in GATT 1947 is available."[12] Full analyses of the outcomes appear to have begun with the Kennedy Round, typically done by the GATT or WTO Secretariat. On the other hand, reports by the Secretariat, and by the United Nations Conference on Trade and Development (UNCTAD), the Organisation for Economic Cooperation and Development (OECD), and various other institutions, indicate the "the achievement during the last 50 years or so in industrial tariff reduction has been impressive. . . ."[13]

V. THE KENNEDY ROUND (1964-1967)

The 1964-67 Kennedy Round was more ambitious and complex than any previous multilateral trade talks. By 1967, there were 76 contracting parties to GATT, though only 32 of them granted tariff concessions in this Round. Nonetheless, a large reduction was achieved on many products.

The *Trade Expansion Act of 1962* gave the American negotiating team the authority to pursue an across-the-board cut of up to 50 percent, and for some product categories an even deeper cut than 50 percent. (The only exceptions to the limitation of the 50 percent cut (*i.e.*, items for which decreases of more than 50 percent were permitted) seem to be for dicyandiamide and limestone, which are employed in the manufacture of cement, to which 19 U.S.C. § 1821(b)(1) did not apply.)

Six factors made the Kennedy Round particularly noteworthy and established trends that continue to the present day. First, the negotiation process for cutting tariffs changed from the traditional product-by-product approach to an across-the-board or linear method. As a general matter, it may be observed there is a tension between reciprocity and across-the-board tariff

---

[12] ANWARUL HODA, TARIFF NEGOTIATIONS AND RENEGOTIATIONS UNDER THE GATT AND THE WTO ¶ J.2 at 70 (2001).

[13] *Id.* ¶ J.6 at 72.

cuts. Reciprocity entails that, with respect to trade barriers on a particular good, contracting party A treats contracting party B in the same way that B treats A. Reciprocity is less demanding, from a free trade perspective, than national treatment, which requires A to treat the goods of B in the same manner as A treats A's own goods. Contracting party A is unlikely to grant across-the-board tariff cuts on goods from contracting party B without reciprocal treatment. In any event, on 21 May 1963, the contracting parties launched the Round by adopting a *Ministerial Resolution* calling for "substantial linear tariff reductions with a base minimum of exceptions which shall be subject to confrontation and justification" among industrialised countries for industrial products.[14] In other words, their goal was a cut of 50 percent on all products, with precious few exceptions that had passed a rigorous test. The contracting parties agreed to this goal for two reasons:

> Two main considerations led to the adoption of the linear approach. First, the item by item, request-offer method adopted in past negotiations, with its *dependence on* the extent to which the principal supplier was *willing to reciprocate* the reduction of duty in a particular product, had led to *very small reductions* which were in some cases worthless in commercial terms. Second, with the increase in the number of contracting parties, the traditional method had become increasingly *cumbersome and unwieldy.*[15]

Also, the *Resolution* recommended addressing disparities in tariff levels, and called for "tariff reductions . . . based upon special rules of general and automatic application."[16]

In the end, after repeatedly pushing back the deadline for completion, the talks finished in May 1967, and the protocol embodying the results was signed on 30 June 1967. (Uruguay Round negotiations finished on the day trade negotiating authority of the American president expired — 15 December 1993. The Kennedy Round package was signed on the last day of that authority. The obvious point is multilateral trade negotiations almost invariably "go down to the wire.") In the end, Kennedy Round negotiators achieved an across-the-board tariff cut of 35 percent:

> During the Kennedy Round, the principal industrialised countries made *tariff reductions on 70 percent of their dutiable imports, excluding cereals, meat, and dairy products.* Although the working hypothesis adopted for industrial products was for a linear cut of 50 percent, because of numerous exceptions, an *effective reduction of 35 percent* was obtained in industrialised countries for these products. The tariff reductions made by the developing countries were *highly selective* and would *not* have made a significant impact on their trade-weighted average tariff.[17]

---

[14] *Ministerial Meeting: Arrangements for the Reduction or Elimination of Tariffs and Other Barriers to Trade, and Related Matters, and Measures for Access to Markets for Agricultural and Other Primary Products*, B.I.S.D. (12th Supp.) at 47-49 (1964) (adopted 21 May 1963).

[15] HODA, *supra* note 12, ¶ B.8 at 30-31 (emphasis added).

[16] *Ministerial Meeting: Arrangements for the Reduction or Elimination of Tariffs and Other Barriers to Trade, and Related Matters, and Measures for Access to Markets for Agricultural and Other Primary Products*, B.I.S.D. (12th Supp.) 47-49 (1964) (adopted 21 May 1963).

[17] HODA, *supra* note 12, ¶ J.3 at 70 (emphasis added).

In practice, "across-the-board" meant 60,000 products were covered by the reduction.

To be more specific, concessions made by the EEC, Japan, Sweden, Switzerland, the United Kingdom, and the U.S. covered 70 percent of dutiable imports (worth about $26 billion) into these countries. Most of their concessions (covering roughly $18 billion of dutiable imports) were tariff cuts of 50 percent or more, some of concessions (covering roughly $5 billion of dutiable imports) were tariff cuts of between 20 and 50 percent, and some concessions (covering roughly $4 billion of dutiable imports) were smaller tariff cuts. On some dutiable imports (worth about $11 billion), these countries granted no concessions. Professor Dam, then, finds the results of this Round disappointing:

> In the end, *30 percent of the dutiable imports of the major participants were left untouched by tariff reductions*, and approximately one-third of the reductions on the remaining imports were of less than the full 50 percent. Just as in earlier rounds the principle equating the binding of a low tariff with the substantial reduction of a high tariff had failed to survive intact the realities of tariff bargaining, so in the Kennedy Round *the across-the-board principle was seriously compromised.*[18]

Still, the across-the-board method of tariff reductions continues to be used.

The second noteworthy feature of the Kennedy Round was coverage of agricultural as well as industrial goods. For example, agreements were reached on grains and on chemical products. Reducing tariff barriers in agricultural trade did not prove easy. "[T]he linear approach to agricultural goods was abandoned completely,"[19] and:

> [i]n addition to excepting individual products [from the linear method of cutting tariffs], it was decided after extensive discussions to *treat the agricultural sector specially.* This special treatment was thought to be justified by the high frequency of quantitative restrictions and other non-tariff barriers in agriculture, a circumstance that tended to make tariffs irrelevant to determining international trade flows for agricultural products. In part, the dispute about agriculture reflected a difference between the national interests of the two major protagonists, the United States and the EEC. *The United States was a major agricultural exporter, and its negotiators were committed politically to the Congress to making the successful conclusion of agricultural negotiations a condition for any concessions on industrial products. The EEC was for many agricultural products a major importer and was pursuing a conscious policy of seeking agricultural self-sufficiency.* The United States, although maintaining that the general linear rules should apply to agricultural tariffs of major significance, was successful in seeking the adoption of *"acceptable conditions of access"* as the goal of agricultural sector negotiations. "Acceptable conditions of access" was open to the interpretation that the United States sought a *guarantee of a certain percentage share of the EEC market,* a

---

[18] KENNETH W. DAM, THE GATT 77 (1970) (emphasis added).

[19] JACKSON, *supra* note 10, § 10.5 at 225.

guarantee that would have been difficult to reconcile with the linear method if not also with the most-favored-nation clause.

In the end, *all agricultural products were excluded from the linear negotiations*. Cereal, meats, and dairy products were the subjects of special discussions oriented toward the creation of international commodity arrangements, and the remaining agricultural products were dealt with through specific offers — that is to say, through *product-by-product negotiations*.[20]

Not surprisingly, efforts to liberalize trade in agriculture continued through the subsequent Tokyo and Uruguay Rounds.

Third, no longer was the U.S. the sole driving force in the negotiating rounds. Japan acceded to GATT in 1955, and the EEC was formed in 1957. During the Kennedy Round, both emerged as key players in negotiations. To this day, the U.S., EU, and Japan remain dominant — and, to many participants and observers hegemonic — powers in multilateral trade discussions. However, Australia, Brazil, Canada, China, India, Korea, and others have joined the rank of powerful counties able to set agendas and shape negotiating outcomes in the multilateral trading system. Roughly 80 percent of the WTO Membership is comprised of developing and least developed countries. In the infrequent instances when they behave as a unified bloc, they, too, can "make" or "break" a deal. In sum, the origins of the dispersion of influence can be traced to the Kennedy Round.

Fourth, the Kennedy Round negotiators discussed the interests of LDCs. The *Ministerial Resolution* of 21 May 1963 launching the Round proclaimed "in the trade negotiations every effort shall be made to reduce barriers to exports of the less developed countries, but that the developed countries *cannot expect to receive reciprocity* from the less developed countries."[21] (Soon thereafter, nearly *verbatim* language would find its way into Article XXXVI:8.) Many LDCs acceded to GATT in the early 1960s. On 1 May 1964, an International Trade Center was created to channel information, and offer advice, to them. (This Centre continues in a new incarnation under WTO auspices.) In February 1965, the Committee on Trade and Development was established. (The Committee also continues to the present in its modern-day incarnation under the WTO).

During the Kennedy Round, LDCs were treated as "nonlinear countries," meaning they participated in tariff reductions through affirmative product-specific offers. They were keenly interested in products such as cereals, dairy, and meat, and the Trade and Development Committee set up working groups to study these commodities. The LDCs did not have to table their offers until they learned about tariff reductions developed countries offered on agricultural products of interest to poor countries.

Many LDCs, pursuant to the non-reciprocity principle, made no tariff reduction commitments. Indeed, because the negotiations among developed countries were rife with confrontation, and so many LDCs were involved in the

---

[20] DAM, *supra* note 18, at 70-71 (emphasis added).

[21] *Ministerial Meeting: Arrangements for the Reduction or Elimination of Tariffs and Other Barriers to Trade, and Related Matters, and Measures for Access to Markets for Agricultural and Other Primary Products*, B.I.S.D. (12th Supp.) 47, 48-49 (1964) (adopted 21 May 1963) (1964) (emphasis added).

negotiations, "in the end, only sixteen countries (counting each member state of the EEC separately) participated in the Kennedy Round as linear countries, while thirty-six were in the nonlinear category."[22] With respect to product coverage, LDCs made no tariff reductions on 21 percent of their dutiable imports, and cuts in their tariffs of less than 50 percent on 26 percent of these imports. LDCs agreed to grant tariff concessions of 50 percent or more on 49 percent of their dutiable items, and cuts of more than 50 percent on 5 percent of these items.

Furthermore, during the Kennedy Round, a new Part IV entitled "Trade and Development" (Articles XXXVI-XXXVIII) was added to GATT. This Part obligates developed countries to give high priority to reducing their trade barriers to products from developing countries, and eschew erection of new barriers against such products. Article XXXVI:8 states developed countries do not "expect reciprocity" from developing countries. By no means have all major countries put into practice fully these requirements. During the Kennedy Round, tariff concessions granted by developed countries tended to cover industrial products of potential, not actual, export interest to LDCs. Specifically, of the dutiable manufactured goods of actual interest to LDCs, 24 percent of the value of these products imported by major developed countries were not subject to any tariff reduction, 29 percent of these products were subject to reductions of less than 50 percent, and 47 percent were subject to reductions of 50 percent or more. By comparison, for all manufactured products, 16 percent were subject to no tariff cut, 29 percent to a cut of less than 50 percent, and 55 percent to a cut of 50 percent or more. To the present, the meaning and implementation of special and differential treatment for developing and least developed countries is a key source of controversy.

Fifth, Kennedy Round negotiators worked to reduce non-tariff barriers, as well as tariffs. To be sure, they were not the first to identify these barriers. In the 1955-56 Geneva Round, the negotiators put on the agenda "certain regulations and protection afforded through the operation of import monopolies."[23] The *Ministerial Resolution* launching the Kennedy Round spoke of "deal[ing] not only with tariffs but also non-tariff barriers."[24] Apparently, the negotiators appreciated the definition of a non-tariff barrier ought not to be circumscribed to import licenses, quotas, and other quantitative restrictions. Rather, the definition should embrace abuse of trade remedies, because that abuse constricts or blocks importation of targeted merchandise. Accordingly, the Kennedy Round negotiators established an AD code. However, it was a plurilateral deal. Congress felt the American trade diplomats did not have delegated authority to negotiate this code, thus the U.S. never joined it, and the code had little practical impact.

The final and perhaps most enduring noteworthy feature of the Kennedy Round is its identification of issues that remain on the multilateral trade

---

[22] DAM, *supra* note 18, at 73.

[23] *Plans for Tariff Reduction and Rules and Procedures for 1956 Tariff Conference, Annex, Section II (Scope of Negotiations)*, B.I.S.D. (4th Supp.) 80 ¶ 4 (1956) (adopted 18 Nov. 1955).

[24] *Ministerial Meeting: Arrangements for the Reduction or Elimination of Tariffs and Other Barriers to Trade, and Related Matters, and Measures for Access to Markets for Agricultural and Other Primary Products*, B.I.S.D. (12th Supp.) 47-49 (1964) (adopted 21 May 1963).

negotiating agenda. Agriculture products and special and differential treatment are two examples. Reducing non-tariff barriers, and expanding the meaning of the term, are a third illustration of efforts at progressive liberalisation of trade. Still another illustration are the discussions that occurred during the Round on customs valuation, leading to an agreement on chemical products and the controversial valuation method used at the time by the U.S. known as the American Selling Price (ASP). (The Kennedy Round deal on chemicals called on Europe to reduce its tariffs on chemical products if the U.S. dropped the ASP valuation method.) Modern day negotiators owe gratitude (or blame) to Kennedy Round negotiators for putting these items squarely on the negotiating table.

VI. THE TOKYO ROUND (1973-1979)

No doubt tariff reductions achieved in the Dillon and Kennedy Rounds stimulated international trade and enmeshed the contracting parties in a growing network of economic interdependence. In fact, from 1950-75, merchandise trade among industrial countries grew at an average rate of 8 percent annually, which was double the growth rate of the gross national product of these countries. However, as impressive as the results of the Dillon and Kennedy Rounds were, more progress was needed on reducing tariff barriers on agricultural goods, managing the special problems of developing countries and — most importantly — combating the spread of non tariff barriers (NTBs).

In early 1972, the U.S., EEC, and Japan called for multilateral, comprehensive GATT negotiations. They did so in the wake of the international monetary crisis of 1971. The crisis prompted President Richard M. Nixon to end convertibility of the U.S. dollar into gold (*i.e.*, to close the "gold window"), and abandon the fixed exchange rate system for currencies established in 1944 by the *Bretton Woods Agreement*. As in the Kennedy Round, many tariff negotiations were conducted on a linear across-the-board basis. However, Tokyo Round talks were even broader and more ambitious than the Kennedy Round talks. They were open to non-contracting parties and, most significantly, dealt expressly with NTB reductions.

In retrospect, the Tokyo Round — if not the Kennedy Round — marks an interesting point in the history of Article XXVIII:1 *bis*. This provision (as discussed earlier) clearly condones the conduct of tariff negotiations. It does not expressly mention multilateral trade negotiations on non-tariff topics. Yet, negotiators in the Tokyo Round (indeed, in the Kennedy Round, if not earlier) were not inhibited by this technicality. Nor should they have been, as they had, and continue to have, the authority to negotiate any matter relevant to GATT under Article XXV:1. Accordingly:

> [i]n the Tokyo Round, while tariff negotiations were important, the negotiations on non-tariff measures were given equal, if not greater, importance. No tariff conference under GATT 1947 was confined purely to tariffs and even the early rounds envisaged negotiations on quotas and the protection afforded through the operation of import and export monopolies. But it was during the Tokyo Round that a successful

attempt was made to negotiate agreements on a range of non-tariff measures.[25]

Emerging from the Tokyo Round was a comprehensive package of agreements adopted by 85 contracting parties.

Not all 85 contracting parties agreed to cuts in their Schedules of Concessions. In the end, only 36 of them, including the 10-member EC, did so. Still, over $300 billion of trade was covered by tariff reductions and bindings phased in during a 7-year period.

Specifically, the weighted average tariff on manufactured goods from the 9 major industrial markets declined from 7 percent to 4.7 percent, causing a 34 percent decrease in customs duties collected:

> During the Tokyo Round, the level of all *industrial* duties in *industrialised* countries (EC, U.S., Canada, Japan, Austria, Finland, Norway, Sweden, and Switzerland) was reduced by *one-third if measured on the basis of customs collection*, and by about *39 percent if based on simple average rates*. In these countries, the *simple average declined from 10.4 to 6.4 percent*, and the *weighted average was reduced from 7.0 to 4.7 percent* (using import data from MFN origin in 1977, except that 1976 was used in the case of Austria, Canada, and Norway). *No comparable estimates are available for developing countries*, again [as in the Kennedy Round] because of the *selective nature of their bindings and reductions*, but a GATT Secretariat study mentions that the coverage of their tariff reductions was $3.9 billion of their imports in 1976 and 1977. As for tariffs facing imports of developing countries, the average MFN reduction on industrial products was shallower than the overall cut, about one-quarter compared with one-third. This reflected the fact that important product groups in the exports of developing countries such as textiles, clothing, footwear, and travel goods were subjected to lower than formula reduction.[26]

Put differently, Tokyo Round reductions on industrial tariffs were similar to that achieved in the Kennedy Round. Even developing countries cut tariffs on $3.9 billion of imports.

How did Tokyo Round negotiators achieve these cuts in industrial tariffs? The *Ministerial Declaration* launching the Round called for the use of "appropriate formulae of . . . general application."[27] In other words, the *Declaration* envisaged an across-the-board method of some sort, not the selective, product-by-product approach of the Early Rounds. A number of contracting parties — notably, Canada, the EEC, Japan, Switzerland, and U.S. — proposed specific formulas, and the Swiss approach was accepted. The "Swiss Formula," as it became known, is:

$$Z = \frac{(\text{coefficient})(X)}{(\text{coefficient}) + (X)}$$

---

[25] HODA, *supra* note 12, ¶ A.6 at 26.

[26] *Id.* ¶ J.6 at 72 (emphasis added).

[27] *Declaration of Ministers Approved at Tokyo*, B.I.S.D. (20th Supp.) 19 (1973) (adopted 14 Sept. 1973).

That is,

$$Z \quad = \quad \frac{(A)(X)}{(A) + (X)}$$

In this formula, the variable "X" represents the initial rate of duty, and the variable "Z" represents the final rate of duty. The contracting parties forge an agreement on the value of the coefficient, which sometimes is abbreviated with the letter "A." There is an inverse relationship between the value of the coefficient and the reduction in tariffs, *i.e.*, the smaller the value of the coefficient, the greater the cut.

In the Tokyo Round, Australia, Austria, the EEC, Hungary, and Nordic countries used 16 as the value in making their tariff cut offers. Czechoslovakia, Japan, Switzerland, and the U.S. used 14. In general, developing countries favoured the Swiss Formula, though they argued for particularized treatment to account for their economic needs. Many of them offered concessions later in the Round, after June 1979 when major developed countries concluded their talks.

As in the Kennedy Round, during the Tokyo Round the application of a linear formula was not truly across-the-board on industrial products. There were three significant departures. First, several contracting parties simply exempted certain product categories from the application of the formula. They did so, even though the Ministerial Declaration launching the Round did not refer to exceptions. Second, Canada was permitted to use an equation other than the Swiss Formula. Third, Iceland, New Zealand, and South Africa applied the product-by-product methodology.

Aside from tariff cuts, four other results of the Tokyo Round stand out. First, some reductions in agricultural tariffs occurred. However, no formula was used. Rather, the traditional, selective product-by-product approach was applied.

Second, agreements on reducing NTBs were achieved. For example, codes on customs valuation, import licensing procedures, government procurement, and technical barriers to trade, were reached. Some of these codes formed the basis, even to the extent of *verbatim* texts, for Uruguay Round accords.

Third, Tokyo Round negotiators drew up accords on trade remedies. They approved a code on subsidies and countervailing duties (CVDs), and they revised the Kennedy Round *AD Code*. They also codified practices and procedures concerning dispute settlement and the use of trade measures to safeguard the external financial and balance of payments (BOP) positions of a contracting party.

Fourth, the legal basis for granting preferential trade treatment to LDCs was made permanent. An *"Enabling Clause"* was agreed to as the legal basis for the Generalized System of Preferences (GSP) offered by developed countries. (The GSP is a non-reciprocal scheme whereby certain exports from beneficiary developing countries receive duty-free treatment.) Until the Tokyo Round, a waiver from GATT obligations like MFN treatment under Article I:1 provided that basis. Technically, the waiver provision, contained in Article XXV, did not afford certainty and predictability. The waiver standard is both rigorous and subject to contextual interpretation. Article XXV:5 calls for a waiver only under "exceptional circumstances." A general preferential scheme like the GSP, which applies to a large number of developing countries, could not pass muster. At least some of them suffer from "exceptional circumstances," but not all, and not in all economic sectors. Additionally, during the Tokyo Round, LDCs were afforded more flexibility in enacting trade measures designed to meet their economic growth interests.

Chapter 2

THE URUGUAY ROUND (1986-1994) AND BIRTH OF THE WTO (1995)

Trade is the natural enemy of all violent passions. Trade loves moderation, delights in compromise, and is most careful to avoid anger. It is patient, supple, and insinuating, only resorting to extreme measures in cases of absolute necessity. Trade makes men independent of one another and gives them a high idea of their personal importance: it leads them to want to manage their own affairs and teaches them to succeed therein. Hence it makes them inclined to liberty but disinclined to revolution.

> —ALEXIS DE TOCQUEVILLE (1805-1859), 2 DEMOCRACY IN AMERICA ch. 21 (1840).

DOCUMENTS SUPPLEMENT ASSIGNMENT

1. GATT Articles XXVI, XXXI-XXXIII, XXXV

2. *Ministerial Declaration* on the Uruguay Round (Punta del Este, 20 September 1986)

3. WTO *Agreement*

4. U.S. Statement of Administrative Action on the *WTO Agreement* (concerning U.S. sovereignty)

I. NEGOTIATING REDUCTIONS IN TRADE BARRIERS

A. Non-Tariff Issues

Despite impressive results in the Tokyo Round, soon after its conclusion the international economic community was faced with sluggish economic growth, rapid inflation, and high unemployment. Economists dubbed the vexing phenomenon "stagflation." Many contracting parties, including the United States, resorted to protectionist measures like voluntary export restraints (VERs). These measures were subtle but discriminating quantitative restrictions that circumvented Tokyo Round disciplines because of their voluntary nature. Not until the Uruguay Round were they banned (specifically, in Article 11:1(b) of the *Agreement on Safeguards*).

Moreover, a built-in danger was embedded in some Tokyo Round outcomes that would not be corrected until the Uruguay Round agreements were signed: free riding. The Tokyo Round codes applied only to signatory countries. Many less developed countries, for example, rejected them. Thus, a two-tier system was created — one tier of signatories, and one tier of non-signatories. Signatories had to resort to legal devices (*e.g.*, statutory provisions in the legislation implementing the codes into domestic law) to ensure that non-signatories did not free ride on the benefits of the codes while eschewing the obligations of those codes.

Why the need for a Uruguay Round? Aside from weaknesses in the GATT dispute resolution system (discussed in Chapter 1), among the most challenging problems faced by the world trading community after the Tokyo Round were substantive issues of market access in key economic sectors. The Round simply had not dealt with certain sectors adequately, or at all, in terms of providing a framework for market liberalization. By the mid-1980s, it was clear a new, even more ambitious, Round was necessary.

For example, the burgeoning trade in services, and barriers to such trade, remained wholly outside the GATT framework. Intellectual property rights required better protection than currently afforded by many NICs and LDCs. Too many contracting parties were protecting their agricultural sectors, through tariffs, NTBs, and subsidies, to too great a degree.

Not surprisingly, then, tariff reductions were not the primary motive for launching the Uruguay Round. Here, again, is an illustration of the Article XXVIII:1 *bis* authorization to start a round of tariff negotiations being used for far wider purposes than just cutting tariffs. What, in particular, prompted trade policy makers to commence the Uruguay Round? There is no single cause. Aside from the residual problems from the Tokyo Round, among the most challenging problems faced by the world trading community after that Round were substantive issues of market access in key economic sectors. The Tokyo Round failed to deal with certain sectors adequately, or at all, in terms of providing a framework for market liberalization. By the mid-1980s, the need for a new, even more ambitious, set of multilateral discussions was evident.

For example, the perspective of developed countries was shaped strongly by the orientation of their economies in favor of service businesses and products embodying intellectual property rights. Barriers to trade in services were a constraint on the international growth of these economies, yet services trade remained wholly outside the GATT framework. These countries also sought better IPR protection than afforded in newly industrialised countries, like Brazil, India, and Korea (and Taiwan (or, technically, "Chinese Taipei"), which acceded to the WTO on 1 January 2002), as well as in many developing countries, such as Egypt, Indonesia, and Thailand (and China, which acceded to the WTO on 11 December 2001).

From the perspective of many developing countries, particularly net agricultural exporters, and developed country members of the Cairns Group, principally Australia and New Zealand, too many contracting parties clung to various forms of protection for agricultural products. (In addition to these two countries, the 17-member Cairns Group consists of Argentina, Bolivia, Brazil, Canada, Chile, Colombia, Costa Rica, Guatemala, Indonesia, Malaysia, Paraguay, Philippines, South Africa, Thailand, and Uruguay.) These forms included high tariff and non-tariff barriers, generous domestic support for their farmers, and significant export subsidies for their farm products.

In addition, many developing and least developed countries were concerned about the global system of quotas for textile and apparel (T&A) products that existed under the 1974 *Multi Fibre Agreement* (*MFA*). These countries sought to make the economic transition from primarily agrarian economies by moving factors of production into low-value added manufacturing sectors, such as ready made garments (RMGs). To one degree or another, they were following the pattern of industrialisation laid out by W.W. Rostow in his 1960 classic work, *The Stages of Economic Growth*. While faulted for specifying a deterministic path on which the categories of development were not always clear-cut (*e.g.*, in what stage would complex economies like those of China or India be placed?), Professor Rostow's work served to highlight the significance access to foreign markets potentially can have in advancing along the development path. The *MFA* quotas, by contrast, blocked export growth in certain T&A products of some countries — and, not surprisingly, raised the cost of clothing to consumers in importing countries.

Certain issues cut across crude categories of "First World" and "Third World." For instance, various contracting parties sought to clarify and amplify trade remedy rules, namely antidumping duties, subsidies and countervailing measures, and safeguards. Finally, while concerns about infringement on sovereignty existed, and continue to the present, many contracting parties felt the time had come for a permanent multilateral infrastructure to promote trade liberalization and deal with the expanding scope of international trade law and policy. In other words, it was necessary to resurrect the ITO, ultimately under a different name — WTO.

The U.S. had a particularly keen interest in the Uruguay Round. It was globally competitive (and in some instances dominant) in services, IP industries, and agriculture. A deal yielding significant market access for American businesses in these sectors was a Round that would be welcome. But, American interests in these sectors were not necessarily consonant with what less developed countries wanted or needed, hence a major North-South confrontation was inevitable.

The Uruguay Round was launched in September 1986 with a *Ministerial Declaration* issued by trade ministers from the contracting parties meeting in Punta del Este, Uruguay. The U.S. successfully advocated the establishment of an agenda for this Round that was even broader and more ambitious than that of the Tokyo Round. The agenda is set forth in the *Declaration*. In contrast, in the Third WTO Ministerial Conference in Seattle, held in November — December 1999, the U.S. was far less successful in pushing forward what at the time was billed a "Millennium Round."

B. Industrial Tariff Cuts

Certainly, Uruguay Round negotiators dealt with tariffs. All contracting parties participated in the Round, in the sense each one of them had to make offers to cut tariffs, *i.e.*, produce a schedule of concessions on goods. For many developing and least developed countries, the "grant" of a tariff concession took the form of an agreement to a ceiling binding, whereas for developed countries there were true tariff cuts. How did negotiators achieve the cuts, in whatever form?

The *Ministerial Declaration* launching the Uruguay Round did not state whether the linear approach would be used (much less present a detailed formula), or whether the traditional item-by-item would be the methodology. However, it did speak to the problem of tariff peaks and tariff escalation, and appeared to back away from the Article XXXVI:8 non-reciprocity rule:

> Negotiations shall aim, by appropriate methods, to reduce or, as appropriate, eliminate tariffs, including the reduction or elimination of *high tariffs* and *tariff escalation*. Emphasis shall be given to the expansion of the scope of tariff concessions among *all* participants. [Emphasis added.]

Switzerland proposed a formula to cut industrial tariffs essentially the same as the equation used in the Tokyo Round, *i.e.*, the "Swiss Formula."

However, Uruguay Round negotiators never agreed on a single formula to be used for all industrial product categories. All they could agree on, which was not insignificant, was a set of guidelines, reached during the 1990 Mid-Term Review Conference in Montreal, Canada. The key points of the *Montreal Guidelines* were:

- The *substantial reduction or*, as appropriate, *elimination of tariffs by all participants*, with a view to achieving lower and more uniform rates, including the *reduction or elimination of high tariffs, tariff peaks, tariff escalation and low tariffs*, with a target amount for overall reductions *at least as ambitious* as that achieved by the formula participants in the *Tokyo Round*.

- A *substantial increase in the scope of bindings*, including bindings at ceiling levels, so as to provide greater security and predictability in international trade.

- The need for an approach to be elaborated to give *credit for bindings*; it is also recognised that participants will receive appropriate recognition for liberalization measures adopted since 1 June 1986.

- The *phasing of tariff reductions* over appropriate periods to be negotiated.[1]

Despite significant efforts after the Montreal Mid-Term Review, the contracting parties could not reach agreement on a single formula. That is, they gave up the effort to set a common modality, and in January 1990, they essentially turned once again to the traditional approach of making requests and offers to reduce or eliminate, and bind, industrial tariffs on a line-by-line basis.

Fortunately, the contracting parties accepted the *Montreal Guidelines*, and their subsequent discussions, implied an overall target to reduce industrial tariffs by one third, *i.e.*, 33 1/3 percent. Without a formula, though, each contracting party could decide how it would cut its tariffs. For instance, the EC, Finland, Norway, and Sweden used a three-tiered formula the EC suggested:

- Least developed contracting parties would not have to cut their tariffs, or only do so to the extent they felt able.

---

[1] Uruguay Round Document MTN.TNC/7(MIN) at 4, *quoted in* Anwarul Hoda, Tariff Negotiations and Renegotiations under the GATT and the WTO ¶ B.23, at 35, ¶ C.10, at 49 (2001) (emphasis added).

- Developing contracting parties would reduce to a ceiling binding of 35 percent any base (initial rate) above 35 percent. For base rates at or below 35 percent, developing countries would negotiate reductions bilaterally in an effort to harmonize duties.

- Developed contracting parties would reduce to a ceiling binding of 20 percent any base rate at or above 40 percent. For base rates less than 40 percent, if the base rate were between 30 and 40 percent, then there would be a flat rate reduction of 50 percent.

The third point can be exemplified as follows.

If the base rate were 38 percent, then it would be cut in half to 19 percent. If the base rate were between zero and 29 percent, then that base would be reduced according to the following formula:

$$R = \text{Base Rate} + 20$$

in which:

"R" stands for the percentage (rate) of reduction applied to the Base Rate.

However, if the base rate were 15 percent, then the rate of reduction would be 35 percent, implying a new tariff of 9.75 percent (the result of 15 percent minus 35 percent of 15 percent, *i.e.*, 15-5.25 percent).

The EC formula attacked the problem of tariff dispersion across countries by requiring deeper cuts on higher tariffs, and not exempting *a priori* any developed or developing contracting party. By contrast, Japan proposed the elimination of all industrial tariffs, with developing countries subject to a less severe obligation (*e.g.*, cutting a proportion of their tariffs). In the end, Japan joined Austria and Canada, and all three contracting parties used a formula proposed by Canada, as follows:

$$R = 32 + \frac{\text{Base Rate}}{5}$$

in which:

"R" stands for the percentage (rate) of reduction applied to the Base Rate, and R cannot exceed 38 percent,

"Base Rate" refers to the initial tariff rate on the product in question, but with all base rates below 3 percent to be eliminated (*i.e.*, reduced to zero) on view that such low tariffs have only a nuisance value but no protective effect, and

the term $\dfrac{\text{Base Rate}}{5}$ is rounded down to the nearest whole number.

Yet another formula, which Australia proposed and used, called for the elimination of any base rate of 2 percent or less. For non-*de minimis* base rates, Australia called for deeper cuts on higher rates:

If the Base Rate exceeds 15 percent, then:

$$R \quad = \quad \frac{(Base\ Rate - 15)}{(Base\ Rate)} \quad x \quad (100)$$

If the Base Rate exceeds 10 percent but is less than or equal to 15 percent, then:

$$R \quad = \quad \frac{(Base\ Rate - 10)}{(Base\ Rate)} \quad x \quad (100)$$

where in both instances:

"R" stands for the percentage (or rate) of reduction applied to the Base Rate.

For example, applying the Australian formulas, if the Base Rate were 50 percent, then the rate of reduction (R) applied to it would be 70 percent, yielding a new bound tariff ceiling of 15 percent. If the Base Rate were 12 percent, then it would be reduced by 16 2/3 percent, producing a new bound tariff level of 10 percent.

Even these formulas were not applied in their pure form. Norway modified the EC formula, and Austria did not apply the maximum 38 percent rate of reduction to any product category. The adulterations are not surprising, given the range of perspectives and objectives animating in the Uruguay Round. From the perspective of different contracting parties, each formula had strengths and weaknesses. For example, contrary to Canada, the EC did not favor the elimination of low tariffs, or at least not if credit were given for such action. The EC claimed they were not mere nuisances, but rather provided a contracting party with a modicum of negotiating leverage.

What about the American methodology on cutting industrial tariffs during the Uruguay Round? As Professor Hoda writes:

> The United States advocated the adoption of a request-and-offer approach. It argued that, after the previous rounds, the tariff regimes of countries which had participated in the formula cuts had already been substantially liberalised and little overall protection remained to justify a linear approach. Further, modern data processing techniques made it possible to conduct request-offer negotiations efficiently. Moreover, such procedures were best suited to address tariff peaks and tariff escalation, the reduction of which was an objective of the negotiations.[2]

Thus, even after the Montreal Mid-Term Review, the United States adhered to the request-offer, item-by-item method. For many industrial product groups, and several industrial sectors, the United States called for the elimination of tariffs. Accordingly, Uruguay Round negotiators considered American-inspired "sectoral proposals," also known as "zero for zero proposals," in areas such as chemicals, clothing and textiles, and non-ferrous metals. On

---

[2] HODA, *supra* note 1, ¶¶ B.16, B.25, at 33, 36 (2001).

selected products, the United States made specific reduction offers (except in two instances, namely, where the principal supplier of a product had not asked the United States for a concession, and where the United States was not negotiating with the country in the Uruguay Round and that country supplied a substantial share of imports to the American market). The United States warned it would fight free rider behavior of some contracting parties by refining its concession offers to benefit only the contracting parties that had made serious proposals.

In the end, following not only the March 1992 "Dunkel Text," but also continuing through the last day of negotiations on 15 December 1993, what did the Uruguay Round negotiators agreed upon with respect to industrial tariffs? In brief, they achieved the following reductions:

- All developed contracting parties met the overall target percentage reduction of 33 1/3 percent, and some of them exceeded this target. In particular, developed countries cut tariffs on industrial products they import from all sources (whether a developed, developing, or least developed country) by 40 percent. The cut was from a pre-Uruguay Round trade-weighted tariff average of 6.3 percent to a post-Round trade-weighted average of 3.8 percent.

- Developed contracting parties were slightly less generous in cutting tariffs on industrial products they import from developing and least developed countries. For industrial products imported by developed countries from developing countries, the cut was 37 percent, from a pre-Uruguay Round trade-weighted average of 6.8 percent to a post-Round 4.3 percent. For such products from least developed countries, the cut was 25 percent, from a pre-Uruguay Round average of 6.8 percent to a post-Round average of 5.1 percent. A few sectors explain the difference between these figures, on the one hand, and the figures on tariff cuts on industrial products from all sources, on the other hand. Developed countries reduced tariffs on clothing and textiles, fish, and fish products — all exports from developing and least developed countries — by a lower average amount than on other products.

- Developed contracting parties agreed to extend the scope of industrial products subject to ceiling bindings. With an increase in the number of bound tariff lines from 78 to 99 percent, virtually every industrial product traded among industrialised countries is subject to a bound rate.

- Developed contracting parties extended the scope of duty-free treatment for industrial products from 20 percent of these goods to 44 percent of them.

- Developed contracting parties agreed to reduce, but not eliminate, tariff peaks above 15 percent. They cut from 7 to 5 percent the proportion of industrial products subject to a tariff peak.

- To some extent, developing countries agreed to increase the scope of product categories subject to ceiling bindings, to reduce bound tariffs in key sectors like clothing and textiles, and to narrow gaps between bound and applied rates. Specifically, developing countries increased from 21 to 73 percent the number of industrial tariff lines subject to bound rates, and transition economies agreed to increase this number from 73 to 98 percent.

- Little progress was made towards reducing or eliminating tariff escalation, *i.e.*, the phenomenon of a higher tariff applicable to a product at a higher stage of processing a lower tariff applicable to the product in its unprocessed or semi-processed state. Measures as the absolute difference between a tariff at the higher end and at the lower end of processing, the average tariffs maintained by developed countries across all industrial products involved escalation both before and after the Uruguay Round. However, the absolute reduction in tariffs were larger for advanced products than for unprocessed products or products at early stages of production.

In sum, the Uruguay Round negotiators produced reasonably impressive results on industrial tariff cuts.

II. THE "GRAND BARGAIN"

Reductions of industrial tariffs achieved during the Uruguay Round are only part of the story of that remarkable eight years (1986-94) of multilateral trade negotiations. The cuts occurred in the broader context of a "Grand Bargain." Essentially, the United States, EU, and other developed countries gained for their cherished services and IP sectors the benefits of the *General Agreement on Trade in Services (GATS)* and the *Agreement on Trade Related Aspects of Intellectual Property Rights (TRIPs Agreement)*. In exchange, they agreed to grant developed and least developed countries improved terms of entry to their agricultural and T&A markets, on a more even playing field than before. They did so through the *Agreement on Agriculture* and the *Agreement on Textiles and Clothing (ATC Agreement)*. Put succinctly, and setting aside the many achievements of the Uruguay Round in areas like dispute settlement and trade remedies, the Grand Bargain was better market access for services and improved IP protection in exchange for more open agricultural markets and an end to global T&A quotas.

Overall, in the context of this Grand Bargain, the Uruguay Round produced an array of agreements. Table 2-1 lists them. What is the relationship between GATT and the WTO? The technical legal answer is that GATT is one of the 13 Multilateral Trade Agreements covering goods listed in Annex 1A to the *Agreement Establishing the World Trade Organization*. As a text annexed to the *WTO Agreement*, GATT is incorporated by reference into the web of multilateral trade rules found in that *Agreement*, and throughout other texts listed in the Annexes. There are four such annexes, with Annexes 1, 2, and 3 containing "Multilateral Trade Agreements" that were part of the single undertaking in the Uruguay Round, and Annex 4 containing "Plurilateral Agreements" that WTO Members could opt into (or not). These Annexes to the *WTO Agreement*, and the specific "covered" agreements contained in the Annexes, are listed in the following Table 2-1.

Of course, to say GATT is an "annexed" agreement and thereby incorporated by reference is to understate its contemporary importance. It remains the central substantive legal document, even the "constitution," of international trade.

TABLE 2-1:
ANNEXES AND AGREEMENTS THEREIN TO THE *WTO AGREEMENT*

Annex	Agreement(s) in Annex
Annex 1	**Annex 1A — Multilateral Trade Agreements on Goods** (1) GATT 1994, which incorporates by reference the entire 1947 GATT text. (2) *Agreement on Agriculture* (3) *Agreement on the Application of Sanitary and Phytosanitary Measures (SPS Agreement)* (4) *Agreement on Textiles and Clothing (ATC Agreement)* (5) *Agreement on Technical Barriers to Trade (TBT Agreement)* (6) *Agreement on Trade-Related Investment Measures (TRIMs Agreement)* (7) *Agreement on Implementation of Article VI of GATT 1994 (Antidumping Agreement or AD Agreement)* (8) *Agreement on Implementation of Article VII of GATT 1994 (Customs Valuation Agreement)* (9) *Agreement on Pre-shipment Inspection (PSI Agreement)* (10) *Agreement on Rules of Origin* (11) *Agreement on Import Licensing Procedures* (12) *Agreement on Subsidies and Countervailing Measures (SCM Agreement)* (13) *Agreement on Safeguards*
	Annex 1B — Services *General Agreement on Trade in Services (GATS)*
	Annex 1C — Intellectual Property *Agreement on Trade Related Aspects of Intellectual Property Rights (TRIPs Agreement)*
Annex 2	*Understanding on Rules and Procedures Governing the Settlement of Disputes (Dispute Settlement Understanding or DSU)*
Annex 3	*Trade Policy Review Mechanism (TPRM)*
Annex 4	**Plurilateral Agreements —** (1) *Agreement on Government Procurement (GPA)* (2) *Agreement on Trade in Civil Aircraft* Note: The *International Dairy Arrangement*, and the *Arrangement Regarding Bovine Meat*, both plurilateral agreements, have expired.

III. THE STRUCTURE OF THE WTO

Below is an excerpt from one of President Bill Clinton's *Statements of Administrative Action* on the Uruguay Round agreements. These *Statements* were submitted to Congress with the 1994 *Uruguay Round Agreements Act.* (This *Act* is codified at 19 U.S.C. Sections 3501-3624. It also amends several other provisions in Title 19)) There is one *Statement* for each of the agreements.

Generally, the *Statements* are worthy of perusal.[3] First, they provide clear expositions of the underlying trade agreement (in the instance below, the *WTO Agreement*). Second, Section 102(d) of the 1994 *Act* (19 U.S.C. § 3512(d)) imparts to them an exalted status: they are the "authoritative expression" by the United States of the underlying agreement and its implementation. In any U.S. judicial proceeding, they are the definitive legislative histories. The *Statement* on the *WTO Agreement* is of particular note, and thus is set out below. It lays out the structure of the WTO. Observe, too, it opens with remarks about American sovereignty.

URUGUAY ROUND TRADE AGREEMENT, *STATEMENT OF ADMINISTRATIVE ACTION, AGREEMENT ESTABLISHING THE WORLD TRADE ORGANIZATION*
H.R. Doc. No. 316, at 659-667 (27 September 1994)

The *Agreement Establishing the World Trade Organization* (*WTO Agreement*) creates a permanent forum for member governments to address issues affecting their multilateral trade relations as well as to supervise the implementation of the trade agreements negotiated in the Uruguay Round. The new World Trade Organization (WTO) will operate in much the same manner as the General Agreement on Tariffs and Trade, which it will replace, while overseeing a wider variety of trade agreements and benefiting from a number of improved decision making procedures.

1. U.S. SOVEREIGNTY

U.S. sovereignty is fully protected under the *WTO Agreement*. The WTO will continue the longstanding GATT practice of making decisions by consensus. The last policy decision made by vote under the GATT — other than approving a waiver or a country's accession to the GATT — was in 1959. However, should a vote be taken on a matter in the WTO, the improved procedures written into the *WTO Agreement* will ensure that there can be no change in U.S. substantive rights and obligations without the agreement of the United States.

The WTO will have no power to change U.S. law. If there is a conflict between U.S. law and any of the Uruguay Round agreements, section 102(a) of the implementing bill [the 1994 Act, 19 U.S.C. § 3512(a)] makes clear that U.S. law will take precedence:

No provision of any of the Uruguay Round Agreements, nor the application of any such provision to any person or circumstance, that is inconsistent with any law of the United States shall have effect.

Moreover, . . . WTO dispute settlement panels will not have any power to change U.S. law or order such a change. Only Congress and the Administration can decide whether to implement a WTO panel recommendation and, if so, how to implement it.

---

[3] Excerpts from several of the *Statements* are set out in the *Documents Supplement*, and, like other primary source materials, are referenced for reading at the outset of the relevant Chapter in the Textbook.

2. Objectives and Principles

The preamble sets forth the objectives of the *WTO Agreement* and the principles that should guide its member governments. The first paragraph of the preamble recognizes the need to achieve the goals of expanding trade and economic development in a manner that allows for the optimal use of the world's resources in accordance with the objective of sustainable development as well as in a manner that seeks to protect and preserve the environment. The preamble also recognizes that agreements to reduce tariffs and other barriers to trade and to eliminate discriminatory treatment can contribute to attaining these objectives.

3. Establishment of the WTO

Articles I and II establish the WTO and specify the various trade agreements that will apply to member governments. Article II provides that by accepting membership in the WTO, each government will automatically become a party to 18 agreements and legal instruments, referred to as "multilateral trade agreements" (MTAs). They are set out in Annexes 1, 2, and 3. One of these — the Trade Policy Review Mechanism (TPRM) — is the continuation of a procedural mechanism that has been in operation since 1989. This mechanism enhances transparency and supplies information regarding the operation of member governments' trade policy.

Certain WTO agreements, referred to as "plurilateral trade agreements" ("PTAs") and included in Annex 4, will apply only between WTO members that accept them. [The most significant PTA is the Agreement on Government Procurement.] . . .

Paragraph 4 of Article II establishes the relationship between the current General Agreement on Tariffs and Trade (GATT 1947) and the General Agreement on Tariffs and Trade that is contained in Annex 1A of the WTO Agreement (GATT 1994). GATT 1947 and GATT 1994 are legally distinct and contain different provisions. Furthermore, GATT 1994 is not considered to be a successor agreement to GATT 1947. Thus, if a government withdraws from GATT 1947 and joins the WTO, it will have no GATT obligations to countries that have not also joined the WTO.

4. WTO Functions and Structure

Article III provides that the WTO will oversee the application of the various WTO agreements and serve as the framework for member governments to conduct their trade relations under those agreements. Article III anticipates future negotiations among WTO members both on matters covered by existing WTO agreements as well as other subjects. Although any negotiations regarding amendments or additions to existing agreements would take place under WTO auspices, the *WTO Agreement* does not preclude negotiations in other fora on subjects related to those agreements, such as shipbuilding subsidies.

In addition, the WTO will administer the TPRM and the *Understanding on Rules and Procedures Governing the Settlement of Disputes (DSU)*, and will cooperate with the International Monetary Fund and the World Bank. [A later Chapter discusses the *DSU*.]

Under Article IV, the "Ministerial Conference," consisting of representatives of all WTO governments will convene at least every other year to carry out WTO functions, including decisions on matters that WTO members may raise concerning a MTA. The Ministerial Conference will establish a Committee on Trade and Development, a Committee on Balance of Payments, a Committee on Budget, Finance and Administration (Budget Committee), and a Committee on Trade and the Environment.

When the Ministerial Conference is not in session, its functions will be carried out by a General Council, also comprising representatives of WTO member governments. (Because it carries out the functions of the Ministerial Conference, references below to the Ministerial Conference should be read to apply to the Council as well.)

When it applies the *DSU*, the Council will convene as the Dispute Settlement Body (DSB). The Council will convene as the Trade Policy Review Body to carry out the functions of the TPRM.

Three subsidiary councils will oversee the functioning of the MTAs. The Council for Trade in Goods will be responsible for the agreements included in Annex 1(A). The Council for Trade in Services will oversee the *General Agreement on Trade in Services* (*GATS*) and the Council for Trade-Related Aspects of Intellectual Property . . . will have responsibility for the *TRIPs Agreement*. Each of these councils may elect to establish subsidiary bodies.

In addition, the various PTAs may establish their own supervisory bodies. Those bodies will be required to keep the General Council informed of their activities.

Article V requires the General Council to make appropriate cooperative arrangements with other intergovernmental organizations that have responsibilities related to those of the WTO. The Council may also consult and cooperate with non-governmental organizations with an interest in WTO matters.

5. THE SECRETARIAT

Article VI provides for a WTO Secretariat, whose Director-General will be selected by the Ministerial Conference. Secretariat personnel will perform their duties pursuant to regulations issued by the Conference. Like other multilateral organizations, the staff of the Secretariat is required to be impartial and member governments may not seek to influence staff actions.

6. BUDGETARY MATTERS

Article VII establishes a three-step annual budgetary process for the WTO. First, the WTO Director-General will present a budget estimate to the Budget Committee. Next, that committee will issue a budget recommendation to the General Council. Finally, the General Council will adopt the annual budget estimate.

The Budget Committee will issue regulations concerning how member contributions are to be apportioned and how to deal with members in arrears. Those regulations are to be based, as far as practicable, on the GATT 1947 regulations and practices.

7. LEGAL STATUS

Under Article VIII, each WTO member is required to accord the WTO sufficient legal status for it to exercise its functions. Each member is also required to accord the WTO, its officials, and representatives from member governments requisite "privileges and immunities," similar to those stipulated in the 1947 U.N. *Convention on the Privileges and Immunities of the Specialized Agencies.*

8. PROCEDURES FOR MAKING DECISIONS

The procedures and rules for decision making on WTO matters are set forth in Articles IX and X of the Agreement. In each area, WTO provisions either strengthen the safeguards against action with which the United States disagrees or maintains current GATT practice.

Article IX establishes rules for issuing waivers and definitive interpretations of the MTAs. The WTO will continue the longstanding GATT practice of attempting to reach such decisions by "consensus" — that is, without formal objection by any member country. However, as has been the rule under the GATT, a matter may be decided by vote in the absence of a consensus. Although GATT 1947 provides for the possibility of resolving matters through voting, there has not been a vote on a policy matter (other than a decision on grant of a waiver or the terms of accession for a new contracting party) since 1959. If there is a vote, the matter will be decided by majority of the votes cast, unless the WTO Agreement or the relevant MTA or PTA provides otherwise.

As has been the case under the GATT 1947, each WTO member will have one vote. There is a special rule for the European Union (which will be a WTO member in addition to its member countries) that ensures that the EU casts only as many votes as it has member countries who are members of the WTO.

The Ministerial Conference and the General Council are the sole WTO bodies empowered to issue authoritative, binding interpretations of the *WTO Agreement* and MTAs. The Conference and Council may not, however, use their authority to issue interpretations that would undermine the amendment provisions set out in Article X.

Interpretations may be adopted by a vote of three-quarters of WTO members, and must be based on a recommendation from the Council charged with overseeing the relevant agreement. For example, the General Council may issue an interpretation of the Agreement on Safeguards only on the basis of a recommendation from the Council on Trade in Goods.

A member government requesting a waiver of a MTA provision must first submit the request to the council in charge of the agreement in question. The council has up to 90 days to consider the request and submit a report to the General Council.

If a member country seeks the waiver of an obligation that is subject to a transition period, such as most of the obligations in the *TRIPs Agreement*, or is subject to staged implementation, such as certain tariff cuts, there must be a consensus to grant the waiver. Waivers for other types of obligations must be agreed to by three-quarters of the members if a consensus is not reached within 90 days after the request is received.

A decision granting a waiver must include: (1) a statement of the "exceptional circumstances" justifying the decision; (2) the terms and conditions governing the application of the waiver; and (3) the termination date of the waiver. If a waiver is granted for more than one year, the General Council will conduct an annual review to determine whether the exceptional circumstances continue to apply and whether the country granted the waiver has met any terms and conditions the General Council attached to the waiver. On the basis of this review, the General Council may extend, modify, or terminate the waiver.

The WTO waiver provisions significantly improve upon the current GATT requirements for grant of a waiver, enhance transparency in the operation of the waiver, and provide greater certainty regarding the duration and scope of the waiver. The consensus provision greatly increases the likelihood that important, but politically difficult, obligations such as those in the *TRIPs Agreement*, will be implemented. Furthermore, the three-quarters majority vote requirement increases the number of members that must agree to the grant of any waiver.

Procedures for interpretations and waivers of the PTAs will be governed by the rules of the relevant agreement.

9. AMENDMENTS

Under Article X, any member may propose that the Ministerial Conference consider amending the *WTO Agreement* or an MTA. In addition, each of the three subordinate Councils (for trade in goods, services, and *TRIPs*) may submit proposals to amend the MTA it oversees.

During the first 90 days that the Ministerial Conference considers a proposed amendment, or any extended period the Conference may establish, it may submit the proposal to the members for domestic ratification only if there is a consensus to do so. If the Conference cannot reach a consensus during this period, two-thirds of the members may vote to submit the proposed amendment to the members for possible ratification.

Article X sets out rules concerning the manner in which certain types of amendments may enter into force and which members will be bound by those amendments. For example, certain provisions of the MTAs may not be amended unless all WTO members agree, and such amendments do not enter into force for any member until all members have agreed to the amendment. These are Articles IX (decision making) and X (amendments) of the *WTO Agreement*; Articles I (MFN) and II (tariff bindings) of GATT 1994; Article II:1 (MFN) of the *GATS*; and Article IV (MFN) of the *Agreement on TRIPs*.

Two general rules apply in other cases. First, amendments affecting member rights and obligations (by far the largest category of likely amendments) become effective on ratification by two-thirds of WTO members, but only for those governments agreeing to the amendment. For example, if the United States does not accept a substantive amendment to the Agreement on Agriculture, that amendment does not apply to the United States.

However, a three-fourths majority of the Ministerial Conference may decide that an amendment of this type is so important that members which refuse to accept it may need to withdraw from the WTO. This rule is based on a longstanding GATT provision of this nature. The GATT rule has never been invoked, despite the fact that a GATT contracting party can be requested to withdraw based on only a two-thirds majority vote.

Second, if the Conference decides by a three-quarters vote that a proposed amendment will not affect member rights and obligations, the amendment will become effective for all members when ratified by two-thirds of WTO governments.

Article X sets out special rules for amending the *DSU* and the TPRM. Any member may propose that the Ministerial Conference consider such an amendment. Conference decisions to approve amendments to the DSU may only be made by consensus. The Conference may amend the TPRM under the normal decision making rules of Article IX:1, that is, either by consensus or, failing a consensus, by majority vote. It should be noted, however, the TPRM is simply a procedural mechanism. A decision to amend the *DSU* or TPRM is effective for all WTO members.

Procedures for amending the various PTAs are set out in those agreements. The Conference may add new PTAs to Annex 4 of the *WTO Agreement* only by consensus of all WTO members. On the other hand, if all members of a PTA request that the agreement be dropped from Annex 4, the General Council may decide to do so by consensus or majority vote.

10. ORIGINAL MEMBERSHIP

Article XI sets three requirements in order for a government to become an original member of the WTO. First, a government must be a party to the GATT at the time the *WTO Agreement* enters into force. Second, the government must have accepted the *WTO Agreement* and the MTAs. Finally, the government must have submitted a "Schedule of Concessions and Commitments" for both the GATT 1994 and the *GATS*.

11. ACCESSION AND NON-APPLICATION

Governments that do not qualify as original WTO members may accede to the *WTO Agreement* and the MTAs, as provided in Article XII. The terms of any such accession will be negotiated between the applicant government and the WTO General Council, which may approve an accession by a two-thirds vote.

Article XIII permits WTO members not to apply the *WTO Agreement*, the MTAs, and the *DSU* to other members, subject to a number of conditions.

First, a government that decides not to apply those provisions to another government may do so only at the time the government invoking non-application or the other government becomes a WTO member. Second, the right of current GATT Contracting Parties to "non-apply" the WTO agreements to other GATT Contracting Parties will be limited to those cases where the governments concerned do not apply the GATT to each other at the time the WTO Agreement enters into force for them. In addition, governments that accede to the WTO must notify the Ministerial Conference before the Conference takes action on the accession request if they intend to "non-apply" the agreement to any WTO member upon accession.

Non-application under the PTAs is governed by specific provisions on that subject in each such agreement.

The *WTO Agreement* provisions regarding non-application significantly improve upon the current GATT, which prohibits a GATT contracting party from engaging in tariff negotiations if it intends to invoke non-application at the time the new entrant accedes. Under Article XIII of the WTO Agreement, a WTO member can engage in such negotiations, ensuring that the acceding government will apply desirable tariff rates to the member government if, at some later date, the member chooses to apply the Agreement to the acceding country.

12. ENTRY INTO FORCE

[The *WTO Agreement* entered into force on 1 January 1995.] . . .

13. WITHDRAWAL

Pursuant to Article XV, a government may withdraw from the *WTO Agreement* — and thus from the MTAs — six months after the government submits written notice to the WTO Director-General. Procedures for withdrawal from the PTAs are set out in those agreements.

14. MISCELLANEOUS PROVISIONS

Article XVI makes certain provisions regarding the transition from the GATT to the WTO. For example, decisions, procedures, and customary practices established by the GATT "CONTRACTING PARTIES" will apply under the WTO. Furthermore, the GATT Secretariat is to become the Secretariat of the WTO "to the extent practicable."

Article XVI also provides that if there is a conflict between a provision of the WTO Agreement and a provision of an MTA, the *WTO Agreement* provision will take precedence to the extent of the conflict.

Paragraph four of Article XVI requires each WTO member to ensure that its governmental measures conform with its obligations under the MTAs. This provision is simply a restatement of the long accepted principle of public international law that countries will abide by their commitments. Paragraph four does not create obligations beyond those imposed by the MTAs.

WTO members are not permitted to file "reservations" (*i.e.*, declare that they will not be bound by certain provisions) under the *WTO Agreement*.

Governments may record reservations under the MTAs only to the extent allowed by the relevant MTA. The use of reservations under the PTAs is governed by each PTA.

15. NOTES AND ANNEXES

The annexes to the *WTO Agreement* incorporate each of the various MTAs and PTAs. Annex 1A, for example, includes each of the various "trade-in-goods" agreements that form part of the overall WTO Agreement. Among the agreements that figure in Annex 1A is the GATT 1994, which is defined to mean the 1947 text of the GATT plus:

- various legal instruments, such as waivers and accession protocols, adopted by the GATT Contracting Parties;

- six Understandings concerning various GATT articles;

- a protocol adopted in Marrakesh when the WTO Agreement was signed;

- changes in certain GATT terms (*e.g.*, changing "contracting party" to read "Member") to make them applicable to the WTO; and

- an exception to Part II of the GATT for the *Jones Act*.

An interpretative note to Annex 1A provides that any conflict between the GATT 1994 and a provision of the other trade-in-goods agreements in the annex will be resolved in favor of the latter.

Annex 1B of the *WTO Agreement* incorporates the *GATS*. Annex 1C sets out the *Agreement on TRIPs*. Annex 2 contains the *DSU* and Annex 3 sets out the Trade Policy Review Mechanism. The PTAs are set out in Annex 4.

IV. THE 1996 *INFORMATION TECHNOLOGY AGREEMENT* AND POST-URUGUAY ROUND DEALS

By no means did the Uruguay Round lead to freer, much less free, trade in all product markets. Notably, duties remained on many agricultural and industrial products, and impediments to services traded still abounded. These matters would have to be addressed in future multilateral negotiations.

However, in the aftermath of the Uruguay Round, various WTO Members sought plurilateral bargains to liberalize trade in specific sectors. The *Information Technology Agreement* (*ITA*) is a case in point. Signed in 1996 by 66 WTO Members, this accord removed tariffs on knowledge-based, high-technology exports. The *ITA* provides duty-free treatment to most computer-related goods. Thereafter, Members added additional products for duty-free treatment, yielding a so-called "*ITA II*" accord.

Some WTO Members also appreciated there were products not invented at the time of the *ITA* and *ITA II*, such as multi-chip integrated circuits (MCPs). An MCP enhances the functions and quality of communication devices (*e.g.*, Blackberry devices, cell phones, and digital cameras) by allowing memory and processing chips to be put in the same package. The U.S. imposed a 2.6 percent tariff on MCPs, the EU a 4 percent tariff, and Korea an 8 percent tariff. (Japan did not impose a tariff on MCPs.) However, in November 2005, the U.S., EU, Japan, Korea, and Taiwan agreed to provide duty-free treatment to MCPs (as of 1 January 2006). This post-Uruguay Round deal is plurilateral. But, the five founding Members account for 70 percent of world MCP production. (Major manufacturers include Intel, Micron, and Texas Instruments.) Once Members accounting for 90 percent of production sign, the deal is considered a multilateral WTO compact.

V. ACCESSION

A. The Original GATT Contracting Parties

Article XXVI of GATT contains provisions on entry into force of the GATT. As specified in Article XXXII, the "contracting parties" are those countries that are original (*i.e.*, founding) parties to GATT or that subsequently acceded to GATT. Article XXVI is relevant to the original contracting parties, whereas Article XXXIII establishes the process of accession for countries that are not founding members. The 23 original contracting parties are:

Australia	Lebanon
Belgium	Luxembourg
Brazil	Netherlands
Burma (Myanmar)	New Zealand
Canada	Norway
Ceylon (Sri Lanka)	Pakistan
Chile	Southern Rhodesia (Zimbabwe)
China	Syria
Cuba	South Africa
Czechoslovakia	United Kingdom
France	United States
India	

Article XXX:1 states that amending GATT requires either a two-thirds or unanimous vote of the Contracting Parties, depending on the provision being amended. A two-thirds vote is required to amend Article XXXIII.

GATT Article XXXIII is minimalist in content, and Article XII of the *WTO Agreement* is little more than an echo of the GATT provision. GATT Article XXXIII says that a government that is not a party to GATT (or a government acting on behalf of a separate customs territory that possesses full autonomy in its external commercial relations) can accede to the GATT. That government must do so on terms agreed to between the government and the Contracting Parties. Then, the Contracting Parties must approve a decision in favor of accession by a two-thirds majority. (The minority of existing members that do not want to deal with the new party have the option of non-application under Article XXXV of the GATT and Article XIII of the *WTO Agreement*.) Over time, GATT practice developed to fill in the details unspoken by Article XXXIII.

B. Joining the GATT—WTO System

Conceptually, and in practice, accession is a two-step process. First, a government seeking accession — the applicant — must negotiate bilateral concession agreements with each WTO Member individually that asks the government to do so. Collectively, the Members requesting bilateral agreements are referred to as an "accession Working Party." The bilateral deals embody promises the applicant makes to individual Members about opening the applicant's market to goods and services from those Members. They should not be confused with previously-negotiated deals that the applicant may have made with Members. At issue here are brand new agreements, or at the least, revisions to existing agreements. These new agreements are the price of admission into the GATT—WTO system.

The need for the first step is not apparent from GATT Article XXXIII, which after all speaks of the joint action of the Contracting Parties. Still, it has become indispensable. What Members will ask for bilateral concession agreements? Those members that have a keen export interest in the applicant's market. Therefore, the first step can be a tedious process. For commercially and politically significant applicants like the People's Republic of China (PRC) and Taiwan, many Members are sure to ask for bilateral deals. Roughly 40 WTO Members asked the PRC for bilateral concession agreements (including Australia, Brazil, Canada, Chile, the EU, Hungary, India, Japan, New Zealand, Norway, Switzerland, and the U.S.), and about 26 Members (including Hong Kong and the U.S.) asked Taiwan for such deals. Saudi Arabia, Iran, and Russia are other examples where many existing Members will want bilateral agreements. The bilateral agreements need not be identical — indeed, it is unlikely they will be. The Members will have some common, and some different, export interests. For example, in August 1998 Taiwan completed its bilateral agreement with the U.S. Taiwan offered greater market-opening concessions to American agricultural products (specifically, beef and port innards, and chicken) than it had agreed to in its deals with the EU and Japan.

The second step is the negotiation of a Protocol of accession with all WTO Members, *i.e.*, with the WTO as a whole. (Technically, the Protocol is not the same thing as the decision of the Contracting Parties referred to in GATT Article XXXIII. The decision is taken, and a separate protocol is drafted and approved. Thus, it could be said that accession actually involves three steps: bilateral deals, the decision, and the protocol.) Obviously, the Protocol will not be agreed to unless the first step is accomplished. Why? Because if the demands of several Members for bilateral concession agreements remain unsatisfied, then why would those Members support accession? (To be sure, if only a few Members remain unsatisfied, then they could invoke the non-application provisions of the GATT and *WTO Agreement*.) At the same time, successful completion of the first step is no guarantee that negotiating a protocol of accession will be easy. To make matters even more complicated, the two steps may overlap.

The Protocol represents the terms of entry into the WTO. It is, in effect, a contract between the acceding party and the Members in their joint capacity (the Contracting Parties, in the language of GATT Article XXXIII). As such, it implies the Members in their joint capacity are a separate legal entity under international law. Many of the arrangements made in the bilateral concession agreements become multilateralized through the protocol. In fact, the bilateral deals are incorporated into a schedule of commitments that is sent with the protocol, along with a report from the Working Party, to the WTO General Council for approval.

In addition, the protocol outlines the applicant's current trade laws and policies, and the differences between that regime and the minimum GATT—WTO requirements. The protocol explains how — and when — the applicant intends to correct these differences. Thus, for example, there might be a gap between the applicant's sanitary rules and the *SPS Agreement*, or its copyright laws and the *TRIPs Agreement*. The protocol will identify these problem areas, and set out the agreed plan of action for dealing with them.

Finally, some applicants may want the protocol to indicate their status as a developing, or even least developed, country so as to take advantage of special and differential treatment afforded by many Uruguay Round agreements for such countries. The PRC, for example, argued vociferously — but, ultimately, unsuccessfully — for across-the-board developing country status. Many WTO Members may see this as a ruse to avoid trade obligations for as long as possible. Indeed, as intimated, aside from the problem of status, the question of "when?" often is crucial. Applicants may want to defer the reduction and elimination of tariff and non-tariff barriers for as long as possible. Extant Members are sure to pursue the opposite goal in the Protocol negotiations.

Amidst these negotiations may be a sense of urgency, particularly by the applicant. The longer the negotiations drag on, the more likely the terms of entry will become more onerous. Why? Because the WTO Members will agree among themselves to new trade liberalizing initiatives. For example, suppose a new trade negotiating round commences and results in a major market-opening deal on agriculture. A country that acceded before the new round would have had the opportunity to shape the terms of this deal, and in particular, make sure it can live with those terms. A country seeking accession after the round will be stuck with the deal negotiated by others. Moreover, to use a track-and-field metaphor, "the bar will get raised." Many of the pre-round concessions the applicant made in bilateral negotiations during the first step of the accession process may, after the round, be deemed inadequate. After all, if the new round leads to greater liberalization among the Members, then more will be expected of the applicant.

In the PRC's case, the sense of urgency spilled over to Taiwan. Taiwan was concerned that if it was not a WTO Member by the time a new multilateral trade round (at the time, billed the "Millennium Round") was supposed to have commenced (early 2000), then the concessions it had made in its bilateral agreements would be deemed inadequate by the WTO Members. Taiwan feared it would have no choice but to liberalize more quickly, and risk the shock that import surges would inflict on its economy that rapid liberalization would entail. Taiwan considered the possibility of backing away from its "down payment" market access measures made to the U.S. if it did not gain WTO membership in the near future. After all, why implement these measures on the assumption of imminent accession if that event was far off? There was the "rub." Politically, Taiwan could not become a WTO Member before the PRC. Thus — somewhat ironically — Taiwan was quite eager to see the PRC accede.

This irony suggests that despite the difficulties and complexities, negotiations on bilateral agreements and the protocol ought not to be analogized to a war, or even a non-violent zero-sum game. With respect to most if not all applicants, there is a shared interest among the applicant and the WTO Members that the applicant be brought into the club. That shared interest may spill over to other applicants waiting in the queue, as in the PRC-Taiwan case. As long as an applicant remains outside the WTO, it bears no multilateral trade obligations whatsoever. The applicant is responsible for performing only those requirements it has previously taken on through regional or bilateral trade and investment treaties. Likewise, the WTO Members bear no multilateral obligations to the applicant, and are liable only for the obligations they have previously assumed through a direct deal with the applicant. By joining the WTO, trade relations between the applicant and WTO Members become stabilized in a legal sense. Each side takes on clear, predictable multilateral obligations towards the other that are almost certain to be far more rigorous, in terms of demanding trade liberalization, than any previous bilateral arrangements. Moreover, there is a dispute resolution mechanism to adjudicate alleged breaches. In brief, the two steps ought to be thought of as a positive-sum game.

The benefits of this game extend beyond trade relations. An oft-made (and quite plausible) argument was that the PRC would be a better neighbor in Asia, and a more responsible world citizen, once it was welcomed into the WTO. To delay accession unnecessarily would be to isolate the PRC. It would punish the PRC's burgeoning middle class, the very people most likely to embrace democracy. Then, the PRC might turn inward, its human rights record might worsen, and its hand in Tibet might be all the heavier. It might also become increasingly hostile to the outside world, more inclined to settle matters — like the possible reunification of Taiwan, problems in Hong Kong, or the dispute over the Spratly Islands with several Asian countries — militarily.

A final point about the GATT—WTO accession concerns GATT Article XXVI:5(c). This provision establishes a different procedure for accession for a customs territory that has full autonomy in the conduct of its external commercial relations. That territory can be sponsored for membership by an existing contracting party responsible for the territory. In 1950, Indonesia, sponsored by its former colonial master, the Netherlands, became the first country admitted under this provision. Starting in 1957 and for several years thereafter, several former colonies — Cambodia, Ghana, Laos, Malaysia, and Tunisia, for example — entered into GATT through the sponsorship procedure.

In contrast to Article XXXIII, the Article XXVI:5(c) procedure does not require a series of bilateral concession agreements, decision of the Contracting Parties, or protocol of accession. Rather, the customs territory/newly independent country obtains membership on the same terms and conditions as those accepted by its former colonial master on its behalf. For example, if the Dutch agreed to bind the tariff on imports of wheat into Indonesia at 12 percent, then as a new contracting party, Indonesia would have a tariff schedule with a 12 percent bound rate for wheat. Significantly, Indonesia would not inherit a concession on wheat if the Dutch had made none. As another example, if the sponsoring contracting party elected to non-apply GATT obligations to another party, then the sponsored entity would be deemed to have elected non-application to the same entity. (This scenario occurred with respect to former British colonies sponsored by the United Kingdom. The British had avoided application of GATT to Japan when Japan acceded, and thus so also did the former British colonies.)

Under GATT Article XXVI:5(c) and procedures adopted during a 1957 GATT meeting, there is a period of *de facto* application of GATT obligations on a reciprocal basis between the contracting parties and the customs territory/newly independent country. During the period, the new country can adjust to the obligations, implement necessary trade policies, and decide for sure whether it desires full GATT membership. Assuming it decides affirmatively, then full membership follows after a prescribed reasonable (though sometimes prolonged) period.

C. Enter the Dragon

The PRC became a WTO Member effective 11 December 2001. For the PRC, the accession process took about 15 years, following its application on 10 July 1986 to join GATT. The critical breakthrough came on 15 November 1999, when the PRC and U.S. reached a bilateral agreement. In that bilateral accord, the commitments made by the PRC — and, specifically, then Vice Premier Zhu Rongji, one of China's great modern reformers — were breathtaking. The two sides agreed on a comprehensive package embodied in 250 pages of text (including about 60 pages of tariff schedules), with many hand-written notations that appeared to be last-minute arrangements. The key points of the deal, which later became multilateralized into terms of entry to the WTO, were as follows:

1. *Tariffs*: The PRC agreed to reduce overall tariffs from an average of 22.1 percent to an average of 17 percent. It promised to slash tariffs on industrial goods from the 1997 average of 24.6 percent to 9.4 percent by 2005, with the majority of cuts by 2003. On industrial products considered by the U.S. to be a priority (*i.e.*, in which the U.S. has a keen export interest), the PRC agreed to reduce tariffs to 7.1 percent. The PRC also agreed to participate in the WTO *Information Technology Agreement* (*ITA*), and thereby committed itself to reducing tariffs on computers, computer equipment, semiconductors, and internet-related equipment from 13.3 percent to zero by 2005.

2. *Quotas*: The PRC agreed to eliminate all import quotas on industrial goods by no later than 2005, with most quotas abolished by 2002. For priority American products (*e.g.*, optic fiber cable), the PRC said it would eliminate quotas immediately upon accession. While still in operation, quotas will grow at a 15 percent annual rate to ensure that market access increases progressively.

3. *Agriculture*: The PRC agreed to reduce the overall agricultural tariffs to 17 percent by January 2004 at the latest. This reduction was considerable, as the PRC's tariffs on farm goods ranged from 20 to 50 percent, with an average rate of 31.5 percent. Moreover, on agricultural products considered by the U.S. to be a priority, the PRC agreed to cut tariffs by January 2004 from an average of 31.5 percent to an average of 14.5 percent. These products included beef (with a pre-agreement rate of 45 percent and a post-agreement rate of 12 percent), cheese (with a pre-agreement rate of 50 percent and a post-agreement rate of 12 percent), poultry (with a pre-agreement rate of 20 percent and a post-agreement rate of 10 percent), and wine (with a pre-agreement rate of 65 percent and a post-agreement rate of 12 percent). The PRC also agreed to liberalize purchases of bulk agricultural commodities by establishing TRQs for barley, corn, cotton, rice, and wheat, and phasing out state trading of soy oil. The quota thresholds in these TRQs is to be high and growing, and the applicable tariff for over-quota shipments is to average between 1-3 percent. A share of the TRQs is to be reserved for private traders. (On some items, such as cottonseed oil, peanut oil, soybean oil, and sunflower-seed oil, the PRC agreed to an immediate elimination of TRQs.) More generally, for the first time, the PRC agreed to permit trade in agricultural goods between private parties. Finally, the PRC pledged to eliminate SPS measures not based on scientific evidence.

4. *Automobiles*: The PRC agreed to reduce tariffs on vehicles from 80-100 percent to 25 percent by 1 July 2006, and to make the deepest cuts within the first few years following accession. It pledged to cut tariffs on auto parts by the same date to an average of 10 percent. The U.S. had hoped for a phase-out period that would end by 2005. It agreed to the extra year in exchange for a Chinese pledge to allow foreign non-bank financial institutions to provide automobile financing immediately upon accession. In addition, the PRC agreed to phase out all quotas on auto imports by 2005. Until then, it committed to a base level quota of $6 billion, and to increasing this level by 15 percent annually until the quotas are eliminated.

5. *Trading Rights*: The PRC agreed to grant foreign firms full rights to import and export goods. There will be no need to trade through a Chinese middleman. The PRC said it would phase in these rights over 3 years.

6. *Distribution Rights*: The PRC agreed to grant distribution rights to foreign exporters and manufacturers for both agricultural and industrial goods, whether imported or made in the PRC, within 3 years following accession. The foreign firms will be able to conduct their own distribution networks. In other words, there will be no need for Chinese middlemen. They will be able to maintain wholesale or retail operations, as well as after-sales services (*e.g.*, repair, maintenance, and transport). However, the PRC maintained some limitations on distribution rights. For example, in the first 3 years after accession, foreign oil companies will be limited to 30 gas service stations in the country, thus inhibiting the distribution of their product.

7. *Services Auxiliary to Distribution*: The PRC agreed to phase out all restrictions on services auxiliary to distribution within 3-4 years following accession. Examples of these services included air corridor, freight forwarding, packing, rental and leasing, storage and warehousing, and technical testing and analysis. After the phase-out period, the PRC promised that foreign firms would be able to establish 100 percent wholly-owned subsidiaries to provide these services.

8. *Textiles*: The U.S. agreed to phase out textile quotas by 2005, as the *ATC Agreement* calls for (corresponding to the expiration of the *Multi-Fiber Agreement*), not 2010 as the American textile lobby had hoped. However, the U.S. retains for 12 years (*i.e.*, until 31 December 2008, which is after the *ATC* expired) after the PRC's accession a special safeguard mechanism aimed at preventing textile import surcharges. The remedy was created especially for use against a rapid increase in Chinese textile imports that cause, or threaten to cause, market disruption (namely, material injury) in the U.S.

9. *Dumping*: For purposes of monitoring possible dumping of Chinese goods, the U.S. will continue to treat the PRC as a non-market economy (NME) for 15 years after its accession. Accordingly, when calculating Normal Value in the computation of the dumping margin (the difference between Normal Value and Export Price or Constructed Export Price), the Department of Commerce is likely to use a proxy, Constructed Value. To arrive at a value for Constructed Value, the Commerce Department will look to data from a third country (such as India, Indonesia, or Thailand — or even Paraguay, as occurred in the past). Respondents in antidumping (AD) cases argue this calculation — in particular, the choice of a third country from which to gather data for Constructed Value — is highly arbitrary and skewed toward finding a positive dumping margin. The USTR pointed out that the NME statute is self-limiting: if a particular sector in a foreign economy, or an entire foreign economy, demonstrates it has become market-oriented, then the rules are not applied to that sector.

10. *Subsidies*: The PRC agreed to eliminate all export subsidies. The elimination of these subsidies on cotton and rice was of particular importance to the U.S. In addition, the U.S. reserved the right for the 15 years following the PRC's accession to take into account the special characteristics of the PRC's economy when applying countervailing duty (CVD) law. In particular, in a case involving a newly privatized company, the U.S. could identify and measure the benefit of a subsidy provided to that firm when it was still a state owned enterprise (SOE), and thereby fashion an argument that the benefit carried through to the post-privatization entity. Finally, the PRC accepted the ability of foreign governments to apply the Uruguay Round *Agreement on Subsidies and Countervailing Measures* (*SCM Agreement*) against Chinese SOEs, when appropriate.

11. *Product-Specific Safeguard*: In addition to the normal WTO safeguard mechanism pursuant to GATT Article XIX and the Uruguay Round *Agreement on Safeguards*, American firms will be permitted to avail themselves of a new and special safeguard remedy, known as the Product-Specific Safeguard. This remedy will be designed to address imports of Chinese goods that are a significant cause, or threat, of material injury to a U.S. industry. The remedy differs from a normal safeguard action in two key respects. First, the U.S. will be allowed to apply import restraints unilaterally based on criteria that are less stringent than those in the *Safeguards Agreement*. Second, it permits the PRC to address import surcharges by imposing voluntary restraint agreements (VRAs) (which are otherwise illegal under Article 11:1(b) of the *Agreement*). The Product-Specific Safeguard will remain in force for the first 12 years of the PRC's WTO Membership.

12. *Telecommunications Services*: The PRC agreed to open, within limits, its telecom market to foreign companies and provide them with national treatment. Through these commitments, the PRC agreed to join the WTO *Basic Telecommunications Agreement*. Consequently, the PRC agreed to implement the pro-competitive regulatory principles set forth in the Agreement, like cost-based pricing, inter-connection rights, the establishment of an independent regulatory authority, and technologically-neutral scheduling (*i.e.*, allowing foreign suppliers to choose which technology to use in providing telecom services). As for the market-opening commitments made by the PRC, they covered two broad areas: FDI in the telecom sector, and geographic restrictions on the provision of telecom services. With respect to FDI, the PRC agreed, effective immediately upon accession, to allow foreign companies to take up to a 49 percent stake in JVs engaged in certain telecom services. (Foreign investment in telecommunications had been barred entirely.) After 2 years of membership, they would be permitted a 50 percent stake in JVs providing value-added and paging services. After 5 years, foreign firms could take up to a 49 percent stake in JVs providing mobile voice and data services. After 6 years, they could own up to 49 percent of a JV providing domestic and international services. Thus, the U.S. dropped its insistence that the PRC allow foreign firms a 51 percent equity interest within 4 or 5 years after accession. In return, the U.S. accepted immediate 49 percent stakes, rising to 50 percent stakes with management control within 2 years. The USTR pointed out that under Chinese law, contractual management and operational participation was possible with a 50/50 ownership structure. As regards geographic limitations on the provision of telecom services by foreign firms, the PRC agreed to phase out all such restrictions for paging, value added, and closed user groups in 3 years, mobile voice, cellular, and data services in 5 years, and domestic wireline and international services in 6 years. The PRC agreed to open its most important telecom corridor (the Beijing — Shanghai — Guangzhou region, which represents 75 percent of all traffic in the PRC), immediately upon accession to all telecom services. The PRC also assured the U.S. it would permit foreign firms to provide telecom services via satellite. Finally, it appeared that PRC authorities accepted the fact that production quotas on mobile phones they had planned would be incongruous with GATT— WTO rules, hence the need to abandon the planned quotas.

13. *Internet Services*: Foreign companies will be allowed to invest in Chinese internet content providers, subject to a 49 percent equity limit. Whether existing foreign investments in excess of this limit would be "grandfathered" was not clear, though arguably such investments fell within the scope of a clause providing for the continuation of existing joint ventures (JVs) in all service sectors.

14. *Banking Services*: The PRC agreed that 2 years after it acceded to the WTO, foreign banks would be allowed to conduct local currency business (*e.g.*, deposit-taking and lending) with Chinese enterprises in specified geographical regions. In other words, 2 years after accession, foreign banks will receive qualified national treatment within those regions. Five years after the accession, the customer and geographic restrictions will be lifted: foreign banks will be able to conduct retail business (principally taking deposits from, and making loans to, Chinese individuals) in local currency, and will be able to establish branches anywhere in the PRC. That is, 5 years after accession, foreign banks will have complete national treatment, because they will be able to handle local currency business of any kind, anywhere.

15. *Securities Underwriting Services*: The PRC agreed to permit foreign brokerage firms to operate in the PRC, subject to fairly tight restrictions. Investment by foreign firms in Chinese securities underwriting companies would have to be through a JV, and the foreign stake would be limited to 33 percent. The JVs would receive national treatment in that they could underwrite domestic equity offerings. In addition, they could underwrite and trade in international equity and all corporate and government debt issues. More generally, the PRC pledged that as the scope of business activities of Chinese securities firms grows, there will be concomitant expansion in the permissible scope for foreign JV securities companies.

16. *Fund Management Services*: The PRC agreed to permit foreign fund managers to operate in the PRC, but also subject to fairly tight restrictions. Foreign investment in JV fund management companies will be limited to 33 percent upon the PRC's accession. Three years following accession, the limit will rise to 49 percent. Thus, over time, foreign financial firms receive national treatment, and experience an expansion in the scope of business concomitant with Chinese firms.

17. *Insurance Services*: The PRC agreed to award licenses to foreign insurance companies to do business in the PRC solely on the basis of prudential criteria. It pledged to abandon economic needs tests (*i.e.*, conditioning the grant of a license on the economic needs of the locality in which the foreign firm proposes to do business), and to eliminate quantitative restrictions on the number of licenses it issued. (The economic needs test had been used to protect domestic insurers that were losing money.) With respect to FDI in specific insurance activities, the PRC agreed to grant foreign insurers the right, effective immediately upon WTO accession, to take up to a 50 percent equity stake in local life insurance companies, up to a 51 percent stake in non-life insurance companies, and up to 100 percent in re-insurance companies. (Non-life insurance products include health, pension, property policies.) These JVs would be empowered to insure large-scale risks, and foreign life insurance firms would be allowed to pick their own JV partners. However, their operations would be restricted to key Chinese cities of priority interest to the U.S. during the first 2-3 years following accession, namely, a dozen cities including Shanghai and Guangzhou. Two years after accession, the PRC pledged it would open up a second dozen cities, including Beijing, and permit foreign non-life and re-insurance companies to form wholly-owned subsidiaries. Five years after accession, the PRC would drop all geographic restrictions on licensing, and permit nation-wide branching. Regarding scope of activities, the PRC agreed to allow foreign property and casualty firms to insure large-scale commercial risks nation-wide immediately upon accession. During a 5-year phase in period, the PRC promised to expand the scope of permissible activities of foreign insurance companies to include group, health, and pension products. (Relaxing restrictions on group insurance activities was of particular interest to foreign insurers. Group products account for the largest and most lucrative market segment. Thus, foreign insurers chafed at being limited to selling policies to individuals.) However, whether foreign insurers could offer group plans to companies not based in the same city as the insurer, and whether these insurers could open branch offices, were left unclear. Significantly, the PRC made no commitments on market access for foreign insurance brokers.

18. *Cultural Industries*: The PRC agreed to allow foreign movie companies to distribute significantly more movies than the pre-agreement limit of 10 annually. In the first year following accession, the PRC promised to permit 40 foreign movies to be distributed, and 50 by the third year. However, of the 40 and 50 movies, respectively, allowed in, the PRC said only 20 would be distributed on a revenue-sharing basis. (As for the rest, presumably, foreign movie companies would be paid a flat fee.) The PRC also agreed to allow foreign companies to establish JVs to distribute audio and video recordings, and software entertainment, to own and operate cinemas, and to hold up to 49 percent of the shares of these JVs.

19. *Travel and Tourism Services*: The PRC pledged that immediately upon accession, foreign-owned hotel companies could establish majority-owned hotels in the PRC. There would be no geographic restrictions on operations. Three years after accession, they could set up 100 percent-owned hotels. In addition, the PRC agreed to allow foreign travel operators to provide the full range of travel agency services, and have access to government resorts.

20. *Accounting Services*: The PRC agreed to eliminate its mandatory localization requirement, thereby promising unrestricted access to individuals licensed in the PRC as Certified Public Accountants (CPAs). It pledged to award accounting licenses in a transparent manner and apply national treatment to foreign and Chinese applicants. Foreigners would be allowed majority control of accounting firms.

21. *Legal Services*: Perhaps lawyers did not get the best of deals! The PRC promised to allow foreigners majority control not only of accounting firms, but also of architectural, computer services, dental, engineering, management consultancy, medical, and urban planning firms. But, not so with law. Like many WTO Members, the PRC declined to allow foreigners to hold majority control in local legal practitioner firms.

Impressive as these commitments were, they were only part of the deal. Upon accession, the PRC assumed all of the obligations in the GATT—WTO regime.

For example, it implemented the *TRIMs Agreement*, and thereby eliminated trade and foreign exchange balancing requirements, and local content requirements. It abandoned the practice of conditioning investment approvals on performance requirements, offsets, and the conduct of R&D activities in the PRC. As another example, it implemented the *TRIPs Agreement*, and hence forswore forced technology transfer. Still another example concerns SOEs. The PRC began ensuring SOEs make purchases and sales based solely on commercial considerations (*e.g.*, price, quality, availability, and marketability), and provide foreign firms with the opportunity to compete for contracts on non-discriminatory terms. Significantly, the PRC agreed to the American demand that purchases and sales by SOEs would not be considered "government procurement," and thus would be subject to normal GATT—WTO disciplines. (Were they considered government procurement, the PRC could avoid signing the *Agreement on Government Procurement* — a plurilateral arrangement — and thereby exempt its massive SOE sector.)

President Clinton, whose USTR, Charlene Barshefsky was principally responsible for the 15 November 1999 bilateral accord, characterized it correctly: it was the "most one-sided trade deal in history." On 25 May 2000, the House of Representatives voted narrowly, but decisively, approved permanent normal trade relations (PNTR) for the PRC. The vote was 237-197. On 19 September, the Senate followed suit and approved PNTR legislation by an 83-15 margin. Through these legislative actions, China no longer was subject to annual review of its human rights record under the *Jackson — Vanik Amendment* to the *Trade Act of 1974*, as a condition to get MFN treatment from the U.S.

Thereafter, China reached bilateral agreements with the few key remaining Members that had sought them. Notably, the EU insisted on better market access terms for luxury goods (a European export specialty) and eased terms of entry for large retail stores (such as Carrefour). Mexico proved to be the last hurdle. It was particularly concerned about competition from Chinese products in third country markets, and obtained concessions (*inter alia*) concerning dumping and other trade remedies.

To be sure, now that China is in the WTO, the debate has shifted from entry commitments to full implementation and vigorous enforcement of those terms. Controversies exist in a number of areas, notably, discriminatory taxation, intellectual property protection, SPS measures, subsidization, and foreign bank entry. Currency valuation, and whether China manipulates its currency by artificially linking it to the U.S. dollar at an over-valued rate, thereby discouraging China from importing U.S. goods and contributing to the giant bilateral trade deficit, is a point of contention. Yet, however heated these debates are, two points must be kept in mind.

First, the world is a long way from a "Red" China implacably hostile to the U.S. The countries may be strategic competitors, but they know well the benefits from cooperation and peaceful economic competition. Fighting about pirated music or software, as opposed to pointing weapons and firing real rounds at one another, is a sign of progress. Second, Chinese leaders have embarked resolutely on a course of economic openness and liberalization. In doing so, they have taken a bet that although reform will mean painful adjustments and uneven development, on balance and in the long run, the Chinese people can compete and win in global trade.

D.   Enter the Kingdom

The Kingdom of Saudi Arabia applied to become a GATT contracting party on 13 June 1993. On 9 September 2005, the Kingdom concluded its bilateral accession agreement with the U.S., the last of roughly 40 such agreements. On 28 October, the Working Party finished its work on the accession package, and on 11 November the WTO General Council adopted the terms of accession. The Kingdom, one of the last major economies not in the WTO, became a Member effective 11 December 2005.

In reviewing the key terms of entry for the Kingdom, below, consider the extent to which China's terms had raised the bar:

1. *Application of Agreements*: The Kingdom will apply the WTO agreements throughout its territory, including immediately the *SPS* and *TRIPs Agreements*.

2. *Market Access for Goods*: The Kingdom will have an average bound tariff level of 12.4 and 10.5 percent for agricultural and non-agricultural products, respectively, by the end of a 10-year implementation period. Most tariff rates, namely, 92.6 percent, are set at the final bound rate as of the date of accession. For the remaining rates, the remaining final bound levels will be implemented in 2008, 2010, or 2015. Final bound individual agricultural tariffs will range from 5-200 percent, with the highest rates on dates and tobacco products. For non-agricultural products, 11 percent will be duty free, and the highest tariff will be on iron, steel, and wood products.

3. *Forbidden Products*: The Kingdom will invoke the GATT Article XX(a) public morality exception to ban entry into the Kingdom of products forbidden by Islamic Law. Such goods are alcohol, pork, pork items, and pornography.

4. *List of Banned Items*: The Kingdom will review, at least once a year, of its list of banned imports, and removal from that list of merchandise the importation of which would not compromise the legitimate objectives of the Kingdom.

5. *Non-Tariff Barriers*: The Kingdom will eliminate all non-tariff barriers inconsistent with WTO rules.

6. *Banking Services*: The Kingdom will permit the commercial presence of foreign banks through a branch of an international bank, or through a locally-incorporated joint stock company, with a 60 percent equity cap on foreign participation in a joint venture. Foreign banks can establish branches in the Kingdom. Only commercial banks may offer financial services, though non-commercial banking financial institutions can provide asset management and advice.

7. *Insurance Services*: The Kingdom will permit commercial presence of foreign insurance companies through a direct branch of a foreign insurer, or through a locally incorporated cooperative insurance joint stock company, in which the foreign equity cap will be 60 percent. Extant foreign insurers have three years following accession to convert to either a direct branch or a Saudi cooperative insurance company, during which time they may continue their operations, and offer new products and services. However, *Shari'a* proscriptions on acceptable insurance products (*takaful*) must be respected.

8. *Telecommunications Services*: Within three years of accession, the Kingdom will permit up to 70 percent foreign equity ownership in the telecommunications sector, specifically, for both basic and value-added telecom services. However, a joint stock company must provide public telecom services.

9. *Distribution Services*: During a 3-year phase out period, the Kingdom will phase out most restrictions on the distribution of goods within its territory.

10. *Fees*: The Kingdom will review, within 2 years of accession, of a fee it charges for authenticating trade documents, to bring this fee into conformity with WTO rules.

11. *Foreign Direct Investment (FDI)*: The Kingdom agreed to broad opening to FDI, based on a Negative List approach (whereby all sectors are open save for those specifically listed), excluding a few key sectors such as upstream petroleum activities.

Consider the Chinese and Saudi accession terms in studying other country case studies, including Russia and Vietnam (which became a WTO Member on 11 January 2007).

VI. CHANGING THE RULES

A. Reservations

Is it possible for a new or existing WTO Member to file a "reservation" to the *WTO Agreement* or its Annexes? That is, could a Member simply declare it will not be bound by certain provisions? After all, reservations are contemplated in the *Vienna Convention on the Law of Treaties*. Moreover, when a country accedes to the WTO, typically it negotiates "reservations," in the form of terms and conditions for entry, in its protocol of accession.

Nevertheless, upon entry, and as regards existing Members, the general answer is "no." Article XVI:5 of the *WTO Agreement* prohibits reservations to that *Agreement*, and permits reservations to a provision in a specific multilateral accord only to the extent allowed for by that accord. Joining and participating in the GATT—WTO regime is, indeed, a single undertaking.

B. Amendments

Multilateral trade rules must be rigorous, but also afford some flexibility. Rigidity in a legal system is likely to lead for the ossification of that system, or a revolution against it. Thus, GATT and the WTO Agreement allow for amendment of their rules. However, as a threshold matter, what is the relationship between GATT Articles XXV:5 and XXX? That is, what is the difference between a waiver from a multilateral trade law obligation, and an amendment of that obligation?

To ask the question is to reveal the answer. In theory, a waiver is a request a WTO Member makes to be relieved from a GATT—WTO obligation. The relief applies only to that Member, and typically just for a short term. It is not a generalized, permanent lessening of an obligation, which would require an amendment. That is, an amendment applies to all Members, or a large portion thereof (*e.g.*, least developed countries), and represents a permanent, or at least long-term, alteration of the obligation. Also, it might be urged a waiver never involves a new obligation, only removal of an existing one.

In practice, however, this distinction may not be so obvious. A Member could request a waiver that is worded in a sufficiently generic manner so as to accommodate other Members, so long as they satisfy the criteria set forth in the waiver. For instance, a waiver for the European Union (EU) to give preferences to over 70 of its former colonies in the African, Caribbean, and Pacific (ACP) countries arguably is tantamount to an amendment. (Nonetheless, the EU gets waivers periodically for ACP preferences.) Moreover, what about waiver criteria, *i.e.*, the terms and conditions to be satisfied in order to get relief from the obligation? Suppose they include notice and reporting requirements, consultation procedures, or economic or financial ratio tests. (Criteria in the first two categories indeed have been set forth in waivers.) Might these criteria constitute new obligations, are they nothing more than requirements tied to the waiver?

Delineating waivers from amendments is important. While the WTO Ministerial Conference is the ultimate decision maker in either instance, the criteria for decision making vary. For example, if there is no consensus on a proposed amendment, then the Ministerial Conference decides by a two-thirds majority whether to submit the amendment to the Members for acceptance. There is no such hurdle on waiver decisions — they are made directly, without the need of a prior decision as to whether to submit the waiver request to the Members. As another example, Article X of the *WTO Agreement* contains a number of details unique to the amendment process. More importantly, in some instances proposed amendments require unanimity.

GATT Article XXX:1 mandates that all contracting parties accept a proposed amendment to Part I of GATT before that proposal takes effect. Part I of GATT contains the first two of the four pillars, *i.e.*, the MFN and tariff binding obligations in GATT Articles I and II, respectively. All other GATT provisions (including the national treatment obligation of Article III, the transparency provisions of Article X, and rule against quantitative restrictions in Article XI) can be amended upon a two-thirds vote of the contracting parties. Article X:2 of the *WTO Agreement* supplements these thresholds. It indicates unanimity of acceptance is necessary not only for proposed changes to GATT Articles I and II, but also for proposed changes to Article IX of the *WTO Agreement* (concerning WTO decision making, including decisions about waivers), Article II:1 of *GATS* (concerning MFN treatment), and Article 4 of the *TRIPs Agreement* (concerning MFN treatment for IPR protection). Likewise, Article X:8 supplements the thresholds in GATT. It mandates that amendments to the *DSU* require consensus.

A proposed amendment to a GATT provision outside of Part I, or to a WTO accord other than the particular aforementioned provisions, takes effect upon acceptance by two-thirds of the WTO Members. (*See* GATT Article XXX:1 and *WTO Agreement* Article X:3.) However, if that amendment affects the substantive rights and obligations of the Members, then it becomes effective only for those Members that accepted the proposal. For the one-third or fewer Members that did not, the substantive amendment is inapplicable unless and until they accept it. Why?

No doubt protection of sovereign interests of the non-approving Members in the face of possible tyranny of the majority is the heart of the answer. Every Member should be allowed to decide whether to incur new obligations, and not have them foisted upon itself by a majority. In contrast, procedural amendments take effect for the entire membership upon acceptance by the two-thirds super-majority. Who decides whether an amendment does or does not affect substantive rights and obligations? The Ministerial Conference, by a three-quarters vote.

Conceivably, the Members approving the amendment might find it so fundamentally important that any non-accepting Member must consider withdrawal from the GATT, or remain as a Member only with the consent of the Ministerial Conference. GATT Article XXX:2 and Article X:3 provide for this instance. Withdrawal is provided for in GATT Article XXXI and WTO Agreement Article XV, and takes effect 6 months after providing notice of that withdrawal. Finally, observe that any WTO Member can propose the Ministerial Conference make an amendment. In addition, each of the Councils of the General Council — the Goods, Services, and TRIPs Council — may submit amendment proposals for the agreements it oversees.

C. Rectifying Tariff Schedules

Evidently, amending a provision of the GATT—WTO regime is difficult, and rightfully so. However, in at least one instance, it is necessary to "get amendments through" quickly and with ease, namely, technical corrections to tariff schedules. Given the thousands of product lines and corresponding numbers, descriptions, and tariff rates, it is inevitable that mistakes will be made in virtually every Member's schedule. The Ministerial Conference would grind to a halt if the amendment process of GATT Article XXX and *WTO Agreement* Article X had to be used for every such correction. Yet, it could be argued that the formal amendment process was required, because GATT Article II:7 makes tariff schedules "an integral part of Part I" of the GATT, hence unanimity would be required for every amendment no matter how minor.

Fortunately, a certification process developed during the pre-Uruguay Round era and continues in use. A minor technical correction — or, in GATT-speak, "non-substantive rectification" — is accepted automatically by all contracting parties so long as they are given notice and raise no objections. On 19 November 1968, the Contracting Parties decided to establish the "Procedures for Modification and Rectification of Schedules." It states a certification not challenged by any contracting party within 60 days' notice of that certification shall take effect. This *Decision* is consistent with customary international law on correction of errors of a purely formal nature in treaties.

Chapter 3

THE DOHA ROUND: LAUNCH AMIDST SCHISMS (NOVEMBER 2001-AUGUST 2004)

[T]he surest path to greater wealth is greater trade.

> —President George W. Bush, Speech to United Nations General Assembly, 14 September 2005.

DOCUMENTS SUPPLEMENT ASSIGNMENT

Ministerial Declaration launching the Doha Round (Doha, Qatar, November 2001)

I. THE SCHISMATIC ENVIRONMENT

A. Categories of Members

The Ministerial Conference in Doha, the capital of Qatar, was the fourth such meeting of the senior-most trade officials from WTO Members. Pursuant to Article IV:1 of the of the *Agreement Establishing the World Trade Organization* (*WTO Agreement*), the Conferences are held at least once every two years. The Ministerial Conference is the highest decision-making body of the WTO, and its composition bespeaks an institutional hallmark, namely, the WTO is Member-driven. Forceful as the personality of a particular Director-General may be, real power lies with the Members, not the head of the WTO Secretariat. Consider the timing and duration of the Conferences, and the principal results for each one is remembered.

As was true in September 1986 in Punta del Este, Uruguay, when the Uruguay Round began, in November 2001 in Doha, when the Doha Round was launched, tariff negotiations were not the primary impulse. Rather, to simplify, there were two catalysts. At Doha, agriculture-exporting countries, particularly among developing and least developed WTO Members, wanted developed countries, especially the U.S., EU, and Japan, to eliminate export subsidies for agricultural products. Conversely, developed countries, which tend to be net exporters of services, sought enhanced market access for their service providers, such as commercial and investment banks, insurance companies, architecture and engineering firms, health care professionals, and (of course!) lawyers.

These catalysts bespeak distinctions among countries that appeared at least as early as the Tokyo Round. The distinctions became chasms during and after the Uruguay Round, and continued through the Doha Round. "Developed" countries are not all like minded. The U.S. and EU are strategic competitors in trade as they are allies. Australia and New Zealand incline toward more pro-free trade positions on agriculture than do Japan or Korea. Moreover, some developed countries have underdeveloped regions in them. In brief, the "First World" is not a monolith.

The "Third World" is not monolithic either. The label "less developed country" (LDC), used through the Tokyo Round, suffices only as a general rubric to capture all "poor" countries. However, "LDC" is a veil over the line between "developing" and "least developed" countries. What is a "developing" versus "least developed" country? Developing countries are self-identified as such. According to socioeconomic criteria, including the famous "dollar a day" standard (*i.e.*, a *per capita* Gross Domestic Product (GDP) or one U.S. dollar a day or less), the United Nations classifies about 50 countries as "least developed." Among them, roughly 41 are WTO Members, several are in the process of acceding to the WTO, and one (Burma) is an original GATT contracting party.

B. Breakdown of the Uruguay Round Grand Bargain?

For developing and least developed countries, the Grand Bargain of the Uruguay Round had broken down. Some suspected they had been hoodwinked. They expected more dramatic reductions of domestic agriculture support, and an end to agriculture export subsidies, pursuant to the WTO *Agreement on Agriculture*. This expectation may have been unrealistic, particularly in light of the many detailed exceptions in that *Agreement* — for example, for Blue Box domestic support (*i.e.*, production set-aside schemes), the exemption of food aid and export credits from the meaning of export subsidies, and the lack of an adamantine commitment to eliminate export subsidies.

Moreover, consider the extent to which developing and least developed countries could take advantage of Uruguay Round opportunities — or, for that matter, of potential benefits from any Round. India is a case in point. With a decrepit physical infrastructure, including road and port facilities, to what degree can Indian farmers or manufacturers seize upon lower tariff and non-tariff barriers abroad? With erratic power supplies, what choice do Indian food processing factories have but to shut down episodically, or incur costs of self-generation power (which erodes their labor and materials cost advantages)?

Brazil affords another illustration. For years under military dictatorship, Brazil constrained its own agricultural sector. It focused on industrial development, using agriculture for resources for this development, and inexpensive food for its growing urban populace. The government set prices (and guaranteed minimum prices to producers), controlled quantities that could be exported, and taxed exports. For instance, it subjected cotton to an export quota to ensure steady, cheap supply to the textile and apparel (T&A) industry. In the late 1970s, farmers and ranchers began migrating from the traditional breadbasket area of the country, the south (*e.g.*, the state of *Mato Grosso do Sul*), to the savannah areas of the center-west, where land is comparatively cheaper. Only in the 1990s, following the dictatorship period, did Brazil abolish the official restrictions, and cut subsidies. Agriculture now accounts for 8.8 percent of Brazil's GDP, but (unlike the usual pattern in other countries) this share is not falling as development in other sectors proceeds.

Agriculture accounts for 40 percent of Brazil's exports, and a huge percentage of its trade surpluses. It is the world's largest exporter of beef, coffee, orange juice, and sugar, and a major participant in world markets for pork, poultry, and soya. Still, Brazil faces infrastructural and other challenges. Only 10 percent of its roads are paved (the figure in Argentina is 29 percent), and its railway network is poor. Some farmers in the south reportedly use genetically modified (GM) soya seeds smuggled from Argentina. Some ranchers in the north allegedly hire laborers from questionable contractors, known as *gatos*, resulting in labor rights violations.

Following the Uruguay Round, poor country advocates produced empirical and case study research on what they alleged were devastating effects of that Round, especially the *Agreement on Agriculture*. For instance, in December 2005, the Forum for Biotechnology & Food Security in New Delhi, India published *Trade Liberalization in Agriculture: Lessons from the First 10 Years of the WTO*.

In this Report, lead author Devinder Sharma and his colleagues examine the experiences of many developing and least developed countries:

1. From 1986-96, *i.e.*, throughout the Uruguay Round period, government spending on agriculture by developing countries fell by roughly 50 percent.

2. Freer trade in agriculture since the Uruguay Round has had negative repercussions for poor countries, essentially creating a new, global farming system that undermines food security in these countries.

3. Specific adverse impacts include (1) surges in imports of staple foods, (2) price depression in domestic agricultural markets, (3) bankruptcies and impoverishment of local farmers, (4) takeovers of small farms by large enterprises (*i.e.*, corporate farming), (5) a shift from producing essential crops to growing cash crops for export, (6) chronic hunger for billions of rural inhabitants, who no longer grow their own food and lack purchasing power to buy food, and (7) environmental degradation caused by developed country farmers, who farm intensively a single crop (often getting a subsidy to do so) rather than engage in crop diversification.

To be sure, the authors are not dispassionate, questioning the intention as well as the effects of agricultural trade liberalization. They indicate the free trade paradigm aims to discourage poor countries from growing staple foods and commercially important commodities like cotton and sugar.

The Indian Report contains provocative recommendations. First, there should be a "Multilateral Agreement Against Hunger" that enshrines a right to food. This right would be primary in all farm trade negotiations, and enhance food security in developing and least developing countries. Second, these countries should be allowed to protect themselves against floods or surges of cheap farm products. Protective actions should include hiking tariffs, imposing quantitative restrictions, and using special safeguard measures. Third, agricultural subsidies should be re-categorized into two boxes — support benefiting small farmers, and support for large agricultural firms and land owners.

In reflecting on the Grand Bargain of the Uruguay Round, developing and least developed countries consider non-agricultural sectors as well. Notably, they study the effects on their T&A industries from the end of the global quota scheme associated with the 1974 *MFA*. The gist of the WTO *Agreement on Textiles and Clothing (ATC)* was a "suicide" (or, the better characterization may be "murder") clause whereby as of 31 December 2004 *MFA* quotas were phased out. Large T&A manufacturing countries like China and India made smaller ones like Bangladesh and Sri Lanka worry foreign garment companies would consolidate their operations in the larger countries. These manufacturers no longer needed to source products from many different locations to conform to the global quota scheme. Free from the distorted incentives of this scheme, they could make as much as they needed in any country. Certainly, the smaller countries had a decade (from the entry into force of the *ATC*, on 1 January 1995, to the final phase out of *MFA* quotas) to figure out how to cope, adjust to a more competitive global clothing trade, and commence diversification into other sectors. The leaders in these countries did not all use the time equally wisely. Still, the adjustment costs in the T&A industries of these countries meant real, human suffering, often for millions of young women working in these industries.

For their part, developed countries are not entirely happy with the outcome of the Grand Bargain. Non-agricultural market access (NAMA) matters both to their beleaguered rust-belt industries and sophisticated manufacturing sectors. These countries seek sought better market access for their service providers, and look for improved concession offers under the *General Agreement on Trade in Services (GATS)*. They demand improved intellectual property (IP) protection and enforcement in the Third World. A number of other issues concern them, and — depending on the precise question — cut across simplistic "First World" and "Third World" categories.

Among these issues are clarifying antidumping (AD) and countervailing duty (CVD) disciplines, delineating the relationship between multilateral agreements on the environment and WTO accords, reforms to the dispute settlement system, resolving at least some of the issues from the 1996 WTO Ministerial Conference in Singapore (the "Singapore Issues," namely, competition policy, customs facilitation, foreign direct investment, transparency in government procurement), and enhancing legal capacity and the rule of law in developing and least developed countries. To clarify or complicate matters (depending on one's side of the debate), some academics push for multilateral trade talks to address substantive authority over a wide array of non-trade or trade-related topics, and in effect become a global governance institution.

II. THE NOVEMBER 2001 DOHA DEVELOPMENT AGENDA

What is astonishing — and heartening — is that less than two months after 9/11, the WTO Members gathered in the heart of the Persian Gulf, in Doha. After much hard and late-night bargaining at this Ministerial Conference, and urged on by the forceful leadership of the WTO Director-General, Mike Moore, the Members agreed to a "Doha Development Agenda" (DDA). Agreement in November 2001 on this Agenda formally launched the Doha Round.

The essential elements of the DDA are as follows. In studying them, as well as negotiating proposals and outcomes, consider a key thematic problem of the Doha Round. Where, and to what extent, is "Development" manifest?

A.   Agricultural Subsidies

Members agreed to negotiations on "reductions of, with a view to phasing out, all forms of export subsidies" for farm products and "substantial reductions in trade-distorting domestic" support schemes, but "without prejudging the outcome" of these talks, and taking into account the need for special and differential treatment for under-developed countries.

B.   Industrial Products

Members agreed to negotiations to eliminate or cut tariff and non-tariff barriers, including tariff spikes (*i.e.*, peaks) on sensitive exports like textiles and apparel (T&A), which are of importance to poor countries. Reduction obligations need not be reciprocal, to allow special and differential treatment for Third World countries.

C.   Services

Members agreed to continue negotiations on (1) market access for financial, telecommunication, and transport services, and (2) easing of immigration rules for employing workers on temporary contracts.

D.   Trade Remedies

In the *Ministerial Declaration* (¶ 28), Members agreed to negotiations on "clarifying and improving disciplines" on AD and CVD rules (including fishing subsidies) as set forth in the Uruguay Round *Antidumping Agreement* and *Agreement on Subsidies and Countervailing Measures* (*SCM Agreement*), while "preserving the basic concepts, principles and effectiveness of these *Agreements* and their instruments and objectives. . . ." The meaning of "instruments" is not entirely clear. The U.S. took the position it refers to trade remedy laws of Members (*e.g.*, U.S. AD and CVD rules). Moreover, the U.S. insisted on disciplines against dumping and illegal subsidization, as distinct from restraints on remedial measures to combat these unfair trade practices.

E.   Regional Trade Agreements (RTAs)

Members agreed to negotiations on "clarifying and improving disciplines and procedures" on free trade agreements (FTAs) and customs unions (CUs).

F.   Electronic Commerce

Members extended until the Fifth Ministerial Conference (September 2003) a ban (initially imposed at the Second Ministerial Conference in Geneva in 1998) on imposing tariffs on certain kinds of electronic commerce.

G. Intellectual Property

Members adopted a *Declaration* that developing countries will be immune from challenge under the Uruguay Round *Agreement on Trade Related Aspects of Intellectual Property Rights* (*TRIPS*) if they seek to obtain medical supplies via compulsory licensing in order to meet a public health crisis. The *Declaration* provides: "*The TRIPS Agreement* does not and should not prevent Members from taking measures to protect public health," and should be understood and enforced in a way "supportive of WTO Members' right to protect public health and, in particular, to promote access to medicines for all."

H. Geographic Indications

Members agreed to discuss protection for geographical indications of certain foods (namely, cheese, ham, rice, and yogurt), and establish a global system for registering and notifying geographical indications on wines and spirits, with the possibility of extending the system to cover other items.

I. Special and Differential Treatment on Subsidies

Members agreed to requests for extension of the period for phasing out export and import substitution subsidies under Article 27:4 of the *SCM Agreement*.

J. The Four "Singapore Issues"

These four issues are foreign direct investment (FDI), trade and competition policy, trade facilitation (*i.e.*, simplifying customs procedures), and transparency in government procurement. Preparatory work to continue under WTO Working Groups established at the First Ministerial Conference in Singapore in 1996. Negotiations on Singapore issues were deferred until after the Fifth Ministerial Conference in 2003, and then only if an "explicit consensus" existed to start. (Any Member could block commencement — an assurance sought at Doha by India, and gained through a statement by the Conference Chairman, Qatar's Youssef Kamal.) Such talks would deal with technical assistance for, and capacity-building in, developing countries.

K. Environment

Members agreed to negotiations on the (1) relationship between WTO obligations and multilateral environmental agreements (MEAs) (*e.g.*, between *TRIPs* and the U.N. *Convention on Biodiversity*, or between WTO obligations and *Cartagena Bio-safety Protocol for Genetically Modified Organisms*), (2) information exchange between the WTO and MEA Secretariats, and (3) reduction of trade barriers to environmentally-friendly goods and services. Whether to discuss eco-labeling and other "green" matters was deferred until the Fifth Ministerial Conference in 2003, but no formal action then.

L. Fishing Subsidies and the Environment

Fish provide 2.6 billion people (many in poor countries) with 20 percent or more of their total animal protein intake. Fish are one of the most traded commodities in the world. Of total world fish production, exports account for 38 percent. The value of fish exports for developing countries ($20.4 billion in 2004) is notably higher than any other commodity, including rice and coffee. Commercial trade in fish products is a $56 billion business (annually, as of 2005). Yet, fishing is a case in point of the interaction between subsidies and the environment. The U.S., along with other Members such as Argentina, Australia, Chile, Ecuador, Iceland, New Zealand, and Peru, worry about the sustainability of this trade. The United Nations Food and Agriculture Organization (FAO) reports (as of 2005) that 75 percent of the fishing stocks in the world are over-exploited, fully exploited, depleted, or recovering from depletion. Government subsidies for the fisheries sector aggregate globally to $30-34 billion per year, with the Japan, the EU, and China being the top three subsidizers. Two-thirds of subsidies support activities that promote over-fishing. That is, 20-25 percent of the value of the commercial fishing trade (*i.e.*, $10-15 billion) is subsidized. In brief, government funds to the fishing industry not only contribute to resource exhaustion, but also wreak havoc on marine ecosystems. The Members agreed to consider ways to eliminate subsidy schemes that cause over-fishing or over-capacity in the fisheries sector. Notably, the U.S. (in May 2007) proposed all WTO Members eliminate subsidies that promote over-capacity.

By design, negotiations on all items were conducted as a single undertaking. No accord on any issue could be final until agreement occurred on all other matters.

III. OPEN ISSUES

The DDA skipped key details of how to liberalize trade in agricultural and industrial products. WTO Members proclaimed terrorism would not stop the launch of a new round to promote global capitalism. They professed faith in peace and prosperity that can come from increased trade. Yet, they failed to chalk out how to proceed.

For example, the Members agreed there ought to be a ban on taxing e-commerce. That ban applies to digitized goods, *i.e.*, goods like printed materials, software, music, films, and video games that could be shipped physically, but are transmitted across the internet. However, assuming many such goods are shipped in digitized form, the top 10 potential losers of tax revenue from this ban, other than the EU (the largest loser in dollar terms of foregone customs duties), Canada (6th), and Israel (10th), would be developing countries: India (2nd); Mexico (3rd); Malaysia (4th), Brazil (5th), China (7th), Morocco (8th), and Argentina (9th). How might such countries address this situation?

By no means was e-commerce the only example of an issue left open from the November 2001 Doha Ministerial Conference. Other significant topics were:

- Intellectual Property and Compulsory Licensing

- Intellectual Property and Generic Imports
- Export Subsidy Phase Outs
- Dispute Settlement Reform

In studying the Doha Round, and the particular topic areas of IP, subsidies, and the *DSU*, consider whether, and the extent to which, these issues were resolved.

In sum, the DDA was both ambitious and ambiguous from the outset. Lest there was any doubt about the difficulties in the road following the November 2001 meeting in Qatar, consider the post-Doha remark of Director-General Moore: "We're setting ourselves up for a difficult fifth ministerial." His prognostication proved spot on correct.

IV. THE SEPTEMBER 2003 COLLAPSE IN CANCÚN

The next major stop on the Doha Round road was the Fifth Ministerial Conference in September 2003, held in Cancún, Mexico. Little progress was made after the Doha Ministerial Conference, as political leaders focused their attention on the War on Terror and its expansion, in March 2003, to Iraq. Accordingly, a successful outcome from the Cancún Conference would do much to advance the Doha Round.

Yet, the groundwork needed for success simply had not been done. Essentially, the Cancún Ministerial Conference collapsed over three main problems. Each is addressed in turn below.

A. Singapore Issues

Led by Brazil and India, several developing countries — whose numbers fluctuated around 20-22, and known alternatively as the "G-20," "G-21," or "G-22" — opposed the EU with respect to Singapore Issues. Developing countries firmly opposed any negotiations on two of them, FDI liberalization and trade and competition policy. Ultimately, the EU abandoned efforts to bring these two issues into the Doha Round.

B. Agriculture

The G-22 opposed efforts led by the U.S. to improve access to their markets for agricultural products without significant cuts in domestic farm subsidies in developed countries, and an end to farm export subsidies provided by those countries. The WTO Members failed to meet a 31 March 2003 deadline for agreement on modalities for agriculture tariff cuts, thereby reducing the likelihood of progress in Cancún. Some Members were counting on others to make offers, and fashioning their own offers in anticipation thereof. Offers might be balanced in a cross-sectoral manner.

Hypothetically, in the run up to the Cancún Conference, New Zealand might have hoped for an offer from Korea on agricultural products. But, if New Zealand did not table an offer on services sector liberalization, then Korea might not make an agricultural trade offer. If neither Member is willing to go first, progress stalls. In turn, a positive outcome at the Conference is jeopardized, because the ground work for a deal has not been laid.

That is precisely what happened. The parameters of an overall deal, which require careful calculations and considerable time before a Ministerial Conference, especially when multiple sectors are at play, did not exist on the eve of the Cancún Conference. At the Conference, the negotiators lacked the time, and many did not have the inclination, to fix the problem. Following the Conference, they continued to breach many Doha Round negotiation deadlines, on agricultural and non-agricultural matters.

C. Services

The initial deadline for tabling offers to liberalize services trade was 1 June 2002. WTO Members failed to meet it, as well as new deadlines, such as 31 March 2003, 1 January 2005, and 31 July 2006. As offers came in during 2003, it was apparent few Members were willing to provide new, commercially meaningful market access. Most proposals simply pledged to bind in the proposing Member's service schedule its existing practices. For example, going into the Doha Round, India had scheduled commitments in 20 percent of all service areas in which a binding liberalization commitment theoretically could be made.[1] Its Doha Round offer increased that figure to just 24 percent. Brazil's offer was of even poorer quality. It offered to increase the scope of its bindings from 10 to 13 percent of total possible liberalization commitments that could be made. By contrast, going into the Round, the U.S. Services Schedule embodied bound commitments on 58 percent of potential coverage.

It proved especially difficult for least developed countries to provide timely, commercially meaningful offers. How fast, and how extensively, to liberalize services trade are technical complexity questions — more so than freeing goods trade. Such countries typically lack domestic legal capacity to negotiate effectively on services matters. After all, there are four different modes of supply and domestic regulatory concerns (discussed in a later Chapter), plus a domestic constituency — which fears foreign competition — to match each services sector and sub-sector.

In some respects, the lack of progress in Cancún on *GATS* issues was emblematic of the deep North — South divide in the WTO. Before the Conference, the EU requested 72 poor countries, including 14 of the 41 least-developed WTO Member countries, to liberalize their regimes for water services. The requests suited the commercial interests of the EU, which boasts leading water service providers such as RWE/Thomas, Suez, and Vivendi. It also was consistent with calls by the World Bank, in the 2002 *World Development Report*, for poor countries to privatize water and environmental services, including provision of potable water. Many poor countries viewed the EU requests, and World Bank advice, as a trap to avoid. Once a country privatizes these services, they become subject to possible *GATS* commitments, and that country comes under significant pressure from the EU to grant European companies market access. Yet, the empirical record emerging from some

---

[1] *See* Daniel Pruzin, *Industry Warns of Impact on Services Talks of Failed Attempt on Farm, NAMA Modalities*, 23 INT'L TRADE REP. (BNA) 1091, 1092 (20 July 2006).

countries and sectors — such as Uganda and water services — suggests privatization and liberalization of water services had disastrous effects on poor people. Efficiency calculations and projections notwithstanding, many Ugandans got reduced access to potable water, and at increased prices.

To be sure, it is simplistic to characterize hesitancy or outright opposition to services trade liberalization at the Cancún Conference as only a rich versus poor issue. Lack of negotiating ambition was a point transcending, to some degree, the rich-poor gap. Requests and offers to open up services markets were not comprehensive. For instance, there were requests on financial services, including health insurance, and on professional services such as dentistry, medicine, nursing, and midwifery. But (as of the spring 2003, as the WTO observed), in the health services sector category, there were no requests.

Overall, there were many dialogues on services at the Conference in which Members heard, but did not listen to, one another. An ideological divide, cutting across the relative wealth of nations, was the common discursive feature. On one side were trade officials who truly believe in the logic of services privatization and progressive liberalization of services trade. On the other side were counterparts who see the logic as a recipe to sell off to corrupt elites valuable state assets, and to carve up of their countries for profit-driven foreign providers. To what extent does this divide remain, and why?

With these issues unresolved, the Cancún Conference ended up with more than well publicized, enthusiastic backslapping and hugs among G-22 delegates (for having blocked the Round), and increased rancor between developed and developing countries (with each group accusing the other of sabotage). The Conference closed — hours before scheduled, an unusual occurrence in trade talks, which typically exhaust or exceed a deadline — with bitter acrimony between two hegemonic powers, the U.S. and EU.

The latter schism is intriguing. At a critical juncture in the Cancún Conference, the U.S. evidently decided to side with the EU and not make serious agricultural trade concessions to the G-20. The U.S. alienated the vast majority of the WTO Members by appearing to oppose developing and least developed country farm interests. In the run-up to the Conference, Oxfam U.K. published a damning report — *Rigged Rules and Double Standards* (2003) — chronicling effects on Third World farmers of U.S. and EU subsidies. Media stories abounded about deleterious repercussions of U.S. cotton subsidies for poor farmers in West African countries — farmers who happened to be Muslim, but who had not yet fallen to extremist tendencies. Oxfam pointed out that from 2001-03, the "Cotton Four" countries — Benin, Burkina Faso, Chad, and Mali — had lost about U.S. 400 million because of America selling subsidized cotton on the world market. Links to global health concerns and the spread of the HIV/AIDS virus were drawn, as policy makers and observers noted some Third World farmers driven off the land by First World agricultural barriers and subsidies became lorry drivers, spreading the virus the length and breadth of their countries if they visit infected prostitutes on their routes.

Had the U.S. failed to see the link between its farm policies and long term-national security and health care risks? Or, had it chosen a short-term, expedient path, namely, avoid alienating the EU in return for EU support, in the United Nations Security Council and other venues, for American-led military operations in Iraq and Afghanistan?

V. THE AUGUST 2004 *FRAMEWORK AGREEMENT*

In the spring and summer 2004, it was by no means certain the Doha Round would succeed, but certain it would not be completed by the initial target of year-end 2005. On 16 July, the Director-General, Dr. Supachai Panitchpakdi of Thailand, and the Chairman of the WTO General Council, Shotaro Oshima of Japan, issued a first draft for a structure to continue the Round. At the end of July 2004, after a week of hard bargaining in Geneva, WTO Members transformed this draft into a 17-page document setting out a road map for the remaining talks. The document on which they agreed, the *"Framework Agreement,"* highlighted the pivotal role of agricultural issues.

A. Agriculture and Development

Nearly half of the *Framework Agreement* deals with these issues, and that portion is called the "Framework for Establishing Modalities in Agriculture." As for the balance of the *Agreement*, it addresses industrial tariffs and an assortment of other topics. Why does the *Agreement* give such extensive coverage to agricultural issues? The question is all the more poignant when two facts are considered: agriculture and food processing comprise roughly 10 percent of world merchandise trade, and less than 4 percent of total world GDP. An easy answer is food is special. It affects every person every day.

A second response concerns food security. The aim of self-sufficiency, even net food exporter status, has been articulated by major developing countries, including China (especially under Chairman Mao Zedong), India (especially under Prime Minister Indira Gandhi), and Pakistan (under various military and civilian rulers). This aim also is of consequence to developed countries. In the wake of deprivations during and following the Second World War, food security was a founding principle of the EU's Common Agricultural Policy (CAP). In Japan, too, food security matters.[2] In a February 2007 report, the Japanese Ministry of Agriculture, Forestry, and Fisheries (MAFF) said abolition of farm tariff and non-tariff barriers would do more than cause a 2 percent decline in GDP, and lead to job losses of 3.75 million workers (5.5 percent of the total labor force). Farm trade liberalization also would reduce Japan's food self-sufficiency from 30 to 10 percent. To be sure, "food security" need not mean complete "self-sufficiency." But, do most notions of the concept mitigate against mutual interdependence, and in favor of farm trade barriers for some measure of self-reliance?

A third reason for the focus of the *Framework Agreement* on agricultural issues is their inherent complexity and technical detail. Markets for primary and processed commodities are among the most distorted in the global economy. In other words, the focus on agriculture in the *Agreement* partly

---

[2] *See Farm Trade Liberalization in Japan to Cost Jobs, Trim Domestic Output, MAFF Estimate Says,* 24 Int'l Trade Rep. (BNA) 310 (1 March 2007).

reflects the simple fact farm trade barriers and subsidies are high. In 2001, the trade-weighted average tariff for agricultural products was over three times the average for merchandise trade. The weighted average bound (*i.e.*, maximum) agricultural tariff rate among Members is 27 percent, while the actual (*i.e.*, applied) agricultural tariff rate is 14 percent. Thus, most WTO Members have considerable room to raise applied tariffs up to bound levels. Conversely, a substantial reduction in those levels is needed if the outcome is to be lower imposed tariffs. About $200 billion of agricultural subsidies are disbursed each year, which equals 15 percent of total world agricultural output (roughly $1.2 trillion). The U.S. and EU each account for one-third, and Japan just below 15 percent, of total world agricultural subsidies.

A fourth answer considers the term "Development" in the rubric for the Round, "Doha Development Agenda." For developed countries, agriculture accounts for just 1.5 to 2 percent of GDP (though GDP in those countries is huge). In the U.S., agriculture accounts for about 1 percent of GDP, and employs about 1 percent of the population. For these countries, Doha Round talks on agriculture involve policy issues about managing adjustment costs and multi-functionality. By contrast, for developing and least developed countries, the share of agriculture in domestic output is far higher than single digit percentages. Over 70 percent of the poor in developing countries live in rural areas. To deal with agriculture through the *Framework Agreement* is to deal directly with the livelihoods of most of the poor in most poor countries. India is a case in point, with 20 percent of its GDP and 60 percent of its people engaged in farming.

Ghana is another example. Agriculture accounts for 30-40 percent of its GDP, and 60 percent of the workforce depends on this sector. Cocoa is the main cash crop. Ghana is the second largest exporter of cocoa in the world (following Côte d'Ivoire), and 40 percent of its export revenues come from cocoa. Yet, 35 percent of its farmers are poor, operating at subsistence. They rely on rain, and only 5 percent of the land in Ghana that could be irrigated actually is. Each year, 1 percent of Ghana's GDP is lost to soil erosion. The government has technical advisors to help, but its budget permits just 1 agricultural agent per 1,300 farms. Tragically, with a decrepit physical and marketing infrastructure, a storage facility shortage, Ghana wastes 30-40 percent of its farm output every year.

Thus, for many farmers and related businesses in poor countries, Doha Round outcomes on agriculture could tip the balance between modest hope for prosperity and depressing confinement to poverty. For net food importing countries, the outcomes raise a long-term concern about food security.

B.   Re-Thinking the Grand Bargain

Possibly the most persuasive reason the August 2004 *Framework Agreement* dwelt on agricultural issues was widespread perception among WTO Members that on those issues, more than any other, the Uruguay Round Grand Bargain had been broken. Members questioned whether they benefited, even in a net sense, from the Bargain. Developing and least-developed countries, and some developed countries (*e.g.*, Canada) complained that self-proclaimed free trading nations were hypocritical on agricultural trade matters. Some developed countries retained high average agricultural import tariffs. The EU average farm tariff (as of March 2007), for instance, was 23 percent.[3] To be sure, there was some hypocrisy in the developing country position. India imposed duties and taxes, in addition to tariffs, on certain non-staples that led to ridiculously high effective rates. Because of add-on levies on wine and spirits, India's true tariff on those products rose from 100 and 150 percent, respectively, to nearly 500 percent.

Worse yet, from a poor country perspective, developed nations stymied the substantial market access gains anticipated in the wake of the Uruguay Round *Agreement on Agriculture*. They limited agricultural imports by maintaining Byzantine rules on the allocation of quotas, imposing technical barriers, deploying sanitary and phytosanitary standards (SPS) for protective (rather than scientific) purposes, filing trade remedy actions against foreign products, entering into RTA preferences, and — of course — not slashing subsidies. For instance, though they experienced benefits from the Uruguay Round, the Canadian beef and pork sectors complained they were victimized by complex administrative rules in the EU, and safeguard actions and SPS measures in Japan.

Not surprisingly, with differing interests, and with differing views of the outcome of the Grand Bargain, WTO Members pursue divergent agricultural policies. For instance, East and South Asian countries tend to protect their farmers through traditional devices, and have the highest agricultural tariffs in the world. In 2001, India, Japan, Korea, Taiwan, Thailand, and Vietnam were in this group, with the average agricultural tariff in each country exceeding 30 percent. (China had been in this group before its WTO accession in December 2001, but its terms of entry called for significant agricultural tariff cuts.) Such developing and least developed countries feel threatened by competition — not only in third countries, but in their own domestic markets — from agri-business in North America and, increasingly, in the EU.

Conversely, the *European Free Trade Association (EFTA)*, the members of which are Iceland, Liechtenstein, Norway, and Switzerland, and EU, and U.S., tend to rely relatively less on tariffs to protect their farmers. At 2.4 percent (in 2001), average U.S. agricultural tariffs are nearly the lowest in the world. Agricultural tariffs among *EFTA* countries, as well as the EU, average 13.9 percent. Instead, developed countries help their farmers with subsidies. Measured as a percentage of total agricultural output (in 2001), *EFTA* countries have the highest subsidy rates in the world. They subsidize the equivalent of between 83 and 140 percent of their overall agricultural production. Measured as a percentage of total agricultural output, the U.S., EU, and Japan spend similar sums on domestic farm support — about 37 percent. But, the EU relies far more than the U.S. on "Amber Box" subsidies (discussed below), which are the most trade-distorting form of support (save for export subsidies). About 50 percent of EU subsidies ($44.7 billion annually) are Amber Box. Only about 20 percent of U.S. support ($14.4 billion in 2001) is in this Box, with 70 percent ($50.67 billion) in the non-trade distorting

---

[3] *See* Vir Singh, *EU's Farm Commissioner Asks India, U.S. to Make Firm Commitments in Doha Round*, 24 INT'L TRADE REP. (BNA) 334-35 (8 March 2007).

category called the "Green Box." Green Box programs include agricultural research, certain types of direct payments to farmers (namely, support decoupled from the amount or type of crop grown), disaster relief, disease control, domestic food aid, environmental protection, infrastructure support, regional assistance, and restructuring aid.

When starting positions in any negotiation are based on divergent policy paradigms, which in turn are supported by domestic constituencies with entrenched interests, reaching consensus is a Herculean task. With different tools for agricultural protection predominating in different WTO Members, by August 2004, positions in the Doha Round talks on how to lower trade barriers were predictable. Spokespersons for developing countries, like South African President Thabo Mbeki, called on the U.S. and EU to end domestic farm subsidies within three years, and agricultural export subsidies within five years. Developed countries pushed developing countries to improve market access for foreign agricultural products by slashing tariffs and quotas. The Round stalled.

VI. THE IMPACT OF U.S. PRESIDENTIAL TRADE NEGOTIATING AUTHORITY

A. The Commerce Clause

With their many, deep schisms, WTO Members were deadlocked as they approached the sixth Ministerial Conference in Hong Kong in December 2005. They downplayed expectations about results they could achieve, urging a basic agreement on modalities would be a success. Perhaps substantive results would be had in 2006. After all, trade talks often go "down to the wire," and the deadline was 30 June 2007, when the authority of the U.S. President to negotiate trade agreements, under the *Trade Promotion Authority (TPA)* legislation of 2002 (19 U.S.C. §§ 3801-3813), would expire.

Every minute counted. To make matters more difficult, technically, the real deadline was midnight Eastern Standard Time (EST) on 31 March 2007. That was because of a *TPA* requirement the President notify Congress 90 days before expiry of negotiating authority he will submit to it a deal under *TPA* procedures. Negotiators for the *Korea — United States Free Trade Agreement*, known as *KORUS*, beat this deadline by 25 minutes, with Korean and American officials signing an accord just before noon on 1 April 2007 in Seoul. The 30th of March fell on a Friday, and negotiators worked the weekend, essentially getting the benefit of an extra 24 hours — Saturday, the 31st, plus the time zone difference between Washington, D.C., and Seoul. Doha Round negotiators were not so lucky. They failed to show notable progress to meet the 90 day notice rule.

Under the Commerce Clause — Article I, Section 3, Clause 8 of the U.S. Constitution — Congress has the power to regulate foreign trade. It delegates this authority, subject to the delegation doctrine, to the President. The authority is bounded by a time limit, and by negotiating objectives. Typically, multilateral trade rounds last at least as long as this time limit. In exchange for accepting the boundaries and objectives set by Congress, the President receives a commitment — manifest in the legislation delegating authority, such as *TPA* — that Congress will consider any negotiating outcome under special procedural rules.

The key such rule is an "up-or-down vote" on a proposed trade deal, without any amendment to that agreement. The prospect of Congress amending a carefully crafted, delicately balanced multilateral trade deal would undermine the President's negotiating credibility with other WTO Members, hence the bargain with Congress in *TPA*-type legislation. During the Uruguay Round, Congress extended the authority — originally granted in 1988, and lapsing in 1991 — for two years, until 15 December 1993. On that date, negotiations actually finished. Yet, the bipartisan consensus in favor of multilateral trade negotiations, which existed for most of the post-Second World War era, degenerated during and after the Uruguay Round. In the late 1990s, President Bill Clinton failed to win renewal of trade negotiating authority, then called "Fast Track," after two attempts. (In 1997, the attempts were Senate Bill 1269 and House Resolution 2621. In 1998, the attempt was Senate bill 2400.) After a lapse, in 2002, President George W. Bush secured *TPA*, but only by one vote. In brief, no American President — and thus no WTO Member — can rest assured Congress will grant trade negotiating authority.

Thus, without a Doha Round deal by the *TPA* expiry date, the President would have to persuade Congress to extend *TPA*. That could prove difficult, if the vote on the *Central American Free Trade Agreement* (*CAFTA*) was prologue. This deal passed on 30 June 2005 in the Senate by a 54-45 vote, but cleared the House of Representatives on 28 July 2005 by a 217-215 vote. The *CAFTA* battle left many House Democrats embittered. They perceived President George W. Bush failed to consult with them on *CAFTA* terms. For them, the protection of worker rights was a key term. They believed the President surrendered strong worker rights provisions (meeting the standards of the International Labor Organization (ILO)), to which Central American countries were willing to adhere, in exchange for a "stand still" commitment to enforce effectively their existing labor laws. And, in November 2006, the Democrats took control of both chambers of Congress.

Pro-labor advocates argued (*inter alia*) *TPA* renewal should be granted only if the core text of an FTA contain an obligation to adopt and enforce ILO standards. The Bush Administration, and many Republican legislators, worried that kind of obligation could be used to challenge U.S. labor laws. They called for a safe harbor exemption. Of course, as the AFL-CIO rightly intoned, a meaningful duty with a large exemption for the U.S. would be blatantly hypocritical. By April 2007, opposition to *TPA* renewal had significant momentum. A coalition of 713 environmental, farm, and labor groups — 102 of them national organizations, and 611 from states and localities — signed a letter to leaders in the U.S. Senate and House of Representatives. The letter stated that even if Democratic Party proposals for enhanced environmental and labor rights, and investor protections, were incorporated into a new *TPA* bill, the fast-track procedure was too broken to be fixed. The legislature of the State of Maine reinforced the message, unanimously adopting (in April 2007) a resolution (SP 649), spearheaded by the Maine Fair Trade Campaign, opposing *TPA* as an undemocratic, exclusive, inside-the-Beltway device yielding bad trade bargains.

This momentum produced a change in presumption. U.S. and foreign trade negotiators had assumed they must finish a deal before *TPA* expired, and notify Congress of one by 31 March 2007. Now, it seemed *TPA* would not be renewed unless they first reached a deal, or clear draft accord, which Congress could accept. That is, the mentality changed from "we need to beat the deadline" to "we need to prove why our negotiating mandate should be renewed." In accord with this shift, in April 2007, at a New Delhi, India meeting of the Group of Four (*i.e.*, WTO G-4 in the WTO, Brazil, India, the EU, and U.S.), negotiators agreed to try to show results in the Doha Round by year-end 2007.

B. The May 2007 Agreement between Congress and the President

In May 2007, after much rhetorical bluster and hard negotiations, a deal was struck, not on *TPA*, but a possible precursor to its renewal.[4] Democrats, in control of Congress following the November 2006 elections, agreed to consider passage of bilateral FTAs negotiated with Panama and Peru — but not necessarily Colombia or Korea. Republicans agreed that henceforth, all trade agreements must include in their core text the following terms:

1. A commitment by each FTA party to "adopt, maintain, and enforce" in its domestic law the 5 ILO core labor standards set out in the 1998 ILO *Declaration on Fundamental Principles and Rights at Work*, namely, the (1) freedom of association (including the right to organize), (2) right to bargain collectively, (3) elimination of all forms of compulsory (*i.e.*, forced) labor, (4) effective abolition of child labor, and (5) elimination of employment and occupational discrimination.

2. Authorization for an FTA party to condition central or sub-central government procurement contracts on adherence to the ILO *Declaration*.

3. A commitment by each FTA party to "adopt, implement, and enforce" in its domestic laws the obligations contained in 7 major multilateral environmental agreements (MEAs), including the *Convention on International Trade in Endangered Species* (*CITIES*) and *International Whaling Convention* (*IWC*).

4. Enforcement of labor and environmental obligations through government (but not private party) action under FTA dispute settlement provisions, with the burden of proof on the complaining government to show the respondent has engaged in a "sustained or recurring course of action or inaction" (*i.e.*, a persistent pattern of violation) in respect of a labor or environmental obligation, which has an impact on trade or investment.

---

[4] *See* Rossella Brevetti, *Democratic, GOP Lawmakers Reach Agreement with Administration on FTAs*, 24 INT'L TRADE REP. (BNA) 674-75 (17 May 2007); Rossella Brevetti, *Administration Drafting Legal Text for Labor/Environment Deal with Congress*, 24 INT'L TRADE REP. (BNA) 675-76 (17 May 2007); Rossella Brevetti, *AFL-CIO, USW Give Cool Response to Labor Deal on FTAs; Teamsters Opposed*, 24 INT'L TRADE REP. (BNA) 676-77 (17 May 2007).

5. A prohibition against an FTA party using inadequate resources, or alternative priorities, as a defense in a case in which it is accused of failing to enforce labor laws relating to the ILO *Declaration*.

6. A conflict of laws provision that bars an FTA party from using as a defense an FTA provision to undermine MEA obligations, in a case in which an MEA affects performance of an FTA obligation.

7. A prohibition against any FTA party lowering labor or environmental laws.

8. Use of penalties for violations of labor or environmental obligations that are the same as for breaches of other FTA duties.

9. Allowance for faster access to generic medicines, especially for poor countries that are parties to an FTA, essentially by (1) modifying data exclusivity period (*i.e.*, the period during which the manufacturer of a generic drug is barred from using clinical test data from the innovating company) to 5 years in most cases (with expiration of the period in an FTA party at the same time as in the U.S., if the period already commenced), (2) ensuring data exclusivity rules do not prevent a party from taking a measure to protect public health, or invoke WTO authorizations, (3) eliminating any requirement that a drug regulatory agency withhold approval of a generic until it certifies marketing of the generic would not violate any existing patent, and (4) removing any rules that obligate an FTA party to extend the term of a patent on a pharmaceutical product to account to delays in the process of approving the patent.

10. Clarification the U.S. has full authority to bar a foreign company from operating an American port, based on national security concerns, and exercise of this authority may not be challenged under the FTA.

Without doubt, the May 2007 deal among Democratic and Republican legislators, and the White House, evinced the declining authority of the U.S. President in setting the trade policy agenda, and concomitant reassertion by Congress of its Constitutional duty to regulate foreign trade.

Indubitably, too, the deal heralded a critical shift from the approach to labor and environmental issues taken in the 1990s and at the turn of the Millennium, as manifest in the *North American Free Trade Agreement* (*NAFTA*) and other U.S. FTAs. Express invocation of the ILO *Declaration* and MEAs, and preclusion of certain defenses, are substantive differences — at least on paper. Query, whether the deal could be a "Trojan Horse"? Might international labor or environmental rules, beyond obligations specifically mentioned, creep into FTAs? Apparently eager to avoid incremental importation of other rules, the U.S. urged the only obligation concerned the ILO *Declaration* (and, presumably, the referenced MEAs), and that it was in full compliance.

Note, finally, the deal includes a Strategic Worker Assistance and Training (SWAT) Initiative. SWAT extends beyond Trade Adjustment Assistance (TAA), to encourage education, training, and portability of health and pension benefits for entire communities injured by the effects not only of trade liberalization, but also technology. This encouragement was not enough to bring major American labor unions to support either FTAs or Doha Round talks. The AFL-CIO, United Steel Workers of America (USW), and Teamsters expressed alarm at job outsourcing associated with trade liberalization, and skepticism about the extent to which enhanced labor provisions would improve meaningfully the lives of workers abroad.

Chapter 4

THE DOHA ROUND: INTRICATE NEGOTIATIONS AND RESULTS (AUGUST 2004-DECEMBER 2007)

You who believe, do not wrongfully consume each other's wealth but trade by mutual consent.

> —The Qur'an, Surah 4, Ayat 29 (M.A.S. Abdel Haleem, trans., 2004)

DOCUMENTS SUPPLEMENT ASSIGNMENT

Ministerial Declaration launching the Doha Round (Doha, Qatar, November 2001)

I. THE DEADLOCK ON AGRICULTURAL ISSUES

A. The October 2005 Portman Proposal, EU Counter-Proposal, G-10 and G-20 Plans

A theme of the WTO *Agreement on Agriculture*, negotiated in the 1986-94 Uruguay Round, is farm trade liberalization should occur in three ways: reduction of tariffs, domestic support (with such support categorized into "Boxes"), and export subsidies. This theme continued in the Doha Round. Yet, on many issues, notably agriculture, the August 2004 *Framework Agreement* for the Doha Round lacked detail. That fact reflected a truism observed by *The Economist*:

> Dismantling subsidy systems and cutting farm tariffs is not easy, given farmers' well-honed political tactics and many countries' sentimental attachment to the idea of food security. Like all disarmament negotiations, however, it is made easier if the great powers are willing to lay down some of their arms.[1]

A new WTO Director-General, Pascal Lamy, who took office in September 2005, and a rising chorus of business interests, called upon Members to fill in details and thereby progress toward successful completion of the Round.

Non-governmental organizations (NGOs), and some WTO Members, vociferously opposed further trade liberalization — each with its own justification. Some practicing and academic lawyers began to question whether the WTO system, or at least the method of multilateral trade negotiations, was dysfunctional. Was the WTO becoming as administratively inflexible and politically

---

[1] *To Doha's Rescue*, THE ECONOMIST, 15 Oct. 2005, at 13.

77

polarized as the United Nations? Thus, a depressingly familiar pattern of efforts at progress obfuscated by, even deliberately entangled with, public posturing set in for the latter half of 2004 and first half of 2005. Some WTO Members offered proposals as much for their theatrical value as trade liberalization purposes. For instance, in September 2005, President George W. Bush offered to cut all agricultural subsidies, but only if the other WTO Members did so, too. Whether Congress would agree to termination of all subsidies was dubious, even if the condition were met. Whether the rest of the world could or would agree was still more dubious. The EU Trade Commissioner, Peter Mandelson, said the offer amounted to "playing to the gallery."

However, in the fall and winter 2005, leading up to the December 2005 Hong Kong Ministerial Conference, at least some WTO Members seriously pursued consensus on details left open by the *Framework Agreement*. The most significant development came in October 2005, when the U.S. made an ambitious proposal to break the deadlock on agricultural issues. Ambassador Rob Portman, the United States Trade Representative (USTR), revealed the proposal in an article he authored in the *Financial Times*.[2] The Proposal represented a modification in American negotiating strategy. Until it was unveiled, the U.S. had insisted it would make deep cuts in agricultural subsidies only if other WTO Members indicated first what reductions they would make to import tariffs and other agricultural trade barriers. As USTR Portman rightly observed, in playing its hand first, the U.S. was "taking a risk." Of course, the risk was calculated. Immediately, the Proposal achieved what no doubt it was designed, in part, to do — make the EU look like the obstructionist in the Doha Round, and split EU states.

EU Trade Commissioner Peter Mandelson managed to respond quickly — on 28 October 2005 — to the Portman Proposal. Yet, reactions to the EU Counter-Proposal were critical. The Brazilian Foreign Minister said there had been "no clear movement by the Europeans on market access," and the Indian Commerce Minister said the EU's tariff suggestions were "more restrictive" than the Portman Proposal.[3] Recriminations flew within the EU. France charged the EU Counter-Proposal exceeded "red lines" on beef, butter, poultry, sugar, and tomatoes. The French Agriculture Minister, Dominique Bussereau, garnered the signatures of Italy, Ireland, Spain, plus 10 other of the 25 EU states, on a memo demanding the EU consult with them before tabling any agriculture concessions, so that national officials in each EU state could scrutinize a prospective offer for its economic and social consequences. One EU trade official observed:

> The EU is trying to present itself as a happy family of 25 member states, driving forward a trade agenda with clearly established priorities. But on agriculture we now seem to have very different visions of the future for European farmers and sometimes sound as if we are on the verge of a real divorce, especially between Britain and France.[4]

---

[2] *See* Rob Portman, *America's Proposal to Kickstart the Doha Trade Talks*, FINANCIAL TIMES, 10 Oct. 2005, at 15.

[3] Daniel Pruzin, *EU Tweaks WTO Farm Subsidy Proposal, Offers 70 Percent Cut in Amber Box Support*, 22 INT'L TRADE REP. (BNA) 1648, 1649 (13 Oct. 2005).

[4] *Small Countries Hope U.S. and EU Clash Will Spark Trade Reform*, FINANCIAL TIMES, 10 Oct. 2005, at 4.

Despite his fractious constituency, Commissioner Mandelson rebuffed the French efforts, saying pre-clearance of every offer by each EU country "would stop the Doha Talks in their tracks," as the EU negotiating team would be weakened fatally, having to bargain simultaneously with EU member states and the rest of the world.[5]

The Portman and EU plans catalyzed movement by other WTO Members. The Group of 10 (G-10) countries offered ideas, as did the Group of 20 (G-20) developing countries. The G-10 includes Iceland, Israel, Japan, Korea, Liechtenstein, Mauritius, Norway, Switzerland, and Taiwan. The G-20, an outgrowth from the September 2003 Cancún Ministerial Conference, includes Argentina, Bolivia, Brazil, Chile, China, Cuba, Egypt, Guatemala, India, Indonesia, Mexico, Nigeria, Pakistan, Paraguay, Philippines, South Africa, Tanzania, Thailand, Uruguay, Venezuela, and Zimbabwe.

Below, features of the Portman Proposal, EU Counter-Proposal, and G-10 and G-20 Plans are set out. Of the offers, the Portman Proposal and EU Counter-Proposal were the most comprehensive, while the G-10 and G-20 Plans left some topics unaddressed.

B. Tariff Reductions

Tariffs are the most obvious border measure restricting movement of farm products. The U.S., EU, G-10, and G-20 offered competing ideas to enhance agricultural market access by cutting tariffs. The Portman Proposal called for reductions in three 5-year stages using a non-linear formula developed by Brazil, India, and others in the G-20. In the first stage, from 2008-13, there would be steep tariff cuts, ranging from 55 to 90 percent. Developed countries with the highest tariffs would make cuts at the higher end of the range. Table 4-1 sets out the progressive, tired approach of the Proposal, as well as the EU Counter-Proposal. The overall average tariff cut would be 75 percent. (Australia made a similarly aggressive offer, also with a 75 percent average cut.)

Anytime a plan for an average tariff cut is tabled, its details, and the nature of the sponsor's tariff schedule, must be examined. A cut to average tariffs, without further disciplines, may not be ambitious in terms of affording new market access. For example, suppose a country agrees to a 50 percent average tariff cut.[6] Suppose, too, it has two tariffs levels — one at 100 percent and one at 1 percent. The country could implement a 50 percent average tariff cut by eliminating the 1 percent tariff, which is a trivial, nuisance duty anyway with no protective effect. It could retain the 100 percent duty. The country could argue it slashed its average tariff by 50 percent: while it did not reduce the 100 percent duty, it eliminated the 1 percent duty. Moving from 1 to 0 percent is a 100 percent cut, and averaged across two tariff levels (100 and 1 percent), the result is a 50 percent overall average cut. This argument is disingenuous, if not specious. The country's post-cut duty rates are 100 and 0 percent, for a 50 percent average. The pre-cut rates were 100 and 1 percent, for 50.5 percent average. The average rate has fallen by 0.5 percent.

---

[5] Raphael Minder & Edward Alden, *French Bid to Curb Mandelson Farm Cuts Rejected*, FINANCIAL TIMES, 19 Oct. 2005, at 2.

[6] *See Sharing Bodily Warmth*, THE ECONOMIST, 27 Jan. 2007, at 75.

TABLE 4-1:
**PROPOSED AGRICULTURAL TARIFF CUTS — PORTMAN PROPOSAL
AND EU COUNTER-PROPOSAL**

Portman Proposal: Existing Bound Tariff Rate Band	Portman Proposal: Cut Required to Bound Tariff	EU Counter-Proposal: Existing Bound Tariff Rate Band	EU Counter-Proposal: Cut Required to Bound Tariff
Between 1 and 19%	55-66% cut	Between 0 and 30% Developing countries permitted a one-third higher band	20% (linear) Developing countries obliged to cut by two-thirds of this amount, *i.e.*, by 13.33%
Between 20 and 39%	65-75% cut	Between 30 and 60 % Developing countries permitted a one-third higher band.	30 %(linear) Developing countries obliged to cut by two-thirds of this amount, *i.e.*, by 20%.
Between 40 and 59%	75-85% cut	Between 60 and 90% Developing countries permitted a one-third higher band	40% (linear) Developing countries obliged to cut by two-thirds of this amount, *i.e.*, by 26.67%
Over 60%	85-90% cut, with maximum tariff of 75%	Over 90%	50 percent (linear), with cap of 100 percent tariff Developing countries permitted a tariff cap of 150%

Under the Portman Proposal, the actual obligatory tariff cut would depend on the extant rate. A higher cut would be required of a tariff at the high end of the band, a lower cut on the lower end, and a medium cut to a tariff in the middle of the band. For example, in the 20-40 percent band, a tariff of 39 percent (the high end of the band) would be slashed by 75 percent, a tariff of 21 percent (the low end) cut by 65 percent, and a tariff of 30 percent (the mid-point) decreased by 70 percent. Requiring disproportionately large cuts from high-tariff countries, such as the EU and Japan, yields less tariff dispersion among WTO Members. The Proposal also called for developing countries to impose a ceiling of 100 percent on their farm tariffs.

The second stage, 2013-2018, laid out by the Portman Proposal would be a five-year *interregnum*, from 2013-2018. During this stage, WTO Members would pause to evaluate the effects of the cuts made in the first stage. In the third stage, from 2018-23, agricultural tariffs would be eliminated entirely. There would be a narrow scope for alternative treatment, *i.e.*, an exemption from deep tariff cuts, for sensitive products. Significantly, no more than 1 percent of the tariff "lines" in the Harmonized Tariff Schedule (HTS) of a Member could be classified as "sensitive." (The term "line" refers to a product category in the HTS designated by a 6 digit classification.) The 1 percent limit would exclude HTS lines at which the bound rate is zero. Obviously, the larger the limit, the greater the extent to which market access commitments are undermined. World Bank research indicated that if just 2 percent of products are spared from tariff cuts, then 75 percent of the benefits of the cuts is eliminated.

The EU could not match the Portman Proposal. The EU Counter-Proposal was for up to a 50 percent reduction in developed country farm tariffs (though some accounts put the steepest cuts at 60 percent). As Table 4-1 shows, it was more complex than the U.S. offer, calling for tiered reductions and special and differential treatment for developing countries. The Counter-Proposal also was less ambitious than Uruguay Round terms in the *Agreement on Agriculture*.

During the Uruguay Round, each developed country committed to an average 36 percent decrease in its agricultural tariff rates. The EU Counter-Proposal would oblige developed countries (including the EU) to cut their tariffs by an average of 38 (or by some accounts, 39) percent, and developing countries to do so by 25 (or by some accounts, 24.5) percent.[7] That hardly was better than the previous Round. It also was manifestly less than demands on the EU by the U.S. and G-20, which, respectively, called for an average EU farm tariff cut of 66 and 54 percent. Observe the U.S. would cut its tariffs by a lesser amount than the EU, because its initial point is lower — the average EU farm tariff exceeds 30 percent, while the U.S. average is 12 percent.

By the EU's calculation, the average cut in its Counter-Proposal is 46 percent, and the resultant average EU farm tariff falls to 12 percent. By January 2007, Commissioner Mandelson claimed the EU might sweeten its farm tariff cut offer from an average of 39 percent to nearly 54 percent — though a majority of EU Agricultural Commissioners rebuked him for doing so, saying he exceeded his negotiating mandate from the EU states.[8] Whatever the precise average cuts, the Proposals did not intersect.

Complicating matters for the EU was a February 2007 WTO study of the Common Agricultural Policy (CAP) highlighting embarrassing facts.[9] First, the average EU farm tariff jumped from 16.5 percent in 2004 to 18.6 percent in 2006 (largely because of a hike in non-*ad valorem* tariffs, *i.e.*, tariffs imposed

---

[7] *See, e.g., France Opposes More Farm Cuts*, FINANCIAL TIMES, 12 Jan. 2007, at 5.

[8] *See* Alan Beattie, *Ministers Inject Fresh Life into Doha Trade Talks*, FINANCIAL TIMES, 29 Jan. 2007, at 3.

[9] *See* Daniel Pruzin, *WTO Report Criticizes EU Barriers to Farm Imports Despite CAP Reforms*, 24 INT'L TRADE REP. (BNA) 260 (22 Feb. 2007).

by the EU without reference to the value of a farm product import, but rather on a volume basis, such as per kilo). Second, the EU has extraordinary tariff spikes — 428 percent on some processed food products, and average MFN tariffs of 55 percent on cereals, 40 percent on sugar, and 25 meat products. Third, the EU increased the number of farm tariff lines subject to tariff rate quotas from 89 in 2003 to 91 in 2006, though the average fill rate (*i.e.*, the amount of actual in-quota imports compared to the quota threshold) was 62 percent (in 2002).

The EU Counter-Proposal envisioned a larger list of sensitive products than the Portman Proposal — 8 percent of tariff lines, meaning exemption for 160 of the EU's 2,000 HTS lines of farm products. Fully 7 percent of these lines had tariffs of more than 100 percent. To be sure, 8 percent was an improvement over earlier EU offers, which designated as "sensitive" 20 percent, *i.e.*, 400 tariff lines. Moreover, in July 2006, the U.S. and EU narrowed the gap. The U.S. said it could accept a cap on sensitive product designations of 3-4 percent of tariff lines, up from its initial position of 1 percent. The EU said it could drop the cap from 8 to 4-5 percent.

However, the EU did not clarify the proportion of aggregate agricultural import value on its sensitive products list. That fact is indispensable to gauge the commercial significance of exemptions. At the same time, the EU called for minimum reductions on tariffs on sensitive products — a minimum 5 percent cut to tariffs on these products between 0-30 percent, 10 percent on tariffs between 30-60 percent, 15 percent on tariffs between 60-90 percent, and 20 percent on tariffs over 90 percent.

In fairness to the EU, its Counter-Proposal manifest two climb-downs by Brussels. First, at negotiations in Paris in September 2005, the EU called for less ambitious cuts than the Counter-Proposal. Its Paris offer was for an average tariff cut of 24.5 to 36.4 percent, across four bands, with a 60 percent cut on the highest tariffs.

Second, the EU abandoned its insistence on a "pivot." The term refers to in-built flexibility when lowering tariffs. A WTO Member can make a less-than-average cut on a particular product in a given band, especially a product that Member designates as "sensitive." In the Paris talks, the EU called for a pivot of 5-10 percent from the agreed tariff cuts. The number of products declared "sensitive" would depend on the tariff cut and pivot. For a given pivot, the higher the cut, the larger the number of products designated as "sensitive." For example, said the EU, an average tariff cut of 26.4 percent, with a pivot of ± 10 percent, would mean designating 162 products "sensitive." A cut of 24.5 percent, with a ± 10 percent pivot, would mean 152 products were "sensitive." A linear cut of 36.4 percent, with no pivot, would mean nearly 400 products were "sensitive."

Unsurprisingly, the U.S. opposed the pivot. The U.S. said it would inject ambiguity, complexity, and uncertainty into market access liberalization, and give the EU an additional layer of protection for sensitive products. The G-20 developing countries agreed with the U.S. But, some G-10 countries embraced the pivot in their plan.

Dropping the pivot, and reducing sensitive products to 8 percent of tariff lines, deeply divided the EU. The French Foreign Trade Minister, Christine

Lagarde, accused the European Commission of exceeding its negotiating mandate agreed in 2003 by EU member states. The French Interior Minister, Nicolas Sarkozy, said in responding to the Portman Proposal, Commissioner Mandelson, had accepted a "fool's bargain."[10] He described sectors such as beef, butter, dairy, sugar, and tomatoes as "strategic."[11] The Agriculture Ministers of Austria, Belgium, Czech Republic, Cyprus, Finland, France, Greece, Hungary, Iceland, Italy, Lithuania, Luxembourg, Poland, and Spain signed a protest letter accusing the Commission of jeopardizing market balances and the reforms to the CAP agreed to in June 2003, which set payments to EU farmers until 2013.[12]

Certainly, it was widely understood that the EU could not continue a strategy of free trade within and protectionism without. It no longer had the economic or political power to dictate terms of trade. Still, protecting the CAP was a crucial goal for some EU states — even if the risk were scuppering the Doha Round. They recalled June 2003 CAP reforms, which lowered Blue Box subsidies.

Under the CAP, farmers traditionally have been guaranteed an "intervention price" for their product (if the world market price was below that price). They also were guaranteed production payments (*i.e.*, funds to produce a certain amount of crop output or livestock head), which were Blue Box subsidies (because they were linked to output). The reforms entailed cutting intervention prices, and reducing Blue Box subsidies by de-coupling payments from production (*i.e.*, de-linking payment of a subsidy, and the amount of the payment, from crop yields or livestock head). The EU committed to replacing existing schemes with less trade distorting direct income subsidies not linked to output. That is, the EU declared it would end price and output-linked supports with a single payment scheme to subsidize directly the income of its farmers.

However, the speed with which the EU is phasing out old schemes and phasing in new subsidies differs from one product to another. De-coupling is an uneven process, slow for some products, fast for others. Even for rapidly reformed sectors, many EU countries worry slashing tariffs — as the Portman Proposal asked — would subject European farmers to competition that would force many of them to abandon farming. Many products remain protected by high tariff walls. In some sectors, such as dairy, these countries said only a gradual weaning away from guaranteed prices could avoid market havoc and considerable damage to farmers. France cited the example of beef: a 20 percent tariff cut on beef would result in 15,000 additional tons of imported beef, and beef prices to fall by half. In both the dairy and beef markets, Argentina, Australia, and New Zealand offer stiff competition that put EU farmers under pressure. France also cited the tomato market. Cutting tomato tariffs by 10 percent would allow foreign producers to sell their tomatoes as low as the price the EU gave to its preferential trading partners in the Mediterranean region.

---

[10] Alan Beattie, Frances Williams, Martin Arnold & Raphael Minder, *EU Under Pressure as Trade Talks are Halted*, FINANCIAL TIMES, 21 Oct. 2005, at 1.

[11] Martin Arnold, Alan Beattie & Jean Eaglesham, *Sarkozy's "Fool's Bargain" Tirade Deepens French Rift with Brussels*, FINANCIAL TIMES, 21 Oct. 2005, at 2.

[12] The Portuguese Agriculture Minister signed too, but later withdrew his name.

In contrast to the EU Counter-Proposal, the G-20 issued a Plan that, in some respects, was the most far-reaching call for farm tariff cuts. Table 4-2 summarizes the G-20 Plan. This Plan, while differentiating developed from developing country obligations, did not include a pivot. It identified four tariff bands and suggested sizeable cuts in each. Under the G-20 Plan, the overall average agricultural tariff cut in developed countries would be 54 percent, and in developing countries 36 (or, by some accounts, 39) percent.

That gap, however, is one reason why a U.S. trade official said the G-20 Plan was "not very enticing." Also, there were questions about the 54 percent figure.[13] The U.S. said the correct number is about 52 percent. Australia said the actual average cut for rich countries would be 40 percent, if the EU hung onto a list of sensitive product exemptions.

The U.S. rejected a G-20 demand, put forth by India, that developing countries be allowed to designate up to 20 percent of their farm tariff lines as sensitive, and do so using self-selected criteria such as food and income security, and rural development. Of these special lines, the G-20 said at least 50 percent would be exempt from any tariff reduction, and the remaining ones should be subject to less-than-agreed cuts. U.S. Agriculture Secretary Mike Johanns countered for some developing countries, a 20 percent designation would mean shielding 94-98 percent of farm imports from duty reductions, and tariffs would be cut below current applied rates for only 14 percent of tariff lines, meaning there would be no real market access improvement for 86 percent of farm products.[14] The U.S. position was special products should be dealt with not by exemptions from tariff reductions, but by encouraging market access through the use of tariff rate quotas (TRQs). With a TRQ, which in-quota shipments of those products may be imported at low duties, and both the duty rates and quota thresholds may be negotiated.

In March 2007, the Group of 33 (G-33) developing countries backed away from an aggressive formula for designating products as sensitive. At a meeting in Jakarta, Indonesia, the G-33 agreed to slash by half (from 24 to 12) the number of criteria on which they rely to identify special product exemptions from tariff cuts. Exactly which other criteria, such as broad indicators of economic development and specific measures like the contribution of a farm product to rural income, they would use, how they would apply them, and their concession would affect market access, was unclear.

The American, European, and G-20 discussions came at a time of growing realization of the importance to developing country income growth and poverty of market access and subsidies. Many, but by no means all, of the subsidies paid by developed country governments to their farmers are for products in which poor countries do not, or cannot, compete. Accordingly, one statistical estimate produced by the World Bank became a mantra for trade liberalizers:

---

[13] *See* Daniel Pruzin, *Doha Round Talks Once Again Facing Moment of Truth at Late July Meetings*, 23 INT'L TRADE REP. (BNA) 1086, 1087 (20 July 2006).

[14] *See* Daniel Pruzin, *India's Nath Unyielding in "Confessional" With Lamy, Repeats Demand for Flexibilities*, 23 INT'L TRADE REP. (BNA) 1089 (20 July 2006); Daniel Pruzin, *WTO Members Still Far From Deal in Doha Negotiations, USTR Schwab Says*, 24 INT'L TRADE REP. (BNA) 65, 66 (18 Jan. 2007); Vir Singh, *U.S. Agriculture Secretary Urges India to Grant Greater Market Access*, 23 INT'L TRADE REP. (BNA) 1687 (30 Nov. 2006).

92 percent of the benefit to poor farmers around the world from agricultural trade liberalization in the Doha Round would come from cuts in farm tariffs by rich countries, not from their subsidy reductions. The World Bank also estimated that, because of the large gap in many countries between bound and applied rates, any tariff cuts of less than 75 percent from bound rates, which did not also have strict limits on product exemptions from the cuts, would be commercially insignificant. Such countries included developing ones, like India. The average bound tariff rate for India on farm products is 114.2 percent, and its average applied rate is 40.8 percent.[15]

TABLE 4-2:
G-20 AGRICULTURAL MARKET ACCESS PLAN

Existing Bound Tariff Rate Band for Developed Country	Cut Required to Bound Tariff for Developed Country	Existing Bound Tariff Rate Band for Developing Country	Cut Required to Bound Tariff for Developing Country
0-20%	45% (linear)	0-30%	25% (linear)
20-50%	55% (linear)	30-80%	30% (linear)
50-75%	65% (linear)	80-130%	35% (linear)
Over 75%	75% (linear) Maximum permissible tariff after cuts = 100%	Over 130%	40% (linear) Maximum permissible tariff after cuts = 150%

How did the EU defend its Counter-Proposal, especially in light of considerably different ones from developing countries, some of which are its former colonies? The EU pointed out it is the largest importer of agricultural products from poor countries. Over 80 percent of food exports from them is sold to the EU, and since the June 2003 CAP reform, the EU imports 10 times more of these products than the U.S. However, this defense — as the *Financial Times* observed — is disingenuous. It is "hardly surprising" a "temperate continent next door to a tropical one" would do so, and yet it does not stop that continent from "expensively producing some laughably inappropriate products such as sugar."[16]

Seemingly oblivious to such points, in October 2005, the G-10 put forth farm tariff cut ideas notably long on complexity and short on ambition. Table 4-3 summarizes them. The G-10 said its Plan would lead to an average cut of 40 percent in developed country tariffs, and two-thirds that amount (26.67 percent) for developing countries.

Essentially, the G-10 called for cuts of just 27-45 percent on developed country farm tariffs ranging across any of four bands, or cuts of 32-50 percent if flexibility were allowed to deviate from agreed cuts in each band. Wider bands and lesser cuts applied to developing countries. The G-10 did not appear to specify the cuts these countries would be obliged to make. However, for both

---

[15] *See* Daniel Pruzin, *G-4 Talks End with Signs of Movement; U.S. Ready to Improve Subsidy Cuts Offer*, 24 INT'L TRADE REP. (BNA) 643-44 (10 May 2007).

[16] *A CAP and Bull Story*, FINANCIAL TIMES, 27 Oct. 2005, at 12.

developed and developing countries, the cuts would be less severe if no pivot existed for sensitive products. Moreover, if the cuts were linear, *i.e.*, if there were no pivot and the reductions applied across the board within a band, then up to 15 percent of tariff lines could be designated as "sensitive." With a pivot, 10 percent of these lines could be labeled "sensitive." Cuts to sensitive products, if any, would be agreed to individually, without applying a tariff-reduction formula. Finally, the G-10 resisted any cap on farm tariff rates, and allowed for 10-15 percent of total tariff lines being designated "sensitive." Unmistakably, the G-10 was less enthusiastic than either the U.S. or EU about agricultural market access liberalization.

TABLE 4-3:
G-10 AGRICULTURAL MARKET ACCESS PLAN

Existing Bound Tariff Rate Band for Developed Country	Cut Required to Bound Tariff for Developed Country	Existing Bound Tariff Rate Band for Developing Country	Cut Required to Bound Tariff for Developing Country
0-20%	If no pivot, 27 percent linear cut. If +/— 7% pivot for sensitive products, then 32% cut.	0-30%	Unclear
20-50%	If no pivot, 31% linear cut. If +/— 8%pivot for sensitive products, then 36%.	30-70%	Unclear
50-70%	If no pivot, 37% linear cut. If +/— 9% pivot for sensitive products, then 42%.	70-100%	Unclear
Over 70%	If no pivot, 45% linear cut. If +/— 10% pivot for sensitive products, then 50%.	Over 100%	Unclear

C. Tariff Rate Quota Enlargements

TRQs are a second measure a country may impose at its border to restrict entry of farm products. Negotiating TRQ parameters is complex, because three variables are at play simultaneously:

- *Sensitivities*

How many products should a country be allowed to designate as sensitive, and protect through a TRQ? Further, what criteria should it be allowed to use in making the designation?

- *Deviations*

How should exporters of a product be compensated by an importing country when that country deviates from the tariff cut agreed upon and applicable to the product, but instead designates the product as sensitive? The answer typically is an increase in the volume of the TRQ, *i.e.*, expansion of the in-quota threshold, the importing country maintains on the sensitive product, possibly coupled with a cap on the in-quota tariff rate.

- *Bases*

If compensation for a deviation from an agreed upon cut is through an increase in a TRQ threshold, then how should the increase be calculated? Should it be premised on agricultural consumption in the importing country, or some other factor?

In respect of all three variables, the U.S., EU, and G-10 offered competing ideas. However, through three devices, the Portman Proposal called for better market access for farm products subject to a TRQ.

First, in-quota thresholds for existing TRQs would rise by 7.5 percent of current domestic agricultural consumption. (In earlier Doha Round talks, the U.S. suggested a 5 percent figure. Hence, the Portman Proposal was an improvement.) Second, tariff rates on in-quota shipments would be cut to zero. Third, tariff rates applicable to out-of-quota shipments would be reduced by 50 percent. In sum, the Proposal suggested trade liberalizing changes to both dimensions of a TRQ — raising quotas and cutting tariffs.

Later, in 2006, the U.S. supplemented its TRQ proposal. Specifically, if a country does not cut the tariff on a sensitive product by the agreed-upon amount, then it should provide compensation to its trading partners by increasing the TRQ applicable to that product. The TRQ increase should be on a sliding scale ranging from at least 4 percent, to as much as 20 percent, depending on the extent of the deviation of the actual from the agreed-upon tariff cut. The U.S. and EU debated over the appropriate quantitative deviation from an agreed-upon tariff cut that would trigger a mandatory in-crease in TRQ volume.[17] The EU said not unless the deviation is 10 percent from the agreed cut should it be obliged to expand a TRQ threshold. The U.S. disagreed, calling for better market access through higher TRQ increases triggered by a lower deviation.

As indicated, generally a TRQ is used to protect a sensitive product (such as beef, dairy, and poultry, over which the U.S. and EU haggled as to the appropriate in-quota threshold increase). As the Cairns Group proposed in March 2007, simplicity and transparency mitigate in favor of only two kinds of deviations from agreed-upon tariff cutting formulas:

(1) For a sensitive product on which the deviation from the agreed-upon tariff cut is small (*e.g.*, an agreed 50 percent tariff cut, and a cut for the product of 40 percent), the TRQ increase need only be correspondingly small.

(2) For a sensitive product on which deviation from the agreed-upon tariff cut is large (*e.g.*, an agreed upon 50 percent cut, but a cut on the item of 5 percent), the TRQ increase should be large to assure enhanced market access.

---

[17] *See* Daniel Pruzin & Lawrence J. Speer, *Key Ministers Meet Amid Growing Discontent With Secrecy in Doha Talks*, 24 INT'L TRADE REP. (BNA) 331-32 (8 March 2007).

Further, a trade-liberalizing approach would call for a cap on in-quota tariffs, with a lower cap on sensitive goods for which deviations from agreed-upon cuts are small.

However, what if a Member seeks to protect a sensitive good that is not subject to a TRQ? The Portman Proposal said the Member could choose among one of three devices to protect the product:

(1) Extended Phase-outs: Phase out agreed-upon tariffs over an extended time period, *i.e.*, one longer than applicable to non-sensitive articles.

(2) Back-loading: Adhere to the regular implementation period for agreed-upon tariffs, but make smaller tariff cuts in the initial period of implementation, and larger tariff cuts later.

(3) Safeguards: Impose a quantity-specific safeguard that would restrict imports in excess of a target volume, but phase out the safeguard over time.

The 1 percent limit on designating products as "sensitive" would circumscribe the use of these devices.

The EU Counter-Proposal on enhanced market access through expanding quantitative restrictions was nearly impenetrable. Australia's Trade Minister, Mark Vaile, quipped "if you can understand it, [it] really hardly opens up the market in most sectors to any new trade flows."[18] The EU said it would expand TRQs according to a formula. Whereas the U.S. formula for increasing a TRQ was based on a percentage of domestic consumption of the product in question, the EU formula to determine the increase appeared to contain five main variables: import volumes; import prices; normal tariff cuts; applied cuts for sensitive products; and level of real market access. The EU claimed TRQ expansion would be up to 37 percent for some goods. The U.S. retorted the likely increase in volume (based on EU domestic consumption) would be 2 percent. For almost every country, domestic agricultural consumption is a figure exceeding import volume. The EU formula, then, would lead to smaller TRQ increases commitments than the Portman Proposal, simply because the EU premised commitments on a smaller base.

The G-20 suggested a minimum increase of TRQ volumes, measured in relation to domestic consumption, of 6 percent.[19] However, the G-20 insisted any increase, and any reduction of in-quota tariffs, be non-discriminatory. Its insistence aimed to thwart American efforts to negotiate guaranteed TRQ enlargements, and tariff reductions, for sectors of keen export interest to the U.S., like beef, corn, pork, and poultry.

For its part, the G-10 suggested a sliding scale for sensitive products subject to a TRQ. The greater the expansion in the in-quota threshold, the lower the obligatory tariff cut. If a TRQ expanded by just 5 percent, then the tariff would

---

[18] Daniel Pruzin, *Portman Disappointed by Ag Market Access Response; Ministers to Regroup Next Week*, 22 INT'L TRADE REP. (BNA) 1614, 1615 (13 Oct. 2005); *see also* Daniel Pruzin, *Doha Round Talks Once Again Facing Moment of Truth in Late July Meetings*, 23 INT'L TRADE REP. (BNA) 1086, 1087 (20 July 2006).

[19] *See* Daniel Pruzin, *WTO Farm Talks in London Stall as Key Players Fail to Make Headway*, 24 INT'L TRADE REP. (BNA) 292-93 (1 March 2007).

have to be cut by 25 percent. If it expanded by 15 percent, then the tariff cut would be 15 percent. If it expanded by 25 percent, then the necessary tariff cut would be just 5 percent. What if a sensitive product is not subject to a TRQ? The G-10 proposed increasing market access for these products either by a dilated period in which to implement linear tariff cuts, or an abbreviated period in which to implement smaller, sliding-scale cuts.

D. Domestic Support

The universe of agricultural subsidies is large and complex. The WTO *Agreement on Agriculture* was a watershed accord in organizing them into different categories, or "Boxes." The Doha Round talks focused on these categories. Yet, to many WTO Members, especially from the Third World, and several NGOs, the talks were about more than details of the categories. Former World Bank President Paul Wolfowitz observes:

> It is trade, not aid, that holds the key to creating jobs and raising incomes. It is trade that will allow poor countries to generate growth; forgiving debt alone will not do that. It is trade that has helped 400 m[illion] Chinese escape poverty in the last 20 years [1985-2005] and the same can happen elsewhere.
>
> . . . .
>
> Above all, there is a *moral argument* [for liberalizing trade]. How can we justify spending $280 bn [billion] on support to agricultural producers in developed countries — nearly the total gross domestic product of Africa and four times the total amount of overseas aid? How can we justify imposing barriers on the poorest 2 bn people that are twice as high as on everyone else? How can we accept a system in which Africa's share of world exports has fallen from 3.5 percent to less than 2 percent in the past 30 years?[20]

Notably, only five products account for nearly half of the $280 billion in annual developed country farm subsidies. Cutting support on these products, such as cotton, dairy, and rice, which tend to be of keen interest to poor country farmers, could make an enormous difference in their livelihood.

What presumption underlies the above moral argument? Is it a principle known in Catholic Social Justice Theory as the preferential option for the poor?[21] According to this principle, first priority ought to be given to attending to the needs of the poor. Yet, that Theory contains a no less compelling principle, namely, the equal dignity of each human person and of work. Do some moral arguments exalt the interests of African farmers over their counterparts in the U.S. and France, in accordance with the preferential option for the poor, but give less dignity to the person and labor of the American and French farmer? Consider these normative matters from a variety of religious and philosophical perspectives, when evaluating farm subsidy proposals.

---

[20] Paul Wolfowitz, *Everyone Must do More for Doha to Succeed*, FINANCIAL TIMES, 24 Oct. 2005, at 13 (emphasis added).

[21] *See* RAJ BHALA, TRADE, DEVELOPMENT, AND SOCIAL JUSTICE chs. 17-22 (2003).

1. Domestic Agricultural Support through *De Minimis* Subsidies

De Minimis subsidies are support that normally would be included in the Amber Box and, therefore, would be subject to reduction commitments for that Box. However, this support is defined in terms of low limits, hence no cut is required to it. Under the Uruguay Round *Agreement on Agriculture*, one limit is for product-specific support, and is up to 5 percent of the total value of agricultural production within a low limit. The other limit is for non-product specific support, and is up to 5 percent of the total value of agricultural production. The 5 percent caps apply to developed countries. For developing countries, the caps on product- and non-product specific support are 10 percent (each). A WTO Member can take advantage of both limits (*i.e.*, there is no trade off between them).

The thresholds may seem trivial. However, the most "water," in the sense of the largest gap between actual and permissible spending, is in the area of *De Minimis* subsidies. Moreover, *De Minimis* subsidies account for 45 percent (as of 2001) of all U.S. agricultural support that is trade-distorting.

Accordingly, under the Portman Proposal, the U.S. agreed to cut *De Minimis* subsidies by 50 percent from the allowed levels, *i.e.*, to 2.5 percent of the value of domestic farm production for a developed country, and 5 percent for a developing country. The reduction would apply to both product-specific and non-product specific support. With a 50 percent cut in the levels, the U.S. could exempt $5 billion of product-specific support, and a further $5 billion of non-product specific support. In 2001, the U.S. spent $6.83 billion on non-product specific *De Minimis* support. Examples of such support were crop insurance, irrigation, and market loan assistance (later superseded by counter-cyclical payments, discussed below). The EU Counter-Proposal indicated a willingness to make cuts as deep as 65 percent in *De Minimis* support.

2. Domestic Agricultural Support through Blue Box Subsidies

The definition of the Blue Box in Article 6:5 of the WTO *Agreement on Agriculture* covers only those subsidy programs that require a limit on production. Thus, the Box essentially is a category for production "set asides" (*i.e.*, payments not to produce, or to limit acreage under production). The ostensible purpose of this category is to assist a WTO Member to reform its farm sector. This Box was designed particularly to help the EU wean farmers off subsidies linked to production, which historically have resulted in over-production. Blue Box subsidies are considered less distorting of trade patterns than Amber Box subsidies, and certainly than export subsidies. Hence, Blue Box subsidies are subject to less strict disciplines and Amber Box or export subsidies.

Counter-cyclical support provides farmers with payments if global commodity prices decline (thus causing the price of their crop to fall), and assures them of a minimum (or floor) price. That is, a counter-cyclical payment compensates a farmer for low market prices, by paying the farmer the amount of the gap between an international price and a government-established target price, whenever the world market price plummets beneath the set price. But, in the U.S., this support is not contingent on a farmer agreeing to set aside part of his land and let that part lie fallow. In other words, it is de-coupled from production. The American commodity loan program is an example of counter-cyclical support the U.S. sought to transfer from the Amber Box category of trade-distorting subsidies to a newly enlarged Blue Box.

Under the August 2004 *Framework Agreement*, WTO Members agreed to a cap on expenditures on Blue Box subsidies. The cap was 5 percent of the overall value of agricultural production of a Member. The U.S. also obtained at least broad wording to the definition of the Blue Box that would allow counter-cyclical payments. The Portman Proposal responded to suggestions from NGOs like Oxfam to lower the ceiling, by calling for a cut of one-half in that ceiling over five years, *i.e.*, a cap of 2.5 percent of the total value of farm production. Initially, the EU declined to endorse this cap, perhaps not surprisingly, because it is the largest Blue Box spender. By December 2006, it agreed in principle to a 2.5 percent limit.

To be sure, the Proposal allowed the U.S. to include counter-cyclical payments to farmers in this Box. Critics charged these payments encourage over-production. Moreover, insofar as the cut would be from bound, not actual, spending levels, some observers questioned the real impact. Thus, Oxfam dubbed the Proposal "smoke and mirrors," noting it would allow for Box-shifting of payments, from the Amber to Blue Box, and necessitate a cut in total U.S. subsidies of only 2 percent (from $74.7 to $73.1 billion at the end of the Doha Round implementation period). That NGO feared for the future of Third World farmers facing competition from U.S. cotton, corn, and rice. The Institute for Agriculture and Trade Policy, based in Minneapolis, observed the U.S. could shift even more subsidies into the unregulated Green Box, and appeared likely to do so in the *2007 Farm Bill*. (U.S. farm legislation, which contains agricultural support provisions, have a five-year pendency.)

To be fair, however, Green Box subsidies are by definition not (or minimally) trade distorting. The *Agreement on Agriculture* intentionally creates this Box to preserve some sovereignty for WTO Members to fashion farm policy. More-over, a reduced Blue Box cap would limit the ability of the U.S. (and other Members) to shift all counter-cyclical payments from the Amber to Blue Box. Such Box-shifting, if permitted, could immunize subsidies from reduction commitments applicable to the Amber Box.

Yet, that immunity presumed — perhaps wrongly — no reduction commit-ments were set for Blue Box programs. Brazil and other G-20 countries, plus Australia and (with a touch of irony) the EU, urged disciplines on Blue Box spending — namely, a limit on product-specific spending, and restrictions on the amount of counter-cyclical compensation to farmers. Still, without any reduction commitments, the Portman Proposal to cut the cap would be significant in itself. In dollar terms, U.S. counter-cyclical payments hovered at $6-7 billion annually, and the applicable cap was $7.6 billion. A cut in the cap to 2.5 percent of total U.S. agricultural production would translate into maximum Blue Box subsidies of just below $5 billion per year.

3. Domestic Agricultural Support through Amber Box Subsidies

Pursuant to the Uruguay Round *Agreement on Agriculture*, a number of WTO Members cut Amber Box subsidies. Programs in the Amber Box, which include direct payments to farmers and price supports, are by nature trade distorting. Between 1998 and 2001, the EU had cut such programs by 15.9 percent (in euro terms), from $52.3 billion to $35.2 billion. (In U.S. dollar terms, the decrease was 32.7 percent, but those terms are misleading, because the euro weakened against the dollar.)

On previous occasions, the EU demanded the U.S. cut trade-distorting, *i.e.*, Amber Box, subsidies by 55 percent. The American Farm Bureau President, Bob Stallman, urged the U.S. not to cut by more than half. The Portman Proposal bested the EU demand by 5 percent, and the Farm Bureau hope by 10 percent, proposing a 60 percent reduction in U.S. domestic farm subsidies over five years, from 2008-13. Thus, in dollar terms, the U.S. would cut its annual Amber Box spending cap, to which it agreed in the Uruguay Round, from a bound level of $19.1 billion to $7.64 billion.

U.S. Amber Box spending was $14.4 billion (in 2001, and estimated at just over $12 billion in 2004, or roughly $16 billion if counter-cyclical payments are included). The $14.4 billion figure excludes counter-cyclical payments, and other support programs established by the U.S. *Farm Security and Rural Investment Act of 2002* (Public Law 107-171, 116 Stat. 134, *i.e.*, the *2002 Farm Bill*, which expired on 30 September 2007). Under the Proposal, the U.S. would cut its ceiling on Amber Box payments to 46.9 percent below actual spending (the percentage difference between $14.4 and $7.64 billion), meaning it would have to make real cuts in farm support. Of the $14.4 billion, the largest sums were paid to support dairy ($4.5 billion), soybeans ($3.6 billion), cotton ($2.8 billion), corn ($1.27 billion), and sugar ($1 billion). The Proposal included spending caps on specific products.

While Canada called for an even larger cut, the 60 percent reduction would be stage one of a three-stage plan. Here, too, the second stage, from 2013-2018 would be a 5-year *interregnum* for evaluation of prior cuts. In the third and final stage, from 2018-23, all trade-distorting support would be eliminated. However, the Portman Proposal insisted on following the harmonization principle (set forth in the *Framework Agreement*). Deeper cuts would be required of higher-subsidizing WTO Members, and there would be three "bands," as Table 4-4 sets out.

Simply put, the EU would have to cut its Amber Box subsidies by 83 percent, because it starts from a higher bound base level than the U.S. The EU also spends roughly three times more than the U.S. on domestic farm support. The result would be a reduction in the allowable Amber Box disparity between the EU and U.S. from 4:1 to 2:1. For the same reason, Japan, too, would be expected to make a cut of more than 80 percent. The Proposal called for cuts of 37 percent for developed countries with Amber Box support of less than $12 billion. It did not expect cuts from developing or least developed countries.

TABLE 4-4:
PORTMAN PROPOSAL FOR HARMONIZING AMBER BOX CUTS

Bound Amber Box Annual Spending Level agreed to in Uruguay Round	Countries Affected (Uruguay Round bound levels)	Cut from Bound Level in Portman Proposal
Above $25 billion	EU ($88 billion) Japan ($35 billion)	83% (for EU) At least 80% (for Japan)
Between $12 and $25 billion	U.S. ($19.1 billion)	60%
Zero to $12 billion	Other developed countries	37%

The EU responded with a 70 percent reduction offer (slightly more generous than the 65 percent it tabled at September 2005 talks in Paris). But, cuts in Amber Box spending from bound levels might not have much impact. The EU's binding for this Box is 67 billion euros (about $88 billion) per year. Later, in 2006, the EU intimated it might agree to a 75 percent cut, but only if the U.S. reduced its Amber Box cap by 65 percent.

The G-20 Plan included domestic support reduction ideas, as in Table 4-5. Not surprisingly, with extensive rural poverty in G-20 countries, this Plan called for deeper cuts than either the Portman Proposal or EU Counter-Proposal. Moreover, the G-20 Plan exempted developing countries from Amber Box reduction commitments, if those countries have not already bound their level of spending in this Box.

TABLE 4-5:
G-20 PLAN FOR AMBER BOX CUTS

Bound Amber Box Annual Spending Level agreed to in Uruguay Round	Countries Affected (Uruguay Round bound levels)	Cut from Bound Level in G-20 Proposal
Over $25 billion	EU ($88 billion) Japan ($35 billion)	80%
Between $15 and $25 billion	U.S. ($19.1 billion)	70%
$15 billion or less	Other developed countries	70%

E.   Export Subsidies

Because they intend to promote exports, or have that effect, agricultural export subsidies are the most trade distorting form of farm support. Their purpose is to change the pattern of trade by stimulating exports of the subsidized primary or processed agricultural product. The *Agreement on Agriculture* called for reductions in export subsidies, but not their elimination. The G-20, and British Prime Minister Tony Blair, previously identified 2010 as the year by which all farm export subsidies should be eliminated. The Portman Proposal accepted this date — three years ahead of the 2013 target set in December 2005 at the WTO Ministerial Conference in Hong Kong. The EU refused to match this resolute offer, and could not possibly do so.

The EU spends more on direct export subsidies ($2 billion annually) than any other WTO Member, and accounts for 90 percent of all export subsidies paid by developed countries. The EU accused the U.S. of using food aid to dump surplus farm output, and reiterated its demand for disciplines on such aid, such as replacing in-kind food shipments with cash-only grants, save for true emergencies. On this point, the Proposal stated the U.S. would tighten rules on food donation to ensure this aid does not displace commercial farm trade, but would not risk reducing aid to the needy.

At the core of the U.S.—EU battle was the definition of what qualifies as a farm "export subsidy." The EU insisted on so-called "parallelism." All forms of export support — direct payments as well as export credits, export credit guarantees, food aid, and insurance — should be included. The EU said export monopolies through State Trading Enterprises (STEs), for instance, in Australia, Canada, and New Zealand, also should be included. Under a thorough definition, the U.S. is the biggest spender — $3 billion per year. To be sure, the U.S. offered to cut the subsidy element of its export credit programs by requiring repayment of export credits within six months. But, the EU called for the U.S. to do more than circumscribe the repayment period. It should require an export credit agency to be self-, not government-funded, and provide export guarantees only to cover risks (not purchases).

F. Overall Agricultural Support

Across all Box categories, during the Uruguay Round the U.S. bound its levels of support at about $48 billion.[22] This aggregate results from $9.6 billion for the Blue Box (calculated according to a new limit of 5 percent of the value of total domestic agricultural output), a further $19.2 billion for *De Minimis* payments (calculated as the sum of just under $10 billion for product-specific support and $10 billion for non-product specific support), and $19.1 for the Amber Box.

The Portman Proposal established a tripartite band for reductions in overall agricultural subsidies, that is, the sum of trade-distorting support, namely, Amber Box, Blue Box, and *De Minimis* programs. The bands reflected non-linearity, *i.e.*, deeper, harmonizing cuts from larger subsidizers. Accordingly, the EU would reduce its overall bound level of subsidies by 75 percent, the U.S. by 53 percent, and Japan and other developed countries by 31 percent. In the August 2004 *Framework Agreement*, the U.S. had agreed to an overall annual cap of $50 billion, so a 53 percent cut would mean cutting the cap to $23.5 billion. The precise figure the U.S. offered was $22.4 billion.

The EU rejected the figure. It said the U.S. ought to limit itself to $15-$17 billion annually. Likewise, India was not impressed with these features of the Portman Proposal, nor by U.S. suggestions for the Amber Box, Blue Box, and *De Minimis* programs. From India's vantage point, the fact the EU could spend, under Uruguay Round commitments, four times more than the U.S. on farm subsidies was less significant than the fact the U.S. is a much larger farm commodity exporter than the EU.

---

[22] *See* Daniel Pruzin, *WTO Ag Chair Urges Members to Consider Scenario for Domestic Farm Support, Tariffs*, 23 INT'L TRADE REP. (BNA) 1722 (7 Dec. 2006).

Seeing 30-40 percent of the price of U.S. farm commodities as comprised of a subsidy, India urged that what flows is not trade, but subsidies, and Indian farmers compete with the U.S. Department of the Treasury. By India's calculation, the U.S. spent almost $21.5 billion per year on trade-distorting domestic farm subsidies, consisting of $14.4 billion in Amber Box support and $7.04 billion in non-product specific *De Minimis* support.[23] Under the Portman Proposal, the U.S. would be able to spend $7.64 billion annually in the Amber Box, $4.9 billion in the Blue Box (through, for example, counter-cyclical payments), $4.9 billion on product-specific *De Minimis* support, and $4.9 billion on non-product specific *De Minimis* support. The total amount would be $22.4 billion, which would imply the U.S. could boost subsidies by about $1 billion.

Moreover, argued India, the Portman Proposal created plenty of room for Box shifting. For example, of the $7.04 billion in non-product specific *De Minimis* spending, most of it took the form of counter-cyclical payments. The U.S. could shift these payments to the Blue Box, and thereby free up spending in both product and non-product specific *De Minimis* spending. With the new room for *De Minimis* spending, the U.S. could shift programs out of the Amber Box, into the *De Minimis* category. Not surprisingly, India scoffed at a maximum permitted subsidy limit on U.S. spending at $22.4 billion. The cap should be $12 billion — but that figure would be a non-starter with the House and Senate Agriculture Committees, and American farm interests.[24]

Conversely, proposed EU cuts — said India — appeared substantive. India estimated EU trade-distorting subsidies at about 66.6 billion euros annually, consisting of 43.6 billion in the Amber Box, 22.2 billion in the Blue Box, and 745 million in *De Minimis* support. With the proposed cuts, EU Amber Box spending would fall to 20.1 billion euros per year, Blue Box spending would decline to 12.3 billion euros annually, and *De Minimis* support could rise to 8.5 billion per year. That total would be 40.9 billion euros, nearly 26 billion less than actual EU spending.

Argentina came to the same conclusion as India about the Portman Proposal. Argentina estimated total U.S. spending in 2001 in the Amber and Blue Boxes, and *De Minimis* support, at $21 billion. Under the Proposal, the ceiling would be $23 billion — allowing the U.S. to increase spending. Similarly, Brazil said the overall level of trade-distorting support matters most, and

---

[23] Actual spending figures can be difficult to come by and compare. Each WTO Member is supposed to report them to the WTO, but does not always do so in a timely fashion. As of 2001, the overall U.S. farm subsidy spending was $71.9 billion. Of this amount, two-thirds, or $50.7 billion, was in the Green Box. The U.S. spent $14.4 billion in the Amber Box, nothing in the Blue Box, $600 million (in 2000) on product-specific *De Minimis* support, and $6.83 billion on non-product specific *De Minimis* support (down from $7.28 billion in 2000). Thus, actual U.S. domestic farm subsidy expenditures in 2000-2001 totaled $24.6 billion. By 2005, the sum of Amber Box, Blue Box, and *De Minimis* spending declined to $19.7 billion. Some estimates (including one by the Canadian government) indicated 2006 for actual U.S. expenditures (in 2006) on overall trade distorting support (OTDS) was about $11 billion.

For the EU, in marketing year (MY) 2003-04, 22 billion euros in the Green Box, 31 billion euros in the Amber Box, and 25 billion euros in the Blue Box. As of July 2007, its OTDS was 110.3 billion euros.

[24] *See* Alan Beattie, *U.S. and EU "Must Give Ground" on Trade*, FINANCIAL TIMES, 25 Jan. 2007, at 3.

called for a far deeper cut in this level than in the Proposal. Not surprisingly, therefore, the G-20, proposed harmonizing cuts in overall subsidies. Table 4-6 summarizes the G-20 Plan. Notably, the G-20 Plan agreed developing countries should be put in separate bands and obliged to make cuts in the sum of their Amber Box, Blue Box, and *De Minimis* support. However, the Plan did not specify what those reductions commitments should be.

TABLE 4-6:
G-20 PLAN FOR CUTS TO OVERALL TRADE — DISTORTING AGRICULTURAL SUBSIDIES

Overall Trade-Distorting Agricultural Subsidies (Annual Spending, Sum of Existing Bound Level of Amber Box, Blue Box, and De Minimis Support)	Countries Affected	Obligatory Reduction to Bound Level of Overall Subsidies
Over $60 billion	EU	80%
Between $10 and $60 billion	U.S.	75%
Less than $10 billion	Other developed countries	70%

G. Cotton Subsidies and the *Peace Clause*

In the run-up to the December 2005 WTO Ministerial Conference in Hong Kong, in addition to offers on agricultural market access and domestic support, WTO Members tabled suggestions on two other key agricultural matters.

1. Cotton Subsidy Elimination

African, along with Caribbean, countries argued strenuously at the September 2003 Cancún Ministerial Conference excessive subsidies to American cotton farmers had a serious adverse effect on their cotton farmers. Oxfam supported the argument, saying U.S. cotton subsidies between 2001-2003 cost African cotton growers about $400 million. Four West African cotton-producing countries — the "Cotton Four," consisting of Bénin, Burkina Faso, Chad, and Mali —threatened to block discussions in the December 2005 Hong Kong Ministerial Conference if developed countries failed to adopt concrete measures to address their concerns. The Cotton Four called for three specific reforms. Led by Brazil, the G-20 backed their demands.

First, West African countries sought identification of a date by which both domestic and export subsidies on cotton would be eliminated. In the U.S., these subsidies totaled $4.2 billion (in crop year 2004-05, double the amount from the 2003-04 crop year). Second, they expected immediate budget assistance and compensation to their farmers who had suffered losses, which they estimated at $350 million in lost export revenue because of world cotton prices depressed by subsidized developed country cotton. Third, they insisted on an action plan to help develop West African cotton trade.

Of the West African demands, the first was the most critical. There are roughly 25,000 cotton farmers in the U.S. There are 2 million cotton farmers in Africa. They are largely unsubsidized, yet are among the most efficient in the world. These facts alone justify the first demand on utilitarian grounds. Consequential reasoning buttresses the insistence of the Cotton Four it would not suffice to reduce cotton subsidies — they must go entirely and immediately. Only then might there be an upward impact on world market cotton prices. In brief, subsidy reform in rich countries is meaningful to farmers in poor countries only if it affects world market prices, and this effect is most likely if reform means termination. That general proposition is true in respect of any good.

Farmers in poor countries do not receive subsidies. By definition, their governments are too poor to fund major subsidy programs. Consequently, these farmers must accept for sales of their crop the world market price for that crop. To assist them, in the sense of boosting revenue and alleviating income poverty, they need higher prices. Small cuts by rich countries on export subsidies do not matter to poor country farmers. For them, the ideal is cessation of all export subsidies on all products. That end is politically infeasible in rich countries. The second best solution is to start with products of keen export interest to poor countries. Cotton is at or near the top of that list.

2. *Peace Clause* Renewal

A particularly intriguing feature of the Portman Proposal was its call for renewal of the *"Peace Clause"* contained in the Article 13 of the Uruguay Round *Agreement on Agriculture*. This *Clause*, which bars use of the WTO *Agreement on Subsidies and Countervailing Measures (SCM Agreement)* to challenge domestic farm support, expired on 31 December 2003. Brazil successfully attacked U.S. cotton subsidies and EU sugar subsidies, thereby creating uncertainty in the two trade giants about the WTO compatibility of many of their farm programs.

The defeat stunned legislators and aides in the Senate and House Agricultural Committees. Had they not drafted the cotton subsidy program to fit squarely within the Green Box, *i.e.*, to qualify as non-trade distorting spending, and thus not subject to reduction commitments associated with the Amber Box? Yet, in the *Upland Cotton* case, the Appellate Body held some U.S. programs were mis-classified in the Green Box, and the *Peace Clause* did not apply to the cotton subsidies. Thus, if the U.S. (and EU) were to make sizeable subsidy cuts commitments in the Doha Round, then they wanted the certainty and predictability that would come from a *Peace Clause* renewal. The Portman Proposal suggested a 5-year term, from the date the Doha Round accords are implemented, and broad immunity for all domestic support that complied with these accords. Not surprisingly, Brazil (the principal complainant in *Upland Cotton*), as well as other G-20 developing countries, scoffed at the suggestion.

Filling in details on other issues, as well as agricultural market access, left open from the August 2004 *Framework Agreement*, remained essential to Doha Round progress. Yet, in advance of the Hong Kong Ministerial Conference, gaps among negotiating positions were wide. Consensus on compromise was far off.

II. THE DEADLOCK ON NON-AGRICULTURAL ISSUES

A. NAMA

For the entire history of GATT and the WTO, both bound (*i.e.*, maximum permissible, or ceiling) and applied (*i.e.*, actual) tariff rates have tended to be considerably higher in the First than Third World. The average bound tariff rate (as of 2005) on industrial products among developing countries is 29 percent. Among the Quad Group — the U.S., EU, Japan, and Canada — that average is 9 percent. In India, the average applied rate on industrial products is 32 percent, and in Brazil, it is 14 percent. Among the Quad, applied rates on industrial products range from 5.4 to 6.9 percent. Thus, in the run-up to the December 2005 Hong Kong Ministerial Conference, developed countries — led by the U.S. and EU — insisted on better market access for their manufactured products.

Business lobbies, such as the U.S. National Association of Manufacturers (NAM), pointed out countries such as Brazil maintain high bound tariff rates on industrial products, but impose actual tariffs at well below the bound rates. That means any cut from bound rates would not result in commercially meaningful NAMA, if the applied rates remain unchanged. The gap between bound and actual rates also means there is considerable room to raise actual rates. Politicians in the U.S. and EU said any cuts in American and European farm tariffs and subsidies would have to be met with reciprocal benefits for their exporters of industrial products, as well as their service providers. In other words, they demanded an "agriculture versus NAMA and services" deal.

Accordingly, on NAMA, the U.S. pressed for a "Swiss Formula" to cut tariffs on industrial products. This kind of Formula requires non-linear reductions — deeper cuts on higher tariffs, and, therefore, increases harmonization among tariff rates. Moreover, the U.S. insisted on applying the Formula to actual, not bound, rates. Developing countries led by Argentina, Brazil, and India (ABI) took the diametric opposite approach.

Under the "ABI" Proposal, the method used to cut tariffs would be less aggressive than the Swiss Formula. Cuts would depend on the average tariff rate of a Member, allowing developing countries to retain relatively higher tariff rates than developed countries. The cuts would apply to bound, not actual, tariffs. The ABI proposal also provided developing countries with generous special and differential treatment — extended periods for implementing tariff cuts, the right to exclude some tariff lines from cuts, and to apply less-than-full formula cuts to some lines.

The EU expressly linked NAMA and agricultural tariff cuts. The EU took a different approach from both the U.S. and ABI on details, however. It called on developed countries to limit tariffs on goods to 10 percent, and for better-off developing countries to make more generous market access offers than poorer countries.

The WTO Members also sparred on an all-important number, namely, the coefficient in the mathematical formula they agreed to use to cut tariffs. In the Swiss Formula, a lower coefficient leads to higher tariff cuts, and its value is the highest allowable tariff rate. The U.S. favored a coefficient in the low single digits, and a modestly higher figure for developing countries. The U.S., EU and, other industrialized Members agreed large developing countries, such as Brazil and India, should accept a coefficient of 15, in exchange for any agreement by them to a coefficient of 10. The U.S. observed a coefficient of 15 would allow Brazil and India to have average industrial tariffs between 4-7 times higher than those of the U.S. Canada declared 15 would " 'barely scratch the surface' of developing country applied tariffs."[25]

Other WTO Members disagreed. They called for a uniform coefficient of 10, with flexibility for developing countries. Still other Members advocated a coefficient of less than 2 for developed countries, and at least 20 for developing countries. A bargaining group of developing countries, called the "NAMA 11," said the difference in coefficients between developed and developing countries should be 25 points. (The NAMA 11 included Argentina, Brazil, Egypt, India, Indonesia, Namibia, Philippines, South Africa, Tunisia, and Venezuela). Only that magnitude (or more) would be consistent with special and differential treatment. Brazil, for example, said it could accept a coefficient of 20, while Malaysia said it would have to be at least 20. India insisted on 30 or more. China demanded one as high as 35 for developing countries, and 5 for developed countries. The NAMA-11 contended a coefficient of 35 would impose 50 percent cuts on their bound tariffs, and 26 percent cuts on their applied tariffs. In sum, the proposed coefficients varied from 0-10 for developed countries, and 10-30 plus for developing countries, and the two sides sparred over the impact their favorite number would have on tariff schedules.

The U.S. could not accept such high coefficients for developing countries. A coefficient of 20 would mean that up to half of the applied tariffs in Brazil and India would not be reduced at all. It also would mean the Brazilian and Indian tariff lines subject to reductions would be cut by an average of just 10 percent.[26] Thus, as late as March 2007, progress on NAMA remained blocked.

One problem was linkage. Several WTO Members refused to table major offers until they saw a deal on agricultural trade liberalization. The U.S. countered, in 2006-2007, with a call to change process. Why not engage in NAMA talks on a sectoral basis? Important sectors included automobiles and auto parts, bicycles and bicycle parts, chemicals, electronics and electronic products, fish and fish products, forestry products, gems and jewelry, raw materials, hand tools, health care products, pharmaceuticals, and sports equipment. Accordingly, the U.S. tried to induce developing countries into NAMA talks on a sector-by-sector basis by discussing various flexibilities that could be afforded to them — in effect, special and differential treatment. The possibilities included:

1.   Extended periods for developing countries in which to eliminate industrial tariffs in certain sectors.

---

[25] Daniel Pruzin, *Major Developing Countries Dig in Heels Against Steeper Tariff Cuts in NAMA Talks*, 24 INT'L TRADE REP. (BNA) 821-22 (14 June 2007).

[26] *See* Daniel Pruzin, *U.S. Industry Looks for Brazilian Support on NAMA Sectorals*, 24 INT'L TRADE REP. (BNA) 407-08 (22 March 2007); Daniel Pruzin, *WTO Chair Says NAMA Talks Blocked Due to Stalemate in Agriculture Negotiations*, 24 INT'L TRADE REP. (BNA) 297-98 (1 March 2007).

2. A zero-for-X arrangement that would require rich countries to eliminate all industrial tariffs in exchange for poor countries cutting their duty rates in certain sectors by more than required by an agreed-upon general formula, but not to zero.

3. Staged implementation periods, or phases, for developing countries to reduce progressively tariffs in certain sectors, eventually going to zero in most sectors, with certain sensitive products reserved.

(The U.S. counseled against having more than one kind of flexibility per tariff line.)

Thus, for example, in April 2007, Japan, Singapore, and Taiwan proposed — and Norway, Switzerland, and the U.S. agreed — to a sectoral initiative that would eliminate duties on 28 categories of sports equipment at the 6-digit Harmonized System (HS) level (*e.g.*, balls, clubs, fishing gear, gym equipment, motor boats, safety headgear, sail boats, skis, and tennis racquets). Because developing countries account for almost 63 percent of all sports equipment exports from WTO Members (and 13 percent of their imports), surely they would have an interest in this initiative.[27] The proposal called for a 5-year tariff phase out period in this sector among developed Members. Developing countries would get a longer period, and could retain tariffs on certain items. A similar proposal — floated the same month by Japan, Singapore, Switzerland, Taiwan, and Thailand — covered bikes and bike equipment. Again the case for developing country interest was strong. They account for 84 percent of bike and bike part exports (and 11 percent of the imports) among WTO Members. China alone makes 60 percent of all bikes in the world (though its merchandise its bike and bike part producers are frequent targets of antidumping (AD) investigations).

Yet, overall, the American effort at NAMA progress through sectoral initiatives did not work — despite warnings from WTO officials, and some Members, that making NAMA offers contingent on progress in agriculture was risky. A breakthrough in farm trade talks would not necessarily mean quick results could be had on industrial sectors — or, for that matter, services. In response, the U.S. suggested a "critical mass" strategy to sectoral negotiations. A proposal to cut tariffs in a particular sector would be deemed accepted if WTO Members accounting for a significant part of the trade in that product (defined, said the U.S., as 80 percent) agreed to that proposal. Developing countries with little or no stake in the sector, therefore, could opt out of talks on that sector.

B. NAMA Dispute Settlement

NAMA involves not only tariff, but also non-tariff, barriers to industrial products. Non-tariff barriers take a variety of forms, depending on the good and country, including import license requirements, import quotas, and other quantitative restrictions. Testing and certification rules, and food, health, and safety requirements, also can be non-tariff NAMA barriers. Should disputes over such barriers be brought under the WTO *Understanding on Rules and*

---

[27] *See* Daniel Pruzin, *Six WTO Members Propose to End Tariffs on Sporting Goods, Bicycles in NAMA Talks*, 24 INT'L TRADE REP. (BNA) 509 (12 April 2007).

Procedures Governing the Settlement of Disputes (Dispute Settlement Under-standing or *DSU)*, or should an alternative mechanism be used?

The question — potentially a heretical one from the vantage point of *DSU* champions — arose in Doha Round talks.[28] Most developing countries initially favored sticking with the *DSU*, whereas the EU called for a mediation process. Later in the Round, the NAMA 11 suggested a NAMA dispute resolution mechanism in which experts, known as facilitators, would be appointed by disputing WTO Members. The facilitators would provide assistance to these Members, and advise them on how to resolve their differences. The EU countered (in March 2007) with its own problem-solving procedure. It would call upon facilitators, imposing on them short deadlines to counsel disputing parties on an appropriate solution.

III. THE DEADLOCK ON SERVICES

A. The Significance of Services

Progressive liberalization of services trade within the architecture of the *General Agreement on Trade and Services (GATS)* is no less difficult than freeing up agricultural trade. It also is no less important. Nearly 70 percent of world Gross Domestic Product (GDP) consists of services, which are higher value-added than agriculture. Roughly the same percentage of the labor force in developed countries is employed in a service sector.

Few issues are of greater commercial significance to the economy of American economy than services trade liberalization. Services account for roughly 75 percent of America's GDP, and 8 out of 10 American jobs are in the services sector. Not surprisingly, the U.S. continued its advocacy, honed in the Uruguay Round, for elimination of services trade barriers that put its service providers at an international competitive disadvantage. High as the values of actual services traded are, however, it is a mistake to think of this trade as the province of developed countries.

First, major developing countries are increasingly involved in a few services markets. India is a well-known case in point, in respect of information technology (*e.g.*, software development), back office operations (*e.g.*, clearing and settlement of financial market transactions), and call centers (*e.g.*, customer assistance). Second, few developing or least developed countries pin their long-term economic growth on agricultural or low-valued added industrial production. They look to the history of present-day developed countries, and seek to climb the value added chain. Third, many developing and least developed countries simply lack capacity to provide essential services such as banking, insurance, telecommunications, and even utilities to their populations. These services are essential if those countries hope to climb the value-added chain.

Consequently, services trade liberalization tends to be a double-edged sword. On the one hand, poor countries recognize the importance of opening

---

[28] *See* Daniel Pruzin, *Slow Progress Made on Core NAMA Issues, Advances on Nontariff Barriers, Chair Says*, 24 Int'l Trade Rep. (BNA) 333 (8 March 2007).

their markets, both to receive the services in the short-term and stimulate growth and maturation of their own globally competitive service providers. On the other hand, too much service sector liberalization, too quickly, may doom local providers, which cannot compete with the likes of world-class American banks, insurers, and telecom companies.

B. Negotiating Progressive Services Trade Liberalization

As with agricultural negotiations, services talks engender tensions between hard commitments and flexibility, between developed and developing countries, and between big emerging countries and smaller, poorer countries. How are these tensions managed? Among the principles governing progressive liberalization of services under *GATS* are:

1. Assuring services trade is liberalized to the mutual advantage of WTO Members.

2. Respecting the policy objectives of each Member, and the right of each Member to regulate services.

3. Accounting for differing stages of economic development among Members, and the need for poor countries to participate in services trade.

4. Appreciating that rapid services liberalization may be difficult for countries that recently acceded to the WTO, as they have taken on a large number of substantive commitments, and face significant economic reform challenges.

However, these principles do not yield specific outcomes.

At negotiations in Paris in September 2005, the U.S., EU, Brazil, and India formed a "Core Group" of WTO Members to advance services negotiations. Other Members in the Group included Argentina, Australia, Canada, Chile, China, Hong Kong, Japan, Korea, Malaysia, Mexico, New Zealand, Singapore, South Africa, and Taiwan. This Group was an eclectic bunch.

In the U.S. and EU, over 50 percent of the services markets are liberalized. In Brazil, the figure is about 10 percent. India has a traditional, socialist-style stance to reserve service sectors for domestic providers, many of which are mollycoddled state-owned enterprises conflicted with the new dynamism of its private entrepreneurial business services and software industries. Yet, India also champions its increasingly prominent status in some services markets, and knows the aspirations of millions of its people are tied to outsourcing back office, call center, and support services from developed countries. Services account for over half of India's GDP.

Expectedly, given this diversity, deep disagreement within the Core Group emerged. The schism, largely between developed and developing countries, was over a proposal called "benchmarking" or "scoring." The conventional method for the negotiations had been "request-offer," whereby a WTO Member puts out a market access request to other Members in which a Member has an actual or potential services trade interest. Those other Members respond to the request with individual offers. Negotiations ensue on a bilateral basis, with the goal being to narrow the difference between the request and offer.

By December 2005, even though roughly 93 WTO Members had tabled offers, the U.S., EU, and other Members seeking aggressive services trade liberalization were frustrated with the poor quality of the offers, and the time-consuming nature of the request-offer process.

Thus, with Korea, Switzerland, and Taiwan, the U.S. and EU said it was time to supplement the request-offer method with minimum commitments on the services trade liberalization and an assessment of the quality of the offers, *i.e.*, benchmarking or scoring. The EU specifically called for identifying priority services sectors, and market access offers in a minimum number of such sectors that were commercially meaningful and no worse than the existing degree of market openness. Switzerland developed a quantitative scale, ranging from zero to 100, to assess the quality of offers.

However, other Core Group members, especially developing countries such as Argentina, Brazil, Malaysia, and South Africa, resisted minimum, across-the-board commitments. They countered with three arguments. First, benchmarking is incompatible with the flexibility contained in *GATS*. A premise of the *GATS* is freedom for each WTO Member to select the service sectors or sub-sectors in which it agrees to make commitments. Second, benchmarking is unfair to developing countries, because it applies across-the-board to all service sectors. These countries have fewer operative service sectors, and fewer service sectors subject to previously made *GATS* commitments, than developed countries. But, if their offers are subject to benchmarking scrutiny, then they will have to make greater market opening commitments sectors than developed countries to pass muster. (To be sure, benchmarking cannot force WTO Members to make better offers.) Third, it might well be pointless to seek minimum commitments from all WTO Members, especially if the minimum is so low as not to result in much improvement in market opening. Instead, why not identify the most important Members, from the perspective of services suppliers, and focus on a deal with them?

In October, the Core Group agreed on a compromise "Supplemental Negotiating Approach." There would be certain broad political objectives about the coverage of Doha Round services liberalization negotiations, and quality of the offers tabled. On coverage, numerical targets could be used to gauge the scope of market access commitments, *i.e.*, the number of sectors and sub-sectors liberalized. But, targets could be individualized for WTO Members, with lower ones for developing countries than for developed countries.

With respect to quality, there would be "modal qualitative parameters" for each of the four modes of services supply identified in the *GATS*, *i.e.*, Mode I (cross-border supply, which includes provision of outsourced services), Mode II (consumption abroad), Mode III (commercial presence, or FDI), and Mode IV (temporary migration of professionals, *e.g.*, via a term assignment). For example, on Mode I, commitments would have to cover increased business opportunities, made possible in part by technological developments. On Mode III, economic needs tests and other market access restraints (*e.g.*, specification of forms of entry, like joint venture) would be removed, and permissible foreign equity levels would be enhanced. On Mode IV, commitments could be both improved and de-linked from commercial presence requirements. Across all four Modes, the Core Group said the number of service sectors exempted from

MFN treatment under *GATS* Article II:1 would be reduced substantially to a minimum level, and new commitments would be scheduled with greater clarity than in the past.

C. A Services Safeguard?

A major sticking point in Doha Round services negotiations was whether to include in *GATS* a safeguard remedy. A general safeguard exists in GATT Article XIX and the Uruguay Round *Agreement on Safeguards*, but it applies only to goods. Following the 1997-99 Asian Economic Crisis, many countries blamed foreign financial services institutions for causing, or exacerbating, monstrous drops in banking, securities, and property markets, and the deleterious knock-on effects. Some WTO Members sought the legal right to limit access to their services markets whenever their domestic services firms were threatened by competition from overseas. At the end of the Uruguay Round, they agreed to multilateral talks on the issue, which were to be finished by the end of 1997. They were not, and eventually were folded into the Doha Round. However, in March 2003 the talks reached a stalemate.

In March 2007, eight of the ten countries in the *Association of South East Asian Nations* (*ASEAN*) — Brunei, Burma (Myanmar), Cambodia, Indonesia, Malaysia, Philippines, Thailand, and Vietnam (but not Laos, which is not a WTO Member, and Singapore, which has strong vested interests in free services trade) — offered a services safeguard proposal:[29]

1. A WTO Member would have the legal right to impose an emergency safeguard against foreign financial services firms if its domestic service firms were in jeopardy from the foreign competition.

2. To invoke the right, the importing Member would have to prove an emergency market condition exists. That would mean showing its domestic services firms are experiencing market conditions that cause serious injury, or threaten serious injury. Such conditions would include a substantial increase in imports of services, a sharp decline in the number of domestic services providers, or a steep drop in their employment, market share, profits, or sales figures.

3. To prove the case, the importing Member would have to conduct an investigation, and adhere to procedures, similar to those in a safeguard relief action against foreign goods.

4. Unlike safeguard relief for goods, where the remedial device is imposition of a tariff or non-tariff barrier, the remedy for services would be positive, aimed at helping domestic firms adjust to foreign competition. Grants and tax preferences would be examples. Only as a last resort would an importing Member be allowed to suspend a *GATS* market access commitment.

5. As with safeguard relief for goods, for services any safeguard remedy would be applied on a most favored nation (MFN) basis. Its duration normally could not exceed three years (one year less

---

[29] *See* Daniel Pruzin, *ASEAN Countries Renew Call for WTO Services Safeguard Rules*, 24 Int'l Trade Rep. (BNA) 370 (15 March 2007).

than the limit for goods). An importing Member would retain its *GATS* Article XXI right to negotiate permanent withdrawal of a concession.

6.   No safeguard could be applied against a developing country Member that constitutes only a small market share of the service at issue.

7.   A service exporting Member, the firms from which are subject to a safeguard, would have a right of reprisal against the importing country imposing the remedy. If the importing Member did not adhere to the rules on imposition, then it could retaliate.

8.   The services safeguard would have a limited scope. It would apply only to service sectors and sub-sectors in which an importing Member has made a *GATS* market access commitment, but not yet fully implemented it. If the sector or sub-sector at issue was unbound, or if foreign firms already had exercised their market access right granted to them under *GATS*, then, no safeguard remedy could be imposed.

Proponents in *ASEAN* said their proposal was carefully calibrated, and that a services safeguard would give them the political safety valve needed to make dramatic trade liberalizing commitments, thus leading to freer trade in services and increased FDI.

Unsurprisingly, reaction from major service exporting countries, especially the U.S., EU, Japan, and Switzerland, was negative. They argued (*inter alia*) the proposal was ambiguous as to defining a domestic service sector supplier (a problem akin to defining "like or directly competitive product" in a safeguards action against goods), and delineating the scope of remedial action. Query whether their reaction might be short-sighted? Is the pattern of comparative advantages in services trade be the same over time?

IV. THE DECEMBER 2005 HONG KONG MINISTERIAL CONFERENCE

A. Protests

A taste of the "passions inspired by globalization," as the *Financial Times* put it, came in the weeks and days before the December 2005 Hong Kong Ministerial Conference. In October, protestors temporarily blockaded WTO Director-General Pascal Lamy as he left a meeting of non-governmental organizations (NGOs) at Hong Kong University. The Sunday before the Conference started, 4,000 demonstrators marched in Hong Kong, chanted "Our world is not for sale," and called for the abolition of the WTO.

Among them were migrant workers from Indonesia and the Philippines, who used their only day of the week off to protest against the WTO. Some donned T-shirts emblazoned with slogans like "Junk the WTO" and "Stop Collusion between Government and Business." Others dressed as chickens. They voiced concerns ranging from the undemocratic way in which WTO officials are elected to overriding the sovereignty of WTO Members to protecting workers and the environment. The medley of NGO groups itself was amazing, and included the ActionAid, Alberta Egg Producers, Canadian Bar Association, Czech-Moravian Confederation of Trade Unions, Focus on the Global South, Friends of the Earth, Istanbul Textile and Apparel Exporters Association, Mexican Pig Breeders Council, Oxfam, South Asia Fisheries for Justice Network (Sea-fish), and the U.S. Semi-Conductor Association.

Korean farmers attracted considerable attention, even sympathy, from the Hong Kong public.

> Raymond and Kimmy Li brought their son, seven, and daughter, 10, to join yesterday's [18 December 2005] march "to teach our children about the WTO and how it affects you," Ms. Li said. "If the protestors did not fight, nobody would know what their problems are."[30]

The problems of the Korean farmers were (*inter alia*) a decision in November 2005 to increase rice imports. Their protests included swimming across Hong Kong harbor.

Unfortunately, towards the end of the Ministerial Conference, protests became more violent than any other in Hong Kong in the previous decade (which encompassed the handover of the former Crown Colony to China, on 1 July 1997 — a moving event your author and his wife had the honor of witnessing). As farmers and their supporters sought to break into meeting halls, Hong Kong police rebuffed them with pepper spray, tear gas, and water canons. In the end, at least 900 protestors were arrested. By contrast, at the 1999 Seattle Ministerial Conference, though the demonstrations were larger than in Hong Kong, over 500 were arrested. Small wonder why WTO Members no longer line up to host these Conferences — indeed, only Mexico and Hong Kong volunteered for the 2003 and 2005 meetings, respectively.

B. Constrained Optimization

By the opening of the Hong Kong Ministerial Conference, 6,000 delegates from 149 Members, 2,000 NGO delegates, 3,000 journalists, and 10,000 activists had descended on Hong Kong. The contours of disagreement, but no resolutions, were sharp.

1. Efficient agricultural exporting countries like the U.S., Australia, and Brazil looked for lower agricultural trade barriers and subsidies. But, less efficient farmers in these countries were not eager to lose tariff protection or subsidies.

2. In exchange for cuts in its own farm tariffs and subsidies, the U.S. sought improved offers from developing countries on NAMA and service sector liberalization, and more significant cuts than the EU had offered in its relatively higher farm tariffs and subsidies. The U.S. also sought market access for certain agricultural products in major markets like India. Cotton, corn, sugar, and rice are examples — but also are sensitive in, and highly subsidized by, India.

3. The EU and Japan joined the U.S. on NAMA and service sector issues, demanding large developing countries like Brazil and India

---

[30] Alexandra Harney, *How It All Ended in Teargas for Hong Kong*, FINANCIAL TIMES, 19 Dec. 2005, at 2.

open their markets to manufactured goods and services. Rich countries offered to compromise on farm trade if poor countries did so on industrial and services trade. Thus, for example, the EU said China needed to cut trade barriers in sectors like automotive. Threatening to file a WTO case, and ultimately doing so, the European Commission observed China favored domestic car producers, imposed investment restrictions, local content requirements — and, to boot, weakly enforced IP rights.

4. The EU and Japan did not join the U.S. in calls for deeper cuts on farm tariffs and subsidies. Japan complained its agricultural interests, protected by some of the highest tariffs in the world, were being ignored. India objected to cutting farm tariffs, which protected hundreds of millions of small, low-productivity farmers.

5. Large developing countries, particularly Brazil, India, China, and South Africa, coalescing in the G-20, sought major cuts in farm tariffs and subsidies from the EU. But, they were cautious of dropping bound tariffs on industrial products or throwing open service sectors, especially in respect of infant industries and service providers. India noted that except for alcoholic beverages, automobiles, and tobacco products, its applied tariffs already were low on products of keen export interest to the U.S. and EU. For instance, India's average applied rates (for the year ended 31 March 2006), excluding the episodic high tariffs, were 5.7 and 6 percent for American and European imports, respectively.[31]

6. Like most poor countries, the large developing countries objected to two assumptions underlying the agriculture-for-manufacturing-and-services deal pushed by the U.S. and EU. First, why should poor countries be satisfied with supplying agricultural products to rich countries, and concede manufacturing and services to the First World? Second, why should poor countries be expected to offer a *quid pro quo*, particularly in light of GATT Article XXXVI:8, concerning non-reciprocity? Poor country advocates observed that, because of high tariffs on processed foods and labor-intensive industrial goods, rich countries collect tariffs four times higher on imports from poor countries than from other rich countries. Poor countries also pointed to the hypocrisy in the proposed deal: rich countries sought increased service market access, but were unwilling to make concessions on the temporary migration of persons from poor countries to provide services in rich countries (so-called "Mode IV" services supply under the *GATS*).

7. Least developed countries feared reductions in trade barriers by the U.S., EU, and other First World countries. Under preferential trade arrangements (PTAs) granted by some developed countries, many of them receive duty-free treatment. (For example, the "Everything But Arms" initiative of the EU provides duty-free treatment to 90 percent of imports from least developed countries.) If developed

---

[31] *See* Vir Singh, *Commerce Minister Nath Says India Willing to Push for Fair Multilateral Trade*, 23 INT'L TRADE REP. (BNA) 1217 (17 Aug. 2006).

countries lowered bound most favored nation (MFN) rates, then the difference — called the "margin of preference" — between those rates and zero tariff treatment would shrink. However, the International Monetary Fund (IMF) released a study, *Africa in the Doha Round* (December 2005), counseling poor countries to liberalize trade and negotiate generous reciprocal reductions in trade barriers, rather than focusing on holding onto trade preferences.

8. Least developed countries producing cotton, namely, Benin, Burkina Faso, Chad, and Mali, sought elimination of cotton subsidies paid to U.S. and other developed country farmers. They were boosted by a study from the Cato Institute, *Boxed In* (December 2005), stating total U.S. trade-distorting subsidies exceeded limits set pursuant to the WTO *Agreement on Agriculture*, and caused serious prejudice to the interests of other Members by suppressing prices in violation of the WTO *Agreement on Subsidies and Countervailing Measures (SCM Agreement)*.

9. Least developed countries that are net food importers feared subsidy cuts by developed countries. Those cuts would raise their food import bill. In its 2005 *Annual Report*, the United Nations Food and Agricultural Office (FAO) explained food security problems tend to be greatest in countries with relatively little trade, and said poor countries would gain more by reforming their agricultural trade policies than from trade liberalization among developed countries. However, the FAO also suggested food supply to net-food importers could become less secure if the cost of subsidized food imports rose dramatically because of subsidy cuts.

One way to characterize these contours of disagreement is "complex linkages." No WTO Member would move unless other Members agreed to do so. If each Member insists on linkage, the result is deadlock. Another way to characterize the contours of disagreement is to view trade negotiations as a problem of constrained optimization. The contours were severe constraints, and an optimal solution — if one existed — for satisfying the constraints was not obvious.

The EU made the linkages or constraints yet more rigid on the eve of the Conference. It proclaimed its refusal to budge on agricultural subsidies without movement from Brazil, India, and other large developing countries on NAMA and services liberalization. The official host of the Conference, Hong Kong's Commerce Secretary, John Tsang, said failure to reach a deal, especially after the collapse of talks in Cancún, "would kill the credibility of the WTO" and possibly cause the whole WTO system to "crumble."[32] That apocryphal scenario did not occur, though the mere articulation of it suggested three questions.

First, how could delegates undermine what the *Financial Times* dubbed "the world's most impressive achievement in multilateral rule-making" — the WTO?[33] At a time of crisis and despair over other international organizations,

---

[32] Victor Mallet, *Credibility of WTO at Stake*, Financial Times, 18 Oct. 2005, at 9.

[33] Martin Wolf, *The World Has Everything to Lose if Trade Liberalization Fails*, Financial Times, 2 Nov. 2005, at 13.

notably the United Nations, the WTO, and its predecessor incarnation, the GATT, stood out as institutions achieving considerable success on a focused mission. Few regions, including East Asia, had effective regional institutions or policies to provide fairness, predictability, and stability. East Asia is an example, with narrow economic integration focusing on intra-company trade in components that are shipped though cross-border supply chains ending up in China, where final assembly occurs, followed by exportation. Unlike the WTO, the *ASEAN* FTA, called *"AFTA"* (*i.e.*, the *Association of South East Asian Nations Free Trade Area*) lacks strong, central institutions and a serious dispute settlement mechanism. Surely, the *ASEAN* countries, and others in regional trade agreements (RTAs), needed the WTO to save them from the limitations of their groupings.

Second, were some linkages or constraints patently unfair, particularly ones developed countries drew between their proposals and offers from most developing countries, and to trade policy reform in least developed countries? Consider the fact if the internal trade of the EU is excluded, then 20 countries account for 82 percent of world imports of goods, and 86 percent of world imports of commercial services (as of 2004). "Fewer than 30 players matter in these [Doha Round] negotiations," observed the *Financial Times*. Surely a deal among major WTO Members with no expectation from the others was worth contemplating.

Third, had delegates to Hong Kong forgotten the context in which the Doha Round started? It was the immediate aftermath of the 9/11 terrorist attacks. Surely, a successful Round would be an even stronger statement against disorder than the *Ministerial Declaration* launching the Round, proof the world community could agree on a liberal, rules-based international political economy.

As the *Financial Times* put it, after the Hong Kong Ministerial Conference, the Doha Round was "still breathing, but only just."[34] With the *Hong Kong Declaration* of 18 December 2005, the negotiators kept the Round on "life support." The *Declaration* contained generalities, and set target deadlines. For example, the *Declaration*:

- Stated there should be four tiers, differing for rich and poor countries, for cutting farm tariffs, a three-band classification system for cutting domestic farm support cuts, and rules to protect Box shifting.

- Set 30 April 2006 as the deadline for agreeing on modalities for agricultural market access and subsidies, and for NAMA. By that date, formulas and figures for cutting tariffs and subsidies were requited.

- Set 31 July 2006 as a date for submitting revised services offers.

None of these points went much beyond the *status quo ante*, *i.e.*, positions on the eve of the Conference.

Described euphemistically, then, the *Hong Kong Declaration* was "modest," covering agricultural export subsidies, a trade-and-aid package, and intellectual property. There was plenty of blame to go around. Major developing

---

[34] *Doha Trade Round is Left on Life Support*, FINANCIAL TIMES, 19 Dec. 2005, at 14.

countries such as Brazil, China, and India would have to make substantial offers on liberalizing their markets to trade in industrial products and services. Some NGOs ill-served poor countries, being "false friends" peddling "economically illiterate" arguments that protected internationally uncompetitive manufacturers, high-cost, low-quality service providers, and corrupt state-owned enterprises. Said the *Financial Times*, there was a risk these NGOs would make "the WTO as ineffective as UNCTAD [the United Nations Conference on Trade and Development]." As for the EU and U.S., the newspaper all but dubbed them selfish. The EU would have to improve "vastly" its offer on agricultural market access, and

> [p]rotection-free market access for the least developed [countries] is the least they deserve. It is a scandal that the U.S. Congress resists this. It is equally shocking that it cannot stop subsidizing U.S. cotton farmers at the expense of poor West African producers.[35]

As for resuscitating the other critical matters, negotiations simply dragged on into 2006.

C. Kicking the Can Down the Road (Again)

A month before the December 2005 Hong Kong Ministerial Conference, the WTO Members abandoned any effort to achieve at the Conference a specific blueprint for negotiations to a final Doha Round bargain. Without an accord on modalities such as formulas, numbers, and dates for cutting tariffs and subsidies, it was evident the Conference would not yield an ambitious deal. To be sure, the WTO Director-General, Pascal Lamy, issued a draft ministerial declaration on 26 November, and a revised draft on 1 December. But, a perusal of the drafts revealed few binding commitments, plenty of ambiguity masked by phrases like "working hypothesis" and "common understanding," and a large number of unsettled issues.

The 18 December *Hong Kong Ministerial Declaration* is little different, save for the topics of agricultural export and cotton subsidies, and trade and aid. On agricultural market access, it restates well-known ideas trotted out in the Portman Proposal, EU Counter-Proposal, and the ACP, G-10, and G-20 Plans of applying graduated tariff cuts across four bands or tiers. That also is true for domestic farm support. The *Declaration* has three reduction bands, with yet-to-be-agreed steepened cuts.

Likewise, on NAMA, the *Declaration* identifies the Swiss Formula, with coefficients for cutting tariffs. But, in these instances the *Declaration* left plenty of ambiguity. For instance, it speaks of "coefficients" in the Swiss Formula, but fixes neither their value nor number. The U.S. had called for two coefficients (one each for developed and developing countries) of low values (to assure deeper tariff cuts). Argentina, Brazil, and India had sought multiple coefficients (to allow for tariff cuts to be set individually for Members depending on the average tariff rate of a Member). The ambiguous word "coefficients" allowed both sides to crow or complain.

For developed countries, the *Declaration* went backwards on services trade liberalization. It restates a commitment to intensify talks "with a view to

---

[35] *Doha Trade Round is Left on Life Support*, FINANCIAL TIMES, 19 Dec. 2005, at 14.

expanding the sectoral and modal coverage of commitments and improving their quality." But, an Annex to the *Declaration* backs away from a call to engage simultaneously in bilateral and plurilateral proposals. The latter method allows for exchanges of collective requests and offers by groups of WTO Members in any service sector, or on any mode of service supply. The Group of 90 Alliance, comprised (*inter alia*) of African countries, objected to the plurilateral approach. The result was watered down language allowing for so-called "friends groups" — *i.e.*, like-minded countries — to bargain plurilaterally in services sectors of importance to them, such as accounting, audiovisual, computer, energy, express delivery, financial, legal, logistics, and telecommunications. The G-90 also succeeded in weakening language on the importance to make better commitments on commercial presence, foreign equity participation, and goals concerning Mode IV (namely, visa and residency requirements for the cross-border movement of professionals).

Perhaps worst of all, the *Hong Kong Ministerial Declaration* lacked ambition, a product of a Conference as much about theater as substantive negotiations. The EU Trade Commissioner, Peter Mandelson, managed an ending line at once ridiculously dramatic and dramatically ridiculous:

> Europe made it happen, and we are pleased to have done so. We said we came to Hong Kong to do business, and this shows we meant it. [36]

To use a different metaphor, on all tough issues, negotiators kicked the can down the road. Indeed, they had done so again. The first kick was in November 2001, when the *Doha Ministerial Declaration* had been long on ideas and short on commitments. The outcome of the Hong Kong Conference was ironic. Only an ambitious deal would justify the investment of time and political capital, and produce major benefits. As former Director-General Dr. Supachai Panitchpakdi said, a "crisis of immobility" plagued the WTO. [37] All that was certain on the eve of the Conference was an accession ceremony for a new Member, the 150th — Tonga, a tiny, South Pacific Island nation.

D. Agricultural Export Subsidies

Doha Round negotiators at the Hong Kong Ministerial Conference were unable to reach agreement on agricultural market access through tariff reduction or TRQ expansion. They also failed to make progress on reducing domestic agricultural support through reductions of *de minimis* and Amber Box subsidies, or reform of the Blue Box. The South African Trade union federation, COSATU, which is a partner in the African National Congress (ANC), declaimed

> The situation will remain that it would be better to be a cow in Japan being subsidized for $7 per day, to being a human being living in Africa. [38]

---

[36] Christopher S. Rugaber & Peter Menyasz, *WTO Ministerial Agrees on Setting Course for Final Stage of Talks; Some Disappointed*, 22 INT'L TRADE REP. (BNA) 2046, 2049 (22 Dec. 2005).

[37] *Wanted: A Sense of Urgency in Doha Talks*, FINANCIAL TIMES, 13 Dec. 2005, at 16.

[38] *Resigned Response to Limited Progress at WTO Talks*, FINANCIAL TIMES, 20 Dec. 2005, at 4.

The one area in which they agree was fixing a date to terminate all export subsidies.

That date is 2013. The agreement came after the EU was isolated by virtually all other WTO Members, and after an all-night negotiating session. Roughly 90 poor countries normally loyal to the EU because of preferential trading arrangements and historical ties joined forces with the G-20 (especially agricultural exporting countries in that Group), Australia, Canada, and New Zealand. They put to the EU a joint demand, buttressed by American support: end agricultural export subsidies by 2010. The EU fired back it would not budge unless the U.S. reformed trade-distorting features of its export-credits and direct-food aid programs, and Australia, Canada, and New Zealand dismantled their trade-distorting STEs. These countries called the EU intransigent, and said it produced no evidence of trade distortion from these arrangements.

In the end, after an all-night negotiating session, the date of 2013 was agreed. However, even this agreement was conditional on meeting a demand of the EU, namely, "parallelism." All export subsidies had to be eliminated in a "progressive and parallel Manner," which meant indirect export subsidies also had to go by 2013. The precise nature and value of this indirect support had yet to be determined. Of particular concern to the EU were export credits, credit guarantees, insurance programs, and STEs. In brief, the EU said it would eliminate its export subsidies only if these other forms of support were subject to parallel treatment.

Accordingly, the EU secured important contingencies in the language of the *Hong Kong Declaration* Export credits, credit guarantees, and insurance programs would have to be "self-financing, reflecting market consistency." The period for ascertaining whether a particular scheme is self-financing would have to be "sufficiently short," otherwise the "real, commercially oriented discipline" on the scheme could be circumvented. The *Declaration* also committed WTO Members to preventing commercial displacement caused by food aid, and ensuring there is "no loophole for continuing export subsidization" by such aid. It calls upon Members to agree to new restrictions on in-kind food aid and cash (or "monetized") food aid. At the same time, the U.S. was successful in pushing forward the idea of a "Safe Box" for *bona fide* food aid in emergencies. As for STEs, the EU insisted their trade-distorting behavior would have to cease. They would have to be disciplined to bar them from exercising their monopoly powers, as the *Declaration* puts it, "in any way that would circumvent the direct disciplines on STEs on export subsidies, government financing, and the underwriting of losses."

Query whether the conditional agreement to end export subsidies by 2013 was a major concession by the EU. Under its June 2003 reforms to the CAP, and the 2007-2013 budget accord, the EU is reducing annual export subsidies from roughly 3 to 1 billion euros by 2013. Though the Hong Kong deal called for "substantial" reductions by 2010 (*i.e.*, by the first half of the implementation period), the EU refused to accelerate all cuts by then. In other words, not unlike other multilateral trade rounds, Doha Round deals are contingent in part on the settlement of the EU's budget. Until the 1980s, this budget was set annually. Now, it is set on a seven-year cycle, which means the timing of WTO obligations is linked to this cycle, just as the schedule for talks over those obligations relate directly to the expiry date of U.S. Presidential *Trade Promotion Authority (TPA)*.

E. Trade, Aid, and Cotton

Eager to find some common ground amidst the deadlocks over agricultural and non-agricultural issues, negotiators from the U.S., EU, and Japan sought agreement on a "trade-and-aid" package for the 50 least developed countries. Accordingly, the 18 December 2005 *Hong Kong Ministerial Declaration* speaks of three inter-related components to the negotiations: "trade," namely, duty-free, quota-free access for exports; "aid," *i.e.*, financial and technical assistance; and elimination of cotton subsidies.

Collectively, least developed countries account for less than 1 percent of world trade. Moreover, the total amount of trade-related aid to all developing and least developed countries is about $3 billion (as of 2005), and a further $10 billion is provided for infrastructure. These figures pale in significance to developed country expenditures on farm subsidies. Thus, an ambitious package not riddled with complex rules of origin or exceptions for products of keen export interest to these countries could help boost the fortunes of the poorest countries. Unfortunately for them, the *Declaration* fell short of earning the descriptive adjective "ambitious."

Regarding "trade," the U.S. gave serious consideration to duty-free, quota-free access for all products from least developed countries, save for sensitive goods. The EU dropped its demand the U.S. remove all barriers to poor country exports, essentially conceding it is politically unfeasible for the U.S. to open its markets completely to textile and apparel (T&A), leather goods, and sugar from developing and least developed countries. The U.S. was especially reluctant to do so from competitive producers of these products, for instance, Bangladesh and Cambodia with respect to T&A.

Canada, too, had sensitivities — dairy, egg, and poultry products. The EU already established an "Everything But Arms" (EBA) initiative, which gives duty free, quota free treatment on nearly universal product coverage. But, the EBA has notable exceptions for bananas, rice, and sugar. For Japan, the sensitive sectors it refused to open to least developed countries were fish, leather goods, and rice. Australia and New Zealand already offered duty-free, quota free access to most, if not all, goods from least developed countries. Evidencing considerable diversity within the Third World, larger developing countries agreed to consider opening their markets to least developed countries goods.

Accordingly, the *Hong Kong Declaration* identifies benefactor countries "facing difficulties at this time." They agreed to provide duty-free, quota-free treatment to 97 percent of all exports from least developed countries. They would do so by 2008, or whenever the WTO Members are supposed to implement a final Doha Round deal. The *Declaration* promises the 97 percent benefactors would take "progressive" steps to offering free trade to 100 percent of least developed country exports. On "aid," the U.S. pledged to ask Congress to double its spending on trade-related assistance over five years (2005-10) from $1.3 to $2.7 billion. The U.S. assiduously noted it is the largest aid-for-trade donor. Its help takes the form not of loans, but grants, especially to small- and medium-sized enterprises (SMEs) and farmers.

Japan announced an integrated trade-and-aid package. The Prime Minister, Junichiro Koizumi, explained the package was based on the "one village, one-product campaign" launched in 1979 in the southern Japanese prefecture of Oita.[39] The essence of the package was to develop the supply chain from production to export, and add value at each step in the chain. Specifically, for any particular agricultural or fisheries product, the chain links farmers, fishermen, and other workers in a small or medium-sized enterprise in a least developed country with consumers in Japan, other developed countries, and developing countries. Through a $10 billion allocation over three years, and the additional financing of 10,000 trainees, Japan said it would help least developed countries improve their infrastructure for production, distribution, and trade. Examples of projects would be enhancing farm productivity through technical cooperation on soil cultivation and irrigation, improving seed varieties, and upgrading the mechanisms to preserve and process agricultural products. Japan would give duty free, quota-free treatment on agricultural imports from least developed countries, but apparently not for fisheries products or leather goods. Prime Minister Koizumi also showcased his country's significance and generosity: Japan is the second largest economy in the world, the largest net importer of agricultural products, provides no agricultural export subsidies, and gave more total aid between 1995-2005 than any other country.

Consensus on a trade-and-aid package did not mean agreement to end cotton subsidies. True, the *Hong Kong Ministerial Declaration* called on, but did not obligate, developed countries to eliminate them by 2006. This call reflects demands of West African cotton producing countries for the U.S. to eliminate its cotton subsidies, which exceed $4 billion annually (in the crop year 2003/04). They also sought an emergency fund to compensate their farmers for depressed world cotton prices they believed were caused by these subsidies. The U.S. touted 11 studies showing the effect of its subsidies were minimal, perhaps depressing world prices by 2-4 percent (according to studies by the IMF and FAO), though other Members said the figure was at least 10 percent.

In "Green Room" negotiations at Hong Kong, the West African countries pushed the U.S. to cut by 60 percent its cotton subsidies by 2007, a further 20 percent cut by 2009, and complete elimination by 2010. (The rubric is after talks involving a subset of WTO Members that occur in the room near the office of the Secretary-General in the WTO Secretariat building in Geneva.) The U.S. refused, saying the talks should transcend cotton subsidies. True, admitted the U.S., the share of world exports accounted for by African products fell from 2.5 percent in 1980 to 0.9 percent in 1999. But, queried the U.S., why? Surely, greater gains to West Africa could come from market access, assistance, and fundamental trade policy reforms in their countries. Overall, between 1983-2003, high-income countries in the Organization for Economic Co-operation and Development (OECD) cut by 84 percent their

---

[39] Junichiro Koizumi, *A Joint Effort is Needed to Eradicate Poverty*, FINANCIAL TIMES, 12 Dec. 2005, at 15.

average applied tariffs, to 3.9 percent. Yet, African countries did so by just 20 percent, to an average applied tariff of 17.7 percent. Some of the highest tariffs they levied applied to goods from other African countries, and they had made little progress on regional integration. African countries also had non-tariff barriers 4 times higher than developed countries.

In the end, the U.S. agreed to dismantle two of its cotton subsidies by April 2006, the "Step 2 Program" and the Export Credit Guarantee Program. Through the Step 2 Program, U.S. cotton millers and exporters received a subsidy to buy higher-priced American rather than imported cotton. Under the Credit Guarantee Program, the U.S. backed the financial creditworthiness of foreign buyers of American cotton. Yet, ending these two Programs hardly was a concession. The U.S. faced an international legal obligation to do so to comply with a 2005 Appellate Body ruling in the *Upland Cotton* case. The Appellate Body held both Programs were illegal export subsidies. As for reform to the rest of the cotton subsidies, the U.S. position was to wait until an overall agricultural trade deal had been agreed, but discuss with West African countries the possibility of faster, deeper cuts to remaining cotton subsidies than other farm products.

Query the significance of two other American concessions on cotton. The U.S. said it would provide West African cotton with unrestricted access into its market. The average out-of-quota (*i.e.*, above quota) tariff on cotton from the Cotton Four countries is 20 percent. Eliminating that border tax is not insignificant. However, to what extent is West Africa concerned about duty-free, quota-free treatment for exports to the U.S.? American spinners use six million bales of cotton annually (as of 2005). Collectively, Chinese, Indian, and Pakistani spinners use 70 million bales per year. To focus on the American market is to miss the mark. Second, the U.S. offered $7 million in assistance to help increase the productivity of West African cotton farmers to expand their export and marketing capacity. Is this a sufficient amount? Moreover, is the U.S. the proper source of it, given that China is the world's largest cotton producer and importer?

Interestingly, more than West African cotton farmers sought cessation of American cotton subsidies. China is both the largest producer and importer of cotton. Cotton is the second most important cash crop in China, following oil seeds. Cotton also is the most labor-intensive agricultural product in China, employing roughly 46.2 million workers. In the week before the Hong Kong Ministerial Conference, Oxfam released a study on Chinese cotton farmers, with data from two of the poorest provinces in China, Gansu and Xinjiang. The study indicated in the 4 years following the accession of China to the WTO on 11 December 2001, imports of American cotton surged 21 times, adversely affecting local production. Presumably, China used some of this cotton to produce T&A, which it shipped to the U.S. (and EU). Yet, in 2005, the U.S. (and EU) negotiated quantitative restrictions on Chinese T&A imports, and in 2004-05 imposed or threatened safeguard remedies against several categories of these imports. In brief, the U.S. was both subsidizing its cotton farmers and protecting its T&A manufacturers.

F.   Special and Differential Treatment

What special and differential treatment did the Hong Kong negotiators afford to poor countries? The "glass is half-full" response is "considerable." The aforementioned deals on agricultural export and cotton subsidies, trade and aid, and IP justify this positive outlook. Another justification might be a seemingly technical provision in the *Declaration* provides developing countries the right to use a special safeguard (SSG) mechanism against agricultural import surges that cross a volume or price trigger.

Article 5 of the WTO *Agreement on Agriculture* creates the SSG mechanism, but it needed elaboration for poor countries to use it. A price trigger is relevant to many poor countries lacking technical capacity to monitor imports on a real-time basis, or at least a timely manner. Without that capacity, they are unaware whether a volume threshold is crossed, and thus whether their producers of a like domestic product face an import surge. Led by Indonesia, the G-33 had pushed for a reference in the *Declaration* to a price trigger. That Group said under a refurbished SSG mechanism, developing countries should be allowed to impose tariffs of up to between 50 and 100 percent on imported farm products. They should be able to apply the remedy either with a trigger volume or trigger price. The relevant data on volumes or prices should be a prior 3 year average.

Poor countries and their NGO advocates found the metaphor of "the glass is half-empty" apt. For them, maybe it was more than half-empty. The *Hong Kong Declaration* does not reflect the GATT Article XXXVI:8 concept of non-reciprocity. Rather, it reflects "less-than-full reciprocity," which means poor countries still have obligations, but modestly less onerous ones than rich countries. For example, developing countries may self-designate special agricultural products that would be subject to lower tariff reductions, or exempt from tariff bindings commitments. (But, the *Declaration* does not specify the number of tariff lines they can designate.) Might it be a conceptual shift occurred after 1964, when the Contracting Parties added Article XXXVI and the rest of Part IV to GATT? If so, did this shift actually begin as early as the Tokyo Round?

V.   INTELLECTUAL PROPERTY ACCOMPLISHMENTS

Two notable results of the Hong Kong Ministerial Conference took place at the intersection of IP and trade, though technically they occurred at a WTO General Council session on 6 December, before the Conference opened.

A.   Extended Transition Periods

First, on 30 November 2005, WTO Members agreed to extend preferential treatment to least developed countries under the WTO *TRIPs Agreement* from 10 to 16 years (counting from the entry into force date, which for developed countries typically was 1 January 1996). That is, recognizing the "special needs" and "economic, financial, and administrative constraints" in the poorest of poor countries, *TRIPs* Article 66:1 affords them a decade-long transition period. Thus, least developed countries were supposed to have implemented all *TRIPs Agreement* obligations by 31 December 2005. As this date approached, many of them asked for more time, such as an additional 15-year general exemption from *TRIPs* obligations, lasting until 2020.

The compromise reached on the even of the Hong Kong Ministerial Conference was to give them until 1 July 2013. Note, however, the compromise does not alter an earlier deal set out in the Doha *Declaration on TRIPs and Public Health*. In that *Declaration*, least developed countries are exempt until 1 January 2016 from protecting pharmaceutical patents. The extended special and differential treatment to 2013 also does not affect new WTO Members, which joined the club after its establishment on 1 January 2005. Those countries, such as China, Kingdom of Saudi Arabia, Russia, and Vietnam, apply *TRIPs* obligations as specified in their accession terms. Generally, the specification calls for immediate compliance. Finally, the 2013 extension does not affect developing or economies in transition from central planning. They already benefited from the Article 65:2-3 grace period of 5 years, which lapsed on 1 January 2000.

B. Dreaded Diseases, Generic Medicines, and the *TRIPs* Amendment

Second, WTO Members agreed to ease restrictions on imports of generic copies of life-saving medicines by poor countries that do not have the capacity to manufacture generics. Such countries cannot take advantage of the compulsory licensing under Article 31 of the *TRIPs Agreement*. This provision allows the government of a Member to issue a compulsory license only if it would be used "predominantly" to supply the domestic market in that country. If a country lacks manufacturing capacity (*e.g.*, Mali), then importing generics is its only viable alternative. But, such importation could imply the exporting Member (*e.g.*, the EU) might not be supplying predominantly its own market. The Doha *Ministerial Declaration* on compulsory licensing did not fix the anomaly. The special *Declaration on TRIPs and Public Health*, while referring to the problem in Paragraph 6 — hence, the rubric "Paragraph 6 issue" — did not fix it either.

Accordingly, in August 2003, the Members agreed to grant three temporary waivers, two from Article 31(f) and one from Article 31(h) of the *TRIPs Agreement*, to deal with the problem of manufacturing capacity. Essentially, they allow a country to issue a compulsory license and thereby override patent rights, and import generic drugs to treat public health matters, including HIV/AIDS, malaria, and tuberculosis.

1. First Waiver from Article 31(f)

Any WTO Member can export generic pharmaceutical products made under a compulsory license to meet the needs of an importing country. However, checks must be established checks to ensure beneficiary countries import generics without undermining the patent systems of developed countries. To ensure a beneficiary is not constrained by burdensome or impractical checks inuring to the benefit of rich countries, the waiver affords that country flexibility. The measures must be "reasonable," within its "means," and "proportionate" to its "administrative capacities." There are three kinds of checks.

First, generic medicines must not be diverted to the wrong markets. Second, while no WTO approval is required, a developing or least developed country invoking the waiver must notify the WTO before importing a generic version of a patented medicine. It must explain what it is importing, in what expected quantities, affirm that it has insufficient or no manufacturing capacity for the product in question, and (if the product is patented in its territory) confirm it has granted a compulsory license in accordance with the *TRIPs Agreement*. Similarly, a developed or developing country that exports pharmaceuticals under a compulsory license must notify the WTO it is doing so. The exporting Member must explain the conditions on (including length of) the license, identify the licensee and product, and state the expected export quantities destinations.

Technically, any Member — rich or poor — can invoke the Article 31(f) waiver. However, in 2003, 23 developed countries declared voluntarily they would not import generic pharmaceutical products. In 2004, the 10 newly acceding countries to the EU added themselves to this list. Thus, the 33 Members abstaining from waiver rights are:

Australia	Greece	New Zealand
Austria	Hungary	Norway
Belgium	Iceland	Poland
Canada	Ireland	Portugal
Czech Republic	Italy	Slovak Republic
Cyprus	Japan	Slovenia
Denmark	Latvia	Spain
Estonia	Lithuania	Sweden
Finland	Luxembourg	Switzerland
France	Malta	United Kingdom
Germany	Netherlands	U.S.

Significantly, 11 additional Members voluntarily declared (in connection with the December 2005 *Statement* of the General Council Chairperson, discussed below) they would use the waiver system to import generics only in a national emergency or other circumstance of extreme urgency:

Hong Kong	Macao	Taiwan
Israel	Mexico	Turkey
Korea	Qatar	U.A.E.
Kuwait	Singapore	

Which Members are the most likely exporters of generics? The answer includes the ones that changed their laws to implement the waiver and permit manufacturing of generics under a compulsory license exclusively for export. These countries include Canada, the EU, India, and Norway. For instance, in 2005, the Indian Parliament amended the country's patent law to make illegal copying patented drugs. Hence, an Indian drug company cannot lawfully supply African countries with an unauthorized version of a patented medicine.

Rwanda was the first WTO Member to invoke the generics import waiver. In July 2007, it notified the Membership it would import (from 2007-09) 260,000 packs of a generic version of a patented medicine. The generic product, TriAvir, is made in Canada by Apotex, Inc. It is a fixed dose admixture of Zidovudine (used to treat HIV), Lamivudine (for HIV and hepatitis B), and Nevirapine (for HIV/AIDS). Rwanda explained it is not able to produce the generic medicine domestically.

2. Second Waiver from Article 31(f)

Developing and least developed WTO Members are not bound by the constraints on exports with respect to exporting in a regional (RTA), as long as at least half of the members of that RTA are least developed (as of August 2003, when the *Medicines Agreement* was forged). This waiver allows such countries to take advantage of economies of scale associated with an FTA or CU in which they participate.

This waiver is inapplicable to *NAFTA*, because no *NAFTA* Party is least developed. It would apply to the *Southern African Customs Union (SACU)*. Would this waiver apply to *CAFTA—DR*, the members of which are Costa Rica, El Salvador, Guatemala, Honduras, Nicaragua, the U.S., plus the Dominican Republic?

3. Waiver from Article 31(h)

A WTO Member importing generic pharmaceuticals made under a compulsory license is not liable for payment of compensation to the patent holder of the medicine subject to the license. Rather, liability is owed by the exporting country. This waiver avoids the possibility of double payment to the right holder, and relieves importing countries, which are likely to be acutely poor, from a possible burden.

Not surprisingly, developing countries sought to make the *Medicines Agreement* permanent. On 6 December 2005, the WTO Members made the waivers permanent. (Technically, they remained temporary until 1 December 2007, the target date by which two-thirds of the WTO Members were to ratify the changes.) The result — a new Article 31 *bis*, which is a direct translation of the waivers, and Annex to the *TRIPs Agreement* — made legal history. It is the first amendment to a Uruguay Round accord. However, the result came about only after considerable controversy.

Led by the U.S., developed countries queried whether the *Medicines Agreement* was a solution searching for a problem. No poor country had invoked Article 31 of the *TRIPs Agreement*. Decrepit distribution systems, dreadful health care, and monstrous corruption are the real impediments to distributing medicines in many parts of the world. Developed countries and their pharmaceutical industries feared export-oriented compulsory licensing would be used to achieve commercial or industrial goals, not for public health reasons. Unscrupulous behavior could occur whereby generics were diverted away from poor people in an intended recipient country to paying customers in rich countries, thereby undermining the market for patented medicines. In response, on 6 December 2005, when the Members adopted the waivers as a "*Decision,*" the Chairman of the WTO General Council issued a "*Statement*" about these concerns.

To make it part of a binding deal with the *Medicines Agreement*, the U.S. and other developed countries sought express reference in the text of the *TRIPs Agreement* to the Chairperson's *Statement*, thus giving it legal status. Led by India (a major source of generics) and Kenya (a large consumer of them), plus Argentina, Brazil, and the Philippines, poor countries objected. They saw the *Statement* as creating "best endeavor" duties, but not hard obligations on monitoring and enforcement. They noted since August 2003 deal, drug prices had fallen by 70-80 percent. In the end, the U.S. dropped its demand for a reference, agreeing to have the *Statement* re-read at the 6 December General Council meeting. Poor countries agreed not to change the *Medicines Agreement*.

In the spring 2007, Thailand became the first country to invoke the compulsory license provisions of the *TRIPs Agreement*, the *Doha Declaration on TRIPs*, and *Medicines Agreement*.[40] Thailand has an ambitious healthcare program to make life-saving treatments for certain diseases available free or at reduced prices. Accordingly, Thailand issued a compulsory license for two HIV/AIDS drugs, efavirenz (also called Stocrin), on which Merck held the patent, and Kaletra, on which Abbott Laboratories held the patent, plus a third compulsory license for a tuberculosis medicine on which Sanofi-Aventis held the patent. Considerable controversy ensued.

In respect of efavirenz, Thailand authorized domestic production of generic versions until 2011, and importation from India of generic copies until it gains manufacturing capacity. The Pharmaceutical Research and Manufacturers of America (PhRMA) castigated Thailand for not consulting or negotiating first with Merck. But, was Thailand obligated to do so for a compulsory license in a public health emergency to be used for a non-commercial treatment program? For Kaletra, Thailand argued Abbott had been selling the non-heat stable version to it at U.S. $2,200 per patient, whereas Abbott sold the drug at $500 per patient in Africa. Abbott said Thailand was using compulsory licensing as a tool for price negotiations. It retaliated by withholding seven drugs from the Thai market, including the heat-stable version of Kaletra, which is widely sought after in hot, humid countries for patients for whom the first-line drug therapies has failed.

Notably, for efavirenz, Brazil asked Merck to cut the price from $1.57 per patient per day to 65 cents — the amount at which Merck sold it in Thailand. Merck refused. Merck distinguished the two countries: AIDS is more prevalent in Thailand than Brazil, and Brazil is larger and wealthier than Thailand. Therefore, Thailand — but not Brazil — is in Merck's category for pricing at cost. Brazil simply can afford to pay more for drugs than a poorer, harder hit country like Thailand. Not persuaded by a utilitarian calculus, in May 2007, Brazil became the second country to invoke compulsory licenses, overriding Merck's efavirenz patent. The drug would be available, sourced from India, at 45 cents. Observe that of 180,000 Brazilians who get free anti-retroviral AIDS medicines from the government, 75,000 Brazilians use efavirenz.

---

[40] *See* Amy Kazmin & Andrew Jack, *Abbott Pulls HIV Drug in Thai Patents Protest*, FINANCIAL TIMES, 14 March 2007, at 7.

VI. THE JULY 2006 COLLAPSE

A. The Lamy 20-20-20 Proposal

The months following the December 2005 Hong Kong Ministerial Conference were dreary ones for WTO negotiators. No country wanted to be blamed for a breakdown in the Doha Round, yet no country appeared willing — political rhetoric notwithstanding — to be the first to make substantive concessions that might heal schisms on agriculture, NAMA, and other issues. On 28 June 2006, in advance of ministerial-level negotiations in Geneva, the WTO Director-General, Pascal Lamy, offered a so-called "20-20-20" formula to catalyze discussions.[41]

The Lamy Proposal suggested a modality around the G-20 Plan. First, the G-20 idea that developed countries cut their average farm tariff by 54 percent would be taken. Second, the U.S. would reduce its overall trade-distorting domestic support (OTDS) in agriculture to below $20 billion annually. Third, developing countries would employ a coefficient for NAMA in the Swiss Formula of 20. But, the U.S. rejected the Proposal.

In particular, the National Association of Manufacturers (NAM) and the National Foreign Trade Council (NFTC) said 20 was too high a coefficient, *i.e.*, it would not result in sufficient market access for U.S. industrial products in developing countries. (The lower the coefficient, the greater the tariff cuts.) The U.S., joined by the EU, called for the G-20 to accept a coefficient of 15. But, Brazil and India insisted on 30.

B. Pre-Collapse Computer Simulations

Efforts were made to move forward using highly technical, hypothetical, statistical estimations of possible bargaining outcomes. The G-10 used computer modeling to simulate the effects of various trade barrier reductions.[42] The simulations were based on proposals for tariff cuts tabled by the U.S., EU, G-20, and various other WTO Members or groupings. For example, a simulation on agricultural market access was run assuming (1) linear cuts would be applied to different bands of tariffs, and (2) no pivot affording flexibility to apply a less-than-agreed cut to a sensitive product would be allowed. These assumptions were contrary, respectively, to U.S. and EU proposals. But, different simulations were run reflecting their proposals.

The simulations also covered NAMA.[43] For instance, depending on special and differential treatment afforded to developing countries on sensitive products, a coefficient of 20 would cut Brazil's average applied industrial tariff rate of 10.97 percent to between 8.7 and 9.2 percent, Egypt's average applied

---

[41] *See* Daniel Pruzin & Nancy Ognanovich, *Lamy Cites Little Progress in "Confessionals," Warns G-8 Leaders Doha Talks Near Failure*, 23 INT'L TRADE REP. (BNA) 1087, 1088 (20 July 2006); Gary G. Yerkey, *World Bank Chief Backs "20-20-20" Plan To Break Impasse in WTO Agricultural Talks*, 23 INT'L TRADE REP. (BNA) 1052, 1053 (13 July 2006).

[42] Daniel Pruzin, *Lamy Sees Signs for Optimism in Doha Talks, Results by April*, 23 INT'L TRADE REP. (BNA) 234-35 (16 Feb. 2006).

[43] *See* Daniel Pruzin, *EU Sounds Warning Over Reticence of Developing Countries in NAMA Talks*, INT'L TRADE REP. (BNA) 751 (31 May 2007).

industrial tariff would drop from 12.5 percent to a 7.6-9.2 percent average, and Malaysia's average applied tariff would drop from 8.6 percent to between 4.2-6.0 percent. A coefficient of 20 would mean India's average applied industrial tariff rate would fall to between 12-17 percent.

Significantly, no computer model was based with the interests of any single Member or bloc in mind. Rather, each model applied a common set of parameters to the simulated tariff cuts. A different letter of the alphabet identified each of models used (*e.g.*, "model A," "model B," and so on). The models estimated the effects of alternative Doha Round proposals on the global trading system. However, apparently for many individual WTO Members, the more important estimation was the impact of a proposal on its own trading interests. Whatever gains the system might experience, what really mattered was the effect at home. Thus, the math exercises failed to yield a set of reduction commitments on which all Members could agree. In other words, no simulation purged enough fear out of enough Members to make concessions to advance the Round.

C. The RAMs and an Accumulation of Flexibilities

Computer modeling could not solve another problem that arose in Doha Round negotiations, namely, demands by Recently Acceded Members — RAMs — for kinder, gentler treatment than would be given by any final deal to developing countries. That is, poor countries were not the only cohort of WTO Members calling for preferential treatment. Countries that recently had joined the club said it would be unfair to ask them to make significant new tariff concessions. The RAMs included

Albania	Kyrgyzstan
Armenia	Macedonia
China	Moldova
Croatia	Oman
Ecuador	Panama
Jordan	Taiwan
Kingdom of Saudi Arabia	Vietnam

(Vietnam was the 150th WTO Member, effective 11 January 2007.) Obliged by their recent terms of accession, they had just cut, or were phasing in cuts, on farm and non-farm tariffs. Not only were their average tariffs significantly lower than before joining, but also they had converted tariff schedules to *ad valorem* rates, *i.e.*, rid the schedules of complicated specific duties. And, they bound the rates on 100 percent of their tariff lines.

Thus, in June 2006, China proposed that new Members should be allowed two kinds of preferential treatment in respect of tariff cutting for NAMA:

1. Apply a higher coefficient in the formula ultimately chosen to reduce industrial tariffs that is 1.5 times higher than the coefficient used by developing countries. (The higher coefficient would result in smaller tariff cuts.)

2. Apply less than the agreed-upon cuts on up to 15 percent of their tariff lines (with reductions of no less than 50 percent of the

agreed-upon cuts), or simply exempt up to 10 percent of the tariff lines from any cuts.

Fairness, newly acceded countries said, applies to services trade, too. WTO entry terms obliged them to liberalize service markets, so why should they have to pay twice?

In March 2007, led by China, the RAMs unveiled a proposal on agricultural trade liberalization.[44] Its key terms and justifications were:

1. RAMs would reduce bound farm tariff levels by 50 percent of the reductions to which developing countries agreed. That would be fair, because the average RAM bound agricultural tariff levels is just over 17 percent, as against a 61 percent average for non-RAM developing countries and 12.5 percent in developed countries. Indeed, China's average bound farm tariff rate is 15 percent, and its highest bound duty, 65 percent, is an above-quota rate on a TRQ for cotton.

2. RAMs would be allowed to exempt up to 10 percent of farm tariff lines from any reductions. That would be fair, because over 7 percent of RAM agricultural tariff lines are set at zero, and nearly 80 percent are bound below 20 percent.

3. RAMs would have a period of no less than 5 years in which to implement their obligations, and get at least 5 years longer than non-RAM developing countries to do so. That would be fair, because during the Uruguay Round developing and least developed countries had a 5-10 year grace period.

4. Any RAM that had bound its trade-distorting agricultural subsidies, namely, Amber Box and *De Minimis* support, would not have to cut its *De Minimis* spending. That would be fair, because non-RAM developing countries have a *De Minimis* support cap of 10 percent of the total value of domestic agricultural production. But, under its accession agreement, China accepted an 8.5 percent limit. Moreover, RAMs do not provide agricultural export subsidies, and do not have STEs, both of which are trade distorting.

5. Small, low-income RAMs that are economies in transition (*i.e.*, former Soviet-bloc countries) would not be obligated to reduce either Amber Box or *De Minimis* support. That would be fair in view of the unique status of these countries.

The appeal to fairness was not persuasive. As with their reaction to China's NAMA offer, to which the U.S. and EU said acceptance would mean an accumulation of flexibilities, developed countries responded to the RAM farm trade proposal with skepticism. When would demands for ever-more special treatment and greater differentiation end?

Manifestly, the coalescence of new WTO Members revealed another schism in the world trading system. Distinctions had moved far beyond the Tokyo Round era line of less developed and developed countries. They traversed the

---

[44] *See* Daniel Pruzin, *China, Other New WTO Members Seek Special Terms on Farm Tariff, Subsidy Cuts*, 24 INT'L TRADE REP. (BNA) 369 (15 March 2007).

Uruguay Round era lines of developed, developing, and least developed countries. Now, there were old versus new Members, be they rich or poor, and old, poor Members versus new, poor Members. What effects do increased delineations among Members, and consequent advocacy for different forms of preferences, have on the theory and praxis of special and differential treatment?

D. A Suspension, Perhaps?

At the end of July 2006, major WTO Members gathered for yet more talks to seek common ground. The outcome was clear before the scheduled end of the discussions. The Indian Commerce Minister, Kamal Nath, left early, saying further negotiations were pointless because of the intransigence of the U.S. and EU to cut farm subsidies and grant agricultural market access, respectively, while insisting on enhanced NAMA from developing countries. Not surprisingly, the revised deadline for submitting revised service market access offers — 31 July 2006 — fell by the wayside. Recriminations ensued, especially between the U.S. and EU. Most international trade lawyers and scholars declared the Doha Round dead or on its death throes, believing it nearly impossible to reach a conclusion before the 30 June 2007 end of presidential trade negotiating authority delegated by Congress (*i.e.*, Trade Promotion Authority, or TPA).

The WTO Director-General, Pascal Lamy, opined the Round had not collapsed, but merely was suspended. Efforts to lift the suspension, or perhaps more accurately, resuscitate it, proved fruitless. The Group of Six (G-6), consisting of the U.S., EU, Australia, Brazil, India, and Japan, tried. In August 2006, the USTR, Susan Schwab, called on China to take a more prominent role, expressing surprise China was willing to allow other developing countries to represent its interests in G-6 talks, and asking rhetorically: "If you were China, with arguably the greatest stake in the world trading system, would you want India and Brazil to be articulating your position [in the G-6]"?[45] That effort proved nothing more than a clumsy, thinly veiled attempt by the Americans to divide developing countries amongst themselves.

VII. REVIVAL EFFORTS

A. Spring 2007 Farm Trade Discussions

With America, and much of the world, pre-occupied with the War on Terror, Iraq, and Congressional elections, no progress — or even serious effort — was made to breathe life into the Doha Round in the late summer and fall of 2006. In December 2006, President George W. Bush referred to the "Doha Round" as the "Darfur Round."[46]

At a January 2007 lunch, in advance of the World Economic Forum, President Bush told his USTR, Susan Schwab, and the EU Trade

---

[45] *See* Richard McGregor, *U.S. Presses China to Take Doha Role*, FINANCIAL TIMES, 30 Aug. 2006, at 4.

[46] *Just Do It*, THE ECONOMIST, 13 Jan. 2007, at 64.

Commissioner, Peter Mandelson "Go to it, Susan. Go to it, Mandelson. Just get it done."[47] Later, around the Davos, Switzerland based Forum, trade ministers took up the mantle again — negotiations the USTR called "three dimension chess."[48] In public discourse, each official tended to say its side was flexible, but needed movement from other sides. The underlying message was if the Doha Round failed, it was the fault of some other country. Each articulated the point that proposals made thus far promised big benefits for many countries, but they could not be realized without agreement on all parts of a deal as a single undertaking. The subliminal point was other countries should be ashamed to abandon the progress made.

To their credit, and continuing with the "what if?" scenarios explored through computer simulations, negotiators considered the following ideas.

- Might the U.S. agree to deep farm subsidy cuts in exchange for deep farm tariff cuts by the EU?

The *Financial Times* reported a deal was at hand whereby the U.S. would cap its overall trade-distorting farm subsidies at $17 billion annually, meaning actual reductions from existing spending of from $19.1 billion.[49] The EU would reduce its average agricultural tariffs by at least 54 percent, and improvement from the current offer of (apparently) 39 percent. Both sides rejected the story. India's Commerce Minister, Kamal Nath, reminded the U.S. that "If the U.S. seeks market access for its subsidized products, it will result in more market access for subsidy flows, not trade flows."[50] France reminded the EU Trade Commissioner, Peter Mandelson, that he had no mandate to increase average farm tariff cut proposal beyond 39 percent.

- Might new 5-year U.S. farm legislation, specifically, the 2007 *Farm Bill*, be both WTO compatible and embody U.S. commitment to a Doha Round deal?

Some features of the *Bill* (initially released as a 181 page document by the USDA in January 2007, and containing over 65 proposed modifications in American agricultural policy) were consistent with the October 2005 Portman Proposal, namely, a cut in annual allowable trade-distorting subsidies from $22.4 to $17 billion, suggesting a roughly 20 percent reduction in federal farm spending over the 5-year life of the *Bill*. Overall, the 2002 *Farm Bill* cost the U.S. government about $97 billion, whereas the 2007 proposed *Bill* had a price tag of $87.3 billion.

Specifically, the 2007 *Bill* suggested a limit on subsidies per farmer to a maximum $360,000 per year, and sharply circumscribed eligibility. Farmers with an annual adjusted gross income (wages and other income less farm expenses and depreciation) in excess of $200,000 would be ineligible for support — a reduction in the income threshold from $2.5 million, meaning about 80,000 producers would lose support. That made sense, as they were

---

[47] *Id.* at 64, 65.

[48] *Id.* at 64.

[49] *See* Eoin Callan & Alan Beattie, *U.S. and EU Near Farm Trade Deal*, FINANCIAL TIMES, 22 Jan. 2007, at 3.

[50] Alan Beattie, *U.S. and EU "Must Give Ground" on Trade*, FINANCIAL TIMES, 25 Jan. 2007, at 3.

relatively wealthy. As of 2005, 60 percent of U.S. farmers got no federal support, while 10 percent of the farmers got 72 percent of it, and over half of the subsidies were concentrated in just 25 of the 435 U.S. congressional districts.[51]

The *Bill* also sought to shift payments from trade- and price-distorting crop subsidies to Green Box direct income support decoupled from prices and production. For example, it called for lower support for dairy farmers and sugar processors, and reduced crop insurance. It also sought removal of the implicit link between the type of crop a farmer produces (namely, eschewing fruits and vegetables) and eligibility for cotton subsidies — a link Brazil successfully attacked as trade-distorting in the 2005 *Cotton* case.

However, other features of the *Bill* suggested only incremental changes in programs that also were the subject of the *Cotton* case. For example, the *Bill* retained the Marketing Loan Program (which pays farmers when the price of their product falls below a set level), making only a modest adjustment to the calculation of the target price level (to take account of actual market prices). In specific, the *Bill* called for a cap on marketing loans for corn at $1.85 per bushel, for cotton at 52.92 cents per pound, for soybeans at $4.92 per bushel, for wheat at $2.58 per bushel — all lower amounts than the previous rates. The *Bill* proposed to set loan rates based on the five-year average price of the commodity in question, but excluding the lowest and highest year prices.

As another example of incremental change, the *Bill* included counter-cyclical payments (whereby farmers are subsidized in inverse proportion to market prices), which the U.S. hoped to include within an enlarged Blue Box, with only a minor adjustment to include national crop yields as well as prices in calculating the amount of subsidy. The *Bill* indicated a conversion from price-based counter-cyclical payments to revenue-based payments. That is, counter-cyclical support for a commodity would be triggered if the actual national revenue per acre for that commodity fell below the national target revenue per acre. With price-based countercyclical payments, farmers experiencing crop loss are under-compensated, and farmers with high output are over-compensated. Revenue-based countercyclical payments are a way to target more precisely support.

Subsidies to U.S. cotton producers were another illustration.[52] Argentina explained the *Bill* would increase their direct payments by 65 percent (in 2008-09, compared to 2006). Countercyclical payments (which compensate farmers when the market price for cotton falls below a government-set target price) would be made at the same loan rate as before. But, farmers would be assured an income boost, because the payments would be calculated on a new base period for production (2002-06).

In brief, the *Bill* was a reminder of U.S. insistence on sovereignty over farm legislation. The *Bill*, the U.S. insisted, would not be written in the WTO, and the U.S. would adhere to the revenue assurance principle — protecting farmers' incomes, if not entirely by price supports, then by a mix of devices. Not

---

[51] *See Uncle Sam's Teat*, THE ECONOMIST, 9 Sept. 2006, at 35.

[52] *See* Daniel Pruzin, *Argentina Says Proposed U.S. Farm Bill Would Violate WTO Cotton Commitments*, 24 INT'L TRADE REP. (BNA) 408 (22 March 2007).

surprisingly, the Directorate-General for Agriculture of the European Commission concluded in a February 2007 analysis of the *Bill* that it was "not encouraging" for future negotiations.[53] It lamented continued reliance on trade-distorting measures (rather than shifting subsidies into the Green Box), and maintenance of large support programs to products like dairy and sugar.

- Might the U.S. and EU agree to enhanced agricultural market access via TRQ reform?

The two sides studied the possibility of higher quota thresholds, and lower out-of-quota tariffs, for beef, other meat products, and dairy goods. The EU said it would increase beef imports by 800,000 metric tons annually, boost the in-quota TRQ volume for poultry from 400,000 to 650,000 metric tons, and increase the in-quota TRQ threshold for butter from 90,000 to 140,000 metric tons. The U.S. retorted the EU offered only a 160,000 ton in quota beef threshold. The balance of its offer was not a bound commitment, but rather merely a forecast of higher import volume that could occur if the EU cut its out-of-quota beef tariff.

B. The April 2007 Falconer "Center of Gravity" Text and Its Aftermath

The Doha Round reached a stage in which virtually all important discussions were between the U.S. and EU, typically shrouded in secrecy. This process created bitter resentment, as Egypt's Trade Minister, Rachid Mohammed Rachid, intoned:

> Africa has been totally neglected. Africa has been dealt with more by threats than by anything else. They have been told: "You should not be the ones blocking this deal. You should be supporting it.[54]

Yet, only if the U.S. and EU could unite with an impressive farm trade offer could they then pressure the G-20, and especially Brazil and India, into better NAMA and service trade proposals. Moreover, the cabal-like negotiations intimated limited results.[55]

The Chairman of the WTO agricultural negotiations, Ambassador Crawford Falconer of New Zealand, set them out in a "Challenges Paper." It was circulated to Members, and posted on the WTO website, in April 2007.[56] He

---

[53] Gary G. Yerkey, *USDA Farm Bill Proposal "Not Encouraging" for WTO Negotiations, New EU Analysis Finds*, 24 INT'L TRADE REP. (BNA) 227-28 (15 Feb. 2007).

[54] Alan Beattie, *Doha Breakthrough Possible in Weeks, Says EU*, FINANCIAL TIMES, 26 Jan. 2007, at 4.

[55] *See* Daniel Pruzin, *Doha Agriculture Chair Finds Silver Lining in Members' Criticisms of "Challenges" Paper*, 24 INT'L TRADE REP. (BNA) 641-43 (10 May 2007); Daniel Pruzin, *WTO Chair Identifies "Center of Gravity" for Doha Round Agreement on Agriculture*, 24 INT'L TRADE REP. (BNA) 606-07 (3 May 2007); Daniel Pruzin, *U.S. to Come Under Pressure to Reveal Bottom Line on Ag Subsidies in Doha Talks*, 24 INT'L TRADE REP. (BNA) 607-09 (3 May 2007).

[56] In May 2007, Chairman Falconer issued a Second Installment of the Challenges Paper, which also was posted on the WTO website, and which covered additional topics not treated in the First Installment of April. In summary, the bluntly worded Second Installment set out the following points:

1.   *Special Safeguards*

(Text continued on page 129)

Developing countries, led by India, Indonesia, and the Philippines, suggested a special safeguard mechanism (SSM) that would permit imposition of 50-100 percent tariffs on an imported agricultural product if (1) imports of that product increase by more than 5 percent (in volume terms) vis-à-vis a recent calendar year, or (2) the price of that product falls in comparison with the average price in a previous 3 year period. There appeared to be consensus that if the SSM in Article 5 of the *Agreement on Agriculture* is retained, then it must afford greater flexibility for developing countries so as to serve its "special" purpose. That object is to respond to the needs of farmers in developing countries, particularly in respect of food security, livelihood security, and rural development. Accordingly, the quantity and price triggers, as well as the duration of the remedy, likely would need amendment.

2.   *Tropical and Diversification Products*

Consensus on a complete list of tropical and diversification products, and the kind of special treatment they should be accorded — such as, for example, a reduction to zero for tariffs of between 0-25 percent, and a tariff cut of 85 percent for tariffs over 25 percent — had not emerged.

3.   *Small, Vulnerable Economies (SVEs)*

It appeared an acceptable definition of an "SVE" was one with an economy that, in the period 1999 to 2004, had an average share of world merchandise trade of 0.16 percent or less, of world trade in non-agricultural products of 0.1 percent or less, and world trade in agricultural products of 0.4 percent or less. This definition was developed by SVEs. There was consensus that their export interests should receive enhanced improvements in market access.

4.   *The Green Box*

No WTO Member suggested an overhaul of the "Green Box" definition, *i.e.*, all agreed it should contain only those support measures that are non-or minimally-trade distorting, and do not have the effect of giving price support to producers. Brazil, India, and other developing countries urged stricter disciplines on this Box to avoid "box shifting," the phenomenon of amending a farm subsidy program so that it qualifies for the Green Box, and thereby is exempt from a reduction commitment, but making no change to the actual level of expenditure. The U.S. and EU resisted this idea, pointing out Green Box programs — such as support for agricultural research, disease control, environmental protection, regional and restructuring assistance, and rural development and infrastructure — are non- or minimally-trade distorting. They also argued stricter Green Box disciplines would undermine current reforms, which are based on Uruguay Round rules.

Thus, the key point of controversy was just how far to enlarge the Green Box, if at all. There was general or considerable support to enlarge the Green Box to include support payments for: (1) land reform programs in developing countries (including associated administration and legal services); (2) acquisition of stocks for food security, (3) acquisition of foodstuffs at subsidized prices when procured from low-income and resource-poor producers in developing countries with the goal of fighting hunger and rural poverty; (4) pilot and new programs in developing countries to cover losses of less than 30 percent of the average production in cases of crop or livestock production for disease control purposes.

5.   *Least Developed Countries*

Developed countries, and developing countries in a position to do so, should give at least 97 percent of agricultural exports from least developed countries duty-free, quota-free treatment, as agreed at the December Hong Kong Ministerial Conference, and they ought to provide the remaining 3 percent that treatment by the end of the applicable implementation period.

6.   *Cotton Market Access*

Developed countries, and developing countries in a position to do so, ought to provide duty- and quota-free access to cotton exports from least developed countries.

7.   *RAMs*

A consensus appears to exist that new WTO Members should qualify for special and differential treatment accorded to developing countries in the areas of agricultural market access, domestic support, and export competition. The Kingdom of Saudi Arabia and Vietnam, in particular, should not be subjected to new Doha Round undertakings, though China should be obligated to make further tariff and subsidy reductions. No RAM, it appeared, would escape cuts in *De Minimis* subsidies, which likely would be 25 percent (5 percent less than the first installment of the Challenges Paper suggested for developing countries). In respect of farm tariff cuts, RAMs summarized bluntly the "center of gravity" around which a farm trade deal could occur:

1. *Overall Average Farm Tariff Cuts*

The overall average tariff cut for developed countries would have to be between 39 and 66 percent, *i.e.*, between the EU and U.S. proposals. Most likely, a 50 percent cut (or somewhat above that) would be acceptable. The reductions should be non-linear, and thereby harmonizing, meaning the highest band of tariffs should be cut by between the EU and U.S. proposals of 60 and 85 percent, respectively, with the most politically feasible deal being a 60-70 percent cut in the top band. For developing countries, the overall cut would have to be a minimum of two-thirds of the figure applicable to developed countries, meaning 33 percent based on a 50 percent compromise. Possibly, for them a simple linear cut in their overall average farm tariff, with a minimum cut on each product, would suffice.

2. *Sensitive Products, TRQs, and Zero Duty Lines*

A compromise would require a limit on the number of farm products a Member could designate as sensitive of between 1 and 5 percent of all tariff lines. To be sure, sensitive products still would be subject to tariff cuts, probably between one-third and two-thirds of the reduction in an agreed-upon formula applicable to non-sensitive items (with the G-20 hoping for just a 20 percent deviation, and the EU arguing for 50 percent). And, TRQs for sensitive products would increase in correlation with the extent of deviation from agreed cuts. There was no agreement as to the exact correlation between TRQ expansion and deviation from tariff cuts. There was some center of gravity around expanding TRQs by 5-8 percent. But, arguments persisted over whether the increase should be calculated relative to domestic consumption (a larger figure, which the U.S. favored, arguing for 6 percent thereof) or import volume (a smaller figure, which the EU favored, urging 2-3 percent thereof). Arguments also raged over whether a farm product subject to a zero tariff should be included in the computation of the maximum number of tariff lines that can be designated sensitive. That technical point has potentially major consequences. Assume the HTS has 700 agricultural tariff lines, and of them, a particular Member gives duty-free treatment on 200. Capping

---

probably would have to concede to a cut for each band that is 5 percent less than the cut generally applicable.

8. *Tariff Escalation*

Little progress existed on this topic. Indeed, the basic issues of identifying instances of tariff escalation and agreeing on a formula to deal with it remained open.

9. *Tariff Simplification*

There was no progress on whether and how to address this topic.

10. *Long-Standing Preferences and Preference Erosion*

Most of the problem of preference erosion exists with respect to a small range of products, namely, sugar, bananas, and a few other fruits and vegetables. Trade-based solutions (such as extended implementation periods to avoid sharp, sudden cuts in the margin of preference) might need to be supplemented with non-trade-based solutions (such as technical assistance programs).

11. *Commodities*

A consensus had yet to emerge on the relationship of GATT Article XX(h) to arrangements by commodity producers.

sensitive products at 3-5 percent, and including zero tariff lines in the cap, means the Member can designate 35 as sensitive. Excluding them means it can reserve 25 lines.

3. *Special Product Designations by Developing Countries*

Developing countries would have to accept a limit on special product designation of between 5 to 8 percent of all tariff lines, assuming developed countries agreed on a 1-5 percent limit on sensitive products. That would mean developing countries would be able to designate a greater number of tariff lines as "special" than the number of lines developed countries could pick as "sensitive." However, tariffs on specially designated products would need to be cut by two-thirds of the reductions by developed countries, *i.e.*, 10-20 percent cuts.

4. *Overall Farm Subsidy Reductions*

The U.S. would have to cut its proposed cap on OTDS from nearly $23 billion annually to a figure between the very low teens and $19 billion. It was inconceivable the U.S. could emerge from the Doha Round with the right to spend more on farm subsidies than its actual expenditures in 2001 when the Round started. The U.S. intimated flexibility to drop its cap to $17 billion, but not to $12 billion (as Brazil and India demanded) or $115 billion (as the EU sought). Yet, whether Congress would accept even a $17 billion cap was uncertain. In June 2007, House Agriculture Committee Chairman Collin Peterson (Democrat — Minnesota) criticized the Bush Administration for making the October 2005 Portman Proposal without consultation, much less input, from Congress, and insisted his Committee would write a Farm Bill for American farmers, not the WTO.[57] As for the EU, it would have to cut its OTDS by 70-80 percent. Japan would have to do so by an amount comparable to U.S. cuts.

5. *Amber Box Cuts*

The U.S. and Japan would have to cut Amber Box subsidies by 60 percent, and the EU by 70 percent. Hence, the U.S. Amber Box spending limit would fall from $19.1 to 7.64 billion annually, and the EU cap from 67 to 20 billion euros.

6. *Base Period*

The U.S. argued for a 1999-2000 as the base period from which to calculate product-specific Amber Box subsidies. That argument was self-serving. U.S. farm spending was far higher (with Amber Box spending reaching a peak then) than in the period other Members, including the G-20, supported, namely, 1995-2000.

7. *Blue Box Cuts*

WTO Members appeared willing to agree to an additional 50 percent Blue Box reduction, *i.e.*, from the 5 percent of the total value of domestic agricultural production, to 2.5 percent of that value. However, they had not agreed whether product-specific caps should be put on the Blue Box, or calculated for the Amber and Blue Box combined. The G-20 called for product-specific

---

[57] *See* Gary G. Yerkey, *House Ag Chair Peterson Says U.S. Negotiating "With Ourself" in WTO Talks*, 24 INT'L TRADE REP. (BNA) 826-27 (14 June 2007).

limits in Blue Box spending, which the U.S. rejected. Also unacceptable was the idea of an "anti-concentration" mechanism: a certain percentage of Blue Box spending would be designated as the maximum limit that could not be exceeded for any single product. The mechanism was a veiled version of product-specific limits.

8. *De Minimis Cuts*

WTO Members also seemed willing to cut by half the limit on *De Minimis* spending, from 5 to 2.5 percent of the total value of domestic agricultural spending.

9. *Export Subsidy Cuts*

WTO Members agreed at the December 2005 Hong Kong Ministerial Conference to eliminate export subsidies by 2013, but not on the precise modality for doing so. The G-20 agreed to a compromise suggestion in the Falconer text that 50 percent of the export subsidies be eliminated by 2010, and the balance phased out during 2011-2013. That agreement was notable because of the initial position of the G-20: 50 percent of the export subsidies should be eliminated in the first year of implementation, and a further 30 percent cut by the middle of that period.

In sum, the Falconer text was an honest "fish-or-cut-bait" document. Not surprisingly, most Members found something to criticize in it.

Japan rejected immediately a 1-5 percent limit on sensitive product designations. The U.S. said the Falconer text ignored economic analyses showing most development gains from farm trade liberalization would come from lower farm tariffs, not U.S. domestic support cuts — though the U.S. hinted at acquiescing to modest OTDS cuts beyond its $23 billion offer. Conversely, the G-20 demanded the U.S. reduce OTDS to around $12 billion, period. Contrary to the U.S. position, there could be no calibration, or exchange rate, between cuts in farm subsidies and expansion of market access through farm tariff cuts. The G-10 countries, notably Japan and Switzerland, adamantly opposed any cap on farm tariffs, and said the lowest level of farm tariff cuts in the text still was too high.

Even a positive reaction from the EU prompted controversy. The EU hinted it might improve its original offer to reduce farm tariffs — from an average decrease of 39 percent, to a figure nearer 54 percent. It could do so by cutting tariffs on tropical products. The U.S. replied significant reductions to the highest tariff band are what matter — they should be 75-85 percent, not 60 percent as the EU sought. The G-20 observed a cut to the highest band of 50 percent, with many sensitive product designations, would be of little value.

Despite the raucous response, the center of gravity identified in the Falconer Challenges Paper was positive. On the theory that compromise means all get something and none gets everything, the text revealed the basis for compromise. Of course, even if it did, compromises were needed on NAMA and services trade, too, and all compromises were inter-related. Unfortunately, those compromises proved elusive.

In late June 2007, the Doha Round collapsed again.[58] The Group of Four (G-4) — Brazil, India, the EU, and U.S. — held make-or-break talks in

---

[58] Eoin Callan, *China's Shadow Looms Over Doha Failure*, FINANCIAL TIMES, 23-24 June 2007, at 3; *A Seat At the Table*, FINANCIAL TIMES, 23-24 June 2007, at 6.

Potsdam, Germany, scene of the last major conference of the Second World War, in 1945. The EU and U.S. did little if anything to improve their offers on agricultural topics. Under heavy pressure from developing countries, Brazil's Foreign Minister, Celso Amorim, backed away from earlier offers. India's Commerce Minister, Kamal Nath, showed up late and — said the EU and U.S. — looked eager to leave. Predictably, the EU and U.S. accused Brazil, India, and the developing world generally of missing an extraordinary opportunity to secure lower farm tariffs and subsidies in developed countries by conceding reductions to trade barriers on industrial products. Brazil, India, and many poor countries offered a one-noun rebuttal: China.

That is, if EU-U.S. proposals for a low NAMA coefficient were implemented, then infant industries in many developing countries would die in competition with Chinese manufacturers. More was at stake from cutting industrial trade barriers than anxiety in Old Europe or the American Rust Belt. Entrepreneurs and factory workers in many poor countries, too, felt uneasy about China, and their countries lacked meaningful trade adjustment assistance beyond family networks. To be sure, some South East Asian countries, and Japan, had strategies to cooperate with and benefit from, the long-term ascendancy of China. But, these positive synergies exacerbated schisms present when the Doha Round was launched in November 2001 — rich and poor, some rich versus other rich, and some poor against other poor.

Query whether blaming anxiety about China is short-sighted? Is the real culprit historical asymmetry in trade barrier reductions in the GATT era, *i.e.,* from 1947-95? In that period, capitalist developed countries made aggressive cuts to barriers against industrial goods trade, but many developing countries pursued policies of Import Substitution, if not outright socialism. By November 2001, was the asymmetry too great to be re-balanced by a grand bargain of "agriculture for industry plus services"? China, then, may be an intervening, but not principal causal, variable.

Consider, too, the signal a Doha Round collapse might send to a reviled group to which the launch of the Round was (at least implicitly) aimed — Islamic extremists. If agreement on a Doha Development Agenda (DDA) in Qatar two months after 9/11 supposedly proved (*inter alia*) violent "bad guys" would not bring down the global economic order, then what would collapse say about peace-loving "good guys"? Would it indicate even the monstrous threat of extremism cannot bring them to get past myopic economic self-interest, nor to formulate a social agenda to promote the common good?

C. A New American Demand on Dumping

Links between a successful Doha Round outcome and the War on Terror apparently were not at the forefront of the American trade negotiating position in respect of a new demand the U.S. raised on 27 June 2007: change the antidumping (AD) rules to permit zeroing, and reject the Chinese proposal on Sunset Reviews of AD orders. (Zeroing and Sunset Review are treated in later Chapters.) Failure to agree would mean the U.S. would not agree to a Doha Round conclusion.

For the Americans, the bottom line was:[59]

- Article 2:4:3 must be added to the WTO *Antidumping Agreement* to nullify a bevy of Appellate Body rulings. The new Article would expressly permit that when AD authorities aggregate results of comparisons between Normal Value and Export Price, they "are not required to offset the results of any comparison in which the export price is greater than the normal value against the results of any comparison in which the normal value is greater than the export price."

- Article 9:3 of the *Antidumping Agreement* must be amended to affirm the amount of an AD duty cannot exceed the dumping margin.

- It must be clear that when checking whether the amount of an AD duty exceeds the dumping margin, authorities "may calculate the margin of dumping on the basis of an individual export transaction or multiple export transactions."

- The 29 June 2007 Chinese proposal on Sunset Reviews must be rejected. That proposal would (1) forbid under all circumstances any AD duty order longer than 10 years, (2) ban self-initiation of these Reviews by governmental authorities, and (3) restrict initiation of these Reviews to domestic producers. (The Antidumping Agreement calls for orders to lapse after 5 years, unless criteria are satisfied for their renewal, and permits self-initiation.)

In essence, there must be no weakening of AD defenses, and if that requires legislatively over-ruling Appellate Body decisions adverse to the U.S. on zeroing, so be it.

Despite tough rhetoric from the Deputy USTR — that zeroing was a "very important issue" to the U.S., and that the U.S. "cannot envisage an outcome to the negotiations without addressing zeroing" — and an admonition to Members "not to leave it to the dispute settlement system to make subjective judgments about what is fair," the Americans got little support.[60] Almost all WTO Members opposed the U.S. position. At an 11 July 2007 meeting of the WTO negotiating group on rules, Argentina, Brazil, Canada, Chile, China, Costa Rica, Japan, Korea, Malaysia, Mexico, Taiwan, and Thailand all spoke openly against the U.S. position. Only Egypt argued zeroing should be permitted, but then only in certain circumstances.

D. The July 2007 Draft Modalities Texts and Their Aftermath

On 17 July 2007, the Chairman of the WTO negotiating groups on agriculture and NAMA (New Zealand's Ambassador Crawford Falconer, and Canada's Ambassador Donald Stephenson, respectively) released texts of agreements intended to serve as a basis for continued Doha Round talks. Unlike the earlier Center of Gravity texts, the draft agreements did not dwell on the

---

[59] Daniel Pruzin, *U.S. Sets WTO Approval of "Zeroing" as Condition of Agreement to Doha Deal,* 24 INT'L TRADE REP. (BNA) 1040-41 (19 July 2007).

[60] *See id.*

personal impressions of their authors as to what concessions would be necessary, or should be made, to finish the Round. Rather, the draft accords were modalities documents, setting out as objectively as possible the points on which consensus had been reached, the remaining areas of controversy, and the range of alternatives suggested by Members to resolve those controversies. Consequently, the July 2007 draft modalities texts essentially summarized the point to which the Doha Round had evolved since November 2001 on agricultural and NAMA issues.

Specifically, the draft texts suggested negotiations should proceed along the lines outlined below. Predictably, the suggestions provoked sharp reactions:[61]

For agricultural market access:

1. On farm tariffs, there would be non-linear cuts to bound rates. Developed countries would cut tariffs in the highest band (duties above 75 percent) by 66-73 percent. That was above the maximum amount the EU had ever publicly declared it could accept — 60-70 percent — but below the U.S. demand of an 85 percent cut. Developed countries would cut tariffs in the lowest band (20 percent or below) by 48-52 percent. The proposed obligations appeared too severe for Japan. Japan said the cuts would translate to slashing its rice and wheat tariffs to 4-6 percent, and the number of its high-tariff farm imports from 200 to 40-60.

2. The obligations on developing countries would be two-thirds those on developed countries. Developing countries would administer a 44-48 percent cut on the highest band of their bound tariffs (duties above 130 percent), and a 32-34 percent cut to their lowest tariff band (30 percent of less). (Because developing countries generally levy higher duties than developed countries on farm products, the band ranges for them would be set at higher levels.) Least developed countries would not be obliged to cut their farm tariffs. The U.S. said these obligations were insufficient to improve access to major developing country agricultural markets.

3. On sensitive product designations, developed countries could identify as sensitive either 4 or 6 percent of their farm tariff lines. But, if a developed country had 30 percent or more of its tariff lines in the highest tariff band (duties above 75 percent), then it could designate 6 or 8 percent of its farm tariff lines as sensitive. Developed

---

[61] *See* Ed Taylor, *Brazilian Farm and Business Sectors Divided in Reactions to Doha Draft Texts*, 24 INT'L TRADE REP. (BNA) 1141-42 (9 August 2007); Daniel Pruzin, *"Intensive" Work Needed on Doha Round in September, WTO Chief Lamy Tells TNC*, 24 INT'L TRADE REP. (BNA) 1105-06 (2 August 2007); Daniel Pruzin, *U.S. Expresses Disappointment with Draft WTO Agriculture Text*, 24 INT'L TRADE REP. (BNA) 1054-55 (26 July 2007); Daniel Pruzin, *U.S. Criticizes Draft NAMA Text, Refutes Developing Nations' Arguments on Tariffs*, 24 INT'L TRADE REP. (BNA) 1062-63 (26 July 2007); Daniel Pruzin, *Brazil's Amorim Says WTO Draft Texts for Agriculture, NAMA Talks Lack Balance*, 24 INT'L TRADE REP. (BNA) 1063-65 (26 July 2007); Toshio Aritake, *Japan's Farm Minister Terms Latest WTO Texts "Improvement" but Still Not Acceptable*, 24 INT'L TRADE REP. (BNA) 1066-67 (26 July 2007); Daniel Pruzin, *WTO Chairman Issue Draft Ag, NAMA Texts Outlining Tough Concessions Needed in Doha*, 24 INT'L TRADE REP. (BNA) 1012-14 (19 July 2007).

countries would have to cut bound tariff rates on sensitive products by between one-third and two-thirds of the agreed formula reduction. India decried the unfairness of no such flexibility for developing countries.

4. The obligation on sensitive products for developing countries would follow the one-third/two-third approach. They could designate as sensitive up to one-third more of their tariff lines than developed countries. Developing countries would have to cut tariffs on sensitive products by two-thirds of the cut required of developed countries.

5. On tariff rate quotas (TRQs), any sensitive product subject to a TRQ would have to apply a minimum in-quota volume threshold increase calculated as a percentage of total domestic consumption of that product. The increase would compensate exporting countries for the protection afforded to a product from a tariff cut by its "sensitive" designation. The amount of TRQ expansion for a product would vary inversely with the deviation from the agreed-upon tariff cut. If a country deviated from the agreed-upon bound tariff cut by two-thirds (the maximum permissible deviation), *i.e.*, it made only one-third of the agreed upon cut, then the percentage TRQ increase would be at least 4, and possibly 6. If the country deviated from the formulaic cut by just one-third (the minimum deviation), *i.e.*, it imposed two-thirds of the agreed cut, then it would expand its TRQ by 3 or 5 percent. The EU said this scheme excessively expanded TRQs for sensitive products, thereby crossing one of its "red lines." Japan ruled out any TRQ expansion for rice, its tariffs on which exceed 100 percent.

6. There would be no fixed cap for any country on the duty rate for a sensitive farm product. But, any country with a tariff exceeding 100 percent on over 5 percent of its farm tariff lines would have to pay compensation to other countries. The compensation would take the form of an additional increased in-quota TRQ threshold for the high-tariff lines.

For agricultural subsidies:

1. The bound level of OTDS would be slashed in a non-linear fashion, with steeper cuts to support levels in higher band ranges. Developed countries with the highest support levels, namely, the EU, would cut OTDS by either 75 or 85 percent. Such cuts would mean an annual OTDS spending cap on the EU of 16.5 billion euros or 27.6 billion euros, respectively. That severe a reduction, said the EU, would cross a "red line." For developed countries with the next highest support levels, *i.e.*, Japan and the U.S., the cuts would be either 66 or 73 percent. Developed countries with OTDS levels in the lowest band ($10 billion or less) would be obliged to cut their level by 50 percent. Consequently, Japan would have to agree to a ceiling on annual OTDS spending of 1.5 trillion yen or 1.9 trillion yen. But, these proposed cuts would translate into figures beyond

what the U.S. had offered. To the U.S., a cut of 66 or 73 percent to OTDS would mean a ceiling on OTDS of $13 or $16.4 billion, respectively. The U.S. offered a $23 billion cap, hinting at best a possible $17 billion ceiling, and rejecting $13 billion. Conversely, the cuts are not nearly as steep as the $12 billion sought by the G-20, led by India and Brazil. The G-20 took the same view in respect of EU and Japanese OTDS.

2. The OTDS reduction obligation on developing countries would be two-thirds that on developed countries. Least developed countries would have no OTDS reduction obligation.

3. Amber Box funding would be disciplined through non-linear reductions, with the highest cuts to the highest support level bands. Developed countries, particularly the EU, with support in the highest band would have to cut Amber Box programs by 70 percent. Countries in the next band, like Japan and the U.S., would impose a 60 percent cut. That reduction commitment would restrict the U.S. to a maximum annual $7.6 billion expenditure on Amber Box support. The EU and Japanese yearly limits would be 20.1 billion euro and 1.6 trillion yen, respectively.

4. There would be product-specific support limits in the Amber Box. No developed country could increase product-specific subsidy by the average amount it had spent to support that product in a base period. The base period to determine the limit would be 1995-2000. But, the U.S. could use 1995-2004 as its base period, as its average spending then was higher than between 1995-2000. (Specifically, the U.S. could take the average of its spending in 1995-2004 and 1995-2000.)

5. The *De Minimis* exception on domestic support, applicable to developed countries, would be cut to either 2 or 2.5 percent of the value of total domestic agricultural production.

6. Blue Box expenditures would be capped at 2.5 percent of total domestic agricultural production, as set out in the August 2004 *Framework Agreement.*

7. Abusive box shifting — specifically, moving a large amount of support programs (such as countercyclical payments in the U.S.) into the Blue Box — would be punished. If a country put more than 40 percent of its OTDS into the Blue Box, then that country would be obliged to apply the same reduction figure to Blue Box support as it must to Amber Box. Further, no country would be allowed to give Blue Box support to a specific product in excess of the average value of subsidies it gave to that product in the base period of 1995-2000.

8. Agricultural export subsidies would be eliminated in accordance with the 2005 Hong Kong Ministerial Conference accord, namely, complete elimination by 2013, and a 50 percent reduction by 2010.

9. New disciplines would apply on export credits, credit guarantees, and insurance, and food aid, as detailed in an annex.

10. STEs, particularly farm export monopolies in Australia, Canada, and New Zealand, would be eliminated by 2013.

11. Trade-distorting cotton subsidies, particularly output-linked support, would be reduced significantly. The U.S. would have to cut them by 82 percent. The U.S. declared this provision to be "unacceptable," as well as duplicative with the product-specific Amber Box restrictions. Non-production linked subsidies would be capped at one-third of their average amount in the 1995-2000 base period.

For NAMA:

1. The critical Swiss Formula coefficient for reducing bound industrial tariff rates would be between 19 and 23 for developing countries. For developed countries, it would be 8-9. The developing country obligation would be considerably stricter than the 35 sought by the NAMA-11 countries. But, it reflects a 25 June 2007 middle-ground proposal from some East Asian and Latin American countries — Chile, Colombia, Costa Rica, Hong Kong, Mexico, Peru, Singapore, and Thailand. Their suggestion was a developing country coefficient in the high teens or low 20s in exchange for a developed country coefficient of below 10. Developing countries rejected the 19-23 range. South Africa insisted a 25 point gap between developing and developing country obligations was necessary to prevent it suffering "massive unemployment and deindustrialization." Conversely, the U.S. and Japan rejected the 19-23 as imposing insufficiently small tariff cuts, especially in respect of T&A, which would make it difficult for the U.S. to agree to reciprocal T&A duty reductions. The U.S. pointed out that, with the 19-23 and 8-9 ranges, under any scenario the average applied industrial tariff rate among roughly 30 developing countries required to make cuts still would be three times higher than the rate in developed countries. The present ratio is 2-to-1, meaning the market access differential would worsen, to the disadvantage of developed countries. Brazil retorted that a coefficient between 19-23 would mean a 53-58 percent reduction in its bound tariffs. A coefficient of 23 would compel it to cut applied tariffs on 4,900 industrial products, including 799 electronic and electrical products, and many T&A and footwear items — all of which were in competition with Chinese merchandise.

2. Developed countries would have 5 years to implement fully their industrial tariff cuts. Developing countries would have 9 years.

3. Developing countries could exempt up to 10 percent of their industrial tariff lines from the full force of agreed-upon cuts. But, they would have to subject them to at least half of those cuts. An alternative flexibility would be to exclude 5 percent of their lines from any reduction.

4. A further flexibility for developing countries, as proposed by Mexico, would be a developing country could boost its Swiss Formula coefficient by as many as 3 points, if it abjured any product

exemptions. Thus, their coefficient would be 22-26. The U.S. rejected such flexibilities. With a coefficient of 19 plus use of a flexibility, some developing countries could maintain their highest tariff at 60 percent. In contrast, the highest American industrial tariff — 58.2 percent on certain footwear — would have to fall to 8 (or 9) percent.

5. No industrial tariff cuts would be expected of least developed countries.

6. For certain RAMs — Armenia, Kingdom of Saudi Arabia, Kyrgyzstan, Macedonia, Moldova, Vietnam — no Doha Round NAMA market access commitments beyond their WTO accession terms would be needed. Two other RAMs — China and Taiwan — would apply the new obligations. But, in two respects, they would get the benefit of a 2-year grace period. First, they would not have to implement Doha Round cuts to industrial product tariffs until 2 years after finishing the implementation of their accession commitments. Second, they would get 2 years, beyond the normal implementation period, to phase in Doha Round obligations.

In a sense, there was nothing to "accept" or "reject" in the draft texts. They articulated the *status quo*, thereby stressing areas in which negotiators had much work to do.

Not surprisingly, to expect the modalities documents would galvanize the Round and bring about its successful conclusion was too much to ask. That might have happened with the Center of Gravity texts. Alas, they did not do so. Weeks before their issuance, the respective Chairs of the agriculture and NAMA negotiating groups jointly warned WTO Members the modalities documents would not be breakthrough agreements. Upon issuance, the draft texts evinced well-known considerable differences and wide bargaining ranges. Ambassador Falconer pointedly remarked:

> I'm in no danger of being hugged to death.
>
> . . . .
>
> Suffice it to say that this document [the agriculture modalities draft] is intended to take everyone out of their [*sic*] comfort zones.[62]

The uncomfortable zones included:

1. Bracketed text, that is, square parentheses, *e.g.*, in the agriculture draft around figures like percentage cuts to be applied to final bound total aggregate measure of support (AMS), base periods for calculating product-specific AMS limits, tariff reductions, and in the NAMA draft on coefficients in the Swiss formula for developed and developing Members).

2. Alternative language on certain provisions, *e.g.*, in the agriculture draft, for the special agricultural safeguard.

3. Uncertainties on certain topics, *e.g.*, in the NAMA draft, on flexibilities for developing countries.

---

[62] Daniel Pruzin, *WTO Chairmen Issue Draft Ag, NAMA Texts Outlining Tough Concessions Needed in Doha*, 24 INT'L TRADE REP. (BNA) 1012-14 (19 July 2007).

4. Yet-to-be-drafted provisions, *e.g.*, in the agriculture draft, on geographical indications (such as for wines and spirits, sought by the EU), special product treatment for developing countries (whereby such products are entirely shielded from tariff cuts), and in the NAMA draft, on non-tariff barriers, sectoral initiatives (advocated by the U.S.), special treatment for environmental goods, and possible extensions of the *Peace Clause* in the WTO *Agreement on Agriculture*.

Urged on by WTO Director-General Pascal Lamy, negotiators pledged to continue their talks through the fall 2007. At a 17 August 2007 speech in Kuala Lumpur, Malaysia, he called successful completion a "political must." Many Members and their domestic political constituencies thought quite the opposite.

Probably the fullest truth came from the President of the Federal Reserve Bank of St. Louis, William Poole. The Doha Round was "on the verge of collapse."[63]

---

[63] Gary G. Yerkey, *WTO Chief Says Deal in Doha Talks "Doable" but Fed's Poole Sees Talks Near Collapse*, 24 INT'L TRADE REP. (BNA) 1198-99 (23 August 2007).

Part Two

ADJUDICATORY FOUNDATIONS OF FREE TRADE

Chapter 5

ADJUDICATION MECHANISMS

The partisan, when he is engaged in a dispute, cares nothing about the rights of the question, but is anxious only to convince his hearers of his own assertions.

—Plato (427-347 B.C.) Dialogues, *Phaedo*

DOCUMENTS SUPPLEMENT ASSIGNMENT

1. *Havana Charter* Articles 41, 47-48, 66, 92-97
2. GATT Articles XXII-XXIII
3. WTO *DSU*
4. U.S. *Statement of Administrative Action* for the *DSU*

I. THE PRE-URUGUAY ROUND DISPUTE SETTLEMENT SYSTEM

A. Is International Trade Law Really "Law"?

It is not a complete answer to the question "why the need for a Uruguay Round" to speak only of the need for substantive market access in services, intellectual property (IP) industries, and agriculture. Weaknesses in the pre-Uruguay Round dispute resolution system also were a cause. It would be an overstatement to say that the Uruguay Round was needed to strengthen the GATT multilateral dispute resolution mechanism — but it would not be that great of an overstatement.

In his 1832 work, *The Province of Jurisprudence Determined*, John Austin espoused a strict brand of legal positivism according to which a rule qualifies as "law" only if the rule is a command issued by a sovereign and is habitually obeyed under threat of punishment. To Austinian positivists, international law was not law at all. Rather, it was a custom or more, with no greater or lesser strength than social or dress fashions. There was, after all, no central sovereign, no habitual obedience, and no enforcement mechanism. Austinian positivists could have pointed to the insufferably weak pre-Uruguay Round dispute settlement system as "Exhibit A." (Positivists following H.L.A. Hart and his 1961 *The Concept of Law* could offer a rebuttal. What would it be?)

B. GATT Articles XXII and XXIII

To appreciate the inherent frailties the Uruguay Round negotiators needed to fix, it is necessary to understand the textual bases for those frailties, namely, GATT Articles XXII and XXIII. Article XXII calls upon each contracting party to accord "sympathetic consideration" to and consult with other contracting parties. Article XXIII establishes a skeletal framework for handling cases where one contracting party believes another contracting party is acting at variance with GATT obligations, technically known as "violation nullification or impairment," or otherwise behaving in a way that denies benefits that should be available, technically known as "non-violation nullification or impairment." The distinction between violation and non-violation nullification or impairment is worth emphasizing, because it is unique.

The labels are indicative. A "violation" claim, authorized by GATT Article XXIII:1(a), means the complainant alleges the respondent has implemented a trade measure that is a violation of some provision of GATT or an agreement negotiated thereunder. In a "non-violation" claim, made pursuant to GATT Article XXIII:1(b), the respondent is not accused of maintaining a trade measure that runs afoul of GATT law. Rather, implementation of the respondent's lawful measure results in denial or disruption of trade benefits to the complainant that the complainant negotiated within the GATT framework. As the distinction between "violation" and "non-violation" claims is built into GATT in Article XXIII, and as GATT remains the foundational document in the post-Uruguay Round era, the distinction remains as relevant as ever.

In the pre-Uruguay Round era, GATT Articles XXII-XXIII were criticized — properly — as insufficiently precise and, therefore, ineffective. Such criticisms were a major impetus behind the Uruguay Round negotiations, and specifically, the *WTO Agreement* and *DSU*. But, these Articles were not the only source of difficulty. After the Tokyo Round, it was not always clear how they related to various Tokyo Round codes. Some of these codes contained dispute settlement procedures. Consequently, there was controversy as to whether a dispute should be governed by the general provisions of Articles XXII-XXIII, or specific procedures established in a Tokyo Round code.

Still another important part of the context to appreciate is the clash of philosophies of dispute resolution evident in the pre-Uruguay Round era. GATT Articles XXII-XXIII, and the dispute settlement system they spawned, reflected a "pragmatic" approach to multilateral dispute resolution, as distinct from a "legalistic" one. American-trained lawyers might prefer a litigation-style approach to dispute resolution that contains precise, rules-based adjudicatory procedures. That way, all parties operate on a level playing field — procedural due process ensures equality. It also operates as a shield against domestic political pressures. But, the pre-*DSU* system was a European-style conciliatory one. The emphasis was on negotiation and diplomacy.

The implicit assumption in the negotiation/diplomacy approach was contracting parties would act nobly toward one another, or at least they would realize that not following the "Golden Rule" in one case would haunt them in a future one. Probably most Austinian positivists, and certainly any adherent of the realist schools of international relations theory, would call that assumption naive — and it was. In case after case, talks between contracting parties to resolve disputes turned into power games that added to trade friction rather than leading to mutually acceptable, balanced solutions. To be sure, the American legalistic approach risked turning GATT adjudication into the worst sort of personal injury circus trials. But, the European pragmatic approach was worse than simply non-transparent, elitist, and effete. It was incongruous with how nation-states interact if they have not bound themselves to a rigorous procedural mechanism for resolving disputes.

In retrospect, perhaps the clash between dispute resolution styles was inevitable. Until the Uruguay Round, the world was not ready for a formal adjudicatory mechanism with the sort of "teeth" that John Austin's austere positivism demanded. Such a mechanism would be law-applying, but it also might wind up being law-creating, thus threatening the sovereignty of nation-states. Keep that point in mind when reading WTO Panel and Appellate Body reports, and ask whether they do not — in effect — amount to an emerging body of international common law on trade.

C. Pre-Uruguay Round Dispute Settlement

How did dispute settlement actually "work" before the *DSU*? The steps outlined below were followed *in seriatim*, though not all of the steps would be used in every case as a settlement could be negotiated at any point.

1st — Informal bilateral consultations. A call by the complaining contracting party upon another contracting party, the respondent, for bilateral consultations. GATT Article XXII:1 obligated the respondent to look "sympathetically" upon the request, and afford opportunities for consultations.

2nd — Informal multilateral consultations. A call by the complaining contracting party, pursuant to GATT Article XXII:2, for multilateral consultations, in the hopes additional interested parties not only would bring pressure to bear on the respondent, but also suggest creative solutions.

3rd — More formal bilateral consultations. The complaining party would trigger the more formal dispute resolution procedures of GATT Article XXIII. Paragraph 1 of that Article calls for more formal bilateral consultations, and identifies violation nullification and impairment (Article XXIII:1(a)) and non-violation nullification and impairment (Article XXIII:1(b)) as justiciable claims.

4th — Request for panel. A request by the complaining party for the formation of a panel pursuant to GATT Article XXIII:2. (Early in GATT history, complaints were heard by the Contracting Parties. Soon, however, it became customary to refer cases to a subset of the membership, *i.e.*, a Working Party that included the complainant and respondent, along with a few other contracting parties. By the mid- to late-1950s, the practice of using panels of 3-5 experts was established, and the practice was codified in the 1979 Tokyo Round Understanding on Dispute Settlement.)

5th — Panel formation. Assuming no blockage (discussed below), a panel would be formed pursuant to GATT Article XXIII:2 by consensus of the GATT Council.

6th — Oral and written submissions. The panel would receive written and oral submissions from the complaining and respondent parties, all in secret.

7th — Panel deliberations and report. The panel would deliberate and prepare its report, again all in secret.

8th — Submission of the report and adoption. The panel would present its report to the GATT Council. Assuming no blockage (discussed below), the GATT Council would adopt the report by consensus. Only if a report were adopted could its recommendations take effect.

9th — Compliance. The losing contracting party was supposed to comply with the recommendations of the adopted report. If the case involved violation nullification and impairment, then the key recommendation would be removal of the offending measure. If the case involved non-violation nullification and impairment, then the key recommendation would be the restoration of the competitive relationship that had been upset because of the measure in question.

10th — Compensation or retaliation, if necessary. If the losing contracting party refused to comply with the panel's recommendations, then it could pay compensation to the winning party. Failing an agreement on compensation, the winning party might seek a consensus from the GATT Council for authorization to retaliate, in the form of suspending or withdrawing GATT obligations owed to the losing party in an amount equal to the trade damage caused by the losing party to the winning party as a result of the measure at issue.

As intimated earlier, these steps were riddled with problems that rendered the entire system insufferably weak. The four key problems were: delays, blockages, compliance, and enforcement through remedial action.

D. Weaknesses in Pre-Uruguay Round Dispute Settlement

Four serious weaknesses plagued the GATT panel system used from 1947 to 1994. First, there were no time periods for the various steps. Any step could go on seemingly interminably. Consequently, cases could — and did — drag on for years. For example, the infamous *Oilseeds* case (in which the U.S. complained about the EC's subsidy payments to processors, and later to farmers, of oilseeds), took 4 1/2 years to resolve. The U.S. first requested a panel in April 1988. In November 1992, after contentious negotiations during the Uruguay Round that threatened to derail the entire Round, the dispute finally was resolved.

Second, any party to a case — typically, it would be the respondent contracting party — could block the formation of a GATT panel. As a result, an adjudicatory body might never be established. Moreover, assuming a panel was agreed to and the panel issued a report, adoption of that report by the Contracting Parties could be blocked. Typically, the losing party would block adoption of either panel formation, report adoption, or both. Even if neither panel formation nor report adoption were blocked, authorization to retaliate in the event of non-compliance could be blocked.

Blockage was possible because under pre-Uruguay Round rules, a consensus among the contracting parties was needed to agree to form a panel or adopt a report. But, in the sometimes perverse lexicology of GATT, "consensus" essentially meant unanimity. If there was an objection from even one contracting party, the action was blocked. To those seeking to advance the international rule of law, this situation was ludicrous: it was as if a defendant in a trial could veto the very holding of a trial and, if one were held, could overturn the verdict.

Thus, for example, in the *Oilseeds* case, the EC (specifically, France) blocked adoption of the second panel report, issued in March 1993, which held that the EC's subsidy payments to farmers constituted a non-violation nullification and impairment of the zero-tariff bindings on oilseeds during the Dillon Round. In the first panel report, issued in November 1989, a panel had found the EC's subsidy payments to processors to be inconsistent with the national treatment obligation of GATT Article III:4, and also a non-violation nullification and impairment of the tariff bindings. The EC responded by altering its subsidy scheme, paying European farmers directly instead of processors. The U.S. challenged the alteration, thus precipitating the second report.

Third, there was no obligation on a losing party to explain to either the winning party, or more generally to the contracting party, how it planned to comply with the recommendations set forth in a panel report. Indeed, assuming no voluntary undertaking by the losing party to comply, whether there was even an obligation under international law to comply with those recommendations was arguable. Certainly, the U.S. had no such obligation under domestic law. Thus, a losing party could — and sometimes did — dither about for months or years, refusing to commit to any plan of action to rectify its trade measures against which a panel had ruled.

If and when the losing party finally did do something, its plan of action might not result in compliance with the panel's recommendation. Indeed, it might be a clever subterfuge. Put more mildly, compliance was somewhat of a self-judging matter: the losing party could alter its disputed trade measure in some way, and declare that it has implemented the recommendation. The EC's response to the first panel report in the *Oilseeds* case is a good example. While that report was issued in November 1989 and adopted in January 1990, the EC did not modify its subsidies scheme until the end of 1991. The modification did not, in the eyes of the U.S., rectify the non-violation nullification and impairment defect of the initial subsidies scheme. But, there was no "court" to judge compliance. Like Sisyphus rolling the rock up the hill one more time, America had to challenge the new scheme.

Fourth, remedial action to enforce compliance was virtually impossible. The only way a winning party could — consistent with its GATT obligations — retaliate was to obtain the approval of the Contracting Parties. But, their approval required a consensus, and once again, that could be blocked by just one contracting party — typically, the losing one. Thus, not surprisingly, in only one pre-Uruguay Round case did the Contracting Parties condone retaliation (a 1952 case in which the Netherlands was authorized to retaliate against the U.S.). Small wonder the U.S. put such great emphasis on Section 301 actions, which it took unilaterally. So exasperated was the Bush Administration with the EC's blockage of the second panel report in the *Oilseeds* case that it announced the unilateral imposition of 200 percent tariffs on European wine, cheese, and other products worth $1 billion in total as of December 1992 if no settlement was reached. Fortunately, the November 1992 Blair House Accord settled the matter (the EC agreed to reduce the number of hectares of European oilseed production eligible for a subsidy) and paved the way toward the Uruguay Round *Agreement on Agriculture*.

The defects in the pre-Uruguay Round dispute settlement system gave credence to the Austinian positivistic position. How could GATT rules be considered "law"? Disputes over the application of the rules might never be adjudicated, and even if they were the losing party might never comply with the result. These weaknesses were more than just theoretical possibilities. Pre-Uruguay Round GATT history is littered with disputes whose resolution was either imperiled or rendered impossible because of them.

E. Is It "Law" Now?

Happily for the multilateral trading system, and more generally for those seeking to advance the international rule of law, all of that history ended with the Uruguay Round. As discussed later, the *DSU* contains tight deadlines for virtually every stage of the dispute resolution process, and disputes generally are resolved within one year. Blockage of formation of a panel is possible for only one meeting of the DSB (the one at which formation is requested); thereafter, a panel must be formed. Blockage of adoption of panel or Appellate Body reports is impossible. The losing party must notify the DSB how it will comply. Failure to comply will trigger remedial action — blockage of authorization to retaliate is impossible. In brief, there is an "automaticity," and there are "teeth," built into the *DSU*. Austinian positivists no longer can look to international trade law, at least, to support their proposition that international law is not "law."

II. THE WTO *DSU*

A. Resolving Pre-Uruguay Round Weaknesses

The *DSU* is one of the principal achievements of the Uruguay Round and a cornerstone of the modern multilateral trading system. The *DSU* applies to all disputes brought after 1 January 1995, even if the facts giving rise to the dispute occurred earlier. The four key frailties of pre-Uruguay Round dispute settlement were delays, blockages, compliance, and enforcement. The *DSU* goes very far indeed in curing these defects.

First, as discussed below, the *DSU* creates a multi-step procedure. There are specific time deadlines associated with each of these stages. There is no prospect of long delays associated with the process, nor of the consequent unlikelihood of obtaining a GATT panel decision in a timely fashion. (This statement should be qualified: conceivably, the WTO could be so flooded with cases and so starved of resources that the panels and Appellate Body could not meet their deadlines.)

Second, the *DSU* also resolves the problem of blockages, by "reversing the presumption" necessary for action. A panel will be formed, a panel or Appellate Body report will be adopted, and retaliation will be authorized, unless there is a consensus *against* doing so. "Consensus" means no formal objection from any WTO Member. Thus, if even one Member opposes the prevention of creating a panel (*i.e.*, wants a panel to be formed), opposes the rejection of a report (*i.e.*, wants the report to be adopted), or opposes the refusal to authorize retaliation (*i.e.*, wants to allow retaliation), then blockage is impossible. Invariably, there always is one such Member — the complainant as to panel formation, and the winning party as to report adoption and retaliation.

What about the third and fourth pre-*DSU* defects, compliance and enforcement? Once a panel or Appellate body report is adopted, the losing WTO Member must notify its intentions as regards implementation of the recommendations contained in the report. If immediate compliance is impracticable, then a "reasonable period" is permitted. The presumptive "RPT," which stands for "reasonable period of time," is not to exceed 15 months. As for enforcement, if the losing Member refuses to comply, then it is supposed to negotiate a mutually acceptable compensation package with the prevailing Member. Failing that, the DSB must authorize trade retaliation by the winning Member.

In general, through the *DSU*, WTO Members commit to eschew unilateral determinations of violations, and unilateral trade actions, on matters dealt with by a GATT—WTO text. That is, an indispensable feature of WTO membership is submission to the *DSU* for all trade disputes to which it applies. Aside from the *DSU*'s cures for delays, blockages, compliance, and enforcement, this submission goes a long way to addressing the skepticism of Austinian positivists about international legal regimes.

All of this is not to say the *DSU* embodies the most sublime multilateral dispute settlement procedures known. No adjudicatory mechanism is perfect, and while the *DSU* is being used regularly, serious concerns exist. For example, consider the following:

    1.   *Quality*: Are the rulings of panels and the Appellate Body likely to be at least as well-reasoned as those of pre-Uruguay Round GATT panels and domestic courts like the CIT and Federal Circuit?

    2.   *Impartiality*: Is the make-up of the panels and the Appellate Body such that the complaining and responding parties are assured an unbiased hearing?

    3.   *Due Process*: To what extent do *DSU* procedures comport with procedural due process rights such as adequate and timely notice, reciprocal discovery, and appeal?

    4.   *Equal Justice*: Do developing countries have the same ability to obtain justice as developed countries? What about least developed countries?

    5.   *Ambiguities*: What ambiguities exist in the *DSU*? How are they, and how should they be, dealt with?

For U.S. implementing provisions on dispute settlement, see 19 U.S.C. §§ 3531-3538.

B. "Nullification or Impairment" and "Adverse Impact"

In addition to curing deficiencies in the pre-Uruguay Round dispute settlement system, the *DSU*, along with WTO Appellate Body jurisprudence, go some way to clarify the GATT Article XXIII concept of nullification or impairment. Uruguay Round negotiators took "violation nullification or impairment" and equated it with the concept of "adverse impact." Article 3:8 of the *DSU* creates a rebuttable presumption a breach by one WTO Member of a rule in a covered agreement, *i.e.*, in any GATT—WTO text, has an adverse impact on other Members. That is, acting inconsistently with an agreement is presumed to nullify or impair benefits accruing to other Members. The rebuttable presumption benefits complainants. The burden to rebut the presumption is on the respondent. What, then, is an "adverse impact"?

The *DSU* does not define the concept. But, subsequent case law is of assistance. For example, in *European Communities — Export Subsidies on Sugar*, WT/DS265/AB/R, WT/DS266/AB/R, WT/DS283/AB/R (adopted 19 May 2005) (complaints by Australia, Brazil, and Thailand), the Appellate Body explained:

> 298. . . . [T]he Complaining Parties [Australia, Brazil, and Thailand] provided evidence to the Panel suggesting that the EC sugar regime [consisting of price regulations and export subsidies] caused them losses, for example, of US $494 million for Brazil and US $151 million for Thailand in 2002. The Panel specifically found that "the European Communities has not rebutted the evidence submitted by the Complainants with regard to the amount of trade lost by the Complainants as a result of the EC sugar regime." The European Communities has not attempted to rebut this evidence on appeal. The European Communities, instead, appears to suggest that, to rebut the presumption of nullification or impairment, it need only demonstrate that the Complaining Parties "could not have expected that the EC would take any measure to reduce its exports of C sugar."

> 299. The text of Article 3.8 of the *DSU* suggests that a Member may rebut the presumption of nullification or impairment by demonstrating that its breach of WTO rules has no adverse impact on other Members. Trade losses represent an obvious example of adverse impact under Article 3.8. Unless a Member demonstrates that there are no adverse trade effects arising as a consequence of WTO-inconsistent export subsidies, we do not believe that a complaining Member's expectations would have a bearing on a finding pursuant to Article 3.8 of the *DSU*. Therefore, the European Communities has failed to rebut the presumption of nullification or impairment pursuant to Article 3.8 of the *DSU*.

The penultimate sentence of the second paragraph is worthy of comment. Whether a complainant expected nullification or impairment, *i.e.*, an adverse effect, is immaterial. What matters is what actually happened.

C. The Multi-Step Procedure

There are four general phases to post-Uruguay Round dispute resolution: (1) consultation; (2) use of a Panel; (3) appeal to the Appellate Body; and (4) surveillance and implementation. Some of these *DSU* phases may be broken down into more specific steps, set out below. Be sure to appreciate some of its finer points contained in these steps, including the tight deadlines.

Step 1: Informal Dispute Resolution Mechanisms

In most cases, a panel is not the first mechanism to be tried. Rather, the use of good offices, conciliation, or mediation — *i.e.*, informal mechanisms — is tried first. (*See DSU* Article 5.) (The use of these mechanisms can be terminated at any time.) How long must consultations last? If consultations fail to settle a dispute within 60 days, or if the parties mutually agree that the dispute cannot be settled by consultation within 60 days, then the complainant can request the establishment of a panel. (*See DSU* Article 4:7.) In an urgent situation, a panel can be established earlier.

Step 2: Recourse to a Panel

If informal mechanisms fail, then a panel can be convened upon request. There is no express requirement that a panel be used after informal mechanisms have been tried and failed. Such a requirement could be inferred from *DSU* Articles 3:4 and 6, plus the desire to carry-over pre-Uruguay Round practice.

Step 3: The Waiting Period Requirement

Assume an aggrieved WTO Member seeks consultations on day 1 and requests conciliation before day 60. The respondent must address the request within 10 days of the request. Consultations should begin within 30 days, though the parties can agree otherwise. Then, the complainant must wait at least 60 days from the day consultations were requested before seeking a panel. (*See DSU* Article 5:4.) The purpose of this 60-day "waiting period" is to assure that consultations are given adequate time to succeed.

However, there are two exceptions to the waiting period requirement. First, both parties to the dispute can jointly agree to the appointment of a panel before the expiration of the waiting period. Second, if no timely response to the request for consultations is offered (*i.e.*, no response is offered within 10 days of the request), or if consultations do not begin within 30 days of the request, then the aggrieved party can seek a panel.

Step 4: Formation of a Panel

When a complainant requests a panel, the panel must be established no later than the first meeting of the DSB following the request. This rule ensures panels are formed expeditiously. (*See DSU* Article 6:1.) The panel must consist of 3 persons, unless the parties agree otherwise within 10 days of its establishment. (*See DSU* Article 8:5.) The panelists must be well-qualified and are drawn from a roster maintained by the WTO Secretariat. (*See DSU* Articles 8:1, 8:4.) If there is no agreement on composition within 20 days of establishing the panel, then the Director-General must pick panelists at the request of either party within 10 days of the request. (*See DSU* Article 8:7.)

Step 5: Operation and Functions of the Panel

As soon as practicable, the panel must fix the timetable for resolution of a dispute. (*See DSU* Article 12:3.) If possible, the timetable should be set within 1 week of the composition of the panel and the establishment of the panel's terms of reference. Thus, the panel must stipulate precise deadlines for written submissions from the parties. However, there is no sanction for failure to provide such deadlines. The panel must issue its report to the complainant and respondent Members within 6 months, or 3 months in an urgent case. (*See DSU* Article 12:7-9.) No extension beyond 9 months is permitted.

Step 6: Suspension of the Panel

The complainant can ask the panel to suspend work for 12 months. That might facilitate settlement in highly complex or politically-charged cases.[1]

Step 7: Adoption of a Panel Report by the DSB

The DSB cannot consider a panel report until 20 days after the report is issued to the Members. Members objecting to the report must do so in writing within 10 days of the DSB meeting. The DSB must adopt the report within 60 days of its circulation to the Members, unless the DSB decides by consensus not to adopt it or a party to the dispute notifies the DSB of its intention to appeal the panel's decision. (*See DSU* Article 16:4.) The entire process — from establishment of a panel to adoption of the report — must take place within 9 months, or 12 months where there is an appeal. (*See DSU* Article 20:1.)

Step 8: Appeal

A party may appeal an adverse panel decision. (*See DSU* Article 17.) The appeal must be confined to issues of law and legal interpretation, hence issues of fact may not be appealed. Query how to differentiate facts from law, and how to handle issues mixed with facts and law. Generally, the Appellate Body must render a decision within 60 days, and in no case longer than 90 days. The DSB must adopt the report within 30 days of its circulation to the Members, unless there is a consensus against adoption. Thus, an appeal adds 90-120 days, *i.e.*, 3-4 months, to the overall 9-12 month process. Put differently, assuming an appeal, the case should be adjudicated fully within 12-16 months.

Step 9: Recommendations

Article 19:1 of the *DSU* requires a panel, or the Appellate Body, to recommend a Member found to have a measure inconsistent with a GATT—WTO agreement bring the offending measure into compliance with the agreement. Compliance may entail amending the measure, or removing it entirely. But, neither the panel nor the Appellate Body is obligated to state precisely how the losing Member should fulfill its obligations. Almost invariably, the "judges of Geneva" avoid infringing on sovereignty by phrasing their "court order"

---

[1] The EU did just this with its complaint against the U.S. over the *Helms-Burton Act*, and a settlement was negotiated involving suspension and waiver of the *Act's* sanctions, and a commitment by the President to seek changes in the *Act*. Suspension of the panel also occurred in the *Boeing — Airbus* dispute between the U.S. and EU over alleged aircraft subsidies.

generically, in the last paragraph of their report, as a "recommendation to bring the inconsistent measure into conformity with the relevant agreement."

In special cases, such as subsidies, the situation is a bit different. *DSU* Article 1:2 says the *DSU* applies subject to additional rules on dispute settlement in covered agreements listed in *DSU* Annex 2. This Annex states (*inter alia*) the *Agreement on Subsidies and Countervailing Measures* (*SCM Agreement*). Article 4:7 of the *SCM Agreement* states if a Member is found to have a prohibited subsidy, then the panel "shall recommend that the subsidizing Member withdraw the subsidy without delay," and "shall specify . . . the time-period within which the measure must be withdrawn."

Step 10: Compliance

In all cases, within 30 days of adoption by the DSB of a panel or Appellate Body report, the losing Member must inform the DSB of its intentions regarding implementation of the recommendations contained in the report. Aside from cases involving an agreement listed in *DSU* Annex 2, neither the panel nor the Appellate Body is required to set out a time frame for implementation. But, generally, compliance is expected within a "reasonable period" not to exceed 15 months. (*See DSU* Article 21:3.)

Step 11: Compensation or Retaliation

If a panel recommendation is not implemented within a reasonable period of time, then the losing Member unable or unwilling to comply with the recommendation must enter into negotiations with the winning Member to develop a satisfactory scheme of compensation. (*See DSU* Article 22). Suppose the offending Member fails to implement a panel's recommendation or ruling and, after 20 days of negotiations, no satisfactory compensation scheme is arranged. In that case, the injured Member has a right to retaliate pursuant to authorization from the DSB. (*See DSU* Article 22:2.)

Retaliation must be limited to the same sector as that in which nullification or impairment occurred, if this is practicable. For example, the injured Member can seek permission from the DSB to suspend concessions in the sector at issue that had been granted previously to the offending Member. (*See DSU* Article 22:3.) The DSB must grant authorization to retaliate within 30 days unless it decides to the contrary by consensus. (*See DSU* Article 22:6.) The Member subject to retaliation may object to the level of retaliation, in which case the matter is referred to arbitration.

In rare instances, a respondent might elect not to contest the facts or arguments set out by the complainant, in effect pleading *nolo contendere* (no contest). Yet, the respondent might not withdraw its case. Why not? The answer is doing so would cut off its future rights, namely, to contest implementation of a panel (or Appellate Body) ruling, and to retaliate if need be.[2] In turn, as no mutually agreeable result has been reached, the panel must fulfill its fundamental obligation under *DSU* Article 11 to make an "objective assessment of the matter." In other words, absent a mutually agreed solution, there

---

[2] This scenario occurred in an antidumping zeroing case. *See* WTO Panel Report, *United States — Anti-Dumping Measure on Shrimp from Ecuador*, WT/DS335/R (issued 30 Jan. 2007).

is no settlement. But, as the basis for its right to expect compliance with, and implementation of, a decision, and its right to retaliate in the event of non-compliance, a complainant needs a favorable judgment in hand.

A Different Step: Arbitration

There is a possibility (under *DSU* Article 25) of using arbitration as an alternative means of dispute resolution. Why is this option offered? Under what circumstances can it be invoked? In what contexts should disputing parties consider it a viable procedure?

D.   Direct versus Indirect Effect

WTO PANEL REPORT, *UNITED STATES — SECTIONS 301-310 OF THE TRADE ACT OF 1974*
WT/DS152/R (adopted 27 January 2000) (Not Appealed)

VII. FINDINGS

. . . .

C. The EC Claim that Section 304 is Inconsistent with Article 23.2(a) of the *DSU*

. . . .

4. *Article 23.(a) of the DSU Interpreted in Accordance with the Vienna Convention Rules on Treaty Interpretation*

. . . .

(c) *". . . the ordinary meaning [of the terms of the treaty] . . . in the light of the object and purpose [of the treaty]*

[Omitted here are the merits of the EU argument that Sections 301-310 of the U.S. *Trade Act of 1974*, as amended.]

7.71 What are the objects and purposes of the *DSU*, and the WTO more generally, that are relevant to a construction of Article 23? The most relevant in our view are those which relate to the creation of market conditions conducive to individual economic activity in national and global markets and to the provision of a secure and predictable multilateral trading system.

7.72 Under the doctrine of direct effect, which has been found to exist most notably in the legal order of the EC but also in certain free trade area agreements, obligations addressed to States are construed as creating legally enforceable rights and obligations for individuals. Neither the GATT nor the WTO has so far been interpreted by GATT/WTO institutions as a legal order producing direct effect. Following this approach, the GATT/WTO did *not* create a new legal order the subjects of which comprise both contracting parties or Members and their nationals.

7.73 However, it would be entirely wrong to consider that the position of individuals is of no relevance to the GATT/WTO legal matrix. Many of the benefits to Members which are meant to flow as a result of the acceptance of various disciplines under the GATT/WTO depend on the activity of individual economic operators in the national and global market places. The purpose of many of these disciplines, indeed one of the primary objects of the GATT/WTO as a whole, is to produce certain market conditions which would allow this individual activity to flourish.

7.74 The very first Preamble to the *WTO Agreement* states that Members recognise

> that their relations in the field of trade and economic endeavour should be conducted with a view to raising standards of living, ensuring full employment and a large and steadily growing volume of real income and effective demand, and expanding the production of and trade in goods and services.

7.75 Providing security and predictability to the multilateral trading system is another central object and purpose of the system which could be instrumental to achieving the broad objectives of the Preamble. Of all WTO disciplines, the *DSU* is one of the most important instruments to protect the security and predictability of the multilateral trading system and through it that of the market-place and its different operators. *DSU* provisions must, thus, be interpreted in the light of this object and purpose and in a manner which would most effectively enhance it. In this respect we are referring not only to preambular language but also to positive law provisions in the *DSU* itself. Article 3.2 of the *DSU* provides:

> The dispute settlement system of the WTO is a central element in providing security and predictability to the multilateral trading system. The Members recognize that it serves to preserve the rights and obligations of Members under the covered agreements. . . .

7.76 The security and predictability in question are of "the multilateral trading system." The multilateral trading system is, per force, composed not only of States but also, indeed mostly, of individual economic operators. The lack of security and predictability affects mostly these individual operators.

7.77 Trade is conducted most often and increasingly by private operators. It is through improved conditions for these private operators that Members benefit from WTO disciplines. The denial of benefits to a Member which flows from a breach is often indirect and results from the impact of the breach on the market place and the activities of individuals within it. Sections 301-310 themselves recognize this nexus. One of the principal triggers for U.S. action to vindicate U.S. rights under covered agreements is the impact alleged breaches have had on, and the complaint emanating from, individual economic operators.

7.78 It may, thus, be convenient in the GATT/WTO legal order to speak not of the principle of direct effect but of the principle of indirect effect.

7.79 Apart from this name-of-convenience, there is nothing novel or radical in our analysis. We have already seen that it is rooted in the language of the

WTO itself. It also represents a GATT/WTO orthodoxy confirmed in a variety of ways over the years including panel and Appellate Body reports as well as the practice of Members.

7.80 Consider, first, the overall obligation of Members concerning their internal legislation. Under traditional public international law a State cannot rely on its domestic law as a justification for non-performance. [*See Vienna Convention on the Law of Treaties*, Article 27.] Equally, however, under traditional public international law, legislation under which an eventual violation could, or even would, subsequently take place, does not normally in and of itself engage State responsibility. If, say, a State undertakes not to expropriate property of foreign nationals without appropriate compensation, its State responsibility would normally be engaged only at the moment foreign property had actually been expropriated in a given instance. And yet, even in the GATT, prior to the enactment of Article XVI:4 of the *WTO Agreement* explicitly referring to measures of a general nature, legislation as such independent from its application in specific instances was considered to constitute a violation. This is confirmed by numerous adopted GATT panel reports and is also agreed upon by both parties to this dispute. Why is it, then, that legislation as such was found to be inconsistent with GATT rules? If no specific application is at issue — if, for example, no specific discrimination has yet been made — what is it that constitutes the violation?

7.81 Indirect impact on individuals is, surely, one of the principal reasons. In treaties which concern only the relations between States, State responsibility is incurred only when an actual violation takes place. By contrast, in a treaty the benefits of which depend in part on the activity of individual operators the legislation itself may be construed as a breach, since the mere existence of legislation could have an appreciable "chilling effect" on the economic activities of individuals.

7.83 It is commonplace that domestic law in force imposing discriminatory taxation on imported products would, in and of itself, violate Article III irrespective of proof of actual discrimination in a specific case. [Of course, as the Panel observes here in footnote 665, the decisive criterion is a change in relative competitive opportunities caused by a measure of general application, whereby imports are disadvantaged in comparison with like domestic products.] Furthermore, a domestic law which exposed imported products to future discrimination was recognized by some GATT panels to constitute, by itself, a violation of Article III, even before the law came into force. Finally, and most tellingly, even where there was no certainty but only a risk under the domestic law that the tax would be discriminatory, certain GATT panels found that the law violated the obligation in Article III. A similar approach was followed in respect of Article II of GATT 1994 by the WTO panel on *Argentina — Textiles and Apparel (US)* when it found that the very change in system from *ad valorem* to specific duties was a breach of Argentina's *ad valorem* tariff binding even though such change only brought about the potential of the tariff binding being exceeded depending on the price of the imported product. [*See Argentina — Certain Measures Affecting Imports of Footwear, Textiles, Apparel and Other Items* (WT/DS56). The panel report was issued on 25 November 1997, and upheld by the Appellate Body. The Appellate Body report, and the panel report as modified by the Appellate Body, were adopted by the DSB on 22 April 1998.]

7.84 The rationale in all types of cases has always been the negative effect on economic operators created by such domestic laws. An individual would simply shift his or her trading patterns — buy domestic products, for example, instead of imports — so as to avoid the would-be taxes announced in the legislation or even the mere risk of discriminatory taxation. Such risk or threat, when real, was found to affect the relative competitive opportunities between imported and domestic products because it could, in and of itself, bring about a shift in consumption from imported to domestic products: This shift would be caused by, for example, an increase in the cost of imported products and a negative impact on economic planning and investment to the detriment of those products. This rationale was paraphrased in the *Superfund* case as follows:

> to protect expectations of the contracting parties as to the competitive relationship between their products and those of the other contracting parties. Both articles [GATT Articles III and XI] are not only to protect current trade but also to create the predictability needed to plan future trade.

[*See United States — Taxes on Petroleum and Certain Imported Substances* ("*US — Superfund*"), GATT B.I.S.D. (34th Supp.) 136 at ¶ 5.2.2 (1988) (adopted 17 June 1987). In this case, a GATT panel found that tax legislation violated certain GATT obligations, even though the legislation had not yet entered into force.] Doing so, the panel in *Superfund* referred to the reasoning in the *Japanese Measures on Imports of Leather* case. [*See Japan — Measures on Imports of Leather*, GATT B.I.S.D. (31st Supp.) at 94 (1985) (adopted 15-15 May 1984)]. There the panel found that an import quota constituted a violation of Article XI of GATT even though the quota had not been filled. It did so on the following grounds:

> the existence of a quantitative restriction should be presumed to cause nullification or impairment not only because of any effect it had had on the volume of trade but also for other reasons, *e.g.*, it would lead to increased transaction costs and would create uncertainties which could affect investment plans.

7.85 In this sense, Article III:2 is not only a promise not to discriminate in a specific case, but is also designed to give certain guarantees to the market place and the operators within it that discriminatory taxes will not be imposed. For the reasons given above, any ambivalence in GATT panel jurisprudence as to whether a risk of discrimination can constitute a violation should, in our view, be resolved in favour of our reading.

III. PROCEDURAL "COMMON LAW"

Try as they might, the Uruguay Round negotiators could not anticipate all of the procedural issues that would arise in cases brought under the *DSU*. Thus, from the outset of its operation, the *DSU* could not possibly be an entirely comprehensive, self-contained rule book. This fact led to an obvious question of immense practical importance: how would procedural questions not addressed in the *DSU* be resolved? The obvious answer was panels and the Appellate Body would have to engage in interstitial rule-making.

And so they did. By 2000, panels and the Appellate Body issued a number of important rulings on procedural issues. Query whether these rulings are precedent — in the *stare decisis* sense of the word — for all WTO Members. (The same question can be asked of panel and Appellate Body holdings on substantive issues.) In a practical, day-to-day sense, the answer seems to be "yes," as several of the rulings are referred to over and over again in subsequent cases.

As just one of many possible examples, the Appellate Body's cites and applies in many subsequent cases the burden of proof rule that it first established in the May 1997 *Wool Shirts* case. It uses the rule in its December 1997 report in its *India — Patent Protection for Pharmaceutical and Agricultural Chemical Products*, in its January 1998 report in *EC Measures Concerning Meet and Meat Products (Hormones)*, and in its June 1998 report in *European Communities — Customs Classifications of Certain Computer Equipment*. Likewise, the Appellate Body relies on its bright line rule on judicial economy, established in *Wool Shirts*, in the *India — Patent Protection* and July 1998 *European Communities — Measures Affecting the Importation of Certain Poultry Products* cases.

In sum, it may be fair to say that a corpus of procedural common law is emerging. The prominent "black letter" rules in this body are discussed below.

A. Standing to Bring a Complaint

In its 1997 Report on *European Communities — Regime for the Importation, Sale and Distribution of Bananas*, the Appellate Body considered the plausible EC argument that the U.S. lacked standing to bring the case. The argument, articulated in the EC's emotive cry "not one banana," was the U.S. has no actual or potential trade interest justifying its claim. Its banana production is minimal, it has never exported bananas, and this situation is unlikely to change due to climactic and economic conditions in the U.S.

The American rebuttal reflected the realities of global production. Whether bananas were imported by the EC from the customs territory of the United States was immaterial. What mattered was whether U.S. companies exported bananas to the EC, regardless of where they grew the bananas. In this case, the U.S. had a significant commercial interest because the ability of two American companies, Chiquita and Dole, to export bananas to the EC was adversely affected by the EC's anti-free market regime.

The American rebuttal was yet more plausible than the European argument. The GATT—WTO regime would be a very unhelpful one indeed if it could be invoked to fight protectionism only after satisfying a territorial test for the movement of goods (or, for that matter, services). The EC's banana preference scheme, while directly impacting banana-growing countries, had a global reach because of the offshore corporate interests in those countries. The U.S. clearly was implying the EC exalted form over substance, whereas the U.S. demanded to be heard based on trading difficulties faced by American firms as a result of the preference scheme. Not surprisingly, therefore, the Appellate Body agreed with the U.S.

The Appellate Body found that Article 3:3 of the *DSU* (concerning the importance of the prompt settlement of disputes) and Article 3:7 (cautioning Members to "exercise . . . judgment" as to whether bringing a case would be "fruitful") did not establish a prerequisite that a complainant have a "legal interest" before requesting a panel. Such a prerequisite was not set forth expressly elsewhere in the *DSU* or the WTO Agreement, nor could it be implied in any other GATT—WTO agreement. The Appellate Body agreed that every WTO Member possesses a good deal of discretion as to whether to bring an action. The matter is self-regulating, with each Member responsible for deciding whether an action would be "fruitful" (the Appellate Body probably did not intend the pun).

The result is only fair, especially from a developing country vantage. To limit dispute settlement to countries with an actual trade interest would be to exclude countries that are potential exporters. Further, a liberal standing, keeping "court house doors" open, as it were, enhances fairness and legitimacy in the WTO adjudicatory system. Finally, there is a shared interest among WTO Members that rules are followed.

B. Ripeness and Mootness

What sort of impact must a trade measure have on a complaining Member before a WTO panel will rule on the legality of that measure? It is clear under both pre-and post-Uruguay Round practice a panel will not consider an issue ripe before the measure actually has been enacted into law. After all, why should panels get involved in theoretical or hypothetical abstractions? Are they not far too busy with "live" cases as it is? But, after enactment, must a panel wait until some definite action has occurred as regards the complaining Member, *i.e.*, must it wait until the measure actually is applied against the complainant and begins to cause some adverse effect to the complainant?

The *DSU* is silent, but pre-Uruguay Round GATT jurisprudence provides guidance. Expectations of contracting parties, not just existing trade relations, must be protected. Why? Because importers and exporters develop expectations and make business decisions based thereon. Put differently, if their expectations are unreliable — more prayer than sound forecast — then they will not have the certain, predictable legal scaffolding on which to build their trade relations. Thus, for example, in the 1985 case of *Japanese Measures on Imports of Leather* (GATT B.I.S.D. (31st Supp.) at 94), the panel issued a ruling even though the trade measure at issue had not been applied against imports. In the 1988 case of *United States — Taxes on Petroleum and Certain Imported Substances* (GATT B.I.S.D. (34th Supp.) at 136), the panel opined even though a domestic law had not yet taken effect.

In the 1997 case of *Argentina — Measures Affecting Imports of Footwear, Textiles, Apparel, and Other Items*, the U.S. challenged Argentina's tariff regime for a range of imports, arguing it violated that country's tariff commitments bound under GATT Article II. Argentina's defense was the issue was not ripe. The U.S. had not proven Argentina actually had imposed a duty in excess of the bound rates, and a mere prospect a duty might exceed these rates did not rise to a violation. The U.S. countered with the argument Argentina's tariff regime was mandatory: the rates must be imposed by Argentine customs authorities — they have no discretion. In other words, said the U.S., it was only a question of time, of "when," not "if," a violation would occur.

The Appellate Body agreed. As long as it is possible to conclude with sufficient certainty a violation will occur, then a measure is actionable. The fact that the measure, while enacted, has not yet taken effect, or that it has not yet had a trade effect on the complainant, is immaterial. Simply adopting the measure changes the competitive relationship between the parties because it has the potential to create a violation, and that alone undermines the certainty and predictability cherished in the multilateral trading system. In brief, the test for ripeness in the GATT—WTO law is not particularly demanding: if the measure necessarily will result in a violation under some conditions, there is no need to wait for those conditions to occur. Put conversely, only if a Member retains discretion to interpret or apply its law in a manner consistent with its GATT—WTO obligations — *i.e.*, only if the measure is not mandatory — would the measure not be considered ripe for review.

What about the "mirror image" of ripeness — mootness? May a panel issue a ruling in a case where the measure in dispute has been withdrawn, or has expired? Again, the *DSU* is silent. Ostensibly, as regards the disputing parties, the ruling would seem to be a waste of time. However, as is observed in the 1998 case of *European Communities — Measures Affecting Importation of Certain Poultry Products*, a terminated measure may have lingering trade repercussions on the export performance of the complaining Member. Thus, the panel in that case rejected the EC's argument that it could not rule on a measure challenged by Brazil. Moreover, consider the interests of non-disputants. If one of them were to consider adoption of a similar measure, then a ruling might be very instructive. In other words, if the dispute is capable of being repeated, why not go forward with the case?

Several pre-Uruguay Round GATT panels took this approach. They tended to issue rulings even after the disputed measure had terminated, but only if the disputed measure was in effect when the terms of reference for the panel were agreed upon, or if there was no objection from either party. The WTO panels and Appellate Body continue this nuanced approach in *Argentina — Footwear* and the 1996 case of *United States — Standards for Reformulated and Conventional Gasoline*. They compare two dates: (1) the date on which the measure has been withdrawn or expired, and (2) the date on which the panel's terms of reference were set by the DSB. If the measure terminated before the terms of reference were set, then the issue is considered moot, and the panel will not rule on it. If the measure was still in effect when the terms were established, then it is "fair game."

Plainly, the date on which a complaining Member asks for a panel is immaterial. The logic is some date must be selected as the formal commencement of the adjudication process, and the date on which a panel's terms of reference is at least as good, if not better, then any other candidate. At that juncture, the imprimatur of the DSB on the settlement process is indelible. Accordingly, for example, in the 1996 case of *Indonesia — Certain Measures*

Affecting the Automobile Industry, the panel rejected Indonesia's defense its National Car Program was immune from scrutiny because it had expired. Indonesia failed to offer this defense until after the deadline for submitting information and arguments, and in any event the complainants disagreed that the Program had lapsed. However, beware of the possibility of strategic — or dare it be said, bad faith? — behavior on the part of a respondent. It could abolish the disputed measure the day before a panel's terms are set, and reinstate it after the panel's ruling.

C. Exhaustion of Domestic Remedies

Must an injured private party exhaust all remedies available to it under domestic law before that party's government can bring an action to the WTO? Put differently, in terms of raising issues, rather than exhausting remedies: must a private party have raised an issue before the relevant domestic judicial and administrative bodies in order for the Member to raise that issue at the WTO? This problem is most likely to arise in trade remedy cases — AD, CVD, safeguards, and IPR protection actions, for example — where countries offer recourse under domestic law. The *DSU* does not address the problem.

Under pre-Uruguay Round GATT practice, panels did not feel inhibited by the "local remedies rule," even though adjudicating a case before it had been aired fully under local law risked affronting the sovereignty of the contracting party in whose jurisdiction the case properly would be heard. However, panels scrupulously limited their review to whatever facts already had been put in front of the relevant domestic court or administrative agency. Likewise, in *Argentina — Footwear*, the WTO panel rejected the argument Argentina could not be held to have violated its tariff binding until importers of the goods in question had exhausted the remedies available to them under Argentine law. The panel stated resolutely that WTO Members are expected to comply with their obligations, regardless of the availability, or lack thereof, of an appropriate remedial mechanism under domestic law. The supporting logic is consequentialist in nature. Demanding exhaustion of local remedies would result in delay (perhaps years) and uncertainty (as to the ultimate rules that will be held valid and enforceable). Those results are the antipodes of what the GATT—WTO regime is trying to promote.

However, the Appellate Body has yet to rule on the problem of raising an issue at the WTO that was not raised at the domestic level. How should the problem be resolved? On the one hand, in some cases, a matter might not be raised under local law simply because it is not an issue under that law. In such cases, what did not transpire at the domestic level should have no bearing on a subsequent WTO case. But, on the other hand, in other cases — those where local law does deal with the matter — failure to raise a matter ought to prejudice efforts to raise it at the WTO level. For instance, suppose in a WTO case a complaint concerns the failure of a domestic court or administrative agency to provide a well-reasoned explanation for its action. The obvious rebuttal would be the complainant never raised the issue, so the local adjudicator never felt a need to amplify its written discourse.

D. Sufficiency of a Complaint

One of the important procedural issues the Appellate Body confronted in the *EC-Bananas* case concerned what in American civil procedure is known as "notice pleading" versus "fact pleading." What are the requirements for a complaining Member's complaint? *DSU* Article 6:2 provides only a sketchy answer, saying that the complainant's request for a panel must be "in writing," "identify the specific measures [of the respondent] at issue," and "provide a brief summary of the legal basis of the complaint sufficient to present the problem clearly."

The EC argued the American complaint against it was "unacceptably vague," thus falling far short of meeting even these skeletal requirements. After all, the U.S. merely listed the provisions of the specific Uruguay Round agreements that the EC allegedly violated. The U.S. did not detail its arguments as to which European measures violated which provisions of which agreements. The Europeans demanded a linkage between particular features of its banana import quota and licensing regime and the relevant laws (an application of the law to the facts, as it were), whereas the Americans had done nothing more than refer to the "banana regime" as the source of all the purported problems. The U.S. offered two rebuttals. First, Article 6:2 did not require "a detailed exposition tying each specific measure to each provision of law to be claimed" as violated. Second, the EC had ample notice of the claims against it during the consultation phase, *i.e.*, information the U.S. had provided during this phase could in effect "cure" any missing pieces from its complaint.

The Appellate Body agreed with the U.S. The American list was enough, it met the "minimum standards" of Article 6:2, and the EC was confusing the fundamental distinction between a claim and an argument supporting a claim, and thus between a complaint and a brief. In the American civil procedure lingo, the Appellate Body was saying notice pleading suffices. A mere listing of the allegedly violated rules of international trade law, without detailed supporting arguments or an indication of which disputed measures relate to which legal provisions, suffices.

The Appellate Body observed the complaint-drafting requirements are kept minimal under *DSU* Article 6:2 for two good reasons. First, the complaint helps in setting the panel's terms of reference. Second, it informs the respondent of the legal basis for the complainant. These purposes are easily met without intricate pleadings. The only caveat the Appellate Body added was that uncertainty as to whether a complaint satisfies Article 6:2 cannot be cleared up, or "cured," by a subsequent submission. The complainant must "get it right" in the complaint itself. But, assuming a complainant says enough to establish terms of reference and give notice, it need say no more.

E. Judicial Economy

Must a panel or the Appellate Body resolve all of the claims made in a case, or may it decide only those claims necessary to dispose of the case? That the Appellate Body had to step in to answer this question is not a surprise.

Nothing in the *WTO Agreement* deals with the problem, and the nearest guidance in the *DSU* is set forth in Article 11:

> The function of panels is to assist the DSB in discharging its responsibilities under this Understanding and the covered agreements. Accordingly, a panel should make *an objective assessment of the matter before it*, including an objective assessment of the facts of the case and the applicability of an conformity with the relevant covered agreements, and make such other findings as will assist the DSB in making the recommendations or in giving the rulings provided for in the covered agreements. (Emphasis added.)

In 1997, the problem came to a head in *United States — Measure Affecting Imports of Woven Wool Shirts and Blouses from India.*

India inferred from Article 11 a right of a complainant to a ruling on each and every claim a complainant raises in a case. The Panel held otherwise.

> [W]e disagree and refer to the consistent GATT panel practice of judicial economy. India is entitled to have the dispute over the contested "measure" resolved by the Panel, and if we judge that the specific matter in dispute can be resolved by addressing only some of the arguments raised by the complaining party, we can do so. We, therefore, decide to address only the legal issues we think are needed in order to make such findings as will assist the DSB in making recommendations or in giving rulings in respect of this dispute.

The Appellate Body agreed with the Panel and, in so doing, relied extensively on prior GATT practice.

That practice set out the circumstances in which a Panel, or the Appellate Body, may exercise judicial economy. As the Appellate Body stated in a 2004 case, *Canada — Measures Relating to Exports of Wheat and Treatment of Imported Grain*, WT/DS276/AB/R (27 September 2004):

> The practice of judicial economy, which was first employed by a number of GATT panels, allows a panel to refrain from making multiple findings that the same measure is *inconsistent* with various provisions when a single, or a certain number of findings of inconsistency, would suffice to resolve the dispute. Although the doctrine of judicial economy *allows* a panel to refrain from addressing claims beyond those necessary to resolve the dispute, it does not *compel* a panel to exercise such restraint. At the same time, if a panel fails to make findings on claims where such findings are necessary to resolve the dispute, then this would constitute a false exercise of judicial economy and an error of law. (original emphasis; footnotes omitted)

In brief, as the Appellate Body indicated in a 1998 case, *Australia — Measures Affecting Importation of Salmon*, WT/DS18/AB/R (adopted 6 November 1998), "judicial economy" means addressing only "those claims on which a finding is necessary in order to enable the DSB to make sufficiently precise recommendations and rulings so as to allow for prompt compliance by a Member with those recommendations and rulings," and thus achieve an effective resolution of disputes to the benefit of all Members.

Judicial economy is premised on more than the need to conserve judicial resources and dispose of matters efficiently. It is a principle of self-restraint. If WTO adjudicators were to decide every issue raised by a complainant, they would be "making" more law than they need to, rather than "finding" just enough law to settle a dispute. That is, they would blur the line between judicial and legislative functions that is drawn by Article 3:9 of the *DSU* and Article IX of the *WTO Agreement*. In turn, they would de-legitimize the dispute resolution process.

That said, appellants in WTO litigation sometimes ask the Appellate Body to "complete the legal analysis" that a Panel failed to finish, because the Panel exercised false judicial economy. The Appellate Body will do so, thereby examining an issue not specifically addressed by the Panel, in order to resolve the dispute between the parties. What constraints exist on the Appellate Body stepping in to "top up" the legal analysis? The Appellate Body summarized them in the 2005 *EC — Sugar* case:

> [T]he Appellate Body has declined to complete the legal analysis where "the factual findings of the panel and the undisputed facts in the panel record" did not provide a sufficient basis for the legal analysis by the Appellate Body. [The Appellate Body cited *European Communities — Measures Affecting Asbestos and Asbestos-Containing Products*, WT/DS135/AB/R (adopted 5 April 2001).] Moreover, as Article 17.6 of the *DSU* limits appeals to "issues of law covered in the panel report and legal interpretations developed by the panel", the Appellate Body has also previously declined to complete the legal analysis of a panel in circumstances where that would involve addressing claims "which the panel had not examined at all." [The Appellate Body cited to its *EC — Asbestos* Report, and also to its Report in *European Communities — Measures Affecting the Importation of Certain Poultry Products*, WT/DS69/AB/R (adopted 23 July 1998).] In addition, the Appellate Body has indicated that it may complete the analysis only if the provision that a panel has not examined is "*closely related*" to a provision that the panel has examined, and that the two are "part of a *logical continuum*." [Here again, the Appellate Body cited to the *EC — Asbestos* case, as well as another one of its Reports, *Canada — Certain Measures Concerning Periodicals*, WT/DS31/AB/R (adopted 30 July 1997).]

Note the accretion of precedent resulting in the constraints.

F. Burden of Proof

Does the complainant or respondent bear the burden of proof in WTO adjudication? This very basic question is not addressed in the WTO Agreement or *DSU*. In retrospect, therefore, it could be only a matter of time before the Appellate Body would have to step in with an interstitial rule. The opportunity came in *United States — Wool Shirts*, in the context of Article 6:2 of the WTO *Agreement on Textiles and Clothing (ATC)*. This Article establishes the right of an importing Member to implement a safeguard action if its textile or apparel producers are damaged by the phase-out of the *Multi-Fiber Agreement*:

> Safeguard action may be taken under this Article when, on the basis of a determination by a Member, *it is demonstrated* that a particular product is being imported into its territory in such increased quantities as to cause serious damage, or actual threat thereof, to the domestic industry producing like and/or directly competitive products. Serious damage or actual threat thereof must *demonstrably* be caused by such increased quantities in total imports of that product and not by such other factors as technological changes or changes in consumer preference. (Emphasis added.)

The highlighted language obviously does not answer the question "who must demonstrate?" the elements set forth in Article 6:2.

In the case, India claimed the U.S. was unjustified in resorting to a transitional safeguard action. Was the burden then on India to prove its claim. Or, was it on the U.S. to justify its action?

India argued the burden ought to be on the Americans, because Article 6:1 of the *ATC* states transitional safeguards "should be applied as sparingly as possible." That is, they are exceptional, and the WTO Member invoking the exception should be required to prove it qualifies for the exception. The U.S. countered with a quasi-precedent argument. GATT practice had been for the complainant to present a *prima facie* case of violation. Hence, India had to show the Americans were unreasonable in determining increased woven wool shirt and blouse imports had caused serious damage or actual threat thereof to domestic producers. The Appellate Body provided the answer.

> [A] party claiming a violation of a provision of the WTO Agreement by another Member must assert and prove its claim. In this case, India claimed a violation by the United States of Article 6 of the *ATC*. We agree with the Panel that it, therefore, was up to India to put forward evidence and legal argument sufficient to demonstrate that the transitional safeguard action by the United States was inconsistent with the obligations assumed by the United States under Articles 2 and 6 of the ATC. India did so in this case. And, with India having done so, the onus then shifted to the United States to bring forward evidence and argument to disprove the claim. This, the United States was not able to do and, therefore, the Panel found that the transitional safeguard action by the United States "violated the provisions of Articles 2 and 6 of the *ATC*."

> In our view, the Panel did not err on this issue in the case.

Put succinctly, the Americans had won the battle, but lost the war. The Appellate Body stuck with GATT practice, as the U.S. had urged, yet still held India had met its burden.

Thus, the burden of proof rule has three steps to be followed *in seriatim*. First, a complainant Member must present a *prima facie* case. Second, if it does, then it creates a rebuttable presumption that the measure complained of is inconsistent with the applicable rule. Third, the burden shifts to the respondent Member to rebut the presumption. Concomitantly, the respondent bears the burden of proof of any affirmative defense.

G. Fact-finding by Panels

A WTO panel is ill-equipped to engage in fact-finding. Still, *DSU* Article 13:1 gives it "the right to seek information and technical advice from any individual or body which it deems appropriate," and says a Member "should respond promptly and fully to any request by a panel. . . ." In speaking of individuals and bodies, the first part of the provision is more aspirational than authoritative. The GATT—WTO agreements are among sovereign states, not individuals, international organizations, or NGOs. The second part of the provision, by using the term "should" rather than "shall," admits that no WTO panel can compel compliance with a fact-finding request.

To be sure, "discovery" of documents, in the common law sense of the term, is unavailable under the *DSU*. The Panel Report in *Argentina — Footwear* makes this point. But, the panel in that case took the occasion of Argentina's refusal to provide documents (specifically, additional customs invoices) to the U.S. to offer *dicta* on fact finding. The panel said a "rule of collaboration" exists in *DSU* adjudication: parties must provide information necessary for the presentation of facts and evidence to the panel. The rule means a respondent Member is obligated to provide a panel with relevant documents in its sole possession. The obligation arises after the complaining Member has done its best to secure the evidence, and produced some *prima facie* evidence in support of its case.

Chapter 6

ADJUDICATION CONTROVERSIES

A judge is a law student who marks his own examination papers.

> —H.L. Mencken (iconoclastic American journalist and writer, 1880-1956)

DOCUMENTS SUPPLEMENT ASSIGNMENT

1. GATT Articles XXII-XXIII
2. WTO *DSU*
3. U.S. *Statement of Administrative Action* for the *DSU*

I. IMPERFECTIONS

By most accounts, WTO dispute settlement is a remarkable success. The *Understanding on Rules and Procedures Governing the Settlement of Disputes* (*Dispute Settlement Understanding*, or *DSU*) is a crowning achievement of the Uruguay Round. Pre-WTO dispute settlement under GATT Article XXIII was a diplomatic system, dominated by clubby insiders sometimes called "old GATT hands," who demographically (as is sometimes said indelicately of international commercial arbitrators) tended to be "pale, male, and stale." The results inclined toward political compromises translated into abstruse legal language. The *DSU* boasts three major gains over former procedures, which also are advantages over the operation of the International Court of Justice (ICJ).

First, there is compulsory jurisdiction. The single undertaking approach to Uruguay Round texts means all WTO Members must adhere to the *DSU*. Second, decisions rendered under the *DSU* are enforceable. To be sure, as the work of the late Professor Robert E. Hudec shows, the record of compliance under the old GATT system was better than sometimes believed. Compromises were reached, after all, and contracting parties were repeat players with reputational interests. Still, that system lacked the rigorous enforcement mechanism characteristic of the *DSU*. Third, the *DSU* affords complainants and respondents are right of appeal. That innovation was strongly urged by the U.S. during the Uruguay Round.

Despite these gains, the *DSU* is not perfect — no human adjudicatory system is. Anticipating problems, Uruguay Round negotiators built in a future negotiating agenda into the *DSU*, and work on it began four years after the *DSU* entered into force (*i.e.*, 1 January 1999). To summarize the consensus of comments from WTO Members on this agenda: "We are happy, the *DSU* works reasonably well, but there are a few minor technical difficulties, on which we all agree." A myriad of substantial proposals for *DSU* reform followed. Unfortunately, work on the in built agenda was unsuccessful because Members could not agree on which proposals to advance.

WTO Members then made what in retrospect proved to be a colossal mistake: they moved the in built agenda into the Doha Round. By creating a built in agenda, the Uruguay Round negotiators clearly telegraphed their intent not to make *DSU* reform subject to the horse trading endemic to multilateral trade talks (*e.g.*, agricultural market access and subsidy cuts in exchange for better non-agricultural market access (NAMA) and General Agreement on Trade in Services (*GATS*) offers). By inserting adjudication rule improvements into the DDA, the topic became part of the single undertaking approach of the Doha Round — nothing could be agreed to on *DSU* changes unless and until all other issues were resolved. In effect, *DSU* reform became hostage to unrelated, politicized matters, and to vicissitudes of the Round. For its part, Taiwan tried to break the logjam on *DSU* reform by taking the topic out of the diplomatic processes of the Round and placing it in the jurisdiction of an *ad hoc* technical committee comprised of former members of the WTO Appellate Body. Taiwan's proposal was not adopted.

II. TRANSPARENCY AND PARTICIPATION

A. Opening the Courtroom?

Why can't the courtroom be open so anyone can observe WTO panel and Appellate Body proceedings? Why must these meetings go on in secret? Why can't all submissions (*e.g.*, briefs) made by disputing Members and third parties be made public? Why is it necessary to rely on the re-production of arguments in a panel or Appellate Body report to understand which Member argued what claim or defense, and why they did so? Why can't *amicus* briefs be accepted routinely? Why must NGOs and other stakeholders in the multilateral trading system face the prospect of their briefs ignored?

To an Anglo-American trained lawyer, the answer is obvious. There is no "downside" to being more transparent, particularly if it will quell criticism of the WTO. Thus, during his speech in Geneva at the occasion of the 50th anniversary of the GATT system, in 1997, President Clinton not only asked these questions, but also called for an open courtroom door, and publication of submissions, and the acceptance of *amicus* briefs. But, the answer is not so obvious to all WTO Members. It is difficult for some Members — particularly developing countries — to accept a level of transparency in WTO adjudication that is far greater than what they permit in their own domestic legal systems. What exists in the U.S. Constitution or the *Administrative Procedures Act* often does not exist in other countries. As another example, the *Uruguay Round Agreements Act of 1994* obligates the United States Trade Representative (USTR) to solicit views of the public in any WTO case to which the U.S. is a party. But, this mandate — which brings a certain degree of democratic openness to the process, at least in terms of the formation of claims and defenses — is not found in the laws of many Members.

In other words, the objection to greater transparency from developing countries is based on more than just an adherence to the traditional secretive habits of international organizations or a view of the WTO as an inter-governmental entity. It is an objection grounded in jurisprudence, political philosophy, and legal culture. Why permit "cameras in the courtroom" in Geneva or access to Members' submissions, and why invite submissions from "outsiders," if there are no such rights permitted at home?

Moreover, greater transparency poses significant logistical questions that veil very different premises. If submissions are to be published, when — immediately upon filing, or after a case concludes? Private-sector lawyers observing the case might like immediate publication so that they can advise their clients better, but it may require a good deal more resources to provide such swift access. If there is to be access to hearings, what form should that access take? Would the publication of a hearing transcript suffice? Or, is physical presence necessary? What about CNN or Court-TV coverage? As for *amicus* briefs, which non-governmental organizations (NGOs) ought to be recognized? There are a large number of entities claiming to represent civil society. In reality, many of them are from western countries, and lobby for western concerns. How, if at all, is the WTO to decide which voices are worth hearing? And, what about *stare decisis*, or some notion of *de facto* precedent? Is it appropriate to speak of an emerging body of common law produced by a system of dubious transparency? The sun shines far more brightly on real precedent setters, the common law courts, than on panels or the Appellate Body.

Still, the very opponents of greater transparency might be among its biggest beneficiaries. Developing countries are in desperate need of technical assistance that would enable them to participate more effectively in the adjudicatory system. To be sure, in the first few years of the operation of the *DSU*, a few developing countries won some impressive victories against the U.S. — Venezuela and Brazil in the *Reformulated Gasoline* case, and India and Costa Rica in cases involving textiles safeguards. But, by "showing up" in the WTO and bringing these cases, developing countries may have made themselves more visible as targets for suits. Frequently, they are respondents. Suppose a developing country could send representatives to observe hearings, study briefs, and file *amicus* briefs in cases in which that country was not involved. Surely that country would learn from this access how to be a better respondent, as well as a better complainant.

B. *Amicus* Briefs, the 1998 *Turtle — Shrimp* Case, and the Aftermath

Can an NGO submit a brief in a WTO adjudicatory proceeding? The *DSU* does not explicitly grant WTO Members the right to submit expert testimony. But, there are no provisions that bar a Member from including this sort of information in written submissions to a panel or the Appellate Body. Moreover, to say NGOs clamor at the WTO gates seeking to be heard is an understatement. Listening sincerely could bolster the legitimacy and credibility of the dispute settlement process. But, listening to everything from everyone would cause the dispute settlement mechanism to collapse in the cacophony — or perhaps more accurately, under the weight of legal briefs submitted.

In its 1998 decision, *United States — Import Prohibition of Certain Shrimp and Shrimp Products*, the Appellate Body held panels should treat a brief of an NGO appended to the brief of a Member involved in a dispute as part of its submission. In other words, NGO briefs attached to party submissions are admissible. Of course, to take advantage of this holding, an NGO must obtain the consent of the Member government involved. That will require negotiation between the NGO and government. No government will affix an NGO brief to its submission that in any way undermines its position. In turn, the NGO seeking to be heard may feel its freedom of speech — specifically, its ability to stake out an independent legal position — is compromised.

What about cameras in the courtroom? While *DSU* proceedings are held in secret, parties may waive secrecy and grant a degree of public access, should they unanimously agree to do so. For roughly the first decade of *DSU* operation, parties did not make use of this relative procedural flexibility, and thus did not address directly a principal criticism of the WTO. But, in September 2005, a shift occurred. In a proceeding concerning the *Beef Hormones* case, the U.S., Canada, and European Communities (EC) all agreed to waive their right to secrecy, and grant the public access to proceedings.

Just how much public access was permitted? The WTO panel meetings were broadcast on closed circuit television into a viewing room at WTO headquarters in Geneva. Seats were made available to the first 400 members of the public who completed and returned a form made available on the WTO website. Third parties to the dispute did not consent to public viewing of their panel meetings. Consequently, they were not broadcast. Might this event prove transformational in public access to *DSU* proceedings?

WTO APPELLATE BODY REPORT, *UNITED STATES — IMPORT PROHIBITION OF CERTAIN SHRIMP AND SHRIMP PRODUCTS*
WT/DS58/AB/R (adopted 6 November 1998)

V. Panel Proceedings and Non-requested Information

99. In the course of the proceedings before the Panel, . . . the Panel received a [joint] brief from the Center for Marine Conservation ("CMC") and the Center for International Environmental Law ("CIEL"). Both are non-governmental organizations. . . . [T]he Panel received another brief . . . from the World Wide Fund for Nature [also an NGO]. The Panel acknowledged receipt of the two briefs, which the non-governmental organizations also sent directly to the parties to this dispute. The complaining parties — India, Malaysia, Pakistan and Thailand — requested the Panel not to consider the contents of the briefs in dealing with the dispute. In contrast, the United States urged the Panel to avail itself of any relevant information in the two briefs. . . .

100. . . . . [T]he Panel did two things. First, the Panel declared a legal interpretation of certain provisions of the *DSU*: *i.e.*, that accepting non-requested information from non-governmental sources would be "incompatible with the provisions of the *DSU* as currently applied." Evidently as a result of this legal interpretation, the Panel announced that it would not take the briefs submitted by non-governmental organizations into consideration. Second, the Panel

nevertheless allowed any party to the dispute to put forward the briefs,or any part thereof, as part of its own submissions to the Panel, giving the other party or parties, in such case, two additional weeks to respond to the additional material. The United States appeals from this legal interpretation of the Panel.

101. . . . [A]ccess to the dispute settlement process of the WTO is limited to Members of the WTO. This access is not available, under the *WTO Agreement* and the covered agreements as they currently exist, to individuals or international organizations, whether governmental or non-governmental. Only Members may become parties to a dispute of which a panel may be seized, and only Members "having a substantial interest in a matter before a panel" may become third parties in the proceedings before that panel. [*DSU* Articles 4, 6, 9-10.] Thus, under the *DSU*, only Members who are parties to a dispute, or who have notified their interest in becoming third parties in such a dispute to the DSB, have a *legal right* to make submissions to, and have a *legal right* to have those submissions considered by, a panel. [*See DSU* Articles 10, 12, and Appendix 3.] Correlatively, a panel is *obliged* in law to accept and give due consideration only to submissions made by the parties and the third parties in a panel proceeding. These are basic legal propositions; they do not, however, dispose of the issue here presented by the appellant's first claim of error. We believe this interpretative issue is most appropriately addressed by examining what a panel is *authorized* to do under the *DSU*.

. . . .

103. In *EC Measures Affecting Meat and Meat Products (Hormones)*, we observed that Article 13 of the *DSU* "enable[s] panels to seek information and advice as they deem appropriate in a particular case." Also, in *Argentina — Measures Affecting Imports of Footwear, Textiles, Apparel and Other Items*, we ruled that:

> Pursuant to Article 13.2 of the *DSU*, a panel may seek information from any relevant source and may consult experts to obtain their opinions on certain aspects of the matter at issue. *This is a grant of discretionary authority: a panel is not duty-bound to seek information in each and every case or to consult particular experts under this provision.* We recall our statement in *EC Measures Concerning Meat and Meat Products (Hormones)* that Article 13 of the *DSU* enables a panel to seek information and technical advice as it deems appropriate in a particular case, and that the DSU leaves "to the sound discretion of a panel the determination of whether the establishment of an expert review group is necessary or appropriate." *Just as a panel has the discretion to determine how to seek expert advice, so also does a panel have the discretion to determine whether to seek information or expert advice at all.*
>
> . . . .

In this case, we find that the *Panel acted within the bounds of its discretionary authority under Articles 11 and 13 of the DSU in deciding not to seek information from, nor to consult with, the IMF.* (emphasis added)

104. The comprehensive nature of the authority of a panel to "seek" information and technical advice from "any individual or body" it may consider

appropriate, or from "any relevant source," should be underscored. This authority embraces more than merely the choice and evaluation of the *source* of the information or advice which it may seek. A panel's authority includes the authority to decide *not to seek* such information or advice at all. We consider that a panel also has the authority to *accept or reject* any information or advice which it may have sought and received, or to *make some other appropriate disposition* thereof. It is particularly within the province and the authority of a panel to determine *the need for information and advice* in a specific case, to ascertain the *acceptability* and *relevancy* of information or advice received, and to decide *what weight to ascribe to that information or advice* or to conclude that no weight at all should be given to what has been received.

105. It is also pertinent to note that Article 12.1 of the *DSU* authorizes panels to depart from, or to add to, the *Working Procedures* set forth in Appendix 3 of the *DSU*, and in effect to develop their own *Working Procedures*, after consultation with the parties to the dispute. Article 12.2 goes on to direct that "[p]anel procedures should provide *sufficient flexibility* so as to *ensure high-quality panel reports* while *not unduly delaying the panel process*." (emphasis added)

106. The thrust of Articles 12 and 13, taken together, is that the *DSU* accords to a panel established by the DSB, and engaged in a dispute settlement proceeding, ample and extensive authority to undertake and to control the process by which it informs itself both of the relevant facts of the dispute and of the legal norms and principles applicable to such facts. That authority, and the breadth thereof, is indispensably necessary to enable a panel to discharge its duty imposed by Article 11 of the *DSU* to "make an objective assessment of the matter before it, including an *objective assessment of the facts of the case* and the *applicability of and conformity with the relevant covered agreements. . . .*" (emphasis added)

107. Against this context of broad authority vested in panels by the *DSU*, and given the object and purpose of the Panel's mandate as revealed in Article 11, we do not believe that the word "seek" must necessarily be read, as apparently the Panel read it, in too literal a manner. That the Panel's reading of the word "seek" is unnecessarily formal and technical in nature becomes clear should an "individual or body" first ask a panel for permission to file a statement or a brief. In such an event, a panel may decline to grant the leave requested. If, in the exercise of its sound discretion in a particular case, a panel concludes *inter alia* that it could do so without "unduly delaying the panel process," it could grant permission to file a statement or a brief, subject to such conditions as it deems appropriate. The exercise of the panel's discretion could, of course, and perhaps should, include consultation with the parties to the dispute. In this kind of situation, for all practical and pertinent purposes, the distinction between "requested" and "non-requested" information vanishes.

108. . . . [A]uthority to *seek* information is not properly equated with a *prohibition* on accepting information which has been submitted without having been requested by a panel. A panel has the discretionary authority either to accept and consider or to reject information and advice submitted

to it, *whether requested by a panel or not*. The fact that a panel may *motu proprio*[by its own force] have initiated the request for information does not, by itself, bind the panel to accept and consider the information which is actually submitted. The amplitude of the authority vested in panels to shape the processes of fact-finding and legal interpretation makes clear that a panel will *not* be deluged, as it were, with non-requested material, *unless that panel allows itself to be so deluged*.

109. Moreover, acceptance and rejection of the information and advice of the kind here submitted to the Panel need not exhaust the universe of possible appropriate dispositions thereof. In the present case, the Panel did not reject the information outright. The Panel suggested instead, that, if any of the parties wanted "to put forward these documents, or parts of them, as part of their own submissions to the Panel, they were free to do so." In response, the United States then designated Section III of the document submitted by CIEL/CMC as an annex to its second submission to the Panel, and the Panel gave the appellees two weeks to respond. We believe that this practical disposition of the matter by the Panel in this dispute may be detached, as it were, from the legal interpretation adopted by the Panel of the word "seek" in Article 13.1 of the *DSU*. When so viewed, we conclude that the actual disposition of these briefs by the Panel does not constitute either legal error or abuse of its discretionary authority in respect of this matter. The Panel was, accordingly, entitled to treat and take into consideration the section of the brief that the United States appended to its second submission to the Panel, just like any other part of the United States pleading.

110. We find, and so hold, that the Panel erred in its legal interpretation that accepting non-requested information from non-governmental sources is incompatible with the provisions of the *DSU*. At the same time, . . . the Panel acted within the scope of its authority under Articles 12 and 13 of the *DSU* in allowing any party to the dispute to attach the briefs by non-governmental organizations, or any portion thereof, to its own submissions.

C. Private Counsel

Can a private legal advisor to a WTO Member participate in a WTO panel or Appellate Body hearing? The *DSU* is silent on this question, and no pre-Uruguay Round GATT panel had addressed it. As on the other issues, on this matter procedural common law from the Appellate Body was needed. However, this issue — more than the others — went to the heart of participation in the *DSU*. Many developing country Members are too poor to maintain a standing army of trade lawyers ready to do battle at the WTO. Resource constraints compel them to hire from the private sectors lawyers as consultants for specific cases as the need arises. These lawyers clearly are not government officials, thus their presence alters the inter-governmental character of the WTO.

The USTR opined private attorneys should not be able to attend panel hearings, much less present arguments to a panel. The USTR fretted over confidentiality and conflicts of interest, saying the presence of outside counsel somehow might lead to problems involving keeping matters confidential or dealing with representation of multiple governments. However, it never quite explained why private lawyers were less able to keep secrets or adhere to the attorney-client privilege rule, or why they were less able to resolve ethical issues, than government counsel. The USTR's other argument, that if it became common practice to hire private counsel, then developing countries would be priced out of the dispute settlement business because they could not afford the legal fees, seemed paternalistic. The USTR also neglected the fact many private attorneys (not to mention law professors) might enjoy taking less developed country (LDC) cases on a *pro bono* basis.

In its 1997 *EC — Bananas* Report, the Appellate Body held a private legal adviser to the government of St. Lucia — which was a third party in the case — is allowed to participate in an oral hearing of the Appellate Body. (The panel had ruled St. Lucia's two private sector attorneys could not be allowed in the hearing room to present St. Lucia's views. The panel wanted to follow pre-Uruguay Round GATT practice, which forbade private attorneys from participation if there were any objections, and in the case the United States objected. Also, the panel feared St. Lucia somehow might gain an unfair advantage if its private counsel were recognized.) The Appellate Body reasoned nothing in the *WTO Agreement* or *DSU* specified who can represent a Member in making presentations at an oral hearing. In so doing, the Appellate Body took a pragmatic approach that was consistent with normal practice in public international law, namely, that each country can decide for itself the composition of its delegation. Thus, a Member is free to employ private sector attorneys to represent it. Moreover, said the Appellate Body, if developing countries are to participate fully and effectively, then they might need private counsel. (The fact the other third parties in the case backing St. Lucia's argument were all less developed countries illustrated the point: Belize, Cameroon, Côte d'Ivoire, Dominica, Dominican Republic, Ghana, Grenada, Jamaica, St. Vincent and the Grenadines, Senegal, and Suriname.) Finally, the Appellate Body highlighted the systemic interest in the best possible counsel representing Members in *DSU* proceedings.

What about oral hearings of WTO panels? The question of private counsel representing Members at the panel stage was not raised in *EC — Bananas*. However, in the *Indonesia — Automobile Industry* case, the panel rejected an attempt by the U.S. to exclude two private lawyers representing Indonesia from the first substantive meeting of the panel with the parties. The *Indonesia* panel essentially followed the decision and logic of the Appellate Body in *EC — Bananas*.

The strongest argument against allowing private counsel to represent Members probably is they might tend to view a case as a "one shot deal." A government presumably considers its long-term interests when it shapes its legal arguments in a case at bar. It might avoid taking an extreme position in that case for fear the arguments it deploys today will come back to haunt it in a future case. Private counsel, it could be argued, are less inclined to consider the long-term ramifications of positions they argue because they think in client-by-client, not sustainable policy, terms. However, the problem with this argument is it assumes WTO Members would not monitor — indeed, approve — the positions taken by their private counsel. The lawyer is not the client, rather the Member is, and thus the Member is supposed to approve legal strategy. As a practical matter, it is not uncommon for the real underlying party in interest in a case — for example, a multinational corporation — to fund the cost of private outside counsel. Often a WTO Member will work with outside counsel paid for by interested private parties.

III. STRUCTURAL AND OPERATIONAL PROBLEMS

Only a view of WTO adjudication through rose-colored lenses would lead to the conclusion the *DSU*, in its practical implementation, has been free from serious problems. To be sure, the system handles a large volume of cases, and in general produces results consistent in terms of jurisprudence and expectations. For the most part, losing Members comply with recommendations within the usual 15-month implementation period.

Perhaps the most significant effect of WTO adjudication is panels and the Appellate Body have the same effect as a police officer on the street: deterrence. In the end, it is not so much which cases are won or lost that matters, but rather Members formulate and modify their trade measures in accordance with GATT—WTO obligations because they know the operation of the *DSU* is a "cop" watching over their behavior.

Still, several difficulties — in addition to interstitial law-making on procedural issues and the problem of compliance — are apparent. These problems have yet to be resolved. Arguably, they are sufficiently serious as to threaten the very operation of the *DSU*, and thereby its ability to deter wrongful conduct.

A. The Consultation Phase

Consultations must be requested, and the disputing WTO Members must meet at least once, before a panel can be convened. Only if a result is not achieved within the prescribed time period does the case move forward to the panel phase. During the first five years of operation, there were on average about 40 consultations per year. About half of these cases did not go beyond the consultation phase for one of two reasons: they were settled, or the complainants abandoned their claims.

The existence of a consultation phase highlights the fact the WTO is not just a court. That initial phase is important and, indeed, is inherited from the pre-Uruguay Round era. It is the phase in which diplomacy — that curious mixture of negotiations and politics — plays a pre-eminent role with the hope of a mutually agreeable solution. As the Appellate Body stated in a Compliance Report, *Mexico — Anti-Dumping Investigation of High Fructose Corn Syrup (HFCS) from the United States — Recourse to Article 21:5 of the DSU by the United States*, WT/DS132/AB/RW, ¶ 58 (adopted 21 November 2001):

> We agree . . . on the importance of consultations. Through consultations, parties exchange information, assess the strengths and weaknesses of their respective cases, narrow the scope of the differences between them and, in many cases, reach a mutually agreed solution in accordance with the explicit preference expressed in Article 3.7 of

the *DSU*. Moreover, even where no such agreed solution is reached, consultations provide the parties an opportunity to define and delimit the scope of the dispute between them. Clearly, consultations afford many benefits to complaining and responding parties, as well as to third parties and to the dispute settlement system as a whole.

(The Appellate Body quoted this language in a major agricultural case, *United States — Subsidies on Upland Cotton*, WT/DS267/AB/R, ¶ 284 (adopted 21 March 2005)). However, in some cases the disputing Members treat the consultation phase as a mere formality, entering the phase with a view it is a useless exercise.

Should, therefore, a more legalistic, pre-trial discovery process replace consultations? The Appellate Body thinks not. In its *Cotton* Report (¶ 287), it appeared content with the *status quo* in which consultations are off limits to WTO adjudication:

> [W]e are inclined to agree with the panel in *Korea — Alcoholic Beverages*, which stated that "[t]he only requirement under the *DSU* is that consultations were in fact held . . . [w]hat takes place in those consultations is not the concern of a panel." [Panel Report, *Korea — Taxes on Alcoholic Beverages*, WT/DS75/R, WT/DS84/R, ¶ 10.19 (adopted as modified by the Appellate Body 17 February 1999).] Examining what took place in the consultations would seem contrary to Article 4.6 of the *DSU*, which provides that "[c]onsultations shall be confidential, and without prejudice to the rights of any Member in any further proceedings." Moreover, it would seem at odds with the requirements in Article 4.4 of the *DSU* that the request for consultations be made in writing and that it be notified to the DSB. In addition, there is no public record of what actually transpires during consultations and parties will often disagree about what, precisely, was discussed.

What factors counsel against replacing GATT-style consultations with American-style pre-trial discovery? Might it be the virtues of discovery would be offset by its vices, and not routinely encourage parties toward settlement, but rather harden both their positions and demeanors, and push them to litigation?

Good faith is a critical problem plaguing the consultation phase. As indicated, the consultation phase is an inheritance from the GATT era, with the idea that the best solution is one that is mutually acceptable and achieved diplomatically — in effect, it is better to agree than to sue. Under the *DSU*, consultations are compulsory. Yet, overall, only about 25 percent of cases are solved through them. Most consultations fail because the complainant and respondent must notify the Dispute Settlement Body (DSB) of their case. That notification generates publicity, and triggers mandatory, formal *DSU* procedures. Not infrequently, publicity is adverse to a settlement, and parties prefer secret talks. Hence, in the WTO, they have taken to circumventing the *DSU* by entering into consultations before lodging a *DSU* notice. That behavior has spawned a pre-filing consultation system. Indeed, some Members view formal consultations as a waste of time. Once they give the requisite notification, they wait the prescribed 8-week period, and then begin litigation. Essentially, the complainant and respondent have a gentleman's agreement they will meet for consultations once, as the *DSU* requires, and then let the two month period tick away, all the while preparing for adversarial proceedings. That conduct seems to violate the good faith obligation in the *DSU*.

Accordingly, two proposals have been floated in the context of *DSU* reform discussions to change the formal consultation phase.

1. Why not force consultations between parties and create a written record of the talks for a *DSU* panel to use, should it be necessary? A panel would have the right to send a case back to the complainant and respondent for consultations, if it decides they have not bargained in good faith. The problem with this proposal is it undermines the presumption that consultations occur without prejudice to the positions of the parties. Consultations are not supposed to be civil discovery.

2. Why not use consultations to find a common factual predicate for a panel, should a case go that far? At least the complainant and respondent will have made some progress through consultations, namely, they can stipulate to the facts. This proposal suffers from the same defect as the first one — consultations are not discovery.

Given the common shortcoming, a third proposal might be to shorten the time frame for consultations to just one month. Though it would not solve the underlying difficulty, at least it would reduce time wasted.

A final important question about the consultation phase intersects with the problem of the right to counsel of choice. As discussed earlier, the *EC — Bananas* and *Indonesia — Automobile Industry* cases clarified the right to counsel, finding if a WTO Member wants to "deputize" certain private sector attorneys, it can. But, what about the use of private sector attorneys in the consultation phase? The evolving practice is if a Member insists strongly enough (as have, for example, Brazil and India), then those lawyers will be allowed in the negotiating room. However, they do not yet seem to be given the privilege of speaking in the consultation sessions.

B.   Panel Selection, Composition, and Overload

Panels are an inheritance from GATT Articles XXII-XXIII provisions, which, in turn, came from the *Havana (ITO) Charter*. These provisions linked GATT dispute settlement to the International Court of Justice (ICJ). Through GATT history, panels evolved from two earlier conceptual states. Initially, Working Groups consisting of the disputing contracting parties and neutral contracting parties met together around a negotiating table to resolve a contested matter. Subsequently, Working Groups split the complainant and respondent, putting them across opposite sides of a table, thus symbolically indicating an adversarial aspect to the otherwise diplomatic procedure. Today, as in pre-*DSU* practice, a panel can consist of 3 or 5 members, though in practice panels have always been the smaller of the two numbers.

Ideally, disputing Members are supposed to agree on panelists to hear their case. Often, they do not. That is, the complainant, respondent, and WTO

Secretariat — specifically, the Legal Affairs Division therein — do not always agree on the panelists. The result is the Director-General must pick panelists. It may be dreadfully unhealthy for the WTO adjudicatory system to have the Director-General involved personally in a large number of cases. Panelists — like arbitrators — are supposed to be selected by the parties, not by the Director-General, except in unusual circumstances. Of course, that conclusion depends on one's view of the system and the role of the Director-General.

Perhaps even more troubling than disagreements on panelists is their dependence on the Secretariat, especially the Legal Affairs Division. Panelists are not nearly so independent as they may appear. In many, if not most, cases, the Legal Affairs Division writes the report — not the panelists. That Division provides legal assistance and research for the panel. Is there, then, a need for greater "professionalization" of panels?

Usually, panelists are government officials, and occasionally, they are academics. Invariably, being a panelist is not a full-time job. Rather, it is a secondary pursuit to which no panelist possibly can devote full attention. Yet, cases are becoming increasingly complex, involving multiple GATT provisions and Uruguay Round agreements, demanding more of each panelist — as evidenced by the extraordinary length of most panel reports. Would the adjudicatory mechanism be better served by a standing panel, or panels, akin to the standing Appellate Body?

The EU (among others) thinks so. The EU has proposed creation of a standing, or permanent, roster of panelists. This registry would consist of 15-20 persons, would be maintained by an independent entity, and 3 persons would be allocated to a panel. The Director-General would not be involved in selecting panelists on a case-by-case basis. There would be an elite cadre of international trade professionals who are full-time panelists. The idea is tempting, but then who would pick the permanent panelists? How would they be selected? Exactly what criteria would be used?

Undoubtedly, a standing panel or panels would have to be equipped to handle the massive caseload that faces — and sometimes buries — current *ad hoc* panels. The ICJ was called upon to adjudicate less than 100 cases in its first 50 years of operation. (The U.S. Court of International Trade (CIT), which has nine judges, issues as many as 200-250 decisions a year.) Within the first few years of the operation of the *DSU*, the case volume surpassed the 100 mark. Furthermore, the volume had increased significantly over the pre-Uruguay Round era. Resources for dispute resolution remain woefully inadequate to handle this volume, and to deal with the many tasks that must be performed aside from adjudication *per se*, for example, translation. Perhaps the WTO mechanism as presently constituted and funded can handle 20-25 cases annually from start to finish. Asked to deal with a considerably larger number, the system may not be able to meet its own deadlines. Indeed, it appears some cases actually take up to 3 years for resolution.

C. Estoppel and the 2005 *EC — Sugar Regime* Case

WTO APPELLATE BODY REPORT, *EUROPEAN COMMUNITIES — EXPORT SUBSIDIES ON SUGAR*
WT/DS265/AB/R, WT/DS266/AB/R, WT/DS283/AB/R (adopted 19 May 2005) (complaints by Australia, Brazil, and Thailand)

[The substantive issue concerned whether the EC provided an illegal export subsidy to sugar exports, in violation of the WTO *Agreement on Agriculture*.]

302. The Panel found that the Complaining Parties "ha[d] acted in good faith in the initiation and conduct of the present dispute proceedings." The Panel emphasized that the Complaining Parties "were entitled to initiate the present WTO proceedings as they did and at no point in time have they been estopped, through their actions or silence, from challenging the EC sugar regime which they consider WTO inconsistent." The Panel explained that:

> . . . it is not possible to identify any facts or statements made by the Complainants where they have admitted that the EC measure was WTO consistent or where they have promised that they would not take legal action against the European Communities. In the Panel's view the "silence" of some of the Complainants cannot be equated with their consent to the European Communities' violations, if any. Moreover, the Complainants' silence cannot be held against other WTO Members who, today, could decide to initiate WTO dispute settlement proceedings against the European Communities.

> . . . .

309. The Panel cautioned that "it is far from clear whether the principle of estoppel is applicable to disputes between WTO Members in relation to their WTO rights and obligations." The Panel added that "[t]he principle of estoppel has never been applied by any panel or the Appellate Body." The Panel went on to opine that, assuming, for the sake of argument, that estoppel could be invoked in WTO dispute settlement:

> Brazil's and Thailand's silence concerning the European Communities' base quantity levels as well as with respect to the ACP/India sugar Footnote does not amount to a clear and unambiguous representation upon which the European Communities could rely, especially considering that, in the Panel's view, there was no legal duty upon the Complainants to alert the European Communities to its alleged violations. Furthermore, it is not possible to identify any facts or statements made by the Complainants where they have admitted that the EC measure was WTO consistent or where they have promised that they would not take legal action against the European Communities. In the Panel's view the "silence" of some of the Complainants cannot be equated with their consent to the European Communities' violations, if any.

310. We agree with the Panel that it is far from clear that the estoppel principle applies in the context of WTO dispute settlement. Indeed, on appeal,

the participants and third participants have advanced highly divergent views on the concept itself and its applicability to WTO dispute settlement.

311. The European Communities argues that estoppel is a general principle of international law, which follows from the broader principle of good faith. As such, estoppel is "one of the principles which Members are bound to observe when engaging in dispute settlement procedures, in accordance with Article 3.10 of the *DSU*." Regarding the content of estoppel, the European Communities argues that "[e]stoppel may arise not only from express statements, but also from various forms of conduct, including silence, where, upon a reasonable construction, such conduct implies the recognition of a certain factual or juridical situation." Australia, in contrast, submits that the principle of estoppel is not applicable in WTO dispute settlement. With respect to the content of estoppel, Australia submits that estoppel cannot "apply as to a statement of a legal situation." Brazil agrees with the Panel that the European Communities' claims regarding estoppel were "without merit." Similarly, Thailand maintains that the Panel was correct in concluding that the principle of "estoppel is not mentioned in the WTO Agreement, or the *DSU*, and that it has never been applied by any panel or the Appellate Body." The United States emphasizes that "[n]owhere in the *DSU* or the other covered agreements is there a reference to 'estoppel'." Moreover, according to the United States, " '[e]stoppel' is not a defense that Members have agreed on, and it therefore should not be considered by the Appellate Body."

312. The principle of estoppel has never been applied by the Appellate Body. Moreover, the notion of estoppel, as advanced by the European Communities, would appear to inhibit the ability of WTO Members to initiate a WTO dispute settlement proceeding. We see little in the *DSU* that explicitly limits the rights of WTO Members to bring an action; WTO Members must exercise their "judgement as to whether action under these procedures would be fruitful", by virtue of Article 3.7 of the *DSU*, and they must engage in dispute settlement procedures in good faith, by virtue of Article 3.10 of the *DSU*. This latter obligation covers, in our view, the entire spectrum of dispute settlement, from the point of initiation of a case through implementation. Thus, even assuming *arguendo* that the principle of estoppel could apply in the WTO, its application would fall within these narrow parameters set out in the *DSU*.

313. With these considerations in mind, we examine the arguments of the European Communities on this issue. Even assuming, for the sake of argument, that the principle of estoppel has the meaning that the European Communities ascribes to it, and that such a principle applies in WTO dispute settlement, we are not persuaded, in the circumstances of this case, that the Complaining Parties would be estopped from bringing claims against C sugar [*i.e.*, sugar produced in Europe above the thresholds established by the for "A" and "B" quotas, and exported pursuant to EC rules].

314. The European Communities argues that the Complaining Parties are estopped from bringing their claims against C sugar because their "lack of reaction to the non-inclusion of C sugar in the base quantity, together with the other undisputed facts and circumstances . . ., clearly represented to the EC that the Complainants shared the understanding that the C sugar regime did not provide export subsidies." Furthermore, according to the European

Communities, it "could legitimately rely upon that shared understanding in order not to include exports of C sugar in the base levels."

315. We observe, first, that the Panel specifically found that "it is *not* possible to identify *any* facts or statements made by the Complainants where they have admitted that the EC measure was WTO consistent or where they have promised that they would not take legal action against the European Communities." We consider this finding to be based on the Panel's weighing and appreciation of the evidence.

316. Secondly, the European Communities suggests that it "could legitimately rely" upon an alleged "shared understanding" between "all the participants in the Uruguay Round" in deciding not to include exports of C sugar in the base quantity levels in its Schedule. We recall that the Panel found no evidence of any such "shared understanding" in this case. Thus, as we see it, the European Communities has no basis on which to now assert that it could have legitimately relied upon such alleged "shared understanding" in deciding not to include exports of C sugar in the base quantity levels in its Schedule.

317. For these reasons, we reject, as did the Panel, the European Communities' allegation that the Complaining Parties were estopped from bringing their claims against C sugar.

D. Legal Capacity in Developing Countries

Most developing, and virtually all least developed, countries are dreadfully ill-prepared for the rigors of WTO adjudication. Precious few members of the Secretariat's staff that are devoted full- or part-time to providing technical legal assistance to less developed countries are WTO Members. How can this situation be rectified?

One possibility would be to increase significantly the Secretariat's resources for technical legal assistance. Any developing country could go to the Secretariat's dedicated division for legal help, whether that country is in the capacity of a complainant, respondent, third party, or observer. In some ways, the Secretariat's staff would function like a Legal Aid Bureau. However, the ultimate goal would be to train less developed Members to help themselves, so in the longer term they would not need legal assistance.

Were the Secretariat to take on this sort of function in a serious way, it would face an enormous challenge. Could it render zealous advocacy on behalf of less developed Members, but at the same time avoid undermining the reputation of the Secretariat as a neutral, unbiased party? Woe unto the WTO if the Secretariat's reputation deteriorates to that of the U.N. Secretariat. Relative to the U.N. (and, perhaps, other international organizations), at any rate, the WTO has been blissfully free of politicization, and hiring decisions tend to be based largely on merit. If that perception changes, then the WTO may face a credibility crisis, which could translate into a funding crisis as legislatures around the world — particularly Congress — will question their contributions.

To avoid unsettling the fragile equilibrium the WTO has struck, might it be better to create an inter-governmental legal aid society for less developed

Members? That organization could be funded by developed country Members, directly or through their contributions to the WTO, and provide needed technical assistance for specific cases, plus training programs to create a cadre of knowledgeable trade lawyers in the trade ministries of developing countries. Perhaps a new inter-governmental organization is not needed. Could an NGO, or even the World Bank, provide the facility on a "sub-contract" basis? Perhaps the legal academy might have a role in long-term human capital development. The WTO could provide scholarships for lawyers to earn J.D. degrees in accredited U.S. law schools. Whatever the mechanics, there is one hurdle to overcome: why should developed Members fund a program that helps developing Members sue, or respond to suits brought by, developing countries?

Significantly, in 1964, in conjunction with the addition of Part IV to GATT on Trade and Development, the Trade Advisory Center was created. The mission of the Center is to help expand legal capacity in developing countries. Specifically, it assists them to prepare and defend cases, and to understand the complexities of multilateral trade agreements. However, the Center is not the darling of all WTO Members, and not all Members contribute financially to it. Some Members, such as the U.S., question why they should fund an entity that helps other Members bring cases against them.

IV. COMPLIANCE AND ENFORCEMENT PROBLEMS

A. The "Three-Year Pass"

It is sometimes remarked, with a dose of cynicism, any WTO Member can get away with any violation of a GATT—WTO obligation for about 3 years. That is because it takes 12-18 months for a case to proceed through the *DSU* mechanism, and the reasonable period for compliance with an adverse decision typically allotted is 15 months. Why not, then, commit a violation, if it is in the interest of a country, its political leaders, or some influential constituency, to do so, and then withdraw the offending measure after 3 years? Indeed, critics of steel safeguards imposed by President George W. Bush on 5 March 2002 noted a built-in sunset date of 3 years (through March 2005). *See* WTO Appellate Body Report, *United States — Definitive Safeguard Measures on Imports of Certain Steel Products*, WT/DS248/AB/R (adopted 10 December 2003).

True as this observation may be, it must be put into perspective. First, 3 years are not always exploited mercilessly. In the steel case, the President removed the safeguard 15 months early, on 4 December 2003. That was one week before the DSB adopted an adverse Appellate Body decision. The revocation followed a mid-term review by the International Trade Commission (ITC). The review showed steel prices had risen and the U.S. steel industry had successfully re-organized. Perhaps most relevant to the timing of the revocation was the completion of the November 2002 mid-term elections?

Second, and more generally, it would be an unfairly high standard to judge the efficacy of WTO adjudication by the standard of perfect compliance. In no legal system beneath the Heavens is there 100 percent, expeditious obedience with judgments. As it so happens, the vast majority of cases result in compliance — sooner or later — by the losing Member. The Table (containing data as of April 2005, thus covering the first 10 years of *DSU* operation, which commenced on 1 January 1995) suggests this fact. Why this general practice occurs is the subject of scholarly debate. The answer may differ depending on the Member, case, and context. Three commonly touted explanations involve game theory, reputation, and fidelity.

First, WTO Members may appreciate they are repeat players in a game, and seek to maximize joint, long-term outcomes. They see each other frequently, so if they expect others to comply with adverse judgments, then they, too, must comply when a Panel or the Appellate Body rules against them. Second, Members may care about their reputation in the world arena, not wanting to be considered unilateralist, much less an outlaw. Third, Members simply may believe in the international legal order, for idealistic or utilitarian reasons, or both. Fidelity to this order, manifest in adherence to WTO adjudicatory outcomes, may help secure their idealistic and utilitarian interests.

To be sure, serious problems of compliance have arisen in WTO cases, but only a minority of them. Two quintessential instances are the 1997 WTO Appellate Body outcome in *European Communities — Regime for the Importation, Sale and Distribution of Bananas*, and the 1998 Appellate Body decision in *EC Measures Concerning Meat and Meat Products (Hormones)* cases. In these instances, the EC lost, yet compliance with Appellate Body recommendations was not forthcoming.

TABLE 6-1:

OPERATION OF THE *DSU* DURING THE FIRST 10 YEARS (1995-2005)

Variable	Number of Cases
Total Cases Brought	335
Mutually Agreed Solutions	50
Settled or Inactive Disputes	29
Panel and Appellate Body Reports Adopted by the DSB	95
Panel and Appellate Body Reports on Compliance Adopted by the DSB	15
Arbitrations on Level of Suspension of Concessions	16
Authorizations by DSB to Suspend Concessions	15

Lest there be any thought the U.S. always wears the "white hat," its compliance with the October 1998 *United States — Import Prohibition of Certain Shrimp and Shrimp Products* decision can be called into question. After it, American government officials visited Panama and warned shrimp exports from that country would not be allowed into the United States pursuant to the very statute the Appellate Body had ruled could not be justified under the *chapeau* to GATT Article XX. The officials discovered many Panamanian shrimp trawlers had been outfitted with turtle-excluder devices (TEDs), but the TEDs had been turned off or intentionally disabled. (The Panamanian fishermen, most of whom are poor, did not like using the TEDs because they reduced their shrimp catch.) About 20 percent of Panama's exports is shrimp to the United States, and the Panamanians were concerned about antagonizing the United States, which was scheduled to return the Panama Canal in December 1999. Thus, they negotiated an agreement with the U.S. rather than worrying about compliance with the Appellate Body ruling and modifying its import ban on shrimp caught on vessels without appropriate TEDs.

The fundamental debate, then, is about the nature of the legal obligation created by a recommendation from a WTO Panel or the Appellate Body and adopted by the DSB. (In keeping with GATT tradition, panels and the Appellate Body phrase their prescriptions for a losing Member not as orders, but as recommendations.) That is, what is the responsibility of a WTO Member once it has lost a case? *DSU* Article 21 indicates the Member is supposed to comply, within a reasonable period of time, with the recommendations of the panel or Appellate Body report. Thus, in a violation nullification and impairment case, the losing Member is supposed to alter its offending trade law or regulation. In a non-violation nullification and impairment case, the losing Member is supposed to reach a mutually satisfactory adjustment with the winning Member.

But, *must* the losing Member take these corrective steps? *DSU* Article 21 states compliance is the preferred result. It also contemplates instances where the losing Member pays compensation or accepts retaliation. Thus, the question is, does the losing Member have an option to (1) comply, (2) pay compensation, or (3) subject itself to retaliation? Or, is the loser legally bound to comply? The *DSU* is not as clear on this point as it might be, and commentators differ on the answer.

The scenario in which this ambiguity becomes obvious is not only the *a priori* case, that is, the case in which a losing Member is deciding what to do. The ambiguity also becomes obvious *post hoc*, *i.e.*, after the losing Member has decided to comply. Suppose a losing Member announces unilaterally "I have implemented," and the prevailing Member replies "No, you have not, and I am now able to retaliate." Who is to judge compliance, and by what standards? This scenario materialized in the *EC — Bananas* case, as well as the *EC — Beef Hormones* case. Certainly, no Member commences a WTO action with the objective of retaliation. Retaliation is an indication of a break down, a failure. But, when a right to retaliate is claimed, inevitably the grander issue of compliance is at play.

On one side of this debate are scholars and practitioners who focus on the text of the *DSU*. It does not expressly obligate losing WTO Members to implement a report's recommendations. These advocates point out if the Uruguay Round negotiators intended to require implementation, they could — and would — have said just that. Rather, the relevant provisions of the *DSU* indicate only a strong preference for compliance over compensation or retaliation:

1. *DSU* Article 3:7: "In the absence of a mutually agreed solution, the first objective of the dispute settlement mechanism is usually to secure the withdrawal of the measures concerned if these are found to be inconsistent with the provisions of any of the covered agreements [*i.e.*, if there is violation nullification and impairment]. The

provision of compensation should be resorted to only if the immediate withdrawal of the measure is impracticable. . . . The last resort . . . is the possibility of suspending the application of concessions or other obligations. . . ."

2. *DSU* Article 19:1: "Where a panel or the Appellate Body concludes that a measure is inconsistent with a covered agreement, it shall recommend that the Member concerned bring the measure into conformity with that agreement."

3. *DSU* Article 21:1: "Prompt compliance with recommendations or rulings of the DSB is essential in order to ensure effective resolution of disputes to the benefit of all members."

4. *DSU* Article 22:1: "Compensation and the suspension of concessions or other obligations are temporary measures available in the event that the recommendations and rulings are not implemented within a reasonable period of time. However, neither compensation nor the suspension of concessions or other obligations is preferred to full implementation of a recommendation. . . ."

5. *DSU* Article 22:8: "The suspension of concessions or other obligations shall be temporary. . . . [T]he DSB shall continue to keep under surveillance the implementation of adopted recommendations or rulings, including those cases where compensation has been provided or concessions or other obligations have been suspended but the recommendations . . . have not been implemented."

6. *DSU* Article 26(b): "[W]here a measure has been found to nullify or impair benefits [*i.e.*, in a non-violation nullification and impairment case] . . . there is no obligation to withdraw the measure. However, in such cases, the panel or the Appellate Body shall recommend that the Member concerned make a mutually satisfactory adjustment. . . ."

In contrast, Article 94 of the U.N. *Charter* states crisply "[e]ach Member of the United Nations *undertakes to comply* with the decision of the International Court of Justice in any case to which it is a party" (emphasis added). Yes, it may be nice, for a variety of policy reasons, to encourage compliance. But, to say obedience is an international legal obligation under the *DSU* is an unjustified "stretch" of the *DSU* language quoted above.

On the other side of the debate are scholars and practitioners who find the *DSU* Article 22:1 language is sufficiently strict to eliminate the possibility of an option. They note a non-implemented panel report remains on the agenda of the DSB, and infer from this implementation is required under international law. They add: (1) nothing in the *DSU* contravenes the rule of Article 26 of the *Vienna Convention on the Law of Treaties*, which requires treaty members to perform their obligations; (2) allowing Members to choose between implementation and compensation would render the provisions of the Uruguay Round agreements that expressly authorize payment of compensation redundant (*e.g.*, Article 26:1(b) of the *DSU*, which states there is no obligation to remove a measure causing non-violation nullification and impairment); (3) most WTO Members assume implementation is required; (4) if losing Members had an option to choose whether to comply or pay compensation, then the dispute settlement system would favor large, rich Members over small, poor Members; and (5) the U.S. favors implementation whenever it is victorious and, therefore, ought not to be hypocritical. Finally, they suggest Members seem quite willing to try to avoid compliance by seeking waivers (*e.g.*, for the *Lomé* and *Cotonou Conventions*) or replacing illegal measures with legal ones that still have a protective effect. Hence, there is no need to encourage such behavior by giving them an option to comply or compensate with a panel or Appellate Body recommendation.

From a policy standpoint, the multilateral dispute settlement system would indeed be stronger if compliance is a mandatory obligation under international law. It also would be more fair, in that developed, developing, and least developed countries would be on a more level playing field. However, it is important to approach the problem unemotionally. The textual basis for arguing an option does not exist is weak, and the fact that *DSU* Article 26 does not contravene the *Vienna Convention* rule about following obligations begs the question of what the obligations are. It may well be the best argument against the "option theory" is emerging custom and practice: most WTO Members, including the U.S., believe compliance is demanded, there is no option to choose among the alternatives of compliance, compensation, or acceptance of retaliation. Eventually, that custom and practice may evolve into customary international law.

This possibility, however, is by no means assured. Perhaps there is an enticing middle ground in the implementation-versus-compensation debate. Put bluntly, it is "who cares whether a losing party implements or compensates as long as the parties to the dispute are satisfied?" All that ought to matter is the achievement of a resolution of whatever sort with which the parties agree. Indeed, *DSU* Article 3:7 says "[t]he aim of the dispute settlement mechanism is to secure a positive solution to a dispute."

Finally, as an historical footnote, during the Congressional debate over the 1994 *Uruguay Round Agreements Act*, Senate Majority Leader Robert Dole (Republican — Kansas) and the Clinton Administration's USTR, Mickey Kantor, reached an accord on America's posture in the event it lost several WTO cases. Essentially, the Administration agreed to support legislation to establish a "WTO Dispute Settlement Review Commission" consisting of 5 federal appellate judges. That Commission would review all WTO cases the U.S. lost to determine whether the panel or Appellate Body had exceeded its authority or acted outside the scope of the relevant trade agreement, added to America's obligations or diminished its rights, acted arbitrarily or capriciously, or engaged in misconduct. If the Commission found three "violations" in a 5-year period, then any member of the House or Senate could introduce a joint resolution to disapprove of America's participation in the WTO. If the resolution were approved, then the U.S. would commence withdrawal. The legislation called for in this Dole — USTR deal of 23 November 1994 never was enacted. Nevertheless, the point had been made: the U.S. was concerned about protecting its sovereignty as regards adverse WTO decisions.

B. Sequencing and Retaliation

If a losing WTO Member fails to comply with an adopted Panel or Appellate Body Report within the reasonable period allotted, then what procedures must the winning Member follow to exercise its right of retaliation? Can the winning Member "pull the trigger" immediately upon expiry of the reasonable period of time? What if the losing Member argues it indeed has complied? The problem, known as "sequencing," is whether the winner must obtain a ruling the loser in fact has failed to comply before retaliating. Specifically, in advance of retaliation, is it necessary to re-submit a dispute about compliance to the original Panel, or may a winning Member proceed directly to obtain authorization to retaliate from the DSB? The question is critical, because it goes to the essence of compliance with and enforcement of international trade law.

In the *Bananas* case, the U.S. and EU argued bitterly over the interpretation of *DSU* Articles 21:5-6 and 22:2, from which the sequencing problem arises. The Uruguay Round drafters of the *DSU* failed to catch a serious inconsistency between *DSU* Articles 21:5-6 and 22:5. The U.S. claimed the right to go straight for DSB authorization under *DSU* Article 22:5. The EC scoffed, citing *DSU* Article 21:5-6.

The EC argued it was impossible to read Article 22:2 without first observing the clear mandate of Article 21:5-6, which was to submit a dispute about compliance to a panel and await a ruling. The U.S. was trying to avoid a key check against unilateral action, namely, to start the dispute settlement process from scratch before retaliating against a losing Member's plan for implementing Appellate Body recommendations. After all, how could a winning Member be allowed to judge compliance? Surely that was the province of a panel.

There was a kernel of logic in the American position. If a fox cannot be trusted to guard a chicken coop, then neither can the chickens be left in charge. Why should compliance by a losing Member be presumed unless and until a panel decides otherwise? That would put the loser in the position of judging its own compliance, with no swift corrective action available to the winner. The loser could delay indefinitely real implementation, by tinkering with its trade regime, submitting to a compliance hearing, making a few more minor adjustments in response to the outcome of the hearing, submitting to another compliance hearing, making a few more minor changes in response, and so on *ad infinitum*.

The specter of a horrible endless loop does not mean events would go on forever without retaliation. Possibly at worst (from the American perspective), under a close reading of *DSU* Articles 21:5 and 22:6 sympathetic to the EC position (*i.e.*, the necessity of going through an Article 21:5 proceeding before retaliating), the winning Member is free to retaliate after the first iteration, *i.e.*, after the original panel has met and found the first minor adjustment to be non-compliant, and after the reasonable period for compliance defined in Article 21:3 has expired. At that juncture, there ought not to be any doubt about the right to retaliate under Article 22:6. However, even though the very right to retaliate has been established, and even with retaliation after the first iteration, good faith implementation by the losing Member is not assured. The losing Member still could protest it is making necessary modifications, and the retaliation is unjust, or at least excessive. It could stress retaliation is occurring against an offending measure — the original measure as modified the first time — that no longer exists, because that measure was altered after the Article 21:5 proceeding. Here, then, would be a potentially endless loop with retaliation triggered after the first round of the battle over compliance. Whether the prospect materializes will depend very much on the persuasiveness of the retaliation.

In any event, at the core of the American position was not only substantive logic, but also procedural fairness. Suppose a panel is called under *DSU* Article 21:5 to adjudicate an issue of compliance. Why should a winning Member have to endure normal dispute resolution procedures, particularly the 60-day consultation period prior to the establishment of a panel, yet again? In all likelihood, more consultations advantage the losing Member: it could delay, still further, compliance. Instead, the original panel ought to be reconvened immediately, it ought to be permitted to rule on a compliance plan that has not yet taken effect, and the decision ought to be issued expeditiously (*e.g.*, within 90 days, as required by Article 21:5, which is half the usual time given for issuance of a panel report). Otherwise, any hope the winner might have of enforcing the initial judgment would be dashed in meaningless negotiations and endless delays.

The American position also had an implication for the allocation of the burden of proof in a *DSU* Article 21:5 hearing. Doubtless the U.S. would contend (in the *Bananas* context, anyway, if an Article 21:5 hearing were necessary) a losing Member that pleads compliance for a measure that has been modified more than once ought to have the burden of proof the measure indeed is in compliance, just as the winning Member has the initial burden of proof the first modification to the measure is not compliant. In other words, it would be for the winning Member to prove the offending measure as modified initially by the losing Member still is insufficient to satisfy the relevant panel or Appellate Body recommendations. At that point, retaliation under *DSU* Article 22:6 is permissible. Assuming the losing Member makes further modifications in response to the retaliation, it will be for that Member to prove these modifications are enough and justify an end to the sanctions.

In the *Bananas* case, the Arbitral Panel found the wording of the two Articles "apparently irreconcilable." It declined to resolve the matter, correctly pointing out a definitive solution was for the WTO to reach under the auspices of its review of the operation of the *DSU*. Nevertheless, the Arbitral Panel tipped its hat in favor of the American position. The Panel agreed a winning Member would be prevented from invoking its Article 22 right of retaliation if it were forced into a new panel proceeding on compliance under Article 21:5. After all, Article 22:2 gives the winning Member just 20 days after the deadline for compliance to request DSB authorization for retaliation, but completion of a new panel case would take considerably longer than that. Thus, insisting on an Article 21:5 hearing would render the Article 22 deadline, and thereby the all-important right attached to it, meaningless.

In the *Bananas* and other cases, the sequencing problem has been resolved in an *ad hoc* manner. Typically, a compromise is reached involving suspension of the right to retaliate until a panel has ruled on compliance. For instance, in the *Bananas* case, the U.S. and EU agreed to await an Arbitral Panel ruling (which came on 6 April 1999). For the fifth time in 6 years, the GATT—WTO published a ruling condemning the EC's preferential trading arrangement for bananas. The latest decision was a near-complete vindication for the U.S. The Arbitral Panel agreed the EC's modifications to its banana import regime fell short of satisfying the Appellate Body's recommendations. In fact, they amounted to nothing more than a re-writing of the old rules in the hopes of avoiding compliance. Consequently, it said, the U.S. was justified retaliating against the EC. The only consolation for the EC was the Panel trimmed the amount of appropriate retaliation, from $520 million down to $191.4 million.

The USTR published (on 9 April) a revised schedule of targeted products, and endured the formality of obtaining DSB authorization for retaliation (on 19 April), and began imposing the 100 percent retaliatory tariff (retroactive to 3 March 1999). The targeted products included: batteries, bath preparations, and lithographs from the United Kingdom; various paper products (*e.g.*, uncoated felt paper and paperboard) and lithographs, mainly from the United Kingdom; handbags from France and Italy; bed linen, largely from France and Italy; and electro-thermic coffee and tea makers from Germany. The DSB authorization was historic: it was the first time the WTO had authorized the use of sanctions. Only once in the pre-Uruguay Round era had sanctions been agreed upon — a 1952 case in which the GATT allowed Netherlands to implement quotas on imports of American wheat flour.

The EC accepted the ruling (quibbling only about the retroactive imposition of retaliatory duties). However, it said it would need at least 8 months — *i.e.*, until early 2000 — to develop a plan for reforming its preferential trading arrangement for bananas. After all, the EC had to please the competing interests of the U.S. (which sought an abolition of the tariff-rate quotas and licensing system), the ACP countries (which were entitled to preferences under the *Lomè Convention*), and other Latin American producers, including the *BFA* countries (which demanded fair market access).

C. Carousel Retaliation

The *Carousel Retaliation Act*, codified at 19 U.S.C. 2416, permits retaliatory trade measures against nations that, in the estimation of the U.S., have not satisfactorily complied with recommendations contained in a panel or Appellate Body report adopted by the DSB. The *Act*, which was a 2000 amendment to Section 306 of the *Trade Act of 1974*, targets exports on a revolving schedule.

Subsection (a) of 19 U.S.C. Section 2416 establishes a general monitoring obligation for the U.S. Trade Representative:

> The Trade Representative shall monitor the implementation of each measure undertaken, or agreement that is entered into, by a foreign country to provide a satisfactory resolution of a matter subject to investigation under this subchapter or subject to dispute settlement proceedings to enforce the rights of the United States under a trade agreement providing for such proceedings.

Paragraph (1) of 19 U.S.C. Section 2416(b) explains what happens if the Trade Representative is unsatisfied:

> [i]f, on the basis of the monitoring carried out under subsection (a) of this section, the Trade Representative considers that a foreign country is not satisfactorily implementing a measure or agreement referred to in subsection (a) of this section, the Trade Representative shall determine what further action the Trade Representative shall take under section 2411(a) of this title.

In addition, Subsection (b)(2)(A) provides:

> [i]f the measure or agreement referred to in subsection (a) of this section concerns the implementation of a recommendation made pursuant to dispute settlement proceedings under the World Trade Organization, and the Trade Representative considers that the foreign country has failed to implement it, the Trade Representative shall make the determination in paragraph (1) no later than 30 days after the expiration of the reasonable period of time provided for such implementation under paragraph 21 of the *Understanding on Rules and Procedures Governing the Settlement of Disputes*. . .

Therefore, following a *DSU* proceeding, when the Trade Representative monitors implementation (or the lack thereof) by a foreign country of a recommendation, and determines the foreign country is not "satisfactorily implementing" the decision in favor of the U.S., then the Trade Representative must take retaliatory action.

Of critical importance is the nature of the retaliation, which Section 2416(b)(2)(B) addresses. Assuming the problem concerns implementation of a WTO decision, then this Section is triggered. It provides:

§ 2416(b)(2)(B) states

> . . . in the event that the United States initiates a retaliation list or takes any other action described in section 2411 (c)(1)(A) or (B) of this title against the goods of a foreign country or countries because of the failure of such country or countries to implement the recommendation made pursuant to a dispute settlement proceeding under the World Trade Organization, the Trade Representative shall periodically revise the list or action to affect other goods of the country or countries that have failed to implement the recommendation.

Evidently, the periodic revision gives rise to the name "Carousel Retaliation." Further, Section 2416(b)(2)(C) requires the Trade Representative to

> 120 days after the date the retaliation list or other section 2411(a) action is first taken, and every 180 days thereafter, review the list or action taken and revise, in whole or in part, the list or action to affect other goods of the subject country or countries.

In effect, the speed at which the carousel turns is 6 months. To make retaliation as effective as possible, Section 2416(b)(2)(D) says that whenever revising the lists,

. . . the Trade Representative shall act in a manner that is most likely to result in the country or countries implementing the recommendations adopted in the dispute settlement proceeding or in achieving a mutually satisfactory solution to the issue that gave rise to the dispute settlement proceeding.

On 5 June, 2000, following signature of the *Carousel Retaliation Act* by President Bill Clinton, the EC sued the U.S. in the WTO. The EC claimed carousel retaliation violates Articles 3.2, 21.5, 22, and 23 of the *DSU*. The EC also argued the *Act* violates Article XVI:4 of the *Agreement Establishing the WTO* (*WTO Agreement*), and GATT Articles I, II and XI. That is because, urged the EC, the *Act* mandates retaliation but fails to obtain authorization from the DSB for a specific retaliatory action. As yet, the case is unresolved.

What is the theory behind the *Act*? Congress passed it in the midst of frustration with the EU's failure to comply in the 1997 *Bananas* case. Neither diplomatic cajoling nor authorized sanctions on a fixed group of products seemed to work in that case. Why not, then, induce compliance by causing widespread uncertainty and fear? The threat of rotating the list of sanctioned products would cause unpredictability among producers in the losing WTO Member. Afraid their merchandise could be "hit" next, they would lobby their government to comply with the adverse WTO decision. Is the theory akin to a war strategy? Is that strategy intentional infliction of casualties on civilians? Or, are all merchandise targets legitimate enemy combatants?

D. Non-Trade Reducing Retaliation

Advanced as *DSU* enforcement appears compared to the ICJ or other international mechanisms, the key tool — trade sanctions — is somewhat primitive. In contrast to the United Nations system, neither the WTO Secretariat, nor the Membership at large, plays a role in setting sanctions. Trade sanctions may not work in the case of a large country (*e.g.*, the U.S.) losing to a small country (*e.g.*, Togo), and even when the case involves two hegemons (*e.g.*, the U.S. and EU), query whether trade retaliation brings about a rapid resolution. Moreover, sanctions are prospective only — they do not date back in time to when an injury occurred.

To be sure, the record of compliance under the *DSU*, like the old GATT system, is good. In most cases, the losing party complies, if for no other reason than, as in the GATT era, countries realize the adjudicatory mechanism they have is all they have got. Non-compliance, occurring in relatively few cases, is most likely in a highly politicized dispute, such as *Bananas*, *Beef Hormones*, *Byrd Amendment*, *Foreign Sales Corporation*, and *Steel*. Nevertheless, to improve the *DSU* enforcement mechanism, four major proposals have been suggested.

1. *Trade Compensation*

A losing party could give additional non-MFN benefits to the winner.

2. *Monetary Compensation*

Another reform suggestion is to allow for monetary compensation, that is, damages (fines). Under this proposal, a losing party would pay a fine to the winning party, and the fine would be calculated both prospectively and retrospectively. There would be an exemption for least developed countries, which cannot afford to pay fines. However, such countries, if they lost a case and refused to comply, would be susceptible to retaliation. A rather one-sided variant of this proposal, offered by several poor countries (including Cuba) would be to employ fines only if they win a case, but calculate damages only prospectively.

3. *Tradeable Remedies*

A winning party could sell its right to retaliate against the losing party to another (third) WTO Member, and thereby get money from the sale proceeds. The other Member could exercise the right to retaliate in favor of one of its industries.

4. *Joint Retaliation*

To encourage (if not bludgeon) compliance, retaliation could be had by a group of WTO Members, or possibly all of them. The idea is akin to collective security in the United Nations system. But, that analogy reveals a key weakness of the proposal. There is a cost to retaliating, so which WTO Members would participate in a case? Would there retaliation discussions become like Security Council sanctions debates? In the end, would one country, or an ad hoc coalition of the willing, take the lead in enforcement? If that scenario materialized, then would the system resemble vigilante justice?

Evidently, a feature common to all the proposals is that trade-shrinking, or trade-reducing, retaliation should be eliminated or sharply circumscribed. The obvious disagreement is over its replacement.

More generally, what ethos should surround use of the *DSU*, including an enforcement tool? Uruguay Round negotiators made clear that use of the *DSU*, including retaliation, should not be considered a hostile act. Yet, when the U.S. first deployed sanctions against the EU — in the *Beef Hormones* and *Bananas* cases — the EU viewed it as a hostile act. The EU Trade Commissioner, Sir Leon Brittan, took his revenge, filing the *Foreign Sales Corporation* case against the U.S.

V. PRECEDENT

A. The Role of Pre-Uruguay Round GATT Panel Reports

What role, if any, should pre-*DSU* panel reports play in cases brought under the *DSU*? This question is narrower than asking whether GATT or WTO reports are "precedent" in the Anglo-American sense of the word, or whether the doctrine of *stare decisis* operates in a *de facto* or *de jure* manner. The focus is whether any use can be made of the earlier reports and, if so, what sort of use.

In the 1996 *Japan Alcoholic Beverages* case (excerpted below), the Appellate Body considered the matter, and drew a distinction between adopted and unadopted GATT panel reports. The Appellate Body concluded adopted panel reports are not binding in a strict sense in a subsequent case, even if the subsequent case involves the same parties and basically the same facts. A holding in an adopted panel report is neither a definitive interpretation of the GATT nor an agreement by the Contracting Parties on the legal reasoning contained in that report. After all, Article IX:2 of the WTO *Agreement* states only the Ministerial Conference and General Council are empowered to adopt definitive interpretations of GATT—WTO texts.

Similarly, a prior holding in an adopted GATT panel report could not be considered "subsequent practice" for the parties to the case by virtue of the decision of the Contracting Parties to adopt the report. Article 31 of the *Vienna Convention on the Law of Treaties* indicates "subsequent practice" is a tool for treaty interpretation. Article 31 of the *Vienna Convention* says "[t]here shall be taken into account, together with the context . . . any subsequent practice in the application of the treaty which establishes the agreement of the parties regarding its interpretation."

Why does this Article, indeed the *Convention*, matter in WTO adjudication? As the Appellate Body explained in its 1996 Report in *United States — Standards for Reformulated and Conventional Gasoline* (WT/DS2/AB/R, adopted 20 May 1996):

> [The] general rule of interpretation [as set out in Article 31(1) of the *Vienna Convention on the Law of Treaties*] has attained the status of a rule of customary or general international law. As such, it forms part of the "customary rules of interpretation of public international law" which the Appellate Body has been directed, by Article 3(2) of the *DSU*, to apply in seeking to clarify the provisions of the *General Agreement* and the other "covered agreements" of the *Marrakesh Agreement Establishing the World Trade Organization* (the *WTO Agreement*).

In brief, the *Vienna Convention* is rendered relevant to WTO cases by *DSU* Article 3:2, which calls for interpretation of GATT—WTO texts in light of the customary rules of interpretation of public international law. But, the Appellate Body apparently feels just one pre-Uruguay Round panel report hardly constitutes "practice."

As for unadopted GATT panel reports, the Appellate Body in *Japan — Alcoholic Beverages* made clear they have no legal status. These reports lack the imprimatur of the Contracting Parties. However, the Appellate Body did not shut the door on their use. Unadopted, pre-*DSU* reports may be guidance for a WTO Panel or the Appellate Body.

B. The 1996 *Japan Alcoholic Beverages* Case

WTO APPELLATE BODY REPORT, *JAPAN — TAXES ON ALCOHOLIC BEVERAGES*
WT/DS10/AB/R, WT/DS11/AB/R (adopted 1 November 1996)

E. Status of Adopted Panel Reports

In this case, the Panel concluded that,

. . . panel reports adopted by the GATT Contracting Parties and the WTO Dispute Settlement Body constitute subsequent practice in a specific case by virtue of the decision to adopt them. Article 1(b)(iv) of GATT 1994 provides institutional recognition that adopted panel reports constitute subsequent practice. Such reports are an integral part of GATT 1994, since they constitute "other decisions of the Contracting Parties to GATT 1947."

Article 31(3)(b) of the *Vienna Convention* states that "any subsequent practice in the application of the treaty which establishes the agreement of the parties regarding its interpretation" is to be "taken into account together with the context" in interpreting the terms of the treaty. Generally, in international law, the essence of subsequent practice in interpreting a treaty has been recognized as a "concordant, common and consistent" sequence of acts or pronouncements which is sufficient to establish a discernable pattern implying the agreement of the parties regarding its interpretation. An isolated act is generally not sufficient to establish subsequent practice; it is a sequence of acts establishing the agreement of the parties that is relevant.

Although GATT 1947 panel reports were adopted by decisions of the Contracting Parties, a decision to adopt a panel report did not under GATT 1947 constitute agreement by the Contracting Parties on the legal reasoning in that panel report. The generally-accepted view under GATT 1947 was that the conclusions and recommendations in an adopted panel report bound the parties to the dispute in that particular case, but subsequent panels did not feel legally bound by the details and reasoning of a previous panel report. [The Appellate Body cited support for this proposition: *See European Economic Community — Restrictions on Imports of Dessert Apples*, B.I.S.D. (36th Supp.) at 93 ¶ 12.1 (1990) (adopted 22 June 1989).]

We do not believe that the Contracting Parties, in deciding to adopt a panel report, intended that their decision would constitute a definitive interpretation of the relevant provisions of GATT 1947. Nor do we believe that this is contemplated under GATT 1994. There is specific cause for this conclusion in the *WTO Agreement*. Article IX:2 of the *WTO Agreement* provides: "The Ministerial Conference and the General Council shall have the exclusive authority to adopt interpretations of this Agreement and of the Multilateral Trade Agreements." Article IX:2 provides further that such decisions "shall be taken by a three-fourths majority of the Members." The fact that such an "exclusive authority" in interpreting the treaty has been established so specifically in the *WTO Agreement* is reason enough to conclude that such authority does not exist by implication or by inadvertence elsewhere.

Historically, the decisions to adopt panel reports under Article XXIII of the GATT 1947 were different from joint action by the Contracting Parties under Article XXV of the GATT 1947. Today, their nature continues to differ from interpretations of the GATT 1994 and the other Multilateral Trade Agreements under the *WTO Agreement* by the WTO Ministerial Conference or the General Council. This is clear from a reading of Article 3.9 of the *DSU*, which states:

> The provisions of this *Understanding* are without prejudice to the rights of Members to seek authoritative interpretation of provisions of a covered agreement through decision-making under the *WTO Agreement* or a covered agreement which is a Plurilateral Trade Agreement.

Article XVI:1 of the *WTO Agreement* and paragraph 1(b)(iv) of the language of Annex 1A incorporating the GATT 1994 into the *WTO Agreement* bring the legal history and experience under the GATT 1947 into the new realm of the WTO in a way that ensures continuity and consistency in a smooth transition from the GATT 1947 system. This affirms the importance to the Members of the WTO of the experience acquired by the Contracting Parties to the GATT 1947 — and acknowledges the continuing relevance of that experience to the new trading system served by the WTO. Adopted panel reports are an important part of the GATT *acquis*. They are often considered by subsequent panels. They create legitimate expectations among WTO Members, and, therefore, should be taken into account where they are relevant to any dispute. However, they are not binding, except with respect to resolving the particular dispute between the parties to that dispute. [In a footnote, the Appellate Body added: "It is worth noting that the Statute of the International Court of Justice has an explicit provision, Article 59, to the same effect. This has not inhibited the development by that Court (and its predecessor) of a body of case law in which considerable reliance on the value of previous decisions is readily discernible."] In short, their character and their legal status have not been changed by the coming into force of the *WTO Agreement*.

For these reasons, we do not agree with the Panel's conclusion . . . that "panel reports adopted by the GATT Contracting Parties and the WTO Dispute Settlement Body constitute subsequent practice in a specific case" [by virtue of the decision to adopt them] as the phrase "subsequent practice" is used in Article 31 of the *Vienna Convention*. Further, we do not agree with the Panel's conclusion . . . that adopted panel reports in themselves constitute "other decisions of the Contracting Parties to GATT 1947" for the purposes of paragraph 1(b)(iv) of the language of Annex 1A incorporating the GATT 1994 into the *WTO Agreement*.

However, we agree with the Panel's conclusion . . . that *unadopted* panel reports "have no legal status in the GATT or WTO system since they have not been endorsed through decisions by the Contracting Parties to GATT or WTO Members." Likewise, we agree that "a panel could nevertheless find useful guidance in the reasoning of an unadopted panel report that it considered to be relevant."

C. *De Facto Stare Decisis?*

Just how persuaded is the WTO Appellate Body of its own reasoning in the *Japan Alcoholic Beverages* case? The *Financial Times* aptly summarized the conventional wisdom about precedent in the international legal system:

> . . .[M]ore and more of the work of trade relations has shifted away from negotiations and towards litigation and arbitration. To its defenders, this trend represents rule and reason constraining power politics. To its critics, it means runaway jurists subverting democracy.
>
> . . . .
>
> Public international law is based on the Roman civil law of continental Europe rather than the English common law tradition. Accordingly, although they [WTO panels and the Appellate Body] take account of decisions in previous cases, rulings are not bound to follow precedent. There is considerable potential for panels to interpret — critics would say make up — the law themselves, particularly under a new system such as the WTO, whose panel[s] and the legal texts [save for GATT] it interprets date only from 1994.[1]

Yet, in actual practice, the extent of its reliance on prior cases is considerable. That fact is evident in many excerpts from Appellate Body Reports in this Textbook. Likewise, in everyday practice, when dispensing advice to clients, drafting legal memos, and writing briefs and other litigation submissions, international trade lawyers treat prior Appellate Body decisions with great care. Depending on the facts and arguments, those decisions are supporting or distinguishable precedents. Indeed, might it be malpractice to neglect them? But, if — in a *de facto* sense — *stare decisis* operates in Appellate Body jurisprudence, then how does that jurisprudence relate to the emerging body of opinions from dispute settlement tribunals under free trade agreements?

D. The Role of the Appellate Body

Technical *DSU* reform issues arising in the appellate phase revolve around remand authority and sequencing. The Appellate Body is a distinguishing feature of the *DSU*, in significant part because it adds a legal veneer over what otherwise might be (and in some cases is) a diplomatic compromise. The Appellate Body is supposed to ensure the soundness of panel holdings and rationale.

However, there is also in *DSU* reform discussions a concern about the role of the Appellate Body. In practice, the Appellate Body increasingly has a view of itself as an international court, and as a contributor to the development of WTO law. To some degree, it seeks to set judicial policy for the WTO, and sees itself as part of an integrated international system in which its charge is to ensure the consistency of WTO law with public international law. Symbolically indicative of the growing independence of the Appellate Body is the fact

---

[1] Alan Beattie, *From a Trickle to a Flood — How Lawsuits Are Coming to Dictate the Terms of Trade*, FINANCIAL TIMES, 20 March 2007, at 11.

it has a building in Geneva (near the World Intellectual Property Organization, WIPO) entirely separate from the WTO Secretariat. In the first several years of the life of the WTO, the Appellate Division was a separate, secure location within the Secretariat.

Part Three

ECONOMIC FOUNDATIONS OF FREE
TRADE

Chapter 7

FREE TRADE THEORY

I have never known much good done by those who affected to trade for the public good.

      —Adam Smith (1723-1790)

DOCUMENTS SUPPLEMENT ASSIGNMENT

1.   *Havana, Charter* Articles 1-10
2.   GATT Preamble
3.   WTO *Agreement* Preamble

I. THE CLASSICAL ATTACK ON MERCANTILISM

A. Mercantilism

The starting point, or close to it, of virtually every contemporary textbook on international economics is a consideration of a basic question: why trade? The invariable answer is the Law of Comparative Advantage. This "Law," or more accurately, economic principle, is associated with the 19th century English political economist, David Ricardo (1772-1823). In Chapter 7 of his classic *On the Principles of Political Economy and Taxation* (1817), Ricardo laid out the case for international trade.

To be complete, it is important to appreciate Adam Smith (1723-1790), in *An Inquiry into the Wealth of Nations* (1776), investigated the benefits of free trade. Smith, the second scholar to hold a professorship in moral philosophy at the University of Glasgow, was a student of Francis Hutcheson (1694-1746), the first holder of the moral philosophy chair at Glasgow, whose primary works were *Inquiry into the Original of Our Ideas of Beauty and Virtue* (1725) and *An Essay on the Nature and Conduct of the Passions and Affections, with Illustrations of the Moral Sense* (1728). Ricardo — the first in England to hold a chair in political economy — built on the ideas of Smith and Hutcheson. Indeed, reading *The Wealth of Nations* at age 27 stimulated Ricardo's interest in economics. Smith wrote partly in response to the prevailing economic orthodoxy of the 17th and 18th centuries, namely, mercantilism.

Contrary to what is often thought, mercantilism is not an anti-trade doctrine. Rather, it is an anti-free trade doctrine that calls for government intervention to generate a trade surplus. Mercantilists sourced the wealth of a nation in its stock of precious metals, such as gold. This stock rose by exporting, because payment for exported goods was received in such metals. This wealth can be used to invest in assets in other countries, and such investments give the surplus country economic and political influence in the other countries. In contrast, imports cost a nation in precious metals, thus diminishing wealth. Accordingly, mercantilists sought to maximize wealth by maximizing exports and minimizing imports, and thereby maximize the net outflow of goods, *i.e.*, the balance of trade, and the net inflow of payments. The mercantilist trade policy called for restrictions, such as high tariffs, on imports, and support, such as subsidies, for exports.

Despite public pronouncements by politicians and trade negotiators, consider whether and to what extent classical and neoclassical economic arguments against mercantilism and in favor of free trade are manifest in negotiated outcomes, *i.e.*, in trade agreements. Free trade rhetoric aside, do officials behave like neo-mercantilists, focusing excessively on a "favorable" trade balance? Do they seek to maximize the net inflow of funds, through net exports, and then invest the funds in foreign financial assets (*e.g.*, stocks, bonds, and real estate)? If so, then is their goal to maximize influence abroad? Conversely, does this goal lead them to fear surpluses in other countries, such as Japan, the Kingdom of Saudi Arabia, and China, which may lead to foreign dominance?

The logic of mercantilism and neo-mercantilism presumes protection and export subsidies can generate a trade surplus. In fact, most economists agree the critical long-run determinant of a country's trade balance is its savings rate — not protectionist measures (or the threat of such measures), because few foreign barriers make a noticeable impact on exports (the Common Agricultural Policy (CAP) of the European Union (EU) is an exception), and even if such measures reduce imports, they do not boost exports. By producing more goods than it consumes, a country creates an exportable surplus, and it can export this excess over what it consumes. Examples are Japan and China, which have high savings rates. With an abysmally low savings rate, the U.S. is a counter-example. Furthermore, arguably, neither the size of a bilateral trade deficit, nor the nationality of the owner of an asset, ought to matter. Rather, overall macroeconomic performance and the quality of management of an asset are, or ought to be, of concern.

For instance, a trade surplus hardly is "favorable" if the material well-being of residents in the net exporting country deteriorates because they are starved of imports. That scenario occurred in Romania in the 1980s, under the Communist ex-dictator Nikolai Ceauscescu. Exports may be viewed as a means of paying for what people want from overseas. Similarly, a trade deficit is not "unfavorable" if it results from imports of capital equipment, such as machine tools, and the capital is put to such good use that the rate of return on it exceeds its cost. This phenomenon is observed in well-run developing countries in South East Asia. In the 1980s, the U.S. ran large trade deficits financed by inflows of foreign savings (*e.g.*, purchases of American treasury securities by Japanese investors). The U.S. used these funds in part to finance military buildups, which in turn assisted in facing down the Soviet Empire and ending the Cold War. Might, then, a trade deficit work in favor of the common good?

B. Adam Smith and Absolute Advantage

In his attack on mercantilism, Adam Smith urged the dominant contributor to national wealth and power is economic growth. In turn, economic growth depends on an efficient division of labor. The mercantilist policy of erecting trade barriers inhibits the expansion of markets. Such barriers limit the size of a market (for example, by preventing one country from selling goods to another country). In turn, the potential for more efficient division of labor, and specialization of production, is choked off. Smith examined the instance of "absolute advantage," which refers to the ability of one country to produce a good using fewer resources than any other country. Trade allows a country to specialize in the production of a good in which it has an absolute advantage, rather than have to generate some output of several goods, which it must do under autarky.

For instance, suppose China can produce one ready-made garment, such as a pair of men's pants, and one ton of a steel product, such as "H" beams, with 10 hours worth of work by textile workers and 20 hours worth of work by steel workers, respectively. India requires 25 labor hours for the textiles, but just 5 labor hours for the steel, to generate the same volume of output in each sector. Table 7-1 sets out these figures.

TABLE 7-1:
ABSOLUTE ADVANTAGE

Output and Country	China	India
	Labor Needed per unit of Output	*Labor Needed per unit of Output*
Textiles — *Unit = 1 men's pants*	10 labor hours	25 labor hours
Steel — *Unit = 1 ton of "H" beams*	20 labor hours	5 labor hours

China has an absolute advantage in the production of textiles, but India holds the absolute advantage in steel. Smith argued international trade would allow for an appropriate division of labor across countries, and thereby allow each country to specialize in the production of the good in which it possesses an absolute advantage. Accordingly, China would focus on textiles, and India on steel.

Table 7-2 illustrates the result from production specialization and attendant international division of labor, and the possibility of trade. Suppose China sacrifices making 1 ton of "H" beams. China can re-allocate to textile production the 20 hours of labor it had dedicated to steel production (assuming labor is mobile between the sectors). With 20 more hours available for textile work, China can generate 2 additional pairs of men's pants. Similarly, suppose India foregoes production of textiles, and re-allocates labor to the steel sector. The 25 labor hours India shifts from making 1 pair of pants can generate an additional 5 tons of steel. The final result is clear: total output as between China and India has risen, but no additional productive resources are consumed. Each country specializes in making the good in which it has an absolute advantage. The result is an efficient international division of labor.

TABLE 7-2:
ABSOLUTE ADVANTAGE, INTERNATIONAL DIVISION OF LABOR, AND TOTAL OUTPUT

Output and Country	China	India
	Labor Needed per unit of Output	*Labor Needed per unit of Output*
Textiles — *Unit = 1 men's pants*	10 labor hours	25 labor hours
Steel — *Unit =1 ton of "H" beams*	20 labor hours	5 labor hours
Total Output under Autarky	1 men's pants and 1 ton of "H" beams	1 men's pants and 1 ton of "H" beams
Total Output with Free Trade	3 men's pants	6 tons of "H" beams
Difference in Total Output with Free Trade versus Autarky	1 additional pair of men's pants	4 additional tons of "H" beams

Therefore, Smith urged, a mercantilist policy, whereby imports are taxed heavily, restricted by quota, or forbidden, makes little sense. Rather, increased output is possible with an international division of labor based on absolute advantage. International trade follows, if neither country consumes all it produces. China can import steel from India that India does not use. India can import surplus textile production from China.

Further, the price at which each country obtains a good from the other, with free trade, is cheaper than the pre-trade autarky price. Why? Consider the pre-trade price ratio of textiles to steel in each country. The price of each good in each country is the wage rate per hour in each country multiplied by the number of labor hours needed:

Price of good	=	(wage rate per hour) $\times$ (number of labor hours)

Thus, in China:

$P^{C}_{textiles}$	=	$W^{C} \times (10 \text{ hours})$
P^{C}_{steel}	=	$W^{C} \times (20 \text{ hours})$

And in India:

$P^{I}_{textiles}$	=	$W^{I} \times (25 \text{ hours})$
P^{I}_{steel}	=	$W^{I} \times (5 \text{ hours})$

The symbol "$P^{C}_{textiles}$" stands for the price of a pair of men's pants, "W^{C}" denotes the hourly wage rate in China, and "P^{C}_{steel}" is the price of 1 ton of "H" beams. Analogous symbols, with "I" for India, apply to the Indian economy. The wage rate in the textile and steel sectors in China is assumed to be the same, because any difference would be eliminated by migration of workers from lower- to higher-paying jobs. The same assumption is made for India (though, of course, W^I and W^C are not necessarily equal). This assumption presumes labor is freely mobile in each country.

The pre-trade price ratio in each country is:

$$\frac{p^{Ctextiles}}{p^{Csteel}} = \frac{W^C \times (10 \text{ hrs})}{W^C \times (20 \text{ hrs})} = 0.5 \text{ in China}$$

$$\frac{p^{Itextiles}}{p^{Isteel}} = \frac{W^I \times (25 \text{ hrs})}{W^I \times (5 \text{ hrs})} = 5 \text{ in India}$$

Calculation of these ratios eliminates wage rates, resulting in the denomination of each good in terms of units of the other. That is, a unit of textiles is priced in terms of units of steel, and conversely a unit of steel is priced in terms of textiles. (As intimated earlier, the units are 1 pair of men's pants and 1 ton of "H" beams.) Accordingly, before trade, 1 unit of textiles costs ½ unit of steel in China, but costs 5 units of steel in India. Textiles are considerably more expensive in India than China. Because of the price differential, there is considerable scope for mutual gain from trade.

Specifically, it is economically rational for India to abandon textile production, focus on steel, and import garments from China. Conversely, steel is relatively expensive in China. One unit of steel is worth 2 textile units in China, but in India 1 unit of steel costs just one-fifth a unit of textiles. So, China ought to specialize in textiles, and import steel form India. With free trade, there is a single world-market price ratio. Depending on the market forces of supply and demand, it is an intermediate level between the autarky ratios of 0.5 and 5. Suppose the world market price ratio of textiles to steel is 3:

$$\frac{p^{textiles}}{p^{steel}} = 3$$

Table 7-3 summarizes the gains from trade with absolute advantage. At this ratio, China exports 1 unit of textiles, which pays for 3 units of steel imported from India. Trade renders both countries better off than before.

Under autarky, China must give up 2 units of textiles to get just 1 unit of steel (or, 3 units of steel would have cost China 6 units of textiles). China's gain may be quantified as the difference in the units of steel it imports against what it must produce on its own, *i.e.*, 3 units versus ½ unit, or 2.5 units. As for India, it too is better off with trade. India exports 1 unit of steel, and imports from China one-third of a unit of textiles. Without trade, a unit of steel fetches just one-fifth of a unit of textiles. India's gain from trade is the difference between one-third and one-fifth of a unit of textiles (²⁄₁₅ of a unit). Significantly, the additional total output associated with free trade suggests consumers in both countries benefit from expanded consumption opportunities. The production gain from trade, wrought by specialization, leads to greater output, which in turn means more goods are available to consumers at a cheaper price than under autarky.

TABLE 7-3:
**ABSOLUTE ADVANTAGE, INTERNATIONAL DIVISION OF LABOR,
AND TOTAL OUTPUT**

Scenario and Country	China	India
Autarky Price Ratio	$\dfrac{P^{Ctextiles}}{P^{Csteel}} = 0.5$	$\dfrac{P^{Itextiles}}{P^{Isteel}} = 5$
Free Trade Price Ratio (by assumption)	$\dfrac{P^{textiles}}{P^{steel}} = 3$	$\dfrac{P^{textiles}}{P^{steel}} = 3$
Results Under Autarky	1 unit of textiles costs ½ unit of steel. Conversely, 1 unit of steel costs 2 units of textiles. China has an absolute advantage in textiles	1 unit of textiles costs 5 units of steel. Conversely, 1 unit of steel costs 1/5 unit of textiles. India has an absolute advantage in steel
Incentives	Textiles are relatively cheaper in China than India (½ unit of steel in China versus 5 units of steel in India) China should export textiles and import steel.	Textiles are relatively more expensive in India than China (5 units of steel in India versus ½ unit of steel in China). India should export steel and import textiles.
Gains From Trade	China exports 1 unit of textiles and imports 3 units of steel. For the 1 unit of textiles, China gains 2.5 extra units of steel, in comparison with autarky (the difference between 3 and ½ units).	India exports 1 unit of steel and imports 1/3 of a unit of textiles. For the 1 unit of steel, India gains an extra 2/15 of a unit of textiles (the difference between 1/3 and 1/5 units).

Absolute advantage is a powerful explanation for international trade in certain markets and among some countries. For instance, why do Brazil and Colombia export coffee, the Kingdom of Saudi Arabia oil, and South Africa diamonds? Absolute advantage, which derives from climatic conditions and natural resource endowments in these countries, is the answer. However, the explanation falls short of explaining a considerable part of trade. What happens if one country (say, China, in the example) has an absolute advantage in the production of both goods (textiles and steel)? In reality, a few major trading countries appear to have an absolute advantage in a large array of goods, and small countries would seem to be helpless. Is a country that nature treats parsimoniously doomed to inauspicious prospects in international trade?

The answer given by many opponents of trade liberalization is "yes." They assert small countries cannot gain from free trade. This assertion is not new. Readers of *The Wealth of Nations* were concerned about the scenario of one country having an absolute advantage in the production of multiple products — and in the late 18th and early 19th centuries, that country was Great

Britain. Under classical and neoclassical economic theory, however, the assertion is false.

David Ricardo addressed the matter with the Law of Comparative Advantage. Ricardo argued international trade is mutually beneficial for countries, even if one has an absolute advantage in the production of all goods, under the following terms:

1. For the country with an absolute advantage in both goods, Ricardo advised specializing in the production of, and exporting, the good in which it has the greatest absolute advantage.

2. For the country with an absolute disadvantage in both goods, Ricardo suggested specializing in the production of, and exporting, the good in which it has the least absolute disadvantage.

This rule is the "Law of Comparative Advantage," which the Nobel Prize winning economist Paul Samuelson calls "the most beautiful idea in economics."

Under the Law of Comparative Advantage, one country will have more of an advantage, or less of a disadvantage, in at least one good, compared with another country. The concept upon which Ricardo relied to evaluate advantage differentials is opportunity cost — how much production of one commodity must be sacrificed to release enough factor resources to make an extra unit of another commodity. Ricardo's insight, then, was to highlight the central role played by relative — not absolute — costs of production in determining the international division of labor, trade flows, and creation of mutual gain.

II. RICARDO'S LAW OF COMPARATIVE ADVANTAGE

A. The Law in Brief

Put succinctly, the Law of Comparative Advantage states the net welfare of a society increases from free trade. The net gain occurs because free trade permits specialization of production, and enhances opportunities for consumption. Economists in the classical tradition of Ricardo and Smith, such as Alfred Marshall (1842-1924), a Cambridge scholar, author of *Principles of Economics* (1890), and dominant British economist of his era, are called "neo-classicists." They elaborate on Ricardo's Law with arithmetic examples and graphs. What is the connection between classical and neoclassical economic analysis, on the one hand, and modern international trade law, on the other hand? Simply stated, the former tends to drive the latter. The Law of Comparative Advantage is the stated logic for negotiating, drafting, implementing, and enforcing rules to liberalize trade on a multilateral, regional, or bilateral basis.

To be sure, the Law of Comparative Advantage is not the only rationale for rules oriented toward freer trade, and by no means is it universally accepted. Other supporting rationales exist, as do many critics of the Law — including economists — who fault its underlying assumptions, practical feasibility, and effects. Even among supporters do not adhere faithfully and at all times to the Law. Trade negotiators, including (reputedly) the United States Trade Representative (USTR), confess (privately) the hypocrisy that they are free traders until they get to the negotiating table, at which point they become mercantilists. Nevertheless, Comparative Advantage is the major economic paradigm for international trade law. Consequently, thorough familiarity with it, and the arithmetic and graphical proofs of the Law, is essential.

B. The Classical Arithmetic Demonstration

Consider, first, an arithmetic demonstration, akin to the presentation classical economists give. In Ricardo's proof, the example was Portuguese wine and English cloth. Portugal held an absolute advantage in both goods, because it produced both more cheaply than England. However, Portugal's climate and soil gave it a comparative advantage in wine. That is, Portugal could produce wine more cheaply and efficiently than cotton. Hence, Ricardo showed, Portugal would benefit more by specializing in wine and importing English cloth than producing both wine and cotton. Here, as with the hypothetical case of absolute advantage, the countries are China and India, and the goods are textiles (a unit of which is one pair of men's pants) and steel (a unit of which is 1 ton of "H" beams). Table 7-4 sets forth comparative advantage as a basis for trade.

TABLE 7-4:
COMPARATIVE ADVANTAGE

Output and Country	China	India
	Labor Needed per unit of Output	*Labor Needed per unit of Output*
Textiles — *Unit = 1 men's pants*	3 labor hours	12 labor hours
Steel — *Unit = 1 ton of "H" beams*	6 labor hours	8 labor hours

"Comparative advantage" is a situation in which the price of a good in a country, before trade, is less than the price of the same good in the rest of the world. The country has a comparative advantage in that good, because of the lower relative pre-trade price.

From Table 7-4, it is evident China has an absolute advantage in the manufacture of both goods. China requires 3 labor hours to make a unit of textiles, whereas India needs 12 hours. China needs 6 labor hours to make a unit of steel, whereas India needs 8 hours. However, the strength of China's absolute advantage in the two sectors is not the same. China is 4 times more efficient than India in textile production, because China can generate 1 pair of men's pants in 3 labor hours instead of 12 labor hours. In contrast, China is only $\frac{1}{3}$ more efficient than India in steel production, because China needs 6 labor hours to India's requirement of 8 labor hours (and $\frac{2}{6}$ reduces to $\frac{1}{3}$).

In this scenario, Ricardo's Law calls for China to specialize in textile production. China has the greatest absolute advantage in this sector. India ought to specialize in making steel, as it has the least absolute disadvantage in this sector. China then can export its surplus textiles to India in exchange for surplus Indian-made steel. No new factor of production, specifically, no more labor, is required in either country. But, each country must shift labor from one sector to the other. Thus, assume China cuts steel production by 1 unit (*i.e.*, makes one fewer ton of "H" beams). China re-allocates the six labor hours from the steel to the textile sector. The result is an increase in textile output of two units (*i.e.*, two more pairs of men's pants), because China requires three labor hours per unit of textiles. Conversely, suppose India cuts textile production by one unit (*i.e.*, makes 1 fewer pairs of men's pants). The 12 labor hours freed from textile production shift to making steel, and leads to production of 1.5 units of steel (*i.e.*, a further 15 tons of steel). That is because India needs eight labor hours per unit of steel (and 12 divided by 8 is 1.5.).

Table 7-5 summarizes the gains from trade. It is assumed the single world market price ratio is 1.

$$\frac{P^{textiles}}{P^{steel}} = 1$$

With trade barriers dismantled, 1 pair of men's pants can be exchanged across the Sino — Indian border for 1 ton of "H" beams. Depending on world market supply and demand forces, the price ratio with trade could settle anywhere between the autarky ratios in each country, namely, 0.5 in China and 1.5 in India. These ratios are calculated as follows:

$$\frac{P^{Ctextiles}}{P^{Csteel}} = \frac{W^C \times (3 \text{ hrs})}{W^C \times (6 \text{ hrs})} = 0.5 \text{ in China}$$

$$\frac{P^{Itextiles}}{P^{Isteel}} = \frac{W^I \times (12 \text{ hrs})}{W^I \times (8 \text{ hrs})} = 1.5 \text{ in India}$$

(Each symbol is defined in the same manner as earlier in this Chapter.)

Even though there is no increase in factors of production (*i.e.*, no more labor), and even though China holds an absolute advantage in both goods, there is a boost to total — or world — output. With more overall output, resulting from specialization based on comparative advantage, each country is better off by trading its exportable surplus. In turn, consumption possibilities in each country are greater through trade than under autarky. Thus, free trade benefits the supply side of an economy by increasing productive efficiency and income through production specialization. It benefits the demand side of an economy by enhancing the availability of goods for consumption. Of course, free trade does not equalize the standard of living across countries. But, it is a positive sum (not zero sum or negative sum) game. Both trading partners experience a net gain through specialization in production and expansion of consumption opportunities.

TABLE 7-5:
COMPARATIVE ADVANTAGE AND THE GAINS FROM TRADE

Output and Country	China	India
	Labor Needed per unit of Output	*Labor Needed per unit of Output*
Textiles — *Unit = 1 men's pants*	3 labor hours	12 labor hours
Steel — *Unit = 1 ton of "H" beams*	6 labor hours	8 labor hours
Autarky Price Ratios	$\dfrac{P^{Ctextiles}}{P^{Csteel}} = 0.5$	$\dfrac{P^{Itextiles}}{P^{Isteel}} = 1.5$
Free Trade Price Ratio *(by assumption)*	$\dfrac{P^{textiles}}{P^{steel}} = 1$	$\dfrac{P^{textiles}}{P^{steel}} = 1$
Domestic Results under Autarky	Textiles cost China 3 labor hours per unit. Steel costs China 6 labor hours per unit. China makes 1 textiles unit and 1 steel unit.	Textiles cost India 12 labor hours per unit. Steel costs India 8 labor hours per unit. India makes 1 textiles unit and 1 steel unit.
Total Production under Autarky *(China and India combined)*	2 textile units (1 each from China and India). 2 steel units (1 each from China and India).	As in column to left.
Results from Specialization based on Comparative Advantage	China continues to make 1 textile unit, but forgoes production of 1 steel unit, which frees up 6 labor hours for production of 2 more textile units. Thus, China makes 3 textile units total. World textiles output is 3 units, with production concentrated in China. China can trade 1 unit of textiles for 1 unit of steel.	India continues to make 1 steel unit, but forgoes production of 1 textile unit, which frees up 12 labor hours for production of 1.5 more steel units. Thus, India makes 2.5 units of steel total. World steel output is 2.5 units, with production concentrated in India. India can trade 1.5 units of steel for 1.5 units of textiles.
Production Gains from Free Trade *(compared to Autarky)*	Higher output: 1 extra textile unit is produced. With trade, China makes 3 textile units, but India forgoes production of 1 textile unit. Under autarky, both countries combined for 2 units.	Higher output: 0.5 extra steel unit is produced. With trade, India makes 2.5 steel units, but China forgoes production of 1 steel unit. Under autarky, both countries combined for 2 units.
Consumption Gains from Free Trade *(compared to Autarky)*	Lower price: Chinese steel consumers get steel at a cost of 1 textile unit, rather than 2 textile units.	Lower price: Indian textile producers get textiles at a cost of 1 steel unit, rather than 1.5 steel units.

Specifically, under autarky assume China and India made 1 unit of textiles and steel, hence world (China plus India) output of each product was 2 units. With trade, the world market price ratio is 1. China still can make 1 textile unit, but it forgoes 1 unit of steel production, thereby freeing up 6 labor hours. China can allocate this work to the textile sector, and generate 2 additional units (because it takes China 3 hours per textile unit), for a total of 3 units. By specializing in textiles, China produces a net gain of 2 textile units in comparison with autarky. However, with specialization in steel, India gives up textile production, so the loss of its 1 unit must be counted against China's increase of 2 units. The result is a net world output increase of 1 unit.

Given the world price ratio of 1, China can trade one or both of its extra textile units to India for 1 or 2, respectively, units of steel. Suppose China trades 1 textile unit for 1 steel unit. It would have taken China 6 labor hours to generate 1 unit of steel. Thus, China gets 1 steel unit for the 3 labor hours it used to make the traded good — textiles — rather than the 6 labor hours it would have needed to make the steel itself. Put differently, China gets the steel at a lower opportunity cost (*i.e.*, the cost associated with foregone alternatives) to itself by trading for the steel rather than producing it domestically.

Similarly, India can continue to produce 1 unit of steel, but scale back textile production by 1 unit, thus freeing up 12 labor hours. India can channel this factor into steel production, and generate 1.5 additional units of steel (because it takes India 8 hours per unit of steel) compared with what it did as a closed economy. That result is a net increase in Indian steel output of 1.5 units. Total Indian output is 2.5 units (the sum of the 1 unit India continues to make and 1.5 new units). But, with China now specializing in textiles, it no longer produces a textiles unit. This diminution must be counted against India's gain of 1.5 units. The net result is an increase in world steel output of 0.5 units.

India can trade steel for textiles at the world price ratio of 1. For instance, if India trades 1.5 units, then it will receive 1.5 units of textiles in return. It would have taken India 18 labor hours to generate 1.5 textile units (12 hours for 1 unit, plus 6 for an additional half unit). Thus, India gets 1.5 units of textiles for the 12 labor hours it used to make the good it exported — steel — rather than the 18 hours it would have needed to make the textiles itself. Stated equivalently, India gets the textiles at a lower opportunity cost to itself by trading for the textiles rather than producing them domestically.

Observe, also, the benefit from trade based on comparative advantage to Chinese and Indian consumers. Chinese steel consumers have steel available to them at a cheaper price (1 textile unit, instead of the autarkic price of 2 textile units). Further, there is a larger output of steel from India available to China, given India's extra output. Similarly, Indian textile consumers can obtain textiles at a cheaper cost (1 unit of steel, instead of the autarkic cost of 1.5 units of steel). These consumers also gain from having more textiles available to them, because of China's extra output.

A key assumption underlying the argument for free trade based on comparative advantage is the mobility of factors of production, especially labor. Contrary to the exuberant rhetoric of some pro-free trade politicians and policy officials, it is simplistic to say free trade creates new jobs. Rather, free trade creates income by re-allocating factors of production from less to more productive sectors within an economy. Economists dub this transfer of resources "allocative efficiency." By increasing average productivity of the factors in an economy, income rises. In this process, jobs are lost in the less productive sector, and expansion in the more productive sector results in additional jobs. What, if anything, can and ought to be done to assist workers in either or both sectors? This question raises issues concerning Trade

Adjustment Assistance programs, and the relative abilities of rich and poor countries to fund such programs.

III. ASSUMPTIONS UNDERLYING COMPARATIVE ADVANTAGE

A. The Assumptions Explained

Like most economic "laws," the Law of Comparative Advantage rests on a number of assumptions. They facilitate the analysis of the effects of trade liberalization. Also, these assumptions are needed for three important theorems (discussed later) that follow from the Law of Comparative Advantage, namely, the Factor Price Equalization Theorem, the Heckscher-Ohlin Theorem (also called the Factor Proportions Theorem), and the Stopler-Samuelson Theorem:

1. *Rationality*

Each economic agent, whether a producer or consumer, acts in a rational manner. Producers seek to maximize profits, and consumers seek to maximize their level of satisfaction, or "utility."

2. *Two Countries*

There are two countries in the world. In the examples, India and Iran are the focus. However, it is possible to group all countries other than Iran (or India) together and label them "Rest of world" (ROW).

3. *Two Commodities*

There are two commodities in the world. In the first hypothetical, the goods are carpets and tea. However, it is possible to group all goods other than tea (or carpets) into a bundle, or basket, called "All other goods" (AOG). In the second hypothetical, the goods are oil and pharmaceuticals. Again, it is possible to substitute AOG for pharmaceuticals (or oil). The two commodities produced, and the trade-offs in production, are depicted using a diagram called a "Production Possibilities Frontier."

4. *No Money Illusion (Relative Prices)*

Economic agents do not suffer from "money illusion." That is, when a producer or consumer makes a decision based on a change in the price of one item, the economic agent also takes into account the prices of other items. For example, if all prices rise, or if all of them fall, then a producer or consumer is not fooled by examining only one or a few prices. Rather, the agent looks for real, not just nominal, prices. In particular, the agent looks at relative prices — the relationship of one price to another.

5. *Fixed Factor Endowments*

In each country, the endowments of factors of production are fixed in the short term (*i.e.*, during the next one year). The "factors of production," or "resources," are labor (*i.e.*, workers), land (*i.e.*, real property and fixtures), physical capital (*i.e.*, capital equipment, like machine tools), human capital (*i.e.*, knowledge), and technology (*e.g.*, computers). These factors are used to produce goods. In the medium term (2-5 years) and long term (more than 5 years), factor endowments can change.

6.   *Homogenous Factors*

Factors of production are homogeneous from one country to another. For instance, labor in one country is identical to labor in another country. Likewise, capital in the two countries is identical.

7.   *Different Factor Endowments*

The two countries do not have identical proportions of each factor of production. Rather, the relative proportionate endowments vary. One country may have relatively more labor, but relatively less capital, than the other country. Of significance is not the absolute amount of each factor in each country. Rather, what matters is the proportion of one factor to another (or all others) within a country, and the comparison of that proportion from one country to another. That is, factor endowments are measured by the ratio of one factor to another factor (or to all other factors). Thus, a country is "capital abundant" if the ratio of capital to labor (or capital to all other factors) is greater than the ratio in the other country. This abundance is "relative" in the sense of a comparison of the ratios between the two countries. A country is "labor abundant" if the ratio of labor to capital (or labor to all other factors) is greater than the ratio in the other country. This labor abundance is relative, in a proportionate sense, between the countries.

8.   *Technology Availability*

Each country has equal access to technology needed to produce each commodity. That is, the technology available to each country is the same.

9.   *Intensiveness*

As between the two commodities, one is capital intensive and one is labor intensive. Intensiveness is a measure of the proportion of one factor of production used to make a good in relation to another factor (or all other factors). A good is "capital intensive" if the most important resource used in its production, as measured by the ratio of capital to labor (or capital to all other factors), is capital. A good is "labor intensive" if the predominant resource used to make the good, gauged by the ratio of labor to capital (or labor to all other factors), is labor.

10.   *Perfect Competition in Commodities Markets*

In the sectors in which each of the two commodities is produced, competition among producers is perfect. There are no instances of monopoly or oligopoly. In other words, there are many buyers and sellers of the goods, so that no one purchaser or producer can control the price of either good — buyers and sellers are "price takers." Thus, the supply of, and demand for, each commodity determines its price. Further, there are no externalities (unaccounted costs, *e.g.*, pollution, or benefits) from production of either good. Consequently, the market price of a good reflects its true social, or opportunity, cost of production. Also, the marginal cost of production (*i.e.*, the cost of making the last unit) equals the value of the resources needed to make it, plus a normal profit. In the long run, the price of a good equals the cost of production of that good.

11. *Perfect Competition Among Factors of Production*

In the markets for factors of production, there is perfect competition. No single resource provider, be it labor, land, physical capital, human capital, or technology, can control the price at which is supplies the resource. That is, many laborers, landowners, and capitalists, and human capital and technology are readily available. Likewise, on the demand side, there are many buyers of these resources, so no one buyer can set the price. Sellers and buyers of factors of production are "price takers." Consequently, the supply of, and demand for, each factor determines the price of that factor.

12. *Perfect Factor Mobility Domestically*

Factors of production are perfectly mobile domestically. There are no barriers to the re-allocation of a factor from employment in one sector to another, in response to changes in prices, within a single country. Factors will move from one sector to another based on payments they receive — wages to labor and human capital, rents to owners of land and physical capital, and royalties to owners of technology. Consequently, within one country, in each of the two commodity sectors, these factor returns will be the same. For example, each industry will pay the same wage rate to workers and same rents to capital, otherwise factors would migrate until any difference is eliminated.

13. *Factor Immobility Internationally*

Factors of production cannot move from one country to the other. For example, workers cannot migrate from one country to another, and capitalists cannot move their equipment across borders. As a result, differences in wage rates, returns to capital, and other factor payments (when measured in the same currency) can exist between the two countries, even after trade commences. Without this assumption, the Production Possibilities Frontier of one or both countries would change (either in terms of shape or location), because of migration.

14. *Constant Returns to Scale*

The assumption about "constant returns to scale" states a proportionate change in factors of production yields a proportionate change in output. For example, if production of a commodity requires labor and capital, and the amount of each resource is doubled, then constant returns to scale would mean the amount of output correspondingly doubles. However, as with the first assumption, this assumption is not essential to the Law — it simply allows for a more dramatic illustration of the impact of opening a country to international trade than would be true otherwise. Typically, it is relaxed in advanced demonstrations of the Law, because in reality, diminishing returns to scale occur.

15. *Consumer Preferences*

It is possible to represent the tastes and preferences of all consumers in a society using a diagram called an "Indifference Curve." Moreover, the consumers in each country have equal tastes and preferences. For example, if the price of one commodity, measured in terms of the units of the other commodity, is the same in both countries, then consumers in each country will consume the same proportion of each commodity.

16. *No Trade Barriers*

There are no barriers to trade, in the form of transportation costs, other kinds of transactions costs, tariffs, or non-tariff measures. In other words, when trade commences between the countries, it is free trade. Consequently, with international trade, there is a single world market price for each commodity.

17. *Incomplete Specialization*

Each country continues to produce at least a small quantity of both commodities. Under autarky, both countries produce both goods. When trade occurs between the countries, neither country specializes entirely in the production of only one commodity.

18. *Trade Balances*

In each country, exports pay for imports, hence trade is balanced. This assumption simplifies the analysis by ruling out the possibility of net flows of funds between the countries. Each country pays for its imports with what it exports.

19. *Further Assumptions*

Some demonstrations of the Law of Comparative Advantage rely on two further assumptions. The first one is based on the Labor Theory of Value, in which classical economists believed. This assumption states the only relevant factor of production, with respect to costs of production or productivity, is labor. Put differently, the assumption is that while two (or more) resources may be used, such as labor and capital, both are used in production in the same ratio in a country — the mix of factors is the same within an industry in a particular country, though not necessarily across countries.

For instance, two workers per machine may be the ratio in one country, but the ratio could be three workers per machine in the other country. According to the Labor Theory of Value, under autarkic conditions, the amount of labor needed to make a good is the determinant of the price of that good. (Classical economists took a holistic view, including in the labor calculation the amount of labor going into making capital equipment used in production of the final good.) This assumption is obviously false, as many goods with the same price embody different quantities of labor. It is used, however, to simplify the analysis, but relaxing it does not undermine the Law of Comparative Advantage.

The second assumption sometimes used is about costs of production, namely, that they are constant costs of production. This assumption means the amount of production of one commodity that a country must forego to produce an additional unit of the other commodity remains the same at all levels of production. For example, to produce six instead of five units of the second commodity, a country must sacrifice three units of output of the first commodity. With constant costs, to produce seven instead of six units of the second commodity (or, for that matter, twenty instead of nineteen units), it must sacrifice three units of output of the first commodity. In brief, with constant costs of production, the opportunity cost of increasing output of one good stays the same. In contrast, if production costs decrease, then the number of units of the first commodity that must be sacrificed with increased output of the second commodity fall (*e.g.*, to two units, and then one unit). If production costs increase, then the number of units that must be sacrificed rises with higher levels of production of the second commodity (*e.g.*, three units, then four units, then five units, and so forth).

The assumption of constant costs of production results in a Production Possibilities Frontier that is a straight line sloping downward to the right. Without constant returns to scale, the Production Possibilities Frontier is a curve concave to the origin of the graph on which it is drawn. The constant costs assumption is not essential to the demonstration of the Law of Comparative Advantage.

Finally, observe some assumptions are further from reality than others. Consider the implications for net gains from trade when one or more assumptions are relaxed.

B. New Trade Theory and Increasing Returns to Scale

The Law of Comparative Advantage rests in part on the assumption of constant returns to scale. According to this Law, international trade results from differences in factor endowments among countries, which generate comparative advantage. However, the "New Trade Theory" offers an additional, complimentary explanation of why trade occurs and may be mutually beneficial. This Theory drops the assumption of constant returns to scale. It observes that in reality, increasing returns to scale often occur.

Two contexts in which they occur are intra-industry trade and inter-industry trade. First, at the level of a firm, there may be increasing returns to scale, known as internal scale economies. Second, at the level of an economy (in a national or regional sense), there may be increasing returns to scale, called external scale economies. Intra-industry trade is observed in many markets. For example, the U.S., EU, and Japan trade cars and watches. (To be sure, there is a debate to be had about the definition of "industry." Is there one automobile market, and a single watch market, or is it more appropriate to consider separate markets based, for instance, on product features?) Comparative advantage does not well explain this phenomenon, yet such trade is not insignificant. About 25 percent of trade of industrial countries is considered intra-industry. However, the effects of economies of scale, along with monopolistic competition (*i.e.*, product differentiation to secure a niche in a market), may help explain the occurrence.

Unfortunately, at the micro (*i.e.*, plant) level, some models do not make predictions about the relationship between economies of scale and intra-industry trade. Other models suggest a negative correlation between the two variables, that is, greater scale economies correlate with less intra-industry trade. It is possible to rationalize this suggestion by saying large plants tend to dominate industries in which the goods produced are fairly homogeneous (*e.g.*, steel). In such industries, in contrast to industries in which there is imperfect competition through differentiated products, there is little room for intra-industry trade.

At the macro (*i.e.*, national or regional) level, the evidence appears stronger than at the micro level that increasing returns to scale help explain trade (whether intra- or inter-industry). A pioneering study by business school scholar Michael Porter, *The Competitive Advantage of Nations* (1990) highlighted the importance of agglomeration. Using the case-study method, he found many instances of countries gaining a competitive advantage in an international market through a domestic cluster of firms. The concentration in Dalton, Georgia, of production of American carpets, and similarly of European carpets in Flanders, are illustrations of geographically localized industries that appear to be driven by external economies of scale, which in turn promotes trade.

IV. KEY MICROECONOMIC CONCEPTS FOR COMPARATIVE ADVANTAGE

A. Overview

To understand the graphical presentation of the Law of Comparative Advantage, five basic microeconomic concepts are needed. They are:

1. Production Possibilities Frontier (PPF).

2. Marginal Rate of Transformation (MRT).

3. Societal Indifference Curve (IC).

4. Marginal Rate of Substitution (MRS).

5. Relative Price Line depicting terms of trade (TOT).

These concepts are explained in turn below.

B. Production Possibilities Frontier and Marginal Rate of Transformation

A PPF is a diagram of the alternative combinations of two goods that one country can produce with all its factors of production. That is, a PPF shows the maximum amount of one good that can be produced, while making a specific amount of another good. When a country employs fully all factors of production in the most efficient manner, then that country operates on its PPF (such as at Point A). To say factors are deployed "efficiently" means they are engaged in making a combination of goods at the lowest cost with the existing available technology. Graph 7-1 shows a PPF for India.

GRAPH 7-1:
PRODUCTION POSSIBILITIES FRONTIER FOR INDIA

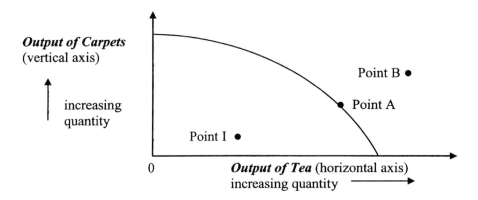

The goods in question are carpets (on the vertical axis) and tea (on the horizontal axis). Movement upward or rightward along the axes reflects increasing quantities of carpets or tea, respectively. When a resource is idle, or when a resource is unemployed or underemployed, or not used efficiently, then the country operates at a point inside its PPF. (Point I, on Graph 7-1, would be such an instance.) A country cannot operate beyond its PPF (for example, at Point Y on Graph 7-1.) Over time, a PPF shifts outward, as the stock of one or more resources in a country grows (*e.g.*, more labor because of population growth or immigration, more land through land reclamation, more physical capital through investment, higher human capital through education, or improved technology). If one or more factors shrink, then the PPF can shift in.

The MRT is a microeconomic concept that answers the following question: What does the slope of the PPF indicate? The slope of the PPF is the MRT. Arithmetically, the slope of any line is computed as follows:

$$\text{Slope of Line} \quad = \quad \frac{\text{Change in Vertical Axis}}{\text{Change in Horizontal Axis}} \quad = \quad \frac{\Delta Y}{\Delta X}$$

where "Δ" means "change in," "Y" is the symbol for the vertical axis, and "X" is the symbol for the horizontal axis.

Thus, the formula for the MRT:

$$\text{MRT} \qquad = \qquad \frac{\Delta Y}{\Delta X}$$

Intuitively, the MRT reflects the opportunity cost of production between two goods. The concept of "opportunity cost" refers to sacrifice, namely, what amount of production of one item must be sacrificed to produce another item. Embedded in this concept is the re-allocation of factors of production from making one good to making another good. Significantly, therefore, the PPF, via the MRT, reveals trade-offs for a society, *i.e.*, the opportunity cost to a society of manufacturing one versus another commodity.

C. Societal Indifference Curves and Marginal Rate of Substitution

The third microeconomic concept, an IC, exhibits the tastes and preferences of an individual, or society. Consequently, it alleviates the need for an assumption that a choice among alternative combinations of goods that could be consumed reflects "given" tastes and preferences that are exogenous (*i.e.*, not explained by the model at hand). Accordingly, an IC represents the different combinations of goods an individual consumer, or a society, could have to yield a particular level of material satisfaction.

Graph 7-2 depicts an IC map for a country, India. The goods in question are, again, carpets and tea. An IC is drawn as a downward-sloping curve that is convex (*i.e.*, bowed inward) to the origin of the graph on which it is plotted. (The "origin" is the zero point, at which the vertical and horizontal axes intersect). The level of satisfaction, or utility, is the same on an IC. Each IC — on a map of them — reflects different levels of utility. Along any single IC, the level of satisfaction is the same. What changes in moving along an IC is the precise combination of goods.

GRAPH 7-2:
SOCIETAL INDIFFERENCE CURVES FOR INDIA

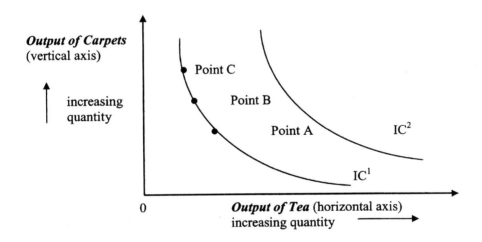

For instance, in moving along IC^1 from Point A to Point B, Indians consume fewer carpets and more tea at Point B than at Point A. However, they are indifferent as to consuming at Point A or B, because each point yields the same level of utility. Literally, an IC shows combinations of carpets and tea Indian society could consume to obtain a given level of satisfaction and among which they are indifferent. Movement from Point A to Point B is nothing more than a substitution of one good for another. The rate at which Indian consumers are willing to substitute between the two goods is the Marginal Rate of Substitution (MRS). The MRS is the slope of an IC at a particular point on that IC.

The closer an IC is to the origin of a graph, the lower the level of satisfaction associated with the combinations of goods represented by that IC. Conversely, the further away an IC is from the origin, the higher the utility level obtained from the alternative combinations of goods reflected in that IC. Thus, IC^1 represents a lower level of satisfaction than IC^2. In other words, a movement upward and to the right in a map of ICs, from one IC to another, means increases in consumer satisfaction. By assumption, economic actors — whether individuals, groups, or countries — seek to attain the highest possible IC, and thereby the greatest level of utility.

ICs do not intersect. If they did, then it would mean the same combination of goods yields two different levels of utility. That result would be illogical. It also would be contrary to the characteristic of an IC map that the further an IC is from the origin, the higher the level of satisfaction reflected by that curve.

As intimated, an IC can represent the tastes and preferences of a country. Technically, the correct label for such an IC is a "Social Indifference Curve." By assumption, IC^1 and IC^2 are social ICs. Social ICs have the same character-istics as individual ICs. However, a Social IC is not established simply by summing up all tastes and preferences embodied in the individual ICs of each person in a country. Income distribution matters, because different distribu-tions within a county lead to different IC maps. For instance, if a country liberalizes its trade laws, then some individuals may benefit (*e.g.*, exporters), while others suffer (*e.g.*, producers of products that are like, or compete directly with, imports). Trade liberalization will not have an even effect across all individuals. To account for the distributional effects of freer trade, economists rely on the "Compensation Principle." Social welfare potentially increases from a policy change like trade liberalization if the gainers take part of their gain to compensate the losers, so that everyone has the potential to become better off. In sum, a Social IC map involves not just the aggregation of individual ICs, but also use of the Compensation Principle.

The fourth microeconomic concept, MRS, is analogous to the MRT. Just as the slope of the PPF is the MRT, the slope of an IC is the MRS. In Graph 7-3, clearly, IC^1 has a steeper slope at Point B than at Point A.

GRAPH 7-3:
MARGINAL RATES OF SUBSTITUTION ALONG SOCIAL
INDIFFERENCE CURVE FOR INDIA

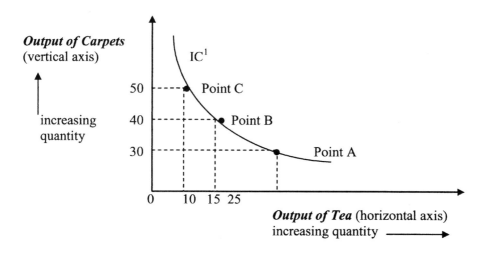

As India moves along IC^1 upward and to the left, from Point A to Point B, from Point B to Point C, and so forth, the MRS decreases, which arithmetically means the MRS becomes a larger negative number. The arithmetic fact that MRS decreases with movement up and to the left of an IC reflects the economic concept of diminishing marginal utility. Essentially, the more of one good an individual or society consumes of that good, the less utility derived from each incremental unit of that good. (Imagine the difference in satisfaction between the first and second slice of pizza, and the fifth and sixth slice of pizza. The diminution in marginal satisfaction illustrates diminishing marginal utility from pizza. If asked to trade off glasses of fine red wine for the second slice of pizza, a consumer might be willing to give up two glasses. But, having eaten five slices, asked about how much red wine a consumer would be willing to give up to get a sixth slice, the likely answer would be less than half a glass!) Diminishing marginal utility also accounts for why ICs are convex to the origin (zero point) of a graph.

For a fuller appreciation of MRS and diminishing marginal utility, recall that the slope of any line is computed as follows:

$$\text{Slope of Line} \quad = \quad \frac{\text{Change in Vertical Axis}}{\text{Change in Horizontal Axis}} \quad = \quad \frac{\Delta}{\Delta X}$$

where "Δ" means "change in," "Y" is the symbol for the vertical axis, and "X" is the symbol for the horizontal axis.

Thus, the formula for MRS is the same as that for MRT, namely:

MRS   = Slope of IC at a point   = $\dfrac{\Delta Y}{\Delta X}$

Accordingly, as shown in Graph 7-3, in moving from Point A to Point B, India consumes less tea (15 instead of 25 units) and more carpets (40 instead of 30 units):

MRS in moving from $\dfrac{\Delta Y}{\Delta X}$ $\dfrac{40-30}{-(25-15)}$ = -1
Points A to B

(The slope is negative, because the denominator reflects a diminution in consumption of tea.) Intuitively, to consume 10 more units of carpets, India has to forego consumption of 10 units of tea. To Indians, there is a one-to-one trade off between carpets and tea.

The trade-off changes if India moves from Point B to Point C. As Graph 7-3 shows, with increased consumption of another 10 carpets (from 40 to 50 units), India's consumption of tea again drops — but by 5 units (from 15 to 10), rather than 10 units as in the movement from Points A to B:

MRS in moving from $\dfrac{\Delta Y}{\Delta X}$ $\dfrac{50-40}{-(15-10)}$ = -2
Points B to C

Intuitively, to consume another 10 units of carpets, India is willing to forego only 5 units of tea. Why? At such a high consumption level of carpets (50 units, at Point C), Indian consumers do net get much utility from the incremental carpet they consume. They will not be induced to consume one more carpet if they have to forego much tea. The diminishing MRS in moving from points A to C, *i.e.*, the increase in the negative number, from — 1 to — 2, is the arithmetic statement of diminishing utility to India from consuming ever-larger amounts of carpets.

D. Relative Price Line

The fifth and final microeconomic concept needed to demonstrate the Law of Comparative Advantage is a Price Line. This concept is not different from the MRS or MRT. Essentially, it is a straight line, and the focus of attention is on the slope of the line (defined earlier). On a graph, if the vertical (y) axis measures units of quantity of one good produced or consumed, and horizontal (x) axis gauges units of a second good produced or consumed, then the numerator and denominator of the slope formula (ΔY and ΔX, respectively) obviously consist of quantities of goods. Those quantities reflect a trade-off between production or consumption of one good versus another. That is, the slope is a ratio of exchange between the two goods.

A ratio of exchange between goods is the same as the relative price between goods. True, the ratio is constructed using quantities. So, the relative price is not in terms of a currency, but rather in terms of units of one good exchangeable for another good. However, that kind of trade is barter (or, more generally, counter-trade), which occurs in various markets and contexts. Economists frequently measure relative prices in terms of the ratio of product quantities, they call the relative price line the "terms of trade" (TOT), and they do this for all kinds of goods. The generic formula for a TOT index is:

$$\text{TOT} = \frac{\text{Index of Export Prices}}{\text{Index of Import Prices}} \times 100$$

As its name suggests, the TOT are the relative prices at which two countries trade goods or services, or more specifically, the terms, in the sense of price, which one country receives (from another country) for its exports (to that other country) in relation to the price that country pays (to the other country) for imports.

Thus, to take one example, consider oil and pharmaceuticals. The relative price of these commodities would be:

$$\text{Relative Price} = \frac{\text{Change in barrels of oil}}{\text{Change in bottles of pills}} = \frac{\Delta Y}{\Delta X} = \frac{P^{OIL}}{P^{PILL}}$$

The symbol "P^{OIL}" stands for the price of oil, and "P^{PILL}" is the price of pharmaceuticals.

Another way to explain this point is as follows. Suppose a barrel of oil costs U.S. \$50, and a bottle of pills cost \$25. Then, the relative price of oil to pills, in terms of nominal (or money) prices would be

$$\frac{\$50}{\$25} = 2$$

Consequently, 1 barrel of oil could be sold to purchase 2 bottles of pills. To generalize, if

$$\frac{P^{OIL}}{P^{PILL}} = k \text{ (where } k = 2, \text{ in the example)}$$

Then, 1 unit of oil equals k (*e.g.*, 2) units of pills.

Graph 7-4, called "Relative Price Lines," shows two different TOTs.

GRAPH 7-4:
RELATIVE PRICE LINES

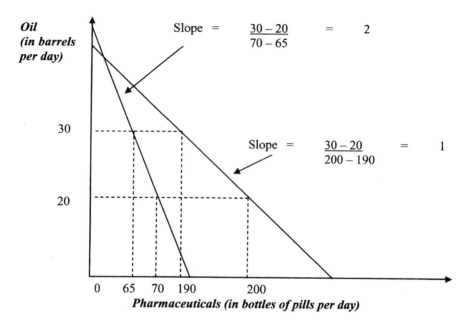

The steeper Line, with a slope of 2 (technically, — 2), shows oil is twice as dear as medicine. That is because 2 bottles of pills must be sacrificed for 1 barrel of oil. The second, flatter Line has a slope of 1 (or — 1). Here, 1 barrel may be traded for 1 bottle.

As an added feature, the end points of a Relative Price Line show what quantity of a good could be consumed if all income were spent on that good. For example, where the Relative Price Line intersects with the vertical axis, all income is spent on oil. Where a Relative Price Line intersects with the horizontal axis, all income is spent on pharmaceuticals. This insight suggests a Line also reveals a budget constraint. That is because it depicts the maximum amount of either good, or alterative combinations of a good, which can be purchased. The further the Line from the origin of Graph 7-4 (where the axes intersect), the higher the budget.

E. Summary

In Graph 7-5, all of the aforementioned concepts are combined, using India, oil, and pharmaceuticals as an example:

GRAPH 7-5:
BASIC MICROECONOMIC CONCEPTS FOR LAW OF COMPARATIVE ADVANTAGE — INDIAN OIL AND PHARMACEUTICAL PRODUCTION

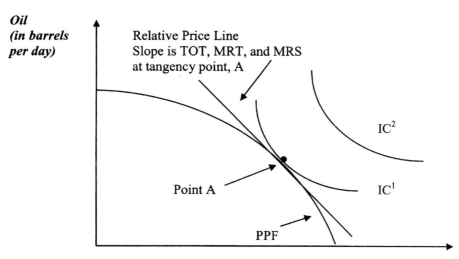

Pharmaceuticals (in bottles of pills per day)

That is, a PPF with a Societal ICs, one of which is tangent to (*i.e.*, just touching) the PPF, is mapped. Alternative Relative Price Lines, including one through the tangency point, are shown. The slope of a Relative Price Line tangent to the PPF not only reflects the TOT at the tangency, Point A, but also the MRT at that point. Likewise, the slope of a Line tangent to a Societal IC is both a TOT and the MRS at the tangency.

V. THE NEOCLASSICAL GRAPHICAL DEMONSTRATION OF COMPARATIVE ADVANTAGE

A. Conditions under Autarky

Graph 7-6 exhibits a PPF, ICs, and a Price Line for a country. By hypothesis, the country is India before 1991. This Graph is titled "India under Autarky." This term refers to an economic policy of not participating in international trade, *i.e.*, not importing or exporting any goods (or, presumably, services). An autarkic economy is a closed one. The proof, elaborate as it may at first appear, is designed to make a powerful point: with a fixed stock of factors of production, free trade based on the specialization of production in a good in which a country has a comparative advantage expands consumption opportunities in the country beyond the limits of what that country can produce under autarky. In brief, free trade generates a net benefit to the country, in the form of a production gain and a consumption gain.

The word "net" requires careful attention. The word connotes what comparative advantage says and does not say. Many politicians knowingly or unwittingly ignore this distinction, and thereby oversell the benefits of free trade. The proof is not free trade benefits all interest groups in society, *i.e.*, all producers, all consumers, and the government. Some groups, most notably, the government (which collects tariff revenue), and certain producers (namely, ones producing a product that is like or directly competitive with imports, or which benefit from quota rents) suffer when trade barriers like tariffs and quotas are dropped. Not surprisingly, then, certain interest groups argue for protection. Likewise, the proof is not the whole world is helped by trade liberalization. Rather, the proof is on balance, a country that dismantles its trade barriers, even unilaterally, is better off than it had been when closed to trade.

GRAPH 7-6:
INDIA UNDER AUTARKY

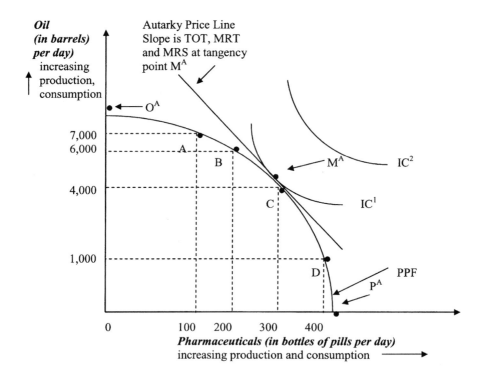

Before 1991, the Indian economy was not autarkic. But, neither did India pursue aggressive trade liberalization — quite the contrary. Few are the cases of pure or nearly pure autarky, with Burma from 1962-88, China from

1949-79, and North Korea after 1953, among them. However, from Independence on 15 August 1947 through 1991, India pursued socialist policies championed by Prime Minister Jawaharlal Nehru (1889-1964) and his daughter, Prime Minister Indira Gandhi (1917-1984), as well as self-reliance, a philosophy advocated by Mohandas K. ("Mahatma") Gandhi (1869-1948). These policies included high tariff barriers, many quotas, and licensing for imports and exports. Thus, for instance, India sought (and, with the help of the Green Revolution in the 1960s, eventually attained) self-sufficiency in food, even becoming a net exporter of grains.

As the axes of Graph 7-6 illustrate, the two commodities at issue are oil (*i.e.*, crude oil), on the vertical axis, and pharmaceuticals (*i.e.*, medicines), on the horizontal axis. Upward movement on the vertical axis indicates increasing quantity of oil produced and consumed (typically measured in barrels per day). Rightward movement on the horizontal axis indicates increasing quantity of pharmaceuticals produced and consumed (measured in terms of bottles of pills per day). The PPF is the arch sloping downward from the top left of the vertical axis to the far right of the horizontal axis. At the top left, where the PPF intersects the vertical axis, Point O^A (for "oil under autarky), India produces and consumes only oil. At the bottom right, where the PPF intersects with the horizontal axis, Point P^A (for "pharmaceuticals under autarky"), India produces and consumes only pharmaceuticals. In the middle of the PPF, at Point M^A (for "mix under autarky"), India produces a 50-50 mix of oil and pharmaceuticals. Movement down and to the right of the PPF means India produces and consumes less oil and more pharmaceuticals, and movement up and to the left suggests the reverse pattern.

India is a diversified economy, producing and consuming more than just oil and medicine. It is possible to depict graphically more than just two commodities. To do so, the axes measure bundles of goods. For instance, the vertical axis could depict a bundle of durable goods (*i.e.*, goods the life of which typically exceeds one year, such as cars and refrigerators), and the horizontal axis could gauge non-durable goods (*i.e.*, merchandise with a less-than-one year life, such as most food items). Using oil and pharmaceuticals is an assumption to simplify the analysis, but broadening the number of commodities does not change the demonstration of the Law of Comparative Advantage.

Why is the PPF shaped like an arch concave (*i.e.*, bowed out) from the origin, Point O, where the axes intersect? The answer is increasing costs of production, specifically, opportunity costs. To make more pharmaceuticals, India must give up production of oil. That is, India must release some factors of production dedicated to oil and re-allocate them to making medicines. The more pharmaceuticals India seeks to produce, the more oil production it must forego. That is, India must forego ever-increasing quantities of one good to produce more of the other good. Stated in economic terms, India faces increasing opportunity costs of production.

For instance, to move from producing 100 bottles of medicine per day to 200 bottles, India must give up production of 1,000 barrels of oil per day. This shift is from Points A to B on the PPF. However, if India wants to increase pharmaceutical production further, from 200 to 300 bottles per day, then it must give up 2,000 barrels of oil per day. This shift is shown from Points B to C on the PPF. If India wants to boost output of medicines from 300 to 400 bottles per day, then it must forego 3,000 barrels of oil per day. This change is from Points C to D on the PPF. In brief, increasing production costs mean for each successive increment in the production of one unit of a good, it is necessary to forego an ever-larger number of units of production of the other good.

Re-allocating resources from the oil to pharmaceutical sector assumes the resources indeed are mobile. In reality, there are likely to be barriers to mobility, as well as transaction costs. Workers may not want to leave their homes and communities, particularly if they have to migrate far from their families to locations where a different language is spoken or religion is practiced. Capital equipment and technology needed to explore and drill for oil, pump it, and transport it to refineries is not readily convertible to making medicine. Thus, for a country to take advantage of trade liberalization, it often is necessary to implement complementary reforms to allow factors migration to optimally efficient uses based on a new set of world market forces.

In the example, the MRT is the opportunity cost India faces as it selects a particular combination of oil and pharmaceuticals to produce and consume. If production costs are constant, then the MRT is the same at all points on the PPF. After all, the slope of the Line is the same at all points. But, if (as in the Graph) costs are increasing, then MRS changes. At each point on the PPF, MRS is different from each other point, because the slope of a straight line tangent to a point differs from other points. In specific, with movement down and to the right, MRT increases. The increases reflect growing costs of production — *i.e.*, foregoing ever-larger amounts of oil to make another bottle of pills.

From the Graph, the MRS at different points is apparent. Moving from Points A to B means increasing output of pharmaceuticals from 100 to 200 bottles, but foregoing 1,000 barrels per day of oil. Therefore, the MRS (slope) is:

$$\frac{\Delta Y}{\Delta X} \quad = \quad \frac{-(1,000)}{200 \; - \; 100} \quad = \quad -10$$

(The sign on the numerator is negative, because oil production falls.) To shift from points B to C, meaning an increased pharmaceutical output from 200 to 300 but a drop in oil production by 2,000 barrels per day, would imply a greater MRS (steeper slope):

$$\frac{\Delta Y}{\Delta X} \quad = \quad \frac{-(2,000)}{300 \; - \; 200} \quad = \quad -20$$

Finally, the shift from points C to D imply yet another boost in output of medicines by 100 bottles per day, but a steeper drop than before in oil output — India forgoes 3,000 barrels per day. The MRS (slope) is:

$$\frac{\Delta Y}{\Delta X} \quad = \quad \frac{-(3,000)}{400 \; - \; 300} \quad = \quad -30$$

Clearly, the MRS increases from -10 to -30, bespeaking increased production costs.

The scenario of increasing production costs is more realistic than imposing an assumption India faces constant costs of production. In fact, most countries have to forego making more of one commodity if they attempt to produce ever-increasing amounts of another commodity. It is possible (indeed, easy) to represent a PPF with constant costs of production — the PPF is a straight line. To say costs are "constant" means the number of units of output of one good a country such as India must forego in order to make an additional unit of another good remains the same. If the PPF in the Graph were a straight line, from points O^A to P^A, then it would mean India faces constant costs of production as between oil and medicines. The straight-line PPF would indicate India gives up the same amount of oil production, for example, 1,000 barrels per day, to produce more pharmaceuticals, whether the increase is from 100 bottles of pills per day to 200 bottles, or from 300 bottles per day to 400 bottles.

The critical insight to obtain from the Graph is a country under autarky can consume only what it produces. It cannot specialize in the production of one good, generate a surplus for export, and exchange that exportable surplus for imports. After all, the country is closed to trade. At what point will India produce and consume? It can choose any point on, or within, its PPF. It will make the choice based on societal preferences, which are represented by ICs. In the Graph, by assumption India chooses Point M^A. It is confined to producing a mix of goods on its PPF, and it cannot achieve a level of consumer satisfaction beyond that PPF (such as at IC^2).

B.   Conditions with Free Trade

In 1991, India undertook serious economic reforms. This policy shift reflected business realities, and had geopolitically strategic implications. Some of India's growth is in the intellectual property (IP) sector, including medicines. India makes generic drugs cheaply and in large volumes, and exports them to countries that lack the same manufacturing capacity, such as many Sub-Saharan African nations. As for oil, India now competes, along with China and other big emerging economies, with the U.S., EU, Japan, and established powers to satisfy growing domestic energy demand. Industrialization and rising lifestyle expectations drive that demand.

Accordingly, Graph 7-7 continues the example, showing post-1991 India. Entitled "India with Free Trade," this Graph depicts the effect on India of opening to importation and exportation of goods (and, again, services). India cannot produce enough oil to satisfy domestic needs, and the gap between its own output and consumption grows as does the Indian economy and incomes of Indians. Thus, the Graph shows India imports oil. By hypothesis, its source is Iran. About 60 percent (as of December 2007) of proven oil reserves in the world are located in the Middle East. The Kingdom of Saudi Arabia is home to the largest share, 22 percent of all proven reserves, Iran roughly 11 percent, and Iraq nearly 10 percent. However, at the 2004 rate of production in the Kingdom, Saudi Arabia will exhaust its reserves in 68 years, whereas Iran's reserves will last 89 years. In sharp contrast, India has just 19 years of remaining reserves.

Of course, in reality, India relies on a variety of foreign sources, and it is possible to group them together under the banner "Rest of World" (ROW). That is, ROW could be India's trading partner. Iran is chosen, however, to emphasize the complex nexus between security and trade, and test the proposition of peace through trade.

To get Iranian oil (and natural gas), India uses a newly constructed pipeline, which crosses Pakistani territory. Relying for some energy needs on a pipeline that traverses its traditional nemesis, Pakistan, is for India both a security risk and a strategic opportunity for better relations with Pakistan. From the U.S. perspective, stability on the Indian Subcontinent — where both India and Pakistan are armed with deliverable nuclear weapons, and fight over Kashmir — is only part of the calculus. Many among the best and brightest in America's foreign policy elite look askance at India cozying up to Iran. They are wary of Iran's nuclear ambitions, and suspicious of its support for extremist causes. The dreadful bilateral relations date not just to November 1979, when militants seized the American Embassy in Tehran (and held 52 Americans hostage for 444 days). They go at least as far back as 1953, to a U.S.-inspired *coup d'etat* of Iran's democratically elected Prime Minister, Mohammed Mossadegh (1882-1967). Accordingly, the U.S. maintains sanctions on the world's only *Shi'ite* theocracy. The 1996 *Iran and Libya Sanctions Act* (which President George W. Bush renewed in respect of Iran) discourages through a secondary boycott other countries from investing in Iran's energy sector. Thus, trade reform in India is not just about trade.

GRAPH 7-7:
INDIA WITH FREE TRADE

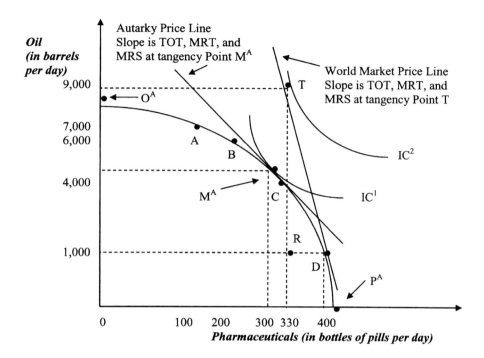

What does India export in return for Iranian oil? The answer is pharmaceuticals, particularly generic drugs. India produces far more bottles per day than it can consume. In contrast, Iran — which has an excess supply of oil — is more than eager to trade oil to India in exchange for medicines, which (by assumption) it needs. On the Graph, this exchange is depicted by what economists dub the "Trade Triangle," TRD. Essentially, India exports RD units of pharmaceuticals in exchange for imports of RT units of oil.

From trade, India is better off than under autarky, as Table 7-6 shows. Specialization of production in a commodity in which India has a comparative advantage, plus a higher level of consumer satisfaction, are why India is "better off" than before.

TABLE 7-6:
SUMMARY OF GAINS FROM FREE TRADE

	Oil (barrels per day)	Pharmaceuticals (bottles of pills per day)
Production Under Autarky	4,000	300
Production with Free Trade	1,000	400
Production Gain or Loss with Trade (compared to Autarky)	3,000 barrels per day less produced. Specialization out of oil, in which India lacks a comparative advantage.	100 additional bottles of pills per day produced. Specialization into pharmaceuticals, in which India has a comparative advantage. Also, Indian producers obtain a higher price for their product.
Consumption under Autarky	4,000	300
Consumption with Free Trade	9,000	330
Production (Exportable) Surplus or Consumption Deficit	Deficit of 8,000	Surplus of 70
Consumption Gain from Trade (compared to Autarky)	Indians consume an additional 5,000 additional barrels of oil per day. Also, Indians get oil at a lower price.	Indians consume an additional 30 bottles of pills per day.

These reasons also would justify India's interest in trade with Iran. While the U.S. and its allies may have political motives for isolating Iran from the global economy, these motives may be incongruous with India's economic interests. It is interesting to re-calculate matters from an American perspective. Might increased trade between India and Iran enhance American national security interests? Indeed, in his *Principles of Political Economy and Taxation* (1817), Ricardo signaled the civilizing benefits from commercial intercourse:

> Under a system of perfectly free commerce, each country naturally devotes its capital and labor to such employments as are most beneficial to each. This pursuit of individual advantage is admirably connected with the universal good of the whole. By stimulating industry, by rewarding ingenuity, and by using most efficaciously the peculiar powers bestowed by nature, it distributes labor most effectively and most economically: while, *by increasing the general mass of productions, it diffuses general benefit, and binds together, by one common tie of interest and intercourse, the universal society of nations throughout the civilized world.* It is this principle which determines that wine shall be made in France and Portugal, that corn shall be grown in

America and Poland, and that hardware and other goods shall be manufactured in England. . . . [Emphasis added.]

Put squarely, is the conflict between American politics and Indian economics a false one?

C. The General Lesson

To sum up, and to generalize the lesson, there are four critical points to appreciate about the Graph and Table:

1. *Production Gains from Trade*

Following the Law of Comparative Advantage, India specializes in pharmaceutical production. It moves from Point M^A to Point D on its PPF, thereby expanding pharmaceutical output from just under 300 bottles per day to 400 bottles per day. It scales back oil output, from just over 4,000 barrels per day to 1,000 barrels per day. This shift reflects the TOT India faces with economic reform via trade liberalization.

2. *Consumption Gains from Trade*

Indian consumers can achieve a higher level of material satisfaction with free trade than under autarky. They will seek to attain a consumption level at the highest possible Societal ICs, but subject to the TOT set by the world market. At the TOT dictated by the World Market Price Line, they can reach IC^2. That is, they move from Point M^A to Point T on IC^2. At this level of material well being, Indian consumers do not purchase all the pharmaceuticals India produces. India makes 400 bottles per day (at Point D), but its people consume 330 bottles per day, leaving 70 bottles per day of surplus. But, Indians would like more oil than India pumps and refines, as domestic demand is 9,000 barrels per day, but domestic output is just 1,000 barrels per day. How does India rectify this situation of excess demand for oil? The answer is international trade. With the extra pharmaceutical production, India has an excess supply of that product. It ships this surplus to Iran, in exchange for the necessary oil.

3. *World Market Price*

The World Market Price Line embodies the TOT India faces with free trade. What will the TOT, a single international trade equilibrium, be? World market forces of supply and demand in the two commodity markets, oil and pharmaceuticals, decide the answer. These forces are, at a human level, the decisions of millions (if not hundreds of millions) of producers and consumers in Indian, Iranian, and other markets. Undoubtedly, the equilibrium will be an intermediate level between the autarky prices in India and Iran. Intuitively, this result makes sense. Indian pharmaceutical companies would not sell pills to Iran at a price cheaper than they could receive in India. Conversely, Iranian oil companies would not sell oil to India at a barrel price cheaper than what they could sell on their home market. Consumers in each country react in the same manner. Indian consumers would not by oil from Iran at a higher price than they can receive domestically, and Iranian consumers would not get their medicines from India if domestic equivalents were available at a lower price.

To appreciate this point in arithmetic and graphical terms, recall the Autarky Price Line and World Market Price lines are sloped downward. Technically, their slopes are denominated by a negative number, but what matters is the absolute value and the trade-off this value represents. A smaller absolute value (such as 1 in comparison with 2), reflects a less steep slope than a larger absolute value (such as 2 in comparison with 1).

Assume, then, the TOT under autarky at Point M^A is 1. In other words, 1 barrel of oil is equal to 1 bottle of pills. Therefore, Indian pharmaceutical companies can sell in India 1 bottle of pills and receive 1 barrel of oil. As the Graph depicts, the World Market Price line is steeper than the Autarky Price Line. That steepness must be reflected in a larger number than 1. So, assume the slope is 2. The implication is that at Point D, 2 barrels of oil are equal to (*i.e.*, may be traded for) 1 bottle of pills. Therefore, Indian pharmaceutical companies can sell Iranian consumers one bottle and receive two barrels of oil. Clearly, the Indian pharmaceutical companies will prefer trade to autarky, because with trade their product commands a higher price than under autarky. Intuitively the result makes sense. Demand for their product rises with trade, as both Iranian and Indian consumers are buying their product.

From the perspective of Indian consumers, trade is beneficial. Under autarky, Indians paid for one barrel of oil with one bottle of pills. With trade, at Point T, they get two barrels for a bottle of pills. Put differently, the currency with which Indian consumers pay for imports commands more goods than under autarky. Again, intuitively, this result makes sense. With trade, the oil supply available to Indian consumers expands to include Iranian output, leading to a drop in price.

4. *Economic Democracy and Efficiency*

There is a kind of economic democracy associated with free trade. Under autarky, the decision of what to produce, and how much, typically is dictated by central government planners. Under free trade, producers respond to free market signals. Likewise, under autarky, consumers are stuck with consumption trade-offs set by the planners. Under free trade, they adjust their consumption to world market prices. Most importantly, from an economic perspective, rational responses to such signals are efficient. To be sure, not everyone has equal access to participate in import-export transactions. Market participation is part of the evaluation of the democratic nature of trade liberalization. But, under autarky, equality is hardly assured. Indeed, history records some of the most grossly unequal — and poor — societies are ones with autarkies.

Notwithstanding these benefits from free trade, there is an important concern left out in the analysis: which country, India or Iran, gains more from trade? That is, how are the gains from trade distributed between the two countries?

The answer depends on the international equilibrium price, *i.e.*, the world market price ratio, or TOT. The closer the TOT is to the price under autarky for one country, the less the gains from trade for that country, and the greater the gains from trade for the other country. For example, if the autarky price ratio of oil to pharmaceuticals for India is 1 and Iran is 3, and the TOT is

2, then the two countries split the gain equally. But, if the TOT of oil to medicines is 1.5, then Iran captures a larger share of the gain from India. Intuitively, the reason is producers do not get a much higher price for their product with trade than under autarky, and consumers cannot buy a product at a much cheaper price with trade than under autarky, if the TOT and autarky price ratios are nearly the same.

A logical follow-up question is in what instances will the gains from trade be split relatively equally? Economists suggest a roughly 50-50 sharing occurs when countries are roughly equal in size (*e.g.*, in their economies), and their consumers have broadly the same tastes and preferences. If two countries are quite unequal in size, then the big country is likely to obtain a lesser proportion of the gain than the small country. That suggestion seems counter-intuitive, but it makes sense. The small country is unlikely to be able to satisfy the large consumption demand in a big country, much less world demand, for a particular product. As a result, the big country will continue to produce a considerable volume of that product, even thought it may lack a comparative advantage in the product. Economists dub this scenario the "importance of being unimportant," meaning that in trade with big countries, small countries are likely to capture most of the gains from trade. This scenario has practical importance for the debate about whether, and how, developing and least developed countries can benefit from open trade.

VI. CONTEMPORARY ARGUMENTS FOR FREE TRADE[1]

A. Static versus Dynamic Models

Classical and neoclassical arguments for free trade highlight static changes. However, significant net static efficiency gains are from trade liberalization, there may be equally or more impressive gains accruing over time from trade-related changes. Static gains are one-time, following from world-market price signals and factor re-allocation. For instance, trade liberalization increases long-run level of *per capita* income. But, in a static Smith-Ricardo style model, it is not possible to discern whether, to what extent, and how trade liberalization might induce growth effects, such as long-run increases in the rate of growth of *per capita* income. In such a model, growth occurs only by a transition from one *per capita* income level to the next, made possible by savings and investment. In brief, to focus only on static gains is to understate the full benefits from trade.

Consequently, in many economic models of economic growth developed since the Smith — Ricardo era, including so-called "endogenous growth models," the spotlight is on dynamic gains from trade. Dynamic gains occur over a sustained period, and are compounded from one year to the next. In the

---

[1] *See, e.g.*, UNITED STATES INTERNATIONAL TRADE COMMISSION, THE DYNAMIC EFFECTS OF TRADE LIBERALIZATION: AN EMPIRICAL ANALYSIS, INVESTIGATION NUMBER 332-375, (Pub. No. 3069, Oct. 1997); Paul Krugman, *Empirical Evidence on the New Trade Theories: The Current State of Play*, *in* NEW TRADE THEORIES: A LOOK AT THE EMPIRICAL EVIDENCE (Bocconi University, Milan ed. 1994); Keith E. Maskus, *Using the International Trading System to Foster Technology Transfer for Economic Development*, 2005 MICH. ST. L. REV. 219-41.

contemporary models, effects of trade liberalization are neither transitional nor felt only on the level of *per capita* income. They are permanent, and affect the rate of growth of income. These results follow from a theoretical consideration of sources affecting growth that are not included in the classical and neoclassical models — learning by doing, human capital, and knowledge capital.

The exploration by modern economists begins with the following question: does a country that adopts policies encouraging freer trade experience more rapid rates of growth in *per capita* income than a country that does not engage in trade liberalization? This question matters because even small differences in income growth rates (*e.g.*, a few tenths of a percentage point annually), over a sustained period and compounded over time, translate into large differences in standards of living. As a dramatic example, consider El Salvador and Japan. In the mid-1950s, the two countries had about the same level of *per capita* income. By 1993, the income of one Japanese person equaled the income of 24 Salvadorans. Why? Japan maintained over 38 years a difference of less than 9 percent in economic growth per person. The point is that if trade liberalization has a positive impact on growth rates, even a modest one, then it also is likely to have a positive effect on living standards.

In a static, classical model of an economy, and in neoclassical growth models, the traditional sources of economic growth, *i.e.*, of increases in *per capita* income, are long-run phenomena, namely,

1. savings and investment, which allow for capital accumulation,

2. population growth, which results in an expanded labor supply, and

3. technological change, which results in greater efficiency and productivity, by permitting a greater level of output per unit of inputs.

These phenomena cause an outward shift in the PPF of a country, resulting in expanded output and trade opportunities. But, in the classical model, savings, population growth, and technological change are exogenous. That is, they are not determined by the model, but rather are assumed given and set by variables for which the model does not account.

B. Trade Liberalization, Savings, and Investment

In contemporary models of economic growth, the traditional determinants — labor, capital accumulation — play an important role. There is increasing empirical evidence that trade liberalization stimulates growth indirectly by operating on traditional factor accumulation. In particular, trade liberalization stimulates domestic savings. In 1968, the economist Alfred Maizels tested the trade — savings link using annual data from 1950-60 for 11 countries (Australia, Burma, Iceland, India, Ireland, Jamaica, Malawi, Rhodesia, South Africa, Trinidad and Tobago, and Zambia). He asked whether export income has a higher power to explain gross domestic savings than non-export income (*i.e.*, Gross Domestic Product (GDP) excluding exports).

The answer was "yes." A change in exports has associated changes in domestic savings. There is a positive relationship between exports and savings rates. Maizels offers three explanations for this result: the propensity to save is higher in the export sector than other sectors; government revenues depend on tariffs on foreign trade; and sustained growth in exports raises the marginal propensity to save (MPS) in other sectors.

At least two subsequent empirical studies confirm Maizels' overall results. In 1971, Jaymin Lee used a larger sample of data (28 countries, 20 of which were developing and 8 developed) over a longer period (15 years) than Maizels' data set. Lee showed export income played a more significant role in determining savings than non-export GDP. Lee also demonstrated this result for both primary exporting countries and non-primary exporting countries. In 1982, P.S. Laumas confirmed the hypothesis that the MPS out of export income is greater than the MPS out of non-export income for primary exporting countries, though not for non-primary exporting countries.

However, like many debates in economics, empirical evidence exists on both sides of the trade — savings link. In 1989, a study by A.K. Lahiri showed no consistent, statistically significant relationship between savings and exports. The somewhat mixed results may reflect different model specifications (particularly with respect to the savings function) and different data sets (*e.g.*, the countries and time period investigated).

The reason a trade — savings link is so important is the further connection to investment. If trade stimulates savings, then it means the pool of funds available for investment in capital equipment enlarges. In turn, with more physical capital, an economy can grow more rapidly than before. In brief, trade may stimulate the rate of *per capita* income growth by positively impacting savings and, therefore, investment. As a related point, there is a broad consensus among economists that trade liberalization stimulates foreign direct investment (FDI), which in turn boosts growth.

C. Trade Liberalization and Additional Sources of Growth

Newer models of economic growth expand the list of sources of growth to include (at least) three further independent variables. These variables are endogenous, *i.e.*, explained by the model:

1. *Learning by doing*

This variable refers to experience gained by workers in the production process. Through such experience, workers accumulate technological knowledge, and thereby become more productive. This accumulation occurs along with capital accumulation. Both lead to a social pool of knowledge on which other firms in an economy can draw. Stated differently, there are "knowledge spillover effects" among firms. Such effects help firms overcome diminishing returns to capital.

2. *Human capital accumulation*

Production requires not only physical capital, but also human capital — that is, skilled workers. Such workers are more productive than unskilled workers. Workers become skilled in part by formal education, which is costly in that it requires investment (*i.e.*, allocations of capital and labor) in the education industry for the benefit of future workers, and the temporary withdrawal of current workers from the labor force. Workers with more human capital tend to accumulate human capital more easily than those with less human capital, which is to say skilled workers tend to learn more readily than unskilled workers. Human capital accumulation, like learning by doing, is related to the accumulation of physical capital, and leads to a pool of general knowledge on which all workers can draw. Also like learning by doing, increases in human capital help counteract diminishing returns to physical capital.

3. *Knowledge capital accumulation*

This variable also is called "R&D" capital, meaning research and development. R&D activity leads to technological advances, product differentiation, and improvements in the quality and sophistication of products. As with learning by doing and human capital accumulation, there are positive spillover effects, which help mitigate diminishing returns to capital equipment. There also are externalities, whereby an industry different from the one in which R&D occurred initially benefits from the R&D outcome.

These variables all affect the dependent variable, the rate of economic growth. More experienced, smarter workers, and R&D, all stimulate the rate of growth of *per capita* income. But, what is the role of international trade in contemporary growth models?

More specifically, does trade liberalization increase or decrease the rate of economic growth? There is no single answer or clear theoretical prediction. The role of trade varies, depending on the model. The channels through which trade liberalization operates may be complex. Consequently, the role of trade is a matter left for empirical testing. Overall, however, the effect of trade on learning by doing, human capital, and knowledge capital, is positive. Trade seems to boost economic growth by operating through these variables. But, the nexus is indirect, and ambiguities and trade-offs exist.

As for learning by doing, workers who gain experience in production can be more productive. Through trial-and-error, they develop techniques that increase output per labor hour. Trade liberalization can encourage, at least indirectly, this process, or create an incentive to learn on the job. Exactly how, why, and the extent to which this occurs depends on the country and sector in question.

As a related matter, trade liberalization leads to specialization. In turn, specialization leads to increased efficiency, lower costs, and higher income levels. For instance, greater efficiency can result in the production of a finished good by using specialized parts and machinery. As another illustration, a production process may be more efficient as a result of breaking that process down into several highly specialized tasks. Indeed, two forms of specialization — "product specialization" and "process specialization" — accompany trade liberalization. "Product specialization" refers to specializing parts and machinery in production. "Process specialization" refers to specializing the stages of the production process. Both kinds of specialization lead to greater efficiency in production. Moreover, specialization also results in increased innovation and product variety for consumers.

With respect to human capital, trade liberalization may increase returns to human capital by increasing the efficiency of production, and by increasing the demand for goods produced by skilled workers. Indeed, there is empirical evidence that human capital has a greater effect on *per capita* income growth in open economies than in closed economies. However, this effect may vary between rich and poor countries. In countries relatively well endowed with skilled labor, such as the U.S., trade liberalization tends to shift output toward goods that use intensively in their production skilled labor. That shift creates an incentive to accumulating human capital, and higher human capital stimulates the rate of economic growth. In countries relatively well endowed with unskilled labor, such as Bangladesh, trade liberalization tends to shift output to unskilled-labor-intensive goods. Abstracting from other forces, that shift may reduce incentives to accumulate human capital, and, in turn, the rate of growth.

Finally, international trade is connected to knowledge capital accumulation, generally appearing to spur the rate of technical innovation. Trade entails commercial contacts among countries, and firms in those countries. Such contacts involve exchanges of information about products and production processes, and of technological information itself. Through foreign direct investment (FDI), technology transfer also occurs, particularly in the context of the life cycle of a product. Under the "Product Life Cycle Hypothesis, innovations are transferred from developed to developing countries as the market for a product, in which technology is embedded, in a developed country becomes saturated and the production process becomes routine and cheap. The Austrian economist Joseph Schumpeter (1883-1950) referred to the process by which imitation and competition erodes market power, and induces new inventions, as "creative destruction." The point is that trade facilitates the creative destruction process, and possibly shortens the life cycle of some products.

At the same time, two aspects of the international trade law regime — enhanced intellectual property (IP) protection (*e.g.*, in terms of time length and geographic scope) and stronger enforcement of IP rights — may benefit certain countries at the expense of others. They may contribute growth in developed countries, yet do little for many developing and least developed countries. Moreover, while trade liberalization expands market opportunities for firms to sell their products, it also increases competition among firms. If such competition erodes the retained earnings of a company, and those earnings are the main source of R&D funding for that company, then trade may be said to have had a negative effect on the knowledge capital accumulation of that company.

In sum, contemporary growth models suggest the possibility that the dynamic effects of trade liberalization may far outweigh the static effects. They consider endogenously more determinants of *per capita* income than do classical and neoclassical models. However, the extent of the contribution of trade liberalization to increases in growth rates is not clear, nor are the precise causal mechanisms by which trade operates through variables like learning by doing, human capital, and knowledge capital. Addressing these uncertainties has practical policy implications.

For example, suppose the contribution of trade to growth, through these three variables, is weak. Then, a country might choose to emphasize increases in traditional factors of production, and non-trade measures to boost total factor productivity (TFP). In contrast, if trade manifestly and positively affects the three variables, which in turn boost the rate of growth, then the preferred policy would be free trade, along with the promotion of on-the-job training programs, support for education, and encouragement of R&D. Interestingly, part of the debate about how and why the post-Second World War "East Asian Miracle" occurred reflects these concerns.

Some economists argue this "Miracle" was nothing more than growth caused by increases in traditional factors like labor and capital, with TFP playing only a modest contributory role. East Asian countries, they urged, had not experienced rates of technological progress greater than the rates in the OECD or Latin America, and faced diminishing returns to capital, particularly insofar as labor and capital were not easily substitutable. Other economists pointed out that trade-friendly policies in most East Asian countries stimulated investment rates, staved off diminishing returns to capital, and boosted *per capita* income growth. Questions also were raised about how open to trade these countries actually had been, and whether other, non-economic factors, such as good governance and low corruption, were key ingredients in the "Miracle."

Chapter 8

QUESTIONING FREE TRADE THEORY

All economic theory involves untrue simplifying assumptions.

> —Paul Krugman, *Empirical Evidence on the New Trade Theories:
> The Current State of Play, in* NEW TRADE THEORIES: A LOOK AT THE
> EMPIRICAL EVIDENCE 12-23 (Bocconi University, Milan ed. 1994)

DOCUMENTS SUPPLEMENT ASSIGNMENT

1. *Havana Charter* Articles 1-10
2. GATT Preamble
3. WTO *Agreement* Preamble

I. DOES COMPARATIVE ADVANTAGE MAKE SENSE?

A. Questionable Assumptions

Many assumptions on which free trade theory, and in particular the Law of Comparative Advantage, rest (put politely) dubious. First, are factors of production truly homogeneous? "Of course not" is the answer. True, in groups of countries at relatively comparable developmental stages, there may be broad similarities among factors. Yet, overall, factors differ across countries. Indeed, workers seek to differentiate themselves from others in skill levels. To the extent factors are not homogeneous, the goods and services they produce may be dissimilar. (For example, is a Toyota vehicle originating in Japan, Thailand, and the U.S. identical?) Might that explain intra-industry trade?

Second, are factors of production immobile across borders? Again, the answer is "surely not." Factors of production are mobile across borders — and land can be reclaimed from the sea, as in the Netherlands and Singapore. Multinational corporations (MNCs) facilitate not only labor migration, but also movement of physical and human capital, and technology. Consequently, the Production Possibilities Frontier for a country may shift expeditiously, changing the nature of comparative advantages of that country. (For example, a net inward migration of unskilled or semi-skilled Central American workers into the U.S. might boost America's manufacturing competitiveness). Might these shifts lead to changes in the pattern of trade, *i.e.*, what a country exports and imports?

Third, how realistic is it to presume a balance of trade? On the one hand, some countries, notably the U.S., run persistent large trade imbalances. On the other hand, for many countries, exports and imports are roughly equal. Further, if an exporter receives money for merchandise shipped abroad, then it is likely the exporter will not hold those funds indefinitely. Rather, it will purchase other goods (possibly from overseas), or invest them in a financial asset.

Fourth, are transportation costs zero? Here, too, the answer is obviously "no." In fact, if they are too high in relation to the price of a good or service, then that item will not be traded. It may be cheaper to buy mangoes in India or get a haircut in China. But, given transportation costs, a consumer in Kansas would not fly to New Delhi or Beijing solely for the reputed king of fruit or chic Asian coiffure.

B. Infant Industry Protection

Among many arguments made against free trade over the centuries, one in which economists (though not all of them) are inclined to put some faith concerns infant industries. In his 1791 *Report on Manufactures*, Alexander Hamilton urged that young American industry requires protection from experienced foreign competition. The argument is an industrialized economy has advantages over a non-industrialized one that render it difficult for the less developed economy to set up sustainable industries.

For example, it is unreasonable to expect Mali or Sri Lanka simultaneously to practice free trade in information technology (IT) and spawn a computer software industry to rival Microsoft. By protecting infant industries — *i.e.*, nascent industries that poor countries seek to foster — a government gives them some time, or breathing space, to get "up to speed" and competitive. Without this time, a software start-up company in Timbuktu or Colombo would be wiped out by head-to-head competition with Microsoft. Thus, protection of an infant industry is a defensive measure. In contemporary hands, the argument has an added poignant point about hypocrisy. At various points in their history, the U.S. and other modern-day developed countries employed protection to help their infant industries. It is unfair to demand free trade now of struggling countries. Ought not they be able to protect their infant industries until maturity?

Compelling as the argument is, it is problematical. First, who decides what infants get protection, and thus an enhanced chance at life? Presumably the answer is industries in which a country likely will develop a comparative advantage. But, how is this probability appraised in advance? Are government officials good at "picking winners"?

Second, for how long will protection last? The ideal answer is "temporarily." As the philosopher John Stuart Mill said, protection should be a temporary measure to test whether a country develops a comparative advantage in a protected industry. Once that test is passed, and the industry is ready for foreign competition, the protective measures should cease. Yet, in reality, protection has a nasty way of becoming rather permanent. In part, permanence follows from dependence that mollycoddles rather than strengthens an infant. It also follows from corruption, whereby government officials are cajoled, in one form or another, into continuing the protective measures.

Third, how is infant industry protection delineated from strategic trade policy? In theory, protective measures for infants are defensive, whereas strategic trade policy is offensive. In practice, that line is easy to blur.

C. Revitalizing Ailing Domestic Industries

Another argument against the Law of Comparative Advantage is that operation of the Law might make it impossible for ailing industries to revitalize. A loss of comparative advantage in an industry may not be permanent. Perhaps protection would enable an industry to adjust to changed competitive circumstances, and flourish once again. Protective measures would give it time to compete effectively. The industry can adopt more efficient production processes, resulting in better, cheaper products.

There is an alternative scenario, too. Protection would allow for gradual contraction of an ailing industry that cannot revitalize. Without protection, there would be a chaotic collapse, which would entail massive job losses and, possibly, social unrest. As a result, the transfer of productive resources — especially labor — to other pursuits is not so jarring. In brief, protection is needed not for revitalization, but for orderly termination.

As with the infant industry argument, serious questions must be put to the revitalization argument. First, does empirical evidence support it? Generally, the answer is "no." A November 1986 Congressional Budget Office Study, *Has Trade Protection Revitalized Domestic Industries?*, assessed effects of quotas imposed to help four industries mount a comeback: automobiles, footwear, steel, and textiles and apparel. The Study showed domestic industries are not revitalized under protection. Specifically, quotas do not cause an increase in investment in the steel or textiles and apparel industries, and probably are not a factor in increased in investment in the auto industry. True, quotas led to more investment in the footwear industry. But, labor productivity did not grow sufficiently to close the huge gap in costs between U.S. and foreign shoe companies. To be fair, query whether the protection is sufficient to revitalize an affected industry.

Second, is protection the correct policy tool to revitalize a domestic industry? Arguably, cost-saving measures are needed. An industry may require better capital equipment to cut expensive labor, or to improve human capital and technology to boost production efficiency. To be sure, protection might give an industry the ability to make cost-reducing investments that it could not make with free trade because of a lack of resources. But, it could equally well create complacency in the industry. Or, protection could lead to a "moral hazard" problem whereby the industry is not careful in the selection of its investments because it has the "safety net" of tariff and non-tariff barriers.

Third, is it wise to second-guess Wall Street, *i.e.*, financial markets? If these markets function well, then allow a government to cast doubt on professional financial judgment? Private sector analysts specialize in critiquing financial performance and prospects of companies and industries, and price credit accordingly. If a firm or industry cannot afford financing under a liberalized trade regime, then is it wise to provide funds in a sheltered environment? In brief, should politicians "pick winners"? As with the infant industry argument, the revitalization argument (or its orderly contraction version) casts them in the role of choosing what lives and what suffers. Evidently, that is not a role for which most government officials have the training or temperament. Further, it invokes a debate in political philosophy about the proper role of government.

The infant industry and revitalization arguments, as well as the scenario of orderly contraction, involve a fundamental concern — the nexus between trade liberalization, on the one hand, and jobs and wages, on the other hand. Indeed, the specter of job growth and wage gains emboldens free traders every bit as much as the specter of job loss and wage declines motivates anti-free traders. The heated rhetoric is particularly evident in the context of multilateral trade negotiations, such as the Doha Round, controversial WTO rulings involving trade remedies like anti-dumping and countervailing duties, and free trade agreements. Each side hurls empirical studies — often produced by Washington, D.C.-based think tanks with ideological sympathies on one side or the other — about the effects of jobs and wages. Unfortunately, however, what is lost in the shouting are the economic theorems that address the links among trade, jobs, and wages. Those theorems, most notably, are the Factor Price Equalization Theorem and the Stopler-Samuelson Theorem.

II. MARX, LENIN, AND TRADE

A. A Powerful Critique

It is all too easy to read the term "Marxism" in a pejorative sense. It is all too easy to think Marxism is a bankrupt ideology in light of the collapse of communism virtually everywhere. (In a number of countries where communism has not yet collapsed, such as Laos and Vietnam, there is a growing "disconnect" between official state ideology and everyday reality in the marketplace. Into that gap the interests of the poor often tumble.) Just as it is bad lawyering to underestimate the opposition, it is bad scholarship to dismiss prematurely an entire paradigm that may still yield some provocative insights. As Niall Ferguson, an Oxford history professor, observes in London's *Financial Times*:

> As a prophet Marx was, of course, a washout. He was also a class traitor, taking the side of the proletariat when he himself was the quintessential 19th century bourgeois. His socialist utopia turned out to be a corrupt tyranny, which expropriated the wealth of the middle class only in order to enrich a new class of apparatchiks.
>
> *Even so, Marx's insights into capitalism can still illuminate. . . .*
>
> This may read like heresy, especially in the pages of the *Financial Times*. But a little reflection on the current crisis of capitalism will show otherwise. . . .
>
> For Marx, the defining characteristics of capitalism in his own time included "the centralization of capital," "the expropriation of the mass of the people by a few usurpers," and "the entanglement of all peoples in the net of the world-market, and with this, the international character of the capitalistic regime" [quoting chapter 32 in volume I of *Das Kapital* (1867)]. In other words, *widening inequality and globalisation*.
>
> Forget Marx's utopian prophecy that capitalism would be succeeded by socialism, with all property redistributed according to the workers'

needs. *The real point is that many of the defects he identified in 19th century capitalism are again evident today.*[1]

Indeed, many lawyers who have toiled away in multinational law firms for long hours at highly specialized and repetitive tasks, not receiving the full value of their labor input, and feeling alienated from clients, might be surprised at just how many passages from the works of Karl Marx (1818-1883) or Vladimir I. Lenin (1870-1924) correctly capture their work life. In brief, whether they are right or wrong, and whether one agrees with them or not, neither of them can be dismissed as "stupid." To the contrary, it is worth inquiring whether aspects of their critique of capitalism have enduring value.

B. Exploitation and Surplus

Do the wealthy countries talk like free traders, but at the negotiating table behave like mercantilists, with the goal of maximizing market access for their own MNCs? Never mind that investment by MNCs tends rather strongly to occur among developed countries — Africa, for example, captures less than 0.7 percent of global foreign direct investment (FDI). In the Marxist paradigm, the answer is a resolute "yes."

In 1867, Karl Marx published the first volume of *Das Kapital*. Before then, he had written about various aspects of the nature of capitalism in *Economic and Philosophical Manuscripts of 1844*. Between these two dates, he (sometimes co-authoring with Friedrich Engels) produced a large body of work in which he developed his critique. One of Marx's works that clearly and concisely expresses his ideas is *Wage Labor and Capital*. This essay began as a series of lectures Marx delivered in Brussels in December 1847, which were published in 1849.

The basic story line in Marx's classic critique of capitalism is clear enough: competition among capitalists ultimately dooms their economic system. The chain of causation, said Marx, was inevitable — historically determined, as it were. Marx urged in that process, capitalists exploit rather mercilessly not only workers in their own countries, but also workers in poor countries, and indeed the poor countries themselves. In this story line, perhaps, lie the origins of contemporary claims that the rules of international trade are adverse to the interests of poor countries.

Marx's critique of capitalism posits two key factors of production: labor and capital. "Labor," of course, refers principally to workers on a factory assembly line. "Capital" means physical capital, such as machine tools on that line. The model does not ascribe much importance to other factors, such as land or human capital. In the model, "capitalists" are the class of businessmen who own the capital, and who employ labor to work with the capital in the production of goods. The goal of capitalists — as free-market economists champion in their classical and neoclassical models — is to maximize profits. In Marxist terminology, this equates to a relentless drive for "surplus labor."

---

[1] Niall Ferguson, *Full Marx*, Financial Times, Aug. 17-18, 2002, at Weekend I (emphasis added); *see also* Leo XIII, Encyclical Letter, Rerum Novarum ("On the Condition of the Working Classes") ¶¶ 1-6 (15 May 1891).

Occasionally, Marx is rather imprecise in some of his terminology, and here we happen upon an example. He speaks of "surplus," which at least in a loose sense we can equate as conceptually the same thing as "profits" and "returns to capital." How so?

Every capitalist has to pay his workers. Likewise, every capitalist has to invest money "up front" in a machine. The capitalist wants to generate as much money over and above the wages he must pay his workers, and over and above previous investment expenditures in machines. In other words, every capitalist is motivated to maximize "profit," in the sense of the amount of money earned from selling products made by labor and capital, less the amount he must pay to workers and for the machines. Put squarely in the language of modern-day economic theory, every capitalist wants to maximize profits, which is done by maximizing gross revenues from sales, and by minimizing variable and fixed costs of production.

However, capitalists do not have much control over sales revenues. In the long run, they cannot generate higher returns to capital by raising prices. So, said Marx, there is cut-throat competition. (A renowned Marxist famously remarked that when it comes time to hang capitalism, the capitalists will compete to sell you the rope!) The point is that in their competition with one another, capitalists ineluctably over-produce. Capitalists tend to saturate — and eventually super-saturate — the markets in which they sell their goods. The inevitable result is a decline in prices for those goods.

The way out of this spiral of over-production and price declines is to expand the size of the market. But, the market in any one country is only so large (particularly in the short- and medium-term, and where population size is not growing rapidly). Capitalists seek to expand their markets by finding new ones overseas. Here, then, is where capitalists become imperialists.

The more intense the competition in their domestic markets, the more voracious their appetite to find new consumers in new markets. Indeed, they may unite on one point — entry into an unholy alliance with their governments and military to force open foreign markets. That unity breaks down when the military-industrial complexes of the great powers fight among themselves over the spoils from newly opened foreign markets.

It is precisely on this point that V.I. Lenin expounds in his 1916 classic, *Imperialism: The Highest Stage of Capitalism*.[2]

> The building of railways seems to be a simple, natural, democratic, cultural and civilizing enterprise; that is what it is in the opinion of bourgeois professors, who are paid to depict capitalist slavery in bright colors, and in the opinion of petit-bourgeois philistines. But as a matter of fact the capitalist threads, which in thousands of different inter-crossings bind these enterprises with private property in the means of production in general, have converted this work of construction into an instrument for oppressing *a thousand million* people (in the colonies and semi-colonies), that is, more than half the population

[2] V.I. LENIN, IMPERIALISM: THE HIGHEST STATE OF CAPITALISM 4-5 (Junius Publications Ltd. ed. 1996) (1916) (emphasis original).

of the globe, which inhabits the subject countries, as well as the wage slaves of capitalism in the lands of "civilization."

Private property based on the labor of the small proprietor, free competition, democracy, *i.e.*, all the catchwords with which the capitalists and their press deceive the workers and the peasants — are things of the past. Capitalism has grown into a world system of colonial oppression and of the financial strangulation of the overwhelming majority of the people of the world by a handful of "advanced" countries. And this "booty" is shared between two or three powerful world marauders armed to the teeth (America, Great Britain, Japan), who involve the whole world in *their* war [the First World War] over the sharing of *their* booty.

With a few changes in words — *e.g.*, from "building of railways" to "forging of international trade routes" — it is easy (though, again, perhaps not correct normatively) to translate Lenin's classic into a modern critique of the WTO and international trade law.

Thus, in Marxist-Leninist terms, the accession to the WTO of new Members from the Third World is all about is market access. Market access for whom? Not so much for China and other developing countries, Marx would reply, as for the hegemonic trade powers that already are in the club. China is a case in point. Even the U.S. President could not help but admit that the 15 November 1999 bilateral concession agreement between the U.S. and China was the most lopsided trade deal in history. American MNCs won nearly everything. American producers subject (or potentially subject) to competition from like or directly competitive products from China gave very little. All that was left was for China to implement its WTO commitments. As this task has proved quite controversial in some sectors of keen interest to American enterprise (*e.g.*, banking and intellectual property), the U.S. now insists in accession negotiations that would-be WTO Members actually enact and enforce their commitments before gaining accession. Examples include accession negotiations with the Kingdom of Saudi Arabia and Russia.

In any event, there remains a small conceptual leap from the concept of surplus and the need to open up markets overseas, on the one hand, and Lenin's conclusion quoted above, on the other hand. The bridge between the two sides is Marx's proposition that the capitalists' "surplus" is formed from accumulated labor.

In the Marxian paradigm, capitalists might not have much control over the cost of capital. They have to buy machines for the factory assembly lines at whatever price prevails, and eventually they must recoup that investment if they are to avoid insolvency. Thus, says Marx, the essential source of surplus (*i.e.*, profits) is labor. Specifically, he means that a capitalist's profit really is a surplus generated by accumulated labor. But, what does this proposition mean?

To maximize profit, the capitalist minimizes the one variable over which he has some control — wages. The capitalist produces more and more, and endeavors to raise the productivity of capital, through greater division of labor. Laborers work on ever-more narrow, and thus ever-less satisfying, tasks. They use machinery that enable them to produce more in a given period of time, so the scale of production expands (hence the consequences of over-production and price depression). As the workers' tasks are divided, they are by definition simplified.

Marx argues that as workers compete with one another for employment that is monotonous, wage rates in this repulsively unskilled labor market inevitably fall. The capitalist is only too eager to pay workers only subsistence wage, or as near thereto as possible. That way, the "return on capital" — another way of describing "surplus" or "profit" — is larger. (The meaning of "return on capital," or "return to capital," in the Marxian paradigm is a bit different from that in the modern-day capitalist sense. Whereas Marx was rather imprecise in this terminology, the Wall Street analyst would consider it to be the rate of return that an owner of machine earns from the funds he invested to buy that machine. In other words, it refers to the return on invested capital, which is a narrower concept than "profits.") Accordingly, from a Marxist — Leninist perspective, neither the WTO nor international trade law does enough to protect the rights of workers in developing countries.

Marx argues the source of surplus is "accumulated" labor. What does the adjective "accumulated" mean? It refers to Marx's famous labor theory of value, which the following example illustrates. Suppose a worker at IBM requires 10 hours to produce a personal computer (PC). IBM sells the computer for $2,000, a price that reflects ruthless competition in the PC market among a number of producers — IBM, Dell, Gateway, etc. Is the worker paid $2,000 (or anywhere near that amount)?

Of course not, urges Marx. Marx says that IBM will pay a wage that is the minimum amount necessary for the worker to survive — a subsistence wage. Suppose that amount is $100. It ought to be quite apparent why Marx sneers that "[t]o be a productive laborer is, therefore, not a piece of luck, but a misfortune."

So far, this analysis is all quite familiar to students of classical and neoclassical economics. The caveat to add is that Marx assumed there is a large pool of labor — a reserve army of the unemployed — that ensures (along with the division of labor) that wage rates are kept low. As soon as workers lobby for a wage increase, they will be met with the rebuttal from capitalists that there are many outside the factory gates willing to take their jobs. The machinery the capitalists employ in the production process is their ally: it dispenses with the need for muscular power, thereby expanding the pool of eligible workers to include weaker men, plus women and children.

To be sure, there might be an excess demand for workers, based on labor shortages. Marx would reply that such a situation would not endure, that sooner or later, the capitalist business cycle would turn. The tendency of capitalists to over-produce when in competition with one another might lead them, at some point, to cut back temporarily on production. In turn, they would lay off workers, and the redundant workers would staff the reserve army of the unemployed.

At this point, Marx's argument takes a U-turn. He re-visits the production process, and posits that the PC (in my example) embodies 10 hours of labor.

That is, the value of the PC is based on the 10 hours of labor. Yes, that value also reflects other factors of production — capital and land, for example. But, Marx dwells on the labor input, hence the name for his theory of the valuation of goods — the labor theory of value. Moreover, the surplus (*i.e.*, profit) of capitalists is derived from the deliberate failure of the capitalists to return to the worker all 10 hours of value that are embodied in the PC. In the example, the worker toiled for 10 hours, but received only $100. For Marx, that $100 is not anywhere near the full labor value embodied in the product. It might translate into, say, 4 hours worth of work, assuming a subsistence wage of $25 per hour (and assuming the worker were paid the time value of his labor). In other words, the capitalist obtained a surplus from the worker of 6 hours.

Here, then, is the explanation for the statement that the surplus generated by capitalists is "accumulated" labor. For every PC IBM sells, it accumulates 6 hours of labor in the sense that it does not return this portion of the value of the product to the worker who made it. The repeated phenomenon of paying workers less than the labor value embodied in their work is accumulated surplus. As Marx writes in *Das Kapital*,

> The value of a commodity is, in itself, of no interest to the capitalist. What alone interests him, is the surplus-value that dwells in it, and is realizable by sale. . . .
>
> The shortening of the working-day is, therefore, by no means what is aimed at, in capitalist production, when labor is economized by increasing its productiveness. It is only the shortening of the labor-time, necessary for the production of a definite quantity of commodities, that is aimed at. The fact that the workman, when the productiveness of his labor has been increased, produces, say 10 times as many commodities as before, and thus spends one-tenth as much labor-time on each, by no means prevents him from continuing to work 12 hours as before, nor from producing in those 12 hours 1,200 articles instead of 120. Nay, more, his working-day may be prolonged at the same time, so as to make him produce, say 1,400 articles in 14 hours. . . . The object of all development of the productiveness of labor, within the limits of capitalist production, is to shorten that part of the working-day, during which the workman must labor for his own benefit, and by that very shortening, to lengthen the other part of the day, during which he is at liberty to work gratis for the capitalist. . . .
>
> . . . .
>
> The directing motive, the end and aim of capitalist production, is to extract the greatest possible amount of surplus-value, and consequently to exploit labor-power to the greatest possible extent.[3]

It is this fact, urges Marx, that makes capitalism inherently exploitative. The conditions in which this fact is manifest alienate the worker from the fruits of his labor. Simply changing a few words in the above-quoted package would suffice to make it appear to be a contemporary attack on global

---

[3] KARL MARX, DAS KAPITAL, *in* THE MARX-ENGELS READER 383-85 (Robert C. Tucker ed., 2nd ed. 1978)

production and trade, the evils of which are felt by workers in poor countries, yet which are effectively protected in good measure (so the claim goes) by the WTO and its rules.

Marx takes the point one step further, saying capital itself is accumulated surplus. His point is capitalists may re-invest the accumulated surplus generated by the difference between the labor value of a product (in the above example, 10 hours), on the one hand, and the return to labor (in the above example, 4 hours), on the other hand. Specifically, they re-invest in physical capital, buying more machines and building more assembly lines. In fact, capitalists need to re-invest the surplus in order to expand production, and thereby become larger and stronger in their competition with one another. Hence, for Marx, the source of not only profit, but also of capital, is accumulated surplus from labor.

C. The Search for New Markets

What does the Marxist-Leninist argument have to do with trade in the modern-day multilateral trading system, and how is it the starting point for the now-fashionable proposition that developed countries block full and fair participation in this system? The answer is Marx and Lenin offer three key points about international trade that remain relevant to the present day.

First, in their never-ending efforts to maximize surplus in the face of intense competition in exhausted domestic markets, capitalists inevitably look for new markets overseas. Marx makes this point in various works, including *The German Ideology*:

> With the advent of manufacture the various nations entered into competitive relations, a commercial struggle, which was fought out in wars, protective duties and prohibitions, whereas earlier the nations, insofar as they were connected at all, had carried on an inoffensive exchange with each other. Trade had from now on a political significance.
>
> . . . .
>
> In spite of these protective measures large-scale industry universalized competition . . ., established means of communication and the modern world market, [and] subordinated trade to itself. . . . By universal competition it forced all individuals to strain their energy to the utmost. It destroyed as far as possible ideology, religion, morality, etc., and, where it could not do this, made them into a palpable lie. It produced world history for the first time, insofar as it made all civilized nations and every individual member of them dependent for the satisfaction of their wants on the whole world, thus destroying the former natural exclusiveness of separate nations.[4]

It seems quite apparent that Mr. Marx is commenting on globalisation and its pernicious effects long before the critics of the WTO and international trade law.

---

[4] THE GERMAN IDEOLOGY, *in* THE MARX-ENGELS READER, *supra* note 3, at 77, 81.

In the 18th, 19th, and early 20th centuries, the search for new markets led to overt colonialism. The expression "trade followed the flag" meant that a colonial power could open up new trading markets by sending in its navy first. In fact, Lawrence James' examination of colonial history suggests that the opposite actually occurred in many instances — the flag followed trade in order to secure and reinforce trade routes that merchants had pioneered. Even Marx suggested the possibility of a few salutary effects, however unintended they may have been, of British colonialism in India, namely, the destruction of the age-old and oppressive village system that was the foundation of Oriental despotism. But, these debates are for another time and place.

In the late 20th and early 21st centuries, it is not uncommon to hear it said that businesses from developed countries are the new agents of colonialism, and international trade law is written to serve MNC interests. Critics point out that the bargaining power to open up new markets is asymmetric. That is, except where a developing country is large and powerful — Brazil, China, Mexico, or India, for instance — corporations (or their official representatives, such as the United States Trade Representative (USTR)) are largely able to dictate terms of market access.

D. Extracting Surplus

The second key point in the Marxist-Leninist trade argument relates to labor surplus. As capitalists open new markets overseas, they also locate production facilities their, especially in colonies or former colonies — FDI, in modern parlance). After all, why not make goods in these Third World countries, in which labor costs are relatively lower than in home countries of major corporations? Then, returns to labor are minimized, and profits maximized. In so doing, capitalists extract surplus from Third World laborers — a colonial, or neo-colonial, surplus.

This extractive process, Marx argued, is inherently exploitative. Developing countries need the surplus to re-invest in their own economies (e.g., in new production facilities). Precisely because they are poor countries, they lack a large endowment of resources to use as a basis for industrialization. Draining what surplus they do have from their workers makes their growth process all the more difficult.

Unfortunately for the poor countries, the principal source of investment comes from abroad — FDI. The FDI generates accumulated surpluses that MNCs repatriate to the bank accounts of capitalists that run these firms from plush offices in developed countries. (From time to time, workers in the home countries of MNCs tire of their exploitation, and threaten industrial action. Then, the capitalists can take some of the labor surplus extracted from developing countries, and use it to increase the wages of the restless workers. Of course, the increase would be the minimum amount necessary to stave off the threatened action.) The result is a continued, indeed ever-growing, gap between rich and poor countries:

> Of the former European colonies, many have experienced some development, but only a tiny handful have joined the developed world. A considerable number in Africa have experienced not progress but

catastrophic decline, with steep falls in living standards and services, and in some cases the complete collapse of the state.

. . . .

Latin America is a particularly striking example of the triumph of hope over experience. Several states have achieved very real progress, and are of course vastly richer than they were a century ago. But very few indeed have achieved western standards of living and levels of democracy. Argentina was probably closer to such a breakthrough a century ago than it is today. . . .

Objectively, the centres of successful capitalism remain today what they were 100 years ago: western Europe, its overseas white colonies and its immediate European periphery; and Japan. Since 1945, to this group have been added two former Japanese colonies already developed under Japanese rule — South Korea and Taiwan — and a handful of international *entrepôts* such as Singapore.[5]

Contemporary critics of the multilateral trading system would add simply WTO rules — such as the WTO *Agreement on Trade Related Investment Measures (TRIMs)* — actually protect (or reinforce) this exploitative process.

E.   Unholy Alliances

The third key insight into world trade offered by Marx and Lenin concerns the relationship between politics and economics in both rich and poor countries. As the argument goes, capitalists advocate free trade policies vis-à-vis developing countries. They push for open markets overseas as an outlet, or vent, for their excess production. Simultaneously, they lobby their governments for protection from foreign imports, so as to avoid exacerbating competitive pressures in domestic markets. Here is a double standard that amounts not to pure free trade, but rather mercantilism in new garments.

Worse yet, there is nothing in the logic of capitalism to put an end to the hypocrisy. Marx and his adherents observed the declining rates of return to capital in developed country markets, caused by over-production and ferocious competition, coupled with cheap labor overseas, mandate a push to pry open Third World markets. Yet, independent of this mandate is another: natural resources. Some Third World countries have minerals and raw materials to fuel the engines of capitalist production.

Accordingly, so goes the Marxist critique, capitalists push to secure these sources of supply for their factories. For the Third World country, the result is over-investment in its natural resource sector. Rather than focus on giving birth to, and nurturing, infant industries, the country is "encouraged" by MNCs and their governments to pursue a free trade policy that allows foreigners to invest in this sector, and assures them of a steady source of supply from it. Depending on the geographic location and political structure of a particular Third World country, it may be impossible to safeguard these sources and trade routes without military help. Hence, now as in the avowedly colonial era of the past, an unholy military — industrial alliance is established.

---

[5] Anatol Lieven, *The Road to Riches Discredited*, FINANCIAL TIMES, 12 Aug. 2002, at 11.

A particularly intriguing feature of this alliance is identified by a formerly famous development economist of the mid-20th century — Paul Baran. In his 1957 classic, *The Political Economy of Growth*, Baran inquires why workers in developed countries generally decline to unite with their cohorts in less developed countries, and why they tend not to protest against the exploitation by a military-industrial complex. Baran's argument is workers in a developed country often benefit from the alliance.

Suppose the supply of natural resources from developed countries were restricted or cut off, and re-directed to infant industries in the Third World. Would the developed country workers be better off? Hardly, says Baran. They would lose their jobs, because absent this supply of natural resources, which were essential inputs in the goods they made, their factories would have no option but to close down. The most obvious example of the clash of interests was between workers in defense industries in developed countries, on the one hand, and workers in emerging industries in the Third World, on the other hand. It was no small clash, given the economic importance and political prominence of defense and defense-related industries in developed countries.

In sum, the third link is this: developed countries hamper integration of developing countries into the multilateral trading system by nearly dictating free trade policies to them, yet limiting their access to developed country markets. They are unable to grow into robust players, because the playing field is not level. They cannot protect their infant industries. Their agricultural and industrial sectors are exposed to stiff foreign competition in their own domestic markets, and they have few overseas opportunities. Even small producers and local industries — from handicrafts to textiles — are destroyed.

Worse yet, goes the Marxist-influenced argument, in some developing countries the power elite (rulers and their families, the land-owning aristocracy, and well-connected businessmen) connive with foreign powers against the interests of the poor. This elite class enjoys luxury items made and exported by foreign MNCs. Cars and washing machines are examples. Members of the elite class also are quite happy to see the MNCs produce luxury goods locally, which they could afford.

Thus, wrote the renowned Brazilian development economist, Celso Furtado, serious income inequality within a Third World country can, and does, lead to an alignment of interests between local elites and foreign capitalists. Why would these elites advocate a more level playing field for multilateral trade, if that would entail (1) limiting luxury good imports (in order to preserve precious foreign exchange reserves for imports essential to the poor, or to emerging industries), (2) a re-orientation of domestic production away from luxury goods consumed by local elites and toward basic goods in which there was a broader societal interest, and (3) maybe even formal income redistribution? Conversely, why would foreign capitalists seek radical change, when (1) they profit from exporting luxury items to a power elite in developing countries, and (2) their own home markets spilling over with excess production? To the contrary, the local power elite and foreign capitalists have every incentive to maintain extant trade patterns.

Not surprisingly, therefore, after winning independence from their former colonial masters, and particularly after the Second World War when a number of development theories arose that condoned one form or another of protection-ism to assist in the growth process, many Third World countries turned inward. China's and India's socialist policies (different in nature and severity, to be sure), and much of Latin America's import substitution policies, are examples. Some theories were rather pessimistic about the possibility of ever achieving a level playing field within a capitalist paradigm. They called for a restructuring of economic and social relationships, along non-capitalist lines, and these calls found outlets in various United Nations declarations.

III. STRATEGIC TRADE POLICY AND MANAGED TRADE

Arguably, neither free trade nor protectionism best explains reality. Rather, strategic trade policy and managed trade do.[6] Neither extreme, in the pure economic sense, exists. All trade occurs pursuant to some government strategy or management. Most governments try to manage trade in certain strategic or sensitive sectors.

"Strategic trade policy" is the creation through government intervention of competitive advantages for companies in which economies of scale can be realized. An "economy of scale" may be internal or external. An "internal" economy of scale means the reduction of costs per unit as output of a firm rises. It occurs via R&D, the fruits of which increase efficiency, and sheds wastage, in production. In turn, internal economies of scale can lead to an imperfectly competitive market, *i.e.*, a monopoly or oligopoly. An "external" economy of scale is where costs per unit of production depend not on the size of a company, but on that of an industry. It explains why many companies in the same industry locate near one another (*e.g.*, clusters of life sciences companies in Kansas City).

The focus of strategic trade policy is what a government can do to boost internal economies of scale in an industry. The idea is one government (*e.g.*, the EU) must act, because if it does not then another government (*e.g.*, China) will act. Because internal economies of scale may yield a monopoly or oligopoly position, once a foreign industry is at that commanding height, it is hard for domestic firms, much less new entrants, to compete. (With monopolistic competition, product differentiation may be the key to entry.) In sum, strategic trade policy is limited government industrial policy.

What is the distinction between the two concepts — between strategic trade policy and managed trade? There are common points. Both presume interna-tional trade is a zero-sum game. Both presume a consensus can be reached on the industries that a government ought to support. Both are "offensive" policies designed to stimulate an industry, not defensive policies to protect or revitalize a declining one.

However, strategic trade policy uses subsidies, rather than tariffs or quotas. Being unilateral, it does not entail, or require, trade negotiations with foreign governments. Manifestly, through government intervention to support a chosen industry, it is an activist approach. Managed trade focuses on bilateral

---

[6] *See* PAUL KRUGMAN, THE AGE OF DIMINISHED EXPECTATIONS 110-12 (1990); Peter A.G. Van Bergeijk & Dick L. Kabel, *Strategic Trade Theories and Trade Policies*, 27 J. OF WORLD TRADE 176-77, 180-85 (1993).

negotiations with foreign governments to achieve market access commitments. It is a dance between two countries to regulate trade for the mutual benefit of favored industries. Numerical targets or expectations are set. That intervention aside, the government does not directly support an industry.

Are these policies sound? The answer depends on who is asked. Likewise, whether strategic trade policy works depends on who is consulted. A sizeable body of evidence points to limited effects, even in sectors a consensus agrees are strategic. Examples include commercial aircraft, semiconductors, and telecommunications equipment. Even if it "works," there is a threshold problem of who decides what industries are "strategic." There also is a risk of error in identifying "strategic" industries. That judgment presumes an uncanny ability to prognosticate future national security needs. Even if these problems are met, strategic trade policy in one country can be met with retaliation by others, thereby eroding the multilateral trading system.

Chapter 9

TRADE PATTERNS AND FACTORS OF PRODUCTION

It won't help this country however much we bang our heads on the ground. All we know is how to scream, pray, and fight. But the prayers are worth nothing if we don't work. We can't just sit and wait for God's mercy.

> —ÅSNE SEIERSTAD, THE BOOKSELLER OF KABUL 45
> (Ingrid Christophersen trans., 2003)

DOCUMENTS SUPPLEMENT ASSIGNMENT

1. *Havana Charter* Articles 1-10
2. GATT Preamble
3. WTO *Agreement* Preamble

I. THE TERMS OF TRADE

A. The Net Barter TOT

Does participation in the international trading system help or hinder a country's economic growth? One statistic often examined is the "Terms of Trade" (TOT). Economists define TOT as the ratio of export to import prices. That is,

$$\text{TOT} = \frac{\text{Index of prices of merchandise exported by a country}}{\text{Index of prices of merchandise imported by a country}}$$

$$= \frac{P_{EX}}{P_{IM}}$$

The TOT measures the purchasing power of a country, in the sense of how much it can buy (import) from what it sells (exports). Thus, the TOT as defined above also are known as the "net barter terms of trade."

The TOT of a country are "unfavorable" or "deteriorating" if prices of imported merchandise rise, prices of exported merchandise fall, or both. The intuition is readily apparent. Import prices are akin to expenditures, and export prices are akin to revenue, whether of a household or firm. High or rising expenses, low or falling revenues, or both can imperil a family or business. So, too, it is for a country. One ill effect of unfavorable TOT is a decline in the share of world trade accounted for by a country.

Advocates of Export Orientation policy argue the TOT of a country rise through trade. In contrast, advocates of Import Substitution, being export pessimists, point out instances in which increased trade led to deteriorating

TOT of a country. Notwithstanding this policy debate, TOT are a useful tool to explore the effects of trade on an economy.

B. The Income TOT

Economists sometimes rely on a statistic known as the "Income TOT," which is closely related to the Net Barter TOT. The arithmetic formula for Income TOT is:

$$\frac{P_{EX} \times Q_{EX}}{P_{IM}}$$

where Q_{EX} is the quantity of goods exported, hence the numerator represents export revenues (the price of exports multiplied by the volume of those exports). Studying Income TOT is it reveals export revenues generated by a country, which the country can use to pay for imports. That is, it gives a more direct sense than Net Barter TOT of what a country earns from trade and, thereby, what it can afford to spend.

II. THE PATTERN OF TRADE

Classical and contemporary arguments for free trade, while often put to the test empirically, are grand in scope. They ask whether trade liberalization is a "good thing" in a general sense. The logic is deductive: reasoning from general principles, arguments are built. But, economists are (for the most part) a savvy lot. They appreciate the importance of inductive logic, of reasoning from the specific to the general. Ask the proverbial "average person in the street" whether free trade is a good thing, mostly the responses hinge on that person's perception of how free trade affects her. Thus, economists spend a good deal of time considering the effects of free trade on a variety of variables — patterns, infant industries, labor, the environment, and even national security and sovereignty. The expectation (or, at least, hope) a few generalizations about free trade can be drawn from these effects. Of course, the reality is these studies hardly resolve the issue. Rather, the debate between free-traders and protectionists continues as an epic intellectual struggle.

If trade liberalization occurs, what is the effect on the patterns of trade? Put differently, what determines whether a country imports or exports a particular product? The traditional answer is based on Ricardo's law of comparative advantage. If a country has a comparative advantage, in terms of cost, in producing a good, then it will export that good. If not, then it will import the good. Yet, this answer fails to account for shifts in an endowment of factors of production. There are changes in land (e.g., through land reclamation, desertification, or soil erosion), labor (e.g., through population growth or immigration), physical capital (e.g., through investment), human capital (e.g., through education), and technology (e.g., through research and development).

A. The Heckscher-Ohlin Theorem

In the 1930s, the Swedish economists Eli Heckscher and Bertil Ohlin attempted to rectify this defect in the classical model and devised what is known as the Heckscher-Ohlin Theorem. It is set forth in Ohlin's 1935 classic, *Interregional and International Trade*. (Ohlin was awarded the 1977 Nobel Prize in Economics.) Heckscher and Ohlin agreed with Ricardo; international trade is based on differences in comparative costs. But, they sought to uncover the reasons for cost differentials — a point Ricardo largely ignored.

Their answer? Factor endowments. Heckscher and Ohlin predicted international trade is based on — indeed, caused by — differences in factor abundance across countries. Thus, for example, a country would export labor-intensive goods if it has an abundance of labor. (By "intensity," economists mean a higher proportion of labor than of capital will be used in production. This definition depends on the ratio of factors used in production, not on the ratio of the overall availability of factors. Of course, the Theorem links the two ratios.) In contrast, a country relatively better endowed with land will specialize in the production and export of primary products.

Why? Differences in relative factor endowments mean differences in comparative production costs, the focus of Ricardo's attention. A labor-abundant country can produce labor-intensive goods cheaply, and a land-abundant country can produce land-intensive goods cheaply. Think China and Canada, respectively, to see the importance of plentiful versus scarce factors for the price of goods that use intensively in their production those factors and, in turn, on pattern of inter-industry trade.

To reach their result, Heckscher and Ohlin needed to make several simplifying assumptions, two of which were particularly critical. First, countries differ in their factor endowments. Some countries have plenty of labor (*e.g.*, China and India), some have an abundance of land (*e.g.*, Australia, Canada, and Russia). Others have a surplus of capital (*e.g.*, Japan and the U.S.). Still others concentrate on human capital (*e.g.*, Singapore) and technology (*e.g.*, Germany, United Arab Emirates).

Second, production functions for different goods make use of factors of production in different proportions. (A production function is a microeconomic mathematical relationship between factors of production, which are the independent variables, and output of a particular product, which is the dependent variable. There is a coefficient associated with each independent variable that represents the importance of its contribution in the production process.) For example, more labor is used in the production of Persian carpets than in growing wheat, but more land is used in harvesting wheat than weaving carpets. However, third, Heckscher and Ohlin assumed that for any particular good (*e.g.*, carpets or wheat), the production function was the same in every country in which that good was produced. Thus, the production function for Persian carpets was the same in Iran, Turkey, and Pakistan, and the production function for wheat was the same in the U.S., Canada, and Australia. Another way to put this assumption is that each country has the same production technology for a particular good.

Despite mixed empirical evidence for the Heckscher-Ohlin Theorem, it remains a celebrated predictive tool for the effects of trade liberalization on trade patterns. For good reason. It is logically compelling, *i.e.*, it makes good common sense. Stated succinctly, the Theorem posits a country will specialize in the export of goods whose production uses intensively the factors with which the country is relatively well endowed. The country will import those goods that use intensively in their production the factors with which the country is not relatively well endowed. Professor Melvin Krauss puts it nicely:

> The fundamental idea is that, both for the world as a whole and its constituent nations, it is more efficient for each country to concentrate on the commodity that uses its relatively abundant factor intensively in its production and to import the other good than for each country to attempt to produce large amounts of both goods. The labor-abundant country should concentrate its production on the labor-intensive good and import the land-intensive good, and vice versa for the land-abundant country. In other words, the gains from international trade result from the correct matching of land-intensive and labor-intensive production technologies of goods with different factor supply or endowment ratios between countries.[1]

To follow up on Professor Krauss' rendition, assume the U.S. has relatively more physical capital than China, while China has relatively more labor than the U.S. The Heckscher-Ohlin Theorem predicts the U.S. will export capital-intensive goods to China, and China will export labor-intensive goods to the U.S. Sometimes, the Theorem is called the "Factor Proportions Theory." The logic of that appellation now is clear: the Theorem emphasizes the interplay of (1) proportions of different factors of production in each country, and (2) proportions in which each factor is used to make different goods.

As intimated earlier, the intuitive reasoning behind this prediction is simple and harkens back to Ricardo. Differences in the relative prices of goods are the consequence of differences in relative factor endowments. In a capital-abundant country, capital will be relatively cheaper than labor, and in a labor-rich country, labor will be relatively cheaper than capital. Because capital is cheaper than labor in the capital-abundant country, that country can produce a capital-intensive good more cheaply than the labor-rich country. Thus, because the U.S. has an abundance of capital relative to China, it can produce capital-intensive goods more cheaply than China. With trade liberalization, the U.S. will do so, and export them to China. As for China, because it is better endowed with labor than the U.S., China can make labor-intensive goods more cheaply than the U.S. Trade liberalization will cause China to do just that, and export these goods to the U.S. in return for capital-intensive goods made in America.

Or, consider the U.S. and Japan. Obviously, the U.S. has far more agricultural land available than Japan. (Roughly 60-70 percent of Japan is mountainous or otherwise not arable.) If free trade in agricultural products were to exist between the two countries, the Heckscher-Ohlin Theorem would predict America would be a net exporter of fruits, vegetables, and meats to Japan. What would the Japanese export in return, assuming free market access? Herein lies a small knot in the Theorem. Both countries are well endowed with labor, physical capital, human capital, and technology. The Theorem would appear to predict two-way trade in goods that use intensively in their production these factors. Japan would, therefore, export manufactured and

---

[1] MELVIN KRAUSS, THE NEW PROTECTIONISM 5 (1978).

high-tech goods to the U.S., but so too would the U.S. to Japan. It is difficult to say, however, precisely which manufactured or high-tech goods would be traded in which direction.

B. The Leontief Paradox and Empirical Tests of the Heckscher-Ohlin Theorem

Unfortunately, empirical tests of the Heckscher-Ohlin Theorem have not always lent solid support. In 1953, Russian-born economist Wassily Leontief used input-output analysis to test the Theorem. In this methodology, an input-output table is constructed that details the sales of every industry to all other industries in an economy. The result is a giant spreadsheet of rows and columns, or, in mathematical terms, of linear algebraic equations. Communist planners used such tables to develop central plans. Professor Leontief developed the methodology (which won him the 1973 Nobel Prize). Using data from 200 American industries for the year 1947, Professor Leontief came to the conclusion America exported labor-intensive goods and imported capital-intensive goods.

The conclusion was startling. The U.S. in 1947 was capital abundant. Thus, the Heckscher-Ohlin Theorem would predict America's export industries would be capital-intensive, and its import-competing industries would be labor intensive. Fittingly, the conclusion is memorialized as the "Leontief Paradox."

Some economists suggest the test was the most famous one in the history of economic thought, and the findings were among the most puzzling and troubling ever produced by an economist. Economists had thought they had the explanation for trade patterns in the Heckscher-Ohlin Theorem, and since its development in the early 1930s, the Theorem had become one of the most revered general equilibrium theory in all of economics. Now, it appeared the Theorem could not even explain the ostensibly clear case of the U.S. To make matters worse, when Professor Leontief repeated his test with data from 1951, the Paradox remained. Professor Robert Baldwin looked at data for 1962, and again found the Paradox. Leontief-like tests for Japan using data from the 1950s, Canada, and India all showed the Paradox.

Even Professor Leontief was worried. He tried immediately to resurrect the Heckscher-Ohlin Theorem. He suggested the importance of American labor was understated in his model because U.S. workers are three times as productive as foreign workers. If their superior productivity was included in the calculation — *i.e.*, if each unit of labor were multiplied by three — then the U.S. would come out as a labor-abundant country. The pattern of labor-intensive exports would be consistent with the Theorem.

It was a nice try. But, the sad truth is the productivity of American workers is not as superior as Professor Leontief would have it. Possibly, Professor Leontief did not include natural resources or human capital in his calculations. Indeed, in accounting for these missing factors, studies by two economists, Jaroslav Vanek and Donald Keesing, are particularly renowned. In 1959, Professor Vanek called attention to the importance of non-agricultural land — *i.e.*, raw materials — in American imports. He argued physical capital and land are complementary factors with respect to the production of raw materials. (As a simple example, coal mining is made possible by both land and proper equipment.) Professor Leontief had urged America's import-competing industries were capital-intensive. But, because his model posited two factors of production — physical capital and labor — it was unrealistic. Maybe there was more than just "capital" in his capital factor. Maybe a third factor, non-agricultural land, was embedded in it as well. That is, Professor Vanek suggested the apparent importance of capital-intensive output in America's import-competing industries might reflect the land-intensive nature of that production. Professor Leontief had too simplistic a model, and had not sufficiently dis-aggregated the data, to capture this effect.

In 1966, Professor Donald Keesing argued it is misleading to treat labor as a single factor. Professor Keesing's analysis of the Leontief Paradox is similar to that of Professor Vanek, but concerns a different variable. Whereas Professor Vanek focused on capital, Professor Keesing focused on labor, but both said the Paradox resulted from an all-too-simple model with insufficiently dis-aggregated data. Professor Keesing divided the American labor force according to skill levels, and found that export production is more skill-intensive than import-competing production. Accordingly, the U.S. should be seen as a skill — *i.e.*, human-capital, abundant country. When Professor Keesing examined the data in this way, the Paradox was reversed: the U.S. exported capital-intensive goods.

Whatever the reason for the Paradox, it has not spelled the end for the Heckscher-Ohlin Theorem. That Theorem renders a fairly accurate account for some inter-industry trade among less developed countries (LDCs). It also is correct in respect of the pattern of trade in manufactured goods between developed countries, on the one hand, and newly industrialized countries (NICs) and LDCs, on the other hand. For instance, the U.S. tends to export skill-intensive products to Thailand, a NIC, which tends to export low-value added products to the U.S. In comparison with Thailand, the U.S. is relatively well-endowed with skilled labor, so this pattern of trade is consistent with the Theorem. Of course, trade between developed and developing countries accounts for a small (albeit growing) percentage of world trade, thus resurrecting the Theorem solely on the basis of this trade is not sufficient.

What about the mixed empirical results? Perhaps some can be explained. Consider the test for Japan using data from the 1950s. At that time, Japan was labor abundant, yet the test showed Japan to be exporting capital-intensive goods and importing labor-intensive goods. But, on closer inspection, Japan was capital-intensive relative to many of its trading partners, especially those in Asia. Likewise, the test for Indian exports to the U.S. showed them to be more capital-intensive than Indian imports from the U.S. Yet, the same test also showed that, overall, Indian exports tended to be labor-intensive — a conclusion clearly consistent with the Heckscher-Ohlin Theorem.

What about Leontief's original test for the pattern of American exports? In his 1984 book *Sources of International Comparative Advantage: Theory and Evidence*, Edward E. Leamer argued Leontief had taken an insufficiently comprehensive view of America's factor endowments. Professor Leamer argued the Heckscher-Ohlin Theorem cannot be tested on a country-by-country basis, nor will it do to guess about the position of a particular country. Rather, it is necessary to examine many countries simultaneously, and actually measure their relative factor endowments. Professor Leamer reasoned that it would be right to call the U.S. capital rich only if it has a larger share of the world's capital stock than of other factors of production. Therefore, he collected data on a large number of countries, examining each country's factor endowments in comparison with the world stock of those factors. While his results are complex, among them is a finding that countries with large shares of the world's capital stock tend to be net exporters of capital-intensive goods (as long as statistical adjustments are made for the relative abundance in those countries of natural resources and skilled labor).

What is the bottom line? The most appropriate view of the Heckscher-Ohlin Theorem probably is a balanced one: use it with care and realize its limitations. It remains the — or, at least, one of the — most logically tight economic explanations of trade patterns. Yet, the Leontief Paradox nags. Moreover, the Theorem fails to explain or predict much of the intra-industry trade (such as the exchange of manufactured goods for other manufactured goods) among industrialized countries. Contemporary trade relations in the U.S. — Japan are a case in point.

Most importantly, the bottom line is the Heckscher-Ohlin is a starting point, not the finishing line, for explanations of the effect of free trade on the patterns of trade. Economists are seeking ways to re-cast the Heckscher-Ohlin Theorem. In particular, they are dropping the grossly simplifying assumption of the Theorem that each country uses the same production technology. Economists know that with a given set of inputs, some countries can produce more output than others. The different outcomes are a result of "factor augmentation" — factors like labor are helped in some countries by better technology, whereas other countries lack that technology. The result is one American worker may be worth five Portuguese workers, and eight Bangladeshi workers, in terms of output per labor-hour, simply because the American worker has access to state-of-the-art technology. (Imagine writing a research paper without a computer to underscore the point.) Much empirical testing has yet to be done along these lines. So far, when economists examine differences in factor endowments without assuming identical technologies, but instead adjusting for factor augmentation, they seem to account quite accurately for the observed pattern of world trade.

C. The Theory of Monopolistic Competition

The mixed — some might say disappointing — empirical results from tests of the Heckscher-Ohlin Theorem catalyzed a search for alternative explanations of trade patterns. In fact, one such explanation pre-dates the Theorem. Recall the Heckscher-Ohlin Theorem cannot account for intra-industry trade, that is, trade in the same item between two countries. Such trade has expanded rapidly since the Second World War. Why, for example, do the U.S. and Europe export automobiles to each other? One explanation might be differentiated consumer preferences. Many Americans prefer imported cars. They perceive the imports to be of superior quality, and they have a snob appeal to boot. The English economist, Edward H. Chamberlin, offered a second reason — monopolistic competition — in the early 20th century.

The neoclassical theory of perfect competition relies on the assumption competing firms produce identical products that may be substituted for one another. In his classic book, *The Theory of Monopolistic Competition: A Reorientation of the Theory of Value*, Chamberlin points out this assumption is sheer folly. In reality, firms compete by attempting to differentiate their products. Through product differentiation, firms gain monopoly power, and imperfect or "monopolistic" competition results. For instance, the cars America imports from Europe are different from those it exports to Europe.

Finally, the Heckscher-Ohlin Theorem says nothing about two other post-Second World War phenomena: intra-firm and inter-firm trade. The former refers to trade within different constituent parts of a single multinational corporation. The latter concerns trade within several firms cooperating in a joint venture or sub-contracting relationship. To explain such trade, it is necessary to study the rise of multinational oligopolies, as well as the globalization of production through FDI.

D.   The Product Life Cycle Hypothesis

A business school theory of international trade patterns that seems to accord more accurately with reality than the Heckscher-Ohlin Theorem is the Product Life Cycle Hypothesis. Professor Raymond Vernon put it forth in 1966. The U.S. (and other developed countries) often change from being a net exporter to a net importer of a particular good when production of that good becomes standardized. Radios, televisions, video cassette recorders (VCRs), and semi-conductors are examples of this phenomenon. How does this transformation occur? Professor Vernon studied the process by which a product is invented, and subsequently becomes standardized as consumers and producers alike become acquainted with the features of the product.

A technologically advanced product is introduced first by a company (or companies) in the U.S. primarily for domestic consumption. In this early stage of product development and marketing, it is important for the producer to be close to the market in order to receive feedback about the product from consumers, and make necessary modifications to the product based on this feedback. The market niche may consist of relatively high-income consumers. The producer is concerned more with perfecting the product than profits, market share, or export opportunities.

Soon, however, product development stabilizes, and production costs correspondingly level off or even decline owing to economies of scale. Accordingly, the product is mass-marketed, and profitable export opportunities are investigated and seized. In particular, consumers in NICs and LDCs develop a taste for the product as a result of marketing efforts made by the American producer. Soon the product is exported from the U.S. to meet burgeoning demand in these countries — assuming, of course, there are no barriers to trade in that product market. At this early juncture in the life cycle, the country in which the product is invented — here, the U.S. — has the comparative advantage in making and exporting it.

However, as time passes, the product and production technology become even more standardized and labor intensive. Companies in highly populated

NICs and LDCs realize they can make the same or a similar product more cheaply than the American producer — in part because of relatively lower wage levels in those countries — and they begin to do so. Hence, the American producer becomes less successful in competing with these low-cost foreign producers. Alternatively, the American producer may decide to close production facilities in the U.S. and open them in the low-wage countries. Plainly, the comparative advantage starts shifting to these countries.

As a result, producers in NICs and LDCs mass produce the product. They market it not only to domestic consumers, but also to consumers in developed countries such as the U.S. Eventually, again assuming no trade barriers, the U.S. becomes a net importer of the good. The shift from net exporter to net importer status often is accompanied by a transfer of production technology from the American producer to producers in the NICs and LDCs. At this point, the product has gone through its complete life cycle, and comparative advantage has shifted completely. The American producer must invent a new product, or develop a significant variation of the mature product, to remain competitive. Accordingly, a critical concern of the American producer is sure to be its ability to protect its intellectual property rights.

Three points are worth noting about the Product Life Cycle Hypothesis. First, its applicability is limited to trade in the manufacturing sector, or more accurately, in certain types of products. There must be a degree of technical sophistication — invention, followed by design, followed by development — in the product for it to have a life cycle.

Second, the Hypothesis does not explain trade patterns in all sophisticated products. The U.S. has not surrendered its comparative advantage in advanced products like aircraft, medical instruments, and some computer equipment and pharmaceuticals. These are mature products, yet the U.S. remains the world leader in their production. The problem, then, is the Hypothesis is of limited generalizability. It cannot predict well either (1) when or (2) to what products the location of comparative advantage will shift.

Third, the Hypothesis can be used to explain (in part) the Leontief Paradox. The U.S. is an innovative country, creating many new products a year. By definition, production of newly designed products is not yet standardized and, therefore, is quite labor-intensive. Businesses prefer not to invest in physical capital equipment for a new product until its features are settled, the exact market identified, and the best way to automate production determined. Until production is standardized, exports of the product will be labor-intensive. Perhaps Professor Leontief's data reflected this phenomenon.

III. RETURNS TO FACTORS OF PRODUCTION

A. Links among Trade, Jobs, and Wages

One of the most hotly debated topics in international trade policy is the effect of trade liberalization on jobs and wages, and one of the most outspoken commentators on the subject is Professor Paul Krugman. In *Pop Internationalism* (1996), he says stagnation in American wages after 1973 (that is, the decline in real earnings of blue-collar workers in most years since 1973) is not due to free trade. He takes head on the thesis of another prominent economist, Ravi Batra, who in *The Myth of Free Trade* (1993) puts the blame for post-1973 earning and employment loss squarely on free trade. Professor Batra points out in 1973, the trade/GNP ratio (the ratio of imports plus exports as a percentage of GNP) took off, soaring soon thereafter about 20 percent and never to fall below that threshold again. Professor Batra argues 1973 was the year when the carnage in manufacturing jobs and real wages began. He urges that the phenomenon cannot be explained by a fall in the productivity of the American worker. To the contrary, productivity rose steadily in the post-1973 period (albeit at a declining rate of growth).

How does Professor Krugman proceed with, and defend, his counter-argument? First, Professor Krugman points out compensation for highly educated workers has risen. He also points out that wages of the average American worker more than doubled between 1945 and 1973. Thus, the phenomenon of wage stagnation labor union leaders are fond of recalling every time a new trade liberalization bill is proposed is really a discrete one, both in terms of the sector affected and the duration of the effect.

Second, he debunks the conventional wisdom post-1973 blue-collar wage stagnation is due to a decline in the competitiveness of the American worker, that somehow foreign produces have eroded the American manufacturing base, resulting in mass lay-offs in manufacturing industries, particularly among less skilled worker. It is wrong, he says, to blame the imports made by huge reserves of unskilled labor in the Third World for the problem. International trade has only a small role to play in causing the U.S.'s manufacturing difficulties. It is simply a mistake in logic to construct a causal relationship between a rise in imports and shrinkage of the industrial sector. After all, during the 1970-1990 period, when manufacturing imports rose, so too did manufacturing exports. Many American industrial companies may have laid off workers, but many added employees to produce for new overseas market opportunities.

Put differently, a dollar's worth of imports of manufactured goods may displace a dollar of sales of a like domestic product. But, a dollar of manufactured exports obviously is a dollar of sales revenue to a U.S. exporter. The question, as Professor Krugman points out, is the net effect of a simultaneous growth in manufactured exports and imports — has the trade deficit in manufactured goods been increasing as a percentage of GDP? In 1970, the U.S. had a trade surplus in manufactured goods. Measured as a percentage of GDP, manufactured exports exceeded manufactured imports by 0.2 percent. Since then, the U.S. has had a manufacturing trade deficit. In 1986, it reached a peak: manufacturing imports minus manufacturing exports, divided by GDP, equaled 3.1 percent of GDP. But, by 1990 the trade deficit in manufacturing had fallen to just 1.3 percent of GDP.

Even more significantly, says Professor Krugman, are statistics on the decline in the U.S. trade position in manufactured goods compared with the fall in the share of those goods in GDP. Between 1970-90, the share of manufacturing in GDP fell by 6.6 percent. By how much did the manufacturing trade position as a percentage of GDP decline during that same 20 years? Just 1.5 percent. By correcting for the manufacturing trade deficit thusly (*i.e.*, seeing it in the context of the broader manufacturing story), the bottom line is obvious: "if trade in manufactured goods had been balanced from 1970 to 1990, the downward trend in the size of the manufacturing sector would not have been as steep as it actually was, but most of the de-industrialization would still have taken place."[2] In sum, even if between 1970-90 the U.S. had not been importing more manufactured goods than it had exported, the decline in manufacturing still would have occurred.

What, then, explains this ineluctable de-industrialization if not international trade? Professor Krugman says the immediate reason is a change in the composition in domestic spending. Americans simply do not buy as many manufactured goods as they once did. In 1970, 46 percent of American consumption went on goods that were manufactured, grown, or mined, and 54 percent on services. By 1991, those shares had changed to 40.7 and 59.3 percent, respectively. What had Americans decided to spend more money on? Health care, travel, entertainment, legal services, restaurants, etc. Small wonder, intones Professor Krugman, that manufacturing is less important in the American economy.

But, this explanation leads to another question. Why did (and are) Americans spending less income on manufactured goods? Professor Krugman's answer is these goods are cheaper, relative to the price of services. During 1970-90, the price of goods relative to services fell 22.9 percent. Why are manufacturing goods cheaper? Because productivity has grown faster in the manufacturing than in the services sector. This growth translates into lower consumer prices. Herein is an irony: it is the productivity of American labor that contributes to the declining importance of the manufacturing sector.

> Does this irony suggest we should wish for slower productivity growth?
>
> . . . [C]onsider a world in which productivity (output per worker-hour) increases by the same amount in every nation around the world — say, 3 percent a year. Under these conditions, all other things remaining equal, workers' real earnings in all countries would tend to rise by 3 percent annually as well. Similarly, if productivity grew at 1 percent a year, so would earnings. (The relation between productivity growth and earnings growth holds regardless of the absolute level of productivity in each nation; only the rate of increase is significant.)
>
> Concerns about international competitiveness, as opposed to low productivity growth, correspond to a situation in which productivity growth in the U.S. falls to 1 percent annually while elsewhere it continues to grow at 3 percent. If real earnings in the U.S. then grow at 1 percent a year, the U.S. does not have anything we could reasonably call a competitive problem, even though it would lag other nations. The rate of earnings growth is exactly the same as it would be if other countries were doing as badly as we are.
>
> The fact that other countries are doing better may hurt U.S. pride, but it does not by itself affect domestic standards. It makes sense to

---

[2] PAUL KRUGMAN, POP INTERNATIONALISM 38 (1996).

> talk of a competitive problem only to the extent that earnings growth falls by more than the decline in productivity growth.[3]

In other words, focus on whether earnings growth keeps pace with productivity growth.

What about the blue-collar earnings carnage said to result from foreign competition? As an empirical matter, Professor Krugman estimates wage loss in 1990 from de-industrialization caused by foreign competition at less than 0.07 percent of national income. He concedes this competition can affect adversely TOT: the burgeoning supply of foreign manufactured goods can provoke a decline in prices of like domestic products. This effect works through the exchange rate, as the dollar depreciates relative to foreign currencies, and the price of imports rises. In the end, real earnings in the U.S. can fall, because Americans must sell their manufacturing output more cheaply, and they must pay more for manufactured imports. He even concedes between 1970 and 1990, the U.S. TOT deteriorated, as the ratio export to import prices fell by over 20 percent. (Put equivalently, Americans had to export 20 percent more to pay for the same import quantity.) But, he eschews ascribing too much blame to foreign competition. Professor Krugman points out during the 1970s and 1980s, real earnings grew roughly 6 percent. Suppose U.S. TOT had not deteriorated in those decades — would earnings have grown faster? His answer is yes, but the growth rate would have been only about 8 percent.

As persuasive as Professor Krugman's analysis may be, it may strike some as cold. Surely less-educated workers in the U.S. are not helped by cheap foreign competition. As he acknowledges, this view is grounded on

> . . . a familiar concept in the theory of international trade: factor price equalization. When a rich country, where skilled labor is abundant (and where the premium for skill is therefore small), trades with a poor country, where skilled workers are scarce and unskilled workers abundant, the wage rates tend to converge. The pay of skilled workers rises in the rich country and falls in the poor one; that of unskilled workers falls in the rich country and rises in the poor nation.
>
> Given the rapid growth of exports from nations such as China and Indonesia, it seems reasonable to suppose that factor price equalization has been a major reason for the growing gap in earnings between skilled and unskilled workers in the U.S.[4]

However, Professor Krugman rejects this factor price equalization rationale. In a telling sentence, he writes: "We have found that increased wage inequality, like the decline of manufacturing and the slowdown in real income growth, is overwhelmingly the consequence of domestic causes."[5]

How could Professor Krugman possibly reject a theorem so powerful as factor price equalization? He returns to the

> underlying logic of factor price equalization, first explained in a classic 1941 paper by Wolfgang F. Stolper and Paul A. Samuelson. The

---

[3] *Id.* at 41-42.

[4] *Id.* at 43-44.

[5] *Id.* at 44.

principle of comparative advantage suggests that a rich country trading with a poor one will export skill-intensive goods (because it has a comparative abundance of skilled workers) and import labor-intensive products. As a result of this trade, production in the rich country will shift toward skill-intensive sectors and away from labor-intensive ones. That shift, however, raises the demand for skilled workers and reduces that for unskilled workers. If wages are free to rise and fall with changes in the demand for different kinds of labor (as they do for the most part in the U.S.), the real wages of skilled workers will rise, and those of unskilled workers will decline. In a poor country, the opposite will occur.

All other things being equal, the rising wage differential will lead firms in the rich country to cut back on the proportion of skilled workers that they employ and to increase that of unskilled ones. That decision, in turn, mitigates the increased demand for skilled workers. When the dust settles, the wage differential has risen just enough to offset the effects of the change in the industry mix on overall demand for labor. Total employment of both types of labor remains unchanged.

According to Stolper and Samuelson's analysis, a rising relative wage for skilled workers leads all industries to employ a lower ratio of skilled to unskilled workers. Indeed, this reduction is the only way the economy can shift production toward skill-intensive sectors while keeping the overall mix of workers constant.

This analysis carries two clear empirical implications. First, if growing international trade is the main force driving increased wage inequality, the ratio of skilled to unskilled employment should decline in most U.S. industries. Second, employment should increase more rapidly in skill-intensive industries than in those that employ more unskilled labour.[6]

Here lies the rub. The empirical implications of the Stopler-Samuelson Theorem are not borne out:

. . . Between 1979 and 1989 the real compensation of white-collar workers rose, whereas that of blue-collar workers fell. Nevertheless, nearly all industries employed an increasing proportion of white-collar workers. Moreover, skill-intensive industries showed at best a slight tendency to grow faster than those in which blue-collar employment was high. . . .

Thus, the evidence suggests that factor price equalization was not the driving force behind the growing wage gap. The rise in demand for skilled workers was overwhelmingly caused by changes in demand *within* each industrial sector, not by a shift of the U.S.'s industrial mix in response to trade.[7]

It is folly to blame manufactured goods from developing countries. The fact, says Professor Krugman, is the bulk of America's imports of manufactured

---

[6] *Id.* at 45-46.

[7] *Id.* at 46-47.

products comes from developed, not developing, countries. Workers in those countries have similar skill levels, and paid comparable (and in some instances higher) wages, as American workers.

What, then, is the reason for declining relative demand for less skilled workers? Here, Professor Krugman admits uncertainty. Echoing Lester Thurow's analysis in *The Future of Capitalism* (1996), Professor Krugman blames technological change. Less skilled workers are left behind by the digital economy, *i.e.*, the digital divide is a real.

> The share of manufacturing in GDP is declining because people are buying relatively fewer goods; manufacturing employment is falling because companies are replacing workers with machines and making more efficient use of those they retain. Wages have stagnated because the rate of productivity growth in the economy as a whole has slowed, and less skilled workers in particular are suffering because a high-technology economy has less and less demand for their services.[8]

Yet, the key point is all of this — to one degree or another — would have happened with or without international trade.

B. The Factor Price Equalization Theorem

Economists are not blind to the effects of trade liberalization on wage rates. Indeed, for some time they have offered two theorems concerning these effects. Like most economic theorems, they are not always borne out by empirical testing. Nevertheless, the logic — indeed, simple common sense — behind the theorems makes them compelling. It might even be argued the failure of trade policy makers and legislators to come to grips with these theorems — for example, through a meaningful trade adjustment assistance program is a major reason for widespread resistance to, and persistent anxiety about, trade liberalization.

Consider the U.S., a capital-abundant country, and Mexico, a labor-abundant country. Obviously, they are members of a free trade agreement (FTA) — the *North American Free Trade Agreement (NAFTA)*. Assume, however, factors of production could not flow freely across the U.S. — Mexican border: capital in the U.S., and labor in Mexico, stayed put. No matter. The free trade occurring between the two countries is a substitute for the free mobility of factors of production.

How so? First, consider an autarkic scenario. In the absence of any trade, wage rates in the U.S. will be high, because labor is scarce, and the U.S. is not efficient at producing labor-intensive goods. However, physical capital is cheap, because it is in abundance, and thus so also are capital-intensive goods. Conversely, in Mexico, the returns to capital are extraordinary, because capital is scarce in Mexico and, therefore, commands a high price. But, labor is cheap because it is abundant, and goods that are labor-intensive can be purchased for a bargain.

Now, along comes *NAFTA*. Recall the Heckscher-Ohlin Theorem predicts a country will specialize in the production of, and export, that good which uses

---

[8] *Id.* at 48.

intensively in its production the factor with which the country is relatively well endowed. Thus, the Theorem predicts the U.S. will export capital-intensive goods to Mexico (*e.g.*, cars and medical instruments), and Mexico will export labor-intensive goods to the U.S. (*e.g.*, low-value added products like brooms, ceramics, or simple shoes and toys). Consider, then, the impact on the factor markets in each country. In the U.S., demand for capital will rise, and demand for labor will fall. Factor resources, specifically, capital, shift to the advantaged export sector. After all, in response to demand from Mexico, businesses will make more capital-intensive goods. Thus, U.S. businesses will need more machine tools, and less labor. Returns to capital will rise, but the price of labor (*i.e.*, wages) will fall.

In Mexico, the opposite reactions will occur. Factor resources, in particular, labor, shifts to the advantaged labor-intensive export sector. After all, in response to demand from the U.S., Mexican businesses will concentrate on producing and exporting labor-intensive goods. Their demand for labor will rise, causing an increase in wages, but the demand for capital will fall, causing a drop in the return to capital.

Observe the Heckscher-Ohlin Theorem does not require complete specialization. Quite the contrary. Incomplete specialization is most likely. Each country continues to produce some of each good. The U.S. still makes some labor-intensive goods, and Mexico still produces some capital-intensive goods. Specialization, then, is a focus or emphasis, but not an all-or-nothing proposition. Why not?

Because of increasing opportunity costs. Production in the advantaged industry continues to increase as long as the relative cost of this expansion is lower than, or just equal to, the relative price. But, eventually, the relative cost of producing a product begins to exceed the relative price obtained from selling that product, thus making further increases in output in the favored industry economically irrational. Ultimately, even in the advantaged sector, the law of diminishing returns must apply. At some point, adding more and more of the abundant factor of production will yield less-than-proportional increases in output, suggesting that the additions of the input are not paying off. Better to keep those inputs in the other industry. Hence, the other industry will survive, in a diminished state, and still compete with imports. There would be complete specialization only in the highly unusual case where the price of a country's exported good rises to such a high level that all of that country's factors are attracted to producing exportables.

Now, juxtapose the pre- and post-*NAFTA* scenarios. Before *NAFTA*, labor commanded a premium in the U.S., whereas capital did not. After *NAFTA*, American wage rates fell, but owners of capital enjoyed higher returns. In Mexico, the opposite events occurred. The end result is a convergence — ultimately, an equalization — of factor prices. Mexican wages rise, while American wages fall, and the two eventually equalize. Returns to capital in the U.S. rise, while in Mexico they fall, and eventually move to the same level. This is factor price equalization: in the absence of free mobility of factors of production across geo-political boundaries, free trade causes a long-run convergence in the incomes of each factor of production. In each country, the price of the abundant factor goes up, and the price of the scarce factor falls, because free trade impels each country to use its abundant factor all the more. Or, to put it concisely: free trade is a perfect substitute for factor mobility and leads to the equivalence of factor prices.

Why is it justified to say that factor incomes will *equalize*? Why not just stop with the less strong proposition that they will *tend* to converge? The answer is that free trade ought to result in a common world-market price for a product. In every country, the American-made, capital-intensive good will cost the same, and likewise, there will be a single, world-wide price for the Mexican-made, labor-intensive good. (Observe the critical hidden assumptions here necessary for this result: an absence of trade barriers, perfectly competitive markets, use of the same production technology, and identical products.) Because each country continues to produce some of each good (*i.e.*, there is incomplete specialization), and because each good is produced at the same cost using the same technology, returns to each factor should equalize.

Another way of explaining the justification for equalization is to consider what the goods exported by each country embodies. The answer is the abundant factor of production. When the U.S. exports capital-intensive goods to Mexico, it is exporting some of its abundance of capital. The Americans are letting the Mexicans have use of some of their abundant factor — not by selling it directly, but by exporting the good that is produced with a high ratio of capital to labor. Conversely, when Mexico exports labor-intensive goods to the U.S., it is exporting some of its abundance of labor. The Mexicans are letting the Americans use some of their generous endowment — again, not by direct sales, but by exports of the good that uses labor intensively in the production process. In brief, when countries trade, they do more than exchange goods. They exchange the factors of production embodied in those goods.

Thus, if the U.S. is "exporting" some of its capital to Mexico, through the embodiment of capital in the capital-intensive good, then it is reasonable to expect the return to capital in Mexico to fall. In effect, the "supply of capital" in Mexico increases, but demand for capital has not picked up — indeed, it has fallen with trade liberalization. The income earned by Mexican owners of capital must, therefore, fall. Likewise, if Mexico is "exporting" some of its labor to the U.S., through the embodiment of labor in the labor-intensive good, then wages in the U.S. must fall. The practical effect is that the "supply of labor" in the U.S. increases. Given that demand for labor in the U.S. falls with trade liberalization, American wages are sure to drop.

Interestingly, there is some empirical evidence to support the Factor Price Equalization Theorem. In 1993, Professor Dan Ben-David published the results of his analysis of the effects of lowering trade barriers in western Europe following the creation of the EU. He found a dramatic reduction in the dispersion of incomes across countries.

As another example, before 1970, many developing countries exported raw materials to the U.S. and EU. However, since 1970, some developing countries have been exporting manufactured goods to the U.S. that use unskilled labor intensively in the production processes. These exporting countries are NICs such as Korea and Brazil, and their exports include textiles and apparel, and shoes. In return, the U.S. and EU have exported products that are skill-intensive, capital-intensive, such as chemical and aircraft. What has the effect of this NIC-developed country trade pattern been on wages of highly skilled and unskilled workers in developed countries?

The answer is wages of highly skilled workers have risen, but wages of unskilled workers have fallen. For instance, from 1970-89, the real wage of American male workers in the 90th percentile (*i.e.*, those earning more than the bottom 90 percent) rose by 15 percent, but the real wage of American male workers in the 10th percentile fell by 25 percent. This fact is what the Factor Price Equalization Theorem predicts. NICs export less-skill-intensive manufactured goods, because they are abundant in unskilled workers. The Theorem forecasts the wages of unskilled workers in the U.S. and EU (workers employed in import-competing industries) will fall. In contrast, the U.S. and EU export high-skill-intensive goods, because they are abundant in human capital. The Theorem says demand and, hence, wages, of highly skilled U.S. and EU workers will rise.

Still, complete factor price equalization has not occurred in the U.S. or EU. Nor has it occurred as a result of *NAFTA*, much less as a result of the Uruguay Round agreements. A particular interesting fact is that the growing wage inequality between skilled and unskilled workers in the U.S. and EU also is occurring in NICs. Skilled workers in China, for instance, are doing very well, yet the Factor Price Equalization Theorem would predict a drop in their wages. Why have factor prices not equalized?

One obvious answer is that trade between NICs and developed countries is insufficiently large in volume to influence income distribution. Most trade occurs among developed countries. Another possibility is that the explanation has nothing to do with trade. The reason for growing wage inequality, at least, is technology: workers who know how to use it win, those who do not are left behind.

However, part of the answer must lie in the assumptions underlying the Factor Price Equalization Theorem. They simply do not hold as true in reality as economists might like. First, complete free trade is needed. After all, if prices of goods cannot equalize, then factor returns cannot equalize. However, this assumption is patently false. Tariff and non-tariff barriers remain the world over, and even when they fall, remedial actions often are taken to re-impose barriers. Even so-called FTAs, like *NAFTA*, have their share of barriers. Preferential rules of origin are a case in point.

Second, there must be no transport costs (or, at least, they must be negligible). That assumption remains a shipper's dream. Most of world trade moves by ocean freight. Depending on trade volumes and routes, freight charges vary. During and after the 1997-99 Asian economic crisis, when currencies were devalued, and depreciated, relative to the U.S. dollar, exports from the Far East to America surged. Freight charges and container rates were cheap on voyages from the U.S. back to the Far East. However, during oil price shocks, wars, or other civil unrest, these costs can skyrocket. The point is, transports costs are rarely, if ever, negligible.

Third, there must be no factor reversals, *i.e.*, there must be no differences in the rankings of countries with respect to the factor requirements needed for a particular good. For example, suppose that in the U.S., producing cars is capital intensive and growing soybean is land intensive. A factor reversal would exist if, in another country that also made cars and soybeans, cars were less capital-intensive than soybeans. If the U.S. exported soybeans, and the other country exported cars, both countries would appear to be specializing in a non-capital-intensive product. It would, then, be impossible to draw any general conclusions about trade patterns from the data of these two countries. However, whether this assumption is true is an empirical question. It depends on the countries involved and, more specifically, on their technologies of production. The Factor Price Equalization Theorem assumes that production technologies are the same. But, this need not be true in all instances, particularly if factors are substitutable in the production process of a particular good. For example, Californian farmers use considerable machinery to grow rice, whereas Thai and Vietnamese farmers use a labor-intensive process.

Fourth, the Theorem relies on the assumption that relative factor endowments across countries are not wildly different. If they were, then either or both countries might produce only one good. Suppose the U.S. had a huge amount of capital and very little labor, and Mexico had an enormous population size but no capital. The U.S. might produce only capital-intensive goods, and Mexico might produce only labor-intensive goods. When the two countries traded, the issue of the equalization of factor prices would have no practical importance. In fact, there are cases where factor endowments are not at all close. India and Russia, with tremendous differences in labor and land, or Burma and Singapore, with tremendous differences in natural resources and human capital, are examples.

All of this is not to say the Factor Price Equalization Theorem is either utterly quixotic or a mere intellectual curiosity. It is useful, if for no other reason than it lends insight into what might happen if the economist's dream of real trade liberalization came true. In turn, it should catalyze thought as to how to handle adjustment costs that might arise after a free trade deal is signed.

C. The Stopler-Samuelson Theorem

The Theorem — as it would come to be labeled — published in 1941 by Professors Stopler and Samuelson is all about the income distribution effects of trade liberalization. In political terms, it is about the winners and losers from free trade. As such, it helps explain why certain groups support, and others oppose, free trade. The Stopler-Samuelson Theorem follows logically from the Factor Price Equalization Theorem, just as the Factor Price Equalization Theorem emerges straight out of the Heckscher-Ohlin Theorem. Like the other Theorems, the Stopler-Samuelson Theorem focuses on inter-industry, not intra-industry, trade.

The question Professors Stopler and Samuelson began with is this: If free trade occurs, what is the effect on the price of the scarce factor of production? Their answer: that price must fall. The intuitive reasoning is simple.

In the example of U.S. and Mexico, America is accurately assumed to be blessed with plenty of capital, but a scarcity of labor, relative to Mexico.

Mexico faces the opposite situation. When trade liberalization occurs because of *NAFTA*, Mexicans demand capital-intensive goods from the U.S. Professors Stopler and Samuelson knew the U.S. has a comparative cost advantage, based on relative factor endowments, in these goods. They also knew Americans seek labor-intensive goods from Mexico, because Mexico produces these more cheaply than the U.S., given Mexico's abundance of labor.

The result is captains of American industry stock up on physical capital, but not labor. They buy more of the factor with which their country is relatively well endowed. Demand for capital-intensive goods, which Mexico fuels, is increasing. Given this export demand, the price of capital-intensive goods must rise, and thus so too must returns to capital. After all, an increase in the price of capital-intensive goods must lead to an increase in the income of the factor used intensively in the production of that good.

As for American wage rates — the returns to the scarce factor of production — they will tumble. The captains of American industry know better than to try and compete with Mexico in the production of a labor-intensive good, *i.e.*, a good in which America lacks a comparative cost advantage, given the differences in relative factor endowments. In contrast, in Mexico, businesses hire workers, knowing America has an appetite for Mexican labor-intensive goods. Given this export demand, the price of Mexico's labor-intensive goods inevitably rises. There is a concomitant increase in the returns to the factor used intensively in producing those goods — Mexican labor, *i.e.*, Mexican wages must rise. But, Mexican businesses do not increase their demand for capital. Returns to capital — Mexico's scarce factor of production — thus tumble.

Complete specialization does not occur in reality. Even with free trade between the U.S. and Mexico, there are some American businesses hiring labor for labor-intensive goods. And, some Mexican businesses employ capital for capital-intensive goods. What is the long-term fate of these enterprises? Not good, if free market forces operate.

American workers making labor-intensive goods will face stiff import competition, as will Mexican capital that produces capital-intensive goods. Neither of these groups will be able to exploit their "scarcity power" in their respective countries if they are forced to compete with their cohorts across the border. Not surprisingly, American labor and Mexican capital will oppose free trade. They may demand protection, and they may get it if they have sufficient lobbying clout or if they happen to be making a product deemed strategic. At the least, American labor and Mexican capital may demand adjustment assistance packages to cope with vicissitudes.

Here, then, is the Stopler-Samuelson Theorem. Trade liberalization leads to an increase in the relative price of labor in the labor-abundant country (*e.g.*, Mexico), and a decrease in the relative price of labor in the capital-abundant country (*e.g.*, U.S.). These results occur because of the effect of trade liberalization on the relative demand for factor inputs. In the labor-abundant country, demand for labor rises, and demand for capital falls. Conversely, in the capital-abundant country, demand for capital rises, and demand for labor falls. In brief, free trade helps the abundant factor and harms the scarce factor. It increases the income of a country's plentiful factor, because it is used intensively in the export sector, but it lowers the income of the country's scarce factor, which is used by domestic producers that compete with imports.

One clear implication of the Stopler-Samuelson Theorem is that the share of each factor of production in a country's national income accounts will change. In the example, the share of Mexico's GDP accounted for by labor will rise, while the share accounted for by capital will fall. In the U.S., the share of capital in national income will rise, whereas the share of labor will fall.

What are obvious lessons to draw from the Stopler-Samuelson Theorem? If you are counsel to one of the scarce factors of production — American labor, for example — then demand protection. A tariff on Mexican labor-intensive goods would raise the cost of those goods, and allow American businesses producing labor-intensive goods to raise their prices to the higher level resulting from the tariff. When the price of their product rises, American workers will realize higher wages. But, if you are the attorney for one of the plentiful factors of production — Mexican labor, for example — then lobby for free trade. You want to avoid tariffs and other protective measures that inevitably interfere with market-based income distribution outcomes.

While those lessons are "obvious," they are not exclusive. If you want to make the case for free trade to representatives of the scarce factor of production — for example, American unions — then you will have to come up with a mechanism for helping them weather the nastier effects of free trade. Fiscal compensation from the government, in the form of trade adjustment assistance is the conventional mechanism. Recall the central insight of Ricardo's Classical Model: free trade results in a *net* gain to the countries involved, because each country specializes in the production of what it can produce most efficiently (cheaply), and each country consumes a bundle of goods that is unattainable under autarky. Therefore, it ought to be possible for the winners from free trade to transfer some of their gain to the losers as compensation. Still a bolder proposal to make the world safe for free trade and yet retain a compassionate disposition to the losers might be to focus on human capital development. What better way to cope with the vicissitudes of the global economy than to re-conceptualize education as a life-long process, and for the government to provide (directly or indirectly) subsidized training? After all, better to give workers a fishing pole for life than a fish for today.

IV. COMPENSATING "LOSERS" FROM FREE TRADE

A. The Evolution of Trade Adjustment Assistance

Even staunch free trade advocates ought to admit that trade liberalization results in *net* gains to an economy. There are "winners" and "losers," and the benefits accruing to the winners more than offset the injury experienced by the losers. But, this net gain is little comfort to a worker who experiences real wage declines, or unemployment, as a result of fair foreign competition. Nor is it much comfort to a firm forced to downsize significantly or declare bankruptcy, or the community in which the firm is located, which experiences the economic and social externalities associated with the firm's contraction. How can the net gain from free trade be realized while at the same time assuring that injuries to workers, firms, and communities caused by free trade are redressed? One possibility — that appears efficient from a positive perspective, and fair from a normative perspective — is to transfer some of the net gain from free trade to injured workers, firms, industries, and perhaps even communities. As one economist writes:

> Economic theory has long taught that international trade governed by the principle of comparative advantage, or relative factor endowments, will, over the long run, provide maximum benefit to all trading parties. These benefits will generally consist of higher returns to the factors of production, lower prices, and a wider range of choices to consumers than would exist in the absence of this trade. The theory recognizes, however, that overall economic and social benefits may be accompanied by adverse short-term economic and social effects on selected parts of a national economy. Inasmuch as the social benefits from the trade are thought to be widespread throughout the economy, it is generally accepted that an adjustment assistance program designed to ease the adverse impact of rising imports on workers, firms, and regions is a vital concomitant to lowered trade restrictions.[9]

Thus, the winners could compensate the losers through a redistribution scheme that is a non-protectionist alternative to import restrictions.

In thinking about non-protectionist choices, recall that protectionist measures (*i.e.*, tariffs and non-tariff barriers) are an expensive way to save jobs. In *Measuring the Costs of Protection in the United States*,[10] Gary Clyde Hufbauer and Kimberly Ann Elliott estimate it costs American consumers a staggering $170,000 to protect a job. Hufbauer and Elliott use 1990 data for 21 sectors of the American economy ranging from ball bearings to women's hand bags. Their figure of $170,000 represents the average the amount of consumer surplus lost as a result of protectionist measures in these 21 sectors. They find that in 4 of the 21 sectors, the amount is $500,000. (In the steel sector, there are estimates as high as $1 million for each job saved.) When Hufbauer and Elliott take the gain to producers benefiting from protection (*i.e.*, increased producer surplus) into account, the average net national welfare cost per protected job is about $54,000. Accordingly, part of the rationale for trade adjustment assistance is a worker can be re-trained for far less than $170,000, or even $54,000.

Nothing in the GATT—WTO regime obliges a Member to implement a redistribution scheme, nor does the regime set out parameters with which such a scheme must comply. (To be sure, GATT Articles XXXVI-XXXVIII urge developed countries to adopt measures that help expand trade from less developed countries. But, it is difficult to infer from these provisions an obligation to implement a domestic structural adjustment program.) The first efforts at developing a scheme to compensate parties injured by free trade were in Europe. The establishment of the European Economic Community in 1957 resulted in hardship for many workers and firms because of reduced

---

9 Samuel M. Rosenblatt, *Trade Adjustment Assistance Programs: Crossroads or Dead End?*, 9 L. & POLICY IN INT'L BUS. 1065, 1066 (1977).

10 GARY CLYDE HUFBAUER & KIMBERLY ANN ELLIOTT, MEASURING THE COSTS OF PROTECTION IN THE UNITED STATES 11-13 (1994).

trade barriers. Adjustment assistance was provided to dislocated workers and firms.

Between 1954-1960, many bills were proposed in Congress to establish a program for American workers and firms, but none was enacted. The first American Trade Adjustment Assistance (TAA) program was authorized by the *Trade Expansion Act of 1962* to help workers dislocated as a result of a federal policy to reduce barriers to foreign trade. President Kennedy articulated this link:

> I am also recommending as an essential part of the new trade program that companies, farmers, and workers who suffer damage from increased foreign import competition be assisted in their efforts to adjust to that competition. When considerations of national policy make it desirable to avoid higher tariffs, those injured by that competition should not be required to bear the full brunt of the impact. Rather, the burden of economic adjustment should be borne in part by the Federal Government. [11]

However, the programs were not widely used because of strict eligibility criteria set forth in the *Trade Expansion Act of 1962*. In fact, no adjustment assistance was granted until 1969. Under the *1962 Act*, workers or firms were eligible for assistance only if 4 criteria were met:

1. Imports of a product like or directly competitive with the product they produced were increasing;

2. The increased imports were in major part a result of trade agreement concessions;

3. The firm was seriously injured, or threatened with serious injury (or the workers were unemployed or threatened with unemployment); and

4. The increased imports were the major factor in causing the serious injury (or unemployment).

Congress attempted to liberalize the eligibility criteria (and increase the amount of benefits) through changes to the programs made by the *Trade Act of 1974*, as amended.

For example, the second criterion quoted above was abolished. The serious injury test in the third criteria was replaced with requirements that a significant number of workers have been (or are threatened with the possibility of being) laid off and sales or production of the firm have decreased. Finally, the causation threshold was reduced. Instead of showing that increased imports were a "major factor" in causing serious injury, it was necessary to show they "contributed importantly" to declining sales or production. The current statutory authorization for the programs remains in Title II of the *1974 Act*, and the eligibility criteria are discussed more fully below.

---

[11] *Hearings Before the House Comm. on Ways and Means on H.R. 9900: A Bill To Promote the General Welfare, Foreign Policy and Security of the United States Through International Trade Agreements and Through Adjustment Assistance to Domestic Industry Agriculture and Labor, and for Other Purposes*, 87th Cong., 2d Sess. 8 (1962) (message from President John F. Kennedy relative to the Reciprocal Trade Agreements Program).

Unfortunately, the TAA programs seem to have little positive impact in helping the workers and firms that lose from free trade. One practitioner observes that "[a]s the *1974 Act* program developed it proved to be no more effective in facilitating adjustment than the *1962 Act* program had been," and that the TAA program for firms "has not functioned" since 1987.[12] Two reasons why adjustment assistance has been ineffectual are evident from the discussion of the TAA programs below: obtaining TAA is a nightmarishly complex process, and the amount of assistance is meager.

Two other reasons also may account for the disappointing results: money and policy. First, funding for the programs is provided from general federal revenues and, therefore, subject to the politics of budget cutting in an era of deficit reduction. From 1975-79, many workers and some firms obtained assistance. Payments to workers surged to $1.6 billion in 1980, the highest level ever, and amounted to $1.4 billion in 1981. These large sums prompted the Reagan Administration to propose the abolition of the TAA programs. Congress responded by tightening eligibility requirements and decreasing benefits in the *Omnibus Budget Reconciliation Act (OBRA)* of 1981 and subsequent budget legislation. In the *OBRA* of 1993, Congress re-authorized the TAA programs for workers and firms through fiscal year 1998, with assistance to terminate on September 30, 1998. In that *Act*, the Congress also reduced the cap on funding for re-training from $80 million to $70 million for the 1997 fiscal year.

Congress again re-authorized the TAA program, and funded it, via its October 1998 omnibus spending package (H.R. 4328, § 1012). That package ensured continuation through 30 June 1999. In June 1999, Congress was poised to grant an extension through 30 September 2001. But, the trade bill with the embedded extension got bogged down in the politics of the Generalized System of Preferences (GSP), Caribbean Basin Initiative (CBI), trade preferences for sub-Saharan Africa, and fast-track trade negotiating authority. Thus, TAA expired on 30 June 1999. Not until November 1999 did Congress pass a renewal bill, and did so retroactively. A separate *NAFTA Worker Security Act* in 1993 established a TAA regime for workers harmed by implementation of *NAFTA*.[13]

The *Trade Adjustment Assistance Reform Act of 2002 (2002 TAA Reform Act)* brought a much needed "shot in the arm" for the TAA programs through consolidation, expanded coverage, and much larger funding appropriation. This legislation incorporated the *NAFTA* TAA program, which had been separate since inception. The coverage now includes workers affected by a shift in production realized under any FTA, or under the *African Growth and Opportunity Act (AGOA), Andean Trade Preference Act (ATPA)*, or *Caribbean Basin Economic Recovery Act (CBERA)*. As with previous TAA legislation, the *2002 Act* continues eligibility for two classes of potential beneficiaries — firms, or groups of former employees. (Technically, the application process and funding sources are distinct.) Essentially, for former employees lodging a

---

[12] Bruce E. Clubb, I United States Foreign Trade Law § 24.9.2, at 797.

[13] *See North American Free Trade Agreement Implementation Act*, Pub. L. 103-182 §§ 501-06 (8 Dec. 1993).

petition, at least three workers at a firm must be adversely affected by a covered trade agreement to be eligible for TAA.

Significantly, the *2002 TAA Reform Act* expands the scope of eligibility to include "secondary workers," a term that means workers employed by an upstream supplier (*i.e.*, a firm providing inputs into a finished product made by a firm that already has been certified as eligible for TAA), or with a downstream producer (*i.e.*, a firm using in its product components made by a firm already certified as eligible). The *Act* has provisions for health coverage through a Federal tax credit, a demonstration project for Older Workers (over 50 years old), and aid for farmers and livestock producers (including fisherman) managed by the Department of Agriculture (USDA). The *Act* maintains TAA for firms as well. The overall funding for the TAA program in 2005 was $1.057 billion (of which $12 million is for firms, and $90 million for farmers and livestock producers).

B. The Policy of Trade Adjustment Assistance

TAA programs are a readily apparent government expense, the benefits of which are not necessarily visible to those other than the targeted beneficiaries. In contrast, the costs of protection to limit import competition fall on a diffuse and typically poorly organized group of consumers. Moreover, if a tariff is imposed, then the government earns revenue. Thus, it is often easier to take a protectionist route than the prudent course.

Interestingly, in the *Omnibus Trade and Competitiveness Act of 1988* Congress urged the President to undertake negotiations in the Uruguay Round to allow any country to impose a small, uniform fee of not more than 0.15 percent on all imports in order to fund a country's adjustment assistance scheme. (Unilateral imposition of the fee could violate existing GATT obligations on MFN treatment, tariff bindings, and non-discrimination.) No such deal was reached. The *1988 Act* authorized the President to impose an import fee either after completing the Uruguay Round, or two years following enactment of the *Act*, unless it was "not in the national economic interest" to do so. President George H. W. Bush decided the import fee was not in the national interest.

Second, TAA programs raise serious policy concerns. For example, why should the government prefer to assist workers or firms dislocated by free trade as opposed to any other economic phenomenon? Further, what is to prevent adjustment assistance from becoming a subsidy to inefficient workers and firms? Conversely, is adjustment assistance "burial insurance" for workers and firms? To what extent are the same or similar benefits available through other federal or state entitlement programs? Finally, and perhaps most fundamentally, is adjustment assistance "industrial policy"? This term generally refers to policies "that affect the allocation of a country's resources in terms of industrial sector, region, and time." A key objection to industrial policy is that government plays an inappropriately large, even dominant, role. The forces of the free market lead to more efficient allocations of resources than government decisions. Hence, the argument runs, government bureaucrats should not promote certain domestic industries over others through the provision of adjustment assistance. Of course, a counter-argument is that many governments — including those of some of our important Asian trading partners such as the governments of Japan and Korea — actively engage in planning and support activities with respect to certain sectors of their economies to ensure that these sectors remain internationally competitive.

Third, consider the twin facts of economic uncertainty in the U.S. in 2002, when the *TAA Reform Act* was passed, and congressional elections that year. To what degree would it matter that many populous states (*e.g.*, California, Florida, and Ohio) are hard hit by increased foreign competition and factory closings? Is relief promised by TAA an election cycle political smoke screen shielding incumbents from constituents disillusioned by trade liberalization?

C. Funding Problems

Funding for all TAA program benefits, as well as *NAFTA* transitional adjustment assistance, is provided by the federal government — *i.e.*, general tax revenues — and dispensed by states. For instance, TRA payments are funded as a general federal entitlement associated with the Federal Unemployment Benefit Account of the Department of Labor (DOL). The amount of such funding is modest: in fiscal 1995, for example, $274.4 million was appropriated for TRA payments and related administrative expenses. In fiscal 1997, $276.1 million was appropriated for them. The fact Congress essentially did not increase funding between 1995 and 1997, in spite of the implementation of the Uruguay Round agreements and *NAFTA*, underscores a lack of commitment to, and the uncertain future of, TAA. The expenses of re-employment services are defrayed by federal grants to states. Similarly, training, job search, and relocation allowances are paid for by means of an annual appropriated entitlement under the Training and Employment Services account of the DOL. The 2002 *TAA Reform Act* increased funding for the program to levels not seen since the early 1980s.

D. Efficacy

In the years since the *Trade Adjustment Assistance Reform Act of 2002* was passed, the Government Accountability Office (GAO) analyzed the success of TAA, especially with its new features.[14] The GAO research indicates while some benefits are being realized, overall TAA is not utilized to its full extent by workers certified to apply.

1. A September 2004 report (GAO-04-1012) finds workers apply more quickly for benefits, but only because of an increase in the productivity of the DOL in processing petitions — from 238 days to 38 days, a dramatic time decrease necessitated by a new 40 day maximum guideline. States report more workers in training programs. That is because of a 2002 requirement that a worked be enrolled either (1) 8 weeks after petition certification, or (2) 16 weeks after the worker is laid off, whichever is later. States struggle

---

[14] Its reports, submitted to Congress, are *available at* www.gao.gov (under "trade adjustment assistance").

to meet administrative demands, and often to find training funds to meet the needs of workers.

2.   A January 2006 report (GAO-06-43) examines 5 plant closings. In them, 75 percent or more of workers received some reemployment assistance, and a majority was either working elsewhere or had retired. The Health Care Tax Credit (discussed below) was the most underutilized benefits, with only 12 percent of workers claiming it. They were unaware of it, had other coverage, or found coverage too expensive even with the tax break. Only half of older workers knew a wage subsidy benefit existed, and no more than 20 percent of them obtained it.

3.   An April 2006 report (GAO-06-496) finds states are, in general, under-reporting participation in the TAA program. It also highlights the desire among states to share lessons about TAA, and improve statistical collection and quality.

4.   A December 2006 report (GAO-07-201) reviews the USDA TAA program. It concludes fisherman receive far more of the benefits than farmers. Salmon and shrimp fisherman receiving approximately 92 percent of all funds paid. The Foreign Agricultural Service (FAS) reviews the petitions under the same 40 day limit as the DOL. Yet, participation is low, with just 101 petitions submitted petitions in fiscal years 2004-2006. Among other crops certified for TAA benefits are lychees, olives, catfish, Concord grapes, potatoes, and blueberries.

In sum, TAA benefit petitions are increasing. But, there is a lack of information about new benefits, and coordination between DOL and states needs improvement. Put succinctly, access to TAA has been improved, but the benefits are not fully utilized.

V.   LEGAL CRITERIA FOR COMPENSATION

A.   Worker Eligibility for Trade Adjustment Assistance

The U.S. TAA program for workers is set forth in Sections 221-250 of the *Trade Act of 1974*, as amended. *See* 19 U.S.C. §§ 2271-2331. The program offers compensation in the form of Trade Readjustment Allowances (TRA) (*i.e.*, cash benefits), re-employment services, training, and additional allowances while in training. *See* 19 U.S.C. §§ 2291-2298. Reforms under the 1981 *OBRA* shifted focus from income compensation for temporary layoffs to return to work through retraining and other adjustment measures for the long-term unemployed. The *Deficit Reduction Act of 1984* boosted worker training allowances, and job search and relocation benefits. The *1988 Act* modified significantly the eligibility criteria for cash benefits, and put greater emphasis on worker retraining. For example, the *1988 Act* amendments require a worker to be enrolled in, or complete, training as a condition for receiving a TRA. *See* 19 U.S.C. § 2291(a)(5).

Federal and state authorities jointly administer the TAA program. Therefore, workers seeking TAA must deal with two phases and two layers of government. First, they must apply to the federal government for certification for eligibility. Second, if they receive certification, then they must apply to their state government for benefits. Each state has a cooperative agreement with the DOL on administration.

At the federal level, the DOL operates TAA through the Employment and Training Administration (ETA). (The USDA administers the program for farmers.) The ETA processes petitions for eligibility submitted by workers, and issues certifications or denials. Only workers adversely affected by increased imports are eligible for benefits. (Obtaining federal certification for eligibility is a complicated process. A group of 3 or more workers, a union, or an authorized representative of a group of workers may file a petition with the ETA for certification for eligibility. *See* 19 U.S.C. § 2271(a). The ETA must determine that: (1) a significant number or proportion of the workers in a firm have been or are threatened to be totally or partially separated (*i.e.*, laid off); (2) the firm's sales or production have decreased in absolute terms; and (3) increases in like or directly competitive imported products "contributed importantly" to both the layoffs and decline in sales or production. *See* 19 U.S.C. § 2272(a)(1)-(3); *Former Employees of Home Petroleum Corp. v. United States*, 16 CIT 778, 779 (slip op. 92-156) (CIT 1992); *Former Employees of Bass Enter. v. United States*, 706 F. Supp. 897 (CIT 1989). The ETA must make the eligibility determination within 60 days after a petition is filed.

Applying the third criterion is problematic. There is a threshold question of what constitutes a "like or directly competitive" product. *See, e.g., Former Employees of North American Refractories Co. v. United States*, 16 CIT 166, 167-68 (slip op. 92-37) (CIT 1992). Once that decision is made, the causation issue must be tackled. Imports "contribute importantly" if they are "a cause which is important but not necessarily more important than any other cause." 19 U.S.C. § 2272(b). Plainly, this standard is easier for a petitioner to meet than the "substantial cause" standard associated with Section 201 relief. Still, defining "important" is not easy, as a court noted in an early TAA case under the *1974 Act, United Glass and Ceramic Workers of North America v. Marshall*, 584 F.2d 398, 407 (D.C. Cir. 1978). In *Former Employees of Johnson Controls v. United States*, the court defined "important" as a "causal nexus" between (1) import penetration and (2) separation of a worker and firm: "[a] causal nexus exists where there is a *direct and substantial* relationship between increased imports and a decline in sales and production." 16 CIT 617, 618 (slip. op. 92-114) (CIT 1992) (*citing Former Employees of Health-Tex, Inc. v. United States*, 14 CIT 580 (CIT 1990)) (emphasis added).

The phrase "direct and substantial" seems misleading. It obfuscates an already fuzzy distinction between TAA and Section 201 escape clause causation tests. Suppose imports of a product decline nationwide, but imports by competitors of a firm at which workers are laid off increase. Are the increased imports "important"? The Court in *United Rubber Cork, Linoleum and Plastic Workers of America, Local 798 v. Donovan* gives an affirmative reply. *See* 652 F.2d 702 (7th Cir. 1981).

Secondary workers (*i.e.*, employees of upstream or downstream firms) follow a similar petition certification process. They must satisfy 3 conditions:

1. A significant number or proportion of workers in the firm (or subdivision) are totally or partially separated, or are threatened with total or partial separation;

2. The workers' firm (or subdivision) is a supplier or downstream producer to a firm (or subdivision) that employs a group of workers who received (already) certification of eligibility for a primary firm, and the supply or production is related to the article that is the basis for the (prior) certification; and

3. Either (1) the workers' firm is a supplier and the component part it supplies to the firm (or subdivision) comprises at least 20 percent of production or sales of the workers' firm, or (2) a loss of business by the workers' firm with the other firm contributed importantly to the workers' actual or threatened separation.

Note the causation standard in the third criterion. What constitutes an "important" contribution? That issue is the subject of litigation in the CIT and Federal Circuit.

The three-pronged test to get certified suggests many workers are unlikely to qualify. Some statistics support this expectation. Overall (based on 1990s data), the odds are about two-in-three a petition will be certified and worker will be covered.

At the state level, certified workers apply for TAA benefits at the nearest office of the State Employment Security Agency. In effect, the state acts as a federal agent to give information, process applications, determine individual eligibility for benefits, issue payments, and provide re-employment services and training opportunities. *See* 19 U.S.C. §§ 2311(a), 2313(a). States apply specified criteria for TRA cash benefits, re-employment services, and training. In addition to these tasks, states must give written notice to each worker to apply for TAA, in cases where the worker is covered by a federal certification of eligibility, and publish each certification in a newspaper in the area in which certified workers reside. Finally, states must advise each adversely affected worker at the time the worker applies for unemployment insurance of the TAA program, and counsel each worker to apply for training when the worker seeks a TRA.

B. Qualifying Requirements and Limits on Benefits

Qualifying for a TRA cash benefit is hard, because five criteria must be met. The first criterion concerns the timing of the "qualifying separation" between a worker and firm, *i.e.*, the lay off that generates eligibility for a TRA. The worker must be laid off on or after the "impact date" set out in a certification for that worker. This date is when total or partial layoffs begin, or threaten to begin. It is never more than 1 year before the date a certification petition is filed. Also, the worker must be laid off within 2 years after the date the certification is issued. Hence, a certified worker has 2 years to apply for a TRA.

Second, the worker must have been employed for 1 year before the first qualifying separation, and must have earned at least $30 per week for at least 6 months. Third, the worker must be entitled to unemployment insurance but exhausted all rights to this entitlement, including extended benefits. Consequently, she cannot obtain both unemployment insurance and a TRA — the TRA essentially serves as a continuation of unemployment insurance. Fourth, the worker must not be disqualified from receiving unemployment insurance extended benefits because she has accepted a new job. Finally, as mentioned above in connection with the *1988 Act* amendments, the worker must be enrolled in or have completed a training program.

If these criteria are met, then a worker may receive a TRA. But, the level and duration of this cash benefit are limited. As to the level, the worker can get cash for each week of unemployment equal to the most recent weekly benefit amount of unemployment insurance the worker received after her first qualifying separation and before exhausting this insurance. The TRA is reduced by the amount of any training allowance provided. In essence, the amount of a TRA is limited to the amount of unemployment insurance for which a worker qualifies. *See* 19 U.S.C. §§ 2291-2293. This limitation was introduced by the *OBRA* of 1981 to reduce the cost of the TAA program to the federal government.

In respect of the duration of a TRA, there is a 1-year limit linked to the period during which unemployment insurance is received. *See* 19 U.S.C. § 2293(a)(1). A worker can get unemployment insurance followed by a TRA for a maximum of 52 weeks. Thus, a worker who gets unemployment insurance for 30 weeks could thereafter obtain a TRA for at most 22 weeks. However, the TRA may be extended for an additional 26 weeks if the worker participates in training. A TRA for 52 weeks or less is called the "basic TRA," while an extension of the cash benefit associated with training is the "additional TRA."

In addition to limits on level and duration, the attractiveness of a TRA is reduced because of the lag time between the first qualifying separation and receipt of a TRA. Evidence from 1974-1979 indicates on average workers receive their first TRA payment 14-16 months after becoming unemployed. Notwithstanding regular unemployment compensation from the state within the first 2 weeks of separation, their income support may be insufficient when they most need it, namely, while out of work and looking for a job. Yet, equity demands not only prompt administrative action on a TRA application, but also a full, fair analysis of each case.

Regardless of whether a certified worker exhausts unemployment benefits and is eligible for TRA payments, she may receive re-employment services and training through an appropriate state agency. *See* 19 U.S.C. § 2295. These services are counseling, vocational testing, and job search and placement. A job search allowance is available if a certified worker cannot obtain suitable employment within her commuting area. The allowance is limited to 90 percent of necessary job search expenses, up to a maximum $800. A relocation allowance is available to a worker obtaining suitable employment outside her commuting area. Its cap is 90 percent of reasonable moving expenses, plus a lump sum payment of three times her average weekly wage up to a maximum $800.

Traditionally, training referred to the development of new skills. As a result of the *1988 Act* amendments, it now includes remedial education. The costs of training are covered directly by the federal government (through the relevant state agency), or through a voucher system. The *1988 Act* also converted training from an entitlement contingent on the availability of appropriated funds to an entitlement without regard to the availability of funds to pay the costs of training.

However, limits on availability of funding for training exist. For example, the *1988 Act* established an annual aggregate ceiling on training costs of $80 million. *See* 19 U.S.C. § 2296(a)(2)(A). Moreover, training is given only if 6 conditions are satisfied. *See* 19 U.S.C. § 2296(a)(1). First, there must be no suitable employment available. Second, it is clear the worker would benefit from appropriate training. Third, the worker must be qualified to undertake and complete the training. Fourth, the training is reasonably available from government or private sources. Fifth, the training is offered at reasonable cost. Sixth, there is a reasonable expectation of employment after finishing the training.

Ironically, TRA payments may operate at cross-purposes with re-employment services and training. This irony arises from the fact that many workers find that their previous job offered better pay and benefits than any new job available through training. Consequently, workers may elect to postpone retraining or a job search in the hope that they will be recalled to their old job. Moreover, they are likely to have many incentives to avoid moving to a new community for a job, *e.g.*, a spouse with a local job, children in nearby schools, family in close proximity, ownership of real property, long-standing ties to the community, etc. Put simply, TRA payments may exacerbate the adjustment problem. Indeed, data from 1974-1979 indicate this phenomenon occurred.

C. Health Care Tax Credit

The 2002 *TAA Reform Act* ushered in a Federal tax credit to subsidize private health care coverage for displaced workers who are certified to receive TAA benefits. The Internal Revenue Service (IRS) administers the Health Care Tax Credit (HCTC). The HCTC covers 65 percent of premiums a worker pays for qualified health insurance. The tax credit can be refunded if a worker has no tax liability. It can be advanced to apply to insurance purchases, obviating the need to wait to receive it until filing a tax return.

The HCTC can be applied toward purchase of 3 kinds of policies:

1. *Consolidated Omnibus Budget Reconciliation Act of 1985 (COBRA)* continued employer-sponsored health insurance.

2. An individual health insurance policy (if already covered by an individual policy 30 days before becoming unemployed).

3. A group policy offered through a spouse's employer.

The Federal tax credit can apply to certain types of State provided coverage.

D. Trade Adjustment Assistance for Firms

Sections 251-264 of the *1974 Act* added a TAA program for firms adversely affected by import competition. *See* 19 U.S.C. §§ 2341-2355. The Economic Development Administration (EDA) of the Department of Commerce administers this program. Compensation to certified firms consists exclusively of technical assistance to develop and implement an economic recovery strategy. Amendments to the program made in 1986 under the *COBRA* eliminated financial assistance benefits, which had included direct loans and loan guarantees. *See* 19 U.S.C. § 2344(d).

E. Trade Adjustment Assistance for Farmers and Fishermen

Farmers and agricultural commodity producers (including livestock producers and people employed in the fishing industry) are covered under the *TAA Act of 2002*. The Secretary of Agriculture manages this program, which is designed to help compensate farmers whose incomes have dropped from levels in the past year. The USDA can compensate farmers for up to half of the difference between (1) 80 percent of the average national price for a commodity over the preceding 5 years, and (2) the average national price in the current year. The amount any one farmer can receive under this program is capped at $10,000 per 12 month period. The payment also cannot exceed the limitation on counter cyclical payments in the *Food Security Act of 1985* (Section 1001(c)).

F. Why Not Outsourced Software Workers?

In the technology sector, many software developers have seen their jobs offshored or outsourced to countries like India. Petitions to certify software firms have confounded the DOL. Is software code an "article" the TAA program covers? For example, former employees of Computer Sciences Corporation (CSC), Electronic Data Systems (EDS), and International Business Machines (IBM) filed petitions with the DOL for certification of benefits due to software "source code" development that was offshored. Initially, the DOL discounted "code" as an "article." Its logic was "code" is not stored on a tangible medium, but rather transmitted electronically.

The Court of International Trade (CIT) disagreed. It said the HTSUS lists electronically transmitted computer software. Hence, software is an article, even though it is exempt from duty. *See Former Employees of International Business Machines, Global Services Division v. United States Secretary of Labor*, 462 F. Supp. 2d 1239 (CIT 2006). The CSC case is even more egregious. The plaintiffs endured five negative petition reviews by the DOL, and two visits to the CIT with a stern warning the second time from Judge Nicholas Tsoucalas that "Labor is stubbornly arguing its position that software code must be embodied on a physical medium. . . . The plain language of the *Trade Act* does not require that an article must be tangible." *Former Employees of Computer Sciences Corporation v. United States Secretary of Labor*, 414 F. Supp. 2d 1334, 1343 (CIT 2006). In April 2006, the DOL acquiesced, expanding the definition of "article" to cover non-physical-medium products. *See* 71 Fed. Reg. 18,355 (11 April 2006).

Why is the DOL challenged by outsourcing of software jobs? Does it presume TAA benefits are for factory workers and farmers, but not white collar workers? Is the presumption that losers from trade are only in dying industries, not infant industries, which may be taking global hold far more rapidly than to what people can react? Evidently, the CIT is compelling the Department to rethink its paradigm.

Chapter 10

ECONOMICS OF TRADE BARRIERS

Good fences make good neighbors.
> —Robert Frost (1874-1963), *Mending Wall*

DOCUMENTS SUPPLEMENT ASSIGNMENT

1. *Havana Charter* Articles 1-10
2. GATT Preamble, Articles I-II, XI
3. WTO *Agreement* Preamble

I. TARIFF BASICS

A. Types of Tariffs

A tariff is a tax on the importation of a good or service. It is distinct from a so-called "direct" tax, which is a tax on income. The accrual of income triggers the application of an income tax. A tariff is also distinct from a so-called "indirect," or "internal," tax, which is a levy on a particular economic transaction other than the cross-border provision of a good or service or the accrual of income. For example, a tax may be imposed on the sale of a product, known as a "sales" or "consumption" tax, or on the addition of value to a product, known as a "value-added" tax (VAT). A tariff, then, is triggered by transfer of a good or service across an international boundary.

Tariffs come in one of three types: *ad valorem*; specific; or hybrid. As the Latin term suggests, an *ad valorem* tariff is a charge on the value of the imported good or service. The charge is expressed as a set percentage of the price of a good or service. For example, levies of 2.5 percent of the value of a car, or 25 percent of the value of a truck, are *ad valorem* tariffs. A specific duty is an assessment based not on the value, but the volume, of the good or service imported. The volume is expressed in terms of the physical units by which industry custom and practice measures the good or service. For example, a charge of $1.23 per bushel of wheat, or $4.56 per ton of steel, would be specific duties. Finally, a hybrid tariff combines both ad valorem and specific duty features. A charge of 5 percent plus 78 cents per dozen eggs would be a hybrid tariff.

Implicit in cataloging of tariff types is the importance of customs valuation. Tariff liability, that is, the amount of tariff owned on a good or service by the importer of record of that good or service, depends on two variables: the tariff amount, and the value or weight of the product. If the tariff is an *ad valorem* rate, then for any given rate, the higher the tariff value, the higher the tariff liability. If the tariff is a specific duty, then for any given level of duty, the larger the volume by weight imported, the higher the liability.

In truth, tariff liability depends on a third variable — customs classification, which is a decision implicit in the tripartite catalogue of tariffs. How do customs officials and the importer of record know the correct tariff to apply to a good or service? The answer is customs classification. Imported merchandise must be classified properly according to a standard scheme for classifying products known as the "Harmonized System" (HS).

Any of the aforementioned kinds of tariffs may be "non-discriminatory" or "discriminatory." A non-discriminatory rate indicates an importing country applies a stated tariff to all like products regardless of origin. An example is the MFN tariff rate is a non-discriminatory one, as all like products from WTO Members. Significantly, different countries — including WTO Members — may (and typically do) have different tariffs on a particular item. The rice tariff in Japan is notoriously high, whereas in other countries it is far lower. The point about non-discrimination is the importing country, *e.g.*, Japan, applies the same tariff to like-product rice from all other countries.

In contrast, a discriminatory tariff indicates the like product attracts a different tariff rate from an importing country, depending on the country of origin. For example, if Japan charges a 100 percent duty on Thai rice, but 25 percent on Indian rice, the tariff discriminates against Thai rice, and the overall scheme confers a margin of preference of 75 percent to Indian rice (the difference between 100 and 25 percent). Discriminatory tariffs are permissible, under certain circumstances, namely, the application of trade remedies (such as antidumping or countervailing duties, or safeguards), regional trade agreements (RTAs), preferential schemes (like the Generalized System of Preferences (GSP)), and the treatment of non-WTO Members.

B. Tariff Peaks, Escalation, and Inversion

As its rubric suggests, a tariff "peak" is a high tariff, namely, a tariff that is particularly high given the other tariffs, or average tariff, in the Schedule of Concessions of a particular country. No standard definition of a tariff "peak" exists. However, a commonly accepted benchmark is 15 percent for a developed country. Developing and least developed countries tend to have considerably higher average tariffs than developed countries. For some poor countries, 15 percent would be a low or average rate. Hence, for such countries, demarcating a tariff peak requires a higher figure than 15 percent.

Tariff escalation and tariff inversion are phenomena occurring within the Schedule of Concessions of several countries — they are mirror images. With tariff escalation, the applicable duty rate on a product increases as processing of that product advances. The rates on the raw materials needed to make the product are zero or low. The rates on intermediate (*i.e.*, semi-finished) inputs are relatively higher than, or at least the same as, duties on raw materials. The rate on the finished product is high. In Table 10-1, data collected by the WTO from the late 1990s illustrate tariff escalation. A number of product categories are affected by tariff escalation, including fruit, leather, rubber, tobacco, and wood. In such categories, the *ad valorem* duties rise directly with the stage of processing.

To give a specific example, suppose the EU provides duty-free treatment on cocoa from Ghana, a 10 percent duty on cocoa that is semi-processed by adding sugar, and a 15 percent duty on chocolate candies. Clearly, as the stage of processing advances, the tariff rises. The implications of this tariff escalation ought to be obvious. On the one hand, chocolate candy producers in some EU states benefit from zero- or low-duty rates on inputs, and from protection against imports of the finished like product. On the other hand, Sub-Saharan African countries that would like to diversify away from dependence for export revenues on primary commodities like cocoa face stiffer tariffs on processed goods. Indeed, in general, tariff escalation is adverse to efforts by developing and least developed countries to industrialize.

TABLE 10-1:
TARIFF ESCALATION IN THE SCHEDULES OF DEVELOPED COUNTRIES (LATE 1990s)

Type of Product And Average Tariff Rate Imposed by Developed Countries	All Manufactured Goods Except for Petroleum	All Natural Resource-Based Goods Except for Petroleum
Raw Materials	0.8	2.0
Semi-manufactured items	2.8	2.0
Finished Goods	6.2	5.9

During the 1960s, scholars and advocates for poor countries called for preferential trading arrangements with developed countries to rectify the tariff escalation problem. One result was creation of the Generalized System of Preferences (GSP), which authorizes (but does not require) any country to provide duty-free, or low-duty, access to products, including manufactured items, from less developed countries. The GSP is plagued by a number of difficulties that limit its efficacy, and tariff escalation continues to be observed in the Schedules of some developed countries.

Tariff inversion also is observed. Here, the tariff rate varies inversely, not directly, with the stage of processing. Higher tariffs protect against imports of raw materials and inputs, and lower tariffs are imposed on finished goods. Tariff inversion creates an artificial incentive for producers to source inputs domestically, rather than rely on imported raw materials and intermediate goods. It may be part of a strategy to diminish dependence on foreign sources, or more generally associated with import substitution.

Developing and least developed countries, to the extent they rely on exports of primary commodities or semi-finished items, are affected adversely by tariff inversion in developed countries. Exports of the items in which they have a keen interest face stiff tariffs, thus making it difficult for them to generate large export revenues. In turn, their efforts at industrialization, by leveraging off of their comparative advantage in primary products, are impeded. Presumably, they could use the revenues from primary commodity exports to invest in enterprises making finished products. Not surprisingly, therefore, scholars and advocates point to the untoward effects on poor countries of tariff inversion as well as tariff escalation.

C. The Effective Rate of Protection

Schedules of Tariff Concessions can be deceiving. The degree of protection afforded to a domestic industry, and the extra charge importers must pay, is not always apparent from looking at an *ad valorem* tariff rate in a Tariff Schedule. To get an accurate picture of the degree of protection, economists rely on the concept of "Effective Protection" and its implementing formula for the "Effective Rate of Protection."

The basic formula for the Effective Rate of Protection is as follows:

$$\text{Effective Rate of Protection} = \frac{\begin{array}{c}(\text{Value Added of a Good at Tariff-distorted Price}) \\ - \\ (\text{Value Added of the Good at World Market Price})\end{array}}{\text{Value Added of the Good at World Market Price}}$$

or, to simplify using arithmetic symbols,

$$\text{ERP} = \frac{VA_{TP} - VA_{WP}}{VA_{WP}}$$

The term "value added" is meant to connote the value of an article of merchandise as added at a particular stage in the production process. Generally, these stages are raw (unfinished), intermediate (semi-finished), or final (finished).

Consider a simple example. Suppose Japan imports sugar from Brazil and milk from New Zealand to make rice pudding. Japanese rice pudding producers rely on domestically grown rice for their product. They sell the rice pudding domestically, and export it overseas. Obviously, rice pudding is the final product. The imported components, as it were, are sugar and milk. Because Japan has an FTA with New Zealand, it imports milk duty free. However, it has no special trade arrangement with Brazil, so it imposes the MFN duty rate on Brazilian sugar. Suppose, further, that Japan also imports rice pudding from India, *i.e.*, Indian producers are major competitors producing a like product. The MFN tariff rate on rice pudding imports is 10 percent.

What protection is afforded to Japanese rice pudding producers? The natural inclination is "50 percent," because that is the *prima facie* tariff Japan puts on imported rice pudding. This answer is not necessarily correct. Indeed, it is wrong. It understates the true level of protection, if there is a tariff only on imported rice pudding, but not on any components, like sugar or milk. It also is wrong, in that it overstates the true level of protection, if there is a tariff on any imported component used by Japanese producers to make rice pudding. The correct answer depends on the *ad valorem* tariff on the imported like product, namely, Indian rice pudding, in relation to the *ad valorem* tariff on components, namely, sugar. Table 10-2 summarizes the answer.

Table 10-2 relies on a few additional assumptions. First, the price of one container of Japanese rice pudding is (expressed in Japanese *yen*, ¥) is ¥ 2,000.

That also is the price of Indian rice pudding, sold in Japan, if Japan imposed no duty on this imported product. In brief, these figures are free-trade prices. Second, if Japan imposes no duty on sugar imports, then the cost of Brazilian sugar needed per container of Japanese rice pudding is ¥ 800. In other words, this figure is the free trade price of sugar. Clearly, using world market (*i.e.*, free trade) prices, 40 percent of the value added in the finished product comes from sugar, and the remaining 60 percent from the addition of milk from New Zealand and further processing in Japan.

Third, to highlight the impact on prices of imposing a tariff on inputs (*e.g.*, sugar) into finished goods (*e.g.*, rice pudding) that are consumed domestically and exported, the Table lays out 8 distinct policy alternatives for Japan:

1. Free Trade: Japan imposes no tariff either on the finished product (the like product, *i.e.*, imported rice pudding), or the input (imported sugar).

2. 10 Percent Duty on Finished Good (the like product, *i.e.*, imported rice pudding) Only: Japan imposes a tariff only on imports of rice pudding, the like product in competition with Japanese-made rice pudding.

3. 10 Percent Duty on Finished Good (the like product, *i.e.*, imported rice pudding), and 25 Percent Duty on Input (imported sugar).

4. 10 Percent Duty on Finished Good, and 50 Percent Duty on Input.

5. 10 Percent Duty on Finished Good, and 75 Percent Duty on Input.

6. 10 Percent Duty on Finished Good, and 100 Percent Duty on Input.

7. 10 Percent Duty on Finished Good, and 150 Percent Duty on Input.

8. 10 Percent Duty on Finished Good, and 200 Percent Duty on Input.

Clearly, the key difference in the scenarios, particularly the instances of 50 percent protection on the finished product, is the degree of protection on the input.

As Table 10-2 evinces, the higher the level of protection, in terms of the *ad valorem* rate, for inputs, the lower the ERP. That is, the ERP for a finished product varies inversely with the level of protection imposed on its inputs. True, the producer of the finished product — Japanese rice pudding makers — benefit from the 50 percent duty on the like product imported from other countries like India. But, that benefit is undermined by the higher price the Japanese rice pudding makers must pay for a key component — sugar from Brazil — because of the tariff. With no sugar tariff, the ERP is a whopping 600 percent. But, with a 200 percent sugar tariff, the ERP is negative 200 percent.

Clearly, the ERP for a finished product turns negative with tariff escalation. If a finished product uses one or more imported components intensively in production, and if tariffs on these components are higher than the protection for the finished good, then ERP becomes negative. Stated differently, the imported finished product (Indian rice pudding) becomes cheaper than the domestic competitor (Japanese rice pudding), because tariffs on the components used by domestic producers have driven up their costs of production to render them uncompetitive against the imports.

TABLE 10-2:
ILLUSTRATING EFFECTIVE PROTECTION — JAPAN, FINISHED GOOD (RICE PUDDING), AND INPUT (SUGAR)

Policy Option	Price of Finished Good (Rice Pudding)	Cost of Imported Inputs (Sugar)	Value Added at Tariff-Distorted Prices by Japanese Producers of Rice Pudding, VA_{TP} (Difference between Price of Finished Good and Cost of Imported Inputs)	Effective Rate of Protection (ERP) (VA_{TP} minus VA_{WP} divided by VA_{WP})
Free Trade (*i.e.*, World Market Prices)	¥ 2,000.	¥ 800.	¥ 200. This figure is VA_{WP}, not VA_{TP}, because in this Policy Option there is no tariff distortion.	None. There is no tariff protection on the finished good or input.
10% Duty on Finished Good (Rice Pudding)	¥ 2,200. Free trade price plus 10% tariff.	¥ 800. Zero percent duty on sugar.	¥ 1,400. This figure is VA_{TP}, because of price distortion the tariff causes.	600%. The difference between ¥ 1,400 and ¥ 200, divided by ¥ 200.
10% Duty on Finished Good (Rice Pudding) 25% Duty on Input (Sugar)	¥ 2,200. Free trade price (¥ 2,000) plus 10% tariff.	¥ 1,000. Free trade price (¥ 800) plus 25% duty (¥ 200).	¥ 1,200. This figure is VA_{TP}, because of price distortions the tariffs cause.	500%. The difference between ¥ 1,200 and ¥ 200, divided by ¥ 200.
10% Duty on Finished Good 50% Duty on Input	¥ 2,200. Free trade price (¥ 2,000) plus 10 percent tariff.	¥ 1,200. Free trade price (¥ 800) plus 50 percent duty (¥ 400).	¥ 1,000. This figure is a VA_{TP}, because of the price distortions the tariffs cause.	400%. The difference between ¥ 1,000 and ¥ 200, divided by ¥ 200.
10% Duty on Finished Good 75% Duty on Input	¥ 2,200. Free trade price (¥ 2,000) plus 10 percent tariff.	¥ 1,400. Free trade price (¥ 800) plus 75 percent duty (¥ 600).	¥ 600. This figure is a VA_{TP}, because of the price distortions the tariffs cause.	300%. The difference between ¥ 600 and ¥ 200, divided by ¥ 200.
10% Duty on Finished Good 100% Duty on Input	¥2,200. Free trade price (¥2,000) plus 10% tariff.	¥1,600. Free trade price (¥ 800) plus 100% duty (¥ 800).	¥400. This figure is VA_{TP}, because price distortions the tariffs cause.	200%. The difference between ¥400 and ¥200, divided by ¥200.
10% Duty on Finished Good 150% Duty on Input	¥ 2,200. Free trade price (¥2,000) plus 10% tariff.	¥ 2,000. Free trade price (¥ 800) plus 150% duty (¥1,200).	¥ 0. This figure is VA_{TP}, because of price distortions the tariffs cause.	—100%. The difference between ¥0 and ¥200, divided by ¥200.
10% Duty on Finished Good 200% Duty on Input	¥ 2,200. Free trade price (¥2,000) plus 10% tariff.	¥ 2,400. Free trade price (¥800) plus 200 percent duty (¥1,600).	— ¥ 200. This figure is VA_{TP}, because of price distortions the tariffs cause.	—200%. The difference between —¥200 and ¥200, divided by ¥200.

An important policy insight from this fact is a country must have a coordinated strategy toward its Tariff Schedule. On the one hand, positive ERPs are sensible if they are intended to encourage assembly and finishing operations within a country whose producers use global sourcing of the cheapest possible inputs. In turn, positive ERPs are consistent with an Export Orientation policy, *i.e.*, a policy of industrialization an economic growth stimulated in part, possibly large part, by exports. In the example, Japan's goal might be to develop an international comparative advantage in processed agricultural products like rice pudding. However, the end result can be dependence on foreign source inputs, like Brazilian sugar. The higher the ERP, the greater the risk of dependence on imported parts.

On the other hand, negative ERPs are sensible if they are intended as an incentive to rely on domestic, rather than foreign, inputs. For instance, Japan might intend the ERP for rice pudding producers to be negative, because it wants them to use domestically-produced sugar or sugar substitutes. Accordingly, negative ERPs are consistent with an Import Substitution policy, *i.e.*, a policy of industrialization and economic growth by government intervention to promote selected domestic industries and restrict imports. In other words, Japan may be trying to develop a local sugar or sugar substitute industry, encourage input sourcing from this industry, and divert it from Brazilian sugar plantations. Yet, if ERPs are "too" negative, then the local producers cannot compete with the foreign like product, and the aim of Import Substitution is defeated.

II. CLASSICAL AND NEOCLASSICAL ECONOMIC ANALYSES OF A TARIFF

In Chapter 7 of his 1817 classic, *The Principles of Political Economy and Taxation*, David Ricardo explains why a country is better off with international trade than under its opposite, autarky. The country experiences net economic benefits from a unilateral (and, therefore, unconditional) reduction (indeed, elimination) of tariff barriers. The gist of Ricardo's argument is the country is able to specialize in production of a commodity in which it has a comparative cost advantage. He illustrates the argument with the England and Portugal, and commodities such as cotton and wine. Economists depict production specialization with a graph of a country's "production possibilities frontier." This frontier delineates the maximum amount the country can produce with its existing stock of factors of production (*i.e.*, labor, land, human capital, physical capital, and technology). By identifying the terms of trade for a country with a line that is drawn tangent to the frontier and reflects the world market prices of one commodity against another, economists identify the theoretical point of production specialization.

In turn, argued Ricardo, a country can trade its exportable production surplus for an imported commodity in which it does not enjoy a comparative cost advantage. The cross-border exchange allows consumers in the country to realise a higher level of consumption than they had before, when their country engaged in an autarky. In accordance with their preferences, which economists express on a graph with "societal indifference" curves, the consumers can have more of the goods that interest them. Put succinctly, Ricardo's law of comparative advantage holds that trade liberalization allows for net social gains to a country that dismantles its tariff barriers because that country can specialize in the production of what it is best at, in terms of relative cost, and it can consume a larger quantity of commodities on better terms.

Ricardo's law of comparative advantage remains a fundamental economic paradigm in which to argue for trade liberalization. Ricardo argued, using arithmetic examples, that this law held even if one country had an absolute advantage, *i.e.*, it could produce more of every product more cheaply than another country. Essentially, his reasoning was there always would be at least one commodity in which a country had a relatively larger comparative cost advantage, and that would be the product in which it should specialize. As for the other product, the prospective trading partner had the relative cost advantage in that, and should specialise in its production.

While this paradigm is dominant in the minds of many free trade advocates, the economic costs and benefits of a tariff, and tariff reduction, are not always spelled out with precision. It is worth doing so, because those benefits are the economic rationale for binding tariffs at lower levels under Article II of GATT. In other words, what justifies multilateral tariff cuts is Ricardo's law of comparative advantage, and more precisely, the economic analysis of a tariff.

To illustrate the economics of a tariff, consider the following not-so-hypothetical example. Burma (Myanmar), which is a founding contracting party to GATT, gained independence from Britain in 1948, at which time it was the wealthiest country in South East Asia. From 1948-62, this ethnically diverse nation was a fledgling democracy. However, in 1962, General Ne Win took power in a *coup d'etat*, and pursued autarkic trade policies between 1962-88. The General espoused a "Burmese Way of Socialism," which would lead to greater self reliance. He was deposed by a group of military officers who named their ruling junta the "State Law and Order Restoration Commission," and later renamed it with the euphemism the "State Peace and Democracy Commission." Contrary to calls by the Nobel Peace Prize winning head of Burma's National League for Democracy, Aung Sung Suu Kyi, who has supported an international boycott against the military junta, the rulers seek greater trade and investment with the outside world.

Accordingly, the military junta proposes to adopt trade liberalisation policies, including the reduction or elimination of tariffs and non-tariff barriers on various categories of imported merchandise. One such non-tariff barrier is an import ban on foreign-produced jade, which (by assumption) has been protecting Burmese jade producers for years. However, the generals encounter stiff resistance from domestic jade producers. These producers lobby the generals to impose a 25 percent *ad valorem* tariff rate to protect them from foreign competition once the junta eliminates the import ban. Burmese jade producers fear free trade because of competition from Chinese jade, hence the Burmese producers oppose the move. Burmese jade is arguably the best in the world, being of a uniquely high quality and pure color, and thus is not necessarily "like" Chinese jade. Still, Burmese producers worry about losing domestic market share, because of import competition from imports, the price of which will drop with free trade.

From an economic perspective, the argument of Burmese jade producers is narrow and self-interested. It neglects the net benefit to Burma that will result from dismantling the tariff. This result is evident from Graph 10-1, the key points of which Table 10-3 summarizes.[1] To begin, a tariff is a tax on imports

---

[1] Note that the intersection of domestic demand and supply curves represents equilibrium price and quantity conditions in Burma under autarky.

that, at given world prices, raises the internal (or domestic) price of imported merchandise. The amount of increase is in proportion to the rate at which the tariff is imposed. So, for example, if Burma imposes a 25 percent tariff on imported jade, then a $1,000 shipment of jade from China would cost, to Burmese consumers, $1,250. Imposition of a tariff affects three distinct constituencies in an importing country — consumers, producers, and the government.

Generally speaking, domestic consumers suffer from a tariff. They must pay a higher price for imported merchandise. Domestic producers of a like, directly competitive, or substitutable produce (*i.e.*, of any good that may be consumed in lieu of the imported good) benefit from a tariff. They receive a higher price for their output than would be the case if free trade were pursued. To be sure, the price of a domestic good — such as jade produced in Burma — need not rise, because obviously it is not subject to the tariff. However, domestic producers may respond to tariff protection by raising their prices to some degree to gain extra revenue. Presumably, domestic producers would not raise their prices to the same levels as imported merchandise (as they would lose the benefit of tariff protection). As for the government of the importing country, it gains from imposing a tariff insofar as it collects tariff revenues. This gain is particularly significant for poor countries that rely heavily on tariffs to fund government programs.

GRAPH 10-1:
NEO-CLASSICAL ECONOMIC ANALYSIS OF A TARIFF

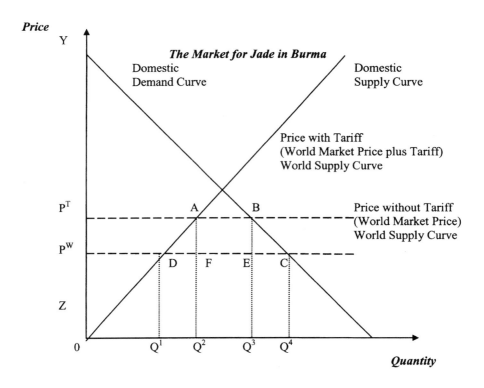

Indubitably, this group-by-group accounting is simplistic. It does not consider whether domestic producers, if they raise their prices, will behave in a far-sighted manner. Will they re-invest the added revenues to enhance their efficiency and prepare for international competition if, and when, protection is removed? As for the government, what will it do with the tariff revenue? Might it invest the funds in education and infrastructure projects that support economic growth, or will it apply them to transfer payment obligations (*e.g.*, welfare) or use them to pay down official debt?

Put succinctly, the standard neoclassical economic analysis of a tariff is static. It does not measure the uses to which higher domestic producer revenues or government tariff revenues are put over time. The analysis also is insular. It leaves out the effect on exporters in a foreign country — like jade producers in China — of a tariff in one market. Similarly, it leaves out knock-on effects. Perhaps Chinese producers, dissuaded by the tariff from exporting large volumes to Burma, divert some of their trade to Thailand and Vietnam. The Burmese tariff has changed the pattern of Chinese jade exports, but the above analysis does not examine the effects of those exports on third countries.

TABLE 10-3:
SUMMARY OF NEO-CLASSICAL ECONOMIC ANALYSIS OF A TARIFF

Constituency within Burma	Domestic Price *before* Tariff is Imposed (same as World Market Price) and Quantity of Imports without Tariff (domestic demand minus domestic supply)	Domestic Price *after* Tariff is Imposed (World Market Price plus Tariff) and Quantity of Imports with Tariff (domestic demand minus domestic supply)	Amount of Surplus or Revenue *before* Tariff is Imposed (area)	Amount of Consumer or Producer Surplus, or Government Revenue, *after* Tariff is Imposed (area)
Consumers	P^W $Q^4 - Q^1$	P^T $Q^3 - Q^2$	YCP^W	YBP^T
Producers			ZDP^W	ZAP^T
Government			None	ABEF
Net Effects from Imposing Tariff				Consumers lose BCP^WP^T surplus. Producers gain ADP^WP^T. Government gains ABEF tariff revenue. Burma loses BCE (consumption cost) plus AFD (production cost).

Setting aside these shortcomings, the analysis does furnish useful insights. It highlights the source of loss to consumers, and of gains to producers and the government. In turn, it provides a visual depiction of the net welfare cost of a tariff. These insights come from an appreciation of the demand and supply curves, and the price lines.

On any chart measuring price (on the vertical axis) and quantity (on the horizontal axis), the demand curve for any normal good slopes downward, *i.e.*, there is an inverse relationship between price paid and quantity demanded. Domestic consumers are willing and able to consume a larger quantity of the good as its price falls. Put simply, consumers will buy more of a good if it is cheaper (assuming, of course, it is directly substitutable with other goods, which implies competition among goods is based on price, not on other criteria like quality or product differentiation).

Conversely, the supply curve slopes downward, *i.e.*, there is a direct relationship between price received and quantity supplied. Domestic producers are willing and able to increase output as the price they obtain for their work rises. The upward slope of this, or any, supply curve also reflects increasing costs of production — as output increase, production costs increase (though, with economies of scale, per unit long run average costs may decline). That is why producers require a higher price to coax out more production. The intersection between the domestic demand and supply curves represents a market equilibrium point. At this point, assuming autarkic conditions, producers will meet consumptive demand in exchange for a particular price.

To continue the illustration, assume Burma's economy opens to international trade, and the world market price for the good in question — jade — is below the autarkic equilibrium. That price is depicted in the Graph as P^W, and no tariff is yet imposed. The horizontal line emanating from P^W is, in effect, the world supply of jade. It is made up of all jade production around the world — Chinese, Burmese, Thai, and so forth. The line is horizontal to reflect that Burmese consumers are "price takers" in the world market. This line presumes Burma is a small country player in the world jade market. Burmese consumers do not have sufficient market power, in the sense of being large buyers of jade relative to other countries, to influence the world market price. Rather, consumers in Burma must accept whatever price is set on the world market, which in turn depends on aggregate global production and consumption.

Burmese consumers would like to buy an amount of jade represented by Q^4, which corresponds to point C on their demand curve. Burmese producers prefer to supply an amount of jade represented by Q^1, which corresponds to point D on their supply curve. Foreign producers must supply the difference between these two quantities, which is Q^4 minus Q^1, and which corresponds to the gap between points C and D. Thus, at the given world market price, P^W, Burma will import $Q^4 - Q^1$ jade from countries like China.

Significantly, there are many jade consumers in Burma who are willing and able to pay a price higher than P^W for jade. They are represented on the demand curve as the portion of that curve from point X to point C. Theoretically, the demand curve is made up of thousands, or millions, of individuals, and the willingness and ability of each one to pay a certain price in exchange for a specific quantity is reflected at a particular point on that curve. The demand curve simply aggregates all these individual scenarios. Every consumer on the demand curve above point C would be willing and able to pay more than P^W to obtain a corresponding quantity of jade. With free trade, however, these consumers need not do so; rather, they need pay only P^W. In that sense, they get a "surplus" from trade, a benefit quantified by the difference between the higher value they could and would pay, and the amount, P^W, which they actually pay. This amount, for all consumers above point C, is called "consumer surplus." It is depicted on the Graph as the triangle whose points are XCP^W. This triangle reflects the price gap (between P^W and X) and the quantity demanded (between C and P^W).

It is possible to see this result by looking at areas underneath the demand curve. Burmese consumers spend CQ^40P^W on jade, which consists of the quantity they purchase (Q^4) multiplied by the price at which they purchase the jade (P^W). Of this total expenditure, they spend DQ^10P^W on jade manufactured in Burma, and CQ^4Q^1D on imported jade. That is because $Q^4 - Q^1$ jade is imported, and Q^1 jade is produced in Burma. However, Burmese consumers are willing and able to spend YCQ^40 on jade. That is, there are consumers willing to pay a price for jade higher than P^W, yet they do not have to. For these consumers, the area underneath the demand curve is surplus, once the actual amount they do pay (CQ^40P^W) is subtracted.

A similar analysis exists for jade producers in Burma. Some of them are willing and able to produce a specified quantity of jade at a price below P^W. They are represented on the supply curve between the points Z and D. With free trade, these producers receive P^W, which exceeds the amount they actually could and would insist upon to produce. Accordingly, they obtain a benefit from trade, which is called "producer surplus." It is depicted by the triangle whose points are ZDP^W. This triangle reflects the price gap (between P^W and Z) and the quantity supplied (between Z and D).

Another way to appreciate why the triangle ZCP^W represents producer surplus is to consider the meaning of the rectangle DQ^10P^W. It represents total revenue earned by Burmese jade producers, consisting of the quantity of jade they sell (Q^1) multiplied by the price at which they sell the jade (P^W). From this rectangle, to calculate their profit, producers must subtract costs. The area underneath the supply curve, which is DQ^10Z, represents those costs. Subtracting it from the total revenue rectangle leaves the surplus of ZDP^W, *i.e.*, the triangle above the supply curve.

Observe both consumer and producer surplus are an area on the Graph. Consumer surplus logically is the area below the demand curve to the prevailing price (implying a saving in expenditure between what consumers on the higher end of the demand curve are willing and able to pay and what they actually have to pay). Producer surplus logically is the area above the supply curve up to the prevailing price (implying a gain from selling output at a price above that at which they were willing and able to produce).

As for the third constituency, the government, its "benefit" takes the form of tariff revenue. The quantity of imports at the world market price, P^W, is the difference between domestic demand and supply, Q^4 minus Q^1. However, with free trade, no tariff is imposed on these imports, hence tariff revenue is zero.

Continuing the hypothetical, suppose Burma's military junta gives into its domestic jade producers. There are a variety of reasons why it might do so. First, producers are a concentrated lobby. Benefits of protection are focused on them. Conversely, consumers are a diffuse lot. Benefits of free trade are spread among tens of thousands of individuals. They may not be organized into an effective political lobbying group. Thus, while a minority, the voice of the producers resonates loudly and clearly in the relevant government ministries. Indeed, that voice may promise political support for the ruling junta. That suggests a second reason for giving into the demand for tariff protection — cozy, if not corrupt, relationships.

On the Graph, imposition of a tariff is depicted by the horizontal line at the level P^T. This level is the world market price, P^W, plus the amount of the tariff (*e.g.*, 25 percent *ad valorem*). The result of the tariff is to increase the price of jade paid by Burmese consumers in proportion to the amount of the tariff. This increase is the difference between P^T and P^W. Stated differently, the world supply curve of jade (both Burmese and foreign) Burmese consumers face rises to the horizontal line emanating from P^T, and that level is the new price Burmese consumers must pay. It is worth highlighting that the world price remains at P^W. It is assumed Burma cannot change this price by imposing a tariff, because Burma is an insufficiently small player — consumer — in the world market to move world market prices. But, the domestic price Burmese consumers must pay rises to P^T. Therefore, the tariff creates a differential between world and domestic jade prices.

Because of the inverse relationship between price and quantity demanded, consumers of jade in Burma scale back their consumption from point C to point B, that is, from Q^4 to Q^3. With the rise in price faced by domestic consumers from P^W to P^T, they cut consumption from point C, corresponding to quantity Q^4, to point B, corresponding to quantity Q^3. The effect on consumer welfare of this price rise obviously must be adverse, and it is. With free trade, Burmese consumers had spent CQ^40P^W on jade. With the tariff, consumers spend BQ^30P^T. The difference between these two areas is the rectangle BEP^WP^T, plus the small triangle BCE. They sum up to the total loss incurred by consumers because of the tariff, and each of these areas has significance.

The rectangle BEP^WP^T reflects additional funds consumers in Burma must pay for jade owing to the tariff. That is, this rectangle represents income redistribution from consumers to the other two constituencies in society. As explained below, of this rectangle, the area ADP^WP^T is an income transfer to producers in Burma, and the area ABEF is an income transfer to the Burmese government. Domestic producers boost output in response to the tariff, from Q^1 to Q^2, and (again, as explained below), the result is an inefficient allocation of productive resources into jade production, shown by the triangle AFD. The government collects tariff revenue, in the amount of ABEF.

As for the triangle BCE, it reflects lost consumption opportunities. These losses are measured by the amount of the decrease in consumption multiplied by the value of jade in terms of the willingness and ability of each Burmese consumer to pay. Consumers would have paid a price for units between Q^4 and Q^3 reflected by their demand curve, specifically the portion of the curve between points C and B. Thus, the consumption cost of the tariff is demarcated by the triangle BCE.[2] Put differently, because Burmese consumers no longer face the world market price P^W, they cannot buy $Q^4 - Q^3$ units of jade at that price. They must accept Q^3 units at the higher price P^T.

---

[2] Technically, it could be argued the proper measurement of the consumption cost is to consider the area BCE and the area CQ^4Q^3E. That argument would be based on the simple subtraction of areas, namely, the pre-tariff consumption expenditure of CQ^40P^W minus the post-tariff consumption expenditure of BQ^3P^T. The difference is BEP^WP^T, which reflects the transfer of income from consumers to producers (ADP^WP^T) and to the government (ABEF), plus BCQ^4Q^3. Following this argument, the triangle BCE and the rectangle CQ^4Q^3E together represent lost, or foregone, consumption opportunities from the tariff. However, a distinction could be made between the triangle BCE, which is opportunity cost, in a pure sense, and the rectangle CQ^4Q^3E, which represents money Burmese consumers no longer have to spend for Chinese jade. They were spending this money previously when they were importing $Q^4 - Q^1$ Chinese jade. Now, they import the difference $Q^3 - Q^2$, which is less, in volume terms. Hence, Burmese consumers are saving money. The money saved is a benefit to them, so the net loss to consumers from lost consumption is the triangle above the rectangle, namely, BCE.

In brief, the total loss for consumers is the area BCP^WP^T. Of this area, BCE symbolizes a decrease in consumption. The remaining area, BEP^WP^T represents an income transfer, of which ABP^WP^T goes to producers, and ABEF goes to the government.

What about the implications of the tariff for jade producers in Burma? Imposition of the tariff affords them the opportunity to fetch a higher price for their output, which they are wont to do as far as possible without pricing their jade above imported jade. They may, then, raise their prices from P^W to P^T. Because of the direct relationship between price and quantity supplied, producers of jade in Burma eagerly shift factors resources into jade mining and boost output. They expand product from D to A on the supply curve, that is, from Q^1 to Q^2. The gap between domestic demand and supply narrows from $Q^4 - Q^1$ to $Q^3 - Q^2$. Thus, imports fall to $Q^3 - Q^2$. Burmese jade producers fulfill a larger amount of domestic consumption than before, which is precisely the expected effect of the tariff.

Not surprisingly, as a result of increased output and per unit price, total revenue for Burmese jade producers jumps from DQ^10P^W to AQ^20P^T. Their cost of production rises from DQ^10Z to AQ^20Z. But, with the increase in total revenue, their surplus also rises from ZDP^W to AZP^T. The change in producer surplus is a gain of ADP^WP^T, the predictability of which helps explain why the Burmese jade industry support the tariff. In sum, the tariff encourages more production (indeed, as explained below, over-production) of the local import substitute, and conversely reduced consumption (indeed, under-consumption) of the imported item.

As intimated above, the Burmese government obtains revenue from the tariff in the amount of the tariff multiplied by the volume of imports. On the Graph, this amount is the rectangle ABEF, which is the tariff (P^T minus P^W) multiplied by import volume (Q^3 minus Q^2). Here, then, is one constituency that gains from the tariff.

Producers of jade in Burma also gain. For them, surplus expands from ZDP^W to ZAP^T. The difference is the shape ADP^TP^W. A larger number of domestic producers are willing and able to produce jade at the price P^T than were willing to do so at the price P^W, simply because P^T exceeds P^W. These producers are reflected on the supply curve between the points D and A. They enter the jade market because of the higher price caused by the tariff. Put differently, the tariff creates an artificial incentive for some Burmese factors of production to re-deploy into the jade sector.

As before without the tariff, there is another method — using subtraction of graphic areas — to compute producer surplus. Consider the meaning of the rectangle AQ^20P^T. It represents total revenue earned by Burmese jade producers, consisting of the quantity of jade they sell (Q^2) multiplied by the price at which they sell the jade (P^T). From this rectangle, to calculate their profit, producers must subtract costs. The area underneath the supply curve, AQ^20Z, represents those costs. Subtracting it from the total revenue rectangle leaves the surplus of ZAP^T, *i.e.*, the triangle above the supply curve.

Clearly, domestic producers benefit from tariff protection in the amount of increased producer surplus, ADP^TP^W. That is not true for domestic consumers.

Because they face a higher price, many of them scale back consumption. On the Graph, they are consumers lying on the demand curve between points C and B. Correspondingly, consumer surplus falls from XCP^W to XBP^T. The difference is BCP^WP^T. The contrasting ramifications of the tariff have technical economic labels associated with them, namely, an "income distribution" (or "income transfer") effect and a "resource allocation" effect.

That is, first, any tariff (be it on jade imports into Burma or petroleum imports into the U.S.) redistributes, or transfers, income away from consumers toward producers. Consumers give up some of their surplus, and they give it up to producers. On the Graph, of the loss in consumer surplus of BCP^WP^T, a portion, specifically, DAP^TP^W, is transferred to producers. Put bluntly, this portion is money out of the pockets of Burmese consumers and into the coffers of producers.

A second portion of lost consumer surplus of BCP^WP^T, namely ABEF, signifies a transfer from consumers to the government. To be sure, the government collects tariff revenue directly from importers, but consumers foot the bill in the form of the higher price, P^T. In brief, by increasing the domestic price of imports by comparison with their levels under free trade, a tariff causes income to be redistributed among groups within an economy, notably, from consumers to producers and the government.

As for the second ramification, resource allocation, any tariff causes domestic producers to make too high a level of the import substitute (*e.g.*, Burmese jade), and concomitantly forces domestic consumers to purchase too low a volume of imported merchandise (*e.g.*, Chinese jade). In other words, a tariff induces too much domestic output and too little domestic consumption of the import, with the result being an inefficient allocation of domestic factors of production dedicated to produce the import substitute. In sum, in the illustration of Burma, too much Burmese jade is produced in lieu of importing Chinese jade, and too little imported Chinese jade is consumed.

What does "too much" mean? With respect to domestic production, it means that given the world market price of Chinese jade undistorted by the Burmese tariff, it would be cheaper for Burma to import Chinese jade than to produce more jade at home. With respect to domestic consumption, "too little" means that given the world market price of Chinese jade undistorted by the Burmese tariff, it would be socially optimal to consume more of the Chinese jade.

Significantly, the income and resource allocation effects are largely hidden from the eyes of the public in the importing country. For instance, when a consumer in Burma purchases jade jewelry, the jeweler provides the customer with a bill that does not include, as a separate itemised item, the tariff. Rather, the bill provides a sub-total, any applicable sales or other taxes or fees, and a total price. The amount of the income of the consumer being redistributed to jade producers in Burma, through the tariff, is not transparent to the consumer. Similarly, the change in domestic production patterns, specifically the reallocation of factors to the jade sector and away from other areas of the Burmese economy, is not readily apparent to the public. To the contrary, it is most evident to the laborers changing jobs from, say, mining sapphires to mining jade.

An obvious question is why the Burmese government eschews transparent redistribution of income in favour of domestic jade producers. The answer is equally obvious: that action would be too controversial politically. Direct income transfers are not only more transparent to the public, but also avoid imposing welfare costs on consumers (in the form of lost consumer surplus) because (unlike a tariff) it has no effect on domestic prices, and thus are favoured by economists over trade protection. Yet, a direct income transfer, in lieu of a tariff, must be funded in some way. That is, a tariff yields revenue to the government, whereas income redistribution is — from the perspective of a government — a subsidy that must be funded from some source. More ominously, the virtue of transparency can be, from the perspective of a government, a vice. The visibility of the income transfer may cause individuals and businesses in transferor sectors (*i.e.*, those economic agents from which money is being redistributed) to protest. The protests may be socially disruptive, and could de-stabilise the government. Why not, take the "quieter" road of a tariff? — or, so the thinking in official circles goes.

The income and resource allocation effects also relate to a second, and fundamental, question about any tariff, namely, what is its net effect? Invariably, the answer is that consumers lose surplus, which is offset by the gains to producers of surplus and to the government of revenue. However, the offset is partial, as there is a net loss to society represented by two triangles in a graphical analysis. In other words, in virtually all instances, the amount domestic consumers lose as a result of a tariff exceeds the sum of the gains to domestic producer and the government, hence the overall effect on the economy of the importing country is negative.

From the Graph, two triangles, BCE and AFD, symbolize the net loss to Burma. They are, respectively, the "consumption cost" and "production cost" of the tariff.

> • The triangle BCE, which is the consumption cost of the tariff and, therefore, the income transferred from domestic jade consumers to domestic jade producers. Specifically, the consumption cost arises from the fact the tariff leads to higher prices in the domestic economy (from P^W to P^T) and reduced consumption of the imported product (from the difference between Q^4 and Q^1 to the difference between Q^3 and Q^2).This artificial distortion sends a signal to consumers to scale back consumption from the optimal level. That level, at point C, is where the marginal social value of jade, measured by CQ^4, equals its marginal social cost, also CQ^4. The scale back in consumption is to a sub-optimal level, namely, point B. This point is sub-optimal, because the marginal social value of jade, which is measured by BQ^3 and corresponds to the tariff-induced price, P^T, exceeds the marginal social value of the good, which is EQ^3 and corresponds to the undistorted world market price, P^T. Social welfare would rise if consumers could boost their consumption by the difference between Q^4 and Q^3 units, but they are unwilling and unable to do so, because of the tariff.

> plus

> • The triangle AFD, which is the production cost of the tariff and, therefore, the resources reallocated to domestic jade production.

Specifically, the production cost arises from the fact the tariff leads to higher prices in the domestic economy (from P^W to P^T) and reduced imports (from the difference between Q^4 and Q^1 to the difference between Q^3 and Q^2). his artificial distortion sends a signal to factor resources, inducing labor, land, human capital, physical capital, and technology to shift to the protected sector (evidenced by the movement on the supply curve from D to A), and boost output of the import substitute (from Q^1 to Q^2).

To recap the illustration, Burmese jade producers gain DAP^TP^W in surplus, the Burmese government gains ABEF in tariff revenue, and Burmese consumers lose BCP^WP^T in surplus. Their loss outweighs the gains, with a net loss to society measured by a consumption cost of BCE and a production cost of AFD.

A highly relevant follow-up question is how neoclassically inclined economists are so sure the total loss to consumers (on the Graph, BCP^WP^T) must outweigh the total gain to producers (on the Graph, ADP^WP^T). The short answer is domestic consumption is greater under free trade than domestic production.

Yet, the calculation of overall economic welfare rests on key implicit assumptions. One such assumption is each constituency in a society is of equal value. That is, the interests of consumers, producers, and the government are given equal importance. If, to the contrary, the interest of any one or two of the groups is elevated over the remaining group or groups, then the net conclusion may change.

A second assumption is that but for the tariff, factor resources would have remained in more productive endeavours than increasing output of the import substitute. For example, suppose Burmese resources used to expand jade production are drawn from rice paddies. To call this shift economically inefficient presumes the resources are better deployed in paddy fields than jade mines. It could well be the resources were underemployed, or even of zero marginal productivity (*i.e.*, labor surplus), in those fields. The judgment also presumes the resources would not have been allocated to an even less efficient activity than jade mining.

Another way to characterise the argument about productive inefficiency is to consider the relationship between factor returns, especially wages to laborers, and productivity. Neoclassical economic theory teaches that wage levels reflect productivity levels, *i.e.*, workers get paid a wage reflecting their output per hour worked. Free trade is a discipline on management and labor, because it compels them to keep wage claims in line with productivity growth. Consider the following modification of the hypothetical illustration involving Burma and the jade market.

Suppose productivity of Burmese jade miners increases by 10 percent, but their wages rise by 15 percent. The price of Burmese jade will rise. But, this price will not be justified by either an increase in the quantity or quality of Burmese jade. Consequently, Burmese jade will be less competitive, on the world market, in comparison with Chinese jade. What occurs to the link between wage claims and productivity when an industry, like Burmese jade, is granted protection through a tariff? The succinct answer is the link is de-coupled, or broken. Wages can grow more rapidly than productivity, and profits can be abnormally high, because of the trade barrier to the substitute foreign good. Thus, in the hypothetical example, imposing a tariff to help Burmese jade producers actually encourages higher costs and inefficiencies.

There is a third implicit assumption in the neoclassical analysis of a tariff. It is that the importing country is a price taker in world markets. However, the so-called "optimum tariff argument," or "terms of trade argument," indicates a country may benefit from imposing a tariff. This argument is discussed below.

III. THE TERMS OF TRADE ARGUMENT

The standard neoclassical analysis of tariffs assumes that an importing country contemplating imposition or retention of a tariff is an insufficiently important consumer in the world market for the product in question to affect the price of that product. In fact, that assumption may be untrue. Graph 10-2 illustrates the optimum tariff argument, also known as the terms of trade argument. Table 10-4 summarizes the results from the Graph.

From the outset, it must be stressed the instances in which the optimum tariff argument holds are rare. They occur only when consumption of imports by a particular country accounts for a large share of aggregate world consumption. Consequently, a change in domestic consumption patterns can influence world market prices. Stated differently, the market for the product in question is not a perfectly competitive one characterised by a large number of undifferentiated consumers, no one of which is powerful enough to influence prices. Rather, in that market, the country is a "price maker," *i.e.*, the country is a large enough consumer to affect world market prices by curtailing its demand for imports through imposition of a tariff. The effect is a decrease in the world market price, and thus an improvement in the country's terms of trade (*i.e.*, a lower price of imports in relation to the price of exports).

GRAPH 10-2:
THE OPTIMUM TARIFF ARGUMENT

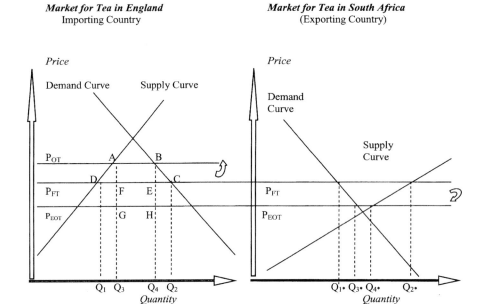

Market for Tea in England
Importing Country

Market for Tea in South Africa
(Exporting Country)

The intuition behind the optimum tariff argument is simple. As Professors Husted and Melvin explain:

> Suppose that the country that imposes a tariff is a large country in the sense that it is a significant importer (or exporter) of the product in question. In that case, . . . the imposition of a tariff could lead to a welfare improvement for the country, relative to free trade. In essence, because the country has market power, by imposing a tariff it is able to obtain the goods it continues to purchase at a lower world price. *By forcing down the world price, the tariff-imposing country, in effect, shifts some of the burden of the tariff onto the exporting country.*[3]

In other words, once an importing country imposes a tariff, the country consumes less of dutiable merchandise. The resulting diminution in demand is significant, in the sense the country makes up a large percentage of world market demand. When its consumption of the merchandise falls, the world market feels the impact, namely, a lower world market price for the imported merchandise. The drop in the world market price adversely affects exporters of the product, thus shifting some of the burden of the tariff from consumers in the importing country (who, in the normal scenario, suffer from higher prices caused by the tariff) to exporters (who, in the optimal tariff scenario, suffer from lower prices for their product). What is ironic about this outcome is it is brought on by the tariff.

---

[3] STEVEN HUSTED & MICHAEL MELVIN, INTERNATIONAL ECONOMICS 168-69 (4th ed. 1998) (emphasis added).

The Graph of the optimal tariff argument consists of two panels, one for the importing country, on the left hand, and one for the exporting country, on the right hand. Assume the product in question is tea, the importing country is England, and the exporting country is South Africa. (Choosing Sri Lanka as the exporting country would be obvious, but it is the largest tea exporter in the world and that fact would complicate the illustration. England, of course, is a renowned importer of tea, and in colonial times set up many tea plantations, including in Ceylon.) The left-hand panel of the Graph shows the market for tea in England, combining both a demand and supply curve. The right-hand panel of the Graph shows the market for tea in South Africa.

The Graph is similar, but not identical, to the Graph of a normal tariff scenario.[4] The demand curve in each country reflects willingness and ability of consumers to purchase alternative quantities of tea at a given array of prices. The supply curve in each country reflects willingness and ability of producers to offer alternative quantities of tea at an array of prices. The supply curve in each country is an aggregate one, reflecting both domestic tea production and imported tea. The critical point to appreciate about the supply curve in the English market is it slopes upward because the price of tea to English consumers is not constant. Rather, because England — by hypothesis — is a large country consumer of tea, the price of tea depends on the quantity of tea bought in England.

With free trade (*i.e.*, no tariffs), the equilibrium price is P_{FT}. While this price would be the intersection of the English demand and supply curves if England were the only tea consumer in the world, it is not at that point because there are other countries importing tea. Accordingly, P_{FT} lies at a level below the intersection of English demand and supply, and at that level England imports tea in the amount of the difference between Q_2 and Q_1. This difference corresponds to the difference between Q_{2*} and Q_{1*} in the South African market. (The English import volume of $Q_2 - Q_1$, and the South African export volume of $Q_{2*} - Q_{1*}$, would be identical if England imported only from South Africa, which may or may not be the case.) However, at P_{FT}, South Africa is a net exporter of tea, and the position of its supply and demand curves relative to those curve for England reflect this fact. The difference between Q_2 and Q_1 in the South African market is an exportable surplus, and South Africa exports this amount to England.

---

[4] Note imposition of an optimum tariff raises the domestic price in England from the free trade price P_{FT} to P_{OT}, but depresses the world market price. Hence, exporters get a price below the free trade price, namely, P_{EOT}.

TABLE 10-4:
SUMMARY OF KEY POINTS ON THE OPTIMUM TARIFF

Constituency in England (Importing Country) or South Africa (Exporting Country)	Domestic Price *before* Optimum Tariff is Imposed (same as Free Trade Price) and Quantity of Imports without Optimum Tariff (domestic demand minus domestic supply)	Domestic Price *after* Optimum Tariff is Imposed (Free Trade Price as affected by Tariff) and Quantity of Imports with Optimum Tariff (domestic demand minus domestic supply)	Change in Surplus as a Result of the Optimum Tariff (area)
Consumers	P_{FT} $Q_2 - Q_1$	P_{OT} in England PE_{OT} in South Africa $Q_4 - Q_3$	Decrease of $P_{OT}BCP_{FT}$
Producers			Increase of $P_{OT}ADP_{FT}$
Government			Tariff Revenue of ABHG
Net Effects of Optimum Tariff			Consumption cost of BCE. Production cost of AFD. Overall tariff revenue of ABHG. English consumers pay ABEF of tariff. South African exporters pay EFGH of tariff. England shifts some of the burden of tariff to South Africa.

Suppose England imposes an optimal tariff on tea imports. It does so as a large country consumer of tea, *i.e.*, a price maker, not a price taker. (This fact is evidenced in part by the upward slope of the supply curve for tea England faces.) As a result of the optimal tariff, there is a rise in the domestic price of tea, from the initial free trade price of P_{FT} to P_{OT}. Clearly, consumption of tea in England falls from point C on the demand curve to point B. Correspondingly, tea production rises from point D to point A. As a result, imports decline from the difference between Q_2 and Q_1 to that between Q_4 and Q_3.

In England, as a result of the optimal tariff, consumers experience a loss of their surplus. This loss is the area $P_{OT}ABCP_{FT}$. However, English tea producers garner an increase in their surplus in the amount of $P_{OT}ADP_{FT}$. The difference between these two areas on the Graph is the shape ABCD. The area BCE is the consumption cost of the tariff, and the area AFD is the production cost of the tariff. Accordingly, to this point, the graphical analysis is essentially the same as for the non-optimal tariff scenario.

At this point, the analysis changes. What price do South African tea exporters receive? The answer is not the same price paid by English consumers. If it were, then it would imply Her Majesty's Government takes all the tariff revenue and hands it over to South African tea planters. The answer is also not the free trade price. If it were, then it would contradict the initial assumption England is a large-country consumer with influence on world market prices. By assumption, England's tariff pushes down the world market price. Thus, the price South African planters receive must be below P_{FT} — and it is, at the level P_{EOT} (standing for the exporters' price with the optimum tariff).

At the price P_{EOT}, England imports the difference between Q_4 and Q_3. Thus, Her Majesty's Government gains the area ABHG in tariff revenue. (That is a larger block of revenue than if the scenario is a non-optimum tariff.) Does this tariff revenue outweigh the consumption cost of the tariff (BCE) plus the production cost of the tariff (AFD)? From the Graph itself, the answer is indeterminate, *i.e.*, the net welfare effect on England of imposing the optimum tariff could be positive or negative. In practice, the answer depends on the relative sizes of the tariff revenue, on the one hand, and the consumption and production costs, on the other hand. In turn, those relative sizes depend on the slopes of the demand and supply curves and the size of the tariff imposed by England.

Two points are clear. First, South African exporters pay part of the optimum tariff revenues of ABHG. (Technically, as a legal matter, tea importers in England are liable, but economists presume the importers pass on the tariff to their suppliers overseas, if the two entities are distinct). Specifically, South African exporters pay EFGH of the tariff. Why is this so? Before the tariff, they received a price of P_{FT} for their tea. With the tariff, the price drops to P_{EOT}. Accordingly, they bear the brunt of the decline from the free trade price to P_{EOT}. Similarly, but conversely, with free trade, English consumers paid P_{FT}, and with the optimum tariff, they pay P_{OT}. Therefore, English consumers bear the brunt of the price rise, from P_{FT} to P_{OT}. In brief, the tea exporters suffer from the lower price for their product, and the tea drinkers suffer from the higher price for their purchases. The "bottom line" is England has sufficient market power to shift some of the burden of the optimum tariff to South African exporters.

The second point that is clear from the Graph goes to the concept of an optimal tariff. It is optimal not in the sense that it unequivocally raises net welfare in the importing country every time. Again, that result depends on demand and supply conditions, and the level at which the tariff is set. Rather, the tariff is "optimal" in comparison with the level of welfare under free trade conditions. In England's case, the goal of Her Majesty's Government is to set the tariff at a level that maximises the difference between the tariff revenue it collects, ABGH, and the consumption and production costs of the tariff (BCE and AFG) respectively. To be more precise, the Government seeks to maximize the difference between the area EFGH and the consumption and production costs. That is because EFGH is tariff revenue the Government gains in the optimal tariff scenario that it does not get in the normal (non-optimal) scenario (because the free trade price is unaffected in that scenario).

The second point is the key insight from the argument, namely, that an importing country in the position of England in the example can set the tariff at a level that enhances that country's net welfare relative to its net welfare with free trade. The effects of a drop in world market price counter-balance the usual adverse effects associated with a tariff (namely, a decline in consumer surplus that offsets gains in producer surplus and tariff revenue). The tariff is set to induce a drop in world market price that offsets the rise in price caused by the tariff. For instance, normally, a 25 percent tariff would lead to a rise in the domestic price of up to 25 percent, but have no effect on the world market price. In the optimal tariff scenario, a 25 percent tariff causes a 25 percent drop in both domestic and world market prices (which are the same). In this example, the tariff has no effect on prices, and thus there is no change in either consumer or producer surplus.

There are three rebuttals to the optimum tariff argument. First, in the vast majority of markets, any one country is too small a consumer of a product to affect the world market price of that product. Few countries are large enough consumers of a good to affect its world market price. Second, even in the rare instance of a price-making country, there is no assurance the government of that country has the technical capacity to set a tariff at an optimum level. To do so requires a large amount of data about domestic and world market demand and supply conditions, and prices. In the above example, it is possible a country sets the tariff at too high or too low a level. Third, even assuming the price-making country "calculates it right," there is the possibility of retaliation. The trading partners of that country may increase their own tariffs to protect their agricultural and industrial producers. The overall economic result, for the world, of increased protectionism would be negative. The "bottom line" is the optimum tariff argument is a weak one against multilateral tariff reductions under the auspices of GATT and the WTO.

IV. NEOCLASSICAL ECONOMIC ANALYSIS OF A QUOTA

There seems to be no limit to the types of non-tariff barriers — "NTBs" for short — governments can concoct to protect favored sectors. Quantitative restrictions in the form of a quota constrict supply and raise the price of merchandise subject to the quota. In consequence, Consumer Surplus declines, Producer Surplus rises, and quota rents are generated. The other two ramifications do not offset the decline in Consumer Surplus. Therefore, a dead weight loss occurs, as the conventional neoclassical analysis predicts.

Graph 10-3 depicts this analysis using the U.S. sugar market. (The analysis may be generalized to any market in any country.) Historically, imports into this market have been subject to quotas. As usual, the demand curve slopes downward, reflecting an inverse relationship between the price of merchandise and the quantity of it consumers are willing and able to buy. This curve shows demand for sugar by U.S. consumers. The supply curve slopes upward, intimating a direct relationship between the price of merchandise and its quantity producers willingly and ably make and sell. This curve represents sugar grown, processed, and refined in the U.S.

Consumer Surplus is the area underneath a demand curve, and above the market price of the good. The area is "surplus," because consumers on the relevant portion of the demand curve are willing and able to spend a price for merchandise higher than the prevailing market price. As these particular consumers pay less for the good than they theoretically would be willing and able to, they reap a "surplus." Producer Surplus is the area above a supply curve, and below the market price of merchandise. The area is "surplus" to producers, because businesses are willing and able to make and sell a good for a price lower than the prevailing market price. As these particular producers get a higher price for their output than they theoretically seek, they receive a "surplus."

GRAPH 10-3:
WELFARE EFFECTS OF A QUOTA

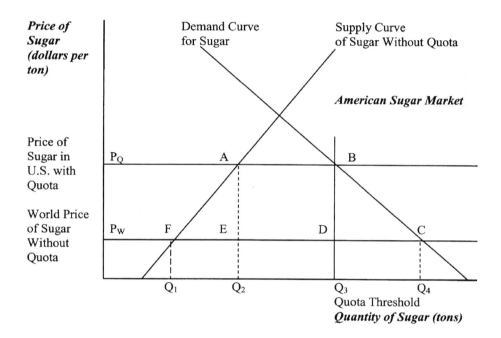

Assume the world market price of sugar without a quota is P_W. This price prevails in the U.S. market if no quota regime exists, *i.e.*, if there is free trade in sugar. At this price, the quantity Americans demand, Q_4, exceeds the available supply from American producers, Q_1. The gap, $Q_4 - Q_1$, must be made up by imports. In effect, the points C and F are the free trade equilibrium domestic supply and demand amounts, respectively.

Suppose American producers lobby successfully for protection from imports in the form of a quota. The effective supply curve changes from the upward sloping one to one that, at the quota threshold, becomes a vertical line. The hypothesized quota amount is Q_3. No sugar may be lawfully imported in excess of Q_3. With supply constricted at a quantity less than necessary to satisfy demand, the price of sugar rises from P_W to P_Q. At the new, higher price, some consumers find sugar too expensive, and demand falls from Q_4 to Q_3. Therefore, the gap between demand and supply falls from $Q_4 - Q_1$ to $Q_3 - Q_2$.

This gap is satisfied by imports, *i.e.*, $Q_3 - Q_2$ is imported. The price differential of $P_Q - P_W$ generates a profit per unit, or Quota Rent received by any entity possessing the right (*e.g.*, in the form of a license) to import and re-sell sugar. In effect, points B and A represent the new equilibrium domestic demand and supply, respectively, with the quota.

The price increase from P_W to P_Q has three ramifications. First, Consumer Surplus declines by the area $P_Q BCP_W$. With the higher price, P_Q, fewer consumers are willing and able to purchase sugar, *i.e.*, fewer consumers would buy sugar at a price higher than the prevailing price, P_W. That reduction entails lost Consumer Surplus. The decrease in Consumer Surplus is akin to the increase that occurs through tariff protection, where the tariff results in a price P_Q. The consumers that remain in the market do not have the option of turning to foreign suppliers beyond the quota threshold quantity Q_2.

Second, Producer Surplus increases by the amount $P_Q AFP_W$. Because American sugar producers receive a higher price for their output — P_Q instead of P_W — they gain. This gain takes the form of a jump in the number of producers willing and able to participate in the market at the prevailing price in comparison with the price indicated by their position on the supply curve. The increase in Producer Surplus is akin to the increase that occurs through tariff protection, where the tariff results in a price P_Q. In both instances, it is essentially higher profits obtained by domestic producers than received without protection. That is, Producer Surplus increases because of reduced competition from imports of a like product, which enables domestic producers to raise their prices without the risk of losing customers to foreign suppliers.

Third, a Quota Rent is generated. Succinctly put, a "Quota Rent" is a profit arising because a quota artificially raises the price of imported merchandise. The area ABDE represents this Rent. The area is the volume of sugar allowed into the U.S. under the quota, $Q_3 - Q_2$, multiplied by the price differential between the quota price, P_Q, and the world market price, P_W. The Quota Rent, or artificial gain, accrues to any entity holding the right to import sugar and sell the imported sugar. For example, the right could be obtained by licensees, assuming the quota is effected through a licensing regime. If the U.S. government gives licenses to existing domestic sugar producers, then these producers obtain all of the Rent (*i.e.*, all of ABDE), and this Rent essentially supplements their increased Producer Surplus. If the government gives the licenses to foreign companies exporting the merchandise, then those companies capture the entire Rent. The Rent takes the form of a gain from being able to sell sugar at a price artificially inflated by the quota. The gain is at the direct expense of American consumers. Put differently, it is a redistribution of income from consumers to the entities holding the quota right.

If an importing country government gives licenses in a quota to foreign exporters, and the government negotiates the import threshold with those exporters, then the regime is a Voluntary Export Restraint (VER). The welfare analysis is the same as for a quota.

Had protection of the domestic sugar market taken the form of a tariff, and the tariff resulted in a price P_Q, then ABDE would have been tariff revenue accruing to the U.S. government. Not surprisingly, then, economists encourage the conversion of quotas into tariffs, *i.e.*, tariffication, and in some instances

— such as Article 4:2 of the WTO *Agreement on Agriculture*, this conversion is mandatory. To calculate the tariff equivalent of a quota, the difference between the price of merchandise subject to a quota and the world market price is divided by the world market price. That is:

$$\text{Tariff Equivalent of Quota} = \frac{(\text{Price of Merchandise Constrained by a Quote}) - (\text{World Market Price of the Merchandise})}{(\text{World Market Price of the Merchandise})} \times (100)$$

For example, if the per unit quota-constrained price is \$15, and the world market price \$10, then the Tariff Equivalent would be

$$\frac{(15-10)}{(10)} \times (100) = 50 \text{ percent}$$

In brief, a "Tariff Equivalent" refers to the replacement of a quota with a tariff set at a rate that provides the same degree of restriction on imports as the quota.

It is incorrect to state categorically (as do Professors Matsushita, Schoenbaum, and Mavroidis) that "a tariff raises revenue for the importing government, while an import quota creates revenue for foreign producers," and "[t]his excess profit is not collected by the importing country but accrues to the foreign producers of the product."[5] In the hypothetical, there is one way the U.S. government (or any government in its position) could capture all or part of the Quota Rent. Rather than give away licenses to foreign sugar producers (or to governments, which then allocate them to private producers), the U.S. could auction licenses to import and re-sell sugar. With a competitive bidding process, the license price, multiplied by the number of licenses, may approximate the Quota Rent of ABDE. Yet, few developed WTO Members use competitive auction systems to allocate quota shares.

One reason why an importing country government might not want the public to know the amount private individuals or businesses would be willing to pay for a license is if they did, then the cost to consumers of the quota regime (the decrease in Consumer Surplus) would be transparent. Another reason is the bureaucratic expenses associated with administering an auction system. Even if a government captures ABDE in Quota Rent, to compute its profit, it must subtract from this gross revenue its expenses in running the license regime. A third reason why a government may avoid a competitive auction system is its aim to keep any quota protection temporary. Should it capture a Quota Rent, then it may become dependent on that Rent to finance a special program, and interests in the program may vest.

Still another reason a government of an importing country is loathe to inform exporting country governments it is auctioning off licenses to import merchandise from their country and capturing the Quota Rent. The exporting country governments might protest against the rent-seeking behavior, and outright profiteering, to the detriment of their exporters (assuming the

---

[5] Mitsuo Matsushita, Thomas J. Schoenbaum & Petros C. Mavroidis, The World Trade Organization — Law, Practice, and Policy 124 (2003).

exporters would have received the quota licenses). Perhaps not surprisingly, then, GATT Article XIII calls for allocation of shares in a quota by agreement with principal supplying countries, or failing such an agreement, by allotment according to trade shares in a recent representative period. Other means entail legal risks, as the European Communities (EC) found out in the 1997 *Bananas* case.

As for the size of the Quota Rent, it depends on where the quota threshold is set and the consequent price increase, and this increase depends in part on the relative elasticities of supply and demand. Professors Husted and Melvin report that in the mid-1980s, the U.S. could have obtained between $3.7 and $6.8 billion annually by auctioning licenses on quotas then in place on steel, and on textiles and apparel. As another illustration, Professors Dunn and Mutti explain:

> If quota rights are allocated to importers, they receive the windfall profit. Suppose oil can be purchased on the world market at $1.50 per barrel and shipped to the East Coast of the United States for $0.75 per barrel for a total landed cost of $2.25; at the same time a U.S. quota is being used to protect an internal price of approximately $3.50. Those allowed to import oil into the United States receive a gift of $1.25 per barrel. They land oil at a cost of $2.25, and it is immediately worth $3.50. This example is not accidental. It was the situation prevailing from the 1950s into the 1960s in the United States, and it produced enormous monopoly rents for the major oil companies that were allocated quota rights by Washington.
>
> [A] key assumption of the oil example . . . is that U.S. importers are able to buy foreign goods at a world price that does not rise as a result of U.S. actions. This outcome is particularly likely when there are many foreign producers who are not organized in any way to take advantage of the scarcity of the product in the U.S. market.[6]

Likewise, Professors Husted and Melvin recall oil import quotas imposed by the U.S. in the 1960s, which were designed to increase the competitiveness of American oil fields.[7] The U.S. government gave American oil companies the quota, and set a low import threshold. As a result, companies were able to import oil from the Persian Gulf at $1.85 per barrel, and sell it in the U.S. at a 67 percent mark-up, or $3.10 per barrel. In 1966, the companies obtained $620 million in Quota Rent (or $2.6 billion in 1993 dollars).

What is the net welfare effect of the quota? The triangles AEF and BDC are the answer. The first triangle, AEF, represents an inefficient allocation of factors of production in the American economy to sugar production. Under world market price conditions, less land, labor, physical capital, human capital, and technology would be dedicated to growing, refining, and processing sugar than is allocated under the quota regime. By constricting supply and raising price, the quota distorts the domestic market and creates an artificial incentive to over-produce sugar in the U.S. The over-production is ironic,

---

[6] ROBERT M. DUNN JR. & JOHN H. MUTTI, INTERNATIONAL ECONOMICS 130-31 (5th ed. 2000).

[7] *See* STEVEN HUSTED & MICHAEL MELVIN, INTERNATIONAL ECONOMICS 168-69 (4th ed. 1998) (emphasis added).

because it still is not enough to satisfy domestic demand. The second triangle, BDC, represents lost consumption opportunities. A segment of American buyers cannot afford sugar, and are knocked out of the market by the quota.

Taken together, the two triangles, AEF plus BDC, are dead weight loss from the quota. This loss is the net effect of the quota: the decline in Consumer Surplus, plus the increase in Producer Surplus and Quota Rents. The dead weight loss is akin to the net affect of protection via a tariff, where the tariff results in price P_Q. Professors Krugman and Obstfeld, citing early 1990s data on the U.S. sugar import quota regime, observe:

> The sugar quota illustrates in an extreme way the tendency of protection to provide benefits to a small group of producers, each of whom receives a large benefit, at the expense of a large number of consumers, each of whom bears only a small cost. . . . [T]he yearly consumer loss amounts to only about $6 *per capita*, or perhaps $25 for a typical family. Not surprisingly, the average American voter is unaware that the sugar quota exists, and so there is little effective opposition.

> From the point of view of the sugar producers, however, the quota is a life-or-death issue. The U.S. sugar industry employs only about 12,000 workers, so the producer gains from the quota represent an implicit subsidy of about $90,000 per employee. It should be no surprise that sugar producers are very effectively mobilized in defence of their protection.

> Opponents of protection often try to frame their criticism not in terms of consumer and producer surplus, but in terms of the cost to consumers of every job "saved" by an import restriction. Economists who have studied the sugar industry believe that even with free trade, most of the U.S. industry would survive; only 2,000 or 3,000 workers would be displaced. Thus, the consumer cost per job saved is more than $500,000.[8]

However, an important caveat must be issued. This net welfare analysis implicitly assumes equal weighting of consumer, producer, and government interests. Depending on the country, market, and cultural, social, and political circumstances, the interest of one sector may be exalted. Consider the sugar market in a small Latin American country. Many poor families depend on sugar plantations for livelihood. Immediate, uncompensated removal of quota protection could doom them economically, leaving them with a devil's choice as to whether to rely on illicit activities for meager income, education, and health care.

---

[8] Paul R. Krugman & Maurice Obstfeld, International Economics: Theory and Policy 202-03 (4th ed. 1997).

Part Four

LEGAL PILLARS OF FREE TRADE

Chapter 11

THE FIRST PILLAR: MFN TREATMENT AND GATT ARTICLE I

He who has a thousand friends has not a friend to spare, and he who has one enemy will meet him everywhere.

— 'Ali ibn Abu Talib, A hundred Sayings (cousin and son-in-law of the Prophet Mohammed (PBUH), 4th caliph, and key figure in *Shi'ite* Islam)

Documents Supplement Assignment

1. *Havana Charter* Articles 15-16, 43-45, and 98-99
2. GATT Articles I, XX, XXI, XXIV, and XXXV
3. 1979 Tokyo Round *Enabling Clause*

I. THE MFN OBLIGATION

A. Overview

The most favored nation (MFN) obligation in GATT Article I:1 may be most famous rule in international trade. What is the substantive nature of the obligation? Briefly put, the rule demands non-discrimination. No WTO Member is to discriminate on measures affecting international trade against another or other WTO Members.

To take an example, consider tea trade among the U.S., India, and Sri Lanka. Assume the teas traded are like products. In negotiations between the U.S. and Sri Lanka, the U.S. commits to reducing its tariff from 10 to 5 percent, and eliminate any applicable quantitative restrictions (such as import licenses and quotas), on Sri Lankan grown tea. The U.S. cannot keep the tariff at 10 percent, or maintain quantitative restrictions, on Indian tea (or, for that matter, tea originating in any other WTO Member, such as Kenya). Rather, the U.S. must extend the same concession to India, and must do so right away without conditions. Immediate, unconditional extension to India of the best trade treatment the U.S. affords is what the MFN obligation commands.

This synopsis raises at least as many questions as it answers. The text of the MFN obligation is nuanced. It is risky to underestimate the power of the obligation. A careful reading of GATT Article I:1 reveals there is more to it than giving equal tariff treatment to imported goods. However, continued reading points up limitation on this potency. Article I:2 is an illustration, which benefited colonial preference schemes, such as Britain's Imperial Preference System, and similar links between France and Belgium and their former colonies. Still other limitations on the duty to confer MFN treatment exist for preferential trading arrangements for poor countries (in the Tokyo Round *Enabling Clause*), regional trade agreements (RTAs) (in Article XXIV), and a so-called "laundry list" of reasons (in Article XX).

B. "Likeness" and "Products"

Manifestly, non-discriminatory tariff treatment applies only if "like products" are at issue, and only if such products are imported from another, or other, contracting parties — *i.e.*, WTO Members. What is a "like product"?

That issue has been the subject of considerable litigation. Much of the case law arises under the national treatment obligation of GATT Article III, as the term "like product" is used in both the sentence of Article III:2 (the national treatment obligation for fiscal measures, namely, internal taxes), and in Article III:4 (the national treatment obligation for non-fiscal measures). The key test, set out by the WTO Appellate Body in the 1996 *Japan Alcoholic Beverages* case, calls for examination of the physical characteristics of a good, consumer tastes concerning the good, and end uses of the good.

The word "product" means Article I:1 covered goods, whether agricultural or manufactured items. Does the obligation extend to services or intellectual property (IP)? "No," is the answer. But, there are analogous MFN provisions for services and IP, respectively, Article II of the WTO *General Agreement on Trade in Services and Article 4 of the WTO Agreement on Trade Related Aspects of Intellectual Property Rights*.

C. Scope: The 1948 *India — Tax Rebates on Exports and 1952 Belgian Family Allowances* Cases

Assuming "likeness" of "products," what is the scope of the MFN obligation? That is, precisely what conduct is barred, and how far does the obligation apply? Article I:1 refers to "any advantage, favour, privilege or immunity" granted by one WTO Member to goods imported from any other country (whether or not an original GATT contracting party or WTO Member). Yet, neither Article I, nor the attendant Interpretative Notes, define measures in this critical phrase. Early GATT Panels stepped in to offer guidance, and took literally the word "any" — to means "any."

An early, relevant case, *India — Tax Rebates on Exports*, dates from 1948. *See Application of Article I:1 to Rebates on Internal Taxes*, Ruling by the Chairman on 24 August 1948, II GATT B.I.S.D. 12 (1948). The facts are unsurprising in the context of the regrettable Post-1947 Partition history of the Indian Subcontinent. India granted rebates of excise taxes with respect to products exported to GATT contracting parties, except for exports from Pakistan. In so doing, India conferred an obvious "advantage," "favour," and "privilege" extended to Indian exports to all GATT countries other than Pakistan. The Chairman of the Working Group deciding the case found the Indian measure incongruous with Article I:1. The adversaries settled the case.

Observe, then, application of the MFN obligation is not limited to importation of goods from overseas. The rule covers exportation of goods to an overseas destination. From the GATT Article I:1 text, the scope of the rule encompasses rendering payment for imports or exports, as long as the payment transaction crosses an international boundary. In brief, imports, exports, and cross-border payments for them are covered.

Governments can be (and many are) devilishly clever in articulating a measure, disguising it to be facially neutral. Suppose a government defines a rule in terms of goods with certain characteristics. Might the actual or potential result be discrimination against goods based on their origin? The answer is "yes, especially if the correlation is high between physical characteristics and a particular country of origin." Consequently, the MFN mandate covers instances of *de facto*, as well as *de jure*, discrimination against goods imported from one or more particular countries.

There is early supporting case law, albeit modest. In a 1952 decision, *Belgian Family Allowances (Allocations Familiales)*, a GATT Panel considered a special charge Belgium imposed on purchases by public agencies of Danish and Norwegian imports. *See* II GATT B.I.S.D. (1st Supp.) 59 (1953) (adopted 7 November 1952). Belgium did not apply the charge to goods from four other countries. Rather, whether it levied the charge hinged on whether Belgium judged the country of export had a welfare system to support families similar to that of Belgium. Evidently, Belgium considered Denmark and Norway did not have sufficiently similar systems. Hence, the Belgians imposed the charge on their exports, and used the proceeds for family allowances (and, presumably, to pressure the Danes and Norwegians to implement a Belgian-comparable system).

The GATT Panel ruled Belgium's family allowance levy illegal under Article I:1, stating:

> 3. According to the provisions of paragraph 1 of Article I of the General Agreement, any advantage, favour, privilege or immunity granted by Belgium to any product originating in the territory of any country with respect to all matters referred to in paragraph 2 of Article III shall be granted immediately and *unconditionally* to the like product originating in the territories of all contracting parties. *Belgium has granted exemption from the levy under consideration to products purchased by public bodies when they originate in Luxembourg and the Netherlands, as well as in France, Italy, Sweden and the United Kingdom.* If the General Agreement were definitively in force in accordance with Article XXVI, it is clear that that exemption *would have to be granted unconditionally to all other contracting parties (including Denmark and Norway). The consistency or otherwise of the system of family allowances in force in the territory of a given contracting party with the requirements of the Belgian law would be irrelevant* in this respect, and the Belgian legislation would have to be amended insofar as *it introduced a discrimination between countries having a given system of family allowances and those which had a different system or no system at all, and made the granting of the exemption dependent on certain conditions.* [Emphasis added.]

The italicized language indicates the Panel condemned the Belgian levy as discriminating against imports depending on family allowance schemes in an exporting country.

Stated differently, the Belgian measure amounted to conditional MFN treatment. Its imposition depended on the family allowance schemes of the exporting country. The Belgian tax distinguished among countries of origin, but veiled their distinctions with a characteristic supposedly attendant to a product, namely, family welfare benefits. There appeared to be no *de jure* discrimination against Danish or Norwegian goods, indeed the Belgian measure was prima facie neutral. But, the measure entailed *de facto* discrimination, namely, prejudicial treatment was the effect of enforcing the tax.

What Belgium sought was a distinction among goods based on characteristics of the country of origin of the goods. That must be forbidden. It is a form of conditionality. A succinct way to summarize the rule for which *Belgian Family Allowances* stands for is characteristics of goods themselves may be the basis for a distinction among goods. However, characteristics of the country of origin of those goods may not be the basis for differentiating among the goods. Lest there be doubt about the sagacity of this rule, consider the proverbial slippery slope that would occur without it.

D. Countries Covered: WTO Members Versus "Other" Countries

The MFN obligation not to discriminate against certain foreign imports, exports to certain foreign countries, or payments rendered for certain imports or exports, it applies only if the foreign country at issue is a WTO Member. The like product at issue must originate from within the territory of that Member, and origination cannot be taken for granted in every instance. Neither Article I:1, nor the rest of GATT, offer specific rules to determine whether a product originates in another GATT territory. At both the 1946 and 1947 Preparatory Conferences in London and Geneva, respectively, the drafters consciously eschewed efforts to define the meaning of "originating in."

To do so, they feared, would be to compromise the overall project, as the topic was sure to be involved. The result is rules of origin are left to an importing country, *i.e.*, each retains sovereignty to determine whether a product comes from another. In turn, the potential for monstrous heterogeneity in rules of origin exists. Multilateral efforts to bring order, consistency, and predictability to non-preferential rules of origin (*i.e.*, where no preferential trading arrangement benefits are at stake) have met with modest success. The latest endeavor is under the auspices of the WTO *Agreement on Rules of Origin*.

Of course, depending on facts in a case, origin determinations can be not only technically intricate, but also politically explosive. Taken, then, a hypothetical case of dress shirts sewn from yarn spun in Libya, which is from cotton grown in Egypt. The shirts are designed in Lebanon, and cut and sewn in Syria. Final assembly occurs in Jordan, where buttons from Israel also are affixed to the shirts, as well as pockets from the West Bank and Gaza Strip. Is this shirt a product of a non-WTO Member (Lebanon, Libya, Palestine, or Syria), or a Member (Egypt, Israel, or Jordan)? The answer depends on the applicable rule of origin for this apparel product. That rule is formulated and implemented by the country of importation. If that country has strategic interests in the Middle East, and if the differential between the MFN and non-MFN rate for dress shirts imported into that country is marked, then assuredly the origin determination, and the rule of origin itself, is seen as much for its political ramifications as technical accuracy.

That said, the political logic of using territory to measure the boundaries of the MFN obligation ought not to be doubted. There are not only rules to being a part of any club, but also benefits. One key benefit of being in the WTO club is receipt of MFN treatment. To extend this benefit to non-Members would be to allow them to free-ride on the club, in that they would not also be obliged to apply the MFN rule (or, for that matter, any other GATT obligation) to the Members. At the same time, MFN treatment may be required through legal vehicles other than GATT.

To take a hypothetical case involving Iran, which is not yet a WTO Member, suppose the U.S. agrees to drop its MFN duty on imported pistachios from 15 to 5 percent. The 5 percent rate applies to all pistachio-exporting countries that are WTO Members. But, Iran's pistachios (which are the world's best) still attract the 15 percent duty. A cursory reading of GATT Article I:1 misses subtleties of this kind. Further, while the U.S. does not owe Iran MFN treatment under Article I:1, suppose the U.S. were to enter into a bilateral agreement with Iran, or to include Iran in a *Middle East Free Trade Area* (*MEFTA*) — even though Iran has not acceded to the WTO. Under terms of the bilateral deal, or *MEFTA*, the U.S. agrees to a 10 percent tariff on pistachios from Iran. Is there any circumstance under which Iran, as a *MEFTA* country but not a WTO Member, could claim MFN benefits under Article I:1, *i.e.*, the 5 percent duty?

The answer is a qualified yes. If *MEFTA* contained an MFN clause, and if that clause does not exclude MFN treatment provided under GATT, then Iran could make the claim, albeit under *MEFTA*. Iranian pistachios then would be entitled to the MFN rate of 5 percent, yet Iran would not have had to provide any trade concession to WTO Members. That blatant free-riding surely would motivate the U.S. to insist on an MFN clause in *MEFTA* that would not incorporate Article I:1 benefits, and thereby ensure Iranian pistachios get the *MEFTA* rate of 10 percent.

To illustrate another subtlety, consider a variation in the hypothetical example. In multilateral trade negotiations, the United States agrees to drop its original MFN tariff on pistachios from 15 to 5 percent, but grants duty-free treatment to Iranian pistachios under *MEFTA*. This situation is the converse of the initial fact pattern: initially, the MFN rate was below the non-MFN rate, whereas now the MFN rate exceeds the *MEFTA* rate. Must the U.S. extend the zero-tariff treatment to pistachios from, say, Turkey (a WTO Member, but — hypothetically — not a party to *MEFTA*)? The answer is yes — indeed, not just "yes," but "yes, immediately, and unconditionally." The obligation implicates advantages, favors, privileges, and immunities extended to any other country, whether or not that other country is a WTO Member. In fact, at the 1947 Geneva Conference, the suggestion to limit MFN obligation only to contracting parties was rejected.

Because of Article I:1, Turkey's like product is entitled to the best treatment the U.S. gives to any other country, whether or not that other country is a WTO Member. Were that not true, then every WTO Member could undermine the multilateral trade liberalization process by giving MFN tariff concessions through rounds of WTO negotiations, but granting still better concessions to non-Members. To put the point differently, the MFN obligation ensures Members free ride on non-Members, but not the other way around. Here, then, is just one incentive to join the WTO.

Significantly, the Turkish pistachios are entitled to non-discriminatory treatment from the U.S., which means more than mere entitlement to the best treatment the U.S. gives to a like product from any other country. The word "unconditional" means what it says — Turkey need not have done, nor do, anything for its pistachios to receive MFN treatment. The U.S. cannot demand "effective access," or an "equivalent competitive opportunity," for a class of its exports to Turkey. Put differently, reciprocity is not permitted in this contextual dimension. So, for instance, if Turkey's MFN tariff rate on pistachios is 20 percent, then Turkish pistachio exports to the U.S. are entitled to America's MFN rate — notwithstanding Turkey's own 20 percent duty. That duty is irrelevant to the obligation of the U.S. to extend its MFN rate to Turkish exports.

Reciprocal granting of concessions on tariff and non-tariff barriers is the central feature of most negotiations on liberalizing trade in goods (and services). But, that is a matter to be dealt with at the bargaining stage, not at the subsequent stage of applying agreed-upon concessions. Negotiations are the opportunity for the U.S. to attempt to persuade Turkey to lower its 20 percent rate. If the U.S. is dissatisfied with the Turkish response, then it can elect not to finalize, or even offer, an unrequited concession. Of course, in that scenario, all pistachio exporting countries potentially suffer from Turkey's stubbornness, so Turkey may find itself pressured to liberalize access to its markets from more trading partners than the U.S. Again, the critical legal point about unconditionality is that when negotiations are done, and it is time to implement MFN treatment, it is illegal under Article I:1 to condition that treatment on any reciprocal concession.

II. THE 1998 *INDONESIA CAR* CASE AND FOUR ANALYTICAL QUESTIONS

Subsequent decisions from GATT and WTO adjudicators confirm the potency of the MFN obligation. For instance, a 1998 WTO Panel ruled that the National Car program sponsored by the government of Indonesia blatantly violated Article I:1, stating:

> The Appellate Body, in *Bananas III*, confirmed that *to establish a violation of Article I, there must be an advantage, of the type covered by Article I and which is not accorded unconditionally to all "like products" of all WTO Members. Following this analysis, we shall first examine whether the tax and customs duty benefits are advantages of the types covered by Article I. Second, we shall decide whether the advantages are offered (i) to all like products and (ii) unconditionally.*[1]

---

[1] WTO Panel Report, *Indonesia — Certain Measures Affecting the Automobile Industry*, WT/DS54/R, ¶¶ 14.137-138 (adopted 23 July 1998, not appealed) [hereinafter *Indonesia Car* Panel Report] (emphasis added).

The italicized language in the *Indonesia Car* Panel Report reveals four analytical questions at the heart of every MFN problem:

1. Whether there is an advantage created by a measure?

2. Whether the products affected by the measure are "like"?

3. Whether the disputed measure is a type regulated by the MFN provision?

4. Whether the advantage is offered to all like products unconditionally?

Only if the answer to the first three questions is "yes," and to the fourth question "no," is there a violation of Article I:1.

In the *Indonesia Car* case, the Panel answered "yes" easily to the first two questions. (The Panel applied the same "like product" analysis under Article I as under Article III, holding National Cars and their parts imported from Korea are "like" any motor vehicle and parts and components imported from other WTO Members.) As to the third question, the Panel queried whether tax and customs duty benefits of the February and June 1996 car programs are advantages covered by Article I? It replied:

> The *customs duty benefits* of the various Indonesian car programmes are *explicitly covered by the wording of Article I*. As to the *tax benefits* of these programmes, we note that *Article I:1 refers explicitly to "all matters referred to in paragraphs 2 and 4 of Article III."* We have already decided that the *tax discrimination aspects of the National Car programme were matters covered by Article III:2* of GATT. Therefore, the customs duty and tax advantages of the February and June 1996 car programmes are of the type covered by Article I of GATT.[2]

As the italicized language indicates, a key issue in any Article I case is whether the MFN obligation is applicable to the type of measure at issue. The Panel separately identified the benefits at issue — tax treatment and customs duties. The first clause of Article I:1 expressly mentions customs duties. So, those benefits are subject to scrutiny under the Article. Tax treatment is not expressly mentioned in this Article. But, Article I:1 does state it covers all matters subject to Article III:2 and III:4. Tax treatment is explicitly mentioned in Article III:2, hence it also is subject to scrutiny under Article I:1.

On the final question, the Panel found Indonesia did not confer unconditionally to all like products the advantages from its customs duty and tax treatment measures:

> 14.143 We now examine whether the advantages accorded to National Cars and parts and components thereof from Korea are unconditionally accorded to the products of other Members, as required by Article I. The GATT case law is clear to the effect that any such advantage (here tax and customs duty benefits) cannot be made conditional on any criteria that is not related to the imported product itself. [The Panel quoted from the 1952 *Belgian Family Allowances* case.]

---

[2] *Indonesia Car* Panel Report, *supra* note 1, at ¶ 14.139 (emphasis added).

. . . .

14.145 Indeed, it appears that the design and structure of the June 1996 car programme is such as to allow situations where another Member's like product to a National Car imported by PT PTN from Korea will be subject to much higher duties and sales taxes than those imposed on such National Cars. For example, *customs duties as high as 200% can be imposed on finished motor vehicles while an imported National Car benefits from a 0% customs duty. No taxes are imposed on a National Car while an imported like motor vehicle from another Member would be subject to a 35% sales tax.* The distinction as to *whether one product is subject to 0 % duty and the other one is subject to 200% duty or whether one product is subject to 0% sales tax and the other one is subject to a 35% sales tax, depends on whether or not PT TPN had made a "deal" with that exporting company to produce that National Car,* and is covered by the authorization of June 1996 with specifications that correspond to those of the Kia car produced only in Korea. *In the GATT/WTO, the right of Members cannot be made dependent upon, conditional on or even affected by, any private contractual obligations in place.* [On this point, the Panel cited to the GATT Panel Report in the *Canada — Administration of the Foreign Investment Review Act* case, B.I.S.D. (30th Supp.) (adopted 7 February 1984).] The existence of these conditions is inconsistent with the provisions of Article I:1 which provides that tax and customs duty benefits accorded to products of one Member (here on Korean products) be accorded to imported like products from other Members "immediately and unconditionally." [Citation omitted.]

14.146 We note also that *under the February 1996 car programme the granting of customs duty benefits to parts and components is conditional to their being used in the assembly in Indonesia of a National Car.* The granting of tax benefits is conditional and limited to the only Pioneer company producing National Cars. And there is also a third condition for these benefits: *the meeting of certain local content targets.* Indeed under all these car programmes, customs duty and tax benefits are conditional on achieving a certain local content value for the finished car. The existence of these conditions is inconsistent with the provisions of Article I:1, which provides that tax and customs duty advantages accorded to products of one Member (here on Korean products) be accorded to imported like products from other Members "immediately and unconditionally."

14.147 For the reasons discussed above, we consider that the June 1996 car programme which *introduced discrimination between imports in the allocation of tax and customs duty benefits based on various conditions and other criteria not related to the imports themselves and the February 1996 car programme which also introduce discrimination between imports in the allocation of customs duty benefits based on various conditions and other criteria not related to the imports themselves,* are inconsistent with the provisions of Article I of GATT.[3]

---

[3] *Indonesia Car* Panel Report, *supra* note 1, at ¶¶ 14.143, 14.145-147 (emphasis added).

Finally, the untenable legal position of Indonesia is worthy of remark. Legal argumentation — a proposition followed by a rebuttal — is dialectical. A key to understanding future implications of many international trade disputes, and fashioning winning legal arguments, is to understand the losing argument, and why it failed.

In the *Indonesia Car* case, the theory of Indonesia's argument was the public — private distinction. Indonesia argued receipt of tariff and sales tax exemptions is a private sector choice. A firm is free to choose where to locate its factory, and to decide how much local content to use, not government direction. Because the decision to receive these benefits is a private choice, the benefits were not subject to scrutiny under GATT. After all, GATT regulates only public (*i.e.*, official or governmental) measures. Consistent with the general erosion in both international and U.S. law of the public-private distinction, the Panel rejected Indonesia's defense. Its findings in the *Indonesia Car* case were not appealed.

III. THE 2000 *CANADA AUTO PACT* CASE AND *DE FACTO* DISCRIMINATION

WTO APPELLATE BODY REPORT, *CANADA — CERTAIN MEASURES AFFECTING THE AUTOMOTIVE INDUSTRY* WT/DS139/AB/R (adopted 19 June 2000)

II. THE MEASURE AND ITS BACKGROUND

7. The Canadian measure [*i.e.*, the import duty exemption] at issue in this appeal is duty-free treatment provided to imports of automobiles, buses and specified commercial vehicles ("motor vehicles") by certain manufacturers under the Customs Tariff, the Motor Vehicles Tariff Order, 1998 (the "MVTO 1998") and the Special Remission Orders (the "SROs"). The conditions under which eligibility for the import duty exemption is determined are set out in the MVTO 1998, the SROs and certain Letters of Undertaking (the "Letters").

8. The MVTO 1998 has its origins in the [1965] *Agreement Concerning Automotive Products Between the Government of Canada and the Government of the United States of America* (the "*Auto Pact*") [published at 4 INTERNATIONAL LEGAL MATERIALS 302], which was implemented domestically in Canada by the MVTO 1965 and the Tariff Item 950 Regulations. These legal instruments were replaced by the MVTO 1988 and later by the MVTO 1998. The MVTO 1998 is in effect today.

9. Under the MVTO 1998, the import duty exemption is available to manufacturers of motor vehicles on imports "from any country entitled to the Most-Favored-Nation Tariff," if the manufacturer meets the following three conditions: (1) it must have produced in Canada, during the designated "base year," motor vehicles of the class imported; (2) the ratio of the net sales value of the vehicles *produced in Canada* to the net sales value of all vehicles of that class *sold* for consumption *in Canada* in the period of importation must be "equal to or higher than" the ratio in the "base year," and the ratio shall

not in any case be lower than 75:100 (the "ratio requirements"); and (3) the amount of Canadian value added in the manufacturer's local production of motor vehicles must be "equal to or greater than" the amount of Canadian value added in the local production of motor vehicles of that class during the "base year" (the "CVA requirements"). [The beneficiaries of the MVTO 1998 totaled 33 firms, of which 4 were automobile manufacturers, 7 bus manufacturers, and 27 manufacturers of specified commercial vehicles.]

. . . .

14. In accordance with its obligations under the *CUSFTA*, since 1989, Canada has not designated any additional manufacturers to be eligible for the import duty exemption under the MVTO 1998, nor has Canada promulgated any new SROs. Also, the MVTO 1998 specifically excludes vehicles imported by a manufacturer which did not qualify before 1 January 1988. Thus, the list of manufacturers eligible for the import duty exemption is closed.

. . . .

IV. Issues Raised in This Appeal

63. This appeal raises the following issues:

(a) whether the Panel erred in concluding that Canada acts inconsistently with Article I:1 of the GATT 1994 by according the advantage of duty-free treatment to motor vehicles originating in certain countries, pursuant to the MVTO 1998 and the SROs, which advantage is not accorded immediately and unconditionally to like products originating in the territories of all other WTO Members;

. . . .

[Omitted is the discussion of whether Canada violated the WTO *Agreement on Subsidies and Countervailing Measures (SCM Agreement)* and *General Agreement on Trade in Services (GATS)*.]

V. Article I:1 of the GATT 1994

. . . .

69. On appeal, the issue before us is whether the import duty exemption accorded by this measure is consistent with Canada's obligations under Article I:1 of the GATT 1994. We are confronted with the daunting task of interpreting certain aspects of the "most-favored-nation" ("MFN") principle that has long been a cornerstone of the GATT and is one of the pillars of the WTO trading system.

70. In examining the measure in issue, we note that the import duty exemption is afforded by Canada to imports of some, but not all, motor vehicles. We observe, first of all, that the Canadian Customs Tariff provides that a motor vehicle normally enters Canada at an MFN tariff rate of 6.1 per cent. This is also the bound *ad valorem* rate in Canada's WTO Schedule of Concessions. The MVTO 1998 and the SROs modify this rate by providing

the import duty exemption for motor vehicles imported by certain manufacturers meeting certain ratio requirements and CVA requirements. The MVTO 1998 accords the import duty exemption in the form of a "reduced rate of customs duty," established in the amended Canadian Customs Tariff as "free." The SROs accord the import duty exemption in the form of a full duty "remission."

71. Although the measure on its face imposes no formal restriction on the *origin* of the imported motor vehicle, the Panel found that, in practice, major automotive firms in Canada import only their own make of motor vehicle and those of related companies. Thus, according to the Panel,

> . . .General Motors in Canada imports only GM motor vehicles and those of its affiliates; Ford in Canada imports only Ford motor vehicles and those of its affiliates; the same is true of Chrysler and of Volvo. These four companies all have qualified as beneficiaries of the import duty exemption. In contrast, other motor vehicle companies in Canada, such as Toyota, Nissan, Honda, Mazda, Subaru, Hyundai, Volkswagen and BMW, all of which also import motor vehicles only from related companies, do not benefit from the import duty exemption.

. . . .

72. Therefore, the Panel considered that, in practice, a motor vehicle imported into Canada is granted the "advantage" of the import duty exemption only if it originates in one of a small number of countries in which an exporter of motor vehicles is affiliated with a manufacturer/importer in Canada that has been designated as eligible to import motor vehicles duty-free under the MVTO 1998 or under an SRO.

73. Since 1989, no manufacturer not already benefiting from the import duty exemption on motor vehicles has been able to qualify under the MVTO 1998 or under an SRO. The list of manufacturers eligible for the import duty exemption was closed by Canada in 1989 in fulfilment of Canada's obligations under the *CUSFTA*.

74. Thus, in sum, while the Canadian Customs Tariff normally allows a motor vehicle to enter Canada at the MFN duty rate of 6.1 per cent, the same motor vehicle has the "advantage" of entering Canada duty-free when imported by a designated manufacturer under the MVTO 1998 or under the SROs.

75. In determining whether this measure is consistent with Article I:1 of the GATT 1994, we begin our analysis, as always, by examining the words of the treaty. . . .

76. The applicability of certain elements of Article I:1 is not in dispute in this case. First, the parties do not dispute that the import duty exemption is an "advantage, favour, privilege or immunity granted by any Member to any product." Second, it is not disputed that some, but not all, motor vehicles imported from certain Members are accorded the import duty exemption, while some, but not all, like motor vehicles imported from certain other Members are not. Third, the Panel's interpretation that the term "unconditionally" refers to advantages conditioned on the "situation or conduct" of exporting countries has not been appealed.

77. One main issue remains in dispute: has the import duty exemption, accorded by the measure to motor vehicles originating in some countries, in which affiliates of certain designated manufacturers under the measure are present, also been accorded to like motor vehicles from all other Members, in accordance with Article I:1 of the GATT 1994?

78. In approaching this question, we observe first that the words of Article I:1 do not restrict its scope only to cases in which the failure to accord an "advantage" to like products of all other Members appears *on the face* of the measure, or can be demonstrated on the basis of the words of the measure. Neither the words *"de jure"* nor *"de facto"* appear in Article I:1. Nevertheless, we observe that Article I:1 does not cover only "in law," or *de jure*, discrimination. As several GATT panel reports confirmed, Article I:1 covers also "in fact," or *de facto*, discrimination. Like the Panel, we cannot accept Canada's argument that Article I:1 does not apply to measures which, on their face, are "origin-neutral."

[Following the penultimate sentence in Paragraph 78, in footnote 70, the Appellate Body cited precedent:

We note, though, that the measures examined in those reports differed from the measure in this case. Two of those reports dealt with "like" product issues: panel report, *Spain — Tariff Treatment of Unroasted Coffee*, L/5135, adopted 11 June 1981, BISD 28S/102; panel report, *Canada/Japan — Tariff on Imports of Spruce, Pine, Fir (SPF) Dimension Lumber*, L/6470, adopted 19 July 1989, BISD 36S/167. In this case, as we have noted, there is no dispute that the motor vehicles subject to the import duty exemption are "like" products. Furthermore, two other reports dealt with measures which, on their face, discriminated on a strict "origin" basis, so that, at any given time, either every product, or no product, of a particular origin was accorded an advantage. See panel report, *Belgian Family Allowances*, G/32, adopted 7 November 1952, BISD 1S/59; panel report, *European Economic Community — Imports of Beef from Canada*, L/5099, adopted 10 March 1981, BISD 28S/92. In this case, motor vehicles imported into Canada are not disadvantaged in that same sense.]

79. . . . Article I:1 requires that *"any advantage*, favour, privilege or immunity granted by any Member to *any product* originating in or destined for any other country shall be accorded immediately and unconditionally to the like product originating in or destined for the territories of *all other Members*."* (emphasis added) The words of Article I:1 refer not to *some* advantages granted "with respect to" the subjects that fall within the defined scope of the Article, but to *"any advantage*;" not to *some* products, but to *"any product"*; and not to like products from *some* other Members, but to like products originating in or destined for *"all other"* Members.

80. We note also the Panel's conclusion that, in practice, a motor vehicle imported into Canada is granted the "advantage" of the import duty exemption only if it originates in one of a small number of countries in which an exporter of motor vehicles is affiliated with a manufacturer/importer in Canada that has been designated as eligible to import motor vehicles duty-free under the MVTO 1998 or under an SRO.

81. Thus, from both the text of the measure and the Panel's conclusions about the practical operation of the measure, it is apparent to us that "[w]ith respect to customs duties . . . imposed on or in connection with importation. . .," Canada has granted an "advantage" to some products from some Members that Canada has not "accorded immediately and unconditionally" to "like" products "originating in or destined for the territories of *all other Members*." (emphasis added) And this, we conclude, is not consistent with Canada's obligations under Article I:1 of the GATT 1994.

82. The context of Article I:1 within the GATT 1994 supports this conclusion. Apart from Article I:1, several "MFN-type" clauses dealing with varied matters are contained in the GATT 1994. [These clauses are for internal mixing requirements (Article III:7), cinema films (Article IV(b)), transit of goods (Articles V:2, V:5-6), marks of origin (Article IX:1); quantitative restrictions (Article XIII:1), measures to assist economic development (Article XVIII:20), and measures for goods in short supply (Article XX(j)).] The very existence of these other clauses demonstrates the pervasive character of the MFN principle of non-discrimination.

83. The drafters also wrote various exceptions to the MFN principle into the GATT 1947 which remain in the GATT 1994. [Most notably, Articles XX (general exceptions), XXI (security exceptions) and XXIV (customs unions and free trade areas).] Canada invoked one such exception before the Panel, relating to customs unions and free trade areas under Article XXIV. This justification was rejected by the Panel, and the Panel's findings on Article XXIV were not appealed by Canada. Canada has invoked no other provision of the GATT 1994, or of any other covered agreement, that would justify the inconsistency of the import duty exemption with Article I:1 of the GATT 1994.

84. The object and purpose of Article I:1 supports our interpretation. That object and purpose is to prohibit discrimination among like products originating in or destined for different countries. The prohibition of discrimination in Article I:1 also serves as an incentive for concessions, negotiated reciprocally, to be extended to all other Members on an MFN basis.

85. The measure maintained by Canada accords the import duty exemption to certain motor vehicles entering Canada from certain countries. These privileged motor vehicles are imported by a limited number of designated manufacturers who are required to meet certain performance conditions. In practice, this measure does not accord the same import duty exemption immediately and unconditionally to like motor vehicles of *all* other Members, as required under Article I:1 of the GATT 1994. The advantage of the import duty exemption is accorded to some motor vehicles originating in certain countries without being accorded to like motor vehicles from *all* other Members. Accordingly, we find that this measure is not consistent with Canada's obligations under Article I:1 of the GATT 1994.

86. We, therefore, uphold the Panel's conclusion that Canada acts inconsistently with Article I:1 of the GATT 1994 by according the advantage of the import duty exemption to motor vehicles originating in certain countries, pursuant to the MVTO 1998 and the SROs, which advantage is not accorded immediately and unconditionally to like products originating in the territories of all other WTO Members.

IV. JUSTIFYING THE MFN OBLIGATION

A. The Free Rider Problem

What justifies an MFN obligation, particularly one that is immediate and unconditional? The ineluctable free rider problem caused by the preclusion of conditions on extending MFN treatment to another WTO Member renders the question all the more poignant. For instance, once one Member — say, India — extracts reciprocal concessions from another Member — say China — in a negotiating session, India is not at liberty to limit its best tariff and non-tariff barrier treatment only to China. To the contrary, India must extend the same best treatment to all other Members automatically, regardless of whether they granted concessions to India.

Arguably, a conditional, and maybe gradual, extension of non-discriminatory treatment would be a savvy, and fair, basis on which to liberalize trade. After all, to continue with the illustration, other WTO Members — such as Malaysia — might hold back from offering concessions. Other Members might understate intentionally their willingness to "pay" for India's concessions, because they anticipate India will grant concessions in its negotiations with China. Why should Malaysia bother paying? In effect, Malaysia believes India cares so much about market access in China for the products under negotiation that India will make the concessions to China necessary to secure that access for Indian exporters, and India will do so not minding that Malaysian exporters will benefit from the same concessions India makes for Chinese exports.

But, consider the view from New Delhi. Suppose India perceives (or, better yet, foresees) Malaysia is free riding on its concessions to China. India might elect not to make concessions in the first instance — at least, not unless Malaysia enters into discussions too. Why not, then, relax the MFN obligation, so India is induced to make big concessions in its talks with China? China might be eager for this outcome, especially if it is an inefficient producer, in relation to other WTO Members, of merchandise subject to trade talks. From Beijing's vantage, any environment in which India grants relatively less efficient Chinese producers market access is positive, especially weighed against the possibility India refuses any concessions in order to thwart would-be free riders.

The free rider problem thus exemplified means a rationale for the immediate, unconditional MFN obligation is essential. The illustration suggests this obligation inhibits a WTO Member from offering trade concessions. A logical step would be to re-assess the methodology by which trade concession negotiations proceed. However, it is insufficient to dismiss the problem by changing from a product-by-product method to an "across-the-board" method. True, the free rider problem is acute if WTO Members discuss tariff cuts on apples, then bananas, then cauliflower, then the (odious) durian fruit, and so on. It is less apparent if they agree to a linear approach whereby each nation cuts tariffs on all imports (or, at least, on large categories, such as all fruits and vegetables, or all primary agricultural commodities) by 50 percent.

Yet, the second methodology still manifests the problem. Members with higher initial average tariff levels are left with higher tariff levels even after the cuts. Suppose Malaysia's initial tariff on bananas is 30 percent, and China's is 20 percent. After the 50 percent reduction, the respective rates are 15 and 10 percent. Malaysia still has a relatively higher level of protection. Put differently, it free rides in the amount of 5 percent (the difference between its and China's banana tariff). An across-the-board methodology does not resolve the problem, if that method is not truly across-the-board in its coverage. If there are exceptions from the cuts, then Members with excepted products are free riders. The longer the list of their exceptions, the greater the free riding.

B. Preserving Concessions

Even if a trade negotiating methodology eliminates entirely the free rider problem, the need to justify the MFN obligation is not excused. One rather obvious justification is the central role the obligation plays in preserving the benefits of trade concessions. Indeed, a 1909 article on the MFN clause spells out this justification:

> Every state has a two-fold object in its international politico-commercial arrangements: to gain and to preserve the greatest possible advantages, and to *guard against present or future disadvantages and discriminations*. In making treaties with this object in view, the clause of the most-favored-nation has been found one of the most convenient and effective instruments, especially for the attainment of the latter end. . . .
>
> . . . .
>
> Not only did this clause [when it entered into widespread use in the 17th Century] generalize previous provisions [contained in earlier negotiated commercial treaties], it performed a more important function, namely, to safeguard the state in whose treaties it appeared *against future discriminations*.[4]

Consider once again, trade negotiations between India and China.

Suppose the MFN obligation does not exist, and India grants concessions to China. Because China does not owe MFN treatment to India, once its deal with India is sealed, China could enter into a trade accord with Pakistan in which China grants lower duties, and more generous quotas, to Pakistani merchandise than China provides to like products from India under its agreement with India. From India's perspective, the value of the concessions India granted to China is eroded. India made concessions to get improved access to the Chinese market. Yet, Pakistan now has access on better terms (lower tariffs and larger quotas) than India. In contrast, if an MFN obligation exists, then India can rest assured the value of its concessions is preserved.

C. Historical and Political Rationales

Satisfying as the "preservation of concessions" rationale may be, there are deeper justifications for the obligation. After all, savvy Indian trade

---

[4] S.K. Hornbeck, *The Most Favored-Nation Clause*, 3 AMERICAN J. OF INT'L L. 395, 397, 399, 422 (1909).

negotiators could hedge against the risk of erosion by inserting a guarantee in their deal with China that ensures the value of their concessions are preserved. Of course, that guarantee might look uncannily like an MFN clause, and would presume the Indians could monitor all the future trade deals entered into by China.

In pursuit of a deeper justification, consider the history of the obligation, its implications for trade relations, and more generally for peace and security. What might occur if a different rule existed? In justifying legal doctrines, a common recourse is to tradition (*i.e.*, history). It is not simply the law always has been as such, but that the stability of the rule has meant certainty and predictability for parties governed by the rule. So, a way to rationalize the MFN obligation is to point out an embryonic version of it existed as early as 1417, namely, an agreement between King Henry V of England and Duke John of Burgundy, signed in Amiens on 17 August 1417, known as the *Treaty for Mercantile Intercourse with Flanders*. An even earlier version of the MFN clause existed in a treaty dated 8 November 1226. Through the clause in that *Treaty*, "the Emperor Frederick II conceded to the City of Marseilles the privileges previously granted to the citizens of Pisa and those of Genoa," apparently for "political" reasons.[5]

D. The Economic Rationale

There are two dimensions to an economic analysis of the MFN obligation in GATT Article I:1. First, countries stand to gain from the international economic order if they can realize their comparative advantages through trade, as distinct from suffering within their production possibilities frontier under autarky. Through trade, they can focus factors of production in the specialization of products in which they have a relative cost advantage, and export surplus production in exchange for imports of products in which they have a comparative disadvantage. Those imports allow citizens to consume large quantities of more products than would be possible under autarky. The political implication of specialized production and increased consumption is citizens, and their government, will see gains accruing from trade, and seek to preserve opportunities for further gains by avoiding military conflict with trading partners. Put bluntly, violent confrontation is based on country of origin (namely, of the troops), whereas unconditionality means country of origin is irrelevant to receiving MFN treatment (as long as the country is a party to GATT).

In respect of the second economic dimension, unconditional treatment is akin to insurance for the benefit of a bargain from concessions granted. Unconditionality gives a trading partner legal certainty the concessions it is granted (presumably, in exchange for reciprocal concessions) are not undermined by the grantor country subsequently offering better treatment to a third country. That certainty is commercially relevant when a third country exports to the same market, i.e., to the grantor country. To take an example, because of Article I:1, India can rest assured if Australia offers it a tariff reduction on wheat from 30 to 15 percent, and thereafter offers Pakistan duty-free

---

[5] *See id.* at 398-99.

treatment for its wheat, then Indian wheat also will receive zero-tariff treatment.

Of course, this example is deceptively simple, because it implicates an important exception to the MFN obligation, namely, the GATT Article XXIV:5 authorisation to form a regional trade agreement (RTA), specifically, a free trade agreement (FTA) or customs union (CU). If Australia and Pakistan are not in an RTA, then India's legal certainty is real. However, if the two nations form an FTA or CU, the accord covers wheat, and the coverage calls for duty-free two-way trade, then Indian wheat farmers will be disadvantaged compared to their Pakistani competitors. In other words, the specter of an RTA eroding the value of tariff concessions is a ubiquitous legal uncertainty.

V. CRACKS IN THE FIRST PILLAR

A. Cracks Created by GATT Article XX General Exceptions

All pillars of GATT, and indeed all other GATT—WTO obligations, are subject to a general set of exceptions set forth in Article XX. The grand free trade principle on which GATT stands — the pillars — are not without cracks. This "laundry list," albeit incomplete, generates some of the most hotly and frequently debated problems in the multilateral trading system.

Premiere examples are Articles XX(b) and (g), which encompass restrictions on imports to promote environmental interests, *i.e.*, sanitary and phytosanitary (SPS) measures and natural resource protection. Cases involving those two exceptions have spawned important jurisprudence on how to read Article XX, and a practical two-step test. In brief, the Appellate Body teaches that an importing WTO Member adopting a trade-restrictive measure and invoking an Article XX defense must first prove the measure fits within one of the ten Paragraphs in the Article. If it does, then the measure must pass muster under the requirements set forth in the *chapeau* to Article XX. Examine that *chapeau* and be sure to identify the critical language.

Paragraph (e) is another example of an important item on the general exceptions list. Article XX(e) permits derogations from GATT—WTO obligations, such as a ban on imports of prison-labor products. The U.S. has maintained a prohibition on prison-labor products that even pre-dates GATT. Whether that provision has been circumvented has been the subject of great controversy in the context of America's trade relations with China. For instance, in 1993 and 1994 in connection with the renewal of China's MFN status, the U.S. accused China of exporting products made by convicts, including political prisoners. To the present day, many American trade officials and observers believe China is not complying with a *Memorandum of Understanding* (*MOU*) between the two countries to prevent prison-labor exports.

What of the other items on the Article XX laundry list? Paragraph (d) contains a potentially large exception, one for any measure that is necessary to secure compliance with a law or regulation that is itself not inconsistent with the GATT. In other words, given an acceptable law, a trade measure that violates GATT would be permissible if it is necessary to ensure the law is obeyed.

Article XX also contains three specific, less-often invoked exceptions. Paragraph (c) covers measures on gold or silver exports, Paragraph (f) focuses on measures to protect national artistic, historic, or archaeological treasures, and Paragraph (h) permits measures in pursuance of inter-governmental commodity arrangements. Article XX(h) allows for production and export quotas on goods managed by international commodity cartels, such as the Organization of Petroleum Exporting Countries (OPEC).

As the "OPEC exception" suggests, with respect to all items on the Article XX list, because of the broad wording of the *chapeau*, the trade measures embraced include restrictions on exports as well as imports. Thus, for example, suppose Syria — like Jordan — is at WTO Member. Jordan is plagued by pilfering of artifacts in Petra by Bedouins from Syria. The Bedu tribes people abscond with their booty and contribute to a vibrant secondary market that flourished in Syria. Jordan could invoke Paragraph (f) to justify a ban on exports of its artifacts from Petra to Syria — a ban that, because it does not apply to exports to all other Members, runs afoul of the MFN obligation of GATT Article I:1.

B. A Crack for Morality and Islamic Implications

From an interdisciplinary perspective, perhaps the most intriguing exception on the Article XX list is the first. Paragraph (a) condones derogations from GATT—WTO obligations for trade measures necessary to protect public morals. The U.S. has a pre-GATT statute for precisely this purpose. *See* 19 U.S.C. § 1305; *U.S. v. Various Articles of Obscene Merchandise*, 705 F.2d 41 (2d Cir. 1983) (discussing Constitutional tests for "obscenity" in the context of magazines imported from Germany).

Some Islamic countries have invoked the Article XX:(a) exception to ensure their trade rules comport with the *Shari'a* (Islamic Law). The Kingdom of Saudi Arabia, for instance, cited this Paragraph in its 2005 WTO terms of entry to justify its ban on imports of alcohol, pork, pork products, and pornography. However, the Saudi approach, undoubtedly dictated by the *Wahhabi* school of *Sunnite* jurisprudence, is by no means widely accepted within the Islamic world. Egypt (the largest Arab Muslim country), Malaysia (the most developed Muslim country), and Indonesia (the world's largest Muslim country) do not invoke Article XX:(a). Rather, they focus on the substantive nature of what the *Shari'a* forbids — consumption (not importation or sale) of certain products, and the spirit of the *Shari'a*, namely, that decisions about such consumption are best left to the individual devotee and the relationship between that devotee and God (Allah). Their approach also tends to the pragmatic, namely, imposition of a high tariff on products like alcohol, which has potential to yield revenues that can be put to good ends.

C. Trade Preferences and the 1979 Tokyo Round *Enabling Clause* Exception

Special and differential (S&D) treatment for poor countries is an obvious violation of the MFN obligation. However, an immunity for preferential trade programs (or, at least some of them) for poor countries from GATT Article I:1 exists. A waiver granted from Article I obligations was made permanent in the Tokyo Round *Decision on Differential and More Favourable Treatment, Reciprocity and Fuller Participation of Developing Countries* — widely referred to as the *Enabling Clause* — of 28 November 1979. (*See* B.I.S.D. (26th Supp.) 203-05 (1980).) Until that point, the waiver had been granted episodically by joint action of the GATT Contracting Parties. Paragraph 1 of this *Clause* contains the operative MFN waiver: "Notwithstanding the provisions of Article I of the General Agreement, contracting parties may accord differential and more favourable treatment to developing countries [including, via footnote 1 to the *Clause*, developing territories], without according such treatment to other contracting parties."

Paragraph 2 of the *Enabling Clause* lists four programs that qualify for the waiver. The first three programs are designed to stimulate "North-South" trade (especially from the South to the North). Developed WTO Members can offer to less developed Members: preferential tariff treatment under the Generalized System of Preferences (GSP) (item a); differential and more favorable treatment concerning non-tariff measures (item b); and special treatment to least developed countries within the context of measures to help less developed countries (item d). The fourth scheme (item c) is designed to boost "South-South" trade. Less developed Members can form regional or global arrangements that cut or eliminate tariffs, and (in accord with conditions the WTO Members may prescribe) non-tariff measures, on products imported from one another.

Thus, to take an hypothetical example, assume the U.S. grants duty-free treatment to rice from Laos, which is not yet a WTO Member. The U.S. does so because Laos is a less developed country in need of help. The U.S. makes the same decision, for the same reason, for rice from Cambodia, which is a WTO Member. The normal MFN rate of 15 percent continues to apply to rice imported by the U.S. from Japan, which also is a WTO Member. Would Japan have an Article I:1 grievance against the American decision? The answer is "no." The U.S. can grant duty-free treatment to developing countries under its GSP program, whether they are WTO Members or not. Paragraph 1 of the *Enabling Clause* provides the general MFN waiver, and Paragraph 2(a) specifically lists GSP programs as qualifying for the waiver.

That answer is reinforced by the 2004 Appellate Body decision in the EC GSP case. Suppose, however, the U.S. makes further distinctions among poor rice exporting countries, giving some — but not all — preferences, based on whether they support American foreign policy or national security goals. The *EC GSP* case addresses what might be called "extra-special special and differential treatment."

D. Trade Remedies

A number of exceptions to the MFN obligation, and indeed other GATT pillars, arise from trade remedies. When a country imposes an antidumping (AD) duty, a countervailing duty (CVD), or safeguard measure, or takes action in response to a balance of payments (BOP) crisis, it almost always is trespassing against the MFN rule — and other GATT—WTO commitments, too. However, there are built-in exceptions for trade remedies, namely:

1. GATT Article VI and the WTO the *Antidumping Agreement*, for AD duties.

2. GATT Articles VI and XVI, and the WTO *SCM Agreement* for CVDs.

3. GATT Article XIX and the WTO *Agreement on Safeguards*, for general safeguards.

4. GATT Articles XII and XVIII, and the Uruguay Round *Understanding on the Balance of Payments Provisions of the General Agreement on Tariffs and Trade 1994*, for BOP safeguards.

5. Article 5 of the WTO *Agreement on Agriculture*, for special safeguards on farm products.

Accordingly, and briefly put, neither AD duties nor CVDs need be imposed on an MFN basis. After all, these remedies are targeted against merchandise subject to investigation (*i.e.*, "subject merchandise"), and that merchandise comes from one or a few countries alleged to be the source of dumping or illegal subsidization. However, in contrast, a safeguard remedy must be imposed on an MFN basis, though this requirement stems not from Article XIX. Rather, Article 2:2 of the WTO *Agreement on Safeguards* states "[s]afeguard measures shall be applied to a product being imported irrespective of its source." Must BOP safeguards be applied in an MFN manner?

VI. A CRACK FOR HUMAN RIGHTS AND THE RESURRECTION OF IMMANUEL KANT?

It could well be few drafters of GATT digested (as much as one ever can) the philosophical works of Immanuel Kant. Or, if they did, they were unmoved. Nowhere in GATT is there an exception to obligations for advancing the cause, or protesting the abuse, of human rights. The silence looms throughout Uruguay Round texts. The GATT—WTO system is quintessentially state-centered, pre-supposing the irreducible elements in multilateral trade law are sovereign states, not individuals. If "justice" is, as Plato says, a conception of a Right Order, then the regime seems not to have a vision of that Order beyond a general aim of trade liberalization under fair conditions.

Only the exception in GATT Article XX(e) for prison labor products veers closely to a human rights concern, though there are good reasons to believe even this provision was spawned by fear that prison labor products were a form of unfair competition. Forget about possible mistreatment of prisoners. What really mattered was that their products were made for free, aside from the cost of the prisoners' upkeep at around subsistence level — or, sometimes horrifyingly below that. Hence, prison labor products could be analogized to illegally subsidized goods, and they could easily be dumped.

The rising chorus of protest voices traditionally excluded or not heard loudly at the WTO — individual and NGO voices — may signal a resurrection of Kant's thesis that an international legal regime is just insofar as it makes the normative state of the individual its central concern. As Kant argues in his 1795 essay (revised slightly in 1796), *Toward Perpetual Peace: A Philosophical Sketch*, it will not do to divorce the business of international law, and the concern for justice in the international realm, from injustice in the domestic sphere. The very legitimacy of international law is not derived exclusively from whether each government that participates in the creation of international rights and obligations controls the people in its territory. That is far too cold an approach. Rather, says Kant, the legitimacy of international law depends very much on how each state treats the people in its territory.

To Kant, a morally legitimate international legal system is based not just on (1) the allegiance of states to the international rule of law, nor simply on (2) the derivation of mutually advantageous benefits from peaceful intercourse. Legitimacy also demands as a building block for the international legal order (3) a shared commitment among states to individual freedom. The chain of logic in these three Kantian Definite Articles is thus: international law is morally legitimate if states are morally legitimate; states are morally legitimate if they adhere to a liberal conception of democracy and human rights, *i.e.*, domestic justice; hence, international law is legitimate if the states in the international legal system are committed to a just domestic order.

And so, perhaps, it goes with international trade law. If the GATT—WTO regime is a just one, in the sense of Kant or his modern-day apostles of liberal democratic theory, then the central focus of this regime must be on the protection and service of the individual. Put bluntly, human rights — and, by extension, democratic civil liberties, labor rights, and environmental rights — must be a, if not the, normative priority for GATT and the WTO if the multilateral trading system is "legitimate." It will not do to hide behind the veil of sovereignty. That dirty "S" word, under the traditional state-centric paradigm of international law, presumes that virtually every established government represents its people, that every state is free to adopt any form of political, social, and economic organization. That approach counsels against intervention of one state in the affairs of another state, even a far more authoritarian one. In contrast, the Kantian argument is not every state is as sovereign as every other. Only just states — those committed to domestic justice — are entitled to the shield of sovereignty. In brief, in the Kantian universe, there is no room for a WTO Member to say "trade is trade, but human rights are a wholly unrelated matter for each Member to address individually as it sees fit."

What should be made of this universe? No doubt it is a realm for the noble, the passionately committed defenders who hear the cry of the individual in the face of inexorable globalization. But, consider the universe from a dispassionate distance. First, does the Kantian thesis mask an underlying intolerance of all domestic conceptions of justice other than a liberal democratic one? Is it an attempt, albeit philosophical elegant, to force upon the rest of the world a western conception of how to run a polity? If so, how could the WTO be a vehicle for the extraterritorial application of one set of political values without tearing the institution apart? Should it be that vehicle in the first place? Have the WTO and its previous incarnation, the GATT, been successful in liberalizing world trade because they have defined and focused their mission in a narrow, precise manner? Why not leave the grander — and perhaps insoluble — conflict about linking international and domestic justice to the UN, which already is half-wrecked anyhow?

Second, is the Kantian thesis internally flawed? What of the positivist response, which divorces moral from legal obligations, and teaches that the foundation of international law is the consent of states, and that consent is based on each state's self-interest? Is that not a more accurate explanation of the GATT—WTO regime? One strain of this positivist perspective — reciprocal entitlements theory — holds that even when a state has a selfish incentive to breach a rule, it might not do so in order to help preserve the international legal order from which the state derives, over the long run, many benefits. Does that help explain why WTO Members typically comply with panel and Appellate Body recommendations? To be sure, there is a latent normativity in positivism — that actors are motivated by self-interest. But, that latent assumption permits escape from the central paradox of a Kantian-style democratic liberalism, namely, the intolerance of all other "illiberal" systems. (This paradox is an example of a fundamental conundrum in philosophy: tolerance does not allow intolerance.)

Third, what of the application of the argument of John Rawls to international trade law, namely, that it is folly to exclude a hierarchical or communal state — like China or Iran — from the international legal order? These states, while not based on liberal principles, are based on concepts that are rational in their own domestic contexts. Since when is it the white man's burden to denigrate those concepts and try to compel changes in those contexts? Short of irrationality — i.e., tyranny of the most abominable kind that cannot be ignored — it is simply not "just" for liberal states to coerce these other states. In brief, can we say with Rawls that core human rights are contingent western liberal rights that are not enforceable under international law?

This question is all the more poignant in view of the fact that deep-seated religious beliefs and traditions sometimes are the roots of so-called "illiberal" systems. To what extant can — and, more importantly, should — the multilateral trading system be the fiat for western-style democratic political reform, when such reform necessitates a change in underlying religious doctrine and culture? Consider a government measure to ban imports from countries in which women wear a *hijab* (veil). The exporting country takes the case to the WTO, claiming this sartorial code is not listed in GATT Article XX as a basis for deviating from Article XI:1. The respondent importing country argues women's rights are accepted under international law as human rights, and the *hijab* represents the denial of those rights. In the WTO hearing room, the respondent holds up pictures of Afghan women as "Exhibit A," and solemnly declares it does not want to support such oppression by doing business with such countries.

The WTO panel is faced with a dilemma. It can focus on the language of the GATT, and thereby support religious freedom, but thereby risk triggering condemnation for its narrow-minded support of corporate interests. Or, it can incorporate into that language a human rights exception of its own making, but thereby risk undermining its own legitimacy by judicial activism that infringes on sovereignty. The obvious point is that defining and enforcing human rights law sometimes becomes inextricably intertwined with religious values. Is the GATT—WTO regime really supposed to handle such matters, and at the same time not lose focus on its core mission of trade liberalization? Or, is that core mission inevitably a broad messianic one that leads to normative decisions about religious values?

In answering these questions, it is ever so difficult to think objectively, as a world citizen. *A propos* the example of the *hijab*, most westerners would be shocked to learn that women in Iran are enfranchised from the age of 15, and that they obtained the right to vote before their sisters in Switzerland (the home of the WTO). More generally, they would be stunned by the insights into Iranian society and the condition of women provided by Robin Wright of *The Sunday Times* (London). She contends much of the most profound discourse in the Islamic world is taking place in Iran.

Finally, if Kant and his followers are so confident of the superiority of western enlightenment values, then why not stand aside and watch the international legal order evolve naturally toward a greater focus on individuals? If the values are superior, then surely even most octagenarian despots and firebrand *mullahs* will figure that out, perhaps with a little nudging from domestic constituencies. As people and businesses in those constituencies trade with people and businesses in democratic states, liberal political, economic, and social ideas will flow across borders, along with goods and services. Put simply, will Engagement through trade — market forces — lead inevitably to the realization of Kant's vision of legitimacy?

VII.   NON-APPLICATION AND GATT ARTICLE XXXV

A.   Syria, Lebanon, and the Meaning of Non-Application

Suppose Syria accedes to the WTO. Is Syria legally entitled to have every WTO Member extend all multilateral trade obligations to it? The short answer is "yes, but. . ." Syria has this right, but any Member can invoke non-application. Suppose Lebanon is a WTO Member, having acceded before Syria. Assume, too, many Syrian exports are shipped abroad through Lebanese ports, such as Beirut and Tyre, and many imports come through these facilities. However, political relations between Syria and at least some constituencies in Lebanon are poor. The question is whether the existing Member of the club, Lebanon, can opt not to treat the newly joining Member, Syria, as a Member?

The qualified affirmative answer — "yes, but" — is incongruous with multilateralism. Surely the right answer, if multilateral trade obligations are to be taken seriously, is there is no possibility of Lebanon treating Syria as anything but a full WTO Member. Yet, the specter of non-application necessitates qualification. Non-application is not a new concept. The GATT drafters dedicated Article XXXV to it, and the Uruguay Round negotiators added to the *WTO Agreement* a complimentary provision, Article XIII, which is based on the GATT Article. These developments occurred for good reason.

What exactly does "non-application" mean? In brief, it is an opt-out from extending GATT—WTO benefits. Non-application is a unilateral right of either a contracting party (Member) or an acceding government to determine whether to apply GATT—WTO rules to each other. In practice, non-application means Members in question do not enter into multilateral trade law relations with one another. The scope of non-application is as broad or narrow as desired by the new or existing Member invoking it. At one extreme, non-application can mean denial of all GATT—WTO obligations. At the other extreme, it can mean denial of just one obligation, such as MFN treatment under Article I:1, or tariff concessions under Article II:1(b). Non-application also allows for the converse scenario, whereby a new Member elects not to extend GATT—WTO obligations to an extant Member. Both scenarios arise only if the WTO Member invoking the non-application option satisfies certain criteria set forth in Article XXXV and Article XIII of GATT and the *WTO Agreement*, respectively. What, precisely, are those criteria?

B. The New Accession Scenario

Taking these two provisions together, non-application is possible in either of two scenarios. The scenarios may be labeled, respectively, and "grandfathering" and "new accession." The first scenario is of historical import only. It relates only to founding WTO Members that had invoked Article XXXV of GATT before the birth date of the WTO. That is, non-application via grandfathering no longer is an option. As of the entry into force of the *WTO Agreement*, 1 January 1995, a GATT contracting party had to have invoked Article XXXV against another contracting party. Assuming both contracting parties carried through as WTO Members, then the non-application as between them that pre-dated the WTO also carries through. The scenario, then, is one in which a contracting party affirmatively wants to deny not only GATT rights, but also all benefits flowing from the *WTO Agreement* and its Annexes, to another contracting party after 1 January 1995. That desire is given legal effect through grandfathering.

As its rubric connotes, the second non-application scenario pertains to accessions of governments that were not original Members of the WTO. Suppose an existing Member, such as Lebanon in the hypothetical, decides it does not want to extend the rights and privileges of Membership to a newly acceding Member, like Syria. Practically speaking, that decision means Lebanon will not apply the *WTO Agreement*, nor the accords annexed to it. How does Lebanon go about effecting this decision?

The existing WTO Member (Lebanon) must invoke the non-application at the time the other government (Syria) accedes to Membership. Lebanon must announce it will not apply GATT—WTO rules to Syria at the time Syria accedes to the WTO. To wait beyond that accession point is to forfeit the option of non-application. The same rule applies to the converse situation. Should Syria elect not to apply the rules to Lebanon, it had better make this announcement before acceding, or it loses the option of treating Lebanon as a non-Member. Specifically, in both instances, the announcement of intention to invoke non-application must be made through notification to the WTO Ministerial Conference before the Conference takes final action on the accession request.

Critically, an existing WTO Member cannot defer its decision about non-application regarding a newly acceding Member, and *vice versa*. This prerequisite for non-application is eminently sensible. If deferral were permitted, then the multilateral effect of the *WTO Agreement* and its Annexes could be undermined at any time. The multilateral trading system would be akin to a sand castle awaiting the right tide to erode it from underneath and around its sides. The WTO might become something akin to the International Court of Justice (ICJ), which is enervated by countries opting in or opting out of compulsory jurisdiction based on national interest. Better, the logic is, to limit the period during which non-application is an option to the time before accession.

C. The 2005 Case of Israel and Saudi Arabia

To be sure, non-application is a potentially serious restraint on multilateralism, particularly if it occurs among large, commercially significant countries. A powerful domestic constituency in one country with its own political, social, or economic justification (*bona fide* or not), or a caustic, unilateralist leader in a country, might stir up trouble by deciding to pull out from GATT—WTO obligations with a target Member.

Happily, that did not happen between Israel and the Kingdom of Saudi Arabia. Israel publicly declared it would not invoke non-application in connection with the accession (which occurred on 11 December 2005) of the Kingdom of Saudi Arabia to the WTO (so long as the Kingdom withdrew from participation in the Arab Boycott of Israel.) Why cast an even longer, darker shadow over multilateralism by extending the time to invoke non-application indefinitely into the future?

D. The 2007 Case of Vietnam and the Americans

Not all invocations of non-application are sinister, even as between former warring countries. In November 2006, just before the WTO General Council approved the terms of accession of Vietnam, the U.S. invoked it in respect of Vietnam, even though the two countries had signed a bilateral trade agreement, and the U.S. supported Vietnam's accession. (The accession occurred on 11 January 2007.) The U.S. did so because of an admixture of technical legal reasons and domestic politics. A Cold War Era trade statute, the *Jackson-Vanik Amendment* (19 U.S.C. 2431) to the *Trade Act of 1974* required Presidential certification of human rights criteria (especially freedom of emigration for religious minorities) for the U.S. to grant normal trade relations (NTR) — *i.e.*, MFN treatment — to Communist countries. (The certification was subject to Congressional over-ride.) If the U.S. treated Vietnam as a WTO Member, it would have to give Vietnam permanent, immediate, and unconditional MFN treatment — otherwise, Vietnam could sue the U.S. under the DSU. Yet, because of the *Jackson-Vanik Amendment*, the U.S. could not offer such treatment until Congress removed Vietnam from Jackson-Vanik reviews, and granted it permanent NTR (*i.e.*, PNTR) status.

Given the November 2006 election, seating of a new Congress, and change in control of political power of both the House and Senate, Congress did not get around to granting Vietnam PNTR status until 8 December 2006. Indeed, Congress refused to do so until the administration of President George W. Bush agreed to establish a program by which the U.S. Department of Commerce (DOC) would monitor textile imports from Vietnam and self-initiate antidumping (AD) petitions if the DOC thought Vietnam dumped clothes into the U.S. (Vietnam, of course, complained the contingency was unfairly discriminatory.) The President signed the bill on 29 December, and the U.S. withdrew its non-application the day before Vietnam became a WTO Member.

E. Modified Prerequisites

A key legal question, with important policy ramifications, is whether Article XIII of the *WTO Agreement* modifies the pre-requisites in Article XXXV of GATT for invoking non-application. A cursory comparison might indicate the *WTO Agreement* inherits the GATT requirements. But, that indication is wrong. Professor Wang's research points up this error.[6] He asks whether, as a matter of law, it is easier to achieve non-application under *WTO Agreement* Article XIII in comparison with GATT Article XXXV. He responds it is easier to achieve under Article XIII.

That is because GATT Article XXXV contains two pre-requisites before a contracting party can non-apply multilateral trade obligations to another contracting party. First, in Article XXXV:1(a), neither contracting party must have entered into tariff negotiations with the other. Once contracting parties enter into tariff negotiations, they cannot deny application of GATT obligations to each other. What does "enter into tariff negotiations" mean? Essentially, it means delegations from the contracting parties have held their first meeting, and exchanged lists of offers of tariff concessions.

Second, under Article XXXV:1(b), either contracting party must withhold consent to the application of GATT (or Article II thereof) at the time the applicant becomes a contracting party. Whereas the first pre-requisite is about talks, the second pre-requisite is about timing. The acceding party and the extant contracting parties lose recourse to the non-application clause upon accession. Therefore, non-application can occur only between contracting and acceding parties.

What does Article XIII of the *WTO Agreement* demand? Simply put, the first pre-requisite in GATT Article XXXV:1(a) no longer exists. The lack of tariff negotiations is not a condition for resorting to non-application. A WTO Member and an acceding party can engage in tariff concession negotiations without prejudice to the right of either the Member or party to invoke the non-application clause with respect to the other.

---

[6] *See* Lei Wang, *Non-Application Issues in the GATT and the WTO*, 28 J. OF WORLD TRADE 49 (1994).

There are two points of continuity between the GATT and *WTO Agreement* on this subject. First, there never has been a need for a contracting party (Member) to state its purpose for non-application. The government invoking this option can be as secret or transparent as it wants about its motivations. Second, there never has been a requirement that a government invoking the option get approval from the Contracting Parties (or WTO Members). The option always has been unilateral in every sense.

F. Policy Illogic?

What policy rationale justifies non-application, *i.e.*, why give the option to extant and newly acceding WTO Members? With non-application, two governments that have joined the same multilateral trade package are allowed not to enforce the rules in the package as between them. Put indelicately, why not say "grow up, act like adults, and treat everyone in the club, including each other, as an equal"?

The answer relates to the link between non-application under GATT Article XXXV and accession under Article XXXIII. In drafts of GATT discussed in the 1946 London and 1947 Geneva Preparatory Conferences, Article XXXIII implicitly required unanimous consent of existing contracting parties to the accession of a new contracting party. The original text of the Article referred only to the accession of a new government on terms agreed to by that government and the Contracting Parties — hence the implication of a unanimous consensus. But, certainly by the March 1948 Havana Conference, the drafters understood this implication might mean the barrier for some potential new contracting parties would be insurmountable. Thus, in that Conference, to encourage broad participation, the Contracting Parties agreed to change the implicit unanimity rule for accession to an explicit rule of consent by a two-thirds majority.

Smart as this change was, it created a political problem. One or more existing contracting parties might find themselves bound by trade obligations to which they had not consented, because they were in the one-third minority opposing accession of the new government. The problem was not merely theoretical. India and Pakistan, both original contracting parties and signers of the *Protocol of Provisional Application* in June 1948, agreed on one point: neither wanted trade relations with South Africa (also an original contracting party). The reason, essentially, was the deplorable policy of apartheid in that country. Non-application under Article XXXV was the device to satisfy the Indian and Pakistani concerns, and each government invoked it against South Africa. Interestingly, the scope of India's invocation extended to all GATT obligations, whereas Pakistan declared it would deny only MFN obligations to South Africa.

The June 1948 use by India and Pakistan of Article XXXV against South Africa bespeaks the intentionally political nature of non-application. The opt-out option, as originally conceived, is for dissenters from a two-thirds vote for accession. The entry can occur, hence the two-thirds of governments seeking to engage constructively the new government can do so, and possibly thereby alter offensive conditions. The other countries can elect not to soil their hands or consciences by eschewing trade relations entirely or in part. Simply put, Article XXXV is intended for governments politically opposed to a new contracting party, not for advancing commercial aims. To be sure, that opposition may mollify domestic political constituencies, echoing their voice.

Of course, the logic of non-application — a political exception for dissenters from a particular accession — is weaker after the Uruguay Round. Professor Wang's point is the number of pre-requisites for invoking non-application has shrunk from two under Article XXXV of GATT to one under Article XIII of the *WTO Agreement*. Critically, the pre-requisite dropped by Uruguay Round negotiators was, pursuant to Article XXXV:1(b), that an extant contracting party (Member) must not have entered into trade negotiations with the applicant government. Under Article XIII, all that is required is a declaration before accession occurs. Consequently, an extant Member can enter into full-blown negotiations with the applicant and hold out the possibility of denying one or more GATT—WTO obligations if the applicant does not provide acceptable concessions.

This possibility may create considerable pressure on an applicant, depending on the political and economic context in which the negotiations take place. That is, the pressure makes a negotiation table that already is un-level in many accession negotiations even more tilted against the applicant. Most importantly, the failure to carry Article XXXV:1(b) of GATT into Article XIII of the *WTO Agreement* means the justification for non-application may not always be political, much less noble, as when India and Pakistan took the option against South Africa in June 1948. Rather, non-application may be an economic tool — in contravention of the original intent of the GATT drafters.

Alternatively, might it be said non-application never was about "just" politics? Consider Japan, when it acceded to GATT in 1955, and faced non-application by 15 contracting parties, including Australia, France, and the United Kingdom. (Years later, after hard bargaining on market access, they withdrew this status.) Were the reasons hard feelings from the Second World War, fear of Japan's rising economic might, or both?

Chapter 12

THE SECOND PILLAR: TARIFF BINDINGS AND GATT ARTICLE II

A prince never lacks legitimate reasons to break his promise.

      —Niccoló Machiavelli (1469-1527), The Prince ch. 18 (1514)

DOCUMENTS SUPPLEMENT ASSIGNMENT

1. *Havana Charter* Article 17
2. GATT Articles II, XX, XXXV, XXVIII *bis*, and XXX
3. WTO *Agreement* Articles IX-XI

I. BOUND VERSUS ACTUAL RATES

Tariffs may be *ad valorem* (*i.e.*, imposed on the value of an article), specific (*i.e.*, imposed on the units of an article, such as its weight), or hybrid (*i.e.*, a combination of *ad valorem* and specific). A 25 percent tariff is an *ad valorem* duty, a levy of $25 per kilo is a specific duty, and an imposition of 25 percent plus $25 per kilo is a hybrid duty.

Regardless of the type of tariff imposed, a distinction exists between an "applied" and "bound" tariff. An "applied" tariff, is also sometimes called an "actual" tariff, though neither term is found in Article II or Article XXVIII *bis*. Rather, the relevant portions of Article II, specifically, Paragraph 1(b)-(c), speak of "ordinary customs duties." Likewise, Article II:1(b)-(c) does not use the term "bound" duty, but rather a wordier formulation about duties set forth in a Schedule of Concessions of an importing country. However, Article XXVIII:2(a) *bis* employs the term "binding." Moreover, the nearly universally used terms are "applied" (or "actual") and "bound."

What, then, is the difference between these two tariffs? An "applied" rate is the rate a WTO Member actually imposes on a category of imported merchandise, whereas a "bound" tariff is a level of protection a Member has agreed not to exceed. That is, assuming a WTO Member has committed to a particular level of protection, such as Bangladesh setting forth a 90 percent tariff on imported luxury passenger cars in its Schedule of Concessions, that commitment is called the "bound" rate. The rubric is apt, because the Member is bound to keep the rate as a maximum level of protection. (To be sure, there are exceptions, as also discussed later on.) The Member has made a promise and is legally bound by that promise. In brief, a bound rate is the highest level of protection the country may impose on a category of merchandise. That suggests another reason the word "bound" is apt. It connotes the image of an upper boundary — or, to use a related metaphor, of a ceiling. Accordingly, "bound" rates are sometimes colloquially referred to as maximum, or ceiling, rates.

There arises in "GATT speak" a distinction between the words "bound" and "binding." All of the product categories listed in a Schedule of Concessions (discussed below), for which a contracting party or WTO Member has made a tariff concession, are considered "bound." Any individual tariff commitment is considered a "binding." However, the distinction is not absolute, and in practice occasionally is blurred.

II. SCHEDULES OF CONCESSIONS

Regardless of the manifestation of tariff a WTO Member imposes on a category or merchandise, every Member sets forth its bound tariffs (of whatever type, including TRQs) in a document called the "Schedule of Concessions." (The adjective "every" is subject to a modest qualification, discussed below, implicating Article XXVI:5(c), about the accession of a dependent customs territory and succession.) This document is better known as a "Tariff Schedule" or "Tariff List." After all, the document contains an item-by-item list of product categories (harmonized according to the "Harmonized System" (HS) run by the World Customs Organization (WCO)), followed by the tariff imposed on that product. However, the label "Schedule of Concessions" — and in particular the word "Concessions" — is technically more accurate than the casual term.

First, the Schedule of Concessions of each WTO Member records its bound tariffs. A tariff list could be a separate document providing actual, but not bound, tariffs. In other words, a Member's Schedule reveals the maximum (not minimum, and not necessarily actual) rates the Member possibly may apply to a particular product.

Second, the bound tariffs reflect give-and-take sessions among Members in which reciprocal trade offs occur. Those trade offs are, in fact, concessions granted to one another. In turn, the WTO publishes the Schedules of Concession of all Members in what, not surprisingly given the 6,000 plus HS product classification scheme and the roughly 150 Members, are thick volumes. As the WCO adjusts this scheme to accommodate new products (for example, high-technology items), and as Members negotiate reductions in bound rates, the Schedules are updated.

The published Schedules have real legal significance. They are an integral part of GATT, and are made so by Article II:7. In other words, Paragraph 7 incorporates by reference the Schedules into GATT, ensuring the bound rates are not only promises to be kept, but also international legal obligations.

The statement "every" WTO Member has a tariff schedule needs a modest qualification. Under Article XXVI:5(c) of GATT, some geopolitical entities that were not sovereign states became contracting parties. At the time of their accession to GATT, they were customs territories, and they had full autonomy in the conduct of their external commercial relations. But, they were, in one way or another, dependent territories of existing contracting parties. Typically, these territories had a colonial link to a "mother" country. An existing contracting party accepted GATT on behalf of a territory, and when the territory gained full independence, its membership in GATT continued. That is, it succeeded as a contracting party. (Accordingly, Article XXVI:5(c) sometimes is referred to as the provision by which accession is by "route of succession."[1]

When the existing contracting country sponsored them for GATT membership, they acceded with the Schedule of their sponsor. That is to say, they did not have a separate Schedule for themselves. However, upon independence, they published a Schedule in their own right based on what their sponsor had negotiated for them. One instance stands out as an exception. Upon its independence, Gabon repudiated the Schedule France had negotiated for it when it was a dependent territory.

Two separate, but far more relevant, topics concerning Schedules of Concessions are how they are organized and what they "look like." On the first question, bound series of volumes, published by the WTO, set out the Schedules. The sizeable Membership of the WTO means many commodious volumes are needed to accommodate the Schedules of all Members. The Schedule of each Member is identified with a Roman numeral. The Roman numerals are assigned to the Schedules in a logical fashion, namely, the order of accession of each Member. Thus, the newest Member of the WTO will have its Schedule published in the volume with the highest Roman numeral. If two or more Members accede simultaneously, then the numerals are assigned in alphabetical order of the country names of these new Members.

As for what a Schedule looks like, it is comprised of four basic Parts, as follows. The first two Parts have compromised a Schedule ever since GATT was founded. The third and fourth Parts were added after 1947:

1. Part I covers MFN concessions. This Part contains the bound MFN tariff rates to which a WTO Member has committed to all other Members.

2. Part II contains preferential concessions. This Part lists preferences, most notably the special and differential tariff treatment given by developed country Members to certain developing and least developed country Members.

3. Part III chronicles concessions on non-tariff measures.

4. Part IV, added as a result of the WTO *Agreement on Agriculture* reached during the Uruguay Round, states the binding commitments of each Member on the level of domestic support it will provide to its farmers and farm products (most notably, its Amber Box subsidies, which relate to its Total Aggregate Measure of Support, less its Blue and Green Box subsidies), and the level of export subsidies it will provide to its primary and processed agricultural goods.

In any Part of a Schedule, there may exist for a particular product, group of products, or as a generally applicable statement, an insertion known as a "Note." Essentially, a Note is a reservation negotiated specially by a WTO

---

[1] ANWARUL HODA, TARIFF NEGOTIATIONS AND RENEGOTIATIONS UNDER THE GATT AND THE WTO ¶ C.5, at 19 (2001).

Member to clarify, modify, or qualify in some way a concession granted by that Member.

If Schedules of Concessions contain bound rates, then what document sets out applied rates? The answer is (somewhat confusingly, given the overlapping labels) is a "Tariff Schedule." However, this Schedule is published not by the WTO. Rather, each individual Member puts out its list of actual rates in a Schedule.

III. SPECIFIC MINIMUM DUTIES AND THE 1998 *ARGENTINA FOOTWEAR* CASE

WTO APPELLATE BODY REPORT, *ARGENTINA — MEASURES AFFECTING IMPORTS OF FOOTWEAR, TEXTILES, APPAREL AND OTHER ITEMS*
WT/DS56/AB/R (adopted 22 April 1998)

I. INTRODUCTION: STATEMENT OF THE APPEAL

1. Argentina appeals from certain issues of law covered and legal interpretations developed in the Panel Report, *Argentina — Measures Affecting Imports of Footwear, Textiles, Apparel and Other Items* (the "Panel Report"). The Panel was established to consider a complaint by the United States against Argentina concerning certain measures maintained by Argentina affecting imports of textiles, apparel, footwear and other items, in particular, measures imposing specific duties on various textile, apparel or footwear items allegedly in excess of the bound rate of 35 per cent *ad valorem* provided in Argentina's Schedule LXIV. . . .

2. Argentina approved the results of the Uruguay Round of multilateral trade negotiations through Law No. 24.425, promulgated on 23 December 1994, and the bound rate of 35 per cent *ad valorem* included in its Schedule LXIV became effective on 1 January 1995. This binding was generally applicable to imports, with a number of exceptions that are not relevant in this case. In parallel, Argentina maintained a regime of Minimum Specific Import Duties (*"DIEM"*) [in Spanish, *Derechos de Importación Específicos Mínimos*] as from 1993 in respect of textiles, clothing and footwear through a series of resolutions and decrees commencing with Resolution No. 811/93 of 29 July 1993 (concerning textiles and apparel) and Resolution No. 1696/93 of 28 December 1993 (concerning footwear), with subsequent extensions and modifications. The DIEM were revoked in respect of footwear on 14 February 1997 through Resolution No. 225/97 of the Argentine Ministry of Economy and Public Works and Services, and the Panel decided not to review the consistency with the *WTO Agreement* of the DIEM with respect to footwear. . . . [As the Panel explained, the stated purpose of the minimum specific import duties was to counteract injury allegedly suffered by Argentine manufacturers as a result of imports of textiles, apparel and footwear at prices lower than the production costs in the countries of origin or lower than international prices. In brief, the system worked as follows. For each relevant

HS tariff line of textiles, apparels and footwear, Argentina calculated an average import price. Once it had determined this price for a particular category, Argentina multiplied that price by the bound rate of 35 per cent, resulting in a specific minimum duty for all products in that category. Upon the importation of covered textiles, apparel or footwear, depending on the customs value of the goods concerned, Argentina applied either the specific minimum duty applicable to those items or the *ad valorem* rate, whichever was higher.]

. . . .

IV. Interpretation of Article II of the GATT 1994

A. The Type of Duty

. . . .

41. Argentina appeals . . ., arguing that the Panel erred in its interpretation that Article II of the GATT 1994 does not permit a Member to apply a type of duty other than that provided for in that Member's Schedule. Argentina maintains that the Panel should have taken into account whether the level of protection to domestic products ensuing from the application of the actual duty imposed is, or is not, higher than the level of protection resulting from the duty bound in the Member's Schedule. In Argentina's view, a Member is free to choose the type of duty applied, provided that the maximum level of protection specified in that Member's Schedule is not exceeded.

. . . .

44. The legal issue before us here is whether the application by a Member of a type of duty other than that provided for in its Schedule is, in itself, inconsistent with Article II of the GATT 1994. We now turn to an examination of this question, first, in the light of the terms of Article II:1 of the GATT 1994 and, second, in the context of Argentina's *DIEM* system at issue in this case.

45. The terms of Article II:1(a) require that a Member "accord to the commerce of the other Members treatment no less favourable than that provided for" in that Member's Schedule. Article II:1(b), first sentence, states, in part: "The products described in Part I of the Schedule . . . shall, on their importation into the territory to which the Schedule relates, . . . be exempt from ordinary customs duties in excess of those set forth and provided therein." Paragraph (a) of Article II:1 contains a general prohibition against according treatment less favourable to imports than that provided for in a Member's Schedule. Paragraph (b) prohibits a specific kind of practice that will always be inconsistent with paragraph (a): that is, the application of ordinary customs duties in excess of those provided for in the Schedule. Because the language of Article II:1(b), first sentence, is more specific and germane to the case at hand, our interpretative analysis begins with, and focuses on, that provision.

46. A tariff binding in a Member's Schedule provides an upper limit on the amount of duty that may be imposed, and a Member is permitted to impose a duty that is less than that provided for in its Schedule. The principal obligation in the first sentence of Article II:1(b), as we have noted above, requires

a Member to refrain from imposing ordinary customs duties *in excess* of those provided for in that Member's Schedule. However, the text of Article II:1(b), first sentence, does not address whether applying a *type* of duty different from the *type* provided for in a Member's Schedule is inconsistent, in itself, with that provision.

47. In accordance with the general rules of treaty interpretation set out in Article 31 of the *Vienna Convention*, Article II:1(b), first sentence, must be read in its context and in light of the object and purpose of the GATT 1994. Article II:1(a) is part of the context of Article II:1(b); it requires that a Member must accord to the commerce of the other Members "treatment no less favourable than that provided for" in its Schedule. It is evident to us that the application of customs duties *in excess* of those provided for in a Member's Schedule, inconsistent with the first sentence of Article II:1(b), constitutes "less favourable" treatment under the provisions of Article II:1(a). A basic object and purpose of the GATT 1994, as reflected in Article II, is to preserve the value of tariff concessions negotiated by a Member with its trading partners, and bound in that Member's Schedule. Once a tariff concession is agreed and bound in a Member's Schedule, a reduction in its value by the imposition of duties in excess of the bound tariff rate would upset the balance of concessions among Members.

48. We turn next to examine whether, by applying the *DIEM* instead of the *ad valorem* duties provided for in its Schedule, Argentina has acted inconsistently with Article II:1(b), first sentence, of the GATT 1994.

49. . . . [T]he Argentine methodology of determining the *DIEM* is, first, to identify a representative international price for each relevant tariff category of textile and apparel products. Once this representative international price has been established, Argentina then multiplies that price by the bound rate of 35 per cent, or by the actually applied rate of less than 35 per cent, to arrive at the *DIEM* for the products in that category. Customs officials are directed, in a specific transaction, to collect the higher of the two values: the applied *ad valorem* rate or the *DIEM*.

50. To grasp the meaning and implications of the Argentine system, it is important to keep in mind that for any specific duty, there is an *ad valorem* equivalent deduced from the ratio of the absolute amount collected to the price of the imported product. Thus, the *ad valorem* equivalent of a specific duty varies with the variation in the price of imports. It is higher for low-priced products than for high-priced products. To illustrate, a specific duty of $10 collected on all imported products in a certain tariff category, is equivalent to 10 per cent *ad valorem* if the price of the imported product is $100; however, it is equivalent to 20 per cent *ad valorem* if the price is only $50.

51. Thus, under the Argentine system, whenever the amount of the specific duty is determined by applying the bound rate of 35 per cent to the representative international price in a certain tariff category, the *ad valorem* equivalent of the specific duty is greater than 35 per cent for all imports at prices below the representative international price; it is less than 35 per cent for all imports at prices above the representative international price. Therefore, collecting the higher of the two values means applying the bound tariff rate of 35 per cent *ad valorem* to the range of prices above the representative international

price, and applying the minimum specific import duty with an *ad valorem* equivalent of more than 35 per cent to the range of prices below the representative international price.

52. In cases where the amount of the *DIEM* is determined by applying a rate of *less than* 35 per cent — for example, 20 per cent — to the representative international price in a certain tariff category, the result would be as follows. For the range of prices *above* the representative international price, the *ad valorem* equivalent of the specific duty would be less than 20 per cent. With respect to the range of prices *below* the representative international price, a distinction should be made between two zones. As to a certain zone of prices immediately below the representative international price, the *ad valorem* equivalent of the specific duty would be greater than 20 per cent but less than 35 per cent. However, for products at prices below that zone, the *ad valorem* equivalent of the specific duty would be greater than 35 per cent.

53. In the light of this analysis, we may generalize that under the Argentine system, whether the amount of the *DIEM* is determined by applying 35 per cent, or a rate less than 35 per cent, to the representative international price, there will remain the possibility of a price that is sufficiently low to produce an *ad valorem* equivalent of the *DIEM* that is greater than 35 per cent. In other words, the structure and design of the Argentine system is such that for any *DIEM*, no matter what *ad valorem* rate is used as the multiplier of the representative international price, the possibility remains that there is a "break-even" price below which the *ad valorem* equivalent of the customs duty collected is in excess of the bound *ad valorem* rate of 35 per cent.

54. We note that it is possible, under certain circumstances, for a Member to design a legislative "ceiling" or "cap" on the level of duty applied which would ensure that, even if the type of duty applied differs from the type provided for in that Member's Schedule, the *ad valorem* equivalents of the duties actually applied would not exceed the *ad valorem* duties provided for in the Member's Schedule. However, no such "ceiling" exists in this case. The measures at issue here, as we have already noted, specifically and expressly require Argentine customs officials to collect the greater of the *ad valorem* or the specific duties applicable, with no upper limit on the level of the *ad valorem* equivalent of the specific duty that may be imposed. Before the Panel, Argentina argued that its domestic challenge procedure (recurso de impugnación), in combination with the precedence and direct effect of international treaty obligations in the Argentine national legal system, operated as an effective legislative "ceiling" to ensure that a duty in excess of the bound rate of 35 per cent *ad valorem* could never actually be imposed. The Panel did not accept this argument, and Argentina has not appealed from that finding of the Panel. In this case, therefore, there is no effective legislative "ceiling" in the Argentine system which ensures that duties in excess of the bound rate of 35 per cent *ad valorem* will not be applied.

55. We conclude that the application of a type of duty different from the type provided for in a Member's Schedule is inconsistent with Article II:1(b), first sentence, of the GATT 1994 to the extent that it results in ordinary customs duties being levied in excess of those provided for in that Member's Schedule. In this case, we find that Argentina has acted inconsistently with

its obligations under Article II:1(b), first sentence, of the GATT 1994, because the *DIEM* regime, by its structure and design, results, with respect to a certain range of import prices in any relevant tariff category to which it applies, in the levying of customs duties in excess of the bound rate of 35 per cent *ad valorem* in Argentina's Schedule.

56. We modify the Panel's findings . . . accordingly. [The Appellate Body upheld the finding of the Panel that the U.S. adduced sufficient evidence to establish a *prima facie* violation of GATT Article II:1 for 940 relevant tariff categories for textile and apparel products in the *Nomenclatura Común MER-COSUR* ("N.C.M.") of Argentina, even though the U.S. submitted average calculations for 118 tariff categories. In other words, the Appellate Body agreed with the Panel that data submitted by the U.S. on the average import price of certain products in relation to the total amount of duties collected ". . .provides *reliable information* that, on a tariff line basis, duties above the bound rate of 35 per cent *ad valorem* have been imposed" (emphasis added by Appellate Body). Appellate Body Report, ¶ 61. The Appellate Body also agreed with the Panel and U.S. that ". . . if an average calculation shows duties above 35 per cent, this is *evidence of a sufficient number of transactions* which were subject to duties imposed above the 35 per cent *ad valorem*" (emphasis added). Id.]

IV. LEGITIMATE EXPECTATIONS, TARIFF BINDINGS, AND THE 1998 *EC LAN* CASE

WTO APPELLATE BODY REPORT, *EUROPEAN COMMUNITIES — CUSTOMS CLASSIFICATION OF CERTAIN COMPUTER EQUIPMENT*
WT/DS62/AB/R, WT/DS67/AB/R, WT/DS68/AB/R
(adopted 22 June 1998)

I. INTRODUCTION

1. . . . . The Panel was established to consider complaints by the United States against the European Communities, Ireland and the United Kingdom concerning the tariff treatment of Local Area Network ("LAN") equipment and personal computers with multimedia capability ("PCs with multimedia capability"). The United States claimed that the European Communities, Ireland and the United Kingdom accorded to LAN equipment and/or PCs with multimedia capability treatment less favourable than that provided for in Schedule LXXX of the European Communities ("Schedule LXXX") and, therefore, acted inconsistently with their obligations under Article II:1 of the *General Agreement on Tariffs and Trade* 1994 (the "GATT 1994").

. . . .

V. "LEGITIMATE EXPECTATIONS" IN THE INTERPRETATION OF A SCHEDULE

74. The European Communities . . . submits that the Panel erred in interpreting Schedule LXXX, in particular, by:

(a) reading Schedule LXXX in the light of the "legitimate expectations" of an exporting Member; and

(b) considering that Article II:5 of the GATT 1994 confirms the interpretative value of "legitimate expectations." . . .

75. Schedule LXXX provides tariff concessions for ADP [automatic data processing] machines under headings 84.71 and 84.73 and for telecommunications equipment under heading 85.17. The customs duties set forth in Schedule LXXX on telecommunications equipment are generally higher than those on ADP machines. . . . Schedule LXXX does not contain any explicit reference to "LAN equipment" and . . . the European Communities currently treats LAN equipment as telecommunications equipment. The United States, however, considers that the EC tariff concessions on ADP machines, and not its tariff concessions on telecommunications equipment, apply to LAN equipment. The United States claimed before the Panel, therefore, that the European Communities accords to imports of LAN equipment treatment less favourable than that provided for in its Schedule, and thus has acted inconsistently with Article II:1 of the GATT 1994. The United States argued that the treatment provided for by a concession is the treatment reasonably expected by the trading partners of the Member which made the concession. On the basis of the negotiating history of the Uruguay Round tariff negotiations and the actual tariff treatment accorded to LAN equipment by customs authorities in the European Communities during these negotiations, the United States argued that it reasonably expected the European Communities to treat LAN equipment as ADP machines, not as telecommunications equipment.

. . . .

80. We disagree with the Panel's conclusion that the meaning of a tariff concession in a Member's Schedule may be determined in the light of the "legitimate expectations" of an exporting Member. First, we fail to see the relevance of the *EEC — Oilseeds [i.e., European Economic Community — Payments and Subsidies Paid to Processors and Producers of Oilseeds and Related Animal-Feed Proteins, GATT B.I.S.D. (37th Supp.) at 86 ¶ 148 (adopted 25 January 1990)] panel report with respect to the interpretation of a Member's Schedule in the context of a violation complaint made under Article XXIII:1(a) of the GATT 1994. The EEC — Oilseeds panel report dealt with a non-violation complaint under Article XXIII:1(b) of the GATT 1994, and is not legally relevant to the case before us. Article XXIII:1 of the GATT 1994 provides for three legally-distinct causes of action on which a Member may base a complaint; it distinguishes between so-called violation complaints, non-violation complaints and situation complaints under paragraphs (a), (b) and (c). The concept of "reasonable expectations", which the Panel refers to as "legitimate expectations", is a concept that was developed in the context of non-violation complaints. As we stated in India — Patents, for the Panel to use this concept in the context of a violation complaint "melds the legally-distinct bases for 'violation' and 'non-violation' complaints under Article XXIII of the GATT 1994 into one uniform cause of action," and is not in accordance with established GATT practice. [See Report of the Appellate Body, India — Patent Protection for Pharmaceutical and Agricultural Chemical Products, WT/DS50/AB/R. ¶¶ 36, 41-42 (adopted 16 January 1998).]*

81. Second, we reject the Panel's view that Article II:5 of the GATT 1994 confirms that "legitimate expectations are a vital element in the interpretation" of Article II:1 of the GATT 1994 and of Members' Schedules. It is clear from the wording of Article II:5 that it does not support the Panel's view. This paragraph recognizes the possibility that the treatment *contemplated* in a concession, provided for in a Member's Schedule, on a particular product, may differ from the treatment *accorded* to that product and provides for a compensatory mechanism to re-balance the concessions between the two Members concerned in such a situation. However, nothing in Article II:5 suggests that the expectations of *only* the exporting Member can be the basis for interpreting a concession in a Member's Schedule for the purposes of determining whether that Member has acted consistently with its obligations under Article II:1. In discussing Article II:5, the Panel overlooked the second sentence of that provision, which clarifies that the "contemplated treatment" referred to in that provision is the treatment contemplated by *both* Members.

82. Third, we agree with the Panel that the security and predictability of "the reciprocal and mutually advantageous arrangements directed to the substantial reduction of tariffs and other barriers to trade" is an object and purpose of the *WTO Agreement*, generally, as well as of the GATT 1994. However, we disagree with the Panel that the maintenance of the security and predictability of tariff concessions allows the interpretation of a concession in the light of the "legitimate expectations" of exporting Members, *i.e.*, their *subjective* views as to what the agreement reached during tariff negotiations was. The security and predictability of tariff concessions would be seriously undermined if the concessions in Members' Schedules were to be interpreted on the basis of the subjective views of certain exporting Members alone. Article II:1 of the GATT 1994 ensures the maintenance of the security and predictability of tariff concessions by requiring that Members not accord treatment less favourable to the commerce of other *Members* than that provided for in their Schedules.

83. Furthermore, we do not agree with the Panel that interpreting the meaning of a concession in a Member's Schedule in the light of the "legitimate expectations" of exporting Members is consistent with the principle of good faith interpretation under Article 31 of the *Vienna Convention*. [Article 31(1) of the *Vienna Convention* provides that "[a] treaty shall be interpreted in good faith in accordance with the ordinary meaning to be given to the terms of the treaty in their context and in the light of its object and purpose."] Recently, in *India — Patents*, the panel stated that good faith interpretation under Article 31 required "the protection of legitimate expectations." We found that the panel had misapplied Article 31 of the *Vienna Convention* and stated that:

> The duty of a treaty interpreter is to examine the words of the treaty to determine the intentions of the parties. This should be done in accordance with the principles of treaty interpretation set out in Article 31 of the *Vienna Convention*. But these principles of interpretation neither require nor condone the imputation into a treaty of words that are not there or the importation into a treaty of concepts that were not intended.[*See* Appellate Body Report, *India — Patents* at ¶ 45.]

84. The purpose of treaty interpretation under Article 31 of the *Vienna Convention* is to ascertain the *common* intentions of the parties. These

common intentions cannot be ascertained on the basis of the subjective and unilaterally determined "expectations" of *one* of the parties to a treaty. Tariff concessions provided for in a Member's Schedule — the interpretation of which is at issue here — are reciprocal and result from a mutually-advantageous negotiation between importing and exporting Members. A Schedule is made an integral part of the GATT 1994 by Article II:7 of the GATT 1994. Therefore, the concessions provided for in that Schedule are part of the terms of the treaty. As such, the only rules which may be applied in interpreting the meaning of a concession are the general rules of treaty interpretation set out in the *Vienna Convention*.

85. Pursuant to Article 31(1) of the *Vienna Convention*, the meaning of a term of a treaty is to be determined in accordance with the ordinary meaning to be given to this term in its context and in the light of the object and purpose of the treaty. Article 31(2) of the *Vienna Convention* stipulates that:

> The context, for the purpose of the interpretation of a treaty shall comprise, in addition to the text, including its preamble and annexes:
>
> (a)   any agreement relating to the treaty which was made between all the parties in connexion with the conclusion of the treaty;
>
> (b)   any instrument which was made by one or more parties in connexion with the conclusion of the treaty and accepted by the other parties as an instrument related to the treaty.

Furthermore, Article 31(3) provides that:

> There shall be taken into account together with the context:
>
> (a)   any subsequent agreement between the parties regarding the interpretation of the treaty or the application of its provisions;
>
> (b)   any subsequent practice in the application of the treaty which establishes the agreement of the parties regarding its interpretation;
>
> (c)   any relevant rules of international law applicable in the relations between the parties.

Finally, Article 31(4) of the *Vienna Convention* stipulates that:

> A special meaning shall be given to a term if it is established that the parties so intended.

86. The application of these rules in Article 31 of the *Vienna Convention* will usually allow a treaty interpreter to establish the meaning of a term. However, if after applying Article 31 the meaning of the term remains ambiguous or obscure, or leads to a result which is manifestly absurd or unreasonable, Article 32 allows a treaty interpreter to have recourse to:

> . . . supplementary means of interpretation, including the preparatory work of the treaty and the circumstances of its conclusion.

With regard to "the circumstances of [the] conclusion" of a treaty, this permits, in appropriate cases, the examination of the historical background against which the treaty was negotiated.

87. In paragraphs 8.20 and 8.21 of the Panel Report, the Panel quoted Articles 31 and 32 of the *Vienna Convention* and explicitly recognized that these fundamental rules of treaty interpretation applied "in determining whether the tariff treatment of LAN equipment . . . is in conformity with the tariff commitments contained in Schedule LXXX." . . . [T]he Panel, after a textual analysis, came to the conclusion that:

> . . . for the purposes of Article II:1, it is impossible to determine whether LAN equipment should be regarded as an ADP machine purely on the basis of the ordinary meaning of the terms used in Schedule LXXX taken in isolation.

Subsequently, the Panel abandoned its effort to interpret the terms of Schedule LXXX in accordance with Articles 31 and 32 of the *Vienna Convention*. In doing this, the Panel erred.

88. . . . [T]he Panel referred to the context of Schedule LXXX as well as to the *object and purpose of the WTO Agreement* and the GATT 1994, of which Schedule LXXX is an integral part. However, it did so to support its proposition that the terms of a Schedule may be interpreted in the light of the "legitimate expectations" of an exporting Member. The Panel failed to examine the context of Schedule LXXX and the object and purpose of the *WTO Agreement* and the GATT 1994 in accordance with the rules of treaty interpretation set out in the *Vienna Convention*.

89. We are puzzled by the fact that the Panel, in its effort to interpret the terms of Schedule LXXX, did not consider the *Harmonized System* and its *Explanatory Notes*. We note that during the Uruguay Round negotiations, both the European Communities and the United States were parties to the *Harmonized System*. Furthermore, it appears to be undisputed that the Uruguay Round tariff negotiations were held on the basis of the *Harmonized System's* nomenclature and that requests for, and offers of, concessions were normally made in terms of this nomenclature. Neither the European Communities nor the United States argued before the Panel that the *Harmonized System* and its *Explanatory Notes* were relevant in the interpretation of the terms of Schedule LXXX. We believe, however, that a proper interpretation of Schedule LXXX should have included an examination of the *Harmonized System* and its *Explanatory Notes*.

90. A proper interpretation also would have included an examination of the existence and relevance of subsequent practice. We note that the United States referred, before the Panel, to the decisions taken by the Harmonized System Committee of the WCO in April 1997 on the classification of certain LAN equipment as ADP machines. . . . The European Communities observed that it had introduced reservations with regard to these decisions and that, even if they were to become final as they stood, they would not affect the outcome of the present dispute for two reasons: first, because these decisions could not confirm that LAN equipment was classified as ADP machines in 1993 and 1994; and, second, because this dispute "was about duty treatment and not about product classification." We note that the United States agrees with the European Communities that this dispute is not a dispute on the *correct* classification of LAN equipment, but a dispute on whether the tariff treatment accorded to LAN equipment was less favourable than that provided

for in Schedule LXXX. However, we consider that in interpreting the tariff concessions in Schedule LXXX, decisions of the WCO may be relevant; and, therefore, they should have been examined by the Panel.

91. We note that the European Communities stated that the question whether LAN equipment was bound as ADP machines, under headings 84.71 and 84.73, or as telecommunications equipment, under heading 85.17, was not addressed during the Uruguay Round tariff negotiations with the United States. We also note that the United States asserted that:

> In many, perhaps most, cases, the detailed product composition of tariff commitments was *never* discussed in detail during the tariff negotiations of the Uruguay Round . . . (emphasis added)

and that:

> The US-EC negotiation on Chapter 84 provided an example of how two groups of busy negotiators dealing with billions of dollars of trade and hundreds of tariff lines relied on a *continuation of the status quo.* (emphasis added)

This may well be correct and, in any case, seems central to the position of the United States. Therefore, we are surprised that the Panel did not examine whether, during the Tokyo Round tariff negotiations, the European Communities bound LAN equipment as ADP machines or as telecommunications equipment.

[The Appellate Body also faulted the Panel for the way in which it examined EC classification practice, during the Uruguay Round, of LAN equipment. This practice is a supplementary means of interpretation, within the meaning of Article 32 of the *Vienna Convention*. But, said the Appellate Body, the Panel did not treat the practice as a supplement. The purpose of treaty interpretation is to establish a common intention of the parties, yet the practice the Panel examined was that only of the EC. The Panel erroneously determined American classification practice, during the Uruguay Round, of LAN equipment to be irrelevant. Thus, the Panel wrongly based its conclusion about common intention on just one party's practice — the EC.]

V.   CRACKS IN THE SECOND PILLAR: LIMITATIONS ON BINDINGS

The reduction or elimination of tariffs is the classic device to promote free trade. Article II of GATT, Article 302 of *NAFTA*, and other tariff provisions of free trade agreements (FTAs) embody the principle of tariff concessions and binding tariff commitments. No doubt these provisions are significantly responsible for major decreases in levels of protection. The Uruguay Round Multilateral Trade Agreements (MTAs) yielded an average tariff reduction of 40 percent, and *NAFTA* resulted in the creation of a cross-border duty-free market. Both regimes cover agricultural as well as industrial products.

Yet, as Professor Kenneth W. Dam pointed out long ago in *The GATT* (1970), tariff concessions are subject to various limitations. Consequently, the cause of free trade is rarely promoted through a dramatic, immediate, and comprehensive reduction or elimination of tariffs on all imports. Rather, trade relations among countries often are managed through tariff reductions that are carefully calculated and circumscribed, and often undermined.

Exceptions to and limitations on tariff bindings suggest an important question to consider when beginning an inquiry into the provisions of a trade-liberalizing agreement. Do not be mesmerized by a grand, market-opening provision. Wait to see what exceptions exist. Consider carefully the extent to which the grand provision is eroded by exceptions (sometimes, a veritable laundry list of them).

A. Waivers

1. Waiver Contexts

Requests for waivers may arise in not only *post hoc, i.e.*, after an adverse adjudication, but also a *priori, i.e.*, before a case has been litigated. Indeed, typically, that is the more common context. For instance, a WTO Member facing a balance of payments (BOP) crisis may believe temporary relief from a GATT—WTO duty would help address that crisis. Perhaps a tax on imports from certain countries would work, though absent a waiver it would violate a tariff binding, or other pillar obligations. Perhaps an across-the-board tariff surcharge is needed, yet without a waiver the action would violate Article II. Sometimes, a Member may want the ability to manage agricultural imports, at least to ensure these imports do not undermine domestic price support schemes. (The waiver obtained by the U.S. to impose restrictions on agricultural imports if need be is an example, and one that has had a major impact on world trade. *See Waiver to the United States Regarding the Restrictions under the Agricultural Adjustment Act*, B.I.S.D. (3rd Supp.) 32 (1955)). Still other contexts in which waivers have been provided are for fiscal reform, introduction of new tariff nomenclature, and continuation of preferential treatment for a newly independent territory that had been provided before independence.

Surely in the long run, the multilateral trading system has an interest in providing episodic relief by means of waiver. Absent a mechanism for obtaining a waiver, the alternative may be the complete withdrawal of the Member from the WTO system, or the brazen, unilateral declaration of non-compliance by the Member. But, should waivers become too easy to obtain, then obligations may be observed more in the breech. Put differently, if multilateral trade obligations are solemn ones — if the pillars are not to develop cracks that will cause them to topple — then obligations must not be easily waived. In sum, small cracks can afford flexibility, but big ones can cause collapse.

2. Waiver Criteria

It is, indeed, possible to obtain a waiver from multilateral trade obligations. "Possible" does not mean "easy." Rules on waivers of obligations are set forth in GATT Article XXV:5 and Article IX:3 of the *WTO Agreement*. While Article IX:3 contains more detail than Article XXV:5, the two rules contain the same key criteria, namely, that a waiver (1) can be granted only in "exceptional circumstances," and (2) only upon the approval by a super-majority of the WTO Members.

What circumstances might be "exceptional"? No broad definition is provided, nor is an illustrative list. GATT Article XXV:5 speaks of exceptional circumstances "not elsewhere provided for in this agreement," so presumably a context contemplated by another GATT Article would not be "exceptional." It would seem, therefore, that a waiver concerning a proposed regional trade agreement (RTA) would be inappropriate, unless the proposal is for an entity short of a full-fledged free trade agreement (FTA) or customs union . After all, an exception for RTAs is set forth in GATT Article XXIV:5-10. In fact, the waiver power has been used for proposed RTAs that do not rise to the level of an Article XXIV:10 FTA or customs union. (A good example is the 1965 waiver granted to the U.S. and Canada for their agreement on automotive products. *See* B.I.S.D. (14th Supp.) at 37 (1966).)

In addition, Article IX:4 of the *WTO Agreement* requires any favorable waiver decision to state the "exceptional circumstances" that justify the waiver, as well as any terms and conditions attached to the waiver. But, surely there ought to be more to the concept of "exceptional circumstances" than obtaining the necessary votes at the WTO based on a set of justifications that the club finds politically acceptable? Surely there ought to be some judgment that granting a waiver to one Member now will somehow advance the long-term interests of the Membership, of the GATT—WTO system, or at least is not entirely incongruous with those interests?

Perhaps a clue as to the meaning of "exceptional circumstances" is provided by the preference in Article IX:4 for waivers of less than one year. Any waiver granted for longer than one year must be reviewed annually to ensure that the exceptional circumstances justifying it still exist, and to verify that any terms and conditions attached to the waiver have been met. Based on that annual review, the waiver may be extended, modified, or terminated. Thus, it might be inferred that "exceptional circumstances" are short-term ones.

As for the voting threshold, GATT Article XXV:5 contains a two-pronged test. First, of the contracting parties voting on the question of whether to grant the applicant contracting party a waiver, at least two-thirds must vote in favor of the waiver. Second, this super-majority of contracting parties agreeing to the waiver must constitute more than half of all contracting parties. Interestingly, clause (i) of Article XXV:5 permits Members, using these same voting tests, to define certain categories of "exceptional circumstances" for which different voting requirements would apply. In other words, conceivably the Members could change the voting requirements for a specific type of "exceptional circumstance," but they could do so only by meeting the base-line "two-thirds" and "50-percent plus" tests.

Significantly, the two-pronged test in GATT Article XXV:5 was changed by the WTO Agreement. Article IX:3 mandates a simple "three-fourths" rule. Any waiver to an obligation created under an MTA, which of course includes the GATT itself, must be approved by a decision of three-quarters of the entire WTO membership. In addition, Article IX:3(a) specifies that the decision is to be made at a Ministerial Conference, and that the normal practice of decision-making by consensus is to be used. If a consensus cannot be reached, then a vote is taken, and the three-fourths rule is used. Also, Article IX:3(b) contemplates a role in considering waiver requests for the Councils for Trade in Goods, Trade in Services, and TRIPs — *i.e.*, the Councils overseeing Annexes 1A, 1B, and 1C to the *WTO Agreement*, respectively. Initially, an applicant Member submits its waiver request to the relevant Council, which must submit a report to the Ministerial Conference on the request within 90 days. Then, the Conference takes over the matter. Likewise, it is the Conference that is responsible for stating the "exceptional circumstances" that justify a waiver, setting out any terms and conditions attached to a waiver, reviewing waivers exceeding one year in duration, and deciding whether to extend, modify, or terminate long-term waivers. In all these respects, the Conference plays the role that the GATT Council played in the pre-Uruguay Round era.

Plainly, the straightforward "three-fourths" voting threshold in Article IX:3 is considerably stricter than the old GATT Article XXV:5 rule, *i.e.*, than the "two-thirds" and "50 percent plus" voting tests. Assume 150 contracting parties (WTO Members), and suppose 100 of them cast a vote on the waiver. Of the 100 voting, assume 75 contracting parties vote in favor of granting the applicant a waiver. Of the votes cast (100), clearly the applicant has satisfied the super-majority rule of two-thirds: it needed 66. However, the applicant failed to clear the 50 percent-plus hurdle. By assumption, there are 150 contracting parties, so the applicant needed 76 contracting parties to vote in favor of the waiver. Yet, 76 is considerably fewer than the 113 required under the rule in Article IX:3 of the *WTO Agreement*. In brief, a waiver applicant must persuade many Members of the appropriateness of the deviation from an obligation.

In one other respect, the *WTO Agreement* raises the bar to obtain a waiver. Suppose the subject of a waiver concerns a transition period, or a period for a staged implementation of obligations. Several Uruguay Round agreements (*e.g., the Agreements on Agriculture, Subsidies and Countervailing Measures, and Trade-Related Aspects of Intellectual Property Rights*) contain special and differential treatment for developing and least developed countries in the form of transition or phase-in periods. Any waiver of an obligation subject to a transition or phase-in period must be approved by a consensus of the Ministerial Conference. A three-quarters majority will not do. Thus, in practice, that means there must be no objection, which in turn means it is nearly impossible to obtain the waiver. Third World countries may be particularly "hard hit" by this demanding rule, and be forced either to implement politically and economically difficult obligations, or to avoid performance of the obligation and suffer the likelihood of a WTO suit.

B. Modifications and Withdrawals

1. GATT Article XXVIII Procedures

Perhaps the most obvious crack in the GATT pillar on bindings is set forth in Article XXVIII. Following the procedures laid out in that Article, a WTO Member may modify or even withdraw permanently the tariff concessions bound in its schedule.

Article XXVIII:1 lays out those procedures in brief. It calls for a negotiation and agreement between, on the one hand, A WTO Member seeking to modify or withdraw its tariff concession (known as the "applicant") and, on the other hand, the Member with which the concession initially was negotiated, plus any other Member with a "principal supplying interest" in the product. Consultation is required with any Members deemed by the WTO membership to have a "substantial interest in . . . [the] concession." Article XXVIII:2 indicates that the negotiations and agreement may include provisions for compensatory adjustments with respect to other products. So, for example, setting aside concerns about equivalence in volume or value of trade, Egypt might be permitted to withdraw a tariff binding on papyrus, resulting in an increase from 5 to 10 percent, if it agrees to reduce its bound rate on dates from 20 to 10 percent. Article XXVIII:2 also sets forth the key criterion for modification or withdrawal: the Members "shall endeavor to maintain a general level of reciprocal and mutually advantageous concessions not less favorable to trade than that provided for" before the negotiation. In other words, the overall level of protection is not supposed to rise.

Suppose no agreement is reached. Then, under either Article XXVIII:3(a) or 4(d), the applicant Member is free to modify or withdraw its concession unilaterally. But, the other concerned Members can withdraw "substantially equivalent concessions" from the applicant. (Whether Article XXVIII:3(a) or 4(d) is relevant depends on the exact procedure used by the applicant. If the normal 3 year cycle contemplated in Article XXVIII:1 is used, then paragraph 3(a) is relevant. If the application for modification or withdrawal is made at any other time in special circumstances, then paragraph 4 is applicable.) Likewise, even if an agreement is reached, if a particular Member has a substantial interest that has not been satisfied, then it may take action under Article XXVIII:3(b) or 4(b), *i.e.*, withdraw substantially equivalent concessions vis-à-vis the applicant. Finally, observe that Article XXVIII:5 enables Members to reserve the right to modify or withdraw concessions, and authorizes other Members to counter with modifications or withdrawals of their own.

2. Differences between GATT Articles XXVIII and XIX

It is important to appreciate the differences between modification or withdrawal under GATT Article XXVIII, on the one hand, and an escape clause action under GATT Article XIX, on the other hand. There are four principal differences: scope; duration; timing; and substantive standards.

1. Through Article XXVIII a Member can renegotiate several unrelated concessions, or conceivably even its entire tariff schedule. In contrast, Article XIX is episodic. A WTO Member can invoke it only one concession at a time, or perhaps a few concessions relating to a single industry. Thus, an Article XXVIII action could potentially affect a greater volume of trade than an Article XIX action. However, Article XIX allows for the suspension of not only tariff concessions, but also other types of GATT obligations. Indeed, this possibility applies to both an initial Article XIX action and subsequent retaliation. Article XXVIII is limited to the suspension of tariff concessions.

2. An Article XXVIII action results in a permanent change in a tariff schedule. In contrast, an Article XIX action leads to a temporary remedy.

3. It is not possible for a Member to resort to Article XXVIII whenever it likes. It can do so only at a point that is a transition between successive periods of continued application (unless "special circumstances" justify "out-of-season" negotiations). In contrast, a Member can bring an Article XIX remedial action anytime.

4. Article XXVIII contains none of the substantive standards set forth in Article XIX. The safeguard provision, of course, has important prerequisites regarding import volume, causation, and injury.

To be sure, there are some similarities between Articles XXVIII and XIX.

For example, neither provision mandates that an importing-country Member compensate exporting-country Members. Article XXVIII:2 states that an agreement between the Member that takes an Article XXVIII and other affected Members may include a compensation arrangement. It also urges Members to maintain the general level of concessions that existed among them before the Article XXVIII action. Similarly, compensation is a voluntary matter under Article XIX and Article 8 of the Uruguay Round *Agreement on Safeguards* (though the *Agreement* provides a right of retaliation, waived for the first 3 years a safeguard action is in effect, if affected Members are not compensated for trade displaced by the safeguard action).

C. Surcharges, Specific Duty Conversions, and Reciprocity

In spite of tariff bindings achieved under GATT Article II, GATT contracting parties succeeded in applying tariff surcharges. The inflation-devaluation provision in GATT Article II:6 is another limitation on tariff bindings. Still another instance in which protection can rise is when a WTO Member converts a specific duty to an *ad valorem* tariff. The answer to the question "what is the *ad valorem* equivalent (AVE) that matches the level of protection of the specific duty?" is the distinction among more, less, or the same amount of protection.

A very practical limitation on reducing tariff barriers is the principle of reciprocity. A WTO Member is discouraged from reducing its tariffs without — to use contract law terminology — adequate, bargained-for consideration. The disincentive is reinforced by the fact that any reduction will apply to all Members by virtue of Article I. Of course, reciprocity is both a shield against and a sword for cutting tariffs: when consideration is received, benefits spread on a multilateral basis under the MFN principle.

Limitations on *NAFTA* Article 302 (and analogous provisions in other FTAs) exist as well. First, it is not true all tariffs on all goods imported by the U.S., Canada, and Mexico automatically were eliminated. Duty-free treatment applies only to originating goods, that is, goods that originate from one of the *NAFTA* parties. Rules of origin, set forth in Chapter 4 of *NAFTA*, distinguish originating from non-originating goods. They effectively set strict limits on the scope of duty-free treatment. Second, even for many originating goods, duty-free treatment did not begin immediately with the entry into force of *NAFTA* on 1 January 1994. Rather, goods were placed into one of four categories. Depending on the category of the good, either the applicable tariff was eliminated immediately, or phased out over a 5, 10, or 15 year period.

D. Balance of Payments Restrictions, Tariff Surcharges versus Quota Rents, and the 1989 _Korea Beef_ Case

GATT PANEL REPORT, _REPUBLIC OF KOREA — RESTRICTIONS ON IMPORTS OF BEEF (COMPLAINT BY THE UNITED STATES)_
B.I.S.D. (36th Supp) 268, 270-271, 273-278, 301, 304-306
(1988-1989) (adopted 7 November 1989)

FACTUAL ASPECTS

. . . .

(a) General

12. Since its accession in 1967, Korea has maintained balance-of-payments (BOP) measures on various products. Since that year, and to date, Korea's BOP restrictions have been subject to regular review by the BOP Committee. During this period, Korea had abandoned or relaxed restrictions on some products. By 1988, restrictions for which Korea claimed BOP cover were still maintained on 358 items, including beef. In 1979, the Korean tariff on beef was reduced from 25 per cent to 20 per cent and bound at that level. Korean beef imports increased from 694 tons (product weight) in 1976 to 25,316 tons in 1981, 42,329 tons in 1982 and 51,515 tons in 1983. Increased beef supplies, due to rising domestic production and the higher level of beef imports, resulted eventually in falling prices on the Korean domestic market and mounting pressures from Korean beef farmers for protection from the adverse effects of beef imports.

13. In October 1984, Korea ceased issuing tenders for commercial imports to the general market, and in May 1985 orders for imports of high-quality beef for the hotel market also ceased, leading to a virtual stop of commercial beef imports. These measures were neither notified to, nor discussed in, the BOP Committee. Between May 1985 and August 1988, no commercial imports of beef took place. Korea partially reopened its market in August 1988, permitting up to 14,500 tons (product weight) of beef to be imported before the end of the year. For 1989, a quota of up to 39,000 tons had been announced.

(b) Korea's Balance-of-Payments Consultations

14. At the last meeting of the BOP Committee in December 1987, "the Committee took note with great satisfaction of the improvement in the Korean trade and payments situation since the last full consultation." "The prevailing view expressed in the Committee was that the current situation and outlook for the balance of payments was such that import restrictions could no longer be justified under Article XVIII:B. . . ."

15. Therefore, the BOP Committee "stressed the need to establish a clear timetable for the early, progressive removal of Korea's restrictive trade measures maintained for balance-of-payments purposes. It welcomed Korea's

willingness to undertake another full consultation with the Committee in the first part of 1989. . . ."

16. Economic indicators in Korea since its latest BOP consultations showed a continuation of the favourable economic situation of the recent past. . . .

. . . .

(d) Korean Beef Import Regime

. . . .

(ii) Current Import System

22. On 1 July 1987, [Korea enacted] . . . the *Foreign Trade* Act. A new organization was established by the Korean Government, the Livestock Products Marketing Organization (LPMO). . . . This organization administered on an exclusive basis the importation of beef within the framework of quantitative restrictions set by the Korean Government. According to its current by-laws. . . the LPMO was to:

— stabilize the prices of livestock products through smooth adjustment of supply and demand, supporting thereby, and at the same time, both livestock farmers and consumers; and

— contribute to improving the balance of payments.

The main function of the LPMO was the administration of the quota restrictions set by the government. . . .

23. Under the current import arrangements, the MAFF [Ministry of Agriculture, Forestry, and Fisheries] sets a maximum import level on the basis of various criteria such as estimated domestic beef production and estimated domestic consumption. In 1988, the LPMO imported the beef through a system of open tenders and resold a major part of it by auction to the domestic market.

24. Before reselling the imported beef either through the wholesale auction system (61.2 per cent of total volume) or directly (38.8 per cent), for instance to hotels, the LPMO added its costs and a profit margin. Between August and October 1988, the LPMO imposed an announced base price under which the meat was not sold at the wholesale auction. Since October, no explicit base price had been announced on the understanding that a certain base price level had to be respected. After having deducted its overhead, the difference between the import contract price and the auction price (or derived direct sale price) was paid into the Livestock Development Fund. This difference varied from one month to another, and also for different types of beef, but was on average approximately 44 per cent of the contract price in the period August to November 1988.

MAIN ARGUMENTS

General

. . . .

Article II

34. The *United States* claimed that the LPMO was levying surcharges on imported beef, which averaged 36 per cent, for the purpose of equalizing import prices with high domestic prices. After negotiations with the United States, Korea bound its tariff on meat during the Tokyo Round of Multilateral Trade Negotiations. The concession was set out in Schedule LX. By agreement with the United States, Korea reduced its tariff on meat of bovine animals (0201.01) from 25 per cent to 20 per cent *ad valorem* and bound it at that rate. The imposition of surcharges on imported meat was plainly inconsistent with Article II:1(b).

35. The United States also argued that the LPMO appeared to have as its purpose, and had taken concrete steps to afford, protection for Korean beef farmers. As such, it was fundamentally inconsistent with Article II:4. Article II:4 barred a contracting party from using import monopolies to restrict trade or afford protection in excess of a bound tariff concession. As shown by the *Canadian Liquor Boards Panel* report [*see Canada — Import, Distribution and Sale of Alcoholic Drinks by Canadian Provincial Marketing Agencies*, B.I.S.D. (35th Supp.) at 37 (1989) (adopted 22 March 1988) (focusing on alleged violations of GATT Articles II:4 and XI:1); *see also Canada — Import, Distribution and Sale of Certain Alcoholic Drinks by Provincial Marketing Agencies*, B.I.S.D. (39th Supp.) at 27 (1993) (adopted 18 February 1992) (focusing on alleged violations of GATT Articles III:4 and XI:1], a government-sponsored import monopoly was not permitted to charge differential mark-ups on imported goods, much less generalized import surcharges. The imposition of such mark-ups constituted additional protection in violation of Article II:4. A state-trading organization was limited by Article II:4 to charging the landed costs, plus transportation, distribution, and other expenses incident to the purchase, sale or further processing, plus a reasonable margin of profit. In particular, the margin of profit charged was limited to a margin that would prevail under normal conditions of competition and had to be the same on average for domestic and imported goods.

36. The United States believed that the LPMO's practices fell squarely within the rule adopted in the *Canadian Liquor* Boards case. The LPMO was setting minimum bid prices that involved mark-ups of up to 56 per cent on United States boxed beef and up to 136 per cent for Australian carcass beef. These surcharges were far in excess of the "reasonable profits" permitted by Article II:4 and nullified or impaired the 20 per cent Tokyo Round tariff binding negotiated by the United States. In the view of the United States, the clear purpose and intent of the surcharges imposed by the LPMO was to afford extra protection to Korean beef farmers over and above the GATT-bound tariff in violation of Article II:4.

37. *Korea* replied that the United States reliance on the *Canadian Liquor Board* Panel case was misplaced. In that case, the panel was not concerned with the administration of a GATT-consistent import restriction. Rather the panel reviewed the import, distribution and sales practices of a state-trading monopoly that operated independently from any restriction. Canada did not impose any quantitative restrictions which its liquor boards were supposed to administer. In respect of beef products, the operation of the LPMO in no way resulted in surcharges that were far in excess of the "reasonable profits" permitted by Article II:4.

. . . .

39. . . . Korea recalled that virtually all imported beef was resold through wholesale market auctions or at prices that were equivalent to or lower than an auction-based priced average for imported beef. Korea argued that the real grievance of the United States was that the auction-based system operated by the LPMO in buying and reselling imported beef allowed Korea to capture the "quota rents." Quota rents were the price increases produced by the quantitative restrictions on imported beef. The United States mistakenly referred to these price increases as mark-ups or surcharges. Yet, quota rents simply represented the economic impact of quantitative restrictions. They did not constitute additional trade restraints, such as surcharges or mark-ups that were impermissible under Article II. Nothing in the GATT, particularly Article XIII, prevented the importers (or the foreign suppliers, as the case might be) from collecting these price increases. Moreover, it had long been recognized that the auction method was superior to any other in achieving a non-discriminatory allocation of quota shares, consistent with Article XIII.

40. Consequently, assuming that Korea was entitled to maintain quantitative restrictions under Article XVIII:B, then the LPMO's administration of these restrictions was subject to two GATT requirements: first, the LPMO had to administer these consistent with Article XIII; second, the LPMO could not impose surcharges on beef imports that exceeded Korea's tariff on beef which had been bound pursuant to Article II. These were the relevant standards, according to Korea, for this Panel's review of the LPMO's operation. Korea explained that quota shares were allocated to the foreign suppliers who submitted the lowest bid to the tender which the LPMO had issued. When the successful bidder then exported the beef to Korea, it was subject to the bound customs duty of 20 per cent. In addition, 2.5 per cent was levied pursuant to the National Defence Tax Law. This extra levy was not inconsistent with the GATT because the levy applied across the board, to foreign and domestic goods alike, and even to the income of wage earners. No other taxes, levies or charges were applied on imports of beef. Thus, in Korea's view, the LPMO's operation was also consistent with Article II. In conclusion, because it met the requirements of both Article II and Article XIII, the LPMO's operation was consistent with the General Agreement.

. . . .

FINDINGS AND CONCLUSIONS

. . . .

Article II

124. The Panel noted that the LPMO was a beef import monopoly established in July 1988, with exclusive privileges for the administration of both the beef import quota set by the Korean Government and the resale of the imported beef to wholesalers or in certain cases directly to end users such as hotels. The Panel examined whether the mark-ups imposed on imported beef, in combination with the import duties collected at the bound rate, afforded "protection on the average in excess of the amount of protection provided for" in the Korean Schedule in violation of the provisions of paragraph 4 of Article II, as claimed by the United States. The Panel noted Korea's view that the operation of the LPMO was consistent with the provisions of Article II:4.

125. The LPMO bought imported beef at world market prices through a tender system and resold it either by auction to wholesalers or directly to end users. A minimum bid price at wholesale auction, or derived price for direct sale, was set by the LPMO with reference to the wholesale price for domestic beef.

126. In examining Article II:4, the Panel noted that, according to the interpretative note to Article II:4, the paragraph was to be applied "in the light of the provisions of Article 31 of the *Havana Charter*." Two provisions of the *Havana Charter*, Articles 31:4 and 31:5 were relevant. Article 31:4 called for an analysis of the import costs and profit margins of the import monopoly. However, Article 31:5 stated that import monopolies would "import and offer for sale such quantities of the product as will be *sufficient to satisfy the full domestic demand* for the imported product. . ." (emphasis added). In the view of the Panel, Article 31:5 clearly implied that Article 31:4 of the *Havana Charter* and by implication Article II:4 of the General Agreement were intended to cover import monopolies operating in markets not subject to quantitative restrictions.

127. Bearing in mind Article 31:5 of the *Havana Charter*, the Panel considered that, in view of the existence of quantitative restrictions, it would be inappropriate to apply Article II:4 of the General Agreement in the present case. The price premium obtained by the LPMO through the setting of a minimum bid price or derived sale price was directly afforded by the situation of market scarcity arising from the quantitative restrictions on beef. The Panel concluded that because of the presence of the quantitative restrictions, the level of the LPMO's mark-up of the price for imported beef to achieve the minimum bid price or other derived price was not relevant in the present case. Furthermore, once these quantitative restrictions were phased out, as recommended by the Panel in paragraph 131 below, this price premium would disappear.

128. The Panel stressed, however, that in the absence of quantitative restrictions, an import monopoly was not to afford protection, on the average, in excess of the amount of protection provided for in the relevant schedule,

as set out in Article II:4 of the General Agreement. Furthermore, in the absence of quantitative restrictions, an import monopoly was not to charge on the average a profit margin which was higher than that "which would be obtained under normal conditions or competition (in the absence of the monopoly)." . . . The Panel therefore expected that once Korea's quantitative restrictions on beef were removed, the operation of the LPMO would conform to these requirements.

129. The Panel then examined the United States contention that Korea imposed surcharges on imported beef in violation of the provisions of paragraph 1(b) of Article II and noted that Korea claimed that it did not impose any surcharges in violation of Article II:1(b). The Panel was of the view that, in the absence of quantitative restrictions, any charges imposed by an import monopoly would normally be examined under Article II:4 since it was the more specific provision applicable to the restriction at issue. In this regard, the Panel recalled its findings in paragraph 127 above. It concluded, therefore, that it was not necessary to examine this issue under Article II:1(b).

. . . .

RECOMMENDATIONS

131. In the light of the findings above, the Panel suggests that the Contracting Parties recommend that:

(a) Korea eliminate or otherwise bring into conformity with the provisions of the General Agreement the import measures on beef. . . .

(b) Korea hold consultations with the United States and other interested contracting parties to work out a timetable for the removal of import restrictions on beef justified since 1967 by Korea for balance-of-payments reasons and report on the result of such consultations within a period of three months following the adoption of the Panel report by the Council.

Chapter 13

THE THIRD PILLAR: NATIONAL TREATMENT AND GATT ARTICLE III

". . . you shall love your neighbor as yourself. . . ."
——The Gospel According to Matthew, Chapter 19, Verse 19

Documents Supplement Assignment

1. *Havana Charter* Articles 18-19, 29, 46-54
2. GATT Articles III, XV:4, XV:9, XVII, and XXIV:12
3. Interpretative Notes, *Ad Article III* and *Ad Article XV*
4. WTO *Agreement on Trade Related Investment Measures (TRIMs Agreement)* Articles 2-3, and Annex
5. WTO *Agreement on Government Procurement (GPA)*, Article III
6. *NAFTA* Chapter 3, and Article 1102
7. Relevant provisions in other FTAs

I. NATIONAL TREATMENT ON FISCAL MEASURES UNDER GATT ARTICLE III:1-2

A. Internal Taxes, "Like Products," and Japan's Liquor Market

Japan is the second largest market in the world for American distilled spirits. Under Japan's Liquor Tax Law, certain imported alcoholic beverages — such as brandy, cognac, genever, gin, liqueurs, rum, vodka, whiskey, and other spirits — were subject to an internal tax. However, domestically produced *shochu* (a distilled white spirit) was subject to a much-reduced tax. For example, the tax on *shochu* was between one-fourth and one-seventh of the tax on imported brandy and whiskey, and two-thirds of the tax on imported rum and vodka. Not surprisingly, between 1989-96, the share of *shochu* in the Japanese market for distilled spirits grew from 61 to 74 percent. Further, whereas other industrialized countries import an average of 30 percent of such beverages consumed, Japan imports only 8 percent.

The complainants in the 1996 *Japan Alcoholic Beverages* case — the U.S., EU, and Canada — alleged the Japanese tax scheme violated GATT Article III:2. They claimed a violation of both the first and second sentences of Article III:2. Contrary to the first sentence, Japan applied different tax rates to like products. Contrary to the second sentence, it distorted the relative prices of imports and *shochu*, and consequently distorted consumer choice between these categories of alcoholic beverages.

The first sentence of Article III:2 calls for non-discriminatory treatment with respect to internal taxes or other internal charges as between imports and "like" domestic products. Related to Article III:2 is a critical Interpretative Note, *Ad Article III, Paragraph 2*, which says: "[a] tax conforming to the requirements of the first sentence of paragraph 2 [of Article III] would be considered to be inconsistent with the provisions of the second sentence [of Article III:2] only in cases where competition was involved between, on the one hand, the taxed product and, on the other hand, a *directly competitive or substitutable product* which was not similarly taxed" (emphasis added).

Thus, on each claim, the complainants faced a threshold problem. As regards the first sentence of Article III:2, are imported spirits and *shochu* "like products"? If not, then there could be no violation of this sentence, because it expressly refers to "like domestic products." As regards the second sentence, are imported spirits and *shochu* "directly competitive and substitutable products"? If not, this sentence is inapplicable, because the Interpretative Note expressly refers to "directly competitive and substitutable products." In brief, only if *shochu* were a "like" or a "directly competitive and substitutable product" would the complainants qualify for protection under the Article III:2 national treatment principle.

Japan countered that imported spirits are neither like products, nor are they directly competitive or substitutable. Hence, neither the first nor the second sentence of Article III:2 matters. Japan advocated a highly restrictive definition of "like" product, namely, one that was more-or-less the same product. Japan's fallback position was that even if *shochu* were a competitive or substitutable product, no violation of Article III:2 occurred, at least not of the second sentence, simply because the Liquor Tax law was not designed to protect domestic production. Japan argued its pure-hearted motivation was relevant because the second sentence of Article III:2 references Article III:1 which, in turn, frowns upon internal taxes applied so as to afford domestic production.

The WTO Panel rejected Japan's restrictive approach to defining a "like" product. It took a flexible, eclectic approach to defining a "like" product and a "directly competitive or substitutable product." There could be no one precise, uniform, or absolute definition of either term. Rather, the terms are to be interpreted on a case-by-case basis. That is, the meaning of "likeness" and "directly competitive or substitutable" depends dearly on the context in which these terms were used in a particular GATT &mdash WTO text. The Panel did not mean to imply its approach lacked substance. It affirmed the nature of the term "like" means that "like products" need not be identical in all respects, though they ought to have essentially the same physical characteristics and end uses. "Directly competitive or substitutable products" need not even physically resemble one another, though they ought to have common end uses as illustrated by elasticities of substitution. The Panel also felt confident pointing out that "like products" are a narrower class of products than "directly competitive or substitutable products," because the first and second sentences, coupled with the Interpretative Note, differentiate between these two classes.

The Panel held *shochu* is a "like" domestic product vis-à-vis vodka, and Japan's tax scheme violated the first sentence of Article III:2 by taxing the latter in excess of the former. The Panel also concluded that *shochu*, brandy, genever, gin, liqueurs, rum, and whisky are "directly competitive or substitutable products." On this basis, the Panel concluded Japan violated the second sentence of Article III:2, as the dissimilar treatment of *shochu* and these imports affords domestic protection to *shochu* producers. Accordingly, the Panel recommended Japan equalize the taxes, either by raising the tax on *shochu* or lowering it on imported spirits.

B. Key Findings in the 1996 *Japan — Alcoholic Beverages* Case

WTO APPELLATE BODY REPORT, *JAPAN — TAXES ON ALCOHOLIC BEVERAGES*
WT/DS8/AB/R, WT/DS10/AB/R, WT/DS11/AB/R
(adopted 1 November 1996)

A. INTRODUCTION

Japan and the United States appeal from certain issues of law and legal interpretations in the Panel Report. . . . That Panel (the "Panel") was established to consider complaints . . . against Japan relating to the Japanese Liquor Tax Law (*Shuzeiho*), Law No. 6 of 1953 as amended (the "Liquor Tax Law").

. . . .

C. ISSUES RAISED IN THE APPEAL

The appellants . . . have raised the following issues in this appeal:

. . . .

1. Japan

   (a) whether the Panel erred in failing to interpret Article III:2, first and second sentences, in the light of Article III:1;

   (b) whether the Panel erred in rejecting an "aim-and-effect" test in establishing whether the Liquor Tax Law is applied "so as to afford protection to domestic production";

   (c) whether the Panel erred in failing to examine the effect of affording protection to domestic production from the perspective of the linkage between the origin of products and their treatment under the Liquor Tax Law;

   . . . .

   (e) whether the Panel erred in interpreting and applying Article III:2, second sentence, by equating the language "not similarly taxed" in *Ad* Article III:2, second sentence, with "so as to afford protection" in Article III:1; and

   (f) whether the Panel erred in placing excessive emphasis on tariff classification as a criterion for determining "like products."

2. United States

. . . .

    (b)   whether the Panel erred in failing to find that all distilled spirits are "like products";

    (c)   whether the Panel erred in drawing a connection between national treatment obligations and tariff bindings;

. . . .

    (g)   whether the Panel erred in finding that the coverage of Article III:2 and Article III:4 are not equivalent; and

. . . .

D. TREATY INTERPRETATION

Article 3.2 of the *DSU* directs the Appellate Body to clarify the provisions of GATT 1994 and the other "covered agreements" of the *WTO Agreement* "in accordance with customary rules of interpretation of public international law." Following this mandate, in *United States — Standards for Reformulated and Conventional Gasoline* [WT/DS2/9, adopted 20 May 1996] we stressed the need to achieve such clarification by reference to the fundamental rule of treaty interpretation set out in Article 31(1) of the *Vienna Convention [on the Law of Treaties]*. We stressed there that this general rule of interpretation "has attained the status of a rule of customary or general international law." There can be no doubt that Article 32 of the *Vienna Convention*, dealing with the role of supplementary means of interpretation, has also attained the same status.

. . . .

Article 31 of the *Vienna Convention* provides that the words of the treaty form the foundation for the interpretive process: "interpretation must be based above all upon the text of the treaty." The provisions of the treaty are to be given their ordinary meaning in their context. The object and purpose of the treaty are also to be taken into account in determining the meaning of its provisions. A fundamental tenet of treaty interpretation flowing from the general rule of interpretation set out in Article 31 is the principle of effectiveness (*ut res magis valeat quam pereat*) [As the Appellate Body indicated in a footnote, the Latin expression means: "When a treaty is open to two interpretations one of which does and the other does not enable the treaty to have appropriate effects, good faith and the objects and purposes of the treaty demand that the former interpretation should be adopted."] In *United States — Standards for Reformulated and Conventional Gasoline*, we noted that "[o]ne of the corollaries of the 'general rule of interpretation' in the *Vienna Convention* is that interpretation must give meaning and effect to all the terms of the treaty. An interpreter is not free to adopt a reading that would result in reducing whole clauses or paragraphs of a treaty to redundancy or inutility."

. . . .

F. Interpretation of Article III

The *WTO Agreement* is a treaty — the international equivalent of a contract. It is self-evident that in an exercise of their sovereignty, and in pursuit of their own respective national interests, the Members of the WTO have made a bargain. In exchange for the benefits they expect to derive as Members of the WTO, they have agreed to exercise their sovereignty according to the commitments they have made in the *WTO Agreement*.

One of those commitments is Article III of the GATT 1994. . . .

. . . .

The broad and fundamental purpose of Article III is to avoid protectionism in the application of internal tax and regulatory measures. More specifically, the purpose of Article III "is to ensure that internal measures 'not be applied to imported or domestic products so as to afford protection to domestic production.' " [The quotation is from *United States — Section 337 of the Tariff Act of 1930*, B.I.S.D. (36th Supp.) at 345 ¶ 5.10 (1990) (adopted 7 November 1989).] Toward this end, Article III obliges Members of the WTO to provide equality of competitive conditions for imported products in relation to domestic products. [The Appellate Body cited two cases in support of this proposition: *United States — Taxes on Petroleum and Certain Imported Substances*, B.I.S.D. (34th Supp.) at 136 ¶ 5.1.9 (1988) (adopted 17 June 1987); *Japan — Customs Duties, Taxes and Labeling Practices on Imported Wines and Alcoholic Beverages*, B.I.S.D. (34th Supp.) at 83 ¶ 5.5(b) (1988) (adopted 10 November 1987) ("*1987 Japan — Alcohol*").] "[T]he intention of the drafters of the Agreement was clearly to treat the imported products in the same way as the like domestic products once they had been cleared through customs. Otherwise indirect protection could be given." [Here, the Appellate Body quotes from *Italian Discrimination Against Imported Agricultural Machinery*, B.I.S.D. (7th Supp.) at 60 ¶ 11 (1959) (adopted 23 October 1958).] Moreover, it is irrelevant that "the trade effects" of the tax differential between imported and domestic products, as reflected in the volumes of imports, are insignificant or even non-existent; Article III protects expectations not of any particular trade volume but rather of the equal competitive relationship between imported and domestic products. [For this point, the Appellate Body cited *United States — Taxes on Petroleum and Certain Imported Substances, supra*, at 136 ¶ 5.1.9.] Members of the WTO are free to pursue their own domestic goals through internal taxation or regulation so long as they do not do so in a way that violates Article III or any of the other commitments they have made in the *WTO Agreement*.

The broad purpose of Article III of avoiding protectionism must be remembered when considering the relationship between Article III and other provisions of the *WTO Agreement*. Although the protection of negotiated tariff concessions is certainly one purpose of Article III, the statement in . . . the Panel Report that "one of the main purposes of Article III is to guarantee that WTO Members will not undermine through internal measures their commitments under Article II" should not be overemphasized. [In support of the first clause of this proposition, the Appellate Body cited two cases: *1987 Japan — Alcohol, supra*, at 83 ¶ 5.5(b); *Canada — Import, Distribution and Sale of*

Certain Alcoholic Drinks by Provincial Marketing Agencies, B.I.S.D. (39th Supp.) at 27 ¶ 5.30 (1993) (adopted 18 February 1992).] The sheltering scope of Article III is not limited to products that are the subject of tariff concessions under Article II. The Article III national treatment obligation is a general prohibition on the use of internal taxes and other internal regulatory measures so as to afford protection to domestic production. This obligation clearly extends also to products not bound under Article II. [As support, the Appellate Body cited three cases: *Brazilian Internal Taxes*, B.I.S.D. II at 181 ¶ 4 (1952) (adopted 30 June 1949); *United States — Taxes on Petroleum, supra*, at 136 ¶ 5.1.9; *EEC — Regulation on Imports of Parts and Components*, B.I.S.D. (37th Supp.) at 132 ¶ 5.4 (1991) (adopted 16 May 1990).] This is confirmed by the negotiating history of Article III.

G. ARTICLE III:1

The terms of Article III must be given their ordinary meaning — in their context and in the light of the overall object and purpose of the *WTO Agreement*. Thus, the words actually used in the Article provide the basis for an interpretation that must give meaning and effect to all its terms. The proper interpretation of the Article is, first of all, a textual interpretation. Consequently, the Panel is correct in seeing a distinction between Article III:1, which "contains general principles," and Article III:2, which "provides for specific obligations regarding internal taxes and internal charges." Article III:1 articulates a general principle that internal measures should not be applied so as to afford protection to domestic production. This general principle informs the rest of Article III. The purpose of Article III:1 is to establish this general principle as a guide to understanding and interpreting the specific obligations contained in Article III:2 and in the other paragraphs of Article III, while respecting, and not diminishing in any way, the meaning of the words actually used in the texts of those other paragraphs. In short, Article III:1 constitutes part of the context of Article III:2, in the same way that it constitutes part of the context of each of the other paragraphs in Article III. Any other reading of Article III would have the effect of rendering the words of Article III:1 meaningless, thereby violating the fundamental principle of effectiveness in treaty interpretation. Consistent with this principle of effectiveness, and with the textual differences in the two sentences, we believe that Article III:1 informs the first sentence and the second sentence of Article III:2 in different ways.

H. ARTICLE III:2

1. First Sentence

Article III:1 informs Article III:2, first sentence, by establishing that if imported products are taxed in excess of like domestic products, then that tax measure is inconsistent with Article III. Article III:2, first sentence does not refer specifically to Article III:1. There is no specific invocation in this first sentence of the general principle in Article III:1 that admonishes Members of the WTO not to apply measures "so as to afford protection." This omission must have some meaning. We believe the meaning is simply that the presence of a protective application need not be established separately from the specific requirements that are included in the first sentence in order to show that a tax measure is inconsistent with the general principle set out in the first sentence. However, this does not mean that the general principle of Article III:1 does not apply to this sentence. To the contrary, we believe the first sentence of Article III:2 is, in effect, an application of this general principle. The ordinary meaning of the words of Article III:2, first sentence leads inevitably to this conclusion. Read in their context and in the light of the overall object and purpose of the *WTO Agreement*, the words of the first sentence require an examination of the conformity of an internal tax measure with Article III by determining, first, whether the taxed imported and domestic products are "like" and, second, whether the taxes applied to the imported products are "in excess of" those applied to the like domestic products. If the imported and domestic products are "like products," and if the taxes applied to the imported products are "in excess of" those applied to the like domestic products, then the measure is inconsistent with Article III:2, first sentence.

This approach to an examination of Article III:2, first sentence, is consistent with past practice under the GATT 1947. [Here, the Appellate Body cited four cases: *Brazilian Internal Taxes, supra*, at 181 ¶ 14; *1987 Japan — Alcohol, supra*, at 83 ¶ 5.5(d); *United States — Taxes on Petroleum, supra*, at 136 ¶ 5.1.1; and *United States — Measures Affecting the Importation, Internal Sale and Use of Tobacco*, B.I.S.D. (41st Supp. vol. 1) at 131 (1997) (adopted on 4 October 1994).] Moreover, it is consistent with the object and purpose of Article III:2, which the panel in the predecessor to this case dealing with an earlier version of the Liquor Tax Law [*1987 Japan — Alcohol*] . . . rightly stated as "promoting non-discriminatory competition among imported and like domestic products [which] could not be achieved if Article III:2 were construed in a manner allowing discriminatory and protective internal taxation of imported products in excess of like domestic products." [*See Japan — Alcohol, supra*, at 83 ¶ 5.5(c).]

(a) *"Like Products"*

Because the second sentence of Article III:2 provides for a separate and distinctive consideration of the protective aspect of a measure in examining its application to a broader category of products that are not "like products" as contemplated by the first sentence, we agree with the Panel that the first sentence of Article III:2 must be construed narrowly so as not to condemn measures that its strict terms are not meant to condemn. Consequently, we agree with the Panel also that the definition of "like products" in Article III:2, first sentence, should be construed narrowly.

How narrowly is a matter that should be determined separately for each tax measure in each case. We agree with the practice under the GATT 1947 of determining whether imported and domestic products are "like" on a case-by-case basis. The Report of the Working Party on *Border Tax Adjustments*, adopted by the Contracting Parties in 1970, set out the basic approach for interpreting "like or similar products" generally in the various provisions of the GATT 1947:

> . . . the interpretation of the term should be examined on a case-by-case basis. This would allow a fair assessment in each case of the different elements that constitute a "similar" product. Some criteria were suggested for determining, on a case-by-case basis, whether a product is "similar": the product's end-uses in a given market; consumers' tastes and habits, which change from country to country; the product's properties, nature and quality. [Report of the Working Party on *Border Tax Adjustments*, B.I.S.D. (18th Supp.) at 97 ¶ 18 (1972) (adopted 2 December 1970).]

This approach was followed in almost all adopted panel reports after *Border Tax Adjustments*. [The Appellate Body cited six cases to prove its point: *The Australian Subsidy on Ammonium Sulphate*, B.I.S.D. II at 188 (1952) (adopted on 3 April 1950); *EEC — Measures on Animal Feed Proteins*, B.I.S.D. (25th Supp.) at 49 (1979) (adopted 14 March 1978); *Spain — Tariff Treatment of Unroasted Coffee*, B.I.S.D. (28th Supp.) at 102 (1982) (adopted 11 June 1981); *1987 Japan — Alcohol, supra*, at 83; *United States — Taxes on Petroleum, supra*, at 136; and *United States — Standards for Reformulated and Conventional Gasoline*, WT/DS2/9 (adopted on 20 May 1996).] This approach should be helpful in identifying on a case-by-case basis the range of "like products" that fall within the narrow limits of Article III:2, first sentence in the GATT 1994. Yet this approach will be most helpful if decision makers keep ever in mind how narrow the range of "like products" in Article III:2, first sentence is meant to be as opposed to the range of "like" products contemplated in some other provisions of the GATT 1994 and other Multilateral Trade Agreements of the *WTO Agreement*. In applying the criteria cited in *Border Tax Adjustments* to the facts of any particular case, and in considering other criteria that may also be relevant in certain cases, panels can only apply their best judgment in determining whether in fact products are "like." This will always involve an unavoidable element of individual, discretionary judgment. We do not agree with the Panel's observation . . . that distinguishing between "like products" and "directly competitive or substitutable products" under Article III:2 is "an arbitrary decision." Rather, we think it is a discretionary decision that must be made in considering the various characteristics of products in individual cases.

No one approach to exercising judgment will be appropriate for all cases. The criteria in *Border Tax Adjustments* should be examined, but there can be no one precise and absolute definition of what is "like." The concept of "likeness" is a relative one that evokes the image of an accordion. The accordion of "likeness" stretches and squeezes in different places as different provisions of the *WTO Agreement* are applied. The width of the accordion in any one of those places must be determined by the particular provision in which the term "like" is encountered as well as by the context and the circumstances that prevail in any given case to which that provision may apply. We believe that, in Article III:2, first sentence of the GATT 1994, the accordion of "likeness" is meant to be narrowly squeezed.

The Panel determined in this case that *shochu* and vodka are "like products" for the purposes of Article III:2, first sentence. We note that the determination of whether vodka is a "like product" to *shochu* under Article III:2, first sentence, or a "directly competitive or substitutable product" to *shochu* under Article III:2, second sentence, does not materially affect the outcome of this case.

A uniform tariff classification of products can be relevant in determining what are "like products." If sufficiently detailed, tariff classification can be a helpful sign of product similarity. Tariff classification has been used as a criterion for determining "like products" in several previous adopted panel reports. [The Appellate Body cited three cases here: *EEC — Measures on Animal Feed Proteins, supra*, at 49; *1987 Japan — Alcohol*, at 83; and *United States — Reformulated Gasoline, supra*.] For example, in the *1987 Japan — Alcohol* Panel Report, the panel examined certain wines and alcoholic beverages on a "product-by-product basis" by applying the criteria listed in the Working Party Report on *Border Tax Adjustments*,

> . . . as well as others recognized in previous GATT practice (*see* B.I.S.D. 25S/49, 63), such as the Customs Cooperation Council Nomenclature (CCCN) for the classification of goods in customs tariffs which has been accepted by Japan.

Uniform classification in tariff nomenclatures based on the Harmonized System (the "HS") was recognized in GATT 1947 practice as providing a useful basis for confirming "likeness" in products. However, there is a major difference between tariff classification nomenclature and tariff bindings or concessions made by Members of the WTO under Article II of the GATT 1994. There are risks in using tariff bindings that are too broad as a measure of product "likeness." Many of the least-developed country Members of the WTO submitted schedules of concessions and commitments as annexes to the GATT 1994 for the first time as required by Article XI of the *WTO Agreement*. Many of these least-developed countries, as well as other developing countries, have bindings in their schedules which include broad ranges of products that cut across several different HS tariff headings. For example, many of these countries have very broad uniform bindings on non-agricultural products. This does not necessarily indicate similarity of the products covered by a binding. Rather, it represents the results of trade concessions negotiated among Members of the WTO.

It is true that there are numerous tariff bindings which are in fact extremely precise with regard to product description and which, therefore, can provide significant guidance as to the identification of "like products." Clearly enough, these determinations need to be made on a case-by-case basis. However, tariff bindings that include a wide range of products are not a reliable criterion for determining or confirming product "likeness" under Article III:2.

With these modifications to the legal reasoning in the Panel Report, we affirm the legal conclusions and the findings of the Panel with respect to "like products" in all other respects.

(b) *"In Excess Of"*

The only remaining issue under Article III:2, first sentence, is whether the taxes on imported products are "in excess of" those on like domestic products.

If so, then the Member that has imposed the tax is not in compliance with Article III. Even the smallest amount of "excess" is too much. "The prohibition of discriminatory taxes in Article III:2, first sentence, is not conditional on a 'trade effects test' nor is it qualified by a *de minimis* standard." [In support, the Appellate Body cited *United States — Measures Affecting Alcoholic and Malt Beverages*, B.I.S.D. (39th Supp.) at 206 ¶ 5.6 (1993) (adopted 19 June 1992); *Brazilian Internal Taxes, supra*, at 181 ¶ 16; *United States — Taxes on Petroleum, supra*, at 136 ¶ 5.1.9; *1987 Japan — Alcohol, supra*, at 83 ¶ 5.8.] We agree with the Panel's legal reasoning and with its conclusions on this aspect of the interpretation and application of Article III:2, first sentence.

2. Second Sentence

Article III:1 informs Article III:2, second sentence, through specific reference. Article III:2, second sentence, contains a general prohibition against "internal taxes or other internal charges" applied to "imported or domestic products in a manner contrary to the principles set forth in paragraph 1." . . . Article III:1 states that internal taxes and other internal charges "should not be applied to imported or domestic products so as to afford protection to domestic production." . . . *Ad Article III:2* [explains Article III:2, second sentence, applies to competition between a taxed imported product and a domestic "directly competitive or substitutable product" that is not similarly taxed]

. . . .

Article III:2, second sentence, and the accompanying *Ad* Article have equivalent legal status in that both are treaty language which was negotiated and agreed at the same time. The *Ad* Article does not replace or modify the language contained in Article III:2, second sentence, but, in fact, clarifies its meaning. Accordingly, the language of the second sentence and the *Ad* Article must be read together in order to give them their proper meaning.

Unlike that of Article III:2, first sentence, the language of Article III:2, second sentence, specifically invokes Article III:1. The significance of this distinction lies in the fact that whereas Article III:1 acts implicitly in addressing the two issues that must be considered in applying the first sentence, it acts explicitly as an entirely separate issue that must be addressed along with two other issues that are raised in applying the second sentence. Giving full meaning to the text and to its context, three separate issues must be addressed to determine whether an internal tax measure is inconsistent with Article III:2, second sentence. These three issues are whether:

(1)   the imported products and the domestic products are "directly competitive or substitutable products" which are in competition with each other;

(2)   the directly competitive or substitutable imported and domestic products *are "not similarly taxed"*; and

(3)   the dissimilar taxation of the directly competitive or substitutable imported domestic products *is "applied . . . so as to afford protection to domestic production."*

Again, these are three separate issues. Each must be established separately by the complainant for a panel to find that a tax measure imposed by a Member of the WTO is inconsistent with Article III:2, second sentence.

(a) *"Directly Competitive or Substitutable Products"*

If imported and domestic products are not "like products" for the narrow purposes of Article III:2, first sentence, then they are not subject to the strictures of that sentence and there is no inconsistency with the requirements of that sentence. However, depending on their nature, and depending on the competitive conditions in the relevant market, those same products may well be among the broader category of "directly competitive or substitutable products" that fall within the domain of Article III:2, second sentence. How much broader that category of "directly competitive or substitutable products" may be in any given case is a matter for the panel to determine based on all the relevant facts in that case. As with "like products" under the first sentence, the determination of the appropriate range of "directly competitive or substitutable products" under the second sentence must be made on a case-by-case basis.

In this case, the Panel emphasized the need to look not only at such matters as physical characteristics, common end-uses, and tariff classifications, but also at the "market place." This seems appropriate. The GATT 1994 is a commercial agreement, and the WTO is concerned, after all, with markets. It does not seem inappropriate to look at competition in the relevant markets as one among a number of means of identifying the broader category of products that might be described as "directly competitive or substitutable."

Nor does it seem inappropriate to examine elasticity of substitution as one means of examining those relevant markets. The Panel did not say that cross-price elasticity of demand is *"the* decisive criterion" for determining whether products are "directly competitive or substitutable." The Panel stated the following:

> In the Panel's view, the decisive criterion in order to determine whether two products are directly competitive or substitutable is whether they have common end-uses, *inter alia*, as shown by elasticity of substitution.

We agree. And, we find the Panel's legal analysis of whether the products are "directly competitive or substitutable products" . . . to be correct.

  . . . .

[The Appellate Body also concluded, in favor of the United States, that the Panel erred in law in limiting its conclusions on "directly competitive or substitutable products" to *shochu*, whisky, brandy, rum, gin, genever, and liqueurs. The self-imposed limitation was inconsistent with the Panel's Terms of Reference, which covered "all other distilled spirits and liqueurs falling within HS heading 2208" too.]

(b) *"Not Similarly Taxed"*

To give due meaning to the distinctions in the wording of Article III:2, first sentence, and Article III:2, second sentence, the phrase "not similarly taxed" in the *Ad* Article to the second sentence must not be construed so as to mean the same thing as the phrase "in excess of" in the first sentence. On its face, the phrase "in excess of" in the first sentence means *any* amount of tax on imported products "in excess of" the tax on domestic "like products." The phrase "not similarly taxed" in the *Ad* Article to the second sentence must therefore mean something else. It requires a different standard, just as "directly competitive or substitutable products" requires a different standard as compared to "like products" for these same interpretive purposes.

Reinforcing this conclusion is the need to give due meaning to the distinction between "like products" in the first sentence and "directly competitive or substitutable products" in the *Ad* Article to the second sentence. If "in excess of" in the first sentence and "not similarly taxed" in the *Ad* Article to the second sentence were construed to mean one and the same thing, then "like products" in the first sentence and "directly competitive or substitutable products" in the *Ad* Article to the second sentence would also mean one and the same thing. This would eviscerate the distinctive meaning that must be respected in the words of the text.

To interpret "in excess of" and "not similarly taxed" identically would deny any distinction between the first and second sentences of Article III:2. Thus, in any given case, there may be some amount of taxation on imported products that may well be "in excess of" the tax on domestic "like products" but may not be so much as to compel a conclusion that "directly competitive or substitutable" imported and domestic products are "not similarly taxed" for the purposes of the *Ad Article* to Article III:2, second sentence. In other words, there may be an amount of excess taxation that may well be more of a burden on imported products than on domestic "directly competitive or substitutable products" but may nevertheless not be enough to justify a conclusion that such products are "not similarly taxed" for the purposes of Article III:2, second sentence. We agree with the Panel that this amount of differential taxation must be more than *de minimis* to be deemed "not similarly taxed" in any given case. And, like the Panel, we believe that whether any particular differential amount of taxation is *de minimis* or is not *de minimis* must, here too, be determined on a case-by-case basis. Thus, to be "not similarly taxed," the tax burden on imported products must be heavier than on "directly competitive or substitutable" domestic products, and that burden must be more than *de minimis* in any given case.

In this case, the Panel applied the correct legal reasoning in determining whether "directly competitive or substitutable" imported and domestic products were "not similarly taxed." However, the Panel erred in blurring the distinction between that issue and the entirely separate issue of whether the tax measure in question was applied "so as to afford protection." Again, these are separate issues that must be addressed individually. If "directly competitive or substitutable products" are *not* "not similarly taxed," then there is neither need nor justification under Article III:2, second sentence, for inquiring further as to whether the tax has been applied "so as to afford protection." But if such products are "not similarly taxed," a further inquiry must necessarily be made.

(c) "So As To Afford Protection"

This third inquiry under Article III:2, second sentence, must determine whether "directly competitive or substitutable products" are "not similarly taxed" in a way that affords protection. This is not an issue of intent. It is not necessary for a panel to sort through the many reasons legislators and regulators often have for what they do and weigh the relative significance of those reasons to establish legislative or regulatory intent. If the measure is applied to imported or domestic products so as to afford protection to domestic production, then it does not matter that there may not have been any desire to engage in protectionism in the minds of the legislators or the regulators who imposed the measure. It is irrelevant that protectionism was not an intended objective if the particular tax measure in question is nevertheless, to echo Article III:1, "*applied* to imported or domestic products so as to afford protection to domestic production." [Emphasis added.] This is an issue of how the measure in question is *applied*.

In the *1987 Japan — Alcohol* case, the panel subsumed its discussion of the issue of "not similarly taxed" within its examination of the separate issue of "so as to afford protection":

> . . . whereas under the first sentence of Article III:2 the tax on the imported product and the tax on the like domestic product had to be equal in effect, Article III:1 and 2, second sentence, prohibited only the application of internal taxes to imported or domestic products in a manner "so as to afford protection to domestic production." The Panel was of the view that also small tax differences could influence the competitive relationship between directly competing distilled liquors, but the existence of protective taxation could be established only in the light of the particular circumstances of each case and there could be a *de minimis* level below which a tax difference ceased to have the protective effect prohibited by Article III:2, second sentence.

To detect whether the taxation was protective, the panel in the 1987 case examined a number of factors that it concluded were "sufficient evidence of fiscal distortions of the competitive relationship between imported distilled liquors and domestic *shochu* affording protection to the domestic production of *shochu*." These factors included the considerably lower specific tax rates on *shochu* than on imported directly competitive or substitutable products; the imposition of high *ad valorem* taxes on imported alcoholic beverages and the absence of *ad valorem* taxes on *shochu*; the fact that *shochu* was almost exclusively produced in Japan and that the lower taxation of *shochu* did "afford protection to domestic production"; and the mutual substitutability of these distilled liquors. The panel in the 1987 case concluded that "the application of considerably lower internal taxes by Japan on *shochu* than on other directly competitive or substitutable distilled liquors had trade-distorting effects affording protection to domestic production of *shochu* contrary to Article III:1 and 2, second sentence."

As in that case, we believe that an examination in any case of whether dissimilar taxation has been applied so as to afford protection requires a comprehensive and objective analysis of the structure and application of the measure in question on domestic as compared to imported products. We believe it is possible to examine objectively the underlying criteria used in a particular tax measure, its structure, and its overall application to ascertain whether it is applied in a way that affords protection to domestic products.

Although it is true that the aim of a measure may not be easily ascertained, nevertheless its protective application can most often be discerned from the design, the architecture, and the revealing structure of a measure. The very magnitude of the dissimilar taxation in a particular case may be evidence of such a protective application, as the Panel rightly concluded in this case. Most often, there will be other factors to be considered as well. In conducting this inquiry, panels should give full consideration to all the relevant facts and all the relevant circumstances in any given case.

In this respect, we note and agree with the panel's acknowledgment in the *1987 Japan — Alcohol* Report:

> . . . that Article III:2 does not prescribe the use of any specific method or system of taxation. . . . [T]here could be objective reasons proper to the tax in question which could justify or necessitate differences in the system of taxation for imported and for domestic products. The Panel found that it could also be compatible with Article III:2 to allow two different methods of calculation of price for tax purposes. Since Article III:2 prohibited only discriminatory or protective tax burdens on imported products, what mattered was, in the view of the Panel, whether the application of the different taxation methods actually had a discriminatory or protective effect against imported products.

We have reviewed the Panel's reasoning in this case as well as its conclusions on the issue of "so as to afford protection." . . . We find cause for thorough examination. The Panel began . . . by describing its approach as follows:

> . . . if directly competitive or substitutable products are not "similarly taxed", and if it were found that the tax favours domestic products, then protection would be afforded to such products, and Article III:2, second sentence, is violated.

This statement of the reasoning required under Article III:2, second sentence is correct. However, the Panel went on to note:

> . . . for it to conclude that dissimilar taxation afforded protection, it would be sufficient for it to find that the dissimilarity in taxation is not *de minimis*. . . . [T]he Panel took the view that "similarly taxed" is the appropriate benchmark in order to determine whether a violation of Article III:2, second sentence, has occurred as opposed to "in excess of" that constitutes the appropriate benchmark to determine whether a violation of Article III:2, first sentence, has occurred.

. . . [T]he Panel added:

> (i)   The benchmark in Article III:2, second sentence, is whether internal taxes operate "so as to afford protection to domestic production", a term which has been further interpreted in the Interpretative

Note *Ad Article III:2, Paragraph 2*, to mean dissimilar taxation of domestic and foreign directly competitive or substitutable products.

And, furthermore . . . the Panel concluded that:

(ii)   *Shochu*, whisky, brandy, rum, gin, genever, and liqueurs are "directly competitive or substitutable products" and Japan, by not taxing them similarly, is in violation of its obligation under Article III:2, second sentence, of the General Agreement on Tariffs and Trade 1994.

Thus, having stated the correct legal approach to apply with respect to Article III:2, second sentence, the Panel then equated dissimilar taxation above a *de minimis* level with the separate and distinct requirement of demonstrating that the tax measure "affords protection to domestic production." . . . [A] finding that "directly competitive or substitutable products" are "not similarly taxed" is necessary to find a violation of Article III:2, second sentence. Yet this is not enough. The dissimilar taxation must be more than *de minimis*. It may be so much more that it will be clear from that very differential that the dissimilar taxation was applied "so as to afford protection." In some cases, that may be enough to show a violation. In this case, the Panel concluded that it was enough. Yet in other cases, there may be other factors that will be just as relevant or more relevant to demonstrating that the dissimilar taxation at issue was applied "so as to afford protection." In any case, the three issues that must be addressed in determining whether there is such a violation must be addressed clearly and separately in each case and on a case-by-case basis. And, in every case, a careful, objective analysis, must be done of each and all relevant facts and all the relevant circumstances in order to determine "the existence of protective taxation." [The Appellate Body again cited the 1987 *Japan — Alcohol* case.] Although the Panel blurred its legal reasoning in this respect, nevertheless we conclude that it reasoned correctly that in this case, the Liquor Tax Law is not in compliance with Article III:2. As the Panel did, we note that:

. . . the combination of customs duties and internal taxation in Japan has the following impact: on the one hand, it makes it difficult for foreign-produced *shochu* to penetrate the Japanese market and, on the other, it does not guarantee equality of competitive conditions between *shochu* and the rest of "white" and "brown" spirits. Thus, through a combination of high import duties and differentiated internal taxes, Japan manages to "isolate" domestically produced *shochu* from foreign competition, be it foreign produced *shochu* or any other of the mentioned white and brown spirits.

Our interpretation of Article III is faithful to [in the words of *DSU* Article 3:2] the "customary rules of interpretation of public international law." WTO rules are reliable, comprehensible and enforceable. WTO rules are not so rigid or so inflexible as not to leave room for reasoned judgments in confronting the endless and ever-changing ebb and flow of real facts in real cases in the real world. They will serve the multilateral trading system best if they are interpreted with that in mind. In that way, we will achieve the "security and predictability" sought for the multilateral trading system by the Members of the WTO through the establishment of the dispute settlement system.

I. CONCLUSIONS AND RECOMMENDATIONS

For the reasons set out in the preceding sections of this report, the Appellate Body has reached the following conclusions:

> . . .
>
> (b) the Panel erred in law in failing to take into account Article III:1 in interpreting Article III:2, first and second sentences;
>
> . . . and
>
> (d) the Panel erred in law in failing to examine "so as to afford protection" in Article III:1 as a separate inquiry from "not similarly taxed" in the *Ad* Article to Article III:2, second sentence.

With the modifications to the Panel's legal findings and conclusions set out in this report, the Appellate Body affirms the Panel's conclusions that *shochu* and vodka are like products and that Japan, by taxing imported products in excess of like domestic products, is in violation of its obligations under Article III:2, first sentence. . . . Moreover, the Appellate Body concludes that *shochu* and other distilled spirits and liqueurs listed in HS 2208, except for vodka, are "directly competitive or substitutable products," and that Japan, in the application of the Liquor Tax Law, does not similarly tax imported and directly competitive or substitutable domestic products and affords protection to domestic production in violation of Article III:2, second sentence. . . .

The Appellate Body *recommends* that the Dispute Settlement Body request Japan to bring the Liquor Tax Law into conformity with its obligations under the General Agreement on Tariffs and Trade 1994.

C. Subsequent Applications of the Precedent

In cases following *Japan — Alcoholic Beverages*, challenges have been made to the liquor tax regimes in various WTO Members, including Chile, Korea, and India. In such cases, the application of the holdings in *Japan — Alcoholic Beverages* has become nearly axiomatic. *See, e.g.*, the Appellate Body Reports in *Korea — Taxes on Alcoholic Beverages*, WT/DS75/AB/R, WT/DS84/AB/R (adopted 18 January 1999), *Chile — Taxes on Alcoholic Beverages*, WT/DS87/AB/R, WT/DS110/AB/R (12 January 2000). Many challenges also have been made to discriminatory internal taxes on non-alcoholic beverages, such as soft drinks sweetened with high fructose corn syrup, or with beet sugar, instead of domestically-produced cane sugar. Given the precedents, the results have been predictable.

II. NATIONAL TREATMENT ON NON-FISCAL MEASURES UNDER GATT ARTICLE III:4

A.   Canada's *Foreign Investment Review Act*

GATT PANEL REPORT, *CANADA — ADMINISTRATION OF THE FOREIGN INVESTMENT REVIEW ACT*
B.I.S.D. (30th Supp.) 140, 142-147 (adopted 7 February 1984)

2. Factual Aspects

. . . .

2.2. *The Foreign Investment Review Act.* In December 1973 the Parliament of Canada enacted the *Foreign Investment Review Act.* According to Section 2(1) of this *Act*, the Parliament adopted the law "in recognition that the extent to which control of Canadian industry, trade and commerce has become acquired by persons other than Canadians and the effect thereof on the ability of Canadians to maintain effective control over their economic environment is a matter of national concern" and that it was the[re]fore expedient to ensure that acquisitions of control of a Canadian business or establishments of a new business by persons other than Canadians be reviewed and assessed and only be allowed to proceed if the government had determined that they were, or were likely to be, of "significant benefit to Canada."

2.3. Section 2(2) lists five factors to be taken into account in assessing whether a proposed investment is or is likely to be of significant benefit to Canada. These are:

(a)   the effect of the acquisition or establishment on the level and nature of economic activity in Canada, including, without limiting the generality of the foregoing, the effect on employment, on resource processing, on the utilization of parts, components and services produced in Canada, and on exports from Canada;

(b)   the degree and significance of participation by Canadians in the business enterprise of new business and in any industry or industries in Canada of which the business enterprise or new business forms or would form a part;

(c)   the effect of the acquisition or establishment on productivity, industrial efficiency, technological development, product innovation and product variety in Canada;

(d)   the effect of the acquisition or establishment on competition within any industry or industries in Canada; and

(e)   the compatibility of the acquisition or establishment with national industrial and economic policies, taking into consideration industrial and economic policy objectives enunciated by the government or legislature of any province likely to be significantly affected by the acquisition or establishment.

2.4. *Written undertakings given by investors.* The *Act* provides that investors may submit written undertakings on the conduct of the business they are proposing to acquire or establish, conditional on approval by the Canadian government of the proposed acquisition or establishment. The submission of undertaking is not required under the *Act* but, as the administration of the *Act* evolved, they are now routinely submitted in support of nearly all larger investment proposals. Many undertakings are the result of negotiations between the investor and the Canadian government. Undertakings given by investors may deal with any aspect of the conduct of a business, including employment, investment, research and development, participation of Canadian shareholders and managers, productivity improvements as well as practices with respect to purchasing, manufacturing and exports. There are no pre-set formulas or prescriptions for the undertakings.

2.5. *Purchase undertakings.* Undertakings with respect to the purchase of goods have been given in a variety of forms:

— some involve best efforts to seek Canadian sources of supply;

— some specify a percentage or amount of purchases of Canadian products;

— some envisage replacement of imports with Canadian-made goods in a specific dollar amount;

— some refer to the purchase of Canadian products, others only to the purchase from Canadian suppliers (whether of domestic or imported goods);

— some involve a commitment to set up a purchasing division in the Canadian subsidiary; and

— some involve a commitment to consult with [a] federal or provincial industry specialist in drawing up tender lists.

Undertakings on purchases are often but not always conditional on goods being "available," "reasonably available" or "competitively available" in Canada with respect to price, quality, and delivery or other factors specified by the investor.

2.6. *Manufacturing undertakings.* Some firms have given undertakings to manufacture in Canada products or components of a product used or sold by the firm.

. . . .

2.8. *Statistics on the undertakings.* The *Act* came into force on 9 April 1974 with respect to acquisitions and on 15 October 1975 with respect to new businesses. From April 1974 to September 1982, the Government of Canada has rendered decisions on 4,103 investment proposals, of which 2,448 were from the United States. Approximately 90 per cent of the reviewable investment proposals on which the government has taken a decision have been judged to be of significant benefit to Canada and have, therefore, been allowed. The Panel asked questions about the frequency with which the various types of undertakings have been given. In order to answer these questions the Canadian government reviewed a sample of 181 investments allowed in the month of November in the years 1980, 1981 and 1982. . . . In this sample, 55 of the investors or 30 per cent of the total gave no undertakings relating

5.6. The Panel carefully examined the Canadian view that the purchase undertakings should be considered as private contractual obligations of particular foreign investors vis-à-vis the Canadian government. The Panel recognized that investors might have an economic advantage in assuming purchase undertakings, taking into account the other conditions under which the investment was permitted. The Panel felt, however, that even if this was so, private contractual obligations entered into by investors should not adversely affect the rights which contracting parties, including contracting parties not involved in the dispute, possess under Article III:4 of the General Agreement and which they can exercise on behalf of their exporters. This applies in particular to the rights deriving from the national treatment principle, which — as stated in Article III:1 — is aimed at preventing the use of internal measures "so as to afford protection to domestic production."

5.7. The Panel then examined the question whether less favourable treatment was accorded to imported products than that accorded to like products of Canadian origin in respect of requirements affecting their purchase. For this purpose the Panel distinguished between undertakings to purchase goods of Canadian origin and undertakings to use Canadian sources or suppliers (irrespective of the origin of the goods), and for both types of undertakings took into account the qualifications "available," "reasonably available," or "competitively available."

5.8. The Panel found that undertakings to purchase *goods of Canadian origin* without any qualification exclude the possibility of purchasing available imported products so that the latter are clearly treated less favorably than domestic products and that such requirements are therefore not consistent with Article III:4. This finding is not modified in cases where undertakings to purchase goods of Canadian origin are subject to the qualification that such goods be "available." It is obvious that if Canadian goods are not available, the question of less favourable treatment of imported goods does not arise.

5.9. When these undertakings are conditional on goods being "competitively available" (as in the majority of cases) the choice between Canadian or imported products may frequently coincide with normal commercial considerations and the latter will not be adversely affected whenever one or the other offer is more competitive. However, it is the Panel's understanding that the qualification "competitively available" is intended to deal with situations where there are Canadian goods available on competitive terms. The Panel considered that in those cases where the imported and domestic product are offered on equivalent terms, adherence to the undertaking would entail giving preference to the domestic product. Whether or not the foreign investor chooses to buy Canadian goods in given practical situations is not at issue. The purpose of Article III:4 is not to protect the interests of the foreign investor but to ensure that goods originating in any other contracting party benefit from treatment no less favourable than domestic (Canadian) goods, in respect of the requirements that affect their purchase (in Canada). On the basis of these considerations, the Panel found that a requirement to purchase goods of Canadian origin, also when subject to "competitive availability," is contrary to Article III:4. The Panel considered that the alternative qualification "reasonably available" which is used in some cases, is *a fortiori* inconsistent with Article III:4, since the undertaking in these cases implies that preference has to be given to Canadian goods also when these are not available on entirely competitive terms.

5.10. The Panel then turned to the undertakings to buy from *Canadian suppliers*. The Panel did not consider the situation where domestic products are not available, since such a situation is not covered by Article III:4. The Panel understood the choice under this type of requirement to apply on the one hand to imported goods if bought through a Canadian agent or importer and on the other hand to Canadian goods which can be purchased either from a Canadian "middleman" or directly from the Canadian producer. The Panel recognized that these requirements might in a number of cases have little or no effect on the choice between imported or domestic products. However, the possibility of purchasing imported products *directly* from the foreign producer would be excluded and as the conditions of purchasing imported products through a Canadian agent or importer would normally be less advantageous, the imported product would therefore have more difficulty in competing with Canadian products (which are not subject to similar requirements affecting their sale) and be treated less favourably. For this reason, the Panel found that the requirements to buy from Canadian suppliers are inconsistent with Article III:4.

5.11. In case undertakings to purchase from Canadian suppliers are subject to a "competitive availability" qualification, as is frequent, the handicap for the imported product is alleviated as it can be obtained directly from the foreign producer if offered under more competitive conditions than via Canadian sources. In those cases in which Canadian sources and a foreign manufacturer offer a product on equivalent terms, adherence to the undertaking would entail giving preference to Canadian sources, which in practice would tend to result in the purchase being made directly from the Canadian producer, thereby excluding the foreign product. The Panel therefore found that requirements to purchase from Canadian suppliers, also when subject to competitive availability, are contrary to Article III:4. As before (paragraph 5.9), the Panel considered that the qualification "reasonably available" is *a fortiori* inconsistent with Article III:4.

. . . .

6. Conclusions

6.1. . . . [T]he Panel concluded that the practice of Canada to allow certain investments subject to the *Foreign Investment Review Act* conditional upon written undertakings by the investors to *purchase* goods of Canadian origin, or goods from Canadian sources, is inconsistent with Article III:4 of the General Agreement according to which contracting parties shall accord to imported products treatment no less favourable than that accorded to like products of national origin in respect of all internal requirements affecting their purchase. . . .

6.3. The Panel is aware that inconsistency with Article III:4 was not intended by the *Foreign Investment Review Act*, which does not require the submission of undertakings, but that this practice developed as the administration of the *Act* evolved, to the point that "they are now routinely submitted in support of nearly all larger investment proposals." . . . This evolution may partly reflect the need for foreign investors to demonstrate, by this and other means, to the Canadian administration that their proposed investment would be of significant benefit to Canada. The Panel sympathizes with the desire of the Canadian authorities to ensure that Canadian goods and suppliers would be given a fair chance to compete with imported products. However, the Panel holds the view that the purchase requirements under examination do not stop short of this objective but tend to tip the balance in favour of Canadian products, thus coming into conflict with Article III:4.

6.4. The Panel recognizes that purchase requirements may reflect plans which the investors would have carried out also in the absence of the undertakings; that undertakings with such provisos as "competitive availability" have an adverse impact on imported products only in those cases in which imported and Canadian goods are offered on equivalent terms; and that the undertakings are enforced flexibly. Many of the undertakings, though technically in violation with the General Agreement, therefore possibly do not nullify or impair benefits accruing to the United States under the General Agreement. However, under standing GATT practice, a breach of a rule is presumed to have an adverse impact on other contracting parties, and the Panel also proceeded on this assumption.

6.5. As to the extent to which purchase requirements reflect plans of the investors, the Panel does not consider it relevant nor does it feel competent to judge how the foreign investors are affected by the purchase requirements, as the national treatment obligations of Article III of the General Agreement do not apply to foreign persons or firms but to imported products and serve to protect the interests of producers and exporters established on the territory of any contracting party. Purchase requirements applied to foreign investors in Canada which are inconsistent with Artic[l]e III:4 can affect the trade interests of all contracting parties, and impinge upon their rights.

. . . .

6.7. Taking into account all the above considerations, the Panel considered what scope might exist for modifications of administrative practices under the *Foreign Investment Review Act* so as to bring them into conformity with Canada's obligations under the General Agreement. . . .

. . . [T]he Panel considers that the Canadian authorities might resolve the problem by ensuring that any *future* purchase undertakings will not provide more favourable treatment to Canadian products in relation to imported products. The Panel's findings also apply to *existing* purchase undertakings. However, the Panel recognizes that an immediate application of its findings to these undertakings might cause difficulties in the administration of the *Foreign Investment Review Act*. Consequently, the Panel suggests that the Contracting Parties recommend that Canada bring the existing purchase undertakings as soon as possible into conformity with its obligations under the General Agreement. . . .

C. Foreign Direct Investment and the WTO *Agreement on Trade-Related Investment Measures*

Treating domestic and imported products alike, at least in substance if not identically, is a key means to promote freer trade. "The foreigner shall be treated like the local" — that, is in crude terms, what this idea of non-discrimination is all about. It is an equal protection clause, akin to the 14th Amendment to the United States Constitution, but set in a global context and applied to commodities. The lofty principle is embodied in several parts of GATT Article III.

Notably, national treatment is the hallmark of the Uruguay Round *Agreement on Trade Related Investment Measures (TRIMs)*. Article 2 of the *TRIMs Agreement* incorporates by reference GATT Article III. Consider the WTO Panel Report in *Indonesia — Certain Measures Affecting the Automobile Industry*, WT/DS54/R (adopted 23 July 1998, not appealed). What did the Panel say about the relationship between GATT Article III and the *TRIMs Agreement* Article 2, and how did these rules to the local content obligations of Indonesia's National Car Program?

To be sure, not all FDI problems are national treatment. Frequent issues include expropriation (or the risk thereof), compensation for nationalized assets, repatriation of earnings, and corruption. (On the latter topic, as a matter of legal compliance and ethical behavior, international trade counsel should be familiar with the U.S. *Foreign Corrupt Practices Act* and OECD Bribery Convention.) Such topics are properly covered in an FDI course. Still, as the *Canada Foreign Investment Review* case suggests, many issues arising from FDI involve discrimination vis-à-vis domestic competitors.

National treatment also is a cornerstone of U.S. free trade agreements (FTAs), such as the *North American Free Trade Agreement (NAFTA)*. The general obligation is in Article 301 of *NAFTA*, which incorporates GATT Article III by reference. In respect of FDI, what national treatment rule does *NAFTA* Chapter 11 set out?

III. DOMESTIC SOURCING AND GATT ARTICLE III:5

A. American Tobacco Support

GATT PANEL REPORT, *UNITED STATES — MEASURES AFFECTING THE IMPORTATION, INTERNAL SALE AND USE OF TOBACCO*
B.I.S.D. (41st Supp. Vol. l.) at 131-134, 136-139, 159 (1997)
(adopted 4 October 1994)

II. Factual Aspects

General

6. On 10 August 1993, the United States enacted the 1993 Budget Act [the *Omnibus Budget Reconciliation Act of 1993*, Pub. L. No. 103-66, 107 Stat. 318,

August 10, 1993] which included the Agricultural Reconciliation Act of 1993 containing, in Section 1106, . . . a Domestic Marketing Assessment ("DMA") [concerning tobacco]. . . . The U.S. tobacco programme had for many years comprised production controls and price supports for tobacco produced in the United States. Control of the domestic supply of tobacco was provided for to the extent that producers of an individual kind or type of tobacco had approved such controls. Production controls had been approved for 98 per cent of all tobacco grown in the United States, including the two principal kinds, burley and flue-cured tobacco. However, according to law, a group of growers could, by majority vote, decide not to form a producer co-operative and could thereby "opt out" of both the price-support and the production-control provisions of the law. For instance, Maryland tobacco was not subject to production controls or price supports, because its producers voted to eliminate controls in 1966. Production controls were currently enforced through the use of poundage quotas, which limited the number of pounds that could be marketed both nationally and from a particular domestic farm. Only those farms with a poundage quota could market without penalty tobacco of the kind or type to which the quota applied. The U.S. Secretary of Agriculture set a national poundage quota under formulas established by law and differing by tobacco kind. Poundage quotas acted as licenses to market tobacco. These "licenses" were strictly limited, and generally held only by farms with a production history.

7. The current tobacco programme also provided for price support, the level of which was set by the Secretary of Agriculture on an annual basis and which was available only to producers who had approved production controls. Price support was provided through non-recourse government loans. [The loans were non-recourse, because tobacco served as collateral to satisfy the loan amount, and there was no further recourse to the producer.] Instead of selling their tobacco to a private buyer, farmers subject to production controls could pledge their tobacco as collateral for a price support loan under the price support programme. Because the farmer would not normally sell the tobacco for less than the loan amount, the loan value of the tobacco acted as a floor price for domestic tobacco. The price support programme operated through special "area marketing associations", first created in 1938, which maintained the inventory of the pledged tobacco. The producer owned area marketing associations existed solely to perform functions connected with the price support interests of producers. The loans were made available through funds supplied by the Commodity Credit Corporation (CCC) of the United States Department of Agriculture (USDA). CCC tobacco outlays were repaid by the proceeds of the sale of inventory tobacco by the area marketing associations. With the inauguration of the "no-net-cost program" . . . producers and purchasers had to pay "assessments" to cover any losses incurred by the CCC.

Domestic Marketing Assessment (Section 1106(a))

8. Beginning after the end of 1994, the *1993 Budget Act* required that designated "Domestic Manufacturers of Cigarettes", *i.e.* those manufacturers that individually contributed at least 1 per cent of all cigarettes produced and sold in the United States, certify the percentage of domestic tobacco used in

the cigarettes they had produced in the United States for the year. Six companies in the United States were considered as Domestic Manufacturers of Cigarettes under the *Act*, and these manufacturers accounted for more than 99 per cent of all cigarettes produced in the United States in the period 1986-1990. If a Domestic Manufacturer of Cigarettes failed to certify the quantity used, it was presumed to have used only imported tobacco. If a Domestic Manufacturer of Cigarettes's use of domestic tobacco was less than 75 per cent of its total tobacco use per year, it had to pay to the CCC a non-refundable marketing assessment and make supplementary purchases from the burley and flue-cured tobacco area marketing associations up to the amount of the shortfall, which could be used in the following year. The requirement applied equally to cigarettes that were exported. The assessment per pound was equivalent to the difference between: (1) the average of domestic burley and flue-cured tobacco market prices during the preceding calendar year; and (2) the average market prices for imported unmanufactured tobacco during the preceding calendar year. Penalties were due from Domestic Manufacturers of Cigarettes which failed to pay an outstanding assessment, or which did not make the purchases from the area marketing associations.

B. Key Findings in the 1994 *U.S. Tobacco* Case

GATT PANEL REPORT, *UNITED STATES — MEASURES AFFECTING THE IMPORTATION, INTERNAL SALE AND USE OF TOBACCO*
B.I.S.D. (41st Supp. Vol. l.) 131, 160-162, 176-177 (1997)
(adopted 4 October 1994)

V. Findings

. . . .

Domestic Marketing Assessment (DMA)

63. The Panel noted that the issues in dispute with respect to the DMA arose essentially from the following facts. The DMA legislation, Section 1106(a) of the 1993 Budget Act, required each "domestic manufacturer of cigarettes" . . . to certify to the Secretary of the U.S. Department of Agriculture (USDA), for each calendar year, the percentage of domestically produced tobacco used by such manufacturer to produce cigarettes during the year. A domestic manufacturer that failed to make such a certification or to use at least 75 per cent domestic tobacco was subject to penalties in the form of a non-refundable marketing assessment (*i.e.* the DMA) and was required to purchase additional quantities of domestic burley and flue-cured tobacco.

. . . .

Article III:5

. . . .

66. The Panel . . . recalled the complainants' claim that the DMA was inconsistent with both the first and second sentences of this provision.

67. As to the applicability of Article III:5, first sentence, to the DMA, the Panel considered that it first had to determine whether the United States had established an "internal quantitative regulation relating to the mixture, processing or use of products in specified amounts or proportions. . . ." The Panel noted the following in this respect:

(a) First, the DMA was established by an Act of the U.S. Congress, Section 1106(a) of the *1993 Budget Act*, and was implemented through regulations of USDA. The effective date for the DMA was 1 January 1994. It thus constituted a *regulation* within the meaning of Article III:5.

(b) Second, the Panel noted that the opening sentence of the DMA legislative provision, Section 1106(a) of the *1993 Budget Act*, stated:

> "CERTIFICATION. A *domestic manufacturer* of cigarettes *shall certify* to the Secretary, for each calendar year, the percentage of the quantity of tobacco used by the manufacturer to produce cigarettes during the year that is produced in the United States." *(emphasis added)*

The DMA was thus an *internal* regulation imposed on domestic manufacturers of cigarettes.

(c) Third, the Panel noted that the second sub-paragraph of the DMA legislative provision stated:

> "PENALTIES. In General. Subject to subsection (f) [exception for crop losses due to natural disasters], a *domestic manufacturer of cigarettes that has failed*, as determined by the Secretary after notice and opportunity for a hearing, to *use in the manufacture of cigarettes* during a calendar year a *quantity of tobacco grown in the United States that is at least 75 percent of the total quantity of tobacco used* by the manufacturer or to comply with subsection (a) [certification requirement], *shall be subject to* the requirements of subsections (c), (d) and (e) [*penalties* in the form of a nonrefundable marketing assessment and a required purchase of additional quantities of domestic burley and flue-cured tobacco]." *(emphasis added)*

The DMA was thus a *quantitative* regulation in that it set a minimum *specified proportion* of 75 per cent for the use of U.S. tobacco in manufacturing cigarettes.

(d) Fourth, the DMA was an internal quantitative regulation relating to the *use* of a product, in that it *required the use* of U.S. domestically grown tobacco.

The Panel thus found that the DMA was an "internal quantitative regulation relating to the . . . use of products in specified amounts or proportions. . .," within the meaning of the first part of the first sentence of Article III:5.

68. The Panel then turned to a consideration of whether the DMA "requires, directly or indirectly, that any specified amount or proportion of any product which is the subject of the regulation must be supplied from domestic sources", as provided in the second part of the first sentence of Article III:5. The Panel noted the following in this respect:

(a) The DMA required each domestic manufacturer of cigarettes to certify to the Secretary of USDA, for each calendar year, the percentage of the quantity of tobacco used by the manufacturer to produce cigarettes during the year that was produced in the United States.

(b) Subject to an exception dealing with crop losses due to disasters, a domestic manufacturer that failed to make the required certification or to use at least 75 per cent domestic tobacco was subject to penalties including the required purchase of additional domestic tobacco.

The Panel thus *concluded* that the DMA was an internal quantitative regulation relating to the use of tobacco in specified amounts or proportions which required, directly or indirectly, that a minimum specified proportion of tobacco be supplied from domestic sources, inconsistently with Article III:5, first sentence.

69. The Panel next turned to a consideration of whether the DMA was inconsistent with Article III:5, second sentence, as claimed by the complainants. On this point, the Panel noted that the second sentence of Article III:5 is subsidiary to the first sentence thereof, as the second sentence only becomes relevant where a contracting party is "*otherwise* apply[ing] internal quantitative regulations in a manner contrary to the principles set forth in paragraph 1", *i.e.*, "so as to afford protection to domestic production." The Panel was therefore of the view that, in light of the finding of inconsistency of the DMA with Article III:5, first sentence, it would not be necessary to examine the consistency of the DMA with Article III:5, second sentence.

. . . .

VI. Conclusions and Recommendations

125. On the basis of the findings set out above, the Panel *concludes* that:

(a) the Domestic Marketing Assessment (Section 1106(a) of the *1993 Budget Act*) was an internal quantitative regulation inconsistent with Article III:5. . . .

. . . .

126. The Panel recommends that the Contracting Parties request the United States to bring its inconsistent measures into conformity with its obligations under the General Agreement.

IV. CRACKS IN THE THIRD PILLAR

A. Direct Taxation

Like the MFN and tariff concession principles, the obligation to provide national treatment principle is not unqualified. For instance, under both GATT Article III:2 and *NAFTA* Article 301:1, national treatment applies to indirect but not direct taxes. Suppose an Indian food company sells its *mithai* (traditional sweets) in Pakistan. Assume the Pakistani tax authority has jurisdiction over the company (perhaps because the company has an office in Lahore). The Pakistani tax authority imposes a higher income tax (a direct tax) on the Indian company than on Pakistani *mithai* producers. There is no violation of the MFN, tariff concession, or national treatment obligations.

This hypothetical example begs the question of what delineates a "direct" from an "indirect" tax. The fact that an "indirect" tax also is called an "internal" tax is misleading, because it suggests only a post-border (i.e., post-customs clearance) levy would be an "indirect" or "internal" tax. Where a tax is imposed — at or after the border — is irrelevant to distinguishing "direct" from "indirect" taxes. Another irrelevancy is the rubric applied to a tax by the taxing authority. A government might call a levy an "internal" tax, when in fact it is a tariff. Its motive for the label might be to avoid application of GATT Article II tariff binding rule to the levy, because its overt tariff plus the levy exceed the bound rate. Calling the levy an "internal" tax would take it out from Article II scrutiny. Yet, if the levy is collected at the time, and on condition of entry, into an importing country, and not applied to domestic products, then it is squarely a tariff subject to the discipline of Article II, not an "indirect" or "internal" tax subject to the discipline of Article III.

The simplest and most practicable distinction between a "direct" and "indirect" tax is that the former is a tax on income and the latter is not. A "direct" tax applies to the earnings of a taxpayer and is levied on the producer or vendor. An "indirect" tax is levied on a product or a transaction, namely, the value thereof. That is, the difference is the taxable entity. A "direct" tax is borne by a producer or seller, which generates income from economic activity. An "indirect" tax is borne by a consumer of the goods or services associated with that activity. Thus, a tax on gross income, adjusted for various items (i.e., credits and deductions) is "direct." A tax on sales or value added is "indirect."

Consider whether this distinction, based on incidence of the tax makes sense in reality? Do producers and vendors pass on at least a portion of their income taxes to consumers through higher prices? Do they also sometimes absorb sales and value added taxes through lower prices? Consider, too, why GATT Article III carves out direct taxes from the discipline of national treatment? Would even the original 23 GATT contracting parties have agreed to multilateral regulation of income taxes?

B. Exchange and Sub-Central Taxation

Some categories of taxation do not fit easily into the "direct" — "indirect" distinction. For example, are exchange taxes, which apply to foreign exchange transactions, covered by Article III:1-2? The hedged answer is "not necessarily." The argument that they are would be made under GATT Article XV:4, the Interpretative Note to it, *Ad Article XV, Paragraph 4*, and Article XV:9. What would be the arguments for and against requiring exchange taxes to comport with national treatment?

Are taxes imposed by state or local governments subject to national treatment? Here the answer is more firm. If discriminatory, then they are problematical under GATT, particularly because of the Interpretative Note, *Ad Article III, Paragraph 1* (last sentence) and Article XXIV:12. Consider the terms in these provisions that would be used to attack such taxes. Without doubt, state and local taxation is covered by the national treatment principle of *NAFTA* Article 301:1 plainly applies to them by virtue of Article 301:2. Note also, as regards *NAFTA*, Article 301.3 explains that Annex 301.3 details exceptions taken by the *NAFTA* Parties to the national treatment principle. These exceptions pertain to tariffs and measures applicable to specific types of imports.

C.   Subsidies and Government Procurement

How is it legally permissible for a WTO Member to provide a subsidy to one of its nationals, but not to foreigners? For example, suppose the Indian government offers its farmers subsidized water and kerosene, the Argentine government offers its people subsidized bread, and the U.S. and EU governments offer support payments for certain crops grown by their producers. Assume these schemes discriminate against foreigners. Indeed, for budgetary reasons, they must — governments are unwilling, unable, or both to subsidize the entire world. The discrimination is excused by GATT Article III:8(a). Here, then, is a clear limitation on national treatment.

Until the plurilateral Uruguay Round *Agreement on Government Procurement* (*Government Procurement Agreement*, or *GPA*), the national treatment principle did not apply to government procurement by virtue of GATT Article III:8(b). Article III of the *GPA* obligates the parties to accord national treatment to products, services, and suppliers of other parties. However, once again this obligation is heavily qualified. The WTO Members that are parties to the Agreement are entitled to take, and indeed have taken, derogations as set forth in Appendix I to the *GPA*. The Member-parties specifically list their public sector entities that abide by the *GPA*. Thus, for example, the U.S. elected to eschew application to certain purchases of the Departments of Agriculture, Commerce, or Defense, and to purchases by certain sub-federal governments like the State of Kansas.

V.   A CRACK FOR CULTURE?

A.   Cultural Industries and Canadian Magazines

1.   Cultural Protection versus Free Trade?

Of English language magazines circulating in Canada, half are foreign. Eighty percent of magazines sold at Canadian news stands are foreign, mostly American. Of the 1,400 magazines Canadian publishers produce, over half have no operating profit. Do these data bespeak a threat to Canadian culture, or a triumph of a free market for ideas?

To be sure, many of American magazines are split-run editions, *i.e.*, an edition is produced for the Canadian market containing advertisements directed at this market and extra pages for local editorial content. But, most of the editorial content remains American. Moreover, the parent publisher is an American company with the advantage of vast economies of scale.

Worst of all from the Canadian perspective is that split-run editions siphon off scarce advertising revenues. Every dollar of an advertising budget spent on placing an ad in an American or other foreign magazine directed at the Canadian market is one less dollar available for expenditure on an ad in a Canadian magazine. The result is that Canadian magazines are starved for advertising revenues. Indeed, the foreign parents find split-run editions to be effective ways to raise advertising revenues in local markets. In brief, to many in the Canadian magazine industry, a split-run edition is an essentially American product paid for by Canadian advertisers.

2. Canada's Protective Measures

To preserve its domestic magazine market, on 15 December 1995 Canada enacted legislation — "Part V.I of the Excise Tax Act," the "Tax on Split-run Periodicals" — slapping an 80 percent excise tax on advertising revenues of split-run editions of foreign magazines. That is, Part V.I required imposition, levy, and collection of a tax equal to 80 percent of the value of all the advertisements in a split-run edition of a periodical. Tax liability lay with the publisher, or person connected with the publisher (*e.g.*, through an equity interest of 50 percent or more), or the distributor, printer, or wholesaler. To ensure collection, Canada imposed the tax on whichever of these persons resided in Canada, with joint and several liability for the tax operating between publisher and person connected with it, and also operating among distributor, printer, and wholesaler.

Clearly, a key term in Part V.I was "split run." Under Part V.I, a "split run" edition was defined as one (1) distributed in Canada, (2) in which more than 20 percent of the editorial material is the same or substantially the same as the editorial material that appears in one or more excluded editions of the periodical, and (3) contains an advertisement that does not appear in identical form in the excluded editions. There was an exemption for grandfathered periodicals, essentially those distributed in Canada before 26 March 1993. Part V.I also contained an exemption from the meaning of "split run" for any edition that is primarily circulated outside of Canada. Finally, it exempted from the definition any edition with identical advertisements in the Canadian and non-Canadian issues, so long as the circulation outside Canada exceeded the circulation within Canada. (Canada also excluded from the definition of "periodical" any catalog made up substantially of advertisements.)

Part V.I defined the value of all advertisements in a split-edition to be the total of all the gross fees for all the advertisements contained in the edition, and it applied the tax on a per-issue basis. Canada added an anti-avoidance provision to its tax code to make sure advertising expenses in a split-run edition of a foreign-owned magazine were not deductible from taxable income. These measures did not affect regular editions of foreign magazines distributed in Canada.

The U.S., which initiated both a Section 301 investigation and WTO case, argued the periodicals tax amounted to a virtual ban on the entry of split-run magazines into the Canadian market: 80 percent is so high, it makes operation economically unfeasible. It also argued the tax was discriminatory.

Canada pointed out the tax would apply equally to a domestic publisher with a split run edition containing foreign content and Canadian advertising. Moreover, the tax closed a loophole created by electronic publishing. Time-Warner, Inc. had declared its intention to produce a Canadian edition, with mostly American editorial content, of *Sports Illustrated* that would be transmitted electronically into Canada for printing. This transmission would circumvent Tariff Code 9958, a special restriction blocking importation into Canada of split-run periodicals.

Canada enacted Tariff Code 9958 in 1965. It applied to any special edition periodical (including a split-run edition or regional edition) containing an advertisement "primarily directed" to a market in Canada that did not also appear in identical form in all editions of that issue of the periodical distributed in the country of origin of the periodical. Tariff Code 9958 prohibited imports of these editions. To determine whether an advertisement was "primarily directed" at the Canadian market, the Canadian government took a number of factors into consideration. These included (1) specific invitations to Canadian consumers only, (2) listing of Canadian addresses as opposed to foreign addresses, (3) whether there were enticements to the Canadian market, and (4) references to Canada's goods and services tax. In addition, Tariff Code 9958 applied to any edition of a periodical in which more than 5 percent of the advertising content consisted of advertisements "directed" at the Canadian market. Advertisements were considered "directed" to the Canadian market if they indicated specific sources of product or service availability in Canada, or if they had specific terms or conditions relating to the sale of goods or services in Canada. Naturally, the U.S. argued Tariff Code 9958 violated the GATT XI:1 rule against prophylactic restrictions on imports.

The U.S. also was irked by Canadian postal subsidies to its domestic publishing sector. These subsidies took the form of low rates charged by Canada Post Corporation, a crown corporation, to magazines produced in Canada by Canadian-owned companies. (In 1989, the value of the subsidy peaked at $172 million; by 1998 it had fallen to about $35 million.) Specifically, Canada had three categories of postal rates for publications:

(1) "funded" rates, which were subsidized by the Canadian government, and which were available only to periodicals edited, printed, and published in Canada that were Canadian-owned and controlled, and which met certain editorial and advertising requirements (*e.g.*, the subject of the periodical had to be news, commentary, religion, science, agriculture, literature or the arts, criticism, health, or academic/scholarly matters, and no more than 70 percent of the space in the periodical could be devoted to advertising);

(2) "Canadian" rates, which were available to Canadian-owned and controlled periodicals that were edited, printed, and published in Canada, and which to such periodicals that did not qualify for a funded rate; and

(3) "international" rates, which applied to all foreign publications mailed in Canada.

The funded rates program aimed to promote Canadian culture by reducing distribution costs for Canadian periodicals. Canada said this "subsidy" was the most efficient way to provide assistance. The U.S. retorted that because it was not provided directly by the Canadian government, it violated WTO rules.

3. The WTO Panel and Appellate Body Reports

Curiously, Canada did not invoke the cultural industry exemption provisions of *NAFTA* (Article 2106 and Annex 2106), in spite of American provocation to do so. Indeed, neither side availed itself of the *NAFTA* Chapter 20 forum. The U.S. urged that as a cultural product, a magazine should be considered in the same way as any merchandise. It accused Canada of using "culture" as an excuse to favor domestic firms. Canada said the matter was purely domestic, hence *NAFTA* was irrelevant. At bottom, Canada knew that invoking the *NAFTA* exemption would create the possibility of U.S. retaliation, which the exemption specifically authorizes.

In March 1997, a WTO panel ruled against Canada, upholding most of the American arguments. In *Canada — Measures Prohibiting or Restricting Importation of Certain Periodicals*, the Panel said the periodicals tax violated the GATT Article III:2 national treatment obligation, and the 1965 tariff prohibiting imports of split-run editions violated the Article XI rule against import bans. The preferential postal rates did accord less favorable treatment to imported magazines than to like Canadian magazines, thus violating the national treatment provision of GATT Article III:4. But, said the panel, the preference was a subsidy under GATT Article III:8(b), hence the violation was excused.

Canada appealed the ruling, arguing the controversial measures were directed at a service — advertising in foreign magazines — not the magazines *per se*. In July 1997, the WTO Appellate Body rejected this argument. Its Report is excerpted below. Essentially, the Appellate Body upheld the findings of the Panel, though it reversed the panel's conclusion on the postal subsidy issue, concluding postal rates did not constitute a subsidy under GATT Article III:8(b). Presumably, therefore, they violated Article III:4.

B. The 1997 *Canada Periodicals* Case

WTO APPELLATE BODY REPORT, *CANADA — CERTAIN MEASURES CONCERNING PERIODICALS*
WT/DS31/AB/R (adopted 30 July 1997)

V. Article III:2, First Sentence, of the GATT 1994

With respect to the application of Article III:2, first sentence, we agree with the Panel that:

> . . . the following two questions need to be answered to determine whether there is a violation of Article III:2 of GATT 1994: *(a)* Are imported "split-run" periodicals and domestic non "split-run" periodicals like products?; and *(b)* Are imported "split-run" periodicals subject to an internal tax in excess of that applied to domestic non "split-run"

periodicals? If the answers to both questions are affirmative, there is a violation of Article III:2, first sentence. If the answer to the first question is negative, we need to examine further whether there is a violation of Article III:2, second sentence.

[Citing its Report in *Japan — Alcoholic Beverages*, the Appellate Body observed in a footnote that it

> need not examine the applicability of Article III:1 separately, because, as the Appellate Body noted in its recent report, the first sentence of Article III:2 *is*, in effect, an application of the general principle embodied in Article III:1. Therefore, if the imported and domestic products are "like products," and if the taxes applied to the imported products are "in excess of" those applied to the like domestic products, then the measure is inconsistent with Article III:2, first sentence. (emphasis original)]

A. LIKE PRODUCTS

We agree with the legal findings and conclusions in . . . the Panel Report [concerning the "like produce" analysis]. In particular, the Panel correctly enunciated, in theory, the legal test for determining "like products" in the context of Article III:2, first sentence, as established in the Appellate Body Report in *Japan — Alcoholic Beverages*. We also agree with the second point made by the Panel. As Article III:2, first sentence, normally requires a comparison between imported products and like domestic products, and as there were no imports of split-run editions of periodicals because of the import prohibition in Tariff Code 9958, which the Panel found (and Canada did not contest on appeal) to be inconsistent with the provisions of Article XI of the GATT 1994, hypothetical imports of split-run periodicals have to be considered. As the Panel recognized, the proper test is that a determination of "like products" for the purposes of Article III:2, first sentence, must be construed narrowly, on a case-by-case basis, by examining relevant factors including:

(i)   the product's end-uses in a given market;

(ii)   consumers' tastes and habits; and

(iii) the product's properties, nature and quality.

However, the Panel failed to analyze these criteria in relation to imported split-run periodicals and domestic non-split-run periodicals. Firstly, we note that the Panel did not base its findings on the exhibits and evidence before it, in particular, the copies of *TIME*, *TIME Canada* and *Maclean's* magazines, presented by Canada, and the magazines, *Pulp & Paper* and *Pulp & Paper Canada*, presented by the United States, or the *Report of the Task Force on the Canadian Magazine Industry* (the *"Task Force Report"*).

Secondly, we observe that the Panel based its findings that imported split-run periodicals and domestic non-split-run periodicals "can" be like products, on a single hypothetical example constructed using a Canadian-owned magazine, *Harrowsmith Country Life*. However, this example involves a comparison between two editions of the same magazine, both imported products, which could not have been in the Canadian market at the same time. Thus, the discussion . . . [in] the Panel Report is inapposite, because the example is incorrect.

> The Panel leapt from its discussion of an incorrect hypothetical example to . . . conclude that imported "split-run" periodicals and domestic non "split-run" periodicals *can* be like products within the meaning of Article III:2 of GATT 1994. In our view, this provides sufficient grounds to answer in the affirmative the question as to whether the two products at issue *are* like because, . . . the purpose of Article III is to protect expectations of the Members as to the competitive relationship between their products and those of other Members, not to protect actual trade volumes. (Emphasis added)

It is not obvious to us how the Panel came to the conclusion that it had "sufficient grounds" to find the two products at issue *are* like products from an examination of an incorrect example which led to a conclusion that imported split-run periodicals and domestic non-split-run periodicals *can be* "like."

We therefore conclude that, as a result of the lack of proper legal reasoning based on inadequate factual analysis, . . . the Panel could not logically arrive at the conclusion that imported split-run periodicals and domestic non-split-run periodicals are like products.

We are mindful of the limitation of our mandate in Articles 17.6 and 17.13 of the *DSU*. According to Article 17.6, an appeal shall be limited to issues of law covered in the Panel Report and legal interpretations developed by the Panel. The determination of whether imported and domestic products are "like products" is a process by which legal rules have to be applied to facts. In any analysis of Article III:2, first sentence, this process is particularly delicate, since "likeness" must be construed narrowly and on a case-by-case basis. We note that, due to the absence of adequate analysis in the Panel Report in this respect, it is not possible to proceed to a determination of like products.

We feel constrained, therefore, to reverse the legal findings and conclusions of the Panel on "like products." As the Panel itself stated, there are two questions which need to be answered to determine whether there is a violation of Article III:2 of the GATT 1994: (a) whether imported and domestic products are like products; and (b) whether the imported products are taxed in excess of the domestic products. If the answers to both questions are affirmative, there is a violation of Article III:2, first sentence. If the answer to one question is negative, there is a need to examine further whether the measure is consistent with Article III:2, second sentence.

Having reversed the Panel's findings on "like products," we cannot answer both questions in the first sentence of Article III:2 in the affirmative as is required to demonstrate a violation of that sentence. Therefore, we need to examine the consistency of the measure with the second sentence of Article III:2 of the GATT 1994.

B. Non-Discrimination

In light of our conclusions on the question of "like products" in Article III:2, first sentence, we do not find it necessary to address Canada's claim of "non-discrimination" in relation to that sentence.

VI. Article III:2, Second Sentence, of the GATT 1994

We will proceed to examine the consistency of Part V.1 of the Excise Tax Act with the second sentence of Article III:2 of the GATT 1994.

A. JURISDICTION

Canada asserts that the Appellate Body does not have the jurisdiction to examine a claim under Article III:2, second sentence, as no party has appealed the findings of the Panel on this provision. [The Appellate Body rejected this argument, essentially because (1) the legal obligations in the first and second sentences of Article II:2 are closely linked, (2) the Panel made findings legal findings concerning the first sentence, one of which the Appellate Body reversed, and (3) it would be remiss of the Appellate Body not to complete the analysis of Article III:2.]

. . . .

B. THE ISSUES UNDER ARTICLE III:2, SECOND SENTENCE

In our Report in *Japan — Alcoholic Beverages*, we held that:

> . . . three separate issues must be addressed to determine whether an internal tax measure is inconsistent with Article III:2, second sentence. These three issues are whether:
>
> (1) the imported products and the domestic products *are "directly competitive or substitutable products" which are in competition with each other*;
>
> (2) the directly competitive or substitutable imported and domestic products are *"not similarly taxed"*; and
>
> (3) the dissimilar taxation of the directly competitive or substitutable imported domestic products *is "applied . . . so as to afford protection to domestic production."*

1. Directly Competitive or Substitutable Products

In *Japan — Alcoholic Beverages*, the Appellate Body stated that as with "like products" under the first sentence of Article III:2, the determination of the appropriate range of "directly competitive or substitutable products" under the second sentence must be made on a case-by-case basis. The Appellate Body also found it appropriate to look at competition in the relevant markets as one among a number of means of identifying the broader category of products that might be described as "directly competitive or substitutable," as the GATT is a commercial agreement, and the WTO is concerned, after all, with markets.

According to the Panel Report, Canada considers that split-run periodicals are not "directly competitive or substitutable" for periodicals with editorial content developed for the Canadian market. Although they may be substitutable advertising vehicles, they are not competitive or substitutable information vehicles. Substitution implies interchangeability. Once the content is accepted as relevant, it seems obvious that magazines created for different markets are not interchangeable. They serve different end-uses. Canada draws attention to a study by the economist, Leigh Anderson, on which the *Task Force Report* was at least partially-based, which notes:

> U.S. magazines can probably provide a reasonable substitute for Canadian magazines in their capacity as an advertising medium, although some advertisers may be better served by a Canadian vehicle. In many instances however, they would provide a very poor substitute as an entertainment and communication medium.

Canada submits that the *Task Force Report* characterizes the relationship as one of "imperfect substitutability" — far from the direct substitutability required by this provision. The market share of imported and domestic magazines in Canada has remained remarkably constant over the last 30-plus years. If competitive forces had been in play to the degree necessary to meet the standard of "directly competitive" goods, one would have expected some variations. All this casts serious doubt on whether the competition or substitutability between imported split-run periodicals and domestic non-split-run periodicals is sufficiently "direct" to meet the standard of *Ad* Article III.

According to the United States, the very existence of the tax is itself proof of competition between split-run periodicals and non-split-run periodicals in the Canadian market. As Canada itself has acknowledged, split-run periodicals compete with wholly domestically-produced periodicals for advertising revenue, which demonstrates that they compete for the same readers. The only reason firms place advertisements in magazines is to reach readers. A firm would consider split-run periodicals to be an acceptable advertising alternative to non-split-run periodicals only if that firm had reason to believe that the split-run periodicals themselves would be an acceptable alternative to non-split-run periodicals in the eyes of consumers. According to the United States, Canada acknowledges that "[r]eaders attract advertisers" and that, ". . . Canadian publishers are ready to compete with magazines published all over the world in order to keep their readers, but the competition is fierce."

According to the United States, the *Task Force Report* together with statements made by the Minister of Canadian Heritage and Canadian officials, provide further acknowledgment of the substitutability of imported split-run periodicals and domestic non-split-run periodicals in the Canadian market.

We find the United States' position convincing, while Canada's assertions do not seem to us to be compatible with its own description of the Canadian market for periodicals.

. . . .

The statement by the economist, Leigh Anderson, quoted by Canada and the *Task Force Report*'s description of the relationship as one of "imperfect substitutability" does not modify our appreciation. A case of perfect substitutability would fall within Article III:2, first sentence, while we are examining the broader prohibition of the second sentence. We are not impressed either by Canada's argument that the market share of imported and domestic magazines has remained remarkably constant over the last 30-plus years, and that one would have expected some variation if competitive forces had been in play to the degree necessary to meet the standard of "directly competitive" goods. This argument would have weight only if Canada had not protected the domestic market of Canadian periodicals through, among other measures, the import prohibition of Tariff Code 9958 and the excise tax of Part V.1 of the Excise Tax Act.

Our conclusion that imported split-run periodicals and domestic non-split-run periodicals are "directly competitive or substitutable" does not mean that all periodicals belong to the same relevant market, whatever their editorial content. A periodical containing mainly current news is not directly competitive or substitutable with a periodical dedicated to gardening, chess, sports, music or cuisine. But news magazines, like *TIME*, *TIME Canada* and *Maclean's*, are directly competitive or substitutable in spite of the "Canadian" content of *Maclean's*. The competitive relationship is even closer in the case of more specialized magazines, like *Pulp & Paper* as compared with *Pulp & Paper Canada*, two trade magazines presented to the Panel by the United States.

The fact that, among these examples, only *TIME Canada* is a split-run periodical, and that it is not imported but is produced in Canada, does not affect at all our appreciation of the competitive relationship. The competitive relationship of imported split-run periodicals destined for the Canadian market is even closer to domestic non-split-run periodicals than the competitive relationship between imported non-split-run periodicals and domestic non-split-run periodicals. Imported split-run periodicals contain advertisements targeted specifically at the Canadian market, while imported non-split-run periodicals do not carry such advertisements.

We, therefore, conclude that imported split-run periodicals and domestic non-split-run periodicals are directly competitive or substitutable products in so far as they are part of the same segment of the Canadian market for periodicals.

2. Not Similarly Taxed

Having found that imported split-run and domestic non-split-run periodicals of the same type are directly competitive or substitutable, we must examine whether the imported products and the directly competitive or substitutable domestic products are not similarly taxed. Part V.1 of the Excise Tax Act taxes split-run editions of periodicals in an amount equivalent to 80 per cent of the value of all advertisements in a split-run edition. In contrast, domestic non-split-run periodicals are not subject to Part V.1 of the Excise Tax Act. Following the reasoning of the Appellate Body in *Japan — Alcoholic Beverages*, dissimilar taxation of even some imported products as compared to directly competitive or substitutable domestic products is inconsistent with the provisions of the second sentence of Article III:2. In *United States — Section 337*, the panel found:

> . . . that the "no less favourable" treatment requirement of Article III:4 has to be understood as applicable to each individual case of imported products. The Panel rejected any notion of balancing more favourable treatment of some imported products against less

favourable treatment of other imported products. [GATT B.I.S.D. (36th Supp.) at 345 ¶ 5.14 (adopted 7 November 1989).]

With respect to Part V.1 of the Excise Tax Act, we find that the amount of the taxation is far above the *de minimis* threshold required by the Appellate Body Report in *Japan — Alcoholic Beverages*. The magnitude of this tax is sufficient to prevent the production and sale of split-run periodicals in Canada.

3. So as to Afford Protection

The Appellate Body established the following approach in *Japan — Alcoholic Beverages* for determining whether dissimilar taxation of directly competitive or substitutable products has been applied so as to afford protection:

> . . . we believe that an examination in any case of whether dissimilar taxation has been applied so as to afford protection requires a comprehensive and objective analysis of the structure and application of the measure in question on domestic as compared to imported products. We believe it is possible to examine objectively the underlying criteria used in a particular tax measure, its structure, and its overall application to ascertain whether it is applied in a way that affords protection to domestic products.
>
> Although it is true that the aim of a measure may not be easily ascertained, nevertheless its protective application can most often be discerned from the design, the architecture, and the revealing structure of a measure. The very magnitude of the dissimilar taxation in a particular case may be evidence of such a protective application, . . . Most often, there will be other factors to be considered as well. In conducting this inquiry, panels should give full consideration to all the relevant facts and all the relevant circumstances in any given case.

With respect to Part V.1 of the Excise Tax Act, we note that the magnitude of the dissimilar taxation between imported split-run periodicals and domestic non-split-run periodicals is beyond excessive, indeed, it is prohibitive. There is also ample evidence that the very design and structure of the measure is such as to afford protection to domestic periodicals.

The Canadian policy which led to the enactment of Part V.1 of the Excise Tax Act had its origins in the *Task Force Report*. It is clear from reading the *Task Force Report* that the design and structure of Part V.1 of the Excise Tax Act are to prevent the establishment of split-run periodicals in Canada, thereby ensuring that Canadian advertising revenues flow to Canadian magazines. Madame Monique Landry, Minister Designate of Canadian Heritage at the time the *Task Force Report* was released, issued the following statement summarizing the Government of Canada's policy objectives for the Canadian periodical industry:

> The Government reaffirms its commitment to protect the economic foundations of the Canadian periodical industry, which is a vital element of Canadian cultural expression. To achieve this objective, the Government will continue to use policy instruments that encourage

the flow of advertising revenues to Canadian magazines and discourage the establishment of split-run or "Canadian" regional editions with advertising aimed at the Canadian market. We are committed to ensuring that Canadians have access to Canadian ideas and information through genuinely Canadian magazines, while not restricting the sale of foreign magazines in Canada.

Furthermore, the Government of Canada issued the following response to the *Task Force Report*:

> The Government reaffirms its commitment to the long-standing policy of protecting the economic foundations of the Canadian periodical industry. To achieve this objective, the Government uses policy instruments that encourage the flow of advertising revenues to Canadian periodicals, since a viable Canadian periodical industry must have a secure financial base.

During the debate of Bill C-103, An Act to Amend the Excise Tax Act and the Income Tax Act, the Minister of Canadian Heritage, the Honourable Michel Dupuy, stated the following:

> . . . the reality of the situation is that we must protect ourselves against split-runs coming from foreign countries and, in particular, from the United States.

Canada also admitted that the objective and structure of the tax is to insulate Canadian magazines from competition in the advertising sector, thus leaving significant Canadian advertising revenues for the production of editorial material created for the Canadian market. With respect to the actual application of the tax to date, it has resulted in one split-run magazine, *Sports Illustrated*, to move its production for the Canadian market out of Canada and back to the United States. Also, *Harrowsmith Country Life*, a Canadian-owned split-run periodical, has ceased production of its United States' edition as a consequence of the imposition of the tax.

We therefore conclude on the basis of the above reasons, including the magnitude of the differential taxation, the several statements of the Government of Canada's explicit policy objectives in introducing the measure and the demonstrated actual protective effect of the measure, that the design and structure of Part V.1 of the Excise Tax Act is clearly to afford protection to the production of Canadian periodicals.

VII. Article III:8(b) of the GATT 1994

. . . .

Both participants agree that Canada's "funded" postal rates involve "a payment of subsidies." The appellant, the United States, argues, however, that the "funded" postal rates programme involves a transfer of funds from one government entity to another, *i.e.*, from Canadian Heritage to Canada Post, and not from the Canadian government to domestic producers as required by Article III:8(b).

As we understand it, through the PAP, Canadian Heritage provides Canada Post, a wholly-owned Crown corporation, with financial assistance to support special rates of postage for eligible publications, including certain designated domestic periodicals mailed and distributed in Canada. This programme has been implemented through a series of agreements, the MOA [*i.e.*, the Memorandum of Agreement Concerning the Publications Assistance Program Between the Department of Communications and Canada Post Corporation], between Canadian Heritage and Canada Post, which provide that in consideration of the payments made to it by Canadian Heritage, Canada Post will accept for distribution, at special "funded" rates, all publications designated by Canadian Heritage to be eligible under the PAP. The MOA provides that while Canadian Heritage will administer the eligibility requirements for the PAP based on criteria specified in the MOA, Canada Post will accept for distribution all publications that are eligible under the PAP at the "funded" rates.

The appellant, the United States, cited four GATT 1947 panel reports as authorities for its interpretation of Article III:8(b). However, these panel reports are not all directly on point. In *Italian Agricultural Machinery* [GATT B.I.S.D. (7th Supp.) at 60 (adopted 23 October 1958)] and *EEC — Oilseeds* [GATT B.I.S.D. (37th Supp.) at 86 (adopted 25 January 1990)], the panels found that subsidies paid to purchasers of agricultural machinery and processors of oilseeds were not made "exclusively to domestic producers" of agricultural machinery and oilseeds, respectively. In *United States — Malt Beverages* [GATT B.I.S.D. (39th Supp.) at 206 (adopted 19 June 1992)] and *United States — Tobacco* [GATT B.I.S.D. (37th Supp.) at 86 (adopted 25 January 1990)], the issue was whether a reduction in the federal excise tax on beer or a remission of a product tax on tobacco constituted a "payment of subsidies" within the meaning of Article III:8(b). In *United States — Malt Beverages*, the panel found that a reduction of taxes on a good did not qualify as a "payment of subsidies" for the purposes of Article III:8(b) of the GATT 1994. In *United States — Tobacco*, having found that the measure at issue was not a tax remission, the panel concluded that it was a payment which qualified under Article III:8(b) of the GATT 1994.

In *EEC — Oilseeds*, the panel stated that "it can reasonably be assumed that a payment not made directly to producers is not made 'exclusively' to them." This statement of the panel is *obiter dicta*, as the panel found in that report that subsidies paid to oilseeds processors were not made "exclusively to domestic producers," and therefore, the EEC payments of subsidies to processors and producers of oilseeds and related animal feed proteins did not qualify under the provisions of Article III:8(b).

A proper interpretation of Article III:8(b) must be made on the basis of a careful examination of the text, context and object and purpose of that provision. In examining the text of Article III:8(b), we believe that the phrase, "including payments to domestic producers derived from the proceeds of internal taxes or charges applied consistently with the provisions of this Article and subsidies effected through governmental purchases of domestic products" helps to elucidate the types of subsidies covered by Article III:8(b) of the GATT 1994. It is not an exhaustive list of the kinds of programmes that would qualify as "the payment of subsidies exclusively to domestic producers," but those words exemplify the kinds of programmes which are exempted from the obligations of Articles III:2 and III:4 of the GATT 1994.

Our textual interpretation is supported by the context of Article III:8(b) examined in relation to Articles III:2 and III:4 of the GATT 1994. Further-more, the object and purpose of Article III:8(b) is confirmed by the drafting history of Article III. In this context, we refer to the following discussion in the Reports of the Committees and Principal Sub-Committees of the Interim Commission for the International Trade Organization concerning the provi-sion of the Havana Charter for an International Trade Organization that corresponds to Article III:8(b) of the GATT 1994:

> This sub-paragraph was redrafted in order to make it clear that nothing in Article 18 could be construed to sanction the exemption of domestic products from internal taxes imposed on like imported products or the remission of such taxes. At the same time the Sub-Committee recorded its view that nothing in this sub-paragraph or elsewhere in Article 18 would override the provisions of Section C of Chapter IV. [Interim Commission for the International Trade Organi-zation, Reports of the Committees and Principal Sub-Committees: ICITO I/8, Geneva, September 1948, p. 66. As the Appellate Body stated in footnote 73 of its Report, Article 18 and Section C of Chapter IV of the Havana Charter for an International Trade Organization correspond, respectively, to Article III and Article XVI of the GATT 1947.]

We do not see a reason to distinguish a reduction of tax rates on a product from a reduction in transportation or postal rates. Indeed, an examination of the text, context, and object and purpose of Article III:8(b) suggests that it was intended to exempt from the obligations of Article III only the payment of subsidies which involves the expenditure of revenue by a government.

We agree with the panel in *United States — Malt Beverages* that:

> Article III:8(b) limits, therefore, the permissible producer subsidies to "payments" after taxes have been collected or payments otherwise consistent with Article III. This separation of tax rules, *e.g.*, on tax exemptions or reductions, and subsidy rules makes sense economically and politically. Even if the proceeds from non-discriminatory product taxes may be used for subsequent subsidies, the domestic producer, like his foreign competitors, must pay the product taxes due. The separation of tax and subsidy rules contributes to greater transpar-ency. It also may render abuses of tax policies for protectionist purposes more difficult, as in the case where producer aids require additional legislative or governmental decisions in which the different interests involved can be balanced.

As a result of our analysis of the text, context, and object and purpose of Article III:8(b), we conclude that the Panel incorrectly interpreted this provision. For these reasons, we reverse the Panel's findings and conclusions that Canada's "funded" postal rates scheme for periodicals is justified under Article III:8(b) of the GATT 1994.

Chapter 14

THE FOURTH PILLAR: NON-TARIFF BARRIERS AND GATT ARTICLE XI

I against my brother.

I and my brother against our cousin.

I, my brother, and our cousin against the neighbors.

All of us against the foreigner.

> —Bedouin Proverb (*quoted in* BRUCE CHATWIN, THE SONG LINES, ch. 30 ("From the Notebooks") (1987))

DOCUMENTS SUPPLEMENT ASSIGNMENT

1. *Havana Charter* Articles 4, 6, 13, 20-21, 38-39
2. GATT Articles X, XI, and XVIII:B
3. WTO *TBT Agreement*
4. *NAFTA* Chapters 9, 18
5. Relevant provisions in other FTAs

I. QUANTITATIVE RESTRICTIONS, THE SCOPE OF GATT ARTICLE XI:1, AND THE 1988 *JAPAN SEMICONDUCTORS* CASE

GATT PANEL REPORT, *JAPAN — TRADE IN SEMI-CONDUCTORS*
B.I.S.D. (35th Supp.) 116, 118-122, 151-158 (1989)
(adopted 4 May 1988)

VII. FINDINGS

96. The Panel understood the complaint of the EEC to be that:

— the measures applied by the Japanese Government to exports of semi-conductors at prices below company-specific costs to certain third countries to implement its Arrangement concerning Trade in Semi-Conductor Products with the United States, restricted exports of semi-conductors and therefore contravened Article[ ] . . . XI. . . .

. . . .

A. *The Third Country Market Monitoring*

99. The Panel considered the following facts as central to its examination of this part of the EEC's [European Economic Communities'] complaint. After

having concluded the [2 September 1986] *Arrangement with the United States concerning Trade in Semi-Conductors*, the Japanese Government:

— requested Japanese producers and exporters of semi-conductors covered by the *Arrangement* not to export semi-conductors at prices below company-specific costs;

— collected data on company and product-specific costs from producers; introduced a statutory requirement, reinforced by penal servitude not exceeding six months or a fine not exceeding Y 200,000, for exporters of semi-conductors to report data on export prices;

— systematically monitored company and product-specific cost and export price data on semi-conductors which were sold for export to certain contracting parties other than the United States;

— instituted quarterly supply and demand forecasts and communicated to manufacturers its concern about the need to accommodate their production levels to the forecasts as compiled by MITI [Japan's Ministry of International Trade and Industry, now called "METI" for "Ministry of the Economy, Trade, and Industry."]

[The *Arrangement*, reprinted at 25 INTERNATIONAL LEGAL MATERIALS 1408 (November 1986), had associated with it a confidential Side Letter, the contents of which became public only after the *Arrangement* was unveiled. In the Letter, the U.S. articulated a goal for market access. Within 5 years, *i.e.*, by 1991, foreign (not just American) semiconductor producers should have at least a 20 percent share of the Japanese market. The use of a specific numerical target for a chosen sector was a bald attempt at managed trade. Japan responded to the Side Letter by agreeing to "recognize" this goal, and to "welcome" its realization. Whether these words indicated a legal commitment to a 20 percent share of the Japanese market for foreign chip producers would remain a point of contention for the duration of the *Arrangement*. Query whether, when, and how the Letter was revealed to the GATT Panel. What ethical rules would affect this question?

The *1986 Arrangement* lapsed after 5 years, and was succeeded by a new one of the same name, signed and effective on 1 August 1991. *See* 31 INTERNATIONAL LEGAL MATERIALS 1074 (September 1992). The *1991 Arrangement* incorporated the essential language of the 1986 Side Letter, namely, that Japan

recognizes that the U.S. semiconductor industry expects that the foreign market share will grow to more than 20 percent of the Japanese market by the end of 1992 and considers that this can be realized.

But, Japan hastened to add that its recognition was "neither a guarantee, a ceiling nor a floor [*sic*] on the foreign market share." No numerical target was set for years after 1992. Whereas the *1986 Arrangement* failed to defined "market share, the *1991 Arrangement* did so via two formulas, which themselves engendered controversy.

The *1991 Arrangement* terminated in 1996, and was not renewed. Rather, the Administration of President Bill Clinton signed a *Joint Statement by the*

Government of the United States and the Government of Japan Concerning Semiconductors on 2 August 1996. The *Joint Statement*, with a 3-year lifespan and terminating on 31 July 1999, contained neither numerical targets nor an expectation about market share. It simply called for private sector data collection on the semiconductor market (including market share), and annual meetings between the two governments. It was superseded in 1996 by another *Joint Statement*, but this time a plurilateral declaration involving the EU, Korea, and Taiwan, as well as the U.S. and Japan. The *1996 Joint Statement* was renewable as of 1 August 2004.

To the present day, the foreign market share of the Japanese chip market is a closely watched statistic. Interestingly, when the *1986 Agreement* was signed that share was 8 percent. By 1997 (second quarter), it was 35.8 percent, and for the remainder of the 20th century hovered at or about 30 percent. Had managed trade worked?]

. . . .

104. The Panel examined the parties' contentions in the light of Article XI:1. . . . The Panel noted that this wording [of Article XI:1] was comprehensive: it applied to all measures instituted or maintained by a contracting party prohibiting or restricting the importation, exportation or sale for export of products other than measures that take the form of duties, taxes or other charges.

105. The Panel noted that the Contracting Parties had decided in a previous case that the import regulation allowing the import of a product in principle, but not below a minimum price level, constituted a restriction on importation within the meaning of Article XI:1. . . . [*See EEC — Programme of Minimum Import Prices, Licenses and Surety Deposits for Certain Processed Fruits and Vegetables*, B.I.S.D. (25th Supp.) at 68, 99 ¶ 4.9 (1979) (adopted 18 October 1978)]. The Panel considered that the principle applied in that case to restrictions on imports of goods below certain prices was equally applicable to restrictions on exports below certain prices.

106. The Panel then examined the contention of the Japanese Government that the measures complained of were not restrictions within the meaning of Article XI:1 because they were not legally binding or mandatory. In this respect the Panel noted that Article XI:1, unlike other provisions of the General Agreement, did not refer to laws or regulations but more broadly to measures. This wording indicated clearly that any measure instituted or maintained by a contracting party which restricted the exportation or sale for export of products was covered by this provision, irrespective of the legal status of the measure.

107. Having reached this finding on the basis of the wording and purpose of the provision, the Panel looked for precedents that might be of further assistance to it on this point. It noted that the Contracting Parties had addressed a case relating to the interpretation of Article XI:2(c) in the report of the Panel on *Japan — Restrictions on Imports of Certain Agricultural Products* (L/6253). Under Article XI:2(c), import restrictions might be imposed if they were necessary to the enforcement of "governmental measures" restricting domestic supplies. The complaining party argued in the earlier

panel proceedings that some of the measures which Japan had described as governmental measures were in fact "only an appeal for private measures to be taken voluntarily by private parties" and could therefore not justify the import restrictions. Japan replied that "to the extent that governmental measures were effective, it was irrelevant whether or not the measures were mandatory and statutory," that the governmental measures "were effectively enforced by detailed directives and instructions to local governments and/or farmers' organizations" and that "such centralised and mutually collaborative structure of policy implementation was the crux of government enforcement in Japan. . . ." The Panel which examined that case had noted that "the practice of 'administrative guidance' played an important role" in the enforcement of the Japanese supply restrictions, that this practice was "a traditional tool of Japanese government policy based on consensus and peer pressure" and that administrative guidance in the special circumstances prevailing in Japan could therefore be regarded as a governmental measure enforcing supply restrictions. The Panel recognized the differences between Article XI:1 and Article XI:2(c) and the fact that the previous case was not the same in all respects as the case before it, but noted that the earlier case supported its finding that it was not necessarily the legal status of the measure which was decisive in determining whether or not it fell under Article XI:1.

108. The Panel recognized that not all non-mandatory requests could be regarded as measures within the meaning of Article XI:1. Government-industry relations varied from country to country, from industry to industry, and from case to case and were influenced by many factors. There was thus a wide spectrum of government involvement ranging from, for instance, direct government orders to occasional government consultations with advisory committees. The task of the Panel was to determine whether the measures taken in this case would be such as to constitute a contravention of Article XI.

109. In order to determine this, the Panel considered that it needed to be satisfied on two essential criteria. First, there were reasonable grounds to believe that sufficient incentives or disincentives existed for non-mandatory measures to take effect. Second, the operation of the measures to restrict export of semi-conductors at prices below company-specific costs was essentially dependent on Government action or intervention. The Panel considered each of these two criteria in turn. The Panel considered that if these two criteria were met, the measures would be operating in a manner equivalent to mandatory requirements such that the difference between the measures and mandatory requirements was only one of form and not of substance, and that there could be therefore no doubt that they fell within the range of measures covered by Article XI.1.

110. On the first criterion, the Panel considered the background against which the measures operated. The Panel noted that the Government of Japan had formally concluded in September 1986 an *Arrangement with the Government of the United States*, one of the main provisions of which was for the Japanese Government to monitor costs and export prices to third country markets in order to prevent dumping. Following bilateral consultations, the Government of Japan assured the United States in April 1987 that it had

taken "appropriate action to ensure that Japanese semi-conductor exports are being sold at not less than their costs in third country markets." In the light of this, the Panel considered that at least by April 1987, there would certainly have been no doubt in the minds of relevant Japanese producers and exporters that the Japanese Government had made an undertaking to the United States to ensure that a certain class of sales did not take place. They would also have known that any such action would have led to the Government of Japan being unable to fulfill a commitment which it had given to the United States, and therefore would have adverse consequences for Japan. They would also have been aware that the Government had the fullest information available to identify any producers or exporters selling at prices below costs.

111. The Panel considered that, in the above circumstances, the Japanese Government's measures did not need to be legally binding to take effect, as there were reasonable grounds to believe that there were sufficient incentives or disincentives for Japanese producers and exporters to conform. The Panel did not consider that these circumstances were, of themselves, sufficient to ensure compliance. Indeed, events showed that despite the existence of the Arrangement, a certain number of Japanese producers and exporters had pursued their original course of production and sales. What was required to ensure compliance were additional Government measures.

112. The Panel went on to consider the second criterion regarding the manner in which the measures operated in this case. To begin with, the Panel noted the Japanese Government's own description of its measures as provided to the United States in its Position Paper of April 1987, notably that "Japan exercised administrative guidance to achieve production cut-backs and adopted more stringent export licensing practices" and that "actions have been taken aimed at reducing supplies and squeezing out grey market transactions." It referred also to the measures taken as "recently-ordered production cut-backs," and that "the measures (*i.e.*, those relating to production and export administration) taken by the Japanese Government have as their exclusive purpose and effect avoiding below cost sales of semi-conductors in third country markets."

113. The Panel further examined the structure and elements of the measures adopted. It noted that Japanese producers were required to submit detailed information on costs on a regular basis. It also noted the importance of the statutory requirement for exporters to supply information on export prices and of the heavy penalties attached for failure to comply with that requirement. The objective of identification in the monitoring measures was clear. For instance, in cases where the exporter was not a producer, the origin of the transaction had to be declared and identified. The Panel noted that this gave the Japanese Government a comprehensive basis for precise identification of the source of any below cost pricing. It also observed that any producer or exporter would have been aware that the Japanese Government would be in a position to have this information. The preparedness of the Japanese Government to request, and to continue requesting, for below cost sales to cease was also evident.

114. The Panel examined the operation of the supply and demand forecasts. It noted that MITI had instituted regular meetings of the Supply and Demand

Forecasts Committee, involving producers, upon which its forecasts were drawn up. The Panel considered that the Government of Japan played a decisive role in the entire operation. Indeed it was stated by Japan that "the Japanese Government, in consideration of large inventories of products, made an attempt to restore balance in supply and demand." Thus in the first and second quarters of 1987, the Government of Japan compiled the supply and demand forecasts "to get production levels reflective of actual demand." The Panel recalled the statement quoted in paragraph 112 above concerning the production cut-backs and the avoidance of below cost sales of semi-conductors in third country markets. On the basis of these, the Panel considered that the Government of Japan had intervened to facilitate the reduction of the production levels of semi-conductors through the operation of the supply and demand forecasts. The Panel further considered that if Japanese producers and exporters were subject to any measure restricting the exportation or sale for export of semi-conductors, they would have to adjust their production levels accordingly. The Panel therefore considered that the operation of the supply and demand forecasts had facilitated the reduction of the production levels, strengthening the effectiveness of the other measures adopted.

115. The Panel then considered whether the operation of the measures was essentially dependent on Government action. The complex of measures was, in the Panel's view, so dependent. The period between September 1986 and January 1987 gave an interesting indication of how Japanese firms were disposed to operate where they were subject to less constraint. It was apparent that they had been prepared to produce and sell up to a quantity which included what was later termed "false demand" in the context of the revised supply or demand forecast in February 1987. The Panel considered that the disposition to produce and sell was what the Government of Japan by its complex of measures intended to control, by the strengthening of the monitoring measures, lowering of the minimum export amount requiring an export licence to 50,000 yen, requests to producers not to export at prices below company-specific costs, and the revisions of the supply and demand forecasts.

116. The Panel also considered that the series of statements quoted in paragraph 112 above were relevant in this context. In addition to these, the Panel noted that Japan had stated in the proceedings of the Panel that "although monitoring by MITI was limited in scope, it was still meaningful because MITI represented a neutral and objective figure overseeing the entire industry while taking into account costs and prices among competing companies in Japan. Monitoring also helped to stamp out suspicion among companies that others were cheating or resorting to dumping." Japan had further stated that "if the semi-conductor manufacturers were to pursue their own profits and ignore MITI's concern, the whole dumping prevention mechanism would collapse," and that "the administration presents (firms) with objective facts and considerations and others that are usually not obtainable by one firm alone." The Panel considered that these statements concerning the way in which the Government exercised its authority were a further confirmation of the fact that the Government's involvement was essential to the prevention of sales below company-specific costs.

117. All these factors led the Panel to conclude that an administrative structure had been created by the Government of Japan which operated to

exert maximum possible pressure on the private sector to cease exporting at prices below company-specific costs. This was exercised through such measures as repeated direct requests by MITI, combined with the statutory requirement for exporters to submit information on export prices, the systematic monitoring of company and product-specific costs and export prices and the institution of the supply and demand forecasts mechanism and its utilization in a manner to directly influence the behaviour of private companies. These measures operated furthermore to facilitate strong peer pressure to comply with requests by MITI and at the same time to foster a climate of uncertainty as to the circumstances under which their exports could take place. The Panel considered that the complex of measures exhibited the rationale as well as the essential elements of a formal system of export control. The only distinction in this case was the absence of formal legally binding obligations in respect of exportation or sale for export of semi-conductors. However, the Panel concluded that this amounted to a difference in form rather than substance because the measures were operated in a manner equivalent to mandatory requirements. The Panel concluded that the complex of measures constituted a coherent system restricting the sale for export of monitored semi-conductors at prices below company-specific costs to markets other that the United States, inconsistent with Article XI.1.

118. The Panel then reverted to the issue raised by the EEC concerning the delays of up to three months in the issuing of export licences that had resulted from the monitoring of costs and export prices of semi-conductors destined for contracting parties other than the United States. It examined whether the measures taken by Japan constituted restrictions on exportation or sale for export within the meaning of Article XI:1. It noted that the Contracting Parties had found in a previous case that automatic licensing did not constitute a restriction within the meaning of Article XI:1 and that an import licence issued on the fifth working day following the day on which the licence application was lodged could be deemed to have been automatically granted. . . . [*See EEC — Program of Minimum Import Prices, supra*, at 95 ¶ 4.1.] The Panel recognized that the above applied to import licences but it considered that the standard applicable to import licences should, by analogy, be applied also to export licences because it saw no reason that would justify the application of a different standard. The Panel therefore found that export licensing practices by Japan, leading to delays of up to three months in the issuing of licences for semi-conductors destined for contracting parties other than the United States, had been non-automatic and constituted restrictions on the exportation of such products inconsistent with Article XI:1.

II. QUANTITATIVE RESTRICTIONS, SCHEDULES OF TARIFF CONCESSIONS, AND THE 1989 *AUSTRALIA SUGAR* CASE

GATT PANEL REPORT, *UNITED STATES — RESTRICTIONS ON IMPORTS OF SUGAR*
B.I.S.D. (36th Supp.) 331-338, 341-344 (1989)
(adopted 22 June 1989)

2. FACTUAL ASPECTS

2.1. In the Annecy Round in 1949, the United States negotiated and included in Schedule XX tariff concessions on raw and refined sugar subject to a provision relating to Title II of the *Sugar Act of 1948* or substantially equivalent legislation. Title II of the *Sugar Act of 1948* required the Secretary of Agriculture to establish quotas on the importation and domestic production of sugar on the basis of his yearly determination of the amount of sugar needed to meet consumers' requirements in the continental United States.

2.2. This provision, enlarged to authorize the President of the United States to proclaim a rate of duty and quota limitation on imported sugars if the Sugar Act or substantially equivalent legislation should expire, was reflected in Schedule XX following the Torquay Round in 1951 and, with some modification, following the Kennedy Round in 1967 and the Tokyo Round in 1979. By Proclamation 3822 of 16 December 1967, the President of the United States added to the TSUS the Head Note reflecting this provision.

2.3. In 1988 the United States modified its GATT Schedule in accordance with the harmonized system. Since then, the provision has been contained in Chapter 17 of GATT Schedule XX (United States), and reflected in the corresponding portion of the Harmonized Tariff Schedule of the United States (HTSUS). The provision reads as follows:

> 2.   The rates in subheadings 1701.11, 1701.12, 1701.91.20, 1701.99, 1702.90.30, 1702.90.40, 1806.10.40 and 2106.90.10, on 1 January 1968, shall be effective only during such time as Title II of the Sugar Act of 1948 or substantially equivalent legislation is in effect in the United States, whether or not the quotas, or any of them, authorized by such legislation, are being applied or are suspended:

Provided,

> (a) That, if the President finds that a particular rate not lower than such 1 January 1968 rate, limited by a particular quota, may be established for any articles provided for in the above-mentioned subheadings, which will give due consideration to the interests in the United States sugar market of domestic producers and materially affected contracting parties to the General Agreement on Tariffs and Trade, he shall proclaim such particular rate and such quota limitation, to be effective not later than the 90th day following the termination of the effectiveness of such legislation;

(b) That any rate and quota limitation so established shall be modified if the President finds and proclaims that such modification is required or appropriate to give effect to the above considerations; and

(c) That the 1 January 1968 rates shall resume full effectiveness, subject to the provisions of this note, if legislation substantially equivalent to Title II of the *Sugar Act of 1948* should subsequently become effective.

2.4. The *Sugar Act of 1948* expired on 31 December 1974 and was not replaced by substantially equivalent legislation. The President of the United States established, by Proclamation 4334 of 16 November 1974, import quotas and rates of duties on raw and refined sugar on the basis of the Head Note. Subsequent Presidential Proclamations modified the applicable duties and quota amounts.

2.5. On 5 May 1982, the President of the United States, pursuant to his authority under the Head Note, established, by Proclamation 4941, an emergency import quota programme to regulate imports of sugar into the United States market, according to which the size of the global import quota is determined and announced quarterly or for other periods by the Secretary of Agriculture and allocated between the different supplying countries according to their past performance during a previous representative period. Australia retained a share of 8.3 per cent of the total United States import sugar market.

. . . .

2.6. Since 1982, the global import quota has generally been set on an annual basis. . . . Although Australia's share of the base quota remained at 8.3 per cent, Australia's actual share of the total United States market for imported sugar declined to less than 7.9 per cent in 1987-1988 due to minimum shipment provisions provided in the quota arrangements for small quota countries.

2.7. Production of sugar in the United States . . . increased from 5.9 million short tons in 1982 to 7.3 million short tons in 1987. . . .

3. MAIN ARGUMENTS

. . . .

Article XI

3.3. *Australia* claimed that the import restrictions on sugar maintained by the United States pursuant to Presidential Proclamation 4941 of 5 May 1982 were inconsistent with the provisions of Article XI:1. . . .

3.4. Australia noted that paragraph 2 of Article XI provided for exemptions from the provisions of paragraph 1 of that Article, but argued that the import restrictions on sugar maintained by the United States did not qualify for any of the requirements in the relevant sub-paragraphs of Article XI:2. In particular, Australia recalled that Article XI:2(c)(i) required that, for the exemption from the provisions of Article XI:1, the import-restricting measures must be "necessary to the enforcement of governmental measures which operate: to restrict the quantities of the like domestic product permitted to be marketed or produced. . . ." It also required that the restrictions ". . . shall not be such as will reduce the total of imports relative to the total of domestic production, as compared with the proportion which might reasonably be expected to rule between the two in the absence of restrictions."

3.5. Australia maintained that the United States import restrictions on sugar did not meet either of these requirements. Regarding governmental measures in force, Australia recalled that . . . the United States had confirmed that the United States sugar programme did not contain any provisions designed to limit or restrict quantities of cane or beet sugar produced domestically or to limit the quantities eligible for support under the Price Support Loan Program. Similarly, United States sugar import quotas and total sugar imports had declined significantly since the introduction of restrictive quotas in 1982, whereas the United States domestic sugar production had increased over this period. . . .

3.6. The *United States* pointed out that these restrictions were in accordance with a negotiated provision of a tariff concession which was an integral part of the General Agreement. Therefore, the United States considered that Article XI was not relevant to the matter examined by the Panel as one provision of the General Agreement could not overrule another. . . .

Article II

3.7. The *United States* recalled that the import restrictions on raw and refined sugar examined by the Panel were administered pursuant to a provision which was part of a tariff concession first negotiated in the Annecy Round in 1949. The United States maintained that this provision was consistent with Article II:1(b) which, *inter alia*, permitted contracting parties to subject tariff concessions to "the terms, conditions or qualifications set forth" in their Schedules of Concessions. Pursuant to Article II:7, these Schedules were annexed to the General Agreement and were made an integral part of it. The United States concluded that the terms, conditions and qualifications applicable to particular tariff concessions, including the import restrictions at issue in the present case, were an integral part of the General Agreement. Therefore, they could neither be challenged nor overruled by another part or provision of the General Agreement.

3.8. *Australia* did not question the United States argumentation that qualifications to tariff concessions were permissible under the provisions of Article II:1(b). However, Australia claimed that qualifications to concessions could neither justify the application of measures contrary to other provisions of the General Agreement, nor could they provide a derogation from contracting parties' obligations under specific provisions of the General Agreement. Australia pointed out that Article II, unlike other GATT Articles which provide for derogations from the provisions of the General Agreement, contained no mechanism, explicit or implicit, for escape from those provisions. Article II dealt simply with concessions to other contracting parties, not rights to exempt specific goods from provisions of the General Agreement. Australia noted that the *Sugar Act of 1948* allowed for quotas on both domestic production and imports . . . which made it a system which might, if challenged in the GATT, have had elements necessary for *prima facie* conformity with Article XI:2. . . .

3.9. Australia recalled that at the 9th Session in 1955, the Contracting Parties had adopted the report of the Review Working Party on Other Barriers to Trade. . . . This report contained, *inter alia*, an agreement that matters which might affect the practical effects of tariff concessions could be negotiated and incorporated into the appropriate schedule annexed to the General Agreement "provided that the results of such negotiations should not conflict with other provisions of the Agreement." . . .

3.10. Australia said that contrary to the United States argumentation . . . it was not Australia but the United States which claimed that one part of the General Agreement could overrule another as it was arguing that a provision contained in its Schedule annexed to Part I overrode any obligations the United States might have under Part II of the General Agreement. In Australia's view, the question of one part of the General Agreement overriding another should not arise, as Schedules in Part I could not contain provisions which, in their operation, were inconsistent with those set out in other parts of the Agreement. . . .

3.11. The *United States* [argued that the] . . . Working Party on Other Barriers to Trade was limited by its terms of reference to consideration of proposals submitted with respect to (a) subsidies, countervailing and anti-dumping measures, and (b) state trading, surplus disposal, disposal of non-commercial stocks and the general exceptions to the Agreement. It did not set out to make recommendations on Article II which was the subject of another working party, the Working Party on Schedules and Customs Administration also established as part of the 1955 review process. The United States noted that the statement cited by Australia would not support Australia's claim even if it were read to apply to matters other than subsidies. In that statement, the Working Party agreed that contracting parties "should" avoid agreeing to subsidies provisions in their Schedules which might not be consistent with other provisions of the General Agreement. In the United States view, this was clearly nothing more than a policy recommendation and not a legal requirement.

. . . .

3.14. The United States maintained that . . . the Head Note explicitly authorized a quota on imports of sugar. The United States said that, by raising this claim, Australia was requesting the Panel to declare that actions taken by the United States in conformity with a negotiated tariff provision were not permissible. In other words, Australia was seeking to terminate or to modify a United States tariff concession not by negotiation, but by the operation of a dispute settlement panel.

3.15. Furthermore, the United States recalled that in many instances both the Schedules negotiated in 1947 and those now in effect contained terms, conditions and qualifications other than tariffs. If Australia's claim was correct, all these non-tariff conditions, including those in Australia's own Schedule, would not be permissible. But if a contracting party could do under a

Schedule qualification only what it could do under another provision of the General Agreement, then there would be no need to have schedule qualifications and Article II:1(b) would be, to a great extent, meaningless.

3.16. *Australia* replied that it was not attempting to alter the GATT Schedule of the United States through the dispute settlement process, but only to have the United States sugar import regime brought into conformity with the GATT obligations of the United States. Australia stressed that, although a contracting party could unilaterally modify its Schedule, if the argumentation made by the United States was accepted, it would be open to any contracting party to have included in its GATT Schedule provisions which gave it wide derogations from its obligations under any other provisions of the General Agreement it considered appropriate. And once such provisions were in the Schedule, they would not be open to challenge by another contracting party.

3.17. Australia sought clarification from the United States on its interpretation of its tariff concession on sugar. Australia noted that, failing clarification to the contrary, it understood that with the expiry of the *Sugar Act of 1948* and in the absence of substantially equivalent legislation, the United States claimed to be able to set tariffs at any rate above 0.6625 cents a pound and quotas at any level (including possibly a zero level). If this understanding was correct, the concessions operated in a manner contrary to the purpose of Article II. Moreover, Australia assumed that the United States claimed to have exemption not only from Article XI, but also from Articles I and XIII of the General Agreement.

. . . .

5. FINDINGS

5.1. The Panel noted that the basic issue before it was as follows. The United States maintains quantitative restrictions on the importation of certain sugars described in its GATT Schedule of Concessions (Schedule XX). The maintenance of quantitative restrictions is inconsistent with Article XI:1 of the General Agreement which provides, *inter alia*, that:

> "No restrictions . . . made effective through quotas . . . shall be . . . maintained by any contracting party on the importation of any product of the territory of any other contracting party."

Article II:1(b) of the General Agreement provides that the products described in the Schedules of Concessions of the contracting parties

> "shall, on their importation into the territory to which the Schedule relates, *and subject to the terms, conditions or qualifications set forth in that Schedule*, be exempt from ordinary customs duties in excess of those set forth and provided for therein." (emphasis added).

The *United States* argues that the proviso "subject to the terms, conditions or qualifications set forth in that Schedule" in Article II:1(b) permits contracting parties to include qualifications relating to quantitative restrictions in their Schedule. The United States had made use of this possibility by reserving in its Schedule of Concessions the right to impose quota limitations on imports of sugar in certain circumstances. Since the restrictions on the importation of sugar conformed to the qualifications set out in the Schedule of the United States, and the Schedules of Concessions were, according to Article II:7, an integral part of the General Agreement, the restrictions were consistent with the United States obligations under that Agreement. *Australia* argues that qualifications to concessions made in accordance with Article II:1(b) cannot justify measures contrary to other provisions of the General Agreement, in particular not quantitative restrictions inconsistent with Article XI:1. . . .

5.2. The Panel first examined the issue in the light of the wording of Article II. It noted that in Article II:1(b), the words "subject to the . . . qualifications set forth in that Schedule" are used in conjunction with the words "shall . . . be exempt from ordinary customs duties in excess of those set forth in [the Schedule]." This suggests that Article II:1(b) permits contracting parties to qualify the obligation to exempt products from customs duties in excess of the levels specified in the Schedule, not however to qualify their obligations under other Articles of the General Agreement. The Panel further noted that the title of Article II is "Schedules of Concessions" and that the ordinary meaning of the word "to concede" is "to grant or yield." This also suggests in the view of the Panel that Article II permits contracting parties to incorporate into their Schedules acts yielding rights under the General Agreement but not acts diminishing obligations under that Agreement.

5.3. The Panel then examined the issue in the light of the purpose of the General Agreement. It noted that one of the basic functions of the General Agreement is, according to its Preamble, to provide a legal framework enabling contracting parties to enter into "reciprocal and mutually advantageous arrangements directed to the substantial reduction of tariffs and other barriers to trade." Where the General Agreement mentions specific types of negotiations, it refers to negotiations aimed at the reduction of barriers to trade (Articles IV(d), XVII:3 and XXVIII *bis*). This supports in the view of the Panel the assumption that Article II gives contracting parties the possibility to incorporate into the legal framework of the General Agreement commitments additional to those already contained in the General Agreement and to qualify such additional commitments, not however to reduce their commitments under other provisions of that Agreement.

. . . .

5.5. The Panel then examined the issue in the light of the practice of the Contracting Parties. The Panel noted that the Contracting Parties adopted in 1955 the report of the Review Working Party on Other Barriers to Trade, which had concluded that

> "there was nothing to prevent contracting parties, when they negotiate for the binding or reduction of tariffs, from negotiating on matters, such as subsidies, which might affect the practical effects of tariff concessions, and from incorporating in the appropriate schedule annexed to the Agreement the results of such negotiations; *provided that the results of such negotiations should not conflict with other provisions of the Agreement*." (emphasis added). . . .

Whether the proviso in this decision is regarded as a policy recommendation, as the United States argues, or as the confirmation of a legal requirement, as Australia claims, it does support, in the view of the Panel, the conclusion that the Contracting Parties did not envisage that qualifications in Schedules established in accordance with Article II:1(b) could justify measures inconsistent with the other Articles of the General Agreement.

5.6. The Panel finally examined the issue in the light of the drafting history. It noted that the reference to "terms and qualifications" was included in a draft of the present Article II:1(b) during the Second Session of the Preparatory Committee of the United Nations Conference on Trade and Employment. The original draft had referred only to "conditions." This amendment was proposed and adopted "in order to provide more generally for the sort of qualifications actually provided in the form of notes in the specimen Schedule. A number of these notes are, in effect, additional concessions rather than *conditions* governing the tariff bindings to which they relate." . . . Schedule provisions qualifying obligations under the General Agreement were not included in the specimen Schedule nor was the possibility of such Schedule provisions mentioned by the drafters. The Panel therefore found that the drafting history did not support the interpretation advanced by the United States.

5.7. . . . [T]he Panel found that Article II:1(b) does not permit contracting parties to qualify their obligations under other provisions of the General Agreement and that the provisions in the United States GATT Schedule of Concessions can consequently not justify the maintenance of quantitative restrictions on the importation of certain sugars inconsistent with the application of Article XI:1.

III. CRACKS IN THE FOURTH PILLAR

A. Cracks Embedded in GATT Article XI:2

As in the other pillars of GATT (MFN and national treatment, and tariff bindings), in the quantitative restrictions pillar there are cracks. That is, there are exceptions to the broad trade-liberalizing obligation for which the pillar stands. Some of the cracks are embedded in the pillar itself. Article XI:2(a) creates an exception to the prophylactic ban of Article XI:1 on quantitative restrictions that is for "critical shortages." Article XI:2(b) is a "classification and grading exception." Article XI:1(c) is an "agriculture" exception. Examine each exception to appreciate how it applies.

Some free trade agreements (FTAs) exhibit a GATT-like pattern. For example, GATT Article XI:2(b) condones certain technical barriers to trade (TBTs), permitting quantitative restrictions "necessary to the application of standards or regulations for the classification, grading or marketing of commodities." Similarly, *NAFTA* Annex 301:3 contains exceptions to Article 309:1 in addition to those in GATT Article XI:2 that are already incorporated by reference. Overall, to what extent do the GATT Article XI:2 and FTA exceptions, such as in *NAFTA* Annex 301.3, undermine the proscriptive rule? Is a pro-free trade rule followed by an exception allowing for managed trade?

In respect of Article XI:(c), observe that in the 1989 *Dessert Apples* case, a GATT Panel gave this exception a narrow interpretation.[1] From

---

[1] *See* GATT Panel Report, *EEC — Restrictions on Imports of Dessert Apples*, B.I.S.D. (36th Supp.) at 93 (adopted 22 June 1989) (complaint by Chile).

April-August 1988, the EEC imposed a quantitative restriction, in the form of an import license requirement, on foreign dessert apples in excess of a prescribed (or "reference") quantity. The EEC also intervened in the dessert apples market to boost prices, and thus incomes, of farmers in EEC states, and if necessary could impose further barriers to imports. The schemes violated Article XI:1, but the EEC defended, with Article XI:(c)(i)-(ii), a suit by Chile. The GATT Panel essentially held that Article XI:(c)(1) is not intended to permit a protective remedy. To interpret it as such would mean it could be used to undermine the value of a tariff concession previously granted. The exception applies only to an import restriction necessary to enforce a domestic program that clearly is set out to limit domestic marketing or production. Further agreeing with Chile, the Panel held under Article XI:2(c)(ii) that the term "temporary" means just that, and in the case the surplus of dessert apples in the EEC was chronic and a substantial, structural one.

B. Cracks Anticipated by GATT Articles XII and XVIII:B for Balance of Payments Crises

Article XI:1 of GATT purports to promote free trade by taking a hard line against quantitative restrictions on imports. Certain FTAs take the same hard line. For example, *NAFTA* Article 309:1 incorporates Article XI:1 by reference. However, the proscriptive rule is subject to several exceptions in Article XI:2, as well as in FTAs. One of the most important and widely used exceptions to the rule against quantitative restrictions concerns a disequilibrium in a country's BOP. GATT Article XII applies to a WTO Member that must safeguard its external financial position and BOP.

1. BOP Crises and Foreign Exchange Controls

The scenario contemplated is not always one in which a WTO Member invokes GATT Article XII immediately. Indeed, typically the imposition of foreign exchange (FX) controls is the first response. The scenario is simple to explain, but frequently nightmarishly complex to resolve. A Member has a serious current account deficit and is depleting its hard currency reserves to pay for imports. A "hard" currency is one that is freely convertible and widely accepted as a means of payment. U.S. dollars, British pound sterling, EU euro, Japanese yen, Conversely, a "soft" currency is one that may or may not be freely convertible, but in either case is not widely accepted as a means of payment. Indonesian rupiah, Pakistani rupees, Turkish lira, and United Arab Emirate dirhams are examples. Exporters from a WTO Member with a soft currency will prefer payment in a hard currency. They need hard currency to pay for raw materials and other imported inputs into their production processes. Moreover, to the extent domestic inflation is unacceptably high, the value of their soft currency is eroded.

In this scenario, a Member may administer FX controls to preserve precious hard currency reserves. One such control involves the central bank of the Member. Exporters are required to deposit a portion of their hard currency earnings with the central bank. The export earnings are withdrawn by the exporter only in local currency at an official exchange rate. Invariably, that rate is better for the central bank than the "black market" rate, which is closer to the true market equilibrium value. For example, suppose an exporter earns $1 million and the black market rate is 10 units of the local, soft currency per $1. The exporter is entitled to 10 million units of the local currency. The official rate, however, is set at 7.5 units per $1, so the central bank gives the exporter just 7.5 million units of the local currency (*i.e.*, $1 million multiplied by 7.5 instead of 10). Small wonder why some exporters in this situation try to evade the currency controls by "under invoicing." Behaving illegally and unethically, the exporter presents a false invoice to its central bank, customs, and tax authorities, which understates the true amount of earnings — say, $600,000, not $1 million, in the hypothetical. The exporter arranges with the importer of its goods to receive the rest of the payment from the importer — $400,000 — in hard currency in an offshore account hidden from the authorities.

In any event, export earnings, which are hard currency reserves held in accounts at the central bank, are used by importers to pay for imports. Typically, a Member determines what may be imported, preferring essential raw materials, intermediate goods, and finished products over expenditures of precious reserves on luxury goods. (Of course, a corrupt regime will ensure the "right" senior officials get their luxury items.) The Member requires importers to convert at an official exchange rate the local soft currency into the hard currency they need to make payment for permissible imports.

2. Invoking GATT Article XII

But, what if a WTO Member has a BOP deficit so serious that FX controls prove insufficient to preserve reserves? Evasion of the controls, along with capital flight, may be rampant. The importers' demand for hard currency may far exceed hard currency export revenues, and the Member cannot obtain even essential items. As a "rule of thumb," a country ought to have hard currency reserves equivalent in value to at least 3 months' worth of imports. That way, if export revenues were completely shut off, the country could obtain what it needed for 12 weeks, and during that time re-arrange its finances and seek assistance from other countries and from multilateral and regional lending facilities. What if a Member's reserves are dangerously close to the 3 month minimum, as occurred in Pakistan in 1999, when after trading nuclear tests with India the level was at two weeks worth of imports?

Under GATT Article XII, a Member may elect to enact quantitative barriers to imports that would otherwise run afoul of Article XI:1. For example, importers in the contracting party may be required to obtain a license from the government in order to import goods. In addition, import quotas may be placed on certain products. Imports of certain products, such as toys for the rich, may be banned completely. The restrictions may be drafted in terms of the quantity or value of imports.

There are six parameters within which a quantitative barrier scheme must operate.

    1.   First, under Article XII:2, quantitative barriers must "not exceed those necessary" to stem an "imminent" foreign exchange reserves crisis or to achieve a "reasonable" rate of increase in reserves.

2. Second, under Article XIII:1, the barriers must be applied to all countries in a non-discriminatory fashion, *i.e.*, in an MFN manner. No one Member's exports can be singled out for restrictive treatment. (Article XII:4(c)-(d) makes clear the disciplines of Article XIII apply to BOP restrictions taken under Article XII:1.)

3. Third, under Article XIII:2, the distribution of trade in a product subject to import restrictions must approximate the distribution that would occur without the restriction. In effect, there must be no distortion of the pattern of trade.

4. Fourth, Article XIII:3 requires transparency in the establishment and administration of import licensing and quota programs. The restrictions must be published and information must be made available to interested parties.

5. Fifth, Article XIII:4 requires the Member to consult with other WTO Members, upon request, about adjusting the import restrictions.

6. Finally, under Article XII:5, "persistent and widespread" use of import restrictions that indicates a "general disequilibrium which is restricting international trade" will trigger discussions among WTO Members with a view to removing the underlying causes of the disequilibrium.

(The infamous and now classic case on GATT Article XIII is the 1997 *Bananas* dispute.)

Notably, the parameters in GATT Article XIII that constrain Article XII BOP restrictions are themselves subject to an important exception in Article XIV. A Member may deviate from Article XIII in respect of a "small" part of its trade "where the benefits to the contracting party . . . substantially outweigh any injury which may result to the trade of other contracting parties." What, then, is the "bottom line" on deviating from Article XI:1 under the authority of BOP restrictions Article XII:1 condones?

The obligations of a Member adopting quantitative restrictions may be summarized as follows:

(1) Restrictions shall be progressively relaxed as conditions permit;

(2) Measures should avoid uneconomic employment of productive resources;

(3) As far as possible, measures should be adopted that expand rather than contract international trade;

(4) [Measures should] [a]void unnecessary damage to commercial or economic interests of any other contracting parties;

(5) [Measures should] [a]llow minimum commercial quantities of each description of goods so as to avoid impairing regular channels of trade;

(6) [Measures should] [a]llow imports of commercial samples;

(7) [Measure should] [a]void restrictions that prevent compliance with "patent, trademark, copyright, or similar procedures;"

(8)   But imports of certain products deemed more essential may be pre-
      ferred over other imports.[2]

3.   Developing Countries and GATT Article XVIII:B

A special exception to GATT Article XI:1 is provided for developing countries
in GATT Article XVIII:B. (This exception is dealt with in a major WTO
dispute, the 1999 *India — Quantitative Restrictions* case.) In brief, GATT
Article XVIII:B establishes a BOP exception to the rule against quantitative
restrictions for less developed countries (LDCs). As Article XVIII:4(a) makes
clear, the exception applies specifically to WTO Members with an "economy
. . . [that] can only support low standards of living and is in the early stages
of development." The BOP exceptions in GATT Articles XII and XVIII are not
mutually exclusive, and some distinctions exist between the two Articles.

For example, Article XVIII does not speak of an "imminent" reserves crisis
and, therefore, seems to contemplate that a LDC may face a chronic problem
and need to implement quantitative restrictions for long periods. Moreover,
Article XVIII:9 indicates that quantitative restrictions may be used "to ensure
a level of reserves adequate for the implementation of its [*i.e.*, the LDC's]
program of economic development. . . ." Thus, evaluating an LDC's right to
invoke Article XVIII:B requires an examination of its development plans.
Finally, a Member imposing a quantitative restriction for BOP reasons under
Article XII must enter into annual consultations with the rest of the Membership. If the basis for the restriction is Article XVIII:B, then such consultations
must be biennial. Significantly, pursuant to Article XIV, an Article XVIII BOP
exception may be applied in a discriminatory fashion.

IV.   TECHNICAL BARRIERS TO TRADE AND THE 2002
PERU SARDINES CASE

A.   Another Kind of Non-Tariff Barrier

By no means are conventional quantitative restrictions, like quotas and
import licenses, the only kind of non-tariff barrier to trade. Technical barriers
to trade (TBTs) can, and indeed are, non-tariff barriers to trade. So, too, are
some sanitary and phytosanitary measures (SPS). SPS measures concern risks
to human, animal, or plant life or health from disease or disease-bearing
agents. TBT measures do not address threats from these causes, but rather
concern matters like product safety and quality standards, and the prevention
of consumer fraud. Not until the Uruguay Round, however, did the multilateral trading community agree upon credible disciplines to TBT and SPS
measures. The *Agreements on Technical Barriers to Trade* (*TBT Agreement*)
and *Sanitary and Phytosanitary Measures* (*SPS Agreement*) establish criteria
to delineate legitimate from protectionist TBT and SPS measures,
respectively.

In March 2001, Peru brought a complaint against the European Communities (EC). Peru alleged Regulation (EEC) 2136/89 prevented its exporters from

---

[2] JOHN H. JACKSON, WORLD TRADE AND THE LAW OF GATT 685 (1969).

using the trade description "sardines" for their products shipped to the EC. The relevant *Codex Alimentarius* standards (specifically, STAN 94-181, revised 1995, abbreviated as "Codex Stan 94") lists the species "*sardinops sagax sagax*" as among the species that can be traded as "sardines." Thus, argued Peru, the EC Regulation was an unjustifiable barrier to trade in breach of GATT Article XI:1 and Article 2 of the WTO *Agreement on Technical Barriers to Trade (TBT Agreement)*. In its May 2002 Report, the Panel agreed with Peru. The European Regulation breached Article 2:4 of this *Agreement*.

The EC appealed. The Appellate Body upheld the finding of the Panel that the Regulation is properly characterized as a "technical regulation" under the *TBT Agreement*. It also upheld the Panel's conclusion about the temporal application of Article 2:4 of the *Agreement*. The provision applies to measures adopted before 1 January 1995 (when the *Agreement*, like other Uruguay Round texts, entered into force), but which have not lapsed, as well as to extant technical regulations. In other words, the Appellate Body agreed the *Agreement* applied retroactively as well as prospectively to the EC Regulation.

The Appellate Body then turned to two issues, also arising under Article 2:4 of the *TBT Agreement*, namely

1. Whether to uphold the finding of the Panel that Codex Stan 94 is a "relevant international standard"?

2. Whether to uphold the Panels' finding that the EC failed to use Codex Stan 94 "as a basis for" the EC regulation?

The Appellate Body also had to decide whether it should uphold the Panel's finding that the respondent EC had the burden of proof to show Codex Stan 94 is an "ineffective or inappropriate means for the fulfillment of the legitimate objectives pursued." Here, in contrast to the first two issues, Peru lost. The Appellate Body held the Panel should have allocated to Peru the burden to show Codex Stan 94 is an "effective and appropriate" way to fulfill "legitimate objectives." Fortunately for Peru, the Appellate Body held it adduced sufficient evidence and legal arguments to prove Codex Stan 94 is not "ineffective or inappropriate" to fulfill the "legitimate objectives" of the EC Regulation.

B. Using International Standards for Legitimate Objectives

WTO APPELLATE BODY REPORT, *EUROPEAN COMMUNITIES — TRADE DESCRIPTION OF SARDINES*
WT/DS231/AB/R (adopted 23 October 2002) (complaint by Peru)

I. Introduction

. . . .

2. This dispute concerns the name under which certain species of fish may be marketed in the European Communities. The measure at issue is Council Regulation (EEC) 2136/89 (the "EC Regulation"), which was adopted by the Council of the European Communities on 21 June 1989 and became applicable

on 1 January 1990. The EC Regulation sets forth common marketing standards for preserved sardines.

3. Article 2 of the EC Regulation provides that:

Only products meeting the following requirements may be marketed as preserved sardines and under the trade description referred to in Article 7:

— they must be covered by CN codes 1604 13 10 and ex 1604 20 50;

— *they must be prepared exclusively from fish of the species "Sardina pilchardus Walbaum";*

— they must be pre-packaged with any appropriate covering medium in a hermetically sealed container;

— they must be sterilized by appropriate treatment. (emphasis added)

4. *Sardina pilchardus* Walbaum ("*Sardina pilchardus*"), the fish species referred to in the EC Regulation, is found mainly around the coasts of the Eastern North Atlantic Ocean, in the Mediterranean Sea, and in the Black Sea.

5. In 1978, the *Codex Alimentarius* Commission (the "*Codex* Commission"), of the United Nations Food and Agriculture Organization and the World Health Organization, adopted a world-wide standard for preserved sardines and sardine-type products, which regulates matters such as presentation, essential composition and quality factors, food additives, hygiene and handling, labelling, sampling, examination and analyses, defects and lot acceptance. This standard, CODEX STAN 94-1981, Rev.1-1995 ("Codex Stan 94"), covers preserved sardines or sardine-type products prepared from the following 21 fish species:

— *Sardina pilchardus*

— *Sardinops melanostictus, S. neopilchardus, S. ocellatus, S. sagax[,] S. caeruleus*

— *Sardinella aurita, S. brasiliensis, S. maderensis, S. longiceps, S. gibbosa*

— *Clupea harengus*

— *Sprattus sprattus*

— *Hyperlophus vittatus*

— *Nematalosa vlaminghi*

— *Etrumeus teres*

— *Ethmidium maculatum*

— *Engraulis anchoita, E. mordax, E. ringens*

— *Opisthonema oglinum.*

6. Section 6 of Codex Stan 94 provides as follows:

  6. LABELLING

In addition to the provisions of the Codex General Standard for the Labelling of Prepackaged Foods (CODEX STAN 1-1985, Rev. 3-1999) the following special provisions apply:

6.1 NAME OF THE FOOD

The name of the product shall be:

6.1.1

     (i)   *"Sardines" (to be reserved exclusively for Sardina pilchardus (Walbaum)); or*

    (ii)   *"X sardines" of a country, a geographic area, the species, or the common name of the species in accordance with the law and custom of the country in which the product is sold, and in a manner not to mislead the consumer.*

6.1.2   The name of the packing medium shall form part of the name of the food.

6.1.3   If the fish has been smoked or smoke flavoured, this information shall appear on the label in close proximity to the name.

6.1.4   In addition, the label shall include other descriptive terms that will avoid misleading or confusing the consumer. (emphasis added)

7. Peru exports preserved products prepared from *Sardinops sagax sagax* (*"Sardinops sagax"*), one of the species of fish covered by Codex Stan 94. This species is found mainly in the Eastern Pacific Ocean, along the coasts of Peru and Chile. *Sardina pilchardus* and *Sardinops sagax* both belong to the *Clupeidae* family and the *Clupeinae* subfamily. As their scientific name suggests, however, they belong to different genus. *Sardina pilchardus* belongs to the genus *Sardina*, while *Sardinops sagax* belongs to the genus *Sardinops*. . . .

   . . . .

VII. The Characterization of Codex Stan 94 as a "Relevant International Standard"

A. *The European Communities' Argument that Consensus is Required*

219. The European Communities argues that only standards that have been adopted by an international body by consensus can be *relevant* for purposes of Article 2.4 [of the *TBT Agreement*]. The European Communities contends that the Panel did not verify that Codex Stan 94 was not adopted by consensus, and that, therefore, it cannot be a "relevant international standard."

220. However, in our view, the European Communities' contention is essentially related to whether Codex Stan 94 meets the definition of a "standard" in Annex 1.2 of the *TBT Agreement*. The term "standard", is defined in Annex 1.2 as follows:

2. *Standard*

Document approved by a recognized body, that provides, for common and repeated use, rules, guidelines or characteristics for products or related processes and production methods, with which compliance is not mandatory. It may also include or deal exclusively with terminology, symbols, packaging, marking or labelling requirements as they apply to a product, process or production method.

Explanatory note

The terms as defined in ISO/IEC Guide 2 cover products, processes and services. This *Agreement* deals only with technical regulations, standards and conformity assessment procedures related to products or processes and production methods. Standards as defined by ISO/IEC Guide 2 may be mandatory or voluntary. For the purpose of this Agreement standards are defined as voluntary and technical regulations as mandatory documents. *Standards prepared by the international standardization community are based on consensus. This Agreement covers also documents that are not based on consensus.* (emphasis added)

221. The European Communities does not contest that the Codex Commission is an international standardization body, and that it is a "recognized body" for purposes of the definition of a "standard" in Annex 1.2. The issue before us, rather, is one of *approval*. The definition of a "standard" refers to documents *approved* by a recognized body. Whether approval takes place by consensus, or by other methods, is not addressed in the definition, but it is addressed in the last two sentences of the Explanatory note.

222. The Panel interpreted the last two sentences of the Explanatory note as follows:

> The first sentence reiterates the norm of the international standardization community that standards are prepared on the basis of consensus. The following sentence, however, acknowledges that consensus may not always be achieved and that international standards that were not adopted by consensus are within the scope of the *TBT Agreement*.[86] This provision therefore confirms that even if not adopted by consensus, an international standard can constitute a relevant international standard.

We agree with the Panel's interpretation. In our view, the text of the Explanatory note supports the conclusion that consensus is not required for standards adopted by the international standardizing community. The last sentence of the Explanatory note refers to "documents." The term "document" is also used in the singular in the first sentence of the definition of a "standard." We believe that "document(s)" must be interpreted as having the same meaning in both the definition and the Explanatory note. The European Communities agrees. Interpreted in this way, the term "documents" in the

---

[86] The record does not demonstrate that Codex Stan 94 was not adopted by consensus. In any event, we consider that this issue would have no bearing on our determination in light of the explanatory note of paragraph 2 of Annex 1 of the *TBT Agreement* which states that the *TBT Agreement* covers "documents that are not based on consensus."

last sentence of the Explanatory note must refer to standards *in general*, and not only to those adopted by entities *other than* international bodies, as the European Communities claims.

223. Moreover, the text of the last sentence of the Explanatory note, referring to documents not based on consensus, gives no indication whatsoever that it is departing from the subject of the immediately preceding sentence, which deals with standards adopted by international bodies. Indeed, the use of the word "also" in the last sentence suggests that the same subject is being addressed — namely standards prepared by the international standardization community. Hence, the logical assumption is that the last phrase is simply continuing in the same vein, and refers to standards adopted by international bodies, including those not adopted by consensus.

224. The Panel's interpretation, moreover, gives effect to the *chapeau* of Annex 1 to the *TBT Agreement*, which provides:

> The terms presented in the sixth edition of the ISO/IEC Guide 2:1991, General Terms and Their Definitions Concerning Standardization and Related Activities, shall, when used in this *Agreement*, have the same meaning as given in the definitions in the said Guide . . .

> For the purpose of this *Agreement*, *however*, the following definitions shall apply . . . (emphasis added)

Thus, according to the *chapeau*, the terms defined in Annex 1 apply for the purposes of the *TBT Agreement* only if their definitions *depart* from those in the ISO/IEC Guide 2:1991 (the "ISO/IEC Guide"). This is underscored by the word "however." The definition of a "standard" in Annex 1 to the *TBT Agreement* departs from that provided in the ISO/IEC Guide precisely in respect of whether consensus is expressly required.

225. The term "standard" is defined in the ISO/IEC Guide as follows:

> Document, established by *consensus* and approved by a recognized *body*, that provides, for common and repeated use, rules, guidelines or characteristics for activities or their results, aimed at the achievement of the optimum degree of order in a given context. (original emphasis)

Thus, the definition of a "standard" in the ISO/IEC Guide expressly includes a consensus requirement. Therefore, the logical conclusion, in our view, is that the *omission* of a consensus requirement in the definition of a "standard" in Annex 1.2 of the *TBT Agreement* was a deliberate choice on the part of the drafters of the *TBT Agreement*, and that the last two phrases of the Explanatory note were included to give effect to this choice. Had the negotiators considered consensus to be necessary to satisfy the definition of "standard," we believe they would have said so explicitly in the definition itself, as is the case in the ISO/IEC Guide. Indeed, there would, in our view, have been no point in the negotiators adding the last sentence of the Explanatory note.

226. Furthermore, we observe that the Panel found that, in any event, the European Communities did *not* prove that Codex Stan 94 was *not* adopted by consensus. Instead, the Panel found that, "[t]he record does not demonstrate that Codex Stan 94 was not adopted by consensus."

227. Therefore, we uphold the Panel's conclusion . . . that the definition of a "standard" in Annex 1.2 to the *TBT Agreement* does not require approval by consensus for standards adopted by a "recognized body" of the international standardization community. We emphasize, however, that this conclusion is relevant only for purposes of the *TBT Agreement*. It is not intended to affect, in any way, the internal requirements that international standard-setting bodies may establish for themselves for the adoption of standards within their respective operations. In other words, the fact that we find that the *TBT Agreement* does not require approval by consensus for standards adopted by the international standardization community should not be interpreted to mean that we believe an international standardization body should not require consensus for the adoption of its standards. That is not for us to decide.

B. *The European Communities' Argument on the Product Coverage of Codex Stan 94*

228. We turn now to examine the European Communities' argument that Codex Stan 94 is not a "*relevant* international standard" because its product coverage is different from that of the EC Regulation.

229. In analyzing the merits of this argument, the Panel first noted that the ordinary meaning of the term "relevant" is "bearing upon or relating to the matter in hand; pertinent." The Panel reasoned that, to be a "relevant international standard," Codex Stan 94 would have to bear upon, relate to, or be pertinent to the EC Regulation. The Panel then conducted the following analysis:

> The title of Codex Stan 94 is "Codex Standard for Canned Sardines and Sardine-type Products" and the EC Regulation lays down common marketing standards for preserved sardines. The European Communities indicated in its response that the term "canned sardines" and "preserved sardines" are essentially identical. *Therefore, it is apparent that both the EC Regulation and Codex Stan 94 deal with the same product, namely preserved sardines.* The scope of Codex Stan 94 covers various species of fish, including *Sardina pilchardus* which the EC Regulation covers, and includes, *inter alia*, provisions on presentation (Article 2.3), packing medium (Article 3.2), labelling, including a requirement that the packing medium is to form part of the name of the food (Article 6), determination of net weight (Article 7.3), foreign matter (Article 8.1) and odour and flavour (Article 8.2). The EC Regulation contains these corresponding provisions set out in Codex Stan 94, including the section on labelling requirement. (emphasis added; footnote omitted)

230. We do not disagree with the Panel's interpretation of the ordinary meaning of the term "relevant." Nor does the European Communities. Instead, the European Communities argues that, although the EC Regulation deals *only* with preserved sardines — understood to mean exclusively preserved *Sardina pilchardus* — Codex Stan 94 *also covers* other preserved fish that are "sardine-type."

231. We are not persuaded by this argument. First, even if we accepted that the EC Regulation relates only to preserved *Sardina pilchardus*, which we

do not, the fact remains that section 6.1.1(i) of Codex Stan 94 also relates to preserved *Sardina pilchardus*. Therefore, Codex Stan 94 can be said to bear upon, relate to, or be pertinent to the EC Regulation because both refer to preserved *Sardina pilchardus*.

232. Second, . . . although the EC Regulation expressly mentions only *Sardina pilchardus*, it has legal consequences for other fish species that could be sold as preserved sardines, including preserved *Sardinops sagax*. Codex Stan 94 covers 20 fish species in addition to *Sardina pilchardus*. These other species also are legally affected by the exclusion in the EC Regulation. Therefore, we conclude that Codex Stan 94 bears upon, relates to, or is pertinent to the EC Regulation.

233. For all these reasons, we uphold the Panel's finding . . . that Codex Stan 94 is a "relevant international standard" for purposes of Article 2.4 of the *TBT Agreement*.

VIII. Whether Codex Stan 94 Was Used "As a Basis For" the EC Regulation

234. We turn now to whether Codex Stan 94 has been used "as a basis for" the EC Regulation. It will be recalled that Article 2.4 of the *TBT Agreement* requires Members to use relevant international standards "as a basis for" their technical regulations under certain circumstances. The Panel found that "the relevant international standard, *i.e.*, Codex Stan 94, was not used as a basis for the EC Regulation." The European Communities appeals this finding.

. . . .

240. With this understanding of this international standard in mind, we turn to the requirement that relevant international standards must be used "as a basis for" technical regulations. We note that the Panel interpreted the word "basis" to mean "the principal constituent of anything, the fundamental principle or theory, as of a system of knowledge." In applying this interpretation of "basis" to the measure in this dispute, the Panel contrasted its interpretation of section 6.1.1(ii) of Codex Stan 94 as setting forth "four alternatives for labelling species other than *Sardina pilchardus*" that all "require the use of the term 'sardines' with a qualification," with the fact that, under the EC Regulation, "species such as *Sardinops sagax* cannot be called 'sardines' even when . . . combined with the name of a country, name of a geographic area, name of the species or the common name in accordance with the law and custom of the country in which the product is sold." In the light of this contrast, the Panel concluded that Codex Stan 94 was *not* used "as a basis for" the EC Regulation.

[In respect of the "four alternatives," the Appellate Body is speaking of the Peruvian argument, accepted by the Panel, that section 6.1.1(ii) is properly interpreted as follows: a species other than *Sardina pilchardus* may be marketed as "X sardines," where "X" is one of the following four alternatives — (1) a country, (2) a geographic area, (3) the species, or (4) the common name of the species.]

. . . .

242. The question before us, therefore, is the proper meaning to be attributed to the words "as a basis for" in Article 2.4 of the *TBT Agreement*. In *EC — Hormones* [i.e., *EC Measures Concerning Meat and Meat Products (Hormones)*, WT/DS26/AB/R, WT/DS48/AB/R (adopted 13 February 1998)], we addressed a similar issue, namely, the meaning of "based on" as used in Article 3.1 of the *SPS Agreement*, which provides:

Harmonization

1. To harmonize sanitary and phytosanitary measures on as wide a basis as possible, Members shall *base their sanitary or phytosanitary measures on international standards*, guidelines or recommendations, where they exist, except as otherwise provided for in this *Agreement*, and in particular in paragraph 3. (emphasis added)

In *EC — Hormones*, we stated that "based on" does not mean the same thing as "conform to." In that appeal, we articulated the ordinary meaning of the term "based on," as used in Article 3.1 of the *SPS Agreement* in the following terms:

A thing is commonly said to be "based on" another thing when the former "stands" or is "founded" or "built" upon or "is supported by" the latter.[150]

The Panel here referred to this conclusion in its analysis of Article 2.4 of the *TBT Agreement*. In our view, the Panel did so correctly, because our approach in *EC — Hormones* is also relevant for the interpretation of Article 2.4 of the *TBT Agreement*.

243. In addition, as we stated earlier, the Panel here used the following definition to establish the ordinary meaning of the term "basis":

The word "basis" means "the principal constituent of anything, the fundamental principle or theory, as of a system of knowledge."[90]

Informed by our ruling in *EC — Hormones*, and relying on this meaning of the term "basis," the Panel concluded that an international standard is used "as a basis for" a technical regulation when it is used as the principal constituent or fundamental principle for the purpose of enacting the technical regulation.

244. We agree with the Panel's approach. In relying on the ordinary meaning of the term "basis", the Panel rightly followed an approach similar to ours in determining the ordinary meaning of "based on" in *EC — Hormones*. In addition to the definition of "basis" in *Webster's New World Dictionary* that was used by the Panel, we note, as well, the similar definitions for "basis" that are set out in the *The New Shorter Oxford English Dictionary* [1993 ed., vol. I, p. 188], and also provide guidance as to the ordinary meaning of the term:

---

[150] L. Brown (ed.), *The New Shorter Oxford English Dictionary on Historical Principles* (Clarendon Press), Vol. I, p. 187.

[90] [*Webster's New World Dictionary*, (William Collins & World Publishing Co., Inc., 1976)], p. 117.

3. [t]he main constituent. . . . 5. [a] thing on which anything is constructed and by which its constitution or operation is determined; a determining principle; a set of underlying or agreed principles.

245. From these various definitions, we would highlight the similar terms "principal constituent," "fundamental principle," "main constituent," and "determining principle" — all of which lend credence to the conclusion that there must be a very strong and very close relationship between two things in order to be able to say that one is "the basis for" the other.

246. The European Communities, however, seems to suggest the need for something different. The European Communities maintains that a "rational relationship" between an international standard and a technical regulation is sufficient to conclude that the former is used "as a basis for" the latter. According to the European Communities, an examination based on the criterion of the existence of a "rational relationship" focuses on "the qualitative aspect of the substantive relationship that should exist between the relevant international standard and the technical regulation." In response to questioning at the oral hearing, the European Communities added that a "rational relationship" exists when the technical regulation is informed in its overall scope by the international standard.

247. Yet, we see nothing in the text of Article 2.4 to support the European Communities' view, nor has the European Communities pointed to any such support. Moreover, the European Communities does not offer any arguments relating to the context or the object and purpose of that provision that would support its argument that the existence of a "rational relationship" is the appropriate criterion for determining whether something has been used "as a basis for" something else.

248. We see no need here to define in general the nature of the relationship that must exist for an international standard to serve "as a basis for" a technical regulation. Here we need only examine this measure to determine if it fulfils this obligation. In our view, it can certainly be said — at a minimum — that something cannot be considered a "basis" for something else if the two are *contradictory*. Therefore, under Article 2.4, if the technical regulation and the international standard *contradict* each other, it cannot properly be concluded that the international standard has been used "as a basis for" the technical regulation.

255. Thus, we need only determine here whether there is a *contradiction* between Codex Stan 94 and the EC Regulation. If there is, we are justified in concluding our analysis with that determination, as the only appropriate conclusion from such a determination would be that the Codex Stan 94 has not been used "as a basis for" the EC Regulation.

. . . .

256. We accept the European Communities' contention that the EC Regulation contains the prescription set out in section 6.1.1(i) of Codex Stan 94. However, . . . the analysis must go beyond section 6.1.1(i); it must extend also to sections 6.1.1(ii) and 2.1.1 of Codex Stan 94. And, a comparison between, on the one hand, sections 6.1.1(ii) and 2.1.1 of Codex Stan 94 and, on the other hand, Article 2 of the EC Regulation, leads to the inevitable conclusion that a contradiction exists between these provisions.

257. The effect of Article 2 of the EC Regulation is to prohibit preserved fish products prepared from the 20 species of fish other than *Sardina pilchardus* to which Codex Stan 94 refers — including *Sardinops sagax* — from being identified and marketed under the appellation "sardines", even with one of the four qualifiers set out in the standard. Codex Stan 94, by contrast, permits the use of the term "sardines" with any one of four qualifiers for the identification and marketing of preserved fish products prepared from 20 species of fish other than *Sardina pilchardus*. Thus, the EC Regulation and Codex Stan 94 are manifestly contradictory. To us, the existence of this contradiction confirms that Codex Stan 94 was not used "as a basis for" the EC Regulation.

258. We, therefore, uphold the finding of the Panel . . . that Codex Stan 94 was not used "as a basis for" the EC Regulation within the meaning of Article 2.4 of the *TBT Agreement*.

IX. The Question of the "Ineffectiveness or Inappropriateness" of Codex Stan 94

. . . .

B. *Whether Codex Stan 94 is an Effective and Appropriate Means to Fulfill the "Legitimate Objectives" Pursued by the European Communities Through the EC Regulation*

. . . .

1. The Interpretation of the Second Part of Article 2.4

285. The interpretation of the second part of Article 2.4 raises two questions: first, the meaning of the term "ineffective or inappropriate means;" and, second, the meaning of the term "legitimate objectives." As to the first question, we noted earlier the Panel's view that the term "ineffective or inappropriate means" refers to two questions — the question of the *effectiveness* of the measure and the question of the *appropriateness* of the measure — and that these two questions, although closely related, are different in nature. The Panel pointed out that the term "ineffective" "refers to something which is not 'having the function of accomplishing,' 'having a result,' or 'brought to bear,' whereas [the term] 'inappropriate' refers to something which is not 'specially suitable,' 'proper,' or 'fitting.'" The Panel also stated that:

> Thus, in the context of Article 2.4, an ineffective means is a means which does not have the function of accomplishing the legitimate objective pursued, whereas an inappropriate means is a means which is not specially suitable for the fulfilment of the legitimate objective pursued. . . . The question of effectiveness bears upon the *results* of the means employed, whereas the question of appropriateness relates more to the *nature* of the means employed. (original emphasis)

We agree with the Panel's interpretation.

286. As to the second question, we are of the view that the Panel was also correct in concluding that "the 'legitimate objectives' referred to in Article 2.4

must be interpreted in the context of Article 2.2," which refers also to "legitimate objectives", and includes a description of what the nature of some such objectives can be. Two implications flow from the Panel's interpretation. First, the term "legitimate objectives" in Article 2.4, as the Panel concluded, must cover the objectives explicitly mentioned in Article 2.2, namely: "national security requirements; the prevention of deceptive practices; protection of human health or safety, animal or plant life or health, or the environment." Second, given the use of the term *inter alia* in Article 2.2, the objectives covered by the term "legitimate objectives" in Article 2.4 extend beyond the list of the objectives specifically mentioned in Article 2.2. Furthermore, we share the view of the Panel that the second part of Article 2.4 implies that there must be an examination and a determination on the legitimacy of the objectives of the measure.

2. The Application of the Second Part of Article 2.4

287. With respect to the application of the second part of Article 2.4, we begin by recalling that Peru has the burden of establishing that Codex Stan 94 is an effective *and* appropriate means for the fulfillment of the "legitimate objectives" pursued by the European Communities through the EC Regulation. Those "legitimate objectives" are market transparency, consumer protection, and fair competition. . . .

288. This being so, our task is to assess whether Peru discharged its burden of showing that Codex Stan 94 is appropriate and effective to fulfill these same three "legitimate objectives." In the light of our reasoning thus far, Codex Stan 94 would be *effective* if it had the capacity to accomplish all three of these objectives, and it would be *appropriate* if it were suitable for the fulfillment of all three of these objectives.

289. We share the Panel's view that the terms "ineffective" and "inappropriate" have different meanings, and that it is conceptually possible that a measure could be effective but inappropriate, or appropriate but ineffective. This is why Peru has the burden of showing that Codex Stan 94 is both *effective* and *appropriate*. . . . [H]owever, . . . in this case, a consideration of the *appropriateness* of Codex Stan 94 and a consideration of the *effectiveness* of Codex Stan 94 are interrelated — as a consequence of the nature of the objectives of the EC Regulation. The capacity of a measure to accomplish the stated objectives — its *effectiveness* — and the suitability of a measure for the fulfillment of the stated objectives — its appropriateness — are *both* decisively influenced by the perceptions and expectations of consumers in the European Communities relating to preserved sardine products.

290. . . . [T]he Panel concluded that "Peru has adduced sufficient evidence and legal arguments to demonstrate that Codex Stan 94 is not ineffective or inappropriate to fulfill the legitimate objectives pursued by the EC Regulation." . . . We note, in particular, that the Panel made the factual finding that "it has not been established that consumers in most member States of the European Communities have always associated the common name 'sardines' exclusively with *Sardina pilchardus*." We also note that the Panel gave consideration to the contentions of Peru that, under Codex Stan 94, fish from

the species *Sardinops sagax* bear a denomination that is distinct from that of *Sardina pilchardus*, and that "the very purpose of the labelling regulations set out in Codex Stan 94 for sardines of species other than *Sardina pilchardus* is to ensure market transparency." We agree with the analysis made by the Panel. . . .

290. We, therefore, uphold the finding of the Panel . . . that Peru has adduced sufficient evidence and legal arguments to demonstrate that Codex Stan 94 is not "ineffective or inappropriate" to fulfill the "legitimate objectives" of the EC Regulation. . . .

V. TRANSPARENCY AND GATT ARTICLE X: THE FIFTH PILLAR?

A. Why Transparency Matters

Other than by luck, it is impossible to compete effectively, much less successfully, in a game the rules of which one is ignorant. Where rules are made available to some, but not all, competitors, the playing field is not level. Put conceptually, non-transparency of rules is a non-tariff barrier to free, fair competition in two respects. First, some players — those "not in the loop" — are disadvantaged relative to players that understand the rules. Second, potential players — ones seeking entry into the game — are disadvantaged relative to players that understand the rules. Transparency is all about providing the opportunity to learn the rules to all existing and potential competitors on a non-discriminatory basis. It is not about the equality of result. Transparency does not demand that every existing or potential competitor actually understand and apply the rules to an equally masterful degree. Transparency also is not the same as participation. Transparency merely demands that every current or prospective player have the chance to learn the rules, not that all of them have a voice in shaping the rules.

To say transparency "merely" demands equality of opportunity is beguilingly simple. The object is to ensure international trade laws are sufficiently transparent so as to avoid constituting a non-tariff barrier. But, what does it mean, in practice, to say that a set of rules — like the body of international trade law in a WTO Member, or indeed the GATT—WTO regime itself — is "transparent"? GATT Article X:1 provides some guidance, requiring prompt publication in such a manner as to allow governments and traders to become acquainted with the law. Article X:2 calls for enforcement of laws only after they have been officially published. Thus, for example, in *EEC — Restrictions on Imports of Apples* (B.I.S.D. (36th Supp.) at 135, 166-67 ¶¶ 5.20-5.23 (1989)), at issue was an EEC import quota allocation scheme that was announced in April 1988. Yet, the quota covered the period February-August 1988. Because the quota was back-dated two months before it was published, the GATT panel ruled that it ran afoul of Article X. Finally, Article X:3 speaks of the uniform, impartial, and reasonable administration of laws, the use of independent adjudicatory tribunals.

But, even this minimalist list of transparency variables is problematical. First, consider GATT Article X:1. How prompt is "prompt" publication — a day, week, month, year? What sort of publishing vehicle is needed to allow the players to familiarize themselves with the law? Is it enough for the government of the Kyrgyzstan to print copies of a new antidumping regulation in the Russian language and make the copies available on a table in a ministry office in downtown Bishkek (the capital city)? Or, must the Kyrgyz government publish the regulation in all of the official United Nations languages (Arabic, Chinese, English, French, Russian, and Spanish) on the Internet at a website with a server that is accessible 24 hours a day from around the world?

Further, exactly what is the scope of Article X:1. That is, what must be published? In *Japan — Measures Affecting Consumer Photographic Film and Paper*, WT/DS44/R (adopted 22 April 1998) (the infamous *Kodak-Fuji* case), the U.S. claimed Japan violated Article X:1. Japan did not publish administrative rulings on two subjects, enforcement actions by Japan's antitrust regulator (the Japan Fair Trade Commission (JFTC)), and guidance given to regional offices of the Ministry of International Trade and Industry (MITI) and to local authorities on the administration of a law on large retail stores. The Panel held Article X:1 does not require publication of administrative rulings addressed to specific entities, and the U.S. failed to prove the unpublished JFTC enforcement actions and MITI guidance resulted in changes in law. The U.S. did not appeal.

As for Article X:2, ought there be some minimum time between publication and enforcement? After all, not all the players will see new laws as soon as they are published — it may take some time for knowledge of it to filter out into the market place. Moreover, what if a WTO Member shares information about an impending change in law with some players, but not others, before actual publication? The case of *Canada — Import, Distribution and Sale of Certain Alcoholic Drinks by Provincial Marketing Agencies* (B.I.S.D. (39th Supp.) at 27, 85-86 ¶ 5.34 (1993)) illustrates both issues. The U.S. complained Ontario's legislative assembly announced a new pricing policy for beer only 5 days before its entry into force. The U.S. also charged the liquor board of British Colombia shared information about pricing policy with Canadian brewers before making that same information available to American authorities. Surely, these acts meant favoritism for Labatts and Molson (Canadian brands), and discrimination against Budweiser and Miller (American brands). Yet, the GATT Panel found no violation of Article X. That Article, said the Panel, did not mandate any waiting period between publication and application of a new trade rule, nor did it obligate a contracting party to share information simultaneously with foreign and domestic producers. The Panel thereby condoned the practice of helping domestic producers adjust to an impending change in law by telling only them of it early, and then making adjustment more difficult by enforcing the new law shortly after publication on unsuspecting foreign competitors.

Consider, finally, Article X:3. It cannot be interpreted literally. Rather, its language ought to be read as embodying an ideal type. As long as laws are administered by humans, they will not be applied in an entirely uniform, impartial, and reasonable manner, and no adjudicatory tribunal will be entirely independent. To advocate American-style separation-of-powers for every other WTO Member is unrealistic, and possibly even wrong-headed insofar as the doctrine arose and evolved in the unique American context. It is also naive to believe the separation is as great in practice as the doctrine would have it in theory. The real question is the permissible degree of variance among WTO Members from the ideal type.

Perhaps even more problematical than the items on the GATT Article X list are the omissions. What about all of the procedural due process protections that are so familiar in American administrative law? Ought WTO Members be obligated to provide opportunity for a public hearing on any proposed new trade law? Ought they to offer a 90 day notice and comment period, *i.e.*, to publish any proposed regulation and invite suggestions from the players during a review period, before re-publishing the regulation in final form? These sorts of questions raise deeper issues about the democratic character of a government. What American-trained lawyers may regard as a birthright for their importer and exporter clients may be seen in other political cultures as an expensive luxury, even an arrogant privilege.

Doha Round negotiators, like their Uruguay and Tokyo Round predecessors, understood the importance of transparency to free and fair trade. The Uruguay Round negotiators affirmed the use of the *Trade Policy Review Mechanism* (*TPRM*) to review systematically and periodically the trade laws and policies of each Member. In the *Ministerial Decision on Notification Procedures* (a partial successor document to the 1979 Tokyo Round *Understanding Regarding Notification, Consultation, Dispute Settlement, and Surveillance*, B.I.S.D. (26th Supp.) at 210 (1979)), Uruguay Round negotiators emphasized the importance of each Member notifying and publishing its trade measures, and agreed to create a central registry at the WTO to file notifications. The Council for Trade in Goods was allocated responsibility of reviewing notification obligations and procedures under WTO texts. Finally, several texts contain their own transparency provisions that supplement general obligations in GATT Article X. Examples of built-in complementary or supplementary transparency rules include:

1.   Article 2:9 of the *Agreement on Technical Barriers to Trade* (*TBT Agreement*)

2.   Articles 2(g) and 3(e) of the *Agreement on Rules of Origin*

3.   Article 25 of the *Agreement on Subsidies and Countervailing Measures* (*SCM Agreement*)

4.   Article 12 of the *Agreement on Safeguards*

5.   Article 7 of the *Agreement on Sanitary and Phytosanitary Measures* (*SPS Agreement*)

6.   Article 63 of the *Agreement on Trade Related Aspects of Intellectual Property Rights* (*TRIPs Agreement*)

7.   Article 18:2-3 of the *Agreement on Agriculture*

8.   Article 6:1 of the *Agreement on Trade Related Investment Measures* (*TRIMs Agreement*)

9.   Article III of the *General Agreement on Trade in Services* (*GATS*)

What Doha Round processes or results (if any) enhanced transparency?

Just how serious the Uruguay Round negotiators were is hardly evident from the subsequent operation of the WTO itself. The Organization is criticized severely for being staffed by faceless, secretive bureaucrats who follow procedures only they and a handful of outsiders understand, and circulate restricted documents amongst themselves but are hesitant (if not loathe) to publish those documents. How fair is this criticism?

The WTO's website contains an enormous amount of information, and delays in making materials publicly available surely are due in part to the chronic triangular problem of excess work, short staffing, under funding — and, most of all, politically correct but practically ridiculous demand to translate everything into French and Spanish. Still, as long as there are legitimate concerns about the transparency of the WTO itself, there will be a pharisaical ring in its calls for greater transparency among the Members.

The post-Uruguay Round case of *EC — Poultry Products* (excerpted below), involves a claim of violation of GATT Article X. To be sure, many more issues were at stake, most notably critical questions about the non-discriminatory administration of tariff-rate quotas under GATT Article XIII (a matter discussed later in the context of the *Bananas* case). The large number of disputed issues, coupled with the obtuse nature of the textual provisions involved, mean the case makes for difficult reading (a common problem among many agriculture cases for the same reasons).

Essentially, a dispute arose out of a 1994 bilateral agreement, known as the *"Oilseeds Agreement,"* negotiated between Brazil and the EC concerning, *inter alia*, trade in poultry under the authority of GATT Article XXVIII (which concerns the modification of tariff schedules through negotiation and agreement by the WTO Members). This *Agreement* was negotiated after the Contracting Parties adopted a panel report, *European Economic Community — Payments and Subsidies Paid to Processors and Producers of Oilseeds and Related Animal-feed Proteins* — the infamous *EEC — Oilseeds* case that threatened to derail a successful conclusion to the Uruguay Round. (*See* GATT, B.I.S.D. (37th Supp.) at 86 (1989-90) (adopted 25 Jan. 1990)). In the wake of that case, the Contracting Parties authorized the EC to negotiate with interested parties under GATT Article XXVIII. The EC did so with respect to Brazil and nine other parties. Thus, the *Oilseeds Agreement* referred to in *EC — Poultry*, which is technically a set of Agreed Minutes signed on 31 January 1994, is the outcome of the EC-Brazil bilateral talks.

The *Oilseeds Agreement* authorized the EC to impose a duty-free global annual tariff-rate quota (TRQ) of 15,500 tons for frozen poultry meat imports. All imports under the quota were subject to presentation of an import license, though it was not necessary to show a license for an out-of-quota shipment. The EC Tariff Schedule indicated the TRQ, along with base duty rates for out-of-quota amounts. Also in its Schedule, the EC reserved the right to impose a special safeguard, in accord with Article 5 of the Uruguay Round *Agreement on Agriculture*. That remedy would result in an additional duty on out-of-quota imports, assuming the price of these imports fell below a trigger price pre-set and published by the EC. The import price would be measured as either a "representative price" (determined by accounting for third-country prices, "free-at-Community offer prices," and prices of imported products at various stages of marketing in the EC), or, at the request of the importer, the "cost, insurance, and freight" (c.i.f.) price.

Brazil quarreled with a number of aspects of the way in which the EC implemented and administered the tariff-rate quota scheme. In addition to Brazil's transparency claim under GATT Article X, Brazil argued the EC had violated GATT Articles II (concerning tariff bindings), III (concerning non-discriminatory treatment between imports and like domestic products), and XIII (concerning the non-discriminatory administration of quantitative restrictions). On these substantive claims, the Panel ruled against Brazil. Brazil, however, prevailed with respect to some of its arguments that the EC had not implemented the TRQ in accordance the Uruguay Round *Agreement on Import Licensing Procedures*, and with respect to its argument the EC's definition of the CIF price had not complied with the *Agriculture Agreement*.

On appeal, Brazil raised a host of substantive issues, including whether a tariff-rate quota resulting from negotiations under GATT Article XXVIII must be administered in a non-discriminatory manner consistent with Article XIII, *i.e.*, whether the quota must be applied on an MFN basis. On this issue, the Appellate Body upheld the panel's ruling. For its part, the EC appealed the Panel's ruling that Article 5:1(b) of the *Agriculture Agreement* requires an import price to be the CIF price plus ordinary customs duties. Its appeal was successful, as the Appellate Body overturned the Panel ruling.

Interestingly, underlying much of the substantive debate in *EC — Poultry Products* is a significant difference in how Brazil and the EC viewed the *Oilseeds Agreement*. To Brazil, the *Agreement* was a means for the EC to negotiate with it separately from other frozen poultry meat exporters. Rather than pursue a strategy of compensating all exporters on a common, MFN basis, Brazil characterized the *Agreement* as a way the EC could give variable compensatory solutions, *i.e.*, *sui generis* solutions to specific Members. The *Agreement*, Brazil said, embodied a country-specific package for Brazil, and did not require MFN application of the tariff-rate quota share for Brazil.

Thus, for instance, it was not necessary for Brazil's share in the duty-free global annual quota of 15,500 tons to be the same as set forth in other bilateral agreements the EC might make with other WTO Members (*i.e.*, it was not necessary for shares to be allocated, as GATT Article XIII:2(d) suggests, among Members with a substantial interest based on proportions of imports into the EC during a previous representative period). Conversely, the EC — agreeing with the panel's finding — did not believe anything in GATT Article XXVIII (concerning modification of tariff schedules), or, for that matter, the *WTO Agreement*, waived the MFN obligations of Articles I and XIII.

The clashing characterizations of the *Oilseeds Agreement* were motivated by conflicting trade interests. Brazil would benefit from a larger, non-MFN share of the EC's TRQ, as opposed to a smaller, MFN share. Allocation of shares to non-Members would reduce Brazil's slice of the in-quota amount. Conversely, the EC would benefit from adherence to the MFN principle, because Brazil would reach its in-quota limitation more quickly than if it had an "extra" amount. In turn, the EC could apply a protectionist safeguard measure under the *Agriculture Agreement* sooner rather than later. At the least, the EC would garner the tariff revenue from over-quota shipments.

Likewise, were the EC to allocate shares to non-Members, then Members like Brazil would be more likely to reach their reduced quota allotments more quickly than otherwise would happen.

B.   The 1998 *EC — Poultry Products* Case

WTO APPELLATE BODY REPORT, *EUROPEAN COMMUNITIES — MEASURES AFFECTING THE IMPORTATION OF CERTAIN POULTRY PRODUCTS*
WT/DS69/AB/R (adopted 23 July 1998)

VI. ARTICLE X OF THE GATT 1994

110. With respect to Article X, the Panel found:

> . . . that Article X is applicable only to laws, regulations, judicial decisions and administrative rulings "of general application" . . . licences issued to a specific company or applied to a specific shipment cannot be considered to be a measure "of general application." In the present case, the information which Brazil claims the EC should have made available concerns a specific shipment, which is outside the scope of Article X of GATT.
>
> In view of the fact that the EC has demonstrated that it has complied with the obligation of publication of the regulations under Article X regarding the licensing rules of general application, without further evidence and argument in support of Brazil's position regarding how Article X is violated, we dismiss Brazil's claim on this point.

111. Article X:1 of the GATT 1994 makes it clear that Article X does not deal with specific transactions, but rather with rules "of general application." It is clear to us that the EC rules pertaining to import licensing . . . are rules "of general application." The Panel found that with respect to these rules of general application, the European Communities had complied with its publication obligations under Article X. Brazil does not appeal this finding.

112. Brazil, however, argues that the Panel erred in law in assessing measures of general application in Article X of the GATT 1994 and that the Panel also misinterpreted Brazil's submissions relating to Article X. According to Brazil, the generally applicable rules of the European Communities relating to imports of frozen poultry meat do not allow Brazilian traders to know whether a particular shipment will be subject to the rules governing in-quota trade or to rules relating to out-of-quota trade, and Brazil maintains that this is a violation of Article X.

113. The approach to Article X of the GATT 1994 advocated by Brazil would require that a Member specify in advance the precise treatment to be accorded to each individual shipment of frozen poultry meat into the European Communities. Although it is true, as Brazil contends, that any measure of general application will always have to be applied in specific cases, nevertheless, the particular treatment accorded to each individual shipment cannot be considered a measure "of general application" within the meaning of Article X. The

Panel cited the following passage from the panel report in *United States — Restrictions on Imports of Cotton and Man-made Fibre Underwear* [WT/DS24/R, adopted as modified by the Appellate Body report on 25 February 1997]:

> The mere fact that the restraint at issue was an administrative order does not prevent us from concluding that the restraint was a measure of general application. Nor does the fact that it was a country-specific measure exclude the possibility of it being a measure of general application. If, for instance, the restraint was addressed to a specific company or applied to a specific shipment, it would not have qualified as a measure of general application. However, to the extent that the restraint affects an unidentified number of economic operators, including domestic and foreign producers, we find it to be a measure of general application.

We agree with the Panel that "conversely, licences issued to a specific company or applied to a specific shipment cannot be considered to be a measure 'of general application'" within the meaning of Article X.

114. It is inherent in the nature of a tariff-rate quota that imports over the threshold quantity specified in the rules of general application will not benefit from the terms of the tariff-rate quota. Within the framework of the rules of general application that establish the terms of the tariff-rate quota for frozen poultry meat, the detailed arrangements concerning the importation of a particular shipment of frozen poultry into the European Communities are made primarily among private operators. These arrangements will determine whether a particular shipment falls within or outside the tariff-rate quota, and will consequently determine whether the rules relating to in-quota trade or those relating to out-of-quota trade will apply to a given shipment. These arrangements among private operators have been generally left to them by the government of the Member concerned. Article X of the GATT 1994 does not impose an obligation on Member governments to ensure that exporters are continuously notified by importers as to the treatment particular impending shipments will receive in relation to a tariff-rate quota.

115. Article X relates to the *publication* and *administration* of "laws, regulations, judicial decisions and administrative rulings of general application", rather than to the *substantive content* of such measures. In *EC — Bananas* [WT/DS27/AB/R, adopted 25 September 1997], we stated:

> The text of Article X:3(a) clearly indicates that the requirements of "uniformity, impartiality and reasonableness" do not apply to the laws, regulations, decisions and rulings *themselves*, but rather to the *administration* of those laws, regulations, decisions and rulings. The context of Article X:3(a) within Article X, which is entitled "Publication and Administration of Trade Regulations", and a reading of the other paragraphs of Article X, make it clear that Article X applies to the *administration* of laws, regulations, decisions and rulings. To the extent that the laws, regulations, decisions and rulings themselves are discriminatory, they can be examined for their consistency with the relevant provisions of the GATT 1994.

Thus, to the extent that Brazil's appeal relates to the *substantive content* of the EC rules themselves, and not to their *publication* or *administration*, that appeal falls outside the scope of Article X of the GATT 1994. The WTO-consistency of such substantive content must be determined by reference to provisions of the covered agreements other than Article X of the GATT 1994.

116. For these reasons, we uphold the Panel's finding . . . that "the information which Brazil claims the EC should have made available concerns a specific shipment, which is outside the scope of Article X of GATT."

C. Challenging Substance and the 2006 *EC — Customs* Case

It seems hard to believe poor pleading and argumentation by the U.S. in the *European Communities — Selected Customs Matters*, WT/DS315AB/R (adopted 11 December 2006) would overcame facts so much in its favor that America would lose the case. But, essentially, that happened, particularly in respect of framing the terms of reference of the Panel that heard the case. After all, anyone traveler to more than one EU country knows the EU does not have a harmonized customs service. The EU states do not necessarily administer, in every instance, harmonized approaches to classification, valuation, judicial review, audits, and penalties, so as to guarantee the same outcome. An exporter, therefore, of an identical product to two or more EU states must gird itself for the possibility of divergences in the manner in which the states may apply their rules. Rarely would those divergences — hence the American challenge under Article X:3(a).

The *EC — Customs* case arose partly from different classifications of the same liquid crystal display (LCD) flat monitors with a digital video interface by various states in the European Communities (EC). The facts for the U.S. side were compelling. Some states classified the monitors under Harmonized System (HS) 8471 of the EC Common Customs Tariff as computer monitors. The consequence was zero duty treatment, because computer monitors fall under the *Information Technology Agreement* (*ITA*).[3] But, other EC states (such as The Netherlands) classified the goods as video monitors, with the result they were subject to a 14 percent duty under HS 8528. The essence of the American argument was the EC manner of administering its laws, regulations, decisions and rulings, as described in GATT Article X:1, is not uniform, impartial and reasonable, and is therefore inconsistent with Article X:3(a). As Professor David Gantz observes,

> Had the United States been fully successful in its broad challenge, based on Article X:3 of the GATT, the Appellate Body might have decreed, and the EC have been forced to adopt, a centralized customs decision review mechanism, which would have ensured a prompt, quasi-automatic centralized mechanism for review and coordination of the determinations of the national offices, and perhaps their auditing, in matters of classification, valuation and penalties, among others.

---

[3] *See Ministerial Declaration on Trade in Information Technology Products*, 13 Dec. 2006, *available at* www.wto.org.

However, that didn't happen. Instead, the Appellate Body, even though sympathizing with the United States' assertions on appeal that it had in fact been challenging broadly the EC customs administrative system, declined to "complete the analysis" for lack of a proper factual record. At best, the decision leaves open the possibility that the United States, with more extensive evidence, could launch a new attack on the EC customs administrative system, with much more extensive evidence as to how individual EC member country decisions resulted in a system that is inconsistent with the requirements of Article X.[4]

To be sure, the Appellate Body affirmed the Panel's finding that the classification divergence was a "non-uniform administration within the meaning of Article X:3(a) of the GATT 1994."[5]

But, that affirmance was not the key feature of the decision. Rather, as Professor Gantz suggests, the Appellate Body offered a significant innovation, namely,

> [a] somewhat broader interpretation of GATT Article X:3(a), which instead of limiting challenges to the *application* of a Member's laws (as suggested by earlier decisions), leaves open the possibility of a challenge to "the substantive content of a legal instrument that regulates the administration" of customs related laws and regulations, to the manner in which a legal instrument is administered, provided that the claimant meets the burden of showing "how and why those provisions necessarily lead to impermissible administration of the legal instrument of the kind described in Article X:1."
>
> . . . .
>
> . . . [T]he problem for the Appellate Body [in the *Customs* case] is that . . . two prior rulings, *EC — Bananas* and *EC — Poultry*, give at least the appearance of barring challenges under Article X:3(c) to the substance of the laws and regulations. In *EC — Bananas III*, the Appellate Body stated that "Article X applies to the *administration* of laws, regulations, decisions and rulings. To the extent that the laws, regulations, decisions and rulings themselves are discriminatory, they can be examined for their consistency with the relevant provisions of the GATT 1994." [*European Communities — Regime for the Importation, Sale and Distribution of Bananas*, WT/DS27/AB/R, ¶ 200 (adopted 25 September 1997)]. Similarly, in *EC — Poultry*, the Appellate Body concluded that to the extent the Brazilian appeal "relates to the *substantive content* of the [EC] rules themselves and not to their *publication or administration*, that appeal falls outside the scope of Article X of GATT 1994." [*European Communities — Measures Affecting the Importation of Certain Poultry Products*, WT/DS69/AB/R, ¶ 115 (adopted 23 July 1998).]

In a critical passage in its *EC — Customs* decision, the Appellate Body distinguished the earlier precedents. Its prior statements

---

[4] Raj Bhala & David Gantz, *WTO Case Review 2006*, 24 Ariz. J. Int'l & Comp. L. (2007).

[5] Appellate Body Report, *EC — Customs*, ¶ 260.

do not exclude, however, the possibility of challenging under Article X:3(a) the substantive content of a legal instrument that regulates the administration of a legal instrument of the kind described in Article X:1 . . . While the substantive content of the legal instrument being administered is not challengeable under Article X:3(a), we see no reason why a legal instrument that regulates the application or implementation of that instrument cannot be examined under Article X:3(a) if it is alleged to lead to a lack of uniform, impartial or reasonable administration of that legal instrument. [Appellate Body Report, *Customs*, ¶ 200.]

What must one Member show to challenge successfully not simply the administration of trade laws, but the substantive rules governing the administration of laws?

> . . . [T]he burden on the claimant wishing to prevail on such allegations is substantial. It must show that the challenged legal instrument "necessarily leads to a lack of uniform, impartial or reasonable administration." It won't be enough for the claimant just to cite the legal instrument; it "must discharge the burden of substantiating how and who those provisions necessarily lead to impermissible administration of the legal instrument of the kind described in Article X:1."[6]

Manifestly, the jurisprudence on transparency is evolving, and may do so in the context of customs unions like the EU and *MERCOSUR*. Should GATT Article XXIV should excuse transgressions against Article X:3(a)?

---

[6] Bhala & Gantz, *supra* note 4 (*quoting* Appellate Body Report, *Customs*, ¶ 201).

Chapter 15
ADMINISTERING QUANTITATIVE RESTRICTIONS AND GATT ARTICLE XIII

Do not do unto others as you would that they should do unto you. Their tastes may not be the same.

—George Bernard Shaw (1856-1950), MAN AND SUPERMAN
(*Maxims for Revolutionists: The Golden Rule*, 1903)

DOCUMENTS SUPPLEMENT ASSIGNMENT

1. *Havana Charter* Articles 22-23
2. GATT Articles XI, XIII-XIV

I. EUROPEAN REGULATION OF BANANA IMPORTS

A. Origins of the EC Import Regime

On 1 July 1993, the EC introduced a common market organization for all banana imports, wherever sourced, through Council Regulation (EEC) 404/93 (Regulation 404/93). EC legislation, regulations, and administrative measures supplemented the Regulation. The common market organization replaced the EC's consolidated tariff of 20 percent *ad valorem* on banana imports, which had been in effect since 1963. It also replaced a hodgepodge of banana import regimes of individual member states.

Those regimes were bilateral arrangements each member state had with developing countries in the African, Caribbean, and Pacific (ACP). The individual regimes entailed a combination of quantitative restrictions and licensing requirements. Some regimes were very strict. Of course, in keeping with the common market, member states permitted duty-free entry from other member states. But, the particularities of the bilaterally arranged regimes as regards imports differed significantly.

Spain, for example, maintained a *de facto* prohibition on imports of bananas, and met its consumption requirements almost exclusively with domestic production from the Canary Islands. France relied principally on bananas from its overseas departments, Guadeloupe and Martinique, and bestowed preferential access on its former colonies, the ACP countries of Côte d'Ivoire and Cameroon. The United Kingdom imported bananas on preferential terms from its former colonies in the Caribbean, particularly the ACP countries of Jamaica and the Windward Islands (Dominica, Grenada, St. Lucia, and St. Vincent and the Grenadines).

Interestingly, a few EC member states relied on banana imports not from ACP countries, but rather from Latin American countries — so-called "dollar bananas." These member states included Belgium, Denmark, Germany, Luxembourg, Ireland, and the Netherlands. Except for Germany, these states relied on the consolidated 20 percent tariff as the sole protective measure against banana imports. Germany permitted duty-free imports up to the level of estimated domestic consumption. The seeds of strain within the EC that would emerge during the *Bananas* War thus were apparent. France and the United Kingdom would prove far more committed to the defense of preferential arrangements for ACP bananas than would the northern European or Benelux countries.

The banana import regimes of individual EC member states hardly went unnoticed by the banana exporting countries denied preferential access. The assorted bilateral preferential regimes were the subject of a complaint brought under the pre-Uruguay Round dispute resolution procedures by Colombia, Costa Rica, Guatemala, Nicaragua, and Venezuela. It resulted in a GATT Panel Report issued on 3 June 1993, *EEC — Members States' Import Regimes for Bananas* (DS32/R) It is sometimes called the "first" *Banana* Panel Report, or *Bananas I*. While the Report recommended various changes to the bilateral import regimes, the Contracting Parties did not adopt it.

The new common market organization regime the EC commenced in 1993 implemented a preferential trading arrangement (PTA) for *Lomé Convention* countries. The EC had negotiated this *Convention* in 1975 with approximately 71 ACP developing countries — the so-called "ACP" or "Lomé" countries. The First *Convention*, signed in Yaoundé, Cameroon, in 1963, like the *Lomé Convention*, set forth a means for the EC to aid the ACP countries, partly through a system of trade preferences (*e.g.*, lower tariffs or duty-free treatment). Many of the Lomé countries are former European colonies. Thirty-nine of the Lomé countries are among the world's 48 poorest countries.

The Fourth *Lomé Convention* was signed on 15 December 1989 by the EC and the ACP countries, many of which are now WTO Members. This edition contained a protocol concerning bananas, implemented fully in 1993. Consuming about 4 million tons of bananas annually, the EC is the second largest importer of bananas in the world, after the U.S. Domestic EC producers supply only between 645,000 and 750,000 tons of the bananas consumed in the EC. Their producing areas are in the Azores and Algarve, Canary Islands, Crete, Guadeloupe, Lakonia, Madeira, and Martinique.

Obviously, then, the EC needs imports to satisfy the balance of consumer demand. For example, the EC imports at least 2.1 million tons of bananas from Latin America, particularly Colombia, Costa Rica, Ecuador, Honduras, and Panama, and up to 727,000 tons from ACP countries. Among the ACP suppliers are Belize, Cameroon, Côte d'Ivoire, Colombia, Dominica, Dominican Republic, Jamaica, and St. Lucia.

The EC's PTA for bananas obviously violates Article I:1 of GATT — the most-favored nation (MFN) clause — because it treats bananas from ACP countries (particularly from 12 traditional ACP supplying countries) more favorably than bananas from other countries of origin. However, as a general matter, the violation could be excused by virtue of a Waiver from the EC's Article I:1 obligations. The Waiver, requested by the EC, was granted on 9 December 1994 by a decision of the GATT Contracting Parties. It allowed the

EC to deviate from the MFN clause "to the extent necessary . . . to provide preferential treatment for products originating in ACP states as required by . . . the Fourth *Lomé Convention*, without being required to extend the same preferential treatment to like products of any other contracting party." On 14 October 1996, the WTO General Council agreed to extend the Waiver until 29 February 2000.

Once again, European preferences for ACP bananas became the subject of controversy. Once again, the complaining parties were the same as those in the first *Bananas* case: Colombia, Costa Rica, Guatemala, Nicaragua, and Venezuela. Employing the pre-Uruguay Round dispute resolution procedures, they objected to the discriminatory nature of the EC's market organization for bananas. Once again, they essentially won on the merits. A GATT Panel issued its Report, *EEC — Import Regime for Bananas* (DS38/R), on 11 February 1994. However, the Report in this second *Bananas* case — *Bananas II* — was not adopted by the Contracting Parties. The non-adoption, coupled with EC resistance to make changes in the ACP preference scheme, may explain in part why Colombia, Costa Rica, Nicaragua, and Venezuela negotiated the *Banana Framework Agreement* (*BFA*) with the EC. But, once again, the complainants' effort to achieve what they regarded as fair market access — a more level playing field — was denied.

Bananas II, like *Bananas I*, thus was hardly akin to a smoldering ember. To use that metaphor would suggest a dying fire. These early cases were more akin to serious border exchanges in a war soon to break out.

B.   Three Import Categories and Associated Tariff-Rate Quotas

The *Bananas* War itself — a WTO action — was fought over the PTA set forth in Regulation 404/93. This Regulation established three categories of banana imports:

(1) "Traditional ACP bananas." These are bananas traditionally imported by the EC from 12 ACP countries. These countries of origin are known as the "12 traditional ACP countries." They are Belize, Cameroon, Cape Verde, Côte d'Ivoire, Dominica, Grenada, Jamaica, Madagascar, Somalia, St. Lucia, St. Vincent and the Grenadines, and Suriname, the so-called "traditional" ACP countries.

(2) "Third-country bananas." These are imports from any third country, *i.e.*, from any non-ACP country. The most prominent examples are imports from the America's co-complainants in the WTO action, Ecuador, Guatemala, Honduras, and Mexico.

(3) "Non-traditional ACP bananas." These bananas are defined to come from two sources: (a) quantities of bananas in excess of the quantities traditionally supplied by (*i.e.*, the country-specific quota allotments for) the 12 traditional ACP countries, and (b) quantities supplied by ACP countries that are not traditional suppliers to the EC (such as the Dominican Republic, Ghana, and Kenya).

Under its PTA, the EC provided a different tariff treatment for each category. Table 15-1, and the discussion after it, explain these categories and related treatment.

TABLE 15-1:
THE THREE IMPORT CATEGORIES AND ASSOCIATED
TARIFF-RATE QUOTAS

EC TREATMENT PURSUANT TO COUNCIL REGULATION 404/93	TRADITIONAL ACP BANANAS	THIRD-COUNTRY BANANAS	NON-TRADITIONAL ACP BANANAS
Definition of Category	Bananas imported into the EC from the 12 traditional ACP supplying countries, namely: Belize, Cameroon, Cape Verde, Côte d'Ivoire, Dominica, Grenada, Jamaica, Madagascar, Somalia, St. Lucia, St. Vincent and the Grenadines, and Suriname.	Bananas imported into the EC from any non-ACP country (*e.g.*, U.S. co-complainants, Ecuador, Guatemala, Honduras, and Mexico).	Bananas imported into the EC from any of the 12 traditional ACP supplying countries in excess of the traditional quota allocation for these countries of 857,700 tons annually. Also, all bananas imported into the EC from any non-traditional ACP supplying country (*e.g.*, Dominican Republic, Ghana, Kenya).
Tariff-rate Quota Amount (in terms of tons annually, net weight)	In-quota amount of 857,700 (not bound).	In-quota amount is known as "basic tariff quota" (bound). The EC set it at 2 million in 1993, 2.1 million in 1994, and 2.2 million in 1995. The EC increased the basic tariff quota by 353,000 (unbound) to accommodate consumption and supply needs of three newly acceded EC members (Austria, Finland, and Sweden).	The EC set aside 90,000 (bound) of the basic tariff quota for non-traditional ACP bananas.

Country-Specific Allocations, and "Others" Category (in terms of tons annually, net weight, or percentage)	The EC allocated the 857,700 in-quota amount among the 12 traditional ACP suppliers:
	
	Belize, 40,000; Cameroon, 155,000;
	Cape Verde, 4,800;
	Côte d'Ivoire, 155,000;
	Dominica, 71,000;
	Grenada, 14,000;
	Jamaica, 105,000;
	Madagascar, 5,900;
	Somalia, 60,000;
	St. Lucia, 127,000;
	St. Vincent and the Grenadines, 82,000;
	Suriname, 38,000.
		The EC allocated percentage shares in the basic tariff quota (which it originally set at 2 million, as noted above, plus an increase of 353,000 for the three new EC members) to the four *BFA* countries (Colombia, Costa Rica, Nicaragua, and Venezuela).
		
		In addition, the EC put non-*BFA*, non-ACP countries into an all "others" category in which there were no country-specific allocations.
		
		Thus:
		
		Costa Rica, 23.4 %;
		Colombia, 21 %;
		Nicaragua, 3 %;
		Venezuela, 2 %;
		Others, 46.32 %
		  (in 1994), 46.51 %
		  (in 1995).
		
		The EC set aside the remaining share of the basic tariff quota, equaling 90,000, for non-traditional ACP bananas.
			The EC allocated 30,000 of the 90,000 of the basic tariff quota to 3 of the 12 traditional ACP suppliers for quantities in excess of the traditional amounts they supply:
			
			Belize, 15,000;
			Cameroon, 7,500;
			Côte d'Ivoire, 7,500.
			
			The EC allocated the remaining 60,000 of the 90,000 to non-traditional ACP countries:
			
			Dominican Republic, 55,000;
			Other non-traditional ACP suppliers (*e.g.*, Ghana, Kenya), 5,000.

Tariff Applicable to In-Quota and Out-of-Quota Imports (ECU per ton)	Duty-free for in-quota amount. ECU 693 for out-of-quota amount (in 1996-97).	ECU 75 up to basic tariff quota (applied on an MFN basis). ECU 822 for out-of-quota amount (in 1995), ECU 793 for out-of-quota amount (in 1996-97), and ECU 680 (in 2000) (bound and applied on an MFN basis).	Duty-free entry for non-traditional ACP bananas up to the country-specific allocations of the 90,000 set-aside. ECU 722 for out-of-quota amount (in 1995), and ECU 693 for out-of-quota amount (in 1996-97).

For the first category, the EC calculated each year 857,700 tons of bananas traditionally were supplied by the 12 ACP countries listed in Table 15-1. These "traditional" supplying countries began exporting bananas to the EC before 1991. Accordingly, the EC granted duty-free entry to up to 857,700 tons annually from these countries. The EC divided the 857,700 limit among the

12 traditional ACP countries into country-specific quantitative limits. For example, the largest allocation went to Cameroon and Côte d'Ivoire (155,000 tons annually each), while the smallest allocations went to Madagascar (5,900 tons annually) and Cape Verde (4,800 tons annually). Interestingly, the EC did not bind country-specific quantities in its Schedule, and there is no provision in the EC regulations to increase the level of traditional ACP allocations.

The EC excluded bananas from Latin America from the PTA for traditional ACP supplying countries. Indeed, the category of "third-country bananas" encompasses banana imports from all non-ACP countries. It includes major Latin American banana producers (such as Ecuador, Guatemala, Honduras, and Mexico, the U.S. co-complainants). The EC set forth in its Schedule a bound tariff-rate quota, called the "basic tariff quota," for all third-country bananas. It adjusted the basic tariff quota amount each year on the basis of a "supply balance," a figure it calculated from production and consumption forecasts for the upcoming year.

Initially, in 1993, the EC set the basic tariff quota at 2 million tons (net weight) of third-country bananas. The EC raised it to 2.1 million tons in 1994, and to 2.2 million tons in 1995. The EC bound its basic tariff quota in its GATT Article II Uruguay Round Schedule. Following the accession of Austria, Finland, and Sweden to the EC on 1 January 1995, the EC increased — but, did not bind — the in-quota threshold by 353,000 tons to account for the consumption and supply needs of these new member states.

The EC established an MFN tariff of ECU 75 per ton for in-quota shipments, *i.e.*, imports of bananas from third countries within the basic tariff quota (*e.g.*, in 1995, 2.2 million tons plus 353,000 tons, or 2.535 million tons). To out-of-quota shipments, *i.e.*, banana imports in excess of the basic tariff quota (*e.g.*, in 1995, above 2.535 million tons), the EC applied an MFN tariff of ECU 822 per ton (as of 1 July 1995). Pursuant to its Uruguay Round commitments, the EC cut this amount to ECU 792 per ton (effective 1 July 1996), still about 10 times higher than for in-quota shipments. At the end of the 6-year period to implement those commitments (*i.e.*, in 2000), the EC's final bound MFN rate was ECU 680 per ton. The reduction from ECU 822 to ECU 680 may seem impressive, but the final amount is still almost ten times as high as the tariff for in-quota shipments. In other words, it is a major barrier to third-country bananas.

Significantly, four banana-exporting countries in Latin America — Colombia, Costa Rica, Nicaragua, and Venezuela — realized they could not obtain free market access to the EC. The GATT Panel Report in the second *Bananas* case they (along with Guatemala) had brought against the EC had neither been adopted by the Contracting Parties nor otherwise forced any meaningful changes to the EC's PTA. Consequently, these four dollar banana exporting countries negotiated with the EC for better treatment than other dollar banana supplying countries. In 1994, they and the EC entered into a *Framework Agreement on Bananas* (commonly referred to as the "*BFA*"). The *BFA* took effect on 1 January 1995, and expired on 31 December 2002. To be sure, the *BFA* countries did not get better-than-average treatment for free. They surrendered a valuable right, namely, they agreed not to sue the EC in the WTO before 2002.

Under the *BFA*, the EC allocated in its GATT Article II Schedule to each of the four exporting countries specific shares of the bound basic tariff quota. That is, these privileged countries were guaranteed a slice of the tariff-rate quota for dollar bananas. Costa Rica, for instance, was given a 23.4 percent share, Colombia received a 21 percent share, Nicaragua a 3 percent share, and Venezuela a 2 percent share. In total, the EC reserved for *BFA* countries a whopping 49.4 percent of its basic tariff quota.

Non-ACP, non-*BFA* countries were not so fortunate. The EC put them in an "Others" category. In 1994, this catch-all grouping equaled 46.32 percent of the overall in-quota amount of the basic tariff quota. In 1995, it was 46.51 percent. Moreover, whenever the EC raised its basic tariff quota (*e.g.*, from 2.1 million tons annually to 2.2 million tons annually between 1994 and 1995), it allocated the increase to *BFA* countries (including countries in the "others" category) in accord with these proportionate shares.

Plainly, because of the *BFA*, *i.e.*, because of the exclusion of all but four of the Latin American banana exporting countries, the EC did not treat all third-country banana producers alike. Indeed, the pattern should now be emerging. The EC gave country-specific shares in a tariff-rate quota to 12 of its former colonies, and country-specific shares in its basic tariff quota to four dollar banana exporters. All other countries were left to fight over the scraps of the basic tariff quota.

The third and final category of banana imports created by the EC is an offspring of the second category. "Non-Traditional ACP Bananas" covers two sub-categories of banana imports: (1) bananas exported by the 12 traditional ACP countries in excess of the 857,700 ton allotment already allocated to them; and (2) all bananas exported by non-traditional ACP countries. In other words, this category embraced all ACP countries, differentiating between historical ACP suppliers, on the one hand, and countries not traditionally supplying the EC, on the other hand. Pursuant to the *BFA*, the EC carved out from the basic tariff quota 90,000 tons annually. It then divided the 90,000 ton carve-out between these two sub-categories of non-traditional ACP bananas, and bound this amount in its GATT Article II Schedule. All 90,000 tons were admitted duty-free.

Why would the *BFA* countries agree to the reservation of 90,000 tons of the basic tariff quota for non-traditional ACP countries? After all, the *BFA* countries are not ACP countries, thus any subtraction from the basic tariff quota for the ACP countries would come at their expense (unless the EC took the 90,000 tons only from the "others" category of third-country bananas). One possibility is because the EC bound the 90,000 ton figure in its schedule, the *BFA* countries felt assured there would be no more "leakage" of in-quota amounts from them to the ACP. That is, the EC would not take away any more of the basic tariff quota for the ACP. To be sure, the fact the EC bound the 90,000 ton figure meant it agreed not to lower the amount. Conceivably, the EC might be more generous to the ACP, but apparently the *BFA* felt that scenario was unlikely. A second answer is the *BFA* countries had to accept the 90,000 ton reservation for non-traditional ACP countries as a *quid pro quo* for country-specific percentage share allocations of the basic tariff quota the *BFA* countries were guaranteed by the EC.

The EC divided the 90,000 ton limit into country-specific allocations: 15,000 tons to Belize, a traditional ACP supplier; 7,500 tons to Cameroon, a traditional ACP supplier; 7,500 tons to Côte d'Ivoire, a traditional ACP supplier; 55,000 tons to the Dominican Republic, a non-traditional ACP supplier; and 5,000 tons to all "other" non-traditional ACP supplying countries (for example, Ghana and Kenya). The EC based the allocations to the three traditional ACP suppliers, Belize, Cameroon, and Côte d'Ivoire, on the best-ever pre-1991 export volumes of these countries to the EC.

What about out-of-quota shipments? The EC subjected them to a per ton duty adjusted each year. In 1995, it was ECU 722, fully ECU 100 less than the ECU 822 the EC charged to out-of-quota shipments of bananas from third countries. In 1996-97, the EC charged a tariff of ECU 693 per ton on over-quota amounts of bananas from non-traditional ACP suppliers. This tariff was clearly more preferential than the ECU 793 per ton rate applicable to out-of-quota shipments from third countries that took effect on 1 July 1996. The margin of preference, of course, reflected the distinction between ACP and non-ACP countries. Here, then, we see one more part of the pattern: discrimination in favor of ACP countries vis-à-vis non-ACP countries.

C. Licensing Requirements

The facts of the *Bananas* War would be considered difficult, but not excessively so, if there were no more to recount. But, beyond the EC's tripartite categorization, what elevates the factual predicate from the level of "difficult" to "nearly incomprehensible" is the EC's licensing system. Still, having a try at the licensing scheme is needed to comprehend several battles of the War.

The EC subjected bananas from traditional ACP, third-country, and non-traditional suppliers to licensing procedures. Only an importing company that held a license was permitted to import bananas into the EC. To get this cherished authorization, an importer filed an application with the competent authority in each EC member state into which the importer sought market access. That authority administered the EC's license allocation procedures in cooperation with the EC office in the member state.

The relevant licensing requirements are those applicable to banana imports from third countries and non-traditional ACP suppliers at the preferential tariff rate for in-quota shipments. The EC applies three cumulatively applicable procedures: (1) operator category rules; (2) activity function rules; and (3) export certificate requirements for Colombia, Costa Rica, and Nicaragua.

First, the EC allocates licenses among "operator categories." There are three such categories, A, B, and C, which Table 15-2 below summarizes, and in which any company seeking to import bananas into the EC is placed. Category C licenses are not transferable to A or B operators, but Category A or B licenses may be traded among operators from any category. Every applicant for a license to import bananas from a third country or a non-traditional ACP country is placed in one of these three categories. The categories differ from one another according to the past import activities of the applicant, namely, the (1) countries (if any) from which it has been importing bananas, and (2) length of time it has been importing bananas.

Category C operators are newcomers. They started marketing bananas from origins other than EC or traditional ACP countries in 1992 or after. As an example, an importer that began marketing third-country or non-traditional ACP bananas in 1993 would be put in Category C. The EC allocates 3.5 percent of the import licenses available for third-country and non-traditional ACP bananas at in-quota rates to Category C operators. Because they are newcomers, there are no data on the quantities of bananas each Category C operator historically has imported. Therefore, the EC divides licenses among these operators on a *pro rata* basis. The EC derives the 3.5 percent figure by studying the volume of license applications for the newcomer portion of the in-quota amount of the tariff-rate quota.

Category B operators have not marketed third-country or non-traditional ACP bananas before, but they have been marketing EC and traditional ACP bananas. They are trying to add third-country or non-traditional ACP bananas to their portfolio of business interests (or perhaps to switch entirely to bananas from other sources). We might, then, call them the "diversifiers." The EC gives them 30 percent of the licenses to import third-country and non-ACP bananas at in-quota rates. Why 30 percent? The EC looked at the average quantity of bananas from the EC and traditional ACP supplying countries that Category B operators marketed during the most recent three-year period for which data were available. In other words, the EC picked the 30 percent figure based on recent import trends. Notice, then, it is permissible for an importer with a license to import traditional ACP bananas to obtain, in addition, a license to import third-country and non-traditional ACP bananas. That importer would, of course, be placed in Category B.

Table 15-2:
Operator Categories in the EC's Tariff-Rate Quota for Imported Bananas from Third or Non-Traditional ACP Countries

Operator Category	Definition of Operator Category	Allocation of Licenses to Each Operator Category for Bananas to be Imported at In-Quota Tariff Rates from Third or Non-Traditional ACP Countries (Expressed as a Percentage of Total Import Licenses)	Basis for Determining the Percentage Allocation of Licenses Among Operators within Each Category
Category A	"Old hands" Any operator that has been marketing bananas since before 1992 from third countries and/or non-traditional ACP countries.	66.5 percent	The EC divides the 66.5 percent license allocation among Category A operators based on the average quantities of third-country and/or non-traditional ACP bananas that the operator has imported during the most recent three year period for which data exist. Essentially, operators that have been importing larger volumes receive a more generous allocation than operators that have been handling smaller volumes.
Category B	"Diversifiers" Any operator that has marketed bananas from the EC and/or traditional ACP countries during a preceding 3 year period.	30 percent	The EC divides the 30 percent license allocation among Category B operators based on the average quantities of EC and/or traditional ACP bananas the operator has marketed in the most recent three-year period for which data exist. Essentially, operators that have been importing larger volumes receive more generous allocations than operators that have been handling smaller volumes.
Category C	"New-comers." Any operator that started marketing bananas from other than the EC and/or traditional ACP countries in 1992 or after.	3.5 percent	No data are available because Category C operators are newcomers. The EC divides the 3.5 percent allocation among applicants on a *pro rata* basis.

Notice also Category B operators are not as favored as Category A operators, discussed next, who get the largest percentage share of licenses.

Category A operators have been marketing third-country and/or non-traditional bananas since before 1992. They are — in contrast to the newcomers of Category C and the diversifiers of Category B — the "old hands." They receive from the EC the lion's share of the allocation of all import licenses for third-country and non-traditional bananas: 66.5 percent. How did the EC come upon this figure (which, of course, it considered generous)? The EC used the same basis for determining entitlement to Category A licenses as for Category B licenses, namely, recent import data. Specifically, the EC checked the average quantities of bananas from third-countries and/or non-traditional ACP countries marketed in the three most recent years for which data were available. It decided that Category A operators ought to be entitled to receive 66.5 percent of the licenses for importation of bananas from third countries and non-traditional ACP countries at the in-quota rates.

In sum, conceptually, the EC does not immediately allocate import licenses directly to individual operators. First, it gives them to import operator categories. Then, based on activity functions, it allocates them to individual operators within the categories. Regarding its allocation to categories, the EC grants the vast majority to Category, A, populated by companies that have been importing third country and non-traditional ACP bananas since before 1992. The category representing companies that have only just begun importing bananas from outside the EC and traditional ACP countries, *i.e.*, have done so only since 1992, get a tiny fraction — 3.5 percent — of the licenses. The category representing companies that have focused their efforts on bananas from the EC and traditional ACP suppliers are better off, with a 30 percent allocation.

Is it fair to say the "old hands" at importing from third countries and non-traditional ACP countries are the "chosen ones," because the EC license allocation scheme favors importers that have been in that market for a sustained period with a 66.5 percent allocation? Not necessarily. To be sure, the 66.5 percent figure suggests the scheme favors the *status quo* and makes it tough for companies trying to break into the third-country and non-traditional ACP banana import market to do so. But, Category B operators are more accurately dubbed the "chosen ones." Consider exactly who they are. Critics of the EC's preference scheme emphasize Category B operators tend to be European (especially British and French) companies. Consequently, these licensees get a sizeable chunk — 30 percent — of the licenses to import non-traditional ACP and third country bananas, even though that market niche has not been their forte. Consequently, Category B operators have a significant degree of control over the price paid to producers of dollar bananas, and the EC retail price. The spread between the two prices often is large — as much as $12 per box of bananas, reflecting a payment of $4 to the Latin producer and a re-sale price of $16. Thus, Category B importers have a significant vested interest in seeing the way the EC doles out licenses does not disrupt the *status quo*.

What does the term "marketing" bananas mean? How does the EC determine the amount of bananas an individual operator is licensed to import, *i.e.*, the "individual operator reference quantities"? These areas of uncertainty created by the operator category rules are resolved by the so-called "activity function" rules. Table 15-3 summarizes the rules, which are the second of the cumulatively applicable EC procedures to allocate licenses to import bananas from third countries and non-traditional ACP countries. Based on activity functions, the EC allocates fixed percentages of licenses required for the importation of bananas from these sources at in-quota tariff rates.

Activity function rules pertain only to Category A and B operators, not Category C. To qualify for Category A or B, an importer must have performed at least one of the "marketing" activities — (a), (b), or (c) — during the three-year data period that determines the reference quantities of bananas. Activity

(a) functions are associated with a "primary importer." An operator performs activity (a) if it purchases green bananas from producers in third countries, traditional ACP countries, or non-traditional ACP countries, or if it produces bananas in these countries, and subsequently sells the bananas in the EC. An operator performs activity (b) if it acts as a "secondary importer" or "customs clearer." It does so by, as an owner, supplying and releasing green bananas for free circulation, with a view to subsequent marketing of the bananas in the EC, and takes on the risk of spoilage or loss. Finally, an operator performs activity (c) if it acts as a "ripener," *i.e.*, as an owner, it ripens and markets green bananas within the EC.

Associated with each activity is a weighting coefficient. This coefficient is applied to the average quantity of bananas marketed by an operator in the 3 most recent data years. The result of the multiplication is the individual operator's reference quantity. In turn, the EC uses that quantity to set the individual operator's annual entitlement to licenses. That is, an operator's license claim is based on its reference quantity. This quantity depends on the product of the operator's (1) historical banana import volumes, and (2) the weighting coefficient as determined by its type of activity.

TABLE 15-3:
ACTIVITY FUNCTIONS UNDER THE EC'S TARIFF-RATE QUOTA FOR IMPORTED BANANAS FROM THIRD AND NON-TRADITIONAL ACP COUNTRIES

Activity Function	Type of the Activity	Definition of the Activity	Weighting Coefficient (Reflects the Level of Commercial Risk Borne by Operator in Connection with the Activity, and is Used to Determine Each Operator's Individual Reference Quantity)
(a)	Primary Importer	Purchasing green bananas from producers in third countries, traditional ACP countries, or non-traditional ACP countries, or producing such bananas in these countries, and subsequently selling them in the EC.	57 percent
(b)	Secondary Importer (*i.e.*, Customs Clearer)	As an owner, supplying and selling green bananas with a view to their subsequent marketing in the EC, while bearing the risk of spoilage or loss.	15 percent
(c)	Ripener	As an owner, ripening green bananas and marketing them in the EC.	28 percent

On what are the values of the weighting coefficients based? Risk. The weighting coefficients differ depending on the level of commercial risk borne by the operators for the different activities. The idea is greater risk, greater reward. The EC as licensor is in the business of granting licenses to operators that have undertaken commercial risk at some point in the marketing chain. It rewards risk-taking, because the amount of bananas from third countries and non-traditional ACP countries that these licenses authorize an operator to import depends on the riskiness of the activities the operator has performed.

Logically, those firms engaging in riskier activities should have a larger entitlement to licenses, and the EC's activity function rules are designed to implement this logic. Primary importation is seen as the riskiest activity, so it has the highest weighting coefficient, 57 percent. Secondary importation is viewed as the least risky of the three activities, so its weighting coefficient is 15 percent. In between these two activities in terms of risk levels is ripening, which carries a 28 percent coefficient. If an operator performs more than one activity, then it gets the benefit of the weighting coefficients associated with those activities. An operator performing all three activities would have a weighing coefficient of 100 percent.

The preceding paragraphs imply an operator's individual reference quantity is not necessarily identical in amount with the amount of third country and ACP bananas the operator is licensed to import. Rather, the individual reference quantity is a key figure the EC uses to decide (1) the operator's claim for a license, and (2) the amount of bananas the license represents. Conceptually, calculation of the individual reference quantities is the penultimate step. The final step is translation of these quantities into actual license grants for specific amounts to individual operators. How the EC performs the final step is not entirely apparent from either the Panel or Appellate Body Report, from which it is difficult to fathoming the precise details. (It was said, half-jokingly, perhaps three or four people at the EC in Brussels could explain what is going on, though not necessarily in a satisfactory manner. Fortunately, understanding them does not seem to be essential to understanding the legalities of the *Bananas* War.)

Another way to comprehend weighting coefficients is to realize they represent the percentage of Category A and B licenses to which an importer engaged in a certain activity has access for the importation of bananas from third countries and non-traditional ACP countries. Primary importers may obtain access to "A" and "B" licenses equivalent to 57 percent of their past import volumes (assuming they do not also perform customs clearance and ripening activities). Customs clearers get 15 percent of the "A" and "B" licenses, and ripeners are eligible for 28 percent (again, assuming no further activities).

A greatly simplified hypothetical example might help clarify how the operator category and activity function rules work in practice. Assume the EC sets the in-quota amount — the basic tariff quota — for bananas from third countries and non-traditional ACP supplying countries at 2 million tons (net weight). Thus, the total in-quota amount of bananas from third countries and non-traditional ACP supplying countries for which the EC will distribute licenses is 2 million tons.

Based on average quantities of third-country and/or non-traditional ACP bananas marketed in the three most recent years for which data are available, the EC decides to allocate 66.5 percent of these licenses to Category A operators. Based on the average quantities of EC and/or traditional ACP bananas marketed in the three most recent years for which data are available, the EC allocates 30 percent of the licenses to Category B operators. Accordingly, the licenses the EC grants to Category A importers to import bananas from third countries and non-traditional ACP suppliers at the in-quota tariff will represent 66.5 percent of the 2 million ton quota, or 1,300,000 tons. Thirty percent of the licenses, representing 600,000 tons, will go to Category B. Operators in Category C will be authorized to import 100,000 tons in total at the in-quota tariff rate.

But, how does the EC determine the amount of bananas permitted to be imported by an individual operator, *i.e.*, the "individual reference quantity," of that operator? The EC has to look to the activity category of that importer. Therefore, consider three license applicants, Zabars, HyVee, and Freshfields. Suppose Zabars has never marketed third-country or non-traditional ACP bananas in the EC. Therefore, it falls in Category C. The EC allocates Zabars a portion of the 3.5 percent of the licenses available for Category C operators.

How big is the allocation, and thus how many tons of bananas is Zabars entitled to import from third countries and non-traditional ACP countries? The answer depends on a *pro rata* license allocation among Category C applicants.

Suppose HyVee has marketed traditional ACP bananas. Specifically, it has ripened and sold these bananas within the EC. Accordingly, it is a Category B operator, and has been engaging in activity (c). The EC allocates to HyVee a portion of the 30 percent of import licenses for in-quota third-country and non-traditional ACP bananas. Suppose, for the sake of argument, HyVee has imported on average 200,000 tons of traditional ACP bananas during the most recent three-year data period. (Obviously, not all of these imports have been at the in-quota amount. This figure represents both in-quota and out-of-quota amounts.) What is HyVee's individual reference quantity?

The answer — again, in this over-simplified example — is 56,000 tons. This answer results from the application of the weighting coefficient for activity (c), in which HyVee is engaged, to the 200,000 ton average quantity of bananas HyVee has marketed. The coefficient is 28 percent, and the product of it and 200,000 tons is 56,000 tons. Given this individual reference quantity, we can say that we would not expect the EC to grant HyVee a Category B operator license to import any more than 56,000 tons of bananas from third countries and non-traditional ACP countries at the in-quota amount. In other words, the 56,000 ton figure sets an upper boundary.

Precisely what amount of such bananas does the EC authorize HyVee to import? The answer depends on HyVee's individual reference quantity. Notice, therefore, the individual reference quantity determines entitlement to import a specified amount of third-country and ACP bananas. But, it is not necessarily the licensed amount itself. The license, of course, entitles HyVee to receive the benefit of the lower tariff rate on bananas up to the licensed amount. Bananas from these countries of origin in excess of this individual reference quantity are subject to the higher tariff for out-of-quota shipments.

Suppose HyVee was engaged in activity (a), primary importing. The EC deems that riskier than ripening, as is evident from the 57 percent weighting coefficient. Therefore, HyVee's individual reference quantity would be higher: 114,000 (*i.e.*, the product of the 200,000 ton average quantity of traditional ACP bananas Well Spring had been marketing and the coefficient.) In turn, HyVee is entitled to a Category B license authorizing it to import more third-country and non-traditional ACP bananas than would be the case if HyVee were engaged only in ripening. Here, too, the individual reference quantity to serve as an upper limit on the precise tonnage entitlement, *i.e.*, the entitlement will not exceed 114,000 tons. What is the logic behind the larger entitlement HyVee gets as a primary importer as opposed to a ripener? Again, greater risk assumed in the past entitles an importer to greater return, in the form of a more generous import license, for the future. Because HyVee has been engaged in the riskier business of primary importation of traditional ACP bananas, the EC rewards HyVee with a license to import a larger quantity of third-country and non-traditional ACP bananas than would be the case if HyVee had been a mere ripener of traditional ACP bananas.

Finally, consider the position of Freshfields. Suppose it has marketed third-country and (or) non-traditional ACP bananas for many years (in particular, since before 1992), and thus fits into Category A. Assume Freshfields has acted as a primary importer, *i.e.*, engaged in activity (a), so the applicable weighting coefficient is 57 percent. Suppose further the average quantity of bananas, both in-and out-of-quota, that Freshfields imported from third countries and (or) non-traditional ACP countries in the most recent three years is 400,000 tons. Therefore, its individual reference quantity for these imports is 228,000 tons (*i.e.*, the product of this amount and the coefficient). Given this reference quantity, Freshfields is entitled to a Category A import license authorizing it to bring into the EC a set amount of bananas, not to exceed 228,000 tons, at the in-quota tariff rate from third countries and non-traditional ACP countries. Any amount in excess of what the EC authorizes is subject to the out-of-quota rate.

Here again, the "greater risk, greater reward" logic can be seen by way of example. If Freshfields had engaged in only secondary market activities, *i.e.*, if it had acted only as a customs clearer, then its individual reference quantity would be far lower — the product of 15 percent and 400,000 tons, or 60,000 tons. In turn, the EC would set an in-quota amount for Freshfields as regards the importation of third-country and ACP bananas commensurate with this lower reference quantity.

Allocating licenses to import bananas from third countries and non-traditional ACP supplying countries involves multiple steps that the EC undertakes *in seriatim*. Step 1 results in the placement of importers into operator categories A, B, and C, and the assignment of percentage shares of licenses to those categories. Step 2 results in the calculation of individual reference quantities, and on the basis thereof, the allocation of licenses for importation at the in-quota tariff rate to each company in Category A and B. Step 3, explained here, concerns an additional requirement that must be satisfied in order to receive an import license for bananas from any one of the *BFA* countries.

The EC reserved for *BFA* countries specific shares in the basic tariff quota for duty-free imports of bananas from non-traditional ACP supplying countries and third country suppliers. Among the *BFA* countries, the EC granted Colombia a 21 percent share in the tariff-rate quota, Costa Rica a 23.4 percent share in the tariff-rate quota, Nicaragua a 3 percent share, and Venezuela a 2 percent share. These country-specific reservations are not, however, the only special treatment *BFA* provides to these exporting countries. In addition, the *BFA* authorizes these four countries to issue special export certificates for up to 70 percent of their country-specific allocations.

The export certificates are a device by which a *BFA* country can decide which companies can take advantage of the country-specific shares and export bananas to the EC. Without an export certificate, exportation is forbidden. Of the four *BFA* countries, Colombia, Costa Rica, and Nicaragua — but not Venezuela — chose to issue export certificates. In turn, the EC required by regulation a Category A or C (but not B) operator to obtain a certificate in order to be eligible to receive from the EC a license to import bananas from Colombia, Costa Rica, and Nicaragua.

II. FINDINGS IN THE 1997 *BANANAS* CASE

WTO APPELLATE BODY REPORT, *EUROPEAN COMMUNITIES — REGIME FOR THE IMPORTATION, SALE AND DISTRIBUTION OF BANANAS*
WT/DS27/AB/R (adopted 25 September 1997)

I. Introduction

1. The European Communities and Ecuador, Guatemala, Honduras, Mexico and the United States (the "Complaining Parties") appeal from certain issues of law and legal interpretations in the Panel Reports, *European Communities — Regime for the Importation, Sale and Distribution of Bananas* (the "Panel Reports"). . . .

2. The Panel issued four Panel Reports [one for the U.S., Ecuador, and Mexico, and one for Guatemala and Honduras combined] . . .

[The Panel's findings with respect to the complaints of Ecuador and Mexico were identical. It also made the same findings, except for the *GATS* claims, which were not in issue, with respect to the complaints of Guatemala and Honduras. Omitted are the portions of the Appellate Body Report dealing with the *GATS*. In brief, the U.S. prevailed in its claim the EC's banana import regime ran afoul of the MFN and national treatment principles in *GATS* Articles II and XVII, respectively. Observe, as the Appellate Body stated in ¶ 255(p), that there is no legal basis for an *a priori* exclusion of a trade measure from the scope of the GATT *and GATS*. Depending on the measure in question, both regimes may overlap simultaneously.]

. . . .

IV. Issues Raised in this Appeal

129. The appellant, the European Communities, raises the following issues in this appeal:

. . . .

(d) Whether the EC's allocation of tariff quota shares, whether by agreement or by assignment, to some, but not to other, Members not having a substantial interest in supplying bananas to the European Communities, is consistent with Article XIII:1 of the GATT 1994; and whether the tariff quota reallocation rules of the *BFA* are consistent with the requirements of Article XIII:1 of the GATT 1994;

. . . .

(f) Whether the existence of two separate EC regimes for the importation of bananas is legally relevant to the application of the non-discrimination provisions of the GATT 1994 and the other Annex 1A agreements of the *WTO Agreement*;

. . . .

(i) Whether the application of the EC activity function rules to imports of third-country and non-traditional ACP bananas, in the absence of the application of such rules to imports of traditional ACP bananas, is consistent with Article I:1 of the GATT 1994; and whether the EC export certificate requirement for the importation of *BFA* bananas is consistent with the requirements of Article I:1 of the GATT 1994;

(j) Whether the EC import licensing procedures are within the scope of Article III:4 of the GATT 1994; and, if so, whether the EC practice with respect to hurricane licenses is consistent with the requirements of Article III:4 of the GATT 1994. . . .

[Omitted is the Appellate Body's discussion of issues (i) and (j). In respect of licensing requirements, what ought the outcome to be on these issues? Check ¶ 255(n)-(o) below. Also excludes is the Appellate Body's treatment of the following issues the EC raised. Whether: (1) the U.S. had standing to bring GATT claims; (2) the requirements of *DSU* Article 6:2 for establishment of a panel were met; (3) Articles 4:1 and 21:1 of the WTO *Agreement on Agriculture* prevailed over the EC's GATT Article XIII obligations; (4) the EC was required under the *Lomé Convention* to allocate shares in its tariff-rate quota to traditional ACP countries, and to maintain licensing procedures for bananas from third countries and non-traditional ACP countries; (5) the WTO *Agreement on Import Licensing Procedures* are relevant to tariff-rate quotas; and (6) the EC's licensing system ran afoul of GATT Article X:3(a). These five issues are not central to the case, in contrast to the GATT Article XIII claim. As noted earlier, the discussion of all *GATS* issues also is excluded. Finally, omitted is the discussion of the complainants' argument as to whether the *Lomé Convention* waiver for the EC that covers GATT Article I also covers Article XIII. In brief, the Appellate Body found the waiver did not embrace breaches of Article XIII.]

B. Multilateral Agreements on Trade in Goods

. . . .

2. *Article XIII of the GATT 1994*

159. The European Communities raises two legal issues relating to the interpretation of Article XIII of the GATT 1994. The first is whether the allocation by the European Communities of tariff quota shares, by agreement and by assignment, to some Members not having a substantial interest in supplying bananas to the European Communities (including Nicaragua, Venezuela, and certain ACP countries in respect of traditional and non-traditional exports), but not to other such Members (including Guatemala), is consistent with Article XIII:1. The second is whether the tariff quota reallocation rules of the *BFA* are consistent with the requirements of Article XIII:1 of the GATT 1994.

. . . .

161. In administering quantitative import restrictions or tariff quotas, Members must also observe the rules in ArticleXIII:2. . . . Article XIII:2(d) provides specific rules for the allocation of tariff quotas among supplying

countries, but these rules pertain only to the allocation of tariff quota shares to Members "having a substantial interest in supplying the product concerned." Article XIII:2(d) does not provide any specific rules for the allocation of tariff quota shares to Members not having a substantial interest. Nevertheless, allocation to Members not having a substantial interest must be subject to the basic principle of non-discrimination. When this principle of non-discrimination is applied to the allocation of tariff quota shares to Members not having a substantial interest, it is clear that a Member cannot, whether by agreement or by assignment, allocate tariff quota shares to some Members not having a substantial interest while not allocating shares to other Members who likewise do not have a substantial interest. To do so is clearly inconsistent with the requirement in Article XIII:1 that a Member cannot restrict the importation of any product from another Member unless the importation of the like product from all third countries is "similarly" restricted.

162. Therefore, on the first issue raised by the European Communities, we conclude that the Panel found correctly that the allocation of tariff quota shares, whether by agreement or by assignment, to some, but not to other, Members not having a substantial interest in supplying bananas to the European Communities is inconsistent with the requirements of Article XIII:1 of the GATT 1994.

163. The second issue relates to the consistency of the tariff quota reallocation rules of the *BFA* with Article XIII:1 of the GATT 1994. Pursuant to these reallocation rules, a portion of a tariff quota share not used by the *BFA* country to which that share is allocated may, at the joint request of the *BFA* countries, be reallocated to the other *BFA* countries. These reallocation rules allow the exclusion of banana-supplying countries, other than *BFA* countries, from sharing in the unused portions of a tariff quota share. Thus, imports from *BFA* countries and imports from other Members are not "similarly" restricted. We conclude, therefore, that the Panel found correctly that the tariff quota reallocation rules of the *BFA* are inconsistent with the requirements of Article XIII:1 of the GATT 1994. Moreover, the reallocation of unused portions of a tariff quota share exclusively to other *BFA* countries, and not to other non-*BFA* banana-supplying Members, does not result in an allocation of tariff quota shares which approaches "as closely as possible the shares which the various Members might be expected to obtain in the absence of the restrictions." Therefore, the tariff quota reallocation rules of the *BFA* are also inconsistent with the *chapeau* of Article XIII:2 of the GATT 1994.

. . . .

4. *The "Separate Regimes" Argument*

189. It has been argued by the European Communities that there are two separate EC import regimes for bananas, the preferential regime for traditional ACP bananas and the *erga omnes* regime for all other imports of bananas. . . . The European Communities argues . . . the non-discrimination obligations of Articles I:1, X:3(a) and XIII of the GATT 1994 . . . apply only *within* each of these separate regimes. The Panel found that the European Communities has only one import regime. . . .

190. The issue here is not whether the European Communities is correct in stating that two separate import regimes exist for bananas, but whether the existence of two, or more, separate EC import regimes is of any relevance for the application of the non-discrimination provisions of the GATT 1994. . . . The essence of the non-discrimination obligations is that like products should be treated equally, irrespective of their origin. As no participant disputes that all bananas are like products, the non-discrimination provisions apply to *all* imports of bananas, irrespective of whether and how a Member categorizes or subdivides these imports for administrative or other reasons. If, by choosing a different legal basis for imposing import restrictions, or by applying different tariff rates, a Member could avoid the application of the non-discrimination provisions to the imports of like products from different Members, the object and purpose of the non-discrimination provisions would be defeated. It would be very easy for a Member to circumvent the non-discrimination provisions of the GATT 1994, . . . if these provisions apply only *within* regulatory regimes established by that Member.

191. Non-discrimination obligations apply to all imports of like products, except when these obligations are specifically waived or are otherwise not applicable as a result of the operation of specific provisions of the GATT 1994, such as Article XXIV. In the present case, the non-discrimination obligations of the GATT 1994, specifically Articles I:1 and XIII, apply fully to all imported bananas irrespective of their origin, except to the extent that these obligations are waived by the *Lomé [Convention]* Waiver. We, therefore, uphold the findings of the Panel that the non-discrimination provisions of the GATT 1994, specifically, Articles I:1 and XIII, apply to the relevant EC regulations, irrespective if there is one or more "separate regimes" for the importation of bananas.

. . . .

V. Findings and Conclusions

255. For the reasons set out in this Report, the Appellate Body:

. . . .

(e) upholds the Panel's finding that the allocation of tariff quota shares, whether by agreement or by assignment, to some, but not to other, Members not having a substantial interest in supplying bananas to the European Communities is inconsistent with Article XIII:1 of the GATT 1994;

(f) upholds the Panel's finding that the tariff quota reallocation rules of the *BFA* are inconsistent with Article XIII:1 of the GATT 1994, and modifies the Panel's finding by concluding that the *BFA* tariff quota reallocation rules are also inconsistent with the *chapeau* of Article XIII:2 of the GATT 1994;

. . . .

(k) upholds the Panel's findings that the non-discrimination provisions of the GATT 1994, specifically, Articles I:1 and XIII, apply to the relevant EC regulations, irrespective of whether there are one or more "separate regimes" for the importation of bananas;

. . . .

(n) upholds the Panel's conclusions that the EC activity function rules and the *BFA* export certificate requirement are inconsistent with Article I:1 of the GATT 1994;

(o) upholds the Panel's findings that Article III:4 of the GATT 1994 applies to the EC import licensing procedures, and that the EC practice with respect to hurricane licenses is inconsistent with Article III:4 of the GATT 1994; . . . .

III. HELPING OR HURTING THE THIRD WORLD?

One of the most regrettable aspects of the *Bananas* War was the rhetoric about helping developing countries. The EC was particularly vocal in asserting that it had their interests at heart. Anything less than a vigorous defense of the preferential trading scheme for bananas would be a betrayal of the poor farmers in ACP countries, to whom the Europeans owed a special obligation given the colonial past. What about, for example, Belize, where bananas account for one in every 10 jobs?

The U.S. fired back with its own high-minded contention: in addition to the 4,000 Americans who lost their jobs with Chiquita as a result of the illegal EC preference regime, what about the poor banana growers in Latin America? Ten percent of Ecuador's population was employed in the banana growing industry. In other words, the EC's PTA hurt other developing countries. For example, ten percent of the population of Ecuador, which is the leading Latin banana supplier to the EC and produces 30 percent of the world's bananas, is engaged in growing bananas.

Both sides hid the real driving forces behind their cases: their own banana companies. After all, since when do hegemonic powers fight a trade war solely over developing country interests? The preferential trading system for bananas benefited — in effect if not design — European producers, and Chiquita and Dole calculated accurately that its destruction would benefit them. Dividing banana producing-countries into ACP and non-ACP camps, and causing them to do battle through their hegemonic benefactors, might well have been a neo-colonialist manifestation of the old "divide and conquer" strategy. But, suspicion and conspiracy theory is for another time and forum. Did a veil hiding each side's true motivations extend to the underlying economics of the world banana market and, consequently, inhibited a dialog about how to help banana producers?

There are three essential facts about the world banana market that were lost amidst the rhetoric. First, ACP bananas are more expensive than dollar bananas. Differences in production costs are the reason for the price differential. ACP bananas from the Caribbean are grown on small farms set amidst hilly terrain. In contrast, dollar bananas are grown on large plantation farms benefiting from economies of scale and low wages. Production costs are on average about one-third lower than in the Caribbean. The differential can be even greater: whereas ACP production costs can be as high as $515 per ton, Ecuador, for example, produces bananas at $162 per ton.

Second, given the production cost gap, representatives of the Caribbean banana industry freely admit they could not survive without the EC's PTA for bananas. In fact, preferential access plays a significant role in many Caribbean economies. About 60 percent of the foreign exchange revenue of the four Windward Islands comes from banana exports to the EC. (In St. Vincent, 70 percent of the population is dependent on the banana industry.) In some Caribbean economies, banana exports account for 60 percent of all exports. Caribbean farmers say they do not possess the technology to grow other crops, and in any event a banana crop blown down from a hurricane (a not infrequent occurrence) recovers in just nine months. Caribbean banana producers also warn that if the EC preference scheme were dismantled, trade in associated products (*e.g.*, avocados and citrus fruits) would be damaged, because banana boats would no longer visit their ports. The island farmers then would have no choice but to shift to lucrative crops such as cocaine.

Third, the EC's PTA is rotten for European consumers, and provides far less succor to ACP countries than is commonly realized. The World Bank puts it more delicately, calling the arrangement highly inefficient. However stated, the point is that Europeans pay far more than they need to for bananas, and banana plantation workers in poor countries get far less. The microeconomic distribution effects of the EC's arrangement are entirely incongruous with its noble rhetoric. The *Financial Times* rightly observed that EC consumers pay at least 10 times more for bananas, through prices made artificially high by the preference scheme, than the benefit that redounds to banana producers. Likewise, *The Economist* incisively pointed out that

> the European banana regime is a rich man's racket, not a boon for the poor. It costs European consumers around $2 billion a year — 50 cents per kilo of bananas. Of that, around $1 billion goes to the distributors. Banana growers in the poor countries that the Europeans claim to care about gain only $150 m[illion] a year.

If French carpenters and Belgian dentists are paying so much for bananas, and Caribbean growers are getting so little, who is capturing all the rent? As *The Economist* suggests, none other than European fruit companies. The "insider" European companies — particularly those Category B operators — awarded import licenses collect monopoly rents at the expense of the ostensible beneficiaries of the arrangement, the ACP countries. In sum, the scheme hardly serves as a ladder out of poverty for ACP countries, yet such a ladder is the altruistic metaphor used to justify its existence.

What are we to make of these three facts? If the U.S. and EC are not disingenuous in their concern for developing countries, and if they care at all about consumers, then they will work together not only to dismantle entirely the PTA for bananas, but also to devise an adjustment assistance mechanism for banana producing countries. To retain the arrangement in virtually any conceivable form is to sell short consumer interests in favor of those of a cabal of corporations. To liberalize trade in the world's banana market without a compensatory mechanism for countries damaged by that liberalization would be heartless. To fail to take both steps would reveal a lack of commitment to, and understanding of, free trade theory.

Even the most staunch advocates of free trade must admit that trade liberalization results in *net* gains to an economy. There are "winners" *and* "losers" from free trade, as Adam Smith and David Ricardo, the avatars of free trade, pointed out. Yes, the benefits accruing to the winners more than offset the injury felt by the losers. But, this net gain is little comfort to a worker who experiences real wage declines, or unemployment, as a result of fair foreign competition. Nor is it much comfort to a firm, or an industry, forced to downsize or go bust. And, what of the communities in which these workers and firms are located? They suffer economic and social dislocations.

The central challenge for trade officials on both sides of the Atlantic is, therefore, not to convince themselves and the public that liberalizing the world banana market would be a "good" thing. That is axiomatic. Rather, the central challenge is to persuade producer interests likely to be injured by free trade that a creative solution exists to deal with the damage. To be sure, nothing in international trade law — specifically, the GATT or the Uruguay Round agreements — compels a country to develop a program for helping workers. Still, if American and European trade officials are to avoid the unsavory epithet of "uncompassionate," then they must have an answer to ACP countries at risk of being left behind by a new trade deal that is, on balance, in the global interest.

The most obvious, efficient, and fair possibility is to transfer some of the net gain from free trade to injured workers. In other words, direct aid whereby the "winners" compensate the "losers" by sharing a bit of their gain. It is an old idea stemming from an understanding of what Adam Smith and David Ricardo themselves knew: that free trade based on the law of comparative advantage is, on balance, beneficial for society, and some of this benefit can be channeled to those who need help to face the challenges posed by free trade. If ACP, particularly Caribbean countries, do not have a comparative advantage in banana production, then there is no point in perpetuating their dependence on this industry through a PTA that wreaks havoc on consumer interests and channels rents to special corporate interests. The wise long-term strategy is to provide financial and technical assistance to these countries to transfer their productive resources into endeavors where they have, or can gain, a comparative advantage.

Exactly what endeavors these might be is for economic, business, agricultural, and industry experts to determine. Perhaps the Caribbean countries of the ACP ought to focus on different crops, on light industry, or on certain service sectors. Perhaps the answer differs from one country to the next. Exactly how to finance the new endeavors is also a matter for the experts. It may be crippling for some countries to service debt; for them, outright grants will be needed. Other countries may be good candidates for "soft" (*i.e.*, long-term, low interest rate) loans. The U.S. and EC can provide answers through an *ad hoc* bilateral working party. Or, they can pool their expertise with that of the WTO and World Bank, two institutions that have pledged to work together to assist developing countries. In the end, if a successful transition adjustment assistance program is devised, it might serve as a model for future cases in which trade liberalization adversely affects certain developing country producers. As such, it may embolden trade officials in benefactor and beneficiary countries to dismantle their more protectionist preferential schemes and face up to free trade.

Critics of a trade adjustment assistance scheme for developing countries doubtless will make two arguments. First, the scheme smacks of a 1970s-style "new international economic order" in which massive resources are transferred from First to Third World countries. The scheme may be aimed at smoothing the transition to free trade. But, this end cannot justify by the means, namely, a socialist re-distributive mechanism. A resource transfer would be nothing short of a bail-out for countries plagued by mis-management and corruption. In turn, at best it would encourage the adoption of industrial policies by developing country governments. At worst, it would create a moral hazard problem, encouraging bad behavior by other developing country governments. Only the hard discipline imposed by global economic forces will strengthen these countries.

Second, trade adjustment assistance for workers, firms, industries, and communities has been largely unsuccessful in developed countries. If a single rich country like the U.S. cannot make it work within its own borders for literate, well-fed, but out-of-luck recipients, then how can it possibly be made to work on a much larger scale — the principal export industry of an entire country? Certainly, two international bureaucracies — the WTO and World Bank — are no more efficient, and have no more market sense, than the American government.

The criticisms cannot be ignored, but equally, they must not be overstated, for that would lead to paralysis. On the first point, whether trade adjustment assistance amounts to a bail-out and spawns a moral hazard problem depends on how it is structured. If the assistance is simply a wire transfer of funds to a country's treasury, then the critics' worst fears may be realized. But, if funds are disbursed only after careful conditions have been agreed upon, and then only to a special administrator acting independently of the government, they stand a better chance of being put to good use. The conditions ought not to be a template imposed by a WTO — World Bank team on every country. Rather, they ought to be based on an adjustment plan initially drafted by the recipient country's government in consultation with overseas and domestic experts.

The heart of that plan should be a specific strategy to transfer factors of production — labor, land, human capital, physical capital, and technology — from one sector (e.g., bananas) to another. It must identify barriers to factor mobility within the country, and explain how to reduce them. In respect of labor and human capital, it ought to explain what sort of worker re-training will be necessary. For land, physical capital, and technology, the plan ought to set forth tax and other financial incentives needed to make the necessary shifts. Overall, the plan must be realistic in its time frame. Perhaps most importantly, the plan ought to make clear that no assistance is to be provided to reluctant factors of production. Assistance must reward entrepreneurship.

The second criticism, the poor record of adjustment assistance in the U.S., is not unfair. But, the reasons for that record need to be examined. A case can be made politicians have not given the various trade adjustment assistance programs a fair chance. In many fiscal years, the programs have been under-funded, and some have been cut back or eliminated. Equally relevant is the fact that eligibility for assistance depends on a complex web of criteria that are difficult to administer, in large part because they try to identify the cause of injury. Only if import competition is the cause is an applicant eligible. If, for instance, a worker is displaced because of technological change, then her only recourse is regular unemployment insurance.

In both of these critical respects, assistance for a developing country trying to wean itself off of bananas or some other industry in which it lacks a comparative advantage need not be like domestic trade adjustment assistance. If the U.S. and EC are serious about helping ACP countries reduce their dependence on a single, uncompetitive crop, and more generally if the WTO and World Bank are serious about smoothing the transition for developing countries undergoing trade liberalization, then the assistance program for countries ought to be adequately funded. Perhaps the "gain" accruing to the "winners" could be taxed in a non-discriminatory way to provide funds for the program (*e.g.*, a small, temporary surcharge on the income of multinational fruit companies).

The point is the cause of free trade is damaged rather considerably if the developed countries and multilateral organizations promise a compassionate brand of free trade and then deliver far less than their promise. That may be incentive enough to "get it right." Likewise, the mistake of nightmarish eligibility criteria need not be repeated at the international level. For countries, the cause of injury is already clear — trade liberalization as a result of, for example, the dismantling of a preferential arrangement. Thus, establishing and navigating a myriad of rules about injury causation are unnecessary. As proposed above, the focus ought to be on a plausible adjustment plan.

In sum, one lesson from the *Bananas* War is important underlying economic facts on which sound policy should rest tend to be forgotten or hidden in nasty trade disputes. The losers are not the workers predicted by the Law of Comparative Advantage. Rather, they are the people one or both sides in the dispute claim to help. The winners are, again, not who Ricardo's Law forecasts, but rather insiders. A trade policy stance that matches rhetoric would have two uncompromising principles. First, developing countries ought not to be pitted against one another in trade battles between hegemons. The days of using them as pawns in some greater crusade should have ended with the Cold War. Second, developing countries should not be encouraged through PTAs to remain dependent on an uncompetitive industry. Rather, through meaningful, incentive-oriented, assistance, they ought to be encouraged to meet the challenges of free trade. Fidelity to these principles might reduce trade friction and help create healthy trading partners.

IV. DOMESTIC POLITICS AND PUBLIC CHOICE THEORY

Does the *Bananas* War illustrate Public Choice Theory? Why did the U.S. bring the case, and why did the EC defend its PTA so vigorously? The consistent answer from practitioners is corporate lobbying influence: Chiquita and Dole in the U.S., and large fruit companies in the EC, such as the Irish banana distributor Fyffes Plc. For instance, *The Economist* was hardly the only influential publication covering the *Bananas War* to observe Carl Lindner, Chairman of Chiquita, was politically well-connected, had actively lobbied the Clinton Administration, and was a major donor to both the Democratic and Republican Parties. Not surprisingly, EC officials voiced their concern that Mr. Lindner has undue influence over American trade policy as regards bananas. This brutally realistic — indeed, rather cynical — answer suggests public choice theory may be powerful in explaining how the War started, and once it started, why it dragged on for so long. The answer also suggests a sinister irony: if American fruit companies are so influential in the White House and Capitol Hill, is the U.S., which used to "buy" Central American "banana" republics, the new "banana" republic?

In brief, public choice theory is microeconomic logic applied to politics. Politicians are viewed as suppliers of a product, namely, policy initiatives. Voters are viewed as consumers of that product. Votes are the currency they use to "pay" political officials for new policies. Accordingly, there is an upward-sloping supply curve for policy initiatives — more votes, more policies. There is a downward-sloping demand curve for these initiatives — the cheaper the cost, in terms of votes, the greater the demand. Where the two curves intersect, equilibrium is reached.

But, voters do not all weigh in with equal force. Some voters — well-organized, well-financed groups that work through sophisticated lobbyists — are more influential in pressing their case to political officials. Those groups provide a large number of votes in exchange for favorable policy initiatives. Thus, they have a particularly strong influence on policy. To the "inside-the-beltway" crowd in Washington, D.C., these points are hardly surprising. Public Choice Theory merely dresses up the obvious in a sophisticated, if antiseptic, jargon. The point is simply America has no trade policy; rather, it has clients. Nevertheless, the Theory is used to explain the rationale for certain international trade statutes. Jargon notwithstanding, the application of the theory to trade is entirely reasonable. If the Law of Comparative Advantage were translated literally into multilateral trade agreements and domestic trade statutes, those agreements and statutes would be far shorter than they are now. The essential language would be, simply, that "all tariff and non-tariff barriers are hereby abolished," and thereafter would follow a broad definition of "tariffs" and "non-tariff barriers." In reality, of course, agreements and statutes contain trade-liberalizing commitments, followed by pages and pages of exceptions thereto, plus a host of remedies to combat unfair, and sometimes fair, import competition. How can the exceptions and remedies be explained? Public choice theory provides an answer: they are the product of interest-group pressure on trade officials.

This explanation is a plausible one for the *Bananas* War. Consider how the War started? The U.S. is not a banana exporter. But, two prominent American multinational corporations — Dole and Chiquita Brands — produce bananas in Latin America for export to third countries like EC member states, as well as to the U.S. Dole and Chiquita, along with Del Monte, owned by Jordanian interests, are the largest banana companies in the world. They account for roughly two-thirds of world trade in bananas, and have 42 percent of the EC market. In contrast, bananas produced in the ACP account for just 19 percent of total EC banana imports. (Caribbean bananas, in particular, account for only 7 percent of the EC market, and only 3 percent of the world banana exports.)

ACP countries seized on these statistics to support their view dollar bananas hardly are prejudiced by the EC's PTA. More importantly for public choice theory is that defenders of the arrangement highlight that powerful executives of some of the American-based multinational fruit companies have contributed handsome sums to influential political organizations. The allegation is these executives were successful in persuading the Clinton Administration to champion the corporate cause of making war on the EC's arrangement. It is exactly the allegation public choice theory would suggest.

Given that the U.S. does not export a single banana, ACP countries, especially in the Caribbean, were incensed when it brought a WTO complaint that jeopardized their economies. Consistent with Public Choice Theory, they claimed pressure from politically important firms, not U.S. economic self-interest, concern for developing countries, or legal principle, motivated the suit. So influential were corporate interests that they persuaded U.S. trade officials to use (abuse?) the country's economic largesse to beat up on struggling Caribbean democracies. In 1992, the combined gross domestic product (GDP) of 3 of the 4 Windward Islands (Dominica, St. Lucia, and St. Vincent and the Grenadines) was less than $1 billion, just one-quarter of Chiquita's gross revenue that year. The combined GDP of the 7 principal Caribbean nations (the 4 Windward Islands plus Belize, Jamaica, and Suriname) is less than 0.4 percent of U.S. GDP.

Does corporate lobbying influence explain the tenacity with which the EC defended its PTA? British and French firms were said to have particular clout. They were the most vocal advocates of a no-compromise position after the Appellate Body issued its Report. In contrast, other EC states in which there are no such corporate interests — Germany, for example — took a much softer line, advocating full-scale reform, or even dissolution, of the arrangement.

Part Five

CUSTOMS LAW

Chapter 16

ORIGIN AND ENTRY

The Guardian of the Gates led them through the streets until they came to a big building, exactly in the middle of the City, which was the Palace of Oz, the Great Wizard. There was a soldier before the door, dressed in a green uniform and wearing a long green beard.

"Here are the strangers," said the Guardian of the Gates to him, "and they demand to see the Great Oz."

"Step inside," answered the soldier, "and I will carry your message to him."

> —L. FRANK BAUM, THE WIZARD OF OZ 177
> (1900, Centennial ed. 2000)

DOCUMENTS SUPPLEMENT ASSIGNMENT

1. *Havana Charter* Articles 33, 35-37
2. GATT Articles V, VIII, IX:6
3. WTO *Agreement on Rules of Origin*

I. COUNTRY OF ORIGIN MARKINGS

A. Why Mark Origin?

If a country of origin marking is accurate, then the purpose acknowledged in the last clause of GATT Article IX:2 is served, namely, assisting consumers. But, it may be inquired whether this purpose is worthy. That is, do consumers care where merchandise is made, *i.e.*, is origin a factor in consumption decisions? The short answer is that in most cases, it depends on the product. Pencils? No. Eyeglass frames? Not usually. Red wine? Absolutely. Oriental carpets? No question. Cars? Probably. Toys? Maybe. These illustrations suggest a factor as or more important than origin — brand name.

The illustrations also beget examples in which brand name may not matter. Consider the potential benefits to consumers of labeling in the context of a 1988 American case decided by the Court of International Trade (CIT), *Koru North America v. United States.*[1] Arguably, the decision in this case cuts against consumers who would like to know all the countries that derive a material economic benefit from the sale of imported merchandise.

In *Koru*, fishing vessels chartered to a New Zealand corporation and flying the flags of New Zealand, the former Soviet Union, and Japan caught fish outside of the territorial waters of New Zealand, but within the Exclusive

---

[1] 701 F. Supp. 229 (CIT 1988).

483

Economic Zone of that country. The fish were cleaned and frozen in this Zone, and then taken to New Zealand for shipment to South Korea. In Korea, the fish were processed and frozen and shipped as fillets to the U.S. The United States Customs Service argued the fish are the product of New Zealand, the Soviet Union, and Japan, whereas the plaintiff claimed they are the product of New Zealand alone. The CIT arrived at a third solution, finding they are the product of Korea. Some American consumers might prefer the position of the Customs Service, because it provides them with the greatest amount of information. It lists all countries involved in the production process, and thus identifies the economic beneficiary countries.

However, the problem with the Customs Service's argument was its parameters were unclear. Under what circumstances will a country be listed as a country of origin? Must a certain percentage of total value added occur in that country? Or, is any country involved in even the slightest way in the production process a beneficiary? The argument of the Customs Service did not address directly these matters, nor did it have to in *Koru*.

Whatever the interest level and motivation of an individual consumer regarding the country of origin of particular merchandise, the fact is marking requirements are premised on the theory that the ultimate purchaser of an import has a right to know where the item she might buy is made. The markings are data to analyze and synthesize along with other information. In consequence, the consumer should be in a position to make an informed purchase decision. For certain merchandise made in some countries, markings are important for ethical reasons. For example, a prospective purchaser may eschew Persian carpets woven in Pakistan out of concern that child labor is used to weave the carpets. (That concern, for other purchasers, is offset by the possibility the earnings from part-time child labor help a family educate its kids at good quality private schools rather than extremist Islamic schools, *i.e., madrassahs*.[2]) Or, a consumer may wish to avoid toys made in China, perhaps because of allegations they are made by prison labor. Similarly, a prospective purchaser may have in mind environmental issues, such as supporting sustainable development in a particular country, when examining an origin marking.

However, could marking requirements also reinforce consumer stereotypes and prejudices about products from certain countries? For example, a consumer may believe televisions made in Japan are superior in quality to those made in Korea and, accordingly, look for Japanese-made TVs. Yet, Korean TVs may indeed be as good as those from Japan. Worse yet, could the markings have protectionist repercussions? No doubt some consumers intentionally search for articles stamped or labeled "Made in U.S.A." and eschew those indicating a foreign origin for reasons that cross the line between patriotic pride and bellicose nationalism.

Interestingly, the intent of the U.S. marking statute — Section 304 of the *Tariff Act of 1930*, as amended (19 U.S.C. § 1304) — appears to include the protection of American industries. This Statute pre-dates GATT, and permits the "ultimate purchaser" in the U.S. to choose between a domestic and

---

[2] *See* Raj Bhala, *Poverty, Islam, and Doha*, 36 INT'L LAW. 159, 188-92 (2002).

foreign-made product, or between the products of different foreign countries. Quoting from a 1940 case, the U.S. Court of International Trade (CIT) observed:

> the primary purpose of the country-of-origin marking statute is to "mark the goods so that at the time of purchase the ultimate purchaser may, by knowing where the goods were produced, be able to buy or refuse to buy them, if such marking should influence his will." (Congress, of course, had in mind a consumer preference for *American made* goods.)[3]

In a 1939 decision, the United States Court of Appeals for the Second Circuit rejected the claim of an appellant who had pled guilty to criminal charges associated with removing a country of origin marking that the country of origin statute was unconstitutional. Interestingly, the Court stated:

> The requirement that goods at the time of importation bear marks indicating the country of origin appeared first in the Tariff Act of 1890 (26 Stat. 613) and has been included in all later tariff acts. The purpose was to apprise the public of the foreign origin and thus *to confer an advantage on domestic producers* of competing goods. Congress was aware that many consumers prefer merchandise produced in this country.[4]

Here, then, is judicial recognition of an uncomfortable fact: the purpose of the American marking statute, and by inference Article IX, is based on a false premise. Quite possibly, modern consumers in the international economy do not care about country of origin labels.

As intimated, from the perspective of many consumers around the world, products are increasingly global in nature. Name brand matters. Bulgari and Chanel, Coca-Cola and Pepsi — such are the labels about which consumers tend to care most. To be sure, from time to time consumer fads arise in certain countries — a "Made in U.S.A." label becomes "cool" in Russia after the collapse of the Soviet Union, or a "Made in France" label is reviled in the midst of a dispute about conflict in Iraq. Nevertheless, in general what may be more important than a country of origin marking is irrelevant is the ability to rely on the authenticity of the merchandise, *i.e.*, not a pirated copy, hence the importance of enforcing intellectual property rights.

Moreover, most consumers are aware (indeed, increasingly so) of the reality of multi-country production, that many products are made in, or using inputs from, more than one country. Suppose a "global" product — a car, computer, or TV — is comprised of components from many countries. Again, the country of origin label may be irrelevant to many consumers. Here, too, consumers care little about the country of origin. They focus on brand name. Choices are based on perceptions of quality associated with firms that have differentiated their product in part through name-brand marketing, not on where the product is made. Typically, it is more important to a consumer to drive a

---

[3] National Juice Products Association v. United States, 628 F. Supp. 978, 988 n.14 (CIT 1986), *quoting* United States v. Friedlaender & Co., 27 CCPA 297, 302, C.A.D. 104 (1940) (emphasis added).

[4] *See* United States v. Ury, 106 F.2d 28, 29 (2d Cir. 1939) (emphasis added).

Honda, work on an Apple computer, and run in Adidas shoes than to know the outcome of applying a complicated origin test (*e.g.*, substantial transformation or value added). Indeed, insofar as a rule of origin imposes compliance costs on a manufacturer or importer that raise retail prices, the consumer may be harmed. In sum, a key issue is whether a country of origin marking requirement and attendant non-preferential rules of origin serve a purpose in an era of globalized, name-brand product differentiation.

Indubitably, manufacturers appreciate these points, as they envision a global market for their wares. The aforementioned brand names sell products in over one hundred countries. In the same or similar product markets, the companies compete with one another in part by differentiating their product through brand name identification. The competition is imperfect, as economists would say, as each producer uses brand recognition as a strategy to acquire some degree of monopoly power. There may be minor deviations in the product a manufacturer sells in one country versus another country. For example, the famous but secret "7X" formula for Coke may be altered for the Chinese market to make the beverage sweeter to accommodate Chinese tastes. Yet, these deviations have no bearing on country of origin. They are important only in differentiating certain export markets on the basis of consumer preferences.

B. Marking Requirements

U.S. CUSTOMS AND BORDER PROTECTION, *IMPORTING INTO THE UNITED STATES, A GUIDE FOR COMMERCIAL EXPORTERS*
97-104 (November 2006)

35. Country-of-Origin Marking

U.S. customs laws require that each article produced abroad and imported into the United States be marked with the English name of the country of origin to indicate to the ultimate purchaser in the United States what country the article was manufactured or produced in. These laws also require that marking be located in a conspicuous place as legibly, indelibly and permanently as the nature of the article permits. Articles that are otherwise specifically exempted from individual marking are also an exception to this rule. These exceptions are discussed below.

Marking Required

If the article — or its container, when the container and not the article must be marked — is not properly marked at the time of importation, a marking duty equal to 10 percent of the article's customs value will be assessed unless the article is exported, destroyed or properly marked under CBP [U.S. Customs and Border Protection, officially called the "Customs Service" until 1 March 2003] supervision before the entry is liquidated.

Although it may not be possible to identify the ultimate purchaser in every transaction, broadly stated, the "ultimate purchaser" may be defined as the last person in the United States who will receive the article in the form in which it was imported. Generally speaking, when an article is imported into and used in the United States to manufacture another article with a different name, character or usage than the imported article, the manufacturer is the ultimate purchaser. If an article is to be sold at retail in its imported form, the retail customer is the ultimate purchaser. A person who subjects an imported article to a process that results in the article's substantial transformation is the ultimate purchaser, but if that process is only minor and leaves the identity of the imported article intact, the processor of the article will not be regarded as the ultimate purchaser.

When an article or its container is required to be marked with the country of origin, the marking is considered sufficiently permanent if it will remain on the article or container until it reaches the ultimate purchaser.

When an imported article is normally combined with another article after importation but before delivery to the ultimate purchaser, and the imported article's country of origin is located so that it is visible after combining, the marking must include, in addition to the country of origin, words or symbols clearly showing that the origin indicated is that of the imported article, and not of any other article with which it has been combined. For example, if marked bottles, drums, or other containers are imported empty to be filled in the United States, they shall be marked with such words as "Bottle (or drum or container) made in (name of country)." Labels and similar articles marked so that the name of the article's country of origin is visible after it is affixed to another article in this country shall be marked with additional descriptive words such as "label made (or printed) in (name of country)" or words of equivalent meaning.

In cases where the words "United States" or "American" or the letters "U.S.A." or any variation of such words or letters, or the name of any city or locality in the United States, or the name of any foreign country or locality in which the article was not manufactured or produced, appear on an imported article or container, and those words, letters, or names may mislead or deceive the ultimate purchaser about the article's actual country of the origin, there shall also appear, legibly, permanently and in close proximity to such words, letters or name, the name of the country of origin preceded by "made in," "product of," or other words of similar meaning.

If marked articles are to be repacked in the United States after release from CBP custody, importers must certify on entry that they will not obscure the marking on properly marked articles if the article is repacked, or that they will mark the repacked container. If an importer does not repack, but resells to a repacker, the importer must notify the repacker about marking requirements. Failure to comply with these certification requirements may subject importers to penalties and/or additional duties.

Marking Not Required

The following articles and classes or kinds of articles are not required to be marked to indicate country of origin, *i.e.*, the country in which they were grown, manufactured, or produced. However, the outermost containers in which these articles ordinarily reach the ultimate purchaser in the United States must be marked to indicate the English name of the country of origin of the articles.

Art. . .

. . . .

Bags, jute,

. . . .

Bearings, ball, 5/8-inch or less in diameter,

. . . .

Bolts, nuts, and washers,

. . . .

Briquettes, coal or coke,

Buckles, one inch or less in greatest dimension,

. . . .

Buttons,

Cards, playing

Cellophane and celluloid in sheets, bands, or strips,

Chemicals, drugs, medicinals, and similar substances, when imported in capsules, pills, tablets, lozenges, or troches,

Cigars and cigarettes,

. . . .

Effects, theatrical,

Eggs,

Feathers,

Firewood,

Flooring, not further manufactured than planed, tongued and grooved,

Flowers, artificial, except bunches,

Flowers, cut,

Glass, cut to shape and size for use in clocks, hand, pocket, and purse mirrors. . .

. . . .

Hooks, fish (except snelled fish hooks),

. . . .

Livestock,

Lumber, except finished,

Lumber, sawed,

Metal bars except concrete reinforcement bars, billets, blocks, blooms, ingots, pigs, plates, sheets, except galvanized sheets, shafting, slabs, and metal in similar forms,

. . . .

Monuments,

Nails, spikes, and staples,

Natural products, such as vegetables, fruit, nuts, berries, and live or dead animals, fish and birds; all the foregoing which are in their natural state or not advanced in any manner further than is necessary for their safe transportation,

. . . .

Paper, newsprint, [stencil, or stock]

. . . .

Plants, shrubs, and other nursery stock,

. . . .

Poles, bamboo,

. . . .

Rope, including wire rope, cordage, cords, twines, threads, and yarns,

. . . .

Screws,

. . . .

Skins, fur, dressed or dyed, [and raw fur skins],

. . . .

Sponges

. . . .

Tiles, not over one inch in greatest dimension,

. . . .

Trees, Christmas,

Weights, analytical and precision, in sets,

Wicking, candle,

Wire, except barbed.

Unless an article being shipped to the United States is specifically named in the foregoing list, it would be advisable for an exporter to obtain advice from CBP before concluding that it is exempted from marking. If articles on the foregoing list are repacked in the United States, the new packages must be labeled to indicate the country of origin of the articles they contain. . . . If they do not package, but resell to repackagers, they must notify repackagers about these marking requirements. Failure to comply with these certification requirements may subject importers to penalties and marking duties.

Other Exceptions

The following classes of articles are also exempt from country-of-origin marking. (The usual container in which one of these articles is imported will also be exempt from marking.)

- An article imported for use by the importer and not intended for sale in its imported or any other form.

- An article to be processed in the United States by the importer or for his account other than for the purpose of concealing the origin of the article and in such manner that any mark of origin would necessarily be obliterated, destroyed, or permanently concealed.

- An article that the ultimate purchaser in the United States, by reason of the article's character or the circumstances of its importation, must necessarily know the country of origin even though the article is not marked to indicate it. The clearest application of this exemption is when the contract between the ultimate purchaser in the United States and the supplier abroad insures that the order will be filled only with articles grown, manufactured, or produced in a named country.

The following classes of articles are also exempt from marking to indicate country of origin:

- Articles incapable of being marked,

- Articles that cannot be marked prior to shipment to the United States without injury,

- Articles that cannot be marked prior to shipment to the United States except at a cost economically prohibitive of their importation,

- Articles for which marking of the containers will reasonably indicate their country of origin,

- Crude substances,

- Articles produced more than 20 years prior to their importation into the United States,

- Articles entered or withdrawn from warehouse for immediate exportation or for transportation and exportation.

Although the articles themselves are exempted from marking to indicate country of origin, the outermost containers in which they ordinarily reach the ultimate purchaser in the United States must be marked to show the articles' country of origin.

When marking an article's container will reasonably indicate its country of origin, the article itself may be exempt from such marking. This exemption applies only when the article reaches the ultimate purchaser in an unopened container. For example, articles that reach the retail purchaser in sealed containers marked clearly to indicate the country of origin fall within this exception. Materials to be used in building or manufacture by the builder or manufacturer who will receive the materials in unopened cases also fall within the exemption. The following articles, as well as their containers, are exempt from country-of-origin marking:

- Products of American fisheries that are free of duty,

- Products of United States possessions,

- Products of the United States that are exported and returned,

- Articles valued at not more than $200 (or $100 for *bona fide* gifts) that are passed without entry.

Goods processed in *NAFTA* countries are subject to special country-of-origin marking rules that can be found in . . . [Title 19 of the Code of Federal Regulations (CFR)].

36. Special Marking Requirements

The country-of-origin marking requirements are separate and apart from any special marking or labeling required on specific products by other agencies. It is recommended that the specific agency be contacted for any special marking or labeling requirements.

Certain articles are subject to special country of origin marking requirements: Iron and steel pipe and pipe fittings; manhole rings, frames, or covers; and compressed gas cylinders must generally be marked by one of four methods: die-stamped, cast-in-mold lettering, etching (acid or electrolytic) or engraving. In addition, none of the exceptions from marking discussed above are [*sic*] applicable to iron and steel pipe and pipe fittings. [Additional articles subject to special marking requirements include knives and laboratory, scientific, and surgical instruments. Watches are yet another example. Their cases and movements must bear the manufacturer or purchaser, as well as country of origin, and the movements must state the number of jewels serving a mechanical purpose as frictional bearings.]

37. Marking — False Impression

Section 42 of the *Trademark Act of 1946* (15 U.S.C. 1124) provides, among other things, that no imported article of foreign origin which bears a name or mark calculated to induce the public to believe that it was manufactured in the United States, or in any foreign country or locality other than the country or locality in which it was actually manufactured, shall be admitted to entry at any customhouse in the United States.

In many cases, the words "United States," the letters "U.S.A.," or the name of any city or locality in the United States appearing on an imported article of foreign origin, or on the containers thereof, are considered to be calculated to induce the public to believe that the article was manufactured in the United States unless the name of the country of origin appears in close proximity to the name which indicates a domestic origin.

Merchandise discovered after conditional release to have been missing a required country of origin marking may be ordered redelivered to CBP custody. If such delivery is not promptly made, liquidated damages may be assessed against the CBP bond. . . .

An imported article bearing a name or mark prohibited by Section 42 of the *Trademark Act* is subject to seizure and forfeiture. However, upon the filing of a petition by the importer prior to final disposition of the article, the CBP port director may release it upon the condition that the prohibited marking be removed or obliterated or that the article and containers be properly marked; or the port director may permit the article to be exported or destroyed under CBP supervision and without expense to the government.

Section 43 of the *Trademark Act of 1946* (15 U.S.C. 1125) prohibits the entry of goods marked or labeled with a false designation of origin or with any false description or representation, including words or other symbols tending to falsely describe or represent the same. Deliberate removal, obliteration, covering, or altering of required country-of-origin markings after release from CBP custody is also a crime punishable by fines and imprisonment (19 U.S.C. 1304[l]).

C. Geographic Indications

Suppose Joe's Jerseys of Tulsa, Oklahoma imports baseball jerseys made in Thailand. The front of the jerseys says "Kansas City Royals" and, like authentic Royals jerseys, are blue and white in color. The jerseys do not have a country of origin marking, which in itself may violate relevant country of origin marking rules. An additional problem is the jerseys may create a false impression. The name "Kansas City Royals" may be calculated to cause prospective buyers to believe the jerseys are made in the U.S. The lack of a country of origin label in close proximity to the geographic name means it is impossible to discern the true origin of the jerseys. Further, the jerseys may violate Section 42 of the United States *Trade-Mark Act of 1946* (15 U.S.C. § 1124). That Section provides that violating goods may not be admitted into the U.S. If the jerseys already were admitted, then the CBP could that they be re-delivered to the custody of the CBP. The jerseys could be subject to seizure and forfeiture. Joe's Jerseys may petition the CBP to release the jerseys on the condition they are properly labeled "Made in Thailand."

While the drafters of GATT surely were not all baseball fans, they appreciated the issue presented by this illustration — the need to protect consumers from being misled by a geographic name on an article of merchandise, in a label affixed to the article, or both. That is, the drafters foreshadowed one of the modern controversies lying at the intersection of international trade law and intellectual property (especially trademark) protection. Their thoughts on the matter are set out in GATT Article IX:6, which concerns a "geographic indication," also called an "appellation of origin."

These interchangeable terms connote a label revealing the place of origin of a good that has characteristic qualities resulting from that origin. In other words, it is the place name, or the words associated with a place, used to identify merchandise. Geographic indications bespeak (or purport to) a particular quality, reputation, or other characteristic based on the origin of the merchandise. Famous examples would be "Beaujolais," "Bordeaux," "Burgundy," "Champagne," "Pilsen," "Roquefort," and "Tequila." Another illustration of disputes that can arise is a battle lasting over 100 years about the use of the name "Budweiser" between a Czech brewery, Budejovicky Budvar AS, and Anheuser-Busch of St. Louis, Missouri.

In at least 100 lawsuits across roughly 30 countries, the two sides have contested who has the trademark right, based on an appellation of origin, to sell beer called "Budweiser" or "Bud." In January 2007, in the case of

Anheuser-Busch Inc. v. Portugal (application No. 73049/01), the Grand Chamber of the European Court of Human Rights (ECHR) agreed with Anheuser-Busch that, as a conceptual matter, an intellectual property right (IPR), such as the right to use a trademark or appellation of origin, is a form of right protected by the 1950 *European Convention on Human Rights.*[5] Forty-six countries, including every EU member, are party to the *Convention*, and ECHR decisions are binding on all of them. But, on a 15-2 vote, the ECHR held Anheuser-Busch had no right to re-establish its trademark in Portugal, essentially refusing to second guess a decision of Portugal's Supreme Court that was neither arbitrary nor manifestly unreasonable. (Query whether a reasonable agreement might be one in which Anheuser-Busch would use the name "Budweiser" in North America and the United Kingdom, but "Bud" in continental Europe so as to differentiate it clearly from the Czech "Budweiser" product.) Anheuser-Busch now holds the distribution rights to the Czech beverage in the U.S., causing some beer connoisseurs to wonder whether it might pressure the Czech brewery to alter its strict standards on ingredients and fermentation.

The EU is particularly interested in seeing tighter regulation on the use of place names, especially on wine. At least as to wine, Australia, Canada, New Zealand, and the U.S. support the *laissez-faire status quo* in which a winery can use a place name for its product regardless of where it makes the wine. (The only multilateral accord in place on the use of geographic indications for wine is the 1957 *Lisbon Agreement*, which is administered by World Intellectual Property Organization (WIPO). The *Agreement* obligates countries simply to register with WIPO their use of place names for wine.) Nevertheless, a number of developing and least developed countries complain developed countries benefit from geographic indications by pursuing them aggressively and obtaining some kind of IP protection for them. They are especially concerned about companies from developed countries engaging in such practices with respect to products from developing and least developed countries. The Doha Round was one of many forums in which this concern has been expressed. What proposals were made in this Round, why, and for whose benefit?

To take a not-so-hypothetical example, an EU fashion company obtains silk from Rajshahi, Bangladesh, or an EU art dealer buys silkscreen prints from Rajasthan, India. These companies negotiate exclusive arrangements, market the product as "Rajshahi Silk" or "Rajasthani Prints," respectively, and thereby garner monopoly-type profits from sales. The losers in this game, say developing and least developed countries, are the artisans and craftsmen in Bangladesh and India, who do not receive the full value of the product that bears their geographic indication. The rebuttal, of course, is that those countries failed to establish an economic climate, legal system, and entrepreneurial culture in which the artisans and craftsmen could identify geographically indicated products, export them, and obtain the profits for themselves. In other words, developed countries respond, what kept developing and least developed countries waiting until multinational corporations figured out the value of the products?

---

[5] *See* Arthur Rogers, *Anheuser-Busch Hails European Court Ruling That Trademark Applications Get Protections*, 24 INT'L TRADE REP. (BNA) 72-73 (18 Jan. 2007).

In GATT Article IX:6, the drafters create no "hard" law. The command conveyed by the auxiliary verb "shall" is followed by the intransitive verb "cooperate." The "softness" of Paragraph 6 is further apparent from the second sentence. The same auxiliary verb ("shall") is used, yet followed by "accord full and sympathetic consideration" to geographic indication issues. In brief, under Paragraph 6, WTO Members are to work together to fight the use of a trade name that misrepresents the true origin of a product to the detriment of a distinctive geographical name in a Member that is protected by the law of that Member.

To be sure, a "soft" law obligation is not meaningless, particularly if it is paired with another obligation of equal or greater firmness. That is the case with Article IX:6, because it must be read in conjunction with GATT Article XX(d). Paragraph (d) is the "administrative exception" in the laundry list of general exceptions to GATT obligations. It permits deviation from a GATT obligation if (1) "necessary to secure compliance with laws or regulations," (2) the law or regulation itself is consistent with GATT, and (3) the requirements of the *chapeau* to Article XX are satisfied. (The *chapeau* bars a trade measure applied in a way that would constitute "arbitrary or unjustifiable discrimination . . . or a disguised restriction on international trade. . . .") An express example of a trade measure that might qualify under Article XX(d) is one protecting patents, trademarks, copyrights, or preventing deceptive practices. Thus, a measure adversely affecting certain imports, but necessary to protect geographical indications, might pass muster under the associated provisions of Article IX:6 and XX(d).

The express prerequisite in Article IX:6 for cooperation is a Member has "legislation" to protect a particular geographical indication. Whether by "legislation" the GATT drafters meant any regulation or rule, or whether they intended the narrow connotation of a bill passed by a legislature and signed by an executive authority, is not clear. That ambiguity aside, there also is an implicit prerequisite in Article IX:6. There must be a credible allegation of infringement, *i.e.*, merchandise bearing a misleading geographic indication is sufficiently like or similar to a *bona fide* item that producers of the latter item are harmed. Significantly, Paragraph 6 does not contain a *mens rea* element. Whether misrepresentation of the true origin of a product is intentional, or arises from negligence of one form or another, does not matter. Put in Anglo-American torts lingo, the drafters saw geographical indication infringement as a strict liability offense.

II. NON-PREFERENTIAL RULES OF ORIGIN

A. Contexts for Rules of Origin

GATT does not say much about the substantive test or tests to be used to ascertain the country from which a good came, *i.e.*, about how to decide whether a good is from overseas. All efforts in early GATT history to concoct a harmonized definition of "origin" failed. As yet, there is no single harmonized definition of "origin," though efforts are underway pursuant to the WTO *Agreement on Rules of Origin*. As for proof or origin, here again, GATT says essentially nothing, *i.e.*, of what evidence should be presented to demonstrate convincingly the true origin of merchandise. Routinely, customs officials around the world rely on statements presented in shipping documents, most notably, a certificate of origin. Yet, that reliance merely shifts the burden of work from the government to the private sector. The task for international trade counsel advising exporters is to figure out what to declare in a certificate of origin. Put bluntly, neither Article IX nor any other provision of GATT lays out a rule, or rules, of origin.

It should be clear there are two contexts in which a rule of origin is needed. Consider the following example. Assume (as is true) this edition of the Textbook is written at the University of Kansas, as well as in Hong Kong, China, New Delhi, India, and Singapore, and then edited in New York and New Jersey. Assume, too, paper is imported from Canada, and the ink from Russia. The paper and ink are processed in the Netherlands. The Textbook then is imported into the U.S., for sale globally.

Of what country is the Textbook a product? The answer is found by applying a rule of origin. The purpose of any rule of origin is to determine the country of origin of an imported good. That is, a rule of origin is the criterion employed to identify the "nationality" of a product. One context in which this identification is necessary is where no preferential trade benefits, such as duty-free treatment under the *North American Free Trade Agreement (NAFTA)*, the *Central American Free Trade Agreement — Dominican Republic (GATT— WTO)*, or the bilateral U.S. (*FTAs*), such as with Australia, Bahrain, Chile, Israel, Jordan, Morocco, and Singapore are at issue. What matters is simply affixing the proper country of origin marking on the article being imported, in keeping with the requirements of GATT Article IX.

In this first context, the rules of origin are accurately called "non-preferential" rules of origin. The importance of such rules cannot be over-emphasized:

> An erroneous determination of the country of origin of imported merchandise can have disastrous consequences for the parties involved in the transaction. For example, merchandise marked with the incorrect country of origin may be subject to seizure or an assessment of supplemental marking duties. The Customs Service may also impose substantial monetary or criminal penalties against the importer if Customs suspects that the importer purposefully obscured, removed, or altered the country of origin mark. Finally, the *Trademark Act of 1946* [15 U.S.C. §§ 1051-1127] prohibits the importation of articles of foreign origin which display a name or mark intended to persuade the public to believe that an imported product was manufactured in the United States or in "any foreign country or locality other than the country or locality in which it was in fact manufactured." An article imported in violation of this statute may be detained, seized, or forfeited.[6]

In addition, non-preferential rules of origin are needed when countries agree to restrict imports from or exports to certain countries, such as a voluntary

---

[6] Michael P. Maxwell, *Formulating Rules of Origin for Imported Merchandise: Transforming the Substantial Transformation Test*, 23 GEO. WASH. J. INT'L L. & ECON. 669, 670 (1990).

restraint agreement (VRA, also called a "voluntary export restraint," or VER) governing steel or car exports from Japan to the U.S. The rule of origin determines whether a steel or car shipment is from Japan and, therefore, subject to the VRA. (Of course, most VRAs are not permitted under Article 11:1(b) of the WTO *Agreement on Safeguards.*)

Non-preferential rules of origin are required to enforce effectively antidumping (AD) and countervailing duty (CVD) orders. For example, suppose an AD or CVD order is issued by Mexico's Ministry of the Economy against the Tianjin Toy Company (TTC) of Tianjin, China. By means of a rule of origin, Mexican customs authorities will determine whether toys imported into the U.S. are the product of TTC and, therefore, subject to the remedial duty. Suppose TTC establishes an assembly operation in Lahore, Pakistan and ships toys to Mexico from that factory. TTC could be attempting to circumvent the duty order by making toy components in China and simply assembling the components in Pakistan. A rule of origin serves as an anti-circumvention device.

In the second of two contexts in which a rule of origin is needed, special trade treatment is at stake. Illustrations include duty-free treatment under a customs union (CU) or FTA, or under a program of special and differential treatment for poor countries, like the Generalized System of Preferences (GSP) or *African Growth and Opportunity Act (AGOA)*. The purpose of "preferential" rules of origin is to determine eligibility for tariff preferences and manage the problem of transshipment. It is interesting, and of some practical significance, to consider whether and to what extent non-preferential and preferential rules of origin differ from each other. It may be argued that in a large number of instances, in either context, the origin test essentially is a value added computation, *i.e.*, a country-by-country calculation of the value added to the imported article.

B. Types of Non-Preferential Rules of Origin

A myriad of different, specific non-preferential rules of origin exists. (That also is true of preferential rules.) However, in broad, conceptual terms, there are three basic categories of non-preferential rules of origin.

1. *Goods Wholly Obtained*

The country of origin of imported merchandise is the country in which the article was manufactured, produced, or grown. This rule is relatively straightforward, but it works only where the agricultural or industrial process is not multi-jurisdictional.

2. *Substantial Transformation*

If merchandise is produced in two or more countries, then its country of origin is the country in which the last "substantial transformation" of the merchandise occurred. This rule has been the subject of much litigation in the U.S., as case law adduces.

3. *Value Added*

An article is deemed to originate in the country in which a specified percentage of its total value is contributed. Careful attention must be paid to what counts in summing up the value.

In studying non-preferential rules of origin, consider the relationships among the tests, and especially whether — in practice — an examination of substantial transformation ends up being a value added test.

American courts have not found the term "substantial transformation" to be unconstitutionally vague. They have rejected the suggestion that reasonable businessmen would find it ambiguous. As the U.S. Court of Appeals stated in a 1980 decision:

> "Substantial transformation," while not a term or sub-term in common use, is composed of two words in common use. "Transformation," whether or not modified by an adjective, means a *fundamental* change, not a mere alteration, in the form, appearance, nature, or character of an article. As is indicated by its first syllable, it means a change which carries an article or other object *across* from one class to another class. When used to aid in the determination of the appropriate rate of duty under a tariff schedule it means such a change as to move the article either from one to another of the classes established by official tariff schedules, or from one to another of the classes of goods, wares, and merchandise commonly recognized in the commercial markets where such articles are traded. As a modifier of "transformation," "substantial" means more than "fundamental" because if that were its only meaning it would be redundant; it means a very great change in the article's "real worth, value." [Citation omitted.] Hence, . . . "substantial" has an *economic* meaning. The adjective "substantial" informs us that the degree of change is to be measured with reference to economic value, and the degree must be very great.
>
> When read, as it should be, as a unified expression, not as two separate words . . . we hold that the sub-term "substantial transformation" means a fundamental change in the form, appearance, nature, or character of an article which adds to the value of the article an amount or percentage in comparison with the value which the article had when exported from the country in which it was first manufactured, produced, or grown.
>
> That meaning . . . is the one which would naturally occur to a person of common education and common sense who realized, as he should from reading the whole of [the relevant Customs rule in the Code of Federal Regulations] . . . that the general rule was to treat the country where an article was produced as the "country of origin." . . .[7]

Without doubt, the landmark case on the definition of "substantial transformation" is a 1908 decision of the United States Supreme Court in *Anheuser — Busch Brewing Association v. United States*.[8] There, the Court defined "substantial transformation" in terms of a "name, character, or use" test that is applied to this day. To change the country of origin, said the Court, "[t]here

---

[7] United States v. Murray, 621 F.2d 1163, 1168-69 (1st Cir. 1980).
[8] 207 U.S. 556, 562 (1908).

must be transformation; a new and different article must emerge 'having a *distinctive name, character, or use.*'"[9]

For example, suppose bamboo is imported from Thailand to Australia. Coffee tables are made from the bamboo in Australia. The tables are exported to the U.S. Certainly, they are an Australian product, because all three prongs of the test are met (though satisfying one is sufficient) — the name, character and use of the bamboo were changed in Australia. However, like many Supreme Court efforts at clarifying the law, the name, character, or use test is straightforward as a theoretical matter, but difficult to apply in practice:

> In determining whether merchandise has emerged from a manufacturing process with a new name, character, or use, the courts consider (1) the value added to the merchandise at each stage of manufacture, (2) the degree and type of processing that occurred in each country, (3) the effect of processing on the article, (4) the markets in which the article was sold at each stage of production, (5) the capital costs of the processing, (6) the manner in which the article was used before and after processing, (7) the durability of the article before and after processing, (8) the lines of distribution in which the article was sold, (9) the article's name or identity in commerce before and after processing, and (10) the tariff classification of the merchandise before and after processing.[10]

Given the range of potential factors a court might examine, importers have little certainty as to the origin of their merchandise. The fact the design and production of goods is increasingly global in nature further complicates the practical application of the substantial transformation test.

C. Made in Taiwan?: The 1992 *National Hand Tool* Case

The existence of a non-preferential rule of origin for a particular article hardly guarantees a non-contentious outcome. Applying the substantial transformation test illustrates this point. Consider the 1992 case of *National Hand Tool Corp. v. United States.*[11]

The National Hand Tool Corporation (NTH) imports nine kinds of components of mechanics' hand tools from Taiwan. The components are further processed and assembled in the U.S. into flex sockets, speed handlers, and flex handles. These tools are used for tightening and loosening bolts, and use is predetermined at the time of importation into the U.S.

In addition, the Court of International Trade (CIT), which heard and decided the case, was presented with the following facts:

1. In Taiwan, the components are either cold-formed or hot-forged into their final shape before importation, except for speed handler bars, which are reshaped by a large power press after importation.

2. The grip components of flex handles are knurled in the U.S. by turning a grip portion of the handle against a set of machine dies

---

[9] *Id.* (emphasis added).

[10] Maxwell, *supra* note 6, at 673.

[11] 16 C.I.T. 308, 1992 Ct. Int'l. Trade Lexis 60 (1992).

that form a cross-hatched diamond pattern. This pattern yields a safe and comfortable gripping service.

3. Some components are heat-treated in the U.S., while others are undergo heat treatment in Taiwan. The heat treatment is designed to strengthen the steel by carburization (*i.e.*, the strengthening of the surface of steel by increasing its carbon content). The heating process changes the micro-structure of the material, but there is no change in the chemical composition of the material.

4. After the heat treatment, the components are cleaned by sand-blasting, tumbling, and/or chemical vibration. The cleaning process for some components occurs in Taiwan, while for other components it occurs in the U.S.

5. The components are electroplated with nickel and chrome to resist rust and corrosion. Some components are electroplated in Taiwan, while others are electroplated in the U.S.

6. In the U.S., the components are assembled into finished machine tools through a manual assembly operation.

The U.S. Customs Service argued the components should bear a "Made in Taiwan" marking. NTH protested, saying the components are substantially transformed in the U.S. and, therefore, need not bear a country of origin marking, *i.e.*, they are an American product. NTH also argued the value added to the components in the U.S. is relatively significant when compared to the operation in the U.S.

The CIT agreed with the Customs Service. The Court found the pre-importation processing of cold-forming and hot-forging (the first bullet point fact above) is a more complicated function than the post-importation processing. Specifically, the post-importation processing of the components of mechanics' hand tools does not result in a "substantial transformation." The Court found that the name, character, or use did not change, so the components should be marked with a "Made in Taiwan" label.

The CIT reasoned, first, that the components imported into the U.S. had the same name as the completed machine tool. Second, there was no change in the character of the imported components as a result of heat treatment, electroplating and assembly in the U.S. Except for the speeder handle bars, each component was either hot-forged or cold-formed into its final shape in Taiwan. Third, there is no change in the use of the components after importation. The use is predetermined at the time of importation.

Interestingly, the CIT rejected the argument of NTH regarding the value added in the U.S. NTH wanted the court to consider

(1) the invoice purchase price of imported components with the proportionate value of components in its sale price of finished machine tools to U.S. customers, and

(2) all of NTH's costs and profits.

The Court stated if these factors were relevant, then there would be inconsistent marking requirements for importers who perform exactly the same process on imported merchandise but sell at different prices. To avoid such ludicrous results, the Court noted only the character, name, or use test, not a value added test, is appropriate.

D. Policy Neutrality?

What is, and ought to be, the relationship between non-preferential rules of origin and their policy purpose? In particular, to what extent, if any, are these rules "policy neutral"? Consider the following hypothetical illustration.

Assume the U.S. Congress is about to enact steel import quotas for Japanese and Korean steel. The bill requires a rule of origin to determine whether steel is from Japan or Korea and thereby subject to the quota. Should this non-preferential rule of origin be related directly to the underlying purpose of the statute, or should it be policy neutral?

It has been argued rules of origin should be "keyed" to the underlying purpose of the statute that calls for such rules.[12] Thus, a rule of origin for a steel import quota should be different from the rule of origin for computers or agricultural products:

> At present, the substantial transformation test is used to determine the country of origin for purposes of administering restraint agreements for steel, textiles, and machine tools. The test is also applied for marking goods with their country of origin, and in determining the identity of the constituent goods in merchandise eligible for duty-free treatment pursuant to the Generalized System of Preferences and the Caribbean Basin Initiative. The different goals animating these programs should be reflected in the criteria used to govern the country of origin determinations. Country of origin criteria under the marking statute should reflect the desire to accurately inform purchasers of the country from which articles are imported. In contrast, the country of origin for products subject to quota agreements should reflect the purpose of the negotiated agreements — to prevent evasion of quotas. Finally, country of origin determinations under trade preference programs should be made in a manner that ensures that the developing nations for which these programs are intended achieve real economic development.[13]

In sum, the argument is rules of origin should not be policy neutral. Accordingly, some courts view the "essence" test as biased in favor of a particular policy. In contrast, such courts find a rule of origin based on the name, character, or use of a product as policy neutral.[14]

---

[12] Maxwell, *supra* note 6, at 670.

[13] Maxwell, *supra* note 6, at 677.

[14] *Compare* Ferrostaal Metals Corp. v. United States, 664 F. Supp. 535 (CIT 1987) *with* National Juice Products Association v. United States, 628 F. Supp. 978 (CIT 1982).

III. MARKING DISPUTES

A. Where Are the Shoes From?: The 1982 *Uniroyal* Case

UNIROYAL, INC. v. UNITED STATES
United States Court of International Trade
542 F. Supp. 1026, 1027-1030 (1982), *aff'd* 702 F.2d 1022
(Fed. Cir. 1983)

MALETZ, JUDGE.

Footwear uppers consisting of complete shoes except for an outsole are manufactured by plaintiff in Indonesia and imported by it into the United States. After importation, plaintiff sells the uppers to the Stride-Rite Co., which completes the manufacturing process by attaching pre-shaped outsoles to the uppers and then markets the finished shoes to retail establishments.

This case involves 82 pairs of footwear uppers of the type specified above which plaintiff manufactured in Indonesia from leather and other materials of United States origin. Plaintiff sought to import these uppers and sell them to Stride-Rite so that it could attach the outsoles and market the completed shoes in accordance with its normal practice. However, on January 26, 1982, the uppers were excluded from entry when the Customs Service refused to permit them to be withdrawn from warehouse for consumption on the ground that they were not marked with the country of origin as required by section 304 of the Tariff Act of 1930, as amended (19 U.S.C. 1304). Given these considerations, the question is whether Stride-Rite is the ultimate purchaser of the imported uppers so as to exempt them from the country of origin marking requirements. This in turn depends on whether the manufacturing process in which Stride-Rite attaches the outsoles to the imported uppers effects a "substantial transformation" of the uppers.

. . . .

The Facts

. . . [E]xcept for the absence of an outsole, the upper in its condition as imported is a complete shoe. Thus in its condition as imported, the upper has been substantially transformed in Indonesia from sheets of leather into a substantially complete shoe. And having been "lasted" in Indonesia the upper has already attained its ultimate shape, form and size. In appearance, the upper resembles a moccasin save that it has a stitched seam, and roughing on the bottom to facilitate the attachment of the outsole. Because of these latter characteristics, the upper is not marketable at retail as a complete shoe.

Prior to exportation to the United States, the uppers are packed in cartons which are marked "Made in Indonesia." However, the uppers themselves are not marked with the country of origin.

Subsequent to importation into the United States, plaintiff sells the uppers to Stride-Rite in the cartons marked "Made in Indonesia." Stride-Rite then attaches pre-shaped and pre-sized outsoles to the uppers, cleans and polishes the uppers, and thereafter sells the completed shoes to retail stores under the trade name "Sperry Topsiders."

In the process of attaching the outsole to the upper, Stride-Rite relasts the leather upper, applies cement to the bottom of the upper to provide a temporary bond for the outsole, temporarily bonds the outsole to the upper by an outsole press, removes the last, and then attaches the outsole to the upper by stitching on a "Littleway" machine.

The purpose of relasting — which consists of reinserting a last into the previously completed and lasted upper — is not to give the upper shape, form or size. Rather, it is to hold the upper steady and so facilitate the alignment and temporary cementing of the outsole to the upper. Relasting, though convenient, is not necessary to the attachment of the outsole to the upper inasmuch as hand pressure alone is sufficient to press the upper and outsole together to provide a temporary bond.

The process of combining the uppers to the outsoles is significantly less time consuming than the process of manufacturing the upper. Thus the record shows that it takes more than eight times the amount of time to manufacture the upper than to attach the outsole to the upper. In this connection, a time study shows that it takes some four hours to manufacture twelve pairs of uppers similar to the imported merchandise whereas only one-half hour is required to attach twelve pairs of uppers to the outsoles.

The process of combining the uppers to the outsoles is also significantly less costly than the process of manufacturing the upper, with the record indicating that the cost of direct labor in the manufacture of the upper is about eight times greater than the cost of the direct labor required to attach the outsole to the upper. Also, the cost to Stride-Rite for the imported upper is significantly greater than the cost of the outsole.

In addition, manufacture of the upper requires at least five highly skilled operations including cutting the leather, skiving, stitching the collar, setting up the hand lasting and hand sewing the upper. In contrast, the only highly skilled operation necessary in combining the upper and outsole is the Littleway stitching.

Opinion

Section 304 of the *Tariff Act of 1930*, as amended, requires that with certain specified exceptions, every article of foreign origin imported into the United States be marked with its country of origin in such a manner that its ultimate purchaser in the United States will be aware of the country of origin. The legislative purpose of this enactment . . . was "to enable the *'ultimate purchaser'* of the goods to decide for himself whether he would 'buy or refuse to buy them.'"

Given the statute and its legislative purpose, plaintiff contends that the uppers are not required to be marked-this on the asserted basis that Stride-Rite is the ultimate purchaser of the uppers. . . . Stride-Rite, plaintiff argues, is the ultimate purchaser because it allegedly effects a substantial transformation of the uppers into new articles having a different name, character and use, *i.e.*, shoes.

. . . .

. . . [T]he test to be applied is whether the imported article has undergone a "substantial transformation" which results in an article having a name, character or use differing from that of the imported article. If such substantial transformation occurs, then the manufacturer is the ultimate purchaser and the consumer need not be informed of the country of origin. On the other hand, if the manufacturing or combining process is merely a minor one which leaves the identity of the imported article intact, a substantial transformation has not occurred and an appropriate marking must appear on the imported article so that the consumer can know the country of origin.

. . . .

Examining the facts in the present case, the conclusion is clear that a substantial transformation of the upper has *not* occurred since the attachment of the outsole to the upper is a minor manufacturing or combining process which leaves the identity of the upper intact. Thus the upper — which in its condition as imported is already a substantially complete shoe — is readily recognizable as a distinct item apart from the outsole to which it is attached. And the manufacturing process performed by Stride-Rite is a minor assembly operation which requires only a small fraction of the time and cost involved in producing the uppers.

The fact is that the manufacturing operation performed by Stride-Rite in attaching the outsole to the upper is conceptually no different than (for example) attaching buttons to a man's dress shirt or attaching handles to a finished piece of luggage. To consider attachments of this kind to be a "substantial transformation" would be to open the door wide to frustration of the entire purpose of the marking statute. Thus in the present case it would be misleading to allow the public to believe that a shoe is made in the United States when the entire upper — which is the very essence of the completed shoe — is made in Indonesia and the only step in the manufacturing process performed in the United States is the attachment of an outsole.

B. Where Is the Juice From?: The 1986 *National Juice Products* Case

NATIONAL JUICE PRODUCTS ASSOCIATION v. UNITED STATES
United Sates Court of International Trade
628 F. Supp. 978, 980-981, 989-991 (1986)

RESTANI, JUDGE.

This case involves a United States Customs Service (Customs) ruling that country-of-origin marking requirements apply to frozen concentrated orange juice and reconstituted orange juice that contain imported concentrated orange juice for manufacturing. . . . This ruling is being challenged by plaintiffs, the National Juice Products Association (NJPA) and Citrus World, Inc., Coca-Cola Foods, a Division of the Coca-Cola Company, Lykes Pasco Packing Company, and TreeSweet Products, individually and as members of NJPA. . . .

. . . .

The controversy underlying this action began on January 16, 1985, when Customs national import specialist, Officer W.J. Springer of the New York Seaport, sent a directive to various Customs ports advising them of his opinion that orange juice products using the imported ingredient of concentrated orange juice for manufacturing (manufacturing concentrate) be marked to indicate foreign origin. . . .

. . . .

The Customs' ruling at issue involved manufacturing concentrate processed from oranges grown in foreign countries. This manufacturing concentrate is then blended with domestic concentrate. Ratios of 50/50 or 30/70 (foreign/ domestic) were represented to be "common." Customs ruled that for purposes of country of origin marking, the manufacturing concentrate is not "substantially transformed" after undergoing the further processing in the United States. Under Customs' ruling, retail packages of frozen concentrated orange juice and reconstituted orange juice must be marked to indicate that the products contain foreign concentrate.

This "name, character, or use" test was applied by Customs in finding that no substantial transformation occurs in the production of retail orange juice products from manufacturing concentrate. Customs' ruling must stand unless it is shown to be arbitrary, capricious, or otherwise not in accordance with the law. . . .

In its ruling, Customs addressed each of the factors, name, character, and use, in turn. Plaintiffs argued that the name change from "concentrated orange juice for manufacturing" to "frozen concentrated orange juice" and "orange juice from concentrate" was significant to a finding of substantial transformation. The court agrees with Customs' conclusion that these names, derived from the FDA's [Food and Drug Administration's] standards of identity, "merely refer to the same product, orange juice, at different stages of production." [In footnote 15 of its opinion, the court observed the plaintiffs made much of the fact that the imported and retail products at issue have distinct standards of identity under the Food and Drug Administration's ("FDA") regulations. For instance, the plaintiffs pointed out that the imported product is called "concentrated orange juice for manufacturing" and the retail products are known and labeled as "frozen concentrated orange juice" and "orange juice from concentrate." However, for two reasons, the court did not find this argument persuasive and concluded the FDA standards do not bind the Customs Service in determining whether a substantial transformation has occurred. First, the regulations of the FDA and Customs Service are promulgated under completely different statutes. Hence, as a technical matter one agency's regulations could not bind the other agency's regulations. Second, the policies underlying the regulations of the FDA and Customs Service are different. The policy underlying the FDA standards of identity are designed to inform the consumer about ingredients in a product, but not to identify the origin of the product as a whole. The policy underlying the country-of-origin marking statute and the Customs Service's regulations is to facilitate consumer purchasing decisions and to protect American industry. Consequently, the interests of one agency's regulations would not be furthered by relying on the other agency's regulations.] In any case, a change in the name of the product is the weakest evidence of a substantial transformation. *See Uniroyal, Inc. v. United States*, 3 CIT 220, 542 F. Supp. 1026 (1982), *aff'd*, 702 F.2d 1022 (Fed.Cir.1983) (fact that this imported product was called an "upper" and final product called a "shoe" did not affect the court's finding of no substantial transformation). . . .

Customs also found that the fact that the imported concentrate is sold to producers whereas the retail product is sold to consumers does not constitute a sufficient change in character and use to render the concentrate substantially transformed. Plaintiffs rely on the *Midwood* decision, in which this court's predecessor, the Customs Court, emphasized this transition from producers' goods to consumers' goods in finding that steel forgings are substantially transformed into flanges and fittings. *Midwood Industries, Inc. v. United States*, 313 F. Supp. 951, 957, *appeal dismissed*, 57 CCPA 141 (1970). . . . As noted by Customs, however, the significance of this producers' good — consumers' good transformation in marking cases is diminished in light of this court's recent decision in *Uniroyal, Inc. v. United States* [excerpted above]. . . . In *Uniroyal*, the imported article was a leather shoe upper to which an outsole was attached in the United States. Although the upper is not a consumers' good in that it cannot be worn as a shoe, the court found that there was no substantial transformation. . . . Under recent precedents, the transition from producers' to consumers' goods is not determinative. Plaintiffs must demonstrate that the processing done in the United States substantially increases the value of the product or transforms the import so that it is no longer the essence of the final product. *United States v. Murray*, 621 F.2d 1163, 1170 (1st Cir. 1980) (Chinese glue blended with other glues in Holland were not substantially transformed because although it was transformed from a processors' good to an end-users' good there was no evidence that the glue had increased in value); *Uniroyal* . . . (imported upper was "the very essence of the completed shoe," court also found the attachment of uppers to outsoles "significantly less costly" than the process of manufacturing the upper).

Plaintiffs in the instant case offer evidence that they claim demonstrates that domestic manufacturing substantially increases the value of the product from the manufacturing concentrate stage to the retail product stage. Contrary to plaintiffs' claim, however, the evidence offered indicates that the manufacturing concentrate constitutes the majority of the value of the end products. In fact, according to plaintiffs' evidence, the values added to the products involved here by the addition and blending of the orange essences, orange oil, and water, and related production range from 6.68 to 7.57%. This increase in value may be significant with regard to other products, but here the sum of all of the activities contributing to the added value are relatively minor, much like the addition of the outsoles in *Uniroyal*. In fact, plaintiffs' evidence shows that the addition of the oils and essences, the primary basis for plaintiffs' claim that substantial transformation has occurred, contributes only 1.75 to 1.86% to the value of the end products.

. . . .

It is unclear whether plaintiffs contend that the addition of water constitutes a substantial change. The court believes it does not, in and of itself, constitute such a change in the context of the products under discussion. The court, however, did consider the value added by the addition of water together with the oils, essences and the overall blending process. Considering the process as a whole, the court concludes that Customs could rationally determine that the major part of the end product, when measured by cost, value, or quantity, is manufacturing concentrate and that the processing in the United States is a minor manufacturing process.

The court also finds reasonable Customs' conclusion that the manufacturing concentrate "imparts the essential character to the juice and makes it orange juice" . . . Thus, as in *Uniroyal*, the imported product is "the very essence" of the retail product. . . . The retail product in this case is essentially the juice concentrate derived in substantial part from foreign grown, harvested, and processed oranges. The addition of water, orange essences, and oils to the concentrate, while making it suitable for retail sale, does not change the fundamental character of the product, it is still essentially the product of the juice of oranges. The court concludes that Customs' ruling that manufacturing juice concentrate is not substantially transformed when it is processed into retail orange juice products is not arbitrary or capricious, but is in accordance with applicable law. The orange juice processors are not the ultimate purchasers of the imported product because consumers are the last purchasers to receive the product in essentially the form in which it is imported. In accordance with 19 U.S.C. § 1304, the retail packaging must bear an appropriate country-of-origin marking.

C. Who Is the Ultimate Purchaser and Is the Label Conspicuous?: The 1986 *Pabrini* Case

PABRINI, INC. v. UNITED STATES
United States Court of International Trade
630 F. Supp. 360, 361-363 (1986)

Dicarlo, Judge.

Umbrellas from Taiwan entered at Port of Los Angeles were assessed country of origin marking duties of ten percent ad valorem pursuant to Section 304 of the Tariff Act of 1930, as amended, 19 U.S.C. § 1304 (1982), when liquidated in April, 1982 by the United States Customs Service (Customs). Section 304 requires that all imported merchandise be marked in a manner "conspicuous" to the "ultimate purchaser." Plaintiff protested assessment of the marking duties and filed this action following denial of the protest. . . .

. . . Plaintiff contends that (1) the umbrellas need not be individually marked since they were distributed as gifts by a donor who was the "ultimate purchaser" and was aware of the country of origin, and (2) a small label sewn to one of the seams inside the umbrellas sufficiently identifies the country of origin. The Court disagrees with both contentions. . . .

"Ultimate purchaser"

Plaintiff alleges that the umbrellas were distributed without further charge to patrons of the Hollywood Park Race Track paying the regular admission fee. Plaintiff argues that the "ultimate purchaser" of the umbrellas within the meaning of Section 304 was not the racetrack patron, but the racetrack, which was aware of the umbrellas' country of origin, and the umbrellas are therefore excepted from the marking requirement. . . .

The current language of the first paragraph of Section 304 was enacted as part of the *Customs Administrative Act of 1938.* . . . Previously, the marking statute did not mention an end user or "purchaser" of the article. The statute provided simply that "[e]very article imported into the United States . . . shall be marked. . . ." The principal purpose of the 1938 revision of Section 304 was to eliminate the previous requirement that the article, its immediate container, and the outer package all be marked with the country of origin.

"As in all cases involving statutory construction, 'our starting point must be the language employed by Congress.'" *American Tobacco Co. v. Patterson,* 456 U.S. 63, 68 (1982). . . (quoting *Reiter v. Sonotone Corp.,* 442 U.S. 330, 337 (1979). . .). *Webster's Second New International Dictionary* 2015 (1934), published four years before the enactment of the statute, defines "purchaser" as "one who purchases," and "purchase" as "to obtain (anything) by paying money or its equivalent." Thus, the question before the Court is whether by paying admission to the racetrack the racetrack patrons obtained the umbrellas by paying "money or its equivalent."

Under federal common law at the time the statute was enacted, consideration was defined as "some . . . benefit or advantage conferred upon the promisor . . . or any detriment . . . suffered or undertaken by the promisee." *Cuneo Press v. Claybourn Corp.,* 90 F.2d 233, 236 (7th Cir.1937). . . . By purchasing a ticket to the racetrack, the patrons paid one consideration for two promises by the racetrack: admission to the racetrack and transfer of an umbrella.

The Court holds that racetrack patrons receiving the umbrellas as a condition to payment of the regular price of admission were not donees of gifts but "ultimate purchasers" of the imported merchandise within Section 304. . . .

"Conspicuous place"

Plaintiff also contends that a label sewn to one of the seams inside the umbrella measuring approximately 1 d inches by d inches printed with the words "100% NYLON MADE IN TAIWAN" is "conspicuous" within the meaning of the statute.

. . . .

Whether the marking is conspicuous is a question of fact.

. . . .

The Court finds as a matter of fact that the small label cannot be seen easily and without strain. The label cannot be seen unless the umbrella is opened, and even then it is difficult to find. The Court holds that the marking is not "conspicuous" within the meaning of Section 304. . . .

Since the Court finds that the umbrellas were not marked in a manner conspicuous to the ultimate purchaser, summary judgment for defendant is granted. . . .

IV. ENTRY OF MERCHANDISE

A. Entry for Consumption

U.S. CUSTOMS AND BORDER PROTECTION, *IMPORTING INTO THE UNITED STATES, A GUIDE FOR COMMERCIAL EXPORTERS*
11-13 (November 2006)

When a shipment reaches the United States, the importer of record (*i.e.*, the owner, purchaser, or licensed customs broker designated by the owner, purchaser, or consignee) will file entry documents for the goods with the port director at the goods' port of entry. Imported goods are not legally entered until after the shipment has arrived within the port of entry, delivery of the merchandise has been authorized by CBP, and estimated duties have been paid. It is the importer of record's responsibility to arrange for examination and release of the goods.

Pursuant to 19 U.S.C. 1484, the importer of record must use reasonable care in making entry.

. . . In addition to contacting CBP, importers should contact other agencies when questions arise about particular commodities. For example, questions about products regulated by the Food and Drug Administration should be forwarded to the nearest FDA district office . . . or to the Import Division, FDA Headquarters. . . . The same is true for alcohol, tobacco, firearms, wildlife products (furs, skins, shells), motor vehicles, and other products and merchandise regulated by the other federal agencies for which CBP enforces entry laws. . . .

. . . .

Goods may be entered for consumption, entered for warehouse at the port of arrival, or they may be transported in-bond to another port of entry and entered there under the same conditions as at the port of arrival. Arrangements for transporting the merchandise in-bond to an in-land port may be made by the consignee or by a customs broker or by any other person with an interest in the goods for that purpose. . . .

Goods to be placed in a foreign trade zone are not entered at the customhouse. . . .

Evidence of Right to Make Entry

Goods may only be entered by their owner, purchaser, or a licensed customs broker. When the goods are consigned "to order," the bill of lading, properly endorsed by the consignor, may serve as evidence of the right to make entry. An air waybill may be used for merchandise arriving by air.

In most instances, entry is made by a person or firm certified by the carrier bringing the goods to the port of entry. This entity (*i.e.*, the person or firm certified) is considered the "owner" of the goods for customs purposes.

The document issued by the carrier for this purpose is known as a "Carrier's Certificate." . . . In certain circumstances, entry may be made by means of a duplicate bill of lading or a shipping receipt. When the goods are not imported by a common carrier, possession of the goods by the importer at the time of arrival shall be deemed sufficient evidence of the right to make entry.

Entry for Consumption

Entering merchandise is a two-part process consisting of: (1) filing the documents necessary to determine whether merchandise may be released from CBP custody, and (2) filing the documents that contain information for duty assessment and statistical purposes. Both of these processes can be accomplished electronically via the Automated Broker Interface (ABI) program of the Automated Commercial System (ACS).

Entry Documents

Within 15 calendar days of the date that a shipment arrives at a U.S. port of entry, entry documents must be filed at a location specified by the port director. These documents are:

- Entry Manifest (CBP Form 7533) or Application and Special Permit for Immediate Delivery (CBP Form 3461) or other form of merchandise release required by the port director,
- Evidence of right to make entry,
- Commercial invoice or a pro forma invoice when the commercial invoice cannot be produced,
- Packing lists, if appropriate,
- Other documents necessary to determine merchandise admissibility.

If the goods are to be released from CBP custody at the time of entry, an entry summary for consumption must be filed and estimated duties deposited at the port of entry within 10 working days of the goods' entry.

Surety

The entry must be accompanied by evidence that a bond has been posted with CBP to cover any potential duties, taxes, and charges that may accrue. Bonds may be secured through a resident U.S. surety company, but may be posted in the form of United States currency or certain United States government obligations. In the event that a customs broker is employed for the purpose of making entry, the broker may permit the use of his bond to provide the required coverage. [Notably, in 2006, bond limits were raised to cover potential antidumping (AD) or countervailing duty (CVD) liability, even absent a preliminary affirmative dumping margin or subsidy determination.]

Entry Summary Documentation

Following presentation of the entry, the shipment may be examined, or examination may be waived. The shipment is then released if no legal or regulatory violations have occurred. Entry summary documentation is filed and estimated duties are deposited within 10 working days of the entry of the merchandise at a designated customhouse. Entry summary documentation consists of:

- Return of the entry package to the importer, broker, or his authorized agent after merchandise is permitted release,

- Entry summary (CBP Form 7501),

- Other invoices and documents necessary to assess duties, collect statistics, or determine that all import requirements have been satisfied. This paper documentation can be reduced or eliminated by using features of the ABI.

B. Immediate Delivery

U.S. CUSTOMS AND BORDER PROTECTION, *IMPORTING INTO THE UNITED STATES, A GUIDE FOR COMMERCIAL EXPORTERS* 13-14 (November 2006)

An alternate procedure that provides for immediate release of a shipment may be used in some cases by applying for a special permit for immediate delivery on CBP Form 3461 prior to arrival of the merchandise. Carriers participating in the Automated Manifest System can receive conditional release authorizations after leaving the foreign country and up to five days before landing in the United States. If the application is approved, the shipment will be released expeditiously after it arrives. An entry summary must then be filed in proper form, either on paper or electronically, and estimated duties deposited within 10 working days of release. Immediate-delivery release using Form 3461 is limited to the following types of merchandise:

- Merchandise arriving from Canada or Mexico, if the port director approves it and an appropriate bond is on file,

- Fresh fruits and vegetables for human consumption arriving from Canada or Mexico and removed from the area immediately contiguous to the border and placed within the importer's premises within the port of importation,

- Shipments consigned to or for the account of any agency or officer of the U.S. government,

- Articles for a trade fair,

- Tariff-rate quota merchandise and, under certain circumstances, merchandise subject to an absolute quota. Absolute-quota items require a formal entry at all times,

- In very limited circumstances, merchandise released from warehouse followed within 10 days by a warehouse withdrawal for consumption,

- Merchandise specifically authorized by CBP Headquarters to be entitled to release for immediate delivery.

C. Entry for Warehouses

U.S. CUSTOMS AND BORDER PROTECTION,
IMPORTING INTO THE UNITED STATES, A GUIDE FOR COMMERCIAL EXPORTERS
14 (November 2006)

If one wishes to postpone release of the goods, they may be placed in a CBP bonded warehouse under a warehouse entry. The goods may remain in the bonded warehouse up to five years from the date of importation. At any time during that period, warehoused goods may be re-exported without paying duty, or they may be withdrawn for consumption upon paying duty at the duty rate in effect on the date of withdrawal. If the goods are destroyed under CBP supervision, no duty is payable.

While the goods are in the bonded warehouse, they may, under CBP supervision, be manipulated by cleaning, sorting, repacking, or otherwise changing their condition by processes that do not amount to manufacturing. After manipulation, and within the warehousing period, the goods may be exported without the payment of duty, or they may be withdrawn for consumption upon payment of duty at the rate applicable to the goods in their manipulated condition at the time of withdrawal. Perishable goods, explosive substances, or prohibited importations may not be placed in a bonded warehouse. Certain restricted articles, though not allowed release from custody, may be warehoused.

Information regarding bonded manufacturing warehouses is contained in section 311 of the *Tariff Act* [*of 1930*, as amended] (19 U.S.C. 1311). [Note there are several different classes of bonded warehouse, including a specific class for duty-free shops at airports and other ports of entry. Precisely what kind of economic activity can be done in a warehouse depends, in part, on the category of that warehouse.]

D. Transportation of Merchandise in Bond

U.S. CUSTOMS AND BORDER PROTECTION,
IMPORTING INTO THE UNITED STATES, A GUIDE FOR COMMERCIAL EXPORTERS
16-17 (November 2006)

Not all merchandise imported into the United States and intended for domestic commerce is entered at the port where it arrives. The importer may prefer to enter the goods at a different location in the United States, in which case the merchandise will have to be further transported to that location. In order to protect United States revenue in these cases, the merchandise must travel in a bonded status from the port of arrival to the intended port of entry. This process is referred to as *traveling under Immediate Transportation procedures* and is accomplished by the execution of CBP Form 7512 (Transportation Entry and Manifest of Goods Subject to CBP Inspection and Permit). The merchandise is then placed with a carrier who accepts it under its bond for transportation to the intended destination, where the normal merchandise entry process will occur.

E. Manufacturing in a Warehouse and the 1992 Tropicana Case

TROPICANA PRODUCTS, INC. v. UNITED STATES
United States Court of International Trade
789 F. Supp. 1154, 1155-1159 (1992), *aff'd without opinion*
983 F.2d 1001 (Fed. Cir. 1992)

NEWMAN, SENIOR DISTRICT JUDGE.

Introduction

Presented for determination is the dutiable status of frozen concentrated orange juice for manufacturing ("manufacturing concentrate") imported from Brazil in 1981 by Tropicana Products, Inc. ("Tropicana") and processed in its "Class 8" Customs bonded warehouse.

. . . The merchandise was entered at the port of Tampa, Florida in 1981, and after processing in and withdrawal from Tropicana's bonded warehouse was assessed with duties at the rate of 35 cents per gallon as "concentrated" fruit juices. . . .

The importer insists that . . . Customs should have classified the imports as "not concentrated" (their condition as withdrawn from bonded warehouse), dutiable . . . at the lower rate of 20 cents per gallon.

Under 19 U.S.C. § 1562 . . . with Customs' permission, imported goods may be entered in a bonded warehouse and "cleaned, sorted, repacked, or *otherwise changed in condition, but not manufactured*" (emphasis added). If the statute has been complied with, Customs must classify the imports in conformity with their condition as withdrawn from the warehouse rather than in their condition as they arrived in the United States.

On August 7, 1981 the Customs Service promulgated a ruling that Tropicana's bonded warehouse processing of its manufacturing concentrate was a "manufacture for purpose of 19 U.S.C. 1562 and is not a permissible manipulation." C.S.D. 82-24, 82 Cust. Bull. 713 (1982). Tropicana protested, [the] . . . protests were denied, and this action followed.

. . . .

Findings of Fact

. . . .

1. The manufacturing concentrate at issue was produced in Brazil by removing water from natural strength fresh juice extracted from oranges having a Brix value (measure of the concentration of soluble solids) of 11.8°, concentrating the juice to a Brix value of 65°, and then freezing the concentrate. [Brix, calibrated in degrees and symbolized by a small circle (°),

measures the concentration of dissolved solids in a liquid. In specific, it measures the mass ratio of dissolved sucrose, *i.e.*, sugar, to water in a particular fluid. For example, a liquid with a Brix value of 30° means that per 100 grams of solution, there are 30 grams of sugar and 70 grams of water. Brix value is used (*inter alia*) to measure the amount of sugar in fruit juices, soda, and wine. For instance, a fruit juice with 1° Brix value, which indicates 1-2 percent sugar by weight, is considered appropriately sweet.]

2. The frozen manufacturing concentrate was shipped to Tropicana in 55 gallon drums. When Tropicana's 65° Brix value manufacturing concentrate arrived at the port of entry, Tampa, Florida, its condition was concededly "concentrated" . . . .

3. The imports comprised identifiable lots of manufacturing concentrate with varying chemical characteristics affecting taste, such as Brix to acid ratios (a measure of the sweetness of the juice). . . .

. . . .

5. Unblended manufacturing concentrate is the basic orange juice raw material, which by blending of lots having different Brix to acid ratios and dilution (with treated water or single strength juice) to reduce the Brix value, several orange juice products are produced for the retail market: 41.8° Brix value frozen concentrated orange juice (from which a retail consumer makes a single strength orange juice by adding three cans of water to the retail package), and 11.8° Brix value orange juice from concentrate (a single strength juice consumed directly from the retail package without further dilution with water). . . .

6. Tropicana used the imported manufacturing concentrate to produce an 11.8° Brix value orange juice from concentrate for sale at retail in an essentially two phase production process, utilizing a bonded warehouse for the initial phase and unbonded facilities to complete the product for retail sale. The initial phase — processing in the bonded warehouse — is the focus of this case.

7. In the initial, or bonded warehouse, phase . . . Tropicana produced essentially an intermediate product, a 17.3° Brix value partially reconstituted precursor of the retail 11.8° Brix value orange juice from concentrate product. . . .

8. In producing the 17.3° Brix value precursor, Tropicana performed two distinct steps in its bonded warehouse — blending and dilution — which, if not independently, surely in combination, constituted "manufacturing" for purposes of § 1562:

    (a) *Blending*: After thawing the frozen imported concentrate to make it processable, Tropicana selected identifiable lots having varying Brix to acid ratios and other chemical composition characteristics for quality controlled blending to create the desired characteristics (flavor, density and sweetness, as measured by an index) of the end or finished product — orange juice from concentrate. When imported, these lots were distinguishable by color coded barrel tops. Typically two to ten lots were blended. Tropicana's assertion that this quality controlled blending to specification was simple, unsophisticated "mixing" is facetious.

(b) *Dilution*: In the second major phase of the bonded warehouse operations, domestically purchased water that was specially treated and filtered was added to be blended 65° Brix value manufacturing concentrate diluting its concentration to a Brix value of 17.3°, thus producing an intermediate stage partially reconstituted orange juice from concentrate precursor for further processing in Tropicana's unbonded facilities.

9. At the time of the entries in issue (1981), orange juice was classified by Customs under either of two items of the TSUS, dependent upon the Brix value of the imported product: [o]range juice having a Brix value 17.32° or less was classifiable as "not concentrated," dutiable under item 165.30; orange juice having a Brix value of more than 17.32° was classified as "concentrated," dutiable under item 165.35.

10. Tropicana's 17.3° Brix value precursor product withdrawn from its bonded warehouse was made to precise specifications and subjected to stringent quality controlled highly automated blending and dilution processes designed to accomplish *two objectives*: (1) duty reduction by conformance with the 17.32° Brix value threshold concentration for classification of the juice as "not concentrated" (item 165.30) when withdrawn from the bonded warehouse; and (2) compatibility of the intermediate 17.3° Brix product in the standard of quality and specifications for subsequent advancement to the 11.8° Brix retail orange juice from concentrate product.

11. Tropicana's bonded warehouse processing effected a fundamental change in the character and use of the imported manufacturing concentrate.

12. The 17.3° Brix value partially reconstituted product of the bonded warehouse was not a standard orange juice product or marketable by Tropicana, but required certain finishing operations. In Tropicana's unbonded facilities, the 17.3° precursor was further diluted with treated water to 11.8° Brix, ingredients of minor value (orange oils, and occasionally pulp and essences for flavoring) were added, the orange juice from concentrate was then Pasteurized, chilled and packaged for sale at retail.

Conclusions of Law and Discussion

1. Under the tariff provision captioned "Manipulation in warehouse," 19 U.S.C. § 1562, imported "merchandise may [with Customs' permission and supervision] be cleaned, sorted, repacked, or otherwise changed in condition, *but not manufactured*, in bonded warehouses" (emphasis added).

2. Except for scouring or carbonizing of wool, which § 1562 expressly excludes from the term "manufactured," the latter term was left undefined by Congress. The provisions of § 1562 have been administered by Customs for some 70 years and the agency has been regularly required to determine on a case by case basis whether a myriad of manipulations performed in bonded warehouses constitute "manufacturing." As used in § 1562, . . . the term "manufactured" has not previously been construed by the courts, and hence this case involves an issue of first impression.

3. Tropicana posits and defendant disputes that the "substantial transformation" test long applied by the courts to country of origin, drawback, Generalized System of Preferences and other tariff provisions should now be applied to construing the term "manufactured" in § 1562. Citing *National Juice Products Association v. United States* 628 F. Supp. 978 (1986) [excerpted above], . . . Tropicana argues that its bonded warehouse operations did not result in a "substantial transformation" of the imported merchandise and therefore it did not "manufacture" in its warehouse. Defendant and counsel for *Amicus Curiae* Florida Citrus Mutual, on the other hand, maintain that the "substantial transformation" test applied in *National Juice* for purposes of country-of-origin marking is inapplicable to the term "manufactured" as used in § 1562; and, even if applicable, there was a substantial transformation of the imports in the bonded warehouse. The court agrees, on both counts, with defendant's contentions.

4. "Substantial transformation is a concept of major importance in administering the customs and trade laws. ***: There must be transformation; a new and different article must emerge, 'having a distinctive name, character, or use.' The criteria of name, character and use continue to determine when substantial transformation has occurred ***." *Ferrostaal Metals Corp. v. United States*, 664 F. Supp. 535 (1987). . . .

5. The substantial transformation test itself may lead to differing results "where differences in statutory language and purpose are pertinent." *National Juice*. . . . "[C]ourts have been reluctant to lay down specific definitions in this area [manufacturing] other than to discuss the particular facts of cases *under the particular tariff provisions involved*." *Belcrest [Linens v. United States]*, 741 F.2d 1368 [(CAFC 1984)] (emphasis added). . . .

The short of the matter: the criterion of whether goods have been "manufactured" serves different purposes under different statutes, particularly § 1562 on the one hand and statutes concerned with country-of-origin marking, Generalized System of Preferences and drawback on the other; substantial transformation criteria cannot be applied indiscriminately in the identical manner across the entire spectrum of statutes for which it is necessary to determine whether merchandise has been "manufactured."

6. To interpret "manufacturing" — an expressly prohibited manipulation under § 1562 — as requiring a high threshold of transformation (*viz.*, a substantial transformation as stringently required in country of origin and drawback cases), would negate the evident legislative intent of the statute to permit only very minor or rudimentary manipulations in bonded warehouses — akin to the exemplars (cleaning, sorting and repacking). Hence, in the context of § 1562, the prohibited manipulation, manufacturing, may be contravened at a relatively low threshold of "transformation."

7. Acceptance of Tropicana's broadly expansive construction of a permissible "change in condition" under § 1562, coupled with its restrictive construction of prohibited "manufacturing" as contravened only at a substantial or high threshold of transformation, would make the statute's exemplar rudimentary manipulations (cleaned, sorted, repacked) meaningless.

8. While the term "manufactured" commonly connotes a "transformation" of an import to a "new and different article" *(Anheuser-Busch Brewing Assn.*

v. United States, 207 U.S. 556 (1908). . .), for purposes of the particular statute here under consideration a low threshold of transformation satisfies the meaning of "manufactured." . . .

9. For purposes of § 1562, merchandise may be "manufactured" even if transformation results in merely a material for further manufacture. . . .

10. "While to constitute an article a manufacture, it may be necessary to convert the article into an entirely different article, *it is only necessary that the article be so processed that it be removed from its crude or primary state, though it remain a variety of the original material, to be manufactured.*" *United States v. C.J. Tower & Sons*, 44 CCPA 1, C.A.D. 626 (1956) (emphasis added). . . .

11. Under § 1562, an intermediate material in process or precursor product resulting from a "transformation" of an imported raw material, although requiring further processing or fabrication to produce a finished article of commerce, may itself be regarded as "manufactured" for purposes of § 1562.

12. The fact that Tropicana's 17.3° Brix partially reconstituted orange juice from concentrate was a nonstandard and unmarketable product and not an "article of commerce," does not preclude "transformation" and thus manufacture of the imported manufacturing concentrate into a new article for purposes of § 1562. In tariff parlance, there is a fundamental differentiation between the terms "manufactured" and "manufactures of." The former describes a processing operation while the latter refers to a completed article of commerce.

13. Tropicana's duty-reduction motivation for its bonded warehouse processing of the manufacturing concentrate is neither proscribed by § 1562 nor any other provision of the tariff laws. In that connection, the court observes the fundamental right of an importer to so fashion his goods as to obtain the lowest possible rate of duty, absent any fraud, deception or artifice concerning the condition of the goods. . . .

14. Although under § 1562 the tariff classification of imported merchandise may be changed by permissible manipulations in a Customs bonded warehouse, an importer may not fashion his goods or change their condition in a bonded warehouse to obtain a lower rate of duty by impermissible manipulations. In this case, Tropicana "fashioned its merchandise" in its bonded warehouse by manufacturing, which is expressly prohibited.

15. Under the rule of *ejusdem generis* (where the statute's particular words of description are followed by general terms), the scope of permissible manipulations falling within the language "otherwise changed in condition," must be construed not only with reference to the immediately following qualifying language, "but not manufactured," but also in the context of the common characteristic of the statute's antecedent specific permissible exemplars, "cleaned, sorted, repacked." . . . The exemplars are, obviously, all very rudimentary forms of manipulation that do not alter the merchandise *per se*. Tropicana's bonded warehouse operations . . . are not literally, analogous to or *ejusdem generis* with "cleaned, sorted, repacked," and therefore are not within the scope of "otherwise changed in condition."

. . . .

Conclusion

Based on the record before the court, the particular language and evident purpose of § 1562, Tropicana's 17.3° Brix value product was "manufactured" in its Class 8 Customs bonded warehouse for purposes of § 1562, whether or not "substantially transformed" for purposes of country of origin marking, drawback, GSP and other unrelated statutory provisions. The imported merchandise was, therefore, properly assessed with duties at the rate of 35 cents per gallon as concentrated juices. . . .

V. FOREIGN TRADE ZONES

A. Nature and Supervision

The *Foreign Trade Zones Act of 1934*, as amended (19 U.S.C. §§ 81a-81u), authorizes the establishment of foreign trade zones (FTZs). An FTZ is a special, enclosed, secure area located within or adjacent to a U.S. port of entry. For example, an FTZ may be located at an industrial park or in a terminal warehouse facility. Its purpose is to attract and promote international trade transactions.

With certain exceptions, any foreign or domestic merchandise can be brought into a FTZ for a variety of purposes:

- Assembly
- Breaking up

- Cleaning
- Distribution
- Destruction
- Exhibition
- Grading
- Further manipulation or processing

- Manufacturing
- Mixing with foreign or domestic merchandise

- Repacking
- Sale
- Sorting
- Storage
- Testing

Indeed, in 1970 the United States Court of Appeals in *Armco Steel Corp. v. Stans*, 431 F.2d 779 (2d Cir. 1970), validated the use of FTZs for manufacturing in order to avoid customs duties. Foreign merchandise may be brought into an FTZ from overseas or from a bonded warehouse (though if it is transferred from a bonded warehouse, it must be re-exported, destroyed, or stored permanently in the FTZ, and cannot be imported into the United States customs territory). Significantly, it may remain in the FTZ for an unlimited period of time. There is no deadline for importing foreign merchandise in an FTZ into U.S. customs territory, or for re-exporting or destroying the merchandise.

Every officially designated U.S. port of entry is entitled to at least one FTZ. A corporation or political subdivision (*e.g.*, a state) may apply for permission to establish a "general purpose" FTZ or a "sub-zone." The application is reviewed by the Foreign Trade Zone Board, which consists of the Secretary of Commerce, who serves as the chairperson, and the Secretary of the Treasury. A general purpose FTZ allows more than one company to operate in the zone, whereas a sub-zone is used by an individual firm. Only a previous grantee of a general purpose FTZ can apply to establish a sub-zone. A sub-zone helps a firm that cannot take advantage of an existing general purpose FTZ because, for example, it cannot relocate its operations to the general purpose zone.

Thus, a general purpose FTZ must be within 60 miles or 90 minutes' driving time from the supervising office of the Customs Service. But, there is no such limit on a sub-zone. Indeed, typically sub-zones are located in the private facility of the individual user firm. In general, the Foreign Trade Zones Board approves applications to establish a general FTZ or sub-zone so long as the intended operations are not detrimental to the public interest. Unless local domestic industries or labor groups are sensitive to imports, an application is not controversial.

The CBP supervises the operation of FTZs. Specifically,

> CBP is responsible for activating foreign-trade zones, securing them, controlling dutiable merchandise moving in and out of them, protecting and collecting the revenue, assuring that there is no evasion or violation of U.S. laws and regulations governing imported and exported merchandise, and assuring that the zones program is free from terrorist activity.[15]

However, technically every FTZ is outside the customs territory of the U.S. for purposes of customs entry procedures. Therefore, foreign merchandise brought into a FTZ is not subject to a duty, quota, or formal entry procedure unless and until it is subsequently imported into the customs territory. In other words, the fundamental legal advantage associated with an FTZ is that foreign merchandise is brought into the zone without being subject to U.S. customs laws. (To be sure, the merchandise is subject to all other federal laws, *e.g.*, the *Food, Drug, and Cosmetic Act.*)

B. Privileged versus Non-Privileged Status

In respect of tariff treatment of foreign merchandise brought into an FTZ, CBP makes a critical threshold inquiry: is the merchandise "privileged" or "non-privileged"? The status of merchandise as privileged or non-privileged is relevant to its tariff treatment if and when it is subsequently imported into the U.S. The CBP renders a determination on the basis of an application filed by the importer of the merchandise. In general, only foreign merchandise that has not yet been manipulated or manufactured so as to effect a change in its HTS tariff classification is eligible for privileged status. In contrast, foreign merchandise in an FTZ that already has been manipulated or manufactured, recovered waste, and merchandise that no longer can be identified as domestic merchandise are deemed to be non-privileged foreign merchandise.

The CBP appraises and classifies foreign privileged merchandise when merchandise enters an FTZ. Accordingly, the importer of privileged merchandise pays a previously determined tariff when bringing the merchandise into U.S. customs territory. The fact the merchandise may have been manipulated,

---

[15] UNITED STATES CUSTOMS AND BORDER PROTECTION, IMPORTING INTO THE UNITED STATES 152 (2006).

even manufactured, in the FTZ does not alter the amount of the tariff for which the importer ultimately is liable, *i.e.*, any alteration or production of the privileged merchandise with other foreign privileged merchandise, or domestic merchandise, does not affect tariff liability. Simply put, privileged status means the rate of duty and tariff classification is frozen at the time, and based on the condition, of the merchandise when it is admitted to the FTZ. Subsequent work on the merchandise in the FTZ does not un-freeze the duty or classification, regardless of when the merchandise is withdrawn from the FTA and entered into the U.S. customs territory. (As intimated earlier, domestic merchandise — other than wine, beer, distilled spirits, and a few other items — can be taken into an FTZ and combined with, or made part of, other articles. As long as the identity of the domestic merchandise is maintained in accordance with CBP regulations, it can be returned to U.S. customs territory free of duty.) Consequently, the dutiable value of a finished product that is processed in an FTZ is the value attributable to the foreign components that entered and were used in the FTZ, not the value added in the FTZ.

Conversely, non-privileged merchandise (*e.g.*, merchandise composed entirely of foreign non-privileged or domestic merchandise, or of a combination of privileged and non-privileged merchandise) is appraised and classified by CBP when it is transferred out of an FTZ. Therefore, tariff owed on non-privileged merchandise depends on its classification and valuation when it is imported into the U.S. customs territory, not when it enters an FTZ.

C. Tariff Minimization and Other Advantages

Ultimately, election of privileged or non-privileged status is left to the importer. Typically, it makes the choice at the time of admitting goods into an FTZ. If the importer does not want privileged status for foreign merchandise, then it will not file an application for this status with CBP when it brings the merchandise into an FTZ. The flexibility afforded the importer is significant because it means the importer can pay duty either on components and raw materials, or on a completed article. That is, the FTZ allows the importer to minimize its duty liability — an obvious goal of every importer. Note, however, CBP may require certain commodities to be placed in privileged status because of a trade remedy at issue, such as an antidumping (AD) duty or countervailing duty (CVD).

Suppose an importer faces an inverted tariff, which is common with respect to high technology merchandise. An inverted tariff occurs when the tariff applicable to components or raw materials is higher than the duty on a completed article. The importer can minimize its tariff liability by (1) bringing higher-duty foreign components into an FTZ, (2) not filing an application for privileged status with the Customs Service, and (3) manufacturing or assembling the higher-duty components in the FTZ into a lower-duty product.

There is another way in which an importer of foreign merchandise may save money by using an FTZ. When merchandise enters a FTZ, it may contain moisture, dirt, or broken contents. If the merchandise were imported directly into U.S. customs territory, then these imperfections might lead to a higher tariff bill — for example, because they increase the amount (in terms of weight or volume) of the shipment. While in an FTZ, drying, evaporation, cleaning, and so forth can occur. In addition, the ultimate purchaser of the merchandise may complain, and the importer might have to provide the buyer with replacement merchandise. In contrast, while in the FTZ, the importer can remove imperfections in its merchandise and, possibly, avoid such problems.

In addition to minimizing tariff liability, FTZs serve four further purposes. First (as indicated at the outset), they expedite and encourage foreign commerce. For instance, an importer (or foreign exporter) that plans to begin or expand operations in the U.S. might bring its merchandise into an FTZ and await the development of a favorable market in the country. By bringing the merchandise to the threshold of the American market, the importer ensures it can deliver the merchandise to buyers immediately, thereby avoiding the risk that buyers might cancel their purchase orders owing to shipping delays. (This same advantage exists with respect to merchandise destined ultimately for a nearby country, say Canada or Mexico.) Further-more, FTZs encourage importers to market foreign merchandise.

Second, FTZs facilitate marketing. An importer may display merchandise within an FTZ for the benefit of interested buyers. That is, exhibiting merchandise within an FTZ for an unlimited time period, with no requirement of exportation or duty payment, is permitted. (The merchandise exhibited is held under a bond posted by the exhibit operator.) Retail trade is prohibited, but the importer may sell from stock in the FTZ in wholesale quantities.

Third, FTZs promote assembly and manufacturing operations in the U.S. In turn, American workers are employed in such operations. In fact, in 1996 Congress amended the *Foreign Trade Zones Act* (via the *Miscellaneous Trade and Technical Corrections Act*, Pub. L. 104-295) to permit deferral of payment of duty on certain production equipment admitted into an FTZ. (Technically, merchandise imported into an FTZ that is to be used therein, such as production equipment or construction materials, must be entered for consumption before it is taken into the FTZ. Accordingly, without the amendment, tariffs would be owed.) The tariff on imported production equipment and components installed in an FTZ is not due until the equipment and components are ready to be placed into use for production. Consequently, a manufacturer can assemble, install, and test the equipment and components before duties are owed — thus encouraging production in the FTZ.

Fourth, suppose a finished product is made for the American market from foreign and domestic components. Conducting assembly or manufacturing operations in a FTZ means there is no need to bear costs (*e.g.*, freight) and risks (*e.g.*, loss, damage, or delay, or political risk) of shipping domestic components to an overseas production facility.

Judging from the number of FTZs, it appears these purposes have been served. In 1970 there were 7 general purpose FTZs and 3 sub-zones. By 1987, there were 138 general purpose FTZs, and 101 sub-zones. As of 2007, there were 250 general purpose FTZs and 450 sub-zones. However, with respect to all of the aforementioned advantages, query what benefits exist from an FTZ for goods originating in a country with which the U.S. has a free trade agreement (FTA)?

Notably, Kansas City is one of the largest zone operators, in the country, with over 17.6 million square feet. Kansas City is a distributed zone, which includes several zones and sub-zones in the area. The Kansas City trade zone handles more volume than the FTZs of Chicago, Dallas, Denver, Minneapolis, and St. Louis. Among the companies with warehouses in the Kansas City FTZ are Bayer, Ford, Kawasaki, Midwest Quality Gloves, Pfizer, and Yulshin USA.

Chapter 17
TARIFF CLASSIFICATION

In spite of significant progress in recent years and the dazzling success stories of open markets and free trade exemplified by Hong Kong and Singapore, the march toward worldwide free trade has had its stumbling blocks. Old habits die hard; protectionism dates back centuries and of course exists today. Customs administrations in many countries represent the first and last line of defense for those who would sacrifice the economic prosperity brought about by free trade for the apparent short-term gain of protecting uncompetitive industries.

—MICHAEL H. LANE, CUSTOMS MODERNIZATION AND THE
INTERNATIONAL TRADE SUPERHIGHWAY x (1998)

DOCUMENTS SUPPLEMENT ASSIGNMENT

1. *Havana Charter* Articles 33, 35-37

2. GATT Article VII

3. *General Rules of Interpretation for the Harmonized Tariff Schedule (GRI)*

4. *NAFTA* Chapter 5

5. Relevant provisions in other FTAs

I. THE HARMONIZED SYSTEM

HOUSE COMMITTEE ON WAYS AND MEANS, 109th CONGRESS, 1st SESSION, *OVERVIEW AND COMPILATION OF U.S. TRADE STATUTES*
Part I, 1-3 (Committee Print, June 2005)

Historical Background

The Harmonized Tariff Schedule of the United States (HTS [or HTSUS]) was enacted by subtitle B of title I of the *Omnibus Trade and Competitiveness Act of 1988* [Public Law 100-418, approved 23 August 1988] and became effective on January 1, 1989 [via Presidential Proclamation Number 5911, 19 November 1988]. The HTS replaced the Tariff Schedules of the United States (TSUS), enacted as Title I of the *Tariff Act of 1930* (19 U.S.C. 1202) by the *Tariff Classification Act of 1962* [Public Law 87-456, approved 24 May 1962]; the TSUS had been in effect since August 31, 1963. [For a pre-Uruguay Round discussion of the TSUS and HTS, see Peggy Chaplin, *An Introduction to the Harmonized System*, 12 NORTH CAROLINA JOURNAL OF INTERNATIONAL LAW & COMMERCIAL REGULATION 417 (1987).]

The HTS is based upon the internationally adopted Harmonized Commodity Description and Coding System (known as the Harmonized System or HS) of the Customs Cooperation Council [now World Customs Organization, or WCO]. Incorporated into a multilateral convention effective as of January 1, 1988, the HS was derived from the earlier Customs Cooperation Council Nomenclature, which in turn was a new version of the older Brussels Tariff Nomenclature. The HS is an up-to-date, detailed nomenclature structure intended to be utilized by contracting parties as the basis for their tariff, statistical, and transport documentation programs.

The United States did not adopt either of the two previous nomenclatures but, because it was a party to the convention creating the Council, and because of the potential benefits from using a modern, widely adopted nomenclature, became involved in the technical work to develop the HS. Section 608(c) of the *Trade Act of 1974* [Public Law 93-618, approved 3 January 1975] directed the U.S. International Trade Commission (ITC) to investigate the principles and concepts which should underlie such an international nomenclature and to participate fully in the Council's technical work on the HS. The ITC, Customs and Border Protection (which represents the United States at the Council), and other agencies were involved in this work through the mid-and late-1970's; in 1981, the President requested that the ITC prepare a draft conversion of the U.S. tariff into the nomenclature format of the HS, even as the international efforts to complete the nomenclature continued. The Commission's report and converted tariff were issued in June 1983. After considerable review and the receipt of comments from interested parties, legislation to repeal the TSUS and replace it with the HTS was introduced. Following the August 23, 1988 enactment of the *Omnibus Trade and Competitiveness Act*, the United States became a party to the HS Convention, joining over 75 other major trading partners.

Structure of the HTS

Under the HS Convention, the contracting parties are obliged to base their import and export schedules on the HS nomenclature, but the rates of duty are set by each contracting party. The HS is organized into 21 sections and 96 Chapters, with accompanying general interpretive rules [*i.e.*, the General Rules of Interpretation, or GRI] and legal notes. [In studying the HS, consider what status the GRI and legal notes have in a domestic legal setting, such as in U.S. litigation.] Goods in trade are assigned in the system, in general, to categories beginning with crude and natural products and continue in further degrees of complexity through advanced manufactured goods. These product headings are designated, at the broadest coverage level, with 4-digit numerical codes and are further subdivided into narrower categories assigned 2 additional digits. The contracting parties must employ all 4-and 6-digit provisions and all international rules and notes without deviation; they may also adopt still narrower subcategories and additional notes for national purposes, and they determine all rates of duty. Thus, a common product description and numbering system to the 6-digit level of detail exists for all contracting parties, facilitating international trade in goods. Two final Chapters, 98 and 99, are reserved for national use (Chapter 77 is reserved for future international use).

The HTS therefore sets forth all the international nomenclature through the 6-digit level and, where needed, contains added subdivisions assigned 2 more digits, for a total of 8 at the tariff-rate line (legal) level. Two final (non-legal) digits are assigned as statistical reporting numbers where further statistical detail is needed (for a total of 10 digits to be listed on entries). Chapter 98 comprises special classification provisions (former TSUS schedule 8), and Chapter 99 (former appendix to the TSUS) contains temporary modifications pursuant to legislation or to presidential action.

Each Section's Chapters contain numerous 4-digit headings (which may, when followed by 4 zeroes, serve as U.S duty rate lines) and 6-and 8-digit subheadings. Additional U.S. notes may appear after HS notes in a Chapter or Section. Most of the general headnotes of the former TSUS appear as general notes to the HTS set forth before Chapter 1, along with notes covering more recent trade programs (and the non-legal statistical notes). These notes contain definitions or rules on the scope of the pertinent provisions, or set additional requirements for classification purposes. In addition, the HTS contains a table of contents, an index, footnotes, and other administrative material, which are provided for ease of reference and, along with the statistical reporting provisions, have no legal significance or effect.

The HTS is not published as a part of the statutes and regulations of the United States, but is instead subsumed in a document produced and updated regularly by the ITC entitled "Harmonized Tariff Schedule of the United States: Annotated for Statistical Reporting Purposes." Changes in the TSUS became so frequent and voluminous that its inclusion in title 19 of the U.S. Code effectively ceased with the 1979 supplement to the 1976 edition. The Commission is charged by section 1207 of the *1988 Omnibus Trade and Competitiveness Act* (19 U.S.C. 3007) with the responsibility of compiling and publishing, "at appropriate intervals," and keeping up to date the HTS and any related materials. The initial document appeared as USITC Publication 2030. That document, and subsequent issuances, have included both the current legal text of the HTS and all statistical provisions adopted under section 484(f) of the *Tariff Act of 1930* (19 U.S.C. 1484(f)). It is presented as a looseleaf publication so that pages being issued in supplements to modify the Schedule's basic edition for any year edition may be inserted as replacements. Two or more supplements may appear between the publication of each basic edition.

Unlike the TSUS, which applied exclusively to imported goods, the HTS can, for almost all goods, be used to document both imports and exports, with a small number of exceptions enumerated before Chapter 1, which require particular exports to be reported under Schedule B provisions. That Schedule, which prior to 1989 served as the means of reporting all exports, has been converted to the HS nomenclature structure. For certain goods that are significant U.S. exports, variations in the desired product description and detail compel the use of Schedule B reporting provisions that cannot be accommodated in the HTS under the international nomenclature structure.

[There is a critical conceptual, and often practical, distinction between a bound tariff and an applied tariff. Does the HTS contain bound or actual rates? What document contains the bound rates to which WTO Members have agreed through multilateral trade negotiations?]

II. READING A TARIFF SCHEDULE

HOUSE COMMITTEE ON WAYS AND MEANS, 109th CONGRESS, 1st SESSION, *OVERVIEW AND COMPILATION OF U.S. TRADE STATUTES*
Part I, 3-10 (Committee Print, June 2005)

The HTS, like its predecessor the TSUS, is presented in a tabular format containing 7 columns, each with a particular type of information. A sample page of the HTS is set forth [below]. . . . [As originally reprinted by the Ways and Means Committee, the Table erroneously omitted the columns found in the actual HTS. The Table reproduced here, taken from the HTS, includes the columns found therein.]

The first column, entitled "Heading/Subheading," sets forth the 4-, 6-, or 8-digit number assigned to the class of goods described to its right. It should be recalled that 8-digit-level provisions bear the only numerical codes at the legal level which are determined solely by the United States, because the 4- and 6-digit designators are part of the international convention.

The second column is labeled "Stat. Suffix," meaning statistical suffix. Wherever a tariff rate line is annotated to permit collection of trade data on narrower classes of merchandise, the provisions adopted administratively by an interagency committee under Section 484(f) of the *1930 Act* (19 U.S.C. 1484(f)) are given 2 more digits which must be included on the entry filed with Customs officials. Where no annotations exist, 2 additional zeroes are added to the 8-digit legal code applicable to the goods in question. The goods falling in all 10-digit statistical reporting numbers of a particular 8-digit legal provision receive the same duty treatment. The third column, "Article Description," contains the detailed description of the goods falling within each tariff provision and statistical reporting number.

The third column, "Article Description," contains the detailed description of the goods falling within each tariff provision and statistical reporting number.

In the fourth column, "Units of Quantity," the unit of measure in which the goods in question are to be reported for statistical purposes is set forth. These units are administratively determined under Section 484(f) of the *Tariff Act of 1930*. In many instances, the unit of quantity is also the basis for the assessment of the duty. For many categories of products, two or three different figures in different units must be reported (*e.g.*, for some textiles, weight and square meters; for some apparel, the number of garments, value, and weight), with the second unit of quantity frequently being the basis for administering a measure regulating imports, such as a quota. If an "X" appears in this column, only the value of the shipment must be reported.

The remaining columns appear under the common heading "Rates of Duty" and are designated as Column 1 (subdivided into "General" and "Special" sub-columns) and Column 2. These Columns contain the various rates of duty that apply to the goods of the pertinent legal provision, depending on the source of the goods and other criteria. Their application to goods originating in particular countries is discussed below under the heading "Applicable duty treatment."

Harmonized Tariff Schedule of the United States (2005)
Annotated for Statistical Reporting Purposes

Heading/ Subheading	Stat. Suffix	Article Description	Units of Quantity	Rates of Duty		
				1		2
				General	Special	
		I. PRIMARY MATERIALS; PRODUCTS IN GRANULAR OR POWDER FORM				
7201	00	Pig iron and spiegeleisen in pigs, blocks or other primary forms:				
7201.10.00	00	Nonalloy pig iron containing by weight 0.5 percent or less of phosphorus.............	t...........	Free		$1.11/t
7201.20.00	00	Nonalloy pig iron containing by weight more than 0.5 percent of phosphorus..........	t...........	Free		$1.11/t
7201.50	00	Alloy pig iron; spiegeleisen:				
7201.50.30	00	Alloy pig iron......	t...........	Free		$1.11/t
7201.50.60	00	Spiegeleisen.......	t...........	Free		0.5%
7202	00	Ferroalloys:				
		Ferromanganese:				
7202.11	00	Containing by weight more than 2 percent of carbon:				
7202.11.10	00	Containing by weight more than 2 percent but not more than 4 percent of carbon......	kg........ Mn kg	1.4%	Free (A, AU, CA, CL, E, IL, J, JO, MX, SG)	6.5%

A rate of duty generally has one of three forms: *ad valorem*, specific, or compound. An *ad valorem* rate of duty is expressed in terms of a percentage to be assessed upon the customs value of the goods in question. A specific rate is expressed in terms of a stated amount payable on some quantity of the imported goods, such as 17 cents per kilogram. Compound duty rates combine both *ad valorem* and specific components (such as 5 percent *ad valorem* plus 17 cents per kilogram).

Chapter 98 comprises special classification provisions permitting, in specified circumstances, duty-free entry or partial duty-free entry of goods which would otherwise be subject to duty. The article descriptions in the provisions of this Chapter enunciate the circumstances in which goods are eligible for this duty treatment. Some of the goods eligible for such duty treatment include: articles re-imported after having been exported from the United States; goods subject to personal exemptions (such as those for returning U.S. residents); government importations; goods for religious, educational, scientific, or other qualifying institutions; samples; and articles admitted under bond.

Chapter 99 contains temporary modifications of the duty treatment of specified articles in the other chapters. Additional duties and suspensions or reductions of duties enacted by Congress are included, as are temporary modifications (increases or decreases in duty rates) and import restrictions (quotas, import fees, and so forth) proclaimed by the President under trade agreements or pursuant to legislation. Separate sub-chapters contain temporary special duty treatment for certain goods of countries having a free trade agreement with the United States. However, antidumping and countervailing duties imposed under the authority of the *Tariff Act of 1930*, as amended [to eliminate the unfair advantage of under-priced or subsidized imports, respectively] are not included and are instead announced in the *Federal Register*.

Applicable Duty Treatment

Column 1 — General. — The rates of duty appearing in the "General" sub-column of Column 1 of the HTS are imposed on products of countries that have been extended normal trade relations (NTR), which was previously called most-favored-nation (MFN) or non-discriminatory trade treatment, by the United States, unless such imports are claimed to be eligible for treatment under one of the preferential tariff schemes discussed below. The general duty rates are concessional and have been set through reductions of full statutory rates in negotiations with other countries, generally under the GATT and the WTO.

Column 1 — Special. — General Note 3 to the HTS sets forth the special tariff treatment afforded to covered products of designated countries or under specified measures. These programs and the corresponding symbols by which they are indicated in the "Special" sub-column, along with the appropriate rates of duty, are as follows:

Generalized System of Preferences (GSP) . . . . . . A, A*, or A+
United States — Australia Free Trade Agreement . . . . . . AU
Automotive Products Trade Act [of 1965, between the
    U.S. and Canada, Public Law 89-283, 19 U.S.C.
    Sections 2001 *et seq.*] . . . . . . B
Agreement on Trade in Civil Aircraft C
North American Free Trade Agreement:
                    Goods of Canada, under
                        the terms of General Note
                        12 to this Schedule . . . . . . CA
                    Goods of Mexico, under the
                        terms of General Note 12

to this Schedule	. . . . . .	MX
African Growth and Opportunity Act	. . . . . .	D
United States — Chile Free Trade Agreement	. . . . . .	CL
Caribbean Basin Economic Recovery Act[CBERA]	. . . . . .	E or E*
United States — Israel Free Trade Area	. . . . . .	IL
Andean Trade Preference Act [ATPA] or Andean Trade		
Promotion and Drug Eradication Act	. . . . . .	J, J*, or J+
United States — Jordan Free Trade Area		
Implementation Act	. . . . . .	JO
Agreement on Trade in Pharmaceutical Products	. . . . . .	K
Uruguay Round Concessions on Intermediate		
Chemicals for Dyes	. . . . . .	L
United States — Caribbean Basin Trade		
Partnership Act	. . . . . .	R
United States — Singapore Free Trade Agreement	. . . . . .	SG

[Note that in light of recent FTAs, the designation "BH" refers to the *U.S. — Bahrain FTA*, "MA" refers to the *U.S. — Morocco FTA*, and "P" or "P+" refers to the *Central American Free Trade Agreement* (including the Dominican Republic).]

The presence of one or more of these symbols indicates the eligibility of the described articles under the respective program. In the case of the GSP (when in effect), a symbol followed by an asterisk indicates that, although the described articles are generally eligible for duty-free entry, such tariff treatment does not apply to products of the designated beneficiary countries specified in General Note 4(d). In the case of *CBERA* and the *ATPA*, the asterisk indicates that some of the described articles are ineligible for duty-free entry. [It is the duty of the importer to show eligibility for a conditional exemption from tariff liability based on one of these programs.] . . .

Column 2. — The Column 2 rates of duty apply to products of countries that have been denied NTR status by the United States (see General Note 3(b)) [namely, Cuba and North Korea]; these rates are the full statutory rates, generally as originally enacted through the *Tariff Act of 1930* [*i.e.*, the highly restrictive Smoot-Hawley tariffs]. . . .

[Is Iran a Column 1 or 2 country? President Bill Clinton's Executive Order Number 13059 of 19 August 1997 confirmed that virtually all trade and investment with Iran by United States persons was banned. In March 2000, the Clinton Administration eased trade sanctions on Iran to allow imports of carpets and food products, including dried fruits, nuts, and caviar. Actual or prospective importers needed to know whether Iran was a Column 2 country.

Whether Iranian products get Column 1 or 2 treatment appears (as of March 2007) to depend on which part of the U.S. government is asked. For CBP, Iran is a Column 1 country. Iran does not appear in General Note 3(b) to the HTS. Moreover, in a ruling on pistachios, CBP informed a California-based importer the applicable rate of duty is a Column 1 rate, namely, 0.9 cents per kilo for in-shell pistachios (HTS 0802.50.20), and 1.9 cents per kilo for shelled pistachios (HTS 0802.50.40). *See* Letter from Robert B. Swierupski, Director, National Commodity Specialist Division, United States Customs and Border

Protection to Mr. Ahmad Foroutan Zymex Industries, Inc., dated 19 December 2005, Index Number NY L88981, available at http://rulings.customs.gov.

However, for the International Trade Administration (ITA) division of the Department of Commerce (DOC), Iran is a Column 2 country. In a Sunset Review of an antidumping (AD) order on raw, in-shell pistachios from Iran, the DOC states the 2005 tariff rate for in-shell pistachios from Iran is the Column 2 duty. The DOC observes (in footnote 5 to Table I-4) that Column 2 rates "appl[y] to imports from a small number of countries that do not enjoy normal trade relations duty status, applicable to imports from Iran." The Column 2 rate is 5.5 cents per kilo. *See* United States International Trade Commission, Investigation No. 731-TA-287 (Review) (Publication No. 3824, December 2005.]

Special Duty Exemptions and Preferences

Certain notable provisions in Chapter 98 of the HTS grant duty-free entry to various categories of American goods returned from abroad and allow U.S. tourists to import foreign articles free of duty. Other provisions in the General Notes of the HTS provide duty-free treatment to imports from the U.S. insular possessions, to imports of Canadian auto products under the *Automotive Products Trade Act*, and to articles imported for use in civil aircraft under the [plurilateral WTO] *Agreement on Trade in Civil Aircraft*.

American goods returned (HTS subheading 9801.00.10). — American goods not advanced or improved abroad may be returned to the United States free of duty under HTS subheading 9801.00.10. The courts have interpreted this provision to allow duty-free entry of American goods which had been exported for sorting, separating (*e.g.*, by grade, color, size, etc.), culling out, and discarding defective items and repackaging in certain containers, so long as the goods themselves were not advanced in value or improved in condition while abroad.

American goods repaired or altered abroad (HTS subheading 9802.00.40). — HTS subheading 9802.00.40 provides that goods exported from the United States for repairs or alterations abroad are subject to duty upon their re-importation into the United States (at the duty rate applicable to the imported article) only upon the value of such repairs or alterations. The provision applies to processing such as restoration, renovation, adjustment, cleaning, correction of manufacturing defects, or similar treatment that changes the condition of the exported article, but does not change its essential character. The value of the repairs or processing for purposes of assessing duties is generally determined, in accordance with U.S. Note 3 to sub-chapter II of Chapter 98, by —

(1) the cost of the repairs or alterations to the importer; or

(2) if no change is made, the value of the repairs or alterations, as set out in the customs entry.

However, if the customs officer finds that the amount shown in the entry document is not reasonable, the value of the repairs or alterations will be determined in accordance with the valuation standards set out in Section 402 of the *Tariff Act of 1930*, as amended [19 U.S.C. § 1401a].

. . . .

American components assembled abroad (HTS subheading 9802.00.80).
— Articles assembled abroad from American-made components may be
exempt from duty on the value of such components when the assembled article
is imported into the United States under HTS subheading 9802.00.80. This
provision enables American manufacturers of relatively labor-intensive products to take advantage of low-cost labor and fiscal incentives in other countries
[usually developing or least developed countries] by exporting American parts
for assembly in such countries and returning the assembled products to the
United States, with partial exemption from U.S. duties. [The *maquiladora*
plants along the U.S. — Mexico border are a prime example.]

Subheading 9802.00.80 applies to articles assembled abroad in whole or in
part of fabricated components, the product of the United States, which —

> (1)   were exported in condition ready for assembly without further
>   fabrication;
>
> (2)   have not lost their physical identity in such articles by change in
>   form, shape, or otherwise; and
>
> (3)   have not been advanced in value or improved in condition abroad,
>   except by being assembled and by operations incidental to the
>   assembly process such as cleaning, lubricating, and painting.

The exported articles used in the imported goods must be fabricated U.S.
components, *i.e.*, U.S.-manufactured articles ready for assembly in their exported condition, except for operations incidental to the assembly process.
Integrated circuits, compressors, zippers, and precut sections of a garment are
examples of fabricated components, but uncut bolts of cloth, lumber, sheet
metal, leather, and other materials exported in basic shapes and forms are
not considered to be fabricated components for this purpose.

To be considered U.S. components, the exported articles do not necessarily
need to be fabricated from articles or materials wholly produced in the United
States. If a foreign article or material undergoes a manufacturing process in
the United States resulting in its "substantial transformation" into a new and
different article [*i.e.*, having a distinctive name, character, or use], then the
component that emerges may qualify as an exported product of the United
States for purposes of subheading 9802.00.80.

The assembly operations performed abroad can involve any method used
to join solid components together, such as welding, soldering, gluing, sewing,
or fastening with nuts and bolts. Mixing, blending, or otherwise combining
liquids, gases, chemicals, food ingredients, and amorphous solids with each
other or with solid components is not regarded as "assembling" for purposes
of subheading 9802.00.80. Special rules apply to certain goods receiving
preferential benefits under the *African Growth and Opportunity Act*, the
Caribbean Basin Trade Partnership Act, and the *Andean Trade Promotion and
Drug Eradication Act*. . . .

The rate of duty that applies to the dutiable portion of an assembled article
is the same rate that would apply to the imported article. The assembled
article is also treated as being entirely of foreign origin for purposes of any

import quota or similar restriction applicable to that class of merchandise, and for purposes of country-of-origin marking requirements. . . .

An article imported under subheading 9802.00.80 is treated as a foreign article for appraisement purposes. That is, the full appraised value of the article must first be determined under the usual appraisement provisions. The dutiable value, however, is determined by deducting the cost or value of the American-made fabricated components from the appraised value of the assembled merchandise entered under subheading 9802.00.80.

Personal (tourist) exemption. — Sub-chapter IV of Chapter 98 of the HTS sets forth various personal exemptions for residents and nonresidents that arrive in the United States from abroad. The relevant customs regulations are set forth at 19 CFR 148 *et seq.* In particular, HTS subheading 9804.00.65 provides that U.S. residents returning from a journey abroad may import up to $800 of articles free of duty, an increase from $400 recently made in the *Trade Act of 2002* (Public Law 107-210). [A lower threshold applies to nonresidents entering the U.S.] The articles must be for personal or household use and may include not more than 1 liter of alcoholic beverages, not more than 200 cigarettes, and not more than 100 cigars.

[The personal exemption presumes articles are carried by the returning U.S. citizen or resident. Goods imported separately go through the usual customs clearance process. The $800 exemption applies on a per person basis, hence a family of three traveling together is entitled to a $2,400 exemption. Moreover, the tariff rate on the first $1,000 in excess of the exemption amount is a flat 10 percent. So, for instance, an individual bringing a rug from Turkey worth $1,100 would pay a tariff $70 (10 percent times the difference between $1,100 and $400). Finally, as any American who has returned from abroad knows, a declaration of the value of articles bought overseas and carried back is made on a Customs Declaration Form with the cheerful heading "Welcome to the United States." Failure to make a truthful declaration can lead to civil and criminal penalties.]

III. CLASSIFICATION METHODOLOGIES

A. The Duty Owed Formula

As regards the payment of tariffs, there are two essential steps an importer undertakes with respect to imported merchandise: classification and valuation. Classification is the process whereby the article is placed in the correct HTS category. There are approximately 5,000 articles described by headings (identified by 4 digits) or sub-headings (identified by 6 digits) in the first 96 of the 98 Chapters of the HTS. A particular tariff is associated with each heading and sub-heading. Hence, classification is essential in order to determine the tariff applicable to the article.

Naturally, classification assumes familiarity with the HTS. That requirement is not as demanding as it seems, despite the size of the HTS. An importer engaged in trading particular merchandise ought to, and typically does, know all of the potentially relevant classifications for the merchandise. Moreover, the importer always has the option of utilizing the services of a customs broker for assistance in clearing shipments.

Valuation is the process of appraising the value of the article. In the case of *ad valorem* duty rates, the tariff is applied to this value. Thus, the process of establishing the duty owed is determined by the following simple arithmetic formula:

Duty Owed = [Tariff Applicable to Article Properly Classified]
         ×
        [Value of Article]

The first term on the right-hand side of the equation is established by properly classifying the article in the HTS. That classification yields an *ad valorem*, specific, or hybrid duty. The second right-hand term is established by an appropriate valuation method, which in most cases, is the transaction value — in effect, the commercial invoice price.

An important practice tip is that "if in doubt, ask." CBP provides a wealth of information on request concerning the classification and valuation process. Moreover, it is possible to obtain an "advance ruling" from CBP, essentially by setting forth the relevant facts and asking how it would treat the matter in question.

As intimated, classification and valuation are — at least initially — the responsibility of the importer, not CBP. Indeed, allocating the responsibility in this manner reflects a policy known as "informed compliance." To be sure, there are instances in which CBP may question an importer's declarations in the entry documents filed by the importer. The importer will then be put to the test as to the classification, valuation, and possibly even the country of origin of the merchandise.

First, the importer may be a "newcomer," one unbeknownst to the CBP. There is no track record of dealings between the customs officials at the local port of entry and this importer. Hence, there is no basis for trusting the importer's declaration.

Second, the importer may fit a "profile" developed by CBP, possibly in cooperation with domestic and foreign law enforcement and intelligence agencies, of international traders whose merchandise should be checked. The profile may reflect the ongoing effort to interdict shipments of unlawful goods (namely, narcotics), combat illegal trans-shipments (*e.g.*, of textiles), and fight terrorism. Perhaps a particular importer is a rather suspicious character or company. Or, perhaps the importer may be bringing in goods from a suspicious country. In either event, CBP is likely to question the importer's declarations. Your Casebook author ostensibly fit into the second category when he returned from Burma (Myanmar). That country, along with Laos and Thailand, is part of the infamous "Golden Triangle," from which a large percentage of certain drugs (*e.g.*, heroin) come. Carrying several bottles of pills reinforced the profile, even though they were filled with salubrious — and legal — herbs like gingko and ginseng. It took about an hour to sort matters out.

B. The General Rules of Interpretation

Conceptually, an article may be classified in the HTS in one of four different ways. That is, the HS — and, in turn, the HTS — relies on four kinds of provisions to classify merchandise:

1. a general description;

2. an *eo nominee* description (*i.e.*, a description according to the commonly used name of the article);

3. a description according to component material; or

4. a description by actual or principal use (*i.e.*, a description that includes reference to how the article is used).

The HTS General Rules of Interpretation (GRI) are used to help place an article in the proper classification.

Rule 1 of the GRI states that headings (*i.e.*, the 4 digit HTS categories), and sub-headings (*i.e.*, the 6 digit HTS categories), not titles of chapters, sub-chapters, or sections, should be used to classify and article. For instance, Chapter 62 of the HTS is entitled "Articles of Apparel and Clothing Accessories, Not Knitted or Crocheted." This rubric is irrelevant with respect to classifying coats.

The traditional label for Rule 2(a) of the GRI is the "Doctrine of the Entireties." Under this Doctrine, reference to an article in an HTS heading (or sub-heading) includes three forms of that article, namely, the:

1. complete, finished, and assembled form of the article;

2. complete, finished form of the article that is unassembled or disassembled; and

3. incomplete, unfinished form of the article where this form has the "essential character" of the complete, finished article.

Consider, for example, heading 6201 is "men's or boy's overcoats, carcoats, capes, cloaks, anoraks (including ski-jackets), windbreakers and similar articles (including padded, sleeveless jackets), other than those of heading 6203 [which covers suits and blazers]."

Suppose L.L. Bean imports men's parkas from Canada. The parkas are down-filled and have four pockets. Plainly, this heading covers the imported parkas if they arrive in complete, finished, and assembled form. The heading also covers the parkas if each parka is imported in three pieces — namely, two arms and a body — and the pieces subsequently are assembled at an L.L. Bean factory in Freeport, Maine. Finally, this heading should cover the parkas even if they are imported into the U.S. without the down filling or pockets and the filling is injected, and pockets attached, later in the factory. Arguably, the incomplete, unfinished items have the essential character of a parka. After all, there is no other conceivable use for the items. Note that anoraks, including ski-jackets of man-made fibers "[c]ontaining 15 percent or more by weight of down and waterfowl plumage and of which down comprises 35 percent or more by weight" is HTS item 6201.93.10. This article carries a bound rate of duty of 4.4 percent. The pre-Uruguay Round rate was 4.7 percent.

The Doctrine of the Entireties is important because it prevents an importer from structuring the way in which it imports articles to avoid a tariff that should logically apply. Structuring could take the form of importing components of the article and assembling them in the U.S. to take advantage of lower tariffs on the components than the assembled article. It could also take the form of deliberately omitting a component (or a few components) from the article in order to remove the article from a higher-tariff category and place it in a lower tariff category. In both cases, the complete, finished, and assembled form of the article is apparent from the items that are imported. Neither the lack of assembly nor a missing component should defeat an otherwise appropriate tariff classification.

Rule 2(b) of the GRI indicates that a reference in the HTS to an article of a given material or substance includes reference to an article that consists wholly or partly of such material or substance. Thus, both a "pure" and "mixed" (i.e., "composite") article is covered by the heading. Consider HTS item 6201.93, which is anoraks including ski jackets, of man-made fibers. This item covers anoraks that are wholly or partly of man-made fibers. Here, the Rule serves to prevent structuring the composition of an article to avoid an otherwise appropriate classification.

What if an article can be placed in two or more HTS classifications? GRI Rules 3 and 4 of the GRI address this issue. It is of immense practical importance when different tariffs are specified for the various relevant classifications. Rules 3 and 4 contain four tools for choosing the correct classification. These tools are to be used *in seriatim*. The first tool, Rule 3(a), is traditionally known as the "Rule of Relative Specificity." It establishes a preference for the heading that provides the most specific description of the article. A description by use is more specific than an *eo nominee* description or a general description. An *eo nominee* description is more specific than a general description.

For instance, take iron and steel springs. The description by use classification "[l]eaf springs and leaves therefor: [s]uitable for motor-vehicle suspension: [t]o be used in motor vehicles having a G.V.W. not exceeding 4 metric tons" is HTS item 7320.10.30. (It carries a post-Uruguay Round tariff of 3.2 percent, reduced from 4 percent.) This classification is more specific than the alternative general description classification "other [leaf springs and leaves therefor]" (HTS item 7320.10.60, which carries the same pre-and post-Uruguay Round tariff rates).

As another example, consider apricot products. The *eo nominee* classification "apricot pulp" (HTS item 2008.50.20, which carries a post-Uruguay Round tariff of 10 percent, reduced from 12.5 percent) is more specific than the general description "apricots" (HTS item 0809.10.00, which carries a post-Uruguay Round tariff of 0.2 cents per kilogram, reduced from 0.4 cents per kilogram).

Rule 3(a) also states that if two or more headings each describe only part of the materials or substances used in a mixed or composite article, then such headings are deemed to be equally specific. Similarly, if two or more headings each describe only some of the items in an article that is comprised of a set of items, then such headings are deemed equally specific. In these cases, Rule 3(a) does not yield a classification, and the second tool must be used.

For example, suppose Mediterranean Market in Lawrence, Kansas, imports packages of dried fruits. Each package contains prunes, figs, papayas, and cherries. They are sold as a single article, namely, a gift pack. (Because they are suitable for immediate consumption, HTS heading 0812, which concerns dried fruit not suitable for immediate consumption, is inapplicable.) According to HTS item 0813.50.00, which covers mixtures of nuts and dried fruits, the applicable post-Uruguay Round bound tariff rate is 14 percent (reduced from a previous rate of 17.5 percent). However, suppose each gift pack also contains brazil nuts, pecans, and almonds. HTS item 2008.19.85 concerns mixtures of fruits and nuts and specifies a post-Uruguay Round bound tariff rate of 22.4 percent (reduced from a previous rate of 28 percent). Both HTS items — 0813.50.00 and 2008.19.85 — describe only some of the items in the gift packs. Thus, both are deemed equally specific under Rule 3(a).

The second tool, Rule 3(b), is the "essential character" test. It is used if application of Rule 3(a) fails to achieve a classification for a mixed article or a set. Classification is based on the materials in the mixed article, or items in the set, that give the article its essential character.

This analysis sometimes requires creative argument. Consider a desk set sold as a single article. It is comprised of a pencil, eraser, paper, and ruler. What item gives the set its essential character? Arguably, the paper imparts the essential character because the other items operate on the paper: the pencil is used to write on the paper, the eraser is used to eliminate marks from the paper, and the ruler is used to draw lines on the paper. Accordingly, the correct classification for the article under Rule 3(b) could be paper. But, the application of Rule 3(b) may not yield a classification. Consider again the Mediterranean Market gift packs. What item gives the pack its essential character?

If both Rules 3(a) and 3(b) fail to yield a classification, then the third tool, found in Rule 3(c), must be employed. It simply states the article should be classified according to the heading that occurs last in numerical order among the headings of the HTS that equally merit consideration. Applying Rule 3(c) to the Mediterranean Market gift packs, HTS item 2008.19.85 would be the correct classification. It appears in Chapter 20 of the HTS, which clearly comes after HTS item 0813.50.00, which appears in Chapter 8.

Finally, if none of the aforementioned tools works, then Rule 4 of the GRI instructs that the problematical article must be classified in the heading for the goods to which the article is most akin.

There is an important overlay on the GRI: a large body of common law — both case law and administrative precedents — applying the GRI from the CIT and Federal Circuit. That law can help guide importers on classification questions.

IV. LIQUIDATION OF ENTRIES

U.S. CUSTOMS AND BORDER PROTECTION, *IMPORTING INTO THE UNITED STATES, A GUIDE FOR COMMERCIAL EXPORTERS*
83-84 (November 2006)

CBP officers at the port of entry or other officials acting on behalf of the port director review selected classifications and valuations, as well as other required import information, for correctness or as a proper basis for appraisement, as well as for agreement of the submitted data with the merchandise actually imported. The entry summary and documentation may be accepted as submitted without any changes. In this situation, the entry is liquidated as entered. Liquidation is the point at which CBP's ascertainment of the rate and amount of duty becomes final for most purposes. Liquidation is accomplished by posting a notice on a public bulletin board at the customhouse. . . .

CBP may determine that an entry cannot be liquidated as entered for one reason or another. For example, the tariff classification may not be correct or may not be acceptable because it is not consistent with established and uniform classification practice. If the change required by this determination results in a rate of duty more favorable to an importer, the entry is liquidated accordingly and a refund is authorized for the applicable amount of the deposited estimated duties. On the other hand, a change may be necessary which imposes a higher rate of duty. For example, a claim for an exemption from duty under a free-rate provision or under a conditional exemption may be found to be insufficient for lack of the required supporting documentation. In this situation, the importer will be given an advance notice of the proposed duty rate increase and an opportunity to validate the claim for a free rate or more favorable rate of duty.

If the importer does not respond to the notice, or if the response is found to be without merit, entry is liquidated in accordance with the entry as corrected, and the importer is billed for the additional duty. . . .

V. CLASSIFICATION CONUNDRUMS

A. Protests

U.S. CUSTOMS AND BORDER PROTECTION, *IMPORTING INTO THE UNITED STATES, A GUIDE FOR COMMERCIAL EXPORTERS*
84 (November 2006)

After liquidation, an importer may still pursue, on CBP Form 19 (19 CFR 174), any claims for an adjustment or refund, for entries filed before 12-18-06, by filing a protest within 90 days after liquidation. The protest period has been extended to 180 days for entries filed on or after 12-18-06. In order to apply for a Headquarters ruling, a request for further review must be filed with the protest. The same Form 19 can be used for this purpose. If filed separately, application for further review must still be filed within 90 days of liquidation. However, if a ruling on the question has previously been issued in response to a request for a decision on a prospective transaction or a request for internal advice, further review will ordinarily be denied. If a protest is denied, an importer has the right to litigate the matter by filing a summons with the U.S. Court of International Trade within 180 days after denial of the protest. The rules of the court and other applicable statutes and precedents determine the course of customs litigation.

While CBP's ascertainment of dutiable status is final for most purposes at the time of liquidation, a liquidation is not final until any protest which has been filed against it has been decided. Similarly, the administrative decision issued on a protest is not final until any litigation filed against it has become final.

Entries must be liquidated within one year of the date of entry unless the liquidation needs to be extended for another one-year period not to exceed a total of four years from the date of entry. CBP will suspend liquidation of an entry when required by statute or court order. A suspension will remain in effect until the issue is resolved. Notifications of extensions and suspensions are given to importers, surety companies, and customs brokers who are parties to the transaction.

B. Substantial Completeness and the 1989 *Simod* Case

SIMOD AMERICA CORP. v. UNITED STATES
United States Court of Appeals for the Federal Circuit
872 F.2d 1572, 1573-1579 (1989)

NICHOLS, SENIOR CIRCUIT JUDGE.

Simod America Corp. ("Simod") appeals from the judgment of the United States Court of International Trade holding that its shoe components imported from Italy in 1980-84 are dutiable as footwear under items 700.35 and 700.67 of the Tariff Schedules of the United States (TSUS). *Simod America Corp. v. United States*, 693 F. Supp. 1172 (Ct. Int'l Trade 1988) (Re, C.J.). We reverse and remand.

Background

Simod imported partially constructed athletic shoes from Italy. As imported, the articles included an upper, the portion of the shoe that covers the top of the foot ("the shoe top"), and a thin piece of fabric, called an underfoot, which is sewn in the location where the shoe sole was ultimately to be placed and remained there on completion of the shoe. Some of the shoe tops had an exterior of more than 50 percent leather and others did not.

The manufacturing performed in Italy was begun by applying a cutting die to a sheet of textile or leather materials. Leather materials were cleaned and skived (pared) before proceeding to the production line. The pieces of cut material were then stitched together and ornamented. Next, eye stays were applied to the shoe material and then metal eyes were attached with the use of a fully automated machine, and a thermosetting machine. Finally, an underfoot was attached to the shoe top in the location where the sole was ultimately to be placed. The underfoot is a necessary preparation for lasting.

The shoe tops were imported into the United States where they were lasted and provided with shoe soles and manufactured into finished athletic shoes at a factory in Middletown, Rhode Island. The soles manufactured at the Middletown plant were of a type produced by injecting liquid polyurethane into a mold and allowing it to harden. The polyurethane injection process was skillfully demonstrated to this court and the trial court by way of a videotape.

The process of making the polyurethane shoes soles centers around a machine known to the trade as a Desma 513/24. The Desma is a massive piece of equipment costing $800,000 to one million dollars. The machine has 24 stations, each station having a mold which forms the shoe sole and a last which is used to shape the shoe top into an appropriate form. Because the shoes come in different sizes, 30 to 40 pairs of different size lasts are required. The lasts are individually hand-crafted, and one set of 30 to 40 lasts takes approximately an entire year to produce. Thus, before even a beginning of the shoe sole injection process, significant start-up time and start-up costs were incurred.

The shoe sole manufacturing process began by heating the polyol and isocyanate chemicals which make up the polyurethane shoe soles in separate ovens at differing temperatures for 24 and 48 hours, respectively. The polyol material was then dyed with a coloring suspension, a procedure which required 20 to 40 minutes time. The molds at each station of the Desma machine were thoroughly cleaned to remove remnants of polyol from prior injections and then sprayed with releasing agents.

Next, the imported merchandise was mounted onto the last and mold at each station and secured in place by the underfoot. The shoe top was hammered by hand to take the shape of the last. Cement was applied to the bottom and sides of the shoe top, and polyurethane was then injected into the mold to form the outsole of the shoe.

The Desma has a control panel which regulates many of the machine's operations. A timer is set to control the duration of the injection; a counter regulates the quantity of polyurethane injected into the mold and the ratio of polyurethane to isocyanate. The quantity of material injected is varied by the control panel according to the size of the shoe being made.

A first injection of polyurethane was shot into a mold at each station to form the shoe outsole. After the first injection was completed, the mold release agent was removed from the shoe outsole. Failure completely to remove the release agent would have prevented the second injection from adhering properly and ruined the partially constructed merchandise. Once the release agent was completely removed from the outsole, a second injection was shot into each mold to create the shoe midsole. The mold had to be properly sealed to the shoe top as improper sealing between the shoe top and the mold causes the polyurethane to seep out and create a defective shoe. After the second injection was successfully performed, the shoe soles required between 12 and

24 hours to harden. After hardening, the shoes were passed through a finishing line where they were trimmed, cleaned, and otherwise touched up through the use of both hand and machine labor. The operations performed on the finishing line took approximately 20 minutes per pair.

. . . .

The imported merchandise was classified by the Customs Service ("Customs") as unfinished "footwear" under items 700.35 and 700.67, and that classification was sustained by the Court of International Trade.

Issue

Whether the trial court clearly erred in determining that the imported merchandise is properly classified under the "footwear" provisions.

Discussion

I.

General Interpretative Rule 10(h) of the TSUS provides, in pertinent part, that:

> unless the context requires otherwise, a tariff description for an article covers such article, whether assembled or not assembled, and whether finished or not finished.

Customs contends that the imported merchandise was properly classified as unfinished footwear pursuant to Rule 10(h). In order to pass on the correctness of this proposition, we must first examine the definition of unfinished footwear and determine whether the imported merchandise fits that definition.

The trial court defined unfinished footwear as "substantially complete" footwear. . . . Neither party contends that this definition is in error nor do we. . . .While Simod asserts error in the trial court's failure to establish a definition of footwear, the definition of a classification term is a question of law which we are free to determine for ourselves by resort to lexicographic and other materials. . . . Tariff terms are construed according to their common and commercial meanings which are presumed to be the same. *Webster's Third New international Dictionary, Unabridged*, at 886 (1976) defines footwear as:

> wearing apparel for the feet (as shoes, boots, slippers, overshoes) usu. excluding hosiery.

It is not disputed that at the completion of the manufacturing process, the imported articles will be wearing apparel for the feet; therefore, the key issue is whether the imported articles are "substantially complete" wearing apparel for the feet, or "substantially complete" footwear.

While the meaning of a classification term is a question of law, the issue of whether particular imported articles come within the definition of a classification term is a question of fact subject to the clearly erroneous standard of review. . . . The classification of the Customs Service is presumed to be correct and the burden of proof is upon the party challenging its classification. . . .

Our predecessor court fashioned a test for determining substantial completeness in *Daisy-Heddon, Div. Victor Comptometer Corp. v. United States*, 600 F.2d 799 (CCPA 1979), recognizing, however, that not all of the factors of the test will be applicable to a particular importation, and additional unstated factors may bear on the issue. The *Daisy-Heddon* factors are:

> (1) comparison of the number of omitted parts with the number of included parts; (2) comparison of the time and effort required to complete the article with the time and effort required to place it in its imported condition; (3) comparison of the cost of the included parts with that of the omitted parts; (4) the significance of the omitted parts to the overall functioning of the completed article; and. (5) trade customs, *i.e.*, does the trade recognize the importation as an unfinished article or as merely a part of that article.

600 F.2d at 803.

With regard to the first factor, the trial court properly found that 25 parts are assembled in Italy to comprise the imported article. With the addition of only four omitted parts, the shoes would be complete. This factor weighs in favor of finding substantial completeness.

Turning to the second factor, we compare the time and effort required to complete manufacture of the article after importation with the time and effort required to place the article in its imported condition. The trial court found:

> In contrast to the labor-intensive craftsmanship demonstrated at the Italian stitching rooms, the Middletown factory procedure was highly industrialized. *** None of these tasks [performed in the Middletown factory] involved considerable skill. The workers at the Italian stitching rooms, however, performed most of their work by hand. The workers employed at the Italian stitching rooms were more skilled than Simod's factory workers. Hence, Simod expended more time and effort in the production of the shoes into their imported condition than in finishing them at the Middletown factory.

> . . . .

The operations performed in Italy were carried out with the aid of equipment markedly less sophisticated than the Desma machine, but requiring more hand labor. There were machines but of the individually operated tabletop variety. The Middletown factory required relatively little hand labor, but employed sophisticated and expensive equipment requiring intensive supervision and maintenance. The fact that the Middletown operation was largely mechanized does not detract from the substantial nature of the manufacturing efforts undertaken there. In its analysis, the trial court ignored the capital-intensive nature of the Middletown manufacturing plant. The expensive and sophisticated nature of the equipment used at the Middletown plant indicates to this court it is clear error to hold that a substantial effort is not needed to place the imported articles into a completed condition.

It is a principle of Customs law that imported merchandise is dutiable in its condition as imported, except in the instance (not here involved) of deception, disguise, or artifice resorted to for the purpose of perpetrating a fraud of the revenue; what is going to be done with it afterwards is not relevant. . . . If this writer may speak out of personal knowledge, the principle is so basic it hardly needs to be mentioned in any discussion of a classification problem by judges, officials, or lawyers having any serious involvement in such matters. The well-informed CCPA that promulgated *Daisy-Heddon, supra*, was well aware of it . . . and in using, as a test of substantial completeness, the comparison of the labor required before importation, and for full completion after importation, it did not intend a breach of the basic rule. It would be a startling breach if two identical entries were classified differently because, after importation, one was destined for completion in a labor-intensive operation, and the other in a capital-intensive operation. The purpose of the *Daisy-Heddon* tests is to determine the extent the imported article is the completed article, unfinished, and that is the same in either of the cases supposed above. Accordingly, it is implicit in the *Daisy-Heddon* tests, and explicit so far as the occasional necessity of other unstated tests is there recognized, that labor-intensivity alone cannot be made a test of completeness where there is a great difference in the extent of capital intensivity in the manufacturing operation before and after importation. After all, one does not have to be a disciple of Karl Marx to recognize that somebody's labor at some time made possible the capital-intensive operation that eliminates recourse to much direct labor in the United States phase of production of the involved footwear. As the learned Chief Judge overlooks this, his analysis is clearly erroneous.

Apart from the costly equipment needed to process the imported articles, the time required to transform them into completed footwear is significant. The trial court found that the Desma machine produced 1,200 shoes in an 8-hour shift and that each shoe required less than one minute on the Desma machine. There is uncontradicted evidence that each shoe remained in its mold on the Desma machine for approximately two minutes after the two polyurethane injections were shot. In the face of this evidence, the finding that each shoe required less than one minute on the Desma machine is clearly erroneous.

Further, the trial court improperly focused on the output rate of the Desma machine without considering the fact that it processes many articles simultaneously. The relevant inquiry is not how many shoes can be produced per day. The relevant inquiry is how much time is spent to complete manufacture of each imported article. *See Daisy-Heddon*, 600 F.2d at 803 ("the time and effort required to complete the article"). The Desma machine simultaneously processes 24 articles, and the output rate must be appropriately adjusted. Using the trial court's output rate findings, the process time *per shoe* is:

$$\frac{8 \text{ hours}}{1,200 \text{ shoes}} \quad \times \quad 24 \text{ stations} \quad = \quad 9.6 \text{ minutes per shoe}$$

or 19.2 minutes of processing time per pair. In addition to the time on the Desma machine, the shoes required between 12 and 24 hours to harden and 20 minutes on the finishing line.

The Italian stitching rooms required approximately 17 minutes (15 minutes processing time plus 2 minutes cutting time per pair) to prepare the imported merchandise. Clearly, the time required to complete manufacture of the imported articles is greater than that required to place them in their imported condition.

Considering the substantial time and effort invested in completing construction of the athletic shoes, the trial court clearly erred in finding that "Simod expended more time and effort in the production of the shoes into their imported condition than in finishing them at the Middletown factory." . . .

The third *Daisy-Heddon* factor involves the cost of the imported article compared to the cost of the omitted parts. Due to the capital-intensive nature of the Middletown operation, the cost of adding the omitted shoe sole would properly include the indirect cost of using the Desma machine. Certainly the machine depreciates as each shoe comes off the production line. The record reveals the following direct costs of producing the shoe soles:

polyurethane	$1.40
insole	.21
laces	.11
mold release	.15
labor	.66
TOTAL	$2.53

The trial court apparently relied upon the above figures, as it found that the cost of producing the shoe soles was $2.50 or less. . . . No evidence was introduced reflecting the indirect cost of using the Desma machine. In the absence of that information, the comparison of the cost to produce the imported articles with the cost to complete their manufacture in Middletown is not probative.

The fourth *Daisy-Heddon* factor focuses on the significance of the omitted parts. The absence of an essential part does not preclude a finding of substantial completeness, *Channel Master, Div. of Avnet, Inc. v. United States*, 856 F.2d 177, 179 (Fed.Cir.1988); *Daisy-Heddon*, 600 F.2d at 802-803, but it does tip the balance away from such a finding.

The fifth and final inquiry specified in *Daisy-Heddon* is whether the trade recognizes the article as unfinished footwear or merely a component of footwear. The evidence on this issue was vigorously disputed on both sides and the trial court did not make any specific finding on this issue, nor do we think one is needed for our decision.

As the trial court aptly noted, the merchandise itself is often a potent witness in classification cases. . . . We have examined the exhibits representing the imported merchandise and while it clearly is embryo footwear, it is also clearly in the infant stages of manufacture. It does not tell us it is substantially complete. In *Channel Master, supra*, the importer urged that the imported articles were not substantially complete, because they were missing certain component parts. The court deemed the merchandise substantially complete owing to the "relatively quick, simple, and costless steps required for untrained consumers to insert" the missing parts into the merchandise. Here, the time, effort, and cost to complete the merchandise is not insignificant. Based upon our examination of the merchandise as its own witness, as well as the above-discussed analysis, we are left with the definite and firm conviction that a mistake has been committed and therefore reverse the trial court's finding that the footwear is substantially complete as imported.

Thus, we have determined that the involved articles were not "unfinished footwear" and could not properly have been classified under TSUS items 700.35 and 700.67. On the other hand, we are unable on the present record, and in the absence of findings by the Court of International Trade, to discern what the true classification should have been. This would formerly have required affirmance of the erroneous classification since under former law, the importer had a dual burden to establish the error of the Customs classification, and the correctness of a classification properly claimed by it. By *Jarvis Clark Co. v. United States*, 733 F.2d 873 (1984), . . . this unique rule has been held repealed by Congress. The original classification having been tested and found wanting on our review, the case can now be remanded to the Court of International Trade to find a correct answer, whether previously claimed or not claimed by the importer. If need be, a further remand to the Customs Service for consideration by it is also permissible under the *Jarvis Clark* rules. The correctness of Customs classifications is too important a matter to be made the subject of word games any longer, and the courts are too burdened with cases for the same or similar entries to be litigated and relitigated over and over again.

C. Proper Classification and the 1994 *Marubeni* Case

MARUBENI AMERICA CORP. v. UNITED STATES
United States Court of Appeals for the Federal Circuit
35 F.3d 530 (1994)

RICH, CIRCUIT JUDGE.

The United States (the government) appeals the May 14, 1993, judgment of the Court of International Trade (CIT) . . . holding that 1989 and 1990, two door, two-wheel and four-wheel drive, Nissan Pathfinder (Pathfinder) vehicles are correctly classified under heading 8703.23.00 (8703) of the Harmonized Tariff Schedule of the United States (HTSUS) as motor vehicles principally designed for the transport of persons. [Marubeni America Corp. imports the Pathfinder, but Nissan Motor Corporation U.S.A. is the real party in interest and is treated as such in the opinion.] We affirm.

I. Background

A. *The Merchandise*

The merchandise at issue is a two door, two-wheel or four-wheel drive, dual-purpose or multipurpose passenger vehicle, generally referred to as a compact sports utility vehicle. The Pathfinder does not have a cargo box or bed like a truck. Instead, its body is one unit that is configured much like an ordinary station wagon in that it has rear seats that fold forward, but not flat, for extra cargo space. These seats, however, are not removable. The spare tire is housed within the cargo space or alternatively, it may be attached outside the vehicle on the rear hatch. The rear hatch operates like those on a station wagon; it has a window that may be opened to place small packages in the cargo area without opening the tailgate. The Pathfinder is mechanically designed for both on-and off-road use.

. . . .

B. *Proceedings Below*

The Pathfinder was classified by the United States Customs Service (Customs) under 8704.31.00 (8704) of the HTSUS as a "motor vehicle for the transport of goods." Pursuant to 9903.87. 00 of the HTSUS a 25% *ad valorem* duty was assessed.

Nissan administratively protested this decision . . . claiming that the Pathfinder should be classified as "motor cars and other motor vehicles principally designed for the transport of persons . . . including station wagons" under 8703 HTSUS. This protest was denied. Nissan then brought an action in the CIT. The CIT conducted a three week trial *de novo* . . . that included test driving the Pathfinder and comparison vehicles, videotape viewing, and extensive presentation of both testimonial and documentary evidence. The government argued that the Pathfinder is more like a pick-up truck; therefore, it was "motor vehicle for the transport of goods." The CIT concluded that Customs' classification of the Pathfinder under 8704 HTSUS, "motor vehicle for the transport of goods" was incorrect, and that the correct classification was under 8703 HTSUS, "motor vehicle principally designed for the transport of persons." The duty assessed under 8703 HTSUS is 2.5% *ad valorem*. The United States now appeals from the judgment of the CIT. . . .

II. Analysis

The issue is whether the Pathfinder has been classified under the appropriate tariff provision. Resolution of that issue entails a two step process: (1) ascertaining the proper meaning of specific terms in the tariff provision; and (2) determining whether the merchandise at issue comes within the description of such terms as properly construed. The first step is a question of law which we review *de novo*, and the second is a question of fact which we review for clear error.

The government asserts that the CIT erred by applying improper and inconsistent standards, and that the Pathfinder is not primarily designed for the transport of persons based on the practice of Nissan and the industry.

A. *Proper Meaning*

It is well settled that "the ultimate issue, whether particular merchandise has been classified under an appropriate tariff provision, necessarily depends on the meaning of the terms of that provision, which is a question of law subject to *de novo* review." *Lynteq, Inc., v. United States*, 976 F.2d 693, 696 (Fed. Cir. 1992). To determine the proper meaning of tariff terms as contained in the statute, the terms are "construed in accordance with their common and popular meaning, in the absence of contrary legislative intent." *E.M. Chemicals v. United States*, 920 F.2d 910, 913 (Fed. Cir. 1990). "To assist it in ascertaining the common meaning of a tariff term, the court may rely upon its own understanding of the terms used, and it may consult lexicographic and scientific authorities, dictionaries, and other reliable information sources." *Brookside Veneers, Ltd. v. United States*, 847 F.2d 786, 789 . . . *cert. denied*, 488 U.S. 943 (1988). . . .

The two competing provisions of the HTSUS are set forth below.

8703   Motor cars and other motor vehicles principally designed for the transport of persons (other than those of heading 8702), including station wagons and racing cars.

8704   Motor vehicles for the transport of goods.

There are no legally binding notes to these headings that are relevant to the classification of dual-purpose vehicles such as the Pathfinder; therefore, we need only look to the common meaning of the terms as they appear above.

By the express language of 8703, "motor vehicle principally designed for the transport of persons," it is clear that the vehicle must be designed "more" for transport of persons than goods. *Webster's Third New International Dictionary of the English Language, Unabridged* (1986) defines "principally" as "in the chief place, chiefly;" and defines "designed" as "done by design or purposefully opposed to accidental or inadvertent; intended, planned." Thus, if the vehicle is equally designed for the transport of goods and persons, it would not be properly classified under 8703 HTSUS. There is nothing in the legislative history that indicates a different meaning.

The government argues that "the correct standard to be utilized in determining the principal design of any vehicle must be its construction — its basic structure, body, components, and vehicle layout — and the proper question to be asked is whether that construction is uniquely for passenger transportation." This standard is clearly at odds with Customs' interpretation in its March 1, 1989, memorandum providing guidance in applying these headings to sports utility vehicles. Customs stated:

> Design features, whether they accommodate passenger transport or cargo transport, or both, are of two types both of which are relevant in determining the proper classification of a sports-utility vehicle. First are what may be regarded as structural, or integral design features such as basic body, chassis, and suspension design . . . style and structure of the body [control access to rear]. The second type of design features, auxiliary design features are also relevant when determining whether, on the whole, the transport of persons was the principal design consideration. *Neither type by itself can be considered determinative on the issue of the purpose for which the vehicle was principally designed.* (emphasis added)

Thus, "requiring that the resulting product be uniquely constructed for the purpose of transporting persons to," the exclusion of any other use, is a constrictive interpretation of the terms with which we cannot agree.

There is nothing in the statute, legislative history, or prior Customs decisions that would indicate that "principally designed" refers only to a vehicle's structural design as asserted by the government. To answer the question, whether a vehicle is principally a particular purpose, not uniquely designed for a particular purpose, one must look at both the structural and auxiliary design features, as neither by itself is determinative.

The government's exclusionary construction fails on another point. Heading 8703 HTSUS specifically includes "station wagons," which are not uniquely designed for transport of persons, rather, they are designed as dual-purpose vehicles for the transport of goods and persons. The Pathfinder, like a station wagon, is a vehicle designed with a dual-purpose — to transport goods and persons.

The specific mention of "including station wagons" in 8703 can affect proper classification when dual-purpose vehicles are at issue. The Explanatory Notes define "station wagon" as "vehicles with a maximum seating capacity of nine persons (including the driver), the interior of which may be used, without structural alteration, for the transport of both persons and goods." Customs Co-operation Council (CCC), 4 HARMONIZED COMMODITY DESCRIPTION AND CODING SYSTEM, *Explanatory Notes, Heading No. 87.03* (1st ed. 1987). As noted by the CIT, the Pathfinder meets the literal definition of a station wagon. Even so, the CIT accorded proper weight to the definition offered by the CCC when it stated that the "Explanatory Note definition of station wagons should not be read too literally." As above, we can look to Customs interpretations for instruction on the intended meaning of "including station wagons." Again in its March 1, 1989, memorandum Customs stated:

> Given the wording of the heading and corroborating indications in the working papers of the Customs Cooperation Council, the correct reading that the phrase "*including station wagons*" was not intended to expand upon or be an exception to the requirement that articles are classifiable in heading 8703 only if they are "*principally designed for transport of persons.*" It should be emphasized that this interpretation does *not* read the station wagon reference out of the statute; its inclusion is necessary to clarify that the cargo-carrying capacity of dual-purpose vehicles does *not* foreclose a finding that they are principally designed to carry persons. (emphasis added)

Therefore, notwithstanding the fact that a vehicle may fit the definition of a station wagon and that the term is expressly included in 8703 HTSUS, that vehicle is not automatically included in or excluded from 8703 HTSUS classification. It necessarily follows that correct interpretation of 8703 HTSUS requires a determination of whether or not the vehicle was "principally designed for the transport of persons," and not merely a finding that it is within the definition of a "station wagon," unless of course it is unquestionably a station wagon. The Pathfinder is not the latter.

In summary, we find that the proper meaning of "motor vehicle principally designed for the transport of persons" to be just that, a motor vehicle principally designed for the transport of persons. While we find it unnecessary to assign a quantitative value to "principally," the statutory language is clear that a vehicle's intended purpose of transporting persons must outweigh an intended purpose of transporting goods. To make this determination, we find that both the structural and auxiliary design features must be considered.

This construction comports with Customs' interpretations and the CIT's analysis; and it is equally consistent with the common and popular meaning of the terms.

B. *Proper Classification*

While the meaning of a classification term is a question of law, the issue of whether merchandise comes within the definition of a classification term is a question of fact subject to the clearly erroneous standard of review. *Simod America Corp. v. United States*, 872 F.2d 1572, 1576 (Fed. Cir. 1989). . . . Customs' classification of imported merchandise is presumed to be correct, 28 USC § 2639(a)(1) (1988), and the party challenging the classification has the burden of overcoming this presumption. *Id*. To overcome this presumption, the court must consider "whether the government's classification is correct, both independently and in comparison with the importer's alternative." *Jarvis Clark Co. v. United States*, 733 F.2d 873, 878 (Fed. Cir. 1984). . . . . . .

If the Pathfinder satisfies the requirements of 8705 HTSUS, there is no need to discuss 8704 HTSUS because under the General Rules of Interpretation (GRI) when an article satisfies the requirement of two provisions, it will be classified under the heading giving a more specific description, here 8703 HTSUS. GRI 3(a). Conversely, if the Pathfinder does not fall within 8703 HTSUS, it falls into 8704 HTSUS.

The CIT conducted a three week trial *de novo*, to determine whether the Pathfinder was principally designed for the transport of persons or goods. The CIT looked at both design intent and execution, evaluating both structural and auxiliary design features. The CIT limited evidence to the vehicle models in the entries currently under consideration with the exception of evidence that was provided for comparison with vehicles that were readily accepted as trucks or passenger cars. These included the Nissan Hardbody truck and the Nissan Maxima sedan.

It is evident that the CIT carefully applied the proper standards in making its decision. In reaching its conclusion, the CIT evaluated the marketing and engineering design goals (consumer demands, off the line parts availability, etc.), the structural design necessary to meet both cargo and passenger carrying requirements for both on-and off-road use, as well as interior passenger amenities.

The CIT also recognized that the Pathfinder was basically derived from Nissan's Hardbody truck line yet, the Pathfinder was based upon totally different design concepts than a truck. The CIT correctly pointed out these differences and more importantly, the reasons behind the design decisions, including the need for speed and economy in manufacturing to capture the changing market, a market into which Nissan was a late entrant. Specifically, the designers decided to adopt the Hardbody's frame side rails and the cab portion from the front bumper to the frame just behind the driver's seats so that they could quickly and economically reach the market. The front suspension system was also adopted from Nissan's truck line but the rear suspension was not. The fact that a vehicle is derived in-part from a truck or from a sedan is not, without more, determinative of its intended principal design objectives which were passenger transport and off-road capability.

Substantial structural changes were necessary to meet the design criterion of transporting passengers. The addition of the rear passenger seat required that the gas tank be moved to the rear and the spare tire relocated. This effectively reduces the cargo carrying capacity. Of particular importance was the design of a new rear suspension that was developed specifically to provide a smooth ride for passengers. New and different cross beams, not present on the Hardbody frame, were added to the Pathfinder's frame to accommodate the above changes.

Other design aspects that point to a principal design for passengers include: the spare tire and the rear seat when folded down intrude upon the cargo space; the cargo area is carpeted; a separate window opening in the pop-up tailgate accommodates passengers loading and unloading small packages without having to lower the tailgate. In contrast, the Hardbody truck bed can accommodate loading with a fork lift, clearly a design feature for cargo. The CIT also found that the cargo volume is greatly reduced when the rear seat is up to accommodate passengers. Moreover, the axle and wheel differences are minor and consistent with the Pathfinder's off-road mission, particularly in the loaded condition. The Pathfinder has the same engine size as the Maxima passenger car.

Auxiliary design aspects, in addition to those merely relating to the structural derivation of the Pathfinder, that indicate passenger use over cargo use include: vehicle height was lowered 50 millimeters; the seat slides were improved yet similar to those on two door passenger sedans. Other auxiliary design features that point to transport of passengers include: rear seats that recline, are comfortable, and fold to make a fairly flat cargo bed but are not removable; rear seat stereo outlets, ashtrays, cubbyholes, arm rests, handholds, footwells, seat belts, child seat tie down hooks and operable windows. The CIT noted that there is not much more that can be done to accommodate passengers in the rear seat. Moreover, the testimony of the three primary design engineers as well as the contemporaneous design development documents support the finding that the Pathfinder was principally designed for the transport of persons.

The non-tariff regulations (NHTSA and EPA regulations) are not dispositive for purposes of tariff classification. . . . The government concedes this point. Nonetheless, the government goes on to argue that "the fact that safety, emission and fuel design changes required by those regulations are an element of the design process . . . should afford greater import to Nissan's decisions of what features to incorporate under the . . . regulatory schemes" and that these regulations are in accord with the motor vehicle industry. As noted by the CIT, the government's assessment that these regulatory schemes contain language that is substantially the same as the statutory language in the HTSUS, therefore affording these regulations greater relevance, is misplaced. The reasoning is baseless because those regulations include a category for Multipurpose Passenger Vehicles (MPV), a category that is not specifically delineated in the HTSUS.

In its March 1, 1989, memorandum referred to above Customs has drawn what appears to be a line between two door and four door versions of sports utility vehicles. Customs' conclusion, however, that vehicles that lack rear side passenger access doors are to be classified under 8704, is de facto affording determinative weight to this feature. This line, classifying two door dual-purpose vehicles for the transport of goods while classifying the four door version as principally designed for transport of persons, appears to be arbitrary.

Passenger cars with two doors also have restricted entry into the rear seat but this fact does not take these vehicles out of 8703 classification. Two door passenger cars are equipped with a seat slide mechanism that effectively slides the front seat forward to provide easier access to the rear seat. The doors of two door passenger cars are generally wider as well. The CIT found that the Pathfinder has both of these features so that passengers can be easily accommodated. Therefore, the two door Pathfinder accommodates passengers in the rear seat as well as two door passenger cars, if not as easily as four door sports utility vehicles. Consequently, the number of doors on a vehicle should not be determinative.

Conclusion

We hold that the court applied the correct legal standards, and that the evidence of record supports the CIT's decision that the Pathfinder is principally designed for the transport of persons.

Accordingly, we affirm the decision of the Court of International Trade in holding that the Pathfinder vehicle at issue is correctly classified under 8703.23.00. . . .

Chapter 18

TARIFF VALUATION

That which costs little is less valued.

> —MIGUEL DE CERVANTES (1547-1616), DON QUIXOTE, Part 1,
> Book 4, Chapter 7 (1605, P. Motteux, trans.)

DOCUMENTS SUPPLEMENT ASSIGNMENT

1. *Havana Charter* Articles 33, 35-37
2. GATT Article VII
3. WTO *Customs Valuation Agreement*
4. U.S. *Statement of Administrative Action* on the WTO *Agreement on Customs Valuation*
5. WTO *Agreement on Pre-Shipment Inspection (PSI Agreement)*
6. U.S. *Statement of Administrative Action* on the *PSI Agreement*
7. *NAFTA* Chapter 5
8. Relevant provisions in other FTAs

I. PRE-URUGUAY ROUND PROTECTIONISM AND DISHARMONY

A. The Skeletal GATT Article VII Framework

One customs law practitioner remarks:

> The problem of valuation is inherently difficult. No one solution yields the right answer. Whether it is a taxing authority assessing property, an executor dealing with a family business or a businessman setting the price of a new product, there is simply no one way to determine the "true" value of something. Nor does a "true" value exist somewhere out there — if only we could find it. The problem is compounded in designing a customs valuation code, for the valuation formula must fit every kind of merchandise, every kind of transaction and every country — and still be easy to administer.[1]

Until the Tokyo Round *Valuation Code* (more formally known as the *Agreement on Implementation of Article VII of the General Agreement on Tariffs and Trade*), there was no single framework governing customs valuation methodology among GATT contracting parties. To be sure, GATT Article

---

[1] Saul L. Sherman, *Reflections on the New Customs Valuation Code*, 12 L. & POL'Y INT'L BUS. 119 (1980).

VII:2(a) states that duty should be assessed on the "actual value" of imported merchandise, not on an "arbitrary or fictitious" value, nor on a value based on the "national origin" of the merchandise.

But, GATT Article VII:2(a) proved to be more of an exhortation than a uniform standard. The definition of "actual value" in Article VII:2(b) is somewhat ambiguous and manipulable. Little specific guidance for customs officials is found elsewhere in Article VII. In addition to this GATT provision, a Brussels Definition of Value existed and was used by roughly 100 nations. Neither the U.S. nor Canada followed the Brussels Definition. They maintained their own valuation systems.

B.   Protectionism and the American Selling Price Methodology

Until the *Trade Agreements Act of 1979*, which implemented the Tokyo Round *Valuation Code*, the valuation system the U.S. used was particularly complex. Two separate valuation standards actually existed side-by-side. The first system, called the "old" system, was set forth in Section 402a of the *Tariff Act of 1930*, as amended (19 U.S.C. § 1402). (This section was repealed by Section 201(b) of the *Trade Agreements Act of 1979*). It established a hierarchy of valuation methods, namely,

> (1)   Foreign Value (which is based on the value of merchandise sold in foreign markets) or Export Value, whichever is higher,
>
> (2)   United States Value, and
>
> (3)   Cost of Production.

The old system also called for the use of the American Selling Price (ASP) to appraise certain designated articles like benzenoid chemicals and footwear.

The ASP method was not based on the value of the imported product, but rather on the value of a domestically produced product. The ASP was used because the United States Tariff Commission (the ITC's predecessor) and the President found that "the statutory duties did not equalize the difference in cost of production between the domestic and foreign producer of like or similar articles."[2] Thus, the ASP was a blatantly protectionist effort to eliminate comparative cost advantages in certain industries.

In the early 1950s the Department of the Treasury attempted to eliminate Foreign Value as a basis of appraisement because Export Value data were more readily available. Moreover, by eliminating Foreign Value, the valuation process would be streamlined. There would be no need to determine simultaneously Foreign Value and Export Value in order to ascertain which is the higher figure. As a result, Congress enacted the *Customs Simplification Act of 1956*. The *1956 Act* created the "new" law, codified in Section 402 of the *Tariff Act of 1930*, as amended (19 U.S.C. § 1401a). The Foreign Value was eliminated, and Export Value was the primary basis of appraisement. The United States Value and Cost of Production, renamed "Constructed Value," remained the first and second alternative standards, though their definitions were altered.

---

[2] *Id.* at 123 n.13.

The key effect of the new law was the reduction in duties for many articles. Accordingly, Congress was unwilling to apply the new law to all imported articles. The Secretary of the Treasury prepared a list of those articles which, if appraised under the new law, would be valued at 95 percent or less of the amount at which they had been valued under the old law, *i.e.*, a list of articles whose dutiable value was reduced by 5 percent or more as a result of the new law. The so-called "Final List" was published on 20 January 1958 in Treasury Decision 54521. All articles on the Final List continued to be appraised under the old law.

In sum, after the *1956 Act*, there were nine separate bases for customs valuation: five under the old law (Foreign Value, Export Value, United States Value, Cost of Production and ASP), which applied to articles on the Final List, and four under the new law (Export Value, the modified United States Value, the modified Constructed Value and ASP), which applied to articles not on the Final List. Not only was this customs valuation system complex, but also it was unique. America's system differed from the methodologies used in other countries. Further, the ASP irked many of America's trading partners.

> The most immediate and controversial of these factors [that led to the adoption of a uniform code on valuation during the Tokyo Round] was the elimination of the bitterest legacy left in the wake of the Kennedy Round — the American Selling Price (ASP) system — which arose out of a valuation provision in the U.S. *Tariff Act*. [19 U.S.C. Sections 1336(a) and (b), 1401a(a)(4) and (e), and 1402(a)(4) and (g) (1976).] This debacle, more than any other single factor, placed valuation in the limelight during the earliest days of the Tokyo Round. [According to the ASP,] the value of the imported product is measured by the price of the competing domestic product. In other words, the importer's duty value is set by his (usually high-priced) domestic competitor. Europeans, whose chemical industry was the prime target of ASP, found this approach offensive in principle, and the issue generated a great deal of emotion during the Kennedy Round negotiations (1964-67). The parties to that Round reached a side agreement on ASP, under which tariff rates on the affected products were to have been increased substantially in exchange for the abolition of ASP and reversion to the usual valuation standards. Protectionist forces in the United States were so strong, however, that this side agreement was never presented to Congress for a vote, and ASP continued as before.

> By 1975, however, the emotional sting had been taken out of the ASP issue. The U.S. chemical industry was ready to accept the demise of ASP, seeking only compensatory duty rate adjustments. The industry apparently realized only after that it was too late to reverse gears that the side agreement rejected in 1967 had entailed so large a compensatory rate increase that it probably would have been better to accept it and drop ASP. In addition, structural changes in both domestic and foreign chemical companies made ASP less beneficial to the domestic industry. Perhaps most important, ASP was a rather outrageous protectionist device and simply could not be expected to survive another round of GATT negotiations.

. . . .

The elegant strategy for dispatching ASP adopted by the European negotiators was to call for a uniform international code on customs valuation. ASP was such an inappropriate system that no one could seriously suggest that it be applied universally under an international agreement. Thus, the *Valuation Code* was designed largely to give ASP a decent burial. . . .[3]

Thus, the Tokyo Round *Valuation Code* marked the demise of ASP, and the harmonization of valuation standards.

C. Harmonization at Last in the Uruguay Round

The Uruguay Round *Agreement on Implementation of Article VII of the General Agreement on Tariffs and Trade 1994* (*Agreement on Customs Valuation*) is virtually identical to the 1979 Tokyo Round Code. Accordingly, no change in U.S. statutes or CBP regulations were needed to implement the *Agreement*. The *Agreement* augurs greater uniformity in valuation methodology, but not necessarily uniform values. The aim of the *Agreement*, like its predecessor, is to ensure that different customs officials in the WTO Members use the same approach to determine the value of an article for purposes of applying a tariff. The goal is not to ensure that they always reach the same value with respect to a given article.

A variety of economic factors may cause the price of a particular article, in dollar terms, to vary from one country to another, and from one week to the next. For example, an exporter in Country A may sell an article to a unrelated company in Country B and to an affiliate in Country C. The price of the article paid by the two companies is likely to differ. The *Nissho Iwai* case raises this point. Related-party transactions may call for a different valuation methodology from the one used for arms-length sales. Related parties are broadly defined (in 19 U.S.C. § 1401a(g)) to include:

1. members of the same family;

2. partners;

3. an employer and employee;

4. an officer or director of an organization and such organization;

5. an officer and director of an organization and an officer or director of another organization if each individual is an officer or director in the other organization;

6. any person (including a corporation, partnership or other business association) that directly or indirectly owns, controls or holds with the power to vote, 5 percent or more of the outstanding voting stock of any organization and such organization; and

7. two or more persons directly or indirectly controlling, controlled by, or under common control with, any person.

Foreign exchange rates are another example of why valuations may differ. These rates change not just from week to week, but from minute to minute.

---

[3] *Id.* at 123-24.

This volatility may affect the dollar-denominated price of an article. Note carefully the currency conversion rules.

Finally, and perhaps most importantly, valuations can differ simply because an exporter may charge different prices for its product in different countries. After all, distinct local market conditions lead to differential pricing strategies for the same product sold in multiple countries. But, of course, anyone who has purchased a Big Mac at McDonald's franchises in different countries is aware of this phenomenon.

II. VALUATION METHODOLOGIES

A. Method #1: Transaction Value

U.S. CUSTOMS AND BORDER PROTECTION, *IMPORTING INTO THE UNITED STATES, A GUIDE FOR COMMERCIAL EXPORTERS*
84-90 (November 2006)

The entry filer is responsible for using reasonable care to value imported merchandise and provide any other information necessary to enable the CBP officer to properly assess the duty and determine whether any other applicable legal requirement is met. The CBP officer is then responsible for fixing the value of the imported merchandise. The valuation provisions of the *Tariff Act of 1930* are found in section 402, as amended by the *Trade Agreements Act of 1979.* . . .

Generally, the customs value of all merchandise exported to the United States will be the transaction value for the goods. If the transaction value cannot be used, then certain secondary bases are considered. The secondary bases of value, listed in order of precedence for use, are:

- Transaction value of identical merchandise,
- Transaction value of similar merchandise,
- Deductive value,
- Computed value.

The order of precedence of the last two values can be reversed if the importer so requests in writing at the time of filing the entry. . . .

Transaction Value [Elements]

The transaction value of imported merchandise is the price actually paid or payable for the merchandise when sold for exportation to the United States, plus amounts for the following items if they are not included in the price:

- The packing costs incurred by the buyer,
- Any selling commission incurred by the buyer,
- The value of any assist,

- Any royalty or license fee that the buyer is required to pay as a condition of the sale,

- The proceeds, accruing to the seller, of any subsequent resale, disposal, or use of the imported merchandise.

The amounts for the above items are added only to the extent that each is not included in the price actually paid or payable and information is available to establish the accuracy of the amount. If sufficient information is not available, then the transaction value cannot be determined and the next basis of value, in order of precedence, must be considered for appraisement. . . .

Packing costs consist of the cost incurred by the buyer for all containers and coverings of whatever nature and for the labor and materials used in packing the imported merchandise so that it is ready for export.

Any selling commission incurred by the buyer with respect to the imported merchandise constitutes part of the transaction value. Buying commissions do not. A selling commission means any commission paid to the seller's agent, who is related to or controlled by, or works for or on behalf of, the manufacturer or the seller.

The apportioned value of any assist constitutes part of the transaction value of the imported merchandise. First the value of the assist is determined; then the value is prorated to the imported merchandise.

An assist is any of the items listed below that the buyer of imported merchandise provides directly or indirectly, free of charge or at a reduced cost, for use in the production or sale of merchandise for export to the United States.

- Materials, components, parts, and similar items incorporated in the imported merchandise,

- Tools, dies, molds, and similar items used in producing the imported merchandise,

- Merchandise consumed in producing the imported merchandise,

- Engineering, development, artwork, design work, and plans and sketches that are undertaken outside the United States.

"Engineering. . .," will not be treated as an assist if the service or work is:

- Performed by a person domiciled within the United States,

- Performed while that person is acting as an employee or agent of the buyer of the imported merchandise, and

- Incidental to other engineering, development, artwork, design work, or plans or sketches undertaken within the United States.

In determining the value of an assist, the following rules apply:

- The value is either: (a) the cost of acquiring the assist, if acquired by the importer from an unrelated seller, or (b) the cost of the assist, if produced by the importer or a person related to the importer.

- The value includes the cost of transporting the assist to the place of production.

- The value of assists used in producing the imported merchandise is adjusted to reflect use, repairs, modifications, or other factors affecting the value of the assists. Assists of this type include such items as tools, dies, and molds.

For example, if the importer previously used the assist, regardless of whether he acquired or produced it, the original cost of acquisition or of production must be decreased to reflect the use. Alternatively, repairs and modifications may result in the value of the assist having to be adjusted upward.

- In case of engineering, development, artwork, design work, and plans and sketches undertaken elsewhere than in the United States, the value is:

    1. The cost of obtaining copies of the assist, if the assist is available in the public domain,

    2. The cost of the purchase or lease, if the assist was bought or leased by the buyer from an unrelated person,

    3. The value added outside the United States, if the assist was reproduced in the United States and one or more foreign countries.

So far as possible, the buyer's commercial record system will be used to determine the value of an assist, especially such assists as engineering, development, artwork, design work, and plans and sketches undertaken elsewhere than in the United States.

Having determined the value of an assist, the next step is to prorate that value to the imported merchandise. The apportionment is done in a reasonable manner appropriate to the circumstances and in accordance with generally accepted accounting principles. By the latter is meant any generally recognized consensus or substantial authoritative support regarding the recording and measuring of assets and liabilities and changes, the disclosing of information, and the preparing of financial statements.

Royalty or license fees that a buyer must pay directly or indirectly as a condition of the sale of the imported merchandise for exportation to the United States will be included in the transaction value. Ultimately, whether a royalty or license fee is dutiable will depend on whether the buyer had to pay it as a condition of the sale and to whom and under what circumstances it was paid. The dutiable status will have to be decided on a case-by-case basis.

Charges for the right to reproduce the imported goods in the United States are not dutiable. This right applies only to the following types of merchandise:

- Originals or copies of artistic or scientific works,

- Originals or copies of models and industrial drawings,

- Model machines and prototypes,

- Plant and animal species.

Any proceeds resulting from the subsequent resale, disposal, or use of the imported merchandise that accrue, directly or indirectly, to the seller are dutiable. These proceeds are added to the price actually paid or payable if not otherwise included.

The price actually paid or payable for the imported merchandise is the total payment, excluding international freight, insurance, and other c.i.f. charges, that the buyer makes to the seller. This payment may be direct or indirect. Some examples of an indirect payment are when the buyer settles all or part of a debt owed by the seller, or when the seller reduces the price on a current importation to settle a debt he owes the buyer. Such indirect payments are part of the transaction value.

However, if a buyer performs an activity on his own account, other than those that may be included in the transaction value, then the activity is not considered an indirect payment to the seller and is not part of the transaction value. This applies even though the buyer's activity might be regarded as benefiting the seller; for example, advertising.

Exclusions

The amounts to be excluded from transaction value are as follows:

- The cost, charges, or expenses incurred for transportation, insurance, and related services incident to the international shipment of the goods from the country of exportation to the place of importation in the United States. [These foreign inland freight, and related charges, must be identified separately.]

- Any reasonable cost or charges incurred for:

    1. Constructing, erecting, assembling, maintaining, or providing technical assistance with respect to the goods after transportation into the United States, or

    2. Transporting the goods after importation.

- The customs duties and other federal taxes, including any federal excise tax, for which sellers in the United States are ordinarily liable.

. . . .

Limitations

The transaction value of imported merchandise is the appraised value of that merchandise, provided certain limitations do not exist. If any of these limitations are present, then transaction value cannot be used as the appraised value, and the next basis of value will be considered. The limitations can be divided into four groups:

- Restrictions on the disposition or use of the merchandise,

- Conditions for which a value cannot be determined,

- Proceeds of any subsequent resale, disposal or use of the merchandise, accruing to the seller, for which an appropriate adjustment to transaction value cannot be made,

- Related-party transactions where the transaction value is not acceptable.

The term "acceptable" means that the relationship between the buyer and seller did not influence the price actually paid or payable. Examining the circumstances of the sale will help make this determination.

Alternatively, "acceptable" can also mean that the transaction value of the imported merchandise closely approximates one of the following test values, provided these values relate to merchandise exported to the United States at or about the same time as the imported merchandise:

- The transaction value of identical merchandise or of similar merchandise in sales to unrelated buyers in the United States,
- The deductive value or computed value for identical merchandise or similar merchandise.

The test values are used for comparison only, they do not form a substitute basis of valuation. In determining whether the transaction value is close to one of the foregoing test values, an adjustment is made if the sales involved differ in:

- Commercial levels,
- Quantity levels,
- The costs, commission, values, fees, and proceeds added to the transaction value (price paid) if not included in the price,
- The costs incurred by the seller in sales in which he and the buyer are not related that are not incurred by the seller in sales in which he and the buyer are related.

As stated, the test values are alternatives to an examination of the circumstances of the sale. If one of the test values is met, it is not necessary to examine the circumstances of the sale to determine if the relationship influenced the price.

B.   Method #2: Transaction Value of Identical or Similar Merchandise

U.S. CUSTOMS AND BORDER PROTECTION, *IMPORTING INTO THE UNITED STATES, A GUIDE FOR COMMERCIAL EXPORTERS* 90-91 (November 2006)

When the transaction value cannot be determined, then an attempt will be made to appraise the imported goods under the transaction value of identical merchandise method. If merchandise identical to the imported goods cannot be found or an acceptable transaction value for such merchandise does not exist, then the next appraisement method is the transaction value of similar merchandise. In either case the value used would be a previously accepted customs value.

The identical or similar merchandise must have been exported to the United States at or about the same time that the merchandise being appraised is exported to the United States.

The transaction value of identical or similar merchandise must be based on sales of identical or similar merchandise, as applicable, at the same commercial level and in substantially the same quantity as the sale of the merchandise being appraised. If no such sale exists, then sales at either a different commercial level or in different quantities, or both, can be used but must be adjusted to take account of any such difference. Any adjustment must be based on sufficient information, that is, information establishing the reasonableness and accuracy of the adjustment.

The term "identical merchandise" means merchandise that is:

- Identical in all respects to the merchandise being appraised,
- Produced in the same country as the merchandise being appraised,
- Produced by the same person as the merchandise being appraised.

If merchandise meeting all three criteria cannot be found, then identical merchandise is merchandise satisfying the first two criteria but produced by a different person than the producer of merchandise being appraised.

. . . Merchandise can be identical to the merchandise being appraised and still show minor differences in appearance.

- *Exclusion*: Identical merchandise does not include merchandise that incorporates or reflects engineering, development, art work, design work, or plans and sketches provided free or at reduced cost by the buyer and undertaken in the United States.

The term "similar merchandise" means merchandise that is:

- Produced in the same country and by the same person as the merchandise being appraised,
- Like the merchandise being appraised in characteristics and component materials,
- Commercially interchangeable with the merchandise being appraised.

If merchandise meeting the foregoing criteria cannot be found, then similar merchandise is merchandise having the same country of production, like characteristics and component materials, and commercial interchangeability but produced by a different person.

In determining whether goods are similar, some of the factors to be considered are the quality of the goods, their reputation, and existence of a trademark.

- *Exclusion*: Similar merchandise does not include merchandise that incorporates or reflects engineering, development, art work, design work, and plans and sketches provided free or at reduced cost to the buyer and undertaken in the United States.

It is possible that two or more transaction values for identical or similar merchandise, as applicable, will be determined. In such a case the lowest value will be used as the appraised value of the imported merchandise.

C. Method #3: Deductive Value

U.S. CUSTOMS AND BORDER PROTECTION, *IMPORTING INTO THE UNITED STATES, A GUIDE FOR COMMERCIAL EXPORTERS*
91-94 (November 2006)

If the transaction value of imported merchandise, of identical merchandise, or of similar merchandise cannot be determined, then deductive value is the next basis of appraisement. This method is used unless the importer designates computed value as the preferred appraisement method. If computed value was chosen and subsequently determined not to exist for customs valuation purposes, then the basis of appraisement reverts to deductive value.

Basically, deductive value is the resale price in the United States after importation of the goods, with deductions for certain items. In discussing deductive value, the term "merchandise concerned" is used. The term means the merchandise being appraised, identical merchandise, or similar merchandise. Generally, the deductive value is calculated by starting with a unit price and making certain additions to and deductions from that price.

Unit Price. One of three prices constitutes the unit price in deductive value. The price used depends on when and in what condition the merchandise concerned is sold in the United States.

1. **Time and Condition:** The merchandise is *sold in the condition as imported at or about the date of importation of the merchandise being appraised.*

Price: The price used is the unit price at which the greatest aggregate quantity of the merchandise concerned is sold at or about the date of importation.

2. **Time and Condition:** The merchandise concerned is *sold in the condition as imported but not sold at or about the date of importation* of the merchandise being appraised.

Price: The price used is the unit price at which the greatest aggregate quantity of the merchandise concerned is sold after the date of importation of the merchandise being appraised but before the close of the 90th day after the date of importation.

3. **Time and Condition:** The merchandise concerned is *not sold in the condition as imported and not sold before the close of the 90th day* after the date of importation of the merchandise being appraised.

Price: The price used is the unit price at which the greatest aggregate quantity of the merchandise being appraised, after further processing, is sold before the 180th day after the date of importation.

This third price is also known as the "further processing price" or "superdeductive."

The importer has the option to ask that deductive value be based on the further processing price.

Under the superdeductive method the merchandise concerned *is not sold in the condition as imported and not sold before the close of the 90th day* after the date of importation, but is sold before the 180th day after the date of importation.

Under this method, an amount equal to the value of the further processing must be deducted from the unit price in determining deductive value. The amount so deducted must be based on objective and quantifiable data concerning the cost of such work as well as any spoilage, waste or scrap derived from that work. Items such as accepted industry formulas, methods of construction, and industry practices could be used as a basis for calculating the amount to be deducted.

Generally, the superdeductive method cannot be used if the further processing destroys the identity of the goods. Such situations will be decided on a case-by-case basis for the following reasons:

- Sometimes, even though the identity of the goods is lost, the value added by the processing can be determined accurately without unreasonable difficulty for importers or for CBP.

- In some cases, the imported goods still keep their identity after processing but form only a minor part of the goods sold in the United States. In such cases, using the superdeductive method to value the imported goods will not be justified.

The superdeductive method cannot be used if the merchandise concerned is sold in the condition as imported before the close of the 90th day after the date of importation of the merchandise being appraised.

Additions. Packing costs for the merchandise concerned are added to the price used for deductive value, provided these costs have not otherwise been included. These costs are added regardless of whether the importer or the buyer incurs the cost. "Packing costs" means the cost of:

- All containers and coverings of whatever nature, and

- Packing, whether for labor or materials, used in placing the merchandise in condition, packed ready for shipment to the United States.

Deductions. Certain items are not part of deductive value and must be deducted from the unit price. These items are as follows:

- Commissions or profit and general expenses. Any commission usually paid or agreed to be paid, or the addition usually made for profit and general expenses, applicable to sales in the United States of imported merchandise that is of the same class or kind as the merchandise concerned, regardless of the country of exportation.

- Transportation/insurance costs.

  (a) The actual and associated costs of transportation and insurance incurred with respect to international shipments concerned from the country of exportation to the United States, and

  (b) The usual and associated costs of transportation and insurance incurred with respect to shipments of such merchandise from the place of importation to the place of delivery in the United States, provided these costs are not included as a general expense under the preceding item. . . .

- Customs duties/federal taxes. The customs duties and other federal taxes payable on the merchandise concerned because of its importation plus any federal excise tax on, or measured by the value of, such merchandise for which sellers in the United States are ordinarily liable.

- Value of further processing. The value added by processing the merchandise after importation, provided that sufficient information exists concerning the cost of processing. The price determined for deductive value is reduced by the value of further processing only if the third unit price (the superdeductive) is used as deductive value.

For purposes of determining the deductive value of imported merchandise, any sale to a person who supplies any assist for use in connection with the production or sale for export of the merchandise shall be disregarded.

D.   Method #4: Computed Value

U.S. CUSTOMS AND BORDER PROTECTION, *IMPORTING INTO THE UNITED STATES, A GUIDE FOR COMMERCIAL EXPORTERS*
94-96 (November 2006)

The next basis of appraisement is computed value. If customs valuation cannot be based on any of the values previously discussed, then computed value is considered. This value is also the one the importer can select to precede deductive value as a basis of appraisement.

Computed value consists of the sum of the following items:

- The cost or value of the materials, fabrication, and other processing used in producing the imported merchandise,

- Profit and general expenses,

- Any assist, if not included in bullets 1 and 2,

- Packing costs.

Materials, Fabrication, and Other Processing. The cost or value of the materials, fabrication, and other processing of any kind used in producing the imported merchandise is based on (a) information provided by or on behalf of the producer, and (b) the commercial accounts of the producer if the accounts are consistent with generally accepted accounting principles applied in the country of production of the goods.

. . . If the country of exportation imposes an internal tax on the materials or their disposition and refunds the tax when merchandise produced from the materials is exported, then the amount of the internal tax is not included as part of the cost or value of the materials.

Profit and General Expenses

- The amount is determined by information supplied by the producer and is based on his or her commercial accounts, provided such accounts are consistent with generally accepted accounting principles in the country of production.

- The producer's profit and general expenses must be consistent with those usually reflected in sales of goods of the same class or kind as the imported merchandise that are made by producers in the country of exportation for export to the United States. If they are not consistent, then the amount for profit and general expenses is based on the usual profit and general expenses of such producers.

- The amount for profit and general expenses is taken as a whole.

Basically, a producer's profit could be low and his or her general expenses high, so that the total amount is consistent with that usually reflected in sales of goods of the same class or kind. In such a situation, a producer's actual profit figures, even if low, will be used provided he or she has valid commercial reasons to justify them and the pricing policy reflects usual pricing policies in the industry concerned.

Under computed value, "merchandise of the same class and kind" must be imported from the same country as the merchandise being appraised and must be within a group or range of goods produced by a particular industry or industry sector. Whether certain merchandise is of the same class or kind as other merchandise will be determined on a case-by-case basis.

In determining usual profit and general expenses, sales for export to the United States of the narrowest group or range of merchandise that includes the merchandise being appraised will be examined, providing the necessary information can be obtained.

If the value of an assist used in producing the merchandise is not included as part of the producer's materials, fabrication, other processing, or general expenses, then the prorated value of the assist will be included in computed value. It is important that the value of the assist not be included elsewhere because no component of computed value should be counted more than once in determining computed value.

. . . The value of any engineering, development, artwork, design work, and plans and sketches undertaken in the United States is included in computed value only to the extent that such value has been charged to the producer.

The cost of all containers and coverings of whatever nature, and of packing, whether for labor or material, used in placing merchandise in condition and packed ready for shipment to the United States is included in computed value.

III. VALUATION CONUNDRUMS

A. No Method Works

What happens if none of the standard valuation methods can be used for a particular shipment of merchandise? The answer is appraisal occurs based on one of the standard methods. However, reasonable adjustments as necessary are made to that method. Moreover, appraisal is based to the greatest extent possible on previously determined values.

For example, CBP may

(1)   interpret flexibly the requirement that identical or similar merchandise be exported at or about the same time as the merchandise being appraised,

(2)   look to a third country, other than the country of exportation, as a basis for valuation, or

(3)   consider prior appraisals of identical or similar merchandise using deductive or computed value.

What facts and circumstances might lead to the need to improvise?

B.   Currency Conversion

U.S. CUSTOMS AND BORDER PROTECTION, *IMPORTING INTO THE UNITED STATES, A GUIDE FOR COMMERCIAL EXPORTERS*
84 (November 2006)

The conversion of foreign currency for customs purposes must be made in accordance with the provisions of 31 U.S.C. 5151(e). This section states that CBP is to use rates of exchange determined and certified by the Federal Reserve Bank of New York. These certified rates are based on the New York market buying rates for the foreign currencies involved.

In the case of widely used currencies, rates of exchange are certified each day.

The rates certified on the first business day of each calendar quarter are used throughout the quarter except on days when fluctuations of five percent or more occur, in which case the actual certified rates for those days are used. For infrequently used currencies, the Federal Reserve Bank of New York certifies rates of exchanges upon request by CBP. The rates certified are only for the currencies and dates requested.

For CBP purposes, the date of exportation of the goods is the date used to determine the applicable certified rate of exchange. This remains true even though a different rate may have been used in payment of the goods. Information as to the applicable rate of exchange in converting currency for customs purposes in the case of a given shipment may be obtained from a CBP port director.

C. Related Parties and the 1992 *Nissho Iwai* Case

NISSHO IWAI AMERICAN CORP. v. UNITED STATES
United States Court of Appeals for the Federal Circuit
982 F.2d 505, 506-511 (1992)

LOURIE, CIRCUIT JUDGE.

Nissho Iwai American Corporation (NIAC) appeals from the judgment of the United States Court of International Trade granting the government's cross-motion for summary judgment and counterclaim on NIAC's challenge of a valuation determination by the United States Customs Service. *Nissho Iwai American Corp. v. United States*, 786 F. Supp. 1002 (1992). [Omitted is the discussion of the counter-claim.] In granting summary judgment, the trial court held that the transaction value of the imported merchandise at issue, as defined in 19 U.S.C. § 140la(b)(1) (1988), was properly based on the price of the sale from the middleman to the ultimate United States purchaser. Because the transaction value in this case must be based on the price of the sale from the foreign manufacturer to the middleman, we reverse the trial court's grant of summary judgment. . . .

Background

This appeal concerns the proper dutiable value of 205 rapid transit passenger cars imported to the United States from Japan during 1983-1985. The vehicles at issue were imported pursuant to a three-tiered distribution arrangement involving a manufacturer, Kawasaki Heavy Industries Ltd. (KHI), a middleman, Nissho Iwai Corporation (NIC), and a purchaser, the Metropolitan Transportation Authority of New York City (MTA). NIC and KHI are independent corporations organized under the laws of Japan. The MTA is a public benefit corporation of the State of New York.

In 1981, NIC and KHI conducted preliminary negotiations regarding the possible manufacture of subway cars by KHI for the MTA. By means of a contract dated March 17, 1982, the MTA agreed to purchase 325 passenger cars from NIAC, a wholly-owned U.S. subsidiary of NIC, for use in the New York City Transit System. Article VI-C of the contract specified that "the passenger cars to be furnished hereunder will be manufactured and produced by Kawasaki Heavy Industries, Ltd., Japan." The contract also stipulated that the vehicles would be manufactured using components from both the United States and Japan. The MTA purchased the cars at the unit price of $844,500 per car as provided in Article VII-A(a) of the contract. On the same day the contract was entered into by the MTA and NIAC, NIAC assigned all of its rights and obligations under the contract to NIC pursuant to Article VI-A. KHI also signed a warranty of performance to the MTA and NIAC on that date.

Pursuant to a contract dated March 23, 1983, NIC placed an order with KHI for the production of the 325 passenger cars subject to the NIC/NIAC-MTA contract of March 17, 1982. Under the KHI-NIC agreement, KHI agreed to manufacture the 325 vehicles in Japan in accordance with the specifications of the NIC/NIAC-MTA contract, said vehicles to be delivered to NIC "FOB, Kobe Japan." ["FOB" is an international contract law term standing for "free on board."] The vehicles manufactured and delivered by KHI were specifically intended for sale to the MTA and could not be used for any other purpose. The payment by NIC to KHI was negotiated to be ¥ [Japanese yen] 80,002,100 per vehicle, plus escalation and change order payments determined under a formula specified in the NIC/NIAC-MTA contract.

The 325 passenger cars subject to the NIC/NIAC-MTA and KHI-NIC contracts were imported in sixteen entries from August 18, 1983 through June 27, 1985. Upon entry, the imported vehicles were classified under item 690.10, Tariff Schedules of the United States (TSUS), dutiable (at the rate in effect at the time of each entry) on the full value of the imported merchandise less the cost or value of products of the United States included in such value pursuant to item 807.00, TSUS. [The HTS took effect on 1 January 1989. Neither party disputed either the applicability of the TSUS or the specific classification thereunder.]

Duties were assessed by Customs on the basis of the "transaction value" of the imported vehicles, as that term is defined in 19 U.S.C. § 140la(b)(1). The transaction value of the first 120 passenger cars (the first eleven entries) was determined on the basis of the KHI-NIC sales price. The entry of those vehicles is not at issue. The remaining 205 cars, however, were appraised by Customs at the price paid by the MTA to NIC/NIAC, less certain deductions which Customs considered appropriate. Specifically, Customs determined that each of the imported vehicles at issue had a dutiable value of "US$542,036.45, per unit less appropriate duties net." Upon making the necessary duty deductions, the final dutiable value per vehicle was assessed at $497,737.61 for vehicles entered in 1983, $500,495.16 for vehicles entered in 1984, and $503,751.17 for vehicles entered in 1985.

On August 4, 1983, NIAC protested Customs' appraisals of the value of the imported merchandise and requested that Customs issue a ruling holding that the dutiable value of the vehicles should be based on the price paid by NIC to KHI. Customs responded that it "was [initially] refraining from issuing a ruling in this case," because the issue whether the KHI-NIC sales price could represent the "relevant sale for exportation to the United States under 19 U.S.C. § 140la(b)(1)" was "involved in a case which [was then] currently pending" before the Court of International Trade. That case was *American Air Parcel Forwarding Co. Ltd. v. United States*, 664 F. Supp. 1434 (1987), . . . rev'd sub nom. *E.C. McAfee Co. v. United States*, 842 F.2d 314 (Fed. Cir. 1988).

The entries at issue were finally liquidated in December 1985. Customs adhered to its determination that the transaction value of the imported vehicles was represented by the contract price between the MTA and NIC/NIAC. NIAC commenced an action in the Court of International Trade for re-liquidation of the imported vehicles based upon the price paid by NIC to KHI. NIAC argued that this court's decision in *McAfee* mandates that the appraisal of the value of the imported vehicles be based on the price paid by the middleman to the manufacturer, *i.e.*, the KHI-NIC price.

Before the trial court, the parties filed cross motions for summary judgment on the re-liquidation claim. Following the analysis of *Brosterhous, Coleman & Co. v. United States*, 737 F. Supp. 1197 (Ct. Int'l Trade 1990), the court determined that the contract between the MTA and NIC/NIAC "was the contract which most directly caused the goods to be exported to the United States" and thus held that the value of the vehicles was properly based on the NIC/NIAC-MTA contract. . . .

Discussion

On appeal to this court, NIAC argues that the trial court failed to follow the holding in *McAfee* that the price of the initial sale from the manufacturer to the middleman must be used for appraisal, not the price of the sale from the middleman to the purchaser. . . .

I. *Transaction Value*

The parties do not dispute that the imported vehicles must be appraised on the basis of "transaction value." The transaction value of imported merchandise is defined in Section 402(b)(1) of the *Tariff Act of 1930*, as amended by section 201 of the *Trade Agreements Act of 1979*, codified at 19 U.S.C. § 140la(b)(1), as the "price actually paid or payable for the merchandise when sold for exportation to the United States," subject to certain additions and deductions as noted earlier. The primary issue here is whether the trial court erred in determining that the NIC/NIAC — MTA contract price is the price actually paid or payable for the imported vehicles when sold for exportation to the United States.

McAfee similarly involved a three-tiered system for distributing custom-made clothing assembled in Hong Kong to purchasers in the United States. Under this system, purchasers' orders for the clothing were taken by a distributor who then contracted with tailors in Hong Kong to produce the clothing. Upon receipt of the completed clothing, the distributor imported the items into the United States and forwarded them to the purchasers. The clothing entries were liquidated pursuant to an assessment of transaction value based on the price to the U.S. purchasers rather than the price paid by the distributor to the Hong Kong manufacturers.

The principal issue addressed by the court in *McAfee* concerned the proper transaction value of the imported merchandise. In resolving that issue, the court in *McAfee* essentially addressed two separate questions: (1) whether the sale between the manufacturer and the middleman involved merchandise that was "for exportation to the United States," and if so, (2) which of the two possible sales prices (*i.e.*, the price paid by the middleman or the price paid by the purchaser) was proper for valuation purposes.

Regarding the first question, the court determined that "[w]here clothing is made-to-measure for individual United States customers and ultimately sent to those customers, the reality of the transaction between the distributors and the tailors is that the goods, at the time of the transaction between the distributors and tailors, are 'for exportation to the United States.' " . . . Upon concluding that the merchandise sold by the manufacturers to the middleman was made for exportation to the United States, the court was then faced with deciding which price should be used as the basis for appraising the transaction value.

In addressing that question, the court found guidance from *United States v. Getz Bros. & Co.*, 55 CCPA 11 (1967), a decision binding upon us in which the determination of transaction value of imported merchandise in the context of a three-tiered distribution was also involved. As the court in *McAfee* succinctly stated:

> [t]he issue in *Getz* was whether valuation of certain plywood should be at the manufacturer's price to a foreign middleman or that middleman's price to the United States customer. Two holdings in that case are significant here. First, a sale need not be to purchasers located in the United States to provide the basis for valuation. Second, *if the transaction between the manufacturer and the middleman falls within the statutory provision for valuation, the manufacturer's price, rather than the price from the middleman to his customer, is used for appraisal.* [Citations omitted.]

McAfee, 842 F.2d at 318, (emphasis added). Following the holdings of *Getz*, the court in *McAfee* held that the transaction value of the imported garments should have been determined on the basis of the Hong Kong tailors' assembly price, rather than on the basis of the price paid by the U.S. purchasers to the distributor.

Although the court in *McAfee* recognized that "[a] determination that goods are being sold or assembled for exportation to the United States is fact-specific and can only be made on a case-by-case basis" . . . that caveat pertains specifically to determining whether a certain sales price falls within the statutory definition of transaction value under 19 U.S.C. § 140la(b)(1). However, once it is determined that both the manufacturer's price and the middleman's price are statutorily viable transaction values, the rule is straightforward: the manufacturer's price, rather than the price from the middleman to the purchaser, is used as the basis for determining transaction value. Indeed, the court noted that

> . . . if the importer establishes that his claimed, lower valuation falls within the statute, the importer is entitled to the benefit of that valuation even though Customs' valuation also satisfies the same statutory requirements. While an argument could be made that Customs should have the option to impose the higher duty in such circumstances, . . . precedent is to the contrary.

Id. at 318.

The government argues that the so-called "first sale" rule of *Getz* and *McAfee* should not apply to every case where there is a manufacturer, a middleman, and a purchaser, regardless of the facts involved. We agree. Conceivably, mechanical application of the rule whenever there is a three-tiered distribution system could lead to inequitable results where the manufacturer's price is set artificially low. However, the rule only applies where there is a legitimate choice between two statutorily viable transaction values. The manufacturer's price constitutes a viable transaction value when the goods are clearly destined for export to the United States and when the manufacturer and the middleman deal with each other at arm's length, in the absence of any non-market influences that affect the legitimacy of the sales price. As the government itself recognizes, that determination can only be made on a case-by-case basis. In this case, the vehicles that were the subject of the KHI — NIC contract were manufactured for a specific United States purchaser, the MTA. They were unquestionably intended "for exportation to the United States" and had no possible alternative destination.

At trial, the government argued that the transaction between KHI and NIC did not fall within the statutory definition of transaction value because the sales price negotiated between KHI and NIC was not the product of arm's length bargaining. The trial court, however, rejected the government's allegations that KHI and NIC were "related parties" under 19 U.S.C. § 140la(g) and that there was no sale for exportation between KHI and NIC. The court determined that the "agreements between NIC and KHI were [not] of a different nature from the foreign transactions in . . . *Getz* and *McAfee*" . . . .

On appeal, the government contends that the price paid by NIC to KHI under the KHI — NIC contract cannot represent the correct appraised transaction value of the imported vehicles because that contract did not involve the sale of complete vehicles. According to the government, KHI did not "own" the U.S.-made components found in the imported vehicles and thus the contract between KHI and NIC only involved the sale of the vehicles' Japanese-made components. In support of its position, the government relies on Article 3 of the KHI-NIC contract, which provided that the price negotiated between KHI and NIC of ¥ 80,002,100 per vehicle was subject to change with any change in the quantity of Japanese-made components as compared to U.S.-made components. We reject the government's contention.

Under the KHI — NIC contract, KHI agreed to manufacture 325 rapid transit passenger vehicles in accordance with the contract between NIC/NIAC and the MTA, and NIC agreed to pay for them. Although KHI was required to use a specified quantity of U.S.-made components in the fabrication of the vehicles, that requirement did not render the contract as merely one for the sale of components made in Japan. A breakdown between the Japanese and American content of the vehicles was necessary for purposes of establishing financing credit from the Export — Import Bank of Japan. Any change in the content ratio would have an effect on such credit, and thus the KHI — NIC contract provided for compensatory price adjustments. The government has failed to establish that the use of U.S.-made components in the manufacture of the imported vehicles in any way undermined the legitimacy of the price negotiated between KHI and NIC for the purchase of the completed vehicles or that the sales price did not accurately reflect the price that would exist in a true arm's length transaction.

Accepting that both the manufacturer's price and the middleman's price may serve as the basis of transaction value, the critical issue on appeal here centers upon which price is legally proper. In view of the controlling and binding authority of *McAfee*, we hold that the transaction value of the imported passenger cars at issue must be based on the KHI — NIC contract price.

The trial court, however, determined that *McAfee* was distinguishable from the instant case and thus did not consider it controlling authority in appraising the transaction value of the imported vehicles. Instead, the court employed the analysis set forth in *Brosterhous* . . . in determining that the transaction value should be based on the price paid by the purchaser. We agree with NIAC that the trial court committed reversible error in failing to follow the controlling authority of *McAfee*.

. . . .

The ultimate issue in *McAfee* was whether the assembly price of the imported merchandise, rather than the price paid by the purchaser, should serve as the basis for determining transaction value. Similarly, the critical issue here is whether the sales price paid by NIC to KHI should serve as the basis for appraising the transaction value of the imported vehicles. *McAfee* speaks directly to that question and answers it in the affirmative. That case is not only applicable here, it is dispositive.

In the interest of clarifying the law, we consider it necessary to examine the case of *Brosterhous, Coleman & Co. v. United States* . . . upon which the trial court relied in reaching its decision. The court in *Brosterhous* held that where there are two transactions that can be considered to be sales for importation to the United States, "Customs policy is that transaction value should be calculated according to the sale which most directly caused the merchandise to be exported to the United States." . . .

The U.S. Customs Service issued a seminal ruling in C.S.D. 83-46, 17 Cust.B. 811 (January 21, 1983) in which it stated its position that "the transaction to which the phrase 'when sold for exportation to the United States' refers when there are two or more transactions which might give rise to a transaction value, is the transaction which most directly causes the merchandise to be exported to the United States." . . . In so ruling, Customs acknowledged that under 19 U.S.C. § 140la(b), as it existed before amendment by the *Trade Agreements Act of 1979*, "it was possible to use as the sale for exportation to the United States for purposes of determining statutory export value a sale from a foreign seller to a foreign buyer, who in turn sold the merchandise to a United States importer." However, Customs departed from that view because the *Trade Agreements Act* replaced "export value" with "transaction value" as the primary basis for valuation. Thus Customs concluded that "[c]ases decided under the prior law are not, therefore, necessarily precedent under the [*Trade Agreements Act*]." . . .

We reject the Customs Service's rationale as being legally unsound. A similar argument was rejected by the court in *McAfee*, which recognized that "the language of the earlier statute is not significantly different from the . . . provision of the current statute." . . . We agree with NIAC that the 1979 amendment did not change the operative language of the statutory provision for valuation which requires that the sale be "for exportation to the United States." Further, we can discern nothing in the legislative history of the 1979 amendment that suggests that Customs, in determining the transaction value of imported merchandise, should undertake an investigation focusing on which of two transactions most directly caused the exportation. The "Customs policy" followed by *Brosterhous* proceeds from an invalid premise. To the extent

Brosterhous is inconsistent with this court's decision in *McAfee* by requiring a weighing of the relative importance of two viable transactions, it is overruled.

IV. DRAWBACK

U.S. CUSTOMS AND BORDER PROTECTION, *IMPORTING INTO THE UNITED STATES, A GUIDE FOR COMMERCIAL EXPORTERS*
80-81 (November 2006)

Drawback is a refund of monies — customs duties, certain internal revenue taxes and other fees — that were lawfully collected at the time of importation. [Generally, the amount refundable is 99 percent of the duties or taxes collected on imported merchandise. The Continental Congress established drawback in 1789 [under the first tariff act] to create jobs in the new United States and to encourage manufacturing and exporting.

[Since 1789, drawback has been a mainstay of U.S. customs law. However, what is the value of drawback if MFN rates fall through multilateral trade negotiations? Query, too, what effect FTAs and developing country preference schemes have on drawback.]

For drawback to be paid, the imported merchandise must be exported or destroyed under CBP supervision after importation.

Types of Drawback

Although Section 1313, Title 19, of the United States Code provides for several types of drawback, there are three primary types of drawback of interest to most importers:

- Manufacturing drawback,
- Unused-merchandise drawback, or
- Rejected-merchandise drawback.

Manufacturing drawback is a refund of duties paid on imported merchandise specifically designated for use in manufacturing articles that are subsequently exported or destroyed. For example: two-inch speakers are imported and are incorporated into a certain model clock radio. The speakers themselves are not altered, just used in the production of a new and different article.

Manufacturing operations to produce the new and different article must take place within three years receipt by the manufacturer or producer of the merchandise. The drawback product must be exported or destroyed within five years from the date of importation. Drawback can be paid on merchandise used to manufacture or produce a different article if it was not the merchandise imported but is commercially interchangeable, *i.e.*, of the same kind and quality, or if it falls under the same eight-digit Harmonized Tariff Schedule number as the merchandise to which it is compared, and the party claiming drawback has had possession of it for three years. This is called "substitution."

Unused-merchandise drawback is a refund of any duty, tax, or eligible fees paid on imported merchandise that is exported or destroyed without undergoing any manufacturing operations and that is never used in the United States. The imported merchandise must be exported within three years of the date it was imported.

Rejected-merchandise drawback is refund of duties on imported merchandise that is exported or destroyed because it:

- Did not conform to sample or specifications,
- Was shipped without the consignee's consent, or
- Was defective at time of importation.

To qualify for rejected-merchandise drawback, the merchandise in question must be returned to CBP custody within three years of the date it was originally released from CBP custody.

. . . .

. . . Rejected merchandise drawback was amended in 2004 to permit limited substitution of imported merchandise. The import merchandise on which drawback is claimed must be classified under the same 8-digit HTSUS subheading and have the same specific product indicator (such as a part number, product code or sku) as the merchandise that is exported or destroyed and must have been imported within one year of the export or destruction.

[Must imported merchandise be used in the manufacturing process in the U.S., *i.e.*, incorporated into a finished product that is exported, to support a drawback claim? Obviously, the answer is "no." Congress authorized unused merchandise drawback, also known as *same condition drawback*, in 1980, thereby removing a constraint that had exited in the *Tariff Act of 1930*. Same condition drawback allows for drawback on imported merchandise that is subsequently exported, even the merchandise was not manufactured into another article. Must exactly the same merchandise, on which an import duty was paid, be exported in order to support a drawback claim? Again, the answer is "no." Section 202 of *Trade and Tariff Act of 1984*, 19 U.S.C. Section 1313(j)(2), essentially allows for *substitution, same condition drawback, i.e.*, a refund on merchandise of the same kind or quality as imported merchandise, in effect, fungible articles. However, must a claimant for drawback on substitution, same condition merchandise be the exporter of that merchandise? In other words, must the claimant be in possession of this merchandise? For a case answering "no," see *Central Soya Co., Inc. v. United States*, 761 F. Supp. 133, *aff'd* 953 F.2d 630 (Fed. Cir. 1992).]

V. PRE-SHIPMENT INSPECTION

A. False Invoicing and Other Incentives for PSI

Closely related to the problem of customs valuation is the matter of pre-shipment inspection. Pre-shipment inspection is

> an examination, on behalf of a foreign government or other contracting principal, of the quality and quantity of goods exported to that country

or principal and an evaluation of whether or not the transaction value of the goods corresponds, within acceptable limits, to the export market price generally prevailing in the country of origin of the goods. The examination is conducted by private inspection companies [known as pre-shipment inspection, or PSI, companies] retained for that purpose by the governments of many developing countries to perform quantity and quality inspections and price comparisons on their imports. These inspections are generally conducted within the country of export [*e.g.*, at a seaport or airport].[4]

Typically, a developing or least developed country employs pre-shipment inspection to check the value of merchandise to be imported into its country to ensure this value corresponds with the value the exporter lists on the invoice to the importer.

A government, and particularly a central bank, of a poor country is especially likely to care about accurate valuation if the country lacks hard currency and the imported merchandise must be paid for in such currency. To obtain hard currency to pay an exporter, an importer in a poor country may be required to apply to the central bank. Because hard currency reserves are precious, the central bank wants to be sure that it does not give the importer any more than necessary to pay for the imports. Pakistan, shortly after testing nuclear devices in May 1998, saw its hard currency reserves at the dangerously low level of two weeks worth of imports.

However, not infrequently in developing countries, the central bank maintains an official exchange rate. The official rate deliberately over-values the local currency relative to the hard currency, in order to make imports cheap and avoid spending precious hard currency reserves. Hence, there is a *de facto* dual exchange rate, a higher official rate and a lower unofficial or "black market" rate. This duality creates an arbitrage possibility for importers.

Importers can — and some do, despite the illegality and immorality of the behavior — submit a false invoice to their central bank, *i.e.*, an invoice showing a price for the imported merchandise higher than its true transaction value. If a central bank acts on the false invoice, then it enables the importer to get more hard currency than is needed to pay the exporter. In turn, the importer can sell the hard currency on the black market for its own local currency, and profit from the difference (or spread) between the official and black market rates.

A simple example illustrates the point. Suppose a Pakistani furniture company wants to import small coffee tables from the U.S. The true transaction value of each coffee table is $100, and the official Indian rupee — U.S. dollar exchange rate administered by the National Bank of Pakistan (NBK) is 30 rupees to the dollar. However, the black market rate is 40 rupees to the dollar, thus the NBK rate clearly overvalues the rupee by 10 rupees per dollar. The Indian importer submits a false invoice to the NBK stating a unit transaction value is $125. Assume the NBK acts on this false invoice. Accordingly, based on the official exchange rate of 30 rupees to the dollar, the

---

4 I THE GATT URUGUAY ROUND: A NEGOTIATING HISTORY (1986-1992), at 738-39 (Terence P. Stewart ed., 1993).

importer buys $125 from the NBK at a cost of 3,750 Indian rupees for each coffee table it plans to import. The importer then uses $100 of the $125 to pay the American exporter for each table. The importer sells the remaining $25 on the black market at the rate of 40 rupees per dollar. The black-market sale garners 1,000 rupees for the importer. (If the importer colludes with the exporter to persuade the exporter to provide a false invoice, then possibly the importer will split the 1,000 rupees with the exporter.) Thus, the importer bought more dollars from the NBK than needed to pay for the coffee tables using rupees at an overvalued rate of 30 rupees per dollar, and then sold the excess dollars in the black market for 40 rupees per dollar, pocketing the spread of 10 rupees per dollar. Put simply, it bought hard currency from the NBK at a cheap price (in rupee terms), and sold hard currency at a higher price (in rupee terms) on the black market.[5]

It is precisely this arbitrage that creates an incentive for a developing country government to conduct a PSI. In the above example, inspectors from the government of Pakistan, or a private company it hires, would check the shipment of coffee tables in the U.S., before that shipment leaves for Pakistan, to see if the transaction value really is $125. To be sure, it may be hard for the inspectors to foil a well-planned, well-executed scheme concocted by the Pakistani importer and American exporter. Nonetheless, given the importance of hard currency to many the treasuries of developing and least developed countries, the PSI effort may be worthwhile.

No doubt the real culprit is the lack of free convertibility of the developing country currency, *i.e.*, the poor country creates the incentive to submit false invoices by its exchange controls. However, the 1997-99 Asian Economic Crisis illustrates that developing country governments often are resistant to devaluing their currency and, ironically, will spend billions of dollars worth of hard currency reserves to maintain an over-valued peg. The response of the Thai, Malaysian, Philippine, and Indonesian governments illustrates the point. Thus, until developing countries accept realities in the foreign exchange market with respect to the true value of their currency, pre-shipment inspection is likely to continue. Significantly, as President Pervez Musharraf recounts in his autobiography, *In the Line of Fire* (2006), Pakistan accepted these realities in the late 1990s and early 2000s, liberalizing foreign currency restrictions. Yet, given the overhang of their sovereign debt-servicing obligations initially incurred in the 1970s and 1980s, and denominated in hard currencies, and given their need to import capital equipment, pharmaceuticals, and other items necessary to develop economically and raise living

---

[5] Over-invoicing also could be achieved in a slightly different manner. The importer might import merchandise of inferior quality, *i.e.*, the falsity in its invoice might not be the transaction value, but rather the description of the goods being imported. For example, the Pakistani importer might submit an invoice for $125 for small cherry wood coffee tables, which is the correct transaction value for such tables, but in fact intend to import small pine coffee tables at a price of $100. Still another way to over-invoice is to import a smaller quantity of merchandise than is set forth in the invoice. For instance, the Pakistani importer might submit an invoice for $125 for 100 coffee tables, but intend to import only 90 tables. In both of these alternatives, if the NBK accepts the false invoice, the Indian importer will obtain an allocation of U.S. dollars from the NBK in excess of the correct amount due for payment of the shipment to be received from the American exporter.

standards, many Third World governments are reluctant to undergo "shock therapy" and let their currencies float freely on the world market.

It should also be noted certain developing countries may create an incentive for their importers to under-invoice. This incentive arises from very high tariffs owed on imported merchandise. By submitting an invoice with an erroneously low transaction value, the importer may save on its tariff bill. Another way to circumvent the high tariff is to manipulate not the transaction value of imported merchandise, but rather its customs classification. The importer can mis-classify the merchandise in a lower-tariff category. An importer in a developing country with both high tariffs and currency controls undoubtedly will weigh the benefits from over-invoicing (in terms of currency gains) against the benefits from under-invoicing (in terms of duties saved), and choose the appropriate strategy. Under-invoicing could, of course, trigger an antidumping investigation that might result in the imposition of antidumping duties.

In any event, the incentive to under-invoice and consequent loss of tariff revenue is another reason why a developing country may engage in PSI. Once again, the source of the problem may be government international economic policy. A protectionist tariff regime, coupled with heavy reliance on tariffs for revenue, may create an incentive for non-compliance. (To be sure, as Alfred E. Eckes, Jr., ably points out in *Opening America's Market* (1995), the U.S. pursued protectionist policies for much of its early history.)

B. PSI as a Potential Non-Tariff Barrier

Unfortunately for exporters from developed countries, pre-shipment inspection is not necessarily an innocuous matter. Depending on the nature of the inspection procedures, the process can amount to a non-tariff barrier to trade.

1. First, the inspection process may impose administrative costs on developed country exporters. Their personnel need to respond to information requests from the inspectors.

2. Second, the inspection process may cause delays in shipments. An August 1987 study of pre-shipment inspection programs by the International Trade Commission (ITC) finds that 40 percent of shipments subject to pre-shipment inspection are delayed by an average of 20 days.[6]

3. Third, inspectors may demand confidential or sensitive business information, such as pricing data (*e.g.*, price relationships with suppliers of intermediate products), cost data (*e.g.*, the cost of manufacturing the merchandise to be shipped), or intellectual property material (*e.g.*, documents pertaining to an application for a patent, trademark, or copyright). The inspectors may not be careful with such information.

4. Fourth, the methods used by the pre-shipment inspectors may not be transparent. For example, they may reject a claimed transaction value simply because it falls outside of a certain range, but not explain how that range is determined.

---

[6] *See* U.S. International Trade Commission, *Pre-shipment Inspection Programs and Their Effects on U.S. Commerce*, ITC Inv. No. TA-332-242, U.S. ITC Pub. 2003 (1987).

5. Fifth, the exporter may have no right to appeal a decision of the inspector. If a transaction value is rejected, then it simply may have to live with the rejection.

In an effort to deal with the problem of pre-shipment inspection as a non-tariff barrier to trade, Uruguay Round negotiators reached an *Agreement on Pre-shipment Inspection*.

C. The WTO *PSI Agreement*

The *PSI Agreement* is suitably broad in scope. It covers "pre-shipment inspection activities," which Article 1:3 defines as "*all* activities relating to the verification of the *quality*, the *quantity*, the *price*, including currency exchange rate and financial terms, and/or the customs *classification* of goods to be exported to the territory of the user Member [*i.e.*, the WTO Member mandating or contracting for the use of pre-shipment inspection] [emphasis added]." The *Agreement* is designed to ensure PSI is reasonable and not an undue interference on legitimate trade. No changes to U.S. law were necessary to implement the *Agreement*. There are five aspects of the *Agreement* worth highlighting.

First, Articles 2:1-8, 3, 5, and 9 are "fairness" provisions. They require, *inter alia*, WTO Members using PSI to employ objective, transparent procedures, and apply these procedures in a non-discriminatory manner with respect to all affected exporters. For instance, exporters must be provided with all information necessary to comply with pre-shipment inspection requirements, relevant laws and regulations must be published before they take effect, and absent an emergency, additional requirements should not be applied unless an exporter is given advance notice. Members engaging in PSI activities must notify the WTO of their laws and regulations immediately after they are published.

Second, Article 2:15-19 seeks to minimize unreasonable delays. In general, the inspection process should be complete within five working days. By the end of this period, the inspector is required to issue either a clean report of its findings, or an explanation as to why it cannot issue such a report. Upon request of the exporter, the inspector must undertake a preliminary verification, and promptly inform the exporter of the results, with respect to the price of the merchandise and applicable exchange rate.

Third, Article 2:9-13 attempts to ensure confidential exporter information is protected. Inspectors are supposed to treat non-public information they receive as confidential, and governments employing private inspection firms must safeguard the information they receive from the firms. Additionally, inspectors should not request an exporter to provide information about manufacturing data, unpublished technical data, internal pricing, manufacturing costs, profits, or (unless required to conduct an inspection) information about contract terms between the exporter and its supplier.

Fourth, Article 2:20 requires inspectors to use a uniform price verification methodology. For example, inspectors must base their price comparisons on the price of identical or similar merchandise offered for export from the same country of exportation under comparable conditions of sale. These comparisons must conform to customary commercial practices, and include any standard discounts or other factors affecting price. It is not permissible for an inspector to base a price comparison on the selling price of merchandise produced in the country of importation, the price of merchandise from a country other than the actual country of exportation, or an arbitrary or fictitious value.

Finally, exporters are given a chance to appeal in writing decisions of pre-shipment inspectors under Article 2:21. The inspectors must establish procedures and designate a local representative to receive, consider, and render prompt decisions on any written appeal or grievance, lodged by an exporter. Under Article 4, grievances that cannot be resolved through the appeals process are to be dealt with through binding arbitration administered jointly by the Independent Entity (created by the WTO in 1996 as a subsidiary body of the Council for Trade in Goods), International Chamber of Commerce (ICC) and International Association of Pre-shipment Inspection Companies. In brief, a three-member arbitral panel is used, with one panelist selected by each side, plus an independent trade expert. Panel decisions must be rendered within eight working days of the request for arbitration, unless the parties agree to extend this deadline.

Chapter 19

TRADE CONTROLS

For whosoever commands the sea commands the trade; whosoever commands the trade of the world commands the riches of the world, and consequently the world itself.

> —Sir Walter Raleigh (c. 1554-1618), *A Discourse of the Invention of Ships, Anchors, Compass, &c., in* 8 THE WORKS OF SIR WALTER RALEIGH, KT. 325 (1829, reprinted 1965)

DOCUMENTS SUPPLEMENT ASSIGNMENT

1. *Havana Charter* Articles 16, 45:1(a)(ii), 99
2. GATT Articles I, XXI
3. *NAFTA* Chapters 5, 21
4. Relevant provisions in other FTAs

I. THE NATIONAL SECURITY EXCEPTION

A. The Need for GATT Article XXI

Article XXI is the exception in GATT for national security. While rarely invoked, this exception is highly significant, all the more so after the terrorist attacks of 11 September 2001. Following 9/11, the U.S. added several dramatic devices to its arsenal of border protections. But for Article XXI, inevitable clashes would occur between, on the one hand, unilateral measures adopted under these statutes, and on the other hand, pillar GATT obligations, and various duties under other WTO agreements.

Could these clashes be managed by Article XXXV:1(b), which allows for non-application of the GATT, and thereby the imposition of economic measures such as bans or boycotts? Obviously not. Non-application under Article XXXV:1 must be invoked by a WTO applicant against a WTO Member at the time the applicant joins the WTO. Or, conversely, a Member must invoke it against an applicant at the time the applicant joins the WTO.

Could Article XXV:5 manage the clashes? Again, certainly not. This provision explains how to obtain a waiver of obligations in "exceptional circumstances not elsewhere provided for in" GATT. To obtain a waiver, this Article requires a two-thirds majority vote involving more than half of the WTO Members. There is no exception to this requirement for unilaterally-imposed national security measures. Thus, it is Article XXI that provides the indispensable textual basis in GATT for such measures.

B. Scope and Self-Judgment

The all-embracing scope of Article XXI, as an exception to GATT obligations, is manifest from the first word of the Article, "[n]othing." Once a WTO Member relies on Article XXI to implement a measure against another Member, there is no GATT obligation to which the sanctioning Member must adhere with respect to the target Member. This point is further reinforced by a 1949 *Decision* of the Contracting Parties in a case brought under Article XXIII of GATT by the former Czechoslovakia against the U.S.[1]

Czechoslovakia argued the U.S. breached its obligations under Articles I and XIII by reason of its administration of export licensing and short-supply controls. The controls, instituted in 1948, discriminated among destination countries. The U.S. defended the controls under Article XXI(b)(ii), arguing they were necessary for security purposes, and they applied only to a narrow group of exports of goods that could be used for military purposes. The Contracting Parties rejected the Czech claim, voting 17 to 1, with 3 abstentions. In so doing, "the Chairman indicated that Article XXI 'embodied exceptions to the general rule contained in Article I.' "[2] Most of the other fundamental GATT obligations were not at issue in the case. But, it is reasonable to infer from this statement that if the Article I MFN rule is excepted, so too would be the other duties.

Indubitably, the most important and controversial portion of Article XXI is Article XXI(b). The word "it" means sole discretion to determine whether an action conforms to the requirements set forth in Article XXI(b) rests with the WTO Member invoking sanction measures. The plain meaning of this word indicates no other Member or group of Members, and no WTO panel or other adjudicatory body, has any right to determine for a sanctioning Member whether a measure satisfies the requirements. This interpretation is evident, for example, in the confident statement of the representative from Ghana concerning Ghana's boycott of Portuguese goods when Portugal acceded to GATT in 1961: "each contracting party was the sole judge of what was necessary in its essential security interest [and] [t]here could therefore be no objection to Ghana regarding the boycott of goods as justified by security interests."[3]

C. Four Controversial Corollaries

If it is correct that Article XXI(b) allows each WTO Member to decide for itself what its "essential security interests" are, then what legal implications follow? Arguably, four corollary propositions may be advanced:

1. *No Prior Notice*:

A sanctioning Member need not give any prior notice of impending national security sanctions, nor need it give notice upon or after the imposition of sanctions. It was, for example, Cuba, not the U.S., which informed GATT

---

[1] *See* I World Trade Organization, Guide to GATT Law and Practice — Analytical Index 602, 606 (6th ed. 1995); *Decision of 8 June 1949*, II B.I.S.D. 28 (1952), GATT/CP.3/SR.22.

[2] GATT Analytical Index, *supra* note 1, at 606.

[3] *Id.* at 600.

contracting parties of the trade embargo imposed on Cuba in February 1962 by the Kennedy Administration, and thereafter the Administration invoked Article XXI as its justification. In contrast, the Reagan Administration informed the contracting parties of its May 1985 prohibition on imports of all Nicaraguan goods and services, and its ban on exports to Nicaragua of all American goods and services other than those destined for the organized democratic resistance.

2. *No Justification*:

A sanctioning Member need not justify its determination to the WTO or its Members.

3. *No Approval or Ratification*:

A sanctioning Member need not obtain the prior approval or subsequent ratification of the WTO or its Members.

The first three propositions are manifest in a GATT Council discussion about trade restrictions on imports from Argentina imposed between April and June 1982 as a result of the Falklands Islands War by European Economic Community (EEC) members, Canada, and Australia. The EEC representative stated that the exercise of Article XXI rights "required neither notification, justification nor approval [*sic*], a procedure confirmed by thirty-five years of implementation of the General Agreement."[4] The U.S. representative made the point in even bolder terms: "The General Agreement left to *each contracting party* the judgment as to what *it* considered to be necessary to protect its security interests. The Contracting Parties had *no power* to question that judgment."[5]

4. *Threat versus Actual Danger*:

The fourth corollary principle concerns threatened versus actual dangers. A sanctioning Member may determine that its essential security interests are, in the words of the representative from Ghana in the 1961 debate about Ghana's boycott of Portuguese goods, "threatened by a *potential* as well as an actual danger."[6] As discussed more fully below, nothing in Article XXI(b) requires a sanctioning Member to face a danger that has manifest itself in a concrete sense, such as a physical invasion or armed attack, before imposing a national security measure.

If the four corollary propositions are correct, then they surely place Article XXI(b) among the GATT provisions coming closest to allowing a Member to act unilaterally.

D. Two Possible Restraints

What checks exist against unrestrained, cowboy-like behavior under Article XXI? Arguably, at least two — giving prior notice in the hope of engendering support, or at least minimizing opposition, to national security sanctions, and using the critical terms in the introductory *chapeau* to Article XXI(b) as a

---

[4] *Id.* at 600.

[5] *Id.* at 600.

[6] *Id.* at 600 (emphasis added).

gauge of the reasonableness of such sanctions. Neither is a fail safe device against abusive invocations of Article XXI(b), and the corrosive effect on multilateralism from them.

First, in most cases it is politically prudent for a sanctioning Member at least to give prior notice to other WTO Members, and possibly also attempt to garner a critical mass of multilateral acquiescence, if not *de facto* support, before using Article XXI. Thus, on 30 November 1982, after discussing the Falklands Islands crisis, the Contracting Parties adopted a *Decision Concerning Article XXI of the General Agreement* setting forth two points about the invocation of Article XXI.

> 3. Subject to the exception in Article XXI:a [concerning the right to withhold sensitive information], contracting parties should be informed *to the fullest extent possible* of trade measures taken under Article XXI.

> 4. When action is taken under Article XXI, all contracting parties affected by such action retain their full rights under the General Agreement.[7]

To be sure, the first paragraph is nothing more than a procedural recommendation. It is not an obligation to give notice to the WTO or its Members because of the phrase "to the fullest extent possible," and the sanctioning Member decides whether notice is "possible." Moreover, there is no preference expressed as between *a priori* or *post hoc* notice. But, the first paragraph of the *Decision* reflects a consensus view that giving prior notice is not just a matter of courtesy and respect for trading partners, but also a way of reducing friction. Presenting the international community *fait accompli* with national security sanctions inevitably leads to quarrels among political allies, with countries opposing the sanctions typically arguing they share the same end as the sanctioning country, but disagree with sanctions as a means to achieve that end. These quarrels have exploded into major trade rows because the U.S. has taken to the use of secondary boycotts of a target country, thus penalizing entities from third (including allied) countries that trade with or invest in the target.

The second restraint on cowboy behavior is contained in the introductory *chapeau* to Article XXI(b). A sanctioning Member is supposed to make sure that its measure is "necessary" for the "protection" of that Member's "essential security interests." For the most part, GATT contracting parties exercised restraint in interpreting these terms, and most WTO Members similarly have been cautious. Overall, the number of express or implicit invocations of Article XXI remains relatively small. Nevertheless, the potential for abuse exists, and the considerable criticism of recent American sanctions laws would lead some observers to doubt the power of these terms to continue to act as a restraint on cowboy behavior. After all, these terms are broad enough to encompass a variety of circumstances, and their application to a particular set of facts is subjective. At the same time, these terms are a gauge by which the world trading community can opine on a sanctioning Member's use of Article XXI(b).

---

[7] *Id.* at 606 (emphasis added).

Put differently, they can help shape world opinion as to whether a sanctioning Member is "crying wolf."

Consider Sweden's global import quota system for certain footwear, in effect from November 1975 to July 1977. Sweden argued the

> decrease in domestic production has become a critical threat to the emergency planning of Sweden's economic defense as an integral part of the country's security policy. This policy necessitates the maintenance of a minimum domestic production capacity in vital industries. Such a capacity is indispensable in order to secure the provision of essential products necessary to meet basic needs in case of war or other emergency in international relations.[8]

In fairness to the Swedish argument, it is true that, as one contracting party said during the discussion of the 1949 action brought by Czechoslovakia against the U.S., Article XXI covers "goods which were of a nature that *could contribute to war potential.*"[9] But, on reflection, the gauge suggested reveals why Sweden's argument is outrageous: it is a slippery slope. Would buttons for military uniforms be "necessary" for the "protection" of Sweden's "essential security interests" on the grounds that troops are disadvantaged if they lack appropriate attire?

More generally, is Article XXI(b) really designed for potential non-military (*i.e.*, economic) threats? If so, then America's Big Three automakers (General Motors, Ford, and Chrysler) could argue that Japanese auto imports should be banned or severely restricted because of the threat they pose to market share in the vital passenger car industry. Likewise, India could argue (as it has) it must enact extraordinary measures against imported food to ensure it maintains self-sufficiency in food, especially given its long-standing border conflicts.

These arguments, however, would stretch beyond recognition Article XXI(b), making it a commercial as well as national security exception. In terms of these arguments, the central thrust behind Article XXI(b) is the requirement of showing a link between the American passenger car industry and a national security threat, or between India's food needs and its traditional nemeses, Pakistan and China. But, these arguments pre-suppose such a link and thus become self-fulfilling. To be sure, there are cases in which commercial and national security interests are so intertwined that a bright line between the two interests cannot be drawn. Nonetheless, it must be remembered that regular trade remedies condoned under other articles of GATT, most notably the escape clause permitted by Article XIX, exist to deal with non-military threats posed by fair foreign competition.

As another illustration of how the gauge can be helpful in delimiting Article XXI(b), consider an argument made by Nicaragua in an action it brought against the U.S. relating to a trade embargo imposed by the Reagan Administration in May 1985 against Nicaragua. Nicaragua urged that the key terms in the Article XXI(b) *chapeau* amount to a self-defense requirement, *i.e.*, they mean that a Member can invoke Article XXI(b) only after it has been subjected

---

[8] *Id.* at 603.

[9] *Id.* at 602.

to aggression. In the unadopted 1986 report, the GATT Panel felt its strict terms of reference prevented it from ruling on this argument. However, Nicaragua's argument cannot be right. If the drafters of GATT meant to include only self-defense cases, then it is likely they would have said so expressly and, perhaps even referenced the language in Article 51 of the United Nations Charter.[10] Instead, they used terms that would balance competing interests, as is evident from the statement of one of the drafters of the *Havana Charter* about the meaning of "essential security interests."

> We gave a good deal of thought to the question of the security exception which we thought should be included in the Charter. We recognized that there was a great danger of having too wide an exception and we could not put it into the Charter, simply by saying: "by any Member of measures relating to a Member's security interests," because that would permit anything under the sun. Therefore we thought it well to draft provisions which would take care of real security interests and, at the same time, so far as we could, to limit the exception so as to prevent the adoption of protection for maintaining industries under every conceivable circumstance. . . . [T]here must be some latitude here for security measures. It is really a question of balance. We have got to have some exceptions. We cannot make it too tight, because we cannot prohibit measures which are needed purely for security reasons. On the other hand, we cannot make it so broad that, under the guise of security, countries will put on measures which really have a commercial purpose.[11]

Moreover, clauses (i), (ii), and (iii) that follow the *chapeau* to Article XXI(b) indicates actual aggression is not a prerequisite — the point the Ghanian Representative made.

These clauses envision the invocation of Article XXI(b) to deal with nuclear weapons material, arms trafficking, or an international relations emergency. If a sanctioning Member had to wait until a hostile power acquires nuclear weapons, a destabilizing number or type of non-nuclear arms, or a physical invasion, then it would be too late for trade sanctions to have any protective effect. In addition, the threat may be orchestrated by a "military establishment," a term broad enough to include not just sovereign governments, but also major terrorist organizations or drug cartels.

At the same time, however, implicit in clauses (i), (ii), and (iii), and in the words "necessary," "protection," and "essential security interests," must be the concept of a *credible* threat from these dangers. Simply "crying wolf" will not do, because Article XXI could not have been designed to protect a hyper-sensitive government anymore than many standards of care in tort law do not protect the hyper-sensitive plaintiff. Rather, the test should be an objective

---

[10] Article 51 provides that "[n]othing in the present Charter shall impair the inherent right of individual or collective self-defense if an armed attack occurs against a Member of the United Nations, until the Security Council has taken measures necessary to maintain international peace and security." 59 Stat. 1031, done at San Francisco, 26 June 1945, entered into force on 24 October 1945.

[11] GATT ANALYTICAL INDEX, *supra* note 1, at 600.

one, namely, whether a "reasonable" government faced with the same circumstances would invoke Article XXI. In sum, it is the implicit concept of a credible threat judged from the objective standpoint of a reasonable, similarly-situated government, coupled with the articulation of specific types of dangers that track one or more of the three clauses, and not Nicaragua's unduly restrictive self-defense argument, that can be a restraint on cowboy behavior.

II. TRADE SANCTIONS

A. Basic Statutory Authorizations

HOUSE COMMITTEE ON WAYS AND MEANS, 109TH CONG., 1ST SESS., *OVERVIEW AND COMPILATION OF U.S. TRADE STATUTES* 217-19, 228-31 (Committee Print June 2005)

International Emergency Economic Powers Act

In 1977, Congress passed the *International Emergency Economic Powers Act* (*IEEPA*) [50 U.S.C. §§ 1701-1706]. The *Act* grants the President authority to regulate a comprehensive range of financial and commercial transactions in which foreign parties are involved, but allows the President to exercise this authority only in order "to deal with an unusual and extraordinary threat, which has its source in whole or in part outside the United States, to the national security, foreign policy, or economy of the United States, if the President declares a national emergency . . . with respect to such threat."

Background

Public Law 95-223 [approved 28 December 1977], of which [the] *IEEPA* constitutes title II, redefined the President's authorities to regulate international economic transactions in times of national emergency, until then provided by section 5(b) of the *Trading with the Enemy Act* (*TWEA*) (50 App. U.S.C. § 5(b)), by eliminating *TWEA's* applicability to national emergencies and instead providing such authorities in a separate statute of somewhat narrower scope and subject to congressional review.

The authorities granted to the President under *IEEPA* broadly parallel those contained in section 5(b) of the *TWEA*, but are somewhat fewer and more circumscribed. While under the *TWEA* the existence of any declared national emergency, whether or not connected with the circumstances requiring emergency action, was used as the basis for such action, the *IEEPA* allows emergency measures against an external threat only if a national emergency under the *National Emergencies Act* [Public Law 94-412, 50 U.S.C. §§ 1601 *et seq*.] has been declared with respect to the same threat. Nevertheless, the President's authorities under the *IEEPA* still remain extensive and, as noted below, were further enhanced in 2001 by the *USA Patriot Act* [Public Law 109-56, approved 26 October 2001]. . . . Under [the] *IEEPA*, the President may "by means of instructions, licenses, or otherwise . . . investigate, regulate, prevent, or prohibit" virtually any foreign economic transaction, from import or export of goods and currency, to transfer of exchange or credit. The only international transactions exempted from this authority are personal communications not involving a transfer of anything of value; charitable donations of necessities of life to relieve human suffering (except in certain circumstances); the importation to or expatriation from any country of information and informational materials, such as publications, not otherwise controlled by export control law or prohibited by espionage law; or personal transactions ordinarily incident to travel.

[The] *IEEPA* was amended by section 106 of the *USA Patriot Act* . . . to enhance its authorities. First, the *Patriot Act* clarified that the broad authorities granted to the President in the *IEEPA* include the power to block property during the pendency of an investigation. It also allows the President to confiscate and vest property of any foreign country or foreign national that has planned, authorized, aided, or engaged in armed hostilities with or attacks against the United States. In addition, the *USA Patriot Act* provides that in any judicial review of a determination made under the authorities section of [the] *IEEPA*, if that determination was based on classified information, such information may be submitted to the reviewing court *ex parte* and *in camera*.

[The] *IEEPA* requires the President to consult with Congress, whenever possible before declaring a national emergency, and while it remains in force. Once a national emergency goes into effect, the President must submit to Congress a detailed report explaining and justifying his actions and listing the countries against which such actions are to be taken, and why. The President is also required to provide Congress periodic follow up reports every six months with respect to the actions taken since the last report, and report any change in information previously reported. [The] *IEEPA* programs are established pursuant to a Declaration of National Emergency under the *National Emergencies Act*. They can be terminated by the President, and are typically continued annually on the anniversary date of the declaration of the national emergency, if the President determines it is necessary.

Application

Since its enactment, the authority conferred by [the] *IEEPA* has been exercised on various occasions and for different purposes. For example, [the] *IEEPA* has been used to impose a variety of economic sanctions on foreign countries, as well as to block property and prohibit transactions with specially designated persons, such as persons who commit, threaten to commit, or support terrorism; persons indicted as war criminals by the International Criminal Tribunal for the former Yugoslavia [ICTFY]; persons who threaten international stabilization efforts in the Western Balkans; and persons undermining democratic processes or institutions in Zimbabwe. In addition, [the] *IEEPA* has been used to continue in force the authority of the *Export Administration Act* during several periods when statutory authority has lapsed. . . .

Iran

In response to the seizure of the American Embassy and hostages in Teheran, President Carter, using *IEEPA* authority, on November 14, 1979, declared a national emergency and ordered the blocking of all property of the government of Iran and of the Central Bank of Iran within the jurisdiction of the United States. The measure and its later amendments were implemented through Iranian Assets Control Regulations (31 C.F.R. §§ 535). Sanctions against Iran were broadened on April 7, 1980, and April 17, 1980, to constitute eventually an embargo on all commercial, financial, and transportation transactions with Iran, with minimal exceptions. The trade embargo was revoked by President Carter on January 19, 1981 [following signature of the Algiers Accords, which (*inter alia*) created the Iran — U.S. Claims Tribunal in The Hague, Netherlands], after the release of the Teheran hostages, but the national emergency has remained in effect and has been extended.

[On 29 October 1987, President Ronald Reagan re-imposed an embargo on imports of goods and services from Iran. His action followed Iranian attacks on American flag ships during the Iran — Iraq War, and was under the authority of the *International Security and Development Cooperation Act of 1985*, 22 U.S.C. § 2349aa-9, and implemented via Iranian Transactions Regulations set out at 31 CFR Part 560. The embargo remains in force, though it was eased in 2000 to allow some agricultural trade [*e.g.*, caviar, dried fruit, foodstuffs, and nuts, as well as carpets]. *See* 31 C.F.R. § 560.535. In 2004, certain publishing activities between the U.S. and Iran were allowed to resume. *See* 31 C.F.R. §§ 515.577, 538.529, and 560.538.]

President Clinton invoked his authority under [the] *IEEPA* and other statutes on March 15, 1995 to prohibit the entry of any U.S. person or any entity controlled by a U.S. person into a contract involving the financing or overall supervision and management of the development of the petroleum resources located in Iran. The President imposed additional sanctions on May 8, 1995. [Specifically, in Executive Order Number 12959, 60 Fed. Reg. 24757, President Clinton prohibited trade in goods and services of Iranian origin, the export of goods, technology or services to Iran, and providing financing for those transactions, including the provision or use of other financial services with respect to such transactions. The re-exportation to Iran from third countries of goods or technology which had before been controlled for export to Iran is also prohibited. Transactions such as brokering and other dealing by U.S. persons in Iranian goods and services is prohibited, as well as new investments by U.S. persons in Iran or in property owned or controlled by the government of Iran. Finally, U.S. companies are prohibited from approving or facilitating their subsidiaries' performance of transactions that they themselves are prohibited from performing.] The sanctions were then amended in 1997 [by Executive Order 13059]. [Additional sanctions were imposed on Iran through the *Iran and Libya Sanctions Act of 1996* (*ILSA*), which Congress renewed with respect to Iran in 2006. The Office of Foreign Assets Control (OFAC) of the Department of the Treasury administers the sanctions.]

Additional Applications

Further examples of the use of the *IEEPA* include: by President Reagan in May 1985 against Nicaragua (specifically, the Sandinista government), in October 1985 against the apartheid regime of South Africa, in January 1986, and in 1992, against the government of Colonel Muammar Qaddafi of Libya (for support of terrorism), and in April 1988 against Panama (namely, the regime of Manuel Antonio Noriega of Panama); by President George H.W. Bush in August 1990 against Iraq (in response to its invasion of Kuwait), in October 1991 against Haiti (in response to the overthrow of a democratically elected government), and in 1992 against Serbia and Montenegro (because of actions in Croatia and Bosnia-Herzegovina); and by President Bill Clinton in June 1998 against Serbia and Montenegro (because of actions in Kosovo), in 1993 against Angola (owing to actions by the National Union for the Total Independence of Angola — UNITA), in 1995 against terrorists disrupting the Middle East peace process, in May 1997 against Burma (because of oppression of democratic opposition), in November 1997 against Sudan (because of support for terrorism, efforts to destabilize neighboring governments, and human rights abuses), in July 1999 against the Taliban regime in Afghanistan, and in 2001 against Sierra Leone and Liberia (because of illicit trade in diamonds). In October 2000, Congress enacted legislation — the *Trafficking Victims Protection Act of 2000* — authorizing the President to invoke the *IEEPA* in cases of trafficking in persons.]

. . . .

Trading With the Enemy Act

The *Trading With the Enemy Act* (TWEA) [Public Law 65-91, Chapter 106, 50 U.S.C. App. §§ 1-44] prohibits trade with any enemy or ally of an enemy during time of war. From enactment in 1917 until 1977, the scope of the authority granted to the President under this *Act* was expanded to provide the statutory basis for control of domestic as well as international financial transactions and was not restricted to trading with "the enemy." In response to the use of the *Act's* authority under section 5(b) during peacetime for domestic purposes that were often unrelated to a pre-existing declared state of emergency, Congress amended the *Act* in 1977. In 1977 Congress removed from the *TWEA* the authority of the President to control economic transactions during peacetime emergencies. Similar authorities, though more limited in scope and subject to the accountability and reporting requirements of the *National Emergencies Act*, were conferred upon the President by the *International Emergency Economic Powers Act*. . . . Presidential authority during wartime to regulate and control foreign transactions and property interests were retained under the *Trading With the Enemy Act*. In addition, the 1977 legislation authorized the continuation of various foreign policy controls implemented under the *Trading With the Enemy Act*, such as trade embargoes and foreign assets controls. The retention of such existing controls, however, was made subject to one-year extensions conditioned upon a presidential determination that the extension is in the national interest.

Background

The *Trading With the Enemy Act* was passed in 1917 "to define, regulate, and punish trading with the enemy." The *Act* was designed to provide a set of authorities for use by the President in time of war declared by Congress. In its original 19 sections, the *TWEA* provided general prohibitions against trading with the enemy; authorized the President to regulate and prohibit international economic transactions by means of license or otherwise; established an office to administer U.S.-held foreign property; and set up procedures for claims to such property by non-enemy persons, among other provisions. The original 1917 *Act* appeared not to authorize the control of domestic transactions and limited its use to wartime exigencies.

Over the years, through use and amendment of section 5(b), the basic authorizing provision, the scope of presidential actions under the *TWEA* was greatly expanded. First, the *Act* was expanded to control domestic as well as international transactions. Second, the authorities of the *Act* were used to apply to presidentially declared periods of "national emergency" as well as war declared by Congress. From 1933, when Congress retroactively approved President Roosevelt's declaration of a national banking emergency by expanding the use of section 5(b) to include national emergencies, until 1977, when Congress amended section 5(b), . . . the President was authorized in time of war or national emergency to:

(1) regulate or prohibit any transaction in foreign exchange, any banking transfer, and the importing or exporting of money or securities;

(2) prohibit the withdrawal from the United States of any property in which any foreign country or national has an interest;

(3) vest, or take title to, any such property; and

(4) use such property in the interest and for the benefit of the United States.

The *Trading With the Enemy Act* did not provide a statement of findings and standards to guide the administration of section 5(b). There was no provision in the *Act* for congressional participation or review, or for presidential reporting at specified periods for actions undertaken under section 5(b). There was no fixed time period for terminating a state of emergency. Nor was there any practical constraint on limiting actions taken under emergency authority to measures related to the emergency.

Application

By 1977 a state of national emergency had been declared by the President on four occasions and left unrescinded. In 1933 President Roosevelt declared a national emergency to close the banks temporarily and to issue emergency banking regulations. In 1950 President Truman declared a national emergency in connection with the Korean conflict. President Nixon declared a national emergency in 1970 to deal with the Post Office strike and another in 1971 based on the balance-of-payment crisis. As one measure to remedy this crisis, President Nixon at the same time imposed an import surcharge without specifically referring to section 5(b), but later did take recourse to it as an additional authority when the action was challenged in court.

[The case is *United States v. Yoshida International, Inc.*, 526 F.2d 560 (C.C.P.A. 1975). President Nixon's action was held to be constitutional, and in any event he terminated the surcharge after a little over 4 months. Further illustrations of invocation of the *TWEA* include by President Roosevelt against the Axis Powers in the Second World War, by President Lyndon B. Johnson with respect to China, North Korea, Cambodia, and North and South Vietnam. The ban on virtually all transactions with Cuba also is based on Section 5(b) of the *TWEA*.]

B. Conventional Normative and Empirical Issues

Sanctions, and more generally international trade law and policy, are a subset of American foreign policy. Sanctions are one way in which America interacts — or does not interact — with the rest of the world. Ronald Steel argues in his excellent little book, *Temptations of a Superpower* (1996), the central unresolved problem in America's post-Cold War foreign policy is translation of unparalleled military might built up during the Cold War into political influence. In May 1998, for example, America was embarrassingly unable to dissuade Pakistan from testing nuclear devices in response to India's nuclear tests. This problem is manifest whenever sanctions are used, particularly when they are deployed by the U.S. — as typically occurs — unilaterally. Through sanctions instead of military force, America is not simply expressing displeasure, but more importantly seeking to change the behavior of another country's government, or even cause the downfall of that government.

Debate about sanctions rightly is interdisciplinary. Lawyers, diplomats, economists, political scientists, historians, philosophers, offer a variety of perspectives, along with human rights activists, environmentalists, and other concerned lobbying groups and citizens. Despite this motley collection of voices, nearly the entire debate is focused on just two issues.

1. Is the *normative* purpose for invoking the sanction appropriate? Is it, for example, a proper policy to use sanctions to pry open an overseas market on behalf of a domestic business? To combat human rights abuses? Genocide? Religious persecution? To confront or contain a stubborn dictator? To prevent nuclear proliferation? Perhaps these cases are easy. But, what about using sanctions to combat corruption, or discourage abortion? The normative issue, then, is one of drawing lines, of delineating legitimate purposes without sliding down a slippery slope of indefensible sanctions.

2. Are sanctions *efficacious*, *i.e.*, do they work, in the sense of inducing changed behavior? If so, do sanctions work only after imposing an unacceptably large opportunity cost on domestic businesses (especially workers)? After all, these businesses would otherwise (1) offer goods and services to trade with the target country, (2) win lucrative procurement contracts from the target country's government, and (3) engage in profitable foreign direct investments in the target country. Even if the opportunity cost is not unacceptable, what

about the strain on relations with trading partners? Overall, the heart of this issue is whether the cost of sanctions exceeds their benefits based on historical experience.

Both issues have a corollary, namely, the danger of overuse. Even if a proposed sanction rests on well-grounded and is likely to achieve a desired outcome, the proposal still needs to be examined in the overall context of extant and possible future sanctions. There is a legitimate fear that too frequent deployment of the sanctions weapon will render it ineffective. Potential targets will be nonplused by the threat of sanctions. They will build that threat into their rational calculus when considering a course of conduct at which the sanction-imposing country is sure to look askance.

C. A Generic Analytical Framework

Setting aside the normative issue of purpose and the empirical issue of efficacy, how might an international trade lawyer confront *any* existing or proposed sanctions legislation? Might it be possible to develop a conceptual framework — or put less pretentiously, an algorithm — that can be used generically? The short answer is "yes."

The Table below offers a seven-step model to help understand what any unfamiliar, complex sanctions legislation says, and what it purports to do. The model is positivist in nature: it seeks to reveal legal doctrine and consequences, and eschew the interesting but messy and over-played normative debate about the content of the law. All seven steps rely heavily on conventional legal reasoning, and in particular, endeavor to draw careful, critical distinctions. The seven steps can be remembered by the simple acronym, "*MRS. WATU*" (a common Indonesian surname!).

The right-hand column indicates the *MRS. WATU* model is not limited to analyzing what a particular piece of sanctions legislation says and does. The model also reveals why one sanction regime could be more controversial than another. Typically, the explanation is cast in terms of normative purposes or empirical effects. It might be said, for instance, the 1996 *Helms-Burton Act* is controversial because sanctions are not the way to deal with the Castro government.[12] Or, sanctions formerly imposed against India and Pakistan under the *Nuclear Proliferation Prevention Act of 1994 (Nuclear Proliferation Act)* might have been pointless, as the "nuclear genie was out of the bottle," and hypocritical because of a different standard set for Israel.[13]

---

[12] The formal name of the *Helms-Burton Act* is the *Cuban Liberty and Democratic Solidarity (LIBERTAD) Act of 1996*, Pub. L. No. 104-114, 110 Stat. 785, codified as amended at 22 U.S.C. §§ 6021-6091. Guidelines and implementing regulations for the *Helms-Burton Act* exist. *See Cuban Assets Control Regulations; Indirect Financing in Cuba, Civil Penalties*, 61 Fed. Reg. 37,385 (1996) (codified at 31 C.F.R. pt. 515) (bringing existing Cuban asset control regulations into conformity with the Act); *Guidelines Implementing Title IV of the Cuban Liberty and Democratic Solidarity Act*, 61 Fed. Reg. 30,655 (1996) (implementing provisions of the *Act* and authorizing the Secretary of State and Attorney General to deny visas to certain foreigners); *Summary of the Provisions of Title III of the Cuban Liberty and Democratic Solidarity (LIBERTAD) Act of 1996*, 61 Fed. Reg. 24,955 (1996) (summarizing the *Act* and discussing persons who knowingly and intentionally traffic in confiscated property).

[13] For the *Nuclear Proliferation Act*, see Pub. L. No. 103-236, April 30, 1994, 108 Stat. 507, codified as amended at 22 U.S.C. §§ 6301-6305, and amending various other sections of titles 12 and 22 of the U.S.C.

Notably, after the 9/11 terrorist attacks, on 22 September 2001, President George W. Bush issued a Presidential Determination in which he waived non-nuclear arms export control sanctions against both India and Pakistan. The President lifted nuclear sanctions against India following a nuclear energy deal, to which Congress agreed, in December 2006.[14] Nuclear sanctions remain in force against Pakistan, which the U.S. justifies in part on the relatively poorer record of Pakistan (evidenced, for instance, by the A.Q. Khan scandal) than India in respect of non-proliferation. The deal with India, though, prompted outcries of a double standard for favored American allies in the War on Terror, and in respect of Israel, and accusations the U.S. was scuppering the July 1968 *Nuclear Non-Proliferation Treaty (NPT)*.

---

[14] *See Henry J. Hyde United States — India Peaceful Atomic Energy Act of 2006*, Pub. L. 109-401, 18 December 2006.

TABLE 19-1:
SYNOPSIS OF THE *MRS. WATU* MODEL

Acronym/Step	Issue for Examination	Possible *a priori* Expectation Regarding Controversy from Sanction
M — *M*ethod(s) of Sanction(s)	What method(s) of sanction(s) is used?	A larger number of methods affects more constituencies and suggests greater force, thus it is likely to cause greater controversy.
R — *R*ight of Action	Is there a private right of action?	A private right of action is almost certain to cause controversy because it is private and extraterritorial.
S — *S*econdary Boycott	Is there a secondary boycott (*i.e.*, one against not only direct trade transactions with the target — the primary boycott — but also against third parties or countries trading with the target)?	A secondary boycott is almost certain to cause controversy because it is seen as bullying and an infringement on sovereignty, and it is likely to evoke blocking legislation.
W — *W*aiver Authority	Who (if anyone) has the authority to waive the sanction, and what are the waiver criteria?	Waiver decisions are inherently political, and the degree of controversy is likely to depend partly on the wording of the criteria.
A — *A*im of Sanction	Is the sanction aimed at a regime or commodity, or possibly a production process?	A sanction aimed at a commodity or at a production process may be particularly controversial, because of substitution effects and perceived protectionism, respectively.
T — *T*ermination Criteria	What criteria, if any, exist to terminate the sanction?	A lack of termination criteria will be controversial in the long term, and if they exist, then the degree of controversy is likely to depend partly on their wording.
U — *U*nilateral Nature	Is the sanction imposed unilaterally?	A *de jure* and *de facto* unilateral sanction is almost certain to be particularly controversial.

In any event, *MRS. WATU* provides an *independent basis* for understanding why a sanction regime is controversial, or relatively more controversial than another. This basis is neither normative nor empirical, but doctrinal. *MRS. WATU* focuses on what the law says and does, not its underlying policy or economic efficacy. Hence, conclusions about controversies surrounding different sanctions schemes may be drawn without basing them on the purpose, economic effect, or policy success of those schemes.

III. PHILOSOPHICAL ARGUMENTS ON THE MORALITY OF SANCTIONS

Is the imposition of trade sanctions morally defensible? Is a decision not to impose trade sanctions morally defensible? If there is disagreement over economic analyses of sanctions, *i.e.*, whether they work, *a fortiori* there is disagreement over philosophical evaluations of sanctions, *i.e.*, whether they are "good." It is impossible to forge unanimity on these inherently normative questions. Why? Because they beg a question on which there is certain to be disagreement: what are the criteria for judging morality? Put differently, whether one views a sanctions regime, or a sanctions-free regime, as "just" hinges critically on one's approach to the most fundamental question in all of jurisprudence: what is "justice"?

Yet, herein lays another example of why international trade law is such a fascinating subject: this fundamental question cannot be avoided. It exists in the sanctions context, and then crops up again in the contexts of the treatment of developing countries, workers' rights, and environmental rights. It goes without saying that no book on jurisprudence, and certainly no textbook on international trade law, can define "justice" satisfactorily for all times and places. However, it is possible to outline here three competing conceptions of justice that are manifest in the context of trade sanctions: utilitarian (or more generally, teleological) theory, Just War theory, and Kantian (or more generally, deontological) theory.[15]

A. Utilitarian Theory

The utilitarian, or consequentialist, analysis of sanctions focuses on whether sanctions produce their desired effect, and whether that effect is on balance positive. Accordingly, the first question to ask is "what is the goal of the sanctions regime?" In the vast majority of cases, the goal is a change in the behavior of the target government. For example, the U.S. might seek to persuade Iran from arming Hizbullah guerrillas in southern Lebanon, or to discourage China from handpicking a successor to the Dalai Lama. Once the specific goal of a sanctions regime is ascertained, then the next step is to ask whether it was achieved. Did Iran stop shipping high-technology missiles to Hizbullah? Did the Tibetans pick their own Dalai Lama? The third and most important step is to consider the net effect of the sanctions regime. If it achieved its goal, then at what cost? If it was unsuccessful, then were the costs nonetheless worth incurring?

The first step is an exercise in statutory analysis and legislative history. In most cases, the law itself, and the preparatory work in support of it, will reveal the purpose — or purposes — of a sanctions regime. However, it is important to appreciate the possibility of purposes other than, or in addition to, inducing or compelling a target country to alter its behavior or cast off its leaders. Sanctions may be designed to defend against or deter an illegal or

---

[15] *See* FERNANDO R. TESON, A PHILOSOPHY OF INTERNATIONAL LAW (1998); GEOFFREY THOMAS, AN INTRODUCTION TO ETHICS 71-74 (1993); Frank Garcia, *A Philosophy of International Law*, 93 AM. J. INT'L L. 746, 747-49 (1999) (reviewing FERNANDO R. TESON, A PHILOSOPHY OF INTERNATIONAL LAW (1998)).

aggressive action, to exact retribution from (*i.e.*, simply punish) the target country, or to send a symbolic message to the target about international standards of conduct. Often, are designed very much with the soul of the country imposing them in mind, *i.e.*, they are a device to renounce complicity with evil (*e.g.*, the exploitation of child labor), regardless of whether the evil is legal in some technical sense.

Likewise, a healthy dose of cynicism is needed in this step. What legislators and politicians say about a regime is not always the real truth, the whole truth, or the lasting truth. Consider the American-led sanctions regime before the first Gulf War. Its stated purpose was to drive Saddam Hussein's forces from Kuwait. The regime failed to end that occupation, so coalition forces drove out Iraqi troops. Having achieved that objective by force, why did sanctions become so important after cessation of hostilities? The answer is the purpose of the regime changed, from the oft-repeated one of liberating Kuwait to the noble sounding one of protecting Kurds in northern Iraq and marsh Arabs in southern Iraq — hence the "no-fly zones." Or, to be more cynical but perhaps more accurate, was their underlying purpose all along to "contain" Iraq by toppling Saddam and destroying its chemical, biological, and (purported) nuclear weapons capabilities? Clearly, any inquiry into the purpose of a sanctions regime can lead to some jarring contradictions that complicate a utilitarian cost-benefit analysis.

The second step is an empirical investigation. Interestingly, one of the leading analysts of sanctions and their effects — Dr. Gary Hufbauer — argues sanctions achieve their goal in only about 34 percent of the cases.[16] Often sanctions produce a "rally-around-the-flag effect" in the target country, *i.e.*, civilians mobilize in support of their otherwise distasteful leadership simply because they perceive themselves to be facing a common external threat. The final step, however, is where utilitarian analysis is most poignant.

The most famous utilitarian principle, which is associated with the work of the 19th century philosopher Jeremy Bentham, is the "greatest good for greatest number" criterion. It is a principle of "*act* utilitarianism," meaning an action is right if and only if it maximizes welfare. In other words, only if an action produces more welfare, in a net sense, than any other possible course of action, is that action "good" or "just." Thus, in the present context, an act utilitarian analysis would hold that a sanctions regime is morally defensible if its benefits exceed its costs, and thus it maximizes welfare. But, this begs two questions: what is meant by "welfare" (*i.e.*, how are "benefits" and "costs" defined and measured), and whose welfare is relevant?

On the first question, is "welfare" satisfaction of material wants? For example, a sanctions regime might be thought unjust because it leads to unspeakable deprivations among children and the elderly in a target country. Alternatively, is "welfare" happiness in a deep spiritual sense? A sanctions regime may be deemed just because consumers in the sanctioning country have "no blood on their hands," because they are not buying toys for their children made by prison workers in China. On the second question, is the relevant focus the welfare of the country imposing the sanctions (*e.g.*, all

---

[16] *See* GARY C. HUFBAUER ET AL., ECONOMIC SANCTIONS RECONSIDERED (2d ed. 1990).

Americans), the target country (*e.g.*, all Iraqis), or both? How are the welfare effects to be aggregated? Should the welfare of some sub-groups of people (*e.g.*, women and disabled persons in the target country) be accorded greater weight than the welfare of other sub-groups (*e.g.*, American companies that lose business opportunities in the target country)?

Another prominent 19th century English philosopher, John Stuart Mill, offers a different utilitarian criterion — *rule* utilitarianism. Under a rule utilitarian analysis, an action is right only if it is in conformity with a rule, and by following that rule more welfare is produced than by following any other rule. The calculation of welfare on a particular occasion is not important. What matters is that across a large number of cases, a rule is followed, and following that rule in case after case leads to welfare maximization. The clear focus is on practices and behavior, and the moral requirement for a rule utilitarian is to follow the rule routinely, because by doing so ensures benefits exceed costs by the greatest possible amount. Observe, then, why rule utilitarianism sometimes is called "indirect" utilitarianism — because decision-making in an individual case is not governed by a cost-benefit calculation in that case.

Thus, rule utilitarianism would call for the establishment of sanctions policy that covers all instances of a defined type of egregious behavior by foreign governments. Once that behavior is manifest, the sanctions regime would be triggered automatically. There would be no calculation of the costs to businesses from the sanctioning country in terms of lost profitable opportunities, or of the costs to innocent civilians in the target country. Nor would the anticipated benefits in the particular case matter. Rather, at the time the policy was established, a determination would have been made that the automatic rule — imposing sanctions to combat the offensive behavior — is the welfare-maximizing one. To be sure, the same problems of definition, *i.e.*, what is "welfare," whose welfare matters, and how should the welfare of different sub-groups be aggregated, that plague an act utilitarian analysis are endemic here too.

Moreover, there is the additional problem of calculating at the policy formation stage that the proposed rule indeed will maximize welfare. Rule utilitarianism does not demand that sanctions work in every instance — maybe they work against South Africa and the former Rhodesia to bring down apartheid, but not against the Taliban in Afghanistan to force equal treatment of women. But, the criterion does demand that over the long-term, when the bulk of cases are considered, welfare is maximized. In other words, rule utilitarianism is more demanding than act utilitarianism in a critical respect: it requires the *a priori* formulation of the ideal rule.

Forming an ideal rule is easier with knowledge of historical patterns. In this respect, some of Dr. Hufbauer's empirical findings is noteworthy. In looking at a large number of sanctions regimes, he says sanctions tend to produce their desired result only if they lead to a fall in GNP of at least 2.5 percent. To cause that serious a recession indeed requires keeping the sanctions in place for at least about 3 years. Conversely, sanctions are almost certain to fail if all they do is cause a 1 percent contraction in GNP. Against which countries are sanctions most likely to produce the requisite GNP declines? Obviously, against countries with economies smaller than the sanctioning powers. In brief, these sorts of finding would be relevant in the rule formation stage when calculating the costs of an automatic sanctions rule.

A final concern about a rule utilitarian approach is whether all similarly situated parties must follow the rule in like cases. Must France, Japan, Russia, and the United Kingdom behave the same way with respect to an extremist Islamic state, and to the proliferation of nuclear, chemical, and biological weapons? Possibly, welfare — defined in a global sense — cannot be maximized unless the rule is the same for everyone. Thus, the U.S. might accomplish little in terms of welfare maximization if the other trading powers do not pursue the course of action. Why might there be this divergence in response to egregious behavior? Because some governments may follow rule utilitarianism, whereas others follow act utilitarianism.

B.   Kantian Theory

It was that giant of philosophy, Immanuel Kant, who counseled in his essay, *Perpetual Peace*, that the center of the international law must be the normative status of the individual, that it is wrong to conceive of international law as concerned only with the rights and duties of states as the fundamental unit of that law without also examining each state's domestic political system and its treatment of its citizens.[17] Kant's thesis is contrary to the traditional state centrism of international law. Sovereign nation states are not the atoms on which the matter of international law is constructed. What happens at the sub-atomic level — inside nation states — is important. To Kant, the business of international law was inextricably linked to the question of domestic justice. International law — and one can extend this to international trade law — is legitimate only if it is founded on an alliance of separate, free nations united by their moral commitment to individual freedom, not merely by their allegiance to the international rule of law and the mutual benefits of peaceful intercourse.

In other words, in the Kantian paradigm, it will not do to care only about whether a government controls its people, or to say that so long as the government exercises control, it can participate as a sovereign entity in a "just" international legal system. Rather, *how* a government treats *its own* people matters in the evaluation of the "just-ness" of the international legal order. The international law created and practiced by nation states cannot be considered morally defensible if those states fail to behave in a just manner with respect to the people living inside their boundaries. Thus, for Kant there is little if any room for the defense commonly offered for alleged human rights abuses: "back off, it is our own internal matter." (China is well known for this defense, but recall that the U.S. offers an essentially similar response to criticism of its widespread use of the death penalty.)

Put bluntly (as many did at the 1999 WTO Ministerial Meeting in Seattle), whether the GATT—WTO regime is "legitimate" (*i.e.*, "just" or "morally

---

[17] *See* Immanuel Kant, *To Perpetual Peace, in* PERPETUAL PEACE, AND OTHER ESSAYS ON POLITICS, HISTORY, AND MORALS 107 (Ted Humphrey trans. 1983); Heiner Bielefeldt, *Autonomy and Republicanism: Immanuel Kant's Philosophy of Freedom*, 25 POL. THEORY 524, 547-48 (1997).

acceptable") depends very much on whether the WTO Members are committed to domestic justice in the realms of human, labor, and environmental rights. Why? Because for Kant — and liberal theorists generally — the purpose of a nation state is to protect and serve its people. Only to the extent a nation state serves this purpose is it morally acceptable. If the WTO consists of a large number of states that do not serve this purpose, then much of the Membership is illegitimate, and any trade law they write or practice must also lack legitimacy. In brief, justice in international trade law cannot be separated from justice at the domestic level of WTO Members.

From a Kantian perspective, perhaps the "World Trade Organization" really is a "Sovereign State Trading Organization." Perhaps it is right to attack it for producing decisions that, however persuasive in terms of GATT Article XX:(b) and (g), horrify environmentally-minded observers. After all, how is one to deal with the fears of labor and human rights activists, who see their interests as the next ones to be sacrificed at the altar of MFN, national treatment, tariff bindings, non-discriminatory application of quotas, or some other trade-liberalizing principle. However noble that principle may be on the black boards of neoclassical economists, in the equations of game theorists, or in the theories of positivist philosophers, obviously it is not universally persuasive. How, then, is one to agree the *DSU* process is "legitimate" if much of that process excludes important voices, if much of that process is hidden from our eyes, if that process does not always call upon the best and brightest specialists to help resolve a dispute?

This same sort of Kantian reasoning can be applied in the sanctions context. Sanctions are to be evaluated not on teleological grounds. Whether they are efficacious is irrelevant, because acting on the basis of a moral principle is what matters. Nor is it permissible for a nation state to hide behind the traditional public international law principle of non-intervention in order to rationalize infringements on justice within its territory. In other words, without going so far as to label Kant an interventionist (a point that is in dispute), a reasonable inference to draw from his anti-statist approach is that sanctions may well be appropriate in certain cases. Precisely which cases is a matter for judgment on a deontological ground, namely, to what extent do they place the *normative status of the individual* at the center of attention?

That question, which is premised on a view that people are moral rather than economic agents, begs another one: who ought that "individual" to be? A good guess is a person (or identifiable group of persons) oppressed in a country targeted for sanctions. In other words, the focus ought to be on anyone whose human, labor, or environmental rights are being violated systematically by the target country's government. Any sanctions regime that takes aim at correcting the violation would be morally justifiable.

Kantian reasoning can be taken to a yet deeper level. The best-known of Kant's many insights is his categorical imperative: one ought to act as if the principle on which one is acting would become a universal law. That is, to decide whether a particular course of action is morally right, consider the principle underlying it. Would you wish all others to adhere to the same principle, and thereby pursue the same course of action in the same circumstances? If so, then the principle is morally defensible, and the action correct.

Plainly, the orientation is humanitarian, not utilitarian. It is a sort of golden rule.

In the sanctions context, the same question can be asked. What is the principle motivating a country to consider imposing sanctions? Is it a principle the country would want all other countries to adopt — including, of course, instances in which roles are reversed and foreign countries debate sanctions against the first country? Suppose the principle is the protection of human rights. If that is the principle the sanctioning country thinks ought to be universalized, then it is morally correct to follow the principle by implementing sanctions. It does not matter whether other countries actually join in the sanctions regime in a particular case, or even whether their present governmental policies are in accord with the principle. What matters is whether the sanctioning country believes the principle ought to be a universal one. Clearly, under this logic, there is plenty of room for the U.S. (or any other sanctioning country) to be a lone voice.

There is at least one very obvious danger with taking the Kantian thesis too far. It can become a fancy philosophical device to assert the superiority of western liberal values over all others. No universal conception of human nature is tolerated, except that articulated by Enlightenment philosophers and their intellectual progeny, like America's founding fathers. The result is, as Professor Garcia succinctly points out, the central paradox of western liberalism. The Kantian-style liberal logic impels one toward an intolerant stance vis-à-vis all countries not viewed as "liberal." Is this not precisely the stance many Americans take toward, for example, Iran and Syria? In brief, the pure-hearted Kantian approach runs amuck and becomes an empty-headed fighting liberalism that succumbs readily to constant use of sanctions.

In a 1993 essay, American philosopher John Rawls offers a way out of this problem.[18] For him, the world is not "either-or," "black or white." He eschews condemnation of nation states that do not follow western-style values as "illiberal." Rather, his work suggests a three-part classificatory system and a spectrum of legitimacy. At one end of the spectrum, there are some countries that adhere to western liberal values. The U.S. is the quintessential example. At the other end, there are truly tyrannical states that go about violating those human rights that all informed observers would agree are core rights. North Korea and any other outlaw country would be at this end. What exactly are these core human rights? The right to life, personal property, equality before the law, and freedom from enslavement. Liberal democratic rights, such as freedom of worship or speech, are not included.

In between these two extremes, there are "hierarchical/communal" states. These are "decent" states. To some significant degree, their governments represent the preferences of their citizens. Moreover, the societies are premised on rational principles. To be sure, these countries are not American-style democracies, as they are not founded on a western liberal political values. Theocratic states are examples. But, the fact they embody the preferences of their people, coupled with the fact that there is a comprehensible logic to explain why they are structured in a certain way, gives hierarchical/communal

---

18 *See* JOHN RAWLS, THE LAW OF PEOPLES (2000); John Rawls, *The Law of Peoples*, 20 CRITICAL INQUIRY 36 (1993).

states a certain degree of legitimacy. Possibly, Iran and Singapore would be examples. The bottom line implication? Sanctions against hierarchical/communal states are not morally justifiable. Accordingly, the Rawlsian critique helps avoid the danger of over-using sanctions that can occur when a Kantian position is taken too far.

C. Just War Theory

In an already classic work, *Just and Unjust Wars*, American philosopher Michael Walzer formulates a theory of when it is morally defensible to go to war.[19] That theory can be, and has been, applied to the use of sanctions. It is not necessarily a perfect fit, because Just War theory is designed for analyses of wartime sieges and blockades, whereas sanctions are a lesser (and hopefully alternative) form of conflict. Still, six criteria can be drawn from the tradition of Just War theory, which taken together provide a test for whether a sanctions regime is morally justified. (These criteria are not necessarily set forth in order of importance. Indeed, it may be queried whether there is — or should be — a hierarchy among the criteria.)

First, are sanctions being used as a penultimate measure? The ultimate measure is, of course, the use of force. Sanctions are more easily justified in a moral sense if they are taken after all less coercive measures have been tried and failed, and if they are the last step to avert armed conflict. President Wilson made the point when he tried unsuccessfully to persuade the U.S. to join the League of Nations:

> A nation boycotted is a nation that is in sight of surrender. Apply this economic, peaceful, silent, deadly remedy and there will be no need for force. It is a terrible remedy. It does not cost a life outside the nation boycotted, but it brings pressure upon the nation that, in my judgment, no modern nation could resist.[20]

Put conversely, sanctions ought to be a more *humane* alternative to the certain death and destruction that a downward spiral to "total war" would bring. At the same time, they ought to be sufficiently resolute so as to be something more than a pusillanimous consolation for inaction or indifference.

Second, are sanctions a *sincere* alternative to force? It may be that resort to sanctions is disingenuous, that in fact the country imposing sanctions intends all along to go to war. Sanctions thus become a prelude to war — a morally indefensible policy. This accusation is made of the U.S. in its pre-first Gulf War sanctions policy to Iraq. Sanctions take time to work, as Dr. Hufbauer's research mentioned above suggests. Yet, the first Bush Administration gave sanctions barely half a year to work (August 1990-January 1991), and spent those six months building up an overwhelming strike force in the Gulf area. Critics charge that Administration was bent on war soon after Iraq invaded Kuwait. Arguably, sanctions were less of a threshold for peace than

---

[19] *See* MICHAEL WALZER, JUST AND UNJUST WARS (2d ed. 1992); Jack T. Patterson, *The Political and Moral Appropriateness of Sanctions, in* ECONOMIC SANCTIONS 89-96 (David Cortright & George A. Lopez eds., 1995).

[20] Drew Christiansen & Gerard F. Powers, *Economic Sanctions and Just-War Doctrine, in* ECO-NOMIC SANCTIONS 97-117 (David Cortright & George A. Lopez eds., 1995).

a trap door for war. To be sure, the rebuttal in this instance is that every "extra" day given for sanctions was a day for Saddam Hussein to "dig in," thus increasing the chance for a longer, bloodier battle, and also another day of hell for the Kuwaiti people.

One way to discern whether the second criterion is satisfied is to ask: are good faith negotiations underway during the period in which sanctions are imposed? If sanctions are the penultimate step to armed conflict, and if the country imposing them sincerely desires to avert death and destruction, then the sanctioning country will do its best to come to a deal with the target country. It will search for a compromise that resolves the pattern of behavior it is sanctioning in a fair manner. Again, the U.S. has been criticized for failing to negotiate in good faith with Saddam during the prelude to the first Gulf War.

The third criterion for evaluating sanctions drawn from Just War theory is proportionality. Are the sanctions imposed proportionate to the behavior of the target country? Clearly, the animating principle is fairness — a punishment should fit a crime. It exists in Articles 22:6-7 of the WTO *Dispute Settlement Understanding (DSU)*. A WTO Member that loses a case and is alleged not to comply with a Panel or Appellate Body recommendation or pay compensation to the winning Member can complain to an arbitrator that it is the victim of excessive retaliation by the winning Member.

In the sanctions context, there are likely to be heated debates about whether measures against a target are excessive. It is scarcely possible to change a persistent pattern of behavior of a foreign government — say, persecution of a religious group — with a limp-wristed sanction like suspending shipments of luxury cars. Only if the target feels, or feels threatened by, real pain might it reconsider its conduct. Thus, Professor Damrosch argues sanctions-induced reductions in the standard of living of the target population are morally tolerable so long as they do not cause a significant segment of that population to fall below subsistence level.[21] Yet, the pain of teetering around that level may be precisely the grounds for arguing sanctions are unjust because they are too sharp.

It may be ventured as a general proposition that no sanctions regime is morally defensible if it leads to the denial of fundamental human rights. Most importantly among such rights would be the right to life. The economic coercion deliberately wrought by sanctions should not to threaten or lead to the loss of life. Therefore, there must be a humanitarian exception to the sanctions. A blockage of food or medicines would be unconscionable, but an embargo that denies travel visas, freezes assets, ceases military cooperation, and causes job losses would not be. The Clinton Administration's decision in 1999 to remove such items from the scope of some of its sanctions regimes can be justified in this light. Another way to put the general proposition is that sanctions are morally unjustifiable if they inflict irreversible and grievous harm to innocents, and such harm is best conceptualized in terms of core human rights.

---

[21] *See* Lori Fisler Damrosch, *The Civilian Impact of Economic Sanctions, in* ENFORCING RESTRAINT: COLLECTIVE INTERVENTION IN INTERNAL CONFLICTS 281-84 (Lori Fisler Damrosch ed., 1993).

Fourth, is the deployment of sanctions on a unilateral, plurilateral, or multilateral basis? Just War theory suggests that the larger the number of countries imposing sanctions, the more likely the sanctions regime is morally defensible. There is strength in numbers, particularly when those numbers encompass a diverse array of cultures, religions, and philosophies that have come to an agreement voluntarily. In other words, the consensus should be both broad and deep so that the sanctions regime has credibility, and it should not be based on one or a few dominant players effectively bribing others to join in. Conversely, sanctions imposed by the U.S. alone, for instance, or imposed by several countries that have been promised economic and military aid by the U.S., is harder to justify on moral grounds against charges of self-serving, bully-like behavior.

Fifth, Just War theory indicates it is appropriate to ask about the humanitarian cost of sanctions. It establishes a principle of civilian (*i.e.*, non-combatant) immunity, namely, innocent civilians ought not to be victimized by sanctions. A sanctions regime hardly is moral if it afflicts a civilian population like a bombing campaign (be it one with precision-guided weapons or not). After all, civilians — especially women, children, the elderly, the disabled, and the poor — are likely to be remote from the wrongdoing in the target country. Accordingly, President Eisenhower's famous Secretary of State, John Foster Dulles, opposed boycotts other than arms embargoes and specific measures that would embarrass the government of the target country. Similarly, sanctions against Iraq that deny basic medicines to children and the elderly cannot easily be defended. Sanctions must not only take aim at the individuals and institutions in a foreign country responsible for egregious behavior, but also they must hit those targets, without "collateral damage." Such damage may reinforce the ruling elite of a country, if it leads to a rally-around-the-flag effect, or helps weaken or dispose of opponents of that elite.

As regards the fifth criterion, only in two instances does it become morally defensible to lift the immunity for civilians. First, the civilians themselves in the target country ask foreign powers to impose sanctions on their country. The head of Burma's National League for Democracy, and winner of the Nobel Peace Prize, Aung Sung Suu Kyi, did precisely this — encourage the U.S. and other countries to isolate the ruling military junta in Rangoon. Thus, in this instance the civilians assent to the possibility that they, too, will feel the pain of sanctions.

There is, of course, a question whether civilians calling for sanctions are the ones whose counsel ought to be followed. The voice of a Mahatma Gandhi or Nelson Mandela is more credible than the voice of the president of a steel company or steel workers' union. A Gandhi or Mandela has nothing to gain materially and everything to lose, from the imposition of sanctions. But, sanctions might be a windfall for the steel executive or union boss. Foreign steel competition is withdrawn from the market, thereby instating or re-instating a dominant market position for the domestic producers. More generally, human rights advocates in the target country are more likely to be attuned to the effects of sanctions on the most vulnerable and least powerful segments of the civilian population. Given that they are double victims — victims of their own country's government and soon-to-be victims of the sanctions — their call for sanctions is a powerful one indeed.

Second, if civilians in a target country are not "innocent," then sanctions that adversely affect their lives may be judged as morally defensible. This instance occurs when civilians, as well as their leaders, are to blame for egregious behavior. Perhaps ordinary citizens willingly participate in acts of violence against a racial or ethnic minority. Or, perhaps they simply "rally around the flag," and thus become collaborators with a heinous regime. Targeting civilians for sanctions as well as their leaders is particularly justified if the country has a reasonably well-functioning democracy (*e.g.*, Israel). Because a large block of civilians voted in their rulers, they are liable for aiding and abetting heinous conduct against vulnerable populations (*e.g.*, Palestinians).

The obvious problem with both exceptions to the principle of civilian immunity is to discern a clear message from the civilians in a target country. What if some civilian leaders call for sanctions, while others do not? What if some civilian leaders work hand-in-glove with an authoritarian or totalitarian government, while others form an underground resistance? In brief, what voices should be heard, and how much weight should be given to each voice? The dilemma of identifying legitimate, authoritative voices is particularly acute when, as is typically true in target countries, there is no democratic means of deciding who represents the population. Circumstances in the target country obviously will not permit a free and fair plebiscite on sanctions policy. Indeed, civilian groups may bicker — or worse — among themselves and show little interest in achieving a unified strategy. Kurdish and Palestinian leaders are cases in point.

The sixth and final criterion is both the most important and elusive. The first word in "Just War theory" is "just." Accordingly, any sanctions regime should be premised on a conception of justice. What is the vision of a rightly ordered world that demands the imposition of sanctions? The question goes to the purpose of a sanctions regime. It is important, because if sanctions are a sincere alternative to war (the first two criteria), then they ought to be a morally superior alternative to war — or else why bother going through the sanctions exercise?

An answer to the question is elusive. One could offer as a general principle that Right Order is not one in which grave evils (*e.g.*, tyrants like Hitler or genocides like Rwanda) are allowed to flourish. Hence, sanctions become a response to a grave injustice, a violation of a fundamental international law or norm. But, that proffered answer is too easy. It defines things negatively, saying what Right Order is not, rather than what it *is*. Socrates devoted his life to learning about what is "right," and his travails produced the greatest philosophical dialogues in history. That they continue to be a source of lively debate is proof that the lesser politicians who govern countries are quite unlikely to come to philosophical agreement on a global Right Order. But, they might reach a political compromise that, like watching an ancient Roman ruin come into focus in a desert as a sand storm abates, bears some semblance to a conception of what is Good.

Consider, for example, a political compromise that holds for sanctioning Iraq, Iran, or both in order to maintain western control over the flow of oil through the Straits of Hormuz. Is this really just another power play by hegemonic powers, another instance of big countries bullying small ones for self-interested ends. Or, might the compromise be justified on the ground that to surrender this control would be to risk catastrophic economic deprivation in the developed world, of which the oil crises of 1974 and 1979 were only a glimpse? In turn, a collapse of the western and Japanese economies would afflict the Third World, because developed countries no longer would be viable export markets for its goods. In brief, rich people would become poor, and poor people would become poorer. Whatever the good life is, it is not economic chaos.

Among the many interesting features of Just War theory is that it seems to be a hybrid. It combines elements of the teleological and deontological approaches. For instance, in asking about the proportionality of sanctions measures and articulating a principle of civilian immunity, it seems to take on the rule utilitarian concern of finding a strategy that across the broad spectrum of cases will maximize welfare. The proportionality principle itself can be conceived of in act utilitarian terms, insofar as it involves a weighing to the harm caused by sanctions against the good that might result from them. Likewise, the interest in humanitarian costs, which is embedded in the civilian immunity principle, would be an element in an act utilitarian calculation. On the other hand, that very concern, and the principle itself, indicate a focus on the normative status of individuals in the target country. This suggests a distinctly deontological flair. Sanctions are demanded simply as a principle of natural justice raised by the abhorrent behavior of a target country in the case at hand.

IV. EXPORT CONTROLS

A. Legal Points

Since 1940, the U.S. government has applied export controls continuously. Thus, navigating through and complying with export controls is an important area in the practice of many international trade lawyers, and for some a full time job. Briefly put, there are three significant control programs, differentiated by the type of export at issue. Under all three programs, a license is required before exportation of the merchandise, technology, or service in question is lawful. The types of licenses, and the licensing authorities, differ depending on the category of proposed export:

    1. *Nuclear Materials and Technology —*

Pursuant to the *Atomic Energy Act*, the responsible licensing authority is the Nuclear Regulatory Commission (NRC).[22]

    2. *Defense Articles and Services —*

Pursuant to the *Arms Export Control Act* the Department of State is the responsible licensing agency.[23] Defense articles and services requiring a license are indicated on the Munitions Control List (MCL), which the State Department maintains.

---

[22] *See* 10 C.F.R. § 110.

[23] *See* 22 U.S.C. § 2778.

3. *Non-Military Dual Use Goods and Technology —*

Pursuant to the *Export Administration Act*, as amended (discussed below) the Bureau of Industry and Security (BIS) of the Department of Commerce is responsible for licensing commercial goods and technical data that are susceptible to civilian or military use. (Via internal order, on 18 April 2002, the DOC changed the name of its "Bureau of Export Administration" to the BIS. The switch is regrettable at least from the standpoint of intruding on a venerable international central banking organization, the Bank for International Settlements, or BIS, in Basle, Switzerland.) Dual use goods are set out on the Commerce Control List (CCL), which the BIS maintains. Exportation is illegal unless authorized by a BIS-granted license.

It is worth elaborating on the third category, as it generates considerable daily work.

For dual use items, two types of licenses exist — an individual validated license, which permits a single shipment, or a bulk license, which condones multiple shipments. What criteria do BIS apply when considering license applications? First, it considers the intended end use of the article or technology. Second, it evaluates the probability and likely effect of diversion of the article or technology to military use. The Secretary of Defense is authorized to review a license application if it evokes a national security concern, while the Secretary of State may check a particular application for foreign policy reasons.

It is critically important for both U.S. and foreign attorneys to realize the licensing rules apply extraterritorially. Both exportation and re-exportation of a U.S.-origin commodity or technical data, on the CCL list, from a foreign country to another country require a license. Indeed, a foreign-made product containing components or technology of U.S. origin, which are on the CCL list, needs a license before that product can be exported from a foreign country to another country.

What principles of jurisdiction under public international law justify the long arm of U.S. export controls on dual use items? The answer appears to be the nationality principle. Extraterritorial application affects a company located overseas that is owned or controlled by a U.S. person. What constitutes ownership or control? Might another jurisdictional principle — the subjective territorial principle of an act occurring outside U.S. borders having effects inside the U.S. — justify the long arm? Compare the extraterritorial application of U.S. export controls with U.S. antitrust law and securities regulation.

For all three kinds of export controls, the lists of controlled items are not lapidary. They change, sometimes frequently. Memorizing those lists would be a task both time-consuming and pointless. However, two key points should be appreciated. First, the burden of deciding whether merchandise cannot be exported without a license lies with the exporter. The general presumption in U.S. international trade law is that no merchandise needs an export license unless that item is on an export control list, or is destined for a target country. Therein lays the responsibility of the exporter — to determine whether its merchandise fits in a product category needing a license, or will wind up in a target country.

Second, failure to comply with applicable export restrictions may result in criminal sanctions. The punishments can be severe, and create multiple criminal liabilities. For example, violation of export control rules is a specified unlawful activity for purposes of money laundering laws under the *Money Laundering Control Act of 1986*. (*See* 18 U.S.C. §§ 1956-57.) There is no shortcut for painstaking legal research, including consultation with appropriate federal authorities, to meet the burden of compliance and avoid penalties. In particular, the Department of State administers export control rules on military technology, and the Department of Commerce (specifically, the Bureau of Industry and Security, formerly known as the Bureau of Export Affairs) deals with rules for dual-use technology. They provide an export license, if one is needed, and may be of service to prospective exporters and their clients. The Departments of Energy and the Treasury (in particular, OFAC) also are involved in certain licensing decisions.

B. Policy Rationales

There is no hiding the fact U.S. export controls serve — or, are supposed to serve — three policy purposes. They are (not necessarily in order or priority):

1. *Protect Commodities in Short Supply*

Interestingly, this policy provided the initial basis for export controls in 1940. During the Second World War, the U.S. needed to restrict exports to avoid or mitigate scarcity of critical articles, and sought to assure their equitable distribution in the U.S. and to the Allied Powers. Expectations following the War were that the controls would terminate, especially as commodity shortages eased. But, the Cold War provided a new policy justification, and Congress enacted the *Export Control Act of 1949* (Public Law 81-11, approved 26 February 1949) to restrict all American exports to Communist countries. This rationale resonates in subsequent statutes (*e.g.*, the *1979 Act*, discussed below) by, for example, allowing the President to impose an export control to protect the U.S. economy from a drain of scarce materials or reduce the inflationary impact of foreign demand.

2. *Protect National Security*

During the Cold War Era, this rationale meant fighting Communism in part by restricting exports to Communist countries. In the post-Cold War, post-9/11 period, it means (*inter alia*) combating terrorism and isolating rogue regimes. Both meanings, discussed below, are relevant not only to military articles and technologies, but also to items that could be diverted from civilian use to upgrade significantly the military capabilities of an actual or potential adversary.

3. *Advance U.S. Foreign Policy Interests*

Foreign policy controls are particularly controversial. Two examples occurred during the Cold War, when Presidents Jimmy Carter and Ronald Reagan, in 1979 and 1981, respectively, invoked export control authority for foreign policy purposes. President Carter embargoed grain exports to the former Soviet Union after it invaded Afghanistan. President Reagan banned sales to the Soviet Union by American firms, and their foreign subsidiaries, of commodities and technology relating to oil and gas transmission. The idea was to inhibit the Soviets from building a natural gas pipeline to Western Europe, thereby denying them energy revenues and the opportunity to create dependent clients.

In neither case was a military article at issue. Dubbing grain a dual use article, on the logic that soldiers eat bread or pasta, is a stretch. The ban aroused the ire of — and inflicted considerable pain on — farmers in the American Midwest and Great Plains region. Not surprisingly, the *1985 Act* (discussed below) circumscribed the ability of the President to impose export controls on agricultural products. As for energy supplies, the pipeline was built anyway, and supplies Germany, Poland, and other EU members. It bears the rubric "Friendship Pipeline," which is rather ironic. Occasionally, Russia battles with Belarus (or other former Soviet bloc countries) though which the pipeline runs, over schemes hatched in Minsk to tax trans-shipment flows, especially in response to export taxes imposed by Moscow. Russia also alleges Belarus occasionally siphons off, without paying, oil and natural gas. To be sure, each side needs the other. In January 2007, Russia briefly turned the spigot off on the Druzhba oil pipeline. But, it relies heavily on energy sales to the west, and thus transshipment. Transit countries get subsidized oil and natural gas from Russia.

There are two obvious, and continuing, examples of export controls rationalized by U.S. foreign policy interests. First, the U.S. subjects to these controls crime control and detection instruments. It looks askance at efforts to export this equipment to countries that may engage in persistent, gross human rights violations. Of course, in the post-9/11 world of renditions and secret prisons, query whether controls on this merchandise are relegated to higher *realpolitik* priorities. Second, shipments of goods and technology, exclusive of humanitarian supplies, to certain countries are banned. Those countries are the usual suspects — Cuba, Iran, Syria, North Korea, and Sudan. Query here whether constructive engagement might be preferable to economic isolation.

In reviewing all three export control policy goals, consider the extent to which close allies, or countries the U.S. is cultivating to join that camp, may share these purposes. Is it accurate to say that the ultimate choice of what and how to control is an American decision?

C. Statutory Framework

To effect the policy goals discussed above, Congress — beginning with the *Export Control Act of 1949* (Pub. L. 81-11, 26 February 1949) — has set up and occasionally adjusted a statutory framework. The *1949 Act* authorized controls of items in short supply, but with a view to advancing American foreign policy goals, particularly scrutinizing proposed exports to Communist countries that might have a military application. That *Act* remained in force for 20 years, and was renewed by Congress in 1951, 1953, 1956, 1958, 1960, 1962, and 1965. Subsequently Congress replaced it by the *Export Administration Act of 1969* (Public Law 91-184, approved 30 December 1969), which was amended in 1972, 1974, and 1977. Later, the *Export Administration Act of*

1979 (Public Law 96-72, 29 September 1979, codified at 50 U.S.C. App. §§ 2401 *et seq.*) replaced the *1969 Act.*

The *1979 Act* was extended thrice, in October 1983, December 1983, February 1984, and March 1984, as Congress debated major overhauls in the law. During certain *inter regnum* when authority under the *1979 Act* lapsed, President Ronald Reagan invoked the *IEEPA*, and issued an Executive Order (Number 12470 of 30 March 1984) to continue the control regime. Through the *Export Administration Amendments Act of 1985* (Public Law 99-64), and the *Omnibus Trade and Competitiveness Act of 1988* (Public Law 100-418, Title II, Subtitle D, approved 23 August 1988, codified at 50 U.S.C. §§ 2403 *et seq.*), Congress re-authorized and further amended the *1979 Act.*

Throughout the many legislative amendments and sagas involving Capitol Hill and the White House, the basic export control regime and its three policy rationales have been constant. However, Congress has added notable complementary and supplementary features to the regime, including:

(1)   The *1969 Act* countenanced removal of export controls on goods and technologies that were freely available and of marginal military value.

(2)   The 1977 amendments to the *1969 Act* expanded export controls extraterritorially, thereby authorizing the DOC to control foreign-origin goods and technical data re-exported by a U.S.-owned or U.S.-controlled company overseas.

(3)   The 1977 amendments also strengthened U.S. anti-boycott rules. These rules bar U.S. persons from taking any action with the intent to comply with, or support, any foreign country boycott (*e.g.*, that of the Arab League) aimed at a country (*e.g.*, Israel) friendly to the U.S.

(3)   The *1979 Act* provided formal authorization to U.S. participation in the Coordinating Committee on Multilateral Export Controls (CO-COM) (discussed below).

(4)   The *1979 Act* also established, for the first time, separate and distinct criteria and procedures to impose export controls for two long-standing policy purposes (discussed below) — protecting U.S. national security and furthering U.S. foreign policy interests. The *Act* laid out time deadlines for processing export license applications, mandated creation of a Militarily Critical Technologies List (MCTL) to ensure the CCL of goods and technology maintained by the DOC is both adequate and focused narrowly on items most militarily important, and introduced foreign availability of a good controlled by the U.S. as a criterion in making a licensing decision.

(5)   The *1985 Act* articulated the enhancement of U.S. export competitiveness as a factor in export controls. The *Act* sought to reduce export disincentives, and ease the burden on American exporters, which had been one of total licensing. Accordingly, the *Act* eliminated the need to obtain a license to export certain relatively low-technology articles, obligated the Secretary of Commerce to revise the CCL list at least annually, streamlined the license application

and approval process, created a process to decontrol goods widely available (either *per se* or via competing products) in foreign countries and thus not susceptible to U.S. control, and required the President to consult with industry (as well as Congress) before imposing controls for foreign policy purposes. Interestingly, the *Act* also curtailed the ability of the President to impose a foreign policy control on goods or technology already subject to an existing export contract. Only if prohibiting performance on those contracts is instrumental to remedy a situation posing a direct threat to U.S. strategic interests is that kind of control possible.

(6)   The *1985 Act* also identified credible enforcement as a goal of the American export control regime. Toward that end, the *Act* clarified the Customs Service (now CBP) — not the DOC — has primary responsibility for enforcing export controls at all U.S. ports of entry and exit, and overseas. The *Act* also created new criminal offences against illegal diversions of controlled goods, and strengthened penalties on existing violations.

(7)   Continuing a theme from the *1985 Act*, the *1988 Act* contained provisions to cut export disincentives. The *1988 Act* called for further cuts on the CCL, increased efficiency in both the license application procedures and determinations about foreign availability. This *Act* also authorized distribution licenses for multiple exports to China.

(8)   The *1988 Act* also continued the theme of the *1985 Act* concerning enforcement. The *1988 Act* barred persons convicted of an export control or *IEEPA* violation — or anyone affiliated with such persons, whether by ownership, control, or position of responsibility — from applying for or using an export license. To use a baseball metaphor, the prohibition amounted to "one strike and out," and extended to the dugout.

On 30 September 1990, the *Export Administration Act* expired. Several efforts at renewal failed, including on account of a November 1990 pocket veto by President George H.W. Bush of reauthorizing legislation.

Thereafter, in the early 1990s, Congress occasionally extended the *Act* (namely, in March and July 1994). It did so again in November 2000, effective until August 2001. However, since then (*i.e.*, in every legislative session including and since the 104th Congress), there has been no agreement, either on Capitol Hill or between legislators and the White House, on a long-term extension, much less a modified one, which would give a sound statutory foundation for the U.S. export control regime.

Of course, that regime remains in place. The statutory basis cited by the Executive Branch for the regime is the *IEEPA*. Essentially, under the *IEEPA*, the President announces an emergency to continue the existing export control regime (as President Bill Clinton did in August 1995, August 1996, and August 1997). Typically, the President also issues an Executive Order, which is published in the *Federal Register*, saying the national emergency continues, and thus so too must the regime.[24]

In respect of export control statutory reauthorization, over what issues have officials in the Legislative and Executive Branches sparred? One technical, product-specific example concerns high performance computers (HPCs). Beginning in 1998 with the *National Defense Authorization Act* (Public Law 105-85, Section 1211, approved 18 November 1997), Congress mandated use of a benchmark for gauging computing ability of an HPC, namely, millions of theoretical operations per second (MTOPS). The DOC organized HPC destination countries into four tiers, and applied MTOPS thresholds. In brief, an export license for an HPC is not necessary for a Tier 1 country, whereas a Tier 4 country is subject to an embargo. The key Tier is the third. A dual-control system applies to Tier 3 countries, in which civilian versus military end users and end users are distinguished. An exporter is obligated to give the DOC notice before shipping an HPC above the MTOP threshold to a Tier III country. Further, export to a Tier III country of an above-threshold HPC is subject to approval from the Secretaries of Commerce, Defense, Energy, and State. If the exportation occurs, then post-shipment verification is needed. Congress also requires the President to notify it of any adjustment in MTOP thresholds.

However, by 2001, and continuing at least through May 2003, Congress considered repealing the obligation to use MTOPS as a benchmark. Aside from HPCs, what other matters impede passage of a new iteration of the *Export Administration Act*?

D. Post-Cold War Tendencies

Since the end of the Cold War, there has been a major shift in the locus of decision-making as to what articles are, or ought to be, subject to export controls. Succinctly put, that shift is from multilateralism to unilateralism. During the Cold War Era, from the late 1940s until early 1990s, the U.S. made these determinations in partnership with its non-Communist allies in Western Europe, Japan, and other parts of the world. An informal body, COCOM, served as a multilateral forum for cooperation on export control matters. The Cold War focused attention on the need for cooperation and coordination to prevent or restrict sensitive technology shipments to Communist countries. Thus, from 1950-94, Japan, and all countries in the North Atlantic Treaty Organization (NATO), save for Iceland, participated in COCOM, meeting periodically to set policy, publish lists of controlled items, and develop effective procedures. Notably, the *1979 Act* directed the President to negotiate with COCOM partners on ways to cut the scope of export controls.

Few, if any, would doubt the end of the Cold War was a welcome development. But, it has created a void in which two tendencies are manifest. One (intimated in the above policy discussion) is that individual governments, notably the U.S., can and do establish unilateral solutions to export issues.

---

[24] *See, e.g.*, President Bill Clinton's Executive Order Number 12924, 19 Aug. 1994, *Continuation of Export Control Regulations*, 59 Fed. Reg. 43,437 (23 Aug. 1994), and President George W. Bush's Executive Order Number 13222, 17 Aug. 2004, 66 Fed. Reg. 44,025 (22 Aug. 2001).

They do so because authority over export control regulation is devolved, both across countries and within the government of a particular country, over export controls. This trend may displease prospective exporters, insofar as it creates an "exporter beware scenario," because it suggests all merchandise may be exported unless prohibited, but creates uncertainty as to what specific articles or technology may be prohibited. However, the rules are supposed to serve over-arching interests of the country imposing them.

The second post-Cold War Era tendency concerns the proliferation of bad actors, some of them non-state entities. Groups like Al Qaeda (which in Arabic means "the base") seek to obtain weapons of mass destruction (WMDs) and put them to wicked ends. Ironically, the second tendency may reinforce the first, yet the first tendency may be a less effective way of dealing with the second one than a rigorous multilateral export control regime. To be sure, the Wassenaar Arrangement of 1996 established a new international group to perform many of the same functions as COCOM. But, what are its strengths and weaknesses? Remember, too the erosion of multilateralism in the export control arena when studying post-9/11 U.S. border security measures. Has the same shift occurred with respect to importation?

Finally, every export restriction, as well as every border security measure, potentially pits the government against the business community. Is tension between traders seeking efficiency and regulators seeking control an immutable feature of these kinds of trade restrictions? To what extent is the discourse characterized by the public sector arguing it knows best, based on secret intelligence, what to regulate and who to ostracize, and the private sector retorting that open trade (and investment) relations, which create interdependence, are the best long-term guarantee of peace and security?

Chapter 20

BORDER SECURITY

To the size of states there is a limit as there is to other things, plants, animals, implements; for none of these retain their natural power when they are too large or too small, but they either wholly lose their nature or are spoilt.

> —ARISTOTLE, POLITICS (*quoted in* JOSEPH PEARCE, SMALL IS STILL BEAUTIFUL 116 (2006))

DOCUMENTS SUPPLEMENT ASSIGNMENT

1. *Havana Charter* Articles 16, 45:1(a)(ii), 99
2. GATT Articles I, XXI
3. *NAFTA* Chapters 5, 21
4. Relevant provisions in other FTAs

I. OVERVIEW OF U.S. CUSTOMS

A. A Proud Tradition

Tariff legislation, and the U.S. Customs Service, are nearly as old as the American Republic.[1] The introduction to the *Second Act* of the First Congress — the *Tariff Act (Duty Act)*, dated July 4, 1789 — stated its purpose was

> for laying a Duty on Goods, Wares, and Merchandises imported into the United States.

That is, responding to the urgent need for funds, the First Congress passed, and President George Washington, signed the *Tariff Act of July 4, 1789*. This *Act* authorized the collection of duties on imported goods. The news media of the day called it "the Second Declaration of Independence." The *Third Act* of the First Congress — called the *Act Imposing Duties on Tonnage*, dated July 20, 1789 — established duties on all ships and vessels. Those duties were a levy on the weight of incoming crafts, whether American or foreign.

Two weeks later, on July 31, 1789, the *Fifth Act* of the First Congress established port districts in each state, and staffing for each port. In effect, the *Fifth Act* created the Customs Service and authorized ports of entry. The Customs Service — born in July 1789 — is the oldest American government agency. Two months later, in September 1789, Congress created the Department of the Treasury, and put the Customs Service in that Department.

---

[1] *See* U.S. Treasury Fact Sheet, www.ustreas.gov/education/duties/bureaus/uscustoms.shtml; Customs and Border Protection, www.cbp.gov/xp/cgov/toolbox/about/history/history.xml.

Thus, of the first five pieces of legislation passed by the young American Congress, three of them dealt squarely with international trade.[2] Money helps explain the immediate attention Congress gave to the Customs matters. Shortly after the American revolutionaries declared independence, the nation teetered on the brink of bankruptcy. For the first 125 years of American history, tariffs were the primary source of government revenue. Funding most of the budget, tariffs allowed for:

1. Purchase of the territories of Louisiana (from France in 1803) and Alaska (from Tsarist Russia in 1867 — a transaction dubbed "Seward's Folly").

2. Acquisition of Oregon (through the 1818 *Treaty of Ghent*, with Great Britain, plus a further agreement with Britain in 1846 removing any British claims to the American West) and Florida (through the 1819 *Adams — Onís Treaty* with Spain).

3. Construction of the National Road between 1811 and 1820 from Cumberland, Maryland, to Wheeling, West Virginia.

4. Construction of the Transcontinental Railroad, from 1853 to 1869, which stretched from sea-to-sea.

5. Building the nation's lighthouses, starting in 1716, before Independence, and continuing to 1910.

6. Building the U.S. military and naval academies at West Point (in 1802) and Annapolis (in 1845), respectively.

7. Building the City of Washington, D.C., following the British burning of it on 24 August 1814, during the War of 1812.

Impressively, by 1835, Customs revenue alone had reduced the national debt to zero.

In fact, not until 1916, when the U.S. Supreme Court held an income tax to be constitutional under the 16th Amendment, did the relative importance of tariffs decrease.[3] This pattern — Customs fueling the lion's share of the budget while an income tax system is non-existent or inchoate — is typical of countries as they develop. Today, duty collection accounts for approximately 1 percent of U.S. government revenue (specifically, 1.09 percent in 2005). Still, it is 1 percent (amounting to $23 billion in 2005) of a huge figure. Moreover, with growing trade volumes (albeit generally lower tariff rates), Customs is

---

[2] The first five *Acts* of the First Congress are:

1.   1 Cong. Ch. 1, June 1, 1789, 1 Stat. 23 (entitled *Time and Manner of Certain Oaths*).

2.   1 Cong. Ch. 2, July 4, 1789, 1 Stat. 24.

3.   1 Cong. Ch. 3, July 20, 1789, 1 Stat. 27.

4.   1 Cong. Ch. 4, July 27, 1789, 1 Stat. 28 (concerning the establishment of the Department of Foreign Affairs, the precursor to the modern-day Department of State).

5.   1 Cong., Ch. 5, July 31, 1789, 1 Stat. 29.

Observe, then, that of the first 5 *Acts*, 4 of them concerned international relations.

[3] In 1895, the Supreme Court ruled the federal statutory income tax unconstitutional. *See* Pollock v. Farmers' Loan & Trust Co., 157 U.S. 429, 158 U.S. 601 (1895). The process for ratifying the 16th Amendment was completed in 1913. Three years later, the Court affirmed the constitutionality of that Amendment. *See* Brushaber v. Union P.R. Co., 240 U.S. 1 (1916).

a growing source of revenue for the Federal government, and the Customs Service is profitable — returning over $16.00 to the taxpayer for every dollar appropriated by Congress.

B. A Day in the Life of Customs

The specific functions formed by the Customs Service have not remained the same during its proud history. The Customs Service was the parent or forerunner to several other government agencies. For instance, in the early years of American history, the Customs officers —

    i. Administered military pensions;

    ii. Collected import and export statistics;

    iii. Supervised revenue cutters; and

    iv. Established standard weights and measures.

Now, officials from the Departments of Veterans Affairs, Bureau of Census, U.S. Coast Guard, and National Bureau of Standards, respectively, perform these functions. In addition, the Customs Service used to collect hospital dues to help sick and disabled seamen, a function Public Health Service officials later performed.

Of course, throughout its history, the core business, as it were, of the Customs Service has been, and remains, the following:[4]

Trade Revenue and Administrative Functions:

    i. Assessing and collecting duties, excise taxes, fees, and penalties due on imported merchandise, and thereby protecting revenue. On a typical day, the Customs Service collects $84,400,000 in tariffs, duties, and fees, and approves for entry 85,300 shipments of goods.

    ii. Processing persons, baggage, cargo and mail, and administering certain navigation laws. On a typical day, the Customs Service processes a million passengers and pedestrians, including 680,000 aliens, 240,737 incoming international air passengers, 71,151 passengers and crew arriving by ship, 327,042 incoming privately-owned vehicles, and 70,900 truck, rail, and sea containers.

    iii. Collecting accurate data on imports and exports for compilation in international trade statistics. For this function, the 9th and 10th digits in the Harmonized Tariff Schedule of the United States (HTSUS) — the statistical suffix — are useful.

Trade Remedy Functions:

    i. Protecting holders of U.S. intellectual property rights (IPRs) by enforcing remedies, such as Section 337 of the *Tariff Act of 1930*, as amended, that allow for the exclusion of merchandise infringing on an IPR, or seizure of such merchandise.

    ii. Protecting American labor rights by enforcing remedies, particularly the prohibition on importation of convict-made goods under Section 307 of the *Tariff Act of 1930*, as amended.

---

[4] *See* U.S. Customs and Border Protection, *Typical Day*, *available at* www.cbp.gov/xp/cgov/toolbox/about/accomplish/day.xml. The statistics above are as of December 2006.

iii. Enforcing other remedies against unfair trade practices, namely, implementing antidumping (AD) and countervailing duty (CVD) orders on subject merchandise.

Law Enforcement and Border Control Functions:

i. Enforcing import and export laws and regulations at U.S. ports of entry, ensuring all merchandise imported into or exported from the Customs territory of the United States conform to U.S. import-export laws.

ii. Ensuring (along with the Immigration and Naturalization Service) persons attempting to enter the U.S. are doing so lawfully. On a typical day, the Customs Service makes 63 arrests at ports of entry, and 2,984 apprehensions between ports for illegal entry. It refuses entry at ports of entry to 574 non-citizens, and 63 criminal aliens, and intercepts 20 smuggled aliens trying to enter the U.S. The Customs Service also rescues 8 illegal migrants per day on average in distress or dangerous conditions between ports of entry.

iii. Combating smuggling, including the interdiction and seizure of contraband items, such as child pornography or illegally trans-shipped textiles and apparel.

iv. Combating fraud aimed at circumventing Customs laws, including the interdiction and seizure of illegally trans-shipped textiles and apparel or merchandise with false country of origin labeling. On a typical day, the Customs Service seizes $646,900 worth of fraudulent commercial merchandise at ports of entry, and intercepts 71 fraudulent documents.

v. Serving as the first line of defense in the war on drugs at ports of entry, and specifically, interdicting and seizing narcotics and other illegal drugs. On a typical day, the Customs Service seizes 1,769 pounds of narcotics in 63 seizures at ports of entry, and a further 3,788 pounds of narcotics in 20 seizures between ports of entry.

vi. Assisting in the investigation, apprehension, and conviction of persons engaged in counterfeiting and money laundering. On a typical day, the Customs Service seizes $157,800 in undeclared or illicit currency.

vii. Enforcement of over 400 provisions of law, other than import-export rules, on behalf of at least 40 other government agencies, including provisions on quality of life, notably, environmental regulations on motor vehicle safety and emissions, water pollution, pesticides, freon smuggling, and endangered species protection, and provisions on agriculture, public health, and consumer safety. On a typical day, the Customs Service seizes 4,462 prohibited meat, plant materials, or animal products, including 147 agricultural pests, at ports of entry

National Security Functions:

i. Controlling the import and export of merchandise, particularly with respect to imports or exports of controlled merchandise, such as military or dual-use technologies, and critical technology that might be used to make weapons of mass destruction (WMDs).

  ii. Intercepting persons trying to enter the U.S. who pose a national security risk to the country. On a typical day, the Customs Service intercepts 1.5 travelers because of terrorism or other national security concerns.

Obviously, the Customs territory of the United States, around which the Customs Service must perform these protective functions, is vast. There are:

  i. 5,000 miles of border with Canada.

  ii. 1,900 miles of border with Mexico.

  iii. 95,000 miles of shoreline

  iv. 325 ports of entry

  v. 20 sectors with 33 border checkpoints between the ports of entry.

Not surprisingly, therefore, the Customs Service requires a large, well-trained, and dedicated staff. It boasts approximately 42,000 employees, including 18,000 officers, 12,300 Border Patrol agents, 2,000 agriculture specialists, and 650 air and marine officers. On an average day, the Customs Service deploys 8,075 vehicles, 260 aircraft, 215 watercraft, and 202 equestrian patrols, as well as 1,264 canine enforcement teams.

II. THE POST-9/11 PARADIGM SHIFT

A. Good Goods and Good People

Overall, the Customs Service has been, and continues to be, the indispensable authority to facilitate the lawful cross-border movement of goods and people. This pre-9/11 paradigm, in which Customs authorities the world over are, first and foremost, international trade players with law enforcement and border patrol functions related directly to trade, is reflected in international Customs agreements from before that day. Generally speaking, pre-9/11 Customs treaties addressed:

  1. The Publication of Customs tariffs;

  2. The Establishment of an international body headquartered in Brussels, the Customs Cooperation Council (CCC), now called the World Customs Organization (WCO);

  3. Container conventions;

  4. Importation of samples, and temporary importation of professional equipment, with a view to generating new business;

  5. Harmonization of procedures; and

  6. Non-preferential rules of origin.

In the pre-9/11 world, facilitating trade was of primary importance, and the key law enforcement challenge was limiting illegal drug imports. However, after 9/11, this business plan for the Customs authorities, indeed the whole paradigm in which they operate, appears to have changed.

Nowhere better is that shift manifest than in the name change. Following 9/11, the U.S. Customs Service was newly christened "Customs and Border Protection" (CBP). The essence of the new paradigm appears not to be trade *per se*, or facilitating trade, but securing trade. The lodestar for the CBP is to allow entry into the U.S. only for "good" goods and "good" people. Likewise, from an international perspective, the thrust of Customs treaties may well have altered, with their focus on secure movement of goods and people. Thus, the paradigm seems to have shifted from a focus on collecting tariffs and stopping drugs to securing the borders. The CBP now is a weapon in the War on Terror, which happens to retain its historical trade and trade-related functions. If, indeed, this characterization is correct, then query what impact CBP is having in the War.

B. Homeland Security

As just indicated, the most obvious titular manifestation of the change from Customs-as-a-trade agency to Customs-as-a-security agency is the abandonment of the name "Customs Service" in favor of CBP. The most obvious organizational manifestation of the paradigm shift is the creation of the Department of Homeland Security (DHS), a post-9/11 cabinet-level, Executive Branch department. The two events are connected. When DHS was born, the new term CBP was created, and the CBP moved from the Department of the Treasury to DHS. The legislative instrument effecting these changes is the *Homeland Security Act of 2002* (Public Law 107-296, 25 November 2002, codified in scattered titles and sections of the U.S.C.).[5]

The *Homeland Security Act* has nine titles. Title I of the *Act* creates the "Department of Homeland Security" and gives it a three-pronged mission:

(1)   Prevent terrorist attacks within the U.S.

(2)   Reduce vulnerability of the U.S. to terrorism.

(3)   Minimize damage, and assist in recovery, from terrorist attacks that do occur in the U.S.

To fulfill its mission, the DHS has five primary responsibilities:

(1)   Information Analysis and Infrastructure Protection (Title II).

(2)   Chemical, Biological, Radiological, Nuclear, and Related Countermeasures (Title III).

(3)   Border and Transportation Security (Title IV).

(4)   Emergency Preparedness and Response (Title V).

(5)   Management and coordination with other executive agencies, state and local governments, and the private sector (Titles VI and VII).

The final two Titles (VIII and IX) concern transition arrangements and conforming and technical amendments.

---

[5] The paradigm shift is manifest in many other ways not directly connected to international trade, and effected through other statutes, namely, the *Patriot Act 2001* (Pub. L. 107-56, 115 Stat. 272), *Patriot Act Renewal 2005* (Pub. L. 109-177, 120 Stat. 192), and *Secure Fence Act 2006* (Pub. L. 109-367, 120 Stat. 2638).

Naturally, CBP is charged with the third responsibility. Hence, Title IV of the *Homeland Security Act* is especially important for international trade lawyers. The salient features of this Title are:

Title IV assigns to CBP the responsibilities of —

(1) Preventing the entry of terrorists and the instruments of terrorism from entry into the U.S.

(2) Securing U.S. borders, territorial waters, ports, terminals, waterways, and air, land, and sea transportation systems, including the managing and coordinating of government activities at points of entry.

(3) Administering U.S. immigration and naturalization laws of the U.S.

(4) Administering U.S. Customs laws.

(5) Ensuring the speedy, orderly, and efficient flow of lawful traffic and commerce.

To implement these responsibilities, Title IV establishes a new body — Immigration and Customs Enforcement (ICE). Born in March 2003, ICE is the largest investigative branch in the DHS. In essence, ICE is a combination of the law enforcement arms of the pre-9/11 Immigration and Naturalization Service (INS) and Customs Service. As such, ICE focuses on enforcement of immigration and Customs laws, and protection from terrorist attacks. ICE executes this mission by targeting illegal immigrants, namely, the people, money, and materials that support terrorism and other criminal activities. Lest it be thought the ICE overlaps with other law enforcement agencies, the sharing of responsibilities is a deliberate post-9/11 strategy. That strategy, called "layered defense," is designed to create a thick barrier against bad people and bad goods from entering the U.S., and bad acts from occurring within the country.

Also to implement these responsibilities, Title IV of the *Act* transfers various agencies into the DHS, namely:

(1) *Customs Service (CBP)*

As indicated earlier, the Customs Service no longer is part of the Department of the Treasury. (*See* Section 402 (1) of the *Act*, 6 U.S.C. § 202, and Treasury Department Order No. 100-16, Appendix to 19 CFR Part 0.) Note, then, Congress shifted the delegation of general authority over traditional, indeed historic, Customs revenue functions from their obvious home — the Treasury Department — to DHS. However, in doing so, Congress allowed for a few exceptions.

In particular, the Secretary of the Treasury retains sole authority to approve any new regulations concerning

i.   Import quotas or trade bans

ii. User fees

iii. Marking

iv. Labeling

v.   Copyright and trademark enforcement

vi.   Completion of entry or substance of entry summary, including duty assessment and collection

vii.   Classification

viii.   Valuation

ix.   Application of the Harmonized Tariff Schedule of the United States (HTSUS)

x.   Eligibility or requirements for preferential trade programs

xi.   Establishment of recordkeeping requirements

Exactly where authority to review, modify, or revoke any determination or ruling that falls within these areas is not clear, but is under consideration. (*See* 19 U.S.C. §§ 1516 and 1625(c).) To facilitate coordination between DHS and the Treasury Department, particularly with respect to these areas, Title IV of the *Act* creates an Advisory Committee on Commercial Operations of the Customs Service. Its members are jointly appointed, and meetings presided over by, the Secretaries of the Treasury and Homeland Security.

Notably, there is an "exception to the exception." In the event of an overriding, immediate, and extraordinary security threat to public health and safety, the Secretary of Homeland Security may take action in one of the areas otherwise reserved to the Secretary of the Treasury, without prior approval of the Secretary of the Treasury. However, immediately after taking such action, the Secretary of Homeland Security shall certify in writing the specific reasons for the action, and deliver the report to the Secretary of the Treasury, as well as Congress (specifically, the Chairman and Ranking Member of the Senate Committee on Finance). Unilateral action by the DHS Secretary must terminate within 14 days, unless the Secretary of the Treasury approves its continuation and provides notice thereof to the DHS Secretary.

(2)   *Immigration and Naturalization Service (INS)*

The INS is transferred from the Department of Justice (DOJ).

(3)   *Animal and Plant Health Inspection Service*

This Service is transferred from the U.S. Department of Agriculture (USDA).

(4)   *Coast Guard*

The Coast Guard is transferred from the Department of Transportation (DOT).

Title IV also transferred the Transportation Security Administration (TSA) from the DOT to DHS, and moved the Federal Protective Service of the GSA to DHS.

III.   POST-9/11 U.S. TRADE SECURITY INITIATIVES

A.   Statutory Overview

For most international trade lawyers, and their clients, involved in importation into the U.S., the greatest post-9/11 shift affecting their daily transactions concerns port and container security.[6] In part, the shift shows how seriously authorities take the Tom Clancey novel, *The Sum of All Fears* (1991), which became a 2002 movie thriller. The nightmarish plot involves smuggling, amidst lawful merchandise imported into the U.S., a nuclear device, and detonating it at the Super Bowl. Nuclear weapons are not the only WMDs worrying authorities. Biological weapons pose a risk, which the U.S. Congress addressed through the *Bioterrorism Act* (*BTA*). The five Titles of the *BTA* (discussed below) aim to secure U.S. food and drug supplies, and drinking water, against the threat of a bioterrorist attack, and enhance preparedness in the event of such an attack.

Accordingly, increased port and container security to guard against entry of WMDs, as well as other contraband items, is a key component of an overall national security strategy to manage risks and target threats. There are several elements to post-9/11 port and container security. They include (as explained below) the *Container Security Initiative* (*CSI*) and *Customs — Trade Partnership Against Terrorism* (*C-TPAT*) (explained below), as well as schemes such as "Screening" (*i.e.*, evaluating the import risk of all incoming vessels, and assigning the appropriate level of scrutiny based on the risk level), the "24 Hour Rule" (*i.e.*, mandating a minimum of 24 hours prior notice for importation of articles into the U.S. by water-based vessel, or 4 hours for air-based vessels, so CBP has the chance for screening), "Canines" (*i.e.*, using dog bomb and drug detection teams), and "High Tech" (*i.e.*, deploying advanced technology).

Initially, some of these elements were laid out directly, or countenanced by, the *Homeland Security Act of 2002*.[7] Many, however, were administrative fiat, that is, initiatives of the CBP. Thus, in October 2006, Congress enacted the *CSI* and *C-TPAT* programs into law.[8] Congress did so through the *Security and Accountability for Every Port Act of 2006*, which has the clever acronym the "*SAFE Port Act*."[9] Until their codification, the *CSI* and *C-TPAT* had been

---

[6] *See* Port Security Fact Sheet, *available at* www.cbp.gov/linkhandler/cgov/newsroom/fact_sheets/port_security/port_security.ctt/port_security.pdf.

[7] The 24 Hour Rule was set out in the *Trade Act of 2002*, Pub. L. 107-120, and is found at 19 C.F.R. Parts 4 (water-borne vessels), 24 (administrative procedures and fees), and 122 (aircraft).

[8] *See* U.S. Customs and Border Protection, Frontline News, 20 October 2006, *available at* www.cbp.gov/newsroom/).

[9] *See* H.R. 4954, 109th Cong., 2d Sess., Pub. L. 109-347. There are 8 parts to the *Act*:

(1)   Security of United States Seaports

(2)   Security of International Supply Chain

(3)   Administration

(4)   Agency Resources and Oversight

(5)   Domestic Nuclear Detection Office

(6)   Commercial Mobile Service Alerts

(7)   Other Matters

(8)   Unlawful Internet Gambling Enforcement

Observe the last part is a response to the WTO Appellate Body decision in the 2005 *Antigua Gambling* case.

The *CSI* is codified at 6 U.S.C. § 945, and *C-TPAT* is codified at 6 U.S.C. §§ 961-973.

administrative programs without a clear statutory basis. The *SAFE Port Act* also contained new security mandates, including a requirement that the 22 busiest ports in the U.S. implement radiation detection technology.

B. Fighting Bioterrorism with the *BTA*

Surely a bioterrorist attack is among the "worst nightmare" scenarios of security officials around the world. One response of the U.S. to this threat is the *Public Health Security and Bioterrorism Preparedness and Response Act of 2002* (Public Law 107-188, 12 June 2002, codified at 42 U.S.C §§ 201 *et seq.*) Known as the *Bioterrorism Act* (*BTA*), it is a complement to the *Homeland Security Act of 2002*.

While it consists of a large number of provisions affecting many parts of the U.S. government, the *BTA* is neatly organized into five Titles. The names of the first four Titles intimate strongly the policy objectives of the legislation. (Title V concerns additional provisions unrelated to bio-terrorism.)

Title I:	National Preparedness for Bioterrorism and Other Public Health Emergencies
Title II:	Enhancing Controls on Dangerous Biological Agents and Toxins
Title III:	Protecting Safety and Security of Food and Drug Supply
Title IV:	Drinking Water Security and Safety

In studying the *BTA*, consider whether its specific measures will achieve the policy objectives.

C. Securing Ports and Containers with the *CSI*

The *Container Security Initiative* (*CSI*), which the U.S. government announced in January 2002, has four core features to create and enforce a security regime for global shipping into the U.S.:[10]

    (1)   Identify high risk containers.

    (2)   Prescreen and evaluate containers before they are shipped.

    (3)   Use technology to prescreen.

    (4)   Use smarter, more secure, containers.

"Containers," of course, refers to the twenty-foot equivalent unit (TEU) hollow rectangles, or similar large box-like receptacles, for holding merchandise being shipped from an exporter to an importer.

Under the *CSI*, a team of CBP officers is deployed to foreign ports — ports of shipment for goods destined for the U.S. At those ports, the officers work jointly with foreign officials to screen — in effect, pre-screen — containers departing for the U.S. Roughly 50 foreign ports participate in pre-screening (as of February 2007). They are considered "operational" for *CSI* purposes, and designated as "*CSI* ports." The key advantage of pre-screening at a *CSI*

---

[10] *See* U.S. Customs and Border Protection Fact Sheet CSI (26 Sept. 2006), *available at* www.cbp.gov/xp/cgov/border_security/international_activities/csi/.

port is expedited processing. That is, if a container is pre-screened, then, upon arrival at the U.S. border, the cargo in it is processed in an expedited manner.

A key aspect of CSI is a "24 Hour Rule." Exporters must file manifest declarations 24 hours before loading a container on a vessel bound for the U.S. Consider the impact on developing and least developed country exporters. Does compliance increase administrative expenditures, or simply shift back in time by one day the actual expenditure? Might enhanced logistical efficiency (*e.g.*, alacritous processing) be a positive externality of compliance? What is the cost of failure to comply when the cargo is a perishable commodity, which a typical poor country exports?

D.   Securing Global Supply Chains with *C-TPAT*

As its rubric suggests, *C-TPAT* is a government instigated joint venture with the private sector to enhance international trade security.[11] The program focuses on fighting terrorism by making the cross-border commercial supply chain through which merchandise is imported into the U.S. as safe, secure, and efficient as possible. *C-TPAT* has five goals, which it seeks to achieve through a close partnership between the CBP and businesses committed through their practices to trade security and trade law compliance. The five goals are:

(1)   *Enhancing the Security of Supply Chains*

Ensure *C-TPAT* partners improve the security of their international supply chains pursuant to specified security criteria, working with stakeholders in that chain, and thereby enhance U.S. border security. In particular —

    a.   Certify security profiles and information provided by *C-TPAT* partners.

    b.   Enhance validation selection procedures by relying on risk factors, and expand the scope and volume of validations. "Validation" itself refers to the process by which CBP meets with company representatives, and visits domestic and foreign sites to verify company statements about security. A company is selected for validation based on the risk in its import supply chain. In turn, risk is assessed based on factors such as security-related anomalies, strategic threats posed in particular geographic regions, and import volumes.

    c.   Formalize requirements for *C-TPAT* to be a self-policing tool, and implement periodic self-assessment checks.

    d.   Require the partners to engage on security matters with all business entities in a supply chains.

(2)   *Increasing the Efficiency of Supply Chains*

Provide incentives and benefits to include expedited processing of *C-TPAT* shipments to *C-TPAT* partners, thus increasing the efficiency, as well as security, of international supply chains. In particular —

---

[11] *See* websites www.cbp.gov/linkhandler/cgov/import/commercial_enforcement/ctpat/ ctpat_strategicplan.ctt/ctpat_strategicplan.pdf;   and   www.cbp.gov/xp/cgov/import/ commercial_enforcement/ctpat/ctpat_faq.xml.

a. Develop a *C-TPAT* secure communication platform.

b. Conduct supply chain security training seminars and targeted outreach programs for certified partners and the trade community.

c. Share information, including on "security best practices," among the partners.

d. Develop minimum security practices, especially applicable to the point of origin, point of stuffing (*i.e.*, the time and place at which cargo is put into a container and then sealed), and smarter, more secure cargo containers.

e. Provide expedited processing benefits to the partners.

(3) *Internationalizing Security Standards*

Internationalize the core principles of *C-TPAT* through cooperation and coordination with the international community. In particular —

a. Work with the international trade community to secure global supply chains.

b. Partner with domestic Customs administrations (*e.g.*, Mexican Customs officials in Kansas City) to coordinate anti-terrorism efforts.

c. Support the World Customs Organization (WCO) to develop a WCO framework to secure and facilitate global trade through Customs-private sector partnerships.

d. Coordinate with other international organizations to improve the security and integrity requirements of their membership.

(4) *Supporting CBP*

Support other CBP security and facilitation initiatives. In particular —

a. Help implement and expand the *Free and Secure Trade* (*FAST*) program.

b. Assist in developing and implementing a smarter and more secure container.

c. Complement the *CSI*.

d. Reinforce other CBP and DHS anti-terrorism efforts.

(5) *Bettering Administration*

Improve administration of the *C-TPAT*. In particular —

a. Implement a human capital plan.

b. Expand the structured training program for supply chain specialists.

c. Coordinate with the CBP Modernization Office to enhance *C-TPAT* data collection and information management capabilities.

Observe the integrated approach to global commodity chains underlying *C-TPAT*. Each step in the process of bringing merchandise into the U.S. is viewed not in isolation, but as part of an overall transaction, any link of which could be vulnerable to terrorist infiltration.

Note also the third goal. The rhetoric surrounding the program is distinctly multilateral. It emphasizes "partnership," "support," "cooperation," and "coordination." But, consider the extent to which initiatives of the WCO are catalyzed or channeled by U.S. security policy.

The public-private partnership is an essential foundation of *C-TPAT*. Consider the alternative to the government obtaining the assistance of private industry to ensure increased vigilance throughout international supply chain. The government — CBP — takes full charge of security by rigorous inspections of virtually every container crossing into the U.S. That regime would cost an astronomical sum in government resources, impose high — even prohibitive — expenses on importers and suppliers, cause trade to grind to a halt, and have deleterious knock-on effects throughout the economies of the U.S. and its trading partners. In other words, there is no viable alternative. Yet, as a partnership between the public and private sectors, *C-TPAT* is voluntary. The program admits CBP can provide the highest level of cargo security only through close cooperation with the ultimate owners of international supply chain. Those owners are businesses — importers, carriers, consolidators, licensed Customs brokers, exporters, and manufacturers. Essentially, then, *C-TPAT* is a means by which CBP asks them to ensure the integrity of their security practices, and communicate and verify the security guidelines of their business partners in the supply chain.

Observe that both *CSI* and *C-TPAT* endeavor to extend the zone of security around the U.S. Where possible, they push that zone to the point of origin of a shipment and merchandise. What are the *C-TPAT* security criteria on which CBP makes designation decisions?

Necessarily, the security guidelines adjust to threat types and levels. Currently (as of February 2007), they address a broad range of topics, including:

  i.   Personnel
  ii. Physical and procedural security access controls.
  iii. Education, training and awareness.
  iv. Cargo manifest procedures.
  v.   Conveyance security threat awareness.
  vi. Documentation processing.

Any company that applies for *C-TPAT* designation must sign an agreement with CBP committing itself to these guidelines. In addition, a *C-TPAT* partner must agree to leverage its business and service providers to increase their security practices. In that way, *C-TPAT* influences positively the security practices of thousands of companies located around the globe not enrolled in the program. Interestingly, many companies demand of the entities with which they do business that these entities enroll in *CTPAT*, or at least adhere to its security guidelines. They do so, for example, by conditioning their business relationships on compliance.

What types of businesses may apply to be a *C-TPAT* partner? The answer is somewhat predictable. There is open enrollment (as of February 2007) for the following business types related to cargo handling and movement in the U.S. import supply chain:

  i.　U.S. importers of record

 ii.　U.S./Canada highway carriers

iii.　U.S./Mexico highway carriers

 iv.　Air, rail, or sea carriers

  v.　U.S. Marine Port Authority or Terminal Operators

 vi.　U.S. Air Freight Consolidators, Ocean Transportation Intermediaries and Non-Vessel Operating Common Carriers (NVOCC)

vii.　Mexican and Canadian manufacturers

viii.　Certain invited foreign manufacturers

 ix.　Licensed U.S. Customs brokers

CBP established these "enrollment categories," which is logical given its responsibility for screening all import cargo transactions. Utilizing risk management principles, CBP determined that *C-TPAT* should seek to enroll compliant, low-risk companies that are directly responsible for importing, transporting, and coordinating commercial import cargo into the U.S. A decision to enroll a particular company depends on that company being a trusted import trader with good supply chain security procedures and controls, which will allow for reduced screening of its imported cargo. In turn, CBP resources are liberated to focus screening efforts on import cargo transactions involving unknown or high-risk import traders.

Assuming a company is eligible to participate in *C-TPAT*, to become a partner it must apply. The application is online (at www.cbp.gov), and requires submission of

 (1)　corporate information,

 (2)　a supply chain security profile, and

 (3)　acknowledgement that participation is voluntary.

In essence, the application allows CBP to designate qualified companies as low risk. Shipments from or to such companies are less likely to be examined than non-designated companies — a benefit discussed below. The designation is based on the Customs compliance history and security profile of a company, and on validation of a sample international supply chain involving that company. CBP conducts domestic and foreign site visits to examine whether companies adhere to security "best practices," and evaluates weaknesses along their international supply chains.

Obviously, the second item in the application is critical. To complete a security profile, an applicant must conduct a comprehensive self-assessment of its supply chain security procedures using the *C-TPAT* security criteria (or guidelines jointly developed by CBP and the trade community for the specific enrollment category to which the applicant belongs). The criteria cover —

 1.　Business Partner Requirements

2. Procedural Security

3. Physical Security

4. Personnel Security

5. Education and Training

6. Access Controls

7. Manifest Procedures

8. Information Security

9. Conveyance Security

Not all companies are in a position to meet *C-TPAT* minimum security criteria. These criteria are not intended to impose additional costs on companies, but they are unlikely to do so only if a company already satisfies them.

Interestingly, all information on supply chain security submitted by *C-TPAT* applicants is kept confidential. Moreover, CBP does not disclose whether a company participates in *C-TPAT*. However, query whether, and the extent to which, CBP may share confidential information with other parts of the U.S. government, and with foreign governments? Might the prospect of intra-or inter-governmental data sharing be a concern even to law-abiding companies? Might it be a concern among rejected applicants?

Of course, a threshold question for an eligible company and its international trade counsel is why bother applying to join the first world-wide supply chain security initiative, a program that might change considerably with experience? That is, what benefits accrue from *C-TPAT* participation? After all, from a legal perspective, whether a company participates in *C-TPAT* or not makes no liability difference, *i.e.*, *C-TPAT* is not intended to add to, or detract from extant obligations under U.S. trade laws and regulations. And yet, joining *C-TPAT* obviously commits a company to follow through on actions specified in an agreement signed with CBP. These actions include self-assessing security systems, submitting security questionnaires, developing security enhancement plans, and communicating *C-TPAT* guidelines to other entities in the supply chain. If a company, after joining *C-TPAT*, fails to meet the minimum security criteria, then its status as a certified partner is suspended, or even removed — as are the aforementioned benefits. That status, and the benefits, may be reinstated when the company implements corrects its security deficiencies.

One answer to "why join?" is *C-TPAT* offers a trade-related business an opportunity to play an active role in the war against terrorism. That answer, in itself, hardly appeals to economic self-interest. Rather, it is a call to patriotism. Another, more commercially meaningful, response is that by participating, a company ensures its employees, suppliers, and customers are part of a transactional chain with enhanced security and efficiency. Tangibly, that means benefits for certain certified *C-TPAT* member categories, including:

1. A reduced number of CBP inspections, and thus reduced border delays.

2. Priority processing for CBP inspections, *i.e.*, front-of-the-line processing for inspections when possible.

3. Assignment (upon satisfactory completion of the online application) of a *C-TPAT* Supply Chain Security Specialist (SCSS), who works with a company to validate and enhance security throughout its international supply chain.

4. Potential eligibility for the CBP Importer Self-Assessment (ISA) program, which emphasizes self-policing instead of CBP audits.

5. Eligibility to attend *C-TPAT* supply chain security training seminars.

To be sure, weighing these benefits against costs is especially important for small and medium sized enterprises (SMEs). *C-TPAT* is not designed to be a "big company program," nor could it be to achieve widespread success. SMEs account for a large volume of import transactions every day. What special considerations might affect SMEs in deciding whether to participate in *C-TPAT*? What advantages, if any, might be gained from complying with *C-TPAT* level security criteria, but not being a formal partner?

E.   Securing *NAFTA* Trade with *FAST* and *SENTRI*

Free and Secure Trade (FAST) is an initiative of the Parties to the *North American Free Trade Agreement (NAFTA)* Parties — the U.S., Canada, and Mexico — in the form of an accord among the respective governments.[12] This accord is neither part, nor an outgrowth, of that free trade agreement (FTA). Rather, it is a response to the post-9/11 environment, whereby the Parties seek to build on the economic successes of their FTA, while also addressing security concerns they did not foresee when *NAFTA* entered into force on 1 January 1994.

Through the *FAST* accord, the *NAFTA* Parties commit themselves to coordinate border processes using a common set of risk management principles, supply chain security systems, advanced technology, and partnerships with industry. In effect, *FAST* is an effort to harmonize border security procedures. Different sets of security procedures in the U.S., Canada, and Mexico can create inefficiencies that hamper importers and carriers, and vulnerabilities that terrorists and narcotics traffickers exploit. The logic is that harmonization helps avoid these insalubrious outcomes. However, as with *CSI* and *C-TPAT*, query whether "harmonization" winds up being "Americanization."

After all, *FAST* essentially leverages on *C-TPAT*. Specifically, *FAST* is a clearance process at the *NAFTA* borders. Under the *FAST* program, a *C-TPAT* importer may be designated as a *FAST* entity, if it uses *C-TPAT* approved carriers. A separate application and approval process is necessary for a *C-TPAT* approved carrier to be designated a "*FAST* Highway Carrier." Once this designation is obtained, known low risk cargo importers may select a *FAST* Highway Carrier to ship its merchandise. The practical result is merchandise of that importer can cross the border through a separate *FAST*-designated lane in a swifter manner than others. Across the U.S. — Canada and U.S. — Mexico border, several *FAST* crossing points exist (*e.g.*, Sweetgrass,

---

[12] *See* www.cbp.gov/xp/cgov/import/commercial_enforcement/ctpat/fast/.

Montana; Coutts, Alberta; El Paso, Texas; and Ciudad Juarez, Chihuahua), with additional ones planned.

Incongruous with the harmonization principle is the fact that somewhat different requirements and procedures exist at the northern and southern *NAFTA* borders. That is true not only for obtaining certification as a *FAST* Highway Carrier, but also for an individual driver qualifying for a "*FAST* Pass," *i.e.*, a valid *FAST* Commercial Driver Card adducing eligibility to use *FAST* clearance.

     1.   Northern Border —

To qualify for *FAST* Highway Carrier status between the U.S. and Canada, there are two separate applications, one for the U.S. *FAST* Processing Center, and the other for the Canadian *FAST* Processing Center. Each Center independently performs a risk assessment, and issues approvals. The U.S. requires a *FAST* approved carrier to satisfy all *C-TPAT* standards by or through the *FAST* registration process.

As regards the *FAST* Commercial Driver Card, an individual must complete a *FAST* Commercial Driver Application for the U.S. and Canada. The application first is subjected to a risk assessment by a Canadian consortium of the Canada Border Service Agency (CBSA), Citizenship and Immigration Service for Canada (CIC), and Canada Revenue Agency. Upon approval from Canada, CBP conducts a full risk examination at its risk assessment center in St. Albans, Vermont. Note, then, U.S. authorities do not grant automatic recognition to the Canadian risk assessment. An applicant CBP identifies as "low risk" reports to an enrollment center, where that driver is interviewed, has his or her original identification and citizenship documents reviewed, is fingerprinted, and is digitally photographed. Successful applicants are issued a *FAST* Pass.

     2.   Southern Border —

To qualify for *FAST* Highway Carrier status between the U.S. and Mexico, an applicant must prove it has a history of complying with all relevant legislative and regulatory requirements set forth by CBP. The applying carrier must commit itself to *C-TPAT* security-enhancing business practices. Further, it must use drivers who are in possession of a valid *FAST* commercial driver card when using *FAST* clearance.

The procedure for a *FAST* Commercial Driver Card for the southern border is similar to that for the northern border. However, the *FAST* driver application is submitted to the Mellon Financial Corporation in Pittsburgh, Pennsylvania. Thereafter, it is forwarded to the CBP risk assessment center in St Albans, Vermont.

Consider these differences when studying the *NAFTA* Mexican Trucking dispute.

As indicated, *FAST* eligible shipments benefit from expedited border crossing procedures. How exactly is incoming cargo released under the *FAST* program to save time and enhance efficiency? There are two cargo release methods: paperless processing and the pre-arrival processing system (PAPS). With paperless processing, shipping documents are transmitted through electronic data interchange (EDI) and transponder technology. Just as e-mail is a faster velocity communication method than paper mail, this transmission speeds up Customs clearance. In contrast, PAPS utilizes barcodes located on commercial invoices and manifests. A Customs broker references the barcodes in the Automated Commercial System (ACS), which is an electronic database for filing Customs entry documentation electronically. Thus, when a *FAST* truck comes to the border, a Customs officer can scan the barcode, and thereby retrieve automatically entry documentation and allows for faster port processing of incoming cargo.

Not all *NAFTA* border crossings involve commercial-grade shipments of merchandise. Everyday, millions of motorists cross at points such as Windsor — Detroit on the U.S. — Canadian border, and Juraez-El Paso on the U.S.-Mexican border. They may do so for work or pleasure. These motorists are not interested in, and indeed may be ineligible for, a *FAST* Commercial Driver Card, and do not necessarily work for carriage companies with or seeking *FAST* Highway Carrier status. Yet, two facts about them are clear. First, they are important, if not indispensable, to the operation of the *NAFTA* economies. Second, there is a security risk a terrorist might lurk among the honest motorists. The *Secure Electronic Network for Travelers Rapid Inspection (SENTRI)* program is another effort emblematic of the dual nature of the mission of CBP, namely, to facilitate expeditious border crossings by legitimate travelers while screening out evildoers from crossing the frontiers.[13] As with *CSI*, *C-TPAT*, and *FAST*, the *SENTRI* program leverages off high technology.

The *SENTRI* program actually pre-dates 9/11. It was first implemented at the Otay Mesa passenger port of entry in California in 1995. The program was extended periodically, typically for two-year intervals, but in October 2006, for a 5-year period (*i.e.*, through 2011). The program has been popular, for reasons anyone who has stood in a long immigration queue at an airport understands. Individual motorists who are *SENTRI* members have access to a dedicated commuter lane — the *SENTRI* lane — that allows faster processing at ports of entry. They are trusted travelers — trusted, that is, by the U.S. government. To qualify, an applicant must undergo voluntarily a background check, in-person interview, and fingerprinting — and pay a fee (U.S. $129 as of February 2007) to cover administrative expenses. (The fee is non-refundable, even if the applicant is rejected!)

F. Good Goods, Good People, and Good Countries

1. Domestic Politics and Implementing the 9/11 Commission Recommendations

"Six years after the terrorist attacks of 9/11 and three years after the bipartisan and independent 9/11 commission delivered to the American people a road map for security that the Republican Congress has failed to pass into law, the Democratic Congress is about to deliver to the President a bill for

---

[13] *See SENTRI* Press Release, 30 Oct. 2006, *CBP Launches SENTRI Program Improvements: Five-Year Membership Extension and New Online Application System Announced, available at* www.cbp.gov/xp/cgov/newsroom/news_releases/102006/10302006_4.xml.

his signature to make the American people safer."[14] This remark, from Speaker of the House Nancy Pelosi (Democrat-California), indicates the political controversy surrounding the topic of trade and security. Passage of the new bill, entitled *Implementing Recommendations of the 9/11 Commission Act of 2007*, Pub. L. 110-53, 121 Stat. 266, 3 August 2007, was at the top of the priority list of the new, Democratic-controlled, 110th Congress.[15] The bill was House Resolution 1, and Senate Resolution 4.

Immediately, the practical impact of the *2007 Act* was felt worldwide. That is because its provisions ratchet up American security requirements for essentially all imports into the U.S. The bill is voluminous. It boasts 24 titles and 284 pages of text covering the following topics:

    i.   Financial grants for Homeland Security (Sections 101-104), and for Emergency Management Performance projects (Sections 201-202).

    ii.   Communications improvement for first responders (*i.e.*, the first officials to respond to an emergency, such as medical staff, fire-fighters, and police) and interoperability (among different communications systems at the federal, state, tribal, and local levels, in the event one fails) in emergency situations. (Interestingly, the 2006 *SAFE Port Act* did not mention funding for interoperability in respect of tribal areas.) (Sections 301-302, 401-410.)

    iii.   Intelligence sharing among government agencies (Sections 501-541) and Congressional oversight (Sections 601-605).

    ix.   Prevention of terrorist travel, including international collaboration on border security, enhanced identification document security, modernization of visa waiver schemes, model ports of entry programs (Sections 701-725), plus privacy and civil liberties protection (Sections 801-804).

    x.   Prevention of terrorist attacks including critical infrastructure reinforcement (Sections 1001-1003), upgrading defenses against nuclear and radiological weapons of mass destruction (WMDs) (Section 1101-1104), bio-surveillance against a "biological event of national concern" (Section 1102), transportation security (Sections 1201-1310), including public transport (Section 1401-1415), railroads (Section 1511-1528), aviation (*e.g.*, construction of blast-proof airplane cargo holds) (Section 1601-1618), trucking (Section 1531-1542), and hazardous material transport (*e.g.*, to ensure "hazmats" are moved around, not through, urban areas) (Section 1551-1558).

    xi.   100 percent container screening (Section 1701).

    xii.   Fighting terrorism through (*inter alia*) education in "predominantly Muslim countries" (Sections 2011-2014), democracy advancement

---

[14] Demetri Sevastopulo & Robert Wright, *U.S. to Screen All Foreign Ship Cargoes*, FINANCIAL TIMES, 26 July 2007, at 8 (quoting Nancy Pelosi).

[15] The official title of the Report is *The 9/11 Commission Report — Final Report of the National Commission on Terrorist Attacks Upon the United States*. Thomas H. Kean (the former Republican Governor of New Jersey) was the Chair and Lee H. Hamilton (the former Democratic Congressman from Indiana) served as Vice Chair.

in the "Broader Middle East" region (Section 2021), and "Reaffirming United States Moral Leadership" (Sections 2031-2034).

xiii.   Specific efforts in Afghanistan (Section 2041), Pakistan (Section 2042), and the Kingdom of Saudi Arabia (Section 2043).

Time will tell whether the *Act* actually enhances America's national security, or impedes trade and adds transaction costs.

2. A Triple Play

Essential to understanding the *2007 Act* is its clear thrust to continue the post-9/11 paradigmatic shift in Customs law from traditional functions like tariff collection (through classification, valuation, and origin determination) and statistics gathering (*e.g.*, on Harmonized Tariff Schedule (HTS) and Balance of Payments (BOP) matters), to the securing America's supply chain globally amidst the War on Terror. Only "good goods" and "good people" should move across America's borders.

Also essential to understanding the *Act* is it broadens the thrust. "Good countries" are a criterion for distinguishing among sources of imports. Not only must a good be "good," and a person be "good," if entry is to be permitted, but also the source of the good or person had better be a "good" country. In brief, the *2007 Act* is about "good goods, good people, and good countries."

How, exactly, does the *2007 Act* seek to make this triple play? A number of features of the triple play are worth highlighting.

3. Good Goods and Good People

Several topics in the *2007 Act* elaborate on the "good goods, good people" paradigm shift wrought by earlier, post-9/11 reforms. Project grants, emergency communications efforts, and intelligence gathering are found in the *2002 Homeland Security Act*. The anti-terrorist attack provisions continue efforts by the CBP and *2006 SAFE Port Act* to address vulnerabilities in America's large transportation network.

The *2007 Act* essentially funds the pre-existing programs, albeit with some broadening of them. Notably, the funding allows individual Congresspersons to demonstrate the relevance of their state to their constituents in the War on Terror. Less euphemistically, critics might charge the funding is old-fashioned, pork barrel politics.

4. Good Countries, Too

The *2007 Act* extends the immediate post-9/11 trade security paradigm beyond goods and people to countries. That is most evident in three topical areas: the container security requirement; efforts to re-assert America's moral leadership in the world; and programs aimed at key countries.

5. Screening

The container security, or screening, requirement is that all containers must be scanned in a foreign country port of discharge before they are shipped to the U.S. Section 1701(b)(1) of the *2007 Act* states:

> A container that was loaded on a vessel in a foreign port shall not enter the United States (either directly or via a foreign port) unless the container was scanned by nonintrusive imaging equipment and radiation detection equipment at a foreign port before it was loaded on a vessel.

Effectively, scanning must occur at the point of stuffing, after which a container is sealed. Conceptually, the key point is that "good" goods had better come from "good" countries, with a "good" country being one whose ports provide 100 percent container screening.

While adroit ports like Hong Kong raised little or no objection to this requirement, the general foreign reaction was outcry. Some Asian countries indicate they suffer the brunt of the 100 percent screening rule. That is because they account for most of America's imports. While only 1.8 million containers travel from Europe to the U.S. (in 2006), 13.7 million come from Asia.[16]

European countries complain the "unilateral action by the U.S. would force Europe's taxpayers to foot the bill for America's security," and explain they rather would have continued the "risk based" assessment scheme. Under it, only a sample of containers (not every single container) was screened, based on origin.[17] Surely the U.S. had not given risk assessment — which it created under the *CSI* — enough time to prove its merit. Surely, too, the Congressional Democrats were too eager to score political points. The previous Republican-controlled Congress passed the *SAFE Port Act* in October 2006, hardly a month before the watershed election. A few months later, the *2007 Act* appeared.

Nevertheless, with fear a WMD might be smuggled into a container gripping the American psyche, the only rational response is to check every container. That said, there are circumstances under which the 100 percent screening requirement is relaxed. First, the obligation is not immediate. The *Act* establishes an implementation date of 3-5 years, finishing on 1 July 2012, or possibly earlier if the Secretary of Homeland Security deems it possible based on pilot programs. That date can be pushed out further, in 2-year increments, on a port-specific basis, if the Secretary presents Congress with written justification. The *Act* sets out 6 possible justifications, 2 or more of which must exist in a port for a postponement of implementation of 100 percent screening in that port:[18]

(1) Scanners are not available for purchase and installation.

(2) Scanners yield too many false positives (*i.e.*, false alarms) to be effective.

---

[16] Andrew Bounds, *Brussels Attacks American Plan to Scan Shipping Containers*, FINANCIAL TIMES, 3 Aug. 2007, at 6.

[17] *Id.*

[18] The *2007 Act* uses the term "systems to scan containers," which effectively means scanners.

Any extension would take effect 60 days from the date the Secretary presented a report, and the Secretary must inform Congress the following year if this granted extension is to be renewed again after the 2-year period expires.

(3)   The port does not have the physical characteristics to install a scanner.

(4)   Scanners cannot be integrated with existing facilities at a port.

(5)   Scanners will significantly impact trade capacity and flow of cargo.

(6)   Scanners do not give automated alerts of questionable or high-risk cargo.

Second, two categories of imports are exempt from the screening requirement: Department of Defense military shipments into the U.S., and military cargo of foreign countries, are exempt. Third, Congress mandated that the Secretary implement the 100 percent container screening obligation in a manner that does not violate international trade rules, especially ones of the World Customs Organization (WCO).

6. Moral Leadership

Animating through parts of the *2007 Act* is the presumption a "good" country is one that respects, and to some degree follows, American moral principles. One sub-title in the *2007 Act*, "Reaffirming United States Moral Leadership," is telling.[19] Some provisions in this sub-title are thinly veiled efforts at converting "bad" to "good" countries. Other provisions work to ensure certain countries stay on a "good" behavioral trajectory. Accordingly, the sub-title encourages increased pro-American media broadcasts abroad, especially in times of a foreign crisis. The Broadcasting Board of Governors is tasked with the responsibility of providing Arabic and Persian translations of news broadcasts to Congress, and the public, via its website. The Department of State is to develop strategies for scholarship and scholarly exchanges with, and library collection building in, Muslim countries.

Even more thinly veiled are the attempts to convert countries to democracy. Under the *Advance Democratic Values, Address Non-democratic Countries and Enhance Democracy Act of 2007 (ADVANCE Democracy Act)*, which is embedded in the *2007 Act*, the Department of State is to evangelize democracy around the world. Its mission instruments are (1) a new "Democracy Liaison Officer" corps, (2) a special office for democracy development, (3) upgraded training of Foreign Service Officers, (4) handing out awards for pro-democracy movements, and (5) an enhanced website that touts success stories on promoting democracy. The irony that these attempts — were the United States not a democracy — would be dubbed "propaganda" is difficult to miss. In the long run, American deeds impress even the least sophisticated foreigners more than American words. Fortunately, the *ADVANCE Democracy Act*

---

[19] In one sense, the incongruity between American values and American human rights practice during the Iraq War, particularly following the Abu Ghraib prisoner abuse scandal, the rubric is misleading. "Reclaiming" might be more accurate than "reaffirming." The *9/11 Commission Report* states the U.S. should work with "friends to develop mutually agreed upon principles for the detention and humane treatment of captured international terrorists." The *2007 Act* follows up, seeking a modicum of reclamation. The *Act* says the "sense of Congress" is the Secretary of Homeland Security should develop a common coalition approach to comply with Common Article 3 of the *Geneva Conventions*. The Secretaries of Defense and State, and the Attorney General had to present a progress report on this approach within 6 months of enactment of the *Act*.

calls on the President to investigate human rights violations, and pursue country-specific strategies to promote democracy.

7. Key Country Initiatives

The third manifestation of the paradigmatic shift in post-9/11 U.S. Customs law toward "good countries" is in provisions targeting certain categories of, or specific, nations. For instance, the U.S. continues its visa waiver program for friends in the War on Terror. They are "good" countries. Hence, their people need not undergo strict scrutiny before entering the U.S. Never mind the obvious vulnerability here — a threat posed by "home grown" terrorists in Europe, perhaps individual British Muslims of Pakistani origin, or German converts to Islam. To look beyond an EU passport and scrutinize religion or national origin would be politically, and probably legally, unacceptable.

Education to help countries be "good" is another example. The *Act* distinguishes two regions — "Predominantly Muslim Countries" and the "Broader Middle East." Labels aside, the first category is the broader one, as it presumably includes any country in any region with an Islamic population of 50 percent or more. The "Broader Middle East" covers Afghanistan, Algeria, Bahrain, Egypt, Iran, Iraq, Jordan, Kuwait, Lebanon, Libya, Morocco, Oman, Pakistan, Qatar, Saudi Arabia, Syria, Tunisia, United Arab Emirates (UAE), West Bank and Gaza, and Yemen. Notably, this second category excludes Turkey and Israel, and does not extend northward into Central Asia.

Predominantly Muslim Countries are the beneficiary of funding for "modern basic public education," including English language training, and creation of an International Muslim Youth Opportunity Fund. These two schemes aim to discourage financing of *madrassas* (Islamic religious schools) that simultaneously neglect fundamental cognitive and skills training necessary for success in the global economy and emphasize memorization of the *Qur'an* and extreme Islamic doctrines.

For the Broader Middle East, the *2007 Act* authorizes a Middle East Fund, to offer grants, technical assistance, and training to support civil society, education reform, and human rights (including women's rights), foster an independent media and political participation, create economic opportunities for citizens, and enforce the rule of law.

Front-line allies in the War on Terror — Afghanistan, Pakistan, and Saudi Arabia — get special attention. Afghanistan is funded to train its civilian police force. The program for Pakistan is wide-ranging. The President is to develop a strategy to help it:

(1) Curb nuclear proliferation.

(2) Fight corruption.

(3) Reduce poverty.

(4) Improve governance and governmental authority, especially in the North West Frontier Province (NWFP), Federally Administered Tribal Areas (FATA), Waziristan, and parts of Balochistan.

(5) Secure its borders, especially with Afghanistan and Iran to block Taliban and other terrorist group movements.

(6)   Resolve its long-standing Kashmir dispute with India.

(7)   Generally advance the rule of law.

Held out to Pakistan is the promise of funds if it demonstrates a "clear commitment to building a moderate democratic state." The *Act* highlights Saudi Arabia — not Afghanistan or Pakistan — as having an "uneven record in the fight against terror." It does recognize Royal family efforts to fight terrorists, including private financing for them (*e.g.*, the 9/11 hijackers).

8. The Power Game

The *2007 Act* is as much about power between Congress and the Executive Branch over foreign economic policy, and specifically the trade — national security nexus, as it is about shifting the Customs law paradigm to make Americans more secure. The *Act* bolsters Congressional oversight, relative to the Executive Branch, on a topic the White House championed itself as the pre-eminent authority. Until the *Act*, the Republican-dominated Congress left the nexus to the President, who in turn delegated authority to the CBP. There was little challenge to Executive Branch initiatives such as the *2002 Act*, the *BTA, 2006 Safe Port Act*, and programs such as *CSI* and *C-TPAT*.

Many Democrats, however, specifically asked why recommendations in the *9/11 Commission Report* went un-enacted, and upon taking control of Congress, put them into legislation. In so doing, Congress also inserted throughout the *2007 Act* metrics to measure progress toward goals it establishes, and obligations on the President or State Department to report to it on those metrics. In that respect, a sub-title about reaffirming America's moral leadership veils an intra-governmental power play. Congress can reaffirm its power relative to the Presidency by working to reaffirm American values.

For example, by setting out specific goals, and tying funding to their realization, on democracy and human rights, Congress demonstrates to the White House its determination to set priorities and evaluative metrics. As another example, for the country-specific programs, in respect of all three front-line countries, the President (or the State Department) must report on their social, economic, legal, and political development — or lack thereof. The State Department is supposed to list each predominantly Muslim country as to the seriousness of its efforts to support the U.S. schemes. For Afghanistan, progress reports are expected to gauge the success of that training. For every 6 months through 2009, it must receive reports from the Executive on Pakistani progress. The *Act* requires the President to provide Congress with a written analysis of Saudi progress in the fight against terrorism, as well as on economic, political, and social reform, and improved religious freedom, and assess Saudi membership in the *International Convention for the Suppression of the Financing of Terrorism*, and evaluate the work of the Saudi Nongovernmental National Commission for Relief and Charity Work Abroad.

IV. THE INTERNATIONAL IMPACT OF U.S. SECURITY PROGRAMS: EXPORTING U.S. POLICY TO THE WORLD CUSTOMS ORGANIZATION?

The post-9/11 American security initiatives, such as *CSI* and *C-TPAT*, predate an international regime for securing global trade against terrorist threats. To what extent does the U.S. — by design or effect — export its Customs rules on security, unilaterally drawn up and implemented, to other countries? Does the U.S. essentially take its security regime as its negotiating position in the World Customs Organization (WCO)?

One approach to this question is to consider the timing and nature of work undertaken by the WCO. In June 2005, the WCO published a *Framework of Standards to Secure and Facilitate Global Trade*. Query whether this *Framework* (*inter alia*) legitimizes *CSI* and *C-TPAT*. The Framework states that enhanced security must rest on two pillars — "Customs to Customs" and "Customs to Business." In reviewing the synopsis of these pillars below, consider the extent to which they resemble, respectively, *CSI* and *C-TPAT*.

1.   Standards for Customs to Customs Security Enhancements —

The *Framework* calls on WCO member countries to evaluate global supply chains in an integrated manner. They should upgrade cargo inspections, partly by using modern technology, better risk management systems, identifying high risk cargo or containers, obtaining advanced electronic information, targeting, and communicating with different governmental authorities. They also should articulate performance measures, conduct periodic security assessments, and emphasize the importance of integrity among Customs officials. The *Framework* highlights the importance of outbound security inspections, a provision obviously in the interest of major importing countries like the U.S.

2.   Standards for Customs to Business Security Enhancements

The *Framework* manifests the need for public-private partnerships to address security risks, facilitate trade, and build open communication channels between the two sectors. These partnerships can be forged with low-risk importers and carriers, designating as authorized economic operators (AEOs) on the basis of sound security criteria. The partnerships can take advantage of advanced technology, not only in security procedures (*e.g.*, infrared detection equipment), but also in applying and maintaining AEO designations (*e.g.*, on line applications)

Building on these pillars, the *Framework* contains several specific provisions, many of which resemble U.S. rules. For example, Note 1.3.6 in the *Framework* is redolent of the CBP "Prior Notice Rule." This Note states

> The exact time at which the Goods and Cargo declarations have to be lodged with the Customs administration at either export or import should be defined by national law after careful analysis of the geographical situation and the business processes applicable for the different modes of transport, and after consultation with the business sector, and other Customs administrations concerned.[20]

The *Framework* establishes minimum prior notice deadlines based on the transport mode — 24 hours before port arrival for maritime, 4 hours for air, 2 hours for rail, and 1 hour for road.

To be sure, the *Framework* does not establish a mandatory set of rules. Rather, it amounts to a set of suggestions, *i.e.*, recommendations as to best

---

[20] WORLD CUSTOMS ORGANIZATION, FRAMEWORK OF STANDARDS TO SECURE AND FACILITATE GLOBAL TRADE 22 (2005).

standards and practices that signatories ought to implement into their respective laws, as well as a commitment to "endeavor to secure the full cooperation of business" and report back to WCO on their progress.[21] Bluntly put, the WCO does not have the enforcement capabilities of the WTO *Dispute Settlement Mechanism (DSU)*, and the U.S. cannot force its will on other WCO countries. Yet, as the pre-eminent multilateral Customs law body — the one, for instance, responsible for the Harmonized System (HS) — its power of suggestion is considerable. As a practical matter, probably the biggest constraint on that power is capacity in developing and least developed countries. Without assistance, they cannot acquire the requisite sophisticated, automated security systems needed to implement the *Framework* standards — even if they have the political will to do so.

---

[21] *Id.* at 41-42.

Part Six

FREE TRADE AGREEMENTS

Chapter 21
ECONOMIC ASPECTS OF FTAs

If economists could manage to get themselves thought of as humble, competent people on a level with dentists, that would be splendid.

—John Maynard Keynes (1883-1946), Essays in Persuasion, Ch. 5, *The Future* (1931)

Documents Supplement Assignment

1. *Havana Charter* Articles 43-45
2. GATT Article XXIV
3. Relevant provisions in FTAs

I. TERMINOLOGICAL DISTINCTIONS AND BASIC FACTS

A. "RTA" and "PTA"

To be technically precise, there is a distinction among the terms "Regional Trade Agreement" (RTA), Free Trade Agreement (FTA), and Customs Union (CU). The term RTA is an umbrella covering both FTAs and CUs. Sometimes, the term "Preferential Trade Agreement" (PTA), is used as a synonym for RTA. The term RTA can be misleading. That is because it suggests all the countries that are members of an FTA or CU in question are located in the same geographic region. The U.S. and Bahrain are not in the same region, yet have an FTA. That also is because RTA intimates all countries in a region are members of an RTA. Belize and Panama are not members of the *Central American Free Trade Agreement (CAFTA*, or *CAFTA—DR*, where "DR" stands for Dominican Republic).

The term PTA avoids this misconception. However, "PTA" can be confused with preferential arrangements for developing and least developed countries, such as the Generalized System of Preferences (GSP) and *African Growth and Opportunity Act (AGOA)*. Thus, there is no perfect term or acronym to cover FTAs and CUs.

Among RTAs, the balance of attention of many international trade lawyers and scholars, and the business media, focuses on FTAs. Accordingly, this and subsequent Chapters frequently employ the rubric of "FTAs." However, many of the legal and policy principles are applicable to CUs, and where appropriate, attention is dedicated to them.

B. "FTA"

The distinction between an FTA and CU is embedded in GATT Article XXIV:8. This provision not only provides the exemption from the MFN obligation of GATT Article I:1 necessary to create an RTA, but also defines the two creatures. An FTA is an arrangement between two or more countries removing all, or substantially all, barriers to trade between or among them. The arrangement may be bilateral, *i.e.*, between two countries, such as the *U.S. — Israel FTA* and *U.S. — Bahrain FTA*. Or, an FTA may be plurilateral, *i.e.*, among a group of countries, such as the *North American Free Trade Agreement* (*NAFTA*), which covers Canada, Mexico, and the U.S., *Common Market for Eastern and Southern Africa* (*COMESA*, which as an FTA with aspirations to be a CU), which covers 20 African nations, and *CAFTA—DR*, which covers the U.S., Costa Rica, El Salvador, Guatemala, Honduras, Nicaragua, plus the Dominican Republic.

Each member of an FTA retains its sovereignty as to setting trade barriers vis-à-vis products originating from third countries (*i.e.*, non-FTA members). For example, assume neither the U.S. nor Bahrain has an FTA with Japan. The U.S. might impose a 2.5 percent tariff on passenger automobiles from Japan, whereas Bahrain retains a 5 percent duty on the same vehicles. Under the *U.S. — Bahrain FTA*, however, the FTA members have agreed to the same duty on vehicles trade between them — zero.

C. Trade Treaty for the Peoples

Interestingly, inspired partly by some socialist-oriented Latin American leaders during the first decade of the new millennium, such as Bolivian President Eva Morales and Venezuelan President Hugo Chavez, "PTA" may have taken on yet another meaning — "Peoples Trade Agreement." (The Spanish acronym is "TCP," for *El Tratado de Comercio entre los Pueblos*, *i.e.*, "Trade Treaty for the Peoples"). A PTA in this new sense is an economic alternative and political challenge to an FTA. In April 2006, Bolivia and Venezuela joined Cuba in signing a 10-point PTA. The first point says the trilateral accord

> is a response to the failed neo-liberal model, based as it is on deregulation, privatization and indiscriminate opening of markets.[1]

Accordingly, the PTA aims to promote

> a model of trade integration between people that limits and regulates the rights of foreign investors and multinationals so that they serve the purpose of national productive development.[2]

What motivated Bolivia, Venezuela, and Cuba to sign a PTA?

One answer is they resurrected — consciously or not — socialist-style trade policies popular in Latin America in the 1950s and 1960s. These policies, advocated by leading economists like Paul Baran, Raul Prebisch, and Hans Singer. Another answer is a genuine sense a conventional market capitalist FTA will not work for them. President Morales vowed in March 2006 that Bolivia "never" would negotiate an FTA with the U.S, and in August 2006 Bolivian Vice President Alvaro Garcia Linera explained:

---

[1] Lucien O. Chauvin, *Venezuela, Bolivia, and Cuba Sign Alternative "Trade Treaty for the Peoples"*, 23 INT'L TRADE REP. (BNA) 692 (4 May 2006).

[2] *Id.* at 692.

Bolivia wants trade relations with the entire world. I traveled to the United States to try to advance a trade pact. But, we can't just have free trade under the old rules, because it is too aggressive for our economy.

For example, how is a small farmer in Bolivia going to compete with farmers from countries that use the latest tractors and other technologies? Its like trying to make the 2nd century compete with the 21st century. The same goes for our urban small businesses. How are we going to compete with giant factories under such conditions?[3]

Interestingly, a third answer is soybean economics provoked the Bolivia — Venezuela — Cuba PTA. When Colombia signed an FTA with the U.S. on 27 February 2006, it agreed to purchase a 600,000 ton quota of American soybeans. Until that point, Bolivia had shipped 500,000 tons of soybeans to Colombia, worth $166 million (in 2005). The *U.S. — Colombia TPA* thus diverts soybean trade away from Bolivia and toward America. Bolivian President Morales responded immediately with the PTA proposal. Andean region politics reinforced his call.

The Community of Andean Community (CAN) — founded in 1969, and comprised of Bolivia, Colombia, Ecuador, Peru, and Venezuela — had been disintegrating. Not only Colombia, but also Peru (in April 2006), signed FTAs with the U.S. Further, in December 2005, *MERCOSUR* admitted Bolivia and Venezuela to full membership, and in April 2006, Venezuelan President Chavez announced his country was withdrawing from CAN — and called the Peruvian President, Alejandro Toledo — a traitor to South America for signing an FTA with the U.S.

D. An Overview of U.S. FTAs

No international trade lawyer (or teacher!) possibly can know every detail of each FTA.[4] However, every international trade lawyer (and teacher!) should memorize the countries with which the U.S. has an FTA, and thereby be able to spot when an FTA issue actually or potentially arises.

In brief, the U.S. is a party to the following FTAs:

1. *U.S. — Israel FTA*, effective 30 August 1985.

2. *Canada — U.S. FTA (CUFTA)*, effective 1 January 1989, but legally most provisions suspended by *NAFTA*.

3. *North American Free Trade Agreement (NAFTA)*, effective 1 January 1994.

4. *U.S. — Jordan FTA*, effective 17 December 2001.

5. *U.S. — Singapore FTA*, effective 1 January 2004.

---

[3] James Langman, *Bolivia Looks for New Kind of Trade Pace With U.S., While Seeking ATPDEA Extension*, 23 INT'L TRADE REP. (BNA) 1198-2000 (10 Aug. 2006).

[4] The *Dictionary of International Trade Law* accompanying this Textbook contains extensive Tables on legal and political facts about the FTAs in which the U.S. is involved, and on the substantive market access provisions concerning goods, services, and government procurement in those FTAs.

6. *U.S. — Chile FTA*, effective 1 January 2004.

7. *U.S. — Australia FTA*, effective 1 January 2005.

8. *U.S. — Morocco FTA*, effective 1 January 2006.

9. *Central American Free Trade Agreement — Dominican Republic (CAFTA—DR)*, effective 1 March 2006 with El Salvador, and 1 April 2006 with Guatemala, Honduras, and Nicaragua, but not implemented in Costa Rica or Dominican Republic as of December 2007.

10. *U.S. — Bahrain FTA*, effective 1 August 2006.

11. *U.S. — Oman FTA*, effective no earlier than 1 January 2007.

12. *U.S. — Peru FTA*, signed 12 April 2006 but not implemented as of December 2007.

13. *U.S. — Colombia FTA*, signed 22 November 2006 but not implemented as of December 2007.

14. *U.S. — Panama FTA*, signed December 2006, but with the labor provisions left open pending guidance from Congress, and not implemented as of December 2007.

15. The FTA between Korea and the U.S., called *KORUS*, signed in March 2007, but not implemented as of December 2007.

Further, every international trade lawyer (and teacher!) should be aware that a number of intriguing features are evident from these FTAs, which provoke many questions. Consider for instance:

a. The time between commencing negotiations and entry into force. What factors affect the gap?

b. The votes in the U.S. Congress on each FTA, including the overall vote and "no" vote by political party, and political control in Congress at the time of the vote. Is there anything left of the famed post-Second World War bipartisan consensus in favor of free trade?

Obviously, there are an enormous number of FTAs — planned, in negotiations, and implemented — not involving the U.S.

For instance, Australia, Japan, Mexico, New Zealand, and Singapore have FTA "dockets," as it were, differing in activity, history, and purpose. So, too, does the EU. Indeed, the EU has entered into, and continues to pursue, "association agreements." These free-trade deals are more than an economic link. They are designed as the first step toward accession into the EU, at least for some of the former Soviet bloc countries. However, it is dubious as to whether the EU ever would admit all of the countries in the Mediterranean region with which it has such agreements.

E. "CU"

A CU is one step deeper than an FTA in terms of economic integration. The members of a CU — which may be bilateral or plurilateral — agree to delete all, or substantially all, barriers to internal trade between or among them. In that sense of internally free movement of goods, and an attendant set of rules to determine origin within the grouping, a CU is like an FTA. However, the CU members also agree to a Common External Tariff (CET), which means they establish the same trade barriers on the same categories of products in the Harmonized System (HS) — a unified set of customs laws and procedures. In brief, a CU is a single market both as among the members and vis-à-vis the rest of the world.

Of course, it is not easy for countries to agree on a unified tariff schedule, and harmonize their non-tariff barriers. They must not only coordinate their foreign economic policy, but also integrate this homogenous outlook with their domestic commercial, financial, and investment needs and interests. No one country can impose its trade policies on the others in the grouping. That is as true for customs duties as it is for non-tariff barriers (such as technical standards), investment rules, and intellectual property (IP) protection. Not surprisingly, therefore, there are fewer examples of CUs in the world than there are FTAs, and often countries seeking an RTA start with an FTA, and then articulate a desire to move to a CU in the future.

The most obvious and successful example of a CU is the European Union (EU). However, it actually is a step beyond a CU, insofar as most of the EU members (with the notable exceptions of the United Kingdom and Denmark) have accepted a common currency — the euro. In other words, the EU boasts not only a single market that is the hallmark of a CU, but also monetary union. Such union necessitates prior agreement on convergence criteria, for example, permissible government budget deficits. In addition to the EU, other examples of CUs include *MERCOSUR* and the *Southern African Customs Union (SACU)*.

F. An Arab Islamic CU: The GCC

While the Near East boasts an ancient history of trading, among Arab countries for most of the 20th century, trade languished. Conflict, imprudent economic policies, outright corruption, plus the lingering effects of colonialism, are among the culprits. However, Arab countries have made efforts to foster regional trade. Indeed, an illustration of a CU in the Arab Islamic world was formed in 1981 in Riyadh, Kingdom of Saudi Arabia. Six Arab countries in the Gulf (that is, the Persian or Arabian Gulf) region — Bahrain, Saudi Arabia, Kuwait, Oman, Qatar, Saudi Arabia, and the United Arab Emirates (UAE) — agreed to form the "Cooperation Council for the Arab States of the Gulf." The group commonly is known as the "Gulf Cooperation Council" (GCC). As a Persian country, Iran is not a member. The other two Gulf Arab nations, Iraq and Yemen, also did not join, though Yemen (as of 2006) seeks membership.

The purpose of the GCC is to promote stability and economic cooperation in the region. Thus, in 1991, during the first Gulf War, the GCC formed a regional military force with Egypt and Syria, which was used to liberate Kuwait and is available for peacekeeping purposes. The GCC also has a fund for Arab development. Most notably from a trade perspective, in January 2003, the GCC eliminated tariff and many non-tariff barriers on trade among member states, and established a CU.

Specifically, at a December 2001 GCC Heads of State Summit, GCC leaders agreed to an across-the-board CET of 5 percent on imports originating from non-GCC countries, with implementation in January 2003. Considerable challenges face the GCC, such as agreement on a list of products as to which a tariff higher than the 5 percent CET will apply. Some GCC countries have tariffs of 15-20 percent or more on certain products — Bahrain, for instance, has a 20 percent duty on 12-millimeter steel bars. Some of them impose a duty of 100 percent or more on goods the consumption of which is forbidden under Islamic Law (*Shari'a*), namely, alcohol, pork, and pork products. On alcohol, Bahrain puts a 125 percent duty, and Oman and Qatar a 100 percent duty, but the Kingdom of Saudi Arabia bans importation of all these goods under GATT Article XX(a). Most GCC countries impose a 100 percent tariff on tobacco products. Additional challenges the GCC faces in achieving a CU include agreement on the distribution of revenues and setting common technical standards.

Notably, like the EU, the GCC aspires to create a common currency, and thus achieve monetary union. The target date is 1 January 2010, and the new currency is to float freely by 2015. To meet this deadline, Kuwait agreed in January 2003 to end its 27 year-long link to a basket of currencies. (Kuwait was the only GCC country to peg its currency to a unit other than the U.S. dollar. The other GCC countries linked their currencies to the dollar.) Still, the GCC did not meet its 2005 deadline for agreement on convergence criteria, especially inflation rates, which vary considerably in the Gulf Region. Given the real-world experience of the EU in forming a monetary union, the European Central Bank (ECB) (among other entities) provides technical assistance on convergence criteria, including the formation of a common currency, the name of such currency, and the location of a central bank. In September 2006, the GCC agreed to put its Central Bank in Abu Dhabi. As for the currency name, it might be "*karam*" — the Arabic word for "generosity."

II. JOB CREATION OR DESTRUCTION?

A. Theoretical Points

RTAs are far more than economic creatures. The reality they also are political bodies is evident from watching events on Capitol Hill. Sometimes, economic issues dominate the debate. Dairy and sugar lobbies had serious reservations about the *U.S. — Australia FTA*. But, often other factors enter into the legislative process. *NAFTA* almost was derailed by a 10-10 authorizing vote in the Senate Finance Committee, the *U.S. — Jordan FTA* was held up for a year over ideology, and labor rights and social issues loomed large in the row over the *Central American Free Trade Agreement (CAFTA or CAFTA—DR)*. Moreover, RTAs may be about the cultural identity of a region. By integrating governments and communities of the members, they may give them a collective voice in the global economy. For instance, former Malaysian Prime Minister Mahathir Muhammad adamantly opposes U.S. membership in the FTA of the *Association of South East Asian Nations (ASEAN)*. Were the far larger U.S. a member of the *ASEAN FTA (AFTA)*, it would drown out the distinct voice of the smaller South East Asian countries, and meddle in their internal and regional affairs.

Thus, it is unfair to judge the success of RTAs solely on neoclassical economic grounds. Nevertheless, whether they "are good" or "make sense" depends very much on their economic performance. The analysis is both theoretical and empirical in nature. To begin, as a general economic benefit RTA advocates say that in virtually all countries with which the U.S. has entered into an FTA, there has been an increase in *per capita* GNP, and sometimes an acceleration in the rate of growth of *per capita* GNP. The elimination of trade barriers — that is, deeper cuts in tariff and non-tariff barriers than occur in a multilateral trade round under GATT—WTO auspices — by a fewer number of countries at least correlates with the *per capita* income changes. Whether this elimination is a statistically significant causal factor, much less the most important one, in boosting income, is another question. Even if it is, changes in income distribution and poverty levels are a critical and hotly contested matter.

The effects of RTAs on income levels, growth, and distribution are connected with a bottom-line question that virtually all workers, whether blue or white collar, whether in agriculture, manufacturing, or services, ask — or ought to ask — when their government contemplates an RTA: what will this mean for my job? In the most general sense, the answer is that an RTA presents both risks and opportunities. Hence, the appetite of any individual for an RTA may depend on her risk profile.

Knowing that this question resonates in the minds of many workers, much of the empirical economic research focuses on whether more jobs are created than are lost in each of the member countries of an RTA. Free trade theory is misinterpreted if it is believed that there are no "losers" from trade liberalization. The reduction of tariff and non-tariff barriers is supposed to reward industries that have a comparative advantage, and punish those that do not. In turn, productive resources (labor, land, human capital, physical capital, and technology) are supposed to be reallocated from the "losing" to the "winning" sectors.

Moreover, recall the Stopler-Samuelson Theorem predicts trade liberalization will lead to a reduction in the returns to labor in the labor-scarce country. That is, wages will fall in that country, and rise in the labor-surplus country. The reason is that the labor-scarce country will specialize in the export of goods that use intensively in their production other factors (such as land and capital) in which that country has a surplus. In contrast, the labor surplus country will export labor-intensive goods, thereby capitalizing on its comparative advantage derived from its labor surplus position. Thus, the demand for labor will fall in the labor-scarce country, causing a drop in wages, while it will rise in the labor-surplus country, causing a rise in wages.

Politicians have their own version of the Stopler-Samuelson Theorem. During the 1992 presidential campaign, candidate Ross Perot warned of a "giant sucking sound." He meant that *NAFTA* would cause a net loss of American jobs to Mexico, and forecast the loss would be on the order of 5.9 million. In 1995, and again in 1998, perennial presidential candidate Patrick Buchanan warned the real income of American workers would continue to erode as *NAFTA* forced them to compete with Mexican laborers earning a tenth of their wages. The Administrations of Presidents George H.W. Bush and Bill Clinton countered with rosy forecasts about hundreds of thousands of new jobs resulting from freer trade with Mexico and Canada, which in turn would stimulate American economic growth. Both sides lacked common sense. On the one hand, as the *Wall Street Journal* pointed out in 1997, Americans had been losing jobs long before *NAFTA* was invented. On the other hand, how could it possibly be that freer regional trade alone — and not macroeconomic, technological, or demographic forces — would produce so many new jobs?

B. **Empirical Research**

The effects of an FTA on jobs and wages are not the only repercussions of importance. Has an FTA boosted overall economic growth? Advocates of *NAFTA* assert the Mexican economy outperforms economies in the rest of Latin America. Critics charge there are other non-*NAFTA* causes at play, and the period of investigation can make all the difference in reaching a result like "the Mexican economy grew by 3 percent while other Latin economies grew by 2.5 percent." Has an FTA affected migration patterns? Advocates of *NAFTA*, like former Mexican President Salinas, said the U.S. would get both more tomatoes and tomato workers. Opponents said migration is driven more by demographic trends than an FTA. Has an FTA had negative externalities? Advocates and opponents of *NAFTA* argue about implications of the accord on the environment, labor, and narcotics trafficking.

Nevertheless, in the minds of most average citizens in most countries, the job and wage effects of an FTA loom the largest. For all the opportunity it creates, trade liberalization also causes anxiety. The American public is deeply skeptical about job and wage effects of FTAs. In a 1998 NBC/*Wall Street Journal* poll, 58 percent of Americans surveyed said foreign trade had been bad for America because cheap imports have led to wage declines and job losses. The skepticism persists to the present day. No doubt such polls, read by politicians, help explain close votes on Capitol Hill on many trade deals, such as *CAFTA—DR*. In many countries, the public shares the skepticism of Americans about trade liberalization. Is this sentiment, and hard-fought political battles, warranted?

That is, what do the empirical analyses about job creation versus destruction — most of which use *NAFTA* as their case in point — say? Some economists counsel that studying the "job count" effects of an FTA is a fool's errand. That advice has not put a halt to the research. So numerous are the studies that even a brief synthesis of the majority of them is impossible. Moreover, *NAFTA* is different from all other U.S. FTAs because of the trade shares involved, *i.e.*, it is so much larger than other deals. However, a peek at just a few, conducted in the wake of *NAFTA*, suggests the difficulty in providing an unambiguous answer.

In 1996, the North American Integration and Development Center at the University of California at Los Angeles (UCLA) published the results of a comprehensive study funded by the U.S. government. It found *NAFTA* created about 49,000 jobs through exports to Mexico. Imports from Mexico had cost more than 38,000 jobs. The net effect was 11,000 new jobs, an insignificant amount among roughly 125 million U.S. jobs. In other words, the UCLA study said that both sides were wrong. Significantly, the study stressed that the 1995 Mexican peso crisis, during which the value of the Mexican peso fell dramatically relative to the U.S. dollar, had more to do with boosting Mexican exports to the U.S. than did *NAFTA*. Interestingly, in 1997 the Toronto-based C.D. Howe Institute reached a similar conclusion with respect to Canada: neither *NAFTA* nor its predecessor, *CUFTA*, had produced a dramatic effect on Canadian jobs, hence free trade between Canada and the U.S. could not be blamed for Canada's disappointing labor market performance.

In 1997, the Institute for Policy Studies, an independent center, teamed with the Great Cities Institute of the College of Urban Planning and Public Affairs at the University of Illinois at Chicago. They issued a report rebutting Clinton Administration claims that export growth resulting from *NAFTA* and the Uruguay Round agreements would translate into new jobs. The study pointed out the global economy was dominated by MNCs, which have no incentive to create jobs in the U.S. vis-à-vis any other location. That is, there was no guarantee that MNCs would use additional profits earned through increases in exports of their product to finance new jobs in the U.S. To the contrary, MNCs might use these profits to finance activities that actually lower employment (and wages) in the U.S., *e.g.*, mergers, outsourcing, and downsizing. However, the Illinois study did not provide much in the way of empirical assessments. It also seemed somewhat undercut by a 1998 survey released by the Center for Strategic and International Studies, a Washington, D.C. think tank. That survey found the vast majority of North American businesses polled either employed more workers, or kept the same number of workers, since *NAFTA* entered into force on 1 January 1994. Of 361 American, Canadian, and Mexican businesses, only 11 percent reported fewer employees since *NAFTA* took effect, and only one such company blamed *NAFTA* for job losses.

A 1997 study by the Economic Policy Institute (EPI) did stake out a position on the actual effect of *NAFTA* on American employment. The EPI is a non-profit research group funded by labor unions and corporations. A *NAFTA* critic, it teamed up with some other critics (the Institute for Policy Studies, International Labor Rights Fund, Public Citizen's Global Trade Watch, Sierra Club, and U.S. Business and Industrial Council Educational Foundation) to produce a report entitled *The Failed Experiment — NAFTA at Three Years* (June 1997). The report said America's trade deficit with Mexico and Canada rose dramatically since *NAFTA*'s entry into force. In consequence, the U.S. lost 420,000 jobs — 251,000 Americans lost their jobs because of the worsened trade balance with Mexico, and 169,000 Americans were thrown out of work because of the deterioration in the bilateral trade balance with Canada. The EPI study was careful to point out *NAFTA* hardly was the only, or even major, cause of the bilateral trade deficits. The Mexican peso crisis, and depreciation of the Canadian dollar relative to the U.S. dollar, were key factors, too. Thus, the stunning 420,000 figure could not be pinned entirely on *NAFTA*. In November 1999, the EPI updated its analysis. In the new study, *NAFTA*'s *Pain Deepens*, the EPI reported job losses of more than 440,000 as a result of *NAFTA* and attendant trade deficit. (California was the biggest job loser — 44,132.) Displaced workers who did manage to find new jobs took an average 16 percent pay cut.

In 1997, the Clinton Administration weighed in on the empirical effects of *NAFTA*. Not surprisingly, its report — *Study on the Operation and Effects of the North American Free Trade Agreement* (July 1997) — contended that 2.3 million American jobs depended on exports to Mexico and Canada. Of these, roughly 90,000 to 160,000 were newly created jobs as a result of *NAFTA*. Also in 1997, the ITC said that the effects of *NAFTA* on domestic employment could not be discerned because of the high employment rate in the U.S. since *NAFTA* entered into force. These two studies, while hardly supporting *NAFTA*'s critics, suggested the Bush and Clinton Administrations had over-sold the positive effects of *NAFTA* on jobs. Paper agreements, it must be remembered, cannot create socioeconomic miracles.

The studies continued into the new millennium, of course. In 2000, the North American Integration and Development Center at UCLA reported *NAFTA* created somewhere in the range of 130,000 to 208,980 new jobs. In July 2001, the EPI issued another study claiming NAFTA had cost America jobs. This study, which assumed trade deficits remain the same, put the job loss figure at 733,060. In 2003, a study associated with the *NAFTA* Trade Adjustment Assistance program examined data from 1994-2002. It recorded 413,123 job dislocations. That suggests a rate of dislocation of about 50,000 per year. However, this study has been criticized for both over- and under-counting.

Is there an empirical "bottom line"? Probably not. During the first several years after *NAFTA* entered into force (on 1 January 1994), empirical estimates of its impact on aggregate employment range from gains of 160,000 jobs to losses of 420,000 jobs. Almost certainly, neither extreme is accurate. Truth lies somewhere in between. A 1997 study by the ITC, *The Impact of the North American Free Trade Agreement on the U.S. Economy and Industries: A Three-Year Review* (U.S. ITC Pub. 3045, June 1997), confirmed this point. It found no discernible impact of the agreement on aggregate American employment. A number of studies have shed light on the impact of *NAFTA* on specific sectors. For example, U.S. corn exports have put Mexican corn farmers under serious pressure, and Oxfam reported Mexico lost 1.3 million farm jobs in the first decade of *NAFTA*. But, the overall impression from sectoral analyses is "it depends," namely, on the sector, researcher and methodology, and period of investigation.

This last variable is important. Opponents of *NAFTA* sometimes speak as if job loss is permanent unemployment. In many, if not most, instances, that is not true. Job loss typically is temporary dislocation. Further, depending on the period, a certain set of exchange rates will prevail. It is difficult for an exporter to compete with over-valued exchange rates. That is true even if that exporter otherwise has a global comparative advantage. Change the period of research, and the exchange rate may change, too, yielding different results.

Fortunately, the *Financial Times* of London has kept its wit amidst the confusion sewn by economists. In 1997, it queried:

> Which of the following have been caused by the *North American Free Trade Agreement*?
>
> 1.   The loss of 500,000 U.S. jobs.
>
> 2.   A 2 m[illion] rise in Mexican unemployment.
>
> 3.   The peso crisis.
>
> 4.   More hepatitis and chronic diarrhea in Mexico.
>
> 5.   Two armed uprisings south of the Rio Grande.
>
> 6.   Malfunctioning toilets at the office of the U.S. Trade Representative.
>
> Answer: None or all of the above, depending on whom you ask.[5]

Obviously, trade policy on RTAs might be simpler to formulate if statistics and econometrics all pointed in one direction, job creation or job destruction. They do not, and perhaps never will. Each study is unique in the exact issue it addresses, assumptions it makes, data sets it uses, and methodologies it applies. No study is entirely free from seepage of researcher bias, or bias of the entity that funds the study, into the analysis.

Most importantly, the effect of *NAFTA* — or, for that matter, any RTA, or trade liberalization in general — on jobs should not be overestimated. There are a range of macroeconomic factors (*e.g.*, monetary policy, exchange rate movements), technological developments (*e.g.*, labor-saving devices), and demographic conditions (*e.g.*, aging and immigration) that affect employment trends. Beware of pundits that point only to trade as a cause of job gains or losses. Beware, also, of the difference between (1) aggregate employment effects and (2) localization of job losses in certain sectors (*e.g.*, textiles and apparel) in which the U.S. may have lost its comparative advantage. Perhaps, then, there is practical bottom line: statistics and econometrics can help inform the debate about RTAs, but they ought not to drive it, or be relied upon as dispositive.

III.   TRADE CREATION OR DIVERSION?

A.   Viner's 1950 Study

Asking whether entry into an RTA results in a net job gain or loss to a country assumes the perspective of an individual RTA member country. A second critical question is asked from a "bird's eye" view of the entire RTA: does the RTA stimulate more trade than it diverts, that is, does the "trade creation" effect overwhelm, or is overwhelmed by, the "trade diversion" effect? In 1997, the WTO opined that Mexico's trade was too biased in favor of *NAFTA*. Complex rules of origin, for instance, had diverted trade toward the U.S. and Canada, and away from more efficient suppliers. In 1992, just before *NAFTA*

---

[5] Nancy Dunne, Stephen Fidler & Patti Waldmeir, *Old Wounds to Reopen: An Imminent Report on NAFTA Could Affect Future U.S. Trade Policy*, Financial Times, 30 June 1997, at 21.

entered into force, the share of Mexico's merchandise trade with the U.S. was 75 percent. In 1996, shortly after the agreement took effect, the share had risen to 80 percent. The WTO advised that Mexican industry would be better off if concessions granted to the U.S. and Canada were extended to all of Mexico's trading partners. The WTO's advice — sensible as it may be — also reflects its role as the flagship institution to advance multilateral trade liberalization.

The WTO's concern about trade creation versus diversion is hardly new. The problem was identified, in conceptual terms, as far back as 1950 by the famous economist Jacob Viner, in a book entitled *The Customs Union Issue*. To be sure, by definition an RTA means that preferential treatment is given to suppliers in member countries, so increased trade activity among the preferred suppliers is bound to occur. But, asked Viner, will it occur to an adverse degree? Following the approach of Viner and his successors, the application of neoclassical economic tools provides a model of the trade creation versus diversion issue. By "trade creation," Viner meant a shift in demand for imports from an inefficient to an efficient source. By "trade diversion," he meant a shift of imports from an efficient to an inefficient source.

Consumers enjoy a greater range of goods at lower prices when their country joins an RTA. After all, as the member countries of the RTA reduce trade barriers among themselves, the price of intra-regional imports falls, which then stimulates demand for these imports. Thus, trade creation ought to result from demand stimulation caused by the drop in trade barriers. Certainly, there are hidden assumptions here: consumers are motivated solely (or primarily) by price in deciding what to buy, and the goods produced within and outside the RTA are substitutes. Whether these assumptions are valid depends on two key empirical measures: the elasticity of demand, and the elasticity of substitution, respectively. Nonetheless, the basic insight is that trade creation through an RTA entails a shift from home country production to imports from a partner country as a result of a decline in the price of the good in question.

As for trade diversion, this effect is expected because of the elimination of barriers among only the RTA member countries. Non-members do not benefit from the intra-regional tariff cuts. Consumers in the member countries are likely to shift to the now lower-priced intra-regional imports, and away from the relatively higher priced substitute products they formerly bought from non-member countries. In other words, what was imported from non-members before will be imported from members. The shift of imports from outside the RTA to a partner country is, of course, trade diversion from the outside countries. Again, this effect assumes that price is the only (or, at least a significant) determinant of consumer preference, and that the goods produced within and outside the RTA are alike.

Interestingly, not all economists worry about trade diversion. Former U.S. Treasury Secretary and Harvard President Lawrence Summers finds it "surprising that this issue is taken so seriously — in most other situations, economists laugh off second best considerations and focus on direct impacts." Part of what motivates this comment is a belief that trade diversion is a minor nuisance. However, Professor Jagdish Bhagwati, Arvind Panagariya, and others reject Summers argument. They challenge the premise that economists do not pay attention to second-best solutions. In practice, economists do study these solutions. Moreover, the first-best solution, non-discriminatory trade liberalization — *i.e.*, movement toward a multilateral free-trade regime — is by definition ruled out (at least for the short term) when a group of countries bands together to form an RTA. In other words, RTAs are an inherently second-best solution to the problem of trade liberalization. Because they are a widely used alternative, their potential effects — including trade diversion — demand attention.

Related to the long-standing controversy about trade creation and diversion is the problem of bilateral trade deficits. Does entry into an RTA mean a member will experience a trade deficit with another or other members? The question is especially poignant if the member enjoys a surplus with another member before the RTA takes effect, as the U.S. did vis-à-vis Mexico before *NAFTA* entered into force on 1 January 1994. *NAFTA* critics cite the post-*NAFTA* bilateral deficits as evidence the accord is not working to the advantage of the U.S. Similar concerns surround the *U.S. — Israel FTA* and *U.S. — Jordan FTA*: have these deals helped Israel and Jordan, respectively, more than the U.S.? If the yardstick is percentage increases in export growth, then critics of these *FTAs* can point to data showing (for example) Israeli exports to the U.S. grew by 10 percent (but U.S. exports to Israel grew by a smaller amount), and Jordanian exports to the U.S. tripled (but not so with flows in the other direction). Of course, this criticism depends on the period from which data are extracted.

One resolution to the problem of bilateral trade deficits among RTA partners is to question the question. Do bilateral trade deficits really matter? If so, then why do they matter? Assuming bilateral trade deficits are important (and not all economists would agree on that point), and assuming there are no advantages from an RTA to offset a deficit (a dubious assumption), then a second response is "it depends." Many factors affect a trade balance, other than trade barriers. Exchange rates, savings rates, consumption trends, and product innovation (partly because of technological change) are among the variables. These variables fluctuate over time, again underscoring the importance of the period of investigation.

B. The Neoclassical Economic Analysis

Both the trade creation and trade diversion effects can be represented graphically, as below. Suppose 4-door, non-sport utility passenger automobiles with V-6 engines are made in Argentina. They are not made in great supply, because the industry is an infant one. Still, suppose it is an industry Argentina hopes to develop. The Graph depicts the market for these cars in Argentina, and the Table summarizes the effects of two alternative regimes: a tariff on all imports, and an FTA (or CU) favoring imports from a member country but discriminating against third country merchandise.

The line DD represents demand for this product in Argentina. SS represents domestic supply of these cars in Argentina. Assume Argentina trades cars with two other countries, Brazil and Japan. Both countries manufacture cars that, while not identical with, are substitutable for the Argentine product. Brazil is especially eager to develop its car industry further, because like Argentina, it sees this industry as central to its economic future. This belief is common in the developing world, as China, India, Indonesia, Malaysia, and Vietnam evince. However, history manifests its patent falsity. Countries like Finland, Norway, Singapore, and Switzerland all developed without a domestic car industry. The belief also is economically misguided, because there is tremendous over-capacity in the world car market.

GRAPH 21-1:
THE ARGENTINE CAR MARKET

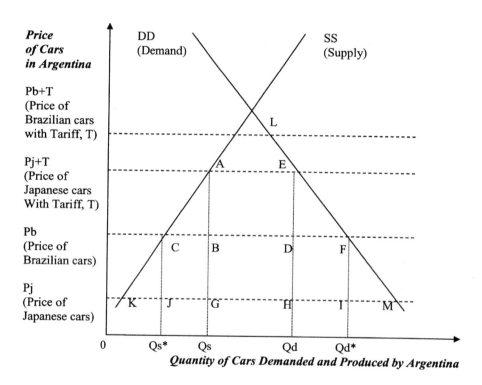

In any event, the price of the Brazilian cars is P_b. The Japanese model is price P_j. They are free trade prices. Obviously, Japan is a more efficient producer than Brazil, because P_j is less than P_b. Thus, *ceteris paribus* (*i.e.*, all other things being equal), Argentina will import more Japanese than Brazilian cars. Observe the intersection of the demand and supply curves corresponds to a price level above the prices of Brazilian and Japanese cars. After all, Argentine cars (reflected by SS) are relatively uncompetitive.

TABLE 21-1:
SUMMARY OF EFFECTS OF AN FTA (OR CU)

Variable	With Tariff, T, Imposed by Argentina on Brazilian and Japanese Cars	With FTA (or CU) involving Argentina and Brazil, but not Japan
		(No Tariff on Brazilian Cars. Tariff remains on Japanese Cars. If customs union, Tariff is a Common External Tariff.)
Argentine Demand	Qs Relevant price is Pj+T, reflecting consumer preference for cheaper Japanese cars over Brazilian cars.	Qd* Relevant price is Pb, reflecting consumer preference for duty-free Brazilian cars over Japanese cars, to which the Tariff, T, applies. Argentine consumers demand more cars at lower price Pb than at Pj+T.
Argentine Supply	Qd Based on price Pj+T for Argentine cars.	Qs* Based on price Pb for Argentine cars. Argentine producers make fewer cars at lower price Pb than at Pj+T. Gap filled by trade creation (imports from Brazil).
Imports	Qd — Qs All imports from Japan.	Qd* — Qs* All imports from Brazil.
Tariff Revenue	AEHG To Argentine government, equal to Tariff, T, multiplied by import quantity.	None (foregone). Possibly de minimis amount collected on small number of Japanese imports.
Trade Creation	None	Increase in imports, which is the difference between from Qs* — Qs and Qd* — Qd.
Trade Diversion	None (assuming Tariff is applied on MFN basis)	
Change in Consumer Surplus	Not applicable If compare against free trade, where relevant price is Pj, then loss of EMPjPj+T	Increases by EFPbPj+T
Change in Producer Surplus	Not applicable If compare against free trade, where relevant price is Pj, then gain of AKPjPj+T.	Decreases by ACPbPj+T
Difference between Changes in Consumer and Producer Surplus	Not applicable If compare against free trade, where relevant price is Pj, then AEMK.	EFCA
Net Welfare Effect	Not applicable If compare against free trade, where relevant price is Pj, then AGK and EHM, which is AEMK minus the tariff revenue, AEHG.	ABC and DEF Tariff revenue AEHG is foregone. ABC reflects lower prices. DEF reflects expanded consumption opportunities.
Dead Weight Loss	Not applicable. If compare against free trade, where relevant price is Pj, then AGK is dead weight loss because of inefficient Argentine production encouraged by the Tariff, T, and EHM is dead weight loss because of diminished consumption opportunities.	BDHG Graphically, BDHG is the difference between EFCA (which reflects the Consumer and Producer Surplus changes) and AEHG (foregone tariff revenue). Conceptually, BDHG suggests Argentina would be better off under free trade, i.e., by eliminating the Tariff, T, on all car imports. Then, the Price would be Pj, and the quantity imported Qd* — Qs*

Suppose Argentina has in place a tariff on all imported automobiles, including the cars from Japan and Brazil. The value of the tariff is T, and it is plainly designed to protect domestic car producers. The price of the Japanese cars rises to $P_j + T$, and the value of the Brazilian model increases to $P_b + T$. Again, the price of the Japanese cars remains relatively lower, so Argentina will import more Japanese than Brazilian cars. Indeed, it may be safe to say that the tariff compels Argentina to import from Japan, not Brazil, *i.e.*, the tariff will have priced the Brazilian model out of the market.

How many cars will Argentina import? The answer depends on the number of cars produced in Argentina. The price of the cars made by their Japanese competitors, inclusive of the tariff, is $P_j + T$. At that price, Argentine car companies have an incentive to produce the quantity Q_s. Likewise at that price, Argentine consumers will demand the quantity Q_d cars. Plainly, Argentine demand outstrips Argentine supply by the amount $Q_d - Q_s$. Therefore, Japanese cars are needed to plug the gap. Argentina will import $Q_d - Q_s$ cars from Japan at a price of $P_j + T$. Notice the Argentine government will collect a tariff revenue of AEHG, which reflects the quantity imported $(Q_d - Q_s)$ multiplied by the amount of the tariff (the increase from P_j to $P_j + T$, *i.e.*, T).

Now suppose opposition from Argentine car producers (and, probably, other groups) is overcome, and Argentina enters into a free trade area with Brazil, but not Japan. Eventually, Argentina and Brazil hope to become a customs union, but they agree to start with the creation of an internal free market before implementing a common external tariff. The central obligation each of the three countries must perform to give birth to a free trade area is to eliminate tariffs on goods traded among them. Thus, Argentina must drop its tariff, T, on cars from Brazil. The tariff remains in effect for cars from non-member countries, *i.e.*, countries outside the free trade area like Japan.

The trade diversion effect is evident from the fact that the price of cars from Brazil falls to P_b, but the price of cars from Japan remains at $P_j + T$. P_b is less than $P_j + T$, hence Argentine consumers are likely to switch, *ceteris paribus*, from the higher-priced Japanese car to the now cheaper Brazilian model. In other words, the gap between Argentine supply and demand, $Q_s - Q_d$, used to be filled by Japanese cars. Now, the Brazilians take over. The change is, of course, a diversion of trade from a non-member of the free trade area (Japan) to a member of that area (Brazil).

The trade creation effect also is apparent from the Graph. The price of imported cars has fallen from $P_j + T$ to P_b. The fall in the import price should generate additional imports, and indeed it does. At P_b, Argentine companies produce Q_s^* cars, but Argentine consumers demand Q_d^* cars. The domestic demand-supply gap has yawned from $Q_d - Q_s$ to $Q_d^* - Q_s^*$. The difference between Q_s^* and Q_s, and between Q_d^* and Q_d, is trade creation. The trade created from Q_s to Q_s^* results from the fact that Argentine companies produce fewer cars at the lower price, P_b. The trade created from Q_d to Q_d^* follows from the increased demand among Argentine consumers for cars at that lower price. Thus, Brazilian car companies not only fill the $Q_d^* - Q_s^*$ void, but the quantity they export to Argentina exceeds the quantity Japanese companies previously had exported.

Trade diversion and creation are not the only effects the Graph shows. Most obviously, Argentina loses the tariff revenue, AEHG, which it previously collected. After all, no longer is Argentina importing $Q_d - Q_s$ cars from Japan at a price of $P_j + T$ inclusive of the tariff T. Now, it imports $Q_d^* - Q_s^*$ cars from Brazil at a price of P_b. To be sure, Japanese cars remain available at a price of $P_j + T$, but it is assumed they are not imported in significant quantities because of their much higher price relative to the Brazilian models. Accordingly, any tariff revenues from Japanese imports are *de minimis*.

There is another subtle, but important, lesson from the Graph. At the lower import price, P_b, Argentine consumers gain. Their gain is represented by the triangles ABC and DEF. The gain of triangle ABC arises because Argentine consumers no longer have to pay higher prices to Argentine car companies. Instead of buying Q_s cars from them at a price $P_j + T$ (assuming the Argentine car companies charged the same price as the Japanese producers plus the tariff), Argentine consumers reduce purchases of Argentine cars to Q_s^*, and pay P_b instead of $P_j + T$. The gain of triangle DEF can be thought of as a consequence of the fact Argentine consumers can buy more imported cars at a cheaper price. Their demand has grown from Q_d to Q_d^*, and they pay P_b instead of $P_j + T$.

Another way to see that the triangles ABC and DEF represent a gain to Argentine consumers is to consider the changes in consumer and producer surplus. The demand curve DD represents the quantity of cars Argentine consumers are willing and able to buy at a given range of prices. It slopes downward because as the price of cars falls, consumers want more cars, *ceteris paribus*. Points on the demand curve, but above the actual price, are points at which consumers buy cars for a price that is less than the amount that they are willing and able to pay — *i.e.*, the consumers operating on these points of DD "get a good deal." For example, consider point L. A consumer operating at this point is willing and able to pay a price for cars higher than $P_j + T$, namely, $P_b + T$. But, she need not pay this exorbitant amount because the going price is $P_j + T$. She is happy, and more generally, the points beneath DD and above the actual price constitute the zone of consumer surplus, because consumers save money when they buy. "Consumer surplus" is the difference between the price that consumers are willing to pay for a product, and the price they actually pay.

As for the supply curve SS, it represents the quantity of cars Argentine producers are willing and able to manufacture at a given range of prices. It slopes upward because as the price of cars rises, producers are willing to make more cars (again, *ceteris paribus*). A point on SS above the going price for cars is a "good deal" for producers. Producers operating at such a point manufacture cars that fetch a price that is higher than the price they require in order to coax them to manufacture. For example, consider point K. Argentine producers are willing and able to manufacture cars and sell them for a low price, P_j. But, they need not do so, because the actual price is $P_j + T$. They benefit from the difference between what they would have sold for, and what they actually received. Put differently, points above SS comprise the zone of producer surplus, because producers make extra money. "Producer surplus" is the difference between the price at which producers would like to supply a product, and the price at which they actually supply it.

To see how the triangles ABC and DEF represent a gain to consumers from the creation of the free trade area, compare consumer and producer surplus before and after the creation. First, what areas represented consumer and producer surplus when Argentine consumers faced a price of $P_j + T$, and Argentine producers charged this price? For consumer surplus, the answer is the large area marked off by point E, across to the left to $P_j + T$, and upwards to the demand curve DD. For producer surplus, the answer is the large area demarcated by point A, across to the left to $P_j + T$, and downwards to the supply curve SS.

As explained above, when Argentina joins the free trade area and removes the tariff, T, on Brazilian cars, the price of these imports falls to P_b. When that occurs, consumer surplus expands, and producer surplus contracts. Consumer surplus becomes the area from point F, across to P_b, and up to the demand curve DD. The increase in consumer surplus is $EFP_bP_j + T$. Producer surplus falls to the area from point C, across to P_b, and down to the supply curve SS. The decrease is $ACP_bP_j + T$. The difference between the increase in consumer surplus ($EFP_bP_j + T$) and the decrease in consumer surplus ($ACP_bP_j + T$) is the trapezoid EFCA.

Of this trapezoid, it was established earlier that AEHG is tariff revenue that the Argentine government no longer collects after entry into the free trade area. The difference between the trapezoid EFCA and the forgone tariff revenue AEHG is the triangle ABC and the triangle DEF, and the rectangle BDHG. Thus, the difference between the increase in consumer surplus, on the one hand, and the decline in producer surplus plus the lost tariff revenue, on the other hand, includes the net gain to consumers, the triangles ABC and DEF.

What about the rectangle BDHG? It represents still another subtle but interesting lesson from the Graph. We can say that it is part of the "dead weight loss" that arises as a result of the free trade area. The trade diversion effect that occurs when Argentina and Brazil enter into the accord is not necessarily healthy, certainly not in the short-run anyway. Brazil is an inefficient producer relative to Japan, yet the free trade area diverts trade in Brazil's favor. From the standpoint of economic welfare, Argentina would have been better off had it eliminated the tariff, T, for all car imports regardless of their origin. Then, the price of cars sold in Argentina would be P_j, that is, the price of the most efficient producer, Japan. Because Argentina imports from a higher-cost producer, Brazil, Argentine consumers pay P_b instead of P_j. The difference between these prices, P_b-P_j, multiplied by the quantity imported, Q_d^*-Q_s^*, is the extra cost of importing from the higher-cost producer. It is represented by the rectangle CFIJ, which includes BDHG.

The general point to keep in mind, then, is that a free trade area always is less satisfactory, from a neoclassical economic perspective, than a complete free trade regime. The reason is that only in a free trade regime are imports assuredly coming from the cheapest-cost producer. In a free trade area, imports may be sourced from an inefficient producer, resulting in foregone opportunities or savings, collectively known as a dead weight loss. As Professors Bhagwati and Panagariya conclude: "our analysis enables us to examine and reject the much-cited claim that it is wrong to worry about trade diversion and that PTAs are generally as good as non-preferential trade liberalization."[6] Put succinctly, not all forms of trade liberalization are equal.

---

[6] Jagdish Bhagwati & Arvind Panagariya, *Preferential Trading Areas and Multilateralism — Strangers, Friends, or Foes?*, *in* THE ECONOMICS OF PREFERENTIAL TRADE AGREEMENTS 1-55 (Jagdish Bhagwati & Arvind Panagariya eds., 1996).

A final subtle lesson from the Graph is aesthetic. Neoclassical economic graphs are like some of Mondrian's paintings. Both have plenty of nice, neat lines that make up squares, rectangles, triangles, trapezoids, etc. As a very general rule, in the economic graphs, welfare effects on consumers and producers are triangular in shape. Tariff revenue effects are rectangles. As for Mondrian paintings . . . well, perhaps that is why they are art.

So, what is the "bottom line" of the neoclassical economic analysis of the free trade area between Argentina and Brazil? If the question invites comparison with pure free trade, then the answer was just revealed. If, however, the question asks for an evaluation of the free trade area on its own merits, then the answer is uncertain. True, as a general matter, the consensus of economic studies on RTAs show the gains from trade creation outweigh losses from trade diversion. But, a complete evaluation requires an inquiry into whether, excluding the loss of government tariff revenue, the net welfare effect of an RTA is negative. The answer, graphically, is the consumer gain of ABC + DEF minus the cost of buying from an inefficient producer, CFIJ. It is not possible to say whether the gain outweighs the loss without knowing more about three empirical facts: the shape of the demand curve, the shape of the supply curve, and the height of the tariff. That is, figures for the elasticities of demand and supply, and the size of the tariff, T, are needed.

Moreover, the search for a "bottom line" conclusion based on one sector is rather artificial. Argentina and Brazil are diverse economies, and any RTA can be trade-creating in one sector, and trade-diverting in another sector. To determine the implications of an RTA in an aggregate sense, a more comprehensive and nuanced analysis is needed. Multi-sectoral, computable general equilibrium (CGE) and "gravity" models provide this sort of analysis. (Interestingly, CGE models give lower predictions on the increases in trade caused by an FTA than do gravity models.) An even broader answer would include the effect on sectors and countries around the world, *i.e.*, a world welfare analysis.

C. The Tariff Redistribution Effect

As intimated, the aforementioned "bottom line" based on simple neoclassical analysis is not the full story. Suppose in the Argentina-Brazil free trade area, there is more trade creation than trade diversion, so the consumer gain outweighs the cost of buying from an inefficient producer. Can it be said unequivocally that Argentina is better off? No. The neoclassical analysis above neglects income distribution effects that arise from the re-distribution of tariff revenue. Because of this effect — a re-distribution of tariff revenue from Argentina to Brazil — it is quite possible that Argentina experiences a net welfare loss, even if trade creation overwhelms trade diversion (indeed, even if there is no trade diversion at all).

When Argentina eliminates its tariff, T, on Brazilian cars, the terms of trade between Argentina and Brazil in the car sector change in favor of Brazil. That is, Brazil exports more cars to Argentina, and thus Brazilian car producers earn more profits. At the same time, the Argentine government loses tariff revenue, which in absence of corruption presumably was put to use for the benefit of the Argentine people through appropriate fiscal expenditures.

Income is thus distributed from Argentina to Brazil: less is collected by the Argentine government and spent on the Argentine polity, and more is earned by Brazilian car manufacturers.

How large is this income re-distribution? The answer depends on the size of the initial tariff, T, the initial volume of car exports from Brazil to Argentina, and the extent to which Argentina opens its market to Brazilian cars. The greater the initial tariff, the greater the volume of Brazilian car exports before the creation of the RTA, and the larger Argentina's market opening, the greater the potential loss to Argentina. A greater initial tariff and import volume means that Argentina had been collecting a large amount of tariff revenue before it joined the RTA. (Recall tariff revenue is calculated as the amount of the tariff multiplied by the quantity of imports.) A large market opening means Argentina risks being flooded with Brazilian cars. The corollary, then, to the ostensible "bottom line" is that a country can lose from liberalizing trade under a preferential trade arrangement, even if that arrangement creates more trade than it diverts.

D. Dynamic Considerations and Margins of Preference

Aside from the controversial assumptions on which it rests, one of the central difficulties of the neoclassical analysis of trade creation and diversion, even as supplemented by an examination of income re-distribution, is that it is static. For example, over time, Brazilian car companies can reap economies of scale that, in turn, may allow them to increase their efficiency. The elimination of the tariff as between Argentina and Brazil will mean that Brazilian producers no longer are hamstrung by the dis-economies inherent in a single modest market, but rather can take advantage of the combined Argentine-Brazilian market.

However, whether Brazilian car companies actually become more efficient, or whether they produce in the cozy free trade arrangement without cutting costs and boosting output, remains to be seen. If barriers to FDI are low, then Japanese car companies may respond to the free trade area by building factories in Brazil. The presence, or even the threat, of these factories may motivate Brazilian auto executives and workers. It may even result in joint ventures between Brazilian and Japanese producers, which in turn results in technology transfer from the Japanese to the Brazilian partners. However, at the outset it is not at all clear that Brazil should be in the car business, and any dynamic gains will by definition not materialize for some time.

In addition, the neoclassical economic analysis does not explicitly account for margins of preference. This term refers to the difference between an MFN tariff and the preferential (*e.g.*, duty-free) rate associated applicable to a particular category of merchandise. The higher the MFN tariff, the greater the margin of preference. In turn, the greater the margin, the greater the trade (and investment) diversion effects of an RTA. Finally, the greater the diversion, the greater the potential damage to less developed countries not included in an RTA or other preferential trading arrangement (*e.g.*, countries receiving special and differential treatment pursuant to the Tokyo Round *Enabling Clause*, and countries like Bangladesh that are not beneficiaries of the *African*

Growth and Opportunity Act (*AGOA*)). Therefore, if MFN tariff rates decrease through multilateral trade rounds, or if new RTAs enter into force that embody broader, deeper tariff cuts than extant accords, the margins of preference diminish.

E.   *MERCOSUR* and Alleged Trade Diversion

The graphical example used above concerning the car trade in Latin America is not entirely hypothetical. In 1996-97, one of the most publicized real-world examples of the trade diversion question materialized. The conventional wisdom about *MERCOSUR* was it had created billions of dollars worth of trade among its members, and simultaneously paved the way for the members to compete in the global economy. An unpublished study, leaked to the press by the principal economist in the World Bank's international trade division, Alexander J. Yeats, challenged the conventional wisdom. It argued *MERCOSUR* was repeating the policy folly of autarky and import substitution, which crippled Latin economies in the 1950s and 1960s, at a regional level.

The very title of the Yeats study bore all the marks of controversy, differing significantly from the normally soporific rubrics of World Bank research. Yeats called it *Does MERCOSUR's Trade Performance Justify Concerns About the Global Welfare Reducing Effects of Regional Trading Arrangements? YES!* The study concluded that inefficient industries were prospering behind high trade walls built by *MERCOSUR*. The sectors in which intra-*MERCOSUR* trade had grown most rapidly were capital-intensive goods like cars, buses, agricultural machinery, and refrigerators. But, these goods were produced inefficiently by the *MERCOSUR* members: the goods were too expensive, and of too poor a quality, to sell to anyone but *MERCOSUR* members.

The auto sector was a prime example. In 1988, trade in motor vehicles among Argentina, Brazil, Paraguay, and Uruguay was just $207 million. (In December 2005, Bolivia and Venezuela joined these four countries as full *MERCOSUR* members.) By 1994, intra-*MERCOSUR* trade in autos exploded to $2.1 billion. In part, the explosion resulted from the separate — and very significant — barriers that *MERCOSUR* members maintained individually to third-country auto imports, despite their commitment to formation of a customs union. Brazil imposed tariffs as high as 70 percent on imported vehicles, and Argentina and Uruguay had quotas on foreign vehicle imports. To be fair to Brazil and Argentina, it ought to be understood that as a result of *MERCOSUR* obligations, tariffs on autos had fallen from as high as 100 percent to 20 percent. Predictably, auto imports into *MERCOSUR* surged, and Brazilian car producers cried they would collapse without protection. They got it, in the form of 70 percent tariffs (though by 1998 the duty had fallen to 49 percent for autos produced by companies without Brazilian subsidiaries). Argentina, however, kept a lid on its tariffs, at around 30 percent. Likewise, Uruguay's rate was 23 percent, and Paraguay's rates ranged from 10 to 15 percent. Starting on 1 January 2000, *MERCOSUR* implemented a unified auto import policy consisting of a CET of 35 percent. This rate applies to passenger cars, trucks, and buses. (Lower rates, between 14-18 percent, apply to auto parts.) The common external tariff was reached only after considerable squabbling between Brazil, which seeks to develop a car industry, and its *MERCOSUR* partners members, which do not and thus did not want to raise their auto tariffs to the 35 percent level.

Three adverse effects resulted from the protection of inefficient industries behind *MERCOSUR's* trade walls. First, and most obviously, *MERCOSUR* consumers were harmed. They paid more, but got less in terms of quality, for capital-intensive goods. In microeconomic tools, there was a large loss of consumer surplus. Insofar as many of the goods were intermediate ones used in the production process for other products, producers of the other products were injured.

Second, factors of production were being misallocated away from more competitive industries. When *MERCOSUR's* CET ultimately fell, the very industries most likely to succeed in the global economy would not have received the necessary labor, land, physical capital, human capital, and technology to ensure world-class performance. Conversely, there would have been over-investment in the very industries least likely to succeed on the global playing field.

Third, non-*MERCOSUR* countries that produced capital-intensive goods were damaged. The cheaper, higher quality items produced by third-country suppliers were not admitted into *MERCOSUR* in the volumes, and at the prices, that free trade logic would dictate. This effect, along with the misallocation of *MERCOSUR's* productive resources, amounted to trade diversion. The discrimination against these third-country products in favor of intra-*MERCOSUR* trade distorted the normal, free-market pattern of international trade flows. *MERCOSUR* members were concentrating on selling products, which were not internationally competitive, to one another. This concentration on the wrong products, and on each other's markets, plainly was caused by the higher tariff and non-tariff barriers *MERCOSUR* maintained on third-country products than on products from its members.

Concomitant with this trade diversion was investment diversion. Japanese and American auto producers scrambled to build plants in *MERCOSUR* countries so as to get inside the fortress. Absent the need to leap-frog *MERCOSUR's* CET, this flow of foreign direct investment might well have been channeled elsewhere.

The WTO added a fourth adverse effect *MERCOSUR* was having on the economies of its member countries, particularly Uruguay, that might just as easily have been included in the Yeats study. In a 1998 *Trade Policy Review Mechanism (TPRM)* report, the WTO warned that Uruguay relied too heavily on trade with its *MERCOSUR* partners. For instance, between 1992-98, more than half of all of Uruguay's merchandise exports went to a *MERCOSUR* country, with Brazil alone accounting for almost 40 percent of the shipments. Deliveries to the rest of the world had declined. By not diversifying its export customers and import sources, Uruguay was vulnerable to vicissitudes in Argentina, Brazil, and Paraguay. A safer strategy was to hedge against regional downturns by having significant export and import ties with third countries. Insofar as *MERCOSUR*-induced trade diversion inhibited diversification, it was not in Uruguay's long-term economic interest.

The Yeats study was a political headache for the World Bank, and the Bank proceeded to create a public relations disaster for itself. Officially, it supported *MERCOSUR*, and its policy is to avoid public criticism of World Bank members. Brazil accused Yeats in thinly veiled terms of using his position to draw public attention to his views. The Bank felt compelled to distance itself from the study, saying it was iconoclastic and did not represent official policy. It refused to release the study (though in 1997 it apparently reversed course and published it as Policy Research Working Paper 1729), and forbade Mr. Yeats from speaking to the press. Critics of the study said Yeats was wrong to have drawn the inference of trade diversion from data on exports. They pointed out imports from other *MERCOSUR* countries had grown faster than imports from third countries, but the gap was not significant, and certainly far less great than that between the growth of intra-*MERCOSUR* exports versus third-country exports. Still, the Bank appeared to be stifling honest intellectual discourse that was in the best interests of developing countries. One *Wall Street Journal* editor asked sarcastically: "So we have an economist in the international trade division at the World Bank who is not supposed to have professional opinions about world trade. What is he supposed to do?"

The Yeats study should compel consideration of yet one more adverse repercussion: the effects of regionalization on the multilateral trading system. Does *MERCOSUR's* experience challenge the integrity of the multilateral trading system? How might that integrity be preserved? It is difficult to argue that the criteria of GATT Article XXIV are sufficiently strict to ensure that the formation of an FTA or CU does not undermine multilateral trade liberalization. Yet, WTO Members have done nothing to impose new strictures on the formation of RTAs. Low intra-regional barriers, coupled with high external ones and protectionist preferential rules of origin, characterize trade in various sectors of some RTAs. The current lax criteria help explain why there are now over 100 regional trade groupings, and virtually every WTO Member belongs to at least one of them.

IV. STEPPING STONES OR FORTRESSES?

A. The Stepping Stones Argument and Related Advantages

An important issue in the controversy generated over the position and role of RTAs in the world trading system is their effects on that system. Do they lead to broader, deeper integration among a larger number of countries? Or, do they become endpoints? If negotiating an RTA is a precursor to, or catalyst for, multilateral trade talks, so much the better.

Advocates of FTAs and CUs have some historical evidence in their favor. Consider European integration. To be sure, its purpose was to put a stop to European wars, not catalyze multilateral trade efforts. Yet, three important steps in the integration process seem to have had a salubrious effect on them. First, the creation of the European Community (EC) by the 1957 *Treaty of Rome* led to the 1962 *Trade Expansion Act* in the U.S., and the 1964-67 Kennedy Round. Second, EC expansion in 1973 to include the United Kingdom contributed to momentum for the 1976-79 Tokyo Round. Third, deepening amalgamation (including monetary union) through the 1992 *Treaty of Maastricht*, though finalized near the end of the Uruguay Round, reinforced multilateral trade liberalization efforts.

Another example comes from "Down Under." In January 1983, the original *Closer Economic Relationship (CER)* between Australia and New Zealand entered into force. At that time, the *CER* did not include services. In 1988, they added a *CER Services Protocol* to cover all services sectors. That development helped position the two countries for multilateral negotiations on the *General Agreement on Trade in Services (GATS)*.

As still another example, Chapters in *NAFTA* are one intellectual origin of some WTO agreements. One story about the genesis of *NAFTA* is the U.S. was frustrated by its inability in 1982 to persuade other countries to commence a new round of multilateral trade negotiations. Therefore, the U.S. shed its reluctance to make use of GATT Article XXIV, and sought trade liberalization on a regional level. Having done this, it pursued multilateral trade talks, beginning in 1986, and on a more-or-less parallel track. Consequently, some Uruguay Round texts read similarly to Chapters of *NAFTA*. Many provisions in the *Agreement on Trade Related Aspects of Intellectual Property Rights (TRIPs)* look like Chapter 17 in *NAFTA*, on Intellectual Property. There also is a reasonably close correspondence between provisions in the *GATS*, on the one hand, and the *NAFTA* Chapters (12 and 14) on Services and Financial Services (respectively). The resemblances suggest the *NAFTA* Parties took their FTA agreement as a basis, if not model or precedent, for a multilateral bargain. That should not be a surprise. Having negotiated an FTA, they hardly would want to see it undermined by a WTO deal.

RTA advocates also point out negotiating an FTA or customs union is a process that yields learning-by-doing. Negotiators become educated and experienced. They can leverage off their enhanced legal capacity to negotiate RTA expansions or WTO deals — contexts in which the issues may be more complex than before. Mexican and Korean trade negotiators are examples. Some Mexican negotiators helped Central American officials prepare for *CAFTA—DR* talks with the U.S. by providing training courses on their experience with the U.S. and *NAFTA*. Korean negotiators worked on trade deals with New Zealand and Singapore, before "big league" talks with the U.S. and Japan. The capacity building effect is especially important for developing and least developed countries. As the number of countries with a team of savvy, sophisticated negotiators expands, reaching a multilateral bargain ought, in theory, to be a more efficient process with better outcomes than otherwise would have occurred.

B. The Fortress Argument and Related Drawbacks

RTAs do not necessarily lead to grander trade liberalization. Indeed, the claim of competitive liberalization — that pursuing freer trade on any one level (bilateral, regional, or multilateral) stimulates and reinforces that pursuit on the other two levels — has not been put to a serious test. That is because a large number of RTAs (perhaps most in the world), especially FTAs, entered into force since Uruguay Round negotiations concluded on 15 December 1993.

Accordingly, what if members of an FTA or CU become self-satisfied with their arrangement, and retreat into it? Then, they effectively undermine the multilateral trading system. Consider, for example, the fact that while *CUFTA* preceded *NAFTA*, *NAFTA* has not led to an *FTAA* — *i.e.*, *NAFTA* has yet to lead to hemispheric integration. Similarly, the many RTAs the U.S. negotiated and signed between 2000 and 2004, namely, with Australia, Bahrain, *CAFTA—DR*, Chile, Jordan, Morocco, and Singapore, did not contribute to a successful outcome in the Doha Round. To the contrary, they were a hedge against the failure of that Round. Another way to put the question is as follows: Are negotiations for an RTA and multilateral trade liberalization dependent on or independent of one another? That is, what relationship, if any, exists between the time paths of the two sets of negotiations?

If they are dependent, then each negotiation could be a spur for the other. There could be a domino effect, whereby non-members seek to join the RTA for fear of a loss of competitiveness. This effect could stimulate multilateral talks, as more and more non-members seek to maintain or enhance their competitive positions. However, if RTA and multilateral talks are not related, then formation of an RTA could be the end of the line for many years. Economists like Professor Jagdish Bhagwati fear exactly this independence. RTAs, they say, are more often than not stumbling blocks to broader trade liberalization. Once created, they become economic fortresses. In some instances, member countries may feel their RTA market is large enough internally, and covers a sizeable enough percentage of export markets. They have little incentive, at least in the short or medium turn to expand the RTA or pursue a multilateral trade round. Likewise, industries in the member countries may be successful in lobbying their governments to eschew further, progressive trade liberalization that might expose them to competition from third country producers.

With RTAs pursued independently of, and undermining, multilateral trade liberalization, the result is a proliferation in legal complexity. That is most evident in the area of preferential rules of origin. Each RTA will have its own such rules. The result is a global trading system that, to use Professor Bhagwati's metaphor, looks like a spaghetti bowl. Trade barriers (including, possibly, Sanitary and Phytosanitary Standards (SPS) and Technical Barriers to Trade (TBT)), and thus market access, vary depending on the country of origin of the imported article — a *prima facie* incongruity with the MFN concept. In turn, the tariff and non-tariff barriers to market access rely on monstrously complex preferential rules of origin, which is good work for customs lawyers, but distasteful to exporters and importers.

Spaghetti, of course, is not what businesses — especially multinational corporations — order. They engage in global production, attempting to source inputs based on comparative costs so as to realize economic efficiencies. At the top of their menu is clear soup. They consider whether the margin of preference accorded by an RTA vis-à-vis the otherwise-applicable MFN rate for their merchandise is a benefit that offsets the cost of compliance with the rules of origin of the RTA. The lower the margin of preference, and the more onerous the rules, the more likely they will elect to pay the MFN rate.

As an historical point, the inconsistency of RTAs with America's MFN policy since the Inter-War Period is worth highlighting. The U.S. followed a conditional MFN strategy from the birth of the republic through the 1920s. The result was discrimination against certain countries. In 1924, the Economic Advisor to the U.S. Secretary of State wrote a memo to the Secretary advocating an end to conditional MFN treatment. The memo argued conditionality creates antagonism, promotes discord, and discourages commerce. By the time of the GATT negotiations, in 1946-47, the U.S. was firmly committed to an unconditional MFN policy. Similarly, the U.S. understood that discrimination in favor of RTA partners meant discrimination against the rest of the world. By being selective in economic friends, the U.S. risked making economic — and political — enemies. (Of course, in the post-Second World War era, the EU took the opposite approach. The very creation of this customs union led to the greatest discrimination against non-European countries in history. Hence, membership in the EU is a highly contentious affair.) However, the aggressive FTA policy the U.S. has pursued since roughly the late 1990s, which has created a patchwork of bilateral and regional FTAs, undermines the unconditional MFN pillar of GATT.

Still another concern about both FTAs and CUs, which borrows from the rubric of "trade diversion," is "attention diversion." Do RTA negotiations create a disincentive to pursue multilateral reform because of the resources they consume? Does the large size of the EU as a customs union make reform of the Common Agricultural Policy (CAP) more difficult, and increasingly so with EU expansion, than would be true in pursuing agricultural reform with just one European country? Even for a relatively well-lawyered body like the USTR, negotiating an RTA consumes time and energy. There may be some learning-by-doing, and thus efforts to use a template from prior agreements. But, there are *sui generis* features to every RTA.

Moreover, completion of an FTA or CU is only the beginning. Monitoring compliance with any RTA obligation is necessary, which consumes precious government resources. Interestingly, during the Clinton Administration, the U.S. brought an average of 10 cases per year to the WTO as a complainant. As of May 2003, during the Bush Administration, that average had dropped to about 2 cases per year. Might a reason for the decrease be a pre-occupation with FTA deals? Overall, to what extent is this resource allocation justified if other FTA members are not commercially significant? Perhaps the answer hinges on whether the FTA serves an important non-commercial purpose. For example, Israel accounts for roughly 1 percent of total U.S. trade. Jordan accounts for about 2/10 of 1 percent of total U.S. trade. By contrast, trade with America's *NAFTA* partners, Canada and Mexico, accounts for 30 times (or more) than with Israel or Jordan. Yet, the Trade Representative devotes more than one percent of its resources to administering the FTAs with Israel and Jordan. The same point can be made with the *U.S. — Singapore FTA* and *U.S. — Chile FTA*. While Singapore and Chile are diversified economies in terms of their imports and exports (though Singapore does not export agricultural products), Singapore and Chile account for only about 2 percent of total U.S. trade.

"Negative precedents" are another potential drawback of RTAs. Suppose an RTA contains weak disciplines (*e.g.*, it permits certain kinds of discriminatory treatment) and a poor dispute settlement mechanism (*e.g.*, it is slow and lacks strong enforcement tools). Suppose, further, partial sectoral coverage and product exclusions diminish its commercial significance. This kind of RTA, comprised of "WTO minus" commitments (*i.e.*, below the levels set by extant WTO accords), is not a benchmark agreement for multilateral trade liberalization. Rather, it is a negative precedent for future WTO rounds. Put differently, from a global systemic perspective, an RTA containing "WTO plus" rights and obligations would be preferable.

A serious worry is whether an FTA or CU evolves from a trade fortress into a military fortress. If so, then they may create peace and security within their bloc, but not spreading the "peace through trade" effect outside the bloc? In the 1930s, President Franklin Roosevelt's visionary Secretary of State, Cordell Hull, sensed a great danger from trade blocs. A division of the world into such blocs was a threat to international prosperity and security. Global prosperity hardly was likely if countries retreated behind regional fortresses. They might facilitate militarism on a regional basis, and their trade fortresses might go to war with one another when they felt their markets were threatened. Hull read the history of the 19th and early 20th century very much in this fearsome light. He believed passionately a free, open global trading system was the best guarantor of international prosperity and security. His belief was translated into Anglo-American plans for the post-Second World War trading system.

Whether RTAs are stepping stones or fortresses depends in part on relative negotiating dynamics. By definition, any RTA discussions involve fewer countries than the number of WTO Members. Negotiations almost surely are easier with a relatively smaller number. Though that is no guarantee of success, *prima facie* the time and energy of bargaining among, say, five likeminded countries are reduced, and the logistics easier, than talks among 150 countries. During the Doha Round, neither the U.S. nor the EU relished the prospect of repeated confrontations with developing and least developed countries, and the business communities in both the U.S. and EU often seemed content with the RTA deals their governments concluded. Small wonder, then, why — during this Round — the two trade hegemons aggressively pursued RTAs with a select number of countries. However, that pursuit exacerbated rich — poor tensions in the Round. Engaging in RTA negotiations with some countries sewed resentment among countries not invited to the table. Thus piqued, the excluded countries — many of which were developing and least developed — were both less committed to a successful multilateral outcome, and less inclined to compromise with the U.S. and EU in multilateral talks.

V. THE DIVERSITY OF FTAS: BREADTH, DEPTH, AND TIMING

Conventional wisdom holds "globalization" is the word defining the present era of international trade history. Paradoxically, interest and activity in regionalism has rarely if ever been higher than today. From a multilateralist perspective, RTAs are supposed to be an exception to the rule of MFN treatment. Yet, are they the rule, and MFN treatment the exception? That is, are FTAs and CUs proliferating to a degree that puts the WTO at risk of being a WTO a sideshow and talk shop? It is tempting to infer an affirmative answer simply from the large and increasing number of RTAs. That answer troubles advocates of multilateralism. However, five points ought to qualify this answer.

First, many FTAs (and CUs) are under negotiation. Many of them never will come to fruition. Second, a large number of FTAs are between or among former Soviet republics. The extent to which these accords are operative varies. Third, at the WTO, there may be some double counting of FTAs. Once an FTA is notified to the WTO, it is counted once under Article XXIV of GATT. It also may be counted a second time under Article 5 of the *General Agreement on Trade and Services* (*GATS*). Fourth, more than half of the FTAs involve less developed countries, and about one quarter of the FTAs involving these countries are between or among them and the EU. Accordingly, proliferating regionalism — if indeed the adjective is accurate — has development implications. Fifth, and perhaps most importantly, not all FTAs are alike.

Rather, FTAs vary considerably according to their economic ambition. Three key variables gauge this ambition: breadth, depth, and timing. "Breadth" refers to how comprehensive an FTA is, *i.e.*, its scope — wide or narrow. Does it cover all sectors and products in the economies of the member countries? Or, does it exempt a large number of sectors? Does it leave out a few sensitive sectors or products that account for a large volume or value of trade? The extreme free-trade possibility is complete coverage of all goods and services. In practice, however, coverage is always less than 100 percent, at least in the immediate and short term.

For example, the 1 January 1983 *Closer Economic Relationship* (*CER*) between Australia and New Zealand, and 1994 *NAFTA*, are comprehensive FTAs. The May 2003 *U.S. — Singapore* and June 2003 *U.S. — Chile FTAs* boast even more features than *NAFTA*. (Likewise, the EU is a thorough customs union.) Indeed, the U.S. now insists on comprehensive FTAs, *i.e.*, deals that cover goods, services, and intellectual property (IP). The U.S. points out its approach respects GATT Article XXIV, which requires that an FTA or CU cover substantially all trade.

Even with comprehensive accords, there is room for broader integration. Regarding *NAFTA*, in energy and energy services, especially oil and gas, restrictions on cross-border investment exist, and in security, risk management issues remain. But, that room is small in comparison with many FTAs involving less developed countries. These deals tend to contain exceptions so extensive it is almost laughable to call them "free trade" agreements. The FTAs between the EU and Mexico, Chile and Mexico, and Colombia and Mexico are all less ambitious than *NAFTA*. The *EU — Mexico FTA* leaves out agriculture. The FTA of the *Association of South East Asian Nations* (*ASEAN*), called *AFTA* (for *ASEAN Free Trade Area*) omits services, leaves out major agricultural products, and allows some members — those with national car projects like Indonesia and Malaysia — to maintain trade barriers on autos and auto parts. Consider, then, whether any EU-type FTA or association agreement satisfied the GATT Article XXIV obligation? Would *NAFTA* and the EU itself be among the precious few instances of compliance?

"Depth" refers to the extent of reduction of tariff and non-tariff barriers — deep or shallow? For each merchandise category, the extreme free-trade possibility is complete elimination of all barriers. Does the FTA slash all tariffs to zero, eradicate all quantitative restrictions, and move aggressively against abuse of technical barriers to trade (TBT) and sanitary and phytosanitary (SPS) measures? Or, is the FTA shallow in these respects? That is, does it allow for non-zero tariffs on some merchandise, and the re-imposition of tariffs (sometimes called "tariff snap backs") under certain circumstances? Does it leave plenty of room to deploy TBT and SPS measures for protectionist purposes?

"Timing" concerns the speed with which an FTA liberalizes trade — fast or slow? The extreme free-trade possibility is immediate elimination of all tariff and non-tariff barriers on all goods and services. In practice, that speed never is reached. Rather, FTAs create staging categories, and slot products into the categories. Barriers fall at different rates, depending on the category of the merchandise in question. Timing also refers to the realization of benefits from an FTA. Static gains, profiled in neoclassical economic analysis of RTAs, emphasize increased imports and exports. But, dynamic gains, too, may be achieved. For example, if an FTA creates a better business climate and stimulates foreign and domestic investment, then capital formation and productivity may increase.

As intimated, the three variables — breadth, depth, and timing — are manifest in detailed provisions, which fall into three categories:

1. *Concession Exclusions*:

Goods or sectors agreed upon as "sensitive" are excluded from trade liberalizing concessions. The exclusion may be permanent or for a sustained, definite period, or it may be subject to negotiation after a certain date.

2. *Tariff Phase Outs*:

Goods or sectors not rising to the level of "sensitive," but still of concern, are excluded from immediate duty-free treatment. Tariff reduction schedules are set, with longer durations for goods of greater concern.

3. *Tariff Contingencies*:

Goods or sectors — whether or not sensitive or of concern — may be subject to a contingent tariff program. One such program is a tariff rate quota (TRQ), on which the U.S. insists in its FTAs. Another example is a special safeguard. Using this remedial device, MFN duties may be re-imposed on a product category if imports in that category from an FTA partner are below a threshold price or above a threshold volume.

Where in an FTA are these kinds of provisions found? The truth is they are not always "in" the text of the FTA. For political reasons, governments sometimes place them in not-so-transparent side letters to an FTA.

The three variables determine the significance of economic benefits an FTA generates. Succinctly put, an FTA is less economically meaningful if it is (1) narrow in coverage, (2) shallow in barrier reductions, and (3) slow in phasing out barriers. In turn, an FTA that is not economically meaningful, in terms of bringing about economic benefits both in the short and long term, is not sustainable. In other words, it will fail to generate economic gains. That is true even if political and national security factors commend the FTA. To the extent political and national security aims depend on economic gains, they will not be realized.

Further, an FTA that lacks economic ambition indicates irresolute political behavior. Such an FTA suggests difficult domestic political decisions in each of the member countries are not being made. That is, the governments are not pursuing full economic reform, but rather exempting certain preferred constituencies. An FTA lacking in ambition also may become obsolete shortly after it is signed. It may not be an enduring model agreement that can be used as a "boilerplate text." Rather, with new economic developments, there are likely to be demands for new and different accords, stylized to fit the idiosyncrasies of a business climate that, too, will change.

Chapter 22

POLITICAL AND SECURITY ASPECTS OF FTAs

We rail at trade, but the historian of the world will see that it was the principle of liberty; that it settled America, and destroyed feudalism, and made peace and keeps peace; that it will abolish slavery.

  —Ralph Waldo Emerson (1803-82), JOURNALS (1909-14)
  (entry for January 1844)

DOCUMENTS SUPPLEMENT ASSIGNMENT

1. *Havana Charter* Articles 43-45
2. GATT Article XXIV
3. Relevant provisions in FTAs

I. COMPETITIVE LIBERALIZATION AND ITS DEFECTS

Does the strategy of competitive liberalization work in practice? Allegedly, former Singaporean Prime Minister Lee Kuan Yew developed the strategy in 1993, in the context of the Asia Pacific Economic Cooperation (APEC) forum. In the context of a domestic economy, it means implementing economic reforms to enhance international competitiveness. To help achieve this goal, trade liberalization is necessary at three levels — multilateral, regional, and bilateral. In turn, developing FTAs and customs unions, on a regional or bilateral basis, can lead to liberalization multilaterally through the WTO.

Prime Minister Lee argued that if the U.S. were serious about competitive liberalization of its domestic economy, then it would invite any Asian country to join *NAFTA* that also was committed to deregulation. There would be tension with some Asian countries, in which changing economic structures and policies is a slow process (*e.g.*, Japan). But, within five years any recalcitrant Asian country would acquiesce, liberalize expeditiously, because it could not afford to stay out of an FTA with the U.S.

In brief, competitive liberalization means moving as aggressively as possible toward the goal of global free trade by pursuing trade liberalization on three levels — multilateral, regional, and bilateral — simultaneously. In theory, at least, this pursuit is mutually reinforcing. For example, an FTA can encourage movement in WTO negotiations, and vice versa, as Susan Schwab explains:

> My experience as U.S. Trade Representative [for President George W. Bush] is that they [bilateral, regional, and multilateral trade deals] are in fact mutually reinforcing. The negotiated bilateral and regional deals are gold-standard agreements. They are very deep in that

virtually everything opens up. It's not a way of negotiating around sensitivities but a way of coming to grips with sensitivities. Here in these bilateral negotiations, you develop a precedent that could at some point be translated in a multilateral setting. In some cases, you really need a multilateral approach to get at issues like piracy and counterfeiting. I have found in Geneva our very best allies for a strong Doha Round have been current and former [free trade] partners.[1]

Thus, none other than a leading advocate of competitive liberalization, Fred Bergsten, the Director of the Institute for International Economics in Washington, D.C., urged creation of a *Free Trade Agreement of the Asia Pacific Region (FTAAP)* in August 2006, right after the Doha Round negotiations collapsed in July.[2]

His argument is two-pronged. First, an *FTAAP* would revive the Doha Round, the way the first summit of the Asia Pacific Economic Cooperation (APEC) forum shocked Uruguay Round negotiators into completion of that Round, after they missed an initial 1990 deadline. They missed it because of EU obstinacy against reform of the Common Agricultural Policy (CAP). When EU negotiators learned the November 1993 APEC summit yielded a commitment to free trade (which APEC leaders reiterated at their 1994 summit), they agreed to CAP reforms — knowing the alternative to a failed Uruguay Round was a vast FTA in the Asia Pacific region. In brief, Bergsten urged that even the prospect of an *FTAAP* is leverage to complete a multilateral trade round. After all, the 21 APEC members account for over half of world GNP and nearly half of world trade. Better to have a successful multilateral round than be left out of an *FTAAP*. The gains from an *FTAAP* would be for members, and non-members would suffer trade diversion.

However, Guy de Jonquières of the *Financial Times* casts serious doubt on the Bergsten argument:

> [T]he argument is tenuous, being based on a version of history subscribed to in Washington but nowhere much else.
>
> It holds that the Uruguay Round came to closure in 1993 because APEC leaders scared a recalcitrant Europe into resuming negotiation by making a vague, U.S.-inspired call for closer intra-regional links. But if Europe was swayed at all it was because it feared the U.S. was preparing to unplug itself from multilateralism — not because it seriously believed a grouping as formless, disparate and strife-ridden as APEC could agree on much. The conventional explanation of the Uruguay Round's endgame remains the most plausible: Europe's internal agricultural reforms allowed it to offer just enough on farm trade to escape blame for scuppering the talks, while the U.S. settled for a far weaker deal than it had been holding out for.[3]

---

[1] Renuka Rayasam, *Free-Trade Evangelist*, U.S. NEWS & WORLD REPORT, 21 Aug. 2006, at 22 (Q&A: Susan Schwab).

[2] Fred Bergsten, *Plan B for World Trade: Go Regional*, FINANCIAL TIMES, 16 Aug. 2006, at 9.

[3] Guy de Jonquières, *Do-it-Yourself is Free Trade's Best "Plan B"*, FINANCIAL TIMES, 24 Aug. 2006, at 9.

The best alternative to multilateralism, then, is not bilateralism or regionalism, but unilateralism — that is, unilateral dismantling of trade barriers, exactly as David Ricardo's law of comparative advantage suggests, and as Australia, Chile, China, Hong Kong, Singapore, and to a lesser degree, India, all have done in recent decades, with ensuing net welfare gains. Moreover, neither the quote from Ambassador Schwab nor the *FTAAP* idea mentions underlying domestic catalysts — or retardants — for competitive liberalization. In truth, competitive is driven — or held back — by domestic-level economic reforms, *i.e.*, deregulation and the advancement of a free market system. Might it, then, be more accurate to call the strategy "complimentary liberalization," or (as it euphemistically is sometimes dubbed) "parallel liberalization"?

Labels aside, it is necessary to examine domestic-level reform strategies and visions, neither of which is homogeneous or static across countries. For many countries, including some APEC members, the important part of the rubric "Doha Development Agenda" was the middle word. Would competitive liberalization advance development, and in particular, would address growing income disparities? Consider Asian free trade bastions like Singapore:

> The social contract under which Singaporeans gave up certain civil liberties in return for prosperity is under threat.
>
> . . . .
>
> Shortly after the [May 2006 general] election [in which the ruling People's Action Party (PAP) experienced an 8 percentage point drop in support], the government revealed that the income gap was bigger than at any time since independence in 1965. The bottom 30 percent of households have seen incomes fall since 2000.
>
> Singapore's Gini coefficient, a measure of income inequality, places the city state at 105th in the world, between Papua New Guinea and Argentina.
>
> "A two-speed, dual economy appears to be emerging in Singapore," said Citigroup.
>
> "Globalization, for a small open economy, may be having a disproportionately large impact."[4]

China faces the same problem on a much larger scale.[5] A time series analysis of relevant statistics, including Gini coefficients, indicates in 1986, income distribution in China resembled Germany and Sweden. By 2006, the rich-poor gap had widened to a degree making China more unequal than Russia or the U.S., and approaching Brazil and Mexico. Why? China's development model, which favored investment on the coast, a large number of labor surplus workers shifting from non-productive work in the rural sector into manufacturing and service jobs, and corruption were among the culprits. Aggressive trade liberalization may well have been at least a handmaiden.

---

[4] John Burton, *Singapore's Social Contract Shows Signs of Strain*, Financial Times, 19-20 Aug. 2006, at 3.

[5] Richard McGregor, *China Seeks to Reduce Gap Between Rich and Poor*, 8-9 July 2006, at 2.

Whatever label is used for "competitive liberalization," the policy presumes shared interests within and among countries in freer trade at bilateral, regional, and multilateral levels. In turn, it presumes interests are impelled by shared, or at least complementary, visions of desirable domestic policies and the role of each country in the trading system.

Competitive liberalization also suffers from conceptual and practical problems. Consider the following questions:

1. *Integration of Reforms*:

How does trade liberalization feed back to domestic-level reforms? This question is particularly acute in special or sensitive sectors like agriculture and textiles and apparel (T&A).

2. *The Bicycle Theory*:

How do multilateral, regional, and bilateral trade liberalization efforts relate to one another? In particular, is the "Bicycle Theory" of trade negotiations correct, whereby these efforts must continue (as a cyclist must keep pedaling to move forward) or they will come to a halt (as a cyclist would stop, even fall off)? Competitive liberalization presumes there are three bicycles, and trade talks at the multilateral, regional, or bilateral level will spur such talks on another level, or the other two levels. But, the right metaphor for trade negotiations may be not a bicycle but a hedge. The *Financial Times'* Guy de Jonquières puts the concern this way:

> Washington has claimed . . . that its use of muscular bilateral trade diplomacy will re-energize the multilateral trading system by unleashing a wave of "competitive liberalization." The Doha [Round] debacle has exposed that theory for what it is. In practice, bilateralism has fed off itself, intensifying the rush into preferential deals while draining energy from the Doha talks, polarizing the U.S. Congress and further diminishing its appetite for trade initiatives of all descriptions.[6]

Moreover, a reverse causal directional arrow may exist: stalled or failed talks at one level (*e.g.*, the Doha Round) may bring out calls for talks at another level (*e.g.*, bilateral FTAs).[7] There is plenty of evidence in favor of a reverse directional arrow. Israel, for example, began pursuing FTA negotiations with *MERCOSUR* in December 2005, the month of the unsuccessful WTO Hong Kong Ministerial Conference, and talks continue apace.[8] India boasted FTAs with Singapore, Sri Lanka, and Thailand. In light of the July 2006 collapse of Doha Round negotiations, India announced it would pursue FTAs vigorously, including with the EU and Japan. Even Chile, well disposed to unilateral trade barrier reduction, has not sat on the sidelines. It has FTAs with China and South Korea, a "Partial Scope Agreement" with India, and

---

[6] Jonquières, *supra* note 3, at 9.

[7] *See, e.g.*, Christopher Swann & Edward Alden, *Focus on Bilateral Trade Deals, Bush is Urged*, FINANCIAL TIMES, 4 April 2006, at 7 (discussing advice to President George W. Bush from Rep. Bill Thomas, Chairman, House Ways & Means Committee, to focus efforts on FTAs, because the U.S. and EU have irreconcilable differences in the Doha Round).

[8] David Haskel, *MERCOSUR, Israel to Exchange Duty-Free List of Products for Inclusion in Free Trade Pact*, 23 INT'L TRADE REP. (BNA) 542 (6 April 2006).

(as of June 2006) is discussing a comprehensive "Economic Association Agreement" with Japan.

3. *The Collective Action Problem*:

WTO Members did not commit themselves to ensuring regional integration compliment their Doha Round negotiations. They could have entered into an "RTA Peace Clause," whereby they placed a standstill on all new FTAs and CUs until they completed the Round. Instead, they raced each other to seal RTA deals.

Does this behavior suggest it would be easier for the roughly 150 WTO Members to reach consensus in a multilateral trade round if they did not have the option of joining an FTA? That is, does this option give them an exit strategy, which in turn creates a collective action problem — namely, no one Member is willing to forego the RTA option unless all other Members do, but each Member passes the responsibility to others to take the lead in exerting discipline.

4. *Erosion of the Global Economic Order*:

Is competitive liberalization a fair concept, particularly when it discriminates through an RTA, within the context of non-discriminatory treatment under GATT—WTO rules, and results in elaborate preferential rules of origin in each FTA or CU? Arguably, competitive liberalization means competitive discrimination, trade diversion, and erosion of the global economic order. That is precisely the argument of the Asian Development Bank, which in *The Routes for Asia's Trade* (2006) warned FTAs undermine global trade liberalization and exacerbate divisions within Asia, leaving the poorest countries worst off.[9]

To take a technical example, suppose under *NAFTA*'s yarn-forward origin rule, the U.S. accords duty-free treatment to cotton shirts imported from Mexico, but only if they are made from yarn spun into cotton fabric in Mexico. The U.S. imposes a tariff on the same kind of shirts if the yarn is spun into fabric in Pakistan. Logically, Mexican garment manufacturers will source the input (yarn) from within *NAFTA*. Economically, the U.S. has exported its tariff to Mexico, *i.e.*, the effect of the origin rule is as if Mexico imposed a tariff on the Indian input. That effect undermines any previously agreed multilateral tariff reduction on the input.

The foundation of the global economic order is the multilateral trading system, characterized by non-discriminatory treatment and the progressive lowering and binding of barriers. A preference granted to one country is discrimination visited on all other countries. Because discrimination is incongruous with the multilateral trading system, it erodes the global economic order. Nonetheless, WTO Members, and GATT contracting parties before them, have entered into FTAs and CUs — under the cover of GATT Article XXIV and *GATS* Article V.

---

[9] *See* Asian Development Bank, The Routes for Asia's Trade (2006), *available at* www.adb.org/Documents/books/ado/2006/documents/ado2006-part3.pdf; Jonathan Hopfner, *ADB Suggests Asian Nations Face Risks with Pursuit of Bilateral Free Trade Deals*, 23 INT'L TRADE REP. (BNA) 611-12 (20 April 2006).

Consider the example of Mongolia. As of August 2006, this country was the only WTO Member not to have joined an RTA. As Damedin Tsogtbaatar of the Mongolian Development Strategy Institute explains, Mongolia has put more into the WTO than it has obtained from it, because it "chose, ironically, a rather Buddhist path of self-perfection and good WTO-consistent behavior, without regard to whether other countries were doing the same."[10] Yet, query whether this "Buddhist path" is precisely what other WTO Members ought to follow, and thus whether competitive liberalization is a road for apostates. Indeed, if every one of the 149 WTO Members struck a bilateral FTA with every other Member, then there would be 11,026 bilateral deals.

5. *The International Rule of Law*:

How does competitive liberalization contribute to the international rule of law?

On the one hand, adjudicatory mechanisms and outcomes under an RTA may prove useful as guidance, even path-breaking in legal theory or rationale, for WTO panels and the Appellate Body. They also may provide for forum selection, and contribute to healthy competition among adjudicators in different bodies by encouraging them to better quality proceedings and outcomes. On the other hand, RTA dispute settlement schemes may lead to forum shopping. They also may present an un-level dispute settlement playing field. Would, for example, it be preferable to resolve alleged trade violations of China through *ASEAN* or through the WTO *DSU*?

6. *Alignment of Benefits*:

Does competitive liberalization fail to align properly economic and non-economic benefits from trade liberalization? Consider rents from tariffs in comparison with rents from intellectual property rights (IP). Tariff rents arise from government collection of tariff revenue. IP rents are associated with the ability of a patent, trade or service mark, or copyright owner to exclude all others from manufacturing, distributing, or licensing the good or service embodying the IP, and thus to hold a monopoly position with respect to that good or service.

Suppose competitive liberalization were extended to the extreme through RTAs, whereby the U.S. had an FTA with every country in the world. Rents from tariffs would disappear. That is because with all trade accorded duty-free treatment, neither the U.S. nor its FTA partners gain tariff revenue. Would IP rents disappear?

The answer is "no." Holders of patents, trade and service marks, and copyrights — from Adidas to Sony Pictures, from Amazon.com to Roche — assuredly would press the U.S. and its FTA partners for textual provisions to ensure strict IP protection and enforcement. Thus, exporters and importers of goods would enjoy the disappearance of tariff rents. IP holders would enjoy the maintenance of IP rents. This alignment could create tension.

The first group (exporters and importers) would focus on the economic dimensions of the FTAs. The second group (IP rights holders) would be keenly sensitive to IP infringement, and urge rigorous prosecution and penalties. The

---

[10] *Least Favored Nation*, THE ECONOMIST, 5 Aug. 2006, at 68.

first group would prefer diplomatic peace to preserve its economic benefits. The diplomatic interests of the second group might call for confrontation to enforce their IP rights, possibly with some disruption in the economic *status quo*. In brief, competitive liberalization in the extreme might not necessarily bring into alignment all economic and non-economic features of RTAs.

> 7. *Administration*:

Finally, competitive liberalization suffers from an administrative problem. It is a strategy only rich countries can pursue effectively. It requires a considerable number of talented international trade lawyers to pursue three-track negotiations, and the lawyers on each track must coordinate with the lawyers on all other tracks. That is a challenge even for the USTR, and *a fortiori* it is a close-to-insurmountable task for trade ministries in the Philippines, Suriname, or Togo.

Clearly, then, from a systemic perspective, competitive liberalization is at best an imperfect justification for an active FTA policy.

That said, the fundamental point to observe is that competitive liberalization itself is not a purely economic strategy. As suggested, encouraging trade negotiations on three tracks simultaneously is a self-interested hedge against the political risk of failure on one or two of the tracks. In American terms, it avoids the U.S. "putting all its trade eggs in the multilateral basket." More bluntly, it ensures U.S. efforts to obtain market access in other countries are not subject to a veto by any one country, such as France or India, or by any one domestic constituency, such as steel or T&A interests. If blockage occurs on one level, then progress might be made on another level.

II.   CHOOSING FTA PARTNERS

What priorities ought to govern the decision to enter into negotiations for an FTA or customs union? That is, what are the criteria by which to decide potential RTA partners? For much of GATT history, with the notable exception of economic integration in Europe beginning in 1950, FTAs and CUs were somewhat of a sideshow in the international trade arena. However, as of May 2003, there were 155 FTAs notified to the WTO, and an additional 83 that had been concluded but not notified. At that time, the U.S. was a partner in 3 of the 155 (and 2 of the 83), and the EU (or the *European Free Trade Area*, *EFTA*), a partner in 59 of the 155 (and 6 of the 83).

These figures continue to grow. Overall, there are roughly 300 FTAs and CUs in the world (and dozens more planned or under negotiation). This number is roughly double the number of WTO Members, and about one-third more than the number of countries in the world. If the global trading system is characterized by regionalism and bilateralism, then which actual and potential RTAs ought to be highest on the negotiating agenda for a country? As the number of RTAs suggests, these questions are relevant to most countries. Mexico, for example, is said to have more FTAs than any other country — 42. Indeed, the country has had a post-*NAFTA* FTA binge — Mexico had just one FTA, with Chile, in 1994.

No less than two dozen countries have asked the U.S. for an FTA. How should the U.S. pick among them? Should the criteria be exclusively, or primarily, economic? What would the specific criteria be, and how would they apply in particular contexts? For example, how might an FTA between the U.S. and Thailand benefit each country economically? Thailand is a major production base for Japanese and other foreign auto and auto parts producers. What would be the effect of an FTA on the auto industry in each country, and third countries? Conversely, what factors are or should be relevant from the perspective of other countries in contemplating, negotiating, and implementing an FTA with the world's superpower?

Economic research, starting with Jacob Viner's classic study, *The Customs Union Issue* (1950), has evaluated the complex effects of RTAs on trade activity. For the consensus of mainstream economists, the general theoretical conclusions are:

i.   It is better to liberalize trade unilaterally, even without reciprocal concessions from trading partners. This conclusion follows from the standard Smith — Ricardo arguments for free trade.

ii. It is better to negotiate trade liberalization through a multilateral forum, rather than regional or bilateral fora. This conclusion follows from the analysis of trade creation versus trade diversion.

Obviously, these conclusions do not dispose of efforts to enter sub-multilateral trade deals. There may be practical economic blessings and curses — what might be called "political economy" factors — from an RTA. In turn, once political calculations enter into RTA decisionmaking, then so also do national security considerations.

III. POLITICAL CRITERIA

Evidently, the plethora and dispersion of actual and potential RTAs means they are more than just economic creatures. Political factors may impel countries to a deal. An obvious example is direction from a legislature or domestic constituencies. Article I, Section 8, Clause 3 of the U.S. Constitution gives Congress the power to regulate trade with foreign nations. Congress may delegate that power to the Executive Branch, and thereby authorize the President to conduct trade negotiations at the multilateral, regional, or bilateral level. Such delegations typically entail Congressional guidance as to countries with which the President should seek an FTA.

That is the case for the *Caribbean Basin Initiative* (*CBI*), an ongoing initiative created under the 1983 *Caribbean Basin Economic Recovery Act* (*CBERA*) (which was expanded in 1990 and amended in 2000). The *CBI* calls for negotiations with Central and Southern American nations. Similarly, through the 2000 *African Growth and Opportunity Act* (*AGOA*) (as subsequently amended), Congress pushed for FTAs in Sub-Saharan Africa. In both instances, FTAs with the U.S. create the potential to support regional integration. Immigrant communities in the U.S. — Central Americans and Africans, respectively — helped to support *CBI* and *AGOA*.

Notably, America's first FTA with a sovereign nation came in April 1985 when it signed an accord with Israel. (The *Canada — U.S. Auto Pact* of 1965 obviously precedes this accord, but it covers only trade in auto and auto parts.)

The *U.S.— Israel FTA* came a decade after the EU signed a free trade accord with Israel, in 1975. It also helped unblock a debate in Congress over trade delegation authority to the President for what would be the Uruguay Round. In October 2000, the U.S. signed an FTA with Jordan. Both countries were members of the GATT—WTO system when their FTAs occurred: Israel acceded to GATT on 6 April 1962, and Jordan joined the WTO on 11 April 2000. These FTAs are unambiguous examples of trade policy being used as a tool of foreign policy. That is, America's foreign policy interests in Israel and Jordan outweigh any domestic economic sensitivity to particular imports from these countries.

At the same time, the *Israel* and *Jordan FTAs* exemplify the way in which a politically driven bargain can broaden ties among the member countries. Before these deals, political and military affairs dominated the relationships between the U.S. and Israel, and the U.S. and Jordan. After the FTAs took effect, indeed as they were negotiated, tomato growers and sweater producers became interested in the relationships. In other words, an FTA can expand the range of constituencies actively engaged in a foreign linkage. That expansion can yield not only net economic benefits among the members, but also reinforce mutual political and military ties.

A. Case Study: Taiwan

Since 1979, when President Jimmy Carter normalized relations with the People's Republic of China (PRC), and de-recognized the Republic of China (Taiwan), the U.S. has pursued a policy toward the two entities that sometimes is characterized as strategic ambiguity. On the one hand, the 1979 *Taiwan Relations Act* (22 U.S.C. §§ 3301 *et seq.*) reaffirms America's commitment to a "One China Policy," a product of the famous February 1972 *Shanghai Communiqué* worked out between Chinese Premier Zhou Enlai and U.S. Secretary of State Henry Kissinger. On the other hand, the same *Act* commits the U.S. to providing military and economic assistance to Taiwan.

Strategic ambiguity certainly has not inhibited commercial relations between the U.S. and Taiwan, and in 1994 the two sides signed a *Trade and Investment Framework Agreement (TIFA)*. (The U.S. suspended talks under the TIFA in 1998, displeased at three aspects of Taiwan's trade policy: reluctance to open its rice market; slow progress on opening service markets; and poor enforcement of IP rights). Taiwan is the eighth largest trading partner of the U.S. Indeed, U.S. trade with Taiwan far exceeds trade with any other potential FTA partner in the Far East, except Korea. For the U.S., the largest export benefit from an FTA with Taiwan would be in the auto and auto parts sector. But, U.S. auto and auto producers suspect an FTA would make little difference in practice, because Taiwan eventually would eliminate its ban on imports from China of these products.

Suppose auto and auto parts could be exported directly from China to Taiwan. U.S. producers in China would benefit — without an FTA with Taiwan. For Taiwan, the U.S. is the most important trading partner (measured in terms of two-way trade, *i.e.*, exports plus imports), though exports from Taiwan to China are increasingly important. The biggest export gain for

Taiwan from an FTA with the U.S. would be concentrated in the T&A sector, in which it holds a clear comparative advantage over the U.S. Neither country would see agriculture as a major issue in an FTA with the other, largely because Taiwan is not a major agricultural exporter, and thus not a threat to American farmers.

What, then, would be the logic of a *U.S. — Taiwan FTA*? In a study of the potential benefits from such an accord, the U.S. ITC suggested the overall economic gains would be modest. As the American Chamber of Commerce (AmCham) in Taipei pointed out in a May 2006 *Taiwan White Paper*, many benefits could be had without an FTA, but rather through removing restrictions on transactions across the Taiwan Strait. Such restrictions inhibit imports into Taiwan from the Mainland of certain products, investment in the Mainland, travel from the Mainland to Taiwan by employees of multinational (including Taiwanese) companies, transfer from Taiwan to the Mainland of commercial technology, and direct air and shipping links between Taiwan and the Mainland. In turn, cross-Strait integration is retarded, and Taiwan segregates itself from Greater China and the global economy.

By inference, therefore, geopolitical calculus would be the logic of a *U.S. — Taiwan FTA*. An agreement between the two sides would have significant political benefits. It would formalize the close relationship between the U.S. and Taiwan, and suggest the former regards, or at least treats in a *de facto* way, the latter as an independent nation. It also would challenge the efforts of China to isolate Taiwan, both diplomatically and in international trade. And, U.S. leadership might embolden allies. For years, Taiwan was tried to conclude bilateral trade accords with Australia, Japan, and Singapore, but they have been standoffish, fearful of annoying China. In other words, a *U.S. — Taiwan FTA* would be less about trade between the parties and more about a stark political statement to the giant country across the Formosa Straits.

Should, then, the criteria for choosing RTA partners include, even be dominated by, political factors? An FTA or CU can broaden and deepen links among member countries. Such integration can, in turn, be furthered through monetary and political union — as the EU shows. No longer is the remark of American Secretary of State Henry Kissinger — to the effect, when you want to speak to "Europe," whom do you call? — accurate. Europe, generally, speaks with one voice on an array of political issues.

Taiwan does not sit forlornly hoping for an FTA with the U.S. Rather, it has an active FTA policy, including negotiated bilateral deals with Guatemala, Nicaragua, and Panama, and in May 2007, after 1 year of bargaining, it signed its first "multilateral FTA" with El Salvador and Honduras.[11] Under the *Taiwan-El Salvador-Honduras FTA*, which took effect on 1 January 2008, 57.1 percent of Taiwanese exports to El Salvador (3,590 products), and 61.9 percent of its exports to Honduras (3,881 products) have duty free treatment. Among the delighted constituencies are Taiwanese producer-exporters of certain agricultural items, electronics, golf clubs, hand tools, home appliances, rubber products, screws and nuts, and tires. Conversely, Taiwan accords duty free

---

[11] Yu-Tzu Chiu, *Taiwan Signs Free Trade Pact with El Salvador and Honduras*, 24 INT'L TRADE REP. (BNA) 700 (17 May 2007).

status to 64.4 percent of El Salvadorean imports (5,688 products), and 69.4 percent of Honduran imports (6,135 products).

Possibly, Taiwan could benefit economically from the *FTA* in conjunction with closer trade relations between the U.S. and Central America under the *Central American Free Trade Agreement — Dominican Republic (CAFTA—DR)*. How might Taiwanese producer-exporters use the *FTA* and *CAFTA—DR* to facilitate access for their products into the U.S. market? Observe the *FTA* is clever for Taiwan for diplomatic reasons, too. It is an opportunity for a modicum of influence in a world in which a dwindling number of countries grant it official recognition.

B. Case Study: Panama

Few, if any, FTA stories are entirely happily. Political factors can be a significant impediment to, and even vitiate (temporarily, if not permanently), a proposed FTA. Negotiations between the U.S. and Panama, conducted between April 2004 and December 2006 are an example. The two countries, sharing a common destiny through the Canal Zone, seemed well poised for an easy FTA negotiation. Panama — unlike the *CAFTA* countries — has a small agricultural sector, and thus poses little challenge to entrenched U.S. lobbying interests in sectors like sugar. Further, even without an FTA, over 95 percent of Panamanian exports enjoyed duty-free access to the U.S. market (many through preferences like the GSP and CBI). Nevertheless, three issues almost proved politically insurmountable in the FTA talks — Sanitary and Phytosanitary Standards (SPS), labor rights, and lobbying.

First, the U.S. insisted Panama sign a side letter on SPS measures that obligated Panama to recognize all American testing procedures and measures for food and beverage products. Bitter historical experience, albeit from when Panama was under military dictatorship, in which American exports were blocked for political reasons veiled by SPS concerns, impelled the U.S. to take this position. The U.S. asserted other countries with which it had or was negotiating an FTA, such as Colombia and Oman, had agreed to an SPS side letter. Panama countered with a demand to see the other side letters, which the U.S. refused, forcing Panama to attempt to get them directly from the other countries. In February 2006, Panama further countered with a request to visit the U.S. to review the food safety and inspection system of the U.S. Department of Agriculture. The logic was that if the U.S. demands Panama accept American SPS standards, then Panama would like first to see what the system is and how well it works. Surprisingly, the initial American response was negative, but the U.S. ultimately relented. Interestingly, Panama urged the U.S. to put a negotiated text on the recognition of SPS measures not in a side letter, but in the FTA document itself. The U.S. refused.

From the political angle of Panama, the side letter was the SPS equivalent of dollarization, *i.e.*, dropping its own currency, adopting the U.S. dollar, and thus being entirely subject to monetary policy set by the Federal Reserve. The government of Panama would have to accept for Panamanian citizens whatever food and beverage risk assessment testing the U.S. government set for American citizens. To be sure, the U.S. levels might well be higher than all or almost all Panamanian levels. Yet, politically, Panamanian leaders would have to defend the delegation, if not abdication, of the sovereign right to set SPS standards — a right guaranteed by the WTO *Agreement on Sanitary and Phytosanitary Standards* — to the giant country to the north. Indeed, in early 2006, the Panamanian Agriculture Minister, Laurentino Cortizo, resigned, saying an FTA would increase the risk of his country importing animal diseases.

Also from a Panamanian political vantage point, the U.S. failed to differentiate among Central American nations. Pursuant to *CAFTA—DR* negotiations, the U.S. was largely successful in obtaining recognition from the likes of El Salvador to accept the equivalency of U.S. meat and poultry inspection and other SPS standards. The U.S. refused to implement *CAFTA—DR* with respect to El Salvador on the target date of 1 January 2006, because that country had not recognized the American standards as equivalent. Only when with recognition did implementation follow, on 1 March 2006. But Panama is not El Salvador, which is poorer, more agrarian, and weaker. Thus, Panama is less susceptible than El Salvador to American pressure in the form of "do this or we don't implement." Of course, the American side had its own political concerns: in the Trade Promotion Authority (TPA) legislation by which Congress delegated power to the President to conduct FTA talks, Congress required the U.S. export its equivalency standards. Might it be inferred as a general proposition that the deal, if any, trade negotiators bring home depends in large part on negotiating parameters set by their political masters?

Second, the U.S. told Panama it would have to change its labor law, which meant a possible change to its constitution, to grant workers in the Panama Canal Zone the right to strike. Panama responded Canal Zone jobs are among the most highly sought after in the country. That is because of their relatively higher pay, benefits, and working conditions. Workers there have little or no interest in that right, but even if they did, Panama could not afford granting this right. Trade through the Canal Zone accounts for a significant percentage of economic activity and national income in Panama, not to mention 5 percent of world trade. By 2014, Panama plans to add a $5.25 billion third lane (specifically, two large flights of three locks), and widen and deepen the 50-mile Canal. Its goal is to increase capacity and allow the largest and most modern container vessels to sail directly from Asia to the U.S. Eastern Seaboard. (When the Canal opened in 1914, the 12 locks could handle the biggest ships of the day.) In part, China's rise as a producer and exporter of manufactured goods necessitates expansion, as the Canal (as of June 2006) operates at 90 percent capacity. Expansion means the Canal could accommodate ships that are up to 366 meters wide and 49 meters wide, and which can carry 12,000 twenty-foot equivalent units of containers — *i.e.*, ships larger than currently exist, and twice the size of the biggest vessels now able to use the Canal.

Any strike or serious labor disruption not only could hamper expansion plans, but also cripple operations in the Canal Zone, with adverse knock-on effects for the country and world trade. For example, if a vessel is too large for the Canal, or if the Canal is closed, the alternative Asia-to-East Coast route is through the Suez Canal — which is further, longer, and entails political risks associated with transport in the Middle East — or from Asia to the West Coast, and then across America by rail. Quite rightly, Panama asked, did the U.S. — indeed the world trading community — seriously believe a right to strike, in the special context of the Canal Zone, would be a responsible economic, political, and national security gesture? From an historical perspective, the American position was ironic: an American-engineered revolution in Colombia led to Panamanian independence in 1903, and Panama obtained full control of the Canal from the U.S. on 31 December 1999.

Third, the U.S called upon Panama to persuade the American Congress to accept a *U.S. — Panama FTA*. This demand came at a time when a former Congressman from Ohio — Ambassador Robert Portman — held the position of USTR. Skilled in Capitol Hill Politics, the USTR appreciated the significant opposition to FTAs, especially from Democratic Party members. However, from Panama's vantage point, the USTR was calling on its government to do the work of the USTR. If Panama agreed, then it would be in the position of negotiating not with one executive branch agency (the USTR), but with dozens of different interest groups embodied in 435 House members and 100 Senators. The Panamanian response was firm and called for reciprocity. If the Panamanian Ambassador to the U.S. had to lobby Democrats on the Hill for an FTA, then the American Ambassador to Panama would have to lobby Panamanian lawmakers.

Evidently, with that response, the FTA talks ended in the spring 2006. For Panama, prospective economics benefits from a deal were less than the political costs associated with American demands. Roughly three-quarters of Panamanian exports go to the U.S., even without an FTA. The average MFN tariff imposed by these exports is quite low, especially if T&A products are excluded. Thus, for most of its exports, the margin of preference Panama would gain from an FTA is modest. As for T&A, with competition from China, India, and Vietnam, Panama appreciates its future is not in this sector. It encourages adjustment of factor resources to other sectors, especially services, which account for 70 to 80 percent of its GDP.

Similarly, for the U.S., political costs outweighed prospective economic gains. An FTA with Panama would provide American manufacturers with another platform from which to export, based on relatively cheap labor. But, politically, no American administration can articulate openly FDI overseas as a reason for establishing an FTA. That would translate as factory closures (or non-openings) in the U.S., and thus job loss (or non-creation) for Americans. Accordingly, only significant concessions from Panama that could be touted publicly would persuade a skeptical Congress to pass an FTA.

Surprisingly, a few days before Christmas 2006, the USTR announced it had struck a deal with Panama. Panama accepted U.S. SPS standards on meat and poultry, and apparently had agreed to do some lobbying on Capitol Hill, too. Over 50 percent of U.S. farm exports (including beef, certain processed goods, poultry, soybeans, wine and distilled spirits) receive duty-free treatment upon entry into force of the FTA, as do Panamanian T&A articles — if they use U.S. or Panamanian yarn or fabric. U.S. financial providers also obtain enhanced market access, U.S. government contractors benefit from greater transparency, and U.S. investors are guaranteed national treatment

— all important with respect to the Panama Canal expansion, for example. Notably, in February 2007, while the FTA was before Congress, Panamanian President Martín Torrijos traveled to Washington, D.C., and personally called on the leadership of the House Ways and Means Committee — the third time he had met with the Committee Chairman (Charles Rangel, Democrat-New York). Clearly, Panama had conceded it would have to share the burden of proof that Congress should pass the FTA.

When is a deal truly complete? When negotiators inked the Panama FTA in December 2006, they left open its chapter on labor standards. Pending guidance from Congress, labor issues had to be resolved. Whether the story would end happily was not clear.

IV. POLITICAL ECONOMY CRITERIA

A. Sensitive Sectors and Legislative Support

In reality, it is not always easy to separate political and economic factors. Trade policy initiatives, including FTA and CU proposals, may arise from an mixture of the two. An obvious example concerns sensitive sectors and the link to selling a deal to national legislatures.

The U.S. consciously examines the pattern of exports of a prospective RTA partner before considering whether to commence discussions with that country. The "hard" case is a pattern revealing the other country has a keen interest in access to the American market for products the U.S. regards as sensitive. Assuredly, any FTA with that country will be difficult to sell to domestic producers of the like product regarded as sensitive by the U.S. Those producers will exert influence against the FTA on Capitol Hill. To overcome their opposition, the U.S. will need to show enormous gains on other fronts, meaning that the other country will have had to make correlating concessions. Such concessions, however, may create political headaches for that country.

Conversely, the "easy" case, of course, is a country with an export interest in few if any sensitive products. Opposition may arise from civil society, that is, from non-governmental organizations (NGOs), including activists for labor and environmental rights, and for religious freedom. But, few if any domestic economic constituencies will mobilize against the deal. The U.S. may not need to press relentlessly for full and immediate market access in every goods and services sector (although a template-like approach to FTA negotiations that is both ill-considered and insolent may lead the USTR to do so.) Assuming NGO opposition is addressed through appropriate provisions in the FTA, or in acceptable, transparent side letters, then legislators on Capitol Hill may have little trouble supporting the deal.

B. Locking in Reform in a Coalition of the Well Performing

Another clear manifestation of the political economy of RTAs concerns liberalization. Sustaining momentum for, and solidifying, economic and political reforms are potential gains from an RTA. A country politically serious about real economic liberalization is likely to be a country serious about an RTA. The link between an RTA and reform may be especially apparent when negotiations pair a relatively larger and smaller country, or a developed and developing country. The RTA can be both a catalyst and *raison d'être* for reform in a smaller or developing country, and thus a persuasive tool against recalcitrant traditionalism.

Thus, in evaluating countries, the U.S. considers whether top political leadership of a prospective FTA partner is fully committed to reform, and both willing and able to deliver on legal commitments. Three indicators of this commitment are:

1. *WTO Performance*:

Has a would-be FTA partner been slack in implementing multilateral trade commitments? If so, then why would the U.S. expect it to behave differently in an FTA? However, is it appropriate for the U.S. to demand that the country commit to cooperating with the U.S. in the WTO? Calling upon the country, as an equal WTO partner, to take a problem-solving approach to multilateral trade controversies is one thing. Conditioning an FTA on that country supporting American positions in the WTO is quite another thing.

2. *Negotiation Team*:

How capable and skillful is the trade negotiating team of a country that is a would-be FTA partner with the U.S.? Sending a team lacking in legal capacity is a poor harbinger of life after an FTA. It suggests the team may make commitments it neither understands fully nor appreciates how to implement rigorously.

3. *TIFAs*:

Has a would-be FTA partner entered into a *Trade and Investment Framework Agreement* with the U.S.? These modest documents are frameworks on which the U.S. prefers to build (and sometimes insists on building) an FTA. Morocco, Bahrain, Egypt, Indonesia, the Philippines, and Thailand are among the many countries that have signed *TIFAs*.

In sum, in selecting countries for an FTA, the U.S. seeks a "coalition of the well performing," with the U.S. setting criteria for performance and judging its quality.

Consider whether *NAFTA* helps lock in reforms in Mexico. No longer does Mexico experience pendulum-like swings between economic liberalization and nationalization and state planning. Mexico has used *NAFTA* successfully to complement domestic economic liberalization, and thereby attract foreign direct investment (FDI) from developed countries. Observe, then, a corollary point: competition for FDI is an incentive for a poor country to eschew isolationism and push for an FTA.

Such competition is nearly pointless if a poor country retains high trade barriers, discriminatory standards, and import substitution policies. Conversely, an FTA is a statement about commitment to economic reform and the rule of law. Two other examples of how an RTA can help catalyze and sustain political momentum for economic reforms are the U.S. FTAs with Israel (signed in April 1985) and Jordan (signed in October 2000).

C. Case Study: Egypt

Egypt has an approximately U.S. $100 billion economy (as of May 2003). Its largest trading partners are the EU and U.S. Why is Egypt a viable potential FTA partner for the U.S.? The obvious response might emphasize the national security purposes a *U.S. — Egypt FTA* could serve. Arguably, however, political and economic factors justify Egypt as an FTA partner for the U.S.

Politically, Egypt has long been a (if not the) leader in the Arab world, and a uniquely influential country in the Middle East. Egypt hosted the Arab League when that body was founded in 1945. It was the first country to sign a peace treaty with Israel, the 1979 Camp David Accords brokered by President Jimmy Carter. Egypt has exported political ideas, including in 1958 socialism and pan-Arabism through the ultimately unsuccessful United Arab Republic. It also exports its culture around the Middle East, including the Egyptian dialect of Arabic, through cinema, music, and television. Egypt also exports its human capital. There are roughly two million Egyptians working in the Middle East outside of their home country, many as teachers, including law professors at Arab law faculties.

Economically, Egypt is not Chile but seems to want, and need, to be. The *per capita* GNP of Egypt (at just U.S. $1,500 in May 2003) is considerably lower than that of Chile. Unlike Chile, Egypt has not completed economic liberalization, and hardly is a model reform country. Some American trade policy officials argue that a country ought to reform economically first, and then enter into FTA negotiations. However, that stance potentially pre-empts an FTA, because if a country has implemented meaningful reforms, then it might not need an FTA. In other words, an FTA can accelerate a reform process that is inchoate in a country like Egypt.

Egypt took some important stabilization measures in the 1990s. It reduced its fiscal (budget) deficit from 20 to 1 percent of national income. It unified its foreign exchange rates into a single rate, devalued its currency (the Egyptian pound), anchored the exchange rate, and finally floated the currency. The Egyptian central bank tamed inflation (to a rate of about 5 percent in the 1990s), and has shifted its monetary policy to target inflation.

To be sure, there are political and economic factors mitigating against rash conclusion of a *U.S. — Egypt FTA*. The U.S. criticized the way in which Egypt handled its fall 2005 presidential elections, including suppression of opposition candidates (some of which were fielded by the Muslim Brotherhood), its conviction (on charges of forgery) of Ayman Nour, the runner up in these elections, and its postponement of municipal elections (which had been slated for April 2006). Structural reform in the Egyptian economy is lagging. Privatization of state-owned enterprises (SOEs) is needed, and exchange rate deviation from purchasing power parity (PPP) needs to be addressed. Trade laws require further liberalization. Egypt has virtually eliminated all of its import bans, implemented the WTO *Agreement on Customs Valuation*, and joined both the *Basic Telecommunications Agreement* and the *Information Technology Agreement (ITA)*. But, many of its WTO commitments are weak. Query, then, would an FTA encourage broader and deeper reform of the political economy, or should it be a pre-condition to a deal?

D. Case Study: Korea and *KORUS*

Another manifestation of political economy criteria in relation to an FTA is a potential bargain between the U.S. and Korea, called "*KORUS*." Formal negotiations commenced between the two countries in June 2006. The two sides signed the deal in Seoul, on 1 April 2007, within 25 minutes of expiry of the deadline under U.S. *Trade Promotion Authority* (*TPA*) for notifying Congress of an agreement. The negotiators deftly took advantage of a weekend, plus the difference between Korean and Eastern Standard Time. (It was 11:35 p.m. EST on 31 March when they inked the deal.)

In the world (as of 2005), Korea is the 10th largest economy, 11th largest market, 7th largest goods exporter and importer, 10th largest services exporter, and 6th largest services importer. Korea is America's 7th largest trading partner (with $72 billion in two-way trade goods, and $14 billion in two-way services trade, in 2005), and 6th largest market for U.S. farm goods. Conversely, importing 17 percent of Korea's global exports, America is Korea's 3rd largest market. Overall, imports and exports account for roughly two-thirds of Korea's Gross Domestic Product (GDP).

Thus, *KORUS* is the most commercially significant FTA the U.S. has, save for *NAFTA*. In announcing negotiations, however, President George W. Bush made clear more than economics were at stake: "[The two countries] have a strong alliance and are bound together by common values and a deep desire to expand freedom, peace, and prosperity throughout Asia and the world."[12] Once North Korea successfully tested a nuclear device, in October 2006, it was obvious an FTA ought to be viewed in geopolitical terms. *KORUS* is a device to merge trade and security issues, and a tool to strengthen the economic and military alliance between the two countries that began over a half century ago when President Harry S. Truman intervened in the Korean War.

For the U.S., most economic gains from an FTA with Korea are likely to come from improved terms of trade (*i.e.*, cheaper import prices and higher export prices). Gains might also come from enhanced market access through lowering tariffs. On agricultural products, Korea's trade-weighted average duty rate is 64.1 percent (the simple average is 52 percent), with tariffs as high as 500 percent (as of 2005). (America's average farm tariff is 12 percent (as of 2005)). On industrial goods, the trade-weighed average is 4.5 percent, but on autos it is 8 percent (in contrast with the U.S. rate of 2.5 percent) — on top of an engine displacement tax the U.S. contended discriminates against foreign-produced cars because the amount of the tax depends on engine size, and foreign cars have larger-sized engines than Korean cars. Among OECD countries (of which Korea is one), imported cars account for 40 percent of the market, but in Korea the figure is just 2.7 percent (as of 2005). Notably, under *KORUS*, in the auto sector, Korea agreed to:

  i.   Drop immediately the 8 percent tariff on 2 of the 3 major auto import categories covering U.S. priority passenger vehicles and trucks.

---

[12] Christopher S. Rugaber, *U.S., Korea Launch FTA Talks, Will Seek To Reach Agreement by End of This Year*, 23 INT'L TRADE REP. (BNA) 207-09 (9 Feb. 2006).

ii.	Eliminate the engine displacement based taxes (*e.g.*, Korea's Annual Vehicle Tax, Special Consumption Tax, and Subway/Regional Development Bond).

iii.	Establish an Automotive Working Group to review auto-related regulations, promote good regulatory practices in Korea, ensure Korea shares the same information on technical standards with U.S. automakers as it does with Korean companies, and serve as an early warning system against possible future market access barriers.

iv.	Create an enhanced dispute settlement mechanism for controversies over auto-related measures, requiring a decision by a panel within 6 months of commencing a case, and allowing the winning country to snap back the tariff at issue to the pre-*KORUS* MFN level.

For its part, the U.S. agreed to phase out its 2.5 percent car tariff, and 25 percent truck tariff, on Korean vehicles across 10 years (beginning with small-engine capacity cars, in which Korea has a keen export interest).

Finally, gains to the U.S. from *KORUS* are likely to come from removing non-tariff barriers, especially opaque, unpredictable, and discriminatory regulations, and anti-competitive practices of the giant industrial conglomerates, or *chaebols*. Such barriers plague agricultural products. For example:

i.	Quotas raise rice imports from 4 to just 8 percent of domestic consumption between 2005-15.

ii.	Korean sanitary and phytosanitary (SPS) measures shut out U.S. beef, starting in December 2003, over concerns about mad cow disease (with a partial reopening in September 2006 for boneless beef from cattle less than 30 months old, followed in April 2007 by import clearance from Korea's National Veterinary Research and Quarantine Service of a 6.4 metric ton shipment of beef from Creekstone Farms of Kansas). Korea had been the third largest market for U.S. beef exports, but during the closure Australian beef imports into Korea soared.

iii.	A Korean Ministry of Health and Welfare rule (effective 1 January 2007) mandates all restaurants with a floor space of 300 square meters or more display on menu boards and signs the country of origin of beef they serve, with criminal penalties of up to a $31,200 fine and 3 year prison term for violation.

Non-tariff barriers also impede market access for autos (*e.g.*, Korea-specific emission standards), as well as banks, insurance companies, pharmaceutical firms, software businesses, and telecommunications providers. Overall, with coverage of farm and auto trade, the net welfare gains from *KORUS* should prove significant. (There also could be significant trade diversion.) Conversely, had *KORUS* excluded the agricultural sector alone, then over half of all forecast gains would have disappeared. However, significantly, *KORUS* does not cover rice — Korea insisted upon its exclusion. Moreover, Korea made no formal commitment on SPS measures in respect of U.S. beef.

Manifestly, a central challenge facing the U.S. in negotiating FTAs with North East Asian countries — Japan as well as Korea, in particular — are agricultural barriers imposed by them. With 3.5 million farmers who make themselves heard through bodies like the Korean Advanced Farmers Federation, Korea had a three-pronged strategy in FTA talks:

(1) exclusion of sensitive agricultural commodities;

(2) long-term tariff reduction schedules for some farm products; and

(3) contingent tariff programs, such as tariff rate quotas (TRQs) and special safeguards for other products.

Services, too, posed a hurdle to *KORUS* negotiations.

Korea was willing to concede only gradual liberalization in sectors in which the U.S. holds a comparative advantage. In the end, Korea conceded to a Negative List approach to liberalizing services trade (whereby access is provided in all sectors unless specifically exempted). Accordingly, it granted enhanced market access for audio-visual (AV) and broadcasting services, e-commerce, legal, and telecommunications services (including 100 percent U.S. ownership of telecom operations in Korea within 2 years of the effective date of *KORUS*, an increase from the 49 percent cap), and transparency guarantees. The AV sector is a curious one. Korea maintains a screen quota requirement. Formerly, all movie theaters had to reserve 40 percent of their screen time (equivalent to 146 days) for Korean movies. Korea announced in January 2006 it would lower the requirement (as of July 2006) to 20 percent (73 days), which satisfied the USTR. Korea also agreed to allow (within 3 years of the entry into force of *KORUS*) U.S. firms to own 100 percent of program providers. Korean viewers might agree domestic movies are improving — becoming more competitive with Hollywood competitors. Such improvement makes it easier for Korean movie theaters to meet the quota rule profitably — though perhaps not as profitably as a free-trade-in-movies regime.

For Korea, most economic gains likely will arise from improved allocative efficiency, *i.e.*, the deployment of factors of production in a more efficient manner than before. Notably, most of the Korean business community supported the idea of an FTA with the U.S. They included exporters of autos, cell phones, computer chips, and other consumer goods. They advocated coverage of e-commerce, and non-discriminatory, duty-free treatment for digital products. But, they complained of not only American tariff barriers, but also non-tariff barriers such as complex technical regulations and sanitary measures, inefficient customs procedures, and of protectionist government procurement practices. An FTA could address their complaints. A March 2006 study by the Korea Institute for Economic Policy showed a net gain from an FTA of 2 percent in Korea's GDP, and a net employment boost of 0.36 percent (equal to 100,000 jobs).

Not surprisingly, there also was significant opposition within Korea to *KORUS*. The Korean International Trade Association (a business association representing over 90,000 companies) listed 312 tariff lines — or 33.4 percent of Korea's total imports — as sensitive. Opposition was especially strong among agricultural constituencies, which virtually ruled out full, immediate, duty free coverage of this sector. For instance, Korea ultimately agreed to eliminate its 40 percent tariff on beef, but only over 15 years.

The Korean government subsidizes heavily its farm sector. The Korean Rural Economic Institute said in a March 2006 study that an FTA would cause a U.S. $1 billion decrease in Korean agricultural production, an increase in imports from $1.9 to $2.3 billion, and a decline from 140,000 to 20,000 jobs. While the farm sector is not globally competitive, it is politically powerful. Over time, that power is likely to wane. The contribution of agriculture to the Korean economy (measured as a percentage of GNP) is shrinking. Korean farmers are aging — over 70 percent of them are over age 50. In part to address this opposition, the Korean Ministry of Commerce, Industry, and Energy (MOCIE) announced in April 2006 it would implement rules to provide trade adjustment assistance worth $3 billion over the first decade of operation of an FTA with the U.S. The help would include a corporate turnaround fund, job placement, and subsidized loans.

Interestingly, in April 2004 Korea's first FTA — with Chile — took effect. The deal, signed on 15 February 2003, includes agricultural products (albeit non-threatening products). Korea negotiated with Chile, and for coverage of agriculture, as a strategy for developing an FTA with Japan. It hoped the *Korea — Chile FTA* might be a useful precedent for a deal with Japan. However, Korea did not have an easy time in negotiating agricultural trade liberalization with Chile. Among other products, Chile exports apples and grapes. Korea produces a modest volume of apples. Still, Korean apple farmers banded together with other domestic farmers, and joined forces with labor unions. This organized heterogeneity opposed not only the FTA with Chile, but also with Japan. They even opposed an FTA with Singapore, which is not an agricultural exporter. In brief, the *Korea — Chile FTA* galvanized disparate opponents in Korea, and the FTA did not prove to be an easy entrée into further FTAs. The same phenomenon occurred in Japan, with respect to an FTA with Singapore. Japanese economic reformers focused on an FTA with Singapore, presuming or hoping it would not engender domestic agricultural opposition. In fact, Japanese farmers saw through the Korean-style strategy — that one FTA would be used as leverage for another, and the next one would materially affect their interests. Consequently, they opposed the *Japan — Singapore FTA*. They could not block it, and it was signed on 13 January 2002 and entered into force on 30 November 2002.

To be sure, there are domestic political interests in the U.S. that made *KORUS* politically difficult, even if it would be economically rational. One example is the T&A industry, which sought a yarn-forward rule of origin to ensure virtually the entire production process occur in Korea for a T&A product to qualify as originating within the *KORUS* region. Their views were heard, as *KORUS* includes a yarn forward rule (meaning Korean producers must use Korean or U.S. yarn and continue thereafter with originating materials and processes), as well as a special textile safeguard remedy for temporary relief from Korean T&A articles shown to damage U.S. producers.

American steel producers are another example, as are some manufacturers, especially of electronics. They tend to be less competitive than their Korean counterparts, oppose free trade with Korea. They are wont to deploy trade remedies against these competitors. Korea argues the U.S. is too zealous in using antidumping (AD) and countervailing duty (CVD) remedies, especially against Korean semiconductor and steel producers. For instance, in May 2003 there were 23 American AD and CVD orders against Korea. (Interestingly, about 18 of them were against steel and steel products, suggesting Korea does not have a "trade remedy problem" with the U.S., but rather a "steel problem.") From the Korean perspective, an FTA with the U.S. ought to discipline use of trade remedies. To ask how that perspective would be regarded on Capitol Hill is to intimate the obvious answer.

Overall, there is considerable trade friction between the U.S. and Korea. In its 2003 *National Trade Estimate Report on Foreign Trade Barriers* (*NTE*), the USTR published 23 pages of complaints — more than any other country with which the U.S. contemplated an FTA, and behind only Japan, China, and the EU. Moreover, there is significant anti-American sentiment in Korea. In 1989, the U.S. International Trade Commission (ITC) conducted a study on a *KORUS*. The ITC concluded the idea was a bad one, because it would provoke a large increase in anti-American sentiment in Korea. Roughly two decades later, that sentiment has increased. It is a political guess as to whether the FTA might bring exacerbate emotions, or might reduce them by linking the countries closer economically.

V. NATIONAL SECURITY CRITERIA

A. No Bright Line

It is difficult to put the national security case for an FTA more directly than did Humayun Akhtar Khan, Pakistan's Minister of Commerce, to the U.S. authorities in August 2006. A bilateral deal would be

> part of the global "war on terror." [That is because] an agreement with the U.S. would create thousands of jobs in Pakistan, and be a powerful weapon in the "international fight against extremism."[13]

Minister Khan was re-stating a proposal for a *U.S. — Pakistan FTA* first raised by President Pervez Musharraf with President George W. Bush in December 2004. As Minister Khan said in August 2006,

> President Musharraf is very clear that the long-term solution to ending the extremism problem in Pakistan is to economically improve [*sic*] Pakistan.[14]

The U.S. has countered that establishing "Reconstruction Opportunity Zones," or "ROZs," on the border between Afghanistan and Pakistan might resolve the problem. The U.S. would give products originating in an ROZ duty-free treatment from the U.S. Is an ROZ a better, or distant second-best, solution to an FTA with a country on the front lines in the war on terror?

If the case — which, put succinctly, is the adage that idle hands are the devil's playmate — is so compelling, then why do FTAs between the U.S., on the one hand, and the likes of Afghanistan, the Kingdom of Saudi Arabia,

---

[13] Krishna Guha, *Pakistan Hopeful of U.S. Trade Pact*, Financial Times, 7 Aug. 2006.

[14] Christopher S. Rugaber, *Pakistani Commerce Minister Urges U.S. To Consider Pakistan Free Trade Agreement*, 23 Int'l Trade Rep. (BNA) 1195 (10 Aug. 2006).

Yemen, as well as Pakistan, not yet exist? One obvious answer is opposition from American producers that make products like or directly competitive with foreign goods. In 2006, Gary C. Hufbauer published *Sustaining Reform With a U.S. — Pakistan Free Trade Agreement*, a book on the possible economic effects of a bilateral deal. Each country imposes high tariffs on imports from the other country, and a bilateral deal might boost two-way trade by 40-50 percent. The T&A sector in Pakistan would be a key beneficiary — its exports could rise by U.S. $1 billion, and 200,000 new jobs in that sector could be created. Because many Pakistan workers support up to 6 family members, over 1 million Pakistanis might experience positive knock-on effects. But, opposition from the American T&A industry would be stiff. Should that opposition block a deal that looks to be in America's national security interest? Or, might it be said American jobs are the security interest at stake?

Another, albeit partial, consideration may be extracted from FTA examples. There is no bright line between an economic, political, and national security assessment of an RTA. That is especially true for the U.S. Accounting for roughly 25 percent of world GNP (and higher on PPP terms), the U.S. has economic — and concomitant political — interests in every region of the world. It must pursue balance among different regions in establishing and strengthening its FTA networks. Put bluntly, the global superpower must not be a regional FTA player, and must fashion its FTA policy in conjunction with its national security interests. It may be ventured that every FTA or CU the U.S. even contemplates has a national security dimension. In the post-9/11 world, the U.S. is explicit that it expects from any prospective FTA partner cooperation — or better — on foreign policy and security matters.

Consider the *U.S. — Peru Trade Promotion Agreement* (*PTPA*), signed in April 2006. One argument for the deal was it would support Peru in the Andean region, which is plagued by economic and political instability, including narco-terrorism, which threaten U.S. security. The causal nexus is the *PTPA* would be part of a strengthened, transparent legal framework for trade and FDI, and such economic activity would generate employment opportunities in Peru, enlarging the number of people with a stake in the *status quo*. The same argument was made by the U.S. in favor of the *U.S. — Colombia TPA* concluded in February 2006.

As another example, consider *KORUS*. It implicates not only the economic, political, and political economy criteria discussed earlier, but also strengthen the military alliance between the two nations. What effect might it have on containing North Korea, or on reunification of the Korean Peninsula? In May 2006, preparing for the first round of FTA talks with the U.S., held in June, the Korean Ministry of Foreign Affairs and Trade (MOFAT) declared it would call for rules of origin that could facilitate reunification. Specifically, it said the U.S. should recognize as of South Korean origin merchandise any goods made in Kaesong.

Kaesong is a city and large inter-Korean industrial zone close to, but on the North Korean side of, the demilitarized zone (DMZ). It is about one hour drive from Seoul, across the DMZ. About 40 South Korean companies (as of August 2006) have built factories in the Kaesong Industrial Complex, which was set up in June 2003. The Kaesong factories produce consumer goods, including clothing and kitchenware. Labor costs are far cheaper there than in South Korea. In June 2006, the South Korean government decided to provide state-backed credit guarantees to firms that do so. A South Korean firm can get receive a payment guarantee for up to U.S. $10.4 million for establishing production facility in Kaesong. The terms are generous.[15] The guarantee costs between 0.5 and 3 percent of the amount of the secured loan. The guarantee period is up to 7 years for a bank loan that funds up to 70 percent of an investment expenditure.

In FTA talks during 2006, American negotiators told Korea it would apply any accord only to U.S. and South Korean territory, and not allow products made in North Korea to receive preferential treatment. In an August 2006 C-SPAN television interview, the USTR, Susan Schwab, rather rudely intoned: "It won't happen, can't happen. That won't change."[16] Following the October 2006 North Korean nuclear test, South Korea indicated some flexibility. As Tae-Sik Lee, South Korea's Ambassador to the U.S. said:

> When we started these negotiations, we wanted to include it [Kaesong] in the FTA, but as time goes by we have noticed that the atmosphere has been shifting rather negatively against this idea. That is why we are squeezing our wisdom to find some way out.[17]

Query whether the hard line American position is a cause or consequence, that is, whether it exacerbates or is the effect of differences between the U.S. and North Korea over not only nuclear weapons, but also human rights. Is the "wisdom" to be "squeezed" really about the long-standing theoretical debate over whether to constructively engage an enemy or isolate a country on the axis of evil? Further, is the U.S. position consistent?

Ultimately, Korea and the U.S. reached a compromise for Kaesong. The *KORUS* rules of origin forbid Kaesong products from entry. However, *KORUS* creates a bilateral commission, which meets annually, to consider "outward processing zones." One such zone could be Kaesong. The commission considers whether conditions on the Korean Peninsula warrant preferential treatment for products from a zone. The commission establishes criteria — including labor practices — that a product from a zone must meet before qualifying as originating, and then recommends to Congress and the Korean National Assembly that *KORUS* be amended to include goods from the appropriate zone.

The *U.S. — Singapore FTA* has a precedent for inclusion of special economic zones (SEZs) outside the territory of the parties. In that *FTA*, goods made on Batam and Bintam Islands, Indonesia, just off the coast of Singapore, may qualify for preferential treatment. Finally, is the American position politically tenable, given that Korea successfully negotiated an extension of duty-free treatment for Kaesong goods in its FTA with Singapore in 2004, its FTA with the *European Free Trade Association (EFTA)* in 2005, and *ASEAN* in 2006?

[15] *See* James Lim, *South Korea Plans to Extend Guarantees To Firms in North Korean Industrial Zone*, 23 Int'l Trade Rep. (BNA) 983 (29 June 2006).

[16] Gary G. Yerkey, *U.S. Rejects South Korean Bid to Include North Korean Products in Free Trade Pact*, 23 Int'l Trade Rep. (BNA) 1255 (24 Aug. 2006).

[17] Krishna Guha, *Trade Pact Urged for U.S. and S. Korea*, Financial Times, 23 Oct. 2006, at 2.

National security is more than just a criterion for establishing an FTA. It also may be an over-riding exception to all obligations in an FTA. In the 2006 *U.S. — Bahrain* and *U.S. — Oman FTAs*, the following "Essential Security" provision exists:

> [Nothing in the agreement] shall be construed . . . to preclude [either party to the FTA] from applying measures that it considers necessary for the fulfillment of its obligations with respect to the maintenance or restoration of its international peace or security or the protection of its own essential security interests.[18]

This language also exists in the U.S. FTAs with Bahrain, Chile, and Morocco, and in *CAFTA—DR*. The U.S. considers the Essential Security provision to be self-judging, and thus applicable unilaterally. No doubt this provision will be part of any future FTA, for example, with the United Arab Emirates (UAE). Its key terms appear to be self-judging, and thus could apply in a wide range of contexts. Consider the March 2006 dispute over the ultimately unsuccessful takeover by Dubai Ports (DP) World of several port management facilities in several east coast ports. Would the above language immunize from legal action the U.S., were it to block acquisition of its port facilities by a foreign company?

B.   Case Studies: *MEFTA*, Morocco, and Australia

To what extent do and should national security criteria predominate, or at least play a role in, choosing RTA partners? The American strategy, articulated in May 2003 by President George W. Bush, to achieve a *Middle East Free Trade Area (MEFTA)* by 2013, certainly follow this logic. Underlying these *MEFTA* is a belief in a causal nexus leading from free trade to economic growth, then to social and political stability, and then to political reform. As envisioned by President George W. Bush, a MEFTA could bring prosperity and democracy to a region in which Islamic extremists define a future that resembles the Dark Ages of Europe. Toward this end, the U.S. has built a network of FTAs with the likes of Bahrain, Jordan, and Morocco.

Consider, for instance, the *U.S. — Morocco FTA*. Morocco is a middle-income developing country, with roughly the same *per capita* GNP as Egypt (U.S. $1,300). Morocco is not a large market for U.S. products. But, American exporters certainly prefer duty-free access to that market than the average MFN tariff Morocco imposes of 34 percent. In fact, such treatment puts the Americans on a level playing field with their European competitors. Because of an association agreement between the EU and Morocco, all tariffs on industrial trade between the EU and Morocco are scheduled to fall to zero by 2012.

Still, from the American side, national security was a (if not the) prime criterion, in the FTA. Morocco has a long history of friendship with the U.S., which the FTA cements. For decades, Moroccan foreign policy has urged restraint by Israelis and Palestinians. Morocco also has a demonstrable record of fighting terrorism. For the U.S., the FTA logic was to help accelerate economic development, and thereby alleviate economic conditions that may

---

[18] *See Bahrain FTA*, Chapter 20 (Exceptions), Article 20:2; *Oman FTA*, Chapter 21 (Exceptions), Article 21:2.

breed extremist behavior. Ultimately, whether the logic is fanciful depends on domestic economic and political reform, infrastructure development, and the enhancement of legal capacity, in Morocco itself. Without such change, the full benefits of an FTA are not attainable.

Interestingly, from the perspective of Morocco, an FTA with the U.S. satisfied more than national security criteria. Morocco saw an FTA with the U.S. as an opportunity to gain leverage with the EU. The largest trading partners for Morocco (as of May 2003) are France (to which Morocco ships 34 percent of its exports, and from which Morocco obtains 24 percent of its imports), Spain (13 and 10 percent, respectively, of exports and imports), and the U.S. (3 and 6 percent, respectively). Consequently, the prospect of an FTA with the U.S. created for Morocco the risk of trade diversion from the EU to the U.S., and a loss of tariff revenue collected on American products. Morocco viewed this scenario as an opportunity, however. It could bargain more aggressively with the EU, at least subtly playing it and the U.S. off against each other.

National security also is the logic of the post-9/11 U.S. deal with Australia. The "Lucky Country" is a key American ally in the War on Terror, and in countering if not containing Chinese expansionism. That is, it is naïve to see the *U.S. — Australia FTA* as something other than a device for America to cement a strategic military relationship. Indeed, sometimes it is bluntly observed that Australia has embraced the role scripted for it by the U.S. — Deputy Sheriff in the Asia-Pacific region. In contrast, New Zealand was not included in these *FTA* talks. New Zealand's stance on the Iraq War, and its desire to remain nuclear free, explain why. New Zealand did not support the U.S. position in 2003 in the United Nations Security Council with respect to the use of force in Iraq. Moreover, New Zealand prohibits U.S. Navy ships that are nuclear powered or nuclear armed from docking in its ports. Similarly, the *U.S. — Singapore FTA* was signed at the White House on 6 May 2003. While the *Chile FTA* was ready for signature, the U.S. deferred signature for a month, until 6 June 2003. Chile did not support the U.S. position in the Security Council on war in Iraq. The diplomatic affront had little practical effect, however, as both FTAs entered into force on 1 January 2004. Is it wise to define FTA policy by opposition to a specific war or nuclear weapons generally?

VI. COMPETITIVE IMPERIALISM

A. U.S. — EU Competition

Emphasis in American trade policy on FTAs is more than merely curious. Possibly, it is a watershed shift in U.S. foreign policy. Before the Uruguay Round, the U.S. regarded RTAs as the work of the devil, and the GATT as the exorcist. American leadership guaranteed the multilateral trading system as the foundation of the global economic order, and consistently pushed for non-discriminatory trade relations and progressive lowering and binding of trade barriers. However, since that Round, and especially since the late 1990s, the U.S. has pursued FTAs with the zeal of a recent convert.[19] From the U.S. perspective, the EU started the FTA race and continues to sprint.

For example, in May 2006, the EU launched FTA talks with Central America, and pushed for an FTA with the 10-country *Association of South East Asian Nations (ASEAN)*.[20] It also pursued strengthened trade links with the Andean Community, consisting of Bolivia, Colombia, Peru, Ecuador, and (until April 2006) Venezuela. In September 2006, EU Trade Commissioner Peter Mandelson called for a "Global Europe Strategy" that entails a "more 'activist' approach to opening foreign markets by negotiating FTAs, particularly with Asian nations" such as India, Korea, as well as *ASEAN*.[21] French Foreign Trade Minister Christine Lagarde not only echoed his call, urging a "more active, more pragmatic, and better prepared" FTA policy than in the past, but added a key reason for the change: the U.S. is "aggressively pursuing bilateral and regional deals, so France and Europe must join in, or risk being left behind."[22]

Put aside the inconvenient chronology in some instances that might undermine the American case for zeal in reaction to European perfidy, including a de facto moratorium on bilateral deals the EU implemented after violent anti-free trade protests at the November 1999 WTO Ministerial Conference in Seattle.[23] In March 2006 the *Central American Free Trade Agreement (CAFTA or CAFTA—DR)* entered (partially) into force, suggesting the EU may be sprinting to catch up. Indeed, in October 2006 EU governments and European businesses expressed concern they were falling behind the U.S. in the race to sign developing countries up to FTAs.[24] In other instances, the race might be rather too close to call. In December 2005, the U.S. completed FTA negotiations with Peru, and did so with respect to Colombia in February 2006.

These deals, in the words of Venezuelan President Hugo Chavez, "mortally wounded" the Community.[25] In one technical sense, he was correct. Those *FTAs* complicated the efforts of the Community to adopt a common tariff. Without a common tariff, it would be unlikely it could negotiate a trade accord with the EU. Had the U.S. effectively blocked EU efforts by dividing and

---

[19] Among the countries the website of the United States Trade Representative lists as ones with which the U.S. is pursing FTAs as of March 2007 are several Arab Muslim countries, plus Korea (negotiations commenced in 2004), Malaysia (negotiations commenced in June 2006), and Thailand (negotiations commenced in 2004).

[20] Jason Gutierrez, *Mandelson Says European Union to Discuss Free Trade Agreement with ASIAN Members*, 23 INT'L TRADE REP. (BNA) 763-64 (18 May 2006); David Haskel, *EU, Central America Agree to Start Talks On Free Trade; Mercosur, Andean Talks Stall*, 23 INT'L TRADE REP. (BNA) 766-67 (18 May 2006).

[21] Gary G. Yerkey, *EU Needs to Take More "Activist" Approach To Trade, Launch New FTAs, Mandelson Says*, 23 INT'L TRADE REP. (BNA) 1366 (21 Sept. 2006).

[22] Lawrence J. Speer, *France to Push EU for Bilateral, Regional Trade Deals as WTO Talks Founder*, 23 INT'L TRADE REP. (BNA) 1407 (28 Sept. 2006).

[23] *See* Juliane von Reppert-Bismark, *EU Is To Focus on Bilateral Deals After Failed Global Trade Talks*, WALL ST. J., 2 Oct. 2006, at A4.

[24] *See id.*

[25] Lucien O. Chauvin, *Ecuador Disrupted by Free Trade Talks with United States; Andean Pact Threatened*, 23 INT'L TRADE REP. (BNA) 640 (6 April 2006).

conquering the Andes? In August 2006, the U.S. signed a *Trade and Investment Framework Agreement (TIFA)* with *ASEAN*.[26] The following month the EU approved exploratory FTA talks with *ASEAN*, launching them formally in May 2007. In sum, it is open to question whether U.S. moves are preemptive or reactive. The best answers probably are "both" and "it depends on the case." Never mind, however, from an official U.S. perspective: the truth is or must be EU behavior justifies American zeal for FTAs.

For the U.S., then, traditionally, RTAs were a tool of the weak, like the original European Community (EC) nations. Now, it is a tool in the hands of a large, potent counterweight to the U.S. on the world stage. So, it must also be in the toolkit of the largest and most powerful economy, the U.S. The need to counter preferential inroads of others, particularly major industrial countries, now is a lodestar of American trade policy.

Should "pre-emption" or "rebuttal" (depending on the vantage point) be a criterion for entering into an FTA? That is, should countering the trade strategy of another country be a motive for negotiating an FTA? To put the question provocatively, are FTAs a tool used by hegemonic trading nations in their race against one another to create neo-colonialist spheres of influence in developing and least developed regions, and thereby vie for economic and political influence with one another? The *Financial Times*, hardly leftist leaning, suggests the possibility, commenting that bilateral trade deals "have tended to be heavily tilted in favor of the powerful and decked out like Christmas trees with provisions for special interests."[27] In brief, do competitive liberalization and economic, political economy, political, and national security criteria explain FTAs? Or, are FTAs really about competition among imperialist powers?

Overall (as of May 2003), the EU has approximately 30 RTAs, with at least four additional accords under active negotiations. For example, in the Middle East, EU RTA policy proceeds on three tracks:

1. *Euro-Med Agreements*:

These association agreements are between the EU and individual countries in the Mediterranean region, including Algeria, Egypt, Israel, Jordan, Lebanon, Morocco, the Palestinian Authority, and Tunisia. They are streamlined so as to be similar in substantive content, thereby establishing a template-like arrangement between each country and the EU.

2. *The Agadir Agreement*:

This *Agreement* is between the EU, on the one hand, and Egypt, Jordan, Morocco, and Tunisia, on the other hand. It bears some resemblance to the *Euro-Med Agreement*, and in effect constitutes a subset of them. However, the *Agadir Agreement* is structured to form the basis of an FTA among the four countries. Whether the EU plans to be part of this FTA is unclear.

---

[26] *See* Jonathan Hopfner, *ASEAN, U.S. Ink Trade, Investment Pact; Pledge to Work for Breakthrough on Doha*, 23 International Trade Reporter (BNA) 1296-97 (7 September 2006); John Burton, *Washington Signs Pact with ASEAN Nations*, Financial Times, 26-28 August 2006, at 5.

[27] *Bilateral Trade Deals: A Dangerous Affair*, Financial Times, 27 July 2006, at 12.

3. *GCC FTA*:

This FTA, which the EU pursues, is a traditional one between the EU and GCC.

Given EU activism in the RTA field, American companies feel disadvantaged, and demand of their government a leveling of the competitive playing field. Arguably, *MEFTA*, a vision articulated by President George W. Bush in May 2003, and U.S. negotiations with the *Southern African Customs Union (SACU)*, consisting of Botswana, Lesotho, Namibia, South Africa, and Swaziland, launched in 2003, are a response to this call, and thereby an effort to counter European economic (and, in turn, political) influence in the Islamic and developing world. To be sure, official U.S. rhetoric often casts RTAs as in the self-interest of poor countries. Seventy percent of the tariffs paid by developing countries are paid to other developing countries. Surely, then, the USTR does poor countries a favor by pushing a zero-tariff regime.

Maybe, depending partly on whether those countries can offset the loss of tariff revenue with other sources of government funding, such as income taxes. Questions of structural reform aside, the fact is the job of the USTR is to promote American economic interests. An FTA with the U.S. is neither an entitlement nor an act of charity. It must (or ought to) be a net benefit to each party. As for American economic interests, they are a component of a larger foreign policy agenda. That is true for the EU. In the Mediterranean region, EU RTAs are motivated strongly by geo-political and economic factors, and EU trade policy has out run and out maneuvered U.S. trade policy.

Notably, the EU has an association agreement with Egypt. Under the EU — Egypt deal, Egypt is phasing out its tariffs on EU products over 3, 9, 12, and 15 years (depending on the merchandise). Obviously, if and when fully implemented, this and other such accords will supplement the already considerable economic, and concomitant political, influence of the EU in the Arab world. The U.S. cannot remain idle.

American exporters would be disadvantaged if only their European competitors had duty-free market access to these regions. Likewise, U.S. producers needing inputs from these regions would face higher costs relative to foreign competitors if the competitors, but not them, could import inputs free of duty. One end result would be a diminution of political leverage in the Middle East relative to the EU. Political realists and energy strategists would point out the importance of such leverage, especially as China and India add themselves in the mix with the EU and U.S. as competitors for strategic resources held by some Middle Eastern nations — oil and natural gas.

A similar argument can be made with respect to U.S. negotiations with *SACU*, namely, that they are designed to counter economic (and, in turn, political) influence of the EU in this resource-rich part of the Third World. The EU and Asia heavily dominate the pattern of trade of Southern African countries, with *NAFTA* a distant third. The EU has long-standing preferential arrangements in place with most Sub-Saharan African countries, including the *Lomé* and *Cotonou Conventions*. In 1999, the EU and *SACU*, which is comprised of Botswana, Lesotho, Namibia, South Africa, and Swaziland, entered into an FTA — though the deal is not a comprehensive one.

Here, again, the U.S. cannot stand idly by. Aside from foreign policy benefits of a *SACU FTA*, there are potential economic benefits for the U.S. From *SACU*, the U.S. imports auto parts, diamonds, and platinum for catalytic converters. An FTA would introduce the discipline of rules of origin for such imports. U.S. exports to *SACU* have not grown much. An FTA might help boost exports. To be sure, the margin of preference would decline, because *SACU* members are reducing their tariffs, and incline toward free-trade orientation, as many of their exports are sold outside Southern Africa. The U.S. also might see greater access to services markets and enhanced IP protection. The latter point suggests consumers in *SACU* could be obligated to pay higher prices for IP products that their governments now allow them to buy at cheap prices, or even provide for free. In effect, they would pay the rents to U.S. IP holders, which the U.S. would regard as a condition for increased market access for *SACU* exports (especially T&A), and which would give the U.S. increased economic influence in *SACU*.

How would *SACU* benefit from an FTA with the U.S., especially if the U.S. does not maintain its July 2005 commitment to exercise flexibility in the negotiations? If *SACU* adroitly leverages negotiations with the EU and U.S., then it might win better market access concessions for agricultural and non-agricultural goods, and obtain reasonable provisions on IP protection, from both powers than it would have from isolated talks. An FTA with the U.S. also would be a hedge for *SACU* against expiration of the *African Growth and Opportunity Act (AGOA)*, the U.S. trade preference program for Sub-Saharan Africa.[28] Finally, *SACU* members would gain duty free access for T&A exports to the U.S. Such access would help them in view of the 31 December 2004 expiration of quotas under the *Multi-Fibre Agreement (MFA)*, pursuant to the WTO *Agreement on Textiles and Clothing (ATC)*. T&A exports from *SACU* to the U.S. were not quota-constrained, but MFA expiry meant the loss of guaranteed market access and competition with the likes of China and India.

In practice, however, whether *SACU* realizes the full potential of an FTA depends on two important questions. First, will *SACU* dedicate itself to internal reform, especially expanding its regime to include agriculture, services, and government procurement? American businesses have a keen interest in exporting farm products, and providing services, overseas. Yet, *SACU* provides duty-free treatment only for goods. That is, *SACU* is a common policy on industrial tariffs. If *SACU* as a group does not enlarge its regime, then the undesirable result may be hub-and-spoke arrangements with the U.S., with the U.S. at the hub, and specific spoke arrangements tailored for individual *SACU* members on agriculture and services. Also, American businesses are interested in bidding on government procurement projects abroad. Traditionally, *SACU* has shown a strong preference for doling out contracts to local suppliers in a non-transparent manner.

Second, will *SACU* build the institutional and legal capacity to follow through on its own commitments, and enforce obligations incumbent on the U.S.? Poor capacity is a great constraint on Sub-Saharan African development. Preferential rules of origin are just one illustration in which *SACU* will need

---

[28] *See* Gary G. Yerkey, *U.S., SACU Agree to Create "Framework" But Free Trade Agreement Now Longer Term*, 23 INT'L TRADE REP. (BNA) 621-22 (20 April 2006).

an expanded cadre of trade lawyers. With the 1999 *EU — SACU FTA*, an accord between *SACU* and the *Southern African Development Community* (*SADC*), and an FTA with the U.S., exporters and importers will need sound counsel on three different sets of origin rules to take advantage of duty free treatment.

These two questions are poignant in light of a theme emerging from some economic analyses, including by the World Bank, of the effects of the Uruguay Round on the Third World. That theme is most of the positive economic benefits from the Round came from liberalization entered into by developing and least developed countries. In other words, internal reforms, not gains through greater exports, are the predominant source of benefits from a Round — and, by extension, an FTA.

Consider, too, trade coverage of the U.S. FTAs — with Canada and Mexico through *NAFTA*, most Central American countries (Costa Rica, El Salvador, Guatemala, Honduras, Nicaragua, plus the Dominican Republic) via *CAFTA—DR*, and bilaterally with Australia, Bahrain, Chile, Israel, Morocco, Jordan, and Singapore. These FTAs cover roughly one-third of total American trade (mostly accounted for by *NAFTA*). The U.S. has pursued additional FTAs that would push the figure up to about half of its total trade. Query whether the strategy is to develop a two-tier structure whereby MFN rates apply to European products, and preferential rates apply to merchandise from the FTA partners. Lest the question sound preposterous, consider the fact the EU has done just that with respect to the U.S. The number of RTAs and preferential arrangements in which the EU is involved is so large the EU has MFN relations with only seven countries. That is, for imports into the EU, MFN rates apply only to goods from Australia, Canada, China, Japan, New Zealand, Taiwan, and the U.S. Goods from the rest of the world enter under an RTA or an assistance scheme for poor countries.

As another example of one trade power using an FTA to rebut another, consider the *U.S. — Chile FTA*, signed in June 2003. Chile has a unified and uniform MFN tariff rate of 6 percent. (Admirable as that is to free traders, Singapore has no tariffs on most items.) U.S. Exporters wanted to eliminate this duty on merchandise they shipped to Chile. They were losing market share to Canadian exporters, under an FTA already in existence between Canada and Chile. For example, Caterpillar, Inc., complained to the USTR that one of its machines imported into Chile was disadvantaged by about U.S. $13,000-14,000, relative to Canadian like products, because of the Chilean duty. The disadvantage also hurt Idaho potato farmers in their competition with Canadians to export their merchandise — used, of course, in French fries — to Chile. Not surprisingly, the U.S. responded with an FTA with Chile.

B. Competition from Japan

Yet another example of competition for FTAs among major trading nations is a dramatic alteration by Japan of its historic and exclusive emphasis on multilateralism. In the late 1990s, Japan began to explore, both informally and formally, FTAs. In 2002, Japan and *ASEAN* signed a "Comprehensive Partnership." Japan has a keen interest building with *ASEAN* an East Asian

FTA (*EAFTA*), which would link it with China, (including Hong Kong), Korea, and Taiwan — and, possibly, Australia, New Zealand, and India.[29] Surely, Japan took note of the lack of progress toward an FTA with the U.S., coupled with U.S. pursuit of deals with countries other than Japan. In April 2006, Japan proposed creation of an East Asian economic and trade area that would easily rival the sizes of *NAFTA* and EU by embracing 16 East Asian countries, including all 10 members of *ASEAN*, thereby covering about one half of the global population.[30] These efforts have led to FTAs between Japan and Singapore, Malaysia, the Philippines, and Thailand.

Significantly, in May 2007, Japan reached a basic FTA with *ASEAN*, which the countries signed in November of that year.[31] Under the *ASEAN — Japan Economic Partnership Agreement* (*EPA*), Japan agreed to eliminate tariffs on 92 percent of *ASEAN* goods. However, it excluded rice, sugar, and other sensitive agricultural products. The *ASEAN* nations, except for the four newest and poorest ones — Burma (Myanmar), Cambodia, Laos, and Vietnam — agreed to eliminate tariffs on 90 percent of imports from Japan within 10 years. Vietnam pledged to do so within 10-15 years, and Burma, Cambodia, and Laos promised to phase out the tariffs on a 15 year schedule. The *EPA* modifies preferential rules of origin to stimulate intra-*ASEAN* trade and investment by qualifying traded components as originating. Suppose a Japanese manufacturer exports and processes an industrial part to Thailand, and then exports the processed product to Malaysia. Before the *EPA*, Malaysia deemed the finished good originating outside *ASEAN*. With the *EPA*, Malaysia counts it as originating in the bloc, subjecting it to the intra-*ASEAN* duty rate of zero to 5 percent.

Most notably, in respect of competitive imperialism, the *ASEAN — Japan EPA* is an FTA with 650 million people — larger than either *NAFTA* or the EU. The fact Japan excludes intentionally the U.S. is testament to its competition with the U.S., and perhaps also to America's declining influence in East Asia. Indeed, Japan explicitly seeks to enlarge the *EPA* to include China and Korea, which would result in a massive counterweight to the U.S., *NAFTA*, and EU. Interestingly, the *EPA* also spotlights Sino — Japanese competition. In 2006, for the first time since the Second World War, China (excluding Hong Kong) overtook the U.S. as Japan's largest trading partner.[32] (With Hong Kong counted, China did so in 2004.) The trade is diversified, with China exporting to Japan clothes, computers, and certain electronics, and Japan sending China communications equipment, other types of electronics, and organic compounds. But, Japan could not watch China deepen its integration with *ASEAN*, and obtain preferential access through a possible FTA with *ASEAN*, without seeking that same access.

---

[29] *See* Jonathan Hopfner, *ASEAN Ministers Cool to Japanese Proposal to Begin Studying Regional Free Trade Zone*, 23 INT'L TRADE REP. (BNA) 1297-98 (7 Sept. 2006).

[30] *See* Toshio Aritake, *Japan to Propose Economic, Trade Area to Rival NAFTA, European Union*, 23 INT'L TRADE REP. (BNA) 572 (13 April 2006).

[31] *See* Toshio Aritake, *Japan, ASEAN Strike "Basic" Free Trade Deal to Abolish 90 Percent of Tariffs in 10 Years*, 24 INT'L TRADE REP. (BNA) 650 (10 May 2007).

[32] *See* Toshio Aritake, *China Overtakes U.S. as Japan's Top Trade Partner in Fiscal 2006*, 24 INT'L TRADE REP. (BNA) 624 (3 May 2007); Michiyo Nakamoto, *China Overtakes U.S. in Trade with Japan*, FINANCIAL TIMES, 26 April 2007, at 5.

Also significant is the fact Japan's FTA strategy is global. Japan has a bilateral economic partnership agreement with Mexico. In September 2006, Japan and Chile agreed to a framework for an FTA that would eliminate tariffs on most products, covering 92 percent of bilateral trade (by value), with the notable exception of agriculture, over 10 years.[33] Also that month, Japan commenced FTA negotiations with the GCC.[34] Japan obtains all of its crude oil from abroad, 75 percent of which comes from the GCC. It also exports a sizeable volume of industrial products, including autos, appliances, and electronics, to the GCC. The outlines of a deal were apparent: Japan could abolish its tariffs on crude oil, as well as refined oil products, and the GCC could eliminate the 5-10 percent tariffs it levies on Japanese products.

The Philippine accord, signed in September 2006 after negotiations commenced in February 2004, is commercially noteworthy for its coverage, and its treatment of sensitive sectors and immigration.[35] Upon entry into force, the *Japan — Philippines FTA* immediately lifts duties on 97 percent of Japanese exports to the Philippines, including apples, grapes, pears, and other fruit, and 60 percent of Japanese steel imports. It cuts to zero immediately duties on 92 percent of Philippine exports to Japan — a significant boon to Japanese companies, for which the Philippines is a manufacturing base for semi-finished goods. Those companies make electrical products and machinery in the Philippines, and then export them to Japan (or third countries) for further work. The *FTA* gives Japan 10 years to phase out tariffs on Philippine bananas, and allows Japan to set a tariff-free quota for pineapples of 1,000 tons annually (growing to 1,800 tons in 5 years). The *FTA* also gives Japan 5 years to eliminate duties on tuna and bonito fish, as well as cut tariffs and set low-tariff quotas on chickens and sugar. The Philippines can retain until 2010 its 30 percent tariff on vehicles with an engine size of 3 liters or less, with renegotiations on the rate in 2009, but must eliminate duties on vehicles of larger engine sizes by 2010. The Philippines is entitled to send laborers, including an initial number of 1,000 nursing care assistants, to Japan.

Of course, countering China sometimes impels U.S. trade policy proposals. In 1993, China announced its desire to join *ASEAN*, including the *ASEAN FTA*, also called "*AFTA*." Fearing American dominance, *ASEAN* excludes the U.S. In 2002, China came to an accord on *ASEAN* and *AFTA* membership. President George W. Bush reacted with an "Enterprise for *ASEAN* Initiative." Yet, the "EAI" has been ineffectual.

C. Who Divides?

If competition among imperial powers underlies the drive for FTAs, then is there a danger it becomes enmeshed with, or at least perceived as, a "Divide and Conquer" strategy reminiscent of empires past? For example, would

---

[33] Toshio Aritake, *Japan, Chile Reach Framework For FTA on 92 Percent of Goods*, 23 INT'L TRADE REP. (BNA) 1411-12 (28 Sept. 2006).

[34] *See Japan, UAE to Try Speed Up EPA with GCC*, 24 INT'L TRADE REP. (BNA) 632 (3 May 2007); *Japan, GCC To Hold First FTA Meeting This Week*, KHALEEJ TIMES (UAE), 20 Sept. 2006, at 49.

[35] *See* Toshio Aritake, *Japan, Philippines Sign Free Trade Agreement After Differences Resolved*, 23 INT'L TRADE REP. (BNA) 1335 (14 Sept. 2006).

MEFTA — by design or effect — effectively vitiate the customs union envisaged by the GCC? Likewise, would a *Free Trade Area of the Americas* (*FTAA*) offset the power of *MERCOSUR*, and Brazil in particular? Competition even with Mexico, a *NAFTA* partner, may figure in the calculus. Mexico has a large number of FTAs, covering most of its export markets in Latin America, and is working on an accord with *MERCOSUR*.[36]

Or, to apply the phrase of Sir James Robertson, the British Civil Secretary, who in December 1951 wrote in his diary in the context of the Mahdist-Anti-Mahdist rivalry in the Sudan, would it be accurate to say: "They divide and we rule"?[37] In other words, if the major trading powers of today use RTAs as an instrument for prominence, and sometimes dominance, then what countries — the ruling or the ruled — do the dividing?

VII. THE *CAFTA—DR* CONCATENATION

It would be a grave error to believe the same criteria motivate all countries in every proposed or actual FTA or CU to negotiate with one another, and enter into a deal. In fact, any one country may have multiple justifications for seeking an RTA. Or, in the same RTA, one dominant motive may impel one country, whereas another reason may drive its partner in the bargain. In brief, a concatenation of economic and non-economic criteria may explain the genesis of, and be the sustenance for, an FTA or CU. To illustrate this point, consider *CAFTA—DR*.

The Presidents of five Central American countries — Costa Rica, El Salvador, Guatemala, Honduras, and Nicaragua — proposed the idea of an FTA when President Bill Clinton visited the region in 1997. Those Presidents called for enhanced benefits under the *Caribbean Basin Initiative* (*CBI*), a preferential trading arrangement sponsored by the U.S., or *NAFTA* parity, as a short-term measure, and an FTA as a long-term strategy. President Clinton explained to them that FTA negotiations were not possible at that juncture, given his lack of delegated trade negotiation authority from Congress. In 2002, during a visit to the Organization of American States (OAS), President George W. Bush announced he would pursue an FTA — and, by then, had the authority to do so.

Arguably, an FTA with the U.S. was the most significant pro-development idea to emerge from Central America in decades. Central America has a history of failure to achieve economic integration, dating as far back as independence from Mexico in the 1920s. The region has established every possible institution and accompanying bureaucracy to link the national economies closely, but none has generated substantive results. Border disputes stretching back decades occasionally turn into bloody clashes.

In every material respect, Costa Rica, El Salvador, Guatemala, Honduras, and Nicaragua are tiny relative to the U.S. These 5 countries (as of May 2005) have 12 percent of the population of the U.S., 4.5 percent of the territory of

---

[36] *See* Michael O'Boyle, *Mexico, Argentina Sign Accord to Expand Limited Free Trade, Will Continue Talks*, 23 INT'L TRADE REP. (BNA) 917 (15 June 2006).

[37] GLEN BALFOUR-PAUL, THE END OF EMPIRE IN THE MIDDLE EAST — BRITAIN'S RELINQUISHMENT OF POWER IN HER LAST THREE ARAB DEPENDENCIES 4 (1991).

the U.S., and 0.5 percent of the GDP of the U.S. Their combined GDP is about $59 billion, below that of Chile. From their perspective, the U.S. market is critical. Remittances from their expatriate workers (legal and illegal) in the U.S. are a significant source of income, and for some countries the largest source. The 5 countries ship 50 percent of their exports to the U.S., and 45 percent of their imports come from the U.S. The converse is not true. For the U.S., which is the fifth largest Spanish-speaking nation in the world, the 5 countries are commercially insignificant. They represent about 1 percent of total U.S. trade (exports and imports).

By suggesting an FTA, the Central American leaders signaled their interest in broad, deep integration with the U.S. and each other, as opposed to a five bilateral hub-and-spoke link with the U.S. as the hub, and their commitment to economic and legal reform. To be sure, an FTA never is or can be a panacea for poverty. Proper macroeconomic management, infrastructure development, pro-competitive policies, salubrious education and social policies, and legal capacity building are indispensable if trade liberalization is to assist in income generation and poverty reduction. What use, for example, is duty-free access to the giant American market if there is not enough reliable electricity to power factories to make goods for export, if workers are insufficiently trained to perform even semi-skilled manufacturing tasks, road networks from factories to ports are better suited for mules than container-carrying trucks, and the ports themselves are bedeviled with antiquated cranes and corrupt officials? Observe the link between this question and government procurement. A Chapter in *CAFTA—DR* on government procurement that encourages transparency in bidding and brings top-notch providers of infrastructure goods and services to the region would contribute to economic growth. Does *CAFTA—DR* provide for this result?

From the outset, Panama was not involved in the *CAFTA—DR* negotiations. It is relatively richer than the Costa Rica, El Salvador, Guatemala, Honduras, and Nicaragua. Ranked by the Human Development Index (HDI) among 173 countries (as of May 2003), the U.S. is 6, Costa Rica is 43, and El Salvador, Guatemala, Honduras, and Nicaragua all are below 100. Indeed, save for Panama and Costa Rica, poverty rates are higher in Central America than the rest of Latin America. Moreover, being service-oriented, the economy of Panama is structurally quite different from the rest of Central America. Services (such as banking and finance, and transportation) account for a far greater percentage, and agriculture and T&A far lesser percentages, of employment and GDP in Panama than in the other Central American economies. The Canal Zone, and importance it plays in world trade and the Panamanian economy, also accounts for the unique situation of the country. Finally, psychologically and culturally, Panama sometimes considers itself part of Central America, and sometimes part of South America. Panama is not part of the Central American Common Market, an RTA created in the 1960s which remains inchoate, and which lacks a CET on some products. But, the Dominican Republic is not part of this Common Market either, and it is a *CAFTA—DR* member. Query whether *CAFTA—DR* envisages the possibility of Panama docking onto the accord, and whether it is possible for *CAFTA—DR* itself to dock onto *NAFTA*.

Thus, for Costa Rica, El Salvador, Guatemala, Honduras, and Nicaragua, economic criteria dictated the choice of each other and the U.S. as FTA partners. The specific negotiating objectives of the Central American countries included:

    i.   Secure guaranteed, duty-free, quota-free access to the largest market in the world (the U.S.), particularly for products of keen export interest, such as T&A.

    ii.   Create a hedge against unilateral preference grants by the U.S., such as the CBI.

    iii.   Enhance overall economic development.

However, the mismatch in material positions meant economics had little power to explain the U.S. interest in *CAFTA—DR*. Neither did generosity toward five poor countries play a role. To the contrary, geopolitical and security objectives motivated the American side.

America's history pre-*CAFTA—DR* with Central America resonates between the extremes of benign neglect and over-engagement. In the 1990s, more illegal immigration into the U.S. originated from Central than South America, despite the fact the former region has a considerably smaller population base than the latter region. Central America also devolved into a base for drugs, narco-terrorism, and money laundering. From the U.S. vantage, as long as Central America remains poor, it is unstable and insecure, and the U.S. vulnerable. That is because poverty creates conditions hostile to peace. It swells the ranks of persons willing or susceptible to engage in bad acts. Surely something is amiss when (as was true as of May 2003) Norway and Mongolia each pay the same amount of tariff duty to the U.S. — about $23 million — but Norway has $5.2 billion of exports to the U.S., and Mongolia just $132 million. U.S. tariffs on goods that matter to Third World countries — such as cotton, footwear, peanuts, and T&A — are high, in the range of 40 to 60 percent. Thus, an FTA with Central America made sense for U.S. political and security objectives. It could strengthen Central America by helping each country achieve its economic objectives. Specifically, by improving terms of entry for Central American products to the U.S. market, employment in export-sectors of Central America could increase, leading to rising living, labor, and environmental standards.

Consider the legal obligations created by *CAFTA—DR*. To fulfill its criteria, did the U.S. have to make major concessions? To what extent is it an optimal negotiating strategy for the U.S. to try extracting maximum economic concessions from Central American countries? Might undue U.S. pressure put both sides in a mercantilist position? Evidently, the criteria motivating the Central American countries and U.S., while different, proved complimentary. The economic development interests of the 5 tiny countries meshed with political and security goals of their giant partner. In July 2006, the accord passed the House of Representatives, albeit by the slimmest margin of any trade deal in U.S. history — 217 to 215 (with 2 Congressmen not voting) — and cleared the Senate by a 55-to-45 margin. *CAFTA—DR* took effect on 1 March 2006.

Chapter 23

MULTILATERAL DISCIPLINES ON FTAs

Politicians tell you that when they sign a bilateral agreement with a pal, they get on TV. When they are the 149th minister around the table at the WTO, they don't get on TV.

> —Pascal Lamy, Director-General, World Trade Organization, *in* Alan Beattie & Andrew Bounds, *Sceptics Fear Political Ties That Bind Free Trade*, FINANCIAL TIMES, 5 October 2006, at 8

DOCUMENTS SUPPLEMENT ASSIGNMENT

1. *Havana Charter* Articles 43-45
2. GATT Article XXIV
3. Uruguay Round *Understanding on the Interpretation of Article XXIV*

I. THE WEAK DISCIPLINE OF GATT ARTICLE XXIV

WORLD TRADE ORGANIZATION, *REGIONALISM AND THE WORLD TRADING SYSTEM*
5-17, 19-20 (April 1995)

1. The MFN clause and regional integration agreements

In essence, MFN ensures that the principles of GATT and the commitments made in the course of trade negotiating rounds are uniformly applied by each country to its trading partners, which contributes to securing and realizing the economic benefits of international trade, both for importers and for exporters. Equal treatment of imports from different origins helps ensure that these are purchased from the lowest-cost foreign suppliers, thereby reinforcing comparative advantage in the world market and minimizing the cost of protection at home. Exporters can expect new multilateral trading opportunities to result from the multitude of bilateral bargains negotiated during GATT rounds and to be protected from having those new opportunities impaired by subsequent discrimination between sources of supply. In terms of domestic political considerations, the requirement to treat all signatories equally is a restraint on the temptation to discriminate against imports from particular sources, especially small or politically weak countries. More generally, by limiting the extent to which a country can play favorites, and thus de-politicizing trade, the MFN principle helps smaller trading nations realize their desire to be treated equally in their economic relations with their more powerful trading partners. In these and other ways, non-discrimination contributes greatly to the regularity, orderliness and predictability which form the essence of a rules-based international trading order.

. . . .

With the case for non-discrimination so strong, the question naturally arises as to why the founders of GATT included provisions permitting customs unions and free trade areas. One part of the answer is political realism. Customs unions have a long history, . . . and many countries would not have signed an agreement that prohibited future such arrangements with neighbours. But it also seems likely that *genuine* customs unions and free trade areas were viewed as compatible with the principle of non-discrimination, as distinct from the various forms of *ad hoc* and partial discrimination that were evident in the inter-war period. Dismantling restrictions on all (or most) trade represents an important step in the direction of carrying out economic activity with one or more partners on the same basis as, say, between different states or provinces of the same country. The founders of GATT recognised, in other words, that economic integration between several countries has or can have an economic rationale analogous to the process of integration within a single sovereign state, which in turn means that regional integration agreements do not pose an *inherent* threat to efforts to promote continued integration on a world-wide basis.

GATT rules on customs unions and free trade areas reflect the drafters' desire to provide for such agreements, while at the same time ensuring that the trading interests of third countries are respected and, more generally, that such agreements are compatible with a rules-based and progressively more open world trading system. For this reason, the provisions on customs unions and free trade areas establish a number of conditions which the agreements must satisfy, as well as transparency requirements in order to monitor whether those conditions are being met.

The principal GATT rules on regional integration agreements . . . are contained in Article XXIV. . . . In addition, Article XXV (waivers) has provided the GATT basis for several past agreements. . . .

2. The origins of Article XXIV

Paragraph 2 of Article I of the GATT explicitly exempts ("grandfathers") from the MFN requirement preferential arrangements in force at the time the GATT came into effect. These included the existing British Imperial Preferences, preferences in force in the French Union, preferences given by the Benelux countries and by the United States, those exchanged between Chile and its neighbours, and the preferences granted by the Lebano-Syrian Customs Union to Palestine and Transjordan. However, these preferences were "capped" by the requirement that they could not be raised above existing levels (generally those in force in April 1947), and their significance in world trade has been steadily reduced . . . by successive rounds of tariff negotiations.

The introduction of MFN, with existing preferences tolerated but capped, laid the foundations for future growth of world trade on the basis of non-discrimination. This was a central goal, in particular, of the United States.

Nevertheless, even the United States, vigorously opposed to preferences, accepted from the beginning the case for *customs unions* in which participating countries would adopt a common trade policy, including a common external tariff. A provision for customs unions was thus included, subject to conditions, in the United States' proposals of 1945, which launched the negotiations that eventually led, via the draft *Charter* for the stillborn International Trade Organization (ITO), to the GATT. The concept was strongly supported by several European governments, notably France and the members of the recently established Benelux customs union.

The United States' proposals did not, however, mention *free trade areas*, nor provide for *interim agreements* leading to customs unions or free trade areas. The practical need for interim agreements, on the grounds that participants in customs unions could not be expected to move overnight to mutual free trade and common trade policies, was accepted during preparatory negotiations on the GATT and reflected in Article XXIV of the original General Agreement signed in October 1947.

Drafting of the *ITO Charter* continued during the United Nations Conference on Trade and Employment held in Havana from November 1947 to March 1948. At the end of the Conference, a First Session of the GATT contracting parties was held, at which recognition was given to the concept of a free trade area in which members would remove their mutual trade barriers but maintain their individual national trade policies towards non-members. The proposal was introduced by Lebanon and Syria, with support from several other developing countries, on the grounds that avoidance of the requirement for a common external trade policy — which required the further step of an agreement on the harmonization of trade policies — made the free trade area technique better suited to the needs of integration among developing countries. The proposal, championed by France, was accepted as a means of blunting developing-country demands for a legitimization of preferences. These changes were incorporated into the General Agreement in 1948. Article XXIV has remained essentially unchanged since (the Uruguay Round on Article XXIV clarifies certain provisions, but does not change the rules).

3. The provisions of Article XXIV

Under Article XXIV, customs unions and free trade area agreements are a permitted exception to the cardinal principle of non-discrimination because it is recognized that such agreements have the potential to further economic integration without necessarily adversely affecting the interests of third countries. Paragraph 4 sets out the parameters of trade liberalization both internally and externally:

> the purpose of a customs union or of a free trade area should be to facilitate trade between the constituent territories and not to raise barriers to the trade of other contracting parties with such territories.

Paragraph 8 of Article XXIV defines the characteristics of customs unions and free trade areas. Summarizing and simplifying slightly, it states that parties to customs unions and free trade areas must eliminate duties and other restrictive regulations of commerce with respect to substantially all the trade between their constituent customs territories. The requirement to eliminate duties and other restrictions on mutual trade is not absolute, however. Apart from the flexibility implicit in the "substantially-all-trade" requirement, members may still "where necessary" exercise their rights to maintain duties or restrictions under GATT Articles XI (quantitative restrictions), XII (restrictions applied for balance-of-payments purposes), XIII (non-discriminatory administration of quantitative restrictions), XIV (exceptions to the rules of non-discrimination), XV (exchange arrangements) and XX (general exceptions). A further criterion which applies only to customs unions is that its members must apply substantially the same duties and other regulations of commerce to trade with non-members (in other words, have a common external tariff and more generally a common trade policy). [Query whether, as a practical matter, most FTAs do not meet the "substantially all trade" requirement. To the extent an FTA does not satisfy it, the potential for trade and investment diversion is considerable. Indeed, are the exclusions from coverage by an FTA are most likely to be in important sectors susceptible to trade diversion?]

An important rationale for the substantially-all-trade requirement is that it helps governments resist the inevitable political pressures to avoid or minimize tariff reductions in inefficient import-competing sectors. A wider sectoral coverage enhances the trade-creating effect of such agreements. The requirement also ensures that regional agreements are limited to those which have sufficient political support in member countries to overcome protectionist opposition to more or less complete free trade among the participants, and that agreements are not misused as a cover for narrow (sectoral) discriminatory arrangements. The criterion thereby helps "differentiate between politically unavoidable and containable deviations from the most-favoured principle" by determining "the point where trade policy is allowed to give way to foreign policy." Recast to emphasize its incentive effect, the argument is that "the rules of Article XXIV attempt to limit discrimination by imposing a high (political) cost on it: strictly interpreted, they would only allow it when the parties are really serious about favoring each other (free trade among the partners for most products) . . . [thus] the high political cost of establishing such preferential arrangements acts as a deterrent to their formation."

Paragraph 5 of Article XXIV spells out the conditions to be met by customs unions and free trade areas so as to avoid adverse effects on the trade of third countries. A major constraint placed on customs unions is the requirement that the common external tariff, and other trade measures imposed at the time of the formation of a customs union, be set at a level that is not "on the whole" higher or more restrictive than was imposed by the constituent territories prior to its formation. If the level of the common external tariff is such that any of its individual members' bound tariffs are raised, paragraph 6 states that "the procedures set forth by Article XXVIII shall apply." This procedure provides for the withdrawal or modification of previously negotiated tariff concessions, with the possibility for compensatory tariff reductions, . . . taking into account the new market access opportunities created for the same product by decreases in tariffs of other members of the customs union. Members of free trade areas, even though they do not adopt a common external tariff or common trade policy, are subject to similar obligations.

Paragraph 7 contains requirements to ensure transparency of *proposed* agreements. Agreements are to be promptly notified to GATT for examination by the contracting parties, which may make recommendations. Because customs unions and free trade areas are normally established over a fairly long period to avoid the economic dislocations of a rapid move to free trade among the members, Article XXIV provides explicitly for *interim* agreements. To avoid the danger that such interim agreements are used as a pretext for introducing discriminatory preferences, paragraph 5(c) requires that they include a "plan and schedule for the formation of such a customs union or such a free trade area within a reasonable length of time." If the contracting parties, acting jointly, find that the plan and schedule in the interim agreements are not likely to lead to the formation of the customs union or free trade area, or not to do so within a reasonable period, the contracting parties are to make recommendations. The agreement is not to be maintained or put into force unless it is amended in accordance with such recommendations.

In 1972, it was decided that notification should be made following the signature of the agreements. The practice has been for parties to the agreement to provide trading partners with a text of the agreement, so that they may consider in detail its implications for their trade and economic interests. In practice, again, notification is generally followed by the establishment of a working party with the terms of reference "to examine in the light of the relevant GATT provisions, [name of the agreement], and to report to the [GATT, now WTO General] Council." Participation in working parties is open, and the countries who are parties to the agreement are always members of the working party and have the same status as other delegations. The working party's report to the Council, the governing body of the contracting parties, represents the views of all participants and therefore records different views if necessary. The report of the working party is adopted by the Council, and may form the basis on which the contracting parties acting jointly may take a final decision on conformity of the agreement with Article XXIV or formulate recommendations to members of interim agreements.

. . . Article XXIV provides in several instances for "recommendations" and "findings" to be made by the contracting parties, in particular as regards interim agreements. Article XXV:4 provides that "decisions of the contracting parties shall be taken by a majority of the votes cast." By tradition, however, decisions in GATT which have required a positive action to be taken by a contracting party or parties have been taken by consensus. This condition has been deemed to be met if no formal objection to the decision is made by a delegation at the meeting when the issue is taken up.

Paragraph 10 states that proposals for free trade areas or customs unions not meeting the criteria described above may be approved by a two-thirds majority of the contracting parties, provided that such proposals eventually lead to the formation of a customs union or free trade area. The drafting history indicates that this provision was intended to provide for the supervision of free trade areas and customs unions in which not all participants were GATT contracting parties.

4. Issues of interpretation

For most of GATT's first decade of existence, the General Agreement's rules on regional agreements were little used, and remained — as had been envisaged by the drafters — a minor element in world trade relations. This changed in 1957, with the notification to GATT of the *Treaty of Rome* creating the European Economic Community (EEC). The birth of the Community, an event of prime political and economic importance, required the GATT contracting parties to interpret certain provisions of Article XXIV for the first time, and involved, again for the first time, important trade and economic interests on all sides. The member states of the proposed EEC, on the one side, and many of their trading partners, on the other, found themselves unable to reach agreement on the consistency of the *Treaty* with Article XXIV, or on compensation for changes in the bound tariffs of EEC member states. It has been argued that, in the ensuing attempt to reconcile GATT provisions with a political development of over-riding importance, compromises and interpretations were put forward that subsequently undermined the authority and clarity of the GATT rules on regional integration agreements.

Although the *Treaty of Rome* was drafted with the GATT rules in mind, its examination in GATT revealed diametrically opposed views among different parties on the compatibility of several of its provisions with Article XXIV. Questions were raised regarding the trade implications for non-members of the application of a simple, un-weighted arithmetic average of the tariffs applied by each of the EEC member states as of 1 January 1957. Third countries argued that this approach would lead to a substantial increase in tariffs affecting products of current export interest, thereby conflicting with the requirement of paragraph 5 of Article XXIV that the common external tariff not be set at a level that was on the whole higher than previously. Strong objections were voiced regarding the association between the Community and the "Overseas Territories", mainly former colonies and territories of France and of members of the Benelux Union. This association, although presented as a collection of bilateral free trade areas, was seen by non-members as effectively dismantling the ceiling placed on preferences in force at the time the GATT was established, thereby creating a new and wider preferential system. As a result, no agreement was reached on the compatibility of the *Treaty of Rome* with Article XXIV, and the contracting parties agreed that because "there were a number of important matters on which there was not at this time sufficient information . . . to complete the examination of the Rome Treaty . . . this examination and the discussion of the legal questions involved in it could not be usefully pursued at the present time." The examination of the EEC agreement was never taken up again.

The inconclusive nature of the examination of the Treaty of Rome set a pattern which was to dominate virtually all future examinations of agreements notified under Article XXIV. Summing up this experience, the Chairman of the Working Party on the *Canada-United States Free Trade Agreement* (*CUFTA*) introduced the report to the GATT Council in 1991 by observing that

> Over fifty previous working parties on individual customs unions or free trade areas had been unable to reach unanimous conclusions as to the GATT consistency of those agreements. On the other hand, no

such agreements had been disapproved explicitly. . . . One might . . . question what point was there in establishing a working party if ("no one") expected it to reach consensus findings in respect of specific provisions of such agreements, or to recommend to the participants how to meet certain benchmarks. It might not be irrelevant that the Working Party on the [*Canada — United States Free Trade*] *Agreement* commenced work only after a delay of more than two years. As further agreements came along, there might be a risk that they would be treated increasingly superficially and that contracting parties would lose — if they had not already done so — the ability to distinguish between agreements of greater or lesser GATT consistency. . . .

In adopting the Report of the Working Party, the Council agreed to consider how examinations of agreements submitted under Article XXIV might be improved. At the December 1992 session of the contracting parties, the Chairman observed that "the time is now ripe for a substantial review of the way in which working parties fulfill their remits under Article XXIV, especially to ensure that the results of their efforts are both clear and meaningful." This question remained on the agenda of the GATT contracting parties in 1993 and 1994, but no review took place. In view of the fact that the improvements agreed to in the Uruguay Round . . . do not alter existing procedures for examination, the question of the working party's examination of agreements will also figure on the agenda of the WTO.

A principal concern, especially in the light of an increasing number of regional integration agreements, is that such initiatives and the world trading system can and should be mutually supportive. Leaving aside for the time being the question of whether agreements since the creation of the GATT have met this goal, it is evident that the interpretation of the obligations and the application of the procedures relating to Article XXIV have encountered a number of serious problems. . . . At the interpretative level, these problems are mainly due to the imprecise language of Article XXIV in a setting that does not invite consideration of systemic aspects of such processes but where, instead, third countries concentrate on the specifics of the case in hand and seek to limit the trade diversionary effects of regional integration agreements, . . . and of course to maintain their GATT rights. In turn, as a result driven at least partially by the procedures themselves, third countries have generally withheld their approval of particular agreements, leading to an inconclusive examination process. . . .

(a) *Interim agreements: notification, plans and schedules for completion*

. . . [A] contracting party entering into a customs union or free trade area is required to promptly notify [*sic*] the contracting parties. With respect to interim agreements, especially, Article XXIV provides for the contracting parties to make recommendations to the parties to the agreement if, after having studied the plan and schedule for its completion, they find that such agreement is not likely to result in the formation of a customs union or of a free trade area within the period contemplated or that the period is not a reasonable one. The parties to the interim agreement shall not maintain or put into force the agreement if they are not prepared to modify it in accordance with these recommendations.

Most notified agreements have been interim agreements, and the practice of participants in terms of the timing of notification has varied. In the first decade of GATT's history, notification was made with the intention of seeking the approval of the contracting parties before the first actions were taken under the agreement. The *Treaty of Rome*, for instance, was signed on 25 March 1957 and notified to the contracting parties immediately thereafter, with the Treaty entering into force on 1 January 1958. . . .

Since these early years of the GATT, however, there have been few instances in which the working party completed its examination of an agreement prior to its entry into force. For agreements notified since 1980, the period between the date of entry into force and the adoption of the working party's report has ranged from 3 months to over 4 years. Partly, this is due to sometimes very short intervals between signature and entry into force, but in other cases, notification has occurred only after ratification of the agreement by the domestic legislatures, leaving little time for examination prior to entry into force. Recently, the *NAFTA* was ratified by Canada, Mexico, and the United States in 1993 and entered into force on 1 January 1994, while its members agreed to the establishment of a working party only in January 1994. Similarly, the enlargement of the European Union on 1 January 1995 to include Austria, Finland and Sweden preceded the establishment of a working party. In practice, the examination of agreements by the contracting parties has become *ex post*, when there is little or no opportunity for third country concerns raised in the working party to be taken into account by members of the agreement.

In discussions among participants in working parties, the provisions of interim agreements have raised issues of interpretation. Article XXIV requires that interim agreements include "a plan and schedule for the formation of a customs union or of a free trade area within a reasonable time." However, no definitions of the terms "interim agreements", "plan and schedule" and "a reasonable length of time" are provided. This absence of agreed definitions has led to controversy in certain cases regarding whether a particular interim agreement qualified as such, in that it clearly and unambiguously would lead to the establishment of a customs union or free trade area, within a well-defined period of time. In several instances, third countries were of the opinion that there was no definite end-point to the period of transition since no reference dates were provided for in the text of the agreement. This issue has arisen less frequently in interim agreements notified recently, however, which have included plans and schedules with fixed transition periods.

Another area of difficulty has been the reporting obligations of members of regional agreements subsequent to the working party's examination. In 1971, the contracting parties acting jointly instructed the GATT Council of Representatives to establish a calendar fixing dates for the examination every two years of reports on preferential agreements. The effectiveness of this exercise was undermined by the absence of an agreed format for reports — reflecting the different opinions on the objective of this reporting obligations among contracting parties — and the contracting parties claiming to have completed the implementation of free trade areas or customs unions (for example, the European Economic Community, the *European Free Trade Association* and the Australia — New Zealand *Closer Economic Relations Trade Agreement*) did not submit reports. A calendar for such reports has not been set by the Council since 1987. [Apparently, a WTO calendar existed in 2004.]

(b) *The "substantially-all-trade" requirement*

Differences of opinion among participants in working parties regarding the interpretation of the "substantially-all-trade" requirement in Article XXIV have been a major reason why working parties have not reached a consensus on the GATT consistency of individual agreements.

This requirement refers to the scope of liberalization to be achieved by members of a customs union or free trade area. Discussions in GATT working parties have centered on whether this concept should be understood in qualitative terms (no exclusion of major sectors) or in quantitative terms (percentage of trade of the members covered). With regard to the *qualitative* perspective, third countries have questioned whether agreements that explicitly excluded trade in unprocessed agricultural products — the case of most agreements — met the substantially-all-trade requirement. For example, the working party which examined Sweden's free trade agreements with the Baltic States would have agreed on the full conformity of these agreements with Article XXIV, the rest of whose contents and provisions received broad acceptance, had some members of the working party not claimed that the exclusion from the agreements proper (and separate treatment) of agricultural trade prevented full conformity of the Agreements with the obligations of Article XXIV.

The signatories defending their agreement in this particular instance, and more generally members of agreements which exclude agricultural products have maintained that the criterion of Article XXIV is that obstacles be eliminated on substantially all the trade between the parties and not on trade in substantially all products or sectors. These members thus believe that this language does not preclude the exclusion of a sector of economic activity such as agriculture, provided that the overall trade coverage of the agreement meets the criterion laid down in Article XXIV. This *quantitative* interpretation of the relevant provision of Article XXIV:8(b) thus argues that the percentage of trade on which obstacles are eliminated by the agreements should be considered as determining whether the provision has been respected. The counter-argument is that the observed value of trade in a given sector may be low as a result of impediments to trade, and not because of its having an intrinsically lesser economic or trade importance. These differences of opinion demonstrate the subjective nature of the interpretation of Article XXIV:8(b) in the absence of further guidance or agreed interpretations.

Another issue on which differences of opinion have been frequent is the *scope of liberalization in the notified agreement in terms of measures rather than sectors covered*, in particular the extent to which non-tariff as well as tariff measures on intra-area trade are dismantled. . . . Article XXIV:8

specifically provides that members of a free trade area or customs union may exercise their rights to maintain duties or restrictions on intra-area trade under a list of certain GATT Articles. If this were to be interpreted as being an exhaustive list, it would disqualify agreements where members have retained the right to apply restrictions on intra-member trade under GATT provisions not explicitly mentioned in the list, such as safeguard measures (under Article XIX) or restrictions for national security reasons (under Article XXI) or even to apply anti-dumping or countervailing measures (Article VI). In this regard, the EEC argued, before the Committee which examined the Treaty of Rome, that national security (Article XXI) was not mentioned in the list but "it would be difficult, however, to dispute the right of contracting parties to avail themselves of that provision which related, *inter alia*, to traffic in arms, fissionable materials, etc."

A related issue is whether parties to a free trade area or customs union are entitled (or, indeed, can be required) to exempt the other members from safeguard actions in the form of quantitative restrictions (for example, under Article XIX), which would otherwise be administered in a non-discriminatory manner according to historical trade shares (Articles XIII and XIV). Is a member of an agreement permitted to introduce such restrictions only on imports from non-members even though the alleged source of the problem is imports from all sources? In practice, members of certain free trade agreements have sometimes exempted regional trade partners from safeguard actions. However, third countries have often taken issue with an interpretation of Article XXIV that permits a departure from all GATT obligations requiring non-discriminatory treatment.

(c) The "not-on-the-whole-higher-or-more-restrictive" requirement

A major constraint placed on customs unions under paragraph 5 of Article XXIV is the requirement that the common external tariff and other restrictive regulations imposed at the time of the formation of the union not be on the whole higher or more restrictive than those imposed by the constituent territories before the formation. . . . [T]he method in which the common external tariff of a customs union is elaborated from individual member tariffs — for example, simple averaging, trade-weighted averaging or alignment at the lowest tariff — has important effects on the *ex post* market access opportunities of third-country suppliers. A closely related issue is whether it is necessary, for the purpose of making a comparison between *ex ante* and *ex post* market access opportunities of third-country suppliers, for the purpose of making a comparison between *ex ante* and *ex post* market access opportunities, that a country-by-country and product-by-product examination of the effect of increases in tariffs be undertaken. In the examination of the Treaty of Rome, third countries argued that members of a customs union or free trade area should not raise barriers to the trade of *any* individual third country, while the EEC was of the view that such an interpretation would be inconsistent with the requirement that the duties and other regulations imposed at the institution of the union should not *on the whole* be higher or more restrictive than the general incidence prior to the formation of the union. The requirement has been interpreted by the EEC to apply to third countries as a group rather than individually, and to not preclude the raising of barriers to trade in a sector or sub-sector of merchandise trade provided barriers are lowered in other sectors or sub-sectors. Third countries have repeatedly raised their concerns regarding the operation of this provision in the working parties established to examine subsequent enlargements of the EEC.

As regards bound rates, if a contracting party proposes to increase a bound rate of duty on joining a customs union, the normal GATT procedures for the modification of schedules apply, as set forth in Article XXVIII. In providing for compensatory adjustment, paragraph 6 of Article XXIV states that due account is to be taken of the compensation already afforded by the reductions brought about in the corresponding duties of the other members of the union. However, controversy exists as to when the negotiations for compensation should be carried out (before or after the establishment of the customs union), the nature of compensation, and whether account must also be taken of tariff reductions by the members of the customs union on other items. The negotiations on compensation that followed the submission of the common external tariff of the EEC (the 1961 Dillon Round), proved sufficiently complex and disappointing for third countries that some were led to threaten retaliation.

A particularly controversial issue in examinations of free trade areas has been their rules of origin, which are the criteria established for products to receive free trade area treatment in instances in which intermediate goods imported from third countries are used in the production process. Since there are more and less restrictive ways of designing and administering rules of origin, third countries have been concerned that such rules create new trade barriers to their trade with member countries. Third country members of the working parties on the 1973 free trade agreements between the EC and individual *EFTA* member states, for example, indicated that the effect of their rules of origin would be to raise barriers to third-country trade in intermediate products, and that the rules of origin were so complex and cumbersome as to be a barrier to trade in and of themselves. Another view was that the absence of GATT guidelines on rules of origin for regional integration agreements left contracting parties free to adopt whatever rules they may deem appropriate.

. . . .

(e) *GATT status of agreements notified under Article XXIV*

. . . Working parties were established to examine virtually all notified agreements. In recent years, the large volume of agreements notified under Article XXIV has led to a practice of grouping, where possible, the examination of several agreements under a single working party. . . . .. . .Conformity with Article XXIV has been explicitly acknowledged by the working party, through the requisite consensus, in the case of only six agreements: the Southern Rhodesia — South Africa Customs Union Agreement; the El Salvador-Nicaragua Free Trade Area and the Participation of Nicaragua in the Central American Free Trade Area; the Caribbean Free Trade Agreement and the later Caribbean Community and Common Market (CARICOM); and the Czech Republic-Slovak Republic Customs Union.

. . . .

In the remaining cases — the vast majority — the conclusions of the reports submitted by the working parties generally note the divergent views expressed by participants regarding the conformity of the agreement in question with the GATT, with members of the agreement upholding the latter's conformity with Article XXIV, and with one or more third countries taking an alternative view or withholding any definite view on the question. Thus, while there have been very few unanimous conclusions or specific endorsements that all the legal requirements of Article XXIV have been met, the working parties have also never reached the conclusion that the legal requirements had *not* been met. In other words, and this needs to be emphasized, *making no pronouncement on the key matters they were charged to examine has been the rule for Article XXIV working parties*. The absence of such recommendations has been interpreted by several contracting parties as meaning that it must therefore be presumed that the agreement in question is in conformity with Article XXIV, while others have considered that, in the absence of any final decision by the contracting parties acting jointly on the conformity of a particular agreement with the provisions of Article XXIV, the legal status of such an agreement remains open.

. . . .

6. Article XXV (Waivers)

Article XXV permits the contracting parties acting jointly to grant waivers from obligations under the General Agreement. The provision has on occasion been used to authorize regional agreements. In 1948, France obtained a waiver from Article I:1 for a proposed customs union with Italy, which was not at the time a signatory to the General Agreement. Later, the European Coal and Steel Community, which could not qualify as a customs union because of its limited product coverage, was authorized by a waiver in 1952. Similarly, the United States obtained a waiver in 1965 for its agreement with Canada on free trade in automotive products. However, a majority of the 28 waivers from Article I granted since the inception of GATT have involved preferences granted by developed to developing countries on a non-reciprocal basis, in most instances for the stated purpose of promoting economic development through increased export earnings. A recent example is the waiver granted in December 1994 to the European Community for preferential treatment on imports from ACP states under the Fourth *Lomé Convention* [and, still more recently, a waiver granted on 23 June 2000 for the successor agreement, the *Cotonou Convention*].

7. The WTO: revised and extended rules for regional agreements

. . . .

While the *TRIPS Agreement* [i.e., Agreement on Trade-Related Aspects of Intellectual Property Rights] does not contain provisions specific to regional agreements, the multilateral agreements on goods and services do. First, in *goods*, the WTO takes over existing GATT provisions (Article XXIV, the Enabling Clause and other relevant decisions of the GATT Contracting

Parties), supplemented by the Uruguay Round *Understanding on Article XXIV.*

. . . .

The *Understanding* clarifies several aspects of the operation of paragraph 5 of Article XXIV by providing guidelines on the methods to be followed in comparing the overall level of tariffs and charges on imports before and after the formation of a customs union. In particular, the assessment will be based on a weighted average of tariff rates and customs duties collected, using applied rates. . . . A reasonable length of time for the formation of a customs union or a free trade area is deemed to be ten years, except for exceptional circumstances, where a full explanation is required.

The negotiations on compensation provided for under paragraph 6 of Article XXIV, where needed, must begin before the common external tariff is implemented. This is important to third countries because the short-term trade diversionary effects of the establishment of a customs union are easier to mitigate when the new common external tariff already includes compensatory adjustments. In these negotiations, when one or more constituent members of the customs union is required to raise its tariff on a particular product, due account must also be taken of reductions in the tariff on that product by other members, in deciding on compensatory tariff reductions on other products. The *Understanding* therefore makes it clear that negotiating partners are *required to* take into account reductions of duty only on the same tariff line. While the text does not preclude acceptance of any incidental reductions in tariffs on other products as part of the compensation, third countries cannot be required to accept them. . . .

Regarding transparency, the *Understanding* requires that *all* agreements notified under Article XXIV be examined by a working party. If an interim agreement is notified without a plan and schedule, the working party shall in its report recommend a plan and schedule. The *Understanding* also confirms the biennial reporting requirement for members of regional agreements.

The *Understanding* also clarifies the relationship between the invocation of the dispute-settlement provisions of the WTO, and the examination of agreements under Article XXIV. The *Understanding* states that the dispute-settlement provisions "may be invoked with respect to any matters arising from the application of Article XXIV." This was intended to resolve uncertainty as to whether a panel can consider issues arising from an agreement that had already been examined by a working party established under Article XXIV, it having been at times argued that only an Article XXIV working party can properly do this.

While the purpose of the *Understanding* on Article XXIV is to clarify certain of the areas where the application of Article XXIV had given rise to controversy in the past, and particularly as regards the external policy of customs unions, it fell short of addressing most of the difficult issues of interpretation. . . . For example, no consensus emerged in the Uruguay Round Negotiating Group on GATT Articles concerning proposals made by several participants (notably Japan), to clarify the substantially-all-trade requirement. It is evident, therefore, that most of the problems that have plagued the working party process were not solved in the Uruguay Round. There is, it should be added, a recognition in the Preamble of the *Understanding* that the contribution to the expansion of world trade of customs unions and free trade areas is "increased if the elimination between the constituent territories of duties and other restrictive regulations of commerce extends to all trade, and [is] diminished if any major sector is excluded."

II. *GATS* ARTICLE V PARAMETERS

A. Five Modest Requirements

Akin to GATT Article XXIV is *General Agreement in Trade in Services* (*GATS*) Article V. The latter provision, entitled Economic Integration, tries to subject the inevitable efforts to forge FTAs and CUs to multilateral disciplines, without applying disciplines so tight they stifle the efforts — or, are simply ignored. Article V is needed simply because modern FTAs and CUs contain provisions on service sector liberalization. What are its disciplines? Aside from Article V:7 requirements concerning notification and reporting to the WTO Council for Trade in Services, there are five essential disciplines. Are they more or less light-handed than the disciplines of GATT Article XXIV?

First, Article V:1(a) says an FTA or CU treating services must have "substantial sectoral coverage." The footnote to Article V:1(a) defines "substantial" in terms of the number of sectors, the volume of trade affected, and modes of service supply, and counsels against *a priori* exclusion of any mode of supply. Observe the footnote does not prohibit *a priori* exclusion of certain sectors from foreign service providers — such as, for example, upstream energy exploration in a Gulf Arab country, or commercial banking in the U.S.

Second, Article V:1(b) requires an FTA or CU to eliminate "substantially all discrimination" between or among its members in the covered sectors. That means the FTA or CU must eliminate existing discriminatory measures, and prohibit new ones. Article V:1(b) reinforces — and, indeed, expressly refers to — the national treatment rule of *GATS* Article XVII. However, there exist several exceptions. They include *GATS* Articles XI-XII and XIV-XIV *bis*. What do they say? Curiously, Article V:2 says that in considering whether an FTA or CU wipes out "substantially all discrimination," account may be taken of the relationship between the accord and the "wider process of economic integration or trade liberalization among the countries concerned." Is this statement a further exception to the demands of national treatment? Observe, too, the special and differential treatment in Article V:3(a). This provision affords "flexibility" to developing country WTO Members in satisfying Article V:1(a) and (b). But, when is flexibility so elastic it scuppers a discipline? Is it wise public policy to grant these countries flexibility in service sector liberalization through FTAs and CUs?

Third, Article VI:4 contains a two-pronged mandate. First, the design of an FTA or CU must be to "facilitate trade" between or among parties to the accord. That would seem obvious enough, but how is "facilitation" is judged, short of a sector-by-sector review of the rules? Second, an FTA or CU must not "raise the overall level of barriers to trade in services" against third countries (*i.e.*, non-parties) that are WTO Members. The second prong applies to covered sectors, and requires a comparison of the barriers before and after the FTA or CU entered into force.

Fourth, Article V:6 is a kind of conditional MFN rule. It ensures the benefits of service sector liberalization through an FTA or CU apply to a third-country service supplier that is a juridical person in the territory of a member of the FTA or CU and doing business in that territory. For example, suppose the *U.S. — Jordan FTA* liberalizes trade in legal services. A law firm from the United Kingdom, which also is established and engaged in substantive business operations in Kansas City, Kansas, seeks to provide legal services in Amman. As long as the law firm is a juridical person constituted under the laws of the U.S. and the state of Kansas, then it is entitled to treatment provided for in the *Jordan FTA*. This discipline encourages providers from non-members to use the FTA or CU as a platform for exporting their services. At the same time, it prevents them from trans-shipping their services, because of its two conditions — juridical personhood and substantive business operations.

Interestingly, Article V:3(b) supplements the discipline with special and differential treatment. Service providers that are juridical persons in (or owned or controlled by natural persons of) a developing country WTO Member that is a party to an FTA or CU may be given more favorable treatment in that FTA or CU, as long as the accord involves only developing countries, than service providers from countries (developed or developing) that are not parties. In effect, Article 3(b) waives for developing country WTO Members the conditional MFN requirement. For example, a British law firm with an office in Dhaka would not be entitled to the benefits from an FTA between Bangladesh and India.

Fifth, Article V:5, which works in tandem with Article XXI:2-4, puts a price tag on the conclusion, expansion, or modification of service trade rules in an FTA or CU. If a WTO Member changes or withdraws any service trade liberalization commitment in an FTA or CU to which it is a party, then it may have to pay compensation to affected non-party WTO Members. A general level of mutually advantageous commitments that is not less favorable to services trade than existed under the status quo ante is to be maintained. Compensatory adjustments are made following negotiations on an MFN basis, or via arbitration if no agreement is reached among the concerned WTO Members.

The first use of these provisions was in the context of EU enlargement. The U.S. asked the EU for a compensatory adjustment. Several new EU members — namely, Austria, Cyprus, Czech Republic, Estonia, Finland, Hungary, Latvia, Lithuania, Malta, Poland, Slovak Republic, Slovenia, and Sweden — had made *GATS* concessions before joining the EU. But, they modified their service sector laws and regulations to harmonize them with EU rules. The modifications were inconsistent with their previous *GATS* commitments. Joined by Brazil, Canada, Hong Kong, Japan, and 16 other WTO Members, and following 3 years of negotiations, in September 2006 the EU agreed to a compensation package. Under it, the EU affords enhanced market access, especially in advertising, computer services, engineering, and finance.

Note Article V:8 limits the scope of Article V:5 to third-country WTO Members. A party to an FTA or CU cannot seek compensation under *GATS* for benefits accruing to another FTA or CU member. Thus, for example, France could not get compensation for EU service schedule changes made owing to enlargement. That limitation is sensible enough, for such compensation — if any — is a matter for the parties to the FTA or CU to work out amongst themselves.

B. A *GATS* Plus Approach?

Might it be said *GATS* Article V embodies a "*GATS* Plus" approach. Services commitments in an FTA or CU can be more liberal than what a WTO Member puts in its *GATS* Schedule. At the least, the RTA commitment must be no less liberal than the multilateral obligation. Article V also authorizes a Member not to offer MFN treatment on a "better-than-*GATS* commitment" in an FTA or CU. Typically, this "no MFN" limit is put in the RTA itself. The *New Zealand — Singapore Closer Economic Partnership* (*CEP*), an FTA between the two countries, furnishes an interesting example of a GATS Plus commitment, but it is a limitation on market access, and it concerns local culture.

In its *GATS* Schedule, New Zealand took a national treatment qualification for the *Treaty of Waitangi*. Via that maneuver, New Zealand reserved the right to discriminate in favor of Maori individuals on a commercial or industrial undertaking. This qualification could be subject to litigation under the *DSU*. In the *New Zealand — Singapore CEP*, New Zealand took a broader qualification than what it inserted in its *GATS* Schedule. The *CEP* reservation embraces "matters covered by this *Agreement* [the *CEP*], including in fulfillment of its [New Zealand's] obligations under the *Treaty of Waitangi*." This qualification is not subject to litigation under the *DSU*, nor under the dispute settlement provisions of the CEP. (Under the CEP, Singapore could request an arbitration panel in the event of a dispute over the reservation).

III. CASE STUDY: THE 1999 *TURKEY — TEXTILES* CASE

A. Subject Matter Jurisdiction over FTAs

The WTO Committee on Regional Trade Agreements, formed in 1995, is supposed to examine any FTA or CU in relation to GATT—WTO standards. As of May 2003, it had failed to complete a review of any FTA or CU, because of a lack of consensus. Of the 283 RTAs in existence (at that time), only about 60 ever had "passed" through formal multilateral review. In practice, what multilateral body has, or should have, subject matter jurisdiction over FTAs and CUs?

Might the answer be, and ought it to be, the Appellate Body? Consider its opinion in the 1999 *Turkey Textiles* case below. Consider, too, the administrative resource constraints in the WTO — both the Appellate Division and the Committee on RTAs — in relation to the large, growing, and increasingly complex network of RTAs. Does the Appellate Body offer any significant jurisprudence on the meaning of key terms in GATT Article XXIV?

B. India's Problem with Turkey's Quotas

WTO PANEL REPORT, *TURKEY — RESTRICTIONS ON IMPORTS OF TEXTILE AND CLOTHING PRODUCTS*
WT/DS34/R (adopted as modified by the Appellate Body, 19 Nov. 1999) (complaint by India)

II. FACTUAL ASPECTS

. . . .

B. Turkey's Trade Relations with the European Communities

1. *Association between Turkey and the European Communities, and the GATT/WTO process*

2.10 On 12 September 1963, Turkey and the Council and member States of the then European Economic Community ("EEC") signed the *Ankara Agreement*, which entered into force on 1 December 1964. The *Ankara Agreement* formed the basis of the Association (in the sense of Article 228 of the *Treaty of Rome*) between Turkey and the European Communities envisaging that its objectives would be reached through a customs union which would be established in three progressive stages: preparatory, transitional and final. Article 28 of the *Ankara Agreement* also left open "the possibility of the accession" of Turkey to the EEC. The *Ankara Agreement* itself contained the modalities of the preparatory stage of the Association.

2.11 The terms and conditions for the implementation of the transitional stage were defined in the 1970 *Additional Protocol* to the *Ankara Agreement* and in the 1971 *Interim Agreement*. The provisions of the *Interim Agreement* entered into force on 1 September 1971 and the *Additional Protocol* entered into force on 1 January 1973. These texts provided for an extended transitional period running over 22 years and foresaw the establishment of a customs union by the end of 1995. The *Additional Protocol* provided for an asymmetrical liberalization of intra-trade, because of the disparity in levels of development between the parties: the European Communities were to abolish all duties and QRs [quantitative restrictions, such as quotas] on imports of industrial products from Turkey as from September 1971, while Turkey was to do so over the transitional period, according to a timetable. The *Protocol* also contained provisions designed to ensure the alignment of Turkey on EC policies in many areas (commercial policy, standards, competition, state aids, trade in services, etc.).

. . . .

2.13 Starting in 1973, Turkey embarked in the gradual alignment of its customs duties to the EC Common Customs Tariff ("CCT"), as scheduled. The implementation of Turkey's obligations arising out of its Association with the European Communities was interrupted during a number of years, due *inter alia* to the crisis in which the Turkish economy was engulfed following the oil shocks of 1973 and 1979. In 1987, when Turkey requested accession to the

European Communities, completion of the customs union was seen as part of a package of measures designed to help Turkey prepare for membership. In 1988, Turkey resumed the reduction of its customs duties and alignment on the CCT.

2.14 The *Ankara Agreement* and the subsequent instruments concluded in the context of the Association between Turkey and the European Communities during the 1970s were notified to the GATT Contracting Parties under Article XXIV:7 of GATT 1947. The GATT entrusted three separate working parties with the task of examining the different agreements in light of those provisions. . . .

2.15 As agreed at a meeting of the Turkey-EC Association Council ("Association Council") held in November 1992, negotiations were initiated between the two parties on the modalities for the completion of the customs union, *i.e.*, for the final phase of the Association. These negotiations were conducted from 1993 to 1995.

2.16 On 6 March 1995, the Association Council took Decision 1/95, to enter into force on 1 January 1996. Decision 1/95 set out the modalities for the final phase of the Association between Turkey and the European Communities. In addition to the elimination of customs duties and alignment on the CCT, it contained provisions for the harmonisation of Turkey's policies and practices in all areas covered by the Association where this was deemed necessary "for the proper functioning of the Customs Union." . . . Decision 1/95 was submitted to the European Parliament for its approval and subsequently formally adopted by the Association Council on 22 December 1995. On 22 December 1995, the Association Council also adopted Decision 2/95, in pursuance of Article 15 of Decision 1/95. Decision 2/95 defined the coverage of products for temporary exception from Turkey's application of the CCT in respect of third countries, and fixed the timetable for their alignment to the CCT (from 1 January 1996 to 1 January 2001).

2.17 The entry into force of "the final phase of the Customs Union" between Turkey and the European Communities was notified to the WTO on 22 December 1995, under Article XXIV of GATT. The texts of Decision 1/95 and Decision 2/95 were distributed to Members on 13 February 1996. On 29 January 1996, the CTG [WTO Council for Trade in Goods] adopted standard terms of reference for the examination of the "Customs Union between Turkey and the European Community" ("Turkey-EC customs union"), and referred such examination to the CRTA [WTO Committee on Regional Trade Agreements].

. . . .

2.19 . . . The CRTA met twice to examine, in the light of the relevant provisions of GATT, the Turkey-EC customs union: on 23 October 1996 and on 1 October 1997. Additional written questions from Members were also replied to by the parties. To date, the CRTA has not yet finalized its examination.

. . . .

2. *Synopsis of recent developments in Turkey-EC trade*

2.21 The European Communities [*i.e.*, the EC-15] has traditionally constituted the major single market for Turkish goods and Turkey's major supplier, accounting for around 50 per cent of both Turkey's exports and imports. . . .

C. Quantitative Limits in Respect of Turkey's Imports of Certain Textile and Clothing Products

1. *Historical background*

. . . .

2.29 Turkey became a member of the *MFA*, as an exporting country, in 1981. Since 1979, Turkish textile and clothing products were subjected to restraints in the EC market under the provisions of Article 60 of the *Additional Protocol* to the *Ankara Agreement*.

2.30 On 31 December 1994, one day before the *ATC* came into force, Turkey did not maintain QRs on imports of textile and clothing products. Its exports of certain textile and clothing products were at that time under restraint in the European Communities and other countries' markets under the *MFA*.

2. *Recent background*

. . . .

2.34 Early in 1995, in its endeavour to complete Decision 1/95 requirements for the "completion of the Customs Union," Turkey sent proposals to the relevant countries (*i.e.*, those whose imports of textiles and clothing were under restraint in the EC market), including India, to reach agreements for the management and distribution of quotas under a double checking system. A standard formula was proposed for calculating the levels of QRs on textile and clothing products to be introduced by Turkey vis-à-vis all third countries concerned.

2.35 On 31 July 1995, Turkey forwarded to the Indian authorities a draft Memorandum of Understanding on trade in the categories of textile and clothing products on which Turkey intended to introduce QRs. India was invited to enter into negotiations with Turkey, with the participation of the European Communities, to conclude, prior to the completion of the Customs Union, an arrangement covering trade in those products which would be similar to the one already existing between India and the European Communities. India maintained that the intended restrictions were in contravention of Turkey's multilateral obligations and declined to enter into discussions on the conditions proposed by Turkey.

2.36 Agreements providing for restraints similar to those of the European Communities were negotiated by Turkey with 24 countries (WTO Members and non-Members). As provided for in Article 12 of Decision 1/95, the EC Commission cooperated with the Turkish authorities in the preparation of negotiating positions and generally participated in the negotiations themselves. As from 1 January 1996, unilateral restrictions or surveillance regimes were applied to imports originating in another 28 countries (WTO Members and non-Members), including India, with which Turkey could not reach agreement. These restrictions only affected products whose export to the European Communities was also under restraint.

2.37 The quantitative limits established by Turkey . . . [were published in the Official Gazette and set quarterly or bi-annual bases, depending on the year].

3. *Quantitative limits imposed on certain Turkey's imports of textile and clothing products from India*

2.38 Turkey applies QRs [quantitative restrictions], as of 1 January 1996, on imports from India of 19 categories of textile and clothing products. . . .

2.39 In the case of India, the formula used by Turkey to fix the level of the QRs corresponded to either (i) the arithmetical average of imports into Turkey from India for the category of products during the period 1992-1994; or (ii) an amount based on total EC imports for the category of products in question multiplied by the percentage of the basket exit threshold laid down in the bilateral agreement between the European Communities and India in force in 1994, multiplied by the percentage share of Turkish GDP in EC-15 total GDP (*i.e.*, 2.5 per cent), whichever was the higher. To this amount the corresponding growth rates in force in quota years 1994 and 1995 had been added to arrive at a level for 1996. . . .

4. *Statistical analysis of Turkey's imports of textile and clothing products under restraint*

(a) Imports of 61 textile and clothing product categories under restraint

. . . .

2.42 For the 61 categories of textiles and clothing under restraint, Turkey's imports from all non-EC countries (including India) accounted for 4.5 and 5 per cent of its total imports from those countries in 1994 and 1995, respectively, (*i.e.*, prior to the introduction of the restraints) and for less than 4 per cent of the corresponding totals in 1996 and 1997. The share of imports of those same product categories in Turkey's total imports from the EC-15 increased from 1.7 per cent in 1994 to 3 per cent in 1997.

(b) Imports of the 19 textile and clothing product categories under restraint for India

2.43 Statistics provided by India show that the value of its exports to Turkey of the 19 product categories under restriction dropped in 1996 and continued to decline in the following year, albeit less markedly; in 1995, exports under those categories had virtually trebled over their level in 1994. Such fluctuations were mainly due to variations in exports of restricted textile products to Turkey. A different behaviour is observed in India's exports to Turkey of other — unrestricted — products during the period 1994-1997: their share in India's total exports of textiles and clothing to Turkey has increased throughout the period, from 32 per cent in 1994 to 87 per cent in 1997. . . .

2.44 Data derived from trade statistics supplied by Turkey on its imports from India of the restricted 19 product categories in 1994 to 1997 differ in magnitude or movement from those provided by India. Nevertheless, they point at similar overall trends, both with respect to imports of product categories under restraint and with respect to imports of other textile and clothing products. . . .

2.45 [B]ased on Turkish statistics, . . . [i]mports from all origins into Turkey of the 19 product categories under restraint for India accounted in both 1994 and 1995 for 24 per cent of Turkey's total imports of textiles and clothing, this share declining to 19 per cent in 1997.

. . . .

2.46 Turkey's imports of the 19 categories of textiles and clothing under restraint for India from all non-EC countries (including India) accounted for less than 3 per cent of Turkey's imports of all products (including textiles and clothing) from those countries in both 1994 and 1995, and for less than 2 per cent of the corresponding totals in 1996 and 1997. The share of imports of the same 19 product categories in Turkey's imports of all products (including textiles and clothing) from the EC-15 doubled from 0.5 per cent in 1994 to 1.1 per cent in 1997.

C.   GATT Article XXIV as a Defense

WTO APPELLATE BODY REPORT,
TURKEY — RESTRICTIONS ON IMPORTS OF TEXTILE AND CLOTHING PRODUCTS
WT/DS34/AB/R, (adopted 19 Nov. 1999) (complaint by India)

IV. Issue Raised in this Appeal

41. This appeal relates to certain quantitative restrictions imposed by Turkey on 19 categories of textile and clothing products imported from India. Turkey adopted these quantitative restrictions upon the formation of a customs union with the European Communities. The Panel found these quantitative restrictions to be inconsistent with Articles XI and XIII of the GATT 1994 and Article 2.4 of the *ATC*. The issue raised by Turkey in this appeal is whether these quantitative restrictions are nevertheless justified by Article XXIV of the GATT 1994.

V. Article XXIV of the GATT 1994

42. In examining Turkey's defence that Article XXIV of the GATT 1994 allowed Turkey to adopt the quantitative restrictions at issue in this appeal, the Panel looked, first, at Article XXIV:5(a) and, then, at Article XXIV:8(a) of the GATT 1994. The Panel examined the ordinary meaning of the terms

of these provisions, in their context and in the light of the object and purpose of the *WTO Agreement*. The Panel reached the following conclusions:

> With regard to the specific relationship between, in the case before us, Article XXIV and Articles XI and XIII (and Article 2.4 of the ATC), we consider that the wording of Article XXIV does not authorize a departure from the obligations contained in Articles XI and XIII of GATT and Article 2.4 of the ATC.
>
> . . . .
>
> [Paragraphs 5 and 8 of Article XXIV] do not . . . address any specific measures that may or may not be adopted on the formation of a customs union and importantly they do not authorize violations of Articles XI and XIII, and Article 2.4 of the ATC. . . . We draw the conclusion that even on the occasion of the formation of a customs union, Members cannot impose otherwise incompatible quantitative restrictions.

Consequently, the Panel rejected Turkey's defence that Article XXIV justifies the introduction of the quantitative restrictions at issue. Turkey appeals the Panel's interpretation of Article XXIV.

43. . . . [I]n its findings, the Panel referred to the *chapeau* of paragraph 5 of Article XXIV only in a passing and perfunctory way. The *chapeau* of paragraph 5 is not central to the Panel's analysis, which focuses instead primarily on paragraph 5(a) and paragraph 8(a). However, we believe that the *chapeau* of paragraph 5 of Article XXIV is the key provision for resolving the issue before us in this appeal. . . .

44. To determine the meaning and significance of the *chapeau* of paragraph 5, we must look at the text of the *chapeau*, and its context, which, for our purposes here, we consider to be paragraph 4 of Article XXIV.

45. First, in examining the text of the *chapeau* to establish its ordinary meaning, we note that the *chapeau* states that the provisions of the GATT 1994 "*shall not prevent*" the formation of a customs union. We read this to mean that the provisions of the GATT 1994 *shall not make impossible* the formation of a customs union. [The Appellate Body cited the definition of "prevent" in *The New Shorter Oxford English Dictionary* (1993).] Thus, the *chapeau* makes it clear that Article XXIV may, under certain conditions, justify the adoption of a measure which is inconsistent with certain other GATT provisions, and may be invoked as a possible "defence" to a finding of inconsistency.

46. Second, in examining the text of the *chapeau*, we observe also that it states that the provisions of the GATT 1994 shall not prevent "*the formation of a customs union*." This wording indicates that Article XXIV can justify the adoption of a measure which is inconsistent with certain other GATT provisions only if the measure is introduced upon the formation of a customs union, and only to the extent that the formation of the customs union would be prevented if the introduction of the measure were not allowed.

47. It follows necessarily that the text of the *chapeau* of paragraph 5 of Article XXIV cannot be interpreted without reference to the definition of a

"customs union." This definition is found in paragraph 8(a) of Article XXIV. . . .

48. Sub-paragraph 8(a)(i) of Article XXIV establishes the standard for the *internal trade* between constituent members in order to satisfy the definition of a "customs union." It requires the constituent members of a customs union to eliminate "duties and other restrictive regulations of commerce" with respect to "substantially all the trade" between them. Neither the GATT Contracting Parties nor the WTO Members have ever reached an agreement on the interpretation of the term "substantially" in this provision. It is clear, though, that "substantially all the trade" is not the same as *all* the trade, and also that "substantially all the trade" is something considerably more than merely *some* of the trade. We note also that the terms of sub-paragraph 8(a)(i) provide that members of a customs union may maintain, where necessary, in their internal trade, certain restrictive regulations of commerce that are otherwise permitted under Articles XI through XV and under Article XX of the GATT 1994. Thus, we agree with the Panel that the terms of sub-paragraph 8(a)(i) offer "some flexibility" to the constituent members of a customs union when liberalizing their internal trade in accordance with this sub-paragraph. Yet we caution that the degree of "flexibility" that sub-paragraph 8(a)(i) allows is limited by the requirement that "duties and other restrictive regulations of commerce" be "eliminated with respect to substantially all" internal trade.

49. Sub-paragraph 8(a)(ii) establishes the standard for the trade of constituent members *with third countries* in order to satisfy the definition of a "customs union." It requires the constituent members of a customs union to apply "substantially the same" duties and other regulations of commerce to external trade with third countries. The constituent members of a customs union are thus required to apply a common external trade regime, relating to both duties and other regulations of commerce. However, sub-paragraph 8(a)(ii) does *not* require each constituent member of a customs union to apply *the same* duties and other regulations of commerce as other constituent members with respect to trade with third countries; instead, it requires that *substantially the same* duties and other regulations of commerce shall be applied. We agree with the Panel that:

> [t]he ordinary meaning of the term "substantially" in the context of sub-paragraph 8(a) appears to provide for both qualitative and quantitative components. The expression "substantially the same duties and other regulations of commerce are applied by each of the Members of the [customs] union" would appear to encompass both quantitative and qualitative elements, the quantitative aspect more emphasized in relation to duties.

50. We also believe that the Panel was correct in its statement that the terms of sub-paragraph 8(a)(ii), and, in particular, the phrase "substantially the same" offer a certain degree of "flexibility" to the constituent members of a customs union in "the creation of a common commercial policy." Here too we would caution that this "flexibility" is limited. It must not be forgotten that the word "substantially" qualifies the words "the same." Therefore, in our view, something closely approximating "sameness" is required by Article XXIV:8(a)(ii). We do not agree with the Panel that:

. . . as a general rule, a situation where constituent members have "comparable" trade regulations having similar effects with respect to the trade with third countries, would generally meet the qualitative dimension of the requirements of sub-paragraph 8(a)(ii).

Sub-paragraph 8(a)(ii) requires the constituent members of a customs union to adopt "substantially the same" trade regulations. In our view, "comparable trade regulations having similar effects" do not meet this standard. A higher degree of "sameness" is required by the terms of sub-paragraph 8(a)(ii).

51. Third, in examining the text of the *chapeau* of Article XXIV:5, we note that the *chapeau* states that the provisions of the GATT 1994 shall not prevent the formation of a customs union *"Provided that."* The phrase *"provided that"* is an essential element of the text of the *chapeau*. In this respect, for purposes of a "customs union", the relevant proviso is set out immediately following the *chapeau*, in Article XXIV:5(a). It reads in relevant part:

> with respect to a customs union . . ., the duties and other regulations of commerce imposed at the institution of any such union . . . in respect of trade with contracting parties not parties to such union . . . shall not on the whole be higher or more restrictive than the general incidence of the duties and regulations of commerce applicable in the constituent territories prior to the formation of such union . . .;

52. Given this proviso, Article XXIV can, in our view, only be invoked as a defence to a finding that a measure is inconsistent with certain GATT provisions to the extent that the measure is introduced upon the formation of a customs union which meets the requirement in sub-paragraph 5(a) of Article XXIV relating to the "duties and other regulations of commerce" applied by the constituent members of the customs union to trade with third countries.

53. With respect to "duties", Article XXIV:5(a) requires that the duties applied by the constituent members of the customs union *after* the formation of the customs union "shall *not* on the whole be *higher* . . . than the *general incidence*" of the duties that were applied by each of the constituent members before the formation of the customs union. Paragraph 2 of the *Understanding on Article XXIV* requires that the evaluation under Article XXIV:5(a) of the *general incidence of the duties* applied before and after the formation of a customs union "shall . . . be based upon an overall assessment of weighted average tariff rates and of customs duties collected." Before the agreement on this Understanding, there were different views among the GATT Contracting Parties as to whether one should consider, when applying the test of Article XXIV:5(a), the *bound* rates of duty or the *applied* rates of duty. This issue has been resolved by paragraph 2 of the *Understanding on Article XXIV*, which clearly states that the *applied* rate of duty must be used.

54. With respect to "other regulations of commerce", Article XXIV:5(a) requires that those applied by the constituent members *after* the formation of the customs union "shall *not* on the whole be . . . *more restrictive* than the *general incidence*" of the regulations of commerce that were applied by each of the constituent members *before* the formation of the customs union. Paragraph 2 of the *Understanding on Article XXIV* explicitly recognizes that

the quantification and aggregation of regulations of commerce other than duties may be difficult, and, therefore, states that "for the purpose of the overall assessment of the incidence of other regulations of commerce for which quantification and aggregation are difficult, the examination of individual measures, regulations, products covered and trade flows affected may be required."

55. We agree with the Panel that the terms of Article XXIV:5(a), as elaborated and clarified by paragraph 2 of the *Understanding on Article XXIV*, provide:

> . . . that the effects of the resulting trade measures and policies of the new regional agreement shall not be more trade restrictive, overall, than were the constituent countries' previous trade policies.

and we also agree that this is:

> an "economic" test for assessing whether a specific customs union is compatible with Article XXIV.

56. The text of the *chapeau* of paragraph 5 must also be interpreted in its context. In our view, paragraph 4 of Article XXIV constitutes an important element of the context of the *chapeau* of paragraph 5. The *chapeau* of paragraph 5 of Article XXIV begins with the word "accordingly," which can only be read to refer to paragraph 4 of Article XXIV, which immediately precedes the *chapeau*. . . .

57. According to paragraph 4, the purpose of a customs union is "to facilitate trade" between the constituent members and "not to raise barriers to the trade" with third countries. This objective demands that a balance be struck by the constituent members of a customs union. A customs union should facilitate trade within the customs union, but it should *not* do so in a way that raises barriers to trade with third countries. We note that the *Understanding on Article XXIV* explicitly reaffirms this purpose of a customs union, and states that in the formation or enlargement of a customs union, the constituent members should "to the greatest possible extent avoid creating adverse affects on the trade of other Members." Paragraph 4 contains purposive, and not operative, language. It does not set forth a separate obligation itself but, rather, sets forth the overriding and pervasive purpose for Article XXIV which is manifested in operative language in the specific obligations that are found elsewhere in Article XXIV. Thus, the purpose set forth in paragraph 4 informs the other relevant paragraphs of Article XXIV, including the *chapeau* of paragraph 5. For this reason, the *chapeau* of paragraph 5, and the conditions set forth therein for establishing the availability of a defence under Article XXIV, must be interpreted in the light of the purpose of customs unions set forth in paragraph 4. The *chapeau* cannot be interpreted correctly without constant reference to this purpose.

58. Accordingly, on the basis of this analysis of the text and the context of the *chapeau* of paragraph 5 of Article XXIV, we are of the view that Article XXIV may justify a measure which is inconsistent with certain other GATT provisions. However, in a case involving the formation of a customs union, this "defence" is available only when two conditions are fulfilled. First, the party claiming the benefit of this defence must demonstrate that the measure

at issue is introduced upon the formation of a customs union that fully meets the requirements of sub-paragraphs 8(a) and 5(a) of Article XXIV. And, second, that party must demonstrate that the formation of that customs union would be prevented if it were not allowed to introduce the measure at issue. Again, *both* these conditions must be met to have the benefit of the defence under Article XXIV.

59. We would expect a panel, when examining such a measure, to require a party to establish that both of these conditions have been fulfilled. It may not always be possible to determine whether the second of the two conditions has been fulfilled without initially determining whether the first condition has been fulfilled. In other words, it may not always be possible to determine whether not applying a measure would prevent the formation of a customs union without first determining whether there *is* a customs union. In this case, the Panel simply assumed, for the sake of argument, that the first of these two conditions was met and focused its attention on the second condition.

60. More specifically, with respect to the first condition, the Panel, in this case, did not address the question of whether the regional trade arrangement between Turkey and the European Communities is, in fact, a "customs union" which meets the requirements of paragraphs 8(a) and 5(a) of Article XXIV. The Panel maintained that "it is arguable" that panels do not have jurisdiction to assess the overall compatibility of a customs union with the requirements of Article XXIV. We are not called upon in this appeal to address this issue, but we note in this respect our ruling in *India — Quantitative Restrictions on Imports of Agricultural, Textile and Industrial Products* on the jurisdiction of panels to review the justification of balance-of-payments restrictions under Article XVIII:B of the GATT 1994. The Panel also considered that, on the basis of the principle of judicial economy, it was not necessary to assess the compatibility of the regional trade arrangement between Turkey and the European Communities with Article XXIV in order to address the claims of India. Based on this reasoning, the Panel assumed *arguendo* that the arrangement between Turkey and the European Communities is compatible with the requirements of Article XXIV:8(a) and 5(a) and limited its examination to the question of whether Turkey was permitted to introduce the quantitative restrictions at issue. The assumption by the Panel that the agreement between Turkey and the European Communities is a "customs union" within the meaning of Article XXIV was not appealed. Therefore, the issue of whether this arrangement meets the requirements of paragraphs 8(a) and 5(a) of Article XXIV is not before us.

61. With respect to the second condition that must be met to have the benefit of the defence under Article XXIV, Turkey asserts that had it not introduced the quantitative restrictions on textile and clothing products from India that are at issue, the European Communities would have "exclud[ed] these products from free trade within the Turkey/EC customs union." According to Turkey, the European Communities would have done so in order to prevent trade diversion. Turkey's exports of these products accounted for 40 per cent of Turkey's total exports to the European Communities. Turkey expresses strong doubts about whether the requirement of Article XXIV:8(a)(i) that duties and other restrictive regulations of commerce be eliminated with respect

to "substantially all trade" between Turkey and the European Communities could be met if 40 per cent of Turkey's total exports to the European Communities were excluded. In this way, Turkey argues that, unless it is allowed to introduce quantitative restrictions on textile and clothing products from India, it would be prevented from meeting the requirements of Article XXIV:8(a)(i) and, thus, would be prevented from forming a customs union with the European Communities.

62. We agree with the Panel that had Turkey not adopted the same quantitative restrictions that are applied by the European Communities, this would not have prevented Turkey and the European Communities from meeting the requirements of sub-paragraph 8(a)(i) of Article XXIV, and consequently from forming a customs union. . . . [T]he terms of sub-paragraph 8(a)(i) offer some — though limited — flexibility to the constituent members of a customs union when liberalizing their internal trade. As the Panel observed, there are other alternatives available to Turkey and the European Communities to prevent any possible diversion of trade, while at the same time meeting the requirements of sub-paragraph 8(a)(i). For example, Turkey could adopt rules of origin for textile and clothing products that would allow the European Communities to distinguish between those textile and clothing products originating in Turkey, which would enjoy free access to the European Communities under the terms of the customs union, *and* those textile and clothing products originating in third countries, including India. In fact, we note that Turkey and the European Communities themselves appear to have recognized that rules of origin could be applied to deal with any possible trade diversion. Article 12(3) of Decision 1/95 of the EC-Turkey Association Council, which sets out the rules for implementing the final phase of the customs union between Turkey and the European Communities, specifically provides for the possibility of applying a system of certificates of origin. A system of certificates of origin would have been a reasonable alternative until the quantitative restrictions applied by the European Communities are required to be terminated under the provisions of the *ATC*. Yet no use was made of this possibility to avoid trade diversion. Turkey preferred instead to introduce the quantitative restrictions at issue.

63. For this reason, we conclude that Turkey was not, in fact, required to apply the quantitative restrictions at issue in this appeal in order to form a customs union with the European Communities. Therefore, Turkey has not fulfilled the second of the two necessary conditions that must be fulfilled to be entitled to the benefit of the defence under Article XXIV. Turkey has not demonstrated that the formation of a customs union between Turkey and the European Communities would be prevented if it were not allowed to adopt these quantitative restrictions. Thus, the defence afforded by Article XXIV under certain conditions is not available to Turkey in this case, and Article XXIV does not justify the adoption by Turkey of these quantitative restrictions.

IV. CASE STUDY: THE 2006 *MEXICO — HFCS* CASE

A. The U.S.-Mexican Sugar War

Mexican restrictions on imports of artificial sweeteners and sugar substitutes, most notably high fructose corn syrup (HFCS), and on imports of beverages containing HFCS, largely through tax measures, has been the subject of a battle between Mexico and the United States dating to 1997. Indeed, sugar has been perhaps the most contentious product in the booming trade between the two countries, and given rise in the legal literature to the term "Sugar War" or "Sugar Wars." One battle in the War was an antidumping (AD) action, whereby Mexico imposed AD duties on HFCS from the United States. (In 1997, Mexico calculated preliminary duties at $55 to $175 per ton of HFCS. In 1998, it finalized these amounts.) Following adverse decisions by panels under Chapter 19 of the *North American Free Trade Agreement* (*NAFTA*) and the WTO *Understanding on Rules and Procedures Governing the Settlement of Disputes* (*Dispute Settlement Understanding*, or *DSU*), Mexico revoked the AD duties in 2001.

The next year, Mexico — specifically, its Congress — launched another battle in the Sugar War, firing a battery of tax measures (explained below). Correctly perceiving those measures as discriminatory, the United States fired back with a WTO action. Mexico again had a sour experience with a WTO panel. The United States prevailed, as the *HFCS* Panel held Mexico's taxes on soft drinks and other beverages that use any sweetener other than cane sugar were illegal under GATT Article III:2 (first and second sentences) and Article III:4.

Mexico appealed. Three Mexican measures, in specific, were in dispute:

1. *Soft Drink Tax*:

A 20 percent tax imposed on the transfer or importation of soft drinks and other beverages that use any sweetener other than cane sugar. In effect, this measure was a 20 percent imposition on imported soft drinks sweetened with high fructose corn syrup (HFCS) or beet sugar.[1] The levy did not apply to soft drinks sweetened with cane sugar, which tended to be Mexican beverages.

2. *Distribution Tax*:

A 20 percent tax on specific services when provided for the purpose of transferring products such as soft drinks and other beverages that use any sweetener other than cane sugar. Examples of such services include agency, brokerage, commission, consignment, distribution, mediation, and representation). This measure, in essence, was a 20 percent levy on services relating to imported soft drinks sweetened with high fructose corn syrup (HFCS) or beet

---

[1] Three types of sweeteners are used in soft drinks and syrups. Cane sugar, which is a form of sucrose, is the first type. It is a disaccharide comprised of 50 percent glucose and 50 percent fructose, and these parts are bonded together. The second type of sweetener is beet sugar. While it is a distinct form of sucrose, as it is derived from a different source, it is chemically and functionally identical to cane sugar. The third sweetener is, of course, HFCS, which comes from corn starch. That is, HFCS is a corn-based liquid sweetener, high in fructose relative to regular corn syrup, and made through a multi-stage production process.

sugar. The levy did not apply to soft drinks sweetened with cane sugar, which tended to be Mexican beverages.

3. *Bookkeeping Requirements*:

Obligations imposed on taxpayers subject to the Soft Drink or Distribution Tax. These obligations did not apply to domestically-manufactured beverages that used cane sugar as a sweetener.

Mexico implemented these measures beginning in 2002.

1. Aim and Effect

While aim is not relevant to a GATT Article III case, manifestly, Mexico designed these measures to protect its domestic sugar producers — and, of course, grab the attention of the United States and try to force a settlement in the Sugar War. Precious little HFCS is made in Mexico; most of it comes from the giant country to the North. Conversely (as even a brief tour around Veracruz, or a drive from Xalapa to Veracruz evinces), Mexico has plenty of cane sugar plantations. They are not altogether efficient, nor are Mexican sugar refineries. Unsurprisingly, before imposition of the tax, HFCS accounted for 99 percent of Mexico's imports of sweeteners.

Notably, the Mexican market in this product category is dominated by foreign multinational corporations. The Panel, with realism and a touch of sarcasm, observed that was so "in other parts of the world," too. Coca Cola controls 71.9 percent of the Mexican carbonated soft drink market, and Pepsi Cola has a 15.1 percent share of that market. A Peruvian company, Kola Real, holds 4 percent, and Cadbury Schweppes about 2 percent. However, the Mexican tax measures were not aimed at MNCs *per se*, *i.e.*, they were not aimed at excluding foreign soft drinks. Rather, their focus was on the sweetener used by the MNCs, seeking to discourage American HFCS and encourage use of local sugar.

Similarly, while proof of actual injury is unnecessary to prevail in a GATT Article III claim, there was little doubt the 20 percent tax caused damage to American producers of HFCS. Mexico was America's largest market for HFCS before the tax. The industry group for American HFCS producers, the Corn Refiners Association, said the tax cost their members $944 million in annual lost sales, equal to 168 million bushels of corn. Absent the tax, and with full restoration of the Mexican market for HFCS exports from the U.S., the Association estimated the price per bushel of corn in the United States likely would increase by 10 cents in major corn states, and 6 cents nationally.

2. The Two Mexican Defenses

At the Panel stage, the United States prevailed in its arguments that the Mexican measures violated the national treatment obligations of Article III:2 (first and second sentences) and Article III:4. On these points, Mexico did not appeal the Panel's findings. (The American arguments raise a matter on which some comment is worth making, below.) The unsuccessful Mexican defense was twofold.

First, the American complaint in the WTO was inextricably linked to a dispute between the United States and Mexico arising under *NAFTA*. The two sides battled over how to interpret *NAFTA* Section 703:2 and Annex 703:2. Invoking these provisions, Mexico claimed the United States has not provided its cane sugar producers with the market access to which they have a right under the free trade accord. For example, between 1995-2001, Mexico imported 3 million tons of sweeteners from the United States, but the United States allowed in only 224,000 tons of sugar from Mexico.

Specifically, Mexico said *NAFTA* permits Mexico to sell its surplus sugar in the American market free of duty, *i.e.*, as long as Mexico qualifies as a "surplus producer" under Section 703:2 and Annex 703:2 (paragraphs 13-22), then it can ship all excess sugar production to the United States duty free. The United States disagreed, asserting there is a limit (until free trade in sugar supposedly occurs in 2008 under *NAFTA*) as to how much sugar Mexico can ship duty free. The United States pointed to a Side Letter the two countries signed in 1993. The Side Letter limits access to the U.S. market, and reportedly states (in essence) that

> Mexico's domestic consumption of HFCS must be considered when calculating Mexico's net sugar market access to the U.S. market, and . . . Mexico will be determined to be a net surplus producer only when production of sugar exceeds consumption of sweeteners, including both sugar and HFCS.[2]

Further, the Side Letter limits Mexican sugar imports into the United States at a zero duty rate to 250,000 tons annually. Mexico retorted the Side Letter is invalid, because the Mexican Senate never approved it.

Thus, Mexico brought a *NAFTA* Chapter 20 case. However, its *NAFTA* Section 703:2 right had no effective *NAFTA* remedy. The United States, argued Mexico in the WTO action, had obstructed that case from going forward. Exasperated, Mexico took recourse (unilaterally, to be sure) to the Soft Drink and Distribution Tax measures, and the Bookkeeping Requirements, essentially because of America's breach of its *NAFTA* obligations. Thus, Mexico asked the Panel to decline to exercise its jurisdiction, and recommend the Parties pursue both of their actions before a *NAFTA* Chapter 20 Panel.

Second, as a fall back position in the WTO case, Mexico argued Article XX(d) justified any Article III violations. This exception is for administrative necessity. It condones a measure inconsistent with a GATT—WTO obligation, but only if it is necessary to implement a rule that is, itself, consistent with multilateral trade rules. If the Panel were to render a decision, then Mexico asked it to ensure explicitly that its decision does not prejudice its rights in the *NAFTA* case. In other words, said Mexico, if the Panel is going to bisect what is really one Sugar War into two battles, then it should bisect them into completely different theaters of combat that do not relate to one another.

---

[2] John Nagel, *U.S. Executive Urges Sweetener Accord with Mexico, Outlines Important Points*, 20 INT'L TRADE REP. (BNA) 393 (27 Feb. 2003).

3. The Panel, Consequentialism, and Morality

Unfortunately for Mexico, the Panel rejected its primary argument that the United States wrongly bisected what is one case. The Panel not only said it lacked the discretion to decide whether or not to exercise jurisdiction over a case properly before it, and thus did exercise this jurisdiction, but also held against the Article XX(d) defense. The Soft Drink Tax, Distribution Tax, and Bookkeeping Requirements hardly were necessary to secure compliance by the United States with other laws or regulations. That set the stage for a simple appeal — was the Panel right to exercise jurisdiction rather than defer to a *NAFTA* dispute settlement action, and if so, was it right to rule against the Article XX(d) defense?

The readily apparent problem with the Mexican strategy is that it was, at bottom, tit-for-tat. That results in the law of the jungle governing international economic relations. But, Mexico's strategy was poor on more than consequential grounds. It was morally dubious.

Victimized as Mexico probably was by poor American behavior in respect of *NAFTA*, it took a deliberately illegal act (violating a pillar of GATT) and sought to justify that act with the positive consequences the act might produce (better behavior by the United States). In international trade relations, as in all aspects of life, even an unambiguously good outcome causally linked to a serious wrong does not justify the wrong. Much of the *Mexico — HFCS* case, then, can be read as the Appellate Body, like the Panel before it, looking (consciously or not) for the technically correct legal bases on which to manifest these consequential and normative principles.

B. *NAFTA*, the WTO, and Judicial Abstinence

WTO APPELLATE BODY REPORT, *MEXICO — TAX MEASURES ON SOFT DRINKS AND OTHER BEVERAGES*
WT/DS308/AB/R (adopted 24 March 2006)
(complaint by United States)

I. Issues Raised in This Appeal

39. The following issues are raised in this appeal:

   (a) whether the Panel erred in concluding that a WTO panel "has no discretion to decide whether or not to exercise its jurisdiction in a case properly before it" and, if so, whether the Panel erred in declining to exercise that discretion in the circumstances of this dispute;

   (b) whether the Panel erred in concluding that Mexico's measures do not constitute measures "to secure compliance with laws or regulations", within the meaning of Article XX(d) of the GATT 1994. . . .

[On the third issue, the Appellate Body held the Panel did make an objective assessment of the facts of the case, as required by *DSU* 11.]

IV. The Panel's Exercise of Jurisdiction

. . . .

B. *Analysis*

44. . . . "Mexico does not question that the Panel has jurisdiction to hear the United States' claims." Moreover, Mexico does not claim "that there are legal obligations under the *NAFTA* or any other international agreement to which Mexico and the United States are both parties, which might raise legal impediments to the Panel hearing this case." Instead, Mexico's position is that, although the Panel had the authority to rule on the merits of the United States' claims, it also had the "implied power" to abstain from ruling on them, and "should have exercised this power in the circumstances of this dispute." Hence, the issue before us in this appeal is not whether the Panel was legally precluded from ruling on the United States' claims that were before it, but, rather, whether the Panel could decline, and should have declined, to exercise jurisdiction with respect to the United States' claims under Article III of the GATT 1994 that were before it.

45. Turning to Mexico's arguments on appeal, we note, first, Mexico's argument that WTO panels, like other international bodies and tribunals, "have certain implied jurisdictional powers that derive from their nature as adjudicative bodies," and thus have a basis for declining to exercise jurisdiction. We agree with Mexico that WTO panels have certain powers that are inherent in their adjudicative function. Notably, panels have the right to determine whether they have jurisdiction in a given case, as well as to determine the scope of their jurisdiction. In this regard, the Appellate Body has previously stated that "it is a widely accepted rule that an international tribunal is entitled to consider the issue of its own jurisdiction on its own initiative, and to satisfy itself that it has jurisdiction in any case that comes before it." Further, the Appellate Body has also explained that panels have "a margin of discretion to deal, always in accordance with due process, with specific situations that may arise in a particular case and that are not explicitly regulated." For example, panels may exercise judicial economy, that is, refrain from ruling on certain claims, when such rulings are not necessary "to resolve the matter in issue in the dispute." The Appellate Body has cautioned, nevertheless, that "[t]o provide only a partial resolution of the matter at issue would be false judicial economy."

46. In our view, it does not necessarily follow, however, from the existence of these inherent adjudicative powers that, once jurisdiction has been validly established, WTO panels would have the authority to decline to rule on the entirety of the claims that are before them in a dispute. To the contrary, we note that, while recognizing WTO panels' inherent powers, the Appellate Body has previously emphasized [in *India — Patent Protection for Pharmaceutical and Agricultural Chemical Products*, WT/DS50/AB/R ¶ 92 (adopted 16 January 1998)] that:

> Although panels enjoy some discretion in establishing their own working procedures, *this discretion does not extend to modifying the substantive provisions of the DSU. . . . Nothing in the DSU gives a*

*panel the authority either to disregard or to modify . . . explicit
provisions of the DSU.* (emphasis added)

47. . . . Mexico argues that "[t]here is nothing in the *DSU* . . . that
explicitly rules out the existence of" a WTO panel's power to decline to exercise
its jurisdiction even in a case that is properly before it.

48. We first address Article 7 of the *DSU*, which governs the terms of
reference of panels. . . . The Panel in this dispute was established with
standard terms of reference, which instructed the Panel to "examine" the
United States' claims that were before it and to "make findings" with respect
to consistency of the measures at issue with Article III of the GATT 1994.

49. The second paragraph of Article 7 further stipulates that "[p]anels shall
address the relevant provisions in any covered agreement or agreements cited
by the parties to the dispute." The use of the words "shall address" in Article
7.2 indicates, in our view, that panels are required to address the relevant
provisions in any covered agreement or agreements cited by the parties to the
dispute.

. . . .

51. Article 11 of the *DSU* states that panels *should* make an objective
assessment of the matter before them. The Appellate Body has previously held
[in *Canada — Measures Affecting the Export of Civilian Aircraft*, WT/DS70/
AB/R, ¶ 187 (20 August 1999), which quoted *The Concise Oxford English
Dictionary*] that the word "should" can be used not only "to imply an exhortation, or to state a preference", but also "to express a duty [or] obligation." The
Appellate Body has repeatedly ruled that a panel would not fulfil its mandate
if it were not to make an objective assessment of the matter. [The Appellate
Body cited to its Reports in *Canada — Aircraft*, ¶¶ 187-88, *European Communities — Export Subsidies on Sugar*, WT/DS266/AB/R, ¶¶ 329, 335 (adopted
19 May 2005), *EC Measures Concerning Meat and Meat Products (Hormones)*,
WT/DS26/AB/R, WT/DS48/AB/R, ¶ 133 (adopted 13 February 1998).] Under
Article 11 of the *DSU*, a panel is, therefore, charged with the *obligation* to
"make an objective assessment of the matter before it, including an objective
assessment of the facts of the case and the applicability of and conformity with
the relevant covered agreements." Article 11 also requires that a panel "make
such other findings as will assist the DSB in making the recommendations
or in giving the rulings provided for in the covered agreements." It is difficult
to see how a panel would fulfil that obligation if it declined to exercise validly
established jurisdiction and abstained from making any finding on the matter
before it.

52. Furthermore, Article 23 of the *DSU* states that Members of the WTO
shall have recourse to the rules and procedures of the *DSU* when they "seek
the redress of a violation of obligations . . . under the covered agreements."
As the Appellate Body has previously explained [in *United States — Sunset
Review of Anti-Dumping Duties on Corrosion-Resistant Carbon Steel Flat
Products from Japan*, WT/DS244/AB/R ¶ 89 (adopted 9 January 2004)],
"allowing measures to be the subject of dispute settlement proceedings . . .
is consistent with the comprehensive nature of the right of Members to resort
to dispute settlement to 'preserve [their] rights and obligations . . . under the

covered agreements, and to clarify the existing provisions of those agreements'." We also note in this regard that Article 3.3 of the *DSU* provides that the "prompt settlement of situations in which *a Member considers* that any benefits accruing to it directly or indirectly under the covered agreements are being impaired by measures taken by another Member is essential to the effective functioning of the WTO." The fact that a Member may initiate a WTO dispute whenever it considers that "any benefits accruing to [that Member] are being impaired by measures taken by another Member" implies that that Member is *entitled* to a ruling by a WTO panel.

53. A decision by a panel to decline to exercise validly established jurisdiction would seem to "diminish" the right of a complaining Member to "seek the redress of a violation of obligations" within the meaning of Article 23 of the *DSU*, and to bring a dispute pursuant to Article 3.3 of the *DSU*. This would not be consistent with a panel's obligations under Articles 3.2 and 19.2 of the *DSU*. We see no reason, therefore, to disagree with the Panel's statement that a WTO panel "would seem . . . not to be in a position to choose freely whether or not to exercise its jurisdiction."

54. Mindful of the precise scope of Mexico's appeal, we express no view as to whether there may be other circumstances in which legal impediments could exist that would preclude a panel from ruling on the merits of the claims that are before it. In the present case, Mexico argues that the United States' claims under Article III of the GATT 1994 are inextricably linked to a broader dispute, and that only a *NAFTA* panel could resolve the dispute as a whole. Nevertheless, Mexico does not take issue with the Panel's finding that "neither the subject matter nor the respective positions of the parties are identical in the dispute under the *NAFTA* . . . and the dispute before us." Mexico also stated that it could not identify a legal basis that would allow it to raise, in a WTO dispute settlement proceeding, the market access claims it is pursuing under the *NAFTA*. It is furthermore undisputed that no *NAFTA* panel as yet has decided the "broader dispute" to which Mexico has alluded. Finally, we note that Mexico has expressly stated that the so-called "exclusion clause" of Article 2005.6 of the *NAFTA* had not been "exercised." We do not express any view on whether a legal impediment to the exercise of a panel's jurisdiction would exist in the event that features such as those mentioned above were present. In any event, we see no legal impediments applicable in this case.

55. Finally, as we understand it, Mexico's position is that the "applicability" of its WTO obligations towards the United States would be "call[ed] into question" as a result of the United States having prevented Mexico, by an illegal act (namely, the alleged refusal by the United States to nominate panelists to the *NAFTA* panel), from having recourse to the *NAFTA* dispute settlement mechanism to resolve a bilateral dispute between Mexico and the United States regarding trade in sweeteners. Specifically, Mexico refers to the ruling of the Permanent Court of International Justice (the "PCIJ") in the *Factory at Chorzów* case, and "calls into question the 'applicability' of its WTO obligations towards the United States in the context of this dispute."

[As the Appellate Body recounted in a footnote, the passage of the ruling to which Mexico referred states:

. . . one party cannot avail himself of the fact that the other has not fulfilled some obligation, or has not had recourse to some means of redress, if the former party has, by some illegal act, prevented the latter from fulfilling the obligation in question, or from having recourse to the tribunal which would have been open to him.

(Permanent Court of International Justice, *Factory at Chorzów (Germany v. Poland)* (Jurisdiction), 1927, PCIJ Series A, No. 9, p. 31) (underlining added by Mexico omitted)]

56. Mexico's arguments, as well as its reliance on the ruling in *Factory at Chorzów*, is misplaced. Even assuming, *arguendo*, that the legal principle reflected in the passage referred to by Mexico is applicable within the WTO dispute settlement system, we note that this would entail a determination whether the United States has acted consistently or inconsistently with its *NAFTA* obligations. We see no basis in the *DSU* for panels and the Appellate Body to adjudicate non-WTO disputes. Article 3.2 of the *DSU* states that the WTO dispute settlement system "serves to preserve the rights and obligations of Members under the *covered agreements*, and to clarify the existing provisions of *those agreements*." (emphasis added) Accepting Mexico's interpretation would imply that the WTO dispute settlement system could be used to determine rights and obligations outside the covered agreements. In light of the above, we do not see how the PCIJ's ruling in *Factory at Chorzów* supports Mexico's position in this case.

[In a footnote, the Appellate Body further observed that

. . . the ruling of the PCIJ in the *Factory at Chorzów* case relied on by Mexico was made in a situation in which the party objecting to the exercise of jurisdiction by the PCIJ was the party that had committed the act alleged to be illegal. In the present case, the party objecting to the exercise of jurisdiction by the Panel (Mexico) relies instead on an allegedly illegal act committed by the other party (the United States).

Should this difference matter? Or, is the real weakness in the Mexican argument that the U.S. has not prevented Mexico from fulfilling its GATT obligations?]

57. For all these reasons, we *uphold* the Panel's conclusion . . . "under the *DSU*, it ha[d] no discretion to decline to exercise its jurisdiction in the case that ha[d] been brought before it." Having upheld this conclusion, we *find* it unnecessary to rule in the circumstances of this appeal on the propriety of exercising such discretion.

C. *NAFTA* and Administrative Necessity under GATT Article XX(d)

WTO APPELLATE BODY REPORT, *MEXICO — TAX MEASURES ON SOFT DRINKS AND OTHER BEVERAGES* WT/DS308/AB/R (adopted 24 March 2006)

V. Article XX(d) of GATT 1994

. . . .

B. *Analysis*

68. The central issue raised in this appeal is whether the terms "to secure compliance with laws or regulations" in Article XX(d) of the GATT 1994 encompass WTO-inconsistent measures applied by a WTO Member to secure compliance with another WTO Member's obligations under an international agreement.

69. . . . [W]e consider it more helpful to begin our analysis with the terms "laws or regulations" in Article XX(d) (which we consider to be pivotal here) rather than to begin with the analysis of the terms "to secure compliance," as did the Panel. The terms "laws or regulations" are generally used to refer to domestic laws or regulations. As Mexico and the United States note, previous GATT and WTO disputes in which Article XX(d) has been invoked as a defence have involved domestic measures. Neither disputes that the expression "laws or regulations" encompasses the rules adopted by a WTO Member's legislative or executive branches of government. We agree with the United States that one does not immediately think about international law when confronted with the term "laws" in the plural. Domestic legislative or regulatory acts sometimes may be intended to implement an international agreement. In such situations, the origin of the rule is international, but the implementing instrument is a domestic law or regulation. In our view, the terms "laws or regulations" refer to rules that form part of the domestic legal system of a WTO Member. Thus, the "laws or regulations" with which the Member invoking Article XX(d) may seek to secure compliance do not include obligations of *another* WTO Member under an international agreement.

70. The illustrative list of "laws or regulations" provided in Article XX(d) supports the conclusion that these terms refer to rules that form part of the domestic legal system of a WTO Member. This list includes "[laws or regulations] relating to customs enforcement, the enforcement of monopolies operated under paragraph 4 of Article II and Article XVII, the protection of patents, trade marks and copyrights, and the prevention of deceptive practices." These matters are typically the subject of domestic laws or regulations, even though some of these matters may also be the subject of international agreements. The matters listed as examples in Article XX(d) involve the regulation by a government of activity undertaken by a variety of economic actors (*e.g.*, private firms and State enterprises), as well as by government agencies. For example, matters "relating to customs enforcement" will generally involve rights and obligations that apply to importers or exporters, and

matters relating to "the protection of patents, trade marks and copyrights" will usually regulate the use of these rights by the intellectual property right holders and other private actors. Thus, the illustrative list reinforces the notion that the terms "laws or regulations" refer to rules that form part of the domestic legal system of a WTO Member and do not extend to the international obligations of another WTO Member.

71. Our understanding of the terms "laws or regulations" is consistent with the context of Article XX(d). As the United States points out, other provisions of the covered agreements refer expressly to "international obligations" or "international agreements." For example, paragraph (h) of Article XX refers to "obligations under any intergovernmental commodity agreement." The express language of paragraph (h) would seem to contradict Mexico's suggestion that international agreements are implicitly included in the terms "laws or regulations." The United States and China [a third party participant] also draw our attention to Article X:1 of the GATT 1994, which refers to "[l]aws, regulations, judicial decisions and administrative rulings" and to "[a]greements affecting international trade policy which are in force between a government . . . of any Member and the government . . . of any other Member." Thus, a distinction is drawn in the same provision between "laws [and] regulations" and "international agreements." Such a distinction would have been unnecessary if, as Mexico argues, the terms "laws" and "regulations" were to encompass international agreements that have not been incorporated, or do not have direct effect in, the domestic legal system of the respective WTO Member. Thus, Articles X:1 and XX(h) of the GATT 1994 do not lend support to interpreting the terms "laws or regulations" in Article XX(d) as including the international obligations of a Member other than that invoking the provision.

72. We turn to the terms "to secure compliance," which were the focus of the Panel's reasoning and are the focus of Mexico's appeal. The terms "to secure compliance" speak to the types of measures that a WTO Member can seek to justify under Article XX(d). They relate to the design of the measures sought to be justified. There is no justification under Article XX(d) for a measure that is not designed "to secure compliance" with a Member's laws or regulations. Thus, the terms "to secure compliance" do not expand the scope of the terms "laws or regulations" to encompass the international obligations of another WTO Member. Rather, the terms "to secure compliance" circumscribe the scope of Article XX(d).

73. Mexico takes issue with several aspects of the Panel's reasoning related to the interpretation of the terms "to secure compliance." . . . [A]ccording to the Panel, "[t]he context in which the expression is used makes clear that 'to secure compliance' is to be read as meaning to enforce compliance." The Panel added that, in contrast to enforcement action taken within a Member's legal system, "the effectiveness of [Mexico's] measures in achieving their stated goal — that of bringing about a change in the behaviour of the United States — seems . . . to be inescapably uncertain." Thus, the Panel concluded that "the outcome of international countermeasures, such as those adopted by Mexico, is inherently unpredictable."

74. It is Mexico's submission that the Panel erred in requiring a degree of certainty as to the results achieved by the measure sought to be justified.

Mexico also asserts that the Panel, in its reasoning, incorrectly relied on the Appellate Body Report in *U.S. — Gambling* [*i.e., United States — Measures Affecting the Cross-Border Supply of Gambling and Betting Services*, WT/DS285/AB/R ¶ 317 (adopted 20 April 2005).] We agree with Mexico that the *US — Gambling* Report does not support the conclusion that the Panel sought to draw from it. The statement to which the Panel referred was made in the context of the examination of the "necessity" requirement in Article XIV(a) of the *General Agreement on Trade in Services*, and did not relate to the terms "to secure compliance." As the Appellate Body has explained previously [in *Korea — Measures Affecting Imports of Fresh, Chilled and Frozen Beef*, WT/DS161/AB/R, WT/DS169/AB/R, ¶ 164 (adopted 10 January 2001)], "the contribution made by the compliance measure to the enforcement of the law or regulation at issue" is one of the factors that must be weighed and balanced to determine whether a measure is "necessary" within the meaning of Article XX(d). A measure that is not suitable or capable of securing compliance with the relevant laws or regulations will not meet the "necessity" requirement. We see no reason, however, to derive from the Appellate Body's examination of "necessity", in *US — Gambling*, a requirement of "certainty" applicable to the terms "to secure compliance." In our view, a measure can be said to be designed "to secure compliance" even if the measure cannot be guaranteed to achieve its result with absolute certainty. Nor do we consider that the "use of coercion" is a necessary component of a measure designed "to secure compliance." Rather, Article XX(d) requires that the design of the measure contribute "to secur[ing] compliance with laws or regulations which are not inconsistent with the provisions of" the GATT 1994.

75. Nevertheless, while we agree with Mexico that the Panel's emphasis on "certainty" and "coercion" is misplaced, we consider that Mexico's arguments miss the point. Even if "international countermeasures" could be described as intended "to secure compliance," what they seek "to secure compliance with" — that is, the international obligations of another WTO Member — would be outside the scope of Article XX(d). This is because "laws or regulations" within the meaning of Article XX(d) refer to the rules that form part of the domestic legal order of the WTO Member invoking the provision and do not include the international obligations of *another* WTO Member.

. . . .

77. . . . Mexico's interpretation of Article XX(d) disregards the fact that the GATT 1994 and the *DSU* specify the actions that a WTO Member may take if it considers that another WTO Member has acted inconsistently with its obligations under the GATT 1994 or any of the other covered agreements. As the United States points out, Mexico's interpretation of the terms "laws or regulations" as including international obligations of another WTO Member would logically imply that a WTO Member could invoke Article XX(d) to justify also measures designed "to secure compliance" with that other Member's WTO obligations. By the same logic, such action under Article XX(d) would evade the specific and detailed rules that apply when a WTO Member seeks to take countermeasures in response to another Member's failure to comply with rulings and recommendations of the DSB pursuant to Article XXIII:2 of the GATT 1994 and Articles 22 and 23 of the *DSU*. Mexico's interpretation would allow

WTO Members to adopt WTO-inconsistent measures based upon a *unilateral* determination that another Member has breached its WTO obligations, in contradiction with Articles 22 and 23 of the *DSU* and Article XXIII:2 of the GATT 1994.

78. Finally, even if the terms "laws or regulations" do not go so far as to encompass the WTO agreements, as Mexico argues, Mexico's interpretation would imply that, in order to resolve the case, WTO panels and the Appellate Body would have to assume that there is a violation of the relevant international agreement (such as the *NAFTA*) by the complaining party, or they would have to assess whether the relevant international agreement has been violated. WTO panels and the Appellate Body would thus become adjudicators of non-WTO disputes. As we noted earlier [at Paragraph 56, excerpted earlier], this is not the function of panels and the Appellate Body as intended by the *DSU*.

79. For these reasons, we agree with the Panel that Article XX(d) is not available to justify WTO-inconsistent measures that seek "to secure compliance" by another WTO Member with that other Member's international obligations. In sum, while we agree with the Panel's conclusion, several aspects of our reasoning set out above differ from the Panel's own reasoning. First, we conclude that the terms "laws or regulations" cover rules that form part of the domestic legal system of a WTO Member, including rules deriving from international agreements that have been incorporated into the domestic legal system of a WTO Member or have direct effect according to that WTO Member's legal system. Second, we have found that Article XX(d) does not require the "use of coercion" nor that the measure sought to be justified results in securing compliance with absolute certainty. Rather, Article XX(d) requires that the measure be designed "to secure compliance with laws or regulations which are not inconsistent with the provisions of" the GATT 1994. Finally, we do not endorse the Panel's reliance on the Appellate Body's interpretation in *US — Gambling* of the term "necessary" to interpret the terms "to secure compliance" in Article XX(d).

80. Therefore, we *uphold*, albeit for different reasons, the Panel's conclusion . . . that Mexico's measures do not constitute measures "to secure compliance with laws or regulations," within the meaning of Article XX(d) of the GATT 1994.

Chapter 24

PREFERENTIAL RULES OF ORIGIN

Tell me this: who begot thee?

—William Shakespeare, Two Gentlemen of Verona,
act 3, sc 1

DOCUMENTS SUPPLEMENT ASSIGNMENT

1. *NAFTA* Chapter 4
2. Rules of Origin in other FTAs

I. WHY PREFERENTIAL RULES OF ORIGIN ARE INDISPENSABLE

Suppose Countries A, B, C, and D, all WTO Members, form a free trade agreement (FTA) or customs union (CU). As a result, goods from any one of these countries may be imported into any other country in the regional trade agreement (RTA) duty-free. Suppose Country E, but not Country F, is a WTO Member. It should be clear that there are three distinct tariff regimes in Countries A, B, C, and D.

First, preferential duty-free treatment applies to goods originating from within the FTA or CU. Second, MFN rates, negotiated and bound as a result of previous GATT—WTO rounds, apply to goods of E imported into Countries A, B, C, or D. Third, non-MFN rates apply to goods from F imported into Countries A, B, C, or D.

How does a customs official in Countries A, B, C, or D determine whether a good is from (1) the FTA or CU, (2) Country E, or (3) Country F? Customs officials in the *North American Free Trade Agreement (NAFTA)* Parties — countries analogous to A, B, C, and D — face this dilemma. Country E is akin to any WTO Member, while Country F is akin to North Korea. Preferential rules of origin resolve the dilemma. Such rules establish the country of origin of a good to determine whether it is from the FTA or CU in question. In essence, a "rule of origin" is a genealogical rule about a category of merchandise. The rule is "preferential" in the sense that depending on the genealogy of the article, duty-free or other special treatment may be accorded to that article.

There would be no need for such rules if all goods from all countries were imported at MFN rates, regardless of the origin of the goods. But, as the above example illustrates, a "true" MFN system does not exist. In practice, the origin of goods matters because the international trade community is divided into customs unions and free trade areas. Because they assign a nationality to a good that is treated differently for tariff purposes according to its country of origin, preferential rules of origin are the cornerstone of any customs union or FTA. They ensure that only goods originating from a country in a preferential trading arrangement receive duty-free treatment. After all, the countries that are party to the arrangement have a legitimate interest in seeking to limit the benefits of the arrangement to themselves, *i.e.*, in avoiding free riders. But, the key issue is whether the preferential rules of origin concocted by the member countries to delineate their goods from the goods of all other countries are unacceptably trade-distorting.

Preferential rules of origin also are of paramount importance in resolving the problem of "trade deflection." This term refers to re-routing of products originating in a third country that do not have preferential access to the market of one country. They lack duty-free access because the third country is not a member of the same FTA or CU as the other country. Goods are re-routed through a second country that does have preferential access, because the second country is a member of the relevant FTA or CU. While "trade deflection" is largely synonymous with "trans-shipment," in fact deflection can occur through other than simple trans-shipment, *i.e.*, export from one country and subsequent re-export to another country. In particular, the goods can undergo a basic operation, such as re-packaging, cleaning, or sorting, when they are re-routed in the second country. Rules of origin of an FTA or CU are designed to counteract trade deflection by either means, barring preferential treatment for non-originating deflected goods.

For example, suppose Countries R, S, and T are WTO Members, but Country Z is not a Member. Country Z exports basketballs to Country R. In turn, Country R exports the basketballs to Country S. No change is made to them in R. Or, alternatively, they are repackaged, cleaned, or sorted. Thus, the basketballs are deflected from Z to S through R. Assume Country S levies a 20 percent tariff on the basketballs trans-shipped through Country R, and R protests. Country R points out that as a result of previous negotiations conducted under GATT—WTO auspices, the binding tariff commitment made by Country S with respect to basketballs is 15 percent. It further points out that S imposes a 12 percent duty on basketballs imported directly from Country T. Thus, Country R argues it is entitled to either the 15 percent tariff by virtue of the binding commitment, or the 12 percent rate by virtue of the MFN clause in GATT Article I. Country R's argument must fail because the basketballs are the product of Country Z.

A slight alteration in the facts may radically change this outcome in Country R's favor. Assume the goods in question are not basketballs but copper. While the copper is in Country R, it is melted down, processed, and made into copper wire. s the copper wire the product of Z or R? Mere trans-shipment, or even re-packaging, cleaning, and sorting does not result in a change in the country of origin of the good, as the basketball example illustrates. However, transformation of the good into another good may result in a change in the country of origin. Making copper wire out of copper may be a sufficient transformation to justify Country R's argument it is entitled to the bound or MFN rate, because the copper wire truly is a product of R and is categorized differently, and thus a different duty rate applies.

II. THREE CATEGORIES OF PREFERENTIAL RULES OF ORIGIN

In spite of the global disharmony, preferential rules of origin may be placed in one of three general categories: (1) the substantial transformation test; (2) the value added test; and (3) the hybrid approach. These categories are based in part on the work of the 1953 GATT drafting group and the 1974 *Kyoto Convention*.

Category 1: The Substantial Transformation Test and Change in Tariff Classification Rule

Under the "substantial transformation" test, merchandise becomes the product of the most recent exporting country in which a "substantial" transformation of the input goods imported from another country occurred. For example, transforming copper into copper wire might be considered "substantial."

This test still begs the question of what is "substantial." A reasonably precise and objective answer is a transformation is substantial if it results in a change in the HTS classification of the good. Specifically, the 4 digit HTS category in which the good is placed is different from the category (categories) of the material(s) used to make the good. In other words, if a finished product falls under a tariff classification at the 4 digit level that is different from any of the materials used to make the product, then a shift at the 4 digit level has occurred. This method is sometimes called the "change in tariff heading" (CTH), or simply "tariff shift," rule. If the rule calls for a change at the 6 digit HTS category, *i.e.*, at the level of sub-heading rather than heading, then that rule is technically a "CTSH" rule — a change in tariff sub-heading.

For any particular product, a CTH rule may be phrased in positive or negative terms. The positive construction takes the form of saying origin is conferred if there is "a change from any other heading to heading . . . to Chapter __. . . ." The negative construction takes the form of saying origin is conferred if there is "a change from any other heading, except for the headings of Chapter __ to . . . ." Consider the negative construction in relation to specified manufacturing processes (discussed below). Can a negative CTH rule be written to have the same effect as a specified process rule?

Consider the above example involving copper and Countries R, S, T, and Z. Suppose copper appears in one 4 digit HTS classification, while copper wire appears in a different 4 digit heading. The copper is mined in Country Z and exported to Country R, where operations are performed on the copper that result in copper wire. Subsequently, the copper wire is trans-shipped through Country S to Country T. Because of the tariff shift at the 4 digit level, the operations performed in Country R on the copper are "substantial" transformation. Thus, the copper wire is a product of R, not Z.

The CTH rule is particularly helpful in harmonizing rules of origin because it relies on the HTS. As of 2006, 169 countries, representing 98 percent of world trade, use the HTS. (These figures are up from 1993, the year the Uruguay Round concluded, when the HTS covered about 120 countries and 90 percent of world trade.) In turn, the HTS is structured in a way that facilitates the application of the CTH rule:

The Harmonized System comprises 21 Sections, 96 Chapters and 1,241 headings. [More recently, in the U.S. Tariff Schedule, a 22nd Section was introduced for "special classifications." There are now 99 Chapters, with Chapter 77 reserved for future use.] Of these 1,241 headings, 930 are sub-divided into 2,449 sub-headings, which are further sub-divided into 2,258 two-dash sub-headings, thereby providing a total of 5,018 separate categories of classification of goods in the Harmonized System. Classification of goods under these headings or sub-headings is governed by the heading or sub-heading text, supported by General Rules for the interpretation of the Harmonized System, Section Notes, Chapter Notes and Sub-heading Notes.

. . . .

The first feature [of the Harmonized System that makes it suitable for use in determining country of origin] is the basic classification division according to industrial sector. [G]oods . . . are first grouped in 21 Sections and then in 96 Chapters which, in principle, are established by industrial sector. This is one of the most important requirements for a nomenclature to qualify for use in the determination of the country of origin, given that the country of origin is determined on the basis of the substantial transformation concept in so far as the goods have been manufactured in two or more countries.

The second feature is the order of headings within a Chapter. There are 1,241 headings . . . which constitute the most important level for tariff classification as well as for origin purposes. [H]eadings are placed within a Chapter in the order based upon the degree of processing. For example, Chapter 72 which covers iron and steel begins with pig iron (heading 72.01) and the heading number increases as a product is further processed; ingot (heading 72.04), semi-finished products (heading 72.06), flat-rolled products (headings 72.08 to 72.12), bars and rods (headings 72.13 to 72.15), angles, shapes and sections (heading 72.16), wire (heading 72.17). The order of headings within a Chapter generally reflects the degree of processing a product has undergone. This structure makes the Harmonized System a suitable device for applying the concept of substantial transformation in determining the country of origin.[1]

Still, the CTH rule poses some difficulties.

One difficulty is that headings in certain chapters of the HTS do not reflect the degree of processing. For example, there is no processing associated with the live animals listed in Chapter 1. Accordingly, the rule may not always mesh with the HTS. This difficulty reflects the more general fact that the HTS was not designed as a methodology to confer origin. When product-specific rules of origin (PSROs) are based on the HTS, clever businesses and their attorneys can figure out CTH requirements that best suit their interests, regardless of the underlying economic integrity of those requirements.

---

[1] Hironori Asakura, *The Harmonized System and Rules of Origin*, 27 J. WORLD TRADE 5, 9, 12 (1993).

A second problem is certain manufacturing or processing operations are deemed insubstantial, even though they result in a change in tariff classification. That is, even a change in tariff classification from one chapter to another may not result in a substantial transformation. For example, a change to a preparation of vegetables, fruits, or nuts — *i.e.*, items listed in HTS Chapter 20 — from the vegetable products listed in Chapters 6-14 as a result of freezing, canning in water or natural juices, or roasting is not substantial.

Consider HTS Chapter 7, which covers edible vegetables. The first nine headings (07.01 to 07.09) list fresh and chilled vegetables. Subsequent headings specify frozen vegetables (heading 07.10), provisionally preserved vegetables (heading 07.11) and dried vegetables (heading 07.12). Have frozen, provisionally preserved, and dried vegetables truly been "substantially" transformed from fresh vegetables? In such cases, countries frequently list exceptions to the CTH rule. Indeed, *NAFTA*'s rules of origin, which are contained in Section B of Annex 401, contain several dozens of such exceptions. With respect to vegetables, to obtain the status of the country of origin, "a change to heading 07.10 through 07.14 from any other chapter" is required:

> In other words, the change in tariff heading method is not applicable to the classification change within a chapter but is applied only to the classification change from *outside* the chapter. The same is applied in the NAFTA in respect to some other chapters, *i.e.*, 1 (animals), 2 (meat), 3 (fish), 5 (animal products, n.e.s. (not elsewhere specified)), 6 (plants), 8 (fruits and nuts), 9 (coffee, tea, spices), 10 (cereals), 11 (milling industry products), 12 (oil seeds), 13 (vegetable saps and extracts), 16 (preparations of meat, fish, etc.), 25 (salt, sulphur, etc.), 49 (products of the printing industry), 69 (ceramics), 82 (tools of base metal) and 97 (works of art).[2]

A third concern with the CTH rule follows from the second problem.

Exceptions to the rule necessarily result in protection for certain domestically produced goods. For example, assume Austria exports fresh carrots to Mexico. In Mexico, the carrots are frozen. The frozen carrots are exported to the U.S. Because a change in tariff classification from fresh vegetables to frozen vegetables is deemed not to be a substantial transformation under *NAFTA*, the frozen carrots are a product of Austria, not Mexico. Therefore, they do not qualify for duty-free treatment under *NAFTA*, but rather receive the appropriate MFN rate. This result helps protect U.S. farmers and domestic vegetable processors from competition from non-*NAFTA* agricultural and food producers. The many exceptions to the CTH rule identified in the above-quoted passage suggest protection is afforded to a significant number of industries. To be sure, the result also helps protect *NAFTA* farmers from non-*NAFTA* farmers and food processors who alter slightly their goods to obtain *NAFTA* benefits that the *NAFTA* Parties have not extended to the non-*NAFTA* countries.

A fourth problem is the converse of the second problem. In certain cases, a substantial transformation may occur even though there is no change in tariff classification between the inputs and final product. This phenomenon

---

[2] *Id.* at 17 (emphasis added).

occurs with respect to chemicals, and in classifications that include finished goods and their constituent parts.

Finally, the concepts of "essential character" and substantial transformation must operate in a consistent manner. As one scholar puts it, "one of the fundamental questions when using the Harmonized System to determine the country of origin of goods manufactured or processed in two or more countries is how to ensure the conceptual fusion of essential character and substantial transformation." The HTS GRI rely on the assumption that every good has an essential character. Thus, the doctrine of the entireties set forth in GRI Rule 2(a) states that reference to an article includes reference to the incomplete or unfinished form of the article, as long as that form has the essential character of the complete or finished article.

Consider a car that is made in Japan and exported to Canada without tires. In Canada, tires are placed on the car, and the vehicle is then exported to the U.S. Is the vehicle a product of Japan, in which case the MFN tariff rate applies, or Canada, in which case *NAFTA* duty-free treatment applies? The HTS contains General Explanatory Notes that provide examples of processing that does not alter the essential character of a good. The General Explanatory Note to HTS Chapter 87, which covers vehicles, indicates that a motor vehicle not yet fitted with tires or a battery, or not yet equipped with an engine, still has the essential character of a motor vehicle and is classified as such. Adding tires, a battery or an engine will not result in a change in tariff heading and, therefore, no substantial transformation will occur.

In spite of these difficulties, the WTO *Agreement on Rules of Origin* advocates the CTH rule as the primary criterion for determining origin. It states origin is to be conferred where the last substantial transformation took place, not where the most significant substantial transformation occurred. By focusing on the last, not the most significant, substantial transformation, the *Agreement* fosters certainty and predictability. That focus also is easier for customs officials, who can disregard previous operations and need not make judgments about which among multiple substantial transformations was the most significant.

The *Agreement* establishes a Technical Committee that must work in conjunction with the CCC to design a specific system of changes in HTS headings and sub-headings that qualify as substantial transformations. The Technical Committee and CCC also must determine what alternative rules of origin — such as a value-added test or list of manufacturing and processing operations — should be applied to goods for which a CTH rule is unworkable. The scope of the Agreement is limited: it does not apply to preferential trading arrangements, *i.e.*, FTAs or CUs, nor does it apply to preferential trading policies such as the GSP.

Category 2: The Value Added Test

Under the "value added" test, a good becomes the product of the most recent exporting country only if a specified percentage of value was added to the good in that country. A comparison is made between the ex-factory cost of the product upon exportation, and the cost of all materials used to make the product in the country from which it is exported. To continue with the above example, suppose Country S has a 50 percent value added test, and only 49 percent of the value of materials and processing associated with the manufacture of copper wire is added in Country R. Then, the copper wire would be a product of Country Z, not Country R.

Value added tests are common in U.S. customs law. One example is the 35 percent value added test in the GSP program. A second example is the 35 percent value added test in the *Caribbean Basin Initiative (CBI)*. A third example is the 35 percent value added test in the *U.S. — Israel FTA*. This test is derived from the *CBI* rule of origin. Under the *FTA*, a good that is wholly the growth, product, or manufacture of the exporting country (*i.e.*, the U.S. or Israel), or that is a new or different article that is grown, produced, or manufactured in the exporting country, qualifies for preferential treatment as a product of the U.S. or Israel if two conditions are met. First, the good is imported directly from Israel into the U.S., or vice versa. Second, at least 35 percent of the appraised value of the good is attributable to the cost of the materials and processing operations performed in the exporting country.

As a practical matter, it is important to know what criteria are used to calculate value. That is, first, what are the elements that enter into the value of the product? Do overhead expenses that are allocable to different articles qualify, and if so, how are they apportioned among merchandise? Is the calculation an ex-works cost, Second, what valuation method is used? Standard international commercial terms published by the International Chamber of Commerce, *INCOTERMS*, articulate a range of possibilities, including ex-works, fob (free on board), cif (cost, insurance, and freight), ex-factory (which includes cost of production and producer's profit), and so on. The answer to both questions typically is found in the rules of origin of the relevant FTA or CU, and implemented by the customs officials in the FTA or CU member countries. Observe that methods such as cif, which are higher-value because they are more inclusive, are thereby more restrictive on the use of non-originating inputs than other methods.

Two other practical points are notable about a value added preferential rule of origin. First, an importer of a good for which it seeks preferential treatment, or the producer or exporter of that product, had better keep good records of the production costs. In the event customs authorities seek proof of the costs, or audit relevant facilities, documentary evidence may be dispositive in proving the applicable value added test was satisfied. This problem afflicts developing countries that make many products using a single input. For instance, crude palm oil from Malaysia is imported by several developing countries, from which they make soap, margarine, and refined cooking oil. Accurate record-keeping and accounting methods are needed to calculate the input cost for each finished good.

Second, exchange rate movements can affect whether a product does, or does not, qualify as originating. The Table below summarizes an example of a product made in Bahrain for which the importer in the U.S. seeks duty-free treatment under the *U.S. — Bahrain FTA*. The example presumes the good produced in Bahrain requires local and imported inputs, labor, capital goods (*i.e.*, machinery), and allocated factory overhead expenses. The example also presumes the imported inputs are from Japan, and thus non-originating, *i.e.*, the applicable *FTA* rule of origin excludes them from counting in the value added calculation.

In Scenario 1, the exchange rate is U.S. $1 to 4 Bahraini *dinars*. In Scenario #2, the exchange rate is U.S. $1 to 8 Bahraini *dinars* — a 100 percent depreciation in the Bahraini currency. Almost certainly, the *dinar* is not static against third country currencies, *i.e.*, if it falls against the dollar, it is likely to tumble against other currencies, too. Suppose the Bahraini producer-exporter relies on inputs from Japan. The *dinar* depreciates not only against the dollar, but also against the Japanese *yen*. Thus, if the producer-exporter spends 2,000 *dinars* for the Japanese inputs before the exchange rate change, and if the *dinar* depreciates by 80 percent against the yen, then the producer-exporter will have to spend 3,600 *dinars* (80 percent above 2,000 *dinars*) to pay for the inputs. To be sure, 100 and 80 percent depreciations are enormous, and would put any economy into a crisis were they to occur quickly. Over the long term, however, such movements (for some currencies) observed and (for some countries) salubrious.

Critically, there is no change in the nature of economic activity in Bahrain. The same inputs and factors of production are used before and after the exchange rate shifts. The example, therefore, highlights how these shifts can affect entitlement to preferential treatment. Might this fact lead the Bahraini producer-exporter to change its source of inputs? For instance, might it source inputs from Bahrain or the U.S. — even if they are costlier and of lesser quality than the Japanese inputs? If this sourcing change occurs, then has the operation of the value added rule of origin artificially distorted trade patters?

Finally, suppose non-originating inputs are substantially transformed in Bahrain, under an applicable rule of origin (such as CTH or CTSH), so that they can be included in the value added calculation for the finished product. What effect might exchange rate movements of the Bahraini *dinar* against the *yen* have on the value added calculation?

Category 3: The Hybrid Test

The final category of rules of origin is a synthesis of the aforementioned approaches. A rule of origin may be a hybrid of the substantial transformation and value added tests. It may specify both a tariff shift and value added percentage. *NAFTA* contains hybrid tests for automotive goods.

TABLE 24-1:
EXAMPLE — VALUE ADDED TESTS, EXCHANGE RATE
FLUCTUATIONS, AND THE *U.S. — BAHRAIN FTA*

Item (denominated in dinars unless otherwise noted)	Cost in Bahraini *dinars* in Scenario #1 (U.S. $1 = 4 Bahraini dinars)	Cost in Bahraini *dinars* Scenario #2 (U.S. $1 = 8 Bahraini dinars)
Originating inputs (*i.e.*, materials from the U.S. or Bahrain)	600	600
Non-originating inputs (*i.e.*, from third countries)	2,000	3,600 (assumes 80% depreciation in *dinar* against *yen*)
Non-originating inputs (*i.e.*, from third countries) denominated in U.S. dollars	$500	$450
Labor (wages)	500	500
Machinery (depreciation of capital equipment)	400	400
Allocable Factory Overhead Expenses	300	300
Total Cost (ex-factory) in *dinars*	3,800	5,400
Total Cost (ex-factory) in dollars	$950	$675
Value Added in Bahrain in *dinars*	1,800 (3,800 minus the non-originating inputs)	1,800 (5,400 minus the non-originating inputs)
Value Added in Bahrain in U.S. dollars	$450 ($950 minus the $500 non-originating inputs)	$225 ($675 minus the $450 non-originating inputs)
Percentage Value Added in Bahrain (Value Added in Bahrain divided by Total Cost)	47.37%	33.33%
Would a 35% Value Added Test for preferential treatment be met?	Yes	No

III. PROBLEMS WITH PREFERENTIAL RULES OF ORIGIN

A. Non-Uniformity and Attempts at Harmonization

In general, the critical issue associated with the application of preferential rules of origin is how much must a good be transformed to effect a change in country of origin. The GATT does not resolve this issue. The matter rests with each WTO Member. Consequently, there is no uniform rule of origin to delineate the threshold transformation needed to alter the country of origin of an article. Moreover, GATT Article XXIV, which permits the creation of FTAs and CUs, says nothing about the rules of origin that an area or union may establish. Countries in an FTA or CU have unfettered discretion in establishing preferential rules of origin.

Not surprisingly, one observer reports "[t]here exist fourteen different preferential rules [of origin] in the European Communities, six in the United States and one in Japan" and adds that "the number may vary depending on the method of counting used." For example, *AFTA* has made use of a value-added rule of origin that states that a good is a product of a member country if at least 40 percent of its content is from any member country. The Andean Community relied on a change in tariff classification rule of origin, supplemented by a 50 percent value added rule. The rules of origin used in the *EFTA* consist of specified process lists and a 50 percent value added test for certain products.

Non-uniformity also exists within particular countries. A former Deputy Assistant Secretary of the Treasury remarked that

> [u]nfortunately, courts in the United States have not developed a rational, consistent set of principles for determining the origin of goods. Consequently, case-by-case origin determinations made by both the courts and customs officials have been inconsistent and contradictory, and have offered little guidance on which the international trade community can rely.[3]

The truth of this observation is apparent from case law on non-preferential rules of origin.

The lack of uniformity at both the international and domestic level is not a result of a lack of effort at harmonization. Various attempts have been made to develop a harmonized system of rules of origin.

For example, in October 1953 the GATT contracting parties studied a resolution submitted by the International Chamber of Commerce that called for uniformity. A drafting group established by the contracting parties prepared a two-part definition of "origin." First, a good resulting exclusively from the materials and labor of a single country was the product of the country where the good was harvested, manufactured, or otherwise brought into being. Second, a good resulting from the materials and labor of two or more countries was the product of the country in which the goods underwent the last "substantial transformation." This term was defined to mean processing that resulted in "a new individuality being conferred on the goods." Eleven countries favored the adoption of the drafting group's definition, but nine (including the U.S.) wanted to amend it, and eight opposed adoption. Thus, no action was taken. (*See* GATT B.I.S.D. (2d Supp) at 56 (1954).) The heart of the argument against uniformity — one still heard today — is that each country ought to be free to establish rules of origin, because these rules are inextricably tied up with national economic policies. In particular, they are a non-neutral tool for those policies, not merely a set of technical, objective, and de-politicized devices.

---

[3] John P. Simpson, *North American Free Trade Agreement — Rules of Origin*, 28 J. WORLD TRADE 33, 33-34 (1994).

In September 1974, the CCC adopted the *International Convention on the Simplification and Harmonization of Customs Procedures*, commonly called the *"Kyoto Convention."* (The EC adopted it in 1977. The U.S. did so in 1983, but declined to accept the rules of origin provisions. The Convention was amended in June 1999 and February 2006.) Annex D.1 to the *Kyoto Convention* establishes a similar two-part methodology to determine the country of origin. A good "wholly produced" in a country originates in that country. An example is a natural resource product that is extracted from a particular country. Where two or more countries are involved in production, the good is said to originate in the country where "substantial transformation" occurred — that is, the country in which the last substantial manufacturing or processing took place so as to impart the essential character to the good.

All countries agree a simple assembly or cosmetic processing of a product, such as packaging, should not qualify as a substantial transformation. However, most cases are not so obvious. The drafters of the *Kyoto Convention* were aware the second part of the definition would be particularly controversial, because it would be difficult to apply the abstract concept of "substantial transformation" in practice. Accordingly, the *Convention* suggests practical rules indicating a transformation occurs if any of the following three circumstances occurs: (1) there is a change of tariff classification; (2) a manufacturing or processing operation identified on an agreed-upon list has been used; or (3) a specific *ad valorem* percentage of materials or value added is reached.

In general, however, the *Kyoto Convention* delegates substantial discretion to domestic customs authorities. Hence, there is room for material discrepancies among rules of origin in different countries. One observer concludes that:

> The vagueness of the *Kyoto Convention* and the lack of GATT discipline have allowed countries a great deal of discretion. The consensus appears to be that there is no ideal system of origin, as arguments can be found in the literature in favour and against each rule that is used in practice. Whatever rule is used, transparency and predictability will be maximized if it is applied uniformly and consistently. In practice, however, few countries apply a uniform rule of origin. Indeed, the plethora of existing rules suggests that many countries are not convinced that a uniform rule is preferable.[4]

The Uruguay Round *Agreement on Rules of Origin* does not establish a uniform preferential rule of origin.

Rather, that *Agreement* focuses on non-preferential rules. The *Agreement* established a 3-year plan of action for WTO Members leading toward global harmonization of non-preferential rules of origin for roughly 5,500 product tariff lines:

> The *Agreement* applies to rules used in connection with the differential application of commercial policy instruments on the basis of origin, such as tariffs or anti-dumping and countervailing measures or safeguard measures. It aims to establish harmonized rules of origin

---

[4] Bernard Hoekman, *Rules of Origin for Goods and Services — Conceptual Issues and Economic Considerations*, 27 J. WORLD TRADE 81, 85 (1993).

among Members of the WTO within three years through the completion of a detailed work program, and in the transition period, provides for transparency and procedural rights for exporters. Although the *Agreement* explicitly does not cover the design of rules of origin elaborated under free trade agreements, the fact that rules of origin will be harmonized by WTO Members under the work program, is likely to influence the rules of origin elaborated in future free trade areas, since there will be a multilateral standard against which the free trade area rules of origin may be assessed. While the design of rules of origin for free trade areas is not covered, Annex 11 of the *Agreement* provides for enhanced transparency of such origin rules.[5]

Thus, the aim of the *Agreement* is a universal approach to the challenges of defining when goods originate or are wholly obtained in one country, and identifying what operations or processes do not confer origin, outside of the context of FTAs and CUs.

Unfortunately, the original deadline of July 1998 was missed and pushed back until November 1999, because agreement had been reached on harmonized rules for only 1,300 tariff lines. Controversial sectors, like textiles, barely had been discussed. Significantly, under Section 132 of the *1994 Uruguay Round Agreements Act* (19 U.S.C. § 3552), the U.S. may elect not to be bound by the results of the harmonization work. The second and subsequent deadlines also could not be met. Nevertheless, work continues. Even when it is completed, it is entirely possible — indeed, likely — that Members will disagree from time to time on how to interpret and apply the harmonized rules, and on how to classify certain products. Thus, harmonized origin determinations is in some sense an ideal type that never can be realized for all products at one time. The question is really one of minimizing disharmony, and thereby attacking protectionism.

The *Agreement* also imposes certain disciplines that Members must observe, before and after such harmonization is achieved, regarding rules of origin. Two examples are noteworthy. First, rules must not be used to pursue trade policy objectives, distort trade flows or discriminate against certain Members. Rather, they must be used as a technical device.

Second, all rules of origin must be clearly defined, and more generally, they must be highly transparent (*e.g.*, they must be published, new or modified rules must not be applied retroactively, any interested person must have the right to request an advanced, binding assessment of a rule, and the right to independent judicial review of administrative determinations about rules). Relatedly, until harmonized system is in place, Members are not supposed to apply "negative" rules, *i.e.*, rules that state only what does not constitute a substantial transformation (discussed below), but which do not state what does count as a substantial transformation. Negative rules are especially pernicious, because they create uncertainty for exporters, and leave undue discretion in the hands of customs officials in the importing country.

---

[5] WORLD TRADE ORGANIZATION, REGIONALISM AND THE WORLD TRADING SYSTEM 20 (1995).

B. Complexity and Cost of Compliance

No RTA can function without rules of origin. Such rules determine whether merchandise originates within a member country and, therefore, is eligible to the preferential treatment accorded by the FTA or CU. Such rules also are the playground for protectionist interests in the members. The difficulty in qualifying as an originating good varies directly with the strictness of the rules and their technical complexity, and inversely with the transparency of the rules. In some RTAs, the very articulation of the rules is intimidating. Rules of origin in the FTA between the EU and Poland take up 81 pages. In *NAFTA*, the origin rules consume about 200 pages.

Consequently, perhaps the most important point about preferential rules of origin to appreciate at the outset is they can defeat the entire purpose (or purposes) that motivated countries to enter into an RTA. Put simply and generally, in preferential rules of origin lurk the devil of protectionism. Teams of lawyers are needed to fight that devil, to counsel exporters and importers how to navigate the rules to qualify merchandise as originating within the RTA. The direct costs associated with rule of origin compliance are roughly 3-5 percent of the value of a shipment in question. If the cost of complying with the rules of origin is too high, then why bother claiming duty-free treatment?

For instance, up to 25 percent of goods eligible for duty-free treatment in the EC and *EFTA* do not receive such treatment. These importers willingly allow their merchandise to be treated as if it came from outside the EC or *EFTA* and, therefore, pay the MFN rate applicable to their goods. The importers simply do not want to struggle with complex rules of origin, nor do they wish to bother with the paperwork required by the rules. As another example, less than 5 percent of exports from Albania to the EU, which are eligible for preferential treatment granted by the EU, actually obtain that treatment. The reason is the high cost of complying with the EU's origin rules. (Happily for Albania, as a step toward full EU membership, in September 2006 the European Parliament assented to an FTA between the EU and Albania within 10 years.)

The point is preferential rules of origin may be so complex that manufacturers, exporters, and importers simply ignore them. Clearly, when this phenomenon occurs, the efficacy of a preferential trading arrangement diminishes. Further, the development objective of establishing regional production linkages and networks between or among the FTA or CU countries may be defeated is lost. In any RTA, the specific tipping point is when compliance costs exceed versus margin of preference benefits. As indicated, compliance costs vary directly with rule complexity. The margin of preference is the difference, for a particular category of merchandise, between the MFN tariff rate and the preferential rate. Suppose legal fees to research the manufacturing process associated with a type of merchandise, and the potentially relevant rules of origin, and to prepare certificates of origin amount to 3 percent of the value of a shipment of that merchandise. If the preference to gain is duty-free treatment, but the MFN rate is 3 percent or less, then the compliance costs exceed the potential gain.

C. Perverse Incentives, Cumulation, and Tolerance Levels

Preferential rules of origin can create perverse incentives. For example, might a value added rule discourage a company from investing in new property, plant, and equipment that would increase production efficiency, but drop the cost of manufacturing? Would, and should, the answer depend on that drop in relation to the tariff saved from qualifying for preferential treatment?

Even more plausible is a scenario in which a preferential rule of origin chooses among input suppliers. In an era of globalized manufacturing, absent the prospect of preferential treatment under an FTA or CU, producer-exporters are wont to source inputs from the lowest-cost, best-quality supplier. Such rules, however, may be an incentive to purchase inputs from within the FTA or CU. Insofar as the rules are difficult to modify, they cannot possibly accommodate frequent changes in global industrial configurations. In turn, trade diversion away from more efficient input suppliers can vitiate efforts by industries in the FTA or CU region to achieve economies of scale.

Perhaps, then, the following points from a World Bank publication are both unsurprising and troubling:

> There is no evidence that strict rules of origin over the past 30 years have done anything to stimulate the development of integrated pro-duction structures in developing countries. In fact, such arguments have become redundant in the light of technological changes and global trade liberalization, which have led to the fragmentation of production processes and the development of global networks of sourcing. Globalization and the splitting up of the production chain does not allow the luxury of being able to establish integrated produc-tion structures within countries. Strict rules of origin act to constrain the ability of firms to integrate into these global and regional produc-tion networks and in effect to dampen the location of any value-added activities. In the modern world economy, flexibility in the sourcing of inputs is a key element in international competitiveness. Thus, it is quite feasible that restrictive rules of origin, rather than stimulating economic development, will raise costs of production by constraining access to cheap inputs and undermine the ability of local firms to compete in overseas markets.[6]

In other words, the rules may be injurious to the long-term goal of becoming globally competitive. Why comply with them — save for the short-term benefit of duty-free treatment?

To be sure, there are ways to combat the problem of perverse incentives. In particular, two factors — cumulation rules and *de minimis* thresholds — can help preserve market-based decision making. "Cumulation" refers to the legal ability of a producer to import inputs without altering the origin of the good it makes, and thus without vitiating the entitlement of that good to preferential treatment. Consider, for instance, *CAFTA*. To what extent can

---

[6] P. Brenton & H. Imagawa, *Rules of Origin, Trade and Customs, in* CUSTOMS MODERNIZATION: A HANDBOOK 36 (L. de Wulf & J. Sokol eds., 2004).

a Honduran company incorporate non-*CAFTA* inputs and still obtain duty-free treatment from the U.S. for the finished product it exports to there?

A rule of "bilateral cumulation" allows inputs from only Honduras or the U.S. to qualify as originating inputs. All other imported inputs, whether from El Salvador or India, would not qualify. A "diagonal cumulation" rule allows inputs from any *CAFTA* country to qualify. Obviously, diagonal cumulation is more in keeping with the spirit of an FTA with more than two countries than bilateral cumulation. Significantly, at least four preferential arrangements allow for diagonal cumulation. They are the *ASEAN* FTA (*i.e.*, AFTA), Andean Community, Generalized System of Preferences (GSP), including the EU's Everything But Arms (EBA) initiative, and South Asia Association for Regional Cooperation (SAARC). Thus, for instance, under the EBA, a preferential scheme for least developed countries, the EU allows a least developed country to source inputs from other such countries, and not thereby destroy the ability of a finished product to obtain duty-free or low-tariff treatment upon shipment to the EU.

A rule of "full cumulation" allows inputs from any country, whether or not it belongs to *CAFTA*, to qualify. The inputs themselves need not undergo a substantial transformation in Honduras, though the finished good must satisfy an applicable rule of origin. Interestingly, the EU's rules of origin under its *Cotonou Agreement*, a preferential scheme for African, Pacific, and Caribbean (ACP) countries, allow for full cumulation among ACP countries. That is, one ACP country can source inputs from another ACP country, produce a finished product, export that product, and expect the EU to treat the product as made entirely of parts from the producing-exporting country.

De minimis thresholds also are called "tolerance" levels. They allow a certain percentage of non-originating materials to be incorporated into a good without altering the origin of that good. The obvious purpose is to afford flexibility in the administration of rules of origin. The EU permits a 15 percent tolerance level in the *Cotonou Agreement*, meaning that up to 15 percent of the value of a product can originate from a non-ACP country and not disentitle the product from duty-free treatment by the EU. By contrast, in its General Preferential Tariff (GPT), the Canadian GSP program, Canada sets a 60 percent *de minimis* threshold for least developed country exports, and 40 percent for developing country exports.

D.   Middle East Politics and QIZs

Preferential rules of origin can have important political ramifications. That is most apparent when they are drafted to favor merchandise from constituencies in a RTA member country, and discriminate against like products from third countries. For example, as the WTO Appellate Body case in *Canada Auto Pact — Certain Measures Affecting the Automotive Industry*, WT/DS139/AB/R (complaint by Japan) and WT/DS142/AB/R (complaint by EC) (19 June 2000) suggests, the Pact favored American and Canadian auto and auto parts suppliers, and discriminated against European and Japanese competitors. Another instance is the May 1985 *U.S. — Israel FTA*, and the 1975 *EU — Israel FTA*.

At the time of the U.S. deal, Palestinians did not have a widely recognized state. Effectively, the *U.S. — Israel FTA* discriminated against products made in the Occupied Territories, particularly the West Bank and Gaza Strip (less so the Golan Heights, to which Syria lays claims). Similarly, the EU deal excludes from preferential treatment merchandise made in the Occupied Territories. That exclusion operates to ensure Israeli goods are not from those Territories, though controversies between EU and Israel have arisen as to whether some merchandise entered in the EU as "Israeli" actually is.

Significantly, on 17 October 1995, the U.S., Israel, and Palestinian Authority exchanged letters agreeing to elimination of duties on articles originating in the West Bank and Gaza Strip. The Palestinian Authority made three pledges: to give American products duty-free access; to prevent illegal trans-shipment of non-Israeli and non-Palestinian origin goods, which are ineligible for duty-free treatment; and to support every effort at ending the Arab economic boycott of Israel. In May 1996, the U.S. and Israel agreed to amend their *FTA*, whereby they established "Qualified Industrial Zones" (QIZs) between Jordan and Israel. The QIZs are designed to rectify discriminatory effects of the *U.S. — Israel FTA* on Palestinians. To implement the October 1995 side letters and the QIZ arrangement, in October 1996, Congress amended the *United States — Israel Free Trade Implementation Act of 1985* by adding a new section to give the President authority to eliminate tariffs on products from the West Bank or Gaza Strip. The legislation applies to products from areas designated as industrial parks. They are located between the West Bank and Israel, and the Gaza Strip and Israel. It also provides for duty-free treatment for products in QIZs between Israel and Jordan and Israel and Egypt.

Thus, the U.S. accords articles originating in designated industrial parks and QIZs receive the same tariff treatment as Israeli products under the *FTA*. Obviously, these benefits are designed to encourage Arab — Israeli economic and social cooperation. Preferential rules of origin are a legal device for this encouragement. The same preferential rules of origin as exist in the *U.S. — Israel FTA* apply to all products from the industrial parks or QIZs. However, there must be a minimum amount of Israeli, Palestinian, Jordanian, or Egyptian content to qualify for duty free treatment.

By way of comment, the prospect of duty-free access to the U.S. is a characteristically American solution to the Arab — Israeli conflict. If enough money is dangled in front of the Palestinians, in the form of duty-free treatment to the consumer market of last resort, the U.S., then surely they will follow rational economic decision-making patterns. They will shift their attention to exports. Sadly, the solution has done little to stem violence throughout Israel and the Occupied Territories. How far can preferential rules of origin go to bring about peace? Might they even exacerbate tensions?

Consider the fact that duty-free treatment for articles from Israeli — Jordanian QIZs created a new problem. Products originating in Jordan did not receive duty-free treatment, and thus were discriminated against relative to like Palestinian merchandise. To address it, and to reward Jordan for signing a peace treaty with Israel in 1994, in 1996 the U.S. and Jordan agreed to a QIZ program whereby companies in American-approved industrial parks may export their goods duty-free to the United States. The QIZs (as of February 2007) are:

On the Northern Jordanian — Israeli Border: The Gateway QIZ.

In Amman: The Al-Qastal Industrial Zone, Al-Tajamouat Industrial Estate, and Mushatta International Complex.

In Aqaba: The Aqaba Industrial Estate.

In Irbid: The Al-Hassan Industrial Estate and the Jordan Cyber City.

In Kerak: The Kerak Industrial Estate.

In Zarqa: The Ad-Dulayl Industrial Park and the El-Zai Readywear Manufacturing Company.

Even more significantly, the U.S. addressed the problem — and rewarded Jordan for its support of Israeli — Palestinian peace negotiations (especially the 1993 *Oslo Accords*) — by entering into FTA negotiations with Jordan, signing a deal in October 2000.

No less than four questions may be asked about Jordan's QIZs, each one suggesting an irony:[7]

    i.   Who are the real beneficiaries? The QIZs boast 114 companies (as of February 2007). But, most of them are foreign entities, specifically, non-Jordanian and non-Israeli, with a large contingent from China. Of the 54,000-60,000 workers in the QIZs, about 18,000 — a third — are Jordanian. Bluntly put, many Jordanian citizens are unwilling to take a low-paid QIZ job, meaning non-Jordanians workers, especially from the Indian Sub-Continent, hungrily snap up the jobs.

    ii.   Are QIZs in the Middle East a divide-and-conquer strategy by hegemonic powers, or at least is pitting one Arab country against another their effect? Egyptian QIZs enjoy two comparative advantages over Jordanian QIZs. Egypt boasts relatively lower labor costs, and the access to its famed cotton is immediate.

    iii.   In the short-and medium-term, is a QIZ beneficial if manufacturing continues in sunset industries? Jordan, for example, has not provided much governmental support in the form of vocational training, nor created conditions for technology transfer. Thus, products made in the QIZs tend to be low-value added items like textiles and apparel, not so-called "new economy" products.

    iv.   What long-term value is a QIZ anyway if an FTA exists? A QIZ may be an irrelevancy, once duty-free treatment is possible through an FTA. Indeed, when the *Jordan FTA* fully frees up trade between the U.S. and Jordan (in 2010), there will be no need to include Israeli components in merchandise to obtain duty-free entry into the U.S.

A final irony is the impact — whatever their intent — of QIZs on Palestinians. Have Palestinians been helped by the various QIZs, and if not, why not?

---

[7] *See* Sharmilla Devi, *U.S. Trade Pact with Jordan Under A Cloud*, FINANCIAL TIMES, 27 Oct. 2006, at 3.

Consider the fact Israeli garment manufacturers generally prefer to outsource work to a Jordan, instead of contracting for Palestinian workers in the Occupied Territories. Might it be inferred that the presence of a QIZ in Jordan or Egypt creates an alternative for foreign enterprises to employing Palestinians?

Relations between the U.S. and Central America, and among Central American countries, furnish another example of political ramifications from preferential rules of origin. Assume a leading goal of *CAFTA—DR* is broader, deeper linkages among the members. Yet, suppose different rules of origin apply to trade between the U.S. and its *CAFTA—DR* partners, depending on the partner. For example, suppose a 50 percent value added test is used for wood handicrafts from Costa Rica, but the like product from Guatemala requires only 35 percent value added to qualify as originating in *CAFTA—DR*. Would genuine trade integration among preferred countries be possible without harmonized preferential origin rules? In turn, would heterogeneity in the rules exacerbate not only economic differences, but also political squabbles, among exporters?

E. Non-Tariff Barriers

The earlier example regarding *NAFTA*'s vegetable rules of origin and carrots from Australia suggests that rules of origin can be non-tariff barriers to trade. If the definition of "substantial transformation" is sufficiently restrictive, or the percentage value added requirement is sufficiently high, then imports will not qualify for preferential tariff treatment associated with a customs union or free trade agreement, or bound or MFN rates associated with the GATT—WTO regime. In 1974, for example, the U.S. argued rules of origin in FTAs between the EC and certain non-EC European countries were protectionist. The U.S. complained the rules favored parts and partly manufactured goods from non-EC European countries over such goods from the U.S. because of a 95 percent value added requirement. More generally, rules of origin can be subtle ways of managing trade in certain goods. As one trade negotiator states:

> The inescapable fact is that rules of origin are tools of discrimination. They have no other purpose. They are used to implement national and international laws that confer special benefits on goods of some countries and special penalties on goods of other countries.

> Those who suggest that rules of origin should be merely technical, and entirely divorced from policy considerations, simply misunderstand why rules of origin exist at all.

> . . . .

> [R]ules of origin are at best a necessary evil. They are needed to allow us to implement, with minimal disruption of trade, national laws that discriminate between goods based on their country of origin. Until the nations of the world achieve a stage of enlightenment that allows non-discriminatory trade, we must work together to ensure that rules

of origin required to implement discriminatory laws do not themselves become trade barriers.[8]

Perhaps the response to this stark reality is that as an increasing number of countries realize the benefits of free trade, they will become ever more vigilant against the abuse of rules of origin.

IV. CASE STUDY: PREFERENTIAL RULES OF ORIGIN IN *NAFTA* AND OTHER FTAs

It is instructive to consider some of the difficult, real-world problems tackled, or avoided, by negotiators in an FTA such as *NAFTA*. Their bargaining illustrates many of the pros and cons of different types of preferential rules of origin. The outcomes indicate the in-the-trenches origin work in which international trade lawyers engage.

During their negotiations with Mexican trade representatives in 1991-92, American and Canadian officials were concerned that *NAFTA* would facilitate trans-shipment of third-country goods through Mexico and thereby avoid American and Canadian trade barriers. In particular, they feared Mexico would become an "export platform" — a point of entry into the vast North American market — for Hong Kong, Malaysia, the Philippines, and other Far East countries. At the same time, as *NAFTA* Article 102:1(a) states, the fundamental purpose of the accord is to liberalize trade.

Accordingly, the challenge faced by *NAFTA* negotiators was to steer a middle course, avoiding both lax preferential rules of origin that would cause their fears to be realized and strict rules that were protectionist. Did the negotiators fail in their endeavor? Two critics argue

> . . . the main area where the *NAFTA* is open to criticism is its enumeration of restrictive rules of origin. These arcane trade provisions have been aptly labeled "tools of discrimination": they are used to determine which goods qualify for preferential treatment under the *NAFTA* and to deny *NAFTA* benefits to those goods that contain significant foreign-sourced components.
>
> . . . .
>
> The impact of rules of origin in limiting trade liberalization is suggested by comparing actual and hypothetical duty collections on U.S. imports from Canada. Based on 1991 data, duty collections from Canada will eventually drop to about 18 percent of the most-favored-nation (MFN) duty rates rather than the zero level that would occur without rules of origin. In other words, about 18 percent of US imports from Canada will not benefit from the [*Canada — U.S.*] FTA.[9]

A third critic predicts:

> In the near future, *NAFTA*'s rules of origin will encourage increased foreign investment in North America as foreign multinationals are

---

[8] John P. Simpson, *North American Free Trade Agreement — Rules of Origin*, 28 J. World Trade 33, 40-41 (1994).

[9] Gary Clyde Hufbauer & Jeffrey J. Schott, Nafta — An Assessment 5 (rev'd ed. 1993).

forced to locate not only "screwdriver" assembly plants but also input manufacturing plants within the region. This re-sourcing of production inputs and assembly plants will be most pronounced in industries whose products face large external tariffs — textiles, for example — or significant non-tariff barriers to trade. On a second level, this forced relocation of production facilities to countries within the free trade area will hamper the economic growth of developing countries that do not have equal terms of access to a large consumer market such as the European Community (EC) or the United States. On a third level, *NAFTA*'s restrictive rules of origin threaten to "obliterate" many of the touted benefits of *NAFTA*. Because *NAFTA*'s rules of origin only apply to goods that cross borders within *NAFTA*, foreign corporations will have a strong incentive to avoid them by sourcing their assembly plants within the ultimate market (*i.e.*, the U.S.), thereby frustrating the free trade agreement's goal of promoting greater efficiency within North America through the pursuit of comparative advantage.[10]

The merits of the criticism that the negotiators failed to steer a middle course between permissiveness and protectionism must be judged by analyzing carefully the nature and effects of the rules. The devil truly is in the details.

To summarize what follows below, Article 302 of *NAFTA* calls for progressive elimination of tariffs on "originating goods." Under Article 201, a good is "originating" (*i.e.*, it is the product of a *NAFTA* Party) if it satisfies a rules of origin set forth in Chapter 4 of *NAFTA*. That Chapter indicates the negotiators settled on eight broad types of rules of origin. Subsequent FTA negotiators followed and built on these categories. Thus, many, if not all, of these kinds of preferential rules of origin are found in other FTAs to which the U.S. is a party. In all instances — *NAFTA* and the other U.S. FTAs — the rules are set forth in lengthy, complex annexes to the agreements, and rendered effective in the U.S. through the legislation implementing the agreement in question.

Significantly, even if one of the rules of origin is satisfied with respect to a particular good, that good can be disqualified from preferential treatment. For example, *NAFTA* Article 411 explains an originating good will be disqualified if it is trans-shipped, that is, "undergoes further production or any other operation outside the territories of the Parties, other than unloading, reloading or any other operation necessary to preserve it in good condition or to transport the good to the territory of a Party." In addition, under Article 412(b), if the purpose of a production process simply is to circumvent *NAFTA*'s rule of origin, then goods subject to that process will be disqualified.

In studying preferential rules of origin, whether in *NAFTA* or any FTA or CU, consider whether and how they can function, by design or effect, as "covenants not to compete." Some economists argue the rules distort production decisions in FTAs and CU. There is an incentive for a producer of finished goods in an FTA or CU to select sources of raw materials and intermediate

---

[10] Joseph A. LaNasa III, *Rules of Origin Under the North American Free Trade Agreement: A Substantial Transformation into Objectively Transparent Protectionism*, 34 HARV. INT'L L.J. 381, 401-02 (1993).

inputs based on eligibility for preferential treatment rather than, or in addition to, efficiency criteria like cost. In turn, the producer may become less efficient, and consumers ultimately may suffer by paying higher prices. This argument suggests that preferential rules of origin have a detrimental impact not only on third-country suppliers (*i.e.*, those whose raw materials and inputs are ineligible for preferential treatment), but also on certain groups within the preferential trading area.

A. The Goods Wholly Obtained Rule

The first preferential rule of origin found in *NAFTA* relies on the concept of "goods wholly obtained." Under *NAFTA* Article 401(a), a good that is wholly obtained or produced in a *NAFTA* Party qualifies for preferential treatment. This rule covers extracted mineral goods, agricultural goods, fish products, and goods from the seabed. (*See NAFTA* Article 415.) This justification for origination is both basic and obvious. Hence, it is found in all FTAs. Thus, for example, Article 4:1(1)(a) of the *Chile FTA* states that a good is originating if it is "wholly obtained or produced entirely in the territory of Chile, the United States, or both." Article 3:1(a) of the *Singapore FTA* contains the same rule, as does Article 5:1(a) of the *Australia FTA* (referring to Singaporean and Australian territory, respectively, of course). Likewise, Article 5:1(a) of the *Morocco FTA* states that a good originates within the territory of Morocco or the U.S. if it is "wholly the growth, product, or manufacture of" either or both countries.

The Goods Wholly Obtained Rule is adapted from Rule 2 of the 1974 *Kyoto Convention*. That Rule lists 10 types of goods that must be considered to be produced wholly within one country. One innovation introduced by *NAFTA* is that a good taken from outer space by a *NAFTA* Party is deemed to be wholly obtained in that Party.

What is not so obvious is that whether an agricultural or fisheries product is "wholly obtained" in one country is not a binomial matter. Rather, there are many possibilities along a continuum of free trade and protectionism. Suppose corn grown in Mexico is from seed imported from Brazil. That seed is genetically modified, using scientific procedures developed at collaborating labs in the Australia and Japan. The Mexican farmers use fertilizer from India. Their irrigation equipment is from the U.S., and water services are provided by a partially-privatized company the owners of which include German and Swiss conglomerates. The Goods Wholly Obtained Rule cuts off the inquiry about origin with the soil — the corn is Mexican because it was planted, grew, and harvested in Mexican soil.

The point is, as with the origin of the cosmos, for primary commodities, the origin inquiry can be taken back many steps. The number of steps taken, and the step or steps chosen to confer origin, are policy choices. For example, if a goal of *NAFTA* were to protect domestic corn farmers in each of the Parties, then the goods Wholly Obtained Rule would insist that seed — and maybe the fertilizer, too — come from the U.S., Canada, or Mexico. The only real limits on tracing the origin of a product are practical. Do reliable records exist for each step in the production process? Is it cost-effective, in relation to the benefits of duty-free treatment, to trace back several steps up the commodity chain?

B.   The Originating Materials Rule

Article 401(c) of *NAFTA* is a logical extension of the Goods Wholly Obtained Rule. It indicates a good is originating if produced entirely in a *NAFTA* Party exclusively from originating materials. For example, suppose a pen is made in Canada from plastic, metal, and ink, all of which are from the U.S. or Mexico. Because the materials are originating, the pen is an originating good. Like the Goods Wholly Obtained Rule, the Originating Materials Rule is basic and obvious. It, too, is common to FTAs.

For example, it exists in the *U.S. — Israel FTA*. To be "Israeli," an article must be grown or manufactured in, or the product of, Israel, which can occur if the product is made in Israel, the U.S., or both, exclusively from originating materials. Likewise, under the *Chile FTA*, a good is considered originating if it is produced entirely in Chilean or American territory, or both, exclusively from originating materials. That also is true, with respect to Singaporean and American territory, under the *Singapore FTA*, and Australian and American territory under the *Australia FTA*.

C.   The Substantial Transformation Rule

The third rule, set forth in *NAFTA* Article 401(b), relies on the concept of "goods substantially transformed." The Substantial Transformation Rule applies to cases where a good contains non-originating materials. If each non-originating material is transformed by production that occurs entirely within one or more *NAFTA* Parties so that each such material undergoes a change in tariff classification, then the good is an originating good. Consequently, this rule sometimes is called the "Tariff Shift" Rule or "CTH" Rule (for "change in tariff heading or sub-heading"). As noted later with respect to tomato paste and tomato catsup, protectionist impulses may motivate some Tariff Shift Rules.

Globalization demands a Substantial Transformation Rule. Specifically, multi-jurisdictional sourcing and production — sometimes called global commodity or supply chains — mean many articles are not entirely grown or produced in one country. Thus, the first two rules would render them ineligible for preferential treatment. In turn, an FTA would be under-inclusive in coverage, and fail to maximize the potential net gains from trade liberalization. Accordingly, FTAs typically contain a Substantial Transformation Rule. For example, under the *U.S. — Israel FTA*, if an article is made of foreign materials, then to be "Israeli," it must be substantially transformed into a new or different article that is grown, manufactured, or produced in Israel. Qualifications in the *Israel FTA* ensure a minor pass-through operation is not enough to transform substantially an article.

In fact, FTAs typically contain dozens, even hundreds, of Substantial Transformation Rules. Each one is specific to a product category in the HTS, demanding some degree of change in tariff classification from one stage of production to another. CTH. For example, the *Chile FTA* states that a good qualifies as originating, even if the materials used to produce the good are not themselves originating, if those non-originating materials are transformed in such a way as to cause their tariff classification to change (or meet other requirements). The *Singapore* and *Australia FTAs* also contain Tariff Shift Rules. Typically, a lengthy, detailed annex to an FTA sets out the shift in the HTS categorization required for a transformation of non-originating materials into a new and different article to be considered "substantial." In *NAFTA*, it is Annex 301, in the *Chile FTA*, it is Annex 4.1, in the *Singapore FTA*, it is Annex 3A, and in the Australia FTA is it Annexes 4-A and 5-A. The *Morocco FTA*, too, has product-specific rules of origin set out in Annex 5-A.

As a general proposition, the larger the shift in tariff classification demanded, the more protectionist the rule. For instance, a Substantial Transformation Rule that calls for a CTH at the 4 digit HTS classification level demands a greater degree of economic activity with respect to transformation of an article than a CTH at the 6 or 8 digit level. Not surprisingly, during FTA negotiations lobbyists trying to protect domestic industries vie with free trade advocates for the attention of trade officials.

Protectionist forces tend to seek Substantial Transformation Rules for their clients that require considerable manufacturing activity to qualify a product as originating in the FTA area. That way, most like products will be deemed to originate in third countries, and will receive MFN tariff, not duty-free, treatment. Free traders fight for minimalist CTH obligations, so as to allow their consumer and importer clients access to a wide array of merchandise that qualifies for a zero duty. The battle is fought in the trenches — the 4, 6, and 8 digit HTS product categories. The results are published in long, obscure annexes to the FTA that contain product-specific Substantial Transformation Rules referring back to HTS codes.

NAFTA negotiators found the Tariff Shift Rule to be problematical. They sought to differentiate simple from complex assembly operations. For example, the negotiators elected to create new tariff provisions covering major components of products in HTS Chapter 84 and establish a rule to distinguish simple and complex assembly:

> In Chapter 84, in order to develop an origin rule for machine tools that distinguishes between simple and complex assembly, we created new tariff provisions for four major components:
>
> i. the main engine;
>
> ii. hydraulics (that is, the pumps);
>
> iii. the numerical controller; and
>
> iv. major weldments or casting (that is, the major structural components of the machine).
>
> Under the rule of origin we created for machine tools, if at least three of these four major components are produced within the *NAFTA* and the final assembly occurs within the free trade area, the machine tool is considered to be eligible for tariff preference.
>
> On the other hand, if two or more of the major components are produced outside the free trade area, mere final assembly of the

machine tool from those components is not recognized as resulting in a product eligible for tariff preference.[11]

A related problem the negotiators tackled was how to treat a complex assembly of a good from small parts versus a simple assembly from major components:

> In [HTS] Chapter 85, in order to develop an origin rule for electric ranges and ovens, we created new tariff provisions within sub-heading 8516.90, the sub-heading for parts of electric ranges and ovens. In the breakouts we cover the following parts of electric ranges and ovens:
>
> i. cooking chambers, whether or not assembled;
>
> ii. top surface panels, with or without heating elements or controls;
>
> iii. door assemblies, incorporating at least two of the following: inner panel; outer panel; window; insulation.
>
> Assembly of complete ovens and ranges from smaller parts (regardless of the origin of smaller parts), is recognized as resulting in a product eligible for tariff preference. On the other hand, assembly of final products from the major components, described in the new provisions, does not result in a product eligible for preference if those components were produced outside the free trade area.[12]

Similar solutions were devised for other products listed in HTS Chapters 84, 85 and 90 like fax machines, paging devices, and other telecommunications equipment, printers, data processing equipment and radar equipment.

While the *NAFTA* negotiators considered assembly issues, they appear to have avoided the question of whether to adopt a single, general CTH Rule. To be sure, the principle advantage of any CTH Rule is that it provides certainty and predictability to manufacturers, exporters, and importers because it can be articulated clearly and learned quickly. However, the key disadvantage is that different CTH Rules apply to different goods, as the discussion of assembly issues illustrates. In fact, Annex 401 of *NAFTA*, where *NAFTA*'s rules of origin are located, has 148 pages. It is estimated that these pages contain over 11,000 rules of origin. This estimate suggests a proliferation in CTH Rules of origin. In *CUFTA*, *NAFTA*'s predecessor, 1,498 rules of origin were set forth in 20 pages. Interest group politics — in fancy academic jargon, "Public Choice Theory" — appears to be the leading explanation for this proliferation:

> The case of tomato catsup and tomato paste offers an example. Catsup (*salsa de tomate*) is classified in chapter 21 of the HTS, under item 2103.20, while tomato paste (*pasta de tomate*) is classified in chapter 20, under HTS item 2002.90. The [*Canada-United States*] *FTA* rule of origin provides that the operations necessary to convert a product classified in any chapter other than chapter 21 into a product classified in that chapter will confer preferential origin on the chapter 21 product. Thus, when imported tomato paste (chapter 20) is

---

[11] Simpson, *supra* note 8, at 38.

[12] *Id.* at 39.

processed into tomato catsup (chapter 21), the catsup qualifies for the FTA preference.

Under *NAFTA*, however, the rule is different. Conversion of tomato paste imported from outside *NAFTA* into tomato catsup within *NAFTA* will not confer origin on the catsup for preferential purposes. The formulation of the rule is that a change to item 2103.20 (tomato catsup) from any other chapter, *except* subheading 2002.90 (tomato paste), will confer origin. Under *NAFTA*, then, the tomato paste itself must be produced within the territory of a *NAFTA* member if the tomato catsup is to receive preferential treatment.

. . . .

This absence of a general rule or principle for determining origin is perhaps the major shortcoming of CTH, one that would be no surprise to political "realists" or to economists of the public choice persuasion. It renders CTH susceptible to capture by industries interested in minimizing their exposure to competition. In *NAFTA*, in the case of tomato catsup, it apparently was easy for an industry interested in minimizing competition from tomato paste outside the three-country area to fashion a product-specific rule denying the preference to catsup made from the imported tomato paste. There is no other apparent reason for the change in *NAFTA* from the *FTA* rule. In 1992, it so happens, Chile was the leading foreign supplier of tomato paste to the United States. Thus Chilean tomato paste can be used in catsup that will enjoy preferential treatment under the *FTA*, but none of it will have that privilege under *NAFTA*. It so happens that Mexico was the second leading supplier of tomato paste in the United States in 1992.

These facts would seem to justify the tentative assumption that the rule was changed at the behest of the Mexican producers of tomato paste who presumably would benefit at the expense of their competitors in Chile. . . .

The very fact that we are able only to speculate about the "policy" behind this particular rule illustrates the ease with which CTH may be captured by specific companies or industries. The stated rules are, superficially, comprehensible to all, but their rationale rarely is. . . .

. . . The hundreds of pages and thousands of lines of a tariff schedule offer countless opportunities for similar rules, rules that sometimes may amount to a covenant not to compete.[13]

These sorts of games, which seem to compromise the dignity of international trade law, call forth an obvious question: Why not apply one CTH Rule to all items in the HTS?

For example, suppose the policy goal is that only a major manufacturing and processing operation should count as a substantial transformation. Then, the CTH Rule could be that a change in the HTS tariff classification at the

---

[13] N. David Palmeter, *Pacific Trade Liberalization and Rules of Origin*, 27 J. WORLD TRADE 49, 51-52 (1993).

2 digit level is a substantial transformation. Alternatively, if the goal is that a minor operation suffices, then the CTH Rule could be that a change at the 6 (or even 8) digit level qualifies as a substantial transformation. A uniform rule might de-politicize the process of formulating rules of origin by barring special rules for industries with lobbying power.

D.   The Value Added Test

Value Added Tests are easy to articulate. A specified percentage of the total value of a product must be added in a country for the product to be considered a product of that country. They are common in FTAs. For example, the *U.S. — Israel FTA* has a 35 percent value added rule for many articles. To qualify as "Israeli," at least 35 percent of the total value of that article must come from (1) materials produced in Israel plus (2) the direct cost of processing operations performed in Israel.

Typically, the U.S. negotiates for what might be dubbed an American Content Provision. This Provision allows a certain percentage of the materials to come from the U.S. itself, rather than from the partner country, yet still qualify toward the threshold. In the *Israel FTA*, up to 15 percent of the content of an article may be from the U.S., which means that in calculating whether 35 percent of the value added of an article is Israeli, up to 15 percent of American-origin material will count.

NAFTA contains a Value Added Test. However, *NAFTA* negotiators faced four difficulties with this kind of preferential rule of origin. First, they "found that value-added rules of origin are difficult to design, and are unpredictable because of the instability of the cost elements that go into value added." Suppose a Mexican car manufacturer buys Japanese engines, Indonesian tires, and Thai batteries and exports finished vehicles to the U.S. The manufacturer will pay its suppliers in *yen*, *rupiah*, and *baht*. The exchange rates for *yen-peso*, *rupiah-peso*, and *baht-peso* inevitably fluctuate. The manufacturer will pay its Mexican workforce in *pesos*. The manufacturer's export revenues are denominated in dollars. The dollar-*peso* exchange rate fluctuates, often quickly and dramatically. Thus, the cost of inputs and export revenues, when translated into pesos, will change. Exchange rate fluctuations can affect determinations of origin made on a value added basis.

Second, suppose in the above example all inputs were denominated in *pesos*. Surely the prices of these inputs will change. Such changes will affect the value added calculation. Similarly, the Mexican manufacturer is likely to adjust the sale price of the vehicles in response to changes in American market conditions, which in turn may affect the value added calculation.

Third, the Value Added Test lacks reciprocity and thereby discriminates against low-wage countries. Suppose athletic shoes are made from Mexican rubber soles, Canadian leather and American plastic. Consider two opposite scenarios. In Case 1, these parts are transformed into a finished product in Mexico. Subsequently, the shoes are exported to Canada or the U.S. In Case 2, they are transformed into a finished product in either Canada or the U.S., and then exported to the U.S. Because wage rates are lower in Mexico than Canada, the value added in Mexico may be lower than in Canada. As a result, in Case #1, a threshold established in a value added test may not be satisfied, hence the shoes may fail to qualify for duty-free treatment. In Case 2, because of the higher value added resulting from higher labor costs in the U.S. or Canada, the shoes are more likely to meet the threshold. More generally, the value added calculation may be manipulated by altering the location of production processes. Of course, in many instances such alterations may be difficult, or any consequent tariff savings may not be offset by other costs.

Finally, enforcing a Value Added Test is difficult. Customs officials must verify value added calculations submitted by importers. Such verification requires an examination of the financial records of the manufacturer. These records may be located overseas and based on accounting principles other than U.S. Generally Accepted Accounting Principles (GAAP). The foreign manufacturer may not want to divulge the information, particularly in a situation where the importer of the product is not affiliated with the manufacturer. It is also possible that the manufacturer simply does not want to assume the burden of such record keeping.

In spite of these difficulties, *NAFTA* makes use of the Value Added Test for certain products. The Regional Value Content Rule for the automobile industry (discussed below) is a significant example. Other instances are fishing reels, toy electric trains, and certain other products that are placed in the same HTS category as their constituent parts. Because the parts and finished goods are in the same category, even a complex assembly operation cannot cause a change in tariff classification. Thus, a CTH Rule is unhelpful, and a Value Added Test is used.

Some post-*NAFTA* FTAs rely on Value Added Tests. For instance, the *U.S. — Morocco FTA* has a general 35 percent Test not unlike the Test in the *Israel FTA*. A good qualifies as originating in the territory of Morocco or the U.S. if it is a new or different article, it has been grown, produced, or manufactured in Morocco, the U.S., or both, and the value of the (1) materials produced plus (2) direct cost of processing operations performed in either or both countries is 35 percent or more of the appraised value of the article. Query when the value is appraised, and by whom?

E. The Hybrid Rule

The *NAFTA* Parties consider certain industries, such as automobiles, chemicals, plastics, machinery, footwear, and electronics, to be sensitive. A subtle phrase in Article 401(b) — "and the good satisfies all other applicable requirements of this Chapter" — is the clue that for these sectors, special hybrid rules of origin exist. The Hybrid Rules are set forth in Annex 401.1.

For example, to qualify for preferential treatment an automotive product must satisfy two tests. First, it must meet a CTH Rule. Second, the value of the components of the good from *NAFTA* Parties must meet a specified percentage — called the "Regional Value Content" (RVC). The RVC is, therefore, a measure of the value of the content of a good that is added in or derived from one or more *NAFTA* Parties. Conceptually, the formula for RVC is:

$$\text{RVC} = \frac{\text{(Total Value of the good)} - \text{(Value of non-originating materials in the good)}}{\text{(Total value of the good)}} \times 100$$

(Note that an alternative to the RVC test applies to some goods, namely, they must include specified components.)

The RVC for cars, light trucks, engines, and transmissions is 62.5 percent. It is 60 percent for other vehicles and parts. (*See NAFTA* Article 403:5. These RVCs were phased in over an 8-year period.) Thus, to receive duty-free treatment, at least 62.5 percent of the value of the content of an assembled car exported from one *NAFTA* Party to another must be from a *NAFTA* Party. Interestingly, under *Canada-U.S. FTA* the RVC was 50 percent. Thus, *NAFTA* has a stricter — and, therefore, more protectionist — rule of origin for cars than previously existed for the U.S. and Canada.

For most goods, manufacturers may calculate RVC using either the "transaction value" or "net cost" method. (*See NAFTA* Article 415.) The basis of the former method is the price actually paid or payable for the good. In contrast, the latter method relies on the total cost of the good with deductions for sales promotion, marketing cost, royalties, and packing and shipping. Thus, in practice the formulas for RVC are:

$$\text{RVC} = \frac{\text{(Transaction Value of the good)} - \text{(Value of non-originating materials in the good)}}{\text{(Transaction Value of the good)}} \times 100$$

$$= \frac{\text{(Net Cost of the good)} - \text{(Value of non-originating materials in the good)}}{\text{(Net Cost of the good)}} \times 100$$

(*See NAFTA* Article 402:2-3.)

Automobile manufacturers do not have a choice regarding calculation methodology. They must use the net cost formula. (*See NAFTA* Article 402:5(d).) This method may have additional protectionist effects because it contains a tracing requirement for 69 specified automobile parts, including engines, transmissions, bumpers, and mirrors. The make-up of a part is scrutinized to determine whether the part itself is made up of foreign inputs. The value of any foreign content in the part must be subtracted when calculating the net cost of a vehicle, *i.e.*, the foreign content value of a part cannot be included in the RVC calculation. (*See NAFTA* Article 403:1-2.)

The tracing requirement is designed to rectify a "roll-up" problem that existed with the *Canada — U.S. FTA*. The problem was that the full value of a good was counted as originating or non-originating even though the good contained a mixture of originating and non-originating materials. For example, assume a car is made in Canada and Thailand. The value added in Canada is 51 percent, while 49 percent of the assembly occurs in Thailand. During the Thai assembly operation, a part whose value is 49 percent Thai is included in the car. Under the net cost method articulated in the *Canada — U.S. FTA*, the part was counted as 100 percent regional (*i.e.*, originating in the U.S. or Canada) on the ground that its domestic value exceeded 50 percent of its total value. In effect, the foreign contribution to the value of the part was "rolled up" into, or neglected in favor of, the domestic value. Because of the *NAFTA*'s tracing test, 49 percent of the value of this part must be deducted in the net cost calculation of RVC. Indeed, the non-originating value remains non-originating through every stage of assembly to the time of calculating the RVC. Annex 403.1 of *NAFTA* contains a list of automotive parts for passenger and light vehicles that are subject to the tracing requirement.

The tracing requirement has a significant adverse consequence. It encourages auto producers to source fully from within *NAFTA*. No producer wants to be audited by a customs authority, and using inputs only from *NAFTA* Parties minimizes the risk of an audit. It also eliminates the necessity of keeping records to satisfy a tracing inquiry from customs officials. In turn, the actual RVC may be raised to over 62.5 — and possibly 100 — percent. More generally, the RVC and tracing requirements may create perverse economic incentives. Producers in *NAFTA* may be compelled to purchase their inputs from less efficient suppliers in *NAFTA* instead of choosing a supplier based strictly on cost and quality considerations. In effect, trade in inputs may be diverted from certain non-*NAFTA* suppliers in favor of *NAFTA* suppliers. The result may be that the global competitiveness of some *NAFTA* producers is undermined.

F. The Assembled Goods Rule

Suppose that with respect to an assembled product, the following two circumstances exist. First, the product and its constituent parts are listed in the same HTS sub-heading. Therefore, the product does not satisfy a CTH Rule. Second, one or more of the constituent parts are non-originating. Hence, the Goods Wholly Obtained Rule is inapplicable. For example, a bicycle assembled in Mexico cannot meet the CTH Rule because the parts of the bicycle — the tires, handle bar, chain, and seat — are placed in the same HTS category as an assembled bicycle. If any of the parts are non-originating, then the bicycle does not satisfy the Goods Wholly Obtained Rule. Should the bicycle qualify as an originating good?

The answer is provided in *NAFTA* Article 401(d), which calls for the use of an RVC test. Article 401(d) indicates that a finished product that is made of one or more non-originating materials and does not undergo a change in tariff classification because the product and its materials are in the same HTS heading qualifies as an originating good if it meets an RVC test. That test is a 60 percent RVC where the transaction value method is used, or a 50 percent RVC where the net cost method is used. Thus, in the example of the assembled bicycle, if the value of at least 60 percent of its parts are derived from a *NAFTA* Party, then the bicycle is an originating good.

A major exception to the Assembled Goods Rule, discussed below, is that it does not apply to textiles and apparel merchandise.

G. The Specified Process Rule

One mechanism for determining whether a "substantial transformation" occurs is to agree upon specific manufacturing operations and processes that cause such a transformation. Like the Substantial Transformation Rule and Value Added Test, a Specified Process Rule for origination can be stated with clarity so that it provides precise guidance for manufacturers, exporters, and importers. However, a key disadvantage stems from the relative knowledge of trade negotiators and industry officials about manufacturing and production. Industry officials will know more than trade negotiators and, therefore, are in a position to influence negotiators because of their knowledge. They may lead negotiators to adopt rules that restrict rather than liberalize trade.

A second disadvantage is it may be costly and time consuming to maintain an up-to-date list of manufacturing operations and production processes. Inevitably, these operations and processes will change with technological developments that yield greater efficiency. Finally, Specified Process Rules, unlike CTH Rules, are not based on a uniform foundation like the HTS. Hence, there is room for substantial disharmony across different countries.

In spite of these disadvantages, *NAFTA* negotiators agreed to use Specified Process Rules for certain goods, particularly ones considered sensitive. These Rules are a balance — to put it diplomatically — between free trade and protectionism. A notable class of sensitive goods, indeed of a sensitive sector, is textiles and apparel. Thus, textiles and apparel are the quintessential context in which specified process rules are used.

The *NAFTA* negotiators devised a special rule of origin based on manufacturing operations and production processes for the textile and apparel sector. Like the intricate provisions for automobiles, the so-called "fiber-forward" and "yarn-forward" rules of origin in *NAFTA* for textiles and apparel are highly restrictive and less liberal than the *Canada — U.S. FTA* rules. To understand them, it is first necessary to appreciate the basic steps involved in textile and apparel production. The Diagram below shows them.

The *Canada — U.S. FTA* established a "double transformation" test. A finished garment qualified as originating, and thereby got duty-free treatment under *CUFTA*, if garment parts were cut and sewn into the finished garment in either Canada or the U.S. Whether the yarn or other fabric used to make the garment was foreign (*i.e.*, from a non-*CUFTA* country) was irrelevant. Likewise, the country of origin of the fiber, from which the yarn is spun, and in turn from which fabric is made, was irrelevant.

In contrast, *NAFTA* sets forth a triple transformation test. Under this test, a finished garment must be made from (1) yarn spun into fabric a *NAFTA* Party, (2) fabric cut into pieces in a *NAFTA* Party, and (3) pieces sewn together in a *NAFTA* Party. Thus, the basic rule of origin for textile and apparel products is called the "yarn-forward" rule. It means yarn must be spun in the *NAFTA* region, and all subsequent processing — creating fabric, cutting, sewing, and final assembly — must occur in that region. (*See NAFTA* Annex 401 Section XI.) The only irrelevancy is the origin of the fiber used to spin the yarn.

DIAGRAM 24-1:
BASIC STEPS IN TEXTILE AND APPAREL MANUFACTURING

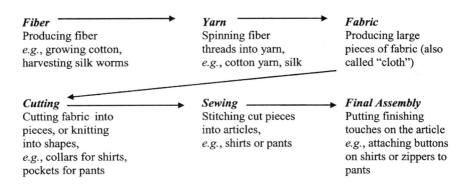

Fiber
Producing fiber
e.g., growing cotton,
harvesting silk worms

Yarn
Spinning fiber
threads into yarn,
e.g., cotton yarn, silk

Fabric
Producing large
pieces of fabric (also
called "cloth")

Cutting
Cutting fabric into
pieces, or knitting
into shapes,
e.g., collars for shirts,
pockets for pants

Sewing
Stitching cut pieces
into articles,
e.g., shirts or pants

Final Assembly
Putting finishing
touches on the article
e.g., attaching buttons
on shirts or zippers to
pants

Similarly, under the *U.S. — Singapore, U.S. — Chile, U.S. — Australia,* and *U.S. — Morocco FTAs*, for textile and apparel merchandise, the Tariff Shift Rule is a Specified Process Rule, and the basic such Rule is yarn forward. (*See, e.g., Australia FTA*, Chapter 5:1 and Rule 1 in Chapters 61-62 of Annex 4-A, and *Morocco FTA*, Articles 4-5 and Rule 1 in Chapters 61-62 of Annex 4-A.) For a textile or apparel article to qualify as "Made in Singapore," "Made in Chile," "Made in Australia," or "Made in Morocco," and receive preferential tariff treatment from the U.S., the article must be cut (or knit to shape) and sewn (or otherwise assembled) in Singapore, Chile, Australia, or Morocco from yarn, or fabric made from yarn, which originates in Singapore, Chile, Australia, Morocco or the U.S. *CAFTA—DR* contains a similar rule. Observe that the origin of the thread used to assemble a garment can matter, too. Under *CAFTA—DR*, the thread must be wholly formed and finished either in a *CAFTA—DR* country or the U.S. Put simply and generally, a yarn forward rule means using third-country yarn (*e.g.*, non-Singaporean, non-Chilean, non-Australian, non-Moroccan, non-*CAFTA—DR*, non-American yarn) disqualifies an article from duty-free treatment under the respective *FTA*.

To be sure, the impact of a yarn forward rule may be softened by the exemption of certain types of fabrics from the triple transformation test associated with such a rule. For example, *NAFTA* exempts 16 fabrics. The exempted fabrics need not pass through three transformations in order to qualify for preferential treatment:

Less demanding rules of origin govern certain knitted underwear, brassieres, and shirts made from fabric in short supply in North America, and textile and apparel articles made from fabric not commonly produced in North America. For example, silk and linen apparel articles follow a single-transformation instead of a "yarn-forward" rule. Thus, silk blouses are considered originating even if made from non-originating fabric, provided the fabric is cut and sewn in one or more *NAFTA* countries. [Because the fabric must be cut and sewn in the *NAFTA* region, it might be more precise to call the rule a "double" transformation one.] These exceptions give producers flexibility to import materials not widely produced in North America.[14]

Sometimes, the exemptions reflect consumer preferences, as among Anglophilic Americans for Harris tweed.[15] The general yarn-forward rule means a coat is not "Mexican" if it is made from non-*NAFTA* (*e.g.*, Indian) yarn or fabric, or if it is sewn together with thread imported from outside the *NAFTA* region. However, an exception exists for coats made from Harris tweed, where such tweed is hand-woven using a loom less than 76 centimeters wide, and imported from Britain into Mexico.

The protectionist impact of a yarn-forward rule is further softened by the fact *NAFTA* establishes tariff preference levels (TPLs) for apparel that fails to satisfy the yarn-forward rule. Such apparel can receive preferential treatment up to the applicable TPL. That is, the TPL is a tariff-rate quota: *NAFTA*'s preferential duty applies to imports up to the TPL, and the MFN rate applies to imports in excess of that level. Unfortunately, the TPLs are not only a loophole in the rule of origin, but also create incentives for fraud, trans-shipment, and other kinds of abuse. Moreover, there are no TPLs established for 14 categories of apparel. (*See NAFTA* Schedule 3.1.2.)

The *U.S. — Morocco FTA* contains another example of softening the otherwise strict yarn forward rule. Article 4:3:11 of this *FTA* contains an exception to this rule for 30 million square meter equivalents of apparel that does not satisfy the yarn forward rule. ("Square meter equivalents," or "SMEs," is a standard way of measuring quantity of apparel.) However, the exception applies only for the first decade the FTA is in effect, *i.e.*, 1 January 2006 until 31 December 2016. Moreover, the threshold is phased down from 30 million to zero SMEs over this decade. What is the purpose of this time-bound exception? Might it be to give Moroccan garment manufactures a transition period to adjust their supply sources to meet the yarn forward test?

Notably, in some U.S. trade accords, and for certain textile and apparel merchandise, the Specified Process Rule may be even more strict than a yarn-forward rule. For instance, under *NAFTA*, a "fiber-forward" rule is used for products made of fibers that are produced in abundance in the *NAFTA* region. Examples include man-made fiber sweaters and fabrics knitted from cotton. Under the fiber-forward rule, it is not sufficient that the yarn (or other material) from which an article is made is from a *NAFTA* Party. The yarn must be spun from fiber that itself is from a *NAFTA* Party. That is, the (1)

---

[14] United States Customs Service, NAFTA — Guide to Customs Procedures 17 (1994).

[15] *See Least Favored Nation*, The Economist, 5 Aug. 2006, at 68.

fiber that is the basic element from which all subsequent operations occur must originate in a *NAFTA* Party, (2) yarn must be spun from that fiber in a *NAFTA* Party, (3) article must be cut in a *NAFTA* Party, and (4) article must be sewn in a *NAFTA* Party. In effect, the rule is a "quadruple" transformation test.

The restrictive specified process rules for textile and apparels industries should not overshadow specified process rules for other industries that clearly result in trade liberalization. For example, a computer qualifies as an originating good if its circuit board is made in a *NAFTA* Party and this board is transformed so that its tariff classification changes (perhaps from a circuit board to a partly-assembled computer). In addition, a low common external tariff exists for computers and related parts. Thus, *NAFTA* essentially establishes a truly free market for computer products.

Observe that not every production process will cause an article to become an originating good. For example, *NAFTA* Article 412(a) indicates that merely diluting a good with water where there is no material alteration in the good does not qualify as an operation resulting in an originating good.

H. The *De Minimis* Test

The final type of rule of origin found in *NAFTA* is a *De Minimis* Test. Under Article 405:1, a good that fails to satisfy the applicable rules of origin nevertheless is an originating good if the value of the non-*NAFTA* materials used to make the good is no more than 7 percent of the price or total cost of the good. For textiles and apparel, the *De Minimis* test is based on the weight of the components of the garment in question. Other FTAs tend to contain *De Minimis* Tests, though the threshold levels may vary from one accord to another.

V. THE 2006 *CUMMINS* CASE

CUMMINS INCORPORATED v. UNITED STATES
United States Court of Appeals for the Federal Circuit
454 F.3d 1361-66 (2006)

Mayer, Circuit Judge.

Cummins Inc. appeals the United States Court of International Trade's grant of summary judgment, which held that the crank shafts imported by Cummins into the United States did not originate in Mexico and were not entitled to preferential treatment under the *North American Free Trade Agreement* ("*NAFTA*"). *Cummins Inc. v. United States*, 377 F. Supp. 2d 1365 (Ct. Int'l Trade 2005). We affirm.

Background

Under the United States' tariff laws, products that "originate in the territory of a *NAFTA* party" are entitled to preferential duty treatment. General Note 12(a)(ii), Harmonized Tariff Schedule of the United States ("HTSUS"); *see also*

19 U.S.C. § 3332 (2000). One way a product may so originate is if it is "transformed in the territory" of a *NAFTA* party. General Notes 12(b)(i)-(iv), HTSUS. One manner in which a good can be transformed, as is relevant to this case, is by undergoing a "change in tariff classification" "to subheading 8483.10 from any other heading." General Notes 12(b)(ii)(A),12(t)/84.243(A), HTSUS. Here, Cummins contends that the crankshafts it imports into the United States undergo such a tariff shift in Mexico from heading 7224 to subheading 8483.10.30, and are thereby entitled to preferential duty treatment.

The facts surrounding the production of the crankshafts are undisputed. Production begins in Brazil, where Krupp Metalurgica Campo Limpo creates a forging having the general shape of a crankshaft. This forging is created from a closed-die forging process, which involves forging alloy steel between matrices. After forging, the excess material that was squeezed out of the matrices, called "flash," is removed by a process called trimming. The trimming is done on a separate machine within approximately ten seconds of the forging press operation. Because the process of trimming can distort the forging, the forging is then coined. Coining involves applying pressure to the forging, which is still hot and malleable, in a closed die. After coining, the forging is subjected to shot blasting. Shot blasting uses abrasive particles to strike the surface of the forging to remove dirt and oxide from its surface. The forging is then cooled, and its ends are milled so that it can be securely clamped into machines in Mexico for final machining operations. The last manufacturing process performed in Brazil is mass centering, in which the forging's center of balance is determined and locator center points are machined into each end.

After these processes are performed in Brazil, the forging is imported into Mexico by Cummins de Mexico, S.A. ("CUMMSA"), a wholly owned subsidiary of Cummins. As imported, the forging has the general shape of, but cannot yet function as, a crankshaft. After importation into Mexico, CUMMSA performs at least fourteen different steps on the forging that cover over 95% of its surface area resulting in a useable crankshaft, which Cummins imports into the United States. It is undisputed that the crankshaft imported into the United States is classifiable under subheading 8483.10.30 of the HTSUS, which covers "[t]ransmission shafts (including camshafts and crankshafts) and cranks. . . ."

The Court of International Trade addressed nearly identical facts in an earlier case involving the same crankshafts. *Cummins Engine Co. v. United States*, . . . 83 F. Supp. 2d 1366 (Ct. Int'l Trade 1999) ("*Cummins I*"). The crankshaft manufacturing process there was nearly identical to the one here, except that a grease pocket was milled into the forging in Brazil. The court held that machining the grease pocket in Brazil precluded classification under heading 7224 upon importation in Mexico, because it was further working the product beyond roughly shaping it by forging.

After *Cummins I*, Cummins filed for an amended advance ruling letter from the United States Customs and Border Protection ("Customs"), based on the grease pocket being machined in Mexico instead of Brazil. Despite the change in the manufacturing process, Customs determined that the crankshafts did not originate in Mexico. . . . Prior to issuing its decision, Customs submitted the question to the World Customs Organization ("WCO"), which issued a classification opinion, approved by the member states 31 to 1, determining that the proper classification of the forgings imported into Mexico was under heading 8483, not heading 7224. . . . However, Customs did not expressly rely upon the WCO decision in denying Cummins preferential treatment.

In response to Customs' advance letter ruling, Cummins filed an action in the Court of International Trade under 28 U.S.C. § 1581(h). [Under Section 1581(h), the CIT may review pre-importation Customs' rulings if the party commencing the action demonstrates that "he would be irreparably harmed unless given an opportunity to obtain judicial review prior to such importation."] While that action was pending, Cummins imported into the United States a test shipment of three finished crankshafts marked as originating in Mexico, which Customs classified under subheading 8483.10.30, HTSUS. Cummins protested this classification, arguing that the proper classification was (MX)8483.10.30. [The prefix "MX" signifies an article is a product of Mexico, and thereby accorded *NAFTA* preferential treatment.] After protesting Customs' classification of the test shipment, Cummins filed an action under 28 U.S.C. § 1581(a). The trial court consolidated the two actions, but later found the section 1581(h) action moot in light of the one under section 1581(a).

The court determined on summary judgment that the articles imported into Mexico were properly classified under subheading 8483.10.30, not heading 7224, and accordingly did not undergo a tariff shift and were not entitled to preferential treatment under *NAFTA*. Cummins appeals the trial court's grant of summary judgment, and we have jurisdiction under 28 U.S.C. § 1295(a)(5).

Discussion

We review the trial court's grant of summary judgment on tariff classifications *de novo*. . . . A classification decision involves two underlying steps: determining the proper meaning of the tariff provisions, which is a question of law; and then determining which heading the disputed goods fall within, which is a question of fact. . . . However, when the nature of the merchandise is undisputed, as it is here, the classification issue collapses entirely into a question of law. . . . Although our review is de novo, we accord deference to a Customs' classification ruling in proportion to its "power to persuade" under the principles of *Skidmore v. Swift & Co.*, 323 U.S. 134, . . . (1944). . . . In addition, "Customs' relative expertise in administering the tariff statute often lends further persuasiveness to a classification ruling, entitling the ruling to a greater measure of deference." . . .

It is undisputed that the crankshafts imported into the United States are properly classified under subheading 8483.10.30. The disputed issue is whether the crankshafts undergo a tariff shift in Mexico. That is, do the crankshafts enter Mexico under a different tariff heading than they leave Mexico? The trial court concluded that the crankshafts do not undergo a tariff shift as they are classified under subheading 8483.10.30 upon import into and export out of Mexico. Cummins contends that this classification was error, and the proper classification of the product upon import into Mexico is under heading 7224, which covers "[o]ther alloy steel in ingots or other primary forms; semifinished products of other alloy steel."

"The General Rules of Interpretation (GRI) govern the classification of goods within the HTSUS." *Hewlett-Packard Co. v. United States*, 189 F.3d 1346, 1348 (Fed. Cir. 1999). Under GRI 1, the classification "shall be determined according to the terms of the headings and any relevant section or chapter notes." As noted above, Cummins contends that the goods imported into Mexico are properly classified as "semifinished products of other alloy steel" under heading 7224. Chapter 72's notes expressly define "semifinished," in pertinent part, as "products of solid section, which have not been further worked than . . . roughly shaped by forging, including blanks for angles, shapes or sections." Chapter 72, Note 1(ij), HTSUS. Thus, if the product imported into Mexico has been further worked beyond being roughly shaped by forging, it does not fall within heading 7224. The parties dispute the meaning of the term "further worked."

Cummins relies on Additional U.S. Note 2 to Chapter 72, which defines "further worked" as subjecting the product to one of several expressly listed surface treatments. [Additional U.S. Note 2 to Chapter 72, HTUS, says that unless the context provides otherwise, " 'further worked' refers to products subjected to any of the following surface treatments: polishing and burnishing; artificial oxidation; chemical surface treatments such are [*sic*] phosphatizing, oxalating and borating; coating with metal; coating with nonmetallic substances (*e.g.*, enameling, varnishing, lacquering, painting, coating with plastics materials); or cladding."] It is undisputed that none of these surface treatments are [*sic*] performed in Brazil, and Cummins contends that so long as none of these specific operations are performed prior to importation into Mexico, the product has not been "further worked." The trial court rejected this argument in *Cummins I*, and we do so now.

The definition of "further worked" in Chapter 72 is expressly inapplicable where "the context provides otherwise." Here, to read the term "further worked" as referring to only these specific treatments would lead to a nonsensical result. In particular, this definition would render the phrase "than . . . roughly shaped by forging" meaningless and contravene the well-established principle that a statute should be construed "if at all possible, to give effect and meaning to all the terms." *Bausch [v. United States]*, 148 F.3d [1363] at 1367 [Fed Cir. 1998].

Absent an applicable express definition or contrary legislative intent, we must construe the term "further worked" "according to [its] common and commercial meanings, which are presumed to be the same." *Carl Zeiss, Inc. v. United States, 195 F.3d 1375, 1379 (Fed. Cir. 1999)* (citing *Simod Am. Corp. v. United States, 872 F.2d 1572, 1576 (Fed. Cir. 1989))*. Here, the plain meaning of "further worked, "when read in context, means working the product beyond the point of roughly shaping it by forging. The trial court, relying in part on *Winter-Wolff, Inc. v. United States, . . .* 996 F. Supp. 1258, 1265 (Ct. Int'l Trade 1998) (construing "further worked" in the context of subheading 7607.11.30), defined "further worked" more precisely as "to form, fashion, or shape an existing product to a greater extent." We agree that this definition is suitable in the context before us.

Here, the product was forged and then trimmed, coined, shot blasted, milled, and mass centered in Brazil. Cummins suggests that these are steps within the "forging process." However, the relevant language is not "further worked beyond the forging process" but "further worked than roughly shaped by forging." The government cites evidence that the act of forging is understood in the industry as being distinct from the additional operations performed by Cummins in Brazil. In particular, the Forging Handbook provides that trimming occurs "[u]pon completion of the forging operation." *Forging Handbook Forging Industry Association, Forging Handbook* 153 (Thomas G. Byrer 1985). This *Handbook* also describes coining as a "finishing operation." . . . Significantly, Cummins agreed that trimming (and hence every step thereafter) takes place "after forging." Moreover, milling the ends of the forging product is outside of the forging process and constitutes working the product beyond roughly shaping it by forging, namely forming, fashioning, or shaping it to a greater extent. Thus, the product imported into Mexico from Brazil cannot be classified under heading 7224.

. . . .

We agree with the trial court that the forging is properly classified under heading 8483 upon importation into Mexico. GRI 2(a) provides that "[a]ny reference in a heading to an article shall be taken to include a reference to that article incomplete or unfinished, provided that, as entered, the incomplete or unfinished article has the essential character of the complete or finished article." In addition, the Explanatory Notes [II] to GRI 2(a) provide that this rule applies "to blanks unless these are specified in a particular heading. The term 'blank' means an article, not ready for direct use, having the approximate shape or outline of the finished article or part, and which can only be used, other than in exceptional circumstances, for completion into the finished article . . . ." . . . Here, the product imported into Mexico had the general shape of a crankshaft and was intended for use only in producing a finished crankshaft. In fact, certain operations done in Brazil, such as milling the forgings' ends, were done solely to simplify the operations in Mexico in completing the crankshaft. As such, the forged product imported into Mexico was properly classified under subheading 8483.10.30. Accordingly, it did not undergo a tariff shift and was not entitled to preferential treatment under *NAFTA* when imported into the United States.

Finally, Cummins contends that the trial court erred by improperly relying upon the WCO classification opinion. While such an opinion is not given deference by United States courts, it can be consulted for its persuasive value, if any. *Cf. Sanchez-Llamas v. Oregon*, 548 U.S. __, 126 S. Ct. 2669 . . . (2006) (rejecting the argument that U.S. courts are obligated to comply with interpretations of the *Vienna Convention* by the International Court of Justice (ICJ)); *Corus Staal BV v. Dep't of Commerce*, 395 F.3d 1343, 1349 (Fed. Cir. 2005) (observing that World Trade Organization decisions are accorded no deference); *Timken Co. v. United States*, 354 F.3d 1334, 1343-44 (Fed. Cir. 2004). The Supreme Court has rejected any notion of deference or obligation to a foreign tribunal's decisions. In so doing, it observed, "If treaties are to be given effect as federal law under our legal system, determining their meaning as a matter of federal law 'is emphatically the province and duty of the judicial department,' . . . ." *Sanchez-Llamas*, 2006 U.S. LEXIS 5177 at*39 (quoting *Marbury v. Madison*, 5 U.S. 137, 1 Cranch 137, 177, 2 L. Ed. 60 (1803)). Like the ICJ's interpretation of the treaty terms in *Sanchez-Llamas*, the WCO opinion is not binding and is entitled, at most, to "respectful consideration." *Id*. It is not a proxy for independent analysis.

Here, the court accorded no deference to either the WCO opinion or the categorization by Mexico's Customs authority. Instead, it independently construed "further worked, "based solely on the tariff terms and the principles set forth in the GRIs, and consulted the WCO opinion and Mexican categorization only as persuasive authority. The court properly construed the statutory terms as they are written. *See Corus Staal*, 395 F.3d at 1349; *cf. Suramericana de Aleaciones Laminadas v. United States*, 966 F.2d 660, 668 (Fed. Cir. 1992) ("While we acknowledge Congress's interest in complying with U.S. responsibilities under the GATT, we are bound not by what we think Congress should or perhaps wanted to do, but by what Congress in fact did.").

Conclusion

Accordingly, the judgment of the United States Court of International Trade is affirmed.

VI. CASE STUDY; THE *NAFTA* CERTIFICATE OF ORIGIN AND 2006 *CORRPRO* CASE

How does a customs official of the U.S., Canada, or Mexico know an article is an "originating good" as defined in Article 201 and Chapter 4 of *NAFTA* and, therefore, qualifies for preferential treatment under Article 302 of *NAFTA*? The exporter of the article provides the answer.

NAFTA Article 501 obligates every American, Canadian, and Mexican exporter to complete and sign a Certificate of Origin indicating whether the article it is exporting to another *NAFTA* Party is an originating good. The importer is entitled to rely on the Certificate. If the exporter does not manufacture the article, then it is entitled to complete the Certificate based on its knowledge of whether the article qualifies as an originating good, or on information provided by the manufacturer. However, the exporter, not the manufacturer, is obligated to furnish the Certificate. (*See NAFTA* Article 501:3-4.) *NAFTA* establishes a standard Certificate form and obligates exporters to retain all records relating to the origin of their article for five years. (*See NAFTA* Article 505:(a).)

The importer claims duty-free treatment by making a written declaration, based on the Certificate, which the importer keeps in its possession and shows to customs officials upon request, stating that the article is an originating good. The importer must retain a copy of the Certificate for 5 years. (*See NAFTA* Article 505:(b).) If the importer has reason to believe that the Certificate on which the declaration is based contains incorrect information, then duties (if applicable) must be paid. (*See NAFTA* Article 502.)

If customs officials suspect that an article is not an originating good in spite of a claim for treatment as such, they may undertake an "origin verification."

This procedure entails an extraterritorial investigation. *NAFTA* Article 506:1 authorizes customs officials to send written questionnaires to the exporter or producer of the article, and to visit the premises of the exporter or producer to examine relevant records and observe production facilities. If the exporter or producer does not consent to a verification visit, then customs officials in the importing country may deny preferential treatment to the article in question. (*See NAFTA* Article 506:4.)

Under what circumstances might customs officials doubt a claim about origin? One instance is where the exporter is a new entrant into the market, one with which the officials are not familiar, and thus has no "track record." A second instance is where the exporter "fits a profile" of false claimants. To what degree might use by a new shipper of a customs broker known to customs officials help mitigate any doubts?

CORRPRO COMPANIES, INC. v. UNITED STATES
United States Court of Appeals for the Federal Circuit
433 F.3d 1360 (2006)

LOURIE, CIRCUIT JUDGE.

The United States appeals from the decision of the United States Court of International Trade denying the government's motion to dismiss for lack of jurisdiction, granting Corrpro Companies, Inc.'s ("Corrpro's") motion for summary judgment, and classifying the subject merchandise under Harmonized Tariff Schedule of the United States ("HTSUS") MX 8543.40.00, duty-free. *Corrpro Cos. v. United States*, 2004 Ct. Intl. Trade LEXIS 114, slip op. 2004-116 (Ct. Int'l Trade Sept. 10, 2004) ("Decision"). Because Customs did not make a protestable decision as to *North American Free Trade Agreement* ("*NAFTA*") eligibility giving rise to jurisdiction in the Court of International Trade under 28 U.S.C. § 1581(a), we reverse.

Background

This case arises from Corrpro's attempt to claim preferential treatment under *NAFTA* for certain entries of sacrificial magnesium anodes. Enacted on December 8, 1993, *NAFTA* is an agreement between the United States, Canada, and Mexico to promote the free flow of goods through a reduction or phased elimination of tariffs and non-tariff barriers to trade. 19 U.S.C. § 3312 (1994) (approving and implementing *NAFTA*). *See Xerox v. United States*, 423 F.3d 1356, 1359 (Fed. Cir. 2005). Preferential tariff treatment under *NAFTA* allows importers to enter qualified goods into the United States free of duty.

Under *NAFTA*, an importer's right to preferential tariff treatment for qualifying goods does not vest automatically on entry. . . . As provided in Articles 501(1) and 503(1) of *NAFTA*, implemented in 19 C.F.R. § 181.21(a), an importer seeking preferential tariff treatment under *NAFTA* must make a written declaration that the goods qualify for *NAFTA* treatment and must base that declaration on a properly executed *NAFTA* "Certificate of Origin" that covers the goods being imported. 19 C.F.R. §§ 181.11(a), 181.21(a) (2005)

("A Certificate of Origin shall be employed to certify that a good being exported either from the United States into Canada or Mexico or from Canada or Mexico into the United States qualifies as an originating good for purposes of preferential tariff treatment under the *NAFTA*.")

However, an importer is not required to submit a written declaration and the appropriate *NAFTA* Certificates of Origin immediately upon entry of the subject goods. *Xerox*, 423 F.3d at 1361. Under Article 502(3) of *NAFTA*, codified at 19 U.S.C. § 1520(d), an importer who does not make a *NAFTA* claim at the time of entry may nevertheless apply for a "refund of any excess duties paid" on a good qualifying for *NAFTA* treatment by submitting a written declaration and the appropriate Certificates of Origin "within 1 year after the date of importation." 19 U.S.C. § 1520(d) (2000). In this case, Corrpro claims that its imported goods are entitled to *NAFTA* treatment even though it did not make a *NAFTA* claim at the time of entry or within one year of entry.

On August 16, 1999, Corrpro began importing magnesium anodes into the United States. . . . The United States Bureau of Customs and Border Protection ("Customs") classified the goods under HTSUS 8104.19.00 as "magnesium and articles thereof, including waste and scrap: Unwrought magnesium: Other" at the rate of 6.5 percent *ad valorem*. . . . Corrpro did not make a claim for *NAFTA* treatment at the time of entry under 19 C.F.R. § 181.21(a). . . . On June 30, 2000, Customs liquidated the subject merchandise under 19 U.S.C. § 1500. Customs did not accord the goods any preferential treatment under NAFTA because Corrpro had not yet raised the issue. . . .

Corrpro also did not claim preferential treatment under *NAFTA* within one year of the date of importation under 19 U.S.C. § 1520(d). However, on September 12, 2000, Corrpro filed protests to Customs' liquidation under 19 U.S.C. § 1514(a), arguing that the goods were classifiable as HTSUS MX 8543.30.00, free of duty under *NAFTA*. . . . Section 1514(a) is a procedural mechanism by which an importer may protest Customs' decision pertaining to the classification, rate, and amount of duties, but it does not specifically relate to *NAFTA* eligibility. . . .

Corrpro claimed preferential treatment under *NAFTA* in its 19 U.S.C. § 1514(a) protest without filing a written declaration or Certificates of Origin substantiating its assertion of *NAFTA* eligibility. On August 13, 2001, Customs denied Corrpro's protests in full. . . . Later in 2002, for the first time, Corrpro submitted to Customs Certificates of Origin covering the goods, after it had filed a complaint in the Court of International Trade. . . . [The parties dispute whether the Certificates of Origin were filed on February 4, 2002, as stated in the affidavit attached to the Certificates, or on June 27, 2002, the date indicated on the certificates themselves.]

Corrpro had filed its complaint in the Court of International Trade seeking preferential duty treatment for the imported goods on September 6, 2001. In its complaint, Corrpro asserted that the trial court had jurisdiction under 28 U.S.C. § 1581(a) because of its 19 U.S.C. § 1514(a) protest challenging the "classification and the rate and amount of duties chargeable." . . . Corrpro then moved for summary judgment that the subject merchandise was entitled to preferential duty treatment under *NAFTA*. . . . On September 10, 2004, the Court of International Trade held that it had jurisdiction to entertain the action and granted Corrpro's motion for summary judgment.

In determining whether Customs had made a protestable decision that conferredjurisdiction over Corrpro's *NAFTA* claims, the trial court first held that Customs' initial classification of the goods was a decision on *NAFTA* eligibility that could be protested, even though Customs had not expressly considered the question of preferential treatment under NAFTA at that time. . . . The trial court reasoned that this inference was warranted because Corrpro had been precluded by Customs Headquarters Ruling Letter ("HQ") 557046 from making a *NAFTA* claim at the time of entry. . . . HQ 557046, which provides that anodes classifiable in HTSUS 8104.19.00 are not eligible for duty-free treatment under the Generalized System of Preferences, was issued on May 17, 1993, prior to the enactment of *NAFTA* (although it was retracted on October 10, 2001). The trial court therefore concluded that Corrpro had acted properly under a standard of reasonable care in not seeking *NAFTA* treatment at the time of entry or within one year of entry. . . . Second, the trial court held that Corrpro's post-importation submission of *NAFTA* Certificates of Origin met the procedural requirements of 19 C.F.R. § 10.112 because Corrpro's delay in submission had resulted from its adherence to Customs' classification ruling. . . . Third, the trial court held that the subject merchandise satisfied *NAFTA*'s rules of origin and thus was eligible for preferential treatment under *NAFTA* as a matter of law. . . .

The government timely appealed. . . .

Discussion

We review the Court of International Trade's jurisdictional ruling based on its interpretation of 19 U.S.C. §§ 1514 and 1520(d) *de novo*. *Xerox v. United States*, 423 F.3d 1356, 1359 (Fed. Cir. 2005). We also review that court's grant of summary judgment *de novo*. *Int'l Trading Co. v. United States*, 412 F.3d 1303, 1307 (Fed. Cir. 2005).

. . . .

We agree with the government that the Court of International Trade lacked jurisdiction over the complaint for lack of a protestable decision by Customs. 28 U.S.C. § 1581(a) establishes jurisdiction over protestable decisions, providing that the "Court of International Trade shall have exclusive jurisdiction of any civil action commenced to contest the denial of a protest, in whole or in part, under section 515 of the *Tariff Act of 1930*." However, we recently held in Xerox that Customs' liquidation of an importer's entries was not a protestable decision with respect to preferential treatment under *NAFTA* because "Customs at no time considered the merits of *NAFTA* eligibility, nor could it [have] without a valid claim by [the importer] for such eligibility." 423 F.3d at 1363 (emphasis added). We observed, "in the absence of a proper claim for *NAFTA* treatment, either at entry or within a year of entry . . . Customs cannot make a protestable decision to deny an importer preferential *NAFTA* treatment." *Id*. at 1365. We concluded that because "the existence of a protestable decision of the type enumerated in 19 U.S.C. § 1514(a) is a condition precedent for jurisdiction to lie in the Court of International Trade under section 1581(a)," Xerox's appeal of an invalid protest was properly dismissed for lack of jurisdiction. *Id.* Accordingly, under our precedent, there is a protestable decision as to *NAFTA* eligibility that confers jurisdiction in the Court of International Trade under 28 U.S.C. § 1581(a) only when the importer has made a valid claim for *NAFTA* treatment, either at entry or within a year of entry, with a written declaration and Certificates of Origin presented in a timely fashion, and Customs has engaged in "some sort of decision-making process" expressly considering the merits of that claim. *Id.* at 1363 (*quoting U.S. Shoe Corp. v. United States*, 114 F.3d 1564, 1569 (Fed. Cir. 1997)).

Corrpro concedes that it did not make a post-importation *NAFTA* claim within a year of entry under 19 U.S.C. § 1520(d). Corrpro argues, however, that its late submission is excused because, under a standard of reasonable care, it could not make a *NAFTA* claim until after HQ 557046 was revoked. We will not decide that question; even assuming that Corrpro could have made a valid claim after the expiration of the one-year time limit, Corrpro cannot establish that Customs engaged in some sort of decision-making on the merits of a valid *NAFTA* claim. In order to make a valid *NAFTA* claim, an importer must submit a written declaration and the appropriate Certificates of Origin. 19 C.F.R. §§ 181.11(a), 181.32. An importer may not circumvent these statutory and regulatory requirements. Corrpro did not submit the appropriate Certificates of Origin until 2002. Thus, neither Customs' initial classification decision, made in 1999, nor its liquidation of goods, made in 2000, could have been a decision on the merits of a valid *NAFTA* claim, as no valid *NAFTA* claim existed at that time. As we held in Xerox, "there is simply no basis for attributing to Customs a decision denying [a *NAFTA*] claim that did not exist." 423 F.3d at 1363. Moreover, there is no evidence that Customs in fact considered Corrpro's *NAFTA* claim after the Certificates of Origin were submitted in 2002, while Corrpro's action was pending in the Court of International Trade. Therefore, Customs did not make a protestable decision establishing jurisdiction under 28 USC § 1581(a).

In holding that it had jurisdiction over Corrpro's claim, the Court of International Trade erred in concluding that the initial classification decision by Customs in 1999 was a protestable decision. We recognize, of course, that Xerox was decided after the trial court rendered its decision in this case. In any event, the trial court's reasoning assumed that Corrpro had made a valid *NAFTA* claim at the time of entry, even though Corrpro had not yet raised that issue. But we cannot attribute to Customs a decision on a *NAFTA* claim that did not yet exist. Because Customs could not have considered and did not consider the merits of *NAFTA* eligibility in the initial classification decision, it did not make a protestable decision at that time. For the same reason, we disagree with Corrpro's argument that Customs' liquidation of the goods is a protestable decision. Customs could not have engaged in any sort of decision-making as to *NAFTA* eligibility in liquidating the goods because Corrpro had not yet raised the *NAFTA* issue.

. . . .

Conclusion

Because Corrpro did not satisfy the statutory requirements in order to make a valid *NAFTA* claim until 2002, Customs could not have and did not consider the merits of that claim in its initial classification decision or liquidation. Accordingly, there was no protestable decision conferring jurisdiction on the Court of International Trade under 28 U.S.C. § 1581(a). The decision of that court denying the government's motion to dismiss and granting summary judgment for Corrpro is therefore *reversed*.

VII. CASE STUDY: TRANS-SHIPMENT AND THE *U.S. — SINGAPORE FTA*

Generally, trans-shipment of a good through a party to an FTA does not confer origin on that good. To the contrary, preferential rules of origin help screen out trans-shipped goods. These rules differentiate them from products that underwent meaningful economic activity in the territory of one or more FTA parties. Further, FTAs tend to contain a "direct shipment requirement" as a complement to preferential rules of origin, meaning the product for which duty-free treatment is sought must move directly from one FTA party to another. However, is there any instance of an FTA that permits trans-shipment to confer origin and, therefore, authorize duty-free treatment?

The answer is "yes." The *U.S. — Singapore FTA*, in Annex 3B, contains a list of goods that are deemed to originate in Singapore. To qualify for the list and thus duty-free entry into the U.S., these goods, as finished, must be imported from Singaporean to American territory. Annex 3B uses the term "itself, as imported," with respect to a good shipped from Singapore to the U.S. Significantly, this term means a good is deemed to originate in Singapore only if that good is trans-shipped through Singapore. If a good is incorporated into another product as a component thereof, then that good is not considered "originating" in Singapore, and does not qualify for Annex 3B.

There is an unsurprising exception: a component not trans-shipped through Singapore, and incorporated in another product there, originates in Singapore if that component is shipped first from the U.S. to Singapore. In other words, components count if they come from the U.S., but non-American components do not qualify for Annex 3B. Note the effect of this exception on RVC Rules in the *Singapore FTA*. (Section 202(d) of the *United States-Singapore Free Trade implementation Act* sets out these Rules.) A component does not qualify as "originating" in the RVC calculation, unless shipped from the U.S. to Singapore, and then in Singapore incorporated in a final product.

What kinds of goods does Annex 3B of the *Singapore FTA* contain? This Annex covers the "Integrated Sourcing Initiative" (ISI), and the listed goods — called ISI goods — are, for the most part, information technology (IT) goods. As a member of the WTO *Information Technology Agreement*, an outgrowth of the Uruguay Round, the U.S. accords duty-free MFN treatment to such products. Thus, from the U.S. perspective, accepting trans-shipped IT products from Singapore for duty-free treatment was no major concession in the FTA negotiations. Why might Annex 3B be in the interests of Singapore? Might the reasons lie in Singapore's interest in being both a leading center for high technology and obtaining trans-shipment business for its famed Port of Singapore Authority?

Chapter 25

TYPICAL FTA OBLIGATIONS: MARKET ACCESS

Ultimately, the question that confronted us was whether to accept a very, very good, albeit less perfect agreement, or to lose the agreement because Korea refused to move on rice.

—Karan Bhatia, Deputy United States Trade Representative (2 April 2007), *in* Amy Tsui & James Lim, Korea, *U.S. Reach Free Trade Agreement; Lawmakers Express Opposition to Approval*, 24 Int'l Trade Rep. (BNA) 474-75 (5 April 2007)

DOCUMENTS SUPPLEMENT ASSIGNMENT

For goods —

1. *Havana Charter* Article 44
2. GATT Article XXIV
3. *NAFTA* Chapters 1-3
4. U.S. *Statement of Administrative Actions* for *NAFTA* Chapter 8
5. Relevant provisions in other FTAs

For services —

1. *NAFTA* Chapters 10-14
2. U.S. *Statements of Administrative Action* for *NAFTA* Chapters 10, 12, 13, and 14
3. Relevant provisions in other FTAs

I. A "CHECKLIST"

Evidently, a regional trade agreement (RTA), be it a free trade agreement (FTA) or customs union (CU), is an economic entity, central to which are market access opportunities. No less evidently, however, an RTA is borne of and sustained by political, political economic, national security, and even cultural factors. Of course, for international trade lawyers and scholars, every RTA also is a legal phenomenon.

That is so in two senses. First, any FTA or CU exists within the multilateral trading system, specifically, within the framework of GATT Article XXIV and various WTO provisions (assuming any of the FTA or CU countries is a WTO Member). Second, an FTA or CU creates legal rights and duties for the members. In effect, it is a contract among a subset of the world's trading nations designed to work to the mutual advantage of the contracting states. This second sense is the present subject.

Ultimately, the most legally correct, way to study RTAs is to read them carefully. In the present context, that kind of thorough, "bottom-up" review is impossible. Only a dedicated work, possibly with multiple volumes, can do justice to all of America's FTAs, much less the FTAs and customs unions involving other countries. Perhaps the second-best solution is a conceptual, "top-down" approach. Rather than chronicle the details of what each and every FTA and customs union says, consider the essential features common to all of them, and the typical variations observed among those features. Put differently, what framework ought a trade lawyer to have in mind when opening up an RTA — what can she expect to see, or not see, in that text?

The obvious starting point is to appreciate what countries are party to the RTA in question. Instances in which borders are in controversy, and merchandise might originate in a disputed territory, can pose legal issues. An example is Israel and the Occupied Territories. Another, albeit hypothetical, illustration would be an FTA between India and Pakistan in which neither side agreed to admit duty-free products from Kashmir, the borders of which have been hotly contested since the British Partition of 15 August 1947.

Sometimes, a country not included in a particular RTA may have preferential treatment under an accord with one (or more) of the members of that RTA. The Dominican Republic is an illustration. In the initial *CAFTA—DR* negotiations, it was excluded from coverage. However, its merchandise was eligible for preferential treatment under the *Caribbean Basin Initiative* (*CBI*), a manifestation of special and differential treatment for poor countries. During the *CAFTA—DR* talks, concerns arose that its benefits should not exceed those the *CBI* provides. An integrated market in Central America and the Caribbean, especially in the agriculture and textile and apparel (T&A) sectors, with harmonized rules, was considered desirable. Eventually, the Dominican Republic was added to *CAFTA—DR*, hence the acronym *CAFTA—DR*.

Similarly, FTAs may be crafted in a way to allow — to use a science fiction metaphor — "docking on" of new countries. The *U.S. — Australia FTA* is an illustration, as its drafters knew that one day, New Zealand might join this FTA. This example — and plenty of others, including the enlargement of the EU customs union, associate memberships in *MERCOSUR*, and new countries in the FTA of the *Association of South East Asian Nations Free Trade* (*ASEAN*), called *AFTA* — suggests a trade lawyer never should take the membership of an RTA as immutable.

Of course, generally speaking, parties to an RTA, and their geo-political boundaries, are self evident and uncontroversial. What is germane is the political economy mixture among members. *NAFTA* is the first FTA major developed countries (the U.S. and Canada) signed with a developing country (Mexico). *CAFTA—DR* is the first FTA the U.S. negotiated with least developed countries. Members such as Honduras, Nicaragua, and Guatemala qualify for this status, and among *CAFTA—DR* members about 65 percent of the population in each country is engaged in agriculture. How might the diversity in levels of economic development affect trade liberalization rules of the RTA? Is an RTA with poor countries inherently more about development than commerce, as least in the short and medium term? Is such an RTA likely to prove contentious, because these countries typically specialize in products developed countries regard as sensitive? As for political systems represented in the RTA, they may range from democracies to kingdoms. Is one form of government an easier type for negotiation and implementation? Are there differences as to building legitimacy among a populace for trade liberalization?

To these questions, consider the interactive effects of economics and politics. Trade policy, especially its economic dimensions, can affect trade politics. If the policies underlying an RTA are sound, and if they are formulated transparently and explained honestly to the public, then can political polarization be avoided? If so, then perhaps the make-up of RTA members matters less than how the government of each member manages — and sometimes leads — its domestic constituencies.

Indubitably, in an FTA or CU a trade attorney will find market access obligations, and exceptions to them for sensitive sectors. These obligations will include goods. Depending on the RTA, they may include services and electronic commerce (e-commerce) as well. The attorney also will find process-type duties, notably transparency rules. The attorney may observe the RTA creates new institutions, or adds to or modifies the responsibilities of existing institutions, and establishes one or more dispute settlement mechanisms. In addition, the attorney should be prepared for Chapters on special sectors, like agriculture and intellectual property, on special concerns, like environmental and labor rights. Trade remedies — special rules on antidumping (AD), countervailing duty (CVD), and safeguards cases — also are likely to appear in an RTA text.

Should a trade attorney also anticipate coverage of broad and fundamental social matters? The answer depends on the FTA. The U.S. FTAs tend to eschew these topics. In contrast, all of the newer association agreements and RTAs of the EU contain language on sustainable development and human rights. That language may be in the geopolitical interests of the EU, but undoubtedly is also embodies European social values.

The aforementioned issues might be grouped under the rubric of a "Check List." Below, issues on the List are discussed. No Check List is failsafe, however. Some RTAs cover topics not dealt with by WTO agreements. *NAFTA*, for example, has provisions (Chapter 15) on trade and competition policy. That fact suggests that, as a compliment to the Check List, it may be useful to consider whether obligations created by an RTA are "WTO Plus." That is, does the RTA go beyond what a WTO text covers or requires? To take one example, *NAFTA* Chapter 17, on IP, has a reciprocity rule on secondary broadcasting rights. (*See* Article 1703). There is no analogous provision in the WTO *Agreement on Trade Related Aspects of Intellectual Property Rights (TRIPs)*.

Legal aspects of RTAs is as rapidly evolving an area of international trade law as any other specialty in the field. Mastery of an FTA or CU comes from the intimate knowledge gained, in part, through perusal of the primary source text. Yet, then, a new RTA is signed, the features of which are not entirely taken from the template of previous deals. To illustrate the point, an attorney could not be satisfied with a sound knowledge of the IP rules of *NAFTA*. Within a decade of that deal, the U.S. negotiated FTAs with Singapore and Chile. These accords contain innovative methods for protecting digital IP rights. Evidently, RTA law is a stimulating area of trade law practice and scholarship.

II. ELIMINATING TRADE BARRIERS

A. How Comprehensive?

Perhaps the first and most obvious legal question about an FTA, other than the identity of the members and the effective date, is how comprehensive the deal is. In August 2006, Chile signed an FTA with China. The match was literally natural: China needs copper and other natural resources to fuel its growth, and Chile is a major supplier of these resources. The *Chile — China FTA* frees 92 percent of Chile's exports to China from Chinese tariffs, eliminates Chilean tariffs on 50 percent of China's exports to Chile, and phases out over 5-10 years certain other tariffs. Is this deal "comprehensive"?

The starting point to address the question is to think about market access. "Market access" has the same meaning in the context of trade liberalization negotiations at the multilateral, regional, and bilateral level. The term connotes the extent to which, and under what conditions, goods and services from one country may enter into the commercial stream of another country. Consequently, while the negotiating dynamics differ among the three levels, the negotiating points are similar. They include the following issues that may be raised with respect to any existing or potential FTA:

   1.   *Tariff Barriers*:

Scope —

To what extent does the FTA eliminate tariffs on trade among the member countries?

Speed —

How fast does the FTA eliminate tariffs, *i.e.*, what is the phase-out period?

Sensitivities —

If the FTA does not accord duty-free treatment to all goods, then how many exceptions from tariff elimination for so-called "sensitive" products does it contain?

Phase Out Periods —

If the FTA does not provide duty-free treatment immediately to all products, then how fast will tariffs be reduced, and on how many products?

E-Commerce —

Does the FTA extend (sooner or later) duty-free treatment to e-commerce, or restricted to traditional physical commerce?

   2.   *Non-Tariff Barriers*:

Scope —

To what extent does the FTA eliminate or reduce non-tariff barriers, such as quotas, import licenses, other quantitative restrictions, customs procedures, and non-transparency in trade rules or administration?

Sanitary and Phytosanitary Standards (SPS) and Technical Barriers to Trade (TBT) —

Does the FTA impose strict disciplines against the abuse of SPS and TBT measures for protectionist purposes?

Speed —

How fast does the FTA eliminate or reduce non-tariff barriers?

    3. *Services*:

Scope —

Does the FTA reduce or eliminate barriers to all services trade, or does it cover only some service sectors and sub-sectors? For example, are service sector commitments made using a "Negative List" approach, whereby all sectors are presumed covered unless specifically protected by exemption, or a "Positive List" approach, which implies the reverse presumption, and is relatively less trade-liberalizing?

Modes —

Will there be any restrictions in the four modes of service supply — Mode I (cross border trade), Mode II (consumption abroad), Mode III (establishment, *i.e.*, FDI), and Mode IV (temporary migration)? (These Modes are set out in the *General Agreement on Trade in Services (GATS)*.) If so, then what restrictions will apply, and to what specific service sectors and sub-sectors?

    4. *Government Procurement*:

Scope —

To what extent does the FTA open government procurement markets to cross-border goods and services? For example, does the FTA cover sub-central as well as central government entities? Does it cover quasi-governmental entities? Does the FTA use a Negative List approach or a Positive List approach?

Thresholds —

What monetary value must a prospective contract have for it to be subject to government procurement disciplines in the FTA?

    5. Non-Discriminatory Treatment:

Coverage —

Does the FTA mandate that each party accord non-discriminatory treatment to all goods, services, and government procurement from all other member countries?

Exceptions —

In what, if any, instances does the FTA permit a party to discriminate in favor of its own businesses or industries?

Depending on the answers to these questions, an RTA is more or less economically ambitious — that is, comprehensive in terms of its breadth and depth of economic coverage.

B. Case Study: The *U.S. — Singapore* and *U.S — Chile FTAs*

The *U.S. — Singapore* and *U.S. — Chile FTAs*, both implemented on 1 January 2004, are examples of deals more comprehensive than even *NAFTA*.

All three accords cover agricultural and industrial products, and services, insist on phased reductions in tariff and non-tariff barriers depending on the product category, and mandate considerable opening of many service sectors and sub-sectors. But, for example, the *Chile FTA* eliminated immediately (as of the date of entry into force, 1 January 2004), tariffs on 85 percent of U.S. tariff lines. In other words, it created truly free trade overnight on 85 percent of the product categories listed in the U.S. Harmonized Tariff Schedule (HTS). The extended liberalization period applied to agriculture and wine.

The *Singapore* and *Chile FTAs* are said to contain preferential rules of origin that are easier to administer — at least in their design — than the *NAFTA* origin rules. This broad characterization must be qualified with the remarks that rules on specific categories of merchandise may be complex, and *NAFTA* itself is a high benchmark for complexity. Nonetheless, unlike *NAFTA*, the *Singapore* and *Chile FTAs* contain obligations covering the following areas:

    i.   E-commerce.

    ii.   Customs procedures.

    iii. Services using a "Negative List" approach, whereas *NAFTA* employs a "Positive List" method, and all 4 "Modes" of supply. (These approaches and Modes are discussed later.)

    iv. Government procurement, using a "Negative List" approach, whereas *NAFTA* employs a "Positive List" method.

The *Chile FTA* also terminates Chile's status as a GSP beneficiary, which makes sense because the FTA effectively makes permanent duty-free treatment that would otherwise occur under the GSP. Each of the above obligations is significant.

Even the casual Internet shopper for books on Amazon.com or baseball products on MLB.com (like your textbook author) appreciate the burgeoning value and volume of e-commerce. Similarly, any shopper who has crossed an international boundary lawfully can appreciate the potential non-tariff barrier posed by customs procedures, and is aided in advance of the border crossing by transparency in customs rules (*e.g.*, publication on the Internet, which the *U.S. — Singapore FTA* mandates). With a Positive List, trade liberalization occurs only in service sectors and government procurement specifically stated on the list. The presumption is against open markets, unless otherwise indicated. With a Negative List, trade liberalization occurs in all service sectors and government procurement, except for areas excluded by putting them on the list. The presumption is in favor of open markets, unless otherwise said. Embracing Modes I, II, III, and IV of supplying services across borders means that access through one Mode will not be offset by restrictions in another Mode.

C. Case Study: The *U.S — Australia FTA*

Another comprehensive bargain is the *U.S. — Australia FTA*. There is (as of 2003) about $21 billion in two-way goods trade between the U.S. and Australia, and $6.6 billion in their services trade, with Australia having a bilateral trade deficit against the U.S. Roughly 11 percent of Australian exports go to the U.S., but less than 2 percent of U.S. exports are shipped to Australia. Bilateral foreign direct investment (FDI) is important to each country. American FDI in Australia (as of 2003) approximated $141.5 billion (with U.S. affiliates located Down Under selling $65 billion), and Australian investment in the U.S. was $70.4 billion (with Aussie affiliates in the U.S. generating $56 billion in sales revenues). What were the key negotiating objectives of the two countries?

Negotiators wanted a comprehensive deal. They achieved that result, in part because of their generally similar open economy dispositions. For example, before the *FTA* took effect, their levels of goods protection were similar. The average applied Australian MFN tariff was 4.3 percent. While Australia had an average bound rate of 10.5 percent, it unilaterally decided to drop its bound rate. The average U.S. MFN rate was 5.4 percent. Each country had some sectors in which they had a keen export interest, or, a particular sensitivity.

More specifically, the American objectives concerning market access for goods and services included:

1. *Agricultural Single Desks*:

The "single desk" refers to a government body, *i.e.*, a state owned enterprise (SOE) or state trading enterprise (STE), which has a monopoly on importation of the product in question, and from which domestic buyers must purchase the product. Australia operated single desks for barley, sugar, and wheat. With a keen export interest in these products — Kansas, for instance, typically is the largest wheat producing American state — the U.S. wanted Australia to end this import monopoly and allow its wheat farmers to sell directly to Australian buyers. Australia resisted reforms, recalling that after it had eliminated its single desk for wool imports, its domestic wool market collapsed.

2. *Entertainment*:

The U.S. urged Australia to eliminate its screen quotas, which apply to TV programming (in contrast to Korea's quotas, which apply to movies). The issue proved not to be too contentious. Australian news and cultural programs easily fill up the quota time.

3. *Government Procurement*:

The U.S. hoped to pry open Australian government procurement markets.

4. *Mode IV Services Supply*:

The U.S. sought business visa facilitation, *i.e.*, eased requirements and procedures concerning business visas.

Logically, Australia sought enhanced market access for certain products in which it had a keen export interest. These products included:

1. *Light Trucks*:

Australia sought elimination of the 25 percent MFN tariff imposed by the U.S. on light trucks, which could occur immediately through an FTA.

    2. *Beef*:

Australia desired meaningful access to the American market for its exports of beef, dairy, and sugar. Whether the U.S. would treat these three farm products alike, however, was dubious. Australia understood that in FTA negotiations with Chile, the U.S. had agreed to treat Chilean beef exports more favorably than Chilean dairy or sugar exports. In the *U.S. — Chile FTA*, the U.S. agreed to liberalize its TRQs (and phase in lieu of them tariffs) across 5 years on beef, but across 12 years for dairy and sugar.

    3. *Dairy Products*:

Australia held only a small share of the U.S. dairy products market. Australia hoped to export high-value added products (such as cheese), rather than low value added products (such as milk powder). Accordingly, Australia believed its negotiating objectives were not averse to the U.S. dairy support program.

    4. *Sugar*:

As with beef and dairy products, Australia sought a quick end to American TRQs on sugar. Yet, whether Australia could benefit from free trade in sugar was unclear. The Australian state of Queensland produces sugar, but less efficiently than Brazilian competitors. Brazilian sugar exports might still fare well against Queensland products, even if the latter were not subject to a TRQ. The issue never came to fruition, as sugar is not included in the *U.S. — Australia FTA*.

The specific bargaining objectives of the U.S. and Australia highlight two points that may be inferred from all FTA negotiations.

First, where the parties end up — what kind of RTA they get — depends critically on what they seek. The more ambitious their aims to liberalize trade, and the more hesitant they are to carve out protections, the more comprehensive the market access their accord will provide. Second, the degree of contention in negotiations is not necessarily evident from the initial stated positions. If protective measures opposed by one party are not, in fact, administered strictly, then the party maintaining the measures may not cling to them in the face of this opposition.

III. SENSITIVE PRODUCTS AND SECTORS

A. How Many Sensitivities?

The Doha Round negotiations involved hard bargaining over the number of tariff lines in the Harmonized Tariff Schedule (HTS) a WTO Member could designate as "sensitive" and, therefore, exempt the product category represented by that line from tariff cuts. Typically, FTA and CU negotiations also involve intricate, give-and-take on how many, and which, products each prospective party can protect, what protective methods can be used, and for how long these methods are available.

Several of the existing FTAs to which the U.S. is a party provide illustrations of sensitive products and sectors. They are as follows, arranged chronologically according to the date of entry into force. Of what legal moment is identification of a product or sector as "sensitive"?

The mere designation results in placement of the sensitive product into a special category. That category is special, because products in it do not receive duty free treatment immediately upon the entry into force of the FTA. The key questions are the date when such products do receive duty-free treatment, and the formula for phasing out tariffs on those products.

Obviously, the longer the phase out period, the more extended the period of protection. Less obvious is the impact of the tariff reduction methodology. Typically, tariffs are phased out in equal annual installments. For instance, if the sensitive product is corn, the Mexican tariff is 30 percent, and *NAFTA* calls for a 15-year phase out, then the reduction methodology would be to cut 2 points off the tariff in each of the 15 years. At the end of the first year, the Mexican tariff would be 28 percent, and at the end of the 15th year, it would be zero. An accelerated schedule would call for bigger cuts up front, perhaps 20 percentage points cut in the first five years. In contrast, a back-ended methodology would be protectionist approach. It would permit the steepest cuts occur toward the end of the phase-out period (*e.g.*, cutting 20 points from the 30 percent tariff in the last five years of the 15 year period).

B. Case Study: Agricultural Products and Textile and Apparel

The best guess for designation of a sensitive product, and for establishment of a special remedy, is a primary or processed agricultural product. Virtually every FTA into which the U.S. has entered designates multiple such products, and includes some kind of special remedial provision. T&A are the next best guess.

- 30 August 1985 *U.S. — Israel FTA*:

When originally signed on 22 April 1985, this *FTA* did not cover either agriculture or services. A side agreement, signed on 4 November 1996, was added to cover agriculture. It lapsed in 2002, but then was extended twice, through 31 December 2002 and 31 December 2003. Renewal of the side agreement was negotiated, and signed on 27 July 2004, effective through 31 December 2008.

The *U.S. — Israel FTA* allows for emergency relief for perishable agricultural products. The provision is modeled after the CBI, and contained in Section 404 of the *Trade and Tariff Act of 1984*. A U.S. petitioner may file with the Secretary of Agriculture for relief against perishable imports from Israel. The criteria are that the product is being imported in such increased quantities as to be a substantial cause of serious injury, or threat thereof, to a U.S. industry. The Secretary of Agriculture has 14 days to render a determination and report to the President, who then has 7 days to decide whether to take emergency action. That action could consist of re-imposition of the original (*i.e.*, pre-*FTA*) MFN rate on the product in question.

- 1 January 1994 *NAFTA*:

While this accord is one of America's most comprehensive RTAs, *NAFTA* did not liberalize trade in all sectors with equal alacrity. Rather, goods were divided into three categories, and tariff and non-tariff barriers phased out immediately, or over 5, 10, or 15 year periods. Trade in the most sensitive goods — in the "C +" category, noted in *NAFTA* Annex 302:2 — was not freed up for 15 years after *NAFTA* entered into force. Specifically, duties on these goods were removed in 15 annual stages commencing on 1 January 1994, with duty free treatment effective 1 January 2008.

A, if not the, quintessential example, particularly for the U.S., is sugar. It is subject to special protections, in effect for 14 years after *NAFTA* entered into force. They are in Chapter 7, entitled Agriculture and Sanitary and Phytosanitary Measures, specifically Paragraphs 13-22 of Section A of Annex 703:2. Observe the obscurity of the placement of these protections, not to mention their complexity, which becomes apparent upon even a glance at them. Reputedly, there exist one or more side letters on sugar restrictions. Yet, they are difficult to obtain — or, as one *NAFTA* attorney put it to your textbook author, good luck if the side letters ever see the light of day.

Is protecting the sugar growing and harvesting industry (both cane and beet) in the U.S. through *NAFTA* and other FTAs, or by simply excluding it from coverage, as in the *U.S. — Australia FTA*, a dubious policy? That policy is reinforced by agricultural legislation, such as the *2002 Farm Bill*, which:

(1)   Continued a quota system on imported sugar limiting foreign sugar to 15 percent of the U.S. market share,

(2)   Required the Department of Agriculture to operate a loan program (whereby producers receive loans at minimum price levels) at no cost to the taxpayer,

(3)   Set minimum domestic prices for sugar at prices substantially higher than the world market level, and

(4)   Had marketing allotments for sugar produced domestically.

When the effects of protection on sugar-consuming product businesses are considered, the answer is "yes." These businesses are called "sugar-containing product (SCP) manufacturers," and the three most significant of them are chocolate and chocolate confectionary, non-chocolate confectionary, and breakfast cereal. In February 2006, the U.S. Department of Commerce published *Employment Changes in U.S. Food Manufacturing: The Impact of Sugar Pricing.*[1] This study points out:

(1)   Over the last quarter century (1980-2005), the wholesale price of refined sugar in the U.S. has been two to three times higher than the world price. In 2004, the U.S. price was 23.5 cents per pound, but the world price was 10.9 cents per pound.

(2)   Over 10,000 American jobs were lost in the SCP manufacturing sector between 1997-2002 because of the high cost of sugar.

(3)   The job loss occurred through SCP manufacturers closing facilities in the U.S. and relocating their plants to Canada, where sugar

---

[1] *See* ita.doc.gov/media/Publications/pdf/sugar06.pdf; Rossella Brevetti, *Commerce Study Says 10,000 Jobs Lost Because of High U.S. Sugar Prices*, 23 INT'L TRADE REP. (BNA) 266-67 (23 Feb. 2006); *see also* Competitive Enterprise Institute, *Is the U.S. Sugar Problem Solvable?* (April 2006), *available at* www.cei.org/pdf/5263.pdf (arguing sugar protection has a negative impact on the environment).

prices average less than half of U.S. prices, or Mexico, where the prices average two-thirds of U.S. prices.

(4) In 1997, the SCP manufacturers employed 987,210 people, whereas 61,000 worked in growing and harvesting sugar cane and beet, hence the protectionist policy benefits a group less than 10 percent of the size of the group it injures.

(5) For every job in the growing and harvesting sector the protectionist policy saves, it costs about three jobs in the confectionary producing area.

What was the counter-argument of sugar growers and harvesters, led by the American Sugar Alliance (ASA)? First, the world market prices the Commerce Department examined were artificially depressed, because of sugar dumping by foreign countries, and excluded transportation and storage costs. Second, without support like the loan program, the industry would be in a sour position. Sugar producer prices have fallen 30 percent since 1996. Third, plants leave the U.S. because of high wages, taxes, rental, and health care costs. Concerned about the persuasiveness of their rebuttal, the ASA welcomed creation of a Sugar Caucus in the House of Representatives, dedicated to their protection.

From Mexico's perspective, two examples in the C + category are beans and white corn. They are staples in the Mexican diet. Following *NAFTA*, Mexican bean and corn farmers had lobbied their government not only for this delay, but also for help in competing with subsidized U.S. farm products. In March 2006, Mexico sought approval from the USTR to delay opening the Mexican market for these products. In June 2006, the USTR rejected Mexico's request, and also ruled out the possibility of direct American assistance to small Mexican bean and corn farmers, whose output was at risk of being displaced by U.S. products.

● 17 December 2001 *U.S. — Jordan FTA*:

The general origin rule in the *Jordan FTA* for T&A merchandise is yarn forward. This *FTA* is concerned with all T&A articles, but has notably restrictive special origin rules for certain products that effectively deny them preferential treatment. Wool scarves are an illustration, to which the yarn forward rule does not apply. Wool sweaters also appear to be a case in point. The abstruse prose used to cover these sweaters is in Paragraph 9(b)(iii) of the rules of origin in Annex 2:2:

> . . . except for goods classified under such headings as of cotton or of wool or consisting of fiber blends containing 16 percent or more by weight of cotton, if the fabric in the goods is dyed and printed, when such dyeing and printing is accompanied by 2 or more of the following finishing operations: bleaching, shrinking, fulling, napping, decating, permanent stiffening, weighting, permanent embossing, or moireing.

To what is this reference? The answer is articles within this description — such as wool sweaters — are not subject to the general yarn forward rule. Rather, these articles are entirely outside of the *Jordan FTA*, because this "except clause" takes them out of otherwise applicable rules that would confer origin on them. Hence, they are not accorded duty-free treatment. Put bluntly, they remain protected, and thus an example — albeit obscure, of how an FTA does not create true free trade in all goods.

- 1 January 2004 *U.S. — Singapore FTA*:

It might be too strong to affix the label "protectionist" to T&A market access rules in the *Singapore FTA*. This merchandise receives duty-free treatment — but, only if it meets applicable preferential rules of origin. Such treatment applied immediately, upon entry into force of the *FTA*. Of course, Singapore is neither a major T&A exporter, nor an important source of components for T&A articles. Not surprisingly, then, the *FTA* permits a limited amount of T&A to be admitted duty free each year, even if they contain third country (*i.e.*, non-U.S., non-Singaporean) yarns, fibers, or fabrics. In other words, given the realities of the Singaporean economy, a generous third-country T&A provision in the *FTA* almost was a necessity.

That said, the *FTA* contains tough monitoring and anti-circumvention rules. They include reporting requirements, licensing rules, and allowance for unscheduled factory checks. From an American perspective, they ensure only Singaporean T&A receive tariff preferences. The President authorized to exclude from entry any T&A merchandise from any enterprise in Singapore that does not permit a site visit requested by U.S. Customs officials, or that engages intentionally in circumvention. From a Singaporean vantage, these rules help minimize the instances in which the major port facility in Singapore, the Port of Singapore Authority (PSA), is a conduit for illegal T&A trans-shipment.

- 1 January 2004 *U.S. — Chile FTA*:

This *FTA* includes agricultural products and wine, in which Chile has a significant export interest. However, this merchandise receives duty-free treatment not immediately, but over an extended period. As a southern hemispheric country, Chile supplies grapes, plums, and other produce to the U.S. and other countries in the northern hemisphere from roughly November to May. During the "out-of-season," farmers in these countries are not harvesting and selling their crop. Thus, Chilean farmers do not compete head-to-head with their U.S. counterparts. This complementary, counter-cycle suggests free trade "over night" in agricultural products ought to be easy to negotiate.

Not so, as the *Chile FTA* liberalizes agricultural trade with lags of 8 and 12 years, depending on the product. Specifically, horticultural products obtained immediate duty free treatment. But, the *FTA* phases out tariffs on dairy and meat across 8 years. For grain, livestock, processed products, and sugar, it phases out tariffs across 12 years. What factors explain these product-specific tariff deferments?

One point about American tariffs on Chilean farm products is the semi-transparency of the duty rates. Chapter 7 of the HTS covers unprocessed vegetables and fruit, while Chapter 20 of the HTS covers processed vegetables and fruit. Tariffs on such products ought to be listed in these Chapters, as they are — for example — for spinach (Chapter 7) and tomato paste (Chapter 20) imported from Canada and Mexico under *NAFTA*. However, for the *Chile FTA*, tariffs on many unprocessed and processed vegetables and fruit are in

Chapter 99 of the HTS. Thus, for instance, the American tariff on Chilean tomato paste, listed in Chapter 99, is 11.6 percent. In contrast, it is duty-free for Mexican tomato paste. But, this contrast is hard to see without flipping through the HTS Chapters. The clue to connecting the Chapters is to read the footnotes within the duty schedule in Chapters 7 and 20. Observe that seasonally counter-cyclical farm products are listed (based on products) in the HTS, and tomato paste is not one of them. Who, then, might the 11.6 percent tariff protect? Might Mexican tomato paste producers be the answer, given that they are largest exporter of this product to the U.S. (as of 2005)? In turn, might it then be said that one FTA (*Chile FTA*) is used to protect third country interests under another FTA (*NAFTA*)?

As for T&A, they qualify for immediate duty-free treatment if they satisfy the applicable rule of origin. Like the *Singapore FTA*, the *Chile FTA* contains a third country source provision. A limited amount of T&A containing fiber, yarn, or fabric that is not from the U.S. or Chile may be admitted duty free.

Finally, the *Chile FTA* contains special rules on capital controls, a non-trade issue not dealt with in most other RTAs, but which raises important international financial policy questions. Before the 1997-99 Asian Economic Crisis, the International Monetary Fund (IMF) strongly encouraged developing countries to liberalize fully their capital accounts. It, and free-market oriented economists, argued opening the capital account (1) allows a poor country to access more easily foreign funds (*e.g.*, investment in local equity and debt instruments), (2) makes the process of allocating capital more efficient by subjecting it to market forces (*i.e.*, decisions of international investors), and (3) broadens the sharing of risks associated with developing countries by enlarging financing sources.

One lesson from Asian countries in the Crisis is developing countries cannot benefit from full capital account liberalization unless they have in place sound institutions and mature domestic financial markets. In particular, they need a well-functioning legal system, strong corporate governance, macroeconomic discipline, and appropriate exchange rate policies before opening the capital account. Another lesson, especially from countries like Malaysia, which rejected IMF assistance during the Crisis, is that capital account liberalization renders a country vulnerable to speculative financial flows that, if large and fast enough, can wreak havoc on an economy.

Chile paid careful attention to the debate about how quickly, and under what conditions, to open a capital account, and to the Asian experience. In its negotiations with the U.S., it sought a mechanism to insulate itself from volatile movements in financial flows and the untoward knock-on effects of such flows in the real economy. The result was a compromise. The *U.S. — Chile FTA* makes controls on the flow of financial capital illegal. Concerned Chile might be tempted to restrict capital, the U.S. insisted upon this obligation. But, Chile won an exception to the obligation.

- 1 January 2005 *U.S. — Australia FTA*:

Impressively from a free trade perspective, Australia committed to eliminating duties on all U.S. agricultural exports immediately upon entry into force of the *U.S. — Australia FTA*. Less impressively from that perspective, the

U.S. agreed to phase out duties on Aussie agricultural imports over a 4-18 year phase out period. Still less impressively, each country preserves protections on a limited number of sensitive farm products. The U.S. maintains tariff rate quotas (TRQs) on beef, dairy products, and sugar. Indeed, the *FTA* excludes sugar entirely. The American side gave its beef sector the most extended protection — a TRQ regime lasting 18 years. Australia maintains TRQs on cheese and tobacco. (The TRQs are preferential, implying higher in-quota thresholds, lower above-quota tariffs, or both.) Special safeguards also apply to these products. Further examples of sensitive products, to which TRQs or special safeguards apply, are cotton, peanuts, and other horticultural products.

The two countries also restrict FDI and certain kinds of transactions. For example, the U.S. applies the *Jones Act* restrictions against foreign vessels engaging in cabotage (carriage of goods between U.S. ports). Because Australia makes "fast ferries," it is not pleased by this ban. For its part, Australia maintains restrictions on media ownership, and local content requirements for broadcasting — neither of which appeal to the U.S. entertainment industry. Because Australia is not a member of the WTO *Agreement on Government Procurement* (a plurilateral accord), it refused to open its government procurement market to the U.S.

- 1 March 2006 *CAFTA—DR*:

Not surprisingly, as with *NAFTA*, treatment of agricultural products — especially sugar — proved to be the most controversial market access issue in *CAFTA—DR* negotiations. The agricultural sector (as of May 2003) employs 30-40 percent of the Central American labor force, but about 1 percent of American workers. This sector accounts for about 17 percent of the GDP of Central America, but about 1-2 percent of the U.S. national income. There is a dualism in Central American agriculture. One part of the sector is traditional, highly protected, and domestically oriented. For it, *CAFTA—DR* was more of a threat than opportunity. The other part, comprised of major, internationally competitive farms, is modern. For it, *CAFTA—DR* was less of a threat and more of an opportunity. This kind of dualism also exists in U.S. agriculture. Sugar was the bitter battleground, with American producers lobbying ferociously to defeat the deal entirely.

In brief, *CAFTA—DR* regulates sugar imports into the U.S. by a TRQ system. During the first year of operation, it allows a maximum additional 107,000 metric tons of sugar. The figure rises to 151,000 tons over 15 years. The latter figure is just 1.2 percent of sugar consumption in the U.S. (as of 2006), and in 15 years is projected to be only 1.7 percent.

Not surprisingly, *CAFTA—DR* also regulates T&A imports into the U.S. It does so in part through the use of "Tariff Preference Levels," or "TPLs."[2] For example, the TPL for Nicaragua is 100 million square meters of apparel. This amount may enter the U.S. duty free for the first 5 years during which *CAFTA—DR* is operative, even though the apparel may be made of yarn or fabric from third countries, *i.e.*, ones not members of *CAFTA—DR*. Up to 100

---

[2] *See* Christopher S. Rugaber, *Senate Approves Promised Textile Changes To CAFTA—DR as Part of Pension Legislation*, 23 INT'L TRADE REP. (BNA) 1198 (10 Aug. 2006).

million meters of apparel made of Chinese fabric could qualify. However, after 5 years this TPL is eliminated. Further, to get the benefit of the TPL, Nicaragua had to agree to purchase trouser fabric from the U.S. in an amount equal to its use of the TPL. Hypothetically, if Nicaragua uses 2 million square meters of such fabric from India, then it had better purchase this amount from an American source, too.

The technique of regulating T&A imports through TPLs reflects a tug-of-war between foreign manufacturers and domestic producers of a like or directly competitive product. Manufacturers located in a *CAFTA—DR*, which may be American, Canadian, European, Chinese, or other non-*CAFTA—DR* firms operating in production facilities in Central American, seek the freedom to source inputs like yarn and fabric from the cheapest price, highest quality source. The likes of China and India are obvious candidates. Conversely, domestic producers seek to limit duty-free treatment only to products containing components from *CAFTA—DR* members. They — and their industry association, the National Council of Textile Organizations (NCTO) — point out the *CAFTA—DR* region is the second largest market in the world for American-made yarns and fabrics. The NCTO also explains that whereas the content of clothing imported into the U.S. from Central American is about 70 percent "Made in the U.S.A.," for Chinese apparel is just 1 percent U.S. content. Query, then, whether for the NCTO and its members, *CAFTA—DR* may not be so much about free trade in T&A, but fair trade — "fair" in the sense of protecting the input relationships with Central America.

IV. SENSITIVITIES AND SAFEGUARDS

A. Any Bilateral or Special Safeguards?

Beyond separate (or non-existent) phase-out periods for trade barriers on "sensitive" products and sectors, the possibility of a special remedy is a second legal ramification of the label "sensitive." That is, an FTA may establish a remedy for action against imports of sensitive products. However, this protective possibility is not necessarily limited to sensitive products. It could apply just to designated products, or to any imported article.

The special action is legally distinct from an AD, CVD, or general safeguard remedy, and it is one of the surest challenges to market access, and strongest tools for managing trade. Conceptually, and sometimes by title, safeguard provisions in FTAs are dubbed "bilateral safeguards" or "emergency action," if they apply to all product types, or "special safeguards" or "product-specific safeguards," if they apply only to designated types. Whatever the label, the remedy allows an importing country that is an FTA member to put back — or snap back — the pre-FTA MFN tariff on a sensitive product, or to suspend any further scheduled tariff reductions on the product.

For any FTA safeguard, the key question concerns the legal criteria for imposing relief. Under what conditions may one FTA partner "hit" a category of imports from another partner? The first option is to use trigger price and trigger volume criteria fixed by an arithmetic formula. The second, and possibly more frequently used option, is to articulate elastic textual criteria modeled after global safeguard relief pursuant to GATT Article XIX and the WTO *Agreement on Safeguards*. As a general pattern, the first option is used for special agricultural safeguards. The second option is used for bilateral safeguards, and T&A safeguards. This pattern is not invariant. The *CAFTA—DR* T&A safeguard is based on a trigger threshold (which for the first time, in July 2006, the U.S. threatened to use against Honduran socks). What explains this pattern and deviations?

Thus, for example, the *U.S. — Jordan FTA* permits the U.S. to impose a bilateral safeguard under criteria akin to the global safeguard remedy in the GATT — WTO regime. The ITC must decide whether, as a result of the reduction or elimination of a duty, a Jordanian article is being imported into the U.S. in such increased quantities, and under such conditions, that the imports alone are a substantial cause of serious injury or threat thereof to a domestic industry producing an article that is like or directly competitive with the Jordanian import. Upon an affirmative ITC determination, the President must provide necessary import relief. The relief could include suspension of any further duty reduction, or an increase in the rate of duty.

The *U.S. — Chile FTA* has a special safeguard provision, designed for certain agricultural products, known as "agricultural safeguard goods." It calls for automatic assessment of a duty on such a good if the unit import price of that good upon entry to the U.S. is less than the trigger price for that good set out in the FTA. The *U.S. — Australia FTA* has an elaborate special agricultural safeguard remedy, which is contained in Article 3:4 and Annex 3-A. Article 3:4 authorizes the U.S. to impose a safeguard, namely, an additional duty, on Australian agricultural imports listed in Annex 3-A. There are three categories of potentially targeted goods:

1. *Horticulture Safeguard*:

For certain horticultural goods.

2. *Quantity-Based Beef Safeguard*:

For certain beef imports imported into the U.S. above specified quantities between 1 January 2013 and 31 December 2022.

3. *Price-Based Beef Safeguard*:

For the same categories of beef as the Quantity-Based remedy, but applicable to beef imported into the U.S. after 31 December 2022, above a specified quantity, if the monthly average index price in the U.S. falls below a specified trigger price.

Note, then, the legal criteria for the beef safeguard are trigger volume and trigger price, not GATT — WTO type language. The remedy under any special safeguard is an additional duty. But, the sum of that additional duty and the applied rate in the U.S. Tariff Schedule may not exceed the lesser of the MFN rate imposed by the U.S. when the Australia *FTA* entered into force. In other words, the tariff cannot snap back to a level higher than what existed when the two countries commenced "free" trade on 1 January 2005.

Redolent of the *U.S. — Australia FTA*, the *U.S. — Morocco FTA* has a price-based safeguard for some horticultural products. Under Article 3:5 and Annex 3-A of the *Morocco FTA*, the U.S. can impose an agricultural safeguard, namely, an additional duty, on certain Moroccan horticultural goods. The U.S. Schedule to Annex 3-A of the *FTA* lists these goods. The *Singapore, Chile, Australia,* and *Morocco FTAs* also have a T&A safeguard.[3] So, too, does *CAFTA—DR.* In the U.S., the Committee for Implementation of Textile Agreements (CITA) has authority over these special safeguards.

An interested party may ask the President to determine whether, because of duty elimination under the relevant FTA, a Singaporean, Chilean, Australian, Moroccan, or *CAFTA—DR* T&A article, is being imported into the U.S. in such increased quantities and under such conditions as to cause serious damage, or actual threat thereof, to a domestic industry. The *Singapore FTA* requires causation to be substantial. Evidence CITA requires to show injury includes data on imports, market share, and production. The increase in imports may be absolute, or relative to the domestic market for that article. The domestic industry must produce a product that is either like, or directly competitive with, the imported article. The second possibility broadens considerably the range of potentially interested parties. The petitioner — an "interested party" — could be any entity, whether a firm, certified union, group of workers, or trade association, which represents a domestic producer of a like or directly competitive article, or which represents a domestic producer of a component used in the production of a like or directly competitive article. This second possibility — to include upstream, or input, producers — further broadens the range. CITA also may self-initiate a petition.

The relief under the *Singapore* and *Chile FTAs* is to suspend duty reduction on T&A merchandise (if the tariff is not already zero), or re-impose the MFN rate for the article at the time relief is granted. Under the *Australia* and *Morocco FTAs*, the relief appears different: suspension of any remaining duty reduction, or imposition of the lesser of the MFN rate (1) extant at the time of the remedy or (2) rate when the *FTA* entered into force. That also is the rule under Article 3:23 of *CAFTA—DR.* What explains the distinction from the *Singapore* and *Chile FTAs,* and is it a material difference?

If an FTA creates a safeguard — be it bilateral (*i.e.*, general, as most FTAs do) or special (as is common in FTAs for agricultural goods, T&A) — then how does that remedy relate to global safeguard actions under the GATT — WTO regime? Theoretically, multilateral rules ought to be pre-eminent, and perhaps even pre-empt any regional action. That is not the position U.S. FTAs take. They allow exemption from a global safeguard for imports from an FTA partner, if the ITC determines those imports are not the substantial cause of serious injury or threat to a U.S. industry. This exemption is a kind of rule against double jeopardy that ensures the U.S. does not impose both a global and FTA safeguard against the same merchandise from the same country. For instance, suppose the U.S. imposes safeguard relief under GATT Article XIX, the WTO *Safeguards Agreement,* and Section 201 of the *Trade Act of 1974,* as amended, to protect certain phosphate products. The *Jordan FTA* requires the ITC to consider whether phosphate articles of Jordanian origin are

---

[3] *See* Section 322(a) of the *United States-Singapore Free Trade Implementation Act,* Section 322(a) of the *United States-Chile Free Trade Implementation Act,* and Section 322(a) of the *United States-Australia Free Trade Implementation Act,* Section 322(a) of the *United States-Morocco Free Trade Implementation Act.*

responsible for damage to American producers of a like or directly competitive product. Following a negative ITC determination, the President may exclude the Jordanian merchandise from the global safeguard action. Consider, then, the interaction of the global and regional safeguard provisions. Does the "no double jeopardy" protection found in FTAs violate GATT — WTO provisions?

Similarly, the *Singapore, Chile, Australia*, and *Morocco FTAs* contain a bilateral safeguard. The rules authorize the President, after an investigation and affirmative determination by the ITC, to impose import relief. The legal criteria to provide relief track GATT Article XIX and the WTO *Safeguards Agreement*. It must be the case that a Singaporean, Chilean, Australian, or Moroccan product is imported into the U.S. in such increased quantities, and under such conditions, as to be the substantial cause of serious injury, or threat thereof, to the domestic industry.[4] If these criteria are satisfied, then the ITC renders an affirmative determination and recommends to the President relief necessary to remedy or prevent serious injury, and facilitate the efforts of the petitioning domestic industry to make a positive adjustment to competition posed by the target foreign good. The relief is to increase the applicable duty to the lesser of the existing MFN rate, or the MFN rate imposed when the relevant *FTA* entered into force, or to suspend duty reductions if they have not yet been fully implemented.

Significantly, FTAs contain grounds for exempting merchandise from a safeguard action. The question is whether the grounds are pre-or post-investigation. Pre-investigation exemption means an imported article is not subject to investigation — in effect, a "no double jeopardy" rule. Generally, under the *Chile, Singapore*, and *Australia FTAs*, any article already subject to import relief under a global (*i.e.*, GATT — WTO) safeguard, or under the bilateral safeguard created by the *FTA*, is immune from a special safeguard investigation under the *FTA*. Further, any article subject to a bilateral safeguard once is exempt from another investigation, meaning relief cannot be provided twice in respect of the same article. The exemption also covers T&A merchandise targeted for relief under the special safeguard provisions in the *FTA*, or an agricultural product subject to special safeguard relief under Article 5 of the WTO *Agreement on Agriculture*.

As for post-investigation exemptions, FTAs typically provide for Presidential discretion in remedy decisions. First, under the *Singapore, Chile*, and *Australia FTAs*, the President need provide import relief only to the extent he determines necessary to remedy or prevent injury and facilitate positive adjustment by the relevant domestic industry. Accordingly, the President could depart from an ITC recommendation, in particularly, by imposing a less potent remedy than urged by the ITC.

Second, FTA general and special safeguards contain outright waiver authority. Under the *Jordan FTA*, the President can waive the otherwise mandatory imposition of a bilateral safeguard if it is not in the U.S. national interest to block imports, or if extraordinary circumstances exist and providing relief

---

4 *See* Sections 311-316 of the *United States-Singapore Free Trade Agreement Implementation Act*, Sections 311-316 of the *United States-Chile Free Trade Agreement Implementation Act*, Sections 311-316 of the *United States-Australia Free Trade Agreement Implementation Act*, Sections 311-316 of the *United States-Morocco Free Trade Agreement Implementation Act*.

would cause serious harm to U.S. national security. The paragon context for waiver is if the imported product is in short supply in the U.S. and needed for defense purposes. The *Singapore, Chile, Australia,* and *Morocco FTAs* authorize the President not to provide bilateral safeguard relief, even if the legal criteria for it are satisfied, if relief would not provide greater economic or social benefits than costs. This standard gives the President considerable discretion, and affords plenty of room for political factors to enter into the calculus. The *Australia FTA* permits the USTR to waive application of the quantity-or price-based beef safeguard if extraordinary market conditions indicate a waiver would be in the American national interest. Exercise of this waiver requires prior notice and consultation with the House Ways & Means and Senate Finance Committees, and private sector advisory bodies.

FTAs also are likely to place a cap on the period of safeguard relief. For the bilateral and T&A safeguard, the *Chile FTA* limits relief to 3 years. A 3-year limit exists for the bilateral and T&A safeguard under the *Morocco FTA.* However, the relief period may be extended, up to an aggregate maximum duration of 5 years. The *CAFTA—DR* limit is a maximum of 3 years. But, if the initial relief period is less than 3 years, then CITA may extend it to 3 years if needed to (1) remedy or prevent serious injury, or actual threat of serious injury, and (2) facilitate adjustment to import competition by the domestic industry. The industry must show it is making positive adjustment. Under the *Singapore* and *Australia FTAs*, relief under the bilateral or T&A safeguard may not exceed 2 years. But, this period may be extended once under certain circumstances, yielding a maximum aggregate relief period of 4 years. The *Australia* and *Morocco FTAs* specify that any bilateral safeguard relief lasting longer than one year must be subject to progressive liberalization over the course of its application.

Query why a limit of 3 years (or less) is common in safeguards? Might the reason relate to Article 8:3 of the *WTO Agreement on Safeguards*? This provision defers for 3 years the right of one WTO Member to suspend substantially equivalent concessions granted to another Member, where the latter has adopted a safeguard measure based on an absolute increase in imports from the former Member. In other words, does a 3-year cap on safeguard relief under an FTA help ensure a "3 year pass" under WTO rules?

Three further notable features of special safeguards in U.S. FTAs are critical circumstances, compensation arrangements, and sunset dates. First, the *Singapore* and *Chile FTAs* allow for provisional relief and critical circumstances in respect of bilateral safeguards. What are they and how do they work? Does the bilateral safeguard in the *Australia FTA* have an analogous provision? The T&A safeguard in the *Australia FTA* permits provisional relief for up to 200 days in the event clear evidence is adduced to show critical circumstances exist. What circumstances might be "critical"? Do the T&A safeguards in the other accords have this provision?

Second, FTAs tend to authorize the President to compensate an FTA party against which the U.S. takes a safeguard action. Both the bilateral and T&A safeguards of the *U.S. — Singapore* and *U.S. — Chile FTAs* contain this authority. Similarly, Article 9:4 of the *Australia FTA* and Article 8:5 of the *Morocco FTA* call for compensation to a target country for a safeguard imposed against one of its exports. Article 2:23:6 of *CAFTA—DR* requires "mutually agreed trade liberalizing compensation" to a target country, *i.e.*, the country whose T&A article is subject to a safeguard. The compensation takes the form of concessions by the country imposing the safeguard that have substantially equivalent trade effects, or are equivalent in value, to the additional customs duties expected from remedial action. These provisions are consistent with the compensation principle in GATT Article XIX and Article 8 of the WTO *Agreement on Safeguards*. The multilateral disciplines call for the safeguard-imposing country to provide the target country with concessions substantially equivalent to the adverse effects of the relief. Of course, there may be considerable debate as to whether concessions are substantially equivalent. That is especially true when, as often occurs, compensation is in a different sector from the targeted article. What if the safeguard-imposing and target countries cannot agree on the value of trade-liberalizing compensation? Then, the FTAs tend to provide the target with the right to increase customs duties on imports from the imposing country.

Third, bilateral and special FTA safeguard provisions tend to have a sunset rule. The *Singapore FTA* discontinues any safeguard relief 10 years from the date of entry into force of the *FTA*, unless Singapore consents. The *Chile FTA* states no bilateral safeguard relief may be given after 10 years from the date of entry into force (or 12 years if that is the relevant period for tariff elimination). For the T&A safeguard, the sunset date is 8 years after entry into force. The *CAFTA—DR* sunset date for the T&A safeguard is 5 years from the date on which the accord takes effect.

Sunset rules are not as trade liberalizing as they appear. The *Australia and Morocco FTA* sunset rules are less free-trade oriented than analogs in the other *FTAs*. That is because of the date on which the clock for the sunset starts to tick. Whenever that date is after the entry into force, the sunset is postponed. For the bilateral safeguard, the *Australia FTA* specifies 10 years, *i.e.*, the remedy ceases to exist on 1 January 2015, unless tariff elimination for the article in question exceeds a decade, in which case the remedy terminates as soon as zero duty treatment starts. For the special T&A safeguard, the sunset period is 10 years, but measured from the date on which duties on the merchandise in question are eliminated. Thus, hypothetically, if duties on 100 percent cotton sleeveless dresses is eliminated on 1 July 2012, then safeguard remedy is available to protect a domestic industry making a like or directly competitive article until 30 June 2022. The *Morocco FTA* employs the same deferred sunset rule for its bilateral and T&A safeguards. No such safeguard action may be taken after 5 years (for the bilateral safeguard) or 10 years (for the T&A safeguard) from the date on which duties on the good in question are eliminated. For the special agricultural safeguard in the *Australia FTA*, the sunset date depends on the product. The horticulture safeguard ends when duty-free treatment on the horticultural good in question is phased in. That also is the rule for the quantity-based beef safeguard. But, the price-based beef safeguard never terminates, meaning the free-trade value of the agreement in the beef sector always is in peril.

As a final note about bilateral and special safeguards, what must not be lost amidst technical legal criteria is the role politics associated with very specific products can play in a case. Pockets for apparel are one illustration. To get support for *CAFTA—DR* from legislators representing textile producing states, the administration of President George W. Bush promised to change rules of origin on pockets.[5] It did just that, with the Senate passing legislation (H.R. 4) by a vote of 93-5 in August 2006. The change ensures that material used to make pockets must be made in the U.S., or in another *CAFTA—DR* country, for the apparel product to receive duty-free treatment. That is, using third-country material in pockets vitiates trade benefits.

Honduran socks are another example of writing product-specific rules to get votes.[6] To help secure passage of *CAFTA—DR*, the Bush Administration, in a July 2005 letter, told Representative Robert Aderholt (Republican-Alabama) it would enforce aggressively the T&A safeguard under *CAFTA—DR* (as well as the China-specific remedy in China's terms of WTO accession). The Administration also promised to renegotiate a *CAFTA—DR* rule eliminating immediately U.S. tariffs on socks, and substitute a decade-long phase out of tariffs, or at least tighten the rule of origin for socks to require they be finished in the U.S. to receive duty free treatment. Significant sock manufacturers are located in Congressman Aderholt's Alabama district. With these promises, he voted for *CAFTA—DR*, which passed the House of Representatives by the narrowest of margins.

In July 2006, before *CAFTA—DR* was implemented in all members, the Administration threatened Honduras with the first use of the safeguard. After all, sock imports from the tiny country had increased 49.9 percent in June 2006, and a Canadian company was constructing a sizeable new sock production facility there. Was the threat pressure on Honduras to change its stance against lengthening the phase-out of sock tariffs, and against tightening the rule of origin? What implications would there be, including for *NAFTA*, of action against socks made in the Canadian company's facility?

B. Case Study: The 1998 *NAFTA Broom Corn Brooms* Dispute

A safeguard remedy created by an FTA need not be restricted to a sensitive sector. *NAFTA* Chapter 8 is a case in point, providing for emergency action in any sector. A key case brought under it is the *Broom Corn Brooms* dispute. According to *NAFTA* Article 801:1 and the definition of "domestic industry" in Article 805, the "domestic industry" must produce a "like or directly competitive good." This prerequisite is the same as the elements of GATT Article XIX and Section 201 of the *Trade Act of 1974*, as amended. It is the prerequisite at issue in the 1996-98 *Broom Corn Brooms* dispute. The U.S. and Mexico hotly contested application of the phrase "like or directly competitive product." In its determinations, the ITC excluded straw brooms and plastic brooms from its definition of the U.S. corn broom industry. Mexico contended straw and plastic brooms are like or directly competitive with corn brooms.

---

[5] Christopher S. Rugaber, *Senate Approves Promised Textile Changes to CAFTA—DR as Part of Pension Legislation*, 23 INT'L TRADE REP. (BNA) 1198 (10 Aug. 2006).

[6] *See* Christopher S. Rugaber, *U.S. Preparing to Use CAFTA Safeguard to Restrict Sock Imports from Honduras*, 23 INT'L TRADE REP. (BNA) 1139 (27 July 2006).

Four aspects of the *Broom Corn Brooms* case are noteworthy. First, the case may well prove to be a leading decision on the prerequisite that a competitive industry produce a "like or directly competitive good." Second, the case is of historical interest in its own right because it was the first significant dispute between *NAFTA* Parties. As the *International Herald Tribune* put it, it was "the first case since the trade agreement began that has resulted in one of the three nations taking economic revenge against another."[7] Third, the case highlights the perils of a free trade agreement for marginal industries, and the propensity of these industries to seek escape clause relief when threatened by such an agreement. Fourth, the case illustrates the tandem operation of the *NAFTA* bilateral escape clause and Section 201.

The *Broom Corn Brooms* dispute was a direct result of *NAFTA* tariff elimination. The U.S. offered duty-free treatment to imports of most categories of broom corn brooms from Mexico, and slashed tariffs from 33 percent to 22 percent on certain other corn broom categories. In March 1996, the U.S. Corn-broom Task Force filed a petition against Mexican producers and exporters of broom corn brooms under both *NAFTA* Chapter Eight and implementing American law, and Section 201, the conventional escape clause. (American law authorizes submission of a petition under *NAFTA* Chapter Eight, Section 201, or both laws. *See* § 19 U.S.C. § 3357.) Imported corn brooms account for about 60 percent of the American market, with Mexican brooms capturing the single biggest share. The *NAFTA* complaint was directed at broom corn broom imports from Mexico, *i.e.*, it called for a bilateral escape clause action. The Section 201 complaint was directed at imports from all sources, including Mexico. To be sure, "[j]ust 382 [American] jobs and less than $10 m[illion] of imports are involved [in the broom corn brooms dispute] out of two-way [U.S.-Mexican] trade totaling $140 b[illio]n."[8] However, the employees in these jobs make the case heart-rending: "because corn brooms are so labor intensive, broom-weaving has been a popular product for American companies founded to employ the blind."[9] The American employees felt that "Mexican brooms, which sold for less than their U.S. counterparts, threatened to put them out of business."[10]

Where complaints are brought under both laws, the ITC conducts the investigation jointly, but renders separate determinations in accordance with the differences in the prerequisites for remedial action, and the more limited duration and nature of remedial measures under Chapter Eight. Accordingly, following the *NAFTA* investigation, in August 1996, the ITC rendered a 5-1 affirmative determination that because of a *NAFTA* duty elimination or reduction, broom corn brooms from Mexico are being imported into the U.S. in such increased quantities such that the imports alone are a substantial cause of serious injury or threat thereof to the domestic industry. The ITC

---

[7] Molly Moore, *Fight Sweeps Through NAFTA*, INT'L HERALD TRIBUNE (London), 14-15 Dec. 1996, at 12.

[8] Leslie Crawford & Nancy Dunne, *Spirit of NAFTA Is Swept Under the Carpet*, FINANCIAL TIMES, 19 Dec. 1996, at 8. The *International Herald Tribune* (*see supra* note 7) estimated roughly 600 jobs at small plants in various states were at stake.

[9] *Id.*

[10] Moore, *supra* note 7, at 12.

(specifically, the Chairman and two commissioners) recommended that President Clinton increase the duty on Mexican broom corn brooms to the prevailing MFN rate for 3 years, which is the maximum relief allowable under Chapter Eight.

Following the Section 201 investigation, the ITC rendered a 4-2 affirmative determination in August 1996 that broom corn brooms are being imported into the U.S. in such increased quantities as to be a substantial cause of serious injury or threat thereof to the domestic industry. In this investigation, the ITC Chairman and one Commissioner recommended a 4-year tariff increase encompassing Mexico, and products from the Caribbean Basin Initiative and Andean Pact countries (but not against Canadian or Israeli products). They called for a duty increase to the MFN rate, plus 12 percent *ad valorem* in the first year, 9 percent *ad valorem* in the second year, 6 percent *ad valorem* in the third year, and 3 percent *ad valorem* in the fourth year. Their recommendation encompassed the relief indicated in the *NAFTA* investigation, so they pointed out that there would be no need to engage in a separate *NAFTA* remedy if the duty increase plus a surcharge were implemented. Two other Commissioners called for a 4-year tariff increase on broom corn brooms other than whisk brooms to, in general, 40 percent *ad valorem* in the first year, 32 percent *ad valorem* in the second year, 24 percent *ad valorem* in the third year, and 16 percent *ad valorem* in the fourth year.

In September 1996, President Bill Clinton elected to seek a negotiated settlement in lieu of adopting the various remedial measures recommended by the ITC. The President correctly observed that a broader range of remedies is available under Section 201 than *NAFTA* Chapter Eight, and that the period in which remedies may remain in effect is longer under Section 201 than Chapter Eight. (Section 201 permits non-tariff as well as tariff remedies, whereas Chapter Eight focuses only on tariff measures. Section 201 remedies may remain in effect for up to eight years, whereas Chapter Eight measures generally are limited to three years). Therefore, he reserved the ability to raise tariffs in an amount equal to or greater than the ITC's recommendations.

When negotiations between the USTR and Mexican officials failed after several months, President Clinton announced in December 1996 increased tariffs under Section 201. For one tariff classification of corn brooms (HTS sub-heading 9603.10.60), he raised tariffs from 22.4 percent to 33 percent. For another tariff classification of corn brooms (HTS sub-heading 9603.10.50), he raised tariffs from zero to 33 cents per broom. These increases in tariffs were phased out by the 2000, at which time the applicable rate was at or below the 1996 rates. For a third category of corn brooms (HTS sub-heading 9603.10.40, which encompasses brooms with a value of less than 96 cents), the President continued duty-free treatment, but imposed a global tariff rate quota of 121,478 dozen per year. Imports in excess of this amount were subject to a tariff.

Not surprisingly, the Mexican government and broom makers were angry. The Mexican corn broom industry employs about 2,000 workers, and 60 percent of its brooms are exported to the U.S. The Mexicans argued President Clinton's action has devastated the small town of Cadereyta, capital of the Mexican corn broom industry, which lies just outside the northern city of Monterrey, on the road to Texas.

. . . .

Mr. Jorge Trevino, president of the Mexican Corn Broom Manufacturers' Association, believes the U.S. protectionist measures have imperiled thousands of jobs in and around Cadereyta.[11]

In essence, the U.S. action led to sorrow in the Mexican industry. It also led to retaliation.

In December 1996, Mexico imposed tariff increases on almost two dozen American imports. For example, Mexico imposed a tariff increase of 20 percent on brandy and bourbon whiskey, wine and wine products (*e.g.*, wine coolers), and flat glass, a tariff increase of 12-14 percent on wood office and bedroom furniture, a 12.5 percent tariff increase on all chemically-pure sugar, fructose, and syrup products, and a 10 percent tariff increase on certain notebooks (*e.g.*, telephone agendas). Mexico valued its retaliation at about $1 million, the amount raised by the American safeguard action, and thereby argued it was substantially equivalent to that action. The Mexican authorities expressly invoked *NAFTA* Article 802:6 as authority to take the retaliatory action.

In January 1997, these authorities also requested a dispute resolution panel pursuant to *NAFTA* Chapter 20. They alleged President Clinton's action was not in conformity with *NAFTA*, and that the ITC investigation misapplied the *NAFTA* Article 805 definition of a "domestic industry" as one that produces a like or directly competitive product. The U.S. could have argued *NAFTA* is inapplicable, because the American action ultimately was taken pursuant to Section 201. Of course, this argument would suggest the U.S. is insincere about Chapter Eight, and will resort to Section 201 whenever convenient. Interestingly, this suggestion might not be entirely inaccurate. Are there certain limitations on Chapter Eight bilateral actions that (at least from a petitioner's perspective) are worrisome?

In February 1998, the *NAFTA* Chapter 20 Panel issued a ruling in favor of Mexico. *See U.S. Safeguard Action Taken on Broomcorn Brooms from Mexico*, U.S.A.-97-2008-01, available on the U.S. *NAFTA* Secretariat website, www.nafta-sec-alena.org. (The report actually was issued on 30 January 1998.) The Panel found the American safeguard measure against broom corn brooms was inconsistent with *NAFTA* Article 803 Annex 803:3(12). That provision mandates the administering authority (the ITC) provide reasoned conclusions on all pertinent issues of law and fact in making a determination. The Panel concluded the ITC failed to explain how it defined "directly competitive" in finding that plastic brooms were not part of the domestic industry. Accordingly, the Panel recommended the U.S. bring its conduct into compliance with *NAFTA*. American and Mexican officials met to plan a course of action. What did they decide?

Presumably, one option would have been for the ITC to re-open its investigation and render a new decision that satisfies *NAFTA* Article 803 Annex

---

[11] Crawford & Dunne, *supra* note 8, at 8.

803:3(12). On 3 December 1998, President Clinton announced the removal of the safeguard measure against Mexican broom corn brooms. He emphasized the removal was because of an August 1998 ITC report that the U.S. broom corn broom industry had not made adequate efforts to make a positive adjustment to import competition. *See Broom Corn Brooms: Efforts of Workers and Firms in the Industry to Make a Positive Adjustment to Import Competition*, Inv. No. 332-394, U.S. ITC Pub. 3122 (August 1998). Conspicuously absent from the justification was the fact compliance with the Panel Report demanded removal. Indeed, perhaps removal, and the reasons for it, were disingenuous. Recall the safeguard measure had been in place for a full two years (December 1996-December 1998), the panel had issued its report in January 1998, and the ITC report came in August 1998. Had the U.S. dragged out the case so as to afford protection as long as possible?

V. MANAGED TRADE IN GOODS?: THREE GENERAL POINTS

It is possible to infer three general points about RTAs, be they FTAs or CUs.[12] First, in any RTA negotiation, both sides are highly likely to count agriculture, or at least certain agricultural products, as sensitive. Beef, rice, and sugar are classic examples. Only when negotiating an RTA with a city-state (and there are few of them aside from Singapore and the Holy See), or with a country that lacks an export interest in agriculture, is agriculture not an issue. The negotiating points include (1) the number of primary and processed agricultural commodities is each country allowed to designate as sensitive, (2) the precise identification of which products qualify as sensitive, and perhaps why, (3) the extent to which tariff and non-tariff barriers will be reduced on sensitive products. The third point concedes freer trade will come later rather than sooner on sensitive products. How much deviation will be permitted from the trade liberalization rules that apply to non-sensitive sectors?

One temptation to avoid is a monolithic stereotype of the agricultural sector in any country. Not all farmers are protectionists, nor are all free traders. For example, at the risk of simplification, in the U.S. there are two broad groups of farmers: (1) big field crop farmers, and (2) small crop farmers. The first category includes corn, cotton, soybean, and wheat. Traditionally, many of them — including the Great Plains wheat farmers in states like Kansas — have been ardent free traders. They relied on export markets to take their surplus production. However, they tend to receive most of the approximately $19 billion (annually) in U.S. Department of Agriculture subsidies. It is not easy for this first group to give up their subsidy payments in a multilateral trade round, such as the Doha Round, unless they obtain at least an equivalent guaranteed value in market access to developing country markets, as well as to the EU.

Similarly, they may be skeptical of an RTA, if its rules fail to mandate accelerated reductions in barriers to their commodities. The second group

---

[12] These points are adduced in detail in tables set out in the *Dictionary of International Trade Law* that accompanies this textbook.

includes farmers producing dairy products, peanuts, and sugar. Their domestic market — particularly dairy and sugar — is regulated, putting them in a privileged position. Indeed, their political clout puts them there, and they can wring promises from political candidates to preserve barrier and subsidy levels. Like the first group, the second group insists on equivalency in WTO talks, *i.e.*, equivalent levels of protection to ensure equivalent market access, and equivalent subsidy levels to ensure equivalent support. But, dairy, peanut, and sugar producers may be relatively less enthusiastic about a multilateral or RTA deal that provides equivalence. That is, they may be especially prepared to use trade remedies such as antidumping (AD), if equivalence actually occurs and threatens their position.

Two other issues are increasingly important: safeguard mechanisms and SPS measures. Will a special safeguard remedy exist for agricultural products? If so, what legal criteria must be satisfied to trigger the safeguard? Should the safeguard have a sunset date (*i.e.*, should the remedy terminate after a certain number of years), and if so, what should the date be? As for SPS measures, what will they be, and how will disputes in specific cases be resolved?

Second, in most RTA negotiations, T&A are likely to be of importance — but, not necessarily for the same reasons. That is especially true if the RTA involves economies at different stages of economic development. Of course, the sector is not contested if the prospective members do not produce or export this merchandise. Developed countries with declining T&A sectors are wont to put as many protections in an RTA against competing imports as possible. Developing and least developed countries will take the opposite position. Thus, hard bargaining is foreseeable over the following topics: (1) tariff rates, (2) quota thresholds, (3) both tariff rates and quota thresholds if tariff-rate quotas (TRQs) are relevant, (4) periods for phasing in tariff rate reductions or quota growth, and (5) periods for phasing out tariffs, quotas, and TRQs.

Also, rules of origin on T&A merchandise will be contested. Developed countries generally prefer more restrictive rules, which call for origination based on activity as early as possible in the production chain (*e.g.*, fiber forward or yarn forward rules, which mandate, respectively, that the fiber — such as cotton — or yarn come from within the RTA, and all subsequent activity occur within the RTA). Developing and least developed countries push for rules that allow more inputs to be sourced from, and processing to be done, outside the RTA (*e.g.*, a sewing forward rule, which allows all inputs to come from third countries, including fiber, yarn spun from the fiber, fabric made from the yarn, and allows cutting of pieces to occur in a third country). Further, as with agriculture, almost assuredly T&A products raise a debate about whether to insert in an RTA a special safeguard mechanism for them. If one is inserted, then the debate shifts to the technical criteria for applying the remedy. And, the matter of a sunset date must be considered.

The third general point concerns the rubric "FTA," and is an inference from the first three points. May it be stated with confidence that the "F" word in this acronym ought to be "freer," not "free"? A truly "free trade agreement" would state that all tariff and non-tariff barriers on all merchandise traded are eliminated as of the date of entry into force. That never happens. Duty elimination invariably occurs on less than 100 percent of the trade between or among FTA partners. Always there are a few, sometimes many, product categories — or even entire sectors — scheduled for deferred duty elimination. The deferral periods typically are cast in terms of "staging categories," such as "A," "B," "C," "D," and so forth. Products in the first category receive immediate duty free treatment as of the date of entry into force of the FTA. But, products in remaining categories are not subject to free trade for years from that date — such as 5 years for Category B, 10 years for Category C, 15 years for Category C, and so on.

Obviously, each derogation from the simple but quixotic obligation — "all tariff and non-tariff barriers are eliminated effective on the date of entry into force" — is a step away from comprehensive free trade. Given the large number of derogations in practice, it may be asked not only whether the term "free trade agreement" is accurate, but also, and more fundamentally, whether there is anything such thing as a "free trade" outside of the minds of economists?

VI.   LIBERALIZING SERVICES TRADE OR ENDANGERING SAFETY?: THE *NAFTA* CROSS BORDER TRUCKING DISPUTE

Trucking is big business in *NAFTA*. About 80 percent of trade between the U.S. and Mexico occurs over roads. The roots of the *Mexican Cross Border Trucking Services* date to the early 1980s. In 1982, Congress passed the *Business Regulatory Reform Act*, which (*inter alia*) imposed a two-year moratorium issuing new licenses to foreign carriers operating in the U.S. By Executive Order on 20 September 1982, President Ronald Reagan lifted the moratorium for Canada, but preserved it for Mexico. This Order was extended in 1984, 1986, 1988, 1990, 1992, and 1995.

NAFTA entered into force on 1 January 1994, and the provisions in Annex 1 to it (entitled "Reservations for Existing Measures and Liberalization Commitments"), which covers cross border services, took effect on 18 December 1995. Under them, Mexican commercial trucks were to have full access to 4 U.S. border states in 1995, and access throughout the U.S. in 2000. Likewise, U.S. trucks were to be allowed to deliver goods into Mexico. Instead, the Administration of President Bill Clinton, pointing to concerns about the safety of Mexican trucks and drivers, suspended these provisions. U.S. trucks were shut out of Mexico. Mexican trucks were restricted to making deliveries only into a 20-25 mile commercial zone on the U.S. side of the border between the two countries, adjacent to border crossings. Then, they had to transfer their cargo to a U.S. entity within the post-border buffer zone.

The *NAFTA* Annex 1 provisions also allow for applications for new licenses, from Mexico and Canada, to operate a truck or other vehicle to carry freight across the U.S. border in the same truck or vehicle. However, since 1982, the U.S. has issued no licenses to Mexican applicants. On the day the Annex took effect, Mexico's Secretary of Commerce and Industry (formerly called "SECO-FI," and now called the *Secretaría de Economía*, *i.e.*, the *Ministry of the Economy*, or "*Economía*"), Herminio Blanco, wrote a letter to then USTR

Mickey Kantor, requesting consultations. Consultations were held on 19 January 1996, but with no resolution to the basic Mexican complaint against the U.S. refusal to issue licenses to Mexican trucking firms. Two years later, on 24 July 1998, Secretary Blanco wrote again to USTR Charlene Barshefsky asking for a *NAFTA* Free Trade Commission (FTC) meeting. He expanded the claim: not only did the U.S. reject cross-border trucking licenses for Mexican firms, but also it denied Mexican investors the right to invest in American trucking enterprises. On 19 August 1998, the FTC met, but failed to resolve either issue. On 22 September 1998, the Mexican government called for formation of an arbitral panel to decide both issues. Over a year later (on 10 December 1999), the U.S. asked for consultations with Mexico over its reciprocal decision to refuse to allow American trucking companies into the Mexican market.

The two countries were in a classic tit-for-tat spat, and a *NAFTA* Chapter 20 Panel was formed on 2 February 2000, with a final decision issued a year later. The Final Report in the case, *Cross Border Trucking Services*, was issued 6 February 2001. *See* File No. USA-MEX-98-2008-1, www.nafta-sec-alena.org. The principal legal issue before the Panel was whether the U.S. violated *NAFTA* by failing to phase out restrictions on cross border trucking services and Mexican investment in the U.S. trucking industry. The U.S. defense was its interpretation of "in like circumstances" in *NAFTA* Article 1202. This Article concerns national treatment, while Article 1203 concerns MFN treatment. Article 1202 mandates that each Party "accord to service providers of another Party treatment no less favorable than that it accords, *in like circumstances*, to its own service providers" (emphasis added). The U.S. used the italicized language to justify a "blanket ban," because Mexico lacked the same rigorous truck safety rules as the U.S. or Canada.

Not so, held the Panel. They found the U.S. violated *NAFTA* (specifically Annex 1) obligations, and said the defective regulatory environment in Mexico was an insufficient defense. The "blanket ban" was at issue, not the pursuit of legitimate regulatory objections, hence the Panel advised the U.S. to bring their practices into compliance. Furthermore, regulatory issues should not affect investment recommendations, as the Parties agreed investment does not affect safety. The Panel did not mean to say the U.S. must ignore safety regulations in considering licenses for cross border services. Rather, the Panel insisted the U.S. must afford Mexican (and Canadian) service providers equal treatment in their application review process. In effect, the Panel ruled the U.S. discriminated against Mexican applicants, violating both the national treatment obligation (based on differential treatment of Mexican and American trucking companies), and MFN obligation (based on differential treatment of Mexican and Canadian providers).

Throughout the remainder of 2001, obstinacy was the American response to the adverse Chapter 20 Panel decision. It was no secret the Teamsters Union did not want competition from cheap Mexican truckers. Worse yet for the Mexican side, the 11 September terrorist attacks galvanized Congress to pass legislation heightening border security. Only after mid term elections in late November 2002 did President George W. Bush issue an Executive Order implementing the Panel decision, and thereby lift the ban.

Unfortunately for Mexican trucking interests, that Executive Order engendered another controversy. Environmental groups sued the U.S. government. They argued the President lacked the right to issue the Order without an environmental impact study on the effect of Mexican trucking on the U.S. environment. In June 2004, the Supreme Court ruled the President had authority to issue the Order, holding the Federal Motor Carrier Safety Administration (FMCSA) was not under any obligation to evaluate the environmental effects of cross-border trucking, because the FMCSA lacks the power to prevent cross-border trucking services. *See Department of Transportation v. Public Citizen*, 541 U.S. 752 (2004). This narrow holding is seen as based on the general presumption the President has the right (delegated by Congress) to regulate foreign trade.

The ban, then, on issuing licenses to Mexican trucking companies to carry freight into the U.S., and on Mexican investment in U.S. trucking interests, is over. Yet, difficulties remain. The U.S. is concerned about terrorism infiltrating any borders, illegal immigration and narcotics flows across its southern border, and the effect on the environment of Mexican trucks hauling freight around the U.S. Conversely, Mexico has wondered whether the victory in the Chapter 20 case might be Pyrrhic. If there is a *bona fide* cross-border trucking services market in the *NAFTA* region, then can its companies compete with more efficient, better financed American firms? The U.S. often implements new customs regulations, including requiring the electronic filing of cargo manifests (which list the contents of a shipment, and serves as a security check, and which differs from an entry summary, which is used for tariff purposes). Some Mexican companies cannot meet the new rules as easily as their U.S. and Canadian counterparts — or at all.

Not surprisingly, freight still is transferred at the border between American- and Mexican-owned trucks in the 20-25 mile commercial zone. Literally, cargo is handed off from a Mexican truck to an American truck, and then heads north. The reverse also is true — cargo is physically moved from a U.S. to a Mexican truck, and the recipient truck heads south. In this transaction, repeated thousands of times daily, the real winners are drayage companies that perform the work of transferring cargo from truck to truck. Who are the losers in this relay? Among them are *maquiladoras*, which compete with low- or lower-cost companies making like products in China, and border trade hubs like San Antonio, which do not realize the benefits of expanded trade *NAFTA* should bring. The largest loser may be *NAFTA* itself, and the faith of each Party in the Chapter 20 dispute resolution process. When studying Chapter 20, consider whether, following a favorable adjudicatory outcome, Mexico or Canada can enforce a judgment against the U.S.?

To be sure, in September 2004, Congress passed legislation giving Mexican trucking companies and their drivers two years to meet American safety standards. Those standards included:

i.   Possessing a valid commercial driving license.

ii. Showing medical fitness.

iii. Complying with maximum hours-of-service rules.

iv. Proving the ability to understand questions and directions in English.

v.   Carrying insurance with a U.S.-licensed insurer.

vi.   Passing in-person audits and safety inspections.

In February 2007, the U.S. Secretary of Transportation, Mary E. Peters, announced creation of a 1-year pilot program to allow a select group of 100 Mexican trucking companies to make deliveries beyond existing restricted commercial zones, which vary in size from 3-25 miles inland on the U.S. side of the border. (Even anointed companies could make only international deliveries. They could not deliver goods between U.S. cities, nor carry hazardous materials or passengers.) In April, opposition to the pilot program in Congress, as well as by the Teamsters Union and environmental groups, was so fierce the Department of Transportation (DOT) had to suspend the program.

There is no way, opponents complained, to be sure a Mexican truck driver complies with U.S. safety regulations on hours of service (*i.e.*, that the driver has not been operating for longer than a safe, reasonable period). After all, only 5 percent of Mexican trucks entering the U.S. are inspected. Moreover, the zone serves a law enforcement purpose. As long as Mexican trucks are kept within a 25 mile zone, and required to offload cargo to U.S. carriers, then any illicit items — such as narcotics or weapons — may be detected at that point.

On its side, Mexico said it would consider license applications from U.S. firms seeking to operate in Mexico, but would license only about 100 of them. Whether, and when, there will be free trade in trucking services remains uncertain — all the more so because of approval (by a 411-3 vote) in May 2007 by the House of Representatives of the *Safe American Road Act* (H.R. 1773). The *Act* not only limits participation in any pilot program to 100 Mexican motor carriers and 1,000 commercial motor vehicles, but also has stricter parameters than the DOT envisaged.

VII.   MANAGED TRADE IN SERVICES?

Market access rules on services suggest the same or similar general points as for goods. Is free trade the regime, or is it really managed trade?[13] Evident are the sensitivities in services areas. To be sure, as a September 2006 WTO Working Paper, highlights, the general pattern on Modes I and III (cross-border supply and temporary migration of persons) is that FTA pledges go beyond scheduled *GATS* commitments.[14]

The U.S., in particular, obtains better service market access through FTAs — largely because of its use of a Negative List approach — than under *GATS*. In the U.S. FTAs with Bahrain, the *CAFTA* countries and Dominican Republic, Chile, Colombia, Morocco, Oman, Peru, and Singapore, over 80 percent of all services sub-sectors are covered by trade-liberalizing commitments in Modes I and III. Under *GATS*, the figure is less than 50 percent. Through

---

[13] The *Dictionary of International Trade Law* accompanying this textbook contains Tables detailing these obligations for each FTA to which the U.S. is a party.

[14] *See* Martin Roy, Juan Marchetti & Hoe Lim, *Services Liberalization in the New Generation of Preferential Trade Agreements (PTAs): How Much Further than the GATS?* (ERSD-2006-07) (Sept. 2006), *available at* www.wto.org.

its FTAs, the U.S. is able to focus on access in areas in which it has a keen interest, such as audiovisual, educational, express delivery, and financial, and telecommunications services.

That said, even FTAs involving the U.S. do not reflect full free trade in services. Manifest in the details of the market access commitments on services in every FTA is that no FTA accords across-the-board free trade in services. Were the FTAs to do so, then the rules would occupy just a page or two. As with goods, there are sensitivities in services — and, for that matter, government procurement. Market access rules may obligate FTA members to give MFN and national treatment to service providers and government contractors. In practice, though, these rules may be undermined by corollary concerns, such as environmental degradation, labor rights, and national security.

Accordingly, it must be asked with respect to services, is the term "Free Trade Agreement" a misnomer for services as well as goods? To be sure, Adam Smith and David Ricardo studied trade in goods. Yet, inspired by their paradigm, may it be said with considerable accuracy that every services deal about managed trade?

Chapter 26

TYPICAL FTA OBLIGATIONS: FURTHER COMMITMENTS

Merchants have no country. The mere spot they stand on does not constitute so strong an attachment as that from which the draw their gains.

> —President Thomas Jefferson (1743-1826), *Letter* dated 17 March 1814

DOCUMENTS SUPPLEMENT ASSIGNMENT

1. *Havana Charter* Articles 3, 7, 46-54, 87

2. *NAFTA* Chapters 7A, 10-17, 19-22

3. U.S. *Statements of Administrative Action* for *NAFTA* Chapters 7A, 17, and 19

4. Relevant provisions in other FTAs

I. GOVERNMENT PROCUREMENT

A. Economic Significance

Roughly 20 percent of world trade consists of government procurement. At all levels — federal (central), sub-central (state or provincial), or local — governments around the world must buy goods and services to function, and to provide goods and services themselves. Frequently, the vendors are private companies. Whether they are domestic or foreign businesses, however, depends on a complex array of legal and business considerations. Roughly 20 percent of world trade consists of government procurement, and private companies poised to compete successfully in cross-border sales of goods and services to foreign government would like to see this figure increase.

However, procurement from non-local companies — though often economically efficient, in terms of low costs and high quality — raises two major difficulties. First, should local companies get preference in selling goods and services to a government? GATT Article III:8(a) allows for derogation from the national treatment obligation for government procurement. Second, is it in the national security interest of a government to rely on a foreign company for a particular good or service? The answer depends in part on the availability of domestic substitutes (*e.g.*, how quickly, and in what quantities, and with what quality, can they be produced?), the home country of the foreign company (*i.e.*, is it a friend, foe, or neutral nation?), and the good or service in question (*e.g.*, is it a guidance system for an advanced fighter jet, or generic paint for the jet?).

On a multilateral level, an *Agreement on Government Procurement* (*GPA*) exists. It was produced during the Uruguay Round. However, not all Uruguay Round negotiators agreed to commit their countries to government procurement liberalization. Hence, the WTO *GPA* is a plurilateral agreement, set forth in Annex 4 to the *WTO Agreement*. To be sure, there are an impressive number of signatories to the *GPA*, including the U.S., EU, Korea, Hong Kong, and Israel. Moreover, that number is rising. China, for example, agreed to join the *GPA* in connection with its accession to the WTO. However, the number of WTO Members that have signed on to the *GPA* is a minority of the total Membership. Further, the *GPA* uses a Positive List approach to government procurement liberalization, which is inherently less ambitious than a Negative List method.

Thus, much of the action in government procurement liberalization occurs at the level of a free trade agreement (FTA) or customs union (CU). The U.S. places considerable importance on government procurement provisions in its FTAs, which is not surprising given the competitive position of many American businesses to offer goods and services to foreign governments.

B. Case Study: Social Engineering and Malaysia

Emphasis on liberalized government procurement sometimes conflicts with another reason government procurement is significant. In some countries, it is an instrument of social policy. Malaysia is a case in point.

Following ethnic and race riots in 1969, in which Malays protested against economic dominance by Chinese and Indians, the Malaysian government implemented a New Economic Policy (NEP). Essentially, the NEP is affirmative action for the majority Malays (who account for about 60 percent of the population). The NEP creates special privileges — such as job preferences, equity share distribution rights, low-interest mortgages, reserved seats universities and study-abroad scholarships — for Malays. In FTA negotiations with Malaysia during 2006-07, the U.S. called for a Negative List approach to government procurement. Malaysia not only insisted on a Positive List, but also on the reservation for Malays of certain Malaysian government contracts.

Social engineering through government procurement is not unknown in the U.S., which has reservations for small and minority owned businesses. How many concessions ought the U.S. to make to Malaysia for ethnic-and race-based reservations?

C. Managed Trade Again?

Not surprisingly, the higher the monetary threshold for coverage by FTA rules, the greater the degree of protection conferred on local government procurement providers.[1] That is because government procurement contracts valued at below the threshold are exempt from the market access rules of the FTA in question. Further, the extent to which market access in government procurement is liberalized depends not only on the contract thresholds, but

---

[1] The *Dictionary of International Trade Law* accompanying this Textbook contains a detailed table on market access rules on government procurement and services in U.S. FTAs.

also on two other factors — use of a Negative List (which is inherently more liberalizing than a Positive List), and the number and prominence of government entities subject to the market access rules.

Consider, then what, if any, patterns appear? Would it be accurate or fair to say the U.S. proposes, if not imposes, a template on other countries with which it negotiates FTAs? Or, are the variations in procurement thresholds sufficient to suggest real bargaining? Overall, is the story in the government procurement area — as with private goods and services — managed trade? Would an even better characterization be "micro-managed trade"?

II. INTELLECTUAL PROPERTY

A. Exporting American Standards and *"TRIPs* Plus" Commitments

Even America's first FTA, with Israel in 1985, spoke of IP rights. That accord reaffirmed the commitment of the two countries to existing bilateral obligations on IP rights. It did not advance the cause of IP protection, in the sense of establishing new or higher-than-extant duties. But, it provided a minimum, or floor, ensuring neither country would tolerate a lowering of commitments. In *NAFTA* Chapter 17, the U.S., Canada, and Mexico committed themselves to IP protection at the level provided by the leading world conventions and treaties on patents, trademarks, and copyrights. The strong, comprehensive rules in this Chapter served as a basis, even template, for the WTO *Agreement on Trade Related Aspects of Intellectual Property Rights (TRIPs)*.

Invariably, the minimum commitment in an FTA with the U.S. allows for the creation, maintenance, and enforcement of patents, trademarks, and copyrights. Typically, the FTA partner must agree not to promulgate such laws, or to make amendments where necessary — it must have done so already before the FTA is implemented. A promise of future legislative or regulatory reforms will not do, because once the negotiations are over, the U.S. loses considerable leverage to influence legal reform in the FTA partner. Additionally, enforcement is essential to secure the interests of the American IP sector — and, therefore, to U.S. trade negotiators. Put bluntly, whining from developing or least developed countries about a lack of judicial or law enforcement resources will fall on deaf ears.[2] It may be met with an argument that IP piracy in those countries may well be benefiting a corrupt elite.

Many of America's newer FTAs, especially accords negotiated after the Uruguay Round, call upon partner countries to go beyond IP protection and enforcement measures set out in the *TRIPs Agreement*. In part, that reflects America's bitter experience with lax IP enforcement in major markets like China. U.S. trade negotiators relied, to the detriment of the American IP sector, on promises made by China of future implementation and enforcement

---

[2] *See generally* Margaret Chon, *Intellectual Property and the Development Divide*, 27 Cardozo L. Rev. 2821-2912 (2006) (articulating developing country perspectives); Sue Ann Mota, *TRIPs: Ten Years of Disputes at the WTO*, 9 Comp. L. Rev. & Tech. J. 455-78 (2005) (discussing WTO adjudications on IP matters).

during talks for China's WTO accession, which culminated in a November 1999 U.S. — China bilateral agreement, and entry effective 11 December 2001. The subsequent history, from the U.S. vantage point, was one of failure to adhere to the promises. One lesson learned by U.S. trade negotiators was to insist on results — actual implementation and enforcement — before accession. They drilled the point in WTO accession talks with the Kingdom of Saudi Arabia, which culminated with a bilateral accord in the fall of 2005, and accession on 11 December 2005.

A second lesson from the adverse experience with China was to use FTAs as a vehicle to go beyond the *TRIPs Agreement*, *i.e.*, to demand *TRIPs* Plus commitments from a would-be FTA partner. Consider the following examples:

    i.   In the *U.S. — Jordan FTA*, Jordan agreed to ratify and implement within two years two IP agreements that are not part of its *TRIPs* obligations: the World Intellectual Property Organization (WIPO) *Copyright Treaty*, and the WIPO *Performances and Phonograms Treaty*. The aim of these agreements, which are known as "Internet Treaties," is to protect copyrighted works in a digital network environment. Thus, for example, they provide a creator with the exclusive right to make its creative works available online. The same *TRIPs* Plus provisions, incorporating the most up-to-date international copyright protection standards, exist in the *U.S. — Morocco FTA*.

    ii.   In the *U.S. — Chile FTA* and *U.S. — Singapore FTA*, Chile and Singapore agreed to *TRIPs* Plus commitments not only for patents, trademarks, and copyrights, but also for trade secrets. The two countries also accepted the obligation of ensuring its legal system contains meaningful penalties for piracy and counterfeiting.

    iii.   In negotiations for a *U.S. — Australia FTA*, the U.S. had two key objectives concerning IP. First, it sought better IP protection, especially with respect to grey (parallel) market products. The U.S. achieved this objective through provisions in the FTA that not only complement, but also enhance, existing international standards for both protection and enforcement of IP rights. These *TRIPs* Plus provisions include strong penalties for counterfeiting and piracy. Second, the U.S. opposed the Australian pharmaceutical benefits scheme of pricing. On this point, agreement proved difficult and the end result — though *TRIPs* Plus — was nebulous.

The two countries affirmed their shared objectives of (1) maintaining high quality healthcare and (2) improving public health standards. They agreed on three principles in pursuit of these objectives: (1) the importance of innovative pharmaceuticals, (2) the significance of research and development in the pharmaceutical industry, with appropriate governmental support including IP protection, and (3) the need for timely and affordable access to innovative pharmaceuticals through procedures that value objectively pharmaceuticals based on their therapeutic relevance. The sticking point was the procedures by which a federal health care program lists and prices new pharmaceuticals for reimbursement. Both sides agreed the procedures should demand transparency and accountability. But, how could the U.S. be certain

Australia would not discriminate against drugs from U.S. pharmaceutical companies when listing and pricing medicines in its Pharmaceutical Benefits Scheme? From Australia's perspective, how could its consumers be assured they would have access to effective U.S. drugs at non-astronomical prices?

The *FTA* establishes a Medicines Working Group to continue the conversation between the two countries on pharmaceutical issues, and creates in Australia an independent review process for listing decisions. The conversation indeed continues on this and other controversies. For example, when approving the FTA, the Australian Parliament added an "Anti-Evergreening" amendment to Australian law.[3] This change blocks a pharmaceutical company from evergreening a patent or using the judicial process to preclude introduction of a generic medicine. The U.S. opposes the amendment.

In June 2006, NGOs — 416 of them, including the AFL-CIO, Citizens Trade Campaign, Communications Workers of America, Friends of the Earth, National Farmers Union, Sierra Club, and United Steel Workers — signed a letter urging Congress to reject the *U.S. — Oman FTA* (which Congress ultimately passed that summer.) They argued the accord not only lacked meaningful labor and environmental protections, but also would hurt poor and sick Omanis. The *FTA* IP provisions benefited large pharmaceutical companies by protecting their "unprecedented monopoly rights" of large pharmaceutical companies, forbidding for extended periods competition from generic products, and limiting access to affordable medicines.[4]

In the *U.S. — Colombia TPA*, signed in February 2006, but not implemented as of February 2007, Colombia agreed to join the WTO *Information Technology Agreement (ITA)*.[5] The *ITA*, an outgrowth of the Uruguay Round, lists a large number of computer and computer-related products subject to duty-free, quota-free treatment. However, it is a plurilateral accord, hence joining is required neither by *TRIPs* nor any other WTO accord.

In January 2006, the U.S. and Thailand were engaged in FTA negotiations, which commenced in June 2004. U.S. insistence on *TRIPs* Plus IP commitments contributed to large-scale protests in Chiang Mai, Thailand, against an FTA, and brought talks to a halt. (In January 2006, your Textbook author and his family personally witnessed their peaceful demonstration while on holiday staying at the Sheraton Chiang Mai, where a round of the FTA negotiations happened to be held.) Four specific *TRIPs* Plus controversies arose:[6]

(1) The U.S. insisted on 25-year span for patent protection, beyond the *TRIPs Agreement* norm of 20 years.

(2) The U.S. called for compensatory patent extensions by the Thai government to pharmaceutical companies, if the government

---

[3] *See* Christopher S. Rugaber, *Portman Raises Drug Patent Issues in Meeting with Australian Trade Minister*, 23 INT'L TRADE REP. (BNA) 361-62 (9 March 2006).

[4] Christopher S. Rugaber, *Baucus Slams Administration for Omission of Forced Labor Amendment from Oman FTA*, 23 INT'L TRADE REP. (BNA) 1034 (6 July 2006).

[5] *See* Rossella Brevetti, *Colombia and U.S. Reach FTA After Resolving Agriculture Issues*, 23 INT'L TRADE REP. (BNA) 318-19 (2 March 2006).

[6] *See* Amy Kazmin, Andrew Jack & Alan Beattie, *Patent or Patient? How Washington Uses Trade Deals To Protect Drugs*, FINANCIAL TIMES, 22 Aug. 2006, at 9.

"unreasonably" delayed either the grant of a drug patent, or approval of a drug for market use. The *TRIPs Agreement* does not contain this mandate.

(3)   The U.S. sought a data exclusivity provision not found in the *TRIPS Agreement*. This provision would preclude manufacturers of generic drugs (which, of course, tended to be Thai companies) from using clinical trial data, or other scientific information, from any other company (*e.g.*, an American pharmaceutical giant), to prove its generic product was safe and effective after the product had entered the market. Thailand's Government Pharmaceutical Organization (GPO) objected. The GPO provides "first line" anti-retroviral medicines (*i.e.*, older ones, some of which the patent had lapsed) to 80,000 AIDS patients (as of 2006), and sought to expand this program to 150,000 patients (by 2008). The GPO planned to offer generic "second line" drugs (*i.e.*, newer, more sophisticated medicines still subject to a patent). Data exclusivity would inhibit its ability to do so. Further, data exclusivity would apply even to an unpatented drug, where no patent had been sought because the market for the drug was thought to be too small.

(4)   The U.S. required tight language that would limit the terms and conditions under which the GPO could effect a compulsory license of a new drug. The U.S. offered a side letter assurance that the language would be consistent with the November 2001 Doha Ministerial Conference *Declaration on TRIPs and Public Health*. Again, the GPO replied the language would adversely affect its ability to provide drugs to Thai AIDS patients.

Thousands of Thai health care workers, AIDS victims, and activists — fearful of high-priced medicines should their government "cave" to the demands — demonstrated noisily, but peacefully (in front of the Sheraton Chiang Mai!) for about two days. Farmers, who were upset at U.S. demands concerning agricultural trade (*e.g.*, that Thailand reduce rice tariff barriers), joined them. The U.S. team left the Sheraton as inconspicuously as possible, through a side door behind the concierge desk, into an unmarked van, and down a side street. The USTR blamed the ensuing stall in negotiations on Thai political unrest.[7]

The FTA between Korea and the U.S., *KORUS*, calls on Korea to adhere to patent, trademark, and copyright protection and enforcement consistent with U.S. IP standards, including a 70 year period for copyright protection (rather than the 50 year *TRIPs* mandate), and strong protections for data and digital products (*e.g.*, music text, software, and videos). That is, U.S. law, not *TRIPs*, is the benchmark.

Not surprisingly, some international trade law scholars offer persuasive arguments for the proposition that *"TRIPs* Plus" is *"TRIPs* Minus" for poor countries. For example, Professor Mohammed El-Said of the University of Central Lancashire argues *TRIPs* Plus commitments in deals like the *U.S.*

---

[7] *See* Christopher S. Rugaber, *U.S. — Thailand FTA Talks On Hold, But U.S. Not "Giving Up,"* 23 INT'L TRADE REP. (BNA) 801-02 (25 May 2006).

— *Morocco* and *U.S.* — *Bahrain FTA* end up doing greater harm than good to the U.S. partners, hence rendering those countries worse off than under WTO disciplines.

To be sure, arguments about *TRIPs* Plus commitments are not all one way. As a general matter, to the extent a country is an actual or potential producer of goods and services embodying patents, trademarks, and copyrights, such commitments may redound to the benefit of its economy. IP protection is necessary to ensure inventors make sufficient returns on their investment in research and development, without which the financial incentive for creativity would be gone. Innovation, in turn, is a healthy dynamic influence on economic growth and competitiveness. Moreover, generic manufacturers may produce drugs sub-par in quality, and may lack the capacity to meet market demand. There also is the harsh truth that in some developing and least developed countries, the real enemy to efficacious delivery of medicines is not high prices charged by American pharmaceutical companies, but decrepit infrastructure and rampant corruption.

What is the empirical record? U.S. trade negotiators insist there is no proof *TRIPs Plus* commitments either injure the pharmaceutical industry of an FTA partner or limit access to medicines in that partner. They point to Jordan, claiming that since the *U.S.* — *Morocco FTA* took effect, the number of new innovative pharmaceuticals launched has increased, and Jordanian generic manufacturers have thrived. Of course, the Jordanian market is small, relative to Thailand, not to mention China or India. Indeed, when confronted with a compulsory license threat in a large country, is the official American reaction noticeably stronger?

Consider the 2005 case of the AIDS drug Kaletra, invented by Abbott Laboratories of the U.S.[8] To ensure low-cost provision of Kaletra to patients, Brazil nearly issued a compulsory license. It backed off, allegedly because of phone calls from the White House and Congress, and threats of retaliation. Brazilian President Luiz Inácio da Silva compromised on a deal in which Abbott would keep its patent but offer Kaletra for 6 years at a reduced price.

Another example where pressing for *TRIPs* Plus commitments engenders heated debate arose in the *U.S.* — *Korea FTA* negotiations. In June 2006, the Korean Ministry of Health and Welfare announced it would adopt a "Positive List" system for reimbursement of pharmaceuticals. Only medicines explicitly put on the List would be eligible for reimbursement. With a Negative List, reimbursement is provided for all medicines, except those drugs not on the List. It is inherently a more free-trade policy than a Positive List approach, which potentially discriminates against foreign pharmaceuticals. Fixated on market access for its big drug companies, the U.S. expressed "grave concern" at the announcement.[9] Surely the Ministry had in mind its responsibility, and Korea's sovereign right, to design a system that would avoid sending Koreans

---

[8] *See* Amy Kazmin, Andrew Jack & Alan Beattie, *Patent or Patient? How Washington Uses Trade Deals To Protect Drugs*, FINANCIAL TIMES, 22 Aug. 2006, at 9.

[9] Rossella Brevetti, *Early Progress in U.S. — Korea FTA Talks Bodes Well for Completion, U.S. Official Says*, 23 INT'L TRADE REP. (BNA) 907 (15 June 2006); *see also* Christopher S. Rugaber, *U.S. — Korea FTA Talks Remain On Track, U.S. Trade Official Says*, 23 INT'L TRADE REP. (BNA) 1134 (27 July 2006).

needlessly to their graves, and would control costs to ensure their access to affordable medicines. Yet, when Korean negotiators stuck to their position in July 2006, American negotiators simply walked out of the pharmaceutical talks.[10] Fortunately, the next month the two sides agreed to discussions on the basis of a Positive List, but with coverage of transparency, non-discriminatory pricing, and reimbursement.

Equally touchy is the subject of the rate at which Korea's National Health Insurance (NHI) reimburses generic pharmaceuticals. Roughly 73 percent of reimbursement expenses are on generics. The reimbursement rate is about 70 percent of the price of the original brand-name medicine, in contrast to the rate in the U.S. for generics — 20-30 percent of the original drug.[11] U.S. lobbyists, notably the Pharmaceutical Research and Manufacturers of America (PhRMA), say the high rate paid to firms that imitate, not innovate, is disguised industrial policy to hinder foreign firms seeking to expand business, investment, and research and development (R&D) in Korea. These lobbyists called for the same WTO-Plus provision on independent board review that exists in the *U.S. — Morocco FTA* to prevent systematic over-valuation of generics and undervaluation of new medicines. They were successful, as *KORUS* establishes a Medicines and Medical Devices Committee to monitor relevant commitments.

B.   Relations to Other FTA Obligations

As a final point, consider how IP commitments might relate to other obligations in an FTA. Securitization of IP could be one context. "Securitization" refers to the issuance of financial instruments, typically bonds, based on revenue streams expected from an underlying financial asset of the issuer, like mortgages held, credit card receivables, or car loan payments. Roughly two-thirds of the total value of the balance sheets of American companies is the implied value of intangible assets, like patents, trademarks, and copyrights. Seeing this value, ingenious Wall Street investment bankers created bonds backed by IP royalty payments. Trademarks are a good example. In May 2006, Dunkin' Donuts issued $1.7 billion in bonds secured (*inter alia*) by royalties it expects from its franchisees. Earlier, in 1997, the British rock star David Bowie issued $55 million in "Bowie Bonds." They were backed by future sales of his music.

Obviously, if IP rights are not enforced, then the revenue streams needed to repay securitized bonds could be compromised. Less obvious is the ability of investment banking, accounting, and legal services to provide securitization products. An FTA can assist on both counts. It not only can mandate IP enforcement, but also open services markets so the bankers, accountants, and lawyers can devise and offer innovative financial instruments the underlying value of which depends on IP.

---

[10] *See* Christopher S. Rugaber, *U.S., Korea Agree on "Way Forward" On Pharmaceuticals in Free Trade Talks*, 23 INT'L TRADE REP. (BNA) 1225-26 (17 Aug. 2006).

[11] *See* Christopher S. Rugaber, *U.S., South Korea Aim for Quick Start To FTA Talks; Will Exchange Text in May*, 23 INT'L TRADE REP. (BNA) 411-12 (16 March 2006).

III. FDI AND COMPETITION POLICY

Cross-border investment flows are a major feature of globalization. These flows typically dwarf in value cross-border trade in goods, and are concomitants — indeed, catalysts — for trade in both goods and services. A sizeable percentage of trade in goods and services occurs between or among business affiliates, such as between a Japanese parent corporation and its Chinese subsidiary. In an historical sense, the world in which Adam Smith and David Ricardo hypothesized about one enterprise producing goods in one country and exporting it to consumers in another country no longer exists. Global production and inter-affiliate trading are predominant modern realities. Of course, even in bygone eras, there were multinational enterprises such as the British East India Company. In brief, trade and investment are integrally linked.

That fact may be inferred from *NAFTA* Chapter 11, which both liberalizes restrictions on foreign direct investment (FDI) and affords protections to investors. The *NAFTA* negotiators appreciated that securing the right to invest, protecting all forms of investment — such as concessions, contracts, debt, enterprises, and IP — and ensuring regulatory transparency is essential to attracting overseas capital. So, too, is giving foreign investors the right to establish, acquire, and operate investments on an equal footing with domestic entities. Chapter 11 covers these topics. While less ambitious, the later-in-time WTO *Agreement on Trade-Related Investment Measures (TRIMs)* affords certain investor protections, namely, national treatment. Consider the extent to which *NAFTA* Chapter 11, and FDI sections in other FTAs, contain obligations that go beyond *TRIMs* mandates — *i.e.*, that are "*TRIMs* Plus."

Remarkably, *NAFTA* Chapter 11 also contains an investor-state dispute settlement mechanism. That is, it authorizes investor-state legal action, *i.e.*, the *NAFTA* Parties essentially waive sovereign immunity and allow themselves to be sued by private parties on a claim relating to Chapter 11. A three-member panel of independent arbitrators, not the domestic court system of the host country, handles the claim using procedures set out in Chapter 11. A number of Chapter 11 disputes have been adjudicated, yielding both written opinions and a robust body of scholarship about the cases.

To be sure, whether FDI rules are necessary in an FTA depends on the parties. For example, if the parties have in place a Bilateral Investment Treaty (BIT), then they may be unnecessary. The *U.S. — Morocco FTA* does not have an investment chapter, given the 1997 BIT between the two countries. Still, following *NAFTA*, a number of U.S. FTAs contain rules to liberalize FDI, and thereby complement trade-liberalizing rules. For example, under the *U.S. — Singapore FTA*, Singapore protects all forms of investment, unless specifically exempted, offers national treatment to U.S. investors, and — like *NAFTA* — uses a Negative List approach to FDI access. This generosity to foreign investors is unsurprising, given Singapore's desire and need to attract FDI. The scope of the *U.S. — Morocco FTA* stands rather in between the two extremes of zero and full coverage of FDI in the *Jordan* and *Singapore FTAs*, respectively. The *Morocco FTA* provisions protect all American investment in Morocco, except investment covered by an existing agreement, of which there are two kinds — agreements on natural resources, and agreements on assets controlled by the Moroccan government.

Negotiations for the *U.S. — Morocco FTA* yielded another example of FDI treatment. The U.S. opposed Australia's foreign investment review process. In practice, however, the issue proved not to be too controversial. Few U.S. businesses complained about the process, as Australia routinely granted FDI approval. What result did the negotiators achieve? The answer is all American investment in new businesses is exempt from screening by Australia's Foreign Investment Review Board. The *Australia FTA* also raised significantly thresholds imposed by Australian law for acquisitions in almost all sectors by U.S. investors. Why do countries like Australia — and Canada — reserve the right to review foreign investments? Candidly, is it to ensure their economies are not dominated by investment from one country, such as the U.S.? Is national security, either through overall dominance or a single investment in a sensitive area, a factor? Observe the U.S. does not have a completely open or transparent investment regime. The Committee on Foreign Investment in the United States (CFIUS), and the *Exon-Florio Amendment*, provide the means to block foreign acquisitions of U.S. companies. Acquisitions of firms that export military or dual-use goods, or that engage in significant classified government contracting, pose particular concerns. In addition to these devices, loud, unwelcome Congressional attention, not to mention prejudice, can make prospective acquirers go away, as happened in the spring 2006, when Dubai Ports World dropped its bid to acquire ports on the Eastern Seaboard.

Interestingly, the *Australia FTA* has no analog to *NAFTA* Chapter 11. There are no provisions for allowing investors to arbitrate disputes with host countries. That is because of the trust each side has in the security and predictability of the legal framework of the other side, and the long-standing economic relations between the two countries. Put indelicately, in the *NAFTA* context, many American (and Canadian) investors recoil at the prospect of suing the Mexican government in Mexican court. They are dubious as to the ability of the Mexican court system to afford them procedural and substantive protections. But, suing the Australian government in an Australian court is acceptable (though the *Australia FTA* permits re-visitation of the topic, should circumstances warrant). Again, bluntly, investor protection concerns probably explain why the *Morocco FTA* has an investor-state dispute settlement provision.

Also of note is that a Negative List approach to liberalizing FDI is not used by the EU in its trade agreements. The EU prefers a progressive strategy. Under it, restrictions on the entry, establishment, and operation of investments are removed over time. What might explain the EU preference, and what are the pros and cons of the two methods?

Suppose an FTA liberalizes trade and investment regimes, so that businesses have open access to markets of the member countries. What might be the next concern of a businessperson? A likely answer is that market access would be undermined by anti-competitive behavior. If one of the parties does not have a strong (or, indeed, any) antitrust regime, then provisions in an FTA against anti-competitive practices may be needed. *NAFTA* negotiators anticipated this concern, and agreed upon provisions — in Chapter 15 — concerning competition policy, and the behavior of lawful monopolies and state-owned enterprises (SOEs).

Again following *NAFTA*, U.S. FTAs are likely to contain competition policy obligations. For instance, before the *U.S. — Singapore FTA*, Singapore lacked an antitrust regime. In the *FTA*, Singapore committed to enact a law regulating anticompetitive practices, and create a competition policy, by January 2005. Similarly, the *U.S. — Morocco FTA* contains competition policy provisions obligating Chile to maintain laws enforcing antitrust rules, including laws prohibiting anti-competitive business conduct, and controlling state owned enterprises (SOEs) and officially designated monopolies. The *U.S. — Morocco FTA* forbids anticompetitive business conduct and mandates enforcement against it. This *FTA* contains rules against harmful conduct by government-designated monopolies, and against abuse by SOEs of their official position that would harm the interests of American companies or discriminate against them in the sale of goods or services. The *Australia FTA* also calls for cooperation between the two countries on consumer protection and mutual recognition and enforcement of certain monetary judgments to provide restitution to consumers or investors who suffered economic injury due from deceitful, fraudulent, or misleading practices.

IV. LABOR AND THE ENVIRONMENT

In all of America's FTA negotiations with developing and least developed countries, no topics have been more controversial, and stirred more passion, than labor and the environment. The GATT—WTO frameworks for these matters are inchoate, which creates considerable room for maneuver in FTA negotiations. Put simply, if simplistically, the U.S. — typically urged by labor and environmental groups — is wont to demand rigorous obligations and meaningful enforcement mechanisms. Developing and least developed countries may see such demands as an effort to rob them of a comparative advantage, namely, cheap labor. They also decry efforts to infringe on their sovereign right to fashion rules suitable to their level of development. The invariable response is an FTA will create opportunities to bring people in those countries out of poverty and into the middle class, at which point they naturally will demand enhanced labor and environmental protections.

The practical consequence of the heated debates, in terms of legal texts, is there are semblances among FTAs, but there is no single pattern, no iron template, used in every instance on labor and the environmental. Rather, there exists an evolving menu of options. Not surprisingly, then, with respect to virtually any FTA, there is a robust debate as to whether it contains substantively meaningful obligations, whether disputes about those obligations are susceptible to fair and efficient adjudication, whether dispute resolution outcomes are enforceable in an effective manner, and whether any transition periods to phase in or phase out rules are reasonable.

A. "Enforce Your Own Laws" and Other Obligations

The *NAFTA Labor and Environmental Side Agreements*, and *U.S. — Morocco, U.S. — Singapore, U.S. — Morocco, U.S. — Morocco, U.S. — Morocco, U.S. — Bahrain, U.S. — Oman FTAs*, the *U.S. — Peru* and *U.S. — Colombia TPAs*, *CAFTA—DR*, and *KORUS* contain provisions on labor and the environment. The essential obligation in each *FTA* is to enforce effectively the labor and environmental laws that exist in the member countries. Thus, for example, Article 6 of the *Jordan FTA* mandates the U.S. and Jordan each enforce its own regime. For many labor and environmental groups, and many Congressmen and Senators, the "enforce your own laws" obligation is too weak. That is because the "your own" refers to a country with abysmal laws, and they are under no enforceable obligation to improve.

The U.S. agreements contain a range of additional provisions on labor and the environment. For instance, in the *U.S. — Morocco FTA*, each side:

    i.   Re-affirms its support for core labor standards adopted by the International Labor Organization (ILO) in 1998 in its *Declaration on Fundamental Principles and Rights at Work.*

    ii.   Strives to ensure its law recognizes and protects international labor standards, including the right of workers to organize, bargain collectively, and strike, to have acceptable working conditions, particularly as to minimum wages, hours of work, and occupational safety and health, and to be free from compulsory labor.

    iii.   Re-affirms its belief in the principle of sustainable development.

    iv.   Agrees it is inappropriate to lower labor or environmental standards to encourage trade.

    v.   Pledges to strive to improve its own labor laws

    vi.   Pledges to maintain high levels of environmental protection, and improve environmental laws.

    vii.   Agrees to eliminate tariffs on environmental goods and services, and liberalize restrictions (particularly in Jordan) on environmental services.

Similarly, the *U.S. — Singapore, U.S. — Morocco, U.S. — Morocco, U.S. — Morocco, U.S. — Oman FTAs*, and the *U.S. — Peru*, and *U.S. — Colombia TPAs* include the following commitments:

    i.   Manifest internationally recognized labor principles in domestic labor laws.

    ii.   Ensure environmental laws provide for high levels of protection.

    iii.   Strive to continue to upgrade domestic labor and environmental laws.

    iv.   Avoid of weakening domestic labor or environmental laws.

    v.   Recognize that it is inappropriate to weaken or reduce domestic labor or environmental laws to encourage trade or FDI, *i.e.*, to engage in a "race to the bottom."

    vi.   Utilize dispute settlement procedures established by the FTA for labor and environmental controversies.

To what extent are these additional provisions declarative and aspirational — "soft" versus "hard" law?

B. Case Study: Labor Reform and the *U.S. — Oman FTA*

It is critically important to appreciate the definition of what qualifies as a "labor" or "environmental" law, and thus what must be enforced effectively as the essential obligation, may be open to question. For instance, the President of the Teamsters Union, James P. Hoffa, criticized the labor provisions in the *Peru FTA*, saying they are based on the flawed *CAFTA—DR* model. One flaw is anti-employment discrimination rules are not within the definition of "labor laws" in the *Peru FTA*. Hence:

> [t]he many women who compose much of the workforces in export sectors in Peru and in the Andean region, where sexual harassment has been well documented, would be unprotected from employment and workplace discrimination.[12]

It also is important to realize that in some countries, the aforementioned commitments mean major changes to local law. The AFL-CIO went beyond the boundaries of labor law, casting doubt on the wisdom of an FTA between the U.S. and Colombia because of criminal violence. In a June 2006, *Justice for All: The Struggle for Worker Rights in Colombia*, the AFL-CIO Solidarity Center said since the mid-1980s roughly 4,000 trade unions have been murdered, with more than 2,000 since 1991, mostly because of their participation in labor disputes.

Consider Oman, which commenced labor law reform in 2003, ratifying several ILO and United Nations conventions. In a May 2006 letter from Oman's Minister of Commerce and Industry to the USTR, Oman agreed its labor law commitments fall within the jurisdiction of Chapter 16 of the *U.S. — Oman FTA*, *i.e.*, "as matters arising" under that Chapter, and thus subject to Article 16:6 consultations. In July 2006, Sultan Qaboos bin Said issued a Royal Decree (which Ministerial Decisions supplemented) to implement ILO Conventions 87 and 98, which concern unionization and child labor. In the Omani legal system, a Royal Decree takes precedence over any previously enacted inconsistent measure. The Decree (74/2006):

  i.   Removes governmental involvement in activities of workers' representative committees (*i.e.*, labor unions), and allows more than one committee to be formed to represent workers at a specific enterprise.

  ii. Forbids employee dismissal for lawful activity in a union, and penalizes anti-union discrimination.

  iii. Increases (by 5 times for a first offense, and 2 times for a second offense) dissuasive penalties for violating Omani rules against child labor or the improper use of female labor.

  iv. Prohibits forced or coerced labor, and penalizes violation of this ban (with fines of up to U.S. $1,300 per violation, imprisonment, or both, and a doubling of the penalty for repeat offenders).

  v.   Endorses collective bargaining.

---

[12] Rossella Brevetti, *State Department Report Warns On Labor Rights Problems in Peru*, 23 INT'L TRADE REP. (BNA) 413-14 (16 March 2006).

- Permits the right to strike as a collective bargaining technique, and ensures technical requirements for strikes are consistent with ILO standards.

Not all American politicians were persuaded the reforms, however well intentioned, went far enough. For instance, the Decree did not bar employers in Oman from withholding documents that release a foreign worker (*e.g.*, from the Indian Subcontinent) from an employment contract.

In May 2006, during mark up sessions of the *Oman FTA*, the Senate Finance Committee passed 18-0 an amendment to prevent goods made by slave labor, or with the benefit of human trafficking, from receiving duty free treatment. The USTR opposed the "Conrad-Bingaman-Kerry Amendment" (named after its sponsors, Senators Kent Conrad (Democrat-North Dakota), Jeff Bingaman (Democrat-New Mexico), and John Kerry (Democrat-Massachusetts), saying it was redundant with existing U.S. import restrictions on prison, forced, or indentured labor, and violated *Trade Promotion Authority (TPA)* legislation that allows Congress to suggest only "necessary and appropriate" changes to implement trade deals. The administration of President George W. Bush refused to include the Amendment in the implementing legislation.

To what extent is this kind of resistance to an FTA justified in the case of Oman? Oman is a moderate nation, the only one dominated by the *Ibadhi* sect (which is neither *Sunni* nor *Shi'ite*), has been a loyal U.S. ally for 170 years, and overlooks the strategic Straits of Hormuz near the mouth of the Persian Gulf. Are these facts relevant, and if so, how, to a labor amendment in a trade accord? What about Bahrain, which is not a signatory to ILO conventions on strikes, but is headquarters for the U.S. Navy Fifth Fleet? In November 2006, not even 4 months after the *U.S. — Bahrain FTA* took effect, Bahrain banned strikes and demonstrations at vital establishments, at which national security could be disrupted. The locations are air and sea ports, civil defense installations, hospitals, health centers, and pharmacies, electricity and oil and gas facilities, telecommunication and water areas — and bakeries and educational firms, to boot.

C. Dispute Settlement Mechanisms and Enforcement

Labor and environmental sections of FTAs to which the U.S. is a party tend to create a mechanism to resolve disputes about labor and environmental enforcement, and mandate use of this mechanism. The *NAFTA Labor* and *Environmental Side Agreements* follow — indeed, helped set — this pattern. Article 17 of the *Jordan FTA* sets up a five-stage procedure:

  i.   Consultations, for 60 days, during which the two sides try to settle the matter.

  ii. Joint Committee proceedings, which either party may trigger if consultations fail, and which are to finish in 90 days.

  iii. Dispute settlement panel proceedings (assuming the Joint Committee fails to resolve the dispute), which issues a non-binding report.

  iv. Joint Committee review, which checks the panel report and makes a final effort to resolve the case.

    v.   Imposition by the aggrieved party of "any appropriate and commensurate measures," including economic sanctions, if no satisfactory outcome is reached.

With respect to *CAFTA—DR*, the Secretariat for Central American Economic Integration (SIECA) houses an independent body established by Chapter 17 of the agreement to review allegations a *CAFTA—DR* member fails to enforce effectively its environmental law. The Environmental Chapter of *CAFTA—DR*, Chapter 17, allows members of the public to submit allegations of such failure to an independent body. Article 17:7 specifies filing requirements.

Some FTAs also create non-adjudicatory bodies to cooperate on technical labor or environmental matters. Examples include the U.S. — Moroccoian Joint Forum on Environmental Technical Cooperation, under the *Jordan FTA*, and three cooperative mechanisms in the *U.S. — Morocco FTA* — one for environmental protection, a second for promotion of the ILO *Declaration on Fundamental Principles and Rights at Work*, and a third for compliance with ILO Convention 182 on the *Worst Forms of Child Labor*.

There is, of course, a distinction between adjudication and enforcement. Consider the five Central American countries of *CAFTA—DR* — Costa Rica, El Salvador, Guatemala, Honduras, and Nicaragua. Problems concerning labor and the environment go beyond low standards. Attention is needed to fund enforcement. For example, these countries, like Chile, have signed most or all of the International Labor Organization (ILO) conventions. But, they simply cannot enforce compliance with the conventions. What, then, are the enforcement mechanisms created by FTAs to promote compliance?

The short answer is there is no single approach. Enforcement mechanisms differ considerably across agreements. The *NAFTA Side Agreements* create Commissions on Labor Cooperation, Environmental Cooperation, and Border Environmental Cooperation. These *Side Agreements* authorize trade retaliation, after dispute settlement procedures through the relevant Commission are followed. The financial penalty collected is channeled into a fund, managed by the relevant Commission, to improve labor and environmental conditions. The *U.S. — Morocco FTA*, does not specify fines for a country that fails to adhere to its labor and environmental rules. Beyond the "enforce your own laws" obligation in *CAFTA—DR*, the U.S. provides financial assistance to Central American countries to enhance their labor law regimes.

In contrast, the *Singapore, Chile, Australia*, and *Morocco FTAs* embody the principle of "equivalence," meaning the same remedies exist for commercial, labor, or environmental disputes. The *Singapore FTA* would appear to meet the so-called "equivalency standards" test set forth in U.S. *Trade Promotion Authority (TPA)* for labor and environmental issues. What is this test, and do other FTAs satisfy it? Moreover, the *Singapore, Chile, Australia*, and *Morocco FTAs* are innovative in creating the option of a monetary fine in lieu of imposing a trade sanction, and in channeling proceeds from the fine for labor and environmental initiatives. For example, if a country fails to live up to its own labor and environmental laws, then — after consultations — any financial penalty imposed may be reinvested to boost the enforcement capacity of the sanctioned country. If the losing party in a case fails to pay the fine, then the winning party can resort to the conventional remedy of suspending tariff benefits.

D. Case Study: Labor Conditions in Jordan and the *U.S. — Morocco FTA*

Whatever mechanisms exist in an FTA to adjudicate and enforce labor or environmental disputes, they almost certainly need supplementation and amendment after the FTA operates for a few years. For example, in May 2006 the National Labor Committee (NLC), a New York-based workers' advocacy group, said some apparel manufacturers in Jordan, and contractors that supplied them with workers from Bangladesh, were engaged in human trafficking. The group said Bangladeshi workers suffered 20 hour work days, went unpaid for months, and were imprisoned if they complained. Jordan took the complaints seriously, responding in June 2006 by:

  i.   Creating an inter-ministerial committee to respond to the complaints, plus a separate labor subcommittee under the *U.S. — Morocco FTA* Joint Committee to ensure proper enforcement.

  ii. Forming nine inspection teams to check factories in Jordan, thereby boosting the number of labor inspectors from 88.

  iii. Establishing telephone hot lines in Bengali and other languages spoken by foreign workers for them to make complaints.

  iv. Consulting directly with the government of Bangladesh.

  v.   Shutting down three textile factories, and pledging to take further action.

The NLC alleged Bangladeshi workers, as well as workers from China, the Philippines, and Sri Lanka, are abused physically and psychologically, sexually harassed and raped, and put in unsanitary living conditions.

Also in June, the Jordanian Minister of Trade, Sharif Al Zu'bi, met personally with each of the companies operating in Jordan's Qualified Industrial Zones (QIZs) to explain worker abuse would not be tolerated. "Our inspection regime may have failed us, and may have failed us miserably," he remarked.[13] Also, said the Minister: "We want trade and investment, but not at any price. We want clean investors. . . . They either shape up or ship out. . . . [Jordan will continue to] "do the right thing" [and] "flush out" [the] "bad apples," which he estimated at about 10 percent of all companies operating in Jordan making textile and apparel (T&A) for the American market.[14] Subsequently, Jordan went further:

  i.   In August 2006, the Jordanian Minister of Labor oversaw the transfer of 623 Bangladeshi workers from 7 textile companies in Qualified Industrial Zones (QIZs) implicated in worker rights violations to seven other firms.

---

[13] Gary G. Yerkey, *Jordan Cracks Down on Firms Exploiting Foreign Workers in Violation of Trade Pact*, 23 INT'L TRADE REP. (BNA) 1075, 1076 (13 July 2006).

[14] *Quoted in* Gary G. Yerkey, *U.S., Jordan Sign Agreement to Cooperate In Crackdown on Workers' Rights Violations*, 23 INT'L TRADE REP. (BNA) 1310-11 (7 Sept. 2006).

ii. In September 2006, Jordan and the U.S. signed an agreement to collaborate on, via independent assessment, compliance with internationally recognized workers' rights in QIZs.

The key point is all of Jordan's measures go beyond the basic requirements in the *Jordan FTA*, namely, to consult with the U.S. and, if consultations fail, to entertain "appropriate and commensurate" measures, meaning trade sanctions.

Nevertheless, the U.S. National Textile Association (NTA) was not impressed. In September 2006, it filed with the USTR the first *Jordan FTA* Article 17 case. The NTA alleged Jordan's labor inspectors are underpaid and known to take bribes from employers to overlook labor violations, and faulted Jordan's labor code for the following rules:[15]

i. Only workers of Jordanian nationality can join a trade union.

ii. Government employees, domestic servants, and most agricultural workers cannot join a trade union.

iii. Workers under 25, any person convicted of a criminal offense, or anyone convicted of a misdemeanor involving dishonorable or immoral conduct, cannot join a trade union.

iv. A union cannot be formed by less than 50 workers.

v. The government may decide which industries may unionize, and no more than one union is permitted per industry.

vi. A worker cannot run for office in a union without having been a member for at least two years

vii. The Ministry of Interior both endorses candidates and keeps tabs on activities of unions and union office candidates.

viii. Unions must establish a general confederation, which the government subsidizes and audits.

ix. Unions must give employers 14 days' notice before a strike, and 28 days' notice if the work is related to a public service, but in practice they must obtain government authorization as well, and the government typically declares proposed strikes illegal.

x. The Ministry of Labor can seek judicial dissolution of a union for a labor code violation, or instigation of an illegal work stoppage.

Further, alleged the NTA, Jordanian law mandates a government license for any organization seeking to hold a public rally or meeting, forbids newspapers from publishing encouragement for an unauthorized work stoppage, and bars individual or collective action intended to change Jordan's economy or society. To be sure, the NTA had an economic motivation for its case. In 2000, the last year before the *FTA* took effect, Jordan exported to the U.S. $43 million worth of T&A exports. In 2005, after 4 years of operation, exports of this merchandise had increased to $1.083 billion.

---

[15] *See* Susan J. McGolrick, *AFL-CIO, Textile Producers Accuse Jordan of Violating Trade Pact with U.S.*, 23 Int'l Trade Rep. (BNA) 1416-18 (28 Sept. 2006).

E. Placement of Labor and Environmental Provisions

An issue somewhat related to enforcement is the placement of labor and environmental provisions — and, in those provisions, the dispute settlement mechanism — in an RTA, be it an FTA or CU. The *U.S. — Morocco FTA* accord is the first instance in which the U.S. put the labor and environmental provisions in the text of the accord. (As indicated earlier, the analogs in *NAFTA* are in side agreements.) The essential obligation — application of existing labor and environmental rules — is the same as it is in the *NAFTA Labor* and *Environmental Side Agreements*, and in the *Singapore, Chile, Australia, Morocco, Bahrain*, and *Oman FTAs*, and the *Peru* and *Colombia TPAs*. The object is to prevent a "race to the bottom" among the members, with each country lowering its labor and environmental rules in the hopes of luring trade and investment away from other countries. *CAFTA—DR* contains the same obligation, and an arguably "*Jordan* Plus" provision allocating funds to improved labor conditions in Central America.

Thus, placement of the provisions appears to be important not as a legal matter, but as a political symbol. This variation is not random, but rather a political evolution. Since *NAFTA*, or perhaps partly because of it, many NGO constituencies have lobbied effectively for central placement of their favored provisions. They prevailed with respect to Jordan, and the *Jordan FTA* appears to have set a precedent. The labor and environmental provisions in subsequent U.S. FTAs, including the *Singapore, Chile, Australia, Morocco, Bahrain, Oman FTAs*, and the *Peru* and *Colombia TPAs*, and *CAFTA—DR*, also are in the core text of the accord. For the foreseeable future, Congressional passage of an FTA without this core placement seems nearly impossible.

F. Case Study: The *NAFTA Labor Side Agreement*

1. Origins of the *Labor Side Agreement*

It is commonly thought the origins of the *NAFTA Labor Side Agreement* — officially entitled the *North American Agreement on Labor Cooperation* — lie in Bill Clinton's 1992 presidential campaign. Candidate Clinton was hesitant to endorse *NAFTA*, which the incumbent President, George Bush, and his USTR, Carla Hills, had negotiated. After all, he was running against the President, and he needed to court the traditional Democratic labor vote. In truth, the genesis of the *Labor Side Agreement* was a "May 1 Plan" offered by President George H.W. Bush on 1 May 1991 to respond to the labor and environmental activists who were campaigning against extending *CUFTA* to Mexico.

President George H.W. Bush sought an extension of fast track negotiating authority under the *Omnibus Trade and Competitiveness Act of 1988* until 1 June 1993 to complete a deal with Mexico and Canada.

> Labor and environmental organizations were among the most vocal of these groups [opposing President Bush's request for an extension of fast track authority]. During the fast track debate, labor groups argued that a free trade agreement with Mexico would erode U.S. wages and encourage industrial flight to Mexico, thereby costing U.S. jobs. Environmental and

consumer organizations argued that a free trade agreement would increase unsustainable growth in Mexico, and compromise the ability of the United States to enact and maintain adequate environmental, health, and safety laws. Together, these two communities joined to advance a regulatory competitiveness argument against the fast track extension, arguing that Mexico's failure to enact and enforce a host of labor, worker protection, environmental, health, and safety laws would provide companies operating in Mexico with a competitive advantage over U.S. industries. Relying upon these arguments, many groups formed coalitions to petition Congress to reject fast track and to further consider [sic] the ramifications of a trade agreement that fast track would allow.[16]

President Bush aimed to keep *NAFTA* negotiations focused on what he viewed as singularly trade matters, and to avoid cluttering the accord. Not surprisingly, except for the Preamble to *NAFTA* — which states the Parties are resolved to create new employment opportunities and improve working conditions, and to protect, enhance, and enforce workers' rights — the agreement is silent on labor rights issues. *NAFTA* contains no mechanisms to implement, monitor, or enforce the goals set forth in the Preamble.

President George H.W. Bush responded by dividing the opposition. In his May 1 Plan, he proposed labor and environmental concerns should be dealt not in the text of an FTA, but rather, separately on a "parallel track." Some opponents agreed, while others did not, and President Bush's request for fast track extension was approved by Congress. *See* 137 Cong. Rec. H3588 (daily ed. May 23, 1991); 137 Cong. Rec. S6829 (daily ed. May 24, 1991). Thus was born the idea for a side deal on labor matters.

The President implemented the idea by negotiating three separate MOUs with Mexico. First, on 13 May 1991, the labor secretaries of the U.S. and Mexico signed a 5-year MOU on labor that called for increased cooperation (*e.g.*, information sharing on child labor, worker health and safety, and employment statistics) and joint action (*e.g.*, procedures for resolving labor conflicts). On 14 September 1992, the U.S. and Mexico supplemented this MOU with a bilateral agreement that extended the term of the MOU beyond 5 years and established a consultative commission on labor matters to provide a forum for discussing labor matters. Second, in October 1991, the Office of Management and Budget entered into an MOU with its Mexican counterpart on cooperation in generating statistical data on labor matters. Third, on 7 February 1992, the Occupational Safety and Health Administration entered into an MOU with its Mexican counterpart on the monitoring and enforcement of workplace safety laws.

The fact these MOUs were in place was lost amidst the 1992 presidential campaign rhetoric. Hence, there was little discussion about their substantive merits, and the debate that did occur about the need for a further side agreement on labor was artificial. Yet, the fact was the MOUs helped nurture a culture of social justice as regards Mexican employment practices. True, the MOUs did not deal with adversarial labor-management relations in Mexico.

---

[16] Robert F. Housman & Paul Orbuch, *Integrating Labor and Environmental Concerns into the North American Free Trade Agreement: A Look Back and A Look Ahead*, 8 Am. U. J. Int'l L. & Pol'y 719, 724-25 (1993).

But, it is hard to expect this nearly intractable problem could be solved through an MOU, and in any event the *Labor Side Agreement* also glosses over the problem. Candidate Clinton merely capitalized on the possibility of a new side deal to justify his ultimate lukewarm endorsement of *NAFTA*.

> *NAFTA* did, in fact, put . . . Clinton in a difficult position. Although Clinton had said that he was in favor of free trade, he also wanted the support of both organized labor and the environmental community, and *NAFTA* was a critical issue for securing their support. . . . Clinton did not want to adopt a campaign position that might . . . endanger a *NAFTA*. In an attempt to balance these interests, Clinton-Gore campaign representatives consulted with both Mexican officials and members of the environmental and labor communities in developing Clinton's position. Ultimately, Clinton adopted a compromise position in his October 4, 1992 speech given in Raleigh, North Carolina. . . . Candidate Clinton's compromise approach sought to differentiate from the Bush approach by focusing additional attention on the environmental and labor concerns with *NAFTA*. . . . Rather than renegotiate the *NAFTA*, the Clinton plan entailed substantial use of certain unilateral measures [such as adjustment assistance for U.S. workers adversely impacted by *NAFTA*] and "supplemental agreements" to address the perceived environmental and labor flaws.[17]

Accordingly, when Clinton became President, it fell upon his USTR, Mickey Kantor, to negotiate a side deal somewhat more elaborate than the three earlier MOUs that might fulfill a campaign promise to labor voters.

2. Cross-Border Harmonization of Labor Laws

How one appraises the outcome of the Clinton Administration's labor negotiations with Mexico and Canada depends very much on one's initial expectations. In brief, if cross-border harmonization of labor law is expected, then one is sure to be disappointed. But, if one is looking for better enforcement of the existing labor laws of each *NAFTA* Party, then perhaps the dispute resolution procedures set forth in the *Labor Side Agreement* offer some comfort.

The *Labor Side Agreement* sets forth lofty goals for worker rights. The Preamble states the *NAFTA* Parties are committed to raising the standard of living of workers, promoting investment that is consistent with labor laws, and maintaining workplace health and safety standards. However, given the different stages of economic development of the U.S. and Canada, on the one hand, and Mexico, on the other hand, it is not surprising that labor laws are not harmonized among the Parties. Indeed, the incongruity between the lofty goals stated in the *Labor Side Agreement* and the actual accomplishments of the *Agreement* is stark.

To say the *Labor Side Agreement* does not harmonize labor laws among the *NAFTA* Parties is not much of an overstatement. There is no commitment in *NAFTA* toward upward harmonization, nor is there even an obligation to make labor standards compatible. There is only an agreement to cooperate on labor standards.

---

[17] *Id.* at 793-94.

To be sure, the *Agreement* makes a half-hearted attempt to encourage harmonization. In Article 1(b) and Annex 1, the *NAFTA* Parties committed themselves to promoting 11 guiding principles:

(1) protecting freedom of association and the right to organize;

(2) protecting the right to freely engage in collective bargaining on matters concerning the terms and conditions of employment;

(3) protecting the right to strike so that workers may defend their collective interest;

(4) prohibiting and suppressing all forms of forced labor, except those forms that are generally considered acceptable, such as compulsory military service;

(5) placing restrictions on the employment of children and young persons to safeguard their physical, mental, and moral development;

(6) establishing minimum employment standards, such as minimum wages and overtime pay;

(7) eliminating employment discrimination "on such grounds as race, religion, age, sex, or other grounds, subject to certain reasonable exceptions";

(8) providing equal pay for women and men for equal work in the same establishment;

(9) establishing standards to prevent occupational injuries and illnesses;

(10) compensating workers and their dependents in cases of occupational injuries, accidents, or fatalities that arise during the course of employment; and

(11) providing the same protection to migrant workers as domestic workers with respect to working conditions.

However, Annex 1 makes plain that the extent to which these principles are implemented depends on each Party's domestic law, and each Party "in its own way" will have developed an appropriate legal framework. Thus, the principles "do not establish common minimum standards for their domestic law."

Moreover, a careful review of the eleven principles suggests both ambiguity and controversy. For example, with respect to the seventh principle, should discrimination on the basis of a worker's sexual orientation be outlawed." How is "equal work" to be defined in the eighth principle? With respect to the tenth principle, should compensation be provided for repetitive motion injuries, such as carpal tunnel syndrome? Furthermore, while Article 2 calls on the Parties to adopt "high labor standards, consistent with high quality and productivity workplaces," it also affirms the right of each Party to "establish its own domestic labor standards." In sum, there are no legal obligations in the *Labor Side Agreement* to compel harmonization of labor laws among the *NAFTA* Parties.

Perhaps Articles 3-7 provide the greatest hope for cross-border harmonization. Article 3:1 obligates each *NAFTA* Party to "promote compliance with and effectively enforce its labor law through appropriate government action." What is noteworthy about this obligation is its specificity. Article 3:1-2 suggests to Parties how they might enforce their laws, namely, by appointing and training inspectors, requiring record keeping, monitoring compliance, investigating suspected violations including on-site inspections, initiating proceedings to seek appropriate sanctions to remedy violations, and giving due consideration to a request for an investigation of an alleged violation made by private parties. This obligation is directed particularly at Mexico, in part to placate its labor critics who fear American job losses if the Mexican government entices American companies to relocate to Mexico through lax enforcement of Mexican labor laws.

Article 4 requires that the private parties have "appropriate access to administrative, quasi-judicial, judicial or labor tribunals for the enforcement" of labor laws. Again, this provision is aimed especially at Mexico. Traditionally, its legal system has been more restrictive with respect to private party access than that in the other *NAFTA* Parties. The thrust of Articles 5-7 is the harmonization of administrative law at the national level. Under Article 5, the *NAFTA* Parties guarantee procedural rights in labor law proceedings. These rights involve due process, public access, presentation of evidence, and publication of adjudicatory decisions. Articles 6 and 7 are aimed at improving the transparency of labor laws.

Yet, not too much should be made of Articles 3-7. It is clear from Article 5:8 that decisions of judicial, quasi-judicial, or administrative tribunals of the *NAFTA* Parties on labor matters are not subject to review under the *Labor Side Agreement*. Therefore, while there may be some procedural harmonization in labor adjudication, there is no supra-national body to ensure consistency in substantive adjudicatory outcomes in like cases arising in different *NAFTA* Parties. The rationale for Article 5:8 is the "greater certainty" afforded when labor decisions in the U.S. or any other Party are not subject to review at a supra-national level. This rationale is ironic. No doubt it was evaluated and rejected by the Parties with respect to Chapter 19 dispute resolution procedures in AD and CVD cases, and more generally with respect to the WTO dispute settlement mechanism.

3. Background on Dispute Resolution

i. *The Right to Complain about Lax Enforcement*

What does the *Labor Side Agreement* accomplish? The answer is it primarily serves to establish a dispute resolution mechanism for cases where it is alleged a *NAFTA* Party is not enforcing its own labor laws. Suppose one *NAFTA* Party feels another Party has failed to enforce the provisions of the *Labor Side Agreement*. Articles 27-29 specify the complaining Party has the right to bring an enforcement proceeding against any other Party that allegedly exhibits a "persistent pattern of failure" to enforce its "occupational safety and health, child labor or minimum wage technical labor standards."

In two respects, this right is remarkable. First, exercise of the right implies a sort of "extraterritorial" enforcement. To be sure, exercise of the right does not entail any loss of sovereignty. For example, no *NAFTA* Party or body created by the *Labor Side Agreement* can force the U.S. to change its labor laws. Only Congress and the President can effect such a change. Nonetheless, it is hardly commonplace in international trade law to witness one sovereign state obtaining a "judgment" from an international tribunal that another sovereign state has been lax in enforcing its domestic laws. Yet, the theory underlying the *Labor Side Agreement* is each *NAFTA* Party has a vested interest in labor law enforcement in the other Parties, and that such enforcement is integrally related to trade among the Parties. There are two bases for that interest: a humanitarian concern that workers not be exploited; and a pragmatic concern that worker exploitation not be used as a means of maximizing a comparative advantage or securing direct foreign investment.

Second, the *Labor Side Agreement* allows for the use of trade sanctions — namely, retaliation in the form of suspension of *NAFTA* benefits — against a Party that fails to enforce effectively its labor laws. (*See* Article 41.) Here too, it is relatively rare to observe trade law remedies used to combat labor law problems. Traditionally, such problems were not viewed as related to trade and, therefore, were said to be outside the ambit of trade remedies. Indeed, the *Labor Side Agreement* is the first deal on labor issues crafted specifically in the context of, and designed to join, a trade accord.

However, in three other respects, the importance of the right of one *NAFTA* Party to complain about labor law enforcement in another NAFTA Party is inflated. First (as explained below), the *Labor Side Agreement's* dispute resolution mechanism is intricate, and the time deadlines seem overly generous. It can take 3 1/2 years before a complaining Party can retaliate against a Party that has exhibited a persistent pattern of failure to enforce effectively its labor laws.

Second, there is no private right of action against another Party. (*See* Article 43.) For instance, American trade unions cannot sue directly the Mexican government. As the *GE* and *Honeywell* cases (discussed below) suggest, the access of private parties is limited to their National Administrative Office (NAO). It does not extend to the dispute resolution mechanism.

Third, an individual labor case decided under the law of a *NAFTA* Party cannot be reviewed under the *Labor Side Agreement*. Moreover, with the exception of ministerial consultations (discussed below), the dispute resolution mechanism established in the *Agreement* may not be used to resolve disputes about the rights to associate, organize, or bargain collectively. (*See* Articles 23:2, 27:1, 33:3, and 49.) These facts suggest the scope of application of the *Agreement* is rather narrow.

ii. *Some Critical Terminology*

The definitions of key terms set forth in Article 49 are critical to understanding the enforcement provisions of the *Labor Side Agreement*. However, there are uncertainties associated with some of these terms.

First, a "persistent pattern of practice" means one that is "sustained or recurring," and "does not include a single instance or case."

The term "persistent pattern" was not chosen lightly. The U.S. initially proposed that a "persistent and unjustifiable pattern" of non-enforcement would trigger sanctions. The U.S. proposal did not define these terms. Canada proposed that a "consistent pattern" of non-enforcement would trigger consultations and evaluation by a Panel that could issue non-binding recommendations. Although the Canadian proposal did not define the operative terms "a consistent pattern of violations," the same terms were used in the Canadian proposal for the environmental side agreement and were defined in that proposal by stating that a "consistent pattern of violations does not mean a single violation of this agreement but a pattern of reliably documented violations.". . . Thus, the Parties combined the U.S. and Canadian proposals by first defining a pattern of practice in a manner reflective of the Canadian proposal for a "consistent pattern" and then requiring that the violations also be "persistent." By adopting this framework the Parties have ensured that only the most egregious and continuing violations will ever raise the possibility of binding arbitration and sanctions.[18]

In spite of insights provided by the definition of and history behind the language, there are unresolved questions. For example, can it be inferred that a single, recent, major domestic enforcement action is sufficient to rebut a claim that a persistent pattern of failure exists? There is no numerical test — such as failure to investigate more than 50 percent of complaints submitted during a specified period — to resolve this dilemma.

Second, "technical labor standards" are a subset of those items listed in the Article 49 definition of "labor law." Yet, this subset corresponds to the last eight of the eleven general principles set forth in Annex 1. (Freedom of association and protection of the right to organize, the right to bargain collectively, the right to strike, and the prohibition of forced labor are the first four principles not included as "technical labor standards.") In effect, Articles 27:1, 28, 29, and 49 convert eight general principles into "technical" labor standards. Accordingly, the scope of the dispute settlement mechanism may be not only rather narrow, but also unclear. Quite obviously, there are ambiguities inherent in many of these standards.

Third, Article 49 provides the respondent in an enforcement action with a defense. A *NAFTA* Party has not failed to enforce effectively its standards if its action or inaction reflects a reasonable exercise of official governmental discretion, or a *bona fide* decision to allocate resources to enforcement of other labor matters to which a higher priority is given. Without this defense, one Party could invoke the *Labor Side Agreement* to challenge the failure of another Party to take action simply as a consequence of limited resources and discretionary choices of appropriate authorities.

---

[18] Stanley M. Spracker & Gregory M. Brown, *Labor Issues Under the NAFTA: Options and Resolutions, in* THE NORTH AMERICAN FREE TRADE AGREEMENT 351, 370 (Judith H. Bello et al. eds., 1994); *see also* BARRY APPLETON, NAVIGATING NAFTA 181, 186 (1994); LESLIE ALAN GLICK, UNDERSTANDING THE NORTH AMERICAN FREE TRADE AGREEMENT 121 (2d ed. 1994).

iii. *The Institutional Infrastructure*

What are the mechanics of an enforcement proceeding brought under the *Labor Side Agreement*? To answer this question, it is first necessary to comprehend the institutional infrastructure created by the *Agreement*. Article 8 establishes a Commission for Labor Cooperation, which has three components: a (1) ministerial Council, comprised of the labor ministers of the *NAFTA* Parties; (2) 15 member permanent Secretariat, which is located in Dallas, Texas; and (3) National Administrative Office (NAO) in each Party, which is funded by the respective Parties. (*See* Articles 8:2 and 9-16. The U.S. NAO is housed in the DOC in Washington, D.C.) While the Council is the governing body of the Commission, the Council's day-to-day work is performed by the Secretariat. The NAOs play a significant early role in resolving disputes.

> These Offices specifically serve as points of contact and sources of information for the Council and Secretariat. Further, each office is responsible for receiving and investigating public communications or complaints related to labor law issues in the territorial domain of another Party. The decision to initiate a formal review of such complaints depends upon the discretion of the Secretary of the National Administrative Office. [Accordingly,] . . . review by a National Administrative Office offers citizens, businesses, and other non-governmental organizations a public forum where they may present a complaint against a *NAFTA* member nation. . . .[19]

Thus, with respect to dispute resolution, the purpose of an NAO review is to collect information, which may ultimately trigger formal proceedings, and consult with NAOs in other *NAFTA* Parties.

There are eight broad steps associated with an enforcement proceeding. That is, the *Labor Side Agreement* establishes an eight-level dispute resolution mechanism for resolving allegations that a *NAFTA* Party is not enforcing its labor laws.

4. The Eight Levels of Dispute Resolution

i. Level One: NAO Consultations

Suppose an NAO elects to review complaints submitted by private petitioners. While it can issue a report of its findings, it is not empowered to invoke formal dispute resolution proceedings against a *NAFTA* Party. Rather, under Article 21, an NAO can enter into consultations with the NAO of the other *NAFTA* Party. The NAOs are obligated to share publicly available information with each other. No time limit is established for NAO consultations.

The first request for a formal review submitted to a NAO was made on 14 February 1994.[20] The U.S. NAO received petitions from the International

---

[19] Michael J. McGuinness, Recent Development, *The Protection of Labor Rights in North America: A Commentary on the North American Agreement on Labor Cooperation*, 30 STAN. J. INT'L L. 579, 584 (1994); *see also* Lance Compa, *International Labor Rights and the Sovereignty Question: NAFTA and Guatemala, Two Case Studies*, 9 AM. U. J. INT'L L. & POL'Y 117, 134 (1993).

[20] *See* UNITED STATES INTERNATIONAL TRADE COMMISSION, THE YEAR IN TRADE — OPERATION OF THE TRADE AGREEMENTS PROGRAM, U.S. ITC Pub. 2894, at 49 (July 1995).

Brotherhood of Teamsters (IBT) and the United Electrical, Radio and Machine Workers of America (UE). The UE complaint was brought against a General Electric (GE) motor plant. It accused GE of violating the first, sixth, and ninth principles in Annex 1 of the *Labor Side Agreement* (concerning freedom of association, minimum employment standards, and prevention of workplace injuries, respectively) by firing union activists, and allowing salary, safety, and health standards to fall below minimally acceptable standards. UE's petition also alleged GE's actions violated Mexican labor law. The petition called for the NAO to review Mexico's enforcement of its labor laws. GE stated the workers were fired for violating company work rules. The IBT petition, brought against Honeywell, Inc., focused only on anti-union activities in Honeywell's Chihuahua, Mexico facility. IBT alleged Honeywell fired 20 production workers for trying to form an independent union. Honeywell stated the workers were laid off as a result of downsizing.

On 20 April 1994, the U.S. NAO agreed to review the UE and IBT petitions. It was satisfied the petitions related to labor matters in Mexico and furthered the objectives of the *Labor Side Agreement*. However, after conducting its review, the NAO declined to recommend that the Secretary of Labor pursue ministerial consultations with Mexico under Article 22 of the *Agreement*. In its 12 October 1994 report, the NAO stated the petitioners had not exhausted fully Mexico's own dispute resolution mechanisms, hence the NAO could not conclude Mexico had failed to enforce its labor laws.

ii. *Level Two: Ministerial Consultations*

The second level of the dispute resolution scheme is specified in Article 22. A complaining Party can request consultations between the labor ministers of the complaining and responding Parties. Any matter within the scope of the *Labor Side Agreement* may be the subject of such consultations. No time limit is set for these consultations.

The first case to reach this level of the dispute resolution scheme was filed with the U.S. NAO in August 1994 by American and Mexican labor unions against Sony's Magneticos subsidiary in Mexico. One charge concerned union registration. After a public hearing, the NAO issued its report on 11 April 1995, recommending that consultations be held between the American Secretary of Labor and Mexican Minister of Labor. These consultations led to an agreement on 12 June 1995 on a series of programs that would educate Sony's workers about their union registration rights. Because the matter concerned freedom of association and protection of the right to organize, it is unlikely it could have been taken to subsequent levels in the dispute settlement scheme.

iii. *Level Three: The ECE*

If the labor ministers are unable to resolve a dispute through consultations, then either consulting Party may ask the Council to appoint an Evaluation Committee of Experts (ECE) to investigate the dispute. The ECE consists of three members, with the chairperson selected by the Council from a roster of experts developed in consultation with the ILO. (*See* Articles 24:1(a)-(b),

45.) The members must be labor experts, objective, and independent of the disputing Parties and the Secretariat. (*See* Article 24:1(c).)

The Council can appoint an ECE only if the matter in dispute is "trade-related" *or* "covered by mutually recognized labor laws." (Article 23:3.) What is the rationale for these criteria? They hedge against one Party using the dispute resolution process to impose its own labor standards on another Party. Thus, for example, suppose a Party is not fulfilling its obligation to enforce labor standards. But, suppose also its failure has nothing to do with companies or sectors in that Party competing against imported goods or services from another Party. In this scenario, only consultations are possible. There can be no further steps in the process, because the matter is not trade related.

Despite this rationale, the limits create uncertainties. No test is set forth to determine whether a dispute is "trade related." Consider workers in a factory where 5 percent of the factory's output is exported. Is a labor-management dispute in this factory "trade-related"? Article 49 teaches that a "mutually recognized" labor law of a *NAFTA* Party is one that addresses the same general subject matter as the law of the other Party to the dispute. Suppose Canada provides medical care treatment at the government's expense for workers who develop repetitive stress injuries on the job. In the U.S., some state's general workers' compensation laws might be interpreted as encompassing such injuries. Is the Canadian law "mutually recognized"? More generally, does this term mean "equivalent," or "reasonably analogous"?

If the disputing Parties disagree as to whether the criteria for appointing an ECE are satisfied, then an expert may be appointed to rule on the dispute within 15 days. (*See* Annex 23.) Assuming an ECE is appointed, its job is to analyze the "patterns of practice" in a Party's enforcement of its "occupational safety and health or other technical labor standards." (Article 23:2.) Curiously, this language omits reference to child labor or minimum wage standards. Thus, it would appear the ECE cannot consider such matters.

Each Party's NAO is obligated to provide publicly available information to the ECE to help the ECE in its work. (*See* Article 16:2(d).) The ECE must present a final report to the Council within 180 days after it is established. (It must present a draft report within 120 days. The remaining 60 days allows the disputing Parties to comment on the draft and the ECE to prepare the final version. *See* Articles 25-26.) Significantly, this report is not binding on the Parties to the dispute. The ECE's final report is published 30 days after it is presented to the Council, and the disputing Parties must give comments on it to the Secretariat within 90 days of its publication. (*See* Article 26:2-3.) The Council may then consider the final report and comments at its next meeting. (*See* Article 26:4.)

iv. *Level Four: Direct Consultations*

Following the presentation to the Council of a final ECE evaluation report, Article 27:1 indicates that the disputing Parties may again engage in consultations "regarding whether there has been a persistent pattern of failure" by one Party in the effective enforcement of "occupational safety and health, child labor or minimum wage technical labor standards" with respect to "the general subject matter addressed in the report." No doubt the wording of Article 27:1 is confusing, and the result is anomalous. On the one hand, there is an express reference to child labor and minimum wage standards. On the other hand, the language of Article 27:1 expressly refers to the subject matter of the ECE's report. By virtue of Article 23:2, that report can cover only occupational safety and health or technical labor standards. Thus, whereas the ECE could not consider such matters, the Parties are free to consult in these areas. However, without the benefit of an ECE report on child labor and minimum wage standards, what distinguishes direct consultations (Level Three) from consultations between labor ministers (Level One)?

v. *Level Five: Special Session of the Council*

If after 60 days direct consultations fail, either consulting Party may call for a special session of the Council under Article 28 in order to take advantage of the Council's informal dispute settlement tools. (*See* Article 28:1.) The Council must convene within 20 days of the request. (*See* Article 28:3.) Further, it must "endeavor to resolve the dispute promptly." Its tools include calling upon technical advisors, creating expert groups, using its own good offices, providing conciliation or mediation services, and making recommendations. (*See* Article 28:3-4.)

vi. *Level Six: The Arbitral Panel*

Suppose a dispute remains unresolved after a further 60 days. Then, either disputing Party may ask the Council to convene a five-member arbitral panel under Article 29. (*See* Article 29:1.) Because a panel is appointed upon a two-thirds vote of the Council, it is impossible for any *NAFTA* Party to block commencement of arbitration proceedings. The panel's members are drawn from a roster maintained by the Council of 45 experts representing the Parties. (*See* Articles 30-32.) The individuals listed on the roster must be experts in labor law, have experience in resolving international disputes, or possess other relevant credentials. (*See* Articles 30:2, 31:1.)

The disputing Parties are charged with the responsibility of agreeing to a chair of the arbitral panel within 15 days after the Council votes to convene the panel. (*See* Article 32:1(b).) If they cannot agree to a chair within 15 days, then by lot a chair is selected within an additional 5 days. (Article 32:2(b) specifies a different period when there are more than two disputing parties.) Within 15 days after the chair is chosen, each disputing Party must select two panelists who are citizens of the other disputing Party. (*See* Article 32:1(c). Again, Article 32:2(c) specifies a different period and procedure when there are more than two disputing parties.) The panel's terms of reference are standard and set forth in Article 33:3, namely, to investigate whether there has been a "persistent pattern of failure" by the responding Party "to effectively enforce [*sic*] its occupational safety and health, child labor or minimum wage technical labor standards."

At first glance, Article 29:1, which concerns a request for an arbitral panel, and 23:3, which pertains to the establishment of an ECE, seem redundant. In fact, they are not. Whereas Article 23:3 uses the disjunctive "or," Article 29:1 indicates that an arbitral panel cannot be convened unless the dispute is trade-related "and" covered by mutually recognized labor laws. What is the point of this requirement? It ensures an arbitral panel is not used as a vehicle to coerce one Party to adopt labor standards that are not mutually recognized between or among the Parties. Also, it circumscribes the scope of application of mutually recognized labor standards to cases involving competition in a goods or services sector between or among the Parties.

Use of the conjunctive "and" in Article 29:1 suggests the eight levels in the dispute resolution scheme may be conceptualized as a pyramid. As the disputing Parties ascend through the levels, the requirements to invoke a particular mechanism become more stringent. As another example of this phenomenon, recall that ministerial consultations may concern any matter covered by the *Labor Side Agreement*, but an ECE can consider only occupational safety and health or other technical labor standards. (*See* Articles 22:1, 23:2.)

Within 240 days of its formation, an arbitral panel must submit to the Council a report that states the panel's judgment as to whether the responding Party exhibits a persistent pattern of failure to enforce effectively its labor laws. (A draft report, on which the complaining and responding Parties may comment, is due within 180 days of its formation. *See* Article 36:2. During the remaining 60 days, the panel receives comments and drafts the final report. *See* Article 37.) The final report, which is binding on the disputing Parties, must be transmitted along with comments from the complaining and responding Parties within 15 days of presenting it to the disputants (*See* Article 37:2.)

If an arbitral panel renders an affirmative finding, then it also must recommend a remedy. An affirmative panel report, including the recommended remedy, is implemented by incorporating the report into an "action plan" agreed to by the disputing Parties. (*See* Article 38.) The plan should be agreed to within 60 days of the date the panel issues its final report. (*See* Article 39:1(b).)

vii. *Level Seven: Reconvening the Arbitral Panel*

What if the disputing Parties cannot agree to such a plan? Or, what if the complaining Party believes the responding Party has not implemented the plan? In these instances, either disputing Party may ask the Council to reconvene the arbitral panel. (*See* Article 39:1.)

Where no action plan was agreed to, the request to reconvene an arbitral panel must be made no earlier than 60 days, and no later than 120 days, after the date of the panel's final report. (*See* Article 39:2.) The reconvened panel determines an action plan and imposes a "monetary enforcement assessment," *i.e.*, a fine. (Article 39:4(b).) The panel must make its determination and impose a fine within 90 days of the date it is reconvened. (*See* Article 39:4.) Payment of any fine is due within 180 days of its imposition. (*See* Article 41:1(a).)

Where it is alleged the responding Party has not implemented an action plan, the request to reconvene the panel cannot be made any earlier than 180 days after the disputing Parties agreed to the plan. (*See* Article 39:3(a).) (This time period ensures the responding Party has a chance to implement the plan.) The reconvened panel has 60 days to determine whether the respondent has failed to implement fully the action plan. (*See* Article 39:5.) If the reconvened panel finds the respondent has not complied with the action plan, then it must impose a monetary enforcement assessment against the respondent. (*See* Article 39:5(b).) Presumably to ensure compliance with an action plan is obtained, Article 40 provides the complaining Party with a right to reconvene again the arbitral panel within 180 days of the panel's finding of non-compliance to determine whether the responding Party is fully implementing the action plan. (In effect, it seems that the responding Party gets a "second chance," in the form of a second 180-day period, to implement the plan.) The panel must make its decision within 60 days.

During the first year in which *NAFTA* was effective, *i.e.*, 1994, the maximum fine that could be imposed was $20 million. Since then, the cap has been set at 0.007 percent of the total trade in goods among the *NAFTA* Parties. (*See* Annex 39:1.) Fines are paid into a fund established by the Council and used to improve labor law enforcement in the responding Party. (*See* Article 39:3.)

viii. *Level Eight: Retaliation*

What if the responding Party fails to pay the fine (either in a case where no action plan was agreed to, or where the plan was not implemented)? It is subject to retaliation, namely, the complaining Party may suspend *NAFTA* benefits (*e.g.*, duty-free treatment) otherwise owed to the respondent in an amount equal to the fine. (*See* Article 41.) Special procedures are set forth in Annex 41 and 41A for sanctioning Canada. The Canadian government modified its laws to ensure that any fine imposed by a *NAFTA* arbitral panel is given the same force and effect as an order of a Canadian court, and hence is immediately enforceable in Canada. Accordingly, rather than suspending trade benefits against Canada, a complaining Party would collect a fine and enforce an action plan in an appropriate Canadian court.

5. Justice Delayed and, Therefore, Denied?

i. *An Hypothetical*

How long might it take before retaliation occurs? To answer this question, consider an hypothetical dispute between two *NAFTA* Parties about one of the Party's enforcement of its labor laws. Three assumptions are useful.

First, the maximum time periods specified above are applicable, but there is no time lag associated with moving from one level in the dispute resolution pyramid to the next level. Second, NAO consultations under Article 21 fail to achieve a solution. Third, ministerial consultations under Article 22 end unsuccessfully on Day 1. No assumption is made about how long Level One NAO consultations or Level Two ministerial consultations take. The period for such consultations must be factored into the bottom line calculation.

The answer to the question "how long?" is calculated as follows:

1. *Level Three — The ECE*:

On Day 1, an ECE is established. However, one of the disputing Parties contends that the matter is either not trade-related, or not covered by mutually recognized labor laws. (*See* Article 23:3.) Thus, an independent expert is appointed to resolve this matter. (*See* Annex 23:1.) On Day 15, the expert determines that both criteria are met. (See Annex 23:2.) On Day 195 (180 days after the expert's determination), the ECE issues a final report and presents it to the Council. (*See* Articles 25:1, 26:1.) This report is published on Day 225 (30 days after it is presented to the Council). (*See* Article 26:2.) The disputing Parties transmit comments on the final report to the Secretariat on Day 315 (90 days after the report is published). (*See* Article 26:3.)

2. *Level Four — Direct Consultations*:

On Day 315, one of the disputing Parties requests consultations with the other disputing Party. (*See* Article 27:1.) The consultations are held until Day 375 (using the full 60-day period), but are unsuccessful. (*See* Article 28:1.)

3. *Level Five — Special Council Session*:

On Day 375, one of the disputing Parties requests a special session of the Council. (*See* Article 28:1.) The Council convenes on Day 395 (within 20 days of the request). (*See* Article 28:3.) The special session is held until Day 455 (again using the full 60-day period), yet the dispute still is not resolved. (*See* Article 29:1.)

4. *Level Six — The Arbitral Panel*:

On Day 455 the Council votes to convene an arbitral panel. (*See* Article 29:1.) However, the disputing Parties are unable to agree upon a chair for the panel by Day 470 (15 days after the Council vote). On Day 475, a chair is selected by lot (5 days after the deadlock concerning the chair). On Day 490, each disputing Party selects two panelists from the other Party (using the maximum 15 days allotted). (*See* Article 32:1(b).) The panel issues a report on Day 730 (240 days after it was convened). (*See* Articles 36:2, 37:1.) On Day 790, the disputing Parties agree to an action plan (using the full 60-day period). (*See* Articles 38, 39:1(a).)

5. *Level Seven — Arbitral Panel Reconvened*:

However, the disputing Parties cannot agree on whether the responding Party has implemented fully the action plan. (*See* Article 39:1(b)(i).) On Day 970 (180 days after the action plan was agreed to) the complaining Party requests the arbitral panel be reconvened. (*See* Article 39:3.) The reconvened panel renders a decision on Day 1030 (60 days after it has been reconvened). (*See* Article 39:5.) It orders the respondent to implement the plan and imposes a fine. By day 1210 (180 days after the reconvened panel acted), it appears the respondent has failed in both respects. Accordingly, on Day 1210, the complaining Party requests that the arbitral panel again be reconvened. The reconvened panel renders its determination on Day 1270 (60 days after it is reconvened for the second time). (*See* Article 40.) It holds the responding Party has, indeed, failed to meet its obligations.

6. *Level Eight — Retaliation*:

On Day 1270 — which is about 3 1/2 years after the ministerial consultations ended unsuccessfully — the complaining Party is entitled to retaliate by suspending *NAFTA* benefits with respect to the responding Party.

Observe this calculation does not include time used for NAO or ministerial consultations.

ii. *Workers as Victims*

It might be argued 3 1/2 years is about the same time it would take to obtain a comparable remedy (assuming there is one) under the domestic law of a *NAFTA* Party. This argument amounts to nothing more than an apology for the *Labor Side Agreement*. It merely says the *Agreement* is no worse than existing domestic adjudicatory mechanisms, which most would agree are inefficient, expensive, and uncertain. The ultimate losers could be the workers in the responding Party. For 3 1/2 years, they may have been exploited because their government failed to enforce its own labor laws.

Given the *Labor Side Agreement's* dispute resolution scheme is a protracted, torturous one, what defense did the Clinton Administration make of it during the Congressional debate over *NAFTA*? President Clinton's Labor Secretary Robert Reich testified as follows.

> I want to stress one other point — we continue to have Section 301 authority. We continue to have the authority to impose unilaterally trade sanctions against any nation that violates internationally accepted rules with regard to labor — labor treatment, labor relations. Nothing in NAFTA takes away from that authority we already have under Section 301 of the international trade laws to unilaterally stop trading [*sic*] with a nation that we feel abrogates those basic rights.[21]

Manifestly, this argument elides the merits of the *Labor Side Agreement*. It shifts the focus to the most controversial weapon in America's trade arsenal, Section 301 of the *Trade Act of 1974*, as amended. Worse still, the argument is self-defeating. A Section 301 action against another *NAFTA* Party would undermine whatever credibility the *Labor Side Agreement* may possess.

A different argument in defense of the *Labor Side Agreement* is suggested by considering whether labor issues should be addressed at all in the *NAFTA* context. Is the *Agreement* an instance of thinly-veiled protectionism that seeks to repeal the law of comparative advantage? Is it disingenuous for American labor unions to complain about the plight of Mexican workers — the very workers who are the beneficiaries of *NAFTA*? If the answer to these questions is "yes," then ironically all of the aforementioned weaknesses of the *Labor Side Agreement* may be strengths: a protectionist in free trader's garb will have difficulty in attacking Mexico under the *Agreement*.

---

[21] *NAFTA Labor Issues: Hearings Before the Senate Finance Committee*, 103d Cong., 1st Sess. 8 (21 Sept. 1993).

G.   Case Study: The *NAFTA Environmental Side Agreement*

1.   Trade Promotion, Environmental Protection, and the FTA Context

It is a bland truism to say there is an increased understanding of a nexus between environmental law and international trade law. Certain environmental problems cannot be resolved by one country alone. Global warming, ozone depletion, pollution on contiguous borders, and protecting endangered species are obvious examples. Trade laws can affect the pattern of environmental protection. For example, the environment is less protected in a "pollution haven" country that aggressively encourages the growth of export industries. That kind of environmentally unfriendly trade regime does not lead to sustainable development, because it risks destroying the resource base on which trade occurs.

Thus, from a global systemic perspective, there is a legitimate concern environmental regulations may have a negative impact on trade. Such a regulation may be a disguised barrier to trade, and simply burden trade too much — "too much" as against the degree of environmental protection it affords. At the same time, it is not in the interests of the international trade community to see certain countries become pollution havens. Aside from long-term negative environmental damages wrought by such havens, in the short term they would enjoy huge comparative cost advantages. As yet, there is no WTO agreement on the environment. Thus, the tension between trade promotion and environmental protection plays out in FTA negotiations.

2.   Background to the *NAFTA Environmental Side Agreement*

As with labor, *NAFTA* deals with environmental issues — save for sanitary and phytosanitary standards (SPS) through a side agreement. While post-*NAFTA* accords treat these matters in the core text of the agreement, the *NAFTA Side Agreements* are significant for three reasons. First, of U.S. FTAs, *NAFTA* itself is the commercial colossus. For the U.S., and most American states, the bulk of trade is conducted with Canada and Mexico. Second, as a consequence of the first reason, a labor or environmental dispute is especially likely to arise under *NAFTA*. While labor and environmental concerns exist in other FTA partners, the sheer transactional value and volume ensures disputes arise in these areas among the NAFTA Parties. Third, the *Side Agreements* established standards for the future. From these precedents, as it were, the U.S. developed and refined its negotiating stance on both the text and placement of labor and environmental provisions.

The *NAFTA Environmental Side Agreement* is formally titled the *North American Agreement on Environmental Cooperation* (and sometimes abbreviated "*NAAEC*"). What concerns — or, better put, fears — motivated the *Side Agreement*? The U.S. believed:

> i.   Mexican economic growth, stimulated by *NAFTA*, might give rise to ever-larger volumes of air pollution blowing north, and ever-larger volumes of raw sewage floating north.

ii.   Lower trade restrictions achieved by *NAFTA* could lead to pesticide-laden Mexican vegetables being sold in the U.S.

iii. Some U.S. companies might be attracted to Mexico because of its low environmental standards, and lax enforcement of these low standards, translating into not only lower operating costs for the companies, but also a massive shift of jobs from the U.S. southward.

iv.   Other U.S. companies would not be able to compete with Mexican companies that benefit from escaping from tough, expensive pollution standards, *i.e.*, they cannot match Mexican companies, which engage in "environmental dumping" — polluting Mexican plants that sell goods more cheaply than clean U.S. plants, thereby driving high-cost "environmentally good" U.S. production of business by low-cost "environmentally bad" Mexican production.

Mexico, too, had worries:

i.   The U.S. and Canada could, or would, not empathize with Mexico's plight as a developing country.

ii.   The U.S. and Canada did not appreciate the huge disparities of income between Mexico, on the one hand, and themselves, on the other hand, and thus would not be tolerant toward Mexico's policy priorities, only one of which was addressing local pollution problems to prevent cross-border environmental degradation.

iii. The U.S. would cater to domestic environmental lobbies and use *NAFTA* to impose American environmental solutions on local Mexican problems, rather then allowing local pollution problems to be addressed locally.

The U.S. and Mexico addressed these matters not only through a Clinton Administration *Report on NAFTA Environmental Issues*, and *NAFTA* Chapter 7B, but also through the *Environmental Side Agreement*.

3. The Seven Parts of the *NAFTA Environmental Side Agreement*

What, then, does the *NAFTA Environmental Side Agreement* say? As follows, it consists of seven parts with certain key provisions — and ambiguities:

Part One: Objectives (Article 1)

This Part sets out 10 broadly worded aims, including "support [for] the environmental goals and objectives of the *NAFTA*." It is unclear what, precisely, the "goals and objectives" are.

Part Two: Obligations (Articles 2-7)

This Part contains general commitments, which include most notably (in Article 5:1), "each Party shall effectively enforce its environmental laws and regulations through appropriate governmental action. . .," with enforcement procedures to include remedies for violations, such as the cost of containing or cleaning up pollution, and private access to remedies (such as the right to seek an injunction to obey an environmental law, if the local law provides this right). What constitutes "effective enforcement" is not clear.

The general commitments also include assessing environmental impacts of *NAFTA*, promoting "education in environmental matters," using "economic instruments for the efficient achievement of environmental goals," considering the prohibition on exports of pesticides or toxic substances when one Party bans such substances, ensuring that laws provide for "high levels of environmental protection," and striving "to continue to improve those laws." Again, several key terms are left undefined.

Part Three: Commission for Environmental Cooperation (Articles 8-19)

This Part establishes the Commission for Environmental Cooperation (CEC) to "strengthen cooperation on the development and continuing improvement of environmental laws and regulations. . . ." A Council governs the CEC. The Council operates by consensus, which effectively means unanimity. The exception is a decision (for which it is responsible) to establish an arbitral panel. That decision may be made by a two-thirds vote. The Council consists of cabinet-level environmental ministers from the *NAFTA* Parties, which cooperates with the *NAFTA* Free Trade Commission (FTC) and is assisted by a Joint Public Advisory Committee of five members from each of the Parties, and which has a Secretariat led by an Executive Director. Day to day work of the CEC is conducted by a Secretariat, which is headed by an Executive Director.

Part Four: Cooperation and Provision of Information (Articles 20-21)

This Part commits the *NAFTA* Parties to cooperate on environmental matters, including the sharing of information (when not prohibited by local law).

Part Five: Consultation and Resolution of Disputes (Articles 22-36)

This Part, the longest of the *Side Agreement*, concerns dispute resolution. It authorizes the CEC Council to convene an arbitral panel to consider an allegation from one *NAFTA* Party that another Party is not effectively enforcing its environmental laws. The Council may convene a panel, but only after the issue in question is not resolved pursuant to an investigation by the Council. The Council chooses the panel from a roster of persons expertise and experience.

A "persistent pattern" exists if there is "sustained or recurring course of action or inaction." Part Five does not explain how an arbitral panel should ascertain whether a "persistent pattern" exists. For instance, submissions to arbitral panels under the *Environmental*, as well as *Labor*, *Side Agreement* are strictly government-to-government. Private parties are not directly involved. It is unclear whether a panel may entertain *amicus curiae* briefs, though a panel may — if the disputing Parties agree — seek advice from outside experts. The Panel cannot decide there has been ineffective enforcement (*i.e.*, the Party complained against has as a defense) if the respondent Party (1) engaged in a "reasonable exercise" of its investigatory, prosecutorial, or regulatory discretion, suggesting that nothing in the *Side Agreement* strips a Party of its discretion, or (2) made a *bona fide* decision to allocate resources to enforce higher priority environmental matters, indicating nothing in the

Side Agreement commits a *NAFTA* party to increase agency enforcement budgets.

Four limits exist on the subject matter jurisdiction of an arbitral panel. First, if the issue is the subject of domestic adjudication, then it cannot come before the CEC — and thus an arbitral panel. Preclusion provides some protection against parallel proceedings. Second, the alleged failure to enforce environmental laws must relate to goods traded in North America. Third, "environmental law" is defined narrowly to mean only rules whose "primary purpose" concerns the conditions for harvesting natural resources. Query whether laws affecting coastal fishing, energy extraction, strip mining, and timber harvesting fit within this definition. Fourth, laws concerning wildlife outside the territory of a party are not subject to review. There is no extraterritorialism beyond the *NAFTA* Parties. For instance, the controversial U.S. bans on tuna caught using the purse-seine method, or on shrimp obtained without turtle excluder devices would not be subject to review under the *Side Agreement* if the underlying facts transpired outside of U.S., Canadian, and Mexican waters.

An arbitral panel must issue a written report. The disputing Parties — but not the public — get the opportunity to comment on the draft report. If the panel finds in the affirmative, then it may propose an "action plan" to rectify the persistent pattern. Specifically, if the panel finds the respondent Party is engaged in a persistent pattern of ineffectively enforcing its environmental laws (and has not reasonably exercised discretion or allocated a funds to a higher budget priority), then the disputing Parties try to agree upon a plan. This plan has the advantages of (1) providing an objective way to measure enforcement, (2) serving as an excuse for an environmental agency in a Party to argue that it needs a larger enforcement budget, and (3) embarrassing a *NAFTA* Party into mending its ways. Interestingly, the action plan was the idea of environmental groups, not the USTR. These groups supported it because they felt Mexico lacked the infrastructure needed to enforce its laws. In that context, Mexico needed plans, not financial penalties.

Suppose the prevailing *NAFTA* Party feels the losing Party is not implementing the action plan? Then, it may reconvene the panel, and if the panel agrees, then the panel must impose a "monetary enforcement assessment." In effect, the assessment is a fine, the amount of which the panel has broad discretion to set, and which is paid to the CEC for use in improving the environment or enforcement of environmental law. What if, despite the fine, the losing Party still does not implement the action plan? Continued failure to implement the action plan empowers the prevailing Party, with panel approval, to increase tariffs up to the amount of the fine on goods from the violating Party. The tariff increase is a trade sanction designed to collect an unpaid fine. Notably, this scenario applies only if the violator is the U.S. or Mexico. Canada negotiated an exemption from being targeted for trade sanctions, because it committed to treating a panel decision an "order of the court."

Throughout the process, strict deadlines apply. For example, an arbitral panel must render a written opinion as to whether a "persistent pattern" of failure to enforce effectively "environmental law" exists. The panel has 180 days after formation to prepare a draft report. The Panel's final report must be issued within 60 days of the initial report. If the disputing Parties cannot agree on an action plan within 60 days, then the Panel is reconvened, and within 90 days the panel proposes a plan. If the Panel decides that the defendant Party is not implementing the Action Plan, then the Panel must impose a fine within 60 days.

Still, the total time for completion (from complaint to trade sanction) is a minimum of 755 days. Observe this figure — about 2 years — is only marginally swifter than under the *Labor Side Agreement*. In sharp contrast to both *Side Agreement* dispute resolution timeframes, the regular *NAFTA* Chapter 19 dispute settlement process is 240 days.

Part Six: General Provisions (Articles 37-45)

This Part contains general provisions and definitions.

Part Seven: Final Provisions (Articles 46-51)

This Part contains final provisions typical of an international agreement, dealing with entry into force, amendments, accession, withdrawal, and authentic texts.

Following these Parts are several annexes, two of which pertaining specifically to Canada. Annex 36A, on Canadian Domestic Enforcement and Collection, contains the trade sanction exemption (noted above), and explains that a panel decision "shall become an order of the [i.e., treated as if it were issued by a Canadian] court." Annex 41 states that *Environmental Side Agreement* obligations apply only to matters under Canadian federal jurisdiction, and not to matters within the jurisdiction of a Canadian province.

4. A Success?

Is the *NAFTA Environmental Side Agreement* is a "success"? To be sure, it is positive for the *Environmental Side Agreement* to establish a lofty commitment, namely, each *NAFTA* party shall ensure that its laws provide for "high levels" of environmental protection and strive to continue to improve those levels. The central enforcement obligation — enforcing existing environmental laws — also is noteworthy. It is significant the *Agreement* requires each *NAFTA* Party provide for procedural guarantees in its administrative, quasi-judicial, and judicial systems, and that eschew proceedings that are unnecessarily complicated or unreasonably delayed (problems plaguing some American proceedings). No less important is the effort of the Parties to give arbitral decisions "teeth" by subjecting recalcitrant respondents to fines and trade retaliation.

Notwithstanding these advantages, there are weighty reasons to believe the *NAFTA Environmental Side Agreement* is not a "success." For example, Professor Steve Charnovitz writes:

> First, the NAAEC enforcement procedures only apply to domestic laws and therefore do not apply to international obligations that are not self-executing as domestic law. Thus, the one substantive obligation in the NAAEC, to provide for "high levels" of environmental protection is not subject to dispute settlement under the NAAEC or the *NAFTA*.

Second, neither the NAAEC Secretariat nor the dispute panels have subpoena power. . . .

Whether the absence of subpoena power impedes the panels will depend on whether they search for patterns of inadequate enforcement in the practices of regulatory agencies or in actual pollution levels. Whether the panel will be able to compel governments to provide information from regulatory agencies is unclear. The lack of subpoena power may prove to be a significant constraint on actual pollution level information if governments are not forthcoming with information.

Third, the NAAEC relies exclusively on *ad hoc* panels. In contrast, the European Community has an on-going Court that develops case law for Community-wide rules. Over time, this Court has developed useful environmental norms, but whether useful norms will emerge from the NAAEC's narrow procedures remains to be seen.[22]

This critique is worth pondering. On the first point, of what value is a commitment regarding "high levels" of environmental protection that is vague? To supplement the first and second points, might it be argued that the focus on environmental enforcement, however sloppy that enforcement may be in practice, has diminished efforts toward making specific policy commitments? If a *NAFTA* Party need only enforce the laws existing on its books, then the recipe is for a "stand still," not progress. That is, the *Side Agreement* has a retrogressive focus, namely, the domestic standards of each *NAFTA* Party. Turning to the third point, is the emphasis in the *Side Agreement* on domestic standards in an international agreement is inappropriate. Perhaps the parochial laws of a country may be inadequate for the country's own environmental needs, as well as for the rest of North America. If those laws are inadequate, then enforcement of them does not matter.

A number of additional critical points may be made suggesting the *NAFTA Environmental Side Agreement* is flawed. For instance:

1. Independence of the CEC?

To what extent is the CEC truly independent of the governments of the *NAFTA* Parties? Arguably, it is semi-independent at best. The Council governing the CEC consists of senior cabinet officials, thus ensuring top-level representation of the Parties. But, if its members served fixed terms, and were not answerable to their home country governments, then its independence would be enhanced. Moreover, the CEC is no financially self-sustaining. It has no fiscal powers to raise revenue. Instead, it must submit its annual program and budget to the Council for approval.

2. Private Enforcement?

Does the *Environmental Side Agreement* create a meaningful private right of action? Arguably, the answer is "no" Private parties must work through the relevant governmental trade bureaucracies. Thus, private parties must go through the USTR. Further, the CEC Secretariat has broad discretion to

---

[22] Steve Charnovitz, *The NAFTA Environmental Side Agreement: Implications for Environmental Cooperation, Trade Policy, and American Treaty Making*, 8 TEMP. INT'L & COMP. L.J. 257, 260-83 (1994).

disregard any submission it considers aimed at "harassing industry" rather than promoting enforcement. Finally, even where a case is brought, complaints are against a *NAFTA* Party for failing to enforce effectively its environmental laws. That is, claims are not made against individual companies for despoiling the environment. Yet, as a practical matter, private companies often are culprits.

3. Flaws in the System Design?

Questions about sovereignty, defenses, and remedies cast doubt on the design of the dispute resolution system. On sovereignty, is it more difficult for an international arbitral panel to determine whether a government is complying with its own law than for a court in the defendant country to determine whether a government is complying with its own law (assuming the judiciary is independent)? If the answer is "yes," then why not focus efforts on upgrading the domestic enforcement procedures in each *NAFTA* Party? Would it be less intrusive on the sovereignty of each Party to agree on a set of regional environmental standards for panels to enforce, rather than charge panels with the responsibility of deciding cases about local law? As to defenses, are the justifications of "reasonable discretion" and "higher budget priority environmental enforcement matter" so broad that it is hard to find a respondent Party guilty of a persistent pattern of ineffective enforcement? Concerning remedies, are trade sanctions, if imposed, a useful tool, given they harm consumers in the prevailing Party by raising prices (by the amount of the punitive tariff) on imports from the losing Party? While spending proceeds of a fine on environmental improvement rehabilitates the environment, is there any deterrent value to paying a fine to the CEC? Is the process itself too protracted?

4. Harmonization and Trade Barriers?

Consider whether environmental standards are disguised barriers to trade. Should environmental laws be harmonized so the U.S., Canada, and Mexico deal with the same standards? The trans-boundary reality of pollution counsels an affirmative answer. Yet, many U.S. environmentalists oppose harmonization. They view American laws to be so far ahead of all other countries that harmonization would mean diminution for the U.S. Moreover, harmonization is not thorough even within each *NAFTA* Party. For example, U.S. environmental laws are not harmonized themselves. As California vehicle emission standards illustrate, assuming there is no pre-emptive federal regulation, some state laws may be stricter than others.

Of course, *NAFTA* does not require harmonization of either environmental or labor laws. If it did, would the resulting regime provide better insurance against the abuse of such laws for protectionist purposes? Observe *NAFTA* Chapter 9 concerns technical barriers to trade (TBT). This Chapter provides that if a law has a "legitimate environmental purpose" — *i.e.*, protection of the environment — then an arbitral panel cannot overturn it. Only a showing that the law is a disguised barrier to trade will result in an adverse decision. Under what conditions may a panel overturn a sanitary or phytosanitary standard (SPS)? The criterion is not proof the SPS measure has "no legitimate purpose." That test is too high in this context, and *NAFTA* leaves each Party free to decide and choose, based on a scientific method, its own risk levels.

Observe, in the SPS context, penalties for an offending measure are fines of U.S. $20 million, or trade sanctions, but not striking down the measure.

V. INSTITUTIONS AND DISPUTE RESOLUTION

A. Transparency

Of the most notable commitments concerning the process by which trade is liberalized and institutions consider, promulgate, and enforce trade rules, surely transparency ranks at the top. Not surprisingly, therefore, RTAs are likely to contain some rules on the topic. The easiest such rule is to insist on application of GATT Article X and WTO standards on transparency. That rule effectively "piggy backs" on the multilateral system. It may be the safest such rule, too, for an RTA partner that is not a democracy and whose regime is reluctant to go beyond international standards.

There are, however, RTAs with WTO-Plus commitments on transparency. Two examples are the *U.S — Singapore* and *U.S. — Chile FTAs*. Their provisions go beyond both GATT—WTO and *NAFTA* rules. For instance, the *Singapore FTA* demands transparency in dispute settlement through open public hearings and public access to submissions. It also creates opportunities for participation, allowing third parties to make submissions.

B. Categories of Mechanisms

Dispute resolution procedures in RTAs share common points and boast distinctive features. To approach these similarities and differences, it is useful to start by identifying what the mechanisms are. They can be divided into two broad categories:

    1. *General Dispute Resolution*: Does the RTA contain a general mechanism to resolve disputes among the member countries about the meaning an interpretation of the terms of the accord?

    2. *Topical Dispute Resolution*: Does the RTA contain a special mechanism applicable to a specific subject matter?

In most FTAs, the answer to both questions is "yes." That answer leads to two follow up questions.

First, does the RTA in question create private rights of action, and private remedies? Traditionally, the answer was "no." Older U.S. FTAs, such as the *U.S. — Israel FTA*, create no such rights. That answer also is true with respect to some dispute settlement mechanisms in other FTAs. However, the newer FTAs tend to create room for private rights and remedies, albeit in limited subject matter contexts. The quintessential example is *NAFTA* Chapter 11, which allows private investors to sue host governments.

The second follow up question concerns the infrastructure for dispute resolution. What institutions does an FTA create to perform dispute resolution, and possibly other, functions? It is possible to write an entire book (or multivolume series) in response to this question. Indeed, some such works exist. While there is no substitute for examining individually each FTA, case studies may be instructive. Consider *NAFTA*, which has six different dispute settlement mechanisms.

NAFTA Chapter 20 is the general mechanism, discussed later in this Chapter. The most prominent case brought under this procedure involved the right of Mexican truckers to carry freight on U.S. roadways. *NAFTA* has five topical dispute resolution mechanisms. Chapter 11 deals with investor-state disputes over FDI. There number of Chapter 11 cases is large, which generally result in well-reasoned opinions. Chapter 14 deals with financial services, though there have been few if any cases. Chapter 19 covers AD and CVD issues. Effectively, *NAFTA* Chapter 19 extends the bi-national panel system created by the *U.S. — Canada FTA*. In addition, *NAFTA* has rules on safeguards, contained in Chapter 8. They distinguish regional (*i.e.*, *NAFTA*-based) from global (*i.e.*, WTO-based) safeguards. Finally, the *Environmental Side Agreement* and the *Labor Side Agreement* each have mechanism to deal with the central obligation in each *Side Agreement*, namely, to enforce effectively existing environmental or labor laws. Many observers feel the *Side Agreement* mechanisms have been a disappointment.

NAFTA Chapter 19 is particularly noteworthy. It provides for review of national determinations in AD or CVD cases, in lieu of judicial review in the domestic court system of the relevant *NAFTA* Party (though constitutional issues may be appealed back to that system). The Chapter 19 case volume has been large, including hotly contested disputes over softwood lumber, sugar, and wheat, and many cases have been settled. While the quality of decisions appears reasonably high, the process can be slow. For instance, a dispute between the U.S. and Mexico over cement dumping took 16 years to resolve. There have been few "extraordinary challenges," which are made to an Extraordinary Challenge Committee (ECC) — also a mechanism that existed in the *Canada FTA*.

Likewise, the *U.S. — Morocco FTA* has a general dispute resolution mechanism in Chapter 22. This *FTA* also contains three major topical mechanisms: Chapter 12 on Financial Services, Chapter 18 on Labor, and Chapter 19 on Environment. Unlike *NAFTA*, the *Chile FTA* does not speak about AD or CVD issues, nor contain a special dispute settlement mechanism for them. Rather, the *Chile FTA* states only that each member country reserves the right to apply its own AD or CVD rules. A different pattern exists in the *U.S. — Singapore* and *U.S. — Morocco FTAs*, which set out a general prohibition from taking any trade remedy, except in accordance with GATT rules. Of course, the U.S. did not take a leap of faith regarding AD or CVD rules in its FTA partner countries. As all the partners are WTO Members, those rules are (or should be) certain and predictable, in the sense they conform to GATT Article VI, the WTO *Antidumping Agreement*, and the WTO *Agreement on Subsidies and Countervailing Measures*. The *Chile, Singapore, Australia*, and *Morocco FTAs* dispute settlement mechanisms promote compliance through consultation and remedies that enhance trade, instead of a conventional sanctions-based approach. Thus, these *FTAs* allow for "equivalent" remedies in commercial, as well as labor and environmental, disputes, and allow a winning party to opt for a monetary assessment to enforce obligations.

C. Similarities and Differences

Most RTA dispute settlement mechanisms use arbitration-style procedures. They call for the establishment of a panel of experts. The complainant and respondent present oral and written arguments to the panel. The panel is supposed to render a reasoned decision. Time deadlines are set for each step, or at least each phase, of a case. How effective these deadlines are in practice varies.

One complaint is the arbitral-style procedures in the *NAFTA* mechanism take too long and cost too much, and thus are of less value than had been hoped when *NAFTA* entered into force on 1 January 1994. Moreover, whether the decision may be appealed depends on the FTA and mechanism. For instance, as alluded to above, *NAFTA* contains an "extraordinary challenge" procedure, which has been used thrice, once in a Chapter 19 case involving alleged conflicts of interest by a panelist.

A second complaint about arbitration procedures — indeed, any type of dispute settlement mechanism in an FTA — is that it may be abused for protectionist purposes. Bringing a case can itself be a trade barrier. Addressing this concern is partly a matter of legal culture: if FTA partners tend toward litigiousness in their domestic arenas, then they shall have to adjust their approach to each other in trade disputes. Precisely that pledge was made on 23 July 2001, when the U.S. and Jordan exchanged official letters stating the intention of each side not to apply formal dispute settlement mechanisms in a way that would block trade. They stated a preference for informal mechanisms, specifically bilateral consultations, to secure compliance with obligations in the *U.S. — Morocco FTA*, lieu of seeking formal trade sanctions. Accordingly, only if the two sides have failed to resolve a dispute after consultations is recourse made to a dispute settlement panel. The panel may issue legal interpretations of the FTA. Notably, as with decisions by a panel under the *U.S. — Israel FTA*, decisions by a *U.S. — Morocco FTA* panel are not binding. A similar arrangement exists under the *U.S. — Morocco FTA*, namely, anticipation that most interpretative questions would be resolved by informal or formal government-to-government contacts, and recourse made to a dispute settlement panel, which could issue legal interpretations, only if consultations fail.

How, then, if decisions of an FTA arbitral panel are recommendations, are obligations enforced in the event of non-compliance? Any dispute resolution mechanism holds little value if it does not contain a rigorous enforcement device in the event of non-compliance by the losing party. The conventional device is retaliation, which must be appropriate and proportional. That device exists, for instance, in the *U.S. — Morocco FTA*. Generally, retaliation preferably occurs in the same sector as the dispute. If same-sector sanctions are not feasible, then cross-sectoral retaliation may be authorized. Significantly, in recent U.S. FTAs, there is a choice offered between retaliation and paying monetary damages.

D. Case Study: *NAFTA* Chapter 20

1. The FTC and Secretariat

NAFTA Chapter 20 establishes two institutions, the Free Trade Commission (FTC) and the Secretariat. They are charged with administering *NAFTA* and settling disputes among *NAFTA* Parties.

The FTC is the central institution of *NAFTA* and is loosely akin in structure and function to a hybrid between the WTO Ministerial Conference and the General Council. Like the Ministerial Conference, the FTC is comprised of cabinet-level representatives — namely, the trade ministers — from each *NAFTA* Party. As Article 2001:2 explains, the FTC supervises the implementation of *NAFTA*, resolves disputes about its interpretation and application, and oversees the work of committees and working groups established under *NAFTA*. At the WTO level, these tasks are performed on a day-to-day basis by the General Council, with ultimate authority lying in the Conference. The FTC's interpretive rulings about *NAFTA* are binding on *NAFTA* dispute resolution panels, though not on the courts of the *NAFTA* Parties. The FTC meets at least once a year, and the *NAFTA* Parties alternate as chairperson of these meetings. Article 2001:4 specifies that unless the FTC opts otherwise, it takes decisions by consensus.

The Secretariat is staffed and supported by the Parties and has three national Sections, one for each *NAFTA* Party. (*See NAFTA* Article 2002.) It provides administrative assistance to the FTC and committees and working groups established by the FTC. It also provides administrative assistance to *NAFTA* dispute resolution panels, panels and committees established under *NAFTA* Chapter 19 for the resolution of antidumping and countervailing duty disputes.

2. Two Scenarios for the Use of Chapter 20

In general, the *NAFTA* dispute settlement mechanism is used in two instances. The first scenario is where a *NAFTA* Party disagrees with another Party's interpretation or application of *NAFTA*. That is, in this scenario one Party has taken, or proposes to take, an action potentially inconsistent with *NAFTA*. The second scenario is when a Party challenges a measure (which is defined in Article 2001 to include any "law, regulation, procedure, requirement or practice") that is inconsistent with *NAFTA*, or nullifies or impairs a benefit that the complaining Party reasonably could expect to accrue to it under *NAFTA*. The "nullification or impairment of benefits" standard in *NAFTA* Article 2004 plainly is lifted from GATT Article XXIII:1. How is a nullification or impairment complaint proven? The complainant Party must show that (1) an otherwise *NAFTA*-consistent measure adopted by the respondent Party has resulted in the impairment of an expected *NAFTA* benefit, and (2) at the time *NAFTA* was negotiated, it was not reasonably foreseeable the respondent would adopt the measure. In contrast to the first scenario, the second scenario covers instances where there is no *prima facie* violation of a *NAFTA* obligation.

The Chapter 20 dispute resolution mechanism is mandatory in that a Party cannot enforce a provision of NAFTA against another Party in a domestic court. Rather, *NAFTA's* provisions are enforced by the dispute mechanism NAFTA itself creates.

3. Steps in a Chapter 20 Case

There are three broad steps in a *NAFTA* Chapter 20 adjudication: consultation, review by the FTC, and arbitration. To promote efficiency and ensure a result is obtained, there are strict time limits associated with each step. The steps are designed so that a dispute can be resolved within eight months.

Only *NAFTA* Parties — *i.e.*, governments, not private parties — have standing to use the dispute settlement mechanism. Further, Article 2021 bars the Parties from creating a private cause of action under *NAFTA*. Thus, as is true with respect to the *DSU*, a private business or individual can bring an action only indirectly, by petitioning or otherwise inveighing upon its government to file suit. No doubt this restriction is a source of concern for "Kantian-minded" international trade lawyers. They would like to see the normative status of individuals as the primary focus of trade law, if the trade law regime is to be judged "legitimate." In turn, they would favor direct access for individuals to an adjudicatory mechanism, because that is likely to be the best way to ensure claimed wrongs about the normative status of individuals are heard.

The first step, consultation, is intended to be the primary way to resolve disputes. Consultation may entail inter-governmental meetings. (*See NAFTA* Article 2006.) Special consultative devices exist under Chapter 7B for disputes about SPS measures and Chapter 9 for disputes about standards. These devices are procedurally similar to, but a substitute for, Chapter 20 consultation and involve technical expert advice.

If a dispute remains unresolved after 30-45 days of consultation (or, in the case of perishable agricultural products, 15 days), then either the complaining or responding Party may request a meeting of the FTC. Interestingly, because the FTC acts by consensus, it is effective at resolving a dispute only when all three governments agree on a course of action. Thus, *NAFTA* gives the FTC broad latitude in fashioning an appropriate dispute resolution strategy. For example, the FTC may rely on experts and technical advisors, convene a working group, or make use of an alternative dispute resolution technique such as conciliation or mediation.

If the FTC is unable to resolve the dispute within 30 days, then any consulting Party may request the establishment of a five-member arbitral panel. (*See NAFTA* Articles 2008:1 and 2011.) (The Parties may agree to extend the period for the second step.) A third party with a substantial interest in the dispute can join as a complaining party. *NAFTA* Article 2006:5 makes clear panel proceedings cannot be commenced until the FTC has unsuccessfully attempted to resolve the dispute through conciliation.

The operation of the *NAFTA* arbitral panel is similar to that of a WTO panel. For example, panel members are chosen from a long roster comprised of experienced experts; there is at least one hearing; each Party may offer written initial and rebuttal statements; the panel may rely on experts for advice on environmental, health, safety, and scientific matters; and the panel must issue initial and final reports within a specific time frame. (*See NAFTA* Articles 2009, 2012, and 2016-1017.)

Once a panel issues its report, the disputing Parties must agree on the way to resolve the dispute in conformity with the panel's determinations and recommendations. The preferred means of conformity is to remove any measure that the panel finds inconsistent with that Party's *NAFTA* obligations or impairs another Party's benefits under *NAFTA*. An alternative means is payment of compensation to the aggrieved Party.

If the violating Party fails to conform to a panel's determination or report, then the aggrieved Party — and only it — is entitled to retaliate. Retaliation entails suspension of the application of benefits under *NAFTA* that were previously extended to the violating Party. (*See* NAFTA Article 2019:1.) For example, suppose the U.S. establishes a quota on imports of lumber from Canada, which a panel finds violate *NAFTA*, and the U.S. does not comply with the panel's report. Canada, but not Mexico, could retaliate by limiting the same value of U.S. exports of a different product, perhaps beer. The violating Party that is the target of retaliation can seek panel review of the retaliatory measures if it believes they are manifestly excessive. (*See NAFTA* Article 2019.) What is the justification for this right? It is simply to serve as a check against potential excesses that inhere in any instance when international law condones unilateral retaliation.

Plainly, retaliation involves a trade-distorting action that is otherwise inconsistent with *NAFTA* obligations to offset a *NAFTA* violation. Does this reflect an "eye for an eye" approach? Could retaliation be criticized by saying that "two wrongs don't make a right"? Observe that retaliation is supposed to occur in a sector that is closely related to the one in which the violation occurred, yet cross-retaliation (*i.e.*, retaliation against a different sector) is permissible. Observe also the violating Party may apply to the FTC to establish a panel to determine whether the suspension of benefits is manifestly excessive.

Many obligations established by *NAFTA* resemble or are identical to GATT—WTO obligations. If a complaining Party alleges another Party has violated both sets of obligations, then the complainant can choose to bring its action in either the *NAFTA* or GATT forum. Under certain circumstances, the responding Party, or an affected third Party, can insist that the dispute be resolved by a *NAFTA* panel.

4. Modifications

In three types of cases, the paradigmatic *NAFTA* dispute resolution mechanism may be modified: investor-state disputes brought under Chapter 11 before an arbitral panel; financial services disputes brought under Chapter 14; and reviews of AD and CVD actions conducted under Chapter 19. *NAFTA* Chapter 11 concerns FDI. Such investment is broadly defined to include an equity, debt security, loan, profit-sharing, asset-sharing, real estate acquisition, capital commitment or other interest taken by an investor in one *NAFTA*

Party in the territory of another *NAFTA* Party. An example is the purchase or construction by an individual or firm in one *NAFTA* Party of a factory in another Party. In general, Chapter 11 obliges a *NAFTA* Party that hosts direct foreign investments to accord foreign investors and their investments MFN and national treatment, and to comply with certain minimum standards regarding treatment. (*See NAFTA* Articles 1102-1104.) Failure to do so may trigger a Chapter 11 dispute.

Significantly, only private parties have standing to bring an investor-state claim against a *NAFTA* Party government. In this regard, Chapter 11 is a break with international legal tradition, which accords only to sovereign states the right to bring an action against another state. The "Kantian-minded" trade lawyer can take some satisfaction in this departure. Individuals have the opportunity to shape jurisprudence to a greater extent under Chapter 11 than any other international agreement.

NAFTA Chapter 14 modifies the paradigmatic Chapter 20 dispute resolution mechanism outlined above in three respects. First, disputes may be resolved not only by the FTC or an arbitral panel, but also by an investor-state tribunal under Chapter 11 with the permission of the Financial Services Committee. (*See NAFTA* Articles 1412 and 1415.) The Committee's critical task is to determine whether the exception for prudential measures set forth in *NAFTA* Article 1410 provides a defense against the investor's claim. (That Article enshrines the right of a *NAFTA* Party to adopt prudential measures — for example, regulations related to the safety and soundness of commercial banks — in order to safeguard its financial system.) The Committee must make its decision within 60 days. If the Committee decides the disputed measure, in whole or in part, falls outside the prudential capacity of government, then it will convene an investor-state tribunal. Second, the roster from which an arbitral panel is chosen is comprised of experts in financial services. (*See NAFTA* Article 1414:3.) Third, there are restrictions on cross-retaliation (*i.e.*, on an aggrieved party's right to retaliate outside of the financial services sector). (*See NAFTA* Article 1414:5.)

Chapter 19 establishes binational review panels as an alternative to domestic judicial review of AD and CVD determinations made by administrative agencies like the DOC and ITC. It also establishes an extraordinary challenge procedure to ensure a binational panel review is handled properly. Finally, under Chapter 19 a special committee may be established to determine whether a Party's domestic law hinders operation of the panel or implementation of one of the panel's decision.

Part Seven

REMEDIES AGAINST "UNFAIR" TRADE: ANTIDUMPING LAW

Chapter 27

HISTORICAL AND ECONOMIC FOUNDATIONS OF AD LAW

The future ain't what it used to be.

— YOGI BERRA, THE YOGI BOOK 118 (1998) (Hall of Fame Baseball Player and Manager)

DOCUMENTS SUPPLEMENT ASSIGNMENT

1. *Havana Charter* Article 34
2. GATT Article VI
3. WTO *Antidumping Agreement*

I. GATT ARTICLE VI AND THE DEFINITION OF "DUMPING"

Article VI:1 of GATT states dumping occurs when a producer-exporter sells its product in a foreign market at less than normal value. In general, this practice occurs when the price at which the company exports its product is lower than the price it charges in its home country. The difference between the foreign and domestic market prices is commonly referred to as the "dumping margin." Thus, a generic formula for calculation of the dumping margin is:

Dumping Margin = Normal Value — Export Price

where:

Normal Value	=	domestic price, *i.e.*, the price the exporter charges in its home market.
Export Price	=	foreign price, *i.e.*, the price the exporter charges in the importing country in which dumping is alleged.
If the Dumping Margin is:		positive, then dumping occurs, if zero or negative, then no dumping occurs.

In certain instances, Constructed Export Price is used as a proxy for Export Price. Often, dumping margins are expressed in percentage terms, namely, as a percentage of the Export Price. The formula then becomes:

$$\text{Dumping Margin} = \frac{\text{Normal Value} - \text{Export Price}}{\text{Export Price}} \times 100$$

Expressing a dumping margin in percentage terms is useful, because it facilitates comparison among different cases. How is it known, for example, whether Jordan is more egregious in its alleged dumping of hummus than Turkey? If the margin for Turkey is 138.6 percent, and Jordan 68.2 percent, then the question is answerable. The percentage expression also is useful for a rule of thumb it furnishes. Generally, the Department of Commerce (DOC) is unlikely to be interested in pursuing a case unless the percentage dumping margin is at least in the high double digits. Exactly how high is hard to say, but an 18.9 as opposed to 88.9 percent margin signals a weaker case.

Dumping is primarily a matter of cross-border price discrimination. Consumers of allegedly dumped merchandise in the importing country are segregated from consumers of the like product in the exporter's home country. There is no leakage of dumped goods back to the home market. Consequently, the exporter is able to reap high profits from home market sales. Such profits may subsidize lower profits earned, or losses incurred, from selling the product at a cheap price in the importing country.

Why is dumping recognized in GATT Article VI as a harmful unfair trade practice? If you like hummus (as does your author), then why not enjoy cheaper dumped prices? The answer is the practice is not viewed with consumers of dumped merchandise in mind. Domestic producers of a like product are the group whose interests are exalted.

> Firms [that dump their products in an overseas market] are unfairly able to obtain or hold market share which they otherwise would not enjoy by selling their products at below fair market value. This can occur either because of the lack of a competitive market in the domestic market of the dumping industry (for example due to restrictive business practices) or the firm is simply structurally able to absorb losses. Domestic firms in the importing country must either lower their prices to match the dumped price, or attempt to maintain their prices while conceding market share to imports. The results of dumping in the U.S. have been serious. There has been wholesale withdrawal of U.S. companies from industries experiencing dumping, such as the semiconductor and steel industries. This has resulted in a concomitant loss of tens of thousands of jobs.[1]

However, not all dumping is evil. Article VI condemns only injurious dumping.

That is, dumping is actionable only if it causes material injury to an industry in the importing country. More technically, if dumping causes, or threatens to cause, material injury to an established industry in the importing country that competes with the exporter, or if it materially retards the establishment of an industry in the importing country that would compete with the exporter, then it is actionable. Pursuant to Articles VI:1(a) and VI:2, an antidumping (AD) duty may be imposed by authorities in the domestic market. The amount of the duty is calibrated to offset the dumping margin. The result is — supposedly — a leveling of the competitive playing field.

---

[1] Michael H. Stein, *The Uruguay Round and the Trade Laws: Antidumping, Countervailing Duties, Common Provisions*, I THE COMMERCE DEPARTMENT SPEAKS ON INTERNATIONAL TRADE AND INVESTMENT 881 (1994).

II. EARLY GATT CASES

Are the foundations of AD law incongruous with economic theory? Generally, international trade negotiators have not questioned whether dumping should be actionable. During the *Havana Charter* negotiations, no delegates challenged the right of a government to impose AD duties. Indeed, until the Kennedy Round, negotiators paid little attention to AD law.

Before the Kennedy Round there was only one AD case — in 1955, involving Sweden's imposition of AD duties on Italian exports of nylon stockings — that resulted in a GATT Panel Report. (*See Swedish Anti-dumping Duties*, GATT B.I.S.D. (3d Supp.) at 81 (1955) (adopted 26 February 1955).) The Panel found Sweden's AD regulations did not violate Article VI, and in any event the dispute was resolved when Sweden revoked the regulations. The Report failed to yield any clear-cut interpretations of Article VI. However, the Report is significant in two respects.

First, it establishes a clear rule on the determination of "normal value." The Report authorized a fixed price system whereby the price in the importing country of an allegedly dumped good is compared not to the actual price of that good in the exporter's home country, but rather some minimum price. Under the system, that minimum price must be equal to or lower than the price in the home market of the lowest cost producer of the good. No relationship between the minimum price and either costs of production or actual sales prices is required. Second, the Report indicates administration of AD law must not lead to delays and uncertainties. For example, a decision on the status of allegedly dumped goods must be made in a matter of days of the arrival of the goods in an importing country, otherwise the regime may discriminate against low-cost producers.

Another early GATT Panel Report on AD law provided important guidance on Article VI. In a 1962 case involving exports of potatoes to Canada, a Panel ruled absent a showing of cross-border price discrimination, an AD claim must fail. (*See Exports of Potatoes to Canada*, GATT B.I.S.D. (11th Supp.) at 88 (1963) (adopted 16 November 1962).) Canada could not prove a difference existed between the price of potatoes consumed in the U.S. and price of potatoes exported to Canada. That is, in respect of the dumping margin calculation, Canada did not appreciate the language in Article VI:1(a) concerning "the comparable price . . . for consumption in the exporting country" imposes an affirmative duty on the petitioner to prove price discrimination and, therefore, determine two prices. A sale cannot be at less than Normal Value (*i.e.*, there is no dumping margin) unless the (1) price of allegedly dumped merchandise in the importing country is less than (2) price of the like product destined for the exporter's home market.

Since these early GATT Panel Reports, the volume of AD cases has exploded. Today, AD cases are a mainstay of international trade law practice. Many result in significant — if highly technical — rulings.

III. THE 1967 KENNEDY ROUND AND 1979 TOKYO ROUND *ANTIDUMPING CODES*

The WTO *Antidumping Agreement* was not the first effort at a multilateral accord on AD law. Kennedy Round negotiators produced an *Antidumping Code* in 1967, which entered into force on 1 July 1968. The *Code* sought to ensure AD actions would not be abused. American negotiators were the impetus for putting AD issues on the Kennedy Round agenda. They feared American exports might face discrimination under the guise of AD proceedings. Indeed, an increasing number of GATT contracting parties worried AD law was being or could be used as a non-tariff barrier (NTB). Ironically, the U.S. Congress rejected the *Code*, essentially because AD matters strayed beyond authority Congress had delegated to the Administration of President Lyndon B. Johnson.

Tokyo Round negotiators also produced an *Antidumping Code*. Like its predecessor, the Tokyo Round *Code* contained rules about the conduct of AD investigations in an attempt to ensure they were not used as unjustifiable impediments to trade. Unlike its predecessor, the Tokyo Round *AD Code*, which took effect on 1 January 1980 and succeeded its predecessor, was implemented into U.S. law. (Congress did so through Section 2(a) of the *Trade Agreements Act of 1979*.) However, this *Code* was not part of a single undertaking. Rather, it was a plurilateral accord.

IV. THE 1994 WTO *ANTIDUMPING AGREEMENT*

A. Overview

Major changes in AD law, accepted by all GATT contracting parties as part of the Uruguay Round single undertaking, resulted from the WTO Antidumping Agreement — formally entitled the *Agreement on the Implementation of Article VI of the General Agreement on Tariffs and Trade 1994*. This *Agreement*, which entered into force on 1 January 1995 when the WTO was born, contains far more specific rules than the Tokyo Round AD *Code* in areas such as calculation of the dumping margin (Article 2), determination of injury (Article 3), evidence (Article 6), and duration of AD duties (Article 11). Sections 201-234 of the *1994 Act* implement the *AD Agreement* in U.S. law. This legislation represents the most significant changes in that since the *1979 Act*.

True, substantive standards for the U.S. International Trade Commission (ITC) to make an injury determination — namely, material injury, threat of material injury, or material retardation of the establishment of an injury — remain the same. But, how the DOC calculates a dumping margin dramatically changed. For cases arising after 1 January 1995, when the *Act* took effect, pre-Uruguay Round jurisprudence on injury may be relevant, but pre-Uruguay Round case law on dumping margin calculations is of less value. The *North American Free Trade Agreement (NAFTA)*, and associated implementing legislation, the *1993 North American Free Trade Implementation Act*, also ushered in key changes in U.S. AD law. In particular, Chapter 19 of *NAFTA* established a binational panel review process for cases involving U.S., Canadian, or Mexican parties. This process applies both to AD and countervailing duty (CVD) cases.

B. Standard of Review

One significant effect of the WTO *AD Agreement* pertains to resolution of AD disputes. What standard of review should a WTO dispute settlement panel apply when examining the decision rendered by the DOC or ITC (or, for that matter, any official responsible for administering AD laws in a particular Member)? This issue is important for exporters that may be accused of dumping in a Member that does not provide respondents in AD actions full participation or appeal rights. It also helps avoid infringements on a Member's sovereignty by ensuring WTO panels do not routinely overturn decisions rendered by national authorities. On this matter, a 1990 GATT Panel Report, which was not adopted, raised serious concerns.

In *Seamless Stainless Steel Hollow Products from Sweden* (ADP/47, decided 20 August 1990), the Panel held the DOC's practice of assuming an American industry supports an AD petition is inconsistent with the Tokyo Round *AD Code*. U.S. courts had found the relevant statutory language ambiguous and, therefore, deferred to the DOC interpretation. In contrast, the GATT Panel not only substituted its reading for that of the DOC, but also recommended the DOC revoke its AD order. Further, it said the scope of panel reviews might not be limited to facts and issues raised before a domestic body like the DOC or ITC. Rather, panels might engage in *de novo* review. U.S. negotiators were troubled by this holding and wanted to ensure WTO panels could not "second guess" factual determinations and legal interpretations of the DOC or ITC.

Article 17:6 of the WTO *AD Agreement*, which was finalized after extensive negotiations, indicates WTO panels must apply a standard of review that discourages the reversal of reasonable decisions rendered by authorities in a Member country. A panel cannot overturn a factual determination of a national authority, such as the DOC, if that authority's establishment of the facts was "proper" and its evaluation "unbiased and objective," even if the panel might have reached a different conclusion. A panel cannot overturn a legal determination of a national authority if the relevant provision of the *Agreement* allows for more than one permissible interpretation and the authority's determination rests on one of those interpretations. This Article did not necessitate a change in American AD law. Indeed, it appears similar to the famous *Chevron* standard of review in American administrative law.

Interestingly, this standard of review applies only to AD disputes. Uruguay Round negotiators from many countries preferred a stronger standard of review and, therefore, were unwilling to incorporate Article 17:6 into the WTO *SCM Agreement*. As a result, negotiators could agree only on a declaration AD and CVD cases should be resolved in a consistent manner. Most notably, many American critics of the WTO fault panels and the Appellate Body for exceeding their authority under Article 17:6. Unsurprisingly, they point to cases in which the U.S. lost.

C. Remedies in Theory and Practice

What remedies should be recommended by a WTO panel (or the Appellate Body) that disagrees with a DOC or ITC decision? Unfortunately, the WTO *AD Agreement* does not resolve this issue. Given this void, consider four classes of possible remedies: retroactive, specific, exclusive, and prospective. The WTO *Dispute Settlement Understanding* (*DSU*) plainly condones only the last class.

First, a retroactive remedy, which punishes a violator through monetary compensation to the victim for past economic loss the violator caused, is disfavored:

> Traditionally, GATT dispute settlement has been remedial and pro-spective in nature, the object being to end a situation in which one government is violating the obligations owed to another. GATT dispute settlement has not operated to punish a government for past behavior, nor has it sought to compensate private parties.[2]

Second, a specific remedy is one which recommends a particular course of action, such as revocation of an AD order. On the one hand, specific remedies are disfavored because they are seen as an encroachment on the sovereignty of WTO Members. The relevant authority within a Member should have discretion to decide the best manner to conform its factual determination or legal interpretation to an adverse panel (or Appellate Body) report. A WTO panel (or the Appellate Body) should focus on systemic flaws in a Member's AD regime. On the other hand, the absence of a specific remedy may make WTO dispute resolution less attractive to an aggrieved Member. Moreover, neither the *DSU* nor the *AD Agreement* bars a panel from recommending a specific remedy.

Third, an exclusive remedy is one that indicates it is the only way for a losing Member to comply with an adverse decision. This remedy is disfavored because a panel (or the Appellate Body) may lack expertise in the domestic law of the losing Member. That law may provide for more suitable remedies than the exclusive remedy recommended by the panel (or Appellate Body). Arguably, a panel (or Appellate Body) should confine itself to determining whether a violation occurs, and then give discretion to the losing Member to determine curative measures. Article 19:1 of the *DSU* seems to look askance at exclusive remedies. It indicates that the panel "may" suggest a remedy that the losing Member "could" implement.

Finally, a prospective remedy is designed to obtain relief in the future by alleviating the offending act. *DSU* Article 3:7 calls for prospective remedies, explaining the "first objective" of dispute resolution is "to secure the with-drawal of the measures concerned. . . ." *DSU* Article 19:1 instructs a panel to recommend the losing Member in a dispute bring its measure into confor-mity with the legal provision in question.

V. DUMPING AND PROTECTIONISM

A. The Risk of Protectionist Abuse

The central challenge facing AD law is its articulation to prevent abuse by an industry or workers in an importing country to obtain protection from relatively more efficient foreign companies. If reduction of tariffs and NTBs is not to be offset by protectionist abuse of trade remedies, then these remedies

---

[2] William D. Hunter, *WTO Dispute Settlement in Antidumping and Countervailing Duty Cases, in* I The Commerce Department Speaks on International Trade and Investment 557-85, at 579 (Practicing Law Institute ed., 1994).

must not operate as NTBs. Because of the Byzantine complexity involved in dumping margin calculations and injury determinations, and the delay sometimes associated with these procedures, there is ample opportunity for abuse. That risk is a source of uncertainty for traders, and traders hate uncertainty.

To be sure, all trade remedies — when imposed — afford protection to a domestic producer of a product that is like the merchandise subject to the remedy. However, "protectionist abuse" suggests that a producer has lost its international competitive advantage, *i.e.*, it no longer cost-competitive in the global marketplace. The petitioner is unwilling or unable to reduce its cost structure to meet global competitive pressures, fails to incorporate technological innovations in its manufacturing process and product design, or is insensitive to changes in consumer tastes. Its strategy for survival is to restore the *status quo ante* by raising the cost of imported merchandise through an AD duty.

Indeed, the *in terrorem* effect on a respondent of a preliminary affirmative dumping margin determination is real. That determination triggers suspension of liquidation of entries and collection of estimated duties. The respondent may react by raising prices quickly, and settling with a suspension agreement. That may be the whole point, for petitioner, of filing the action, *i.e.*, to coerce the respondent to join a price cartel. Evidence suggests AD law is a tool for producers in an importing country to maintain a price agreement (which, of course, may be a tacit one).

In such instances, imposition of a trade remedy is at odds with free trade theory. For three reasons, differentiating legitimate dumping cases from cases motivated by protectionism has remained the central challenge since the Kennedy Round.

  i.   In the 1940s and 1950s only a few contracting parties — most notably the U.S. and Canada — had active AD enforcement programs. Today, every WTO Member has an AD law and attendant enforcement scheme. Yet, AD law across Members is not seamlessly harmonious, nor is implementation always consistent.

 ii.   As a result of several successful GATT negotiating rounds, tariffs have fallen dramatically. With respect to many products, they are not capable of serving as the principal means of protection, and other means must be sought.

iii.   Also following successful rounds, it is increasingly difficult to impose NTBs. Indeed, many NTBs have fallen. AD law is an increasingly attractive vehicle to achieve protectionist aims. Domestic industries that have lost their international comparative advantage (*e.g.*, major American steel companies, as distinct from mini-mills) lobby governmental authorities to uphold their dumping petitions.

Thus, the GATT—WTO regime, translated into domestic AD laws, must balance two competing interests. On the one hand, it must acknowledge the legitimacy of AD actions in some instances. On the other hand, it must strike out attempts to use the remedy as a non-tariff barrier to protect companies whose misfortunes are due largely to grand changes in the global economy, the stupidity of its senior management and directors, or some combination thereof.

For four reasons, a complaint brought by New Zealand that is the subject of a 1985 GATT Panel Report exemplifies the use of AD law for protectionist purposes. (*See New Zealand — Imports of Electrical Transformers from Finland*, GATT B.I.S.D. (32nd Supp.) at 55 (1984-85) (adopted 18 July 1985).) First, a New Zealand company on whose behalf the complaint was brought was upset its bid to supply transformers to the New Zealand government was rejected in favor of a bid submitted by a Finnish company. The Finnish company appears to have been a lower-cost producer than the New Zealand company. The Finnish company contended its winning bid was adequate to cover production costs, overheads, and profits. The Finnish company noted that, in contrast, during the period of alleged dumping, the New Zealand company simultaneously experienced increased sales and losses.

Second, the complainant, New Zealand, attempted to manipulate the definition of "industry." It sought to divide the transformer market into 4 segments in a way not necessarily used by other countries. Its purpose was to increase the likelihood of finding injury caused by dumped imports and obtaining relief for specific lines of production.

Third, it was implausible to argue the New Zealand transformer industry was materially injured by competition from Finland. The relevant company accounted for 92 percent of the share of the New Zealand transformer market (measured in terms of total 1983 domestic production). In contrast, Finnish imports accounted for only 2.4 percent of the market (measured in terms of total sales in the New Zealand transformer industry). In addition, only 2.4 percent of transformers imported into New Zealand were from Finland. Finally, while imports increased by 250 percent between 1981-82 and 1982-83, Finnish transformers represented only 3.4 percent of this increase. In sum, plainly Finnish transformers played an insignificant role in the New Zealand market.

Fourth, New Zealand's argument "any given amount of profit lost" amounts to "injury" was patently absurd. So, too, was its argument a threat of material injury existed. The Finnish company had no plans to export additional transformers to New Zealand.

The risk an AD action can be used as a NTB might be reduced if GATT Article VI were not such a generally worded provision. However, it was designed to accommodate U.S. AD law as it existed in 1947. It was not drafted to differentiate with precision abusive from legitimate AD petitions. Perhaps the best example of the ambiguity in Article VI is the term "normal value." As GATT Article VI:1 itself suggests, dumping occurs when products of one country are exported to another country at less than Normal Value. The meaning of that key term hinges on the meaning of other key terms in Article VI:1, such as "comparable price," "ordinary course of trade," "like product," "reasonable addition," "cost of production," and "due allowance." What do they mean? Further, tracking the Article VI:1 language, when is a domestic price "absent"? What "third country" should be used to obtain a comparable price? How should cost of production be calculated? Unless such ambiguities are resolved with precision, dumping margin calculations are fated to be inconsistent and imprecise.

Might the risk of protectionist abuse be reduced if GATT Article VI imposed an affirmative obligation on contracting parties to refrain from dumping? Nothing in Article VI requires a WTO Member to ensure its exporters do not dump abroad. To the contrary, Article VI tacitly assumes the practice will occur. In contrast, there are affirmative obligations on WTO Members to refrain from providing certain types of subsidies. Certainly, banning dumping would provide a stricter discipline than offsetting a dumping margin through an AD duty. However, might a duty to abstain from dumping be problematical? An outright ban could result in attempts to equate prices of like products in different countries where genuine differences in market conditions or production efficiencies lead to justified price distinctions. That is, banning cross-border price discrimination could amount to an attempt to repeal the law of comparative advantage.

B. Batting Averages

Generally speaking (based on statistics from the 1980s and 1990s), the DOC renders an affirmative dumping margin determination in about 90 percent of cases. The ITC renders an affirmative injury determination in about 50 percent of cases. With these kinds of batting averages, it is not surprising AD law is a preferred bat by petitioners with which to hit at foreign imports. Many respondents do not bother to expend time and money battling a dumping margin determination, simply because of the poor odds. Rather, they choose to concentrate on the injury determination. Notably, petitioners around the world — such as China and India — are picking up the bat and having a go at American imports.

Surely, free traders would have thought, even if the drafters of GATT are forgiven for failing to anticipate the proliferation of AD law as a protectionist device, the ambitious, free trade oriented Uruguay Round negotiators were supposed to dismantle the weapon — or, at least, discipline its use. Fortunately, for protectionists seeking undeserved protection from competitive imports, the AD weapon was not neutralized. Quite the contrary, the WTO *Antidumping Agreement* ensures AD remains a weapon of choice for protectionist purposes. Likewise, Title II, Subtitle A of the *Uruguay Round Agreements Act of 1994* (*1994 Act*) implements the *Agreement* into American law by amending the *Tariff Act of 1930* (*1930 Act*), and similar legislation exists (or is supposed to) in every WTO Member. Protectionist abuse remains possible because of textual ambiguities, and inconsistencies with microeconomic insights, namely, the importance of considering the relationship between pricing strategy and costs of production.

VI. NEOCLASSICAL ECONOMIC ANALYSIS OF AD LAW

A. International Price Discrimination and Its Conditions

The strengthening of AD law as a trade remedy occurred in the Uruguay Round despite howls from free trade oriented economists. Accordingly, before delving into that law, consider how neoclassical economists view dumping. The legal discussion is then more fruitful, as the incongruity between law and economic theory becomes clear.

Dumping is international price discrimination. It occurs when an exporter sells merchandise in an importing country at a price below that at which it sells like merchandise in its home country (or, if the home market of the exporter is not viable, then in a third country, or if there is no third country, then at below a constructed value):

> Dumping is, in general, a situation of *international price discrimination*, where the price of a product when sold to the importing country is less than the price of the same product when sold in the market of the exporting country. It is generally accepted in the multilateral trading system that if dumping takes place, it might result in *unfair* trade as the domestic industry of the importing country might suffer harm as a result of the dumping.[3]

(Observe "unfairness" is presumed without recourse to a theory of fairness.)

A more restrictive definition of "dumping" is it occurs when an exporter sells merchandise in an importing country at below the cost of production of that exporter. In either event, if dumping causes or threatens to cause material injury to an established industry making a like product in the importing country, or if dumping materially retards the establishment of an industry in that country, then the practice is actionable. The importing country may impose an AD duty on the dumped merchandise in the amount of the dumping margin, *i.e.*, the difference between the prices in the home market of the exporter and importing country.

Authorities in the U.S. and a handful of other countries (*e.g.*, in certain situations, Canada and Mexico), impose AD duties retroactively. That means an exporter (or, typically, the importer) of dumped merchandise must pay an AD duty on all such goods, going backward in time to a relevant date such as the filing date of the AD petition (or, in critical circumstances, even before the filing date) or the date of a preliminary affirmative determination of a dumping margin. Most other countries, and the EU, follow the system Great Britain established, which affords only prospective relief. That means customs authorities in an importing country collect AD duties going forward from a relevant date, such as the date of a final affirmative finding of dumping.

How is it possible for an exporter to pursue a bifurcated, cross-border price strategy? Neoclassical economists respond with 3 necessary and sufficient conditions:

1. *Market Segregation*

The home market of an exporter and the market in the importing country are segregated from one another. Merchandise does not flow between the markets. Tariff and non-tariff barriers in the exporter's home market buttress a higher home market price, and consumers face significant costs in traveling to the other market. Consequently, the cross-border price differential persists

---

[3] JUDITH CZAKO, JOHANN HUMAN & JORGE MIRANDA, A HANDBOOK ON ANTI-DUMPING INVESTIGATIONS 1 (2003) (emphasis added).

because of the impracticability of arbitrage, *i.e.*, it is not commercially feasible to buy the product in the cheaper market and sell it in the more expensive market. The market segregation may result from, or be reinforced by, trade barriers in the home market of the exporter. That is, the government in this market may protect through high tariff or non-tariff barriers the good produced and sold by the exporter. Restrictive business practices in the exporter's home market also may account for, or buttress, the distinctiveness of that market.

2. *Imperfect Competition*

An exporter does not face perfect competition in both markets. It has sufficient market power in at least one market to influence prices therein. If it lacked such power, then any price differential for merchandise in the different markets would not be in its control. In an extreme case, the exporter is a monopolist in its home market and perfect competitor in the market of the importing country. This condition follows logically from the first one. Because of market segregation, there is no leakage of the dumped product to the exporter's home market. The exporter need not contend with the competition arbitrage would provide, and can reap high profits from home market sales. In some instances, the exporter may use super-normal profits to subsidize sales at "unfairly" low prices in the importing country, enabling it to suffer lower profits, or even losses, in that country. The first and second conditions also are related through the fact each may result from, or be reinforced by, trade barriers and restrictive business practices.

3. *Relative Elasticities*

An exporter faces a relatively more elastic demand curve for merchandise in the market of the importing country, and a relatively less elastic demand curve for like merchandise in its home market. (Elasticity measures the sensitivity of consumer demand to price fluctuations, and arithmetically is the percent change in quantity demanded divided by the percent change in price. An elasticity value exceeding one means "elastic," a value less than one means "inelastic." Depicted on a graph, the demand curve in the home market is steeper than the demand curve in the importing country.) Again, the differential may result from trade barriers that protect the exporter in its home market and shield it from competition in that market. Absent the differential in the price elasticity of demand, the price charged by the exporter in the importing country would equal or exceed the price charged in its home market. Hence, there would be no dumping.

When all three conditions exist in a market, the environment is conducive to cross-border price discrimination.

B. Harmless?

Significantly, economists generally agree except for predation, dumping is basically harmless for the importing country. Consumers in that country benefit from the lower price of imported goods. They are beneficiaries of price discrimination because they have access to cheaper merchandise. If they use that merchandise as an input into production of a finished good, then the final product is cheaper than it otherwise would be. Semiconductor chips used in consumer electronics, pasta used in frozen food, steel used in chain link fences, wood used in furniture or homes — all are examples. Why not, save for the exaltation of producer over consumer interests, allow consumers to enjoy the cheaper dumped price?

Producers of a like product in the importing country may be injured by the low-price competition, or may have a legitimate fear of this competition. Still, the net benefit to the importing country may be positive. Indeed, the analysis of imposition of an AD duty is conceptually the same as that of any tariff. (The very same graphical analysis may be used.) Producers gain through increased surplus, and the government of the importing country gains from a tariff revenue, but these gains typically are more than offset by the loss of consumer surplus. The net result is a dead weight loss, consisting of lost consumption opportunities plus inefficient allocation of factors of production to domestic output in the protected sector.

Empirical evidence strongly supports this neoclassical economic theory. It indicates the gain from obtaining dumped merchandise outweighs the cost to producers in the importing country (measured by reduced profits) and their employees (in terms of reduced employment). The policy implication is not to impose an AD duty, otherwise the net gain is wiped out. Indeed, one economist conducting a welfare analysis of 8 AD proceedings in the U.S. in 1989-90 concluded:

> such duties are an extremely costly way to improve the profitability of U.S. producers or employment in U.S. industries. In these eight cases, the consumer cost per dollar of increased profits ranged from 2.40 to 25.10 dollars, with an average cost of 8.00. The cost to the U.S. economy per dollar of profit ranges from 0.20 to 10.80 dollars, with an average value of 3.60 dollars. The minimum consumer cost per job created was 113,800 dollars, while the minimum cost to the economy to create an additional job was 14,300 dollars.[4]

No less an authority than the ITC considered the counterfactual question of what the economy-wide welfare effects would be if all outstanding AD and CVD orders in 1991 had been removed. These orders affected $9 billion out of $491 billion, or 1.8 percent, of all American merchandise imports. The ITC concluded AD and CVD orders imposed a net welfare cost on the U.S. economy of $1.59 billion, or 0.03 percent of the American GDP ($5.725 trillion). The loss to consumers in the form of higher prices far outweighed the benefit to petitioning industries in the form of increased output and employment.

Certainly, defects plague this kind of neoclassical economic analysis. First, it is static in nature. It may understate — or overstate — effects of AD and CVD orders across time. That is because it amounts to a snapshot of their effects at a moment, or a specified period. Perhaps more damaging is the analysis is narrow.

That is because of a singular focus of the effects of a trade remedy from the perspective of only the importing country imposing an AD order. When both the exporter's and importer's country are considered, it is impossible to

---

[4] Keith B. Anderson, *Antidumping Laws in the United States: Use and Welfare Consequences*, 27 J. WORLD TRADE 99, 115 (1993).

show conclusively *a priori* the welfare effects of cross-border price discrimination are, on balance, negative. Consumers in the exporter's home market are harmed by a higher price. But, the source of the evil is not dumping. Rather, it is the exporter's monopoly power. Such power enables the exporter to garner monopoly rents by charging a price above its marginal cost of production. These extra profits do not offset the welfare loss to consumers. The same logic applies to the less extreme situation where the exporter charges a high (but not monopoly) and low (but not perfectly competitive) price in the home and importing countries respectively. Whether the benefits from cheaper prices in the importing country offset the net loss from monopoly prices in the exporter's country is uncertain. Thus, Professor Dam concludes:

> The fact that governments act against dumping only when the low price is charged in their own territory reveals that governments are concerned with the welfare of their own enterprises rather than the protection of their citizens from discriminatorily high prices charged by monopoly sellers. If the problem were really the discrimination itself, then presumably governments would be more concerned to attack high prices than low prices. Where an exporter sold at home at higher prices than he sold abroad, it would be the exporter's government, not the importer's government, that would take coercive action. The General Agreement, like the governments themselves, views the impact in the low-price country as the harmful aspect of dumping. . . .
>
>   . . . .
>
> *The concern with dumping is therefore a concern with the protection of domestic industry from international competition.*[5]

Consider, then, two hypothetical inquiries, each of which illustrates the fallacy of assuming dumping is evil.

First, suppose AD laws are repealed and conditions that facilitate dumping are eliminated. In theory, prices in the home (*i.e.*, exporting) and importing countries converge because of cross-border arbitrage. Consumers in the home country benefit from lower prices. Yet, consumers in the importing country are harmed by higher prices and the exporter's profits decline. Whether the benefits to the winners outweigh the losses of the losers is uncertain. The net welfare effect of the repeal can only be forecast as positive if the exporter's monopoly position in the home country is completely undermined, and it behaves like a perfect competitor in the importing country.

Second, suppose an AD duty is imposed to level the competitive playing field between subject merchandise imports and a domestic like product. The clear losers are consumers. They must pay a higher price for the import, because of the duty. Also, they may have to pay a higher price for the like product, because domestic companies can competitively raise prices to match the price of imports. One observer points out between 1980 and 1989, "almost all foreign companies investigated for alleged dumping [in the U.S.] were found guilty" and concludes:

> While many people consider dumping an arcane subject, dumping penalties have forced Americans to pay more for photo albums, pears,

---

[5] Kenneth W. Dam, The GATT 168 (1970) (emphasis added).

mirrors, ethanol, cement, shock absorbers, roof shingles, codfish, televisions, paint brushes, cookware, motorcycle batteries, bicycles, martial art uniforms, computers and computer disks, telephone systems, forklifts, radios, flowers, aspirin, staplers and staples, paving equipment, and fireplace mesh panels. Dumping laws increasingly prevent American businesses from getting vital foreign supplies and machinery. Commerce Department officials now effectively have direct veto power over the pricing policies of . . . foreign companies. Dumping law constitutes potential political price controls. . . .[6]

In sum, application of AD law makes the playing field less competitive when interests of consumers of dumped merchandise are considered.

C. Predation?

What about predation, where an exporter tries to drive competitors in an importing country out of business and subsequently raise prices? AD law holds the exporter's conduct unfair, and thus affords protection to its competitors. But, the law is clumsy. Because it neglects the efficiency — specifically, the cost structure — of the exporter, it confuses predatory and non-predatory behavior. As long as the exporter's marginal revenue from sales in the importing country exceed its marginal cost of production, the exporter is behaving in an economically rational fashion.

Further, an exporter selling merchandise in an importing country at a price above its average variable cost of production is not engaging in predatory behavior. Protecting the exporter's competitors from a rational, non-predatory exporter means competitors are not challenged to reduce their cost structures to remain competitive with the exporter. The development of a perfectly or nearly-perfectly competitive market in the importing country is throttled, and consumers are denied the benefit of lower prices:

> [i]n using the predation rationale for AD, purportedly the interests of consumers are being advanced, not those of import-competing firms. Yet in the absence of successful predation, the imposition of AD duties can only harm domestic consumers. As AD actions cause exporters to recoil from the foreign market, competitive pressures are diminished and domestic prices move upward. It is rather paradoxical that vigilant and enthusiastic application of AD by policy officials tends to promote the result that it is supposed to combat under the predation justification: monopoly pricing.[7]

In brief, predation is not a persuasive economic argument in favor of retaining AD laws.

Put differently, AD law ought to be grounded on microeconomic theory. It ought to draw on the theory of the cost structure of a firm, and isolate and

---

[6] James Bovard, The Fair Trade Fraud 108 (1991). *But see* Greg Mastel & Andrew Szamosszegi, Leveling the Playing Field: Antidumping and the U.S. Steel Industry 35-45, 47-51 (1999).

[7] Bernard M. Hoekman & Michael P. Leidy, *Antidumping and Market Disruption: The Incentive Effects of Antidumping Laws*, in The Multilateral Trading System: Analysis and Options for Change 155, 162 (Robert M. Stern ed., 1993).

sanction predation cases. GATT Article VI, the WTO *Antidumping Agreement*, and U.S. implementing legislation fail this criterion. Hence, the 1983 statement of the Court of Appeals for the Federal Circuit in *Smith-Corona Group v. United States* remains true:

> Antidumping duties are imposed on the basis of differences in value, *not* differences in cost. The importation of foreign merchandise can occur at a price greater than cost, yet *still generate liability* for an antidumping duty. The language of the statute would impose a duty on a foreign producer who "eats" either costs or profits in the American market relative to the home market. Thus, cost criteria alone will not redress the full margin of dumping to which Congress sought to attach an antidumping duty. Value must be considered under the statute.
>
> . . . .
>
> Congress sought to afford the domestic manufacturer strong protection against dumping, seeming to indicate that the Secretary [of Commerce] *should err in favor of protectionism.*[8]

Of course, whether this kind of reform — or revolution — in AD law will occur dubious.

D. Repeal?

Skepticism about the economic effects of AD law prompts arguments for its repeal. Four lines of attack exist. First, AD law is redundant. The *Robinson-Patman Act* proscribes price discrimination. Section 2 of the *Sherman Act* outlaws predatory pricing. This redundancy violates the national treatment clause of GATT Article III. AD law does not apply to the domestic context, *i.e.*, a domestic company engaged in price discrimination or predatory pricing only in its home country may run afoul of antitrust, but not AD, law. Of course, a rebuttal is AD law is deliberately designed as an alternative to antitrust laws governing price discrimination and, for that matter, predation:

> [o]ver time, antidumping policy and antitrust policy have diverged strikingly. Antidumping law and policy have evolved along a path of ever-increasing protection for U.S. firms from imports and decreasing concern for consumers and the economy as a whole. Antitrust law relating to predatory pricing, at least in recent decades, has taken a path of increasing concern for consumers and the economy as a whole and decreasing concern for firms suffering intense competition.
>
> Antidumping law no longer acts primarily against predatory pricing. It acts against international price discrimination (sales at a lower price in the United States than in the home country of the exporter) and sales below cost, regardless of whether the sales are predatory or not. Yet, the relevant provisions of the antitrust laws prohibit only predatory pricing; they do not prohibit selling below cost or price discrimination analogous to that prohibited by the antidumping laws except in cases where it is predatory.

---

[8] 713 F.2d 1568, 1575-76 (Fed. Cir. 1983), *cert. denied*, 465 U.S. 1022 (1984) (emphasis added).

This difference is important. Predatory pricing is detrimental to economic welfare because it leads to monopolies, which cause economic inefficiency and raise concerns about social equity. It seldom occurs, however, because it is rarely a profitable strategy and is usually not possible. By contrast, non-predatory price discrimination and sales below cost generally provide net benefits to the country receiving the lower price, and both are relatively common. Moreover, seldom do cases of price discrimination or selling below cost have anything to do with predatory pricing.[9]

Curiously, on the subject of below costs sales, a 1961 GATT *Report of Group of Exports* concluded selling imported merchandise at a loss to obtain a foothold in an importing country market does not constitute dumping under Article VI.[10] Nonetheless, the point is AD law is a practical and political alternative necessary in a world in which cross-border price discrimination is possible because of protection in home markets.

The second line of economic attack is AD law is unnecessary. Injury to an industry in an importing country caused by imports can be addressed by safeguard actions under GATT Article XIX. They condone assistance to companies and workers who suffer from fair foreign competition. Applying it in the context of dumping is legitimate because dumping is not necessarily unfair. One rebuttal to this line of attack is in practice adjustment assistance is difficult to obtain and meager in amount.

Third, AD law cannot address the source of the problem of alleged unfair pricing. While AD law may serve as a bargaining chip to pry open a closed foreign market, its central aim is not to dismantle the duties and NTBs in an exporter's home market that ensure market segmentation. If these barriers are removed, then 1 of the 3 necessary and sufficient conditions for dumping would not exist, hence dumping would be impossible. But, Section 301 of the *Trade Act of 1974*, not AD law, is the unilateral tool to compel market access. Of course, use of Section 301 is constrained by the GATT—WTO regime.

Fourth, AD law creates one of two perverse incentives for an exporter. To minimize the risk of being named a respondent in an AD action, it may reduce exports and increase home-market sales. In turn, the price of its merchandise in the importing country may rise, thereby reducing competitive pressure on producers in that country, while the price of its merchandise in its home country falls. In this instance, AD law thus distorts marketing decisions. Alternatively, if the importing country represents a significant market, the exporter may relocate its production facilities to that importing country. Here, AD law distorts decisions about foreign direct investment (FDI). As one skeptic puts it, "[e]conomic xenophobia is the foundation of U.S. antidumping law."[11]

However, this lesson is akin to being told "rain is wet" when what is needed is advice on the nearest umbrella vendor. AD law persists, indeed thrives. The

---

[9] CONGRESSIONAL BUDGET OFFICE MEMORANDUM, A REVIEW OF U.S. ANTIDUMPING AND COUNTERVAILING-DUTY LAW AND POLICY 2-3 (1994).

[10] GATT, *Report of Group of Exports, Antidumping and Countervailing Duties* at 11 (1961), *reprinted at* B.I.S.D. (9th Supp.) 194-201, at 199 (1961) (adopted 27 May 1960).

[11] BOVARD, *supra* note 6, at 107.

call for repeal is quixotic. For approximately a century — long before GATT entered into force — the international trading community condemned dumping. On 4 major occasions in the 20th century (and countless less heralded opportunities), GATT contracting parties had the chance to ban AD law: in 1947 (when GATT was finalized), 1964-67 (when the Kennedy Round *AD Code* was drafted), 1974-79 (when the Tokyo Round *AD Code* was reached) and 1986-94 (when the WTO *Antidumping Agreement* was produced). Each time, they affirmed dumping as an unfair, and use of AD duties as a remedy.

That is not surprising, as AD law pre-dates modern multilateral trade law. Canada appears to have enacted the first AD legislation in 1903. (Possibly, the *Wilson Bill of 1894* (extended in 1897), in the U.S., qualifies, as it concerned discriminatory pricing of imports. But, it authorized CVDs, not AD duties, in the event of bounty dumping, which referred to government subsidies.) In 1916, the U.S. enacted an *Antidumping Act* (which, roughly 90 years later, the WTO ruled illegal). In the 1920s, the League of Nations gave some attention to AD law, but hardly took steps to curtail or eliminate it. In its proposal for an *ITO Charter*, the U.S. offered a draft text, which, with modification, became GATT Article VI.

Manifestly, AD law has a long history, little of which is characterized by serious, widespread efforts to abolish it. Whether AD law is economically justified is irrelevant. The practical inquiry is whether meaningful circumscribing of that law, to minimizing the risk of protectionist abuse, is possible. Trade negotiators generally dodge that question. They permit ambiguities in applicable texts, which petitioners exploit to use AD law as an NTB. Decades ago, this situation was anticipated. In the 1946 London Preparatory Conference, GATT drafters, including the delegate from the United Kingdom, articulated concern the AD remedy would become a NTB to trade. Periodically thereafter, such worries have been expressed but not assuaged.

Chapter 28

PROCEDURES

We are not here to laugh.

> —Charles de Gaulle (1890-1970), *in*, THE INDEPENDENT (London),
> 21 April 1990

DOCUMENTS SUPPLEMENT ASSIGNMENT

1. *Havana Charter* Article 34
2. GATT Article VI
3. WTO *Antidumping Agreement* Articles 3, 5, 14, 17
4. *NAFTA* Chapter 19
5. Relevant provisions in other FTAs

I. THE PERIOD OF INVESTIGATION

A. The May 2000 WTO *Recommendation*

Neither Article VI of GATT nor Article 5:2 of the WTO *Antidumping Agreement* specifies the period of investigation (POI) in an antidumping (AD) or countervailing duty (CVD) case. Yet, in every case, the POI is critical. Data on alleged dumping, subsidization, and injury or threat of injury are collected relating to a POI. Selection of the starting and ending dates in the POI can strengthen, or destroy, claim. If the claim is successful, then the POI also is the basis for a remedial duty, both in the sense of the timing of assessment of the duty and scope of merchandise on which the duty is imposed.

In May 2000, the WTO adopted a *Recommendation Concerning the Periods of Data Collection for Anti-Dumping Investigations*. The *Recommendation* sets 12 months as the normal POI in a dumping margin investigation, but in no instance less than 6 months. What should the POI be when investigating alleged unlawful subsidization? For injury or threat investigations, the *Recommendation* calls for a POI of at least 3 years, and an overlap between this period and the POI in a dumping margin investigation. Thus, the most recent 12-month, and 3-year, period from which reliable data are attainable are, in practice, the POIs in most dumping margin and injury or threat investigations. Why is a longer period needed in an injury or threat investigation? The answer is more economic variables are studied in it than in a dumping margin inquiry, which involves prices.

The *Recommendation* explains a WTO Member is not supposed to collect data on dumping relating to the time after initiating a dumping margin investigation. However, some Members collect post-initiation data on injury or threat. Why? Might the answer lie in a time lag between dumping as a cause of injury or threat and the manifestation of deleterious effects of dumping? If an investigation takes 12-18 months, then limiting injury or threat data to the pre-initiation period might understate the true effects of dumping. However, might post-initiation data be distorted by the effect of the investigation itself in the market for subject merchandise or a foreign like product?

B. Positive Evidence, Selecting Particular Periods, and the 2005 *Mexico Rice* Case

WTO APPELLATE BODY REPORT, *MEXICO — DEFINITIVE ANTI-DUMPING MEASURES ON BEEF AND RICE, COMPLAINT WITH RESPECT TO RICE*
WT/DS295/AB/R (adopted 20 December)

I. Introduction

. . . .

2. The Mexican Rice Council filed an anti-dumping petition on 2 June 2000 with the Ministry of Commerce and Industrial Development ("SECOFI"), Mexico's investigating authority at that time. The investigation was initiated in December 2000 by the Ministry of Economy ("*Economía*"), which succeeded SECOFI as Mexico's investigating authority. The notice of initiation, a copy of the petition and attachments thereto, and the investigation questionnaire were sent to the Government of the United States and to the two exporters that were specifically identified in the petition as the "exporters," Producers Rice Mill, Inc. ("Producers Rice") and Riceland Foods, Inc. ("Riceland"). Two additional exporters, The Rice Company and Farmers Rice Milling Company ("Farmers Rice"), came forward following the initiation of the investigation and before the preliminary determination, and requested copies of the questionnaire.

3. The period of investigation for the purpose of the dumping determination was 1 March to 31 August 1999. For the purpose of the injury determination, *Economía* collected data for the period March 1997 through August 1999, but based its analysis on the data for 1 March to 31 August for the years 1997, 1998, and 1999 and issued its final affirmative determination on 5 June 2002. *Economía* found that Farmers Rice and Riceland had not been dumping during the period of investigation and consequently imposed a zero per cent duty on these exporters. With respect to The Rice Company, *Economía* determined a dumping margin of 3.93 per cent and imposed a duty in that amount. *Economía* also imposed on the remaining United States exporters of the subject merchandise, including Producers Rice, a duty of 10.18 per cent, calculated on the basis of the facts available.

V. Economía's Injury Determination

A. *The Period of Investigation and the Terms of Reference*

147. . . . The investigation [by *Economía*] was initiated on 11 December 2000, 15 months after the end of the period of investigation. Final anti-dumping measures were imposed on 5 June 2002, just less than three years after the end of the period of investigation.

. . . .

B. *The Use of a Period of Investigation Ending in August 1999 and the Criterion of Positive Evidence*

. . . .

159. The Panel found that, by choosing to base its determination of injury on a period of investigation that ended more than 15 months before the initiation of the investigation, Mexico failed to comply with the obligation to make a determination of injury based on positive evidence. As a consequence, the Panel found that Mexico acted inconsistently with Articles 3.1, 3.2, 3.4, and 3.5 of the *Anti-Dumping Agreement*. . . .

160. Mexico challenges the Panel's findings regarding *Economía's* use of a period of investigation ending in August 1999. . . . According to Mexico, the Panel erred in finding that there is an "inherent real-time link" between the investigation and the data on which it is based. Mexico alleges that this "real-time link" requirement is inconsistent with the option of using a past period as the period of investigation. Mexico also argues that the Panel contradicts itself because the Panel acknowledged that it is impossible that the period of investigation used for purposes of data collection coincide exactly with the time period in which the investigating authority conducts its investigation. For Mexico, the content of Article 3.1 of the *Anti-Dumping Agreement* does not focus on how remote the investigation period is, but on the applicability of the data used.

. . . .

162. The Panel considered that the [May 2000] recommendation adopted by the Committee on Anti-Dumping Practices — the *Recommendation Concerning the Periods of Data Collection for Anti-Dumping Investigations* (the "*Recommendation*") — provides useful support for the correct interpretation of the obligations found in the text of the *Anti-Dumping Agreement*. . . .

. . . .

164. The Panel described "positive evidence" as evidence that is relevant and pertinent with respect to the issue to be decided, and that has the characteristics of being inherently reliable and creditworthy. The Panel was of the view that, under the positive evidence criterion of Article 3.1, the question whether the information at issue constituted "positive evidence" — that is to say, was relevant, pertinent, reliable, and creditworthy — had to be assessed with respect to the current situation.

165. We agree with the Panel that evidence that is not relevant or pertinent to the issue to be decided is not "positive evidence." We also agree with the Panel that relevance or pertinence must be assessed with respect to the existence of injury caused by dumping at the time the investigation takes place. Under Article VI of the GATT 1994 and its "application" in the *Anti-Dumping Agreement*, the conditions for imposing an anti-dumping duty — injury caused by dumping — should obtain at that time. Article VI:2 of the GATT 1994 provides that anti-dumping duties are imposed "to offset or prevent" dumping. The term "offset" suggests that the scheme established in Article VI of the GATT 1994, and applied through the provisions of the *Anti-Dumping Agreement*, fulfils a corrective function: Members are permitted to take corrective measures in order to counter the injurious situation created by dumping. Under the logic of this corrective scheme, the imposition of anti-dumping duties is justified to the extent that they respond to injury caused by dumping. To use the Panel's terminology, anti-dumping duties "counterbalance[]" injury caused by dumping. Because the conditions to impose an anti-dumping duty are to be assessed with respect to the current situation, the determination of whether injury exists should be based on data that provide indications of the situation prevailing when the investigation takes place.

166. This, of course, does not imply that investigating authorities are not allowed to establish a period of investigation that covers a past period. . . . [T]he Panel did not state that the *Anti-Dumping Agreement* requires a coincidence in time between the investigation and the data used therein. On the contrary, the Panel recognized that "it is well established that the data on the basis of which [the determination that dumped imports cause injury] is made may be based on a past period, known as the period of investigation." In order to determine whether injury caused by dumping exists when the investigation takes place, "historical data" may be used. We agree with the Panel, however, that more recent data is likely to provide better indications about current injury.

167. We agree with Mexico that using a remote investigation period is not *per se* a violation of Article 3.1. In our view, however, the Panel did not set out such a principle, as its findings relate to the specific circumstances of this case. The Panel was satisfied that, in this specific case, a *prima facie* case was established that the information used by *Economía* did not provide reliable indications of current injury and, therefore, did not meet the criterion of positive evidence in Article 3.1 of the *Anti-Dumping Agreement*. The Panel arrived at this conclusion on the basis of several factors. The Panel attached importance to the existence of a 15-month gap between the end of the period of investigation and the initiation of the investigation, and a gap of almost three years between the end of the period of investigation and the imposition of final anti-dumping duties. However, these temporal gaps were not the only circumstances that the Panel took into account. The Panel, as trier of the facts, gave weight to other factors: (i) the period of investigation chosen by *Economía* was that proposed by the petitioner; (ii) Mexico did not establish that practical problems necessitated this particular period of investigation; (iii) it was not established that updating the information was not possible; (iv) no attempt was made to update the information; and (v) Mexico did not provide any reason — apart from the allegation that it is Mexico's general practice to accept the

period of investigation submitted by the petitioner -why more recent information was not sought. Thus, it is not only the remoteness of the period of investigation, but also these other circumstances that formed the basis for the Panel to conclude that a *prima facie* case was established. In the light of the general assessment of these other circumstances carried out by the Panel as trier of the facts, we accept that a gap of 15 months between the end of the period of investigation and the initiation of the investigation, and another gap of almost three years between the end of the period of investigation and the imposition of the final anti-dumping duties, may raise real doubts about the existence of a sufficiently relevant nexus between the data relating to the period of investigation and current injury. Therefore, we have no reason to disturb the Panel's assessment that a *prima facie* case of violation of Article 3.1 was made out.

. . . .

169. Mexico also argues that the Panel erred because it based its finding that the period of investigation used by *Economía* was inconsistent with the *Anti-Dumping Agreement* on the *Recommendation.* . ., a non-binding document adopted by the Committee on Anti-Dumping Practices. The *Recommendation* stipulates, *inter alia*, that the period of data collection should end as close to the date of initiation of the investigation as is practicable. We disagree with Mexico's argument. The Panel took care to recall that this *Recommendation* is a "non-binding guide" that "does not add new obligations, nor detract from the existing obligations of Members under the [*Anti-Dumping Agreement*]." It appears to us that the Panel referred to the *Recommendation*, not as a legal basis for its findings, but simply to show that the *Recommendation*'s content was not inconsistent with its own reasoning. Doing so does not constitute an error of law. In any event, we note that the *Recommendation* was not a decisive factor that led the Panel to conclude that the criterion of "positive evidence" in Article 3.1 was not met.

. . . .

171. . . . . The Panel had to decide whether the information relating to a period of investigation ending in August 1999 constituted an appropriate basis for making a determination of injury. The issue before the Panel centred on the manner in which *Economía* conducted the injury analysis, not the interpretation of a specific provision of the *Anti-Dumping Agreement*. Furthermore, . . . the Panel expressed the view that the data on the basis of which a determination of injury caused by dumping is made may relate to a past period, to the extent this information is relevant with regard to the current situation. It appears to us that the Panel's view is compatible with Mexico's own reading of the *Anti-Dumping Agreement*, according to which using data relating to a past period does not, *per se*, entail a violation of that Agreement. For these reasons, we are of the view that Mexico's argument regarding Article 17.6(ii) of the *Anti-Dumping Agreement* is without merit.

172. Accordingly, we *uphold* the Panel's finding . . . that *Economía's* use of a period of investigation ending in August 1999 resulted in a failure to make a determination of injury based on "positive evidence" as required by Article 3.1 of the *Anti-Dumping Agreement*. As a result of this finding, we also *uphold*

the Panel's finding . . . that by choosing this period of investigation, Mexico acted inconsistently with Articles 3.2, 3.4, and 3.5 of that *Agreement*.

C. *The March-August Period*

173. We turn now to the issue whether the Panel erred in finding that, in limiting the injury analysis to the March-August period of 1997, 1998, and 1999, *Economía* failed to make a determination of injury that involves an "objective examination" as required by Article 3.1 of the *Anti-Dumping Agreement*.

174. For the purposes of examining the injury to the domestic industry, *Economía* collected data for a continuous period of three years covering 1997, 1998, and 1999. However, *Economía* limited its analysis to data for the months of March to August of these years; data from the period September to February of each of these years were disregarded. In the Panel's view, such an examination, made on the basis of an incomplete set of data and characterized by the selective use of certain data for the injury analysis, could not be "objective" within the meaning of Article 3.1 of the *Anti-Dumping Agreement*, unless a proper justification were provided. In this respect, the Panel noted that Mexico's only argument was that it was necessary to examine data relating only to the six months from March to August because this was also the six-month period chosen for the analysis of the existence of dumping. The Panel considered that this did not constitute a proper justification for ignoring half of the data concerning the state of the domestic industry. For the Panel, the *Anti-Dumping Agreement* does not require that "a period of investigation [for] the injury analysis should be chosen to fit the period of investigation for the dumping analysis in case the latter . . . covers a period of less than 12 months."

175. The Panel also underscored that, in the petition submitted in June 2000, the domestic producers suggested that the six-month period of March to August should be used because it reflected the period of highest import penetration. Thus, according to the Panel, this period would show the most negative side of the state of the domestic industry. . . . The Panel explained that, although *Economía* was discussing the imports of paddy rice — the raw material for the production of the subject long-grain white rice — *Economía* nevertheless "clearly accepted the link made between production of paddy rice and the imports of the final product which the applicant points out is mainly imported in the period March-August." Thus, the Panel noted that the Preliminary Determination referred to the petitioner's claim that the main import activity of the final product takes place within the period March to August, during which period "paddy rice is not harvested and for that reason this period adequately reflects the import activity."

176. The Panel found that the injury analysis of *Economía*, which was based on data covering only six months of each of the three years examined, did not allow for an "objective examination," as required by Article 3.1 of the *Anti-Dumping Agreement*, for two reasons: first, whereas the injury analysis was selective and provided only a part of the picture, no proper justification was provided by Mexico in support of this approach; and secondly, *Economía*

accepted the "period of investigation proposed by the applicants because it allegedly represented the period of highest import penetration and would thus show the most negative side of the state of the domestic industry." . . .

. . . .

180. The Panel expressed the view that, under Article 3.1, an injury analysis can be "objective" only "if it is based on data which provide an accurate and unbiased picture of what it is that one is examining." This view is consistent with the Appellate Body's statement in *US — Hot-Rolled Steel* [Appellate Body Report, *United States — Anti-Dumping Measures on Certain Hot-Rolled Steel Products from Japan*, WT/DS184/AB/R, (adopted 23 August 2001)] regarding the requirement to conduct an "objective examination" under Article 3.1 of the *Anti-Dumping Agreement*:

> [A]n "objective examination" requires that the domestic industry, and the effects of dumped imports, be investigated in an unbiased manner, without favouring the interests of any interested party, or group of interested parties, in the investigation. The duty of the investigating authorities to conduct an "objective examination" recognizes that the determination will be influenced by the objectivity, or any lack thereof, of the investigative process. (footnote omitted)

Therefore, the question to be decided is whether the Panel erred in finding that the data used by *Economía* in the injury analysis, which relate to the same six-month period in 1997, 1998, and 1999, did not provide an "accurate and unbiased picture" of the injury suffered by the domestic industry.

181. We note that the Panel's finding is based not only on *Economía's* selective use of the information gathered for the purpose of the injury analysis. Indeed, in reaching the conclusion that the data used by *Economía* did not provide an "accurate and unbiased picture," the Panel also relied on another factor: the acceptance by *Economía* of the period of investigation proposed by the petitioner, knowing that the petitioner proposed that period because it allegedly represented the period of highest import penetration. . . . [T]hese two factors, considered together, were sufficient to make out a *prima facie* case that the data used by *Economía* did not provide an "accurate and unbiased picture."

. . . .

183. In *US — Hot-Rolled Steel*, the Appellate Body stated that, from the definition of injury provided in footnote 9 of the *Anti-Dumping Agreement*, "[i]t emerges clearly . . . that the focus of an injury determination is the state of the 'domestic industry.'" We fail to see how, in the present case, the use of data relating to the whole year, as opposed to the March to August period, would have introduced "distortions" of the assessment of the "state of the domestic industry." Rather, . . . examining data relating to the whole year would result in a more accurate picture of the "state of the domestic industry" than an examination limited to a six-month period. Moreover, the explanation put forward by Mexico implies that the dumping determination and the injury determination are integrated. This is not the case; although injury and dumping must be linked by a causal relationship, these determinations are two separate operations relying on distinct data seeking to determine different

things. Accordingly, we see no reason to disagree with the Panel that the explanation provided by Mexico with respect to *Economía's* choice of a limited period of investigation for purposes of the injury analysis was not a "proper justification" sufficient to refute the *prima facie* case that the data used by *Economía* did not provide an "accurate and unbiased picture" of the state of the domestic industry. We therefore agree with the Panel that the data used by *Economía* in the injury analysis, relating to the March to August period of 1997, 1998, and 1999, did not provide an "accurate and unbiased picture" of the state of the domestic industry and, thus, did not result in an "objective examination" as required by Article 3.1. . . .

184. On appeal, Mexico's objections to the Panel's reasoning are not, in substance, different from the arguments it submitted before the Panel. Mexico argues that the proposition that the March to August period is the period of highest import penetration is an unsubstantiated assumption that reflects a "mere opinion." We disagree. In its reasoning, the Panel referred to the petitioner's position that the main import activity of long-grain white rice takes place within the March to August period — during which paddy rice is not harvested in Mexico — and that, for this reason, this period adequately reflects the import activity. Making such a reference is not, in our view, making an unsubstantiated assumption that reflects a "mere opinion."

185. Nor can we accept Mexico's argument that the Panel created a presumption that an injury analysis based on data relating to only parts of years is not objective. We note, first, that the Panel underscored that its "ruling should not be read as to imply that there could never be any convincing and valid reasons for examining only parts of years." Secondly, the Panel's finding is not based exclusively on the fact that *Economía* was selective as regards the data it used in the injury analysis. It is the combination of this factor with another — "the acceptance of a period of investigation proposed by the applicants because it allegedly represented the period of highest import penetration and would thus show the most negative side of the state of the domestic industry" — that led the Panel to consider that a *prima facie* violation of Article 3.1 had been established. Mexico had an opportunity to refute the *prima facie* case by presenting a "proper justification" for the use of the March to August period; however, it failed to do so.

186. Mexico submits that the methodology used was not flawed because six-month periods with the same structure were compared. We agree with Mexico that it was not improper for *Economía* to make comparisons with previous years. The Panel, however, did not find that *Economía* could not make comparisons with previous periods in the injury analysis. The Panel discussed a different question, namely, whether *Economía's* methodology was flawed because segments of years were compared instead of full years.

187. . . . Mexico also contends that the domestic production of long-grain white rice is independent of the production cycles of paddy rice. . . . Mexico questions what it alleges are the premises on which the Panel based its assertion that the period March to August shows the most negative side of the state of the domestic industry. Mexico's allegations refer to facts concerning import patterns of long-grain white rice and the relationship between the production of long-grain white rice and that of paddy rice. Contrary to what Mexico

suggests, the Panel's reasoning was not centred on an assessment of the import patterns of long-grain white rice or the relationship between the production of long-grain white rice and that of paddy rice. On these questions of fact, the Panel did not make any finding, because it considered it was unnecessary to do so. Rather, the Panel's position was based on the findings that *Economía* selected the same period of investigation as that put forward by the petitioner, and that the petitioner proposed this period because the months March to August allegedly represent the period of highest import penetration. . . . [T]he Panel did not err by taking into account this factor in its analysis.

188. For these reasons, we *uphold* the Panel's findings . . . that, in limiting the injury analysis to the March to August period of 1997, 1998, and 1999, Mexico failed to make a determination of injury that involves an "objective examination," as required by Article 3.1 of the *Anti-Dumping Agreement*. Accordingly, we also *uphold* the Panel's findings . . . that, in limiting the injury analysis to the March to August period of 1997, 1998, and 1999, Mexico acted inconsistently with Article 3.5 of that *Agreement*.

C. Different Trade Remedies and the 2005 *Nucor* Case

What happens if, during the POI in an AD or CVD investigation, a different trade remedy is applied, such as a safeguard action under the Escape Clause (Section 201 of the *Trade Act of 1974*, as amended)? The *Nucor* case deals with this issue.

NUCOR CORPORATION v. UNITED STATES
United States Court of Appeals for the Federal Circuit
414 F.3d 1331, 1334-42 (2005)

BRYSON, CIRCUIT JUDGE.

The appellants, United States Steel Corporation and Nucor Corporation, are domestic steel producers. Along with other domestic producers, they petitioned the International Trade Commission to investigate imports of cold-rolled steel products to determine if those imports were causing material injury to the domestic steel industry. *See* 19 U.S.C. §§ 1671d(b)(1), 1673d(b)(1). Upon completion of its investigations, the Commission issued final determinations that the domestic steel industry was not materially injured by reason of the imports. The appellants and other domestic producers filed an action in the Court of International Trade challenging the Commission's negative material injury determinations. The Court of International Trade sustained the Commission's determinations. *Nucor Corp. v. United States*, 318 F. Supp. 2d 1207 (Ct. Int'l Trade 2004). U.S. Steel and Nucor appeal. We affirm.

I

Section 201 of the *Trade Act of 1974*, 19 U.S.C. § 2251(a), authorizes the President to take appropriate action to protect domestic industries from substantial injury due to increased quantities of imports. In June 2001, the President requested that the Commission conduct a *Section 201* investigation of steel products imported between January 1997 and June 2001. Following its investigation, the Commission determined that cold-rolled steel products "were being imported into the United States in such increased quantities as to be a substantial cause of serious injury to the domestic industry" and recommended that safeguard tariffs be imposed on steel products. Consequently, in March 2002 the President imposed safeguard tariffs on steel products, including cold-rolled steel products, of 30 percent for the first year, 24 percent for the second year, and 18 percent for the third year.

In September 2001, a number of domestic steel producers petitioned the Commission to conduct the antidumping and countervailing duty investigations that gave rise to this case. The Commission's antidumping and countervailing duty investigations, which were directed to certain cold-rolled steel products, overlapped the *Section 201* investigation and the subsequent imposition of tariffs on cold-rolled steel products.

. . . .

The Commission issued final determinations on all of the subject investigations in September and November 2002. In those determinations, the Commission found that the "*Section 201* investigation and the President's remedy fundamentally altered the U.S. market for many steel products, including cold-rolled steel." The Commission found that imports of those products declined sharply and that domestic prices increased significantly in the period after the imposition of the *Section 201* tariffs. The Commission further reported that, according to purchasers, the reduction in imports due to the *Section 201* tariffs had led to "higher prices, supply shortages, and some broken or renegotiated contracts." Based on the results of its investigation, the Commission concluded that the *Section 201* relief was the principal reason for the sharp decline in imports near the end of the investigation period. The Commission further found that, as of the conclusion of the antidumping and countervailing duty proceedings, "the domestic cold-rolled steel products industry is neither materially injured nor threatened with material injury by reason of subject imports." Because the Commission determined that the domestic industry was not suffering present material injury or a threat of material injury as a result of the subject imports, no antidumping or countervailing duties were imposed.

In the Court of International Trade, the domestic producers argued that the Commission's negative material injury determinations were flawed because, among other reasons, the Commission failed to consider the effects of imports in the early portion of the investigation period; it failed to make a determination regarding the significance of importers' underselling on domestic producers; and it erred in its determinations regarding the volume of imports and their impact on domestic prices. . . . [T]he trial court sustained the Commission's determinations.

[Omitted are the portions of the Federal Circuit's decision on the (1) significance of underselling by importers, (2) volume of imports, and (3) impact of volume on prices. On these issues, the Federal Circuit upheld the CIT.]

II

U.S. Steel and Nucor argue that the Commission erred by failing to consider the effects of products imported prior to the imposition of *Section 201* tariffs when it determined that the domestic industry was not suffering current material injury because of imports. In particular, they contend that the requirement in 19 U.S.C. §§ 1671d(b)(1) and 1673d(b)(1) that the Commission determine whether the domestic industry is suffering material injury "by reason of imports" mandated that the Commission consider the effects of imports throughout the period of investigation and not confine its consideration to the effects of current imports. Because, in the appellants' view, the Commission based its material injury determinations solely on current imports, the appellants argue that the Commission's material injury determination was legally flawed.

The trial court held that the Commission had reasonably construed the phrase "by reason of imports" in 19 U.S.C. §§ 1671d(b)(1) and 1673d(b)(1) to allow it to focus its investigation on the most recent import data. The court explained that the Commission had investigated imports for the entire period of investigation. Although the Commission had focused mainly on current imports, it had also considered imports during the early portion of that period in assessing the volume of imports, their effects on price, and the overall impact of imports on the domestic industry. The Commission's particular focus on current imports, according to the trial court, was "in accord with the remedial purpose of duties which are intended merely to prevent future harm to the domestic industry by reason of unfair imports that are presently causing material injury." The court also found that although the Commission did not state explicitly that past imports were not causing present material injury, it implicitly made that determination. According to the court, the Commission properly assessed the effects of imports early in the investigation period in light of the evidence that there was a steep decline in imports near the end of the investigation period.

Sections 1671d(b)(1) and 1673d(b)(1) state that the Commission must determine whether a domestic industry "is materially injured . . . by reason of imports." They do not specify how the Commission should weigh imports early in the period of investigation as compared to imports closer to the date of decision, nor do they provide any guidance as to the considerations that should influence the weight the Commission assigns to data from different portions of the investigation period. Because the statutes are silent on those issues, and because the Commission, together with the Commerce Department, is charged with the responsibility of administering the antidumping and countervailing duty statutes, the Commission's construction of those statutes is entitled to deference under the principles of *Chevron U.S.A. Inc. v. Natural Res. Def. Council, Inc.*, 467 U.S. 837, 81 L. Ed. 2d 694, 104 S. Ct. 2778 (1984). . . .

We agree with the trial court that it was reasonable for the Commission to interpret the statutory language to permit it to accord different weight to imports during different portions of the period of investigation depending on the facts of each case. In particular, the Commission acted reasonably in construing the statutory language to permit it to focus on the most recent imports and pricing data. That construction is reasonable for several reasons. First, the purpose of antidumping and countervailing duty laws is remedial, not punitive or retaliatory, see *Chaparral Steel Co. v. United States*, 901 F.2d 1097, 1103-04 (Fed. Cir. 1990), and current data typically is the most pertinent in determining whether remedial measures are necessary, see *Chr. Bjelland Seafoods A/S v. United States*, 19 Ct. Int'l Trade 35, 44 n. 22 (1995). Second, Section 1677(7)(B)(i) provides that, in making the material injury determination required by Sections 1671d(b)(1) and 1673d(b)(1), the Commission shall consider, *inter alia*, the effects of the subject imports on domestic producers. Section 1677(7)(C)(iii) in turn requires the Commission, in determining the impact of the subject imports on domestic producers, to "evaluate all relevant economic factors which have a bearing on the state of the industry in the United States." As the trial court explained, in most cases the most recent imports will have the greatest relevance to the current state of the domestic industry. Third, the Commission has broad discretion with respect to the period of investigation that it selects for purposes of making a material injury determination. As the Court of International Trade has explained, because the statute "does not expressly command the Commission to examine a particular period of time . . . the Commission has discretion to examine a period that most reasonably allows it to determine whether a domestic industry is injured by [less than fair value] imports." *Kenda Rubber Indus. Co. v. United States*, 10 C.I.T. 120, 630 F. Supp. 354, 359 (Ct. Int'l Trade 1986). Since the Commission has broad discretion to choose the most appropriate period of time for its investigation, it would be nonsensical to hold that once the Commission has chosen an investigation period, it is required to give equal weight to imports throughout the period it has selected. For these reasons, both this court and the Court of International Trade have typically upheld the Commission's exercise of its discretion to focus on imports during particular portions of the investigation period, especially imports during the most recent portion of that period. See *Chaparral Steel*, 901 F.2d at 1103; *Taiwan Semiconductor Indus. Ass'n v. United States*, 93 F. Supp. 2d 1283, 1294 n. 13, 105 F. Supp. 2d 1363, 24 Ct. Int'l Trade 220 (Ct. Int'l Trade 2000), *aff'd*, 266 F.3d 1339 (Fed. Cir. 2001); *Angus Chem. Co. v. United States*, 20 C.I.T. 1255, 944 F. Supp. 943, 947-48 (Ct. Int'l Trade 1996), *aff'd*, 140 F.3d 1478 (Fed. Cir. 1998).

In this case, the fact that *Section 201* tariffs were imposed during the period of investigation made the recent data far more probative than earlier data as to whether the industry was suffering present material injury as a result of imports. The Commission found that the *Section 201* relief "was having a major impact in the U.S. market for cold-rolled steel and was the overwhelming factor in the sharp decline in subject imports during the most recent period examined." Substantial evidence in the record supports that finding, and the appellants do not challenge the trial court's determination in that regard. Because the imposition of *Section 201* tariffs had such a dramatic impact on the industry, it was reasonable for the Commission to conclude that the most recent data was the most reliable indicator of whether the industry was suffering material injury as a result of the subject imports and whether the imposition of additional duties would be consistent with the remedial purposes of the antidumping and countervailing duty laws.

The appellants argue that the Commission did not simply assign greater weight to current imports, but that it improperly focused exclusively on current imports and failed to give any consideration to whether the domestic industry was suffering material injury by reason of past imports. They contend that the record does not support the trial court's conclusion that the Commission examined imports over the entire investigation period in making its determination that the subject imports were not causing present material injury.

In making the statutory determination that the domestic cold-rolled steel industry was not suffering material injury by reason of the subject imports, the Commission explained that it focused principally on "the current volume of subject imports and the increase in domestic prices in 2002." The Commission concluded that the present condition of the domestic industry was not "attributable in any material respect to the current subject imports" and that "subject imports are not adversely affecting domestic prices to a significant degree." Its ultimate finding was that there was no "material injury currently being experienced by the domestic industry . . . by reason of the subject imports," *i.e.*, the imports during the period of investigation. The Commission thus explained that its material injury determination, although focusing mainly on current imports, was not restricted solely to current imports but encompassed all "subject imports" during the investigation period.

The appellants do not argue that past imports continued to cause material injury at the end of the investigation period because of accumulated inventories. Nor could they, as the evidence showed that by the end of that period there were widespread supply shortages in the industry, and many producers had been placed on allocation. Instead, the appellants argue that the Commission ignored the continuing price effects of earlier imports resulting from the fact that the prices set in contracts made earlier in the period of investigation were generally "locked in" at the time of contract formation and continued in effect throughout the later portions of the investigation period. Contrary to the appellants' contention, however, the Commission took those facts into consideration; it simply did not find that they were sufficiently important to alter the ultimate material injury determination. Thus, the Commission noted that past imports "continue[d] to have an effect on the industry's contract prices negotiated before the *Section 201* relief was effective," but it nonetheless concluded that imports were not adversely affecting domestic prices to a significant degree "based on the current volume of subject imports and the increase in domestic prices in 2002." In light of that statement and other portions of the Commission's opinion, the trial court ruled that although the Commission did not explicitly state that earlier imports were not causing present material injury, it was reasonable to infer that the Commission so concluded. In particular, the trial court rested its conclusion with respect to that issue on what it referred to as the Commission's "continued discussion of the effects that subject imports entered earlier in the [period of investigation] had on the domestic industry and its ultimate conclusion that the domestic industry was not suffering present material injury."

We concur in the trial court's analysis. The Commission may not have stated explicitly that earlier imports were not causing material injury, but that conclusion was implicit in its analysis. The clear implication of the Commission's findings on that issue is that the prices fixed by contracts that were negotiated earlier in the investigation period may have suppressed the overall average price of domestic products throughout the period, but in light of the decrease in the current volume of imports and the increase in domestic prices in 2002, the effect of those past imports was not significant. We therefore uphold the trial court's decision with regard to the adequacy of the Commission's treatment of the subject imports from early in the investigation period.

II. STEPS IN AN AD OR CVD CASE

A. Overview

The principal American statute covering antidumping (AD) and countervailing duty (CVD) law is the *Tariff Act of 1930*, as amended. Clearly, the statute predates GATT. Many of the amendments made to the *1930 Act* have helped conform U.S. law to GATT—WTO obligations. Conversely, many American negotiating positions in multilateral trade talks have been an effort to legislate, *i.e.*, export, provisions of the *1930 Act* overseas, and thereby ensure new WTO accords are as close as possible to extant U.S. law.

The CVD provisions are set forth in 19 U.S.C. §§ 1671 *et seq.* The AD provisions are in 19 U.S.C. §§ 1673 *et seq.* The overlap intimates commonality among AD and CVD law. Procedures for filing a petition and standing, as well as by preliminary and final determinations, evidence the correctness of that intimation.

By way of synopsis, the *1930 Act* mandates assessment, imposition, and collection of AD or CVD duties after two final administrative determinations. Observe:

  i. "Assessment" refers to a determination of liability, in effect, the estimation of an AD duty or CVD.

  ii. "Imposition," as used in 19 U.S.C. § 1677a(c)(1(C), refers to calculation of the amount of the liability, *i.e.*, of the duty that is or will be levied because the DOC issued an AD or CVD order. Thus, "imposition" presumes issuance of an order, and estimation of the duties. *See, e.g.*, *Dupont Teijin Films U.S.A. v. United States*, 407 F.3d 1211, 1217 (Fed. Cir. 2005).

  iii. "Collection" refers to garnering the duty.

The conceptually distinct steps this terminology embodies should not imply a large time gap between issuance and imposition. As the U.S. Court of International Trade (CIT) said in the *Dupont Teijin Films* case, "it is reasonable for the Department [of Commerce] to consider a countervailing duty to be *'imposed' upon the issuance* of the countervailing duty order." *Dupont Teijin Films U.S.A. v. United States*, 297 F.Supp.2d 1367, 1373 (CIT 2003) (emphasis added), affirmed *Dupont Teijin Films U.S.A. v. United States*, 407 F.3d 1211, 1219 (Fed. Cir. 2005). Interestingly, this ruling is in the context of an adjustment to Export Price in a dumping margin calculation. The Court of Appeals upheld the CIT's interpretation that "imposed" requires issuance of a CVD before the CVD can be used to offset (*i.e.*, deducted from) Export Price in a dumping margin calculation.

Obviously, final determinations occur after preliminary determinations. That means in a U.S. AD or CVD investigation, the procedure is bifurcated into preliminary and final stages. Bifurcation also is true in another sense, namely, there are two federal authorities involved: the U.S. Department of Commerce (DOC) and the U.S. International Trade Commission (ITC). The DOC sits within the Executive Branch, and the Secretary of Commerce is a member of the President's Cabinet. Within the DOC, a division called "Import Administration" (or "IA") handles AD and CVD investigations. The ITC is an independent agency within the Executive Branch. It consists of 6 Commissioners, appointed by the President, with no more than three from one political party. In the event of a tie vote among Commissioners, the determination is deemed to be in favor of petitioners — a result injecting a pro-petitioner bias in AD and CVD injury determinations (and, for that matter, Section 201 Escape Clause cases, as the ITC also is responsible for them).

In both senses, bifurcation is not universal. Some WTO Members require preliminary and final determinations. Others use a unified procedure. In some WTO Members, there are two central governmental authorities involved in AD and CVD cases. In others, there is only one unit. Almost invariably, the ministry responsible for commerce or international trade (which, typically, is the same ministry) is involved. Whether bifurcated or unified, and whether one authorities or two, investigations are almost sure to be complex and contentious. What are the pros and cons of bifurcation?

In an AD case, the responsibility of the DOC is to determine whether the allegedly dumped imports, known as "subject merchandise" (*i.e.*, the "class or kind of merchandise subject to investigation," as they were called under pre-Uruguay Round law) is sold in the U.S. at less than fair value (LTFV). That is, the DOC makes preliminary and final determinations as to the magnitude of the dumping margin — the extent (if any) of cross-border price discrimination. In a CVD case, the DOC is charged with deciding whether a foreign exporter or producer is receiving (or received) an unlawful subsidy and, if so, the amount of that subsidy. The term "subject merchandise" in the CVD context refers also refers to imports under investigation, though the inquiry focuses on subsidization by the government of the home country of the exporter or producer, not dumping. As in an AD case, in a CVD case the renders a preliminary and final determination. In either kind of case, prior to a preliminary determination of dumping or subsidization, the DOC may be called upon to assess whether so-called "critical circumstances" (discussed later) exist.

In both AD and CVD investigations, the job of the ITC is to consider injury or threat thereof to a domestic (*i.e.*, U.S.) industry posed by subject merchandise. In rare instances, the ITC examines whether establishment of a domestic industry is materially retarded because of dumped or illegally subsidized merchandise. The ITC makes preliminary and final determinations as to whether subject merchandise materially injures or threatens to injure a U.S. industry, or materially retards its establishment.

Only if both the dumping margin or subsidization determination by the DOC and the injury determination by the ITC are affirmative is an AD or CVD order issued. The DOC is responsible for issuing the order, which it does to the U.S. Customs and Border Protection (CBP), known in the pre-9/11 era as the "Customs Service." The DOC issues an AD or CVD order to the CBP calling for the collection of a duty equal to the dumping margin or illegal subsidization rate. The CBP collects the duty on a company-specific basis on imports of subject merchandise.

Under pre-Uruguay Round law, an AD or CVD order remained in place, and duties were collected by the Customs Service, for an indefinite period. In the U.S., the average length tended to be a little over 8 years. Because of mandatory "Sunset Reviews," instigated under Article 11 of the WTO *Antidumping Agreement*, an order is presumed to terminate no later than 5 years of the date of its imposition. Other kinds of reviews, specifically "Administrative Reviews" and "Changed Circumstances Reviews," can lead to modification or termination of an AD or CVD order.

Overall, then, an AD or CVD case may be dissected into 10 procedural steps:

Step 1:	Filing an AD or CVD Petition.
Step 2:	Standing and Sufficiency Determination.
Step 3:	Preliminary ITC Injury Determination.
Step 4:	Preliminary DOC Dumping Margin or Subsidization Determination. (Possible "critical circumstances" allegation.)
Step 5:	Final DOC Dumping Margin or Subsidization Determination.
Step 6:	Final ITC Injury Determination.
Step 7:	Issuance of AD or CVD Order.
Step 8:	Reviews of AD or CVD Order.
Step 9:	Appeals (if any).
Step 10:	WTO Adjudication (if any).

Steps 1 through 7 are discussed in turn in detail below. The kinds of Reviews involved in Step 8 (Sunset, Administrative, and Changed Circumstances), and WTO controversies (especially about Sunset Reviews) are discussed briefly below. Steps 9 and 10 involve possibilities of:

    i.   Appeal to the U.S. Court of International Trade, and, thereafter, the Court of Appeals for the Federal Circuit. In rare instances, AD or CVD cases are appealed to the Supreme Court, which hardly ever accepts such appeals.

    ii.   appeal to a tribunal associated with a Regional Trade Agreement (RTA), such as a *NAFTA* Chapter 19 Panel (*i.e.*, a 3-member panel created pursuant to Chapter 19 of the *North American Free Trade Agreement*).

    iii.   An action arising under the *Dispute Settlement Understanding* (*DSU*).

The last two Steps are discussed briefly below.

At any point in an AD or CVD case, settlement may occur. If the petitioner withdraws its petition, then either the DOC or ITC may terminate the investigation. If the investigation was self-initiated, then the DOC has the discretion to terminate. Or, an investigation may be suspended because of settlement. Article 8 of the WTO *Antidumping Agreement* countenances undertakings to suspend investigations. Under what conditions does suspension occur?

In an AD case (pursuant to 19 U.S.C. § 1673c), the DOC may suspend an investigation if it reaches one of three kinds of agreement with exporters accounting for substantially all of the subject merchandise.

a. An agreement to cease exports of subject merchandise within 6 months of suspending the investigation. Essentially, the exporters exit the U.S. market.

b. An agreement to revise prices to eliminate completely all LTFV sales. In effect, exporters commit to change their pricing strategy in the U.S., which means raising the price of subject merchandise through a price undertaking.

c. An agreement to revise prices to eliminate completely the injurious effects of exports of subject merchandise on American producers. Again, the undertaking concerns boosting the price of subject merchandise.

Observe that unless the country of exportation is a non-market economy (NME), a promise to impose a quantitative restriction (*e.g.*, to limit exports of subject merchandise via a quota) would not suffice as a basis for suspension. In all instances, the DOC must be sure termination or suspension of an investigation is in the public interest and it is practicable to be monitored.

In a CVD case (pursuant to 19 U.S.C. § 1671c), the DOC may suspend an investigation based on one of three types of agreements with a foreign government, or with exporters accounting for substantially all imports of subject merchandise:

a. An agreement to eliminate the subsidy completely, or offset it completely within 6 months of suspension of the investigation.

b. An agreement to cease exportation of the subject merchandise within 6 months of suspension of the investigation.

c. An agreement to eliminate completely the injurious effects of subsidized exports (*e.g.*, through a quantitative restrictions, a possibility not available under AD law unless the country of exportation is an NME).

In both the AD and CVD contexts, the agreement to suspend an investigation is called a "Suspension Agreement." In effect, the Agreement is a contract involving the petitioner, respondent or respondent's home-country government, and DOC. The DOC promises to end an AD or CVD investigation, in exchange for changed behavior by the other side.

The DOC cannot enter into a Suspension Agreement without first publishing notice of its intent to suspend an investigation and giving interested parties an opportunity to comment. The DOC can decide not to accept a proposed Agreement, but then must explain why to the exporters involved and give them the chance (if practicable) to comment. If the DOC chooses to proceed with an Agreement, it must first issue an affirmative preliminary dumping margin or subsidy determination, and publish notice of the suspension. Even if the DOC elects to accept an Agreement, both sides — a domestic interested party, and exporters accounting for a significant proportion of exports of the subject merchandise — have 20 days after publication of the notice of the Agreement to call for continuation of the investigation. The DOC and ITC must honor this request.

The effect of a Suspension Agreement goes beyond termination of an investigation by the DOC into dumping or subsidization. The ITC, too, suspends its injury investigation. Moreover, the suspension of liquidation of entries of subject merchandise (which, as explained below, follows an affirmative preliminary dumping or subsidy determination) terminates. Any deposits of estimated AD duties or CVDs are refunded, and any bonds posted as security for these duties are released. The DOC is responsible for monitoring compliance with any Suspension Agreement, and an intentional violation of an Agreement is a civil offence punishable by fines.

B.   Steps 1 and 2: Filing a Petition, Standing, and Sufficiency

Technically, the DOC may initiate an AD or CVD investigation. However, self-initiated cases are rare. Section 609 of the *Trade and Tariff Act of 1984*, codified at 19 U.S.C. § 1673a(2) allows the DOC to monitor imports from additional supplier countries for up to 1 year to determine whether persistent dumping occurs with respect to a particular product and, in turn, whether it should self-initiate an AD investigation. (There is no analogous provision for "persistent subsidization" in CVD cases.) Nonetheless, in almost every instance, it is an "interested party" that files a petition. An "interested party" is one that acts "on behalf of" the allegedly affected U.S. industry and is defined in terms of the following categories of petitioners:

i.   A manufacturer, producer, or wholesaler in the U.S. of a like product.

ii. A certified or recognized union or group of workers that is representative of the affected industry.

iii. A trade or business association with a majority of members producing a like product.

iv. A coalition of firms, unions, or trade associations in which a majority of the individual members have standing.

v.   A coalition or trade association representative of processors, or processor and growers, in cases involving processed agricultural products.

An AD or CVD petition is filed simultaneously with the DOC and ITC. Within 20 days after filing, the DOC must determine whether the petition is legally sufficient to commence an investigation. For small and medium sized enterprises (SMEs), the DOC is required to give technical assistance in preparing and filing a petition. As a practical matter, counsel for petitioners is well-advised to meet informally with the DOC on a possible draft petition. At that juncture, the DOC cannot render a formal decision about the legal sufficiency of a draft, it may be able to provide useful tips as to how it might view certain aspects of that petition.

Observe that while the universe of "interested parties" is large, it is bounded. Individuals or groups not involved in producing a like product are excluded. For example, suppose the subject merchandise is personal computers. Producers of upstream components, such as semi-conductors (*i.e.*, chips), would not be "interested parties." Similarly, producers of downstream products, such as USB hubs, would not have standing as petitioners.

It is critical to appreciate the filing of a petition by a U.S. industry against a foreign exporter or manufacturer, targeting the goods of that foreign company, can have serious adverse effects for the company. At a minimum, it has a certain *in terrorem* effect. It can lead to the company agreeing quickly to raise its prices in the U.S. Indeed, an ulterior motive for filing a petition may be to coerce a foreign exporter or manufacturer into a tacit price cartel, the members of which are the petitioners (and, possibly, other foreign companies).

To provide some safety that an AD or CVD petition is a *bona fide* representation of the sentiments of a domestic industry, Article 5:4 of the WTO *Antidumping Agreement* contains two quantitative metrics to determine whether a petition is filed "by or on behalf of" that industry, or whether the petition would amount to protectionist abuse. They are called the "25 Percent Test" and the "50 Percent Test." Each Test must be satisfied for a petitioner to have standing. Both tests ensure the support of a critical mass of domestic producers in the importing country.

The DOC is responsible for administering these tests as part of its initial determination as to the legal sufficiency of a petition. Significantly, once standing is decided, it may not be challenged before the DOC (or ITC) as the case proceeds through the preliminary and final review steps. However, standing may be challenged in a subsequent court action.

Do the 25 Percent and 50 Percent Tests, which are designed to ensure a petition is supported by a domestic industry, gauge the common good, *i.e.*, the broad public interest? The answer is a clear "no." They measure industry interest, not the public interest. Might there be overlap between industry and public interest? That depends on the case, and the extent to which "industry" is defined to include at least some of the consumers of the subject merchandise.

The 25 Percent Test focuses on the absolute size, measured in terms of output of the domestic like product, of producers or workers supporting an AD or CVD petition. Under this Test, more than 25 percent of the total industry output — whether in support of the petition, in opposition to the petition, or abstaining (no view) — must be in favor of the petition. That is, producers expressing support for the petition must account for at least 25 percent of the total domestic production of the like domestic product, regardless of whether the output is made by a producer supporting or opposing the petition.

As for the 50 Percent Test, it focuses on the relative size of domestic producers (or workers) supporting versus opposing an AD or CVD petition.

Under this Test, more than 50 percent of the output of the domestic like product made by producers (or workers) that have a view (have taken a position) on the petition — whether in support of or in opposition to the petition — must be in favor of the petition. Producers who support the petition must account for more than 50 percent of the total output of the product made by those producers who either support or oppose the petition. Succinctly put, of the producers expressing a position on the petition, more producers must support than oppose it, otherwise the petition does not represent the industry.

Observe the 50 Percent Test measures support and opposition in terms of output of producers that "yes" or "no" to a petition. The total of supporters and opponents, in terms of output, may not equal the total output of the industry, because several producers may have no view on the petition (in effect, they abstain). Suppose the management of a particular company and the workers employed there take oppositional positions on a petition? Under the *Statement of Administrative Action* accompanying the WTO *Antidumping Agreement*, the DOC treats output of that firm as neither support for nor opposition to the petition. Moreover, if the 50 Percent Test is not satisfied (and assuming the 25 Percent Test is met), then DOC must poll the industry. In the event of such polling, the DOC has 40 days to determine whether to initiate an investigation.

As an example, suppose a petition alleges dumping or illegal subsidization of sugar from the European Union (EU). American sugar cane plantation owners in Florida file the petition, as do some Louisiana plantation owners. There is one plantation in Mississippi, on which field workers support the petition, but the owners do not. No sugar beet producer, from which sugar also is derived, agrees with the action. They are located in western states such as Wyoming. Assume American sugar (whether from cane or beet) is considered "like" the EU import, and total domestic (*i.e.*, American) output in the relevant period is 1 million tons. Output of producers supporting the petition is 400,000 tons. Of this figure, 50,000 tons are from the Mississippi plantation. Output of producers opposing the petition is 200,000 tons. Do the petitioners have standing?

The answer is "yes." The petitioners pass both Tests. Output from the Mississippi plantation does not count in favor of the petition, because of the split views between owners and management. By inference, 400,000 tons of output abstains, expressing no view on the petition. Accordingly, calculation of the 25 Percent Test is as follows:

$$= \frac{\text{Output of Petition Supporters}}{\text{Total Output of Domestic Industry}} = \frac{390,000}{1,000,000} = 39 \text{ percent}$$

The first Test is met, as the benchmark is at least 25 Percent. As for the 50 Percent Test, it is checked as follows:

$$= \frac{\text{Output of Petition Supporters}}{\text{Output of Petition Supporters } + \text{ Output of Petition Opponents}} = \frac{390,000}{390,000 \ + \ 200,000} = 66.1 \text{ percent}$$

This figure is more than 50 percent, the relevant threshold, hence the 50 Percent Test is passed. As both Tests are met, the petitioners have standing.

Observe from this example the location of the plantations is irrelevant, as is the interests of American sugar consumers. What matters is the vote in favor or against the petition, weighted by quantity of output. However, suppose owners of several Florida plantations are citizens of, or reside in, Brazil. Should their output be counted in favor of the petition, or might they be biased by virtue of their link to Brazil? Would the answer matter if Brazil, as part of *MERCOSUR*, had a free trade agreement (FTA) with the EU?

In at least one respect, the 25 and 50 Percent Tests are welcome innovations. There were no such harmonized standing requirements in pre-Uruguay Round law. In the U.S., a petitioner was assumed to have standing to file a petition on behalf of an industry, unless another member of the relevant industry challenged that standing. That regime was legally ambiguous, and outcomes depended on circumstances. The Tests offer bright-line rules, with the attendant features such rules provide — certainty and predictability.

Yet, are there conceptual shortcomings associated with the Tests? Do the Tests afford enhanced possibilities for protectionist abuse, especially because they rely on an antediluvian distinction between "foreign" and "domestic" production? To be sure, Articles 4 and 5 of the WTO *Antidumping Agreement* do not require a domestic industry on behalf of which a petition is filed to be owned or controlled by a party in the importing country. But, the Tests depend on an underlying assumption manufacturing operations are neatly divided along territorial lines between a petitioner in the importing country and respondent in a foreign country. In reality, many finished products are the result of a global chain of raw materials, factor inputs, and intermediate goods. That is, in many industries, it is erroneous to think of 100 percent

American producers facing wholly foreign competitors. Such industries are, in effect, demographically mixed.

Furthermore, do practical flaws bedevil the 25 and 50 Percent Tests, with the result being it is easier to file an AD or CVD petition? Consider the fact that Article 5:4 of the WTO *Antidumping Agreement* broadens the universe of potential petitioners. Footnote 14 to Article 5:4 states "Members are aware that in the territory of certain Members, *employees* of domestic producers of the like product or *representatives* of those employees, may make or support an application for an investigation. . . ." Read literally, the footnote means not only labor unions or other worker associations, but also individual employees or *ad hoc* groups of workers, can file a petition. In the U.S., the effect of this language is to place management and workers on an equal footing with respect to supporting or opposing a petition. There are reasons to favor giving *ad hoc* groups of workers standing. But, those reasons presume (1) the prospect of more AD and CVD cases filed against foreign competitors is positive, and (2) *ad hoc* groups of workers can be trusted to file meritorious claims. There may be doubts as to whether an industry that has lost its comparative advantage can avoid grasping at protective measures.

Moreover, all such reasons in favor of expanding the universe of petitioner to include *ad hoc* worker groups would have to remember that successful American firms could be the targets of (*i.e.*, respondents in) AD or CVD cases brought by *ad hoc* groups of workers in foreign countries. In the U.S., there is a historical tendency to think of trade remedy cases in a one-way direction, usually offensively from a petitioner perspective. Under the pre-Uruguay Round law of some GATT contracting parties, unions (much less individual employees) may not have had standing to file a petition. Under the *Antidumping Agreement*, both organized and *ad hoc* groups have standing. Consequently, successful U.S. exporters could be vulnerable to attack in such actions.

As another possible practical flaw, query what entities may express an opinion on an AD or CVD petition. Under Article 4:1(i) of the *Antidumping Agreement*, domestic producers related to a respondent are conditionally disenfranchised from expressing an opinion on a petition. There is a perverse burden of proof for a determination of industry support for a petition. To appreciate this point, consider the following example.

Suppose Nippon Steel Corporation (NSC) has a U.S. subsidiary, Nippon U.S.A., to which it exports steel. Nippon U.S.A., which as a subsidiary of NSC obviously is related to NSC, manufactures both steel and steel-based products like tubing, ball bearings and chain-linked fences. Nippon U.S.A. opposes an AD (or CVD) petition filed by Bethlehem Steel, a U.S. producer, filed against NSC. Bethlehem Steel is a competitor of Nippon U.S.A. The Salina Steel Company, a Kansas-based company, is unrelated to the exporter. Salina imports and uses steel directly from NSC. Salina purchases steel and steel-based products from NSC Japan directly, and from Bethlehem Steel. Salina opposes the petition. The Diagram depicts these facts. At issue is whether the DOC considers the opposition of Nippon U.S.A. and SSC when determining industry support for the petition.

In this situation, the DOC can exclude both Nippon U.S.A. and Salina Steel Company from both the 25 and 50 Percent Tests. Indeed, the DOC must exclude Nippon U.S.A., because this entity is considered an opposing domestic producer related to the exporter. As for Salina Steel, the DOC has the discretion to exclude it. That is, the DOC is empowered to exclude from application of both Tests an unrelated importer of subject merchandise. These exclusions make it easier for the petitioner to meet these tests.

DIAGRAM 28-1:
HYPOTHETICAL CASE ON STANDING

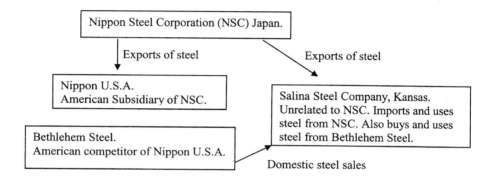

The only instance in which a related producer and unrelated importer can be included is if they show an AD or CVD order would adversely affect their interests. (Pre-Uruguay Round law contained no such rule or exception.) Plainly, the presumption of exclusion conditionally disenfranchises an affiliate of an exporter, and unaffiliated importer. It is an inherent pro-petitioner bias. In the example, to overcome the presumption, Nippon U.S.A., an affiliate of the exporter (NSC), must prove to the DOC:

(1)   it uses steel from NSC in the production of steel-based products,

(2)   it would be harmed by an increase in the price of steel caused by an AD duty, and

(3)   no reliable domestic substitutable steel exists (or it is prohibitively expensive.

Otherwise, Nippon USA will have no voice in the 25 and 50 Percent Tests. Salina Steel Company, an unaffiliated importer, must make the same showing, if it wants a voice.

What is the rationale for putting this burden on affiliates of an exporter and on an unaffiliated importer? One answer is to ensure that foreign producers like NSC, which would not normally be expected to support a petition, are not allowed to prevent investigations from going forward simply by directing or encouraging (implicitly or explicitly) their affiliates in the U.S. to oppose a petition. Is this rationale unfair?

Arguably, it is. First, it is unclear how a related domestic producer that imports subject merchandise can meet the burden of proof. How, for example, can Nippon U.S.A. show its interests as a domestic producer would be adversely affected by imposing an AD or CVD order? Must Nippon U.S.A. demonstrate that it would have to close down production because of the increased cost of imported materials resulting from an AD duty or CVD? Or, would a modest decline in the profits of Nippon U.S.A. a sufficient adverse effect? These ambiguities mean Bethlehem Steel has ample room to argue a remedial action would have no adverse effect on Nippon U.S.A. Bethlehem Steel could try arguing Nippon USA cannot possibly be hurt by an AD order, because Nippon USA always can get its steel from its Japanese parent at a non-arm's length price.

Second, the burden of proof operates in a discriminatory manner. The burden is on a related domestic producer, and unrelated importer, to show harm from an AD order. But, no burden is placed on an unrelated domestic producer (or, for that matter, a related importer). Suppose, for example, the Patriot Steel Corporation, a U.S. company unrelated to NSC, manufactures steel and steel products. To register its opposition to Bethlehem Steel's petition with the DOC, Patriot Steel need not prove it would be injured by an AD or CVD order. Placing the burden on Nippon U.S.A., but not Patriot Steel, assumes corporate affiliation alone determines the position a company takes in an AD action and essentially treats a foreign-owned company as guilty until proven innocent.

Of course, it may be countered a U.S. subsidiary is unlikely to challenge its foreign parent. Would that improbability justify the discrimination? To minimize the risk of protectionist abuse, would it be wise to reverse the burden of proof? That would mean the presumption is Patriot Steel (as well as Nippon U.S.A. and Salina Steel) is enfranchised. The petitioner would have to prove these entities should be excluded on the ground that, with respect to Nippon U.S.A., it assesses its interests not from the viewpoint of its U.S. operations, but instead from that of its Japanese parent. Reversing the burden might also force the DOC to consider expressly the possible positive effects of steel imports at allegedly dumped prices, rather than on the claims of Bethlehem Steel.

C. Steps 3 and 4: Preliminary Determinations

Assuming an AD or CVD investigation is commenced, what is the target? Technically, the answer is imports of a particular product from a particular exporting country, called "subject merchandise." Not surprisingly, companies responsible for making and bringing into the importing country the subject merchandise regard themselves as the targets. They are the respondents in the investigation. Petitioners tend to name as many possible respondents as they can — *i.e.*, the exporters, producers, and importers of the merchandise on which they seek to have an AD duty or CVD imposed.

The first preliminary determination is made by the ITC as to whether there is a "reasonable indication" of material injury, or threat thereof, to a domestic producer of a like product. That this determination occurs first is logical enough. If there is no "harm," then there is no "foul." The ITC must make the finding within 45 days of the day a petition is filed. Its decision is based on information available (IA) to it at that time. If the ITC's determination is negative, then the petition is dismissed and the case ends.

Only with an affirmative preliminary injury determination does the investigation shift back to the DOC. In an AD case, that Department must make a preliminary dumping margin determination. Specifically, the DOC considers whether there is a "reasonable basis to believe or suspect" subject merchandise is, or is likely to be, sold at LTFV, *i.e.*, whether it is dumped. Accordingly, the DOC must ascertain Normal Value and Export Price (or Constructed Export Price), and consider adjustments to these figures to provide a fair comparison. In a CVD case, the DOC decides whether there is a "reasonable basis to believe or suspect that a countervailable subsidy is being provided," *i.e.*, whether subject merchandise benefits (or benefited) from an unlawful subsidy provided by a foreign government (*i.e.*, the government of an exporting country).

The DOC must make its preliminary dumping decision within 140 days after an investigation is initiated, and its preliminary subsidy determination within 65 days after initiation. But, it cannot do so before the ITC makes a preliminary affirmative determination of injury. As with the ITC's determination, the DOC uses IA at the time. In two instances, expedited consideration is possible. First, the DOC may make a preliminary finding within 90 days of initiation, based on IA from the first 60 days. To do so, the information must be sufficient, and the petitioner and respondent must agree to the expedited procedure and waive the need for verification of the evidence available. In a CVD case, an expedited determination is possible under the same conditions, using IA from the first 50 days. Second, in an AD case, a preliminary determination may be made for short-life cycle merchandise (*e.g.*, perishable products), if the foreign producer has been subject to a prior affirmative dumping determination on a similar product.

Conversely, postponements are possible. A preliminary dumping margin determination can be delayed until 190 days after initiation, at the request of the petitioner or if the DOC finds the circumstance are extraordinarily complicated. In a CVD case, either at the petitioner's request or if the DOC finds the issues extraordinarily complicated, extension is possible for 130 days after initiation. Also, in a CVD case, the preliminary subsidy determination can be extended for 250 days if an upstream subsidy is at issue. (An "upstream subsidy" is a financial contribution or benefit, other than an export subsidy, paid by a governmental authority on an input product used in the same country as the authority to manufacture subject merchandise. Under U.S. CVD law, an upstream subsidy is countervailable if it bestows a "competitive benefit" on the merchandise, and has a "significant effect" on the cost of production.)

If the DOC makes a preliminary affirmative dumping margin or subsidy determination by the DOC, then three important effects follow.

1. *Estimation*:

The DOC calculates an estimate of the average amount by which NV exceeds EP (or CEP), *i.e.*, of the average dumping margin. In a CVD case, the DOC estimates the net countervailable subsidy, that is, the amount of the unlawful subsidy provided by the government of the exporting country. The figure becomes the estimated duty rate.

2. *Suspension*:

The DOC directs the CBP to suspend liquidation of all entries of merchandise subject to the affirmative preliminary determination. The suspension applies to shipments of foreign merchandise covered by the investigation from the date the DOC publishes its preliminary decision (which appears in the *Federal Register*). "Liquidation" means completion of all documentation associated with an entry of a shipment of merchandise, and requires final computation of the duties and fees due on an entry. Thus, suspension of liquidation means the CBP defers calculation of the amount and rate of tariff duty applicable to each individual entry until a later. The merchandise may enter the U.S. (or be entered into a warehouse, foreign trade zone, or put in temporary importation in bond). But, as that entry is not liquidated, liability remains for final payment of duties (if any).

3. *Security*:

For each entry, and subsequent entries, of subject merchandise, the respondent must post with the CBP a cash deposit, bond, or other appropriate security equal to the estimated dumping margin or estimated net countervailable subsidy the DOC calculates in its preliminary determination. The "coughing up" of funds must occur at the time the merchandise is imported. The obligation to post security is not a mere down payment. It is collateral for (and sometimes equal to) the full amount in question. This security is required to assure payment of remedial duties, in the event final affirmative dumping or subsidy and injury decisions are rendered and an AD or CVD order is issued.

The third effect is particularly dramatic. Posting security for estimated duties is costly for the respondent — the importer, producer, and/or exporter of subject merchandise. The respondent also is faced with price uncertainty in its business operations. Should the cost of depositing the estimated duties be passed on to the consumers of the merchandise, assuming they can bear this cost? What if no final AD or CVD duty order is issued, or, what if a final order is issued, but it assesses a duty rate different from the estimated duty rate? The respondent must make important price decisions in a legally uncertain environment. It also must consider whether, in an AD case, the motivation of the petitioner is to compel it to raise its prices. Is the petitioner trying to force it to join a cartel? If so, is a price cartel unlawful?

Clearly, then, the process is designed to allow the CBP to start collecting security for AD duties or CVDs as soon as the ITC and DOC have preliminarily determined, respectively, that imports are causing or threatening to cause injury, and are being sold at LTFV. The estimated dumping margin or net countervailable subsidy is the relevant figure for collecting the requisite cash deposit or bond following the preliminary determination, and also following final DOC and ITC determinations (if both are affirmative). This figure, or rate, applies to existing entries of subject merchandise, and prospectively to subsequent entries. The estimate may be recalculated during an Administrative Review, otherwise the liability of the importer of record of the merchandise is fixed at the estimated rate.

Furthermore, following an affirmative preliminary dumping margin or subsidy determination from the DOC, the ITC begins a final injury determination. The DOC must provide the ITC with IA relevant to an injury or threat determination. In the meantime, the DOC proceeds directly to a final determination.

Suppose the DOC's preliminary determination is negative. The above three effects do not occur, and the ITC does not start a final injury determination. Rather, the DOC proceeds to a final determination, and the ITC awaits the outcome. The ITC never commences or completes a final determination based only on a negative preliminary determination by the DOC. The ITC begins a final determination only after an affirmative preliminary or final determination from the DOC. Finally, another dramatic event that can occur at the preliminary investigation stage involves "critical circumstances." Petitioners may allege these exist, and if successful, obtain retroactive relief.

D. Steps 5 and 6: Final Determinations

Regardless of the outcome of a preliminary dumping margin or subsidy determination, the DOC proceeds to render a final determination. Essentially, its job is to look again at whether LTFV sales are occurring, and check the magnitude (if any) of the dumping margin. Thus, in an AD case, it scrutinizes the calculation of Normal Value and Export Price (or Constructed Export Price), considers adjustments needed to these price figures to ensure a fair comparison, and establishes a figure for Normal Value and Export Price. In a CVD case, the DOC studies the alleged illegal subsidy and its magnitude, and decides upon the net countervailable subsidy.

If the DOC's final dumping margin or subsidy determination is affirmative, then it comes up with a final estimated dumping margin or final estimated net countervailable subsidy. Further, the DOC orders the CBP to suspend liquidation of entries, and to post a cash deposit, bond, or other security (assuming these actions were not already taken — they would not have been if the preliminary determination had been negative). Further, with an affirmative final determination, the ITC completes its final injury determination, and the DOC awaits notice of this result.

If the DOC's final determination is negative, then the ITC ends its final injury inquiry. An AD duty or CVD follows only after final DOC and ITC determinations. A negative final dumping margin or subsidy determination terminates the investigation and ends a case, as does a negative final injury determination. Any suspension of liquidation of entries ends, *i.e.*, subject merchandise is liquidated. All estimated duties are refunded, and all bonds or other security released.

The DOC must issue a final dumping margin or subsidy determination within 75 days of its preliminary decision. In an AD case, upon acceptance of a timely request, this period can be extended to up to 135 days from the prior determination. In a CVD case involving upstream subsidies, there are special extended time limits. In a case of both AD and CVD claims about the same subject merchandise, the petitioner can request the DOC postpone its final subsidy determination until the date of the final AD determination.

How much time does the ITC have to complete its final injury determination? The answer depends on the outcome of the DOC's dumping or subsidy investigation. If the preliminary determination by the DOC is negative, but is followed by an affirmative determination, then the ITC has 75 days after that final affirmative determination. If the preliminary determination by the DOC is affirmative, then the ITC must make its final determination within the longer of (1) 120 days from an affirmative preliminary determination by the DOC, or (2) 45 days from an affirmative final determination by the DOC. If the ITC's final injury determination is negative, then the case is terminated and estimated duty deposits are refunded. But, if the ITC's final injury determination is affirmative, then the DOC issues an AD order within 7 days of the ITC's determination.

The legal criteria applied in final injury determinations are set forth in the Article 3 of the WTO *Antidumping Agreement*, Articles 5-6 of the *Subsidies and Countervailing Measures (SCM) Agreement*, and U.S. law. In brief, the ITC looks to see whether a domestic producer of a like product (*i.e.*, like the subject merchandise) is, by reason of dumped imports, materially injured, or threatened with material injury, or (in rare instances), whether the establishment of an industry in the U.S. is materially retarded. In an *SCM Agreement* case brought by one WTO Member against another Member under the *DSU*, the grounds for injury are broader, including not only (1) injury to the domestic industry of another member, but also (2) nullification or impairment of benefits accruing to another Member, or (3) serious prejudice to the interests of another Member. Collectively, these three grounds are called "adverse effects."

E. Step 7: Remedial Orders and Limits

Following an affirmative final dumping margin or subsidy determination by the ITC, and a final injury determination by the ITC, the DOC must issue an AD or CVD order. It must do so within 7 days of notice of the final injury determination by the ITC. Significantly, issuance of an AD or CVD order is automatic after the requisite determinations. Neither the Secretary of Commerce nor the President is authorized to block issuance of the order. Put differently, political influences do not — or, at least, are not supposed to, enter into a case at this stage.

An AD or CVD order is issued to the CBP. Either kind of order describes the goods to which it applies, namely, the subject merchandise and future entries of merchandise. In an AD order, the DOC:

    i.   directs the CBP to assess an AD duty equal to the amount Normal Value exceeds Export Price (or Constructed Export Price), *i.e.*, equal to the dumping margin,

    ii.   requires deposit of estimated AD duties until the entries of merchandise to which the order applies are liquidated, and

    iii.   requires deposit of normal customs duties (*e.g.*, the MFN tariff).

The final determination by the DOC of the dumping margin not only is the basis for assessing an AD duty on previous entries of subject merchandise, but also for deposits of estimated duties on future entries of merchandise covered by the order.

Similarly, in a CVD order, the DOC:

    i.   directs the CBP to assess a CVD equal to the net countervailable subsidy amount,

    ii.   requires deposit of estimated CVDs until the entries of merchandise to which the order applies are liquidated, and

    iii.   requires deposit of normal customs duties (*e.g.*, the MFN tariff).

The final determination by the DOC of the net countervailable subsidy not only is the basis for assessing a CVD on previous entries of subject merchandise, but also for deposits of estimated duties on future entries of merchandise covered by the order.

In both AD and CVD cases, the importer of record technically is liable for the deposits. This party is the entity importing the dumped or unlawfully subsidized product. This party is not necessarily a respondent in a case. When might it not be, and what legal steps should such an importer take to protect itself from "holding the bag"?

Also in both cases, with respect to previous entries of subject merchandise, there is the possibility of a difference between estimated and final duties. Suppose after an affirmative preliminary or final dumping margin or subsidy determination, the cash deposit or bond posted as security for the estimated AD duty or CVD, respectively, is greater than the amount of the duty assessed in the AD or CVD order. The difference between the (1) deposit (or bond) and (2) amount of the final duty is refunded. Does the refund come with interest, too? The answer depends on when merchandise was entered. For merchandise entered before notice of the final injury decision, no interest accrues on an overpayment. For entries of merchandise after this notice, the difference between estimated and final duties is refunded with interest on the amount of the overpayment.

What if the estimated AD duty or CVD is less than the final amount in the order? Must the deficiency in the cash deposit or bond posted be covered? Must interest be paid on the underpayment? Again, the answer depends on the timing of the entries. For merchandise entered before notice of the final injury determination, the difference between estimated and final duties is disregarded, and no interest accrues. In effect, the underpayment is excused. But, for entries after notice of the final injury determination, the difference between lower estimated duties and higher final duties is collected, along with interest on the underpayment. Why is notice of the final injury determination the key point for determining how to handle differences between estimated and final duties?

What is the scope of an AD or CVD order? The short answer is "prophylactic." It applies to all entries of subject merchandise, past, present, and future, commencing from a specific date indicated in the order. Moreover, an order applies countrywide. It includes all exporters, whether or not investigated, unless the DOC determines a specific exporter is selling its product at a non-dumped price, or is not benefiting from an illegal subsidy. For instance, generally in an LTFV investigation, the DOC attempts to include exporters accounting for 60 percent of U.S. imports of subject merchandise. Hence, the 40 percent not investigated still are subject to an AD order. Finally, an AD or CVD order also covers merchandise from a new shipper, *i.e.*, an exporter that did not ship merchandise at the time the original order was issued but, thereafter, began exportation.

Note the relevance of the principle of proportionality, and other disciplines, which constrain AD and CVD orders. GATT Article VI, and the WTO Antidumping and SCM Agreements, state that an AD duty is limited to the margin of dumping, and a CVD is supposed to offset the amount of a subsidy. Moreover, these specifications effectively pre-empt other kinds of remedies. For instance, the WTO Appellate Body ruled against the U.S. *Antidumping Act of 1916*, and against the *Byrd Amendment* — both of which created remedies beyond the scope of the GATT—WTO regime. *See* WTO Appellate Body Report, *United States — Anti-Dumping Act of 1916*, WT/DS136/AB/R (adopted 26 September 2000), and WTO Appellate Body Report, *United States — Continued Dumping and Offset Act of 2000*, WT/DS217/AB/R (adopted 8 January 2003).

F. Step 8: Reviews

There are three kinds of reviews of AD or CVD orders: Sunset Reviews, Changed Circumstances Reviews, and Administrative Reviews. (New shippers also are subject to review.) The criteria for, and application of, Sunset Reviews have generated WTO adjudication. In brief, under Article 11 of the WTO *Antidumping Agreement*, an AD or CVD order presumptively terminates (*i.e.*, sunsets) after 5 years from the date of its imposition. The exception is if, through a Sunset Review, a WTO Member finds expiry of an AD or CVD order likely would lead to continuation or recurrence of dumping or subsidization, respectively, and material injury. To rebut the presumption of a sunset, there must be evidence dumping or unlawful subsidization has not ceased, or a reasonable indication dumping or unlawful subsidization likely would occur again. The point of a Sunset Review is to ensure orders do not take on a lengthy, perhaps interminable, life of their own, as they did in some GATT contracting parties before the Uruguay Round.

The DOC publishes notice of initiation of a Sunset Review no later than 30 days of the fifth anniversary of an AD or CVD order (or Suspension Agreement). Any party interested in maintaining the order (or Agreement) must respond by giving the DOC and ITC evidence about the likely effects of revocation. The DOC has 240 days from the date of initiation to complete the Review, and the ITC has 360 days. Extensions are possible if the case is extraordinarily complicated.

In a Sunset Review of an AD order (or Suspension Agreement), the DOC's charge is to decide whether revoking the order (or terminating the Agreement) would be likely to lead to continued or recurred dumping. The DOC examines:

    i.   the weighted average dumping margin calculated in the original investigation, and in any subsequent Administrative or Changed Circumstances Review,

    ii.   the volume of imports of subject merchandise before and after the order was issued (or Agreement accepted), and

    iii.   with good cause, a list of other factors.

The DOC then informs the ITC of its estimated dumping margin likely to exist if the AD order is revoked (or Agreement terminated). Similarly, in a CVD case, the DOC considers whether revoking an order (or terminating a Suspension Agreement) likely would lead to continued or recurred unlawful subsidization. The DOC checks:

    i.   the net countervailable subsidy calculated in the original investigation, and in any subsequent Administrative or Changed Circumstances Review,

    ii.   any change in the subsidy program of the foreign government involved, and whether such change is relevant, and

    iii.   with good cause, a list of other factors.

The DOC then provides the ITC with a re-calculated net countervailable subsidy figure the DOC prognosticates on the assumption the CVD order is revoked (or Agreement terminated).

For its part, the ITC considers whether revoking an AD or CVD order (or terminating a Suspension Agreement) likely would lead to continued or recurred material injury within a reasonably foreseeable period. The ITC studies:

    i.   the likely volume, price effect, and impact of subject merchandise on the industry from revocation of the order (or termination of the Agreement),

    ii.   its earlier injury determinations,

    iii.   whether the state of the domestic industry has improved,

    iv.   whether that industry is vulnerable to material injury,

    v.   in an AD Sunset Review, the magnitude of the dumping margin, and

    vi.   in a CVD Sunset Review, the magnitude of the net countervailable subsidy rate and the nature of the subsidy (namely, whether the subsidy is prohibited as a "Red Light" under Article 3 of the *SCM Agreement*, or is a "Dark Amber" subsidy actionable under Article 6:1 of this *Agreement*).

May the ITC assess cumulatively the volume and effects of imports of subject merchandise from all countries subject to a Sunset Review to determine if these imports likely would compete with each other, and with domestic like products in the U.S.? The answer is yes, unless there is no discernible adverse impact on the affected U.S. industry. Cumulation is potentially significant. Imports from any one country might not justify continuation of an AD or CVD order. By aggregating imports from multiple countries, it may be possible to show a likelihood of continued or recurred material injury.

Unlike Sunset Reviews, Changed Circumstances Reviews are not mandatory. They apply to an affirmative final determination resulting in an AD or CVD order (or to a Suspension Agreement). They occur only if the DOC or ITC receives information, or a request from an interested party, showing (in the language of 19 U.S.C. § 1675(b)(1)) "changed circumstances sufficient to warrant a review of" the final determination (or Agreement). Without good cause, a Changed Circumstances Review cannot be done within 24 months of the notice of a final determination (or Suspension Agreement). It is the party seeking revocation of an AD or CVD order that bears the burden of persuasion to show circumstances exist to warrant the Review and, ultimately, revocation of the order. What kinds of circumstances might justify the Review? In an AD case, would changes in market prices — *e.g.*, lower Normal Values, or higher Export Prices — suffice? In a CVD case, would changes in subsidization policy in the exporter's home country be persuasive? Or, in both kinds of cases, would it be necessary to show the petitioner in the original investigation no longer is injured or threatened with injury?

Though not mandatory, Administrative Reviews are of great practical significance during the life of an AD or CVD order. (These Reviews also apply to Suspension Agreements.) Each year, in the anniversary month in which the DOC issued an order, either party may ask it to review whether the estimated duty rate is accurate or should be adjusted to yield a new amount applicable to the prior 12 months of imports. In the first year following the order, the estimated duty rate is derived from the dumping margin or net countervailable subsidy calculated by the DOC in the preliminary and final determinations. That is, these estimates yield the final AD duty or CVD liability for the previous year, Year 1. At the end of Year 1, the petitioner and respondent can decide whether to seek re-calculation through an Administrative Review. If neither party requests a Review, then the same estimates remain the basis for estimated duty liability in Year 2. At the end of Year 2, if no Review is requested, then these estimates are finalized — and, these estimates are used as the estimated AD duty or CVD duty for Year 3.

However, upon request of either side, the DOC conducts an Administrative Review. In an AD case, the DOC re-calculates the dumping margin, *i.e.*, Normal Value, Export Price (or Constructed Export Price). In a CVD case it re-computes the net countervailable subsidy. Suppose this Review occurs after Year 1, and it results in a different AD duty or CVD rate than estimated in the preliminary and final determinations. The new amount serves as the final figure for the previous 12 months (Year 1), *i.e.*, for assessment of duties on all entries of merchandise subject to the Review. The new amount also serves as the basis for deposit of estimated duties for all entries subsequent to the period of the Review (*e.g.*, Year 2).

Once again, there may be a difference between estimated deposits and final assessed duties. If the DOC determines in an Administrative Review a higher amount is appropriate, then the respondent is liable for the difference between the old estimated and new final amounts, plus interest. If a lower amount is right, then the respondent receives a refund for the difference, with interest. In either event, the new final AD or CVD rate stays in effect until the next Administrative Review, *i.e.*, the new rate is the deposit rate until completion of the next Review. Thus, a new calculation of the dumping margin or net countervailable subsidy serves two purposes. First, it is the final AD duty or CVD rate for subject merchandise covered by the order in the previous 12 months. Second, it is the estimated amount for the deposit of an AD duty or CVD in the next year.

The dual purposes are why U.S. AD and CVD remedies are dubbed both retrospective and prospective. In contrast, in many WTO Members, the remedies are only prospective. In cases under the *DSU*, remedies are prospective. Does a retrospective dimension raise concerns under Article 10 of the WTO *Antidumping Agreement*?

Consider this question where a petitioner alleges "critical circumstances." In an AD case, the DOC applies (based on IA at the time) a 3-pronged test so see if these circumstances exist:

    i.   there is a history of dumping and material injury, in the U.S. or elsewhere, of the subject merchandise,

    ii.   the importer knew or should have known (1) the merchandise was being sold at LTFV, and (2) there was likely to be material injury because of such sales, and

    iii.   there are massive imports of subject merchandise over a relatively short period.

In a CVD case, the DOC (again, using IA) applies a slightly different 3-pronged test:

    i.   subject merchandise originates in a "country under the Agreement" (*i.e.*, a WTO Member country, or a country with which the U.S. has an agreement for unconditional MFN treatment but does not expressly allow for trade remedy actions under the GATT—WTO accords or import restrictions to counter unfair practices),

    ii.   the alleged countervailable subsidy violates the WTO *Agreement on Subsidies and Countervailing Measures* (*SCM Agreement*), and

    iii.   there are massive imports of subject merchandise over a relatively short period.

If all 3 prongs are satisfied, then the DOC deems the circumstances "critical." It may make this determination before a preliminary dumping margin decision or injury ruling.

If the DOC finds critical circumstances, the remedial implication is dramatic. Any suspension of liquidation of entries the DOC orders applies retroactively to un-liquidated entries of merchandise entered up to 90 days before the date on which the DOC ordered the suspension. That is, the respondent must post security for estimated AD or CVD duties on merchandise technically not subject to the investigation, but which was imported "close enough" to the time of the investigation, where "close enough" is defined as entry within 90 days of the suspension order applying to subject merchandise.

What constraints do Article VI of GATT and Article 11:3 of the WTO *Antidumping Agreement* impose on Sunset Reviews? *See* WTO Appellate Body Report, *United States — Sunset Reviews of Anti-Dumping Measures on Oil Country Tubular Goods from Argentina*, WT/DS268/AB/R (adopted 29 November 2004).

G. Steps 9 and 10: Appeals and WTO Adjudication?

Frequently, an interested party is unhappy with the outcome of an AD or CVD investigation. Judicial review of a final AD or CVD determination may be obtained by filing a summons and complaint, within 30 days of publication of the determination, with the U.S. Court of International Trade (CIT) in New York. The CIT is statutorily bound to apply to the administrative action the following standard of review: whether "substantial evidence on the record" supports the determination, or whether the determination is "otherwise not in accordance with law."

An interested party may appeal a DOC decision not to initiate an investigation, or a negative preliminary injury determination by the ITC. In that appeal, the CIT considers whether the action is "arbitrary, capricious, [or] an abuse of discretion, or [is] otherwise not in accordance with law." It also is possible to appeal the result of a Sunset, Changed Circumstances, or Administrative Review of an AD or CVD order. If a litigant is unsatisfied with a decision of the CIT, then it may appeal to the U.S. Court of Appeals for the Federal Circuit. From there, appeal is possible to the Supreme Court, though review at that level is improbable. Is an affirmative preliminary injury determination, or a preliminary dumping margin or subsidy determination, reviewable by the CIT?

Certain RTAs provide for review of domestic AD or CVD orders. *NAFTA* Chapter 19 is a quintessential example. A *NAFTA* Chapter 19 panel may review a final AD or CVD decision if subject merchandise originates in *NAFTA* Parties. A *NAFTA* panel must apply the law and standard of review of the country in which the AD or CVD case occurred. Thus, in reviewing a DOC or ITC determination, a panel must apply U.S. law and judicial review standards. Once appeal is made to a Chapter 19 panel, it is not possible to return to a domestic court system (*e.g.*, the CIT or Federal Circuit). The only exception, set forth in *NAFTA* Article 1905:1(d), is if a constitutional issue is at stake.

Private parties are involved directly in *NAFTA* Chapter 19 cases. The panels have produced a large and growing body of jurisprudence, and a considerable literature has developed commenting and analyzing the cases. Some of the litigation has been highly contentious, such as the *Softwood Lumber* CVD case, while other disputes have centered around technical matters such as the use of information available.

Observe that not every RTA creates special tribunals for AD and CVD cases. For instance, there are no such provisions in the U.S. free trade agreements (FTAs) with Australia, Bahrain, Chile, Singapore, Jordon, Israel, Morocco, or Oman — in other words, *NAFTA* Chapter 19 is unusual in the American array of FTAs. Somewhat unique are RTAs that ban the use of AD rules. One example is the 1983 *Australia — New Zealand Closer Economic Relations Trade Agreement* (the *ANZCERTA*, or *CER* for short). Article 15 of the 1983 *CER* permits AD actions. However, in 1988, Australia and New Zealand agreed to a *Protocol* to the *CER*. Article 4 of the *Protocol* bans the use of the AD remedy. Another instance is the FTA between Singapore and the members of the *European Free Trade Area* (*EFTA*), which was signed in 2002 and entered into force in 2003. Article 16 of this FTA forbids AD actions between Singapore and the *EFTA* members. A third instance is *EFTA* itself — Article 36 proscribes AD actions among the *EFTA* members.

Some AD or CVD cases generate a dispute between WTO Members. There are two basic sources of conflict. First, one Member may challenge an AD or

CVD law maintained by another Member as inconsistent with one or more GATT—WTO obligations. Second, one Member may argue the process or outcome of a particular AD or CVD investigation violates one or more GATT—WTO obligations. Whether the dispute is a "statutory" or "investigation" challenge, it is handled according to *DSU* procedures. AD and CVD disputes take up a sizeable percentage of the docket of WTO panels and Appellate Body. The jurisprudence is both considerable and evolving. Must all remedies under local law be exhausted before an AD or CVD matter can be brought under the *DSU*?

What happens not if, but when, a WTO panel or the Appellate Body finds an action by the DOC or ITC is inconsistent with U.S. obligations in the GATT—WTO regime? Section 129(a) of the 1994 *Uruguay Round Agreements Act*, codified at 19 U.S.C. § 3538, provides the answer. For a DOC action, the United States Trade Representative (USTR), after consulting with Congress, may request the DOC to issue a determination that would not be inconsistent with the WTO panel or Appellate Body findings. The USTR also may direct the DOC to implement its revised determination, effective for liquidated entries of subject merchandise on or after the date of this direction. As for the ITC, the USTR may ask it to issue an advisory report as to whether the relevant statute permits it to take steps to render its determination not inconsistent with the WTO panel or Appellate Body findings. If the ITC provides an affirmative report, then the USTR may ask it to make a new determination. If the result is an AD or CVD order no longer is justified, then the USTR — after checking with Congress — may direct the ITC to revoke the order, effective for liquidated entries of subject merchandise entered on or after this direction. Interestingly, the President, after consulting with Congress, may reduce, modify, or terminate an ITC action.

A critical, unresolved set of issues concerns interaction among various levels of review. To what extent, if any, must a *NAFTA* Chapter 19 panel pay attention to a ruling by a WTO panel or the Appellate Body? To what extent, if any, must the CIT or Federal Circuit Court take into account a Chapter 19 panel, WTO panel, or Appellate Body decision? Consider the same questions, but change the verb from "must" to "should."

III. THIRD COUNTRY DUMPING

Suppose there is fierce competition in Brazil between rice exports from India and Thailand. The Thai rice farmers accuse their Indian competitors of dumping rice in Brazil. They do not, however, allege the Indians are dumping rice in Thailand. What recourse, if any, do the Thai rice farmers have against dumping in Brazil?

The hypothetical example illustrates "third country dumping," where the third country is Thailand, the importing country is Brazil, and India is the alleged dumper. Article 14 of the WTO *Antidumping Agreement* creates a claim for AD action on behalf of a third country. Under it, Thai government authorities are entitled to apply to the Brazilian AD authority and request Brazil take action against the Indian rice. Article 14:2 requires the Thai action be supported by price information showing the Indian rice is, in fact, being dumped in Brazil, and the dumping causes injury to Thai rice farmers.

It is the third country producers (Thai rice farmers), not domestic producers in the importing country (*e.g.*, rice farmers in Brazil) alleging injury. Article 14:4 makes clear the importing country has sole discretion on proceeding with the case. Why might Brazil choose to bring the action, especially if it has no domestic sector claiming injury? One answer is good citizenship. If Brazil expects serious consideration when it approaches other countries to take up AD claims on its behalf, then it had take the claims of other countries seriously. Put differently, Brazil might anticipate being a "repeat player" in third country AD cases, sometimes as the importing country, and sometimes as the complainant third country. However, might Brazil also have to weigh its trade, investment, and financial relations with the respondent, India?

The standard requirements in a conventional AD case must be met a third country case. Proof is needed of a positive dumping margin, as well as injury caused by dumping. The threshold test of comparability of products — namely, the third country product (*e.g.*, Thai rice) is like the allegedly dumped product (*e.g.*, Indian rice) — must be passed.

In the U.S., a domestic industry exporting goods to another country alleging injury from dumping in that other country must petition the USTR. (For instance, California rice farmers exporting to Brazil might petition the USTR for relief from Indian rice dumped in Brazil.) If the USTR agrees a reasonable basis for the claim exists, then it applies to the appropriate authority in the importing country requesting action be taken on behalf of the U.S. The DOC and ITC assist the USTR in preparing the application (*e.g.*, to provide price and injury data). Here, the U.S. is the third country seeking relief. Suppose authorities in the importing country reject the American application. Then, the USTR must consult with the petitioning industry on whether other action could be taken. What remedy might there be? Would unilateral trade retaliation under Section 301 work?

Conversely, the USTR has discretion to initiate an AD investigation upon request by a third country. It consults with the DOC and ITC about the merits of the petition, and obtains approval from the WTO Council for Trade in Goods before commencing the action. Consider the second sentence of Article 14:4 of the *Antidumping Agreement*. Does this sentence mean Council approval is mandatory, or simply best practice?

Chapter 29

THE DUMPING MARGIN CALCULATION

Protection is not a principle but an expedient.

> —Benjamin Disraeli (1804-81), *Speech to the House of Commons,* 17 March 1845 (having taken the opposite position in a 25 April 1843 speech)

DOCUMENTS SUPPLEMENT ASSIGNMENT

1. *Havana Charter* Article 34
2. GATT Article VI
3. WTO *Antidumping Agreement* Articles 1-2

I. THE LESS THAN FAIR VALUE DETERMINATION

A. The Dumping Margin Formula

"Dumping" refers to the sale or likely sale of imported merchandise at less than fair value (LTFV). What is "fair value," and against what is it gauged? The answer is the standard definition of the term. It is found in Article VI:1 of GATT and Article 2:1 of the WTO *Antidumping Agreement.*

A product is dumped if its "Export Price" (EP) is less than "Normal Value" (NV). Hence, the formula for the absolute dumping margin is:

Dumping Margin = NV — EP

Expressed in percentage terms, the formula is:

$$\text{Dumping Margin} = \frac{NV - EP}{EP} \times 100$$

If a positive dumping margin exists, and dumped merchandise causes or threatens to cause material injury to a producer of a like product in the importing country, then that country may impose a duty on the dumped merchandise. That duty is on top of the normal MFN tariff (or otherwise applicable rate), and may be up to the full amount of the dumping margin. The U.S. imposes an antidumping (AD) duty in the full amount of the dumping margin, whereas the European Union (EU) adheres to the "Lesser Duty Rule," imposing an AD duty just high enough to rectify the dumping. The punitive duty is the remedy for the unfairness of selling at below fair value — or, so the justification goes.

925

Appearances notwithstanding, the study and practice of AD law is not formulaic. The definition and formulas for the dumping margin raise three questions:

1. What is "Normal Value"?

2. What is "Export Price"?

3. What steps are taken ensure Normal Value and Export Price are comparable?

The answers to these questions, in turn, spawn a myriad of questions that make AD law both intellectually fascinating and technically complex. Further, calculation of the dumping margin is only the first of three phases in an AD case. The second phase is the injury determination, and third phase involves a review of an outstanding AD order.

B. Normal Value

To begin, "Normal Value" is a foreign home market price, specifically, the price of a foreign like product sold in the ordinary course of trade (*i.e.*, not to a related party or below-cost) for consumption in the country of the exporter (or producer). Under pre-Uruguay Round terminology used in the U.S., Normal Value was called "Foreign Market Value, or "FMV." Table 29-1 summarizes pre-and post-Uruguay Round dumping terms.

The exporter (or producer) refers to the entity alleged to be dumping merchandise in an importing country. Thus, if China is the importing country, and the exporter is an American company, then Normal Value is the price of the foreign like product sold in the U.S. This scenario is increasingly common. Decades ago, few countries other than the U.S. and EU brought AD cases. In the decade after the Uruguay Round, China, India, and other developing countries became increasingly aggressive about bringing AD cases.

TABLE 29-1:
PRE- VERSUS POST-URUGUAY ROUND TERMINOLOGY IN AD LAW

Pre-Uruguay Round Expression	Post-Uruguay Round Expression
Less Than Fair Value (LTFV)	Less Than Fair Value (LTFV)
Dumping Margin (DM)	Dumping Margin (DM)
Foreign Market Value (FMV)	Normal Value (NV)
United States Price (USP) (referring either to Purchase Price or Exporter's Sales Price)	No equivalent term. Must specify either Export Price or Constructed Export Price
Purchase Price (PP)	Export Price (EP)
Exporter's Sales Price (ESP)	Constructed Export Price (CEP)
Class or kind of merchandise subject to investigation	Subject merchandise
Like product	Domestic like product
Such or similar merchandise	Foreign like product

Reference to a "foreign like product" connotes a threshold likeness issue. Is allegedly dumped imported merchandise, known as the "subject merchandise" (because it is the goods subject to investigation) "like" the product the exporter sells in its home country? That is, in every AD case, there are three categories of goods involved:

i. The foreign like product, which is the good foreign exporter or producer sells in its home country.

ii. The subject merchandise, which is the allegedly dumped import.

iii. The domestic like product, *i.e.*, the product made in the importing country that is allegedly victimized by dumping.

The foreign like product must be compared to subject merchandise for purposes of calculating Normal Value (based on foreign like product sales) and Export Price (or, as explained below, Constructed Export Price). If the foreign like product and subject merchandise are different, then it is inappropriate to compare prices from their sales. In addition, subject merchandise must be compared with the domestic like product. If these goods differ, then it is inappropriate to base an injury determination relating to the domestic un-like product on dumping of subject merchandise.

For instance, suppose Caterpillar, Inc. is accused of dumping tractors in China. To calculate the dumping margin, sales in the U.S. on which Chinese AD authorities base Normal Value must be of tractors that are like tractors allegedly dumped in China, from which the authorities derive Export Price. To determine whether dumped tractors cause or threaten injury, those dumped tractors must be like Chinese-made tractors.

C. Proxies for Normal Value

It cannot be presumed Normal Value exists in every instance. To continue the example, suppose Caterpillar does not sell the same kind of tractors in the U.S. as in China. Rather, it sells those models in third countries, such as Australia, Japan, and Mexico. Or, suppose it sells the same model in the U.S., but in the period of investigation (POI) by Chinese AD authorities, the number of American sales is small. As still another possibility, suppose the sales by Caterpillar in the U.S. are sufficient in number, but below the cost of production. In such instances — no home market sales, an insufficient number of home market sales, or below cost sales — price data from the U.S. are unavailable or unreliable. Consequently, a proxy for the exporter's home market — here, a substitute for the U.S. — must be found. Chinese AD authorities might look to Caterpillar tractor sales in a market that resembles, as far as possible, the U.S. — such as Australia.

These instances can be related. Suppose some sales of the foreign like product made in the home country of the exporter or producer are made at below cost of production. Depending on the facts — namely, whether below-cost sales are in the ordinary course of trade, and the volume of below-cost sales — some or all sales may be disregarded as a basis to calculate Normal Value. If all of them are tossed out, then the home country is not a viable market in which to determine Normal Value. It becomes necessary to consider alternatives, *i.e.*, to find a proxy for Normal Value. The opposite situation can arise, namely, where there are a large number of sales in the exporter's home country (or where a large number of adjustments must be made to Normal Value). In that case, averaging or sampling techniques may be used to calculate Normal Value.

When a country other than the exporter's home market is used, then price data from that country may be used as the basis for a proxy for Normal Value. In other words, third country sales generate the Normal Value proxy, the proxy is known as "Third Country Price," and the dumping margin formula becomes:

Dumping Margin = Third Country Price — Export Price

Essentially, Third Country Price is the price of the foreign like product in a third country.

In some instances, there is no viable third country market from which to derive a price, *i.e.*, there is no third country in which sales of a foreign like product exist to form an adequate basis for comparison against sales of the allegedly dumped merchandise. Then, the proxy for Normal Value is Constructed Value, and formula becomes:

Dumping Margin = Constructed Value — Export Price

When either proxy is used, the dumping margin still may be expressed as a percentage, by dividing the difference by Export Price and multiplying the result by 100.

In contrast to Normal Value and Third Country Price, which are market-observed prices, Constructed Value is a bottom-up calculation of the foreign like product price. It is the sum of the cost of production (*e.g.*, factor inputs and materials that go into the product), plus figures for selling, general, and administrative (SG&A) expenses, and for profits. Article 2:2:2 of the WTO *Antidumping Agreement* mandates that SG&A expenses be actual production and sales data in the ordinary course of trade, But, if they are unavailable, the Article allows for the use of surrogates.

Article 2:2:2 permits three alternative sources from which to derive data are permissible. First, data may come from sales of merchandise in the domestic market of the country of origin, where the merchandise is in the same general category of products as the like product. Second, it is possible to use a weighted average of actual amounts incurred and realized of SG&A expenses, and profits, respectively, by other exporters or producers with respect to the like product as sold by them in the domestic market of the country of origin. Third, any other reasonable method may be used, as long as the amount adjusted for profit does not exceed the profit normally realized by other exporters or producers on sales of products in the same general category in the home market.

There is a clear order of preference, with Normal Value the first choice. Only if Normal Value is unavailable or unreliable is recourse made to Third Country Price. In turn, only if that Price is unavailable is Constructed Value used as a last resort proxy for Normal Value. Whenever Normal Value or Third Country Price is used, observe it is a single value expressed in U.S. dollars.

Moreover, this value is a weighted average of prices in the exporter's home country, or a third country, during the POI.

D. Export Price and Constructed Export Price

What is "Export Price"? It is the price at which subject merchandise is purchased (or agreed to be purchased) before the date of importation into the country in which this merchandise is allegedly dumped. Critically, Export Price must be an arm's length price between unrelated parties. Those parties are the purchaser (*e.g.*, importer) in the importing country and exporter (or producer). Thus, Export Price sometimes is defined simply as the price of subject merchandise between an exporter and unrelated buyer.

If the buyer and seller are related, then a substitute figure — "Constructed Export Price" (CEP) must be used. Constructed Export Price is the price at which subject merchandise is sold (or agreed to be sold) in the importing country before or after importation, where the sale is by or for the account of the exporter (or producer) to the first unrelated purchaser. Put succinctly, Constructed Export Price is sometimes defined as the first sale to an unrelated party in the importing country.

In a world populated by multinational corporations, intra-corporate trade is significant. Hence, related party pricing issues are common. An exporter might sell subject merchandise to a related party (*e.g.*, an importer that is an agency, branch, or subsidiary of the exporter) at a below-market price. The motive of the exporter could be to maximize profits of the affiliate, because applicable tax rates are lower in the importing country than exporting country. If tax rates are higher in the importing country, the exporter might charge its affiliated importer an above-market price, and thereby drain profits from the affiliate. Related-party pricing may have important tax consequences. From the perspective of AD law, if a price between an exporter and related party importer is off-market, then it cannot be used as a basis for a fair comparison to Normal Value. That is because Normal Value (or its proxy) is derived from open market transactions.

Are there instances in which an exporter and importer are related, yet Export Price rather than Constructed Export Price may be used? The answer is "yes." Suppose the purchaser of subject merchandise is a processor of sales-related documentation, but plays no role in setting the price to the first unrelated buyer. Here, the relationship between purchaser and exporter does not affect the price charged to an unaffiliated customer. The purchaser is a pass-through entity. The price is set by arm's length bargaining between exporter and customer. Then, that price is an acceptable basis for Export Price.

E. Comparing Apples to Apples

On the third question posed at the outset about the dumping margin calculation, a variety of steps are needed to ensure what practitioners call an "apples-to-apples" comparison between Normal Value and Export Price (or Constructed Export Price). In seeking fairness, it is essential to inquire whether any term in the dumping margin formula requires one or more adjustments to ensure comparability. In principle, adjustments ought to lead to scientific-like precision of comparability. In practice, arguing about adjustments is common, with *post hoc* rationalization of an addition or subtraction to serve the interest of the petitioner or respondent.

Thus, as GATT Article VI:1 and Article 2:4 of the WTO *Antidumping Agreement* indicate, adjustments are made to Normal Value account for differences in

- Merchandise.
- Quantities sold.
- Circumstances of sale (COS).
- Levels of trade (LOT) at which sales occur.

Adjustments Export Price (or Constructed Export Price) help obtain an *ex-factory* price (*i.e.*, the price of subject merchandise when it leaves the factory door in the home country of the exporter or producer). These adjustments include subtractions for:

- Delivery expenses.
- Import duties.

Some adjustments are made uniquely to Constructed Export Price. They include deductions for

- Selling commissions.
- Indirect selling expenses.
- Expenses and profit for further manufacturing (if any) in the importing country.
- Related-party profit (if any) earned from the sale of subject merchandise through a related distributor to an end-use in the importing country.

(The last deduction is linked to the LOT adjustment to Normal Value.)

In theory and practice, adjustments are a zero-sum game. Any adjustment either widens a dumping margin, which benefits petitioners, or narrows the margin, which pleases respondents. Each side tends to employ a formidable team of accountants and economists to run computer-based dumping margin calculations with different hypothetical adjustments. The simulation best suited to interests of a side — maximizing the margin for petitioners, or minimizing (or eliminating it entirely) for respondents — is sure to be favored by that side. To the extent there is supporting evidence, the adjustments in the "winning" simulation may be justified — *post hoc* — as appropriate.

Observe the LOT adjustment can prove especially tricky. The *Uruguay Round Agreements Act of 1994* (codified at 19 U.S.C. §§ 3501-3624, and amending several other Title 19 provisions) and the accompanying Clinton Administration *Statement of Administrative Action* changed LOT adjustment methodology. The U.S. Department of Commerce (DOC) should deduct from Normal Value any price difference between two levels of trade, if it is proven sales occur at different levels. Ostensibly, this adjustment ensures both Normal Value and Export Price (or Constructed Export Price) are derived from wholesale prices, or from retail prices, and eschews comparing wholesale prices in one market (*e.g.*, the exporter's home country) and retail prices in the other market (*e.g.*, the importing country). However, the intent behind the change is to provide a Normal Value counterpart to a Constructed Export Price adjustment. The relevant adjustment to Constructed Export Price is a deduction for related party profits (*i.e.*, profits earned by a party affiliated with the exporter). Supposedly, the effect is comparison of a sale in the exporter's home market with one in the U.S. at the same point in the commercial chain.

F.   Best Information and *De Minimis* Thresholds

Two of problems, in addition to the issues outlined above, at the outset of a dumping margin calculation concern the choice of information about price data and the need to check whether *de minimis* thresholds are crossed. The first issue is epistemological: how does an investigating authority know the information about Normal Value and Export Price (or Constructed Export Price) is reliable? Ultimately, the authority may have to conduct a "verification" visit in the home country of a respondent to check data from which Normal Value is derived. Likewise, some kind of verification of data about sales transactions in the importing country may be needed.

Generally, an investigating authority seeks to use the best information available, or "BIA." It asks a respondent to complete a lengthy questionnaire, which calls (*inter alia*) for information about pricing. If the respondent fails to fill it out, or if the responses are incomplete or untimely, then the BIA may be data the petitioner provides. Many disputes arise from whether a respondent failed to comply with requirements of the questionnaire, and thus whether reliance on the petitioner's data was reasonable. For a *NAFTA* Chapter 19 Panel Report on BIA, see *Fresh Cut Flowers from Mexico, Final Results of Antidumping Administrative Review*, USA-95-1904-05 (16 December 1996).

One revision to U.S. AD law made by the *1994 Act*, pursuant to the WTO *Antidumping Agreement*, is a change in terminology. "Facts otherwise available" — or, simply "facts available" — replaced "BIA." (*See* 19 U.S.C. § 1677e.) The concept remained the same. The *Statement of Administrative Action* for the *Agreement* observes that neither the DOC nor International Trade Commission (ITC) "must prove that the facts available are the best alternative information. Rather, the facts available are information or inferences which are reasonable to use under the circumstances." The administering agencies are supposed to balance all evidence in a record, and from it draw reasonable inferences. They cannot possibly be expected to demonstrate their inferences are the same as those they would have made if they had perfect information.

De minimis thresholds are another issue arising at the outset. Article 5:8 of the WTO *Antidumping Agreement* establishes a two-part *de minimis* inquiry.

    a.   Is there a volume of imports of subject merchandise below which authorities should ignore alleged dumping? The answer is "yes, 3 percent." (Under pre-Uruguay Round law, there was no *de minimis* volume test.)

b. Is there a value, *i.e.*, a level below which a dumping margin should be ignored? The answer is "yes, 2 percent *ad valorem*." (Under pre-Uruguay Round, the *de minimis* margin threshold was 0.5 percent.)

If either the volume or margin is *de minimis*, then an AD investigation is terminated.

The 3 percent *de minimis* volume test means an investigation starts if the volume subject merchandise is less than 3 percent of total imports of like merchandise from all countries. There is a built-in exception for cases in which more than one country exports subject merchandise. If the total volume of exports from such countries collectively exceeds 7 percent, then an investigation may start, even though no one exporting country's share exceeds 3 percent and is, therefore, negligible. The 2 percent *de minimis* margin test means a dumping margin of 2 percent or less is too small to bother about, and no investigation ensues. Are these *de minimis* thresholds sufficiently high to help mitigate the risk of protectionist abuse of AD law? Would 10 percent be better?

II. HOME MARKET VIABILITY AND NORMAL VALUE

A. The 5 Percent Test

Suppose the number, or nature, of sales of a foreign like product in the home market of an exporter or producer is insufficient to ascertain Normal Value. By "number," the implication is the volume of sales may be low, or even zero. By "nature," the suggestion is sales may be — to use the language of Article 2:2 of the WTO *Antidumping Agreement* — outside of "the ordinary course of trade in the domestic market of the exporting country." In either instance, one of two proxies for Normal Value must be used — a Third Country Price or Constructed Value.

However, the supposition about sufficiency of number and nature presumes a legal test for "insufficiency." How does an administering authority ascertain whether home market sales are, in fact, deficient in some way? The technical term for this issue is "home market viability." This rubric evinces the matter concerns capability of price data from the home market to germinate Normal Value. A footnote to Article 2:2 of the WTO *Antidumping Agreement* addresses the topic by providing a home market viability test.

Briefly put, if sale transactions in the home market of an exporter (or producer) are less than 5 percent of its sales to the importing country (*i.e.*, the one in which dumping is alleged), then "normally" those sales are deemed too small in quantity to render the home market viable. Then, export prices to a third country may be used in lieu of the home market price. Failing an acceptable Third Country Price, Constructed Value is used. Accordingly, the formula for home market viability is:

$$\text{Home Market viability} = \frac{\text{Quantity of sales by Exporter in its Home Market}}{\text{Quantity of sales by Exporter in the Importing Country}} \times 100$$

If this ratio exceeds 5 percent, then the home market is viable. In the U.S., until the Uruguay Round, the formula used bore the same numerator, but a different denominator. The pre-Uruguay Round formula was

$$\text{Home Market viability} = \frac{\text{Quantity of sales by Exporter in its Home Market}}{\text{Quantity of sales by Exporter in All Countries Except the Importing Country}} \times 100$$

The pre- vs. post-Uruguay Round denominator change was from sales excluding the rest of the world to sales excluding the importing country (*e.g.*, the U.S.), *i.e.*, from measuring the home market against the market in the importing country to measuring the home market against markets in the rest of the world (except the U.S.).

The rationale for an ostensibly minor technical change was to prevent reliance on price data to calculate Normal Value from "thin" (*i.e.*, a small volume of) home market sales. If the DOC uses sales figures from countries other than the U.S. in which the volume of sales is low, then the size of the denominator is reduced. In turn, the probability of satisfying the benchmark for viability, and thus using a Normal Value based on thin home market sales, increases. By preventing this outcome, calculation of the dumping margin is said to be less susceptible to manipulation by petitioners.

B. Viability, Product Parts, and the 1991 *NMB Singapore* Case

NMB SINGAPORE LTD. v. UNITED STATES
United States Court of International Trade
780 F. Supp. 823 (1991)

TSOUCALAS, JUDGE.

Plaintiffs, NMB Singapore, Ltd., Pelmec Singapore, Ltd. and NMB Corporation (collectively, "NMB") . . . contest the final determinations of the Department of Commerce, International Trade Administration ("Commerce" or "ITA") in *Final Determination of Sales at Less Than Fair Value: Ball Bearings and Parts Thereof From Singapore*, 54 Fed. Reg. 19,112 (1989). . . . [P]laintiffs contend that the ITA erred in including ball bearing parts in its calculation of the viability of the Singapore home market for NMB's ball bearings. Plaintiffs also assert that the ITA improperly included related party transfers of parts in the viability calculations when there were no comparable sales of parts to unrelated parties.

Background

Defendant-intervenor The Torrington Company ("Torrington") filed a petition . . . requesting that the ITA impose antidumping duties on all imports of antifriction bearings and parts thereof, except for tapered roller bearings, from a number of countries, including Singapore. In the course of the ensuing investigation, the ITA determined that NMB's home market for ball bearings in Singapore was not an appropriate market to compare to the United States market for purposes of calculating the dumping margin. Thus, the ITA resorted to using NMB's sales in a third country, Japan, to determine the margin. . . . [T]he ITA published an antidumping duty order for ball bearings and parts thereof from Singapore, setting an estimated weighted average margin of 25.08% on NMB's merchandise.

Discussion

. . . .

I. Inclusion of Parts in Viability Calculations

. . . .

Home market sales generally are considered too small if they constitute less than five percent of the quantity sold in countries other than the United States. In that case, since the home market is not "viable," FMV [Foreign Market Value, *i.e.*, Normal Value] must be calculated by alternative means, that is, by using either third country sales or constructed value.

Plaintiffs' complaint is that the ITA wrongly included parts of bearings in its calculation of the viability of NMB's home market for ball bearings; that is, the ITA considered ball bearing parts to be merchandise which is "such or similar" to finished ball bearings, and that this caused NMB's home market sales to fall below the regulatory benchmark of 5% of its non-U.S. sales.

The government's response is that it tested viability based on the five classes or kinds of bearings under investigation (ball bearings, spherical roller bearings, cylindrical roller bearings, needle roller bearings and spherical plain bearings) rather than on the such or similar merchandise [*i.e.*, foreign like product] categories normally compared. The reason was that the variations in characteristics of the such or similar merchandise selected by Commerce would have made it "necessary to conduct several hundred viability tests."

Consequently, all sales of antifriction bearings fitting within one of the five classes of bearings, as well as all sales of parts of those bearings, were compared together. Thus, sales of ball bearings and parts of ball bearings in Singapore were divided by sales of ball bearings and parts of ball bearings in all non-U.S. markets, and the resulting percentage was less than 5%.

NMB claims this was unfair and improper because almost all of its sales of ball bearing parts were to its Thai sister company, NMB/Pelmec Thailand, and NMB did not sell parts in the home market. Since each part was treated as if it was equal to each finished bearing, dividing home market sales by non-U.S. sales yielded a figure of less than 5%. The government asserts that it tested parts with finished bearings under each of the five classes of bearings because it would have been wrong to recognize the distinction between finished bearings and parts, and not recognize the hundreds of permutations among bearings based on other characteristics such as outside diameter.

. . . The Court concurs that, given the large number of variations in merchandise and the unique complexity of the bearings investigations, testing viability based on the five classes was appropriate. However, within each class or kind, the ITA should have tested parts separately from finished bearings, where there was no uniform indication of how many parts comprise a bearing, and where the sale of each part was treated the same as the sale of each bearing. The distinction between a finished product and its component parts is fundamental and it would not have sabotaged the class distinctions favored by Commerce for the ITA to have tested parts and finished bearings separately.

. . . .

While the "complex facts" of this case permit Commerce to test viability based on the five classes of bearings, they do not justify the decision not to test parts separately from finished bearings. The result would have been just five more viability tests, not "several hundred," and a more accurate determination of the status of the home market would have ensued. Given the lack of data as to how many parts comprise an average bearing, and the consequent equation of one part to one bearing, the decision to treat parts and completed bearings as such or similar merchandise was not reasonable and was not in accordance with either the letter or the spirit of 19 U.S.C. § 1677b(a)(1)(A).

However, during the investigations, Commerce did in fact respond to the complaints of the few importers whose home markets of finished bearings and parts thereof were found to be non-viable, by testing the viability of finished bearings alone. NMB was such an importer, and the results of the re-testing were that NMB's home market sales of *finished* ball bearings constituted more than 5% of its total non-U.S. sales of finished ball bearings.

Nonetheless, the ITA decided to disregard these results and use NMB's third country data in the price comparisons. The first reason given was that NMB's "submissions on value and volume of sales data were inconsistent with respect to which parts were reported and on what basis (*i.e.*, date of shipment vs. date of purchase order) they were reported." . . . Second, the ITA stated that the increase in the home market's percentage of total non-U.S. sales was not significant, even though the percentage went from under the 5% benchmark to over it. The ITA explained that, because of these reasons, it could not be confident of the viability of the home market and thus third country data from Japan was used instead.

. . . The fact that the increase in the home market's share of total sales was only slight is not a compelling reason [for departing from the U.S. AD statute, the *Tariff Act of 1930*, as amended, and DOC regulations], where the percentage [of 5 percent] did surpass the regulatory benchmark.

The other reason, that the home market data was ambiguous and inconsistent, is a more potent argument. However, the *Final Determination* indicates that the "inconsistent" reporting was only with regard to the sales of parts. . . . Once parts are removed from the equation, this inconsistency will dissipate. Therefore, this reason is inapplicable to the viability of the home market for finished ball bearings. . . .

. . . [T]he Court remands this case to the ITA with instructions that it use NMB's home market sales data for finished ball bearings from Singapore in the price comparisons for purposes of the less than fair value determination. The ITA shall also determine the viability of NMB's home market for ball bearing parts in a separate calculation. . . .

II. Related Party Transfers

NMB also asserts that the ITA improperly used related party transfers in the viability calculations. . . .

All of plaintiffs' sales of parts were to a related party. Thus, plaintiffs assert that these sales should be disregarded since there were no sales to unrelated parties which could serve to determine if the related party transfers were at arm's length.

The *Tariff Act* makes no mention of related party transfers in the context of the viability analysis. . . . Related party transfers *must* be excluded only from actual price comparisons, not from the home market viability tests. This is because the viability test seeks only to determine the level of market activity in a given country, not whether that activity was at arm's length. The arm's length determination is relevant only to the LTFV comparisons. Hence, the ITA's decision to include related party transfers in the viability computations was in accordance with law and is affirmed.

C. Sample, Sporadic, and Related Party Sales and the 1999 *NSK* Case

NSK LTD. v. UNITED STATES
United States Court of Appeals for the Federal Circuit
190 F.3d 1321-35 (1999)

MICHEL, CIRCUIT JUDGE.

This consolidated appeal concerns the Department of Commerce, International Trade Administration's ("Commerce's") fourth annual administrative review of the antidumping order on certain antifriction bearings and parts thereof (the "antifriction bearings"). See *Antifriction Bearings (Other Than Tapered Roller Bearings) and Parts Thereof From France, et al.; Final Results of Antidumping Duty Administrative Reviews, Partial Termination of Administrative Reviews, and Revocation in Part of Antidumping Duty Orders*, 60 Fed. Reg. 10,900 (Dep't Commerce, 1995) (*"Final Results"*). On appeal, the Court of International Trade granted in part and denied in part various parties' motions for judgment on the agency record and remanded to Commerce for various re-determinations in accordance with its opinion. *See NSK Ltd. v. United States*, 969 F. Supp. 34 (Ct. Int'l Trade 1997) (*"NSK I"*). Commerce made the re-determinations as ordered on remand. *See Final Results of Redetermination Pursuant to Court Remand, NSK Ltd., et al. v. United States*, 969 F. Supp. 34, slip op. 97-74 (1997), (Dep't Commerce Apr. 28, 1998) (*"Remand Results"*). The Remand Results were subsequently affirmed by the Court of International Trade in their entirety. *See NSK Ltd. v. United States*, 4 F. Supp. 2d 1264, slip op. 98-77 (Ct. Int'l Trade 1998) (*"NSK II"*).

Plaintiffs-Appellants Koyo Seiko Co., Ltd. and Koyo Corporation of U.S.A. (together "Koyo Seiko"), Plaintiffs-Appellants NTN Bearing Corporation of America, American NTN Bearing Manufacturing Corp., NTN Corporation, NTN Driveshaft, Inc., and NTN-Bower Corporation (collectively "NTN"), and Defendant-Cross Appellant The Torrington Company ("Torrington") now appeal and cross appeal to this court from various aspects of *NSK I* and *NSK II*. We affirm the judgment of the Court of International Trade with respect to NTN's appeal because we find no error, legal or factual, with regard to (i) Commerce's inclusion of certain sample sales and sales with a sporadic sales history as home market sales in its calculation of foreign market value ("FMV") [*i.e.*, Normal Value (NV)]; (ii) Commerce's exclusion of related party sales from the home market sales used in its calculation of FMV; (iii) Commerce's refusal to adjust FMV to take account of NTN's reported home market discounts; and (iv) Commerce's comparison of sales across different levels of trade in its calculation of FMV. However, with respect to the Court of International Trade's rejection of the home market warranty expense factor reported by Koyo Seiko and accepted by Commerce as a "circumstances of sale" adjustment to FMV, we reverse on the grounds that Commerce's acceptance of the adjustment was based upon a reasonable interpretation of the governing statute, accorded with applicable precedent, and its rejection by the court was therefore error. Finally, we affirm with respect to Torrington's cross appeal of the determination of the United States price of the antifriction bearings bought and resold by Defendants-Appellees Honda Motor Co., Ltd., American

Honda Motor Co., Inc., Honda of America Mfg., Inc. and Honda Power Equipment Mfg., Inc (collectively, "Honda"). Like the Court of International Trade, we hold that Commerce reasonably interpreted the term "reseller" in the governing antidumping statute and that substantial evidence supports Commerce's determination that Honda constitutes such a "reseller" with regard to its sales of subject antifriction bearings.

[Omitted is the Court's discussion of NTN's appeal of issues (iii) and (iv). Omitted, too, is the Court's discussion of the appeal by Koyo Seiko concerning the circumstances of sale adjustment (COS) to Foreign Market Value.]

BACKGROUND

The fourth annual administrative review of the antidumping order at issue covered antifriction bearings entered during the period May 1, 1992, through April 30, 1993. Although the review concerned imports from eight countries, the judgments on appeal here concern only imports from Japan. Because the review was initiated prior to January 1, 1995, the applicable antidumping law and regulations are those that were in effect prior to the changes made by the Uruguay Round Amendments [*sic* — the correct word is "Agreements"] Act, Pub. L. No. 103-465, 108 Stat. 4809 (1994) (the *"URAA"*). See *URAA* § 291(a)(2), (b); *Cemex, S.A. v. United States*, 133 F.3d 897, 899 n.1 (Fed. Cir. 1998).

. . . .

. . . NTN argues (i) that substantial evidence does not support Commerce's inclusion in its FMV [Foreign Market Value, *i.e.*, Normal Value] calculation of certain sales identified by NTN as sample sales and sporadic sales; [and] (ii) that Commerce unreasonably excluded from its calculation of FMV certain of NTN's home market sales to related parties. . . .

. . . .

DISCUSSION

. . . .

II. NTN's Appeal

A. The Alleged Sample and Sporadic Sales

Under 19 U.S.C. § 1677b(a)(1)(A) (1988), FMV is the price "at which such or similar merchandise [*i.e.*, foreign like product] is sold or, in the absence of sales, offered for sale in the principal markets of the country from which exported, . . . in the ordinary course of trade for home consumption" (emphasis added). As defined by statute:

> The term "ordinary course of trade" means the conditions and practices which, for a reasonable time prior to the exportation of the merchandise which is the subject of an investigation, have been normal in the trade under consideration with respect to merchandise of the same class or kind.

19 U.S.C. § 1677(15) (1988).

In the *Final Results*, Commerce included as home market sales in the ordinary course of trade certain sales identified by NTN as sample sales and sales with sporadic sales histories. Commerce reasoned that NTN's mere designation of certain sales as sample sales did not satisfy its burden of proving that the sales were made outside of the ordinary course of trade. . . . Similarly, Commerce rejected NTN's claim that certain sales of small quantities of products with sporadic sales histories were outside of the ordinary course of trade, explaining that "such sales histories are typical of certain types of products." . . .

In *NSK I*, the Court of International Trade remanded to Commerce for a re-determination in light of this court's ruling in *NSK, Ltd. v. United States*, 115 F.3d 965, 973-75 (Fed. Cir. 1997), that samples given without consideration do not constitute sales under the antidumping statute. In its *Remand Results*, Commerce explained that certain of the transactions labeled by NTN as "sample and other similar transfers" were, in fact, transfers in which monetary consideration was paid for the bearings. Consequently, the Court of International Trade amended its prior ruling in *NSK I* to order Commerce only to exclude those transactions for which NTN received no consideration. Commerce complied with this instruction on remand and its determinations were sustained by *NSK II*.

We are not persuaded that substantial evidence does not support Commerce's determination that NTN failed to meet its burden to prove that the alleged sample and sporadic sales were sales outside of the ordinary course of trade. The evidence submitted by NTN consisted of its records indicating sales of samples under the term "SAMPLEH" and sporadic sales under the term "NORDCH." The sales designated by NTN as sporadic were simply those in which there were seven or less transactions in the total review period with three or less units per transaction. No evidence was submitted that the process of ordering or shipping these alleged sample or sporadic sales differed from "ordinary" sales. Nor was evidence submitted that any of these sales required, for example, unique engineering specifications. Moreover, no evidence was submitted that the alleged sample sales for which monetary consideration was paid, differed in any material respect, other than by their designation as "SAMPLEH," from "ordinary" sales of the same merchandise for monetary consideration. Thus, given our deferential standard of review, we cannot say that Commerce's finding of a failure of proof was unsupported by substantial evidence.

B. The Related Party Sales

Under 19 U.S.C. § 1677b(a)(3) (1988), Commerce may base FMV on related party transactions. To implement this statute, Commerce promulgated a regulation requiring importers to demonstrate that their sales to related parties are comparable in price to unrelated party transactions. Specifically, the regulation provides:

> If a producer or reseller sold such or similar merchandise to a person related as described in section 771(13) of the *Act*, the Secretary

ordinarily will calculate foreign market value based on that sale only if satisfied that the price is comparable to the price at which the producer or reseller sold such or similar merchandise to a person not related to the seller.

19 C.F.R. § 353.45(a) (1993).

In the fourth annual administrative review, NTN responded to Section C of Commerce's questionnaire by listing its sales and annotating them with a "1" or a "2" to indicate whether they were, respectively, related or unrelated party sales. After conducting an "arm's-length test" using weighted average prices for each class of merchandise to determine whether the prices that NTN charged related parties were representative of market prices, Commerce excluded the reported related party sales of ball and cylindrical roller bearings due to the related party prices being lower than the corresponding unrelated party prices. . . . However, Commerce included the reported related party sales of spherical roller bearings due to the reported prices not being less than the corresponding prices to unrelated parties. . . . In *NSK I*, the Court of International Trade affirmed, reasoning that NTN had presented no evidence that Commerce's test was unreasonable. . . .

On appeal, NTN argues that Commerce's use of weighted averages to compare related and unrelated party sales unreasonably distorted the comparison. To illustrate, NTN provides a hypothetical example in which the actual per unit price to both the related and unrelated parties is the same but, because different quantities are sold to the related and unrelated parties, the weighted average price for the goods sold to the unrelated party is higher.

In light of "the substantial discretion accorded Commerce when interpreting and applying its own regulations," *Torrington Co. v. United States*, 156 F.3d 1361, 1363 (Fed. Cir. 1998), we are unpersuaded that Commerce's use of weighted averages was unreasonable. . . . Commerce's methodology was reasonable because, without the use of weighting, small sales that might be "outliers" could be given undue weight in the calculation. Without employing such a weighting, Commerce's approach would be susceptible to the "perceived danger that a foreign manufacturer will sell to related companies in the home market at artificially low prices, thereby camouflaging true FMV and achieving a lower antidumping duty margin." *NEC Home Elecs., Inc. v. United States*, 54 F.3d 736, 739 (Fed. Cir. 1995). Moreover, although NTN's hypothetical suggests a potential anomaly of using a weighted average test, NTN has not provided evidence, nor even suggested, that such an anomalous result occurred here. Thus, NTN's hypothetical does not demonstrate that Commerce's test was unreasonable as applied to NTN's actual situation, only, at the very most, to circumstances not here present.

D. Below-Cost Sales and the 1984 *Southwest Florida Winter Vegetable* Case

SOUTHWEST FLORIDA WINTER VEGETABLE GROWERS ASSOCIATION v. UNITED STATES
United States Court of International Trade
584 F. Supp. 10 (1984)

CARMAN, JUDGE.

This case presents a novel issue of whether Commerce may disregard a substantial number of below cost sales, reflecting the perishable nature of produce, in determining whether sales were made at less than fair value under our antidumping laws. It is an important determination not only to the parties to this action but to the domestic and Mexican produce industries as a whole. . . .

Plaintiffs filed a petition with the United States Treasury Department (Treasury) . . . alleging certain fresh winter vegetables — tomatoes, squash, eggplant, bell peppers and cucumbers — were imported from Mexico . . . and were being sold in the United States at less than fair value. [At the time of filing, Treasury was an administering authority.] The petition of plaintiffs alleged that Southern Florida and the State of Sinaloa, Mexico, provided the source of virtually all fresh winter vegetables for markets in the United States and that Nogales, Arizona, was the point of importation for over 95 percent of all winter vegetables from Mexico.

. . . Treasury issued . . . a *Tentative Determination of Sales at Not Less Than Fair Value.* . . . Subsequently, the antidumping investigation was transferred to Commerce. . . . Treasury's preliminary negative determination was treated as though it had been issued by Commerce. . . .

. . . Commerce issued a *Final Determination of Sales at Not Less Than Fair Value.*

. . . .

. . . Plaintiffs' contentions in essence are: (1) Commerce erred in using the third country sales methodology rather than the constructed value methodology in determining foreign market value because a substantial number of third country sales at below cost existed making the valuation inaccurate; [and] (2) Commerce improperly refused to disregard a substantial amount of below cost sales. . . . [Omitted are the Plaintiffs' contentions regarding the DOC's adjustments and use of regression analysis.]

Defendant has responded to plaintiffs' arguments, noting: (1) the *1979 Act* [*i.e.,* the *Trade Agreements Act of 1979*, which implemented the Tokyo Round agreements] establishes a general preference for the use of third country sales over constructed value; [and] (2) the decision to include up to 50 percent below cost sales is supported by uncontroverted evidence and is authorized by statute. . . .

I. Methodology Employed

To determine whether sales at less than fair value occurred, Commerce had to calculate the "fair value" of the subject merchandise pursuant to the procedures specified for determining foreign market value. Three methods are available for this calculation: (1) the sales price of the merchandise in the country of export (home market sales), (2) the sales price of the merchandise in a country other than the United States (third country sales), or, (3) the "constructed value" of the merchandise (sum of costs for material, fabrication, general expenses and profit).

Before 1979, the third country sales methodology instead of constructed value methodology was required by statute where the home market sales methodology was not available. . . . Although the mandatory preference for third country sales is no longer required, the legislative history and relevant regulations indicate, nevertheless, a preference for third country sales where there is adequate confirmation subject to timely verification. . . . The criteria employed in selecting the third country sales methodology are in order of significance: similarity of product, volume of sales, and similarity of market from an organizational and development point of view. . . .

If Commerce is unable to establish foreign market value based on home market prices (*e.g.*, where there is no home market) or upon third country sales (*e.g.*, where there is inadequate information that can be verified within the time required), then the constructed value methodology may be employed.

In this case, the home market sales methodology was not employed because an insufficient domestic Mexican market existed for fresh winter vegetables. Commerce utilized the third country (Canada) sales method of comparison instead of the constructed value method noting the general preference for third country sales and its greater accuracy in the case at hand. Furthermore, as noted by Commerce, use of constructed value would be wholly unsuitable to the economic realities presented in this case. A principal characteristic of the fresh winter vegetable market is wide price fluctuations, both within a day and over the season. As the Commerce determination reflects, it is a necessary practice for many individual sales to be below the average cost of production. Profitability depends on sales over the course of a season. The use of a price arrived at by constructed value would necessarily give the appearance of dumping even though sellers would be acting in a normal, indeed in a necessary, manner in light of industry demands. Thus, the constructed value methodology is inappropriate because it would require finding that an economically necessary business practice is unfair. As the Senate Report noted: "[T]hird country prices will normally be preferred over constructed value if presented in a timely manner and if adequate to establish foreign market value." . . .

Plaintiffs argue that third country price data in this case is inadequate for the fair value comparison because of the presence of price volatility and the existence of a significant number of sales below the cost of production. This court cannot agree.

First, the proportion of Canadian sales to United States sales (*i.e.*, Canadian sales are approximately 20 percent of United States sales) affords an adequate basis for comparison in using third country sales and is within established administrative guidelines. Second, plaintiffs conceded in their administrative petition that the two markets are almost identical. And third, the record reflects substantial evidence to support the conclusion of price equality.

Furthermore, plaintiffs' contention that constructed value should have been utilized because (1) some growers had too few or no Canadian sales; (2) on some days, growers had sales to the United States, but none to Canada; and, (3) some growers had insufficient above-cost sales to Canada, is without merit. There is no support for the proposition that Commerce was required to utilize constructed value for those transactions that could not be matched with United States transactions for the same grower's product, size and day.

Based on the general preference for the use of third country sales over constructed value, and the existence of adequate data for third country sales, this court cannot find Commerce erred in its use of this methodology.

II. Treatment of Below Cost Sales

. . . Commerce concluded that "it would be appropriate to disregard below-cost Canadian sales only if such sales constituted 50 percent or more of a grower's total sales to Canada of the type of produce under consideration.". . . Plaintiffs argue this 50 percent benchmark resulted in the erroneous consideration of a significant number of below cost sales in the determination by Commerce of foreign market value. Neither the statute nor its legislative history, however, supports this contention by plaintiffs.

. . . Commerce is required to disregard below cost sales only when they have been made in substantial quantities over an extended period of time, and are not at prices that permit recovery of all costs within a reasonable period of time in the normal course of trade. As legislative history reflects, "[s]tandards would not require the disregarding of below-cost sales in every instance, for under normal business in both foreign countries and the United States, it is frequently necessary to sell obsolete or end-of-model year merchandise at less than cost. . . . [I]nfrequent sales at less than cost, or sales prices which will permit recovery of all costs based upon anticipated sales volume over a reasonable period of time would not be disregarded." . . .

Commerce found that the fresh winter vegetable markets, in contrast to markets for industrial products or agricultural products with a relatively longer shelf life, normally experience below cost sales, and such sales are common and expected.

Commerce determined that Mexican producers do not have the ability to control their short-term output and cannot store their products. They look to make profits over the season as a whole, and do not expect to recover full costs on individual sales. The record reflects that it is not uncommon for some sales by foreign and domestic producers of fresh winter vegetables to be as much as 50 percent below the cost of production.

In short, the statute permits the consideration of below cost sales made in the normal course of trade at prices that permit full cost recovery within a reasonable period of time, and there is substantial evidence in the administrative record to support Commerce's determination that below cost sales in this case up to 50 percent were made in the normal course of trade and at prices that permit full cost recovery within a reasonable period of time. Commerce, therefore, properly regarded the below cost sales in its determination of foreign market value.

E.   Comparing Merchandise and the 1997 *NTN Bearing* Case

NTN BEARING CORPORATION OF AMERICA v. UNITED STATES
United States Court of Appeals for the Federal Circuit
127 F.3d 1061-65 (1997)

RADER, CIRCUIT JUDGE.

. . . NTN Bearing Corporation of America, American NTN Bearing Manufacturing Corporation, and NTN Corporation (collectively, NTN) dispute [the Department of] Commerce's calculation of the fair market value for TRBs [tapered roller bearings]. Because substantial evidence supports Commerce's actions, this court affirms.

I

. . . TRBs are a type of antifriction bearing made up of an inner ring (cone) and an outer ring (cup). Cups and cones sell either individually or as a preassembled "set."

Commerce's fundamental task in an antidumping investigation is to compare the United States price of imported merchandise with the value of "such or similar merchandise" [*i.e.*, foreign like product] in the [exporter's] home market, 19 U.S.C. § 1677 (16) (1988), and assess a duty, known as a dumping margin, for any deficiency. [As the Court explained in a footnote: "This section was amended on December 8, 1994. As both Commerce's administrative review and the Court of International Trade's adjudicatory proceeding were conducted under the statute as written prior to the 1994 amendment, we will refer to the statute in its pre-amended form. The amendment does not affect the outcome in this case."] When Commerce identifies "such" or identical home market merchandise, the comparison between matched goods is easy and accurate. Without identical goods for value comparison, Commerce must find "similar" home market merchandise to make a proper comparison with the imports.

Commerce has established methods to determine the constructed value of "similar" merchandise in the home market. . . . First, Commerce "splits" sales of TRB sets sold in Japan into their component cups and cones. Next, Commerce compares the cups and cones with their imported counterparts using five physical criteria: (1) inner ring bore (inside diameter); (2) outer ring diameter; (3) width; (4) load rating; and (5) "Y," factor (measure of thrust load capability). Finally, Commerce uses a "sum of deviations" method, coupled with a twenty percent difference-in-merchandise test, to find the best matching TRB model.

After assessment of duties, NTN appealed to the Court of International Trade challenging eleven actions by Commerce. . . . In April 1996, the trial court denied in all respects NTN's motion for judgment on the agency record. *NTN Bearing Corp. of Am. v. United States*, 924 F. Supp. 200 (Ct. Int'l Trade 1996). Specifically, the Court of International Trade held that Commerce's set-splitting method prevents an importer from manipulating home market calculations.

Conceding that Commerce may split sets to calculate fair market value, NTN raises only one issue on appeal, namely, the judgment upholding Commerce's splitting of certain "unsplittable" TRB sets. NTN claims that because it never separately sells the cups and cones of certain bearing models — TRB units, TRB double row models, TRB thrust bearings, TRB flanged bearings, and TRB high precision models — Commerce cannot calculate fair market value based on the constituent parts of these bearings. NTN contends that Commerce exceeded its discretion by applying its setsplitting methodology to these unsplittable sets.

II

. . . .

. . . [T]he relevant inquiry is whether the trial court properly sustained Commerce's use of its set-splitting method to split "unsplittable" sets in arriving at a value for similar merchandise." The *Tariff Act of 1930*, as amended . . . broadly defines the phrase "such or similar" as applied to goods for comparison under the antidumping test. Because it does not specify a method for matching a U.S. product with a suitable home-market product, the *Act* has implicitly authorized Commerce to choose a way to identify "such or similar" merchandise. . . .

. . . .

This court has previously upheld Commerce's set-splitting and sum of deviations methods to identify "such or similar" goods for the antidumping comparison. *See, e.g.*, id. at 1204 [*i.e., Koyo Seiko Co. v. United States*, 66 F.3d 1204 (Fed. Cir. 1995)]. These earlier decisions have stressed that Commerce possesses discretion to calculate the fair market value based upon a "close-as-possible" matching of physical characteristics of separate cups and cones. This method does not require an identical match of home market and imported cups and cones. Rather, Commerce remains within its discretion when it strives to find price data for closely analogous bearing components.

The five unsplittable sets at issue always sell as sets in the Japanese market. However, as part of its efforts to match imported components with similar goods sold in the home market, Commerce split the Japanese market sets into their component cups and cones. Commerce then performed a critical physical analysis on each cup and cone, placing the Japanese components into a "pool" of potential "such or similar" home market TRB cups and cones. Commerce used this pool in its "sum of the deviations" methodology and twenty percent difference-in-merchandise test to determine the best matching TRB model components in Japan to compare with the imported cups and cones.

Because it was unable to identify "such" or identical home market goods after a reasonable search for a match to the imported parts, Commerce reasonably applied its splitting methodology to unsplittable sets sold in the home market to identify "similar" goods for a value comparison. This reasonable method was, therefore, in accord with the statute. . . . The antidumping act simply does not require the sale of "similar" merchandise in the same manner in both the United States and home markets. Likewise, the act does not prohibit the separation of unsplittable sets. (In fact, unsplittable sets is a bit of a misnomer. This term includes sets sold in Japan that are easily, but not currently, split, and sets that are assembled into housings that make physical splitting into components difficult.) Acceptance of NTN's argument that Commerce may not split into components products sold only as sets in the home market would allow importers to circumvent the law. An importer could manipulate Commerce's determinations by depriving it of a pool of similar products sold in the home market with which it could compare the imported goods. In the absence of a statutory prohibition against splitting these sets, Commerce's actions are reasonable.

Thus, the Court of International Trade properly upheld Commerce's actions as supported by substantial evidence and in accordance with law.

III.   THIRD COUNTRY PRICE AND CONSTRUCTED VALUE

A.   Choice of Proxy and the 1995 *Floral Trade Council* Case

FLORAL TRADE COUNCIL v. THE UNITED STATES
United States Court of Appeals for the Federal Circuit
74 F.3d 1200-04 (1995)

NIES, CIRCUIT JUDGE.

. . . .

BACKGROUND

This court action commenced with FTC's [*i.e.*, plaintiff-petitioner Floral Trade Council] and *Asocolflores's* [*i.e.*, defendant-respondent *Asociacion Colombiana De Exportadores de Flores (Asocolflores)*] challenge to the final results of an International Trade Administration (ITA) antidumping duty review respecting certain fresh cut flowers from Colombia. 55 Fed. Reg. 20,491 (1990). FTC contested, *inter alia*, ITA's use of constructed value for the foreign market value (*i.e.*, Normal Value) as opposed to using third country prices. *Asocolflores* objected, *inter alia*, to ITA's selection of monthly instead of annual average U.S. prices.

The trial court upheld ITA's use of constructed value, finding reasonable ITA's interpretation of its governing statute that third country prices may be abandoned if there is an adequate factual basis in the record for doing so. Further, that court credited the factors underlying the ITA conclusion that using constructed value was proper because reliance on European prices for third country prices would produce misleading results due to differences between the floral markets in Europe and the United States. The trial court was also persuaded that monthly averaging of U.S. prices was an appropriate compromise, whereas annual averaging would mask dumping. *Floral Trade Council v. United States*, 15 C.I.T. 497, 775 F. Supp. 1492, 1497, 1500 (Ct. Int'l Trade 1991). After remand on grounds not pertinent to this appeal, judgment was entered upholding ITA's review and the parties appealed to this Court. . . .

ANALYSIS

The ITA determinations under review must be upheld unless the determinations are "unsupported by substantial evidence on the record, or otherwise not in accordance with law." *Tariff Act of 1930*, § 516A, 19 U.S.C. § 1516a(b)(1)(B) (1988); *Rhone Poulenc, Inc. v. United States*, 899 F.2d 1185, 1189, 8 Fed. Cir. (T) 61, 65 (Fed. Cir. 1990). Substantial evidence "means such relevant evidence as a reasonable mind might accept as adequate to support a conclusion." *Matsushita Elec. Indus. v. United States*, 750 F.2d 927, 933 (Fed. Cir. 1984) (citing *Universal Camera Corp. v. NLRB*, 340 U.S. 474, 477 . . . (1951)). Moreover, under traditional principles of judicial deference to agency interpretation of statutes the agency administers, our review questions whether the agency's interpretation is reasonable. *Chevron U.S.A. v. Natural Resources Defense Council*, 467 U.S. 837, 844 . . . (1984). . . .

I

Constructed Value

On appeal, FTC argues that ITA unlawfully abandoned third-country prices as the basis for foreign market value. Citing statutes and regulations expressing a preference for third-country prices, FTC contends that ITA could not depart from that preference in this case. FTC asserts that verified third country prices were available and that no unusual facts justified ITA's rejection of them.

The *Tariff Act of 1930*, as amended in 1979, directs ITA to determine the foreign market value based on (1) the price at which similar merchandise is sold in the country from which exported (here Colombia); or (2) if the exporter's home market consumption is low or nonexistent, then the price at which the merchandise is sold for exportation to a third country. 19 U.S.C. § 1677b(a)(1). ITA's own regulations announce a clear preference for third country prices if adequate and verifiable information is available. . . . However, the statute also gives ITA the discretion to construct a value when home market prices cannot be determined. . . .

. . . ITA determined that it could not determine the price under the first statutory directive and, due to extraordinary circumstances, it chose to use a constructed value rather than third country prices. ITA reasoned that the United States and European markets are not positively correlated and that this negative correlation could mask dumping in certain instances or exaggerate it in others. First, ITA determined that the European market for flowers is mature with a constant demand, whereas the United States market exhibits extreme volatility due to sporadic gift-giving. Second, Colombian growers are not a constant participant in the European flower auction houses and, therefore, Colombian growers sell flowers in Europe only occasionally. Third, European and United States holidays often do not coincide, resulting in different peak periods in the two markets. Last, Colombians plan their production cycles on the U.S. market and, therefore, sell excess flowers in markets where they did not necessary plan to sell, which adds an element of chance to prices obtained for those flowers.

FTC takes issue with ITA's exercise of discretion in choosing to use a constructed value rather than using third country prices. We are unpersuaded of factual or legal error in ITA's selection of constructed value or of an abuse of discretion. We find no restriction either in the statute or the regulations limiting use of constructed value to situations where verified information is not available for third country prices. Further, ITA's explanation for rejecting such prices was reasonable.

FTC also attacks the evidence underlying the factors on which ITA relied. Both *Asocolflores* and the government amply demonstrate that substantial evidence exists to support ITA's findings. More than ten years ago, we faced a similar evidentiary challenge and stated:

> That [FTC] can point to evidence which detracts from the evidence which supports the [ITA's] decision and can hypothesize a reasonable basis for a contrary determination is neither surprising nor persuasive. It is not the function of a court to decide that, were it the [ITA], it would have made the same decision on the basis of the evidence. Our role is limited to deciding whether the [ITA's] decision is "unsupported by substantial evidence on the record, or otherwise not in accordance with law."

Matsushita Elec., 750 F.2d at 936. "The possibility of drawing two inconsistent conclusions from the evidence does not prevent an administrative agency's finding from being supported by substantial evidence." *Id.* at 933 (quoting *Consolo v. Federal Maritime Comm'n*, 383 U.S. 607, 619-20 . . . (1966)). Here, FTC asks us to accept its view of the facts, which we decline to do.

. . . [W]e affirm ITA's use of constructed value on the facts of this case.

II

Monthly Averaging

Asocolflores's appeal challenges ITA's selection of monthly, instead of annual, average U.S. prices as unsupported by substantial evidence. Asserting that ITA's reasoning for selecting a monthly average is merely speculative, *Asocolflores* states that ITA's choice is not based on any evidence and is inadequate as a matter of law. *Asocolflores* notes that ITA's internal analyses all support an annual averaging. Further, *Asocolflores* claims that the constructed value for foreign market value is based on an annual average, so that comparing monthly U.S. prices to a constructed annual value will necessarily establish dumping anytime the Colombian grower does not meet its average annual profit. With perishable flowers, growers must occasionally sell at a loss, but at other times the growers sell at a great profit, so that their annual profit balances the peaks and valleys of selling. Last, *Asocolflores* notes that ITA's reasoning for rejecting an annual average for U.S. prices directly contradicts its reasoning for rejecting third country prices for foreign market value.

The *Tariff Act* empowers ITA to use averaging in determining United States price. 19 U.S.C. § 1677f-1(b). The determination to select averages *rests exclusively* with the ITA if the averages are "representative of the transactions under investigation." *Id.* Because ITA has discretion to use averages, *Asocolflores's* challenge must be directed to whether the averages are "representative" of the transactions under investigation.

In its preliminary determination, ITA found averaging was necessary to account for perishability. Growers do not control when flowers will be sold nor the price at which they will be sold. With flowers having such a limited life span, growers cannot await a better market by warehousing nor may growers regulate production in the short term. Growers must sell what their plants produce when the plants produce. In its final determination rejecting economic reports submitted by the growers, ITA stated that annual averaging would mask dumping by balancing high prices in peak months with low prices in other months. ITA also rejected FTC's proposal to use a daily or weekly averaging because ITA wanted a long enough period to account for both distress and non-distress sale prices. Reasoning that flowers can last more than one week and that perishability is a function of variables other than merely time, ITA selected a monthly period for averaging.

The trial court noted: "No period accounts for the legitimate concerns of all parties. Monthly averaging is one acceptable compromise. ITA averaged over what it considered the shortest period possible to ensure that dumping was not obscured entirely, and at the same time, to account for as many perishability factors as possible." *Floral Trade Council*, 775 F. Supp. at 1500. The government argues in its brief that 19 U.S.C. § 1675(a)(2)(A) directs ITA to compare each entry of merchandise subject to the antidumping order, whereas *Asocolflores's* annual averaging would violate that mandate by masking individual instances of dumping. Under an annual averaging, dumping would only be found if the annual aggregate sales of a foreign seller were at less than fair value.

. . . [W]e agree with the government that an annual average would mask dumping related to individual sales. Although some dumping would also be masked under a monthly average, Commerce chose to use a monthly average as representative of the U.S. price to account for perishability of the flowers. Even *Asocolflores* admits that "in general, shorter averaging periods are preferable to longer averaging periods." Basing the U.S. price on an annual average in this market would completely eviscerate determining dumping on the statutorily mandated "each entry of merchandise." Yearly averaging is clearly not more "representative" of the U.S. price than monthly averaging in the circumstances of this case.

In sum, Asocolflores has not persuaded us that ITA abused its discretion, committed an error of law nor made its determination of the amount of dumping unsupported by substantial evidence.

B. Taxes, Interest Expenses, and the 1998 *AIMCOR* Case

AIMCOR v. THE UNITED STATES
United States Court of Appeals for the Federal Circuit
141 F.3d 1098 (1998)

SCHALL, CIRCUIT JUDGE.

This antidumping action stems from the investigation of ferrosilicon imported from Brazil. [As the Court explains in a footnote, "[f]errosilicon is a ferroalloy produced by combining silicon and iron through smelting in a submerged-arc furnace." Its primary use is as an alloying agent in the production of steel and cast iron. Also, in the steel industry, it is used as a deoxidizer and a reducing agent, cast iron producers use it as an inoculant.] Plaintiffs/Cross-Appellants, AIMCOR, Alabama Silicon, Inc., American Alloys, Inc., Globe Metallurgical, Inc., and American Silicon Technologies (collectively "AIMCOR"), are United States ferrosilicon producers, manufacturers, or resellers. Defendant/Appellant, *Companhia Ferroligas Minas Gerais-Minasligas* ("*Minasligas*"), is a Brazilian producer and exporter of ferrosilicon. *Minasligas* appeals the decision of the United States Court of International Trade sustaining the determination of the International Trade Administration, United States Department of Commerce ("Commerce"), that *Minasligas* had sold ferrosilicon at less than fair value and imposing an antidumping order. *See AIMCOR v. United States*, 1996 Ct. Intl. Trade LEXIS 88, No. 94-03-00182, 1996 WL 276955, at *2 (Ct. Int'l Trade May 21, 1996). Specifically, *Minasligas* challenges the inclusion of Brazilian value-added taxes as part of the cost of materials in determining constructed value pursuant to 19 U.S.C. § 1677b(e)(1)(A) (1988). *See AIMCOR*, 1996 Ct. Intl. Trade LEXIS 88, 1996 WL 276955, at *1. AIMCOR cross-appeals, challenging the interest rate used by Commerce to calculate *Minasligas*' imputed negative, United States credit expenses. We affirm.

[In a footnote, the Court observes the AD statutes were amended by the *1994 Act*, and that this *Act* does not apply to investigations initiated before 1 January 1995. The investigation here was initiated prior to that date, and all citations are to the 1988 edition of the U.S. Code.]

. . . .

II

. . . [O]n January 12, 1993, AIMCOR; Silicon Metaltech Inc.; United Autoworkers of America Local 523; United Steelworkers of America Locals 12646, 2528, 5171, and 3081; and Oil, Chemical & Atomic Workers Local 389 (collectively "petitioners") petitioned Commerce, alleging that ferrosilicon from Brazil was being sold or was likely to be sold in the United States at less than fair value. . . . The petitions were filed on behalf of the United States industry and the employees producing, manufacturing, and reselling material like the product at issue. . . . The period of inquiry was from July 1 through December 31, 1992. . . . On August 16, 1993, Commerce issued its preliminary determination, finding dumping and suspending liquidation of ferrosilicon from Brazil. *Preliminary Determination of Sales at Less Than Fair Value: Ferrosilicon From Brazil*, 58 Fed. Reg. 43,323, 43,327 (Aug. 16, 1993) ("*Preliminary Determination*"). On January 6, 1994, Commerce issued its final determination, finding that *Minasligas* had not sold ferrosilicon at less than fair value. *Final Determination of Sales at Less Than Fair Value: Ferrosilicon From Brazil*, 59 Fed. Reg. 732, 739-40 (Jan. 6, 1994) ("*Final Determination*").

In making its *Final Determination*, Commerce based *Minasligas'* United States price on purchase price [*i.e.*, Export Price] because its ferrosilicon was sold to unrelated purchasers in the United States prior to importation and other circumstances did not indicate the exporter's sales price. . . . As far as foreign market value [*i.e.*, Normal Value] was concerned, since petitioners had alleged that *CBCC's* [*i.e.*, *Cia Brasileira Carbureto de Calcio*, a Brazilian exporter of ferrosilicon] and *Minasligas'* home market sales were made at less than the cost of production ("COP") and that foreign market value should be based on constructed value, Commerce initiated COP investigations of *CBCC* and *Minasligas* prior to making its Final Determination. . . . In a COP investigation, Commerce compares the cost of production n6 of the goods at issue to home market sales. . . . [I]f Commerce determines that a sufficient quantity of home market sales were made at prices below the cost of production, Commerce bases foreign market value on constructed value. In making its Final Determination, Commerce determined that *CBCC's* and *Minasligas'* home market sales were viable bases for calculating foreign market value. In its *Final Determination*, it therefore did not base foreign market value upon constructed value. . . .

[As the Court explains in footnotes, first, "[c]ost of production consists of the cost of materials and fabrication; selling, general, and administrative expenses; and inventory carrying costs." Second, "[g]enerally, if more than ninety percent of domestic sales are made at prices below the cost of production, Commerce will use constructed value as the basis for determining foreign market value. Third, Commerce used Constructed Value to set Foreign Market Value for one of *CBCC's* sales because data were insufficient to base foreign market value on home market sales in this instance.]

In conducting the COP investigations of *CBCC* and *Minasligas* and in arriving at its *Final Determination* that home market sales were viable bases for calculating foreign market value, Commerce determined that Brazil's economy was hyperinflationary during the period of inquiry. [In a footnote, the Court states "Commerce generally defines a hyperinflationary economy as one in which the annual inflation rate exceeds fifty percent, causing the value of the relevant currency to rapidly decline in relatively short periods of time."] . . . Consequently, Commerce calculated monthly values for foreign market value, cost of production, and constructed value to eliminate the distortive effects of inflation. . . . In the COP investigations, Commerce included Brazilian value-added taxes as a cost of materials in the cost of production, for purposes of determining whether home market sales were made at prices above the cost of production. Commerce also included these taxes in calculating constructed value. . . . This decision to include the value-added taxes for purposes of the COP investigations was relevant to *CBCC* and *Minasligas* to the extent that it determined whether Commerce would base foreign market value on home market sales or constructed value.

However, in determining whether value-added taxes should be included in determining constructed value, if this method eventually was used to determine foreign market value, Commerce stated:

> When using [constructed value] as a surrogate for home market prices we must determine if in fact the entity under investigation is able to recover all of the taxes paid on inputs (raw materials) from its domestic sales of subject merchandise. If domestic sales of subject merchandise fully recover all of the domestic taxes paid on inputs, then these taxes would appropriately be excluded from the margin analysis. However, if the producer is not able to recover all input taxes from its sales of subject merchandise, then these actual costs must be reflected in the [Constructed Value].

Final Determination, 59 Fed. Reg. at 737 (citing *Camargo Correa Metais, S.A. v. United States*, 17 C.I.T. 897, 911 (1993)). This meant that value-added taxes would only be included in constructed value if the taxes paid on input materials were not fully recovered through the taxes collected on domestic sales. Since Commerce concluded in the *Final Determination* that *Minasligas'* home market sales were made at prices above the cost of production, the decision to include value-added taxes as a cost of materials in the COP investigations did not directly affect *Minasligas*. Since the foreign market value of *Minasligas'* goods was being based on home market sales, and not constructed value, the possibility of including the taxes in constructed value did not affect *Minasligas*. The possibility of including these taxes in determining constructed value was directly pertinent to *CBCC*, though, because Commerce was basing a portion of its foreign market value on constructed value. However, Commerce excluded the value-added taxes paid by *CBCC* on input materials from the cost of materials, and therefore constructed value, the reason being that these taxes were fully offset by taxes collected by *CBCC* on domestic sales of the subject merchandise. . . .

In determining foreign market value for *Minasligas*, Commerce made circumstances of sale adjustments for differences in *Minasligas'* credit expenses pursuant to 19 U.S.C. § 1677b(a)(4)(B) and 19 C.F.R. § 353.56(a) (1997). . . . Commerce made such adjustments for finance charges, warehousing, and quality control expenses. . . . Commerce also imputed negative credit expenses to offset the interest revenue *Minasligas* could earn on advance payments received by *Minasligas* prior to shipping export orders, as more fully explained below. . . .

In response to comments alleging errors in connection with the *Final Determination*, Commerce issued an amended final determination on February 23, 1994. *Notice of Amended Final Determination of Sales at Less Than Fair Value: Ferrosilicon From Brazil*, 59 Fed. Reg. 8598 (Feb. 23, 1994) ("*Amended Final Determination*"). Commerce determined that it had erred in its COP investigations and revised its analysis, using constructed value as the measure of foreign market value for *CBCC's* and *Minasligas'* ferrosilicon. . . . At this time, Commerce's previous decision to include value-added taxes paid on input materials as a cost of materials in determining constructed value, if not fully offset by taxes collected on domestic sales, became directly applicable to *Minasligas* because the foreign market value of its ferrosilicon was now being calculated using constructed value, rather than home market sales. However, as with *CBCC*, Commerce determined that *Minasligas* had fully recovered the value-added taxes paid on input materials through taxes collected on domestic sales. . . . Therefore, Commerce did not include these value-added taxes in the cost of materials in calculating constructed value. . . . Correcting its errors, Commerce determined that *Minasligas* had sold ferrosilicon at less than fair value. . . .

Two Brazilian value-added taxes are at issue in this appeal: (1) the *imposto sobre produtos industrializados* ("*IPI*"), and (2) the *imposto sobre circulacao de mercadorias e servicos* ("*ICMS*"). The *IPI* is a value-added *ad valorem* excise tax, levied at varying rates on manufactured products. The *ICMS* is a value-added sales and service tax levied on sales or the physical movement of goods, freight, transportation and communications services, and electric energy. Most products exported from Brazil are exempt from both taxes. For each tax, a manufacturer offsets taxes paid by it on monthly purchases of raw materials or component parts against taxes collected by it from domestic sales of manufactured products.

Minasligas documents taxes paid on raw materials used in its production process and taxes collected from its sales of finished products in separate accounting ledgers. These ledgers are balanced each month to determine the amount of tax owed to the Brazilian government. If taxes collected from domestic sales exceed the taxes paid on raw materials, *Minasligas* forwards the excess to the Brazilian government. If taxes paid on raw materials exceed the taxes collected from domestic sales, *Minasligas* carries a tax credit forward to the following month and makes no payment to the Brazilian government.

In making its determination that *Minasligas* had made sales at less than fair value, Commerce nevertheless rejected the petitioners' claims that it had erroneously imputed negative credit expenses to *Minasligas* and had incorrectly used a *cruzeiro*-denominated interest rate to calculate those credits. [The *cruzeiro* is a Brazilian currency unit.] . . . The petitioners had sought to eliminate the imputed negative credit expenses, which had the effect of lowering foreign market value, and therefore, the dumping margin. The petitioners had also challenged the use of a *cruzeiro*-denominated interest rate in calculating imputed negative credit expenses, their underlying rationale being that an alternative interest rate would lower the negative credit expenses, thereby increasing foreign market value and the dumping margin.

Negative credit expenses are explained as follows: *Minasligas* financed United States sales of ferrosilicon through the use of United States advance exchange contracts ("AECs"). Under the AECs, which were between *Minasligas* and a bank, the bank would advance *Minasligas* a portion of the value of new export contracts, prior to actual execution of the contract. Commerce determined that *Minasligas* was earning "negative credit expenses" by receiving these advance payments before shipping the subject ferrosilicon.

Commerce's established practice is to calculate credit expenses from the date of shipment to the date payment is received from the customer. . . . *Minasligas* incurred negative credit expenses (or earned credit revenue) from the United States AECs because the advances were received prior to shipment of the ferrosilicon by *Minasligas* and prior to actual payment by the customer. This allowed *Minasligas* to use the money prior to shipment of the ferrosilicon or payment by the customer. *Id.* Commerce determined that the date *Minasligas* received advanced funds was equivalent to receipt of payment from the customer. . . . Commerce computed the imputed negative credit expenses by multiplying the time between receipt of the AEC advances by *Minasligas* and the actual shipment of the ferrosilicon by *Minasligas* by a *cruzeiro*-denominated interest rate.

[In footnotes, the Court explains, first:

A company effectively extends credit to purchasers when it ships merchandise prior to payment, *i.e.*, "during this period, the seller incurs additional expenses through the process of borrowing funds pending receipt of payment or through the fact that funds are tied up due to the existence of accounts receivable." ANTIDUMPING MANUAL, ch. 8, at 18. Commerce uses credit expenses to account for these extensions of credit. Since *Minasligas* received payment prior to shipment, in computing foreign market value, Commerce imputed a negative credit expense, as part of a circumstances of sale adjustment, to account for the interest *Minasligas* could earn on this money between receiving the advance and the actual shipment of the ferrosilicon. See id. at 19. As the Court of International Trade explained, "payment received prior to shipment provides an additional transactional benefit to the seller." *AIMCOR*, 19 C.I.T. 966, 1995 WL 431186, at *6.

Second, "Commerce adds . . . credit expenses to constructed value, thus leading to a higher foreign market value that accounts for the cost of extending credit to purchasers and carrying accounts receivable. This higher foreign market value increases the possibility of a dumping determination and the size of any dumping margin." Third, "[w]hen Commerce adds imputed negative credit expenses to constructed value, a lower foreign market value results, thus reducing the possibility of a dumping determination and the size of any dumping margin."]

III

AIMCOR and *Minasligas* appealed to the Court of International Trade . . . challenging various aspects of the *Final Determination* and the *Amended Final Determination* and seeking judgment upon the agency record. . . . AIMCOR asserted that Commerce had erred in excluding Brazilian value-added taxes from the cost of materials in determining constructed value because these taxes were not remitted or refunded upon exportation of the merchandise within the meaning of 19 U.S.C.§ 1677b(e)(1)(A). . . . *Minasligas* conceded that the *IPI* and *ICMS* value-added taxes were not remitted or refunded upon exportation of the subject ferrosilicon. . . . Noting that the statute requires that constructed value include the cost of materials "at a time preceding the date of exportation of the merchandise," 19 U.S.C. § 1677b(e)(1)(A), the court held that *Minasligas* might be able to show that the value-added taxes paid on input materials did not in fact constitute a cost of materials because these taxes were fully offset by taxes collected on domestic sales prior to exportation of the subject merchandise. . . .The court remanded for Commerce to determine if *Minasligas* had fully recovered value-added taxes paid on inputs prior to exportation of the subject ferrosilicon. . . .

At the same time, the court upheld Commerce's COP analysis. . . . The court also upheld Commerce's analysis of negative credit expenses, resulting from the AECs, but remanded with instructions that Commerce apply a United States dollar-denominated interest rate to the amounts at issue, rather than a Brazilian *cruzeiro*-denominated interest rate. . . .

Commerce issued its final remand determination on January 17, 1996, after comment from the parties. *Final Redetermination of Remand in Ferrosilicon from Brazil*, at 1 ("*Final Remand Determination*"). In the *Final Remand Determination*, Commerce included value-added taxes, the *IPI* and *ICMS*, as a cost of production in calculating constructed value because *Minasligas* could not show that the taxes were fully recovered prior to exportation. . . . Commerce required a sale-specific correlation between taxes paid on input materials and taxes recovered on the products produced from those materials:

> During the remand proceeding, [Commerce] requested that *Minasligas* and *CBCC* provide, for each U.S. sale, the date and amount of the *ICMS* and *IPI* taxes paid on the material inputs used in the production of merchandise sold to the United States, and evidence that these specific taxes were completely recovered prior to exportation for each U.S. sale. However, because each U.S. sale was exported on a unique date, the only way to determine, on a sale-specific basis, whether the taxes paid on the inputs used to produce the merchandise were recovered prior to exportation is to track the specific taxes paid for each input and measure whether these taxes were fully recouped by domestic sales revenue. The parties failed to submit this data. Indeed, they said they were unable to provide this data. The only information they did provide was monthly totals of taxes paid and collected. It is not possible to determine from this data whether the taxes paid on inputs were fully recovered. Accordingly, we find insufficient evidence to conclude that these taxes were fully recovered.

. . . In the *Final Remand Determination*, Commerce also announced that it was revising its general policy concerning Brazilian value-added taxes, stating that it should have included those taxes in its earlier determinations because the taxes were not remitted or refunded prior to exportation, as required by 19 U.S.C. § 1677b(e)(1)(A). . . . Under its revised policy, Commerce assumes that the taxes paid on input materials are recouped by being included in the price of the exported products. Commerce stated its intention to include Brazilian value-added taxes as a cost of materials in constructed value in future investigations unless these taxes are remitted or refunded upon exportation. . . .

In the *Final Remand Determination*, Commerce rejected the use of United States dollar-denominated interest rates from the AECs as evidence of the rate at which *Minasligas* could borrow money. . . . Commerce refused to use these interest rates in computing the negative credit expenses because *Minasligas* received the advances, pursuant to the AECs, in *cruzeiros*. [In a footnote, the Court explains "Commerce normally uses United States interest rates for calculating imputed credit expenses when a respondent has actual United States dollar borrowings. . . . Since *Minasligas* received *cruzeiros* pursuant to the AECs, Commerce determined that the AECs did not constitute United States dollar borrowings."] . . . Instead, Commerce used an aircraft lease with an interest rate denominated in United States dollars to determine the interest rate for calculating the negative credit expenses because this was *Minasligas*' only evidence of United States dollar borrowings and it reflected the credit terms *Minasligas* would encounter when borrowing United States dollars. [The Court observes in a footnote "the actual transaction referred to was the financing of an aircraft purchase," "[t]he interest rate in this 'lease' was the interest rate associated with the loan to finance the aircraft purchase," and "[f]or consistency, we refer to the financing agreement as the 'aircraft lease.'"] . . .

On May 21, 1996, the Court of International Trade ruled on the *Final Remand Determination*. In so doing, the court sustained Commerce's treatment of the value-added taxes. *AIMCOR, 1996 Ct. Intl. Trade LEXIS 88, 1996 WL 276955*, at *1. The court held that *Minasligas* had failed to carry its burden of proving that its pre-exportation cost of materials did not include value-added taxes. . . . The court also held that Commerce's decision to use the aircraft lease as evidence of *Minasligas*' United States dollar-denominated interest rate for purposes of recalculating the negative credit expenses was rational and well within Commerce's discretion. . . . The court rejected AIMCOR's contention that the interest rate in the aircraft lease was not short-term. [In a footnote, the Court explains "[a] short-term borrowing rate is generally used as the interest rate for imputed credit expenses because this rate is most suited for the short-term extension of credit between a buyer and a purchaser."] . . . Since AIMCOR failed to raise before Commerce the issue of whether the chosen interest rate was annual or monthly, the court refused to address this contention by AIMCOR. . . .

Minasligas appeals to us challenging the inclusion of value-added taxes as a cost of materials in calculating constructed value. AIMOCR cross appeals challenging Commerce's use of the aircraft lease to determine the United States dollar-denominated interest rate applicable to the negative credit expenses. . . .

DISCUSSION

. . . .

III

Commerce included the *IPI* and *ICMS* value-added taxes, paid by *Minasligas* on input materials, as a cost of materials in calculating constructed value. . . . *Minasligas* argues that this was error because these taxes were fully recovered through taxes collected on domestic sales. AIMCOR and the government support Commerce's decision, claiming that the taxes were not remitted or refunded prior to exportation, as required by 19 U.S.C. § 1677b(e)(1)(A), and arguing alternatively that *Minasligas* failed to show that taxes paid on inputs were fully recovered prior to exportation.

Under 19 U.S.C. § 1677b(e)(1)(A), in determining constructed value, "any internal tax applicable in the country of exportation directly to such materials or their disposition, but remitted or refunded upon the exportation of the article in the production of which such materials are used" is excluded from the "cost of materials" component of constructed value. Words in a statute are deemed to have their ordinary meaning. . . . "Refund" means "to give or put back . . . to return (money) in restitution, repayment, or balancing of accounts," and "remit" means "to let go back, send back." WEBSTER'S THIRD NEW INTERNATIONAL DICTIONARY 1910, 1920 (1986). It is undisputed that the *IPI* and *ICMS* taxes are not remitted or refunded upon exportation within the meaning of the statute. . . . In other words, these taxes are not paid back to *Minasligas* upon exportation of the ferrosilicon produced from the raw materials on which *Minasligas* paid taxes. Instead, as discussed above, *Minasligas* maintains ledgers in which it records on a running basis taxes it pays and collects. Then, each month, it "settles up" with the Brazilian government.

Commerce's position in the *Final Determination* was that "if in fact the entity under investigation is able to recover all of the taxes paid on inputs (raw materials) from its domestic sales of subject merchandise . . . then these taxes would appropriately be excluded from the margin analysis." . . . The Court of International Trade concurred, stating, "[A] respondent that has fully recovered value-added taxes upon input costs prior to exportation, has not in fact incurred the value-added tax as a 'cost of materials.'" . . .

Using this interpretation, Commerce gave *Minasligas* the opportunity, during the remand proceedings, to provide evidence that the taxes paid on inputs were recovered prior to exportation through taxes collected on domestic sales of the merchandise produced from those inputs. . . . This was consistent with *Camargo*, in which Commerce was to develop a method to account for the economic reality that taxes paid on inputs are not a cost of materials if fully recovered through taxes collected on domestic sales. . . . In this case, Commerce sought from *Minasligas* a sale-specific correspondence between the taxes paid on input materials (raw materials) and the taxes collected on the sale of the product (ferrosilicon) produced from those inputs. . . .

The only evidence *Minasligas* produced on remand consisted of monthly totals of value-added taxes collected and paid. . . . While *Minasligas'* evidence, two tax ledgers containing taxes paid and taxes collected, is regularly inspected by the Brazilian government and conforms to Brazil's generally accepted accounting principles, this evidence is insufficient to show that *Minasligas* fully recovered the value-added taxes prior to exportation. *Minasligas* admitted that it was unable to provide the type of sale-specific correspondence between taxes paid on inputs and taxes collected on domestic sales of the products produced from those inputs that Commerce sought. . . . Even the monthly totals of taxes paid on input materials and taxes collected on domestic sales of finished products did not show that the value-added taxes were fully recovered. We agree with the Court of International Trade that *Minasligas* failed to meet its burden of proving that value-added taxes were fully recovered and that its pre-exportation cost of materials did not include value-added taxes. . . .

Minasligas argues that Commerce effectively denied it the opportunity to prove that the value-added taxes were fully recovered prior to exportation. In the *Final Remand Determination*, Commerce announced that, in future investigations, it would include Brazilian value-added taxes as a cost of materials in calculating constructed value unless the taxes were "remitted or refunded upon exportation," as expressly stated in 19 U.S.C. § 1677b(e)(1)(A). . . . *Minasligas* argues that Commerce, in effect, applied this construction of the statute to it. It claims that because ferrosilicon is produced through a continuous process where raw materials are continuously loaded into electric furnaces to produce a liquid product it is not possible to provide the sale-specific correspondence Commerce sought. We reject this argument. Commerce gave *Minasligas* the opportunity to show that value-added taxes were fully recovered prior to exportation. Even in a continuous process, such as the production of ferrosilicon, we believe it is possible to maintain records that show to some degree that taxes paid on input materials are offset by taxes collected from the domestic sale of products produced from those materials. Essentially, *Minasligas* is arguing that since generally accepted accounting principles in Brazil do not require these sale-specific records, it should not be faulted for not having the records. We cannot agree. The failure to track the taxes on input materials and the taxes recovered from the sale of the merchandise produced from those materials rests solely with *Minasligas*. *Minasligas* had a meaningful opportunity to present evidence, and the evidence it presented was insufficient.

We decline to address whether we would accept the interpretation of 19 U.S.C. § 1677b(e)(1)(A) announced by Commerce in its final remand determination. This interpretation was not applied to *Minasligas* in this case and is not properly before this court. Any statement on this future methodology would constitute an advisory opinion, which we decline to provide. We simply hold that, in this case, the Court of International Trade correctly sustained Commerce's methodology and inclusion of the *IPI* and *ICMS* value-added taxes in the cost of materials in calculating constructed value.

IV

. . . Commerce imputed negative, United States credit expenses to *Minasligas* to account for its receiving payment, prior to shipment of the subject ferrosilicon, pursuant to the AECs. . . . These negative credit expenses account for the additional benefits the seller receives from obtaining payment prior to shipment. . . . In this case, the negative credit expenses were used to offset credit expenses in determining foreign market value. [In a footnote, the Court states "[c]redit expenses are the costs associated with carrying accounts receivable on the books and the expenses related to extending credit to purchasers for the interim between shipment and payment," and "Commerce accounts for these credit expenses by making circumstances of sale adjustments to foreign market value."] . . . Commerce originally used a *cruzeiro*-denominated interest rate to calculate the negative credit expenses, but switched to a United States dollar-denominated rate in the *Final Remand Determination*, as instructed by the Court of International Trade. . . . Commerce rejected the interest rates stated in the AECs and based its calculations on the interest rate in an aircraft lease submitted by *Minasligas*. . . . In its cross-appeal, AIMCOR argues that Commerce incorrectly used this aircraft lease in determining *Minasligas'* imputed negative credit expenses. AIMCOR argues that the AECs principal amounts and interest rates were expressed in United States dollars and that the Court of International Trade erred in concluding that the AEC advances were not United States dollar borrowings because *Minasligas* converted them to *cruzeiros*.

Commerce's stated policy is to use an interest rate tied to the currency in which future payments are expected:

> When sales are made in, and future payments are expected in, a given currency, the measure of the company's extension of credit should be based on an interest rate tied to the currency in which its receivables are denominated. Only then does establishing a measure of imputed credit recognize both the time value of money and the effect of currency fluctuations on repatriating value.

Final Determination of Sales at Less Than Fair Value: Oil Country Tubular Goods From Austria, 60 Fed. Reg. at 33,555. . . . Commerce requires evidence of actual United States dollar borrowings to support a proffered United States dollar-denominated interest rate. . . . Commerce uses a short-term borrowing rate to calculate imputed credit expenses.

Commerce refused to apply the AEC interest rates, which were expressed in United States dollars, in calculating negative credit expenses because *Minasligas* actually received the AEC advances in *cruzeiros*. . . . Consistent with its stated policy of using the interest rate in which receivables are denominated, Commerce sought a United States dollar-denominated interest rate to apply to the negative credit expenses because *Minasligas'* receivables were denominated in United States dollars, *i.e.*, *Minasligas'* customers were to pay for the ferrosilicon in United States dollars. Given that Brazil's economy was hyperinflationary during this period, . . . and the *cruzeiro* was declining at a rate of 25 to 30 percent per month, Commerce did not err in rejecting the AEC interest rates which were tied to advances received in *cruzeiros*. Commerce's decision to reject the AEC interest rates because *Minasligas* was paid in *cruzeiros* and its receivables were denominated in United States dollars is supported by substantial evidence on the record.

The only other evidence of United States dollar-denominated borrowings that *Minasligas* submitted was an aircraft lease. . . . Commerce relied on this lease to determine the interest rate for the imputed negative credit expenses. Commerce did not err in using this rate because it was the only evidence of record of *Minasligas'* United States dollar borrowings. The Court of International Trade rejected AIMCOR's objection that the interest rate in the aircraft lease was not a short-term interest rate. . . . Given that Commerce's first priority is to match the denomination of the interest rate to that of receivables, we uphold the court's decision sustaining Commerce's choice of interest rate. We reject AIMCOR's argument that the AECs were United States dollar borrowings, the reason being that *Minasligas* borrowed, and was paid in, *cruzeiros*.

. . . .

CONCLUSION

The Court of International Trade did not err in sustaining the *Final Remand Determination* of Commerce that included Brazilian value-added taxes paid on input materials as a cost of materials in calculating the constructed value of ferrosilicon, because *Minasligas* failed to show that the taxes were fully recovered prior to exportation of the ferrosilicon that was produced from the taxed raw materials. The court also did not err in sustaining Commerce's choice of interest rate for determining imputed negative, United States credit expenses. . . .

C. Cost of Production, the Major Input Rule, and 2004 *NTN Bearing* Case

NTN BEARING CORPORATION OF AMERICA v. UNITED STATES
United States Court of Appeals for the Federal Circuit
368 F.3d 1369-78 (2004)

LINN, CIRCUIT JUDGE.

NTN Bearing Corporation of America, American NTN Bearing Manufacturing Corporation, and NTN Corporation (collectively "NTN"), and NSK, Limited and NSK Corporation (collectively "NSK") appeal from a judgment of the United States Court of International Trade, in which the court reviewed the final determination of the Department of Commerce ("Commerce") relating to antidumping duties on the import of tapered roller bearings from Japan and China. *NTN Bearing Corp. of Am. v. United States*, 186 F. Supp. 2d 1257 (Ct. Int'l Trade 2002) ("*NTN Bearing I*"). The Timken Company ("Timken") cross-appeals. . . . [W]e affirm.

BACKGROUND

Commerce initiated an antidumping duty administrative review of several manufacturers and exporters of tapered roller bearings from Japan in 1996. . . . Commerce issued questionnaires to the affected parties, including both NTN and NSK, and based its preliminary determination in part on their responses. . . .

Commerce gave the interested parties an opportunity to comment on the preliminary results and then issued final results that took those comments into account. *See Tapered Roller Bearings and Parts Thereof, Finished and Unfinished, From Japan, and Tapered Roller Bearings, Four Inches or Less in Outside Diameter, and Components Thereof, From Japan*, 63 Fed. Reg. 2558 (Dep't Commerce January 15, 1998) (final admin. review) (*"Final Results"*). In these results, . . . Commerce: (1) employed affiliated-party cost data in (a) determining whether "foreign like products" were merchandise similar to U.S. tapered roller bearing models, (b) calculating the difference in merchandise ("difmer") adjustment for non-identical U.S. and home-market matches, and (c) recalculating NSK's reported U.S. inventory carrying costs . . .; (2) relied on facts available to adjust NTN's reported home market billing adjustments . . .: (3) relied on its own sampling of affiliated-party inputs to adjust NTN's reported cost of production ("COP") and constructed value ("CV") for those inputs . . .; (4) rejected Timken's argument that NTN's warehousing expenses were incorrectly allocated . . .; and (5) rejected NTN's argument that zero-priced transactions should be excluded from the margin calculations, ...

. . . .

[Omitted are three portions of the appellate court opinion, which concern facts available, inclusion of transactions adjusted to a zero price, and warehousing expenses.]

ANALYSIS

. . . .

B. Use of Affiliated Supplier Cost Data and 19 U.S.C. § 1677b(f)

In the course of its administrative review, Commerce requested that NSK provide cost data for major inputs received from affiliated parties and used to produce the tapered roller bearings that were the subject of the review. NSK duly provided the data, but protested Commerce's request on the ground that 19 U.S.C. § 1677b(f)(3) permits Commerce to request such data only where it "has reasonable grounds to believe or suspect that an amount represented as the value of [a major] input is less than the cost of production of such input," 19 U.S.C. § 1677b(f)(3) (2000), and Commerce had no such reasonable grounds. Commerce noted that it "had found home market sales below the cost of production (COP) in [its] most recently completed final results for NSK," and conducted a cost test to determine if any of NSK's home market sales in this review were similarly below COP. Based on the result of this test, Commerce used NSK's affiliated supplier cost data to recalculate NSK's total cost of manufacturing ("TCOM"), which the agency then used to recalculate NSK's inventory carrying costs in the United States. Commerce also employed the recalculated TCOM data in determining the difmer adjustment. The agency used this value, which represents differences in physical characteristics between merchandise sold in the United States and that sold abroad, . . . to control which U.S. and home market tapered roller bearings would be compared: Commerce "used a 20 percent [difmer] cost deviation cap as the maximum difference in cost allowable for similar merchandise." . . .

NSK challenges Commerce's use of the affiliated supplier cost data to calculate these variables. In particular, NSK argues that Commerce violated 19 U.S.C. § 1677b(f), which permits the use of these data for "purposes of *subsections (b)* and *(e)*." Those provisions relate to the calculation of COP and

CV, respectively. . . . Citing *FAG Italia, S.p.A. v. United States*, 291 F.3d 806 (Fed. Cir. 2002), NSK argues that the grant of authority to Commerce to use these data for COP and CV calculations implies that Commerce does not have the authority to use the data for other purposes. We disagree.

Section 1677b(f) is entitled "special rules for calculation of cost of production and for calculation of constructed value." NSK sees in this, together with the reference to "purposes of *subsections (b)* and *(e)*" in the statutory text, confirmation that Congress intended the use of affiliated supplier cost data to be limited to these two purposes. The statute does not, however, contain words of restriction limiting the data's use solely to the calculation of COP and CV. NSK thus relies in essence on the maxim *expressio unius est exclusio alterius* ["the expression of one thing is the exclusion of another"] arguing that the expression of subsections (b) and (e) in Section 1677b(f) permits an inference that Congress intended to preclude use of affiliated supplier cost data for any other purpose.

In focusing exclusively on Section 1677b(f) to the exclusion of the other statutory provisions governing Commerce's actions, NSK stretches this well-worn maxim too far. The maxim is not applied where, *inter alia*, "its application would thwart the legislative intent made apparent by the entire act." NORMAN J. SINGER, SUTHERLAND STATUTES AND STATUTORY CONSTRUCTION § 47:25 (6th ed. 2000). We believe that such is the case here.

Commerce's calculation of the adjustments at issue in this case is governed only secondarily by Section 1677b(f); the agency's authority derives directly from other statutory provisions. Similar merchandise, or "foreign like products" in the terms of the statute, is defined by 19 U.S.C. § 1677(16)(B)(ii) as merchandise "like [the subject] merchandise in component material or materials and in the purposes for which used." Commerce is required to determine what merchandise is a "foreign like product" for purposes of, *inter alia*, determining normal value. . . . Similarly, Commerce derives its authority to calculate a difmer adjustment from 19 U.S.C. § 1677b(a)(6), and derives its authority to account for inventory carrying costs from 19 U.S.C. § 1677a(d). Because these statutes provide authority to Commerce to calculate the values in question, we look to the text of these statutes in the first instance for Congress' intent as to how the values are to be calculated. None of these provisions preclude Commerce's use of affiliated supplier cost data in the calculation of these values. NSK's reliance on a maxim of dubious applicability to interpolate restrictions on the use of affiliated supplier cost data into statutes that are silent on the question is unconvincing.

Nor is *FAG Italia* dispositive in this situation. That case involved a statutory grant of authority to Commerce to conduct duty absorption inquiries "during any review . . . initiated 2 years or 4 years after the publication of an antidumping duty order." 19 U.S.C. § 1675(a)(4) (2000). Commerce claimed that this provision did not preclude it from conducting a duty absorption inquiry in the second year after the January 1, 1995 "deemed issuance date" of a transition order (*i.e.*, an antidumping order originally issued before the date that the *Uruguay Round Agreements Act* amendments came into force), which was seven years after the publication of the antidumping duty order in question. . . . We rejected the agency's argument on the grounds that "the absence of a statutory provision cannot be the source of agency authority," . . . and that "statutory provisions governing annual reviews for Commerce do not confer general authority that might include the power to consider duty absorption," . . . . However, we recognized that other more general statutory provisions might provide such authority, but we declined to "reach the question whether Commerce might have been authorized to conduct duty absorption inquiries as part of" another provision. . . .

In this case, . . . authority to calculate the values at issue does not derive from Section 1677b(f), but rather from other statutory provisions. Commerce noted that it "does not rely on a respondent's reported costs solely for the calculation of COP and CV," . . . and concluded that it would be distortive to adjust those costs only for those calculations, but not for others in which they were used. . . . We concur with Commerce's analysis and hold that it did not err in interpreting these provisions to permit it to employ affiliated supplier cost data to calculate cost deviations to limit the definition of similar merchandise, the difmer adjustment, and inventory carrying costs.

C. Validity of 19 C.F.R. § 351.407(b)

NTN challenges Commerce's use of available record information to increase the transfer prices of "major inputs" from affiliated suppliers that NTN used to calculate COP and CV, in order to reflect market value. The statutory scheme that governs calculation of cost of production and constructed value is set forth in 19 U.S.C. § 1677b(f):

> (2) Transactions disregarded
>
> A transaction directly or indirectly between affiliated persons may be disregarded if, in the case of any element of value required to be considered, the amount representing that element does not fairly reflect the amount usually reflected in sales of merchandise under consideration in the market under consideration. If a transaction is disregarded under the preceding sentence and no other transactions are available for consideration, the determination of the amount shall be based on the information available as to what the amount would have been if the transaction had occurred between persons who are not affiliated.
>
> (3) Major input rule
>
> If, in the case of a transaction between affiliated persons involving the production by one of such persons of a major input to the merchandise, the administering authority has reasonable grounds to believe or suspect that an amount represented as the value of such input is less than the cost of production of such input, then the administering authority may determine the value of the major input on the basis of the information available regarding such cost of production, if such cost is greater than the amount that would be determined for such input under paragraph (2).

Under its authority to administer this statutory scheme, . . . Commerce has formulated a regulatory interpretation under which it uses the highest of transfer price, market value and the affiliated supplier's cost of production:

For purposes of Section 773(f)(3) of the *Act*, the Secretary normally will determine the value of a major input purchased from an affiliated person based on the higher of:

(1)   The price paid by the exporter or producer to the affiliated person for the major input;

(2)   The amount usually reflected in sales of the major input in the market under consideration; or

(3)   The cost to the affiliated person of producing the major input.

19 C.F.R. § 351.407(b) (1998).

NTN maintains that it provided Commerce with both COP and transfer price information and argues that under the "major input rule" set forth in Section 1677b(f)(3), Commerce can only resort to information available regarding the COP of an element if Commerce has reason to suspect that the transfer price is less than the affiliated supplier's COP. In NTN's view, "subsection (2) does not . . . apply specifically in the case of an affiliated party transaction in which one of the parties has produced a major input for the merchandise under consideration," and therefore is inapplicable to the valuation of major inputs, which is governed solely by subsection (3). NTN states that on the basis of the COP and transfer price information it supplied, Commerce had no basis for a belief that the transfer price was below the COP for many of the inputs, and alternative valuation methods should not have been used for those inputs, in accordance with Section 1677b(f)(3).

. . . .

The statutory scheme is not a model of clarity, particularly with respect to the question of the applicability of subsection (2) to the valuation of major inputs. We must therefore determine whether Commerce's interpretation of the statute is permissible. . . . NTN seeks to persuade us that it is not; according to NTN, subsection (2) is simply inapplicable here, and if the transfer price is greater than the cost of production, that transfer price must be accepted as the valuation for the major input. The statute does not compel the construction that NTN forces upon it. Section 1677b(f)(3) itself references subsection (2). See 19 U.S.C. § 1677b(f)(3) (mandating the use of COP for the valuation of major inputs "if such cost is greater than the amount that would be determined for such input under paragraph (2)"). This suggests subsection (2) is of no applicability in considering the valuation of major inputs. Rather, it is reasonable to conclude that where the transfer price is less than market value, per subsection (2), or the cost of production, per subsection (3), the transfer price is abandoned in favor of the higher of those two values. Commerce's interpretation of the statute, under which it simply uses the highest value among the transfer price, market value, and cost of production, is neither arbitrary, capricious, nor manifestly contrary to the statute, see *Chevron [U.S.A., Inc. v. Natural Resources Defense Council, Inc.*, 467 U.S. 837 (1984)], 467 U.S. at 844, and we accordingly affirm that interpretation.

Chapter 30

ADJUSTMENTS TO NORMAL VALUE

In times of confusion every active genius finds the place assigned him by Nature. . . .

> —EDWARD GIBBON, THE DECLINE AND FALL OF THE ROMAN EMPIRE
> Ch. V (A.D. 248-285) 173 (The Thirty Tyrants)

DOCUMENTS SUPPLEMENT ASSIGNMENT

1. *Havana Charter* Article 34
2. GATT Article VI
3. WTO *Antidumping Agreement* Articles 1-2

I. OVERVIEW OF ADJUSTMENTS

A. The Zero Sum Game

No more complicated aspect of antidumping (AD) law exists than adjustments in a dumping margin calculation. How nice it would be if the price of an allegedly dumped product — subject merchandise — as sold in the importing country could be compared straight away with the price of the foreign like product as sold in the home market. The difficulty is the two prices are not necessarily comparable.

Perhaps the price in one market is wholesale, while the price in the other market is retail. Perhaps the price in one market contains the cost of containers, as well as freight charges, while the price in the other market does not have them. Perhaps in one or both markets there are expenses directly and indirectly related to selling the product, items like warranties or guarantees, rebates, advertising, and commissions. Perhaps the allegedly dumped product is not identical to the foreign like product, *i.e.*, there are distinguishing physical features. Perhaps there are differences in the way in which subject merchandise and the foreign like product are taxed. Perhaps there are differences in the normal volume sold of the allegedly dumped product and the foreign like product. And so on.

Each possibility shows the naïveté of a straightforward comparison of home and importing country market prices. To ensure an "apples-to-apples" analysis, adjustments are made to observed prices to account for differences in packaging and freight, levels of trade, circumstances of sale, physical features of the merchandise, taxation, volume, and a number of other factors. Indeed, GATT Article VI:1 and Article 2:4 of the WTO *Antidumping Agreement*, plus U.S. antidumping (AD) law (19 U.S.C. §§ 1673 *et seq.*), demand due allowance be taken for differences affecting price comparability.

Once all adjustments are done, it is safe — or, at least, safer — to say "apples" in the home market are being compared to "apples" in the importing country. That is, the comparison is more likely to be a "fair" one only if adjustments are made. And, "fairness" is the standard Article 2:4 of the WTO *Antidumping Agreement* and U.S. law (19 U.S.C. § 1677b(a) set. Thus, Normal Value and Export Price (or Constructed Export Price) are not based solely on raw data on observed prices in two markets. Those data are adjusted to arrive at figures that assure a better degree of comparability.

Only a Textbook dedicated solely to AD law could convey the details of all possible adjustments in a dumping margin calculation. (The book would be of dubious popularity!) After all, only seasoned AD lawyers are conversant with the gamut of adjustments. But, it is possible here to introduce the key adjustments. Before that, it is critical to understand the motivations of the players, petitioner and respondent. Table 30-1 summarizes them. They are diametrically opposed, for the players are locked in a zero-sum game. In theory, at least, an administering agency, such as the U.S. Department of Commerce (DOC), is the impartial referee standing between them to assure fairness.

TABLE 30-1:
SUMMARY OF MOTIVATIONS OF PETITIONER AND RESPONDENT IN ANY DUMPING MARGIN CALCULATION

Item	Petitioner's Motivation	Respondent's Motivation
Overall Dumping Margin, Normal Value – Export Price (or Constructed Export Price)	Maximize the Dumping Margin	Minimize the Dumping Margin
Value of Normal Value	Maximize Normal Value	Minimize Normal Value
Adjustments to Normal Value	Maximize Normal Value by adding to it as many adjustments as possible. Avoid adjustments that are deductions from Normal Value.	Minimize Normal Value by avoiding adjustments that increase Normal Value. Seek as many adjustments as possible that are deductions from Normal Value.
Value of Export Price (or Constructed Export Price)	Minimize Export Price (or Constructed Export Price)	Maximize Export Price (or Constructed Export Price)
Adjustments to Export Price (or Constructed Export Price)	Minimize Export Price (or Constructed Export Price) by advocating adjustments that are deductions. Avoid adjustments that are additions.	Maximize Export Price (or Constructed Export Price) by advocating adjustments that are additions. Avoid adjustments that are deductions.

Adjustments to Normal Value and Export Price (or Constructed Export Price) are made for a variety of reasons, but they take only two forms: an addition or a deduction. That is, some adjustments to Normal Value are additions to the raw data value (or starting point) for Normal Value, while others take the form of deductions. When all the additions and subtractions to the starting point are completed, the result is a final figure for Normal Value. Likewise, some adjustments to Export Price (or Constructed Export Price) are additions to the raw data value, while others are deductions from that starting point. When all the additions and subtractions are made, the result is a final amount for Export Price (or Constructed Export Price). Then, the dumping margin is simply the difference between Normal Value and Export Price (or Constructed Export Price). As a percent, the margin is the difference divided by Export Price (or Constructed Export Price).

As Table 30-1 indicates, a petitioner wants to maximize the dumping margin by maximizing the size of Normal Value and minimizing the size of Export Price (or Constructed Export Price). The respondent wants just the opposite. Better yet, for the respondent, is no dumping margin at all. How does the petitioner play the game? It argues for adjustments to Normal Value that are additions, and against any adjustments that are deductions. The petitioner also argues in favor of adjustments to lower Export Price (or Constructed Export Price), *i.e.*, in favor of deductions from Export Price (or Constructed Export Price), and opposes additions thereto.

The respondent engages in strategic behavior that is a mirror image of what the petitioner does. The respondent seeks to prove adjustments to Normal Value that decrease Normal Value are appropriate, and that adjustments to Export Price (or Constructed Export Price) that increase Export Price (or Constructed Export Price) are proper. Thus, the respondent tries to fit the facts of the case into deductions from Normal Value and additions to Export Price (or Constructed Export Price), and argues against facts that would mitigate in favor of additions to Normal Value or deductions from Export Price (or Constructed Export Price).

B. Tabular Summary of Major Adjustments

What, then, are the major adjustments commonly found in practice? The Tables below summarize them, organized according to the price variable and whether the potential change is an addition to, or subtraction from that variable. Table 30-2 lists additions to Export Price (or Constructed Export Price). Table 30-3 lists deductions from Export Price (or Constructed Export Price). Table 30-4 lists deductions unique to Constructed Export Price. Tables 30-5 and 30-6 list additions to, and deductions from, Normal Value, respectively. Table 30-7 lists adjustments to Normal Value that may be additions to, or deductions from, that variable, depending on the facts of the case. No adjustment need be made if it already is included in the starting point for Normal Value or Export Price (or Constructed Export Price). For example, if data already include overseas packing costs, then there is no need to add them to a variable.

All of the Tables list analogous adjustments (if any). That is, the Tables concerning adjustments to Export Price and Constructed Export Price present any corresponding adjustments to Normal Value. Likewise, the Tables concerning adjustments to Normal Value set out any corresponding adjustments to Export Price and Constructed Export Price.

TABLE 30-2:
ADDITIONS TO EXPORT PRICE (OR CONSTRUCTED EXPORT PRICE)

Addition to Export Price (or Constructed Export Price)	Statutory Reference in 19 U.S.C.	Analogous Adjustment to Normal Value?	Rationale?
Overseas packing costs. Containers, coverings, and all other costs incident to packing subject merchandise for shipment to U.S.	§ 1677a(c)(1)(A)	Addition to Normal Value for overseas packing costs. § 1677b(a)(6)(A)	Helps ensure an "apples-to-apples" comparison with Normal Value. Also, a similar addition is made to Normal Value.
Rebated or uncollected import duties. Any import duties imposed by exporting country rebated or not collected because subject merchandise is exported to U.S. (*e.g.*, drawback.)	§ 1677a(c)(1)(B)	None. Because foreign like product is not exported, no analogous adjustment expected.	Helps ensure an "apples-to-apples" comparison with Normal Value. Drawback is not available for a foreign like product sold in the home market (it is offered only upon export). It is properly part of the price of the foreign like product.
Countervailing duties (CVDs) imposed on subject merchandise.	§ 1677a(c)(1)(C)	None. No analogous adjustment expected, because CVDs are not imposed on foreign like product.	Helps achieve a more accurate price for subject merchandise, based on what a buyer pays for it.

TABLE 30-3:
DEDUCTIONS FROM EXPORT PRICE
(OR CONSTRUCTED EXPORT PRICE)

Deduction from Export Price (or Constructed Export Price)	Statutory Reference in 19 U.S.C.	Analogous Adjustment to Normal Value?	Rationale?
Overseas freight charge. Any additional costs incident to bringing subject merchandise from place of shipment in exporting country to place of delivery in U.S.	§ 1677a(c)(2)(A)	Deduction from Normal Value for internal freight charge. § 1677b(a)(6)(B) (ii)	Helps achieve an *ex-factory* price for subject merchandise. Also, a similar deduction is made from Normal Value.
Export taxes. Any tax imposed by exporting country upon exportation of subject merchandise to U.S.	§ 1677a(c)(2)(B)	None.	Helps ensure an "apples-to-apples" comparison with Normal Value. Export taxes would not be included in price of foreign like product sold in the home market. Because that product is not exported, it bears no export tax. Also, helps achieve an *ex-factory* price for subject merchandise.

TABLE 30-4:
FURTHER DEDUCTIONS FROM (AND UNIQUE TO) CONSTRUCTED EXPORT PRICE

Deduction from Constructed Export Price	Statutory Reference in 19 U.S.C.	Analogous Adjustment to Normal Value?	Rationale?
Selling commissions. Commissions for selling subject merchandise in U.S.	§ 1677a(d)(1)(A)	None.	Helps achieve an *ex-factory* price for subject merchandise.
Direct selling expenses. (Such as credit expenses, guarantees, and warrantees).	§ 1677a(d)(1)(B)	None.	Helps achieve an *ex-factory* price for subject merchandise.
Selling expenses paid by seller on behalf of purchaser.	§ 1677a(d)(1)(C)	None.	Helps achieve an *ex-factory* price for subject merchandise.
Indirect selling expenses. Any other selling expenses not included above. The amount of such other expenses establishes the "Constructed Export Price offset cap."	§ 1677a(d)(1)(D)	"Constructed Export Price offset," by which indirect selling expenses are deducted from Normal Value, but are capped at the amount deducted from Constructed Exported Price. § 1677b(a)(7)(B)	Helps achieve an *ex-factory* price for subject merchandise. The CEP offset accounts for at least some indirect selling expenses incurred in home market, up to the amount of such expenses incurred in U.S.
Cost of further manufacture or assembly. Labor and additional material, in effect, value added in U.S. to subject merchandise.	§ 1677a(d)(2)	None.	Helps achieve an *ex-factory* price for subject merchandise.
Profits allocated to any of the above expenses.	§ 1677a(d)(3)	None.	Helps achieve an *ex-factory* price for subject merchandise.

TABLE 30-5:
ADDITIONS TO NORMAL VALUE

Addition to Normal Value	Statutory Reference in 19 U.S.C.	Analogous Adjustment to Export Price (or Constructed Export Price)?	Rationale?
Overseas packing costs. Cost of all containers, coverings, and expenses to place subject merchandise in condition for shipment to U.S.	§ 1677b(a)(6)(A)	Addition to Export Price or Constructed Export Price for overseas packing charge. § 1677a(c)(1)(A)	Helps ensure an "apples-to-apples" comparison with Export Price (or Constructed Export Price). The price of subject merchandise, because it has been imported into U.S, would entail an overseas packing charge. If none is included, then an addition is made to Export Price (or Constructed Export Price).

TABLE 30-6:
DEDUCTIONS FROM NORMAL VALUE

Deduction from Normal Value	Statutory Reference in 19 U.S.C.	Analogous Adjustment to Export Price (or Constructed Export Price)?	Rationale?
Internal packing charges. Cost of all containers and coverings, and all other costs, to place foreign like product in condition ready for shipment to place of delivery to purchaser.	§ 1677b(a)(6)(B)(i)	None.	Helps achieve an *ex-factory* price for foreign like product.
Internal freight charge. Any costs associated with bringing the foreign like product from the original place of shipment to place of delivery to purchaser.	§ 1677b(a)(6)(B)(ii)	Deduction from Export Price (or Constructed Export Price) for overseas freight charge. § 1677a(c)(2)(A)	Helps achieve an *ex-factory* price for foreign like product. Similar adjustment made to Export Price (or Constructed Export Price).
Rebated or uncollected taxes. Any taxes imposed directly on foreign like product that is rebated, or not collected, on subject merchandise, to the extent such tax is included in the price of foreign like product.	§ 1677b(a)(6)(B)(iii)	None. Under pre-Uruguay Round law, this adjustment took the form of an addition to Export Price (or Constructed Export Price).	Helps achieve an *ex-factory* price for foreign like product.
Constructed Export Price Offset. Deduction for indirect selling expenses incurred in the home market based on sales of foreign like product. Applied only under certain conditions, namely, Normal Value is based on a more advanced stage of distribution than the level of trade (LOT) of Constructed Export Price, but available data do not permit a LOT adjustment to Normal Value. Capped at the amount of indirect selling expenses incurred in U.S.	§ 1677b(a)(7)(B)	Constructed Export Price offset to CEP for indirect selling expenses incurred in U.S. associated with subject merchandise. § 1677a(d)(1)(D)	Helps achieve an *ex-factory* price for foreign like product. Accounts, up to the amount of the cap, for indirect selling expenses incurred in home market.

TABLE 30-7:
ADDITIONS TO OR DEDUCTIONS FROM NORMAL VALUE
(DEPENDING ON THE FACTS OF THE CASE)

Addition to or Deduction from Normal Value	Statutory Reference in 19 U.S.C.	Analogous Adjustment to Export Price (Or Constructed Export Price?	Rationale?
Quantity adjustment. Adjustment for differences in the quantity sold between foreign like product in home market, and subject merchandise in U.S.	§ 1677b(a)(6)(C)(i)	None.	Helps explain some of the difference between Normal Value and Export Price (or Constructed Export Price).
Quality adjustment. Adjustment for differences in the quality of foreign like product and subject merchandise. This "difference in merchandise" (DIFMER) adjustment is made when foreign like product used to determine Normal Value is not identical in physical characteristics with, and produced in the same country by the same person, as subject merchandise.	§§ 1677b(a)(6)(C)(ii) and 1677(16)(B)-(C)	None.	Helps explain some of the difference between Normal Value and Export Price (or Constructed Export Price).
Circumstance of Sale. Known as a "COS" adjustment, it encompasses a variety of circumstances.	§ 1677b(a)(6)(C)(iii)	None.	Helps explain some of the difference between Normal Value and Export Price (or Constructed Export Price).
Level of trade. Known as a "LOT" adjustment, it is made when there is a difference in the level of trade between Normal Value and Export Price (or Constructed Export Price), which involves (1) different selling activities, and (2) demonstrably affects price comparability based on a consistent pattern of price differences.	§ 1677b(a)(7)(A)	None.	Helps explain some of the difference between Normal Value and Export Price (or Constructed Export Price.

The adjustments listed in the Tables are self-explanatory only to a limited degree. It is necessary to read the statutory provisions, and case law elaborations, for a fuller understanding of a particular adjustment. For now, three points are worth observing.

1. *Applicability to Proxies:*

The adjustments potentially available in calculating Normal Value also exist when using a proxy for Normal Value. That is, generally speaking, they apply in Third Country Price or Constructed Value scenarios. However, exceptions exist — for instance, in respect of difmer and Constructed Value.

2. *Unifying Theme:*

To the extent there is any common theme unifying all of the adjustments, any common policy logic, it is this: the adjustments are designed to ensure the comparison between Normal Value and Export Price (or Constructed Export Price) is fair, a "fair" comparison means an "apples-to-apples" one, and "apples-to-apples" generally is defined in terms of *ex-factory* prices. In other words, for the most part, the adjustments are designed to ensure the figures are prices prevailing when merchandise leaves the factory in which it is made. Indeed, Article 2:4 of the WTO *Antidumping Agreement* makes the point that the comparison between Normal Value and Export Price (or Constructed Export Price) normally is to be at the *ex-factory* level.

3. *Offsets:*

To what extent is the mandate of Article 2:4 of the *Antidumping Agreement* not followed universally? In particular, do non-dumped sales offset dumped sales? Notwithstanding the Appellate Body holdings in zeroing cases, various WTO Members do not permit this type of offset, at least not in certain contexts. Hence, a systematic bias remains in favor of a petitioner.

Suppose a respondent sells merchandise in Tulsa, Oklahoma, and Wichita, Kansas. The sales in Tulsa are at dumped prices, *i.e.*, the dumping margin is positive. Sales in Wichita are at prices above Normal Value. Ideally, the respondent would like to use the negative dumping margins from Wichita sales to offset the positive margins from the Tulsa sales. That is not possible. To be sure, in calculating Normal Value and Export Price (or Constructed Export Price), large volumes of data on home market and United States prices, respectively, are averaged. In this sense, the Wichita sales are included in the overall computation. But, there is no specific "rubbing out" of a dumped sale in Tulsa by a non-dumped sale in Wichita.

C. Dignity and Truth

As technical as dumping margin adjustments are, perhaps they raise a deep jurisprudential issue: do these adjustments, motivated as they are by diametrically opposed interests of the players, undermine the dignity of AD law? It could be argued the whole affair is a game in which "truth" — a comparison of the true prices in the home and importing country markets — is not really the object, or at least not the result. Indeed, the arbitrariness of certain adjustments — both conceptually, in the abstract, and in particular contexts — is a complaint often heard from AD lawyers.

The fact is a petitioner and respondent fight intensely for or against an adjustment simply based on what mathematical effect that adjustment has on the calculation. They attempt to cloak their arguments in technical terms, and try to fit the facts within the parameters of established adjustment categories. Sometimes, the fit is a Procrustean one. The argument for or against an adjustment then crosses the line between a good faith effort to push or circumscribe the boundaries of the category, on the one hand, and a rather ridiculous effort to ignore those boundaries, on the other hand.

The question that ought not to be ducked is: what does the great game of adjustments do to the dignity of international trade law? Armies of lawyers, reinforced by legions of accountants, spend an enormous amount of time and effort calculating the effects of every possible addition and subtraction to the dumping margin. This process hardly is what most people have in mind when they think of the grandeur or majesty of the legal system. Yet, that is exactly what happens every day in the "trenches" of AD law. The stakes of battle are very high. Whether a dumping margin exists, and thus whether a case goes forward, may depend centrally on whether a particular adjustment is made or not made. Small wonder, then, why legal and accounting firms that work on AD cases have sophisticated computer programs to "run the numbers" and check the effects of one adjustment versus another.

In these "trenches," query whether truth and justice are the casualties. Do they wind up as far-off, romantic concepts? Often the outcome of "running the numbers" leads to a claim for (or against) a particular adjustment. A vision of the law as something noble means argumentation ought not be crassly consequential in nature. What is "right," not what works out best in terms of the dumping margin formula, ought to motivate an argument, and ought to carry the day.

II. DIRECT SELLING EXPENSES AND THE 1989 *SKF* CASE

SKF U.S.A., INC. v. INA WALZLAGER SCHAEFFLER KG
United States Court of Appeals for the Federal Circuit
180 F.3d 1370 (1999)

EDWARD S. SMITH, SENIOR CIRCUIT JUDGE.

. . . SKF GmbH is a manufacturer and exporter of AFBs [antifriction bearings] in Germany, and SKF USA, Inc. is a United States importer of German AFBs (collectively "SKF"). SKF appeals from two decisions of the United States Court of International Trade, which sustained [the Department of] Commerce's denial of SKF's billing adjustment two and cash discounts. We agree that Commerce properly disallowed SKF's billing adjustment two and cash discounts because the claimed adjustments were not limited to merchandise within the scope of the antidumping order. We therefore affirm.

BACKGROUND

. . . .

. . . SKF participated as a respondent in Commerce's review of AFB imports. . . . SKF submitted information on its sales of AFBs in the German home market during the period of review, including its sales prices and adjustments to those prices . . . Commerce disallowed two adjustments known as billing adjustment two and cash discounts, that SKF claimed in calculating its FMV [Foreign Market Value, *i.e.*, Normal Value]. . . .

In rejecting SKF's adjustments, Commerce relied upon *Torrington Co. v. United States*, 818 F. Supp. 1563 (Ct. Int'l Trade 1993) ("*Torrington CIT*"), wherein the Court of International Trade held Commerce cannot calculate the FMV of merchandise that is within the scope of an antidumping review ("in-scope" merchandise) using a methodology that includes discounts, rebates, and price adjustments on merchandise outside the scope of the antidumping review ("out-of-scope" merchandise). . . . Commerce denied SKF the requested adjustments because they were not reported in a transaction-specific manner and therefore were not limited to merchandise within the scope of the antidumping review. . . .

SKF filed a complaint with the Court of International Trade alleging among other things that Commerce erred in its calculation of the FMV by disallowing adjustments for SKF's billing adjustment two and cash discounts. . . . SKF claimed that all of the adjustments should be treated as "direct" and allowed as adjustments to the FMV. . . . Commerce had rejected that contention, however, because SKF failed to show that the allocated price adjustments at issue were calculated solely on the basis of merchandise under review. . . .

. . . .

We affirm the decision[] of the Court of International Trade on the basis of the in-scope/out-of-scope rule articulated in *Torrington CIT*, and applied by Commerce in disallowing SKF's billing adjustments in this case.

. . . .

ANALYSIS

. . . .

In determining whether goods are being sold at less than fair value, Commerce may allow adjustments to the FMV for direct selling expenses based on three criteria: (1) differences between quantities sold in the foreign and domestic markets; (2) differences in the circumstances of sales; and (3) differences in physical characteristics of the product. . . . [The Court points out in two important footnotes, #6 and #7, that direct selling expenses "are expenses which vary with the quantity sold," *Zenith Electronics Corp., v. United States*, 77 F.3d 426, 431 (Fed. Cir. 1996), or that are "related to a particular sale." *Torrington v. United States*, 68 F.3d 1347, 1353 (Fed. Cir. 1995). In contrast, indirect selling expenses " 'are those that do not vary with the quantity sold.' " *Zenith Elecs.*, 77 F.3d at 431 . . . or that are "not related to a particular sale," *Torrington*, 68 F.3d at 1353. Commerce may deduct indirect selling expenses from Normal Value under the Constructed Export Price offset rule.] . . .

When this procedure was followed in the instant case, Commerce found that SKF's billing adjustment number two and cash discounts were in the nature of direct expenses because they were allocated adjustments that were not granted as a fixed and constant percentage of sale. SKF's adjustments were granted after sale, apparently to correct billing errors (billing adjustment number two) or to lower the price for a particular customer (cash discounts). Commerce disallowed SKF's billing adjustment number two and cash discounts because they were not reported in a transaction-specific manner and therefore were not limited to merchandise within the scope of the antidumping review. . . .

The Court of International Trade agreed with Commerce's characterization of SKF's billing adjustment number two and cash discounts as being in the nature of direct expenses, and agreed that SKF's failure to report them on a transaction-specific basis precluded treatment of the adjustments as direct expenses. . . .

The In-Scope/Out-of-Scope Rule

The in-scope/out-of-scope rule relied on by Commerce in this case was clearly articulated by the Court of International Trade in *Torrington CIT*. . . . In that case, the foreign manufacturer claimed adjustments to FMV for certain post-sale price adjustments ("PSPAs") and rebates that were granted as an ordinary part of its business but which were not tracked on a product-specific basis. The adjustments at issue were not allocated on a product-specific basis and "no effort was made to eliminate PSPAs and rebates paid on out of scope merchandise." . . . Thus, PSPAs and rebates that had been granted on out-of-scope merchandise had been included in calculating the claimed adjustments.

Commerce allowed the claimed adjustments, treating them as indirect expenses. . . . The Court of International Trade reversed, on the basis that "[m]erchandise which is outside the scope of an antidumping duty order cannot be used in the calculation of antidumping duties." . . .

We agree with the *Torrington CIT* court that antidumping duties must be calculated based solely on merchandise within the scope of the antidumping duty order. This requirement is mandated by statute: "If . . . a class or kind of *foreign merchandise* [called "subject merchandise" in post-Uruguay Round AD law] *is being . . . sold in the United States at less than its fair value*, and [a domestic industry is injured by the dumping], then there shall be imposed upon such merchandise an antidumping duty . . . in an amount equal to the amount by which the foreign market value exceeds the United States price *for the merchandise*." 19 U.S.C. § 1673. . . The statutory language thus requires that the antidumping duty be calculated on the basis of the difference between the FMV and the USP for "the merchandise;" *i.e.*, the "foreign merchandise [which] is being . . . sold in the United States at less than its fair value." . . . Price adjustments granted on goods *outside the scope* of the antidumping duty order are irrelevant to calculating the FMV of goods *within the scope* of the antidumping duty order; they simply play no part in determining the FMV of the in-scope goods themselves. The statutory language therefore precludes the use of price adjustments granted on sales of goods outside the scope of the antidumping duty order in calculating the FMV of goods within the scope of the antidumping duty order.

. . . .

In addition, a rule requiring direct price adjustments to relate exclusively to in-scope merchandise is necessary in order to allow Commerce to calculate the FMV as accurately as possible to determine whether dumping has indeed occurred. To allow adjustments to FMV for direct price adjustments encompassing both in-scope and out-of-scope goods would have the effect of averaging prices, diluting some and inflating others, and thereby reduce the accuracy of Commerce's dumping determinations.

. . . .

Application of the Rule

In this case, SKF requested an adjustment to FMV for its billing adjustment two and cash discounts. SKF reported to Commerce that these post-sale price adjustments generally related to multiple invoices and therefore could not be reported in a transaction-specific manner. . . . Commerce denied the adjustments because "SKF did not demonstrate that [either] adjustment[ ] pertained to subject merchandise only," . . . in that "SKF provided no means of identifying and segregating billing adjustments paid on non-scope merchandise." . . .

The party seeking a direct price adjustment bears the burden of proving entitlement to such an adjustment. . . . Commerce determined in this case that SKF had not carried its burden. . . .

We agree with Commerce and the Court of International Trade that the law requires price adjustments to be calculated solely on the basis of merchandise within the scope of an antidumping duty order. . . . Commerce applied the correct legal standard in requiring SKF to show that the claimed adjustments pertained to subject merchandise only. SKF did not do so, and Commerce appropriately denied the requested adjustments.

III. CIRCUMSTANCES OF SALE AND THE 1998 *TORRINGTON* CASE

THE TORRINGTON COMPANY v. UNITED STATES
United States Court of Appeals for the Federal Circuit
156 F.3d 1361-66 (1998)

MICHEL, CIRCUIT JUDGE.

This appeal continues the enduring saga of the efforts of this American ball bearing manufacturer to obtain relief from certain foreign competitors under the trade laws. Here, The Torrington Company ("Torrington") appeals the judgment of the United States Court of International Trade upholding the final determination of the United States Department of Commerce ("Commerce") in its fourth administrative review [in 1995] of the importation of antifriction bearings from various countries. . . . Defendants-Appellees NMB Thai Ltd., Pelmec Thai Ltd., NMB Hi-Tech Bearings Ltd., and NMB Corp. (collectively, "NMB Thai") were interested party-respondents in the underlying antidumping administrative review and were defendants-intervenors at the Court of International Trade. In this appeal, Torrington contends only that the Court of International Trade erred by upholding the determination of Commerce to adjust the foreign (home) market value [*i.e.*, Normal Value] of the subject antifriction bearings to take account of certain international freight expenses. Because Commerce's decision to allow an adjustment for such freight expenses was based upon a reasonable interpretation of its own regulations and thus was entitled to deference, we affirm.

BACKGROUND

NMB Thai is a producer of antifriction ball bearings in Thailand. These bearings are both sold in Thailand and exported to the United States. The antidumping review encompassed importations of such bearings entered between May 1, 1992, and April 30, 1993. During this period, NMB Thai sold its ball bearings in the Thai market through two distinct channels. "Route A" sales were shipped directly to the customer in Thailand via a domestic route. "Route B" sales, however, were first shipped abroad to a warehouse operated by a related company in Singapore and then back to Thailand. The purpose of this circuitous Route B was to obtain certain favorable tax and duty treatment from the Thai government and, in particular, to avoid government restrictions on sales to Thai customers who were certified by the Thailand Board of Investment but did not have a bonded warehouse.

On May 15, 1989, Commerce published antidumping duty orders on antifriction bearings from Thailand. . . . The Commerce decision at issue in the Court of International Trade was rendered in the fourth administrative review of the antidumping duty order.

In the antidumping review, Commerce determined the "United States price" [i.e., Export Price or Constructed Export Price] and the "foreign market value" ("FMV") of the subject merchandise and used this data to calculate antidumping margins in accordance with 19 U.S.C. § 1675. These margins were then used by Commerce to assess antidumping duties on the entries of merchandise covered by the review as well as to calculate estimates of antidumping duties for future entries. . . .

In determining FMV, Commerce is permitted to make adjustments for certain "circumstances of sale" ("COS"). . . . Such COS adjustments are made when the seller incurs certain costs in its home market sales that it does not incur when selling to the United States market. Such adjustments may be made if "the amount of any price differential is wholly or partly due to such difference [in circumstances of sale]" and "those circumstances . . . bear a direct relationship to the sales compared." 19 C.F.R. § 353.56(a)(1). In addition, adjustments to FMV may also be made for indirect selling expenses "incurred in selling such or similar merchandise up to the amount of expenses . . .incurred in selling the merchandise." 19 C.F.R. § 353.56(b)(2). In the antidumping review, Commerce deducted from FMV the pre-sale freight costs for shipping merchandise from Thailand to Singapore as indirect selling expenses pursuant to 19 C.F.R. § 353.56(b)(2). Commerce also deducted from FMV the post-sale freight expenses of shipping the merchandise from Singapore back to Thailand as direct selling costs pursuant to 19 C.F.R. § 353.56(a)(1).

Before the Court of International Trade, Torrington argued, *inter alia*, that NMB Thai's Route B freight expenses were not "selling expenses" for purposes of 19 C.F.R. § 353.56, but rather were general costs incurred for the purpose of receiving government benefits. The Court of International Trade, however, rejected this contention, explaining that this court had previously held both that the "Route B sales were properly classified as home market sales" and that "Commerce may deduct indirect home market transportation expenses from FMV [subject] to the exporter's sales price . . . offset cap [*i.e.*, the Constructed Export Price offset]." . . .

On appeal to this court, Torrington argues that the plain meaning of the governing statute and regulation both indicate that the Route B freight expenses are not selling costs that may be accepted as downward COS adjustments to FMV and, moreover, that permitting such adjustments would defeat the purpose of the COS provisions because the freight costs were offset by savings in NMB Thai's taxes and duties.

DISCUSSION

Our analysis must begin with the controlling statutory language. Under 19 U.S.C. § 1677b(a)(4), "due allowance shall be made" for "the amount of any difference between the United States price and the foreign market value . . . wholly or partly due to . . . other differences in circumstances of sale." This court has previously explained that "the statute does not define the term 'circumstances of sale' nor does it prescribe any method for determining allowances. Congress has deferred to the Secretary's expertise in this matter." *Smith-Corona Group v. United States*, 713 F.2d 1568, 1575, . . . (Fed. Cir. 1983). Accordingly, under the authority of this statute, Commerce promulgated 19 C.F.R. § 353.56, which sets forth the criteria required for the allowance of COS adjustments to FMV. . . . [S]uch adjustments are permitted to take account both of circumstances bearing "a direct relationship to the sales compared," . . . and indirect expenses "incurred in selling such or similar merchandise" ("selling expenses"). . . .

In light of the substantial deference accorded to Commerce when interpreting and applying its own regulations, we find no error in the Court of International Trade upholding Commerce's decision to make a COS adjustment to FMV to take account of NMB Thai's Route B freight costs. The parties do not dispute that Commerce's regulation, which permits adjustments for, *inter alia*, "selling expenses," is an authorized and reasonable administrative interpretation of the governing statute. Moreover, there is no dispute that such selling expenses may properly include freight costs. *See, e.g., Torrington Co. v. United States*, 68 F.3d 1347, 1356 (Fed. Cir. 1995); *Sharp Corp. v. United States*, 63 F.3d 1092, 1097 (Fed. Cir. 1995). In determining that the two Route B freight costs at issue in this case were selling expenses properly the subject of a COS adjustment, Commerce was simply interpreting its own regulations. We give substantial deference to that interpretation. . . .

Commerce's interpretation of its regulation is not "plainly erroneous or inconsistent with the regulation." *Thomas Jefferson Univ. v. Shalala*, 512 U.S. [504,] at 512 [1994]. Rather, its interpretation is a reasonable one in a complex field in which it has special and unique expertise. To interpret the regulation, as Torrington apparently suggests, to require Commerce to parse all freight costs to determine the intent behind such costs would, moreover, be administratively impracticable. Indeed, it is difficult to comprehend the method by which Commerce could be expected to divine the subjective intent behind the decision to transport merchandise by a particular method or along a particular route. For example, a decision to transport certain goods within the country of manufacture by rail rather than road might be due to government rail subsidies, high gasoline taxes, delivery timing requirements, or a combination of such factors. To expect Commerce to determine the specific business strategy behind the decision to use rail transport under such a scenario would be to expect the unattainable. Thus, under circumstances akin to the instant case, where the freight expenses are found directly or indirectly to support the relevant sales, it is appropriate for Commerce to avoid inquiring into the subjective intent behind the incurring of those expenses. Accordingly, we do not regard Commerce's interpretation of its regulation to be unreasonable when the alternative interpretation proffered by Torrington is utterly unworkable.

We also do not agree with Torrington's assertion that allowing NMB Thai a COS adjustment from FMV for the Route B freight expenses somehow vitiates the statutory and regulatory scheme or its policy goals. In support of this proposition, Torrington contends that by permitting NMB Thai this adjustment, Commerce is permitting an adjustment for an expenditure that does not affect price. However, Torrington does not point to any finding in the record substantiating its factual claim that these Route B freight expenses do not affect price. Indeed, notwithstanding any tax, customs, or bonding benefits, Torrington has not brought forward any evidence suggesting that the Thai customers of NMB Thai do not ultimately pay for the circuitous Route B freight costs. Or, to put it differently, Torrington has not produced any evidence that the Route B shipping route provides a net cost saving to Thai customers, only that the Route B costs are incurred to avoid expending the presumably greater costs associated with the Thai tax penalty, customs, and bonding requirements. Accordingly, it is far from apparent that NMB Thai's customers in Thailand do not bear the expense of the roundabout Route B shipping arrangement and we, therefore, do not regard allowing this adjustment to be inconsistent with the overall statutory and regulatory scheme or its policy goals.

. . . .

ARCHER, SENIOR JUDGE, DISSENTING:

The decision of the Court of International Trade sustaining Commerce's deduction from foreign market value (FMV) of the Route B freight costs as home market selling expenses should in my view be reversed. Torrington is correct in arguing that under the governing statute and regulation Route B freight costs are not normal expenses related to home market sales but rather are additional costs incurred to obtain general benefits for the company, *i.e.*, to preserve favorable VAT tax and export duty exemptions.

In general the antidumping statute and regulations seek to produce a fair, "apples-to-apples" comparison between FMV and United States price (USP). To achieve that end, adjustments are made to the base value of both FMV and USP to permit comparison of the two prices at a similar point in the chain of commerce. . . . The USP is adjusted by deducting expenses incurred in selling the merchandise in the United States. . . . FMV is adjusted by deducting direct selling expenses under the circumstances of sale (COS) provision, . . . Moreover, when the USP is based on the exporter's sales price (ESP), the FMV is reduced by the indirect selling expenses to the extent of the deduction for indirect selling expenses from USP. . . .

Home market transportation costs have been considered by Commerce to be sales related and have been treated as selling expenses. . . . As a result, post-sale transportation costs have been allowed as a COS adjustment. Pre-sale transportation costs (not related to any particular sale) have been allowed as indirect selling expenses when the USP is based on ESP [Exporter's Sales Price, *i.e.*, Constructed Export Price]. . . .

Deductions for transportation costs have previously been made for in-country transportation costs — transportation within the country in the normal course of home market sales. *See Cemex, S.A. v. United States*, 133 F.3d 897, 901 (Fed. Cir. 1998) (in-country transportation for home market sales). . . . There is no evidence that Commerce has previously made an adjustment for transportation costs to and from a point outside the country in which home market sales occurred.

. . . In this case, . . . Commerce's own verification clearly shows that the Route B transportation costs were not incurred in the process of selling, but were incurred in order to obtain import duty and VAT tax benefits for NMB Thai. To this end, the verification shows that these Route B transportation costs were incurred because bearings produced in their bonded factories "continue to carry duty-free status when they are exported" and when shipped back to related or unrelated Board of Investment (BOI) companies in Thailand they are treated as "duty-free" imported raw materials. The verification states that NMB Thai found it much simpler to import raw materials in this way. Because the verification establishes the reasons why NMB Thai used the circuitous transportation route, it was not necessary for Commerce to delve into the "subjective intent behind the decision to transport merchandise by a particular method or along a particular route," which is one of the principal concerns of the majority. In this case, the reasons are clear in the verification record and establish that the added transportation costs cannot properly be classified as a form of selling expense.

It is evident in this case that Commerce did not make an "apples to apples" comparison. By allowing an adjustment for a transportation diversion of the nature and magnitude as here involved, Commerce has not made an adjustment in arriving at FMV which reaches the similar point in the chain of commerce to make a proper comparison with the USP. Torrington correctly argues that the excess transportation costs were in the nature of general and administrative overhead costs "related to the company's overall corporate strategy to reduce costs generally and reduce its tax and duty burdens specifically." Selling expenses are commonly understood to be expenses made to support and promote sales. *See NSK v. United States*, 115 F.3d 965, 974 (Fed. Cir. 1997) (when terms not explicitly defined should be given their "ordinary meaning"). [The Dissent points out in a footnote that "Torrington concedes that an adjustment for some transportation costs might be appropriate if NMB Thai can show what it would have cost to ship directly to Route B customers."] The commonly understood definition of selling expenses was not applied here.

I would, therefore, reverse the decision below and remand the case to Commerce to make a transportation adjustment in an amount that reflects what would be a normal transportation cost to Route B customers of NMB Thai.

IV. DIFFERENCES IN MERCHANDISE AND THE 2001 *MITSUBISHI* CASE

MITSUBISHI HEAVY INDUSTRIES, LTD. v. UNITED STATES
United States Court of Appeals for the Federal Circuit
275 F.3d 1056-66 (2001)

CLEVENGER, CIRCUIT JUDGE.

. . . .

I

BACKGROUND

This case involves large newspaper printing presses exported to the United States from Japan. Although all LNPPs have similar design and function, individual LNPPs are custom-made per the customer's specification. The companies provide their customers with a menu of various components that can be built into the machine, and the customer decides what components to order. As a result, individual orders for LNPPs can vary to a greater or lesser extent, depending on what components the customer chooses. Because Japanese and United States newspapers have somewhat different characteristics in terms of size, use of color, etc., the LNPPs used to produce them also have somewhat different components. Thus, every contract for sale of an LNPP contains different terms — including price terms — because the LNPPs themselves have different components from contract to contract.

Upon a petition by Rockwell Graphics Systems, Inc., a U.S. competitor now known as Goss Graphics Systems, Inc. ("Goss"), the Department of Commerce ("Commerce") launched an antidumping investigation of two manufacturers, MHI [Mitsubishi Heavy Industries] and TKS [Tokyo Kikai Seisakusho]. In due course [in 1996], Commerce issued its final antidumping determination finding sales at less than fair value and announcing a dumping margin of 56.28 percent for TKS, the appellant here. . . . Commerce used constructed value ("CV") to calculate the dumping margin, . . . and it used home market (*i.e.*, Japanese) LNPPs as the foreign like product in its determination of profit, which is one component of CV, see 19 U.S.C. § 1677b(e)(2) (1994), despite having earlier found that direct price-to-price comparisons with home market LNPPs were impracticable as a basis for normal value — a finding that led to its original decision to use CV as a basis for normal value. . . .

TKS and MHI appealed numerous aspects of Commerce's determination in Japan Final, including its foreign like product determination. . . . TKS, in particular, argued that Commerce's reliance upon 19 U.S.C. § 1677b(e)(2)(A) to calculate profit was inappropriate because "the findings that led Commerce to rely on CV rather than home-market sales in calculating normal value constituted evidence that no foreign like product existed in the home market." . . . The profit calculation under § 1677b(e)(2)(A) relies upon sales of "a foreign like product." . . . Because Commerce did not describe adequately its profit calculation so as to permit judicial review, the Court of International Trade remanded the case to Commerce to explain upon which of the three statutory definitions of foreign like product it relied to make its profit calculation. . . . In its remand determination, Commerce explained that it had relied upon the definition of foreign like product in 19 U.S.C. § 1677(16)(C), which requires, *inter alia*, that the foreign like product be merchandise that "the administering authority determines may reasonably be compared with" the exported merchandise subject to the investigation. . . .

TKS and MHI appealed the remand determination, and the Court of International Trade remanded again, this time because Commerce failed to explain the factual basis for its determination that the LNPPs sold in Japan and the United States could "reasonably be compared" as required by 19 U.S.C. § 1677(16)(c)(iii). . . . The Court of International Trade was troubled because in its first remand determination, Commerce made statements that made it appear that it had previously conducted a difmer analysis and concluded that the home market and export LNPPs could not reasonably be compared. . . . In its second remand determination, Commerce clarified that it had not conducted a difmer analysis. . . . In addition, Commerce explained the factual basis for its finding that the home-market LNPPs could "reasonably be compared" with their United States counterparts, which included the common use to which the products are put (*i.e.*, printing newspapers) and TKS's and MHI's responses to detailed questionnaires showing that the Japanese and United States LNPPs share the same set of detailed press characteristics. . . .

[In a footnote, the Court explained difmer adjustments as follows:

When the foreign merchandise is not identical to the exported goods, Commerce may conduct a "difmer" analysis, which "adjusts normal value for the 'difference in cost attributable to the difference in physical characteristics' — the difference in merchandise ('difmer') adjustment." *Mitsubishi Heavy Indus., Ltd. v. United States*, 97 F. Supp. 2d 1203, 1206 n.4 (Ct. Int'l Trade 2000). If the "difmer" exceeds 20 percent, Commerce will make a finding that the merchandise cannot be reasonably compared, unless it can otherwise justify the comparison. In other words, a >20% difmer finding creates a presumption of non-comparability. *Id.* Obviously the difmer analysis is conducted — if at all — prior to a decision to use CV, because the difmer adjustment is made to normal value, not CV.

Query why difmer adjustments do not apply to Constructed Value?]

Based on Commerce's explanation of the factual basis underlying its comparability determination, the Court of International Trade affirmed the dumping determination. . . . The court denied TKS's motion for reconsideration, . . . and this appeal by TKS followed. . . .

II

A

. . . .

On appeal, TKS primarily argues that Commerce's determination that home and United States market LNPPs may reasonably be compared is not supported by substantial evidence. We note that in pursuing this argument, TKS has chosen a course with a high barrier to reversal. The Supreme Court has defined substantial evidence as "such relevant evidence as a reasonable mind might accept as adequate to support a conclusion." *Universal Camera Corp. v. NLRB*, 340 U.S. 474, 477, 95 L. Ed. 456, 71 S. Ct. 456 (1951) (quoting *Consol. Edison Co. v. NLRB*, 305 U.S. 197, 229, 83 L. Ed. 126, 59 S. Ct. 206 (1938)). The conclusion reached by Commerce need not be the only one possible from the record, for "even if it is possible to draw two inconsistent conclusions from evidence in the record, such a possibility does not prevent Commerce's determination from being supported by substantial evidence." *Am. Silicon Techs. v. United States*, 261 F.3d 1371, 1376 (Fed. Cir. 2001). . . . After reviewing the record, we conclude that substantial evidence supports Commerce's determination that home-market LNPPs are a foreign like product.

In its second remand decision, Commerce clarified the evidence underlying its decision to use home-market LNPPs as the foreign like product, explaining that "TKS's home market LNPP may reasonably be compared to its sales of LNPP in the United States based on evidence that LNPP in both markets share detailed product characteristics." . . . Commerce noted that its conclusion was further "supported by the common use — to produce newspapers — to which both home market and U.S. LNPP are employed." . . . During the investigation, both TKS and MHI responded to a questionnaire sent by Commerce asking them to identify both United States and home-market LNPPs using the same set of detailed press characteristics. . . . TKS's and MHI's responses to this questionnaire, which indicated that their United States and home-market LNPPs do in fact share a majority of the same — or highly similar — characteristics, provide the principal factual predicate for Commerce's finding. TKS argues that this evidence is "self-serving" because Commerce prepared the questionnaire itself, forcing TKS and MHI to describe their Japanese and United States products using the same characteristics. To the extent that TKS accuses Commerce of stacking the deck against them, its argument is not well taken. As the agency to which Congress delegated the authority to determine antidumping duties, Commerce is responsible for gathering information to make dumping determinations. Commerce uses the information it collects in order to reach its decision — in this case that the home-market and United States LNPPs are reasonably comparable. Although Commerce is an agent of the United States government, it nevertheless makes its dumping determination based on an impartial analysis of the evidence. Furthermore, administrative acts by Commerce enjoy a presumption of regularity that includes, in this case, impartiality in its decision-making process, and one seeking to rebut that presumption carries a heavy burden. . . . There is no evidence to suggest that Commerce made up its mind in advance and cunningly planned its questionnaire to support its position.

MHI's and TKS's responses to Commerce's information-gathering request provide ample support for Commerce's finding. First, the questionnaire responses confirm "that the LNPP sold in Japan and the LNPP sold in the United States share the detailed press characteristics that [Commerce] set out in its questionnaire." . . . And within each characteristic, the responses indicated that the individual specifications for each press characteristic were also similar. Obviously, because the LNPPs are custom-made, each individual LNPP may contain a different mix of these common characteristics. However, it is apparent that they all reflect a choice from among similar characteristics. Based on the long list of shared features, Commerce could reasonably conclude that Japanese and United States LNPPs could reasonably be compared for calculating CV profit.

TKS retorts that whatever the value of the questionnaire, Commerce did not consider the whole record when making its comparability determination, because the weight of evidence points the other way. First, TKS notes that United States LNPPs often contained significantly more individual components than did their Japanese counterparts. However, because profit is calculated as a percentage of the sale price, the fact that Japanese LNPPs may have fewer components (and thus, perhaps, a lower overall price) is immaterial. The individual differences between the United States and Japanese models that TKS cites are significant (for example, the United States units use "tower printing units" instead of the "satellite printing units" and "spot color units" more prevalent in Japan). However, such differences are unavoidable in customized equipment. That a United States buyer chooses a somewhat different mix of components than does a Japanese one may preclude price-matching the two contracts, but it does not mean that the machines themselves may not reasonably be compared.

TKS also takes umbrage at Commerce's reference to the English-language and Japanese-language Spectrum product brochures that TKS submitted in response to Commerce's demand to provide all brochures relating to the merchandise under investigation. Commerce cited the brochures as an example of an LNPP model — the Spectrum model — marketed in both the United States and Japan, and noted that the Japanese and English versions of the brochure were identical. TKS argues that this brochure does not show that all United States Spectrums have identical characteristics as their Japanese counterparts, and that Commerce erred in citing the brochures as evidence of comparability. But this is simply another way of saying that the Spectrums, like all LNPPs, are custom-made. The critical point is, given that individual differences exist from order to order, can the custom-made merchandise from Japan and the United States be reasonably compared? Commerce, looking at a brochure offering identical menus of features to Japanese and United States purchasers, could reasonably conclude that one Spectrum LNPP described in the brochure would be reasonably — not perfectly, not identically, but reasonably — comparable to any other Spectrum model.

In short, TKS does not provide any compelling evidence to suggest that Commerce neglected its duty to base its decision on the whole record. To the extent that TKS urges that the evidence before Commerce could be open to multiple interpretations, its argument does not require, or even allow, reversal. . . . Obviously, TKS draws a different conclusion from the evidence of the variations between individual product specifications than did Commerce, but that cannot — and does not — mean that Commerce's interpretation should be overturned. Accordingly, we hold that substantial evidence supported Commerce's decision to treat Japanese market LNPPs as the foreign like product for its determination in this case.

Chapter 31

ADJUSTMENTS TO EXPORT PRICE AND CONSTRUCTED EXPORT PRICE

The perplexity of life arises from there being too many interesting things in it for us to be interested properly in any of them.

> —G.K. Chesterton (1874-1936), *The Secret of a Train, in* TREMENDOUS TRIFLES (1909)

DOCUMENTS SUPPLEMENT ASSIGNMENT

1. *Havana Charter* Article 34
2. GATT Article VI
3. WTO *Antidumping Agreement* Articles 1-2

I. AFFILIATES AND THE 2000 *AK STEEL* CASE

AK STEEL CORPORATION v. UNITED STATES
United States Court of Appeals for the Federal Circuit
226 F.3d 1361, 1363-76 (2000)

MICHEL, CIRCUIT JUDGE.

AK Steel Corporation, Inland Steel Industries, Inc., Bethlehem Steel Corporation, LTV Steel Company, Inc., National Steel Corporation, and U.S. Steel Group (collectively "domestic producers" or "appellants") appealed to this court the judgment of the United States Court of International Trade in this anti-dumping duties case. The International Trade Administration, United States Department of Commerce ("Commerce") issued a decision: (1) using a three-part test it adopted informally in 1987 to determine whether certain sales to U.S. buyers of Korean steel by U.S. affiliates of the Korean producers were properly classified as Export Price ("EP") sales rather than Constructed Export Price ("CEP") sales, as defined in 19 U.S.C. § 1677a(a)-(b) (1994) and (2) declining to apply the "fair-value" and "major-input" provisions of 19 U.S.C. § 1677b(f)(2)-(3) (1994) to transfers among affiliated steel producers in Korea that it had treated as one entity for purposes of the anti-dumping determination. [Omitted is the portion o the opinion concerning the fair value and major input provisions. The Court uses short-hand for Korean producer names: "Dongbu" for Dongbu Steel Co., Ltd., "Union" for Union Steel Manufacturing Co., Ltd. ("Union"), "POSCO" for Pohang Iron & Steel Co., Ltd., "POCOS" for Pohang Coated Steel Co., Ltd. ("POCOS"), and "PSI" for Pohang Steel Industries Co., Ltd. ("PSI"). Collectively, they are the "Korean producers" or "Korean manufacturers."] As a consequence of these methods and their application, the duty rates were minimal. The domestic producers then filed suit challenging these methods as contrary to the anti-dumping statute. The trial court, however, upheld Commerce's decision and its methods as consistent with the statute. . . . This court, in an opinion issued February 23, 2000, held that the three-part test employed by Commerce is contrary to the express terms defining EP and CEP in the anti-dumping statute as amended in 1994 and therefore reversed-in-part and remanded for a redetermination of the anti-dumping duties. . . . As to the fair-value and major-input provisions we held that Commerce's decision not to apply those provisions to the transactions in suit was reasonable and within its discretion, and its method consistent with the statute, and therefore we affirmed-in-part. . . . The Korean producers then filed a petition for rehearing and suggestion for rehearing *en banc*. Because the Korean producers raised statutory questions that were not raised in the briefs or at oral argument, the panel took the case on reconsideration to address the statutory arguments. This opinion addresses the Korean producers' statutory arguments; however, the outcome of the case is unchanged.

BACKGROUND

In 1993 Commerce issued an order imposing anti-dumping duties on certain steel products from Korea. *See Certain Cold Rolled Steel Flat Products from Korea*, 58 Fed. Reg. 44,159 (Dep't of Commerce 1993) (hereinafter "*Certain Steel Products from Korea*"). . . . [Administrative Reviews occurred in 1995 and 1997, the latter resulting in *Certain Cold-Rolled and Corrosion-Resistant Carbon Steel Flat Products from Korea*, 62 Fed. Reg. 18,404, 18,434 (Dep't of Commerce 1997) (hereinafter "*Final Results*").]

I

. . . In general, Commerce applies the EP methodology to a sale when the foreign producer or exporter sells merchandise directly to an unrelated purchaser located in the United States. Commerce applies the CEP methodology when the foreign producer's or exporter's steel is sold to an unaffiliated U.S. buyer by a producer-affiliated company located in the United States. If the sale is classified as a CEP sale, additional deductions are taken from the sales price to arrive at the U.S. Price. . . .

[In a footnote, the Court observes "[t]he classification of the sales impacts the determination of the dumping margin because the statute provides for certain deductions from CEP that are not deducted from EP. Specifically, commissions for selling, any expenses from the sale (such as credit expenses), the cost of further manufacture, and the profit allocated to those costs and expenses must be deducted from CEP sales. *See* 19 U.S.C. § 1677a(d). Therefore, use of CEP is more likely to result in a determination of dumping." Also in a footnote, the Court states: "[t]he administrative review at issue in this appeal was initiated after the effective date of the 1994 amendments to the anti-dumping laws contained in the *Uruguay Round Agreements Act* ("*URAA*"). Thus, the statute as amended by the *URAA* applies to this case."]

For the sales of steel produced by each of the appellees challenged here, Commerce calculated the U.S. Price based on an EP classification. In determining whether to classify the sales here as EP or CEP, Commerce applied a three-part test (the *"PQ Test"*) that it developed on a remand from an unrelated 1987 case, *PQ Corp. v. United States*, 11 C.I.T. 53, 652 F. Supp. 724, 733-35 (Ct. Int'l Trade 1987). An agency interpretation of 19 U.S.C. § 1677a(a)-(b), the test has been applied when a foreign manufacturer's affiliated entity in the United States makes a sale to an unaffiliated U.S. purchaser prior to import, as in the case of the sales at issue here. Using the *PQ Test*, Commerce classifies sales made by U.S. affiliates as EP sales if the following criteria are met:

> (1)   the subject merchandise was shipped directly from the manufacturer to the unrelated buyer, without being introduced into the inventory of the related shipping agent;
>
> (2)   direct shipment from the manufacturer to the unrelated buyer was the customary channel for sales of this merchandise between the parties involved; and
>
> (3)   the related selling agent in the United States acted only as a processor of sales-related documentation and a communication link with the unrelated U.S. buyer.

. . . .

All of the sales at issue in the present case were "back-to-back" sales: the Korean producer sold the steel to an affiliated Korean exporter; the exporter sold it to its U.S. affiliate; and finally, the U.S. affiliate sold it to the unaffiliated U.S. purchaser. In most cases, however, the steel was shipped directly to the unaffiliated purchaser without entering the inventory of the U.S. affiliate. In the second administrative review, whether the sales of steel manufactured by the Korean producers satisfied the third prong of the *PQ Test* was one of the principal factual issues in dispute. In classifying the sales at issue, Commerce rejected the domestic producers' argument that the activities of the Korean exporter's U.S. affiliates failed the third prong of the test because they "exceeded those of a mere communications link or processor of documents." . . .

II

Commerce "collapsed" POSCO and its related companies, POCOS and PSI, into one entity for purposes of the anti-dumping analysis and then levied a single anti-dumping duty on the entity. In the second administrative review, Commerce determined that "a decision to treat affiliated parties as a single entity necessitates that transactions among the parties also be valued based on the group as a whole. . . . [Thus] among collapsed entities, the fair-value and major-input provisions are not controlling." . . . Therefore, in its 1995 review, Commerce declined to treat the transfers between the related companies as sales between affiliates, but rather treated them as transfers between divisions of the same company and did not apply the fair-value and major-input provisions of 19 U.S.C. § 1677b(f)(2)-(3).

The domestic producers challenged the *Final Results* by filing suit in the Court of International Trade, calling illegal the *PQ Test* and its application to appellees, the decision to collapse the POSCO affiliates, and the determination that the fair-value and major-input provisions did not apply to transfers among the collapsed companies. The Court of International Trade sustained Commerce's *Final Results*, holding the *PQ Test* to be a reasonable interpretation of the statute and the application in this case to be sustainable. In addition the court held that the decisions to collapse the affiliated producers and not apply the fair-value and major-input provisions were within the agency's discretion. . . . The domestic producers timely appealed to this court those portions of the judgment based on statutory interpretation, challenging the legality of the PQ Test and the decision not to apply the fair-value and major-input provisions, assuming the affiliates were properly collapsed. This court issued an opinion on February 23, 2000 reversing the trial court's decision upholding the *PQ Test* and affirming its decision upholding Commerce's decision to collapse the Korean producers and their affiliates. . . .

The Korean producers filed a timely petition for rehearing and suggestion for reconsideration *en banc* with this court. In that petition the Korean producers argued, for the first time, that language in the URAA implementing act rendered the *Statement of Administrative Action* ("SAA") submitted to Congress with the *URAA* a judicially binding interpretation of the agreement and the implementing statute. The panel granted the motion for reconsideration to more fully address the *SAA*.

. . . .

Discussion

. . . .

II *PQ Test*

The Court of International Trade held that the *PQ Test* did not contradict the statute as amended. The court found that the test was "simply a means to determine whether the sale at issue for anti-dumping duty purposes is in essence between the exporter/producer and the unaffiliated buyer, in which case the EP rules apply." . . . The domestic producers argue that Commerce's *PQ Test* conflicts with the unambiguously expressed intent of Congress because the statute and legislative history make clear that a sale by any producer-affiliated seller in the United States to an unrelated U.S. buyer must be classified as CEP. The appellees argue, however, that the statute is ambiguous about how to classify those sales that occur before importation but that are made by producer-affiliated entities in the United States. Therefore, according to appellees, the *PQ Test* is an appropriate methodology for determining whether EP or CEP classification is applied to those sales.

The language of the statute must be viewed in context. The U.S. Price [*i.e.*, EP or CEP] used in making anti-dumping determinations is meant to be the sales price of an arm's-length transaction between the foreign producer and an unaffiliated U.S. purchaser. The U.S. Price is derived from either EP or CEP sales. To isolate an arm's-length transaction under the current statute, Commerce looks to the first sale to a purchaser that is not affiliated with the producer or exporter. If the producer or exporter sells directly to the U.S.

purchaser, that sale is used because it is considered an arm's-length transaction. In that situation the sale is classified as EP. [In a footnote, the Court observes "the statute appears to allow for a sale made by the foreign exporter or producer to be classified as a CEP sale, if such a sale is made "in the United States." 19 U.S.C. 1677a(a). No such transaction is at issue in this appeal."] If, however, the first sale to an unaffiliated purchaser occurs in the United States, then that sale must be used to determine the U.S. Price. Such a sale will be classified as a CEP sale and have additional deductions made to account for certain expenses of the seller in the United States. The purpose of these additional deductions in the CEP methodology is to prevent foreign producers from competing unfairly in the United States market by inflating the U.S. Price with amounts spent by the U.S. affiliate on marketing and selling the products in the United States. In the administrative review process, the foreign producers submit to Commerce the information about sales to unaffiliated purchasers. Those sales must be classified as either: (1) between an unaffiliated U.S. purchaser and the producer or exporter, and thus EP; or (2) between the unaffiliated U.S. purchaser and another entity in the United States that must, by definition, be related to the producer, and thus CEP. Sales in the United States between unaffiliated purchasers and unaffiliated sellers are never at issue; such a sale could never be the first sale to an unaffiliated purchaser.

The question at the root of this appeal is whether a sale to a U.S. purchaser can be properly classified as a sale by the producer/exporter, and thus an EP sale, even if the sales contract is between the U.S. purchaser and a U.S. affiliate of the producer/exporter and is executed in the United States. Appellees argue that it can, if the role of the U.S. affiliate is sufficiently minor that the sale passes the *PQ Test*. The domestic producers argue that the plain language of the statute prevents such a classification. We agree with the domestic producers.

Commerce's three-part *PQ Test* and much of the Court of International Trade case law reviewing it were created before the enactment of the *URAA* in 1994. Prior to the *URAA*, "purchase price" (now EP) was described as:

> the price at which merchandise is purchased, or agreed to be purchased, prior to the date of importation, from a reseller or the manufacturer or producer of the merchandise for exportation to the United States.

19 U.S.C. § 1677a(b) (1988). The "exporter's sales price" (now CEP) was defined as:

> the price at which merchandise is sold or agreed to be sold in the United States, before or after the time of importation, by or for the account of the exporter.

19 U.S.C. § 1677a(c) (1988). The amendments to the statute most relevant to this issue are the addition of the phrase "outside the United States" to the definition of EP, and "by a seller affiliated with the producer" to the definition of CEP. Thus, the 1994 statute reads:

(a) Export Price

The term "export price" means the price at which the subject merchandise is first sold (or agreed to be sold) before the date of importation by the producer or exporter of the subject merchandise outside of the United States to an unaffiliated purchaser in the United States or to an unaffiliated purchaser for exportation to the United States. . . .

(b) Constructed Export Price

The term "constructed export price" means the price at which the subject merchandise is first sold (or agreed to be sold) in the United States before or after the date of importation by or for the account of the producer or exporter of such merchandise or by a seller affiliated with the producer or exporter, to a purchaser not affiliated with the producer or exporter. . . .

19 U.S.C. § 1677a(a)-(b).

Despite these changes to the definitions of EP and CEP, the *SAA* submitted to Congress with the *URAA* states that the statutory changes did not alter the "circumstances under which export price (formerly purchase price) versus constructed export price (formerly exporter's sales price) are used." H.R. REP. No. 103-316, vol. 1 at 822 (1994), reprinted in 1994 U.S.C.C.A.N. 3773, 4163. This panel was aware of the *SAA* when it prepared its original opinion, now withdrawn. Prior to a petition for panel rehearing none of the parties brought to the court's attention, however, that in the statute itself, Congress declared that the *SAA* is to be considered

an authoritative expression by the United States concerning the interpretation and application of the Uruguay Round Agreements and this Act in any judicial proceeding in which a question arises concerning such interpretation or application.

19 U.S.C. § 3512(d). When confronted with a change in statutory language, we would normally assume Congress intended to effect some change in the meaning of the statute. . . . Here, however, the *SAA* prevents us from making such an assumption and we have revised our opinion primarily to address the authoritative weight given the SAA in the statute.

The *PQ Test* arises from Commerce's interpretation of the pre-1994 statutory language. In interpreting the pre-1994 statute, the Court of International Trade in *PQ Corporation* focused on whether there was an affiliate relationship between the foreign producer and the U.S. importer as the primary factor enabling Commerce to differentiate between the two sales classifications. In response to Commerce's argument that there was no statutory requirement that "the importer must be an independent party in order to apply [EP]," the court held that:

while the statute does not state in so many words that [purchase price] and [exporter's sales price] are to be distinguished by the relationship of the foreign producer to the U.S. importer, the statutory definitions of [purchase price] and [exporters sales price] have been distinguished upon this basis from their inception. . . . The express terms of the statute make it clear that a U.S. importer's relationship to a foreign producer will affect the determination of whether [purchase price] or [exporter's sales price] will apply.

PQ Corp., 652 F. Supp. at 732-33 (emphasis added). Despite the Court of International Trade's emphasis on the relationship between the importer and the foreign producer, however, the test developed by Commerce after the remand in *PQ Corporation* actually does not directly examine the legal relationship between the producer and the importer, but rather seeks to determine the role played by the importer in the transaction. The agency continued to apply the test after the statute was amended in 1994.

We are confronted here with a complex statutory interpretation task. The language of the old and new statutes is not identical, yet it is apparently intended to be applied to the same effect in the same "circumstances." The court opinion in *PQ Corporation* interpreting the old version of the statute relies on the legal relationship between an exporter and importer, while the test developed by the agency in response to that interpretation examines the role the importer plays in the transaction. Confronted with these potential contradictions, we start by examining the current statute, as it is the clearest and most current expression of congressional intent.

A. 1994 Statute

Read without reference to the old statutory language, the plain meaning of the language enacted by Congress in 1994 focuses on where the sale takes place and whether the foreign producer or exporter and the U.S. importer are affiliated, making these two factors dispositive of the choice between the two classifications.

The text of the 1994 definition of CEP states that CEP is the "price at which the subject merchandise is first sold in the United States." 19 U.S.C. § 1677a(a) (emphasis added). In contrast, EP is defined as the price at which the merchandise is first sold "outside the United States." 19 U.S.C. § 1677a(b). Thus, the location of the sale appears to be critical to the distinction between the two categories. Appellees, however, point to a decision of the Court of International Trade holding that the words "outside the United States" were ambiguous, finding that it was unclear whether they described the location of the sale or the location of the producer/exporter. *See Mitsubishi Heavy Indus., Ltd. v. United States*, 15 F. Supp. 2d 807, 812 (Ct. Int'l Trade 1998). We do not perceive the same ambiguity. In any event, the trial court's decision is not binding on us.

When the EP definition is read in conjunction with the CEP definition, the alleged ambiguity in the EP definition disappears. The language of the CEP definition leaves no doubt that the modifier "in the United States" relates to "first sold." The term "outside the United States," read in the context of both the CEP and the EP definitions, as it must be, applies to the locus of the transaction at issue, not the location of the company. Therefore, the critical differences between EP and CEP sales are whether the sale or transaction takes place inside or outside the United States and whether it is made by an affiliate. A sales contract executed in the United States between two entities domiciled in the United States cannot generate a sale "outside the United States." Thus, if "outside the United States" refers to the sale, as the appellees argues in this appeal, one of the parties to the sale or the execution of the contract must also be "outside the United States" for an EP classification to be proper. [In a footnote, the Court adds "[w]hile we can hypothesize a sales contract between two U.S. domiciled entities that is entirely executed outside the United States, we make no determination regarding whether such a sale would be classified as an EP or CEP sale."] Accordingly, the conclusion of the *Mitsubishi* court, that the phrase "outside the United States" ambiguously modifies either the sale or the producer/exporter, is incorrect. In general, a producer/exporter in a dumping investigation will always be located outside the United States. Thus, it must be the locus of the transaction that is modified by "outside the United States" in the EP definition for otherwise the description of the producer/exporter would be pure surplusage. Of course, whether a sale is "outside the United States" depends, in part, on whether the parties are or are not located in the United States. A transaction, such as those here, in which both parties are located in the United States and the contract is executed in the United States cannot be said to be "outside the United States." Thus, such a transaction cannot be classified as an EP transaction. Rather, classification as an EP sale requires that one of the parties to the sale be located "outside the United States," for if both parties to the transaction were in the territory of the United States and the transfer of ownership was executed in the United States, it is not possible for the transaction to be outside the United States.

In the *Final Results*, Commerce attempted to circumvent this geographic restriction on the use of EP sales by stating that when the *PQ Test* was satisfied it "considered the exporter's selling functions to have been relocated geographically from the country of exportation to the United States, where the [U.S. affiliate] performs them." The trial judge's holding that the *PQ Test* does not contradict the statute because it is a means of defining whether a sale is "in essence" between a producer/exporter and the unaffiliated buyer suggests the same point. But it is not a valid point because it departs from the factors Congress put in the statute. As discussed above, the plain language of the EP definition precludes classification of a sale between two U.S. entities (*i.e.*, a U.S. affiliate of the producer and a U.S. purchaser) as an EP sale. Thus, the "relocation" concept produces a result that is contrary to the plain language of the statute.

In addition, the Court of International Trade decision in *PQ Corporation* precludes "relocation" of selling activity by holding that the "statute provides no mechanism for imputing actual sales by an importer to that importer's related 'foreign manufacturer or producer of the merchandise' so that [purchase price (now EP)] will apply." *PQ Corp.*, 652 F. Supp. at 733. Thus, Commerce's decision to redefine the activities occurring inside the United States as occurring outside the United States makes an impermissible end-run around both the plain meaning of the statutory language and the mandate of the Court of International Trade in *PQ Corporation*. Congress has made a clear distinction between the two categories based on the geographic location of the transaction; the agency may not circumvent this geographic distinction by "relocating" the activities of the producer/exporter.

Similarly, the statute also distinguishes the categories based on the participation of an affiliate as the seller. The definition of CEP includes sales made by either the producer/exporter or "by a seller affiliated with the producer or exporter." 19 U.S.C. § 1677a(b). EP sales, on the other hand can only be made by the producer or exporter of the merchandise. See 19 U.S.C.§ 1677a(a). Consequently, while a sale made by a producer or exporter could be either EP or CEP, one made by a U.S. affiliate can only be CEP. Limiting affiliate sales to CEP flows logically from the geographical restriction of the EP definition, as a sale executed in the United States by a U.S. affiliate of the producer or exporter to a U.S. purchaser could not be a sale "outside the United States." The location of the sale and the identity of the seller are critical to distinguishing between the two categories.

Congress provided for only two mutually exclusive categories: EP or CEP sales. In distinguishing the two, Congress opted for what can be seen as a structural approach to defining EP and CEP sales, not the function-driven approach of the *PQ Test*. Congress chose clear and unambiguous words such as "affiliated," "sold," and "in" or "outside" the United States. In no sense did it leave the distinguishing factor to the agency to identify. When, as here, there are contracts showing that the sales at issue took place in the United States between two entities with United States addresses, one of which was an affiliate of the producer/exporter, it is contrary to the plain meaning of the statute for Commerce to nevertheless use the *PQ Test* to define the sales as effectively occurring outside of the United States, and thus EP sales rather than CEP sales.

The sales contracts in evidence plainly prove that the sales to the unaffiliated U.S. purchasers were made by affiliates of the foreign producers or exporters that are located in the United States. If the importer and the producer/exporter are affiliated, then the first sale to an unaffiliated party is necessarily the sale between the affiliated importer and the unaffiliated purchaser (unless there is another intermediate U.S. affiliate involved, which would have no effect on the analysis). Thus, the sales at issue fall squarely within the definition of CEP as articulated in the 1994 version of the statute.

. . . .

The Korean producers argue that it is the question of who is the seller that is left unresolved by the statute. Because the terms "seller" and "sold" are undefined in the statute, they are therefore ambiguous, assert the Korean producers [and deference under the Chevron doctrine should be accorded to the *PQ Test*]. . . . We, however, are not persuaded that this language in the statute is ambiguous.

When a word is undefined in a statute, the agency and the reviewing court normally give the undefined term its ordinary meaning. . . . *Black's Law Dictionary* (6th ed. 1990) defines "seller" as "one who has contracted to sell property . . . the party who transfers property in the contract of sale." As to "sold," this court previously addressed the meaning of that term in the definition of the Exporter's Sales Price (now CEP). *See NSK Ltd. v. United States*, 115 F.3d 965, 973 (Fed. Cir. 1997). In that case we defined "sold" to require both a "transfer of ownership to an unrelated party and consideration." . . . We see no reason to depart from those definitions, and therefore hold that the "seller" referred to in the CEP definition is simply one who contracts to sell, and "sold" refers to the transfer of ownership or title. . . . Rather than impliedly delegating the task of distinguishing between the two types of sales to the agency, Congress did so right in the statute.

The sales activities of the U.S. affiliates of the Korean producers or exporters clearly meet these definitions, as evidenced by the contracts for sales between the U.S. affiliates and the U.S. purchasers. The record in this appeal is not disputed; it was the U.S. affiliates of the Korean producers that contracted for sale with the unaffiliated U.S. purchasers. The title or ownership passed from the U.S. affiliate to the unaffiliated U.S. purchaser. There were no contracts between the Korean producers and the unaffiliated U.S. purchasers. Thus, the U.S. affiliates were the "sellers," as indicated by the plain language of the statute. Commerce does not require a cumbersome test, examining the activities of the affiliate, to determine whether or not the U.S. affiliate is a seller, when the answer to that question is plain from the face of the contracts governing the sales in question. If Congress had intended the EP versus CEP distinction to be made based on which party set the terms of the deal or on the relative importance of each party's role, it would not have written the statute to distinguish between the two categories based on the location where the sale was made and the affiliation of the party that made the sale.

. . . .

When Congress makes such a clear statement as to how categories are to be defined and distinguished, neither the agency nor the courts are permitted to substitute their own definition for that of Congress, regardless of how close the substitute definition may come to achieving the same result as the statutory definition, or perhaps a result that is arguably better. Normally, having determined that the agency's test employs terms that are contrary to those in the statute, our analysis would stop. In this case, however, we are confronted with the *SAA*, which Congress has stated provides a guide to authoritative interpretation of the statute.

B. The *Statement of Administrative Action*

Here, despite the plain meaning of the amended language of the statute, the *SAA* that accompanied the *URAA* declares that the "new section 772 retains the distinction in existing law between 'purchase price' (now called the 'export price') and 'exporters sales price' (now called the 'constructed export price')." The *SAA* goes on to state that "notwithstanding the change in terminology, no change is intended in the circumstances under which export price . . . versus constructed export price . . . are used." H.R. REP. NO. 103-316, vol. 1 at 822 (1994), *reprinted in* 1994 U.S.C.C.A.N. 3773, 4163. Appellees cite to the *SAA* as evidence of congressional intent to endorse the *PQ Test* as a proper interpretation of the new statutory language. We, however, do not so interpret the *SAA*.

First, the *PQ Test* is hardly consistent with the pre-1994 statute, read as a whole. Prior to the 1994 amendments, the statute required only that "purchase price" sales be made "prior to the date of importation" without any explicit reference to where the sales had occurred. 19 U.S.C. § 1677a(b) (1988). The "exporters sales price" (now CEP), however, was defined, as it is today, as the "price at which merchandise is sold or agreed to be sold in the United States." 19 U.S.C. § 1677a(c) (1988). Thus, the distinction based on the location of the sale was already present, although less complete, in the prior version of the statute. Use of the *PQ Test* to "relocate" the sales activity from the producer/exporter to the U.S. affiliate therefore appears inconsistent with the pre-1994 statutory language for the same reasons it is inconsistent with the language of today's statute. In addition, the legislative history of the earliest versions of the anti-dumping statute also indicates that Congress traditionally distinguished between EP and CEP based on the presence of an affiliate in the United States. For example, in hearings before the Senate Committee on Finance discussing Sections 203 and 204 of the *Antidumping Act of 1921*, the equivalent of an EP classification was said to apply if "the merchandise is sold by the foreign seller to an American purchaser having no interest in the business of the foreign seller." EMERGENCY TARIFF AND ANTIDUMPING: HEARINGS ON H.R. 2435. BEFORE THE SENATE COMM. ON FINANCE, 67TH CONG. at 11 (1921). In the same hearings, the Exporters Sales Price (or CEP) was said to apply if "the merchandise is sold, by a foreign seller having an interest in the American purchasing agency." . . .

Second, this court has never endorsed the *PQ Test* as a proper interpretation of the pre-1994 statute. Prior to this case, this court has never considered the legality of the test, much less held that the test is a reasonable interpretation of an ambiguous statute. In fact, when describing the EP/CEP distinction, this court has repeatedly relied on the affiliate relationship between the producer/exporter and the importer. . . . In cases heard prior to the amendments, however, the Court of International Trade did approve application of the test that resulted in a purchase price (now EP) classification despite the fact that a U.S. affiliate processed the orders. . . . Nevertheless, in light of this court's earlier statements on the EP/CEP distinctions and Congress's clarification of the statute in 1994, we do not find the Court of International Trade's endorsement of the *PQ Test* to reflect an accurate interpretation of the pre-1994 statute.

Furthermore, in situations where the Court of International Trade has reviewed the application of the *PQ Test* after the 1994 amendments, it has only upheld applications that resulted in the sales in question being classified as CEP sales, rather than as EP sales. . . . Until this case, the Court of International Trade was not confronted with EP classification of a sale in the United States by an affiliate. In addition, the Court of International Trade itself has expressed reservations about the test, admonishing "this is not an easily administrable test and the court suggests that Commerce attempt to draw some sharper lines." *U.S. Steel Group*, 15 F. Supp. 2d at 903.

Finally, there is no indication in the legislative history that Congress intended to retain the *PQ Test* upon amending the statute because the test is nowhere mentioned. The Korean producers correctly argue that Congress is presumed to know the administrative or judicial interpretation given a statute when it adopts a new law incorporating the prior law. *See Lorillard v. Pons*, 434 U.S. 575, 580-81 . . . (1978). *Lorillard*, however, is limited to those situations where Congress "enacts a statute without change." . . . Here we cannot ignore the fact that Congress indeed changed the language of the statute, particularly because the changes are directly at odds with the *PQ Test*. If Congress had intended to endorse the *PQ Test* it would not have undercut the test by adding the clarifying language to the statute in 1994.

Our review of the pre-1994 statute and the 1994 amendments reveals language that is consistent, although clearer in the amended version. Since the amendment, recent court interpretations of the statute and review of the *PQ Test* have also been consistent in interpreting the statute to require CEP classification when a U.S. affiliate is doing the selling. Indeed, the addition of the word "affiliated" to the CEP sales definition in the 1994 amendments is entirely consistent with the relationship-based distinction first articulated by the Court of International Trade in *PQ Corporation* and repeatedly stated by this court. Similarly, the logical interpretation of Congress's addition in 1994 of the words "outside the United States" to the definition of an EP sale is that Congress intended to codify the traditional distinction between the EP and CEP. The addition of these terms merely echoed the interpretation given by the Court of International Trade in *PQ Corporation* and reinforced the language in the statute prior to the 1994 amendment by emphasizing that the critical question was not the role of the affiliate in the sale but the legal relationship between the seller and the producer/exporter, *i.e.*, whether the U.S. importer is an affiliate of the foreign producer. Since the amendments in 1994, there has been no judicial endorsement of the use of the *PQ Test* to "relocate" the sales activities of the exporters to their U.S. affiliates. Despite earlier endorsement of the test by the Court of International Trade, we find nothing in the pre-1994 statute or the *SAA* to indicate that Congress intended that the distinction between EP and CEP to be based on the activities of the importer rather than the legal relationship between the importer and the producer/exporter. Thus, we will not now hold the *SAA* to be an endorsement of an agency interpretation that is inconsistent with the plain language of the current statute, particularly where it is clear to us that the test was never consistent with the statute or congressional intent.

Accordingly, we hold that if the contract for sale was between a U.S. affiliate of a foreign producer or exporter and an unaffiliated U.S. purchaser, then the sale must be classified as a CEP sale. Stated in terms of the EP definition: if the sales contract is between two entities in the United States, and executed in the United States and title will pass in the United States, it cannot be said to have been a sale "outside the United States;" therefore the sale cannot be an EP sale. Similarly, a sale made by a U.S. affiliate or another party other than the producer or exporter cannot be an EP sale. Thus, we reverse the decision of the Court of International Trade and remand to that court (for remand, if necessary, to the Department of Commerce) for a re-determination of anti-dumping duties that is consistent with this holding.

[What is the definition of "affiliate" under U.S. AD law? *See* 19 U.S.C. § 1677(33).]

II. THE PROFIT ADJUSTMENT TO CEP AND 2005 *SNR ROULEMENTS* CASE

SNR ROULEMENTS v. UNITED STATES
United States Court of Appeals for the Federal Circuit
402 F.3d 1358-63 (2005)

CLEVENGER, CIRCUIT JUDGE.

The United States and The Torrington Company ("Torrington") appeal the decision of the United States Court of International Trade that the Department of Commerce ("Commerce") is statutorily required to include imputed credit and inventory carrying costs in "total expenses" when those costs are included in "total United States expenses" for the purpose of calculating constructed export price profit. . . . Because the Court of International Trade erroneously interpreted 19 U.S.C. § 1677a as not permitting Commerce to use actual expenses instead of imputed expenses to account for credit and inventory carrying costs when determining "total expenses," we reverse its decision and remand the case with the instruction that Plaintiffs [*i.e.*, Torrington] be provided an opportunity to make a showing that their dumping margins were wrongly determined because Commerce's use of actual expenses did not account for U.S. credit and inventory carrying costs in the calculation of total expenses.

I

"Dumping" refers to the sale or likely sale of goods at less than fair value. 19 U.S.C. § 1677 (2000). When reviewing or determining antidumping duties, the administering authority is required to determine "(i) the normal value and export price (or constructed export price) of each entry of the subject merchandise, and (ii) the dumping margin for each such entry." 19 U.S.C. § 1675 (2000). Constructed export price ("CEP") refers to the price, as adjusted pursuant to Section 1677a, at which the subject merchandise is sold in the United States to a buyer unaffiliated with the producer or exporter. The "dumping margin" refers to the amount by which the normal value exceeds export price or CEP. § 1677.

Section 1677a authorizes several adjustments to the price that gives rise to CEP. One adjustment involves reducing the price by the profit ("CEP profit") allocated to the "total United States expenses." 19 U.S.C. § 1677a(d)(3) (2000). Total United States expenses include the following:

> (1) the amount of any of the following expenses generally incurred by or for the account of the producer or exporter, or the affiliated seller in the United States, in selling the subject merchandise (or subject merchandise to which value has been added) —
>
> > (A)   commissions for selling the subject merchandise in the United States;
> >
> > (B)   expenses that result from, and bear a direct relationship to, the sale, such as credit expenses, guarantees and warranties;

(C)   any selling expenses that the seller pays on behalf of the pur-
       chaser; and

(D)   any selling expenses not deducted under subparagraph (A), (B),
       or (C);

(2) the cost of any further manufacture or assembly (including additional material and labor), except in circumstances described in
subsection (e) of this section. . . .

§ 1677a(d). CEP profit is calculated by multiplying the "total actual profit"
by the "applicable percentage," which is obtained by "dividing the total United
States expenses by the total expenses." § 1677a(f). Total expenses

    means all expenses in the first of the following categories which
    applies and which are incurred by or on behalf of the foreign producer
    and foreign exporter of the subject merchandise and by or on behalf
    of the United States seller affiliated with the producer or exporter with
    respect to the production and sale of such merchandise.

§ 1677a(f)(2)(C). The applicable category for purposes of this appeal further
defines total expenses as those

    incurred with respect to the subject merchandise sold in the United
    States and the foreign like product sold in the exporting country if
    such expenses were requested by the administering authority for the
    purpose of establishing normal value and constructed export price.

§ 1677a(f)(2)(C)(i).

II

    In the seventh administrative review [published at 62 Fed. Reg. 61,963 (20
November 1997)] of the antidumping duty order on antifriction bearings,
Commerce determined that Plaintiffs had made sales at less than fair
value. . . .

    Plaintiffs sought judicial review of Commerce's final decision in the Court
of International Trade contending, *inter alia*, that Commerce unlawfully
calculated CEP profit because Commerce included an imputed amount for
credit and inventory carrying costs when calculating total United States
expenses, but relied on actual amounts, to the exclusion of an imputed amount,
when calculating total expenses. . . . In particular, Plaintiffs contended that
19 U.S.C. § 1677a unambiguously requires that an imputed amount be used
in the calculation of total expenses when an imputed amount is used in the
calculation of total United States expenses. Relying for support on *Chevron
U.S.A. Inc. v. NRDC*, 467 U.S. 837, . . . (1984), the Court of International
Trade interpreted Section 1677a as unambiguously establishing that total
United States expenses was a subset of total expenses and that therefore:
"Commerce must include imputed credit and inventory carrying costs in 'total
expenses' when they are included in 'total United States expenses.' " . . .

    The Court of International Trade remanded the case to Commerce, ordering
that it re-determine Plaintiff's margin in accordance with the court's construction of the statute. . . . On remand, Commerce complied, but objected to the

Court of International Trade's understanding of Section 1677a. Commerce explained:

> Since the cost of the U.S. and home-market merchandise includes the actual booked interest expenses, it is not appropriate to include imputed interest amounts as well in total expenses. Doing so double-counts this expense to a certain extent and overstates the cost attributed to sales of this merchandise. This overstatement of cost understates the ratio of U.S. selling expenses to total expenses and consequently understates the amount of actual profit allocated to selling, distribution, and further-manufacturing activities in the United States.

Final Results of Redetermination Pursuant to Court Remand (Oct. 13, 2000). . . .

The Court of International Trade affirmed the remand results, . . .and the government and Torrington appeal. . . .

III

The issue in this case is whether it is lawful for Commerce to account for credit and inventory carrying costs with an imputed expense when calculating total United States expenses and to account for the same costs with the presumption that they are embedded in a respondent's actual expenses when calculating total expenses. Because Section 1677a does not unambiguously address the issue, we hold that Commerce may account for credit and inventory carrying costs using imputed expenses in one instance and using actual expenses in the other provided that Commerce affords a respondent who so desires the opportunity to make a showing that the amount of imputed expenses is not accurately reflected or embedded in its actual expenses.

The parties contend that the analysis set forth in *Chevron* controls the outcome of this case. Under that analysis, when a court reviews an agency's interpretation of a statute the agency administers it applies a two-step analytical paradigm. 467 U.S. at 842-43. First, a court considers whether Congress has directly spoken to the precise question at issue. If so, all that remains is for a court to ensure that the agency gives effect to the unambiguously expressed intent of Congress. Second, however, if Congress has not directly spoken to the precise question at issue, making the statute silent or ambiguous with respect to the specific issue, a court considers whether the agency's interpretation is a permissible construction of the statue. *Id.* The parties here divide on whether this case resolves at step one of the *Chevron* analysis.

Appellants [*i.e.*, Commerce] assert that the language of Section 1677a does not show that Congress directly addressed the issue of the manner in which Commerce may account for credit and inventory carrying costs. Therefore, they argue, the question for this court is whether Commerce's election to use imputed expenses when calculating total United States expenses and actual expenses when calculating total expenses reflects a permissible construction of Section 1677a. According to the government, this construction is permissible because (1) it avoids double counting of interest expenses and (2) Commerce interprets the statute to require that actual expenses be used to calculate total expenses.

Appellees [*i.e.*, Torrington] deny that we have authority to consider whether Commerce's interpretation is permissible because, they argue, when Congress drafted Section 1677a it made crystal clear that all expenses "incurred with respect to the subject merchandise sold in the United States" are to be included in the calculation of total expenses. Thus, Appellees contend, because U.S. credit and inventory carrying costs are literally "expenses, "if an imputed number is used to account for these expenses when calculating total United States expenses, Congress has unambiguously stated that Commerce must add that number to the calculation of total expenses even if some or all U.S. credit and inventory carrying costs are already accounted for in a respondent's actual expenses.

Appellees' contention that in Section 1677a Congress has unambiguously and directly spoken to the precise issue in this case is implausible. The statute describes CEP profit as the product of total actual profit multiplied by the applicable percentage. § 1677a(f)(1). The applicable percentage is calculated by "dividing the total United States expenses by the total expenses." § 1677a(f)(2)(A). Total United States expenses are defined as those expenses enumerated in Section 1677a(d)(1) and (2). § 1677a(f)(2)(B). Finally, total expenses in this case include "expenses incurred with respect to the subject merchandise sold in the United States." § 1677a(f)(2)(C)(i). These statutory subsections contain no mention of what manner or form of accounting Commerce is required to use when calculating total United States expenses and total expenses. They also do not state or clearly indicate that Commerce may or may not impute expenses in some calculations and rely on actual expenses in others. Because nothing in the language addresses the question of whether Commerce must use an imputed value when calculating total expenses if it has used an imputed value in calculating total United States expenses, there is no basis to conclude that Congress has provided clear instructions on the issue. . . . Accordingly, the remaining question is whether the agency's interpretation of the section is permissible.

Beyond their arguments directed to the first step of the *Chevron* analysis, Appellees do not seriously dispute that the government's interpretation of Section 1677a is permissible. Our precedent indicates that in antidumping cases, we accord substantial deference to Commerce's statutory interpretation, . . . and this record does not show that Commerce's interpretation is unlawful. In this case, we do not understand the government to argue that Commerce views expenses pertaining to U.S. credit and inventory carrying costs as outside the category of expenses incurred with respect to the subject merchandise sold in the United States. In addition, there is no indication that Commerce interprets Section 1677a to permit the exclusion of expenses pertaining to U.S. credit and inventory carrying costs from its calculation of total expenses. Instead, according to the government and Torrington, when Commerce calculates total expenses it does so under the presumption that using actual expenses in the calculation produces a result that takes into account U.S. credit and inventory carrying costs that were imputed to total United States expenses.

We note, however, that neither the government nor Torrington is unequivocal in this assertion. For instance, the government's brief asserts that "the respondent's interest expenses are included in its actual booked expenses, and these interest expenses already largely account for imputed expenses." Torrington's brief asserts that a respondent's audited financial records "presumptively include all financial expenses, including such financial expenses as might be associated with extending credit to U.S. or home market customers, or in maintaining inventory before sale."

Antidumping laws intend to calculate antidumping duties on a fair and equitable basis. . . . Assuming there are cases where actual expenses do not take into account U.S. credit and inventory carrying costs, it is at least possible that in such cases a respondent's dumping margins are not calculated on a fair and equitable basis. The reason is that the additive increase to the numerator of the applicable percentage fraction may not be adequately reflected in the denominator of the fraction. This may impermissibly distort the CEP profit calculation, and accordingly, the dumping margin.

In this case, the question is whether a respondent is entitled to an adjustment where it can show that expenses imputed to U.S. credit and inventory carrying costs are not reflected or embedded in its actual expenses. We understand the government to concede that an adjustment may be appropriate under normal accounting principles when a respondent can show that CEP profit is unfairly distorted by Commerce's practice of relying on actual amounts for total expenses. In this case, there is no dispute that Plaintiffs-Appellees were not afforded an opportunity to make a showing that Commerce's use of actual expenses did not account for U.S. credit and inventory carrying costs for which imputed values were used in the total United States expenses calculation. Because in appropriate circumstances such a showing may support an adjustment to CEP profit, we remand the case with the instruction that Plaintiffs be provided an opportunity to make a showing that their dumping margins were wrongly determined because Commerce's use of actual expenses did not account for U.S. credit and inventory carrying costs in the calculation of total expenses.

IV

For the reasons stated above, we reverse the Court of International Trade's interpretation of Section 1677a and remand the case with the instruction that Plaintiffs be provided an opportunity to make a showing that their dumping margins were wrongly determined because Commerce's use of actual expenses did not account for U.S. credit and inventory carrying costs in the calculation of total expenses.

III. FURTHER MANUFACTURING, INDIRECT SELLING EXPENSES, THE CEP OFFSET, AND THE 1998 *MITSUBISHI* CASE

MITSUBISHI HEAVY INDUSTRIES, LTD. v. UNITED STATES
United States Court of International Trade
15 F. Supp. 2d 807-824 (1998)

POGUE, JUDGE.

Plaintiffs Mitsubishi Heavy Industries, Ltd. ("MHI") and Tokyo Kikai Seisakusho, Ltd. ("TKS"), respondents in the underlying investigation, and Plaintiff Goss Graphic Systems, Inc. ("Goss"), petitioner in the underlying investigation, filed separate motions challenging various aspects of the [1996] final determination of the International Trade Administration of the United States Department of Commerce ("Commerce" or "ITA") regarding imports of large newspaper printing presses ("LNPPs") from Japan. . . . The motions were consolidated.

The antidumping investigation of LNPPs from Japan was conducted simultaneously with Commerce's [1996] investigation of sales of LNPPs from Germany. . . .

Discussion

I. Constructed Export Price

. . . .

For each of the relevant LNPP sales by MHI and TKS to the United States, Commerce calculated U.S. price based on a CEP methodology. TKS had reported its sales as CEP sales and therefore does not object to Commerce's methodology. However, MHI reported its sales as EP sales. MHI objects to Commerce's decision to reclassify all of its sales as CEP sales. [MHI lost on this argument. Omitted is this portion of the opinion, because the court applies the *PQ* Test for distinguishing EP from CEP — the very Test overturned subsequently in the *AK Steel* case, excerpted above.] MHI also objects to Commerce's decision to treat its installation costs as further manufacturing, Commerce's methodology for allocating general and administrative ("G&A") expenses for MHI's U.S. subsidiary, and Commerce's decision to deduct from U.S. price, indirect selling expenses incurred in Japan. Both TKS and MHI object to Commerce's refusal to grant a level-of-trade ("LOT") adjustment or CEP offset.

. . . .

2. Further Manufacturing by MHI

In calculating MHI's U.S. price, Commerce treated MHI's installation of the subject merchandise as part of further manufacturing "because the U.S. installation process involves extensive technical activities on the part of engineers and installation supervisors and the integration of subject and integral, non-subject merchandise necessary for the operation of LNPPs.". . . According to the statute, CEP is to be reduced by, "the cost of any further manufacture or assembly (including additional material and labor). . . ." 19 U.S.C. § 1677a(d)(2).

MHI maintains that installation expenses should have been treated as movement-related expenses, pursuant to 19 U.S.C. § 1677a(c)(2)(A), which requires Commerce to reduce EP and CEP by "the amount, if any, included in such price, attributable to any additional costs, charges, or expenses . . . which are incident to bringing the subject merchandise from the original place of shipment in the exporting country to the place of delivery in the United States. . . ."

The distinction is significant because Commerce calculates movement-related expenses without imputed profit. Further manufacturing costs, on the other hand, include an imputed profit attributable to the value added by the further manufacturing activities.

. . . .

MHI argues that prior to the *URAA* [*i.e.*, the 1994 *Uruguay Round Agreements Act*], the statute only permitted Commerce to deduct "any increased value, including additional material and labor, resulting from a process of manufacture or assembly performed on the imported merchandise *after the importation of the merchandise and before its sale*. . . ." . . . The current statute does not specify a time period within which the further manufacture or assembly must take place. However, MHI argues, "Congress made it clear . . . that the new provision 'is not intended to effect any substantive change in the deduction made under the current statute for value added from processing or assembly in the United States'. . . ." . . . Because the assembly activities at issue here took place after the sale, MHI argues, they cannot be deducted as further manufacturing.

The Court does not agree. As MHI recognizes, the statute governing the instant investigation does not include any temporal restriction in the definition of further manufacturing. Furthermore, even before the *URAA* took effect, Commerce treated activities occurring after the relevant sales as further manufacturing in certain cases. For example, in *Certain Small Business Telephone Systems and Subassemblies Thereof from Korea*, 54 Fed. Reg. 53,141, 53,151 (Dep't. Commerce 1989) (final det.) ("*SBTS*") the respondent argued specifically that installation occurred after the sale and therefore, could not be considered as value added. Commerce disagreed, explaining, "[w]hether this value is added before or after the sale is irrelevant because, for this product, [respondent's] customers expect the installed system to have the characteristics added by the non-subject merchandise." . . . The physical further manufacturing may have occurred after the sale, but the value added by that further manufacturing was reflected in the sale price of the merchandise. For this reason, *SBTS* was in accordance with the prior statute.

Commerce relied on the same reasoning in this case. " 'Whether value is added before or after the sale is irrelevant because, . . . customers expect the installed system to have the characteristics added by the non-subject merchandise.' " . . . Commerce's explanation is reasonable. LNPPs are custom made to order. Therefore, MHI's installation activities, including the addition of non-subject merchandise would all be included in the sales price of the LNPP agreed upon prior to importation. Furthermore, Commerce's interpretation of the statute has not changed from its pre-*URAA* interpretation. Therefore, Commerce's actions were consistent with the interpretation of the statute articulated in the *SAA* [*i.e.*, the *Statement of Administrative Action* for the *WTO Antidumping Agreement* accompanying the *URAA*].

. . . .

Commerce's decision was consistent with the statute and did not violate any longstanding agency policy. Therefore, the court finds Commerce's action to be in accordance with law.

. . . .

4. Indirect Selling Expenses Incurred in Japan for MHI

The CEP provision requires that Commerce reduce the price of the first sale to an unaffiliated customer in the United States by the amount of selling expenses "incurred by or for the account of the producer or exporter, or the affiliated seller in the United States, in selling the subject merchandise. . . ." 19 U.S.C. § 1677a(d)(1). Indirect selling expenses are a component of selling expenses. *See* 19 U.S.C. § 1677a(d)(1)(D) (requiring that Commerce deduct from CEP any selling expenses not deducted as commissions or direct selling expenses). As part of indirect selling expenses, Commerce included expenses incurred in Japan to support U.S. sales. MHI argues that Commerce should have deducted only those indirect selling expenses incurred by MLP in the United States.

The CEP methodology is intended to determine a U.S. price "calculated to be, as closely as possible, a price corresponding to an export price between non-affiliated exporters and importers." . . . "Accordingly, when ITA makes its CEP adjustments to U.S. price, its objective is to identify indirect selling expenses that would not exist in an EP sale and deduct those expenses. . . ." . . . MHI contends that Commerce should not have deducted expenses incurred by MHI in Japan "for . . . activities that were fully consistent with an EP transaction." . . .

However, once Commerce has decided to rely on CEP, the statute does not require that Commerce examine every potential CEP deduction to determine whether the activity generating the expense would be inconsistent with an EP transaction. The statute contains a list of mandatory deductions, which includes selling expenses incurred in selling the subject merchandise. The statute does not specify as to the location of the activities generating these expenses. Here, Commerce deducted all indirect selling expenses related to respondents' United States sales. This decision was consistent with the statutory CEP provision.

MHI makes a second argument, that the *SAA* specifically limits CEP deductions to "expenses (and profit) associated with economic activities occurring in the United States." . . . MHI interprets this provision to require that the activities generating the deducted costs must occur in the United

States. However, MHI's reading is too narrow. Expenses incurred outside of the United States could still be "associated with" economic activities occurring in the United States. Commerce's approach limited the deductions to those indirect selling expenses "directly associated" with U.S. economic activity. . . . Thus, Commerce's application of the statute was limited enough to be consistent with the interpretation of the statute articulated in the *SAA*.

The petitioner, Goss, objects to Commerce's allocation of respondents' indirect selling expenses incurred in Japan and Germany, arguing that "Commerce undervalued these expenses by deducting only that portion of the indirect selling expenses attributable to U.S. sales when calculating the CEP." . . .

The Court will not address Goss' argument at this time, because in reviewing its allocation of indirect selling expenses to U.S. sales, Commerce came to the conclusion that its methodology overstated the amount of indirect selling expenses to be deducted from CEP. Specifically, Commerce explained that the pool of indirect selling expenses incurred in the home market and allocated to MHI's U.S. sales included "various office and planning expenses . . . [that] are not the type of expenses that ordinarily would be associated with United States economic activity." . . .

. . . .

. . . [I]ndirect selling expenses must be associated with economic activity occurring in the United States. Commerce erred by deducting certain expenses that were not so associated. Therefore, the Court will remand this issue, pursuant to Commerce's request, in order that Commerce may correct its error. Upon remand, Commerce will evaluate whether its allocation methodology either understates or overstates respondent's indirect selling costs. . . .

5. The CEP Offset for MHI and TKS

MHI and TKS both contend that they were entitled to a CEP offset, pursuant to 19 U.S.C. § 1677b(a)(7)(B):

> When normal value is established at a level of trade which constitutes a more advanced stage of distribution than the level of trade of the constructed export price, but the data available do not provide an appropriate basis to determine . . . a level of trade adjustment, normal value shall be reduced by the amount of indirect selling expenses incurred in the country in which normal value is determined on sales of the foreign like product. . . .

Commerce declined to grant the adjustment because, "[i]n this instant investigation, the respondents failed to provide the Department with the necessary data for the Department to consider an LOT [level-of-trade] adjustment. . . . Absent this information, the Department cannot determine whether an LOT adjustment is warranted, nor whether the level of trade in the home market is in fact further removed than the level of trade in the United States."

As the *SAA* makes clear, "if a respondent claims an adjustment to decrease normal value, as with all adjustments which benefit a responding firm, the respondent must demonstrate the appropriateness of such adjustment." . . . In this case, Commerce concluded that neither TKS nor MHI had provided sufficient information to demonstrate the appropriateness of the CEP offset. Specifically, Commerce said, "[r]espondents now contend that there is one home market level of trade to which CEP is being compared, but this claim is not well substantiated. The information we have on the record for sales in the home market does not support this conclusion. . . . For neither TKS nor MHI can we ascertain which selling functions are performed by them and which are provided by leasing companies, trading companies or other entities for each type of home market sale. Thus the minimal amount of information provided does not support the conclusions reached by respondents." . . .

Commerce's conclusion was based upon substantial evidence. . . . In the absence of sufficient information, Commerce's refusal to grant either an adjustment or a CEP offset was appropriate.

IV. REPACKING EXPENSES, LEVELS OF TRADE, THE CEP OFFSET, AND 2004 *NSK* CASE

NSK LTD. v. UNITED STATES
United States Court of Appeals for the Federal Circuit
390 F.3d 1352-61 (2004)

LINN, CIRCUIT JUDGE.

NSK Ltd. and NSK Corp. (collectively "NSK") appeal from the judgment of the Court of International Trade affirming the determinations of the Department of Commerce ("Commerce") holding that NSK's repacking expenses were correctly classified as a selling expense under 19 U.S.C. § 1677a(d)(1)(B) and refusing to grant NSK a partial level of trade adjustment for certain sales comparisons to normal value. . . . Because Commerce's classification of NSK's repacking expenses as selling expenses, and not movement expenses under 19 U.S.C. § 1677a(c)(2)(A), was arbitrary, we vacate and remand that determination. Because Commerce correctly refused to grant NSK a partial level of trade adjustment, we affirm that decision.

I. BACKGROUND

This is an antidumping appeal, pertaining to antidumping duty orders on ball bearings and cylindrical roller bearings imported into the United States from May 1, 1996, through April 30, 1997. . . . NSK Ltd. manufactured and sold the bearings in Japan during the review period; and NSK Corp., a related U.S. corporation, imported them into the United States.

NSK Corp. made deliveries to unaffiliated customers in the United States from various U.S. warehouses it owned and operated. NSK submitted to Commerce a list of expenses incurred in bringing the bearings from Japan to its U.S. customers. These expenses included costs for, *inter alia*, Japanese inland freight, Japanese warehousing, international freight, marine insurance, U.S. inland freight (from port to warehouse, and from warehouse to U.S. unaffiliated customers), U.S. customs duties, U.S. pre-sale warehousing, and

U.S. repacking. Commerce allowed deductions for all the expenses as movement expenses under 19 U.S.C. § 1677a(c)(2)(A), except U.S. repacking expenses, which it treated as direct selling expenses under 19 U.S.C. § 1677a(d)(1)(B). According to NSK, its repacking expenses were incurred when it unpacked merchandise in its warehouse from the international shipping packets into individual or small quantity boxes prior to shipment to unaffiliated U.S. customers.

NSK also submitted to Commerce data about its home market sales. Commerce determined that there were two home market levels of trade: original equipment manufacturers and aftermarket customers. Commerce also found that constructed export price sales constituted a third, distinct level of trade. NSK requested that Commerce calculate a level of trade adjustment measured by price differences between the level of trade found in the home market aftermarket and original equipment manufacturers' levels of trade. Commerce rejected the request, and instead used a "constructed export price offset."

NSK appealed Commerce's classification of repacking expenses and its adjustment as to the level of trade. The Court of International Trade affirmed both of Commerce's determinations, . . . and subsequently dismissed the case. NSK appealed to this court. . . .

II. Discussion

. . . .

B. Repacking Expenses

Section 1677a(c)(2)(A) allows the constructed export price to be reduced by movement expenses. It provides that "the price used to establish export price and constructed export price shall be . . . reduced by":

> the amount, if any, included in such price, attributable to any additional costs, charges, or expenses, and United States import duties, which are incident to bringing the subject merchandise from the original place of shipment in the exporting country to the place of delivery in the United States. . . .

19 U.S.C. § 1677a(c)(2)(A) (2000).

A separate provision provides for different treatment of direct selling expenses, which are also used in calculating the constructed export price: "For purposes of this section, the price used to establish constructed export price shall also be reduced by . . . expenses that result from, and bear a direct relationship to, the sale, such as credit expenses, guarantees and warranties. . . ." *Id*. § 1677a(d)(1)(B).

NSK submitted to Commerce a list of expenses, which included its U.S. repacking expenses. Commerce reduced the U.S. price of the merchandise for all expenses that NSK listed except its repacking expenses. Commerce denied NSK an allowance for the repacking expenses under § 1677a(c)(2)(A), instead treating NSK's repacking expenses as direct selling expenses under § 1677a(d)(1)(B). . . . Commerce reasoned that:

We do not view repacking expenses as movement expenses. The repacking of subject merchandise in the United States bears no relationship to moving the merchandise from one point to another. The fact that repacking is not necessary to move merchandise is borne out by the fact that the merchandise was moved from the exporting country to the United States prior to repacking. Rather, we view repacking expenses as direct selling expenses respondents incur on behalf of certain sales which we deduct pursuant to section 772(d)(1)(B) of the statute [19 U.S.C. § 1677a(d)(1)(B)]. . . .

The Court of International Trade affirmed. . . . The Court of International Trade reasoned that NSK's repacking expenses were properly classified as selling expenses because § 1677a(d)(1)(B) did not provide an exhaustive list and was not limited simply to credit expenses, guarantees, and warranties. . . . The Court of International Trade concluded that it was reasonable to classify the repacking expenses as selling expenses because the repacking was performed on individual products to facilitate their sale to unaffiliated U.S. customers. . . . Moreover, the Court of International Trade found that NSK's repacking expenses were not incidental to bringing the subject merchandise from the original place of shipment to the place of delivery in the United States, and that Commerce thus acted reasonably in refusing to classify the repacking expenses as movement expenses under § 1677a(c)(2)(A). . . .

1. The Parties' Arguments

NSK argues that Commerce erred in classifying its U.S. repacking expenses as selling expenses rather than movement expenses. First, NSK points out that Commerce permitted the constructed export price to be reduced by several other types of similar expenses that it concluded were movement expenses under § 1677a(c)(2)(A). These included: Japanese inland freight (from plant to warehouse, and from warehouse to exit port), international freight, U.S. inland freight (from entry port to warehouse, and from warehouse to U.S. unaffiliated customers) ("U.S. shipping"), Japanese warehousing, marine insurance, U.S. brokerage, U.S. customs duties, and U.S. pre-sale warehousing. NSK argues that if these categories of expenses were deemed movement expenses under § 1677a(c)(2)(A), then U.S. repacking expenses, which are indistinguishable from other pre-sale warehousing, handling, and insurance expenses, should also be categorized as movement expenses.

NSK next argues that Commerce's rationale for treating repacking expenses as transportation expenses cannot withstand scrutiny. NSK contends that whether repacking was required to bring merchandise from Japan to NSK's U.S. warehouse is irrelevant. NSK also argues that the repacking expenses were movement expenses because they were necessary to bring the merchandise to the place of delivery in the United States, e.g., each customer's place of business. NSK points out that repacking was necessary to make the requested quantities of bearings deliverable to U.S. customers. Finally, NSK argues that Commerce's contention that repacking was needed to sell the merchandise to an unaffiliated U.S. customer is inconsistent with its allowance of U.S. inland freight costs as movement expenses, which under Commerce's reasoning also would be "directly related" to specific sales.

Commerce responds that the Court of International Trade properly affirmed its decision that NSK's U.S. repacking expenses were selling expenses. Commerce relies on the following questionnaire response provided by NSK as evidence that its repacking expenses were selling expenses: "Merchandise normally is shipped from the U.S. warehouse in its original containers. In some instances, different pallets were used for shipment to U.S. customers and some repackaging may have occurred to accommodate smaller distributor orders." . . .

Commerce asserts that its rationale is correct that repacking bears no relationship to movement of the merchandise because the merchandise was moved from Japan to the United States prior to any repacking. Commerce further argues that repackaging expenses are distinct from warehousing expenses, because warehousing expenses are associated with storage before or during the movement process. Commerce finally argues that its statutory construction is correct because § 1677a(d)(1)(B) did not limit direct selling expenses to the enumerated credit expenses, guarantees, or warranties.

2. Analysis

. . . .

Neither provision [the movement and sale provisions of the AD statute] mentions repacking specifically. On the one hand, repacking [expenses] could be a movement expense because it could arise "incident to bringing the subject merchandise from the original place of shipment . . . to the place of delivery in the United States." 19 U.S.C. § 1677a(c)(2)(A) (2000). Just as warehousing is considered a movement expense, repacking, especially to enable warehousing, could be deemed a movement expense. On the other hand, repacking could be a selling expense because it could be an "expense[] that results from, and bears a direct relationship to, the sale" to particular customers. *Id.* § 1677a(d)(1)(B). Having received an order, the importer could repack the merchandise to accommodate the customer. Because the movement and selling expense statutes do not unambiguously classify repacking expenses in one category or the other, we must consider Commerce's interpretation under step two of *Chevron* (*i.e.*, *Chevron U.S.A. Inc. v. Natural Resources Defense Council, Inc.*, 467 U.S. 837, 843-44, . . . (1984).)

"If the statute is silent or ambiguous with respect to the specific issue, the question for the court is whether the agency's answer is based on a permissible construction of the statute." *Chevron*, 467 U.S. at 843. We conclude that Commerce's determination that NSK's repacking expenses are properly classified as selling expenses under 19 U.S.C. § 1677a(d)(1)(B) is impermissible. Commerce's classification of repacking expenses as selling expenses is internally inconsistent with its classification of U.S. warehousing expenses and U.S. warehouse-to-customer-shipping expenses as movement expenses.

Commerce's first attempt to explain why repacking is not a movement expense is that "the repacking of subject merchandise in the United States bears no relationship to moving the merchandise from one point to another." . . .

This point is unpersuasive because it is inconsistent with Commerce's treatment of warehousing. If the test is "bearing [a] relationship to moving the merchandise," then U.S. warehousing (*i.e.*, storing goods while awaiting sale to a customer) should not be a movement expense — goods do not move when they are stored.

Commerce next argues that NSK's successful movement of merchandise from Japan to the United States without repacking is evidence that "repacking is not necessary to move merchandise." . . . This rationale is unpersuasive because it too is inconsistent with Commerce's treatment of the U.S. warehousing expense. Under Commerce's rationale, U.S. warehousing also should be excluded from the scope of § 1677a(c)(2)(A) movement expenses because the merchandise, in theory, could be moved from Japan to a U.S. customer without U.S. warehousing, simply by shipping the merchandise directly from Japan to the U.S. customer. However, Commerce considers U.S. warehousing to be a movement expense.

Finally, Commerce implies that even though the statute might allow it to classify repacking as a movement expense, because repacking occurs to enable a sale — whether to satisfy a customer's request for a different lot size or to accommodate shipping — it is a sales expense under § 1677a(d)(1)(B). . . . Once again, Commerce's rationale is internally inconsistent. Treating repacking as a sales expense is inconsistent with treating U.S. shipping as a movement expense. If enabling sales is the test, then U.S. shipping should be a sales expense. Like repacking that enables sales, U.S. shipping occurs after a customer places an order. Indeed, the cost of shipping the merchandise from the U.S. warehouse to the U.S. customer is incurred only because of and in furtherance of the sale. Commerce treats U.S. shipping as a movement expense, however, and fails to explain the inconsistency.

Expenses incurred for U.S. repacking, U.S. warehousing, and U.S. shipping (from the warehouse to particular customers) are analogous. To be consistent, it would appear that Commerce should classify them as the same type of expenses, whether that be as movement expenses or as sales expenses. If Commerce wants to treat these expenses inconsistently, then under *Chevron* we still must defer, but only if Commerce reasonably explains the inconsistency and does not act arbitrarily. . . . Because Commerce did not sufficiently explain the aforementioned inconsistencies, its determination is arbitrary and impermissible. Commerce's classification of NSK's repacking expenses as selling expenses is vacated and remanded for reconsideration consistent with this opinion.

On remand, we caution Commerce to be mindful that repacking may have occurred for a number of different reasons. NSK indicated in its questionnaire response (the only evidence on which Commerce relied in making its decision) that NSK's practice is to bulk ship its merchandise from Japan to U.S. warehouses on pallets used for international shipping. NSK was required to unpack the merchandise from the international shipping pallets, and "in some instances," repack the merchandise into individual or small quantity boxes prior to shipment to U.S. customers. . . . On this record, substantial evidence may not support a determination that NSK's repacking expenses were incurred as a direct result of or in furtherance of sales to particular customers.

Indeed, NSK's counsel noted at oral argument that repacking is sometimes done for other reasons, *e.g.*, to enable warehousing.

C. Partial Level of Trade Adjustment

Commerce is directed by statute to base normal value upon home market sales at the same level of trade as the export price or the constructed export price. 19 U.S.C. § 1677b(a)(1)(B) (2000); *see also Micron Tech., Inc. v. United States*, 243 F.3d 1301, 1303-04 (Fed. Cir. 2001). The same level of trade means comparable marketing stages in the foreign market and in the U.S. market. . . . If Commerce cannot find sales in the foreign market at the same level of trade as in the U.S. market, then it will compare sales in the U.S. and foreign markets at different levels of trade. . . . When comparing sales at different levels of trade, Commerce may make a level of trade adjustment ("LOT adjustment") based on the price differences between the two levels of trade:

> The [normal value] shall also be in creased or decreased to make due allowance for any difference (or lack thereof) between the export price or constructed export price . . . that is shown to be wholly or partly due to a difference in level of trade between the export price or constructed export price and normal value. . . .

19 U.S.C. § 1677b(a)(7)(A) (2000). . . .

In some instances, Commerce will lack sufficient data regarding sales in the two markets to make a LOT adjustment. In those instances, the statutes provide for the application of a constructed export price offset ("CEP offset"), instead of a LOT adjustment. 19 U.S.C. § 1677b(a)(7)(B) (2000) ("When normal value is established at a level of trade which constitutes a more advanced stage of distribution than the level of trade of the constructed export price, but the data available do not provide an appropriate basis to determine under subparagraph (A)(ii) a level of trade adjustment, normal value shall be reduced by the amount of indirect selling expenses incurred in the country in which normal value is determined on sales of the foreign like product. . . ."). . . .

Commerce determined that there were two distinct levels of trade for NSK in the Japanese home market — aftermarket sales and original equipment manufacturer sales — and that these home market levels of trade were at a more advanced stage of distribution than the single constructed export price level of trade in the U.S. market. . . . Commerce found that there was no record evidence to quantify the price difference between the two home market levels of trade and the single U.S. constructed export price level of trade. . . . Thus, Commerce made a CEP offset to the normal value for all of NSK's CEP transactions. . . . Contrary to NSK's arguments, Commerce concluded that it lacked "explicit authority to make a level-of-trade adjustment between two home-market levels of trade where neither level is equivalent to the level of the U.S. sale." . . .

On appeal, the Court of International Trade affirmed Commerce's use of a CEP offset. . . . The Court of International Trade interpreted 19 U.S.C. § 1677b(a)(7)(A) and concluded that a LOT adjustment was to be made to a price-based normal value only for a difference that is shown to be wholly or partly due to a difference in level of trade between the constructed export price or export price and the normal value. . . . Under 19 U.S.C. § 1677b(a)(7)(B), a CEP offset was required when there was no sufficient data to determine a LOT adjustment under § 1677b(a)(7)(A). . . . The Court of International Trade concluded that Commerce's practice at the time, as provided in 19 C.F.R. § 351.412(d) (1998), was to refuse to calculate a LOT adjustment in those cases where the home market data does not demonstrate that a constructed export price level of trade exists with respect to any transactions. . . . The Court of International Trade concluded that Commerce's conclusion that § 1677b(a)(7)(A) did not provide for a LOT adjustment, other than that based upon price differences in the home market between constructed export price and normal value market levels of trade, was reasonable. . . .

1. The Parties' Arguments

On appeal, NSK does not dispute the manner by which Commerce determined the levels of trade of its constructed export price or normal value transactions. NSK objects to Commerce's decision not to calculate what it terms a "partial" LOT adjustment for constructed export price sales matched to aftermarket normal value sales, based on the price differences between original equipment manufacturer normal value sales and aftermarket normal value sales. NSK relies on language in 19 U.S.C. § 1677b(a)(7)(A) that normal value must be adjusted to reflect any difference "that is shown to be wholly or *partly* due to a difference in level of trade between the export price or constructed export price and normal value." (emphasis added). NSK argues that because the language requires a LOT adjustment if it "partly" adjusts for differences in the levels of trade, a "partial" LOT adjustment is mandated in this case.

Commerce responds that it properly rejected NSK's proffered "partial" LOT adjustment. Commerce argues that it correctly interpreted 19 U.S.C. § 1677b(a)(7)(and properly concluded that it lacked statutory authority to make a LOT adjustment using two home market levels of trade where neither level is equivalent to the CEP level of trade.

2. Analysis

We agree that Commerce correctly interpreted 19 U.S.C. § 1677b(a)(7) and properly denied NSK's request for a "partial" LOT adjustment. NSK's statutory interpretation is predicated on the presence of the word "partly" in § 1677b(a)(7)(A). Section 1677b(a)(7)(A) provides:

(A) Level of trade

The price described in paragraph (1)(B) shall also be increased or decreased to make due allowance for any difference (or lack thereof) between the export price or constructed export price and the price described in paragraph (1)(B) (other than a difference for which allowance is otherwise made under this section) that is shown to be wholly or partly due to a difference in level of trade between the export price or constructed export price and normal value, if the difference in level of trade —

  (i) involves the performance of different selling activities; and

  (ii) is demonstrated to affect price comparability, based on a pattern of consistent price differences between sales at different levels of trade in the country in which normal value is determined.

In a case described in the preceding sentence, the amount of the adjustment shall be based on the price differences between the two levels of trade in the country in which normal value is determined.

19 U.S.C. § 1677b(a)(7)(A) (2000) (emphasis added). The word "partly" indicates that a LOT adjustment should be made even when pricing differences between home market levels of trade are only partly attributable to the difference in the level of trade. The partial adjustment must still be between normal value at one level of trade and normal value at the same level of trade as the U.S. sale. Thus, the use of the term "partly" does not mandate a partial LOT adjustment when there are no comparable levels of trade in the home and U.S. markets, and Commerce determines there was insufficient data to make a LOT adjustment. In those instances, 19 U.S.C. § 1677b(a)(7)(B) mandates the use of an alternate adjustment, known as a "CEP offset":

  (B) Constructed export price offset

  When normal value is established at a level of trade which constitutes a more advanced stage of distribution than the level of trade of the constructed export price, but the data available do not provide an appropriate basis to determine under subparagraph (A)(ii) a level of trade adjustment, normal value shall be reduced by the amount of indirect selling expenses incurred in the country in which normal value is determined on sales of the foreign like product but not more than the amount of such expenses for which a deduction is made under section 772(d)(1)(D) [19 U.S.C. § 1677a(d)(1)(D)]. . . .

19 U.S.C. § 1677b(a)(7)(B) (2000) (emphases added). This court noted in *Micron Technologies*:

  In some instances, the level of trade in the home market will constitute a more advanced stage of distribution than the level of trade in the United States, yet Commerce will lack sufficient data regarding the sales in the two markets to make a level of trade adjustment, that is, it will be unable to determine how much to reduce the foreign sale price to arrive at a price comparable to the U.S. price. In those cases, the statute provides for the award of a 'constructed export price offset' [("CEP offset")].

243 F.3d at 1305. A CEP offset is designed to cover situations such as these for which the normal value is at a more advanced stage than the constructed export price level of trade, and for which Commerce determines there is insufficient data to make a LOT adjustment. See 19 U.S.C. § 1677b(a)(7)(B) (2000); see also *Koyo Seiko Co. v. United States*, 22 C.I.T. 424, 8 F. Supp. 2d

862, 866 (Ct. Int'l Trade 1998) ("Commerce's interpretation . . . is reasonable, in light of the existence of the CEP offset to cover situations such as those at issue."). Thus, we conclude that Commerce did not err in applying a CEP offset and denying NSK's request for a "partial" LOT adjustment.

III. Conclusion

Because Commerce's classification of NSK's repacking expenses as a selling expense was arbitrary, we vacate that determination and remand for further proceedings. Because Commerce correctly refused to grant NSK a partial level of trade adjustment, we affirm that portion of its decision.

Chapter 32

DUMPING MARGIN CALCULATION CONTROVERSIES

When you come to a fork in the road, take it.

> —Yogi Berra, The Yogi Book 48 (1998) (Hall of Fame Baseball
> Player and Manager)

Documents Supplement Assignment

1. *Havana Charter* Article 34
2. GATT Article VI
3. WTO *Antidumping Agreement* Articles 1-2

I. CURRENCY CONVERSION

A. Forward Contract Hedging and the 1998 *Thyssen* Case

THYSSEN STAHL AG v. UNITED STATES
United States Court of Appeals for the Federal Circuit
1998 U.S. App. LEXIS 17064 (1998)

Clevenger, Circuit Judge.

In this antidumping action, Thyssen Stahl AG (Thyssen) and its related companies appeal from the decision of the Court of International Trade affirming the decision by the Department of Commerce (Commerce) to use Best Information Available in calculating the ocean transportation costs of the subject products and reversing Commerce's conclusion that Commerce could increase U.S. Price to account for Thyssen's currency hedging gains. . . . We affirm.

I

Thyssen is a German manufacturer of various flat-rolled steel products, including cold-rolled steel and corrosion-resistant steel. Thyssen Inc. (TINC) and Thyssen Steel Detroit Co. (TSD) are related companies that import the subject merchandise produced by Thyssen.

On June 30, 1992, domestic steel producers filed an antidumping petition against Thyssen and other German steel producers. The petition claimed that the German producers were selling cold-rolled and corrosion-resistant, carbon steel products in the United States at less than fair value and thereby causing or threatening material injury to the United States steel industry. Commerce shortly thereafter initiated an investigation of cold-rolled steel and corrosion-resistant steel from Germany. . . .

On August 19, 1992, Commerce issued a questionnaire to Thyssen directing Thyssen to report the sale price associated with each U.S. transaction during the period of review along with all associated charges and adjustments. Two of these charges or adjustments are at issue in this case. The first involves an adjustment to U.S. Price [*i.e.*, Export Price or Constructed Export Price] that Thyssen claimed for currency hedging gains associated with its U.S. sales. The second is the adjustment that Thyssen claimed for ocean freight expenses. [Omitted is the Court's discussion of the second issue.]

. . . .

In response to the questionnaire issued by Commerce, Thyssen claimed an upward adjustment to U.S. Price to account for the currency hedging gains that it incurred with regard to its U.S. sales. Thyssen routinely entered into forward exchange contracts with a private bank, under which it agreed to exchange U.S. dollars for German marks [the currency of Germany before establishment of monetary union in the EU, under the 1992 *Treaty of Maastrich*, resulting in the creation of the euro on 1 January 1999, and its usage on a cash basis as of 1 January 2002] at an established rate in advance of receipt of purchase orders from TINC and TSD. As Thyssen received purchase orders from TINC and TSD, it assigned them to a foreign exchange contract. TINC and TSD paid Thyssen for the steel in U.S. dollars, and Thyssen exchanged those dollars for German marks under the forward contract. Often, the value of the dollar vis-à-vis the mark declined between the date that Thyssen entered the forward contract and the date that Thyssen exchanged its dollars for marks. In these instances, Thyssen experienced a gain in the amount of the difference between the forward contract rate and the spot rate. Thyssen convinced Commerce that these gains were sufficiently attributable to its U.S. sales to warrant an upward adjustment to U.S. Price, which resulted in a decreased dumping margin. Commerce recorded the gains as a negative expense under 19 U.S.C. § 1677a(e) (1988) and 19 C.F.R. § 353.41(e) (1993). The Court of International Trade disagreed with Commerce and concluded that neither the statute nor the regulations contemplated upward adjustments in U.S. Price for currency hedging. . . . [As the Court observed in a footnote, "[u]nder the *Uruguay Round Agreements Act*, Pub. Law. No. 103-465, 108 Stat. 4809 (1994), the U.S. Customs laws were amended to allow for currency conversions at the rate specified in the forward contract. See 19 U.S.C. § 1677b-1(a) (1994). However, the amendment is inapplicable to this case, because the domestic producers filed their antidumping petition before the amendment's January 1, 1995 effective date. . . .] In addition, the court noted that Thyssen's hedging activities were not sufficiently related to its U.S. sales to allow for an adjustment to U.S. Price. See *id.*

. . . .

II

. . . .

. . . Commerce adjusted U.S. Price upward to account for Thyssen's currency hedging gains associated with its U.S. sales. The statute states: "For purposes of this section, the exporter's sales price [*i.e.*, Constructed Export Price] shall also be adjusted by being *reduced* by the amount, if any, of . . . (2) expenses generally incurred by or for the account of the exporter in the United States in selling identical or substantially identical merchandise . . . ." 19 U.S.C. § 1677a(e) (1988) (emphasis added).

The statute clearly contemplates only reductions in U.S. Price to account for expenses, and not increases to account for gains, associated with selling the merchandise. Commerce, however, increased the U.S. Price through linguistic artistry by deeming the gains received by Thyssen on its currency hedging activities "negative expenses." Commerce's interpretation of the statutory section, which would bring both increases and reductions of U.S. Price within the section's reach, contradicts the statute's unambiguous expression of congressional intent, and we therefore owe it no deference. See *Chevron U.S.A. Inc. v. Natural Resources Defense Council, Inc.*, 467 U.S. 837, 842-43 . . . (1984). Commerce's decision to increase U.S. Price for Thyssen's gains received in its currency hedging activity was not in accordance with law, and the Court of International Trade was correct in reversing it. [The Court added in a footnote that is expresses "no view on whether the facts of this case relating to the currency hedging activity would warrant an adjustment under 19 U.S.C. § 1677b(a)(4)(B) (1988) for "other differences in circumstances of sales."]

B. The Post-Uruguay Round Rule

Section 1677b-1(a) of Title 19 of the United States Code states

> In an antidumping proceeding . . ., the administering authority [*i.e.*, the U.S. Department of Commerce (DOC)] shall convert foreign currencies into United States dollars using the exchanger rate in effect on the date of sale of the subject merchandise, except that, if it is established that a currency transaction on forward markets is directly related to an export sale under consideration, the exchange rate specified with respect to such currency in the forward sale agreement shall be used to convert the foreign currency. Fluctuations in exchange rates shall be ignored.

The 1998 *Thyssen* case (excerpted above) transpired before this rule took effect. Is the holding of the case consistent with the post-Uruguay Round rule? The case, like the statute, involved currency hedging through a forward contract. What if the hedging instrument is different, such as a currency swap?

The *Thyssen* case involved a currency conversion for Constructed Export Price (then called Exporter's Sales Price). What rate is used to convert Normal Value? In the U.S., who selects the rate? *See* 19 U.S.C. Section 5151 (concerning certification by the Federal Reserve Bank of New York of the noon buying rate).

II. COMPARISON METHODOLOGIES

What methodologies are used to compare Normal Value with Export Price (or Constructed Export Price)? That is, what kind of comparison should be made between sales transactions of the foreign like product in the home market of an exporter or producer (*i.e.*, Normal Value data) and sales transactions of the subject merchandise in the importing country (*i.e.*, Export Price, or Constructed Export Price)? The answer is a comparison between a weighted average of Normal Value data and Export Price (or Constructed Export Price) data, or between individual transactions.

Article 2:4:2 of the WTO *Antidumping Agreement* indicates the comparison should be between weighted average price data on both sides, or between individual transactions. As a general rule, comparing a weighted average with an individual transaction is not permitted. The reason is obvious. There is a bias in favor of finding a positive dumping margin if the Normal Value figure is an average of many sales transactions, and compared with an Export Price (or Constructed Export Price) figure from a sole transaction. (By analogy, imagine comparing body weight from a one-month average with body weight from a scale reading the day after Thanksgiving.) The rule seeks to avoid this pro-petitioner bias. Usually, the most reliable comparison is between weighted averages, as individual sales transactions may be unrepresentative of a market.

However, Article 2:4:2 is not entirely successful in eliminating the bias. In one instance, it permits comparison between (1) Normal Value, from a weighted average of prices, with (2) Export Price (or Constructed Export Price), from an individual transaction. That instance is where an investigating authority finds evidence of a "pattern" that Export Prices "differ significantly among purchasers, regions or time periods." Accordingly, Section 229 of the 1994 *Uruguay Round Agreements Act* (19 U.S.C. § 1677f-1(d)(1)(A)(ii)) preserves the ability of the DOC to make average-to-individual comparisons. Terms such as "pattern" and "differ significantly" are ambiguous. In practice, the DOC uses the average-to-individual method if neither an average-to-average nor an individual-to-individual comparison will identify targeted dumping. ("Targeted" dumping occurs if dumping is directed at a specific geographic area or time period.)

Moreover, what prevents an investigating authority from disregarding prices above Normal Value when choosing an individual Export Price (or Constructed Export Price) transaction? That is, what rule bars the authority from ignoring non-dumped sales when doing an average-to-individual comparison? For example, suppose a producer sells a foreign like product in its home market at $9, $10 and $11. It would be found to have dumped subject merchandise if there are three sales transactions made at the same prices in the U.S. market. The average Normal Value would be $10 ($30 divided by 3). The result is a $1 dumping margin when compared individually with the $9 U.S. sale. That comparison would mean disregarding the non-dumped sales made at $10 and $11.

As a practical matter, query whether an exporter exercising reasonable care and judgment can determine, at the time it sets its prices for overseas shipments to markets like the U.S., that it risks a dumping charge. For example, suppose a foreign exporter makes its first U.S. sale in January. At that juncture, how can it ascertain what its weighted-average home market prices for the next 6 months, or year, will be? The repercussion of an answer "it cannot" is the exporter is unable to determine *a priori* what prices may lead to an accusation of dumping.

III.   ZEROING AND FAIRNESS

A.   Simple Zeroing, Model Zeroing, and Contexts

When comparing Normal Value to Export Price (or Constructed Export Price), and calculating the dumping margin, what should be done about non-dumped sales? The question raises the controversial practice called "zeroing." Succinctly put, zeroing refers to the artificial assignment of a value of zero to any negative dumping margin. A "negative" dumping margin is one in which Normal Value (or a proxy for it) is lower than Export Price (or Constructed Export Price). Rather than factoring in the negative value into an overall dumping margin calculation, by zeroing the margin is set at zero. Consequently, the negative dumping margin from one transaction, or a group of transactions, does not offset the positive dumping margin from another or other transactions. In turn, the dumping margin is higher than it would be if the zeroing methodology were not used.

Before delving into the jurisprudence on zeroing, it is necessary to appreciate different zeroing methodologies, how they differ from "multiple averaging," and the contexts in which zeroing occurs. There are two basic types of zeroing — Simple and Model — which cover the three ways Article 2:4:2 of the WTO *Antidumping Agreement* articulates for calculating a dumping margin, namely, individual-to-individual, average-to-individual, or average-to-average comparisons of Normal Value and Export Price (or Constructed Export Price), respectively.

1.   Simple Zeroing

This methodology also is called "average-to-individual" or "individual-to-individual" zeroing, because it is used in comparisons of weighted average Normal Value to individual transaction Export Price, or individual transaction-specific comparisons of Normal Value and Export Price. Simple Zeroing entails a comparison between —

> (1)   weighted average Normal Value, derived from multiple sale transactions of a foreign like product, and Export Price, derived from individual sale transactions of subject merchandise, *i.e.*, an "average to individual comparison," or
>
> (2)   Normal Value, derived from individual sale transactions of a foreign like product, and Export Price from individual sales transactions of subject merchandise, *i.e.*, an "individual to individual comparison."

Critically, non-dumped sales of subject merchandise are recorded as zero. That is, in any comparison in which the dumping margin is negative (*i.e.*, average Normal Value is less than individual Export Price, or individual Normal Value is less than individual Export Price), that margin is equated to zero.

The overall dumping margin for subject merchandise is calculated by aggregating the results of all the comparisons. This total dumping margin, which excludes negative amounts by treating them as zero, is expressed as a percentage of the total Export Price, which includes all export transactions. Consequently, the numerator excludes non-dumped sales (by converting any negative values to zero) from any averaging group, while the denominator includes all Export Prices. The numerator is inflated by zeroing. Nevertheless, the importer is liable to pay the final AD duty.

2. Model Zeroing

This methodology also is called "weighted average" zeroing, because it is used in an average-to-average comparison of Normal Value and Export Price within individual averaging groups. Model Zeroing involves the division of subject merchandise and corresponding foreign like product into sub-categories of merchandise. The sub-categories are called "averaging groups," and are established based on the products in them being identical or virtually identical in all physical characteristics, at the same level of trade, sold in the same region, and other relevant factors.

Within each averaging group (*i.e.*, each product sub-category), a weighted average Normal Value and a weighted average Export Price are computed. Weighted average Normal Value is derived from multiple sales transactions of a foreign like product. Weighted average Export Price is derived from multiple sales transactions of subject merchandise. Then, within each group, a comparison is made of weighted average Normal Value against weighted average Export Price. This juxtaposition is an "average-to-average," or "weighted average-to-weighted average" comparison.

Critically, for each averaging group, non-dumped sales of subject merchandise are recorded as zero. That is, for any product sub-category in which the dumping margin is negative (*i.e.*, weighted average Normal Value is less than weighted average Export Price), that Margin is equated to zero.

An overall dumping margin for all averaging groups (*i.e.*, the entire product) is computed by combining the results from the averaging groups, with zeros replacing negative dumping margins. That is, the dumping margins for each averaging groups are summed to establish the dumping margin for the subject merchandise as a whole. This overall margin, of course, reflects zeroing. The overall dumping margin is expressed as a percentage of the total export prices. That is, the formula for the dumping margin expressed as a percentage, has as the numerator the total of the dumping margins, and as the denominator the total of Export Prices.

The numerator excludes non-dumped sales (by converting any negative values to zero) from any averaging group. But, the denominator includes Export

Prices from all averaging groups. The numerator is inflated by zeroing. Of course, the importer is liable to pay the final AD duty.

Finally, and importantly, both Simple and Model Zeroing can — and do — occur in the contexts of an original dumping investigation (at the preliminary or final stage), or a review (such as an Administrative Review, Sunset Review, or New Shipper Review).

B. A Zeroing Hypothetical from the 2004 *Softwood Lumber* Case

An example of Model Zeroing comes from the facts of the *Softwood Lumber* dispute between the United States and Canada. *See* Appellate Body Report, *United States — Final Dumping Determination on Softwood Lumber from Canada*, WT/DS264/AB/R (adopted 31 August 2004). This case sometimes is referred to as "*Softwood Lumber V.*" This stylized example is of Model Zeroing used by the DOC, attacked by Canada, and ruled against by the Appellate Body.

Conceptually, the Model Zeroing the DOC employed has 8 steps. (All prices are in U.S. dollars.) After working through the example, construct an illustration of Simple Zeroing in an individual-to-individual, and an average-to-individual comparison scenario.

Step 1: Division into Product Groups

The subject merchandise, such as softwood lumber, typically consists of several different types of product. While these groups are "like" as products, they may not all be identical. Accordingly, the subject merchandise is divided into groups of identical or broadly similar product types.

Suppose there are 3 product types of softwood lumber:

(1)   Siding Boards:

Boards of dimension 2 inches thick by 4 inches wide, used for the siding of buildings.

(2)   Flooring Boards:

Boards of dimension 2 inches thick by 2 inches wide used for interior floors.

(3)   Deck Posts:

Pressure treated wood of dimension 4 inches thick by 4 inches wide used as posts for exterior decks.

The DOC divides the general like product, softwood lumber, into the 3 groups.

Step 2: Adjustments

Within each product group, raw price data for Normal Value and Export Price (or, if required, Constructed Export Price) is marshaled. Adjustments to Normal Value and Export Price are made. These adjustments assure (or, at least, enhance) the comparability of the price data on Normal Value from the home market of the exporter (here, Canada) and the price data on Export Price of the importing country (here, the U.S.). (In the *Softwood Lumber* case, adjustments were not the prime focus of the appeal. Accordingly, assume all necessary adjustments are made and not controversial.)

Step 3: Computation of Weighted Average Normal Value and Export Price Within Each Group (Multiple Averaging)

Within each product group, a weighted average Normal Value and weighted average Export Price is calculated. This weighting may be for the volume or value of sales within the groups. The weighted average calculation yields Normal Value and Export Price in each group on a per unit basis, *i.e.*, per unit of the product in that group.

Accordingly, the task performed in Step 3 is referred to as "multiple averaging." As the Appellate Body in *Softwood Lumber Zeroing* aptly put it, the task refers to "sub-dividing the product under investigation into sub-groups of comparable transactions and determining a weighted average normal value and a weighted average export price for the transactions in each sub-group."[1]

To continue the hypothetical, assume the results of Step 3 are:

(1)	Siding Boards:		
	Weighted Average Normal Value	=	$200
	Weighted Average Export Price	=	$100
(2)	Flooring Boards:		
	Weighted Average Normal Value	=	$150
	Weighted Average Export Price	=	$100
(3)	Deck Posts:		
	Weighted Average Normal Value	=	$110
	Weighted Average Export Price	=	$250

The fact there are several weighted averages, namely, one set (Normal Value and Export Price) for each product category shows the rationale of the term "multiple averaging."

Step 4: Computation of Dumping Margin within Each Group

Within each product group, a dumping margin, if it exists, is calculated. This calculation is the simple comparison of weighted average Normal Value against weighted average Export Price. The result of Step 4 is multiple values, one for each group, which follow logically from multiple averaging in Step 3. This calculation yields:

(1)	Siding Boards:		
	Weighted Average Normal Value	=	$200
	Weighted Average Export Price	=	$100
	Dumping Margin	=	+ $100
(2)	Flooring Boards:		
	Weighted Average Normal Value	=	$150
	Weighted Average Export Price	=	$100
	Dumping Margin	=	+ $50

---

[1] Appellate Body Report, *Softwood Lumber Zeroing*, ¶ 68.

(3)   Deck Posts:
Weighted Average Normal Value   = $110
Weighted Average Export Price   = $250
Dumping Margin   =   − $140

Here, the multiple values are + $100, + $50, and − $140.

Step 5: Determination as to Whether Dumping Exists

An assessment as to whether dumping occurs — *i.e.*, whether there is a dumping margin — is needed. So, in Step 5, a positive dumping margin, where weighted average Normal Value exceeds weighted average Export Price, is regarded as an instance in which dumping occurs. This occurrence is within a specific product group. A negative dumping margin, where weighted average Normal Value is less than weighted average Export Price, connotes no dumping exists. In such instances, the DOC deems no dumping margin exists for purposes of comparing prices from the investigated transactions.

Taking this approach, in the hypothetical, there is dumping in the first two groups, but not in the third group:

(1)   Siding Boards:
Weighted Average Normal Value   = $200
Weighted Average Export Price   = $100
Dumping Margin   =   + $100   Dumping exists.

(2)   Flooring Boards:
Weighted Average Normal Value   = $150
Weighted Average Export Price   = $100
Dumping Margin   =   + $50   Dumping exists.

(3)   Deck Posts:
Weighted Average Normal Value   = $110
Weighted Average Export Price   = $250
Dumping Margin   =   - $140   No dumping occurs.

Step 6: Volume Weighting

The volume of export transactions is likely to differ from one product group to another. Suppose 75 percent of the transactions are in 1 product category, and 25 percent split between the other 2 categories. The dumping margin (if any) in the high-volume category should have greater weight in a final, overall dumping margin calculation, then the dumping margin in the other categories.

Thus, it is necessary to adjust results from each product group in Step 5 by putting weights on these results commensurate with the export volumes associated with each result. That is the purpose of Step 6. It is achieved by multiplying the difference in each category between weighted average Normal Value and weighted average Export Price, *i.e.*, the Dumping Margin, by the export transaction volume in that category. For simplicity, assume the volume of export transactions in the 3 groups is equal. Therefore, the differences in each category calculated in Step 5 are per unit and reflect volume.

Step 7: Aggregation of Dumping Margins and Zeroing

To arrive at a single, overall dumping margin for subject merchandise (softwood lumber), it is necessary to aggregate the results from the calculation of the differences between weighted average Normal Value and weighted average Export Price (Steps 4 and 5), as corrected for volume (Step 6). That is, it is necessary to sum up results of the dumping margin calculations performed for each product group. This process is "aggregation," because it involves getting one figure for subject merchandise by cumulating results across all groups. The key point here is zeroing occurs in this process.

In particular, for any product category in which the dumping margin is positive, *i.e.*, where weighted average Normal Value exceeds weighted average Export Price, no change is made to that result. However, for any product category in which the dumping margin is negative (or zero), *i.e.*, weighted average Export Price exceeds weighted average Normal Value, the result is set at a zero value. There is no dumping in these groups, as per Step 5, and zeroing literally refers to the change in the negative dumping margin value for such groups to a zero value. As the *Softwood Lumber Zeroing* Panel nicely puts it, "zeroing" is "the process of attributing a 'zero' value to the individual product type comparisons where the weighted average export price is greater than the weighted average normal value for the same product type. . . ."[2]

Consider the example. The result for the first two categories is left alone. But, the result for the third category is zeroed.

(1)   Siding Boards:

Weighted Average Normal Value	=	$200
Weighted Average Export Price	=	$100
Dumping Margin	=	+ $100

Dumping exists. Result left alone.

(2)   Flooring Boards:

Weighted Average Normal Value	=	$150
Weighted Average Export Price	=	$100
Dumping Margin	=	+ $50

Dumping exists. Result left alone.

(3)   Deck Posts:

Weighted Average Normal Value	=	$110
Weighted Average Export Price	=	$250
Dumping Margin	=	- $140

No dumping occurs. Result set to zero.

---

[2] Panel Report, *Softwood Lumber Zeroing*, ¶ 7:186.

With these facts, aggregation produces a dumping margin of + $150, which is the sum of $100 (siding boards), $50 (flooring boards), and zero (deck boards). Without zeroing, the aggregate dumping margin would be + $10. That amount, depending on other facts in the case, might be *de minimis*. Obviously, it also is possible to construct an example, without zeroing, in which the aggregate dumping margin is zero or negative, indicating non-dumped sales of deck posts offset dumped sales of siding and flooring boards.

Step 8: Computation of Overall Dumping Margin

The final stage is computation of a single figure for the dumping margin for the subject merchandise. Step 7 yields an aggregate dumping margin, based on adding the margins of the individual product categories and zeroing any negative margins. However, this aggregate margin is not corrected for the value of export transactions of subject merchandise. It is not clear whether it is based on a billion or a million dollars worth of imports, and thus has to be put into the perspective of the value of all export transactions. Therefore, the formula for the overall weighted average dumping margin is:

$$\text{Overall Weighted Average Dumping Margin} = \frac{\substack{\text{Aggregate Dumping Margin}\\\text{(\textit{i.e.}, sum of price}\\\text{comparisons across all}\\\text{product groups, setting as}\\\text{zero the result of any}\\\text{comparison in which}\\\text{weighted average Export}\\\text{Price exceeds weighted}\\\text{average Normal Value)}}}{\substack{\text{Total Value of all Export}\\\text{Transactions of Subject}\\\text{Merchandise (\textit{i.e.}, sum of}\\\text{the value of transactions in}\\\text{each product group,}\\\text{regardless of the result of}\\\text{price comparisons in the}\\\text{group)}}} \times 100$$

In *Softwood Lumber Zeroing*, the Appellate Body points out the DOC included in the denominator of this formula the value of export transactions from all product categories. In other words, the DOC counted transactions not included in the aggregate dumping margin figure in the numerator by virtue of the zeroing methodology.

In the example, suppose the value of export transactions in each product group is:

Siding Boards:	$500
Flooring Boards:	$300
Deck Posts:	$400

(To be sure, by assumption in Step 6, the volume amounts are the same for each group. The differences in value, therefore, would be due to differences in per unit prices.) Inserting these figures, along with the hypothesized dumping margins for siding and flooring boards, and the zero value for deck posts, into the above formula, the result is:

$$\text{Overall Weighted Average Dumping Margin} = \frac{\$150}{\$500 + \$300 + \$400} \times 100$$

$$\text{Overall Weighted Average Dumping Margin} = 12.5 \text{ percent}$$

Observe if the value of transactions in product groups in which dumping does not occur, *i.e.*, the zeroed groups, is excluded, then the denominator would be smaller. Consequently, the overall dumping margin would increase. In the hypothetical, it would be $800, which would mean an overall margin of 18.75 percent.

In sum, in the *Softwood Lumber Zeroing* case, the DOC applied a weighted average-to-weighted average comparison of Normal Value and Export Price, beginning with a division of subject merchandise into groups of identical or similar softwood lumber products. Within each group, the DOC made multiple comparisons of prices in the home market (Canada) and U.S. To compute weighted averages and a dumping margin, the DOC aggregated results from the individual comparisons. However, using zeroing when aggregating the results, it set a zero value wherever dumping did not occur, *i.e.*, when Normal Value (the Canadian price, converted into U.S. dollars) was below Export Price (the American price).

C. The 2001 *EC Bed Linen* Case

In September 1996, the European Communities (EC) initiated an AD case against imports from India of cotton-type bed linen.[3] It was the first challenge against zeroing, and the catalyst for many subsequent zeroing cases. Interestingly, the European Union (EU) states were split about the case. In 1997, the EU's AD committee recorded a tie vote, 7-7, about the case, with Germany initially postponing, and ultimately casting the tie-breaking vote. The reason for support for the action was clear: protect the EU's fabric-weaving sector from low-priced import competition. Equally obvious was the reason for opposition to the action: job loss in companies that consume the imports, like Britain's Coats Viyella, Lonrho, and the Leeds Group — all of which incurred or faced redundancies from the protective remedy.

"Eurocoton," a federation of associations of European producers of cotton textile products, requested the EC to bring the case. After excluding certain companies, there were 35 remaining petitioner producers, and they represented a major proportion of total EC production of bed linen. The period of investigation (POI) was 1 July 1995 to 30 June 1996, with the injury determination based on data from 1992 to 30 June 1996.

---

[3] *See* WTO Panel Report, *European Communities — Anti-Dumping Duties on Imports of Cotton-Type Bed Linen from India*, WT/DS141/AB/R (adopted as modified by the Appellate Body Report, 12 March 2001); WTO Appellate Body Report, *European Communities — Anti-Dumping Duties on Imports of Cotton-Type Bed Linen from India*, WT/DS141/AB/R (adopted 12 March 2001).

Because there were so many Indian producers and exporters of subject merchandise, cotton-type bed linen, the EC elected to conduct its analysis of dumping on the basis of a sample of Indian companies. In determining the home (*i.e.*, Indian) market price for bed linen sold by the investigated respondents, the EC used Constructed Value as a substitute for Normal Value. The reason for using a proxy for Normal Value was a lack of ordinary course sales in the Indian market. The EC identified 5 types of cotton bed-linen exported to it and also sold in representative quantities in India. However, not all 5 types were sold in India in the ordinary course of trade. Thus, the EC could not base Normal Value on prices from these sales, and had to use Constructed Value.

The EC established Export Price from prices actually paid or payable for cotton-type bed linen in the EC market, and compared Constructed Value with Export Price. This comparison involved weighted averages of Constructed Value and Export Price, computed for each Indian respondent, with the dumping margin being the difference between the weighted average Constructed Value and weighted average Export Price. (That is, for each Indian respondent, the EC calculated a weighted average dumping margin from the weighted average Constructed Value minus the weighted average Export Price.) In the computation, the EC applied a zeroing methodology. It deemed any negative dumping margin (where Export Price exceeds Constructed Value) to be zero.

A notable feature of the way the EC calculated Constructed Value concerned selling, general, and administrative (SG&A) expenses, and profits. One Indian respondent was a company called "Bombay Dyeing." The EC obtained actual SG&A and profit data from Bombay Dyeing, and used these data to calculate Constructed Value for it. In addition, however, the EC used the same data — the SG&A and profit information from Bombay Dyeing — to come up with CV for all the other Indian respondents.

Regarding injury and causation, the EC found evidence of declining and inadequate profitability, and of price depression. Therefore, it reached an affirmative finding of material injury to EC producers. This injury, said the EC, was caused directly by the increased volume of dumped merchandise, and by the dumped prices. The evidence for causation was heavy price undercutting by Indian producers, which in turn led to a significant increase in the market share of Indian bed linen in the EC market, and a concomitant negative effect on sales volumes and prices of European-made bed linen.

In June 1997, the EC imposed provisional AD duties on subject merchandise. It imposed final duties in November 1997. Depending on the Indian respondent, the dumping margins, and hence the duties, ranged from 2.6 percent to 24.7 percent.

India alleged a large number of WTO-inconsistent actions by the EC, mostly pursuant to the WTO *Antidumping Agreement*. Most of India's claims were unsuccessful, and arguably India over-argued the case. For instance, the Panel rejected the charges brought by India under Articles 2:2 and 2:2:2 (alleging improper construction of Constructed Value), Articles 3:1 and 3:4 (alleging improper determination of injury), Article 3:5 (alleging failure to identify and distinguish causal factors in the injury determination), Articles 5:3 and 5:4

(alleging improper initiation of an investigation), and Article 12:2:2 (alleging failure to give public notice). Nevertheless, India won a resounding victory on the technical but important claim under Article 2:4:2 of the *AD Agreement* concerning the EC's zeroing methodology. That triumph was over not only the EC, but also the U.S., which entered the case as a third party and defended the EC's use of zeroing — or, at least, so India and other countries might have believed. The American move was not surprising, in that the DOC, as well as the Canadian administering agency, routinely engages in zeroing. (India also prevailed under Article 2:2:2 of the *AD Agreement*, concerning the proper way to calculate certain types of expenses incurred, and profits realized, by an exporter or producer when computing Constructed Value.)

India successfully argued to the Panel zeroing as employed by the EC breached Article 2:4:2 of the WTO *Antidumping Agreement*. "Zeroing," of course, means equating all non-dumped sales to zero, and thereby preventing non-dumped sales from offsetting dumped sales. In the case, for example, suppose a sale of cotton-type bed-linen in Belgium were made at ECU 10 above Constructed Value (indicating no dumping, or "negative" dumping of 10), while a sale of the subject merchandise in Holland were made at ECU 10 below Constructed Value (indicating a positive dumping margin of 10). In the dumping margin calculation, but for the practice of zeroing, there would be no dumping. The Belgian sale would offset exactly the Dutch sale. Likewise, if the Belgian transaction were at ECU 5 above Constructed Value, but for zeroing, the dumping margin would be reduced (to 5), because the negative dumping in the Belgian sale (-10) would offset in part the positive dumping in the Dutch sale (+10). Obviously, these results would be good news to a respondent like the Indian exporters of cotton-type bed-linen.

Yet, the EC zeroed, deeming all non-dumped sales to have a zero value, no matter how far in excess the sales prices in the EC of subject merchandise (*i.e.*, the Export Prices) were above Constructed Value. So, in the illustration, the EC would treat the Belgian sale as a zero dumping margin. To the EC, whether the sale were made at ECU 10 or ECU 5 above Constructed Value would be irrelevant. In any instance in which Export Price is above Constructed Value (or, for that matter Normal Value or Third Country Price), the EC treats the sale as if Export Price exactly equaled Constructed Value. The effect of that treatment is non-dumped sales cannot offset dumped sales. In the hypothetical, abstracting from a weighted averaging, the dumping margin would be 10, based essentially on the Dutch sale. With a weighted averaging of the Dutch and Belgian sales, the zero value ascribed to the Belgian sale, rather than the true value (-10), would result in an artificially high margin (nearer to +10 than it should be).

India's view was zeroing was contrary to the requirement of Article 2:4:2 of the *Antidumping Agreement*, which not only echoes the need for a "fair comparison" between Normal Value (or its proxy) and Export Price, but also provides guidance on what that constitutes. Article 2:4:2 says that in most cases, a weighted average for Normal Value (or its proxy) must be compared to a weighted average of prices of all comparable export transactions. Alternatively, a comparison can be made between Normal Value and Export Price on a transaction-by-transaction basis. What generally is not permitted is a comparison between a figure for Normal Value determined by a weighted average and export prices from individual transactions. Only where the pattern of Export Prices differs significantly among buyers or regions in the importing country, or time periods — known as targeted dumping — is an average Normal Value-to-individual Export Price comparison justified. The significant differences would justify disregarding certain export prices as distorted or unrepresentative.

To be sure, the zeroing methodology the EC used was Model Zeroing. The EC divided subject merchandise — cotton-type bed linen — into product types (which the Panel called "models"). The EC calculated a weighted average of Normal Value and Export Price for each product type. India did not attack this aspect of the EC's determination. Rather, India's focus was on how the EC treated product types with negative dumping margins. For some of these types, the EC found a positive dumping margin, but for others it found a negative dumping margin. The EC calculated a weighted-average dumping margin for the subject merchandise, *i.e.*, an average dumping margin embracing all types of cotton bed linen. The weighting was based on the volume of imports of each of the product types. What India complained of under Article 2:4:2 was zeroing: in calculating the overall weighted average for cotton bed linen, the EC counted as zero any dumping margin for a product type that, in fact, was negative.

In its Report, the Appellate Body explains with clarity and specificity the contested zeroing methodology:

> [F]irst, the European Communities identified with respect to the product under investigation — cotton-type bed linen — a certain number of different "models" or "types" of that product. Next, the European Communities calculated, for each of these models, a *weighted average* normal value and a *weighted average* export price. Then, the European Communities compared the weighted average normal value with the weighted average export price for each model. For some models, normal value was *higher* than export price; by subtracting export price from normal value for these models, the European Communities established a *"positive* dumping margin" for each model. For other models, normal value was *lower* than export price; by subtracting export price from normal value for these other models, the European Communities established a *"negative* dumping margin" for each model. Thus, there is a "positive dumping margin" where there *is* dumping, and a "negative dumping margin" where there *is not*. The "positives" and "negatives" of the amounts in this calculation are an indication of precisely *how much* the export price is above or below the normal value. Having made this calculation, the European Communities then added up the amounts it had calculated as "dumping margins" for each model of the product in order to determine an *overall* dumping margin for the product *as a whole*. However, in doing so, the European Communities treated any "negative dumping margin" as zero — hence the use of the word "zeroing." Then, finally, having added up the "positive dumping margins" and the zeroes, the European Communities divided this sum by the

cumulative total value of all the export transactions involving all types and models of that product. In this way, the European Communities obtained an overall margin of dumping for the product under investigation.[4]

In effect, the EC did not permit negative dumping margins to offset positive dumping margins. Zeroing was a built-in pro-petitioner bias in the calculation.

How, asked India, could that methodology possibly be said under Article 2:4:2 to be a comparison of a weighted average Normal Value with weighted average or prices in comparable export transactions? In truth, the EC had averaged only within product types (*i.e.*, calculating Normal Value and Export Price within a product type). Once the EC compared product types, its use of zeroing meant the comparison was distorted. Pure, unadulterated weighted averages from the different product types were not compared, because negative dumping margins were excluded from the calculation of an overall weighted average dumping margin, and deemed to be zero dumping margins. The plain meaning of the word "average," said India, anticipates inclusion of all amounts for which the average is being calculated, not a selection of only certain figures to be averaged. This meaning is reinforced by the word "all" in Article 2:4:2, which calls for a "*weighted* average of prices of *all* comparable export transactions." By riding roughshod over this language, the EC overstated the dumping margins for four Indian bed linen companies, and for a fifth company found a dumping margin where one did not, in truth, exist.

The Indian argument against zeroing seems so strong a persuasive rebuttal scarcely seems imaginable. How did the EC try to justify, under Article 2:4:2 excluding negative dumping margins from its calculation of a weighted average dumping margin for cotton-type bed linen? First, the EC said zeroing is directed at dumping, and focuses on types of bed linen where dumping exists as evidenced by a positive dumping margin. Product types that are not dumped still are included in the calculation of an overall weighted average margin, albeit at zero, and thus still pull down the final result. As for the language of Article 2:4:2, it refers to "the existence of margins of dumping." That reference suggests a process of comparing weighted averages of more than one dumping margin. At the same time, the reference leaves to the discretion of each WTO Member the methodology for calculating a single, or overall, weighted average dumping margin. In other words, put more forcefully, Article 2:4:2 does not expressly forbid zeroing.

On appeal, the raised one, straightforward question: was its zeroing methodology consistent with Article 2:4:2 of the *AD Agreement*? The EC defended its practice of zeroing as being consistent, urging this provision demands two steps in the calculation of a dumping margin in any AD case in which the subject merchandise consists of various types of products that are not comparable. First, it is necessary to calculate a weighted average of prices from comparable export transactions (not from all export transactions). The critical aspect of this step, said the EC, was the sub-division of subject merchandise into comparable models, and calculate a dumping margin for each model. Second, an overall weighted average margin — one that encompassed all the

---

[4] *EC Bed Linen* Appellate Body Report ¶ 47 (emphasis original).

models — had to be calculated. In this area, Article 2:4:2 was silent. It was up to each WTO Member country to decide how to go about that second-stage of the methodology, including whether to deem as zero any negative dumping margin.

The EC's defense hinged tightly on the use of the word "comparable" in Article 2:4:2 of the *AD Agreement*. The provision speaks of "comparison of a weighted average normal value with a weighed average of prices of all *comparable* export transactions. . . ." However, the Appellate Body would have none of it, holding that zeroing was entirely inconsistent with this provision.

Why? Characteristically, the Appellate Body began with the relevant text. Nothing in Article 2:4:2 — or any other provision of the WTO *Antidumping Agreement* — remotely suggests a two-stage process for a dumping margin calculation. Moreover, Article 2:4:2 is to be read in light of the basic definition of dumping in Article 2:1: "a *product* is to be considered as being dumped, *i.e.*, introduced into the commerce of another country at less than its normal value, if the export price of the *product* exported from one country to another is less than the comparable price, in the ordinary course of trade, for the like product when destined for consumption in the exporting country." Clearly from the text, a dumping margin is determined on a product-by-product basis, and there is no mandate to subdivide a product under investigation (subject merchandise) into different types or models. In fact, when it did so, the EC behaved hypocritically.

By the EC's own admission, in Commission Regulation (EC) No. 1069/97 of 12 June 1997 imposing a provisional AD duty on imports of cotton-type bed linen originating in Egypt, India and Pakistan, one product was at issue — "bed linen of cotton-type fibres." This product covered pure cotton bed linen, and bed linen of mixed cotton and man-made fiber. It also included bleached, dyed, or printed bed linen. And, significantly, the EC's definition of the subject merchandise included bed sheets, duvet covers, pillow cases, whether packaged as a set or sold separately. In other words, the EC had defined broadly the "product" at issue. The EC even proclaimed in its Regulation that "[n]otwithstanding the *different possible product types* due to different weaving construction, finish of the fabric, presentation and size, packing, etc., *all of them constitute a single product for the purpose of this proceeding* because they have the same physical characteristics and essentially the same use." Its decision, subsequently, to divide this single product into different types, and calculate a dumping margin for each type, was incongruous with its initial proclamation: either the products were comparable, in which case they could be grouped together for a single dumping margin calculation, or they were incomparable. The EC could not have it both ways.

The EC also acted unfairly when it set to zero any negative dumping margins. The plain language of the text of the *AD Agreement* — from which the Appellate Body never departed — is evident. Article 2:4:2 calls for a comparison of a weighted average Normal Value with a weighted average Export Price derived from "*all* comparable export transactions." Whereas the EC stressed the word "comparable," the Appellate Body laid emphasis on the word "all." By excluding the negative dumping margins, the EC did not establish an overall dumping margin on the basis of "all" comparable transactions — and they were comparable, because (again, by the EC's admission), they were one product. That exclusion, in turn, was unfair. Article 2:4, which is expressly referenced in the first sentence of Article 2:4:2, calls for a "fair comparison" of Normal Value and Export Price. How, opined the Appellate Body, could the EC's methodology be judged "fair" when it obviously caused the dumping margin to be inflated?

D. The American Judicial Response in the 2004 *Timken* Case

THE TIMKEN COMPANY v. UNITED STATES
United States Court of Appeals for the Federal Circuit
354 F.3d 1334-47 (2004)

PROST, CIRCUIT JUDGE.

Koyo Seiko Co., Ltd. and Koyo Corporation of U.S.A. (collectively, "Koyo") appeal the decision of the United States Court of International Trade . . . holding that the United States Department of Commerce ("Commerce") properly "zeroed" any negative dumping margins in calculating the weighted-average dumping margin applied to imports of Koyo's tapered roller bearings ("TRBs") from Japan. The Timken Company ("Timken") cross appeals arguing that Commerce, in calculating Koyo's constructed export price ("CEP"), improperly applied the adverse-facts-available rate to the entered value rather than the sales value of Koyo's TRBs. [Omitted is the discussion of the cross appeal.] Because we agree with the Court of International Trade that Commerce properly resolved both issues, we affirm.

I

. . . .

After calculating the dumping margins on the individual U.S. transactions subject to review, Commerce calculates the weighted-average dumping margin "by dividing the aggregate dumping margins determined for a specific exporter or producer by the aggregate . . . constructed export prices of such exporter or producer." . . . When calculating the weighted-average dumping margin, Commerce treats transactions that generate "negative" dumping margins (*i.e.*, a dumping margin with a value less than zero) as if they were zero. *See, e.g.*, *Serampore Indus. Pvt. Ltd. v. Dep't of Commerce*, 11 C.I.T. 866, 675 F. Supp. 1354, 1360-61 (Ct. Int'l Trade 1987). This practice is referred to as "zeroing." Finally, Commerce uses this weighted-average dumping margin to calculate the duties owed on an entry-by-entry basis. 19 U.S.C. § 1675(a)(2).

In this case Commerce initiated an administrative review of alleged sales of TRBs from Japan at less than fair value during the period of October 1, 1998, through September 30, 1999. . . . Based on its review, Commerce calculated preliminary dumping margins of 17.94% on TRBs greater than four inches in diameter and 14.86% on TRBs less than four inches in diameter. . . . Koyo exported both types of merchandise and thus became potentially liable for antidumping duties. . . . [In its briefs, Koyo questioned] . . . *inter alia*, Commerce's zeroing practice. . . .

. . . With respect to Koyo's challenge, Commerce noted that it properly calculated the weighted-average dumping margin by "zeroing" all negative-dumping-margin transactions. Commerce explained that its calculation methodology was derived from the explicit statutory language, and consistent with international obligations. . . . Consequently, it finalized Koyo's company-specific, weighted-average dumping margins. . . .

The Court of International Trade's review of Commerce's *Final Results* dealt with, *inter alia*: (1) Koyo's arguments that Commerce improperly "zeroed" negative dumping margins when calculating Koyo's weighted-average dumping margins, and (2) Timken's arguments that Commerce should have applied the adverse-facts-available rate to the sales value of Koyo's TRBs. . . . As to the first issue, Koyo primarily argued that Commerce's statutory interpretation was unreasonable in light of the World Trade Organization ("WTO") Appellate Body's interpretation of the *Antidumping Duty Agreement* ("*ADA*") in European *Communities — Antidumping Duties on Imports of Cotton-Type Bed Linen from India*, WT/DS/141/AB/R (Mar. 1, 2001) ("*EC — Bed Linen*"). . . . Rejecting the government's threshold argument that § 3512(c) barred Koyo's appeal, the Court of International Trade went on to note that it had previously affirmed zeroing as a reasonable interpretation of 19 U.S.C. § 1673. . . . It also distinguished the *EC — Bed Linen* report because it (1) did not address the U.S. practice of zeroing, and (2) dealt with an antidumping investigation rather than an administrative review. . . . Given that the statute requires Commerce to calculate dumping duties on an entry-by-entry approach and that previous cases determined that zeroing is a reasonable practice under the statute, the Court of International Trade found Commerce's zeroing practice reasonable. . . .

II

. . . .

A

On appeal, Koyo argues that Commerce acted unreasonably in zeroing negative-margin transactions. It contends this practice violates 19 U.S.C. § 1677b(a), which calls for a "fair comparison" of export price ("EP") or CEP and normal value. Koyo relies on the WTO Appellate Body's decision in *EC — Bed Linen*, holding that the practice of zeroing when calculating dumping margins is not a "fair comparison" between EP or CEP and normal value. Thus, because § 1677b(a) specifically implements the "fair comparison" requirements of Article 2.4 of the *ADA*, and because Commerce refused to interpret the statute in a manner consistent with U.S. international obligations by ignoring the holding in *EC — Bed Linen*, Koyo asks that we find that Commerce acted unreasonably in zeroing negative-margin transactions.

Timken and the United States respond that the plain meaning of the antidumping statute calls for Commerce to zero negative-margin transactions, and that the legislative history confirms this reading. Alternatively, even assuming that the statute contains an ambiguous instruction, Timken and the United States argue that Commerce reasonably interpreted the statute and deserves deference. Addressing Koyo's arguments relying on *EC — Bed Linen*, Timken and the United States reiterate the distinctions between that case and this case articulated by the Court of International Trade. Finally, Timken and the United States argue that 19 U.S.C. § 3512(c) and the *SAA* [*Statement of Administrative Action* accompanying the *1994 Uruguay Round Agreements Act*] bar Koyo from bringing this challenge, and that § 3533 precludes us from addressing the implementation of adverse WTO decisions.

We begin by addressing the government's argument that § 3512(c) bars Koyo from bringing this action. Section 3512(c) bars parties from bringing claims directly against the government on the ground that Commerce acted inconsistently with the *Uruguay Round Agreements Act ("URAA")*. 19 U.S.C. § 3512(c). As the Court of International Trade noted, however, Koyo brought this action under U.S. law under the assumption that it would be interpreted so as to avoid a conflict with international obligations. . . . We agree and find that § 3512(c) does not prevent us from addressing Koyo's appeal.

On the merits of Koyo's appeal, we apply a familiar two-part inquiry to determine whether to sustain an agency's interpretation of the statutory scheme it is charged with administering. *See Chevron, U.S.A., Inc. v. NRDC*, 467 U.S. 837, 842-43. . . (1984). First, we determine "whether Congress has directly spoken to the precise question at issue. If the intent of Congress is clear, that is the end of the matter; for the court, as well as the agency, must give effect to the unambiguously expressed intent of Congress." *Id*. "If the statute is silent or ambiguous with respect to the specific issue," however, "the question for the court is whether the agency's answer is based on a permissible construction of the statute." *Id*. at 843. . . . [T]herefore, we must determine whether the statute unambiguously requires providing for zeroing negative margin transactions and, if not, whether Commerce reasonably interpreted the statute to so require.

Turning to the words of the statute, 19 U.S.C. § 1677(35)(A) defines "dumping margin" as "the amount by which the normal value *exceeds* the export price or constructed export price of the subject merchandise." 19 U.S.C. § 1677(35)(A) (emphasis added). Timken and the United States both argue that the use of the word "exceeds" limits the definition of "dumping margin" to positive numbers. . . . [T]hey appropriately cite dictionaries. *Pesquera Mares Australes Ltda. v. United States*, 266 F.3d 1372, 1381 (Fed. Cir. 2001) ("In order to ascertain the established meaning of a [commonly used] term . . . it is appropriate to consult dictionaries."). These dictionaries define "exceeds" as "to be or go beyond (the given or supposed limit, measure, or quantity)," WEBSTER'S NEW TWENTIETH CENTURY DICTIONARY OF THE ENGLISH LANGUAGE UNABRIDGED 636 (2d ed. 1980), or "1. To be greater than; surpass. 2. To go beyond the limits of," THE AMERICAN HERITAGE COLLEGE DICTIONARY 477 (3d 1993).

Recognizing this as a close question, we are reluctant to find these dictionary definitions so clear as to compel a finding that Congress expressly intended to require zeroing. Even using the above "greater than" definitions, the statute does not plainly require consideration of only those dumping margins with a positive value. At least in a mathematical context, "exceeds" does not unambiguously preclude the calculation of a negative dumping margin. We thus disagree with the government's position that Congress deliberately used the word "exceeds" to avoid the calculation of negative dumping margins, instead of using the more open-ended phrase "difference between." Rather, the word "exceeds" could arguably allow for negative dumping margins because it guides the manner in which to set up the mathematical equation — x "exceeds" y = x-y. Similarly, the words "difference between" could arguably be construed as calling for the absolute value of the difference, a positive number — the "difference between" x and y = x-y. Finally, reviewing the legislative history as a whole, we disagree with Timken's argument that the relevant statements, or lack thereof, conclusively demonstrate Congress's adoption of definitions specifically requiring zeroing. Accordingly, we conclude that Congress's use of the word "exceeds" does not unambiguously require that dumping margins be positive numbers.

Because we find that the statute does not directly speak to the issue of negative-value dumping margins, we evaluate whether Commerce's interpretation is based on a permissible statutory construction. Under this second step of the *Chevron* analysis, "any reasonable construction of the statute is a permissible construction." *Torrington v. United States*, 82 F.3d 1039, 1044 (Fed. Cir. 1996). "To survive judicial scrutiny, [Commerce's] construction need not be the only reasonable interpretation or even the most reasonable interpretation. . . . Rather, a court must defer to an agency's reasonable interpretation of a statute even if the court might have preferred another." *Koyo Seiko Co. v. United States*, 36 F.3d 1565, 1570 (Fed. Cir. 1994) (citing *Zenith Radio Corp. v. United States*, 437 U.S. 443, 450, 57 L. Ed. 2d 337, 98 S. Ct. 2441 (1978)). Indeed, we have accorded particular deference to Commerce in antidumping determinations. . . .

We conclude Commerce based its zeroing practice on a reasonable interpretation of the statute. First, while the statutory definitions do not unambiguously preclude the existence of negative dumping margins, they do at a minimum allow for Commerce's construction. Basically, one number "exceeds" another if it is "greater than" the other, meaning it falls to the right of it on the number line. Here, because Commerce's zeroing practice is a reasonable interpretation of the statutory language, we do not question it in light of other reasonable possibilities.

Second, Commerce's methodology for calculating dumping margins makes practical sense. Commerce calculates dumping duties on an entry-by-entry basis. 19 U.S.C. § 1675(a)(2). Its practice of zeroing negative dumping margins comports with this approach. Borrowing Timken's example, suppose a foreign exporter sells the same product to two U.S. customers. The product has a normal value of $0.90, and is sold to the first customer for $1.00 and the second customer for $0.70. Calculated in accordance with § 1677(35)(A), the dumping margin for the first customer is zeroed (0.90 — 1.00 = -0.10 _ 0) and for the second customer is 0.20 (0.90 — 0.70 = 0.20). Assuming sales of 1000 units to each customer, the first customer would not have to pay any dumping duties because it paid a price above normal value, and the second customer would have to pay $200 (1000 transactions x 0.20 dumping margin/transaction =

200) because it paid a price below normal value. This approach makes sense; it neutralizes dumped sales and has no effect on fair-value sales. On the other hand, the approach urged by Koyo, whereby Commerce could not zero negative transactions, would essentially require Commerce to grant the first customer a credit. In the absence of offsetting sales below fair market value, however, Commerce could potentially owe the first customer a payment — a result clearly not contemplated by the statutory scheme.

Third, we note that the Court of International Trade has specifically addressed Commerce's zeroing practice and found it reasonable and in accordance with the law. See *Serampore*, 675 F. Supp. at 1360-61. . . . We find these decisions instructive for purposes of our analysis. Notably, both of these pre-*URAA* cases found zeroing to be a reasonable statutory interpretation given that it legitimately combats the problem of masked dumping, wherein certain profitable sales serve to "mask" sales at less than fair value. *Serampore*, 675 F. Supp. at 1360-61. . . . Although Koyo argues that these decisions addressed the law as it existed prior to the adoption of the *URAA's* "fair comparison" requirements, we find this argument unpersuasive. Neither the pre-*URAA* nor the current definitions unambiguously address the practice of zeroing. The *URAA*-incorporated "fair comparison" requirement, which simply applies to the calculation of normal value under § 1677b(a), does not change this result. The § 1677(35) definitions do, however, lend support to Commerce's statutory construction (as discussed above), even when considered in light of this new "fair comparison" requirement. According Commerce its proper deference, we hold that it reasonably interpreted § 1677(35)(A) to allow for zeroing.

We turn now to Koyo's argument that Commerce unreasonably interpreted § 1677(35) to allow for zeroing, beginning with a review of the WTO's *EC — Bed Linen* report upon which Koyo so heavily relies. *EC — Bed Linen* dealt with a trade dispute between the European Community ("EC") and India. *EC — Bed Linen*, WT/DS141/AB/R . . . . The EC, in investigating and levying duties on the importation of bed sheets from India, engaged in the practice of zeroing negative-margin transactions. . . . India brought an action at the WTO, claiming that the EC practice of zeroing violated Article 2.4.2 of the *ADA*. . . . The WTO Appellate Body evaluated the EC's practice in light of both this article and Article 2.4, which states that one must make a "fair comparison" between the EP or CEP and the normal value when calculating dumping margins. . . . It took the "fair comparison" language to mean that all transactions must be accounted for, whether creating positive or negative dumping margins. . . . Thus, because it was unfair to exclude negative-margin transactions, the WTO Appellate Body concluded that the EC practice of zeroing during an antidumping investigation was impermissible under the *ADA*. . . .

In light of the decision in *EC — Bed Linen*, Koyo asks us to interpret the "fair comparison" language in the U.S. antidumping statute in a manner consistent with U.S. international obligations, thereby adopting the holding in *EC — Bed Linen* and finding Commerce's zeroing practice an unreasonable statutory interpretation. The crux of its argument hinges on the *Charming Betsy* canon of claim construction, according to which courts should interpret

U.S. law, whenever possible, in a manner consistent with U.S. international obligations. *The Charming Betsy*, 6 U.S. (2 Cranch) 64, 118, 2 L. Ed. 208 (1804); *see also Fed. Mogul Corp. v. United States*, 63 F.3d 1572, 1581 (Fed. Cir. 1995) (noting that trade laws are not exempt from the *Charming Betsy* principle); *Luigi Bormioli Corp. v. United States*, 304 F.3d 1362, 1368 (Fed. Cir. 2002) ("The statute must be interpreted to be consistent with [international] obligations, absent contrary indications in the statutory language or its legislative history."). Koyo secondarily relies on its claim that the EC and United States have functionally identical practices that demand similar treatment. Because Commerce has the authority to bring its practice into conformity with U.S. international obligations, Koyo contends, we should find that it was unreasonable for Commerce to continue interpreting the antidumping statute in a non-conforming manner by allowing zeroing.

Koyo's reliance on the "fair comparison" language is misplaced. Section 1677b(a) requires a "fair comparison" as follows: "a fair comparison shall be made between the export price or constructed export price and normal value." . . . Thus, "in order to achieve a fair comparison with the export price or constructed export price," . . . the statute particularly sets out how to calculate "normal value." . . . We agree with the government's position that this is an exhaustive list, and that the "fair comparison" requirement upon which Koyo now relies is specifically defined in the normal-value-calculation instructions. As such, the "fair comparison" requirement of § 1677b(a) does not impose any requirements for calculating normal value beyond those explicitly established in the statute and does not carry over to create additional limitations on the calculation of dumping margins. The *SAA* supports our conclusion. . . . ("To achieve such a [fair] comparison, section 773 [§ 1677b] provides for the selection and adjustment of normal value to avoid or adjust for differences between sales which affect price comparability."). This court has also previously recognized that the explicit statutory adjustments help make a "fair, 'apples-to-apples' comparison" between normal value and EP or CEP. *Micron Tech., Inc. v. United States*, 243 F.3d 1301, 1313 (Fed. Cir. 2001) (quoting *Torrington Co. v. United States*, 68 F.3d 1347, 1352 (Fed. Cir. 1995)).

Further, even assuming that the "fair comparison" language in § 1677b(a) did not limit the analysis to calculating normal value using the statutorily-prescribed adjustments, we would nonetheless find Commerce's continued practice of zeroing reasonable in light of *EC — Bed Linen*. As Koyo acknowledges, the decision is not binding on the United States, much less this court. While Koyo relies on *EC — Bed Linen* for its persuasive value in an effort to convince us of the unreasonableness of Commerce's zeroing practice, we do not find it sufficiently persuasive to find Commerce's practice unreasonable. In light of the fact that Commerce's "longstanding and consistent administrative interpretation is entitled to considerable weight," *Zenith*, 437 U.S. at 450, we refuse to overturn the zeroing practice based on *EC — Bed Linen*.

Finally, we disagree with Koyo's assertion that the Court of International Trade erroneously distinguished *EC — Bed Linen*. . . . [T]he court distinguished *EC — Bed Linen* for two reasons: (1) it did not involve the United States, and (2) it dealt with an antidumping investigation as opposed to an administrative review of dumping. We agree with the Court of International

Trade and find the absence of the United States as a party to be an important distinction.

As to the difference between an investigation and an administrative review, Koyo contends that the distinction is irrelevant — Article 2.4.2 and Article 9.3.1, dealing with investigations and administrative reviews respectively, should be read together. In addition, Koyo argues, the "fair comparison" requirements of § 1677b(a) do not differ depending on the nature of the action. We disagree and find that the Court of International Trade properly distinguished the current case over *EC — Bed Linen*.

Because we find Commerce's zeroing practice to be a reasonable interpretation of the statute, even in light of the decision in *EC — Bed Linen*, we do not address the government's or Timken's arguments that this court is statutorily precluded from reconciling the two under 19 U.S.C § 3533.

E. WTO Zeroing Precedents

By no means did the WTO Appellate Body back down in the face of the 2004 *Timken* decision, nor did that decision dissuade WTO Members from bringing suit against the U.S. over zeroing. In a large number of cases, the Appellate Body ruled consistently — if incrementally — against zeroing. It did so in respect of Simple and Model Zeroing, and in virtually all contexts.[5] In essence, the key violations are:

1. Article 2:4 and 2:4:2 of the *Antidumping Agreement* —

In original investigations, zeroing does not yield a "fair comparison" of Normal Value of a foreign like product to Export Price of subject merchandise. The methodology artificially inflates the dumping margin, because it systematically disregards comparisons in which Export Price exceeds Normal Value.

2. Article 9:3 and 9:5 of the *Antidumping Agreement* and Article VI:2 of GATT —

In Administrative and New Shipper Reviews, zeroing systematically disregards instances in which Export Price exceeds Normal Value, which leads to an assessment of an AD duty that exceeds the actual margin of dumping for a particular exporter. The methodology leads to an artificial inflation of the dumping margin and consequent AD duty established based on that margin. The dumping margin established for an exporter is a ceiling on the total amount of AD duties that can be levied on subject merchandise from that exporter.

3. Article 11:3 of the *Antidumping Agreement* —

In Sunset Reviews, dumping margins calculated with zeroing do not provide a rigorous examination, yield reasoned and adequate conclusions supported by positive evidence, or have a sufficient factual basis.

Query whether there is anything defensible about zeroing, from an international legal perspective, save for its possible use in a targeted dumping case.

---

[5] A Table in the *Dictionary of International Trade Law* that accompanies this textbook summarizes WTO zeroing precedents.

IV. NON-MARKET ECONOMY STATUS

Suppose the home market of an exporter (or producer) of allegedly dumped merchandise is not a market economy. Such an economy is dubbed a "non-market economy" (NME). In computing Normal Value for the dumping margin, price data from an NME are either unavailable or unreliable. By definition, in an NME, prices are set not by market forces of supply and demand, but by government fiat — or, at least, the government plays a major role in establishing prices. It would be unfair to compare Export Price or Constructed Export Price against a non-market price, because these Prices are market-driven values. The comparison would be "unfair" because of the distinct origin and nature of the prices in the importing and exporting countries.

There are three issues arising with NMEs:

     i.   How is an NME defined?

     ii.   What proxy for Normal Value is used when subject merchandise originates in an NME?

     iii.   What are the practical consequences of NME treatment?

The answer to the first question is there are no standard rules in the WTO *Antidumping Agreement*, nor in GATT. Each WTO Member is more or less free to establish criteria for determining whether another Member merits NME treatment. At times, this issue is joined during the accession process. China is a case in point. In its November 1999 bilateral agreement with the U.S., it acquiesced to NME treatment for 15 years following its WTO accession. Vietnam is another illustration.

Interestingly, so too are Russia, Turkey, and Ukraine. In 2002, the EU agreed to grant Russia market-economy status, in November 2005, it did so with respect to Turkey, and the next month it gave this status to Ukraine. In its progress report for Turkey, it highlighted improvements in macroeconomic stabilization, public sector financial managements, banking regulation, and privatization. Yet, it admonished Turkey for not eliminating torture in jails, and called for further progress on acceptance of religious equality, freedom of expression, and rights of women and trade unions.

Applying somewhat different NME criteria from the EU, the U.S. did not follow suit immediately in respect of Russia or Ukraine. The DOC relies on 5 criteria to decide whether a country is a NME. They are:

     1.   *Currency*

Is the currency of the exporting country convertible?

     2.   *Wages*

Are wages in the exporting country determined by free bargaining between labor and management?

     3.   *Investment*

Does the exporting country permit foreign direct investment (FDI) in the country?

4. *Ownership*

To what extent does the government of the exporting country own productive assets and enterprises in that country?

5. *Control*

To what extent does the government of the exporting country control decisions by enterprises about allocating resources, the nature and quantity of output, and the prices of resources and output?

Notably, a DOC determination about NME status is not subject to judicial review.

As for the second question, the proxy used for Normal Value in an NME AD case is a third country. Theoretically, recourse to a third country in this instance is the same as it is when the home market of the exporter is not an NME, but the sales in that market are nonexistent, insufficient, or below cost of production. In both instances, the underlying problem is home market sales do not afford an adequate basis for comparison with Export Price or Constructed Export Price. Thus, in an NME case, a third country is used.

Specifically, to calculate Normal Value, an administering authority takes the factors of production employed in making subject merchandise, such as energy and other utilities, labor, land, human capital, physical capital, raw materials, other representative capital costs, and technology. However, the authority values them at prices in a market economy country. In addition, the authority includes an amount for general expenses, profits, and packing. There is some similarity, conceptually, between this calculation and the calculation of Constructed Value — both are "bottom up" calculations, except that all data in the Constructed Value computation are from the home market of the exporter.

How does the administering authority choose among possible third countries from which to obtain these prices? The authority considers two key factors:

- *Production*: What country is a significant producer of goods comparable to the subject merchandise?

- *Development*: What country is comparable in the level of economic development to the NME for which it would serve as a proxy?

Both criteria leave the authority with plenty of maneuvering room. What metrics define "significant" production? Must the goods be "like," or does mere comparability suffice? What indicators of development define a third country as comparable to the NME — economic variables like *per capita* Gross Domestic Product (GDP), or quality of life factors such as education enrollment and doctors per 100,000, or all of the above? Perhaps most importantly, do the answers to such questions change from NME to NME, and even over time with respect to a particular NME?

The DOC criteria for a NME provoke the third question, about practical effects. The answer many respondents give is hard-bitten, perhaps cynical. They suggest in NME AD cases, an administering authority essentially is free to "make up the numbers." What this comment means is it is easy to inflate Normal Value by choice of a third country, and thereby increase the likelihood of a final affirmative dumping margin determination. If the proxy for the NME is a high-cost country, such as Japan, then Normal Value is likely to be high, especially in comparison with low-cost places such as Indonesia.

Part Eight

REMEDIES AGAINST "UNFAIR" TRADE: COUNTERVAILING DUTY LAW

Chapter 33

HISTORICAL AND ECONOMIC FOUNDATIONS OF CVD LAW

We look upon our epoch as a time of troubles, an age of anxiety. The grounds of our civilization, of our certitude, are breaking up under our feet, and familiar ideas and institutions vanish as we reach for them, like shadows in the falling dusk.

—ARTHUR M. SCHLESINGER, JR., THE VITAL CENTER 1 (1949)

DOCUMENTS SUPPLEMENT ASSIGNMENT

1. *Havana Charter* Articles 25-28, 34
2. GATT Articles VI, XVI
3. WTO *SCM Agreement*
4. U.S. *Statement of Administrative Action* for the *SCM Agreement*

I. THE DEFINITION OF "SUBSIDY"

A. The Problem of Scope

The threshold problem in countervailing duty (CVD) law is defining the term "subsidy." As a theoretical matter, the starting point is the economic concept of a subsidy, which is a "benefit conferred on a firm or product by action of a government."[1] The difficulty with this definition is its potential scope. Read literally, the definition includes activities typically provided by virtually every government in the world: police and fire protection; infrastructure development (*e.g.*, roads, power plants); technological development (*e.g.*, telecommunications), and primary and secondary educational instruction.

These activities confer a benefit on a foreign exporter (or producer) because they reduce its costs. The exporter need not pay (or not pay as much) for its own security and fire officials, basic infrastructure and technology, and training of workers (though it pays for these benefits indirectly through taxes, some of which may be used to fund the subsidy). The same difficulty exists under a different economic approach to defining a subsidy: any cost incurred by or imposed on the granting government. Focusing on cost to define "subsidy" still is overly broad. It includes routine activities every government performs. Also, this focus is misplaced: what should matter is not whether the subsidizing government incurs a cost, but whether the subsidized exporter benefits.

---

[1] JOHN H. JACKSON, THE WORLD TRADING SYSTEM 261 (1989) (citation omitted); *see also id.* at 262-264.

Not surprisingly, therefore, economic approaches to the definition of "subsidy" are of little practical use in CVD law. If that law incorporates a broad economic conception of a subsidy, then an enormous array of foreign government programs will be countervailable. In turn, foreign governments might retaliate by imposing CVDs of their own on central or sub-central government programs. After all, no government wants — or should be required to — give up its ability to support police and fire protection, infrastructural and technological development, and educational services.

In other words, the result of defining "subsidy" in a broad manner that conforms with economic theory would be a deadlock created by (1) exporting countries that use subsidies to further legitimate public policy goals, and (2) importing countries that retaliate against these subsidies with CVDs designed to level the playing field on which domestic producers of a like product must compete with subsidized imports. Virtually every country would fall into both camps: it would retain its subsidy programs, and it would countervail foreign subsidy programs. The multilateral trading system would be highly contentious, and the deadlock might undermine efforts at trade liberalization.

Unfortunately, GATT provides no help in defining the term "subsidy." The term is used blithely in several provisions of Articles VI and XVI. Nowhere in Article VI or XVI (or any other GATT provision) does a definition of "subsidy" or "subsidization" appear. Equally troublesome is the fact Articles VI and XVI are rather generic and to some extent hortatory. Thus, they impose no meaningful discipline on subsidies.

B. Financial Contribution

Given the definitional void in GATT, Article 1 of the Uruguay Round *Agreement on Subsidies and Countervailing Measures (SCM Agreement)* is a welcome development. The definition contains two critical concepts, namely, "financial contribution" and "benefit," that help determine what governmental activities are subsidies. Moreover, the Article 1:1 definition leads to two key devices that help delineate subsidies against which CVD action may be taken from subsidies that are non-actionable. These devices, are a specificity test and a scheme for categorizing subsidies known as the "Traffic Light System." These devices, along with the definition of a "subsidy" as a "financial contribution" that "confers a benefit" are implemented into U.S. CVD law as a result of the *1994 Uruguay Round Agreements Act.*[2]

The definition of "subsidy" in Article 1:1 of the *SCM Agreement* indicates a government program is not a subsidy and, therefore, is not countervailable, unless the government is providing a "financial contribution" to an exporter, producer, group of exporters or producers, industry, group of industries, or to private economic agents in general. Critically, the contribution may be made by "a government or any public body" within that government's territory. Whether the government provides the contribution directly or though an intermediary, including a private body, is irrelevant.

---

[2] *See* 19 U.S.C. § 1677(5A) (concerning specificity, export subsidies, import substitution subsidies, and domestic subsidies), (5B) (concerning non-countervailable subsidies).

In this respect, the language "entrusts or directs" in the Article 1:1 definition, and implemented into U.S. law, is noteworthy. As legislative history to the *1994 Act* makes clear, this language is to be "interpreted broadly to prevent the 'indirect' provision of a subsidy from becoming a harmful loophole to effective enforcement of the countervailing duty law."[3] Accordingly, the U.S. Department of Commerce (DOC) expectedly continues its pre-Uruguay Round practices, evident in famous cases like *Certain Softwood Lumber Products from Canada*, of countervailing alleged foreign government subsidy programs provided through private parties.[4]

What, then, is a "financial contribution"? The Article 1:1 definition of "subsidy" specifies four government practices that constitute a "financial contribution."

i. A direct transfer of funds, such as an equity infusion, loan, or grant, from the government to a firm. This practice is the most obvious type of "financial contribution." But, a potential direct transfer of funds from the government, such as a loan guarantee or assumption of liabilities, also is a "financial contribution."

ii. Foregone or uncollected government revenue, such as a tax credit or tax abatement. For example, the practice of many states and localities to lure business by offering these sorts of tax incentives are clearly "financial contributions." Indeed, it is rather curious why this practice has not caused greater controversy. One reason may be that foreign companies investing in the U.S. often are the beneficiaries of these "financial contributions," and thus foreign governments are hesitant to complain as long as all of the companies from their country have equal access to them along with American competitors. Another likely reason is until a subsidized product is exported, there is no occasion to initiate a CVD proceeding, because no injury from imports yet exists.

iii. Government provision of goods or services other than general infrastructure may be a "financial contribution." Suppose a government provides components at a below-market price that are used to manufacture a finished product. The manufacturer is receiving a "financial contribution" (measured by the reduction from the market price).

iv. Purchase of goods by a government from a firm may be a "financial contribution." Suppose a government buys a finished product from the manufacturer at an above-market price. Plainly, the government is providing the manufacturer with a "financial contribution" (measured by the excess over market price). Likewise, a government scheme to support the income of a firm, or the price of a firm's output, which has the effect of stimulating exports or reducing imports, is a "financial contribution."

Of course, to impose a CVD, it is not enough that a foreign government provide a "financial contribution." Were it sufficient, then any subsidy could

---

[3] SENATE COMMITTEE ON FINANCE, SENATE COMMITTEE ON AGRICULTURE, NUTRITION, AND FORESTRY, AND SENATE COMMITTEE ON GOVERNMENTAL AFFAIRS, URUGUAY ROUND AGREEMENTS ACT, SENATE REPORT NUMBER 412, 103d Congress, 2d Sess. 88, 91 (1994) [hereinafter SENATE REPORT].

[4] *See id.* at 91; HOUSE COMMITTEE ON WAYS AND MEANS, URUGUAY ROUND AGREEMENTS ACT, HOUSE OF REPRESENTATIVES REPORT NUMBER 826, 103d Congress, 2d Sess. 107, 108-09 (1994)

be countervailed. To make a CVD lawful, the contribution must confer a benefit on a specific recipient.

C. Benefit Conferred

Unfortunately, neither the Uruguay Round *SCM Agreement* nor United States CVD law defines expressly the concept of "benefit." Individual WTO Members have some discretion in tailoring their law on when a "benefit" results from a financial contribution. There remains considerable opportunity for WTO panels to develop a body of jurisprudence on this issue.

However, Article 14 of the *SCM Agreement* provides some useful guidance on the issue. It contains four examples of when a benefit is conferred:

1. *Equity capital infusions*:

As Article 14(a) indicates, a "benefit" is conferred where a government provides equity or capital to a recipient that is "inconsistent with the usual investment practice . . . of private investors." The degree of inconsistency is a measure of the value of the benefit.

2. *Loans*:

As Article 14(b) indicates, a "benefit" is conferred when a government provides a loan on more favorable terms than the recipient-borrower could obtain for a comparable loan from a commercial bank. In particular, there is a "benefit" if there is a difference between the amount a borrower (1) pays on the loan from the government, and (2) would pay on a comparable loan from a commercial bank. The value of the benefit conferred equals the difference between these two amounts.

3. *Loan guarantees*:

As Article 14(c) indicates, a "benefit" is conferred on the recipient-borrower if a government provides a loan guarantee that allows the borrower to obtain more favorable terms on a loan from a commercial bank that is guaranteed by the government than the borrower would obtain on a comparable loan from the commercial bank without the government guarantee. That is, a benefit exists if there is a difference between the amount (*i.e.*, surely the total amount, including principal, interest, and fees) the borrower receiving the guarantee (1) pays on the guaranteed loan, and (2) would pay on a comparable loan from a commercial bank absent the guarantee. The benefit conferred equals the difference between these two amounts.

4. *Provision of goods or services*:

As Article 14(d) indicates, a "benefit" is conferred if a government provides goods and services to a recipient for less than adequate remuneration, or purchases goods and services from the recipient for more than adequate remuneration. In other words, if a government provides goods or services at a below-market price, a "benefit" is conferred. The value of the "benefit" equals the difference between (1) the price the government charges for the goods or services and (2) the market price for those same goods or services. Similarly, if a government buys goods or services supplied by a company at an inflated price, then the measurement of the "benefit" is the difference between what the government pays and the prevailing market price for those goods or services.

U.S. CVD law tracks these same four examples. (*See* 19 U.S.C. § 1677(5).) In studying the examples, consider the advantages and disadvantages of the methodology or methodologies an administering authority uses, or should use, to measure the amount of benefit conferred. Is the private sector the best benchmark in all instances?

This list does not expressly state it is non-exclusive, but that is a reasonable reading of Article 14. Moreover, the relevant *Statement of Administrative Action* refers to the Article 14 list as a set of "guidelines," and the U.S. CVD statute uses the word "including" before presenting the list. Hence, there may well be other financial contributions that confer a "benefit" that do not fit neatly within the four examples.

D.   The Specificity Test

Having identified a "subsidy" in the sense of a governmental financial contribution that "confers a benefit," it becomes necessary to consider whether that "subsidy" is directed specifically to certain beneficiaries. Not every "subsidy" is or should be countervailable because governments have a legitimate interest in supporting certain activities, like police and fire services, infrastructure development, and educational services. The Specificity Test in Article 1:2 and 8:1(a) of the *SCM Agreement* (and U.S. CVD law, in 19 U.S.C. § 1677(5)(A), (5A)) is indispensable in delineating lawful (*i.e.*, non-countervailable) from unlawful (*i.e.*, countervailable) subsidies.

The Specificity Test, which is not new in CVD jurisprudence, checks to ensure whether a subsidy is provided to certain enterprises.

> As the Court of International Trade (CIT) made clear in 1983 in the *Carlisle Tire* case, the basic purpose of the specificity test is to serve as a means for differentiating between government assistance that genuinely is available broadly and used widely throughout an economy and subsidies provided to or used by discrete segments of the economy. Thus, while the specificity test is intended to avoid the imposition of countervailing duties in situations where a subsidy is widely available and used throughout an economy, it must not be allowed to serve as a means for avoiding the imposition of duties in other circumstances. The [Senate Finance] Committee welcomes and supports the intention of the Administration, as set out in the *Statement of Administrative Action* [for the *SCM Agreement*], to apply the specificity test "in light of its original purpose, which is to function as an initial screening mechanism to winnow out only those foreign subsidies which truly are broadly available and widely used throughout an economy."[5]

The Specificity Test helps mediate the tension between the legitimate interest of exporting countries to subsidize certain projects and the legitimate interest of importing countries to assure a level competitive playing field for their domestic producers.

---

[5] SENATE REPORT, *supra* note 3, at 92-93.

Accordingly, to be countervailable, a subsidy must be "specific" to an enterprise, industry, or group of enterprises or industries. Conversely, suppose government assistance is both generally available and widely and evenly distributed throughout the jurisdiction of the subsidizing authority. Then, it is not countervailable. Article 2:4 of the *SCM Agreement* requires a specificity determination to be "clearly substantiated on the basis of positive evidence." Thus, contrary to pre-Uruguay Round DOC practice, there is a presumption of non-specificity.

What economic rationale justifies the Specificity Test? In general, a subsidy that is generally available is less likely to create distortions in trade and output patterns than a subsidy that is specific to exporters. Consider, for example, a case where the German government wants to improve economic conditions in the former East Germany. It provides a subsidy to any German company that builds a factory in the former East Germany so long as the factory employs at least 100 workers for 5 years. The subsidy covers the extra costs associated with building a factory in that location, such as roads, extensions of water, sewage, and natural gas pipes, and additional power generation stations. Because the subsidy is available to a company regardless of the type of merchandise it manufactures and regardless of whether it exports its output, no distortion in the pattern of Germany's output or exports should occur, nor should there be any adverse effects on a foreign country.

In this hypothetical, suppose as a matter of practice the subsidy is used only by exporters of certain merchandise. There still may be trade distortive effects. The German government — or any clever drafter of a subsidy program — could make the subsidy generally available, but attach conditions that make it useful only to some exporters. This supposition intimates the need to recognize — and obliterate — any distinction between *de jure* and *de facto* specificity. Both sorts of specific subsidies ought to be actionable. Fortunately, this distinction is explicit in the *SCM Agreement* (and U.S. CVD law).

The Specificity Test works in tandem with the Traffic Light System (discussed in a later Chapter), which places subsidies into one of three categories: (1) "Red Light," or prohibited, subsidies, which are countervailable; (2) "Yellow Light" or "Dark Amber" subsidies, which are collectively called "actionable" subsidies, and which may be countervailed; and (3) "Green Light," or non-actionable subsidies, which (while the category existed) could not be countervailed.

II. NEOCLASSICAL ECONOMIC ANALYSIS OF SUBSIDIES

A. Welfare Effects of a Domestic Production Subsidy

For sound economic reasons, the *SCM Agreement* takes a harder line against export subsidies (and import subsidies) than it does against production subsidies. This "line" is drawn between Part II of the *SCM Agreement* (Articles 3-4) and Part III of the *Agreement* (Articles 5-7). Part II defines "Prohibited" or "Red Light Subsidies" as export (and import substitution) subsidies. Part III defines "Actionable" or "Yellow Light" and "Dark Amber" subsidies. There is an irrebuttable presumption a Red Light subsidy causes an adverse effect

— namely, (1) material injury or threat of material injury, (2) nullification or impairment of GATT benefits, or (3) serious prejudice to the interests of another WTO Member. Accordingly, a CVD may be imposed without needing to show a Red Light subsidy causes an adverse effect. In contrast, a complainant alleging a measure is an Actionable subsidy does not benefit from this presumption, and must show an adverse effect to countervail the subsidy. Not surprisingly, a large number of hard-fought battles in CVD cases are over whether a measure is or is not a Red Light subsidy.

Conceptually, why does the *SCM Agreement* take a hard line against Red Light subsidies? The answer is the welfare effects of export subsidies in comparison with domestic production subsidies. In short, export subsidies are more trade-distorting than non-export subsidies. Indeed, export subsidies are the most trade-distorting of any support measure. That is their purpose, *i.e.*, to alter from free trade equilibrium the pattern of exports or imports, or the world market price, in a particular market for goods (or, presumably, services). In this respect, the term "trade distorting" is a positive concept. But, it also has a normative dimension. "Distortions" arise in connection with the welfare effects of a support measure, and the welfare costs of an export subsidy are worse than those from a production subsidy. Graph 33-1 shows the welfare effects of a domestic production subsidy.

The hypothetical example is the market for rice, and Graph 33-1 portrays that market in Thailand. By assumption, the Thai rice market is competitive. Hence, the Supply and Demand Curves slope upward and downward, respectively. An additional assumption in the neoclassical economic analysis of a domestic production subsidy concerns the size of the subsidizing country. In the example, Thailand is assumed to an important producer of rice. Therefore, its exported output could affect the world market price.

To appreciate fully this and other Graphs, recall the following economic principles:

1. *Demand Curve*:

The line slopped downward to the right represents total demand for a good, whether that good is manufactured domestically or imported. The line slopped upward and to the right is the supply of that good as manufactured by domestic producers. Thus, the two lines depict a product market in a particular importing country.

The Demand Curve captures the various quantities of an imported good and domestic like product that consumers in the country are ready, willing, and able to buy at alternative prices. There is an inverse relationship between quantity demanded, measured on the horizontal or "X" axis, and price, gauged on the vertical or "Y" axis. This inverse relationship reflects the common sense idea that *ceteris paribus*, *i.e.*, all other factors held constant, consumers buy more of a good as the price at which they can purchase it falls.

2. *Consumer Surplus*:

The area underneath the demand line (*i.e.*, to the left and toward the origin of the Graph, "0"), bounded by the equilibrium price of the product, represents "Consumer Surplus." If, for example, that price is P^{WFT}, then Consumer Surplus is the triangular area demarcated by the points P^{WFT}, M, and N, because consumers whose preferences are embodied in the Demand line between points M and N are ready, willing, and able to pay a price for the product higher than P^{WFT}. The fact they need pay only P^{WFT} means they save money, or in economic jargon, obtain a "surplus."

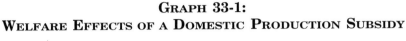

GRAPH 33-1:
WELFARE EFFECTS OF A DOMESTIC PRODUCTION SUBSIDY

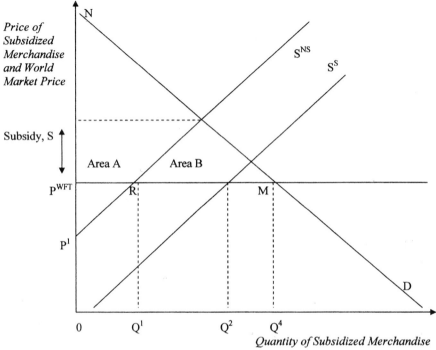

Suppose the price falls from P^{WFT} to some lower level, such as P^1. Then, this surplus would expand accordingly. That would occur because more consumers — reflected in the Demand Curve between a points corresponding to P^{WFT} and the new, lower price level — enter in the market for the product. These consumers start purchasing the product (again, either the imported item or the domestic like product) at the lower price, which is less than the price they would be willing to pay for it (as shown by the higher prices corresponding to the points on the Demand Curve between P^{WFT} and the lower price level). What might cause the price decline from P^{WFT} to P^1? One answer is a subsidy provided by an exporting country's government to companies in manufacturing the product in the foreign country.

1. *Supply Curve (Domestic, Upward Sloping)*:

A Supply Curve illustrates the various quantities of a domestic like product that producers located in the importing country are ready, willing, and able to manufacture at alternative price levels. There is a direct relationship between quantity supplied (also measured on the horizontal axis) and price (again, gauged on the vertical axis). It is based on the common sense idea that *ceteris paribus*, producers will make more of a good as the price at which they can sell the good rises. Significantly, the upward sloping Supply line does not include imported merchandise.

2. *Supply Curve (World, Horizontal)*:

Sometimes, a Supply Curve is depicted as a horizontal line emanating from the vertical (Y) axis. (The Graph later showing welfare effects of export subsidies is an instance.) This line shows supply of imported merchandise. It is horizontal because of an implicit assumption: the importing country is a "price taker." That is, the country cannot affect the world market price of the product. It is not a large enough producer of that product, nor is the product market characterized by monopoly, oligopoly, or other forms of imperfect competition that would translate into an upward sloped world supply line. In other words, the product market is a globally competitive one.

3. *Producer Surplus*:

The area above the supply line (*i.e.*, to the left and away from the origin, "0") is "Producer Surplus" for domestic manufacturers. If the price of the output they sell is P^{WFT}, then their Surplus is demarcated by the points P^{WFT}, R, and P^1. The domestic producers whose interests are embodied on the supply line between points P^1 and R are ready, willing, and able to manufacture and sell the good for a price below P^{WFT}. But, in fact, they receive P^{WFT} when they sell the good. The difference between the price they would have accepted, and the price they obtained, is surplus to them.

What happens if the price falls from P^{WFT} to a price between P^{WFT} and P^1. Producer Surplus declines accordingly. Many domestic producers (specifically, the ones embodied on the Supply Curve between point R and a point corresponding to the lower price level) are not ready, willing, or able to manufacture at the lower price. They are knocked out of the market. Why might the price decline? Again, a foreign government might subsidize merchandise that competes with output of domestic producers.

The support measure at issue is a payment by the Thai government to rice farmers. It is a production subsidy available only to domestic producers, and excepted from the GATT Article III:4 national treatment principle by Article III:8(b). As a practical matter, the Thai subsidy payments could be linked to output, such as 40 baht (about U.S. $1) per kilo of rice produced. Alternatively, the government could fund shifting land from the cultivation of other crops to rice paddy, possibly with the amount of funds disbursed linked to the amount of land re-allocated to rice production (*e.g.*, 4,000 baht per hectare).

Significantly, Thai farmers are eligible for the subsidy whether or not they export their output. (The fact exporters, as well as other beneficiaries, receive a subsidy is enough to qualify the subsidy as export contingent, and thus a Red Light export subsidy under Article 3:1(a) of the *SCM Agreement*. For now, the point is simply the payments are not, in an economic sense, tied directly to exportation.) Also, the payment is not a "set aside," *i.e.*, it is not a payment to cut rice production or take paddy fields out of cultivation. A production-limiting payment, or support de-coupled from production, would not generate the boost in output shown by the Graph.

Before the government in Bangkok intervenes in the domestic rice market with a production subsidy, the prevailing price for rice is P^{WFT}. It is a world market price ("W" stands for "World", and "FT" for "Free Trade.") Next, the Thai government pays the subsidy, S, to rice farmers. As the Graph shows, provision of the subsidy does not change this price. Because there is no change in the price Thai families pay for rice, there is no change in consumer surplus (the area beneath the demand curve down to the price level, which signifies the positive difference between the amount a family is willing and able to pay for rice versus what it actually has to pay).

Predictably, Thai farmers respond by increasing their output of rice, from Q^1 to Q^2. That is the goal of a production subsidy. In effect, the domestic supply of rice shifts outward (to the right) from Supply NS (where "NS" stands for "No Subsidy") to Supply S (where "S" stands for "Subsidy"). The vertical distance between S^{NS} and S^S is the amount of the subsidy. Intuitively, the Supply Curve shifts because the subsidy reduces the average and marginal costs of production. (This response depends on the *ceteris paribus* assumption, *i.e.*, all other relevant variables are unchanged.) There are two obvious welfare consequences:

1.   *Producer Surplus*:

Producer surplus (the area above a supply curve up to the price suppliers received, which denotes the revenue producers obtain above and beyond what they require in order to produce) increases by the area A.

2.   *Government Expenditures*:

Government spending equal the amount of the subsidy, S, multiplied by the output subsidized, which is the difference between Q^2 and the origin, 0. The area A + B shows this transfer to Thai rice farmers.

The net welfare effect is a cost to Thailand, area B. Whereas area A is a pure transfer of Thai taxpayer funds to farmers, area B is a dead weight loss from production inefficiency. The subsidy is an artificially alters the incentives farmers have to deploy land, physical capital, technology, as well as their own labor and human capital, tipping them toward rice production and away from other pursuits.

In a legal dispute, the fact the price of a good is unaffected by a subsidy measure could be critical. It would mean the subsidy does not suppress or depress the world market price, either of which is an adverse effect, namely, serious prejudice, under Article 6 of the *SCM Agreement*. Accordingly, some other adverse effect would have to be proven in order to countervail the subsidy.

Finally, the Graph — when juxtaposed with the welfare effects of a tariff — shows why mainstream economists counsel in favor of an output subsidy over a tariff as a form of government intervention. If there has to be government intervention to help domestic producers, then it ought not to be a tariff. A subsidy does not affect equilibrium domestic consumer prices or consumption levels, but a tariff raises prices, leading to reduced consumption opportunities. Put succinctly, a subsidy is a less inefficient means of boosting output than a tariff, because it intervenes only on the supply side of a market. A tariff has repercussions for both supply and demand sides.

Why, then, do governments resort to tariffs — and, for that matter, quotas? One answer is tariffs (but not quotas) raise money for governments. (Quotas raise no funds for the government, but lead to rents for quota license holders, and consumers tend to view a quota as costless.) Some governments, especially in poor countries with inchoate or corrupt tax systems, rely for a large proportion of their revenue on tariffs. These facts lead to a second answer. A subsidy costs a government money. A third reason concerns a potential benefit of a subsidy. Depending on the nature and amount of a production subsidy, it could lead to lower domestic prices. However, consumers do not necessarily understand this benefit, or if they do, they might not champion it over the expenditure it entails. Finally, a domestic industry might feel politically uncomfortable about receiving a subsidy from the government, especially if the handout is subject to transparent scrutiny through the process of formulating the government's budget. A tariff may be a relatively quieter way of getting the competitive boost sought.

B.   Welfare Effects of an Export Subsidy

Graph 33-2 depicts the effects of an export subsidy. To continue the example from the preceding section — the rice market in Thailand, with the assumptions this market is competitive, and that Thailand is big enough to affect the world price for rice — suppose the government in Bangkok decides to pay a subsidy of 40 baht (approximately U.S. $1) per kilo of rice. This subsidy is paid only for rice grown in and exported from Thailand, not for Thai rice sold domestically. This kind of subsidy is a crude cash payment. There are many kinds of subtle, indirect, or *de facto* export subsidies, some of which are provided by central governments, and others by provincial or local authorities.

The critical point to unlock Graph 33-2 is to appreciate the incentive created for Thai rice farmers by an export subsidy. Because these farmers get paid the 40 baht per kilo only if they export rice, they divert some of their output from sales to domestic consumers, and toward foreign customers. That is, paddy they would have dedicated to Thai sales they re-allocate, for example, to American consumers. The farmers even expand total output, by dedicating more land to paddy fields, or cultivating existing fields more intensively. They sell this extra output overseas. (Observe this response depends on the *ceteris paribus* assumption, *i.e.*, all other relevant variables are unchanged.)

Consequently, Thailand exports more rice than it did before implementing the export subsidy. In turn, rice prices in Thailand drift (or shoot) upward, because of the diversion of rice production from the domestic to overseas markets. But, rice prices overseas — the world market price — could fall. There could be (in the terms of the *SCM Agreement*) price depression. This adverse effect, a form of serious prejudice, would occur if Thailand is a big enough player in the world rice market that its extra rice exports have an appreciable impact on prices. (In fact, Thailand, Vietnam, and California are the world's largest rice producers.) Used in the nontechnical sense, the export subsidy could lead to "dumping" of rice by Thailand on the world market. Even if Thailand is not so large a player, there could be price suppression, as the *SCM Agreement* puts it, which is another form of adverse effect. It means prices cannot rise owing to the subsidy.

Graph 33-2 shows these price movements. The initial world market rice price with free trade is P^{WFT} (where "W" is for "World" and "FT" is for "Free Trade"). This price prevails with no government intervention. At this price, Thai farmers produce Q^1 kilos of rice, and Thai families buy Q^2 kilos. The farmers export their surplus production, which is the difference between Q^2 and Q^1. When the administration in Bangkok promulgates the subsidy, Thai rice farmers respond to the incentive as described. The domestic price of rice, P^D (where "D" stands for "Domestic") rises, and the price on the world market, P^S (where "S" stands for "Subsidy"), falls. The difference between P^D and P^S is the amount of the subsidy, 40 baht per kilo. the rise in the domestic rice price, P^D, is less than the full subsidy amount, because the fall in the rice price in foreign markets is to P^S.

Thai farmers get paid P^D — if they export rice, then they earn P^S from foreign buyers, plus the government subsidy amount. (That is, Thai farmers are willing to accept the lower export price, P^S, because their government makes up the difference between it and the higher domestic price, P^D.) If they sell rice domestically, then they get paid P^D from Thai customers, because the rice price in Thailand is elevated due to the constriction of domestic supply caused by diversion of output to foreign markets. Accordingly, with price PD, Thai rice farmers expand output to Q^4. But, fewer Thai families can afford the higher rice price associated with the export subsidy regime. So, they curtail consumption to Q^3. The gap $Q^1 - Q^3$ is sales diverted abroad. In brief, the increase in Thai rice production from Q^2 to Q^4, coupled with the decrease in Thai rice consumption from Q^1 to Q^2, generate a larger exportable surplus than existed without the subsidy.

The large areas denoted by capital letters on the Graph symbolize the welfare effects of an export subsidy.

1. *Consumer Surplus:*

Consumer surplus in Thailand falls by the amount A + B. Some Thai families are less well off than before. As represented by points on the Demand Curve, fewer families benefit from the gap between P^D and what they are willing and able, as represented by points on the Demand Curve, than the gap between P^{WFT} and that Curve.

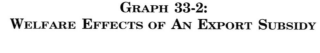

GRAPH 33-2:
WELFARE EFFECTS OF AN EXPORT SUBSIDY

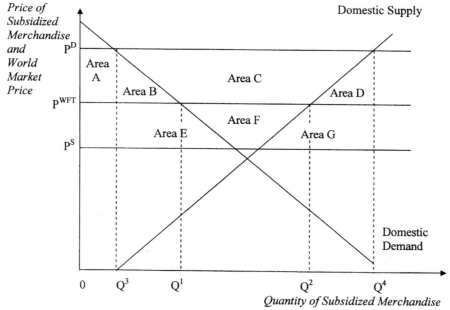

2. *Producer Surplus*:

Producer surplus rises by the amount A + B + C. At P^D, there are more Thai farmers earning above the minimum amount at which they would be willing and able to cultivate rice, as depicted by points on the Supply Curve.

3. *Government Expenditures*:

The Thai government must pay the subsidy on the amount of rice exported. The amount it transfers to farmers is B + C + G + E + F, which equals the amount of the subsidy (P^D — P^S) multiplied by the quantity exported (Q^4 — Q^3).

The net welfare effect is the difference between producer gain and losses to consumers and Thai government, *i.e.*, the area B + D + E + F + G. It is a net loss reflecting:

4. *Production and Consumption Distortions*:

Area B + D is the distortion to consumption and production patterns the export subsidy causes. Area B signifies the diminution in consumption opportunities. But for the subsidy, Thai families would not have to decrease rice consumption from Q^1 to Q^3. Area D bespeaks the rising marginal cost of Thai rice production. That marginal cost exceeds what consumers in other countries pay for Thai rice. Area D shows the inefficient allocation of Thai factors of production to rice paddy. But for the subsidy, the labor, land, human capital, physical capital, and technology Thailand dedicates to expanding rice production from Q^2 to Q^4 would be used in some other endeavor. The consumption and production distortions areas B + D represent are akin to the losses resulting from a tariff.

5. *Terms of Trade (TOT) Effect*:

This effect is different from the instance of a tariff (except in the rare case of an "optimal tariff"). Area E + F + G shows the effect of the export subsidy on the TOT. Insofar as the export subsidy depresses the world market price for rice, from P^{WFT} to P^S, Thailand's TOT (the ratio of its export to import prices) worsen.

To be sure, foreign consumers benefit from a world market price decline — unless their governments impose a CVD. Still, for the exporting country, an export subsidy unequivocally yields costs over benefits. Also, the world price drop hurts rice producers in countries other than Thailand. Therein is an adverse effect under the *SCM Agreement*.

III. NEOCLASSICAL ECONOMIC ANALYSIS OF A CVD

What are the welfare effects of offsetting a foreign government subsidy with a CVD? From a neoclassical economic perspective, the short answer is they are no different from imposing a tariff. More precisely, a CVD is simply a duty on top of the MFN (or otherwise applicable) tariff. Hence, the welfare analysis is the same as increasing a tariff rate. In turn, it is not difficult to appreciate why neoclassical economists look askance at CVDs. Graph 33-3 demonstrates the analysis.

The critical point to appreciate about Graph 33-3 is it portrays the market in the importing country — the country imposing the CVD — for the good (or service) subsidized by a foreign government. It does not depict the effect of the CVD on foreign producers or exporters. Suppose the importing country is the U.S., which decides to countervail a Thai rice subsidy. The Graph shows the effect of the CVD on American consumers of rice, American rice farmers (in California, in particular, which itself is one of the largest rice producing regions in the world), and the U.S. government.

As Graph 33-3 shows, welfare effects of a tariff and CVD are the same. Like a tariff, a CVD lifts the price of subsidized imported goods (subject merchandise) up to its pre-subsidized price. The lift to this level assumes the CVD fully offsets the subsidy, and is not a partial offset in accordance with an EU-style "Lesser Duty Rule" to impose just enough of a CVD to counteract a subsidy. The CVD causes a loss of consumer surplus that outweighs the gain in producer surplus and CVD revenue accrued by the importing country government. The Table below summarizes these results.

The price P^{US} is an unsubsidized price (with "US" meaning "unsubsidized"), while P^S is a subsidized price (with "S" for "Subsidized"). If a foreign government pays a subsidy, directly or indirectly, to farmers or processors of a commodity, or manufacturers of a product located in the territory over which the government has jurisdiction, then those farmers, processors, or manufacturers can sell their output — both in their home market and in overseas markets — at a lower price than they are able to without the subsidy. That certainly could be the case with a Thai rice export subsidy.

GRAPH 33-3:
WELFARE EFFECTS OF IMPOSING A CVD

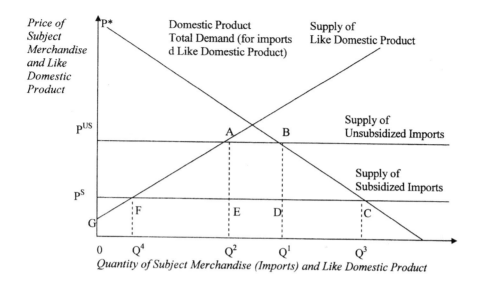

Hence, P^S and its corresponding supply line are beneath PUS and its corresponding supply line. As a result of the subsidy, Consumer Surplus expands by the area $P^{US}BCP^S$, *i.e.*, from P^SCQ^30 (at the unsubsidized price P^{US}) to $P^{US}BCQ^30$ (at the subsidized price P^S). However, Producer Surplus falls by the area $P^{US}AFP^S$, *i.e.*, from $P^{US}AG$ (at the unsubsidized price P^{US}) to P^SFG.

What is the net welfare effect on the importing country of the foreign government subsidy? For context, assume the importing country is the U.S. As depicted, the gain in Consumer Surplus of $P^{US}BCP^S$ outweighs the loss in Producer Surplus of $P^{US}AFP^S$. Points A, B, C, and F, *i.e.*, area ABCF, mark off the difference. In other words, American rice consumers are better off by the increase in their surplus, which more than offsets the damage done to producer interests in that country. Of course, the story does not end here. Producers may well lobby the U.S. government for protection, and file a CVD petition.

Assume the petition is successful, and CVD relief to offset exactly the subsidy is granted. On the Graph, the result is an upward shift in the import supply line, and thus a rise in the price of imported merchandise back to P^{US}. What is the net welfare effect of the CVD? It is redolent of the net welfare effect of a tariff. If domestic producers of the like product (*e.g.*, California rice farmers) take advantage of the protection by raising the price of their product to (or near to) the level of P^{US}, then the effects are as follows.

TABLE 33-1:
SUMMARY OF WELFARE EFFECTS OF A CVD

	Consumer Surplus	Producer Surplus	Tariff Revenue	Net Welfare Effect
Unsubsidized Merchandise Sold at P^{US}	$P*BP^{US}$	$P^{US}AG$	None	Not applicable
Subsidized Merchandise Sold at P^S	Expands by $P^{US}BCP^S$	Declines by $P^{US}AFP^S$	None	Increase in Consumer Surplus outweighs decrease in Producer Surplus by ABCF
Subject Merchandise Sold with CVD imposed at P^{US}	Declines by $P^{US}BCP^S$	Expands by $P^{US}AFP^S$	ABDE	BCD (lost consumption opportunities) plus AEF (inefficient allocation of productive resources)

1. *Consumer and Producer Surplus*:

The gain in Consumer Surplus from the subsidy of $P^{US}BCP^S$ is wiped out, as is the loss in Producer Surplus from the subsidy of $P^{U}AFP^S$. That is, Consumer Surplus declines by $P^{U}BCP^S$, and Producer Surplus expands by $P^{U}AFP^S$.

2. *Government Revenue*:

The U.S. government earns revenue from the CVD imposed on the amount of merchandise subject to the remedy order, which is the difference between Q^1 and Q^2. (Observe without the order, imports are larger, the difference between Q^3 and Q^4, because domestic production of the like product is smaller, at level Q^4 rather than Q^2.) In particular, tariff revenue is ABDE (the amount of the CVD, which is P^U minus P^S, multiplied by the level of imports, Q^1 minus Q^2).

3. *Net Welfare Loss*:

The net welfare loss consists of two triangles on Graph 33-3, BCD and AEF. The triangle BCD reflects lost consumption opportunities ("lost" in that consumers no longer get low subsidized merchandise prices). The triangle AEF is the allocation of productive resources in the importing country to an inefficient activity, namely, production of the like product. It is "inefficient" when compared with subsidized foreign production.

This neoclassical economic analysis proves a CVD damages the welfare of an importing country imposing it. If a foreign government willingly expends resources on a subsidy scheme, and consumers in the importing country benefit (along with producers and exporters of the subsidized good), then why take remedial action?

Even within the paradigm of economics, there are responses focusing on analytical shortcomings. First, the analysis is narrow in scope. It considers welfare effects only in an importing country. An analysis of the effects of the program on the exporting and importing countries, third countries, or the entire trading system, might be insightful.

Second, the analysis is narrow because it is static. A dynamic analysis, *i.e.*, one assessing effects of a subsidy over time, might reveal other implications. For example, a CVD imposed by one country may cause a foreign exporter of subsidized merchandise to re-direct exports to countries with no penalty. The result is elimination of some or most of the revenue previously accruing to the CVD-imposing government, *i.e.*, depicting ABDE as tariff revenue on the Graph is an overstatement.

Third, a number of questionable implicit assumptions underlie the neoclassical critique of CVDs. For instance:

    i.   Product and import markets in the importing country are perfectly competitive. In truth, these markets may be characterized by monopoly, oligopoly, or monopsony. They may not adjust quickly to a dis-equilibriating influence.

    ii.   Subsidized imported merchandise and a domestic like product are perfect substitutes. Often, foreign and domestic firms compete through brand names, and slightly differentiating their products. That is, competition may be imperfect, as firms seek some monopoly power by defining a market niche.

    iii.   Imposition of a CVD is an ineffective tool to deter subsidization. However, the goal of the duty may be not only to remove the offending subsidy, but also to deter future subsidies. The latter goal helps exporters in the importing country that must compete with producers of subsidized merchandise in third countries.

    iv.   Imposition of a CVD will not improve the TOT of the importing country. Albeit rarely, an importing country might account for a sizeable percentage of world consumption of the product in question. (That is, consumers in an importing country might have monopsony power.) Levying a CVD on subject merchandise causes the price of that merchandise in the importing country to rise. Therefore, demand for it in that country falls. This decrease also implies a noticeable drop in world demand for the subsidized merchandise. That occurs because of the importance of the importing country's consumption to world consumption. In turn, with the drop in world demand, the world market price of the subsidized merchandise declines. That drop means the importing country's TOT improves. If this phenomenon occurs, then neoclassical theory suggests a CVD can increase the net welfare of the importing country. Intuitively, the reason is that where a CVD shifts the TOT to the importing country, making imports less expensive than before the duty, part of the tariff revenue accruing to the importing country's government comes out of the producer surplus of foreign exporters. Foreign exporters capture less surplus, because the price of their merchandise falls. In contrast, where the TOT are unaffected by the duty, all of the revenue comes from domestic consumer surplus. Certainly, instances of improved TOT through CVD imposition are unusual, and it is unlikely government officials can carefully calibrate the CVD amount to achieve the desired TOT improvement. Officials risk setting the duty too high, so subsidized merchandise imports are choked off, or too low, so domestic demand for them is not materially affected.

If any assumption is, in fact, incorrect, then the bottom-line conclusions are in doubt.

IV. THE LEVEL PLAYING FIELD ARGUMENT

Whether to impose a CVD is not merely an economic matter. For instance, a pragmatic response to the question "Why impose a CVD?" is "because some domestic producers can." This answer relates to the politics of trade remedies, and implicates a body of analysis known as Public Choice Theory. A CVD may be imposed simply because a petitioning industry can obtain an order. In turn, it is likely to be able to marshal itself into a legal force if it is not too diffuse, and has common interests.

More generally, as with the economic critique of AD law, is their an air of unreality about the neoclassical analysis of CVD law? If the critique sufficed, then CVD law might be abolished for lack of a strong economic foundation. Yet, it persists. It was re-organized and strengthened by the WTO *SCM Agreement*. Governments have legitimate reasons to bestow a subsidy, such as developing a poor region, encouraging research and development, or promoting environmentally-friendly production methods. CVD law has continuing vitality because of widespread perception that some subsidies are a form of unfair competition against which domestic producers must have a remedy. That perception begs a foundational question, namely, what is "fairness" in international trade law?

Leveling the international competitive playing field may be a matter of fairness. A subsidy provided by a foreign government may distort international trade patterns, and that is unfair. Manufacturers of a like product in an importing country cannot compete, and are forced to cut wages or lay off workers. Those actions have ill effects on families and communities. A CVD rectifies the unfairness. Implicit in this response is use of a free, unsubsidized market price as the indicator of "fairness," and a correlative implicit assumption that there is such a thing as a normal trade pattern.

The problem with the defense that a CVD levels the playing field is three fold. First, it exalts property rights and interests of the minority over the majority. Domestic producers, the output of which a CVD protects, gain. But, their gain is the loss of the public, which pays higher prices. Second, a CVD is an artificial interference with property rights. As Professor McGee says in *A Trade Policy for Free Societies* (1994), "fairness" can be defined as non-coercive exchange. So long as an export-import deal is voluntary, with no official tariff, quota, or remedy (which would make trade coercive), then it is "fair."[6] Third, underlying CVD law is a philosophically flawed assumption — trade is a zero sum game. It is, or is supposed to be, a win-win game with mutually beneficial results.

---

[6] *See* ROBERT W. MCGEE, A TRADE POLICY FOR FREE SOCIETIES 6, 15-17 (1994).

Chapter 34

THE SUBSIDY DETERMINATION

Because of their geographical situation and their democratic institutions, Americans have claimed and still claim a large degree of national aloofness and independence; but such a claim could have been better defended several generations ago than it can today. . . . The American nation, just in so far as it believes in its nationality and is ready to become more of a nation, must assume a more definite and a more responsible place in the international system.

—HERBERT CROLY, THE PROMISE OF AMERICAN LIFE 289 (1909)

DOCUMENTS SUPPLEMENT ASSIGNMENT

1, *Havana Charter* Articles 25-29

2. GATT Articles VI, XVI-XVII

3. WTO *SCM Agreement*

4. U.S. *Statement of Administrative Action* for the *SCM Agreement*

I. THE TRAFFIC LIGHT SYSTEM

Articles 1-2 of the WTO *Agreement on Subsidies and Countervailing Measures (SCM Agreement)* defines a "subsidy" as a financial contribution from a government that confers a benefit specific to an enterprise, industry, group of enterprises, or group of industries. Not every "subsidy," however, is illegal under the *Agreement.* How does the *Agreement* differentiate between lawful and unlawful subsidies?

The answer is the Traffic Light system, established (albeit not by name) in Articles 3-9. Arguably, it is one of the most conceptually clear and elegant ways of organizing the confusing universe of subsidies yet devised. Briefly, there are 3 categories of subsidies:

1. *The Prohibited, or Red Light, Category (Articles 3-4)*

There are two Red Light Subsidies, namely:

> (1) Export subsidies, *i.e.*, subsidies contingent *de jure* or *de facto* on export performance), and
>
> (2) Import substitution subsidies, *i.e.*, subsidies contingent on the use of domestic over imported goods.

Annex I to the *SCM Agreement* contains an illustrative list of export subsidies. All Red Light Subsidies are *per se* illegal, irrebuttably presumed to be specific, and irrebuttably presumed to cause an adverse effect.

2. *The Actionable, or Yellow Light and Dark Amber, Category (Articles 5-7)*

Subsidies considered actionable may be countervailed. Yellow Light Subsidies are schemes that do not fit into any other category. In effect, the Yellow Light grouping is the default category. A countervailing duty (CVD) cannot be imposed against a subsidy in this category unless it is proved the subsidy is specific, and causes an adverse trade effect.

Four kinds of support are classified as Dark Amber:

    (1)   more than 5 percent of the value of a product is subsidized;

    (2)   operating losses of an industry is subsidized;

    (3)   operating losses of a firm are subsidized (except for a one-time, non-recurring funding to provide time for the firm to reach a long-term solution and avoid an acute social problem); and

    (4)   direct forgiveness of debt incurred by a firm.

A Dark Amber Subsidy is deemed rebuttably to cause one particular type of adverse trade effect, namely, serious prejudice. However, there is no presumption as to specificity (*i.e.*, specificity must be proven).

3. *The Non-Actionable, or Green Light, Category (Articles 8-9)*

There are three kinds of Green Light Subsidies:

    (1)   support for research and development (R&D) (up to a commercial prototype);

    (2)   assistance to a disadvantaged region (*i.e.*, a poorer area, in terms of income or employment, within a WTO Member); and

    (3)   funds for environmental adaptation (that is, to retro-fit production facilities with equipment needed to comply with new environmental regulations).

All Green Light Subsidies are lawful and non-countervailable. However, as of 31 December 1999, this Category lapsed. Why did the WTO Committee on Subsidies not lift the 5-year sunset rule (1 January 1995 through 31 December 1999) on this Category? What does the lack of a Green Light Category now say about the views of WTO Members on funding R&D, less developed regions, and environmental retro-fitting?

II. GOVERNMENT BAILOUTS AND THE 2005 *KOREA DRAMs* CASE

WTO APPELLATE BODY REPORT, *UNITED STATES — COUNTERVAILING DUTY INVESTIGATION ON DYNAMIC RANDOM ACCESS MEMORY SEMICONDUCTORS (DRAMs) FROM KOREA*
WT/DS296/AB/R (adopted 20 July 2005)

I. Introduction

    1. . . . . The Panel was established to consider a complaint by Korea against the United States regarding the imposition of countervailing duties ("CVDs")

on DRAMS and memory models containing DRAMS [collectively called "DRAMS"] from Korea, following an investigation by the United States Department of Commerce (the "USDOC") and the United States International Trade Commission (the "USITC").

2. The CVD investigation was initiated in November 2002, in response to a petition filed by Micron Technology, Inc. ("Micron"). The Korean companies investigated included Hynix Semiconductor, Inc. ("Hynix") and Samsung Electronics Co., Ltd. ("Samsung"). [Because the countervailable subsidy rate for Samsung was 0.04 percent, which is below the *de minimis* level of 2 percent, the DOC rendered a negative finding of subsidization with respect to Samsung.] The Government of Korea (the "GOK") participated in the investigation as an interested party. The USDOC published a final subsidy determination on 23 June 2003, concluding that Hynix had received financial contributions from the GOK by virtue of, *inter alia*, the GOK's entrustment or direction of Hynix's creditors to maintain the financial viability of Hynix. The USDOC determined that Hynix's countervailable subsidy rate was 44.29 per cent.

3. The USITC published a preliminary injury determination on 27 December 2002 and a final injury determination on 11 August 2003. In its final injury determination, the USITC concluded that the United States DRAMS industry had been materially injured by reason of imports of subsidized DRAMS from Korea. On the basis of these subsidy and injury determinations by the USDOC and the USITC, respectively, the USDOC issued a CVD order on 11 August 2003, imposing CVDs of 44.29 per cent on Hynix, which would be paid by importers as cash deposits at the same time as they would normally deposit estimated customs duties.

. . . .

5. . . . [T]he Panel concluded that:

> . . . the [US]DOC's *Final Subsidy Determination*, the [US]ITC's *Final Injury Determination*, and the *Final Countervailing Duty Order* based thereon, are inconsistent with Articles 1, 2 and 15.5 of the *SCM Agreement*. We therefore conclude that the [United States] is in violation of those provisions of the *SCM Agreement*.

. . . .

V. Interpretation of Article 1.1(a)(1)(iv) of the *SCM Agreement*

A. *Introduction*

. . . .

104. The United States asserts that the Panel's interpretation of the terms "entrusts" and "directs" is erroneous because it fails to "take[] account of the full range of government actions that fall within the ordinary meaning[s] of th[ese] term[s]." . . .

. . . .

B. *Article 1.1(a)(1)(iv) of the SCM Agreement*

1. The Meaning of the Terms "Entrusts" and "Directs"

. . . .

107. Article 1.1(a)(1) makes clear that a "financial contribution" by a government or public body is an essential component of a "subsidy" under the *SCM Agreement*. No product may be found to be subsidized under Article 1.1(a)(1), nor may it be countervailed, in the absence of a financial contribution. Furthermore, situations involving exclusively private conduct — that is, conduct that is not in some way attributable to a government or public body — cannot constitute a "financial contribution" for purposes of determining the existence of a subsidy under the *SCM Agreement*.

108. Paragraphs (i) through (iv) of Article 1.1(a)(1) set forth the situations where there is a financial contribution by a government or public body. The situations listed in paragraphs (i) through (iii) refer to a financial contribution that is provided *directly* by the government through the direct transfer of funds, the foregoing of revenue, the provision of goods or services, or the purchase of goods. By virtue of paragraph (iv), a financial contribution may also be provided *indirectly* by a government where it "makes payments to a funding mechanism," or, as alleged in this case, where a government "entrusts or directs a private body to carry out one or more of the type of functions illustrated in (i) to (iii) . . . which would normally be vested in the government and the practice, in no real sense, differs from practices normally followed by governments." Thus, paragraphs (i) through (iii) identify the types of actions that, when taken by private bodies that have been so "entrusted" or "directed" by the government, fall within the scope of paragraph (iv). In other words, paragraph (iv) covers situations where a private body is being used as a proxy by the government to carry out one of the types of functions listed in paragraphs (i) through (iii). Seen in this light, the terms "entrusts" and "directs" in paragraph (iv) identify the instances where seemingly private conduct may be attributable to a government for purposes of determining whether there has been a financial contribution within the meaning of the *SCM Agreement*.

. . . .

110. The term "entrusts" connotes the action of giving responsibility to someone for a task or an object. In the context of paragraph (iv) of Article 1.1(a)(1), the government gives responsibility to a private body "to carry out" one of the types of functions listed in paragraphs (i) through (iii) of Article 1.1(a)(1). As the United States acknowledges, "delegation" (the word used by the Panel) may be a means by which a government gives responsibility to a private body to carry out one of the functions listed in paragraphs (i) through (iii). Delegation is usually achieved by formal means, but delegation also could be informal. Moreover, there may be other means, be they formal or informal, that governments could employ for the same purpose. Therefore, an interpretation of the term "entrusts" that is limited to acts of "delegation" is too narrow.

111. As for the term "directs," . . . some of the definitions — such as "give authoritative instructions to" and "order (a person) *to do*" — suggest that the person or entity that "directs" has authority over the person or entity that is directed. In contrast, some of the other definitions — such as "inform or guide" — do not necessarily convey this sense of authority. In our view, that the private body under paragraph (iv) is directed *"to carry out"* a function underscores the notion of authority that is included in some of the definitions of the term "direct." . . . In the context of paragraph (iv), this authority is exercised by a government over a private body. A "command" (the word used by the Panel) is certainly one way in which a government can exercise authority over a private body in the sense foreseen by Article 1.1(a)(1)(iv), but governments are likely to have other means at their disposal to exercise authority over a private body. Some of these means may be more subtle than a "command" or may not involve the same degree of compulsion. Thus, an interpretation of the term "directs" that is limited to acts of "command" is also too narrow.

. . . .

113. We recall, moreover, that Article 1.1(a)(1) of the *SCM Agreement* is concerned with the existence of a financial contribution. Paragraph (iv), in particular, is intended to ensure that governments do not evade their obligations under the *SCM Agreement* by using private bodies to take actions that would otherwise fall within Article 1.1(a)(1), were they to be taken by the government itself. In other words, Article 1.1(a)(1)(iv) is, in essence, an anti-circumvention provision. A finding of entrustment or direction, therefore, requires that the government give responsibility to a private body — or exercise its authority over a private body — in order to effectuate a financial contribution.

114. It follows, therefore, that not all government acts necessarily amount to entrustment or direction. . . . [B]oth the United States and Korea agree that "mere policy pronouncements" by a government would not, by themselves, constitute entrustment or direction for purposes of Article 1.1(a)(1)(iv). Furthermore, entrustment and direction — through the giving of responsibility to or exercise of authority over a private body — imply a more active role than mere acts of encouragement. Additionally, we agree with the panel in *US — Export Restraints* that entrustment and direction do not cover "the situation in which the government intervenes in the market in some way, which may or may not have a particular result simply based on the given factual circumstances and the exercise of free choice by the actors in that market." Thus, government "entrustment" or "direction" cannot be inadvertent or a mere by-product of governmental regulation. This is consistent with the Appellate Body's statement in *US — Softwood Lumber IV* that "not all government measures capable of conferring benefits would necessarily fall within Article 1.1(a);" otherwise paragraphs (i) through (iv) of Article 1.1(a) would not be necessary "because all government measures conferring benefits, *per se*, would be subsidies."

115. Furthermore, such an interpretation is consistent with the object and purpose of the *SCM Agreement*, which reflects a delicate balance between the Members that sought to impose more disciplines on the use of subsidies and

those that sought to impose more disciplines on the application of countervailing measures. Indeed, the Appellate Body has said [in *U.S. — Softwood Lumber IV* at ¶ 64] that the object and purpose of the *SCM Agreement* is "to strengthen and improve GATT disciplines relating to the use of both subsidies and countervailing measures, while, recognizing at the same time, the right of Members to impose such measures under certain conditions." This balance must be borne in mind in interpreting paragraph (iv), which allows Members to apply countervailing measures to products in situations where a government uses a private body as a proxy to provide a financial contribution. . . . At the same time, the interpretation of paragraph (iv) cannot be so broad so as to allow Members to apply countervailing measures to products whenever a government is merely exercising its general regulatory powers.

116. In sum, we are of the view that, pursuant to paragraph (iv), "entrustment" occurs where a government gives responsibility to a private body, and "direction" refers to situations where the government exercises its authority over a private body. In both instances, the government uses a private body as proxy to effectuate one of the types of financial contributions listed in paragraphs (i) through (iii). It may be difficult to identify precisely, in the abstract, the types of government actions that constitute entrustment or direction and those that do not. The particular label used to describe the governmental action is not necessarily dispositive. Indeed, as Korea acknowledges, in some circumstances, "guidance" by a government can constitute direction. In most cases, one would expect entrustment or direction of a private body to involve some form of threat or inducement, which could, in turn, serve as evidence of entrustment or direction. The determination of entrustment or direction will hinge on the particular facts of the case.

2. The United States' Appeal

117. The United States alleges that, by equating "entrustment" and "direction" with "delegation" and "command," the Panel failed to interpret those treaty terms in accordance with the customary rules of interpretation codified in the *Vienna Convention on the Law of Treaties*. In this respect, the United States submits that, had the Panel properly interpreted "entrusts" and "directs," it would have recognized that these terms also encompass:

> . . . a government investing trust in a private body to carry out a task, a government giving responsibility to a private body to carry out a task, a government informing or guiding a private body as to how to carry out a task, [and] a government regulating the course of a private body's conduct[.]

. . . .

118. . . . . We explained earlier that the terms "entrusts" and "directs" in Article 1.1(a)(1)(iv) are not limited to "delegation" and "command," respectively. In our view, there may be other means by which governments can give responsibility to or exercise authority over a private body that may not fall within the terms "delegation" and "command," if these terms are strictly construed. . . . [T]he Panel's repeated use of the terms "delegation" and "command," without qualification, in its subsequent analysis, could give the

impression that the terms "entrusts" and "directs" correspond strictly to "delegation" and "command." We do not consider that these words, on their own, convey what we understand by "entrusts" or "directs," as used in Article 1.1(a)(1)(iv), for the terms "delegation" and "command," as we have explained above, are too narrow. Therefore, we *modify* the Panel's interpretation of Article 1.1(a)(1)(iv) of the *SCM Agreement* . . . to the extent that it may be understood as limiting the terms "entrusts" and "directs" to acts of "delegation" and "command."

. . . .

3. Korea's Cross-appeal

120. . . . Korea's cross-appeal . . . challenges the Panel's finding that certain evidence referred to by the USDOC was "sufficient for an objective and impartial investigating authority to properly find government entrustment or direction in respect of KFB [Korea First Bank]." This finding was made in the context of the Panel's examination of the USDOC's reference to alleged threats by the GOK against KFB and another two Korean banks.

121. Korea pointed out to the Panel that "ultimately KFB declined to participate in the Fast Track [Debenture] Programme, and in fact did not participate in the Fast Track [Debenture] Programme, and exercised its appraisal rights in the October restructuring." "KFB's actions," according to Korea, "are hardly consistent with the [United States'] theory of coercion from the [GOK]." The Panel did not find Korea's argument relevant because "[its] analysis at [that] stage [was] concerned first and foremost with the acts of the GOK, rather than private entities' reaction to those acts."

122. On appeal, Korea asserts that the Panel's conclusion regarding entrustment or direction of KFB rests on an incorrect interpretation of Article 1.1(a)(1)(iv) of the *SCM Agreement*. Korea explains that a finding of entrustment or direction under Article 1.1(a)(1)(iv) requires that the private body *carry out* one of the functions listed in that provision. "Mere direction without action," Korea submits, is not sufficient. Korea adds that, in this case, KFB did not carry out the action it was allegedly entrusted or directed to carry out and, therefore, the Panel's finding of entrustment or direction in respect of KFB is incorrect.

123. The United States responds to Korea's appeal by explaining that the Panel's finding in respect of KFB does not relate specifically to KFB's participation in the Fast Track Debenture Programme. It states that "[t]he fact that KFB did not participate in the Fast Track [Debenture] Program was never in dispute." The United States further explains that "the GOK's threats and coercive behavior occurred *because of* 'KFB's failure to participate in the Fast Track [Debenture] Programme.'" The Panel record confirms that KFB participated in the financial transactions that preceded and followed the Fast Track Debenture Programme. We do not read the Panel's finding that the evidence was sufficient to demonstrate GOK entrustment or direction of KFB as necessarily related exclusively to the Fast Track Debenture Programme. Thus, even assuming *arguendo* Korea is correct that a finding of entrustment or direction requires that the function so entrusted or directed be carried out,

we are not persuaded that the basis for the Panel's finding is as narrow as that alleged by Korea.

124. In any event, a finding of entrustment or direction, by itself, does not establish the existence of a financial contribution. Where a government entrusts or directs a private body — by giving responsibility to or exercising its authority over the private body — it is likely that the function that is allegedly entrusted or directed will indeed be carried out. The private body's refusal to carry out the function may be evidence that the government did not give it responsibility for such function, or that the government did not exercise the requisite authority over it such that the private body did not heed the government. It does not, however, on its own, mean that the private body was not entrusted or directed. Depending on the circumstances, a private body may decide not to carry out a function with which it was so entrusted or directed, despite the possible negative consequences that may follow.

125. Still, this does not mean that it is possible to make a finding of a financial contribution under Article 1.1(a)(1)(iv) where a private body does not carry out the function allegedly entrusted or directed to it. Failure by the private body to carry out one of the functions of the types listed in paragraphs (i) through (iii) means that nothing of economic value has been transferred from the grantor to the recipient. [The Appellate Body cited its Report in *Canada — Dairy*, ¶ 87, in which it explained "a 'subsidy' involves a transfer of economic resources from the grantor to the recipient for less than full consideration."] Simply put, if the private body has not carried out the function allegedly entrusted or directed to it, nothing will have changed hands. Therefore, there is no financial contribution and, consequently, there would be no right to apply countervailing measures.

126. For these reasons, we *uphold* the Panel's finding . . . that the evidence was "sufficient for an objective and impartial investigating authority to properly find government entrustment or direction in respect of KFB."

[The Appellate Body found errors in the review by the Panel of the evidence supporting the DOC's subsidy determination on entrustment or direction. The Appellate Body said these errors undermined the Panel's conclusion that the evidence failed to support the DOC's affirmative determination. Therefore, the Appellate Body reversed the conclusion of the Panel, as well as the conclusion of the Panel that the U.S. acted inconsistently with Article 1:1(a)(1)((v) of the *SCM Agreement*. Yet, the Appellate Body could not itself conclude whether the DOC's determination was consistent with this Article. The "bottom line" is there was no final WTO adjudication against the DOC's subsidy determination.]

III.　RED LIGHT SUBSIDIES

A.　Benefit, Export Contingency, and the 1999 *Canada Aircraft* Case

WTO APPELLATE BODY REPORT, *CANADA — MEASURES AFFECTING THE EXPORT OF CIVILIAN AIRCRAFT*
WT/DS70/AB/R (adopted 20 August 1999)

I. Introduction

. . . .

2. The Panel considered claims made by Brazil relating to the activities of the Export Development Corporation (the "EDC"); the operation of Canada Account; the Canada-Quebec Subsidiary Agreements on Industrial Development; Société de Développement Industriel du Quebec; Technology Partnerships Canada ("TPC") and the Defence Industry Productivity Programme, as well as the sale to Bombardier Inc. ("Bombardier"), a Canadian corporation, by the Government of Ontario (through the Ontario Aerospace Corporation) of a 49 per cent interest in de Havilland Holdings Inc. . . . The Panel found "that Canada Account debt financing since 1 January 1995 for the export of Canadian regional aircraft" and "TPC assistance to the Canadian regional aircraft industry" constitute prohibited export subsidies inconsistent with Articles 3.1(a) and 3.2 of the *SCM Agreement*. The Panel rejected all of Brazil's other claims. The Panel recommended that Canada withdraw the prohibited export subsidies "without delay" and, in any event, "within 90 days."

[Specifically, the dispute arose because of various Canadian measures that Brazil alleged to be subsidies inconsistent with Canada's obligations under Articles 3.1(a) and 3.2 of the *SCM Agreement* in that they were contingent (in law or in fact) on export performance. Brazil challenged the following measures: (1) financing and loan guarantees provided by the EDC, including equity infusions into corporations established to facilitate the export of civil aircraft; (2) support provided to the civil aircraft industry by the Canada Account; (3) funds provided to the civil aircraft industry by TPC (and predecessor programs); (4) the sale by the Ontario Aerospace Corporation, an agency or instrumentality of the Government of the Province of Ontario, of a 49 percent interest in a civil aircraft manufacturer (de Havilland Holdings Inc.) to another civil aircraft manufacturer (Bombardier) on other than commercial terms; (5) benefits provided under the Canada-Québec Subsidiary Agreement on Industrial Development; and (6) benefits provided by the Government of Québec under the *Société de Développement Industriel du Québec*. As to measures (2) and (3), the Panel agreed with Brazil's complaint. The Panel rejected Brazil's challenge to the other measures.]

. . . .

IV. Issues Raised in this Appeal

148. This appeal raises the following issues:

(a)   whether the Panel erred in its interpretation of the term "benefit" in Article 1.1(b) of the *SCM Agreement*; [and]

(b)   whether the Panel erred in its interpretation and application of the expression "contingent . . . in fact . . .upon export performance" in Article 3.1(a) of the *SCM Agreement*. . . .

[Omitted is the discussion in which the Appellate Body upheld certain Panel findings about EDC debt financing.]

V. Interpretation of "Benefit" in Article 1.1(b) of the *SCM Agreement*

149. In interpreting the term "benefit" in Article 1.1(b) of the *SCM Agreement*, the Panel found that:

> . . . the ordinary meaning of "benefit" clearly encompasses some form of advantage. . . . In order to determine whether a financial contribution (in the sense of Article 1.1(a)(i)) confers a "benefit," *i.e.*, an advantage, it is necessary to determine whether the financial contribution places the *recipient* in a *more advantageous position than would have been the case but for the financial contribution*. In our view, the only logical basis for determining the position the recipient would have been in absent the financial contribution is the *market*. Accordingly, a financial contribution will only confer a "benefit," *i.e.*, an advantage, if it is *provided on terms that are more advantageous than those that would have been available to the recipient on the market*. (emphasis added)

. . . .

151. Canada appeals the Panel's legal interpretation of the term "benefit" in Article 1.1(b) of the *SCM Agreement*. In Canada's view, the Panel erred in its interpretation of "benefit" by focusing on the commercial benchmarks in Article 14 "to the exclusion of cost to government," . . . .Canada maintains that Annex IV of the *SCM Agreement* supports the view that "cost to government," which is mentioned in Annex IV, is a legitimate interpretation of the term "benefit." . . . Brazil agrees fully with the Panel's interpretation.

. . . .

154. A "benefit" does not exist in the abstract, but must be received and enjoyed by a beneficiary or a recipient. Logically, a "benefit" can be said to arise only if a person, natural or legal, or a group of persons, has in fact received something. The term "benefit," therefore, implies that there must be a recipient. This provides textual support for the view that the focus of the inquiry under Article 1.1(b) of the *SCM Agreement* should be on the recipient and not on the granting authority. The ordinary meaning of the word "confer," as used in Article 1.1(b), bears this out. "Confer" means, *inter alia*, "give," "grant" or "bestow." [Here, the Appellate Body again cited its familiar dictionaries: *The New Shorter Oxford English Dictionary* (Clarendon Press,

1993), *The Concise Oxford English Dictionary*, (Clarendon Press, 1995); and *Webster's Third New International Dictionary* (unabridged), (William Benton, 1966).] The use of the past participle "conferred" in the passive form, in conjunction with the word "thereby," naturally calls for an inquiry into *what was conferred on the recipient*. Accordingly, we believe that Canada's argument that "cost to government" is one way of conceiving of "benefit" is at odds with the ordinary meaning of Article 1.1(b), which focuses on the *recipient* and not on the *government* providing the "financial contribution."

. . . .

156. The structure of Article 1.1 as a whole confirms our view that Article 1.1(b) is concerned with the "benefit" to the recipient, and not with the "cost to government." The definition of "subsidy" in Article 1.1 has two discrete elements: "a financial contribution by a government or any public body" and "a benefit is thereby conferred." The first element of this definition is concerned with whether the *government* made a "financial contribution," as that term is defined in Article 1.1(a). The focus of the first element is on the action of the government in making the "financial contribution." That being so, it seems to us logical that the second element in Article 1.1 is concerned with the "benefit . . . conferred" on the *recipient* by that governmental action. . . .

157. We also believe that the word "benefit," as used in Article 1.1(b), implies some kind of comparison. This must be so, for there can be no "benefit" to the recipient unless the "financial contribution" makes the recipient "better off" than it would otherwise have been, absent that contribution. In our view, the marketplace provides an appropriate basis for comparison in determining whether a "benefit" has been "conferred," because the trade-distorting potential of a "financial contribution" can be identified by determining whether the recipient has received a "financial contribution" on terms more favourable than those available to the recipient in the market.

158. Article 14, which . . . is relevant context in interpreting Article 1.1(b), supports our view that the marketplace is an appropriate basis for comparison. The guidelines set forth in Article 14 relate to equity investments, loans, loan guarantees, the provision of goods or services by a government, and the purchase of goods by a government. A "benefit" arises under each of the guidelines if the recipient has received a "financial contribution" on terms more favourable than those available to the recipient in the market.

. . . .

161. In light of the foregoing, we find that the Panel has not erred in its interpretation of the word "benefit," as used in Article 1.1(b) of the *SCM Agreement*.

VI. "Contingent in Fact Upon Export Performance"

. . . .

167. Article 3.1(a) prohibits *any* subsidy that is contingent upon export performance, whether that subsidy is contingent "in law or in fact." The Uruguay Round negotiators have, through the prohibition against export

subsidies that are contingent *in fact* upon export performance, sought to prevent circumvention of the prohibition against subsidies contingent *in law* upon export performance. In our view, the legal standard expressed by the word "contingent" is the same for both *de jure* or *de facto* contingency. There is a difference, however, in what evidence may be employed to prove that a subsidy is export contingent. *De jure* export contingency is demonstrated on the basis of the words of the relevant legislation, regulation or other legal instrument. Proving *de facto* export contingency is a much more difficult task. There is no single legal document which will demonstrate, on its face, that a subsidy is "contingent . . . in fact . . . upon export performance." Instead, the existence of this relationship of contingency, between the subsidy and export performance, must be *inferred* from the total configuration of the facts constituting and surrounding the granting of the subsidy, none of which on its own is likely to be decisive in any given case.

168. Recognizing the difficulties inherent in demonstrating *de facto* export contingency, the Uruguay Round negotiators provided a standard, in footnote 4 of the *SCM Agreement*, for determining when a subsidy is "contingent . . . in fact . . . upon export performance." . . .

169. Footnote 4 makes it clear that *de facto* export contingency must be *demonstrated* by the *facts*. We agree with the Panel that what facts *should* be taken into account in a particular case will depend on the circumstances of that case. We also agree with the Panel that there can be no general rule as to what facts or what kinds of facts *must* be taken into account. We note that satisfaction of the standard for determining *de facto* export contingency set out in footnote 4 requires proof of three different substantive elements. . . .

170. The first element of the standard for determining *de facto* export contingency is the "*granting* of a subsidy." In our view, the initial inquiry must be on whether the *granting authority* imposed a condition based on export performance in providing the subsidy. In the words of Article 3.2 and footnote 4, the prohibition is on the "*granting* of a subsidy," and not on receiving it. The treaty obligation is imposed on the *granting* Member, and not on the recipient. Consequently, we do not agree with Canada that an analysis of "contingent . . . in fact . . . upon export performance" should focus on the reasonable knowledge of the recipient.

171. The second substantive element in footnote 4 is "tied to." The ordinary meaning of "tied to" confirms the linkage of "contingency" with "conditionality" in Article 3.1(a). Among the many meanings of the verb "tie," we believe that, in this instance, because the word "tie" is immediately followed by the word "to" in footnote 4, the relevant ordinary meaning of "tie" must be to "limit or restrict as to . . . conditions." [Here, the Appellate Body cited *The New Shorter Oxford English Dictionary* and *The Concise Oxford English Dictionary*.] This element of the standard set forth in footnote 4, therefore, emphasizes that a relationship of conditionality or dependence must be demonstrated. The second substantive element is at the very heart of the legal standard in footnote 4 and cannot be overlooked. In any given case, the facts must "demonstrate" that the granting of a subsidy is *tied to* or *contingent upon* actual or anticipated exports. It does *not* suffice to demonstrate solely that a government granting a subsidy *anticipated* that exports would result. The prohibition

in Article 3.1(a) applies to subsidies that are *contingent* upon export performance.

172. We turn now to the third substantive element provided in footnote 4. The dictionary meaning of the word "anticipated" is "expected." [The Appellate Body observed in a footnote that *The New Shorter Oxford English Dictionary* states that a colloquial meaning for "anticipate" is "expect," and *The Concise Oxford English Dictionary* identifies "expect" as a disputed meaning of "anticipate."] The use of this word, however, does *not* transform the standard for "contingent . . . in fact" into a standard merely for ascertaining "expectations" of exports on the part of the granting authority. Whether exports were anticipated or "expected" is to be gleaned from an examination of objective evidence. This examination is quite separate from, *and should not be confused with*, the examination of whether a subsidy is "tied to" actual or anticipated exports. A subsidy may well be granted in the knowledge, or with the anticipation, that exports will result. Yet, that alone is not sufficient, because that alone is not proof that the granting of the subsidy is *tied to* the anticipation of exportation.

173. There is a logical relationship between the second sentence of footnote 4 and the "tied to" requirement set forth in the first sentence of that footnote. The second sentence of footnote 4 precludes a panel from making a finding of *de facto* export contingency for the sole reason that the subsidy is "granted to enterprises which export." In our view, merely knowing that a recipient's sales are export-oriented does not demonstrate, without more, that the granting of a subsidy is tied to actual or anticipated exports. The second sentence of footnote 4 is, therefore, a specific expression of the requirement in the first sentence to demonstrate the "tied to" requirement. We agree with the Panel that, under the second sentence of footnote 4, the export orientation of a recipient may be taken into account as *a* relevant fact, provided that it is one of several facts which are considered and is not the only fact supporting a finding.

174. Canada argues that the Panel erred in stating that "the closer a subsidy brings a product to sale on the export market, *the greater the possibility* that the facts may demonstrate that the subsidy" is "contingent . . . in fact . . . upon export performance" (emphasis added). . . . [T]he Panel added that "the further removed a subsidy is from sales on the export market, *the less the possibility* that the facts may demonstrate that the subsidy" is "contingent . . . in fact . . . upon export performance" (emphasis added). By these statements, the Panel appears to us to apply what could be read to be a legal presumption. While we agree that this nearness-to-the-export-market factor *may*, in certain circumstances, be a relevant fact, we do not believe that it should be regarded as a legal presumption. It is, for instance, no "*less . . . possible*" that the facts, taken together, may demonstrate that a pre-production subsidy for research and development is "contingent . . . in fact . . . upon export performance." If a panel takes this factor into account, it should treat it with considerable caution. In our opinion, the mere presence or absence of this factor in any given case does not give rise to a presumption that a subsidy is or is not *de facto* contingent upon export performance. The legal standard to be applied remains the same: it is necessary to establish each of the three substantive elements in footnote 4.

175. . . . The Panel set out in some detail the various facts that it took into account in concluding that TPC assistance was "contingent . . . in fact . . . upon export performance." Indeed, the Panel took into account sixteen different factual elements, which covered a variety of matters, including: TPC's statement of its overall objectives; types of information called for in applications for TPC funding; the considerations, or eligibility criteria, employed by TPC in deciding whether to grant assistance; factors to be identified by TPC officials in making recommendations about applications for funding; TPC's record of funding in the export field, generally, and in the aerospace and defence sector, in particular; the nearness-to-the-export-market of the projects funded; the importance of projected export sales by applicants to TPC's funding decisions; and the export orientation of the firms or the industry supported.

176. . . . [W]e are unable to agree with Canada that the Panel made the export orientation of the regional aircraft industry the "effective test." In keeping with the standard set forth in footnote 4, the fact of the Canadian industry's export orientation seems to us not to have been given undue emphasis by the Panel. Rather, this fact was simply one of a number of facts that, when considered together, the Panel found demonstrated that the granting of subsidies by TPC was "tied to" actual or anticipated exports.

177. . . . [T]he Panel did not err in taking this nearness-to-the-export-market factor into consideration, together with all the other facts that the Panel considered. Moreover, in our view and in light of all the facts the Panel considered, the Panel would, in all probability, have concluded that TPC assistance to the Canadian regional export industry was "contingent . . . in fact . . . upon export performance," even if it had not taken this factor into account.

. . . .

180. For all these reasons, we uphold the Panel's legal finding that "TPC assistance to the Canadian regional aircraft industry is 'contingent . . . in fact . . . upon export performance' within the meaning of Article 3.1(a) of the *SCM Agreement*."

B. Export-Contingent Tax Exemptions and the 2000 *FSC* Case

WTO APPELLATE BODY REPORT, *UNITED STATES — TAX TREATMENT FOR "FOREIGN SALES CORPORATIONS"*
WT/DS108/AB/R (adopted 20 March 2000)

I. Introduction

1. . . . The Panel was established to consider a complaint by the European Communities with respect to "Sections 921-927 of the Internal Revenue Code and related measures establishing special tax treatment for 'Foreign Sales Corporations' ('FSCs')." . . .

2. . . . [T]he Panel concluded that, through the FSC measure:

(a) the United States has . . . acted inconsistently with its obligations under Article 3.1(a) of the *SCM Agreement* by granting or maintaining export subsidies prohibited by that provision. . . .

[Omitted are portions of the Appellate Body Report dealing with claims and defenses concerning the WTO *Agreement on Agriculture*.]

II. Background

A. *Overview of Relevant United States Tax Laws*

6. For United States citizens and residents, the tax laws of the United States generally operate "on a worldwide basis" [also called "unitary taxation"]. This means that, generally, the United States asserts the right to tax all income earned "worldwide" by its citizens and residents. A corporation organized under the laws of one of the fifty American states or the District of Columbia is a "domestic," or United States, corporation, and is "resident" in the United States for purposes of this "worldwide" taxation system. Under United States tax law, "foreign" corporations are defined as all corporations that are *not* incorporated in one of the fifty states or the District of Columbia.

7. The United States generally taxes any income earned by foreign corporations within the territory of the United States. The United States generally does not tax income that is earned by foreign corporations outside the United States. However, such "foreign-source" income of a foreign corporation generally will be subject to United States taxation when such income is "effectively connected with the conduct of a trade or business within the United States." United States tax laws and regulations provide for the tax authorities to conduct a factual inquiry to determine whether a foreign corporation's income is "effectively connected" income.

8. Many foreign corporations are related to United States corporations. Generally, a United States parent corporation is only subject to taxation on income earned by its foreign subsidiary when such income is transferred to the United States parent in the form of a dividend. The period between the earning of such income by the subsidiary and the transfer to the United States parent company of a dividend is called "deferral" under the United States tax system, because the payment of tax on that income is deferred until the income is repatriated to the United States.

9. The United States has also adopted a series of "anti-deferral" regimes that depart from the principle of deferral and that, in general, respond to specific policy concerns about potential tax avoidance by United States corporations through foreign affiliates. One of these regimes is Subpart F of the United States Internal Revenue Code (the "IRC"), which limits the availability of deferral for certain types of income earned by certain controlled foreign subsidiaries of United States corporations. Under Subpart F, certain income earned by a foreign subsidiary can be imputed to its United States parent corporation even though it has not yet been repatriated to the parent in the form of a dividend. The effect of Subpart F is that a United States parent corporation is immediately subject to United States taxation on such imputed income even while the income remains with the foreign subsidiary.

10. These generally prevailing United States tax rules are altered for FSCs by the FSC measure.

B. *The FSC Measure*

11. FSCs are foreign corporations responsible for certain sales-related activities in connection with the sale or lease of goods produced in the United States for export outside the United States. The FSC measure essentially exempts a portion of an FSC's export-related foreign-source income from United States income tax. The relevant tax regime is comprised of three separate elements, which affect the tax liability under United States law of an FSC as well as of the United States corporation that supplies goods for export. . . .

12. A corporation must satisfy several conditions to qualify as an FSC. To qualify, a corporation must be a foreign corporation organized under the laws of a country that shares tax information with the United States, or under the laws of a United States possession other than Puerto Rico. The corporation must satisfy additional requirements relating to its foreign presence, to the keeping of records, and to its shareholders and directors. The corporation must also elect to be an FSC for a given fiscal year. There is no statutory requirement that an FSC be affiliated with or controlled by a United States corporation. . The FSC measure is, however, such that the benefit to both FSCs and the United States corporations that supply goods for export will, as a practical matter, often be greater if the United States supplier is related to the FSC. As a result, many FSCs are controlled foreign subsidiaries of United States corporations.

13. The foreign-source income of an FSC may be broadly divided into "foreign trade income" and all other foreign-source income. "Foreign trade income" is essentially the foreign-source income attributable to an FSC from qualifying transactions involving the export of goods from the United States. An FSC's other foreign-source income may include *inter alia* "investment income," such as interest, dividends and royalties, and active business income not deriving from qualifying export transactions. This appeal raises a number of issues with respect to the taxation of an FSC's *foreign trade income*. Foreign trade income is in turn divided into *exempt* foreign trade income and *non-exempt* foreign trade income. As explained below, the United States tax treatment of an FSC's *exempt* foreign trade income differs from the United States tax treatment of an FSC's *non-exempt* foreign trade income.

14. An FSC's foreign trade income is its "foreign trading gross receipts" generated in qualifying transactions. Qualifying transactions involve the sale or lease of "export property" or the performance of services "related and subsidiary" to such sale or lease. "Export property" is property manufactured or produced in the United States by a person other than an FSC, sold or leased by or to an FSC for use, consumption or disposition outside the United States, and of which no more than 50 per cent of its fair market value is attributable to imports. In addition, for FSC income to be foreign trade income, certain economic processes relating to qualifying transactions must take place outside the United States, and the FSC must be managed outside the United States.

15. Under the FSC measure, an FSC may, at its option, choose to apply one of three transfer pricing rules in order to calculate its foreign trade income

from qualifying transactions. These pricing rules serve two purposes. First, the transfer pricing rules allocate the income from transactions involving United States export property as between an FSC and its United States supplier. The part of this income attributable to the FSC is its foreign trade income (*i.e.*, exempt and non-exempt foreign trade income). The second purpose of the transfer pricing rules is to determine how much of the income from transactions involving United States export property that is allocated to the FSC as foreign trade income is *exempt* foreign trade income, and how much of it is *non-exempt* foreign trade income. The transfer pricing rule applied to determine the amount of the FSC's foreign trade income must also be applied to determine the division of that foreign trade income into exempt and non-exempt foreign trade income.

C. *Exemptions Provided by the FSC Measure*

16. The FSC measure establishes three main exemptions which affect the United States tax liability of the FSC, of its United States supplier and, possibly United States shareholders. The first exemption relates to the United States tax treatment of the foreign-source income of a foreign corporation. Under United States law generally, the foreign-source income of a foreign corporation engaged in trade or business in the United States is taxable only to the extent that it is "effectively connected with the conduct of a trade or business within the United States." This rule applies whether or not a foreign corporation is controlled by a United States corporation. To determine whether the foreign-source income of a foreign corporation is "effectively connected with the conduct of a trade or business within the United States," a factual inquiry is undertaken by the tax authorities. Under the FSC measure, however, the exempt portion of an FSC's foreign trade income is "treated as foreign source income which is not effectively connected with the conduct of a trade or business within the United States." In other words, the exempt portion of the FSC's foreign trade income is not subject to a factual inquiry to determine if it is "effectively connected with the conduct of a trade or business within the United States." Thus, under this first exemption, a portion of an FSC's foreign-source income is *legislatively determined not to be* "effectively connected" and, therefore, is not taxable in the hands of the FSC — without regard to what conclusion an administrative factual inquiry might come to in the absence of the FSC measure.

17. The second exemption relates to the United States tax treatment of certain income earned by a foreign corporation that is controlled by a United States corporation. Under United States law generally, a United States shareholder in a controlled foreign corporation must include in his gross income each year a *pro rata* share of certain forms of income of the foreign controlled corporation which has not yet been distributed to its United States parent. Such income is known as "Subpart F income." The United States shareholder corporation is immediately subject to United States tax on its Subpart F income, even though it has not yet received the income from its foreign affiliate. Under the FSC measure, however, the foreign trade income of an FSC is generally exempted from Subpart F. Thus, under this second exemption, the parent of an FSC is *not* required to declare its *pro rata* share of the

undistributed income of an FSC that is derived from the foreign trade income of the FSC, and is *not* taxed on such income.

18. The third exemption deals with the tax treatment of dividends received by United States corporations from foreign corporations. Under United States law generally, dividends received by a United States corporation which are derived from the foreign-source income of a foreign corporation are taxable, unless such income has already been taxed under the Subpart F rules. Under the FSC measure, however, United States corporate shareholders of an FSC generally may deduct 100 per cent of dividends received from distributions made out of the foreign trade income of an FSC. Thus, under the third exemption, the parent of an FSC is generally not taxed on dividends received that are derived from the foreign trade income of the FSC.

. . . .

V. Article 3.1 of the *SCM Agreement*

77. . . . Under Article 3.1(a), the Panel determined, first, whether the FSC measure involved a "subsidy" as that term is defined in Article 1.1 of the *SCM Agreement*. The Panel examined, in particular, whether the FSC measure involved the foregoing of "government revenue that is *otherwise due*" under Article 1.1(a)(1)(ii). (emphasis added) The Panel stated:

> . . . we took the term *"otherwise* due" to refer to the situation that would prevail *but for* the measures in question. It is thus a matter of determining whether, absent such measures, there would be a higher tax liability. In our view, this means that a panel, in considering whether revenue foregone is "otherwise due," must examine the situation that would exist but for the measure in question. Under this approach, the question presented in this dispute is whether, if the FSC scheme did not exist, revenue would be due which is foregone by reason of that scheme. (underlining added)

[Omitted is the articulation and adjudication of the American argument concerning the so-called 1981 *Tax Legislation* cases, GATT Article XVI, and the 1981 GATT Council decision.]

. . . .

80. The Panel also examined whether its reading of the term "otherwise due" was affected by footnote 59 of the *SCM Agreement*. The Panel opined:

> . . . even assuming for the sake of argument that footnote 59 is predicated on the assumption that income arising from foreign economic processes is not as a general matter "otherwise due" within the meaning of Article 1.1(a)(1)(ii), we could at most conclude that a decision by a Member not to tax any income arising from foreign economic processes would not represent the foregoing of revenue "otherwise due." There is in our view however nothing in footnote 59 which would lead us to conclude that a Member that decides that it will tax income arising from foreign economic processes does not forego revenue "otherwise due" if it decides in a selective manner to exclude certain limited categories of such income from taxation.

. . . .

86. The United States' appeal from the Panel's specific findings under
Article 3.1(a) is limited to the Panel's treatment of footnote 59. . . . The
United States argues that footnote 59 means that "an exemption of foreign-
source income from taxation, such as that provided by the FSC, does not fall
within the scope of the prohibition [against export subsidies] even where the
exemption in question is limited to income earned in export transactions." The
United States places particular reliance on the second and fifth sentences of
footnote 59. It is "implicit" in the second sentence, argues the United States,
that "foreign-source income may be exempted from tax or taxed to a lesser
extent than domestic-source income." Moreover, the United States contends
that the fifth sentence of footnote 59 allows Members to adopt certain
measures "to avoid double taxation," and that the FSC measure is such a
measure. . . .

. . . .

(a) *Article 1.1 of the SCM Agreement*

90. We turn now to the definition of the term "subsidy" and, in particular,
to Article 1.1(a)(1)(ii), which provides that there is a "financial contribution"
by a government, sufficient to fulfil that element in the definition of a
"subsidy," where "government revenue that is *otherwise due* is foregone or not
collected." (emphasis added) In our view, the "*foregoing*" of revenue "*otherwise
due*" implies that less revenue has been raised by the government than would
have been raised in a different situation, or, that is, "otherwise." Moreover,
the word "foregone" suggests that the government has given up an entitlement
to raise revenue that it could "otherwise" have raised. This cannot, however,
be an entitlement in the abstract, because governments, in theory, could tax
all revenues. There must, therefore, be some defined, normative benchmark
against which a comparison can be made between the revenue actually raised
and the revenue that would have been raised "otherwise." We, therefore, agree
with the Panel that the term "otherwise due" implies some kind of comparison
between the revenues due under the contested measure and revenues that
would be due in some other situation. We also agree with the Panel that the
basis of comparison must be the tax rules applied by the Member in question.
To accept the argument of the United States that the comparator in determining what is "otherwise due" should be something other than the prevailing
domestic standard of the Member in question would be to imply that WTO
obligations somehow compel Members to choose a particular kind of tax
system; this is not so. A Member, in principle, has the sovereign authority
to tax any particular categories of revenue it wishes. It is also free *not* to tax
any particular categories of revenues. But, in both instances, the Member
must respect its WTO obligations. What is "otherwise due," therefore, depends
on the rules of taxation that each Member, by its own choice, establishes for
itself.

91. The Panel found that the term "otherwise due" establishes a "but for"
test, in terms of which the appropriate basis of comparison for determining
whether revenues are "otherwise due" is "the situation that would prevail but

for the measures in question." In the present case, this legal standard provides a sound basis for comparison because it is not difficult to establish in what way the foreign-source income of an FSC would be taxed "but for" the contested measure. However, we have certain abiding reservations about applying any legal standard, such as this "but for" test, in the place of the actual treaty language. Moreover, we would have particular misgivings about using a "but for" test if its application were limited to situations where there actually existed an alternative measure, under which the revenues in question would be taxed, absent the contested measure. It would, we believe, not be difficult to circumvent such a test by designing a tax regime under which there would be *no* general rule that applied formally to the revenues in question, absent the contested measures. We observe, therefore, that, although the Panel's "but for" test works in this case, it may not work in other cases. We note, however, that, in this dispute, the European Communities does not contest either the Panel's interpretation of the term "otherwise due" or the Panel's application of that term to the facts of this case. The United States also accepts the Panel's interpretation of that term as a general proposition.

92. The United States does, however, argue that the Panel erred because the general interpretation of the term "otherwise due" "must yield" to the standard the United States perceives in footnote 59 of the *SCM Agreement*, which the United States contends, is the "controlling legal provision" for interpretation of the term "otherwise due" with respect to a measure of the kind at issue. In the view of the United States, footnote 59 means that the FSC measure is not a "subsidy" under Article1.1 of the *SCM Agreement*. Thus, the United States does not read footnote 59 as providing context for the general interpretation of the term "otherwise due;" rather, the United States views footnote 59 as a form of exception to that general interpretation. . . .

93. Article 1.1 sets forth the general definition of the term "subsidy" which applies "for the purpose of this *Agreement*." This definition, therefore, applies wherever the word "subsidy" occurs throughout the *SCM Agreement* and conditions the application of the provisions of that Agreement regarding *prohibited* subsidies in Part II, *actionable* subsidies in Part III, *non-actionable* subsidies in Part IV and countervailing measures in Part V. By contrast, footnote 59 relates to one item in the Illustrative List of Export Subsidies. Even if footnote 59 means — as the United States also argues — that a measure, such as the FSC measure, is *not* a prohibited *export* subsidy, footnote 59 does not purport to establish an exception to the general definition of a *"subsidy"* otherwise applicable throughout the entire *SCM Agreement*. Under footnote 5 of the *SCM Agreement*, where the Illustrative List indicates that a measure is not a prohibited *export* subsidy, that measure is *not* deemed, for that reason alone, not to be a "subsidy." Rather, the measure is simply *not prohibited* under the *Agreement*. Other provisions of the *SCM Agreement* may, however, still apply to such a "subsidy." . . . [M]oreover, . . . under footnote 1 of the *SCM Agreement*, "the exemption of an exported *product* from duties or taxes *borne by the like product* when destined for domestic consumption . . . shall not be deemed to be a subsidy." (emphasis added) The tax measures identified in footnote 1 as not constituting a *"subsidy"* involve the exemption of exported *products* from *product-based* consumption taxes. The tax exemptions under the FSC measure relate to the taxation of *corporations*

and not *products*. Footnote 1, therefore, does *not* cover measures such as the FSC measure.

94. In light of the above, we do not accept the United States' argument that footnote 59 qualifies the general interpretation of the term "otherwise due." . . .

95. . . . [W]e uphold the Panel's finding that, under the FSC measure, the government of the United States foregoes revenue that is "otherwise due" under Article 1.1(a)(1)(ii) of the *SCM Agreement*. . . .

(b) *Article 3.1(a) of the SCM Agreement*

96. The United States' appeal from the Panel's findings under Article 3.1(a) is limited to its contention that footnote 59 . . . means that the FSC measure is not an "export subsidy." Footnote 59 reads:

> The Members recognize that deferral need not amount to an export subsidy where, for example, appropriate interest charges are collected. *The Members reaffirm the principle that prices for goods in transactions between exporting enterprises and foreign buyers under their or under the same control should for tax purposes be the prices which would be charged between independent enterprises acting at arm's length.* Any Member may draw the attention of another Member to administrative or other practices which may contravene this principle and which result in a significant saving of direct taxes in export transactions. In such circumstances the Members shall normally attempt to resolve their differences using the facilities of existing bilateral tax treaties or other specific international mechanisms, without prejudice to the rights and obligations of Members under GATT 1994, including the right of consultation created in the preceding sentence.
>
> Paragraph (e) is not intended to limit a Member from taking measures to avoid the double taxation of foreign-source income earned by its enterprises or the enterprises of another Member. (emphasis added)

97. We need to examine footnote 59 sentence by sentence. The first sentence of footnote 59 is specifically related to the statement in item (e) of the Illustrative List that the "full or partial exemption remission, or deferral specifically related to exports, of direct taxes" is an export subsidy. The first sentence of footnote 59 qualifies this by stating that "deferral need not amount to an export subsidy where, for example, appropriate interest charges are collected." Since the FSC measure does not involve the *deferral* of direct taxes, we do not believe that this sentence of footnote 59 bears upon the characterization of the FSC measure as constituting, or not, an "export subsidy."

98. The second sentence of footnote 59 "reaffirms" that, in allocating export sales revenues, for tax purposes, between exporting enterprises and controlled foreign buyers, the price for the goods shall be determined according to the "arm's length" principle to which that sentence of the footnote refers. Like the Panel, we are willing to accept, for the sake of argument, the United States' position that it is "implicit" in the requirement to use the arm's length

principle that Members of the WTO are not obliged to tax foreign-source income, and also that Members may tax such income less than they tax domestic-source income. We would add that, even in the absence of footnote 59, Members of the WTO are *not* obliged, by WTO rules, to tax *any* categories of income, whether foreign-or domestic-source income. The United States argues that, since there is no requirement to tax export-related foreign-source income, a government cannot be said to have "foregone" revenue if it elects not to tax that income. It seems to us that, taken to its logical conclusion, this argument by the United States would mean that there could *never* be a foregoing of revenue "otherwise due" because, in principle, under WTO law generally, *no* revenues are ever due and *no* revenue would, in this view, ever be "foregone." That cannot be the appropriate implication to draw from the requirement to use the arm's length principle.

99. Furthermore, we do not believe that the requirement to use the arm's length principle resolves the issue that arises here. That issue is *not*, as the United States suggests, whether a Member is or is not obliged to tax a particular category of foreign-source income. As we have said, a Member is not, in general, under any such obligation. Rather, the issue in dispute is whether, *having decided to tax a particular category of foreign-source income*, namely foreign-source income that is "effectively connected with a trade or business within the United States," the United States is *permitted to carve out an export contingent exemption from the category of foreign-source income that is taxed under its other rules of taxation*. Unlike the United States, we do not believe that the second sentence of footnote 59 addresses this question. It plainly does not do so expressly; neither, as far as we can see, does it do so by necessary implication. As the United States indicates, the arm's length principle operates when a Member chooses not to tax, or to tax less, certain categories of foreign-source income. However, the operation of the arm's length principle is unaffected by the choice a Member makes as to *which* categories of foreign-source income, if any, it will not tax, or will tax less. Likewise, the operation of the arm's length principle is unaffected by the choice a Member might make to grant exemptions from the generally applicable rules of taxation of foreign-source income that it has selected for itself. In short, the requirement to use the arm's length principle does not address the issue that arises here, nor does it authorize the type of export contingent tax exemption that we have just described. Thus, this sentence of footnote 59 does not mean that the FSC subsidies are not export subsidies within the meaning of Article 3.1(a) of the *SCM Agreement*.

100. The third and fourth sentences of footnote 59 set forth rules that relate to remedies. In our view, these rules have no bearing on the substantive obligations of Members under Articles 1.1 and 3.1 of the *SCM Agreement*. So, we turn to the fifth and final sentence of footnote 59. . . .

101. On appeal, the United States maintains that the FSC measure is a measure "to avoid double taxation of foreign-source income" *under footnote 59*. As a consequence, the United States further contends that the FSC measure is excluded from the prohibition against export subsidies in Article 3.1(a) of the *SCM Agreement*. . . . We . . . conclude that the United States did not assert, far less argue, before the Panel that the FSC measure is a

measure "to avoid double taxation of foreign-source income" under footnote 59. . . . It follows, therefore, that this issue was not properly litigated before the Panel. . . .

. . . .

103. Our mandate under Article 17.6 [of the *DSU*] is to address *"issues of law* covered in the panel report and *legal interpretations* developed by the panel." . . . In our view, examination of the substantive issues raised by this particular argument would be outside the scope of our mandate under Article 17.6 of the DSU, as this argument does not involve either an "issue of law covered in the panel report" or "legal interpretations developed by the panel." The Panel was simply not asked to address the issues raised by the United States' new argument. . . . The United States appears in effect to be appealing from the failure of the Panel to make a ruling or legal interpretation concerning the fifth sentence of footnote 59. That failure seems to us due to the failure of the respondent Member properly to litigate the matter before the Panel. We, therefore, decline to examine the United States' argument that the FSC measure is a measure "to avoid double taxation" within the meaning of footnote 59, and we reserve our opinion on this issue.

. . . .

121. In light of all the foregoing, we uphold the Panel's conclusion . . . that the FSC tax exemptions involve subsidies contingent upon export performance that are prohibited under Article 3.1(a) of the *SCM Agreement*.

. . . .

XI. Findings and Conclusions

. . . .

178. The Appellate Body *recommends* that the DSB request the United States to bring the FSC measure that has been found, in this Report and in the Panel Report as modified by this Report, to be inconsistent with its obligations under Articles 3.1(a) and 3.2 of the *SCM Agreement*, . . . into conformity with its obligations. . . .

179. We wish to emphasize that our ruling is on the FSC measure only. As always, our responsibility under the *DSU* is to address the legal issues raised in an appeal in a dispute involving a particular measure. Consequently, this ruling is in no way a judgement on the consistency or the inconsistency with WTO obligations of any other tax measure applied by any Member. Also, this is not a ruling that a Member must choose one kind of tax system over another so as to be consistent with that Member's WTO obligations. In particular, this is not a ruling on the relative merits of "worldwide" and "territorial" systems of taxation. A Member of the WTO may choose any kind of tax system it wishes — so long as, in so choosing, that Member applies that system in a way that is consistent with its WTO obligations. Whatever kind of tax system a Member chooses, that Member will not be in compliance with its WTO obligations if it provides, through its tax system, subsidies contingent upon export performance that are not permitted under the covered agreements.

180. By entering into the *WTO Agreement*, each Member of the WTO has imposed on itself an obligation to comply with *all* the terms of that Agreement. This is a ruling that the FSC measure does not comply with *all* those terms. The FSC measure creates a "subsidy" because it creates a "benefit" by means of a "financial contribution," in that government revenue is foregone that is "otherwise due." This "subsidy" is a "prohibited export subsidy" under the *SCM Agreement* because it is contingent upon export performance. . . . Therefore, the FSC measure is not consistent with the WTO obligations of the United States. Beyond this, we do not rule.

IV. NON-MARKET ECONOMIES AND THE 1986 *GEORGETOWN STEEL* CASE

GEORGETOWN STEEL CORPORATION v. THE UNITED STATES
United States Court of Appeals for the Federal Circuit
801 F.2d 1308-18 (1986)

FRIEDMAN, CIRCUIT JUDGE.

The substantive issue in this case, here on appeal from the Court of International Trade, is whether the countervailing duty provisions in Section 303 of the *Tariff Act of 1930*, as amended, 19 U.S.C. § 1303 (1982), apply to alleged subsidies granted by countries with so-called non-market economies for goods exported to the United States. The International Trade Administration of the Department of Commerce (Administration) held that Section 303 does not apply to non-market economies. The Court of International Trade reversed, holding that the Administration's determination was contrary to law.

We reverse the ruling of the Court of International Trade [CIT] and uphold the Administration's determination. [The Court also held the CIT had no jurisdiction over one of the two cases it decided, because the appeal in that case was not timely filed, and, therefore, reversed part of the order of the CIT, vacated the other part of the order, and remanded with instructions to dismiss part of the case. Omitted are these matters.]

I

A

In November 1983, the appellees, Georgetown Steel Corporation, Raritan River Steel Company, and Atlantic Steel Company (collectively, Georgetown Steel), and Continental Steel Corporation (Continental Steel), filed two countervailing duty petitions with the Administration on behalf of domestic producers of carbon steel wire rod. They alleged that carbon steel wire rod (wire rod) imported into the United States from [the former] Czechoslovakia and Poland, respectively, was "subsidized" and therefore subject to countervailing duties under Section 303. According to them, the subsidies provided for the exported wire rod involved (1) the receipt of exchange rates higher than the official rates, (2) direct payments on goods sold abroad at prices below domestic prices, (3) retention by the exporting entity of part of the "hard currency" obtained from the export sales, (4) application of "trade conversion coefficients" to change the exchange rate and thereby create a more favorable return on the exports, and (5) granting of income tax rebates for such sales.

The Administration instituted countervailing duty investigations based upon those complaints. After hearing, the Administration issued final negative determinations. It held that the Czechoslovakian and Polish exports of wire rod had not received any "bounty" or "grant" within the meaning of Section 303, so that countervailing duties on those items were not applicable.

The Administration concluded that, as a matter of law, Section 303 was inapplicable to non-market economies. 49 Fed. Reg. 19370, 19374 (1984). The Administration defined a "subsidy" as "any action that distorts or subverts the market process and results in a misallocation of resources, encouraging inefficient production and lessening world wealth." *Id.* at 19371, 19375. The agency reasoned that the concept of subsidies, and the misallocation of resources that resulted from subsidization, had no meaning in an economy that had no markets and in which activity was controlled according to central plans. *Id.*

B

While the wire rod cases were pending, Amax-Chemical, Incorporated, and Kerr-McGee Chemical Corporation filed with the Administration petitions alleging that the [former] Soviet Union and the German Democratic Republic [*i.e.*, the former East Germany] had provided subsidies for potash imported into the United States from those countries. The Administration commenced investigations into those complaints. After deciding the wire rod cases, the Administration rescinded its investigations in the potash cases and dismissed those complaints on the ground that both of those countries had non-market economies, and that under its decision in the Polish wire rod case, section 303 was inapplicable to non-market economies. *Id.* at 23428, 23429.

C

Georgetown Steel and Continental Steel sought review in the Court of International Trade of the Administration's negative countervailing duty determinations in the wire rod cases, and Amax Chemical and Kerr-McGee sought review there of the dismissal of their petitions in the potash cases. The court consolidated the cases.

The Court of International Trade reversed the Administration and held that the countervailing duty law covers non-market economies. The court stated that the premise of the Administration "that a subsidy can only exist in a market economy" was "fundamental error." *Continental Steel Corp. v. United States*, 9 C.I.T. 340, 614 F. Supp. 548, 550 (1985). It said that "the only purpose of the countervailing duty law [was] to extract the subsidies contained in merchandise entering the commerce of the United States in order to protect domestic industry from their effect . . . [and that] its effectiveness [was] clearly intended to be complete and without exception." *Id.* at 553. The court remanded the cases to the Administration for further proceedings consistent with its opinion.

. . . .

III

Section 303 of the *Tariff Act of 1930*, as amended, 19 U.S.C. § 1303 (1982), which authorizes the levy of countervailing duties, provides as follows:

> Whenever any country . . . or other political subdivision of government . . . shall pay or bestow, directly or indirectly, any bounty or grant upon the manufacturer or production or export of any article or merchandise manufactured or produced in such country . . . or other political subdivision of government, then upon the importation of such article or merchandise into the United States, whether . . . imported directly . . . or otherwise, . . . there shall be levied and paid, in all such cases, in addition to any duties otherwise imposed, a duty equal to the net amount of such bounty or grant, however the same be paid or bestowed.

The question before us is whether the economic incentives and benefits that the non-market economies of the Soviet Union and the German Democratic Republic have granted in connection with the export of potash from those countries to the United States constitute a "bounty" or a "grant" as those terms are used in Section 303. In its decision in the potash cases, the Administration defined a non-market economy as one that "operates on principles of non-market cost or pricing structures so that sales or offers for sale of merchandise in that country or to other countries do not reflect the market value of the merchandise." 49 Fed. Reg. 23428, 23429 (1984). As the Administration explained in the wire rod cases, in a non-market economy "resources are not allocated by a market. With varying degrees of control, allocation is achieved by central planning." *Id.* at 19371, 19375.

The Administration found in the potash cases that both the Soviet Union and the German Democratic Republic are non-market economies. *Id.* at 23428, 23429. Those findings are not here challenged, and we base our decision upon them.

Congress has not defined the terms "bounty" and "grant" as used in Section 303. [Article 1 of the WTO *Agreement on Subsidies and Countervailing Measures*, or "*SCM Agreement*," which entered into force on 1 January 1995, defines the term "subsidy" as a "financial contribution" that confers a "benefit." Would this *Agreement*, if applicable to the case, make a difference?] We cannot answer the question whether that section applies to non-market economies by reference to the language of the statute. Nor can we answer it, as the Court of International Trade did, by characterizing the statutory language as "abundantly clear" and "the broadest possible," the "plain meaning" of which reflects "an intent to cover as many beneficial acts [for the exporter] as possible," and then concluding that Congress has not attempted to exclude non-market economies from what the court believed to be the sweeping reach of the Section. 614 F. Supp. at 550-52, 555-57.

In its relevant terms, Section 303 is substantially unchanged from the first general countervailing duty statute Congress enacted as Section 5 of the *Tariff Act of July 24, 1897*, 30 Stat. 205. *See Zenith Radio Corp. v. United States*, 437 U.S. 443, 448, 57 L. Ed. 2d 337, 98 S. Ct. 2441 (1978). At the time of the original enactment there were no non-market economies; Congress therefore had no occasion to address the issue before us.

Since that time Congress has reenacted Section 303 six times, without making any changes of significance to the issue before us. *Zenith, id.* n.8; *see Trade Agreements Act of 1979*, Pub. L. No. 96-39, §§ 103, 105(a), 93 Stat. 190, 193, which, after *Zenith*, reenacted the section a sixth time. That fact itself strongly suggests that Congress did not intend to change the scope or meaning of the provision it had first enacted in the last century. *See* S. Rep. No. 249, 96th Cong., 1st Sess. 43 (1979), *reprinted in* 1979 U.S. CODE CONG. & AD. NEWS 381, 429. This conclusion is supported by the fact, discussed in part IIIB below, that Congress on several occasions in other statutes specifically dealt with exports from nonmarket economies.

Since, as the Administration stated in the Polish wire rod case, "Congress never has confronted directly the question of whether the countervailing duty law applies to [non-market-economy] countries. . ., the function of an administrative agency, as well as a court, is 'to discern dispositive legislative intent by "projecting as well as it could how the legislature would have dealt with the concrete situation if it had spoken.'" *Asahi Chemical Industry Co. Ltd. v. United States*, 4 C.I.T. 120, 124, 548 F. Supp. 1261 (1982) (quoting from *District of Columbia v. Orleans*, 132 U.S. App. D.C. 139, 406 F.2d 957, 958 (D.C. Cir. 1968))." 49 Fed. Reg. 19377 (1984). In other words, we must determine, as best we can, whether when Congress enacted the countervailing duty law in 1897 it would have applied the statute to non-market economies, if they then had existed.

Based upon the purpose of the countervailing duty law, the nature of nonmarket economies and the actions Congress has taken in other statutes that specifically address the question of exports from those economies, we conclude that the economic incentives and benefits that the Soviet Union and the German Democratic Republic have provided for the export of potash from those countries to the United States do not constitute bounties or grants under Section 303 of the *Tariff Act of 1930*, as amended.

A

In *Zenith*, the Supreme Court stated the purpose of the *1897 Act* as follows:

> The countervailing duty was intended to offset the unfair competitive advantage that foreign producers would otherwise enjoy from export subsidies paid by their governments.

437 U.S. at 455-56.

Congress thus sought to protect American firms from what it viewed as the unfair competitive advantage a foreign producer would have in selling in the American market if that producer's government in effect assumed part of the producer's expenses of selling here. As the Administration stated in the Polish wire rod case, "in a market economy, scarce resources are channeled to their most profitable and efficient uses by the market forces of supply and demand. . . . In the absence of government intervention, market economies are characterized by flexible prices determined through the interaction of supply and demand. In response to these prices, resources flow to the most profitable and efficient uses." 49 Fed. Reg. 19375 (1984).

American firms were expected and generally were able to compete effectively in the American market against foreign sellers who were subject to the same market pressures and constraints as they were. A foreign seller normally would do business in the American market only because it was profitable for it to do so, and because such sales presumably were at least as profitable, if not more so, than sales elsewhere.

A government subsidy on sales to the United States, however, enabled a foreign producer to sell in the American market in a situation in which otherwise it would not be in the seller's best economic interest to do so. This apparently was what the Administration had in mind when it stated in the Polish wire rod case that "a subsidy (or bounty or grant) is definitionally any action that distorts or subverts the market process and results in a misallocation of resources, encouraging inefficient production and lessening world wealth." *Id.* It was this kind of "unfair" competition, resulting from subsidies to foreign producers that gave them a competitive advantage they otherwise would not have, against which Congress sought to protect in the countervailing duty law.

In exports from a non-market economy, however, this kind of "unfair" competition cannot exist. Although a non-market state may engage in foreign trade through various entities, the state controls those entities and determines where, when and what they will sell, and at what prices and upon what terms. As the Administration explained in the Polish wire rod case,

> the non-market environment is riddled with distortions. Prices are set by central planners. "Losses" suffered by production and foreign trade enterprises are routinely covered by government transfers. Investment decisions are controlled by the state. Money and credit are allocated by the central planners. The wage bill is set by the government. Access to foreign currency is restricted. Private ownership is limited to consumer goods.

Id. at 19376. . . .

In the potash cases the alleged subsidies provided by the Soviet Union and the German Democratic Republic were the receipt on export sales of foreign exchange rates higher than the official rates, direct price equalization payments on exports and, in the case of the Soviet Union, retention by the exporting entities of a portion of the hard currency they earned on foreign sales. Although these benefits may encourage those entities to accomplish the economic goals and objectives the central planners set for them, . . . they do not create the kind of unfair competitive advantage over American firms against which the countervailing duty act was directed.

There is no reason to believe that if the Soviet Union or the German Democratic Republic had sold the potash directly rather than through a government instrumentality, the product would have been sold in the United States at higher prices or on different terms. Unlike the situation in a competitive market economy, the economic incentives the state provided to the exporting entities did not enable those entities to make sales in the United States that they otherwise might not have made. Even if one were to label these incentives as a "subsidy," in the loosest sense of the term, the governments of those non-market economies would in effect be subsidizing themselves. Those governments are not providing the exporters of potash to the United States with the kind of "bounty" or "grant" for which Congress in Section 303 prescribed the imposition of countervailing duties.

B

Further support for our conclusion is furnished by the more recent actions of Congress in dealing with the problem of exports by non-market economies through other statutory provisions. Those statutes indicate that Congress intended that any selling by non-market economies at unreasonably low prices should be dealt with under the antidumping law. There is no indication in any of those statutes, or their legislative history, that Congress intended or understood that the countervailing duty law also would apply.

1.

In the *Trade Act of 1974* (*1974 Act*), Pub. L. No. 93-618, 88 Stat. 1978 (1975), Congress amended the antidumping law, 19 U.S.C. §§ 160-171 (1976) (repealed 1979) (current version at 19 U.S.C. §§ 1673-1673i (1982)) (which was first enacted in 1921, *Antidumping Act, 1921*, ch. 14, §§ 201-212, 42 Stat. 11-15), to deal specifically with exports from non-market economies. Under the antidumping law, when "foreign merchandise [that] is being, or is likely to be, sold in the United States at less than its fair value" threatens to cause or causes actual material injury to a domestic industry or to the establishment of a domestic industry, duties are imposed on that merchandise. 19 U.S.C. § 1673 (1982). The existence and extent of "dumping" are determined on the basis of the excess of the foreign market value of the goods in the country of production over the selling price for the merchandise in the United States. *Id.*

In the *1974 Act*, Congress enacted a special "surrogate country" method for determining whether imports from non-market economies were being "dumped" in the United States. 19 U.S.C. § 164(c) (1976) (repealed 1979). Reasoning that in "State-controlled-economy countries . . . the supply and demand forces do not operate to produce prices, either in the home market or in third countries, which can be relied upon for comparison," S. Rep. No. 1298, 93d Cong. 2d Sess. 174 (1974), *reprinted in* 1974 U.S. CODE CONG. & AD. NEWS 7186, 7311, Congress provided that the foreign market value of goods from non-market economies should be determined on the basis of either a constructed value or the actual selling price of some other market economy country that sells the same or similar merchandise either for home consumption or to other countries. 19 U.S.C. § 164(c) (1976).

In Section 331 of the *1974 Act*, Congress also amended the countervailing duty law. *Trade Act of 1974*, § 331(a), 88 Stat. 2049. There is no indication, however, that in doing so Congress intended to change the scope of that law or believed that it covered nonmarket economies. If Congress had so intended or believed, it is curious that the legislature gave no such indication, particularly in view of the specific changes it made in the antidumping law to deal with the problem.

2.

In the *Trade Agreements Act of 1979 (1979 Act)*, Congress reenacted the special surrogate country antidumping provisions applicable to State-controlled economies that it had previously authorized in the *1974 Act*. Pub. L. No. 96-39, title I, § 101, 93 Stat. 182. The present provision states that if the economy of the exporting country is "State-controlled to an extent that sales or offers of sales of such or similar merchandise in that country or to countries other than the United States do not permit a determination of foreign market value under subsection (a) of this section," the foreign market value of the merchandise shall be determined

> on the basis of the normal costs, expenses, and profits as reflected by either —
>
> (1) the prices, determined in accordance with subsection (a) of this section, at which such or similar merchandise of a non-State-controlled economy country or countries is sold either
>
> > (A) for consumption in the home market of that country or countries, or
> >
> > (B) to other countries, including the United States; or
>
> (2) the constructed value of such or similar merchandise in a non-State-controlled-economy country or countries as determined under subsection (e) of this section.

19 U.S.C. § 1677b(c) (1982).

In the same statute Congress approved the [Tokyo Round] *Subsidies Code*, which a number of countries had adopted to implement the General Agreement on Tariffs and Trade, April 12, 1979, *31 U.S.T. 513*, T.I.A.S. No. 9619. 19 U.S.C. § 2503 (1982). Article 15 of the *Subsidies Code* permitted signatory countries to regulate imports from State-controlled economies based on a surrogate cost methodology under either antidumping or countervailing duty legislation enacted in the particular signatory country. Whichever legislation the signatory country chose to use, it was required to calculate the margin of dumping or the amount of the estimated subsidy by comparison of the export price with:

> (a) the price at which a like product of a country other than the importing signatory [or exporting country] . . . is sold, or
>
> (b) the constructed value of a like product in a country other than the importing signatory [or exporting non-market economy country].
>
> If neither prices nor constructed value as established under (a) or (b) above provide an adequate basis for determination of dumping or

subsidies then the price in the importing signatory, if necessary, duly adjusted to reflect reasonable profits, may be used.

As was the case with the *1974 Act*, in the *1979 Act* Congress also made various changes in the countervailing duty law. Pub. L. No. 96-39, §§ 103, 105(a), 93 Stat. 190, 193. Once again, however, it gave no indication that it understood or intended the latter law to apply to non-market economies. Indeed, Congress' realization, reflected in both the *1974* and *1979 Acts*, that changes in the antidumping law were necessary to make that law more effective in dealing with exports from non-market economies, coupled with its silence about application of the countervailing duty law to such exports, strongly indicates that Congress did not believe that the latter law covered non-market economies.

The Court of International Trade noted that Article 15 of the *Subsidies Code* gave "a country the choice of using subsidy law [countervailing duty law] *or* antidumping law for imports from a country with a state-controlled economy," and that "Congress was informed that countries with non-market economies had participated in the preparation of the Code and that it had been signed, subject to subsequent ratification, by such countries." 614 F. Supp. at 556-57 (footnotes omitted). The court viewed this as "overwhelming evidence that the *1979 Act* show[ed] a definite understanding by Congress that the countervailing duty law covers countries with non-market economies." *Id.* at 557.

The latter conclusion, however, is a *non-sequitur*. It also is inconsistent with our analysis of the Congressional understanding and purpose in enacting the provisions in the *1974* and *1979 Acts* dealing with the application of the antidumping law to non-market economies.

Since the *Subsidies Code* was the product of joint agreement among a number of countries, which had varying laws dealing with selling at unreasonably low prices by foreign producers, it was only natural that the *Code* would merely prescribe the method for determining the existence of a subsidy, and leave it to each country to determine the particular method it would use to deal with the problem. In the United States, as we have held, Congress elected to deal with the problem under the antidumping law and not under the countervailing duty law. The fact that Congress adopted the *Code*, under which the United States also could have proceeded under the countervailing duty law, does not establish that in fact it did so.

. . . .

D.

In *United States v. Zenith Radio Corp.*, 64 C.C.P.A. 130, 562 F.2d 1209, 1219 (CCPA 1977), *aff'd*, 437 U.S. 443, 57 L. Ed. 2d 337, 98 S. Ct. 2441 (1978), the Court of Customs and Patent Appeals, whose decisions we follow, recognized that the agency administering the countervailing duty law has broad discretion in determining the existence of a "bounty" or "grant" under that law. We cannot say that the Administration's conclusion that the benefits the Soviet Union and the German Democratic Republic provided for the export of potash to the United States were not bounties or grants under Section 303 was unreasonable, not in accordance with law or an abuse of discretion. *Chevron,*

U.S.A., Inc. v. Natural Resources Defense Council, Inc., 467 U.S. 837, 842-45, 81 L. Ed. 2d 694, 104 S. Ct. 2778 (1984). . . .

Conclusion

The order of the Court of International Trade is vacated insofar as it reversed the Administration's final countervailing duty determinations in the Czechoslovakian and Polish wire rod cases, and the case is remanded to that court with instructions to dismiss the complaint in those cases for lack of jurisdiction because the complaint was not timely filed. The order of the Court of International Trade is reversed insofar as it set aside the Administration's final actions in the Soviet Union and German Democratic Republic potash cases.

V. PRE-PRIVATIZATION SUBSIDIES

A. The Change in Ownership Methodology and 2000 *British Steel* Case

So important to so many countries is transition from communism or socialism to market capitalism that it is difficult to imagine a WTO trade remedy case more relevant to these countries than *United States — Imposition of Countervailing Duties on Certain Hot-Rolled Lead and Bismuth Carbon Steel Products Originating in the United Kingdom*, WT/DS138/AB/R (adopted 7 June 2000). Known as the *"British Steel"* case, the issue in it is simple to state: when a state owned enterprise (SOE) or state trading enterprise (STE) is privatized, to what extent, if any, do benefits from subsidies the firm previously received while in state hands continue on after the privatization? That is, the issue is whether subsidies continue into the after-life: does the subsidy from the firm's life as an SOE (or STE) carry over into its life as a private business?

In *British Steel*, and in progeny cases, there is no dispute the SOE — *qua* SOE — received state subsides. Nor is there any dispute about what happened next: those subsidies were cut off after privatization. The dispute is whether it right for a country importing goods from the newly-privatized entity to impose a CVD on these goods, on the theory these goods still receive a benefit from the subsidies of yesteryear? If the answer is "yes," imagine how many CVD actions can be brought against imports from transition-economy WTO Members (not to mention Brazil, Mexico, and India). Imagine the possible CVD actions against new Members (*e.g.*, China, Kingdom of Saudi Arabia, and Vietnam), and likely future Members (*e.g.*, Iran, Laos, Syria). If the answer is "no," then imagine the relief among the governments of all these countries — and the consternation in major developed trading countries fighting to retain their industrial base.

Ostensibly, it is ironic this 2000 case involves British Steel plc, and not a company from a more evidently socialist economy than that of England. ("Plc" stands for "public limited company." While in state hands, British Steel plc was the "British Steel Corporation.") But, the irony ends when it is remembered that Thatcher-ism and Blair-ism are relatively recent in Britain. For most of Britain's post-Second World War history, the pre-Blair Labour Party ideals of a large and visible state hand guiding the economy prevailed, and British Steel was a public-sector company. Prime Minister Margaret Thatcher privatized British Steel in December 1988 through a sale of shares. This sale was at an arm's length, and the purchasers paid fair market value for the shares. The Prime Minister also privatized United Engineering Steel (UES) at the same time.

In March 1995, British Steel bought UES, making it a wholly owned subsidiary of British Steel (and, for simplicity, "British Steel" refers to the pre-and post-privatization entity, including the subsidiary.) In October 1999, British Steel merged with a Dutch company, *Koninklijke Hoogvens* NV. The combined Anglo-Dutch entity is called the "Corus Group."

The U.S. alleged Her Majesty's Government provided over $11.2 billion in subsidies to British Steel when it owned the company. These subsidies took the form of equity infusions by the British Government to British Steel between fiscal years 1977-78 and 1985-86. The DOC categorized them as "non-recurring," and spread the presumed benefit from them out over 18 years. That is, the DOC calculated the benefit of the pre-privatization subsidies as of the year in which they were granted. Then, it allocated their benefit over a lengthy period. The DOC said 18 years was the useful life of productive assets in the steel industry. Most importantly, the DOC concluded the benefits of the subsidies during 1977-86 passed through the change in ownership, and thus continued on into the enterprise's new life as a private company.

In March 1993 — clearly after the privatization — the DOC imposed CVDs on imports of certain steel products made by British Steel. This imposition followed a final determination by the DOC of a subsidy rate of 12.69 percent, and a final affirmative injury determination by the ITC. The DOC maintained the CVDs through subsequent administrative reviews in 1995, 1996, and 1997, though the subsidy rates fell with these reviews. (The reviews in other years were not at issue in the case.) The subject merchandise was hot-rolled lead and bismuth carbon steel, commonly known as leaded steel bars, produced by British Steel.

In rendering its decision, the DOC used what is known as the "change-in-ownership" methodology. Under it, the change in ownership effected by privatization does not matter. The benefits of the pre-privatization subsidies continue, or carry over, through to the new corporate incarnation of the former SOE. In effect, the change-in-ownership methodology is a legal presumption — an automatic conclusion about the endurance of benefits that is dreadful for any respondent in a CVD case.

Thus, two extreme and not easily reconcilable perspectives were raised: that all subsidies received from Her Majesty's Government carried over after privatization, and that none of them did. The U.S., emboldened by Senator Orrin G. Hatch (Republican — Utah) and other politicians, urged a mere change in ownership does not affect the application of the CVD remedy. A former SOE can benefit from a carry-over effect of a subsidy received before privatization. After all, the WTO *SCM Agreement* condones imposition of a CVD if a benefit to a recipient is shown. In brief, who owns the recipient is immaterial. What matters is the benefit to the recipient.

In fact, the U.S. argued the premise of CVD law is calculation of a benefit received from a subsidy as of the year of bestowal of the subsidy. This premise is explicit in Article 1:1 of the *SCM Agreement*, which does not speak of examining the continued existence of a benefit. Rather, urged the U.S., Article 1:1 calls for a determination of benefit as of bestowal. It would be neither conceptually correct nor practicable to re-evaluate the benefit conferred by a subsidy every year, year-after-year, and years long after the subsidy initially was granted. Once a benefit at the time of bestowal is shown, the original determination is not to be re-opened. How could it be? CVD law would be nightmarishly difficult to administer if a WTO Member had to demonstrate continually that the benefit originally conferred remained an advantage to the recipient.

The position of the EU was diametrically opposite. Challenging the CVD order, the EU argued the DOC acted contrary to the *SCM Agreement* by failing to consider whether the pre-privatization subsidy provides a benefit after privatization. That is, a pre-privatization subsidy cannot be allocated over time, unless a continued benefit to the recipient is shown. (Interestingly, in February 1995, the U.S. CIT agreed with this argument, made to it by British Steel. But, in October 1997, the Court of Appeals for the Federal Circuit partly reversed the CIT decision. *See British Steel PLC v. U.S.*, 127 F.3d 1471 (Fed. Cir. 1997). The particular provisions under which the EU complained were Articles 10 and 19:4 of the *SCM Agreement*. Article 10 allows imposition of a CVD only after an investigation conducted in accordance with the *SCM Agreement*. Absent proof the targeted imports received the benefit of a subsidy, a CVD may not be imposed. Article 19:4 bars imposition of a CVD in excess of the amount of the subsidy revealed by the investigation. The EU also argued the DOC methodology used by the DOC to calculate the amount of the subsidy lacked any rational basis.

B. Lessons

The U.S. lost the case. Like the WTO Panel before it, the Appellate Body found the DOC was wrong to conclude pre-privatization subsidies received by British Steel were transmitted through the privatization and onto the successor private company. Change in ownership does matter, said the Appellate Body, hence ruling against the change-in-ownership methodology under which pre-privatization subsidies are deemed automatically to yield benefits to a former SOE. The Appellate Body found no validity to a doctrine of automatic pass through, or continuation of benefits, after privatization.

Quite the contrary, said the Appellate Body. What must be shown is the subject merchandise has received, directly or indirectly, a subsidy. Failing to link the pre-privatization subsidies with the imports in question was a violation of Article 10. Given the violation of this provision, the Appellate Body (like the panel) applied the principle of judicial economy and declined to decide the Article 19:4 issue. Significantly, the Appellate Body recommend the Commerce Department regulations and practices be changed in accordance with its ruling.

The Appellate Body rejected the American interpretation of Article 1:1 of the *SCM Agreement*. The United States relied on the present tense of the verb in Article 1:1 — "is conferred," inferring from this tense a necessity to show a benefit only at the time a subsidy is granted. The Appellate Body found no basis for this inference. Nothing in Article 1:1 speaks to the question of when a financial contribution or benefit conferred must be shown to exist. It is simply wrong to draw out of the verb tense in Article 1:1 a benefit from a subsidy is to be shown as of the time a subsidy is bestowed, but no other time thereafter. Lest there be any doubt about this reading of Article 1:1, said the Appellate Body, surely Article 21:1-2 clear up that doubt. These provisions make it quite obvious a renewed inquiry into subsidization — whether or not the subsidy continues to exist — is essential, and if no subsidy is found, then there is no need for a CVD.

Article 21:1 says a CVD is to remain in place for only so long as necessary to counteract effects of subsidization. Article 21:2 calls for establishment of an administrative review mechanism to ensure compliance with Article 21:1. During a review, the DOC (or relevant authority in other Members) is supposed to examine all evidence placed before it by a petitioner and respondent, and that it has obtained. The whole point of an Article 21:2 review is to see whether this evidence constitutes positive information that (1) the subsidizing government has withdrawn its financial contribution, (2) the recipient has repaid the subsidy, or (3) the benefit of the subsidy no longer accrues to the recipient. Thus, the language of Article 21:2 states plainly "[t]he authorities shall review the need for the continued imposition of the duty" and are to "examine whether the continued imposition of the duty is necessary to offset subsidization."

The Appellate Body was every bit as firm in rejecting the American argument the benefits of pre-privatization subsidies passed through to the privatized British Steel firm as it was in rejecting the Article 1:1 contention. There could never be anything more than a rebuttable presumption of a carry over of benefits after privatization; but the presumption must never be an irrebuttable one, as it was under the DOC's change-in-ownership methodology. The U.S. premised its argument in support of this methodology on an interpretation of the text of Article 10 (specifically, footnote 36 thereto) of the *SCM Agreement* and Article VI:3 of GATT, namely, the phrase concerning a subsidy bestowed "upon the manufacture, production or export of any merchandise." The U.S. urged these provisions mean what matters is whether a company's productive operations get the "benefit" of a subsidy. The recipient of interest is not the legal or natural person owning the company, but rather the productive assets of the company. Accordingly, change-of-ownership through privatization is irrelevant — the assets still may be said to receive the benefit of the previously-bestowed subsidies.

Not so, ruled the Appellate Body. First, it cited its own 1999 report from the *Canada — Measures Affecting the Export of Civilian Aircraft* case to support its conclusion a benefit implies a recipient, and a recipient must be a natural or legal person. Second, what matters in deciding whether a "financial contribution" confers a "benefit" is whether a recipient gets that contribution on terms more favorable than those available in the market. In a privatization scenario, it is necessary to consider the value paid for the productive assets and goodwill of the SOE. Was it a fair market value?

Why is this question so important? The underlying rationale of the Appellate Body seems to be as follows. As long as the shares of an SOE are sold to a private company (or the public at large) at a market price, and not an artificially low one, then the privatization is a *bona fide* arm's length one. In turn, it can be inferred no subsidy — no financial contribution to the new owners of the former state-owned productive assets and goodwill-is involved. The new owners are putting the assets and goodwill to work to produce the subject merchandise, but they are not benefiting from any help from the former state owner. In particular, the new owners cannot be deemed to continue to reap the benefits of the pre-privatization subsidy. Consider a contrasting scenario: the new owners buy the SOE at a below-market price from the government. Then, they could be said to receive a benefit. They purchased assets and goodwill at a discount. That discount is the vehicle through which the pre-privatization subsidy passes.

The Appellate Body would have done well to elaborate on the link between Wall Street and receipt of benefits from a pre-privatization subsidy. It reasoned — correctly — the share price (assuming it is a fair market value) of an SOE being privatized incorporates the expected future earnings stream of the company. In turn, that stream reflects the benefit of a subsidy previously received. That is, the stock market accounts for the benefit of a subsidy when it establishes a price for the shares. Presumably, that benefit increases the expected revenue stream and, therefore, increases the share price. If new owners pay this higher price, then they are — in effect — buying, or paying for, the subsidy (or the remaining benefits there from).

For example, suppose the aggregate share price for an SOE that received pre-privatization subsidies is $1 billion. If the share purchasers pay $1 billion, then they are paying back to the government seller that subsidy (or at least the remaining benefits therefrom), and thus buying any lingering benefits from that subsidy. To countervail the products from that privatized entity would be to penalize the new owners twice — the first time was when they paid a share price that included the subsidy benefits, and the second time would be when they pay the CVD. Conversely, suppose the share purchasers pay just $750 million for their shares. Then, they are not paying for the continued benefit of the subsidy (here assumed to be $250 million). Rather, they are receiving that benefit.

In the *British Steel* case, the WTO Panel pointed out the privatization of British Steel occurred at a fair market price, and the U.S. accepted this fact. So, too, did the Appellate Body. Thus, the Appellate Body essentially said a fair market privatization was reincarnation — a new life, not a continuation of an existing life — for an enterprise. If a company purchases an SOE at fair market value, then the SOE is fully reincarnated, and the new owners cannot be subject to duties designed to countervail subsidies bestowed in the last life. Only if they do not pay fair market value is it right to conclude the benefits of pre-privatization subsidies automatically carry over to the new company.

The only point on which the Appellate Body reversed the Panel concerned the nature of an Article 21:2 Administrative Review. Should such a Review of a CVD order be conducted in the same manner as an original subsidy investigation? The Panel said "yes." The Appellate Body said "no." In the investigation, the goal is to determine the existence and extent of a benefit from a subsidy, and all prerequisites in the *SCM Agreement* for imposition of a CVD must be checked. In the Review, only issues an interested party or the administering agency raise need addressing. Quite logically, an investigation is broader in scope than a review.

C. The Modified Change in Ownership Methodology and 2003 *Certain Products* Case

In 2003, the U.S. fought another case on CVDs and pre-privatization subsidies. *See United States — Countervailing Measures Concerning Certain Products from the European Communities*, WT/DS212/AB/R (adopted 8 January 2003) (complaint by the European Communities). As in *British Steel*, in *Certain Products* the Appellate Body was presented with U.S. CVD orders against subject merchandise from foreign producers that had received government subsidies. In both cases, subsidies were paid while the producers were SOEs. But, the subsidies ceased on or before privatization. Privatization meant a change in the ownership of the entities. Thus, in both cases, controversy raged over technical tests of ownership change, with large policy implications.

The tests were used by the U.S. DOC in CVD investigations to determine whether the benefit of a pre-privatization subsidy carries through to a newly privatized entity. Only if the benefit survives the change in ownership could the U.S. lawfully impose a CVD. In particular, according to the change in ownership methodology, the DOC presumed non-recurring subsidies granted to a former producer of a good, before the ownership of this producer changed (*i.e.*, granted while it was a state-owned enterprise) pass through to the current producer of the good after the change of ownership (*i.e.*, after privatization). Put succinctly, the presumption in the methodology is benefits from a pre-privatization subsidy continue after privatization, even though the subsidy itself terminated by the time of privatization, hence it is appropriate to levy a CVD against imports from the privatized entity.

The statute pursuant to which the DOC engaged in the change in ownership methodology is Section 771(5)(F) of the *Tariff Act of 1930*, as amended (codified at 19 U.S.C. § 1677(5)(F)). It says:

> A change in ownership of all or part of a foreign enterprise or the productive assets of a foreign enterprise does not by itself require a determination by the administering authority that a past countervailable subsidy received by the enterprise no longer continues to be countervailable, even if the change in ownership is accomplished through an arm's-length transaction.

In June 2003, the DOC modified its change-in-ownership methodology. It developed a rebuttable presumption, which it described in its regulations:

> The [new] methodology is based on certain rebuttable presumptions. . . . *The "baseline presumption" is that non-recurring subsidies can benefit the recipient over a period of time . . . normally corresponding to the average useful life of the recipient's assets.* However, an

interested party may *rebut this baseline presumption* by demonstrating that, during the allocation period, a *privatization occurred* in which the *government sold* its ownership of *all or substantially all of a company or its assets, retaining no control* of the company or its assets, and that the *sale was an arm's-length transaction for fair market value*.[1]

In effect, the DOC revised methodology was a two-step test:

1. First, the DOC analyzed whether a post-privatization entity is the same legal person as the entity that received the original subsidy before privatization. The factors it checked included the continuity of general business operations, production facilities, and assets and liabilities, and retention of personnel. If these criteria led the DOC to conclude privatization did not create a new legal person, then it stopped its analysis of whether a "benefit" exists. It did not consider whether privatization occurred at arm's length and for fair market value. Rather, the DOC concluded automatically and irrebuttably the subsidy continues to exist for the post-privatization firm, precisely because it is the same person as before.

2. Second, in contrast, suppose the continuity and retention criteria indicated the post-privatization entity was a new legal person, distinct from the entity that received the prior subsidy. Then, the DOC did not impose a CVD on goods produced after privatization on the basis of the pre-privatization subsidy. However, the DOC examined whether any new subsidy had been bestowed upon the new owners of the post-privatization entity as a result of the change in ownership. In particular, the DOC checked whether the sale was at arm's length and for fair market value. If it was not, then the DOC could find a new subsidy had been bestowed, and impose a CVD on that basis.

The "bottom line" was the DOC presumed conclusively that if an SOE and a post-privatized entity are the same legal person, then the benefit received by the SOE automatically continues to accrue to the newly privatized entity. Consequently, the DOC did not investigate the particularities of the case to determine whether a benefit does, in fact, carry through the privatization.

The gravamen of the EC complaint in *Certain Products* was the change in ownership methodology obviates the need for the DOC to establish the essential elements of a countervailable subsidy, namely, the existence of a

---

[1] *Notice of Final Modification of Agency Practice Under Section 123 of the Uruguay Round Agreements Act*, 68 Federal Register 37,125 (23 June 2003) (emphasis added).

Before this innovation, the DOC used a different test, combining the change in ownership methodology with another inquiry, called the "same person" method, thereby creating a two-step test. The DOC developed this "same person change in ownership" methodology following a major decision by the United States Court of Appeals, *Delverde SrL. v. United States*, 202 F.3d 1360 (Fed. Cir. 2000) ("*Delverde III*"), *rehg denied*. In *Delverde III*, the Federal Circuit held it was the intent of Congress, in enacting 19 U.S.C. Section 1677(5)(F), that the DOC examine the particular facts and circumstances of a privatization sale, and determine whether the purchaser received (directly or indirectly) from the government both a financial contribution and a benefit. In June 2003, the DOC dropped the "same person" method, and adopted the above-described methodology.

financial contribution and a benefit from this contribution to the producers under investigation.

That is, framing its arguments under Articles 1:1(b), 10, 14, 19, and 21 of the *SCM Agreement*, the EC said of the revised change in ownership methodology:

> In order to demonstrate that the two companies [an SOE and its privatized successor] are the same person, the DOC maintains that if a firm keeps the same factory, any of the same employees, any of the same customers, any of the same suppliers, this is sufficient reason to presume an automatic pass-through of subsidies.

> [T]he DOC's approach is premised on a preposterous assertion: that subsidies somehow become glued to, live in and then automatically travel with assets wherever they may be sold and regardless of the amount paid for them.

> Thus, under the DOC's approach, if an unsubsidized private company purchases a factory from a prior subsidized owner for 20 times the actual market value of the plant, the DOC would impose countervailing duties on the new owner.[2]

In sum, the EC argued the *British Steel* compelled the Appellate Body in *Certain Products* to find the same person methodology *per se* inconsistent with the *SCM Agreement*. The *Agreement*, as construed in *British Steel*, mandates a new determination of whether a benefit exists when a privatization results in a change of control.

The Appellate Body emphasized two key issues, and held as follows:

1. *Extinction of subsidy benefits through a privatization*:

If a privatization is conducted at arm's length and for fair market value, then does that privatization *systematically* extinguish the benefit from a non-recurring financial contribution bestowed before privatization? Finding the Panel's "yes" answer too rigid, and based on too much faith in equity and debt markets, the Appellate Body overturned the Panel and responded "no."

2. *Legality of the same person methodology*:

Is the DOC change-in-ownership methodology, which effectively involves a same person test, consistent with the *SCM Agreement*? "No," responded the Appellate Body, like the Panel. The DOC's methodology, ruled the Appellate Body, transgressed Article 21:2-3 (covering Administrative and Sunset Reviews of outstanding CVD orders) and its interpretation of this provision in *British Steel*. Under the methodology, if the DOC concluded the pre-and post-privatization entity were the same legal person, then it automatically disregarded information submitted to it to support the contention that no benefit from a prior financial contribution continued to exist. And, the DOC automatically declined to determine whether a benefit continues to exist despite this information. Only if the DOC found a distinct legal person would it study the new information and determine whether a benefit exists — and, even in that

---

2 Joe Kirwin, *EU Will File WTO Challenge to Duties U.S. Imposed on Some EU Steel Imports*, 18 INT'L TRADE REP. (BNA) 1194 (July 26, 2001) (quoting the Commission).

circumstance, the DOC's inquiry would be limited to whether a new subsidy is provided to the owners of the privatized entity. Put succinctly, the methodology led inexorably to a pre-determined conclusion of continued accrual of a benefit from a prior financial contribution, if the DOC found the same person to exist before and after privatization. Because the methodology barred any further analysis whenever the DOC made this threshold finding, it was illegal under Article 21:2.

On balance, the U.S. prevailed on the first issue, but lost on the second issue, which was the key conceptual one.[3]

Consider what rationales support the Appellate Body holdings in *Certain Products*? Consider, too, what facts and holdings distinguish the *British Steel* and *Certain Products* cases? To what extent did the *British Steel* decision establish a precedent for the *Certain Products* case?

VI. THE 2007 U.S. POLICY CHANGE ON CVDs AND NON-MARKET ECONOMIES

One crucial similarity between the 2000 *British Steel* and 2003 *Certain Products* cases was that neither involved a non-market economy (NME). They involved SOEs from market economies. Similarly, in a case in which the U.S. prevailed on claims involving commercial considerations under GATT Article XVII:1 and national treatment under Article III:4, the country at issue — Canada — was a market economy. *See Canada — Measures Relating to Exports of Wheat and Treatment of Imported Grain*, WT/DS276/AB/R (adopted 27 September 2004)

On 30 March 2007, the U.S. Department of Commerce (DOC) announced a dramatic reversal of long-standing policy. No longer would it abstain from applying CVD law to NMEs, as it had for 23 years. The policy of not applying CVD law against NME had two rationales. First, actors in an NME respond to government directives, not subsidies. Second, it is too difficult to calculate accurately the level of subsidization in an NME. What prompted the policy change after 23 years? Was it, as David Spooner, Assistant Secretary of Commerce for Import Administration, said?:

> The China of 2007 is not the Soviet bloc of the mid-1980s, when we formulated our non-market anti-subsidy laws. It would be a divorce from reality if we said there was an absence of market forces in the Chinese economy.[4]

Never mind the fact the Sino-Soviet split occurred in the late 1950s. Is the real reason for the policy reversal a combination of (1) U.S. legal defeats in *British Steel* and *Certain Products*, (2) U.S. concern about new WTO Members, such as China and Vietnam, which are NMEs, as well as NMEs in the queue

---

[3] On a third issue, the legality of the U.S. CVD statute, the Appellate Body held in favor of the U.S.

[4] Kathleen E. McLaughlin, *U.S. Countervailing Duties Against China Could Lead to Further Action, Spooner Says*, 24 INT'L TRADE REP. (BNA) 590 (26 April 2007); *see also Rep. English Says NME-CVD Bill Could Reach House Floor in April*, 24 INT'L TRADE REP. 554-555 (BNA) (19 April 2007).

to join the WTO, and (3) pressure from Congress, manifest in proposed bills to allow the DOC to apply CVD law to NMEs?

The third factor raises the question of authority. *Georgetown Steel* stands for the proposition that the DOC lacks authority to apply CVD laws against NMEs. The CIT, however, thought otherwise, as the Federal Circuit reversed it in that case. Evidently, the CIT never changed its view. In *Government of the People's Republic of China v. United States* (24 ITR 496, 5 April 2007), the CIT held there was no statutory bar to using CVD law against NMEs — effectively the same position it had in the *Georgetown Steel*.

To implement the policy shift, the DOC decided to rely on benchmarks from third countries as a way of measuring subsidies in an NME. (The obvious analogy is with the use of Third Country Price in a dumping margin calculation involving an NME.) Might that reliance be illegal under Article 14 of the WTO *SCM Agreement*? If a Third Country subsidy benchmark is used as a proxy in a case involving China, might that use violate China's terms of accession to the WTO?

Part Nine

INJURY AND CAUSATION IN ANTIDUMPING AND COUNTERVAILING DUTY LAW

Chapter 35

INJURY

_____

Wagner has good moments, but bad quarter-hours.

> —Italian composer Gioacchino Rossini (1792-1868) (referring to
> German composer Richard Wagner (1813-1883))

DOCUMENTS SUPPLEMENT ASSIGNMENT

1. *Havana Charter* Article 34
2. GATT Articles VI, XVI
3. WTO *Antidumping Agreement* Articles 1, 3-6, 15
4. WTO *SCM Agreement* Articles 1, 3-8, 10, 15-16, 27

I. OVERVIEW

An inquiry into injury and causation is an indispensable phase of every
antidumping (AD) case. In an AD case, injury may be actual material injury,
or threat thereof. Similarly, injury and causation are essential features of
every countervailing duty (CVD) case, save for ones involving a prohibited
(Red Light) subsidy. However, in a CVD case, under the WTO *Agreement on
Subsidies and Countervailing Measures (SCM Agreement)*, the relevant
concept is broader than injury — it is adverse effects, which may be material
injury or threat thereof, price depression or suppression, or nullification or
impairment of benefits. Moreover, where a Red Light (*i.e.*, export or import
substitution) subsidy is proven, there is an irrebuttable presumption that
adverse trade effects exist. What rebuttable presumption arises in a case
involving a Dark Amber subsidy?

Evidently, understanding and applying the legal criteria for injury and
causation, both at national and multilateral levels, are critical in the successful prosecution or defense of an AD or CVD case. The drama of this aspect
of the case involves competing stories woven from data. For AD cases, Article
3:1 of the WTO *Antidumping Agreement* demands a determination of injury,
to be consistent with Article VI of GATT, must be based on "positive evidence,"
and "involve an objective examination" of three variables:

  i.   *Volume*, that is, the volume of dumped imports.

  ii. *Price*, that is, the effect of dumped imports on suppressing or
       depressing prices in the importing country of like products (which
       are domestically manufactured merchandise that compete with the
       dumped goods).

  iii. *Effects*, that is, the consequent impact of the dumped imports on
       producers in the importing country of like products.

Significantly, Article 3:4 calls for a broad inquiry into "all relevant economic factors and indices having a bearing on the state of the industry." It lists several indicia, including (1) declines (actual and potential) in sales, profits, output, market share, productivity, return on investments, and capacity utilization, (2) domestic price suppression or depression, (3) the magnitude of the dumping margin, (4) negative effects (actual and potential) on cash flow, inventories, employment, wages, growth, and ability to raise new capital.

As intimated, following a dumping margin or subsidization determination, there is a two-pronged inquiry — into injury, and into causation. Conceptually, that inquiry indeed is in two steps. Are there deleterious repercussions? If so, then are they the result of subject merchandise? In practice, the two steps often are conflated. On causation, both WTO and U.S. law are considerably less precise than on injury. Essentially, as long as injury occurs by reason of dumped merchandise, causation is assumed. Small wonder, then, that in practice, causation winds up being confused with correlation. Clever choice of the period of investigation (POI) helps ensure the time during which merchandise is dumped corresponds to the time of woe as described by a petitioner.

II. KEY TECHNICAL POINTS

At the outset, a few technical details are important to appreciate. Tripping up on them can affect the outcome of an injury investigation, and thereby an AD or CVD case.

A. A Second "Like" Product Determination

While the Department of Commerce (DOC) renders a decision about like products during the dumping margin or subsidy determination phase of an AD or CVD case, respectively, the International Trade Commission (ITC) typically also must do so in the injury-causation phase.[1] The DOC decision is based on a comparison of subject merchandise to a foreign product, asking whether the allegedly dumped or subsidized merchandise is "like" that sold in the home market of the exporting country. The ITC decision entails comparing allegedly dumped or subsidized merchandise with a product made in the U.S. The inquiry is whether the subject merchandise is "like" a domestic one.

B. Circularity in the Definition of "Materiality"

Do not bother looking to the Title 19 of the U.S. Code for a meaningful definition of a key term, namely, "materiality." In a U.S. AD or CVD case, existence of "material" injury typically is alleged. Alleging threat of "material" injury is not uncommon. Yet, the definition of "materiality" is of little help to petitioner or respondent alike (unless either side views ambiguity as an asset). That definition is harm that is not inconsequential, immaterial, or unimportant. (*See* 19 U.S.C. § 1677(7).) Legend has it the definition arose out

---

[1] *See* 19 U.S.C. § 1677(10) (definition of "domestic like product"); Torrington Company v. United States, 747 F. Supp. 744 (CIT 1990), *aff'd* 938 F.2d 1278 (Fed. Cir. 1991).

of Tokyo Round era negotiations involving the U.S. Trade Representative (USTR) in the Carter Administration, Robert Strauss, and the European Communities (EC).

C. Material Retardation

Technically, a third basis on which to render an affirmative injury determination under U.S. AD or CVD law is material retardation of the establishment of a domestic industry. (*See* 19 U.S.C. § 1673b(a)(1)(B)). However, as a practical matter, that basis is rarely if ever successful. The reason is the extraordinarily low threshold for "establishing" an industry, and thus the truly difficult proposition to prove, namely, that dumped or subsidized merchandise are materially retarding that establishment.

It is an overstatement to say the ITC is likely to conclude a domestic industry is set up if the first few steps of implementing a business plan and holding key meetings (*e.g.*, with bankers) have been taken. Any substantial commitment, by the petitioner, to commence production — even if manufacturing has not started — is enough to "establish" an industry. No machinery or facility need be acquired, put into operation, or even contracted for. What if an existing producer (*e.g.*, of dry, salted codfish) seeks a new source of supply for a raw material (*e.g.*, cod from Alaska), but alleges dumping inhibits it from procuring that source? The ITC response is sure to be a new source of supply for an input would not mean a new industry is established, hence the converse situation — no new input — is not one in which creation of a new industry is thwarted.[2]

D. National, Regional, or Multilateral Forums

Save for a statutory ("as such") challenge, as in the WTO Appellate Body cases on the *1916 Act* and the *Byrd Amendment*, AD and CVD cases typically start — and finish — at the national level. Accordingly, they involve private parties arguing before an administrative tribunal (such as the DOC and ITC), and possibly to a formal court (such as the Court of International Trade, in New York). Only if the case raises issues under an applicable free trade agreement (FTA) does it escalate into a regional dispute, such as under Chapter 19 of the *North American Free Trade Agreement (NAFTA)*. Only if the case raises issues under the WTO *Antidumping* or *SCM Agreement* does it lead to a case between sovereigns, namely, the importing and exporting WTO Member countries, under the *Understanding on Rules and Procedures Governing the Settlement of Disputes (Dispute Settlement Understanding, or DSU)*.

---

[2] *See Memorandum to the International Trade Commission from the General Counsel, Legal Issues in Certain Dried Salted Codfish from Canada*, Inv. No. 731-TA-199 (preliminary) (22 August 1984).

III. DEFINING THE INDUSTRY AND MARKET

A. Excluding Related Parties and the 1992 *Torrington* Case

TORRINGTON COMPANY v. UNITED STATES
790 F. Supp. 1161, 1168-69 (CIT 1992), *aff'd* 991 F.2d 809
(Fed. Cir. 1993)

DiCarlo, Chief Judge.

Plaintiff brings this action challenging the negative preliminary determinations of injury by the U.S. International Trade Commission in the antidumping and countervailing duty investigations regarding *Ball Bearings, Mounted or Unmounted, and Parts Thereof, from Argentina, Austria, Brazil, Canada, Hong Kong, Hungary, Mexico, the People's Republic of China, Poland, the Republic of Korea, Spain, Taiwan, Turkey, and Yugoslavia*, 56 Fed. Reg. 14,534 (Int'l Trade Comm'n 1991) (neg. prelim.). . . . The Court affirms the Commission's determinations and holds the Commission did not abuse its discretion . . . by declining to exclude related parties from its consideration of the condition of domestic industry. . . . [The Court also affirmed the ITC's determination that (1) the ITC did not abuse its discretion in relying upon questionnaire data to determine the condition of the industry, (2) there was no reasonable indication of material injury or threat thereof to a domestic industry, and (3) the Commission should not cumulate imports. Omitted are those portions of the opinion.]

. . . .

Discussion

. . . .

B. *The Commission's Decision not to Exclude Related Parties*

Plaintiff contends the Commission erred by failing to exclude from its analysis of the domestic industry related parties who import or are related to exporters of the subject merchandise. *See* 19 U.S.C. § 1677(4)(B). . . . Plaintiff argues financial indicators relevant to the condition of the domestic industry were skewed by inclusion of related parties.

The decision whether to exclude parties who import or are related to exporters of the subject merchandise from consideration of the domestic industry is within the discretion of the Commission. . . . In making this determination, the Commission examines whether there are "appropriate circumstances" for excluding the firm in question from the definition of the domestic industry. . . . The court has upheld the Commission's practice of examining such factors as: (1) the percentage of domestic production attributable to related producers; (2) the reason why importing producers choose to import the subject merchandise (whether to benefit from unfair trade practice or to enable them to continue production and compete in the domestic market), or; (3) the competitive position of the related producer vis-à-vis other domestic producers. . . .

The Commission concluded that appropriate circumstances did not exist to exclude related parties from consideration of the domestic industry. . . . The Commission noted that the ball bearing industry is global in nature and dominated by a small number of multinational companies. . . . Those companies, including plaintiff, operate production facilities in several countries, where production is rationalized to meet the particular needs of each country's market. . . . Since those companies do not find it efficient to produce all ball bearing lines in their U.S. facilities, they import ball bearings or parts from their foreign production operations. . . . The Commission found the related parties' importation was not undertaken principally to benefit from unfair trade practices. . . . The Commission also explained the related parties generally had a longstanding presence as U.S. producers, and that import volume from the subject countries was smaller than U.S. production for each of the related parties and was in most instances quite low. . . . It also noted the related parties collectively account for a substantial proportion of U.S. sales and include some of the largest domestic producers of ball bearings. The Commission determined that exclusion of the related parties could present a distorted view of the industry. . . . The Court finds it was reasonable for the Commission to conclude appropriate circumstances did not exist for exclusion of any of the related parties.

Plaintiff argued the related parties' production rationalization and import practices indicate they shielded their domestic operations from the effects of the imported merchandise. As a result, according to plaintiff, the related parties benefited from unfairly traded ball bearings imported from the subject countries as well as from nine other countries already subject to an antidumping order. Nonetheless, the Commission has the discretion to make a reasonable interpretation of the facts, and the Court will not decide whether it would have made the same decision on the basis of the evidence.

B. Captive Production and the 2001 *Japan Hot-Rolled Steel* Case

Making a like product for a downstream article (which could be a finished article, derivative article, or more advanced version of the article) is called "captive production," and by definition it is not for sale in the merchant market. That is, "captive production" refers to internal transfers of a like product from within different parts of a business enterprise. That production does not enter the open — *i.e.*, merchant market — into which a like product is sold to independent buyers. Obviously, vertical integration is a classic instance in which captive production occurs.

Of the three categories of data an administering authority can use to assess material injury, or threat thereof, in an AD or CVD case, namely, (1) volume, (2) price, and (3) all other relevant economic factors, by far the third category is the largest. Within the third category, one important economic statistic used to assess effects of allegedly dumped or subsidized merchandise on a domestic industry is the Import Penetration Ratio. Conceptually, its formula is:

| Import Penetration Ratio | = | Imports of Subject Merchandise | × | 100 |

Total U.S. Market

The denominator includes both imports of subject merchandise and the domestically-produced like product. The figures in both the numerator and denominator must be from the same POI, and could be in value or volume terms.

However, the market for a domestically-made like product itself consists of two segments:

(1)   The merchant market, wherein buyers of the product are independent of the producer-seller.

(2)   The captive production market, wherein the producer-seller consumes the product at issue, as an input into a finished or derivative article, or a more advanced version of the product.

In the merchant market, a domestic like product competes directly with subject merchandise. In the captive production market, that is not so. The buyer is affiliated with, and relies for supply on, the producer-seller. The quintessential, common instance of this commercial chain is vertical integration.

The obvious question in an injury determination in which the Import Penetration Ratio is studied and captive production exists whether it is fair to include in the denominator of the Ratio data from the captive production market. That is, should the ITC focus solely on the merchant market, when a producer-seller transfers a significant amount of its production of the like domestic product? Articles 3-4 of the WTO *Antidumping Agreement* (detailed as they are) do not answer the question, nor does GATT Article VI (as the GATT drafters almost certainly did not contemplate the issue). However, U.S. law treats the question head on.

Under U.S. AD and CVD law, the short answer is "yes, the ITC should focus on the merchant market." Specifically, Section 222(b)(2) of the *1994 Uruguay Round Agreements Act* (codified at 19 U.S.C. § 1677(7)(C)(iv)) amended U.S. AD and CVD law in respect of market share and other factors affecting the financial performance of a domestic industry. If the ITC finds a domestic like product that is produced internally and consumed captively in a downstream article:

(1)   does not enter the merchant market for that product, *i.e.*, it does not compete with subject merchandise imports, and conversely the domestic like product sold in the merchant market is not generally used to make the downstream article, and

(2)   is the predominant material input in making the downstream article,

then the ITC considers only the merchant market. The ITC must exclude captive production from the denominator of the Import Penetration Ratio.

Manifestly, excluding captive production sales from the denominator will decrease the size of the denominator, thereby boosting the Ratio and strengthening the case for the petitioner. (A higher Ratio suggests subject merchandise has a greater deleterious effect on domestic producers.) Small wonder, then, why Japan sued the U.S. in the WTO, arguing the American statute was inconsistent with the *Antidumping Agreement*, both as such and as applied. *See United States — Anti-Dumping Measures on Certain Hot-Rolled Steel Products from Japan*, WT/DS184/AB/R (adopted 23 August 2001). In the underlying U.S. proceeding, the ITC based an affirmative injury determination on just 30 percent of domestic sales by American steel producers. Because of the statute, the ITC ignored the larger, more profitable, segment of the U.S. steel market, wherein producers consumed hot-rolled steel internally to make other products. Surely the statute precludes a balanced assessment of the economic health of the overall industry. It neglects the plain fact American steel companies do very well for themselves in the captive production market, which is shielded entirely from import competition. To put Japan's argument bluntly, an injury determination that segments a market in this way, dwelling on the segment affected by imports, is biased in in favor of the petitioner.

Both sides scored a partial victory. Japan failed to prove the statute was a *prima facie* violation of GATT—WTO obligations, particularly Articles 3:1 and 3:4 of the *Antidumping Agreement*. That was because the U.S. statute directs the ITC to "focus primarily" on the merchant market. Neither it nor the *Statement of Administrative Action* orders the ITC to focus "exclusively" on that market. But, the U.S. failed to defend the use of the statute by the ITC in the case at bar, because an exclusive focus is precisely what the ITC gave to the merchant market.

In a case such as *Japan Hot-Rolled Steel*, to what extent does the Appellate Body render an interpretation of American trade remedy law, as well as provide an opinion on how the relevant statute is applied by American authorities? Is the interpretation ineluctable? Is it an infringement on sovereignty?

IV. MATERIAL INJURY

A. Evaluating All Factors and the 2001 *Thailand Steel* Case

WTO and FTA case law on injury and causation continues to evolve. One trend is a lack of tolerance for sloppy injury investigations. Rightly so, the Appellate Body has enforced rules in Article 3of the *Antidumping Agreement* requiring a careful, reasoned inquiry into the factors that caused injury in and AD case of adverse trade effects in a CVD case. In the 2001 *Thailand Steel* case, Thailand assessed final AD duties of 27.78 percent on "H beams" from Poland made of iron or non-alloy steel. *See* WTO Appellate Body Report, *Thailand — Anti-Dumping Duties on Angles, Shapes and Sections of Iron or Non-Alloy Steel and H-Beams from Poland*, WT/DS122/AB/R (adopted 5 April 2001).

A key issue on appeal was Article 3:4 of the WTO *Antidumping Agreement*. Must an administering authority examine all economic variables listed therein when making an injury determination? Thailand argued "no," stressing the adjective in Article 3:4 that all "relevant" factors must be checked. (Thailand also interpreted semi-colons and the disjunctive ("or") in Article 3:4 oddly, to suggest that the list of factors in the provision amounted to checking one index in each of the four factor groupings.) Poland emphasized the word "all." The Appellate Body agreed with the Panel, namely, "all" means "all," and the Panel's reasoning in which the Panel relied on customary international legal rules of treaty interpretation, and the Appellate Body's own precedent in Argentina — Safeguard Measures on Imports of Footwear (in which it interpreted a provision on injury determination factors in the WTO *Agreement on Safeguards*, Article 4:2(a), which is akin to Article 3:3 of the *Antidumping Agreement*). In sum, each index associated with each factor listed in Article 3:4 must be checked. Simply put, there are 15 variables in the Article 3:4, and checking each is mandatory.

B. Material Injury Factors and the 1982 *SCM* Case

SCM CORP. v. UNITED STATES
United States Court of International Trade
544 F. Supp. 194, 195-196, 198-201 (1982)

NEWMAN, JUDGE.

I.

Background

This action, brought . . . by SCM Corporation (SCM), a domestic portable typewriter manufacturer, is again before the Court following my remand to, and the responsive Statement of Reasons by, the United States International Trade Commission ("Commission") in *Portable Electric Typewriters From Japan*. . . . Plaintiff has contested the Commission's negative determination of injury, . . . and now before the Court is the Commission's new Statement of Reasons. . . .

. . . .

. . .[O]n remand, the Commission has reexamined the record before it and provided this Court with a new Statement of Reasons. The central issue is whether the Commission's negative injury determination is correct in light of the reasons advanced in its initial and new Statement[s] of Reasons and the record before the Commission. . . . [T]he Commission's negative injury determination is affirmed.

. . . .

II.

Opinion

. . . .

C. *Market Penetration by LTFV Imports*

In its original Statement of Reasons, the Commission majority acknowledged that the LTFV [less than fair value] imports from Japan had obtained a significant share of the domestic market for portable typewriters during the period of . . . investigation (October 1973 — March 1974), but posited that "[i]mport penetration alone is not an adequate basis for determining injury." The Commission majority explained that none of the other tests of injury applied in this case showed injury to the domestic industry, but to the contrary such tests indicated that the domestic industry (*viz.*, SCM) had prospered and was likely to continue expanding.

In its new Statement, the Commission has . . . further elaborated upon its view that market penetration alone is an insufficient basis for an affirmative finding of injury.

The Commission's new Statement on remand cites the facts that the affected domestic industry in this case is represented by a single large firm (SCM) that has no domestic competitors and holds a dominant position in the United States market; that during the period covered by the investigation (1971-74) SCM showed improved performance in all indices of the health of the industry; and that the Commission's view respecting market penetration is consistent with prior Commission precedent. Further, the Commission observed:

> In view of the expanding and increasingly profitable business of the single domestic producer, the mere fact of significant import penetration is not by itself capable of demonstrating injury. This is even more the case since the data show that import penetration dropped sharply in the last year for which information was collected.

And apparently recognizing that the market penetration issue posed by the Court's remand raises essentially a question of law, the Commission stated:

> If increasing penetration alone were adequate to show injury, such a conclusion could be reached by a computer, negating the need for the conceived scheme of economic analysis, and *weighing of all factors* such as production, shipments, capacity utilization, employment and profitability by a collegial body of human beings. [Emphasis added.]

I fully agree with the Commission's rejection of what in essence amounts to a *per se* injury rule based upon significant market penetration. In *Armstrong Bros. Tool Co., et al v. United States (Daido Corporation, Steelcraft Tools Division, Party-in-Interest)*, 483 F. Supp. 312, *aff'd*, 626 F.2d 168 (1980), . . . this Court emphasized the complex multifaceted economic and financial analysis involved in making an injury determination . . . and the broad discretionary authority vested in the Commission. Hence, although significant market penetration by the LTFV imports is obviously a highly relevant factor, the Commission has the discretion — indeed an obligation — to consider and weigh a number of other pertinent economic and financial criteria, and consider all the facts and circumstances, including the health of the domestic industry. That approach is precisely what the Commission followed in this case, eschewing any *per se* injury rule predicated upon significant market penetration.

In view of *Armstrong*, there is now a judicially approved explanation as to the reason why no single economic or financial factor necessarily constitutes injury. . . . Therefore, quite apart from the Commission's rationale expressed in its new Statement of Reasons, the question of law raised on remand pertaining to significant market penetration has been judicially answered in agreement with the rationale applied by the Commission.

Plaintiff's arguments are directed essentially at the relative weight and significance the majority Commissioners accorded to the various factors considered (including market penetration), and also directed at the weight of the evidence. But fundamentally, the relative weight the Commission chose to accord market penetration vis-á-vis other equally pertinent injury criteria considered was a matter of discretion and expert judgment; and as we have seen, it is not the function of the Court in reviewing an injury determination of the Commission . . . to weigh the evidence or to substitute its judgment for that of the Commission. Here, the Commission in making its injury determination acted well within its discretion in giving more weight to the various indices of the health of the domestic industry (supported by substantial evidence) than to the factor of significant market penetration, which market penetration the Commission noted had dropped precipitously in the last year for which information was collected.

D. *Price Suppression*

The Commission's original Statement found the evidence of record insufficient to establish price suppression. Plaintiff argued in its original motion for summary judgment that in determining the existence of price suppression, the Commission should have made a comparison between the wholesale price index for portable typewriters and that for office typewriters, rather than between the index for portable typewriters and that for office and store machines and equipment. In the remand order, . . .the Commission was directed "to reconsider and advise this Court whether there was price suppression, after comparing the wholesale price indexes for portable typewriters and office (electric) typewriters; or to supply this Court with specific reasons why such basis for comparison is inappropriate."

The Commission, in its new Statement, has "upon reevaluation of the record" again found no substantial evidence of price suppression as a result of the LTFV imports of portable electric typewriters. Indeed, on remand the Commission, after comparing the respective wholesale price indexes for portable typewriters and office electric typewriters (the comparison ordered by this Court), found:

> . . . prices for both types of typewriters increased at a similar pace throughout the 1971-1974 period. This information strongly tends to show no suppression of prices by reason of LTFV imports.

In the course of reconsidering its prior finding relative to the absence of price suppression, as required by this Court, the Commission carefully considered and discussed in its new Statement the problem of using certain base years for making a realistic wholesale price-index comparison between office typewriters and portable typewriters. Given all the facts and circumstances taken into account by the Commission, I find the Commission's approach to be rational and supported by substantial evidence. Plaintiff's discussion in its brief of statistical methodology suggesting the re-basing of indexes and assertion of certain facts to challenge the Commission's findings are unsupported by the record.

E. *Lost Sales*

The majority's original Statement of Reasons made no explicit finding of lost sales. However, the dissenting Commissioners apparently reasoned that lost sales were implicit or inferable from SCM's loss of a significant share of the market. However, no evidence of record respecting lost sales is referred to by the dissenters.

My order of remand directed the Commission to "make and report to this Court a specific finding of fact respecting whether there were lost sales as a consequence of market penetration by the Japanese LTFV imports." Responding, the Commission's new statement concluded that "[n]o information in the record of this case offers substantial evidence that the domestic industry lost a significant number of sales, or was injured thereby, as a result of imports of portable electric typewriters from Japan."

Plaintiff maintains that the Commission's new Statement is not responsive to the Court's directive. This contention is plainly untenable. In point of fact, the Commission set forth in detail the basis for its conclusion and specifically addressed plaintiff's contentions.

Thus, the Commission rejected the argument that the increased market share obtained by the Japanese imports must necessarily have been achieved at the expense of the domestic industry in the form of lost sales. The information before the Commission showed that while the percentage of the market attained by the Japanese imports increased during the period of 1971-74, *the market share* in that period for all *imports dropped, and consequently, SCM's own sales increased substantially, both relatively to imports and in absolute terms*. Moreover, the Commission points up that the introduction of lower-priced models from Japan —

> . . . created a vastly increased market for portable typewriters by stimulating demand. As a result, only at most a small portion of the sales of Japanese imports represented a loss to SCM; instead, many represent sales that likely would never have been made in the absence of the low-end models from the market.

The Commission further considered plaintiff's contention that SCM lost specific sales to customers in the mass-merchandising area. On that score, the Commission found the information presented by SCM was "largely speculative and . . . rebutted in part by other information in the record." Specifically, the Commission rejected SCM's claimed losses to three accounts predicated, not on an actual decline in sales, "but on a projection of the amount of sales that SCM might have made in the absence of LTFV imports." In that connection, the Commission observed:

> SCM compares its actual average sales per store for three accounts in 1970 with its sales per store in 1974, measuring its claimed loss

by the difference between the actual 1970 sales and the sales SCM would have made if it had maintained its 1970 ratio of sales per store.

The assumption that each new store added by the three mass merchandisers handled as many portable typewriters as each store did in 1970 is disputed by other testimony in the record. It was pointed out that new stores opened by Kmart in 1973 and 1974 were smaller than prior stores and devoted less display space to typewriters. In addition, one of the three mass merchandisers, in a confidential submission, informed the Commission that SCM's sales to it steadily increased between 1971 and 1973, and that it only began purchasing directly from the Japanese respondents in 1974. It also stated that if its purchases of LTFV imports had any effect on its business with SCM, it was because of (1) SCM's inability to provide it with the beginning price point models that were purchased prior to 1974 from Royal, and (2) SCM's failure to provide it with the full quantity of SCM's innovative cartridge ribbon typewriters that it could have sold. Finally, . . . the underlying assumption that there was a one-to-one relationship between sales of Japanese imports and sales lost by SCM . . . is untenable. *Thus, there is no creditable evidence of record demonstrating significant lost sales by the domestic industry by reason of LTFV imports.* [Footnotes omitted.] [Emphasis added.]

I agree with the Commission's determination that there is no basis in the record for finding that SCM lost significant sales by reason of the LTFV imports. To overturn the Commission's conclusion on this aspect of the case would require the Court to engage in speculative second guessing, and judging the credibility and weight of certain evidentiary matters in the administrative record, which would usurp the Commission's discretion.

V. THREAT OF MATERIAL INJURY AND THE 1988 *GOSS GRAPHICS* CASE

GOSS GRAPHICS SYSTEM, INC. v. UNITED STATES
United States Court of International Trade
33 F. Supp. 2d 1082, 1085, 1089-1102, 1104 (1998)

POGUE, JUDGE.

Plaintiffs Koenig & Bauer-Albert AG and KBA-Motter Corp. ("KBA"), MAN Roland Druckmaschinen AG and MAN Roland Inc. ("MAN Roland"), Mitsubishi Heavy Industries, Ltd. ("MHI") and Tokyo Kikai Seisakusho, Ltd. ("TKS"), respondents in the underlying investigation, seek review of the final determination of the U.S. International Trade Commission ("ITC" or "Commission"), in *Large Newspaper Printing Presses and Components Thereof, Whether Assembled or Unassembled, From Germany and Japan*, Inv. Nos. 731-TA736 & 737, U.S. ITC Pub. No. 2988 (Aug.1996) ("Final Determination"). Specifically, Plaintiffs challenge the ITC's determination that the industry in the United States producing large newspaper printing presses ("LNPPs") is threatened with material injury by reason of imports from Germany and Japan that are sold at less than fair value ("LTFV"). . . .

BACKGROUND

LNPPs are presses that are designed to print major daily papers for large metropolitan newspapers. LNPPs are capable of producing tens of thousands of newspapers per hour. They have a long life-expectancy and must be extremely reliable. LNPPs are individually designed to meet each newspaper's requirements and require sophisticated engineering, programming and manufacturing capabilities. Their design, construction and installation generally require long-term contracts covering all aspects of sale, delivery and construction.

. . . [T]he ITC found that there was a single domestic industry, consisting of all LNPP producers of the domestic like product. Included in the domestic industry were Goss, the petitioner in the underlying investigation, as well as three LNPP producers that are owned or controlled by foreign LNPP manufacturers.

. . . .

DISCUSSION

. . . .

II. The ITC's Threat Determination

A. *The ITC's Consideration of Economic Factors*

In determining whether an industry in the United States is threatened with material injury by reason of imports, (or sales for importation) of the subject merchandise, the ITC is required to consider, "among other relevant economic factors," the following nine factors:

(I)   if a countervailable subsidy is involved, such information as may be presented to it by the administering authority as to the nature of the subsidy. . . .

(II)   any existing unused production capacity or imminent, substantial increase in production capacity in the exporting country indicating the likelihood of substantially increased imports of the subject merchandise into the United States, taking into account the availability of other export markets to absorb any additional exports,

(III)   a significant rate of increase of the volume or market penetration of imports of the subject merchandise indicating the likelihood of substantially increased imports,

(IV)   whether imports of the subject merchandise are entering at prices that are likely to have a significant depressing or suppressing effect on domestic prices, and are likely to increase demand for further imports,

(V)   inventories of the subject merchandise,

(VI)   the potential for product-shifting if production facilities in the foreign country, which can be used to produce the subject merchandise, are currently being used to produce other products,

(VII)   in any investigation under this title which involves imports of both a raw agricultural product . . . and any product processed from such raw agricultural product . . .,

(VIII) the actual and potential negative effects on the existing development and production efforts of the domestic industry, including efforts to develop a derivative or more advanced version of the domestic like product, and

(IX)   any other demonstrable adverse trends that indicate the probability that there is likely to be material injury by reason of imports (or sale for importation) of the subject merchandise (whether or not it is actually being imported at the time).

19 U.S.C. § 1677(7)(F)(i).

Furthermore, the ITC is to "consider the factors set forth [above] as a whole in making a determination of whether further dumped . . . imports are imminent and whether material injury by reason of imports would occur unless an order is issued. . . ." 19 U.S.C. § 1677(7)(F)(ii).

According to the Court of Appeals for the Federal Circuit, "[a]n affirmative injury determination requires both (1) present material injury and (2) a finding that the material injury is 'by reason of' the subject imports." *Gerald Metals, Inc. v. United States*, 132 F.3d 716, 719 (Fed. Cir.1997). The section of the antidumping statute that discusses the threat factors also includes the "by reason of" language. Thus, a positive threat determination also requires a showing of a causal connection between the LTFV goods and the threatened material injury. . . .

Therefore, after considering all relevant economic factors in making a determination of whether further dumped imports are imminent, the Commission must take an analytically distinct step to comply with the "by reason of" standard: the Commission must determine whether these factors as a whole indicate that the LTFV imports made a material contribution to the threat of the material injury. "[E]vidence of *de minimis* (*e.g.*, minimal or tangential) causation of injury does not reach the causation level required under the statute." *Id.* at 722.

Both German and Japanese Plaintiffs oppose the ITC's finding that the domestic industry is threatened with material injury by reason of subject imports. . . . Plaintiffs complain that although the ITC "claimed that it had 'considered, . . . all statutory factors that are relevant to these investigations,'" it never found that further imports were imminent, and never explained "why it was likely, or even possible, that material injury by reason of imports would occur unless an order was issued." . . . The ITC responds that "the Commission was not required to incorporate in its determination language that simply tracked the statutory language. . . ." . . .

While the ITC is correct, in that this court has stated the ITC need not use the precise language of the statute in making its determination, the ITC's statements and analysis must be "sufficient for the Court to infer that the [Commission] found the threat to be real and imminent." *Metallverken Nederland B.V v. United States*, 728 F. Supp. 730, 747 (1989). . . .

The Court addresses the parties' challenges according to the factors as considered by the Commission in making its determination.

1. *Capacity*

Threat factors II and VI both pertain to production capacity. In the underlying administrative proceeding, Plaintiffs argued that they were operating at nearly full capacity and therefore, "they could not make substantial additional sales to the United States." . . .

The Commission rejected this argument, explaining, "although producers may be operating at high capacity utilization rates, they have demonstrated the ability to shift significant future production to the United States from other export markets in the future." . . .

Plaintiffs challenge the Commission's decision, arguing, "[t]he ITC has not provided any cogent rationale why the plaintiffs would expand capacity and divert exports to the United States. . . ." . . . However, Plaintiffs mischaracterize the Commission's position. It is true that the Commission did not find that Plaintiffs *planned* to expand productive capacity or divert exports to the United States. However, it did not claim to have made such a finding. The Commission simply found that Plaintiffs have the ability to compete for and fill U.S. sales orders. . . . Therefore, the Commission concluded, Plaintiffs' high capacity utilization figures did not preclude a threat determination. . . . The Commission never argued that Plaintiffs' capacity data constituted positive evidence that levels of subject imports would increase. The Commission treated Plaintiffs' capacity data as a neutral factor and appropriately attributed less weight to this data than to its other findings. . . .

Plaintiffs also argue, "the ITC took capacity and capacity utilization 'off the table' and presumed that plaintiffs could fill additional orders in the U.S. market despite their reported capacity limitations." . . . However, the commission did not merely presume the Plaintiffs could fill additional orders, the Commission provided substantial evidence demonstrating that "producers are capable of quickly increasing capacity to satisfy new sales," . . . and that "the capacity of the German and Japanese producers appears to vary in correlation with their production figures." . . . These statements are supported by capacity data in the staff report showing that capacity for both German and Japanese Plaintiffs fluctuated widely during the period of investigation. . . .

Based on these data, the Commission reasonably concluded that subject producers' reported capacity figures did not impose strict limits on their ability to increase production and sales. Thus, the ITC's determination that Plaintiffs' high capacity utilization rates did not preclude further imports was supported by substantial evidence.

2. *Home-Country and Third-Country Sales Opportunities*

In considering the statutory factor of "existing unused production capacity or imminent increase in production capacity," the ITC is required to take into account, "the availability of other export markets to absorb any additional exports. . . ." 19 U.S.C. § 1677(7)(F)(i)(II).

Plaintiffs argue that, "the ITC never made any finding that the [Plaintiffs] lack sales opportunities outside the United States or that adverse market conditions outside the U.S. market will cause them to step up efforts in the United States." . . . Furthermore, Plaintiffs claim to have "introduced unrebutted evidence that demand for LNPPs was increasing in Asia, Eastern Europe and Latin America. The ITC is subject to reversal if it ignores affirmative evidence that its predictions of increased imports are improbable or impossible." . . .

. . . .

Because the data provided by Plaintiffs concerning third-country markets was not specific to LNPPs, the Commission's decision to attribute less weight to that data was reasonable. Furthermore, the table relied on by TKS, showing that home market shipments had increased in 1995, and were expected to increase further in 1996 and 1997, also shows that the percentage of shipments going to the United States will be higher in 1997 than in any year during the period of investigation. . . . . . . Thus, the Commission had substantial evidence to support its determination that the third-country and home-market data did not preclude a finding that exports to the United States could increase in the near future.

3. *Increased Imports and Market Prevention*

Regarding Factor III, Plaintiffs argue, "[t]he *Act* [*i.e.*, the *Tariff Act* of 1930, as amended] requires that the ITC shall consider, in making threat determinations, whether there has been a significant rate of increase of the volume or market penetration of imports of the subject merchandise *indicating the likelihood of substantially increased imports*." . . . "Although the ITC claimed to have found 'a significant increase' in the value if import sales in 1994 and 1995," Plaintiffs argue, "it could not have found that this increase was indicative of any similar increase in 1996, since its staff projected that the German and Japanese producers would make no sales in that year. . . ."

Plaintiffs are correct. [Their data] . . . show no sales by German or Japanese producers in 1996. However, this by itself is not conclusive. There is other evidence on the record that tends to support the Commission's conclusion. The record shows that the volume and market penetration of subject imports increased significantly in 1994 and 1995. . . . Furthermore, the Commission found that German and Japanese producers were competing with Goss on more than seventy-five percent of the sales that would be made in the twelve months following the final determination. . . . The evidence also demonstrates that in 1996, German producers submitted bids on approximately two thirds of the bids pending in the market as of August 1, 1996. . . . Similarly, the Japanese producers had submitted bids on approximately half of the sales pending as of August 1, 1996. . . . Thus here, the Commission's finding of a high number of pending contracts for which German and/or Japanese producers had submitted bids was supported by substantial evidence.

As the Commission explained, "[b]ecause the number and value of sales fluctuate considerably from year to year, changes in industry performance on a year-to-year basis may be of limited utility. . ." . . . Thus, the Commission's decision to attribute less weight to the 1996 data was reasonable.

Plaintiffs also argue that because the *Washington Post* sale was the only sale of subject merchandise in 1995, the Commission's determination that subject imports are increasing was unjustified. . . .

The Court agrees with plaintiffs that one sale "does not make a 'trend,'" and that it would have been unreasonable for the ITC to base predictions of future import levels on one sale, even one as large as the *Washington Post* sale. However, the Commission's determination regarding the likelihood of increased future imports was not based solely on the 1995 sales data. In fact . . . the Commission acknowledged the "changes in industry performance on a year-to-year basis may be of limited utility." . . .

"The Commissioners have the discretion to determine the weight to be given factors they consider." *Metallverken Nederland*, 728 F. Supp. at 735. . . . The high number of pending contracts for which German and/or Japanese producers had submitted bids, together with the Commission's findings regarding the subject imports' increasing value and market share in 1994 and 1995, constitute substantial evidence that imports are likely to increase in the near future.

. . . .

4. *Price Effects of the Subject Merchandise*

With respect to the price effects of future imports, Plaintiffs argue that "the proposition that imports had suppressed or depressed prices was contrary to the findings of the ITC's staff." . . . Specifically, Plaintiffs argue,

> [t]he *Staff Report* indicates that "given a particular specification and level of quality, the final installed price to the customer will be a significant deciding factor." . . . However, the Staff recognizes that non-price factors such as technology, quality, service and compatibility with existing presses are more important than price. . . .

. . . Thus, Plaintiffs contend, "[t]he ITC Staff concluded only that price is determinative for *a hypothetical* sale, where technology, quality and other significant non-price factors are assumed to be the same for foreign and domestic bidders." . . . However, Plaintiffs read the ITC *Staff Report* too narrowly. In fact, the ITC Staff found that during the bid process, "the bids are expected to converge," so that by the time of the final bid, "the presses offered by the different makers generally are reasonably similar and meet specifications." . . . This finding supports the Commission's determination that competition during the bid process plays a significant role in determining the sales price of the subject merchandise.

Plaintiffs also argue that a large fraction of the bids were non-competitive and in a significant number of the competitive bids, the bid was not awarded to the lowest bidder. Plaintiffs maintain "[b]oth of these phenomena are inconsistent with a finding that price is the predominant factor driving procurement decisions." . . .

Again, Plaintiffs mischaracterize the Commission's findings. The Commission did not find that price was the *predominant* factor driving procurement decisions. In fact, the Commission stated, "[a]lthough price appears *not* to be the dominant factor in many bid situations, it is nevertheless often an important factor in the purchaser's decision at the final stage of the bid process." . . . Furthermore, the Commission reasonably determined that the fact that bids were not awarded to the lowest bidder in all cases did not necessarily preclude a finding of price suppression or depression by subject imports. As the Commission explained, "purchasers may seek to negotiate more expensive equipment or additional services at the same price level, thereby exacting a higher value product for what appears to be a price similar to that quoted by a different supplier." . . .

In addition, the Court finds, the Commission's findings were supported by substantial evidence. According to the Commission, the "conventional approach to pricing analysis [was] not particularly useful in these investigations," due to, "the nature of the sales process and the relatively unique characteristics of each LNPP or addition sold," as well as, "the fact that price competition occurs primarily during the extensive and highly competitive bid/ negotiation process for LNPP sales. . . ." The Court agrees that because each LNPP is made to customer specifications, a more conventional approach, based, for example, on price trends over time, would not have been useful. Thus, the Commission's decision to rely on anecdotal evidence in evaluating price effects of the subject merchandise was reasonable.

. . . .

Finally, Plaintiffs argue, the ITC's findings as to the price effects of future imports failed to consider the impact of competition among U.S. producers. . . . "To the extent that this competition would have caused the same price effects in the absence of subject imports, it was improper for the ITC to claim that the price suppression or depression it allegedly observed had been caused by subject imports." . . .

. . . [B]ased on the evidence, the Commission could reasonably have concluded that competition among domestic producers alone could not have caused the price effects attributed by the ITC to the subject imports. Both the Plaintiffs and the Commission agree that price effects of competition, to the extent they exist, occur during the period of negotiation after producers have submitted their bids to the purchaser. . . . [I]n a significant number of the competitive contracts awarded during the period of investigation, Goss faced competition only from foreign producers because no other domestic producers submitted bids. . . . Thus, any price effects caused by competition in these sales could not be the result of other domestic producers. Thus, the Commission could reasonably conclude that at least part of the price effect caused by competition would not have occurred in the absence of the subject merchandise.

There is competing evidence on the record that would tend to support Plaintiffs' view that subject imports did not cause depression or suppression of LNPP prices. For example, the evidence indicates that for many purchasers price is "a threshold factor that competing producers must meet for their initial bids to be competitive." . . . The threshold is set, not by the bids offered by competitors, but by the purchaser's budgetary constraints. . . . Thus, even in the absence of subject merchandise, domestic manufacturers would not be able to charge higher prices at this stage, because prices are limited by the purchaser's budget. . . .

. . . .

Nevertheless, the totality of the evidence does not require a single conclusion. "It is not the Court's function to reweigh the evidence, but to decide whether the Commission's determinations are supported by substantial evidence." *Granges Metallverken [AB v. United States]*, 716 F. Supp. [17] at 21 [(1989)]. "[T]he possibility of drawing two inconsistent conclusions from the evidence does not prevent an administrative agency's finding from being supported by substantial evidence." . . . Here, the Court finds substantial evidence supports the Commission's conclusion that the continued participation of producers of merchandise sold at less than fair value in the bidding process is likely to suppress or depress in the imminent future.

5. *Pending Sales*

In its final determination, the Commission stated that

> [the] small number of pending sales, valued . . . [at more than $125 million], will likely result in intense competition among domestic and foreign suppliers for bid awards. Moreover, this intensified competition for a smaller pool of sales opportunities increases the incentive for suppliers of LTFV imports to compete on the basis of price. . . . This smaller value of pending sales also makes it more likely that purchasers will continue to use the LTFV imports to extract price concessions from domestic producers.

. . . .

Plaintiffs contest the Commission's finding that only a small number of LNPP contracts will be awarded in the near future. . . .

The Commission found "the record shows that German and Japanese producers are now in direct competition with domestic producers for bids that are now pending in the LNPP market. While there is evidence of . . . [fewer than twenty] currently pending sales of LNPPs and additions, there is a varying degree of likelihood that contracts will be awarded on these pending sales in the [then near] future." . . . The Commission concluded that only one-third of these sales are likely to occur in the near future — the first half of 1997 or earlier. . . .

In determining which of these pending sales were "imminent," the Commission chose to rely on the expected sales dates reported in its questionnaire responses and confirmed by purchasers.

Plaintiffs challenge the validity of the Commission's process for identifying imminent purchases. . . . Plaintiffs argue that the Commission based its finding on incomplete and unreliable data. . . . Plaintiffs also claim that the Commission did not pursue purchaser information on the status of a small number of pending additions sales on which petitioner was the sole bidder. . . .

To the extent that Plaintiffs' argument rests on the theory that the ITC could have obtained more data, Plaintiffs' argument is irrelevant. The question is not whether the Commission might have obtained additional information, but whether the determination is supported by substantial evidence on the record. . . .

The limits on the ITC's methodology are of a different character. As long as the methodology and procedures are a "reasonable means of effectuating the statutory purpose, and there is substantial evidence in the record supporting the agency's conclusions, the court will not impose its own views as to the sufficiency of the agency's investigation or question the agency's methodology." *Makita Corp. v. United States*, 974 F. Supp. 770, 787 (1997) (*quoting Ceramica Regiomontana, S.A. v. United States*, 636 F. Supp. 961, 966 (1986), *aff'd*, 810 F.2d 1137 (Fed. Cir. 1987)). . . .

The Commission's determination here relied on information from producers, importers and purchasers. The Commission issued several questionnaires requesting data relating to sales pending in the market place. Specifically, the Commission asked the domestic producers and the German and Japanese importers to report all LNPP bid solicitations that were then pending in the marketplace and requested them to submit detailed information describing the status of the bidding process for these bids. Similarly, in its purchaser questionnaire, the Commission asked purchasers to report detailed bid information for sales that had been finalized during the period and for bids that were then pending.

Subsequently, the Commission staff conducted an investigation to determine how many of the bids pending in the market were to be awarded imminently. . . .

Based on this information, the Commission concluded that one-third of these pending sales [*i.e.*, sales of LNPPs that various producers identified as being pending in the market] were more likely to occur in the near future than other pending sales. . . .

Plaintiffs argue that the Commission's finding is contradicted by marketing data presented by them and the petitioner, showing a large number of orders, with a total value of more than $500 million to be awarded in the near future. . . . Plaintiffs misunderstand the nature of the Commission's threat analysis.

The Commission is required to assess whether imports are imminent and material injury would occur in the absence of an order. Because it takes years to complete the bid process, the Commission appropriately concluded that only pending bids, particularly those in which an award was imminent, were relevant to its threat analysis.

Furthermore, the Commission's decision to include among imminent sales only the pending sales that purchasers confirmed were imminent was reasonable. The Commission has the discretion to assess the probative nature of the evidence obtained in its investigation and to determine whether to discount the evidence or to rely on it. . . . Here, the Commission declined to rely on producer estimates of sales dates when it could not obtain confirmations from the purchasers. . . .

. . . .

6. *Research and Development*

Plaintiffs argue that the Commission's findings with respect to the impact of subject imports on domestic producers' research and development (R & D) activities were not supported by the evidence. . . . Specifically, Plaintiffs assert "[b]ased on the ITC's own findings, subject imports were present at what the ITC described as 'a significant level' throughout the POI [period of investigation]. . . . Yet, that did not prevent Goss from spending a relatively constant amount annually on research and development, or from increasing its R & D spending in years that imports increased. . . ." . . . Furthermore, Plaintiffs argue that the ITC's tables show that Goss's sales increased significantly from 1994 to 1995, while its R & D expenditures decreased during the same period. . . .

The Commission found, "there is a relatively direct correlation between a producer's research and development expenditures and its sales revenues." . . . The Commission concluded, "the continued significant presence of the subject imports in the market will significantly hamper the industry's ability to develop the advanced technologies necessary to stay competitive in this market." . . .

The Commission based its finding in part on the testimony of witnesses for the petitioner noting that the petitioner's ability to commit capital to R & D was directly linked to sales revenues. . . . Consistent with this testimony, the other evidence before the Commission shows that annual expenditures on R & D fluctuated in the same direction as annual sales revenues for 1991-95 each year during the period of investigation. . . .

Plaintiffs' arguments appear to ignore the data regarding the industry's R & D expenditures in 1991, which were more than double those in any other year of the period under investigation. . . . In light of the industry's R & D expenditures for 1991, it was reasonable for the Commission to conclude that there was a relatively direct correlation between a producer's R & D expenses and its sales revenues.

Furthermore, the Commission did not neglect the short-term data relied upon by the Plaintiffs. The Commission simply found that "changes in industry performance on a year-to-year basis" is of limited utility. . . . The Commission relied on the correlation between long-term declines in revenue and research spending, and the inverse relationship of these trends with the long-term increase in import penetration. The Commission has the discretion to make reasonable interpretations of the evidence and to determine the overall significance of any particular factor in its analysis.

. . . .

7. *The Commission's Vulnerability Finding*

Plaintiffs argue that the Commission substituted a finding that the domestic industry was vulnerable for an analysis of the appropriate threat criteria. . . .

While the ITC did state that, "[i]n these investigations, the vulnerability of the domestic industry is an important factor in our consideration of the threat of material injury from subject imports," . . . the Commission did not substitute its finding of vulnerability for consideration of a statutory criteria. As summarized above, the ITC considered each of the statutory criteria relevant to this proceeding.

Furthermore, the ITC's consideration of the current state of the domestic industry was appropriate and relevant to this proceeding. . . .

. . . .

8. *The Impact of Possible Changes in the ITA's Dumping Margins*

Plaintiffs also argue that the magnitude of the dumping margins calculated by the ITA heavily influenced the ITC's determination. Plaintiffs have appealed the ITA's determinations in separate cases before this Court. Therefore, Plaintiffs maintain if the ITA changes the dumping margins announced for Plaintiffs as a result of appeal, "the Court should order the ITC to reconsider its determination to account for those changes, and to correct the other errors in its evaluation of the dumping margins." . . . To the extent that Plaintiffs' argument rests on the theory that a subsequent change in margins in and of itself provides an adequate basis for remand to the Commission, Plaintiffs' argument is flawed.

The antidumping statute directs the Commission to consider the "magnitude of the margin of dumping" in its injury analysis in any antidumping proceeding. 19 U.S.C. § 1677(7)(c)(iii)(V). Specifically, the statute defines the "magnitude of the margin of dumping" in a final injury determination as the margin "most recently published by [the Department of Commerce] prior to the closing of the Commission's official record." 19 U.S.C. § 1677(35)(c)(ii).

The statute does not contemplate that a change in margins provides an automatic basis for remand to the Commission. In fact, the *Statement of Administrative Action* accompanying the [1994] *Uruguay Round Agreements Act* recognizes that "[t]he finality of injury determinations would be seriously compromised if the Commission was required to amend or revisit its determination each time the administering authority modified its dumping margin." . . . Therefore, a subsequent change in margins does not automatically mandate a remand to the Commission by this Court.

. . . .

CONCLUSION

For the foregoing reasons, the ITC's Final determination . . . is sustained.

VI.   THE THREE-PRONGED ADVERSE EFFECTS TEST IN CVD CASES

In a WTO CVD action, injury criteria are not exactly the same as in an AD case in that forum. The CVD injury criteria under the WTO *SCM Agreement* are narrower or broader, depending on the kind of alleged illegal subsidy, than under the *Antidumping Agreement*.

They are narrower in the instance of a prohibited, or Red Light, subsidy. Articles 3-4 of the *SCM Agreement* do not require any showing of injury, if a complainant proves the subsidy at issue falls within the Red Light category. That makes sense, because this category contains the two most trade-distorting subsidies of all — export subsidies, and import substitution subsidies. Their very purpose is to boost exports of domestically produced merchandise, and reduce imports of a like product. It is entirely appropriate to deem irrebuttably that injury occurs from such subsidies.

That argument is not as easily made for actionable subsidies, *i.e.*, the Yellow Light and Dark Amber categories. Programs in these categories may distort trade, but whether they do cannot be a matter of irrebuttable presumption. Thus, in the Yellow Light category — which, essentially, is a catch-all for any program that is not Red or Dark Amber — a complainant must prove that adverse effects occur as a result of the subsidy in question. Article 5 of the *SCM Agreement* sets out a three-pronged test for what constitutes an "adverse effect" from a Yellow Light subsidy:

> i. Injury to the domestic industry of the complaining WTO Member.

> ii. Serious prejudice, or threat of serious prejudice, to the interests of the complaining Member, or to the interests of any other Member, with "serious prejudice" meaning (under Article 6:3) any one or more of the following effects from the subsidy:

>> (1) displacing or impeding imports of a like product into the market of the subsidizing Member (the respondent in the case),

>> (2) displacing or impeding exports of a like product in a third country market (because the subsidized goods are exported to the third country market, too),

>> (3) significant price undercutting, price suppression, or price depression in the "same market," or

>> (4) increasing world market share (on a consistent trend during the subsidization period) of the subsidizing Member in respect of the subsidized product (compared with the average share it had in the previous 3 year period).

> iii. Nullification or impairment of benefits accruing directly or indirectly to the complaining Member, or any other Member, under GATT, in particular the benefits of concessions bound under GATT Article II.

The test is phrased in the disjunctive ("or"), hence any single adverse effect will do. Significantly, with a Dark Amber subsidy — defined exclusively as 1 of 4 types, in Article 6:1 of the *SCM Agreement* — a rebuttable presumption arises of serious prejudice.

Here, then, is where the *SCM Agreement* injury criteria are broader than in the *Antidumping Agreement* — serious prejudice or nullification or impairment of benefits never are grounds for showing injury under the latter accord. However, does the *SCM Agreement*, like the *Antidumping Agreement*, allow for threat of material injury? Examine, also, U.S. law as to whether injury criteria in AD and CVD cases are the same.

Finally, the adverse effects scheme of the Traffic Light System creates litigation incentives. Complainants will seek to characterize facts as a Red Light

Subsidy, to alleviate any burden of proving adverse effects. If the facts do not honestly fit that category, then Dark Amber is their next best choice, because they benefit from a rebuttable presumption of serious prejudice. (In both instances, respondents have the diametric opposite incentive.) Failing that, the battleground is in the Yellow Light category, and a critical issue is whether adverse effects exist.

VII.　SERIOUS PREJUDICE, PRICE SUPPRESSION, AND THE 2005 *UPLAND COTTON* CASE

A.　Price Contingent Subsidies

In the 2005 *Upland Cotton* case (excepted below), Brazil challenged an array of subsidy programs that provided $12.9 billion between 1999 and 2002 to American cotton producers. Among them, the four "price-contingent subsidies" at issue were:

1. *Counter-Cyclical Payments*:

Counter-Cyclical Payments are a means of income support to farmers of certain crops (called "covered commodities"). They supplement Direct Payments and Marketing Loan Program Payments. Specifically, Counter-Cyclical Payments fill a gap between (1) the market price (plus any Direct Payment or Marketing Loan Program Payment) and (2) a government-established target price. For cotton, the target price is 72.4 cents per pound. The eligibility requirements and planting flexibility limitations for Counter-Cyclical Payments are the same as those for Direct Payments. As with Direct Payments, the amount of Counter-Cyclical Payments depends on base acres. Like Direct Payments, Market Loss Assistance Payments, and Production Flexibility Contract Payments, Counter-Cyclical Payments did not exist in 1992, the base year for measuring bound levels of support in the *Peace Clause* of Article 13(b) of the *Agreement on Agriculture*.

2. *Market Loss Assistance Payments*:

This measure provided *ad hoc* annual payments to farmers between 1998 and 2001, who also received Production Flexibility Contract Payments. The eligibility criteria for the two types of measures essentially were the same. Market Loss Assistance Payments were designed to be additional help to farmers to make up for losses caused by low commodity prices. Each payment was made pursuant to separate legislation, the last of which was enacted on 13 August 2001 and covered the Marketing Year (MY) 2001 (*i.e.*, 1 August 2001 to 31 July 2002). A Market Loss Assistance Payment was proportionate to the amount of a Production Flexibility Contract Payment, with the actual amount depending on how much was deemed allocated as a Market Loss Assistance Payment. Marketing Loss Assistance Payments, along with Production Flexibility Contract Payments, were the only two disputed subsidy measures in the *Cotton* case that had expired at the time the terms of reference of the Panel were established.

As for Production Flexibility Contract Payments, this measure also provided income support to farmers. It was established by the *Federal Agricultural*

Improvement and Reform Act of 1996 (also called the *FAIR Act of 1996*, or *1996 Farm Bill*) for MY 1996-2002. They were discontinued in May 2002 by the *Farm Security and Rural Investment Act of 2002* (the *FSRI Act of 2002*, or *2002 Farm Bill*), and replaced by Direct Payments. The U.S. funded farmers who had produced historically one (or more) of seven eligible commodities, one of which was cotton. A historical producer would enroll acres on which it had grown cotton during a base period. The U.S. then would allocate to this producer base acres, and a farm-specific yield per acre. The producer would receive a payment dependent on base acreage and yield per acre at a rate specified annually.

The producer was not required to grow cotton to obtain payments. Rather, the U.S. provided support regardless of what the producer chose to grow, or even if the producer opted not to grow any crop. Significantly, however, there was a limitation on this planting flexibility. The U.S. would reduce or eliminate payments if the producer grew fruits or vegetables (other than dry peas, lentils, and mung beans).

Production Flexibility Contract Payments replaced Deficiency Payments. The latter support measure was created by the *FACT Act of 1990*. Deficiency Payments were relevant to calculation of the 1992 level of support, a benchmark under the *Agreement on Agriculture*. Essentially, a Deficiency Payment for cotton depended on the gap between (1) the national average market price for cotton, or the loan rate under the Marketing Loan Program, whichever was higher, and (2) a target price of 72.9 cents per pound of cotton. Whenever the market price or loan rate fell below the target price, a Deficiency Payment would fill the deficit.

3. *Marketing Loan Program Payments*:

Support under the Marketing Loan Program could take one of a variety of forms. However, common to all forms was payments to farmers depended on the difference between the (1) adjusted world price for cotton, which is a reference price tied to the market price of cotton, and (2) so-called "loan rate" fixed periodically under the Program.

4. *User Marketing Payments, also called Step 2 Payments*:

The U.S. maintained Step 2 Payment schemes since 1990. Successive legislation, such as the *FAIR Act of 1996* (the *1996 Farm Bill*), and Section 1207(a) of the *Farm Security and Rural Investment Act of 2002* (the *FSRI Act of 2002*, or the *2002 Farm Bill*), authorize these schemes. Funds are available to both users and exporters of American cotton. In the *Cotton* case, Brazil successfully challenged Step 2 Payments to users as illegal Yellow Light subsidies causing serious prejudice (namely, price depression) under Articles 5-6 of the *SCM Agreement*, and illegal Red Light import substitution subsidies under Article 3:1(b) of that *Agreement*. (Significantly, in February 2006, to comply with the Appellate Body ruling, and to deliver on a promise the USTR made at the December 2005 Hong Kong Ministerial Conference, the House of Representatives agreed to eliminate Step 2 payments. The Senate approved the elimination in late 2005. Effective 1 August 2006, under the *Deficit Reduction Omnibus Reconciliation Act*, signed by President George W. Bush in February 2006, the U.S. repealed the scheme. However, as late as October

2006, Brazil doubted whether the U.S. was canceling other subsidy programs found illegal under WTO rules as causing serious prejudice — especially countercyclical payments, marketing loan payments, and marketing loan assistance payments. Thus, Brazil triggered a WTO compliance complaint.)

Essentially, the CCC issues marketing certificates or cash payments — collectively called "user marketing payments," or simply "Step 2 Payments" — to eligible domestic users and exporters of cotton when certain market conditions exist. Those conditions relate to pricing, namely, when benchmarks for U.S. cotton pricing are exceeded. The cotton must be "eligible," *i.e.*, domestically produced and baled, and the bale must be opened by an "eligible domestic user" or exported by an "eligible exporter." An "eligible domestic user" of cotton is a person regularly engaged in the business of opening bales of eligible cotton to manufacture the cotton into cotton products in the U.S., and has an agreement with the CCC to participate in the Step 2 Payment program. Textile mills are quintessential examples. An "eligible exporter" of cotton is a person, including a producer or cooperative marketing association) who regularly sells eligible cotton for export from the U.S., and has an agreement with the CCC to participate in the program.

As for market conditions in which Step 2 Payments are made, domestic users must have bought for manufacturing use, or exporters must have sold for export, cotton (that is, eligible cotton) in a week following a 4-week period when two price conditions are met. The two price conditions (below) amount to a requirement that the price of U.S. cotton was higher than in Europe, and the world market price for cotton was lower than a U.S.-set target. In turn, if these requirements are met, then a Step 2 Payment ensures U.S. cotton is price competitive vis-à-vis foreign cotton, because the Payment captures the differential between the (lower) prevailing foreign and (higher) U.S. cotton prices.

Each price condition may be expressed arithmetically. The first price condition, which was used for 1996-2001, was:

Lowest U.S. Price Quote for Cotton Delivered to Northern Europe	—	Northern Europe Price Quote	>	1.25 cents per pound

The condition is satisfied if the U.S. cotton price exceeds the Northern European price by more than 1.25 cents per pound. For 2002-05, this price condition was relaxed by eliminating the 1.25 cents per pound threshold. That is, the right-hand side term was zero, meaning this condition was met whenever the U.S. cotton price was higher than the European price, *i.e.*, whenever U.S. cotton was relatively more expensive by any amount. Intuitively, the condition is designed to encourage buying of American cotton when it would not be economically rational to do so, namely, when American cotton is more expensive than non-U.S. substitutes.

Arithmetically, the second price condition is:

Adjusted World Price of Cotton	< or =	(Market Loan Rate)	×	130 percent

This condition occurs when the world cotton price is at or below a threshold defined by the Market Loan Rate, a target price set by the U.S. Government. Under the *1996 Farm Bill*, for 1996-2001, the threshold was 130 percent of the Market Loan Rate. Under the *2002 Farm Bill*, for 2002-05, this price condition was tightened slightly, by raising the threshold to 134 percent of the Rate. Intuitively, the second condition says the world market price is low when it is not more than about one-third above the U.S. target price. If this condition exists, then it suggests it would be economically rational for domestic users, users elsewhere, and exporters to purchase cotton on the world market — not from U.S. cotton farmers. When the second condition obtains, that suggestion is strengthened.

Taken together, the two conditions, if met, mean it is economically rational for a user or exporter to buy cotton quoted in Northern Europe, or on the world market, rather than the relatively more expensive U.S. grown cotton. Herein lies why the two conditions are triggers for a Step 2 Payment. If the conditions exist, then a Step 2 Payment counter-acts them, making it financially viable to buy American cotton. What is the amount of this Payment? Between 1996-2001 (and again starting 1 August 2006), it was the difference between the two price quotes during the fourth week of the four-week period in which the two price conditions are met, *i.e.*, the difference between the U.S. Price and the Northern European Price, minus the 1.25 cents per pound threshold. From 2002-05, it was the difference between the two Prices, with no threshold subtracted.

B.   The Relevant Market and Price

WTO APPELLATE BODY REPORT, *UNITED STATES — SUBSIDIES ON UPLAND COTTON*
WT/DS267/AB/R (adopted 21 March 2005) (complaint by Brazil)

400. Turning to the question of the relevant "market," we observe that Article 6.3(c) of the *SCM Agreement* addresses the situation where "the effect of the subsidy is . . . significant price suppression . . . in the same *market*." (emphasis added) As the Panel suggested, and the parties agree, it is up to the complaining Member to identify the market in which it alleges that the effect of a subsidy is significant price suppression and to demonstrate that the subsidy has that effect within the meaning of Article 6.3(c). Before the Panel, Brazil identified the following as relevant markets for its claim under Article 6.3(c): (a) the world market for upland cotton; (b) the Brazilian market; (c) the United States market; and (d) 40 third country markets where Brazil exports its cotton and where United States and Brazilian upland cotton are found. In contrast, the United States argued before the Panel that the relevant market under Article 6.3(c) must be "a particular domestic market of a Member," and that it cannot be a "world market."

401. The Panel regarded the absence of any geographic limitation or reference to imports or exports in the text of Article 6.3(c), in contrast to Articles 6.3(a) and (b) and 15.2 of the *SCM Agreement*, as indicating that the "same market" under Article 6.3(c) could be a "world market." Applying this

interpretation to the facts of the present dispute, the Panel concluded that a "world market" for upland cotton does exist. The Panel further stated that "[w]here price suppression is demonstrated in [the world] market, it may not be necessary to proceed to an examination of each and every other possible market where the products of both the complaining and defending Members are found." In the present dispute, having found that "price suppression has occurred in the same world market," the Panel decided that it was not "necessary to proceed to any further examination of . . . alleged price suppression in individual country markets." Thus, the Panel's analysis of the world market for upland cotton formed the basis for its finding that the effect of the price-contingent subsidies is significant price suppression within the meaning of Article 6.3(c).

402. On appeal, the United States submits that the Panel erred in interpreting the words "same market" in Article 6.3(c) of the *SCM Agreement* as including a "world market." It also submits that the Panel's finding that a "world market" exists for upland cotton is inconsistent with certain of its other findings. The United States also argues that, in any case, the Panel did not make a finding that United States and Brazilian upland cotton compete in the world market that it had identified for upland cotton. Brazil contends that significant price suppression under Article 6.3(c) "may apply to *any* 'market,' from local to global, and everything in between."

. . . .

404. The Panel described the ordinary meaning of the word "market" as:

> "a place . . . with a demand for a commodity or service;"[1355] "a geographical area of demand for commodities or services;" "the area of economic activity in which buyers and sellers come together and the forces of supply and demand affect prices."[1356]

405. We accept that this is an adequate description of the ordinary meaning of the word "market" for the purposes of this dispute, and we do not understand the parties to dispute it. This ordinary meaning does not, of itself, impose any limitation on the "geographical area" that makes up any given market. Nor does it indicate that a "world market" cannot exist for a given product. As the Panel indicated, the "degree to which a market is limited by geography will depend on the product itself and its ability to be traded across distances."

406. The only express qualification on the type of "market" referred to in Article 6.3(c) is that it must be "the same" market. Aside from this qualification (to which we return below), Article 6.3(c) imposes no explicit geographical limitation on the scope of the relevant market. This contrasts with the other paragraphs of Article 6.3: paragraph (a) restricts the relevant market to "the market of the subsidizing Member;" paragraph (b) restricts the relevant market to "a third country market;" and paragraph (d) refers specifically to the "world market share." We agree with the Panel that this difference may indicate that the drafters did not intend to confine, *a priori*, the market examined under Article 6.3(c) to any particular area. Thus, the ordinary meaning

---

[1355] *The New Shorter Oxford English Dictionary* (1993).

[1356] *Merriam-Webster Dictionary online.*

of the word "market" in Article 6.3(c), when read in the context of the other paragraphs of Article 6.3, neither requires nor excludes the possibility of a national market or a world market. [As the Appellate Body explained in a footnote: "This stands to reason, given that the purpose of the 'actionable subsidies' provisions in Part III of the *SCM Agreement* is to prevent Members from causing adverse effects to the interests of other Members through the use of specific subsidies, wherever such effects may occur."]

407. Turning to the phrase "in the same market," it is clear to us from a plain reading of Article 6.3(c) that this phrase applies to all four situations covered in that provision, namely, "significant price undercutting," "significant price suppression, price depression [and] lost sales." We read the Panel Report and the participants' submissions as endorsing this interpretation. The phrase "in the same market" suggests that the subsidized product in question (United States upland cotton in this case) and the relevant product of the complaining Member must be "in the same market." In this appeal, the Panel and the participants agree that United States upland cotton and Brazilian upland cotton must be "in the same market" for Brazil's claim under Article 6.3(c) to succeed. Furthermore, the participants agree that these are like products.

408. When can two products be considered to be "in the same market" for the purposes of a claim of significant price suppression under Article 6.3(c)? Article 6.3(c) does not provide an explicit answer. However, recalling that one accepted definition of "market" is "the area of economic activity in which buyers and sellers come together and the forces of supply and demand affect prices," it seems reasonable to conclude that two products would be in the same market if they were engaged in actual or potential competition in that market. Thus, two products may be "in the same market" even if they are not necessarily sold at the same time and in the same place or country. As the Panel correctly pointed out, the scope of the "market," for determining the area of competition between two products, may depend on several factors such as the nature of the product, the homogeneity of the conditions of competition, and transport costs. This market for a particular product could well be a "world market." However, we agree with the Panel that the fact that a world market exists for one product does not necessarily mean that such a market exists for every product. Thus the determination of the relevant market under Article 6.3(c) of the *SCM Agreement* depends on the subsidized product in question. If a world market exists for the product in question, Article 6.3(c) does not exclude the possibility of this "world market" being the "same market" for the purposes of a significant price suppression analysis under that Article.

409. According to the United States, if the market examined pursuant to a claim of significant price suppression under Article 6.3(c) is a "world market," then the subsidized product and any like product will necessarily be in that market and the word "same" in Article 6.3(c) would have no meaning. We do not agree with this argument. As we have explained above, there is no *per se* geographical limitation of a market under Article 6.3(c). It could well be a national market, a world market, or any other market. It is for the complaining party to identify the market where it alleges significant price suppression and to establish that that market exists. In doing so, it is

for the complaining party to establish that the subsidized product and its product are in actual or potential competition in that alleged market. If that market is established to be a "world market," it cannot be said, for that reason alone, that the two products are not in the "same market" within the meaning of Article 6.3(c).

410. For these reasons, we agree with the Panel that, depending on the facts of the case, a "world market" may be the "same market" for the purposes of a claim of significant price suppression under Article 6.3(c) of the *SCM Agreement*.

Chapter 36

CAUSATION

I wish I had an answer to that, because I'm tired of answering that question.

—YOGI BERRA, THE YOGI BOOK 83 (1998) (Hall of Fame Baseball Player and Manager)

DOCUMENTS SUPPLEMENT ASSIGNMENT

1. *Havana Charter* Article 34
2. GATT Articles VI, XVI
3. WTO *Antidumping Agreement* Article 3
4. WTO *SCM Agreement Articles* 1, 3, 5-6, 8, 15

I. CAUSATION IN THEORY

A. Why Causation Matters

In an antidumping (AD) case, it does not suffice to prove a dumping margin and injury or threat thereof exists. In a U.S. proceeding, a private petitioner also must prove material injury or threat to a domestic industry occurs "by reason of dumped" imports. Likewise, in a countervailing duty (CVD) investigation, a private petitioner must show more than the existence of an illegal subsidy and material injury or threat. To be successful, the injury or threat must occur "by reason of" the unlawful subsidy. Likewise, in WTO adjudication, a complainant must show the effect of dumping is material injury or threat, or an unlawful subsidy has one of three adverse effects — material injury or threat, nullification or impairment of benefits, or serious prejudice. A noun between two prepositions ("by reason of"), and words that can be nouns or verbs ("effect"), are ambiguous synonyms for a time-honored and fundamental concept animating through every field of law: causation. In brief, it cannot be overemphasized that causation is an indispensable element in any and every AD or CVD investigation.

What does "cause" mean in an AD or CVD case? The same question may be asked of remedies against fair foreign competition, such as a general safeguard action under GATT Article XIX and the WTO *Agreement on Safeguards* ? To what extent must factors causing alleged injury (or threat) be identified and distinguished from one another? No less significant than the rules in Articles 3:1 and 3:4 of the WTO *Antidumping Agreement* on injury is Article 3:5, which concerns causation. Similarly, Article 15:5 of the *Agreement on Subsidies and Countervailing Measures* (*SCM Agreement*) deals with causation.

In brief, Article 3:5 of the *AD Agreement* requires proof dumped imports cause injury to a domestic industry, and of a causal relationship between dumping and injury, from an examination of all relevant evidence. It also calls for consideration of known factors other than dumping that, simultaneously with dumping, are injuring the domestic industry. Article 15:5 of the *SCM Agreement* is essentially a verbatim copy of Article 3:5.

Examples of possible causal factors, other than subject merchandise imports, are competition from non-dumped or non-subsidized merchandise, declines in demand for the domestically-produced like product, changes in consumption patterns, restrictive business practices, technological change, and poor productivity in the domestic industry. Any injury from these factors must not be attributed to injury caused by dumping or subsidization, *i.e.*, the causal effects of each independent variable operating on the domestic industry must be separated from the other.

The Article XIX general safeguard, and Article 4:2 of the *Safeguards Agreement*, also set out a causation standard. Is that standard the same as in the U.S. escape clause, Section 201 of the *Trade Act of 1974*, as amended? Why or why not? Are causation standards for safeguard relief the same as in AD and CVD law? Should they be, or should they be higher than the standards for an AD or CVD remedy? That is, should the causation standards for remedies against fair and unfair trade be the same? What about causation standards for product specific mechanisms, such as agricultural products?

B. Philosophical Perspectives: Aristotle, Hume, Mill, and Hart

Long before the evolution of modern trade remedy law commenced, philosophers explored a topic that would become central to that law — causation. What does it mean to say one event, X, "causes" another, Y? Under what circumstances is it correct to attribute causation, *i.e.*, when is it certain (if ever) that X "causes" Y? How are possible causal factors, such as X, identified in the first place? How is one possible causal factor, X, weighed against others to ascertain the relative importance of X and the other independent variables in "causing" Y? More recently, scholars of jurisprudence have addressed the problem of causation in law, albeit almost exclusively in domestic contexts such as torts.[1]

---

[1] *The Restatement 2d of Torts* defines, at Section 431, legal cause as:

> The actor's negligent conduct is a legal cause of harm to another if (a) his conduct is a substantial factor in bringing about the harm, and (b) there is no rule of law relieving the actor from liability because of the manner in which his negligence has resulted in the harm.

"Substantial," as noted in Comment (a) to Section 431, requires that a

> defendant's conduct ha[ve] such an effect in producing the harm as to lead reasonable men to regard it as a cause, using that word in the popular sense. . . . [In the popular sense] always lurks the idea of responsibility. . . .

This definition essentially equates "causation" with "substantial factor." Thus, it does not provide a basis for a more rigorous, philosophical grounding. Comment (a) to Section 431 essentially eschews any effort at such, distinguishing "substantial cause" from cause in a philosophical sense. The latter, as the Comment indicates,

Modern trade lawyers know well the importance of causation to the outcome of an AD or CVD case, and likewise for a general safeguards case under GATT Article XIX and the WTO *Agreement on Safeguards*. Yet, trade remedy law is underdeveloped, even crude, in respect of its causation criteria. Might the profound explorations of philosophers provide assistance to trade lawyers — and specifically, legislators responsible for drafting the criteria, and judges charged with interpreting and enforcing the criteria? What nuggets might be mined from jurisprudence scholars?

At the risk of gross oversimplification, philosophical insights into causation from a few Ancient and Continental philosophers, and jurisprudential thinkers, are as follows

1. Aristotle (384-322 B.C.) on Causation

The first Ancient Greek philosopher to examine causation, Aristotle encapsulated into four words the entire inquiry: "on account of what?"[2] He responded by delineating four types of causes, which he derived from the four common ways the Ancient Greek word *aition* was used:

(1) *Material Cause — The Substance of a Thing*

In *Physics*, Aristotle wrote about

> that out of which as a constituent a thing comes to be called a cause.[3]

By this he meant the ingredients that make up a thing, X, are the cause of that thing. They are the parts — the material — from which the thing comes into existence. Aristotle's examples were bronze, used to produce a statute, or silver, used to make a cup.

Evidently, material cause for Aristotle is what contemporary international trade lawyers would think about in rule of origin cases. That is because Aristotle equates "Material Cause" with "to be made of." The latter phrase lies at the heart of origination determinations.

(2) *Formal Cause — What It Is To Be a Thing*

Aristotle also wrote that

> [a]ccording to another [meaning], the form or model is a cause; this is the account of what the being would be, and its genera — thus the

---

includes every one of the great number of events without which any happening would not have occurred.

In effect, the Comment equates philosophical cause with "but-for" causation. To be sure, Anglo-American tort law distinguishes

  i.   "but-for" causation (also called "causation in fact," or the "*sine qua non*" formulation), which asks whether a harm would have occurred without an act, from

  ii.   "proximate" causation, which asks a legal policy question about justice and expedience,, essentially inquiring into whether a specific cause in fact ought to be deemed a cause that gives rise to liability for the harm at issue.

Might Anglo-American tort concepts of causation be of assistance in improving causation criteria in trade remedy law?

[2] ARISTOTLE, A NEW ARISTOTLE READER 98 (J.L. Ackrill ed., 1987).

[3] ARISTOTLE, *Physics, The Four Causes*. Aristotle addresses causation in *Posterior Analytics* and *Metaphysics*, but in Physics he deals with the topic in the context of relationships among objects in the natural world.

cause of an octave is the ratio of two to one, and more generally number — and the parts which come into the account.[4]

In other words, "Formal Cause" is simply the form of a thing that gives the thing its essence, and that is recognized as doing so. To answer "what is it to be X?" is to identify the "formal cause" of X.

For instance, the round shape, red seams, white coating, and hard interior give a baseball its form, and thus are the formal cause of the baseball. Equating "Formal Cause" with recognized items that impart essence to a thing is redolent of the essential character test for classification in Customs Law. However, this verbal equation is confusing in modern English parlance. Semantically, "cause" and "what it is to be" are not comprehended as synonyms.

(3) *Efficient Cause — That Which Produces a Thing*

Material and Formal Cause are static, but for Aristotle, Efficient (as well as Final) Cause is dynamic. The first two kinds of causes explain X as it is, and what it is, but not how X came to be X. "[W]hence comes the origin of change" is the Efficient Cause of a thing.[5] Aristotle wrote:

> Again, there is the primary source of the change or the staying unchanged.[6]

By this he meant the Efficient Cause of X is the thing or person that is responsible for X being X. If a change to X, or X staying put, results from the maker of X, then that maker is the Efficient Cause of X. The Efficient Cause is the reason for change or stability in X. Aristotle gave as an example (albeit a gender biased one) of efficient cause that "the father is a cause of the child."[7] That example highlights the fact there may be two efficient causes (mother and father), or more (mother, father, and doctor), of a person (a child). Indeed, for Aristotle, "the man who has deliberated is a cause," which indicates the person(s) who thought about a new child (*e.g.*, grandparents or siblings) are an efficient cause.[8] Notably, to him, every physical substance — including a child — is a combination of matter (which, he said, the mother provides) and form (imparted by the father). Another illustration — one which ought to resonate with lawyers — Aristotle offered of Efficient Cause is an adviser is a cause of the action taken by the advised.

In common contemporary thinking and parlance, the idea of "cause" has been reduced to Efficient Cause. That is a result of the Scientific Revolution. Arguably, this reduction results in a poor, or at least inchoate, conception of causation, particularly because it neglects Aristotle's fourth meaning — Final Cause.

(4) *Final Cause — The Purpose of a Thing*

The teleological meaning of "cause" for Aristotle is conveyed by the term "Final Cause." To identify "what is X for?," that is, what the purpose of X is, why does X exist?, is to delineate the Final Cause of X. As Aristotle puts it:

---

[4] *Id.*

[5] *Id.*, Book II, Chapter 9.

[6] *Id.*, The Four Causes.

[7] *Id.*

[8] *Id.*

[A] thing may be a cause as the end. . . .

. . . .

That is what something is for, as health might be what a walk is for. On account of what does he walk? We answer "To keep fit" and think that, in saying that, we have given the cause. And anything which, the change being effected by something else, comes to be on the way to the end, as slimness, purging, drugs, and surgical instruments come to be as means to health: all these are for the end, but differ in that the former are works and the latter are tools.[9]

As with Efficient Cause, Final Cause poses semantic difficulties for contemporary international trade lawyers. Effectively, Aristotle equates "Final Cause" with a subordinating conjunction in English — "because." However, "because" also is used by them in a phrase like "injury to a domestic industry occurred because of subject merchandise."

Notably, Aristotle never claimed necessity to be an important element in causation. In contrast, Alexander of Aphrodisias (late 2nd and early 3rd centuries A.D.), urged that for a causal relationship, "[it] is necessary that the same effect will recur in the same circumstances, and it is not possible that it be otherwise."[10] "Necessary" is a word found in many international trade laws.

2. Hume (1711-1776) on Causation

In *A Treatise of Human Nature*, Book I, Part III (1739-40) and *An Enquiry Concerning Human Understanding* (1748), the 18th century Scottish philosopher David Hume argued investigations of causation are unproductive, doubted (more so than Rene Descartes) the existence of causal relationships, and rejected the view that

whatever has a beginning must have a cause . . .

. . . .

There is no object, which implies the existence of any other if we consider these objects in themselves, and never look beyond the idea which we form of them.[11]

That is because it is impossible to establish a necessary causal relationship between objects. Hume dissected the notion of causation into three elements — (1) continuity in space and time between cause and effect, (2) priority in time of cause relative to effect, and (3) the necessity of a link between a cause and effect.

---

[9] ARISTOTLE, *supra* note 2, at 98.

[10] RICHARD SORABJI, NECESSITY, CAUSE, AND BLAME: PERSPECTIVES ON ARISTOTLE'S THEORY 64-66 (1980).

[11] BERTRAND RUSSELL, THE HISTORY OF WESTERN PHILOSOPHY 664-65 (1945).

In *An Enquiry Concerning Human Understanding*, Hume explained the first, contiguity in time, as

> an object, followed by another, and where all the objects similar to the first are followed by objects similar to the second.[12]

The second element, he said, means "where if the first had not been, the second never had existed," which suggesting a temporal priority of a cause to its effect.[13] This element sometimes is called the counterfactual definition, or theory, of causation.[14] The first two elements — contiguity and priority — are indispensable features of the contemporary legal concept of proximate (or but-for) causation.[15]

However, it is the third element on which Hume placed the greatest emphasis. To him, the third element is

> an object, followed by another, and whose appearance always conveys the thought to that other.[16]

Said Hume, this element commonly is thought to be "causation." But, the relentless empiricist wrote:

> When we look about us towards external objects, and consider the operation of causes, we are never able, in a single instance, to discover any power or necessary connexion; any quality, which binds the effect to the cause, and renders the one an infallible consequence of the other.[17]

Thus, for example, if one billiard ball, X, strikes another, Y, and Y then moves, it is typically said that X "caused" the motion of Y. Hume disagreed, arguing the statement merely recites what we perceive, indeed what we habitually observe. In truth, staring at X and Y never will produce a sensory perception of a causal connection between them.

That is, for Hume, statements about causation are nothing more than assumptions about necessary connections between supposed causes and effects that spring from our expectations and habits. They are based on impressions, *i.e.*, on what physical senses — sight, sound, taste, and touch — perceive. However, it is impossible to have a sensory impression of a causal connection between events, because a sensory perception of necessity is impossible. Hume famously declares:

> We have no other notion of cause and effect, but that of certain objects, which have always conjoined together.[18]

---

[12] David Hume, An Enquiry Concerning Human Understanding 60 (Tom L. Beauchamp ed., 2000).

[13] *Id.*

[14] *See* David Lewis, *Causation*, *in* Metaphysics: An Anthology 436, 436-43 (Jaegwon Kim & Ernest Sosa eds., 1999).

[15] The Restatement (Second) of Torts 9 (1965), as well as Black's Law Dictionary, refers to "proximate cause" as a cause that directly produces a result, and without which the result would not have occurred.

[16] Hume, *supra* note 12, at 60.

[17] Russell, *supra* note 11, at 660.

[18] *Id.* at 665.

There neither is nor can be such a thing as an impression of a causal connection. What we call causation is not *a priori* knowledge of links between events. Rather, it is *a posteriori* empirical experience of, *i.e.*, constantly witnessing, the conjunction of events.[19] We witness one event following another, and we thereby constantly associate ideas that one event follows another. But, we cannot perceive the critical third element in an ostensible causal relationship — necessity, a necessary connection between cause and effect.

Another way to put the point is Hume views causation as correlation that is psychological in character. That conclusion is unduly pessimistic for international trade lawyers. Hume himself wrote:

> [H]ow must we be disappointed, when we learn, that this connexion, tie, or energy lies merely in ourselves, and is nothing but that determination of the mind, which is acquir'd by custom, and causes us to make a transition from an object to its usual attendant, and from the impression of one to the lively idea of the other? Such a discover not only cuts of all hope of ever attaining satisfaction, but even prevents our very wishes; since it appears that when we say we desire to know the ultimate and operating principle, as something which resides in the external object, we either contradict ourselves, or talk without a meaning.[20]

In brief, Hume's radical empiricist skepticism means a causal link is impossible to prove, and so, too, is proving the falsity of an ascribed causal relationship. Worse yet for trade lawyers, then, is the implication for Sunset Reviews of trade remedy orders. Hume's position means there is no proof conjoined events habitually experienced in the past will occur again. If there is no such thing as subject merchandise caused injury to a domestic industry, then there is no certainty that the effect or removing an AD or CVD order would likely be the re-occurrence of dumping or subsidization.

There has been no philosophically rigorous counter to Hume's demolition of *a priori* views of causation. Yet, the reality of a trade remedy case is it will not do to plead "there is no such thing as causation — Hume says so." But, Hume's conclusion is not pointless. It reminds trade lawyers that we tend to find cause where we want to find it. Thus, it pushes them to think carefully about how and when they use the "C" word, and about the empirical bases for attributing injury to imports of subject merchandise.

---

[19] Immanuel Kant (1724-1804) objected to Hume's narrow empiricism, and his conclusion that causation is illusory. Kant argued in favor of the existence of causation by positing causation as an *a priori* category, *i.e.*, the idea of causation is innate to the human mind. Kant's proof was that we have an idea of causation even when it is not possible for us to observe a causal relationship. For example, causation must exist, because even if we do not watch individual articles of subject merchandise injuring a domestic industry, we know of the possibility of the relationship. Indeed, Kant argues that we cannot help but think in terms of, and know, causal relationships — again, because causation is an *a priori* cognitive category. Further, necessity is an element of this category. Kant wrote it must be the case that

> in that which antecedes and event there be found the condition of a rule, according to which in this event follows always and necessarily.

CRITIQUE OF PURE REASON 130 (1781) (J.M.D. Meiklejohn trans., 1990).

[20] DAVID HUME, A TREATISE OF HUMAN NATURE 266-67 (1739-40) (1978).

3. Mill (1806-1873) on Causation

Less pessimistic about prospects for finding necessary causal relationships, and influenced by scientific views of causation, John Stuart Mill, a successor to David Hume, urged in his work, *System of Logic*, that:

> . . . it is seldom if ever between a consequent and the single anteced-ent that [an] invariable sequence subsists. It is usually between a consequent and the sum of several antecedents, the concurrence of all of them being requisite to produce, that is to certain of being followed by the consequent.[21]

A billiard ball, X, striking another, Y, is an example that rarely exists in nature. No one contends Y moved because of its own substance, or on its own volition. Other factors — such as X — were involved. Yet, in reality, causal relationships are far more complex than two balls. Accordingly, Mill famously defines cause not in the customary but slack way of one event happening immediately before another, but instead as the

> sum total of all the conditions, positive and negative taken together; the whole of the contingencies of every description, which being realized, the consequent invariably follows.[22]

Rarely is a single factor accurately described as a "cause" of an event. If a factor truly is a "cause," then whenever it is manifest, the consequence invariably follows. Reality, observed Mill, is more complex: a consequence results when a set of necessary factors operate in conjunction. That set is properly said to be the "cause" of the effect. Consider whether it is Mill's view of the complexity of causes that comes closest, among philosophical perspec-tives, to causation criteria in modern trade remedy law. Observe, too, both Hume and Mill speak of cause in the Aristotelian sense of "Efficient Cause."

Further, there is a distinction between a "complexity" of causes, which are a set of joint conditions sufficient to bring about an event, and a "plurality" of causes.[23] The latter notion connotes that an event may result from one cause in one time or place, *i.e.*, in one spatio-temporal setting, but occur in another setting from a different cause. In other words, a "plurality" of causes exists whenever there are distinct situations in which different factors produce the same result.

4. Hart (1907-1992) on Causation

One of the foremost legal philosophers of the 20th century, and one influenced both by Hume and post-modernism, was H.L.A. Hart of Oxford University. With his colleague, Tony Honoré, Hart produced what already is a classic in jurisprudence — *Causation and the Law* (1959). Hart delineates three notions of causation that are

> latent in ordinary thought from which the causal language of the lawyer . . . frequently draws its force and meaning."[24]

---

[21] John Stuart Mill, System of Logic, Book III, Chapter V, Section 3 (1843) (Longmans, Green and Co. ed., 1952).

[22] *Id*. at 238.

[23] *Id*. at Book I, Chapter V, Section 3.

[24] H.L.A. Hart & Tony Honoré, Causation and the Law 2 (2d ed. 1985).

The first notion, contingency, is "usually human intervention, which initiates a series of physical changes, which exemplify general connections between types of events."[25] Here, manipulation of factors by a person brings about an intended change. The second notion is an occurrence "whereby one man by words or deeds provid[es] another with a reason for doing something."[26] Underlying this notion is one person inducing or provoking an event. The third notion is an event that violates a breach of a duty, such as the duty to act with reasonable care. The hallmark of this notion is the provision of an opportunity that may be exploited for good or ill.

None of these notions is satisfactory for legal purposes, because lawyers require

> singular statements that [identify] in complex situations certain particular events as causes, effects, or consequences of other particular events. . . .
>
> [Moreover, the] chief concern [of lawyers] with causation is not discoverable connections between types of events, so not as to formulate laws of generalizations, but it is often to *apply* generalizations, which are already known or accepted as true . . . to particular concrete cases.[27]

To be sure, Hart appreciates that while lawyers speak of a factor as the cause of an occurrence, in truth it is never the case that when a

> single event of one kind occurs it is "invariably" followed by some occurrence of another kind.[28]

Accordingly, Hart defines a "cause" as an act that produces an effect if it

> is an intervention in the course of affairs which is *sufficient* to produce the harm without (1) the cooperation of the voluntary actions of others or (2) abnormal conjunctions of events.[29]

In effect, Hart posits cause as a factor that is sufficient to produce a result without an intervening event. That definition relates closely to the second element in Hume's scheme, and thus to the modern legal notion of proximate (or but-for) causation. Interestingly, Hart rejects Mills' concept of "plurality" of causes.[30] He also differentiate moral from legal responsibility.[31] To be held morally responsible for causing harm, one must have indeed caused the harm. Legal liability may be imposed even regardless of cause, as in cases of strict or vicarious liability.

Finally, and critically, in reviewing the above summary, consider whether and how causation criteria in trade remedy law might be put on a stronger, sharper foundation by importing into it the above philosophical and jurisprudential perspectives.

---

[25] *Id.*

[26] *Id.*

[27] *Id.* at 10 (emphasis original).

[28] *Id.* at 17.

[29] *Id.* at 5 (emphasis original).

[30] *See id.* at 20.

[31] *See id.* at 10.

C. One or Two Steps?

UNITED STATES STEEL GROUP v. UNITED STATES
United States Court of Appeals for the Federal Circuit
96 F.3d 1352, 1355-1356, 1359-1362 (1996)

CLEVENGER, CIRCUIT JUDGE.

I.

On June 30, 1992, a group of United States steel companies [led by Bethlehem Steel Corporation] filed a petition with the International Trade Commission alleging that their industry had been harmed by subsidized and "Less Than Fair Value" (LTFV) imports of certain flat-rolled carbon steel products from numerous countries, and seeking the imposition of countervailing and antidumping duties against the subject imports. . . .After affirmative preliminary findings by the Department of Commerce . . . that the imports in question were indeed subsidized or being sold at LTFV, the Commission commenced an investigation to determine whether the imports had caused, or threatened to cause, a material injury to an industry in the United States. . . . In conducting its investigation, the Commission divided the broad category of flat-rolled carbon steel products into four "like products:" (1) hot-rolled products; (2) cold-rolled products; (3) corrosion-resistant products; and (4) cut-to-length plate products. . . . The appeals in this case do not question the Commission's categorization of products, but instead concern only the Commission's determinations with respect to the hot-rolled and cold-rolled categories.

The Commission conducted its investigation over a three-year period, 1990-1992. During that period, the Commission collected large amounts of data concerning the subject imports including detailed information regarding the imports' value, prices, and volume of shipments. In addition, it collected extensive data on the production, capacity utilization, and inventory levels of foreign producers, and carefully examined the patterns of domestic consumption of the subject imports. On the basis of this data, the Commission made its determinations, the majority of which are not contested on this appeal. Of those that are, the Commission determined that most of the subject hot- and cold-rolled imports had not caused, and did not threaten to cause, material injury to a domestic industry. . . .

III.

. . . .

C.

Bethlehem[ ] . . . questions the manner in which the Commission, and in this case, Commissioners Brunsdale and Crawford in particular, determine whether an industry in the United States is materially injured or threatened with material injury by reason of subsidized and/or LTFV imports. A review of the relevant statutes puts Bethlehem's argument in context.

Countervailing and/or antidumping duties may not be imposed on merchandise found to be subsidized and/or dumped unless:

. . . the Commission determines that —

    (A)   an industry in the United States —

        (i)   is materially injured, or

        (ii)   is threatened with material injury

. . . .

by reason of imports of that merchandise.

19 U.S.C. § 1671(a)(2) . . . (for subsidized merchandise); 19 U.S.C. § 1673(2) . . . (for LTFV merchandise). With respect to both subsidized and LTFV imports, "material injury" is defined as "harm which is not inconsequential, immaterial, or unimportant." 19 U.S.C. § 1677(7)(A). . . .

The Commission makes its determinations by tallying the votes of the six individual commissioners, each of whom is obligated to determine whether particular imports cause or threaten to cause the requisite harm. [A sometimes overlooked fact that obviously weighs in favor of industries seeking protection is the following: in the event the ITC is equally divided, *i.e.*, a 3-3 vote, its injury determination (or any review thereof) is deemed affirmative. *See* 19 U.S.C. § 1677(11).] Congress has not left the commissioners at sea in the performance of their individual, and ultimately collective, duties. Instead, Congress has supplied the analytical tools, in the form of statutory tests, some of which must be applied and some of which may be applied before the Commission, acting through its commissioners, arrives at its measurement of the causal effects of particular imports. The statutory tests are many, and specific; in each case, the Commission:

    (i)   shall consider —

        (I)   the volume of imports of the merchandise which is the subject of the investigation,

        (II)   the effect of imports of that merchandise on prices in the United State for like products, and

        (III)   the impact of imports of such merchandise on domestic producers of like products, but only in the context of production operations within the United States; and

    (ii)   may consider such other economic factors as are relevant to the determination regarding whether there is material injury by reason of imports. . . .

19 U.S.C. § 1677(7)(B). . . .

These three general tests are further refined explicitly in the statute. With regard to volume of imports, "the Commission shall consider whether the volume of imports of the merchandise, or any increase in that volume, either in absolute terms or relative to production of consumption in the United States, is significant." 19 U.S.C. § 1677(7)(c)(i). . . . Concerning the effect of imports on price, the Commission must consider whether:

(i)   there has been significant price underselling by the imported
        merchandise as compared with the price of like products of the
        United States, and

(ii)   the effects of imports of such merchandise otherwise depresses
        prices to a significant degree or prevents price increases, which
        otherwise would have occurred, to a significant degree.

19 U.S.C. § 1677(7)(c)(ii). . . .

When considering the impact of LTFV or subsidized imports on the state
of the domestic industry, the specific commands made on the Commission by
Congress are even more detailed:

In examining the impact required to be considered under subparagraph
(B)(iii), the Commission shall evaluate all relevant economic factors which
have a bearing on the state of the industry in the United States, including,
but not limited to —

(i)   actual and potential decline in output, sales, market share, profits,
        productivity, return on investments, and utilization of capacity,

(ii)   factors affecting domestic prices,

(iii)   actual and potential negative effects on cash flow, inventories,
        employment, wages, growth, ability to raise capital, and invest-
        ment, and

(iv)   actual and potential negative effects on the existing development
        and production efforts of the domestic industry, including efforts
        to develop a derivative or more advanced version of the like product.

The Commission shall evaluate all relevant economic factors described in this clause within the context of the business cycle and
conditions of competition that are distinctive to the affected industry.
19 U.S.C. § 1677(7)(c)(iii). . . . [As a result of the 1994 *Uruguay
Round Agreements Act*, a fifth factor was added to this non-exclusive
list: the magnitude of the dumping margin. *See* 19 U.S.C.
§ 1677(7)(c)(iii)(V).] Furthermore, . . . each commissioner is free to
determine whether or not to exclude from the material injury analysis
imports from countries deemed negligible. We note this additional
factor simply to underscore the complicated network of statutory tests
that must or may be employed by each commissioner in deciding
whether the causal effects of particular imports support imposition of
countervailing or antidumping duties.

Over the course of years, differing commissioners have employed differing
methodologies to reach their conclusions on the extent to which LTFV and/or
subsidized imports have harmed, or threatened to harm, domestic industries. . . . [T]he differing methodologies are described as the "one step" and
the "two step" analyses. Under the one-step analysis, a commissioner assesses
in a unitary process both the current state of the domestic industry and
whether that state is materially injured by reason of LTFV or subsidized
imports. Under the two-step analysis, a commissioner first assesses the state
of the relevant domestic industry. If the assessment produces a conclusion that
the industry is materially injured, then the analysis proceeds to its second

step, which is the separate inquiry asking whether the pertinent imports contribute in a non-*de minimis* way to such material injury. Over time, some commissioners have opted for one of these methodologies, and others have preferred the second analytical tool. And in some instances, as with Commissioner Watson in this case, the commissioner simply recites the statutory language, without specifying which of the one- or two-step analyses, or some other analytical construct, has been used to assist the commissioner in fulfilling the statutory requirements.

In this case, Commissioners Brunsdale and Crawford used the one-step analysis in reaching their determinations on material injury. According to Bethlehem, their use of the one-step analysis is forbidden by the relevant statutes, and the two-step method used by the other commissioners in this case must be determined, by this court, to be the only statutorily permitted tool of analysis for rendering material injury determinations. Bethlehem begins with the premise that the statutes require a determination of material injury whenever imports contribute in a non-*de minimis* way to further injury to a domestic industry. Since some commissioners have characterized the effect of the two-step analysis in this manner, Bethlehem urges us to read the two-step analysis into the statute as the only permissible way to assess material injury. Bethlehem argues that the one-step method of analysis violates the statute because it necessarily requires a greater quantum of impact from imports on a domestic industry, in order to find material injury or threatened material injury, than would use of the two-step test. Bethlehem argues that the outcome of this case could change if we were to impose the two-step test on Commissioners Brunsdale and Crawford since it is possible that under the two-step test, they might assess the material injury aspect of the imports differently. Given the votes of other commissioners in this case, additional votes of material injury could tip the scale in Bethlehem's favor.

Bethlehem advanced the same argument in the Court of International Trade, seeking to characterize the difference of modes of analysis of various commissioners as fundamentally different statutory interpretations. The Court of International Trade rejected that characterization, and instead held that the two methods of analysis are simply that, and neither fails to comport with the statutory commands setting forth the manner in which the Commission is to dice a record to reach a material injury determination. Judge Restani, for the Court of International Trade, correctly noted that the two-step method has the virtue of some decision-making efficiencies, but that the statute by its terms does not mandate it as the only method of analysis. She also, rightly, noted that "[t]he statutory language fits very well with a one-step mode of analysis." This is so, in part at least, because of the awkwardness of reading the statute to say that material injury *must* be determined in every case by asking, as Judge Restani put it, "if such imports were a non-*de minimis* contributing cause of the state of the 'materially injured industry.'"

At bottom, Bethlehem seeks a ruling from this court that there should be a single methodology, applicable to each of the commissioners, for determining whether a domestic industry is injured, or threatened with injury, by reason of subsidized and/or LTFV imports. The statute on its face compels no such uniform methodology, and we are not persuaded that we should create one, even were we so empowered.

Congress has crafted an intricate statute, and committed its enforcement to the Department of Commerce and the International Trade Commission. Congress has populated the Commission with six independent commissioners, each confirmed to office by the United States Senate. As Bethlehem candidly and commendably notes in its brief, commissioners are free to attach different weight to the various statutory tests which they are required to employ when evaluating the presence or threat of injury. Also, Bethlehem notes and does not challenge the indisputable proposition that each commissioner is free to attach different weight to factual information bearing on, and determinate of, the many statutory tests; and that commissioners may ultimately reach different factual conclusions on the same record. In the end, of course, the factual conclusions of each commissioner will drive the legal conclusion he or she reaches, namely, whether the requisite injury has been shown. The invitation to employ such diversity in methodologies is inherent in the statutes themselves, given the variety of the considerations to be undertaken and the lack of any Congressionally mandated procedure or methodology for assessment of the statutory tests.

This court has no independent authority to tell the Commission how to do its job. We can only direct the Commission to follow the dictates of its statutory mandate. So long as the Commission's analysis does not violate any statute and is not otherwise arbitrary and capricious, the Commission may perform its duties in the way it believes most suitable. Because we do not believe that the statute compels the commissioners to employ either the one-step or two-step approaches, we disagree with Bethlehem that Commissioners Brunsdale and Crawford employed a causation standard which was contrary to law, and therefore decline to reverse the Commission on this ground.

II. CAUSATION IN PRACTICE

A. Econometrics

Ancient, Continental, and legal philosophers have not crowded out economists in the exploration of causation. Econometricians, in particular, proffer multivariable regression analysis as a method to assess whether a causal relationship exists (*e.g.*, whether tariff reductions stimulate growth in gross domestic product (GDP), and if so, measuring its quantitative impact (*e.g.*, how much of a tariff cut will produce how great an impact on GDP).

A generic (but simplified) formula in this analysis, where three causal factors are posited, is:

$$Y = a + b_1X_1 + b_2X_2 + b_3X_3 + \epsilon.$$

where

Y = dependent variable hypothesized to be caused by the independent variables

X_1, X_2, and X_3 = independent variables

a = a coefficient relating to the intercept of a regression line with the vertical (y) axis when the line is plotted on a graph

b_1 = a coefficient measuring the effect of X_1 on Y

b_2 = a coefficient measuring the effect of X_2 on Y

b_3 = a coefficient measuring the effect of X_3 on Y

ϵ = the error term, which captures the effect of all other factors on Y.

Thus, for example, Y could represent injury to a petitioning industry in a trade remedy case, X_1 could be subject merchandise imports, X_2 technological change, and X_3 interest rate costs. Values for the coefficients b_1, b_2, and b_3 would reflect the relative significant — *i.e.*, statistical causation — of X_1, X_2, and X_3, respectively, to Y. Of course, establishing a persuasive statistic to measure the independent and dependent variables, and gathering reliable data for each statistic is essential. Might these issues unduly influence the choice of a period of investigation (POI)?

Econometricians perform a tests (such as the "t-test") to measure the statistical significance of each independent variable, utilize a statistic (called "R^2" or "R squared") to gauge the explanatory power of the entire regression model. They also check for problems endemic in the model, such as multicolinearity, which occurs when there are causal relationships among the independent variables.

Multivariate regression analysis is widely used not only by academics, but also by economists practicing in investment and commercial banks, government ministries, non-governmental organizations (NGOs) and think tanks, and international organizations. However, multivariable regression analysis is not commonly used in the practice of trade remedy law — yet, at any rate. Trade remedy cases are expensive, and econometric analyses, with expert witnesses to boot, only drive up further those costs. Why incur them, if criteria for causation in AD, CVD, and safeguard law do not demand such sophisticated proof? In particular, if proof that injury to a domestic industry occurs during the POI when subject merchandise is dumped or subsidized, or when fairly traded imports surge, can be offered with arithmetic ratios, graphs, and charts, and such proof suffices, then what incentive exists to go further? As the criteria are presently, correlation tends to suffice as indicative of causation — even though the adage "correlation does not mean causation" is widely understood.

Finally, note the conflicting interests among developing and least developed countries in the debate about the practical costs of upgrading causation criteria. Unless and until sophisticated econometric techniques are cheaply and widely available, then revising the criteria would inhibit their participation in AD, CVD, and safeguard cases. Yet, more rigorous causation standards might well make developed countries think twice before launching a trade remedy case against a poor country.

B.   Defining "By Reason Of" and the 1997 *Gerald Metals* Case

GERALD METALS, INC. v. UNITED STATES
United States Court of Appeals for the Federal Circuit
132 F.3d 716, 717-723 (1997)

RADER, CIRCUIT JUDGE.

The International Trade Commission (Commission) found that Russian, Ukrainian, and Chinese imports of pure magnesium at less than fair value (LTFV) injured the domestic industry. *See Magnesium from China, Russia, and Ukraine*, 60 Fed. Reg. 26,-456-57 (Int'l Trade Comm'n 1995) (final). Gerald Metals, an importer, appealed the injury determination, with respect to the Ukrainian imports, to the United States Court of International Trade. The court affirmed, finding substantial evidence that the domestic industry was materially injured by reason of the LTFV Ukrainian imports. *See Gerald Metals, Inc. v. United States*, 937 F. Supp. 930, 942 (Ct. Int'l Trade 1996). Because, on this record, substantial evidence does not support the Court of International Trade's analysis, this court vacates and remands to the Court of International Trade. . . .

I.

Primary magnesium is decomposed from raw materials into magnesium metal or alloy. The United States Department of Commerce, International Trade Administration (Commerce) divides primary magnesium into two classes, pure and alloy. Pure magnesium encompasses: (1) "pure" products that contain at least 99.8%, by weight, primary magnesium, and (2) "off-specification pure" products that contain at least 50% to 99.8%, by weight, primary magnesium. Alloy magnesium contains 50% to 99.8%, by weight, primary magnesium; however, alloy is mixed with other chemical elements that constitute at least 1.5%, by weight, of the product.

Pure magnesium is both a chemical reagent in the desulfurization and chemical reduction industries and an input in the production of alloy. Pure magnesium has value in the markets for aluminum, steel, magnesium granule, and pharmaceuticals. . . .

Due to the unique characteristics of magnesium production, production — both domestic and foreign — remains relatively steady. Pure and alloy magnesium production requires electrolytic cells that deteriorate if left unused. To avoid the high cost of rebuilding cells and to maximize production efficiency, producers generally maintain continuous and steady production levels of pure magnesium.

. . . .

Much of the record features information about imports from Russia. Specifically, the record shows, in the words of Vice Chairman Nuzum, that "a sizeable portion of the imports from Russia were fairly[-]traded. These imports undersold domestic product almost as frequently as did LTFV imports." . . . Similarly the record shows, in the words of Commissioner Crawford, that "[d]umped Russian imports and fairly[-]traded Russian imports are very close, if not perfect, substitutes for each other.."

All pure magnesium from Russia originates with one of two producers — Avisma Titanium-Magnesium Works (Avisma) and Solikamsk Magnesium Works (SMW). Although trading companies can import Russian pure magnesium from only these two sources, Commerce assigned zero percent dumping margins to some companies, such as Gerald Metals, while assigning margins of 100.25% to other companies. Commerce assigned to all trading companies importing pure magnesium from Ukraine margins greater than zero, ranging from 36.05% to 104.27%. Commerce assigned a margin of 108.26% to all Chinese imports.

Gerald Metals imported both fairly-traded Russian pure magnesium and LTFV Ukrainian pure magnesium. Gerald Metals reasons that because fairly-traded Russian imports are substitutes for LTFV Russian imports, domestic purchasers of magnesium products could fill their demand without resort to LTFV imports. Thus, Gerald Metals argues, the LTFV goods did not cause the injury to domestic industry. Instead, the injury was the result of market forces other than unfair trading.

The Court of International Trade found substantial evidence to support the Commission's determination. . . . Gerald Metals appeals.

II.

This court duplicates the Court of International Trade's review of the Commission's determinations, evaluating whether they are "unsupported by substantial evidence on the record, or otherwise not in accordance with law" [*i.e.*, a *de novo* review]. 19 U.S.C. § 1516a(b)(1)(B)(i). . . .

. . . .

. . . [A] showing that economic harm to domestic industry occurred when LTFV imports are also on the market is not enough to show that the imports caused a material injury. *See United States Steel Group v. United States*, 96 F.3d 1352, 1358 (Fed. Cir. 1996). . . . An affirmative injury determination requires both (1) present material injury, and (2) a finding that the material injury is "by reason of" the subject imports. . . . Hence, the anti-dumping statute mandates a showing of causal — not merely temporal — connection between the LTFV goods and the material injury.

Because this appeal hinges on whether the subject imports caused the injury, this court reviews the record evidence to determine whether substantial evidence supports the Commission's determination that the domestic industry was injured by reason of the subject imports. Substantial evidence is " 'such relevant evidence as a reasonable mind might accept as adequate to support a conclusion.' " *Suramerica* [*de Aleaciones Laminadas, C.A. v. United States*], 44 F.3d [978] at 985 [(Fed. Cir. 1994)] (*quoting Consolidated Edison Co. v. NLRB*, 305 U.S. 197, 229 (1938). . .). However, the substantial evidence standard requires more than mere assertion of " 'evidence which in and of itself justified [the Commission's determination], without taking into account contradictory evidence or evidence from which conflicting inferences could be drawn.'" *Id.* (*quoting Universal Camera Corp. v. NLRB*, 340 U.S. 474, 487 (1951).). Rather "'[t]he substantiality of evidence must take into account whatever in the record fairly detracts from its weight.'" *Id.* (*quoting Universal Camera*, 340 U.S. at 488. . .). . . . .

III.

The central dispute in this case is the Commission's asserted failure to incorporate the undisputed facts about fairly-traded Russian imports into its analysis of the harm caused by reason of the cumulated LTFV imports. Although the record contained surveys of purchaser comparisons of domestic product to the subject imports, there is no similar evidence of product differentiation, non-price differences, or differences in terms and conditions between the two classes of Russian imports-fairly traded and LTFV. . . .

Indeed, only two producers were responsible for all Russian imports. The primary difference in the price and treatment of Russian pure magnesium depended on which trading company imported the product. Pricing by different trading companies, which had dumping margins of either zero percent or 100.25%, determined whether the magnesium arrived as fairly-traded or LTFV. Therefore, only one reasonable conclusion can be drawn from the record: other than differences in the trading company, the Russian imports — both fairly-traded and LTFV — were perfect substitutes for each other, if not the exact same product.

Similarly, Russian and Ukrainian pure magnesium products compete with one another. The Commission noted that the parties to the investigation did not dispute that LTFV imports from Russia and Ukraine competed with one another. Although there was some evidence of product quality differences between these imports, the Commission nonetheless concluded that its supposition was confirmed by other purchasers who stated that they did not differentiate between Russian or Ukrainian magnesium when dealing with the Commonwealth of Independent States (the association of former Soviet Union republics). Thus, the record supports the inference that Russian imports, either fairly-traded or LTFV, are substitutes for LTFV Ukrainian imports.

LTFV Chinese imports were found to compete for sales with the subject imports from Russia and Ukraine. . . . In fact, "numerous . . . purchasers . . . opined that the Chinese magnesium is comparable in quality to and/or can be used for the same uses as the domestic product and as the Russian and Ukrainian imports." . . . Thus, the record shows that the Commission viewed LTFV Chinese imports as close substitutes with both classes of Russian imports and LTFV Ukrainian imports. . . .

These aspects of the record point to a gap in the causal nexus between the LTFV Ukrainian imports and material harm to domestic industry. The Court of International Trade acknowledged this causation problem, but, without citing adequate record support, dismissed this evidence. . . .

First, the Court of International Trade found no evidence supporting Gerald Metals' claim that fairly-traded Russian imports would have replaced all or the greater part of the subject imports. . . . The court stated that Gerald

Metals had premised this argument on the false assumption that producers would switch to different importers trading at fair value in the same way that domestic consumers switch to different trading companies when buying pure magnesium. . . . According to the court, domestic consumers use non-price factors to select a trading partner. . . .

A more reasonable view of the record, however, contradicts these conclusions. At the beginning of the period of investigation, the cumulated LTFV imports had a greater market share than the Russian fairly-traded imports; however, by the end the period, the market share of the fairly-traded Russian imports was greater than that of the LTFV imports. Comparing the quantities purchased by domestic consumers during the entire period reveals that the sales of Russian LTFV product just slightly exceeded that of the fairly-traded Russian product. In fact, the quantity of all Russian pure magnesium sales — including both fairly-traded and LTFV — was three times the combined quantity of sales of LTFV imports from Ukraine and China.

The Court of International Trade apparently failed to evaluate this date in conjunction with the fact that all Russian magnesium originated from only two producers . . . [T]he importer, not the producer, set the price and determined whether Russian magnesium was fairly-traded or LTFV. The domestic consumption and market penetration data reveal that Russian producers sold to fairly-trading importers almost as often as to unfairly trading importers and that domestic purchasers acquired Russian imports from both types of importers in roughly similar amounts.

Indeed, this evidence demonstrates that, contrary to the Court of International Trade's analysis, domestic purchasers were not repelled from the LTFV imports as compared to fairly-traded imports because of non-price factors. This inference is underscored by the fact that the same importer, Gerald Metals, sold fairly-traded Russian product as well as LTFV Ukrainian product to domestic purchasers. Without further explanation, this court cannot adequately review the Court of International Trade's dismissal of the prospect that fairly-traded goods would have replaced LTFV goods.

The Court of International Trade also reasoned that the Commission's injury determination did not rest upon the purported shift of all domestic purchasers of LTFV magnesium to domestic product. In fact, the domestic industry framed its material injury case not in terms of lost sales but in terms of the inability of domestic producers to raise prices without suffering lost sales volume. . . .

After the suspension of LTFV imports of pure magnesium from Canada in 1991-92, the domestic industry apparently expected to raise prices for its pure magnesium. At this time, imports — both LTFV and fairly-traded — entered the United States due in part to liquidation of stockpiles in the former Soviet Union. These imports apparently disrupted the expectation of higher prices for domestic products. The enhanced availability on the world market of magnesium from the former Soviet Union is one of the relevant economic factors influencing both the finding of injury and causation.

Determining the accurate causation of a disrupted market expectation, however, requires careful economic evidence and analysis. The anti-dumping statute requires that the Commission consider all relevant economic factors "within the context of the business cycle and conditions of competition that are distinctive to the affected industry." 19 U.S.C. § 1677(7)(C)(iii). . . . Generally, a sudden increase in world supply in the face of a relatively stable demand results in lower prices. While the statute protects domestic magnesium producers from injury caused by LTFV imports, its scope of protection does not reach so far as to support artificially inflated prices when fairly-traded imports are underselling the domestic product and LTFV imports are readily convertible to fairly-traded product by merely changing importers.

The Court of International Trade erred by applying an incorrect legal test for the amount of contribution to material harm by LTFV goods necessary to satisfy the "by reason of" standard. The Court stated that "[e]ven though fairly-priced imports may have been another cause of injury, the Commission has a statutory obligation not to weigh causes," and "[t]hus . . . correctly did not compare the impact of subject imports to the impact of other factors, like the fairly-traded imports." . . . Thus, the Court followed the reasoning that any contribution constitutes sufficient causation to satisfy the "by reason of" test.

To the contrary, the statute requires the injury to occur "by reason of" the LTFV imports. This language does not suggest that an importer of LTFV goods can escape countervailing [sic] duties by finding some tangential or minor cause unrelated to the LTFV goods that contributed to the harmful effects on domestic market prices. By the same token, this language does not suggest that the Government satisfies its burden of proof by showing that the LTFV goods themselves contributed only minimally or tangentially to the material harm.

The Court of International Trade's review of the record propagates the Commission's misapplication of the "by reason of" test by relying on broad language in the Senate report at the time of enactment of title 19. The report suggested that the Commission need not "contemplate that the effects from the subsidized imports be weighted against the effects associated with other factors . . . which may be contributing to overall injury to an industry[;] [n]or is the issue whether the [LTFV] imports are the principal, a substantial, or a significant cause of material injury." S. Rep. No. 96-249, at 57 (1979), *reprinted in* 1979 U.S.C.C.A.N. 381, 443. . . .

In support of this reasoning, Commerce [sic] cites this court's apparent endorsement of the non-de minimis mode of analysis as one possible way to present sufficient evidence to satisfy the statute's causation requirement. *See United States Steel*, 96 F.3d at 1361-62. In this two-step inquiry, the Commission "first assesses the state of the relevant domestic industry," and if the industry is materially injured, the analysis proceeds "to its second step, which considers whether the pertinent imports contribute in a non-*de minimis* way to such material injury." *Id.* at 1361.

In *United States Steel*, however, this court did not incorporate the relaxed standard of the Senate report into the statute's causation requirement. A careful reading of *United States Steel* reveals that this court did not cite the Senate report nor even endorse *any* specific methodology, including the non-*de minimis* method, for assessing the causation of material injury. . . . Instead, this court hinged the adequacy of a given methodology upon whether it produced sufficient evidence to satisfy the statutory "by reason of" requirement. . . . In fact, contrary to Commerce's [*sic*] view of *United States Steel*, the decision supports the notion that evidence of *de minimis* (*e.g.*, minimal or tangential) causation of injury does not reach the causation level required under the statute.

Hence, the statute requires adequate evidence to show that the harm occurred "by reason of" the LTFV imports, not by reason of a minimal or tangential contribution to material harm caused by LTFV goods. Given the unique circumstances of this case, the record, without more, does not show that LTFV imports of pure magnesium from Ukraine were the reason for the harmful effects to the domestic magnesium industry.

Accordingly, this court concludes that the Court of International Trade failed to consider properly the presence of fairly-traded Russian imports in affirming the Commission's determination of material injury by reason of the LTFV goods.

[On remand, the ITC determined the United States magnesium industry was not materially injured by reason of imports of pure magnesium. The CIT upheld the determination, finding it to be supported by substantial evidence. *See Gerald Metals, Inc. v. United States*, 27 F. Supp. 2d 1351 (CIT 1988).]

C. Attribution and the 2001 *Japan Hot-Rolled Steel* and 2003 *Brazil Iron Tube* Cases

In the 2001 *Japan Hot-Rolled Steel* case, the Appellate Body ruled the U.S. violated Article 3:5 of the WTO Antidumping Agreement. *See United States — Anti-Dumping Measures on Certain Hot-Rolled Steel Products from Japan*, WT/DS184/AB/R ¶¶ 222-23, 233-36 (adopted 23 August 2001). The ITC failed to examine factors other than dumped Japanese steel that also caused injury to the American steel industry, and failed to ascertain whether the injury was attributed to dumped imports. The Appellate Body squarely rejected the interpretation of the Panel on the non-attribution language in Article 3:5. The Panel ruled the language does not require isolation of each potential injury-causing factor, nor does it require a finding that dumped imports alone caused the injury. To the contrary, the Appellate Body held. The Article 3:5 non-attribution wording mandates an investigating authority isolate known injury-causing factors, and carefully ensure injury they cause is not wrongly attributed to dumped imports.

In the 2003 *Brazil Iron Tube* case, the Appellate Body disagreed with Brazil's argument it is necessary to consider injurious factors, other than dumped imports, in aggregate. *See European Communities — Antidumping Duties on Malleable Cast Iron Tube of Pipe Fittings from Brazil*, WT/DS219/AB/R ¶¶ 35, 189 (adopted 18 August 2003). To impose a requirement that all other factors be examined together would be to impose a methodology for non-attribution, which has no basis in the text of the *Antidumping Agreement*. Article 3:5 requires a non-attribution analysis, but does not how to go about it. In consequence, might it be said that the two conceptual stages of (1) identification of potential causal factors and (2) attribution of injurious effects to each causal factors entails, in practice, five steps?

i.   Identifying factors that could be causing injury to the petitioner.

ii. Checking to see whether these factors are operating simulta-
     neously.

iii. Examining all of the factors to see if they do, in truth, have an
     injurious effect.

iv. Differentiating injurious effects of subject merchandise from injuri-
     ous effects of all other known factors.

v.   Ensuring that injury caused by other factors is not erroneously
     attributed to subject merchandise.

Does WTO jurisprudence shed light on whether injurious effects of dumped
or illegally subsidized merchandise must breach a particular threshold to
actionable? What happens if subject merchandise is less than the most
important cause of injury?

D. Price Suppression Caused by a Subsidy and the 2005 *Upland Cotton* Case

WTO APPELLATE BODY REPORT, *UNITED STATES — SUBSIDIES ON UPLAND COTTON*
WT/DS267/AB/R (adopted 21 March 2005) (complaint by Brazil)

[The American cotton support at issue, price-contingent subsidies, are
Counter-Cyclical Payments, Market Loss Assistance Payments, Marketing
Loan Payments, and Step 2 Payments. They are described in a separate ex-
cerpt from the *Upland Cotton* case.]

(c) Meaning of "Significant Price Suppression"

423. A central question before the Panel with regard to Article 6.3(c) of the
SCM Agreement was whether the effect of the subsidy is "significant price
suppression." It is worth setting out the Panel's understanding of the meaning
of the term "price suppression." In explaining this term, the Panel stated:

> Thus, *price suppression* refers to the situation where "prices" — in
> terms of the "amount of money set for sale of upland cotton" or the
> "value or worth" of upland cotton — either are prevented or inhibited
> from rising (*i.e.* they do not increase when they otherwise would have)
> or they do actually increase, but the increase is less than it otherwise
> would have been. *Price depression* refers to the situation where
> "prices" are pressed down, or reduced.[1388]

424. Although the Panel first identified "price suppression" and "price
depression" as two separate concepts. Footnote 1388 of the Panel Report
suggests that, for its analysis, the Panel used the term "price suppression"

[1388] In the remainder of our analysis, we use the term "price suppression" to refer both to
an actual decline (which otherwise would not have declined, or would have done so to a lesser
degree) and an increase in prices (which otherwise would have increased to a greater degree).
(emphasis added)

to refer to both price suppression and price depression. We recognize that "the situation where 'prices' . . . are prevented or inhibited from rising" and "the situation where 'prices' are pressed down, or reduced" may overlap. Nevertheless, it would have been preferable, in our view, for the Panel to avoid using the term "price suppression" as short-hand for both price suppression and price depression, given that Article 6.3(c) of the *SCM Agreement* refers to "price suppression" and "price depression" as distinct concepts. . . .

425. The Panel described its task in assessing "price suppression" under Article 6.3(c) as follows:

> We need to examine whether these prices were suppressed, that is, lower than they would have been without the United States subsidies in respect of upland cotton.

426. As regards the word "significant" in the context of "significant price suppression" in Article 6.3(c), the Panel found that this word means "important, notable or consequential."

427. Article 6.3(c) does not set forth any specific methodology for determining whether the effect of a subsidy is significant price suppression. . . .

(d) Panel's Order of Analysis

. . . .

429. Having determined the relevant products, market, and price, the Panel continued its analysis with respect to Article 6.3(c) in the following order:

Is there "price suppression"?

Is it "significant" price suppression?

"The effect of the subsidy"

430. The United States contests the Panel's decision to address "significant price suppression" before addressing "the effect of the subsidy," arguing that "[a] finding of price suppression *without* any prior finding of 'the effect of the subsidy' would be meaningless; how could one know that prices were lower than they otherwise would have been without knowing what allegedly caused the prices to be lower?" The United States also contends that the Panel used "circular" reasoning by assuming causation in finding price suppression and using its conclusion on price suppression to support its finding on causation (the effect of the subsidy).

431. . . . The text of Article 6.3(c) does not . . . preclude the approach taken by the Panel to examine first whether significant price suppression exists and then, if it is found to exist, to proceed further to examine whether the significant price suppression is the effect of the subsidy. The Panel evidently considered that, in the absence of significant price suppression, it would not need to proceed to analyze the effect of the subsidy. We see no legal error in this approach.

. . . .

434. The specific factors that the Panel examined in determining whether or not "price suppression" had occurred were: "(a) the relative magnitude of

the United States' production and exports in the world upland cotton market; (b) general price trends; and (c) the nature of the subsidies at issue, and in particular, whether or not the nature of these subsidies is such as to have discernible price suppressive effects." In the absence of explicit guidance on assessing significant price suppression in the text of Article 6.3(c), we have no reason to reject the relevance of these factors for the Panel's assessment in the present case. An assessment of "general price trends" is clearly relevant to significant price suppression (although, as the Panel itself recognized, price trends alone are not conclusive). The two other factors — the nature of the subsidies and the relative magnitude of the United States' production and exports of upland cotton — are also relevant for this assessment. We are not persuaded that the fact that these latter factors were also considered in connection with the Panel's analysis of "the effect of the subsidy" amounts to legal error for that reason alone.

435. Turning to the Panel's assessment of the "effect of the subsidy," the Panel addressed the question whether there was a "causal link" between the price-contingent subsidies and the significant price suppression it had found. It then addressed the impact of "[o]ther alleged causal factors." . . . We observe that Article 6.3(c) does not use the word "cause;" rather, it states that "the effect of the subsidy is . . . significant price suppression." However, the ordinary meaning of the noun "effect" is "[s]omething . . . caused or produced; a result, a consequence." The "something" in this context is significant price suppression, and thus the question is whether significant price suppression is "caused" by or is a "result" or "consequence" of the challenged subsidy. The Panel's conclusion that "[t]he text of the treaty requires the establishment of a causal link between the subsidy and the significant price suppression" is thus consistent with this ordinary meaning of the term "effect." This is also confirmed by the context provided by Article 5(c) of the *SCM Agreement* . . . .

436. As the Panel pointed out, "Articles 5 and 6.3 . . . do not contain the more elaborate and precise 'causation' and non-attribution language" found in the trade remedy provisions of the *SCM Agreement*. Part V of the SCM Agreement, which relates to the imposition of countervailing duties, requires, *inter alia*, an examination of "any known factors other than the subsidized imports which at the same time are injuring the domestic industry." However, such causation requirements have not been expressly prescribed for an examination of *serious prejudice* under Articles 5(c) and Article 6.3(c) in Part III of the *SCM Agreement*. This suggests that a panel has a certain degree of discretion in selecting an appropriate methodology for determining whether the "effect" of a subsidy is significant price suppression under Article 6.3(c).

437. Nevertheless, we agree with the Panel that it is necessary to ensure that the effects of other factors on prices are not improperly attributed to the challenged subsidies. Pursuant to Article 6.3(c) of the *SCM Agreement*, "[s]erious prejudice in the sense of paragraph (c) of Article 5 may arise" when "the effect of *the subsidy* is . . . significant price suppression." (emphasis added) If the significant price suppression found in the world market for upland cotton were caused by factors other than the challenged subsidies, then that price suppression would not be "the effect of" the challenged subsidies in the sense of Article 6.3(c). Therefore, we do not find fault with the Panel's

approach of "examin[ing] whether or not 'the effect of the subsidy' is the significant price suppression which [it had] found to exist in the same world market" and separately "consider[ing] the role of other alleged causal factors in the record before [it] which may affect [the] analysis of the causal link between the United States subsidies and the significant price suppression."

438. The Panel's approach with respect to causation and non-attribution is similar to that reflected in Appellate Body decisions in the context of other WTO agreements. In connection with the *Agreement on Safeguards*, the Appellate Body has stated that a causal link "between increased imports of the product concerned and serious injury or threat thereof" [the language of Article 4:2(b) of the *Safeguards Agreement c.f.* Article 3:5 of the *Antidumping Agreement* and Article 15:5 of the *SCM Agreement*] "involves a genuine and substantial relationship of cause and effect between these two elements", and it has also required non-attribution of effects caused by other factors. [On the "genuine and substantial relationship" test, the Appellate Body cited its opinion in *United States — Definitive Safeguard Measure on Imports of Wheat Gluten from the European Communities*, WT/DS166/AB/R, ¶ 69 (adopted 19 January 2001). Concerning non-attribution, the Appellate Body cited its Report in *United States — Definitive Safeguard Measures on Imports of Circular Welded Carbon Quality Line Pipe from Korea*, WT/DS202/AB/R, ¶ 208 (adopted 8 March 2002).] In the context of the [*Antidumping Agreement*], the Appellate Body has stated: "[i]n order that investigating authorities, applying Article 3.5, are able to ensure that the injurious effects of the other known factors are not 'attributed' to dumped imports, they must appropriately assess the injurious effects of those other factors." [The Appellate Body cited its opinion in *United States Antidumping Measures on Certain Hot-Rolled Steel Products from Japan*, WT/DS184/AB/R, ¶ 223 (adopted 23 August 2001).] It must be borne in mind that these provisions of the *Agreement on Safeguards* and the *Anti-Dumping Agreement*, as well as the provisions of Part V of the SCM Agreement, relate to a determination of "injury" rather than "serious prejudice", and they apply in different contexts and with different purposes. Therefore, they must not be automatically transposed into Part III of the *SCM Agreement*. Nevertheless, they may suggest ways of assessing whether the effect of a subsidy is significant price suppression rather than it being the effect of other factors.

(e) Rationale for the Panel's Finding that the Effect of the Price-Contingent Subsidies is Significant Price Suppression

. . . .

449. We now turn to the four main grounds on which the Panel based its conclusion that "a causal link exists between" the price-contingent subsidies and the significant price suppression it had found, which the United States contests. The first reason the Panel provided for finding a "causal link" was the "substantial proportionate influence" of the United States "in the world upland cotton market . . . flow[ing] . . . from the magnitude of the United States production and export of upland cotton." The United States counters that, "absent some analysis of how U.S. cotton competes with cotton from other sources, relative sizes are meaningless." We agree that, in and of itself, the

degree of influence of the United States in the world market for upland cotton may not be conclusive as to the effect of the price-contingent subsidies on prices in that market. However, if the price-contingent subsidies increased United States production and exports or decreased prices for United States upland cotton, then the fact that United States production and exports of upland cotton significantly influenced world market prices would make it more likely that the effect of the price-contingent subsidies is significant price suppression. Accordingly, this fact seems to support the Panel's conclusion. . . .

450. The second reason the Panel provided for finding a "causal link" was its view that the price-contingent subsidies "are directly linked to world prices for upland cotton." This conclusion flowed from the Panel's earlier assessment — in connection with its analysis of significant price suppression — of the *nature* of the price-contingent subsidies. The nature of a subsidy plays an important role in any analysis of whether the effect of the subsidy is significant price suppression under Article 6.3(c). With respect to marketing loan program payments, the Panel found that "[t]he further the adjusted world price drops, the greater the extent to which United States upland cotton producers' revenue is insulated from the decline." As a result, during the 1999-2002 marketing years, United States production and exports remained stable or increased, even though prices of United States upland cotton decreased. The Panel found that Step 2 payments stimulate domestic and foreign demand for United States upland cotton by "eliminating any positive difference between United States internal prices and international prices of upland cotton." The Panel stated that Step 2 payments "result in lower world market prices than would prevail in their absence." Finally, the Panel found that market loss assistance payments and counter-cyclical payments are made in response to low prices for upland cotton and stimulate United States production of upland cotton by reducing the "total and per unit revenue risk associated with price variability." The United States contends that the Panel's analysis of the price-contingent subsidies was "deficient." However, the Panel found that the price-contingent subsidies stimulated United States production and exports of upland cotton and thereby lowered United States upland cotton prices. This seems to us to support the Panel's conclusion that the effect of the price-contingent subsidies is significant price suppression.

451. The third reason the Panel provided for finding a "causal link" was that "there is a discern[i]ble temporal coincidence of suppressed world market prices" and the price-contingent subsidies. The United States describes this as "an exercise in spurious correlation." However, in our view, one would normally expect a discernible correlation between significantly suppressed prices and the challenged subsidies if the effect of these subsidies is significant price suppression. Accordingly, this is an important factor in any analysis of whether the effect of a subsidy is significant price suppression within the meaning of Article 6.3(c). However, we recognize that mere correlation between payment of subsidies and significantly suppressed prices would be insufficient, without more, to prove that the effect of the subsidies is significant price suppression.

452. The fourth reason the Panel provided for finding a "causal link" was the "divergence between United States producers' total costs of production and

revenue from sales of upland cotton since 1997." The United States argues that the Panel should have examined variable rather than total costs in assessing whether "United States upland cotton producers would . . . have been economically capable of remaining in the production of upland cotton had it not been for the United States subsidies at issue."

453. We agree with the general proposition of the United States that variable costs may play a role in farmers' decision-making as to whether to plant upland cotton or some alternative crop, and how much of each crop to plant. From a short-term perspective, variable costs may be particularly important. However, from a longer-term perspective, total costs may be relevant. . . . The Panel found that "the effect of the subsidies was to allow United States producers to sell upland cotton at a price lower than would otherwise have been necessary to cover their total costs." In the circumstances of this dispute, we do not consider that the Panel's reliance on total rather than variable costs of production amounts to an error vitiating the Panel's analysis under Article 6.3(c).

454. Finally, we consider the "other causal factors alleged by the United States" to have had an effect on prices. The United States argues that the Panel erred in addressing upland cotton planting decisions as an "other causal factor," given that the United States maintained that the price-contingent subsidies did not cause price suppression at all. We disagree. We have already addressed the United States' arguments with respect to planting decisions, and we find no fault in the Panel's consideration of the issue of "planting decisions."

455. The United States also argues that United States upland cotton exports increased during 1998-2002 because textile imports increased in the same period, leading to a decline in the use of cotton by domestic mills. The Panel regarded this factor as "concerning support, rather than suppression, of world cotton prices." However, even assuming that increasing textile imports led to increased exports of upland cotton, this does not mean that the price-contingent subsidies did not have the effect of significant price suppression. It was not unreasonable for the Panel to conclude that the "effect" of the price-contingent subsidies was significant price suppression, even if some other factor might also have price-suppressive effects.

456. The remaining three "other causal factors" that the Panel examined were weakness in world demand for upland cotton, the strong United States dollar, and the release by China of government upland cotton stocks between 1999 and 2001. The United States does not specifically address these three factors in its appellant's submission. However, the Panel's discussion of these "other factors" was part of the reasoning leading to the Panel's conclusion under Article 6.3(c), which the United States does appeal. The Panel found that the United States' argument that weak demand caused low prices was inconsistent with the increase in United States upland cotton production and the absence of "pronounced declines" in world upland cotton consumption. With regard to the United States dollar, the Panel stated that exchange rates would affect market prices, but that market prices did not guide "United States producer decisions (except to the extent that, when they are lower than the marketing loan rate, they dictate the magnitude of United States government subsidies to producers)." The Panel pointed to evidence on the record

confirming that marketing loan program payments and Step 2 payments "offset" declines in market prices. With respect to upland cotton stocks released by China, the Panel agreed with the United States (and Brazil) that "an infusion of a large amount of supply onto the market would exert a downward pressure on prices." However, the Panel pointed out that the stock released by the Chinese government "was smaller in magnitude than the United States exports over this period."

457. . . . In sum, the Panel Report shows that it examined the other factors raised by the United States. Although the Panel found that some of them had price-suppressive effects, it did not attribute those effects to the United States' price-contingent subsidies.

III. CUMULATION

A. Cross-Investigation Cumulation and the 1982 *Bingham & Taylor* Case

BINGHAM & TAYLOR DIVISION v. UNITED STATES
United States Court of Appeals for the Federal Circuit
815 F.2d 1482, 1483-1487 (1987)

DAVIS, CIRCUIT JUDGE.

We are called upon to review a decision of the United States Court of International Trade, *Bingham & Taylor Division, Virginia Industries v. United States*, 627 F. Supp. 793 (Ct. Int'l Trade 1986), . . . holding that § 771(7)(c)(iv) of the *Tariff Act of 1930*, as amended (19 U.S.C. § 1677(7)(c)(iv) (1984) [now § 1677(7)(G)(i)]), requires the International Trade Commission (Commission) to assess cumulatively, for purposes of making its preliminary injury determinations, the volume and price effects of imports subject to an antidumping investigation together with imports of like products subject to a countervailing duty investigation. We affirm.

. . . [T]he Commission and the Department of Commerce received a spate of unfair trade petitions filed by the Municipal Castings Fair Trade Council and its individual member companies. Five separate investigations ensued, four of which involved allegations of material injury to the domestic iron construction casting industries by reason of sales at less than fair value (LTFV) of light and heavy construction castings imported from India, Canada, the People's Republic of China and Brazil. The fifth investigation focused on whether imports of subsidized iron construction castings from Brazil were causing material injury to domestic industries manufacturing heavy and light iron construction castings.

. . . .

The Commission arrived at its affirmative injury determinations in the antidumping investigations by cumulating the impact on the domestic industry of imports from the four countries involved. But in reaching its preliminary determinations in the countervailing duty investigation the Commission refused to cumulate the impact of imports subject to the antidumping investigations together with the impact of imports subject to the countervailing duty investigation. This refusal to cross-cumulate led the Commission to different preliminary injury determinations for light iron construction castings from Brazil. In its antidumping investigation, the Commission decided that there was a reasonable indication that these imports were causing material injury to the domestic industry. On the other hand, after examining the identical imports in the context of a countervailing duty investigation, the Commission found no reasonable indication of material injury.

. . . .

. . . Cumulation originated as an administrative practice. Prior to the *1984 Act*, the Commission's cumulation practice was characterized by internal inconsistency and confusion. Without the benefit of a cumulation statute or legislative history, the Commission in effect left the decision whether to cumulate to the discretion of the individual commissioners. Thus, while some commissioners tended to aggregate dumped and subsidized imports in their cumulation analyses, others did not. The Commission as an entity never cross-cumulated.

Congress responded to these variations by enacting as part of the *Trade and Tariff Act of 1984* a new subsection 771(7)(c)(iv) which mandates cumulation in certain circumstances. Although the legislative history of this measure is scant, what does exist supports this court's conclusion that the statute mandates cross-cumulation (at least normally). That Congress sought to inject uniformity into the haphazard application of cumulation is evident from a House Ways and Means Committee report [that is part of the legislative history to the *1984 Act*]:

> The purpose of mandating cumulation under appropriate circumstances is to eliminate inconsistencies in Commission practice and to ensure that the injury test adequately addresses *simultaneous unfair imports from different countries*. Most Commissioners have applied cumulation under certain circumstances but have articulated a variety of differing criteria and conditions. However, cumulation is not required by statute. In additior a few Commissioners have imposed conditions which do not seem justified to the committee.
>
> The Committee believes that the practice of cumulation is based on the *sound principle of preventing material injury which comes about by virtue of several unfair acts or practices* (emphasis added).

H.R. Rep. No. 725, 98th Cong., 2d Sess. at 37, *reprinted in* 1984 U.S. Code Cong. & Admin. News 4910, 5127, 5164. . . .

> In eliminating the Commission's discretion with respect to cumulation, the *1984 Act* directs cumulation whenever the statutory criteria are met. . . . [T]he Committee's use of generic terms collectively describing dumped and subsidized imports in the committee report quoted above suggests that the statutory phrase "subject to investigation" was intended to require cumulation of dumped and subsidized imports. . . . Congress' dual purpose for adopting the cumulation provision was "to eliminate the inconsistencies in the Commission

practice and to ensure that the injury test adequately addresses
simultaneous *unfair imports* from different countries." Cumulation
was viewed as a tool for "preventing material injury which comes
about by virtue of several *unfair acts or practices.*" . . . Obviously,
whether imports are dumped, subsidized, or both does not alter their
status as unfair imports. Further, as the Court of International Trade
noted, it is significant that "Congress did not make any exclusion or
exception for cross-cumulation in the 1984 statute, but rather elected
to mandate cumulation in broad terms."

Nor can it be argued that Congress was unaware of the potential
for cross-cumulation when it drafted the *1984 Act*. During hearings
before the House Ways and Means Subcommittee on Trade, Adolph
J. Lena testified:

> The law now permits the International Trade Commission to com-
> bine or "cumulate" imports from different countries when making
> injury determinations in antidumping and countervailing duty investi-
> gations. Cumulation makes sense; death by one or one hundred blows
> is equally fatal. The ITC, however, has been hesitant to cumulate
> imports at all and extremely reluctant to do so in preliminary injury
> determinations. *There also has been some question about cumulation
> of imports of the same product in separate countervailing duty and
> antidumping cases.* We believe that it would be helpful to amend the
> statute to require cumulation in certain circumstances. Such an
> amendment would help to ensure that domestic industries are not
> denied relief because of an unwise exercise of discretion by the
> Commission.

. . . The matter was thus squarely presented to Congress.

Another indication that the statute ordinarily demands cross-cumulation
is that cross-cumulation fully harmonizes with the pattern of the antidumping
and subsidization aspects of the legislation. . . . First, when Congress added
the cumulation provision in 1984 it did not include that matter in the specific
sections applicable to subsidy and dumping investigations but instead placed
it in the general part of the statute that applies to both types of unfair trade
proceedings. . . . Second, the material injury provisions applicable to the two
types of proceedings are substantially the same, thus showing the complementary nature of both determinations. Third, in the same statute that added
cumulation Congress also provided a method for facilitating the holding of
simultaneous antidumping and subsidy investigations and proceedings with
respect to the same merchandise. . . . This obviously makes cross-cumulation
much easier.

. . . .

. . . [W]e therefore agree with the Court of International Trade's holding
that 19 U.S.C. § 1677(7)(c)(iv) mandates the cumulation of subsidized light
iron construction castings from Brazil with dumped light iron construction
castings from India, Canada, and the People's Republic of China. Particularly
revealing of the need for that decision is the important fact that the Brazilian
imports under investigation in the antidumping proceedings are identical to

those under investigation in the countervailing duty proceedings. That is, all imports from Brazil subject to investigation were both dumped and subsidized. As appellees point out, a finding of material injury with respect to dumped imports from Brazil but not subsidized imports from Brazil would indeed be bizarre where (1) the Brazilian imports at issue in both investigations are identical; and (2) the injury determinations for dumping and subsidy investigations are themselves identical. The same imports subjected to the same tests should naturally yield the same results. A contrary reading of the statute would lead to absurd and mischievous results and thwart Congress' purpose.

[Examine 19 U.S.C. § 1677(7)(G)(i)-(ii). What are the specific requirements for cross-cumulation? Are they defensible in the same manner the Court suggests?]

B. Cross-Country Cumulation and the 1999 *Ranchers-Cattlemen* Case

RANCHERS-CATTLEMEN ACTION LEGAL FOUNDATION v. UNITED STATES
United States Court of International Trade
74 F. Supp. 2d 1353 (1999)

CARMAN, CHIEF JUDGE.

. . . Plaintiffs [the Ranchers-Cattlemen Action Legal Foundation (R-CALF)] contest the negative preliminary injury determination concerning live cattle from Mexico of the United States International Trade Commission (ITC or Commission) in its investigation in *Live Cattle from Canada and Mexico*, 64 Fed. Reg. 3716 (Jan. 25, 1999). . . .

BACKGROUND

. . . .

. . . There are, in general, three developmental stages for cattle prior to slaughter: (1) calves, which are raised and then weaned from their mothers at five to ten months; calves weigh up to 400-650 pounds; (2) yearling/stocker cattle, which have been weaned from their mothers and are fed on forage and roughage feeds or grazed on pasture until they are about 12-20 months old; yearling/stocker cattle generally weigh between 400 to 650-750 pounds; and (3) feeder cattle, which are kept in confined areas for 90 to 150 days and fed on finishing and high-energy rations; feeder cattle weigh up to 1,100 to 1,300 pounds. Once the cattle are sufficiently fed, they are considered fed, fat, or slaughter cattle. Fed, fat, and slaughter cattle are cattle ready for immediate slaughter.

In making its preliminary injury determination concerning live cattle from Mexico, the ITC considered, among other things, issues regarding domestic like product, domestic industry, cumulation, conditions of competition, and reasonable indication of material injury or threat of material injury by reason of the subject imports from Mexico. In consideration of the domestic like product determination, the ITC considered whether live cattle in the primary stages of development should be defined as separate domestic like products from the cattle at more advanced stages of development. The ITC used a semi-finished like product analysis to determine whether the cattle at earlier stages of development are "like" the cattle at more advanced stages of development.

. . . .

Applying the semi-finished like product analysis, the ITC determined that cattle at each stage of development are dedicated to progression to the next stage and will ultimately develop into fed cattle ready for slaughter. Thus, cattle have no independent use or function other than being slaughtered. The ITC found, however, that cattle at different stages of production are not functionally or economically interchangeable since at each stage prior to their final stage, they have not reached their slaughter weight. Moreover, the ITC found that while some operations raise cattle from birth until they are ready for slaughter, it is more common for cattle to be sold at various stages of development. Based on these facts, the ITC defined the domestic "like product" as encompassing all stages of development for live cattle.

In determining the scope of the domestic industry, the ITC found that the domestic industry consists of all U.S. production of the domestic like product, live cattle.

In determining whether to assess cumulatively the volume and effect of imports from Mexico with the imports from Canada pursuant to 19 U.S.C. § 1677(7)(G)(i) . . . the ITC considered whether the imports competed with each other and with the domestic like product in the United States. To determine whether the imports competed with each other, the ITC applied its traditional four-factor test: (1) the degree of fungibility between the imports from the two countries; (2) the presence of sales or offers to sell imports in the same geographic market from the two countries; (3) the existence of common or similar channels of distribution for imports from the two countries; and (4) whether the imports from the two countries were simultaneously present in the market.

In regard to the first factor, the ITC found there was not a sufficient degree of fungibility between the imports from Canada and Mexico. Based on measurement by weight, the ITC found that virtually all subject imports from Canada (95.4 percent by weight) in 1997 weighed over 320 kilograms, or more than 704 pounds, primarily fed cattle ready for immediate slaughter. In contrast, virtually all imports from Mexico (96 percent by weight) in 1997 weighed between 90-320 kilograms, or 198-704 pounds, primarily at the calf or yearling/stocker stages of development. The ITC found the live cattle that have not been fed to slaughter weight are not substitutes for cattle ready for slaughter. As the Commission found cattle in different stages of production are poor substitutes for each other, the ITC determined imports from Canada and Mexico were poor substitutes for each other. Further, the ITC found the cattle imported from Canada were more likely to be British breeds that are likely to produce higher-priced prime and choice quality grade meats. Cattle imported from Mexico, however, were usually Brahman or Brahman cross-breeds which were less likely to produce prime or choice-grade meats. For the reasons stated above, the ITC found limited fungibility existed between the imports of live cattle from Canada and Mexico.

In regard to factor two, geographic overlap, the Commission found there was limited overlap between the markets for the imports from Canada and Mexico. The majority of the subject imports from Mexico entered into four states: Texas, California, New Mexico, and Arizona. The majority of the subject imports from Canada entered into five states: Washington, Utah, Nebraska, Colorado, and Minnesota. The imports from Canada and Mexico overlapped in only five states. Therefore, the ITC found there was limited geographic overlap between the markets for the subject imports from Canada and Mexico.

In regard to factor three, channels of distribution, the ITC found the channels of distribution for the imported cattle depended on the stage of development at purchase. The primary channels of distribution for imports from Mexico were stocker/yearling operators. The primary channels of distribution for imports from Canada were slaughterhouses or packers. Thus, the ITC found there was an insufficient degree of overlap among the channels of distribution to support a finding of competition between the subject imports.

In regard to factor four, simultaneous presence in the U.S. market, the ITC determined live cattle from Mexico and Canada were simultaneously present in the U.S. market during the period of investigation. Based on the above factors, the ITC found the subject imports from Canada and Mexico did not compete with each other, and, therefore, the ITC decided not to cumulate the imports.

In the preliminary injury determination, the ITC found there was no reasonable indication of material injury of the domestic industry by reason of the subject imports from Mexico. The ITC found that the volume and market share of the imports from Mexico were too small throughout the period of investigation to significantly affect the domestic price pursuant to 19 U.S.C. § 1677(7)(c)(ii). . . . Specifically, the ITC found, "the volume and market share of the [] [Mexican] imports [were] declining and [were] at historical low levels." . . . Moreover, the prices for the cattle at the stocker and feeder stages of development in the United States "increased from 1996 to 1998." . . . Thus, the ITC found the small and decreasing volume and market share of imports from Mexico had not had a significant adverse impact on the domestic industry. The ITC attributed any weak performance in the domestic industry to the fact that the domestic industry was in the liquidation phase of the cattle cycle during the period of investigation.

. . . .

DISCUSSION

. . . .

B. Cumulation

In making its preliminary injury determination, the ITC "shall cumulatively assess" the volume and effect of imports of the subject merchandise from all countries for which petitions are filed and/or investigations are self-initiated by the administering authority on the same day if such imports "compete with each other and with domestic like products in the United States market." 19 U.S.C. § 1677(7)(G)(i). In order to satisfy this provision, the ITC must, in part, determine that "a 'reasonable overlap' in competition" exists between the imports from the different countries. *Wieland Werke, AG v. United States*, 718 F. Supp. 50, 52 (1989) (*quoting Granges Metallverken AB v. United States*, 716 F. Supp. 17, 22 (1989)). . . .

In evaluating whether imports from different countries compete with each other, the ITC relies on the following four-factor test [as above]. . . . "While no single factor is determinative, and the list of factors is not exclusive, these factors are intended to provide the Commission with a framework for determining whether the imports compete. . . ." *Goss Graphics Sys., Inc. v. United States*, 33 F. Supp. 2d 1082, 1086 (CIT 1998). . . .

1. *Competition*

One of plaintiffs' core arguments appears to be that the ITC's requirement that subject imports be directly interchangeable *at importation* in order to cumulate the subject imports is contrary to statute and Congressional intent. The plaintiffs' contention, however, is without merit. The plaintiffs' concern essentially involves a question of statutory interpretation. In resolving questions of statutory interpretation, *Chevron* [*i.e., Chevron U.S.A., Inc. v. Natural Resources Defense Council, Inc.*, 467 U.S. 837 (1984)] requires this Court first to determine whether the statute is clear on its face. If the language of the statute is clear, then this Court must defer to Congressional intent. . . . If the statute is unclear, however, then the question for the Court is whether the agency's answer is based on a permissible construction of the statute. . . .

Here, the statutory provision regarding cumulation is unclear. The statute provides . . . that the Commission shall "cumulatively assess the volume and effect" of the imports of the subject merchandise from all countries if "such imports compete with each other and with domestic like products" in the U.S. market. 19 U.S.C. § 1677(7)(G)(i). To include imports in the cumulation equation, the statute requires, among other things, that they "compete with" each other and domestic like products, but it fails to define that phrase. . . . Accordingly, the provision cannot be said to have a plain meaning. . . .

What Congress intended by the phrase "competes with" is not immediately clear from the legislative history of this provision, first added to the law in the *Trade and Tariff Act of 1984*. . . . The Court must, therefore, consider the purpose for enacting the cumulation provision to discern its intended meaning. . . .

Cumulation was mandated "to eliminate inconsistencies in Commission practice and to ensure that the injury test adequately addressed *simultaneous* unfair imports from different countries." HOUSE COMM. ON WAYS AND MEANS, TRADE REMEDIES REFORM ACT OF 1984, H.R. Rep. No. 98-725, at 37 (1984), *reprinted in* 1984 U.S.C.C.A.N. 5127, 5164 (emphasis added). The legislative history's only explicit guidance is that cumulation is designed to take into account "simultaneous unfair imports." *Id.* Because neither the statutory language nor the legislative history conclusively establishes the intended time frame in which the imports are to be considered for competition, the Court assesses the agency's interpretation of the provision to determine whether the agency's interpretation is reasonable and in accordance with the legislative purpose.

In making its competition determination, the Commission found there was insufficient evidence on the record to support a finding of competition between the subject imports from Mexico and Canada in part because when the subject imports were brought into the United States, they were imported at different stages of development. . . . The Commission, therefore, appears to have considered whether the subject imports "competed with" one another at the moment of importation.

Although the statute does not specifically direct the ITC to consider whether the products at issue compete at *importation*, the statute does require that the Commission determine whether the "*imports* compete." As products are U.S. imports when they are "brought in[to] [the United States] from an outside source," WEBSTER'S THIRD NEW INTERNATIONAL DICTIONARY 1135 (1961), . . . consideration by the ITC of whether subject imports compete *at importation* appears to be a reasonable interpretation of the statute. Certainly nothing within the statute *precludes* the ITC from considering competition in terms of the condition of the products at importation. Accordingly, this Court defers to the agency's interpretation of the statute. . . .

2. *Application of Four-Factor Competition Test*

a. *Fungibility*

i. *Fungibility as a Factor of Competition*

Plaintiffs argue the ITC misconstrued the cumulation provision and equated "fungibility" with "competition." Plaintiffs' argument appears, in part, to challenge the ITC's use of "fungibility" as a factor in assessing whether the subject imports compete with each other. This Court, however, has consistently affirmed the Commission's practice of considering four factors — one of which is the degree of fungibility — to assess whether subject imports compete with each other. *See, e.g., Goss Graphics*, 33 F. Supp. 2d at 1086 . . . Thus, to the extent plaintiffs challenge the ITC's use of fungibility in its determination of whether the subject imports compete with each other, this Court holds the ITC's use of fungibility as a factor in determining whether the subject imports competed with each other is reasonable and should not be disturbed.

ii. *Like Products and Competition*

. . . [T]he Commission found the subject imports from Mexico and Canada were like products but found the products did not compete, in part, because they were not sufficiently fungible. R-CALF now uses these findings in an attempt to impugn the Commission's non-cumulation determination. Plaintiffs first allege the ITC's use of a different and more rigorous standard of interchangeability for its cumulation analysis than for its like product analysis is arbitrary and warrants reversal of the ITC's determination. Plaintiffs also argue it was arbitrary for the Commission to give different weight to the finding of a lack of interchangeability in the like product and cumulation analyses.

Plaintiffs' first argument fails because it overlooks the importance of context. The analysis of interchangeability for the purposes of cumulation may vary from that for like product. . . . Such a situation would not necessarily render inconsistent findings regarding interchangeability for the purposes of cumulation and like product analyses arbitrary, capricious, or not in accordance with law.

To the extent plaintiffs' second argument implies the ITC must always find like products compete with each other for the purposes of cumulation, the plaintiffs' argument also must fail. A finding by the ITC of a like product does not control whether the ITC finds competition between the subject imports for the purpose of cumulation. . . . Rather, the ITC must conduct like product and cumulation analyses separately using the factors relevant to each determination. . . .

b. Geographic Overlap

Plaintiffs contend the Commission misidentified the states in which the subject imports overlapped. Specifically, plaintiffs state the ITC "committed error in finding that imports of Mexican and Canadian cattle overlapped in Indiana rather than Idaho." . . . Although plaintiffs acknowledge that the ITC admits it committed this error, plaintiffs assert the error was not harmless as such evidence shows "Mexican cattle were present near the U.S. — Canadian border with Canadian cattle, just as Canadian cattle were present near the U.S. — Mexican border with Mexican cattle." . . .

The Court does not agree with plaintiffs' assertion that the Commission's error is not harmless. In reaching its decision, the Court must be careful not to remand the ITC's preliminary determination for an error of fact unless the Court is in substantial doubt regarding whether the ITC would have reached the same conclusion were the error not to have occurred. . . . Although the ITC erroneously identified one of the states in which the subject imports overlapped, there is other information on the record which supports the ITC's conclusion that there was little geographic overlap between subject imports of live cattle from Canada and Mexico.

Specifically, according to evidence before the ITC, the majority of the imports from Mexico went to four states (California, New Mexico, Texas, and Arizona: 96.3 percent) whereas only 0.51 percent of the imports from Canada went to those same states. . . . In the states in which there was overlap, the imports from one country or sometimes both countries were minimal. . . . Further, as pointed out by the Commission, when corrected for the error, there appears there would have been less of an overlap between Canadian and Mexican cattle than existed when Indiana was incorrectly listed as an overlapping state. . . . Therefore, . . . there is not substantial doubt as to whether the ITC would have reached the same conclusion were it to have correctly identified the overlapping states. . . . [T]his Court finds that the ITC had a rational basis for concluding there was limited geographic overlap between the markets for the subject imports from Canada and Mexico.

c. Channels of Distribution

Plaintiffs allege the ITC erred in concluding that "the purchasers, and thus the channels of distribution, vary depending on the stage of [development of the cattle]." . . .Specifically, plaintiffs state that there was evidence on the record that *feedlots* may acquire stocker cattle as well as feeder cattle and that *packers* (*i.e.*, the slaughterhouses) may acquire *feeder cattle* as well as *fed cattle* ready for slaughter.". . .

Plaintiffs' challenge merits some consideration. Evidence identified by plaintiffs does suggest some packers purchased live cattle at both the fed and feeder stages of development. Nevertheless, there is evidence on the record that the ITC was aware that a limited number of operators in one segment of the market purchased cattle at another stage of development. . . . " 'Absent some showing to the contrary, [the ITC] is presumed to have considered all evidence in the record' " in making its determination. *See, e.g., Connecticut Steel*, 852 F. Supp. at 1065 (*quoting Rhone Poulenc, S.A. v. United States*, 592 F. Supp. 1318, 1326 (1984)). This Court finds the ITC's determination was reasonable and therefore not arbitrary and capricious or an abuse of discretion.

3. Cumulation of Finished and Unfinished Products

Another of plaintiffs' core arguments is that the ITC's determination not to cumulate the subject imports which entered the United States at different stages of development is inconsistent with long-standing agency practice to cumulate finished and unfinished products where both finished products were intended for the same end use. Plaintiffs cite in their brief and in answers submitted in response to the Court's inquiry to several ITC determinations which plaintiffs claim support their assertion. In particular, plaintiffs point to the preliminary investigations of imported pipe fittings from China and Thailand where the ITC cumulated the finished and unfinished pipe fittings even though they were " *'finished by domestic producers. and sold as domestic product.' "* .

The Court does not agree with plaintiffs' assertion that the ITC has a "practice" of cumulating finished and unfinished products. An action by the ITC becomes an "agency practice" when a uniform and established procedure exists that would lead a party, in the absence of notification of change, reasonably to expect adherence to the established practice or procedure. . . . [T]here does not appear to be a "practice" by the ITC of cumulating subject imports where, as here, the products are imported at various stages of development.

Although many of the cases cited by the parties do cumulate finished and unfinished products, the cumulation analysis does not focus on the finished and unfinished nature of the products. Rather, the analysis focuses on the four-factor test used by the ITC in determining whether the imports compete with each other (fungibility, geographic overlap, simultaneous presence in the market, and channels of distribution). Based on these four factors, the ITC appears to make independent, case-by-case decisions regarding whether the imported products must be cumulated. Such a conclusion is consistent with past Court determinations which have required the ITC decisions to be "based upon an independent evaluation of the factors with respect to the unique economic situation of each product and industry under investigation."

Moreover, the subject imports at issue here are distinguishable from subject imports where the ITC has cumulated finished and unfinished products. In the majority of cases cited by plaintiffs, the finishing process for the unfinished products is relatively minor. For example, in the pipe fitting cases, the finishing process is minimal, involving finishing steps such as shot-blasting, heat treatment, machining, etc. . . . . The weighted average cost attributable to the finishing process is only about fourteen percent of the total cost of production. . . . Further, finishing does not significantly alter the function of the fitting. . . .

In contrast, the alleged "unfinished" merchandise at issue here undergoes a "substantial transformation" in the United States. According to Robin L. Turner, attorney for the United States International Trade Commission, of the cattle imported from Mexico, approximately "two-thirds [of the size and weight of the cattle] gets added . . . in the 2United States." . . . Moreover, Mexican cattle "take a year to become beef." . . . The Court finds the degree of transformation and the length of time needed to transform the alleged "unfinished" imports from Mexico into "finished" products distinguishes these products from other products in cases in which the ITC has cumulated finished and unfinished imports. . . .

For the foregoing reasons, the Court finds the ITC's [negative preliminary injury] determination not to cumulate the subject imports from Mexico with those from Canada is not arbitrary or capricious, not an abuse of discretion, and is otherwise in accordance with law.

Part Ten

REMEDIES AGAINST "FAIR" TRADE AND UNILATERAL REMEDIES

Chapter 37

SAFEGUARDS

There is an old saying that to grow grapes for making a good wine the grapevine must suffer.

—DEWEY MARKHAM, JR., WINE BASICS 56 (1993)

DOCUMENTS SUPPLEMENT ASSIGNMENT

1. *Havana Charter* Article 40
2. GATT Articles XII, XVIII, XIX
3. WTO *Agreement on Safeguards*
4. WTO *Agreement on Agriculture*, Article 5
5. WTO *Agreement on Textiles and Clothing (ATC Agreement)*, Article 6:2
6. *NAFTA* Chapter 8
7. Relevant provisions in other FTAs

I. AMERICAN ROOTS OF AND INFLUENCE ON SAFEGUARDS

The roots of the contemporary general safeguard remedy in Article XIX of GATT, sometimes dubbed the "Escape Clause," lie in American trade law of the early 1940s. That is, the safeguard remedy in this law pre-dates Article XIX. Specifically, a 1943 accord between the U.S. and Mexico, a trade agreement negotiated pursuant to the *Reciprocal Trade Agreements Act of 1934* contained the first Escape Clause.[1] It said:

> If, *as a result of unforeseen developments and of the concession granted* on any article enumerated and described in the Schedules annexed to this Agreement, such article is being *imported in such increased quantities* and under such conditions as to *cause or threaten serious injury to domestic producers of like or similar articles*, the Government of either country shall be free to withdraw the concession, in whole or in part, or to modify it to the extent and for such time as may be necessary to prevent such injury.[2]

Escape Clauses like this one were the answer to complaints from Congress about the effects of liberalized trade. For instance, the "[l]egislative history of the 1945 congressional debate on the law that authorized the United States

---

[1] *See* Pub. L. No. 73-474, 48 Stat. 943 (1934), *codified in* scattered sections of title 19.

[2] *Agreement Between the United States and Mexico Respecting Reciprocal Trade*, 23 Dec. 1942, Art. XI, 57 Stat. 833, 845-46 (1943), E.A.S. No. 311 (emphasis added).

to join GATT is replete with congressional complaints of injury to domestic industry through concessions granted in trade treaties."[3] These roots of Article XIX still are vibrant. The critical elements for Escape Clause relief in the language of Article XIX, and in America's statutory versions that have provided for this relief over the decades, are not all that different from the italicized language above.

In February 1947, President Harry S. Truman issued an Executive Order mandating the inclusion of an Escape Clause in every trade agreement negotiated by the U.S. under the authority of the *1934 Act*.[4] Accordingly, the International Trade Commission (ITC) (or its predecessor, the Tariff Commission) has conducted Escape Clause investigations since 1948. President Truman's Order was issued when the U.S. and 21 other nations were in the thick of GATT and *ITO Charter* negotiations. Subsequent Executive Orders have amended the initial one, but the changes did not affect America's fundamental commitment to an Escape Clause. Indeed, in Section 7 of the *Trade Agreements Extension Act of 1951* (Pub. L. No. 82-50, 65 Stat. 72, 74 (1951)) the Escape Clause became a permanent feature of U.S. statutory law.

Given American desires, it is hardly surprising drafters included the multilateral Escape Clause, Article XIX, in GATT. By the time of the 1946 London Preparatory Conference, the U.S. had 3 years of experience with an Escape Clause in its bilateral accord with Mexico. Since those negotiations, the U.S. statutory embodiment of Article XIX, which is Section 201 of the *Trade Act of 1974* as amended,[5] has been amended by the *Trade Expansion Act of 1962*,[6] the *Trade Agreements Act of 1974*,[7] the *Trade and Tariff Act of 1984*,[8] the *Omnibus Trade and Competitiveness Act of 1988*,[9] and the *Uruguay Round Agreements Act of 1994*.[10] ("Section 201" is the generic term covering Sections 201-204, which are codified at 19 U.S.C. §§ 2251-54.) Of course, in a multilateral legal context, Section 201 derives legitimacy from this Article.

The U.S. was more than the principal force behind Article XIX in the GATT negotiations of the mid 1940s. It also advocated for the *Agreement on Safeguards* in the 1986-94 Uruguay Round negotiations. As the Clinton Administration's *Statement of Administrative Action on the Agreement on Safeguards* indicates, the U.S. was concerned that certain topics with which Section 201 dealt remained obscure in Article XIX.

---

[3] JOHN H. JACKSON, WORLD TRADE AND THE LAW OF GATT § 23.1, at 553 (1969).

[4] *See* Executive Order No. 10004, 3 C.F.R. §§ 819-22 (9 Oct. 1948) (revoking Executive Order No. 9832).

[5] *See Trade Act of 1974*, Pub. L. No. 93-618, § 201, 88 Stat. 1978, 2011-14 (3 Jan. 1974), *codified at* 19 U.S.C. § 2251.

[6] *See* Pub. L. No. 87-794, tit. II, § 201, 76 Stat. 872 (11 Oct. 1962).

[7] *See* Pub. L. No. 96-39, tit. I, § 106(b)(3), 93 Stat. 144, 193 (26 July 1979).

[8] *See* Pub. L. No. 98-573, tit. II, §§ 248-49, 98 Stat. 2948, 2998-99 (30 Oct. 1984).

[9] *See* Pub. L. No.100-418, tit. I, § 1401, 102 Stat. 1107, 1225-41 (23 Aug. 1988).

[10] *See* Pub. L. No. 103-465, tit. III, §§ 301-04, 108 Stat. 4809, 4933-38 (8 Dec. 1994).

Accordingly, in the Uruguay Round, American negotiators were successful in persuading their counterparts to incorporate some Section 201 concepts into the WTO *Agreement on Safeguards*. Examples of such concepts include:

   i.   Criteria for determination of increased imports and injury or threat thereof.

   ii. Procedures to ensure transparency.

   iii. An 8-year cap on the duration of an Escape Clause measure.

   iv. Expedited procedures for critical circumstances.

   v.   The progressive liberalization of measures implemented under the Escape Clause (known as "degressivity").

   vi. The right to re-impose safeguard restrictions at a later date.

As also indicated in the *Statement of Administrative Action*, the U.S. was concerned about two provisions in Article XIX:

   a.   The requirement that an Escape Clause measure be applied on a non-discriminatory, MFN basis.

   b.   The ability of countries whose exports are affected by Escape Clause measures to impose retaliatory measures against the country invoking the Clause, if they are not compensated by that country.

The U.S. argued these provisions discouraged use of the general safeguard remedy.

The first provision imposed on a large number of other contracting parties the costs of adjustment to fair foreign competition incurred by an industry in the contracting party invoking the Escape Clause. Thus, the first provision virtually ensured opposition from other contracting parties to an Escape Clause action. The second provision imposed the costs of retaliation or compensation on the contracting party invoking the Clause. Thus, the second provision was a clear disincentive to invoking the Clause.

The individual and combined effects of these provisions, urged the U.S., was contracting parties eschewed Article XIX. Instead, they addressed import surges through so-called gray area measures, *e.g.*, through voluntary export restraints (VERs). Accordingly, "the principal U.S. objective" in the Uruguay Round talks on safeguards "was to develop rules for the application of . . . Article XIX that would encourage WTO members to use rather than by-pass safeguards rules."[11]

The objective was largely achieved. The WTO *Agreement on Safeguards*, which entered into force on 1 January 1995, clarifies some obscurities of Article XIX, including rules on its application. Indeed, the second clause of the Preamble to the *Agreement* declares "the need to clarify and reinforce the disciplines of . . . Article XIX, . . . to re-establish multilateral control over safeguards and eliminate measures that escape such control." Further, Article

---

[11] *See Statement of Administrative Action for the Uruguay Round Agreement on Safeguards*, *in* MESSAGE FROM THE PRESIDENT OF THE UNITED STATES TRANSMITTING THE URUGUAY ROUND TRADE AGREEMENTS, TEXTS OF AGREEMENTS IMPLEMENTING BILL, STATEMENT OF ADMINISTRATIVE ACTION AND REQUIRED SUPPORTING STATEMENTS, H.R. DOC. No. 316, vol. 1, 103d Cong., 2d Sess. 956 (27 Sept. 1994).

11:1(b) of the *Agreement* bans the use of VERs, orderly market arrangements (OMAs), voluntary restraint agreements (VRAs), or any other gray area measures. To be sure, neither GATT Article XIX nor the *Agreement* affects, nor could affect, reach private restraints of trade. That matter is left to the competition law and policy of each WTO Member.

II. PROTECTIONISM AND PROLIFERATION

Why include Article XIX in GATT, and why have a WTO *Agreement on Safeguards*? From a free trade perspective, it is readily apparent safeguards generally, and Article XIX in particular, is incongruous with the fundamental goal of GATT, namely, trade liberalization. They can be characteriszd, not unreasonably, as more than a derogation from the general spirit of GATT that healthy international competition, not interventionist government action, should dictate outcomes.

Worse yet, Article XIX is the most protectionist (though not necessarily the most protective) of all permissible trade remedies. A producer or foreign exporter targeted by an Escape Clause action has done nothing unfair. It is not alleged to have dumped. It is not alleged to have received a subsidy from its government subsidy. It is not alleged to have infringed on an intellectual property right (IPR). Indeed, sometimes it is the failure to obtain relief under one of the unfair import competition laws that prompts an interested party to seek a safeguard remedy. For example, in September 1997, the United States Wheat Gluten Industry filed a Section 201 petition against the European Union (EU) after its effort to seek relief under *Section 301 of the Trade Act of 1974*, as amended, failed.

In an Escape Clause action, all a foreign respondent has done is compete effectively in conformity with free market principles. More or less as a result of the operation of the economic law of comparative advantage, a domestic producer of a like product files a petition in which it claims actual or threatened harm from fair foreign competition. To bow to the petitioner's request is both to over-rule the market and provide a remedy where nothing unjust has occurred. Why, then, bow? That is, what purpose or purposes does safeguard relief serve?

Protectionism is not the only concern about the remedy. From a trade liberalizing perspective, proliferation is a problem, too. A free trade agreement (FTA) involving the U.S. without an Escape Clause is scarcely imaginable. An entire Chapter of the *North American Free Trade Agreement* (*NAFTA*) — Chapter 8 — is dedicated to creating and establishing parameters for the use of the remedy as among the U.S., Canada, and Mexico. What safeguard provisions exist in other U.S. FTAs? To what extent is *NAFTA* Chapter 8 a template for those provisions?

FTAs are not the only mechanism through which safeguards are proliferating. WTO texts themselves are a device. The Uruguay Round *Agreements on Agriculture*, in Article 5, and *Textiles and Clothing* (*ATC*), in Article 6:2, contain product-specific safeguards. That is, they contain trade remedies that may be used in specified sectors, against particular products. Accession agreements with WTO applicants also contain special safeguard mechanisms, which are product-specific and, by definition, country-specific. For example, the 11 January 2007 accession accord for Vietnam contains monitoring and remedial provisions in respect of textile and apparel (T & A) exports from that country. The December 2001 accession agreement for China has both a T & A safeguard, and a product-specific remedy for Chinese merchandise.

Proliferation can occur not only in the sense of creating novel safeguards, but also in terms of the use of extant and new remedies. In the latter respect, the legal criteria for use are critical. Like any weapon, the easier it is use, the more likely it will be used. There are two broad categories of criteria:

1. Verbal formulas, which require proof of an import surge, injury or threat, causation, and (possibly) unforeseen circumstances associated with treaty obligations. Examples include GATT Article XIX and the WTO *Agreement on Safeguards*, and provisions in various FTAs.

2. Arithmetic formulas, which involve application of a "Trigger Price" (*i.e.*, proving imports are sold below a threshold) or "Trigger Volume" (*i.e.*, proving imports are in quantities above a threshold). Examples include the WTO *Agreement on Agriculture*, and provisions in various FTAs.

Depending on the facts, a trigger formula may be easier to apply than a verbal formula. That is because trigger formulas do not require proof of injury or threat to a domestic producer of a like or competitive product, nor do they call for proof that surging imports caused injury or threat. As long as subject merchandise is imported at beneath a trigger price, or above a trigger volume, then the remedy may be imposed. Of course, if neither the price nor volume thresholds are breached, then a petitioner has the option of falling back on a verbal formula, and trying to exploit ambiguities in that formula to its benefit.

III. THE THEORY OF SAFEGUARDS

A. Economic Arguments

Among the leading theoretical economic arguments for safeguard relief are that it helps restore competitiveness, and that it facilitates orderly contraction. In respect of the first argument, it is urged the Escape Clause will give a petitioning industry the protection it needs to get back on its feet, as it were. That is, measures undertaken pursuant to GATT Article XIX and the WTO *Agreement on Safeguards* give an industry hurt by free trade time to adjust to a liberalized trade environment:

> While GATT's primary goal is to establish a more open international trade environment, it recognizes the right of a government to part from free and open trade in certain circumstances. In particular, Article XIX allows a country to "escape" from negotiated tariff reductions, if the increased imports can be shown to "cause or threaten serious injury to domestic producers" of competitive products. In those cases, the country can unilaterally elect to reinstate the trade barrier that was

in effect before the concession. The provision was meant to give industries time to adjust to increased competition.[12]

By providing temporary protection, the relief gives an ailing industry time
to generate profits, and reinvest these profits in factors of production so as
to reduce its costs and thereby regain its competitive edge once protection is
removed. That time may be critical for infant industries, which may have been
exposed prematurely to free trade. In the long run, the international trade
community, especially consumers in different countries, benefit because
efficient competitors re-emerge.

This argument is not without its critics, even from the economically-minded.
One scholar in the law and economics movement, Professor Sykes, states:

> First, it [the restoration of competitiveness argument] relies on the
> questionable assumption that governments can accurately identify
> and protect only those industries that can become "competitive" (or
> "competitive again" in the case of declining industries). The more
> probable outcome is that well-organized producer lobbies will secure
> protection irrespective of the impact such protection is likely to have
> on the "competitiveness" of their particular industry.
>
> Second, even if governments were competent to identify appropriate
> candidates for assistance and would properly exclude poor candidates,
> protection is not necessarily the best way to provide such assistance.
> Direct loans or subsidies to the troubled industry are in theory
> superior to protection, unless such measures entail sufficiently higher
> administrative costs. Loans or subsidies to cover periods of losses can
> be as effective as protection in enabling an industry to become
> "competitive," but they do not introduce the deadweight loss attribut-
> able to the protection-induced distortion of consumer prices.
>
> Finally, and most importantly, government intervention to restore
> "competitiveness" is simply unnecessary, at least in developed coun-
> tries with substantial private capital markets. Private lenders will
> finance efforts to become "competitive" as long as the returns from
> such investments justify the apparent risk. Absent some distortion
> affecting the market rate of interest, therefore, economically worth-
> while investments will be financed without government assistance.
> And, at any rate of interest, investment in industries that are unwill-
> ing or unable to borrow in the capital market diverts resources from
> other investments where the expected returns are greater.[13]

To be sure, this criticism rests on a neoclassical economic perspective of
Article XIX.

From that perspective, a deadweight loss is associated with virtually any
tariff or non-tariff barrier, such as a quota. Either type of barrier causes the
price of an imported good to rise. As a result, for two reasons, consumer
surplus in an importing country erecting a barrier is likely to fall by more

---

[12] CONGRESSIONAL BUDGET OFFICE, HAS TRADE PROTECTION REVITALIZED DOMESTIC INDUS-
TRIES? 3 (1986).

[13] Alan O. Sykes, *Protectionism as a "Safeguard": A Positive Analysis of the GATT "Escape
Clause" with Normative Speculations*, 58 U. CHI. L. REV. 255, 264 (1991).

than the aggregate increase in producer surplus and — assuming a tariff is imposed — government revenue.

1. An increase in the price of an imported good causes some consumers to cease consumption of that good. Because they exit the market, surplus associated with their consumption is lost.

2. Second, an increase in the price of an imported good induces an increase in domestic production of an article that is like or directly competitive with that good. Yet, this output is inefficient because the marginal cost to produce a unit is greater than the price of the import that the unit replaces. As a result, consumers pay a premium for the domestic like product.

Persuasive as this perspective may be, controversial assumptions afflict it. For example, it is a static view, neglecting implications of protection in the medium and long-term. It also is a view from the welfare of the importing country, not the exporting country, or the world economy. And, this perspective assumes safeguards are an economic issue, when in reality they may implicate non-economic concerns.

The second leading theoretical economic argument about the purpose of the safeguard remedy concerns orderly contraction. Surely the Escape Clause facilitates the orderly contraction of industries that cannot regain their competitive edge. Orderly contraction is a different form of adjustment than restoration of competitiveness. Thus, a single "adjustment" analysis is unrealistically broad. Relief prevents shock to factors of production, most notably labor. The protection from imports afforded by the relief slows the rate of contraction in an import-sensitive industry. Workers are not thrown from their jobs, and their wages are not slashed, without warning. Rather, they have time to find new work, or possibly retrain — *i.e.*, to adjust positively to a new global market context.

Stated differently, safeguard relief is a device to allocate costs of market adjustment. Trade liberalization is the consequence of tariff and non-tariff concessions. Products of certain industries are displaced by new, more competitive, imports. At least, mobile factors of a production in a domestic economy should shift to production of goods that can compete with imports in a liberalized trading regime. Yet, moving labor, human capital, and physical capital, and re-allocating or re-claiming land, takes time and money.

These costs have to be allocated in some way between or among countries, and between or among sectors within a country. In all instances, families and communities are at stake. For them, two questions must be addressed. First, should an importing country, exporting country, or both incur the costs of market adjustment? Second, how should these costs be allocated within a particular country?

On the first question, GATT Article XIX and the WTO *Agreement on Safeguards* allow an importing WTO Member to shift at least some market adjustment costs away from an injured domestic industry to an exporter or exporters in another Member. Regarding the second question, Article XIX allows an importing Member to shift at least some of the costs of market adjustment away from an injured domestic injury to domestic consumers (insofar as these consumers pay a higher price for imports, and a lower quantity of imports is made available to them).

Like the restoration of competitiveness argument, the orderly contraction argument is not without critics. Scholars enamored by law and economics urge delaying contraction is an economic vice. Delay means production factors are misallocated in an inefficient industry, one whose marginal cost of production for a unit of output exceeds unit price, for the period of delay. Instead, land, physical capital, labor, and human capital should be redeployed expeditiously to more efficient uses. Better to get pain over with quickly than drag it out. Of course, that prescription is easier to make than take.

B. Political Arguments

Two theoretical political arguments are offered for the safeguard remedy. First, inclusion of an Escape Clause in GATT was a significant reason why Congress agreed to American participation in GATT. That is because Congress appreciated Article XIX could serve as a political safety valve for protectionist pressures.

Suppose a politically powerful industry in complains of injury from a sub-stantial increase in imports, and the increase is due to concessions granted in a trade-liberalizing accord. An Escape Clause allows the government of the importing country to alter unilaterally the accord to aid the affected industry. Absent this political safety valve, the pressures may be manifest in more (perhaps far more) protectionist ways than an Escape Clause petition. Any safeguard remedy affects only a single industry per case, and perhaps just a few firms in that industry. The more trade-restrictive alternative, but for the Clause, would be protectionist legislation. That legislation would affect an entire sector of an economy, and have reverberations throughout many other sectors.

The second justification draws on Public Choice Theory. Surely the Escape Clause encourages a country to enter into a greater number of tariff bindings than it otherwise would. As an American delegate to the original GATT negotiations stated:

> [an Escape Clause would] give more flexibility to the commitments undertaken. . . . Some provision of this kind seems necessary in order that countries will not find themselves in such a rigid position that they could not deal with situations of an emergency character. There-fore, the Article [establishing the Clause] would provide for a modifica-tion of commitments to meet such temporary situation [*sic*]. In order to safeguard the right given and in order to prevent abuse of it, the Article would provide that before any action is taken under an exception, the member concerned would have to notify the organisa-tion and consult with them [*sic*], and with any other interested members.[14]

This view suggests Public Choice Theory helps explain the purpose of safeguards.

---

[14] JACKSON, *supra* note 3, at 554-55 (United Nations Document EPCT/C.II/PV.7, at 3 (1946)).

What is this Theory? Suffice it to say it is nothing more than the application of microeconomic tools to political behavior. As Professor Sykes explains, the Theory

> suggests that policymaking under democratic government depends on the interplay of special interest forces in the political "marketplace." There is generally no reason to expect the democratic process systematically to yield "efficient," "equitable," or otherwise "correct" outcomes by any idealized criterion for measuring the success of policy. Rather, elected officials will pursue their self interest. They will "supply" policy initiatives to interest groups that "demand" them, with the currency of the political marketplace in the form of votes or campaign contributions, for instance. Ultimately, well-organized groups — those most adept at lobbying and most capable of "paying" for policy initiatives — will have their interests vindicated, while diffuse, poorly organized interest groups may suffer.
>
> . . . .
>
> Public choice [theory] predicts that elected officials will concern themselves far more with the impact of trade policy on producer interests than on consumer interests. Individual firms in import-competing or export-oriented industries often have much to gain from specific trade policy measures. And, especially in industries with a relatively small number of large firms, free-rider problems need not seriously impede efforts to influence policy, either because each firm has sufficient incentive to act individually or because interested firms can organize themselves to act collectively through a trade association or lobbying coalition. In contrast, the number of consumers is large and the amount at stake for each consumer on a given trade issue is modest. Consequently, the costs to each consumer of acting individually in an effort to influence the political process will usually exceed the potential gains. Thus, severe free-rider problems will often thwart the task of organizing consumers to act collectively to support liberal trade policies.[15]

Thus, the Theory predicts a politician will focus on concerns of producers adversely impacted by free trade, not of consumers benefited by trade liberalization.

In turn, the essential purpose of GATT Article XIX, the WTO *Agreement on Safeguards*, Section 201, and other safeguard provisions, is to authorize the focus on concerns of allegedly injured producers. As Professor Sykes further explains, it regulates the trade-off between

> trade liberalization *ex ante* [*i.e.*, at the time a trade agreement takes effect] and opportunities to re-impose protection *ex post* [*i.e.*, after a trade agreement enters into force]. When self-interested political officials must decide whether to make trade concessions under conditions of uncertainty about their political consequences, the knowledge that those concessions are in fact "escapable" facilitates initial concessions

---

[15] Sykes, *supra* note 13, at 275-76.

and may reduce the social costs of protection over time. This defense of Article XIX, though conjectural, is nonetheless far more convincing than popular rhetoric about the importance of the escape clause for restoring competitiveness or facilitating an orderly contraction in declining industries, or the hypothesis that escape clause measures provide an *ex post* "safety valve" for protectionist pressures.[16]

In brief, Article XIX relieves a WTO Member of the fear commitments into which it enters are irrevocable.

Lifting this fear helps progressive trade liberalization. If political rewards are sufficient, and the cost of measured retaliation is accepted, then a WTO Member may renege on its commitments. By removing fear at the outset, a Member feels liberated to enter into major trade-expanding deals:

> Although the reduction of protectionist barriers is almost always in the public interest, elected officials or their subordinates may decline to pursue trade liberalization initiatives out of political self-interest, even if the political consequences of liberalization appear favorable at the time of the negotiations. The reason is that unanticipated changes in economic conditions may create circumstances in which the political rewards to an increase in protection (or the political costs of an irrevocable commitment to reduce protection) are great. Consequently, in the absence of an escape clause, trade negotiators may decline to make certain reciprocal concessions for fear of adverse political consequences in the future. But, with an escape clause in place the negotiators will agree on a greater number of reciprocal concessions, knowing that those concessions can be avoided later if political conditions dictate.[17]

In sum, the argument is safeguards ensure flexibility in reducing trade barriers. They boost chances of agreement by accommodating self-interests.

IV. GATT ARTICLE XIX AND THE WTO *AGREEMENT ON SAFEGUARDS*

A. The 1951 *Hatters' Fur* Case and Elements of Safeguard Relief

The 1951 GATT Working Party Report in the *Hatters' Fur* case, the leading early GATT decision on Article XIX, summarizes the elements of an Escape Clause action:

> (a) there should be an abnormal development in the imports of the product in question in the sense that:
>
>   (i) the product in question must be imported in increased quantities;
>
>   (ii) the increased imports must be the result of unforeseen developments and of the effect of the tariff concession; and

---

[16] *Id.* at 259.
[17] *Id.* at 278-79.

(iii) the imports must enter in such increased quantities and under such conditions as to cause or threaten serious injury to domestic producers of like or directly competitive products.

(b) The suspension of an obligation or the withdrawal or modification of a concession must be limited to the extent and the time necessary to prevent or remedy the injury caused or threatened.

(c) The contracting party taking action under Article XIX must give notice in writing to the Contracting Parties before taking action. It must also give an opportunity to contracting parties substantially interested and to the Contracting Parties to consult with it. As a rule consultation should take place before the action is taken, but in critical circumstances consultation may take place immediately after the measure is taken provisionally.[18]

In brief, careful parsing of Article XIX:1(a), and perusal of the *Hatters' Fur* Working Party Report, indicates there are 5 elements to an Escape Clause action:

- The result of unforeseen developments.
- The effect of GATT obligations.
- An increased level of imports (sometimes called a "surge").
- Causation.
- Serious injury or threat of serious injury.

Each element must be present, otherwise relief lawfully cannot be granted.

The WTO *Agreement on Safeguards* contains these elements, and Article 2:1 of the *Agreement* lays particular stress on the third and fourth element. Finally, as per *Hatters' Fur*, other provisions of Article XIX establish procedures to be followed before implementing an Escape Clause remedy, namely, notice and the opportunity for consultations. (As is common among other trade remedies, for safeguard relief there exists an exception to otherwise requisite procedures for critical circumstances.) Articles 3, 12, and 13 of the *Agreement* treat these (and other) procedures.

B. "Like" or "Directly Competitive" Products

Note carefully the kind of product at issue — like or directly competitive. That is, imports of merchandise subject to an investigation (*i.e.*, subject merchandise) must be "like" or "directly competitive with" a product originating in the domestic economy of the importing country in which safeguard relief is contemplated. In an antidumping (AD) or countervailing duty (CVD) action, a "directly competitive" relationship is not close enough. Products must be "like." However, in a national treatment case under GATT Article III:2, second sentence, "substitutability" of products (as per Article III:1, and Ad Article III, Paragraph 2), suffices. Thus, the Escape Clause remedy contemplates a

---

[18] *See Report of the Intersessional Working Party on the Complaint of Czechoslovakia Concerning the Withdrawal by the United States of a Tariff Concession under the Terms of Article XIX of the General Agreement*, Geneva, Nov. 1951 (GATT/CP/106, GATT/CP.6/SR.19, Sales No. GATT/1951-3), B.I.S.D., vol. 2 at 36 (1952) (adopted 27 Sept. 1951).

broader universe of targets than do the AD or CVD remedy, but less so than the national treatment obligation. Does this scheme make sense, particularly in view of the fact the Clause is directed at fairly trade foreign merchandise?

C. Limits on Safeguard Relief

Article XIX:1(a) of GATT, and Articles 2:1-2, 4:2, 5, and 7-8, of the *Agreement on Safeguards*, lay out important boundaries on the Escape Clause remedy, even if where all elements for its application are present:

1. *Scope*:

    The scope of application of remedial measure is restricted to foreign merchandise that is "like" or "directly competitive" with a domestic product.

2. *Nondiscrimination*:

    The remedy must be applied to subject merchandise irrespective of its source, *i.e.*, from all countries, on an MFN basis. This requirement easier to meet if relief is a tariff than a quota or tariff rate quota (TRQ) (because of the problem of quota or TRQ allocation among countries).

3. *Parallelism*:

    The scope of application of a safeguard remedy should be consistent with (*i.e.*, parallel to) the foreign merchandise examined during a safeguard investigation. After all, if an importing Member includes merchandise from all sources in its injury and causation determination, but excludes merchandise originating in certain countries (namely, partners in a FTA or customs union (CU)) from remedial action, then application of the remedy is discriminatory. The problem, however, is that some FTAs and CUs call for exactly this kind of exemption from a global safeguard remedy.

    In the 2000 *Argentina Footwear Safeguard* case, the Appellate Body held Argentina could not rely on its status as a party to *MERCOSUR*, nor on GATT Article XXIV, as a defense for its safeguard remedy applied to footwear imports only from non-*MERCOSUR* countries. In the 2001 *Wheat Gluten* case (in which the U.S. exempted its *NAFTA* partner, Canada, from a safeguard), and 2002 *Line Pipe* case (in which the U.S. excluded both *NAFTA* partners, Canada and Mexico, from a safeguard), the Appellate Body affirmed imports included in an Escape Clause investigation must correspond to imports targeted for remedial action.

4. *Duration*:

    The duration of remedial measure is limited to 4 years, and may be renewed once (for a total of 8 years).

5. *Suspension of the Right to Retaliate*:

    A WTO Member exporting merchandise targeted by a safeguard remedy has the right to receive substantially equivalent concessions from the importing Member, or to suspend such concessions with respect to that Member, unless that Member pays adequate compensation for the adverse effects of the remedy. But, that right is suspended for the first 3 years of a safeguard measure.

These limits on safeguard relief provoke a number of questions.

First, does the 4 year sunset rule provide support for the critique of the WTO dispute settlement mechanism that a *de facto* "Three Year Pass" exists? In other words, can a WTO Member maintain a safeguard inconsistent with GATT—WTO standards for 3 years, not suffer retaliation, and not have to bother too much about an adverse Appellate Body decision?

Second, what is the proper relationship among GATT Article XXIV, Article 2:2 of the *Safeguards Agreement*, and Escape Clause remedies in FTAs and CUs? The Appellate Body has yet to offer a definitive ruling on the question. As a practical matter, how can a WTO Member that also is party to an FTA or CU stay within the bounds of parallelism? In the 2002 *Line Pipe* case, the Appellate Body suggested two possibilities —

 i. Complete exemption, wherein imports from FTA or CU parties are entirely exempt from a global safeguards investigation.

 ii. Non-attribution, whereby imports from FTA or CU partners are included in a global investigation, but imports from non-FTA and non-CU sources are found to be the cause of injury or threat.

Are these scenarios practical to implement?

Third, do the above questions help explain why, as Professor Gantz puts it, the Appellate Body applies "very strict scrutiny" to safeguards relief?[19] What about critical circumstances, which are mentioned, but not defined precisely, in GATT Article XIX:2 and Article 6 of the *Safeguards Agreement*? Should the same limits apply on safeguard actions in those instances, and should they trigger strict scrutiny?

V. GATT—WTO JURISPRUDENCE ON THE ELEMENTS

A. Element #1: Unforeseen Circumstances, the 1951 *Hatters' Fur* Case, Plus Four WTO Appellate Body Precedents

"Unforeseen developments" may be justified by analogy to the public international law principle of changed circumstances, specifically, the doctrine of *rebus sic stantibus* (*i.e.*, in these circumstances, or things staying as they are).[20] This doctrine holds that a treaty ceases to be obligatory upon a fundamental change of the circumstances on which it is based, where the effect of the change is to transform radically the extent of the obligations to be performed under the treaty.[21] Yet, the analogy, begs the central practical question: what are "unforeseen developments"?

---

[19] Raj Bhala & David Gantz, *WTO Case Review 2002*, 20 Ariz. J. Int'l & Comp. L. 143, 179 (2003).

[20] *See* Kenneth W. Dam, The GATT 99, 106 (1970).

[21] *See* I Restatement of the Foreign Relations Law of the United States § 366, at 218 (1987).

• The 1951 *Hatters' Fur* Case:

The enduring value of the 1951 GATT Working Party Report in *Hatters' Fur* (cited earlier) is partly its discussion of the meaning of "unforeseen developments." The dispute arose because in 1950 the U.S., pursuant to its Escape Clause, withdrew a concession on women's fur felt hats and hat bodies it had negotiated in the first Geneva Round of multilateral tariff negotiations in 1947. (The concession involved less than $2 million worth of imports.) The U.S. argued a change of women's hat styles resulted in increased imports, and this change was an "unforeseen development." The former Czechoslovakia challenged the U.S. action, claiming a change in hat styles did not satisfy the Article XIX:1(a) "unforeseen development" prerequisite.

A GATT Working Party was established to consider the Czech complaint. The Working Party, except for the U.S., agreed upon the following definition:

> [T]he term "unforeseen development" should be interpreted to mean developments occurring after the negotiation of the relevant tariff concession which it would not be *reasonable* to *expect* that the *negotiators of the country making the concession* could and should have foreseen at the time when the concession was negotiated.[22]

The *Hatters' Fur* definition of "unforeseen development" is a mixture of objective and subjective factors. The word "reasonable" intimates an objectively reasonable person could not have expected the negotiators of the country concerned to foresee the development. However, the fact "negotiators of the country making the concession" is spelled out suggests this objectively reasonable person must put herself in the position of the negotiators from the country concerned and see matters from their perspective, *i.e.*, understand their subjective position.

The Working Party, save for the U.S., agreed "that the fact that hat styles had changed did not constitute an 'unforeseen development' within the meaning of Article XIX."[23] This conclusion was inevitable. A different outcome would mean any contracting party could invoke the Escape Clause on the pretext imports of a product have increased because of a change in style or fashion. Consumer tastes in the apparel industry change frequently and, therefore, always are foreseeable. Accordingly, the Working Party's Report accepted the Czech argument "it is universally known that fashions are subject to constant changes,"[24] so American negotiators should have anticipated a change in women's hat styles.

Nonetheless, the Working Party — except for Czechoslovakia — found the American Escape Clause action satisfied the "unforeseen developments" prerequisite. The specific facts of the case, "particularly the *degree to which the change in fashion affected the competitive situation*, could not reasonably be expected to have been foreseen by the United States authorities in 1947."[25]

---

[22] World Trade Organization, Guide to GATT Law and Practice — Analytical Index vol. 1, at 517 (6th ed. 1995) [hereinafter GATT Analytical Index] (emphasis added).

[23] *Id.* at 517.

[24] Jackson, *supra* note 3, at 561.

[25] GATT Analytical Index, *supra* note 22, at 517 (emphasis added).

The application by the Working Party of its definition of "unforeseen developments" thus created a subtle, yet dispositive, distinction. A change in fashion always is foreseeable. Hence, such a change itself cannot satisfy the definition. But, the effect of a fashion change on market conditions is not necessarily foreseeable.

Overall, the inference to be drawn from the *Hatters' Fur* case may be, as Professor Dam puts it, that "the 'unforeseen developments' requirement envisages the presence of *very particular changed circumstances* and not merely of a general economic change."[26] After all, whenever tariff or non-tariff barriers are lowered, the possibility of injury or general economic change to the relevant domestic industry should be anticipated. Therefore, only "very particular changed circumstances" ought to satisfy the "unforeseen developments" prerequisite.

For almost half a century — from the 1951 *Hatters' Fur* case until the 2000 WTO action in *Argentina Footwear Safeguard* (cited below), there were few if any notable legal developments relating to the definition of "unforeseen developments." Indeed, the element almost was forgotten as an essentiality in the proper invocation of Article XIX. In the *Argentina Footwear Safeguard* case, however, the Appellate Body made clear the element was as vital as ever. That and subsequent cases contribute — albeit modestly — to the jurisprudence on "unforeseen developments."

- The 2000 *Argentina — Safeguard Measures on Imports of Footwear* Appellate Body Report:[27]

The central issue on appeal concerned the language "as a result of unforeseen developments." The phrase exists in Article XIX:1(a), but not in the WTO *Agreement on Safeguards*. Did the Uruguay Round negotiators mean to extirpate this element from the Escape Clause by omitting it from the *Agreement*, i.e., did the *Agreement* supersede GATT? "No," replied the Appellate Body.

The case arose out of an Argentine safeguard investigation in February 1997. Following the investigation, Argentina imposed provisional measures, in the form of minimum specific import duties, on certain footwear imports. Essentially, Argentina computed for each product an average import price, and then multiplied that price by its bound MFN duty of 35 percent. The result was the specific minimum duty for the product. For each shipment of targeted merchandise, Argentina imposed the higher of the specific minimum duty or the *ad valorem* rate. In July 1997, Argentina's *Commission Nacional de Comercio Exterior (CNCE)* notified the WTO Committee on Safeguards of the *CNCE's* finding of serious injury to the Argentine footwear industry. In September 1997, *CNCE* imposed definitive Escape Clause relief, in the form of specific minimum duties, on imported footwear. (Argentina exempted its partners in *MERCOSUR* — Brazil, Paraguay, and Uruguay — from this relief. Pursuant to the *MERCOSUR* accord, the partners agreed not to impose safeguard relief against one another.) The European Communities (EC)

---

[26] DAM, *supra* note 20, at 102 (emphasis added).

[27] *See* WTO Appellate Body Report, *Argentina — Safeguard Measures on Imports of Footwear*, WT/DS121/AB/R (complaint by European Communities) (adopted 12 Jan. 2000).

challenged the safeguard, arguing Argentina failed to comply with the requirement in Article XIX:1(a) that relief not be granted without proof an increase in imports results from unforeseen developments.

The EC argument rested solely on the proposition GATT and the *Safeguards Agreement* are a single undertaking and constitute an integrated system of disciplines. The EC rejected alternative characterizations, namely, the two documents are in conflict, or the later-in-time *Agreement* supersedes the earlier-in-time GATT. All requirements of both documents had to be met before a WTO Member lawfully could impose a safeguard. One such requirement is "unforeseen developments," which the EC defined according to the ordinary meaning of the phrase, but in a circular fashion, as a sudden change in a course of action, event, or conditions that has not been foreseen. Argentina's rebuttal (with which the U.S., as a third party, agreed), was satisfaction of the elements in the *Agreement* necessarily meant satisfaction of Article XIX:1(a) of GATT. The documents conflicted, as the Uruguay Round negotiators left out the unforeseen developments element, but a *General Interpretative Note* to Annex 1A of the WTO *Multilateral Trade Agreements on Goods* called for giving priority to an MTA over GATT in the event of a conflict.

The WTO Panel, but not the Appellate Body, agreed with the Argentine position. Overturning the Panel's conclusion, the Appellate Body held "unforeseen developments" remains an essential element in an Escape Clause action. It based its holding on Article II of the *Agreement Establishing the World Trade Organization* (*WTO Agreement*). This provision explains all of the accords in Annexes 1, 2, and 3 (and, therefore, includes GATT and the *Agreement on Safeguards*, which are in Annex 1A) are integral parts of the *WTO Agreement*, and all of them are binding on WTO Members. This "one treaty" view of the WTO texts calls for a harmonious interpretation of the equally mandatory provisions in the texts. Articles 1 and 11:1(a) of the *Agreement on Safeguards* reinforce this call, as does the Preamble to the *Agreement*, because they indicate not that the *Agreement* subsumes Article XIX of GATT, but rather that Article XIX remains in full force and effect. Put simply, the EC was right — all of the elements in Article XIX:1(a) and the *Agreement* must exist to support relief.

As for the meaning of "unforeseen developments," the Appellate Body unsurprisingly focused on the ordinary interpretation of these words, settling on the word "unexpected." The developments that lead to merchandise being imported in increased quantities so as to cause or threaten serious injury are "unforeseen" if they are "unexpected." Further, the increased imports are the "effect of obligations" incurred by a WTO Member (an element, like "unforeseen developments," which is set forth in Article XIX:1(a), but omitted from Article 2:1 of the *Agreement on Safeguards*) if the Member has incurred tariff concessions under GATT. In setting "unforeseen" and "unexpected" as synonyms, the Appellate Body expressly put its holding in the line of the 1951 *Hatters' Fur* Report. In that 1951 Report, the GATT Working Party defined an "unforeseen development" as one a contracting party could not reasonably have expected at the time it made a concession.

The Appellate Body did not rule on whether Argentina had satisfied the "unforeseen developments" element. That was because the Argentine safeguard violated Articles 2 and 4 of the *Safeguard Agreement*, and judicial economy rendered it unnecessary to go further.

• The 2000 *Korea — Definitive Safeguard Measure on Imports of Certain Dairy Products* Case[28]

The 2000 *Korea Dairy Safeguard* case stays in the *Hatters' Fur* tradition. As in the *Argentina Footwear Safeguard* case, in the *Korea Dairy Safeguard* case, at the Panel stage the ruling was the Uruguay Round negotiators effectively wrote the "unforeseen developments" element out of Escape Clause law. The Appellate Body reversed the Panel's ruling regarding "unforeseen circumstances." However, the Appellate Body added nothing to its holding in *Argentina Footwear Safeguard*, and tracked its reasoning from that case. Because the Panel said proof of "unforeseen circumstances" was unnecessary, the Appellate Body declined to rule on whether Korea's action embodied this element. To be sure, the *Korea Dairy Safeguard* Report stands equally ably for the proposition this element remains vital in an Escape Clause action, that Article XIX and the *Agreement* are part of an integrated treaty system and the elements of each document must be met, and that the term essentially connotes unexpectedness.

• The 2001 *United States — Safeguard Measures on Imports of Fresh, Chilled or Frozen Lamb Meat from New Zealand and Australia* Case[29]

In 2001, the Appellate Body had another chance to amplify the definition of "unforeseen circumstances." The *Lamb Meat* case arose out of a safeguards investigation by the ITC in October 1998 of lamb meat imports. By a July 1999 Presidential Proclamation issued by President Bill Clinton, the U.S. imposed a TRQ on this product. The TRQ permitted imports at 9, 6, and 3 percent for in-quota shipments during the first three years of relief, respectively, and 40, 32, and 24 percent for above-quota shipments in those years, respectively. Argentina and New Zealand, the two major exporters of lamb meat to the U.S., successfully challenged the Section 201 action.

In *Lamb Meat*, the U.S. offered a novel argument on "unforeseen developments." No specific finding about these developments, or explicit conclusion about them, is required. The ITC did not even consider "unforeseen developments" in its investigation. (The closest it came was a discussion of the change in the pattern of lamb meat imports, but it never explained whether or why this change was an "unforeseen development.") No worries, urged the U.S. All a competent authority need do is establish a factual basis for the existence of unforeseen developments.

Citing the 1951 GATT Working Party Report in *Hatters's Fur*, the U.S. said trade negotiators, when they make a tariff concession, normally do not foresee specific developments in a particular product market that lead to an import surge causing injury to a domestic industry. Essentially, the American

---

[28] *See* WTO Appellate Body Report, *Korea — Definitive Safeguard Measure on Imports of Certain Dairy Products*, WT/DS98/AB/R (complaint by the European Communities) (adopted 12 Jan. 2000).

[29] *See* WTO Appellate Body Report, *United States — Safeguard Measures on Imports of Fresh, Chilled or Frozen Lamb Meat from New Zealand and Australia*, WT/DS177/AB/R (complaint by Australia), WT/DS178/AB/R (complaint by New Zealand) (adopted 16 May 2001).

argument stressed the reality of the mindset of trade negotiators, and the inherent inability to foresee injurious import surges long before they occur. The consequence of the argument was a minimal factual showing of market events should be enough to shift the burden of proof to the complainants — Australia and New Zealand — to prove the tariff negotiators did, in fact, have the requisite foresight. Australia and New Zealand saw through the argument. The ITC report did not contain "reasoned conclusions" on "all pertinent issues of facts and law," as Article 3:1 of the *WTO Agreement on Safeguards* mandated. The argument was nothing more than an *ex post facto* attempt to extract necessary facts from this report.

The Appellate Body did not respond with a holding that clarified "how" to demonstrate the existence of "unforeseen developments," and thus did not go beyond the earlier cases in defining this term. But, it did extend its jurisprudence by explaining "when" and "where" an analysis into unforeseen developments is required. As to "when," the Appellate Body held that a competent authority must render a finding before any Escape Clause relief is granted. That is because "unforeseen developments" is a prerequisite, not concomitant or consequence, of such relief. As to "where," this finding must be in the report of the competent authority.

The Appellate Body understood Section 201 does not require proof of "unforeseen developments." That omission, along with the fact the ITC completed its *Lamb Meat* investigation 7 months before the Appellate Body circulated its Reports in *Argentina Footwear Safeguard* and *Korea Dairy Safeguard*, probably explained why the ITC did not deal with the topic. (The *Lamb Meat* safeguard took effect on 7 July 1999. The Dispute Settlement Body (DSB) adopted the other two Reports on 16 May 2001.) Still, the requirement existed Article XIX:1(a) of GATT, and in *Lamb Meat* the U.S. seemed to concede the requirement remains vital. That concession could be inferred, as the Appellate Body observed, from the change in America's argument from earlier cases. Unlike its position in *Argentina Footwear Safeguard* and *Korea Dairy Safeguard*, in *Lamb Meat* the U.S. did not contend the *Agreement on Safeguards* superseded Article XIX:1(a). Unfortunately for the American position, Appellate Body jurisprudence reaffirming the vitality of the requirement did not come in time for the ITC to adjust its methodology — *i.e.*, to start providing a reasoned, written conclusion.

The particular dispute ended on 31 August 2001, when the Administration of President George W. Bush agreed to implement the Appellate Body Report and remove the TRQs effective 15 November 2001. The American lamb meat industry thus got 2½ years of protection. Yet, no answer to the basic question of the case emerged: does a change in product mix, as occurred in the lamb meat import market, qualify as an "unforeseen development"? The Appellate Body sidestepped this question, because it was not presented with an explicit ITC finding to this effect.

• The 2003 *United States — Definitive Safeguard Measures on Imports of Certain Steel Products* Case[30]

The *Steel Safeguard* case is "infamous" for a number of reasons, including the large number of issues at stake, the acrimony between the respondent and complainants, and the fact it arose in a presidential election cycle. The case began on 28 June 2001, when the ITC commenced an investigation, under Section 201, at the request of the American steel industry and unions. It concluded on 4 December 2003, when President George W. Bush issued a Presidential Proclamation ending relief.

In respect of "unforeseen developments," the Appellate Body rejected the American arguments. The U.S. argued the ITC investigative report went far beyond the explanation the ITC had provided in the 2001 *Lamb Meat* case. The U.S. also emphasized the language of Article 3:1 of the *Agreement on Safeguards*, namely, that "[t]he competent authorities shall publish a report setting forth their findings and reasoned conclusions on all pertinent issues of fact and law." Because this language does not call for an explicit explanation of "unforeseen circumstances," surely it is possible for a competent authority to provide a "reasoned conclusion" without a "reasoned and adequate explanation."

The Appellate Body retorted it was impossible to have a reasoned conclusion, particularly one about an entire context, without reaching the conclusion in a connected, logical manner or expressing the conclusion in a logical form. If a competent authority does not explain its finding, then a Panel — which is barred from conducting a *de novo* review of evidence, and from substituting its judgment for that of the authority — has no choice but to rule the authority failed to conduct a proper analysis.

The Appellate Body also rejected the American argument about aggregate analysis. Contrary to the Panel, the U.S. urged Article XIX:1(a) does not mandate a particular kind of analysis about "unforeseen developments." Thus, it does not require showing imports of each product category subject to Escape Clause action increased because of such developments. Citing its decisions from 2000 in *Argentina Footwear Safeguard* and *Korea Dairy Safeguard*, the Appellate Body said there must be a logical connection between (1) unforeseen developments, and (2) a product subject to relief. In sum, the Appellate Body upheld the Panel's ruling that an "unforeseen developments" analysis must occur on a product-by-product basis. The ITC talked about the overall effects of financial crises in the late 1990s in Russia and Asia, and of the strong American dollar, yet it did not connect the dots, as it were.

On balance, despite several Appellate Body rulings on "unforeseen circumstances." the multilateral trading system has not advanced much beyond the 1951 *Hatters' Fur* Report as to a definition of this term. The definition of "unforeseen circumstances" has stayed at "unexpected" ever since the *Hatters' Fur* case. Some kind of plausible unforeseen development must be identified,

---

[30] *See* WTO Appellate Body Report, *United States — Definitive Safeguard Measures on Imports of Certain Steel Products*, WT/DS248/AB/R, WT/DS249/AB/R, WT/DS251/AB/R, WT/DS252/AB/R, WT/DS253/AB/R, WT/DS254/AB/R, WT/DS258/AB/R, WT/DS259/AB/R (complaints by the European Communities, Japan, Korea, China, Norway, Switzerland, New Zealand, and Brazil) (adopted 10 Dec. 2003).

and some kind of nexus between them and an increase in subject imports must be shown. Yet, exactly how "unexpected" the development should be to qualify as "unforeseen," and exactly how the logical link to increased imports should be made, is not clear.

Two points, in fairness to the Appellate Body, ought to be made. First, it may be that a complete definition of "unforeseen circumstances" is impossible. The term never can connote anything but unexpectedness to be gauged in particular factual settings. Second, the Appellate Body ought not to be accused of changing the rules and applying a new regime retroactively. The "unforeseen developments" requirement is not new or different. Rather, it is as old as GATT itself.

B.   Element #2: GATT Obligations

There is no GATT or WTO jurisprudence on the prerequisite to an Article XIX Escape Clause action that increased imports result from "the effect of the obligations incurred" under the GATT. Indeed, the *Agreement on Safeguards* does not contain this prerequisite. Notably, this element is not found in Section 201. To the extent it is an empty formalism with no real substantive effect in preparing an action, it seems inaccurate to call it a "prerequisite."

C.   Element #3: Increased Imports and the 2003 *Steel Safeguards* Case

An import surge may be measured in either of two ways. That point is not clear from the text of GATT Article XIX(a), but Article 2:1 of the *Agreement on Safeguards* says as much:

1.   Absolute terms, meaning the volume of subject merchandise imports increases without regard to trends in domestic production or consumption of a like or directly competitive product.

2.   Relative terms, meaning the volume of imports rises when gauged against the volume of domestic production (though in absolute terms, that volume may be flat or in decline).

There is, however, little in the way of WTO jurisprudence on increased imports. The leading case is the 2003 *Steel Safeguards* action.

In that case, data indicated that during the 5½ period of investigation (POI), imports of steel products into the U.S. did not increase in a steady trend. The POI was 1996-2000, plus the first 6 months of 2001 compared to the first 6 months of 2000. Most such imports increased in 1996-98, but shipments in some product categories fell in and after 1999, and declined precipitously in the first 6 months of 2001 relative to the first half of 2000.

The Panel disputed the conclusion of the International Trade Commission (ITC) that imports in 5 product categories — certain cold flat-rolled steel (CCFRS), hot-rolled bar, stainless steel rod, stainless steel wire, and tin mill products, had "increased" in an absolute sense. In particular:

i.   CCFRS imports decreased significantly between 2000 and 2001 from 11.5 to 6.9 million short tons. The ITC noted this decrease, but focused on the fact CCFRS imports were higher at the end than the beginning of the relevant period. The Panel stressed the recent, sizeable decline.

ii. Hot-rolled bar imports decreased between 2000 and 2001 by 28.9 percent. The ITC acknowledged but failed to explain this decrease, instead emphasizing two other facts. First, the ITC characterized the increase in these imports from 1999 to 2000 as rapid and dramatic. The Panel observed it was a rise of only 11.9 percent. Second, imports of hot-rolled bar increased 52.5 percent between 1996 and 2000. The Panel pointed out the trend was not consistent, with altering periods of increase and decrease.

iii. Stainless steel rod imports increased from 1996-2000, and by 25 percent from 1999-2000. But, said the Panel, they declined by 31 percent in 2001 in comparison.

Thus, the Panel found violations of Article XIX:1(a) of GATT and Article 2:1 of the *Safeguards Agreement*.

On appeal, the U.S. argued the Panel misinterpreted Article XIX:1(a) and Article 2:1 (especially with respect to CCFRS, hot-rolled bar, and stainless steel rod). The Panel said these provisions require a showing of increased imports that is recent and sudden, and cited the 2000 Appellate Body decision in *Argentina Footwear Safeguard*, in which the Appellate Body opined an increase in imports "must have been recent enough, sudden enough, sharp enough, and significant enough . . . to cause or threaten to cause serious injury." The "increase" in CCFRS imports, concluded the Panel, was not "recent" (having occurred between 1996-98), and the "increase" in imports of stainless steel rod (25 percent in 1999-2000) was followed by a disproportionate decrease (31 percent in 2001 versus 2000). The U.S. objected to the Panel's reading of Article XIX:1(a) of GATT, Article 2:1 of *Agreement*, and *Argentina Footwear Safeguard*. These sources called for a "recent, sudden, sharp, and significant" requirement. Yet, contended the U.S., all that is required is proof the level of imports has increased at the end of the POI in comparison with some unspecified earlier point in time.

Thus, connecting the beginning and endpoints of the POI, the U.S. highlighted the following statistics about imports of 4 major product categories of steel from 1998 to 2000:

i. Carbon and alloy flat products increased 14.1 percent.

ii. Carbon alloy long products increased 64 percent.

iii. Carbon and alloy pipe and tube increased 72 percent.

iv. Stainless steel and alloy tool steel increased 87.6 percent.

Siding with the Panel, the EU countered that the American formulation of how to measure "increased imports" would allow any simple increase to qualify. That kind of formulation glossed over important trends within the POI. Starting in 1999, or the first 6 months of 2000, imports in many steel product categories declined, and for some categories the drop was marked.

The Appellate Body rejected the American formulation. It held the Panel had relied correctly on the *Argentina Footwear Safeguard* precedent. True, neither Article XIX:1(a) of GATT nor Article 2:1 of the *Agreement on Safeguards* contains the words "recent, sudden, sharp, or significant." But, the word "such" precedes the words "increased quantities." In addition, the context of an examination into import trends is set by Article 4:2(a) of the *Agreement*, which calls for an evaluation of "the rate and amount of the increase in imports of the product concerned in absolute and relative terms."

To be sure, the *Argentina Footwear Safeguard* decision does not establish an absolute legal standard. Moreover, the U.S. was correct in its position imports of investigated merchandise need not be increasing at the time of a final determination. Still, ruled the Appellate Body, the American formulation of drawing a line between two points in time is no standard at all. A nuanced analysis of trends is necessary. The American argument that a rise in CCFRS imports from 1996-98 was enough to qualify as an "increase" was not persuasive. That period of time simply was not recent enough, and the U.S. had not provided an explanation of how the 1996-98 trend supported a finding of imports increasing in "such . . . quantities." Regarding hot-rolled bar imports, the Appellate Body said the Panel was right in faulting the ITC for not addressing the relevance of the decrease at the end of the POI. Similarly, the Appellate Body agreed with the Panel that the decrease in stainless steel rod imports at the end of the POI more than offset the earlier — and distant — increases.

Evidently, in proving an increase in imports emerges from the 2003 *Steel Safeguard* case, time is of the essence. Once imports have increased, either in absolute or relative terms, for a few years, then an Escape Clause action should be brought (if at all) immediately. Any delay in commencing the investigation creates opportunity for a new, downward trend in imports. Once the trend has reversed, it will stand out because it is the most recent phenomenon — and that may doom the case.

D. Element #4: Causation and Three Appellate Body Precedents

Article 4:2(b) of the WTO *Agreement on Safeguards* states:

> When factors other than increased imports are causing injury to the domestic industry at the same time, such injury shall not be attributed to increased imports.

That non-attribution should be a requirement before imposing a safeguard is obvious, but the Article 4:2(b) language sidesteps a crucial question about causation: how immediate, direct, and discreet must the "cause" be?

Conceptually, at one extreme, it could be necessary to prove that increased imports were the cause because:

(1)   there is a short time gap between increased imports and the injury,

(2)   the increase leads directly to the injury, and

(3)   no other factor contributes to the injury.

At the other extreme, it could be sufficient to prove simply that increased imports:

(1)   precede the injury, even if the exact gap between the increase and injury is a few years,

(2)   the increase is felt through intermediate factors, which in turn lead to injury, and

(3)   additional factors beyond the increase contribute to the injury.

The first extreme obviously would cut down on the number of successful Escape Clause actions. The second extreme would encourage such actions. Between these two extremes there is a continuum of possibilities.

Article XIX does not pick a point on the continuum, nor are any useful insights provided in the 1951 GATT Working Party Report in *Hatters' Fur*, other than giving the WTO Member that invokes Article XIX "the benefit of any reasonable doubt."[31] Therefore, it is for domestic law to set forth a standard for causation. In Section 201, the U.S. does so with the adjective "substantial" in front of the noun "cause." WTO Appellate Body case law offers some guidance.

● The 2001 *Lamb Meat* Case

In its 2001 *Lamb Meat* decision (cited earlier), the Appellate Body provides some guidance on the element of causation. Australia and New Zealand claimed the analysis by the U.S. ITC, namely, that increased imports caused serious injury to the American lamb meat industry, was flawed. The ITC determined increased lamb meat imports alone were a necessary and sufficient cause of serious injury. The ITC isolated injury from other factors, thereby assuring it did not attribute injury from the other factors to the import surge. However, the complainants said the ITC failed to show it had not wrongly attributed to imports threat of serious injury caused by other factors. The two sides differed over their view and application of the 2001 case of *United States — Wheat Gluten Safeguard*.[32]

Australia said in that case the Appellate Body clearly set out three conceptual steps for a causation analysis. First, injurious effects of imports must be distinguished from injurious effects of other factors. Second, injury caused by other factors must not be attributed to imports. Third, a genuine and substantial relationship of cause and effect must be demonstrated. The U.S. took the view that in *Wheat Gluten*, the Appellate Body reversed the Panel holding that imports have to be isolated from all other causes, and that imports have to be a *per se* cause of serious injury. In *Lamb Meat*, the Panel held the standard for causation means:

---

[31] *Report of the Intersessional Working Party on the Complaint of Czechoslovakia Concerning the Withdrawal by the United States of a Tariff Concession under the Terms of Article XIX of the General Agreement*, Geneva, November 1951 (GATT/CP/106, GATT/CP.6/SR.19, Sales No. GATT/1951-3), B.I.S.D., vol. 2 at 36 (1952) (adopted 27 Sept. 1951), *quoted in* GATT ANALYTICAL INDEX, *supra* note 22, at 518.

[32] *See* WTO Appellate Body Report, *United States — Definitive Safeguard Measures on Imports of Wheat Gluten from the European Communities*, WT/DS166/AB/R (complaint by the European Communities) (adopted 19 Jan. 2001).

(1)   Increased imports are necessary to cause or threaten injury.

(2)   Increased imports also are sufficient to cause or threaten injury.

The injury caused by increased imports is serious enough to be a significant overall impairment in the state of the domestic industry. This three-pronged approach was the same the Panel took in *Wheat Gluten*. But, in *Wheat Gluten*, the Appellate Body rejected it. Not surprisingly, it did so in *Lamb Meat*, too. That is, in both cases the Appellate Body held this approach was too strict.

First, opined the *Lamb Meat* Appellate Body, a causal link can exist between increased imports and serious injury even if there are other factors that contribute simultaneously to the ill condition of a domestic industry. Second, what is crucial is the competent authority does not attribute erroneously serious injury to increased imports when, in fact, the injury results from other causal factors. Thus, held the Appellate Body, there are two conceptual steps in which the authority must engage:

(1)   *Identification:*

It must identify all causal factors contributing to serious injury.

(2)   *Attribution:*

It must separate out and distinguish injurious effects of the different factors.

In *Lamb Meat*, the Appellate Body found the ITC failed to take the second step. To be sure, the ITC did examine six factors, other than increased imports, alleged to contribute to the adverse condition of the American industry. Following Section 201, the ITC considered whether they were a more important cause than imports. In other words, the ITC performed a relative causal analysis. But, that kind of analysis fails to ensure serious injury caused by factors other than increased imports is not attributed to increased imports. Briefly put, a relative causation examination is not the same as a non-attribution analysis, thus the ITC's investigation was inconsistent with Article 4:2 of the WTO *Agreement on Safeguards*.

The Appellate Body did not hold the ITC should have both separated out the injurious effects of imports from other factors, and attach relative weightings to each and every factor. How far must a competent authority go? Once it has identified the distinct factors, and walled off — though some credible statistical or other methodology — the effects of imports from other causes, then it has gotten close to a full analysis. Is all that is left a quantitative measurement of the degree of causal contribution of each factor? If so, then should this final step also be mandatory, especially if the meaning of "cause" is to be take seriously under Article XIX:1(a) and Article 4:2 of the *Safeguards Agreement*?

● The 2002 *United States — Definitive Safeguard Measures on Imports of Circular Welded Carbon Quality Line Pipe from Korea* Case[33]

In the 2002 *Line Pipe* Case, the U.S. imposed Escape Clause relief on imports of line pipe on 18 February 2000 in the form of a TRQ for a period of

---

[33] *See* WTO Appellate Body Report, *United States — Definitive Safeguard Measures on Imports of Circular Welded Carbon Quality Line Pipe from Korea*, WT/DS202/AB/R (adopted 2 March 2002).

3 years and 1 day. Korea challenged the measure, though not the underlying American statute, Section 201. The U.S. set the in-quota threshold at 9,000 tons per year for imports from all sources, including Korea, and did not impose liability for a graduated tariff on shipments under this level. Notably, line pipe from America's *NAFTA* partners, Canada and Mexico, were excluded from the action pursuant to Article 802:1, which states that a global safeguard action will not be applied to a product from another *NAFTA* Party unless that product "contribute[s] importantly to the serious injury, or threat thereof, caused by the imports."

For above-quota shipments, the U.S. applied a graduate tariff of 19, 15, and 11 percent, respectively, in the 3 years of relief. (This relief, effected by Presidential Proclamation of President Bill Clinton, differed from the recommendation of the ITC — a not uncommon occurrence.) The case ultimately settled when the U.S. and Korea agreed to a modification of the TRQ. The U.S. provided Korea with a whopping country-specific in-quota threshold of 17,500 tons of line pipe per quarter.

The Escape Clause action followed a determination by the ITC that imported line pipe was a substantial cause of serious injury to a domestic industry. The ITC came to this conclusion after considering several factors, other than increased imports, alleged to cause injury or threat, and applying the Section 201 standard that increased imports be a cause that is important and not less than any other cause. The other factors included:

(1)   Lower demand for line pipe because of less drilling for oil and gas (*i.e.*, less oil and gas production.

(2)   Increased competition among American manufacturers of line pipe.

(3)   A decline in export markets.

(4)   A shift from the production of oil country tubular goods (OCTG) to the production of line pipe.

(5)   A drop in the cost of raw materials.

Interestingly, three of the six ITC Commissioners agreed the imports were a substantial cause of serious injury to the American industry, two of them agreed they were a threat of serious injury, and 1 Commissioner voted against these findings. The ITC said the first causal factor did contribute to serious injury, increased imports were a more important cause.

The U.S. argued the ITC distinguished properly among the alternative alleged causal factors. Korea did not agree. The WTO Panel seized on this split among the Commissioners, holding it improper to base an Escape Clause action on either serious injury or threat of serious injury, which essentially was the wording of the ITC report. The U.S., intoned the Panel, should pick one or the other, because they are mutually exclusive, and defend its choice as a basis. Applying Article 4:1(a)-(b) of the WTO *Agreement on Safeguards*, the Panel said it is logically inconsistent for serious injury and a clearly imminent threat of serious injury to exist at the same time. The Appellate Body disagreed, finding the language of the *Agreement* flexible enough to accommodate a determination of serious injury, threat, or both in combination.

Moreover, the Appellate Body was reluctant to tell the ITC, or the competent authority in any WTO Member, how to make decisions internally. In other

words, the Appellate Body held it is not necessary to render a discrete either
— or finding. Noting that, by definition, a threat finding allows for relief
without a manifestation of serious injury, the Appellate Body cited the 1951
Hatters' Fur case to support its conclusion that a discrete determination of
either threat or injury was necessary. After all, in *Hatters' Fur*, the GATT
Working Party entertained a single analysis of serious injury or threat, but
not a separate analysis of both.

Further, the Appellate Body interpreted and applied Article 4:2(b) of the
WTO *Agreement on Safeguards* in a way resembling its discussion in the 2001
Lamb Meat case. Two conceptual steps are required for a proper causation
analysis.

   Step   1: A causal link must be demonstrated, which presumes a distinc-
          tion and separation among causal factors.

   Step   2: Injury caused by factors other than an import surge must not
          be attributed to the surge.

In *Line Pipe*, the Appellate Body pointed out Article 3:5 of the WTO *Antidumping Agreement* has language similar to the last sentence of Article 4:2(b) of
the *Safeguards Agreement*. Citing the provisions, and its 2001 Report in *Japan
Hot Rolled Steel*, the Appellate Body explained that in the injury phase of an
antidumping investigation, it is necessary for the competent authority to
identify known factors other than subject merchandise, and provide a satisfactory explanation of the nature and extent of these other factors as distinct
from the injurious effects of the subject merchandise.

The problem with the ITC determination was its lack of an attribution
analysis. The Appellate Body held the ITC failed to ensure it had not
attributed to increased imports the injury caused by factors other than
increased imports. In particular, as Korea pointed out, the ITC simply
asserted it had not conflated causal factors. But, it did not give an explicit,
reasoned, and adequate account of the nature and extent of the injurious
effects of the decline in oil and gas drilling, as distinct from increased line
pipe imports.

   • The 2003 *Steel Safeguard* Case

In the *Steel Safeguard* case (cited earlier), the WTO Panel reviewing the
determination of the ITC said that for seven steel products (certain cold flat
rolled steel (CCFRS), cold-finished bar, fittings, flanges, and tool joints made
of carbon and alloy (FFTJ), hot-rolled bar, stainless steel bar, and welded
pipe), the ITC did not give a reasoned, adequate explanation for a causal link
between increased imports and serious injury. The U.S. appealed, but for
reasons of judicial economy, the Appellate Body declined to rule on the issue.
At the request of the U.S. and several complainants and third-party participants, the Appellate Body — in its unadopted Report — provided guidance
on the issue by referring to its earlier precedents, namely the 2001 *United
States Wheat Gluten* Case, 2001 *Lamb Meat* Case, and 2002 *Line Pipe* Case.

The basic rule from these cases, suggested the Appellate Body in *Steel
Safeguard*, is Articles 2:1, 3:1, and 4:2 of the *Agreement on Safeguards* oblige
a competent authority to prove existence of a causal link between increased
imports and serious injury (or threat) with objective evidence, and provide a

reasoned and adequate explanation to support this demonstration. Without such proof and explanation, applying a remedy is unlawful. The Appellate Body went on to state the attribution analysis of the type done in an AD case, under Article 3:5 of the WTO *Antidumping Agreement*, is required in a safeguards case. That means an examination of the individual effects of other causal factors (*i.e.*, other than imports subject to investigation), but not necessarily of the collective effects of the other factors, on the domestic injury, plus assurance their effects are not erroneously attributed to the increased imports.

E. Element #5: Injury, the 1951 *Hatters' Fur* Case, and Article 4:1-2

Unfortunately, the drafters of GATT did not define "serious" in Article XIX, just as they did not elaborate on the meaning of "material" in Articles VI and XVI. Presumably, "serious" is not "material," as treaty language cannot be read as superfluous. What, then, is "serious"?

On this matter, the 1951 *Hatters' Fur* Working Party Report is of considerable assistance. In that case, the Working Party found evidence to support the American argument of a threat of serious injury to its industry. This evidence took the form of "a large and rapidly increasing volume of imports, while at the same time domestic production decreased or remained stationary." Yet, the Working Party rightly refused to characterize this evidence as conclusive.

> To sum up, the available data support the view that increased imports had caused or threatened some adverse effect to United States producers. Whether such a degree of adverse effect should be considered to amount to "serious injury" is another question, on which the data cannot be said to point convincingly in either direction, and *any view on which is essentially a matter of economic and social judgment involving a considerable subjective element.* In this connection it may be observed that *the Working Party naturally could not have the facilities available to the United States* authorities for examining interested parties and independent witnesses from the United States hat-making areas, and for forming judgments on the basis of such examination. Further, *it is perhaps inevitable that governments should on occasion lend greater weight to the difficulties or fears of their domestic producers than would any international body*, and that they may feel it necessary on social grounds, *e.g.*, because of lack of alternative employment in the localities concerned, to afford a higher degree of protection to individual industries which in terms of cost of production are not economic.[34]

The italicized text is remarkable for its candor and accuracy on three points.

---

[34] GATT ANALYTICAL INDEX, *supra* note 22, at 518. The formal title of the Report is *Report of the Intersessional Working Party on the Complaint of Czechoslovakia Concerning the Withdrawal by the United States of a Tariff Concession under the Terms of Article XIX of the General Agreement*, Geneva, November 1951 (GATT/CP/106, GATT/CP.6/SR.19, Sales No. GATT/1951-3), II B.I.S.D. at 36 (1952) (adopted 27 Sept. 1951).

First, appraising whether injury is "serious" is an art. Second, a multilateral dispute resolution body is in a less favorable position to make the appraisal than domestic authorities because of the constraints on investigative resources available to such a body. Third, domestic authorities may be expected in certain cases to be biased in favor of their ailing local industry and want to minimize or defer the social adjustment costs resulting from import competition.

Further clarification on the meaning of "serious" comes from Article 4:1-2 of the WTO *Agreement on Safeguards*. In brief, Article 4:1(a) defines "serious injury" in terms of a "significant overall impairment," which is intuitively obvious and somewhat circular. Defining "threat of serious injury" in terms of "clearly imminent" serious injury is only a slight improvement in precision. To be fair, however, perhaps these two definitions are about as helpful as can be expected. The key terms are inherently flexible to accommodate different facts and circumstances. Article 4:2(a), however, gives WTO Members specific guidance as to how to measure serious injury or threat thereof by identifying, in a non-exclusive manner, the key variables that ought to be considered.

In the abstract, the effect of most variables identified in Article 4:2(a) on the strength of an Escape Clause case is easy to predict. The greater the absolute or relative rate and amount of increase in imports, the greater the domestic market share taken by imports, and the more dramatic the decline in domestic sales, production, capacity utilization, profits, and employment, the stronger the argument that increased imports have caused serious injury or threat thereof. However, this generalization assumes all other factors are constant (*i.e.*, *ceteris paribus*).

Special care may be necessary when analyzing the variables listed in Article 4:2(a) of the *Safeguards Agreement*. Consider hypothetical trends in productivity in the domestic industry:

1. Suppose productivity as measured by output per person-hour falls. The drop might have little to do with increased imports, particularly if it results from a rise in the number of person-hours worked. This scenario might occur if the domestic industry hires more workers to meet increased demand, but not all of the workers are fully trained and integrated, and thus have not yet reached their maximum efficiency levels. It also might occur where the domestic industry is experiencing diminishing returns with respect to labor, and should invest in other factors of production like physical capital and technology.

2. Alternatively, assume productivity tumbles because output declines. Did increased imports capture market share from domestic production, resulting in a decline in domestic factory orders, which in turn caused the drop in output? That is, are increased imports the culprit?

3. Still another possibility is productivity rises because of downsizing in the domestic industry. The downsizing, which results in a fall of person-hours worked relative to output, may be caused by competition from increased imports.

In sum, analyzing the variables listed in Article 4:2(a) requires attention to how those variables are measured, what other factors bear on them, the extent to which they are correlated or even causally related to one another, and the POI. Generalizations about injury or threat variables should be regarded with some caution.

VI. SECTION 201 ACTIONS

A. Procedures

The key players in an Escape Clause, or Section 201, action are the petitioner, importers and foreign manufacturers, ITC, and President. The ITC is responsible for investigating a case and rendering a determination as to whether a U.S. industry has been seriously injured or threatened with serious injury by imports. If it makes an affirmative determination, then it must recommend to the President the appropriate trade relief needed to alleviate the injury or threat. Whether remedial action is taken is for the President to decide in her sole discretion.

There are 5 basic steps in a Section 201 case. In most cases, the ITC is required to complete its work within 6 months.

Step 1: Petition

An entity which is "representative of an industry," such as a firm, certified or recognized union, group of workers, or trade association, may file a petition "for the purpose of facilitating positive adjustment to import competition." (19 U.S.C. § 2252(a)(1).) The petition is filed with the ITC. "Positive adjustment" refers to (1) the ability of a U.S. industry to compete successfully with imports, or the orderly transfer of that industry's resources to other productive pursuits, and (2) the orderly transfer of dislocated workers in that industry to other productive pursuits. (*See* 19 U.S.C. § 2251(b)(1).) The ITC must forward a copy of the petition to the USTR.. (*See* 19 U.S.C. § 2252(a)(3).) Within 120 days of filing the petition, the petitioner may submit to the ITC and USTR a plan for facilitating positive adjustment. (*See* 19 U.S.C. § 2252(a)(4).)

Most petitions are filed by trade associations or companies, and unions often support a petition. However, a Section 201 case can be commenced in three other manners. First, the ITC may initiate the case on its own motion. Second, the executive branch — specifically, the President or the USTR — may request the ITC to commence a case. Third, the legislative branch may make this request in the form of a resolution from the House Ways and Means Committee or the Senate Finance Committee. (*See* 19 U.S.C. § 2252(b)(1)(A).)

The ITC's regulations specify the contents required for a petition. Generally, a petition must contain: (1) a description of the imported article concerned; (2) the names and addresses of the petitioners and the extent to which the petitioners are representative of a domestic industry (as measured by the percentage of domestic production of the like or directly competitive product accounted for by the petitioners); (3) import data; (4) domestic production data;

(5) data showing injury; (6) a statement relating to the cause of injury; (7) a description of the relief sought; and (8) an explanation of the efforts that are or will be taken to compete with the imported article.

Step 2: ITC Investigation

Upon receiving a petition or request, or adopting a motion, the ITC must commence promptly a Section 201 investigation. It must determine whether a particular article is being imported into the U.S. in "such increased quantities as to be a substantial cause of serious injury, or the threat thereof" to the domestic industry that produces a "like or directly competitive" product. (19 U.S.C. §§ 2251(a), 2252(b)(1)(A).) To obtain relief, there is no requirement a petitioner show a company exporting to the U.S. is engaged in unfair trade practices. To the contrary, Section 201 provides relief from *fair* foreign competition so that an American producer can improve its competitive position relative to foreign companies.

> The underlying rationale for Section 201 is based upon the general concern that as the United States lowers tariff barriers to imports, or grants other trade concessions, domestic industries may, in effect, be caught off guard by the increasing import competition. Section 201 is referred to as the escape clause because it allows the United States to, in effect, escape from its obligations under GATT not to take restrictive actions against imports, absent evidence of unfair trading practices, such as dumping, by foreign manufacturers.[35]

Arguably, in one respect the substantive standards applied by the ITC are inconsistent with GATT Article XIX. This Article establishes a connection between trade liberalization and import protection. It provides that relief is appropriate if "the effect of the obligations incurred" by a Member (as well as "unforeseen developments") result in an increased volume of imports that causes injury. The *1974 Act* severed the connection between trade liberalization and import protection. Suppose there were a challenge in the WTO to the U.S. statutory scheme. What would be the rebuttal? The U.S. could argue that injury can be inferred to result from trade concessions, because these concessions (in the form of tariff concessions) have touched the vast majority of articles.

The ITC must render a determination within 120 days of receiving a petition. (*See* 19 U.S.C. § 2252(b)(2)(A).) The ITC may extend this period to 150 days in an "extraordinarily complicated" case. (19 U.S.C. § 2252(b)(2)(B).) A shorter deadline — 3 months — is prescribed in cases of imports from communist countries. (*See* 19 U.S.C. § 2436(a)(4).) There are special rules for "critical circumstances" cases. (19 U.S.C. § 2252(d)(2)(A).) Critical circumstances exist if a increased imports (either actual or relative to domestic production) are a substantial cause of serious injury, or the threat thereof, to a domestic industry producing an article that is like or directly competitive with the imported article, and a delay in taking action would cause damage to that industry "that would be difficult to repair." (19 U.S.C. § 2252(d)(2)(A).)

---

[35] Thomas V. Vakerics et al., Antidumping, Countervailing Duty, and Other Trade Actions 14 (1987); *see also id.* at 15, 271-72, 274-76.

There also are special rules regarding provisional relief for perishable products. (*See* 19 U.S.C. § 2252(d)(1)(A).) Such products include agricultural products with a short shelf life, growing season, or marketing period. (*See* 19 U.S.C. § 2252(d)(5)(B).)

The ITC must hold public hearings and afford interested parties and consumers the opportunity to be heard. (*See* 19 U.S.C. § 2252(b)(3).) The statute requires the ITC to "take into account all economic factors which it considers relevant," and then provides a non-exhaustive list of such factors. (*See* 19 U.S.C. § 2252(c)(1).) With respect to serious injury, the ITC must consider "the significant idling of productive facilities in the domestic industry," "the inability of a significant number of firms to carry out domestic production operations at a reasonable level of profit," and "significant unemployment or underemployment within the domestic industry." (*See* 19 U.S.C. § 2252(c)(1)(A).) With respect to threat of serious injury, the ITC must consider (under 19 U.S.C. § 2252(c)(1)(B)):

(i)   a decline in sales or market share, a higher and growing inventory (whether maintained by domestic producers, importers, wholesalers, or retailers), and a downward trend in production, profits, wages, productivity, or employment (or increasing underemployment) in the domestic industry,

(ii) the extent to which firms in the domestic industry are unable to generate adequate capital to finance the modernization of their domestic plants and equipment, or are unable to maintain existing levels of expenditures for research and development, [and]

(iii) the extent to which the United States market is the focal point for the diversion of exports of the article concerned by reason of restraints on exports of such article to, or on imports of such article into, third country markets. . . .

"Substantial cause" is defined as one that is "important and not less than any other cause." (19 U.S.C. § 2252(b)(1)(B). Interestingly, a lower causation standard — "significant cause" is applied to imports from communist countries. 19 U.S.C. § 2436(e)(2)(A), (B)(ii).)

> Unlike antidumping or CVD [countervailing duty] cases in which the imports may be one of many causes of injury to a domestic industry, imports in a section 201 action must be shown to be a substantial cause of serious injury, if relief is to be obtained. The injury requirement in a section 201 action is, therefore, *more* stringent, in terms of causation, than is the injury requirement in an antidumping or CVD action.[36]

Under the *1962 Act*, the Escape Clause required a petitioner show that increased imports were a "major" cause of injury. In changing the word "major" to "substantial," the *1974 Act* liberalized the causation element. No adjective appears before the noun "cause" in GATT Article XIX or the WTO *Agreement on Safeguards*, essentially meaning the U.S. causation standard is relatively more difficult to satisfy.

---

[36] *Id.* at 15 (emphasis added).

In two other respects, the *1974 Act* also made it easier for petitioners to obtain relief. First, it eliminated the link between trade concessions and increased imports. Second, it provided that a relative — not necessarily an absolute — increase in imports would suffice. The relative increase concept had been part of the original Escape Clause in the *Trade Agreements Extension Act of 1951*, but was removed in 1962 when the requirements for relief were tightened by the *1962 Act*. The trade-off for the relaxed requirements under the *1974 Act* was the specification import relief was temporary.

An important aspect of the causation analysis is that the ITC cannot "aggregate the causes of declining demand associated with a recession or economic downturn in the U.S. economy into a single cause of serious injury or threat of injury." (19 U.S.C. § 2252(c)(2)(A).) This proscription was added by the 1988 Act after a famous case brought in 1980 by the United Auto Workers and Ford Motor Company. (*See Report to the President on Certain Motor Vehicles and Certain Chassis and Bodies Therefor*, U.S. ITC Inv. No. TA-201-44 (December 3, 1980), 45 Fed. Reg. 85,194 (December 24, 1980).) In this case, the ITC agreed with the petitioners that Japanese auto imports were a cause of the overall decline in consumption of American-made cars. But, it ruled a recession brought about in part by the oil price increase of 1979, which caused a shift in market demand toward smaller cars, was a greater cause of serious injury to American car companies than increased imports. In reaching this decision, the ITC did not isolate each economic factor relevant to the matter of serious injury for the purpose of comparing them with the factor of increased imports. Rather, it aggregated negative economic factors in comparing them with increased imports. The 1988 amendment was motivated in part by a concern that such aggregation would make it virtually impossible for a domestic industry to obtain a favorable ITC determination during in times of recession.

To no one's surprise, the ITC's negative determination in the automobile case led to political controversy. Numerous Congresspersons criticized the decision, and Chairman Charles A. Vanik (D-Ohio) of the Trade Subcommittee of the House Ways and Means Committee called hearings to consider alternative trade action. Senator John C. Danforth (R.-Mo.) introduced legislation, which was not enacted, that would have restricted Japanese car imports from 1981-83 to 1.6 million units — an outright quota that plainly would have run afoul of GATT Article XI:1. (*See* S. 396, 97th Cong., 1st Sess. (1981); 127 Cong. Rec. 1786-87 (1981).)

President Reagan — an otherwise ardent free trader — accomplished via a different vehicle what Senator Danforth's bill would have achieved. In his 1980 Presidential campaign, Ronald Reagan promised relief for the auto industry from foreign competition. (Rich in Republican Party convention delegate votes, and in Electoral College votes, Michigan and Ohio become particularly important states during election seasons!) After the election, the Reagan Administration negotiated a VRA with Japan to limit Japanese car exports to the U.S. The agreement limited Japanese car imports to the U.S. to roughly 1.68 million units annually 1981-83. It was renewed in 1984 at the level of 1.85 million units. In 1985, after record-setting profit and employment data for the American auto industry the previous year, the Reagan Administration decided not seek a fifth year of voluntary quotas. Some scholars argue this saga, coupled with the results of certain other cases from the mid-and late-1970s, have discredited the Escape Clause because the ITC's impartial adjudicatory process is undermined in the political realm.

Step 3: ITC Recommendation

If the ITC makes a negative determination, then the case is terminated. The President has no authority to invoke an escape-clause remedy in the event of a negative determination.

Suppose, however, the ITC renders an affirmative determination that an article is being imported into the U.S. in such increased quantities as to be a substantial cause of serious injury or threat thereof to a domestic industry producing a like or directly competitive product. In this case the ITC must recommend to the President the remedy that would redress the injury and be most effective in helping the industry make a positive adjustment to import competition. (*See* 19 U.S.C. § 2252(e)(1).) The relief is designed only as a temporary measure to help an afflicted domestic industry become more competitive with foreign imports.

The ITC may recommend the adjustment of tariffs, imposition of quotas or tariff-rate quotas, provision of trade adjustment assistance to workers or firms, or any combination thereof. (*See* 19 U.S.C. § 2252(e)(2).) It also may recommend that the President initiate international trade negotiations to address the underlying cause of the increase in the imports and alleviate the injury. (*See* 19 U.S.C. § 2252(e)(4)(A).) The ITC must a hold public hearing regarding its recommendation. (*See* 19 U.S.C. § 2252(e)(5).) The ITC must provide the President with its report and recommendation within 180 days of the day the petition is filed. (*See* 19 U.S.C. § 2252(f)(1). Naturally, a longer period — 240 days — is permitted if the petition alleges critical circumstances exist.) The report must be made public. (*See* 19 U.S.C. § 2252(f)(3).) In addition, if the ITC recommends the provision of adjustment assistance, then the Secretaries of Labor and Commerce must be notified of this recommendation. The Secretary of Labor must give expedited consideration to a petition by workers in a domestic industry for certification of eligibility to apply for adjustment assistance. The Secretary of Commerce must give expedited consideration to a petition from a firm in a domestic industry for certification of eligibility to apply for adjustment assistance. (*See* 19 U.S.C.§ 2252(g).)

Unless the ITC finds "good cause" to reconsider its decision within a year, an Escape Clause proceeding regarding the same article cannot be brought for at least 1 year. (19 U.S.C. § 2252(h).) In *Sneaker Circus, Inc. v. Carter*, 457 F. Supp. 771 (E.D.N.Y. 1978), *aff'd without published opinion*, 614 F.2d 1290 (2d Cir. 1979), the petitioner-plaintiffs were a retailer, wholesaler, and importer of non-rubber athletic footwear covered by two OMAs negotiated by the U.S. with Taiwan and Korea. The OMAs established the number of pairs of such footwear that those countries would export to the U.S. The petitioners alleged the ITC, in making its good cause determination, failed to comply with Section 201. The ITC rendered an affirmative injury determination in September 1975. President Gerald R. Ford determined adjustment assistance, but not other import relief, was the most effective remedy. In September 1976, less than a year after the ITC submitted its report to President Ford, the Senate Finance Committee approved a resolution directing the ITC to institute a new footwear investigation. The resolution indicated that changed circumstances, such as an increase in imports and a rapid deteriorating in economic conditions in the domestic footwear industry, constitute good cause to commence a new investigation. The ITC agreed good cause existed. Ultimately, the Administration of President Jimmy Carter negotiated the two OMAs.

The petitioners challenged the authority of the ITC to consider a good cause issue on the basis of a Senate Finance Committee resolution. They argued the ITC determination was invalid because the ITC can make a good cause determination only after the industry in question presents substantial new evidence. The *Sneaker Circus* court rejected this argument. Not only did it find that Section 201 is silent on the question of who may request a reinvestigation, but also that "there is nothing to indicate that the ITC could not make a good cause determination on its own motion without a request or petition for reinvestigation from some other entity or person."

Step 4: Presidential Action

Within 60 days after the President receives an ITC report that contains an affirmative finding regarding serious injury, or threat thereof, to a domestic industry, the President must "take all appropriate and feasible action" to "facilitate efforts by the domestic industry to make a positive adjustment to import competition. . . ." (19 U.S.C. § 2253(a)(1)(A) and (4). If the President granted provisional relief under critical circumstances, then the time period is 50 days. The President can request additional information from the ITC within 15 days of receiving the report, and it has 30 days to respond. *See* 19 U.S.C. § 2253(a)(5). The President must act within 30 days after receiving any supplemental report. *See* 19 U.S.C. § 2253(a)(4)(B). A different time period exists for a case of critical circumstances in which the President ordered provisional relief.) The action must "provide greater economic and social benefits than costs." (*See* 19 U.S.C. § 2253(a)(1)(A).) If the President follows the ITC recommendation, then the President must set forth a decision and reasons for it in a report to Congress. The report must be made on the date of the decision. (*See* 19 U.S.C. § 2253(b)(1).)

In determining the appropriate relief, the President must consider not only the effectiveness of the relief in facilitating adjustment, but also the cost of the relief on consumers and the economy. The imposition of tariffs, quotas, or tariff-rate quotas take effect within 15 days on which they are proclaimed unless the President also announces her intention to enter into international negotiations. (*See* 19 U.S.C. § 2253(d)(1).) Then, the remedial measures take effect 90 days after the President's decision, and in effect the measures serve as a "bargaining chip."

The President may devise a remedy different from the one recommended by the ITC. Again, a report to Congress is required on the date the decision is made. (*See* 19 U.S.C. § 2253(b)(3).) In *Sneaker Circus*, the petitioners argued that President Carter's remedy was not "commensurate with the injury found by the [International Trade] Commission." This language is found not in Section 201, but in a Report of the Senate Finance Committee concerning the *Trade Act of 1974*. However, the *Sneaker Circus* Court granted substantial deference to the President's negotiating authority. It found "the decision as to the countries with which OMAs should be negotiated is a purely political question," which is "precisely the type of question" that is not reviewable by the courts.

The President also is free to decline to proclaim any remedy, *i.e.*, to find no remedial action is warranted. If the President declines to follow the ITC's recommendation (either because she recommends an alternative remedy or no remedy at all), then Congress could enact a bill implementing the recommendation. (Of course, Congress would need a two-thirds vote of each house to override the expected Presidential veto of the bill.) Upon the enactment of a joint resolution, the recommendation would take effect within 90 days of the date the President transmitted her report to Congress, and the President must proclaim such action. (*See* 19 U.S.C. § 2253(c), (d)(2).)

Unlike the AD or CVD remedies, but like unilateral retaliation under Section 301, the President has considerable discretion in an Escape Clause case. What are the arguments for and against this latitude, as opposed to automaticity, in different kinds of trade remedies?

Step 5: Monitoring, Modification, and Termination of Action

The initial period during which a remedial action is in effect cannot exceed 4 years. (*See* 19 U.S.C. § 2253(e)(1)(A).) This period can be extended, though the total relief period cannot exceed 8 years. (*See* 19 U.S.C. § 2253(e)(1)(B)(ii).) If a trade remedy is in effect for longer than 3 years, then the ITC must issue a report periodically to the President and Congress regarding the progress of workers and firms in the injured domestic industry at making a positive adjustment to import competition. (*See* 19 U.S.C. § 2254(a).) The President may reduce, modify, or terminate the action if she finds that the domestic industry "has not made adequate efforts to make a positive adjustment to import competition" or the remedial action is ineffective because of changed economic circumstances. (19 U.S.C. § 2254(b)(1)(A).) If an action is terminated, then the ITC must report to the President and Congress, and hold public hearings, on the effectiveness of that action at facilitating adjustment. (*See* 19 U.S.C. § 2254(d)(1).) The report is due within 180 days of the termination of the action. (*See* 19 U.S.C. § 2254(d)(3).)

B. Global Production and the 1990 *Certain Cameras* Case

UNITED STATES INTERNATIONAL TRADE COMMISSION, *CERTAIN CAMERAS*
Inv. No. TA-201-62, U.S. ITC Pub 2315 (Sept. 1990)

. . . .

Additional Views of Acting Chairman Anne E. Brunsdale

I concur in the conclusion of my colleagues that increased imports are not a substantial cause of serious injury to the domestic industry producing certain cameras, and I join in their opinion. I present these additional views to elaborate on what I consider the most complex issue in this case — that is, how the Commission should consider the activities and products of U.S. firms that have assembly operations or parts manufacturing facilities abroad. In my view, this is a serious question, less for its bearing on this particular case, than for its likely importance in future cases. Increased globalization of industries is an inevitable consequence of changes in technology, especially in transportation and communications, and the growing integration of the world economy. Therefore, it is important that the Commission grapple with the issue to provide guidance for the future.

In this case, the Commission had to decide how to assess Kodak's domestic operations related to the production of 35mm and 110 cameras that were assembled or partially manufactured in Mexico and Brazil. Further, the Commission had to determine whether those Kodak cameras that are considered to be imports for customs purposes should also be considered imports for the purpose of this investigation. The main argument for using final assembly to determine the country of origin is that final assembly is the stage that transforms parts into the relevant "like or directly competitive article." If all parts are made in the U.S. but assembled abroad then, it is argued, the U.S. is simply a parts manufacturer and not a manufacturer of the like or directly competitive product. Since the court held in *United Shoe Workers of America, AFL-CIO v. Bedell*, a case involving the trade adjustment assistance laws, that parts are not to be considered as like or directly competitive with the finished article, it purportedly follows that final assembly is the critical factor.

I believe that such an argument is simplistic and that a distinction should be made between a mere manufacturer of component parts (as in *United Shoe*) and a manufacturer of the like product, such as Kodak, that has assembly operations abroad. The courts have made clear that firms in upstream industries do not have standing to file a case against imports of a downstream product. In this case, Kodak could not be considered part of the upstream "camera parts" industry, as distinct from the camera industry, because it does not sell parts on the open market and the foreign entities that assemble Kodak cameras abroad do not sell any other brands of cameras on the open market.

While it may make sense for final assembly to be the decisive factor in the determination of an import for customs purposes, it makes little sense for the

Commission to adopt this standard without careful consideration of the consequences. Taken to their extreme, the problems with placing such importance on final assembly become obvious. A domestic screwdriver plant set up only to assemble imported parts would be able to seek relief from products that, except for assembly, are made in the United States. Using a customs standard, we would ignore the fact that the domestic content was substantially higher in the product assembled abroad. Therefore, granting relief to the so-called domestic industry would actually decrease productive activity in the United States. Perversely, the foreign country that supplied parts to the screwdriver plant would be the main beneficiary of such an action. This scenario demonstrates that a simplistic or arbitrary definition of imports or domestic production may prove to be detrimental to U.S. competitiveness in the long run. Therefore, the Commission should look further.

The import relief laws and their legislative history provide limited guidance in this area. While the Commission has addressed similar issues in the past, it has never dealt with this issue explicitly. In a previous 201 case involving motor vehicles, the Commission had to decide how to treat products that had over 50 percent U.S. value-added and were manufactured in Canada by wholly owned subsidiaries of the U.S. firms. While the Commission decided that the products in that case were imports, certain Commissioners expressed the view that products exported for final assembly or minor finishing work should nonetheless be treated as domestic production. [See *Certain Motor Vehicles and Certain Chassis and Bodies Therefor*, Inv. No. TA-201-44, U.S.ITC Pub. 1110 (December 1980) at 15 (Views of Chairman Alberger), and at 101 (Views of Commissioner Stern).] In another 201 case the Commission had to decide if certain producers of motorcycles should be considered part of the domestic industry, despite the fact that their products contained a majority of foreign content. The Commission decided to include those producers in the domestic industry, with their production weighted by the domestic value-added. In explaining their decision, some Commissioners noted the significant productive resources those firms had in the United States. [See *Heavyweight Motorcycles, and Engines and Power Train Subassemblies Therefor*, Inv. No. 201-47, U.S.ITC Pub. 1342 (February 1983) at 9-10 (Views Chairman Eckes) and at 31 (Views of Commissioner Haggart).]

There are also a number of Title VII [*i.e.*, AD and CVD] cases where the Commission had to address similar issues. In a case involving radio pagers, it was decided that even though the pagers were assembled abroad and incorporated foreign parts, they should be considered as part of domestic production. [See *Certain Radio Paging and Alerting Receiving Devices from Japan*, Inv. No. 731-TA-102, U.S.ITC Pub. 1410 (August 1983) at 10 (Views of Chairman Eckes and Commissioner Haggart).] The significant percentage of domestic value-added of the products combined with the fact that domestic activities involved "considerable technical expertise and capital investment" was considered crucial to the determination.

In general, I believe that the Commission has taken a common sense approach and, on a case-by-case basis, has tried to interpret the import relief law at issue in this case in a manner consistent with its fundamental purpose — to provide the U.S. industry with the opportunity to compete in the international arena. Since domestic productive activity is the most important focus of the law, I favor an approach that considers the domestic industry to be all such domestic activity that adds value to the like product. I see no basis for giving greater weight to one kind of value-added activity over another. In addition, I would prefer not to exclude certain domestic productive activity because it contributed an insufficient percentage of domestic value-added to the ensuing final product. After all, there may be more domestic employment and investment generated from a product with a relatively low percentage of domestic value-added than from a product with a relatively high percentage of domestic value-added.

The difficulty with a strict value-added approach is that it cannot be used unless the data are presented in such a way as to allow consideration of all domestic value-added activities. In many cases, it would be impossible to allocate profits and employment in any reliable way. Without such data, Commissioners cannot carry out their statutory obligation to determine the impact of imports on the condition of the domestic industry in a rigorous way. When the data are not available to make a determination based strictly on domestic value-added, I would try to make distinctions for particular products. I would determine whether a good was domestic or imported, initially looking at its share of domestic content, both absolutely and in comparison to the industry average.

In this case, petitioner Keystone contends that the domestic industry should be defined to exclude the operations related to Kodak cameras that have value added in Mexico and Brazil. Kodak, on the other hand, suggests that all of its U.S. camera production activity should be included with the domestic industry, even if the camera is partially manufactured and/or assembled abroad. While I agree with Kodak in principle, the available data do not permit me to evaluate the domestic industry in the manner it suggested. A strict value-added approach in this case would not have allowed Commissioners to address the question of injury to the domestic industry producing conventional cameras. Therefore, I used an alternative approach whereby each product is considered domestic or imported based on its share of domestic content. There were five categories of products to evaluate for domestic content: Keystone cameras, Kodak's domestically produced cameras, Kodak's 110 cameras assembled in Mexico, Kodak's 35mm cameras partially manufactured and assembled in Mexico, and Kodak's 35mm cameras partially manufactured and assembled in Brazil.

Both Keystone and Kodak cameras that are assembled in the United States should be considered as domestic products based on their share of domestic content. [Both companies import foreign components for their cameras that are assembled in the U.S.] Kodak 110 cameras assembled in Mexico should also be considered as domestic products based on their share of U.S. value added, which is comparable to the domestic content of Keystone's cameras. The share of domestic content of Kodak 35mm cameras partially manufactured in Brazil and Mexico was substantially lower than that of the other cameras. Petitioner states, however, that the Commission should be most concerned about final assembly — arguing that it is the true determinant of a domestic product. For the reasons stated above, I do not agree and therefore I find that there is no basis for excluding any Kodak 110 cameras from the domestic industry.

I do not believe that the percentage of domestic content in Kodak's 35mm cameras partially manufactured in Brazil and Mexico is sufficient to consider them as domestic products. Lacking adequate data to isolate and assess the domestic activities attributable to these cameras, to the extent possible I excluded all domestic activities related to production of those cameras from the domestic industry. Including such activities would have only added support to my negative determination.

In view of the increasing globalization of industries, I expect that the Commission will be confronted with this issue many times in the future. The United States is currently pursuing policies that will open markets to foreign trade and investment. Thus, we can expect that U.S. companies will have increased opportunities to open plants and assembly operations in third countries and to benefit from those opportunities abroad, while foreign companies will benefit from increased opportunities in the United States and thereby will contribute to the U.S. economy. Because of increased competition, U.S. firms will be forced to look at alternatives that allow them to remain competitive in the long run. If U.S. firms are successful, this will result in increased employment and output in the United States.

Kodak is a case in point. Historically, Kodak has been a driving force in the domestic camera industry; even petitioner Keystone described itself as operating under Kodak's umbrella through various licensing agreements. Kodak undertakes R&D activity and the manufacturing of camera parts and sub-assemblies in the U.S. and has generated the bulk of employment in the camera industry, particularly if one considers the total wage bill. Kodak stated that some camera models would not be competitive unless a certain portion of their production was done abroad. By assembling those cameras abroad, Kodak has found a way to be competitive in the long run while maintaining significant domestic activity — the very purpose behind this import relief law. Excluding its activities from the domestic industry would undermine the very purpose of this law.

Chapter 38

TRADE RETALIATION

Trade follows the flag.

    —A slogan of the British Empire

I. UNILATERAL TRADE WEAPONS

A. Section 301, Super 301, and Special 301

Section 301 of the *Trade Act of 1974*, as amended, is the most potent and controversial weapon in the American trade remedy arsenal. It is not the only such weapon. "Super 301" and "Special 301" also exist. What are they, and how are they different from "Section 301"? The term "Section 301" commonly is used to include Sections 301-309 of the *1974 Act*, 19 U.S.C. §§ 2411-2419. Super 301 is codified at 19 U.S.C. § 2420. Special 301 is codified at 19 U.S.C. § 2242.

Section 301 authorizes the President to enforce U.S. rights under trade agreements and take action against unfair foreign trade practices. In contrast to antidumping (AD), countervailing duty (CVD), Section 201, and Section 337 cases, where the focus of attention typically is on the behavior of foreign private parties, a Section 301 case solely pertains to the acts, policies, or practices of a foreign sovereign government. Since the 1974 inception of Section 301, the United States Trade Representative (USTR) has undertaken approximately 120 Section 301 investigations. The most common target has been the EU. Japan, Korea, and Taiwan have been the second, third, and fourth most common targets, respectively.

The unilateral nature of Section 301, coupled with the types of retaliatory measures it authorizes, renders it susceptible to the criticism that it is inconsistent with GATT and the *DSU*. Nonetheless, as the USTR itself states, it remains the "principal" statute for addressing allegedly unfair foreign trade practices that affect American exports of goods and services. To appreciate arguments about the GATT consistency of Section 301, it is first necessary to understand the history and operation of the statute. Observe that Super and Special 301 are unilateral weapons, too.

B. Antecedents of Section 301

For over two centuries, the President has had the authority to retaliate against discriminatory foreign trade practices that burden U.S. commerce. To be sure, Article I, Section 8, Clause 3 of the U.S. Constitution — the Commerce Clause — gives Congress the power to regulate foreign trade. However, Congress imparts that power to the Executive branch. Of course, Congress does so subject to the delegation doctrine, which in brief and simplistic terms means Congress must not abdicate its Constitutional duty by giving the President unbounded authority, but rather set parameters on the President's conduct of foreign trade. What are the key delegation doctrine cases arising in the context of international trade, and how has jurisprudence in this area evolved?

Accordingly, for example, Congress empowered by statute President Washington to lay embargoes and other restrictions on imports and exports if he determined foreign countries discriminating against the U.S. A century later, in *Field v. Clark*, 143 U.S. 649 (1892), the Supreme Court upheld an 1890 statute empowering the President to impose retaliatory tariffs on imports from a foreign country if that country imposed duties on American goods that the President deemed reciprocally unequal and unreasonable. The case involved the constitutionality of Congress' delegation of power to the President. The Court's ruling remains good law, and probably would preclude a holding by any court that Congress acted unconstitutionally in delegating power to the President under Section 301. In the *Tariff Act of 1930*, the President was given potent authority to impose tariffs on goods from foreign countries that discriminated against American products. (*See Tariff Act of 1930*, ch. 497, title III, § 303, 46 Stat. 590, 687, codified as amended at 19 U.S.C. § 1303, repealed by the *Uruguay Round Agreements Act of 1994*, Pub. L. 103-465, title II, § 261(a), 8 December 1994, 108 Stat. 4908.) The *Reciprocal Trade Agreements Act of 1934* contained a provision akin to Section 301 authorizing the President to negotiate with, or impose retaliatory duties against, a country whose import restrictions unduly restricted U.S. exports. (*See Act of 1934*, ch. 474, § 1, 48 Stat. 943, 943-44, codified as amended at 19 U.S.C. § 1351.)

More recent origins of Section 301 lie in Section 252 of the *Trade Expansion Act of 1962*, which, in turn, reflected Congressional concern over the enforcement of American trade rights in a dramatically changing international economy. A leading trade scholar, the late Professor Robert Hudec, explains:

> The United States Congress has generally regarded itself as the final (and only true) protector of reciprocity in foreign trade commitments. The Congress harbors a lingering suspicion that the Executive Branch can be persuaded on occasion to sacrifice United States economic interests for the sake of friendly political relations. This suspicion surfaces regularly in congressional appraisal of major GATT tariff negotiations. Each new grant of negotiating authority has typically been preceded by a Congressional tongue-lashing over the one-sided results of the previous negotiations.
>
> By the 1960s, this chorus had grown to include a second theme — the charge that other GATT members had not been living up to their

general legal obligations, and worse, that the eager-to-please Executive Branch had been unwilling to assert United States legal rights against the violators. The criticism led to the enactment of section 252 of the *Trade Expansion Act of 1962*. The section directed the President to seek the removal of illegal restrictions, forbade the President from using tariff concessions to pay for their removal, and authorized retaliation in the event they were not removed. Section 252(c) also authorized retaliation in the case of legal but "unreasonable" restrictions, but in this case the statute instructed the President to have "due regard for the international obligations of the United States."

. . . .

Congressional criticism reemerged after the 1967 Kennedy Round agreement. This time it included an attack on the GATT itself. GATT obligations seemed not to cover some of the new trade practices devised by the EEC; other GATT provisions appeared outdated by more recent wisdom. In addition, there seemed to be a growing reluctance within GATT to enforce those obligations which were clear.

Moral outrage and self-righteousness aside, the criticism had some basis in fact. The economic world of the 1960s had come to include new powers such as Japan, the EEC, and a surprisingly well-organized coalition of developing countries, each with demands not fully anticipated by the 1947 GATT blueprint. The GATT (and particularly the United States) had adjusted to these new demands by deferring, and ultimately shelving, legal objections to some of the new trade practices that had emerged. Instead, the GATT increasingly turned to "pragmatic" solutions that would adjust the competing interests. Viewed from the perspective of the Congress, of course, all these accommodations were violations gone unpunished.

. . . .

Section 301 is a revised and strengthened version of the old section 252. In scope, it covers not only import restrictions, but also other discriminatory acts or policies, export subsidies, and export embargoes. The new section authorizes a greater quantity of retaliation than section 252. Finally, it seems to give the President substantially greater freedom to ignore international obligations when using his retaliatory authority.[1]

Since it enacted Section 301 in 1974, Congress has remained steadfast in its support for the statute. Indeed, it strengthened the statute through Section 1303 of the *Omnibus Trade and Competitiveness Act of 1988*. Section 1303 added Section 182 to the *1974 Act* — the Special 301 provision. Further, the *1988 Act* amended Section 301 to mandate retaliation in certain cases. Finally, that *Act* buttressed Section 301 by adding Super 301. Congress insisted on the threat of unilateral sanctions under Super 301 as a *quid pro quo* for

---

[1] Robert E. Hudec, *Retaliation Against "Unreasonable" Foreign Trade Practices: The New Section 301 and GATT Nullification and Impairment*, 59 MINN. L. REV. 461, 515 (1975). For a case involving the Section 252 of the *1962 Act*, see United States v. Star Industries, Inc., 462 F.2d 557 (C.C.P.A. 1972), *cert. denied*, 409 U.S. 1076 (1972).

extending fast-track trade negotiation authority of President Ronald Reagan. That authority was critical to complete both the Uruguay Round and *NAFTA*.

II. THE OPERATION OF SECTION 301

A. How Section 301 Works

WTO PANEL REPORT, *UNITED STATES — SECTIONS 301-310 OF THE TRADE ACT OF 1974*
WT/DS152/R (adopted 27 January 2000) (Not Appealed)

II. FACTUAL ASPECTS

. . . .

C. PROCEDURES

2.12 Sections 301-310 of the *Trade Act of 1974* [19 U.S.C. §§ 2411-2420] provide a means by which U.S. citizens may petition the United States government to investigate and act against potential violations of international trade agreements. [*See* 19 U.S.C. § 2412(a)(2).] These provisions also authorize the USTR to initiate such investigations at her own initiative. [*See* 19 U.S.C. § 2412(b).] The USTR is a cabinet level official serving at the pleasure of the President, and her office is located within the Executive Office of the President. [*See* 19 U.S.C. § 2171(a), (b)(1).] The USTR operates under the direction of the President and advises and assists the President in various Presidential functions. [*See* 19 U.S.C. § 2171(c)(1).]

2.13 According to Section 302 [19 U.S.C. § 2412], investigations may be initiated either upon citizen petition or at the initiative of the USTR. After a petition is filed, the USTR decides within 45 days whether or not to initiate an investigation. If the investigation is initiated, the USTR must, according to Section 303, request consultations with the country concerned, normally on the date of initiation but in any case not later than 90 days thereafter. [*See* 19 U.S.C. § 2413(a)(1).]

2.14 Section 303(a)(2) [19 U.S.C. § 2413(a)(2)] provides that, if the investigation involves a trade agreement and a mutually acceptable resolution is not reached "before the earlier of A) the close of the consultation period, if any, specified in the trade agreement, or B) the 150th day after the day on which consultation commenced," the USTR must request proceedings under the formal dispute settlement procedures of the trade agreement.

2.15 Section 304(a) [19 U.S.C. § 2414(a)] provides that on or before the earlier of "(i) the date that is 30 days after the date on which the dispute settlement procedure is concluded, or (ii) the date that is 18 months after the date on which the investigation is initiated," "[o]n the basis of the investigation initiated under section 302 and the consultations (and the proceedings, if applicable) under section 303, the Trade Representative shall . . . determine whether" U.S. rights are being denied. If the determination is affirmative,

USTR shall at the same time determine what action it will take under section 301.

2.16 If the DSB adopts rulings favourable to the United States on a measure investigated under Section 301, and the WTO Member concerned agrees to implement that ruling within the reasonable period foreseen in Article 21 of the *DSU*, the USTR can determine that the rights of the United States are being denied but that "satisfactory measures" are being taken that justify the termination of the Section 301 investigation.

2.17 Section 306(a) [19 U.S.C. 2416(a)] requires the USTR to "monitor" the implementation of measures undertaken by, or agreements entered into with, a foreign government to provide a satisfactory resolution of a matter subject to dispute settlement to enforce the rights of the United States under a trade agreement.

2.18 Section 306(b) [19 U.S.C. § 2416(b)] provides:

> "(1) **In general**. — If, on the basis of the monitoring carried out under subsection (a), the Trade Representative considers that a foreign country is not satisfactorily implementing a measure or agreement referred to in subsection (a), the Trade Representative shall determine what further action the Trade Representative shall take under section 301(a). For purposes of section 301, any such determination shall be treated as a determination made under section 304(a)(1).
>
> (2) **WTO dispute settlement recommendations**. — If the measure or agreement referred to in subsection (a) concerns the implementation of a recommendation made pursuant to dispute settlement proceedings under the World Trade Organization, and the Trade Representative considers that the foreign country has failed to implement it, the Trade Representative shall make the determination in paragraph (1) no later than 30 days after the expiration of the reasonable period of time provided for such implementation under paragraph 21 of the *Understanding on Rules and Procedures Governing the Settlement of Disputes. . . .*"

2.19 Section 305(a)(1) [19 U.S.C. § 2415(a)(1)] provides that, "Except as provided in paragraph (2), the Trade Representative shall implement the action the Trade Representative determines under section 304(a)(1)(B), subject to the specific direction, if any, of the President regarding such action" "by no later than . . . 30 days after the date on which such determination is made."

2.20 According to Section 305(a)(2)(A) [19 U.S.C. § 2415(a)(2)(A)], however, "the [USTR] may delay, by not more than 180 days, the implementation" of any action under Section 301 in response to a request by the petitioner or the industry that would benefit from the Section 301 action or if the USTR determines "that substantial progress is being made, or that a delay is necessary or desirable to obtain United States rights or satisfactory solution with respect to the acts, policies, or practices that are the subject of the action."

B. Whether Section 301 Works

There is little debate as to whether Section 301 is efficacious from an empirical standpoint. Reflecting a consensus of scholarly opinion, Professor Taylor rightly points out the statute is not a panacea for America's trade problems.[2] She explains the U.S. used Section 301 between 1985-95 to (1) pursue GATT violations, (2) set the Uruguay Round agenda, and (3) mitigate a persistent trade deficit with Japan. She concludes the practical effects, in these three categories of use, were limited (and potentially conflicted with GATT). Still, no one would contend Section 301 is entirely ineffectual. The consensus seems to be it works — sometimes, in some cases. The open issues are exactly how effective unilateral retaliation is, and why.

Most empirical studies conclude retaliation or threats thereof "work," by which some of them mean an agreement was reached, while others mean a trade liberalization result was obtained, *i.e.*, the target foreign country removed or changed its disputed act, policy, or practice. Possibly the most careful and comprehensive empirical study of unilateral trade retaliation is *Reciprocity and Retaliation in U.S. Trade Policy* (1994), by Thomas O. Bayard and Kimberly Ann Elliott. They analyze 72 cases brought under Section 301, Special 301, and Super 301 between 1975 and June 1994 in which the outcomes were reasonably clear. They define a "successful" outcome as "one in which U.S. negotiating objectives — that is, improved market access for U.S. exporters of goods and services, reduced export subsidies by the European Union and others, and improved protection for intellectual property rights . . . — were at least partially achieved."[3]

Bayard and Elliott conclude unilateral retaliation is reasonably effective as an American trade policy weapon. In spite of frequent, bitter denunciations of Section 301, exercise of the statute seems to have had a net liberalizing effect on world trade. Specifically, in 35 of the 72 cases — about half of the time — the U.S. achieved its negotiating objectives. Interestingly, the success rate has varied over time. Generally, the rate was higher in the mid-1980s, prior to the passage of the *Omnibus Trade and Competitiveness Act of 1988* and Super 301.

What factors contributed to a successful outcome? On the basis of multi-variable regression analysis, Bayard and Elliott find

> a successful outcome is more likely the more dependent the target country is on the U.S. market, the larger the U.S. bilateral deficit with the target is, and the more transparent the targeted trade barrier is. There is some evidence that success is less likely if the target has a record of counter-retaliating against US exports in trade disputes [as, for example, the EU, Canada, and China have done], but the result is not statistically significant. Surprisingly, neither public nor explicit threats . . . appear to affect outcomes in section 301 cases.

---

[2] *See* C. O'Neal Taylor, *The Limits of Economic Power: Section 301 and the World Trade Organization Dispute Settlement System*, 30 Vand. J. Transnat'l L. 209 (1997).

[3] Thomas O. Bayard & Kimberly Ann Elliott, Reciprocity and Retaliation in U.S. Trade Policy 59 (1994).

. . . .

Unexpectedly, GATT procedures do not appear to add much leverage: the success rate for cases in which a GATT panel ruled against a target's policies (54 percent) was not significantly different from that for cases in which there was no GATT ruling or GATT rules were not applicable (47 percent). But, there is still evidence of some deference to GATT rules in these cases. In every case where a GATT panel found a violation or evidence of nullification or impairment, changes in the offending policy were made. In almost half, however, the target country replaced the illegal trade barrier with another type of barrier or disagreed with the U.S. interpretation of what had been agreed.

. . . .

There is also a stronger positive correlation between GATT dispute settlement procedures and success if the European Community is excluded. Cases with GATT rulings, other than those involving the Community, were successful 71 percent of the time (vs. 54 percent overall). Cases involving GATT rulings against the European Community ultimately were judged to be failures on five of eight occasions. Each time the Community changed the offending practice, but it exploited ambiguities in GATT or the bilateral agreements to continue to protect its agricultural producers and processors.[4]

In other words, three variables are critical in predicting the success of an action.

First, Section 301 is an effective tool if the target foreign government is vulnerable because the U.S. is a key destination for its country's exports. In the 35 of 72 successful Section 301 cases, the ratio of the target country's exports to the U.S. as a percentage of the target's Gross National Product (GNP), which is a measure of its export dependence on the U.S., was 7.5 percent. In the 37 of 72 failed cases, the average target country's export dependence was 4.3 percent of its GNP. Obviously, as the share of a target country's GNP accounted for by exports to the U.S. rises, the stakes rise, and American retaliation can inflict serious damage. The practical message for all of America's trading partners is to diversify their export markets, because over-reliance on the American market is dangerous.

Second, the absolute size of the bilateral trade balance between the U.S. and the target foreign country is significant. In successful cases, the average bilateral deficit of the U.S. was $15 billion, while in failed cases it was $2 billion. Why is this variable important? One argument could be the U.S. is more likely to "bargain hard" and take retaliatory action if it faces a greater imbalance, thus a target foreign government perceives threats of retaliation as credible and is more likely to modify its behavior.

Third, the more transparent the act, policy, or practice in question, the more likely that a Section 301 action will be successful. This result seems based on the common sense notion that if the USTR can "see it," then it is easier for the USTR to urge its elimination or modification.

---

[4] *Id.* at 86, 90.

A fourth variable that can influence the outcome of a Section 301 case is whether there are interest groups in the target foreign country that support the U.S. position. For example, do Japanese consumer groups lobby their government to liberalize its import regime with respect to American agricultural goods? Does India seek to replace traditional socialist planning and import substitution policies with market-oriented, trade liberalization policies? Of course, whether a strong reform-oriented constituency exists depends on the degree of political freedom and participation in the target country.

The overall empirical record on Section 301, suggesting the practical utility of this weapon, is philosophically troubling. The probability of success of unilateral retaliation, under the right conditions, elides features unique to each case. Trade disputes are aggregating and assessed into a "win-loss" record — an approach some observers take to participation in *DSU* cases. In other words, empirical studies are motivated by the question "did we win or not?," not by concerns of equity.

Surely procedural and substantive due process ought to matter. First, were results obtained in a fair manner? Ends cannot justify means. Results obtained because of unequal bargaining power are inherently unfair. Asymmetry arises when a target foreign country does not have the ability to strike the U.S. as hard as the U.S. can hit the target. That difference in vulnerability — namely, when there is no market in the target country particularly valuable to American exporters — arises especially when the target is a poor country.

Second, were the results obtained by unilateral retaliation just? Ideally, a target country should abandon or change an act, policy, or practice because it is the right course of action. "Right" not in terms of U.S. economic aims, but because it is an appropriate balance among those aims, the target's legitimate concerns, and the interest of the international community in trade liberalization. Or, "right" simply in a moral sense. Perhaps only when there is a multilateral consensus on "unreasonable" or "discriminatory" measures will it be possible to ensure the outcome in Section 301 investigations (especially under Section 301(b), given the notably ambiguous terms in that statute) is just.

III. THEORIES OF UNILATERAL TRADE RETALIATION

A. Civil Disobedience

The Professor Hudec considered whether Section 301 represents a legitimate form of civil disobedience directed at achieving change given that multilateral dispute resolution in the international trading system is a cumbersome — if not unresponsive — process.

> The obligation not to retaliate without GATT authority presumes that GATT will be able to rule on the disputed legal claim, and, later, on the request to retaliate. If GATT is, in fact, unable to rule, the complainant may be free to resort to "self-help" in some circumstances.[5]

---

[5] Robert E. Hudec, *Thinking About the New Section 301: Beyond Good and Evil, in* Aggressive Unilateralism: America's 301 Trade Policy and the World Trading System 113, 121 (Jagdish Bhagwati & Hugh T. Patrick, eds., 1990).

Put differently, Section 301 is a "disagreeable necessity, a 'lesser evil' chosen to prevent a more damaging outcome."[6] That outcome is the failure of the multilateral trading system because of ineffectual dispute resolution mechanisms.

However, is the premise of justifying Section 301 with civil disobedience theory false? The theory assumes multilateral dispute resolution mechanisms are ineffectual. That is a harsh judgment against the *DSU*. For all its actual or purported flaws — a certain lack of transparency, being overburdened with cases, lacking private party representation, and confusion over how to deal with alleged noncompliance, to name a few — it is hard to say the system is utterly broken. Justice can be, and has been, obtained by many WTO Members in many cases, and few would advocate scrapping the *DSU* in favor of a Thoreau-like retreat to Walden Pond.

B. Game Theory

Economists have long used game-theoretic models to analyze Section 301 negotiations. Recently, this approach has been adopted by legal scholars who adhere to a law and economics perspective on international trade law. For instance, Professor Alan Sykes uses noncooperative game theory to support his argument that the mandatory retaliation provision of Section 301 is a "sensible strategic response to the problem of 'cheating' " under an international trade agreement.[7] A noncooperative game is one in which the players cannot assume that promises always will be kept. The critical underlying assumption is that parties to international trade agreements cannot assume their commitments are binding. Why? Because there is no external authority that can compel the parties to honor their commitments.

Game theory analysis posits a trade agreement between the U.S. and Japan that resembles the well-known Prisoner's Dilemma model. The U.S. promises to reduce the tariff on Japanese widgets to zero in exchange for a Japanese promise to accord duty-free treatment to American gadgets. Each country can choose to comply with the agreement, or cheat on the other country.

> Presumably, the elimination of the tariff on Japanese widgets . . . imposes a political cost on U.S. officials. If tariff reductions are politically advantageous, they will be undertaken unilaterally and trading partners will not need to offer concessions in return. Likewise, the elimination of the tariff on U.S. gadgets no doubt imposes a political cost on Japanese officials. The trade agreement is possible despite these political costs because concessions abroad yield political benefits to officials in each country — exporters gain and "reward" the political officials who are responsible for obtaining the concession. It is also reasonable to suppose that if one country cheats, officials in the other country forfeit most or all of the political gains from obtaining the concession — exporters will not reward officials who obtain concessions on paper that do not materialize in practice. It follows that

---

[6] Hudec, *supra* note 5, at 131.

[7] Alan O. Sykes, *"Mandatory" Retaliation for Breach of Trade Agreements: Some Thoughts on the Strategic Design of Section 301*, 8 B.U. INT'L L.J. 301, 303 (1990).

officials in each country would prefer an environment in which the tariff abroad remained at zero, but the tariff at home was raised ("compliance" by the other country, "cheating" at home). They would then avoid the political costs associated with the concession at home, yet reap the political benefits associated with the concession abroad.

Thus the "payoff structure" for this trade agreement game has the following properties: In each country, officials are better off if both trading nations comply with the agreement than if they both cheat. If only one nation cheats and the other complies, officials in the cheating nation are better off yet, but officials in the complying nation are worse off than if they also cheated.

Figure I illustrates this payoff structure. The numbers are arbitrary, except that they obey the above inequalities.

FIGURE 38-1

		Japanese	*Strategy*
		Comply	Cheat
U.S.	Comply	(10, 10)	(0, 15)
Strategy	Cheat	(15, 0)	(5, 5)

For each possible combination of strategies, Figure I provides an ordered pair representing the payoff to officials in each country. The payoff to U.S. officials is the first number, and the payoff to Japanese officials the second. Thus, for example, if Japan cheats and the U.S. complies, U.S. officials receive a payoff of zero and Japanese officials receive a payoff of 15.[8]

On the basis of the payoff structure, in a single-play game — *i.e.*, where the U.S. and Japan must decide once on a course of action that cannot be modified subsequently in response to the course adopted by the other country — each country will cheat. The numbers in the payoff structure indicate American officials are better off cheating regardless of whether Japan complies or cheats (because 15 > 10 and 5 > 0, respectively). Conversely, Japanese officials are better off cheating regardless of the American course of action (because if the U.S. complies, Japan obtains 15 by cheating but only 10 by complying, and if the U.S. cheats, Japan gets 5 by cheating and zero by complying.) As a result, each country will earn the same payoff (5, 5). No doubt each side would be better off if both countries complied with the agreement, "[b]ut that outcome is untenable because the initial promise to comply is not binding, and because in a single play game neither side can punish the other for cheating in a future period."[9]

What if the game is played repeatedly? After all, a model that is ultimately based on the single play game is not realistic. The U.S. and Japan have a long history of trade relations that includes many moves and countermoves. Their relations are more akin to a chess match that never ends than a single play game. In a multiple-play game, it can be argued that "sustained compliance is by no means assured."[10] Presumably, the U.S. and Japan would

[8] *Id.* at 306.

[9] *Id.* at 307.

[10] *Id.*

announce that if the other party cheats during one period, then it will cheat in the subsequent period. The threat of subsequent retaliatory cheating, however, may not deter cheating in the previous period. In a two-period game,

> [i]n the second period, each player confronts the payoff matrix in Figure I, with no opportunity to punish the other player in the future for cheating (the game will be over). Hence, cheating becomes the dominant strategy for each player in the second period. And, each player can figure this out in the first period — for example, Japan knows that the United States will cheat in the second period regardless of which strategy Japan chooses in the first period. The United States threat to punish cheating is thus an empty one, and would have no deterrent effect on Japan in the first period. Cheating becomes the dominant strategy for Japan in the first period just as in the single-play game. This reasoning also applies to the United States, and so both countries would cheat in both periods.

> Precisely the same logic applies to a game that is repeated four times, five times, and n times, as long as each player knows the number of repetitions. Acting "rationally," both players anticipate that they will each cheat in the last period, and so they have no reason not to cheat in the next to last period, no reason not to cheat in the next to next to last period, and so forth.[11]

Even in an infinite horizon game — one that has no end — the threat to cheat may be one that is potentially credible for an indefinite time. To motivate compliance, a country could employ a "tit-for-tat" strategy, behaving in the current period as the other country did in the previous period. Alternatively, a country may employ a "grim" strategy in which it complies until it discovers the other country is cheating, and thereafter cheats forever. Still another alternative would be a "massive retaliation" strategy whereby a country declares that cheating of the other country abrogates the entire agreement.

In a game-theoretic context, mandatory retaliation under Section 301(a) serves as a credible device to sanction and, therefore, deter cheating on a commitment in a trade agreement. However, the utility of Section 301 is limited in two respects. First, suppose the U.S. retaliates unilaterally in a case where cheating is not blatant, or where the alleged cheater has a legitimate defense (such as under GATT Article XI, XII, XVI, XX, or XXI). Then, the U.S. risks both infamy and counter-retaliation. In turn, its trading partners may be disinclined to negotiate trade deals with the U.S.

Second, the mandatory retaliation provision requires a tit-for-tat, or measured, response. The USTR cannot employ grim and massive retaliation strategies, and this fact undermines the credibility of any retaliatory threat under Section 301. In game theoretic terms, retaliation is credible only if it wipes out the gain that accrues to a cheater from cheating. Otherwise, a cheater will continue to cheat and accept the retaliation. Instead of ruling out *a priori* two strategies, the game theoretic approach suggests that the amount of retaliation should be linked to the amount of the cheater's gain.

---

[11] *Id.* at 307-08.

There are a number of concerns about a game-theoretic analysis of mandatory retaliation under Section 301. Consider the following issues:

1. Is it realistic to assume that parties to international trade agreements do not view their commitments as binding?

2. Is it reasonable to conceptualize international trade agreements as a payoff structure involving two players?

3. Are the predictions of the payoff structure subject to manipulation?

4. What happens if the time horizons of the negotiating parties differ?

5. Should the payoff structure be dynamic?

6. Would preservation of reputation be an incentive to comply?

IV. IS SECTION 301 GATT—WTO CONSISTENT?

WTO PANEL REPORT, *UNITED STATES — SECTIONS 301-310 OF THE TRADE ACT OF 1974*
WT/DS152/R (adopted 27 Jan. 2000) (Not Appealed)

VII. FINDINGS

. . . .

B. Preliminaries

. . . .

2. *The Panel's Mandate*

7.11 The political sensitivity of this case is self-evident. In its submissions, the US itself volunteered that Sections 301-310 are an unpopular piece of legislation. In addition to the EC, twelve of the sixteen third parties expressed highly critical views of this legislation.

7.12 Our function in this case is judicial. . . .

. . . .

6. *The Measure in Question [i.e., Sections 301-310] and the Panel's General Methodology*

7.24 Our mandate in this case is to evaluate the conformity of Sections 301-310 [of the *Trade Act of 1974*, as amended, 19 U.S.C. §§ 2411-2420] with the relevant WTO provisions. . . . Conformity can be ensured in different ways in different legal systems. It is the end result that counts, not the manner in which it is achieved. Only by understanding and respecting the specificities of each Member's legal system, can a correct evaluation of conformity be established.

7.25 Sections 301-310 display some features, common in several jurisdictions, that are typical of much modern complex economic and regulatory legislation. Frequently, the Legislator itself does not seek to control, through statute, all covered conduct. Instead it delegates to pre-existing or specially created administrative agencies or other public authorities, regulatory and supervisory tasks which are to be administered according to certain criteria and within discretionary limits set out by the Legislator. The discretion can be wide or narrow according to the will of the Legislator. Sections 301-310 are part of such a legislative scheme.

. . . .

7.27 The elements of this type of national law are, as is the case here, often inseparable and should not be read independently from each other when evaluating the overall conformity of the law with WTO obligations. For example, even though the statutory language granting specific powers to a government agency may be *prima facie* consistent with WTO rules, the agency responsible, within the discretion given to it, may adopt internal criteria or administrative procedures inconsistent with WTO obligations which would, as a result, render the overall law in violation. The opposite may be equally true: though the statutory language as such may be *prima facie* inconsistent, such inconsistency may be lawfully removed upon examination of other administrative or institutional elements of the same law.

. . . .

C. The EC Claim that Section 304 Is Inconsistent with Article 23.2(a) of the *DSU*

. . . .

3. *The Statutory Language of Section 304 and Member Obligations under Article 23 of the DSU*

. . . .

(a) The Dual Nature of Obligations under Article 23 of the DSU

. . . .

7.38 . . . [W]e conclude as follows:

(a)   It is for the WTO through the *DSU* process — not for an individual WTO Member — to determine that a WTO inconsistency has occurred (Article 23.2(a)).

(b)   It is for the WTO or both of the disputing parties, through the procedures set forth in Article 21 — not for an individual WTO Member — to determine the reasonable period of time for the Member concerned to implement DSB recommendations and rulings (Article 23.2(b)).

(c)   It is for the WTO through the procedures set forth in Article 22 — not for an individual WTO Member — to determine, in the event of disagreement, the level of suspension of concessions or other obligations that can be imposed as a result of a WTO inconsistency, as well as to grant authorization for the actual implementation of these suspensions.

7.39 Article 23.2 clearly, thus, prohibits specific instances of unilateral conduct by WTO Members when they seek redress for WTO inconsistencies in any given dispute. This is, in our view, the first type of obligations covered under Article 23.

. . . .

7.43 Article 23.1 is not concerned only with specific instances of violation. It prescribes a general duty of a dual nature. First, it imposes on all Members to "have recourse to" the multilateral process set out in the *DSU* when they seek the redress of a WTO inconsistency. . . . Members have to have recourse to the *DSU* dispute settlement system to the exclusion of any other system, in particular a system of unilateral enforcement of WTO rights and obligations. This, what one could call "exclusive dispute resolution clause," is an important new element of Members' rights and obligations under the *DSU*. Second, Article 23.1 also prescribes that Members, when they have recourse to the dispute settlement system in the *DSU*, have to "abide by" the rules and procedures set out in the *DSU*. This second obligation under Article 23.1 is of a confirmatory nature: when having recourse to the *DSU* Members must abide by all *DSU* rules and procedures.

(b) Legislation which violates Article 23 of the DSU

7.47 What kind of legislation would constitute a violation of Article 23?

. . . .

7.50 . . . [I]f the USTR were to exercise, *in a specific dispute*, the right thus reserved for him or her in the statutory language of Section 304 and make a determination of inconsistency, the U.S. conduct would meet the different elements required for an individual breach under Article 23.2(a). However, Section 304 does not mandate the USTR to make a determination of inconsistency in violation of Article 23 in each and every specific dispute; it merely sets out in the statutory language itself that the USTR has the power and right to do so. The question here is whether this constitutes a breach of the second type of obligations under Article 23, namely a breach by measures of general applicability such as a general law.

[At the end of the first sentence in ¶ 7.50, the Panel inserted footnote 657. This lengthy sub-text is so important it ought to have been in the main body of the Report. In footnote 657, the Panel explained what would constitute a breach of *DSU* Article 23:2(a). The Panel said if the USTR were to exercise, in a specific dispute, its power under Section 304 to make a determination of inconsistency *before* exhaustion of *DSU* procedures, then the U.S. would violate Article 23:2(a). Why? Because the USTR's action would have met the 4 pre-requisites for a breach of Article 23:2(a). The elements are:

(1)   a Member takes an action "in such cases," as the *chapeau* to Article 23:2 states *i.e.*, in a situation where the Member seeks redress against a violation by another Member of that other Member's

obligations, or against a transgression committed by that other Member which amounts to non-violation nullification or impairment of the first Member's benefits;

(2)   the Member's act is a "determination," *i.e.*, it is not a mere opinion or view expressed before an internal investigation, but rather an action with a high degree of firmness or immutability, and thus essentially is a final decision by the Member concerning the GATT—WTO consistency of a trade measure of another Member;

(3)   the Member's determination is one to the effect a violation has occurred, or its benefits have been nullified or impaired; and

(4)   the Member makes the determination *before* DSB findings in the case have been adopted, *i.e.*, the Member does not make the determination through recourse to the *DSU*, or in a manner consistent with recommendations in a panel or Appellate Body report adopted by the DSB or an arbitration award made under the *DSU*.

The Panel rightly dubbed the conclusion in footnote 657 "of crucial importance," because it "shows that the statutory language of Section 304 reserves the right to the USTR to breach . . . Article 23:2(a)" through an *ad hoc*, specific action in a given dispute.]

7.51 The parties focused much of their arguments on the kind of legislation which could be found to be inconsistent with WTO obligations. The U.S. submitted forcefully that only legislation *mandating* a WTO inconsistency or *precluding* WTO consistency, can, as such, violate WTO provisions. This was at the very heart of the U.S. defence. On this U.S. reading, it followed that since Section 304 never mandates a specific determination of inconsistency prior to exhaustion of *DSU* proceeding nor . . . precludes the U.S. from acting consistently with its WTO obligations in all circumstances, the legislation, in and of itself could not be in violation of Article 23.2(a) of the *DSU*.

7.52 The EC submitted with equal force also certain types of legislation under which a WTO inconsistent conduct is not *mandated* but is *allowed*, could violate WTO obligations. The EC considered that Section 304 is of such a nature.

7.53 . . . [R]esolving the dispute as to which type of legislation, *in abstract*, is capable of violating WTO obligations is not germane to the resolution of the type of claims before us. . . . [T]he appropriate method in cases such as this is to examine with care the nature of the WTO obligation at issue and to evaluate the Measure in question in the light of such examination. The question is then whether, on the correct interpretation of the specific WTO obligation at issue, only mandatory or also discretionary national laws are prohibited. We do not accept the legal logic that there has to be one fast and hard rule covering all domestic legislation. . . . [I]s it so implausible that the framers of the *WTO Agreement*, in their wisdom, would have crafted some obligations which would render illegal even discretionary legislation and crafted other obligations prohibiting only mandatory legislation? Whether or not Section 304 violates Article 23 depends, thus, first and foremost on the precise obligations contained in Article 23.

7.54 We can express this view in a different way:

(a) Even if we were to operate on the legal assumption that, as argued by the U.S., only legislation *mandating* a WTO inconsistency or *precluding* WTO consistency, can violate WTO provisions; and

(b) confirm our earlier factual finding . . . that the USTR enjoys full discretion to decide on the content of the determination,

we would still disagree with the U.S. that the combination of (a) and (b) *necessarily* renders Section 304 compatible with Article 23, since Article 23 may prohibit legislation with certain discretionary elements, and therefore the very fact of having in the legislation such discretion could, in effect, preclude WTO consistency. In other words, rejecting, as we have, the presumption implicit in the U.S. argument that no WTO provision ever prohibits discretionary legislation does not imply a reversal of the classical test in the pre-existing jurisprudence that only legislation mandating a WTO inconsistency or precluding WTO consistency, could, as such, violate WTO provisions. Indeed that is the very test we shall apply in our analysis. It simply does not follow from this test, as sometimes has been argued, that legislation with discretion could never violate the WTO. If, for example, it is found that the specific obligations in Article 23 prohibit a certain type of legislative discretion, the existence of such discretion in the statutory language of Section 304 would presumptively preclude WTO consistency.

7.55 What, then, does such an examination of Article 23 yield?

7.56 . . . [U]nder the statutory provisions of Section 304 each time the USTR exercises the mandatory duty to make a determination, the statutory language gives him or her discretion and reserves to him or her the right to make a determination of inconsistency even in cases where *DSU* proceedings have not been exhausted.

7.57 In our view, the ordinary meaning of the provisions of Article 23, even when read in abstract, supports the position that this aspect of Section 304 constitutes a *prima facie* violation of *DSU* rules and procedures. This interpretation of Article 23 is amply confirmed when we consider, as is our duty under the *Vienna Convention*, the good faith provision in the general rule of interpretation in Article 31 of that *Convention*, and when we evaluate the terms of Article 23 not in abstract, but in their context and in the light of the *DSU's* and the WTO's object and purpose.

[Recall that Article 31:1 of the *Vienna Convention* states: "A treaty shall be interpreted in good faith in accordance with the ordinary meaning to be given to the terms of the treaty in their context and in the light of its object and purpose."]

4. *Article 23.2(a) of the DSU Interpreted in Accordance with the Vienna Convention Rules on Treaty Interpretation*

(a) *"A treaty shall be interpreted . . . in accordance with the ordinary meaning to be given to the terms of the treaty. . . ."*

. . . .

7.59 The text of Article 23.1 is simple enough: Members are obligated generally to (a) have recourse to and (b) abide by *DSU* rules and procedures. These rules and procedures include most specifically in Article 23.2(a) a prohibition on making a unilateral determination of inconsistency prior to exhaustion of *DSU* proceedings. As a plain textual matter, therefore, could it not be said that statutory language of a Member specifically authorizing a determination of inconsistency prior to exhaustion of *DSU* procedures violates the ordinary meaning of Members' obligations under Article 23?

. . . .

7.61 On this reading, the very discretion granted under Section 304, which under the U.S. argument absolves the legislation, is what, in our eyes, creates the presumptive violation. The statutory language which gives the USTR this discretion on its face precludes the U.S. from abiding by its obligations under the WTO. In each and every case when a determination is made whilst *DSU* proceedings are not yet exhausted, Members locked in a dispute with the U.S. will be subject to a mandatory determination by the USTR under a statute which explicitly puts them in that very danger which Article 23 was intended to remove. [Here, the Panel stated in footnote 660 that it rejected "the notion that this danger is removed by virtue of the international obligation alone." In other words, a norm — in the sense of the way a law is or is not used — cannot transform a law from being *prima facie* incongruous with an international legal obligation (like *DSU* Article 23) into a law that is consistent with that obligation.]

(b) "A treaty shall be interpreted in good faith . . ."

7.64 It is notoriously difficult, or at least delicate, to construe the requirement of the *Vienna Convention* that a treaty shall be interpreted in good faith in third party dispute resolution, not least because of the possible imputation of bad faith to one of the parties. We prefer, thus, to consider which interpretation suggests "better faith" and to deal only briefly with this element of interpretation. Applying the good faith requirement to Article 23 may not lead to a conclusive result but impels us in the direction suggested by our examination of the ordinary meaning of the raw text.

7.65 Imagine two farmers with adjacent land and a history of many disputes concerning real and alleged mutual trespassing. In the past, self help through force and threats of force has been used in their altercations. Naturally, exploitation of the lands close to the boundaries suffers, since it is viewed as dangerous terrain. They now sign an agreement under which they undertake that henceforth in any case of alleged trespassing they will abjure self help and always and exclusively make recourse to the police and the courts of law. They specifically undertake never to use force when dealing with alleged trespass. After the entry into force of their agreement one of the farmers erects a large sign on the contested boundary: "No Trespassing. Trespassers may be shot on sight."

7.66 One could, of course, argue that since the sign does not say that trespassers *will* be shot, the obligations undertaken have not been violated. But, would that be the "better faith" interpretation of what was promised? Did they not after all promise *always and exclusively* to make recourse to the police and the courts of law?

7.67 Likewise, is it a good faith interpretation to construe the obligations in Article 23 to allow a Member that promised its WTO partners — under Articles 23.1 and 23.2(a) — that it will generally, including in its legislation, have recourse to and abide by the rules and procedures of the *DSU* which specifically contain an undertaking not to make a determination of inconsistency prior to exhaustion of *DSU* proceedings, to put in place legislation the language of which explicitly, *urbi et orbi* [to the City and to the World] reserves to its Executive Branch the right to make a determination of inconsistency — that which it promised it would not do? This Panel thinks otherwise.

7.68 The good faith requirement in the *Vienna Convention* suggests, thus, that a promise to have recourse to and abide by the rules and procedures of the *DSU*, also in one's legislation, includes the undertaking to refrain from adopting national laws which threaten prohibited conduct.

. . . .

[The Panel then appraised the disputed measure according to the remaining interpretative elements in Article 31 of the *Vienna Convention*, namely, the ordinary meaning of Article 23 in light of the object and purpose, and context, of the *DSU* and this provision. These additional interpretative devices reinforced the Panel's conclusions.]

. . . .

5. *Preliminary Conclusion after the Panel's Examination of the Statutory Language of Section 304*

. . . .

7.96 Consequently, the statutory language of Section 304 — by mandating a determination *before* the adoption of DSB findings and statutorily reserving the right for this determination to be one of inconsistency — must be considered presumptively to be inconsistent with the obligations in Article 23.2(a). The discretion given to the USTR to make a determination of inconsistency creates a real risk or threat for both Members and individual economic operators that determinations prohibited under Article 23.2(a) will be imposed. The USTR's discretion effectively to make such determinations removes the guarantee which Article 23 is intended to give not only to Members but indirectly also to individuals and the market place. . . . [T]he USTR's discretion under Section 304 does not — as the U.S. argued — ensure the consistency of Section 304. On the contrary, it is the core element of the *prima facie* inconsistency of the statutory language of Section 304.

7.97 Therefore, pursuant to our examination of text, context and object-and-purpose of Article 23.2(a) we find, at least *prima facie*, that the statutory language of Section 304 precludes compliance with Article 23.2(a). This is so because of the nature of the obligations under Article 23. Under Article 23, the U.S. promised to have recourse to and abide by the *DSU* rules and procedures, specifically not to resort to unilateral measures referred to in Article 23.2(a). In Section 304, in contrast, the U.S. statutorily reserves the right to do so. . . .

[In footnote 675, following the last sentence of this paragraph, the Panel emphasized its finding did "not require the wholesale reversing of earlier GATT and WTO jurisprudence on mandatory and discretionary legislation." To the contrary, the Panel sought to prove its methodology is not revolutionary. Recalling its discussion in paragraph 7.51, the Panel reiterated the "classical test" of consistency established by previous cases, namely, "only legislation *mandating* a WTO inconsistency or *precluding* WTO consistency could . . . violate WTO provisions. . . ." (emphasis original). The Panel summarized its methodology as examining, "first and with care," the WTO provision in question and the obligation it imposes on Members. Then, the nature of the legislation is studied in relation to the WTO obligation. The Panel said it is wrong to presume the WTO would never prohibit legislation under which a Member would enjoy certain discretionary powers. If a discretionary power granted under domestic law is inconsistent with a WTO obligation, then that law fails the classical test. Why? Because the legislation precludes WTO consistency. Query whether the Panel is expanding the breadth of the classical test in hindsight in order to show it is not reversing a *de facto* precedent.]

6. *The Non-Statutory Elements of Section 304*

(a) *Introduction and Summary of the Panel's Analysis*

7.98 . . . [W]e have deliberately referred to the "statutory language" of Section 304 and likewise we have deliberately concluded that the statutory language creates a *prima facie* violation. We did not conclude that a violation has been confirmed. This is so because of the special nature of the measure in question. The measure in question includes statutory language as well as other institutional and administrative elements. To evaluate its overall WTO conformity we have to assess all of these elements together.

7.99 Therefore, although we found above that the statutory language of Section 304 creates a *prima facie* violation of Article 23.2(a), this does not, in and of itself, establish a U.S. violation. . . .

7.100 . . . The *prima facie* violation was created by the possibility under the statute of the USTR making a determination of inconsistency which negates the assurances that WTO partners of the U.S. and individuals in the market place were entitled to expect under Article 23.

7.101 One can imagine different ways to remove the *prima facie* violation. If, for example, the statutory language itself were modified so that the USTR were not under an obligation to make a determination within the 18 months time-frame, but could, for example, await the making of any determination until such time as *DSU* procedures were completed the guarantee that Article 23 was intended to create would remain intact and the *prima facie* inconsistency would not exist. Likewise, if, by a change in the statutory language, the USTR's discretion to make a determination of inconsistency prior to exhaustion of *DSU* proceedings were curtailed, once again the *prima facie* inconsistency would no longer exist.

7.102 Changing the statute is not the only way to remove the *prima facie* inconsistency. If the possibility of the USTR making a determination of inconsistency prior to exhaustion of *DSU* proceedings were lawfully curtailed in a different manner, the same legal effect would be achieved. The obligation on Members to bring their laws into conformity with WTO obligations is a fundamental feature of the system and, despite the fact that it affects the internal legal system of a State, has to be applied rigorously. At the same time, enforcement of this obligation must be done in the least intrusive way possible. The Member concerned must be allowed the maximum autonomy in ensuring such conformity and, if there is more than one lawful way to achieve this, should have the freedom to choose that way which suits it best.

7.103 Critically, the offending discretionary element has to be *lawfully* curtailed since, as found in WTO case law, conformity with WTO obligations cannot be obtained by an administrative promise to disregard its own binding internal legislation, *i.e.*, by an administrative undertaking to act illegally.

7.104 . . . [W]e find that the *prima facie* violation has in fact in this case been lawfully removed and no longer exists.

7.105 The *Trade Act* in general and Sections 301-310 in particular are part of U.S. legislation which covers the broad range of U.S. trade relations including relations with States that are not WTO Members and including relations with Members that are not covered by WTO obligations.

7.106 The statutory language of Section 304 gives the USTR the broad discretion . . . as regards the entire scope of U.S. trade relations, only a part of which comes within the orbit of WTO obligations. Within the discretion allowed, the statutory language leaves it to the USTR to apply the provisions of the *Trade Act* which relate to the entire gamut of U.S. trade relations in a manner which is consistent with U.S. interests and obligations. The interests and obligations can be different from one group of States to another.

7.107 We find, as a matter of fact, that it is within that broad discretion afforded to the U.S. Administration, notably as regards the content of determinations pursuant to Section 304, lawfully to set out different regimes for the application of Section 304 depending on whether or not it concerns WTO covered situations.

7.108 The language of Section 304 allows the existence of multilateral dispute resolution proceedings to be taken into account. [The Panel referred here in footnote 679, to 19 U.S.C. § 2414, which speaks of an "investigation initiated under section 302 [19 U.S.C. § 2412] and the consultations (*and the proceedings, if applicable*) under section 303 [19 U.S.C. § 2413]" (emphasis added). "The applicable proceedings" are *DSU* procedures.] It also allows for determinations of inconsistency to be postponed until after exhaustion of *DSU* proceedings. This language surely permits the U.S. to limit the discretion of the USTR so that no determination of inconsistency is made before exhaustion of *DSU* proceedings. The discretion granted as to the content of a determination to be made should be interpreted as including the power of the U.S. to adopt an administrative decision limiting the USTR's discretion in a manner consistent with U.S. international obligations. [Interestingly, here in footnote 681, the Panel stated a principal reason it reached this conclusion was "the U.S. constitutional principle of construing U.S. domestic law, where possible, in a way that it is consistent with U.S. obligations under international law."

The Panel accepted the U.S. argument based on the famous *Charming Betsy* case, and quoted from the U.S. brief: "[i]n U.S. law, it is an elementary principle of statutory construction that 'an act of Congress ought never to be construed to violate the law of nations if any other possible construction remains.' *Murray v. Schooner Charming Betsy*, 6 U.S. (2 Cranch 64, 118 (1804))."]

7.109 . . . [W]e find that this is precisely the situation in the present case. Briefly, the U.S. Administration has carved out WTO covered situations from the general application of the [1974] *Trade Act* [*i.e.*, Section 301]. It did this in a most authoritative way, *inter alia*, through a *Statement of Administrative Action* ("*SAA*") submitted by the President to, and approved by, Congress. Under the *SAA* so approved ". . . it is the expectation of the Congress that future administrations would observe and apply the [undertakings given in the *SAA*]." One of these undertakings was to "base any section 301 determination that there has been a violation or denial of U.S. rights . . . on the panel or Appellate Body findings adopted by the DSB." This limitation of discretion would effectively preclude a determination of inconsistency prior to exhaustion of *DSU* proceedings. The exercise of discretion under the statutory scheme is in the hands of the Administration and it is the Administration which has given this undertaking. We recognize of course that an undertaking given by one Administration can be repealed by that Administration or by another Administration. But, this is no different from the possibility that statutory language under examination by a panel be amended subsequently by the same or another Legislator. The critical question is whether the curtailment of discretion is lawful and effective. This Panel finds that it is.

. . . .

[The Panel then elaborated on its finding, examining the portions of the *SAA* concerning Section 301 and statements by the U.S. to the Panel during oral arguments. This evidence clearly indicated Section 304(a)(1) requires the USTR to base a determination of whether U.S. rights have been violated or denied under the relevant trade agreement on results of WTO dispute settlement proceedings, *i.e.*, the USTR cannot make a determination that an act, policy, or practice of a foreign government is inconsistent with a GATT—WTO rule in a manner contrary to *DSU* Article 23:2(a). The Panel also indicated, but did not make a conclusive finding, there was insufficient evidence to support the EC argument that USTR practice under Section 301 violated this Article.]

7. *Summary of the Panel's Analysis and Finding in Respect of the EC Claim under Section 304*

7.131 The overall result of our analysis may be summarized as follows. We found that the statutory language of Section 304 constitutes a serious threat that determinations contrary to Article 23.2(a) may be taken and, in the circumstances of this case, is *prima facie* inconsistent with Article 23.2(a) read in the light of Article 23.1. We then found, however, that this threat had been removed by the aggregate effect of the *SAA* and the U.S. statements before this Panel in a way that also removes the *prima facie* inconsistency and fulfils the guarantees incumbent on the U.S. under Article 23. In the analogy described in paragraph 7.65, the sign "No Trespassing. Trespassers may be shot on sight" was construed by us as going against the mutual promise made among the neighbours always and exclusively to have recourse to the police and the courts of law in any case of alleged trespassing. Continuing with that analogy, we would find in this case that the farmer has added to the original sign which was erected for all to read another line stating: "In case of trespass by neighbours, however, immediate recourse to the police and the courts of law will be made." We would hold — as we did in this case — that with this addition the agreement has been respected.

7.132 This conclusion is based on our reading of Section 304 as part of a multi-layered law containing statutory, institutional and administrative elements. . . .

7.133 First, the *SAA* could be considered not as an autonomous measure of the Administration determining its policy of implementing Section 304, but as an important interpretative element in the construction of the statutory language of Section 304 itself. Whereas the statutory language read on its own does not preclude a determination of inconsistency, as we found above in paragraph 7.31(d), following this alternative methodology, the statutory language read in the light of the *SAA* would have that effect.

7.134 Second, assuming that examination of the statutory language of Section 304 led us to conclude that, because of the broad discretion it gives to the USTR, the statute is in violation of Article 23, we would then need to consider an appropriate remedy, *i.e.*, to consider how the U.S. could restore to its WTO partners the guarantees embodied in Article 23. In our view, any lawful means by which the U.S. Administration could curtail the discretionary element would be sufficient to achieve that goal. In the case at hand, we would then find that the *SAA* and statements of the kind made by the U.S. to the DSB through this Panel effectively provide . . . such a remedy. Therefore, any violation we would thus have found on the basis of the statutory language of Section 304, under this second alternative, would have been remedied.

7.135 . . . [W]e find that Section 304 is not inconsistent with U.S. obligations under Article 23.2(a) of the *DSU*.

Part Eleven

POOR COUNTRIES

Chapter 39

TRADE POLICIES, GROWTH, AND POVERTY

You can't stop terrorism with guns, because it is in the mind. Terrorism is created by a strong feeling of injustice, political or economic, which may be imaginary or real, but when I feel I've been treated badly, when I have no other means at my disposal and when I feel there is no way of winning you over, when I am tiny and you are big, terrorism is the result and I start throwing bombs.

—Muhammad Yunus, 2006 Nobel Peace Prize Winner
(Bangladesh, creator of micro-finance and Grameen Bank),
FINANCIAL TIMES, 9-10 Dec. 2006, at W3.

DOCUMENTS SUPPLEMENT ASSIGNMENT

1. *Havana Charter* Articles 1, 8-15, 24, 55-70

2. GATT Preamble and Articles XVIII, XXXVI-XXXVIII

3. Tokyo Round *Enabling Clause*

4. WTO *Agreement Preamble*

I. TWO POLICY CHOICES

Developing and least developed countries have two basic choices about trade policy: Export Orientation or Import Substitution. The choices are radically different, both in their underlying theory and practical implications.

Export Orientation is premised on Ricardo's Law of Comparative Advantage, and on a presumed causal link between trade and growth. This policy calls for openness to trade, not only to implement the Law and thereby realize the net gains of which Ricardo wrote, but also to boost national income. Through freer trade, a country specializes in production of goods in which it has a comparative cost advantage, leading to an efficient division of labor and allocation of resources. It attains higher levels of social utility from a wider range of consumption choices at cheaper prices than would exist without trade.

Advocates of this policy generally agree with the proposition "the more trade, the better." For them, trade is an engine of growth, a key stimulant for output. Their paragon is the East Asian "Tigers" — Hong Kong, Korea, Singapore, and Taiwan.[1] Their policy is to expand overseas markets, and dismantle domestic trade barriers. They incline toward free trade agreements (FTAs) or customs unions (CUs), and better yet multilateral deals, and look askance at protectionist constituencies.

---

[1] The list of Tigers varies somewhat depending on the study. In a 1993 publication, the World Bank identified seven Tigers, and used yet another acronym, HPAEs, for "High Performing Asian Economies."

In contrast, Import Substitution is premised on a Marxist-oriented view trade with rich nations is inherently exploitative. Such trade reinforces an international division of labor that confines poor countries in agricultural. They plant, grow, and harvest primary products, and extract natural resources, the world market prices of which tend to be low and gyrate. Rich countries benefit from cheap food and natural resources coming from poor countries, and specialize in high-value added manufactured merchandise, as well as services. Whereas Export Orientation advocates agree trade is an engine of growth, Import Substitution proponents are "export pessimists." Export pessimism means trade cannot propel a country to higher levels of growth.

Import Substitution advocates argue that for the Third World, "the more trade, the worse," because it traps poor countries in the role of sending raw materials to the mighty industrial and service economies of the First World. Consequently, they call for tariff and non-tariff barriers against imports, and favor local production over foreign-made goods. That way, infant industries in poor countries have the chance to grow, and the risk of dependence on manufactured items and services from rich nations is minimized. They tout as successful exemplars India and some Latin American countries.

II. EXPORT ORIENTATION

A. Review of the Theory

Export Orientation calls for reliance on international markets to stimulate growth. In contrast to the interventionist role of a government in implementing Import Substitution, with Export Orientation a government takes a neutral stance. Its primary focus is creation and maintenance of an environment favorable to the free market, with key features of this environment being the rule of law and transparency to create as level a playing field as possible for all economic actors (large or small, foreign or domestic).

In particular, a government does not encourage domestic industries to source inputs from in-country suppliers, nor does it promote (*e.g.*, through protection, subsidies, or tax breaks) export-oriented over other industries. It minimizes trade barriers, ensuring tariffs and quotas are low or zero on inputs needed for finished products, and eliminates artificial disincentives to exportation (*e.g.*, export licenses or taxes). The government relies on market forces — particularly world market price signals — to determine the most efficient, profitable allocation of factors of production (capital, human capital, labor, land, and technology). The result is the manufacture of goods in which a comparative advantage exists, or reasonably can be expected through private capital investment.

Export Orientation draws on the intellectual heritage of the classical economist, David Ricardo, and neoclassical economists. They emphasize the net gains to a country from trade liberalization. Specialization of production leads to an efficient allocation of factor resources based on comparative cost advantage. The source of relative cost advantages depends on relative endowments of factor resources among countries. Labor-rich countries will focus on labor-intensive goods, land-abundant countries on land-intensive goods, and so on. Initially, many developing countries will find their comparative advantage in labor-intensive, low-value added manufactured products, along with primary agricultural products. As the skill level of the labor force develops, and as technology is imported, the country should be able to move into higher-value added manufacturing that relies more intensively on human capital than before. Overall, this focus contrasts with Import Substitution, which typically involves production of capital-intensive goods even if a country is not relatively well endowed with capital.

Moreover, Export Orientation takes advantage of a scale effect. The world market for virtually every product is by definition larger than the market in any one country (the rare exceptions being where a product is produced and consumed in only one country). Producers can, therefore, build productive capacity, employ more factors of production, become efficient and develop economies of scale, all with a view to serving a larger world, rather than a smaller domestic, market. In turn, production of an exportable surplus may be traded for products in which a comparative advantage is lacking. To be sure, there is a risk of immiserizing growth, especially as regards primary commodities, if a country is a large enough supplier of a particular commodity (because increased exports of the product could drive down world market prices). The remedy, however, is diversification away from exports of these commodities and into manufactured goods.

Through exportation, an economy advances from an agrarian-based to a modern industrial one. Complementing it is foreign direct investment (FDI), which is attracted to a country in part by the neutral stance of its government, and flows in response to market forces. In keeping with the Product Life Cycle Hypothesis, put forth by a leading scholar of multinational corporations (MNCs), Professor Raymond Vernon, FDI may lead to shifts in the locus of production. After a product is invented and marketed in a developed country, and the manufacturing process becomes standardized, production moves to developing countries. Intellectual property (IP) the product embodies is transferred to local companies (or the original periods of protection expire). In this manner, developing countries move through, at a phase behind developed countries, the Cycle.

As for consumers, they have before them a wider array of alternatives from which to choose, at lower prices, than without trade. The gains from production specialization and higher consumption outweigh losses from tariff revenue or quota rents, which are no longer reaped with free trade, plus losses to producers whose enterprises are shut down or downsized because of a lack of comparative advantage. In principle, the "winners" from trade can compensate the "losers" by agreeing to share some of their gain.

Another point in favor of Export Orientation concerns Terms of Trade (TOT). In theory trade liberalization should improve the TOT of a country. In respect of import prices, PIM, as well domestic like and substitute product prices, they should fall for two reasons. (Recall PIM is the denominator of the TOT ratio.) First, trade liberalization means a drop in tariff and non-tariff barriers. Second, this liberalization leads to increased competition. As regards export prices, PEX, they should rise with freer trade. (Recall PEX is the numerator of the TOT ratio.) The demand of foreign consumers supplements demand by local consumers for the merchandise in question. With more consumers after the same products, the price of the products should rise (assuming all other factors are held constant, *i.e.*, *ceteris paribus*, most notably, product supply). Thus, Export Orientation proponents argue greater openness should improve the TOT of a country.

Not surprisingly, the theory of Export Orientation also relies on the classical and neoclassical economic critique of tariff and non-tariff barriers. To recap, this theory demonstrates such barriers impose a net welfare cost on a country in comparison with the free-trade equilibrium. Tariffs and quotas provide the protected sector with more producer surplus than before (*i.e.*, producer's earn more than the marginal cost of production), and offer the government tariff revenue or the protected sector quota rents. These benefits are outweighed by the loss of consumer surplus, which means there is a decline in the number of consumers willing and able to pay a higher price for the protected product than is charged. Protection raises that price, and consequently cuts into consumer surplus. The net negative effect counsels against increasing trade barriers, and indicates dismantling such barriers, even unilaterally, is economically rationale.

Export Orientation also is backed by the promise of dynamic gains from trade. When a country imports goods, it also imports ideas and IP the goods embody. Domestic entrepreneurs may be encouraged to enter the market and make a like product. Existing producers may be spurred by the competition from overseas. Foreign investors may enter the market to make the product. The result is higher output, which generates surplus income, and thereby savings to be channeled into investment. That new investment can improve production techniques and quality, leading to further output and innovation.

B. Lord Bauer and the Terms of Trade

One of the most provocative economists to comment on development issues is England's Lord Peter T. Bauer, a long-time professor at the London School of Economics and Cambridge University. Born in Budapest in 1915, Lord Bauer wrote in the mid- and latter half of the 20th century and was a fellow of the British Academy. His research, while not all directly bearing on trade, both raises and attempts to rebut criticisms often made about the world trading system, and more generally, of globalization. His perspectives demonstrate the charges and counter-charges heard today are not new.

In *Equality, The Third World and Economic Delusion* (1981), Lord Bauer considers the accusation the First World (*i.e.*, developed nations), manipulate international trade to the detriment of the Third World (*i.e.*, developing and least developed nations). In specific, the First World stands accused of inflicting unfavorable and deteriorating TOT. That is, following the accusation, the First World is charged with orchestrating a decline in the share of international trade held by the Third World. The obvious policy implication from this accusation is Export Orientation is not a viable growth strategy. However, Lord Bauer offers five rebuttals to this accusation.

First, the poorest areas of the Third World have little or no external trade. It makes little sense to blame the First World for manipulating trade against largely autarkic countries. They are poor for domestic reasons, not because of First World manipulation. Virtually any external commercial contracts would be beneficial, *i.e.*, expanded trade would benefit such countries. Indubitably, Lord Bauer would agree with the proposition espoused by former United Nations Secretary General, Kofi Annan, and others, namely, the poor are poor not because of too much globalization, but because of too little.

Second, most countries are developing or least developed, *i.e.*, the bulk of the world is the Third World. Likewise, roughly 80 percent of the WTO Membership consists of such countries. Accordingly, says Lord Bauer, it is not possible to consider the TOT of the Third World in the aggregate. The TOT for any one such country may move favorably during one period, but may deteriorate in another period. Much depends on the period selection for measurement. Countries in the Organization of Petroleum Exporting Countries (OPEC) enjoyed high export prices for their key commodity, oil, in the 1970s, but had to reassess their lavish government spending programs in the late 1990s as those prices — and the revenues from them to fund expenditures — shrank. The point is that generalizing about TOT for the entire Third World makes little sense.

Third, it is simplistic to draw inferences from the TOT alone. Many factors affect the economic performance of Third World countries. For example:

    1.   *Cost of production*:

The TOT cannot be inferred simply from the ratio of import and export prices. This ratio does not take into account the cost of production of exports. The higher the cost of production of exports, the more expensive it is for a Third World country to engage in international trade. High costs of production are based on the cost of factors of production, *i.e.*, land, labor, physical capital, human capital, and technology.

    2.   *Export diversification*:

The diversity of the export base of a country, and quality of its imports, are critical determinants of economic success.

    3.   *Trade volume*:

The volume of trade in which a country is engaged affects its success.

    4.   *Import purchasing power*:

The amount of imports a country can purchase with a unit of domestic resources also affects its success.

Moreover, Bauer argues, Third World countries contribute significantly to their own dismal performance. Corruption, war and conflict, and economic mismanagement are self-inflicted wounds readily apparent in many poor countries. It is difficult to blame developed countries in every instance. For example, the U.S. has had since 1977 the *Foreign Corrupt Practices Act and Antibribery Provisions*, which bars bribery of foreign government officials (codified at 15 U.S.C. §§ 78dd-1 *et seq.*). On 21 November 1997, the OECD agreed to an *Anti-Bribery Convention* (formally, the *Convention Combating Bribery of Foreign Public Officials in International Business Transactions*). Neither the U.S. nor any other OECD country plausibly can be blamed for every war, conflict, or poor policy choice. In sum, there is far more to the problem than TOT.

Fourth, in the vast majority of markets, it is naïve to believe major trading countries can manipulate international prices. Most markets are too broad and deep for price cartels or other anti-competitive practices to work. Prices are the outcome of innumerable individual decisions of market participants. The result is what economists chart as supply and demand curves, not conspiracies to distort TOT.

Fifth, the accusation major powers inflict bad and worsening TOT on the Third World wrongly presumes the share of a country in world trade is, by itself, a gauge of its prosperity or wealth. That share is just one such indicator. Some high-income countries like Brunei, Singapore, Switzerland, and the United Arab Emirates (UAE) have small shares. Still, as a general trend, the Third World share of world trade has increased. By 2004, it approximated 31 percent, the highest figure since 1950, and continues to grow.

A second accusation leveled not directly at the GATT—WTO system, but rather at the related international financial order, concerns external debt. Many developing and least developed countries owe staggering amounts of debt to official creditors (e.g., governments of developed countries), private lending institutions (e.g., commercial banks), and international organizations like the World Bank and IMF. The accusation is this debt reflects exploitation by hegemonic powers of poor countries (if the debtors are sovereign) and businesses in those countries (if the debtors are private enterprises).

The loans, it is said, were thrust on the Third World (particularly in the 1970s, to re-cycle petrodollars deposited by oil exporting countries in western and Japanese financial institutions). The loans help ensure debtor countries buy products from the creditor countries, and thereby remain dependent on them. Many debtors cannot hope to emerge from the burden in a reasonable period of time, and need new funds to repay previously contracted debt. The link to the trade regime is these debtors are forced to use a large portion of their export revenues to repay principal and interest, rather than for reinvestment in productive assets. Not surprisingly, many scholars, governments, think tanks, and so forth have offered proposals since the 1970s, when the debt problem emerged, to alleviate the burden. Serious talk of canceling African debt began in 1987.

Debt forgiveness, advocated by (inter alia) the Holy See and Her Majesty's Government, is the most dramatic proposal. In the summer 2005, British Prime Minister Tony Blair and Chancellor of the Exchequer Gordon Brown persuaded the Group of 8 (G-8, i.e., the rich countries, the G-7, plus Russia) to endorse a plan to cancel all debts of 18 highly indebted poor countries (HIPCs) owed to the World Bank, IMF, and African Development Bank (AfDB). The face value of the debt is $40 billion, on which average service payments are $1 to $1.5 billion. The beneficiaries would be Bolivia, Guyana, Honduras, Nicaragua, and 14 African countries. Nine other debtor-countries may become eligible for relief, and a further 11 countries would be if they reduced ineptitude and corruption. There are two "catches" to the G-8 plan. First, the amount of loans or grants a debtor-country receives from the World Bank or ADB is "adjusted" (i.e., cut) by the amount of money the country saves in debt servicing. For example, in 2006, Rwanda was supposed to pay \$4.5 million to the World Bank and AfDB, and \$2.9 million to the IMF. The G-8 proposal eliminates these repayment obligations. But, it also cuts World Bank and AfDB (but not IMF) funding to Rwanda by \$4.5 million. The net saving to Rwanda, then, is \$2.9 million it does not have to repay the IMF. Second, the G-8 (or any member thereof) could cut funding to the World Bank and AfDB, or their bilateral aid budgets. It is not apparent they all will allocate taxpayer funds to multilateral lenders, as opposed to setting off amounts they might have given against forgiven debt.

Lord Bauer addresses head on the accusation that the external debt of the Third World is the result of exploitation by the West. First, he counters this debt represents resources supplied, namely financial capital from commercial and investment banks, and ultimately saver-investors in the U.S. and other wealthy countries, to the Third World. It is the responsibility of the debtors to channel the funds into productive investments. If they make poor investment choices, or if they allow some of the funds to be skimmed off to corrupt ends, then the creditors hardly are to blame.

To be fair, however, a country receiving \$100 million in aid and paying \$50 million in debt service is not necessarily as well off as a country receiving \$50 million in aid. IMF Chief Economist, Raghuram Rajan, points out the stock of liabilities matters, not just the amount of net inflow of funds. The stock of debt, in particular, can deter FDI. Would-be private investors may be concerned the debtor-government will over-tax their profits to cover debt service obligations. If they elect not to invest, and the investment rate in the debtor-country falls, then growth in the country will fall. In turn, the country will be less able to service its debt than a country that is debt-free.

Second, Lord Bauer explains the difficulties Third World countries have in servicing their debt do not reflect external exploitation generally, nor unfavorable TOT in particular. Rather, the causes lie in

    i.   wasteful use of the funds supplied (*i.e.*, living beyond the country's means),

    ii.   corruption,

    iii.   inappropriate fiscal or monetary policies (*e.g.*, maintaining overvalued exchange rates),

    iv.   the need to import raw materials, intermediate goods, and capital goods (machine tools) to support industrialization.

Regarding the latter cause, Lord Bauer points out as Third World countries industrialize, they typically run large overall BOP deficits (though certain bilateral relationships may be in surplus). Malaysia and China are examples (though, for instance, China has had large trade surpluses with the U.S.). In brief, Lord Bauer's response is to differentiate an exploitative lending relationship from the normal process of economic development, and from bad choices by borrowers.

Finally, Lord Bauer dubs condescending an aspect of the allegation about debt, namely, that imports from major countries ultimately damage people in the Third World. These people exercise free choice to import goods, based on their economic wants. If they did not want the imports, then the goods could not be sold. Yet, they are, and people are willing to produce goods to export and thereby pay for the imports. To allege otherwise is to take no account of the preferences of people in the Third World, and how they organize their economic lives in expressing their preferences.

To these points it is worth adding that most poor countries receive many times more in multilateral, regional, and bilateral aid than they pay in external debt servicing. In the 1990s, reports the World Bank, heavily indebted poor countries received roughly twice as much aid as they paid to service their debts. Mozambique, an extreme example, paid $71.8 million to service its debts in 2003, but got 14 times that amount in aid.

C. Export Processing Zones

An important qualification to the theory of Export Orientation is how this policy is implemented in practice. It would be naïve to think every government takes a wholly laissez-faire approach to building export industries. In fact, many governments adopt modest measures of support. A common example is the creation of Free Trade Zones (FTZs) or Export Processing Zones (EPZs). Led by Premier Deng Xiaopeng, China commenced its movement away from strict socialism in the late 1970s by establishing four "special economic zones" in which market-oriented liberalizations took place.

Generally speaking, an FTZ or EPZ is a geographic location, or a firm or group of enterprises with acknowledged legal standing, to which special governmental treatment applies. This treatment consists of some or all of the following measures:

> 1. *Lower Taxes*:

Tax rates and/or valuations of assets to which tax rates are applied may be reduced or even eliminated. In the alternative, or in addition, tax holidays may be declared whereby no taxes are paid for a certain period (the holiday). Tax deductions from gross income, tax credits against tax liability, and/or accelerated tax write-offs (*e.g.*, depreciation schedules) may be offered.

> 2. *Lower Trade Barriers*:

Tariffs may be reduced or eliminated for goods imported for use as inputs in the production of exported products. Quotas, import licenses, and other non-tariff barriers may be liberalized or eliminated.

> 3. *Rebates*:

Refunds may be offered on all or a portion of certain taxes or tariffs paid, particularly for finished products that are exported.

> 4. *Subsidies*:

Certain infrastructure facilities, such as buildings, and utilities like power and water, as well as training programs for workers, may be subsidized.

The *quid pro quo* for special treatment is, of course, exportation of goods produced in the FTZ or EPZ. In effect, an FTZ or EPZ is a bargain between the public and private sectors. The government hopes to grow the economy and, in the process, create backward linkages and enhance the level of technology in the country. Businesses hope to grow in size and profitability, and gain market access overseas.

Whether this bargain — or, perhaps better put, partnership — between public and private sectors works depends on the overall political, economic, and legal environment of the FTZ or EPZ. In addition to China, Korea and Taiwan are cited as successful examples. However, in certain countries, exploitative working conditions (*e.g.*, long hours, low pay, and occupational health and safety risks), environmental damage, and gender discrimination (namely, excessive reliance on young female workers) have been concomitant with FTZ or EPZs. Moreover, preferences granted can create resentment within a country, and generate concerns about differential, or dualistic, economic development and widening domestic income gaps, as India's experiment with special economic zones (SEZs) under reformist Prime Minister Manmohan Singh suggests.

D. Empirical Evidence

What is the empirical evidence on Export Orientation? The famously cited examples of success are the East Asian Tigers. Within each Tiger, the general cultural, economic, and political environment is favorable to Export Orientation. In particular, the Tigers benefit from a mix of factors:

   1. *Sound Macroeconomic Management*:

Fiscal expenditures are sensible (not profligate or grossly imbalanced), taxation simple and reasonably low (sometimes involving a flat tax), and monetary policy stable to ensure low levels of inflation. Government commitment to these policies is credible, hence businesses can rely on certainty and predictability in macroeconomic management.

   2. *Solid Infrastructure*:

Communication networks, port facilities, transportation links, and utilities accommodate economic growth. And, the government attends to needed upgrades.

   3. *Free Labor Markets*:

Markets for factors of production, particularly labor, are flexible. Government do not impose minimum wages or working conditions, nor employment requirements, on businesses, and discourages (even fights) unionization. Consequently, labor can move fairly quickly to adjust to new incentives associated with changed economic conditions.

   4. *Strong Work Ethic*:

Hard work, dedication, and sacrifice of personal interest for group and national benefits are long-standing cultural values.

   5. *Memories of Suffering*:

Memories of devastation from the Second World War are poignant among survivors. That cohort does not want subsequent generations to suffer as it had.

6. *Anti-Communism*:

The post-Second World War generation does not want to fall victim to communism, and a strong national economy is consistent with a strong defense. Former Singaporean Prime Minister Lee Kuan Yew adds the American defense umbrella, including keeping communism at bay in North Korea and Vietnam, gave the Tigers the breathing space they needed to develop.

7. *Pragmatism*:

With few exceptions (*e.g.*, rice), people do not hold a sentimental attachment to goods or industries. As their country moves up the value-added production chain, they know jobs are lost in one sector, but look forward to new opportunities in others.

Add to these factors a strong scaffolding of the rule of law, and it is hardly surprising the Tigers are "Exhibit A" for successful implementation of Export Orientation.

Also not surprising is the large number of empirical studies about the Tigers, and Export Orientation more generally. Had the Tigers "figured it out"? Is Export Orientation "the way to go"? Among the near-classic studies, which tend to corroborate one another and support Tiger-style Export Orientation are the following:

● *The 1983 Krueger Study on Employment:*

In 1983, Anne O. Krueger, a renowned development economist, examined data on 10 countries for 1960-73.[2] Her focus is the relationship between trade policy and jobs — does Export Orientation generate more jobs than Import Substitution? A key statistic she studied was the ratio of (1) labor per unit of value added to a good that is exported to (2) labor per unit of value added to a good that competes with imports, *i.e.*,

$$\frac{\text{Labor Used per unit of Value Added to Exportable Good}}{\text{Labor Used per unit of Value Added to Import-Competing}}$$

In theory, if Export Orientation generates more jobs than Import Substitution, then the ratio should exceed one, *i.e.*, there is more labor per dollar's worth of exports than labor per dollar's worth of import substitutes. This result should occur for two reasons.

First, export-oriented industries use a greater quantity of labor than import-competing industries. Second, export-oriented industries grow faster than import-substituting industries. To be sure, these ratios do not reveal the occupant profile or nature of the jobs. Happily, there is evidence to suggest in some countries the job-growth associated with Export Orientation benefits women. Unhappily, there is evidence to indicate in some countries the job growth is in low-pay, low-skill work. These shortcomings aside, Krueger's 1983 results are clear: in 9 of the 10 countries studied, the average ratio was 1.57. Moreover, only 1 country had a ratio below one (0.8).

---

[2] *See generally* ANNE O. KRUEGER ET AL., 3 TRADE AND EMPLOYMENT IN DEVELOPING COUNTRIES — SYNTHESIS AND CONCLUSIONS (1983).

- *The 1985 Krueger Study:*

In 1985, Krueger studied the overall economic performance of the East Asian Tigers — Hong Kong, Korea, Singapore, and Taiwan, against that of all countries also considered to be "middle income."[3] Does growth through industrialization and exportation "work"? The answer is clear. The Tigers grew more rapidly than the others in their income cohort. Despite two kinds of difficulties in the 1970s — a change in the TOT against middle income countries, and the oil price shocks of 1973 and 1979 — the Tigers boasted high growth rates and proved more resilient than the other countries. Moreover, income distribution remained fairly equitable in the Tigers.

However, Krueger offers an important caveat. The Tigers commenced their Export Orientation policies in the 1960s, but their success was made possible by more than just these policies. A combination of contributing factors mattered, including — significantly — the international economic climate.

First, for most of the period of the 1960s and after, this climate was favorable to Export Orientation, because international trade in general expanded during this period. In part through successive GATT rounds, such as the Dillon, Kennedy, and Tokyo Rounds, tariff and (eventually) non-tariff barriers fell, especially in the markets of major countries. Conversely, when countries with large populations and purchasing power, like the U.S., EU, and Japan, adopt protectionism policies, particularly in certain product markets through trade remedies like safeguards in response to import surges, export-oriented developing countries may be vulnerable — particularly if their consumer markets are too small to pick up any slack in demand. In other words, the Tigers had access to key markets. This access existed when the Tigers most needed it, namely, when they were developing a comparative advantage — initially, low-value added, labor-intensive products (*e.g.*, shoes and textiles and apparel (T&A)), and later higher-value added, sophisticated products (*e.g.*, cars, consumer electronics, semi-conductors, steel).

Second, the Tigers did not face much competition for most manufactured items in which they sought to develop an international comparative advantage. The world market for such items was not saturated. Dozens of other countries did not simultaneously set up factories to build and export radios, TVs, and other consumer electronic products. Hence, prices were robust, and demand in developed countries was strong. Currently, many countries in the Caribbean, Latin America, and Sub-Saharan Africa remain largely dependent on primary goods for export revenues. Consequently, their revenues and TOT are vulnerable to commodity price movements. Asked about diversifying into manufactured goods, a response they offer is the market for such goods now is crowded.

Third, international banking and securities markets developed, so that the Tigers (and particularly businesses within them) could obtain financial capital from overseas quicker and more cheaply than ever before. While these businesses drew on extended family savings in their early stages, as they grew

---

[3] Anne O. Krueger, *The Experience and Lessons of Asia's Super Exporters, in* EXPORT-ORIENTED DEVELOPMENT STRATEGIES: THE SUCCESS OF FIVE NEWLY INDUSTRIALIZING COUNTRIES 210 (Vittorio Corbo, Anne O. Krueger & Fernando Ossa eds., 1985).

they benefited from the flows of funds from developed countries channeled by the international capital markets. The former Merrill Lynch Dragon Fund was one of many examples of investing savings and retirement funds — at one point, roughly $1.5 billion — from developed countries in equities of approximately 120 East Asian companies.

Fourth, MNCs from developed countries became increasingly prominent actors in developing countries. The MNCs invested directly in countries like the Tigers. These countries had low trade barriers to inputs MNCs needed for production. They encouraged MNCs to source their inputs from them with a generally pro-business climate. As they established production facilities, they boosted local employment and transferred (to some degree) technology.

In sum, Krueger cautions, the Tigers implemented the right policy at the right time. Their experience of the Tigers might well have been different had they tried Export Orientation during an era of declining values and volumes of trade.

- ● *The 1989 Balassa Study on Outward Orientation:*

Bela Balassa, another highly regarded development economist, examines data on a large number of developing countries, classifying them as (1) outward-oriented economies, (2) inward-oriented economies, or (3) nearly closed economies.[4] In the first category are East Asian Tigers, namely, Korea, Singapore, and Taiwan. In the second category are major Latin American countries, including Argentina, Brazil, and Mexico. The third category included Chile, India, and Uruguay. His data covers two periods, 1960-73, and 1973-83. The first oil price shock, engineered by the Organization of Petroleum Exporting Countries (OPEC), occurred at the break point, 1973, and a second OPEC shock occurred in the middle of the second period, 1979. Balassa asks two questions: (1) which kind of economy grew faster, and (2) how did the different kinds of economies react to the oil price shocks?

The answer to both questions is unambiguous. In both periods, countries with outward-oriented economies grew faster than countries with economies in the other two categories. Moreover, outward-oriented economies were able to generate more employment and needed less capital per unit of output (in effect, their ICORs were lower) than the other kinds of economies. To be sure, the oil price shock caused greater economic damage to outward-oriented economies than to other kinds of economies. That result was unsurprising, as an outward-oriented economy by definition is more vulnerable to changes in the prices of energy and major commodities than economies insulated from world markets. But, Balassa finds the outward-oriented economies are more resilient than inward-oriented or essentially closed economies. They rebounded from the 1973 and 1979 shocks relatively quickly, and regained growth rates that were higher than the other types of economies. In fact, they also generated relatively higher savings rates, were less dependent on external borrowing, and had lower inflation rates.

---

4 *See generally* Bela Balassa, *Outward Orientation, in* 2 HANDBOOK OF DEVELOPMENT ECONOMICS 1645-90 (H.B. Chenery & T.N. Srinivasan eds., 1989).

● *The 1987 World Bank Study:*

The World Bank published a study in 1987 of 41 developing countries.[5]
Using Balassa-type categorization, the World Bank slots them along a
continuum:

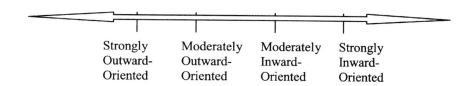

Strongly	Moderately	Moderately	Strongly
Outward-	Outward-	Inward-	Inward-
Oriented	Oriented	Oriented	Oriented

Consistent with the 1985 Krueger and 1987 Balassa studies, the World Bank
finds outward orientation associated with better economic performance than
inward orientation. It concludes the evidence on this point is convincing. Similar follow-up studies show specific positive correlations between, on the one
hand, openness to trade and FDI, and, on the other hand, growth in income,
growth in productivity, investment in human capital, investment in physical
capital, and technology transfer.

● *The 1992 Dollar Study:*

In 1992, David Dollar published the results of his analysis of data from
1976-85.[6] He compared Latin American and African countries against Asian
countries. His question is counter-factual: if the Latin American and African
countries had pursued Export Orientation and other policies similar to the
policies implemented in Asia, what would their performance have been? He
estimates Latin America would have grown 1.5 percent faster, and Africa 2.1
percent faster, than they actually did. Thus, these countries would have been
better off by mimicking pro-trade, Asian-style development strategy.

● *The 1995 Sachs-Warner Study:*

Jeffrey Sachs, a high-profile, controversial economist in his own right, and
Andrew Warner teamed up to publish a study in 1995 in which they developed
criteria for the "openness" of an economy.[7] They asked whether open economies grew faster than closed economies. Their answer was unambiguously
affirmative. Almost all open countries grew faster than closed economies. They
found annual *per capita* GDP growth rate in open economies exceeded that
in closed economies by between 2.2 and 2.5 percent. Sachs and Warner also
considered whether the timing, or extent, of remaining closed made a difference. The answer, again, was affirmative. Countries that maintained closed
economies up until the mid-1970s, or later, were considerably more likely to

---

[5] *See generally* WORLD BANK, WORLD DEVELOPMENT REPORT 1987 ch. 5 (1987).

[6] *See* David Dollar, *Outward-Oriented Developing Economies Really Do Grow More Rapidly:
Evidence from 95 LDCs, 1976-85,* 40 ECON. DEV. & CULTURAL CHANGE 523-44 (1992).

[7] *See* Jeffrey D. Sachs & Andrew Warner, *Economic Reform and the Process of Global
Integration,* BROOKINGS PAPERS ON ECONOMIC ACTIVITY 1995(1), at 1-95 (1995).

suffer from serious macroeconomic problems, even crises, in the 1980s, than countries that were open or abandoned their closed policies by the mid-1970s.

However, arguably, Sachs and Warner define "openness" and "closed" in too rigid a manner. They construct a "dummy" variable (*i.e.*, and on-off indicator, whose value is 1 when a condition such as openness, is true, and 0 when it is false) for "openness." To determine if an economy is "open," they look at tariffs and quotas on intermediate and capital goods, the foreign exchange rate premium in the black (unofficial) market, the existence of export marketing boards, and whether a country was "socialist." They consider "closed" any economy that was not open for 20 years, from 1970 through 1989. Similarly, their data set starts in 1970. Therefore, by definition they exclude countries that benefited from Import Substitution in the 1950s and 1960s, and countries that opened up thereafter. (For instance, South Korea had been open since 1968, but Brazil did not open up until 1991, and India not until 1994.) These concerns lead to a more general one, namely, the lack of standardized definitions of "openness" and "closed." In a June 1996 paper, Lant Pritchett points out there is no correlation among criteria for categorizing economies as outward- or inward-oriented.[8]

To be sure, this large volume of empirical evidence, impressive as it is, has not gone unchallenged. One clever line of argument against it is historical revisionism. Were the East Asian Tigers as free-trade oriented as their advocates, and the evidence they cite, suggests? Among others, Colin Bradford, whose study appeared in 1986, tries to discern fact from fiction.[9] A closer inspection of the policies of the four Tigers shows that only one of them — Hong Kong — followed Export Orientation in its pure form. The other three Tigers intervened to help their export industries, suggesting implementation of Export Orientation does not mean a *laissez-faire* approach to the economy. Among the sins of these three are the following:

i.   Korea pursued some Import Substitution policies, and extended preferential, subsidized credit to export industries.

ii. Singapore gave tax incentives to certain industries engaged in exportation.

iii. Taiwan also gave tax incentives to certain export industries, controlled imports in a way to encourage exportation, and used government enterprises to provide one-third of all fixed investment.

Bradford concludes it is erroneous to give all the credit for the success of the Tigers to Export Orientation. A fuller, more accurate rendition of their history reveals effective public-private partnerships to create conditions in which Export Orientation could be successful. In some instances, such as Korea, trade policy evolved, or switched, from Import Substitution in early stages of growth to Export Orientation in more advanced states. In other instances, trade policy involved a mix of the two policies, with Export Orientation predominating, but Import Substitution used to protect a one or

---

[8] Lant Pritchett, *Measuring Outward Orientation in LDCs: Can It Be Done?*, 49 J. Dev. Econ. 307-36 (1996).

[9] *See* Colin I. Bradford, Jr., *East Asian "Models:" Myths and Lessons, in* Development Strategies Reconsidered 115-28 (John P. Lewis & Valerina Kallab eds., 1986).

a few infant industries. In sum, the Tigers benefited from good governance focused on economic growth, plus a national consensus in favor of making sacrifices to achieve growth.

A second significant thrust at the Export Orientation evidence is methodological and quantitative in nature. Critics point out that much of the evidence is correlative, not causal, in nature. Because growth and other favorable macroeconomic trends accompany trade does not mean trade causes them. In turn, it is unclear exactly how strong the relationship between trade and growth is. That is, it is not easy to attribute a specified percentage of growth to trade, as distinct from other pro-growth factors (like, as in the Harrod-Domar and Solow Models, capital investment).[10]

In fact, the causal direction is not clear. Perhaps growth is associated with, or causes trade. Empirical evidence about Israel and Mexico shows a causal relationship from trade to growth, but from growth to trade in Pakistan. To add to the confusion, evidence concerning some countries (*e.g.*, Colombia and Morocco) shows causation in each direction. Concerning other countries (*e.g.*, Brazil and Korea), data point to the importance of exogenous factors, and industrialization, in boosting trade and growth.

Finally, even if growth causes trade, the precise causal path is not yet certain. Among the leading hypotheses are trade causes growth because trade means (1) competition from imports, (2) greater FDI, (3) improved productivity, (4) more learning (and, therefore, higher human capital), and (5) more efficient allocation of resources. However, the relative importance of these causal chains is not clear. Of course, if the arrow runs in the opposite direction, then these factors, which occur with growth, could generate trade. Ultimately, there may be no single answer for all developing countries.

III. IMPORT SUBSTITUTION

A. Marxist-Oriented Perspectives

Like Export Orientation, Import Substitution has a grand intellectual tradition. The inspiration is Marxist theory, and its various incarnations, which offer a radically different perspective on international trade from capitalist models.

Few better articulated the Marxist maxim that trade is needed by capitalists to obtain inputs for finished goods, and as an outlet for over-production, than Cecil Rhodes, namesake of both Rhodesia (now Zimbabwe) and the Rhodes Scholarship. He declared:

> We must find new lands from which we can easily obtain raw materials and at the same time exploit the cheap slave labor that is available from the natives of the colonies. The colonies would also provide a dumping ground for the surplus goods produced in our factories.[11]

---

[10] These models, as well as the Rostow Stages of Growth Theory and Fei-Ranis Labor Surplus Model, are set out in the *Dictionary of International Trade Law* that accompanies this Textbook. The *Dictionary* also sets out concepts and ways of measuring income poverty, and Amartya Sen's thesis of poverty as capability deprivation and development as freedom.

[11] Edward Goldsmith, *Development as Colonialism, in* THE CASE AGAINST THE GLOBAL ECONOMY 253-66 (Jerry Mander & Edward Goldsmith eds., 1996).

Similarly, in March 1899, a delegate to the French Association of Industry and Agriculture intoned that colonial power must be exercised

> to discourage in advance any signs of industrial development in our colonies, to oblige our overseas possessions to look exclusively to the mother country for manufactured products and to fulfill, by force if necessary, their natural function, that of a market reserved by right to the mother country's industry.[12]

The term "development," urge Marxists, is a euphemism for imperialism and colonialism.

Marxists see continuity between the colonial era of the 1600s through 1960s, and the era of development following the independence of former colonies. For example, the Asian colonial experience included Britain bullying Siam, and France bullying Annam, into signing treaties in 1855 and 1862, respectively, and European powers and Japan carving China up into spheres of influence. Through such arrangements, the colonial powers had access to markets of most Asian coastal regions, special rights for their expatriates working in Asia, and the freedom to build transportation networks and extend their enterprises inland. The renowned English historian, Eric Hobsbawm, reports that in the 1800s, Britain held direct imperial control over one-fourth of the world's surface, the Royal Navy controlled sea lanes to protect trade routes, and London was the world's financial capital. Britain made one-third of all manufactured goods in the world, and produced two-thirds of the world's coal, half its iron, half of the world's factory-made cotton, 40 percent of the world's hardware, and five-seventh's of the world's steel.

What has changed, other than the identities of some bullies and the form of the bullying? MNCs act in lieu of (or as if they were) sovereigns, rely not so much on official "gun boat diplomacy" as on playing off small countries against one another, and if need be bribing officials to extract trade and investment concessions. Exhausted by two world wars, Britain's economic might has declined — but America's has risen. Significantly, like Britain before her, the U.S. preaches the virtues of free trade to achieve commercial goals. These hegemonic powers contend free trade ensures competitiveness.

Marxists also deride free trade for strangling infant industries in the Third World. The European colonial powers made industrial organization among local populations difficult, partly by taxing products consumed by locals, such as alcohol, animals, opium, or salt. To get income to meet their tax obligations, colonized peoples had little choice but to work on plantations or in mines owned by colonial masters. When the colonies gained independence, they lacked diversified economies. With few goods to export, other than primary products, their export revenues were vulnerable to market vicissitudes. They also were not hedged against First World protectionism. Sugar is one example. Poor countries sought to market access for sugar exports, yet the U.S. maintained since the late 1940s tight quantitative restrictions on sugar imports, and encouraged sugar substitutes like artificial sweeteners. The EU subsidized sugar beet production.

---

[12] *Id.*

Countries throughout Latin America, as well as India, resorted to Import Substitution policies in the 1950s through 1980s. Mainstream economists criticized them for doing so. Efforts to prefer local raw materials and intermediate goods, and local production, to imports were inconsistent with the national treatment obligation found in GATT, and their abandonment became a condition for receiving funds from the World Bank. Yet, critics like Walden Bello, in his 1994 study *Dark Victory*, argue a poor country receiving a structural adjustment program loan experiences an increase in commodity exports, but not always an increase in GNP. Why not? Because abandoning Import Substitution led to a net contraction in the domestic economy.

More generally, such critics see lending as a technique of colonialist control. In the mid-1800s, France lent money to the *bey* of Tunis, particularly through bonds, to help the *bey* develop an army and loosen ties with Turkey. (*"Bey"* is a Turkish word for the governor of a province in the Ottoman Empire.) The French bondholders obtained the help of the French Foreign Office to supervise finances in the *bey's* economy. In the great game against the Ottoman Empire for control in the Middle East, the Foreign Office was happy to oblige. In 1869, a Franco-Tunisian Commission imposed stringent conditions on the *bey*, and took the right to collect and distribute state revenues to ensure bondholders were preferred over other creditors. With public finance under foreign control, Tunisia slid into colonial status. When the *bey* needed to raise taxes to pay interest on the bonds and other loans, popular unrest ensured. France responded in predictable fashion. In 1881, to secure its interests, it annexed Tunisia.

Critics charge the formalities of lending are different in contemporary times, but not the underlying control relationships. In exchange for emergency lending to Mexico during the *peso* crisis in 1995, President Bill Clinton imposed similar terms on the Government of Mexico as the French had on the *bey* over a century earlier, namely, conditions to ensure the priority of Wall Street creditors. The IMF and World Bank, through their lending programs, effectively takes over management of the economy of a borrower to ensure timely repayment of principal and interest. The result now is *de facto* colonial control. Conversely, countries such as Singapore and Taiwan, which have been able to minimize external debt, have performed well. Korea, which did take on debt, resisted pressures from the IMF and World Bank to eliminate trade barriers and capital controls until it, essentially, had exported its way out of the debt.

Furthermore, say Marxists, it is hypocritical for the U.S. to advocate free trade given its early history. No less than Alexander Hamilton, in his famous 1791 *Report on Manufacturers*, called for protectionism in the service of economic nationalism. The U.S. maintained high duty rates through 1832, gradually reducing them between 1832 and 1860. To this day, the U.S. resorts to protectionist measures to serve powerful domestic constituencies, as the sugar example indicates.

Even temporary, episodic retreats from free trade did not stop colonialism. Marxists point out that whenever a colonial power implemented protectionist measures, capitalist entrepreneurs simply relied on foreign direct investment (FDI), and the overt colonial control by their home-country governments, to secure new markets. This process occurred in Africa, Asia, Latin America, and the Pacific in the 1870s and 1890s, when economic depression led some European countries (other than Belgium, the Netherlands, and Britain) to raise tariffs. By 1878, Europeans had colonized 67 percent of the land surface of the planet. By 1914, Europeans colonized 84.4 percent.

Within individual poor countries, some scholars surmise this process has resulted in dualistic economic growth. Dualism, or the creation of a dual economy, refers to a phenomenon in which there are two different sectors. Typically, one sector is capital-intensive and relatively wealthy, and the other sector is labor-intensive and relatively poor. The two sectors are not integrated with one another. Writing in the 1950s, the Burmese economist, Hla Myint, argued colonialism led to dualism. He finds the theory explaining exports from developing countries is not Ricardo's comparative advantage principle, but rather a pre-Adam Smith theory known as "vent for surplus." As the rubric suggests, export markets are a "vent" for "surplus" production.

To be sure, at early stages of growth, poor countries have little if any surplus production to export. They lack an integrated national market that would generate sizeable demand for products. But, as foreign businesses enter a country, often as part of a colonial linkage or legacy, they build an infrastructure to support expanded production. They do so because foreign demand would support output growth, *i.e.*, overseas buyers (especially in colonial countries) would consume the surplus. Yet, Myint observes the infrastructure they built does not serve to integrate a labor-intensive agricultural sector with a capital-intensive industrial sector in the host country.

To the contrary, the infrastructure served to integrate one or the other sector directly to the home, *i.e.*, colonial, country (*e.g.*, in Europe, or the U.S.). Specifically, road networks and railway lines, plus attendant communication lines, led directly from farm areas or mines to port facilities to facilitate shipment of crops and natural resources to the home country. The routes were not designed to link these input sources with emerging industrial producers in other parts of the host country. Consequently, the agricultural and natural resource sector generated an exportable surplus, and became the export sector. Products from this sector were land-intensive, and in some instances even capital-intensive. In contrast, industrial production stagnated, hence so too did demand for skilled labor. The end result was two different, non-integrated sectors.

Likewise, the economist Gunnar Myrdal wrote in his classic *Asian Drama* (1968) and in other works, about dualism. He points out it results in increased income inequality within a poor country, as owners of factors of production in the export sector become wealthier, but factor resources in the rest of the economy see no real increases in demand for their services. Classic examples are tea plantation owners in Ceylon (Sri Lanka) and India, palm oil, rubber and tin plantation owners in Indonesia and Malaysia, and mine owners in Sub-Saharan African countries. The large supply of labor in agriculture and mining ensures wage rates are low, and thus profits to owners high. The emphasis on this sector leads to dualistic development, as no integrated national market develops and local industries are neglected, even deliberately suppressed. In turn, dualism means the economy and export base of the poor country remain undiversified — a problem plaguing virtually all least developed countries.

Marxist-oriented scholars view international trade law as part of an overall free-trade framework that creates optimum conditions for First World businesses. From their perspective, this law is a control device in favor of capitalist enterprise, not an empowerment mechanism for the Third World. In most Third World countries, raw power exercised from major trading nations is not necessary to enforce the laws in the framework. The political influence of the hegemons, felt through free-trade oriented rules articulated in and enforced through WTO agreements and FTAs, does the job. Indeed, this legal network is far more extensive than the British Empire ever was.

Ostensibly, this framework is palatable because the field on which trading nations compete is said to be level. Even if it were, the imbalance in political and economic might render the result of any competition unfair. In fact, the field is anything but level. Marxist-oriented critics argue the rules of the GATT—WTO game are designed to create favorable conditions for MNCs. The rights of MNC entry and establishment, removal of restrictions on repatriating earnings, abolition of tariff and non-tariff barriers (particularly for components used by MNCs in production), liberalization of the labor market (to ensure cheap labor unprotected by unions), and national treatment are oft-cited examples of such rules. The favorable conditions are low costs of production, docile laborers, un-enforced environmental standards, and little if any competition. Consequently, roughly 20 to 30 percent of world trade occurs within MNCs (*i.e.*, between different parts of a vertically integrated MNC, such as a parent and one of its subsidiaries). Many world commodity markets are characterized by monopoly or oligopoly conditions, with 40 percent or more of a particular market being controlled by less than 5 companies.

Official U.S. and EU trade delegations consistently advocate for these rules. They do so behind a self-serving veil that the rules are needed to attract trade and FDI, which, in turn, will propel development in poor countries. If and when a poor country resists, the response from representatives of the major powers is "fine, our businesses will go elsewhere." That is, they play poor countries off against one another to tilt the field in their favor. As few such countries are large or powerful enough to continue resisting, the end result is global corporate colonialism protected by international trade law.

Aside from this corpus of law, another feature of the free-trade framework — one that also bespeaks continuity between colonial and post-independence eras — concerns elites. For a capitalist in the First World, what better way to safeguard long-term market access than to have allies in the private and public sectors of the Third World? The British understood the point clearly after the 1857 Indian (or Seapoy) Mutiny, thereafter focusing on the creation of an Anglicized Indian elite that would keep the Indian populace under control and thereby support British commercial interests.

To what extent are the interests of elites in developing and least developed countries any more aligned with the needs of the majority of their countrymen than in the 1800s? Marxists argue the elites of today are akin to the colonial administrators of yesteryear. The large percentage of foreign aid that consists of security assistance of one kind or another (*e.g.*, military training, weapons) is designed to promote the rule of law, not as goal in its own right, but as a means to the fundamental aim of advancing neo-colonial interests. When a Third World leader threatens this aim, the First World — led by the U.S., Britain, other European countries, or some coalition of the interested — takes action. Examples involving the U.S. to which Marxists point include:

1. The American military intervention in Guatemala in 1954, which resulted in the overthrow of a government that nationalized American-owned banana plantations.

2. The American-inspired military *coup d'état* in Brazil in the 1960s, which led to the overthrow of a government that tried to limit the amount of currency a foreign corporation could withdraw from Brazil, initiate a land-reform program that would have returned control of mineral resources from such corporations to locals, and raise wages (leading to higher labor costs for these corporations).

3. Efforts throughout the 1960s and 1970s to remove Fidel Castro from power in Cuba, as he had not only nationalized American business property, but also had agreed to the positioning of Soviet nuclear weapons on Cuban soil.

4. Overt and covert military engagements in Latin America and the Caribbean in the 1980s, including El Salvador, Grenada, and Nicaragua, all of which had Marxist-oriented governments threatening American business interests.

5. High- and low-intensity conflicts in the Middle East, including the 1991 Gulf War and the 2003 Iraq invasion, which at bottom were at least as much about securing oil supplies as fighting terrorism.

Indubitably, each one of these examples, and perhaps any illustration Marxists trot out, is open to considerable debate.

To reduce every instance of the use of force as motivated by a search for new markets, cheap labor, raw materials, or the need to shore up faltering elites is simplistic. Neither the Korean nor Vietnam War is well explained by those rationales, as neither Korea nor Vietnam was a major market or input source at the time of the conflicts. The Marxist perspective also implicitly degrades the contribution of military personnel from the U.S. and its partners. They might be surprised to learn they are helpless, gullible soldiers in the service of an international capitalist conspiracy manipulated by misguided patriotism and rhetoric about spreading peace and democracy abroad.

Nonetheless, the perspective matters, because it resonates in contemporary trade debates. For instance, Marxist-oriented critics fault FTAs, especially for poor countries (*e.g.*, in Latin America) or countries with natural resources (*e.g.*, in the Middle East), as being more about neo-colonialism and less about development. Similarly, FTAs between countries like the U.S. and Australia, or the U.S. and Singapore, are rewards to countries that act as deputy sheriffs to enforce American commercial interests.

B. Frank and Dependency Theory

One of the most provocative schools of thought in development economics to emerge in the 20th century is known as "Dependency Theory." Dependency Theory (in one form or another) resonates in many contemporary debates about trade liberalization and its purportedly salubrious implications. This intellectual debt, however, sometimes goes unrecognized or ignored by economists. For example, while one prominent Textbook (*Economic Development* (2003) by Professor Stuart Lynn of Assumption College) covers the theory, another higher-profile text (*Economics of Development* (4th ed. 1996) by Professor Malcolm Gillis of Rice and Professors Dwight H. Perkins, Michael Roemer, and Donald R. Snodgrass of Harvard) devotes not a word to it.

The father of Dependency Theory is Andre Gunder Frank. Writing in the 1960s, Frank's target was a large one — world capitalist development from the 1400s onwards. Frank studies, along with the work of Immanuel Wallerstein, showed a division of the world into two categories:

     a.   A small number of developed or "metropolitan" countries, collectively called the "center" or "core." The Group of Eight (G-8) countries would be considered the center.

     b.   A large number of un- or under-developed, or "satellite" countries, collectively called the "periphery." Most developing and all least developed countries would be considered the periphery.

This division draws on Marxist-Leninist theory. Marx saw capitalist growth occurring through the accumulation of capital at home and, later, abroad. Lenin argued as capitalists produce ever-increasing amounts of goods and thereby drive down profit rates in their domestic markets, they force themselves to search overseas for new markets.

Frank and other Dependency Theorists elaborate on and extend these ideas. The center drives the development process in the periphery, and that process is a capitalist one. The center uses military power, directly or indirectly, to secure supplies of raw materials and cheap labor for its enterprises. Typically, those enterprises export raw materials back to the center for use in manufacturing, or if engaged in production in the periphery, use labor-intensive methods of production. The enterprises repatriate their profits, or leave them in the hands of local business elites. These elites become a capitalist class in the periphery reliant on the enterprises for their wealth and privileges. Over time, the center gets relatively more developed, taking resources from the periphery, and the periphery relatively less-developed, being drained of those resources. The capitalist class in the periphery facilitates the disparate development.

Frank has a memorable caption for the process — the "development of underdevelopment." The caption embodies the hallmark of Dependency Theory: a peripheral country can develop economically, but only in inverse relation to the strength of its ties to the center. The stronger the ties that bind a peripheral country to the center, the harder it is for the country to develop. The world's least developed regions are the ones with the closest historical ties to Europe and the U.S. Only a large dose of autonomy from the center allows for real development. Hence, the Theory holds that expanded trade is orthogonal to the development interests of poor countries, because it is innately exploitative in favor of rich countries. By implication, the Theory (in contrast to Marxist-Leninist ideology) does not stress class struggle as the force driving historical progress.

This conclusion is entirely contrary to the pro-globalization, pro-free trade tide that has dominated mainstream legal, business, policy, and academic circles in most countries since the end of the Cold War. It suggests developing and least developed countries are foolish to enter FTAs or CUs with developed countries. Yet, the conclusion resonates favorably among an influential group of thinkers and activists in various international and nongovernmental organizations, and in parts of the academy. To be sure, they are not all so radical as to counsel a complete break of economic linkages with the major powers, as ardent Dependency Theorists would. But, they advise a re-balancing of the interactive relationships, and are more patient with Import Substitution, infant industry protection, and trade policies that carve out space for poor countries.

Frank's conclusion, in particular, is based on historical and empirical research focusing on Brazil and Chile. Until the late 1920s, the center-periphery pattern existed, meaning the center countries established the conditions under which peripheral countries developed, or better put, remained underdeveloped. The break from this pattern came when two cataclysmic events distracted the major powers. Between 1929 and 1945, Europe and the U.S. could not dictate the conditions of development, because of the Great Depression and Second World War. During this period, Frank said, the likes of Brazil and Chile were able to develop autonomously. But, when the War ended, dominance by the major powers resumed. Interestingly, Frank also observed in some regions, there were small center-periphery patterns, for example Brazil and its neighbors.

C. The Prebisch-Singer Thesis

Along with the work of Dependency Theorists, the scholarship of the Argentine economist Raul Prebisch provides critical theoretical footing for Import Substitution. Prebisch served with the United Nations Economic Commission for Latin America, and was the first Secretary General for the United Nations Commission on Trade and Development (UNCTAD). Writing in the 1950s, he argued trade causes deterioration in the price of primary products exported by poor countries. In contrast, prices of manufactured goods — the main exports from rich to poor countries — are stable or rising over time. Therefore, the TOT of poor countries deteriorate. Faced with lower export earnings and higher import costs, they are unable to generate savings necessary for capital investment, and thus to industrialize. Participation in trade actually reinforces the international division of labor in which they are trapped in a pattern of producing and exporting primary commodities and natural resources. The research of another economist, Hans Singer, echoes these conclusions. Together, their argument about declining TOT and entrapment in the trading system is called the "Prebisch-Singer Thesis."

This Thesis runs counter to a standard classical and neoclassical prediction in favor of free trade. That prediction is free trade ought to lead to an improvement in the TOT of a country. Increased demand in several other countries for the exports of one country should result in higher prices for those exports. At the same time, lower trade barriers (*i.e.*, a fall in tariffs and quotas) in that country should mean a drop in prices of imported merchandise, as well as in the price of like or directly competitive domestically made goods. Thus, the ratio of export prices, PEX, to import prices, PIM, which is the definition of the TOT, should rise. However, when Prebisch examined data from 1870 to 1936, he found the TOT rose for developed countries, but not developing countries. Singer's findings supported the conclusions Prebisch reached.

Empirical evidence from the 20th century concerning primary product exports, in which developing countries tend to specialize, indicates long-term price declines. Overall, during the First World War (1914-18) and the Great Depression (1929 through the early 1930s), prices of primary commodities fell. They recovered during the Second World War. During the 1950s and 1960s, there was no general trend. In the mid-1970s, these prices spiked, and thereafter remained constant at higher levels during the 1980s and 1990s. In 1997, De Soto published a study of prices of 24 different major commodities from 1900 to 1992. He found the prices trended downward for 17 commodities, increased for 4 commodities, and exhibited no pattern (downward or upward) for 3 commodities. During the same period, prices of merchandise imported by developing countries rose steadily, indicating a TOT decline for many such countries.

Naturally, Prebisch asked why the TOT of developing countries deteriorate as a result of trade. One answer is known as "immiserizing growth." If a country exports a product in sufficiently large volumes, and if those exports account for a substantial share of total world supply of the product, then the exports may cause a fall in the world market price of the product. The country is a large player in the market — such as, for instance, Brazil in the coffee market — and this size redounds to its detriment. The more it exports, the greater the downward pressure on the price of the product, which in turn means PEX deteriorates. Put in graphical terms, the world market supply curve for the product shifts outward, and assuming all other factors are unchanged (*ceteris paribus*), the price falls.

Is it possible to apply the immiserizing growth answer to small developing countries? The response depends on the product in question. Suppose several small developing countries make the same or a substitutable product, and their cumulated exports account for a sizeable portion of world supply. Primary commodities, like banana, cocoa, rubber, and tea provide classic examples. Then, should they increase their exports, the world supply by definition increases substantially, and the product price falls.

Prebisch offered a number of other possible reasons for the decline in developing country TOT associated with trade:

Engel's Law

A well-known principle in microeconomics, which empirical evidence bears out, is as income rises, the portion of income spent on necessities — particularly food — falls. This principle is known as "Engel's Law." Simply put, as people become richer, they spend a smaller percentage of their overall budget on food than they did in the past. Engel's Law is based on a behavioral tendency to consume different goods in different proportions as income rises — in particular, as consumers obtain higher levels of income, their spending patterns shift toward luxury items. Stated in economic terms, there are differences in the income elasticity of demand for products. The income elasticity of demand is the percent change in the quantity demanded of a product that is associated with a given percent change in income. Expressed arithmetically, it is:

$$\text{Income Elasticity of Demand} = \frac{\text{Percentage Change in Quantity Demanded of a Product}}{\text{Percentage Change in Income of a Consumer}}$$

Income inelasticity occurs if the ratio is less than 1, and income elasticity exists if the ratio exceeds 1. Thus, if income rises by 10 percent, and demand increases by more than 10 percent, then the product is said to be "income elastic." If a 10 percent rise in income leads to an increase in demand of less than 10 percent, then it is "income inelastic."

Primary commodities, which are and go into food products, and which are necessity items, tend to be income inelastic. Manufactured goods, which typically are not necessities, tend to be income elastic. Thus, Prebisch argued, as income rises, the demand for products in which developing countries specialize (primary commodities) rises less rapidly than the demand for products in which developed countries specialize (manufactured goods). Increases in income may occur in developed countries (as they get richer), in developing countries (as segments of their society grow richer), or both.

Asymmetric Benefits from Technology

Prebisch alleged technological gains do not have the same impact in developed and developing countries. In developed countries, improved technology helps bolster labor productivity. Wage rates tend to be "sticky downward" for structural reasons, including organized worker groups (*e.g.*, unions). Likewise, product prices tend to remain strong, because of imperfect competition among suppliers (*i.e.*, monopolistic or oligopolistic product markets). In contrast, in developing countries, technological enhancements do more than increase productivity. They also replace labor, and result in lower product prices. Structural features in place to keep wages from sliding do not exist in most poor countries. Some product markets in those countries may be characterized by monopoly or oligopoly, yet the world market for the product is competitive, thereby allowing for price declines with increased exports of the product. Therefore, urged Prebisch, the net effect of technological enhancement on relative TOT is asymmetric. For developing countries, technological improvements lead to a fall in export prices and, hence, falling TOT. For developed countries, these improvements do not put downward pressure on the price of their exports, so there is no adverse effect on their TOT.

Substitution Effects

Prebisch pointed out substitutes have been invented for several products in which developing countries specialize. Examples include petrochemicals (*e.g.*, plastics), which substitute for rubber, and synthetic fibers (*e.g.*, nylon and rayon), which substitute for natural fibers (like cotton). Consequently, the demand in developed countries for the specialty of developing countries has slowed or fallen. In turn, from the perspective of developing countries, the price of that product, PEX, has not increased, and possibly declined. This price is PIM from the perspective of developed countries. The effect on relative TOT is apparent — the TOT of developing countries (where PEX is the numerator of the TOT ratio) is stagnant or drops, and the TOT of developed countries (where PIM is the denominator) stays the same or rises.

Protectionism

Prebisch argued the trade policies of developed countries are to blame, in part, for the failure of the TOT of developing countries to improve with international trade. These policies tend to work against trade liberalization on products of keen export interest to developing countries. Tariff and non-tariff barriers remain high, and tariff escalation exists, on such products. Demand for these products does not increase markedly. Hence, PEX, as viewed by developing countries, does not rise.

The Prebisch-Singer Thesis has not gone without challenge. Three basic categories of questions are put to it. First, as a conceptual matter, is it appropriate to focus on the Net Barter TOT (*i.e.*, the ratio of PEX to PIM) rather than Income TOT (*i.e.*, the ratio of PEX x QEX to PIM, where QEX is the quantity of goods exported, hence the numerator represents export revenues, the price of exports multiplied by the volume of those exports)? Focusing on income TOT reveals export revenues a country generates, which it can use to pay for imports.

Second, how good are the data Prebisch used? A number of problems existed with these data. For example, the period examined, 1870 to 1936, ended during the Great Depression, before world agricultural process recovered. Had the period been different (either shorter, ending before the Depression, or longer, ending after it), prices of developing country exports, PEX, might not have been so low. Further, the price data included transportation costs (*e.g.*, shipping charges), which may have distorted the underlying values for PEX and PIM. Indeed, between 1870 and 1936, transportation costs fell considerably. During this period, the quality of certain goods improved, but these improvements were not necessarily reflected in increased prices. Still another illustration of data problems concerns missing data. Prebisch did not have statistics on exports from Argentina to Great Britain, so he had to infer the value and volume of these exports by examining British statistics on imports from Argentina.

Third, is it insightful to speak of the TOT of developing countries generally? When data are disaggregated by region, not every developing region shows declining TOT. For example, the TOT for Asia are stable or improving. For

Latin America, the trend is improvement in the mid-1970s, followed by long-term decline. The TOT for Middle East countries, particularly oil exporters, depends heavily on oil prices. The point is developing countries are heterogeneous in what they export, and to where. Measuring TOT for this diverse group risks obfuscating success stories with problem cases.

D. Policy Implications of the Prebisch-Singer Thesis

Notwithstanding the challenges to the Prebisch-Singer Thesis, the policy implications of the Thesis are clear: developing countries should diversify their export base by industrialization. That is, rather than rely on exports of agricultural products, they should move into markets for manufactured products — and, by extension of the Thesis, into services. Once they establish a position in certain finished goods markets, these countries can "work backwards" and develop industries in intermediate goods. That is, they can build linkages in their economy, with the end results being vertically integrated industries, improved human capital and technology through industrial development, and less dependence on certain imports from major countries.

Exactly what manufactured products (and services) a particular developing country specializes in depends on its comparative advantages. The Heckscher-Ohlin Theorem may be of assistance. It predicts a country will specialize in the production and export of a product that uses intensively in its production the factor (capital equipment, human capital, labor, land, or technology) with which the country is relatively well endowed. Still, answering "what to export?" is a challenge for many countries.

This question relates directly to market access in developed countries. Suppose a developing country aspires to specialize in refined chocolates (and thereby lessen its dependence on cocoa exports) and dress shoes (and thereby lessen its dependence on leather exports). But, suppose also the tariffs on these products in major markets are high (e.g., there are tariff spikes), or there is tariff escalation (i.e., the tariff on a finished product exceeds that on inputs). The developing country will have little luck in penetrating these markets, unless it can orchestrate barrier reduction through multilateral trade negotiations under WTO auspices, or through talks to form an FTA or CU.

Not surprisingly, in considering "what to export?" a closely related question arises, namely, "how to diversify?" Might it be better for a developing country to eschew trade liberalization temporarily? The logic is that of the infant industry: new industries in a developing country cannot withstand international competition at early stages. In contrast with established industries in developed countries, infant industries in developing countries have not yet achieved low-cost production methods or realized economies of scale (i.e., declining long-run average costs of production), and their output is not of high quality. If faced with direct competition from developed country industries, the infants will not survive, as consumers in developing countries would prefer cheaper, better imports rather than domestically made like or directly competitive products. Private sector financiers would be unwilling to lend funds to the infant industries, because their high costs and low profits render them risky borrowers. In this scenario, a period of protection from import competition will allow the infants to mature, at which point they can compete globally. Financing from development banks, and the government (of the developing country), either directly through grants or "soft" (*i.e.*, low-interest, long-term) loans, or indirectly through guarantees, may be needed.

To be sure, after the American Revolution, no less than Alexander Hamilton, in *Report on Manufactures* (1791), offered this logic for high tariffs. A developing country at the time, America needed to establish an industrial base. Hamilton said it should do so through such protection. In the process, it could gain economic independence from Europe, an aspiration dubbed "economic nationalism." However, free-trade oriented economists point out problems with the infant industry-economic nationalism argument.

First, protection tends not to be removed after its economic purpose is served. Political lobbying from leaders in the protected industry results in mollycoddling long after the infant has matured. The end result of protection may be the creation of a domestic monopoly. As a related matter, the initial imposition of protection, as well as its continuation, presumes the government of the developing country is astute at picking an industry with strong potential to develop an international comparative advantage. Not all such governments, and not all such planners, are skilled at this strategic thinking.

Second, if developing country officials furnish information to private financiers about the long-term viability of infant industries, then they may adjust the tenor of loans. Specifically, lenders may permit long maturity dates sufficient to encompass the time needed to realize economies of scale. Also, a government can subsidize either interest rates or production, and either policy is more efficient than protection.

Third, the challenge infant industries face in some developing countries is not production cost or quality, but infrastructure in a country. Most of the Indian Subcontinent, in contrast to China, is a case in point. Throughout much of the Subcontinent, roads, utilities, and port facilities range from mediocre to decrepit. (Not surprisingly, the Subcontinent attracts service-based businesses like call centers, which rely less on infrastructure than traditional manufacturing.) Protection will not address this challenge. Only government-led initiatives will make a difference. Dismantling trade barriers may facilitate infrastructure improvement, as foreign-based providers of heavy equipment and expertise needed to build roads, utilities, and ports flow in.

E. Empirical Evidence

Export pessimism, Dependency Theory, and the Prebisch-Singer Thesis have been important rationales used by many developing countries to justify Import Substitution. They imposed high tariffs and non-tariff barriers (especially quotas and import licenses) to make imports more expensive or restrict the availability of imports, and thereby gave preference to domestic producers.

Brazil is a notable example. It opted for Import Substitution in response to the Great Depression and Second World War. Table 39-1 shows its consequent shift to domestically made goods. Arguably, because of that strategy, Brazil advanced from reliance on primary products and T&A to intermediate goods. Likewise, Korea employed Import Substitution in the 1950s and 1960s.

Eschewing dependence on foreign firms for technology, Korea honed its own know-how. Table 39-2 shows the impact of the strategy on industrial output and industrial exports. Both statistics rose considerably. Import Substitution proponents point to the strategy as a, if not the, key reason.

TABLE 39-1:
BRAZIL AND IMPORT SUBSTITUTION, 1939-1958

Sector and Year	1939 Percent of Total Industrial Output Accounted for by Sector	1958 Percent of Total Industrial Output Accounted for by Sector
Food and T&A	63%	18%
Intermediate Goods (*e.g.*, equipment, metal goods, machinery, and minerals)	44%	33%

TABLE 39-2:
KOREA AND IMPORT SUBSTITUTION, 1950s AND 1960s

Statistic and Year	1960	1965
Share of Industrial Output in GDP	19%	24%
Share of Manufactured Goods in Total Exports	13%	61%

Obviously, Import Substitution is one strategy in an overall policy mix. A developing country implements it along with policies on exchange rates, interest rates, wages, prices in various markets, and the balance of payments. For example, it may make little sense for a country with a large population, indeed labor surplus, to embark on an Import Substitution strategy that favors capital-intensive production, without further policies to employ the large labor pool and develop its skills. Yet, this result can occur, by design or effect, through exchange rate policies (*e.g.*, keeping them artificially high to facilitate imports of capital equipment) or interest rates (*e.g.*, keeping them artificially low, or subsidizing them, to encourage borrowing for capital equipment purchases). Proper policy coordination, and adaptation of policies to changing economic circumstances, both of which imply a sound policy formation process, are necessary for the right integration of Import Substitution and supporting initiatives.

India is a case in point of good and bad results from Import Substitution. From its Independence on 15 August 1947 to approximately 1991, it pursued this strategy in many sectors. Protection of domestic industries took the form of high tariff rates and the requirement of a license to import. On the one hand, India achieved some degree of independence from imports of certain chemicals, fertilizer, iron, some machinery, petroleum, and steel. Indians are proud (sometimes excessively so) of their innovative and self-reliant economy. On the other hand, corruption abounded with the so-called "License Raj" system, as would-be importers offered bribes to obtain a precious license to import and thereby, in effect, become a monopolist. Moreover, protection led to diversification into product lines in which India lacked a strong potential for comparative advantage, and dependence on some kinds of foreign technology. A domestic producer, once it obtained a license to import technology, was safe from foreign competition for the product in which it incorporated the technology — it had no incentive to innovate.

Nevertheless, for most mainstream economists, the success stories do not amount to persuasive evidence for Import Substitution. They reiterate the well-known classical and neoclassical arguments about the net costs associated with tariffs and quotas: the protection necessary for Import Substitution imposes a dead weight loss caused by inefficient allocation of factors to producing the protected good, and by diminished consumption opportunities. Further, the economic consensus points to counter-evidence on failures in specific countries, and to repeated mistakes associated with this strategy.

As for failed cases, Ghana, Mexico, Pakistan, Tanzania, and Uruguay are among the examples. They experimented with Import Substitution, but implementation was poor and accompanied by inappropriate policies that distorted exchange rates, interest rates and wages, as well as the prices of various imported and domestic goods. Ghana, Mexico, and Pakistan are particularly worthy of note.

Ghana gained independence from Britain in 1957. In 1961, it adopted Import Substitution. The average tariff rate jumped from 17 to 25 percent, and import licenses were mandatory. Table 39-3 shows some near-term results, through 1966. The long-term effects of Import Substitution, which Table 39-4 shows, were unequivocally negative.

TABLE 39-3:
NEAR-TERM EFFECTS OF IMPORT SUBSTITUTION IN GHANA

Statistic and Year	1962	1966
Composition of Imports	Over 50% of imports are consumer goods	30% of imports are consumer goods 65% of imports are capital goods and materials
Growth in Manufacturing	Growth of 10% per year between 1962-66	Growth of 10% per year between 1962-66

TABLE 39-4:
LONG TERM EFFECTS OF IMPORT SUBSTITUTION IN GHANA

Statistic and Year	1950s	1980
Per capita GNP	20 year decline starting in 1950s	20 year decline starting in 1950s
Investment Rate (Investment as a percent of GDP)	20%	5%
Exports (Exports as a percent of GDP)	30%	12%

A *coup d'état* in 1966 changed political leadership. It also ushered in modest trade policy changes, though not until the 1980s did Ghana abandon Import Substitution. Its roughly 20 million people remain poor by any measure — low *per capita* GNP (U.S. $400, ranking it 166 in the world), low life expectancy (57 for men and 59 for women), and low literacy rates with a large gender gap (79 and 61 percent for men and women, respectively).

Why did Ghana fail to grow through Import Substitution? First, tariff rates were not coordinated. Consequently, the Effective Rate of Protection was over 200 percent for some domestic industries, but negative for export industries. Some export industries were faced with the ridiculous situation of having to pay an amount for imported raw materials and components greater than the value of the exported finished product they made. Second, obtaining an import license depended on arbitrary and capricious behavior by government officials. Worse yet, officials solicited — and got — bribes in exchange for licenses. Corruption in license administration, and the trade regime generally, became rampant. Third, the local currency was fixed against foreign currencies. It could not depreciate when Ghana experienced inflation (as market forces would require, because of the increase in supply of local currency that contributed to inflation). With an over-valued exchange rate, exports other than cocoa did not rise. Cocoa export revenues slumped as world market prices for cocoa fell. This environment discouraged entrepreneurs from investing in businesses that could help diversify the export base of the country. Fourth, on manufacturing, two policies encouraged capital-intensive production: minimum wages and interest rate ceilings. Minimum wages raised the cost of labor relative to capital. Credit cost caps encouraged borrowing for capital equipment expenditures. Yet, with a growing population, Ghana needed labor-intensive investments.

Mexico is an important case of policy change. Following Import Substitution for decades, in the early 1980s, Mexico reversed course. It began liberalizing its restrictive trade and investment regime, and withdrawing from state intervention in the economy. In 1986, Mexico acceded to GATT. Commencing free trade negotiations with Canada and the U.S. in the early 1990s, Mexico impressed its partners with its commitment to reform, manifest in new IP protection laws. It became a *NAFTA* Party to the *North American Free Trade Agreement* (*NAFTA*) as soon as *NAFTA* took effect (1 January 1994).

Mexico has over 50 FTAs. They cover its key export markets, including Japan. These accords evince Mexico's dedication to trade liberalization, as they entail international legal commitments to openness and reform. Not surprisingly given their experience and sophistication, Mexican trade officials and practitioners assist countries in Central America in conducting trade negotiations, including with the U.S. on the *Central American Free Trade Agreement (CAFTA)*.

As for Pakistan, Dorosh and Valdes construct a model of its economy.[13] They apply data from 1983-87 to the model, not only on Import Substitution, but also agricultural price and exchange rate policies. They conclude the combined effects of these policies lowered wheat production by 24 percent, and rice production by 52 percent. Posing the counterfactual, if Pakistan had not adhered to Import Substitution and the other policies, then incomes of farmers from 5 major crops would have been 40 percent higher. Another interesting counterfactual is whether and how better economic performance might have altered subsequent history, including the October 1998 military *coup d'etat* by General Pervez Musharraf, and internal battles against Islamic extremism (especially in the North West Frontier Province, Balochistan, and Karachi).

As for often-repeated mistakes with Import Substitution, critics point first and foremost to the political difficulty of removing trade barriers and subjecting domestic industries in developing countries to import competition. The period of protection is one in which captains of the domestic industry become adept at rent-seeking behavior, leading them to lobby for continued protection rather than enhance the competitiveness of their businesses. Insofar as these businesses produce consumer goods, consumers in the developing country are stuck with high-priced, low quality goods. If a developing country has a small market, then it may not be able to support a large number of producers, which reinforces the tendency toward monopoly (or oligopoly). Yet, at the same time, the country remains dependent on imports for capital equipment. To finance such imports, the country may need to borrow from official or private sources, especially if its performance in export markets for consumer goods is lackluster, leading to an increase in foreign debt. In brief, Import Substitution often is a recipe for inefficient, even corrupt, imperfect competition in consumer goods markets, plus increased dependence on foreign physical and financial capital.

A second set of mistakes concerns the relationship of the agricultural to industrial sector. Import Substitution raises the cost of imported seeds, fertilizers, and equipment used by farmers in a developing country. Moreover, this approach sometimes is coupled with maintenance of an overvalued exchange rate. A higher-than-market exchange rate allows a developing country to reduce the cost of imports of approved items, such as capital goods needed for industrialization (because at the higher rate, the country can convert a unit of its currency into more units of foreign currency than the market would justify, and then use the foreign currency to buy needed items). Yet, the overvalued exchange rate makes agricultural exports less attractive to foreign buyers (because they get less units of the developing country currency per unit of their currency than a free currency market otherwise would allow, and thus their purchasing power is reduced).

---

[13] *See* Paul Dorosh & Alberto Valdes, *Effects of Exchange Rate and Trade Policies on Agriculture in Pakistan*, INTERNATIONAL FOOD POLICY RESEARCH INSTITUTE RESEARCH REPORT NO. 84 (Dec. 1990).

The result is TOT deterioration, not internationally, but domestically, namely, between the rural and urban sectors within a country. That is, farmers are worse off because their costs are higher, and sales lower, relative to the industrial sector. This situation, if pronounced or prolonged, can lead to social unrest in rural areas. Economically, it can cause a decline in the balance of trade, and create dependence on borrowing from overseas, thereby leading to (or exacerbating) debt problems.

What, then, is the "bottom line" about Import Substitution versus Export Orientation? The debate is highly contentious, yet it may be said the consensus of economists favor Export Orientation. "Consensus" here does not mean essential unanimity, as it does in WTO decision-making. Rather, it means the majority of economists, and perhaps the caveat should be added that the pool of economists involved is trained in neoclassical economic theory. The consensus would agree trade is not the only engine of growth, but it can be an engine of growth, if other complementary factors exist, not the least of which is good governance and a strong rule-of-law framework.

Chapter 40

SPECIAL AND DIFFERENTIAL TREATMENT

We make a living by what we get, we make a life by what we give.
— Sir Winston Churchill (1874-1965)

Documents Supplement Assignment

1. *Havana Charter* Articles 1, 8-15, 24, 55-70
2. GATT *Preamble* and Articles XXXVI-XXXVIII
3. Tokyo Round *Enabling Clause*
4. WTO *Agreement Preamble*

I. NON-RECIPROCAL TRADE PREFERENCES AND PART IV OF GATT

A. The Intellectual Background: Prebisch and Baran

Part IV of GATT, which was added to GATT in 1966, bears the rubric "Trade and Development." This Part consists of the final three Articles in GATT — XXXVI, XXXVII, and XXXVIII (along with *Ad Articles*). These Articles grew out of concern for development challenges facing Third World countries after the Second World War. The challenges prompted calls to re-balance the trading system to help poor countries.

Specifically, Third World countries called for a complete overhaul of the rules governing world trade. They wanted rules to construct a system that took account of their interests. The unfettered free-flow of goods across borders, prescribed by Adam Smith's logic of absolute advantage and David Ricardo's law of comparative advantage, was unacceptable. Free trade seemed somehow to reinforce inequality between rich and poor countries, and to facilitate neo-colonization, through economic rather than political or military might, of the Third World by the First World.

Leading the calls on behalf of the Third World were the renowned economists, Raúl Prebisch and Paul Baran. In the 1950s and 1960s, Prebisch spoke from two influential positions, Executive Secretary of the United Nations Economic Commission for Latin America (ECLA), and Secretary General of the United Nations Conference on Trade and Development (UNCTAD). In 1964, during Prebisch's tenure (which lasted until 1968) as the first UNCTAD Secretary General, UNCTAD published a highly influential document — *Towards a New Trade Policy for Development*, more commonly known as the "Prebisch Report." Baran was a Stanford University economist and renowned exponent of Marxist-Leninist thinking. Baran issued the call most impressively in writing, publishing *The Political Economy of Growth* in 1957. Now largely forgotten in the American economic academy, at the time it probably was the most widely read book on development in the world.

The likes of Prebisch and Baran argued Third World countries could not compete in the great game of cross-border trade on an equal basis with developed countries. Poor countries needed tariff preferences to ensure access for its goods to developed country markets. Through special market access, poor countries would be able to increase their exports and foreign exchange earnings. In turn, they could use those earnings, and the opportunities, linkages, and know how from increased exports, to diversify their economies. The consequence would be reduced dependence on foreign trade, specifically, on imports from the developed countries of the western world.

In what was a highly charged debate, the Prebisch-Baran side called for six specific reforms to world trade rules, designed as a package to help Third World countries achieve an "attainable minimum" level of participation in the trading system, and thereby of development through that participation:

1. *Market access for primary commodities*: Primary commodities should be given easier access to the markets of major industrial countries. True, some developed countries, such as the U.S., Canada, and Australia, are big exporters of primary commodities. However, many less developed countries are major producers and net exporters of primary commodities.

2. *Purchasing power and price stabilisation*: The purchasing power generated from export earnings of less developed countries should be higher, and it should be stabilised. Stabilisation should occur through two devices: commodity agreements designed to influence prices; and compensatory financing mechanisms. (The first device implicates the exception in Article XX(h) for international commodity agreements). The rationale behind this proposal was many less developed countries rely for foreign exchange earnings on one or a few commodities. The earnings of such countries are adversely affected by swings in the prices of their exports. Of course, commodity price pacts can be fragile, and break apart. (Cases in point are the near-constant controversies in the Organisation of Petroleum Export Countries (OPEC) over production quotas.)

3. *Preferences for industrial products*: There should be preferences for industrial products from less developed countries, particularly from infant industries in these countries. Preferences would assist emerging industries in less developed countries find external markets for their output, and thereby facilitate the industrialization process in these countries. The early rounds of multilateral trade negotiations under GATT auspices succeeded in reducing tariffs on goods produced by developed countries, particularly advanced manufacturers such as cars, machine tools, and computers. However, for lower-value added manufactured items (*e.g.*, textiles, shoes, etc.) trade barriers did not fall so dramatically or rapidly. Developed countries produced these items, but the industries making them were marginally profitable. These industries successfully lobbied for protection from relatively low-cost manufacturers in less

developed countries. Put bluntly, rich countries were reluctant to lower barriers to overseas low-value added manufacturing industries, and sought to protect themselves from low-wage competition. Moreover, in spite of the non-reciprocity rule in Article XXXVI:8, rich countries observed most poor countries had little of value to offer in return for expanded market access for exports from less developed countries.

4. *Import substitution*: Less developed countries should be allowed to protect their industries from foreign competition. Again, the rationale was to assist new industries in those countries, particularly those industries that make components, in securing a customer base among domestic producers of finished products. Moreover, as the rationale went, producers of intermediate goods in less developed countries might benefit from protection from foreign competition in the sense of being able to find external markets for their products.

5. *Trade with socialist countries*: Trade with socialist countries should be expanded under long-term accords. Clearly, this proposal is outdated. It reflected the era in which it was made, when a large number of development thinkers — particularly in the Third World — had faith in state planning.

6. *Trade in "invisibles" and debt servicing*: More attention should be paid to trade in intangible items, and the burden of servicing external debt should be reduced by re-adjusting loan periods and terms. Given the importance of intellectual property (IP) and services, and the continued (indeed worsened) Third World debt problem, this proposal is as relevant today, if not more so, as when offered.

Few of these proposals found their way into "hard law." Developed countries and their advocates rejected (or diluted to the point of meaninglessness) some (cynics would say most) of the proposed reforms. Viewing matters in the context of Cold War politics, they tended to dismiss UNCTAD as a polemical forum for attacking the U.S. and Europe, and to condemn the economic ideology of Prebisch and Baran as leftist and anti-free market.

Still, Prebish, Baran, and their supporters could point to two "hard law" victories. First, in the 1970s, some developed countries implemented preferential tariff schemes for imports from less developed countries. The Generalized System of Preferences (GSP) is the leading example. Second, in 1966, GATT contracting parties elevated special and differential treatment to a new level, adding Part IV to their constitutional document.

B. The 1958 *Haberler Report*

To be sure, more than the work of Baran and Prebisch was behind the second achievement. In November 1957, the Contracting Parties created a three-person group of experts, and appointed Dr. Gottfried Haberler as chair of this Panel. The terms of reference of the Haberler Panel were to examine "past and current international trade trends and their implications." The Panel was to make "special reference" to

> certain trends in international trade, in particular the failure of the trade of less developed countries to develop as rapidly as that of industrialized countries, excessive short-term fluctuations in prices of primary products, and widespread resort to agricultural protection.

The Panel issued a document in October 1958, formally entitled *Trends in International Trade*, but colloquially known as the *"Haberler Report."*

The *Haberler Report* "galvanized" the GATT community "to examine ways in which developing countries could achieve greater access for their exports in world markets." During the next few years, discussions about trade and development intensified, as did negotiations about ways to adjust GATT obligations to ensure trade could realise its full potential in contributing to the economic growth of poor countries. The tangible result of this activity of the late 1950s and early 1960s was Part IV, *i.e.*, Articles XXXVI, XXXVII, and XXXVIII.

On 8 February 1965, in Geneva, the GATT Contracting Parties agreed to the "Protocol Amending the General Agreement on Tariffs and Trade to Introduce a Part IV on Trade and Development." By that Protocol, Part IV was enshrined in GATT, and it entered into force in 1966. (For the U.S., Part IV took effect on 17 June 1966. *See* 17 U.S.T. 1977, 572 U.N.T.S. 320.) In GATT history, it was the largest, most significant, and last amendment.

II. THE SUBSTANTIVE CONTENT OF ARTICLES XXXVI-XXXVIII

A. Overview

Is Part IV of GATT a set of meaningless platitudes? Arguably, "no." There is substantive "hard law" content in its three Articles. Broadly speaking, Articles XXXVI, XXXVII, and XXVIII call for exceptional — or "special and differential" — treatment for "less developed countries." When, in 1966, the Articles were added to GATT, the distinction between "developing" and "least developed" countries was not made. The 1979 *Enabling Clause* formally introduced this distinction into multilateral trade law. Accordingly, the term "less developed countries" is understood as an umbrella one, to refer to both types of poor countries — developing and least developed.

What kind of special and differential treatment for less developed countries does Part IV envision? In brief, Article XXXVI identifies objectives concerning the link between trade and development, distinguishes between earnings generated by primary product exports and market access for industrial products, and establishes the important principle of non-reciprocity. Article XXXVII lays out commitments of developed contracting parties (WTO Members) to less developed contracting parties (Members), and even establishes a skeletal framework for resolving disputes about whether a country in the first category meets its obligations. Article XXXVIII links the objectives set forth in Article XXXVI with by the Contracting Parties (*i.e.*, joint action by the Members), calling for collective action to further those objectives.

B. Non-Reciprocity and GATT Article XXXVI:8

Perhaps the most famous, and likely the most abused, provision in all of Part IV of GATT, which concerns Trade and Development, is Article XXXVI:8. This Paragraph contains a "non-reciprocity rule," or more accurately, a "non-expectation of reciprocity rule." The mandate (and, it is a mandate) is that developed contracting parties *do not expect reciprocity* in trade negotiations to reduce or remove tariffs and other barriers to the trade of less-developed contracting parties. An Interpretative Note, *Ad Article XXXVI Paragraph 8*, reinforces the language of the Paragraph itself, and clarifies the context for the rule is trade negotiations.

The rule is forgotten or neglected in the public pronouncements of plenty of trade policy officials from developed countries, when they opine about what impoverished countries should do. Indeed, the rule has been forgotten or neglected for so long, some less developed country officials seem either unaware of it, or no longer put any hope in it. In practice, now and for many years, is a tendency to adhere to the tradition of conducting and evaluating trade negotiations on the basis of reciprocity. Yet, to forget about Paragraph 8 is to forget about the most significant substantive provision of Part IV, because it is a hard law commitment vis-á-vis less developed countries.

Paragraph 8 is a quintessential example of a rule embodying an unconditional benefit for poor countries. In exchange for whatever a developed country offers, nothing is to be expected. Money is given, though in an indirect manner. Developed countries are obligated not to ask for a reciprocal reduction, or for elimination, in a tariff or non-tariff barrier. When a rich country offers concessions on protectionist measures, Paragraph 8 tells it not to ask for equivalent concessions from poor countries.

Accordingly, rich countries give up a customary and legal right to ask — indeed, to demand or else withdraw their concession offers — for reciprocity. That right is inherent in any kind of negotiations, other than (perhaps) a pure charitable donation. Yet, the fact of legal history is they held onto that right until the 1964-67 Kennedy Round. At that juncture, they took the major step of codifying a new practice through Article XXXVI:8.

Article XXXVI:8 is more than just a rule by which developing countries are obligated to forgo a legal right to insist on reciprocity. It is a rule mandating they acquiesce in continued protectionism by poor countries. To be sure, according to standard capitalist economic theory, including Ricardo's principle of comparative advantage, it is almost never in the interest of a less developed country to maintain high tariff or non-tariff barriers. There are net gains from increased trade, even if the increases result from unilateral dismantling of barriers. Still, Paragraph 8 allows a less developed country to maintain these measures, while developed countries tear down their barriers. Consequently, a less developed country can continue to accrue revenue from tariffs, and reap rents from quotas and other non-tariff barriers (*e.g.*, import licensing requirements). The permitted revenue and rents are a financial transfer from rich to poor countries.

Specifically, they are a transfer of funds from exporters in developed countries (on whose goods tariffs are imposed, or whose goods are affected by quotas or licensing requirements) to the governments of less developed countries. It cannot be assumed these funds will be managed properly or put to good use. Quite possibly, a certain percentage (in some Third World contexts, 10 percent) is vulnerable to misappropriation by unscrupulous behaviour. Corruption aside, accrued revenues and rents are available to the governments to help their countries industrialise. For example, they can be deployed for industry-enhancing infrastructure, like roads, power plants, ports, and schools.

Moreover, it may be argued the protection afforded by the permitted tariff and non-tariff barriers gives time to "infant" industries in the Third World for growth and maturation. During the period of protection, the infants may mature into strong, profitable, job-generating industries. Absent the protection, the infants might die from premature exposure to foreign competition. In effect, foreign competitors incur not only the direct costs of protection (*e.g.*, higher tariff liabilities on their exports to Third World countries), but also an opportunity cost. Lost profits (*i.e.*, potential profits foregone in favour of the infant industries as a result of the protection) are the opportunity cost. Here, then, is another financial transfer.

Significantly, Paragraph 5 of the 1979 Tokyo Round *Enabling Clause* relates closely to Article XXXVI:8. Paragraph 1 of the *Clause* contains the waiver from the Article I:1 MFN principle for contracting parties (*i.e.*, WTO Members) to grant "differential and more favourable treatment to developing countries." Paragraph 2 defines such treatment to include tariff preferences, and specifically mentions GSP programmes, and non-tariff preferences. Tariff and non-tariff preferences are a form of assistance to poor countries. Paragraph 5 of the *Enabling Clause* is a reaffirmation — indeed, reincarnation — of Article XXXVI:8.

Are financial benefits transferred via practice of Article XXXVI:8 obtained by poor countries without any condition whatsoever? The question is rather difficult. A careful reading of Paragraph 8 reveals no condition put upon less developed countries. They are to benefit from "no expectation of reciprocity," regardless of their existing array of tariff and non-tariff barriers, and regardless of their offers (or lack thereof) to reduce these barriers. Simply put, rich countries are not to demand reciprocity, period.

An Interpretative Note to Article XXXVI:8. *Ad Article XXXVI, Paragraph 8* elaborates on what "do not expect reciprocity" means. This *Ad Article* says:

> "do not expect reciprocity" means, in accordance with the objectives set forth in this Article, that the less-developed contracting parties *should* not be expected, in the course of trade negotiations, to make contributions which are *inconsistent* with their individual development, financial and trade needs, *taking into consideration* past trade developments. (Emphasis added.)

The use of the very "should" is sloppy drafting. The main Paragraph uses an imperative construction that creates an obligation (namely, that developed countries "do not expect reciprocity"). Careful drafting of the *Ad Article* would have conveyed the same obligatory sense as the main Paragraph.

Consequently, the *Ad Article* suggests a developed country could expect a less developed country to offer some reciprocal trade concession. Does this suggestion mean the rule in the main Paragraph is conditional? The answer is "no." The suggestion is carefully limited. The *Ad Article* is not an unrestricted license for a developed country to demand concessions of poor countries. It merely allows a developed country to take into account the specific economic circumstances — the "individual development, financial and trade needs" — of the poor country with which it is negotiating. It also allows it to consider past trade developments. In some circumstances, it may be fair for the rich country to ask of the poor country some modest reduction in tariff or non-tariff barriers, subject to the highly significant caveat the reduction is consistent with the specific circumstances and trade trends relevant to that poor country.

Suppose, then, a poor country maintains prohibitive barriers in a particular product market. In a recent three-year period, that country has gained a large share in many foreign markets for the product. Suppose, further, a drop in the barriers to imports of that product from a "prohibitive" level to a "stiff" level (*e.g.*, from a 100 percent tariff to a 20 percent tariff) would not affect adversely the performance of producers and exporters. Would it be reasonable for a developed country to ask for that kind of drop? *Ad Article XXXVI, Paragraph 8* says "yes." Put differently, this Interpretative Note provides some guidance as to when the "do not expect reciprocity" rule of the main Paragraph terminates. It does not make the rule conditional. Rather, it helps identify the outer limits of the scope of application of the rule.

C. Collaboration, GATT Article XXXIII, and the 1980 *Sugar Refunds* Case

Among adopted GATT panel reports attracting little attention, one concerns Part IV, and deals specifically with Paragraph 1 of Article XXXVIII. It is the 1980 case of *EC — Refunds on Exports of Sugar (Sugar Refunds)*. A complaint lodged in November 1978 by Brazil against subsidization by the European Communities (EC) of sugar exports triggered the *Sugar Refunds* case. Australia, Cuba, India, and Peru supported Brazil's complaint. Indeed, Australia had brought a case against the EC on essentially the same facts, and Brazil cited that case in its favor (though the result of that case was somewhat inconclusive). The thrust of Brazil's complaint did not involve Part IV. Rather, Brazil focused on Article XVI:3, arguing refunds on sugar exports granted by the EC resulted in European exporters obtaining more than an equitable share of world export trade in sugar.

Brazil decried the EC's substantial subsidies of sugar, which consistently exceeding international prices of the product. These subsidies were one part of the EC's Common Agricultural Policy (CAP). Brazil alleged the EC was "unrestrained" in its "use of massive subsidies."[1] The EC "had turned from a net importer into a sizeable net exporter of sugar by displacing more efficient producers, mostly less developed countries, at a time of world over-

---

[1] GATT Panel Report, *EC — Refunds on Exports of Sugar*, B.I.S.D. (27th Supp.) 69-98 (March 1981) (adopted 10 Nov. 1980), ¶ 2.6 at 72.

production."[2] (The EC retorted such a change was irrelevant under Article XVI.)

After its six findings under Article XVI, the Panel came to its final conclusion:

> The Panel recognized the efforts made by the European Communities in complying with the provisions of Articles XXXVI and XXXVIII. It nevertheless felt that increased Community exports of sugar through the use of subsidies in the particular market situation in 1978 and 1979, and where developing contracting parties had taken steps within the framework of the *ISA [International Sugar Agreement]* to improve the conditions in the world sugar market, inevitably reduced the effects of the efforts made by these countries. For this time-period and for this particular field, *the European Communities had therefore not collaborated jointly with other contracting parties to further the principles and objectives set forth in Article XXXVI, in conformity with the guidelines given in Article XXXVIII.*[3]

What constitutes joint collaboration? Might it be said that while Article XXXVIII is rarely invoked, when it is used, it can have real significance?

III. THE BOP EXCEPTION FOR DEVELOPING COUNTRIES TO GATT OBLIGATIONS

A. India's Consultations with the GATT—WTO BOP Committee

Like many developing countries during their history, India maintained quantitative restrictions on imports based on a BOP justification. India's restrictions, however, were extensive, affecting 2,714 tariff lines at the 8-digit level of its HS tariff schedule. In May 1997, during consultations, India gave notice of these restrictions to the WTO Committee on Balance-of-Payments Restrictions. It also had given notice in July 1996. Yet, the history of these restrictions and the consultation procedure is far longer than the late 1990s. India had been consulting under GATT Article XVIII:B in the Committee on Balance-of-Payments Restrictions regularly since 1957.

During consultations in November 1994, the Committee stated that it appreciated the courage and sagacity with which India had carried out its economic reform program. It encouraged India to continue implementing its import liberalization program. The Committee noted that, assuming India's BOP showed sustained improvement, India's aim was to move to a regime by 1996-1997, in which import licensing restrictions would only be maintained for environmental and safety reasons. Various members of the Committee welcomed the significant improvement in India's BOP situation since the last consultation but recognized it remained volatile.

During the consultations held in December 1995, the Committee again commended India for the wide-scale economic reforms and comprehensive

---

[2] *Id.* at 72.

[3] *Id.* at 97-98 (emphasis added).

stabilization program over the past 4 years. The policies had led to a robust economic recovery. In particular, the reforms, which included a considerable measure of trade and financial liberalization, exchange rate unification and a move to current account convertibility, had contributed to a large increase in the share of trade in India's GDP. The Committee noted that, since 1992, rapid export growth and capital inflows had been the source of the turnaround in India's external sector and the steady increase in the level of foreign exchange reserves.

To be sure, the Committee took note that, in recent months, there had been a deterioration in the trade balance, investment inflows had slowed and the foreign exchange reserves had declined. In addition, the fiscal deficit and the level of indebtedness remained high. The Committee recalled India's stated aim to move, by 1996-97, to a trade regime under which quantitative restrictions would be retained only for environmental, social, health and safety reasons, provided sustained improvement was shown in its BOP. The Committee also took note of the statement by the IMF that, with continued prudent macro-economic management, the transition to a tariff-based import regime with no quantitative restrictions could reasonably be accomplished within a period of 2 years.

The Committee pointed out since the last full consultation, there had been considerable liberalization of India's import regime, including a gradual increase in the number of consumer items that were freely importable. Nevertheless, almost one-third of tariff lines at eight-digit level under the HS classification remained subject to quantitative restrictions. The Committee noted India's view that, in the context of a deteriorating BOP situation, it would be neither prudent nor feasible to consider the general lifting of quantitative restrictions on imports at this stage. In fact, many WTO Members supported India's continued use of import restrictions under GATT Article XVIII:B for BOP reasons in view of the uncertainty and fragility they perceived in India's BOP position. They felt liberalization and structural reform policies should continue at a pace and sequence suited to Indian conditions.

But, many other WTO Members stated India's BOP position was comfortable, India did not currently face the threat of a serious decline in foreign exchange reserves as set out in Article XVIII:9, and therefore India was not justified in its continued recourse to import restrictions for BOP reasons. They asked India to present a firm timetable for the phasing out of the restrictions, and further information required, before the resumption of the consultations.

The Committee welcomed India's readiness to resume the consultations in October 1996, and to notify the WTO of all remaining restrictions maintained for balance-of-payments purposes soon after the announcement of the 1996/97 Export-Import Policy. Consultations resumed in January 1997. The Committee noted the positive developments in India's economic situation since 1995. It welcomed the continued commitment of Indian authorities to economic reform and liberalization, and gave credit for India's progressive removal of quantitative restrictions notified under Article XVIII:B. The Committee also pointed out the IMF had said India's current monetary reserves were not inadequate and were not threatened by a serious decline. The IMF also expressed the view that the import restrictions could be removed within a relatively short period.

In response, India cautioned its BOP needed close monitoring, and the abrupt removal of import restrictions notified under Article XVIII:B could undermine the stability of its economy and the reform process. The Committee agreed to resume the consultations with India at the beginning of June 1997 to consider a proposal from India on a time-schedule for the elimination of its remaining import restrictions notified under Article XVIII:B and to conclude the consultations consistently with all relevant WTO balance-of-payments provisions.

In May 1997, India notified the Committee of the import restrictions under Article XVIII:B it was maintaining pursuant to its Export-Import Policy for 1997-2002. India also offered a time schedule for the removal of its remaining import restrictions. The schedule was 9 years, from 1 April 1997 to 31 March 2006, divided into three equal phases. India set forth a list of products in respect of which quantitative restrictions on imports maintained under Article XVIII:B had been removed since the last notification of July 1996, as well as the import policy changes announced on 1 April 1997 under its annual Export-Import Policy for 1997-1998.

In June 1997, the Committee resumed consultations with India to discuss the plan. An IMF representative said his position on India's BOP situation had not changed since the January 1997 consultation. During the consultations, all Members expressed their appreciation of India's commitment to eliminate the import restrictions over time and commended India on the comprehensiveness, transparency and timeliness of the plan.

But, many Members voiced concern about the length of the time-schedule. Some agreed India should adopt a cautious approach, others encouraged an acceleration of the phase out. Some Members considered India's BOP situation no longer justified continued recourse to Article XVIII:B. Accordingly, during the June 1997 consultations, India offered to revise the phase-out plan to 7 years. Under the plan, India would eliminate most of the import restrictions in two phases of a length of 3 years each. It would phase out restrictions on a number of items of high sensitivity (or bound at very low rates of duty) during the third phase, reduced from 3 years to 1 year. The Committee could not reach a consensus on India's revised timetable.

B. India's Staggering BOP Restrictions

At issue in the 1999 *India — Quantitative Restrictions* case are a staggering number of import barriers — 2,714. The barriers fell into two broad categories: import restrictions (*i.e.*, tariffs and quotas), and import licensing. All were justified by India under GATT Article XVIII:B as legitimate BOP restrictions. What was the basis under Indian law for the BOP measures? There were several relevant pieces of domestic legislation, described below. They are not unlike the legal authorities found in other developing countries. What makes India particularly instructive is that its domestic legislative framework for regulating imports is a sort of "worst case" scenario. The extensive nature of the framework, combined with endemic corruption associated with license applications and approvals, help explain why many observers of the Indian scene contend the economy is hamstrung by a "license raj" system.

Section 11 of the Customs Act, 1962:

This law provides that the Central Government of India may, by notification in the *Official Gazette*, prohibit (absolutely or subject to conditions), as specified in the notification, the import or export of any goods. The listed purposes for such prohibition include, *inter alia*: Indian security; maintenance of public order and standards of decency or morality; conservation of foreign exchange and safeguarding of BOP; avoiding shortages of goods; prevention of surplus of any agricultural or fisheries product; establishment of any industry; prevention of serious injury to domestic production; conservation of exhaustible natural resources; carrying on of foreign trade in goods by the State or by a State-owned corporation; and "any other purpose conducive to the interests of the general public." Under Section 111(d) of the *Customs Act*, goods imported or exported (or attempted to be imported or exported) contrary to any prohibition are subject to confiscation.

The Foreign Trade (Development and Regulation) Act, 1992:

The *"FTDR Act"* replaced the *Imports and Exports (Control) Act, 1947*. Section 3(2) of the *FTDR Act* authorizes the Central Government to prohibit, restrict, or otherwise regulate the import or export of goods, by Order published in the *Official Gazette*. Under Section 3(3), all goods to which any Order under section 3(2) applies are deemed to be goods the import or export of which Section 11 of the *Customs Act, 1962* prohibits (and thereby subject to confiscation under Section 111(d) of the *Customs Act*).

Section 11(1) of the *FTDR Act* prohibits imports or exports by any person except in accordance with the provisions of the *FTDR Act*, the rules and orders made thereunder and the Export and Import Policy currently in force. Under Section 11(2), when any person makes or abets or attempts to make any import or export in contravention of the *FTDR Act*, any rules or orders made thereunder, or the Export and Import Policy, he is liable to a penalty of up to 1,000 rupees, or 5 times the value of the goods concerned, whichever is greater. Section 7 of the *FTDR Act* states that only persons who have been granted an Importer-exporter Code Number (IEC Number) by the Director General of Foreign Trade (DGFT) may import or export. Under Section 9, the DGFT — who is authorized to grant, renew or deny import and export licenses — may suspend or cancel the IEC Number of any person who has contravened customs laws. (The DGFT is located in India's Ministry of Commerce.)

Section 9 of the *FTDR Act* also requires the DGFT to record reasons in writing if he fails to grant or renew an import license. If a license is granted, it specifies both the value and the quantity of the item that may be imported. The reasons for which the DGFT may deny a license are clearly set forth in Rule 7(1) of the FTR Rules, and include, among others: that an applicant is not eligible for a license in accordance with any provision of the Export and Import Policy, 1997-2002; and, in the case of a license for import, that no foreign exchange is available for the purpose.

Section 15 of the *FTDR Act* provides for an appeal of a decision or order made under the *Act*. This appeal right includes any decision to refuse a license. In the case of an order by an officer subordinate to the DGFT, appeal lies to the DGFT. For an order made by the DGFT, an appeal is to the Central Government. In addition, though Section 15(3) of the *FTDR Act* states "the order made in appeal by the Appellate Authority shall be final. . . .", it can be challenged as violating a legal or constitutional right under Article 226 of the Indian Constitution before the High Court of any State in the Indian Union. Additionally, if an alleged violation is of a fundamental right contained in Part III of the Constitution, it can be challenged under Article 32 of the Constitution before the Supreme Court of India. A challenge would lie, *inter alia*, on the ground the decision is arbitrary, irrational or discriminatory. The decision of a High Court in turn can be challenged in an appeal to the Supreme Court under various Constitutional provisions.

Rules and Orders Promulgated under the FTDR Act:

Section 19 of the *FTDR Act* authorizes the Central Government to make rules for carrying out the provisions of the Act, by notification in the *Official Gazette*. The Foreign Trade (Regulation) Rules, 1993 were issued under the authority of Section 19 of the *FTDR Act*. They provide generally for license applications, license fees, license conditions, refusal, amendment, suspension or cancellation of licenses, and enforcement.

The Export and Import Policy 1997-2002:

Section 5 of the *FTDR Act* authorizes the Central Government to formulate and announce by notification in the *Official Gazette* the export and import policy. The first such policy, the Export and Import Policy 1992-1997, was in effect from 1992 until 31 March 1997. The policy currently in effect at the time of the WTO adjudication was the Export and Import Policy, 1997–2002. India has issued Export and Import Policy statements once every 5 years, effective at the 1 April start of the government fiscal year. Revisions during the 5-year period generally are published on 1 April of subsequent years during the 5-year period, although changes may be made and announced in public notices at any time.

The Export and Import Policy 1997-2002 includes the Negative List of Imports ("Negative List") (discussed below). The List is very important, because it sets forth various prescribed procedures or conditions for imports, and the eligibility requirements including export performance that must be met to qualify for Special Import Licenses.

Section 4:7 of the Export-Import Policy 1997-2002 provides that "[n]o person may claim a license as a right and the Director General of Foreign Trade or the licensing authority shall have the power to refuse to grant or renew a license in accordance with the provisions of the Act and the Rules made thereunder."

In April 1997, India published *The Handbook of Procedures* effective for the period 1997 to 2002. *The Handbook* contains the procedures that must be followed to export or import specific goods, and provides application forms for import licenses. The ITC (HS) Classifications relates the rules set forth in the Export and Import Policy and the *Handbook* to the 8-digit product categories set forth in the HS for commodity classification. For each product listed at the 8-digit level, the *Handbook* indicates 5 types of information in 5 columns: the 8-digit code; the item description, the applicable policy ("prohibited," "restricted," "canalized." or "free"); any conditions relating to the Export and Import Policy (these conditions appear either indicated with the particular item or in licensing notes at the end of the HS Chapter or section thereof); and an indication of whether the product can be imported under a Special Import License.

The Licensing Regime and the Negative List:

India regulates imports by means of the Negative List. If an item is on the Negative List, a prospective importer must apply for a license to the DGFT.

As suggested, the Negative List classifies all restricted imports in one of three categories: "prohibited items," "restricted items," and "canalized items." A "prohibited" item cannot be imported. "Canalized" items may, in principle, be imported only by a designated "canalizing" (government) agency. They are, in effect, the subject of government procurement.

The key part of the Negative List concerns "restricted items." A "restricted" item can be imported only with a specific import license, or in accordance with a public notice issued for that purpose. The most significant "restricted" item on the Negative List is "consumer goods." Naturally, these are items in which American, European, and Japanese exporters are keenly interested.

The Negative List defines the term broadly to include "all consumer goods, howsoever described, of industrial, agricultural, mineral or animal origin, whether in SKD/CKD condition or ready to assemble sets or in finished form." Paragraph 3.14 of the Export and Import Policy further defines "consumer goods" as "any consumption goods which can directly satisfy human needs without further processing and include consumer durables and accessories thereof." Lest there be any doubt, the Negative List also lists 7 product categories to be treated as consumer goods: consumer electronic goods, equipments and systems, howsoever described; consumer telecommunications equipments namely telephone instruments and electronic PABX; watches in SKD/CKD or assembled condition, watch cases and watch dials; cotton, woolen, silk, man-made and blended fabrics including cotton terry towel fabrics; concentrates of alcoholic beverages; wines (tonic or medicated); and saffron.

Suppose a person wants to import a restricted item. The prospective importer must submit an application for an import license to the DGFT, or to an officer authorized by the DGFT (the "licensing authority") with territorial jurisdiction. Import licenses are not transferable. Any person who imports or exports (with or without a license) must have an Importer-Exporter Code (IEC) number, unless specifically exempted. In addition, any person applying for an import or export license must present a Registration-cum-Membership Certificate (RCMC) granted by the Export Promotion Council relating to his line of business, the Federation of Indian Exporters Organisation, or (if the products exported by him are not covered by any Export Promotion Council) the regional licensing authority. The application forms for the RCMC requires the applicant to claim status as a merchant exporter or manufacturer exporter of a specific product or products.

The application form for import of items covered by the Negative List requests information on the applicant's name and address, the type of unit, the applicant's registration number, the end product(s) to be manufactured with licensed capacity, details of the items applied for export, the total CIF (cost, insurance, and freight) value applied for, past production in the previous year, exports done during the previous year, and "justification for import."

Whenever imports require a license, only the "Actual User" may import the goods, unless the Actual User condition is specifically dispensed with by the licensing authority. Paragraph 3.4 of the Export-Import Policy defines "Actual User" as an actual user who may be either industrial or non-industrial. Paragraph 3.5 of the Policy defines "Actual User (Industrial)" as "a person who utilizes the imported goods for manufacturing in his own unit or manufacturing for his own use in another unit including a jobbing unit." Paragraph 3.6 of the Policy defines "Actual User (Non-Industrial)" as "a person who utilizes the imported goods for his own use in (i) any commercial establishment carrying on any business, trade, or profession; or (ii) any laboratory, Scientific or Research and Development (R&D) institution, university of other educational institution or hospital; or (iii) any service industry." The Actual User then cannot legally transfer the imported goods to anyone except with prior permission from the licensing authority concerned, except for a transfer to another Actual User after a period of 2 years from the date of import.

About 10 percent of tariff lines subject to import licensing may also be imported under Special Import Licenses (SILs). Firms receive SILs from the Indian Government in proportion to their exports or net foreign exchange earnings. SILs are issued by the DGFT or regional licensing authorities, and are freely transferable (there are SIL brokers and a resale market for SILs). There are various methods by which a person or firm may apply for a SIL. First, an established private or state-run exporter which meets export performance criteria set forth in Chapter 12 of the Export and Import Policy, and elaborated upon in Chapter 12 of the *Handbook*, can qualify to be recognized by the regional licensing authority or the DGFT as an "Export House," "Trading House," "Star Trading House," or "Super Star Trading House." Such designated exporters automatically qualify for SILs on the basis of entitlement rates set out in paragraph 12:7 of the *Handbook*. Additional bonuses are earned if a designated exporter exports specified products (products made by small-scale industries; fruits, vegetables, flowers or horticultural products; or products made in the North Eastern States) and where over 10 percent of such an exporter's exports are to one or more of 43 listed Central and Latin American countries and territories.

Other exporters can still receive Special Import Licenses equal to 4 percent of the FOB (Free On Board) value of their exports, subject to certain minimum export criteria set out in paragraph 11:11 of the *Handbook*. SILs are also granted to exporters of telecommunications equipment and electronic goods and services; to exporters of diamonds, gems and jewelry; to deemed exporters;

and to small scale exporters holding certain quality certifications of the International Standards Organization (ISO).

C. The Appellate Body's Findings in 1999 *India — Quantitative Restrictions*

WTO APPELLATE BODY REPORT, *INDIA — QUANTITATIVE RESTRICTIONS ON IMPORTS OF AGRICULTURAL, TEXTILE AND INDUSTRIAL PRODUCTS* WT/DS90/AB/R (adopted 22 Sept. 1999)

I. Introduction

1. . . . The Panel was established to consider a complaint by the United States relating to quantitative restrictions imposed by India on imports of agricultural, textile and industrial products.

2. India maintains quantitative restrictions on the importation of agricultural, textile and industrial products falling in 2,714 tariff lines. India invoked balance-of-payments justification in accordance with Article XVIII:B of the GATT 1994, and notified these quantitative restrictions to the Committee on Balance-of-Payments Restrictions (the "BOP Committee"). On 30 June 1997, following consultations in the BOP Committee, India proposed eliminating its quantitative restrictions over a seven-year period. Some of the Members of the BOP Committee, including the United States, were of the view that India's balance-of-payments restrictions could be phased out over a shorter period than that proposed by India. As a result, consensus on India's proposal could not be reached. . . .

. . . .

5. . . . [T]he Panel concluded that:

> (i) the measures at issue applied by India violate Articles XI:1 and XVIII:11 of GATT 1994 and are not justified by Article XVIII:B. . . .

[Omitted it the discussion of the Appellate Body of the Panel's finding that India's BOP measures violated Article 4:2 of the *Agreement on Agriculture*, and nullified or impaired the benefits of the U.S. under GATT and the *Agreement*. Also omitted are the portions of the Appellate Body Report on the competence of the Panel, burden of proof, and objective assessment of the facts under *DSU* Article 11.]

. . . .

V. The Note Ad Article XVIII:11 of the GATT 1994

110. India appeals the Panel's interpretation of the Note *Ad Article XVIII:11* of the GATT 1994 and, in particular, the word "thereupon." India claims that the Panel erred in law in interpreting the word "thereupon" to mean "immediately." According to India, "thereupon":

. . . indicates that there must be a *direct* causal link between the removal of measures imposed [for] balance-of-payments reasons and the recurrence of the conditions defined in Article XVIII:9. (emphasis added)

[The Indian argument, and American rebuttal, on the *Ad* Note issue are worth amplifying. To India, the word "thereupon" is critical because it determines the scope of policy options available to a developing country. It said Note *Ad Article XVIII:11*, in which the word "thereupon" appears, is designed to help a developing country. The *Ad* Note applies in a situation where BOP difficulties have ceased to exist, but there is a threat they might return. India argued its purpose was to authorize a developing country to control the general level of imports over time to ensure imports do not outstrip the country's means to pay for them. By construing "thereupon" as "immediate," the Panel eviscerated the practical applicability of the *Ad* Note.

India said its proposed definition — a less severe one — was more in keeping with the true purpose. By suggesting that "thereupon" means a recurrence of BOP problems must be a *direct* consequence of removing BOP restrictions, India was saying that the removal would lead to a clear, foreseeable rise in foreign exchange expenditure of such a magnitude that foreign exchange reserves no longer would be adequate. (India agreed an "indirect" test would be unworkable, because the indirect consequences of removing BOP restrictions on foreign exchange reserves are too difficult to trace and quantify.) In other words, India feared the Panel's definition of "thereupon" as "immediate" would force developing countries to abandon BOP measures when they could, in fact, foresee serious BOP difficulties on the horizon.

In brief, contended India, there must be a direct link between (1) removal of BOP measures and (2) level of foreign exchange reserve levels. If so, then the measures need not be removed. Put differently, applying India's proposed definition would mean developing countries could remove BOP restrictions gradually, so long as the clear and foreseeable consequence of an immediate removal would be renewed BOP difficulties.

For five reasons, the U.S. backed the Panel's definition. First, it said it was consistent with the interpretive principles of the *Vienna Convention*. Second, the French and Spanish texts of the GATT demanded translation of "thereupon" as "immediately." That is, in these languages, "thereupon" has a temporal — not a causal — meaning. Third, the GATT—WTO texts distinguish between "directly" and "thereupon." For example, the text of the *WTO Agreement* uses the word "directly" in several articles. In contrast, GATT uses "thereupon" in Articles XV:6 and XVIII:18. Fourth, the Panel's definition gives proper effect to the purpose of Note *Ad Article XVIII:11*. That purpose is to ensure remote possibilities are not used as the basis for retaining BOP restrictions when BOP difficulties have ended. Finally, India's proposed definition rested on an implicit assumption that was false. The assumption was that removal of BOP difficulties necessarily would lead to new BOP difficulties. In truth, many developing countries had dis-invoked Article XVIII:B measures without renewed problems.]

111. The Note *Ad Article XVIII:11* provides:

> The second sentence in paragraph 11 shall not be interpreted to mean that a contracting party is required to relax or remove restrictions if such relaxation or removal *would thereupon produce* conditions justifying the intensification or institution, respectively, of restrictions under paragraph 9 of Article XVIII. (emphasis added)

112. The conditions which justify the intensification or institution of balance-of-payments restrictions under Article XVIII:9 (a) and (b) are a threat of a serious decline in monetary reserves, a serious decline in monetary reserves, or inadequate monetary reserves.

113. The Panel found that to maintain balance-of-payments restrictions under the *Ad* Note:

> . . . it must be determined that one of the conditions contemplated in sub-paragraphs (a) and (b) of Article XVIII:9 would appear *immediately after* the removal of the measures, and a *causal link* must be established between the anticipated reoccurrence of the conditions of Article XVIII:9 and the removal. It should be noted that the text requires *more than a mere possibility* of reoccurrence of the conditions ("*would* produce"). The *Ad* Note therefore allows for the maintenance of measures *on the basis only of clearly identified circumstances*, and not on the basis of a general possibility of worsening of balance-of-payments conditions after the measures have been removed. (underlining added [by Appellate Body])

114. We agree with the Panel that the *Ad* Note, and, in particular, the words "would thereupon produce," require a *causal link of a certain directness* between the removal of the balance-of-payments restrictions and the recurrence of one of the three conditions referred to in Article XVIII:9. As pointed out by the Panel, the *Ad* Note demands more than a mere possibility of recurrence of one of these three conditions and allows for the maintenance of balance-of-payments restrictions on the basis only of clearly identified circumstances. In order to meet the requirements of the *Ad* Note, the probability of occurrence of one of the conditions would have to be clear.

115. We also agree with the Panel that the *Ad* Note and, in particular, the word "thereupon," expresses a *notion of temporal sequence* between the removal of the balance-of-payments restrictions and the recurrence of one of the conditions of Article XVIII:9. We share the Panel's view that the purpose of the word "thereupon" is to ensure that measures are not maintained because of some distant possibility that a balance-of-payments difficulty may occur.

116. The Panel considered the various dictionary definitions of the word "thereupon" and came to the conclusion that "the most appropriate meaning should be 'immediately.' " The Panel found support for this interpretation in the context in which the word "thereupon" is used, the objective of paragraphs 4 and 9 of Article XVIII and the *Ad* Note, and the object and purpose of the *WTO Agreement*.

117. We recall that balance-of-payments restrictions may be maintained under the *Ad* Note if their removal or relaxation would thereupon produce: (i) a threat of a serious decline in monetary reserves; (ii) a serious decline in monetary reserves; *or* (iii) inadequate monetary reserves. With regard to the

first of these conditions, we agree with the Panel that the word "thereupon" means "immediately."

118. As to the two other conditions, *i.e.*, a serious decline in monetary reserves or inadequate monetary reserves, we note that the Panel . . . qualified its understanding of the word "thereupon" as follows:

> We do not mean that the term "thereupon" should necessarily mean within the days or weeks following the relaxation or removal of the measures; this would be unrealistic even though instances of very rapid deterioration of balance-of-payments conditions could occur.

119. We agree with the Panel that it would be unrealistic to require that a serious decline or inadequacy in monetary reserves should actually occur within days or weeks following the relaxation or removal of the balance-of-payments restrictions. The Panel was, therefore, correct to qualify its understanding of the word "thereupon" with regard to these two conditions. While not explicitly stating so, the Panel in fact interpreted the word "thereupon" for these two conditions as meaning "soon after." This is also one of the possible dictionary meanings of the word "thereupon." [The Appellate Body here cited *The Concise Oxford English Dictionary* (Clarendon Press, 1995) at p. 1447.] We are of the view that instead of using the word "immediately," the Panel should have used the words "soon after" to express the temporal sequence required by the word "thereupon." However, in view of the Panel's own qualification of the word "thereupon," the use of "immediately" with respect to these two conditions does not amount to a legal error.

120. We, therefore, uphold the Panel's interpretation of the *Ad* Note and, in particular, the word "thereupon."

VI. The Proviso to Article XVIII:11 of the GATT 1994

121. India claims that the Panel erred in law:

. . . by requiring India to use macro-economic and other development policy instruments to meet balance-of-payments problems caused by the immediate removal of its import restrictions.

India argues that such a requirement amounts to a change in its development policy, and is, therefore, inconsistent with the proviso to Article XVIII:11 of the GATT 1994.

. . . .

122. The second sentence of Article XVIII:11 provides that Members:

. . . shall progressively relax any restrictions applied under this Section as conditions improve, maintaining them only to the extent necessary under the terms of paragraph 9 of this Article and shall eliminate them when conditions no longer justify such maintenance;

and adds the following proviso:

> *Provided* that no contracting party shall be required to withdraw or modify restrictions on the ground that a change in its development policy would render unnecessary the restrictions which it is applying under this Section.

123. In reply to a question by the Panel, the IMF stated:

> The Fund's view remains . . . that the external situation can be managed using macro-economic policy instruments alone. Quantitative restrictions (QRs) are not needed for balance-of-payments adjustments and should be removed over a relatively short period of time. . . .

124. In reaching its conclusion that the removal of India's balance-of-payments restrictions will not "immediately" produce the recurrence of any of the conditions of Article XVIII:9 and that the maintenance of these measures is, therefore, not justified under the Note *Ad* Article XVIII:11, the Panel took this statement of the IMF into account.

125. India argues that the Panel required India to change its development policy in order that the removal of the balance-of-payments restrictions would not produce a recurrence of any of the conditions of Article XVIII:9. We disagree. Nothing in the Panel Report suggests that the Panel imposed this requirement. On the contrary, . . . the Panel stated:

> India had in the past used macroeconomic policy instruments to defend the rupee, suggesting that the use of macroeconomic policy instruments as mentioned by the IMF would not necessarily constitute a change in India's development policy.

126. Furthermore, we are of the opinion that the use of macroeconomic policy instruments is not related to any particular development policy, but is resorted to by all Members regardless of the type of development policy they pursue. The IMF statement that India can manage its balance-of-payments situation using macroeconomic policy instruments alone does not, therefore, imply a change in India's development policy.

127. . . . [T]he Panel referred to the following IMF statement:

> The macroeconomic policy instruments would need to be complemented by structural measures such as scaling back reservations on certain products for small-scale units and pushing ahead with agricultural reforms.

128. We believe structural measures are different from macroeconomic instruments with respect to their relationship to development policy. If India were asked to implement agricultural reform or to scale back reservations on certain products for small-scale units as indispensable policy changes in order to overcome its balance-of-payments difficulties, such a requirement would probably have involved a change in India's development policy.

129. We note that the Panel did not take a position on the question whether the adoption of the structural measures of the type mentioned by the IMF would entail a change in India's development policy. The Panel concluded . . . as follows:

> The IMF's suggestions on "structural measures" should not be taken in isolation from the context in which they are made. We recall that the IMF began its reply to Question 3 by stating that India's "external situation can be managed by using macroeconomic policy instruments

alone." Its comments on structural measures appear only at the end of its answer after it has suggested other liberalization measures, such as tariff reductions. The adoption by India of "structural measures" is not suggested as a condition for preserving India's reserve position. Thus, we cannot conclude that the removal of India's balance-of-payment measures would thereupon lead to conditions justifying their re-institution that could be avoided only by a change in India's development policy.

Clearly, the Panel interpreted the IMF statement to the effect that the implementation of structural measures is not a condition for the preservation of India's external financial position. We consider this interpretation to be reasonable.

. . . .

IX. Findings and Conclusions

153. For the reasons set out in this Report, the Appellate Body:

. . . .

    (b)   upholds the Panel's interpretation of the Note *Ad Article XVIII:11* of the GATT 1994 and, in particular, the word "there-upon;" [and]

    (c)   concludes that the Panel did not require India to change its development policy and, therefore, did not err in law with regard to the proviso to Article XVIII:11 of the GATT 1994. . . .

154. The Appellate Body recommends that the DSB request that India bring its balance-of-payments restrictions, which the Panel found to be inconsistent with Articles XI:1 and XVIII:11 of the GATT 1994. . . .

IV. SPECIAL AND DIFFERENTIAL TREATMENT IN WTO AGREEMENTS

Special and differential treatment is not limited to Part IV of GATT. Several WTO texts offer such treatment. However, did the Uruguay Round herald a change in the substantive nature — the generosity — of the treatment?

That is, what patterns emerge from the special and differential treatment afforded by the WTO texts? Does it appear that much of that treatment consists of the length of time a developing or least developed country has to phase in an obligation, or phase out a trade barrier? How does this kind of treatment compare with the treatment afforded by Part IV of GATT? Might it be argued persuasively that GATT provided more generous special and differential treatment than the more recent WTO texts? What would be the basis for such an argument — non-reciprocity, and the relief from obligations, perhaps?

A few WTO texts afford no, or hardly any, special and differential treatment. One example is the *Antidumping Agreement*. Essentially, aside from a higher negligible volume threshold for poor countries, it treats all WTO Members alike.

Other WTO texts were intended to provide considerable assistance to poor countries. The *Agreement on Textiles and Clothing (ATC)* is an example, as it removed (effective 1 January 2005) all quotas on textiles and apparel (T&A). These quotas, set forth under the 1974 *Multi-Fibre Agreement (MFA)*, had regulated global T&A trade, and constrained growth in exports of such merchandise from any one country. Producers sourced merchandise in many countries, so that if the quota for a T&A article (*e.g.*, the American quota on ties from China) were filled, they could ship from another country (*e.g.*, ties from Thailand). Most Third World countries lobbied for, and heralded, the opening of markets — particularly developed country markets — to their T&A articles. It meant exporters could compete in developed country markets based on price and quality, without worrying whether shipments of their merchandise were subject to a quota, and if so, whether the applicable quota had been filled. Finally, as of 1 January 2005, when all *MFA* quotas were abolished, the playing field in the T&A market appeared level.

However, as this date neared, small players like Bangladesh and Sri Lanka realized large players, like China, India, and Vietnam likely would dominate the playing field. No longer needing to spread manufacturing operations across dozens of countries to meet quota limitations, T&A producers responded to the *ATC* by consolidating operations in the large countries. The decision where to open or maintain operations was driven by business concerns (*e.g.*, input sources and transportation costs) and legal risks (*e.g.*, rule of law and the risk of expropriation), not artificial distortions of trade (aside from occasional special safeguard actions, or the threat thereof, particularly against Chinese T&A exports). Had the smaller less developed countries sought and obtained an agreement during the Uruguay Round that now haunted them? Or, had they simply failed to use the decade-long transition period (1 January 1995, when the *ATC* took effect, until 21 December 2004, the last day of *MFA* quotas) wisely by enhancing their attractiveness to multinational producers as a place in which to operate facilities?

V. RECIPROCITY AND EUROPEAN PREFERENCES FOR FORMER COLONIES

In addition to its GSP program, the EU (and its predecessor, the EC), has maintained a PTA for countries in the African, Caribbean, and Pacific (ACP) regions that had been colonies of European powers. The first such program, known as the *Yaoundé Convention*, was signed in 1963 in Yaoundé, Cameroon. The next version was the *Lomé Convention*, signed in 1975 in Lomé, Togo. The preferences afforded by this *Convention* were the subject of the WTO Appellate Body Report in the *Bananas War*. The Convention lapsed in 2000, and was replaced by the *Cotonou Convention*, signed that year in Cotonou, Benin. There are 77 countries, consisting of Anglophone, Francophone, and Lusophone nations, benefiting from the latest *Convention*.

Neither the *Yaoundé* nor *Lomé Convention* required reciprocity of ACP beneficiaries in return for preferential access to the European market. However, the *Bananas War* compelled the EU to re-think discriminatory treatment created by such accords, particularly insofar as poor countries that had not been colonized were disfavored. Accordingly, the *Cotonou Convention* demands

ACP countries cut tariffs on "substantially all" imports from the EU over a "reasonable" period. In practice, "substantially all" may meet two-thirds of EU imports, and a "reasonable" period could be 12 years or more. Failure to follow through means loss of privileges after 2007.

Is reciprocity justified as a condition for benefits? Critics argue "no," partly because it amounts to mercantilism. Interestingly, in March 2005, Her Majesty's Government renounced all "mercantilist" ambitions in British relations with the ACP. Further, reciprocity offends the principle of GATT Article XXXVI:8, and perhaps social justice precepts. But, advocates of reciprocity reiterate the neoclassical economic analysis of free trade, namely, the net benefit accruing to society from tariff reductions, because of the gain to consumers that overwhelms the loss to producers. True, ACP countries faced a significant loss in tariff revenue if they lowered barriers, but perhaps that loss would stimulate advancements, and reduce corruption, in income and sales tax regimes. Advocates also point out three decades after the 1975 *Lomé Convention*, most infant ACP industries had yet to mature. The share held by ACP countries in the EU market had dropped from 8 percent in 1975 to less than 3 percent in 2000.

Does cancellation of one-way preferences catalyze economic reform? A World Bank study by Caglar Ozden and Eric Reinhardt argues "yes," using Chile as an example. In 1988, the U.S. struck Chile from its GSP beneficiary list. Chile dropped its average tariff rate from 20 to 15 percent, partly to cut the cost of imported inputs. Later, Chile embraced an across-the-board 6 percent MFN duty. Coincidence, or cause and effect?

Chapter 41

PREFERENTIAL PROGRAMS

Why is capitalism so robust in some places and failing in others? Why are countries rich in mineral resources often so poor in democratic resources? How can we stimulate economies in developing nations and contain environmental damage at the same time? What simple legal and political steps can we take to harness the tremendous energies of the world's billions of poor?

—President Bill Clinton, *This Conference Will Not Be Like So Many Before It*, FINANCIAL TIMES, 16 September 2005, at 15

DOCUMENTS SUPPLEMENT ASSIGNMENT

1. *Havana Charter* Articles 1, 8-15, 24, 55-70
2. GATT Preamble and Articles XXXVI-XXXVIII
3. Tokyo Round *Enabling Clause*
4. WTO *Agreement Preamble*

I. BACKGROUND TO THE GSP

The idea for a Generalized System of Preferences (GSP) springs from development economics work in the 1950s and 1960s, and particularly in 1964 by the United Nations Conference on Trade and Development (UNCTAD) and its then-Director-General, Raul Prebisch. Tariff preferences granted temporarily and unilaterally by a developed country would increase exports from less developed countries of merchandise in which those countries were not yet competitive. More exports would mean more export earnings (preferably in hard currency, such as U.S. dollars), which less developed countries could use to diversify their economies (*e.g.*, by investing in productive assets in new industries) and reduce their dependence on foreign aid (assuming the revenues are not used for debt servicing or siphoned off by corruption). In the end, the world trading system would become more level, in that all countries could have the opportunity to compete.

By 1968, the U.S. embraced the GSP concept, along with other developed countries. They did so on the understanding that preferences would be subject to safeguard mechanisms to protect domestic industries sensitive to competition from imports that otherwise qualified for tariff-free, quota-free treatment. The U.S. was not the first developed country to establish a GSP program. It did so on 1 January 1976, pursuant to Sub-Chapter V of the *Trade Act of 1974*, as amended, which is codified at 19 U.S.C. §§ 1202, 2461-2467. (The authority provided by the *Act* for duty-free treatment on eligible merchandise from beneficiary developing countries took effect on 3 January 1975, but implementation by the U.S. did not occur for another year.) Earlier, in 1971, both Japan and the European Communities (EC) instituted GSP schemes, and Norway did so in 1972. Canada commenced its General Preferential Tariff (GPT) on 1 July 1974. Indeed, by the early 1970s 19 countries in the Organization for Economic Cooperation and Development (OECD) had GSP schemes.

Accordingly, there is no single or universal GSP program. While each is a nonreciprocal grant of preferences, they differ from one developed country sponsor to the next. In particular, depending on eligibility criteria and margins of preference, some countries are more generous in opening their markets to beneficiary countries than others. The more rigorous the criteria with respect to qualification as a beneficiary and eligible products, the less generous. The smaller the margin of preference, *i.e.*, the difference between duty-free tariff treatment under a GSP program and the normally applied MFN rate, the less generous.

As a preliminary matter, it should be readily apparent nonreciprocal, preferential treatment, such as duty-free and quota-free benefits, for some but not all WTO members violates the MFN obligation in GATT Article I:1. Certain poor WTO Members get the benefits, which are not offered by the developed country Member sponsoring the program to all other WTO Members. That is, there is discrimination against exports originating in a non-beneficiary Member, which are charged the MFN rate and subject to permissible quotas. Without a special dispensation from the WTO Members, or the GATT CONTRACTING PARTIES before them, a GSP-type program would be actionable, regardless of whether or to the extent the program embodies a preferential option for the poor consistent with social justice principles.

Until the Tokyo Round (1974-79), developed countries seeking to sponsor a GSP program dealt with the MFN issue by obtaining a waiver, under GATT Article XXVII, from their Article I obligations. In June 1971, they obtained a 10-year waiver. However, during the Tokyo Round, an *"Enabling Clause"* was drafted, and agreed to, to assure developed and developing countries that the GSP is a permissible exception to the Article I and Article III obligations of GATT. In effect, the *Enabling Clause*, which has no expiry date, made permanent the 10-year waiver granted in June 1971. The *Enabling Clause*, which is contained in the Tokyo Rounds "Texts Concerning a Framework for the Conduct of World Trade," provides the legal basis for "special and differential (S&D) treatment" for developing countries. The *Clause* is known formally as the *Decision on Differential and More Favourable Treatment, Reciprocity and Fuller Participation of Developing Countries*, 28 November 1979.

Significantly, the *Enabling Clause* is not an obligation to establish, maintain, or expand a GSP program. Any Member can do so — or not. Put differently, a GSP program is something of a gift, of varying generosity, not an entitlement, much less unconditional charity. Moreover, the *Enabling Clause* contains the "principle of graduation," whereby less developed countries agree to assume "increased GATT responsibilities as their economies progress."

Conferral of GSP benefits means certain products originating in an eligible country come into the benefactor country (*e.g.*, the U.S.) free of duty or quota. However, the key words are "certain," "originating," and "eligible." Not all countries qualify as beneficiaries. Not all products are eligible. Only an eligible product from a beneficiary that fulfills a preferential rule of origin receives the preference. For example, if gold jewelry from Bangladesh received GSP treatment, then this result would occur because Bangladesh is eligible to be a beneficiary country, gold jewelry is an eligible product, and the shipment of jewelry in question is made in Bangladesh under the applicable rule of origin. Put simply, GSP benefits are akin to a gift that must be earned by fulfilling conditions. Moreover, the gift is temporary. Limitations on the income level of a beneficiary and the market access of a product connote impermanence: the benefits can be withdrawn if a country gets too rich, or a product competes too successfully, in the judgment of the benefactor country.

As indicated at the outset, the American GSP program is set out in Title V of the *Trade Act of 1974*. This legislation has been modified, with important amendments occurring through Section 1111 of the *Trade Agreements Act of 1979*, Title V of the *Trade and Tariff Act of 1984*, and Sections 111(a)-(b) and 114 of the *African Growth and Opportunity Act* (Title I of the *Trade and Development Act of 2000*). Overall, the program is a temporary, unilateral, nonreciprocal grant of preferences to eligible countries on merchandise in sectors of those countries that are not yet competitive internationally. The program includes safeguard mechanisms to protect American industries sensitive to import competition. Hence, there is an underlying tension between extending unilateral assistance to poor countries, on the one hand, and safeguarding American industries, on the other hand. From a practical standpoint, the U.S. Trade Representative (USTR) administers the GSP program.

There are four conceptual steps when representing counsel to a client (*e.g.*, exporter in a developing or least developed country, or importer of merchandise from such a country) seeking GSP benefits for merchandise.

1. *Country Eligibility?*

   Is the country of exportation a Beneficiary Developing Country (BDC)?

2. *Merchandise Eligibility?*

   If the country is a BDC, then is the good a GSP-eligible article?

3. *Origination?*

   If the article is eligible for GSP treatment, does it originate in the country of exportation, under the applicable preferential rule of origin?

4. *General Criteria?*

   Even if a country is a BDC and merchandise is both eligible and originating, are general criteria for extending preferences satisfied?

When in doubt as to any step, the safest legal advice on GSP, as in most customs matters, is to file a ruling request with the Customs and Border Protection (CBP).

At the outset of Sub-Chapter V, 4 general criteria concerning the authority to extend preferences are stated (*See* 19 U.S.C. § 2461).

1. *Effect?*

What effect would granting duty-free status to eligible articles from developing countries have on their economic development, specifically, export expansion?

2. *Other Efforts?*

What comparable efforts (if any) do developed countries other than the U.S. make to assist developing countries by granting preferences on their imports?

3. *Domestic Producers?*

What impact is anticipated on American producers of like or directly competitive products if preferences are extended?

4. *Competitiveness?*

To what extent is a BDC already competitive in respect of an eligible article?

These criteria are general not in the sense of channeling Presidential discretion as to the creation of a GSP program — Congress already has done that. Rather, the criteria are about whether an eligible article from any BDC ought to get GSP treatment. In effect, the criteria presume a country is a BDC, and merchandise from that country is eligible. Put differently, they give interested parties, such as U.S. producers of substitute products, an opportunity to contest against the extension of GSP benefits. The general criteria are one illustration of the less-than-unconditional-generosity that characterizes the GSP program.

A related and significant point is there are two analytical steps in ascertaining eligibility for GSP treatment that do not exist: ownership of an enterprise in a BDC producing eligible merchandise; and distribution of GSP benefits. For example, suppose a major Japanese consumer electronics company, like Sony, produces cameras on the Indonesian island of Batam (off the coast of Singapore, a deep-water port from which the cameras can be exported). Suppose a small family-run business also produces cameras on Batam. Assuming cameras originating in Indonesia are eligible for treatment, the ownership (and, for that matter, structure) of the producer is irrelevant.

Likewise, it does not matter how the benefits of tariff savings from GSP treatment actually are used. Whether Sony and the small Indonesian enterprise pass them to workers, invest them in new capital equipment, or pay them to shareholders in Japan, the U.S., and elsewhere does not affect GSP eligibility. Beyond identification of country and product eligibility, there are no more specifically intended beneficiaries. How, then, is it possible to assure the benefits of GSP treatment flow to people most in need? Or, does that question rest on a misunderstanding of what a GSP program ought to do?

As a practical matter, the GSP program is not permanent. It must be renewed by Congress, which occurs periodically, and which are opportunities for Congress to amend the program. In this respect, there are three general patterns.

First, the renewal periods vary considerably, from a 10 years to 10 months. Second, in some renewal legislation, criteria are added that make receipt of GSP benefits increasingly difficult. Third, the renewal legislation is not always a provision of a trade bill. At times, it is a small piece in a large budget package. Do these observations suggest the U.S. is less than wholeheartedly committed to the GSP concept?

It is quite unlikely the U.S. would abolish its GSP scheme, or that Congress would fail to renew it. However, on a number of occasions, renewal occurs after the sunset date in the statute, and the renewal operates retroactively. To importers, a renewal that is not timely is costly. The CBP typically requires importers to post cash deposit or bond for a shipment of GSP-eligible merchandise, if Congress has yet to renew the program. That way, the CBP is assured duties will be paid if renewal did not occur. When it does occur, CBP returns the deposit to the importer. For small and medium size enterprises (SMEs) that operate on thin profit margins, posting cash deposit or bond can force layoffs or cuts in medical and other benefits. Even getting back the deposit or bond entails the time and expense of proper record keeping, as the CBP must ascertain which importers are owed what amounts.

In 1980, President Jimmy Carter reported to Congress on the progress of the first five years of operation of the GSP program. Since then, the program has been criticized for a number of reasons, including the loss of revenue for the U.S. of tens of millions of dollars. Indeed, budgetary concerns may be the gravest concerns, at least *prima facie*, about the program.

Whenever the program comes up for renewal, respect must be given to the "pay-as-you-go" requirement in Federal budget rules. If the government is going to forego some tariffs on goods from poor countries, then how will it make up the revenue deficiency? Asking this question leads to larger questions about the efficacy of the program, and the criteria under which duty-free treatment is accorded to countries and articles. Such questions were asked, for example, in 1993, when the Clinton Administration lobbied for renewal of the program and extension of GSP benefits to Russia. At the time, Congress (and some members of the Administration) thought seriously about dropping the program.

II. DESIGNATION AS A GSP BENEFICIARY

The authority delegated by Congress to the President to designate a country as a BDC is set forth in Section 502 of the *1974 Act*. (*See* 19 U.S.C. § 2462.) A BDC designation occurs through either an Executive Order or Presidential Proclamation. (*See* 19 U.S.C. § 2467(1).) A BDC can be a country, territory (such as an overseas dependent territory or possession of a foreign country), or group of countries in a free trade area (FTA) or customs union (CU) treated as a single country. (*See* 19 U.S.C. § 2467(2).) For example, on 21 March 1995, President Bill Clinton designated the West Bank and Gaza Strip a BDC. On 7 September 2004, President George W. Bush designated Iraq a BDC (effective 15 days later). The President must notify Congress of any designation (or termination), and give supporting reasons. (*See* 19 U.S.C. § 2462(f)(1).) Once the President grants BDC designation, that country is (along with other

BDCs) listed in General Note 4(a) of the Harmonized Tariff Schedule of the U.S. (HTSUS).

Of course, the delegation from Congress is not unconstrained. There are three kinds of statutory limits on eligibility for BDC designation: income criteria; political considerations; and additional factors:

1. Income Criteria:

The "D" in "BDC" stands for "Developing," so it is logical enough that a country that is not poor is ineligible for GSP treatment. Two criteria assure this result:

(a) Developed Countries.

Developed countries are not eligible for preferential trade treatment under the GSP program. These countries are Australia, Canada, all members of the European Union (EU), Iceland, Japan, Monaco, New Zealand, Norway, and Switzerland. (*See* 19 U.S.C. § 2462(b)(1).) The obvious justification for excluding these countries is they do not need it. However, this justification might be somewhat less persuasive for certain regions with new countries that have joined the EU, and potentially to certain countries or regions therein that might join the EU in the future.

(b) Graduation:

A BDC designee may become a "high income" country as defined by the World Bank. (Indeed, it is hoped a designee does not remain poor.) The cut-off the World Bank used for "high income" is a *per capita* GNP of approximately U.S. $9,206, which covers less than one-sixth of the population of the world (roughly 29 countries with a population of one million or more, totaling 0.9 billion people). If a BDC graduates into this rarified cohort, then the President must terminate its BDC status effective on 1 January of the second year after the World Bank defined it as "high income." (*See* 19 U.S.C. § 2462(e).) Thus, for example, Bahrain, Brunei, Bermuda, and Nauru have been dropped from the list of BDCs, because their *per capita* GNP exceeded the statutory limit.

Query whether there is an argument against the graduation requirement? On the one hand, earlier iterations of the GSP statute did not refer to World Bank cohorts. Rather, the U.S. defined a *per capita* GNP threshold, which periodically adjusted. Reference to the groupings of an international economic organization is less susceptible to domestic political manipulation. On the other hand, the World Bank's cohorts presume an income-based approach to poverty. They say nothing about income distribution or broader measures of development. Thus, a BDC could graduate after crossing into the "high income" cohort, notwithstanding a high and increasing Gini coefficient (indicating greater income inequality) or lower female educational enrollments and labor force participation rates.[1]

---

[1] The *Dictionary of International Trade Law* that accompanies this textbook sets out concepts and ways of measuring income poverty, and Amartya Sen's thesis of poverty as capability deprivation and development as freedom.

2.   Eight Political Considerations:

There is an 8-point list of factors that render a country ineligible for designation by the President as a BDC. This list might be dubbed limitations on eligibility based on the political interests of the U.S.:

(a)   Communism:

A communist country is ineligible. There is one exception: the country, albeit communist, already receives nondiscriminatory (*i.e.*, MFN) treatment from the U.S., is a WTO Member and a member of the IMF, and is "not dominated or controlled by international communism." (19 U.S.C. § 2462(b)(2)(A)(iii).) Until China became a WTO Member effective 11 December 2001, and received permanent normal trade relations (PNTR) status with the U.S., it was ineligible for GSP treatment. Vietnam sought and obtained PNTR status in connection with its bid for WTO Membership (effective 11 January 2007). Could it be said Vietnam is "dominated or controlled by international communism"? Is there any such thing left as "international" communism?

(b)   Cartels:

A country is ineligible if it is a party to an arrangement, the goal of which is "to withhold supplies of vital commodity resources from international trade or to raise the price" of the commodity "to an unreasonable level," and the effect of which is "to cause serious disruption of the world economy." This limitation is for cartels, particularly, the Organization of Petroleum Exporting Countries (OPEC). Insofar as most OPEC members boast high *per capita* incomes, this exception is sensible. However, there are a few notable poor countries in OPEC, such as Nigeria. (*See* 19 U.S.C. § 2462(b)(2)(B).)

(c)   Reverse Preferences:

A country is ineligible if it affords preferential trade treatment to exports from a developed country other than the U.S., and this treatment "has, or is likely to have, a significant adverse effect" on American commerce. This constraint is for "reverse preferences." For example, if a country in the African, Pacific, or Caribbean (ACP) grant duty-free, quota-free treatment to merchandise from the EU, under an accord like the *Cotonou Agreement*, and this grant adversely affects the U.S., then the country is ineligible for GSP treatment. (*See* 19 U.S.C. § 2462(b)(2)(C).)

(d)   Property Rights:

A country is ineligible if it has nationalized or expropriated American property, including intellectual property (IP), or has taken action that is similar in effect to a nationalization or expropriation (namely, nullifying or repudiating an existing contract, or imposing or enforcing taxes or restrictive maintenance or operational conditions). There are three exceptions: the country has provided adequate and effective compensation to the property owner, is in negotiations to provide compensation, or is engaged in arbitration over compensation. This "property rights" limit on eligibility protects not only individual American citizens, but also any corporations, partnerships, or association that is 50 percent or more owned by a citizen. (*See* 19 U.S.C. § 2462(b)(2)(D).) This constraint is redolent of the behavior against which Title III of the *Helms — Burton Act* is aimed, namely, trafficking in American assets confiscated by Fidel Castro's regime in Cuba. That *Act* creates a secondary boycott against, and calls for treble damage liability for, such trafficking.

(e)   Enforcement:

A country is ineligible if it fails to recognize as binding, or enforce, an arbitral award in favor of the U.S. This "arbitration" limit protects individual American citizens, and also any corporation, partnership, or association that is 50 percent or more owned by an American citizen. (*See* 19 U.S.C. § 2462(b)(2)(E).)

(f)   Terrorism:

A country is ineligible if it aids or abets international terrorism (*e.g.*, by granting sanctuary from prosecution for an alleged act), or fails to support the efforts of the U.S. to combat terrorism. (*See* 19 U.S.C. § 2462(b)(2)(F).) This limitation is consistent with the *Iran and Libya Sanctions Act of 1996*, which takes aim at terrorist sponsorship, and at the proliferation of nuclear, biological, and chemical weapons.

(g)   Worker Rights:

A country is ineligible if it fails to afford "internationally recognized worker rights." (19 U.S.C. § 2462(b)(2)(G).) These rights track the 5 most important ones set forth by the International Labor Organization (ILO): the right of association; the right to organize and bargain collectively; a prohibition on forced or compulsory labor; a minimum age for the employment of children (as well as a prohibition on the worst forms of child labor); and acceptable conditions of work (specifically, as to minimum wages, work hours, and safety and health standards). (*See* 19 U.S.C. § 2467(4).) In the GSP context, however, this list is not exclusive. The President must report annually to Congress on the status of internationally recognized worker rights in each BDC. (*See* 19 U.S.C. § 2464.)

(h)   Child Labor:

A country is ineligible if it "has not implemented its commitments to eliminate the worst forms of child labor." (19 U.S.C. § 2462(b)(2)(H).) There are four "worst forms:" slavery in any form (*e.g.*, sale, trafficking, debt bondage, forced or compulsory labor generally or for the armed forces); prostitution and pornography; illicit activities (*e.g.*, narcotics production and trafficking); and work that by its nature "is likely to harm the health, safety, or morals of children." (19 U.S.C. § 2467(6).) The President's annual report on the status of internationally recognized worker rights in each BDC must include discussion of efforts to eliminate the worst forms of child labor in that country. (*See* 19 U.S.C. § 2464.)

Not all political limitations on the President's discretion are equally severe. The President cannot waive the first three limits. However, the President can designate a country as a BDC if it is not in full compliance with any one of the last five restrictions, if that designation "will be in the national economic interest of the United States." (19 U.S.C. § 2462(b).) While the President must report to Congress on what would amount to a waiver of one or more of these eligibility criteria, the words "national economic interest" seem intended to give the President flexibility to escape a restriction. Further, the President must withdraw or suspend designation (by Executive Order or Presidential Proclamation) of any country as a BDC under "changed circumstances," *i.e.*, a country no longer satisfies the political considerations. (19 U.S.C. § 2462(d)(2).)

Interestingly, the list of political considerations has grown longer over time. For instance, Section 412 of the *Trade and Development Act of 2000* added the eighth restriction. Section 4102(a) of the *Trade Act of 2002* prohibited designation of beneficiary status to any country that has not supported the U.S. in combating terrorism. Section 4102(b) of the *Act* added "prohibition on the worst forms of child labor" to the definition of "internationally recognized worker rights." As a general proposition, to what extent is it accurate to say GSP benefits have become more, not less, conditional?

3. Seven Additional Factors:

There are seven further requirements the President must consider in deciding whether to grant BDC status to a particular country. That is, even if a country is not a developed one, and even if it satisfies the aforementioned political considerations, the President must consider the following factors:

(a) Desire?

Has the country expressed a desire to be designated a BDC? (*See* 19 U.S.C. § 2462(c)(1).) In most instances, this factor ought to be a mere formality.

(b) Development Level?

Does the level of economic development of the country, measured by *per capita* GNP, living standards, and other economic factors the President deems appropriate, make it an appropriate designee for BDC status? (*See* 19 U.S.C. § 2462(c)(2).) This factor leaves some room for discretion, as it essentially calls for a decision by the President as to whether the country "is poor enough" for the GSP program.

(c) Other Countries?

Do other major developed countries extend GSP treatment to the country? (*See* 19 U.S.C. § 2462(c)(3).) Arguably, this factor can be used in favor or against a designation of eligibility. On the one hand, getting benefits from other developed countries helps the case of a country for BDC status. It shows other wealthy countries judge the country worthy for such benefits. On the other hand, it hurts the case, because it supports a conclusion the burden of giving is appropriately shared, or that others have done enough.

(d)   Market Access?

To what extent has the country assured the U.S. "it will provide equitable and reasonable access to the markets and basic commodity resources" of the country, and also assured the U.S. "it will refrain from engaging in unreasonable export practices." (19 U.S.C. § 2462(c)(4).) It is difficult to see this factor as other than an expression of self-interest by the U.S., *i.e.*, a kind of *quid pro quo*, contrary to the letter and spirit of GATT Article XXXVI:8, calling for "something in return" for a designation of BDC status.

(e)   IP?

To what extent does the country provide "adequate and effective" IP rights? (19 U.S.C. § 2462(c)(5).) Once again, query the extent to which American self-interest is at play? Query, also, whether this is necessary given the WTO *TRIPs Agreement* and Special 301 in U.S. trade law? Notably, there are lobbying groups carefully monitoring which countries are designated BDCs. For instance, the Coalition for GSP (based in Washington, D.C., and on line at www.tradepartnership.com), is comprised of businesses, trade associations, and consumer organizations. It lobbies for the longest possible extension of the GSP program. However, some of its members have a particular interest in the IP sector (*e.g.*, entertainment and pharmaceutical companies). For them, GSP renewal may be an opportunity to pressure actual or prospective BDCs to tighten enforcement of IPs, by conditioning their support for renewal on such action.

(f)   Investment and Services?

To what extent has the country reduced trade distorting investment practices (*e.g.*, export performance requirements) and barriers to trade in services? (*See* 19 U.S.C. § 2462(c)(6).) The strong U.S. interest in foreign direct investment (FDI) and market access for services again raises the questions of self-interested conditions and insertion of reciprocity into the GSP program. For instance, this factor empowers the President to deny designation of BDC status to a country that offers service schedule liberalization commitments that the President judges insufficient to meet the interests of U.S. financial institutions, telecommunications firms, and other service providers.

(g)   Worker Rights?

To what extent is the country taking steps to afford its workers internationally recognized worker rights? (*See* 19 U.S.C. § 2462(c)(7).) While not to be read as such under basic statutory construction rules, this factor appears superfluous in light of the seventh political consideration above. More generally, it may be queried whether it is appropriate to base GSP eligibility on worker rights criteria. One argument is such rights naturally accrue, or trickle down, as a country grows in prosperity. Oxfam International, however, counters that "[t]he trickle-down discourse of trade incorrectly sees good labor standards as an outcome of economic development, rather than a contributing factor towards it."[2] Accordingly, Oxfam urges "workers' rights and the enforcement of these rights should be seen as crucial determinants of poverty alleviation."[3]

The President may designate particularly poor countries as "least developed beneficiary developing countries" (LDBDCs). To receive this status, a country must be a BDC, and thus must meet all eligibility requirements. (*See* 19 U.S.C. §§ 2462(a)(2), 2467(5).) General Note 4(b) of the HTSUS lists these countries. For example, on 10 January 2003, President George W. Bush designated Afghanistan a BDC (with retroactive effect to 29 January 2001), and an LDBDC (effective 13 February 2003). The benefit (as it were) of LDBDC status is a modestly expanded eligible product list applies to that country.

Summing the limitations above, there are 17 in total — 2 income criteria, 8 political considerations, and 7 additional factors. Are these limitations justifiable, and by what rationale? If the aim of the GSP program is, or ought to be, assistance to poor countries and the promotion of them into healthy trading partners, then what sort of limitations, if any, are justifiable, and why? Should least developed countries have fewer eligibility requirements?

III. GSP — ELIGIBLE ARTICLES

Under authority delegated by Congress to the President, the President may designate articles — *i.e.*, a category of merchandise — as eligible for GSP preferences, namely, duty-free treatment. The designation occurs by Executive Order or Presidential Proclamation. *See* 19 U.S.C. § 2463(a)(1)(A). An article denied designation may not be reconsidered for at least 3 years after the denial. *See* 19 U.S.C. § 2463(a)(1)(C). The President also is authorized to designate eligible articles from LDBDCs.

Procedurally, before any designation of eligibility with respect to articles, public hearings must be held, and advice must be obtained from the International Trade Commission (ITC) (and other Executive Branch agencies) on the probable domestic economic impact of granting eligibility to a particular category of merchandise. This process is an opportunity for lawyers representing exporting countries, importers, domestic producers, and consumers to make arguments in favor or, or against, an eligibility designation. *See* 19 U.S.C. § 2463(a)(1)(A), (e).

For some kinds of merchandise, the room for argument is focused. The GSP statute renders 7 categories of "import sensitive" merchandise as ineligible for duty-free treatment — the "Ineligible List," outlined below. Arguments about eligibility, then, focus on as a factual and legal matter an article is properly classified within an ineligibility category. (*See* 19 U.S.C. § 2463(b)(1).)

Arguments also may focus on whether an article is, in fact, "import sensitive." That is because it is not clear from the statutory language whether

---

[2] Oxfam International, *Stitched Up: How Rich-Country Protectionism in Textiles and Clothing Trade Prevents Poverty Alleviation* 24 (Oxfam Briefing Paper 60, March 2004).

[3] *Id.*

an article properly classified in one of the categories on the Ineligible List is deemed, by virtue of that classification, to be import sensitive. On the one hand, the *chapeau* to the List says "The President may not designate any article as an eligible article . . . if such article is within one of the following categories of import-sensitive articles." That text appears to presume an article within a category is import-sensitive. On the other hand, some of the categories on the List (identified below) repeat the adjective "import-sensitive," which suggests room for an argument about import sensitivity.

Obviously, advocates for preferential treatment (typically, counsel for exporters and importers, and some consumer groups) will argue against a finding of import sensitivity and a classification of ineligibility, and advocates against preferential treatment (typically, counsel for domestic producers) will argue the contrary positions.

The Ineligible List is as follows. Consider the extent to which a BDC may have a keen export interest in articles on the list. (Consider, too, the List in relation to the development model Walt Rostow presents in *The Stages of Economic Growth* (1960).[4]) Is it likely a BDC may have an export interest in ineligible articles as it proceeds from lower-to higher-value added manufacturing? Finally, query whether production of any of these articles in a developed country like the U.S. are worth protecting — is the American comparative advantage in these articles all but lost? If so, then is adjustment assistance to help dislocated American workers, rather than protection against the products made by workers and poor countries, a better policy choice?

1.   Textile and Apparel (T&A) Articles:

All T&A articles are ineligible for GSP treatment. *See* 19 U.S.C. § 2463(b)(1)(A), (4). There are two minor exceptions. First, articles are eligible if they were eligible before a specific date (1 January 1994). In other words, the date operates as a closure — if an article was not eligible as of the date, then it remains ineligible. Second, certain carpets, based on their method of production, are eligible. They are ones that are hand-loomed, hand-woven, hand-hooked, hand-tufted, or hand-knotted and classified under specific 8-digit categories in Chapter 57 of the HTSUS.

2.   Watches:

All watches are ineligible for GSP treatment, with one exception. *See* 19 U.S.C. § 2463(b)(1)(B). A watch entered into the U.S. after a specific date (30 June 1989) is eligible, but only if the President determines it will not cause "material injury" to U.S. manufacturing and assembly operation of watches, watch bands, straps, or bracelets.

3.   Import-Sensitive Electronic Articles:

Any electronic article that is "import sensitive" is ineligible for GSP treatment. 19 U.S.C. § 2463(b)(1)(C). The reference to import sensitivity creates the possibility of arguing a class of electronic merchandise does not affect domestic producers, and thus ought to receive GSP treatment.

---

[4] This and other development models are set out in the *Dictionary of International Trade Law* that accompanies the textbook.

4.   Import-Sensitive Steel Articles:

Any steel article that is "import sensitive" is ineligible for GSP treatment. 19 U.S.C. § 2463(b)(1)(D). Again, reference to import sensitivity creates the possibility of arguing no adverse affect on or threat to affect domestic producers exists.

5.   Import-Sensitive Glass Products:

Any glass (whether semi-manufactured or finished) article that is "import sensitive" is ineligible for GSP treatment. 19 U.S.C. § 2463(b)(1)(F). Once again, the reference to import sensitivity creates the possibility of arguing there is no adverse affect on or threat to affect domestic producers, and thus ought to receive GSP treatment.

6.   Other Import-Sensitive Articles:

Any other article the President determines is "import sensitive" in the context of the GSP program is ineligible. 19 U.S.C. § 2463(b)(1)(G). This "catch all" category of the Ineligible List is a potentially large, as it is unrestricted to the type of merchandise, the production process, or its classification in the HTSUS.

7.   Footwear:

All shoes and other footwear are ineligible for GSP treatment. *See* 19 U.S.C. § 2463(b)(1)(E). There is a minor exception, namely, for footwear that was eligible on or before a specific date (1 January 1995). That is, footwear ineligible as of that date remain ineligible.

8.   Leather Goods:

All leather goods are ineligible for GSP treatment. *See* 19 U.S.C. § 2463(b)(1)(E). Such goods include handbags, luggage, flat goods (*e.g.*, change purses, eyeglass cases, and wallets), and work gloves, as well as apparel and shoes. The same minor exception exists for these goods as for footwear, namely leather goods are eligible if they were eligible on or before a specific date (1 January 1995).

9.   Articles Subject to a Safeguard:

An otherwise eligible article subject to a safeguard action under Section 201 of the *Trade Act of 1974* (*i.e.*, the escape clause, codified at 19 U.S.C. §§ 2251-2254)) is ineligible. *See* 19 U.S.C. § 2463(b)(2). Interestingly, during the Tokyo Round, less developed countries were concerned developed countries would use GATT Article XIX to protect their domestic industries. The U.S. ensures GSP benefits do not undermine safeguard relief by putting articles targeted for this relief on the Ineligible List.

10.   Articles Subject to a National Security Sanction:

Any otherwise eligible article subject to a national security action under Section 232 or 351 of the *Trade Expansion Act of 1962* (codified at 19 U.S.C. §§ 1862, 1981) is ineligible. *See* 19 U.S.C. Section 2463(b)(2).

11.   Agricultural Products:

There is no prophylactic ban on agricultural commodities (either primary or processed) from GSP treatment. However, there are two considerations.

First, appropriate governmental agencies are required to assist BDCs to ensure their agricultural sectors are not oriented to export markets to the detriment of producing foodstuffs for their own people. *See* 19 U.S.C. § 2466. Second, if an agricultural product is subject to a tariff rate quota (TRQ), then any shipment of that product above the in-quota threshold is ineligible for GSP treatment. In other words, over-quota shipments do not get a preference. This restriction affects sugar, which are subject to a TRQ set by the Secretary of Agriculture. Once the Agriculture Secretary establishes the quota quantity that can be entered at a lower-tier duty, the USTR allocates the quantity among sugar exporting countries. These countries get a "Certificate of Quota Eligibility" (CQE), which must be returned with a sugar shipment to receive in-quota treatment. Under the GSP, a sugar-exporting BDC gets duty-free treatment for the in-quota quantity allocated to it, but not for any above-quota shipments.

The fact there are 11 broad categories on the Ineligible List illustrates the proposition that GSP treatment is not about duty-free entry of all merchandise from every poor country. It affords a preference only to certain products, and of course designated ones originating in eligible countries.

Significantly, even if an article is on the Ineligible List, it might be eligible for GSP treatment if the country of origin is a LDBDC. Specifically, six categories of otherwise ineligible merchandise remain ineligible even if they are from a least-developed beneficiary, namely: (1) T&A; (2) watches; (3) footwear; (4) leather goods; (5) articles subject to a safeguard remedy, national security sanction, or emergency tariff adjustment, or (6) agricultural products. *See* 19 U.S.C. § 2463(a)(1)(B). That leaves a few categories from the Ineligible List as eligible if they are from a LDDC — (1) import-sensitive electronics, (2) import-sensitive steel, (3) import-sensitive glass, and (4) other import-sensitive articles. Yet, there is a "catch": the President must be advised by the ITC that the article in question is "not import sensitive in the context of imports from least-developed beneficiary developing countries." *See* 19 U.S.C. § 2463(a)(1)(B). Thus, even with respect to the poorest of countries, product eligibility is highly conditional.

IV. GSP RULES OF ORIGIN

A. The Value Added Test

Even if a country qualifies as a BDC, and even if a merchandise category is eligible, it does not follow automatically a shipment of that merchandise will receive GSP duty-free treatment. The shipment must satisfy a rule of origin to ensure the article is "the growth, product, or manufacture" of a BDC. (19 U.S.C. § 2463(a)(2)(A).) The rule of origin has two prongs.

First, there must be no transshipment. (*See* 19 U.S.C. § 2463(a)(2)(A)(i).) The shipment of merchandise at issue must be imported directly from a BDC into the customs territory of the U.S. Thus, for example, assuming Mauritania is eligible for GSP treatment, Toyota cannot make cars in Japan, ship them to Mauritania, and thereby qualify those cars for GSP treatment. After all, the benefits of the treatment supposedly are directed at a poor country, and designed to encourage meaningful economic activity in that country.

Second, a value added test must be met. This test is designed to answer the question "How much economic activity is 'meaningful'?" The answer is 35 percent. That is, the value added to merchandise in a BDC must be 35 percent or more of the appraised value of the article when it enters the U.S. (*See* 19 U.S.C. § 2463(a)(2)(A)(ii).) The formula for the GSP Minimum Value Added Test is:

If

(1) Cost or value of materials produced in the BDC

+

(2) Direct costs of processing operations in the BDC

= or > 35 percent of total value as appraised by the CBP at time or entry,

then merchandise satisfies the Test. If < 35 percent, then fails.

The extreme cases are easy ones. If all inputs used to produce merchandise are from a BDC, and all processing occurs in the BDC, then the Test is met. Conversely, the GSP statute expressly excludes (1) simple combining or packaging operations, and (2) mere dilution with water or another substance that does not materially alter the characteristics of an article. These operations alone do not qualify an article for originating in a BDC. (*See* 19 U.S.C. § 2463(a)(2)(B).) However, difficulties and disputes arise when sourcing and production is multinational. Then, meaningful economic activity, in the sense of value added to merchandise, occurs both within and outside the BDC.

Should the location in which value is added matter? On the one hand, conferring a GSP preference on merchandise made largely outside of a BDC undermines country eligibility criteria. The 35 percent Value Added Test works in tandem with those criteria. On the other hand, as long as a BDC is not a mere transshipment platform, then at least some useful activity is undertaken there, and at least a few people are employed, even if all they do is minor assembly. By denying GSP treatment because less than 35 percent of the value is added in a BDC, is there a risk no work will be performed in the BDC, and no jobs will be created? Or, does the Test operate to shift — even distort — sourcing and production patterns to take advantage of GSP benefits?

Observe the 35 percent Test does not inquire into the nationality of the workers. It does not matter whether they are legal or illegal residents, or permanent or migrant workers In theory, a group of American law students could be the employees on a farm, or in a factory, in a BDC producing GSP eligible merchandise. Put simply, what is done where, but not who does what, matters.

What happens if materials are imported into a BDC, and then incorporated into the production of an eligible article? Do imported materials qualify toward the 35 percent Test? This question is treated in the 1985 *Torrington* case. In brief, the answer is "yes, but only if the materials imported into a BDC are substantially transformed into a new and different article in that BDC before they are incorporated into the eligible article." Stated differently, there must be (at least) two substantial transformations — of the imported materials into some intermediate product, and then of that product into the finished article, which is eligible for GSP treatment. This requirement is known as the "dual substantial transformation" requirement, and it arises out of the *Torrington* case.

What, then, constitutes "substantial transformation"? Further, what difference should the number of substantial transformations make? Is the rationale, once again, that the U.S. seeks to ensure real economic activity takes place in a BDC, that the BDC is not a mere assembly operation? If so, consider a poor country in which, depending on the type of merchandise, even an assembly operation is a substantial activity.

Suppose two or more BDCs are members of a FTA or CU. An example might be Indonesia and Vietnam, which are in *ASEAN*, and *ASEAN* has an FTA, called "AFTA." Assume an eligible article comes from Vietnam, but components come from Indonesia. Can the Indonesian components qualify in calculating the 35 percent minimum local content requirement? The answer is "yes." Two or more BDCs that are members of the same FTA or CU may be treated as one BDC and cumulated to meet this requirement.

B. Dual Substantial Transformation and the 1985 *Torrington* Case

TORRINGTON COMPANY v. UNITED STATES
United States Court of Appeals for the Federal Circuit
764 F.2d 1563, 1565-1572 (1985)

DAVIS, CIRCUIT JUDGE.

The Government appeals from a decision of the United States Court of International Trade . . . holding that certain industrial sewing-machine needles imported from Portugal by appellee (Torrington) are entitled to enter the United States duty free under the Generalized System of Preferences (GSP). . . . Agreeing that the imported articles meet the prerequisite for duty free entry under the GSP statute, . . . we affirm.

I. Background

The GSP statute . . . represents the United States' participation in a multinational effort to encourage industrialization in lesser developed countries through international trade. The [1974] Act authorizes the President (subject to certain restrictions) to prepare a list of beneficiary developing countries (BDCs), and to designate products of those countries which are eligible for GSP treatment. . . . A designated product imported from a listed country may enter the United States duty free. . . . One problem with this general program is that it could be used to allow a non-eligible country to conduct minimal finishing operations in a BDC, thereby reaping the benefits of the GSP at the expense of American manufacturers, but without the salutory effect of fostering industrialization in the designated country. Congress therefore provided that products from BDCs must meet certain minimum content requirements in order to qualify for duty-free treatment. To this end, 19 U.S.C. § 2463 [re-worded and re-codified at § 2463(a)(2)(A) as a result of amendments in 1996] provides:

> (b) The duty free treatment provided under section 2461 of this title with respect to any eligible article shall apply only —
>
>   . . . .
>
>   (2) If the sum of (A) the cost or value of the materials produced in the beneficiary developing country . . . plus (B) the direct cost of processing operations performed in such beneficiary developing country . . . is not less than 35 percent of the appraised value of such article at the time of its entry in the customs territory of the United States.

    . . . .

    . . . [T]he Customs Service has promulgated regulations interpreting the operative phrase . . . "materials produced in the beneficiary developing country." 19 C.F.R. § 10.177(a) (1984) states that

> the words produced in the beneficiary developing "country" . . . refer to constituent materials of which the eligible article is composed which are either:
>
> (1)   Wholly the growth, product or manufacture of the beneficiary developing country; or
>
> (2)   Substantially transformed in the beneficiary developing country into a new and different article of commerce.

Thus, if the value of the materials described in § 10.177(a)(1) and (2) plus the direct cost of processing operations performed in the BDC account for 35% of the appraised value of the merchandise, the merchandise is entitled to enter duty-free. . . .

The question in this case is whether industrial sewing-machine needles which Torrington imported met these minimum content requirements. . . .

The sewing machine needles at issue were exported from Portugal to the United States by Torrington *Portuguesa*, a manufacturing subsidiary of Torrington. The needles are classifiable under item 672.20 of the Tariff Schedules of the United States (TSUS), "Sewing machines and parts thereof." At the time of the exports, Portugal was designated as a BDC and articles classifiable under item 672.20 were eligible products.

Torrington *Portuguesa* produced the needles from wire manufactured in a non-BDC and brought into Portugal. On this ground the Customs Service denied duty-free treatment to the needles because they did not incorporate any "materials produced" in Portugal, and the direct cost of producing the needles does not account for 35% of their appraised value. In Customs' view the needles failed to meet the minimum content requirements of 19 U.S.C. § 2463(b). Torrington agrees that if Customs' decision not to include the non-BDC wire in the calculation is correct, then the needles do not satisfy the 35%

BDC content requirement. On the other hand, if the other requirements are met, then the 35% BDC content prerequisite is also satisfied.

. . . Initially, the wire runs through a swaging machine, which straightens the wire, cuts it to a particular length, bevels one end of the wire segment and draws out the straightened wire to alter its length and circumference at various points. The result is known in the needle industry as a "swaged needle blank," a "needle blank," or merely a "swage." In an exhibit before the trial court, the parties included a linear drawing of a swage. The first quarter of a swage has roughly the same circumference as the wire segment from which it was made; the second quarter narrows from that size down to roughly half that circumference; the other half then extends straight out from the second quarter. At this point, the swage is useful solely in the production of sewing-machine needles with a predetermined blade diameter, though the resulting needle may vary in other respects (*e.g.*, eye placement, eye size, and needle length).

The next process in the production of needles is "striking." Striking involves pressing an eye into the swage, forming a spot to provide clearance for the thread, and bending the swage at a particular point. At this stage, the articles are known as struck blanks. The struck blank enters a mill flash machine which removes excess material around the eye and forms a groove along the length of the needle which carries the thread while the needle is in use. The merchandise is then pointed (*i.e.*, sharpened) and stamped with a logo or other information. Finally, the needles are hardened, tempered, straightened, buffed, polished, cleaned and plated. Upon completion, the needle has a sharp point at the narrow end, a long groove running down three-quarters of its body ending near the point, and an eye somewhere in the groove with an indentation in the groove near the eye.

. . . In 1973-74, Torrington *Portuguesa* twice shipped large amounts of swages to Torrington to correct production imbalances between the two companies. Torrington *Portuguesa* realized no profit on the exchange, and the transfer was accounted for through appropriate entries in the two companies' inventory and receivables accounts. These are the only transactions in swages in which Torrington (now the only U.S. manufacturer of these needles) has participated.

Based on these facts, the Court of International Trade held the needles to be entitled to duty-free entry under the GSP. . . . [T]he court ruled that, under Customs' regulations, the non-BDC wire must undergo *two* substantial transformations when it is manufactured into a needle if the value of the wire is to be included in the 35% calculation, and that each of these transformations under 19 C.F.R. § 10.177(a)(2) must result in an "article of commerce." The court stated:

> It is not enough to transform substantially the non-BDC constituent materials into the final article, as the material utilized to produce the final article would remain non-BDC material. There must first be a substantial transformation of the non-BDC material into a new and different article of commerce which becomes "materials produced," and these materials produced in the BDC must then be substantially transformed into a new and different article of commerce.

. . . The court noted that the Customs Service and Treasury Department have consistently interpreted the regulations to require a dual transformation (*i.e.*, two successive substantial transformations) in order to be eligible for GSP treatment, and that the requirement of a dual transformation advances the GSP's goals by requiring greater work in the BDC and by thwarting manipulation of the GSP (which the content requirements were designed to avoid).

The court then turned to the question of whether the production of needles in Portugal satisfied the dual transformation requirement. The court determined that a substantial transformation occurs if a manufacturing process results in an article of commerce which has a distinctive name, character, or use. . . . Here, the court held, the swaging process constitutes an initial transformation, and the succeeding processes constitute the second. The swage blanks, the court said, have a distinctive name, a different character from the wire segments from which they are made, and a specific use. Moreover, the swages are "articles of commerce" because, on the two documented occasions set forth in the stipulations, they have been the object of large transactions. Thus, the court concluded that the swaged needle blanks are constituent materials of which the needles are made, and their value (which includes the value of the non-BDC wire) should be included in the 35% value added calculation.

II. The Dual Transformation Requirement

The parties disagree whether the GSP statute and regulations mandate a dual transformation between raw material and finished product if the latter is to be granted duty-free entry. Torrington contends that its transformation of the non-BDC wire into sewing machine needles — even if considered only a single transformation — was in itself sufficient. The Government counters that a single transformation is insufficient to change the non-BDC wire into a material "produced in the developing country" which, if used in the BDC, may then be considered in the BDC-content evaluation.

Like the CIT, we think that the statutory language of 19 U.S.C. § 2463(b) leads to the Government's position. Congress authorized the Customs Service to consider the "cost or value of *materials produced*" in the BDC. (Emphasis added.) [*See* 19 U.S.C. § 2463(a)(2)(A)(ii)(I).] The parties agree that the wire clearly was not a BDC product. As wire, therefore, it may not be considered a BDC material. However, if Torrington Portuguesa transformed the wire into an intermediate article of commerce, then the intermediate product would be an article produced in the BDC, and the value of *that* product (including the contribution of the wire to the value of that intermediate product) would be included.

The legislative history of § 2463 supports this reading. Congress used the content requirement to protect the GSP program from untoward manipulation:

> The percentage . . . assure[s] that, to the maximum extent possible, the preferences provide benefits to developing countries without stimulating the development of "pass-through" operations the major benefit of which accrues to enterprises in developed countries.

. . . In the absence of a dual transformation requirement, developed countries could establish a BDC as a base to complete manufacture of goods which have already undergone extensive processing. The single substantial transformation would qualify the resulting article for GSP treatment, with the non-BDC country reaping the benefit of duty-free treatment for goods which it essentially produced. This flouts Congress' expressed intention to confer the benefits of the GSP fully on the BDC and to avoid conferring duty-free status on the products of a "pass-through" operation.

Moreover, Torrington's contentions, if accepted, would tend to render the 35% requirement a nullity. If only a single transformation were necessary, then the "material produced" in the BDC as a result of this transformation would be the imported product itself. Customs would then face the problem of determining how much of the appraised value of the import resulted from materials produced in the BDC, when the only material produced was the import. The result would always be 100% since the product would always be a constituent material of itself. Congress clearly envisaged some way of separating the final product from its constituent materials, and the dual transformation requirement achieves this end.

. . . .

III. The Swages — Substantial Transformation into a New and Different Article of Commerce

A.

In *Texas Instruments* [*v. United States*, 681 F.2d 778 (CCPA 1982)] . . . the Court of Customs and Patent Appeals adopted the rule, well-established in other areas of customs jurisprudence, that a substantial transformation occurs when an article emerges from a manufacturing process with a name, character, or use which differs from those of the original material subjected to the process. . . . *Anheuser-Busch Brewing Assn. v. United States,* 207 U.S. 556 (1908). . . . The CIT determined here that this substantial transformation test was satisfied when Torrington *Portuguesa* manufactured needle swages from the wire.

. . . Two critical manufacturing steps separate three items (wire, swage and needle) each of which is markedly different from the others. The initial wire is a raw material and possesses nothing in its character which indicates either the swages or the final product. The intermediate articles — the swages — have a definite size and shape which renders them suitable for further manufacturing into needles with various capabilities. At that phase of the production process the material which emerges is more refined, possesses attributes more specifically applicable to a given use, and has lost the identifying characteristics of its constituent material. It is a new and different article.

. . . Manufacturing processes often differ in detail, but we must consider these differences in light of the GSP's fundamental purpose of promoting industrialization in lesser developed countries. Trivial differences in manufacturing processes or techniques will not affect the overall benefit conferred upon the BDCs from the manufacturing conducted in those countries.

. . . .

B.

The CIT also concluded correctly that the swages were "articles of commerce." The Government attacks this determination principally by arguing that the two incidents in which Torrington *Portuguesa* transferred swages to Torrington in this country should not count in deciding whether swages are articles of commerce. We note initially that the phrase "article of commerce" is found only in the regulation, not in the GSP statute, and therefore we interpret the "of commerce" requirement of the regulation in light of the statute's purpose to further BDC industrialization. By emphasizing that the article must be "of commerce," the Customs regulation imposes the requirement that the "new and different" product be commercially recognizable as a different article, *i.e.*, that the "new and different" article be readily susceptible of trade, and be an item that persons might well wish to buy and acquire for their own purposes of consumption or production.

. . . .

Our conclusion is that an "article of commerce" — for the purposes of the pertinent Customs regulation — is one that is ready to be put into a stream of commerce, but need not have actually been bought-and-sold, or actually traded, in the past. Indeed, by requiring proof of actual arms-length transactions by unrelated parties, the Government implies that a new article (never before produced) can never be an article of commerce entitled to GSP treatment — a result not envisaged by Congress. In this instance, we agree with the CIT that the transfer of over four million swaged needle blanks from Torrington *Portuguesa* to Torrington is an adequate showing that swaged needle blanks are articles of commerce. There is no reason to believe that those articles could and would not be sold to other manufacturers of needles who wanted to purchase them for further manufacture into the final product.

IV. The Needles — Substantial Transformation into a New and Different Article

The Government urges that, even if the production of swages from wire constitutes a substantial transformation, the manufacture of the needles from the swages does not. We are referred to . . . the parties' stipulations, in which they note that swages "are dedicated for use solely as sewing machine needles with a predetermined blade diameter. . . . In the majority of cases, a particular type of swaged needle blank becomes only a single particular type of needle." The Government concludes from this that the swages are actually unfinished needles, and do not undergo a substantial transformation into a new article in order to reach their final form. Torrington, also reading from the stipulations, notes that the swages lack the key characteristics of a needle since they have no points or eyes, and that a given swage can be processed into needles with different properties, *e.g.*, eye size.

The Government relies for its position that swages are merely unfinished needles on cases such as *Avins Industrial Products Co. v. United States*, 515 F.2d 782 (1975) . . . and *Lee Enterprises, Inc. v. United States*, 84 Cust. Ct. 208 (1980). These decisions concern the proper classification of imports under the rule that an item in the TSUS covers the article mentioned in finished or unfinished form. The courts ruled that a product is an unfinished form of an article if the product has been manufactured to the point where it is dedicated solely to the manufacture of that article. . . . However, the Government's reliance on these cases is not pertinent. The proper tariff classification is not dispositive of whether the manufacturing process necessary to complete an article constitutes a substantial transformation from the original material to the final product. . . . Instead, we look — keeping in mind the GSP's fundamental purpose of fostering industrialization in BDCs — to the actual manufacturing process by which the intermediate article becomes the final product.

In *Midwood Industries v. United States*, 313 F. Supp. 951 (1970), . . . the Customs Court (now the CIT) determined that forgings for flanges could enter the United States without permanent country-of-origin markings because the importer substantially transformed the forgings in the United States into pipe. In one case, the importer cut the edges; tapered, beveled and bored the ends; and removed die lines and other imperfections from the surface of the final article. . . . The court also heard testimony that, in their imported state, the forgings are useless unless processed into the final flange. . . . The decision in that case was that the importer's efforts resulted in a substantial transformation from the rough forgings into "different articles having a new name, character and use." . . . The court noted that the "imports were *producers'* goods, and the flanges are *consumers'* goods," and held: "While it may be true, as some of the testimony of record indicates, that some of the imported forgings are made as close to the dimensions of the ultimate finished form as possible, they, nevertheless, remain forgings unless and until converted by some manufacturer into *consumers'* goods." . . .

The production of needles from swages is a similar process. The swages are bored (to form an eye), the ridge is carved, and the needle is pointed, cleaned, hardened, plated, etc. The swage is also the approximate size necessary to create the final needle, but, like the forgings in *Midwood,* they are producers' goods. The final needles are consumers' goods. The production of needles from swages is clearly a significant manufacturing process, and not a mere "pass-through" operation as the Government apparently contends. Portugal certainly reaps the benefit of this manufacturing process; indeed, short of manufacturing the wire itself, Torrington *Portuguesa* could do no more than it already does in the production of needles. In these circumstances, we think that Congress intended the GSP statute to apply.

For these reasons, we conclude: (1) that a dual substantial transformation in a BDC is a prerequisite for GSP treatment under the GSP statute and Customs regulations, (2) that the swages which Torrington Portuguesa produced are a separate, intermediate "article of commerce," and (3) that the industrial sewing-machine needles imported by Torrington are entitled to duty-free entry. The decision appealed from is therefore affirmed.

V.   DISCRETIONARY GRADUATION AND COMPETITIVE NEED LIMITATIONS

The President may withdraw, suspend, or limit the application of duty-free treatment as regards a particular article, or indeed all articles from a country (in effect, the entire country). This process is known as "discretionary graduation," and it has occurred annually since 1981 after an inter-agency review. Under amendments to the discretionary graduation rules in the *Trade and Tariff Act of 1984*, the President is required to engage in an annual review of all GSP-eligible products to determine whether they are sufficiently competitive to graduate. For any individual BDC, the outcome can be graduation of just one product (with the other products remaining eligible), or graduation of all products (meaning the country loses its status as a BDC).

In other words, in practice, discretionary graduation can apply to a product, several products, or a whole country. The central question in the review is whether the article still needs GSP treatment, *i.e.*, do they need duty-free treatment to stay competitive in the American market? After all, there may be more worthy products and BDCs to which a preferences should be shifted or focused. Technically, the President must take into account the general factors for GSP treatment, and the seven additional factors for country-eligibility criteria. *See* 19 U.S.C. § 2463(c)(1). In practice, discretionary graduation occurs for certain products from particular BDCs that demonstrate competitiveness, and thus allows a shift of preferences to less-developed countries.

Examples of discretionary graduation of entire countries are Hong Kong, Korea, Singapore, and Taiwan. President George H.W. Bush graduated these countries (on 29 January 1988, effective 2 January 1989) because of their impressive level of economic development and competitiveness. He decided they could sustain their performance without GSP treatment. President Clinton graduated Malaysia (on 17 October 1996, effective 1 January 1997) because of its sufficient advancements in economic development and improved trade competitiveness.

However, discretionary graduation does not impact only newly industrialized countries (NICs) in East Asia. President Clinton also graduated (effective 1 January 1998) Aruba, Cayman Islands, Cyprus, Greenland, Macau, and Netherlands Antilles, as they met the definition of "high income" country set by the World Bank. For the same reason, he also graduated (on 6 July 2000, effective 1 January 2002) French Polynesia, Malta, New Caledonia, and Slovenia. Interestingly, Belarus lost GSP benefits because of its failure to afford its workers internationally recognized worker rights (declared by President Clinton on 6 July 2000). In every instance, the result of withdrawal or suspension of duty-free treatment is re-imposition of the duty otherwise applicable, which in most instances is the MFN rate. That is because Congress — not the President — has the constitutional authority (under the Commerce Clause, Article I, Section 8, Clause 3) to regulate foreign commerce, and thus establish tariff rates.

A major constraint on product eligibility for GSP treatment is known as "competitive need." *See* 19 U.S.C. § 2463(c)(2). If (in any year beginning after

31 December 1995) a BDC exports to the U.S. (directly or indirectly) a product receiving duty-free benefits under the GSP program, and that product becomes competitive in the American market, then the President must terminate duty-free treatment. Termination results in imposition of the normally applied duty, which in most cases is the MFN rate.

The competitive need limits support the same policy goals served by discretionary graduation. First, they establish a benchmark for determining when products are successful in the American market against domestic and other foreign products and, therefore, no longer warrant preferential tariff treatment. Second, they ensure GSP benefits are allocated, or re-allocated, to less competitive articles and less well-off countries. Of course, from the perspective of a BDC, the concern is punishment for market success. Do both discretionary graduation and competitive need limitations serve an ulterior third goal, namely, to provide import protection to domestic producers of like or directly competitive products?

A critical practical question is how the GSP statute defines "competitive needs." Not surprisingly, it calls for an examination of the quantity, value, and relative import penetration of the eligible article shipped to the U.S.:

● *Value Limitation*

The quantity of an eligible article has an appraised value in excess of the applicable amount for the calendar year in which the article is exported. In 1996, the threshold was $75 million. Each year thereafter, the threshold rises by $5 million. Thus, for example, in 2012 the threshold is $155 million, indicating it takes 15 years (from 1996 to 2010) for the threshold to double. *See* 19 U.S.C. § 2463(c)(2)(A)(i)(I), (ii). No adjustment is permitted for the nature of the article. That is, the same threshold applies, whether the merchandise is a low-value added product like woven baskets, or a relatively higher-value added product like batteries. Interestingly, earlier versions of the GSP statute used a different value benchmark, namely, an absolute level (which in 1994 was $114.1 million) adjusted annually in relation to changes in the U.S. GNP.

● *Import Percentage Limitation*

The quantity of an eligible article equals or exceeds 50 percent of the appraised value of total imports of that article into the U.S. in any calendar year. *See* 19 U.S.C. § 2463(c)(2)(A)(i)(II). No adjustment is permitted for the number of other foreign countries exporting the product into the U.S., or for the size of foreign competitors. From the perspective of a BDC avoiding this competitive need limitation, it is better to be one of many small exporters to the U.S. However, the long-term economic interests of the BDC may be to be a major player in the world market for the product.

The two restrictions are simultaneously applicable. Suppose a BDC ships eligible merchandise below the value threshold, but exceeds 50 percent of the total value of imported merchandise. In that scenario, the BDC is not necessarily a large player in the American market, but it is successful in competing in this market against other foreign countries. The consequence is removal of GSP treatment. Termination also is the consequence of the opposite scenario, where the BDC accounts for less than half of American imports of the article, but individually exceeds the value threshold.

Termination under the competitive need limitations occurs no later than 1 July of the year after the BDC breached a limitation. Is termination permanent? The answer is "no," because eligibility can be reinstated to a product if in a later year the competitive need ceilings are not reached. *See* 19 U.S.C. § 2463(c)(2)(C). That is, a BDC that loses GSP eligibility for a particular article can apply for re-designation of benefits. The same eligibility criteria apply as on an initial designation, plus the BDC must have stayed within the competitive need limits in the calendar year preceding re-designation.

Are there exceptions to the competitive need limitations? In other words, is there no choice but to terminate GSP benefits for an eligible product from a BDC that exceeds these limitations? The answer is there is room for maneuver. Indeed, there are two "full" exceptions, and one "partial" exception.

First, neither of the competitive need limitations applies to a LDBDC. *See* 19 U.S.C. § 2463(c)(2)(D). Second, neither limitation applies to a beneficiary Sub-Saharan African country (BSSAC), *i.e.*, a country eligible under the *African Growth and Opportunity Act* for *AGOA* benefits, which also meets the GSP country-eligibility criteria. *See* 19 U.S.C. § 2463(c)(2)(D). There also is a "partial" exception, namely, an exception known as "short supply" to the import percentage limitation. This limitation does not apply to an article if there is no like or directly competitive good produced in the U.S. (as of 1 January 1995). *See* 19 U.S.C. § 2463(c)(2)(E). It would be against the self-interest of the U.S. to deny GSP treatment based on competitive need for an eligible article that not only poses no competitive threat to an American producer, but also is in short supply in the American economy.

A follow-up matter is how much room there is for maneuver. That is, are there circumstances under which the President may waive competitive need limitations? The answer is "yes." There are three waiver possibilities.

First, the President may issue a *de minimis* waiver of the import percentage (but not value) limitation. *See* 19 U.S.C. § 2463(c)(2)(F). Waiver is based on the aggregate appraised value of imports into the U.S. of an eligible article during the preceding calendar year not exceeding a *de minimis* threshold for that year. In 1996, the threshold was $13 million, and for each calendar year thereafter the threshold has been raised by $500,000. Thus, in 2012 the *de minimis* threshold is $21 million. (Earlier versions of the GSP statute implied adjusting the threshold annually with changes in U.S. GNP.)

Observe it takes more than 15 years for the *de minimis* threshold to double to $26 million, and that the absolute dollar value ($500,000) by which the threshold grows is 10 percent of the amount by which the value limit rises ($5 million). Are these facts a basis to claim the threshold is not generous to BDCs? The answer is "probably not." It is important to consider the size of the threshold in relation to the value limitation. In 1996, the threshold was 3.85 percent of the value limitation ($500,000 divided into $13 million). In 2012, the threshold is 13.5 percent of the value limit ($21 million divided into $155 million). In other words, the *de minimis* threshold rises as a percentage of the value limitation. Is this rise consistent over time?

Second, there is what might be called a "self-interest waiver" of the competitive need limitations. *See* 19 U.S.C. § 2463(d)(1)-(2). This waiver involves a two-pronged test:

a. The ITC advises the President (under Section 332 of the *Tariff Act of 1930*, as amended) that an industry in the U.S. would be adversely affected by loss of GSP benefits. For example, short supply induced by loss of the benefits would be relevant. As another example, an industry may rely on duty-free access to an article it uses as an input into production, and would be damaged by the higher cost associated with an MFN tariff imposed on the article.

b. The President must also determine that a waiver of the limitations "is in the national economic interest of the United States." Here again, short supply considerations would be relevant. In making this determination, the President must examine (or reexamine) the country-eligibility criteria, and consider the advice of the ITC. The President also must "give great weight" to two factors: the extent to which the BDC assures the U.S. it "will provide equitable and reasonable access to the markets and basic commodity resources" of that country and "provides adequate and effective protection of intellectual property rights."

These waiver criteria essentially authorize the President to ensure continuous flow of duty-free imports to support domestic needs, and provide leverage on BDCs seeking a waiver to provide American (and other foreign) business interests market access and IP protection.

Third, the President can waive the competitive need limitations if there is a special preferential relationship, and formal agreement, between the U.S. and a BDC. This waiver is designed for possible use with respect to the Philippines. It mandates the Philippines neither "discriminate" against American commerce, nor impose any "unjustifiable" or "unreasonable" barriers to American commerce. *See* 19 U.S.C. § 2463(d)(3). No President has used this waiver.

In sum, there exists considerable room for maneuver in the authority delegated by Congress to the President to waive the competitive need limitations. But, the room is restricted. The President cannot exercise the waiver "too much," and cannot concentrate waivers on just one or a few BDCs. "Too much" and "concentration" are defined according to two quantitative tests:

1. 30 percent restriction:

There is an overall limit on the total value of waivers granted to all BDCs. *See* 19 U.S.C. § 2463(d)(4)(A). In any calendar year (after 1995), total waivers for all BDCs above existing competitive need limitations cannot exceed 30 percent of the aggregate appraised value of all articles imported into the U.S. duty-free under the GSP program in the previous calendar year. Thus, to establish the dollar value of this restriction, it is necessary to calculate the aggregate appraised value in a calendar year of eligible merchandise imported into the U.S., and compute 30 percent of the aggregate appraised value for articles entered duty-free in the previous year. The 30 percent figure from the previous calendar year sets the threshold against which the current calendar year value is measured. The President cannot grant a waiver on an article if doing so would mean the value of articles for which the competitive need limitation is waived crosses the overall 30 percent threshold.

2.   15 percent restriction:

There also is a restriction to ensure waivers of competitive need limitations are distributed among BDCs, rather than being focused on just one or a few beneficiaries. *See* 19 U.S.C. § 2463(d)(4)(B). The President may not grant waivers to more than 15 percent of the aggregate appraised value of all articles imported into the U.S. entered duty-free under the GSP program from BDCs with a *per capita* GNP of $5,000 or more, or from BDCs that account for at least a 10 percent share of total GSP imports. Thus, to establish the dollar value of this restriction, it is necessary to identify these two categories of BDCs, calculate the aggregate appraised value in a calendar year of eligible merchandise imported into the U.S., and compute 15 percent of the aggregate appraised value of articles entered duty-free in the previous calendar year. The 15 percent figure from the prior year sets the benchmark against which current GSP imports are measured. The President cannot grant a waiver on an article if doing so would mean the value of articles for which the competitive need limitation is waived exceeds 15 percent of the value of imports from the two types of BDCs.

Calculating the 30 and 15 percent boundaries can be tricky. *See* 19 U.S.C. § 2463(d)(4)(C). Recall that a competitive need limitation, if imposed, would apply prospectively, specifically, as of 1 July of the following calendar year. Waiver of a competitive need limitation is based on the 30 and 15 percent thresholds, which are calculated using data from the previous calendar year. In that previous calendar year, the article in question received duty-free treatment under the GSP program, and the issue is whether that treatment must be withdrawn in the next year because the competitive need limitation is exceeded — and, if so, whether a waiver is appropriate.

To calculate the waiver thresholds, it is necessary to add three figures:

(1)   the amount of the article that actually entered the U.S. duty-free in the previous year, when the competitive need limitation was inapplicable;

(2)   the amount of the article that would have entered the U.S., had the competitive need limitation applied, and thus the MFN rate imposed; and

(3)   the difference between figures (1) and (2).

In calculating the waiver threshold, the first and third figures — that is, the amount actually entered duty-free, and the extent to which the amount actually entered exceeds what would have been entered had the competitive need limitation been imposed — are both included. The "bottom line" is that it is somewhat easier to reach the waiver threshold because both the first and third figures are included.

There is no time limit on a waiver of competitive need limitations. That is, a waiver lasts until the President determines it is no longer warranted because of "changed circumstances." 19 U.S.C. § 2463(d)(5). What might constitute such circumstances, and thereby call for removal of a waiver?

VI. NONDISCRIMINATORY DISCRIMINATION OR DIVIDE AND RULE?

A. The European GSP Scheme and the War on Drugs

WTO APPELLATE BODY REPORT, *EUROPEAN COMMUNITIES — CONDITIONS FOR THE GRANTING OF TARIFF PREFERENCES TO DEVELOPING COUNTRIES*
WT/DS246/AB/R (adopted 20 April 2004)

I. Introduction

1. . . . . The Panel was established to consider a complaint by India against the European Communities regarding the conditions under which the European Communities accords tariff preferences to developing countries pursuant to Council Regulation (EC) No. 2501/2001 of 10 December 2001 "applying a scheme of generalised tariff preferences for the period from 1 January 2002 to 31 December 2004" (the "Regulation").

2. The Regulation provides for five preferential tariff "arrangements," namely:

   (a) general arrangements described in Article 7 of the Regulation (the "General Arrangements");

   (b) special incentive arrangements for the protection of labour rights;

   (c) special incentive arrangements for the protection of the environment;

   (d) special arrangements for least-developed countries; and

   (e) special arrangements to combat drug production and trafficking (the "Drug Arrangements").

3. All the countries listed in Annex I to the Regulation are eligible to receive tariff preferences under the General Arrangements, which provide, broadly, for suspension of Common Customs Tariff duties on products listed as "non-sensitive" and for reduction of Common Customs Tariff *ad valorem* duties on products listed as "sensitive." . . . The four other arrangements in the Regulation provide tariff preferences *in addition* to those granted under the General Arrangements. [For instance, the tariff preferences include further reductions in the duties imposed on certain "sensitive" products.] However, only some of the country beneficiaries of the General Arrangements are also beneficiaries of the other arrangements. Specifically, preferences under the special incentive arrangements for the protection of labour rights and the special incentive arrangements for the protection of the environment are

restricted to those countries that "are determined by the European Communities to comply with certain labour [or] environmental policy standards," respectively. Preferences under the special arrangements for least-developed countries are restricted to certain specified countries. Finally, preferences under the Drug Arrangements are provided only to 12 predetermined countries, namely Bolivia, Colombia, Costa Rica, Ecuador, El Salvador, Guatemala, Honduras, Nicaragua, Pakistan, Panama, Peru, and Venezuela.

4. India is a beneficiary of the General Arrangements but not of the Drug Arrangements, or of any of the other arrangements established by the Regulation. In its request for the establishment of a panel, India challenged the Drug Arrangements as well as the special incentive arrangements for the protection of labour rights and the environment. However, in a subsequent meeting with the Director-General regarding the composition of the Panel — and later in writing to the European Communities — India indicated its decision to limit its complaint to the Drug Arrangements, while reserving its right to bring additional complaints regarding the two "special incentive arrangements." Accordingly, this dispute concerns only the Drug Arrangements.

5. The Panel summarized the effect of the Drug Arrangements as follows:

> The result of the Regulation is that the tariff reductions accorded under the Drug Arrangements to the 12 beneficiary countries are greater than the tariff reductions granted under the General Arrangements to other developing countries. In respect of products that are included in the Drug Arrangements but not in the General Arrangements, the 12 beneficiary countries are granted *duty free* access to the European Communities' market, while all other developing countries must pay the *full duties applicable under the Common Customs Tariff*. In respect of products that are included in both the Drug Arrangements and the General Arrangements and that are deemed "sensitive" under column G of Annex IV to the Regulation with the exception for products of CN codes 0306 13, 1704 10 91 and 1704 10 99, the 12 beneficiary countries are granted *duty-free* access to the European Communities' market, while all other developing countries are entitled only to *reductions in the duties applicable under the Common Customs Tariff.* (original italics)

6. India requested the Panel to find that "the Drug Arrangements set out in Article 10" of the Regulation are inconsistent with Article I:1 of the *General Agreement on Tariffs and Trade 1994* (the "GATT 1994") and are not justified by the *Decision on Differential and More Favourable Treatment, Reciprocity, and Fuller Participation of Developing Countries* (the "*Enabling Clause*") [GATT Document L/4903, 28 November 1979, BISD 26S/203.] . . .

B. The 2004 *EC GSP* Case

WTO APPELLATE BODY REPORT, *EUROPEAN COMMUNITIES — CONDITIONS FOR THE GRANTING OF TARIFF PREFERENCES TO DEVELOPING COUNTRIES*
WT/DS246/AB/R (adopted 20 April 2004)

[Omitted is the finding of the Appellate Body, upholding that of the Panel, on the relationship between the MFN obligation of GATT Article I:1 and the Enabling Clause. The Appellate Body, agreeing with the Panel, concluded the Clause is an exception to the obligation.

Omitted, too, is the Appellate Body's modification of the finding of the Panel that the EC bears the burden of invoking the *Enabling Clause* and justifying the Drug Arrangements under the *Clause*. The Appellate Body said it was incumbent on India to raise the *Enabling Clause* in forging its claim of inconsistency under the GATT Article I:1 MFN provision. Then, the EC had the burden of proving the Drug Arrangement satisfied the *Clause*. The Appellate Body said India did, to a sufficient extent, invoke the *Clause*, specifically, Paragraph 2(a) thereof.]

V. Whether the Drug Arrangements Are Justified Under the *Enabling Clause*

. . . .

B. *Interpretation of the Term "Nondiscriminatory" in Footnote 3 to Paragraph 2(a) of the Enabling Clause*

. . . .

143. . . . . Paragraph 1 of the *Enabling Clause* authorizes WTO Members to provide "differential and more favourable treatment to developing countries, without according such treatment to other WTO Members." [S]uch differential treatment is permitted "notwithstanding" the provisions of Article I of the GATT 1994. Paragraph 2(a) and footnote 3 thereto clarify that paragraph 1 applies to "[p]referential tariff treatment accorded by developed contracting parties to products originating in developing countries in accordance with the Generalized System of Preferences," "[a]s described in the [*1971 Waiver Decision*], relating to the establishment of 'generalized, nonreciprocal and nondiscriminatory preferences beneficial to the developing countries.'"

144. The *Preamble* to the *1971 Waiver Decision* in turn refers to "preferential tariff treatment" in the following terms:

> *Recalling* that at the Second UNCTAD, unanimous agreement was reached in favour of the early establishment of a mutually acceptable system of *generalized, nonreciprocal and nondiscriminatory* preferences beneficial to the developing countries in order to increase the export earnings, to promote the industrialization, and to accelerate the rates of economic growth of these countries;

Considering that mutually acceptable arrangements have been drawn up in the UNCTAD concerning the establishment of *generalized, nondiscriminatory, nonreciprocal preferential tariff treatment* in the markets of developed countries for products originating in developing countries[.] (original italics; underlining added)

145. Paragraph 2(a) of the *Enabling Clause* provides, therefore, that, to be justified under that provision, preferential tariff treatment must be "in accordance" with the GSP "as described" in the *Preamble* to the *1971 Waiver Decision*. "Accordance" being defined in the dictionary as "conformity," only preferential tariff treatment that is in conformity with the description "generalized, nonreciprocal and nondiscriminatory" treatment can be justified under paragraph 2(a). [Again, the Appellate Body cited to the *Shorter Oxford English Dictionary*.]

146. In the light of the above, we do not agree with European Communities' assertion that the Panel's interpretation of the word "nondiscriminatory" in footnote 3 of the *Enabling Clause* is erroneous because the phrase "generalized, nonreciprocal and nondiscriminatory" in footnote 3 merely refers to the description of the GSP in the *1971 Waiver Decision* and, of itself, does not impose any legal obligation on preference-granting countries. . . .

. . . .

148. Having found that the qualification of the GSP as "generalized, nonreciprocal and nondiscriminatory" imposes obligations that must be fulfilled for preferential tariff treatment to be justified under paragraph 2(a), we turn to address the Panel's finding that:

> . . . the term "nondiscriminatory" in footnote 3 requires that *identical* tariff preferences under GSP schemes be provided to *all* developing countries without differentiation, except for the implementation of *a priori* limitations. (emphasis added)

149. The European Communities maintains that " 'nondiscrimination' is not synonymous with formally equal treatment" and that "[t]reating differently situations which are objectively different is not discriminatory." The European Communities asserts that "[t]he objective of the *Enabling Clause* is different from that of Article I:1 of the GATT."

In its view, the latter is concerned with "providing equal conditions of competition for imports of like products originating in all Members," whereas "the *Enabling Clause* is a form of Special and Differential Treatment for developing countries, which seeks the opposite result: to create unequal competitive opportunities in order to respond to the special needs of developing countries." The European Communities derives contextual support from paragraph 3(c), which states that the treatment provided under the *Enabling Clause* "shall . . . be designed and, if necessary, modified, to respond positively to the development, financial and trade needs of developing countries." The European Communities concludes that the term "nondiscriminatory" in footnote 3 "does not prevent the preference-giving countries from differentiating between developing countries which have different development needs, where tariff differentiation constitutes an adequate response to such differences."

150. India, in contrast, asserts that "nondiscrimination in respect of tariff measures refers to formally equal[] treatment" and that paragraph 2(a) of the *Enabling Clause* requires that "preferential tariff treatment [be] applied equally" among developing countries. In support of its argument, India submits that an interpretation of paragraph 2(a) of the *Enabling Clause* that authorizes developed countries to provide "discriminatory tariff treatment *in favour of the developing countries* but not *between the developing countries* gives full effect to both Article I of the GATT and paragraph 2(a) of the *Enabling Clause* and minimises the conflict between them." India emphasizes that, by consenting to the adoption of the *Enabling Clause*, developing countries did not "relinquish[] their MFN rights [under Article I of the GATT 1994] as between themselves, thus permitting developed countries to discriminate between them."

151. We examine now the ordinary meaning of the term "nondiscriminatory" in footnote 3 to paragraph 2(a) of the *Enabling Clause*. As we observed, footnote 3 requires that GSP schemes under the Enabling Clause be "generalized, nonreciprocal and nondiscriminatory." Before the Panel, the participants offered competing definitions of the word "discriminate." India suggested that this word means " 'to make or constitute a difference in or between; distinguish' and 'to make a distinction in the treatment of different categories of peoples or things.' " The European Communities, however, understood this word to mean " 'to make a distinction in the treatment of different categories of people or things, esp. *unjustly* or *prejudicially* against people on grounds of race, colour, sex, social status, age, etc.' " [In both instances, the Panel quoted from (quoting *The New Shorter Oxford English Dictionary*, L. Brown (ed.) (Clarendon Press, 1993), Vol. 1, p. 689].

152. Both definitions can be considered as reflecting ordinary meanings of the term "discriminate" and essentially exhaust the relevant ordinary meanings. [The Appellate Body, again, pointed to the *Shorter Oxford English Dictionary*.] The principal distinction between these definitions, as the Panel noted, is that India's conveys a "*neutral* meaning of making a distinction," whereas the European Communities' conveys a "*negative* meaning carrying the connotation of a distinction that is unjust or prejudicial." Accordingly, the ordinary meanings of "discriminate" point in conflicting directions with respect to the propriety of according differential treatment. Under India's reading, any differential treatment of GSP beneficiaries would be prohibited, because such treatment necessarily makes a distinction between beneficiaries. In contrast, under the European Communities' reading, differential treatment of GSP beneficiaries would not be prohibited *per se*. Rather, distinctions would be impermissible only where the basis for such distinctions was improper. Given these divergent meanings, we do not regard the term "nondiscriminatory," on its own, as determinative of the permissibility of a preference-granting country according different tariff preferences to different beneficiaries of its GSP scheme.

153. Nevertheless, . . . we are able to discern some of the content of the "nondiscrimination" obligation based on the ordinary meanings of that term. Whether the drawing of distinctions is *per se* discriminatory, or whether it is discriminatory only if done on an improper basis, the ordinary meanings

of discriminate" converge in one important respect: they both suggest that distinguishing among similarly situated beneficiaries is discriminatory. For example, India suggests that all beneficiaries of a particular Member's GSP scheme are similarly situated, implicitly arguing that any differential treatment of such beneficiaries constitutes discrimination. The European Communities, however, appears to regard GSP beneficiaries as similarly situated when they have "similar development needs." Although the European Communities acknowledges that differentiating between similarly situated GSP beneficiaries would be inconsistent with footnote 3 of the *Enabling Clause*, it submits that there is no inconsistency in differentiating between GSP beneficiaries with "different development needs." Thus, based on the ordinary meanings of "discriminate," India and the European Communities effectively appear to agree that, pursuant to the term "nondiscriminatory" in footnote 3, similarly situated GSP beneficiaries should not be treated differently. The participants disagree only as to the basis for determining whether beneficiaries are similarly situated.

[In an edifying footnote following the penultimate sentence of Paragraph 153, the Appellate Body observed:

> We note that the contrasting definitions proffered by the participants, as well as the convergence of those definitions on the fact that similarly situated entities should not be treated differently, find reflection in the use of the term "discrimination" in general international law. In this respect, we note, as an example, the definitions of "discrimination" provided by the European Communities, in footnotes 56 and 57 of its appellant's submission:

> **56** . . . Mere differences of treatment do not necessarily constitute discrimination . . . discrimination may in general be said to arise where those who are in all material respects the same are treated differently, or where those who are in material respects different are treated in the same way.

(*quoting* R. Jennings and A. Watts (eds.), *Oppenheim's International Law*, 9th ed. (Longman, 1992), Vol. I, p. 378)

> **57** . . . Discrimination occurs when in a legal system an inequality is introduced in the enjoyment of a certain right, or in a duty, while there is no sufficient connection between the inequality upon which the legal inequality is based, and the right or the duty in which this inequality is made.

(*quoting* E.W. Vierdag, *The Concept of Discrimination in International Law*, (Martinus Nijhoff, 1973), p. 61).]

154. Paragraph 2(a), on its face, does not explicitly authorize or prohibit the granting of different tariff preferences to different GSP beneficiaries. It is clear from the ordinary meanings of "nondiscriminatory," however, that preference-granting countries must make available identical tariff preferences to all similarly situated beneficiaries.

155. We continue our interpretive analysis by turning to the immediate context of the term "nondiscriminatory." We note first that footnote 3 to

paragraph 2(a) stipulates that, in addition to being "nondiscriminatory," tariff preferences provided under GSP schemes must be "generalized." According to the ordinary meaning of that term, tariff preferences provided under GSP schemes must be "generalized" in the sense that they "apply more generally; [or] become extended in application." [The Appellate Body, here too, cited the *Shorter Oxford English Dictionary*.] However, this ordinary meaning alone may not reflect the entire significance of the word "generalized" in the context of footnote 3 of the *Enabling Clause*, particularly because that word resulted from lengthy negotiations leading to the GSP. In this regard, we note the Panel's finding that, by requiring tariff preferences under the GSP to be "generalized," developed and developing countries together sought to eliminate existing "special" preferences that were granted only to certain designated developing countries. Similarly, in response to our questioning at the oral hearing, the participants agreed that one of the objectives of the *1971 Waiver Decision* and the *Enabling Clause* was to eliminate the fragmented system of special preferences that were, in general, based on historical and political ties between developed countries and their former colonies.

156. It does not necessarily follow, however, that "nondiscriminatory" should be interpreted to require that preference-granting countries provide "identical" tariff preferences under GSP schemes to "all" developing countries. In concluding otherwise, the Panel assumed that allowing tariff preferences such as the Drug Arrangements would necessarily "result [in] the collapse of the whole GSP system and a return back to special preferences favouring selected developing countries." To us, this conclusion is unwarranted. We observe that the term "generalized" requires that the GSP schemes of preference-granting countries remain generally applicable. Moreover, unlike the Panel, we believe that the *Enabling Clause* sets out sufficient conditions on the granting of preferences to protect against such an outcome. . . . [P]rovisions such as paragraphs 3(a) and 3(c) of the *Enabling Clause* impose specific conditions on the granting of different tariff preferences among GSP beneficiaries.

157. As further context for the term "nondiscriminatory" in footnote 3, we turn next to paragraph 3(c) of the *Enabling Clause*, which specifies that "differential and more favourable treatment" provided under the *Enabling Clause*:

> . . . shall in the case of such treatment accorded by developed contracting parties to developing countries be designed and, if necessary, modified, to respond positively to the development, financial and trade needs of developing countries.

158. . . . [U]se of the word "shall" in paragraph 3(c) suggests that paragraph 3(c) sets out an obligation for developed-country Members in providing preferential treatment under a GSP scheme to "respond positively" to the "needs of developing countries." Having said this, we turn to consider whether the "development, financial and trade needs of developing countries" to which preference-granting countries are required to respond when granting preferences must be understood to cover the "needs" of developing countries *collectively*.

159. The Panel found that "the only appropriate way [under paragraph 3(c) of the *Enabling Clause*] of responding to the differing development needs of developing countries is for preference-giving countries to ensure that their

[GSP] schemes have sufficient breadth of product coverage and depth of tariff cuts to respond positively to those differing needs." In reaching this conclusion, the Panel appears to have placed a great deal of significance on the fact that paragraph 3(c) does not refer to needs of "*individual*" developing countries. The Panel thus understood that paragraph 3(c) does not permit the granting of preferential tariff treatment exclusively to a subcategory of developing countries on the basis of needs that are common to or shared by only those developing countries. We see no basis for such a conclusion in the text of paragraph 3(c). Paragraph 3(c) refers generally to "the development, financial and trade needs of developing countries." The absence of an explicit requirement in the text of paragraph 3(c) to respond to the needs of "all" developing countries, or to the needs of "each and every" developing country, suggests to us that, in fact, that provision imposes no such obligation.

160. Furthermore, . . . the participants in this case agree that developing countries may have "development, financial and trade needs" that are subject to change and that certain development needs may be common to only a certain number of developing countries. We see no reason to disagree. Indeed, paragraph 3(c) contemplates that "differential and more favourable treatment" accorded by developed to developing countries may need to be "modified" in order to "respond positively" to the needs of developing countries. Paragraph 7 of the *Enabling Clause* supports this view by recording the expectation of "less-developed contracting parties" that their capacity to make contributions or concessions under the GATT will "improve with the progressive development of their economies and improvement in their trade situation." Moreover, the very purpose of the special and differential treatment permitted under the *Enabling Clause* is to foster economic development of developing countries. It is simply unrealistic to assume that such development will be in lockstep for all developing countries at once, now and for the future.

161. In addition, the *Preamble* to the *WTO Agreement*, which informs all the covered agreements including the GATT 1994 (and, hence, the *Enabling Clause*), explicitly recognizes the "need for positive efforts designed to ensure that developing countries, and especially the least developed among them, secure a share in the growth in international trade commensurate with the needs of their economic development." The word "commensurate" in this phrase appears to leave open the possibility that developing countries may have different needs according to their levels of development and particular circumstances. The *Preamble* to the *WTO Agreement* further recognizes that Members' "respective needs and concerns at different levels of economic development" may vary according to the different stages of development of different Members.

162. In sum, we read paragraph 3(c) as authorizing preference-granting countries to "respond positively" to "needs" that are *not* necessarily common or shared by all developing countries. Responding to the "needs of developing countries" may thus entail treating different developing-country beneficiaries differently.

163. However, paragraph 3(c) does not authorize *any* kind of response to *any* claimed need of developing countries. First, we observe that the types of needs to which a response is envisaged are limited to "development, financial

and trade needs." In our view, a "need" cannot be characterized as one of the specified "needs of developing countries" in the sense of paragraph 3(c) based merely on an assertion to that effect by, for instance, a preference-granting country or a beneficiary country. Rather, when a claim of inconsistency with paragraph 3(c) is made, the existence of a "development, financial [or] trade need" must be assessed according to an *objective* standard. Broad-based recognition of a particular need, set out in the *WTO Agreement* or in multilateral instruments adopted by international organizations, could serve as such a standard.

164. Secondly, paragraph 3(c) mandates that the response provided to the needs of developing countries be "positive." "Positive" is defined as "consisting in or characterized by constructive action or attitudes." [The Appellate Body relied again on the *Shorter Oxford English Dictionary*.] This suggests that the response of a preference-granting country must be taken with a view to *improving* the development, financial or trade situation of a beneficiary country, based on the particular need at issue. As such, in our view, the expectation that developed countries will "respond positively" to the "needs of developing countries" suggests that a sufficient nexus should exist between, on the one hand, the preferential treatment provided under the respective measure authorized by paragraph 2, and, on the other hand, the likelihood of alleviating the relevant "development, financial [or] trade need." In the context of a GSP scheme, the particular need at issue must, by its nature, be such that it can be effectively addressed through tariff preferences. Therefore, only if a preference-granting country acts in the "positive" manner suggested, in "respon[se]" to a widely-recognized "development, financial [or] trade need," can such action satisfy the requirements of paragraph 3(c).

165. . . . . [B]y requiring developed countries to "respond positively" to the "needs of developing countries," which are varied and not homogeneous, paragraph 3(c) indicates that a GSP scheme may be "nondiscriminatory" even if "identical" tariff treatment is not accorded to "all" GSP beneficiaries. Moreover, paragraph 3(c) suggests that tariff preferences under GSP schemes may be "nondiscriminatory" when the relevant tariff preferences are addressed to a particular "development, financial [or] trade need" and are made available to all beneficiaries that share that need.

166. India submits that developing countries should not be presumed to have waived their MFN rights under Article I:1 of the GATT 1994 *vis-à-vis* other developing countries, and we make no such presumption. In fact, we note that the *Enabling Clause specifically* allows developed countries to provide differential and more favourable treatment to developing countries "notwithstanding" the provisions of Article I. With this in mind, and given that paragraph 3(c) of the *Enabling Clause* contemplates, in certain circumstances, differentiation among GSP beneficiaries, we cannot agree with India that the right to MFN treatment can be invoked by a GSP beneficiary *vis-à-vis* other GSP beneficiaries in the context of GSP schemes that meet the conditions set out in the *Enabling Clause*.

167. Finally, . . . pursuant to paragraph 3(a) of the *Enabling Clause*, any "differential and more favourable treatment . . . shall be designed to facilitate and promote the trade of developing countries and not to raise barriers to or

create undue difficulties for the trade of any other contracting parties." This requirement applies, *a fortiori*, to any preferential treatment granted to one GSP beneficiary that is not granted to another. Thus, although paragraph 2(a) does not prohibit *per se* the granting of different tariff preferences to different GSP beneficiaries, and paragraph 3(c) even contemplates such differentiation under certain circumstances, paragraph 3(a) requires that any positive response of a preference-granting country to the varying needs of developing countries not impose unjustifiable burdens on other Members.

168. Having examined the context of paragraph 2(a), we turn next to examine the object and purpose of the *WTO Agreement*. We note first that paragraph 7 of the *Enabling Clause* provides that "[t]he concessions and contributions made and the obligations assumed by developed and less-developed contracting parties under the provisions of the [GATT 1994] should promote the basic objectives of the [GATT 1994], including those embodied in the *Preamble*." . . . [T]he *Preamble* to the *WTO Agreement* provides that there is "need for positive efforts designed to ensure that developing countries, and especially the least developed among them, secure a share in the growth in international trade commensurate with the needs of their economic development." Similarly, the *Preamble* to the *1971 Waiver Decision* provides that "a principal aim of the Contracting Parties is promotion of the trade and export earnings of developing countries for the furtherance of their economic development." These objectives are also reflected in paragraph 3(c) of the *Enabling Clause*, which states that the treatment provided under the *Enabling Clause* "shall . . . be designed and, if necessary, modified, to respond positively to the development, financial and trade needs of developing countries."

169. Although enhanced market access will contribute to responding to the needs of developing countries *collectively*, we have also recognized that the needs of developing countries may vary over time. . . . [T]he objective of improving developing countries' "share in the growth in international trade," and their "trade and export earnings," can be fulfilled by promoting preferential policies aimed at those interests that developing countries have in common, *as well as* at those interests shared by subcategories of developing countries based on their particular needs. An interpretation of "nondiscriminatory" that does not require the granting of "identical tariff preferences" allows not only for GSP schemes providing preferential market access to all beneficiaries, but also the possibility of additional preferences for developing countries with particular needs, provided that such additional preferences are not inconsistent with other provisions of the *Enabling Clause*, including the requirements that such preferences be "generalized" and "nonreciprocal." We therefore consider such an interpretation to be consistent with the object and purpose of the *WTO Agreement* and the *Enabling Clause*.

170. The Panel took the view, however, that the objective of "elimination of discriminatory treatment in international commerce, found in the *Preamble* to the GATT 1994, "contributes more to guiding the interpretation of 'nondiscriminatory'" than does the objective of ensuring that developing countries "secure . . . a share in the growth in international trade commensurate with their development needs." We fail to see on what basis the Panel drew this conclusion.

. . . .

[The Appellate Body considered the relevance of Paragraph 2(d) of the *Enabling Clause* to the interpretation of the term "nondiscriminatory." This Paragraph deals with special treatment of least-developed countries. The Panel characterized Paragraph 2(d) as an exception to Paragraph 2(a), and used Paragraph 2(d) to support its view that paragraph 2(a) requires "formally identical treatment." The Appellate Body found otherwise, stating Paragraph 2(d) is not an exception to Paragraph 2(a), and the reliance of the Panel on Paragraph 2(d) was misplaced. The Paragraphs of the *Escape Clause* are not mutually exclusive, and no one of them is an exception to the other. The critical, independent function of Paragraph 2(d) is to highlight least developed countries as a subcategory of developing countries, and authorize distinct preferences for these poorest-of-the poor countries. Thus, because of Paragraph 2(d), a preference-granting country need not establish that differentiating between developing and least-developed countries is "nondiscriminatory."]

173. Having examined the text and context of footnote 3 to paragraph 2(a) of the *Enabling Clause*, and the object and purpose of the *WTO Agreement* and the *Enabling Clause*, we conclude that the term "nondiscriminatory" in footnote 3 does not prohibit developed-country Members from granting different tariffs to products originating in different GSP beneficiaries, provided that such differential tariff treatment meets the remaining conditions in the *Enabling Clause*. In granting such differential tariff treatment, however, preference-granting countries are required, by virtue of the term "nondiscriminatory," to ensure that identical treatment is available to all similarly situated GSP beneficiaries, that is, to all GSP beneficiaries that have the "development, financial and trade needs" to which the treatment in question is intended to respond.

174. For all of these reasons, we *reverse* the Panel's finding . . . that "the term 'nondiscriminatory' in footnote 3 [to paragraph 2(a) of the *Enabling Clause*] requires that identical tariff preferences under GSP schemes be provided to all developing countries without differentiation, except for the implementation of *a priori* limitations."

. . . .

[The Appellate Body also reversed the Panel holding that the term "developing countries" in Paragraph 2(a) means "all developing countries, except as regards *a priori* limitations." The Appellate Body reasoned that because footnote 3 and Paragraph 3(c) do not ban granting of differential tariffs to different subcategories of GSP beneficiaries, as long as the remaining conditions of the *Escape Clause* are met, the term "developing countries" should not be read to mean "all." In effect, the Appellate Body held "developing countries" can mean less than all of them.]

D. *Consistency of the Drug Arrangements with the Enabling Clause*

. . . .

180. We found above that the term "nondiscriminatory" in footnote 3 to paragraph 2(a) of the *Enabling Clause* does not prohibit the granting of different tariffs to products originating in different subcategories of GSP beneficiaries, but that identical tariff treatment must be available to all GSP

beneficiaries with the "development, financial [or] trade need" to which the differential treatment is intended to respond. The need alleged to be addressed by the European Communities' differential tariff treatment is the problem of illicit drug production and trafficking in certain GSP beneficiaries. . . . [T]herefore, the Drug Arrangements may be found consistent with the "nondiscriminatory" requirement in footnote 3 only if the European Communities proves, at a minimum, that the preferences granted under the Drug Arrangements are available to all GSP beneficiaries that are similarly affected by the drug problem. [In the case, the EU argued the Drug Arrangements are *nondiscriminatory* because designation of beneficiary countries depends only and exclusively on their development needs, and all developing countries that are similarly affected by the drug problem have been included in the Drug Arrangements.] We do not believe this to be the case.

181. By their very terms, the Drug Arrangements are limited to the 12 developing countries designated as beneficiaries in Annex I to the Regulation. Specifically, Article 10.1 of the Regulation states:

> Common Customs Tariff *ad valorem* duties on [covered products] which originate in a country that according to Column I of Annex I benefits from [the Drug Arrangements] shall be entirely suspended.

182. Articles 10 and 25 of the Regulation, which relate specifically to the Drug Arrangements, provide no mechanism under which additional beneficiaries may be added to the list of beneficiaries under the Drug Arrangements as designated in Annex I. Nor does any of the other Articles of the Regulation point to the existence of such a mechanism with respect to the Drug Arrangements. . . . This contrasts with the position under the "special incentive arrangements for the protection of labour rights" and the "special incentive arrangements for the protection of the environment," which are described in Article 8 of the Regulation. The Regulation includes detailed provisions setting out the procedure and substantive criteria that apply to a request by a beneficiary under the general arrangements described in Article 7 of the Regulation (the "General Arrangements") to become a beneficiary under either of those special incentive arrangements.

183. What is more, the Drug Arrangements themselves do *not* set out any clear prerequisites — or "objective criteria" — that, if met, would allow for other developing countries "that are similarly affected by the drug problem" to be *included* as beneficiaries under the Drug Arrangements. . . . Similarly, the Regulation offers no criteria according to which a beneficiary could be *removed* specifically from the Drug Arrangements on the basis that it is no longer "similarly affected by the drug problem." . . . [E]ven if the European Commission found that the Drug Arrangements were having no effect whatsoever on a beneficiary's "efforts in combating drug production and trafficking," or that a beneficiary was no longer suffering from the drug problem, beneficiary status would continue. Therefore, even if the Regulation allowed for the list of beneficiaries under the Drug Arrangements to be modified, the Regulation itself gives no indication as to how the beneficiaries under the Drug Arrangements were chosen or what kind of considerations would or could be used to determine the effect of the "drug problem" on a particular country. . . .

. . . .

186. Against this background, we fail to see how the Drug Arrangements can be distinguished from other schemes that the European Communities describes as "confined *ab initio* and permanently to a limited number of developing countries." As we understand it, the European Communities' position is that such schemes would be discriminatory, whereas the Drug Arrangements are not because "all developing countries are potentially beneficiaries" thereof. In seeking a waiver from its obligations under Article I:1 of the GATT 1994 to implement the Drug Arrangements, the European Communities explicitly acknowledged, however, that "[b]ecause the special arrangements *are only available* to imports originating in [the 12 beneficiaries of the Drug Arrangements], a waiver . . . appears necessary." This statement appears to undermine the European Communities' argument that "all developing countries are potentially beneficiaries of the Drug Arrangements" and, therefore, that the Drug Arrangements are "nondiscriminatory."

187. We recall our conclusion that the term "nondiscriminatory" in footnote 3 of the *Enabling Clause* requires that identical tariff treatment be available to all similarly situated GSP beneficiaries. We find that the measure at issue fails to meet this requirement for the following reasons. First, as the European Communities itself acknowledges, according benefits under the Drug Arrangements to countries other than the 12 identified beneficiaries would require an amendment to the Regulation. Such a "closed list" of beneficiaries cannot ensure that the preferences under the Drug Arrangements are available to all GSP beneficiaries suffering from illicit drug production and trafficking.

188. Secondly, the Regulation contains no criteria or standards to provide a basis for distinguishing beneficiaries under the Drug Arrangements from other GSP beneficiaries. . . . As such, the European Communities cannot justify the Regulation under paragraph 2(a), because it does not provide a basis for establishing whether or not a developing country qualifies for preferences under the Drug Arrangements. Thus, although the European Communities claims that the Drug Arrangements are available to all developing countries that are "similarly affected by the drug problem," because the Regulation does not define the criteria or standards that a developing country must meet to qualify for preferences under the Drug Arrangements, there is no basis to determine whether those criteria or standards are discriminatory or not.

189. For all these reasons, we find that the European Communities has failed to prove that the Drug Arrangements meet the requirement in footnote 3 that they be "nondiscriminatory." Accordingly, we *uphold*, for different reasons, the Panel's conclusion . . . that the European Communities "failed to demonstrate that the Drug Arrangements are justified under paragraph 2(a) of the *Enabling Clause*."

VII. SPECIAL HELP FOR AFRICA?

A. Background on *AGOA*

On 18 May 2000, Congress passed the *"Trade and Development Act of 2000"* (Public Law 106-200, 114 Stat. 251). Signed by President Bill Clinton on this date, the legislation took effect on 1 October 2000. Specifically, Title I is the *"African Growth and Opportunity Act,"* or *"AGOA"* (codified at 19 U.S.C. §§ 3701-3741, with the provisions on trade policy and SSAC benefits in §§ 3701-3724). The function of *AGOA* is to provide preferential trade treatment for certain products originating in eligible SSACs for a limited period. However, the protectionist devil is in the details.

To be sure, the GSP and *AGOA* are not the only scheme of trade preferences the U.S. offers to developing and least developed countries. In 1983, the U.S. enacted the *Caribbean Basin Economic Recovery Act,* commonly known as the *"Caribbean Basin Initiative"* (*CBI*). *See* 19 U.S.C. §§ 2702-2707. The *CBI* provides zero-or low-duty treatment to certain merchandise originating in a beneficiary country. However, the GSP provides the broadest array of benefits (in terms of beneficiary countries and commodities), and *AGOA* concerns the poorest of the poor countries. Accordingly, they merit special attention.

The *AGOA* details concern the words "certain," originating," "eligible," and "limited." The legislation authorizes the President to grant unilateral preferential trade benefits to an SSAC, but only if it pursues economic and political reform, and satisfies other criteria, only with respect to its exports that satisfy an array of technical requirements, and only up through a sunset date. Thus, certain — but not all — T&A merchandise from a Sub-Saharan African country (SSAC) may receive duty-free, quota-free treatment from the U.S. (In addition, eligible SSACs may receive enhanced GSP benefits, such as the waiver of competitive need limits.)

B.   Specified Processes in Textile and Apparel Production

A key set of requirements a Beneficiary SSAC must satisfy under *AGOA* to receive duty-free treatment from the U.S. on T&A shipments are a dizzying array of preferential rules of origin. (There are four additional sets of requirements, concerning documentation, visas, "findings and trimmings," and "interlinings." What are the details of, and justifications for, each of these requirements?) There is little doubt the rationale for such rules is protection of T&A interests in the U.S. producing articles that are like or directly competitive with merchandise from a T&A Beneficiary. To understand the different *AGOA* categories of rules of origin for apparel articles, it is important to recall the six basic steps in making T&A. That is because the *AGOA* T&A rules of origin are specified process rules, not value added rules. In other words, in order for the finished merchandise to qualify for preferential treatment, these rules demand that particular production activity occur in a T&A Beneficiary:

Step 1: Growing cotton or other fiber as raw materials, or manufacturing synthetic fibers, such as nylon or rayon

A rule of origin demanding all production activity from this Step onward occur in one location is called a *"Fiber Forward Rule."* This kind of Rule is the most restrictive of all T&A specified process requirements. All economic activity must occur in one country, otherwise the finished article is considered not to originate in that country and, therefore, is disqualified from preferential treatment. In turn, the more restrictive a preferential rule of origin, the more protectionist it is. By making it difficult to obtain duty-free, quota-free treatment, a tighter rule confers greater protection on domestic (*e.g.*, American) producers of like merchandise.

In theory, a "Seed Forward" or "Fertilizer Forward" Rule could be devised to afford even greater protection than a Fiber Forward Rule. The idea would be to require the seeds used to plant cotton (or other fiber), or the fertilizer used to help the crop grow, to originate in the same country in which all further activity occurs. Failure would mean the finished article would not qualify as originating in that country, hence duty-free, quota-free treatment would be devised. In practice such a Rule does not exist.

Step 2: Spinning yarn from fiber

A requirement that all activity from this Step onward occur in a particular country is a "*Yarn Forward Rule.*" A Yarn Forward Rule is the second most restrictive — and thereby protectionist — type of specified process requirement. In effect, it is used in *AGOA*, for instance, in the first and second of the preference categories, in combination with Assembly Rules (discussed below).

Step 3: Making fabric (also called cloth) from yarn

A mandate that all activity from this Step onward occur in a particular country is a "*Fabric Forward Rule.*" A cursory glance at the first, second, third, seventh, and eighth *AGOA* preferential treatment categories suggests they rely (to varying degrees) on Fabric Forward Rules. However, in fact the categories are constructed in a protectionist manner, because of requirements about yarn.

A garment that is knit does not technically go through the fabric stage. The original *AGOA* legislation did not specify knit-to-shape garments as eligible for duty-free treatment, and the CBP issued draft regulations stipulating they were ineligible. *AGOA II* contained a "knit-to-shape amendment" clarifying knit-to-shape apparel is eligible.

Step 4: Cutting fabric into pieces (or knitting to shape)

A rule calling for all activity from this Step onward to occur in a particular country is called "*Cutting Forward.*" Generally, a Cutting Forward origin rule is more liberal than Fiber, Yarn, or Fabric Forward Rules, because it allows activity in the early stages of the chain of production to occur in countries other than the potential beneficiary of preferential treatment. The second and sixth *AGOA* preference categories use a variant of a Cutting Forward Rule. However (as discussed below), in *AGOA*, the variants are protectionist because of requirements concerning yarn. The fourth *AGOA* preference category also uses a Cutting Forward Rule, albeit for knitting to shape sweaters.

Depending on the garment, cutting may occur in more than one country — so-called "hybrid cutting." The original *AGOA* legislation, did not specify that apparel made in a hybrid cutting process was eligible for duty-free treatment. The CBP issued draft regulations that would have denied eligibility. *AGOA II* contained amendments allowing for preferential treatment for apparel cut both in the U.S. a Beneficiary SSAC.

Step 5: Sewing pieces of cut fabric together

An obligation that all activity from this Step onward to occur in a particular country is a "*Sewing Forward Rule.*" This kind of rule is relatively liberal, *i.e.*, not as protectionist as the previous rules, as it permits all previous Steps to occur in other countries. Sometimes, cutting and sewing are considered parts of the same operation, and the attendant rule is "Cutting and Sewing Forward."

A variation of the Sewing Forward Rule exists in *AGOA*, namely, in the second and sixth preference categories. However, the variations are protectionist. In the second preferential category, the sewing thread must come from the U.S., and in the sixth preferential category, non-American fabric or yarn may be used only if it is in short supply in the U.S.

Step 6: Assembling pieces into a finished article (i.e., final assembly)

A rule calling only for assembly to occur in a particular country — an "*Assembly Rule*" — is the most liberal of all specified process rules, in that it requires the least amount of economic activity to occur in the country seeking preferential treatment. The fourth *AGOA* preference category essentially fits this type. Ostensibly, the first and third categories are Assembly Rules. However (as explained below), strictures embedded in these categories concerning where fabric is from and cutting occurs render them considerably more restrictive than a simple Assembly Rule.

Overall, the *AGOA* preference categories are not pure in the sense of relying entirely on one kind of process forward occurring in a T&A Beneficiary. Rather, as explained in detail below, the categories are hybrids, blending different kinds of specified process rules.

C.   Eight Preferential Rules of Origin

There are 8 categories of apparel articles potentially eligible for duty-free, quota-free treatment under *AGOA*. (*See* 19 U.S.C. § 3721(b)(1)-(6).) (The italicized titles below are unofficial. They are mnemonic aids to summarize the gist of the category.) Apparel from a T&A producer/exporter in a Beneficiary SSAC must fit within a category if, upon entry into the U.S., its apparel exports are to benefit from duty-free, quota-free treatment. Examining each category reveals how the devil operates, and why the rules are properly characterized — from the perspective of T&A Beneficiary SSACs — as a "devil."

Briefly, of the 8 categories, the first 4 of them, and the eighth one, call for some activity to occur in a T&A Beneficiary using inputs from the U.S. (or, in the third and seventh category, from a Beneficiary). The sixth category obviates the need for American inputs only if they are in short supply. The fifth and seventh categories, dealing respectively with sweaters and cultural products, are not as commercially important as the other categories. While the rules of origin are highly technical, the theme emerging from them is evident enough: generosity. Query how generous the U.S. is toward Sub-Saharan Africa. Consider also whether generosity should matter in U.S. trade policy, and if so, why.

In the details of the origin rules of the first, second, third, fourth, sixth, and eighth *AGOA* preference categories, lives (indeed, thrives) the protectionist devil — and, in turn, is manifest America's generosity, or lack thereof, toward T&A Beneficiaries. A donor shows most poignantly its generous spirit in areas in which it faces the largest potential sacrifice, as does America in these categories. Generosity in a preferential trading program does not demand economic martyrdom. But, generosity is greater when it is not convenient or easy for a donor, and when it does not put undue strictures on a beneficiary to suit the commercial self-interest of the donor. Yet, again, the first, second, third, fourth, and sixth categories bear the most restrictive origin rules. Might the explanation lie in the prospect U.S. producers are considerably less likely to produce merchandise that is like or directly competitive with articles in the fifth and seventh categories?

After all, as the examination below reveals, at least *prima facie*, the fifth category appears drafted in a way to exclude sweaters made in a T&A Beneficiary that could substitute for American-made sweaters. Possibly, a rule about using American cashmere or wool whose diameter is 21.5 microns or less does not exist in *AGOA*, because it would be unnecessary, as few (if any) such inputs are made in the U.S. As for the seventh category, while there no doubt are American-made hand-loomed, hand-made, or folklore articles, and ethnic printed fabrics, such production is of small volume and not substitutable with African-made handicraft items. In contrast, precisely where American producers are most likely to be challenged — in the first, second, third, fourth, sixth, and eighth categories, which have the broadest potential array of merchandise — the origin rules are crafted to confer not generosity toward African producer/exporters, but protection for American producers of like or directly competitive products.

It is important to appreciate the particular relevance of the first, second, third, fourth, and sixth categories. Their relevance is evident in terms of commercial potential. These categories may contain the broadest array of T&A merchandise. By definition, the fifth category is limited not just to sweaters, but specifically to sweaters consisting of a certain weight of cashmere, or of a certain weight and diameter of wool. By definition, the seventh category is restricted to handicraft type articles. In contrast, the first, second, third, fourth, and sixth categories may contain articles as diverse as sleepwear for babies and neckties for men. Yet, it is in the categories of greatest potential commercial significance where the rules of origin are tightest.

Category #1 — United States Yarn-Forward with Beneficiary Assembly

Essentially, this category is for apparel articles sewn together in a T&A Beneficiary SSAC using American fabric, which is from American yarn. (*See*

19 U.S.C. § 3721(b)(1); HTSUS Chapter 98, U.S. Note 7(a) at 98-II-3.) Specifically, to qualify for duty-free treatment under this category, an article must meet 5 requirements:

(1)   The article must be sewn (or otherwise assembled) wholly in a T&A Beneficiary (or in multiple such Beneficiaries).

(2)   The article must be made from fabric (cloth) wholly formed in the U.S. (or, if knit, must be from components knit-to-shape in the U.S.). (The article could be made from both fabric and knit-to-shape components.)

(3)   The article must be wholly cut in the U.S. (or, if knit, the components knit-to-shape in the U.S.).

(4)   The fabric itself must be from yarns wholly formed in the U.S. (or, if knit, the components must be from yarns wholly formed in the U.S.).

(5)   Upon entry, the apparel must be classified in either one of two categories in the HTSUS. The first category is subheading 9802.00.80. This subheading appears in Chapter 98, which consists of special classifications for articles exported and returned, having been advanced or improved abroad. Items covered by this Chapter may enter the U.S. duty-free, or partially duty-free, under certain circumstances. These circumstances include re-importation of an article that was exported from the U.S. (without improvement in the condition of the article), articles subject to a personal exemption brought back to the U.S. by a citizen or permanent resident who traveled overseas, government importations, goods used for religious, educational, or scientific institutions, samples, and articles admitted under bond. As for subheading 9802.00.80, it covers articles exported from and returned to the U.S., having been advanced or improved abroad. The second category is Chapter 61, which covers "Articles of Apparel and Clothing Accessories, Knitted or Crocheted," and Chapter 62, which covers "Articles of Apparel and Clothing Accessories, Not Knitted or Crocheted." The second category applies only to apparel that would have been classified in the first category, but for the fact they were embroidered, or subjected to a particular process. The processes include acid washing, enzyme washing, or stone washing, perma-pressing, oven baking, bleaching, garment dyeing, and screen printing. See HTSUS Chapter 98, subheading 9819.11.03 at 98-XIX-4 (concerning these articles).)

This category also includes apparel articles made from fabrics that are not from yarns, as long as the fabrics are wholly formed and cut in the U.S., and the fabrics are classified under heading 5602 or 5603 of the HTSUS. Chapter 56 of the HTSUS deals with T&A articles from "wadding," "felt," "non-wovens," and "special yarns." Heading 5602 contains "felt articles" ("whether or not impregnated, coated, covered, or laminated"). Heading 5603 consists of non-woven articles ("whether or not impregnated, coated, covered, or laminated").

An understandable immediate reaction to this category is to ask why the U.S. insists on a T&A Beneficiary SSAC using American fabric that itself is made of American yarn? One answer is some Beneficiaries do not have the spinning and weaving capacity to produce enough fabric to supply their domestic apparel industry. This scenario is true, for instance, in Bangladesh (in which T&A exports accounted in 2001 for 85.8 percent of merchandise exports, the highest figure in the world). However, even if the same supply constraint exists in a Beneficiary SSAC, it does not follow that *AGOA* must mandate use of American fabric and yarn. Indeed, as Oxfam International points out:

> Rich countries try to justify these heavy requirements [preferential rules of origin for T&A] by saying that they encourage poor countries to develop textile production to supply their clothing sector. However, historical experience and contemporary production patterns undermine this argument. No small, poor country with a significant clothing industry has ever succeeded in developing a matching supply-capacity in textiles.[5]

Why not, then, let apparel producers in the Beneficiary choose input sources based on market considerations like price and quality? Does this query suggest there are deep economic and social justice concerns about the rules of origin?

The Second Preference Category — United States Yarn-Forward with Beneficiary Cutting and Sewing Forward Using American Thread

Essentially, this category is for apparel articles cut in a T&A Beneficiary SSAC from American-made fabric. The fabric must be made of American yarn, and then sewn together in the Beneficiary with American thread. (*See* 19 U.S.C. § 3721(b)(2); HTSUS Chapter 98, subheading 9819.11.06 at 98-XIX-4.) Specifically, to qualify for duty-free treatment under this category, an article must satisfy 5 requirements.

(1) The article must be sewn (or otherwise assembled) entirely in a T&A Beneficiary SSAC (or in multiple such Beneficiaries).

(2) The article must be made from fabric (cloth) wholly formed in the U.S. (or, if knit, must be from components knit-to-shape in the U.S.). (The article could be made from both fabric and knit-to-shape components.)

(3) The fabric itself must be from yarns wholly formed in the U.S. (or, if knit, the components must be from yarns wholly formed in the U.S.)

(4) The fabric must be cut in the T&A Beneficiary SSAC (or in multiple such Beneficiaries).

(5) After cutting, the article must be sewn (or otherwise assembled) using sewing thread from the U.S.

The second preference category also includes apparel articles made from fabrics that are not from yarns, as long as the fabrics are wholly formed (but

---

[5] Oxfam International, *supra* note 2, at 19.

not cut) in the U.S., and the fabrics are classified under heading 5602 or 5603 of the HTSUS (explained above).

The first three requirements are the same as in the first preference category. However, the latter two requirements distinguish the categories. In brief, the second preference category is a cutting forward rule, whereas the first category is an assembly (sewing) forward rule.

In both categories, American fabric made of American yarn must be imported into the T&A Beneficiary SSAC. In the first preference category, the items imported already are cut in the U.S. They can be sewn with or without American thread, but this flexibility comes at a cost — they must satisfy enter into particular HTSUS classifications. In the second preference category, fabric is imported, and cutting goes on in the T&A Beneficiary SSAC. That is advantageous to the Beneficiary, as more goes on there than sewing. However, when it comes time to sew the cut fabric pieces, the thread had better be American. The trade-off for using American thread is no HTSUS classification is mandated for the finished article.

The Third Preference Category — Regional or Other Fabric

The first two preference categories mandate use of American fabric, which in turn is made of American yarn. The third category affords flexibility on the origin of the fabric and yarn, essentially providing duty-free treatment for apparel articles from regional fabric and yarn, but subject to quantitative limits, and only for a limited period. (*See* 19 U.S.C. § 3721(b)(3); HTSUS Chapter 98, subheading 9819.11.09 at 98-XIX-4 (concerning these articles).) In particular, to qualify, an apparel article must satisfy 3 requirements:

(1)   The article must be assembled wholly in a T&A Beneficiary SSAC (or multiple such Beneficiaries).

(2)   The article must be made of fabric (cloth) wholly formed in a T&A Beneficiary SSAC (or multiple such Beneficiaries). The T&A Beneficiary in which assembly occurs need not be the same one as the Beneficiary in which fabric is made.

(3)   The fabric (cloth) must be from yarn originating either in the U.S. or a T&A Beneficiary SSAC (or multiple such Beneficiaries, or a former Beneficiary, *i.e.*, one that is party to an FTA with the U.S.). If the fabric originates in a T&A Beneficiary, then it need not be the same Beneficiary as the one in which the yarn originates.

This preference category is sometimes called "Apparel assembled from regional and other fabric." A more accurate rubric would be "United States Yarn-Forward or Beneficiary Yarn-Forward with Beneficiary Fabric-Forward." By using the words "regional" and "other fabric," this appellation obfuscates the requirement that not all other fabric qualifies.

"Regional" refers only to fabric from yarn spun in a T&A Beneficiary SSAC, and "other" is restricted to fabric from American yarn. For example, men's dress shirts assembled in Kenya from cotton cloth derived from cotton yarn spun either in the same or another Beneficiary, or in the U.S., would qualify. The shirts would not qualify if the cotton cloth came from Egypt or Pakistan, or if the cloth came from a Beneficiary or the U.S., but the yarn came from Egypt or Pakistan.

Significantly, duty-free treatment of articles in this category is subject to an annual quota. In effect, this category is a tariff-rate quota (TRQ), which subjects over-quota shipments to the MFN rate. To what is the cap — the specific percent figure for a particular year — applied? The answer is "square meter equivalents" (SMEs), a denomination that allows for comparison among different kinds of apparel articles, as diverse (for example) as wool sweaters and nylon tights. Thus, for instance, the initial cap, for the 12 months commencing 1 October 2000, was 246,500,393 SMEs. In that year, no more than this amount of apparel from T&A Beneficiary SSACs could obtain preferential treatment in the form of a zero tariff.

The "bottom line," then, is the third preference category is not as generous as it first appears. It promises flexibility to T&A Beneficiary SSACs by allowing them to use fabric made of yarn from either the U.S. or a Beneficiary. But, it imposes serious limits on the volume of apparel made from such fabric, in the form of a TRQ with caps allowed to grow modestly to low ceiling levels. Lest there be any doubt about this verdict, consider the fact that a special safeguard remedy applies to this category.

In particular, if imports from Beneficiaries surge, then the U.S. can remove duty-free treatment. The Secretary of Commerce is authorized to determine whether "there has been a surge in imports of an article [qualifying under the regional fabric preference category] . . . from a" Beneficiary SSAC (19 U.S.C. § 3721(b)(3)(C)(ii)). Specifically, under this provision, the Secretary must decide whether the article

> is being imported in such increased quantities as to cause serious damage, or threat thereof, to the domestic industry producing a like or directly competitive article.

The list of factors the Secretary considers in making an injury determination is open-ended, and includes any economic variable with an effect on imports, such as capacity utilization, domestic production, employment, exports, inventories, investment, market share, prices, profits, and sales. If the answer is affirmative, then the President must suspend duty-free treatment. Any "interested party" can request a ruling from the Secretary. The definition of this term includes not only producers (including workers, unions, and worker groups, as well as trade or business associations) of a like or directly competitive product, but also anyone (producers, workers, unions, and worker groups, and trade or business associations) "engaged in the manufacture, production, or sale of essential inputs for the like or directly competitive article." In other words, the universe of potential claimants with standing to bring a surge mechanism case includes most of the commercial chain, upstream and downstream.

The surge mechanism might be dubbed (diplomatically) "noteworthy." It is a weapon against exports containing regional fabric, yet the weapon targets the apparel sectors of desperately poor countries. The legal aspects of this weapon make it all the more "noteworthy." That is evident by contrasting this mechanism with the legal criteria for an escape clause action under Section

201 of the *Trade Act of 1974* (*See* 19 U.S.C. §§ 2251-2254). These criteria accord (though not completely) with the general safeguard remedy in Article XIX of GATT. The contrast shows the criteria associated with an *AGOA* surge mechanism are less rigorous than the requirements for an escape clause action, meaning it appears comparatively easier to get relief against African apparel.

To invoke the escape clause, increased imports must be "a substantial cause of *serious* injury, or the threat thereof, to the domestic industry producing an article like or directly competitive with the imported article. . . ." The investigation is conducted not by one executive branch official, but rather by an independent agency — the International Trade Commission (ITC). An affirmative determination results in a recommendation to the President for relief, but the President may choose not to raise trade barriers, because such action is "appropriate and feasible." As indicated, the causation test in the surge mechanism is unmodified, *i.e.*, it does not have the descriptive adjective "substantial." Any causal contribution is enough to justify relief. In contrast to a Section 201 case, in a surge mechanism case, it is not necessary to show there is no cause more important than the imports from a Beneficiary.

Also in contrast to a Section 201 case, in a surge mechanism case, one member of the President's cabinet makes the decision. The President has no choice but to suspend duty-free treatment if the decision is positive. Finally, the universe of potential petitioners in a Section 201 case does not expressly include upstream producers, workers, or associations. Rather, the petitioner must be "an entity, including a trade association, firm, certified or organized union, or group of workers, which is representative of an industry." In turn, the industry must be the one subject to actual or threatened serious injury.

The Fourth Preference Category — Third Country Fabric

One dimension of the regional fabric category is, in effect, a separate rule of origin category. There is a special rule for a T&A Beneficiary SSAC designated as "lesser developed," sometimes called the "Third Country Fabric Provision. (*See* 19 U.S.C. § 3721(b)(3)(B); HTSUS Chapter 98, subheading 9819.11.12 at 98-XIX-4 (concerning these articles).) The basic rule for qualifying as "lesser developed" is a *per capita* GNP of less than $1,500 (as of 1998, measured by the World Bank). However, *AGOA* identifies three countries by name as "lesser developed" — Botswana, Namibia, and Mauritius — that have higher *per capita* incomes. Indeed, the *per capita* income of Mauritius, around $10,000, is considerably higher, and that country sometimes is cited as a success story.

The special rule is an apparel article wholly assembled (or knit-to-shape) in a lesser developed Beneficiary (or multiple such Beneficiaries) may qualify for duty free treatment, regardless of the country or origin of the fabric or yarn used to make the articles. In effect, the lesser developed Beneficiary can source inputs from anywhere in the world. However, this special rule is subject to two limitations.

First, the special rule applies only through 30 September 2007, which is just half the length of extension of other *AGOA* benefits. (*See* 19 U.S.C.

§ 3721(b)(3)(B)(i).) Second, there is a cap, which is defined in terms of an "applicable percentage" of SMEs of all apparel articles imported into the U.S. in the previous 12-month period for which data are available. (*See* 19 U.S.C. § 3721(b)(3)(B)(ii).) The cap rises, then falls. In the first year (1 October 2003 through 30 September 2004), the applicable percentage was 2.3571 percent. In the second year, (1 October 2004 through 30 September 2005), it was 2.6428 percent. In the third year (1 October 2005 through 30 September 2006), it peaked at 2.9285 percent. In the final year (1 October 2006 through 30 September 2007), the cap drops to just 1.6071 percent.

The Fifth Preference Category — Beneficiary Knit to Shape-Forward for Certain Sweaters

Certain kinds of sweaters potentially qualify for duty-free treatment. (*See* 19 U.S.C. § 3721(b)(4); HTSUS Chapter 98, subheadings 9819.11.15, 9819.11.18 at 98-XIX-5.) To qualify, the sweaters must satisfy 2 requirements:

    (1)   The sweaters are knit-to-shape in a T&A Beneficiary SSAC.

    (2)   The sweaters are made either of cashmere or fine merino wool.

If the sweaters are cashmere, then their chief weight must consist of cashmere. They also must be classified under sub-heading 6110.10 of the HTSUS, which covers sweaters, pullovers, sweatshirts, waistcoats (*i.e.*, vests), and other similar articles that are knitted or crocheted. If the sweaters are wool, then they must contain 50 percent or more merino wool, and the diameter of that wool must be no finer (*i.e.*, not exceed) 21.5 microns. As indicated earlier, this preference category is narrow and unlikely to be of great commercial significance.

The Sixth Preference Category — Short Supply and NAFTA Parity

Are there any circumstances in which the U.S. will accord duty-free treatment to apparel from a T&A Beneficiary SSAC, which is not a lesser developed country, even though the fabric, or the yarn making up the fabric, is from neither American nor from a Beneficiary? Asked succinctly, can apparel made of third country fabric or yarn qualify? The answer is "yes, under the sixth preference category, the origin or fabric or yarn is irrelevant." (*See* 19 U.S.C. § 3721(b)(5); HTSUS Chapter 98, subheadings 9819.11.21 and 9819.11.24 at 98-XIX-5.)

The usual rubric for this category is the "Third Country Fabric" provision. A full (but cumbersome) title for this category might be "Beneficiary Cutting and Sewing Forward with a *NAFTA* Rule of Origin or with Short-Supply Fabric or Yarn." That is because to qualify, the apparel must be cut (or knit to shape), sewn, and further assembled in a Beneficiary. But, duty-free treatment depends on satisfaction of a short-supply test, plus the applicable *NAFTA* rule of origin. (Generally, *NAFTA* sets out a yarn-forward rule of origin for garments to obtain duty-free, quota-free treatment.)

The short supply test is that the fabric, or the yarn used in the fabric, is "not available in commercial quantities in the United States" (19 U.S.C. § 3721(b)(5)(A)). The exact *NAFTA* rule of origin depends on the customs classification of the apparel article. They are (for the most part) change-in-tariff-heading (CTH) rules, also known as "tariff shift" rules. In theory at least, this kind of rule of origin determines whether a sufficient amount of economic activity occurred in a country to justify conferral of origin in that country. As a general proposition, the greater the shift (*e.g.*, at the 4-digit HTS classification level), the greater the economic activity in a country. Conversely, the smaller the shift (*e.g.*, at the 8-digit level), the more modest the activity.

To apply a CTH rule, two sets of records must be available to answer two questions. First, what HTS classification applied to the imported components before they were manufactured into a finished apparel article? Second, what HTS classification applied to the finished apparel article? The first question concerns customs classification by a Beneficiary (*i.e.*, when the materials imported were imported into the Beneficiary). The second question concerns classification upon entry of the finished article into the U.S. Of course, applying the rule also presumes an exporter in a T&A Beneficiary SSAC has access directly, or through counsel, to *NAFTA*. Annex 401 of *NAFTA* contains the rules of origin (including for Chapters 50-63 of the HTS, which cover T&A merchandise), and they are reproduced in the General Notes to the HTSUS. While this may be true for prominent, well-connected exporters, it is difficult to imagine either *NAFTA* or the HTSUS is a bestseller anywhere on the African continent. Put simply, aside from the complexity of the CTH rules, access to them is difficult, and both problems raise the cost of compliance with *AGOA* to qualify for duty-free treatment.

No less important significant a concern is the oddity of *AGOA* incorporating by reference the Annex 401 origin rules. True, it may be preferable to creating a whole new set of origin rules. But, why give the relatively poorer countries of SSA the same treatment as Mexican apparel exporters? The origin requirement creates a kind of legal parity among two patently unequal categories of exporters whenever fabric or yarn is neither American nor African, subjecting the poorer ones to the same origin strictures as the comparatively better-off ones. Evidently, the scale of relative deprivation plays no role in this preference category.

Implicit in the short-supply test outlined above is permanence, *i.e.*, that the fabric or yarn in question is unavailable in commercial quantities in the U.S. now and in the long run. Silk might be one example of such a fabric. However, what if the fabric or yarn is available, but not immediately, nor in the short or medium term? In that instance, if an "interested party" requests, the President may proclaim duty-free treatment for yarns or fabrics that "cannot be supplied by the domestic industry in commercial quantities in a *timely* manner" (19 U.S.C. § 3721(b)(5)(B)(i) (emphasis added)).

To qualify, such apparel must come from fabric or yarn not available in commercial quantities in the U.S. (the first prong), and that American producers cannot supply in commercial quantities in a timely manner (the second prong). In brief, the apparel qualifies, despite consisting of non-American fabric or yarn, if the inputs are in short supply in the U.S. The President makes the short-supply determination, though in practice the President has delegated this authority to the Office of Textiles and Apparel (OTEXA) at the Department of Commerce. The criteria applied (under 19 U.S.C.

§ 3721(b)(5)(B)(i)) are that the fabric or yarn in question "cannot be supplied by the domestic [American] industry in commercial quantities in a timely manner."

The Seventh Preference Category — Cultural Textile and Apparel

Certain T&A goods, specifically, ones that are hand-loomed, handmade, or folklore articles, or ethnic printed fabrics, potentially qualify for preferential treatment. (*See* 19 U.S.C. § 3721(b)(6); HTSUS Chapter 98, subheading 9819.11.27 at 98-XIX-5.) Conceptually, there are three stages for qualification. First, the prospective T&A Beneficiary SSAC must consult with the U.S. as to the eligibility of the good. Second, the U.S. must decide whether the good indeed qualifies as a hand-loomed, handmade, or folklore article, or an ethnic printed fabric. Third, if the U.S. renders an affirmative determination in the second step, then a competent authority in the beneficiary country must certify the good as an eligible hand-loomed, hand-made, or folklore article, or ethnic printed fabric.

This category poses virtually no competitive threat to any American producer. Almost by definition, African cultural T&A articles do not have like or directly competitive products. Put simply, generosity through duty-free treatment in this category hardly is self-giving. The practical benefit from this generosity, for exporters, depends on the value and volume of exports in this category. Once again, almost by definition, small, cottage-industry-like producers, are among the likeliest of beneficiaries. How significant they are in a national economy, and the role they play in boosting growth, is dubious. After all, few if any countries reached developed country status through a handicrafts industry.

The Eighth Preference Category — Multi-Jurisdictional Apparel

The eighth and final *AGOA* preference category covers apparel assembled in a T&A Beneficiary SSAC from components originating in both a Beneficiary and the U.S. (*See* 19 U.S.C. § 3721(b)(7); HTSUS Chapter 98, subheading 9819.11.30 at 98-XIX-5.) Accordingly, the category might be called "Beneficiary Assembly Forward with Beneficiary or American Components." In specific, sewing may occur in a Beneficiary using American thread, where the components stitched together come from, and are cut in, the U.S. and a Beneficiary (or former Beneficiary) SSAC. The fabric must be American. This fabric must consist of American yarn (or components knit-to-shape in the U.S. and one or more Beneficiary or former Beneficiary, or both).

As an example, suppose the apparel article in question is a 100 percent cotton men's dress shirt. The pockets and sleeves are cut in the U.S., while the body is cut in one Beneficiary. In a second Beneficiary, with American thread, the pockets, sleeves, and body, are stitched together (along with other components, like collars and cuffs, which may come from any country). The pockets, sleeves, and body are from cotton fabric made of cotton spun in the U.S. The article would qualify for duty-free treatment under this category.

This category gives a T&A Beneficiary SSAC a modicum of flexibility in sourcing components. It can choose from multiple jurisdictions, without having to source all components from one jurisdiction. However, it is constrained to choose from the U.S., a fellow Beneficiary, or a domestic source. The insistence on American fabric made of American yarn is a familiar stricture. An essentially similar one exists in the first and second preference category. Thus, the flavor of all three categories is — put colloquially — "you (the Beneficiary) can have duty-free treatment, but only if you use our (American) fabric and yarn."

D. Trade Distortion?

Apparel articles are quintessential examples of low-value added manufactured items economists such as Walt Rostow in his *The Stages of Economic Growth* (1960) identify as significant to countries advancing to and beyond the "take off" for industrialization. For a poor country, these products tend to be ones in which they have a keen export interest, and thus ones for which preferential rules of origin matter greatly.

Trade in T&A constitutes roughly 8 percent of all trade in manufactured goods. The leading example of "high dependence" on T&A (defined as earning more than 50 percent of export revenue from one sector) is Bangladesh, for which T&A account for 85.8 percent of the merchandise export revenue. In India, 20 percent of industrial production comes from T&A, and this sector employs 15 million people. Exports in this sector play prominent roles in many SSACs and North African countries. In all such economies, there are multiplier effects from T&A production and exports. Businesses develop around this activity, from fruit and newsagents to haircutting and pharmacies. There also are significant externalities, including the employment and potential empowerment (as well as exploitation) of women.

To pick up the question of "why?," why is it appropriate to characterize the preferential rules of origin for these articles as "devilish," from the vantage of a prospective Beneficiary SSAC? Surely, the rules are defensible on the ground many SSACs lack the capacity to weave, cut, or assemble fabric, and indeed do not even have significant domestic yarn production. In brief, inputs into apparel articles are not readily available anyway, so what is wrong with rules of origin requiring use of U.S. inputs?

One answer, in brief, is distortion. This response arises out of conventional neoclassical economic theory. These rules create an artificial distortion about sourcing inputs. Consider the reality of global T&A production as seen by Victor Fung, the Chairman of Li & Fung, the major garment supplier in Hong Kong to American and European clothing brands:

> We might decide to buy yarn from a Korean producer but have it woven and dyed in Taiwan. So we pick the yarn and ship it to Taiwan. The Japanese have the best zippers and buttons, but they manufacture them mostly in China. Okay, so we go to YKK, a big Japanese manufacturer, and we order the right zippers from their Chinese plants. Then we determine that . . . the best place to make the garments is Thailand. So we ship everything there. . . . We're not asking which country can do the best job overall. Instead, we're pulling apart the value chain and optimizing each step — and we're doing it

globally. . . . If you talk to the big global consumer-products companies, they are all moving in this direction — toward being best on a
global scale.[6]

Yet, the *AGOA* preferential rules of origin seem either oblivious, or to flout
deliberately, this free market logic. It will not do to criticize SSA for lacking
globally-minded entrepreneurs like Victor Fung, or to castigate African rulers
for bad governance and corruption, without also engaging in introspection.
What technical American trade rules impede the likes of Victor Fung in SSA?
In *AGOA*, the first and third preference categories are not based on pure
assembly rules. Rather, they combine assembly operations in an SSA T&A
beneficiary with yarn-forward requirements. Likewise, the second preference
category is not a pure cutting-forward Rule. Rather, it contains a yarn-forward
requirement. The eighth category suffers from the same problem.

These strictures discourage would-be African entrepreneurs in a T&A SSAC
Beneficiary from obtaining fabric from the cheapest cost or highest quality
sources, and creating an efficient, vertically integrated, global production
chain like that of Li & Fung. Rather, under the first and third categories, they
must pay attention to the country of origin of yarn, not its price or quality.
Under the second category, they must focus on the source of the thread, not
its price and quality. Under the eighth category, they most focus on the source
of fabric, yarn, and thread. If fabric, yarn, or thread is not American, then
any hope of duty-free, quota free treatment from the U.S. is lost. The economic
fact substitute material from a third country, such as Egypt or Pakistan, may
be cheaper or better quality than the American inputs, is legally irrelevant.

One response to the trade distortion critique might be the *AGOA* preferential rules of origin encourage regional development. Some of them allow for
use of fabric or yarn from more than one Beneficiary. The third and eighth
preference categories are illustrations. Such allowance is known as "regional
cumulation," indicating a proportion of the inputs into a finished garment may
come from other countries in the region of the beneficiary, yet not vitiate
eligibility for preferential treatment. Oxfam International dubs regional
cumulation a "flawed trade instrument," stating "there is no development
rationale for promoting *regional* rather than *global* cumulation. It adds:

> The USA's African Growth and Opportunity Act (AGOA) . . .
> contains imperfect rules on cumulation. The Act stipulates that
> apparel exported from African countries to the USA must use either
> US or African fabrics to qualify for *AGOA* benefits, *notably discrimi-
> nating against fabrics produced in Asia*. One recent study [by the
> World Bank] estimates that Mauritius *would have* seen its total
> exports increase by 36 percent between 2001 and 2004 under *AGOA*,
> rather than 5 percent, had restrictive rules of origin *not* been in
> place.[7]

Whether the points Oxfam makes are true generally, or depend on the
industry and regional in question, is a matter best left to development
economists.

---

[6] *Id.* at 20.

[7] *Id.* at 22.

For now, four points should be emphasized. First, not all *AGOA* rules encourage regional development. If they did, then why are they (as Oxfam International puts it) "unreasonably demanding"? Second, the rules are inconsistent, if not disingenuous, in helping SSA. They address development in the American T&A industry as much as in SSA. Arguably because of fears of competition from Asian suppliers, there is no analog to *AGOA* for developing or least developed countries in Asia. Third, whether a rule of origin is an appropriate tool to encourage regional development is questionable. Surely there are more direct, efficient legal instruments. Fourth, and most fundamentally, there may well be strong arguments against promoting regional versus global development.

E. Economic Dependency?

Applying Dependency Theory, rules of origin tie a T&A Beneficiary SSAC to the U.S., or at least encourage that outcome. As Oxfam International observes, "agreements [like *AGOA* and the European "Everything But Arms" (EBA) program] that are supposed to benefit poor countries actually serve to promote the production of textiles in rich countries, to the detriment of the developing world as a whole." In *AGOA* (as intimated earlier), this tying is patent in all but the fifth and seventh preference categories, and effected through hybrid specified process rules of origin. Rather than, for example, a pure assembly rule in the first and third preferential categories, or a pure cutting forward rule in the second and eighth preferential categories, there are added mandates about the American origin of fabric, yarn, or thread. Such mandates encourage a Beneficiary to become dependent on the U.S. for inputs.

This encouragement is ironic. In the aftermath of the Second World War, when the U.S. actively engaged in the drafting of GATT at the 1946 London Preparatory Conference and the 1947 Geneva Preparatory Conference, it argued strongly against the preferential trading arrangements of the European colonial powers. Tying peripheral countries in Africa, Asia, and the Caribbean to the center countries like the United Kingdom and France was incongruous with free trade and the development interests of the poor countries. The American argument was not entirely successful. But, it did at least limit the schemes to the parameters set forth in Article I:2 of GATT, a restricted exception to the most favored nation (MFN) obligation in Article I:1.

Does *AGOA* bespeak an historic reversal of American efforts to resist center — periphery type links? Does it reveal a neo-colonial tolerance (indeed, support) for vertical integration of the T&A production through such links? Why does *AGOA* confer no meaningful reward for economic integration among poor countries, for instance, where a Beneficiary SSAC seeks high-quality, low-cost cotton from Egypt or Pakistan? Is it too cynical a response to say *AGOA* is about divide and rule? These questions are not pleasant to pose, nor should an ideologically driven answer be presumed. But, *AGOA* is not pleasant reading for an international trade lawyer or scholar who believes, perhaps mistakenly or foolishly, that international trade law can be about more than politically-motivated protection, that it can be a policy instrument to assist poor countries.

Another irony about *AGOA* is the first and second rationales may be practically inconsequential. From a legal standpoint, the rules of origin are complex. The cost of understanding and complying with them surely are high, all the more so for an African producer/exporter with limited resources to spend on competent trade counsel (if it even exists nearby). The cost may approach the margin of preference, cut into that margin, or even dwarf it. If compliance costs discourage use of *AGOA* benefits, then neither trade distortion nor dependency occurs. The consequence is "missing preferences" — a poor country does not develop a T&A industry capable of meeting the requirements for duty-free access to the markets of rich countries. Missing preferences is the heart of the irony. The ostensible purpose of *AGOA* — to provide a preference — is unfulfilled.

The problem of missing preferences may be even more likely to arise when an African producer-exporter seeks to ship merchandise to multiple importing countries. Suppose the producer/exporter aspires to gain a foothold not only in the American market, but also the EU market. To gain preferential access, it will be necessary to satisfy *AGOA* origin rules for the American market, and EU origin rules for the European market. To the extent the rules differ, the problem of understanding and applying them increases. If the producer-exporter seeks entry for its merchandise into still more markets, and the importing countries have non-harmonized rules, then the problem is yet worse. Heterogeneous rules of origin are dubbed the "spaghetti-bowl effect." The point is to see the interaction between this effect and missing preferences, as producer-exporters simply — and rationally, from a cost-benefit perspective — elect not to seek preferential access.

F. Social Justice?

To analyze preferential programs like *AGOA* in terms of trade distortion or Dependency Theory is to employ development economics. There is a non-economic basis for critique, indeed, for branding "devilish" on *AGOA* rules of origin for apparel articles. That reason is moral, indeed, religious: these rules are entirely at variance with the preferential option for the poor, which is a tenet of Catholic social justice theory (and, in all likelihood, of justice criteria in other faiths).

This tenet is grounded in Gospel teaching and articulated and elaborated, for example, in the Magisterium of the Roman Catholic Church through (*inter alia*) Papal encyclicals starting in 1891 with *Rerum Novarum* (On the Condition of the Working Classes), by Pope Leo XIII, and emphasized by Pope John Paul II in encyclicals such as *Labourem Exercens* (On Human Work) (1981), *Sollicitudo Rei Socialis* (On Social Concern) (1987), and *Centesimus Annus* (On the Hundredth Anniversary of *Rerum Novarum*) (1991). In brief, it demands primacy in public policy choices be given to the interests of the poor over the well-to-do. America has moved from a generic 35 percent value added test in its GSP program to product-specific rules of origin namely specified processes. Is that move selfish? Is it the case each U.S.-based company can insert into what is or ought to be a charitable program its own special device to make sure generosity stops where its self-interest, however real or remote, begins?

In sharp contrast, Canada adopted in 2003 an "Initiative for Least Developed Countries," making it the only major developed country to fulfill its promise at the Doha Ministerial Conference in November 2001 to provide duty-free, quota-free treatment on T&A articles from least developed countries. This Initiative imposes a two-pronged test to qualify for such treatment, and only one prong need be satisfied. Either:

   i.   An article is made in a least developed country, regardless of value added at the final stage of production (*i.e.*, there is no value-added threshold at that stage), or

   ii. At least 25 percent of the value added to an article occurs in the final stage in a least developed country, but inputs may come from any other country in the world, and there is no dual substantial transformation requirement concerning yarn-to-fabric and fabric-to clothing).

Yet, under *AGOA*, the keen export interest in T&A of Beneficiary SSACs is subordinated to producers of T&A producing like merchandise made in the U.S.

Understandably, the American T&A sector feels besieged by cheaper imports. Hundreds of thousands of jobs have been lost in recent years, as some politicians, especially from the Southeast (the epicenter of the sector), intone. From their vantage, to give GSP treatment to T&A imports exacerbates decline, or at least complicates orderly contraction. The GSP statutory product exemptions are right to calculate generosity to poor countries. The fourth preference category, for the poorest SSA countries, with early its sunset rule and TRQ thresholds, is a good balance. American willingness to give duty-free treatment should extend only to the line of potential threat to U.S. producers.

However, is the socially just response to cut back on generosity toward the poorest countries? Is it to help the shrinking American T&A sector though more generous trade adjustment assistance (TAA)? Ought not generosity to be a positive sum game?

Part Twelve

LABOR AND THE ENVIRONMENT

Chapter 42

TRADE AND LABOR

My grandfather once told me that there are two kinds of people: those who work and those who take the credit. He told me to try to be in the first group; there was less competition there.

— Prime Minister Indira Gandhi (1917-84)

DOCUMENTS SUPPLEMENT ASSIGNMENT

1. *Havana Charter* Articles 1-3, 7, 45:1(a)(vi)

2. GATT Preamble and Article XX(e)

3. WTO *Agreement Preamble*

4. *NAFTA Labor Side Agreement*

5. Relevant provisions in other FTAs

I. DEFINING "INTERNATIONALLY RECOGNIZED WORKER RIGHTS"

Eliding for the moment the problem of defining "worker rights," why do these rights get violated? Oxfam International offers the following five reasons:

   i.   National governments, desperate to attract much-needed foreign investment, offer incentives, including increased labor-market "flexibility" — that is, the denial of fundamental labor rights such as freedom of association, along with the failure to enforce existing legislation.

   ii.   Powerful global buyers, whose business model is based on short-term profit maximization, squeeze the players lower down the supply chain.

   iii.   Producers use cheap labor as their primary competitive advantage, actively discouraging workers from organizing.

   iv.   Lending agencies such as the IMF and World Bank insist on labor-market flexibility as a part of their lending policy.

   v.   Young women and migrants, who constitute a majority of the "flexible, obedient, pliant" workforce, are often not aware of their rights and are highly vulnerable to exploitation (notably including sexual exploitation).[1]

---

[1] Oxfam International, *Stitched Up: How Rich-Country Protectionism in Textiles and Clothing Trade Prevents Poverty Alleviation* 25 (Oxfam Briefing Paper 60, March 2004).

These reasons bespeak the reality of working conditions in the agricultural and industrial sectors of many countries. This reality is not limited to poor countries, nor to those sectors. Service sector workers (including American lawyers!) complain not unreasonably of dreadful working conditions.

These reasons also intimate the parameters of a definition of "worker rights." There are, in fact, an internationally agreed-upon set of such rights.

UNITED STATES INTERNATIONAL TRADE COMMISSION, *TRADE ISSUES OF THE 1990s — PART II*
INTERNATIONAL ECONOMIC REVIEW 18, 19 (1994)

Trade, Employment, and Labor Standards

. . . [B]etween the December 1993 conclusion and the April 1994 signing of the Uruguay Round agreements, the United States sought to have labor standards — also referred to as worker rights — included in discussions of factors affecting trade under the forthcoming WTO regime. However, developing countries were deeply suspicious that such multilateral discussions were likely, at best, to undermine their comparative trade advantage arising out of lower labor costs; at worst, to afford developed countries an issue that could be abused for patently protectionist purposes. [The U.S. tried to have labor topics included on the Doha Development Agenda, but many WTO Members from the developing and least developed world objected.]

U.S. Focus on Worker Rights

The . . . U.S. effort to bring labor standards under multilateral discussion in the trade arena has both a longstanding and a more immediate stimulus. Congressional mandates to pursue "worker rights" have been common as part of the legislative renewal of Presidential trade-negotiating authority since the Eisenhower administration. This mandate was reiterated most recently in Congressional instructions to U.S. negotiators in the *Omnibus Trade and Competitiveness Act of 1988*. Of the 16 negotiating objectives set out in section 101 of the act, no. 14 reads —

(14) Worker Rights. — The principal negotiating objectives of the United States regarding worker rights are —

(A) To promote respect for worker rights;

(B) To secure a review of the relationship of worker rights to GATT articles, objectives, and related instruments with a view to ensuring that the benefits of the trading system are available to all workers; and

(C) To adopt, as a principle of the GATT, that the denial of worker rights should not be a means for a country or its industries to gain competitive advantage in international trade.

. . . The United States has said it supports . . . [labor] rights as a means to raise the living standards of all citizens, including workers. . . . The United

States has stated repeatedly that it in no way seeks to use new labor standards to erect new trade barriers for protectionist purposes.

Although unsuccessful in inserting language concerning worker rights into the *Marrakesh Declaration* in April 1994, the United States did succeed in having trade and labor standards acknowledged by other Round participants as a legitimate subject for consideration . . . [in future WTO projects.]

. . . .

Labor Standards Precursors

In its efforts to raise worker rights as a multilateral issue, the United States pointed out that the Havana Charter of 1948 and, subsequently, the GATT, addressed these rights. The Havana Charter specified —

> The Members recognize that . . . all countries have a common interest in the achievement and maintenance of fair labour standards related to productivity, and thus in the improvement of wages and working conditions as productivity may permit. The Members recognize that unfair labour conditions, particularly in production for export, create difficulties in international trade and accordingly each Member shall take whatever action may be appropriate and feasible to eliminate such conditions within the territory.

The Havana Charter . . . never came into existence as the ITO was never ratified by national legislatures. Although the later preamble to the GATT states that members are joining the General Agreement "Recognizing that their relations in the field of trade . . . should be conducted with a view to raising standards of living," the more specific labor standards of the Havana Charter serve now only as guidelines for present-day negotiators, taken from the collective history of the original negotiation of the General Agreement.

ILO Labor Standards

The United States' campaign to discuss labor standards in relation to trade concentrates largely on five of the most widely recognized labor standards. These five standards are —

1.   The freedom of association;

2.   The right to organize and bargain collectively;

3.   The freedom from forced or compulsory labor;

4.   A minimum age for the employment of children; and

5.   Measures that set forth minimum standards for work conditions.

These standards, as well as others, are internationally recognized by the International Labor Organization (ILO) of the United Nations in its conventions and endorsed by a number of countries.

[The four most significant ILO Conventions are: (1) Number 87, on *Freedom of Association and Protection of the Right to Organize*; (2) Number 98, on the *Right to Organize and Collectively Bargain*; (3) Number 105, on *Abolition of Forced Labor*; and (4) Number 138, on *Minimum Age*. Concerning these and other ILO Conventions, consider which countries have, and have not, ratified them — including the U.S.

On 17 June 1999, the ILO unanimously adopted a Convention 182 on the *Prohibition and Immediate Action for the Elimination of the Worst Forms of Child Labor. See* 38 INTERNATIONAL LEGAL MATERIALS 1215 (1999). Convention 182 defines "child" as anyone less than 18 years old, and identifies the "worst forms" as slavery, debt bondage, forced or compulsory labor (including the use of children in armed conflict), prostitution, pornography, the use of children for illicit activities (*e.g.*, narcotics production and trafficking), and work that is likely to harm the health, safety, or morals of children. ILO members are obligated to take immediate and effective measures to eliminate these practices. Article 10 of the Convention states the Convention enters into force one year after the date on which two ILO members have ratified it. The Seychelles ratified it on 28 September 1999, and Malawi ratified it on 19 November 1999. Thus, the Convention took effect on 19 November 2000. In August 1999, President Clinton sought the advice and consent of the Senate for ratification, and the Senate acted favorably on 2 December 1999. Note, however, the Convention can be viewed as a pragmatic, if not depressing, compromise. Rather than trying to outlaw all forms of child labor, a possibly hopeless effort, it seeks only to rid the globe of the worst forms.]

. . . The United States incorporates these five standards as conditions for affording trade preferences to developing countries under such programs as the Generalized System of Preferences (GSP). In a review of existing trade and labor provisions, prepared for the November 1994 meeting of its governing body, the ILO found that virtually all trade liberalizing agreements lack a "social dimension" or a "labor dimension," particularly concerning the areas covered by the ILO conventions on freedom of association, collective bargaining, prison labor, and forced and child labor. Although the idea is adamantly opposed by developing countries, the paper suggests incorporating some ILO conventions into the WTO rules where the WTO could make decisions concerning trade sanctions following ILO judgment about whether violations had occurred.

II. REALIZING INTERNATIONALLY RECOGNIZED WORKER RIGHTS

ORGANIZATION FOR ECONOMIC CO-OPERATION AND DEVELOPMENT
TRADE AND LABOR STANDARDS 9-17, 19, 21 (1995)

I. *Introduction*

. . . .

Trade and labour market policies are continuously being discussed and reformulated. . . . When does "free trade" give way to "fair trade"? When does the pursuit of one labour standard (*e.g.*, free collective bargaining) take precedence over another (*e.g.*, full employment)?

. . . .

[Below, the following] five questions are raised for consideration:

1. On what basis should labour standards be chosen?

2. Is there such a thing as basic labour rights? If so, should they be harmonized internationally?

3. What labour standards are appropriate beyond the basic level and how might they be achieved?

4. Based on countries' experiences, is it better to promote labour standards directly or indirectly?

5. Are labour standards and international trade substitutes or complements?

II. *The Basis for Deciding on "Appropriate" Labour Standards*

. . . [T]wo extreme positions on labour standards have to be rejected. One is "the more the better." The other is "the fewer the better."

. . . .

How, then, are we to decide which labour standards are appropriate? While it is argued by some that international labour standards are needed in order to prevent countries from competing with one another on the basis of "illegitimate advantages," a different basis for evaluation could be suggested, namely, *basic human rights in the workplace*. The distinguishing criterion one could propose *is whether it is better to have no production at all than to have production using "illegitimate means."*

If this criterion is adopted, it would imply that labour rights would be set at a minimum level appropriate to all working people in rich and poor countries alike and guaranteed by appropriate international agreements. They would be taken out of the realm of benefit-cost comparisons with tradeoffs among desirable goals and would instead be treated as *inviolable* rights.

What are the basic human rights in the workplace for men, women, and children everywhere? Would it be desirable to go beyond these basic labour rights to other labour standards?

III. *Basic Labour Rights and Harmonization of Labour Standards*

It is useful at the outset to distinguish between a "labour standard" and a "labour right"; a "labour standard" is something we would aim towards and rather have than not have, whereas a "labour right" is something that is not to be violated except under the most extreme circumstances. "Labour standards" thus include "labour rights" but go beyond them.

The U.S. Department of Labour has repeatedly upheld the desirability of the following list of labour standards:

1. Freedom of association.

2. The right to organise and bargain collectively.

3. Prohibition on forced or compulsory labour.

4. A minimum age for the employment of children.

5. Guarantee of acceptable working conditions (possibly including maximum hours of work per week, a weekly rest period, limits to work by young persons, a minimum wage, minimum workplace safety and health standards, and elimination of employment discrimination).

Section 502 (b)(8) of the 1984 *Trade and Tariff Act* authorises the President to withhold recognition under the Generalised System of Preferences (GSP) to a country that "has not taken or is not taking steps to afford internationally recognised worker rights to workers in the country (including any designated zone in that country)."

The European Union's "Social Charter," approved by all of the EC Member countries except for the United Kingdom, specifies an even broader list of worker "rights" (which, because they are voluntary, might better be viewed as "targets"):

— Freedom of movement.

— The right to employment and remuneration.

— The improvement of living and working conditions.

— The right to social protection.

— The right to freedom of association and collective bargaining.

— The right to vocational training.

— The right of men and women to equal treatment.

— The right of information, consultation, and participation.

— The right to health and safety in the workplace.

— The protection of children and adolescents in employment.

— The protection of elderly persons.

— The protection of persons with disabilities.

It is sad but true that standards like these are unattainable for most of the world's people. The reason is very basic: most of the world's economies are too poor to assure these standards for the majority of their people, and even in the rich countries, these standards are not guaranteed to everyone. For example, when rural parents in the developing countries must decide between employing their children on the family farm during planting and harvesting season or sending them to school, the children are often made to work long and hard, even though not going to school is known to have potentially negative effects on the children's future opportunities. Or, to take another example of a clash of priorities, when people receive extremely low hourly earnings from wage jobs or self-employment, they will want to work very long work weeks in order to meet their basic subsistence needs; in these circumstances, it would be heartless to limit the work week or compel a weekly rest period. However, the preceding lists are too ambitious and unrealistic for the majority of the world's workers.

Even leading labour officials now recognise the impossibility of guaranteeing "acceptable working conditions" at an internationally uniform level. . . .

[T]he United States' Secretary of Labour [in the Clinton Administration], Robert Reich, said . . .:

> It is inappropriate to dictate uniform levels of working hours, minimum wages, benefits, or health and safety standards. The developing countries' insistence that they must grow richer in order to afford American or European labour standards — and that they must trade if they are to grow richer — is essentially correct.

Along similar lines, the General Secretary of the International Confederation of Free Trade Unions (ICFTU), one of the strongest advocacy groups for labour, wrote:

> The ICFTU-APRO does not think that is possible or desirable to set a world-wide minimum wage. Negotiations between employers, unions, and governments within countries, which take into account productivity and other factors, are the best way to ensure that as trade and development progress, wages and other conditions of work improve.

These statements suggest that a "guarantee of acceptable working conditions" has effectively been removed from current policy debate.

In the spirit of aiming for something that is both attainable and enforceable in *every* country, a set of *basic labour rights for workers throughout the world* can be proposed:

(i)   No person has the right to enslave another or to cause another to enter into indentured servitude, and every person has the right to freedom from such conditions.

(ii) No person has the right to expose another to unsafe or unhealthy working conditions without the fullest possible information.

(iii) Children have the right not to work long hours whenever their families' financial circumstances allow.

(iv) Every person has the right to freedom of association in the workplace and the right to organise and bargain collectively with employers.

Such labour rights are essential for assuring fundamental human rights and that they should, therefore, be adopted around the world as soon as possible. Viewed in this way, the question of whether this four-point programme should be harmonized internationally can be answered easily. Yes, it should be: basic labour rights should be "taken out of competition" and guaranteed everywhere precisely because these rights are basic to all people.

IV. *International Pressure for Additional Labour Standards*

Should international pressure be brought to bear in the pursuit of additional labour standards that go beyond the four basic labour rights just proposed? Here, one would argue that such standards should not be harmonized under the aegis of international organisations even if "deep integration" were possible, which it probably is not. Labour standards should, rather, be left to the individual countries. The reasons for concluding this are several:

1. Although developed countries' concerns for developing countries' labour standards are motivated in part by a humanitarian desire to improve the conditions of work in other countries, they nonetheless strike many in the developing world as unwarranted intrusion into their internal affairs and affronts to their national sovereignty. People in the developing world are offended when they are treated as being incapable of deciding what would be appropriate for themselves, and they rightly regard developing countries' advice as patronising. A remarkable unanimity of views against imposed international labour standards has been expressed by the leaders of developing countries around the world, including the Member states of the Association of South-East Asian Nations and the "Rio Group" of Latin American nations.

2. To many in the Third World, the First World's call for labour standards is protectionism of a badly-disguised sort. Protestations about benevolent motives are regarded with considerable skepticism and, anyhow, motives are not observable. What is observable is that most of the support for labour standards comes from labour unions and labour ministries in some of the developed countries. Not surprisingly, the developing countries often react with anger. Consider this from the [former] Prime Minister of Malaysia [Mahathir]:

Western governments openly propose to eliminate the competitive edge of East Asia. The recent proposal for a world-wide minimum wage is a blatant example. Westerners know that this is the sole comparative advantage of the developing countries. All other comparative advantages (technology, capital, rich domestic markets, legal frameworks, management and marketing networks) are with the developed states. It is obvious that the professed concern about workers' welfare is motivated by selfish interest. Sanctimonious pronouncements on humanitarian, democratic and environmental issues are likely to be motivated by a similar selfish desire to put as many obstacles as possible in the way of anyone attempting to catch up and compete with the West.

3. International standards designed with one problem in mind may make little sense in other contexts. Take the widely urged standard of prohibiting production by forced or convict-labour and banning the trade in such goods. This standard is motivated by abuses in countries which have been found to use political prisoners who are given only meager subsistence and no wages to produce low-cost goods for export. This is indeed outrageous. But would it be any less outrageous if the goods were sold only within those countries? Anyhow, most convicts around the world are imprisoned not for political reasons but because they have been convicted of crimes. To the extent that those who have committed violent or antisocial acts are made to work in prison for their living, why should not the goods they produced be sold abroad, with the proceeds to be used as partial compensation to the home societies (by, for example,

defraying the social cost of maintaining prisons)? The case for banning the export of goods made by prison labour is unconvincing.

4.   It is unlikely that an enforcement mechanism can be found that would be acceptable to all sides, but let us suppose for the moment that one could be. For instance, one of the world's leading advocates for free trade. Professor Jagdish Bhagwati . . . has proposed that U.S. labour laws be applied to subsidiaries of U.S. firms producing in Mexico. Assuming that international labour standards could be enforced in this way, one can reasonably ask whether they should be. Would it be good to apply the U.S. minimum wage to subsidiaries of U.S. firms operating in Mexico, considering the likely adverse employment effects? Should the labour of Mexican children be outlawed even when families rely on that labour for their livelihoods? Would it be right to impose an eight-hour day or a forty-hour week on people who want to work longer? If Mexico were to agree to these standards, how many jobs would move to other countries where these standards are not imposed? How many non-U.S. companies who would not have to meet U.S. labour standards would move into Mexico and replace U.S. companies which would have to meet those standards? It is not obvious what would be good for Mexico: that is not for us to decide, but for them.

. . . .

6.   Finally, it is interesting to note that the ILO itself has *opposed* sanctions against countries that have failed to comply with conventions they have ratified or with the ILO's universal principles. Why? "In addition to implementing sanctions, the mere prospect of sanctions is capable of discouraging ratification, or even membership in the Organisation." And: "[To] link trade concessions (such as access to their markets) to compliance with certain labour standards with a view to combating what they refer to as 'social dumping' . . . [could cause our supervisory machinery to suffer] if the conclusions that result from it are used in a context of coercion."

V. *How to Raise Labour Standards: Push or Pull?*

Assuming that it is left to individual countries to decide when and how to raise labour standards, what lessons might they find helpful from comparative analysis of other countries' experiences? First, it is necessary to be explicit about what is meant by "improved labour standards." Above, it was suggested that higher labour standards might be conceived as enabling workers to achieve higher real earnings at the fullest possible level of employment, and that is the objective that is taken here as given.

Two broad approaches toward raising labour standards can be found:

—   Governments often take direct action aimed at raising labour standards: directly increasing employment, directly raising wages by means of government pay policy for the public sector and minimum wages for the private sector, encouraging and facilitating strong trade unions, instituting ambitious labour codes.

— Labour standards are also promoted indirectly, *via* actions to accelerate economic growth so that improvements in wage and employment opportunities can be afforded. Among the developing countries, the direct approach of pushing up wages and employment has been the dominant one in Latin America and the Caribbean, Africa, and South Asia; by contrast, some Far Eastern economies (Singapore, Hong Kong, Korea, and Taiwan) are noteworthy for their reliance on indirect methods and the virtual absence of direct ones. In the developed world, the European countries might appropriately be classified in an intermediate position.

Setting labour standards directly is a tricky business. . . . [D]ue account must be taken of such predictable consequences as informalisation, partial coverage, and international movement of companies and jobs. . . .

Modern economic theory seeks to justify government intervention in the economy as a response to market failure, but the literature on the labour standards question has not gone very far toward specifying what market failure is being corrected. There are some apparent failures — asymmetric information on the health and safety risks associated with particular jobs (which motivates proposed basic labour standard number (ii) "No person has the right to expose another to unsafe or unhealthy working conditions without the fullest impossible information") and severe limits on international migration as a response to poor labour conditions — but discussion of these is conspicuously missing from the labour standards literature. On the other hand, one "failure" that is sometimes alleged in the literature is the failure of companies to do what is in their own interest, leading some economists and other social scientists to argue that the imposition of labour standards could lead to improved industrial relations practices, more and better worker training, greater purchasing power of labour, and the like, all of which are presumed to be better for firms. This line of reasoning implicitly assumes that firms are not now maximising profits and furthermore that the deviations from profit-maximising behaviour in the absence of enforced labour standards are systematic — too little labour-management cooperation, for example. Neoclassically oriented economists are not likely to be convinced by such claims, implicit or otherwise.

A more convincing argument might be the following: there exist multiple equilibria, the world's economies have somehow got locked into an inferior one because of coordination failures, and the imposition of labour standards on a world-wide scale would cause a shift to a superior equilibrium. This would, however, have to be demonstrated to be applicable to current conditions.

Consider now the alternative of waiting for labour standards to be pulled up by the forces of supply and demand. Have the indirect methods worked? . . . [D]ata [from 1948-90 concerning four East Asian economies, Hong Kong, Korea, Singapore, and Taiwan] show two distinct phases. . . . In the first phase, when these economies were labour-abundant, real labour earnings stayed roughly constant while unemployment fell. In the second phase, once essentially-full employment was attained, real labour earnings rose rapidly while full or nearly-full employment was maintained. The results are astounding: in Taiwan, real wages are eight times higher than they were a generation ago, and in Korea, they are more than six times higher.

The extent to which workers in the Far East shared in their economies' economic growth can be demonstrated in another way. . . . [I]n all four economies in the 1980s, real labour earnings grew at least as fast as real *per capita* GNP. The four Far Eastern economies have had very low rates of unemployment and very low levels of income inequality by international standards. This means that people at the bottom end of the income distribution have benefited proportionately from economic growth, and in this way, growth raised labour standards: real minimum wages were increased, unemployment insurance systems were instituted, social protection systems were created, and collective bargaining grew in importance.

. . . .

These international data suggest that there may be an effective alternative to pushing up wages and other labour standards directly: promoting labour standards indirectly through measures that foster economic growth. This is a call not for inattention to basic labour rights, which have not always been fully honoured in the Far East. It is, rather, a call for careful analysis of which mechanisms would best promote improved labour standards in particular country contexts.

III. BANNING IMPORTS MADE BY FORCED LABOR

A. The GATT Article XX(e) Exception

Given the increased attention galvanized by the anti-globalization movement to the effects of trade liberalisation on labor rights, item (e) is perhaps the most notable of the 10 general exceptions to GATT obligations listed in GATT Article XX. Yet, this exception is not a broad one for all kinds of workers' rights. It is narrowly crafted for "prison" labour. The drafters of GATT had a precedent for their work. A provision in the United States *Tariff Act of 1930* bans importation of prison-made goods.

Why single out prison labor? One justification is economic. Setting aside questions of product comparability or quality, if prison workers are maintained at subsistence level, then their product is akin to unfairly subsidiZed merchandise. Workers in other countries, who are not imprisoned, cannot compete against goods made by prisoners kept barely alive. The price of their output will be higher, in reflection of their higher wages. (To be sure, that higher price also may suggest higher marginal productivity.)

Is this justification persuasive? All too many workers around the world are paid a bare subsistence wage (or less). About one billion people earn one U.S. dollar per day or less, and another one billion people earn two dollars or less per day. Obviously, they are not all in prison. If the rationale for Article XX(e) is to combat an unfair form of competition, then the language of this exception is under-inclusive. Ought it not also cover merchandise for which a worker, jailed or not, is paid less than an agreed-upon threshold? Of course, agreeing on that threshold is nearly impossible, with wealthy WTO Members advocating a high level and poorer Members fearing the higher the level, the greater their loss of comparative advantage.

GATT Article XX(e) is not always easy to implement. For instance, is it possible to determine whether a particular facility in a WTO Member is, in fact, a prison? The Member may be willing to disclose many, even most, of its prisons. For reasons (however dubious) of internal security, it may keep one or a few facilities secret. The 1994 *China Diesel* case raises these matters.

B. Section 307, the 1986 *McKinney* Case, and Defining Who Is Hurt By Forced Labor

McKINNEY v. U.S. DEPT. OF TREASURY
United States Court of Appeals for the Federal Circuit
799 F.2d 1544, 1547-58 (1986)

Archer, Circuit Judge.

Background

Section 307 of the *Tariff Act of 1930*, as amended [19 U.S.C. § 1307], provides that:

> All goods, wares, articles, and merchandise mined, produced, or manufactured wholly or in part in any foreign country by convict labor or/and forced labor or/and indentured labor under penal sanctions shall not be entitled to entry at any of the ports of the United States, and the importation thereof is hereby prohibited, and the Secretary of the Treasury is authorized and directed to prescribe such regulations as may be necessary for the enforcement of this provision. The provisions of this section relating to goods, wares, articles, and merchandise mined, produced, or manufactured by forced labor or/and indentured labor, shall take effect on January 1, 1932; but in no case shall such provisions be applicable to goods, wares, articles, or merchandise so mined, produced, or manufactured which are not mined, produced, or manufactured in such quantities in the United States as to meet the consumptive demands of the United States.

> "Forced labor," as herein used, shall mean all work or service which is exacted from any person under the menace of any penalty for its nonperformance and for which the worker does not offer himself voluntarily.

The United States Department of State, in February 1983, furnished the Congress with a report entitled "Report on Forced Labor in the U.S.S.R." Accompanying this report was a letter of the Undersecretary of State for Political Affairs which stated that forced labor was used to produce large amounts of primary and manufactured Soviet goods for both domestic and export markets.

In September 1983, the Commissioner of Customs sought approval from the Secretary of the Treasury to publish in the *Federal Register* his findings that certain products from the U.S.S.R. may have been produced by forced labor, which would have the effect of prohibiting the entry of such products into the

United States. . . . In May 1984, the Secretary of the Treasury notified the Commissioner that such a determination was not warranted at that time, but should be deferred pending a study by the International Trade Commission.

Thereafter in May 1984, eighty-four members of Congress and several associations petitioned the United States Customs Service to bar importation of goods produced in the U.S.S.R. wholly or in part by forced labor. The Assistant Secretary for Enforcement and Operations of the Treasury subsequently notified these petitioners that the Department of the Treasury would not act on their petition until such time as additional evidence became available.

In January 1985, the Secretary of the Treasury, on the available evidence, determined that there was no reasonable basis upon which to establish a nexus between Soviet forced labor practices and specific imports from the U.S.S.R. or to bar importation of any goods produced in the U.S.S.R. In doing so, the Secretary declined to adopt the Commissioner's proposed findings of late 1983.

Appellants filed the present action on September 26, 1984 seeking declaratory and injunctive relief and filed an amended complaint on February 20, 1985. They alleged that the denial of their May 1984 petition constituted a final agency action . . . which was arbitrary, capricious, an abuse of discretion, or otherwise not in accordance with the law. . . . The appellants further alleged that agency action on their petition was unlawfully withheld or unreasonably delayed. . . .

The court concluded that, with the exception of the congressional appellants in their capacities as workers and producers, none of the appellants possessed standing.

. . . .

On appeal it is argued that all of the appellants in the capacities now asserted have standing, *viz.*, that, either directly or as a representative of their members or constituency, all have suffered injury. As consumers, the injury is that they do not wish to purchase these illegal products and subsidize Soviet human rights violations. They also claim injury "as stockholders in U.S. companies which compete with the illegal imports, as members of the International Longshoremen's Association which are forced to handle these products; as public interest organizations which have a specialized interest in this area; and as Congressmen who are affected by the defendants' actions in their personal, representative and legislative capacities." . . .

Opinion

I.

Fundamentally, the question of standing involves the determination of whether a particular litigant is entitled to invoke the jurisdiction of a federal court to decide the merits of a dispute or of particular issues. . . . The focus is on the qualifications and status of the party seeking to bring his complaint before a federal court and not on the issues he wishes to have resolved. . . .

When the standing of a litigant is placed in issue, the court must undertake a two-step analysis which involves both the constitutional limitations and the prudential limitations that circumscribe standing. . . . As a threshold matter the court must ensure that the litigant satisfies the requirements of Article III of the Constitution. . . . Once the court determines that the litigant satisfies the constitutional aspects, it must consider whether any prudential limitations restrain the court from exercising its judicial power. . . .

Article III confines the role of the federal courts to adjudication of actual "cases" and "controversies." . . . Standing, in the constitutional dimension, is one of the doctrines that clusters about Article III, to define further the case-or-controversy requirement that limits the federal judicial power in our system of government. . . . Those who do not possess Article III standing may not litigate in the courts of the United States. . . .

The principal limitation imposed by Article III is that a litigant seeking to invoke the court's authority must "show that he personally has suffered some actual or threatened injury as a result of the putatively illegal conduct of the defendant." . . . In addition, Article III requires the litigant to establish that there is a causal connection between the litigant's injury and the putatively illegal conduct of the defendant, and that this injury is likely to be redressed should the court grant the relief requested. . . .

The nature of the actual or threatened injury that must be established by the litigant has been described by the Supreme Court variously as: a "judicially cognizable" injury, . . . a "personal" injury, . . . a "distinct and palpable" injury, . . . a "particular concrete" injury, . . . a "concrete" injury, . . . or a "specific present objective harm or a threat of specific future harm." . . . The Court has held that the actual or threatened injury may be either economic or non-economic in nature. . . .

But, the Court has cautioned that "abstract," "conjectural," or "hypothetical" injury is insufficient to meet the Article III requirement for injury. . . . The mere assertion of a right to have the Government act in accordance with the law is not sufficient, in and of itself, to satisfy the injury requirement. . . . Nor is an interest in a problem, no matter how longstanding the interest or how qualified the litigant in matters relating to the problem, sufficient to satisfy the injury requirement. . . .

The Supreme Court has also recognized that an organization may have standing to assert the claims of its members, even where the organization itself has not suffered an injury from the putatively unlawful action. . . . But this doctrine does not vitiate the injury requirement imposed by Article III, for the organization derives its standing in part by showing that its members have incurred an actual or threatened injury.

In addition to the constitutional requirements, the Supreme Court has articulated several prudential limitations that may be relevant in addressing the issue of standing. A litigant must generally assert his own legal rights or interests, and cannot rest his claim to relief on the legal rights or interests of third parties. . . . A litigant must assert an injury peculiar to himself or to a distinct group of which he is a part, rather than an interest shared in substantially equal measure by all or a large part of the populace. . . . And, the litigant's complaint must fall within the "zone of interests" to be protected or regulated by the statute or constitutional guarantee in question. . . .

II.

Appellants have variously alleged standing as consumers, workers and producers, shareholders, handlers, public interest organizations, and legislators who are adversely affected by the importation of Soviet goods in contravention of § 307. . . .

A. *Consumers*

Congressional appellants, in their personal capacities as consumers, have alleged that they are adversely affected by the purchase of, or risk of purchasing, Soviet goods produced by forced labor. The congressional appellants appear to be asserting an alleged Article III injury which they believe reflects both economic injury and non-economic ethical injury. We address both aspects of such alleged injury.

For the purpose of this analysis, it is assumed that the economic detriment alleged is sufficient to satisfy the injury requirement imposed by Article III. We conclude, however, that this court should refrain from exercising jurisdiction over appellants' complaint as it relates to their status as consumers because of the "zone of interests" prudential limitation.

Section 307 was enacted by Congress to *protect* domestic producers, production, and workers from the unfair competition which would result from the importation of foreign products produced by forced labor. No stated or implied intention is evident in the statute or its legislative history to protect the consuming public from the importation of goods produced by forced labor. Although § 307 also *regulates* the importation of products produced by forced labor, it does so in a manner that will afford domestic consumers a supply of such products through importation when there is insufficient domestic production to satisfy consumer demand. Thus, § 307 only affords consumers a legal right or interest to have access to such products by relaxation of the import ban when they are in short supply domestically. This legal interest, however, is not implicated or asserted by any of the appellants claiming consumer status.

The plain language of § 307, accordingly, will not support an interpretation that it was enacted to afford consumers a legal right or interest in preventing, for economic, moral, or ethical reasons, the importation of foreign goods produced by forced labor. Had Congress intended such protection to flow from § 307, it would likely have imposed an absolute bar, *i.e.*, precluding importation of foreign products found to have been produced by forced labor under all conditions, rather than a conditional exclusion to be lifted in the event of unfulfilled domestic demand. . . . The nature and character of the legislation does not support the contention that Congress intended to create a statutory privilege accruing to consumers in the avoidance of purchasing imported goods produced through human rights violations. . . . And though we assume there might be an economic injury to consumers sufficient to meet the requirements of Article III, the economic claim asserted by appellants as consumers is not within the "zone of interests" protected or regulated by § 307. . . .

As to the non-economic injury claimed by appellants as consumers, we do not agree with appellants' assertion that this is the kind of injury that satisfies the Article III requirement. The alleged non-economic injury is founded on the adverse psychological consequences arising from inadvertent support of immoral conduct with which appellants disagree. . . . The ethical injury asserted by appellants is the type of abstract injury, . . . which would transform the federal courts into nothing more than a vehicle for the vindication of value interests of concerned bystanders, . . . and, as such, is not "an injury sufficient to confer standing under Art. III." . . .

Even if this non-economic injury satisfied Article III, prudential limitations counsel against standing for appellants as consumers. In view of the above analysis of economic injury, it is even more unlikely that Congress intended § 307 to shield the psyche of domestic consumers against foreign products produced through human rights violations. Such a conclusion would be anomalous in the face of the exception provided by § 307 for short-supply importation of goods produced by forced labor. Appellants as consumers and their claimed non-economic injury are not within the "zone of interests" protected or regulated by § 307.

Moreover, appellants are also prudentially limited from asserting standing as injured consumers because their injury is not peculiar to a distinct group. . . . Appellants have argued to the contrary, claiming that this non-economic injury is specific to them as a group, but other than a generalized, conclusory statement to this effect they have failed to present any persuasive reasons why they should be so considered. The moral and ethical interest in avoiding the purchase of or boycotting foreign goods produced by forced labor is shared by most, if not all, of the domestic populace. This is the type of wide public concern, amounting to a generalized grievance, which federal courts normally refrain from adjudicating. . . . Appellants' non-economic injury, therefore, cannot serve as a predicate for standing.

B. *Producers*

The WLF [Washington Legal Foundation, one of the appellants] asserts standing on the basis of its members and supporters who include "manufacturers or producers or workers employed by manufacturers or producers of products which are similar to and compete with goods or products being imported unlawfully from the Soviet Union." To rely on derivative or associational standing, the WLF must show that it meets the requirements for standing articulated by the Supreme Court in *Hunt v. Washington State Apple Advertising Commission*, 432 U.S. 333, 343 (1977). . . .

One of the *Hunt* requirements is that an organization must demonstrate that the interests it seeks to protect are germane to the organization's purpose. . . . The WLF, in the amended complaint, avers that it is a "non-profit public interest law firm." The amended complaint does not indicate that a purpose of the WLF is to protect the economic interests of producers and workers generally or to protect its producer and worker members adversely affected by goods imported in contravention of § 307. . . . [T]he WLF has failed to demonstrate a nexus between its organizational purpose and the economic interests of the producers and workers it purportedly represents. . . .

Additionally, WLF has failed to show that its producer and worker members have standing to sue in their own right. . . . A certain degree of specificity in delineating the injury, be it "judicially cognizable," . . . "distinct and palpable," . . . or "concrete" . . . is a prerequisite to Article III standing. WLF, in the amended complaint, has failed to allege sufficient facts to establish an economic injury in fact, leading us to conclude that whatever injury producers and workers may have is, at best, conjectural or speculative. . . . This is not sufficient to satisfy the injury requirement of Article III.

WLF admits in the amended complaint that Soviet forced labor products are "not readily identifiable," although it does mention four broad categories of such products, *viz.*, wood products, refined oil products, gold ore, and farm machinery. The products set forth in the . . . findings of Commissioner of Customs von Raab are likewise not sufficiently specific for the most part to clearly delimit Soviet-made products that would contravene § 307. Even if it is assumed that these products have been satisfactorily identified in the amended complaint, standing for WLF on the basis of its member producers and workers would still have to be denied because the complaint has not "alleged facts sufficient to make out a case or controversy had the members themselves brought suit." . . . The amended complaint does not identify any individuals, industries, producers, or workers in competition with the Soviet products identified by Commissioner von Raab, nor does the complaint provide any information regarding the nature, circumstances, or basis of the injury. Under such circumstances any alleged injury is wholly speculative and conjectural. . . . In the absence of some reasonable delineation of the injury and that it was caused by identified Soviet goods, we hold that WLF may not claim standing based solely upon the allegation that some of its members may be producers or workers.

C. *Shareholders*

Several of the appellants assert standing on the basis of stock ownership in companies that manufacture or produce goods that compete with the Soviet products allegedly made with forced labor. They argue that an allegation of competitive injury to a corporation in which stock is owned is a sufficient basis for shareholders to have standing and, further, that the extent of the competitive injury need not be substantial.

While allegations showing competitive injury may be appropriate to confer standing in appropriate circumstances, . . . appellants have done nothing more than allege competitive injury in the abstract. Article III requires more specific allegations of competitive injury to satisfy the case or controversy requirement. . . . The facts set forth in the complaint must be sufficient for a court to determine, assuming all of the allegations to be true, that a party indeed has suffered, or is likely to suffer, an injury in fact. . . . The amended complaint is grossly deficient in this respect. Appellants allege generally a drop in producers' share prices, . . . but the complaint fails to identify which companies or producers are affected, or to present any information showing a decline in price of shares, or to provide any other relevant information regarding the alleged injury. . . . Appellants' claim of shareholder injury is thus too conjectural and speculative to confer standing. . . . Moreover, a corporation is a legal entity capable of asserting its own legal rights and interests. There has been no demonstration by any of the appellants claiming shareholder status of need or reason for assisting a corporation or for pursuing remedies to which the corporation may be entitled. As a result, the appellants would be prudentially limited from asserting a claim for relief based upon the legal rights or interests of these third parties.

D. *International Longshoremen's Association*

The International Longshoremen's Association, AFL-CIO, (ILA) has asserted standing for itself and through its members on the basis of both economic and non-economic injuries. We have addressed the non-economic injury question . . . and the same reasoning applies with equal force to that type of injury claimed for ILA and its members. Accordingly, we conclude that the ILA does not possess standing on the basis of the alleged non-economic ethical injury, either in itself or derivatively through its members.

. . . .

E. *Public Interest Organizations*

The WLF, the Union Mutual Foundation (UMF), the Constitutional Institute of America (CIA), the Ukrainian Congress Committee of America, Inc. (UCCA), and the Ukrainian Student Association of Michnowsky (TUSM) argue that they are parties having such a personal stake in the outcome of the controversy to assure the concrete adverseness which sharpens the presentation of issues upon which a court so largely depends for illumination of the issues. . . .

. . . .

We find no basis for concluding that the WLF's injury is obviously within the reach of § 307. The question, therefore, is whether this statutory provision, *i.e.*, § 307, can properly be understood as granting a person in the WLF's position a right to judicial relief . . . that is, whether the WLF, as an organization, is within the "zone of interests" to be protected or regulated by the statute. . . . As our discussion *supra* makes evident, § 307 was enacted to protect producers and workers from economic competition from imported products produced by forced labor, and to regulate the importation of forced-labor products for the benefit of consumers when equivalent domestic products are in short supply. . . . The WLF, as an organization, is not within either category to be protected or regulated by § 307. . . . Even though the WLF may have suffered an injury in fact, this prudential limitation bars its claim as an organization to standing.

The UMF, in the amended complaint, avers that it undertakes "activities to protect and promote the welfare of the American worker," and objects to the importation of Soviet forced-labor products. Other than the terse objection to the importation of Soviet products allegedly produced by forced labor, the UMF has singularly failed to set forth any allegation of injury, actual or threatened, as mandated by Article III. . . .

With respect to the CIA the amended complaint states only that it is a joint project of the WLF and the UMF through which these foundations petitioned the Customs Service to prohibit the importation of Soviet forced-labor products. No allegation of injury having been made, there is no predicate for standing for the CIA. . . .

The amended complaint avers that the UCCA and the TUSM, and their members, object to and are adversely affected by the continued importation of Soviet forced-labor products as are the other appellants. . . . The UCCA and the TUSM, however, have not alleged, with any degree of specificity, that as organizations they have been injured or threatened with injury. . . .

The amended complaint also alleges that the Ukrainian appellants "are particularly injured in that a large portion of the political prisoners in labor camps in the Soviet Union are from the Ukraine." Leaving aside the question of whether this alleged injury complies with the injury requirement of Article III, this alleged injury is not causally connected to any conduct, let alone putatively illegal conduct of the Customs Service. . . . The conduct of the Customs Service has nothing whatsoever to do with the alleged fact that Ukrainians are political prisoners in Soviet labor camps, which is the result solely of internal political and policy machinations of the Soviet government. Further, no conceivable relief granted by this court could possibly redress such an alleged injury . . . as rectification of such an alleged injury lies solely within the control of the Soviet government.

. . . .

Affirmed.

C. Section 307, the 1994 *China Diesel* Case, and the Consumptive Demand Exception

CHINA DIESEL IMPORTS, INC. v. UNITED STATES
United States Court of International Trade
870 F. Supp. 347, 348-52 (1994)

RESTANI, JUDGE.

On June 2, 1994, the court denied cross-motions for summary judgment and ordered trial in this matter. . . . The two basic issues set for trial were whether the diesel engines at issue were manufactured by convict or other forced labor, and whether domestic production of a substitute product was sufficient to meet domestic demand.

As to the first issue, the court finds that the subject diesel engines were manufactured by convict labor for the reasons that follow. Both documentary evidence published for internal Chinese consumption and official U.S. government publications are consistent in their description of the basic Chinese penal institutions. Specifically, China has traditional style prison facilities, but it also maintains "Reform Through Labor" facilities, which may be either camps or factories. Persons convicted of crimes are assigned to both types of institutions. In addition, China has "Education Through Labor" facilities, to which persons are assigned following local administrative action. All three facilities are forced labor institutions. The first two, however, are clearly penal, and the inmate workers therein are convicts.

The model 1100 diesel engines at issue were produced by the JINMA Diesel Engine Factory in Kunming, Yunnan Province, China. The JINMA factory is described as a "Reform Through Labor" facility in at least two Chinese publications. . . . It is associated in some undisclosed way with Yunnan Prison No. 1, to which it is adjacent.

In coming to these conclusions, the court has credited most heavily various Chinese government and reference publications, which seem designed to extol production gains or provide reference data, and which appear entirely trustworthy on the issue of the status of the JINMA factory as a penal facility. This information is corroborated by unplanned interviews conducted by a State Department employee with persons living in the vicinity of the JINMA factory. The documents alone, however, would have sufficed. The conclusion is also corroborated by the prevarication of the JINMA factory manager and what the court concludes were staged tours of the facility.

In late October 1992, State Department representatives and plaintiff's representatives visited the JINMA facility on separate trips. The number of workers observed during such visits did not match published data on the number of workers employed. Furthermore, the production observed did not comport with the factory manager's claim of one engine produced every seven minutes. The administration building of four or five floors was reputed to house in excess of 200 employees, yet the production and warehouse workers were said to number only between 100 and 150, spread over three shifts. Obviously, the administration was more in keeping with a greater work force, either on the premises or elsewhere, than was alleged. The court doubts the credibility of the factory manager on this point.

Next, the factory manager defended the plant against "local talk" that it was a prison by explaining that the facility was originally established to provide work for families of prison employees. Thus, the factory was owned by the Ministry of Justice. This does not comport with Chinese publications that place the factory under the Ministry of Justice because it is a "Reform Through Labor" facility. Further, many of the factory buildings were not open to view, even when a request was made.

Other evidence falls in place as well, such as a prison truck observed leaving from the direction of the JINMA gate, a worker hiding her face from the video camera used by plaintiff during one visit, hesitancy about showing the State Department observers the location of the Yunnan No. 1 Prison wall, a blank space on a city map for both the admitted prison and the factory grounds, and the repeated failure to tender any documentation on production and personnel.

The court concludes that CDI has failed to prove that the JINMA model 1100 diesel engine was not made, in whole or in part, with convict labor. While a portion of the production or certain parts may not have been the result of convict labor, CDI has not demonstrated that the convict labor input is *de minimis*.

The court now turns to the second issue. CDI alleges that there are no diesel engines manufactured in the United States capable of providing sufficient reliable continuous power for household use. CDI imports the engines at issue and combines them with alternators to form "generator sets" for sale for such a use. Thus, CDI alleges that the statutory consumptive demand exception in § 1307 is satisfied. The court agrees, to the extent the exception is applicable.

First, U.S.-made gasoline engines are not substitutable. Gasoline engines are not designed to be a continuous power source. If used in this mode, they wear out very quickly. Furthermore, the volatility of gasoline makes it inappropriate, if not illegal, for storage in sufficient quantities to supply continuous power generation, unless one wishes to install an underground tank at considerable expense.

Second, the only American producer of small diesel engines, Onan Corporation, does not market them in normal commercial channels or quantities. Onan captively consumes its production of small diesel engines in the production of generator sets. While a witness from Onan testified that it sells some diesel engines to customers, the witness was not from the sales department. In addition, neither supporting sales documentation nor advertising of such engines for the relevant years was introduced into evidence. To the contrary, post-1987 trade publications, recognized by the Onan witness as reliable, did not list Onan as a producer of small diesel engines. This is corroborated by the original conclusion of a Customs investigator that U.S. producers do not make an equivalent diesel engine. . . . The conclusion was repeated by the Customs investigator at trial.

The consumptive demand exception is intended to benefit consumers of the product at issue. To fulfill this purpose, the product must be available. Defendant argues, however, that mere production capability on the part of the domestic industry suffices to defeat this exception. The court is not persuaded. Given sufficient will, U.S. industry is capable of producing almost any product manufactured elsewhere. Finding the exception inapplicable because of capability to produce would read the exception out of the statute as to manufactured goods, which are specifically covered. . . . Evidence established that a small diesel engine market has existed for at least the past decade, and it is served by merchandise at a variety of prices. If a U.S. manufacturer had the will to enter this market, it would have done so by now. The court concludes that while Onan (or another U.S. manufacturer) might have satisfied domestic demand if it had entered the small diesel engine market in any significant way, it was not a market participant during 1990-92, and its production may not be viewed as available to satisfy such demand.

Third, assuming *arguendo* that Onan's capability must be considered, the ability of the Onan engines to serve the particular purpose at issue is in question. Onan's closest substitute can produce 6 to 7 kilowatts of output on a continuous basis when paired with a suitable alternator. The JINMA model 1100 produces 8 to 9 kilowatts continuously. The 6 to 7 kilowatt range would fulfill most household needs, but some customers may require the higher output on a continuous basis. Because another Onan engine exists that could serve customers with higher demand, and because the testimony is not clear as to the actual kilowatt requirements of CDI's customers and exactly how many customers have such high power needs, CDI has not met its burden of proof on the sub-issue of reasonable commercial substitutability. Nonetheless, because the Onan engines generally were not marketed during the relevant time period, CDI prevails on the over-all consumptive demand issue.

The final question that arises is a legal one. The plain words of the statute indicate that merchandise produced by convict labor is prohibited under any circumstances, and only merchandise produced by non-convict forced labor is subject to the consumptive demand exception. . . . Although the statutory definition of "forced labor" is broad enough to include convict labor, to read the statute in this manner would render the separate specification of "convict labor" redundant. Courts are required to give effect to each word of a statute, whenever possible. . . . Further, the legislative history is consistent with this narrower reading of "forced labor." No court, however, has directly addressed this issue, and CDI alleges that Customs' administrative practice is to apply the exception to both convict and non-convict forced labor.

First, Customs' administrative practice is unclear. Language in one administrative ruling, cited by CDI, supports its view, but only in *dicta*. . . . Also, evidentiary standards developed by Customs for internal guidance purposes do seem to treat convict and non-convict labor identically. . . . The evidentiary standards, however, also count voluntary non-domestic production as available to satisfy domestic demand for purposes of the statute. . . . If the non-domestic production aspect of the standards were applied, CDI's case would also fall, as foreign-made substitutes were available. It seems appropriate to reject both aspects of the standards as ill-considered and inconsistent with the statute, and to rely on the most straightforward statutory interpretation, *i.e.*, the consumptive demand exception does not apply to convict-made goods, and its applicability is unaffected by non-convict or non-forced labor foreign production.

Second, as indicated, the legislative history comports with the plain language of the statute. The convict labor prohibition existed before the statute was amended to cover forced labor and indentured labor under penal sanctions, as well as to provide for a consumptive demand exception. *See Smoot-Hawley Tariff Act of 1930*, Pub.L. No. 361, § 307, 46 Stat. 590, 689 (June 17, 1930). A proposal that would have applied the exception more broadly was not enacted. . . . During the *Smoot-Hawley* debate, concern was expressed that rubber supplies produced with indentured labor should not be interrupted. Any concern about products made with convict labor was not mentioned. . . . Furthermore, discussion in 1931 of a proposed amendment contains specific reference to the non-applicability of the consumptive demand provision to convict labor. . . . This legislative history is so close in time to the original enactment that it has some weight.

Accordingly, the court finds that the JINMA model 1100 diesel engines detained by Customs, which are the subject of this action, are convict-made and are to be excluded from entry into the customs territory of the United States.

[On 7 August 1992, the U.S. and China concluded a "Memorandum of Understanding Between the United States and China on Prohibiting Import and Export Trade in Prison Labor Products" (MOU). The MOU set forth mutual commitments for the exchange of information about American and Chinese prison facilities. Specific terms were included to deal with concerns raised by the Chinese about sovereignty over domestic affairs. Essentially, the MOU allowed each country to request investigations (including visitation) of facilities suspected to be producing goods for export made with prison labor, and to exchange information on relevant laws, regulations, and enforcement. On 13 March 1994, the U.S. signed a Statement of Cooperation on implementing the MOU. The Statement was intended to ensure timely investigation and visitation of prison labor facilities where goods were allegedly made with prison labor. However, American officials continue to complain about the lack of timely and thorough responses from the Chinese government to their requests for information and visits. The State Department said in its 2000 human rights report that China last permitted Customs Service officials to inspect a suspected prison labor facility in 1997. For an account of the MOU and its effects, see United States General Accounting Office, *U.S.-China Trade — Implementation of the 1992 Prison Labor Memorandum of Understanding*, GAO/GGD-95-106 (April 1995).]

Chapter 43

THE JURISPRUDENCE OF GATT ARTICLE XX(B) AND (G)

The preservation of the environment, in which the present as well as the future generations have a right to flourishing social existence, is regarded as a public duty in the Islamic Republic. Economic and other activities that inevitably involve pollution of the environment or cause irreparable damage to it are therefore forbidden.

—Constitution of the Islamic Republic of Iran, Article 50
(Preservation of the Environment), effective 3 December 1979

DOCUMENTS SUPPLEMENT ASSIGNMENT

1. *Havana Charter* Articles 1, 45:1(a)(iii), (viii)
2. GATT Preamble and Article XX(b) and XX(g)
3. WTO *Agreement Preamble*

I. EXTRATERRITORIAL ENVIRONMENTAL MEASURES

A. Primary Boycotts and the 1992 *Tuna — Dolphin I* Case

GATT PANEL REPORT, *UNITED STATES — RESTRICTIONS ON IMPORTS OF TUNA*
B.I.S.D. (39th Supp.) 155, 156-59, 191, 196-201, 205 (1992)
(Not Adopted) (United States-Mexico Dispute)

2. FACTUAL ASPECTS

Purse-Seine Fishing of Tuna

2.1 The last three decades have seen the deployment of tuna fishing technology based on the "purse-seine" net in many areas of the world. A fishing vessel using this technique locates a school of fish and sends out a motorboat (a "seine skiff") to hold one end of the purse-seine net. The vessel motors around the perimeter of the school of fish, unfurling the net and encircling the fish, and the seine skiff then attaches its end of the net to the fishing vessel. The fishing vessel then purses the net by winching in a cable at the bottom edge of the net, and draws in the top cables of the net to gather its entire contents.

2.2 Studies monitoring direct and indirect catch levels have shown that fish and dolphins are found together in a number of areas around the world and that this may lead to incidental taking of dolphins during fishing operations. In the Eastern Tropical Pacific Ocean (ETP), a particular association between dolphins and tuna has long been observed, such that fishermen locate schools of underwater tuna by finding and chasing dolphins on the ocean surface and intentionally encircling them with nets to catch the tuna underneath. This type of association has not been observed in other areas of the world; consequently, intentional encirclement of dolphins with purse-seine nets is used as a tuna fishing technique only in the Eastern Tropical Pacific Ocean. When dolphins and tuna together have been surrounded by purse-seine nets, it is possible to reduce or eliminate the catch of dolphins through using certain procedures.

Marine Mammals Protection Act of the United States (Measures on Imports from Mexico)

2.3 The *Marine Mammal Protection Act of 1972*, as revised (*MMPA*) [16 U.S.C. §§ 1361 *et seq.*], requires a general prohibition of "taking" (harassment, hunting, capture, killing or attempt thereof) and importation into the United States of marine mammals, except where an exception is explicitly authorized. Its stated goal is that the incidental kill or serious injury of marine mammals in the course of commercial fishing be reduced to insignificant levels approaching zero. The *MMPA* contains special provisions applicable to tuna caught in the ETP, defined as the area of the Pacific Ocean bounded by 40 degrees north latitude, 40 degrees south latitude, 160 degrees west longitude, and the coasts of North, Central and South America. These provisions govern the taking of marine mammals incidental to harvesting of yellowfin tuna in the ETP, as well as importation of yellowfin tuna and tuna products harvested in the ETP. The *MMPA* is enforced by the National Marine Fisheries Service (NMFS) of the National Oceanic and Atmospheric Administration (NOAA) of the Department of Commerce, except for its provisions regarding importation which are enforced by the United States Customs Service under the Department of the Treasury [now CBP under the Department of Homeland Security].

2.4 Section 101(a)(2) of the *MMPA* authorizes limited incidental taking of marine mammals by United States fishermen in the course of commercial fishing pursuant to a permit issued by NMFS, in conformity with and governed by certain statutory criteria in sections 103 and 104 and implementing regulations. Only one such permit has been issued, to the American Tunaboat Association, covering all domestic tuna fishing operations in the ETP. Under the general permit issued to this Association, no more than 20,500 dolphins may be incidentally killed or injured each year by the United States fleet fishing in the ETP. Among this number, no more than 250 may be coastal spotted dolphin . . . and no more than 2,750 may be Eastern spinner dolphin. . . . The *MMPA* and its implementing regulations include extensive provisions regarding commercial tuna fishing in the ETP, particularly the use of purse-seine nets to encircle dolphin in order to catch tuna beneath (referred to as "setting on" dolphin). These provisions apply to all persons subject to United States jurisdiction and vessels subject to United States jurisdiction, on the high seas and in United States territory, including the territorial sea of the United States and the United States Exclusive Economic Zone. Although *MMPA* enforcement provisions provide for forfeiture of cargo as a penalty for violation of its regulations on harvesting of tuna, neither the *MMPA* provisions nor their implementing regulations otherwise prohibit or regulate the sale, offer for sale, purchase, transportation, distribution or use of yellowfin tuna caught by the United States fleet.

2.5 Section 101(a)(2) of the *MMPA* also states that "[t]he Secretary of Treasury shall ban the importation of commercial fish or products from fish which have been caught with commercial fishing technology which results in the incidental kill or incidental serious injury of ocean mammals in excess of United States standards." This prohibition is mandatory. Special ETP provisions in section 101(a)(2)(B) provide that importation of yellowfin tuna harvested with purse-seine nets in the ETP and products therefrom is prohibited unless the Secretary of Commerce finds that (i) the government of the harvesting country has a program regulating taking of marine mammals that is comparable to that of the United States, and (ii) the average rate of incidental taking of marine mammals by vessels of the harvesting nation is comparable to the average rate of such taking by United States vessels. The Secretary need not act unless a harvesting country requests a finding. If it does, the burden is on that country to prove through documentary evidence that its regulatory regime and taking rates are comparable. If the data show that they are, the Secretary must make a positive finding.

2.6 The provisions for ETP yellowfin tuna in section 101(a)(2)(B) of the *MMPA* provide special prerequisites for a positive finding on comparability of a harvesting country's regulatory regime and incidental taking rates. The regulatory regime must include the same prohibitions as are applicable under United States rules to United States vessels. The average incidental taking rate (in terms of dolphins killed each time the purse-seine nets are set) for that country's tuna fleet must not exceed 1.25 times the average taking rate of United States vessels in the same period. Also, the share of Eastern spinner dolphin and coastal spotted dolphin relative to total incidental takings of dolphin during each entire (one-year) fishing season must not exceed 15 per cent and 2 per cent respectively. NMFS regulations have specified a method of comparing incidental taking rates by calculating the kill per set of the United States tuna fleet as an unweighted average, then weighting this figure for each harvesting country based on differences in mortality by type of dolphin and location of sets; these regulations have also otherwise implemented the *MMPA* provisions on importation.

2.7 On 28 August 1990, the United States Government imposed an embargo, pursuant to a court order, on imports of commercial yellowfin tuna and yellowfin tuna products harvested with purse-seine nets in the ETP until the Secretary of Commerce made positive findings based on documentary evidence of compliance with the *MMPA* standards. This action affected Mexico, Venezuela, Vanuatu, Panama and Ecuador. On 7 September, this measure was removed for Mexico, Venezuela and Vanuatu, pursuant to positive Commerce Department findings; also, Panama and Ecuador later prohibited their fleets from setting on dolphin and were exempted from the embargo. On 10 October 1990, the United States Government, pursuant to court order, imposed an embargo on imports of such tuna from Mexico until the Secretary made a positive finding based on documentary evidence that the percentage of Eastern spinner dolphins killed by the Mexican fleet over the course of an entire fishing season did not exceed 15 per cent of dolphins killed by it in that period. An appeals court ordered on 14 November 1990 that the embargo be stayed, but when it lifted the stay on 22 February 1991, the embargo on imports of such tuna from Mexico went into effect.

2.8 On 3 April 1991, the United States Customs Service issued guidance implementing a further embargo, pursuant to another court order of 26 March, on imports of yellowfin tuna and tuna products harvested in the ETP with purse-seine nets by vessels of Mexico, Venezuela and Vanuatu. Under this embargo, effective 26 March 1991, the importation of yellowfin tuna, and "light meat" tuna products which can contain yellowfin tuna, under specified Harmonized System tariff headings is prohibited unless the importer provides a declaration that, based on appropriate inquiry and the written evidence in his possession, no yellowfin tuna or tuna products in the shipment were harvested with purse-seines in the ETP by vessels from Mexico, Venezuela or Vanuatu.

. . . .

[Omitted are the factual aspects, main arguments, findings, and conclusions regarding the *Fishermen's Protective Act of 1967* (the *Pelly Amendment*), *MMPA* measures on intermediary country imports, and *Dolphin Protection Consumer Information Act*. Also omitted are the main arguments and submissions by third parties concerning the *MMPA*. Finally, omitted are the Panel's discussion of categorizing the disputed measures as internal regulations under GATT Article III or as quantitative restrictions under Article XI, and its holding — essentially uncontested by the U.S. — that the *MMPA* violated Article XI.]. . . .

5. FINDINGS

. . . .

Article XX

General

5.22 . . . [T]he United States had argued that its direct embargo under the *MMPA* could be justified under Article XX(b) or Article XX(g), and that Mexico had argued that a contracting party could not simultaneously argue that a measure is compatible with the general rules of the General Agreement and invoke Article XX for that measure. . . . [P]revious panels had established that Article XX is a limited and conditional exception from obligations under other provisions of the General Agreement, and not a positive rule establishing obligations in itself. [The Panel cited *United States — Section 337 of the Tariff Act of 1930*, GATT B.I.S.D. (36th Supp.) at 345, 385 ¶ 5.9 (1990) (adopted 7 November 1989), which a later Chapter discusses.] Therefore, the practice of panels has been to interpret Article XX narrowly, to place the burden on the party invoking Article XX to justify its invocation, and not to examine Article XX exceptions unless invoked. Nevertheless, . . . a party to a dispute could argue in the alternative that Article XX might apply, without this argument constituting *ipso facto* an admission that the measures in question would otherwise be inconsistent with the General Agreement. Indeed, the efficient operation of the dispute settlement process required that such arguments in the alternative be possible.

5.23 The Panel proceeded to examine whether Article XX(b) or Article XX(g) could justify the *MMPA* provisions. . . . Article XX provides that:

> Subject to the requirement that such measures are not applied in a manner which would constitute a means of arbitrary or unjustifiable discrimination between countries where the same conditions prevail, or a disguised restriction on international trade, nothing in this Agreement shall be construed to prevent the adoption or enforcement by any contracting party of measures. . .
>
>   (b)   necessary to protect human, animal or plant life or health;
>
>   . . . .
>
>   (g)   relating to the conservation of exhaustible natural resources if such measures are made effective in conjunction with restrictions on domestic production or consumption. . . .

Article XX(b)

5.24 . . . [T]he United States considered the prohibition of imports of certain yellowfin tuna and certain yellowfin tuna products from Mexico, and the provisions of the *MMPA* on which this prohibition is based, to be justified by Article XX(b) because they served solely the purpose of protecting dolphin life and health and were "necessary" within the meaning of that provision because, in respect of the protection of dolphin life and health outside its jurisdiction, there was no alternative measure reasonably available to the United States to achieve this objective. Mexico considered that Article XX(b) was not applicable to a measure imposed to protect the life or health of animals outside the jurisdiction of the contracting party taking it and that the import prohibition imposed by the United States was not necessary because alternative means consistent with the General Agreement were available to it to protect dolphin lives or health, namely international co-operation between the countries concerned.

5.25 . . . [T]he basic question raised by these arguments . . . [is] whether Article XX(b) covers measures necessary to protect human, animal or plant life or health outside the jurisdiction of the contracting party taking the measure, is not clearly answered by the text of that provision. It refers to life and health protection generally without expressly limiting that protection to the jurisdiction of the contracting party concerned. The Panel therefore decided to analyze this issue in the light of the drafting history of Article XX(b), the purpose of this provision, and the consequences that the interpretations proposed by the parties would have for the operation of the General Agreement as a whole.

5.26 . . . [T]he proposal for Article XX(b) dated from the *Draft Charter of the International Trade Organization* (ITO) proposed by the United States, which stated in Article 32, "Nothing in Chapter IV [on commercial policy] of this *Charter* shall be construed to prevent the adoption or enforcement by any Member of measures: . . . (b) necessary to protect human, animal or plant life or health." In the *New York Draft of the ITO Charter*, the preamble had been revised to read as it does at present, and exception (b) read: "For the purpose of protecting human, animal or plant life or health, if corresponding domestic safeguards under similar conditions exist in the importing country." This added proviso reflected concerns regarding the abuse of sanitary regulations by importing countries. Later, Commission A of the Second Session of the Preparatory Committee in Geneva agreed to drop this proviso as unnecessary. Thus, the record indicates that the concerns of the drafters of Article XX(b) focused on the use of sanitary measures to safeguard life or health of humans, animals or plants within the jurisdiction of the importing country.

5.27 . . . Article XX(b) allows each contracting party to set its human, animal or plant life or health standards. The conditions set out in Article XX(b) which limit resort to this exception, namely that the measure taken must be "necessary" and not "constitute a means of arbitrary or unjustifiable discrimination or a disguised restriction on international trade," refer to the trade measure requiring justification under Article XX(b), not however to the life or health standard chosen by the contracting party. [T]his paragraph of Article XX was intended to allow contracting parties to impose trade restrictive measures inconsistent with the General Agreement to pursue overriding public policy goals to the extent that such inconsistencies were unavoidable. The Panel considered that if the broad interpretation of Article XX(b) suggested by the United States were accepted, each contracting party could unilaterally determine the life or health protection policies from which other contracting parties could not deviate without jeopardizing their rights under the General Agreement. The General Agreement would then no longer constitute a multilateral framework for trade among all contracting parties but would provide legal security only in respect of trade between a limited number of contracting parties with identical internal regulations.

5.28 . . . [T]he United States' measures, even if Article XX(b) were interpreted to permit extra-jurisdictional protection of life and health, would not meet the requirement of necessity set out in that provision. The United States had not demonstrated to the Panel — as required of the party invoking an Article XX exception — that it had exhausted all options reasonably available to it to pursue its dolphin protection objectives through measures consistent with the General Agreement, in particular through the negotiation of international cooperative arrangements, which would seem to be desirable in view of the fact that dolphins roam the waters of many states and the high seas. Moreover, even assuming that an import prohibition were the only resort reasonably available to the United States, the particular measure chosen by the United States could in the Panel's view not be considered to be necessary within the meaning of Article XX(b). The United States linked the maximum incidental dolphin taking rate which Mexico had to meet during a particular period in order to be able to export tuna to the United States to the taking rate actually recorded for United States fishermen during the same period. Consequently, the Mexican authorities could not know whether, at a given point of time, their policies conformed to the United States' dolphin protection standards. The Panel considered that a limitation on trade based on such unpredictable conditions could not be regarded as necessary to protect the health or life of dolphins.

5.29 On the basis of the above considerations, the Panel found that the United States' direct import prohibition imposed on certain yellowfin tuna and certain yellowfin tuna products of Mexico and the provisions of the *MMPA* under which it is imposed could not be justified under the exception in Article XX(b).

Article XX(g)

5.30 The Panel proceeded to examine whether the prohibition on imports of certain yellowfin tuna and certain yellowfin tuna products from Mexico and the *MMPA* provisions under which it was imposed could be justified under the exception in Article XX(g). The Panel noted that the United States, in invoking Article XX(g) with respect to its direct import prohibition under the *MMPA*, had argued that the measures taken under the *MMPA* are measures primarily aimed at the conservation of dolphin, and that the import restrictions on certain tuna and tuna products under the *MMPA* are "primarily aimed at rendering effective restrictions on domestic production or consumption" of dolphin. The Panel also noted that Mexico had argued that the United States measures were not justified under the exception in Article XX(g) because, *inter alia*, this provision could not be applied extra-jurisdictionally.

5.31 The Panel noted that Article XX(g) required that the measures relating to the conservation of exhaustible natural resources be taken "in conjunction with restrictions on domestic production or consumption." A previous panel had found that a measure could only be considered to have been taken "in conjunction with" production restrictions "if it was primarily aimed at rendering effective these restrictions." [*Canada — Measures Affecting Exports of Unprocessed Herring and Salmon*, GATT B.I.S.D. (35th Supp.) at 98, 114 ¶ 4.6 (1989) (adopted 22 March 1988).] A country can effectively control the production or consumption of an exhaustible natural resource only to the extent that the production or consumption is under its jurisdiction. This suggests that Article XX(g) was intended to permit contracting parties to take trade measures primarily aimed at rendering effective restrictions on production or consumption within their jurisdiction.

5.32 The Panel further noted that Article XX(g) allows each contracting party to adopt its own conservation policies. The conditions set out in Article XX(g) which limit resort to this exception, namely that the measures taken must be related to the conservation of exhaustible natural resources, and that they not "constitute a means of arbitrary or unjustifiable discrimination . . . or a disguised restriction on international trade" refer to the trade measure requiring justification under Article XX(g), not however to the conservation policies adopted by the contracting party. The Panel considered that if the extra-jurisdictional interpretation of Article XX(g) suggested by the United States were accepted, each contracting party could unilaterally determine the conservation policies from which other contracting parties could not deviate without jeopardizing their rights under the General Agreement. The considerations that led the Panel to reject an extra-jurisdictional application of Article XX(b) therefore apply also to Article XX(g).

5.33 The Panel did not consider that the United States measures, even if Article XX(g) could be applied extra-jurisdictionally, would meet the conditions set out in that provision. A previous panel [in the 1988 *Canada — Herring and Salmon* case] found that a measure could be considered as "relating to the conservation of exhaustible natural resources" within the meaning of Article XX(g) only if it was primarily aimed at such conservation. The Panel recalled that the United States linked the maximum incidental dolphin-taking rate which Mexico had to meet during a particular period in order to be able to export tuna to the United States to the taking rate actually recorded for United States fishermen during the same period. Consequently, the Mexican authorities could not know whether, at a given point of time, their conservation policies conformed to the United States conservation standards. The Panel considered that a limitation on trade based on such unpredictable conditions could not be regarded as being primarily aimed at the conservation of dolphins.

5.34 On the basis of the above considerations, the Panel found that the United States direct import prohibition on certain yellowfin tuna and certain yellowfin tuna products of Mexico directly imported from Mexico, and the provisions of the *MMPA* under which it is imposed, could not be justified under Article XX(g).

B.   Secondary Boycotts and the 1994 *Tuna — Dolphin II* Case

GATT PANEL REPORT, *UNITED STATES — RESTRICTIONS ON IMPORTS OF TUNA*
33 International Legal Materials 839, 887-99 (1994)
(Not Adopted) (United States — EEC dispute)

V. Findings

A. Introduction

. . . .

3. *United States Restrictions Affecting Indirect Imports of Tuna ("Intermediary Nation Embargo")*

5.5 The *Act* [*i.e., Marine Mammal Protection Act*, or *MMPA*] provides that any nation ("intermediary nation") that exports yellowfin tuna or yellowfin tuna products to the United States, and that imports yellowfin tuna or yellowfin tuna products that are subject to a direct prohibition on import into the United States, must certify and provide reasonable proof that it has not imported products subject to the direct prohibition within the preceding six months. This provision, effective 26 October 1992, is an amendment of an earlier provision, interpreted by a United States court to require that proof be made that each country identified as an intermediary nation had itself prohibited the import of any tuna that was barred from direct importation into the United States. . . .

. . . .

F. Concluding Observations

5.42 . . . [T]he objective of sustainable development, which includes the protection and preservation of the environment, has been widely recognized by the contracting parties to the General Agreement. . . . [T]he issue in this dispute was not the validity of the environmental objectives of the United States to protect and conserve dolphins. The issue was whether, in the pursuit of its environmental objectives, the United States could impose trade embargoes to secure changes in the policies which other contracting parties pursued within their own jurisdiction. The Panel therefore had to resolve whether the contracting parties, by agreeing to give each other in Article XX the right to take trade measures necessary to protect the health and life of plants, animals and persons or aimed at the conservation of exhaustible natural resources, had agreed to accord each other the right to impose trade embargoes for such purposes. The Panel had examined this issue in the light of the recognized methods of interpretation and had found that none of them lent any support to the view that such an agreement was reflected in Article XX.

. . . .

VI. CONCLUSIONS

. . . .

[Using analysis redolent of its *Tuna — Dolphin I* Report, the GATT Panel held the primary and intermediary nation embargoes violated GATT Article XI:1 and could not be excused by Article XX(b), (g), or (d). As in *Tuna-Dolphin I*, the Panel recommended the U.S. bring its law into conformity with its GATT obligations.

Is eco-labeling the answer to some trade issues? Does its efficacy depend on the nature and content of, and criteria for, a label, and vigorous enforcement mechanisms? *See, e.g., Earth Island institute v. Hogarth* (9th Cir., 27 April 2007) No. 04-17018, CV-03-00007, in which the U.S. government sought unsuccessfully to weaken labeling rules so as to permit a dolphin-safe label on tuna imports from Mexico and other countries if no dolphins were observed to be killed or maimed. Consider the same questions in respect of "fair trade" labels to certify production in keeping with labor rights.]

II. DIFFERENTIAL ENVIRONMENTAL REGULATIONS AND THE 1996 *REFORMULATED GAS* CASE

A. The *Gasoline Rule*

The "*Gasoline Rule*" is short hand of the Appellate Body for a controversial U.S. Environmental Protection Agency (EPA) regulation. The *Rule* was formally entitled "Regulation of Fuels and Fuel Additives — Standards for

Reformulated and Conventional Gasoline," 40 C.F.R. pt. 80, 59 Fed. Reg. 7,716 (16 February 1994. The EPA promulgated the Rule pursuant to the 1963 *Clean Air Act*, as amended, for reformulated and conventional gasoline. The Rule, which took effect on 1 January 1995, mandated reductions in certain gasoline constituents in order to reduce vehicle emissions. By reducing the harmful constituents in gasoline, exhaust pollution would decrease. Using 1990 figures, the *Gasoline Rule* established baseline "ozone-forming constituent" levels that gasoline could contain.

The *Gasoline Rule* identified nine highly-populated areas — areas most in need of a quick decrease in exhaust pollution. (These were large metropolitan areas that had experienced the worst summertime ozone pollution. In addition to these nine cities, various additional areas were included at the request of certain state governors.) In these so-called "non-attainment areas," only "reformulated" gasoline could be used. Reduction of particularly troublesome constituents (*e.g.*, benzene, oxygen, and Reid Vapor Pressure) was called for between 1995-98. In all other areas of the U.S., "conventional" gasoline — gasoline as clean as gasoline in 1990 — could be used. For conventional gasoline, no specific period for reductions in harmful constituents was set, but all constituents in this type of gasoline ultimately would be subject to regulation.

What exactly were the compositional and performance specifications for "reformulated" gasoline set forth in the *Clean Air Act*? There were three compositional standards: (1) the oxygen content could not be less than 2.0 percent by weight; (2) the benzene content could not exceed 1.0 percent by volume; and (3) the gasoline must be free of heavy metals, including lead and manganese. There were also three performance standards: (1) a 15 percent reduction in the emission of volatile organic compounds (VOCs); (2) a 15 percent reduction in the emission of toxic air pollutants (toxics); and (3) no increase in the emission of nitrogen oxides (NOx). The statute explained the methodologies for satisfying these compositional and performance specifications. It established a "Simple Model" methodology to be used between 1 January 1995 and 1 January 1998, and a "Complex Model" methodology for use thereafter. The Complex Model more accurately predicted emissions performance than the former Model, but it was the Simple Model that was at issue in the dispute.

What about "conventional" gasoline? Congress and the EPA worried that refiners, blenders, and importers might dump pollutants they extracted from reformulated gasoline into conventional gasoline. Therefore, the *Clean Air Act* mandated that all conventional gasoline sole remain at least as clean as 1990 baseline levels. The mandate was strict. The Simple Model for reformulated gasoline covered only certain qualities of that type of gasoline, namely, sulphur, olefins, and T-90. The Simple Model said that these constituents had to remain at or below 1990 levels — a "non-degradation" requirement. However, the non-degradation requirement for conventional gasoline was much broader: it covered not only sulphur, olefins, and T-90, but also all other qualities of that kind of gasoline. There was to be no degradation from the 1990 level for all of the qualities.

How would the EPA judge compliance with the non-degradation mandates for conventional and reformulated gasoline? Each year, it would compare emissions of gasoline sold by domestic refiners, blenders, and importers against emissions from a 1990 baseline. But, that begged the question of how the baselines would be established — and that question was the "rub" of the WTO dispute excepted below. After all, baselines were at the heart of the enforcement process.

B. The Two Step Test

WTO APPELLATE BODY REPORT, *UNITED STATES — STANDARDS FOR REFORMULATED AND CONVENTIONAL GASOLINE*
WT/DS2/AB/R (adopted 20 May 1996)

III. The Issue of Justification Under Article XX(g) of the General Agreement

. . . .

B. *"Relating to the Conservation of Exhaustible Natural Resources"*

The Panel Report took the view that clean air was a "natural resource" that could be "depleted." Accordingly, . . . the Panel concluded that a policy to reduce the depletion of clean air was a policy to conserve an exhaustible natural resource within the meaning of Article XX(g). Shortly thereafter, however, the Panel Report also concluded that "the less favourable baseline establishments methods" were *not* primarily aimed at the conservation of exhaustible natural resources and thus fell outside the justifying scope of Article XX(g).

The Panel, addressing the task of interpreting the words "relating to," quoted with approval the following passage from the panel report in the 1987 *Herring and Salmon* case [*i.e., Canada — Measures Affecting Exports of Unprocessed Herring and Salmon*, GATT B.I.S.D. (35th Supp.) 98 at 114 ¶ 4.6 (1989) (adopted 22 March 1988)]:

> as the preamble of Article XX indicates, the purpose of including Article XX:(g) in the General Agreement was not to widen the scope for measures serving trade policy purposes but merely to ensure that the commitments under the General Agreement do not hinder the pursuit of policies aimed at the conservation of exhaustive natural resources. The Panel concluded for these reasons that, while a trade measure did not have to be necessary or essential to the conservation of an exhaustible natural resource, it had to be *primarily aimed* at the conservation of an exhaustible natural resource to be considered as "relating to" conservation within the meaning of Article XX:(g). (emphasis added by the Panel)

The Panel Report then went on to apply the . . . *Herring and Salmon* reasoning and conclusion to the baseline establishment rules of the *Gasoline Rule* in the following manner:

The Panel then considered whether the precise aspects of the *Gasoline Rule* that it had found to violate Article III — the less favourable baseline establishments methods that adversely affected the conditions of competition for imported gasoline — were primarily aimed at the conservation of natural resources. The Panel saw no direct connection between less favourable treatment of imported gasoline that was chemically identical to domestic gasoline, and the U.S. objective of improving air quality in the United States. Indeed, in the view of the Panel, being consistent with the obligation to provide no less favourable treatment would not prevent the attainment of the desired level of conservation of natural resources under the *Gasoline Rule*. Accordingly, it could not be said that the baseline establishment methods that afforded less favourable treatment to imported gasoline were primarily aimed at the conservation of natural resources. In the Panel's view, the above-noted lack of connection was underscored by the fact that affording treatment of imported gasoline consistent with its Article III:4 obligations would not in any way hinder the United States in its pursuit of its conservation policies under the *Gasoline Rule*. Indeed, the United States remained free to regulate in order to obtain whatever air quality it wished. The Panel therefore concluded that the less favourable baseline establishments methods at issue in this case were not primarily aimed at the conservation of natural resources.

. . . .

A principal difficulty . . . with the Panel Report's application of Article XX(g) to the baseline establishment rules is that the Panel there overlooked a fundamental rule of treaty interpretation. This rule has received its most authoritative and succinct expression in the *Vienna Convention on the Law of Treaties* (the "*Vienna Convention*"), which provides in relevant part:

Article 31
General Rule of Interpretation

1. A treaty shall be interpreted in good faith in accordance with the ordinary meaning to be given to the terms of the treaty in their context and in the light of its object and purpose.

The "general rule of interpretation" set out above has been relied upon by all of the participants and third participants, although not always in relation to the same issue. That general rule of interpretation has attained the status of a rule of customary or general international law. As such, it forms part of the "customary rules of interpretation of public international law" which the Appellate Body has been directed, by Article 3(2) of the *DSU*, to apply in seeking to clarify the provisions of the *General Agreement* and the other "covered agreements" of the *Marrakesh Agreement Establishing the World Trade Organization* (the "*WTO Agreement*"). That direction reflects a measure of recognition that the *General Agreement* is not to be read in clinical isolation from public international law.

Applying the basic principle of interpretation that the words of a treaty, like the *General Agreement*, are to be given their ordinary meaning, in their context and in the light of the treaty's object and purpose, the Appellate Body observes that the Panel Report failed to take adequate account of the words actually used by Article XX in its several paragraphs. In enumerating the various categories of governmental acts, laws or regulations which WTO Members may carry out or promulgate in pursuit of differing legitimate state policies or interests outside the realm of trade liberalization, Article XX uses different terms in respect of different categories:

"necessary"	—	in paragraphs (a), (b) and (d);
"essential"	—	in paragraph (j);
"relating to"	—	in paragraphs (c), (e) and (g);
"for the protection of"	—	in paragraph (f);
"in pursuance of"	—	in paragraph (h); and
"involving"	—	in paragraph (i).

It does not seem reasonable to suppose that the WTO Members intended to require, in respect of each and every category, the same kind or degree of connection or relationship between the measure under appraisal and the state interest or policy sought to be promoted or realized.

At the same time, Article XX(g) and its phrase, "relating to the conservation of exhaustible natural resources," need to be read in context and in such a manner as to give effect to the purposes and objects of the *General Agreement*. The context of Article XX(g) includes the provisions of the rest of the *General Agreement*, including in particular Articles I, III and XI; conversely, the context of Articles I and III and XI includes Article XX. Accordingly, the phrase "relating to the conservation of exhaustible natural resources" may not be read so expansively as seriously to subvert the purpose and object of Article III:4. Nor may Article III:4 be given so broad a reach as effectively to emasculate Article XX(g) and the policies and interests it embodies. The relationship between the affirmative commitments set out in, *e.g.*, Articles I, III and XI, and the policies and interests embodied in the "General Exceptions" listed in Article XX, can be given meaning within the framework of the *General Agreement* and its object and purpose by a treaty interpreter only on a case-to-case basis, by careful scrutiny of the factual and legal context in a given dispute, without disregarding the words actually used by the WTO Members themselves to express their intent and purpose.

. . . .

All the participants . . . in this appeal accept the propriety and applicability of the view of the *Herring and Salmon* report and the Panel Report that a measure must be "primarily aimed at" the conservation of exhaustible natural resources in order to fall within the scope of Article XX(g). Accordingly, we see no need to examine this point further, save, perhaps, to note that the phrase "primarily aimed at" is not itself treaty language and was not designed as a simple litmus test for inclusion or exclusion from Article XX(g).

Against this background, we turn to the specific question of whether the baseline establishment rules are appropriately regarded as "primarily aimed at" the conservation of natural resources for the purposes of Article XX(g). . . . [T]his question must be answered in the affirmative.

The baseline establishment rules, taken as a whole (that is, the provisions relating to establishment of baselines for domestic refiners, along with the provisions relating to baselines for blenders and importers of gasoline), need to be related to the "non-degradation" requirements set out elsewhere in the *Gasoline Rule*. Those provisions can scarcely be understood if scrutinized strictly by themselves, totally divorced from other sections of the *Gasoline Rule* which certainly constitute part of the context of these provisions. The baseline establishment rules whether individual or statutory, were designed to permit scrutiny and monitoring of the level of compliance of refiners, importers and blenders with the "non-degradation" requirements. Without baselines of some kind, such scrutiny would not be possible and the *Gasoline Rule's* objective of stabilizing and preventing further deterioration of the level of air pollution prevailing in 1990, would be substantially frustrated. The relationship between the baseline establishment rules and the "non-degradation" requirements of the *Gasoline Rule* is not negated by the inconsistency, found by the Panel, of the baseline establishment rules with the terms of [GATT] Article III:4. We consider that, given that substantial relationship, the baseline establishment rules cannot be regarded as merely incidentally or inadvertently aimed at the conservation of clean air in the United States for the purposes of Article XX(g).

C. *"If Such Measures are Made Effective in Conjunction with Restrictions on Domestic Production or Consumption"*

The Panel did not find it necessary to deal with the issue of whether the baseline establishment rules "are made effective in conjunction with restrictions on domestic production or consumption," since it had earlier concluded that those rules had not even satisfied the preceding requirement of "relating to" in the sense of being "primarily aimed at" the conservation of clean air. Having been unable to concur with that earlier conclusion of the Panel, we must now address this second requirement of Article XX(g). . . .

The claim of the United States is that the second clause of Article XX(g) requires that the burdens entailed by regulating the level of pollutants in the air emitted in the course of combustion of gasoline, must not be imposed solely on, or in respect of, imported gasoline.

. . . .

There is, of course, no textual basis for requiring identical treatment of domestic and imported products. Indeed, where there is identity of treatment — constituting real, not merely formal, equality of treatment — it is difficult to see how inconsistency with Article III:4 would have arisen in the first place. On the other hand, if *no* restrictions on domestically produced like products are imposed at all, and all limitations are placed upon imported products *alone*, the measure cannot be accepted as primarily or even substantially designed for implementing conservationist goals. The measure would simply be naked discrimination for protecting locally produced goods.

. . . [T]he baseline establishment rules affect both domestic gasoline and imported gasoline, providing for — generally speaking — individual baselines for domestic refiners and blenders and statutory baselines for importers. Thus, restrictions on the consumption or depletion of clean air by regulating the domestic production of "dirty" gasoline are established jointly with corresponding restrictions with respect to imported gasoline. That imported gasoline has been determined to have been accorded "less favourable treatment" than the domestic gasoline in terms of Article III:4, is not material for purposes of analysis under Article XX(g). It might also be noted that the second clause of Article XX(g) speaks disjunctively of "domestic production *or* consumption."

We do not believe, finally, that the clause "if made effective in conjunction with restrictions on domestic production or consumption" was intended to establish an empirical "effects test" for the availability of the Article XX(g) exception. In the first place, the problem of determining causation, well-known in both domestic and international law, is always a difficult one. In the second place, in the field of conservation of exhaustible natural resources, a substantial period of time, perhaps years, may have to elapse before the effects attributable to implementation of a given measure may be observable. The legal characterization of such a measure is not reasonably made contingent upon occurrence of subsequent events. We are not, however, suggesting that consideration of the predictable effects of a measure is never relevant. In a particular case, should it become clear that realistically, a specific measure cannot in any possible situation have any positive effect on conservation goals, it would very probably be because that measure was not designed as a conservation regulation to begin with. In other words, it would not have been "primarily aimed at" conservation of natural resources at all.

IV. The Introductory Provisions of Article XX of the General Agreement: Applying the *Chapeau* of the General Exceptions

. . . .

The *chapeau* . . . prohibits such application of a measure at issue (otherwise falling within the scope of Article XX(g)) as would constitute

    (a)   "arbitrary discrimination" (between countries where the same conditions prevail);

    (b)   "unjustifiable discrimination" (with the same qualifier); or

    (c)   "disguised restriction" on international trade.

. . . .

"Arbitrary discrimination," "unjustifiable discrimination" and "disguised restriction" on international trade may, accordingly, be read side-by-side; they impart meaning to one another. It is clear to us that "disguised restriction" includes disguised *discrimination* in international trade. It is equally clear that *concealed* or *unannounced* restriction or discrimination in international trade does *not* exhaust the meaning of "disguised restriction." We consider that "disguised restriction," whatever else it covers, may properly be read as embracing restrictions amounting to arbitrary or unjustifiable discrimination in international trade taken under the guise of a measure formally within the terms of an exception listed in Article XX. Put in a somewhat different manner, the kinds of considerations pertinent in deciding whether the application of a particular measure amounts to "arbitrary or unjustifiable discrimination," may also be taken into account in determining the presence of a "disguised restriction" on international trade. The fundamental theme is to be found in the purpose and object of avoiding abuse or illegitimate use of the exceptions to substantive rules available in Article XX.

There was more than one alternative course of action available to the United States in promulgating regulations implementing the *CAA* [the *Clean Air Act*, as amended]. These included the imposition of statutory baselines without differentiation as between domestic and imported gasoline. This approach, if properly implemented, could have avoided any discrimination at all. Among the other options open to the United States was to make available individual baselines to foreign refiners as well as domestic refiners. The United States has put forward a series of reasons why either of these courses was not, in its view, realistically open to it and why, instead, it had to devise and apply the baseline establishment rules contained in the *Gasoline Rule*.

In explaining why individual baselines for foreign refiners had not been put in place, the United States laid heavy stress upon the difficulties which the EPA would have had to face. These difficulties related to anticipated administrative problems that individual baselines for foreign refiners would have generated. This argument was made succinctly by the United States in the following terms:

> Verification on foreign soil of foreign baselines, and subsequent enforcement actions, present substantial difficulties relating to problems arising whenever a country exercises enforcement jurisdiction over foreign persons. In addition, even if individual baselines were established for several foreign refiners, the importer would be tempted to claim the refinery of origin that presented the most benefits in terms of baseline restrictions, and tracking the refinery or origin would be very difficult because gasoline is a fungible commodity. The United States should not have to prove that it cannot verify information and enforce its regulations in every instance in order to show that the same enforcement conditions do not prevail in the United States and other countries. . . . The impracticability of verification and enforcement of foreign refiner baselines in this instance shows that the "discrimination" is based on serious, not arbitrary or unjustifiable, concerns stemming from different conditions between enforcement of its laws in the United States and abroad.

Thus, according to the United States, imported gasoline was relegated to the more exacting statutory baseline requirement because of these difficulties of verification and enforcement. The United States stated that verification and enforcement of the *Gasoline Rule's* requirements for imported gasoline are "much easier when the statutory baseline is used" and that there would be a "dramatic difference" in the burden of administering requirements for imported gasoline if individual baselines were allowed.

. . . .

Clearly, the United States did not feel it feasible to require its domestic refiners to incur the physical and financial costs and burdens entailed by immediate compliance with a statutory baseline. The United States wished to give domestic refiners time to restructure their operations and adjust to the requirements in the *Gasoline Rule*. This may very well have constituted sound domestic policy from the viewpoint of the EPA and U.S. refiners. At the same time we are bound to note that, while the United States counted the costs for its domestic refiners of statutory baselines, there is nothing in the record to indicate that it did other than disregard that kind of consideration when it came to foreign refiners.

We have above located two omissions on the part of the United States: to explore adequately means, including in particular cooperation with the governments of Venezuela and Brazil, of mitigating the administrative problems relied on as justification by the United States for rejecting individual baselines for foreign refiners; and to count the costs for foreign refiners that would result from the imposition of statutory baselines. In our view, these two omissions go well beyond what was necessary for the Panel to determine that a violation of Article III:4 had occurred in the first place. The resulting discrimination must have been foreseen, and was not merely inadvertent or unavoidable. In the light of the foregoing, our conclusion is that the baseline establishment rules in the *Gasoline Rule*, in their application, constitute "unjustifiable discrimination" and a "disguised restriction on international trade." We hold, in sum, that the baseline establishment rules, although within the terms of Article XX(g), are not entitled to the justifying protection afforded by Article XX as a whole.

III. SPECIES PROTECTION AND THE 1998 *TURTLE — SHRIPT* CASE

WTO APPELLATE BODY REPORT, *UNITED STATES — IMPORT PROHIBITION OF CERTAIN SHRIMP AND SHRIMP PRODUCTS*
WT/DS58/AB/R (adopted 6 November 1998)

I. INTRODUCTION: STATEMENT OF THE APPEAL

1. This is an appeal by the United States from certain issues of law and legal interpretations in the Panel Report, *United States — Import Prohibition of Certain Shrimp and Shrimp Products.* Following a joint request for consultations by India, Malaysia, Pakistan and Thailand. . ., [these WTO Members] requested . . . that the Dispute Settlement Body (the "DSB") establish a panel to examine their complaint regarding a prohibition imposed by the United States on the importation of certain shrimp and shrimp products by Section 609 of Public Law 101-162 ("Section 609") [16 U.S.C. § 1537] and associated regulations and judicial rulings. . . .

2. . . . The United States issued regulations in 1987 pursuant to the *Endangered Species Act of 1973* [16 U.S.C. §§ 1531 *et seq.*] requiring all United States shrimp trawl vessels to use approved Turtle Excluder Devices ("TEDs")

or tow-time restrictions in specified areas where there was a significant mortality of sea turtles in shrimp harvesting. [*See* 52 Fed. Reg. 24,244 (29 June 1987) — the *"1987 Regulations."*] These regulations, which became fully effective in 1990, were modified so as to require the use of approved TEDs at all times and in all areas where there is a likelihood that shrimp trawling will interact with sea turtles, with certain limited exceptions.

7. . . . . [T]he Panel reached the following conclusions:

> In the light of the findings above, we conclude that the import ban on shrimp and shrimp products as applied by the United States on the basis of Section 609 of Public Law 101-162 is not consistent with Article XI:1 of GATT 1994, and cannot be justified under Article XX of GATT 1994.

. . . .

VI. APPRAISING SECTION 609 UNDER ARTICLE XX OF THE GATT 1994

. . . .

A. The Panel's Findings and Interpretative Analysis

. . . .

117. . . . . The Panel defined its approach as first "determin[ing] whether the measure at issue satisfies the conditions contained in the *chapeau*." If the Panel found that to be the case, it said that it "shall then examine whether the U.S. measure is covered by the terms of Article XX(b) or (g)." The Panel attempted to justify its interpretative approach in the following manner:

> As mentioned by the Appellate Body in its report in the *Gasoline* case, in order for the justification of Article XX to be extended to a given measure, it must not only come under one or another of the particular exceptions — paragraphs (a) to (j) — listed under Article XX; it must also satisfy the requirements imposed by the opening clause of Article XX. We note that panels have in the past considered the specific paragraphs of Article XX before reviewing the applicability of the conditions contained in the *chapeau*. However, *as the conditions contained in the introductory provision apply to any of the paragraphs of Article XX, it seems equally appropriate to analyse first the introductory provision of Article XX.* (emphasis added)

118. In *United States — Gasoline*, we enunciated the appropriate method for applying Article XX of the GATT 1994:

> In order that the justifying protection of Article XX may be extended to it, the measure at issue must not only come under one or another of the particular exceptions — paragraphs (a) to (j) — listed under Article XX; it must also satisfy the requirements imposed by the opening clauses of Article XX. *The analysis is,* in other words, *two-tiered: first, provisional justification by reason of characterization of the measure under XX(g); second, further appraisal of the same measure under the introductory clauses of Article XX.* (emphasis added)

119. The sequence of steps indicated above in the analysis of a claim of justification under Article XX reflects, not inadvertence or random choice, but rather the fundamental structure and logic of Article XX. The Panel appears to suggest, albeit indirectly, that following the indicated sequence of steps, or the inverse thereof, does not make any difference. To the Panel, reversing the sequence set out in *United States — Gasoline* "seems equally appropriate." We do not agree.

120. The task of interpreting the *chapeau* so as to prevent the abuse or misuse of the specific exemptions provided for in Article XX is rendered very difficult, if indeed it remains possible at all, where the interpreter (like the Panel in this case) has not first identified and examined the specific exception threatened with abuse. The standards established in the *chapeau* are, more-over, necessarily broad in scope and reach: the prohibition of the *application* of a measure "in a manner which would constitute a means of *arbitrary* or *unjustifiable discrimination* between countries where the same conditions prevail" or "a *disguised restriction* on international trade" (emphasis added). When applied in a particular case, the actual contours and contents of these standards will vary as the kind of measure under examination varies. What is appropriately characterizable as "arbitrary discrimination" or "unjustifiable discrimination," or as a "disguised restriction on international trade" in respect of one category of measures, need not be so with respect to another group or type of measures. The standard of "arbitrary discrimination," for example, under the *chapeau* may be different for a measure that purports to be necessary to protect public morals than for one relating to the products of prison labour.

121. The consequences of the interpretative approach adopted by the Panel are apparent in its findings. The Panel formulated a broad standard and a test for appraising measures sought to be justified under the *chapeau*; it is a standard or a test that finds no basis either in the text of the *chapeau* or in that of either of the two specific exceptions claimed by the United States. The Panel, in effect, constructed an *a priori* test that purports to define a category of measures which, *ratione materiae* [by reason of the matter involved, *i.e.*, from the nature of the subject matter], fall outside the justifying protection of Article XX's *chapeau*. In the present case, the Panel found that the United States measure at stake fell within that class of excluded measures because Section 609 conditions access to the domestic shrimp market of the United States on the adoption by exporting countries of certain conservation policies prescribed by the United States. It appears to us, however, that conditioning access to a Member's domestic market on whether exporting Members comply with, or adopt, a policy or policies unilaterally prescribed by the importing Member may, to some degree, be a common aspect of measures falling within the scope of one or another of the exceptions (a) to (j) of Article XX. Paragraphs (a) to (j) comprise measures that are recognized as *exceptions to substantive obligations* established in the GATT 1994, because the domestic policies embodied in such measures have been recognized as important and legitimate in character. It is not necessary to assume that requiring from exporting countries compliance with, or adoption of, certain policies (although covered in principle by one or another of the exceptions) prescribed by the importing country, renders a measure *a priori* incapable of

justification under Article XX. Such an interpretation renders most, if not all, of the specific exceptions of Article XX inutile, a result abhorrent to the principles of interpretation we are bound to apply.

122. We hold that the findings of the Panel . . ., and . . . [its] interpretative analysis, constitute error in legal interpretation and accordingly reverse them.

123. Having reversed the Panel's legal conclusion that the United States measure at issue "is not within the scope of measures permitted under the *chapeau* of Article XX," . . . it is our duty and our responsibility to complete the legal analysis in this case in order to determine whether Section 609 qualifies for justification under Article XX. . . .

 . . . .

B. Article XX(g): Provisional Justification of Section 609

125. In claiming justification for its measure, the United States primarily invokes Article XX(g). Justification under Article XX(b) is claimed only in the alternative. . . .

 . . . .

1. *"Exhaustible Natural Resources"*

 . . . .

129. The words of Article XX(g), "exhaustible natural resources," were actually crafted more than 50 years ago. They must be read by a treaty interpreter in the light of contemporary concerns of the community of nations about the protection and conservation of the environment. While Article XX was not modified in the Uruguay Round, the preamble attached to the *WTO Agreement* shows that the signatories to that *Agreement* were, in 1994, fully aware of the importance and legitimacy of environmental protection as a goal of national and international policy. The preamble of the *WTO Agreement* — which informs not only the GATT 1994, but also the other covered agreements — explicitly acknowledges "the objective of *sustainable development*" . . . .

130. From the perspective embodied in the preamble of the *WTO Agreement*, we note that the generic term "natural resources" in Article XX(g) is not "static" in its content or reference but is rather "by definition, evolutionary." It is, therefore, pertinent to note that modern international conventions and declarations make frequent references to natural resources as embracing both living and non-living resources. For instance, the 1982 *United Nations Convention on the Law of the Sea ("UNCLOS")* [done at Montego Bay, 10 December 1982, U.N. Doc. A/CONF.62/122, *reprinted in* 21 INTERNATIONAL LEGAL MATERIALS 1261], in defining the jurisdictional rights of coastal states in their exclusive economic zones, provides:

Article 56
Rights, jurisdiction and duties of the coastal State
in the exclusive economic zone

1. In the exclusive economic zone, the coastal State has:

(a) sovereign rights for the purpose of exploring and exploiting, conserving and managing the *natural resources, whether living or non-living*, of the waters superjacent to the sea-bed and of the sea-bed and its subsoil, . . . (emphasis added)

The *UNCLOS* also repeatedly refers in Articles 61 and 62 to "living resources" in specifying rights and duties of states in their exclusive economic zones. . . . [The U.S. has not joined *UNCLOS*. The Appellate Body proceeded by (1) observing the *Convention on Biological Diversity*, done at Rio de Janeiro, 5 June 1992, UNEP/Bio.Div./N7-INC5/4, *reprinted in* 31 INTERNATIONAL LEGAL MATERIALS 818, which Thailand and the U.S. have signed, but not ratified, and which India, Malaysia, and Pakistan have ratified, uses the concept of "biological resources," (2) explaining *Agenda 21*, adopted by the United Nations Conference on Environment and Development, 14 June 1992, U.N. Doc. A/CONF.151/26/Rev.1, speaks broadly of "natural resources" and in detail about "marine living resources," and (3) quoting from the *Final Act of the Conference to Conclude a Convention on the Conservation of Migratory Species of Wild Animals*, done at Bonn, 23 June 1979, *reprinted in* 19 INTERNATIONAL LEGAL MATERIALS 11, 15, which states migratory species are "living natural resources."]

131. Given the recent acknowledgement by the international community of the importance of concerted bilateral or multilateral action to protect living natural resources, and recalling the explicit recognition by WTO Members of the objective of sustainable development in the preamble of the *WTO Agreement*, we believe it is too late in the day to suppose that Article XX(g) of the GATT 1994 may be read as referring only to the conservation of exhaustible mineral or other non-living natural resources. [Plus, as the Appellate Body stated in footnote 114 of its Report, there is no evidence from the drafting history of an intent on the part of the GATT framers to exclude "living" natural resources from the scope of application of GATT Article XX:(g).] Moreover, two adopted GATT 1947 panel reports previously found fish to be an "exhaustible natural resource" within the meaning of Article XX(g). [*See United States — Prohibition of Imports of Tuna and Tuna Products from Canada*, GATT B.I.S.D. (29th Supp.) at 91 ¶ 4.9 (1983) (adopted 22 February 1982); *Canada — Measures Affecting Exports of Unprocessed Herring and Salmon*, GATT B.I.S.D. (35th Supp.) at 98 ¶ 4.4 (1989) (adopted 22 March 1988).] We hold that, in line with the principle of effectiveness in treaty interpretation, measures to conserve exhaustible natural resources, whether *living* or *non-living*, may fall within ArticleXX(g).

132. We turn next to the issue of whether the living natural resources sought to be conserved by the measure are "exhaustible" under Article XX(g). That this element is present in respect of the five species of sea turtles here involved appears to be conceded by all the participants and third participants in this case. The exhaustibility of sea turtles would in fact have been very difficult to controvert since all of the seven recognized species of sea turtles are today listed in Appendix 1 of the *Convention on International Trade in Endangered Species of Wild Fauna and Flora* ("*CITES*"). The list in Appendix 1 includes "all species *threatened with extinction* which are or may be affected by trade" (emphasis added).

133. Finally, we observe that sea turtles are highly migratory animals, passing in and out of waters subject to the rights of jurisdiction of various coastal states and the high seas. . . . The sea turtle species here at stake, *i.e.*, covered by Section 609, are all known to occur in waters over which the United States exercises jurisdiction. Of course, it is not claimed that *all* populations of these species migrate to, or traverse, at one time or another, waters subject to United States jurisdiction. Neither the appellant nor any of the appellees claims any rights of exclusive ownership over the sea turtles, at least not while they are swimming freely in their natural habitat — the oceans. We do not pass upon the question of whether there is an implied jurisdictional limitation in Article XX(g), and if so, the nature or extent of that limitation. We note only that in the specific circumstances of the case before us, there is a sufficient nexus between the migratory and endangered marine populations involved and the United States for purposes of Article XX(g).

134. . . . [W]e find that the sea turtles here involved constitute "exhaustible natural resources" for purposes of Article XX(g) of the GATT 1994.

2. *"Relating to the Conservation of"*

135. Article XX(g) requires that the measure sought to be justified be one which "relat[es] to" the conservation of exhaustible natural resources. In making this determination, the treaty interpreter essentially looks into the relationship between the measure at stake and the legitimate policy of conserving exhaustible natural resources. . . . [T]he policy of protecting and conserving the endangered sea turtles here involved is shared by all participants and third participants in this appeal, indeed, by the vast majority of the nations of the world. None of the parties to this dispute question the genuineness of the commitment of the others to that policy.

136. In *United States — Gasoline*, we inquired into the relationship between the baseline establishment rules of the United States Environmental Protection Agency (the "EPA") and the conservation of natural resources for the purposes of Article XX(g). There, we answered in the affirmative the question posed before the panel of whether the baseline establishment rules were "primarily aimed at" the conservation of clean air. . . . [The Appellate Body quoted from its holding in that case.] The substantial relationship we found there between the EPA baseline establishment rules and the conservation of clean air in the United States was a close and genuine relationship of ends and means.

137. In the present case, we must examine the relationship between the general structure and design of the measure here at stake, Section 609, and the policy goal it purports to serve, that is, the conservation of sea turtles.

138. Section 609(b)(1) imposes an import ban on shrimp that have been harvested with commercial fishing technology which may adversely affect sea turtles. This provision is designed to influence countries to adopt national regulatory programs requiring the use of TEDs by their shrimp fishermen. . . . There are two basic exemptions from the import ban, both of which relate clearly and directly to the policy goal of conserving sea turtles. First, Section 609, as elaborated in the *1996 Guidelines*, excludes from the import

ban shrimp harvested "under conditions that do not adversely affect sea turtles." Thus, the measure, by its terms, excludes from the import ban: aquaculture shrimp; shrimp species (such as *pandalid* shrimp) harvested in water areas where sea turtles do not normally occur; and shrimp harvested exclusively by artisanal methods, even from non-certified countries. The harvesting of such shrimp clearly does not affect sea turtles. Second, under Section 609(b)(2), the measure exempts from the import ban shrimp caught in waters subject to the jurisdiction of certified countries.

139. There are two types of certification for countries under Section 609(b)(2). First, under Section 609(b)(2)(C), a country may be certified as having a fishing environment that does not pose a threat of incidental taking of sea turtles in the course of commercial shrimp trawl harvesting. There is no risk, or only a negligible risk, that sea turtles will be harmed by shrimp trawling in such an environment.

140. The second type of certification is provided by Section 609(b)(2)(A) and (B). Under these provisions, as further elaborated in the *1996 Guidelines*, a country wishing to export shrimp to the United States is required to adopt a regulatory program that is comparable to that of the United States program and to have a rate of incidental take of sea turtles that is comparable to the average rate of United States' vessels. This is, essentially, a requirement that a country adopt a regulatory program requiring the use of TEDs by commercial shrimp trawling vessels in areas where there is a likelihood of intercepting sea turtles. This requirement is, in our view, directly connected with the policy of conservation of sea turtles. It is undisputed among the participants, and recognized by the experts consulted by the Panel, that the harvesting of shrimp by commercial shrimp trawling vessels with mechanical retrieval devices in waters where shrimp and sea turtles coincide is a significant cause of sea turtle mortality. Moreover, the Panel did "not question . . . the fact generally acknowledged by the experts that TEDs, when properly installed and adapted to the local area, would be an effective tool for the preservation of sea turtles."

141. In its general design and structure, therefore, Section 609 is not a simple, blanket prohibition of the importation of shrimp imposed without regard to the consequences (or lack thereof) of the mode of harvesting employed upon the incidental capture and mortality of sea turtles. Focusing on the design of the measure here at stake, it appears to us that Section 609, *cum* implementing guidelines, is not disproportionately wide in its scope and reach in relation to the policy objective of protection and conservation of sea turtle species. The means are, in principle, reasonably related to the ends. The means and ends relationship between Section 609 and the legitimate policy of conserving an exhaustible, and, in fact, endangered species, is observably a close and real one, a relationship that is every bit as substantial as that which we found in *United States — Gasoline* between the EPA baseline establishment rules and the conservation of clean air in the United States.

142. In our view, therefore, Section 609 is a measure "relating to" the conservation of an exhaustible natural resource within the meaning of Article XX(g) of the GATT 1994.

3. *"If Such Measures are Made Effective in Conjunction with Restrictions on Domestic Production or Consumption"*

143. In *United States — Gasoline*, we held that . . . Article XX(g),

> . . . is appropriately read as a requirement that the measures concerned impose restrictions, not just in respect of imported gasoline but also with respect to domestic gasoline. The clause is a requirement of *even-handedness* in the imposition of restrictions, in the name of conservation, upon the production or consumption of exhaustible natural resources.

In this case, we need to examine whether the restrictions imposed by Section 609 with respect to imported shrimp are also imposed in respect of shrimp caught by United States shrimp trawl vessels.

144. . . . Section 609, enacted in 1989, addresses the mode of harvesting of imported shrimp only. However, two years earlier, in 1987, the United States issued regulations pursuant to the *Endangered Species Act* requiring all United States shrimp trawl vessels to use approved TEDs, or to restrict the duration of tow-times, in specified areas where there was significant incidental mortality of sea turtles in shrimp trawls. These regulations became fully effective in 1990 and were later modified. They now require United States shrimp trawlers to use approved TEDs "in areas and at times when there is a likelihood of intercepting sea turtles," with certain limited exceptions. Penalties for violation of the *Endangered Species Act*, or the regulations issued thereunder, include civil and criminal sanctions. The United States government currently relies on monetary sanctions and civil penalties for enforcement. The government has the ability to seize shrimp catch from trawl vessels fishing in United States waters and has done so in cases of egregious violations. We believe that, in principle, Section 609 is an even-handed measure.

145. Accordingly, we hold that Section 609 is a measure made effective in conjunction with the restrictions on domestic harvesting of shrimp, as required by Article XX(g).

C. The Introductory Clauses of Article XX: Characterizing Section 609 under the *Chapeau's* Standards

146. . . . Having found that Section 609 does come within the terms of Article XX(g), it is not, therefore, necessary to analyze the measure in terms of Article XX(b).

147. Although provisionally justified under Article XX(g), Section 609, if it is ultimately to be justified as an exception under Article XX, must also satisfy the requirements of the introductory clauses — the *"chapeau"* — of Article XX. . . . We turn . . . to the second part of the two-tier analysis required under Article XX.

1. *General Considerations*

. . . .

156. Turning then to the *chapeau* of Article XX, . . . it embodies the recognition on the part of WTO Members of the need to maintain a balance of rights and obligations between the right of a Member to invoke one or another of the exceptions of Article XX, specified in paragraphs (a) to (j), on the one hand, and the substantive rights of the other Members under the GATT 1994, on the other hand. Exercise by one Member of its right to invoke an exception, such as Article XX(g), if abused or misused, will, to that extent, erode or render naught the substantive treaty rights in, for example, Article XI:1, of other Members. Similarly, because the GATT 1994 itself makes available the exceptions of Article XX, in recognition of the legitimate nature of the policies and interests there embodied, the right to invoke one of those exceptions is not to be rendered illusory. The same concept may be expressed from a slightly different angle of vision, thus, a balance must be struck between the *right* of a Member to invoke an exception under Article XX and the *duty* of that same Member to respect the treaty rights of the other Members. To permit one Member to abuse or misuse its right to invoke an exception would be effectively to allow that Member to degrade its own treaty obligations as well as to devalue the treaty rights of other Members. If the abuse or misuse is sufficiently grave or extensive, the Member, in effect, reduces its treaty obligation to a merely facultative one and dissolves its juridical character, and, in so doing, negates altogether the treaty rights of other Members. The *chapeau* was installed at the head of the list of "General Exceptions" in Article XX to prevent such far-reaching consequences.

157. . . . [T]he language of the *chapeau* makes clear that each of the exceptions in paragraphs (a) to (j) of Article XX is a *limited and conditional* exception from the substantive obligations contained in the other provisions of the GATT 1994, that is to say, the ultimate availability of the exception is subject to the compliance by the invoking Member with the requirements of the *chapeau*. This interpretation of the *chapeau* is confirmed by its negotiating history. [The Appellate Body observed in footnote 152 of its Report that Article 32 of the *Vienna Convention* permits recourse to "supplementary means of interpretation, including the preparatory work of the treaty and the circumstances of its conclusion," in order to confirm a meaning resulting from the application of Article 31, or to determine a meaning when the application of Article 31 leaves the meaning ambiguous or obscure, or leads to a manifestly absurd or unreasonable result. The Appellate Body said it was resorting to legislative history to confirm a meaning.] The language initially proposed by the United States in 1946 for the *chapeau* of what would later become Article XX was unqualified and unconditional. Several proposals were made during the First Session of the Preparatory Committee of the United Nations Conference on Trade and Employment in 1946 suggesting modifications. In November 1946, the United Kingdom proposed that "in order to prevent abuse of the exceptions of Article 32 [which would subsequently become Article XX]," the *chapeau* of this provision should be qualified. This proposal was generally accepted, subject to later review of its precise wording. Thus, the negotiating history of Article XX confirms that the paragraphs of Article XX set forth *limited and conditional* exceptions from the obligations of the substantive provisions of the GATT. Any measure, to qualify finally for exception, must also satisfy the requirements of the *chapeau*. This is a fundamental part of

the balance of rights and obligations struck by the original framers of the GATT 1947.

. . . .

159. The task of interpreting and applying the *chapeau* is, hence, essentially the delicate one of locating and marking out a line of equilibrium between the right of a Member to invoke an exception under Article XX and the rights of the other Members under varying substantive provisions (*e.g.*, Article XI) of the GATT 1994, so that neither of the competing rights will cancel out the other and thereby distort and nullify or impair the balance of rights and obligations constructed by the Members themselves in that Agreement. The location of the line of equilibrium, as expressed in the *chapeau*, is not fixed and unchanging; the line moves as the kind and the shape of the measures at stake vary and as the facts making up specific cases differ.

160. . . . . [W]e address now the issue of whether the *application* of the United States measure, although the measure itself falls within the terms of Article XX(g), nevertheless constitutes "a means of arbitrary or unjustifiable discrimination between countries where the same conditions prevail" or "a disguised restriction on international trade." We address, in other words, whether the application of this measure constitutes an abuse or misuse of the provisional justification made available by Article XX(g). . . . [T]he application of a measure may be characterized as amounting to an abuse or misuse of an exception of Article XX not only when the detailed operating provisions of the measure prescribe the arbitrary or unjustifiable activity, but also where a measure, otherwise fair and just on its face, is actually applied in an arbitrary or unjustifiable manner. The standards of the *chapeau* . . . project both substantive and procedural requirements.

2. *"Unjustifiable Discrimination"*

161. We scrutinize first whether Section 609 has been applied in a manner constituting "unjustifiable discrimination between countries where the same conditions prevail." Perhaps the most conspicuous flaw in this measure's application relates to its intended and actual coercive effect on the specific policy decisions made by foreign governments, Members of the WTO. Section 609, in its application, is, in effect, an economic embargo which requires *all other exporting Members*, if they wish to exercise their GATT rights, to adopt *essentially the same* policy (together with an approved enforcement program) as that applied to, and enforced on, United States domestic shrimp trawlers. As enacted by the Congress of the United States, the *statutory* provisions of Section 609(b)(2)(A) and (B) do not, in themselves, *require* that other WTO Members adopt *essentially the same* policies and enforcement practices as the United States. Viewed alone, the statute appears to permit a degree of discretion or flexibility in how the standards for determining comparability might be applied, in practice, to other countries. However, any flexibility that may have been intended by Congress when it enacted the statutory provision has been effectively eliminated in the implementation of that policy through the *1996 Guidelines* promulgated by the Department of State and through the practice of the administrators in making certification determinations.

. . . .

164. . . . [T]he United States also applies a uniform standard throughout its territory, regardless of the particular conditions existing in certain parts of the country. The United States requires the use of approved TEDs at all times by domestic, commercial shrimp trawl vessels operating in waters where there is any likelihood that they may interact with sea turtles, regardless of the actual incidence of sea turtles in those waters, the species of those sea turtles, or other differences or disparities that may exist in different parts of the United States. It may be quite acceptable for a government, in adopting and implementing a domestic policy, to adopt a single standard applicable to all its citizens throughout that country. However, it is not acceptable, in international trade relations, for one WTO Member to use an economic embargo to *require* other Members to adopt essentially the same comprehensive regulatory program, to achieve a certain policy goal, as that in force within that Member's territory, *without* taking into consideration different conditions which may occur in the territories of those other Members.

. . . .

166. Another aspect of the application of Section 609 that bears heavily in any appraisal of justifiable or unjustifiable discrimination is the failure of the United States to engage the appellees, as well as other Members exporting shrimp to the United States, in serious, across-the-board negotiations with the objective of concluding bilateral or multilateral agreements for the protection and conservation of sea turtles, before enforcing the import prohibition against the shrimp exports of those other Members. . . .

167. . . . . First, the Congress of the United States expressly recognized the importance of securing international agreements for the protection and conservation of the sea turtle species in enacting this law. . . . [The Appellate Body quoted generously to this effect from Section 609(a), which *directs* the Secretary of State to enter into bilateral or multilateral agreements to protect and conserve sea turtles.] Apart from the negotiation of the *Inter-American Convention for the Protection and Conservation of Sea Turtles* (the "*Inter-American Convention*") which concluded in 1996, the record before the Panel does not indicate any serious, substantial efforts to carry out these express directions of Congress.

168. Second, the protection and conservation of highly migratory species of sea turtles, that is, the very policy objective of the measure, demands concerted and cooperative efforts on the part of the many countries whose waters are traversed in the course of recurrent sea turtle migrations. The need for, and the appropriateness of, such efforts have been recognized in the WTO itself as well as in a significant number of other international instruments and declarations. . . . [T]he [WTO] *Decision on Trade and Environment*, which provided for the establishment of the CTE [Committee on Trade and the Environment] and set out its terms of reference, refers to both the *Rio Declaration on Environment and Development* and *Agenda 21*. Of particular relevance is Principle 12 of the *Rio Declaration* . . ., which states, in part:

> Unilateral actions to deal with environmental challenges outside the jurisdiction of the importing country should be avoided. *Environmen-*

*tal measures addressing transboundary or global environmental prob-
lems should, as far as possible, be based on international consensus.*
(emphasis added)

. . . [The Appellate Body quoted generously from comparable provisions in
Agenda 21 (para. 2.22(i), the *Convention on Biological Diversity* (Article 5),
and the *Convention on the Conservation of Migratory Species of Wild Animals*
(Annex I).] . . . Furthermore, . . . WTO Members in the Report of the CTE,
forming part of the Report of the General Council to Ministers on the occasion
of the [December 1996] Singapore Ministerial Conference, endorsed and supported [as "best and most effective" multilateral solutions to trans-boundary
or global environmental problems]. . . .

169. Third, the United States did negotiate and conclude one regional
international agreement for the protection and conservation of sea turtles: The
Inter-American Convention. This *Convention* was opened for signature on 1
December 1996 and has been signed by five countries, in addition to the
United States, and four of these countries are currently certified under Section
609. This *Convention* has not yet been ratified by any of its signatories. [The
Appellate Body quoted generously from this *Convention*, too.]

. . . .

171. The *Inter-American Convention* thus provides convincing demonstration that an alternative course of action was reasonably open to the United
States for securing the legitimate policy goal of its measure, a course of action
other than the unilateral and non-consensual procedures of the import
prohibition under Section 609. It is relevant to observe that an import
prohibition is, ordinarily, the heaviest "weapon" in a Member's armoury of
trade measures. The record does not, however, show that serious efforts were
made by the United States to negotiate similar agreements with any other
country or group of countries before (and, as far as the record shows, after)
Section 609 was enforced on a world-wide basis on 1 May 1996. . . .

172. Clearly, the United States negotiated seriously with some, but not with
other Members (including the appellees), that export shrimp to the United
States. The effect is plainly discriminatory and, in our view, unjustifiable. The
unjustifiable nature of this discrimination emerges clearly when we consider
the cumulative effects of the failure of the United States to pursue negotiations for establishing consensual means of protection and conservation of the
living marine resources here involved, notwithstanding the explicit statutory
direction in Section 609 itself to initiate negotiations as soon as possible for
the development of bilateral and multilateral agreements. The principal
consequence of this failure may be seen in the resulting unilateralism evident
in the application of Section 609. . . . [T]he policies relating to the necessity
for use of particular kinds of TEDs in various maritime areas, and the
operating details of these policies, are all shaped by the Department of State,
without the participation of the exporting Members. The system and processes
of certification are established and administered by the United States agencies
alone. The decision-making involved in the grant, denial or withdrawal of
certification to the exporting Members, is, accordingly, also unilateral. The
unilateral character of the application of Section 609 heightens the disruptive

and discriminatory influence of the import prohibition and underscores its unjustifiability.

. . . .

[The Appellate Body went on to point out that transition periods and TED technology sharing by the U.S., under the *1991* and *1993 Guidelines*, discriminated against certain countries.]

176. . . . [W]e find, and so hold, that . . . [the cumulative effect of differences in the means of application of Section 609 to various shrimp exporting countries] . . . constitute "unjustifiable discrimination" between exporting countries desiring certification in order to gain access to the United States shrimp market within the meaning of the *chapeau* of Article XX.

3. *"Arbitrary Discrimination"*

177. We next consider whether Section 609 has been applied in a manner constituting "arbitrary discrimination between countries where the same conditions prevail." . . . Section 609, in its application, imposes a single, rigid and unbending requirement that countries applying for certification under Section 609(b)(2)(A) and (B) adopt a comprehensive regulatory program that is essentially the same as the United States' program, without inquiring into the appropriateness of that program for the conditions prevailing in the exporting countries. Furthermore, there is little or no flexibility in how officials make the determination for certification pursuant to these provisions. . . . [T]his rigidity and inflexibility also constitute "arbitrary discrimination" within the meaning of the *chapeau.*

. . . .

180. . . . [W]ith respect to neither type of certification under Section 609(b)(2) [*i.e.,* under Section 609(b)(2)(A) and (B), or under Section 609(b)(2)(C)] is there a transparent, predictable certification process that is followed by the competent United States government officials. The certification processes under Section 609 consist principally of administrative *ex parte* inquiry or verification by staff of the Office of Marine Conservation in the Department of State with staff of the United States National Marine Fisheries Service. With respect to both types of certification, there is no formal opportunity for an applicant country to be heard, or to respond to any arguments that may be made against it, in the course of the certification process before a decision to grant or to deny certification is made. Moreover, no formal written, reasoned decision, whether of acceptance or rejection, is rendered on applications for either type of certification. . . . Countries which are granted certification are included in a list of approved applications published in the *Federal Register*; however, they are not notified specifically. Countries whose applications are denied also do not receive notice of such denial (other than by omission from the list of approved applications) or of the reasons for the denial. No procedure for review of, or appeal from, a denial of an application is provided.

181. The certification processes followed by the United States thus appear to be singularly informal and casual, and to be conducted in a manner such

that these processes could result in the negation of rights of Members. There appears to be no way that exporting Members can be certain whether the terms of Section 609, in particular, the *1996 Guidelines*, are being applied in a fair and just manner by the appropriate governmental agencies of the United States. It appears to us that, effectively, exporting Members applying for certification whose applications are rejected are denied basic fairness and due process, and are discriminated against, *vis-à-vis* those Members which are granted certification.

. . . .

184. We find, accordingly, that the United States measure is applied in a manner which amounts to a means not just of "unjustifiable discrimination," but also of "arbitrary discrimination" between countries where the same conditions prevail, contrary to the requirements of the *chapeau* of Article XX. The measure, therefore, is not entitled to the justifying protection of Article XX of the GATT 1994. Having made this finding, it is not necessary for us to examine also whether the United States measure is applied in a manner that constitutes a "disguised restriction on international trade" under the *chapeau* of Article XX.

185. In reaching these conclusions, we wish to underscore what we have *not* decided in this appeal. We have *not* decided that the protection and preservation of the environment is of no significance to the Members of the WTO. Clearly, it is. We have *not* decided that the sovereign nations that are Members of the WTO cannot adopt effective measures to protect endangered species, such as sea turtles. Clearly, they can and should. And we have *not* decided that sovereign states should not act together bilaterally, plurilaterally or multilaterally, either within the WTO or in other international fora, to protect endangered species or to otherwise protect the environment. Clearly, they should and do.

186. What we *have* decided in this appeal is simply this: although the measure of the United States in dispute in this appeal serves an environmental objective that is recognized as legitimate under paragraph (g) of Article XX of the GATT 1994, this measure has been applied by the United States in a manner which constitutes arbitrary and unjustifiable discrimination between Members of the WTO, contrary to the requirements of the *chapeau* of Article XX. . . . [T]his measure does not qualify for the exemption that Article XX of the GATT 1994 affords to measures which serve certain recognized, legitimate environmental purposes but which, at the same time, are not applied in a manner that constitutes a means of arbitrary or unjustifiable discrimination between countries where the same conditions prevail or a disguised restriction on international trade. As we emphasized in *United States — Gasoline*, WTO Members are free to adopt their own policies aimed at protecting the environment as long as, in so doing, they fulfill their obligations and respect the rights of other Members under the *WTO Agreement*.

IV.   PASSING THE TWO STEP TEST AND THE 2001 *ASBESTOS* CASE

The Appellate Body Report in the *Asbestos* case — *European Communities — Measures Affecting Asbestos and Asbestos-Containing Products*,

WT/DS135/AB/R (adopted 12 March 2001) — is a cause for both cheer and disappointment. "Cheer," at least among environmentalists, because it is the first instance in which the Appellate Body holds a disputed measure passes muster under both steps in the two-step Article XX test. "Necessity" is not to be interpreted in a highly restrictive manner, but as "reasonable availability," thereby according deference and flexibility to national authorities. "Disappointment," because aside from elaborating on the meaning of "necessity" under Article XX(b), the Appellate Body provides no insights to Article XX — in particular, on how to interpret key terms in the *chapeau*. On appeal, Canada did not raise a challenge under the *chapeau*. Hence, the case is not the quintessential example of successful invocation, following full adjudication, of Article XX(b) and the *chapeau*.

The disputed measure was a French import ban on asbestos and asbestos-containing products. On Step One, Paragraph (b) of Article XX, the Appellate Body asked whether the ban "protected" human life or health, and whether it was "necessary" to do so with a ban. The Panel looked at a large amount of scientific evidence. All four scientific experts it consulted agreed chrysotile asbestos fibres, and cement-based products containing these fibres, constitute a risk to human health. The Panel observed that since 1977, international bodies like the World Health Organisation (WHO) and International Agency for Research on Cancer have acknowledged this risk. Chrysotile, in specific, posed a risk of lung cancer and mesothelioma (another form of cancer) to humans in occupational sectors downstream of production and processing. Cement-based products containing chrysotile posed the same risks for the public in general. As the Panel did not exceed the bounds of its discretion in making these deductions, the Appellate Body found no reason to interfere with them. After all, panels, not the Appellate Body, are the triers of fact.

In the *Asbestos* case, both the Panel and Appellate Body agreed the disputed measure was "necessary," within the meaning of GATT Article XX(b), for protecting human life. There was no reasonably available alternative to banning chrysotile and products containing chrysotile. On appeal, Canada urged the Panel committed legal errors by not quantifying the risk of chrysotile and chrysotile-containing products, and by failing to consider the risk of substitute goods permitted by the French government. Canada also argued the Panel was legally incorrect to hold that controlled use of chrysotile and chrysotile-containing products is not a reasonably available alternative to banning asbestos and products with asbestos. On both arguments, Canada lost.

First, held the Appellate Body, neither Article XX(b), nor any provision of the WTO *Agreement on Sanitary and Phytosanitary Standards* ("*SPS Agreement*"), requires a quantitative measurement of risks to human life or health. Rather, they permit either a quantitative or qualitative evaluation. The Panel looked at the scientific evidence, which indicated no minimum threshold level of exposure or duration has been identified for any risk (except for asbestosis) posed by chrysotile, and which also proved a clear link to cancer. Second, as Canada ought to have known, "it is undisputed that WTO Members have the right to determine the level of protection of health that they consider appropriate in a given situation."[1] France chose to "halt" the spread of asbestos-related health risks, and the word "necessary" in Article XX(b) must not be misconstrued to undermine this sovereign right. True, the substitute good (PCG fibres and cement-based products containing PCG fibres), might pose health risks too. But, these risks are less than those posed by chrysotile asbestos fibres and products containing them. In other words, said the Appellate Body, "it seems to us perfectly legitimate for a Member to seek to halt the spread of a highly risky product while allowing the use of a less risky product in its place."[2]

Canada's argument that the Panel should have found controlled use of asbestos and products containing asbestos is not a reasonably available alternative to banning these products raises the interpretive question of what, at bottom, "necessity" in Article XX(b) means. What factors must be taken into account to determine whether an alternative measure, short of a ban, is "necessary" for the importing country to protect human life or health? In *Reformulated Gasoline* case, the Panel held that an alternative measure is reasonably available even if there are administrative difficulties associated with implementing that measure. As this holding was not appealed, in *Asbestos* the Appellate Body had its first opportunity to opine on the point.

Predictably, the Appellate Body looked to three precedents:

    i.   The 1989 GATT Panel Report, *United States — Section 337 of the Tariff Act of 1930* (B.I.S.D. (36th Supp.) 345 at ¶ 5.26 (adopted 7 November 1989)).

    ii.   The 1990 GATT Panel Report, *Thailand — Restrictions on Importation of and Internal Taxes on Cigarettes* (B.I.S.D. (37th Supp.) 200 (adopted 20 February 1990)).

    iii.   The 2001 Appellate Body Report, *Korea — Measures Affecting Imports of Fresh, Chilled and Frozen Beef* (WT/DS161/AB/R, WT/DS169/AB/R (adopted 10 January 2001)).

In the *Thai Cigarettes* case, the GATT Panel faced the same issue — how to evaluate whether a measure is "necessary" under Article XX(b). The import restrictions on cigarettes imposed by Thailand, said the Panel, could be considered " 'necessary' . . . only if there were *no alternative measure consistent with the General Agreement, or less inconsistent with it*, which Thailand could *reasonably be expected to employ to achieve* its health *policy objectives*."[3]

Parsed carefully, the highlighted language from the *Thai Cigarettes* case contains a four-pronged test for "necessity" under Paragraph (b). The test applies *in seriatim*, *i.e.*, each prong builds on its predecessor.

    i.   First, there must be no measure that is an alternative to the measure in dispute.

---

[1] WTO Appellate Body Report, *European Communities — Measures Affecting Asbestos and Asbestos-Containing Products*, WT/DS135/AB/R, ¶ 168 (adopted 12 March 2001); *see also id.* ¶¶ 157-63.

[2] WTO Appellate Body Report, *European Communities — Measures Affecting Asbestos and Asbestos-Containing Products*, WT/DS135/AB/R, ¶ 168 (adopted 12 March 2001).

[3] B.I.S.D. (37th Supp.) 200 at ¶ 75 (adopted 20 Feb. 1990) (emphasis added).

ii.   Second, assuming there is an alternative measure, it must be either consistent with GATT, or less inconsistent with GATT than the disputed measure.

iii.   Third, assuming there is a GATT-consistent, or less-GATT-inconsistent, alternative measure, it must be reasonable to expect the importing country to employ the alternative.

iv.   Fourth, assuming the first three prongs are met, the alternative measure furthers the health policy goal of the importing country.

The GATT Panel faced nearly the same issue in the *Section 337* case, as did the Appellate Body in *Korea Beef*. What does "necessary" under Article XX(d) mean? The adjudicators established essentially the same test as the *Thai Cigarettes* Panel.

Thus, in *Section 337*, the Panel ruled the proper standard for testing "necessity" under Paragraph (d) is whether

- an alternative measure exists that is available to the importing country,

- it is reasonable to expect the importing country to use the alternative measure, and

- the alternative measure is not inconsistent with other GATT provisions.

In one important respect, the *Section 337* Panel supplemented this test. It considered the possibility no GATT-consistent measure is reasonably available to an importing country. What should the country do? The Panel said the country would be bound to choose from among the alternative measures reasonably available to it the one least inconsistent with other GATT provisions. Put differently, the country would have to choose the least trade restrictive measure, because this least-worst choice would be most consistent with the trade-liberalizing aim of GATT. In *Korea Beef*, the Appellate Body affirmed the *Section 337* test, and did so again in *EC Asbestos*.

Following and building on precedent, the Appellate Body in *Asbestos* the applied the same test for Article XX(b) from *Thai Cigarettes*, and Article XX(d) from *Section 337* and *Korea Beef*. The Appellate Body agreed (1) no alternative measure existed that (2) France could reasonably be expected to employ that (3) was consistent with GATT, or less inconsistent with GATT, than a complete ban on asbestos and asbestos-containing products, which (4) also would achieve France's health policy aim.

Observe, too, the Appellate Body's reiteration of a point it had made in *Korea Beef* about judicial decision-making under Article XX(b) and (d). The "necessity" test requires weighing and balancing to see whether a GATT-consistent, WTO-consistent alternative not only is reasonably available, but also whether it advances a policy goal of the importing country. That country must show how vital the stakes are. The more important the common interests or values at stake, the easier it is to accept a measure is "necessary" to achieve its stated goal. In this regard, the French ban was the perfect case.

The ban was designed to further a value "both vital and important in the highest degree," namely, the preservation of human life and health by eliminating "well-known, and life-threatening health risks posed by asbestos fibres."[4] No alternative measure simultaneously could achieve the same goal and be less restrictive of trade than a prohibition. Canada's proposed alternative — controlled use of asbestos and asbestos-containing products — could not achieve the French aim of halting these risks, but would undermine France's sovereign right to choose its level of health protection.

V. PRODUCTS VERSUS PROCESSES

Is the way in which a product is made — the process and production method (PPM) a justifiable basis for an import restriction? Major jurisprudence under GATT Articles XX(b) and XX(g) — namely, the *Tuna Dolphin I* and *II*, *Reformulated Gasoline*, and *Turtle Shrimp* cases excerpted in an earlier Chapter — all suggest a negative response. None of these cases yields a prophylactic ruling against a particular PPM. The decision in *Beef Hormones*, however, and possibly the *GMO* decision too, suggest use of certain PPMs directly related to the product, and reflected in it, could support an import ban.

Is the difference between a product *per se*, and the way it is grown, raised, harvested, raised, or manufactured, a distinction about the appropriate level at which to regulate? A product embodying a scientifically demonstrable risk of harm is a legitimate target for an import restriction. To ensure protectionism with respect to that product is not afoot, GATT—WTO disciplines apply. But, neither GATT nor the *SPS Agreement on the Application of Sanitary and Phytosanitary Measures* (*SPS Agreement*) is a document designed to deal with harmful production methods that apply to whole categories of merchandise, or that might cause systemic problems like global warming. Those methods are to be regulated through multilateral environmental agreements (MEAs). What role does, and should, preservation of sovereignty play in the product — process distinction?

---

[4] WTO Appellate Body Report, *European Communities — Measures Affecting Asbestos and Asbestos-Containing Products*, WT/DS135/AB/R, ¶ 172 (adopted 12 March 2001).

Chapter 44

SPS MEASURES

Is not disease the rule of existence? There is not a lily pad floating on the river but has been riddled by insects. Almost every shrub and tree has its gall, oftentimes esteemed its chief ornament and hardly to be distinguished from the fruit. If misery loves company, misery has company enough. Now, at midsummer, find me a perfect leaf or fruit.

—Henry David Thoreau (1817-62), *Journals*
(entry for 1 September 1851)

DOCUMENTS SUPPLEMENT ASSIGNMENT

1. WTO *SPS Agreement*
2. U.S. *Statement of Administrative Action* for the *SPS Agreement*
3. *NAFTA* Chapter 7B
4. *NAFTA Environmental Side Agreement*
5. Relevant provisions in other FTAs

I. TRADE AND THE SPREAD OF DISEASE

Surely the deadliest — in a literal sense — argument against free trade concerns the spread of disease. Increased trade increases opportunities for disease to spread. Trade itself is a transmission mechanism for bacteria, viruses, and other threats to human, animal, or plant life and health. In the 14th century A.D., the bubonic plague was spread to Europe in part by fleas on rats on Genovese and Venetian cargo ships bound for Sicily from the Near and Far East. As trade and travel volumes grow in modern times, the opportunity to spread disease expands concomitantly, if not exponentially.

Yet, from time to time to time and country to country, a foreign government may abuse its regulatory authority to protect a favored or politically powerful domestic industry by claiming — without scientific justification — a competing and competitive imported product is a risk to local life or health. Indeed, many American exporters — of apples to Japan or poultry to Russia, for instance — have faced what they regard as abusive sanitary and phytosanitary (SPS) barriers to their shipments.

Aside from the merits of any particular SPS measure, international trade provides three specific mechanisms for disease transmission: goods, vessels, and creatures. First, merchandise that moves across a border may conceal a disease or disease-carrying organism. For example, bulk cargo, such as a shipment of cocoa beans from Côte d'Ivoire, may carry with it a pest. Unless the shipment is fumigated before offloading, the pest will enter the importing country along with the cocoa beans.

1417

Second, a vessel carrying merchandise across a border, or in which merchandise is packed for trans-boundary shipment, may contain a threat. Wooden pallets on which goods are loaded, and wooden crates in which goods are placed, are examples. Untreated wood pallets from China posed a threat because of two pests on them (pine wood nematodes, or "PWN," and the Asian long-horned beetle). In 1998, the U.S. Department of Agriculture (USDA) mandated chemical or heat treatment for wood pallets used to ship merchandise into the country. In 2001, the EU followed suit. The "Pallet Wars" between the U.S. and EU, on the one hand, and China, on the other hand, ensued. From 1998-2001, 38 million wood pallets annually came into the U.S., 80 percent of them from Canada (a major producer-exporter of softwood lumber). China argued the USDA mandate was an unjustifiable SPS measure in view of the disproportionately large percentage of Canadian-origin pallets and the fact pallets are reused in trade. Underlying the Chinese argument was deep concern the SPS measure would stifle Chinese exports in the shadow of the 1997-99 Asian Economic Crisis. On 16 September 2004, the USDA promulgated a final — yet still controversial — regulation on wood pallets.

Third, a person, animal, or plant from one country to another may carry a disease. One example, associated with the movement of persons, is the Sudden Acute Respiratory Syndrome (SARS) epidemic that afflicted much of East Asia from November 2002 to September 2003. Another illustration, connected with bird migration, is the avian flu virus (H5N1). It broke out in Thailand and Vietnam in 2004, and by 2007 had spread to 9 countries, as far west as Egypt and Turkey, and with notable cases in Indonesia and Iraq.

The intersection of international trade and disease transmission is one of the most fascinating areas of evolving WTO jurisprudence. Panels and the Appellate Body must differentiate *bona fide* SPS measures from disguised protectionism. Consequently, they must define what counts as "scientific" evidence, evaluate that evidence, consider whether a disputed measure is justified in proportion to a threat posed, and discern whether a less trade restrictive alternative measure might work. Not all threats are equal.

Indeed, a key fact distinguishing the *Japan Apples* and *Beef Hormones* cases is the nature of the threat. *Japan Apples* concerns an economic threat, that is, the risk a pest might be introduced through apple imports, and that pest would wreak damage to crops in Japan. *Beef Hormones* is about a perceived risk to human health. Does this factual difference suggest the test for the permissibility of an SPS measure should be different? Should a lower threshold be permitted if the threat is to life rather than property? How should potential risks and benefits of genetically modified organisms (GMOs) be assessed and dealt with?

II. THE SUFFICIENCY OF SCIENTIFIC EVIDENCE, GENERAL ARTICLE 2:2 OBLIGATION, AND 2003 *JAPAN APPLES* CASE

A. Japan's Controversial Quarantine

WTO APPELLATE BODY REPORT, *JAPAN — MEASURES AFFECTING THE IMPORTATION OF APPLES*
WT/DS245/AB/R (adopted 10 December 2003)
(complaint by the United States)

II. Background

A. The Disease at Issue

8. . . . . The disease targeted by Japan's phytosanitary measure . . . is called "fire blight," often referred to by the scientific name for its bacterium, *Erwinia amylovora* or *E. amylovora*. Fruits infected by fire blight exude bacterial ooze, or inoculum, which is transmitted primarily through wind and/or rain and by insects or birds to open flowers on the same or new host plants. *E. amylovora* bacteria multiply externally on the stigmas of these open flowers and enter the plant by various openings. In addition to apple fruit, hosts of fire blight include pears, quince, and loquats, as well as several garden plants. Scientific evidence establishes, as the Panel found, that the risk of introduction and spread of fire blight varies considerably according to the host plant.

9. The uncontested history of fire blight reveals significant transoceanic dissemination in the 200-plus years since its discovery. *E. amylovora*, first reported in New York State in the United States in 1793, is believed to be native to North America. By the early 1900s, fire blight had been reported in Canada from Ontario to British Columbia, in northern Mexico, and in the United States from the East Coast to California and the Pacific Northwest. Fire blight was reported in New Zealand in 1919, in Great Britain in 1957, and in Egypt in 1964. The disease has spread across much of Europe, to varying degrees depending on the country, and also through the Mediterranean region. In 1997, Australia reported the presence of fire blight, but eradication efforts were successful and no further outbreaks have been reported. With respect to the incidence of fire blight in Japan, the parties disputed before the Panel whether fire blight had ever entered Japan; but the United States assumed, for purposes of this dispute, that Japan was, as it claimed, free of fire blight and fire blight bacteria.

B. The Product at Issue

[The Appellate Body agreed with the Panel that the product at issue was not only mature, symptomless apples, the sole apple product exported from the U.S. to Japan, but also immature apples and mature, damaged apples.]

C. The Measure at Issue

14. The United States argued before the Panel that, through the operation of various legal instruments, Japan maintains nine prohibitions or requirements imposed with respect to apple fruit imported from the United States. With respect to the United States' description of the requirements for importation of apple fruit from the United States, Japan claimed that two such requirements amounted merely to "procedural steps" common to all phytosanitary measures, and that one of them should actually have been identified as two separate requirements.

15. The Panel decided to regard the multiple requirements imposed on imported apple fruit from the United States as a single measure to be reviewed under the *SPS Agreement* [*i.e.*, WTO *Agreement on the Application of Sanitary and Phytosanitary Measures*]. . . . Therefore, the Panel identified the focus of this dispute to be *a* measure applied by Japan to the importation of apple fruit from the United States, which measure consists of the following ten cumulatively-applied elements:

(a) Fruit must be produced in designated fire blight-free orchards. Designation of a fire blight-free area as an export orchard is made by the United States Department of Agriculture (USDA) upon application by the orchard owner. Any detection of a blighted tree in this area by inspection will disqualify the orchard. For the time being, the designation is accepted only for orchards in the states of Washington and Oregon;

(b) the export orchard must be free of plants infected with fire blight and free of host plants of fire blight (other than apples), whether or not infected;

(c) the fire blight-free orchard must be surrounded by a 500-meter buffer zone. Detection of a blighted tree or plant in this zone will disqualify the export orchard;

(d) the fire blight-free orchard and surrounding buffer zone must be inspected at least three times annually. US officials will visually inspect twice, at the blossom and the fruitlet stages, the export area and the buffer zone for any symptom of fire blight. Japanese and U.S. officials will jointly conduct visual inspection of these sites at harvest time. Additional inspections are required following any strong storm (such as a hail storm);

(e) harvested apples must be treated with surface disinfection by soaking in sodium hypochlorite solution;

(f) containers for harvesting must be disinfected by a chlorine treatment;

(g) the interior of the packing facility must be disinfected by a chlorine treatment;

(h) fruit destined for Japan must be kept separated post-harvest from other fruit;

(i) U.S. plant protection officials must certify that fruits are free from fire blight and have been treated post harvest with chlorine; and

Japanese officials must confirm the US officials' certification and Japanese officials must inspect packaging facilities. (footnote omitted)

[Omitted from the excerpts are the Appellate Body's findings on the following issues: sufficiency of the notice of appeal; the authority of the Panel; and whether the Panel made an objective assessment of the facts under *DSU* Article 11.]

B. Deference to National Authorities?

WTO APPELLATE BODY REPORT, *JAPAN — MEASURES AFFECTING THE IMPORTATION OF APPLES*
WT/DS245/AB/R (adopted 10 December 2003)

VII. Article 2.2 of the *SPS Agreement*

. . . .

[The Appellate Body upheld the Panel's finding concerning apples other than mature, symptomless apples. The Panel found the U.S. satisfied its burden of proof to make a *prima facie* case Japan's quarantine was inconsistent with Article 2:2. The inconsistency, alleged the U.S., was Japan's maintenance of the measure without sufficient scientific evidence. The U.S. case was based on the only kind of apples it ever exported to Japan — mature, symptomless ones. But, this fact did not affect the Appellate Body's view.]

B. Mature, Symptomless Apples

161. . . . Japan contends that the Panel erred in interpreting Article 2.2 of the *SPS Agreement* because the Panel failed to accord a "certain degree of discretion" to the importing Member in the manner in which it chooses, weighs, and evaluates scientific evidence. Japan submitted that, had the Panel accorded such discretion to Japan as the importing Member, the Panel would not have focused on the experts' views. Rather, the Panel would have evaluated the scientific evidence in the light of Japan's approach, which reflects "the historical facts of trans-oceanic expansion of the bacteria" and the rapid growth of international trade, and which is premised on "the fact that the pathways of . . . transmission of the bacteria are still unknown in spite of several efforts to trace them." Japan thus argues that the Panel erred in the application of Article 2.2 of the *SPS Agreement*, as it should have assessed whether the United States had established a *prima facie* case regarding the sufficiency of scientific evidence, not from the perspective of the experts' views, but, rather, in the light of Japan's approach to scientific evidence. According to Japan, had the Panel made such an assessment, it would have been bound to conclude that the United States had not established a *prima facie* case that Japan's measure is maintained without sufficient scientific evidence.

162. We disagree with Japan. As the Panel correctly noted, the Appellate Body addressed, in *Japan — Agricultural Products II* [*Japan — Measures Affecting Agricultural Products*, WT/DS76/AB/R (adopted 19 March 1999)] the

meaning of the term "sufficient," in the context of the expression "sufficient scientific evidence" as found in Article 2.2. The Panel stated that the term "sufficient" implies a "rational or objective relationship" and referred to the Appellate Body's statement there that:

> Whether there is a rational relationship between an SPS measure and the scientific evidence is to be determined on a case-by-case basis and will depend upon the particular circumstances of the case, including the characteristics of the measure at issue and the quality and quantity of the scientific evidence. [*Japan — Agricultural Products II*, para 84.]

The Panel did not err in relying on this interpretation of Article 2.2 and in conducting its assessment of the scientific evidence on this basis.

. . . .

166. In order to assess whether the United States had established a *prima facie* case, the Panel was entitled to take into account the views of the experts. Indeed, in *India — Quantitative Restrictions* [*i.e., India — Quantitative Restrictions on Imports of Agricultural, Textile and Industrial Products*, WT/DS90/AB/R (adopted 22 September 1999), excerpted in an earlier Chapter] the Appellate Body indicated that it may be useful for a panel to consider the views of the experts it consults in order to determine whether a *prima facie* case has been made. Moreover, on several occasions, including disputes involving the evaluation of scientific evidence, the Appellate Body has stated that panels enjoy discretion as the trier of facts; they enjoy "a margin of discretion in assessing the value of the evidence, and the weight to be ascribed to that evidence." Requiring panels, in their assessment of the evidence before them, to give precedence to the importing Member's evaluation of scientific evidence and risk is not compatible with this well-established principle.

167. . . . [W]e reject the contention that, under Article 2.2, a panel is obliged to give precedence to the importing Member's approach to scientific evidence and risk when analyzing and assessing scientific evidence. Consequently, we disagree with Japan that the Panel erred in assessing whether the United States had established a *prima facie* case when it did so from a perspective different from that inherent in Japan's approach to scientific evidence and risk. Thus, we are not persuaded that we should revisit the Panel's conclusion that the United States established a *prima facie* case that Japan's measure is maintained without sufficient scientific evidence.

III. HARMONIZATION OF STANDARDS, ARTICLE 3, AND THE *BEEF HORMONES* CASE

A. The EU's Controversial Hormones Ban

WTO APPELLATE BODY REPORT, *EC MEASURES CONCERNING MEAT AND MEAT PRODUCTS (HORMONES)*
WT/DS48/AB/R (adopted 13 February 1998)

I. INTRODUCTION: STATEMENT OF THE APPEAL

. . . .

2. The Panel [in this case] dealt with a complaint against the European Communities relating to an EC prohibition of imports of meat and meat products derived from cattle to which either the natural hormones: oestradiol-17?, progesterone or testosterone, or the synthetic hormones: trenbolone acetate, zeranol or melengestrol acetate ("MGA"), had been administered for growth promotion purposes. This import prohibition was set forth in a series of Directives of the Council of Ministers that were enacted before 1 January 1995. . . .

. . . .

5. Effective as of 1 July 1997, [European Economic Community (EEC)] Directives 81/602, 88/146 and 88/299 [of 31 July 1981, 7 March 1988, and 17 May 1988, respectively] were repealed and replaced with Council Directive 96/22/EC of 29 April 1996 ("Directive 96/22"). This Directive maintains the prohibition of the administration to farm animals of substances having a hormonal or thyrostatic action. As under the previously applicable Directives, it is prohibited to place on the market, or to import from third countries, meat and meat products from animals to which such substances, including the six hormones at issue in this dispute, were administered. This Directive also continues to allow Member States to authorize the administration, for therapeutic and zootechnical purposes, of certain substances having a hormonal or thyrostatic action. Under certain conditions, Directive 96/22 allows the placing on the market, and the importation from third countries, of meat and meat products from animals to which these substances have been administered for therapeutic and zootechnical purposes.

. . . .

III. ISSUES RAISED IN THIS APPEAL

[Omitted is the Appellate Body's discussion of burden of proof, standard of review, applicability of the *SPS Agreement* to measures enacted before the entry into force of the *WTO Agreement*, objective assessment of the facts under *DSU* Article 11, and selection and use of experts.]

B. A Higher Level of Protection?

WTO APPELLATE BODY REPORT, *EC MEASURES CONCERNING MEAT AND MEAT PRODUCTS (HORMONES)*
WT/DS48/AB/R (adopted 13 February 1998)

X. THE INTERPRETATION OF ARTICLES 3.1 AND 3.3 OF THE *SPS* AGREEMENT

. . . .

159. The . . . conclusion of the Panel has three components: first, international standards, guidelines and recommendations exist in respect of meat and meat products derived from cattle to which five of the hormones involved have been administered for growth promotion purposes; secondly, the EC measures involved here are not based on the relevant international standards, guidelines and recommendations developed by *Codex* [*i.e.*, the *Codex Alimentarius*], because such measures are not in conformity with those standards, guidelines and recommendations; and thirdly, the EC measures are "not justified under," that is, do not comply with the requirements of Article 3.3. *En route* to its . . . conclusion, the Panel developed three legal interpretations, which have all been appealed by the European Communities and which need to be addressed: the first relates to the meaning of "based on" as used in Article 3.1; the second is concerned with the relationship between Articles 3.1, 3.2 and 3.3 of the *SPS Agreement*; and the third relates to the requirements of Article 3.3 of the *SPS Agreement*. . . . [T]he Panel's three interpretations are intertwined.

A. The Meaning of "Based On" as Used in Article 3.1 of the *SPS Agreement*

. . . .

162. We read the Panel's interpretation that Article 3.2 "equates" measures "based on" international standards with measures which "conform to" such standards, as signifying that "based on" and "conform to" are identical in meaning. The Panel is thus saying that, henceforth, SPS measures of Members *must* "conform to" *Codex* standards, guidelines and recommendations.

163. We are unable to accept this interpretation of the Panel. In the first place, the ordinary meaning of "based on" is quite different from the plain or natural import of "conform to." A thing is commonly said to be "based on" another thing when the former "stands" or is "founded" or "built" upon or "is supported by" the latter. [The Appellate Body cited *The New Shorter Oxford English Dictionary on Historical Principles* (L. Brown ed.). vol. I at p. 187.] In contrast, much more is required before one thing may be regarded as "conform[ing] to" another: the former must "comply with," "yield or show compliance" with the latter. The reference of "conform to" is to "correspondence in form or manner," to "compliance with" or "acquiescence," to "follow[ing] in form or nature." [Again, the Appellate Body resorted to the *Oxford English Dictionary*.] A measure that "conforms to" and incorporates a *Codex* standard

is, of course, "based on" that standard. A measure, however, based on the same standard might not conform to that standard, as where only some, not all, of the elements of the standard are incorporated into the measure.

164. In the second place, "based on" and "conform to" are used in different articles, as well as in differing paragraphs of the same article. Thus, Article 2.2 uses "based on," while Article 2.4 employs "conform to." Article 3.1 requires the Members to "base" their SPS measures on international standards; however, Article 3.2 speaks of measures which "conform to" international standards. Article 3.3 once again refers to measures "based on" international standards. The implication arises that the choice and use of different words in different places in the *SPS Agreement* are deliberate, and that the different words are designed to convey different meanings. A treaty interpreter is not entitled to assume that such usage was merely inadvertent on the part of the Members who negotiated and wrote that Agreement. . . .

165. In the third place, the object and purpose of Article 3 run counter to the Panel's interpretation. That purpose, Article 3.1 states, is "[t]o harmonize [SPS] measures on as wide a basis as possible. . . ." The preamble of the *SPS Agreement* also records that the Members "[d]esir[e] to *further the use of harmonized [SPS] measures between Members* on the basis of international standards, guidelines and recommendations developed by the relevant international organizations. . . ." (emphasis added) Article 12.1 created a Committee on Sanitary and Phytosanitary Measures and gave it the task, *inter alia*, of "furtherance of its objectives, in particular with respect to harmonization" and (in Article 12.2) to "encourage the use of international standards, guidelines and recommendations by all Members." It is clear to us that harmonization of SPS measures of Members on the basis of international standards is projected in the *Agreement*, as a *goal*, yet to be realized *in the future*. To read Article 3.1 as requiring Members to harmonize their SPS measures *by conforming those measures with international standards*, guidelines and recommendations, *in the here and now*, is, in effect, to vest such international standards, guidelines and recommendations (which are by the terms of the *Codex recommendatory* in form and nature) with *obligatory* force and effect. The Panel's interpretation of Article 3.1 would, in other words, transform those standards, guidelines and recommendations into binding *norms*. . . . [T]he *SPS Agreement* itself sets out no indication of any intent on the part of the Members to do so. We cannot lightly assume that sovereign states intended to impose upon themselves the more onerous, rather than the less burdensome, obligation by mandating *conformity* or *compliance with* such standards, guidelines and recommendations. To sustain such an assumption and to warrant such a far-reaching interpretation, treaty language far more specific and compelling than that found in Article 3 of the *SPS Agreement* would be necessary.

. . . .

B. Relationship Between Articles 3.1, 3.2 and 3.3 of the *SPS Agreement*

169. . . . [T]he Panel assimilated Articles 3.1 and 3.2 to one another, designating the product as the "general rule," and contraposed that product

to Article 3.3 which denoted the "exception." This view appears to us an erroneous representation of the differing situations that may arise under Article 3, that is, where a relevant international standard, guideline or recommendation exists.

170. Under Article 3.2 of the *SPS Agreement*, a Member may decide to promulgate an SPS measure that conforms to an international standard. Such a measure would embody the international standard completely and, for practical purposes, converts it into a municipal standard. Such a measure enjoys the benefit of a presumption (albeit a rebuttable one) that it is consistent with the relevant provisions of the *SPS Agreement* and of the GATT 1994.

171. Under Article 3.1 . . ., a Member may choose to establish an SPS measure that is based on the existing relevant international standard, guideline or recommendation. Such a measure may adopt some, not necessarily all, of the elements of the international standard. The Member imposing this measure does not benefit from the presumption of consistency set up in Article 3.2; but, . . . the Member is not penalized by exemption of a complaining Member from the normal burden of showing a *prima facie* case of inconsistency with Article 3.1 or any other relevant article of the *SPS Agreement* or of the GATT 1994.

172. Under Article 3.3 . . ., a Member may decide to set for itself a level of protection different from that implicit in the international standard, and to implement or embody that level of protection in a measure not "based on" the international standard. The Member's appropriate level of protection may be higher than that implied in the international standard. The right of a Member to determine its own appropriate level of sanitary protection is an important right. This is made clear in the sixth pre-ambular paragraph of the *SPS Agreement*. . . . . . [T]his right of a Member to establish its own level of sanitary protection under Article 3.3 . . . is an autonomous right and *not* an "exception" from a "general obligation" under Article 3.1.

C. The Requirements of Article 3.3 of the *SPS Agreement*

173. The right of a Member to define its appropriate level of protection is not, however, an absolute or unqualified right. . . .

174. The European Communities argues that there are two situations covered by Article 3.3 and that its SPS measures are within the first of these situations. It is claimed that the European Communities has maintained SPS measures "which result in a higher level of . . . protection than would be achieved by measures based on the relevant" *Codex* standard, guideline or recommendation, for which measures "there is a scientific justification." It is also, accordingly, argued that the requirement of a risk assessment under Article 5.1 does not apply to the European Communities. . . .

175. Article 3.3 is evidently not a model of clarity in drafting and communication. The use of the disjunctive "or" does indicate that two situations are intended to be covered. These are the introduction or maintenance of SPS measures which result in a higher level of protection:

    (a)   "if there is a scientific justification"; or

(b) "as a consequence of the level of . . . protection a Member determines to be appropriate in accordance with the relevant provisions
of paragraphs 1 through 8 of Article 5."

It is true that situation (a) does not speak of Articles 5.1 through 5.8.
Nevertheless, two points need to be noted. First, the last sentence of Article
3.3 requires that "all measures which result in a [higher] level of . . .
protection," that is to say, measures falling within situation (a) as well as those
falling within situation (b), be "not inconsistent with any other provision of
[the *SPS*] *Agreement*." "Any other provision of this *Agreement*" textually
includes Article 5. Secondly, the footnote to Article 3.3, while attached to the
end of the first sentence, defines "scientific justification" as an "examination
and evaluation of available scientific information in conformity with relevant
provisions of this Agreement. . . ." This examination and evaluation would
appear to partake of the nature of the risk assessment required in Article 5.1
and defined in paragraph 4 of Annex A of the *SPS Agreement*.

176. . . . [W]e agree with the Panel's finding that although the European
Communities has established for itself a level of protection higher, or more
exacting, than the level of protection implied in the relevant *Codex* standards,
guidelines or recommendations, the European Communities was bound to
comply with the requirements established in Article 5.1. . . .

IV. PROVISIONAL MEASURES AND ARTICLE 5:7

A. The Precautionary Principle and 1998 *Beef Hormones* Case

WTO APPELLATE BODY REPORT, *EC MEASURES CONCERNING MEAT AND MEAT PRODUCTS (HORMONES)* WT/DS48/AB/R (adopted 13 February 1998)

VI. THE RELEVANCE OF THE PRECAUTIONARY PRINCIPLE IN THE
    INTERPRETATION OF THE *SPS AGREEMENT*

120. We are asked by the European Communities to reverse the finding of
the Panel relating to the precautionary principle. [The Panel held that "to the
extent that this principle could be considered as part of customary international law *and* be used to interpret Articles 5.1 and 5.2 on the assessment
of risks as a customary rule of interpretation of public international law (as
that phrase is used in Article 3.2 of the *DSU*), we consider that *this principle
would not override the explicit wording of Articles 5.1 and 5.2 outlined above,*
in particular since the precautionary principle has been incorporated and
given a specific meaning in Article 5.7 of the *SPS Agreement*." (emphases
original). In turn, the Panel said the precautionary principle did not override
its finding the EC import ban was not based on a risk assessment. Note the
EC stated explicitly it was not invoking Article 5.7.]

. . . .

123. The status of the precautionary principle in international law continues to be the subject of debate among academics, law practitioners, regulators and judges. The precautionary principle is regarded by some as having crystallized into a general principle of customary international *environmental* law. Whether it has been widely accepted by Members as a principle of *general* or *customary international law* appears less than clear. We consider, however, that it is unnecessary, and probably imprudent, for the Appellate Body in this appeal to take a position on this important, but abstract, question. . . .

124. It appears to us important, nevertheless, to note some aspects of the relationship of the precautionary principle to the *SPS Agreement*. First, the principle has not been written into the *SPS Agreement* as a ground for justifying SPS measures that are otherwise inconsistent with the obligations of Members set out in particular provisions of that Agreement. Secondly, the precautionary principle indeed finds reflection in Article 5.7 of the *SPS Agreement*. We agree, at the same time, with the European Communities, that there is no need to assume that Article 5.7 exhausts the relevance of a precautionary principle. It is reflected also in the sixth paragraph of the preamble and in Article 3.3. These explicitly recognize the right of Members to establish their own appropriate level of sanitary protection, which level may be higher (*i.e.*, more cautious) than that implied in existing international standards, guidelines and recommendations. Thirdly, a panel charged with determining, for instance, whether "sufficient scientific evidence" exists to warrant the maintenance by a Member of a particular SPS measure may, of course, and should, bear in mind that responsible, representative governments commonly act from perspectives of prudence and precaution where risks of irreversible, *e.g.*, life-terminating, damage to human health are concerned. Lastly, however, the precautionary principle does not, by itself, and without a clear textual directive to that effect, relieve a panel from the duty of applying the normal (*i.e.*, customary international law) principles of treaty interpretation in reading the provisions of the *SPS Agreement*.

125. We accordingly agree with the finding of the Panel that the precautionary principle does not override the provisions of Articles 5.1 and 5.2 of the *SPS Agreement*.

B.   Sufficient Evidence and the 2003 *Japan Apples* Case

WTO APPELLATE BODY REPORT, *JAPAN — MEASURES AFFECTING THE IMPORTATION OF APPLES*
WT/DS245/AB/R (adopted 10 December 2003)

VIII. Article 5.7 of the *SPS Agreement*

. . . .

170. Article 2.2 of the *SPS Agreement* stipulates that Members shall not maintain sanitary or phytosanitary measures without sufficient scientific evidence "except as provided for in paragraph 7 of Article 5." Before the Panel, Japan contested that its phytosanitary measure is "maintained without sufficient scientific evidence" within the meaning of Article 2.2. Japan claimed,

in the alternative, that its measure is a provisional measure consistent with Article 5.7.

. . . .

172. The Panel found that Japan's measure is not a provisional measure justified under Article 5.7 of the *SPS Agreement* because the measure was not imposed in respect of a situation where "relevant scientific evidence is insufficient."

173. The Panel identified the "phytosanitary question at issue" as the risk of transmission of fire blight through apple fruit. It observed that "scientific studies as well as practical experience have accumulated for the past 200 years" on this question and that, in the course of its analysis under Article 2.2, it had come across an "important amount of relevant evidence." The Panel observed that a large quantity of high quality scientific evidence on the risk of transmission of fire blight through apple fruit had been produced over the years, and noted that the experts had expressed strong and increasing confidence in this evidence. Stating that Article 5.7 was "designed to be invoked in situations where little, or no, reliable evidence was available on the subject matter at issue," the Panel concluded that the measure was not imposed in respect of a situation where relevant scientific evidence is insufficient. The Panel added that, even if the term "relevant scientific evidence" in Article 5.7 referred to a *specific aspect* of a phytosanitary problem, as Japan claimed, its conclusion would remain the same. The Panel justified its view on the basis of the experts' indication that, not only is there a large volume of general evidence, but there is also a large volume of relevant scientific evidence on the specific scientific questions raised by Japan.

. . . .

A. The Insufficiency of Relevant Scientific Evidence

. . . .

176. In *Japan — Agricultural Products II* [*i.e., Japan — Measures Affecting Agricultural Products*, WT/DS76/AB/R at § 89 (adopted 19 March 1999)] the Appellate Body stated that Article 5.7 sets out four requirements that must be satisfied in order to adopt and maintain a provisional phytosanitary measure. These requirements are:

    (i)   the measure is imposed in respect of a situation where "relevant scientific evidence is insufficient;"

    (ii)   the measure is adopted "on the basis of available pertinent information;"

    (iii)   the Member which adopted the measure "seek[s] to obtain the additional information necessary for a more objective assessment of risk;" and

    (iv)   the Member which adopted the measure "review[s] the . . . measure accordingly within a reasonable period of time."

These four requirements are "clearly cumulative in nature;" as the Appellate Body said in *Japan — Agricultural Products II*, "[w]henever *one* of these four requirements is not met, the measure at issue is inconsistent with Article 5.7."

177. The Panel's findings address exclusively the first requirement, which the Panel found Japan had not met. The requirements being cumulative, the Panel found it unnecessary to address the other requirements to find an inconsistency with Article 5.7.

. . . .

B. Japan's Argument on "Scientific Uncertainty"

182. Japan challenges the Panel's statement that Article 5.7 is intended to address only "situations where little, or no, reliable evidence was available on the subject matter at issue" because this does not provide for situations of "unresolved uncertainty." Japan draws a distinction between "new uncertainty" and "unresolved uncertainty", arguing that both fall within Article 5.7. According to Japan, "new uncertainty" arises when a new risk is identified; Japan argues that the Panel's characterization that "little, or no, reliable evidence was available on the subject matter at issue" is relevant to a situation of "new uncertainty." We understand that Japan defines "unresolved uncertainty" as uncertainty that the scientific evidence is not able to resolve, despite accumulated scientific evidence. According to Japan, the risk of transmission of fire blight through apple fruit relates essentially to a situation of "unresolved uncertainty." Thus, Japan maintains that, despite considerable scientific evidence regarding fire blight, there is still uncertainty about certain aspects of transmission of fire blight. Japan contends that the reasoning of the Panel is tantamount to restricting the applicability of Article 5.7 to situations of "new uncertainty" and to excluding situations of "unresolved uncertainty;" and that, by doing so, the Panel erred in law.

183. We disagree with Japan. The application of Article 5.7 is triggered not by the existence of scientific uncertainty, but rather by the insufficiency of scientific evidence. The text of Article 5.7 is clear: it refers to "cases where relevant scientific evidence is insufficient", not to "scientific uncertainty." The two concepts are not interchangeable. Therefore, we are unable to endorse Japan's approach of interpreting Article 5.7 through the prism of "scientific uncertainty."

. . . .

C. The Panel's Reliance on a "History of 200 Years of Studies and Practical Experience"

185. . . . . Japan submits that the Panel was not authorized to rule on the basis of a " 'history' of 200 year[s] of studies and practical experience" because "the United States did not raise any objection to application of Article 5.7 on the basis of [a] 'history' of 200 year[s] of studies and practical experience." In other words, according to Japan, the Panel was not entitled to draw a conclusion regarding Article 5.7 on the basis of such "history" unless the United States had raised an objection based on "history", something that the United States had not done.

186. . . . . [T]he Panel mentioned that, as regards the risk of transmission of fire blight through apple fruit, "scientific studies as well as practical

experience have accumulated for the past 200 years." This statement was relevant to the debate under Article 5.7 and was based on the evidence before the Panel. Accordingly, it was appropriate for the Panel to make such a statement irrespective of whether the United States had explicitly advanced an argument based on "history."

187. . . . [W]e uphold the findings of the Panel . . . that Japan's phytosanitary measure at issue was not imposed in respect of a situation "where relevant scientific evidence is insufficient," and, therefore, that it is not a provisional measure justified under Article 5.7 of the *SPS Agreement*. . . .

V.   RISK ASSESSMENTS UNDER ARTICLES 5:1 AND 5:5

A.   Insufficient Evidence and the 1998 *Beef Hormones* Case

WTO APPELLATE BODY REPORT, *EC MEASURES CONCERNING MEAT AND MEAT PRODUCTS (HORMONES)*
WT/DS48/AB/R (adopted 13 February 1998)

XI. THE READING OF ARTICLES 5.1 AND 5.2 OF THE *SPS AGREEMENT*: BASING SPS MEASURES ON A RISK ASSESSMENT

. . . .

A. The Interpretation of "Risk Assessment"

. . . .

1. *Risk Assessment and the Notion of "Risk"*

. . . .

186. It is not clear in what sense the Panel uses the term "scientifically identified risk." The Panel also frequently uses the term "identifiable risk," and does not define this term either. . . . [In one portion,] the Panel appeared to be using the term "scientifically identified risk" to prescribe implicitly that a certain *magnitude* or threshold level of risk be demonstrated in a risk assessment if an SPS measure based thereon is to be regarded as consistent with Article 5.1. To the extent that the Panel purported to require a risk assessment to establish a minimum magnitude of risk, we must note that imposition of such a quantitative requirement finds no basis in the *SPS Agreement*. A panel is authorized only to determine whether a given SPS measure is "based on" a risk assessment. . . . [T]his means that a panel has to determine whether an SPS measure is sufficiently supported or reasonably warranted by the risk assessment.

2. *Factors to be Considered in Carrying Out a Risk Assessment*

187. Article 5.2 of the *SPS Agreement* provides an indication of the factors that should be taken into account in the assessment of risk. . . . The listing

in Article 5.2 begins with "available scientific evidence"; this, however, is only the beginning. . . . [T]he Panel states that, for purposes of the EC measures in dispute, a risk assessment required by Article 5.1 is "a *scientific* process aimed at establishing the *scientific* basis for the sanitary measure a Member intends to take." To the extent that the Panel intended to refer to a process characterized by systematic, disciplined and objective enquiry and analysis, that is, a mode of studying and sorting out facts and opinions, the Panel's statement is unexceptionable. However, to the extent that the Panel purports to exclude from the scope of a risk assessment in the sense of Article 5.1, all matters not susceptible of quantitative analysis by the empirical or experimental laboratory methods commonly associated with the physical sciences, we believe that the Panel is in error. Some of the kinds of factors listed in Article 5.2 such as "relevant processes and production methods" and "relevant inspection, sampling and testing methods" are not necessarily or wholly susceptible of investigation according to laboratory methods of, for example, biochemistry or pharmacology. Furthermore, there is nothing to indicate that the listing of factors that may be taken into account in a risk assessment of Article 5.2 was intended to be a closed list. It is essential to bear in mind that the risk that is to be evaluated in a risk assessment under Article 5.1 is not only risk ascertainable in a science laboratory operating under strictly controlled conditions, but also risk in human societies as they actually exist, in other words, the actual potential for adverse effects on human health in the real world where people live and work and die.

B. The Interpretation of "Based On"

1. A "Minimum Procedural Requirement" in Article 5.1?

188. Although it expressly recognizes that Article 5.1 does *not* contain any specific procedural requirements for a Member to base its sanitary measures on a risk assessment, the Panel nevertheless proceeds to declare that "there is a minimum procedural requirement contained in Article 5.1." That requirement is that "the Member imposing a sanitary measure needs to submit evidence that at least it actually *took into account* a risk assessment when it enacted or maintained its sanitary measure in order for that measure to be considered as *based on* a risk assessment." . . .

189. . . . [A]s the Panel itself acknowledges, no textual basis exists in Article 5 of the *SPS Agreement* for such a "minimum procedural requirement." . . . We believe that "based on" is appropriately taken to refer to a certain *objective relationship* between two elements, that is to say, to an *objective situation* that persists and is observable between an SPS measure and a risk assessment. Such a reference is certainly embraced in the ordinary meaning of the words "based on." . . . We do not share the Panel's interpretative construction and believe it is unnecessary and an error of law as well.

190. Article 5.1 does not insist that a Member that adopts a sanitary measure shall have carried out its own risk assessment. It only requires that the SPS measures be "based on an assessment, as appropriate for the circumstances. . . ." The SPS measure might well find its objective justification in a risk assessment carried out by another Member, or an international

organization. The "minimum procedural requirement" constructed by the Panel, could well lead to the elimination or disregard of available scientific evidence that rationally supports the SPS measure being examined. . . .

2. *Substantive Requirement of Article 5.1 — Rational Relationship Between an SPS Measure and a Risk Assessment*

. . . .

193. . . . The requirement that an SPS measure be "based on" a risk assessment is a substantive requirement that there be a rational relationship between the measure and the risk assessment.

194. We do not believe that a risk assessment has to come to a monolithic conclusion that coincides with the scientific conclusion or view implicit in the SPS measure. The risk assessment could set out both the prevailing view representing the "mainstream" of scientific opinion, as well as the opinions of scientists taking a divergent view. Article 5.1 does not require that the risk assessment must necessarily embody only the view of a majority of the relevant scientific community. In some cases, the very existence of divergent views presented by qualified scientists who have investigated the particular issue at hand may indicate a state of scientific uncertainty. Sometimes the divergence may indicate a roughly equal balance of scientific opinion, which may itself be a form of scientific uncertainty. In most cases, responsible and representative governments tend to base their legislative and administrative measures on "mainstream" scientific opinion. In other cases, equally responsible and representative governments may act in good faith on the basis of what, at a given time, may be a divergent opinion coming from qualified and respected sources. By itself, this does not necessarily signal the absence of a reasonable relationship between the SPS measure and the risk assessment, especially where the risk involved is life-threatening in character and is perceived to constitute a clear and imminent threat to public health and safety. Determination of the presence or absence of that relationship can only be done on a case-to-case basis, after account is taken of all considerations rationally bearing upon the issue of potential adverse health effects.

195. We turn now to the application by the Panel of the substantive requirements of Article 5.1 to the EC measures at stake in the present case. The Panel lists the following scientific material to which the European Communities referred in respect of the hormones here involved (except MGA):

- the 1982 Report of the EC Scientific Veterinary Committee, Scientific Committee for Animal Nutrition and the Scientific Committee for Food on the basis of the Report of the Scientific Group on Anabolic Agents in Animal Production ("Lamming Report");

- the 1983 Symposium on Anabolics in Animal Production of the *Office international des epizooties* ("OIE") ("1983 OIE Symposium");

- the 1987 Monographs of the International Agency for Research on Cancer ("IARC") on the Evaluation of Carcinogenic Risks to Humans, Supplement 7 ("1987 IARC Monographs");

- the 1988 and 1989 JECFA Reports [*i.e.*, technical reports published in 1988 and 1989 by the Joint FAO/WHO Expert Committee on

Food Additives concerning the evaluation of certain veterinary drug residues in food];

- the 1995 European Communities Scientific Conference on Growth Promotion in Meat Production ("1995 EC Scientific Conference");

- articles and opinions by individual scientists relevant to the use of hormones (three articles in the journal Science, one article in the International Journal of Health Service, one report in The Veterinary Record and separate scientific opinions of Dr. H. Adlercreutz, Dr. E. Cavalieri, Dr. S.S. Epstein, Dr. J.G. Liehr, Dr. M. Metzler, Dr. Perez-Comas and Dr. A. Pinter, all of whom were part of the EC delegation at [the] joint meeting with experts).

. . . .

197. Prescinding from [*i.e.*, leaving aside from consideration] the difficulty raised by the Panel's use of the term "identifiable risk," we agree [with the Panel] that the scientific reports listed above do not rationally support the EC import prohibition.

198. With regard to the scientific opinion expressed by Dr. Lucier at the joint meeting with the experts, . . . this opinion by Dr. Lucier does not purport to be the result of scientific studies carried out by him or under his supervision focussing specifically on residues of hormones in meat from cattle fattened with such hormones. Accordingly, it appears that the single divergent opinion expressed by Dr. Lucier is not reasonably sufficient to overturn the contrary conclusions reached in the scientific studies referred to by the European Communities that related specifically to residues of the hormones in meat from cattle to which hormones had been administered for growth promotion.

199. The European Communities laid particular emphasis on the 1987 IARC Monographs and the articles and opinions of individual scientists referred to above. The Panel notes, however, that the scientific evidence set out in these Monographs and these articles and opinions relates to the carcinogenic potential of entire *categories* of hormones, or of the hormones at issue *in general*. The Monographs and the articles and opinions are, in other words, in the nature of general studies of or statements on the carcinogenic potential of the named hormones. The Monographs and the articles and opinions of individual scientists have not evaluated the carcinogenic potential of those hormones when used specifically *for growth promotion purposes*. Moreover, they do not evaluate the specific potential for carcinogenic effects arising from the presence in *"food,"* more specifically, "meat or meat products" of residues of the hormones in dispute. The Panel also notes that, according to the scientific experts advising the Panel, the data and studies set out in these 1987 Monographs have been taken into account in the 1988 and 1989 JECFA Reports and that the conclusions reached by the 1987 IARC Monographs are complementary to, rather than contradictory of, the conclusions of the JECFA Reports. The Panel concludes that these Monographs and these articles and opinions are insufficient to support the EC measures at issue in this case.

200. We believe that the above findings of the Panel are justified. The 1987 IARC Monographs and the articles and opinions of individual scientists submitted by the European Communities constitute general studies which do

indeed show the existence of a general risk of cancer; but they do not focus on and do not address the particular kind of risk here at stake — the carcinogenic or geno-toxic potential of the residues of those hormones found in meat derived from cattle to which the hormones had been administered for growth promotion purposes — as is required by paragraph 4 of Annex A of the *SPS Agreement*. Those general studies, are in other words, relevant but do not appear to be sufficiently specific to the case at hand.

. . . .

[As regards MGA, the Appellate Body upheld the Panel's finding that there was no risk assessment, because of an almost complete lack of evidence on MGA in the Panel proceedings.]

202. The evidence referred to above by the European Communities related to the biochemical risk arising from the ingestion by human beings of residues of the five hormones here involved in treated meat, where such hormones had been administered to the cattle in accordance with good veterinary practice. The European Communities also referred to distinguishable but closely related risks — risks arising from failure to observe the requirements of good veterinary practice, in combination with multiple problems relating to detection and control of such abusive failure, in the administration of hormones to cattle for growth promotion.

203. . . . Ultimately, the Panel rejects those arguments principally on *a priori* grounds. First, to the Panel, the provisions of Article 5.2 relating to "relevant inspection, sampling and testing methods":

> . . . do not seem to cover the general problem of control (such as the problem of ensuring the observance of good practice) which can exist for any substance. *The risks related to the general problem of control do not seem to be specific to the substance at issue but to the economic or social incidence related to a substance or its particular use* (such as economic incentives for abuse). *These non-scientific factors* should, therefore not be taken into account in a risk assessment but in *risk management.* (underlining added)

Moreover, the Panel finds that . . . the European Communities has not provided convincing evidence that the control or prevention of abuse of the hormones here involved is more difficult than the control of other veterinary drugs, the use of which is allowed in the European Communities. Further, the European Communities has not provided evidence that control would be more difficult under a regime where the use of the hormones in dispute is allowed under specific conditions than under the current EC regime of total prohibition both domestically and in respect of imported meat. The Panel concludes by saying that banning the use of a substance does not necessarily offer better protection of human health than other means of regulating its use.

. . . .

207. The question that arises, therefore, is whether the European Communities did, in fact, submit a risk assessment demonstrating and evaluating the existence and level of risk arising in the present case from abusive use of hormones and the difficulties of control of the administration of hormones for

growth promotion purposes, within the United States and Canada as exporting countries, and at the frontiers of the European Communities as an importing country. Here, we must agree with the finding of the Panel that the European Communities in fact restricted itself to pointing out the condition of administration of hormones "in accordance with good practice" "without further providing an assessment of the potential adverse effects related to non compliance with such practice." . . .

208. . . . [W]e find that the European Communities did not actually proceed to an assessment, within the meaning of Articles 5.1 and 5.2, of the risks arising from the failure of observance of good veterinary practice combined with problems of control of the use of hormones for growth promotion purposes. The absence of such a risk assessment, when considered in conjunction with the conclusion actually reached by most, if not all, of the scientific studies relating to the other aspects of risk noted earlier, leads us to the conclusion that no risk assessment that reasonably supports or warrants the import prohibition embodied in the EC Directives was furnished to the Panel. We affirm, therefore, the ultimate conclusion of the Panel that the EC import prohibition is not based on a risk assessment within the meaning of Articles 5.1 and 5.2 of the *SPS Agreement* and is, therefore, inconsistent with the requirements of Article 5.1.

209. Since we have concluded above that an SPS measure, to be consistent with Article 3.3, has to comply with, *inter alia*, the requirements contained in Article 5.1, it follows that the EC measures at issue, by failing to comply with Article 5.1, are also inconsistent with Article 3.3 of the *SPS Agreement*.

B. Discrimination, Disguised Trade Restrictions, and the 1998 *Beef Hormones* Case

WTO APPELLATE BODY REPORT, *EC MEASURES CONCERNING MEAT AND MEAT PRODUCTS (HORMONES)* WT/DS48/AB/R (adopted 13 February 1998)

XII. THE READING OF ARTICLE 5.5 OF THE *SPS AGREEMENT*: CONSISTENCY OF LEVELS OF PROTECTION AND RESULTING DISCRIMINATION OR DISGUISED RESTRICTION ON INTERNATIONAL TRADE

210. The European Communities also appeals from the conclusion of the Panel that, by adopting arbitrary or unjustifiable distinctions in the levels of sanitary protection it considers appropriate in different situations which result in discrimination or a disguised restriction on international trade, the European Communities acted inconsistently with the requirements set out in Article 5.5 of the *SPS Agreement*.

A. General Considerations: The Elements of Article 5.5

. . . .

213. The objective of Article 5.5 is formulated as the "achieving [of] consistency in the application of the concept of appropriate level of sanitary or phytosanitary protection." Clearly, the desired consistency is defined as a goal to be achieved in the future. To assist in the realization of that objective, the Committee on Sanitary and Phytosanitary Measures is to develop *guidelines for the practical implementation of Article 5.5*, bearing in mind, among other things, that ordinarily, people do not voluntarily expose themselves to health risks. Thus, we agree with the Panel's view that the statement of that goal does not establish a *legal obligation* of consistency of appropriate levels of protection. We think, too, that the goal set is not absolute or perfect consistency, since governments establish their appropriate levels of protection frequently on an *ad hoc* basis and over time, as different risks present themselves at different times. It is only arbitrary or unjustifiable inconsistencies that are to be avoided.

214. Close inspection of Article 5.5 indicates that a complaint of violation of this Article must show the presence of three distinct elements. The first element is that the Member imposing the measure complained of has adopted its own appropriate levels of sanitary protection against risks to human life or health in several different situations. The second element to be shown is that those *levels of protection* exhibit arbitrary or unjustifiable differences ("distinctions" in the language of Article 5.5) in their treatment of different situations. The last element [which arises in part from reading Article 5:1 in the context of Article 2:3 of the *SPS Agreement*] requires that the arbitrary or unjustifiable differences result in discrimination or a disguised restriction of international trade. We understand the last element to be referring to the *measure* embodying or implementing a particular level of protection as resulting, in its application, in discrimination or a disguised restriction on international trade.

215. We consider the above three elements of Article 5.5 to be cumulative in nature; all of them must be demonstrated to be present if violation of Article 5.5 is to be found. In particular, both the second and third elements must be found. The second element alone would not suffice. The third element must also be demonstrably present: the implementing measure must be shown to be applied in such a manner as to result in discrimination or a disguised restriction on international trade. The presence of the second element — the arbitrary or unjustifiable character of differences in *levels of protection* considered by a Member as appropriate in differing situations — may in practical effect operate as a "warning" signal that the implementing *measure* in its application *might* be a discriminatory measure or *might* be a restriction on international trade disguised as an SPS measure for the protection of human life or health. Nevertheless, the measure itself needs to be examined and appraised and, in the context of the differing levels of protection, shown to result in discrimination or a disguised restriction on international trade.

B. Different Levels of Protection in Different Situations

. . . .

218. . . . . [T]he Panel finds that several different levels of protection were projected by the European Communities:

 (i) the level of protection in respect of natural hormones when used for growth promotion;

 (ii) the level of protection in respect of natural hormones occurring endogenously in meat and other foods;

 (iii) the level of protection in respect of natural hormones when used for therapeutic or zoo-technical purposes;

 (iv) the level of protection in respect of synthetic hormones (zeranol and trenbolone) when used for growth promotion; and

 (v) the level of protection in respect of carbadox and olaquindox.

C. Arbitrary or Unjustifiable Differences in Levels of Protection

. . . .

220. The Panel first compares the levels of protection established by the European Communities in respect of natural and synthetic hormones when used for growth promotion purposes (levels of protection (i) and (iv)) with the level of protection set by the European Communities in respect of natural hormones occurring endogenously in meat and other natural foods (level of protection (ii)). The Panel finds the difference between these levels of protection "arbitrary" and "unjustifiable" basically because, in its view, the European Communities had not provided any reason other than the difference between added hormones and hormones naturally occurring in meat and other foods that have formed part of the human diet for centuries, and had not submitted any evidence that the risk related to natural hormones used as growth promoters is higher than the risk related to endogenous hormones. The Panel adds that the residue level of natural hormones in some natural products (such as eggs and broccoli) is higher than the residue level of hormones administered for growth promotion in treated meat. . . . The Panel stresses the very marked gap between a "no-residue" level of protection against natural hormones used for growth promotion and the "unlimited-residue" level of protection with regard to hormones occurring naturally in meat and other foods. Much the same reasons are deployed by the Panel in comparing the levels of protection in respect of synthetic hormones used for growth promotion and in respect of natural hormones endogenously occurring in meat and other foods.

221. We do not share the Panel's conclusions that the above differences in levels of protection in respect of added hormones in treated meat and in respect of naturally-occurring hormones in food, are merely arbitrary and unjustifiable. To the contrary, we consider there is a fundamental distinction between added hormones (natural or synthetic) and naturally-occurring hormones in meat and other foods. In respect of the latter, the European Communities simply takes no regulatory action; to require it to prohibit totally the production and consumption of such foods or to limit the residues of naturally-occurring hormones in food, entails such a comprehensive and massive governmental intervention in nature and in the ordinary lives of

people as to reduce the comparison itself to an absurdity. The other considerations cited by the Panel, whether taken separately or grouped together, do not justify the Panel's finding of arbitrariness in the difference in the level of protection between added hormones for growth promotion and naturally-occurring hormones in meat and other foods.

. . . .

[The Appellate Body also concluded that the difference in the levels of protection set by the EC as regards (1) natural hormones used for growth promotion purposes, and (2) the same natural hormones when used for therapeutic or zoo-technical purposes was neither arbitrary nor unjustifiable. To induce growth promotion, natural hormones are used regularly and continuously, and administered to all herds, and to all members of a herd of cattle. Therapeutic use is selective, and in the context of individual sick or diseased animals. Zoo-technical use maybe for an entire herd, but it occurs only once a year. Thus, growth promotion is a far longer and costlier process that is more difficult to control. The EC requires natural hormones used for therapeutic or zoo-technical purposes to be administered by a veterinarian, and regulates various aspects of this administration. Given the heightened concern about growth promotion, for that purpose even stricter regulation is justified. In effect, the Appellate Body accepted the EC's rationale, as had the Panel.

However, the Appellate Body found the difference in the EC's level of protection with respect to (1) natural and synthetic hormones used for growth promotion, and (2) carbadox and olaquindox (both of which are feed additives, specifically, anti-microbial agents mixed with feed given to piglets), was unjustifiable under Article 5:5 of the *SPS Agreement*. Essentially, the Appellate Body adopted without comment the Panel's rejection of the EC's arguments for the differential treatment.]

D. Resulting in Discrimination or a Disguised Restriction on International Trade

236. In interpreting this last element or requirement of Article 5.5, the Panel recalls the conclusion of the Appellate Body in *United States — Standards for Reformulated and Conventional Gasoline* ("*United States — Gasoline*") [excerpted in a previous Chapter] to the effect that the terms "arbitrary discrimination," "unjustifiable discrimination" and "disguised restriction on international trade" found in Article XX of the GATT 1994, may be read side-by-side and impart meaning to one another. The Panel also recalls our statement in *Japan — Alcoholic Beverages* [also excerpted in an earlier Chapter], and in particular the requirement in Article III:2, second sentence, of the GATT 1994 that dissimilar taxation needs to be "applied . . . so as to afford protection to domestic production." It quotes the passage stating, in part, that "[the dissimilar taxation] may be so much more that it will be clear from that very differential that the dissimilar taxation was applied 'so as to afford protection.' In some cases, that may be enough to show a violation."

. . .

. . . .

239. [W]e disagree with the Panel on two points. First, in view of the structural differences between the standards of the *chapeau* of Article XX of the GATT 1994 and the elements of Article 5.5 of the *SPS Agreement*, the reasoning in our Report in *United States — Gasoline*, quoted by Panel, cannot be casually imported into a case involving Article 5.5 of the *SPS Agreement*. Secondly, in our view, it is similarly unjustified to assume applicability of the reasoning of the Appellate Body in *Japan — Alcoholic Beverages* about the inference that may be drawn from the sheer size of a tax differential for the application of Article III:2, second sentence, of the GATT 1994, to the quite different question of whether arbitrary or unjustifiable differences in levels of protection against risks for human life or health, "result in discrimination or a disguised restriction on international trade."

240. . . . . [T]he degree of difference, or the extent of the discrepancy, in the levels of protection, is only one kind of factor which, along with others, may cumulatively lead to the conclusion that discrimination or a disguised restriction on international trade in fact results from the application of a measure or measures embodying one or more of those different levels of protection. . . . Evidently, the answer to the question whether arbitrary or unjustifiable differences or distinctions in levels of protection established by a Member do in fact result in discrimination or a disguised restriction on international trade must be sought in the circumstances of each individual case.

241. In the present appeal, it is necessary to address this question only with regard to the difference in the levels of protection established in respect of the hormones in dispute and in respect of carbadox and olaquindox.

[The Panel found the "arbitrary or unjustifiable" difference in the EC's level of protection as between (1) hormones and (2) carbadox and olaquindox had resulted in "discrimination or a disguised restriction on international trade." Hence, the Panel held the EC violated Article 5:5. The Appellate Body reversed.]

C. Insufficient Evidence and the 2003 *Japan Apples* Case

WTO APPELLATE BODY REPORT, *JAPAN — MEASURES AFFECTING THE IMPORTATION OF APPLES*
WT/DS245/AB/R (adopted 10 December 2003)

IX. Article 5.1 of the *SPS Agreement*

. . . .

195. Japan challenges three specific aspects of the Panel's analysis of the 1999 PRA [Pest Risk Analysis] under Article 5.1. First, Japan contests the Panel's finding that the 1999 PRA is inconsistent with the requirements of Article 5.1 because it did not focus its analysis on the risk of fire blight entering through *apple fruit*, in particular. Japan contends that the Panel misinterpreted Article 5.1 and misunderstood the Appellate Body's decision in *EC — Hormones* with respect to the requirement of "specificity" of a risk assessment. Secondly, Japan argues that Article 5.1, contrary to the Panel's

interpretation, does not require a consideration of "alternative measures other than [the] existing measures." Finally, Japan claims that its risk assessment should be assessed in the light of evidence available at the time of the assessment, not against evidence that has become available subsequently.

196. We begin our analysis with the text of the relevant provision at issue, Article 5.1 of the *SPS Agreement* [set out in the *Documents Supplement*]. . . . The first clause of paragraph 4 of Annex A to the *SPS Agreement* [also set out in the *Documents Supplement*] defines the "risk assessment" for a measure designed to protect plant life or health from risks arising from the entry, establishment or spread of diseases . . . Based on this definition, the Appellate Body determined in *Australia — Salmon* [*i.e., Australia — Measures Affecting Importation of Salmon*, WT/DS18/AB/R at para. 121 (adopted 6 November 1998)] that:

> . . . a risk assessment within the meaning of Article 5.1 must:
>
> (1) *identify* the diseases whose entry, establishment or spread a Member wants to prevent within its territory, as well as the potential biological and economic consequences associated with the entry, establishment or spread of these diseases;
>
> (2) *evaluate the likelihood* of entry, establishment or spread of these diseases, as well as the associated potential biological and economic consequences; and
>
> (3) evaluate the likelihood of entry, establishment or spread of these diseases *according to the SPS measures which might be applied.* (original italics)

197. . . . [T]he United States does not claim that Japan's risk assessment failed to meet the first of these conditions. The Panel therefore limited its analysis of Japan's risk assessment to the second and third conditions. The Panel found that the 1999 PRA did not constitute a "risk assessment," as that term is defined in the *SPS Agreement*, because it did not satisfy either of those conditions. Japan challenges aspects of the Panel's analysis with respect to both of these conditions.

. . . .

202. We disagree with Japan. Under the *SPS Agreement*, the obligation to conduct an assessment of "risk" is not satisfied merely by a general discussion of the disease sought to be avoided by the imposition of a phytosanitary measure. The Appellate Body found the risk assessment at issue in *EC — Hormones* not to be "sufficiently specific" even though the scientific articles cited by the importing Member had evaluated the "carcinogenic potential of entire *categories* of hormones, or of the hormones at issue *in general*." In order to constitute a "risk assessment" as defined in the *SPS Agreement*, the Appellate Body concluded, the risk assessment should have reviewed the carcinogenic potential, not of the relevant hormones in general, but of "residues of those hormones found in meat derived from cattle to which the hormones had been administered for growth promotion purposes." Therefore, when discussing the risk to be specified in the risk assessment in *EC — Hormones*, the Appellate Body referred in general to the harm concerned (cancer or genetic damage) *as well as* to the precise agent that may possibly cause the harm

(that is, the specific hormones when used in a specific manner and for specific purposes).

203. In this case, the Panel found that the conclusion of the 1999 PRA with respect to fire blight was "based on an overall assessment of possible modes of contamination, where apple fruit is only one of the possible hosts/vectors considered." The Panel further found, on the basis of the scientific evidence, that the risk of entry, establishment or spread of the disease varies significantly depending on the vector, or specific host plant, being evaluated. Given that the measure at issue relates to the risk of transmission of fire blight through apple fruit, in an evaluation of whether the risk assessment is "sufficiently specific to the case at hand," the nature of the risk addressed by the measure at issue is a factor to be taken into account. In the light of these considerations, we are of the view that the Panel properly determined that the 1999 PRA "evaluat[ion of] the risks associated with all possible hosts taken together" was not sufficiently specific to qualify as a "risk assessment" under the *SPS Agreement* for the evaluation of the likelihood of entry, establishment or spread of fire blight in Japan through apple fruit.

204. . . . Contrary to Japan's submission, . . . the Panel's reading of *EC — Hormones* does not suggest that there is an obligation to follow any particular methodology for conducting a risk assessment. In other words, even though, in a given context, a risk assessment must consider a specific agent or pathway through which contamination might occur, Members are not precluded from organizing their risk assessments along the lines of the disease or pest at issue, or of the commodity to be imported. Thus, Members are free to consider in their risk analysis multiple agents in relation to one disease, provided that the risk assessment attribute a likelihood of entry, establishment or spread of the disease to each agent specifically. Members are also free to follow the other "methodology" identified by Japan and focus on a particular commodity, subject to the same proviso.

205. Indeed, the relevant international standards, which, Japan claims, "adopt both methodologies", expressly contemplate examining risk in relation to particular pathways. Those standards call for that specific examination even when the risk analysis is initiated on the basis of the particular pest or disease at issue, as was the 1999 PRA. Therefore, our conclusion that the Panel properly found Japan's risk assessment not to be sufficiently specific, does not limit an importing Member's right to adopt any appropriate "methodology", consistent with the definition of "risk assessment" in paragraph 4 of Annex A to the *SPS Agreement*.

206. We therefore uphold the Panel's finding . . . that Japan's 1999 Pest Risk Analysis does not satisfy the definition of "risk assessment" in paragraph 4 of Annex A to the *SPS Agreement*, because it fails to evaluate the likelihood of entry, establishment or spread of fire blight specifically through apple fruit.

B. Evaluating the Likelihood of Entry, Establishment or Spread of Fire Blight "According to the Sanitary or Phytosanitary Measures Which Might Be Applied"

207. Japan also challenges the Panel's finding that Japan "has not . . . properly evaluated the likelihood of entry 'according to the SPS measures that

might be applied'." According to the Panel, the terms in the definition of "risk assessment" set out in paragraph 4 of Annex A to the *SPS Agreement* — more specifically, the phrase "according to the sanitary or phytosanitary measures which might be applied" — suggest that "consideration should be given not just to those specific measures which are currently in application, but at least to a potential range of relevant measures." Japan acknowledged that it did not consider policies other than the measure already applied. However, according to Japan, this "again relates to the matter of methodology," which is left to the discretion of the importing Member.

208. The definition of "risk assessment" in the *SPS Agreement* requires that the evaluation of the entry, establishment or spread of a disease be conducted "according to the sanitary or phytosanitary measures which might be applied." We agree with the Panel that this phrase "refers to the measures *which might* be applied, not merely to the measures which *are being* applied." The phrase "which might be applied" is used in the conditional tense. In this sense, "might" means: "were or would be or have been able to, were or would be or have been allowed to, were or would perhaps." We understand this phrase to imply that a risk assessment should not be limited to an examination of the measure already in place or favoured by the importing Member. In other words, the evaluation contemplated in paragraph 4 of Annex A to the *SPS Agreement* should not be distorted by preconceived views on the nature and the content of the measure to be taken; nor should it develop into an exercise tailored to and carried out for the purpose of justifying decisions *ex post facto*.

209. In this case, the Panel found that the 1999 PRA dealt exclusively with the " 'plant quarantine measures against *E. amylovora* concerning U.S. fresh apple fruit,' which have been taken by Japan based on the proposal by the US government since 1994." The Panel also found that, in the 1999 PRA, no attempts were made "to assess the 'relative effectiveness' of the various individual requirements applied, [that] the assessment appears to be based on the assumption from the outset that all these measures would apply cumulatively", and that no analysis was made "of their relative effectiveness and whether and why all of them in combination are required in order to reduce or eliminate the possibility of entry, establishment or spread of the disease." Moreover, the Panel referred to "the opinions of Dr. Hale and Dr. Smith that the 1999 PRA 'appeared to prejudge the outcome of its risk assessment' and that 'it was principally concerned to show that each of the measures already in place was effective in some respect, and concluded that all should therefore be applied'." In our opinion, these findings of fact of the Panel leave no room for doubt that the 1999 PRA was designed and conducted in such a manner that *no* phytosanitary policy other than the regulatory scheme *already in place* was considered. Accordingly, we uphold the Panel's finding . . . that "Japan has not . . . properly evaluated the likelihood of entry 'according to the SPS measures that might be applied'."

C. Consideration of Scientific Evidence Arising Subsequent to the Risk Assessment at Issue

210. Finally, Japan argues that "Japan's PRA *was* consistent with Article 5.1 of the *SPS Agreement* at the time of the analysis, because conformity of

a risk assessment with Article 5.1 should be assessed against the information available at the time of the risk assessment." According to Japan, a risk assessment should be evaluated solely against the evidence available at the time of the risk assessment, such that a Member that fulfils the requirement of a risk assessment when adopting a measure is not held to have acted inconsistently with Article 5.1 upon the discovery of subsequently-published scientific evidence.

. . . .

212. The Panel concluded that Japan's measure could not be "based on" a risk assessment, as required by Article 5.1, because the 1999 PRA did not satisfy the definition of "risk assessment" set out in paragraph 4 of Annex A to the *SPS Agreement*. The Panel determined that the definition of "risk assessment" was not satisfied because the 1999 PRA failed to meet the two elements discussed above, namely, that a risk assessment (i) "evaluate the likelihood of entry, establishment or spread of" the plant disease at issue, and (ii) conduct such evaluation "according to the SPS measures which might be applied." . . .

213. . . . . Japan was unable to identify any scientific evidence relied upon by the Panel, but published after the issuance of the 1999 risk assessment, because the Panel did not, in fact, base its finding on such evidence. The Panel's analysis focused almost exclusively on the risk assessment itself to determine whether the 1999 PRA satisfied the legal requirements the Panel found in the *SPS Agreement*. The Panel identified those requirements as the need to assess a risk with a certain degree of "specificity," to evaluate probability rather than possibilities, and to evaluate the likelihood of entry "according to the sanitary or phytosanitary measures which might be applied." . . .

. . . .

216. . . . [W]e uphold the Panel's finding . . . that Japan's 1999 Pest Risk Analysis does not satisfy the definition of "risk assessment" set out in paragraph 4 of Annex A to the *SPS Agreement* because it (i) fails to "evaluate the likelihood of entry, establishment or spread of "the plant disease at issue, and (ii) fails to conduct such an evaluation "according to the SPS measures which might be applied." Furthermore, as the 1999 PRA is not a "risk assessment" within the meaning of the *SPS Agreement*, it follows, as the Panel found . . . that Japan's phytosanitary measure at issue is not "based on" a risk assessment, as required by Article 5.1 of the *SPS Agreement*.

VI. ANOTHER FOOD FIGHT: THE 2006 *GMO* CASE

Still another food fight between the U.S. and EU, one that erupted initially in 1997 and remains unresolved, concerns genetically modified (GM) food. Examples of such food include herbicide-resistant soya beans and vitamin-enhanced oils. Just how safe are GM foods? "Not at all," or at least "not safe enough," is the response of some European consumers — indeed, of consumers in many countries. Starting in June 1999, the EU essentially declined to approve products containing GMOs, despite intense opposition from American biotechnology exporters, and despite the competitive disadvantage imposed on European biotech companies. The U.S. called the EU move illegal discrimination against biotech products on non-scientific grounds. Arguably, however, EU officials had little choice.

That is because part of the dispute over GMOs is about domestic politics rooted in deep-seated cultural preferences. To be sure, Swiss voters in the spring 1998 rejected by a two-thirds majority a referendum proposing to ban genetic modification of plants and animals and their release into the environment. Nonetheless, the fondness for non-GMO and organic products among the European public traditionally is high, perhaps rivaled only in New Zealand and a handful of other countries. Further, even if GMOs were entirely safe, EU officials could not be the bearer of that message to the European public. So badly had they mishandled the problem of bovine spongiform encephalopathy (BSE), *i.e.*, mad cow disease, they had lost credibility on food safety issues with constituents.

In contrast, Americans — ever-optimistic about the power of science to better human life — surely are more tolerant of genetic engineering to yield a sweeter beet or brighter apple than most Europeans. That tolerance may be grounded in American pragmatism. A substantial percentage of America's food supply contains GMOs, and depending on the particular commodity, a large percentage of total output is genetically modified. Roughly half of America's corn production, for instance, contains GMOs. Two other arguments in favor of the biotechnology industry tend to resonate with greater success in the U.S. than the EU.

First, "GM" is a matter of tolerance along a continuum, not binomial definition. As with the term "organic," delineating what is "GM" is a matter of picking a point between 0 and 100 percent. Accordingly, why not select an obvious policy alternative less trade restrictive than a ban — namely, labeling — that leave consumers with as much freedom of choice as possible? Indeed, on 11 January 2000 the EU announced labeling requirements for products containing 1 percent or more GM content (specifically, a 1 percent tolerance level for accidental commingling in corn), and in April 2000 the EU created a "Food Standards Agency" (FSA) to (inter alia) enforce the new rules. These developments followed a 15 May 1997 "Novel Foods Regulation" in the EU. How has the U.S. responded to this new paradigm?

Second, many American agri-businesses laud the economic and even environmental benefits of GMOs, and their potential to be functional foods and therapeutic drugs. They are indispensable to feed a growing world population. Without drought-resistant, pest-resistant, or high-yielding seeds, it would not be possible to produce enough food to meet demand in developing and least developed countries. It is simply naïve to believe the world could get along with organic farming. Indeed, the concept of "organic" is — ironically — artificial. Suppose the mother of a cow from which milk comes once grazed on land to which fertilizer had been applied. Or, suppose the cow's mother once received medicine from a veterinarian. Is that milk organic?

To be sure, Europeans, like-minded citizens outside the EU, and many NGOs, offer rebuttals to both arguments. On the first argument, opponents of GM food remind proponents that defining risk tolerance levels is a sovereign right preserved by the WTO *SPS Agreement*. If the EU, for example, wants to ban any product containing 1 percent or more GM content, as distinct from special labeling of such products, then it is free to do so. "Franken foods," after all, should be forbidden, not simply decried.

On the second argument, critics highlight externalities associated with GMOs. GM seeds may pose phytosanitary risks. A GM product of Monsanto, for instance, might harm the monarch butterfly. In other words, there are potentially adverse fear ecological and physiological consequences from GMOs, for instance, the transference of pesticide resistance from a GMO to a different pest, or the transference of antibiotic resistance from a GMO to bacteria in the human stomach.

Moreover, the seeds create dependence on, if not domination by, American biotech companies. Never mind the fact stifling EU regulation inhibits the competitiveness of a European biotech industry. Leading GMO producers tend to be American, and for some European officials and consumers, that is bad enough. Once a farmer in, say, Sub-Saharan Africa starts planting a field with GM seed, she must rely on inputs — namely, fertilizer — from that same company. The company holds some degree of monopoly position, possibly reinforced by a patent on the seed and fertilizer, and can exploit profitably this status. The farmer becomes hooked on the American supplier, and conversely that supplier has a captive client. Depending on the crop, this dependency-captivity relationship is reinforced annually. Farmers in poor countries must purchase new GM seed each year, because that seed, while pest-resistant, does not produce multiple harvests. Is there a specter of the U.S. and its agribusinesses one day dominate some world food supply markets? Yes, say critics.

The vigorous debate — and the billions of dollars potentially at stake — ensured a fight in the WTO. *See* WTO Panel Report, *European Communities — Measures Affecting the Approval and Marketing of Biotech Products*, WT/DS291/R (adopted 21 November 2006). In August 2003, a panel was established to consider a suit by the U.S. (and other complainants) against the EU. The U.S. claimed the EU:

    i.   Maintained procedures to assess risk that were inappropriate in relation to the actual risk GM products presented.

    ii.   Had not produced sufficient scientific evidence to justify its risk assessment procedures.

    iii.   Applied its risk assessment procedures inconsistently, because it imposed different approval requirements on biotech products and products made using biotech processing aids.

In consequence, the U.S. argued, the EU violated several provisions of the *SPS Agreement*.

Did the U.S. prevail? "Yes and no" is the answer. In its September 2006 Report, the WTO Panel rejected the above three claims. Its rationale was the EU ban on biotech goods was not itself an SPS measure. But, the Panel agreed with the U.S. that the EU action was a *de facto* moratorium on approving GM food, with the consequence of undue delay in certifying 24 products as safe. Thus, said the Panel, the EU violated Article 8 of, and Annex C(1)(a) to, the *SPS Agreement*. The Panel held the U.S. was correct on a second point.

The ban imposed by six EU countries — Austria, France, Germany, Greece, Italy, and Luxembourg — on GM product imports was not founded on proper risk assessment procedures. These import bans were inconsistent with Articles 5:1 and 5:7 of the *Agreement*.

Satisfied with the outcome, the U.S. elected not to appeal. In December 2006, the EU agreed to implement the Panel recommendations. Perhaps both sides were exhausted by the battle, and the ridiculously long Panel Report, which set a WTO record at 1,200 pages.

Might there be an argument GMOs are not covered by the *SPS Agreement* because they represent an alternative to conventional production processes and do not involve additives that could threaten human, animal, or plant life? As such, the governing principle would be national treatment for conventionally-bread and GM products. Of course, that argument would depend on scientific evidence about threats.

Part Thirteen

AGRICULTURE

Chapter 45

MARKET ACCESS

There exists no politician in India daring enough to attempt to explain to the masses that cows can be eaten.

—Prime Minister Indira Gandhi (1917-1984)

DOCUMENTS SUPPLEMENT ASSIGNMENT

1. *Havana Charter* Articles 25-29, 55-70
2. GATT Articles XX(h), XXXVI-XXXVIII
3. WTO *Agreement on Agriculture*
4. *NAFTA* Chapter 7A
5. Relevant provisions in other FTAs

I. TARIFF REDUCTION

A. Tariff Reduction Commitments for Developed Countries

The WTO *Agreement on Agriculture*, a key outcome of the Uruguay Round, consists of commitments in three areas: market access; domestic support; and export subsidies. In all three areas, the Uruguay Round negotiators must be credited with achieving the first comprehensive accord. To be sure, the *Agreement* has many critics, but it was an historic starting point toward free — or freer — trade in the one economic sector that affects every person on the planet, namely, agriculture. The Doha Round negotiations on, and commitments in, all three areas, are based on the structure of the *Agreement*. Thus, to understand the *Agreement* is to appreciate the three-part framework in which agricultural trade liberalization talks proceed.

On market access, in brief, Article 4:1 of the WTO *Agreement on Agriculture*, and attendant documents, call for reductions on tariffs on primary and processed agricultural products. The methodology they employed (discussed below) is known as the "Uruguay Round Approach." More specifically, the obligation to reduce agriculture tariffs is contained in Article 4:1 of the *Agriculture Agreement*. It states simply

> [m]arket access concessions contained in Schedules [of Tariff Concessions of each WTO Member] *relate to* bindings and reductions of tariffs, and to other market access commitments as specified therein. [Emphasis added.]

At first glance, this language seems innocuous. However, the substantive obligations to which it relates are numerical targets for cutting customs duties.

1451

To account for variations in economic development, the Uruguay Round Approach set different targets, as well as different implementation periods, for different classes of WTO Members. Developed countries committed to reduce their agriculture tariffs by an average of 36 percent in value the 6 years following 1 January 1995, *i.e.*, by 1 January 2001, in equal annual installments. For 12 groups of agricultural products, developed countries cut the overall simple average by 37 percent. The range among these groups was, at the low end, a simple average tariff reduction of 26 percent on dairy products. At the high end, it was a simple average cut of 48 percent on cut flowers. For tropical products, which are of keen export interest to many poor countries, developed countries agreed to slash tariffs by an overall simple average amount of 43 percent. In this product grouping, the low-end of the cut was a reduction of 37 percent for tropical fruits and nuts. At the high end, it was a cut of 52 percent for spices, flowers, and plants.

B. Tariff Reduction Commitments for Developing and Least Developed Countries

Developing countries agreed to reduce their duty rates by an average of 24 percent in value (and 14 percent in quantity) over a decade, *i.e.*, by 31 December 2004. Least developed countries are not obliged to make any tariff cuts. Table 45-1 summarizes these targets (as well as the minimum per product cuts). In brief, developing countries are expected to cut their average tariffs on agricultural imports by two-thirds that of developed countries, and are given double the amount of time to do so.

TABLE 45-1:
AGRICULTURAL TARIFF REDUCTION COMMITMENTS MADE IN THE URUGUAY ROUND

Tariff Reduction Commitments	Developed Countries	Developing Countries	Least Developed Countries
Average Cut for All Agricultural Products	36%	24%	Zero
Minimum Cut Per Agricultural Product	15%	10%	Zero
Period for Phasing in the Cuts	6 years, from 1995-2000	10 years, from 1995-2004	Not applicable

Is it striking that any target is set for developing countries? To adherents of Ricardo's theory of comparative advantage, the answer is "no." For them, even unilateral tariff reductions yield a net welfare gain to a society. That gain may be all the greater for a poor country maintaining high barriers, and may boost trade among such countries that slash their barriers. Possibly, for poor countries characterized by labor surplus, reducing barriers to agricultural trade may hasten industrialization (by making the agriculture sectors more competitive, and encouraging a shift of farm workers with zero or low marginal productivity to the industrial sector). In brief, from an economic perspective, it is beneficial for all countries, regardless of their income, to drop their barriers.

However, what the law requires is a different matter. Any obligation imposed on less developed countries to cut tariffs, demanded (however politely) in return for a cut by developed countries, offends the fundamental principle of special and differential treatment embodied in Article XXXVI:8 of GATT.

> The developed contracting parties *do not expect reciprocity* for commitments made by them in trade negotiations to reduce or remove tariffs and other barriers to the trade of less-developed contracting parties. [Emphasis added.]

This principle of non-reciprocity means — or ought to mean — rich countries cut tariffs without asking, expecting, cajoling, or imposing any condition on poor countries. Lest there be any doubt about this meaning, the Interpretative Note to Article XXXVI:8, *Ad Article XXXVI, Paragraph 8*, explains that "do not expect reciprocity" means poor countries

> *should not be expected*, in the course of trade negotiations, *to make contributions* which are *inconsistent with their individual development, financial and trade needs*, taking into consideration past trade developments. [Emphasis added.]

Evidently, some Uruguay Round negotiators forgot, ignored, or altered this meaning, at least with respect to those poor countries for which targeted "contributions" are "inconsistent" with their "needs." To be sure, it is important not to overstate the accusation. The fact negotiators imposed no tariff cut targets on least-developed countries accords fully with the non-reciprocity principle. The argument about incongruity must focus on developing countries, and appraise each such country's "needs" in relation to a 24 percent average cut over 10 years. In the final analysis, the argument likely will be valid for some, but not all, developing countries.

Just how impressive are the 36 and 24 percent targets for cuts in agricultural tariffs under the Uruguay Round Approach, and associated with Article 4:1 of the *Agreement on Agriculture*? Double-digit tariff rate cuts of this magnitude sound ambitious. But, their substantive impact of any tariff cut is impossible to gauge without knowing the initial rates subject to reduction.

C. Base Levels

The level to which a tariff rate falls depends on the level from which it fell. To take two extreme examples, suppose one WTO Member's agricultural tariff rates average 50 percent, while the average duties in a second Member are 5 percent. A 36 percent cut in the first Member's average rates translates into an 18 percent cut, which sounds impressive, but still leaves a high average rate of 32 percent. (Under the *Agreement on Agriculture*, if the Member is a developing country, then the cut is 12 percent, resulting in a formidable 38 percent average rate.) As for the second Member, a 36 percent cut of a 5 percent average duty rate yields a very low average, just 3.2 percent. What, then, was the starting point — the base rate — for measuring the target cuts?

The answer is the tariff in effect on either 1 January 1995 or September 1986, depending on the nature of the rate on the agricultural product at issue. If the duty associated with an individual agricultural product was bound, then the base rate is the bound duty as of 1 January 1995, the date the *Agriculture Agreement* entered into force. If the duty was not bound, then the base rate is the actual duty charged in September 1986, when the Uruguay Round commenced. This distinction affords developing countries the option of binding previously unbound duties. Uruguay Round negotiators agreed these countries could set a bound tariff that would not be subject to further cuts.

The point is there is an opportunity for a disingenuous binding. When converting unbound tariffs on agricultural imports into bound rates during the Uruguay Round, some developing countries decided to set bound tariff ceilings, called "ceiling bindings." Yet, many of them set ceiling bindings on various agricultural imports at rates considerably above previous unbound rates, and they did not commit to declines in these rates over time. To illustrate, suppose Nicaragua's pre-Uruguay Round unbound tariff on corn is 50 percent, and it sets a bound rate of 60 percent. Corn exporters in, for instance, Nebraska have little to cheer about (assuming Nicaragua applies the bound rate, and not some rate below 50 percent). In many developing countries, there is a significant difference between applied and bound agricultural tariff rates. For example, one study observes for 31 developing countries (excluding members of the Cairns Group), the simple (*i.e.*, unweighted) applied agricultural duty is 25 percent, compared to a bound 66 percent rate.

Critics of the *Agreement on Agriculture* charge that, overall, the initial (pre-Uruguay Round) rates are high, hence post-cut rates still are high. While this criticism is fair, an "unbiased" evaluation is impossible. Once again, the end depends in part on the beginning. That is, a proper evaluation hinges on two key factors: (1) selection of a date or period "better" than 1 January 1995 and September 1986, in the sense of lower base rates being in effect; and (2) a standard to determine whether the 36 and 24 percent targeted cuts are ambitious. On the first criterion, no doubt unsatisfied trade liberalizers could point to a date on which agriculture tariffs were low, and thus urge adoption of cuts from a low base. On the second criterion, no doubt they could call for targets more aggressive than 36 or 24 percent. In other words, arguments about the base date and cuts from it rely on criteria, whether made explicit or left as an implicit assumption.

However, the critics have at least one point in their favor — transparency. Neither the tariff reduction targets nor the base rates used to calculate tariff cuts is set forth in the *Agreement*. Rather, to find the tariff reduction targets, it is necessary to go to a side document, dated 20 December 1993, called *Modalities for the Establishment of Specific Binding Commitments Under the Reform Programme*.

This "*Modalities Document*" sets out the ways in which the Uruguay Round negotiators agreed to fulfill their obligations. Annex 3 of the *Modalities Document* deals with market access. The base rates are set forth in a major "*Press Summary*" issued by the GATT Secretariat at the conclusion of the

Uruguay Round negotiations, in April 1994 a few days before signing of the Marrakesh Protocol. They are repeated in a *"Briefing Document"* on trade and agriculture issued by the WTO in October 2002, the month before the Doha Ministerial Conference. The failure of the negotiators to write the starting points into the text only exacerbates suspicions the tariff cuts would be, in terms of substantive importance, less grand than the negotiators proclaimed in enthusiastic official documents like the December 1993 *Press Release.*

The selection of a base rate to commence tariff cuts is not the only way in which to manipulate the ambitiousness of the cuts. A second clever device would be to restrict cuts to certain agricultural products. WTO Members took advantage of the freedom any reduction commitment cast in terms of an "average" inherently allows, namely, the protection of sensitive domestic sectors with below-average reductions. From a free trade perspective, the room for maneuver on per-product cuts is limited. With respect to both developed and developing country WTO Members, Uruguay Round negotiators established minimum tariff cuts for each agricultural product. They did so to ensure a Member did not make all or most cuts on a limited range of products, but leave certain primary commodities or processed items protected with high duty rates, thereby denying market access to foreign exporters of those goods. Thus, developed countries had to reduce the tariff on each agricultural product by a minimum of 15 percent, while the minimum cut on individual products developing countries have to make is two-thirds of the minimum cut required of developed countries, *i.e.*, 10 percent. The same phase-in periods apply for the minimum per product reductions as are generally applicable, namely, equal installments of cuts over six years (1995-2000) for developed countries, and over a decade (1995-2005) for developing countries.

Significantly, for least developed countries, no minimum product-specific tariff reduction targets exist. The *Agriculture Agreement* allows them to maintain their duty rates, and even increase their actual duty rates within their previously-agreed bindings, for as long as they remain least developed. At the same time, the obligation imposed on developing countries to make any minimum reduction hardly amounts to non-reciprocal treatment. Here, as with the 36 and 24 percent tariff cuts, the comment can be made that developed countries are less than charitable in adhering to the mandate in Article XXXVI:8 of GATT.

The targets of 36 and 24 percent cuts would seem sufficiently important to merit express mention in the *Agreement on Agriculture*, perhaps in Article 4 itself. After all, if market access is the first of three methodologies for liberalizing world agricultural trade, and if tariff reduction is the first of three measures associated with this methodology, then surely Uruguay Round negotiators would want to proclaim to the world, in the text of the *Agreement* themselves, the ambitious cuts to which they have committed. Would that incentive be greater for negotiators representing developed countries, at least those eager to show their concern for developed and least developed countries?

How are deviations from the target to be explained? Simply put, by the negotiating process during the Uruguay Round. Also, by definition, a target for some or most members might not be a target for all Members, *i.e.*, some developed or developing country Members might take aim elsewhere. As a hypothetical example, after give-and-take sessions with trading partners, New Zealand might agree to cut its agriculture tariffs by an average of 40 percent (more than the 36 percent target applicable to it), while Nicaragua might agree to cut by 20 percent (less than the 24 percent target applicable to it). (New Zealand offers duty-free treatment to all countries on agriculture products.) The fact the 36 and 24 percent figures are targets, not legal obligations in the text of the *Agreement*, creates the suspicion the figures are "soft." That suspicion matters, especially to farmers and processors, wherever located, looking for signs the multilateral trade negotiation process provides them with meaningful new market access opportunities.

II. TARRIFICATION AND SAFEGUARDS

A. The Chilean Price Band System

The *Price Band* case, *Chile — Price Band System and Safeguard Measures Relating to Certain Agricultural Products*, WT/DS207/AB/R (adopted 23 October 2002, complaint by Argentina), began because Chile implemented two specific measures against farm product imports drawing the ire of Argentina. First, on 30 June 1986, Chile implemented a Price Band System on imported wheat, wheat flour, and edible vegetable oils. Second, Chile imposed provisional and definitive safeguard measures on imported wheat, wheat flour, and edible vegetable oils, and extended those measures. Argentina challenged the first measure under GATT Article II:1, as well as under Article 4:2 of the WTO *Agreement on Agriculture*. Argentina challenged the second measure under GATT Article XIX and various provisions of the WTO *Agreement on Safeguards*.

Chile's bound tariff rate for wheat, wheat flour, and edible vegetable oils was 31.5 percent (though its applied most-favored nation (MFN) rate was much lower, at 8 percent). Argentina claimed the Chilean Price Band System violated GATT Article II:1(b) because it caused Chile, in certain instances, to collect duties in excess of the bound rate. The System, said Argentina, also potentially lead Chile to apply specific duties in violation of the bound 31.5 percent tariff rate. Sometimes, said Argentina, Chile imposed on Argentinian products effective *ad valorem* duties of 64.41 percent on oils, and 60.25 percent on wheat flour.

Of course, Chile disagreed with Argentina, and urged its Price Band System complied with Article II:1(b). At the same time, Chile admitted additional plus regular duties occasionally exceeded its bound rate. Thus, after Argentina brought the WTO action, Chile modified its System to ensure any additional duties applied under it, when added to the normal MFN rate, would not exceed the bound rate of 31.5 percent.

What, exactly, was Chile's Price Band System, and how did it work? Perhaps the best way to understand the Price Band System is to quote directly from the key provision in the 1986 Chilean law in dispute, Article 12 of Law 18.525 of the *Rules on the Importation of Goods* (as amended on 19 November 2001 by Article 2 of Law 19.772, which added the last paragraph):

[Paragraph #1] For the sole purpose of ensuring a reasonable margin of fluctuation of domestic wheat, oil-seeds, edible vegetable oils and sugar prices in relation to the international prices for such products, *specific duties are hereby established in United States dollars per tariff unit, or ad valorem duties, or both,* and rebates on the amounts payable as *ad valorem* duties established in the Customs Tariff, which could affect the importation of such goods.

[Paragraph #2] *The amount of these duties* and rebates, established in accordance with the procedure laid down in this Article, *shall be determined annually by the President* of the Republic, *in terms which, applied to the price levels attained by the products in question on the international markets, make it possible to maintain a minimum cost and a maximum import cost for the said products during the internal marketing season for the domestic production.*

[Paragraph #3] *For the determination of the costs* mentioned in the preceding paragraph, *the monthly average international prices recorded in the most relevant markets during an immediately preceding period of five calendar years for wheat, oil-seed and edible vegetable oils and ten calendar years for sugar shall be taken into consideration.*

[Paragraph #4] These averages shall be adjusted by the percentage variation of the relevant average price index for Chile's foreign trade between the month to which they correspond and the last month of the year prior to that of the determination of the amount of duties or rebates, as certified by the Central Bank of Chile. *They shall then be arranged in descending order and up to 25 per cent of the highest values and up to 25 percent of the lowest values for wheat, oil-seed and edible vegetable oils* and up to 35 per cent of the highest values and up to 35 per cent of the lowest values for sugar *shall be removed.* To the resulting extreme values there shall be added the normal tariffs and costs arising from the process of importation of the said products. The duties and rebates determined for wheat shall also apply to meslin and wheat flour. In this last case, duties and rebates established for wheat shall be multiplied by the factor 1.56.

[Paragraph #5] The prices to which these duties and rebates are applied shall be those applicable to the goods in question on the day of their shipment. The National Customs Administration shall notify these prices on a weekly basis, and may obtain information from other public bodies for that purpose.

[Paragraph #6] *The specific duties resulting from the application of this Article, added to the ad valorem duty, shall not exceed the base tariff rate bound by Chile under the World Trade Organization for the goods referred to in this Article,* each import transaction being considered individually and using the c.i.f. [cost, insurance, and freight] value of the goods concerned in the transaction in question as a basis for calculation. To that end, the National Customs Service shall adopt the necessary measures to ensure that the said limit is maintained.[1]

---

[1] *Price Band* Panel Report, ¶¶ 2.2-2.3 (emphasis added).

In practice, Chile's applied tariff rates were substantially beneath its bound rates. The final above-quoted paragraph, Paragraph #6, mandates that outcome. It places a cap on the combination of (1) an applied *ad valorem* rate and (2) a duty increase resulting from operation of the Price Band System. The cap is the *ad valorem* rate Chile bound in its WTO schedule of concessions. And yet, this cap did not suffice to placate Argentina. What was it about the rather turgid prose that caused controversy? Put differently, what does that prose mean, and how did Chile operate its Price Band System?

As its name suggests, using certain international prices, the Price Band System creates an upper and lower band, or threshold, for import prices of wheat, wheat flour, and oil-seed and edible vegetable oils. Once a year, pursuant to Paragraph #2, the President of Chile issues a decree publishing these upper and lower bands, along with related specific duties. Paragraphs #3 and #4 are all about how the President sets these bands. In brief, the bands are supposed to be calculated on the basis of average monthly prices over the last 60 months (5 years) observed on certain exchanges, adjusted according to an external price index constructed by Chile's Central Bank, and denominated in U.S. dollars. To calculate the Price Band for wheat, Chile used price data for Hard Red Winter No. 2 wheat, f.o.b. (free on board) Gulf, quoted on the Kansas City Board of Trade (KCBT). For oils, Chile examined crude soya bean oil prices, f.o.b. Illinois, quoted on the Chicago Mercantile Exchange. Following paragraph #4 of its Law (quoted above), Chile used the same Price Band to calculate the specific duty (or rebate) for wheat flour as for wheat, and then multiplied the result by 1.56 to obtain the final specific duty (or rebate) for the wheat flour.

Presumably to narrow the potential width of its Price Band, Chile excludes certain adjusted average monthly prices. It lists all of these prices, starting with the highest and descending to the lowest. But, Chile then cuts out up to 25 percent of the highest, and of the lowest, adjusted prices. The result is a narrower range of adjusted prices than otherwise would occur. Then, to the remaining extreme prices, Chile adds normal tariff liabilities, and importation costs, to the remaining prices. In effect, this step means Chile uses c.i.f. prices to establish its Price Band (which is implicit in paragraphs #4 and explicit in paragraph #6). That is, to compute a c.i.f. price, Chile factors in importation costs, such as freight charges, insurance fees, financing (*e.g.*, opening a letter of credit, interest on credit, or taxes on credit), fees for customs agents, unloading charges, costs of transportation to a plant, and wastage costs. The final result is a highest and lowest adjusted price, on a c.i.f. basis, with the most extreme 25 percent of the prices having been excluded from the list. The highest listed price establishes the upper threshold of the Band, and the lowest listed price sets the lower threshold.

Of course, the Price Band is only one component in Chile's overall System. It does no good to have just a Band, without also having target — or, more accurately, "reference" — prices. How would a Chilean customs officer know whether to impose an additional duty if he were conscious only of (1) the Band and (2) the actual import price of a shipment? The officer needs a sense of whether the shipment he is assessing is "too low," "too high," or "just right" in relation to the lower threshold of the Band.

To be sure, one method for giving him that sense would be to use the actual import price as the reference, *i.e.*, the transaction value of the merchandise. (This method characterizes a minimum import price scheme, which is discussed later.) If the transaction value were below the lower band, then the officer would know to slap on an increased duty, *i.e.*, a duty on top of the normal applicable *ad valorem* rate. He would calculate the difference between the transaction value and lower band, and impose a duty on that difference. Conversely, if the transaction value of the imported merchandise were above the upper band, then the officer would know he should grant a rebate. He would calculate the gap between the transaction value and upper band, and provide a rebate based on that gap. (And, if the transaction value fell between the upper and lower thresholds, then he would apply the normal duty, with neither an increase nor a rebate.) In effect, this method makes use of the Price Band and actual import prices, comparing these prices with the upper and lower boundaries of the Band. Plainly, the lower threshold becomes a minimum import price, above which imported merchandise is safe from an extra duty. Consequently, to exporters, it becomes a sort of "target" at or above which to price their merchandise.

However, this straightforward method is not quite what is called for by Chile's above-quoted Law. Instead, paragraph #5 of its Law requires the National Customs Administration to set a "reference price" for wheat, wheat flour, and oil-seed and edible vegetable oils. The Customs Administration does so on a weekly basis, every Friday, by examining prices on foreign markets. The foreign markets it studies are markets of concern to Chile, which for wheat include the U.S., Canada, Australia, and those of the complainant in the case, Argentina. The Customs Administration calculates reference prices by using the lowest f.o.b. prices for wheat, wheat flour, and oil-seed and edible vegetable oils sold in these markets. Whereas in establishing the Price Band Chile computes c.i.f. prices by factoring in typical importation costs, the Customs Administration does not do so when calculating reference prices, *i.e.*, a reference price is an f.o.b. price, but prices in the Band are c.i.f. prices. The reference prices, then, become the gauge by which a Chilean customs officer decides whether to apply an increased duty, grant a rebate, or take neither action. In any particular week, the same reference price applies to all products within a category (*e.g.*, wheat), regardless of the country of origin of the shipment, and regardless of the actual transaction value of the shipment.

Any international transaction lawyer appreciates that for the same merchandise, the c.i.f. price is higher than the f.o.b price. That is because the latter figure excludes costs, insurance premiums, and freight charges, which are built into the former figure. Strictly speaking, then, the two prices are not comparable. All other factors being equal (*ceteris paribus*), by virtue of the c.i.f. prices used to construct it, Chile's Price Band is higher than the f.o.b. reference prices used in connection with the Band. Consequently, the Price Band System has an inherent bias: the reference price for a particular shipment may be below the lower threshold of the Band, because that threshold has importation costs not included in the price.

This fact aside, the methodology explained above means when a shipment of a product subject to the Price Band System — wheat, wheat flour, oil-seed and edible vegetable oils — arrives at the Chilean border, a customs officer calculates the duty liability using a three-step procedure. First, the officer imposes the usual *ad valorem* duty, *i.e.*, the MFN or other applicable rate. Under Chile's simplified, general tariff structure, its applied MFN rate was 8 percent.

In Step Two, the officer identifies the reference price applicable to a particular shipment. As just described, this reference price is not the transaction value of the merchandise. Rather, it is the price the National Customs Administration calculated on a weekly basis. The applicable reference price depends on the date in the bill of lading covering the shipment. That date helps the customs official decide the right week from which to take the reference price. He needs the correct reference price if he is to determine whether an additional duty is required.

Step Three is what Argentina found objectionable about Chile's Price Band System. In this Step, the Chilean customs officer computes the total tariff liability on the shipment of imported merchandise by determining whether he needs to add an additional duty to the usual 8 percent *ad valorem* rate he imposed in Step One. Simply put (with no pun intended), the seeds of controversy were sown between Chile and Argentina when a duty increase — a duty above that imposed in Step One — was triggered. Whenever the reference price pertaining to a shipment of imported wheat, wheat flour, or oil-seed and edible vegetable oil was below the lower threshold of the Price Band, the trigger went off. Essentially, that is what Paragraphs #1 and #5 in the Law say. These Paragraphs instruct the Chilean customs official to compare (1) the reference price pertaining to the shipment in front of him with (2) the upper and lower thresholds in the Price Band. Again, the transaction value of the merchandise is irrelevant (and, for that matter, so are the deductive and computed value of the merchandise).

Suppose the applicable reference price were below the lower threshold of the Price Band. Then, the Chilean customs officer would increase the duty applicable to the imported merchandise. He would apply a specific duty to the merchandise, simply because the reference price is below the lower band. The amount of the specific duty would be the absolute difference between the "reference price" and the lower band. Because the officer would levy the specific duty, on top of the *ad valorem* duty already computed in Step One, the specific duty is an "increase."

What would happen if the reference price relevant to the imported shipment is above the upper threshold of the Price Band? Then, the Chilean customs officer would provide the importer with a rebate. The amount of the rebate would equal the absolute difference between the reference price and the upper band (but could not exceed the applied *ad valorem* rate). In instances in which the reference price fell within the boundaries of the Price Band, the officer would neither impose a specific duty, nor grant a rebate. The only tariff liability would be the standard 8 percent *ad valorem*.

Consider a simplified example of this three-step procedure. Suppose the transaction value of 1,000 kilograms of wheat imported from Argentina to Chile is U.S. $2.00 per bushel, or $2,000 total. Suppose, further, the wheat

Price Band in the Chilean President's decree for the year of importation establishes a lower threshold of $5.00 per bushel, and an upper threshold of $10.00
per bushel. In Step One, a Chilean customs officer would assess an 8 percent
ad valorem duty on the $2,000 shipment, or $160.00.

In Step Two, the customs officer would ascertain the applicable reference
price by checking both the appropriate publication of the National Customs
Administration and the date contained in the bill of lading covering the
Argentine wheat. Assume the date is 24 January 2003, and the "reference
price" determined for that week (*i.e.*, for Friday, 24 January to Thursday, 30
January) is $4.50 per bushel. Clearly, the reference price is 50 U.S. cents below
the lower threshold of the Price Band. Hence, the customs officer must assess
a specific duty in that amount. Assuming, further, the specific duty is levied
on a per bushel basis, then the increased duty would be $500.00 (the product
of 1,000 bushels and $0.50 per bushel). Via Step Three, the total tariff liability
would be $660, comprised of $160, assessed on an *ad valorem* basis, plus an
additional (whopping!) $500 specific duty. Small wonder why Argentine wheat
exporters would be upset.

B. Chilean Safeguard Measures

The transparency of Chile's safeguard law, and the decree implementing
it issued by the Ministry of Finance, was not challenged by Argentina. Chile
had fulfilled its obligation in this respect, notifying the WTO of both legal
instruments on 23 June 1999. Two months later, on 23 August 1999, Chile's
Ministry of Agriculture asked the country's national commission responsible
for investigating alleged distortions in prices of imported goods to self-initiate
a safeguards case on products subject to the Price Band System. (That
commission is known, perhaps rather humorously to some exporters and
importers, as the "Chilean Distortions Commission," or "CDC").

In other words, the Agriculture Ministry, presumably acting with the encouragement of domestic farming interests, sought safeguard protection
against imported wheat, wheat flour, edible vegetable oils, and sugar. Indeed,
the Ministry requested imposition of provisional safeguard measures, pending
final outcome of the investigation. Shortly thereafter, on 9 September, the
National Commission agreed to commence the investigation, though the case
it brought against sugar were not part of the claim Argentina brought to the
WTO. On 22 October, the National Commission recommended to the President
of Chile that he impose provisional safeguards.

Relief came swiftly for Chilean farmers. On 26 November 1999, the President followed through on the recommendation of the National Commission.
He imposed a provisional safeguard on foreign wheat, wheat flour, and edible
vegetable oils. On 7 January 2000, the Commission recommended the relief
be made final, and on 22 January the Ministry of Finance published a decree
doing just that. The relief for domestic producers was definitive, and to last
for one year. The protection took the form of an *ad valorem* tariff surcharge
on imports of the merchandise subject to the Price Band System. On 25 November 2000, the Finance Ministry — upon a recommendation from the
National Commission — agreed to extend the safeguard for another year,

which in practice meant until 26 November 2001. (Chile actually ended the protection for wheat and wheat flour early, on 27 July 2001.) Here, again, transparency was not an issue in the WTO case, as Chile notified the WTO of the measure and its extension.

The way in which Chilean authorities calculated the surcharge was a bit tricky, and it relied in part on the Price Band System. Technically, the surcharge for each import transaction equalled the difference between (1) "the general tariff added to the *ad valorem* equivalent of the specific duty" calculated under the Price Band System, and (2) the tariff "level bound in the WTO" for the relevant product. The Panel explained the calculation as follows:

> The safeguard measures consist of an additional duty on wheat, wheat flour and edible vegetable oils which "shall be determined by the difference between the general tariff added to the *ad valorem* equivalent of the specific duty determined by the mechanism set out in Article 12 of Law 18.525 [quoted earlier] — and its relevant annual implementing decrees — and the level bound in the WTO for these products." Thus, whenever the Chilean PBS [Price Band System] duty exceeds, in conjunction with the 8 per cent applied tariff, the 31.5 per cent bound rate, *the portion of the duty in excess of that bound rate shall be considered to constitute a safeguard measure.* Put another way, *the duty applied pursuant to the safeguard measure is the Chilean PBS duty to the extent it exceeds the 31.5 per cent bound rate.*[2]

Thus, consider the hypothetical 1,000 kilogram shipment of Argentine wheat at U.S. $2.00 per kilogram. The transaction value is $2,000. Assume the bound tariff for wheat is 31.5 percent, as it was in Chile, and further assume the lower and upper bounds of the Price Band System are $5.00 and $10.00, respectively. The general applied *ad valorem* tariff is 8 percent, or $160.00 (the product of the tariff rate and the transaction value). Suppose, again, the reference price for the week in which the shipment occurs is $4.50.

With these parameters, the 50-cent gap between the reference price and the lower threshold is the specific duty (per kilo) under the Price Band System. Applied to a 1,000 kilogram shipment, the additional duty is $500 (the product of 50 cents/kilo and 1,000 kilos). In turn, the total duty owed on the shipment is $660, which is the sum of the general tariff ($160) and the additional specific duty ($500). Based on this total, the amount of the safeguard measure can be determined. It is any excess of this total over the 31.5 percent bound rate. The total duty liability is 33 percent of the transaction value of the shipment. The 33 percent figure is obtained by dividing the $660 liability into the $2,000 transaction value. Clearly, 33 percent is 1.5 percent higher than Chile's bound rate. Consequently, the safeguard measure is considered to be 1.5 percent, or $30.

---

[2] *Price Band* Panel Report, ¶ 7.109 (emphasis added).

III. TEACHINGS OF THE 2002 *CHILE PRICE BAND* CASE

A. Key Issues

At the Panel stage, two legal arguments dominate the *Price Band* case, one about Chile's Price Band System, and the other about its agricultural safeguard measures. Relevant to the first area of dispute were the familiar pillar of GATT, Article II:1(b), concerning tariff bindings, and Article 4:2 of the *Agreement on Agriculture*. Argentina claimed the Price Band System also violated this provision of the *Agriculture Agreement*. Article 4:2 states:

> Members [of the WTO] shall *not* maintain, resort to, or revert to *any* measures of *any* kind which have been required to be *converted into ordinary customs duties* [footnote omitted], *except* as otherwise provided for in Article 5 and Annex 5. [Emphasis added.]

Of course, Chile took the opposite view, urging the System complied with Article 4:2. Regarding this area of dispute, it is worth taking a moment to survey what Article 4:2 says. After all, it is not nearly so widely-known or well-understood as the famous tariff bindings principle in GATT.

The first clause of Article 4:2 of the *Agriculture Agreement* is a prophylactic rule. This clause bans new forms of protection against agricultural products for which "tariffication" — meaning the conversion of a non-tariff barrier to a tariff — is required. The footnote to the first clause, Footnote 1, defines non-tariff barriers as broadly as possible to include

> quantitative import restrictions, *variable import levies*, *minimum import prices*, discretionary import licensing, non-tariff measures maintained through state-trading enterprises, voluntary export restraints, and similar border measures other than ordinary customs duties [emphasis added]. . . .

It does not matter whether the non-tariff barrier is maintained in connection with protections justified under the balance of payments exceptions contained in GATT Articles XII or XVII. The whole point of the first clause of Article 4:2 is to ensure tariffication is not undermined by new, and yet more devious, non-tariff protection. In brief, the six categories of barriers listed in Footnote 1 illustrate the kinds of measures that had to be converted into an ordinary customs duty, by virtue of Article 4:2, to enhance market access opportunities for imports of agricultural products.

However, there are two exceptions to the prophylactic ban on non-tariff barriers against products subject to tariffication. These exceptions are set forth in the first clause of Article 4:2. The second clause of the Article creates both exceptions, by making explicit reference to two other parts of the *Agreement on Agriculture*. The first exception, contained fully in Article 5, concerns special safeguard measures. Simplified, Article 5 allows a Member to invoke a special safeguard against imports of an agricultural product, as long as the volume of imports of an agricultural product exceed an established trigger level, or the c.i.f. price of those imports is below a trigger price level (equalling a reference price that is the average of c.i.f. prices in 1986-88).

The second limitation on the prophylactic rule against non-tariff barriers is set forth in Annex 5 to the *Agreement*. Section A of this complicated Annex lays out certain circumstances in which the prophylactic ban of Article 4:2 is inapplicable. Those circumstances include (1) a *de minimis* level of domestic consumption, (2) the lack of an export subsidy, (3) the existence of effective production-limiting measures, (4) products raising special non-trade concerns (*e.g.*, food security or special environmental concerns), or (5) products subject to minimum access opportunities. Section B explains that the ban on non-tariff barriers does not apply to a primary product that is the predominant staple in the traditional diet of a developing country Member.

Argentina's claim against Chile's provisional and definitive safeguard measures, and the extension of the definitive measures, was based on GATT Article XIX, and various provisions of the WTO *Agreement on Safeguards*. Chile took the position the Panel should not rule on this claim. It explained the provisional and definitive safeguard measures, which were the subject of consultations between the two WTO Members, were not in force. It also said the extension of the measures were not the subject of consultations under WTO auspices. The Panel rejected the Chilean defense.

For seven reasons, the Panel held the Chilean safeguards on wheat, wheat flour, and edible vegetable oils were inconsistent with GATT Article XIX:1(a). Chile did not:

(1) demonstrate the existence of unforeseen developments;

(2) illustrate the likeness, or direct competitiveness, of wheat, wheat flour, and edible vegetable oils made in Chile in comparison with those products imported from Argentina;

(3) define the domestic industry (a consequence of the second reason);

(4) show an increase in imports of merchandise subject to investigation;

(5) prove its domestic industry faced a threat of serious injury;

(6) a causal link between increased imports and the threat of serious injury; and

(7) ensure its safeguards were limited to the extent necessary to prevent injury (or remedy injury) and facilitate adjustment.

On the basis of the same factual predicate, the Panel also found the Chilean measures ran afoul of various provisions of the *Agreement on Safeguards*, namely: Articles 2 and 4 (because Chile failed to demonstrate the products produced in Chile were like or directly competitive with the subject merchandise, and thus failed to identify the domestic industry); Articles 2:1 and 4:2(a) (because Chile failed to demonstrate an increase in imports); Articles 2:1 and 4:2(b) (because Chile failed to demonstrate a causal link between increased imports and threat of serious injury); Article 3:1 (because Chile did not publish the measures in an appropriate medium, nor set out findings and reasoned conclusions); Articles 4:1(a)-(b) and 4:2(a) (because Chile failed to prove the existence of a threat of serious injury); and Article 5:1 (because Chile did not ensure the safeguards were limited to the extent necessary to prevent injury and facilitate adjustment).

Chile did not appeal the Panel's findings on Argentina's safeguards claim. Given the sweeping loss it suffered on this claim, under both GATT Article XIX and the *Safeguards Agreement*, Chile was wise not to do so. The only point Chile managed to score in front of the Panel concerning the safeguard measures was they were not, contrary to Argentina's contention, inconsistent with Article 3:1-2 of the *Safeguards Agreement*. The Panel agreed with Chile it had, in fact, conducted an appropriate investigation by giving Argentina the full opportunity to participate.

But, Chile appealed the Panel's ruling against it in respect of the Price Band System. Specifically, the Panel found against Chile for both reasons Argentina offered. The Panel ruled the additional specific duties Chile imposed under the System qualified as "other duties or charges" within the meaning of the second sentence of GATT Article II:1(b). Therefore, those additional duties were inconsistent with the second sentence. The Panel also held Chile's System violated Article 4:2 of the *Agreement on Agriculture*. The System, found the Panel, was "similar" to a "variable import levy," and also to a "minimum import price system," within the meaning of Footnote 1 to Article 4:2. The additional specific duties imposed by Chile under the System were not "ordinary customs duties" under Article 4:2. Because they were not "ordinary customs duties," and because they resembled two of the items on the list of forbidden non-tariff barriers contained in Footnote 1, they were inconsistent with the prophylactic rule in Article 4:2. On appeal, Chile argued these holdings should be overturned. Instead, the Appellate Body upheld — but with significant modifications — the Panel's conclusions.

B. Key Rulings

Chile urged the Panel erred in assessing the Price Band System under Article 4:2 of the *Agreement on Agriculture*, before doing so under Article II:1(b) of GATT. Chile thought the Panel ought first to have looked at GATT, and then at the *Agriculture Agreement* (an argument mildly reminiscent of the jurisprudence of the Appellate Body on examining the exceptions under, and then the *chapeau* to, GATT Article XX). To this thrust, the Appellate Body responded with a skilful, lawyer-like parrying move. "No," *i.e.*, the Panel acted appropriately in evaluating the System under the *Agriculture Agreement* before doing so under GATT. In consequence, Chile won a reversal of the Panel's finding its Price Band System violated the second sentence of GATT Article II:1(b). But, Chile could not get the Appellate Body to overturn the lower tribunal's decision essentially condemning the measure under Article 4:2 (including Footnote 1 thereto) of the *Agriculture Agreement*. Because the Appellate Body agreed the System violated this Article, it exercised judicial economy in not returning to GATT to consider whether the System violated the first sentence of Article II:1(b).

In specific, one thrust Chile made on appeal concerned the appropriate order in which to analyze a claim an importing country has exceeded its bound rate of tariff with respect to an agricultural product. Should an adjudicator start with GATT Article II:1(b), which the Panel did not do, or should it follow the Panel's example and commence with Article 4:2 of the *Agreement on Agriculture*? Or, is it inappropriate, maybe impracticable, to lay down a general rule of analysis? The Panel's order of analysis was not whimsical. It chose to look to the *Agriculture Agreement* first, because it provides a more specific rule (in Article 4:2) for the facts than does GATT (in Article II:1(b)).

The Appellate Body's parry was gentle — it agreed. The Appellate Body observed the *Agriculture Agreement* is more specific than GATT about agricultural products. GATT deals with all goods, whereas the *Agriculture Agreement* obviously focuses only on farm products. Thus, Article 4:2 of the *Agriculture Agreement* deals more specifically than does GATT with tariff commitments on these products, and on the circumvention of such commitments. The Appellate Body was refreshingly candid in pointing out the weakness of Chile's argument to the contrary, with sentences like "this argument by Chile is flawed,"[3] and "we find no merit in this additional argument by Chile."[4] It also was direct in pointing out the near-irrelevance of Chile's position, saying "[w]e understand Chile to mean by this [Chile's concession that it was not reversible error for the Panel to apply Article 4:2 before applying GATT Article II:1(b)] that the order of analysis would not, taken alone, alter the outcome of the case."[5]

Significantly, the Panel did not develop the order of analysis on its own, but rather applied a precedent set by the Appellate Body. In the *Bananas* case, the Appellate Body upheld the methodology of the panel to examine an issue about import licensing procedures first under the WTO *Agreement on Import Licensing*, and then under GATT transparency rules in Article X. In *Bananas*, the Appellate Body agreed it makes sense to go first to the text that "deals specifically, and in detail" with the issue at hand.[6] Doing so also reinforces the principle of judicial economy. If the issue can be resolved under the first text, then there is no need to look to the second text. Conversely, if the panel had started with GATT, then it would have had to look at the *Agriculture Agreement* too, because Article 21:1 of that *Agreement* mandates GATT applies subject to the provisions of the *Agreement*. Why not choose a methodology that can save a step and thereby conserve judicial resources? Not surprisingly, then, the *Price Band* Appellate Body quoted from its *Bananas* Report, and upheld the Panel's order of analysis.

The most important parry by Chile in the 2002 *Price Band* case was its System was not similar to a "variable import levy" or "minimum import price." Hence, the Panel's analogical reasoning under footnote 1 to Article 4:2 was flawed. "No," was the Appellate Body's parry in response. The Panel's analogy between the System and a variable import levy, and its analogy of the System to a minimum import price, were persuasive.

Conceptually, the most complex and hard-fought of the appeal was the thrust — parry as to whether the Chilean price band was a forbidden measure. Chile lost the match, as it were, because it failed to persuade the Appellate Body that the Panel was wrong in its analogical reasoning. Chile's thrust was its Price Band System "was merely a system for determining the level of

---

[3] *Price Band* Appellate Body Report, ¶ 187.

[4] *Price Band* Appellate Body Report, ¶ 188.

[5] *Price Band* Appellate Body Report, ¶ 189.

[6] *Bananas* Appellate Body Report, ¶ 204 (*quoted in Price Band* Appellate Body Report, ¶ 184).

ordinary customs duties that will be applied up to the 31.5 percent bound rate." The Appellate Body's parry was as follows:

> A plain reading of Article 4:2 and footnote 1 makes clear that, if Chile's price band system falls within any *one* of the categories of measures listed in footnote 1, it is among the "measures of the kind which have been required to be converted into ordinary customs duties," and thus must not be maintained, resorted to, or reverted to, as of the date of entry into force of the *WTO Agreement* [*i.e.,* 1 January 1995, as long as no exception applies].[7]

The judges at both levels agreed Chile's Price Band System was akin to "variable import levies," and to "minimum import prices" within the meaning of Footnote 1 to Article 4:2 of the *Agreement on Agriculture.* That spelled the defeat of Chile.

Put differently, to understand *Price Band* it is critical to appreciate the legal mechanics of how the analogy triggered the application of Article 4:2. It was unnecessary for Argentina to prove Chile's Price Band System actually was a "variable import levy" or a "minimum import price," and neither the Panel nor the Appellate Body held the System constituted such a levy or price *per se.* Rather, it was the analogy that mattered. The Panel held Chile's Price Band System to be a hybrid instrument, which shared most (but not all) of the characteristics of both a variable import levy and minimum import price. The Appellate Body agreed. Likening Chile's Price Band System to a variable import levy or to a minimum import price meant the System was a forbidden "measure." (Recall Article 4:2 is a rule against "measures." Footnote 1 provides a non-exclusive list of examples of "measures," and two of the examples are "variable import levies" and "minimum import prices.") That is, within the language of the rule, Chile's Price Band System was a "measure[] of the kind which ha[s] been required to be converted into ordinary customs duties."

Equally important to understanding *Price Band* is an appreciation of the "big picture." The whole point of Article 4:2 is to ensure the integrity of the process of this conversion. This process — tariffication — is indispensable to enhancing market access for agricultural goods. Article 4:2 ensures its integrity by mandating WTO Members "shall not maintain, resort to, or revert to" any of a wide variety of non-tariff measures. As the Appellate Body helpfully explained:

> . . . As its title indicates, Article 4 deals with "Market Access." During the course of the Uruguay Round, negotiators identified certain border measures which have in common that they restrict the volume or distort the price of imports of agricultural products. *The negotiators decided that these border measures should be converted into ordinary customs duties, with a view to ensuring enhanced market access for such imports.* Thus, *they envisioned that ordinary customs duties would, in principle, become the only form of border protection. As ordinary customs duties are more transparent and more easily quantifiable than non-tariff barriers, they are also more easily compared between trading partners, and thus the maximum amount of such duties can*

---

[7] *Price Band* Appellate Body Report, ¶ 221 (emphasis original).

be more easily reduced in future multilateral trade negotiations. The Uruguay Round negotiators agreed that market access would be improved — both in the short term and in the long term — through bindings and reductions of tariffs and minimum access requirements, which were to be recorded in the Members' Schedules.

. . . Thus, Article 4 of the *Agreement on Agriculture* is appropriately viewed as *the legal vehicle for requiring the conversion into ordinary customs duties of certain market access barriers* affecting imports of agricultural products.[8]

In brief, Article 4:2 states nothing more — or less — than that a Member is not supposed to impose a non-tariff barrier against agricultural imports if it is under an obligation to convert that kind of barrier to a tariff. Without this statement, tariffication could be circumvented by simultaneously changing non-tariff barriers to tariffs, and constructing new non-tariff barriers.

The Appellate Body recognized the wording of Article 4:2 is special. In phrasing the key rule, the provision uses the present perfect tense — "have been required." That is, it states WTO Members are not to implement "*any* measures *of the kind* which *have been required* to be converted into ordinary customs duties. . . ." The Appellate Body understood the *Agreement on Agriculture*, like most other WTO agreements, articulates most other obligations in the present tense, and a rule "expressed in the present perfect tense impose[] obligations that came into being in the past, but may continue to apply at present."[9] The Appellate Body was not being pedantic about English grammar, nor mechanically applying the principles of the *Vienna Convention on the Law of Treaties* concerning plain meaning, object and purpose, and context. Rather, it was considering an argument offered by Chile.

Chile thought the present perfect tense conveys the fact during the 1986-93 Uruguay Round negotiations, no country actually converted a price band system into tariffs (and no country asked Chile to "tariffy" its Price Band System). So, Chile urged, the rule of Article 4:2 applies only to non-tariff measures a country actually converted (or was requested to convert) during the Round. The Appellate Body disagreed.

Appreciating the legal implications of the nuances of grammar, the Appellate Body replied the present perfect tense connotes both (1) the date by which a WTO Member must convert non-tariff measures covered by Article 4:2 into tariffs, and (2) the date from which Members must abstain from non-tariff measures. Contrary to Chile's contention, the conversion process actually did begin during the Uruguay Round. Each country recorded in its draft Schedule of concessions a variety of ordinary customs duties. These tariff concessions compensated for, and replaced, non-tariff barriers that each country had to eliminate. Once the countries formally signed the *Agreement Establishing the World Trade Organization (WTO Agreement)*, on 15 April 1994, the option to replace a non-tariff barrier with an ordinary customs duty in excess of previously-bound rates expired (because the rates became bound as of that date). Further, once the *WTO Agreement* and the covered texts like the

---

[8] *Price Band* Appellate Body Report, ¶¶ 200-01 (footnote omitted, emphasis added).

[9] *Price Band* Appellate Body Report, ¶ 205 (footnote omitted, emphasis added).

Agreement on Agriculture entered into force — 1 January 1995 — each Member was obligated not to impose any non-tariff measures forbidden by Article 4:2. The prohibition applied regardless of whether the Member had converted a measure into a tariff by that date.

The Appellate Body pointed out Chile misread the present perfect tense ("have been required") as the present tense ("are required"). What would be the implication of this misinterpretation, inquired the Appellate Body? It would mean Article 4:2 applies only to non-tariff measures that actually were converted into an ordinary customs duties during the Uruguay Round negotiations (or those measures requested to be converted). In turn, the misinterpretation would suggest a Member that had failed by the end of the Round to convert a measure forbidden by Article 4:2 into a tariff could replace that measure with an ordinary customs duty in excess of its bound tariff rates. That is, misreading "have been" as "are" would remove from the scope of tariff bindings all unconverted measures. A Member could convert the measure to a tariff in excess of the bound rate, and do so with impunity, *i.e.*, without being challenged under the *DSU*. Surely, that result would be wrong — and even Chile had to admit so. Reasoned the Appellate Body, the present perfect tense in Article 4:2 ensures a measure that a Member was supposed to convert to a tariff as a result of the Uruguay Round, but had not yet done so, could not be maintained as of 1 January 1995.

The Appellate Body's rendition of the present perfect tense gives full meaning to the words "any" and "of the kind" in Article 4:2. Moreover, as the Appellate Body observed, its reading is consistent with Footnote 1 to Article 4:2 of the *Agreement on Agriculture*. The Footnote contains a non-exclusive list of forbidden measures, as evidenced by its use of the word "includes." This word means the Uruguay Round negotiators realized there are non-tariff measures they did not specifically identify that have yet to be converted to tariffs. These measures are no less forbidden than the listed examples. Further, the Uruguay Round negotiators knew how to make the distinction between converted and unconverted measures. Whereas Article 4:2 speaks of "have been required to be converted," Article 5:1 uses the phrase measures that "have been converted" (thereby permitting a Member to impose a special safeguard only on agricultural imports in respect of which a non-tariff measure actually has been changed to a tariff). Thus, if the negotiators had wanted to restrict Article 4:2 to measures converted during the Round, then they would have used the past tense, as they had in Article 5:1.

Having explained the legal significance of the present perfect tense for the scope of Article 4:2, the Appellate Body turned to Chile's next contention — that an additional specific duty it applies as a result of the Price Band System already is an "ordinary customs duty" under that Article. Consequently, said Chile, Article 4:2 is irrelevant to the System, because Chile already has done what is required of it, namely, tariffication. Here, too, the Appellate Body disagreed. It found Chile's contention distorted the meaning of the word "convert" in Article 4:2. Adroitly avoiding a metaphysical discussion of the meaning of "conversion," the Appellate Body turned to its favorite lexicographic source, *The New Shorter Oxford Dictionary*. That source says "convert" means "undergo transformation," and "converted" means "changed in their nature" or "turned into something different."[10] Thus, just because a measure results in the imposition of a specific duty does not mean the measure is an ordinary customs duty. The measure leads to the form of a duty, but the nature of the measure itself remains a non-tariff barrier. To close the point, the Appellate Body used both a variable import levy and a minimum price as examples. Each is a non-tariff measure. Each results in a duty. But, neither is a duty.

Putting aside the grammatical and lexicographic debate, Chile's insurmountable problem was it had maintained a non-tariff barrier against agricultural imports even though it was under an obligation to convert that barrier to a tariff. That is, in contravention of Article 4:2 of the *Agreement on Agriculture*, Chile had resorted to a "measure," the Price Band System, which it was supposed to convert to an "ordinary customs duty." To be sure, Chile was able to prove to the Appellate Body that the Panel had not defined "ordinary customs duty" properly. But, that defect did not matter. Chile's appeal hinged far more on the analogies between its System and two of the items listed in Footnote 1 to Article 4:2 (variable import levies and minimum import prices) than on this definition. To see why, suppose the Panel's analogies were wrong. That is, suppose the duties resulting from the Price Band System were "ordinary customs duties." Then, there was nothing for Chile to "convert" to a tariff, because the duties from its System already were tariffs, not "measures" forbidden by Article 4:2. How, asked Chile, could Argentina and the Panel possibly think the additional specific duties applied under the System were non-tariff measures of the kind to be converted to tariffs? They were like any other ordinary customs duty, so Article 4:2 was inapplicable to them because they are what the Article seeks, namely, a converted non-tariff barrier s into tariffs. (As just discussed, Chile made this kind of argument on appeal, but unsuccessfully.)

Thus, quite appropriately, the Appellate Body spent considerable time and effort critically analyzing the analogies. Indeed, one way to understand the appeal is to look past the legal jargon and technicalities associated with the *Agriculture Agreement*. The appeal amounted to a spirited debate over one of the most important tools of a lawyer: reasoning by analogy. Lest there be any doubt about the universality of this tool, that somehow it exists in the toolkit of only common law lawyers, let it be remembered that analogical reasoning is a source of Islamic law. In the Classical Theory of the *Shari'a*, there are four such sources: *kiyaas* (reasoning by analogy) and *ijmaa* (the consensus of the *ulama*) supplement the *Qur'an* and *sunna* of the Prophet (PBUH) as the roots (or "*usuul*") of principles and rules.

How, then, did the Appellate Body reach the conclusion the Panel's analogies between (1) Chile's Price Band System and a variable import levy, and (2) the System and a minimum import price, were persuasive? Citing its opinion in *Beef Hormones*, the Appellate Body observed the Panel rendered a legal characterization when it interpreted the terms "variable import levies" and "minimum import prices," and applied these terms to the facts of the case — even though the Panel itself said its consideration was factual in nature. The Appellate Body did so to dispense with any objection that re-evaluating

---

[10] *Price Band* Appellate Body Report, ¶ 216.

analogies was not properly within its jurisdiction. That said, the Appellate Body re-traced each step in the Panel's analogical reasoning, and essentially agreed the Panel generally had tread correctly. There were four steps on this path.

First, the Appellate Body checked the Panel's definition of "similar." The Appellate Body felt the Panel dwelled on whether the shared characteristics were "fundamental," which set the bar too high. The trusty *New Shorter Oxford English Dictionary* explained two or more items are similar if they some, but not all, common characteristics. There must be some "resemblance or likeness," some indication the items being compared have "the same nature or kind."[11] Of consequence, said the Appellate Body, was "whether two or more things have likeness or resemblance sufficient to be *similar* to each other," and that inquiry "must be approached on an *empirical* basis."[12]

Second, the Appellate Body reviewed the characteristics shared by each of categories of non-tariff barriers listed in Footnote 1 to Article 4:2 of the *Agreement on Agriculture*. The object and purpose of the six categories — (1) quantitative restrictions, (2) variable import levies, (3) minimum import prices, (4) discretionary import licensing, (5) non-tariff measures maintained through a state-trading enterprise, and (6) voluntary export restraints — is to restrict the volume of import products in a manner different from an ordinary customs duty. Moreover, the six categories share the object and effect of distorting the price of agricultural imports in a way different from an ordinary duty. Finally, measures in the six categories disconnect the domestic price of an imported agricultural product from the world market price of that product, and thereby impede the transmission of world market price to the domestic market.

Suppose Chile's Price Band System shared these three features with the other categories. Could it then be classified as a "similar border measure," queried the Appellate Body? The answer is "not so fast," based on the lexicographic definition of "similarity." The Appellate Body said the specific configuration of Chile's System would have to have "sufficient 'resemblance or likeness to,'" or be "'of the same nature or kind'" as, *at least one* of the specific categories of non-tariff measures listed in Footnote 1.[13] Chile did not dispute that the relevant categories were variable import levies and minimum import prices.

It is worth pausing here to observe the implications of Step Two. The Appellate Body was keeping the bar for "similarity" reasonably high. It would not do simply to liken Chile's Price Band System to the generic category of "similar border measure" in Footnote 1 of Article 4:2 of the *Agriculture Agreement*. The Appellate Body insisted, in addition, on a showing the System was akin to one of the six specific categories. Why? That is, why not call it quits with an analogy to the generic category? The most likely reason is such an analogy would beg the question of "similarity," and create circularity: the System would be "similar" to the six specific categories because it would be

---

[11] *Price Band* Appellate Body Report, ¶ 226.

[12] *Price Band* Appellate Body Report, ¶ 226 (emphasis added).

[13] *Price Band* Appellate Body Report, ¶ 227 (emphasis original).

a "similar border measure." In brief, detailed and dry as the Appellate Body reasoning at this step may seem, it certainly was not sloppy.

Third, the Appellate Body observed the Panel was unable to define "variable import levies" and "minimum import prices" using only the tools permitted by Article 31 of the *Vienna Convention on the Law of Treaties*. These terms were undefined in the *Agriculture Agreement*, and no other WTO text provided any clue as to their meaning. The Panel had to rely on "supplementary means of interpretation," which were permissible under Article 32 of the *Vienna Convention*. Using such means, the Panel identified four characteristics (in items (a)-(d) below), which it said were "fundamental," in a variable import levy and minimum import price scheme:

> (a) Variable levies generally operate on the basis of *two prices: a threshold, or minimum import entry price and a border or c.i.f. price for imports. The threshold price may be derived from and linked to the internal market price* as such, *or it may correspond to a governmentally determined* (guide or threshold) *price which is above the domestic market price. The import border or price reference* may correspond to individual shipment prices but is more often an administratively determined *lowest world market offer price.*

> (b) *A variable levy generally represents the difference between the threshold or minimum import entry price and the lowest world market offer price* for the product concerned. In other words, the variable levy changes systematically in response to movements in either or both of these price parameters.

> (c) *Variable levies generally operate so as to prevent the entry of imports priced below the threshold or minimum entry price.* In this respect, that is, *when prevailing world market prices are low relative to the threshold price, the protective effect of a variable levy rises, in terms of the fiscal charge imposed on imports*, whereas this charge declines in the case of *ad valorem* tariffs or remains constant in the case of specific duties.

> (d) *In addition to their protective effects, the stabilization effects* of variable levies generally play a key role in *insulating the domestic market from external price variations.*

> (e) Notifications on *minimum import prices* indicate that these measures *are generally not dissimilar from variable import levies* in many respects, including in terms of their *protective and stabilization effects*, but that their *mode of operation is generally less complicated.* Whereas variable import levies are generally based on the difference between the governmentally determined threshold and the lowest world market offer price for the product concerned, minimum import price schemes generally operate in relation to the *actual transaction value of the imports. If the price of an individual consignment is below a specified minimum import price, an additional charge is imposed corresponding to the difference.*[14]

---

[14] *Price Band* Panel Report, ¶ 7.36 (*quoted in Price Band* Appellate Body Report, fn. 204 at ¶ 229 (emphasis added)).

The Panel identified three additional features common to variable import levies and minimum import prices: they lacked transparency and predictability, and they impeded the transmission of world market prices into the importing country. On appeal, Chile did not quarrel with these characteristics.

In Step Three, the Appellate Body declined to endorse these characteristics as "fundamental." It returned to the customary rules of interpretation under the *Vienna Convention*, namely, the ordinary meaning analysis under Article 31 of the *Convention*. So, once again, the Appellate Body turned to its favorite dictionary, and looked up the words "levy," "import," "variable," and "measure" in *The New Shorter Oxford Dictionary*. The Appellate Body made the unsurprising discovery that inherent in a "variable import levy" is a formula causing an automatic change in the amount of duty, upon the occurrence of certain conditions set forth in the formula, whereas no change happens to an "ordinary customs duty" unless effected by legislative or administrative action. Continuing with its *Vienna Convention* approach, the Appellate Body turned to the object and purpose of Article 4:2. It made the unremarkable observation that the lack of transparency and predictability of variable import levies undermine the object and purpose of this provision — again, a contrast with ordinary customs duties. As for the definition of "minimum import prices," the Appellate Body noted the term meant what it sounded like — the lowest price at which a product can be imported.

What, exactly, in the minds of Appellate Body members made Chile's Price Band System "similar" to a variable import levy or minimum import price? The answer led the Appellate Body to Step Four along the same path the Panel tread. In Step Four, the Appellate Body members explained why Chile's System "shares sufficient features with these two categories of prohibited measures to resemble, or 'be of the same nature or kind' and, thus, also to be prohibited under Article 4:2."[15] First, there was a lack of transparency. Second, there was a lack of predictability. Third, and as a consequence of its opaque and uncertain nature, the System impeded the transmission of international prices into Chile's domestic market. With essentially no discussion, the Appellate Body seemed to agree with Argentina's appellate argument that all three features are associated with paradigmatic variable import levy and minimum import price schemes.

In what way did Chile's Price Band System manifest these features? One instance was the way in which Chile converted the highest and lowest world-market f.o.b. prices it had selected into c.i.f. prices. Chile added "import costs" to the upper and lower thresholds in the Band, but it had no published legislation or regulation setting out how it calculated these costs. Another manifestation of non-transparency, uncertainty, and impeding price transmission existed in how Chile set a weekly reference price for the relevant imported agricultural products. As the Appellate Body explained,

> [u]nder Chile's price band system, the price used to set the weekly reference price is the lowest f.o.b. price observed, at the time of embarkation, in any foreign "market of concern" to Chile for "qualities of products actually liable to be imported to Chile." No Chilean

---

[15] *Price Band* Appellate Body Report, ¶ 240.

legislation or regulation specifies how the international "markets of concern" and the "qualities of concern" are selected. Thus, it is not by any means certain that the weekly reference price is representative of the current world market price. Moreover, the weekly reference price used under Chile's price band system is certainly *not* representative of an average of current lowest prices found in *all* markets of concern. As a result, the process of selecting the reference price is not transparent, and it is not predictable for traders.[16]

In brief, the additional specific duty applicable to a shipment depended on the difference between the lower band and reference price. But, how Chile set the reference price was neither transparent nor predictable.

As for price transmission, the Appellate Body focused on the contrast between how Chile calculated the upper and lower threshold of its Price Band System, as well as the reference prices. Chile did not adjust reference prices for "import costs, and thus did not convert them from an f.o.b. to a c.i.f. basis. Yet, it did so for the upper and lower bands. As mentioned earlier, c.i.f. prices are higher than lower f.o.b. prices — a point the Appellate Body observed. Quite correctly, the Appellate Body explained Chile's comparison of (1) the lower f.o.b. reference price with (2) a higher c.i.f. price band surely inflated the specific duties Chile applied. After all, the amount of the specific duty equalled the difference between (1) and (2), and the gap was artificially large because of the comparison of an f.o.b. with a c.i.f. price. Because of this incongruity, and in particular because of how Chile set reference prices, the Appellate Body felt Chile's Price Band System impeded the transmission of international price developments to Chile's markets, especially in comparison with an ordinary customs duty.

Step Five in the analogical reasoning analysis involved coming to terms with the differences between Chile's Price Band System, on the one hand, and variable import levies and minimum import prices, on the other hand. That is, in Step Five the Appellate Body admitted the analogies were not perfect, agreeing Chile's System was not identical to the two forbidden categories. Table 45-2 summarizes the differences.

Unfortunately, the Appellate Body did not construct a tabular reference. Had it done so, its opinion would have been considerably more accessible to a broader audience. It also would have dispelled the impression that perhaps some Appellate Body members did not feel entirely comfortable with some features of the System, nor with paradigms to which the System was compared — variable import levies and minimum import prices.

---

[16] *Price Band* Appellate Body Report, ¶ 249 (emphasis original).

TABLE 45-2:
ANALOGIZING CHILE'S PRICE BAND SYSTEM TO A VARIABLE IMPORT LEVY AND A MINIMUM IMPORT PRICE

	Chile's Price Band System	Variable Import Levy Scheme	Minimum Import Price Scheme
What two prices are compared?	Chile compares: (1) "lower band," also called the "lower threshold" with (2) "reference price."	The importing country compares: (1) "threshold price," also called the "minimum import entry price," with (2) "reference price," also called the "price reference," or "border price."	The importing country compares: (1) "minimum import price" with (2) actual price of an individual shipment.
What data are used to calculate the lower price (which establishes the minimum price at which a shipment can enter)?	Each year, Chile calculates the lower band using five-year average monthly prices from **world** markets. Chile does not use price data from domestic markets.	The importing country links the threshold price to its **domestic** market, and may set the threshold above domestic market prices. The importing country does not use price data from world markets.	Same as a variable import levy scheme.
What data are used to calculate the second price (which is gauged against the minimum price)?	Each week, Chile calculates the reference price using data from **foreign markets of concern** to Chile. The reference price applies to all products within the same category, regardless of origin or transaction value.	The importing country examines world market prices, and sets the reference price at the lowest **world** market price.	No reference price is calculated. Rather, the importing country compares the price of each shipment to the minimum entry price. The price of each shipment is the actual transaction value of the shipment.
What protection is imposed, in addition to the MFN tariff?	Chile applies an additional specific duty. The amount of the specific duty (in U.S. dollars per unit) equals the difference between the lower band and the reference price. This amount is multiplied by the number of units in a shipment, yielding the additional specific duty. The additional specific duty brings the price of the imported shipment up to the lower band.	The importing country applies a fiscal charge if the reference price is below the threshold price. In practice, the charge is imposed if prevailing world market prices are low relative to the threshold, because the reference price depends on world market price data. The fiscal charge brings the price of the imported shipment up to the "threshold price."	The importing country applies an additional charge if the transaction value is below the minimum import price. The additional charge brings the transaction value up to the minimum import price.
What are the effects of the additional protection?	Imports are not permitted entry at a price below the lower band. Chile's domestic market is insulated from external price variations. Transmission of international prices into Chile is impeded.	Imports are not permitted entry at a price below the threshold price. The domestic market of the importing country is insulated from external price variations. Transmission of international prices into the domestic market is impeded.	Imports are not permitted entry at a price below the minimum import price. The domestic market of the importing country is insulated from external price variations. Transmission of international prices into the domestic market is impeded.

Table 45-2 indicates, in its Price Band System, Chile did not derive a reference price from actual transaction values. Rather, Chile computed reference prices using the lowest prices on world markets (or at least those overseas markets of concern to Chile). In contrast, in a paradigmatic minimum import price scheme, the transaction value of a shipment would be gauged in relation to a specified minimum import price. The government of the importing country would impose an additional duty if the transaction value were below the minimum price. In brief, in Chile's System, a reference price depended on world market prices, whereas in a minimum import price scheme, transaction values of actual shipments mattered. Thus, Chile's System was not identical to a minimum import price scheme.

However, Chile's System resembled a variable import levy scheme. In the paradigmatic levy scheme, two values would be compared: (1) a threshold, *i.e.*, a minimum import entry price, which would be linked to the domestic market, or set by the government at above the domestic market price, and (2) a reference price, which typically would be the lowest world market offer price. If the world market price fell below the threshold, then the importing government would impose a fiscal charge on imports, regardless of the transaction value of the shipments, so as to prevent entry of the imports at below the threshold. Chile's reference prices corresponded to reference prices in the paradigmatic scheme, because both depended on data from overseas markets.

This resemblance, however, also revealed a distinction. Chile's Price Band System differed from a variable import levy in that Chile computed the lower threshold of the Band using world market price data, not data on domestic market prices. In the paradigmatic variable import levy (as well as in a minimum import price scheme), the floor price typically would be derived from or linked to the relevant domestic market price. Often, it would be set above that price (as the Panel explained in its rendition of the terms, quoted earlier). Consequently, the domestic and international markets effectively would be connected. In contrast, as Chile argued in its attack on the Panel's analogy, price bands in its System varied according to world prices, not domestic or target prices. Therefore, urged Chile, its System disconnects price movements in domestic markets from fluctuations in international markets.

Chile failed persuade the Appellate Body. The Appellate Body tracked the work of the Panel, and thereby concluded the lower threshold in Chile's Price Band System did not entirely connect the Chilean and world markets. Frequently, the lower threshold of the System equalled or exceeded the domestic price, principally because of two factors: (1) the way Chile computed the threshold (specifically, its conversion of monthly f.o.b. world-market prices to a c.i.f. basis); and (2) correlation between domestic and world prices. Put simply, said the Appellate Body, even though Chile computed the lower band from world market prices, that band operated like a substitute for domestic target prices. In turn, the Panel was correct to view the threshold as a characteristic of the System similar to a variable import levy or minimum import price.

Step Six was the final step on the Panel's path of analogical reasoning the Appellate Body retraced. In this Step, the Appellate Body weighed the significance of the distinctions it and the Panel had identified in the previous Step. The Appellate Body found they were more or less insignificant. The differences between Chile's Price Band System and the paradigmatic variable import levy or minimum import price did not matter. The Appellate Body not only concluded the System was similar to the variable import levy and minimum import price categories, but also said the System fit within the category of a "similar border measure":

> although there are some dissimilarities between Chile's price band system and the features of "minimum import prices" and "variable

import levies" we have identified earlier, the way Chile's system is designed, and the way it operates in its overall nature, are sufficiently "similar" to the features of both of those two categories of prohibited measures to make Chile's price band system — in its particular features — a "similar border measure" within the meaning of footnote 1 to Article 4:2.[17]

In brief, Chile's System need not be identical to be "similar" to two of the categories in the footnote, and the System certainly fit within the language of "similar border measure." Thus, Article 4:2 of the *Agriculture Agreement* prohibit the System.

With this finding, the thrust—parry match ended. Chile uttered a last gasp before losing: surely, capping the total amount of duties it could levy as a result of its Price Band System at 31.5 percent *ad valorem* — the bound rate in its Schedule — mattered? Chile hoped the cap in the System would differentiate it enough from variable import levy and a minimum import price schemes to save it from condemnation. The Appellate Body extinguished this hope. Nothing in the *Agreement on Agriculture* — either in Article 4:2 itself, in the Article 4:2 context (the Attachment to Annex 5, called "Guidelines for the Calculation of Tariff Equivalents for the Specific Purpose Specified in Paragraph 6 and 10 of this Annex"), or other relevant contexts (especially GATT Articles II:1(b) and XI:1) — suggests a cap would legalize an otherwise prohibited non-tariff barrier.

Like many last-gasp efforts, Chile's lacked logic, and the Appellate Body did not hesitate to highlight three fatal flaws. First, the cap did nothing to enhance the transparency or predictability of the Price Band System. Second, while the cap reduced the extent of trade distortions by limiting the fluctuations of duties, it did not eliminate those distortions. Consequently, with or without the cap, the System was incongruous with the object and purpose of Article 4:2 of the *Agriculture Agreement* — to increase market access for farm products.

Third, if a cap mattered, then the rule of Article 4:2 could be easily circumvented. A WTO Member could sanctify a variable import levy or minimum import price scheme by putting a limit on the *ad valorem* tariff rate applicable under the scheme. Why would the Uruguay Round negotiators, on the one hand, obligate countries to convert non-tariff barriers to ordinary customs duties, and bind those duties, but, on the other hand, allow countries to maintain non-tariff measures and additional duties via these measures? Logically, the availability of the second option would undermine the incentive for a country to take the first option. That is, asked the Appellate Body rhetorically, why would a WTO Member convert a non-tariff measure, if it could keep the measure and simply bind the tariff-equivalent associated with the measure? The match was over.

---

[17] *Price Band* Appellate Body Report, ¶¶ 252.

Chapter 46

DOMESTIC SUPPORT AND EXPORT SUBSIDIES

That which is large enough for the rich to covet . . . is large enough for the poor to defend.

—G.K. Chesterton, The Napoleon of Notting Hill 90-91 (1904)

Documents Supplement Assignment

1. *Havana Charter* Articles 25-28

2. GATT Articles III:8(b), XVI

3. WTO *Agreement on Agriculture*, Articles 6-11, 13, 15, 16, 19-20, Annexes 2, and 3

4. WTO *SCM Agreement* Articles 1, 3, 9

I. DOMESTIC SUPPORT AND THE BOXES

The WTO *Agreement on Agriculture* is a watershed accord in many respects, not the least of which is its system to categorize the large, complex universe of agricultural subsidies. The *Agreement* identifies 3 categories, or "boxes": Amber, Blue, and Green. It identifies 2 further categories, *De Minimis* subsidies and export subsidies. Doha Round negotiators followed the edifice constructed by their Uruguay Round predecessors.

An obvious threshold question is why care about the different Boxes. The short answer is only Amber Box subsidies are subject to reduction commitments. The Aggregate Measure of Support (AMS) is the statistic Uruguay Round negotiators devised to gauge the total amount of subsidy payments a WTO Member provides to its agricultural sector. Subsidy programs differ considerably from Member to Member. As one example, generally speaking, the EU tends to rely more heavily than the U.S. on Blue Box payments. Members also change their programs over time. As an illustration, under the *1996 Farm Bill*, the U.S. did not employ counter-cyclical payments (whereby the payment to a farmer varies inversely with the world market price for the subsidized crop). But, it introduced them in the *2002 Farm Bill*. Given the variances in subsidy programs, the AMS is supposedly a great equalizing statistic. Based on the AMS, WTO Members then make reduction commitments — with two critical caveats.

First, AMS is measured during a base period, which under the *Agriculture Agreement* happens to be 1986-88. During that period, subsidy payments by developed countries were at record highs. Thus, reduction commitments were less impressive, because cuts were applied to an elevated starting point.

Second, Blue Box and Green Box subsidies are excluded from the AMS subject to cuts. In effect, they are taken out of the statistic, meaning cuts apply to a narrower range of programs than the totality. The second caveat is why categorization of subsidy programs is so important. Put bluntly, to immunize a program from subsidy cuts, keep a program out of the Amber Box.

Both caveats help explain why developing and least developed countries feel cheated by the *Agriculture Agreement*. The retort from developed countries is the developing and least developed countries entered freely into the Grand Bargain of the Uruguay Round. The reality, however, is most of them lacked the legal capacity — and many still do — to understand what they were signing.

What, then, are the Boxes? The Blue Box contains agricultural subsidies that are linked to output. These production-linked subsidies take the form of payments to farmers not to produce a certain type or volume of crop. They sometimes are called "production set-asides," meaning that recipients obtain funds by removing, or setting aside, some of their arable land from cultivation. Blue Box subsidies do distort trade, albeit not as egregiously as an export subsidy (which, obviously, is designed to boost exports of a commodity). To the extent a Blue Box subsidy results in a material diminution of output, then (ceteris paribus) it is likely to reduce the available exportable surplus from the subsidizing country. If that reduction is significant enough, and if the country is a major player in the world market for the commodity to which the Blue Box subsidy pertains, then the world market price of that commodity could rise.

The Green Box is the solution Uruguay Round negotiators devised to respond to the central, albeit ambiguous, objection to agricultural trade liberalization. That objection is "agriculture is different." A subsidy program qualifies for the Green Box if it is de-coupled from production (or de-coupled from a lack of production). That is, payments to farmers must not be linked to decisions about the type or volume of crop grown or not grown. Because they are de-coupled from output, they do not influence the availability of farm products in a domestic market, or for export. In other words, Green Box subsidies do not distort trade — the pattern and quantities of farm products imported and exported — or, at worst, they are minimally trade distorting. That being the case, no legal liability under the *Agriculture Agreement* attaches to a Green Box subsidy program.

Like Green Light non-agriculture subsidies under the WTO *Agreement on Subsidies and Countervailing Measures (SCM Agreement)*, Green Box agricultural subsidies are not actionable. Unlike the Green Light category, which lapsed on 31 December 2000, the Green Box category continues in perpetuity. Also unlike its non-agricultural analog, which was restricted to three categories of programs (environmental retrofitting, regional development, and research and development), the Green Box category is not program specific. Thus, for example, if France would like to preserve pretty fields and lovely villages depicted by Impressionist artists, then it can do so through a Green Box program. If the U.S. would like to preserve the family farm by providing direct income payments to farmers, then it likewise can do so. It is only if France or the U.S. link, directly or indirectly, financial support to production decisions does the specter of legal liability arise. Put simply, the Green Box preserves a considerable degree of sovereignty for each WTO Member in its farm policies.

The Amber Box is simply "everything else." It comprises all subsidy programs qualifying neither for the Blue nor Green Box. At the risk of oversimplifying a complex topic, the value of Amber Box payments for a developed or developing country WTO Member as of the defined base period is the basis for the reduction commitment and bound level of support for that Member. Least developed countries are exempt from any reduction commitments.

II. THE GREEN BOX AND THE *UPLAND COTTON* CASE

WTO APPELLATE BODY REPORT, *UNITED STATES — SUBSIDIES ON UPLAND COTTON*
WT/DS267/AB/R (adopted 21 March 2005) (complaint by Brazil)

V. Domestic Support

A. Article 13(a) of the *Agreement on Agriculture* — Planting Flexibility Limitations

1. Introduction

. . . .

311. Production flexibility contract payments were introduced by the *FAIR Act of 1996* [*i.e.*, the *Federal Agricultural Improvement and Reform Act of 1996*, also called the *1996 Farm Bill*]] for the 1996-2002 marketing years, and were made to certain historical producers of seven eligible commodities, including upland cotton. Historical producers could enroll acres upon which upland cotton had been grown during a base period and were allocated upland cotton "base acres" (as well as a farm-specific yield per acre), for which payment would be made at a rate specified each year for upland cotton. The production flexibility contract program dispensed with the requirement that producers continue to plant upland cotton in order to receive payments; instead, payments would generally be made regardless of what the producer chose to grow, and whether or not the producer chose to produce anything at all. However, there were limits to this planting flexibility. Specifically, payments were reduced or eliminated if fruits and vegetables (other than lentils, mung beans, and dry peas) were planted on upland cotton base acres, subject to certain other exceptions.

312. Direct payments were introduced by the *FSRI Act of 2002* [*i.e.*, the *Farm Security and Rural Investment Act of 2002*, or *2002 Farm Bill*]] for the 2002-2007 marketing years. They essentially replaced production flexibility contract payments under the *FAIR Act of 1996*, while also expanding the program to take in historical production of some additional commodities. Both production flexibility contract payments and direct payments were available

for the 2002 crop, but production flexibility contract payments made for that crop were deducted from direct payments made for that crop. Like production flexibility contract payments for upland cotton, direct payments for upland cotton were dependent on base acres allocated by reference to the production of upland cotton during certain base periods. The payments were made each year at a rate fixed for the entire 2002-2007 period at 6.67 cents per pound of upland cotton. As was the case under the production flexibility contract program, producers were not required to grow any particular crop in order to receive direct payments, and could choose to grow nothing at all. In addition to fruits and vegetables (other than lentils, mung beans, and dry peas), wild rice was added to the planting flexibility limitations.

313. The Panel found that the amount of payments under the production flexibility contract program and the direct payment program is "related to the type of production undertaken by the producer after the base period." On this basis, the Panel found that these payments and "the legislative and regulatory provisions that provide for the planting flexibility limitations in the DP programme" do not fully conform to paragraph 6(b) of Annex 2 of the *Agreement on Agriculture*. The Panel concluded that these measures are thus not green box measures, and added that these measures "do not comply with the condition in paragraph (a) of Article 13 of the *Agreement on Agriculture*" and are therefore "non-green box measures covered by paragraph (b) of Article 13."

2. Appeal by the United States

314. The United States appeals the Panel's finding that direct payments, production flexibility contract payments, and the legislative and regulatory provisions that establish and maintain the direct payments program, are not green box measures sheltered from challenge by virtue of Article 13(a) of the *Agreement on Agriculture*. . . .

315. The United States takes issue with the Panel's finding that the planting flexibility limitations mean that the "amount of payments" under the production flexibility contract and direct payment programs is "related to the type of production undertaken by the producer after the base period," within the meaning of paragraph 6(b) of Annex 2 to the *Agreement on Agriculture*. According to the United States, a *negative* direction in respect of production of certain goods — that is, conditioning payment on a producer's *non*-production of certain goods — does not make the amount of payments "related to the type of production." The United States submits that this interpretation serves the "fundamental requirement" found in paragraph 1 of Annex 2 that green box measures "have no, or at most minimal, trade-distorting effects or effects on production."

. . . .

317. Brazil submits that the distinction drawn by the United States between "permitted" (or positive) and "prohibited" (or negative) categories of crops is artificial because the effect of both categories is identical: in both cases, production is channeled *away from* certain "prohibited" crops (for which no payments are made) and *towards* other "permitted" crops (for which payments

are made). Thus, the incentives and disincentives are precisely the same. In both cases, "the amount of" the payment is intrinsically "related to" undertaking production of the "permitted" crops, and not undertaking production of the "prohibited" crops. According to Brazil, the Panel's factual findings support this view because it found that the prohibition on fruits and vegetables (and wild rice in respect of direct payments) imposes "significant constraints" on production decisions and creates incentives for the production of eligible crops rather than those crops that are prohibited.

3. Analysis

. . . .

319. [By virtue of Article 13 of the *Agreement on Agriculture,* the so-called *"Peace Clause,"*] . . . domestic support that conforms fully to the provisions of Annex 2 — that is "green box" support, which is exempt from the domestic support reduction obligations of the *Agreement on Agriculture* — is also exempt, during the implementation period [1 January 1995 through 31 December 2003], from actions based on Article XVI of GATT 1994 and the actionable subsidies provisions of Part III of the *SCM Agreement.*

320. The United States claims that production flexibility contract payments and direct payments are domestic support that conforms fully to the provisions of Annex 2 because they are "[d]ecoupled income support" within the meaning of paragraph 6 of that Annex. . . .

. . . .

322. [T]here is no disagreement between the participants that the amount of payments under the production flexibility contract and direct payment programs depended upon a formula that centred on "base acres," which were established on the basis of the historical production of upland cotton. Nor does the United States dispute that there are limitations on producers' ability to produce certain products, while also receiving production flexibility contract payments or direct payments with respect to upland cotton base acres. Therefore, the question before us regarding the consistency of production flexibility contract payments and direct payments with paragraph 6(b) of Annex 2 is a limited one. It does not concern a measure *requiring* producers to grow certain crops in order to receive payments; it also does not concern a measure with complete planting *flexibility* that provides payments without regard whatsoever to the crops that are grown. Indeed, it does not concern a measure that requires the production of any crop at all; nor does it involve a measure that totally *prohibits* the growing of any crops as a condition for payments. The question before us in this appeal thus concerns a measure with a *partial* exclusion combining planting flexibility and payments with the reduction or elimination of the payments when the excluded crops are produced, while providing payments even when no crops are produced at all.

323. In addressing the question of the consistency of such a measure with paragraph 6(b), we note that under this provision, for income support to be *decoupled,* the "amount of such payments . . . shall not be related to . . . the type or volume of production . . . undertaken by the producer in any year after the base period." It is uncontested that the amount of payments under the

production flexibility contract and direct payment programs may be affected, depending upon whether a producer plants a crop that is permitted under the production flexibility contract or direct payment programs, or a crop that is covered by the planting flexibility limitations. The United States focuses on the term "related to" and contends that the amount of payments under the production flexibility contract and direct payment programs is not "related to" the type of production as proscribed by paragraph 6(b).

324. The ordinary meaning of the term "related to" in paragraph 6(b) of Annex 2 denotes some degree of *relationship* or *connection* between two things, here the amount of payment, on the one hand, and the type or volume of production, on the other. [The Appellate Body cited to the *Shorter Oxford English Dictionary* (2002) and *The New Shorter Oxford English Dictionary* (1993).] It covers a broader set of connections than "based on," which term is also used to describe the relationship between two things covered by paragraph 6(b). Nothing in the ordinary meaning of the term "related to" suggests that the connections covered by this expression may not encompass connections of either a "positive" nature (including directions or requirements to do something) or a "negative" nature (including prohibitions or requirements not to do something) or a combination of both. As the Panel indicated, the ordinary meaning of the term "related to" conveys "a very general notion." Indeed, the United States agrees that, as far as its ordinary meaning in the abstract is concerned, the term "related to" may be broad enough to capture both positive and negative connections, but argues that the context of paragraph 6(b) requires a more limited interpretation of the term, namely, only as covering a "positive" connection between the "amount of . . . payments" and the "type . . . of production." Like the Panel, however, we are of the view that, in the context of paragraph 6(b), the term "related to" covers both positive and negative connections between the amount of payment and the type of production.

325. Paragraph 6 of Annex 2, entitled "[d]ecoupled income support," seeks to decouple or de-link direct payments to producers from various aspects of their production decisions and thus aims at neutrality in this regard. Subparagraph (b) decouples the payments from production; subparagraph (c) decouples payments from prices; and subparagraph (d) decouples payments from factors of production. Subparagraph (e) completes the process by making it clear that no production shall be required in order to receive such payments. Decoupling of payments from production under paragraph 6(b) can only be ensured if the payments are not related to, or based upon, either a positive requirement to produce certain crops or a negative requirement not to produce certain crops or a combination of both positive and negative requirements on production of crops.

326. In contrast to the other subparagraphs of paragraph 6, paragraph 6(e) does explicitly distinguish between positive and negative production requirements, because it prohibits positive requirements to produce. The Panel reasoned that "[i]f paragraph 6(b) could be satisfied by ensuring that no production was required to receive payments, paragraph 6(e) would be redundant." We agree with the Panel that the context provided by paragraph 6(e) indicates that a measure that provided payments, even if a producer

undertook no production at all, would not, for that reason alone, necessarily comply with paragraph 6(b). This is because other elements of that measure might still relate the amount of payments to the type or volume of production, contrary to the requirement of paragraph 6(b).

327. The United States seems to argue that the Panel's interpretation of the relationship between paragraphs 6(b) and 6(e) would subsume paragraph 6(e) within the scope of paragraph 6(b), thereby rendering it redundant. In our view, however, paragraph 6(e) continues to serve a purpose distinct from that of paragraph 6(b). It highlights a different aspect of decoupling income support. In prohibiting Members from making green-box measures contingent on production, paragraph 6(e) implies that Members are allowed, in principle, to require no production at all. Accordingly, payments conditioned on a total ban on any production may qualify as decoupled income support under paragraph 6(e). Even assuming that payments contingent on a total production ban could be seen to relate the amount of the payment to the *volume* of production within the meaning of paragraph 6(b) — the volume of production being nil — giving meaning and effect to both paragraphs 6(b) and 6(e) suggests a reading of paragraph 6(b) that would not disallow a total ban on any production.

328. In addressing the United States' argument on this point, we recall that the measures at issue in this appeal do not provide for payments contingent on a *total ban* on production of *any* crops. The measures at issue here combine payments and planting flexibility in respect of certain covered crops with the reduction or elimination of such payments when certain other excluded crops are produced. The United States argues that, if paragraph 6(e) means that a Member may require a producer not to produce a particular product, "it would not make sense to then prohibit a Member, under paragraph 6(b), from making the amount of payment contingent on fulfilling that requirement." However, in our view, the mere fact that under paragraph 6(e) "[n]o production shall be required in order to receive such payments" does not mean that a partial exclusion of certain crops from payments, coupled with production flexibility regarding other crops, must be consistent with paragraph 6(b).

329. We agree with the Panel that a partial exclusion of some crops from payments has the potential to channel production towards the production of crops that remain eligible for payments. In contrast to a total production ban, the channeling of production that may follow from a partial exclusion of some crops from payments will have *positive* production effects as regards crops eligible for payments. The extent of this will depend on the scope of the exclusion. We note in this regard that the Panel found, as a matter of fact, that planting flexibility limitations at issue in this case "significantly constrain production choices available to PFC and DP payment recipients and effectively eliminate a significant proportion of them." The fact that farmers may continue to receive payments if they produce nothing at all does not detract from this assessment because, according to the Panel, it is not the option preferred by the "overwhelming majority" of farmers, who continue to produce some type of permitted crop. In the light of these findings by the Panel, we are unable to agree with the United States' argument that the planting flexibility limitations only negatively affect the production of crops that are excluded.

330. We are not persuaded otherwise by the United States' reliance upon the terms "amount of such payments" and "undertaken" in the text of paragraph 6(b). According to the United States, the Panel assumes that the "amount of such payments" in paragraph 6(b) can be related to the current type of production because, in some circumstances, a recipient that produces fruits, vegetables or wild rice "receives less payment than that recipient otherwise would have been entitled to." However, for the United States, in that case, the only "amount" of payment that is even arguably "related to" current production is "zero," because those crops are excluded from payment eligibility. The United States further argues, with respect to the phrase "production . . . undertaken by the producer," that the ordinary meaning of the term "undertake" includes to "attempt." In this case, the planting flexibility limitations on a certain range of products, with respect to base acreage, would not relate the amount of payments to production "attempted" by the recipient; rather, the amount of payment is related to or based on the type of production *not* "attempted."

331. In our view, the concepts of "type or volume of production . . . undertaken by the producer" and the "amount of . . . payments" are linked in paragraph 6(b) by the requirement that one "not be related to" the other. This requires a consideration of *the relationship* between the type or volume of production and the amount of payment under a program after the base period. A program that disallows payments when certain crops are produced relates the amount of the payment to the type of production undertaken. The flexibility to produce and receive payment for certain crops covered by a program, combined with the reduction or elimination of such payments when excluded crops are produced, creates a link with the type of production undertaken contrary to paragraph 6(b). This is so because the opportunity for farmers to receive payments for producing covered crops, while less or no such payments are made to farmers who produce excluded crops, provides an incentive to switch from producing excluded crops to producing crops eligible for payments.

332. The United States also contends that its measures, which condition payment on the non-production of certain products, "further the fundamental requirement [in paragraph 1 of Annex 2 to the *Agreement on Agriculture*] that such measures 'have no, or at most minimal, trade-distorting effects or effects on production,'" because their only effects are to reduce production of the prohibited crops. It follows, for the United States, that paragraph 6(b) should not address "negative" prohibitions on the production of certain crops, such as the United States' measures, given that they comply, inherently, with the fundamental requirement. Brazil argues that if paragraph 6(b) is violated, this *ipso facto* violates the fundamental requirement of paragraph 1 of Annex 2 and further analysis is not required.

333. We note that the first sentence of paragraph 1 of Annex 2 lays down a "fundamental requirement" for green box measures, such that they must have "no, or at most minimal, trade-distorting effects or effects on production." The second sentence of paragraph 1 provides that, "[a]ccordingly," green box measures must conform to the basic criteria stated in that sentence, "plus" the policy-specific criteria and conditions set out in the remaining paragraphs of Annex 2, including those in paragraph 6.

334. . . . . [T]he Panel found that the planting flexibility limitations . . . "significantly constrain" production decisions. However one reads the "fundamental requirement" in paragraph 1 of Annex 2, given the factual findings of the Panel, the facts of this case do not present a situation in which the planting flexibility limitations demonstrably have "no, or at most minimal," trade-distorting effects or effects on production.

III. AMS REDUCTION COMMITMENTS, RED LIGHT IMPORT SUBSTITUTION SUBSIDIES, AND THE 2005 *UPLAND COTTON* CASE

WTO APPELLATE BODY REPORT, *UNITED STATES — SUBSIDIES ON UPLAND COTTON*
WT/DS267/AB/R (adopted 21 March 2005) (complaint by Brazil)

2. Panel Findings

518. [An earlier Chapter describes the price-contingent measures, including Step 2 Payments, Brazil successfully attacks in the *Cotton* case.] Before the Panel, Brazil argued that Step 2 payments to domestic users of upland cotton are *per se* import substitution subsidies that are inconsistent with Articles 3.1(b) and 3.2 of the *SCM Agreement*. [As the Appellate Body points out in a footnote: "Before the Panel, Brazil also claimed that Step 2 payments to *domestic users* are contrary to Article III:4 of the GATT 1994 and that they are not justified under Article III:8(b) because they are not exclusively paid to domestic *producers* of cotton, but rather to domestic *users*. The Panel exercised judicial economy in respect of this claim, in the light of the fact that it had already found the same measure to be inconsistent with Articles 3.1(b) and 3.2 of the *SCM Agreement*. Brazil has not appealed the Panel's exercise of judicial economy."] Brazil explained that Step 2 payments to domestic users are "contingent on the use of domestic over imported goods within the meaning of Article 3.1(b) of the *SCM Agreement*" because the payments "are 'conditional' on proof of consumption of domestically produced upland cotton."

519. The United States did not dispute that Step 2 payments are "subsidies" and that to receive a Step 2 payment a domestic user must "open a bale of domestically produced baled upland cotton." The United States, however, asserted that Step 2 payments to domestic users of upland cotton are included, and they comply with, the United States' domestic support reduction commitments pursuant to Article 6.3 of the *Agreement on Agriculture*. As Step 2 payments to domestic users are permitted under the *Agreement on Agriculture*, the United States argued that these payments cannot be contrary to Article 3 of the *SCM Agreement*. This is because the introductory language of Article 3.1 of the *SCM Agreement* makes it clear that that provision applies "[e]xcept as provided in the *Agreement on Agriculture*." The United States additionally asserted that "pursuant to Article 21 of the *Agreement on Agriculture*, all of the Annex 1A agreements (including the *SCM Agreement*) apply subject to the provisions of the *Agreement on Agriculture*."

. . . .

3. Arguments on Appeal

526. On appeal, the United States requests us to reverse the Panel's findings. According to the United States, the Panel's conclusion fails to give meaning to the introductory phrase "[e]xcept as provided in the *Agreement on Agriculture*" of Article 3.1 of the *SCM Agreement*. This phrase not only applies to export subsidies covered by Article 3.1(a) of the *SCM Agreement*, but also to import substitution subsidies covered by Article 3.1(b). The United States contends that Step 2 payments to domestic users are properly classified as domestic support subject to reduction commitments under Article 6 of the *Agreement on Agriculture*. Indeed, paragraph 7 of Annex 3 requires that measures directed at agricultural processors shall be included in the AMS to the extent that such measures benefit the producers of the basic agricultural products. This approach is consistent with the objective of the *Agreement on Agriculture* of providing for substantial progressive reductions in agricultural support and protection sustained over an agreed period of time. . . .

527. Brazil requests that we uphold the Panel's findings. According to Brazil, "[t]he obligations in the *Agreement on Agriculture* and the *SCM Agreement* apply cumulatively, unless there is an exception or a conflict." In Brazil's view, no conflict arises. Under the *Agreement on Agriculture*, WTO Members enjoy a right to grant domestic support in favour of agricultural producers. However, this does not create a conflict with Article 3.1(b) of the *SCM Agreement*, because it is perfectly possible for Members to grant domestic support without making payments contingent on domestic content. In other words, Members can fully enjoy their right to grant domestic support *and* comply with Article 3.1(b).

528. Brazil asserts that this interpretation is consistent with a primary objective of the covered agreements, namely, avoiding discrimination under the national treatment rule. It is also consistent with an adopted 1958 GATT panel report involving a subsidy to agricultural producers that was contingent on purchase of domestic goods. [Brazil's reference was to GATT Panel Report, *Italy — Agricultural Machinery*, para. 16. That Panel, said Brazil, recognized that the GATT contracting parties were entitled to grant support to agricultural producers but found that this could be done without granting domestic content subsidies.] Thus, Brazil states that domestic content subsidies in favour of agricultural producers have been understood to be impermissible since 1958, so there is nothing novel about Brazil's complaint. The *Agreement on Agriculture* did not mark a step back to allowing discrimination and protection that was prohibited under the GATT 1947. Therefore, domestic support under the *Agreement on Agriculture* can and must be granted consistently with Article 3.1(b) of the *SCM Agreement* and Article III:4 of the GATT 1994.

4. Does Article 3.1(b) of the *SCM Agreement* Apply to Agricultural Products?

529. At the outset, we note that the United States did not dispute before the Panel that, if the *SCM Agreement* were applicable, "user marketing (Step 2) payments to domestic users [would] constitute a subsidy conditional or dependent upon the use of domestic over imported goods within the meaning

of Article 3.1(b)" of that *Agreement*. Instead, before the Panel and on appeal, the United States asserts that Article 3.1(b) of the *SCM Agreement* is inapplicable to Step 2 payments to domestic users because these payments are consistent with the United States' domestic support reduction commitments under the *Agreement on Agriculture*.

530. . . . [T]he introductory language of the *chapeau* [of Article 3:1(b) of *SCM Agreement*] makes it clear that the *Agreement on Agriculture* prevails over Article 3 of the *SCM Agreement*, but only to the extent that the former contains an exception.

531. Article 21.1 of the *Agreement on Agriculture* . . . deals more broadly with the relationship between that *Agreement* and the other covered agreements relating to the trade in goods. . . .

532. We agree that Article 21.1 could apply in the three situations described by the Panel, namely:

> . . . where, for example, the domestic support provisions of the *Agreement on Agriculture* would prevail in the event that an explicit carve-out or exemption from the disciplines in Article 3.1(b) of the *SCM Agreement* existed in the *text* of the *Agreement on Agriculture*. Another situation would be where it would be impossible for a Member to comply with its domestic support obligations under the *Agreement on Agriculture* and the Article 3.1(b) prohibition simultaneously. Another situation might be where there is an explicit authorization in the text of the *Agreement on Agriculture* that would authorize a measure that, in the absence of such an express authorization, would be prohibited by Article 3.1(b) of the *SCM Agreement*.

The Appellate Body has interpreted Article 21.1 to mean that the provisions of the GATT 1994 and of other Multilateral Trade Agreements in Annex 1A apply, "except to the extent that the *Agreement on Agriculture* contains specific provisions dealing specifically with the same matter." [The Appellate Body cited to its Report, *EC — Bananas III*, para. 155, and also to its Report in *Chile — Price Band System*, para. 186.] There could be, therefore, situations other than those identified by the Panel where Article 21.1 of the *Agreement on Agriculture* may be applicable.

533. The key issue before us is whether the *Agreement on Agriculture* contains "specific provisions dealing specifically with the same matter" as Article 3.1(b) of the *SCM Agreement*, that is, subsidies contingent upon the use of domestic over imported goods. We, therefore, turn to the relevant provisions of the *Agreement on Agriculture*.

. . . .

539. The United States finds in the second sentence of paragraph 7 of Annex 3 of the *Agreement on Agriculture* an exception to the broad prohibition against subsidies contingent upon the use of domestic over imported goods that is established in Article 3.1(b) of the *SCM Agreement*. We note that Annex 3 sets out instructions on how to calculate WTO Members' AMS. Paragraph 7 is one of 13 paragraphs contained in Annex 3. It reads:

> The AMS shall be calculated as close as practicable to the point of first sale of the basic agricultural product concerned. Measures directed at

agricultural processors shall be included to the extent that such measures benefit the producers of the basic agricultural products.

540. Neither of the two sentences in paragraph 7 of Annex 3 refers to import substitution subsidies. Paragraph 7 of Annex 3 reflects a preference for calculating domestic support as near as possible to the stage of production of an agricultural good. Hence, the first sentence of paragraph 7 of Annex 3 provides that "[t]he AMS shall be calculated as close as practicable to the point of first sale of the basic agricultural product concerned." The second sentence of paragraph 7 recognizes situations where subsidies are not provided directly to the agricultural producer, but rather to an agricultural processor, yet the measures may benefit the producers of the basic agricultural good. This sentence also clarifies that only the portion of the subsidy that benefits the producers of the basic agricultural good, and not the entire amount, shall be included in a Member's AMS.

541. It may well be that a measure that is an import substitution subsidy could fall within the second sentence of paragraph 7 as "[m]easures directed at agricultural processors [that] shall be included [in the AMS calculation] to the extent that such measures benefit the producers of the basic agricultural products." There is nothing, however, in the text of paragraph 7 that suggests that such measures, when they are import substitution subsidies, are exempt from the prohibition in Article 3.1(b) of the *SCM Agreement*. We agree with the Panel that there is a clear distinction between a provision that requires a Member to include a certain type of payment (or part thereof) in its AMS calculation and one that would authorize subsidies that are contingent on the use of domestic over imported goods.

542. The United States argues that, if payments to processors that fall within paragraph 7 are not exempted from the prohibition in Article 3.1(b) of the *SCM Agreement*, paragraph 7 would be rendered inutile. According to the United States, if domestic users were allowed to claim Step 2 payments, regardless of the origin of the cotton, this "would cause the benefit to [domestic] cotton producers to evaporate" and the "subsidy would be transformed from a subsidy 'in favor of agricultural producers' to a simple input subsidy." Rather than "a cotton subsidy," it would become a "textile subsidy." Like the Panel, we do not believe that the scope of paragraph 7 is limited to measures that have an import substitution component in them. There could be other measures covered by paragraph 7 of Annex 3 that do not necessarily have such a component. Indeed, Brazil submits that if the Step 2 payments were provided to United States processors of cotton, regardless of the origin of the cotton, these processors "would still buy *at least* some U.S. upland cotton, so producers would continue to derive *some* benefit." Thus, paragraph 7 of Annex 3 refers more broadly to measures directed at agricultural processors that benefit producers of a basic agricultural product and, contrary to the United States' assertion, it is not rendered inutile by the Panel's interpretation. WTO Members may still provide subsidies directed at agricultural processors that benefit producers of a basic agricultural commodity in accordance with the *Agreement on Agriculture*, as long as such subsidies do not include an import substitution component.

543. In addition to paragraph 7 of Annex 3, the United States draws our attention to Article 6.3 of the *Agreement on Agriculture*. The United States

points out that Article 6.3 explicitly provides that a WTO Member "shall be considered to be *in compliance* with its domestic support reduction commitments in any year in which its domestic support in favour of agricultural producers expressed in terms of Current Total AMS does not exceed the corresponding annual or final bound commitment level." (emphasis added)

544. Like paragraph 7 of Annex 3, Article 6.3 does not explicitly refer to import substitution subsidies. Article 6.3 deals with domestic support. It establishes only a *quantitative* limitation on the amount of domestic support that a WTO Member can provide in a given year. The quantitative limitation in Article 6.3 applies generally to all domestic support measures that are included in a WTO Member's AMS. Article 3.1(b) of the *SCM Agreement* prohibits subsidies that are contingent — that is, "conditional" [citing Appellate Body Report, *Canada — Autos*, para. 123.] — on the use of domestic over imported goods.

545. Article 6.3 does not authorize subsidies that are contingent on the use of domestic over imported goods. It only provides that a WTO Member shall be considered to be in compliance with its domestic support *reduction commitments* if its Current Total AMS does not exceed that Member's annual or final bound commitment level specified in its Schedule. It does not say that compliance with Article 6.3 of the *Agreement on Agriculture* insulates the subsidy from the prohibition in Article 3.1(b). We, therefore, agree with the Panel that:

> Article 6.3 does *not* provide that compliance with such "domestic support reduction commitments" shall necessarily be considered to be in compliance with other applicable WTO obligations. Nor does it contain an explicit textual indication that otherwise prohibited measures are necessarily justified by virtue of compliance with the domestic support reduction commitments.

546. For these reasons, we find that paragraph 7 of Annex 3 and Article 6.3 of the *Agreement on Agriculture* do not deal specifically with the same matter as Article 3.1(b) of the *SCM Agreement*, that is, subsidies contingent upon the use of domestic over imported goods.

547. We are mindful that the introductory language of Article 3.1 of the *SCM Agreement* clarifies that this provision applies "[e]xcept as provided in the *Agreement on Agriculture*." Furthermore, as the United States has pointed out, this introductory language applies to both the export subsidy prohibition in paragraph (a) and to the prohibition on import substitution subsidies in paragraph (b) of Article 3.1. As we explained previously, in our review of the provisions of the *Agreement on Agriculture* relied on by the United States, we did not find a provision that deals specifically with subsidies that have an import substitution component. By contrast, the prohibition on the provision of subsidies contingent upon the use of domestic over imported goods in Article 3.1(b) of the *SCM Agreement* is explicit and clear. Because Article 3.1(b) treats subsidies contingent on the use of domestic over imported products as prohibited subsidies, it would be expected that the drafters would have included an equally explicit and clear provision in the *Agreement on Agriculture* if they had indeed intended to authorize such prohibited subsidies provided in connection with agricultural goods. We find no provision in the *Agreement*

on Agriculture dealing specifically with subsidies contingent upon the use of domestic over imported agricultural goods.

548. Our approach in this case is consistent with the Appellate Body's approach in *EC — Bananas III*. In that case, the European Communities relied on Article 4.1 of the *Agreement on Agriculture* in arguing that the market access concessions it made for agricultural products pursuant to the *Agreement on Agriculture* prevailed over Article XIII of the GATT 1994. [The Appellate Body cited to its Report in *EC — Bananas III*, para. 153.] The Appellate Body, however, found that "[t]here is nothing in Articles 4.1 or 4.2, or in any other article of the *Agreement on Agriculture*, that deals specifically with the allocation of tariff quotas on agricultural products." [The Appellate Body cited to its Report in *EC — Bananas III*, para. 157.] It further explained that "[i]f the negotiators had intended to permit Members to act inconsistently with Article XIII of the GATT 1994, they would have said so explicitly." The situation before us is similar. We have found nothing in Article 6.3, paragraph 7 of Annex 3 or anywhere else in the *Agreement on Agriculture* that "deals specifically" with subsidies that are contingent on the use of domestic over imported agricultural products.

549. We recall that the *Agreement on Agriculture* and the *SCM Agreement* "are *both* Multilateral Agreements on Trade in Goods contained in Annex 1A of the *Marrakesh Agreement Establishing the World Trade Organization* (the "*WTO Agreement*"), and, as such, are *both* 'integral parts' of the same treaty, the *WTO Agreement*, that are 'binding on all Members.' " [The Appellate Body cited to its Reports in *Argentina — Footwear (EC)*, para. 81 (quoting from *WTO Agreement*, Article II:2). (original emphasis).] Furthermore, as the Appellate Body has explained, "a treaty interpreter must read all applicable provisions of a treaty in a way that gives meaning to *all* of them, harmoniously." [The Appellate Body cited to its Reports in *Argentina — Footwear (EC)*, para. 81 and footnote 72 thereto (referring to the Appellate Body Report, *Korea — Dairy*, para. 81; Appellate Body Report, *US — Gasoline*, p. 23, DSR 1996:I, 3 at 21; *Japan — Alcoholic Beverages II*, p. 12, DSR 1996:I, 97 at 106; and *India — Patents (US)*, para. 45). (original emphasis).] We agree with the Panel that "Article 3.1(b) of the *SCM Agreement* can be read together with the *Agreement on Agriculture* provisions relating to domestic support in a coherent and consistent manner which gives full and effective meaning to all of their terms."

550. In sum, we are not persuaded by the United States' submission that the prohibition in Article 3.1(b) of the *SCM Agreement* is inapplicable to import substitution subsidies provided in connection with products falling under the *Agreement on Agriculture*. WTO Members may still provide domestic support that is consistent with their reduction commitments under the *Agreement on Agriculture*. In providing such domestic support, however, WTO Members must be mindful of their other WTO obligations, including the prohibition in Article 3.1(b) of the *SCM Agreement* on the provision of subsidies that are contingent on the use of domestic over imported goods.

551. Turning to the particular measure before us in this dispute, we recall that the United States acknowledged before the Panel that, if the *SCM Agreement* were applicable, "user marketing (Step 2) payments to domestic

users [would] constitute a subsidy conditional or dependent upon the use of domestic over imported goods within the meaning of Article 3.1(b)" of that *Agreement*. The Panel also conducted its own analysis and concluded that:

> The use of United States domestically produced upland cotton is a condition for obtaining the subsidy. User marketing (Step 2) payments to domestic users under section 1207(a) of the *FSRI Act of 2002* are clearly conditional, or dependent upon, such use.

The United States has not appealed this finding and, therefore, we need not review it.

552. Accordingly, we *uphold* the Panel's findings . . . that Step 2 payments to domestic users of United States upland cotton, under Section 1207(a) of the *FSRI Act of 2002*, are subsidies contingent on the use of domestic over imported goods that are inconsistent with Articles 3.1(b) and 3.2 of the *SCM Agreement*.

IV.   AGRICULTURAL EXPORT SUBSIDIES, RED LIGHT EXPORT SUBSIDIES, AND THE 2005 *UPLAND COTTON* CASE

Another remarkable feat of the WTO *Agreement on Agriculture* was its effort, however ineffectual or inchoate, to identify and discipline export subsidies. During the Uruguay Round, the EU capped its export subsidies at roughly $5 billion, and (as of May 2003), spends about $2 billion on such programs. The U.S. capped its export subsidies at $15 million, but understood its export credits and export credit guarantees were not export subsidies. As with other Doha Round agricultural controversies, on export subsidies the negotiators worked within the framework established by their Uruguay Round predecessors. As explained in an earlier Chapter, during the Doha Round, negotiators endeavored to expand and strengthen disciplines on these subsidies. Accordingly, examine what the *Agreement* says about export subsidies to appreciate the Doha Round controversy to end all export subsidies within a reasonable time.

Export subsidies are the most trade-distorting form of support to farmers or processors. Their direct or indirect purpose or effect is to boost exports of a particular product from the subsidizing WTO Member. Depending on the size of the subsidy payments and volume of affected commodity, and the significance of the subsidizing Member, they may displace the like commodity originating in other countries. Displacement may occur in the subsidizing Member, countries producing the like commodity, and third countries. In addition, the subsidy may depress world market prices for the commodity, thereby causing income loss to producers of the like commodity in other countries.

Observe, also, a link between production-linked subsidies in the Amber Box and export subsidies. If farmers are paid to grow a certain crop (as the EU does under the CAP with respect to some commodities), then (ceteris paribus) the volume of that crop available for export increases. Suppose not all of the output is consumed domestically. There are three choices as to what to do with the surplus: let it rot, donate it, or export it. Export subsidies, including export credit programs, help other countries buy the surplus. In effect, one distortion (a subsidy linked to yield) leads to another distortion (overproduction), which is resolved by a third, and trade-distorting subsidy (an export subsidy).

The WTO Appellate Body has been called upon to adjudicate important issues arising from alleged agricultural export subsidies. Excerpted below are portions of Appellate Body Reports in two leading cases, *Upland Cotton* and *EU Sugar*. Brazil brought both challenges in 2004 to U.S. and European farm subsidies, respectively. Its victory put the traditional trade powers on the defensive in Doha Round negotiations, by showing their farm subsidy programs were vulnerable to judicial scrutiny at the WTO. It also highlighted the significant influence of new emerging developing countries, and underscored the diversity of legal interests and capacity within the Third World.

A. Payments to Exporters

WTO APPELLATE BODY REPORT, *UNITED STATES — SUBSIDIES ON UPLAND COTTON*
WT/DS267/AB/R (adopted 21 March 2005) (complaint by Brazil)

567. The issue raised on appeal is whether the Step 2 payments provided to exporters of United States upland cotton, under Section 1207(a) of the *FSRI Act of 2002* [*i.e.*, the *Farm Security and Rural Investment Act of 2002,* also called the *2002 Farm Bill*] are contingent on export performance within the meaning of Article 9.1(a) of the *Agreement on Agriculture* and Article 3.1(a) of the *SCM Agreement*. [Step 2 Payments are described in an earlier Chapter.]

. . . .

570. In previous appeals, the Appellate Body has explained that the WTO-consistency of an export subsidy for agricultural products has to be examined, in the first place, under the *Agreement on Agriculture* [the Appellate Body cited its Compliance Report, *Canada — Dairy (Article 21.5 — New Zealand and US)*, ¶ 123.]; the examination under the *SCM Agreement* would follow if necessary. Turning, then, to the *Agreement on Agriculture*, we note that Article 1(e) of that *Agreement* defines "export subsidies" as "subsidies contingent upon export performance, including the export subsidies listed in Article 9 of this *Agreement*."

571. Although an export subsidy granted to agricultural products must be examined, in the first place, under the *Agreement on Agriculture*, we find it appropriate, as has the Appellate Body in previous disputes, to rely on the *SCM Agreement* for guidance in interpreting provisions of the *Agreement on Agriculture*. Thus, we consider the export-contingency requirement in Article 1(e) of the *Agreement on Agriculture* having regard to that same requirement contained in Article 3.1(a) of the *SCM Agreement*. [The Appellate Body cited its Compliance Report, *United States — Tax Treatment for "Foreign Sales Corporations" — Recourse to Article 21:5 of the DSU by the European Communities*, WT/DS108/AB/RW ¶ 192 (adopted 29 January 2002).]

572. The Appellate Body has indicated, in this regard, that the ordinary meaning of "contingent" is "conditional" or "dependent" and that Article 3.1(a)

of the *SCM Agreement* prohibits subsidies that are conditional upon export performance, or are dependent for their existence on export performance. [The Appellate Body cited its Compliance Report, *Canada — Measures Affecting the Export of Civilian Aircraft — Recourse by Brazil to Article 21:5 of the DSU*, WT/DS70/AB/RW ¶ 47 (adopted 4 August 2000), and its Report, *Canada — Measures Affecting the Export of Civilian Aircraft*, WT/DS70/AB/R ¶ 166 (adopted 20 August 1999).] It has also emphasized that "a 'relationship of conditionality or dependence', namely that the granting of a subsidy should be 'tied to' the export performance, lies at the 'very heart' of the legal standard in Article 3.1(a) of the *SCM Agreement*." [The Appellate Body cited its Compliance Report, *Canada — Aircraft (Article 21.5 — Brazil)*, ¶ 47, which in turn quoted the Appellate Body Report, *Canada — Aircraft*, ¶ 171.] We are also mindful that in demonstrating export contingency in the case of subsidies that are contingent in law upon export performance, the "existence of that condition can be demonstrated on the basis of the very words of the relevant legislation, regulation or other legal instrument constituting the measure."

573. It is clear that the legal provisions pursuant to which Step 2 payments are granted to exporters of United States upland cotton, on their face, apply to exporters of United States upland cotton. Section 1207(a) of the *FSRI Act of 2002* provides that, when certain market conditions exist, the United States Secretary of Agriculture:

> . . . shall issue marketing certificates or cash payments, at the option of the recipient, to domestic users and *exporters* for documented purchases by domestic users and *sales for export by exporters.* (emphasis added)

The regulations [7 C.F.R. § 1427.103(a), 104(a)(2), and 108(d)] define "eligible exporters" as:

> A person, including a producer or a cooperative marketing association . . . regularly engaged in selling eligible upland cotton for exportation from the United States (exporter), who has entered into an agreement with CCC to participate in the upland cotton user marketing certificate program. "Eligible upland cotton" is defined as "domestically produced baled upland cotton which bale is opened by an eligible domestic user . . . or *exported* by an eligible *exporter*."

574. Furthermore, in order to claim Step 2 payments, exporters must submit an application and provide supporting documentation to the CCC, including "proof of export of eligible cotton by the exporter." [*See* 7 CFR Section 1427.108(d).] This provision confirms that the payment is "tied to" exportation. As the Panel explained, "a condition of the receipt of user marketing (Step 2) payments to exporters under section 1207(a) of the *FSRI Act of 2002* will always and inevitably be proof of exportation." Thus, on the face of the statute and regulations pursuant to which Step 2 payments are granted to exporters, the payments are "conditional upon export performance" or "dependent for their existence on export performance." [The Appellate Body cited its Compliance Report, *Canada — Measures Affecting the Export of Civilian Aircraft — Recourse by Brazil to Article 21:5 of the DSU*, WT/DS70/AB/RW ¶ 47 (adopted 4 August 2000).]

575. The United States directed the Panel's attention to the fact that the same statute and regulations also provide for similar payments to domestic users conditioned on the domestic use of United States upland cotton. According to the United States, Step 2 payments to exporters and domestic users are governed by a single legislative provision and a single set of regulations. In addition, the form and payment rate to domestic users and exporters are identical, and the payments are made from a single fund. As Step 2 payments are available to both domestic users and exporters, the United States submits that exportation is not a condition to receive payment and, therefore, the payments are not export-contingent.

576. We are not persuaded by the United States' arguments. Like the Panel, we recognize that Step 2 payments to exporters and domestic users are governed by a single legislative provision and a single set of regulations, that the form and rate of payment to exporters and domestic users are identical, and that the fund from which payments are made is a single fund. Nevertheless, we agree with the Panel that the statute and regulations pursuant to which Step 2 payments are granted do not establish a "single class" of recipients of the payments; rather, the statute and regulations clearly distinguish between two types of eligible recipients, namely, eligible exporters and eligible domestic users.

577. In addition, the statute and regulations establish different conditions that eligible exporters and eligible domestic users must meet to receive Step 2 payments. An eligible domestic user must "open" a bale of cotton to qualify for payment. [See 7 CFR § 1427.103(a).] For its part, an eligible exporter must demonstrate the upland cotton has been exported. These are distinct conditions that the statute and regulations themselves set out for the two distinct recipients of Step 2 payments. Because the conditions to qualify for payment are different, the documentation required from eligible domestic users and eligible exporters is also different. An eligible exporter must submit proof of exportation; an eligible domestic user must provide documentation indicating the number of bales opened. We agree, therefore, with the Panel's view that the statute and regulations pursuant to which Step 2 payments are granted "involve[] payment to two distinct sets of recipients (exporters or domestic users) in two distinct factual situations (export or domestic use)."

578. Furthermore, we agree with the Panel's conclusion that the fact that the subsidy is also available to domestic users of upland cotton does not "dissolve" the export-contingent nature of the Step 2 payments to exporters. The Panel's reasoning is consistent with the approach taken by the Appellate Body in *US — FSC (Article 21.5 — EC)*. [The Appellate Body observed in a footnote the Panel also found support for its reasoning in the Appellate Body's Report in *Canada — Measures Affecting the Export of Civilian Aircraft*, WT/DS70/AB/R (adopted 20 August 1999), which at paragraph 179 states ". . . the fact that some of TPC's contributions, in some industry sectors, are *not* contingent upon export performance, does not necessarily mean that the same is true for all of TPC's contributions. It is enough to show that one or some of TPC's contributions do constitute subsidies "contingent . . . in fact . . . upon export performance." (original emphasis).] In that case, the United States argued that the tax exclusion at issue was not an export-contingent

subsidy because it was available for both (i) property produced within the United States and held for use outside the United States and (ii) property produced outside the United States and held for use outside the United States. The United States asserted that, as the tax exemption was available in both circumstances, it was "export-neutral." [The Appellate Body cited its Compliance Report, Appellate Body Report, *United States — Tax Treatment for "Foreign Sales Corporations" — Recourse to Article 21:5 of the DSU by the European Communities*, WT/DS108/AB/RW ¶ 110 (adopted 29 January 2002).] According to the United States, the panel's separate examination of each situation in which the tax exemption was available "artificially bifurcat[ed]" the measure.

579. The Appellate Body rejected the United States' contention in *US — FSC (Article 21.5 — EC)* because it considered it necessary, under Article 3.1(a) of the *SCM Agreement*, "to examine separately the conditions pertaining to the grant of the subsidy in the two different situations." It then confirmed the Panel's finding that the tax exemption in the first situation, namely for property produced within the United States and held for use outside the United States, is an export-contingent subsidy. In its reasoning, the Appellate Body explained that whether or not the subsidies were export-contingent in both situations envisaged by the measure would not alter the conclusion that the tax exemption in the first situation was contingent upon export:

> Our conclusion that the ETI measure grants subsidies that are export contingent in the first set of circumstances is not affected by the fact that the subsidy can also be obtained in the second set of circumstances. The fact that the subsidies granted in the second set of circumstances *might* not be export contingent does not dissolve the export contingency arising in the first set of circumstances. Conversely, the export contingency arising in these circumstances has no bearing on whether there is an export contingent subsidy in the second set of circumstances.

580. As in *US — FSC (Article 21.5 — EC)*, the Panel in this case found that Step 2 payments are available in two situations, only one of which involves export contingency. The Panel's conclusion, therefore, is consistent with the Appellate Body's holding in *US — FSC (Article 21.5 — EC)* quoted above that "the fact that the subsidies granted in the second set of circumstances *might* not be export contingent does not dissolve the export contingency arising in the first set of circumstances."

581. The United States submits that the facts in this case are similar to those before the panel in *Canada — Dairy*. In that dispute, the complaining parties argued that the provision of milk to exporters/processors under various mechanisms (described as "special milk classes") constituted export-contingent subsidies. The panel in *Canada — Dairy* found, nevertheless, that certain special milk classes were *not* export-contingent because the "milk under such other classes is also available (often exclusively) to processors which produce for the domestic market." [The Appellate Body cited the Panel Report, *Canada — Measures Affecting the Importation of Milk and the Exportation of Dairy Products*, WT/DS103/R and WT/DS113/R ¶¶ 7.41 and fn. 496 at 7.124 (adopted 27 October 1999 as modified by the Appellate Body

Report, WT/DS103/AB/R and WT/DS113/AB/R).] The Panel, in this dispute, did not see any relevance in the Panel Report in *Canada — Dairy* because, in that case, "there was no explicit condition limiting a discrete segment of the payments of the subsidies concerned to exporters." Brazil also seeks to distinguish the factual situation in *Canada — Dairy*, explaining that it involved a single regulatory class of milk instead of two mutually exclusive regulatory categories, as is the case in the present dispute. We agree with the Panel and Brazil that the facts in *Canada — Dairy* differ from those of the present dispute. In this case, we have before us a statute and regulations that clearly distinguish between two sets of recipients — that is, eligible exporters and eligible domestic users — that must meet different conditions to receive payment. In the case of one set of recipients, eligible exporters, exportation is a necessary condition to receive payment.

582. In sum, we agree with the Panel's view that Step 2 payments are export-contingent and, therefore, an export subsidy for purposes of Article 9 of the *Agreement on Agriculture* and Article 3.1(a) of the *SCM Agreement*. The statue and regulations pursuant to which Step 2 payments are granted, on their face, condition payments to exporters on exportation. In order to claim payment, an exporter must show proof of exportation. If an exporter does not provide proof of exportation, the exporter will not receive a payment. This is sufficient to establish that Step 2 payments to exporters of United States upland cotton are "conditional upon export performance" or "dependent for their existence on export performance." [The Appellate Body cited its Compliance Report, referred to above, in *Canada — Civilian Aircraft*, ¶ 47.] That domestic users may also be eligible to receive payments under different conditions does not eliminate the fact that an exporter will receive payment only upon proof of exportation.

583. For these reasons, we *uphold* the Panel's findings . . . that Step 2 payments to exporters of United States upland cotton, pursuant to Section 1207(a) of the *FSRI Act of 2002*, constitute subsidies contingent upon export performance within the meaning of Article 9.1(a) of the *Agreement on Agriculture* and that, therefore, in providing such subsidies the United States has acted inconsistently with its obligations under Articles 3.3 and 8 of the *Agreement on Agriculture*.

584. Having explained that there is no reason to read the export-contingency requirement in the *Agreement on Agriculture* differently from that contained in Article 3.1(a) of the *SCM Agreement*, and having found that Step 2 payments to exporters of United States upland cotton are contingent upon export performance within the meaning of Article 9.1 of the *Agreement on Agriculture*, we also find that such payments are export-contingent for purposes of Article 3.1(a) of the *SCM Agreement*. Consequently, we *uphold* the Panel's findings . . . that Step 2 payments provided to exporters of United States upland cotton, pursuant to Section 1207(a) of the *FSRI Act* of 2002, are inconsistent with Articles 3.1(a) and 3.2 of the *SCM Agreement*.

B. Export Credit Guarantees

One issue in the 2005 *Cotton* case concerned American export credit guarantees for agricultural products. The U.S. has offered Export Credit

Guarantee programs since 1980. Brazil challenged — with success — these measures as illegal Red Light export subsidies under Article 3:1(a) *SCM Agreement*. In specific, it attacked three measures — the General Sales Manager (GSM) 102 and 103 Programs, and the Supplier Credit Guarantee Program (SCGP). (*See* 7 USC § 5622.) The USDA administers export credit guarantee programmes for commercial financing of American agricultural commodities through the CCC.

By statute, the CCC "shall finance or guarantee . . . only United States agricultural commodities." (7 USC § 5622(h).) The statute also sets out percentages of the total amount of export credit guarantees issued for certain fiscal years that promote the export of processed or high-value farm products. The balance of the guarantees is issued to promote bulk or raw agricultural commodity exports. The CCC operates the three Export Credit Guarantee Programs Brazil challenged, GSM 102, GSM 103, and the SCGP.

The stated purpose of these Programs indicates the CCC may use export credit guarantees to "increase exports of agricultural commodities;" "to compete against foreign agricultural exports;" "to assist countries in meeting their food and fiber needs. . .;" and "for such other purposes as the Secretary [of Agriculture] determines appropriate. . . ." (7 U.S.C. § 5622(d).) The statute authorizes the CCC to engage in the following transactions in a manner to benefit directly U.S. agricultural producers:

(1) Under the *GSM 102 Program*, guarantee repayment of credit made available to finance commercial export sales of U.S. agricultural commodities on credit terms of between 90 days and three years.

Specifically, the CCC is authorized to guarantee repayment of credit made available to finance commercial export sales of agricultural commodities from privately owned stocks on credit terms between 90 days and three years. Generally, the CCC covers 98 percent of the principal and a portion of the interest. The CCC selects the commodities according to market potential. The CCC does not provide financing to foreign banks, but rather guarantees payments due from those banks. Only foreign banks approved by the CCC are eligible for guarantees.

To obtain a payment guarantee, once a firm export sale contract is reached, the U.S. exporter applies for a guarantee, and must do so before the date of exportation. The exporter pays a fee that depends on the dollar amount guaranteed, with the relationship between fees and dollar amounts determined according to a schedule of rates applicable to different credit periods. There is a statutory cap on the fee charged of 1 percent of the guaranteed dollar value of the transaction.

Financing occurs when a CCC-approved foreign bank issues an irrevocable letter of credit in favor of the U.S. exporter. Ordinarily, this letter of credit is advised or confirmed by a financial institution in the U.S. that agrees to extend credit to the foreign bank. If the foreign bank fails to make any payment as agreed, then the exporter submits a notice of default to the CCC. The CCC pays the exporter on a valid claim for loss.

(2) Under the *GSM 103 Program*, guarantee repayment of credit made available by financial institutions in the U.S. to finance commercial

export sales of agricultural commodities on credit terms of between 3 and 10 years.

Operation of the GSM Program 103 is similar to the GSM 102 Program. There are four main differences. First, GSM 103 guarantees are "intermediate term credit guarantees," issued for terms from 3 to 10 years. (7 U.S.C. § 5641(b).) Second, only credit extended by a U.S. financial institution is eligible for the guarantee. (The credit risk associated with 3-10 year financing exceeds that for 90 days — 3 year financing, hence the limit to U.S. financial institutions.) Third, the CCC must make additional determinations when issuing a GSM 103 export credit guarantee. In particular, the statute states the CCC

> shall not guarantee . . . the repayment of credit made available to finance an export sale unless the Secretary [of Agriculture] determines such sale will: (1) develop, expand or maintain the importing country as a foreign market, on a long-term basis, for the commercial sale and export of United States agricultural commodities, without displacing normal commercial sales; (2) improve the capability of the importing country to purchase and use, on a long-term basis, United States agricultural commodities; or (3) otherwise promote the export of United States agricultural commodities.

(7 USC § 5622(c). Interestingly, the reference to "a long term basis" does not apply to determinations regarding sales to the independent states of the former Soviet Union.)) Fourth, there is no statutory cap on the origination fees the CCC may charge in connection with a GSM 103 guarantee.

> (3)   Under the *SCGP*, issue guarantees for repayment of credit made available for a period of not more than 180 days by a U.S. exporter to a buyer in another country.

Under this Program, the CCC issues guarantees to repay credit made available for a period not exceeding 180 days, where a U.S. exporter extended credit to a buyer located in a foreign country that purchased an American agricultural commodity. In other words, the exporter negotiates terms of a credit sale with the importer of the commodity. To be eligible for a CCC guarantee, the credit must be secured by a promissory note signed by the importer. That means the importer must issue a dollar-denominated promissory note in favor of the U.S. exporter in the form. The exporter may negotiate an arrangement to be paid, in full or in part, by assigning the right to proceeds that may become payable under the CCC guarantee to a U.S. financial institution.

As with the GSM 102 and 103 Programs, under the SCGP, the CCC does not provide financing. Rather, the CCC guarantees payment due from the importer. Typically, the CCC guarantees a portion (65 percent) of the value of the exports. The guarantee covers principal, but not interest. Once a firm export sale contract exists, the U.S. exporter applies for a payment guarantee, and must do so before the date of exportation. The exporter pays a fee for the guarantee calculated on the guaranteed portion of the value of the export sale. Like the GSM 102 Program, in the SCGP, there is a statutory cap on the fee charged of 1 percent of the guaranteed dollar value of the transaction. If payment is not made on the promissory note, then the exporter (or assignee) submits a notice of default to the CCC. The CCC pays a valid claim for loss.

By statute, the CCC "shall make available" for each relevant fiscal year "not less than $5,500,000,000 in credit guarantees" under these three Export Credit Guarantee Programs. (7 USC § 5641(b)(1).) The CCC retains discretion to allocate the guarantees between short and intermediate terms, and to impose "such terms and conditions as the [CCC] determines to be necessary." (7 USC § 5622(g).)

The statute also sets out restrictions on using credit guarantees. Overall, "the CCC shall not make credit guarantees available in connection with sales of agricultural commodities to any country that the Secretary [of Agriculture] determines cannot adequately service the debt associated with such sale." (7 USC § 5622(f).) Countries eligible for a CCC Export Credit Guarantee Program are categorized according to risk. The risk premium of the country has no impact on premiums payable under a Program.

WTO APPELLATE BODY REPORT, *UNITED STATES — SUBSIDIES ON UPLAND COTTON*
WT/DS267/AB/R (adopted 21 March 2005) (complaint by Brazil)

4. Does Article 10.2 Exempt Export Credit Guarantee Programs from Export Subsidy Disciplines?

. . . .

606. As usual, our analysis begins with the text of the provision in question [Article 10:2 of the *Agriculture Agreement*]. . . .

607. Article 10.2 refers expressly to export credit guarantee programs, along with export credits and insurance programs. Under Article 10.2, WTO Members have taken on two distinct commitments in respect of these three types of measures: (i) to work toward the development of internationally agreed disciplines to govern their provision; and (ii) after agreement on such disciplines, to provide them only in conformity therewith. The text includes no temporal indication with respect to the first commitment. There is no deadline for beginning or ending the negotiations. The second commitment does have a temporal connotation, in the sense that it is triggered only "after agreement on such disciplines." This means that "after" international disciplines have been agreed upon, Members shall provide export credit guarantees, export credits and insurance programs only in conformity with those agreed disciplines. There is no dispute between the parties that, to date, no disciplines have been agreed internationally pursuant to Article 10.2.

608. Article 10.2 does not, however, expressly define the disciplines that *currently* apply to export credits, export credit guarantees and insurance programs under the *Agreement on Agriculture*. The Panel reasoned that "in order to carve out or exempt particular categories of measures from general obligations such as the prevention of circumvention of export subsidy commitments in Article 10.1 of the *Agreement on Agriculture*, it would be reasonable to expect an explicit indication revealing such an intention in the text of the

Agreement." The Panel saw "no language in Article 10.2 which would modify the scope of application of the general export subsidy disciplines in Article 10.1 in the *Agreement on Agriculture* so as to carve out or exempt export credit guarantees from the export subsidy disciplines imposed by that *Agreement.*"

609. We agree with the Panel's view that Article 10.2 does not expressly exclude export credit guarantees from the export subsidy disciplines in Article 10.1 of the *Agreement on Agriculture*. As the Panel observes, were such an exemption intended, it could have been easily achieved by, for example, inserting the words "[n]otwithstanding the provisions of Article 10.1," or other similar language at the beginning of Article 10.2. Article 10.2 does not include express language suggesting that it is intended as an exception, nor does it expressly state that the application of any export subsidy disciplines to export credits or export credit guarantees is "deferred," as the United States suggests. Given that the drafters were aware that subsidized export credit guarantees, export credits and insurance programs could fall within the export subsidy disciplines in the *Agreement on Agriculture* and the *SCM Agreement*, it would be expected that an exception would have been clearly provided had this been the drafters' intention.

. . . .

611. The Panel rejected the United States' submission that Brazil's approach would render Article 10.2 irrelevant. In the Panel's view, "the purpose of any eventual disciplines could be further to facilitate the determination of when export credit guarantee programmes in respect of agricultural products constitute export subsidies *per se* by developing and refining existing disciplines." Put another way, "the work envisaged in Article 10.2 would presumably elaborate further and more specific disciplines that could facilitate identification of the extent to which such export credit guarantee programmes constitute export subsidies, or to what extent export credit guarantee programmes are not permitted." The use of the term "development" in Article 10.2 is consistent with this view. The definitions of the term "development" include: "[t]he action or process of developing; evolution, growth, maturation; . . . a gradual unfolding, a fuller working-out" and "[a] developed form or product . . . an addition, an elaboration." [The Appellate Body cited the *Shorter Oxford English Dictionary*.] This suggests that the disciplines to be internationally agreed will be an elaboration of the export subsidy disciplines that are currently applicable.

612. This interpretation is consistent with the reference in Article 10.2 to internationally agreed disciplines "to govern the provision of" export credits, export credit guarantees or insurance programs; alternatively, Article 10.2 could have referred to internationally agreed disciplines "to govern" export credits, export credit guarantees or insurance programs. The latter formulation ("to govern") would have been broader in scope, whereas the formulation used in Article 10.2 ("to govern the provision") is narrower. If the drafters had intended that currently no disciplines at all would apply to export credit guarantees, export credits and insurance programs, it would have made more sense for them to have chosen the broader formulation "to govern." The drafter's choice of the narrower formulation "to govern the provision of" suggests that export credit guarantees, export credits and insurance programs

are not "undisciplined" in all respects, and that the disciplines to be developed have to do *only* with their *provision*. In other words, export credit guarantees, export credits and insurance programs are governed by Article 10.1 of the *Agreement on Agriculture*, but WTO Members will develop specific disciplines on the provision of these instruments.

613. The Panel's interpretation of Article 10.2, which is based on a plain reading of the text, is confirmed when, in accordance with the customary rules of treaty interpretation codified in Article 31 of the *Vienna Convention*, that provision is examined in its context and in the light of the object and purpose of the *Agreement on Agriculture*, and in particular Article 10, which is entitled "Prevention of Circumvention of Export Subsidy Commitments."

. . . .

615. Although Article 10.2 commits WTO Members to work toward the development of internationally agreed disciplines on export credit guarantees, export credits and insurance programs, it is in Article 10.1 that we find the disciplines that currently apply to export subsidies not listed in Article 9.1. A plain reading of Article 10.1 indicates that the only export subsidies that are excluded from its scope are those "listed in paragraph 1 of Article 9." The United States and Brazil agreed that export credit guarantees are not listed in Article 9.1. Thus, to the extent that an export credit guarantee meets the definition of an "export subsidy" under the *Agreement on Agriculture*, it would be covered by Article 10.1. Article 1(e) of the *Agreement on Agriculture* defines "export subsides" as "subsidies contingent upon export performance, *including* the export subsidies listed in Article 9 of this *Agreement*." (emphasis added) The use of the word "including" suggests that the term "export subsidies" should be interpreted broadly and that the list of export subsidies in Article 9 is not exhaustive. Even though an export credit guarantee may not necessarily include a subsidy component, there is nothing inherent about export credit guarantees that precludes such measures from falling within the definition of a subsidy. An export credit guarantee that meets the definition of an export subsidy would be covered by Article 10.1 of the *Agreement on Agriculture* because it is not an export subsidy listed in Article 9.1 of that *Agreement*.

616. We find it significant that paragraph 2 of Article 10 is included in an Article that is titled the "Prevention of Circumvention of Export Subsidy Commitments." As Brazil correctly points out, each paragraph in Article 10 pursues this aim. Article 10.1 provides that WTO Members shall not apply export subsidies not listed in Article 9.1 of the *Agreement on Agriculture* "in a manner which results in, or which threatens to lead to, circumvention of export subsidy commitments; nor shall non-commercial transactions be used to circumvent such commitments." Article 10.3 pursues the aim of preventing circumvention of export subsidy commitments by providing special rules on the reversal of burden of proof where a Member exports an agricultural product in quantities that exceed its reduction commitment level; in such a situation a WTO Member is treated as if it has granted WTO-*inconsistent* export subsidies for the excess quantities, unless the Member presents adequate evidence to "establish" the contrary. Article 10.4 provides disciplines to prevent WTO Members from circumventing their export subsidy commitments through food aid transactions. Similarly, Article 10.2 must be

interpreted in a manner that is consistent with the aim of preventing circumvention of export subsidy commitments that pervades Article 10. Otherwise, it would not have been included in that provision.

617. The United States submits that Article 10.2 contributes to the prevention of circumvention because it commits WTO Members to work toward the development of internationally agreed disciplines and to provide export credit guarantees, export credits and insurance programs only in conformity with these disciplines once an agreement has been reached. We are not persuaded by this argument. The necessary implication of the United States' interpretation of Article 10.2 is that, until WTO Members reach an agreement on international disciplines, export credit guarantees, export credits and insurance programs are subject to no disciplines *at all*. In other words, under the United States' interpretation, WTO Members are free to "circumvent" their export subsidy commitments through the use of export credit guarantees, export credits and insurance programs until internationally agreed disciplines are developed, whenever that may be. We find it difficult to believe that the negotiators would not have been aware of and did not seek to address the potential that subsidized export credit guarantees, export credits and insurance programs could be used to circumvent a WTO Member's export subsidy reduction commitments. Indeed, such an interpretation would *undermine* the objective of preventing circumvention of export subsidy commitments, which is central to the *Agreement on Agriculture*.

618. The United States submits that, under the Panel's approach, international food aid transactions would be subject to the "full array of export subsidy disciplines" because they are not expressly excluded from Article 10.1. According to the United States, this would adversely affect food security in the less developed world, which cannot be construed as the intent of the drafters. Furthermore, the United States asserts, the Panel's approach would mean that international food aid transactions are subject to both the specific disciplines in Article 10.4 and those in Article 10.1 of the *Agreement on Agriculture*.

619. We are unable to subscribe to the United States' arguments because we do not see Article 10.4 as excluding international food aid from the scope of Article 10.1. International food aid is covered by the second clause of Article 10.1 to the extent that it is a "non-commercial transaction." Article 10.4 provides specific disciplines that may be relied on to determine whether international food aid is being "used to circumvent" a WTO Member's export subsidy commitments. There is no contradiction in the Panel's approach to Article 10.2 and its approach to Article 10.4. The measures in Article 10.2 and the transactions in Article 10.4 are both covered within the scope of Article 10.1. As Brazil submits, "Article 10.4 provides an example of specific disciplines that have been agreed upon for a particular type of measure and that complement the general export subsidy rules" but, like Article 10.2, it does not "establish any exceptions for the measures that [it] covers." WTO Members are free to grant as much food aid as they wish, provided that they do so consistently with Articles 10.1 and 10.4. Thus, Article 10.4 does not support the United States' reading of Article 10.2.

620. The United States also relies on the negotiating history of the *Agreement on Agriculture* to support its position. The Panel identified the drafting

history in the record. It referred to paragraph 22 of the *Framework Agreement on Agriculture Reform Programme* (known as the "DeZeeuw Text"), circulated in July 1990, which envisaged "concurrent negotiations to govern the use of export assistance, including 'disciplines on export credits' ." There was also a "Note on Options in the Agriculture Negotiations" of June 1991, in which the Chairman of the negotiations "requested decisions by the principals on 'whether subsidized export credits and related practices . . . would be subject to reduction commitments unless they meet appropriate criteria to be established in terms of the rules that would govern export competition.'" An addendum circulated in August of 1991 set out an Illustrative List of Export Subsidy Practices and included, as item (i), "[s]ubsidized export credit guarantees or insurance programs." In December 1991, a "Draft Text on Agriculture" was circulated by the Chairman, Article 9.3 of which stated that "[f]or the purposes of this Article, whether export credits, export credit guarantees or insurance programmes provided by governments or their agencies constitute export subsidies shall be determined on the basis of paragraphs (j) and (k) of Annex 1 to the [*SCM Agreement*]." That paragraph was omitted from the "Draft Final Act Embodying the Results of the Uruguay Round of Multilateral Trade Negotiations," which was circulated later that month. Article 10.2 of the Draft Final Act reads as follows:

> Participants undertake not to provide export credits, export credit guarantees or insurance programs otherwise than in conformity with internationally agreed disciplines.

This language was subsequently replaced by the current text of Article 10.2.

621. The Panel did not consider that this negotiating history supported the United States' position that "the drafters intended to defer the application of any and all disciplines on agricultural export credit guarantees." According to the Panel, "[t]he omission of paragraph 3 of Article 9 of the December 1991 Draft Text is consistent with a decision that the words were mere surplusage, because export credits, export credit guarantees and insurance programmes were within the disciplines on export subsidies according to the terms of the agreement captured." "The omission," the Panel added, "is much less consistent with a decision to exclude such programmes from the disciplines altogether, considering the clear textual ability of the disciplines to extend to such programmes and the lack of any attention to an explicit carve-out of such programmes from the disciplines."

622. On appeal, the United States again relies on the drafting history of the *Agreement on Agriculture*, which it considers "reflects that the Members very early specifically included export credits and export credit guarantees as a subject for negotiation and specifically elected *not* to include such practices among export subsidies in the *WTO Agreements* with respect to those goods within the scope of . . . the *Agreement on Agriculture*." The United States adds that "[b]y deleting an explicit reference to export credit guarantees from the illustrative list of export subsidies in Article 9.1, Members demonstrated that they had not agreed in the case of agricultural products that export credit guarantees constitute export subsidies that should be subject to export subsidy disciplines." Finally, the United States takes issue with the

Panel's explanation that draft Article 9.3 was omitted because it was mere surplusage.

623. We agree with the Panel that the meaning of Article 10.2 is clear from the provision's text, in its context and in the light of the object and purpose of the *Agreement on Agriculture*, consistent with Article 31 of the *Vienna Convention*. The Panel did not think it necessary to resort to negotiating history for purposes of its interpretation of Article 10.2. Even if the negotiating history were relevant for our inquiry, we do not find that it supports the United States' position. This is because it does not indicate that the negotiators did not intend to discipline export credit guarantees, export credits and insurance programs *at all*. To the contrary, it shows that negotiators were aware of the need to impose disciplines on export credit guarantees, given their potential as a mechanism for subsidization and for circumvention of the export subsidy commitments under Article 9. Although the negotiating history reveals that the negotiators struggled with this issue, it does not indicate that the disagreement among them related to whether export credit guarantees, export credits and insurance programs were to be disciplined at all. In our view, the negotiating history suggests that the disagreement between the negotiators related to which kinds of specific disciplines were to apply to such measures. The fact that negotiators felt that internationally agreed disciplines were necessary for these three measures also suggests that the disciplines that currently exist in the *Agreement on Agriculture* must apply pending new disciplines because, otherwise, it would mean that subsidized export credit guarantees, export credits, and insurance programs could currently be extended without any limit or consequence.

624. The United States contends that the Panel's interpretation leads to a result that is "manifestly absurd or unreasonable." According to the United States, it "defies logic . . . to take the view of the Panel in which such practices would be treated as already disciplined export subsidies yet not permitted to be included within the applicable reduction commitments expressly contemplated by the text." The Panel's interpretation thus results in an enormous "windfall" for Brazil because the United States would have been permitted to grant export credit guarantees had such measures been listed in Article 9 of the *Agreement on Agriculture*. The United States also submits that exemption of export credit guarantees from export subsidy disciplines of the *Agreement on Agriculture* is further demonstrated by the fact that "no export credit guarantees are reported in the schedules of the United States or any other Members . . . nor are they currently subject to reporting as export subsidies."

625. We do not agree with the United States' submission in this regard. There could have been several reasons why Members chose not to include export credit guarantees, export credits and insurance programs under Article 9.1 of the *Agreement on Agriculture*. One reason, for instance, may be that they considered that their export credit guarantee, export credit or insurance programs did not include a subsidy component, so that there was no need to subject them to export subsidy reduction commitments. There could have been other reasons. Thus, the fact that export credit guarantees, export credits and insurance programs were not included in Article 9.1 does not support the

United States' interpretation of Article 10.2. We also observe that whether WTO Members with export credit guarantee programs have reported them in their export subsidy notifications is not determinative for purposes of our inquiry into the meaning of Article 10.2. In any event, the United States and Brazil disagree about whether such programs are subject to notification requirements.

626. Accordingly, we do not believe that Article 10.2 of the *Agreement on Agriculture* exempts export credit guarantees, export credits and insurance programs from the export subsidy disciplines in the *Agreement on Agriculture*. This does not mean that export credit guarantees, export credits and insurance programs will necessarily constitute export subsidies for purposes of the *Agreement on Agriculture*. Export credit guarantees are subject to the export subsidy disciplines in the *Agreement on Agriculture* only to the extent that such measures include an export subsidy component. If no such export subsidy component exists, then the export credit guarantees are not subject to the *Agreement's* export subsidy disciplines. Moreover, even when export credit guarantees contain an export subsidy component, such an export credit guarantee would not be inconsistent with Article 10.1 of the *Agreement on Agriculture* unless the complaining party demonstrates that it is "applied in a manner which results in, or which threatens to lead to, circumvention of export subsidy commitments." Thus, under the *Agreement on Agriculture*, the complaining party must first demonstrate that an export credit guarantee program constitutes an export subsidy. If it succeeds, it must then demonstrate that such export credit guarantees are applied in a manner that results in, or threatens to lead to, circumvention of the responding party's export subsidy commitments within the meaning of Article 10.1 of the *Agreement on Agriculture*.

627. For these reasons, we *uphold* the Panel's finding . . . that Article 10.2 of the *Agreement on Agriculture* does not exempt export credit guarantees from the export subsidy disciplines in Article 10.1.

. . . .

5. Articles 3.1 and 3.2 of the *SCM Agreement*

630. The United States' argument [that (1) Article 3 of the *SCM Agreement* . . . is subject in its application to Article 21.1 of the *Agreement on Agriculture*, (2) because export credit guarantees are not subject to the disciplines of export subsidies under the *Agreement on Agriculture*, Article 21.1 of that *Agreement* renders Article 3.1(a) of the *SCM Agreement* inapplicable to such measures, and (3) the exemption from action under Article 13(c) is inapplicable, because it only is effective with respect to export subsidies disciplined under the *Agreement on Agriculture*] is premised on the proposition that Article 10.2 of the *Agreement on Agriculture* exempts export credit guarantees from the export subsidy disciplines in that Agreement. The Panel rejected this proposition and we have upheld the Panel's finding in this regard. Therefore, because it is premised on an incorrect interpretation of Article 10.2 of the *Agreement on Agriculture*, we reject the United States' argument. We examine the United States' appeals from other aspects of the Panel's assessment of the export

credit guarantee programs under Article 3 of the *SCM Agreement* in the following section of our Report.

6. Separate Opinion [Dissent]

631. One Member of the Division hearing this appeal wishes to set out a brief separate opinion. At the outset, I would like to make it absolutely clear that I agree with the findings and conclusions and reasoning set out in all preceding Sections of this Report, but one, namely, [the] Section . . . above, which relates to Article 10.2 of the *Agreement on Agriculture*. It is only on the interpretation of Article 10.2 that I must respectfully disagree.

632. First I wish to point out that although Article 10.1 of the *Agreement on Agriculture* covers a range of export subsidies that do not fall within the ambit of Article 9.1 of the *Agreement*, Members considered that it was necessary to carve out three types of programs, namely export credit guarantees, export credits and insurance programs, and to spell out in Article 10.2 their commitments with respect to those three areas. The fact that they chose to deal with these three types of measures in Article 10.2 shows that this special treatment of the three types of measures must be given meaning and weight. Put differently, Article 10.2 is the only provision in the *Agreement on Agriculture* that speaks directly to export credit guarantees, export credits and insurance programs provided in connection with agricultural goods. I read Article 10.2 as saying that WTO Members have committed to two specific undertakings: (1) "to work *toward* the *development*" of international agreed disciplines and (2) to provide export credit guarantees in conformity with these disciplines "*after* agreement on such disciplines." (emphasis added) Thus, the text of Article 10.2 obliges Members to "work toward the *development*" of internationally agreed disciplines to regulate the provision of export credit guarantees, as well as export credits and insurance programs.

633. A specific provision that calls on Members to "work toward the development" of disciplines strongly suggests to me that disciplines do not yet exist. Certainly reference is not made in Article 10.2 to any other disciplines found in the *Agreement on Agriculture* that apply to export credit guarantees, export credits and insurance programs provided in connection with agricultural goods. Furthermore, the second part of Article 10.2 clearly limits the application of disciplines to *after* such time as the international disciplines have been agreed upon. This is a further indication that there are no current disciplines under the *Agreement on Agriculture* that apply to export credit guarantees, export credit and insurance programs.

634. I recognize that the language of this provision is not free from ambiguity. As noted by my colleagues on the Division, the drafters could have — dare I say, should have — made their intentions even more plain. If there were no Article 10.2, then I might concur with my colleagues that to the extent that an export credit guarantee provided an export subsidy then the *Agreement on Agriculture* envisions that that subsidy portion should be addressed by Article 10.1. However, Article 10.2 does exist and the meaning of the words as I read them is entirely prospective, at least with respect to the existence of applicable disciplines.

635. I do not see my reading of Article 10.2 to be inconsistent with the provision's context and with the object and purpose of the *Agreement on Agriculture*. Article 10 is entitled "Prevention of Circumvention of Export Subsidy Commitments." I see the first part of Article 10.1 as setting out a catch-all provision, designed to potentially cover an export subsidy that is used to circumvent the reduction commitments under Article 9. In contrast, as discussed above, Article 10.2 is designed to *specifically* deal [*sic*] with export credit programs, export credits and insurance programs, and its provisions are controlling with respect to any such programs. Although it speaks to prospective development and application of agreed disciplines, Article 10.2 is also consistent with the objective of prevention of circumvention. Its placement in Article 10 suggests a recognition that export credits, export credit guarantees and insurance programs can have the potential to circumvent export subsidy commitments. Article 10.3 pursues the aim of preventing circumvention of export subsidy commitments by providing special rules on reversal of burden of proof when a Member's exports exceed the quantitative reduction commitments, and Article 10.4 itemizes a series of specific commitments or disciplines that apply in the area of international food aid. It is accurate, as my colleagues reason, that the language of Article 10.2 is quite different from that used in Article 10.4. While Article 10.4 establishes disciplines for food aid transactions, Article 10.2 merely foresees that disciplines will be established, in the future, for export credit guarantees, export credits and insurance programs. The fact that a single Article contains commitments with varying degrees of temporal effect and both specific and general provisions, does not support an interpretation that the general undertaking (Article 10.1) overrides the specific and prospective provision (that is, Article 10.2).

636. I also find support for my view in the negotiating history. Of course, care must be taken in relying on negotiating history and I do not wish to imply that resort to Article 32 of the *Vienna Convention* is strictly necessary in these circumstances. [In a footnote, the Dissent recognized "that the negotiating materials referred to by the Panel may not formally constitute *travaux préparatoires* for purposes of Article 32 of the *Vienna Convention*."] Nevertheless, as I read it this history confirms my view that at the end of the Uruguay Round, negotiators had not agreed to subject export credit guarantees, export credits and insurance programs provided in connection with agricultural goods to the disciplines of the *Agreement on Agriculture* or to any other disciplines that existed at that time. Article 10.2, in my view, was intended to reflect this outcome. At one point in the negotiations, there was a proposal for applying to agricultural products the disciplines in the Illustrative List of Export Subsidies annexed to the *SCM Agreement*. [The Dissent elaborated in a footnote as follows: "Specifically, in December 1991, a 'Draft Text on Agriculture' was circulated by the Chairman. Article 9.3 of the draft text stated that '[f]or the purposes of this Article, whether export credits, export credit guarantees or insurance programmes provided by governments or their agencies constitute export subsidies shall be determined on the basis of paragraphs (j) and (k) of Annex 1 to the [*SCM Agreement*]'. . . . Later, the Draft Final Act was circulated and it omitted paragraph 3 of Article 9 that had appeared in the previous draft."] This proposal was dropped in the Draft

Final Act in favour of an "undertak[ing] not to provide export credits, export credit guarantees or insurance programs otherwise than in conformity with internationally agreed disciplines," which in turn was replaced by the current version of Article 10.2. The previous version of Article 10.2 (in the Draft Final Act) reflected an immediate undertaking "not to provide export credit guarantees, export credits or insurance programs otherwise than in conformity with internationally agreed disciplines," whatever those may have been. In contrast, no immediate commitment is evident from the current version of Article 10.2, which instead calls for continued negotiations and for WTO Members to provide export credits, export credit guarantees or insurance programs only in conformity with internationally agreed disciplines *after* agreement on such disciplines. This suggests to me that the negotiators were aware of the need to impose disciplines on export credit guarantees, given their potential as a mechanism for circumvention, but they were unable to agree upon and identify the disciplines that were to apply to such measures until disciplines were developed in the future. Thus, in my view, the negotiating history supports an interpretation that Article 10.2 was inserted to commit WTO Members to continue negotiating on the disciplines that would apply, in the future, and that no disciplines would apply to such measures until such time as disciplines were internationally agreed upon.

637. As noted by my colleagues on the Division, the United States argues that "it defies logic, as well as the obvious object and purpose of the agreement, to take the view of the Panel in which such practices would be treated as already disciplined export subsidies yet not permitted to be included within the applicable reduction commitments expressly contemplated by the text." Brazil argues that the United States was never willing to accept that its export credit guarantee programs constituted an export subsidy and took a calculated risk by not including them under its Article 9 reduction commitments.

638. I agree with my colleagues on the Division that the decisions of WTO Members regarding how to schedule their export subsidy commitments have limited value for purposes of an interpretation of Article 10. However, it seems anomalous that WTO Members with export credit guarantee programs would not have sought to preserve some flexibility to provide subsidies through such programs, which flexibility would have been available to them had such programs been included under Article 9 of the *Agreement on Agriculture*. My colleagues' reading of Article 10 perceives that WTO Members intended to impose upon themselves the more onerous obligation of immediately subjecting export credit guarantees, export credits and insurance programs to the export subsidy disciplines of the *Agreement on Agriculture* rather than the less demanding obligation of working toward the development of such disciplines. We are bound to rely upon what we have before us in the treaty provisions, and I find the same text and context leads me in the opposite direction. Namely, that the absence of reference in Article 9 to export credit guarantees, export credits and insurance programs suggests that it was believed that such measures would not be subject to any disciplines until such time as disciplines were internationally agreed upon pursuant to Article 10.2.

639. In conclusion, for these reasons and particularly my reading of the text, it is my view that, pursuant to Article 10.2, export credit guarantees, export

credits and insurance programs are not currently subject to export subsidy disciplines under the *Agreement on Agriculture*, including the disciplines found in Article 10.1. In the light of Article 21.1 of the *Agreement on Agriculture* and the introductory language to Article 3.1 of the *SCM Agreement*, I am also of the view that export credit guarantees, export credits and insurance programs provided in connection with agricultural goods are not subject to the prohibition in Article 3.1(a) of the *SCM Agreement*.

640. I recognize that this interpretation of Article 10.2 perceives a significant gap in the *Agreement on Agriculture* with respect to export credit guarantees, export credits and insurance programs that apply to agricultural products. This underscores the importance of working "toward the development of international disciplines" as envisioned by Article 10.2.

V. THE EU COMMON AGRICULTURAL POLICY

A. Multi-Functionality

It is easy to lambaste the EU Common Agricultural Policy (CAP). Has it not protected inefficient European farmers for decades from long-needed reforms that free trade would bring about?[1] Has it not driven further into poverty farmers in developing and least developed countries, and jeopardized farmers in other developed countries, by causing overproduction in certain products — mountains of butter and maize, and lakes of wine — and thus price suppression or depression? Are not French farmers, in particular, infamous for being pampered and obstructionist?

Study after study, especially by NGOs, testifies to the greed underlying the CAP, as well as to stark facts such as it is better to be a cow in the EU than a denizen in a least developed country — the cow gets a subsidy larger than the *per capita* income of the sorry chap.[2] Politician after politician, in the U.S. and other agricultural exporting countries, demand an end to the CAP. And yet, for over half a century, the CAP has stood, and even been an organizing principle of the European project. Why? The key to the answer is to consider the role — or roles — of agriculture in a modern society. To what social model of agriculture are EU citizens profoundly and legitimately attached?

But first, appreciate there are two problems with castigating the CAP. The first is philosophical, indeed, theological. Why are the income and work of a farmer in a poor country more important than the livelihood of a farmer in

---

[1] The first common market organization (CMO) under the CAP was established in 1962 for cereals and related goods. In 1964, CMOs for milk and other dairy products were set up. The last CMO, for sugar, was set up in 1968. That year is significant, because continental European leaders, led by France's President, General Charles de Gaulle, sought to have the CAP in place before the United Kingdom joined the European Community (EC) in 1973. Then, and to the present, the United Kingdom inclines toward a more liberalized view of agricultural trade than many continental states, preferring to keep food prices low and thereby bolster the competitiveness of the industrial sector through low labor costs. *See* Gerrit Meester, *European Union, Common Agricultural Policy, and World Trade*, 14 KAN. J.L. & PUB. POL'Y 389, 390-91 (2005).

[2] *See, e.g.*, OXFAM UNITED KINGDOM, RIGGED RULES AND DOUBLE STANDARDS (2002); *see also* ORGANISATION FOR ECONOMIC CO-OPERATION AND DEVELOPMENT AGRICULTURE POLICIES IN OECD COUNTRIES: A POSITIVE REFORM AGENDA (2002), *available at* www.olis.oecd.org.

a rich country? Each farmer has equal human dignity. In a theological paradigm, the source of that dignity is the image of a common creator. Despite this equality, should there be some basis on which to prefer the interests of one over the other? Is one such basis the doctrine, emanating from Catholic Social Justice Theory, of the preferential option for the poor? While all persons have human dignity, the poor deserve special attention simply because they are relatively worse off. As Pope John Paul II put it: "Suffering man belongs to us."[3]

However, are farmers in poor countries relatively worse off? Of course the broadly applicable answer is "yes." This response leads to the second problem: poor, and increasingly vulnerable, farmers in rich countries. Consider the following facts about French agriculture:[4]

   1.   *Fewer Farms*:

For the 50 year period 1955-2005, France lost 100 farms every day. In that half-century, the number of farms shrank from 2.3 million to 545,000.

   2.   *Fewer Farmers*:

In the 25 year period 1970-2005, the number of French farmers fell by two thirds, from 3.3 to 1.1 million. Conversely, in that quarter century, French farms have grown in average size, from 19 to 50 hectares. Overall, French farms are halfway between the large, industrialized farm of Northern Europe and the small, family farms of Southern and Eastern Europe.

   3.   *Poorer Farmers*:

French farmers are becoming poorer. In 1997, 13 percent of them earned less than half of the French median income. By 2003, the figure was 15.9 percent. To boost their income, more of them — and their spouses — are taking non-farm second jobs. In 1997, the share of non-agricultural income in the average French farming household was 19 percent. By 2003, it was 31 percent.

   4.   *Relative Deprivation in the EU*:

Theoretically, the concept of income poverty (as well as the broader concept capability deprivation inspired by Amartya Sen in his book, *Development as Freedom* (1999)) is poignant in a relative sense. Thus, practically, all the more vexing for French farmers is their relative income deprivation. In recent years across the EU generally, the average EU farmer has experienced rising farm income. To be sure, from 2000-2006, the incomes of Belgian, Greek, and Italian — as well as French — farmers fell. But, the incomes of farmers in Germany, Netherlands, and the United Kingdom, and in the 10 new members that joined the EU effective 2005, all rose dramatically.

   5.   *Relative Deprivation within France*:

Between 1997-2003, within France, the average household experienced an income rise of 1.8 percent *per annum*, while the average farm household felt

---

[3] *The Suffering Person Belongs to Us All*, L'osservatore Romano, 17 Jan. 2007, at 3, and in *The Rule for Charity: "Good Should be Done Well!*," L'osservatore Romano, 10 Jan. 2007, at 5.

[4] *See* Martin Arnold, *Poor French Farmers Buck Income Trend*, Financial Times, 11 Jan. 2007, at 3. The data are from INSEE, the official French statistical agency, the French National Institute for Agricultural Research, and Eurostat.

a drop of 1.8 percent. Even if or when the absolute income level of French farm households is equal or slightly above that of non-farm families, the latter cohort is worse off. French farm families tend to be larger than non-farm families (3.2 versus 2.4 members), hence their *per capita* income is lower.

6. *Less Exports*:

While France is the biggest agricultural producer in the EU (in terms of value, as of 2004), its exports are contracting, from a 3.3 percent annual increase in 1999 to a 3.4 percent decrease in 2004.

These facts are all the more poignant because they are French.

Free traders heap blame on French farmers for being among the most recalcitrant constituencies in world trade. Did they not nearly scupper the Uruguay Round, forcing a 1992 Blair House Accord and creation of the "Blue Box" of subsidies for production set-aside payments, and then only after the U.S. had prevailed in the *Oilseeds* case? At the time, the President of the European Commission, Jacques Delors, insisted provocatively: "I'm not going to be an accomplice to the depopulation of the land."[5] Was it not French farmers (among others) persistently and vociferously object to concessions by the EU in the Doha Round on agricultural tariff cuts and trimmings of the sensitive product list?

All true, indeed. French farmers, though they comprise only 3.5 percent of France's population, hold disproportionate political influence. Fourteen percent of French workers depend on agriculture, and France is both the agricultural power in the EU and second largest exporter of farm products in the world.[6] Support from the agro-alimentary industry magnifies the influence of the farmers. Significantly, local officials from 36,000 largely rural communes elect the French Senate.

Indeed, the French farming position is not irrational. To the contrary, it is grounded on a concept of agriculture increasingly accepted even by free trading nations — multifunctionality. Here, then, is the second problem with excoriating the CAP. Agriculture is more than just about growing food in an efficient manner, with production allocated according to the Ricardian paradigm of comparative advantage. It is about food security for a country — indeed, it is about national security. It is about environmental stewardship for children and grandchildren. It is about identity and culture.

Culture, including taste (in the literal sense), is a point articulated passionately by France, which holds dear to a concept of "gastronomic sovereignty." As Christian Ligeard, the head of International Relations for the French Agriculture Ministry, says:

> We don't want to lose self-sufficiency over food supply, which would force French people to eat U.S. beef fed with growth hormones or genetically modified crops from Brazil.[7]

---

[5] *The Farmer's Friend*, THE ECONOMIST, 5 Nov. 2005, at 58.

[6] *See* Daniel Pruzin & Joe Kirwin, *WTO Ministers Step Up Efforts to Secure Breakthrough on Doha*, 24 INT'L TRADE REP. (BNA) 154-156 (quoting French Agricultural Minister Dominique Bussereau).

[7] Martin Arnold, *French Farmers Dig in Against Subsidy Reform*, FINANCIAL TIMES, 8 Dec. 2005, at 7.

Similarly, the cultural image, if not mythology, surrounding the family farm, is strong in France. In November 2005, before the WTO Ministerial Conference in Hong Kong, the French Minister of Trade, Christine Lagarde explained:

> As the recent decision by the United Nations Educational, Scientific and Cultural Organization to adopt a treaty preserving cultural diversity reminds us, *the protection of national distinctiveness is important. For Europeans, particularly the French, agriculture is fundamental to our identity.* The CAP is a cornerstone of this *relationship with our land.* Maintaining it is not just about protecting farmers but defending a *European social model* that balances rural development, food security, and environmental protection.[8]

As in the U.S. and other countries, in France, sentimental attachment is another reason for France's vocal articulation of its agricultural interests. Indeed, for all Europe, quipped *The Economist*, agriculture "is morally good, and support for it is a mark of civilization."[9]

Thus, conventional economic attacks on the CAP miss the mark. They neither rest on a rigorous social justice foundation, nor address the multiple purposes the CAP serves. The CAP was a cornerstone of the post-Second World War unification of Europe into the European Economic Community (EEC), brought about by the 1957 *Treaty of Rome*. Ensuring food security for Europeans was a key purpose for creating the CAP, and it is easy to forget that in the 1940s and 1950s, Europe had food shortages. Article 39 of the *EEC Treaty*, now Article 33 of the *Treaty of the European Union*, articulates 5 specific objectives for the CAP, two of which are clearly about food security:

> To *increase agricultural productivity* by promoting technical progress and by ensuring the rational development of agricultural production and the optimum utilization of the factors of production, in particular, labor.
>
> i. Thus, to ensure a *fair standard of living for the agricultural community*, in particular by increasing the individual earnings of persons engaged in agriculture.
>
> ii. To *stabilize markets.*
>
> iii. To assure the *availability of supplies.*
>
> iv. To ensure that *supplies reach consumers at reasonable prices.*[10]

The first goal is efficiency. The second goal is about fairness, specifically, reduction of rural poverty (which was high in the aftermath of the Second World War), and generally, maintaining the rural way of life. The third goal is about certainty, and indirectly related to food security. The fourth and fifth goals are self-evidently about food security.

As time passes, and the number of Second World War survivors diminishes, it becomes easier to ignore a, if not the, central intent behind the CAP: avoid

---

[8] Christine Lagarde, *Big Cuts in Farm Tariffs Are No Solution to Poverty*, FINANCIAL TIMES, 21 Nov. 2005, at 15 (emphasis added).

[9] *The Farmer's Friend*, THE ECONOMIST, 5 Nov. 2005, at 58.

[10] Meester, *supra* note 1, at 389, 390 (emphasis added).

the food deprivations many Europeans faced during the 1939-45 conflagration and its aftermath. Even today, who recalls the EU was a net importer of some food items (*e.g.*, beef and cereals) in the mid-1950s through the mid-1970s? Yet, citing projections for world population to rise to 9-10 billion by approximately 2025, EU and national-level officials contend the food security motivation of the CAP remains relevant.

Accordingly, the CAP did not begin as an export subsidy program. Rather, it was designed to guarantee high prices to farmers. The mechanism to effect the guarantee, in essence, was government purchasing. The EEC — now EU — agreed to purchase a farm product whenever the price of that product fell below a specific support level. For any particular commodity, if the support level exceeded its world market price, then the possibility existed that consumers might undermine the CAP by importing a like commodity. Thus, the purchasing scheme had to be accompanied by — and still is — significant tariff barriers — initially, a variable import levy — that would offset any difference between prices in the European and world markets. In other words, a restrictive tariff policy was necessary to avoid substitution or arbitrage.

Yet, during and since the 1970s, support prices set by the EU have been far in excess of world prices. Responding not to free trade prices, but CAP price signals, EU farmers have overproduced, *i.e.*, they have supplied the European public with far more food than it possibly can consume. The EU has dealt with the surfeits in two basic ways:

1. *Intervention Buying* — Buying food at a guaranteed support, or intervention, price, which is above world market prices, and storing the so-called "intervention stocks;" and

2. *Export Subsidies* — Providing subsidies to farmers, through a refund scheme to cover the difference between the internal EU market price and lower world market prices, to export food.

As to the first response, in 1985, for example, the EU had to buy 780,000 tons of beef, 1.2 million tons of butter, and 12 million tons of wheat. The second response is supposed to avoid endless increases in food stockpiles.

The choice, which the European Commission (EC) makes, between the purchase/warehouse and export refund options depends on international political and economic factors. There is a balancing act. If export refunds are too high, then world market prices may fall, because of extra EU output on world markets. If support prices are too high, then production surpluses may be too great to stockpile. In trying to balance the variables and deal with overproduction, not infrequently the EC resorts to two other strategies: dumping food on world markets, or donating food to specific countries.

There is another reason criticism of the CAP often misses the mark. It is insufficiently nuanced. Has the EU applied all three CAP instruments — production subsidies (*i.e.*, price support through intervention buying), variable import levies (*i.e.*, tariff protection), and export subsidies (specifically, refunds, which are at issue in the *Sugar* case) — to all farm products? The answer is "no." Table 46-1 shows categories of products to which it traditionally has applied the various instruments. The obvious inference to draw is the CAP does not distort all markets in equal amounts at all times.

TABLE 46-1:
APPLICATION OF CAP POLICY TOOLS TO SPECIFIC
AGRICULTURAL PRODUCTS

CAP Policy Tool	Agricultural Products
All 3 Tools Applied: (1) Production Subsidies (Price Support/Intervention), (2) Import Levy (Tariff Protection), and (3) Export Subsidies (Refunds)	Beef Cereals Dairy Olive Oil Table Wine Sugar
Only 1 or 2 Tools Applied, and Only in Specific Market Situations: For example, just (1) Production Subsidies (Price Support/Intervention), or a combination of (2) Import Levy (Tariff Protection), and (3) Export Subsidies (Refunds)	Eggs Fruit Pork Poultry Vegetables
Coverage Only For Processing (*i.e.*, no support for commodity, but premiums offered to processors)	Oilseeds Protein crops (collectively, along with other products, referred to as "cereals substitutes")
No CAP Coverage (*i.e.*, no support for commodity or processed product)	Consumption and seed potatoes Flowers and flower Bulbs Ornamental Plants

B. The 1992 MacSharry Reform, Agenda 2000, and 2003 De-Coupling

One subsidy does not cure another. The CAP export subsidy regime is one scheme trying to cure a distortion — overproduction — caused by the initial subsidy scheme linking payments to production. The regime only makes matters worse. Higher levels of EU farm exports, encouraged by export subsidies, tend to depress (or suppress) world market prices. In turn, the gap between EU support levels and world market prices yawns (or at least remains large). As the gap grows, the EU pays a larger subsidy, which in turn exacerbates the problem of overproduction — leading to yet greater exportable surpluses. There is a vicious cycle, as it were.[11]

De-linking subsidies from production is an obvious way to deal with the cycle. On a few occasions, the EU has made reforms designed to de-couple payments from output. In 1992, the EU approved the "MacSharry Reform" (named after the EU Agricultural Commissioner who served from 1989-92). This Reform cut support (intervention) prices and mandated production restrictions. The EU eliminated all price support for oilseeds and protein

---

[11] The discussion below draws in part from PAUL R. KRUGMAN & MAURICE OBSTFELD, INTERNATIONAL ECONOMICS: THEORY AND POLICY 198-200 (4th ed. 1997); Meester, *supra* note 1, at 389-412. The Graph is adapted from Professors Krugman and Obstfeld, and Charts from Professor Meester.

crops, and cut it by 20 and 33 percent for beef and cereals, respectively. But, to assist producers, they allowed for direct income payments to farmers. The variables in the formula to determine income compensation are historical areas under cultivation, yield, and livestock units. Such payments are conditional on set asides, *i.e.*, farmers setting taking arable land out of cultivation (for crops), or establishing maximum densities per hectare (for livestock).

The MacSharry Reform heralded a fundamental change in CAP philosophy. As initially conceived, the CAP required farmers to earn income from the market, but the government would intervene as necessary to affect prices. With the Reform, the EU began backing away from intervention, and moving toward direct income support. Following the MacSharry Reform, the EU successfully pushed for creation of a "Blue Box" during Uruguay Round negotiations on the *Agreement on Agriculture*. The 1992 deal creating this Box is known as the "Blair House Accord" (after the Washington, D.C. location where it was reached). Subsidies whereby farmers are paid based on setting aside parts of their fields are exempt from AMS reduction commitments. In other words, the EU's direct, production-limiting income support to farmers goes in the Blue Box.

Bluntly put, without this deal the Uruguay Round would have collapsed. Accordingly, it is sometimes said no multilateral trade round can advance until the EU forges a common negotiating position. The EU cannot do so until it comes to an agreement over hard choices about the CAP.

The MacSharry Reform applied only to beef, cereals, oilseeds, and protein crops. To extend coverage, and to prepare for a new round — the Doha Round — of multilateral trade talks, the EU agreed on "Agenda 2000." Under this amendment to the CAP, the EU applied the MacSharry Reform to the dairy sector, made further cuts in intervention prices, and boosted direct income support. Significantly for farmers, their income payments are in nominal terms, *i.e.*, they are not indexed to inflation, and thus eroded by cost of living increases. Moreover, the Agenda 2000 boost was not directly proportional to the cuts in intervention prices. The EU thought it unnecessary to do so. Because the price of EU farm goods would fall given the CAP reforms, these products would be more competitive on world markets — and EU farmers would make more money the old fashioned way, namely, through free trade at a market price. Also significant for farmers was the express linking of income payments to satisfaction of environmental conditions — a manifestation of multi-functionality.

In June 2003, in connection with the "Mid-Term Review of Agenda 2000," the EU approved further CAP changes. As with prior reforms, the 2003 package aimed to cut output surpluses by lowering intervention prices and de-coupling subsidies from output — in effect, phasing out intervention buying. The EU decreased support prices for butter by 25 percent (across 4 years) and skim milk powder by 15 percent (over 3 years). As with Agenda 2000, increases in income support only partly compensate for these decreases. The EU introduced "modulation" — cuts in income support to large farms so as to fund rural development initiatives. That made sense, because traditionally the CAP was not targeted precisely: the richest 20 percent of farmers received 80 percent of the payments.

Most notably, the EU replaced multiple direct income payments with a single farm payment. The EU entirely de-linked the single farm payment from what a farmer produces. The policy underlying disengaging income subsidies and farm production is to liberate farmers, and thereby increase farm efficiency. Without having to pay attention to support payments, a farmer can make planting, growing, and harvesting decisions based on market signals. Continuing the theme of multi-functionality, in the 2003 reform the EU made the single payment contingent on satisfying not only environmental conditions, but also standards on animal and plant welfare and food safety. These contingencies are known as "cross-compliance."

Not surprisingly, EU officials heard complaints from their rural constituents about the June 2003 reforms. In the mid-1980s, EU farmers received an average subsidy of 80 percent above world market prices. By 2005, the figure had tumbled to one-third above those prices. In the 1980s, subsidies accounted for over two-fifths of the revenues of EU farmers. In 2004, the amount was down to one-third, and headed further down.

To be sure, the details of the June 2003 reforms are complicated and crop specific. For example, that year, the EU stopped all intervention buying of rye. In December 2006, just before two large maize producers, Bulgaria and Romania, joined the EU, the EU announced it was ceasing intervention buying of unsold maize stocks.[12] Eliminating maize intervention buying cut by a third the amount (U.S. $496 million) the EU spends on purchasing unsold cereals, and cut from 18.3 to 10 million tons the amount of maize projected to be in EU warehouses by 2013. Hungarian farmers were worst hit. They account for over 90 percent of maize stocks. Because their country is landlocked, many preferred to sell maize to the EU rather than pay transport costs to sell on the market. The EU said it would sell off remaining maize stocks over five years (2007-2011), and reduced-price corn from Hungary could be exported or used as feed for pigs and poultry.

However, under the CAP reforms, full de-coupling does not occur for all products, and for some products occurs only over a lengthy phase in period. The EU is deregulating the fruit, vegetable, and wine sectors, but not all at once. It is especially important to shift away from production linked subsidies for raisins and tomatoes, which account for large shares of the intervention purchase budget, and the surfeit of which is either donated to charity or buried in a landfill. Ending intervention buying for barley and wheat also is critical — but, politically difficult. France is a large supplier of these products, and tenaciously supportive of the CAP.

Such examples suggest sovereignty of individual EU member states complicates CAP reform. Indeed, the states have discretion to retain some links, on certain products, between income support and output. Therefore, query whether reforms to the CAP are, as yet, sufficiently far-reaching to break the vicious cycle (depicted earlier) and its untoward effects. What is unquestionable, though, is the reformed CAP adduces multi-functionality. Providing direct income support is a policy about rural lifestyle and culture. Cross compliance obviously bespeaks concern about sustainability.

---

[12] *See* Andrew Bounds, *Brussels Set to Bring Down Maize Mountain*, FINANCIAL TIMES, 12 Dec. 2006, at 2.

C. Economics of the CAP

The core of the overproduction problem has been the level at which the EU sets support prices. This level is above not only the world market price that exists outside the EU, and would exist in the EU in the absence of a CAP, with free trade, but also above the price at which domestic EU demand and domestic EU supply would be in equilibrium without any importation of food items. In other words, the level at which the EU commits itself to intervene, and thus guarantees to farmers, is above the EU market-clearing equilibrium price. Consequently, but for the CAP, the EU would be a net importer of food. Of course, that is exactly the situation the founders of the CAP sought to avoid.

The Graph depicts operation of CAP subsidy schemes.[13] The Graph shows alternative price scenarios. The internal EU price, assuming the CAP does not exist and the EU does not import food, is P^{EU} (where "EU" is for "European Union"). At P^{EU}, domestic supply and demand are in equilibrium. At this price, EU farmers produce Q^E, and EU families buy Q^E. The domestic market clears. At P^{CAP}, the EU pays farmers this above-equilibrium level. Farmers have an incentive to produce Q^{SCAP} (standing for "Supply under the CAP"). Yet, EU families buy only Q^{DCAP} (standing for "Demand under the CAP"). The difference between Q^{SCAP} and Q^{DCAP} is what the EU is obligated to buy and store. To avoid purchasing and warehousing this difference, the EU exports it. The EU pays farmers to export this surplus. P^{WM} is the world market price. If this level prevailed in the EU, then the EU would have to import food. That is because EU families would demand Q^{DWM}, but EU farmers would produce only Q^{SWM}. The difference would come from abroad.

---

[13] This Graph closely resembles the neoclassical economic analysis of a generic export subsidy from the perspective of the subsidizing country (presented in an earlier Chapter). In this Graph, for any particular farm product, the EU pays farmers an export subsidy equal to the difference between the price in the EU and world market price.

GRAPH 46-1:
CAP SUBSIDIES, OVER-PRODUCTION. AND EXPORTABLE SURPLUSES

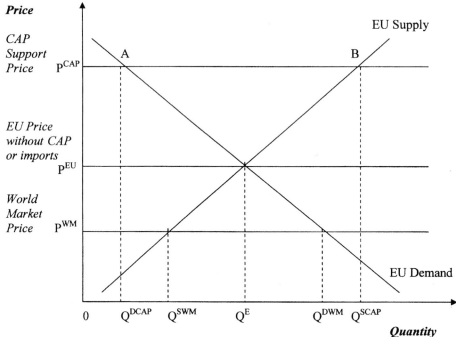

In sum, P^{EU} is a market-clearing autarky price, P^{CAP} is an interventionist price generating an exportable surplus, and P^{WM} is a free trade price in which foreign nations have a comparative advantage in agriculture. Further, the Graph embodies the two kinds of CAP subsidies EU farmers receive. First, they are guaranteed the support price, P^{CAP}. This support is linked to output — in effect, a production subsidy. Second, they receive the difference between the internal price, P^{EU}, and world market price, P^{WM}, for whatever output they ship overseas — in effect, an export subsidy. The EU uses the export subsidy to dispose of the surplus resulting from the production subsidy.

Consequently, the Graph also shows the cost of subsidization to the EU. That cost is the area $ABQ^{SCAP}Q^{DCAP}$. It reflects the quantity exported (Q^{SCAP} versus Q^{DCAP}) multiplied by the value of the total subsidy (P^{CAP} versus P^{WM}, reflecting the production subsidy, P^{CAP} versus P^{EU}, and the export subsidy, P^{EU} versus P^{WM}). Finally, consider the effects on Consumer and Producer Surplus of the different price scenarios. At which price level are EU consumers best off? At which price level are EU farmers best off?

Following the Graph, the two Charts indicate the above analysis can be embellished with important details about the actual operation of the CAP as it developed in the 1960s, and as it has been reformed since then. There are actually four key prices:

    1.   World Market Price, P^{WM} —

The EU gauges the world market price based on c.i.f. (cost, insurance, and freight) prices to principal European harbors.

    2.   Target Price, P^{T} —

The EU Ministers of Agriculture meet annually to establish a desired internal (*i.e.*, domestic EU) price for agricultural products, namely, a Target Price. From the Target Price, P^{T}, with respect to imports into the most significant EU ports (*e.g.*, cereals shipped to Rotterdam), the EU Agriculture Ministers derived a minimum import price, also known as a threshold price.

    3.   Intervention Price, P^{I} —

As indicated earlier, if and when markets for particular farm products in the EU do not clear, the EU purchases and stores the excess supply. Each EU member state has an "intervention office," and this office is legally obligated to buy surplus production at the designated Intervention Price, P^{I}. In the Graph and earlier discussion, this Price is called the "Support Price, P^{CAP}, — a term by which the Intervention Price also is known. In brief, the Intervention Price provides a guaranteed safety net — support — to farmers.[14]

    4.   Internal Market Price, P^{EU} —

In fact, the price in the EU for a particular agricultural product might not exactly equal the desired target, P^{T}. Rather, depending on market conditions, the actual price — P^{EU} — may vary between P^{T} and the Intervention Price. For example, if the EU experiences a deficit in the product in question, then the internal market price equals or exceeds P^{T}. If there is an internal surplus, then the internal market price could be at or below the Intervention Price.

---

[14] In the Graph, P^{CAP} is above P^{EU}, indicating active intervention buying by the EU. In the Chart, P^{I} (akin to P^{EU}) is below P^{EU}, highlighting both the role of P^{I} as a minimum guaranteed floor price, and the reductions in this floor owing to CAP reforms. Furthermore, in the Graph, P^{EU} reflects market clearing under autarky. In contrast, autarky is not assumed in the Charts.

Charts: Operation of the CAP

Chart 46-1: Pre-1992 MacSharry Reform

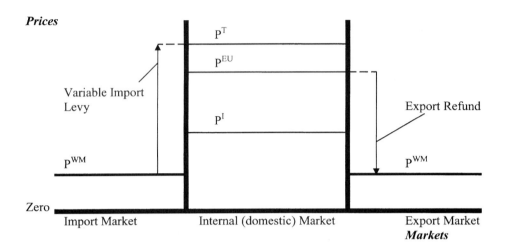

Chart 46-2: After MacSharry Reform, Agenda 2000, 2003
Mid-Term Review

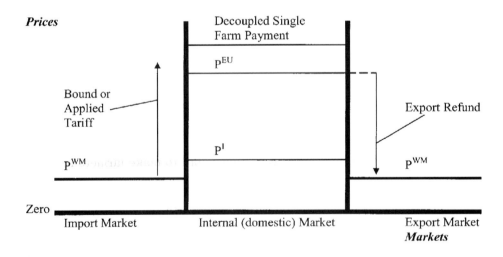

The CAP is designed to keep internal prices high, *i.e.*, P^T above P^{WM}, thus guaranteeing income to farmers and food production for consumers. To assure this differential, tariff protection is a key element of the CAP. Traditionally, the EU imposed a variable import levy, that is, a tariff on farm imports that adjusts with any changes in the gap between internal prices (P^T) and c.i.f. prices (P^{WM}). The EU collects revenue from the tariff, from which it funded agricultural programs costs such as feed and raw materials in exported livestock and other processed products.

Note carefully intervention and export refunds are a cost to the EU, as are direct income payments to farmers. These expenditures — in particular, income support — have grown considerably in recent decades. The whole system, which comes within the EU budget, is operated by the European Guidance and Guarantee Fund for Agriculture. Overall, at about U.S. $52 billion (43 billion euros) annually (as of 2005), the CAP consumes about 40 percent of the EU budget.[15] (The 40 percent figure is whopping in comparison with the European workforce engaged in agriculture — 2 percent.) French farmers get the largest share of CAP outlays — about 20 percent, as Table 46-2 shows. The smallest 76 percent of French farmers get just 20 percent of CAP payments. The largest 10 percent of "French farmers," such as multinational agri-businesses like Cargill and Nestlé, garner over half of the payments.

TABLE 46-2:
DISTRIBUTION OF CAP PAYMENTS (2004)

Country in EU	Percentage of CAP Budget Received
France	22
Germany	14
Italy	12
Spain	12
United Kingdom	9
Greece	6
Ireland	4
All other EU member states (18 countries)	18

CAP spending is not sustainable, and less so as EU membership expands to 27 (as of January 2007) from its base of 6 founding states, and possibly beyond. Indeed, a key factor behind Agenda 2000 was enlargement — consumers in new, Central and Eastern European, member states had less purchasing power than Western European consumers, and could not afford high internal market prices. Conversely, the EU could not afford to make farmers in these states rich by paying high support prices for their output — which, of course, would exacerbate overproduction problems anyway. On 1 May 2004, when the EU expanded by 10 states, farmers in the new members became entitled immediately to CAP market measures. However, their entitlement to direct income payments is phased in across 10 years.

Moreover, funding is co-financed, in part by the EU, and in part by national budgets and rural development schemes at the member state level. That is, in July 2004, the CAP was altered to bifurcate subsidy levels: a basic level of set payments provided by the EU, and an added amount provided at a devolved level, namely, national governments. This reform was essential to

---

[15] *See* Martin Arnold, *Poor French Farmers Buck Income Trend*, FINANCIAL TIMES, 11 Jan. 2007, at 3. The CAP is scheduled for review in 2012 and re-negotiation in 2013.

securing French farming acquiescence to Polish entry into the EU. The concern of the French was that if subsidy payment sources were not split between supra-national and national levels, then the EU would be forced to cut subsidies, because membership enlargement would stretch its budget.

The two Charts illustrate operation of the CAP based on the four aforementioned prices. Chart I is the CAP as initially established, while Chart II shows the shift toward direct income support following the 1992 MacSharry Reform. The Charts bear the following key common points and differences:

i. Each Chart depicts three markets for agricultural products (commodities or processed) — imports into the EU, the internal (domestic) EU market, and exports from the EU.

ii. Movement from left to right on each Chart indicates importation of agricultural products (the left-hand most panel), the EU domestic market (the middle panel), and exportation of agricultural products (the right hand most panel).

iii. On each Chart, upward movement bespeaks rising prices.

iv. In each Chart, in the two external markets, the world market price, P^{WM}, is the only relevant benchmark. At no point does P^{WM} prevail in the internal market. Rather, the internal market is characterized by an actual price, P^{EU}, a government determined Target Price, P^T, which is the highest of all prices, and a government set floor price that, if struck, triggers official purchases and stockpiling, P^I, to support farmers.

v. Regarding imports, the tariff is a variable levy in Chart I, but a fixed duty in Chart II. With a target to preserve, and with a hope of eschewing intervention, the EU adjusts the level of protection, hence the variable levy. The higher P^T in comparison with P^{WM}, the larger the levy. With direct income support, the tariff can be, and is, fixed.

vi. Regarding the internal market, Chart I shows P^T, whereas Chart II displays in its place a level of direct income support. In Chart II, the tariff rate is less important, in a sense, than in Chart I, because the tariff is not centrally aimed at avoiding the undermining of P^T. Also regarding the internal market, both Charts indicate P^I. However, Chart II shows a lower P^I than Chart I, reflecting the cuts in support prices pursuant to CAP reforms.

vii. Both Charts show the World Market Price, P^{WM}. It pertains to imports and exports, being the amount the EU would pay for non-EU farm products, and the amount EU farmers would receive for exporting their goods. However, EU farmers receive a subsidy — the export refund — if they ship their goods overseas. The lower P^{WM} in comparison with P^{EU}, the greater the refund.

In examining the Charts, consider how to place the EU subsidy programs into the Amber, Blue, and Green Boxes of the WTO *Agreement on Agriculture*, and how export refunds would be treated. Consider, too, whether and how any of these programs affect the EU position in, and policy toward, FTA negotiations.

VI. EXPORT SUBSIDIES SUBJECT TO REDUCTION COMMITMENTS AND THE 2005 *SUGAR* CASE

A. The EU Sugar Subsidy Scheme

The 1992 MacSharry Reform, Agenda 2000, and 2003 Mid-Term Review of Agenda 2000 (all discussed earlier in this Chapter) omitted a major agricultural sector — sugar. The combination of long-run, trade-distorting CAP support for sugar and interest among many countries in sugar trade, strong international legal pressure on the EU to change its sugar regime was inevitable. In September 2002, Australia, Brazil, and Thailand successfully challenged the EU system for providing export subsidies to sugar. The WTO Appellate Body Report is excerpted below. It is helpful to put the case in context, namely, the factual predicate to the case and the aftermath of the Report.

Obviously, the common market organization for sugar is part of the CAP. The EU divides sugar produced in its territory into three categories — "A," "B," or "C." Sugar in categories A and B is for internal (*i.e.*, EU) consumption. It is subject to a quota, and the internal price is higher than the world market price. The internal price is a guaranteed minimum figure. Both sugar farmers and processing companies in the EU are eligible to receive at least this floor price. Category C is comprised of sugar produced in excess of the domestic quotas. Category C sugar is sold overseas at the world market price.

Responding to the complaint by Australia, Brazil, and Thailand, in October 2004 a WTO Panel held the sugar subsidy scheme violated limits on export subsidies to which the EU had agreed in the Uruguay Round and set forth in the *Agreement on Agriculture*. The Panel found the EU illegally cross-subsidized Category C sugar exports. It did so by compensating EU sugar producers through the higher guaranteed prices for the Category A and B quota sugar. In April 2005, the Appellate Body upheld the Panel ruling.

The adverse decisions put the EU under pressure to revamp its sugar subsidy scheme. In June 2005, the EU announced it would slash by 39 percent the guaranteed minimum sugar price. The intended effect would be to decrease EU sugar production, partly by forcing less competitive EU sugar farmers and processors out of business, and thereby reducing the amount of Category C sugar exports. Marginal sugar farmers and processors complained, saying a 39 percent cut was too deep. Many such producers were in poorer parts of the EU, or dependent territories. For them, and domestic consumers of their sugar, the EU sugar subsidy provided a measure of food security. By January 2007, sugar production ceased entirely in St. Kitts and Trinidad and Tobago.

During the reasonable period of time (RPT) for compliance with the Appellate Body Report a firestorm arose. In September 2005, the EU said it would give export subsidies to 1.9 million tons of sugar that had been produced for the internal market. That is, the EU declassified 1.9 million tons from the A and B quota Categories, and put this amount into Category C. The declassified sugar had benefited from the high guaranteed minimum internal price, and was being exported — precisely the cross-subsidization found illegal by the WTO Panel and Appellate Body. The three complainant WTO Members said the EU's action undermined the credibility of the WTO, because the EU was raising its subsidized sugar exports during the RPT. The extra 1.9 million tons would raise the total amount of subsidized EU sugar exports to 7.2 million tons, which was about 6 million tons over the annual limit applicable to the EU for subsidized sugar exports. In turn, world market prices likely would fall by over 6 percent. The EU replied with the observation the point of an RPT was to allow for implementation of a ruling, and immediate compliance is impossible.

B. Cross-Subsidization and Government Action

WTO APPELLATE BODY REPORT, *EUROPEAN COMMUNITIES — EXPORT SUBSIDIES ON SUGAR*
WT/DS265/AB/R, WT/DS266/AB/R, WT/DS283/AB/R
(adopted 19 May 2005)
(complaints by Australia, Brazil, and Thailand)

VI. Payments under Article 9.1(c) of the *Agreement on Agriculture*

A. Preliminary Remarks

227. Before the Panel, the Complaining Parties claimed that the EC sugar regime involved various types of "payments on the export of an agricultural product that are financed by virtue of governmental action" within the meaning of Article 9.1(c) of the *Agreement on Agriculture*. The Panel stated that the Complaining Parties claimed that the EC sugar regime:

> . . . involves a series of payments including: (a) payment in the form of below costs C beet sales to C sugar producers/exporters; (b) payment in the form of cross-subsidization resulting from the profits made on sales of A and B sugar used to cover the fixed costs of the production/ export of C sugar; (c) payment in the form of exports of C sugar below total costs of production; and (d) payments in the form of high prices paid by consumers. (footnote omitted)

228. The Panel limited its examination to the first two of the four types of alleged export subsidies set out above. The Panel found, with respect to the first type of "payment," that "C sugar producers receive payment on export by virtue of governmental action through sales of C beet below the total costs of production to C sugar producers." As for the second type of "payment," the Panel found that "producers/exporters of C sugar . . . receive payments on export by virtue of governmental action . . . in the form of transfers of financial resources, through cross-subsidization resulting from the operation of the EC sugar regime." Thus, the Panel found that both types of "payments" examined by it are "payments on the export . . . financed by virtue of governmental action," within the meaning of Article 9.1(c) of the *Agreement on Agriculture*, and that, therefore, they constitute exports subsidies within the meaning of Article 9.1. The Panel then concluded that the European

Communities had not demonstrated, pursuant to Article 10.3 of the *Agreement on Agriculture*, that exports of C sugar exceeding the European Communities' commitment levels since 1995 are not subsidized.

. . . .

B. Do Sales of C Beet Involve Export Subsidies within the Meaning of Article 9.1(c)?

230. The Panel made three distinct findings in concluding that sales of C beet by beet growers to sugar producers constitute an export subsidy within the meaning of Article 9.1(c) of the *Agreement on Agriculture*. The Panel held, first, that sales of C beet involved "payments," because C beet was being sold at prices below its average total cost of production; secondly, that these payments were "*on the export;*" and, thirdly, that these "payments" were "*financed by virtue of governmental action.*" The European Communities does not appeal the first and second of these Panel findings. Rather, the European Communities appeals the third Panel finding, that is, that "payments" in the form of sales of C beet are "financed by virtue of governmental action."

231. In making the contested finding, the Panel stated first that a "demonstrable link" and "clear nexus" between the financing of the payments and the governmental action must be established in order for the "payment" to qualify as a payment "financed by virtue of governmental action." The Panel then found that "a significant percentage of farmers of C beet are likely to finance sales of C beet below the costs of production as a result of [their] participation in the domestic market in selling high priced A and B beet." The European Communities, according to the Panel, controls virtually every aspect of domestic beet and sugar supply and management. In particular, the price and supply of A and B beet are fixed with a view to ensuring a stable and adequate income to beet growers; C beet (which is over-quota beet), generally speaking, can be used only in the production of C sugar, that is, over-quota sugar. Financial penalties are imposed by the European Communities on producers that divert C sugar into the domestic market. The Panel considered this "controlling governmental action" to be "indispensable" to the transfer of resources from consumers and taxpayers to sugar producers and, through them, to A and B beet growers.

. . . .

234. The Appellate Body has previously addressed Article 9.1(c) of the *Agreement on Agriculture* in *Canada — Dairy*, as well as in the compliance proceedings in that dispute, namely, *Canada — Dairy (Article 21.5 — New Zealand and US)* and *Canada — Dairy (Article 21.5 — New Zealand and US II)*. In those disputes, the Appellate Body interpreted the various elements of the phrase "financed by virtue of governmental action."

235. With respect to "governmental action," the Appellate Body found that "[t]he essence of 'government' is . . . that it enjoys the effective power to 'regulate,' 'control' or 'supervise' individuals, or otherwise 'restrain' their conduct, through the exercise of lawful authority." The Appellate Body also held that Article 9.1(c) does not place any qualifications on the types of

"governmental action" that may be relevant under that provision. The governmental action need *not* involve a government "mandate" or other "direction."

236. Addressing the word "financed," the Appellate Body held that this word generally refers to the "mechanism" or "process" by which financial resources are provided, such that payments are made. Article 9.1(c), by stating "whether or not a charge on the public account is involved," expressly provides that the *government itself* need *not* provide the resources for producers to make payments. Instead, payments may be made and funded by private parties.

237. With respect to the words "by virtue of," the Appellate Body has previously held that there must be a "nexus" or "demonstrable link" between the governmental action at issue and the financing of payments. The Appellate Body clarified that not every governmental action will have the requisite "nexus" to the financing of payments. For instance, the Appellate Body held that the "demonstrable link" between "governmental action" and the "financing" of payments would not exist in a scenario in which "governmental action . . . establish[es] a regulatory framework merely *enabling* a third person freely to make and finance 'payments.' " In this situation, the link between the governmental action and the financing of payments would be "too tenuous," such that the "payments" could not be regarded as "financed by virtue of governmental action" within the meaning of Article 9.1(c). Rather, according to the Appellate Body, there must be a "tighter nexus" between the mechanism or process by which the payments are financed (even if by a third person) and governmental action. In this respect, the Appellate Body clarified that, although governmental action is essential, Article 9.1(c) contemplates that "payments may be financed by virtue of governmental action even though significant aspects of the financing might not involve government." Thus, even if government does not fund the payments itself, it must play a sufficiently important part in the process by which a private party funds "payments," such that the requisite nexus exists between "governmental action" and the "financing." The alleged link must be examined on a case-by-case basis, taking account of the particular character of the governmental action at issue and its relationship to the payments made.

238. Turning to the specific circumstances of the present dispute, we note that, in its finding that "payments" in the form of sales of C beet below its total cost of production are "financed by virtue of governmental action," the Panel relied on a number of aspects of the EC sugar regime. The Panel considered, *inter alia*, that: the EC sugar regime regulates prices of A and B beet and establishes a framework for the contractual relationships between beet growers and sugar producers with a view to ensuring a stable and adequate income for beet growers; C beet is invariably produced together with A and B beet in one single line of production; a significant percentage of beet growers are likely to finance sales of C beet below the total cost of production as a result of participation in the domestic market by making "highly remunerative" sales of A and B beet; the European Communities "controls virtually every aspect of domestic beet and sugar supply and management," including through financial penalties imposed on sugar producers that divert C sugar into the domestic market; the European Communities' Sugar Management Committee "overviews, supervises and protects the [European Communities']

domestic sugar through, *inter alia*, supply management;" the growing of C beet is not "incidental," but rather an "integral" part of the governmental regulation of the sugar market; and C sugar producers "*have incentives* to produce C sugar so as to maintain their share of the A and B quotas," while C beet growers "have an incentive to supply as much as is requested by C sugar producers with a view to receiving the high prices for A and B beet and their allocated amount of . . . C beet."

239. We agree with the Panel that . . . all of these aspects of the EC sugar regime have a direct bearing on whether below-cost sales of C beet are financed by virtue of governmental action. As a result, we are unable to agree with the European Communities' first argument on appeal, namely, that the Panel applied a test under which an Article 9.1(c) subsidy was deemed to exist "simply because [governmental] action 'enabled' the beet growers to finance and make payments." Rather, we believe that the Panel relied on aspects of the EC sugar regime that go far beyond merely "enabling" or "permitting" beet growers to make payments to sugar producers. Indeed, in our view, there is a tight nexus between the European Communities' "governmental action" and the financing of payments in the case before us. We have no doubt that, without the highly remunerative prices guaranteed by the EC sugar regime for A and B beet, sales of C beet could not take place profitably at a price below the total cost of production.

. . . .

243. . . . [I] n its analysis of whether the below-cost sales of C beet were "financed by virtue of governmental action," the Panel considered the key aspects of the EC sugar regime and concluded that "C beet growers can use the profits made on the sales of A and B beet to cross-subsidize the sale of C beet" and that "a significant percentage of farmers of C beet are likely to finance sales of C beet below the costs of production as a result of participation in the domestic market in selling high priced A and B beet." The European Communities, . . . is, in essence, challenging the manner in which the Panel weighed and assessed the evidence in coming to the conclusion that C beet growers finance sales of C beet as a result of participation in the highly regulated domestic market. We . . . do not find fault with the Panel's analysis. . . .

244. We now turn to the European Communities' argument that governmental action under the EC sugar regime is "less pervasive" than governmental action in *Canada — Dairy (Article 21.5 — New Zealand and the US II)*. We do not consider it inherently useful to compare the governmental action at issue and the governmental action in the context of a different dispute. The issue before us is not a comparison between two governmental regimes, but rather, whether "payments" under the EC sugar regime are "financed by virtue of governmental action." As the Appellate Body stated in *Canada — Dairy (Article 21.5 — New Zealand and the US)*, "the existence of . . . a demonstrable link [between governmental action and the financing of payments] must be identified *on a case-by-case basis, taking account of the particular governmental action at issue* and its effects on payments made by a third person." In any event, we have already reviewed the aspects of the EC sugar regime on which the Panel relied to make its finding, including the

"European Communities['] control[] [of] virtually every aspect of domestic beet and sugar supply and management," and found the EC sugar regime to be pervasive. Hence, the Panel correctly concluded that the "payments" at issue are being "financed by virtue of governmental action."

. . . .

247. In response to questioning at the oral hearing, the European Communities stated that two "types" of production of C beet exist: one part of the production of C beet is due to "profit reasons," namely, where beet growers are trying to obtain an additional profit because they are able to sell C beet above marginal costs and their fixed costs are covered by sales of A and B beet or of other products; and another part of C beet production, by contrast, is "unintended" and is the result of "other factors," in particular, yield variations. Hence, it is clear that a part of C beet is produced because beet growers are able to obtain "additional profit" by selling such beet below its average total cost of production, but above its marginal costs, while covering their fixed cost by means of sales of A and B beet (or other products).

248. . . . [T]he European Communities did not contest the Panel's finding that production of C sugar represents 11 to 21 per cent of the European Communities' overall production of A and B sugar and that, correspondingly, C beet represents the same proportion of the production of A and B beet. C beet is an important input for C sugar production. We also recall that C beet is being sold at prices that are approximately 60 per cent of the C sugar world market price, which is well below its average total cost of production. In our view, the continued production of such large volumes of over-quota beet, at prices well below its cost of production, could not take place but for governmental action. . . . [T]he Panel found that "the European Communities fails to explain why large numbers of [European Communities'] farmers are engaged in growing C beet if such production only serves to deliver losses" and "the European Communities . . . fails to explain why farmers would maintain, within a mix of farming activities, any sectoral production for which expected revenue is persistently less than the cost of production . . . of C beet."

. . . .

250. For these reasons, we *uphold* the Panel's finding . . . that the alleged payments in the form of low-priced sales of C beet to sugar producers are "financed by virtue of governmental action," within the meaning of Article 9.1(c) of the *Agreement on Agriculture*.

C. Do "Payments" in the Form of "Cross-subsidization" Constitute Export Subsidies within the Meaning of Article 9.1(c)?

1. Introduction

. . . .

253. . . . The Panel found that "cross-subsidization," "in the form of transfers of financial resources from the high revenues resulting from sales of A and B sugar, for the export production of C sugar," constitutes an export subsidy within the meaning of Article 9.1(c) of the *Agreement on Agriculture*.

254. The European Communities argues on appeal that this finding of the Panel is in error because (i) "cross-subsidization" does not constitute a "payment," because it does not involve a "transfer of resources" to the sugar producers; and (ii) the alleged "payment" is not made "on the export" of C sugar, because the sugar producers are not required to produce or export C sugar. . . .

. . . .

2. Whether "Cross-subsidization" Constitutes a "Payment" within the Meaning of Article 9.1(c) of the *Agreement on Agriculture*

257. In finding that "cross-subsidization" constitutes a "payment" within the meaning of Article 9.1(c) of the *Agreement on Agriculture*, the Panel addressed a number of factors. Recalling the Appellate Body's finding in *Canada — Dairy (Article 21.5 — New Zealand and US)*, the Panel used the average total cost of production benchmark for C sugar and noted that C sugar was sold on the world market at prices "well under" the average total cost of production every year from 1992/1993 to 2002/2003. The Panel observed that "the price charged for C sugar does not even remotely cover its cost of production." The Panel also found that "to the extent that the fixed costs of A, B and C [sugar production] are largely paid for by the profits made on sales of A and B sugar, the EC sugar regime provides the advantage which allows EC sugar producers to produce and export C sugar at below total cost of production." The Panel concluded that there was a "payment" "in the form of transfers of financial resources from the high revenues resulting from sales of A and B sugar, for the export production of C sugar, within the meaning of Article 9.1(c) of the *Agreement on Agriculture*."

258. The European Communities argues that the alleged "cross-subsidization" does not involve a "transfer of resources" to the sugar producers, but rather, is: "an internal allocation of each sugar producer's own resources;" the alleged "cross-subsidization" provides no benefit to the sugar producers; and the Panel's interpretation is not supported by the findings of the Appellate Body in the *Canada — Dairy* disputes. The European Communities also submits that the Panel's interpretation turns Article 9.1(c) into "a prohibition of low priced exports" and a "sort of blunt anti-dumping instrument."

259. The Appellate Body interpreted Article 9.1(c) of the *Agreement on Agriculture* in the appeal in *Canada — Dairy*, as well as in the compliance proceedings in that dispute, *Canada — Dairy (Article 21.5 — New Zealand and US)* and *Canada — Dairy (Article 21.5 — New Zealand and US II)*. In those disputes, the Appellate Body held that the word "payment" in Article 9.1(c) denotes "a transfer of economic resources" and that the ordinary meaning of the word "payment" "encompasses 'payments' made in forms other than money." The Appellate Body also found that Article 9.1(c) of the *Agreement on Agriculture* describes an "unusual form of subsidy," in that "payments" can be made by private parties and need not be made by a government. The Appellate Body has also held that the notion of payments covers "a diverse range of practices involving monetary transfers, or transfers-in-kind;" the

"payments" may take place in "many different factual and regulatory settings;" it is necessary to consider the "particular features" of the alleged "payments;" and the standard for determining the existence of "payments" under Article 9.1(c) must be identified after careful scrutiny of the factual and regulatory settings of the measure.

260. In addition, in *Canada — Dairy (Article 21.5 — New Zealand and US)* and *Canada — Dairy (Article 21.5 — New Zealand and US II)*, the Appellate Body held that, in the circumstances of those disputes, the determination of whether payments were made depended on a comparison between the price of a particular product — commercial export milk ("CEM") in those cases — and an "objective standard or benchmark which reflects the *proper value of [that product] to [its] provider*." In those disputes, the Appellate Body found that the standard for determining the proper value of CEM was the average total cost of production, as this standard represented the economic resources the producer invested in the milk that was an input to the production of dairy products. If CEM was sold at less than its proper value — namely, its average total cost of production — "payments" were made, because there was a transfer of the portion of economic resources that was not reflected in the selling price of CEM.

261. In the dispute before us, the Panel applied this benchmark, namely, the average total cost of production for sugar. On appeal, . . . the European Communities does not take issue with the Panel's use of the average total cost of production benchmark in order to ascertain the existence of "payments." Rather, the European Communities argues that the "payments" identified by the Panel are not "payments" within the meaning of Article 9.1(c), because they constitute only an "internal allocation" of the sugar producer's resources and do not provide the sugar producer with new additional resources. The European Communities submits that the existence of a "transfer of resources" implies, by definition, the presence of two different parties, "one which grants the resources and another which receives them."

262. . . . Article 9.1(c) does not qualify the term "payments" by reference to the entity making, or the entity receiving the payment. This may be contrasted with, for instance, Articles 9.1(a) and 9.1(b) of the *Agreement on Agriculture*, which specifically refer to the entities making and also, in the case of Article 9.1(a), to the entity receiving the alleged export subsidy. Moreover, Article 9.1(c), on its face, does not qualify the meaning of the term "payments," other than by requiring that the alleged "payments" be "on the export of an agricultural product" and "financed by virtue of governmental action."

. . . .

264. This, however, does not imply that the term "payment" necessarily requires, in each and every case, the presence of two distinct entities. In other words, contrary to the European Communities' argument, we do not see, *a priori*, any reason why "payments," within the meaning of Article 9.1(c), cannot include, in the particular circumstances of this dispute, transfers of resources within one economic entity. The "payment" in this case is not merely a "purely *notional* "one but, rather, reflects a very concrete transfer of economic resources to C sugar production. In the specific dispute before us,

C sugar is being sold on the world market by European Communities' sugar producers/exporters at a price that does not "even remotely" cover its average total cost of production. In the light of the enormous difference between the price of C sugar and its average total cost of production, we do not see how the "payment" identified by the Panel was "purely notional."

265. The European Communities' approach is, in our view, too formalistic. To illustrate, one could envisage a scenario under which the producers of C sugar are legally distinct from the producers of A and B sugar. In this situation, the European Communities' approach could recognize that a "payment" under Article 9.1(c) could exist because there would be a transfer of economic resources between different parties. If, however, these same producers of A, B, and C sugar were integrated producers and organized as single legal entities, a payment under Article 9.1(c) would not exist, because the transfer would be merely "internal." We do not believe that the applicability of Article 9.1(c) should depend on how an economic entity is legally organized.

266. Accordingly, we do not share the European Communities' objections to the Panel's findings on "cross-subsidization" in the case before us. In this respect, we are also mindful of the fact that, in the ordinary course of business, an economic operator makes a decision to produce and sell a product expecting to recover the total cost of production and to make profits. Clearly, sales below total cost of production cannot be sustained in the long term, unless they are financed from some other sources. This is especially true when the volume of the loss-making sales is substantial. It may be noted that between 1997 and 2002, C sugar exports varied between 1.3 and 3.3 million tonnes, with the sales price not "even remotely" covering the average total cost of production of sugar.

. . . .

268. . . . The European Communities argues that, because the alleged "cross-subsidization" involves no "transfer of resources" to the sugar producers, it confers no *benefit* upon these producers and, therefore, cannot be considered to provide a subsidy. The European Communities disagrees with the Panel's finding that Article 9.1(c) does not require the demonstration of a benefit for a measure to constitute a "payment" within the meaning of that provision.

269. The *chapeau* of Article 9.1 provides: "The following export subsidies are subject to reduction commitments." Hence, Article 9.1 sets forth a list of practices that, by definition, involve export subsidies. In other words, a measure falling within Article 9.1 is deemed to be an export subsidy within the meaning of Article 1(e) of the *Agreement on Agriculture*. We observe that Article 9.1(c) requires no independent enquiry into the existence of a "benefit."

270. For these reasons, we *uphold* the Panel's finding . . . that, in the particular circumstances of this dispute, the production of C sugar receives a "payment on the export financed by virtue of governmental action," within the meaning of Article 9.1(c) of the *Agreement on Agriculture*, in the form of transfers of financial resources through cross-subsidization resulting from the operation of the EC sugar regime.

. . . .

3. Whether "Payment" in the Form "Cross-subsidization" is "On the Export" within the Meaning of Article 9.1(c) of the *Agreement on Agriculture*

272. The Panel concluded that the "payment" in the form of "cross-subsidization" was a payment "on the export" of C sugar within the meaning of Article 9.1(c) of the *Agreement on Agriculture*. The Panel based its finding on the fact that C sugar, unless carried forward, must be exported. The Panel stated that "[b]ecause of that legal requirement, advantages, payments or subsidies to C sugar, that must be exported, are subsidies 'on the export' of that product." The Panel also added that "[t]he only reason why producers of C sugar export C sugar, is because they are prohibited from introducing such sugar into the domestic market, facing heavy penalties pursuant to Article 13 of the EC Regulation [1260/2001] if they do."

273. The European Communities argues that the Panel misinterpreted the requirement that a payment be "on the export" of an agricultural product, as contained in Article 9.1(c). The European Communities argues that this term must be read as meaning "contingent on" exports, rather than "in connection with" or to the "advantage" of exports. The European Communities contends that, under a proper interpretation of the requirement "on the export," this requirement is not satisfied in the present case because "the sugar producers are entirely free to decide whether or not to produce C sugar and, in fact, many do not produce any C sugar at all."

274. . . . . In relation to below-cost sales of C beet, the Panel stated that "payments" "on the export" need not be "contingent on" the export but, rather, need be "in connection" with exports. When analyzing whether "payments" in the form of "cross-subsidization" were "on the export," the Panel did *not* use the same reasoning. Instead, the Panel based its findings on the following reasoning:

> C sugar [can] only be sold for export. If not reclassified, C sugar "may not be disposed of in the Community's internal market and must be exported without further processing." Because of that legal requirement, advantages, payments or subsidies to C sugar, that must be exported, are subsidies "on the export" of that product. (footnote omitted)

275. We agree with the Panel. Under Article 13(1) of EC Regulation 1260/2001, C sugar "must be exported." It follows that payments in the form of "cross-subsidization" are, by definition, "payments" "on the export."

276. The European Communities argues that there is no requirement to *produce* sugar under the EC sugar regime and hence payments in the form of "cross-subsidization" are not "on the export" within the meaning of Article 9.1(c). In our view, the Panel neither suggested that there is a requirement to *produce* C sugar, nor relied on such a requirement for its conclusion that "payments" in the form of "cross-subsidization" are "on the export." Rather, the Panel relied on the fact that, under EC Regulation 1260/2001, C sugar, *once produced*, must be exported.

277. The European Communities refers to the possibility, under EC Regulation 1260/2001, to store and "carry forward" C sugar to the next marketing

year, up to an amount equivalent to 20 per cent of the A sugar quota. We are not persuaded that the possibility to store and "carry forward" C sugar has a bearing on the criterion "on the export" in this dispute. According to the European Commission, C sugar "carried forward" is "treated as A sugar produced by [a producer] as part of that year's production." Moreover, when "carried over" sugar is sold on the European Communities domestic market, the sugar producers must pay to beet growers "the guaranteed prices" that apply only to quota beet and not to C beet. It would appear, therefore, that carrying C sugar forward, for all practical purposes, is in effect a reclassification of C sugar into quota sugar. As a result, we do not believe that the possibility to "carry forward" C sugar invalidates the Panel's finding that "payments" in the form of "cross-subsidization" are "on the export" of C sugar.

278. For these reasons, we *uphold* the Panel's finding . . . that "the payment on C sugar production in the form of [a] transfer of financial resources through cross-subsidization resulting from the operation of the EC sugar regime is *on [the] export* within the meaning of Article 9.1(c) of the *Agreement on Agriculture*." (original emphasis)

279. We wish now to address the European Communities' concern that upholding the Panel's finding that the payments at issue are "on the export" within the meaning of Article 9.1(c) would lead to "blur[ring] the distinction between the disciplines on domestic support and on export subsidies, which is an essential feature of the *Agreement on Agriculture*" and would "allow . . . virtually any form of domestic support" to be "characterize[d] as an 'export subsidy.'" As the Appellate Body has previously stated, WTO Members are entitled to provide "*domestic support*" to agricultural producers within the limits of their domestic subsidy commitments. We observe, however, that the Appellate Body has also held that economic effects of WTO-consistent domestic support may "spill over" to benefit export production. Such spill-over effects may arise, in particular, in circumstances where agricultural products result from a single line of production that does not distinguish between production destined for the domestic market and production destined for the export market.

280. . . . [T]he Appellate Body has cautioned that, "if domestic support could be used, without limit, to provide support for exports, it would undermine the benefits intended to accrue through a WTO Member's export subsidy commitments." . . . [T]hese statements are relevant to the present case. . . . [W]e note that C sugar is produced and exported in huge quantities, and that there is a considerable difference between the world market price and the average total cost of production of sugar in the European Communities. . . . [T]he subsidized production and export of C sugar is not the incidental effect of the domestic support system, but is a direct consequence of the EC sugar regime.

281. We also disagree with the European Communities' argument that the Panel's finding blurs the distinction between domestic support and export subsidies; we disagree, because the European Communities' legislation *requires* the exportation of C sugar, and prices obtained for C sugar on the world market are significantly below the average total cost of production of sugar in the European Communities. In our view, European Communities' legislation leaves the sugar producer wishing to sell C sugar with no choice but to

export, short of the limited option of "carry over." . . . [T]he operation of the EC sugar regime enables sugar producers to cover the fixed costs of producing sugar and to sell C sugar profitably, even though the prices obtained for C sugar are significantly below the average total cost of production of sugar.

Part Fourteen

SERVICES

Chapter 47

SERVICES TRADE NEGOTIATIONS

"Bad, bad!" says the buyer;
but once he has gone his way,
he boasts.

　　　—The Bible, *The Book of Proverbs* 20:14

Documents Supplement Assignment

1. WTO *General Agreement on Trade in Services (GATS)*
2. *NAFTA* Chapters 12-14, 16
3. Relevant provisions in other FTAs

I. SIX THRESHOLD PROBLEMS

Six threshold problems about the *General Agreement on Trade in Services (GATS)* render it no less, and perhaps even more, controversial than GATT.

Problem #1: Coverage

Unlike obligations covering goods under GATT, obligations for services under *GATS* do not apply in a horizontal way. That is, except for a few duties, *GATS* obligations do not apply across the board. In practice, then, most *GATS* obligations are sector-specific and country-specific.

Problem #2: Untested Terrain

The untested nature of *GATS* is evident in a non-legal sense. The economic, social, and cultural effects of services privatization and service trade liberalization have been, are, and will continue to be much debated. With only a handful of Appellate Body reports dealing with claims or defenses under the *GATS*, this agreement remains largely untested legal terrain, too. With GATT, since 1947, there has been a steady development of core rules, in terms of substance and reach. In contrast, *GATS* did not arrive on the desks of international trade lawyers in complete form until 1994. It was the product of complex negotiations in the 1986-93 Uruguay Round. Those negotiations led to a document, *GATS*, that contains many compromises that sometimes lack logic, other than political expediency, partial commitments, inconsistencies and tensions, and ambiguities. The paucity of case law on *GATS* means there are a lot of hypothetical propositions and assumed facts about how the text "ought" to work in practice. But, the legal results are not clear. The only fully and finally adjudicated Appellate Body cases are *EC — Bananas* and *Antigua Gambling* (both excerpted herein), along with application in the *Canada Auto Pact* case of some *Bananas* precedents.

Problem #3: An Evolving Text

The text of GATT is set. Amendments to it have been rare, most recently on 9 June 1966 when Part IV (Articles XXXVI, XXXVII, and XXXVIII) entered into force. Following the Uruguay Round, when "GATT 1994" replaced "GATT 1994," there was no textual change to GATT itself; rather, it was supplemented with various *Decisions* and *Understandings*. In contrast, *GATS* was not entirely complete at the end of the Uruguay Round — negotiators simply could not get the deals done.

Thus, during the first 4 years following the conclusion of that Round (*i.e.*, from 1994-97), provisions were negotiated on liberalizing services trade in a number of sectors.[1] There are six sector-specific Annexes to *GATS*, some of which anticipated post-Uruguay Round negotiations:

Annex on Air Transport Services

Annex on Financial Services

Second Annex on Financial Services

Annex on Negotiations on Maritime Transport Services

Annex on Telecommunications

Annex on Basic Telecommunications

As yet, some Annexes are incomplete. For instance, the *Maritime Services Annex* still is being negotiated. In sum, the text of *GATS* still evolves, resulting in legal uncertainty.

Problem #4: Evolving Services Businesses

The nature of services businesses is changing. The causes include consumer needs and tastes, and advances in information technology. Regulatory policies, particularly with respect to culture, education, energy, environmental sanitation (*e.g.*, garbage collection), finance, health, transportation, and water, also catalyze (and in some instances respond to) changes in service provision. A key question is how *GATS* rules, which themselves evolve through negotiations and decisional law, will apply to a dynamic world of services businesses. While that question applies to GATT rules, arguably most goods markets change relatively less dramatically and quickly than most services markets.

Problem #5: Dominance

In at least some agricultural and industrial markets, developing — and occasionally least developed — countries are regionally if not globally competitive. Ecuador and Ghana are leaders in bananas and cocoa, respectively. India is strong in manufacturing generic medicines, steel, and textiles and apparel. Thailand has attracted considerable foreign investment in the auto and auto parts sectors. While some back office and call center operations have been sent off shore to poor countries, generally these countries are not major players in services markets. That is, it is an inconvenient truth for trade officials from the developed world, who seek to liberalize services trade, that large multinational corporations (MNCs) from these countries — notably the U.S. and EU

---

[1] *See Second Protocol to the GATS*, WTO Document S/L/11 (24 July 1995), *Third Protocol to the GATS*, WTO Document S/L/12 (24 July 1995), *Fourth Protocol to the GATS*, WTO Document S/L/20 (30 April 1996), and *Fifth Protocol to the GATS*, WTO Document S/L/45 (3 Dec. 1997).

— dominate many, if not most, services markets. "Inconvenient" because it makes free trade in services through *GATS* a more difficult proposition to sell to developing and least developed — and, indeed, some developed — countries than free trade in goods through GATT.

Since the 1980s, the World Bank has advocated strongly the privatization of services as a means of delivering more, and better quality, services to the poor, especially in the education, energy, environmental sanitation, health, transportation, utilities, and water sectors. Yet, MNCs from the First World are, or would be with privatization, the providers of these core services to the Third World. What scope would there be in the markets of developing and least developed countries for privatized companies from these countries, and what competitive position might they be in, relative to the MNCs?

Problem #6: Sovereignty

Connected with the problem of dominance is sovereignty. Many GATT obligations concern measures applied at the border, such as tariffs and quotas, to the movement of goods. Some duties, like GATT Article III:1-2, on indirect taxation, and Article X, on transparency, go beyond the border. In comparison, *GATS* deals far more extensively with post-border measures than does GATT. That is because of the nature of services trade. Speaking loosely, tariffs and quotas — *i.e.*, financial or quantitative impositions — may apply to certain modes of services delivery. A fee may be required by the central bank or Ministry of Finance from a foreign bank wishing to open a branch in that country, or an annual limit on the number of licenses the central bank or Finance Ministry gives for opening foreign bank branches may exist. But, in general, trade in services involves much more behind-the-border regulation than does trade in goods.

Consequently, for almost any services sector or sub-sector, trade liberalization raises behind-the-border regulatory issues in the host country. Traditionally, the host country government decides how those issues are resolved. Not infrequently, that government interprets — or misinterprets — pressure to open service markets as pressure to cede sovereignty over its regulatory powers. Is *GATS* an instrument for pushing the host country government out of its own territory, displacing it with MNCs and their powerful home country governments? How can developing and least developed countries effectively manage the tension between (1) preserving regulatory sovereignty and (2) opening services markets to realize greater efficiency and competitiveness?

II. THE EVOLUTION OF *GATS* AND 4 MODES OF SERVICE SUPPLY

The story of how *GATS* came about is both fascinating and complex. One approach to organizing and synthesizing this history is to identify 12 major steps that took the world of multilateral trade law from "nothing" on services to the *GATS*.

Step 1: Conceptual Shift

There had to be a conceptual shift about services, without which *GATS* was impossible. In particular, two paradigmatic shifts occurred in the early and mid 1980s, without which *GATS* would have been impossible:

From Public Service Monopolies to Private Service Suppliers:

A change from viewing services as fundamental social products provided by the public sector, *i.e.*, thinking the government is the key (if not the only) provider in services, to seeing services as a marketplace, and the private sector as the key provider of services. Quintessential examples include electricity, transportation, and water supply.

From Services as Non-Tradeable to Services as Tradeable:

A change from delimiting the scope of international trade to goods to expanding the boundaries of trade to include services, wherein commercial entities could provide services across borders through 4 basic means, known as "Modes," of supply. (These Modes, cross-border supply (I), consumption abroad (II), establishment of commercial presence (III), and movement of national persons (IV), are discussed below.) Leading examples include education, energy, finance. The U.S. pioneered the shift in its free trade agreement (FTA) policy, negotiating provisions in *North American Free Trade Agreement* (*NAFTA*) to liberalize services trade.

Once thinking changed about services provision and trade, three consequences followed.

First, it became widely understood international trade in services is subject to, and inhibited by, non-tariff barriers (NTBs). Second, it became apparent NTBs to services trade could be disciplined by principles borrowed from GATT, such as MFN, national treatment, market access guarantees, and other trade-in-goods type obligations. Third, it became increasingly accepted that NTBs should be subject to these disciplines, *i.e.*, the benchmark for negotiations on disciplines on international services trade should be trade liberalization, meaning free trade. In brief, *GATS* was possible only because of adoption of the idea services could be traded internationally by private enterprises. This shift permitted identification and removal of impediments to services trade.

Why did these paradigmatic movements, and the corollaries, occur? Three causal variables may be identified:

Business Pressure:

In the early 1970s and extending into the 1980s the American financial services sector (*e.g.*, American Insurance Group (AIG), American Express, Bank of America, Citibank, Goldman Sachs, J.P. Morgan, and Merrill Lynch) sought enhanced market access abroad. Seeing tremendous expansion opportunities in countries in which a middle class was emerging and the number of high net worth individuals was growing, this sector began lobbying for removal of barriers to services trade.

Technological Advances:

Also during the 1970s and 1980s, information technology (IT) — commercial computers and satellites — made it possible for services to flow across borders more easily and faster than ever before. The provision of IT itself became a traded service. International transportation technology — especially with the advent of the jumbo jet — improved dramatically. This technology meant goods could be distributed across boundaries easier and faster than before. Distribution itself became a service. It also made travel and tourism services more attractive than before. Better and cheaper audio-visual technology made the transportation of culture and entertainment cheaper and quicker than in any previous era in human history. Entertainment services increasingly became a borderless endeavor.

OECD Preparatory Work:

In the 1970s, the OECD engaged in initial work on services trade. That it was the OECD to do so is not surprising. The OECD, comprised of developed countries, represents the home countries of most MNCs. They are the home countries because for many services, the big markets are in rich, not poor, countries.

No doubt aggressive American advocacy (discussed separately below) was a fourth factor causing the conceptual shift.

Step 2: 1982 — *The First GATT Discussion*

By virtue of the OECD preparatory work, the issue of services trade liberalization was pushed into a broad, multilateral forum — GATT. In 1982, the first discussion of services occurred under the auspices of the contracting parties and GATT Secretariat. Four years before the launch of the Uruguay Round, services trade and liberalization thereof were on the agenda, albeit tentatively, for the contracting parties to discuss.

Step 3: *Aggressive American Advocacy*

No GATT contracting party wanted services trade liberalization on the agenda of any new round of multilateral trade negotiations more than the U.S. American trade negotiators faced significant opposition from their Third World, and especially Indian and Brazilian, counterparts. Deeply suspicious of American intent, they argued that their local services providers would be crowded out by American MNCs. The American side, however, was well prepared for this argument, and succeeded in getting the issue on the GATT agenda.

First, the U.S. collected data on (1) the volume and value of international trade in services, and (2) the types of NTBs to cross-border trade in services, such quotas (limits on the number of service providers allowed in a country), restrictions on FDI (blocking or conditioning the physical establishment of a service provider), limits on access to subsidies for services (*e.g.*, bestowing subsidies only on local providers), and preferences for local service providers over foreign providers (*e.g.*, tax or non-tax advantages). Second, the U.S. proved services indeed were — or could be — trade across borders. The U.S. identified four distinct "Modes" of this trade (discussed below). Having done and having identified NTBs, the U.S. identified negotiating parameters — what was traded, how it was traded, and what impeded trade. Third, the U.S. obtained the support of like-minded countries, *i.e.*, other GATT contracting parties favoring free trade in services. Together, they moved the issue forward through a series of mini-ministerial conferences.

Step 4: The Creation of Precedents

By 1986, the U.S. advocacy succeeded in placing services on the agenda of the Uruguay Round, launched in September of that year in Punta del Este, Uruguay. The U.S. had put the Third World on the defensive as being "protectionist" and "not having clear arguments." Moreover, it made plain there would be no successful outcome to the Round, indeed no Round, if services were left off the negotiating table. As the Round transpired, two important precedents were established for services trade liberalization, thus supporting the American-led effort.

First, in 1988, Australia and New Zealand supplemented their FTA, called the *Closer Economic Relationship (CER)*, with a Services Annex. Unlike *GATS*, the 1988 *CER* Services Annex does not discuss different modes of services supply. Rather, the Annex employs a Negative List approach, which means that all services sectors are presumed to be covered by the *CER* except for those sectors specifically listed as sensitive. This approach is based on a free trade presumption. To be sure, during *GATS* negotiations, no country — save for the U.S. — looked to the Negative List approach as a model for *GATS*. However, the very existence of the *CER* Annex was a stepping stone for multilateral services trade liberalization, even if conducted on a Positive List approach (whereby liberalization occurs only in sectors explicitly listed).

Second, in 1993, the U.S., Canada, and Mexico entered *NAFTA*. Initially, the *NAFTA* Parties called for a Positive List approach to services trade liberalization. Subsequently, the agreed to use a Negative List approach. In turn, in *GATS* negotiations, the U.S. advocated the Negative List approach. That advocacy proved successful.

Step 5: The UNCTAD Counter-Attack

No cohort of contracting parties more fiercely opposed inclusion on the formal GATT agenda of services trade liberalization than Third World countries. They responded to aggressive American advocacy for inclusion by saying there would be no Uruguay Round unless the U.S. and other developed countries agreed to liberalize trade in textiles and farm products, *i.e.*, to reform of the 1974 *Multi-Fibre Agreement*, and to a first-ever *Agreement on Agriculture*. Brazil and India led the counter-attack.

If rich countries had the OECD as their vehicle, then poor countries had the United Nations Conference on Trade and Development (UNCTAD). Cleverly, the latter group invoked UNCTAD, in which Brazil and India held considerable sway, as a forum in which to develop arguments about whether GATT-type concepts and arguments about goods were applicable to the world of services. Surely, thought Brazil, India, and many UNCTAD members, services are a national matter. Surely, the dominant players in domestic services markets are, and ought to be, the public sector.

Significantly, UNCTAD concluded that a services agreement through a GATT multilateral trade round would be nothing more, or less, than an investment agreement. Why did UNCTAD take this view, *i.e.*, why did it equate services with investment? The answer is that the main service providers were (and still are) from the First World. Services trade liberalization would mean investment by these providers into the Third World. Moreover, in the late 1970s and early 1980s, UNCTAD was engaged in a major project on investment — writing of a Code of Conduct on FDI, which would regulate the entry and behavior of MNCs in host countries. The U.S. opposed the draft FDI Code. But, UNCTAD said the U.S. was trying to use GATT as a forum to get what, in effect, would be an agreement on FDI that would facilitate MNC operations across the globe. Indeed, observed UNCTAD, a major advocate in the United States of the services initiative was the American Chamber of Commerce.

Thus, by the mid-1980s, the lines of debate were clear. The U.S. demanded talks on services, and the Third World demanded talks on textiles and agriculture. Each side had its favorite forum, GATT and UNCTAD, respectively. Hoping to advance matters, the Third World advocated a two-tack approach, whereby talks on textiles and agriculture would proceed in a GATT round, and talks on services would be informal (not part of the formal negotiating agenda in the round), and would occur in part through UNCTAD. The U.S. countered successfully with the position that a Uruguay Round must be a "single undertaking." Though this device, it was assured the two tracks (services as well as goods, and agriculture and textiles) were linked, and the ultimate result would be the Grand Bargain of the Uruguay Round.

Step 6: Privatization in the 1980s

Talks on services trade liberalization would have been inconceivable without privatization. Privatization would have been inconceivable without resolute Anglo-American leadership. Throughout the 1980s, President Ronald Reagan and Prime Minister Margaret Thatcher implemented deregulation reforms in the First World, and advocated structural adjustment programs for the Third World. Their position both contributed to and reinforced breathtaking events in former communist countries. Both kinds of reforms — deregulation in the First World, and Third World structural adjustment in the Third World — led to privatization. Once privatization of services was underway, the need for an international agreement on services trade was a logical next step.

Once that step was taken, *i.e.*, once services became a topic in GATT circles, the yardstick for measuring progress and success became free trade. Any GATT contracting party opposing a barrier to services trade could be labeled a protectionist. In the "anyone" category were Brazil, India, and many of their UNCTAD allies.

Step 7: American Identification of 4 Modes of Services Delivery

Perhaps the most critical aspect of U.S. advocacy to place services on the GATT agenda, and set free trade as the benchmark for services trade, was a conceptual. All goods traded across borders move physically — that is the only mode of delivery. But, services are less obvious, even intangible. How could negotiations even begin on liberalizing services trade unless GATT contracting parties had a common understanding as to the ways in which services are provided and traded? The U.S. provided the response. It identified four ways in which services cross international boundaries, known as the four "Modes." So successful was the U.S. response that it is enshrined in *GATS* Article I:2, as follows.

Mode I: Cross-Border Supply
GATS Article I:2(a)

This Mode is pure cross-border trade, as it is defined as providing a service from the territory of one country into the territory of another country. Neither the service supplier, nor the service customer, moves. Rather, the service is produced in one country, consumed in another country, and each side stays put.

A prominent example is a foreign degree program offered by correspondence. The University of London offers a Masters degree (LL.M.) in law, and a student in the U.S. can obtain the degree without going to England. Tele-medicine is another example of Mode I. A patient in Kenya can obtain a diagnosis and treatment through video conferencing with the University of Kansas School of Medicine, without traveling to Kansas City. Tele-dental and tele-veterinary services are further illustrations.

Mode II: Consumption Abroad
GATS Article I:2(b)

This Mode is defined as providing a service in the territory of one country (where the provider is) to a consumer from another country. Hence, it entails movement by a service consumer from its home (or a third) country to the country in which the service supplier is located. The service itself does not travel, rather, the consumer of the service crosses a border into the jurisdiction in which the service is offered.

The many students from overseas who come to the University of Kansas School of Law for a J.D. or S.J.D. degree consume legal education services abroad. Every foreign tourist (*e.g.*, an American consuming services in New Zealand) exemplifies Mode II (*e.g.*, by staying in hotels, eating in restaurants, and attending Maori dance performances). Note tourism counts in balance of payments (BOP) statistics as foreign exchange earnings for the country (*e.g.*, New Zealand) in which a tourist (*e.g.*, an American) consumes the services. Note, too, a small but growing area of Mode II services is medical tourism. A patient journeys from one country to another country for a health service. (An example is the mother-in-law, from Malaysia, of your Textbook author, who came to the U.S. for double knee replacement surgery in the summer 2001). High costs in some developed countries, coupled with rising standards in a few developing countries, appear to contribute to the growth of the medical tourism market.

Mode III: Commercial Presence (FDI)
GATS Article I:2(c)

This Mode is service supply by a foreign entity through direct foreign investment. It is by far the most commonly used method of cross-border service provision. The legal types of entry may vary from one country to another, and from one type of service to another. Choice of form of entry is likely to be determined by host country rules, and affected by strategic business interests. The spectrum of possibilities includes corporate subsidiary, joint venture (JV), branch, agency, representative office, and franchise.

Thus, for example, Islamic Law countries may require formation of a partnership, as corporations are unknown to the *Shari'a*. China may require a JV arrangement in certain fields, especially insurance and telecommunications. Regardless of the type — be it incorporation of a subsidiary, a JV arrangement, a branch, an agency, a franchise, or a simple representative office — the common feature is a parent entity is establishing a physical presence in the jurisdiction of another country. Examples of Mode III delivery abound: a Carrefour store in Muscat and a Wal-Mart store in Beijing; a Citibank branch in Tokyo and a Hong Kong Shanghai Banking Corporation (HSBC) facility in Dubai; an Emirates Airlines office in Colombo and a Qantas Airlines office in Los Angeles; and, of course, franchises outside the U.S. of Kentucky Fried Chicken (KFC), McDonald's, Pizza Hut, and Starbucks.

Mode IV:
Temporary Movement of Natural Persons
(Temporary Immigration)
GATS Article I:2(d)

This Mode refers to the movement of a natural person from one country temporarily across a border into another country for the purpose of supplying a service through the presence of that person in the territory of the second country. A service provider from one country sends one (or more) employees or consultants temporarily overseas to provide a service. A lawyer from Lahore, Pakistan, posted in the Dubai office of her firm, a Turkish law teacher from Bahçeşehir University in Istanbul appointed by the University of Kansas as a Visiting Professor to teach *Comparative Criminal*, and an engineer sent by a German company to India to work on a power project, all are examples of Mode IV delivery. However, the services need not be professional. For example, construction crews from the Indian Subcontinent, or nannies from the Philippines, working in Persian Gulf countries, or laborers from Mexico working in the U.S. on farms or in restaurants, illustrate Mode IV delivery.

Mode IV is a particularly controversial one, especially as it pertains to non-professional services, and tends to divide rich from poor countries. Indeed, unlike the other three Modes, Mode IV is the subject of a special annex to *GATS* — the *Annex on Movement of Persons Supplying Services Under the Agreement*. Notably, *GATS* Article IV calls for increasing participation of these countries in global services trade. With large and growing populations, rising human capital levels, and improving English language skills, many such countries boast a comparative advantage in supplying services through the movement of natural persons. They view themselves as net exporters of temporary workers. However, invariably, Mode IV is the leas open method of service delivery among countries of the Organization for Economic Cooperation and Development (OECD). This group of developed countries imposes tight immigration restrictions. Poor countries retort that the reluctance of rich nations to liberalize Mode IV delivery makes a mockery of *GATS* Article IV. They accuse them of hypocrisy — seeking broad, deep commitments to liberalize Modes I, II, and III, but being loathe to make commitments themselves on Mode IV. They also accuse them of being disingenuous. Is the real reason for Mode IV restrictions national security, or is it fear of wage declines and job loss if unskilled and semi-skilled workers are permitted lawful entry in large numbers? Consider, then, whether and to what extent services trade liberalization is asymmetric.

These four Modes have been — and, as is clear from the above references to *GATS* Article I:2, remain — the basis for categorizing international services trade, and making commitments to free up such trade. Observe, however, that one other basis is needed — a way of classifying the myriad of services actually traded, akin to the Harmonized System (HS) for classifying goods imported across borders.

Step 8: American Identification of Barriers to Services Trade

Were there few barriers to international trade in services, there would be little about which to negotiate. As a practical matter, a key part of the American-led effort to bring services to the GATT agenda, and secure a multilateral services agreement, was identification by the U.S. of the main barriers to services trade. The U.S. concluded all of them were NTBs. Examples included:

  i. On Mode I —

Restrictions on transmitting money out of a country to pay for services, or preferences for the use of domestic service providers.

  ii. On Mode II —

Limits on taking money out of a country, preferring local service providers, or limiting freedom of travel across borders.

  iii. On Mode III —

Rules on FDI, such as requiring a foreign company to have local directors, having 49 percent of its equity held by locals, or mandating investment through a JV.

  iv. On Mode IV —

Restrictions on immigration, especially with respect to visa and work permit requirements.

In highlighting the four Modes, and the fact NTBs were impediments, the U.S. indicated it would be inappropriate to fold services trade into the traditional GATT framework.

Step 9: Uruguay Round Positions

In keeping with its aggressive advocacy, the initial U.S. position in the Uruguay Round was for a comprehensive agreement on free trade in services. Political complexities doomed this position. The European Union (EU), however, presented stiff opposition, arguing for managed trade. Unable to persuade both the EU and the Third World that free, not managed, trade ought to be the goal of the negotiations, the U.S. acquiesced. In consequence, the U.S. bargaining stance effectively shifted to one of aggressive reciprocity — if not every GATT contracting party was willing to open up all of its services sectors, then the U.S. would not open up some of its sensitive sectors.

What were those sensitive American sectors? At the top of the list were aviation, including commercial and cargo transport, finance, including commercial and investment banking, and insurance, maritime transport (especially cabotage). The EU had its own sensitive sectors. France, for example, stressed the importance of protecting cultural industries from an invasion by the likes of Disney and Hollywood.

Once GATT contracting parties tread the path of identifying and seeking exclusions for sensitive service sectors, Uruguay Round negotiations could not be horizontal, *i.e.*, for all sectors. That is, ambitious across-the-board liberalization became impossible. Use of a Negative List approach, with assurances by each country it would keep its List short, looked increasingly unlikely. Rather, negotiations became sector-by-sector — tortuous, inch-by-inch, as it were — and it appeared a Positive List approach would be used. To be sure, liberalization commitments were listed in a Schedule of Services Concessions that contained sector-specific pledges. But, few countries made horizontal commitments. Many commitments they did make were complex.

Complexity arose from four sources. First, commitments applied only to listed sectors or sub-sectors. Second, for each scheduled sector or sub-sector, commitments applied only to certain market access Modes (I, II, III, or IV — but, not all four Modes). Third, commitments were subject to reservations. For instance, a country might agree to open itself up to foreign commercial banks through Mode III. But, this commitment might be followed by reservations allowing the country to impose quantitative restrictions (*e.g.*, it would issue no more than 10 foreign banking licenses per year), geographic restrictions (*e.g.*, licenses would be issued only for operations in two cities), activity restrictions (*e.g.*, foreign banks could not take deposits or make loans in local currency, or engage in foreign exchange trading). Other reservations might concern regulation of the form of entity (*e.g.*, a foreign bank could establish only a subsidiary through a joint venture, but not a wholly owned branch or agency), or ceilings on foreign shareholding (*e.g.*, the foreign bank parent could hold no more than a 49 percent equity stake in the local entity). Fifth, pledges of national treatment were subject to derogations (*e.g.*, the host country could favor local banks, by for example, granting only them the right to be a primary dealer in treasury securities).

Concomitant with complexity in commitments was complexity in rules. Instead of sweeping rules applying horizontally, rules presuming free trade as the base line, Uruguay Round negotiators drafted a text replete with obligations of limited scope and subject to exceptions. They allowed for exemptions from the MFN rule in Article II, for domestic regulations in Article VI, and for discriminatory rather than strict national treatment under Article XVI. (Conditions for imposing an MFN exemption are set out in the *GATS Annex on Article II (MFN) Exemptions*.) Evidently, the result of *GATS* commitments, and the text of *GATS*, would be far from free trade in services.

Whether the American effort toward free trade in services was misguided and improbably from the outset is debatable. What is indubitable is *GATS* cannot be said to be a free trade agreement on services. Rather than a document mandating universal liberalization of trade in services in one shot, *GATS* calls for progressive liberalization — or, less euphemistically, managed trade. Disappointing as that outcome was — and still is — to free traders, at least *GATS* is a beginning, and at least it embodies commitments to ongoing liberalization.

Step 10: Conditional MFN Treatment

As intimated above, once the idea of sector-specific commitments took hold among GATT contracting parties in the Uruguay Round, the next logical question concerned the scope of such commitments. Should a commitment, when it is made and scheduled, apply on an MFN basis, *i.e.*, should it be multilateralized immediately and unconditionally, as would be the requirement for a commitment on a good under GATT Article I:1?

On this issue, the U.S. took a predictable position. If free trade was neither the goal nor the outcome, then the U.S. was going to resist "free riders" — and it did so with success. The MFN rule for services in *GATS* Article II:1 became a conditional obligation. To avoid a country, such as Malaysia, free riding on a pledge by, for example, the U.S., to liberalize trade in a particular sector or sub-sector, without Malaysia providing any commitment roughly equivalent to the American pledge, the MFN rule applies neither automatically nor immediately. In the example, the U.S. could choose whether to grant its commitment to Malaysia, or whether it to hold out until Malaysia makes a substantially equivalent concession.

Step 11: Progress in the Uruguay Round

Two years into the Uruguay Round, at the 1988 mini-Ministerial Conference in Montreal, the GATT contracting parties had made notable progress on services trade liberalization. They agreed:

   i.   No services sector should be excluded *a priori*, *i.e.*, a Negative List approach should be employed.

   ii.   A country could exclude a services sector, but it should do so explicitly, and abstemiously, through careful use of its Negative List.

   iii.   The pillars of GATT — MFN and national treatment, market access through binding commitments, and transparency — plus core principles such as promoting increased participation by less developed countries, and allowing for safeguards — needed to be incorporated into *GATS*.

Not entirely satisfied, the U.S. took aim at contracting parties it viewed as resisting more substantial progress. They were, for the most part, less developed countries. America's trade negotiators adopted what might be dubbed a "Divide and Move" policy, and focused their sights especially on

Brazil, Egypt, and India, which they wished to isolate in the Uruguay Round services talks.

However, these three developing countries pushed back hard. They read the September 1986 Punta del Este *Declaration* launching the Uruguay Round as saying the mandate was only to negotiate a framework for talks on services. Services trade liberalization talks, they said, would occur under an agreed-upon modalities after conclusion of the main Uruguay Round negotiations on goods, including agriculture and textiles. In sharp contrast to the Americans, they did not read the text of the *Declaration* to say there was a mandate to negotiate an actual agreement itself, simultaneously with a deal on goods. From the American perspective, this reading was nothing more than an incarnation of the two-track strategy, already tried and rejected.

Accordingly, and after much hard bargaining, by the 1990 Brussels mini-Ministerial, the GATT contracting parties reached agreement on the following points:

- The structure of a framework text, that is, an actual document containing basic rules on services trade liberalization, ultimately called "*GATS*."

- Annexes would be used to handle leftover items, *i.e.*, issues not covered in the basic *GATS* deal, and also for liberalization commitments in specific sectors in which negotiations could not be finished.

- Each country would have a Schedule of Services, akin to its Schedule of Goods, to embody its trade liberalization commitments.

Services negotiations during the final years of the Uruguay Round tended to focus more on sector and sub-sector requests and offers, and less on the draft of the framework text. That text, along with other draft accords in the Uruguay Round, became known as the "Dunkel Draft," named after the GATT Director-General responsible for producing it, Arthur Dunkel.

Step 12: The Final Outcome

With respect to services, the Dunkel Draft (dated 20 December 1991) was basically the text the GATT contracting parties adopted in December 1993 as the Uruguay Round *GATS*. At that juncture, much business was unfinished. The contracting parties agreed there would have to be Annexes and Schedules for the yet-to-be-agreed on sectors, namely, financial services, maritime transport, and telecommunications.

III. CLASSIFYING SERVICES

A. The Draft United Nations System

Negotiating trade liberalization in services at any level — multilateral, regional, or bilateral — requires more than just agreement on the four Modes of delivery. It also presumes a common classification of the myriad of services traded across borders. Unfortunately, however, there is no Harmonized System (HS) for services, akin to the HS for goods, nor has the task of producing one been assigned to, or taken up by, the multilateral body responsible for the HS — the World Customs Organization (WCO) in Brussels, Belgium. To fill this void, the WTO — and the GATT Secretariat before it — have had to come up with a classification system for services. Their answer is colloquially known as the "W120."

The W120 is the WTO's Services Sector Classification List. In fact, the W120 is drawn from the United Nations Central Product Classification ("CPC") List. The CPC List was not complete when the Uruguay Round ended on 15 December 1993 — the United Nations still was at work refining it. Nevertheless, negotiators in that Round worked off of the CPC List, and it remains the basis for services trade liberalization negotiations among WTO Members. The W120 categorizes services into

- Sectors,
- Sub-sectors, and
- Sub-sub-sectors.

There are 11 standard Sectors:

1. *Business*:

This Sector is huge, covering the range from accountancy to midwifery, and also including legal services.

2. *Communication*:

This Sector also is large, embracing audiovisual, courier, postal, and other such services.

3. *Construction*:

All aspects of building comprise this Sector.

4. *Distribution*:

Any means by which products — goods or services — are distributed are considered distributional services. Thus, wholesale and retail services, and franchising, are included.

5. *Education*:

This Sector is the category for educational services at all four levels — primary, secondary, tertiary, and adult.

6. *Engineering*:

Aeronautical, biomedical, civil, computer, and mechanical engineering services are included in this Sector.

7. *Environment*:

This Sector includes emissions, sanitation, and waste disposal. However, it does not yet (as of March 2003) cover provision of water for human consumption (*i.e.*, potable water services).

8. *Finance*:

This Sector is another capacious category. It embraces commercial banking, insurance, investment banking, portfolio management, securities brokerage, dealing, and underwriting. However, the impact of including commercial banking in the W120 List and CPC, and thereby being subject to *GATS*, is blunted by the *GATS Annex on Financial Services*. There are some "carve out" provisions in the Annex, especially an exemption for prudential supervisory reasons, that limit commitments on commercial banking.

        9.   *Health and Social Services*:

Still another commodious category is this one. It covers a wide range of health services, which may be provided in an institutional context (*e.g.*, nurses in a hospital) or non-institutional context (*e.g.*, home care nurses).

       10.   *Recreation and Culture*:

This Sector covers a diverse array of leisure-related services, such as archives, entertainment, libraries, museums, and sports. The 2004 *Antigua Gambling* case deals with the categorization of gambling services in relation to this Sector.

       11.   *Transportation*:

This category, which is contentious in terms of liberalization, covers air services and maritime services. The fact they are covered is blunted by the existence of Annexes to *GATS* for each sector, which contain carve outs.

As intimated, within each Sector, there are standard Sub-sectors. In turn, within each sub-sector there are standard Sub-sub-sectors.

For example, within the Business Services Sector, one Sub-sector is "Professional." Within the "Professional" sub-sector, there are 6 Sub-sub-sectors: "Accounting," "Dental," Legal," Medical, "Midwifery," and "Nursing." Within the Recreation and Culture Sector, one sub-sector is "Tourism." Within the "Tourism" sub-sector, there are 4 sub-sub-sectors: "Cleaning," "Hotel," "Sports and Recreation," and "Transportation (land, air, sea)." These classifications form the basis for each WTO Member's Services Schedule, negotiations to liberalize trade in services, and recording commitments and reservations on such trade.

Critically, when a country WTO Member negotiates terms in its Schedule, it has to be precise. That is, when it is making a request of another Member for liberalization, or when it is making an offer to another Member, it must clear about exactly which Sector, Sub-sector, or Sub-sub-sector to which the request or offer refers. Likewise, when a Member is contemplating a carve-out (exception) to its offer, or in the offer of another Member, it must be careful to appreciate the sectors, sub-sectors, or sub-sub-sectors to which the carve-out applies. For instance, suppose the U.S. schedules commitments in Professional Services, seeking to liberalize foreign provision in this sub-sector. But, the U.S. seeks to preserve the autonomy of state authorities to regulate bar admission based on examinations. The commitment should make clear it applies to "Business Sector, Professional Services Sub-sector, all Sub-sub-sectors except Legal."

B.   Lingering Classification Issues

Observe four issues concerning the W120 List and CPC scheme. First, the 11 standard sectoral categories are broad. That is evident from a perusal of the sub-sectors and sub-sub-sectors. Many more gradations could be made than exist. For instance, the "Legal" sub-sub-sector could be divided into "Barrister" and "Solicitor" for some common law countries, a special category of "Paralegal" could exist, and gradations could be made on field of law, such as "Antitrust," "Corporate," "International," "Litigation," "Taxation," and so on.

Second, there is nothing eternal about the W120 List or CPC scheme. Since the Uruguay Round, the United Nations has revised the CPC (on at least two occasions, as of March 2003). Countries can, and should, continue to develop categories to suit emerging services markets, and sharpen the lines of categories covering extant markets. Indeed, the List and scheme are not as organized as they might appear. Energy services are one example. There is no separate sector for this globally important area. Rather, energy-related services are strewn across multiple sectoral categories. Not surprisingly, several WTO Members have made proposals to improve classification of energy services.

Environmental services are another example of the need for enhanced classification. Since the end of the Uruguay Round, there has been much liberalization, in the form of privatization, especially of water services. During the Doha Round, the EU favored reclassification of environmental services such that this category would include:

- Water
- Solid waste
- Air
- Noise

Why does the EU take this position? First, it is a provider and net exporter of such services. Second, this scheme is functional, and suits the lines in which EU businesses are engaged.

Third, might "clustering" be a good basis for classifying services? The example of environmental services suggests one strategy for refining categories is to disaggregate them into functional business lines. Clustering calls for like or similar services to be grouped together. Consider the Tourism sub-sector, which includes the sub-sub-sectors of Cleaning, Hotel, Transport (land, sea, and air), and Sports and Recreation. The argument in favor of clustering is that it leads to a pro-free trade outcome. If WTO Members make commitments in one sub-sector, but not in related sub-sectors, then the full practical benefits of the concessions are not realized. To expedite and broaden liberalization, it would be preferable to have commitments on all sub-sectors that are related in practice to one another. However, there are 2 arguments against clustering. First, clustering might inhibit a WTO Member from making any commitment whatsoever. Second, a sub-sector may fit well into either one of two clusters. For example, is the "Postal" better put with air transport services or tourist services?

Fourth, to what extend does, and should, the traditional public — private distinction play a role in services categorization, especially in a world in which many services have been, or are being, privatized? An instructive example comes from the Doha Round, during which New Zealand proposed reclassifications to remove the old fashioned "public — private" distinction, especially for Postal Services. The New Zealand government authority, New Zealand Post, does not have a monopoly, even on the traditional core area business of the letter rate. The government sought to break down the old fashioned ways of describing postal operations, and focus on the function — what is being delivered (*e.g.*, letter, parcel, etc.). The result would be even an implicit public — private distinction. Interestingly, New Zealand's position was motivated in part by its distaste for the Universal Postal Union (UPU), which offers non-MFN benefits in international postal services for Third World countries. Some entrepreneurs have used (or abused) those benefits by setting up operations in a Third World country. New Zealand argued that such behavior undermined the integrity of *GATS*.

IV. READING A SERVICES SCHEDULE

A. Key Terms and the Modes

Reading a Schedule of Concessions on services is more complicated than reading a Schedule of Concessions on goods. That is because of the 4 Modes of delivering services across borders. Trade liberalizing concessions, and exceptions thereto, apply not only to specific Sectors, Sub-sectors, or Sub-sub-sectors, but also to particular Modes of delivery. Thus, in reading a Services Schedule, it is critical to pay attention to the Mode, as well as the kind of service, at issue. Each Modes is indicated by numbers, such as Roman numerals (I, II, III, or IV), or Arabic numerals (1, 2, 3, 4), corresponding respectively to cross-border supply, consumption abroad, FDI, and temporary migration of natural persons.

In theory, any commitment to liberalize services trade may be "horizontal." That means the commitment applies across the board, to all Sectors, Sub-sectors, or Sub-sub-sectors, and to whatever Modes of delivery, indicated by the Member making the commitment. A Horizontal commitment is set out at the start of a Member's Services Schedule. A Horizontal commitment need not be repeated for every sector in the Schedule, precisely because it applies across the board, to all sectors. Notably, a Horizontal commitment can be an exception that applies across-the-board. For example, in its Services Schedule, New Zealand lists as a horizontal exception the *Treaty of Waitangi*. This *Treaty* is critical in preserving Maori rights.

In practice, for most WTO Members, there are few Horizontal commitments. When made, they tend to be promises, and exceptions there to, concerning FDI (Mode III) and movement of natural persons (Mode IV). Most commitments are given on a Sectoral, Sub-sectoral, or Sub-sub-sectoral basis, and on a Mode-by-Mode basis.

Another reason for the relative complexity of a Services Schedule is its peculiar terminology. Among the key words and phrases to understand that typically are found in the Services Schedule of a WTO Member, or in negotiations on requests and offers to liberalize services trade, are:

- The word "Unbound" means a WTO Member makes no commitment in that Sector, Sub-sector, or Sub-sub-sector. That is, "Unbound" indicates no trade liberalization concession has been granted — put colloquially, there are no promises. Thus, the Member can impose any restrictions on the kind of foreign provision at stake. The term is akin to no binding tariff commitment on a product category in a Schedule for goods.

- The word "None" does not mean "no commitments." If it did, then it would be synonymous with "Unbound." To the contrary, "None" is the polar opposite of "Unbound." "None" indicates a WTO Member imposes no restrictions on foreign providers entering its market. Whereas "Unbound" is the most protective indication, "None" is the most pro-free trade commitment. "None" bespeaks total commitment to free trade, in the sense of no limits on trade in the Sector, Sub-sector, or Sub-sub-sector, and through the Modes, indicated.

- When a WTO Member makes a commitment, the technical language it uses is "Unbound, except for. . . ." The promise of trade liberalization is contained in the "except for. . ." clause, and what follows it. In effect, the Member is saying "We make no pledge on trade liberalization for this kind of service, except for the following agreement to open up our market." The words in the "except" clause are critical. They delineate the extent of market access, and ambiguities in it can be the source of dispute. For instance, on Mode 4, if a Member says "Unbound, except for certain employees," then it means the Member makes no pledges on allowing foreign providers to migrate temporarily into that Member, except for "certain employees." But, who are those employees? Are they professional workers, and if so must they be senior managers? Are skilled laborers, semi-skilled laborers, or unskilled laborers included? What parameters define "professional" and "skill" levels?

- The words "Unbound, except for. . ." or "Unbound, except as indicated in the Horizontal Section" mean "there are no binding promises [to liberalize trade in this service], except for the following" or "except as we listed in the Horizontal Section."

- Occasionally, an asterisk (*) appears in a Services Schedule. In particular, a WTO Member may record "Unbound *." The asterisk means it is not possible for that Member to make a binding commitment. Thus, for instance, if a Member states "Cleaning Services (1) Unbound *," then the Member is indicating a foreign provider cannot clean a building by cross-border mode (Mode 1). That, of course, is a physical fact.

Odd as it may seem, in many service fields, for many Modes, and across many WTO Members, no entry appears. What does silence in a Services Schedule mean?

The answer is no entry means a WTO Member has made no commitment at all. That is, if the Member writes nothing for a particular Sector, Sub-sector, or Sub-sub-sector, and a corresponding Mode, then the Member is making no associated trade liberalization commitment. Thus, the legal effect of no entry (silence) is the same as saying "Unbound."

B.   Case Study: New Zealand and Professional Services

To appreciate Services Schedule terminology, and how it interacts with each Mode of service delivery, consider the following example of a portion of the Services Schedule for New Zealand. This example is hypothetical (as in fact, as of March 2003, the New Zealand Schedule had no entries concerning the practice of law).

Note, first, there are three columns in the Schedule. The first column is the service category of issue. In reality, it would also state the number in the W120, which corresponds to the CPC, for the services at issue. The middle column chronicles rules applicable to foreign providers seeking access to the market of the WTO Member to which the Schedule corresponds. The last column displays exceptions to national treatment. Taken together, the three columns tell a story — in *GATS* coded language — about the extent to which a Member is willing to permit free trade for a kind of service.

The left-hand column indicates the Sector or Sub-sector at issue. Here, the concern is Professional Services, which covers 6 Sub-sectors — accounting, dental, legal, medical, midwifery, and nursing.

The middle column shows commitments on market access made by New Zealand for each of the 4 Modes of delivery in the Professional Services sub-sector. For Mode 1, cross-border supply, New Zealand permits free trade, *i.e.*, foreigners can provide professional services via e-mail, tele- and video-conferencing, and short-term visits. However, there is an important exception. Such services may not be provided in the health services area, namely, by dentists, doctors, midwifes, and nurses. Query whether physicians assistants, or X-ray technologists, would be covered by the "except" clause? For Mode 2, consumption abroad, New Zealand permits unconditional free trade. Consumers from New Zealand may travel freely abroad to obtain any Professional Services.

TABLE 47-1:
PORTION OF NEW ZEALAND SERVICES SCHEDULE
(Hypothetical Example)

Sector or Sub-Sector	Limitations on Market Access	Limitations on National Treatment
Business Services Sector, Professional Services Sub-Sector	(1) None, except for Dental, Medical, Midwifery, and Nursing.	(1) None
	(2) None	(2) None
	(3) Unbound, except for Legal, which must be provided in partnership with a New Zealand law firm of which more than 50 percent of ownership is by citizens of New Zealand.	(3) Unbound, except for Legal, which may be provided without passage of the New Zealand Bar Examination, except for representation in New Zealand courts, with the designation "Foreign Legal Consultant."
	(4) Unbound, except for Legal, for which up to 100 one-year work permits may be granted by the Government of New Zealand per year.	(4) Unbound, except for Legal, where preference for one-year work permits may be given to foreign lawyers in specialty fields in which there is no New Zealand citizen practicing in the same geographic market.

For Mode 3, FDI, New Zealand makes no commitment. Thus, for instance, foreign accountants or doctors cannot freely enter New Zealand and establish practices. However, there is a major exception — for lawyers. Foreign attorneys can practice in New Zealand, but must do so in a partnership with New Zealand lawyers, and the partnership must be controlled effectively by those lawyers. For Mode 4, temporary migration, New Zealand again makes no commitment, but subject to an exception for the legal services sub-sub-sector. Each year, the New Zealand government reserves for foreign lawyers up to 100 year-long visas to reside and work in New Zealand.

The right-hand column contains limitations on national treatment imposed by New Zealand on Professional Services trade. On Modes 1 and 2, there are no limitations on national treatment, meaning New Zealand does not reserve the right to prefer domestic providers of a Professional Service over foreign providers. That is, with respect to cross-border supply or consumption abroad, it must treat foreign and New Zealand accountants, health professionals, and lawyers in the same manner. The story is different for Modes 3 and 4. For FDI, New Zealand makes no commitments on Professional Services, other than the legal sub-sub-sector. There, an attorney from overseas, who has not passed the New Zealand bar examination, may practice in New Zealand, but with the special title "Foreign Legal Consultant," and may not appear in a

New Zealand court. Regarding temporary migration, in allocating professional visas, the New Zealand government may give preference to lawyers in specialties where there is no domestic competitor. Query how the government might define a legal "specialty." Would International Trade Law be a specialty, as distinct from International Commercial Law? Query how the government might draw the boundaries of a "geographic market"? Would the city of Auckland market include the Bay of Islands, too?

C. Binding Commitments and the Problem of Ossification

While "*GATS* speak" allows for precision in services trade negotiations and liberalization, it also creates a risk of ossification. For example, suppose in a particular sector New Zealand says that government approval for FDI (Mode 3) is required for any investment of NZ $10 million or more. This threshold is the bound level, and indeed was the commitment made in the Uruguay Round. However, since 1993, when New Zealand bound this level, it has raised the level to NZ $50 million (as of March 2003). Therefore, the applied rate is higher — NZ $50 million. Could New Zealand reduce the applied level to the bound level? Yes. Could it reduce the applied level to below the bound level, say to NZ $5 million? No, as that move would violate its bound commitment.

This illustration shows the relevance of bound commitments under *GATS* Article XVI:2, which are akin to tariff bindings under GATT Article II:1(b). However, the example also suggests a problem with bindings, namely, how can a Services Schedule keep up with changes in domestic legislation and regulation? Another instance is reference in a Schedule to legislation no longer in existence — as in the New Zealand Schedule, which mentions statutes, like the *Dairy Board Act*, that have been repealed. Still another instance of ossification arises when a WTO Member negotiates an FTA.

For example, in 2001, New Zealand and Singapore entered into an FTA. In that deal, New Zealand set NZ $50 million as the threshold for approval of an FDI project. Consequently, a Singaporean investor needs approval from authorities in Wellington only if its proposed project in New Zealand exceeds NZ $50 million. In effect, New Zealand made a "*GATS* Plus" commitment in the FTA. The *New Zealand — Singapore FTA* also says there is no obligation to apply the NZ $50 million threshold on an MFN basis. This exception creates an incentive to an investor from a third country (*e.g.*, the U.S.) to invest in New Zealand through Singapore.

A problem related to ossification is use of terms like "currently," which is found in the New Zealand Schedule. Does that word mean as of 15 December 1993, when Uruguay Round negotiations finished and New Zealand's commitment thus became final, or does it mean today? If "currently" refers to 1993, then a commitment made by one government binds the next and subsequent governments. That is advantageous insofar as it ensures against reneging on the commitments if a different political party comes to power. But, it leaves little room for maneuver. What can a future government do if there is market failure in a services sector in which a government has made a commitment? How might the government withdraw, or modify, its commitment, or take remedial action? Observe *GATS* Article XXI concerns changes to Schedules of Concessions. What does it require?

V. SERVICES TRADE COMMITMENTS (*GATS PREAMBLE,* PARTS I, AND IV-VI)

A. Scope of Coverage

What services are covered by services trade negotiations and the text of *GATS*? Several legal factors delineate the scope.

1. *Key Terms*:

Part I (Article I) of *GATS* explains the scope of the agreement, and it, along with Part VI (Article XXVIII), provides general definitions. Not unlike GATT, throughout *GATS*, the term "measures" (as well as "disciplines") is used. *GATS* applies to any "measures by Members affecting trade in services." Manifestly, the key terms delineating the boundaries are "measures," "affecting," "trade," and "services."

2. *"Measure"*:

A "measure" is defined (in *GATS* Article XXVIII(a)) as any law, regulation, rule, procedure, decision, administrative action, or other device. The breadth of this definition is deliberately intended to identify and discipline all ways governments impede services trade (or try to do so). Examine the final phrase in the definition, "or any other form." Does it cover *de facto*, as well as *de jure*, devices?

3. *"Trade in Services" and the 4 Modes*:

The 4 Modes (discussed above) also are intended to be thorough, embracing all manners by which services are traded across international boundaries, and thereby subject services trade — however it occurs — to *GATS* disciplines. The legal device linking these Modes to scope is the *GATS* Part I definition of "trade in services." That definition, in Article I:2, is constructed on these Modes, *i.e.*, "trade in services" is defined in terms of the 4 modes. The subparagraphs of Article I:2, that is, Article I:2(a)-(d), respectively, set out the 4 Modes.

4. *Sovereignty*:

It is critical to understand WTO Members are asked, but do not have to, make commitments on each Mode. For instance, in a particular services area, such as the Engineering Services Sector, a WTO Member could make a commitment on only one Mode. Simply put, while some Members may come under considerable exogenous or endogenous pressure to liberalize trade in particular Sectors, Sub-sectors, and Sub-sub sectors, as a legal matter *GATS* preserves the sovereignty of each Member to choose, or eschew, commitments.

5. *General Exceptions*:

Exceptions built into *GATS* limit the scope of its coverage. While not gaping holes in the accord, they are not excessively narrow either. Notably, *GATS* Article XIV is entitled "General Exceptions." With five itemized provisions, it is less extensive than its cousin in GATT Article XX, which has ten exceptions. (The considerable freedom of WTO members to choose services on which to make commitments in their Schedules may account for the lesser number, *i.e.*, there may be less need for a laundry list in GATS akin to that in GATT.) Still, Article XIV affords Members to derogate from *GATS* obligations if "necessary" to (1) "protect public morals" or "maintain public order," (2) "protect human, animal or plant life or health," or (3) "secure compliance with laws or regulations" that are not inconsistent with *GATS*. These exceptions are akin to GATT Article XX(a), (b), and (d), respectively. *GATS* Article XIV also affords two tax-based exemptions — to derogate from the (4) national treatment rule (of Article XVII) to secure "equitable and effective" direct taxation, or (5) the MFN rule (of Article II) to implement a tax treaty on avoidance of double taxation. Note that al five exceptions (which are discussed further in the 2005 *Antigua Gambling* case) are subject to a *chapeau*, as are the GATT Article XX exceptions. To what degree are the respective *chapeaux* alike?

6. *Public Services Exemption*:

As part of the definition of "services," *GATS* Article I:3(b) sets out a second exception. Called the "Public Services Exemption," it provides a further limitation on the scope of services trade liberalization and the reach of *GATS* for services not provided on a commercial basis or in competition with the private sector.

7. *Classification*:

Significantly, the range of services subject to liberalization negotiation and *GATS* disciplines is, in practice, a function of the United Nations Classification System — the W120 list and the CPC scheme (discussed earlier). It might be said categorization goes a long way to determining scope, with a direct relationship between the two. That is because the System is used by *GATS*, and is the basis for the Schedules of Services of each WTO Member. Fortunately for free traders, all core services areas are embraced by the System and thus covered by *GATS*.

8. *"Affecting"*:

What about the word "affecting"? What determines whether a measure "affects" any of the wide range of services traded? Must the effect be actual, or is a potential effect enough? *GATS* does not answer these questions. Hence, there is scope for interstitial law making by WTO panels and the Appellate Body

9. *Cooperation*:

GATS Part V contains provisions about institutional structures necessary to implement, monitor, and advance services trade liberalization, notably the Council for Trade in Services (created by Article XXIV). Part V also contains provisions designed to facilitate the involvement of developing country WTO Members in such liberalization. For example, service suppliers are to receive technical assistance through contact points established by developed country Members (Articles IV:2 and XXV). The Members themselves are to work with international organizations involved in services, such as the International Telegraph Union (ITU) and Universal Postal Union (UPU). The extent to which these processes occur and produce meaningful results is open to question, but the basic aim — to expand the scope of services trade liberalization and discipline impediments on such trade — is clear enough.

10.   *Dispute Settlement*:

As the small number of cases dealing with *GATS* suggests, including the 1997 Appellate Body Report in *EC — Bananas* (excerpted in an earlier Chapter), and the 2005 Appellate Body Report in *Antigua Gambling*, the scope of *GATS* is set in part by judges in Geneva. *GATS* Part V requires (in Article XXIII) recourse to the *Dispute Settlement Understanding* (*DSU*), should consultations (under Article XXII), which are the right of each Member to call for, fail to resolve a controversy between or among WTO Members.

11.   *FTAs and CUs*:

Finally, WTO Members may expand the scope of liberalization commitments through negotiations on other services agreements, namely, regional trade agreements (RTAs). However, under *GATS* Article V (discussed in an earlier Chapter), they — free trade agreements (FTAs) and customs unions (CUs) — must be "*GATS* Plus" agreements, or at least consistent with *GATS*. Sub-multilateral deals cannot be used to cut back on multilateral commitments. Conversely, deals made through FTAs and CUs may form the basis for expanded *GATS* commitments in subsequent multilateral bargaining.

What *GATS* does not define, of course, is the factor pre-eminent in determining scope — the ambition of countries to open up markets to free — or freer — trade and subject these markets to *GATS* regulation. That ambition depends on a mix of economic and political logic, both within and among WTO Members.

B.   Requests and Offers

Once the economic and political momentum favors services trade liberalization, how are negotiations actually conducted in practice? Again, *GATS* does not strictly answer the question. Over a period of time relatively short in comparison with the life of GATT, but drawing on the experience of rounds of GATT negotiations, the short answer is on a request-and-offer basis.

First, each WTO Member draws up a list of requests with respect to every other WTO Member of what it would like to see liberalized in that other Member. These requests are based on the assessment of the requesting Member of barriers to services trade in the other Members, and on the export interests of the services providers in the requesting Member. For example, suppose New Zealand asks South Africa to commit all educational services in all Modes of supply. South Africa may have the same request from other WTO Members. Then, South Africa studies the requests and decides what it is prepared to offer.

At this point, an offer is made — or may be made. In the example, South Africa might reply to New Zealand: "Here is what we are prepared to do on educational services liberalization. Are you, New Zealand, prepared to make a commitment on tourism?" The result is an "offer," coupled with a new "request." Suppose New Zealand accepts the new request. The result is a deal.

Significantly, the result is multilateralized. Any bargaining outcomes on services trade liberalization are extended to all WTO Members under the MFN obligation of *GATS* Article II. Therefore, the commitment by South Africa to New Zealand on educational services, and the commitment by New Zealand to South Africa on tour services, is applied to all other WTO Members. Observe, however, the starting point is a bilateral one. That is, a request is made on a bilateral basis, and negotiations and discussions about the request, and any offer, also are on a bilateral basis. The two WTO Members know any request-offer to which they agree will get multilateralized. They also know offers can be withdrawn, and that an exception to the MFN principle could be taken. The bilateral request-offer system can be cumbersome, and led to movement in the Doha Round toward a plurilateral method.

Notably, requests and offers are made in confidence. However, during the Doha Round, WTO Members came under pressure to be more transparent than they had been in the Uruguay Round. The pressure increased in 2001, when the EU requests on environmental services, which it made to 24 other countries, were leaked. The requests were controversial. For example, the EU wanted New Zealand to lift all limits on FDI (Mode III) on environmental services. In response, the EU, as well as the U.S., Australia, and New Zealand began releasing to the public "consultation documents." These texts summarize offers and requests, but are not the actual requests and offers made.

C.   Coverage of Sub-Central Governments

Once a WTO Member agrees to commitments on services trade liberalization, what layers of government are covered by them? The answer is in *GATS* Article I:3(a)(i). Unsurprisingly, the coverage encompasses the central government of the Member. Significantly, it goes beyond that level, to include sub-central and local governments. (Observe there are some countries that have no regional or local government. For example, New Zealand has only a central government.)

Furthermore, Article I:3(a)(ii) states that commitments, and indeed the *GATS* itself, covers any nongovernmental body that exercises regulatory power delegated by a central, regional, or local government. This coverage — to include any delegated authority — represents a major extension of multilateral trade rules by *GATS*. This extension makes sense. Save for it, a covered authority (such as a regional government) could escape from *GATS* obligations by delegating its authority to a nongovernmental body.

It must not go unnoticed that coverage by *GATS* Article I:3(a) of regional and local governments, or their designees, is controversial. That is because *GATS* commitments, set forth in the Schedules of Concessions of each WTO Member, are made by central governments. It is, for example, officials from the USTR making services trade deals, not officials from the Kansas Department of Commerce. The American Bar Association (ABA) and the American Medical Association (AMA), not to mention the State of Kansas, are covered by USTR-led deals. Likewise, a local school board in Dunedin, on the South Island of New Zealand, and even a Maori tribal authority, is covered by commitments made by officials from Wellington. Query whether, and the extent to which, USTR commitments bind Native American tribal authorities? To be sure, central government officials presumably represent interests of sub-central and local governments, and delegated authorities. In practice, their advocacy may be imperfect or incomplete. Nevertheless, their pledges bind lower-level governments. That fact means open, honest communication between a central government and all subordinate bodies is crucial. Otherwise, the latter will resent the former, and *vice versa.*

What does *GATS* Article I:3(a) require the central government of each WTO Member to do vis-à-vis subordinate bodies? The answer is "each Member shall take such reasonable measures as may be available to it to ensure" compliance with obligations and commitments by regional and local governments. What are "such reasonable measures" — what does this mean? Plainly, there is plenty of room for argument. Consider, too, the issue of how this phrase, "such reasonable measures," relates to constitutional issues.

Suppose the New Zealand central government makes a *GATS* commitment on environmental services, specifically, on the number of waste fills (rubbish dumps). New Zealand has made no *GATS* commitments on environmental services (as of March 2003). But, New Zealand did so in its FTA with Singapore, and it did so without consulting the local authorities — like the City Council of Christchurch — in New Zealand. Assume the Christchurch City Council says there can be no more than two dumps, and they must be administered locally. What if the New Zealand *GATS* commitment, thanks to the central government, is there will be more than two dumps, and foreign companies like Waste Management, Inc. from the U.S., may administer the dumps? Assume, further, Christchurch does not change its local rules, and the New Zealand government (for legal reasons, political reasons, or both) cannot force a change in the local rules. What recourse does the U.S. government (acting on behalf of Waste Management, Inc.) have? The answer is to sue New Zealand under the WTO.

With this hypothetical in mind, return to the issue of the meaning of *GATS* Article I:3(a). What steps must New Zealand's central government take to constitute "such reasonable measures"? Is the answer persuasion — would that be enough? Or, is more necessary — is the answer a legislative amendment? Moreover, what New Zealand constitutional limitations are implicated? What if, under that constitution (which is unwritten), the central government cannot override a the local government authority?

D. The Public Services Exception

Depending on the political philosophy and practical inclination of a particular WTO Member, Article I:3(b) may be exploited. This provision offers a potentially generous exception to the scope of *GATS* is for public services. In defining "services," Article I:3(b) manages to be inclusive, ambiguously exclusive, and circular. The word " 'services' includes any service in any sector except services supplied in the exercise of governmental authority." Not surprisingly, the phrase beginning with "except" is called the "Public Service Exception."

The obvious question is what does that critical phrase — "services supplied in the exercise of a governmental authority" — mean? *GATS* Article I:3(c) says it means any service supplied "neither on a commercial basis, nor in competition with one or more service suppliers." Here, then, is a two-pronged opportunity for a WTO Member to get out from the under the definition of "service," and thereby be exempt from *GATS* obligations. At issue must be a service provided on a non-commercial basis, and in a non-competitive manner. Classic examples would be loss-making state owned enterprises (SOEs) providing electricity, local and long-distance phone services, water supply, and other traditional public goods, and doing so as a monopoly.

If the *GATS* Article I:3(b) definitional language is interpreted literally, then the exemption is narrow. In the New Zealand context it would cover a wide array of services, because after the economic deregulation of the 1980s, far fewer services met this exemption than before privatizations that occurred in that decade. For example, in the 1980s, New Zealand, in its tertiary education system, did not charge tuition. University education was free, and there were no private universities. Now, the public sector tertiary education system now fails both Article I:3(b) tests. Tuition fees are charged, so there is a commercial element, and private providers do supply educational services, so the government is in competition with the private sector.

What services would still qualify as "services supplied in the exercise of governmental authority"? Law enforcement, justice, and certain security services (*e.g.*, prison operation) would qualify. A quintessential instance that still would qualify under the Public Service Exemption would be public street lighting. Nonetheless, the trend in New Zealand, and indeed around the world, is unmistakable. With deregulation, which almost by definition means privatization, there are fewer and fewer public goods not supplied on a commercial basis, and not supplied in competition with other providers. Caution is due, however. There is nothing irreversible about deregulation. Some governments — particularly in some Latin American countries — have re-nationalized industries in the first decade of the new millennium, other governments — notably, India — have slowed or cancelled planned privatizations, and still other governments — including in the EU — are searching for an ineffable Third Way between American-style private enterprise and Soviet-style communism. Thus, to different extents at different times, different WTO Members exploit the Public Services Exemption to protect some Sectors or Sub-sectors from foreign competition may.

E. Progressive Liberalization

Part IV of *GATS* reflects the fact complete free trade did not occur in services with the Uruguay Round, any more than it did for goods after the 1947 Geneva Conference when GATT was signed. Thus, Part IV consists of three provisions:

Article XIX:	covering negotiations of specific commitments, memorialized in Schedules of Concessions for Services.
Article XX:	articulating the structure and content of Schedules of Concessions.
Article XXI:	explaining how to modify a commitment in a Services Schedule.

The thrust of Part IV of *GATS* is services trade is to be liberalized progressively. Indeed, "progressive liberalization" is the rubric for the part. But, what "progressive liberalization" mean, when it is in the textual context of a commitment that essentially resists opening up?

Under *GATS* Article XX, a WTO Member, or a newly acceding Member, must list in its Services Schedule the terms, time frame, and effective date of its commitments, and any limitations on or reservations to the commitments, especially any measures it seeks to maintain that are inconsistent with the obligations of Articles XVI (on market access) or XVII (on national treatment). Consider the degree of organization, foresight, and sophistication required to do so. What steps must — or ought — an existing or prospective Member take in formulating a set of *GATS* commitments? Consider:

Step   1: Sector or Sub-Sector?

In what Sector or Sub-sector is the commitment? The answer should be carefully defined, to avoid a misunderstanding later about the breadth of the commitment.

Step   2: Mode of Supply?

What Mode or Modes of supply are covered by the commitment, *i.e.*, I, II, III, and/or IV?

Step   3: Market Access?

What market access commitment under Article XVI should be, and is being, made?

Step   4: Limitations on Market Access?

What restrictions on market access commitments should be, and are being, specified? As per Article XX:2, any qualification to market access must be inscribed in the Schedule column relating to Article XVI (market access)

Step   5: National Treatment?

What national treatment commitments under Article XVII should be, and is being, made?

Step   6: Limitations on National Treatment?

What qualifications on national treatment commitments should be, and are being, made? As per Article XX:2, any qualification to national treatment must be inscribed in the Schedule column relating to Article XVI (market access) — oddly, not the column relating to Article XVII (national treatment).

Assuming an existing or prospective Member takes these steps successfully, it is likely — sooner or later — to seek to modify one or more of its commitments.

At that juncture, Article XXI — which answers the question "How is a *GATS* Schedule changed?" — comes into play. Article XXI:1(a) explains after 3 years (*i.e.*, not until 1 January 1998 or after), a WTO Member — called the "modifying Member" — may modify or withdraw any Schedule commitment in accordance with the rules of Article XXI:1(b). Thus, for the first three years following the entry into force of *GATS* and birth of the WTO, services commitments were frozen. Thereafter, thawing them became possible. To do so, Article XXI:1(b) instructs a modifying Member to notify the Council on Trade in Services no later than within 3 months of the modification. Article XXI:2(a) contemplates the possibility another Member may believe its benefits would be affected adversely by the modification — the "affected Member." If the affected Member wants to discuss the matter, then Article XX:2(a) obligates the modifying Member to negotiate a compensatory adjustment that is "necessary," and Article XX:2(b) mandates making the adjustment on an MFN basis.

"Necessary" does not mean desirable, but whether it means absolutely no other alternative exists is uncertain. Evidently, the *GATS* Article XXI:1-2 scheme relies on the agreement of the modifying Member. To secure that assent, an affected Member must prove prospective injury — in effect, actual threat. In other words, no compensatory adjustment is "necessary" unless the affected Member demonstrates to the satisfaction of the modifying Member that the former would be affected adversely by the move the latter contemplates. How, then, does an affected Member show it would be injured? Should it offer evidence of current earnings? Potential future earnings? Loss of anticipated earnings? Might legitimate expectations be relevant? The answer is unclear. And, what is "necessary"? This term is ambiguous.

It is reasonably clear "compensatory adjustment" does not mean handing over money. The term does not connote a penalty. After all, the modifying WTO Member is not doing anything wrong in seeking to modify its services commitments. Indeed, it has a right to do so. Rather, a "compensatory adjustment" entails opening up an equivalent area of another services market, so that the services suppliers of the affected Member are — in the aggregate — not disadvantaged. The adjustment assures the modifying and affected Members keep the same overall balance of mutually advantageous commitments.

For example, suppose New Zealand wants to alter its audiovisual services commitment by inserting local content quotas for movie theaters in the country (*e.g.*, a rule mandating that at least 10 percent of screen time be allocated to Kiwi productions). New Zealand will have to liberalize trade in a different area, such as postal services (in which New Zealand had no commitments as of March 2003) of equivalent value. The key legal and economic question is how New Zealand and affected Members will measure "equivalence"

Oddly, *GATS* Article XX specifies no period for negotiations. What happens if no agreement is reached on a compensatory adjustment? Article XX:3(a) answers this question, empowering the affected Member to refer the matter — which now is a dispute — to arbitration. Any other affected Member may join in as a party to the arbitration, if it seeks the benefit of the arbitration outcome. Under Article XX:4(a), a modifying Member cannot modify its Services Schedule (*i.e.*, it cannot withdraw its service market access commitment) until it has made a compensatory adjustment in conformity with the arbitration findings. In contrast, Article XX:3(b) says that if no affected Member requests arbitration, then the modifying Member can make the change, without taking any accompanying action.

What if, in the example of New Zealand and audiovisual services (or any comparable hypothetical), New Zealand (or another modifying Member) acts unilaterally? Or, what if New Zealand (or other modifying Member) does not follow the arbitrator's decision? Then, *GATS* Article XX:4(b) authorizes an affected Member to withdraw substantially equivalent benefits in conformity with the arbitrator's decision, and the MFN rule of Article II doe not apply. In other words, there is a tit-for-tat scenario. To play out the scenario, what if an affected Member cannot find equivalent benefits in the same services sector? Then, it can look to another services sector. Article XX:4(b) authorizes cross-services sector retaliation. But, what if there is no equivalence even in another services sector? Then, the affected Member can engage in cross-sectoral retaliation, *i.e.*, it can retaliate against goods imported from the modifying Member.

What is the "bottom line" with respect to modifying service sector liberalization commitments under *GATS* Article XX? Is it that commitments made in Services Schedules are effectively irreversible, because of the specter of compensatory adjustments and arbitration? If so, then a negotiating team had better know what it is doing in advance of making binding commitments. This tough line against modification would be consistent with progressive liberalization of services sector trade.

That liberalization is the purview of *GATS* Article XIX, which mandates ongoing negotiations. Indeed, Article XIX:1 said they had to begin by 1 January 2000 — and they did. Their real economic consequences are open to debate. Article XIX, while titled "Negotiation of Specific Commitments," is known as the "built in negotiations," meaning that the goal of progressively higher levels of services trade liberalization through the modus of post-Uruguay Round negotiations are set in the text of *GATS*. (The WTO *Agreement on Agriculture* also has a built-in agenda.) Significantly, the non-economic effects of the built-in agenda also are disputed. The talks are supposed to reduce or eliminate adverse trade effects on measures designed to provide effective market access. But, what are the implications for (*inter alia*) local and indigenous cultures?

Moreover, if the built-in agenda of services (and agriculture) negotiations means discussions independent of any WTO Ministerial Conference, then what is the relationship between those talks and a multilateral trade round? Should progressive liberalization be conducted separately from a round, part of a grand bargain in the context of a round, or an early harvest of results in services (and agriculture) that facilitates a grand deal? *GATS* Article XIX does not answer this question, nor the related matters of the nature of or pre-conditions for services negotiations. Article XIX:2 speaks of "appropriate flexibility for individual developing country Members for opening fewer sectors, liberalizing fewer types of transactions, progressively extending market access in line with their development situation, and when making access to their markets available to foreign service suppliers, attaching to such access conditions aimed at achieving the objectives . . . in Article IV [namely, increasing developing country participation in world services trade]."

Third World countries point to this passage to support their claim that built-in agenda negotiations must address, and even confer on them, special and differential treatment. First World countries counter by focusing on the word "individual." Surely it means there is no collective recognition of special and differential treatment. Rather, such treatment is on a country-by-country basis. Obviously, this reply is met with disbelief and frustration in poor countries, and they add that the terms of *GATS* Article XIX:3 have not been satisfied. Those terms are that for purposes of establishing guidelines and procedures for on-going negotiations, the Council for Trade in Services must conduct an assessment of services trade in overall terms, and on a sector-by-sector basis, with a view to achieving the objectives of *GATS*, including Article IV:1.

What are the objectives of *GATS*, to which an Article XIX:3 study on services trade ought to direct attention? The answer is in the *Preamble* to *GATS*, which lays out the following goals for services trade liberalization —

    i.   Progressive liberalization.

    ii.   Transparency in services trade.

    iii.   Promotion of liberalization on a mutually advantageous basis.

    iv.   Recognition of rights of WTO Members to regulate, and introduce new regulations on, the supply of services to meet domestic policy objectives.

    v.   Appreciation of the particular need of developing countries to regulate services in accordance with domestic policy goals.

    vi.   Increasing developing country participation in global services trade.

    vii.   Expanding services trade exports from developing countries, in part through improving the efficiency and competitiveness of their domestic services sectors.

    viii.   Understanding the special needs of least developed countries.

To the anger of many Third World countries, these goals are not taken seriously. For example, the asymmetric requests and offers on Modes I-III, versus Mode IV, indicates no overall equilibrium in the rights developing countries obtain against the obligations they incur (or are asked to incur). Observe, however, that under principles of public international law, a preamble to an agreement is not itself binding on the parties to the agreement. The only exception to its legal unenforceability concerns how it may be used. In particular, a preamble may be used to interpret a provision of substance in one of the articles of the agreement.

Equally bad, and contrary to *GATS* Article XIX:3, no assessment has been done (as of December 2007, this work was tied into Doha Round talks). Indeed, the data either do not exist, or have not been collected, and the WTO Secretariat lacks adequate funding to conduct the study. Moreover, at certain turns, the consensus decision-making rule has precluded the Council from moving forward resolutely and taking up its mandate to engage in the study. Accordingly, if a comprehensive, objective investigation occurs, with poor country interests in mind, then it will have to be done by individual WTO Members, or a subset of them.

Given the ambiguities and acrimony over the built-in agenda, some developing countries — led by India — take a hard line position that no further negotiations should be conducted until all the effects of *GATS* thus far are known. Of course, this argument falls on deaf ears in developed countries. Put more aggressively, developing countries are told they have a stark choice — they can be consulted about services trade liberalization, or marginalized from the talks. In sum, negotiating guidelines for services were settled in 2001, but without the *GATS* Article XIX:3 assessment being done.

VI. SCHEDULING *GATS* COMMITMENTS AND THE 2005 *ANTIGUA GAMBLING* CASE

WTO APPELLATE BODY REPORT, *UNITED STATES — MEASURES AFFECTING THE CROSS-BORDER SUPPLY OF GAMBLING AND BETTING SERVICES*
WT/DS285/AB/R (adopted 20 April 2005)

IV. Interpretation of the Specific Commitments Made by the United States in its *GATS* Schedule

158. The Panel found . . . :

. . . the United States' Schedule under the *GATS* includes specific commitments on gambling and betting services under subsector 10.D.

. . . .

159. In the context of the GATT 1994, the Appellate Body has observed that, although each Member's Schedule represents the tariff commitments that bind *one* Member, Schedules also represent a common agreement among *all* Members. Accordingly, the task of ascertaining the meaning of a concession in a Schedule, like the task of interpreting any other treaty text, involves identifying the *common intention* of Members, and is to be achieved by following the customary rules of interpretation of public international law, codified in Articles 31 and 32 of the *Vienna Convention*.

160. In the context of the *GATS*, Article XX:3 explicitly provides that Members' Schedules are an "integral part" of that agreement. Here, too, the task of identifying the meaning of a concession in a *GATS* Schedule, like the task of interpreting any other treaty text, involves identifying the *common intention* of Members. Like the Panel — and, indeed, both the participants — we consider that the meaning of the United States' *GATS* Schedule must be determined according to the rules codified in Article 31 and, to the extent appropriate, Article 32 of the *Vienna Convention*.

161. The contentious issues in this appeal concern whether the Panel erred in the way that it *used* the *Vienna Convention* principles of interpretation in determining the scope of the specific commitments made by the United States in subsector 10.D of its *GATS* Schedule, and whether the Panel erred in the conclusions it drew on the basis of its approach.

A. Interpretation of Subsector 10.D According to the General Rule of Interpretation: Article 31 of the *Vienna Convention*

162. The United States' appeal focuses on the Panel's interpretation of the word "sporting" in subsector 10.D of the United States' *GATS* Schedule. According to the United States, the ordinary meaning of "sporting" includes gambling and betting and the Panel erred in finding otherwise. . . .[T]he interpretative question addressed by the Panel was a broader one, namely "whether the U.S. Schedule includes specific commitments on gambling and betting services notwithstanding the fact that the words 'gambling and betting services' do not appear in the U.S. Schedule." In tackling this question, the Panel turned to Sector 10 of the United States' Schedule to the *GATS*, which Antigua claimed included a specific commitment on gambling and betting services, and the United States claimed did not. The relevant part of the United States' Schedule provides:

[The excerpt is from "The United States of America — Schedule of Specific Commitments, GATS/SC/90, 15 April 1994," called the "United States' Schedule." The "National Treatment" and "Additional Commitments" columns of the U.S. Schedule are omitted from this excerpt.]

Sector or subsector	Limitations on market access
10. RECREATIONAL, CULTURAL, & SPORTING SERVICES	
A. ENTERTAINMENT SERVICES (INCLUDING THEATRE, LIVE BANDS AND CIRCUS SERVICES)	1) None 2) None 3) None 4) Unbound, except as indicated in the horizontal section
B. NEWS AGENCY SERVICES	1) None 2) None 3) None 4) Unbound, except as indicated in the horizontal section
C. LIBRARIES, ARCHIVES, MUSEUMS AND OTHER CULTURAL SERVICES	1) None 2) None 3) None 4) Unbound, except as indicated in the horizontal section
D. OTHER RECREATIONAL SERVICES (except sporting)	1) None 2) None 3) The number of concessions available for commercial operations in federal, state and local facilities is limited 4) Unbound, except as indicated in the horizontal section

163. In considering this section of the United States' Schedule, the Panel stated that it would begin by "examining the ordinary meaning of various key terms used in the U.S. Schedule." The Panel examined the term "Other recreational services (except sporting)" in subsector 10.D, as well as the term "Entertainment services" in subsector 10.A. Having consulted the dictionary

definitions of various words, the Panel found that "the *ordinary* meaning of 'sporting' does not include gambling." The United States submits that the Panel could not have made this finding had it properly followed Article 31(1) of the *Vienna Convention*.

164. Article 31(1) of the *Vienna Convention* requires a treaty to be interpreted "in good faith in accordance with the ordinary meaning to be given to the terms of the treaty in their context and in the light of its object and purpose." In order to identify the ordinary meaning, a Panel may start with the dictionary definitions of the terms to be interpreted. But dictionaries, alone, are not necessarily capable of resolving complex questions of interpretation, as they typically aim to catalogue *all* meanings of words — be those meanings common or rare, universal or specialized.

165. In this case, in examining definitions of "sporting," the Panel surveyed a variety of dictionaries and found a variety of definitions of the word. All of the dictionary definitions cited by the Panel define "sporting" as being connected to — in the sense of "related to," "suitable for," "engaged in" or "disposed to" — sports activities. Some dictionaries also define "sporting" as being connected to gambling or betting, but others do not. Of those that do, several note that the word is mainly used in this sense in the phrase "a sporting man," or in a pejorative sense, and some note that the word is used in this sense only when the gambling or betting activities pertain to sports. Based on this survey of dictionary definitions, as well as the fact that "gambling" does not fall within the meaning of the Spanish and French words that correspond to "sporting," namely "*déportivos*" and "*sportifs*," the Panel made its finding that "the *ordinary* meaning of 'sporting' does not include gambling."

. . . .

B. Interpretation of Subsector 10.D in Accordance with Supplementary Means of Interpretation: Article 32 of the *Vienna Convention*

. . . .

198. Turning to the question of how the subsector 10.D entry "Other recreational services (except sporting)" is to be interpreted in the light of W/120 and the Scheduling Guidelines, we consider it useful to set out the relevant parts of both documents. The relevant section of W/120 is as follows:

SECTORS AND SUB-SECTORS	CORRESPONDING CPC
[. . .]	
10. RECREATIONAL, CULTURAL AND SPORTING SERVICES (other than audiovisual services)	
A. Entertainment services (including, theatre, live bands and circus services)	9619
B. News agency services	962
C. Libraries, archives, museums and other cultural services	963
D. Sporting and other recreational services	964
E. Other	

199. Thus, W/120 clearly indicates that its entry 10.D — "Sporting and other recreational services" — corresponds to CPC Group 964. W/120 does not, however, contain any explicit indication of: (i) whether the reference to Group 964 necessarily incorporates a reference to *each and every sub-category* of Group 964 within the CPC; or (ii) how W/120 relates to the *GATS* Schedules of individual Members.

200. With respect to the first issue, we observe that W/120 sets out a much more aggregated classification list than the one found in the CPC. Whereas W/120 contains 12 sectors (11 and one "other") and more than 150 subsectors, the CPC classification scheme is comprised of 10 Sections, 69 Divisions, 295 Groups, 1,050 Classes and 1,811 Subclasses. The first draft classification list prepared by the GATT Secretariat, W/50, explained that one of the reasons for selecting the CPC as a basis for classification in the services negotiations was that such a product-based system "allows a *higher degree of disaggregation and precision* to be attained should it become necessary, at a later stage." Thus, the CPC's level of disaggregation was one of the very reasons it was selected as a basis for a sectoral classification list. As the CPC is a decimal system, a reference to an aggregate category must be understood as a reference to all of the constituent parts of that category. Put differently, a reference to a three-digit CPC Group should, in the absence of any indication to the contrary, be understood as a reference to all the four-digit Classes and five-digit Sub-classes that make up the group; and a reference to a four-digit Class should be understood as a reference to all of the five-digit Sub-classes that make up that Class.

201. In the CPC, Group 964, which corresponds to subsector 10.D of W/120 (Sporting and other recreational services), is broken down into the following Classes and Sub-classes:

964   Sporting and other recreational services

   9641   Sporting services

      96411   Sports event promotion services

      96412   Sports event organization services

      96413   Sports facility operation services

      96419   Other sporting services

   9649   Other recreational services

      96491   Recreation park and beach services

      96492   Gambling and betting services

      96499   Other recreational services n.e.c.

Thus, the CPC Class that corresponds to "Sporting services" (9641) does *not* include gambling and betting services. Rather, the Sub-class for gambling and betting services (96492) falls under the Class "Other recreational services" (9649).

202. W/120 does not shed light on the issue of how it relates to individual Member's Schedules. That issue is, however, addressed in the 1993 Scheduling Guidelines:

HOW SHOULD ITEMS BE SCHEDULED?

15. Schedules record, for each sector, the legally enforceable commitments of each Member. It is therefore vital that schedules be clear, precise and based on a common format and terminology. This section describes how commitments should be entered in schedules. . . .

A. How to describe committed sectors and subsectors

16. The legal nature of a schedule as well as the need to evaluate commitments, require the greatest possible degree of clarity in the description of each sector or subsector scheduled. In general the classification of sectors and subsectors should be based on the Secretariat's revised Services Sectoral Classification List. [W/120] Each sector contained in the Secretariat list is identified by the corresponding Central Product Classification (CPC) number. Where it is necessary to refine further a sectoral classification, this should be done on the basis of the CPC or other internationally recognised classification (*e.g.*, Financial Services Annex). The most recent breakdown of the CPC, including explanatory notes for each subsector, is contained in the UN Provisional Central Product Classification.

Example: A Member wishes to indicate an offer or commitment in the subsector of map-making services. In the Secretariat list, this service would fall under the general heading "Other Business Services" under "Related scientific and technical consulting services" (see item l.F.m). By consulting the CPC, map-making can be found under the corresponding CPC classification number 86754. In its offer/schedule, the Member would then enter the subsector under the "Other Business Services" section of its schedule as follows:

Map-making services (86754)

If a Member wishes to use its own subsectoral classification or definitions it should provide concordance with the CPC in the manner indicated in the above example. If this is not possible, it should give a sufficiently detailed definition to avoid any ambiguity as to the scope of the commitment. (emphasis added; footnote omitted)

203. The Scheduling Guidelines thus underline the importance of using a common format and terminology in scheduling, and express a clear preference for parties to use W/120 and the CPC classifications in their Schedules. At the same time, the Guidelines make clear that parties wanting to use their own subsectoral classification or definitions — that is, to disaggregate in a way that diverges from W/120 and/or the CPC — were to do so in a "sufficiently detailed" way "to avoid any ambiguity as to the scope of the commitment." The example given in the Scheduling Guidelines illustrates how to make a positive commitment with respect to a discrete service that is more disaggregated than a service subsector identified in W/120. It is reasonable to assume that the parties to the negotiations expected the same technique to be applied to *exclude* a discrete service from the scope of a commitment, when the commitment is made in a subsector identified in W/120 and the excluded service is more disaggregated than that subsector.

204. In our view, the requisite clarity as to the scope of a commitment could not have been achieved through mere omission of CPC codes, particularly where a specific sector of a Member's Schedule, such as sector 10 of the United States' Schedule, follows the structure of W/120 in all other respects, and adopts *precisely* the same terminology as used in W/120. As discussed above, W/120 and the 1993 Scheduling Guidelines were prepared and circulated at the request of parties to the Uruguay Round negotiations for the express purpose of assisting those parties in the preparation of their offers. These documents undoubtedly served, too, to assist parties in reviewing and evaluating the offers made by others. They provided a common language and structure, which, although not obligatory, was widely used and relied upon. In such circumstances, and in the light of the specific guidance provided in the 1993 Scheduling Guidelines, it is reasonable to assume that parties to the negotiations examining a sector of a Schedule that tracked so closely the language of the same sector in W/120 would — absent a clear indication to the contrary — have expected the sector to have the same coverage as the corresponding W/120 sector. This is another way of stating that, as the Panel observed, "unless otherwise indicated in the Schedule, Members were assumed to have relied on W/120 and the corresponding CPC references."

208. In our view, therefore, the relevant entry in the United States' Schedule, "Other recreational services (except sporting)," must be interpreted as *excluding* from the scope of its specific commitment services corresponding to CPC class 9641, "Sporting services." For the same reasons, the entry must be read as *including* within the scope of its commitment services corresponding to CPC 9649, "Other recreational services," including Sub-class 96492, "Gambling and betting services."

. . . .

C. Summary

213. [W]e reject the United States' argument that, by excluding "sporting" services from the scope of its commitment in subsector 10.D, the United States excluded gambling and betting services from the scope of that commitment. Accordingly, we *uphold*, albeit for different reasons, the Panel's finding. . . .

Chapter 48

SUBSTANTIVE SERVICES TRADE OBLIGATIONS

The hijab and bikini don't really go together.

> —Real Estate Developer in Aqaba, Jordan, (who tries to limit the number of devout Muslims in a luxury development)
> (quoted in Sharmila Devi, *Incentives Make Jordanian Port a Haven for Investors*, FINANCIAL TIMES 21-22 October 2006, at 5)

DOCUMENTS SUPPLEMENT ASSIGNMENT

1. WTO *General Agreement on Trade in Services* (*GATS*)
2. *NAFTA* Chapters 12-14, 16
3. Relevant provisions in other FTAs

I. THE RELATIVE STRUCTURE OF *GATS* AND GATT

The *General Agreement on Trade in Services* (*GATS*) is divided into 6 Parts, preceded by a *Preamble*, and followed by a series of Annexes.

Part I: Scope and Definition

Part II: General Obligations and Disciplines

Part III: Specific Commitments

Part IV: Progressive Liberalization

Part V: Institutional Provisions

Part VI: Final Provisions

The preceding Chapter discusses Parts I, and IV-VI, as well as the *Preamble* and Annexes. The focus of the present Chapter is on the substantive obligations affecting services trade liberalization. They are set out in Parts II and III.

Part II addresses the question of what general rules apply to trade in services, delivered through Modes I-IV, and what limited exceptions exist to these rules. Part III concerns the issue of what specific commitments are made in each of the four Modes (I-IV) of delivery, and what exceptions apply to these commitments.

This structure is notably different from that of GATT. GATT consists of 4 Parts containing 38 articles (39 counting Article XXVIII *bis*), and has interpretative notes (*Ad Articles*). Part I of GATT, covering Articles I-II, includes the unconditional MFN and tariff binding obligations, respectively. Part II, boasting Articles III-XXIII, has an array of obligations, such as national treatment, and some institutional and procedural provisions, such as consultation (Article XXII) and nullification or impairment (Article XXIII). Part IV, which has Articles XXXVI-XXXVIII, is the only one with a rubric — "Trade and Development." Additionally, the GATT *Preamble* is shorter than that of *GATS*. And, all of the GATT Annexes (that is, Annexes A-G) concern exceptions or amplifications to the MFN obligation in Article I. The final Annex (H) concerns Japan's long-ago accession to GATT.

What inferences might be drawn from the structural contrasts of the texts aimed at goods versus services? One is that there is no bright-line distinction in GATT, as there is in *GATS*, between general obligations and specific commitments. Broadly, all GATT duties are considered incumbent on all WTO Members. Put differently, *GATS* is structured to be an accord that liberalizes services trade in a contingent and qualified sort of way, whereas the edifice of GATT supports more sweepingly pro-free trade duties.

II. GENERAL OBLIGATIONS AND DISCIPLINES (*GATS* PART II)

A. Analogies to GATT

The general obligations and disciplines that do exist in *GATS* are in Part II. In theory, they apply across the board, *i.e.*, to all service Sectors. In practice, some of the general obligations and disciplines may not apply to all Sectors. That is because exceptions are permitted for certain obligations. Most significantly, an exception is allowed for MFN treatment. (The U.S. invoked this exception in 1993, and again in 1995, in the context of financial services.) The Articles in *GATS* Part II are as follows:

Article II:	Most-Favored Nation Treatment
Article III:	Transparency
Article III *bis*:	Disclosure of Confidential Information
Article IV:	Increasing Participation of Developing Countries
Article V:	Economic Integration
Article V *bis*:	Labor Markets Integration Agreements
Article VI:	Domestic Regulation
Article VII:	Recognition
Article VIII:	Monopolies and Exclusive Services Suppliers
Article IX:	Business Practices
Article X:	Emergency Safeguards
Article XI:	Payments and Transfers
Article XII:	Restrictions to Safeguard the Balance of Payments
Article XIII:	Government Procurement.
Article XIV:	General Exceptions
Article XIV *bis*:	Security Exceptions
Article XV:	Subsidies

A cursory look at the titles of the Articles suggests a number of similarities between *GATS* and GATT. For example:

GATS Article II and GATT Article I set out an MFN obligation.

GATS Article III is redolent of GATT Article X.

GATS Article IV calls to mind GATT Articles XXXVI-XXXVIII.

GATS Article V sets parameters for economic integration, and GATT Article XXIV condones, with some limits, the establishment of free trade agreements (FTAs) and customs unions (CUs).

GATS Article VIII appears to cover state-run enterprises, and GATT Article XVII concerns state trading enterprises (STEs).

GATS Article X seems to be an escape clause, like GATT Article XIX.

GATS Article XI concerns financial transactions, and GATT Article XV covers exchange arrangements.

GATS Article XII is (in truth) an analog to GATT Article XII.

GATS Article XIV and GATT Article XX both list general exceptions (though the *GATS* list is shorter).

GATS Article XIV *bis* and GATT Article XXI both deal with national security.

GATS Article XV (an odd provision in itself) appears akin to GATT Article XVI.

What a cursory glance at *GATS* Part II does not reveal is the extent to which the ostensible likenesses to GATT are, indeed, real. It also does not show two *GATS* provisions remain under negotiation — Articles X and XIII.

Of all Articles in *GATS* Part II, five are of pre-eminent importance. They are Articles II, V, VI, VIII, and XIX. Three of them (Articles II, VI, and VIII) are discussed below. Article V, discussed in an earlier Chapter, imposes modest disciplines on regional trade agreements (RTAs). Article XIX, concerning general exceptions to *GATS* obligations, is discussed later in the present Chapter.

Finally, in the post 9/11 world, special mention should be made of Article XIX *bis*. Its wording is nearly identical to that of GATT Article XXI. As a theoretical matter, what is the point of an exception to trade liberalization of services for national security? As a practical matter, how might the exception work with respect to specific Sectors, Sub-sectors, and Sub-sub sectors?

B. MFN Treatment and Exemptions (*GATS* Article II and Annex)

Article II:1 is the MFN obligation for services, and is akin — but, loosely so — to GATT Article I:1. The *GATS* MFN rule applies both to a service and the service supplier. MFN treatment must be accorded immediate and unconditional MFN treatment to services and service suppliers. But, Article II:2 is a large exception to immediacy and unconditionality. A WTO Member can derogate from the MFN obligation if it lists the exempting measure in its Schedule of Concessions (for Services and Service Providers), and if the measure meets the requirements of the *Annex on Article II Exemptions*. The *Annex on Article II Exemptions* contains instructions for scheduling exemptions from the MFN obligation.

Two of the *Annex* instructions are about timing and circumscribe the extent of deviation possible from immediate, unconditional MFN treatment. First, Paragraph 6 contains a sunset rule. It states "[i]n principle, such exemptions [to MFN treatment under Article II:1] should not exceed 10 years." The decade-long period expired on 31 December 2004. Thus, "in principle," no MFN exemptions should exist. Whether all such exemptions are, in fact, temporary, and have, in fact, lapsed, is a matter for the Council on Trade in Services. The Annex charges this Council with the responsibility of reviewing exemptions (which it continues to do.)

Second, arguably at least, an MFN exemption had to be in place by the conclusion of the Uruguay Round negotiations, *i.e.*, 15 December 1993, and a country had to write the exemption into its Schedule at that time. In other words, the exemption had to be taken as of the end of the Uruguay Round, and listed it in the relevant Schedule. What are the most common exemptions to the Article II:1 MFN obligation taken by WTO Members as of 1993 and inserted into their Schedules? Not surprisingly, they are for air transport, audio-visual, financial, maritime, and telecommunications services.

The difficulty with the second limit on exemptions is it is not readily apparent from the plain meaning of the *Annex*. Where, exactly, does it say in either the *Annex* or Article II itself that an exemption must have been taken in 1993? The answer is nowhere — indeed, not anywhere in *GATS* is an express statement to this effect found. However, some prominent *GATS* commentators suggest this understanding as the rule. For instance, Canada's Pierre Sauvé implies services sector commitments on market access and national treatment made during the Uruguay Round were based on the then-prevailing *status quo, i.e.,* on economic conditions and existing regulations in place in GATT contracting parties involved in *GATS* negotiations during the Round.[1]

The truth is Paragraph 2 of the *Annex* affords the best — but perhaps weak — textual support for this understanding. That Paragraph says "[a]ny new [MFN] exemptions applied for after the entry into force of the *WTO Agreement* [*i.e.*, after 1 January 1995] shall be dealt with under Paragraph 3 of Article IX of that *Agreement.*" It so happens Article IX:3 of the *WTO Agreement* concerns waivers from obligations. The WTO Ministerial Conference may grant such waivers, but only on three-fourths vote of the Members, in "exceptional circumstances," and following consideration by and a report from the Council on Services (assuming the matter concerns services). In brief, taking an MFN exemption no longer is easy. Special permission is needed, thus lending credence to the interpretation that for all practical purposes, an exemption had to be taken before the end of the Uruguay Round. A current or newly acceding Member that failed to take a timely exemption faces improbable odds to insert one into its Services Schedules.

---

[1] *See* PIERRE SAUVÉ, TRADE RULES BEHIND BORDERS: ESSAYS ON SERVICES, INVESTMENT AND THE NEW TRADE AGENDA 41 (2003).

C. Financial Services, the U.S. MFN Exemption, and the December 1997 Deal

When the Uruguay Round negotiations ended on 15 December 1993, agreement was reached on the *GATS*. But, talks on specific market access commitments in the area of financial services — namely, the banking, securities, and insurance businesses — remained unfinished. Accordingly, it was agreed that the time period for talks on financial services would be extended until 30 June 1995. After negotiations failed, the deadline was extended once again, by one month to the end of July 1995.

Significantly, in July 1995, the U.S. exempted itself from applying the *GATS* Article II:1 MFN principle to all other WTO Members in the area of financial services. Its MFN exemption was authorized under Article II:2 and the *Annex on Article II Exemptions*. Why did it take this rather drastic unilateral action?

The U.S. was not satisfied with the market access offers made by other countries, particularly India, Korea, and Malaysia. The tough stance was understandable, given the importance of services to the American economy. Roughly seven out of ten workers in the United States are employed in the services sector, and over two-thirds of America's GDP is accounted for by services. Within the services sector, the U.S. is particularly competitive in banking, securities, and insurance.

Thus, for example, the U.S. was irritated by the fact that, at the time, India's insurance market was closed to foreign insurers. India said it ought not to have to open it until developed countries agreed to relax their restrictions on skilled services workers entering those countries. Nor was the U.S. pleased that, at the time, Korea had a 15 percent limit on foreign ownership of listed financial services. As for Malaysia, it sought to reduce the foreign equity limit on insurance companies to 49 percent, which would have badly damaged the long-standing operation of the American International Group (AIG), which held controlling stakes in local financial service providers. The U.S. feared an expropriation of AIG's interests.

The American MFN exemption did not thwart a global deal. The remaining WTO Members adopted an interim accord, brokered largely by the EU. That accord took effect on 1 August 1996, and lasted until the end of 1997. The United States signed the interim accord, but declined to participate in it fully via its MFN exemption. It was a second-best result, though it did cover roughly 90 percent of world trade in financial services.

Finally, on 12 December 1997 the WTO Members concluded an agreement on a package of financial services commitments. Seventy Members actively negotiated, and 56 Members (counting the EU as one) made new commitments to maintain or expand the market access they provide to foreign financial services providers. (Many other Members already had made commitments in this sector.) The agreement, which entered into force on 1 March 1999, covers more than 95 percent of trade in banking, securities, insurance, and financial information.

That any deal was struck was remarkable. Negotiations took place in the thick of the Asian economic crisis. That crisis could have been used by the likes of Indonesia, Korea, Malaysia, the Philippines, and Thailand as an excuse not to liberalize financial systems. Instead, Asian leaders seemed to agree, more or less, with the assessment of then Secretary of the Treasury, Robert Rubin. He pointed out NICs and LDCs would benefit from service sector liberalization. Their cost of financial capital would be reduced, because there would be more capital suppliers (*e.g.*, banks to make loans, securities firms to underwrite initial public offerings, and insurance companies to issue policies). Moreover, he pointed out that through exposure to foreign competition, domestic financial companies in NICs and LDCs would become more efficient. Thus, for the time being, anyway, much of the world seems willing to try a road different from the tight-fisted restrictions on financial services that characterized most of the latter half of the 20th century.

D. Domestic Regulation and the "Holding Pattern" (*GATS* Article VI)

GATS Article VI, which covers domestic regulation, sets out another important, generic rule. Article VI:1 says that in any Sector in which a "specific commitment" is taken, each WTO Member must assure its domestic regulations are "administered in a reasonable, objective, and impartial manner." The rule applies to any "measure[] of general application affecting trade in services." The basic purpose of the rule is both self-evident and non-controversial.

Observe, however, Article VI:1 is not as generic as it appears at first blush. First, it covers only domestic regulations pertaining to a Sector in which a WTO Member has made a trade-liberalizing commitment. Second, the rule is about the administration of domestic regulations. It is not about their content. Third, the rule is a transitional. Article VI:5(a) says that in a Sectors in which a "specific commitment" is made, until negotiations on permanent disciplines for that Sector are finished, a WTO Member must not apply licensing or qualification requirements, or technical standards, which "nullify or impair" the commitments of that Member in the particular Sector.

The third limit on Article VI:1 applies to licensing regulations, qualification requirements and procedures, and technical standards. An obvious example would be bar examination and admission requirements for lawyers. Another illustration would be certification rules in the health professions. Suppose New Zealand liberalizes its health services provisions through *GATS* commitments, taking no reservation mandating physicians be citizens of the country. Having made this pledge, Article VI:5(a) prevents New Zealand from mandating all doctors be citizens of the country. Query how the Article VI:5(a) constraint on Article VI:1 might affect programs in Gulf Arab countries to replace expatriate with local workers, such as the "Saudi-ization" and "Emirati-ization" schemes in the Kingdom of Saudi Arabia and United Arab Emirates (UAE), respectively.

The text of Article VI:5(a) is rife with interpretative problems, because it is phrased as a triple negative — "not" in the *chapeau*, "not" in sub-paragraph (i), and "not" in sub-paragraph (ii). Essentially, the text says a WTO Member can maintain a domestic regulation affecting trade in services in a Sector in which the Member has made a specific commitment, as long as that measure is neutral, in the sense of how the measure impacts on foreign and domestic suppliers, and foreseeable. The demand for neutrality renders the placement of Article VI:5 appropriate in *GATS* Part II as a general measure.

What does it take for a domestic regulation to be neutral and transparent? The answer, under Article VI:5(a)(i), is a measure meeting all three criteria in Article VI:4(a)-(c), namely, it is

(1) based on objective and transparent criteria,

(2) not more burdensome than necessary to ensure service quality, and

(3) is not a restriction (assuming it is involves licensing) on service supply.

What kind of measure is foreseeable? The answer, under Article VI:5(a)(ii), is a domestic regulation that could reasonably have been expected of the Member imposing it when that Member made the specific commitment in the affected service Sector. As of what time are expectations measured? Article VI:5(b) says when the commitment on the service Sector in question was made. Effectively, that means the conclusion of Uruguay Round negotiations (*i.e.,* 15 December 1993). What is the standard for judging a reasonable expectation? Is it an objective one — the average WTO Member, or the Membership overall? Or, is it a subjective one — an individual Member exporting services in the affected Sector? On these questions, Article VI:5 is silent.

Thus, if a domestic regulation is both neutral and foreseeable, then it does not "nullify or impair" the specific commitment, as the *chapeau* of Article VI:5(a) puts it. Or, if it does, the nullification or impairment does not matter — the regulation still may be implemented and enforced. Conversely, what a Member may not do is maintain a measure that does nullify or impair its commitment by disrespecting the criteria or undermining reasonable expectations. In other words, Article VI:5(a) may be seen as conditional permission to nullify or impair a previous commitment.

For example, suppose New Zealand made a commitment to allow foreign provision through Mode III of construction services during the Uruguay Round. A decade later, it imposes a technical standard for construction services that says a construction company must have 5 years of experience before it can operate in New Zealand. During that decade (1994-2003), foreign construction services providers entered the country, or could have done so, with less than 5 years experience. The new rule nullifies or impairs New Zealand's commitment for certain exporters — service providers with insufficient experience. Still, the rule is neutral under Article VI:5(a)(i) — or, it had better be. If New Zealand had similar experiential requirements for services allied to construction (*e.g.,* electrical, heating, and plumbing) at the time the Round concluded, presumably the new standard also could have been reasonably expected under Article VI:5(a)(ii). Any Member exporting, or contemplating the exportation of, construction services could have checked New Zealand's rules on allied services. Yet, to posit the example is to reveal a difficulty with the foresight requirement. As a practical matter, would a Korean (or Thai) construction company really have done the checking in December 1993 in anticipation of what New Zealand might do in 10 years?

At bottom, Article VI:5(a) embodies a "holding pattern" rule that gives some scope for nullification or impairment of a previous services trade commitment. The rule addresses a concern about subversion of a prior commitment. What happens if a WTO Member applies a domestic regulation adverse to services trade in a Sector in which the Member has made a trade-liberalizing commitment? The answer is "hold still" — not in the sense of barring any new regulations, but in the sense of forbidding a regulation that fails to satisfy the three requirements of Article VI:4, and that could not have been reasonably expected as of the end of the Uruguay Round. If the three neutrality criteria, and the expectancy requirement, are satisfied, then the Member may impose the regulation — even if the regulation nullifies or impairs its prior commitment. This answer is a temporary one. The "holding pattern" ends whenever negotiations on domestic regulations in that Sector achieve permanent disciplines on the scope and nature of those regulations. At that point, Article VI:5(a) "holding measures" may be supplanted or modified by WTO-inspired rules.

The negotiations are to be held under the auspices of the Council on Trade in Services. Its mandate is to develop disciplines on domestic regulations affecting services. Observe the balance of multilateral oversight and WTO Member sovereignty. The multilateral oversight aims to prevent regulations on licensing, qualification requirements, and technical standards from being unnecessary burdens on trade — meaning that objective, transparent criteria should underlie the regulations, they should be no more onerous than needed to upkeep quality, and should not constrict service supply. But, that oversight does not speak directly to the content or purpose of the regulations. What a Member says in its regulations, and its regulatory policies, are for the Member to decide. Is this distinction viable in every instance?

E. Monopolies and Exclusive Suppliers (*GATS* Article VIII)

The reality in many countries — traditionally, and into the present (especially in developing and least developed countries) — is that an array of public services is provided each by a single entity. For example, New Zealand policy calls for electricity throughout the country to be on a single grid. How do monopolies or exclusive service suppliers fit within a WTO framework, the *GATS*, seeking to liberalize trade in services? They are inherently anti- or non-competitive, but free or freer trade means competition on a level playing field among an assortment of domestic and foreign providers.

Article VIII is the *GATS* provision addressing services Sectors, Sub-sectors, or Sub-sub-sectors in which monopoly or exclusive suppliers dominate the market. The Article contains two basic rules:

1. Each WTO Member must ensure any monopoly service provider does not operate in a way that violates Article II (the MFN obligation) or specific services commitments made by that Member.

2. If a monopoly competes directly or through an affiliated company in a market outside the scope of its monopoly, then the monopoly must not abuse its monopoly position to advantage itself in the services area in which it competes.

These rules are set forth in Article VIII:1 and 2, respectively.

To illustrate Article VIII, consider postal services. Historically, in New Zealand (as in other WTO Members), a public sector monopoly has provided postal services. Indeed, in many WTO Members, postal services retain a monopoly on classic letter delivery. An example is the Canadian postal service, Canada Post. A related, and popular, business is courier services. Through *GATS*, many WTO Members have made commitments on courier, but not postal, services. Yet, in many Members, the postal service provider offers courier services too. New Zealand Post offers both, as does the Australian Postal Service and the United States Postal Service. Suppose the United Parcel Service (UPS) mounts a WTO challenge against Canada. UPS alleges Canada Post uses revenue from its core letter delivery service (again, on which Canada Post has a monopoly) to cross-subsidize the courier service Canada Post offers. Canada Post does not have a monopoly, and competes with UPS. Article VIII bars this kind of cross-subsidization. UPS actually made such a challenge under *NAFTA* Chapter 11 in 1999. What was the outcome?

III. SPECIFIC OBLIGATIONS (*GATS* PART III)

A. Examining Commitments and Supply Modes

The commitments in *GATS* Part III, in contrast to Part II, are specific. That is, the obligations in Part III apply to specific services Sectors. Part III has only three Articles:

Article XVI:	Market Access
Article XVII:	National Treatment (*i.e.*, non-discrimination)
Article XVIII:	Additional Commitments (*i.e.*, further pledges about services trade liberalization)

The first two provisions are especially significant. Specific obligations — *i.e.*, commitments — on any service may be made on market access (under Article XVI), national treatment (under Article XVII), or both. The commitments may apply to any one or more of the 4 Modes of supply of a service.

Consequently, for every service Sector (or Sub-sector, or Sub-sub sector), it is necessary to ask—

1st:	What Mode of Supply is at issue? Is it Mode I (cross-border supply), II (consumption abroad), III (FDI), or IV (temporary immigration), or some combination thereof?
2nd:	What specific commitment under *GATS* Part III is made with respect to each Mode? For example, with respect to FDI for commercial banking, is a WTO Member promising market access, or just national Treatment? If a Member promises market access, what kind of access? Does the Member allow for wide-open, essentially free trade? Or, does it hold certain Sectors off limits? For instance, does it restrict certain foreign bank entry through licensing, by limiting foreign banks to operation only in certain geographical areas in the territory of the Member, or by barring foreign banks from certain lines of business?

In sum, *GATS* obligations are divided not only according to the Mode, but also according to the specific obligation agreed upon with respect to each Mode.

B. Market Access (*GATS* Article XVI)

Paragraph 1 of Article XVI says that with respect to market access for each of the 4 Modes of services supply, every WTO Member must give services and service suppliers from all other Members treatment no less favorable than the terms, limitations, and conditions promised in its own Schedule. This rule is the obvious analog to GATT Article II. In both contexts, it is the Member itself that defines the scope of the obligation, namely, by what it promises. Therefore, in its Schedule of Concessions, a Member spells out, in a definite way, its commitments — or lack thereof — for specific Sectors, Sub-sectors, Sub-sub-sectors, and Modes.

Whereas Paragraph 1 tells what a Member shall do, Paragraph 2 reveals what it shall not do. For Sectors (Sub-sectors, or Sub-sub-sectors) in which a WTO Member has made a market access commitment, Article XVI:2 lists the measures a WTO Member promises not to maintain — what it is not supposed to do if it has a scheduled commitment. The "shall not" list is as follows:

   (1)   Limits on Quantity:

Quotas, monopolies, exclusive suppliers, and economic needs tests are all ways to circumscribe the number of providers of a service. Article XVI:2(a) says a WTO Member must not maintain any such limit on this number, *i.e.,* on the number of companies or persons engaged in providing that service.

Suppose New Zealand makes a commitment to open widely to foreign providers its market for English as a Second Language (ESL) and legal education services. It could not subsequently impose a cap of no more than 50 ESL schools in New Zealand, nor could it create a monopoly of one law school. Similarly, suppose the country pledges in the tourism area that foreign providers can operate hotels on the South Island. New Zealand cannot later restrict to one the number of hotels in Queenstown. It also may not require proof by a foreign group, such as Hyatt Corporation (from the U.S.) or Taj Hotels (from India), that Queenstown requires additional hotels. That would be an unlawful economic needs test. Might New Zealand place a limit on the number of casinos, and a requirement that any gambling institution be run by a Las Vegas-based business? The answer could depend on the *GATS* Article XIV public morals exception (discussed later in this Chapter).

   (2)   Limits on Value:

A ceiling on the total value of service transactions a foreign provider may offer is a device to regulate market access by foreign entities. Historically, many Third World governments have set quantitative restrictions on the total value of services foreigners may provide. They do so to maintain foreign exchange controls, fearing an outflow of hard currency revenues, *i.e.,* repatriation of earnings to the home countries of the foreign providers. Another device with the same aim is a numerical asset quota, that is, a ceiling, or floor, on the assets required before a foreign provider may provide a service. Still another such device is an economic needs test.

Article XVI:2(b) forbids all such limits, once a WTO Member has subjected a services Sector to a market access commitment. Thus, for instance, suppose South Africa schedules the health Sector, specifically, heart surgery. Subsequently, it cannot limit cardiac surgeons to grossing (each, annually) 30 million South African rand per practice.

(3)   Limits on Number or Quantity:

Obvious methods to restrict foreign entry into a local service market are limits on the total number of operations or operators, or the total quantity of service output. For example, prescribing the number of medical schools or hospitals that one service supplier may operate, or the number of nurses who may be trained, would be limits on the number of operations and output quantity, respectively. Article XVI:2(c) bars such limits for scheduled Sectors.

(4)   Limits on Natural Persons:

Still another classic device for restricting trade liberalization in services is to limit the total number of natural persons who may be employed in a particular area. A relatively more subtle device is to limit the number of employees necessary to supply the service. For any scheduled Sector, Article XVI:2(d) forbids this kind of restriction, as well as an economic needs test. For example, during the Uruguay Round, New Zealand made a commitment on dentistry, opening to some degree its rolls to foreign-trained dentists. Consequently, New Zealand could not thereafter impose a rule saying "there shall at any one time in the country only 500 practicing dentists total," nor one that restricts dentists to hiring only one hygienist (assuming two are necessary).

(5)   Limits on Form:

Demanding particular vehicles through which to enter a local services market is a common way to protect that market from foreign competition. For instance, until its WTO accession effective 11 December 2001, China required foreign companies, in almost all lines of business, to participate in its market through a joint venture (JV). Entry requirements sometimes are stylized as specifications on the number or percentage of local persons who must be appointed to the board of directors, or senior management positions, of a company. Article XVI:2(e) forbids any limits on entry form for a scheduled Sector.

(6)   Limits on Equity:

One of the most fought over restrictions against services trade liberalization concerns participation by foreign services providers in local suppliers. Governments the world over are wont to impose quantitative ceilings on the percentage of stock, or the total value of stock holding, foreigners may hold in a local entity. In their WTO accession agreements, both China and the Kingdom of Saudi Arabia negotiated — with varying degrees of success, but both tenaciously — foreign equity caps in banking, insurance, and telecommunications. (So, too, did Mexico in *NAFTA* talks with respect to banking and financial services.) The tipping point, of course, is 50.1 percent, which if possible gives control. Once a government schedules a commitment in a particular Sector, Article XVI:2(f) prevents it from backsliding on its pledge by barring any new limits on foreign shareholding or the value (individual or aggregate) of foreign investment.

From the Article XVI:2 "shall not" list, two patterns ought to be evident.

The first pattern concerns the kinds of items on the proscribed list. The first four categories, in Article XVI:2(a)-(d), disallow any caps (limits) on foreign participation in a Sector in which a WTO Member has decided to schedule a commitment. The last two categories, Article XVI:2(e)-(f), disallow any restrictions on how a foreign service supplier enters the local market.

The second pattern, which follows from the first one, concerns the nature of market access pledges under Article XVI. These commitments are definitive. Article XVI says clearly what a market access commitment must cover, by implication from the list of Paragraph 2. The *chapeau* to Paragraph 2 does not read "including, but not limited to. . . ." In other words, to schedule a commitment is a promise both to do something, and not to do certain itemized things. In turn, Article XVI:1-2 puts to every WTO Member three choices for every services Sector and Mode of supply. A Member can opt for free trade, meaning no limitations. It can choose managed trade, in the sense of partial liberalization — it opens certain Sectors and certain Modes to certain degrees, and posts the limits in its Services Schedule. Or, it can choose to make no market access commitments at all, thereby reserving to itself the right to bar foreign participation.

C. National Treatment (*GATS* Article XVII)

Whereas the MFN obligation in *GATS* is a general one, set forth in Part II, Article II, the other great non-discrimination principle — national treatment — is not. It sits in Part III, Article XVII, meaning that national treatment is not an across-the-board duty. Rather, national treatment is obligatory only to the extent a WTO Member chooses to impose it on itself by making a specific commitment in a services Sector (or Sub-sector or Sub-sub-sector). The contrast with GATT and trade in goods is obvious, where Articles I (MFN treatment) and III (national treatment) apply horizontally. Indeed, under *GATS*, a Member is free to schedule a market access commitment under Article XVI, or a national treatment under Article XVII, neither, or both.

What, exactly, does Article XVII mandate? In the simplest theological sense, like GATT Article III, it is a rule to love one's neighbor like oneself. *GATS* Article XVII:1 essentially says foreign and local services providers will be treated equally. Of course, as with GATT Article III, with *GATS* Article XVII:1, the reality of what is required is complex. Article XVII:1 is obligatory only in a Sector in which a WTO Member has made a commitment, and the extent to which it is obligatory is subject to any conditions imposed by the Member. What is required is treatment of foreign services and service suppliers treatment "no less favorable" than that accorded to "like" domestic services and service suppliers.

Two interpretative difficulties leap out from *GATS* Article XVII:1. First, Treatment "no less favorable" is not a command for identical treatment. Rather, substantively equal treatment is the obligation. However, is the jurisprudence of GATT Article III:4 to be applied to the *GATS* context? If so, then equal competitive conditions — regardless of aims — would be the benchmark. Fortunately, Article XVII:2 helps resolve the ambiguity. Formally identical, or formally different, treatment shall be considered to be "less favorable" if it modifies the conditions of competition between foreign services or service suppliers and like domestic services or service suppliers. Therefore, national treatment means providing competitively neutral conditions, *i.e.*, a level playing field.

Second, according to what legal criteria are services to be judged alike? A teaching from the *Japan Alcoholic Beverages* case (excerpted in an earlier Chapter) is that three factors help assess "likeness," and they are applied on a case-by-case basis — physical characteristics, consumer habits and tastes, and end uses. Is this GATT jurisprudence guidance to assess the "likeness" of services? Interestingly, on the third criterion, the general understanding (in scholarly trade literature,) is the test for likeness of services, as with goods, is to consider the perspective of end users. However, why not weigh the potentially differing perspectives of a supplier and consumer? Consider tertiary education. From the point of view of a teacher, face-to-face instruction and correspondence courses are not qualitatively "like" services. But, to a student who cares solely about obtaining a degree or qualification, the two pedagogies are like.

Importantly, the national treatment obligation in *GATS* Article XVII has no itemized list of impermissible limitations, in contrast to the Article XVI:2(a)-(f) list following the market access obligation of XVI:1. Is it reasonable to infer that the lack of a "shall not" list means deviations from national treatment are permitted in scheduled Sectors? If so, then what kind of deviations are allowed, and to what extent? Asked differently, in what kind of *de jure* or *de facto* discrimination might a WTO member seek to engage, *i.e.*, what exceptions to a previously-made national treatment commitment might it want?

GATS Article XVII does not yield a response. However, the so called "*Examples Document*" furnishes an answer. The *Document* is part of the Dunkel Draft of *GATS* and other Uruguay Round texts. At the end of the Round, negotiators were in such a rush they forgot to change the acronym "MTO" (for Multilateral Trade Organization") in the *Examples Document* to the acronym for the institution they created — "WTO." In any event, the *Examples Document* sets out the following list of permissible limitations on national treatment in a scheduled services Sector:

    (1)   Subsidies to Domestic Service Suppliers:

May a foreign services supplier have access to the same subsidies as like domestic suppliers? For example, on tertiary education, should La Trobe University, based in Melbourne, Australia, have access to the same subsidies as the University of Auckland in New Zealand? This question is sensitive. The *Examples Document* answers it by noting that reserving access to subsidies to nationals (*e.g.*, domestic students) is a common reservation in a *GATS* Schedule, and is permitted.

    (2)   Tax Liabilities:

May a heavier tax burden be placed on a foreign company relative to a domestic business? The *Examples Document* says "yes." The permission for differential taxation preserves the sovereignty of WTO Members on direct (income) tax policy.

(3)   License Fees:

May a non-resident service provider be charged a higher license fee than a local resident? The *Examples Document* permits this kind of discrimination.

(4)   Citizenship or Permanent Residency:

May a WTO Member impose a requirement that a particular service be provided only by a citizen or permanent resident of that Member? Such requirements exist, for instance, with respect to government employment and eligibility for government benefits. The *Examples Document* condones these restrictions.

(5)   Bar Admission:

With educational and examination requirements for licensure, legal services hardly are among the most liberalized among WTO Members. Is it permissible for a WTO Member to require a lawyer, for practice certification, to be a graduate of a local university? "Yes," says the *Examples Document*.

(6)   Registration:

Countries typically require foreign entities seeking to operate in their jurisdiction to have a registered office in the jurisdiction. A key reason is the availability of the entity for service of process, and possibly for enforcement of judgments. The *Examples Document* states a WTO Member can require a foreign company to have a registered office in the territory of the Member.

(7)   Local Talent:

As a condition for permission to engage in Mode III supply (FDI), many Third World countries require a commitment by foreign multinational corporations (MNCs) to recruit and develop local human resources. The *Examples Document* indicates local talent strictures on foreign service providers are permissible.

(8)   Land Ownership:

Effective provision of services often requires space. Consider retailing and the footprint America's Wal-Mart or France's Carrefour require — hundreds of thousands of square feet for a store and parking lot. May a WTO Member discriminate against foreign service suppliers by restricting their ability to own or possess land? The *Examples Document* indicates a WTO Member is allowed to restrict foreign ownership of real property.

In some countries, foreign land ownership (especially freehold, or even 99 year leasehold, estates) is a sensitive matter. For instance, in Samoa, an applicant for WTO Membership, roughly 90 percent of tribal lands are owned by the King. In accession negotiations (as of March 2003), notwithstanding the *Examples Document*, the WTO Working Group on Samoa instructed the applicant it must liberalize rules on land ownership to permit foreigners to buy land. Aside from Fiji and Vanuatu, no South Pacific Island country is a WTO Member. To what extent are tribal or other indigenous land ownership patterns, which if unchanged, impinge on services trade liberalization and national treatment commitments, a barrier to Membership in that region?

In sum, all of the above kinds of limitations on national treatment are permissible with respect to scheduled Sectors. The permission comes not directly from Article XVII, but rather from a Dunkel Draft text — the *Examples Document*.

IV. SCHEDULED OBLIGATIONS, KEEPING COMMITMENTS, AND THE 2005 *ANTIGUA GAMBLING* CASE

WTO APPELLATE BODY REPORT, *UNITED STATES — MEASURES AFFECTING THE CROSS-BORDER SUPPLY OF GAMBLING AND BETTING SERVICES*
WT/DS285/AB/R (adopted 20 April 2005)

VI. Article XVI of the *GATS*: Market Access

214. Article XVI of the *GATS* sets out specific obligations for Members that apply insofar as a Member has undertaken "specific market access commitments" in its Schedule. The first paragraph of Article XVI obliges Members to accord services and service suppliers of other Members "no less favourable treatment than that provided for under the terms, limitations and conditions agreed and specified in its Schedule." The second paragraph of Article XVI defines, in six sub-paragraphs, measures that a Member, having undertaken a specific commitment, is not to adopt or maintain, "unless otherwise specified in its Schedule." The first four sub-paragraphs concern quantitative limitations on market access; the fifth sub-paragraph covers measures that restrict or require specific types of legal entity or joint venture through which a service supplier may supply a service; and the sixth sub-paragraph identifies limitations on the participation of foreign capital.

215. The Panel found that the United States' Schedule includes specific commitments on gambling and betting services, and we have upheld this finding. The Panel then considered the consistency of the measures at issue with the United States' obligations under Article XVI of the *GATS*. The scope of those obligations depends on the scope of the specific commitment made in the United States' Schedule. In this case, the relevant entry for mode 1 supply in the market access column of subsector 10.D of the United States' Schedule reads "None." [As the Appellate Body explained in a footnote: "This notation is the opposite of the notation "Unbound," which means that a Member undertakes *no* specific commitment."] In other words, the United States has undertaken to provide full market access, within the meaning of Article XVI, in respect of the services included within the scope of its subsector 10.D commitment. In so doing, it has committed not to maintain any of the types of measures listed in the six sub-paragraphs of Article XVI:2.

. . . .

B. The Meaning of Sub-paragraphs (a) and (c) of Article XVI

221. The *chapeau* to Article XVI:2, and sub-paragraphs (a) and (c), provide:

> In sectors where market-access commitments are undertaken, the measures which a Member shall not maintain or adopt either on the

basis of a regional subdivision or on the basis of its entire territory, unless otherwise specified in its Schedule, are defined as:

(a) limitations on the number of service suppliers whether in the form of numerical quotas, monopolies, exclusive service suppliers or the requirements of an economic needs test; . . .

(c) limitations on the total number of service operations or on the total quantity of service output expressed in terms of designated numerical units in the form of quotas or the requirement of an economic needs test;

9 Subparagraph 2(c) does not cover measures of a Member which limit inputs for the supply of services.

1. Sub-paragraph (a) of Article XVI:2

. . . .

227. The words "in the form of" in sub-paragraph (a) relate to all four of the limitations identified in that provision. It follows, in our view, that the four types of limitations, themselves, impart meaning to "in the form of." Looking at these four types of limitations in Article XVI:2(a), we begin with "numerical quotas." These words are not defined in the *GATS*. According to the dictionary definitions provided by the United States, the meaning of the word "numerical" includes "characteristic of a number or numbers." The word "quota" means, *inter alia*, "the maximum number or quantity belonging, due, given, or permitted to an individual or group"; and "numerical limitations on imports or exports." Thus, a "numerical quota" within Article XVI:2(a) appears to mean a quantitative limit on the number of service suppliers. The fact that the word "numerical" encompasses things which "have the characteristics of a number" suggests that limitations "in the form of a numerical quota" would encompass limitations which, even if not in themselves a number, have the characteristics of a number. Because zero is *quantitative* in nature, it can, in our view, be deemed to have the "characteristics of" a number — that is, to be "numerical."

228. The second type of limitation mentioned in sub-paragraph (a) is "limitations on the number of service suppliers. . . in the form of . . . monopolies." Although the word "monopolies," as such, is not defined, Article XXVIII(h) of the *GATS* defines a "monopoly supplier of a service" as:

. . . any person, public or private, which in the relevant market of the territory of a Member is authorized or established formally *or in effect* by that Member as the sole supplier of that service. (emphasis added)

229. The term "exclusive service suppliers," which is used to identify the third limitation in Article XVI:2(a) ("limitations on the number of service suppliers . . . in the form of exclusive service suppliers"), is defined in Article VIII:5 of the *GATS*, as:

. . . where a Member, formally *or in effect*, (*a*) authorizes or establishes a small number of service suppliers and (*b*) substantially prevents competition among those suppliers in its territory. (emphasis added)

230. These two definitions suggest that the reference, in Article XVI:2(a), to limitations on the number of service suppliers "in the form of monopolies and exclusive service suppliers" should be read to include limitations that are in form *or in effect*, monopolies or exclusive service suppliers.

231. We further observe that it is not clear that "limitations on the number of service suppliers . . . in the form of . . . the requirements of an economic needs test" must take a particular "form." Thus, this fourth type of limitation, too, suggests that the words "in the form of" must not be interpreted as prescribing a rigid mechanical formula.

232. This is not to say that the words "in the form of" should be ignored or replaced by the words "that have the effect of." Yet, at the same time, they cannot be read in isolation. Rather, when viewed as a whole, the text of sub-paragraph (a) supports the view that the words "in the form of" must be read in conjunction with the words that precede them — "limitations on the *number* of service suppliers" — as well as the words that follow them, including the words "*numerical* quotas." (emphasis added) Read in this way, it is clear that the thrust of sub-paragraph (a) is not on the *form* of limitations, but on their *numerical*, or *quantitative*, nature.

[The Appellate Body then examined the context of Article XIV:2(a), specifically the *chapeau* to Article XVI:2, reading it in the light of the object and purpose of *GATS*. The Appellate Body also studied the preparatory work to *GATS*, particularly the 1993 Scheduling Guidelines (which it held to be such work). Both sources — context and preparatory work — reinforced its textual analysis of Sub-paragraph (a).]

. . . .

238. [W]e are of the view that limitations amounting to a zero quota are quantitative limitations and fall within the scope of Article XVI:2(a) [and, therefore, uphold the Panel's finding].

2. Sub-paragraph (c) of Article XVI:2

240. . . . [A]ccording to the Panel, the "correct reading of Article XVI:2(c)" is that limitations referred to under that provision may be: (i) in the form of designated numerical units; (ii) in the form of quotas; *or* (iii) in the form of the requirement of an economic needs test.

241. The Panel then found that, where a specific commitment has been undertaken in respect of a service, a measure prohibiting one or more means of delivery of that service is:

> . . . a limitation "on the total number of service operations or on the total quantity of service output . . . in the form of quotas" within the meaning of Article XVI:2(c) because it . . . results in a "zero quota" on one or more or all means of delivery include[d] in mode 1.

242. The United States asserts that, in so finding, the Panel used an incorrect reading of the French and Spanish texts to arrive at an interpretation that is inconsistent with the ordinary meaning of the English text. Specifically, the Panel relied upon the presence of commas in the French and Spanish versions of the text — but not in the English version — in order to

find that sub-paragraph (c) identifies *three* types of limitations. The United States argues that, when properly interpreted, sub-paragraph (c) identifies only *two* types of limitations. The United States adds that the measures at issue in this case cannot in any way be construed as falling within the scope of either of the *two* limitations defined in sub-paragraph (c).

. . . .

247. In our view, by combining, in sub-paragraph (c), the elements of the first clause of Article XVI:2(c) and the elements in the second part of the provision, the parties to the negotiations sought to ensure that their provision covered certain types of limitations, but did not feel the need to clearly demarcate the scope of each such element. On the contrary, there is scope for overlap between such elements: between limitations on the number of service operations and limitations on the quantity of service output, for example, or between limitations in the form of quotas and limitations in the form of an economic needs test. That sub-paragraph (c) applies in respect of all four modes of supply under the *GATS* also suggests the limitations covered thereunder cannot take a single form, nor be constrained in a formulaic manner. Nonetheless, all types of limitations in sub-paragraph (c) are quantitative in nature, and all restrict market access. For these reasons, we are of the view that, *even if* sub-paragraph (c) is read as referring to only *two* types of limitations, as contended by the United States, it does not follow that sub-paragraph (c) would not catch a measure equivalent to a zero quota.

. . . .

252. . . . [W]e *uphold* the Panel's finding . . . that a measure prohibiting the supply of certain services where specific commitments have been undertaken is a limitation:

> . . . within the meaning of Article XVI:2(c) because it totally prevents the services operations and/or service output through one or more or all means of delivery that are included in mode 1. In other words, such a ban results in a "zero quota" on one or more or all means of delivery include in mode 1.

. . . .

D. Application of Article XVI to the Measures at Issue

257. Having upheld the Panel's interpretation of Article XVI:2(a) and (c), we now consider its application of that interpretation to the measures at issue in this case. . . .

258. . . . It is . . . useful to set out briefly the relevant part of each statute [*i.e.*, the three disputed Federal laws, the *Wire Act*, *Travel Act*, and *Illegal Gambling Business Act* (*IGBA*)], as well as the Panel's finding in respect of that statute. The relevant part of the *Wire Act* states:

> Whoever being engaged in the business of betting or wagering knowingly uses a wire communication facility for the transmission in interstate or foreign commerce of bets or wagers or information assisting in the placing of bets or wagers on any sporting event or contest, or

for the transmission of a wire communication which entitles the recipient to receive money or credit as a result of bets or wagers, or for information assisting in the placing of bets or wagers shall be fined under this title or imprisoned not more than two years, or both. [18 U.S.C. Section 1084(a).]

259. With respect to this provision, the Panel found that "the *Wire Act* prohibits the use of at least one or potentially several means of delivery included in mode 1," and that, accordingly, the statute "constitutes a 'zero quota' for, respectively, one, several or all of those means of delivery." The Panel reasoned that the *Wire Act* prohibits service suppliers from supplying gambling and betting services using remote means of delivery, as well as service operations and service output through such means. Accordingly, the Panel determined that "the *Wire Act* contains a limitation 'in the form of numerical quotas' within the meaning of Article XVI:2(a) and a limitation 'in the form of a quota' within the meaning of Article XVI:2(c)."

260. As regards the *Travel Act*, the Panel quoted the following excerpt:

(a)   Whoever travels in interstate or foreign commerce or uses the mail or any facility in interstate or foreign commerce, with intent to –

    (1)   distribute the proceeds of any unlawful activity; or

    (2)   commit any crime of violence to further any unlawful activity; or

    (3)   otherwise promote, manage, establish, carry on, or facilitate the promotion, management, establishment, or carrying on, of any unlawful activity,

and thereafter performs or attempts to perform—

    (A)   an act described in paragraph (1) or (3) shall be fined under this title, imprisoned not more than 5 years, or both; or

    (B)   an act described in paragraph (2) shall be fined under this title, imprisoned for not more than 20 years, or both, and if death results shall be imprisoned for any term of years or for life.

(b)   As used in this section (i) "unlawful activity" means (1) any business enterprise involving gambling . . . in violation of the laws of the State in which they are committed or of the United States.

[18 U.S.C. § 1952(a)-(b).]

261. The Panel determined that "the *Travel Act* prohibits gambling activity that entails the supply of gambling and betting services by 'mail or any facility' to the extent that such supply is undertaken by a 'business enterprise involving gambling' that is prohibited under state law and provided that the other requirements in subparagraph (a) of the *Travel Act* have been met." The Panel further opined that the *Travel Act* prohibits service suppliers from supplying gambling and betting services through the mail, (and potentially other means of delivery), as well as services operations and service output through the mail (and potentially other means of delivery), in such a way as to amount to a "zero" quota on one or several means of delivery included in

mode 1. For these reasons, the Panel found that "the *Travel Act* contains a limitation 'in the form of numerical quotas' within the meaning of Article XVI:2(a) and a limitation' in the form of a quota' within the meaning of Article XVI:2(c)."

262. The Panel considered the relevant part of the *Illegal Gambling Business Act* to be the following:

(a)   Whoever conducts, finances, manages, supervises, directs or owns all or part of an illegal gambling business shall be fined under this title or imprisoned not more than five years, or both.

(b)   As used in this section—

    (1)   'illegal gambling business' means a gambling business which

        (i)   is a violation of the law of a State or political subdivision in which it is conducted;

        (ii)   involves five or more persons who conduct, finance, manage, supervise, direct, or own all or part of such business; and

        (iii)   has been or remains in substantially continuous operation for a period in excess of thirty days or has a gross revenue of $2,000 in any single day.

    (2)   'gambling' includes but is not limited to pool-selling, bookmaking, maintaining slot machines, roulette wheels or dice tables, and conducting lotteries, policy, bolita or numbers games, or selling chances therein.

[18 U.S.C. § 1955(a)-(b).]

263. The Panel then determined that because the *IGBA* "prohibits the conduct, finance, management, supervision, direction or ownership of all or part of a 'gambling business' that violates state law, it effectively prohibits the supply of gambling and betting services through at least one and potentially all means of delivery included in mode 1 by such businesses;" that this prohibition concerned service suppliers, service operations and service output; and that, accordingly, the *IGBA* "contains a limitation 'in the form of numerical quotas' within the meaning of Article XVI:2(a) and a limitation 'in the form of a quota' within the meaning of Article XVI:2(c)."

. . . .

265. We have upheld the Panel's finding that the United States' Schedule to the *GATS* includes a specific commitment in respect of gambling and betting services. In that Schedule, the United States has inscribed "None" in the first row of the market access column for subsector 10.D. In these circumstances, and for the reasons given in this section of our Report, we also *uphold* the Panel's ultimate finding . . . that, by maintaining the *Wire Act*, the *Travel Act*, and the *Illegal Gambling Business Act*, the United States acts inconsistently with its obligations under Article XVI:1 and Article XVI:2(a) and (c) of the *GATS*.

V. EXCEPTIONS (*GATS* ARTICLE XIV)

A. Comparing GATT and *GATS* Lists

General exceptions to all *GATS* obligations are set forth in Part II, specifically, Article XIX. Thus, Article XIV is akin to GATT Article XX. Four points are readily apparent from a comparison of the two provisions. First, what is the relationship between the itemized lists in each provision, and the *chapeau* to each list? The jurisprudence (discussed in a later Chapter) on the GATT environmental exceptions in Article XX(b) and (g) has evolved considerably, resulting in a two-step test. A measure must be justified provisionally by an itemized exception, and if it is, then must pass muster under the *chapeau* requirements. Is the same two-step test used for *GATS* Article XIV? Consider this question when studying the 2005 *Antigua Gambling* case?

Second, the *chapeaux* to *GATS* Article XIV and GATT Article XX are nearly *verbatim*. Both permit a measure to derogate from an obligation, provided the measure is neither "a means of arbitrary or unjustifiable discrimination between countries," nor "a disguised restriction on trade." The notable difference in the *chapeaux* concerns the similarity of conditions in countries involved in a dispute. GATT Article XX bars discrimination between countries "where the "same conditions prevail." *GATS* Article XIV bars it where "like conditions prevail." Are the words "same" and "like" synonyms?

Third, some *GATS* and GATT exemptions are carbon copies, or nearly so. Article XIV(a)-(b) contains the key *GATS* exceptions, and they illustrate the resemblance. (*GATS* Article XX(c) is an administrative necessity exception, akin to GATT Article XX(d).) Whenever language in one international trade agreement resembles, or is identical to, text in another accord, the obvious question for an adjudicator is whether to borrow jurisprudence. The GATT and *GATS* exceptions require a derogating measure to be "necessary." Should the WTO Appellate Body import into *GATS* Article XIV(a)-(b) the necessity test from GATT Article XX(a)-(b)?

GATS Article XIX(a) permits derogations for a measure "necessary to protect public morals or to maintain public order." What are "public morals"? As for "public order," the footnote accompanying this term says an exception for public order may be invoked "only where a genuine and sufficiently serious threat is posed to one of the fundamental interests of a society." What are such interests, and what might constitute a requisite threat? Surely the answer is different in Singapore, which has vigorous rules about publications on matters of ethnicity, and religion, and the United Kingdom, which is the home of free speech. Do differential local sensitivities suggest regulating media services is a matter best left to individual WTO Members?

Interestingly, GATT Article XX(a) contains the public morals exception, but not the public order exception. Why not? Surely goods or services from overseas might threaten public order. As for "public morals," should this term be interpreted consistently in both GATT and *GATS* contexts? Who should do the interpreting? Consider the following hypothetical.

Assume a measure to ban importation of pornography qualifies under GATT Article XX(a) and *GATS* Article XIV(a). A ban on pornographic magazines would fall under the first provision, and a ban on the cross-border supply of pornographic materials via the internet (Mode I delivery) would fall under the second provision. U.S. Supreme Court jurisprudence leaves the definition of "obscenity" to local communities, but GATT and *GATS* disputes are subject to the *DSU*. What might be a public morals problem in Amarillo almost certainly is not one in Amsterdam. Is it right for the Appellate Body to decide for residents of both cities what is "pornographic," and whether pornography is within the ambit of the public morals exception? In brief, Article XIV(a) becomes highly controversial if a *DSU* adjudication arises in which the Appellate Body overrides a choice by a WTO Member. How might awareness of this fact on the part of Appellate Body members affect their decision-making, either in terms of final outcomes or rationale?

As for *GATS* Article XIV(b), it is identical to GATT Article XX(b). Both are designed to excuse violations that are "necessary to protect human, animal, or plant life or health." Like the public morals — public order exception, this health exception raises controversial questions. For example, would a measure on the qualification of nurses be covered? In New Zealand, a nurse must be trained on "cultural safety." That term, "cultural safety," includes an understanding of the *Treaty of Waitangi* and the Maori people. Is that "cultural safety" "necessary" to human health?

Finally, and probably most obviously, the list of exceptions in GATT is double the length of that in *GATS* — ten bases versus five. Aside from public morality and health, Article XIV does not list the other exceptions found in GATT Article XX. For trade in goods, deviations from general GATT obligations are permitted on major grounds that simply not set out in Article XIV.

1. *Protection of national treasures*:

Why does *GATS* exclude this as a permissible ground for derogation, when it implicates tourism? The desire to see the treasures generates tourism, and foreigners consume tourism services through Mode II, as well as supply it through Mode III. Should services relating to these treasures be protected? Query whether, if they had been a contracting party during the Uruguay Round, China, Iran, Kingdom of Saudi Arabia, Russia, Syria, or Vietnam might have insisted on inserting an exemption into Article XIV for the protection of national treasures.

2. *Conservation of exhaustible natural resources*:

Why does *GATS* fail to list this environmental exemption? After all, the accord covers environmental services. Query whether the countries mentioned above might have sought inclusion of conservation of exhaustible natural resources on the Article XIV list?

3. *Prison labor services*:

Once again, why does *GATS* exclude prison labor services? Is the reason the use of such services in some WTO Members? For example, in some jurisdictions, prisoners do laundry, or staff call centers.

Unfortunately, nothing in the *traveaux* (legislative history) to the *GATS* negotiations explains the GATT — *GATS* differences on general exceptions.

So, how do trade negotiators explain the difference? They say the shorter list of general exceptions in *GATS* is justified because *GATS* takes a Positive

List approach to scheduling services trade commitments. This justification is called the "Scheduling," or the "Positive List" rationale. It means a WTO Member simply can choose not to schedule a service, and thus exempt that service by not making a commitment. The problem with the Scheduling rationale is a WTO Member might make a commitment, either under pressure from other Members, or multinational corporations (MNCs). Or, the Member might agree to liberalize services trade in an area without not fully realizing the implications — particularly in the future — of that commitment. The Scheduling rationale presumes considerable legal capacity and resoluteness on the part of the Member. Especially in least developed and some developing countries, that presumption is invalid.

B. Public Morality and the 2005 *Antigua Gambling* Case

WTO APPELLATE BODY REPORT, *UNITED STATES — MEASURES AFFECTING THE CROSS-BORDER SUPPLY OF GAMBLING AND BETTING SERVICES*
WT/DS285/AB/R (adopted 20 April 2005)
(complaint by Antigua and Barbuda)

C. The Panel's Substantive Analysis Under Article XIV

291. Article XIV of the *GATS* sets out the general exceptions from obligations under that *Agreement* in the same manner as does Article XX of the GATT 1994. Both of these provisions affirm the right of Members to pursue objectives identified in the paragraphs of these provisions even if, in doing so, Members act inconsistently with obligations set out in other provisions of the respective agreements, provided that all of the conditions set out therein are satisfied. Similar language is used in both provisions, notably the term "necessary" and the requirements set out in their respective *chapeaux*. Accordingly, like the Panel, we find previous decisions under Article XX of the GATT 1994 relevant for our analysis under Article XIV of the *GATS*.

292. Article XIV of the *GATS*, like Article XX of the GATT 1994, contemplates a "two-tier analysis" of a measure that a Member seeks to justify under that provision. A panel should first determine whether the challenged measure falls within the scope of one of the paragraphs of Article XIV. This requires that the challenged measure address the particular interest specified in that paragraph and that there be a sufficient nexus between the measure and the interest protected. The required nexus — or "degree of connection" — between the measure and the interest is specified in the language of the paragraphs themselves, through the use of terms such as "relating to" and "necessary to." Where the challenged measure has been found to fall within one of the paragraphs of Article XIV, a panel should then consider whether that measure satisfies the requirements of the *chapeau* of Article XIV.

1. Justification of the Measures Under Paragraph (a) of Article XIV

. . . .

(a) "Measures . . . to Protect Public Morals or to Maintain Public Order"

296. In its analysis under Article XIV(a), the Panel found that "the term 'public morals' denotes standards of right and wrong conduct maintained by or on behalf of a community or nation." The Panel further found that the definition of the term "order," read in conjunction with footnote 5 of the *GATS*, "suggests that 'public order' refers to the preservation of the fundamental interests of a society, as reflected in public policy and law." The Panel then referred to Congressional reports and testimony establishing that "the government of the United States consider[s] [that the *Wire Act*, the *Travel Act*, and the *IGBA*] were adopted to address concerns such as those pertaining to money laundering, organized crime, fraud, underage gambling and pathological gambling." On this basis, the Panel found that the three federal statutes are "measures that are designed to 'protect public morals' and/or 'to maintain public order' within the meaning of Article XIV(a)."

297. Antigua contests this finding on a rather limited ground, namely that the Panel failed to determine whether the concerns identified by the United States satisfy the standard set out in footnote 5 to Article XIV(a) of the *GATS*, which reads:

> [t]he public order exception may be invoked only where a genuine and sufficiently serious threat is posed to one of the fundamental interests of society.

298. We see no basis to conclude that the Panel failed to assess whether the standard set out in footnote 5 had been satisfied. . . . Having defined "public order" to include the standard in footnote 5, and then applied that definition to the facts before it to conclude that the measures "are designed to 'protect public morals' and/or 'to maintain public order,' " the Panel was not required, in addition, to make a separate, explicit determination that the standard of footnote 5 had been met.

299. We therefore *uphold* the Panel's finding . . . that "the concerns which the *Wire Act*, the *Travel Act* and the *Illegal Gambling Business Act* seek to address fall within the scope of 'public morals' and/or 'public order' under Article XIV(a)."

(b) The Requirement that a Measure Be "Necessary" Under Article XIV(a)

300. In the second part of its analysis [*i.e.*, the second part of Step 1 in the two-tiered analysis] under Article XIV(a), the Panel considered whether the *Wire Act*, the *Travel Act*, and the *IGBA* are "necessary" within the meaning of that provision. The Panel found that the United States had not demonstrated the "necessity" of those measures.

301. This finding rested on the Panel's determinations that: (i) "the interests and values protected by [the *Wire Act*, the *Travel Act*, and the *IGBA*] serve

very important societal interests that can be characterized as 'vital and important in the highest degree;' " (ii) the *Wire Act*, the *Travel Act*, and the *IGBA* "must contribute, at least to some extent," to addressing the United States' concerns "pertaining to money laundering, organized crime, fraud, underage gambling and pathological gambling;" (iii) the measures in question "have a significant restrictive trade impact;" and (iv) "[i]n rejecting Antigua's invitation to engage in bilateral or multilateral consultations and/or negotiations, the United States failed to pursue in good faith a course of action that could have been used by it to explore the possibility of finding a reasonably available WTO-consistent alternative."

. . . .

(i) Determining "necessity" under Article XIV(a)

304. . . . . [T]he standard of "necessity" provided for in the general exceptions provision is an *objective* standard. To be sure, a Member's characterization of a measure's objectives and of the effectiveness of its regulatory approach — as evidenced, for example, by texts of statutes, legislative history, and pronouncements of government agencies or officials — will be relevant in determining whether the measure is, objectively, "necessary." A panel is not bound by these characterizations, however, and may also find guidance in the structure and operation of the measure and in contrary evidence proffered by the complaining party. In any event, a panel must, on the basis of the evidence in the record, independently and objectively assess the "necessity" of the measure before it.

305. In *Korea — Various Measures on Beef*, the Appellate Body stated, in the context of Article XX(d) of the GATT 1994, that whether a measure is "necessary" should be determined through "a process of weighing and balancing a series of factors." The Appellate Body characterized this process as one:

> . . . comprehended in the determination of whether a WTO-consistent alternative measure which the Member concerned could "reasonably be expected to employ" is available, or whether a less WTO-inconsistent measure is "reasonably available."

. . . .

308. The requirement, under Article XIV(a), that a measure be "necessary" — that is, that there be no "reasonably available," WTO-consistent alternative — reflects the shared understanding of Members that substantive *GATS* obligations should not be deviated from lightly. An alternative measure may be found not to be "reasonably available," however, where it is merely theoretical in nature, for instance, where the responding Member is not capable of taking it, or where the measure imposes an undue burden on that Member, such as prohibitive costs or substantial technical difficulties. Moreover, a "reasonably available" alternative measure must be a measure that would preserve for the responding Member its right to achieve its desired level of protection with respect to the objective pursued under paragraph (a) of Article XIV.

309. It is well-established that a responding party invoking an affirmative defence bears the burden of demonstrating that its measure, found to be

WTO-inconsistent, satisfies the requirements of the invoked defence. In the context of Article XIV(a), this means that the responding party must show that its measure is "necessary" to achieve objectives relating to public morals or public order. In our view, however, it is not the responding party's burden to show, in the first instance, that there are *no* reasonably available alternatives to achieve its objectives. In particular, a responding party need not identify the universe of less trade-restrictive alternative measures and then show that none of those measures achieves the desired objective. The WTO agreements do not contemplate such an impracticable and, indeed, often impossible burden.

310. Rather, it is for a responding party to make a *prima facie* case that its measure is "necessary" by putting forward evidence and arguments that enable a panel to assess the challenged measure in the light of the relevant factors to be "weighed and balanced" in a given case. The responding party may, in so doing, point out why alternative measures would not achieve the same objectives as the challenged measure, but it is under no obligation to do so in order to establish, in the first instance, that its measure is "necessary." If the panel concludes that the respondent has made a *prima facie* case that the challenged measure is "necessary" — that is, "significantly closer to the pole of 'indispensable' than to the opposite pole of simply 'making a contribution to' " — then a panel should find that challenged measure "necessary" within the terms of Article XIV(a) of the *GATS*.

311. If, however, the complaining party raises a WTO-consistent alternative measure that, in its view, the responding party should have taken, the responding party will be required to demonstrate why its challenged measure nevertheless remains "necessary" in the light of that alternative or, in other words, why the proposed alternative is not, in fact, "reasonably available." If a responding party demonstrates that the alternative is not "reasonably available," in the light of the interests or values being pursued and the party's desired level of protection, it follows that the challenged measure must be "necessary" within the terms of Article XIV(a) of the *GATS*.

(ii) Did the Panel err in its analysis of the "necessity" of the measures at issue?

. . . .

315. In its "necessity" analysis under Article XIV(a), the Panel appeared to understand that, in order for a measure to be accepted as "necessary" under Article XIV(a), the responding Member must have first *"explored and exhausted"* all reasonably available WTO-compatible alternatives before adopting its WTO-inconsistent measure. This understanding led the Panel to conclude that, in this case, the United States had "an obligation to consult with Antigua before and while imposing its prohibition on the cross-border supply of gambling and betting services." Because the Panel found that the United States had not engaged in such consultations with Antigua, the Panel also found that the United States had not established that its measures are "necessary" and, therefore, provisionally justified under Article XIV(a).

. . . .

317. In our view, the Panel's "necessity" analysis was flawed because it did not focus on an alternative measure that was reasonably available to the United States to achieve the stated objectives regarding the protection of public morals or the maintenance of public order. Engaging in consultations with Antigua, with a view to arriving at a negotiated settlement that achieves the same objectives as the challenged United States' measures, was not an appropriate alternative for the Panel to consider because consultations are by definition a process, the results of which are uncertain and therefore not capable of comparison with the measures at issue in this case.

. . . .

321. [T] he Panel erred in assessing the necessity of the three United States statutes against the possibility of consultations with Antigua because such consultations, in our view, cannot qualify as a reasonably available alternative measure with which a challenged measure should be compared. For this reason, we *reverse* the Panel's finding . . . that, because the United States did not enter into consultations with Antigua, [the U.S. could not provisionally justify the three disputed Federal statutes under Article XIV(a), *i.e.*, that these measures did not pass muster in Step 1 of the two-tiered analysis.] . . . .

322. Having reversed this finding, we must consider whether, as the United States contends, the *Wire Act*, the *Travel Act*, and the *IGBA* are properly characterized as "necessary" to achieve the objectives identified by the United States and accepted by the Panel. The Panel's analysis, as well as the factual findings contained therein, are useful for our assessment of whether these measures satisfy the requirements of paragraph (a) of Article XIV.

323. As we stated above, a responding party must make a *prima facie* case that its challenged measure is "necessary." A Panel determines whether this case is made through the identification, and weighing and balancing, of relevant factors, such as those in *Korea — Various Measures on Beef*, with respect to the measure challenged. In this regard, we note that the Panel: (i) found that the three federal statutes protect "very important societal interests;" (ii) observed that "strict controls may be needed to protect [such] interests;" and (iii) found that the three federal statutes contribute to the realization of the ends that they pursue. Although the Panel recognized the "significant restrictive trade impact" of the three federal statutes, it expressly tempered this recognition with a detailed explanation of certain characteristics of, and concerns specific to, the remote supply of gambling and betting services. These included: (i) "the volume, speed and international reach of remote gambling transactions;" (ii) the "virtual anonymity of such transactions;" (iii) "low barriers to entry in the context of the remote supply of gambling and betting services;" and the (iv) "isolated and anonymous environment in which such gambling takes place." Thus, this analysis reveals that the Panel did not place much weight, in the circumstances of this case, on the restrictive trade impact of the three federal statutes. On the contrary, the Panel appears to have accepted virtually all of the elements upon which the United States based its assertion that the three federal statutes are "indispensable."

324. The Panel further, and in our view, tellingly, stated that

. . . the United States has legitimate specific concerns with respect to money laundering, fraud, health and underage gambling that are specific to the remote supply of gambling and betting services, *which suggests that the measures in question are "necessary" within the meaning of Article XIV(a).* (emphasis added [by Appellate Body])

. . .

327. For all these reasons, we *find* that the *Wire Act*, the *Travel Act*, and the *IGBA* are "measures . . . necessary to protect public morals or to maintain public order," within the meaning of paragraph (a) of Article XIV of the *GATS*.

. . . .

3. The *Chapeau* of Article XIV

. . . .

339. The *chapeau* of Article XIV provides:

> Subject to the requirement that such measures are not applied in a manner which would constitute a means of arbitrary or unjustifiable discrimination between countries where like conditions prevail, or a disguised restriction on trade in services, nothing in this Agreement shall be construed to prevent the adoption or enforcement by any Member of measures [of the type specified in the subsequent paragraphs of Article XIV] . . . .

The focus of the *chapeau*, by its express terms, is on the *application* of a measure already found by the Panel to be inconsistent with one of the obligations under the *GATS* but falling within one of the paragraphs of Article XIV. By requiring that the measure be *applied* in a manner that does not to constitute "arbitrary" or "unjustifiable" discrimination, or a "disguised restriction on trade in services," the *chapeau* serves to ensure that Members' rights to avail themselves of exceptions are exercised reasonably, so as not to frustrate the rights accorded other Members by the substantive rules of the *GATS*.

340. The Panel found that:

> . . . the United States has not demonstrated that it does not apply its prohibition on the remote supply of wagering services for horse racing in a manner that does not constitute "arbitrary and unjustifiable discrimination between countries where like conditions prevail" and/or a "disguised restriction on trade" in accordance with the requirements of the *chapeau* of Article XIV.

. . . .

(c) Did the Panel Fail to Take Account of the "Arbitrary" or "Unjustifiable" Nature of the Discrimination Referred to in the *Chapeau*?

. . . .

348. . . . . [T]he Panel found that the United States had not prosecuted certain domestic remote suppliers of gambling services, and that a United States statute (the *Interstate Horseracing Act*) could be understood, on its face,

to permit certain types of remote betting on horseracing within the United States. On the basis of these two findings, the Panel concluded that:

> . . . the United States has not demonstrated that it applies its prohibition on the remote supply of these services in a *consistent manner* as between those supplied domestically and those that are supplied from other Members. Accordingly, we believe that the United States has not demonstrated that it does not apply its prohibition on the remote supply of wagering services for horse racing in a manner that does not constitute "arbitrary and unjustifiable discrimination between countries where like conditions prevail" and/or a "disguised restriction on trade" in accordance with the requirements of the *chapeau* of Article XIV. (emphasis added [by Appellate Body])

. . . .

351. In the light of the arguments before it, we do not read the Panel to have ignored the requirement of "arbitrary" or "unjustifiable" discrimination by articulating the standard under the *chapeau* of Article XIV as one of "consistency." Rather, the Panel determined that Antigua had rebutted the United States' claim of no discrimination *at all* by showing that domestic service suppliers are permitted to provide remote gambling services in situations where foreign service suppliers are not so permitted. We see no error in the Panel's approach.

(d) Did the Panel Err in its Examination of the Alleged Non-Enforcement of the Measures at Issue Against Domestic Service Suppliers?

352. In the course of examining whether the *Wire Act*, the *Travel Act*, and the *IGBA* are applied consistently with the *chapeau* of Article XIV, the Panel considered whether these laws are enforced in a manner that discriminates between domestic and foreign service suppliers. Antigua identified four United States firms that it claimed engage in the remote supply of gambling services but have not been prosecuted under any of the three federal statutes: Youbet.com, TVG, Capital OTB, and Xpressbet.com. Antigua contrasted this lack of enforcement with the case of an Antiguan service supplier that "had modelled [its] business on that of Capital OTB" but was nevertheless prosecuted and convicted under the *Wire Act*. In support of its argument that it applies these statutes equally to domestic and foreign service suppliers, the United States submitted statistical evidence to show that most cases prosecuted under these statutes involved gambling and betting services solely within the United States.

. . . .

354. . . . [N]one of the three federal statutes distinguishes, on its face, between domestic and foreign service suppliers. We agree with the Panel that, in the context of facially neutral measures, there may nevertheless be situations where the selective prosecution of persons rises to the level of discrimination. In our view, however, the evidence before the Panel could not justify finding that, notwithstanding the neutral language of the statute, the

facts are "inconclusive" to establish "non-discrimination" in the United States' enforcement of the *Wire Act*. . . .

. . . .

355. . . . [T]he Panel came to its conclusion — that the United States failed to establish non-discrimination in the enforcement of its laws — on the basis of only five cases: one case of prosecution against a foreign service supplier; one case of "pending" prosecution against a domestic service supplier; and three cases with no evidence of prosecution against domestic service suppliers. From these five cases, the Panel in effect concluded that the United States' defence had been sufficiently rebutted to warrant a finding of "inconclusiveness."

356. . . . [T]he proper significance to be attached to isolated instances of enforcement, or lack thereof, cannot be determined in the absence of evidence allowing such instances to be placed in their proper context. Such evidence might include evidence on the *overall* number of suppliers, and on *patterns* of enforcement, and on the reasons for particular instances of non-enforcement. Indeed, enforcement agencies may refrain from prosecution in many instances for reasons unrelated to discriminatory intent and without discriminatory effect.

357. Faced with the limited evidence the parties put before it with respect to enforcement, the Panel should rather have focused, as a matter of law, on the wording of the measures at issue. These measures, on their face, do *not* discriminate between United States and foreign suppliers of remote gambling services. We therefore *reverse* the Panel's finding . . . that

> . . . the United States has failed to demonstrate that the manner in which it enforced its prohibition on the remote supply of gambling and betting services against TVG, Capital OTB and Xpressbet.com is consistent with the requirements of the *chapeau*.

(e) Did the Panel Fail to Comply with Article 11 of the *DSU* [WTO *Dispute Settlement Understanding*] in its Analysis of Video Lottery Terminals, Nevada Bookmakers, and the *Interstate Horseracing Act*?

. . . .

361. We now turn to the United States' [*DSU*] Article 11 claim [concerning the obligation of a Panel to make an objective assessment of the facts] relating to the *chapeau*. The Panel examined the scope of application of the *Interstate Horseracing Act* ("*IHA*"). [The *IHA* is codified at 15 U.S.C. §§ 3002 *et seq.*] Before the Panel, Antigua relied on the text of the *IHA*, which provides that "[a]n interstate off-track wager *may be accepted* by an off-track betting system" where consent is obtained from certain organizations. Antigua referred the Panel in particular to the definition given in the statute of "interstate off-track wager":

> [T]he term . . . 'interstate off-track wager' means a legal wager placed or accepted in one State with respect to the outcome of a horserace taking place in another State and includes pari-mutuel wagers, where

lawful in each State involved, *placed or transmitted by an individual in one State via telephone or other electronic media and accepted by an off-track betting system in the same or another State*, as well as the combination of any pari-mutuel wagering pools. (emphasis added [by Appellate Body])

Thus, according to Antigua, the *IHA*, on its face, authorizes *domestic* service suppliers, but not *foreign* service suppliers, to offer remote betting services in relation to certain horse races. To this extent, in Antigua's view, the *IHA* "exempts" domestic service suppliers from the prohibitions of the *Wire Act*, the *Travel Act*, and the *IGBA*.

362. The United States disagreed, claiming that the *IHA* — a civil statute — cannot "repeal" the *Wire Act*, the *Travel Act*, or the *IGBA* — which are criminal statutes — *by implication*, that is, merely by virtue of the *IHA's* adoption *subsequent* to that of the *Wire Act*, the *Travel Act*, and the *IGBA*. Rather, under principles of statutory interpretation in the United States, such a repeal could be effective only if done *explicitly*, which was not the case with the *IHA*.

. . . .

364. . . . [T]his aspect of the United States' appeal essentially challenges the Panel's failure to accord sufficient weight to the evidence submitted by the United States with respect to the relationship under United States law between the *IHA* and the measures at issue [*i.e.*, the prohibitions in the *Wire Act*, the *Travel Act*, and the *IGBA*]. The Panel had limited evidence before it, as submitted by the parties, on which to base its conclusion. . . . The Panel found that the evidence provided by the United States was not sufficiently persuasive to conclude that, as regards wagering on horseracing, the remote supply of such services by *domestic* firms continues to be prohibited notwithstanding the plain language of the *IHA*. In this light, we are not persuaded that the Panel failed to make an objective assessment of the facts.

. . . .

(f) Conclusion under the *Chapeau*

367. . . . [T]he Panel expressed its overall conclusion under the *chapeau* of Article XIV as follows:

. . . the United States has not demonstrated that it does not apply its prohibition on the remote supply of wagering services for horse racing in a manner that does not constitute "arbitrary and unjustifiable discrimination between countries where like conditions prevail" and/or a "disguised restriction on trade" in accordance with the requirements of the *chapeau* of Article XIV.

368. This conclusion rested on the Panel's findings relating to two instances allegedly revealing that the measures at issue discriminate between domestic and foreign service suppliers, contrary to the defence asserted by the United States under the *chapeau*. The first instance found by the Panel was based on "inconclusive" evidence of the alleged non-enforcement of the three federal statutes. We have reversed this finding. The second instance found by the

Panel was based on "the ambiguity relating to" the scope of application of the *IHA* and its relationship to the measures at issue. We have upheld this finding.

369. Thus, *our* conclusion — that the Panel did not err in finding that the United States has not shown that its measures satisfy the requirements of the *chapeau* — relates solely to the possibility that the *IHA* exempts only *domestic* suppliers of remote betting services for horse racing from the prohibitions in the *Wire Act*, the *Travel Act*, and the *IGBA*. In contrast, the *Panel's* overall conclusion under the *chapeau* was broader in scope. As a result of our reversal of one of the two findings on which the Panel relied for its conclusion . . ., we must *modify* that conclusion. We *find*, rather, that the United States has not demonstrated that — in the light of the existence of the *IHA* — the *Wire Act*, the *Travel Act*, and the *IGBA* are applied consistently with the requirements of the *chapeau*. Put another way, we uphold the Panel, but only in part.

4. Overall Conclusion on Article XIV

370. . . . The Panel found that the United States failed to justify its measures as "necessary" under paragraph (a) of Article XIV, and that it also failed to establish that those measures satisfy the requirements of the *chapeau*.

371. We have found instead that those measures satisfy the "necessity" requirement. We have also upheld, but only in part, the Panel's finding under the *chapeau*. . . . [T]he only inconsistency that the Panel could have found with the requirements of the *chapeau* stems from the fact that the United States did not demonstrate that the prohibition embodied in the measures at issue applies to both foreign *and* domestic suppliers of remote gambling services, notwithstanding the *IHA* — which, according to the Panel, "does appear, on its face, to permit" *domestic* service suppliers to supply remote betting services for horse racing. In other words, the United States did not establish that the *IHA* does not alter the scope of application of the challenged measures, particularly vis-à-vis domestic suppliers of a specific type of remote gambling services. In this respect, we wish to clarify that the Panel did not, and we do not, make a finding as to whether the *IHA* does, in fact, permit domestic suppliers to provide certain remote betting services that would otherwise be prohibited by the *Wire Act*, the *Travel Act*, and/or the *IGBA*.

372. Therefore, we *modify* the Panel's conclusion . . . . We *find* . . . the United States has demonstrated that the *Wire Act*, the *Travel Act*, and the *IGBA* fall within the scope of paragraph (a) of Article XIV, but that it has not shown, in the light of the *IHA*, that the prohibitions embodied in these measures are applied to both foreign and domestic service suppliers of remote betting services for horse racing. For this reason alone, we *find* that the United States has not established that these measures satisfy the requirements of the *chapeau*. . . .

Part Fifteen

INTELLECTUAL PROPERTY

Chapter 49

INTERESTS AND OBLIGATIONS

Government has no other end but the preservation of Property.

> —John Locke (1632-1704), Second Treatise on Civil Government, Chapter 6 (1681)

Documents Supplement Assignment

1. *Havana Charter* Articles 19, 37:7, 45:1(a)(vii)

2. GATT Articles IV, IX:6, and XX(f)

3. WTO *TRIPs Agreement*

4. U.S. *Statement of Administrative Action* for the *TRIPs Agreement*

5. *NAFTA* Chapter 17

6. Relevant provisions in other FTAs

I. A CLASH OF INTERESTS?

A. Dollars

American dollars are a critical driving force behind the WTO *Agreement on Trade Related Aspects of Intellectual Property Rights* (*TRIPs*), which is contained in Annex 1C to the *WTO Agreement.* That is, the critical catalyst was, and continues to be, profits lost by American companies because of infringements of their intellectual property rights (IPRs) by foreign producers of "pirated" products.[1] It is tempting for such companies, their industry associations, and the American Chambers of Commerce, to point the finger at a few major newly industrialized countries (NICs) and developing countries, notably, China, India, and Russia, along with an assorted bunch of relatively smaller ones, such as Egypt, Thailand, and Vietnam. Hardly a month goes by without publication of a story on rampant piracy of a valid patent, trademark, copyright, or semi-conductor mask work, or on the lack of enforcement of IPRs, in these countries.

Never mind the forgetfulness, if not hypocrisy in these stories. As one senior Eritrean government official once reported (to your Textbook author), the advice she received from a prominent, developed South East Asian nation was

---

[1] *See* Fred Warshofsky, The Patent Wars 90 (1994); World Intellectual Property Organization, Guide to the Berne Convention for the Protection of Literary and Artistic Works 6 *bis.*, 3-6 *bis.* 4 (Paris Act 1971); Karen Kontje Waller, Comment, *NAFTA: The Latest Gun in the Fight to Protect International Intellectual Property Rights*, 13 Dick. J. Int'l L. 347, 348-50 (1995); Richard M. Brenan, *Intellectual Property Aspects of Canada-U.S. Competitiveness in the World Context*, 14 Canada–U.S. L.J. 263, 266 (1989).

to steal as many IPRs as possible before signing the *TRIPs Agreement*. Intellectual property (IP) theft was part of the development history of many of today's rich countries. Never mind, too, the fact that countries such as China, India, and Egypt are increasingly interested in strong, enforceable IP protection — because they are producers and exporters, not just consumers and importers, of merchandise or services embodying IP.

The fact is that economic importance to the U.S. of strong international IP protection cannot be overstated. Roughly $600 billion (in 2005) of the world market for goods consists of pirated or counterfeit goods (up from $150-200 billion in 2001). More than 50 percent of American exports are goods protected by a patent, trademark, copyright, or semiconductor mask work. Of all software used in the world, 35 percent is pirated. In China, 90 percent of software is pirated. Piracy has real-world implications for the labor market. The U.S. auto industry could create an estimated 200,000 jobs if fake auto parts were eliminated.

Consider, as another victim, the American the copyright industry. This industry may be divided into four distinct sectors: (1) the "core" copyright sector, which produces copyrighted works such as newspapers, magazines, books, radio and television broadcasts, records and tapes, movies, plays, advertising, computer software, and data processing; (2) the "partial" copyright sector, which produces goods that are partly copyrighted such as business forms and architectural plans; (3) the "distribution" sector, which distributes copyrighted material to businesses and consumers, such as libraries and wholesale and retail traders; and (4) the "copyright-related" sector, which makes products for use with copyrighted materials such as computers, radios, and televisions. In 1977, the combined share of the U.S. Gross Domestic Product (GDP) accounted for by these four categories was 3.7 percent. By 1993, this share had risen to 5.7 percent. During the same period, the share of GDP accounted for by core copyright industries rose from 2.2 percent to 3.7 percent. These increases implied that from 1977-93, the total copyright industries grew twice as fast as the American economy. Indeed, the core copyright industries grew at 5.6 percent, while the remainder of the economy grew at 2.6 percent.

It is rather stunning to learn that "[t]he core copyright industries contribute more to the U.S. economy and employ more workers than any single manufacturing sector including aircraft manufacturing, primary metals, fabricated metals, textiles, apparel, or chemicals and allied products"[2] The dramatic performance of the copyright industries is due in part to their increasing dominance of markets in other countries. For example, in 1993 foreign sales of the core copyright industries were $45.8 billion, and that figure undoubtedly has risen dramatically. Not surprisingly, the American copyright industries feel seriously threatened by copyright infringements in foreign countries. For instance, it is easy to walk out of one's hotel in Bangkok to a main street and purchase pirated cassette tapes of Michael Jackson, George Michael, Pat Benatar, or any other musician — for roughly $1 a tape! Ironically, it was rumored some American Embassy personnel who were aware of the infringing

---

[2] STEPHEN E. SIWEK & HAROLD FURCHTGOTT-ROTH, COPYRIGHT INDUSTRIES IN THE U.S. ECONOMY: 1977-1993, at iv-v (1995); *see also id.* at 5-6.

tapes actually purchased their favorite tapes for their personal collections, or at least to see whether they enjoyed the music enough to buy an authentic CD.

TRADE AGREEMENTS RESULTING FROM THE URUGUAY ROUND OF MULTILATERAL TRADE NEGOTIATIONS

Hearings before the House Committee on Ways and Means, 103d Cong., 2d Sess. 127-32 (1 February 1994) (Testimony of Eric H. Smith, Executive Director and General Counsel, International Intellectual Property Alliance (IIPA) on Behalf of the IIPA)

Mr. Chairman and Members of the Committee:

. . . .

The IIPA is comprised of . . . trade associations that collectively represent the U.S. copyright-based industries — the motion picture, recording, computer software and music and book publishing industries. . . .

. . . .

These industries represent the leading edge of the world's high technology, entertainment and publishing industries and are among the fastest growing and largest segments of our economy. . . .

. . . IIPA has estimated that the U.S. economy was already losing $15-17 billion in 1992 [the eve of completion of Uruguay Round negotiations, which produced the *TRIPs Agreement*] due to piracy outside this country.

. . . .

While none of our members will seek to oppose the *WTO Agreement* [including the *TRIPs Agreement*,] many of them will not be able to warmly endorse it. However, on careful balance, our members believe that, with the help of a resolute U.S. bilateral trade policy on intellectual property, the impact of the deficiencies in the *TRIPs . . . Agreement*[] can be mitigated.

. . . [T]he final agreement contains many positive elements.

. . . .

[However,] [t]he two major flaws in the final *TRIPs Agreement* . . . detract from these overall well-recognized gains.

1. National Treatment

U.S. negotiators sought in vain to obtain agreement of the European Union to fill the gaps and clarify the ambiguities in the national treatment provisions in the Dunkel text [a prior draft of proposed Uruguay Round trade agreements]. In his testimony last week before the Subcommittee, Ambassador [Mickey] Kantor [President Clinton's first United States Trade Representative (USTR)] emphasized that he was "bitterly disappointed by the European Union's intransigence with respect to national treatment and market access for our entertainment industries." Had the EU been willing to cease its discrimination against U.S. rightholders, the chances of worldwide acceptance of the U.S.' improved proposal (known as Article 14 *bis*) would have been vastly increased. However, notwithstanding the failure to eliminate these gaps and ambiguities, IIPA firmly believes that the existing national treatment obligation in Article 3 of the *TRIPs Agreement* does provide national treatment for many classes of U.S. rightholders.

In some cases, however, WTO members will argue that they are free, without violating their international WTO obligations, for example, to discriminate against U.S. record companies by denying them the critical right to control the public performance and broadcasting of their works by digital means while extending that right to their domestic recording companies. As another example, under this national treatment provision, they could also seek to deny to U.S. record companies the proceeds resulting from blank tape levies to provide some, however inadequate, payment to rights owners for the home taping of their recording. This could happen at the same time as the United States extends full national treatment under its recently adopted blank tape levy on digital recordings to that country's recording companies and performers whose recordings are copied here. The U.S. motion picture industry and U.S. artists and performers could continue to be denied appropriate shares of blank tape video levies on the grounds that the *TRIPs* national treatment provision authorizes this continuing discrimination and subsidy to their own industry. In the end, if these efforts by our trading partners are successful, the U.S. stands to lose millions of dollars in royalties justly due its industries and the American jobs that could be created with those funds will never materialize.

2. Overly Long Transition Periods

The *TRIPs Agreement* continues to permit those countries that qualify as . . . ["developing" or "least developed"] an additional . . . [5 and 10 years, respectively] . . . before they must bring their domestic legislation and enforcement regimes into full compliance with the obligations in the *Agreement*. The countries in transition to market economies also may benefit from this additional transition period. . . . [The extension for developing and transition economy countries ended on 31 December 1999. For least developed countries, the transition period ends on 1 July 2013, by virtue of an extension WTO Members granted on the eve of the 2005 Hong Kong Ministerial Conference. For those countries, in respect of pharmaceutical patent protection, the extension is to 2016 by virtue of the special Doha *Declaration on TRIPs and Public Health*.]

At present, there are a large number of developing countries that, as a result of inadequate legislation or lax enforcement, cause, collectively, billions of dollars in lost jobs and income to the United States. As the result of an aggressive bilateral program using Special 301, Section 301, the Generalized System of Preferences [GSP] Program and similar programs, the U.S. Government has succeeded in bringing many of these countries to within months of compliance with the basic obligations in the *TRIPs Agreement*. Countries like Thailand, Turkey, Egypt, South Korea, Indonesia, Brazil, Venezuela, Philippines, India, and Poland (all GATT members), to name but a few, together account for close to *$1.8 billion* in losses due to piracy of U.S. copyrights [emphasis original]. Were all these countries to take full advantage of their transition period rights under the *Agreement* (and assuming losses remain at the same level as in 1992; though they are likely to increase), the U.S. economy would lose an additional *$7 billion* over that four-year period [emphasis original]. This is a staggering blow to these industries and to the U.S. economy as they seek to add the new high-tech and high-wage jobs necessary for this country to be competitive into the next century.

What is plainly apparent is that none of these ten named countries needs or deserves to take an additional four-year period to deal with the problem of copyright piracy. USTR has been negotiating with each of these countries for well over five years already; many have indicated their commitment to significantly reduce piracy in 1994 or are already in breach of existing bilateral commitments to the United States. For any of these countries to take advantage of their rights under the *TRIPs Agreement* would be an outrage that the United States simply must not tolerate. Unfortunately, the *TRIPs Agreement* could condone such action.

In addition to these two major flaws in the text, the final *TRIPs* text also contains a new concession — this time to the *developed* countries — permitting them to have the benefit of a five-year moratorium on the application of the "nullification and impairment" provisions of the *Agreement*. IIPA has always viewed this remedy, which gets at the "spirit" rather than the letter of the obligations in the *Agreement*, as providing key leverage to ensure that our major trading partners cannot undermine the *Agreement* for protectionist reasons. We regret that this concession was made but believe its absence can be compensated for by a clear and unequivocal U.S. trade policy that would result in punishing any country, at the end of the five-year moratorium, for any actions during the moratorium which had the effect of "nullifying or impairing" any benefit in the *Agreement* which the U.S. had bargained for.

· · · ·

IIPA members are still in the process of evaluating and considering trade and non-trade policy options in the intellectual property area to ensure that our trading partners promptly open their markets to U.S. copyrighted works and avoid taking advantage of actual and potential national treatment loopholes in the *TRIPs Agreement*. Similar consideration is being given to dealing with the issue of broadcast and new technology quotas and similar restrictions faced by our audiovisual industry, particularly in the European Union. Finally, consideration must also be given to ensuring that multilateral obligations in the intellectual property area continue to keep pace with technological developments. Clearly, it will not be possible to secure quickly major changes to the *TRIPs Agreement* which may become necessary due to unforeseen technological developments. A continuing and aggressive bilateral program must also be able to safeguard U.S. interests in this event as well.

· · · ·

While the procedures under Special 301, including the identification of countries that pose IPR problems to the U.S. under Section 182 [19 U.S.C. § 2242] and the commencement of investigations against countries named as Priority Foreign Countries, should continue in effect and should be aggressively used by the Administration, remedies available to the U.S. under its bilateral programs — because of the wider coverage of, and bindings in, the WTO — become more limited. [Mr. Smith noted the IIPA's strong agreement "with statements recently made by Administration officials that where the U.S. national interest is demonstrably at stake, the U.S. should not hesitate to take sanctions even in WTO-bound areas if it would be fruitful in ending the conduct which is damaging to those interests."] However, withdrawal of preferential benefits extended to any country under programs like the GSP, CBI [Caribbean Basin Initiative] and ATPA [Andean Trade Preferences Act, which lapsed] may still occur for failure to meet IPR criteria established for these programs. Countries that unfairly take advantage of the WTO authorized transition period to continue to steal U.S. intellectual property should also be made vulnerable to removal of other trade and non-trade benefits that they receive from the U.S.

Concerted efforts should be made to encourage our trading partners, in appropriate cases, to join the *NAFTA* and adhere to the strong IPR text of this Agreement. We note in particular that the *NAFTA* contains a straightforward national treatment provision of the type the U.S. was unable to achieve in the GATT.

B. Development

As the testimony (above) of Eric H. Smith, Executive Director and General Counsel, International Intellectual Property Alliance (IIPA) indicates, delayed implementation period of the *TRIPs Agreement* for NICs and poor countries undermined the force of the *Agreement*. The NICs had until 1 July 2000, and least developed countries had until 1 July 2006, to implement the *Agreement*. From a cynical perspective, the delays were a license to continue to violate IPRs at the expense of the profits of the rights holders. The Smith testimony suggests ways to combat future IP piracy — direct, even unilateral, action by the U.S. against.

Is special and differential treatment (S&D treatment or SDT) in the *TRIPs Agreement* too generous, as Smith argues? One response of NICs and poor countries to Smith's criticisms bespeaks a radically different perspective on international intellectual property protection. IP is seen as the common heritage of humankind — it is a government-granted privilege, not a natural property right.

> Patents and other intellectual or industrial property are thus statutory rights — benefits created by law by the State. Even to call them "rights" is a misnomer. They are really "privileges" granted by the State by statute — a form of government intervention in the market place, a government subsidy not unlike tax credits, export incentives etc.
>
> Gradually there has been the development of the concept of Science and Technology as a common heritage of mankind but this is now being challenged. In the postwar decades, patents etc. have been garnered by the TNCs [transnational corporations] who have created a monopoly right for themselves. Patent laws were originally established to reward invention and promote industrialisation as well as

prevent import monopolies within the country concerned. However, through efforts to universalise patent laws that give owners the right to exploit the patent at [the] international level (and not only at [the] national level), the industrialised countries are in fact trying to reward export monopolies in the industrial centres which would slow down industrialisation and [the] spread of technology in the Third World.

. . . .

In bringing the issue on the Uruguay Round agenda and by using the term "intellectual property right," the U.S. and other ICs [industrialized countries] have managed to inject some value-loaded words, like "piracy" and "counterfeiting," to describe those who are not prepared to accept their demands. With the help of the media, they have made these terms current coin, confusing the public and legitimising their own demands, and painting those opposing them as indulging in some immoral acts or near criminal conduct. . . .

. . . .

In international trade, "patents" and "trade marks" far from expanding trade are really trade barriers in as much as the owners are given some monopoly import privileges.[3]

This argument seems to underlie the *ordre public* exception to the scope of patentability contained in Article 27:2 of the *TRIPs Agreement*.

The argument also suggests public interests, broadly defined, ought to be given priority over the interest of a private party to obtain and exploit a technological monopoly.

Being a statutorily granted right, the most important consideration in granting IPR protection is public interest — counterbalancing the rights of IPR owners by their obligations to the country granting them such rights, such as through local working, and compulsory licensing in the absence of local working. It may be in the interests of the dominant industrialised nations now to shift the balance more to private rights of their corporations than public interest; but this cannot negate the right of the Third World to maintain this balance and ensure public good and public welfare.[4]

Put bluntly, IP should be used to help improve the lot of poor people, not enrich the coffers of American or European corporations. From this perspective, the *TRIPs Agreement* is biased in favor of private interests from developed countries. Notice the implicit assumption here: NICs, most developing countries, and probably all least developed countries are doomed for the foreseeable future to be net consumers, not net producers, of IP products.

This perspective may be analyzed in economic terms. A key benefit of IPR protection is that it ensures that inventors, artists, writers, and other producers of intellectual property will earn monopoly profits on their work. This assurance is credible because the work is destined to command a price

---

[3] CHAKRAVARTHI RAGHAVAN, RECOLONIZATION: GATT, THE URUGUAY ROUND & THE THIRD WORLD 116-17, 121-22 (1990); *see also id.* at 124-25, 129.

[4] *Id.* at 134.

higher than it would in the absence of protection, and it provides a motivation to create the work. However, monopoly profits represent a transfer of wealth from consumers to producers of IP. Moreover, as in any monopoly situation, the quantity of output and consumption is sub-optimal. The result of this monopoly situation is a deadweight loss, which gives rise to an argument that requiring every country in the world to provide IPR protection might be inefficient. For example, with respect to patents,

> as protection is extended to a larger and larger portion of the world, the marginal benefits of extending it further decline and the marginal costs increase. Therefore if the two are equal for some particular extent of patent protection, then this will be an optimal situation.

> To see that the marginal benefits and costs behave in this way, consider the effect of extending protection to an additional market of some given size. The benefits from doing so arise entirely from the new inventions that this additional market will make profitable but that would not have been profitable to invent with the previous protected market size. The larger the previously protected market, however, the greater will be the number of inventions already invented, and the less desirable will be the ones that remain. Hence, the marginal benefit declines.

> Similarly, the cost of extending patent protection to this additional market is some fraction of the consumer surplus generated in this market by the inventions that would be undertaken anyway. This fraction is the amount by which consumer surplus declines on these goods when consumers are charged a monopoly price, minus the monopoly profits that are earned on the goods. This is therefore a deadweight loss to the world as a whole. The size of this fraction depends on the elasticity of demand for invented goods, and hence on the size of the monopoly markup, but there is no reason to expect this fraction to decline systematically as protection is extended. Therefore, as protection is extended further, and as more and more inventions are therefore stimulated and become subject to this markup, the deadweight loss due to extending to the additional market will grow.

> All of this suggests, therefore, that there will be an optimal geographical extent of patent protection that need not be the whole world.[5]

If, indeed, extension of IPR protection to all countries is not supported by a marginal cost-benefit analysis, then what countries should be exempt from the requirement of providing such protection? Perhaps poor countries should be exempt from patent protection because (1) transfers from poor to rich countries exacerbate income inequality and, therefore, are unfair, (2) patent protection leads to more inventions in developed than less developed countries, because there are more resources in the former than the latter, thus the technology gap between rich and poor countries is worsened, and (3) political

---

[5] Alan V. Deardorff, *Should Patent Protection Be Extended to All Developing Countries?*, *in* THE MULTILATERAL TRADING SYSTEM 443-44 (Robert M. Stern ed., 1993); *see also id.* at 431-32, 435, 438, 443-46.

constituencies in developed countries favor IPR protection, while interest groups in poor countries tend to oppose such protection.

Frederick S. Ringo, an advocate of the High Court of Tanzania, writes about the dilemma facing middle-&thinsip; and low-income countries of sub-Saharan Africa (SSA). He argues the MFN obligation in Article 3 of the *TRIPs Agreement* — whereby each WTO Member must have an MFN clause in its IP law to ensure favored treatment is extended immediately and unconditionally to all other Members — will expand "the legal hegemony. . .of former imperial States over their colonial territories" so that rights holders from other countries can "claim territorial rights" in SSA countries and other poor nations. The transition periods of which Smith (and others) complain actually provides "breathing space" for SSA to develop their technological bases. Ringo's thesis is

> [t]he present era has been hailed as the information age where knowledge constitutes power and a competitive edge over competitors. It is, therefore, in the interest of technology owners that knowledge is not easily dissipated and they have, therefore, pressed for the introduction of *TRIPs* as another barrier to access, and as one of the means of controlling, knowledge.
>
> . . . .
>
> . . . It is perceived by least-developed countries (LDCs) as ironic that the relatively loose international IPR system, which has been in existence for more than one hundred and fifty years and which has served as the basis for the technology transfer, copying, learning and adaptation that permitted the current industrialized countries (not least Japan, but also, at an earlier stage, the United States, France, Germany etc.) to catch up with the technological leaders and to achieve technological parity, is now being made more restrictive in order to make it more costly and difficult for newcomers to enter the field. This does raise questions as to the real intentions of industrial countries in GATT. Further, these moves are in opposition to the internationally accepted transfer-of-technology principles as formulated in the [United Nations] Programme of Action for the Establishment of a New International Economic Order [U.N. General Assembly Resolution 3202, (S-VI), May 1974)]. The one-sided formulations of the *TRIPs Agreement*, which insist on the rights of sellers without juxtaposing the same with the right to economic development of African countries, provide grounds for skepticism as to the acceptability of the *TRIPs Agreement* by these countries despite the legal measures which could be taken.[6]

Does the strength of Ringo's argument vary with the protected product in question?

For example, perhaps trademark protection held by Nike and the National Football League is acceptable to SSA, because athletic shoes and logo apparel are not products central to economic development. In contrast, patents for

---

[6] Frederick S. Ringo, *The Trade-Related Aspects of Intellectual Property Rights Agreement in the GATT and Legal Implications for Sub-Saharan Africa*, 28 J. WORLD TRADE 121, 122-23 (1994).

pharmaceuticals, and trademarks associated with the marketing of pharmaceuticals, may be difficult to justify. Ringo contends:

> Technologies such as those used in the pharmaceutical and chemical industries depend heavily on patents in both products and processes, as well as trade marks in marketing. This sector's moral and commercial practices in LDCs [less developed countries], such as in the SSA countries, have been under close research and criticism. Drugs being a basic need in many LDCs and the costs being exorbitant ensure that many African countries, and some industrial countries, do not offer patent protection to these processes and prefer the use of generic rather than brand-name products. Indeed, some industrial countries have only recently introduced patent protection in pharmaceuticals and chemicals after ensuring the development of their own domestic industries. They have been taken as examples by the LDCs against stricter *TRIPS* enforcement. These measures, which are partly political and partly economic, ensured that needed drugs were acquired at reasonable prices.[7]

There would seem to be at least two difficulties associated with any attempt to justify IP protection on a product-specific basis.

First, delineating products that are crucial to economic development is sure to generate argument. At one extreme, any product that contributes to development as measured by value-added or increases in gross domestic product could be regarded as critical. Thus, athletic shoes and logo apparel would be included. At the other extreme, only those items that impart sustenance to the human body could be regarded as keys to economic development. Examples would include food (particularly species of crops) and medicines, but not clothes or school books (much less law books!). With respect to patent protection for food, Ringo argues:

> Patented plant life in the food industry has resulted in serious food insecurity in some areas and the disappearance of drought-and sickness-resistant strains. The TNC [transnational corporation] agribusiness industries are stated to hold a substantial share of responsibility in this unfortunate event. . . .

> For the agricultural-based economies of the SSA, bio-technologies present a double-edged sword, and several issues will face the WTO and African governments in relation to the *TRIPS Agreement*. First, with the increasing pressures by industrialized countries on African and other LDCs, how can the increased intellectual property rights protection ensure the linking of research to the requirements of the local economies, and the commercialisation of agricultural research results? Second, most SSA countries are being forced to implement World Bank/International Monetary Fund (IMF) structural adjustment programmes (SAPS) with the aim of introducing market economies. These programmes have severely reduced the purchasing capacities of the peoples of these countries. How can bio-technologies be effectively introduced (especially in seed, animal and health sectors)

---

[7] *Id.* at 123-24.

when stronger IPR protection will increase prices, therefore hindering their acceptability? Third, it is well known that the theoretical premises of IPR protection lead to anti-competitive practices which are in conformity neither with internationally agreed principles nor with the aims of SAPS; how can the WTO technically assist SSA countries to counterbalance the adverse effects of such measures in their economies? Fourth, the most challenging aspect facing the WTO in this area is how to shake off the image of GATT as the "rich countries' forum" by ensuring that the *TRIPS Agreement* is not abused by its sponsors, *i.e.*, TNCs and their home governments, to the detriment of the economies of SSA countries. These abuses include using IPRs to create monopoly conditions, destroying bio-diversity, and the destruction of LDC agricultural sectors and environments.[8]

Interestingly, Article 27:3(b) of the *TRIPs Agreement* allows WTO Members to exclude from patentability plants and animals other than micro-organisms. It also authorizes them to exclude from patentability a process that is essentially biological whose purpose is the production of plants or animals. However, Members must allow for protection of plant varieties either by patents or an effective *sui generis* system, or by a combination thereof.

A similar argument could be made with respect to the pharmaceutical and chemical industries. Indeed, before the *TRIPs Agreement* entered into force, Argentina, Brazil, Egypt, Ghana, India, Mexico, Korea, Taiwan, and Thailand did not provide patent protection for pharmaceutical processes. (Interestingly, they were not alone. This protection also was unavailable in Australia, Finland, New Zealand, and Norway.) Chemicals were not patentable in Brazil, Colombia, India, Mexico, and Venezuela. (Here again, the NICs and poor countries were not alone. This protection also was lacking in Japan and Switzerland.) These facts helped generate the *India Patent* case.

Significantly, Article 27:2 of the *TRIPs Agreement* provides a potentially broad exception to the scope of patentable subject matter:

> Members may exclude from patentability inventions, the prevention within their territory of the commercial exploitation of which is necessary to protect *ordre public* or morality, including to protect human, animal or plant life or health or to avoid serious prejudice to the environment, provided that such exclusion is not made merely because their exploitation is prohibited by their law.

In the interest of public health, could a Member decline to provide patent protection for a pharmaceutical company's process for making a particular drug? Could a Member refuse to offer patent protection for an insecticide because it is valuable in protecting the Member's food supply from pests? Because *ordre public* is a vague concept, a Member may interpret it broadly, hence suggesting an affirmative answer to both questions.

However, even some scholars sympathetic to the plight of NICs, developing, and least developed countries question the utility of IP protection for "essential" sectors.

---

[8] *Id.* at 131-32.

Ensuring worldwide rights for processes and products for drugs, it is argued, is essential to encourage new research and discovery of new drugs. But, patents no longer seem to serve their original purpose of innovation of things useful to society and spread of knowledge. In the area of pharmaceuticals, patents and excessive secrecy associated with them appear to be reducing innovation and scientific research, and have not helped produce new drugs needed for the ailments afflicting humanity, particularly the poor.

According to an article in *The Economist* magazine: "Two-thirds of the 50 top selling drugs are retreads of old therapies. Drug research used to be simple. . . Now, biotechnology has made cleverness essential again. . . Unfortunately academic culture and drug-industry culture seem to react as tastelessly as port poured into gin. . . Those scientists who come to the drug industry to get rich and recognised are soon disappointed. Researchers in the industry rarely get a share of the profits from the products they discover."[9]

Moreover, a number of products fall on a continuum between the above two extremes. For example, Ringo asserts that computers and allied products are essential to the development of SSA countries. But, owners of computer technology "are only willing to transfer technology where IPR protection is such that it allows the maximum exploitation of their technological rights," and it is not in the self-interest of SSA countries to develop such legal regimes.[10] Thus, he finds the extension of copyright protection for "literary and artistic works" under the *Berne Convention* to include computer programs irksome.

A second difficulty associated with any attempt to link IP protection to product type concerns the dynamic nature of Third World economic development. The product mix manufactured domestically changes as a country develops. In 1945, who would have thought Japan would mass produce consumer electronics domestically, and subsequently transfer production to Malaysia, Indonesia, Thailand, and Vietnam? More generally, the hidden assumption of Ringo's argument is Third World countries are forever dependent on, and consumers of, foreign technology. Yet, India has its own versions of Silicon Valley in Bangalore and Hyderabad, and Malaysia has impressive hardware and software research facilities in Penang. The inventors of tomorrow who need IP rights and enforcement for creative expression are as likely to come from poor as rich countries.

One interesting omission from the *TRIPs Agreement* concerns the process of checking for counterfeit goods before they are exported. This issue is also not addressed in the WTO *Agreement on Pre-Shipment Inspection*. One reason may be inspection of goods for pirated materials before export is a costly process. Third World countries are unwilling to incur such costs without financial or logistical assistance from First World counterparts.

---

[9] RAGHAVAN, *supra* note 3, at 118.

[10] Ringo, *supra* note 6, at 125.

II. OVERVIEW OF THE *TRIPS AGREEMENT*

A. Purposes and Cornerstones

The *TRIPs Agreement* is an effort to respond to the concerns of not only the American IP industry, but any industry, wherever located, whose product relies on a copyright, semiconductor mask work, patent, or trademark. In fact, it is important to realize that IP can be produced anywhere — wherever there is creative human capital. That means poor countries ought to see themselves not only as consumers of IP products from overseas, but also — sooner or later — as actual or potential producers of IP exports for the rest of the world. Of course, this Janus-faced perspective is not the one that predominates in most parts of the developing and least developed world.

The overall objective of *TRIPs*, stated in Article 7, is to "contribute to the promotion of technological innovation and to the transfer and dissemination of technology, to the mutual advantage of producers and users of technological knowledge and in a manner conducive to social and economic welfare, and to a balance of rights and obligations." Clearly, the *Agreement* is not simply about IP protection. Rather, it is about the tension between such protection, on the one hand, and the need to disseminate knowledge, especially to developing countries that require technology for economic growth, on the other hand.

Articles 3 and 4 are the cornerstones of the *TRIPs Agreement*. Article 3 of the *Agreement* mandates national treatment for intellectual property protection. Article 4 creates an MFN obligation for such protection. But, these cornerstones do not establish a specific level of protection. National or MFN treatment has little value if such treatment provides poor protection. In this regard, it must be remembered the *Agreement* is not the first attempt at cross-border intellectual property protection. There are many pre-Uruguay Round multilateral accords dealing with the protection of specific types of IP that continue in force. The *Agreement* supplements and strengthens the earlier accords and, therefore, presumably harmonizes international IP protection, at a higher level than under previous accords.

B. Special Points about Copyright Protection

For example, in the copyright area, Article 9:1 of the *TRIPs Agreement* requires all WTO Members to comply with the 1971 version of the *Berne Convention for the Protection of Literary and Artistic Works* (*Berne Convention*). (The *Berne Convention* protects copyrights. The U.S. acceded to the *Berne Convention* in 1989.) Interestingly, however, this Article does not require Members to respect the concept of "moral rights" of an author of copyrighted material set forth in the *Berne Convention*. Moral rights, which are recognized by Article 6 bis of the *Berne Convention*, "are author's rights that are separate and distinct from the pecuniary or economic benefits deriving from copyright, which reflect that the author's work is a reflection of the personality of its creator"[11] There are two key moral rights:

---

[11] RICHARD E. NEFF & FRAN SMALLSON, NAFTA: PROTECTING AND ENFORCING INTELLECTUAL PROPERTY RIGHTS IN NORTH AMERICA 17 n.6 (1994)

i.   "the right of paternity," which is the author's right to claim the work
      as her own and put her name on the work, and

ii.   "the right of integrity" (sometimes known as the "right of respect"),
      which is the author's right to object to any distortion, mutilation,
      or derogatory action with respect to the work that would harm the
      author's honor or reputation.

American copyright law does not recognize moral rights. Why not? Observe
they are found in the copyright laws of almost all civil law countries, and
typically they are inalienable by the author.

Significantly, the *TRIPs Agreement* does clarify several ambiguities in the
Berne Convention. First — and perhaps most importantly — disputes arising
under the *Agreement* are subject to the WTO *Dispute Settlement Understanding (DSU)*. As one practitioner points out, this contrasts with the inefficacious
method of dispute resolution under the *Berne Convention*:

> No longer does membership in the *Berne Convention* suffice to protect
> member nations from the perils of copyright non-compliance. An inher-
> ent deficiency plagues enforcement of *Berne Convention* strictures,
> inasmuch as the mechanism of enforcement under the treaty is limited
> to actions brought by one country against another country in the Inter-
> national Court of Justice, a cumbersome procedure which has never
> been invoked. In a world service economy, for which the copyright
> industries produce works that account for billions of dollars of interna-
> tional trade, the lack of effective enforcement mechanisms in the *Berne
> Convention* renders it insufficiently potent to safeguard authors'
> rights.[12]

Second, Article 10:1 states that computer programs and databases must be
given protection as literary works under the *Berne Convention*. Third, Articles
12 and 14:5 essentially require that performers, producers of phonograms, and
authors must receive protection for their works for 50 years. Fourth, both the
Berne Convention and *TRIPs Agreement* confer the exclusive right to authorize
a public performance or broadcast on a performer. (The IPRs of performers,
producers of phonograms, and broadcasting organizations are known as
"neighboring rights.") But, the *Convention* does not provide the performer with
a right to prohibit commercial rentals to the public of originals or copies of
the copyrighted work, unauthorized taping of live performances, or broadcasting of live performances. Under Articles 11 and 14:1-2 of the *TRIPs Agreement*,
performers, producers of phonograms, and authors of computer programs and
films must be permitted to authorize or prohibit commercial rental to the
public of their works. Fortunately for video rental stores and their customers,
Article 11 contains an exception for "cinematographic works unless such
[commercial] rental has led to widespread copying of such works which is
materially impairing the exclusive right of reproduction conferred in . . . [a]
Member on authors and their successors in title." Finally, Article 61 of the
Agreement requires WTO Members to impose criminal penalties for willful
copyright piracy on a commercial scale.

---

[12] David Nimmer, *GATT's Entertainment: Before and NAFTA*, 15 Loy. L.A. Ent. L.J. 133, 135;
see also id. at 143-146.

III. MAILBOXES AND THE 1998 *INDIA PATENT PROTECTION* CASE

A. The Dispute with India

At the conclusion of the Uruguay Round, many developing and least developed countries did not have laws in place to protect patents for pharmaceuticals and agricultural chemicals. India — which, in the past, was one of the world's worst offenders of patent rights — was an example. India granted only process patents. Hence, domestic companies were free to reproduce any new product entering the international marketplace. American pharmaceutical companies complain this piracy costs them $500 million annually.

To be sure, under Article 66:1 of the *TRIPs Agreement*, least-developed country Members were supposed to establish patent laws by 1 January 2006. But, what happened until then, i.e., during the first decade of life of the WTO and *Agreement*? Many pharmaceutical and agricultural chemical companies sought to apply for patent protection in such countries in anticipation of forthcoming patent laws. How could these applicants be confident such countries would recognize their inventions as novel given that legal void? These companies also sought to sell their products in such countries and retain the exclusive right to do so. How could they obtain this right?

The *TRIPs Agreement* answers these questions. Article 70 contains two key transitional rules. First, Article 70:8 requires any WTO Member that did not protect patents for pharmaceuticals and agricultural chemicals to have established by 1 January 1995 a so-called "mail box" system for filing patent applications. Under a mailbox system, the original date on which an applicant files for patent protection pursuant to a yet-to-be-established legal regime is preserved. A mail box applicant will stand a better chance in the future, when the legal regime is in place, of arguing successfully that its invention is novel because its application must be reviewed on the basis of the date it was filed (*i.e.*, placed in the mail box). Second, Article 70:9 requires developing countries to provide exclusive marketing rights for products that are the subject of a mail box patent application.

In December 1994, India implemented temporary rules for a mailbox system through the *Patents (Amendment) Ordinance*. The *Ordinance* expired in March 1995. The Indian government, then led by the Congress Party, also proposed the *Patents (Amendment) Bill of 1995* to amend the *Patents Act of 1970* to make the rules permanent. This proposal also granted exclusive marketing rights for 5 years to newly patented drugs, pharmaceuticals, and agricultural chemicals.

However, writing IP rules in a way that might benefit foreign companies evokes strong emotions in India, a country unusually sensitive about foreign political or economic influence. The government of former Prime Minister Indira Gandhi forced Coca-Cola to withdraw from India in the 1970s when Coke refused to yield its secret "7X" formula. Thus, both the right-wing *Bharatiya Janata Party* (BJP) and the Communist Party — otherwise strange bedfellows — fought the proposed amendment. While the *Lok Sabha*, India's lower house of parliament, approved the proposal, the upper house (the *Rajya*

Sabha) rejected it. Hence, in March 1995 when the temporary mailbox system expired and no exclusive marketing rights system was in place, India was vulnerable to the charge it was in breach of its *TRIPs* obligations.

The U.S. formally made the charge in July 1996. It commenced a Special 301 investigation and a WTO action against India. In September 1997, a WTO Panel ruled in favor of the U.S. In its report, the Panel found India had failed to establish a mail box system. India argued it received mail box applications under an unpublished administrative system. But, the U.S. successfully countered administrative instructions are not legally secure, *i.e.*, not a legally valid mail box, in contravention of Article 70:8. The U.S. doubted the instructions would be upheld under India's *Patents Act*, because drugs, pharmaceuticals, and agricultural chemicals are not patentable under that *Act*.

The Panel also found India ran afoul of two other *TRIPs Agreement* provisions. It violated Article 63:2, because it did not notify the WTO of the legal basis for its administrative mail box scheme, and it violated Article 70:9 by failing to provide for exclusive marketing rights. Not surprisingly, the USTR hailed the decision as an important precedent for the enforcement of American rights. It was the first WTO adjudication under the *TRIPs Agreement*, and it served notice on developing countries to abide by that accord.

India appealed the adverse decision. But, in December 1997 the Appellate Body (whose decision is excerpted below) largely affirmed the Panel report. The Appellate Body upheld the Article 70:8 and 70:9 findings. It overturned the Article 63:2 ruling, on the grounds the Panel had strayed outside of its jurisdiction as the U.S. had not raised this provision when it called for formation of a panel. As it had done with the Panel report, the USTR praised the Appellate Body Report for its precedential value. One of many interesting features of the Report is the extensive discussion of the concept of "legitimate expectations," the difference between violation and non-violation nullification and impairment, and the relevance of this concept and the distinction to the case at bar.

India and the U.S. argued about the time period for implementing the Appellate Body decision. India contended it needed until 16 June 1999 to comply, partly in view of general elections that brought to power a new government led by the BJP. The U.S. hoped for near-immediate implementation, especially in view of the fact India should have amended its law in 1994 in the wake of the Uruguay Round. In April 1998, the two sides agreed to the usual 15 month implementation period, backdated to the date the Dispute Settlement Body adopted the Appellate Body report (16 January 1998). Thus, India was given until 16 July 1999 to bring its legal regime into compliance.

Not only does the case present an interesting mix of the *TRIPs Agreement*, IP protection issues in the Third World context, and domestic Indian politics, but it also underscores the variables affecting foreign direct investment (FDI) flows in the global economy. Ultimately, the BJP seemed to recognize the stakes: India's poor record of IPR enforcement was one reason why it is an unattractive destination for FDI, even (or perhaps especially) in comparison with China. The Indian government also seemed to realize just how important a center of IP activity India had become. It was producing IP products. For the government to view the country as a net consumer of IP products was to see the India of the past, and not imagine the India of the future whose IP entrepreneurs would need *TRIPs* protections abroad.

B. Substantive Outcomes

WTO APPELLATE BODY REPORT, *INDIA — PATENT PROTECTION FOR PHARMACEUTICAL AND AGRICULTURAL CHEMICAL PRODUCTS*
WT/DS50/AB/R (adopted 16 January 1998)

I. Introduction

1. India appeals from certain issues of law and legal interpretations in the Panel Report. . . .

. . . .

(9) Under Indian patent law, patent applications for pharmaceutical or agricultural chemical products made by any person entitled to apply under Section 6 of the *Patents Act 1970* are subject to the same fee as any other patent application being received and allotted a filing date and advertised in the *Official Gazette* with serial number, filing date, name of applicant and title of invention. But, under the administrative arrangements of the Indian patent offices pursuant to the decision taken in April 1995, these applications are unlike other patent applications. They are stored separately and not referred by the Controller to an examiner as specified in Section 12 of the *Act*.

(10) The legal authority for these administrative arrangements that India cited is Article 73(1)(a) of the Indian Constitution, along with the *Indian Patents Act 1970*. Article 73(1) reads as follows:

"*Extent of executive power of the Union.* (1) Subject to the provisions of this Constitution, the executive power of the Union shall extend

(a) to the matters with respect to which Parliament has power to make laws; and

(b) to the exercise of such rights, authority and jurisdiction as are exercisable by the Government of India by virtue of any treaty or agreement:

Provided that the executive power referred to in sub-clause (a) shall not, save as expressly provided in this Constitution or in any law made by Parliament, extend in any State to matters with respect to which the Legislature of the State has also power to make laws."

(11) As for the *Patents Act*, the relevant provisions are:

— Chapter III (Sections 6 through 11) deals with applications for patents. These provisions do not require that applications for patents must be limited to patentable subject matter. They only require that such applications should be for inventions.

— Inventions are defined in Section 2(1)(j) as, *inter alia*, any new and useful substance produced by manufacture, including any new and useful improvement of such a substance.

— Section 5 makes it clear that inventions claiming substances intended for use, or capable of being used, as a food, medicine or drug or relating to substances prepared or produced by chemical processes are not in themselves patentable. But, methods or processes for the manufacture of these products are patentable. Under Section 2(1)(l)(iv) the term "medicine or drug" includes insecticides, germicides, fungicides, weedicides and all other substances intended to be used for the protection or preservation of plants.

— Chapter IV of the *Patents Act* concerns the examination of applications. Section 12 requires that, when the complete specification has been filed with respect to an application for a patent, the application shall be referred by the Controller General of Patents, Designs and Trademarks to an examiner. The examiner shall ordinarily report to the Controller within a period of 18 months on, *inter alia*, whether the application and the specification are in accordance with the requirements of the Act and whether there is any lawful ground for objecting to the grant of the patent under the Act.

— Paragraph 2 of Section 15 states that, if it appears to the Controller that the invention claimed in the specification is not patentable under the Act, he shall refuse the application.

(12) Between 1 January 1995 and 15 February 1997, a total of 1,339 applications for pharmaceutical and agricultural chemical products had been received and registered. Of these applications, American companies had filed 318 applications for pharmaceutical product patents and 45 applications for agricultural chemical product patents. On the day the *Patents (Amendment) Ordinance 1994* had lapsed, 125 applications had been received and filed (41 by American companies). Before 15 February 1997, out of the other 1,214 applications (322 by American companies), 605 had been received and filed prior to the day the *Patents (Amendment) Bill 1995* had lapsed.

(13) The Indian executive authorities do not have the legal powers under present Indian law to accord exclusive marketing rights in accordance with *TRIPs* Article 70:9. No request for grant of exclusive marketing rights was submitted to Indian authorities.]

III. Issues Raised in this Appeal

28. The appellant, India, raises the following issues in this appeal:

  (a) What is the proper interpretation to be given to the requirement in Article 70.8(a) of the *TRIPS Agreement* that a Member shall provide "a means" by which applications for patents for inventions relating to pharmaceutical or agricultural chemical products can be filed?

  (b) Did the Panel err in its treatment of Indian municipal law, or in its application of the burden of proof, in examining whether India had complied with its obligations under Article 70.8(a) of the *TRIPS Agreement*?

  (c) Does Article 70.9 of the *TRIPS Agreement* require that there must be a "mechanism" in place to provide for the grant of exclusive marketing rights effective as from the date of entry into force of the *WTO Agreement*?

[The portion of the Appellate Body report dealing with the alternative U.S. claim under Article 63 is omitted. The Appellate Body reversed the Panel's finding India had violated Article 63:1-2, because the matter was outside of the Panel's terms of reference.]

IV. The *TRIPS Agreement*

29. . . . The dispute that gives rise to this case represents the first time the *TRIPS Agreement* has been submitted to the scrutiny of the WTO dispute settlement system.

30. Among the many provisions of the *TRIPS Agreement* are certain specific obligations relating to patent protection for pharmaceutical and agricultural chemical products [such as in Article 27:1]. . . .

31. However, Article 65 of the *TRIPS Agreement* provides, in pertinent part:

> 1. Subject to the provisions of paragraphs 2, 3 and 4, no Member shall be obliged to apply the provisions of this *Agreement* before the expiry of a general period of one year following the date of entry into force of the *WTO Agreement*.
>
> 2. A developing country Member is entitled to delay for a further period of four years the date of application, as defined in paragraph 1, of the provisions of this *Agreement* other than Articles 3, 4 and 5.
>
> . . . .
>
> 4. To the extent that a developing country Member is obliged by this Agreement to extend product patent protection to areas of technology not so protectable in its territory on the general date of application of this Agreement for that Member, as defined in paragraph 2, it may delay the application of the provisions on product patents of Section 5 of Part II to such areas of technology for an additional period of five years.
>
> 5. A Member availing itself of a transitional period under paragraphs 1, 2, 3 or 4 shall ensure that any changes in its laws, regulations and practice made during that period do not result in a lesser degree of consistency with the provisions of this *Agreement*.

32. With respect to patent protection for pharmaceutical and agricultural chemical products, certain specific obligations are found in Articles 70.8 and 70.9 of the *TRIPS Agreement*. The interpretation of these specific obligations is the subject of this dispute.

. . . .

[Omitted is the Appellate Body's extended discussion, and rejection, in Section V (Paragraphs 33-48) of the Panel's interpretative theory that legitimate expectations always must be considered when appraising the words of the *TRIPs Agreement* — or, by extension, any WTO text. The Panel said protection of legitimate expectations is a well-established principle of GATT, deriving from GATT Article XXIII. The Appellate Body explained the Panel had confused two different strains in prior GATT practice — violation nullification or impairment cases under Article XXIII:1(a), and non-violation nullification or impairment cases arising under Article XXIII:1(b).

Almost all GATT panel cases arose under the first of these provisions. In such cases involving substantive claims under Articles III and XI, panels often would mention the importance of the Articles in protecting legitimate expectations of contracting parties. But, typically, panels made statements only after finding a violation of one of the articles. Only a handful of pre-*DSU* claims were brought under the second provision, and in only 4 of the 14 of them did a GATT panel find non-violation nullification or impairment. The doctrine of protecting reasonable expectations arose under, and is connected with, with non-violation claims. Article 26:1 of the *DSU* imports some GATT Article XXIII:1(b) non-violation concepts. But, Article 64:2 of the *TRIPs Agreement* makes clear that non-violation claims may not be brought under that *Agreement* for the first five years of its life, *i.e.*, between 1 January 1995 and 31 December 1999. The *India Patent Protection* case arose during this period.

In sum, whether legitimate expectations may be used as an interpretative basis is a violation nullification or impairment case is highly dubious, and as a practical matter, impossible in the present dispute.]

VI. Article 70.8

. . . .

54. Article 70.8(a) imposes an obligation on Members to provide "a means" by which mailbox applications can be filed "from the date of entry into force of the WTO Agreement." Thus, this obligation has been in force since 1 January 1995. The issue before us in this appeal is not whether this obligation exists or whether this obligation is now in force. Clearly, it exists, and, equally clearly, it is in force now. The issue before us in this appeal is: what precisely is the "means" for filing mailbox applications that is contemplated and required by Article 70.8(a)? To answer this question, we must interpret the terms of Article 70.8(a).

55. We agree with the Panel that "[t]he analysis of the ordinary meaning of these terms alone does not lead to a definitive interpretation as to what sort of 'means' is required by this subparagraph." Therefore, in accordance with the general rules of treaty interpretation set out in Article 31 of the *Vienna Convention*, to discern the meaning of the terms in Article 70.8(a), we must also read this provision in its context, and in light of the object and purpose of the *TRIPS Agreement*.

56. Paragraphs (b) and (c) of Article 70.8 constitute part of the context for interpreting Article 70.8(a). Paragraphs (b) and (c) of Article 70.8 require that the "means" provided by a Member under Article 70.8(a) must allow the filing of applications for patents for pharmaceutical and agricultural chemical products from 1 January 1995 and preserve the dates of filing and priority of those applications, so that the criteria for patentability may be applied as of those dates, and so that the patent protection eventually granted is dated back to the filing date. In this respect, we agree with the Panel that,

. . . in order to prevent the loss of the novelty of an invention . . .
filing and priority dates need to have a sound legal basis if the
provisions of Article 70.8 are to fulfill their purpose. Moreover, if available, a filing must entitle the applicant to claim priority on the basis
of an earlier filing in respect of the claimed invention over applications
with subsequent filing or priority dates. Without legally sound filing
and priority dates, the mechanism to be established on the basis of
Article 70.8 will be rendered inoperational.

57. On this, the Panel is clearly correct. The Panel's interpretation here is
consistent also with the object and purpose of the *TRIPS Agreement*. The
Agreement [in the Preamble] takes into account, *inter alia*, "the need to
promote effective and adequate protection of intellectual property rights." We
believe the Panel was correct in finding that the "means" that the Member
concerned is obliged to provide under Article 70.8(a) must allow for "the
entitlement to file mailbox applications and the allocation of filing and priority
dates to them." Furthermore, the Panel was correct in finding that the "means"
established under Article 70.8(a) must also provide "a sound legal basis to
preserve novelty and priority as of those dates." These findings flow inescapably from the necessary operation of paragraphs (b) and (c) of Article 70.8.

58. However, we do *not* agree with the Panel that Article 70.8(a) requires
a Member to establish a means "so as to eliminate any reasonable doubts
regarding whether mailbox applications and eventual patents based on them
could be rejected or invalidated because, at the filing or priority date, the
matter for which protection was sought was unpatentable in the country in
question." India is *entitled*, by the "transitional arrangements" in paragraphs
1, 2 and 4 of Article 65, to delay application of Article 27 for patents for
pharmaceutical and agricultural chemical products until 1 January 2005. In
our view, India is obliged, by Article 70.8(a), to provide a legal mechanism
for the filing of mailbox applications that provides a sound legal basis to
preserve both the novelty of the inventions and the priority of the applications
as of the relevant filing and priority dates. No more.

59. But what constitutes such a sound legal basis in Indian law? To answer
this question, we must recall first an important general rule in the *TRIPS
Agreement*. Article 1.1 of the *TRIPS Agreement* states, in pertinent part:

. . . Members shall be free to determine the appropriate method of
implementing the provisions of this Agreement within their own legal
system and practice.

Members, therefore, are free to determine how best to meet their obligations
under the *TRIPS Agreement* within the context of their own legal systems.
And, as a Member, India is "free to determine the appropriate method of
implementing" its obligations under the *TRIPS Agreement* within the context
of its own legal system.

60. India insists that it has done that. India contends that it has established,
through "administrative instructions," a "means" consistent with Article
70.8(a) of the *TRIPS Agreement*. According to India, these "administrative
instructions" establish a mechanism that provides a sound legal basis to
preserve the novelty of the inventions and the priority of the applications as

of the relevant filing and priority dates consistent with Article 70.8(a) of the *TRIPS Agreement*. According to India, pursuant to these "administrative instructions," the Patent Office has been directed to store applications for patents for pharmaceutical and agricultural chemical products separately for future action pursuant to Article 70.8, and the Controller General of Patents Designs and Trademarks ("the Controller") has been instructed not to refer them to an examiner until 1 January 2005. According to India, these "administrative instructions" are legally valid in Indian law, as they are reflected in the Minister's Statement to Parliament of 2 August 1996. And, according to India:

> There is . . . *absolute certainty* that India can, when patents are due in accordance with subparagraphs (b) and (c) of Article 70.8, decide to grant such patents on the basis of the applications currently submitted and determine the novelty and priority of the inventions in accordance with the date of these applications. (emphasis added)

61. India has not provided any text of these "administrative instructions" either to the Panel or to us.

62. Whatever their substance or their import, these "administrative instructions" were not the initial "means" chosen by the Government of India to meet India's obligations under Article 70.8(a) of the *TRIPS Agreement*. The Government of India's initial preference for establishing a "means" for filing mailbox applications under Article 70.8(a) was the *Patents (Amendment) Ordinance* (the "*Ordinance*"), promulgated by the President of India on 31 December 1994 pursuant to Article 123 of India's Constitution. Article 123 enables the President to promulgate an ordinance when Parliament is not in session, and when the President is satisfied "that circumstances exist which render it necessary for him to take immediate action." India notified the *Ordinance* to the Council for *TRIPS*, pursuant to Article 63.2 of the *TRIPS Agreement*, on 6 March 1995. In accordance with the terms of Article 123 of India's Constitution, the *Ordinance* expired on 26 March 1995, six weeks after the reassembly of Parliament. This was followed by an unsuccessful effort to enact the *Patents (Amendment) Bill 1995* to implement the contents of the *Ordinance* on a permanent basis. This *Bill* was introduced in the *Lok Sabha* (Lower House) in March 1995. After being passed by the *Lok Sabha*, it was referred to a Select Committee of the *Rajya Sabha* (Upper House) for examination and report. However, the *Bill* was subsequently not enacted due to the dissolution of Parliament on 10 May 1996. From these actions, it is apparent that the Government of India initially considered the enactment of amending legislation to be necessary in order to implement its obligations under Article 70.8(a). However, India maintains that the "administrative instructions" issued in April 1995 effectively continued the mailbox system established by the *Ordinance*, thus obviating the need for a formal amendment to the *Patents Act* or for a new notification to the Council for *TRIPS*.

63. With respect to India's "administrative instructions," the Panel found that "the current administrative practice creates a certain degree of legal insecurity in that it requires Indian officials to ignore certain mandatory provisions of the *Patents Act*;" and that "even if Patent Office officials do not

examine and reject mailbox applications, a competitor might seek a judicial order to do so in order to obtain rejection of a patent claim."

64. India asserts that the Panel erred in its treatment of India's municipal law because municipal law is a fact that must be established before an international tribunal by the party relying on it. In India's view, the Panel did not assess the Indian law as a fact to be established by the United States, but rather as a law to be interpreted by the Panel. India argues that the Panel should have given India the benefit of the doubt as to the status of its mailbox system under Indian domestic law. India claims, furthermore, that the Panel should have sought guidance from India on matters relating to the interpretation of Indian law.

65. In public international law, an international tribunal may treat municipal law in several ways. Municipal law may serve as evidence of facts and may provide evidence of state practice. However, municipal law may also constitute evidence of compliance or non-compliance with international obligations. For example, in *Certain German Interests in Polish Upper Silesia*, the Permanent Court of International Justice observed:

> It might be asked whether a difficulty does not arise from the fact that the Court would have to deal with the Polish law of July 14th, 1920. This, however, does not appear to be the case. From the standpoint of International Law and of the Court which is its organ, municipal laws are merely facts which express the will and constitute the activities of States, in the same manner as do legal decisions and administrative measures. *The Court is certainly not called upon to interpret the Polish law as such; but there is nothing to prevent the Court's giving judgment on the question whether or not, in applying that law, Poland is acting in conformity with its obligations towards Germany under the Geneva Convention.* (emphasis added) [1926 P.C.I.J. Rep., Series A, No. 7, p. 19]

66. In this case, the Panel was simply performing its task in determining whether India's "administrative instructions" for receiving mailbox applications were in conformity with India's obligations under Article 70.8(a) of the *TRIPS Agreement*. It is clear that an examination of the relevant aspects of Indian municipal law and, in particular, the relevant provisions of the *Patents Act* as they relate to the "administrative instructions," is essential to determining whether India has complied with its obligations under Article 70.8(a). There was simply no way for the Panel to make this determination without engaging in an examination of Indian law. But, as in the case cited above before the Permanent Court of International Justice, in this case, the Panel was not interpreting Indian law "as such;" rather, the Panel was examining Indian law solely for the purpose of determining whether India had met its obligations under the *TRIPS Agreement*. To say that the Panel should have done otherwise would be to say that only India can assess whether Indian law is consistent with India's obligations under the *WTO Agreement*. This, clearly, cannot be so.

67. Previous GATT/WTO panels also have conducted a detailed examination of the domestic law of a Member in assessing the conformity of that domestic law with the relevant GATT/WTO obligations. For example, in *United States*

— *Section 337 of the Tariff Act of 1930*, the panel conducted a detailed examination of the relevant United States' legislation and practice, including the remedies available under Section 337 as well as the differences between patent-based Section 337 proceedings and federal district court proceedings, in order to determine whether Section 337 was inconsistent with Article III:4 of the GATT 1947. [*See* GATT B.I.S.D. (36th Supp.) at 345 (adopted 7 November 1989).] This seems to us to be a comparable case.

. . . .

69. To do so, we must look at the specific provisions of the *Patents Act*. Section 5(a) of the *Patents Act* provides that substances "intended for use, or capable of being used, as food or as medicine or drug" are not patentable. "When the complete specification has been led in respect of an application for a patent," section 12(1) *requires* the Controller to refer that application and that specification to an examiner. Moreover, section 15(2) of the *Patents Act* states that the Controller "shall refuse" an application in respect of a substance that is not patentable. We agree with the Panel that these provisions of the *Patents Act* are mandatory. And, like the Panel, we are not persuaded that India's "administrative instructions" would prevail over the contradictory mandatory provisions of the *Patents Act*. We note also that, in issuing these "administrative instructions," the Government of India did not avail itself of the provisions of section 159 of the *Patents Act*, which allows the Central Government "to make rules for carrying out the provisions of [the] *Act*" or section 160 of the *Patents Act*, which requires that such rules be laid before each House of the Indian Parliament. We are told by India that such rulemaking was not required for the "administrative instructions" at issue here. But this, too, seems to be inconsistent with the mandatory provisions of the *Patents Act*.

70. We are not persuaded by India's explanation of these seeming contradictions. Accordingly, we are not persuaded that India's "administrative instructions" would survive a legal challenge under the *Patents Act*. And, consequently, we are not persuaded that India's "administrative instructions" provide a sound legal basis to preserve novelty of inventions and priority of applications as of the relevant filing and priority dates.

71. For these reasons, we agree with the Panel's conclusion that India's "administrative instructions" for receiving mailbox applications are inconsistent with Article 70.8(a) of the *TRIPS Agreement*.

. . . .

VII. Article 70.9

. . . .

78. India argues that Article 70.9 establishes an obligation to grant exclusive marketing rights for a product that is the subject of a patent application under Article 70.8(a) after all the other conditions specified in Article 70.9 have been fulfilled. India asserts that there are many provisions in the *TRIPS Agreement* that, unlike Article 70.9, explicitly oblige Members to change their domestic laws to authorize their domestic authorities to take certain action

before the need to take such action actually arises. India maintains that the Panel's interpretation of Article 70.9 has the consequence that the transitional arrangements in Article 65 allow developing country Members to postpone legislative changes in all fields of technology except the most "sensitive" ones, pharmaceutical and agricultural chemical products. India claims that the Panel turned an obligation to take action in the future into an obligation to take action immediately.

79. India's arguments must be examined in the light of Article XVI:4 of the *WTO Agreement*, which requires that:

> Each Member shall ensure the conformity of its laws, regulations and administrative procedures with its obligations as provided in the annexed Agreements.

80. Moreover, India acknowledged before the Panel and in this appeal that, under Indian law, it is necessary to enact legislation in order to grant exclusive marketing rights in compliance with the provisions of Article 70.9. This was already implied in the *Ordinance*, which contained detailed provisions for the grant of exclusive marketing rights in India effective 1 January 1995. However, with the expiry of the *Ordinance* on 26 March 1995, no legal basis remained, and with the failure to enact the *Patents (Amendment) Bill 1995* due to the dissolution of Parliament on 10 May 1996, no legal basis currently exists, for the grant of exclusive marketing rights in India. India notified the Council for *TRIPS* of the promulgation of the *Ordinance* pursuant to Article 63.2 of the *TRIPS Agreement*, but has failed as yet to notify the Council for *TRIPS* that the *Ordinance* has expired.

81. Given India's admissions that legislation is necessary in order to grant exclusive marketing rights in compliance with Article 70.9 and that it does not currently have such legislation, the issue for us to consider in this appeal is whether a failure to have in place a mechanism ready for the grant of exclusive marketing rights, effective *as from the date of entry into force* of the *WTO Agreement*, constitutes a violation of India's obligations under Article 70.9 of the *TRIPS Agreement*.

82. By its terms, Article 70.9 applies only in situations where a product patent application is filed under Article 70.8(a). Like Article 70.8(a), Article 70.9 applies "notwithstanding the provisions of Part VI." Article 70.9 specifically refers to Article 70.8(a), and they operate in tandem to provide a package of rights and obligations that apply *during* the transitional periods contemplated in Article 65. It is obvious, therefore, that both Article 70.8(a) *and* Article 70.9 are intended to apply as from the date of entry into force of the *WTO Agreement*.

83. India has an obligation to implement the provisions of Article 70.9 of the *TRIPS Agreement* effective as from the date of entry into force of the *WTO Agreement*, that is, 1 January 1995. India concedes that legislation is needed to implement this obligation. India has not enacted such legislation. To give meaning and effect to the rights and obligations under Article 70.9 of the *TRIPS Agreement*, such legislation should have been in effect since 1 January 1995.

84. For these reasons, we agree with the Panel that India should have had a mechanism in place to provide for the grant of exclusive marketing rights

effective as from the date of entry into force of the *WTO Agreement*, and, therefore, we agree with the Panel that India is in violation of Article 70.9 of the *TRIPS Agreement*.

C. Jurisprudential Considerations

Still another fascinating dimension of the *India Patent* case is jurisprudential. Indeed, it is one of the most fundamental questions in legal philosophy: what is law? India argues its unpublished administrative system is, indeed, "law." The U.S. demands greater formality, looking for a statute with the imprimatur of the Indian Parliament. But, is there not something to the Indian point?

The answer to the question "what is law" may depend on the context of application. Any visitor to India knows there is often quite a difference between the written rule and actual practice. Custom and other informal sources of rules typically are what really matter. Why adhere to formalistic notions about the sources of law grounded in Judeo-Christian tradition when India, and many non-western countries, present a different context?

Moreover, is the American pressure on India hypocritical? Recall that in the *Section 301* case (excerpted in an earlier Chapter), the U.S. "got off the hook" precisely because of the custom and practice surrounding Section 301. The Appellate Body was content with the fact the U.S. did not actually use the discretionary authority granted by statute in a unilateral matter. In other words, even in the developed country context, informalities like actual practice matter. If the behavior and representations of the American government as regards an offending statute counts, then why not count the assurances of the Indian government to fill a void of formal law? Does it boil down to a question of the credibility of the governments involved? If so, is there a presumption favoring First World governments, and is that presumption fair?

IV. RETROACTIVITY, EFFECTIVE PROTECTION, AND THE 2000 *CANADA PATENT TERM* CASE

WTO APPELLATE BODY REPORT, *CANADA — TERM OF PATENT PROTECTION*
WT/DS170/AB/R (adopted 12 October 2000)

I. Introduction

3. Sections 44 and 45 of Canada's *Patent Act* read as follows:

> 44. Subject to Section 46, where an application for a patent is filed under this Act on or after October 1, 1989, the term limited for the duration of the patent is twenty years from the filing date.

> 45. Subject to Section 46, the term limited for the duration of every patent issued under this Act on the basis of an application filed before October 1, 1989, is seventeen years from the date on which the patent is issued.

4. Thus, Section 44 provides for a term of twenty years from the date of *application* for a patent for patent applications filed on or after 1 October 1989, while Section 45 provides for a term of seventeen years from the date of *grant* of a patent for patent applications filed before that date. Patents which are subject to Section 44 are commonly described in Canada as "New Act patents," while those subject to Article 45 are described as "Old Act patents." The Old Act patents are the subject of this dispute.

. . . .

IV. Order of Analysis

49. . . . . As applied by Canada, and as both parties agree, this measure [Section 45] relates to patents for which the applications were filed before 1 October 1989, and which were in force on 1 January 1996, the date on which the *TRIPS Agreement* became applicable for Canada. As in every appeal, a threshold question is whether the measure before us falls within the scope of one of the covered agreements, in this case the *TRIPS Agreement*. For this reason, we begin our analysis of the legal issues raised in this appeal by considering Article 70, because this Article determines the overall applicability of the obligations of the *TRIPS Agreement*, including the obligation found in Article 33, to the measure in dispute. Only if we conclude from addressing Article 70 that the measure before us does fall within the scope of the *TRIPS Agreement* will it become necessary for us to examine the consistency of Section 45 of Canada's *Patent Act* with Article 33 of that Agreement.

V. Articles 70.1 and 70.2 of the *TRIPS Agreement*

. . . .

53. Canada claims that the Panel erred in finding that Article 70.1 does not prevent the obligations of the *TRIPS Agreement* from applying to Old Act patents. In addressing this issue, we look first, as always, at the text of the treaty provision, in accordance with the general rule of interpretation in Article 31 of the *Vienna Convention on the Law of Treaties* (the "*Vienna Convention*" [Done at Vienna, 23 May 1969, 1155 U.N.T.S. 331; 8 International Legal Materials 679.]). . . .

54. Our main task is to give meaning to the phrase "acts which occurred before the date of application" and to interpret Article 70.1 harmoniously with the rest of the provisions of Article 70. We are of the view that the term "acts" has been used in Article 70.1 in its normal or ordinary sense of "things done," "deeds," "actions" or "operations." In the context of "acts" falling within the domain of intellectual property rights, the term "acts" in Article 70.1 may, therefore, encompass the "acts" of public authorities (that is, governments as well as their regulatory and administrative authorities) as well as the "acts" of private or third parties. Examples of the "acts" of public authorities may include, in the field of patents, the examination of patent applications, the grant or rejection of a patent, the revocation or forfeiture of a patent, the grant of a compulsory licence, the impounding by customs authorities of goods alleged to infringe the intellectual property rights of a holder, and the like. Examples of "acts" of private or third parties may include "acts" such as the

filing of a patent application, infringement or other unauthorized use of a patent, unfair competition, or abuse of patent rights.

55. Article 70.1 provides that, where such "acts" "occurred" before the date of application of the *TRIPS Agreement* for a Member, that is to say, where such "acts" were done, carried out or completed before that date, no obligation of the *TRIPS Agreement* is to be imposed on a Member in respect of those "acts." Those "acts" themselves cannot be called in question after the date of application of the *TRIPS Agreement* for a Member. In this regard, . . . the United States has repeatedly emphasized that it is not challenging or complaining against any "act" of any Canadian public authority or private party that took place before 1 January 1996. . . .

56. However, in the realm of intellectual property rights, it is of fundamental importance to distinguish between "acts" and the "rights" created by those "acts." In the field of patents, for example, the grant of a patent (which is clearly an "act") confers at least the following substantive rights on the grantee, according to the provisions of the *TRIPS Agreement*: national treatment (Article 3); most-favoured-nation treatment (Article 4); product and process patents being available in all fields of technology; non-discrimination between imported and domestic products (Article 27.1); the term of protection (Article 33); and "reversal of burden of proof" in the case of process patents (Article 34).

57. . . . [I]f patents created by "acts" of public authorities under the Old Act continue to be in force on the date of application of the *TRIPS Agreement* for Canada (that is, on 1 January 1996), can Article 70.1 operate to exclude those patents from the scope of the *TRIPS Agreement*, on the ground that they were created by "acts which occurred" before that date?

58. The ordinary meaning of the term "acts" suggests that the answer to this question must be no. An "act" is something that is "done," and the use of the phrase "acts which occurred" suggests that what was done is now complete or ended. This excludes situations, including existing rights and obligations, that have *not* ended. Indeed, the title of Article 70, "Protection of Existing Subject Matter," confirms contextually that the focus of Article 70 is on bringing within the scope of the *TRIPS Agreement* "subject matter" which, on the date of the application of the *Agreement* for a Member, is existing and which meets the relevant criteria for protection under the *Agreement*.

59. A contrary interpretation would seriously erode the scope of the other provisions of Article 70, especially the explicit provisions of Article 70.2. Almost any existing situation or right can be said to have arisen from one or more past "acts." For example, virtually all contractual and property rights could be said to arise from "acts which occurred" in the past. If the phrase "acts which occurred" were interpreted to cover all *continuing* situations involving patents which were granted before the date of application of the *TRIPS Agreement* for a Member, including such rights as those under Old Act patents, then Article 70.1 would preclude the application of virtually the whole of the *TRIPS Agreement* to rights conferred by the patents arising from such "acts." This is not consistent with the object and purpose of the *TRIPS Agreement*, as reflected in the preamble of the *Agreement*.

60. We conclude, therefore, that Article 70.1 . . . cannot be interpreted to exclude existing rights, such as patent rights, even if such rights arose through acts which occurred before the date of application of the *TRIPS Agreement* for a Member. We, therefore, confirm the finding of the Panel that Article 70.1 does *not* exclude from the scope of the *TRIPS Agreement* Old Act patents that existed on the date of application of the *TRIPS Agreement* for Canada.

61. Canada also appeals the Panel's determination that Article 70.2 and, therefore, Article 33, applies to Old Act patents. . . . [T]he Panel first found that the "subject matter . . . which is protected" on the date of application of the *TRIPS Agreement* for Canada includes "inventions" protected by Old Act patents. The Panel then found that, under Article 70.2, the *TRIPS Agreement* gives rise to obligations in respect of those patented inventions. Canada does not contest that the "subject matter . . . which is protected" in this case is the patented inventions existing at the time the *TRIPS Agreement* became applicable for Canada. However, Canada does not accept that the obligation in Article 33 applies to Old Act patents.

. . . .

63. In examining the text of this treaty provision [*TRIPs* Article 70:2], the first interpretative issue is whether Old Act patents are "subject matter existing . . . which is protected" on the date of application of the *TRIPS Agreement* for Canada. The second is to determine whether the clause "[e]xcept as otherwise provided," which qualifies Article 70.2, applies to the issue raised in this appeal. We deal with each of these issues in turn.

. . . .

65. We agree with the Panel's reasoning that "subject matter" in Article 70.2 refers, in the case of patents, to *inventions*. . . .

. . . .

67. We now consider whether the qualifying provision at the beginning of Article 70.2 applies in this case. Article 70.2 begins with the words "Except as otherwise provided for in this *Agreement*." Canada argues that Article 70.1 constitutes an exception for "subject matter existing . . . and which is protected" on the date of application of the *TRIPS Agreement* for Canada; that Article 70.1 is, therefore, "otherwise provided," within the meaning of this qualifying provision; and that, accordingly, Article 70.1 overrides Article 70.2. Canada concludes, as a consequence, that the obligation in Article 33 does not apply to Old Act patents.

. . . .

69. Like the Panel, we see Articles 70.1 and 70.2 as dealing with two distinct and separate matters. The former deals with past "acts," while the latter deals with "subject matter" existing on the applicable date of the *TRIPS Agreement*. Article 70.1 . . . operates only to exclude obligations in respect of "acts which occurred" before the date of application of the *TRIPS Agreement*, but does *not* exclude rights and obligations in respect of *continuing situations*. On the contrary, "subject matter existing . . . which is protected" is clearly a continuing situation, whether viewed as protected inventions, or as the patent rights attached to them. "Subject matter existing . . . which is protected" is not

within the scope of Article 70.1, and, therefore, the "[e]xcept as otherwise provided for" clause in Article 70.2 can have no application to it. Thus, for the sake of argument, even if there is a relationship between Article 70.1 and the opening proviso in Article 70.2, Canada's argument with respect to Old Act patents fails nonetheless, as we have concluded that the continuing rights relating to Old Act patents do not fall within the scope of Article 70.1.

70. We wish to point out that our interpretation of Article 70 does not lead to a "retroactive" application of the *TRIPS Agreement*. Article 70.1 alone addresses "retroactive" circumstances, and it excludes them generally from the scope of the *Agreement*. The application of Article 33 to inventions protected under Old Act patents is justified under Article 70.2, not Article 70.1. A treaty applies to existing rights, even when those rights result from "acts which occurred" before the treaty entered into force.

71. This conclusion is supported by the general principle of international law found in the *Vienna Convention*, which establishes a presumption against the retroactive effect of treaties in the following terms:

Article 28
Non-retroactivity of treaties

Unless a different intention appears from the treaty or is otherwise established, its provisions do not bind a party in relation to any act or fact which took place or any *situation which ceased to exist* before the date of the entry into force of the treaty with respect to that party. (emphasis added)

72. Article 28 of the *Vienna Convention* covers not only any "act," but also any "fact" or "situation which ceased to exist." Article 28 establishes that, in the absence of a contrary intention, treaty provisions do *not* apply to "any situation which ceased to exist" before the treaty's entry into force for a party to the treaty. Logically, it seems to us that Article 28 also necessarily implies that, absent a contrary intention, treaty obligations *do* apply to any "situation" which has *not* ceased to exist — that is, to any situation that arose in the past, but continues to exist under the new treaty. Indeed, the very use of the word "situation" suggests something that subsists and continues over time; it would, therefore, include "subject matter existing . . . and which is protected," such as Old Act patents at issue in this dispute, even though those patents, and the rights conferred by those patents, arose from "acts which occurred" before the date of application of the *TRIPS Agreement* for Canada.

73. This interpretation is confirmed by the Commentary on Article 28, which forms part of the preparatory work of the *Vienna Convention*:

If, however, an act or fact or situation which took place or arose prior to the entry into force of a treaty continues to occur or exist after the treaty has come into force, it will be caught by the provisions of the treaty. The non-retroactivity principle cannot be infringed by applying a treaty to matters that occur or exist when the treaty is in force, even if they first began at an earlier date.

This point is further explained by the Special Rapporteur:

The main point . . . was that "the non-retroactivity principle cannot be infringed by applying a treaty to matters that occur or exist when the treaty is in force, even if they first began at an earlier date." In these cases, the treaty does not, strictly speaking, apply to a fact, act or situation falling partly within and partly outside the period during which it is in force; it applies only to the fact, act or situation which occurs or exists after the treaty is in force. *This may have the result that prior facts, acts or situations are brought under consideration for the purpose of the application of the treaty; but this is only because of their causal connexion with the subsequent facts, acts or situations to which alone in law the treaty applies.* (emphasis added)

74. We note that Article 28 of the *Vienna Convention* is not applicable if "a different intention appears from the treaty or is otherwise established." We see no such "different intention" in Article 70. . . .

. . . .

79. . . . [W]e conclude that Article 70.2, and not Article 70.1, of the *TRIPS Agreement* applies to inventions protected by Old Act patents and to the rights conferred by those patents, because they are "subject matter existing . . . and which is protected" on the date of application of the *TRIPS Agreement* for Canada. We, therefore, conclude that Canada is required to apply the obligation contained in Article 33 . . . to Old Act patents.

VI. Article 33 of the *TRIPS Agreement*

. . . .

81. Canada appeals the Panel's finding that Section 45 of Canada's *Patent Act* is inconsistent with Article 33. Canada argues that the Panel misinterpreted Article 33 in two principal ways: first, in finding that there is no textual or contextual support for the view that Article 33 requires Members to provide patent holders with a term of "effective" protection; and, second, in adopting a "specialized, extra-ordinary and obsolete meaning" of the word "available" that excludes consideration of the various administrative steps in Canada's patent-granting procedure from being used to calculate the earliest date on which the term of protection of a patent may expire.

. . . .

85. In our view, the words used in Article 33 present very little interpretative difficulty. The "filing date" is the date of filing of the patent application. The term of protection "shall not end" before twenty years counted from the date of filing of the patent application. The calculation of the period of "twenty years" is clear and specific. In simple terms, Article 33 defines the earliest date on which the term of protection of a patent may end. This earliest date is determined by a straightforward calculation: it results from taking the date of filing of the patent application and adding twenty years. As the filing date of the patent application and the twenty-year figure are both unambiguous, so too is the resultant earliest end date of the term of patent protection.

. . . .

87. The meaning of Section 45 is straightforward. Section 45 defines the term of patent protection in terms of the starting date (the date of "issue" of the patent) and of a duration (seventeen years). These terms are unambiguous. As a result, so too is the end date of patent protection. It is derived through simple calculation: the date of issue of the patent plus seventeen years.

88. Article 33 requires a Member to make a term of protection "available." Canada argues that Section 45 of its *Patent Act* makes "available," on a sound legal basis, a twenty-year term to every patent applicant because, under the Canadian regulatory practices and procedures, every patent applicant has statutory and other means to control and delay the patent-granting process. The Panel rejected this argument, and interpreted the word "available" in the following terms:

> *Black's Law Dictionary* defines the word "available" as "having sufficient force or efficacy; effectual; valid" and the word "valid" in turn means "having legal strength or force . . . incapable of being rightfully overthrown or set aside." The dictionary meaning of the word "available" would suggest that patent right holders are entitled, as a matter of *right*, to a term of protection that does not end before twenty years from the date of filing.

. . . .

90. We agree with the Panel that, in Article 33 of the *TRIPS Agreement*, the word "available" means "available, as a matter of right," that is to say, available as a matter of legal right and certainty.

91. The key question for consideration with respect to the "availability" argument is, therefore, whether Section 45 of Canada's *Patent Act*, together with Canada's related regulatory procedures and practices, make available, as a matter of legal right and certainty, a term of protection of twenty years from the filing date for each and every patent. The answer is clearly in the negative, even without disputing the assertions made by Canada with respect to the many statutory and other informal means available to an applicant to control the patent process. The fact that the patent term required under Article 33 can be a by-product of possible delays in the patent-granting process does not imply that this term is available, as a matter of legal right and certainty, to each and every Old Act patent applicant in Canada.

92. To demonstrate that the patent term in Article 33 is "available," it is not sufficient to point, as Canada does, to a combination of procedures that, when used in a particular sequence or in a particular way, *may* add up to twenty years. The opportunity to obtain a twenty-year patent term must not be "available" only to those who are somehow able to meander successfully through a maze of administrative procedures. The opportunity to obtain a twenty-year term must be a readily discernible and specific right, and it must be clearly seen as such by the patent applicant when a patent application is filed. The grant of the patent must be sufficient *in itself* to obtain the minimum term mandated by Article 33. The use of the word "available" in Article 33 does not undermine but, rather, underscores this obligation.

93. Canada also appeals the Panel's rejection of the view that Article 33 embodies a notion of "effective" protection. This notion, advanced by Canada,

would allow a different end date from that specified in Article 33, so long as the result was equivalent "effective" protection measured from the date of grant of the patent to its expiry.

. . . .

95. The text of Article 33 gives no support to the notion of an "effective" term of protection as distinguished from a "nominal" term of protection. On the contrary, the obligation in Article 33 is straightforward and mandatory: to provide, as a specific right, a term of protection that does not end before the expiry of a period of twenty years counted from the filing date.

96. In support of this notion of "effective" protection, Canada argues that Article 33 must be read conjunctively with Article 62.2, which recognizes the fact that the length of the patent-granting process invariably involves some curtailment of the period of protection. According to Canada, so long as patents are granted "within a reasonable period of time" and there is no "unwarranted curtailment of the period of protection," Article 33, when read with Article 62.2, permits a Member to provide a term of "effective" protection that is equivalent to the nominal term of twenty years from filing prescribed in Article 33. As the American, European and Canadian patent offices take, on an average, from four to five years to grant a patent, this period must, in Canada's view, be regarded as "a reasonable period of time," and, therefore, the term of seventeen years from the grant of the patent that is provided under Section 45 of Canada's *Patent Act* must be regarded as "equivalent" to the term of twenty years from the filing of the patent application that is prescribed by Article 33.

97. We see no merit in this argument of Canada. Article 62.2 deals with procedures relating to the acquisition of intellectual property rights. Article 62.2 does not deal with the duration of those rights once they are acquired. Article 62.2 is of no relevance to this case. This purely procedural Article cannot be used to modify the clear and substantive standard set out in Article 33 so as to conjecture a new standard of "effective" protection. Each Member of the WTO may well have its own subjective judgement about what constitutes a "reasonable period of time" not only for granting patents in general, but also for granting patents in specific sectors or fields of complexity. If Canada's arguments were accepted, each and every Member of the WTO would be free to adopt a term of "effective" protection for patents that, in its judgement, meets the criteria of "reasonable period of time" and "unwarranted curtailment of the period of protection," and to claim that its term of protection is substantively "equivalent" to the term of protection envisaged by Article 33. Obviously, this cannot be what the Members of the WTO envisaged in concluding the *TRIPS Agreement*. Our task is to interpret the covered agreements harmoniously. A harmonious interpretation of Article 33 and Article 62.2 must regard these two treaty provisions as distinct and separate Articles containing obligations that must be fulfilled distinctly and separately.

98. In assessing the consistency of Section 45 with Article 33, we observe that the term of patent protection set out in Section 45 is seventeen years from the date on which the patent is granted, while the term of patent protection required by Article 33 is a minimum of twenty years from the date of filing. Thus, Section 45 will meet the minimum standard prescribed in

Article 33 only if the period between the filing and the issue of the patent (the "pendency period," during which a patent application is examined) is equal to or greater than three years. This may not always be the case, since the "pendency period" may be *less* than three years in many cases. In fact, in this case, Canada has provided uncontested evidence that 66,936 patents existing on 1 January 2000, about 40 per cent of the Old Act patents then in force, end earlier than required under Article 33, by virtue of Section 45.

99. . . . Consequently, we uphold the Panel's finding that a term of protection that does not end before twenty years counted from the date of filing is not available under Section 45 of Canada's *Patent Act*, and that, accordingly, Section 45 is inconsistent with Article 33 of the *TRIPS Agreement*.

Chapter 50

ENFORCEMENT

I know no method to secure the repeal of bad or obnoxious laws so effective as their stringent execution.

    —President Ulysses S. Grant (1822-85), Inaugural Address
    (4 March 1869)

DOCUMENTS SUPPLEMENT ASSIGNMENT

1. *Havana Charter* Articles 19, 37:7, 45:1(a)(vii)
2. GATT Article III:4 and XX(d)
3. WTO *TRIPs Agreement*
4. U.S. *Statement of Administrative Action* for the *TRIPs Agreement*
5. *NAFTA* Chapter 17
6. Relevant provisions in other FTAs

I. INFRINGEMENT, EXCLUSION AND SEIZURE, AND SECTION 337

A. Elements of Section 337 Claim

Section 337 of the *Tariff Act of 1930*, as amended, makes it unlawful to import into the U.S. any article that infringes on a patent, trademark, or copyright that is valid and enforceable in the U.S., or a semiconductor chip that infringes on a registered mask work that is valid and enforceable in the U.S. (*See* 19 U.S.C. § 1337(a)(1)(B)-(D).) As the statute heading intimates, importing infringing articles is considered "unfair." The list of unfair trade practices (and it is a list, not a general theory of fairness) embraces dumping, certain subsidies, and infringement of an intellectual property right (IPR).

The *Omnibus Trade and Competitiveness Act of 1988* (Pub. L. No. 100-418, 102 Stat. 1107) changes an important threshold requirement for Section 337 relief. Before the *Act*, a complainant had to show it constituted or was part of an "efficiently and economically operated" domestic industry. The *1988 Act* eliminates this requirement. Importing infringing articles is unlawful if "an industry in the United States" exists "relating to" articles protected by the patent, trademark, copyright, or mask work at issue. (19 U.S.C. § 1337(a)(2).) That industry is defined to "exist" if there is

    i.   significant investment in plant and equipment,

    ii. significant employment of labor or capital, or

iii.   substantial investment in the exploitation of the patent, trademark, copyright, or mask work as evidenced by expenditures on research, development, or licensing.

(*See* 19 U.S.C § 1337(a)(3).) The third prong of this definition means it no longer is necessary to have extensive production facilities located in the U.S. Yet, the meaning of "significant" and "substantial" is apparent neither from the statute nor legislative history.

Alternatively, because of the *1988 Act* amendments, importing infringing articles is unlawful if an industry in the U.S. relating to a patent, trademark, copyright, or mask work is "in the process of being established." (19 U.S.C. § 1337(a)(2).) Unfortunately, neither the *1988 Act* nor Section 337 has criteria to determine when an industry is "being established." There are few if any analogies from which to reason. Jurisprudence from antidumping (AD), specifically, determinations concerning whether dumping materially retards the establishment of an industry in the U.S., is scant.

Significantly, the *1988 Act* (at § 1341(b)) also eliminates the need to show injury to an industry in the U.S. Congress wanted to make Section 337 "a more effective remedy for the protection of United States intellectual property rights." Thus, the House Ways and Means Committee stated that

> [u]nlike dumping or countervailing duties, or even other unfair trade practices such as false advertising or other business torts, the owner of intellectual property has been granted a temporary statutory right to exclude others from making, using, or selling the protected property. The purpose of such temporary protection, which is provided for in Article I, Section 8, Clause 8 of the United States Constitution, is "to promote the Progress of Science and Useful Arts, by securing for limited Times to Authors and Inventors the exclusive Rights to their respective Writings and Discoveries." In return for temporary protection, the owner agrees to make public the intellectual property in question. It is this trade-off which creates a public interest in the enforcement of protected intellectual property rights. *Any sale in the United States of an infringing product is a sale that rightfully belongs only to the holder or licensee of that property. The importation of any infringing merchandise derogates from the statutory right, diminishes the value of the intellectual property, and thus indirectly harms the public interest.* Under such circumstances, the Committee believes that requiring proof of injury, beyond that shown by proof of the infringement of a valid intellectual property right, should not be necessary.[1]

As one attorney explains, this amendment has an important practical effect.

> Although complainants were denied relief in only a few cases because of a failure to meet these [injury] requirements, it is estimated that over half of the total expenses in litigating section 337 cases were incurred in establishing the injury and other economic requirements.

---

[1] H.R. Rep. No. 40, 100th Cong., 1st Sess., pt. 1, at 156 (1987) (emphasis added).

These expenses tended to make section 337 proceedings inaccessible to prospective complainants with small pocketbooks.[2]

In sum, to establish a violation of Section 337, four elements are necessary:

(1)   a valid and enforceable IPR;

(2)   infringement of that IPR by imports;

(3)   an "industry in the United States" that either "exists" or is "in the process of being established;" and

(4)   a relationship between that industry and the articles protected by the IPR.

In establishing the claim, do the *Federal Rules of Civil Procedure* and *Federal Rules of Evidence* apply? Why or why not?

Notably, Section 337 declares unlawful any unfair method of competition and unfair acts in importation, other than those relating to IP, if the threat of effect of such methods or acts is to (1) destroy or substantially injure an industry in the U.S., (2) prevent establishment of an industry in the U.S., or (3) restrain or monopolize trade and commerce in the U.S. (*See* 19 U.S.C. § 1337(a)(1)(A).) The unfair method or act provision of Section 337 reflects the statute's history: Section 337 was originally enacted in the *Tariff Act of 1922*. Its aim was a panoply of unfair acts not then covered by other unfair import laws. Indeed, the provision was used in antitrust and false advertising cases.

Amendments in the *1988 Act* narrowed the scope of actions that may be brought before the ITC, yet it is still remarkable. The unfair method or act provision in Section 337 remains applicable to allegations such as common law trademark infringement, unfair competition, trade secret misappropriation, trademark dilution, false designation of origin, and gray market importations. Certainly, Section 337 is best known for its use in cases of alleged IPR — especially patent — infringements.

B.   Operation of Section 337

The U.S. International Trade Commission (ITC) has sole authority to investigate alleged Section 337 violations. A case may be commenced by filing a petition with the ITC. (*See* 19 U.S.C. § 1337(b)(1).) Typically, the complainant is a right holder seeking to enforce its IPR against allegedly infringing goods and seeks an order excluding those goods from entry into the U.S. The complainant need not be an American business or citizen. Foreign companies can and do bring Section 337 actions.

Not only are the Japanese improving their U.S. court techniques, but they are learning to play the patent game quite well. In 1992, Japanese companies again led the world in gaining U.S. patents. Canon, Hitachi, and Toshiba ranked one, two, and three, respectively, in the number of American patents received. Number four was IBM. The increase in the Japanese patent portfolio means an inevitable

---

[2] Andrew S. Newman, *The Amendments to Section 337: Increased Protection for Intellectual Property Rights*, 20 L. & PLOL'Y IN INT'L BUS. 571, 576 (1989).

move on the part of the Japanese to litigate in U.S. courts to protect *their* intellectual property.[3]

Alternatively, the ITC may self-initiate a Section 337 action. Under pre-Uruguay Round law, regardless of who initiated a Section 337 investigation, it had to be completed within one year (or 18 months in complicated cases). (*See* 19 U.S.C. § 1337(b)(1) (1994).)

Section 337 is unique among trade remedy laws in that it is the only such law subject to the *Administrative Procedure Act (APA)* (5 U.S.C. §§ 551 *et seq.* 19 U.S.C. § 1337(c). Therefore, all ITC investigations and determinations under Section 337 must be conducted on the record before an administrative law judge (ALJ), after publication of notice and opportunity for hearing in conformity with *APA* requirements. An ALJ decision may be appealed to the ITC and, thereafter, the Court of Appeals for the Federal Circuit. Interestingly, the 1-year (or 18-month) period starts on the day after the ITC publishes a Section 337 investigation notice in the *Federal Register*. It was, and still is, required to publish it upon commencing an investigation. (*See* 19 U.S.C. § 1337(b)(1).) Presumably, the ITC could delay publication of the notice to "buy" itself additional time, though it could not conduct a formal investigation in the pre-notice period.

Section 321(a) of the *Uruguay Round Agreements Act of 1994*, the legislation implementing the Uruguay Round accords, eliminated the one year (and 18 month) time limits on Section 337 actions. (*See Uruguay Round Trade Agreement*, H.R. Doc. No. 316, 103d Cong., 2d Sess., vol. 1, 360 (Sept. 27, 1994).) Presently, the ITC must conclude its investigation and make a determination "at the earliest practicable time after the date of publication of notice of such investigation." (19 U.S.C. § 1337(b)(1).) To promote expeditious adjudication, the statute requires the ITC to set a target date for its final determination. It must set this date within 45 days after initiating an investigation.

C. Temporary Exclusion Orders

Arguably, the defining feature of Section 337 is the ITC's authority to prescribe provisional relief. Infringing imports may pose an imminent threat to a complainant's business. Hence, the complainant may not be able to wait 1 year for a final ITC determination. Instead, the complainant may seek a temporary exclusion order (TEO).

> In 1982, that was the situation faced by the dozen U.S. companies that had created the once-thriving double-sided floppy disk drive industry. "We had a very viable U.S. industry with 12 floppy disk drive companies," recalls Ray Lupo [a private attorney in Washington, D.C.]. "In November 1982, 14 Japanese companies showed up at an American trade show with double-sided floppy disk drives. At the time the drives were selling in the U.S. for $150 to $200. The Japanese were offering theirs for $30 less. Within a year to a year and a half there were only two American companies left — Tandon and Shugart. By the time we

---

[3] FRED WARSHOFSKY, THE PATENT WARS 100 (1994) (emphasis original); *see also id.* at 90, 94-97.

brought the suit [against the Mitsubishi Electric Corporation, TEAC Corporation, Sony Corporation, and other Japanese companies] and obtained a preliminary injunction three months later, there was just Tandon. The whole U.S. industry had been wiped out in the space of just 18 months by the importation of infringing products."[4]

To avoid this result, the ITC is empowered to seal off America's borders to goods that it preliminarily suspects violate an IPR.

In specific, suppose the ITC "determines that there is reason to believe that there is a violation" of Section 337. (19 U.S.C. § 1337(e)(1).) Then it "may direct that the articles concerned . . . be excluded from entry into the United States. . . ." (19 U.S.C. § 1337(e)(1).) As a result of the *1988 Act* amendments to Section 337, the ITC has 90 days (or up to 150 days in complicated cases) to render a decision about preliminary relief. (The 90-or 150-day period begins the day after the date on which the ITC publishes its investigation notice in the *Federal Register*.) When the ITC issues a TEO, it notifies the Secretary of the Treasury of its decision. In turn, the Secretary orders Customs and Border Protection (CBP) to exclude infringing goods from entry into the U.S.

For three reasons, obtaining a TEO order may be difficult. First, even if the ITC suspects an IPR violation, it may decline to impose an order because of an offsetting, and relatively greater, public interest. The ITC makes exceptions if admitting allegedly infringing articles is justified because of the adverse effect exclusion would have on public health and welfare, competitive conditions in the U.S. economy, production of like or directly competitive products, or U.S. consumers. In effect, before imposing a TEO, the ITC does a balancing test, weighing the common good against private gain to the complainant. Even if the exceptions are inapplicable, allegedly infringing goods may be admitted to the U.S. under bond. (*See* 19 U.S.C. § 1337(e)(1); *Biocraft Laboratories, Inc. v. U.S. International Trade Commission*, 947 F.2d 483 (Fed. Cir. 1991).)

Second, as a result of the *1988 Act*, the ITC must apply the same standards to a request for a TEO that a federal district court would apply in a motion for a preliminary injunction. (*See* 19 U.S.C. § 1337(e)(3).) These standards are set forth in the *Federal Rules of Civil Procedure*. Briefly, they concern

(1) the complainant's likelihood of success on the merits,

(2) whether the complainant would suffer irreparable injury during the pendency of the litigation if the temporary relief were not granted,

(3) whether that injury would outweigh harm to other parties if the temporary relief were granted, and

(4) whether temporary relief is in the public interest.

Why is it logical that TEO requisites would follow preliminary injunction criteria?

Third, the ITC may require a complainant to post a bond as a prerequisite to issuance of a TEO. (*See* 19 U.S.C. § 1337(e)(2).) The bond must be forfeited to the government if the complainant is unsuccessful in obtaining the order.

---

[4] *Id.* (emphasis original).

This requirement, also added by the *1988 Act*, raises several practical concerns for complainants.

> The purpose of the provision is to deter complainants from filing frivolous motions for temporary relief. However, it is difficult to envisage the permanent criteria the [International Trade] [C]ommission will use to determine the size of the bond. Will complainants ever be excused from posting a bond? At what time will the bond need to be posted? At what amount should the bond be set? Presumably, the bond should reflect at a minimum the potential gain to the complainant of excluding its competitor's goods during the period of a temporary exclusion order. Moreover, under what circumstances should the bond be forfeited to the U.S. Treasury?[5]

In brief, the bond requirement forces a complainant to engage in a careful risk-return calculation before applying for provisional relief.

D. Permanent Exclusion Orders

If the ITC renders a final determination that Section 337 is violated, then it may order the "permanent" exclusion of the offending articles from entry into the U.S. (*See* 19 U.S.C. § 1337(d).) The aforementioned exceptions for public health and welfare, competitive conditions, production, and consumer interests exist. Thus, the ITC must balance the interest of the complainant in getting complete relief against the interest of the public in avoiding disruption to legitimate trade caused by relief. However, the ITC

> rarely declines to grant relief on public interest grounds, and only when the dual requirements are met that (1) a strong public interest exists in maintaining an adequate supply of the goods under investigation; and (2) either that the domestic industry cannot maintain an adequate supply of the goods or the domestic users of the goods cannot obtain sufficient substitutes. The effect of rising consumer prices due to imposition of a Commission remedy is not sufficient grounds by itself for denying relief.[6]

A "permanent" exclusion order (PEO) remains in effect until the violation ends. (*See* 19 U.S.C. § 1337(k)(1).) Articles subject to such an order that are imported in violation of the order are subject to seizure and forfeiture. (*See* 19 U.S.C. § 1337(i).)

PEOs, which are the primary weapon against infringing imports, take one of two forms. A "limited" exclusion order directs the CBP to bar infringing articles originating from a source the order identifies, such as a specific country or a group of companies within a country. A "general" exclusion order tells the CBP to stop infringing articles regardless of source. The focus is on the nature of an article, not its country of origin or whether the respondent produced it. Thus, a general PEO is the strongest remedy.

---

[5] Newman, *supra* note 2, at 571, 583.

[6] William L. Lafuze & Patricia F. Stanford, *An Overview of Section 337 of the Tariff Act of 1930: A Primer for Practice Before the International Trade Commission*, 25 J. MARSHALL L. REV. 459, 466-67 (1992); *see also id.* at 463, 465-68, 474-90.

Not surprisingly, obtaining a general PEO is difficult. In its 1981 determination in *Certain Airless Paint Spray Pumps and Components Thereof* (*Spray Pumps*), the ITC formulated a high burden of proof. A complainant must prove "both a *widespread pattern of unauthorized use* of its patented invention and *certain business conditions* from which one might reasonably infer that foreign manufacturers other than the respondents to the investigation may attempt to enter the U.S. market with infringing articles." (216 U.S.P.Q. (BNA) 465, 473 (U.S. ITC 1981) (emphasis added).) A variety of facts are potentially relevant:

> Factors relevant to proof of whether a "widespread pattern of unauthorized use" exists include: (1) a Commission determination of unauthorized importation by numerous foreign manufacturers; (2) the pendency of foreign infringement suits based upon the intellectual property right at issue; and (3) other evidence which demonstrates a history of unauthorized foreign use of the patented invention. In order to prove that "certain business conditions" exist which make new foreign entrants into the United States markets likely, the Commission would consider the following: (1) the existence of an established market for the patented product in the United States; (2) the availability of marketing and distributing networks in the United States for potential foreign manufacturers; (3) the cost to foreign entrepreneurs of building a facility capable of producing the article; (4) the number of foreign manufacturers whose facilities could be retooled to produce the patented article; and (5) the cost to foreign manufacturers of retooling their facilities. The "certain business conditions" analysis is essentially an inquiry into barriers to market entry facing the infringing article.[7]

Section 321(a) of the *1994 Act* codified part of the *Spray Pumps* test. (*See Uruguay Round Trade Agreement*, H.R. Doc. No. 316, 103d Cong., 2d Sess., vol. 1, 364 (27 September).) The ITC cannot issue a general PEO unless that order "is necessary to prevent circumvention of an exclusion order limited to products of named persons" and "there is a pattern of violation of. . .section [337] and it is difficult to identify the source of infringing products."

As suggested, it is the CBP that must enforce a TEO or PEO. Accordingly, as a practical matter an individual CBP officer at a port of entry must determine whether an import is infringing on an IPR and, therefore, within the scope of the ITC's order. In many cases this task may be difficult. The officer's decision may be contested in the CIT.

E.   Other Remedies

One other remedy is available to a complainant in the event of a final affirmative Section 337 determination by the ITC. In addition to, or in lieu of, excluding goods from entry, the ITC may issue a temporary or permanent cease and desist order. (*See* 19 U.S.C. § 1337(f)(1).) If IPR violators disobey the order, then the ITC may levy a civil money penalty (*i.e.*, a fine) against them. (*See* 19 U.S.C. § 1337(f)(2).) The reason for the availability of different

---

[7] *Id.* at 459, 468.

remedies is to ensure a complainant can obtain complete relief, and the ITC has broad discretion in selecting an appropriate remedy. (*See, e.g.*, *Viscofan, S.A. v. U.S. International Trade Commission*, 787 F.2d 544, 548 (Fed. Cir. 1986).)

Remedies available under Section 337 are not based on the ITC having *in personam* jurisdiction over a respondent. Instead, Section 337 confers nation-wide *in rem* jurisdiction. As the Court stated in *Sealed Air Corporation v. U.S. International Trade Commission*, 645 F.2d 976, 985 (C.C.P.A. 1981), the statute was "intended to provide an adequate remedy. . .against unfair methods of competition and unfair acts instigated by foreign concerns operating beyond the *in personam* jurisdiction of domestic courts."

F. Presidential Discretion

A TEO, PEO, seizure and forfeiture order, temporary or permanent cease and desist order, or fine is subject to Presidential disapproval. Section 337 requires the ITC to forward a copy of a final determination, and a preliminary determination calling for a TEO, to the President. (*See* 19 U.S.C. § 1337(j)(1)(B).) The President has 60 days to overturn, "for policy reasons," the ITC's determination. (19 U.S.C. § 1337(j)(1)-(2). The 60-day period begins on the day after the day on which the President receives a copy of the ITC determination.) The statute does not delineate the policy reasons that would serve as a basis for overturning an ITC order, hence considerable discretion rests with the President. If the President does not disapprove of the ITC order, then it becomes effective upon publication in the *Federal Register*. The actions taken against the offending articles and culpable parties are effective as provided in the statute. (19 U.S.C. § 1337(j)(3).)

II. THE GATT —WTO CONSISTENCY OF SECTION 337

The GATT consistency of Section 337 is a source of controversy in U.S. —EU trade relations. The controversy escalated to a pre-WTO dispute settlement case, *United States — Section 337 of the Tariff Act of 1930*, B.I.S.D. (36th Supp.) 345 (1990) (adopted 7 November 1989). The EU claimed Section 337 violated GATT Article III:4 and could not be justified as necessary under Article XX(d).

The EU argued, in brief, Section 337 treated foreign merchandise less favourably than American merchandise, because it established different procedures in a patent infringement case if allegedly infringing merchandise is foreign, rather than domestic. Domestic-origin goods could be subject to a Section 337 case or a federal district court action. Foreign-origin goods had to endure a Section 337 action. The EU highlighted critical differences between Section 337 and federal district court actions. The differences included forum, decision-makers, procedural rules, jurisdiction, time limits, counter-claims, public interest considerations, presidential review, remedies, and enforcement.

The Panel, in one of the longest reports in pre-WTO history, accepted the EU argument. In doing so, it made clear Article III:4 applies to procedural as well as substantive law. The Panel also rejected the American defense of administrative necessity under GATT Article XX(d). How did the U.S. respond to the loss? Did compliance become a bargaining chip in the Uruguay Round, *i.e.*, did the U.S. condition amending Section 337 to conform to GATT if *TRIPs Agreement* negotiations proved satisfactory to it? What amendments did it make under the *1994 Uruguay Round Agreements Act*? Do they satisfy the EU? Do they weaken America's defenses against infringing goods?

III. THE GRAY MARKET AND SECTION 337

A. Physical Differences and the 1999 *Gamut* Case

GAMUT TRADING COMPANY v. UNITED STATES INTERNATIONAL TRADE COMMISSION
United States Court of Appeals for the Federal Circuit
200 F.3d 775 (1999)

NEWMAN, CIRCUIT JUDGE.

This action for violation of Section 337 of the *Tariff Act of 1930*, 19 U.S.C. § 1337, was initiated at the United States International Trade Commission ("ITC") on the complaint of the Kubota Corporation, a Japanese company ("Kubota-Japan"), owner of the registered United States trademark "Kubota," and its United States affiliated companies Kubota Tractor Corporation ("Kubota-U.S.") and Kubota Manufacturing of America ("KMA"). Kubota-U.S. is the exclusive licensee of the "Kubota" trademark in the United States, by agreement with Kubota-Japan which provides that the United States trademark and associated goodwill remain the exclusive property of Kubota-Japan.

The respondents are Gamut Trading Company and other entities (collectively "Gamut") that import from Japan and resell in the United States various models of used tractors of under 50 horsepower, all manufactured in Japan by the Kubota Corporation, used in Japan, and bearing the mark "Kubota" that had been properly affixed in Japan. Gamut was charged with violation of Section 337 of the *Tariff Act of 1930*, 19 U.S.C. § 1337, which provides for exclusion of product bearing infringing marks and other remedies, based on asserted infringement of the United States trademark "Kubota":

19 U.S.C. § 1337 Unfair practices in import trade

(a)(1)(C) The importation into the United States, the sale for importation, or the sale within the United States after importation by the owner, importer, or consignee, of articles that infringe a valid and enforceable United States trademark registered under the Trademark Act of 1946.

Describing this case as one of "gray-market goods," the ITC issued a General Exclusion Order against importation of used Japanese tractors bearing the "Kubota" trademark, and Cease and Desist Orders against sale of such tractors that had already been imported into the United States. The principle of gray market law is that the importation of a product that was produced by the owner of the United States trademark or with its consent, but not authorized for sale in the United States, may, in appropriate cases, infringe the United States trademark.

On Gamut's appeal, we now affirm the decision of the ITC.

. . . .

Kubota-Japan manufactures in Japan a large number of models of agricultural tractors, for use in Japan and other countries. Various tractor models are custom-designed for a particular use in a particular country. For example, tractor models that are designed for rice paddy farming are constructed for traction and maneuverability under wet, muddy conditions; these tractors have smaller tire separation in order to make tight turns in rice paddies, and are designed to function with rice paddy tillers, which contain narrow, lightweight blades. No corresponding model is designed for export to the United States.

In contrast, some tractor models that are intended to be used in the United States are specially constructed for lifting and transporting earth and rocks, and to function with rear cutters that contain heavy blades capable of cutting rough undergrowth; these models do not have a direct Japanese counterpart. The tractor models intended for sale and use in the United States bear English-language controls and warnings, and have English-language dealers and users manuals. They are imported by Kubota-U.S. and sold through a nationwide dealership network which provides full maintenance and repair service and maintains an inventory of parts for these specific tractor models. Kubota-U.S. conducts training classes for its dealership employees, instructing them on service and maintenance procedures.

Gamut purchases used Kubota tractors in Japan and imports them into the United States. The majority of the imported tractors are described as between 13 and 25 years old. All bear the mark "Kubota." The Kubota companies state that the importation and its extent came to their attention when United States purchasers sought service and repair or maintenance from Kubota-U.S. dealerships.

The Gray Market

The term "gray market goods" refers to genuine goods that in this case are of foreign manufacture, bearing a legally affixed foreign trademark that is the same mark as is registered in the United States; gray goods are legally acquired abroad and then imported without the consent of the United States trademark holder. *See Kmart Corp. v. Cartier, Inc.*, 486 U.S. 281, 286-87 (1987). . . . The conditions under which gray-market goods have been excluded implement the territorial nature of trademark registration, and reflect a legal recognition of the role of domestic business in establishing and maintaining the reputation and goodwill of a domestic trademark.

Until the Supreme Court's decision in *A. Bourjois & Co. v. Katzel*, 260 U.S. 689 (1923), . . . the prevailing rule in the United States was that the authorized sale of a validly trademarked product, anywhere in the world, exhausted the trademark's exclusionary right; thus the holder of the corresponding registered United States trademark was believed to have no right to bar the importation and sale of authentically marked foreign goods. However, in the *Bourjois* case the Court recognized the territorial boundaries of trademarks, stressing that the reputation and goodwill of the holder of the corresponding United States mark warrants protection against unauthorized importation of goods bearing the same mark, although the mark was validly affixed in the foreign country. In *Bourjois* the foreign-origin goods were produced by an unrelated commercial entity and imported by a third person, although the goods themselves were related in that the United States trademark owner bought its materials from the foreign producer. . . .

Since the *Bourjois* decision, the regional circuits and the Federal Circuit have drawn a variety of distinctions in applying gray market jurisprudence, primarily in consideration of whether the foreign source of the trademarked goods and the United States trademark holder are related commercial entities and whether the imported goods bearing the foreign mark are the same as (or not materially different from) the goods that are sold under the United States trademark, applying a standard of materiality suitable to consider-ations of consumer protection and support for the integrity of the trademarks of domestic purveyors, all with due consideration to the territorial nature of registered trademarks in the context of international trade.

Gamut directs our attention to cases in which the courts have refused to exclude gray market goods. For example, in *NEC Electronics v. CAL Circuit Abco*, 810 F.2d 1506 (9th Cir. 1987), . . . the court held that the importation of genuine NEC computer chips by the defendant, an entity unrelated to any NEC company, did not constitute infringement of the United States "NEC" trademark when there was no material difference between the NEC product imported by the defendant and the NEC product imported by the NEC United States subsidiary; the court distinguished *Bourjois* on the ground that in *Bourjois* the United States trademark owner could not control the quality of the unaffiliated foreign producer's goods, whereas when the companies are commonly controlled there is a reasonable assurance of similar quality.

A similar refusal to exclude was reached in *Weil Ceramics & Glass, Inc. v. Dash*, 878 F.2d 659 (3rd Cir. 1989), . . . wherein the court held that the United States trademark "Lladro" was not infringed by importation and sale of authentic "Lladro" figurines by one other than the trademark holder. The court reasoned that there is no need to protect the consumer against confusion when the goods imported by the defendant are identical to the goods imported by the United States trademark holder. . . . The court also reasoned that when the foreign manufacturer and the United States trademark holder are related companies, there is no need to protect the domestic company's investment in goodwill based on the quality of the trademarked goods, for the foreign manufacturer has control over their quality and the goods (porcelain figurines) are unchanged from their original quality.

However, when there are material differences between the domestic product and the foreign product bearing the same mark, most of the courts that have considered the issue have excluded the gray goods, even when the holders of the domestic and foreign trademarks are related companies, on grounds of both safeguarding the goodwill of the domestic enterprise, and protecting consumers from confusion or deception as to the quality and nature of the product bearing the mark. Thus, in *Societe des Produits Nestlé v. Casa Helvetia, Inc.*, 982 F.2d 633 (1st Cir. 1992), . . . the court held that the foreign owner of the United States trademark "Perugina" and its Puerto Rican subsidiary that imported Italian-made "Perugina" chocolate could prevent the importation of "Perugina" chocolate made under license in Venezuela, because the product is materially different in taste; the court referred to the likelihood of consumer confusion and loss of goodwill and integrity of the mark.

Similarly in *Original Appalachian Artworks v. Granada Electronics*, 816 F.2d 68, 73 (2d Cir. 1987), . . . the court held that the United States owner of the "Cabbage Patch" mark can prevent importation of "Cabbage Patch" dolls that were made and sold abroad under license from the United States owner, on the ground that the foreign dolls were materially different from the dolls authorized for sale in the United States because their instructions and adoption papers were in the Spanish language. . . .

These decisions implement the reasoning that the consuming public, associating a trademark with goods having certain characteristics, would be likely to be confused or deceived by goods bearing the same mark but having materially different characteristics; this confusion or deception would also erode the goodwill achieved by the United States trademark holder's business. Thus the basic question in gray market cases concerning goods of foreign origin is not whether the mark was validly affixed, but whether there are differences between the foreign and domestic product and if so whether the differences are material.

The courts have applied a low threshold of materiality, requiring no more than showing that consumers would be likely to consider the differences between the foreign and domestic products to be significant when purchasing the product, for such differences would suffice to erode the goodwill of the domestic source. As explained in *Nestlé*, "any higher threshold would endanger a manufacturer's investment in product goodwill and unduly subject consumers to potential confusion by severing the tie between a manufacturer's protected mark and its associated bundle of traits." . . . This criterion readily reconciles cases that have permitted parallel importation of identical goods, such as the Lladro figurines in *Weil Ceramics* (consumers not deceived, and no erosion of goodwill) and those that have barred importation based on material differences, such as the "Perugina" chocolate in *Nestlé*. This criterion was applied by the Commission in reviewing the used "Kubota" tractor importations.

The "Kubota" Importations

The ALJ [Administrative Law Judge] found that twenty-four models of the "Kubota" Japanese tractors imported by Gamut were materially different from any corresponding tractor imported by Kubota-U.S., and that one model was substantially the same. The ALJ found that the twenty-four tractor models differed in at least one of the following characteristics: structural strength, maximum speed, power take-off speed, wheel-base and tread-width dimensions, existence of a power take-off shield, and existence of a hydraulic block outlet. The ALJ found that certain parts for these models were not available in the United States, that the service necessary for these tractors differed from the service available for the United States models, that the used Japanese tractors lacked English warning labels and instructions, and that the Kubota-U.S. dealers did not have English-language operator or service manuals for the Japanese models. Finding these differences to be material, the ALJ found that these used tractors bearing the trademark "Kubota" infringed the United States "Kubota" trademark.

The ALJ found that one used tractor model, the Kubota L200, was not materially different from a corresponding model imported and sold by Kubota-U.S., and that although the labels and instructions on the tractor were in Japanese, the English language instruction and service manuals, warning labels, and parts available for the corresponding United States model were applicable to the Japanese Kubota L200. The ALJ concluded that the imported used Kubota L200 tractor did not infringe the "Kubota" United States trademark.

The Commission adopted the ALJ's Initial Decision as to the twenty-four models found to be infringing, and reversed the determination of no infringement by the Kubota L200. The Commission also found infringement by twenty additional tractor models not reviewed by the ALJ. For the Kubota L200 and the twenty additional models, the Commission found that the absence of English-language warning and instructional labels constituted a material difference from the "Kubota" brand tractors sold in the United States by Kubota-U.S., giving rise to trademark infringement by these unauthorized imports and violation of Section 337.

The Question of Material Differences

Gamut argues that the ITC erred in finding that there are material differences between their imported tractors and those imported by Kubota-U.S. Gamut points out that materiality of product differences is determined by the likelihood of confusion of those whose purchasing choice would be affected by knowledge of the differences, . . . and that its purchasers know that they are purchasing a used Japanese tractor. Gamut states that a purchaser of a used tractor bearing Japanese labels would not be deceived into thinking that he/she is buying a new tractor designed for the United States market. Gamut states that any differences between the imported models and the United States models are readily apparent, and thus can not be a material difference.

The ITC rejected this argument, finding that it is not reasonable to expect that purchasers of used Kubota tractors will be aware of structural differences from the United States models and of the consequences of these differences for purposes of maintenance, service, and parts. This finding was supported by substantial evidence. Indeed, the marking of these tractors with the "Kubota" mark weighs against an inference that purchasers would be expected to be aware of or expect structural differences.

As precedent illustrates, differences that may be readily apparent to consumers may nevertheless be material. In *Nestlé*, the court found differences in quality, composition, and packaging to be material. In *Martin's Herend* the court found differences in the color, pattern or shape of porcelain figures to be material, although they would be apparent to an observer of the products side-by-side. [*See Martin's Herend Imports, Inc. v. Diamond & Gem Trading USA*, Co., 112 F.3d 1296 (5th Cir. 1997).] Differences in labelling and other written materials have been deemed material, on the criteria of likelihood of consumer confusion and concerns for the effect of failed consumer expectations on the trademark holder's reputation and goodwill. . . .

The Commission found that the imported used "Kubota" tractors lacked English instructional and warning labels, operator manuals, and service manuals. Labels are attached at various places on the tractor to instruct the user on the proper operation of the tractor and to warn of potential hazards, and include instructions on the direction of the engine speed hand throttle, the function of the transmission, the four-wheel drive, the power take-off speed, hydraulic power lift, and other controls on the tractor. The Commission found that such labels are necessary to safe and effective operation. The authorized "Kubota" tractors bear these labels in English; the permanent labels on the used imported tractors are in Japanese.

While it would be obvious to the purchaser that the warning and instructional labels are in Japanese, there was evidence before the ITC of consumer belief that the used tractors were sponsored by or otherwise associated with the Kubota-U.S. distributorship/service system. The ALJ heard evidence that a purchaser of such a used tractor knew the tractor bore Japanese labels, but did not realize that he was not buying an authorized tractor or that service and parts were not available from the Kubota-U.S. dealerships. Gamut contends that Kubota-Japan and Kubota-U.S. form a single enterprise and thus that Kubota-U.S. can and should provide any parts, service, maintenance, and repairs required by these used tractors. The ALJ found that in order to service the Gamut-imported tractors in the same manner as Kubota-U.S. provides for its authorized tractors, the dealerships and service agencies would require an additional inventory of parts for the various Japan-only models, English-language operator manuals and service manuals that do not now exist, and additional service training as to the different models. There was testimony from a Kubota-U.S. dealer that he had tried to service several of the imported used tractors in order to preserve the reputation and goodwill of the mark, but that he was unable to do so satisfactorily since he had neither technical information nor replacement parts. He testified to customer dissatisfaction and anger with his dealership. The ALJ heard testimony that it would cost millions of dollars to provide equivalent support in the United States for the tractors that are made for use only in Japan. Gamut disputes these assertions and argues that most of the used tractors could be readily serviced without extraordinary effort. However, the record contains substantial evidence in support of the ALJ's findings. Further, materiality does not turn on whether extraordinary effort would be required for Kubota to service the Gamut-imported tractors; the threshold is not so high or the burden of establishing materiality so heavy.

The Kubota companies are not required to arrange to provide service to Gamut's imports in order to ratify these importations by mitigating their injury to the goodwill associated with the "Kubota" trademark. Whether or not the Kubota companies could arrange to service these tractors does not convert an otherwise infringing activity into an authorized importation. . . .

In addition to the differences in labelling, service, and parts, the ALJ found that many of the tractors designed by Kubota for use in the United States are stronger structurally than the corresponding tractors made for use in Japan. For example, the ALJ found that some of the intended United States tractors were made with stronger front and rear axles, front axle brackets, chassis, power trail, and parts contained in the transmission, such as gears. . . . The ALJ heard evidence that these structural differences significantly increase the likelihood of breakdowns of the less strong Japanese models. Although Gamut points to the absence of evidence of actual breakdown, the conceded or established differences in structural strength are relevant to the finding of material differences, and were properly considered by the Commission, along with the evidence concerning labelling, warnings, service, and parts.

Gamut raises the additional argument that in all events the Commission erred in law by applying the material differences test with the low threshold of precedent, because the imported tractors are not new but used. Gamut states that the Commission should have applied a more stringent test, namely, that differences which are easily ascertained by the consumer can not be material. Gamut also argues that the Commission erred in ruling that differences that are easily apparent to the consumer, such as differences in structural strength and availability of parts and service, are material. We conclude that the Commission applied the correct standard, for this standard implements the two fundamental policies of trademark law: to protect the consumer and to safeguard the goodwill of the producer. . . .

Substantial evidence supports the Commission's finding that consumers would consider the differences between the used imported tractors and the authorized Kubota-U.S. tractors to be important to their purchasing decision, and thus material.

Effect of the Fact that the Goods Are Used

Gamut argues that this is not a "gray market" case because the imported tractors are simply durable used goods, rendering it irrelevant whether the trademark owner authorized their sale in the United States. Gamut also argues that imported goods must be sold in competition with the goods of the owner of the United States trademark in order for authentic foreign-marked goods to infringe any trademark rights, citing *Kmart v. Cartier*. . . . Gamut asserts that because Kubota-U.S. sells new tractors in the United States and the respondents sell only used tractors, the goods are not in direct competition and the imported used tractors can not be held to be infringing gray market goods.

Direct competition between substantially identical goods is a factor to be considered, but it is not a prerequisite to trademark infringement. In *Safety-Kleen Corp. v. Dresser Indus.*, 518 F.2d 1399, 1404 (CCPA 1975), . . . the court explained that "While the similarity or dissimilarity of the goods or service should, in appropriate cases, be considered in determining likelihood of confusion . . . the law has long protected the legitimate interests of trademark owners from confusion among noncompetitive, but related, products bearing confusingly similar marks." Similar reasoning applies to products of the gray market.

As we have discussed, trademark law as applied to gray market goods embodies a composite of likelihood of consumer confusion as to the source of the goods, likelihood of consumer confusion arising from differences between the foreign and the domestic goods, impositions on the goodwill and burdens on the integrity of the United States trademark owner due to consumer response to any differences, and recognition of the territorial scope of national trademarks. Various of these factors acquire more or less weight depending on the particular situation. Although it is relevant to consider whether the imported product is new or used, other factors that may affect the reputation and the goodwill enuring to the holder of a trademark are not overridden by the fact that the product is known to be second-hand.

Courts that have considered the question and concluded that used goods can be gray market goods include *Red Baron-Franklin Park, Inc. v. Taito Corp.*, 883 F.2d 275 (4th Cir. 1989) (used circuit boards purchased abroad and imported into the United States without the copyright holder's consent were gray market goods); . . . *Sims v. Florida Dep't of Highway Safety and Motor Vehicles*, 862 F.2d 1449, 1451 (11th Cir. 1989) (used Mercedes Benz automobiles were gray market goods under definition of Clean Air and Safety Act); . . . *Sturges v. Clark D. Pease, Inc.*, 48 F.2d 1035, 1038 (2d Cir. 1931) (barring importation of used HISPANO SUIZA automobile because it bore United States registered trademark).

The ALJ found that Kubota-U.S. has established a reputation for safety, reliability, and service that consumers associate with the "Kubota" mark, and that the used tractors bearing the "Kubota" mark undermine the investment that Kubota-U.S. made in consumer goodwill for "Kubota" products. These findings are supported by substantial evidence. The fact that the imported tractors are used does not prevent a finding of infringement of the United States "Kubota" trademark.

Goodwill of the United States trademark

Gamut points out that according to the trademark license agreement, Kubota-Japan owns the "Kubota" trademark in the United States and associated goodwill. Gamut argues that there can be no infringement of the United States trademark unless Kubota-Japan, as the trademark owner, demonstrates that it "has developed domestic goodwill, that is, independent of the goodwill associated with the mark world wide." The goodwill of a trademark is developed by use of the mark. The ALJ found that Kubota-U.S., through its large network of authorized dealers in "Kubota" — brand products, had established a reputation for product quality and service throughout the United States, establishing use of the mark accompanied by goodwill. This goodwill enures to the benefit of the trademark owner. Gamut's challenge to the standing of the complainants is not well founded.

Remedy

The ALJ recommended imposition of a general exclusion order as to the infringing tractor models, barring their importation and sale unless the tractors bore a permanent, non-removable label alerting the consumer to the origin of the used tractors and containing other information deemed necessary to mitigate consumer confusion. The ALJ also recommended that cease and desist orders be issued to bar the respondents from selling infringing used tractors already imported unless the tractors were appropriately labelled. The Commission, on giving full review to the ALJ's Initial Decision, including various modifications thereof, affirmed the ALJ's ruling that the vinyl decal label that was proposed by Gamut would not eliminate the likelihood of consumer confusion because of the high likelihood that the labels would be removed after importation and prior to sale.

. . . .

An exclusion order is the Commission's statutory remedy for trademark infringement. 19 U.S.C. § 1337(d). In addition, the Commission may issue cease and desist orders when it has personal jurisdiction over the party against whom the order is directed. 19 U.S.C. § 1337(f). There is no dispute that the Commission has personal jurisdiction over the named respondents. Whether every actual or potential dealer in infringing goods was joined in this action does not excuse those over whom the Commission had jurisdiction.

B. Non-Physical Differences and the 2005 *SKF* Case

In *Gamut*, the Court did not face the issue of whether the distinction between domestic and gray market goods must be physical in nature to satisfy the "material difference test." The respondent, Gamut, infringed on Kubota's trademark because the 24 models of the "Kubota" tractors it imported from Japan did not have English language warning labels, and Kubota-U.S. dealers did not have English language operator or service manuals for them. The labelling, service, and parts differences were material as between authorized and gray market merchandise, thus supporting the invocation of Section 337. The issue of non-physical differences was presented on first impression in *SKF USA Inc. v. ITC*, 27 ITRD 1705 (Fed. Cir. 2005) (No. 04-1460).

In *SKF*, the Federal Circuit (per Circuit Judge Lourie) upheld the finding of the ITC that differences between authorized and gray market goods need not be physical, *i.e.*, need not be manifest in the product or its packaging, to be material. Differences in sellers of the product, or the services offered by sellers, may be material and thus establish a trademark infringement. That is because trademarked goods may have non-physical characteristics originating with the trademark owner. But, consumers may believe similar goods lacking those characteristics also originate with the owner. That erroneous impression could mislead consumers and damage the goodwill of the trademark owner.

The *SKF* Court stressed its reasoning, while "a step further" than in *Gamut*, simply made "explicit what may have only been implicit in *Gamut*." Notably, the *Gamut* court used the term "material differences," not "physical differences," and relied on prior case law in which non-physical material differences were held sufficient to avoid trademark infringement. In sum, to establish a Section 337 case based on trademark infringement in the context of the gray market, it does not matter whether differences — so long as they are material — between authorized, domestic goods and imported merchandise are physical or non-physical.

IV. REFUSING PROTECTION AND THE 2002 *HAVANA CLUB* CASE

A. Family, Business, and Political Intrigue

The facts of the *Havana Club* case are an amalgam of family, business, and political intrigue fit for a novel or movie. Until 1960, the Arechabala family owned the name "Havana Club" and applied it to its product, white rum. In 1960, with the Communist Revolution in Cuba, Fidel Castro expropriated the name. In 1994, a joint venture (JV) between a Cuban distiller and a French company, Pernod-Ricard, was established. The JV is called "Havana Club Holdings SA." The JV produces white rum in Cuba, and sells it globally under the "Havana Club" brand name. Exports of the rum are managed by Cubaexport, a state-owned rum enterprise. Because of the U.S. trade embargo against Cuba, importation into the U.S. is prohibited.

Pernod-Ricard says it was in 1994 the Cuban government gave it the right to the Havana Club brand. Notably, even before the Revolution, the Arechabala family let lapse its rights in the "Havana Club" name in some countries. In 1974, the family failed to renew its trademark registration in the U.S., a process that would have cost just $25. In contrast, Pernod-Ricard and Cubaexport registered the Havana Club brand in many countries, including the U.S., without protest from family. There were 8 such registrations between 1995-2000 under Section 44 of the U.S. *Lanham Act* (15 U.S.C. § 1126). Pernod-Ricard says two factors account for the success of the brand, and make it necessary for its products to have a stamp of authenticity and thereby avoid misleading customers: it uses Cuban sugar cane and a special distillation process established in Cuba.[8]

In 1994, Arechabala family sold the name "Havana Club" (the trademark and associated goodwill) to another company, Bacardi Ltd., a private company owned by over 200 descendants of the Bacardi founder. The Bacardi company is based in the Bahamas and has a subsidiary in the U.S. The American subsidiary sells a brand of rum in the U.S. called "Havana Club." According to Bacardi, Pernod-Ricard tried unsuccessfully to buy the rights to "Havana Club" from the Arechabala family shortly after it formed the JV — a clear indication, says Bacardi, Pernod-Ricard recognized the family as the rightful owner of the mark. Bacardi tried to register the mark in the U.S., and began selling the product in 1996. (It distills rum in the Bahamas to avoid any difficulties with the U.S. embargo on imports of Cuban products.)

In 1998, the U.S. enacted a budget bill (the *Omnibus Consolidated and Emergency Supplemental Appropriations Act*), which (*inter alia*) contained

---

[8] *See PTO Cancels Cuban "Havana Club" Mark; Bacardi Set to Sell Rum Under Same Mark,* 23 INT'L TRADE REP. (BNA) 1216-17 (17 Aug. 2006).

Section 211. The bill was signed into law on 21 October 1998. Section 211 states no trademark or trade name of Cuban origin can be protected by law in the U.S. if that mark or name had been used in connection with a business confiscated by the Castro regime. That is, registration or renewal in the U.S. of a trademark is forbidden, if the mark previously was abandoned by its owner whose business and assets were confiscated under Cuban law. Moreover, Section 211 prohibits an American court from recognizing or enforcing any assertion of such trademark rights. Consequently, no court in the U.S. can recognize or enforce an assertion of rights by a Cuban national related to a mark that is the same or similar to a mark used by a business confiscated by Cuba. The only exception is where the original trademark owner expressly agrees to the use of the trademark or trade name.

In 1996, Havana Club Holdings SA commenced litigation in federal court in New York against Bacardi to stop Bacardi from using the "Havana Club" name to sell rum in the U.S. (Bacardi suspended sales, pending outcome of the case.) The plaintiff argued it had been assigned the world-wide rights to the "Havana Club" trademark by the Cuban government, and Bacardi was using its mark illegally. Based on Section 211 of the *Omnibus Appropriations Act*, the U.S. District Court in April 1999 threw out the case. The plaintiff accused Bacardi of deploying lobbying power to effect a change in U.S. law for its sole benefit. It said the case was about Bacardi's desperate attempt to hold onto 50 percent of the American rum market, and Congress' desire to "get tough" on Castro.

In February 2000, a federal appeals court upheld the right of Bacardi to use the "Havana Club" rum label in the U.S., affirming the district court's ruling that the Cuban —French JV had no rights to the trademark in the U.S. *See Havana Club Holding, S.A. v. Galleon S.A.*, 203 F.3d 116 (2d Cir. 2000); *Havana Club Holding, S.A. v. Galleon S.A.*, 62 F. Supp. 2d 1085 (S.D.N.Y. 1999). The Second Circuit Court of Appeals rested its holding on two bases. First, in 1960, the Cuban government illegally confiscated the Havana Club rum distillery from its rightful owner, the Arechabala family. Second, the efforts of Pernod-Ricard to protect the mark violate Section 211.

Did Bacardi abandon the "Havana Club" name? Is Bacardi trying to seize control of the name to fend off competition from Pernod? Section 211 was applied against Havana Club International retroactively — is that unfair? The New York litigation was brought in 1996, the law was enacted in 1998, and the courts applied it in 1999. To be sure, the arguments are not all one way. One argument for Bacardi is Section 211 is no different from legal rights the EU established to protect property expropriated by the Nazis during the Second World War, or by communist regimes during the Cold War.

In July 1999, the EU and Cuba took up the cause of Havana Club Holdings SA, lodging against the U.S. a WTO complaint. Canada, Japan, and Nicaragua reserved third party rights, and only with the intercession of the WTO Director-General was a panel composed. The complainants, led by the European Communities (EC), argued Section 211 of the *Omnibus Appropriations Act* violated *TRIPs Agreement* provisions:

     i.   Article 2, which incorporates by reference relevant provisions of the 1967 *Paris Convention for the Protection of Industrial Property*, as amended by the *Stockholm Act of 1967*.

ii. Article 3, which guarantees national treatment with respect to IP protection.

iii. Article 4, which guarantees MFN treatment with respect to IP protection.

iv. Articles 15-21, which set out obligations for the protection of trademarks.

v. Article 41, covering general obligations about the enforcement of IP rights.

vi. Article 42, dealing with fair and equitable procedures in IP enforcement.

vii. Article 62, on acquiring and maintaining IPR and related *inter partes* (between two or more parties) procedures.

The Panel rejected most EC claims. But, it agreed Section 211(a)(2) inconsistent with *TRIPs Agreement* Article 42. That is because it restricts, in certain circumstances, effective access to, and availability of civil judicial procedures, for IPR holders.

The EC appealed in October 2001, and the Appellate Body rendered a decision in January 2002. That decision presents far more mixed results for the U.S. than the Panel's findings. In brief, the Appellate Body reached the following conclusions:

1. First, it affirmed the Panel's conclusion Section 211 does not violate the U.S. obligations under Article 2:1 of the *TRIPs Agreement* in conjunction with Article 6*quinquies* A(1) of the 1967 *Paris Convention*.

2. Second, it agreed with the Panel Section 211 does not violate *TRIPs Agreement* Articles 15 and 16.

3. Third, as to Section 211(b), it upheld the Panel's finding under Article 42 of the *TRIPs Agreement* of consistency between the two provisions. However, the Appellate Body reversed the Panel's holding Section 211(a)(2) violates Article 42 of the *TRIPs Agreement*. The Appellate Body said Article 42 contains procedural obligations, while Section 211 affects substantive trademark rights.

4. Fourth, in respect of trademark protection, it said Sections 211(a)(2) and (b) violate the national treatment and MFN obligations in the *TRIPs Agreement*, as well as the analogous provisions in the *Paris Convention* (1967). Thus, it reversed the Panel's contrary findings on *TRIPs Agreement* Articles 2, 3, and 4.

5. Fifth, it reversed the Panel's finding that trade names are not a category of IP the *TRIPs Agreement* protects The Appellate Body completed the analysis, reaching the same conclusion for trade names and trademarks. The Appellate Body also ruled Sections 211(a)(2) and (b) are not inconsistent with Article 2:1 of the *TRIPs Agreement* in conjunction with Article 8 of the *Paris Convention*.

Portions of the Report concerning the first and fourth results are excerpted below.

Following the January 2002 Appellate Body Report, the U.S. and EC, along with Cuba, reached an agreement on a reasonable period of time (RPT) for compliance — a maximum of 1 year (until 3 January 2003). Yet, in 2002, to the consternation of the EC and Cuba, the administration of President George W. Bush announced it was unnecessary to clarify Section 211 does not apply to cases in which a trademark has been abandoned by its original owner. The EC said U.S. officials had assured the Panel, and the Panel accepted the assurances, that Section 211 would not apply to a new trademark after a former trademark, to which the Section might have applied, had been abandoned. The obvious problem was American federal courts disagreed. They took the opposite view, applying Section 211 to trademarks succeeding abandoned trademarks. Thus, urged the EC and Cuba, there was legal uncertainty, and any solution to the dispute had to address the issue of abandoned trademarks. After the verbal scuffle, the parties agreed to repeated RPT extensions — to 30 June 2003, 31 December 2003, 31 December 2004, and 30 June 2005. In July 2005, the EU agreed to refrain from seeking WTO authorization to retaliate.

In July 2006, the U.S. Office of Foreign Assets Control (OFAC), which administers the Cuban trade embargo, and which the Department of the Treasury houses, denied an application by Cubaexport a license to renew U.S. registration of the "Havana Club" trademark.[9] (In 1995, OFAC had granted Cubaexport the necessary license — but later revoked it.) In turn, in August 2006, the U.S. Patent and Trademark Office (PTO) declared the "Havana Club" trademark of Pernod-Ricard "cancelled/expired." The PTO rejected the argument of Pernod-Ricard: regardless of OFAC's decision, Pernod-Ricard lodged a timely application with the PTO to renew the trademark; and, the PTO should focus solely on the status of the trademark in evaluating the right to renewal (not bring in other political issues). The PTO also rejected the argument it should not void the trademark until a U.S. court has the opportunity to review the legitimacy of OFAC's denial in respect of the Cubaexport application. Of course, Pernod-Ricard also intoned the PTO's took its decision to cancellation its trademark under Section 211 — which the WTO Appellate Body ruled illegal under Article 42 of the *TRIPs Agreement*.

Was Pernod-Ricard caught between two parts of the U.S. government in a pincer-like move? Alternatively, was there official confusion as to what mattered more — enforcing the Cuban trade embargo, or maintaining the integrity of IPR protection? Did international law matter in the case, and if so, how? What solution was reached?

---

[9] *See PTO Cancels, supra* note 8.

B. Key Findings

WTO APPELLATE BODY REPORT, *UNITED STATES —*
SECTION 211 OMNIBUS APPROPRIATIONS ACT OF 1998
WT/DS176/AB/R (adopted 2 January 2002)

I. Introduction

. . . .

3. . . . Section 211 states as follows:

(a) (1) Notwithstanding any other provision of law, no transaction or payment shall be authorized or approved pursuant to section 515.527 of title 31, Code of Federal Regulations, as in effect on September 9, 1998, with respect to a mark, trade name, or commercial name that is the same as or substantially similar to a mark, trade name, or commercial name that was used in connection with a business or assets that were confiscated unless the original owner of the mark, trade name, or commercial name, or the bona fide successor-in-interest has expressly consented.

[(a)] (2) No U.S. court shall recognize, enforce or otherwise validate any assertion of rights by a designated national based on common law rights or registration obtained under such section 515.527 of such a confiscated mark, trade name, or commercial name.

(b) No U.S. court shall recognize, enforce or otherwise validate any assertion of treaty rights by a designated national or its successor-in-interest under sections 44 (b) or (e) of the *Trademark Act of 1946* (15 U.S.C. 1126 (b) or (e)) for a mark, trade name, or commercial name that is the same as or substantially similar to a mark, trade name, or commercial name that was used in connection with a business or assets that were confiscated unless the original owner of such mark, trade name, or commercial name, or the bona fide successor-in-interest has expressly consented.

. . . .

4. Section 211 applies to a defined category of trademarks, trade names and commercial names, specifically to those trademarks, trade names and commercial names that are "the same as or substantially similar to a mark, trade name, or commercial name that was used in connection with a business or assets that were confiscated" by the Cuban Government on or after 1 January 1959. [The terms "trade name" and "commercial name" are synonymous under federal law.] . . . Section 211(d) [specifically, Section 211(d)(1)] states that the term "designated national" as used in Section 211 has the meaning given to that term in Section 515.305 of Title 31, Code of Federal Regulations ("CFR"), and that it includes "a national of any foreign country who is a successor-in-interest to a designated national." The term "confiscated" is defined [in Section 211(d)(2)] as having the meaning given that term in Section 515.336 of Title 31 CFR. Part 515 of Title 31 CFR sets out the *Cuban Assets Control Regulations* (the "*CACR*"), which were enacted on 8 July 1963 under the *Trading*

with the Enemy Act of 1917 [50 U.S.C. App. Sections 1 ff]. Under these regulations, "designated national" is defined [in 31 C.F.R. Section 515.305-306] as Cuba, a national of Cuba or a specially designated national. "Confiscated" is defined [in 31 C.F.R. Section 515.336] as nationalized or expropriated by the Cuban Government on or after 1 January 1959 without payment of adequate and effective compensation.

 5. Section 211(a)(1) relates to licensing regulations contained in the *CACR*. The *CACR* are administered by the Office of Foreign Assets Control ("OFAC"), an agency of the United States Department of the Treasury. Under United States law, all transactions involving property under United States jurisdiction, in which a Cuban national has an interest, require a licence from OFAC. [*See* 15 U.S.C. Sections 1051ff.] OFAC has the authority to grant either of two categories of licences, namely general licences and specific licences. A general licence is a general authorization for certain types of transactions set out in OFAC regulations. Such a licence is, in effect, a standing authorization for the types of transactions that are specified in the *CACR*. A specific licence, by contrast, is one whose precise terms are not set out in the regulations, so that a person wishing to engage in a transaction for which a general licence is not available must apply to OFAC for a specific licence.

 . . . .

 7. On 10 May 1999, some six months after the entry into force of Section 211, the *CACR* were amended by adding a new subparagraph (a)(2) to Section 515.527, which effectively prohibits registration and renewal of trademarks and trade names used in connection with a business or assets that were confiscated without the consent of the original owner or *bona fide* successor-in-interest. This provision reads:

> (a) (2) No transaction or payment is authorized or approved pursuant to paragraph (a)(1) of this section with respect to a mark, trade name, or commercial name that is the same as or substantially similar to a mark, trade name, or commercial name that was used in connection with a business or assets that were confiscated, as that term is defined in section 515.336, unless the original owner of the mark, trade name, or commercial name, or the bona fide successor-in-interest has expressly consented.

The effect of Section 211, as read with the relevant provisions of the *CACR*, is to make inapplicable to a defined category of trademarks and trade names certain aspects of trademark and trade name protection that are otherwise guaranteed in the trademark and trade name law of the United States. In the United States, trademark and trade name protection is effected through the common law as well as through statutes. The common law provides for trademark and trade name creation through use. The *Trademark Act of 1946* (the "*Lanham Act*") [15 U.S.C. Sections 1051 ff.] stipulates substantive and procedural rights in trademarks as well as trade names and governs unfair competition. Section 211(b) refers to Sections 44(b) and (e) of the *Lanham Act*.

 . . . .

III. Issues Raised in this Appeal

. . . .

98. . . . [I]n this appeal, we examine the WTO-consistency of Section 211 on its face. The question of the WTO-consistency of the *Havana Club Holding* decisions [in U.S. Courts] is not before us. However, as the European Communities has argued and as the United States has agreed, the *Havana Club Holding* decisions are relevant as evidence of how Section 211(b), as the European Communities has put it, "operates in practice." We agree. [How might, and should, the U.S react to an adverse Appellate Body decision if this case were more than a statutory challenge, *i.e.*, if it were a direct challenge to U.S. federal court decisions? Consider the reaction to the Appellate Body decisions on the U.S. Department of Commerce practice of zeroing in dumping margin calculations.]

99. Therefore, the measure at issue in this dispute consists of subsections (a)(1), (a)(2) and (b) of Section 211.

. . . .

V. Article 6*quinquies* of the *Paris Convention* (1967)

122. . . . Article 6*quinquies* A(1) reads:

> Every trademark duly registered in the country of origin shall be accepted for filing and protected *as is* in the other countries of the Union, subject to the reservations indicated in this Article. Such countries may, before proceeding to final registration, require the production of a certificate of registration in the country of origin, issued by the competent authority. No authentication shall be required for this certificate. (emphasis added)

123. Article 6*quinquies* forms part of the *Stockholm Act* of the *Paris Convention*, dated 14 July 1967. The *Stockholm Act* is a revision of the original *Paris Convention for the Protection of Industrial Property*, which entered into force on 7 July 1884. [The original *Paris Convention* was concluded in 1883.] The parties to the *Paris Convention*, who [*sic*] are commonly described as the "countries of the Paris Union," are obliged to implement the provisions of that *Convention*.

124. Article 2.1 of the *TRIPS Agreement* provides that: "[i]n respect of Parts II, III and IV of this *Agreement*, Members shall comply with Articles 1 through 12, and Article 19, of the *Paris Convention* (1967)." Thus, Article 6*quinquies* of the *Paris Convention* (1967), as well as certain other specified provisions of the . . . *Convention* . . ., have been incorporated by reference into the *TRIPS Agreement* and, thus, the *WTO Agreement*.

125. Consequently, WTO Members, whether they are countries of the Paris Union or not, are obliged, under the *WTO Agreement*, to implement those provisions of the *Paris Convention* (1967) that are incorporated into the *TRIPS Agreement*. . . .

. . . .

130. . . . [T]he *Paris Convention* (1967) provides two ways in which a national of a country of the Paris Union may obtain registration of a trademark in a country of that Union other than the country of the applicant's origin: one way is by registration under Article 6 of the *Paris Convention* (1967); the other is by registration under Article 6*quinquies* of that same *Convention*.

131. Article 6(1) of the *Paris Convention* (1967) provides:

> The conditions for the filing and registration of trademarks shall be determined in each country of the Union by its domestic legislation.

132. Article 6(1) states the general rule, namely, that each country of the Paris Union has the right to determine the *conditions* for filing and registration of trademarks in its domestic legislation. This is a reservation of considerable discretion to the countries of the Paris Union — and now, by incorporation, the Members of the WTO — to continue, in principle, to determine for themselves the conditions for filing and registration of trademarks. Thus, in our view, the general rule under the *Paris Convention* (1967) is that national laws apply with respect to trademark registrations within the *territory* of each country of the Paris Union, subject to the requirements of other provisions of that *Convention*. And, likewise, through incorporation, this is also now the general rule for all WTO Members under the *TRIPS Agreement*.

. . . .

136. By virtue of Article 6*quinquies* A(1), WTO Members are obliged to confer an exceptional right on an applicant in a Paris Union country other than its country of origin, one that is over and above whatever rights the other country grants to its own nationals in its domestic law. A national who files for registration of a trademark in his own country must comply *fully* with the conditions for filing and registration as determined by the national legislation of that country. But, if that country is a Member of the Paris Union — and, now, of the WTO — then an applicant from another WTO Member who seeks registration in that country of a trademark duly registered in its country of origin has the *additional rights* that WTO Members are obliged to confer on that applicant under Article 6*quinquies* A(1).

137. The participants to this dispute disagree on the scope of the requirement imposed by Article 6*quinquies* A(1) to accept for filing and protect trademarks duly registered in the country of origin "as is." Looking first to the text of Article 6*quinquies* A(1), we see that the words "as is" (or, in French, "*telle quelle*") relate to the trademark to be "accepted for filing and protected" in another country based on registration in the applicant's country of origin. [In a footnote, the Appellate Body quoted Article 29(1)(c) of the *Paris Convention* (1967), which says: "In case of differences of opinion on the interpretation of various texts, the French text shall prevail."] The ordinary meaning [From *The New Shorter Oxford English Dictionary*] of the words "as is" is "in the existing state." The French term "*telle quelle*" can be defined as "sans arrangement, sans modification" [*i.e.*, as it stands, without adjustments or modifications.] This suggests to us that the requirement of Article 6*quinquies* A(1) to accept for filing and protect a trademark duly registered in the

applicant's country of origin relates at least to the *form* of the trademark as registered in the applicant's country of origin. The question before us is whether the scope of this requirement also encompasses other features and aspects of that trademark as registered in the country of origin.

. . . .

139. . . . To resolve this question, we look to the context of Article 6*quinquies*A(1). We find that there is considerable contextual support for the view that the requirement to register a trademark "as is" under Article 6*quinquiesA*(1) does *not* encompass all the features and aspects of that trademark. . . . Article 6(1) of the *Paris Convention* (1967) reserves to the countries of the Paris Union the right to determine the *conditions* for filing and registration of trademarks by their domestic legislation. Article 6(1) confirms that the countries of the Paris Union did not relinquish their right to determine the conditions for filing and registration of trademarks by entering into the *Paris Convention* (1967) — subject, of course, to the other obligations of Paris Union countries under the *Paris Convention* (1967). Clearly, if Article 6*quinquies* A(1) were interpreted too broadly, the legislative discretion reserved for Members under Article 6(1) would be significantly undermined.

. . . .

141. . . . [I]t does not seem credible to us to contend — as the European Communities does — that many of those very same countries intended more than a century ago, in concluding the *Paris Convention*, or on the occasion of one of the subsequent Revision Conferences of the *Paris Convention* [*e.g.*, the Revision Conference of Lisbon (1958)], to establish a global system for determining trademark ownership that could circumvent, and thereby undermine, a domestic regime of trademark ownership based on use.

. . . .

145. Finally, we look to an agreed interpretation adopted at the conclusion of the original *Paris Convention* in 1883. The *Final Protocol of the Paris Convention* (1883) was considered [as per Paragraph 7 of the *Protocol*] to form an integral part of that *Convention*. Paragraph 4 of that *Final Protocol* in 1883 explained that the provision, which later became Article 6*quinquies* A(1):

> . . . should be understood in the sense that no trademark may be excluded from protection in one of the States of the Union for the sole reason that it does not comply, with regard to the signs of which it is composed, with the conditions of the laws of that State, provided it complies on this point with the laws of the country of origin and that it has been properly filed there. Subject to this exception, *which only concerns the form of the mark*, and subject to the provision of the other Articles of the Convention, *each State shall apply its domestic law.* (emphasis added)

146. As the European Communities has observed, this agreed interpretation was omitted at the Washington Revision Conference of 1911. Yet, . . . no delegation to that Conference expressed the view at that time that this omission should change the meaning of the provision. Indeed, as one WIPO publication states, "it is generally believed that such omission did not alter the intended sense of *'telle quelle'* as it was made explicit in 1883." [*See* World

intellectual Property Organization, *Paris Centenary, 1983* (Pub. No. 875).] On this, we simply observe that our interpretation of Article 6*quinquies*A(1) is not inconsistent with this interpretation.

147. We . . . agree with the Panel that Section 211(a)(1) is a measure dealing, in the particular circumstances in which it applies, with the ownership of a defined category of trademarks. We also agree that the obligation of countries of the Paris Union under Article 6*quinquies* A(1) to accept for filing and protect a trademark duly registered in the country of origin "as is" does not encompass matters related to ownership.

148. For these reasons, we uphold the finding of the Panel . . . that Section 211(a)(1) is not inconsistent with Article 2.1 of the *TRIPS Agreement* in conjunction with Article 6*quinquies* A(1) of the *Paris Convention* (1967).

. . . .

IX. Article 2(1) of the *Paris Convention* (1967) and Article 3:1 of the *TRIPS Agreement*

233. We turn now to the issue of national treatment. In this appeal we have been asked to address, for the first time, this fundamental principle of the world trading system as it relates to intellectual property. There are two separate national treatment provisions that cover trademarks as well as other intellectual property rights covered by the *TRIPS Agreement*. The European Communities claims, on appeal, that Sections 211(a)(2) and (b) violate both.

234. One national treatment provision at issue in this appeal is Article 2(1) of the *Paris Convention* (1967), which states:

> Nationals of any country of the Union shall, as regards the protection of industrial property, enjoy in all the other countries of the Union the advantages that their respective laws now grant, or may hereafter grant, to nationals; all without prejudice to the rights specially provided for by this Convention. Consequently, they shall have the same protection as the latter, and the same legal remedy against any infringement of their rights, provided that the conditions and formalities imposed upon nationals are complied with.

235. . . . [T]he *Stockholm Act* of the *Paris Convention*, dated 14 July 1967, is but the most recent version of that important international intellectual property convention. Article 2(1) was part of the *Paris Convention* in 1883. Since that time, it has remained a treaty obligation of all the countries that have been party to the *Paris Convention*.

236. The parties to this dispute are not unacquainted with the national treatment obligation and other protections for trademarks and other forms of industrial property provided by the *Paris Convention*. Every one of the fifteen Member States of the European Union has long been a country of the Paris Union. Most of the current Member States of the European Union became party to the *Paris Convention* in the 1880's. The most recent did so in 1925 — seventy-seven years ago. Likewise, the United States has, from almost the very beginning, been a country of the Paris Union. The United States became a country of the Paris Union on 30 May 1887. . . .

237. Thus, the national treatment obligation is a longstanding obligation under international law for all the countries directly involved in this dispute, as well as for many more countries of the Paris Union that, like the parties to this dispute, are also Members of the WTO. If there were no *TRIPS Agreement*, if there were no WTO, the parties to this dispute would be bound, nevertheless, under Article 2(1) of the *Paris Convention* (1967), to accord national treatment to other countries of the Paris Union.

238. . . . . [W]hat *is* new is that, as a consequence of the Uruguay Round, Article 2(1) of the *Paris Convention* (1967) was made part of the *WTO Agreement*. . . . [B]y virtue of Article 2.1 of the *TRIPS Agreement*, Article 2(1) of the *Paris Convention* (1967), as well as certain other specified provisions. . ., have been incorporated into the *TRIPS Agreement* and, thus, the *WTO Agreement*. Consequently, these obligations of countries of the Paris Union under the *Paris Convention* (1967) are also now obligations of all WTO Members, whether they are countries of the Paris Union or not, under the *WTO Agreement*, and, thus, are enforceable under the *DSU*.

239. In addition to Article 2(1) of the *Paris Convention* (1967), there is also another national treatment provision in the *TRIPS Agreement*. The other national treatment provision at issue in this appeal is Article 3.1 of the *TRIPS Agreement*. . . .

240. . . . . [I]n drafting the *TRIPS Agreement*, the framers of the *WTO Agreement* saw fit to include an additional provision on national treatment. Clearly, this emphasizes the fundamental significance of the obligation of national treatment to their purposes in the *TRIPS Agreement*.

. . . .

242. . . . . [T]he national treatment obligation is a fundamental principle underlying the *TRIPS Agreement*, just as it has been in what is now the GATT 1994. The Panel was correct in concluding that, as the language of Article 3.1 of the *TRIPS Agreement*, in particular, is similar to that of Article III:4 of the GATT 1994, the jurisprudence on Article III:4 of the GATT 1994 may be useful in interpreting the national treatment obligation in the *TRIPS Agreement*.

243. As articulated in Article 3.1 of the *TRIPS Agreement*, the national treatment principle calls on WTO Members to accord no less favourable treatment to non-nationals than to nationals in the "protection" of trade-related intellectual property rights. The footnote to Article 3.1 clarifies that this "protection" extends to "matters affecting the availability, acquisition, scope, maintenance and enforcement of intellectual property rights as well as those matters affecting the use of intellectual property rights specifically addressed" in the *TRIPS Agreement*. . . . [N]either the *TRIPS Agreement* nor the *Paris Convention* (1967) requires WTO Members to adopt any particular "ownership regime."

244. The European Communities claims that Sections 211(a)(2) and (b) violate the national treatment obligation in both Article 2(1) of the *Paris Convention* (1967) and Article 3.1 of the *TRIPS Agreement* by treating non-United States nationals less favourably than United States nationals in two different situations to which the measure applies: first, that of successors-in-interest or *bona fide* successors-in-interest to original owners; and, second,

that of original owners. The European Communities contends that this discrimination occurs in different ways in these two different situations, but, in each situation, they see a violation of the fundamental obligation of national treatment.

. . . .

249. . . . [B]efore the Panel, the United States argued that Section 211(a)(2) does not apply to United States nationals because, under the *CACR*, United States nationals are prohibited from owning or having an interest in property that was confiscated by the Cuban Government and, therefore, cannot become successors-in-interest. The United States acknowledged that OFAC has the discretion administratively to authorize specific licences with respect to certain transactions that would enable United States nationals to deal with such property. The United States asserted, however, that this discretion has little practical effect because OFAC has never issued such a licence to a United States national for purposes of becoming a successor-in-interest to a confiscating entity. The United States submitted further to the Panel that there is no reason to believe that OFAC would ever issue such a licence, and that, therefore, as a matter of law, the Panel should not assume that OFAC, an agency of the executive branch, would take an action that might put the United States in violation of its international obligations. For these reasons, the United States maintained that it does not provide more favourable treatment to United States nationals than to Cubans and other non-nationals.

250. The Panel accepted this argument by the United States with respect to successors-in-interest. . . .

251. . . . [T]he Panel focused on the discretionary authority enjoyed by OFAC. In so doing, the Panel relied on the report of the panel in *United States Measures Affecting the Importation, Internal Sale and Use of Tobacco* ("*US — Tobacco*") [B.I.S.D. (41st Supp. I) at 131, para. 118 (adopted 4 October 1994)], and on our Report in *United States — Anti-Dumping Act of 1916*("*US — 1916 Act* ") [WT/DS136/AB/R, para. 200 (adopted 26 September 2000)] concerning the issue of discretionary authority. Based on those previous Reports, the Panel concluded that, where discretionary authority is vested in the executive branch of a WTO Member, it cannot be assumed that that Member will exercise that authority in violation of its obligations under any of the covered agreements.

252. The Panel found, as a matter of fact, that OFAC has never granted a specific licence to allow any United States national to become a successor-in-interest to a "designated national." Further, the Panel found that the European Communities had not demonstrated that, in exercising its discretionary authority, OFAC had acted in a manner that was inconsistent with the national treatment obligation in Article 2(1) of the *Paris Convention* (1967) and Article 3.1 of the *TRIPS Agreement.*

. . . .

254. The European Communities appeals these findings. The European Communities does not dispute that OFAC can deny United States nationals the specific licences required under the *CACR* to become successors-in-interest to "designated nationals." Nor does the European Communities dispute that,

to date, OFAC has never granted such a specific licence to United States nationals. Rather, the European Communities argues that the offsetting effect of this admittedly longstanding OFAC practice does not cure the discrimination in Section 211(a)(2) with respect to successors-in-interest who are *not* United States nationals.

255. According to the European Communities, the discriminatory treatment in favour of successors-in-interest who are United States nationals and against successors-in-interest who are *not* United States nationals continues to exist because of what the European Communities sees as an "extra hurdle" that non-United States nationals face procedurally under United States law.

256. That "extra hurdle" is this. United States nationals who are successors-in-interest must go successfully only through the OFAC procedure. In the circumstances addressed by Section 211, they are not subject to the constraints imposed by Section 211(a)(2). In contrast, non-United States successors-in-interest not only must go successfully through the OFAC procedure, but also find themselves *additionally* exposed to the "extra hurdle" of an additional proceeding under Section 211(a)(2). In sum, United States nationals face only *one* proceeding, while non-United States nationals face *two*. It is on this basis that the European Communities claims on appeal that Section 211(a)(2), as it relates to successors-in-interest, violates the national treatment obligation in the *TRIPS Agreement* and the *Paris Convention* (1967).

. . . .

260. . . . . [T]he Panel . . . should have gone on and considered the argument made by the European Communities about the "extra hurdle" faced by non-United States successors-in-interest. For this reason, we do so now.

261. We note, as did the Panel, the report of the panel in *U.S. — Section 337* [GATT, B.I.S.D. (36th Supp.) 345 (adopted 7 November 1989), excerpted in a later Chapter. As the Appellate Body explained in a footnote: "Central to that dispute was a situation where the proceedings that were applicable to imported products alleged to infringe United States patents were different in a number of respects from those applicable before a federal district court when a product of foreign origin was challenged on the grounds of patent infringement.]. That panel [at para. 5.11] reasoned that "the mere fact that imported products are subject under Section 337 to legal provisions that are different from those applying to products of national origin is in itself not conclusive in establishing inconsistency with Article III:4."

262. That panel stated further [at para. 5.12] that:

> [I]t would follow . . . that any unfavourable elements of treatment of imported products could be offset by more favourable elements of treatment, provided that the results, as shown in past cases, have not been less favourable. *[E]lements of less and more favourable treatment could thus only be offset against each other to the extent that they always would arise in the same cases and necessarily would have an offsetting influence on the other.* (emphasis added)

263. And that panel, importantly for our purposes, concluded [at para. 5.19] that:

. . . while the likelihood of having to defend imported products in two fora is small, the existence of the possibility is inherently less favourable than being faced with having to conduct a defence in only one of those fora. (emphasis added)

264. We agree with this approach and consider it to be particularly relevant to this appeal. It is not disputed that Section 515.201 of the *CACR* imposes a limitation — a "hurdle" — on both successors-in-interest who are United States nationals and successors-in-interest who are not. It is also not disputed that Section 211(a)(2) applies only to successors-in-interest who are *not* United States nationals. It is likewise not disputed that, under Section 211(a)(2), in *every individual situation* where a non-United States successor-in-interest seeks to assert its rights without the express consent of the original owner or its *bona fide* successor-in-interest, the United States courts are required not to recognize, enforce or otherwise validate any assertion of rights. . . . [T]his situation exists under the statute *on its face*, and that, therefore, unlike the situation with respect to the granting of a special licence to United States successors-in-interest by OFAC, this situation assumes no action by OFAC or by any other agency of the United States Government.

265. The United States may be right that the likelihood of having to overcome the hurdles of both Section 515.201 of Title 31 CFR and Section 211(a)(2) may, echoing the panel in *U.S. — Section 337*, be *small*. But, . . . even the *possibility* that non-United States successors-in-interest face two hurdles is *inherently less favourable* than the undisputed fact that United States successors-in-interest face only one.

266. . . . [T]he United States has submitted that Section 211 is a statutory articulation of the longstanding doctrine of non-recognition of foreign confiscation that is recognized in "virtually every jurisdiction." Thus, the United States argues that, in the unlikely event that a United States national did somehow succeed in getting a specific licence from OFAC, this longstanding doctrine would be applied by United States courts to prevent such a national from enforcing its rights as a successor-in-interest. The United States argues, therefore, that the prohibition imposed by Section 211(a)(2) with respect to non-United States successors-in-interest would also be applied to United States successors-in-interest. We are not persuaded by this argument.

267. The United States has not shown, as required under the national treatment obligation, that, in every individual case, the courts of the United States would not validate the assertion of rights by a United States successor-in-interest. Moreover, even if there is, as the United States argues, a *likelihood* that United States courts would not enforce rights asserted by a United States successor-in-interest, the fact remains, nevertheless, that non-United States successors-in-interest are placed by the measure, *on its face*, in an inherently less favourable situation than that faced by United States successors-in-interest. And, even if we were to accept the United States argument about the doctrine of non-recognition of foreign confiscation, presumably that doctrine would apply to those who are not nationals of the United States as well as to those who are. Any application of this doctrine would therefore not offset the discrimination in Section 211(a)(2), because it would constitute yet another, separate obstacle faced by nationals and non-nationals alike. Hence,

it would not offset the effect of Section 211(a)(2), which applies only to successors-in-interest who are not United States nationals.

268. Accordingly, we conclude that Section 211(a)(2) imposes an additional obstacle on successors-in-interest who are not nationals of the United States that is not faced by United States successors-in-interest. And, therefore, we conclude that, by applying the "extra hurdle" imposed by Section 211(a)(2) only to non-United States successors-in-interest, the United States violates the national treatment obligation in Article 2(1) of the *Paris Convention* (1967) and Article 3.1 of the *TRIPS Agreement*.

269. For this reason, we reverse the Panel's conclusion . . . that "[b]ecause US nationals are unable to obtain licences so as to become a successor-in-interest and OFAC has not granted any such licence for such purpose . . . Section 211(a)(2) is not inconsistent with Article 3.1 of the *TRIPS Agreement* and Article 2.1 of the *TRIPS Agreement* in conjunction with Article 2(1) of the *Paris Convention* (1967)."

270. The European Communities also raised claims at the level of successors-in-interest against Section 211(b). . . .

271. We agree with the Panel that Section 211(b) applies to successors-in-interest of *any origin*, including United States nationals and that, consequently, Section 211(b) does not accord less favourable treatment to non-United States nationals than to United States nationals.

272. Therefore, we uphold the Panel's conclusion . . . that — at the level of successors-in-interest — Section 211(b) is not inconsistent with Article 2.1 of the *TRIPS Agreement* in conjunction with Article 2(1) of the *Paris Convention* (1967) and Article 3.1 of the *TRIPS Agreement*.

273. We turn now to the European Communities' claims relating to Sections 211(a)(2) and (b) with respect to the other form of discrimination alleged by the European Communities — that of discrimination among *original owners*.

274. On this, the Panel found with respect to Sections 211(a)(2) and (b):

> In respect of original owners, Section 211(a)(2) does not accord a treatment less favourable to foreign original owners than it accords to original owners who are US nationals with respect to protection of intellectual property rights.
>
> . . . .
>
> Similarly, in respect of original owners, Section 211(b) does not accord a treatment less favourable to foreign original owners than it accords to original owners who are US nationals.

In contrast to its reasoned explanation on alleged discrimination relating to successors-in-interest, the Panel gave no further explanation for its conclusion on alleged discrimination among original owners.

275. On appeal, the European Communities argues that the Panel erred in its conclusion about discrimination among original owners. The European Communities maintains that, on their face, both Sections 211(a)(2) and 211(b) violate the national treatment obligation under the *TRIPS Agreement* and the *Paris Convention* (1967) because they provide less favourable treatment to

Cuban nationals who are original owners than to United States nationals who are original owners. The European Communities supports this position by relying on a particular set of circumstances that exists under the statute that, according to the European Communities, illustrates how Sections 211(a)(2) and (b), on their face, discriminate in favour of United States nationals who are original owners and against Cuban nationals who are original owners. The European Communities believes this situation demonstrates the discriminatory treatment implicit in Sections 211(a)(2) and (b).

276. Specifically, the European Communities asks us to consider the following particular set of circumstances that exists under the statute. There are two separate owners who acquired rights, either at common law or based on registration, in two separate United States trademarks, before the Cuban confiscation occurred. Each of these two United States trademarks is the same, or substantially similar to, the signs or combination of signs of which a trademark registered in Cuba is composed. That same or similar Cuban trademark was used in connection with a business or assets that were confiscated in Cuba. Neither of the two original owners of the two United States trademarks was the owner of that same or similar trademark that was registered in Cuba. Those two original owners each seek to assert rights in the United States in their two respective United States trademarks. The situation of these two original owners of these two United States trademarks is identical in every relevant respect, but one. That one difference is this: one original owner is a national of Cuba, and the other original owner is a national of the United States.

277. . . . . The European Communities argues that, on the face of the statute, in this situation, the original owner who is a Cuban national is subject to Sections 211(a)(2) and (b), and the original owner who is a United States national is not. This alone, as the European Communities sees it, is sufficient for us to find that Sections 211(a)(2) and (b) violate the national treatment obligation of the United States.

278. Like the European Communities, we see this situation as critical to our determination of whether the treatment of original owners under Section 211 is consistent with the national treatment obligation of the United States under Article 2(1) of the Paris Convention (1967) and Article 3.1 of the *TRIPS Agreement*.

279. The situation highlighted by the European Communities on appeal exists because Sections 211(a)(2) and (b) apply to "designated nationals." A "designated national" is defined in Section 515.305 of Title 31 C.F.R. [Code of Federal Regulations] as "Cuba and any national thereof including any person who is a specially designated national." [The definition also includes successors-in-interest, discussed earlier by the Appellate Body.] Thus, Sections 211(a)(2) and (b) apply to original owners that are Cuban nationals. Original owners that are United States nationals are not covered by the definition of "designated national" and, thus, are not subject to the limitations of Sections 211(a)(2) and (b).

280. Thus, in our view, the European Communities is correct on this issue. Sections 211(a)(2) and (b) are discriminatory *on their face*.

281. We conclude, therefore, that the European Communities has established a *prima facie* case that Sections 211(a)(2) and (b) discriminate between Cuban nationals and United States nationals, both of whom are original owners of trademarks registered in the United States which are composed of the same or substantially similar signs as a Cuban trademark used in connection with a business or assets that were confiscated in Cuba.

282. The United States attempts to rebut this argument by the European Communities by maintaining that Sections 211(a)(2) and (b) are not applicable to original owners, regardless of their nationality, because original owners are always in a position to consent expressly to their own assertion of rights under Sections 211(a)(2) and (b). Section 211(a)(2), when read together with Section 211(a)(1), and Section 211(b) do indeed provide an exception for designated nationals who have the express consent of "the original owner of the mark, trade name, or commercial name, or the bona fide successor-in-interest." However, the United States erroneously assumes in its argument on this issue that the Cuban original owner of the United States trademark is necessarily the same person as the original owner of the same or substantially similar Cuban trademark used in connection with a business or assets that were confiscated. This is by no means necessarily the case, as is demonstrated in the specific situation posed by the European Communities. In that situation, the Cuban national who holds the trademark rights in the United States would be unable to use its own consent to avoid the court's denial of any assertion of rights under Sections 211(a)(2) and (b) because it was not the original owner of the same or similar Cuban trademark.

283. The United States also argues in rebuttal that Section 211(a)(2) does not apply to Cuban nationals in the situation posed by the European Communities because Section 515.527 of the *CACR* was not in effect when the original owners in this situation obtained their trademark rights in the United States. . . . Section 211(a)(2) refers to the assertion of rights "based on common law rights or registration obtained under such section 515.527." Thus, it is clear from the text of Section 211(a)(2) that the reference to Section 515.527 relates to rights based on registration, and not to common law rights. Indeed, the United States conceded as much in response to our questions at the oral hearing. Thus, this argument may address the discrimination against Cuban nationals who are original owners of trademark rights in the United States *based on registration*. But it does not address the discrimination against Cuban nationals who are original owners of trademark rights in the United States *based on common law*.

284. For trademark rights based on registration, it is true that, in the situation posed by the European Communities, Section 515.527 of the *CACR* would not have been in effect when the Cuban original owner obtained its trademark rights in the United States, namely before the Cuban confiscation. However, . . . Section 515.527 . . . applies not only to the registration, but also to the *renewal* of registered trademarks. Although the Cuban national's initial registration, carried out before the Cuban confiscation, would not have been obtained pursuant to Section 515.527, a renewal of such registration would come within the purview of that provision. Hence, Section 211(a)(2) could apply to a Cuban national who registered a United States trademark before confiscation *and renewed it after that date*.

285. For trademark rights based on common law, the United States contends that the Cuban original owner could not have maintained its rights in the United States trademark because it would not have been able to import the trademarked goods from Cuba and, thus, would not have been able to continue using the trademark "in commerce." Yet, this argument assumes that the Cuban national who owns the trademark in the United States could have imported the trademarked goods *only from Cuba*. . . . [T]he Cuban holder of common law trademark rights in the United States could import the trademarked goods from a country other than Cuba. The United States did not deny this at the oral hearing. We are, therefore, not persuaded by this argument.

286. On this point, the United States replied as well that the Cuban original owner could be "unblocked" under the OFAC regulations, an argument that the United States did not make before the Panel or in its written submissions in this appeal. The relevant regulation is Section 515.505 of the *CACR*, which lists those persons that are "licensed as unblocked nationals" or who may apply to be "unblocked." According to the United States, as an "unblocked national," such a Cuban original owner would have the same status as a United States national. Yet, to fulfill the national treatment obligation, less favourable treatment must be offset, and thereby eliminated, in *every* individual situation that exists under a measure. Therefore, for this argument by the United States to succeed, it must hold true for *all* Cuban original owners of United States trademarks, and not merely for *some* of them.

287. Accordingly, we examine three possible situations to determine whether the discrimination is eliminated in every individual instance that might arise under Section 515.505. The first example involves a Cuban original owner residing in the United States. The second involves a Cuban original owner residing in a country other than the United States or Cuba. The third involves a Cuban original owner residing in Cuba.

288. According to the United States, a Cuban original owner residing in the United States is, in fact, "unblocked" by Section 515.505(a)(2) of the *CACR*. We agree with this reading of Section 515.505(a)(2). This eliminates the less favourable treatment of this Cuban original owner. The other examples, however, yield a different result.

289. A Cuban original owner residing in a country other than the United States or Cuba, for example, in the European Communities, could apply to OFAC to be "specifically licensed as [an] unblocked national[]." This is pursuant to Section 515.505(b) of the *CACR*, because the United States does not impose sanctions on the European Communities and, therefore, the European Communities would be considered part of the "authorized trade territory" described in . . . the *CACR*. This could eliminate less favourable treatment *in practice*. Yet, the very existence of the additional "hurdle" that is imposed by requiring application to OFAC is, in itself, inherently less favourable. Sections 211(a)(2) and (b) do not apply to United States original owners; no application to OFAC is required. But Cuban original owners residing in the "authorized trade territory" must apply to OFAC. Thus, such Cuban original owners must comply with an administrative requirement that does not apply to United States original owners. By virtue alone of having to apply to OFAC, even Cuban original owners that reside in the "authorized trade

territory" . . . are treated less favourably than United States original owners. So, in this second situation, the discrimination remains.

290. A Cuban original owner residing in Cuba is discriminated against as well. Cuba is not part of the "authorized trade territory" because it is subject to sanctions administered by OFAC under the *CACR*. . . . [A] Cuban national who resides in Cuba could not, under any circumstances, be "unblocked." . . . Nor has the United States suggested otherwise. Thus, in this third situation, the discrimination remains as well.

. . . .

[The Appellate Body considered an American argument concerning a different provision of the *CACR*, namely, 31 C.F.R. Section 515.201, which lists transactions that are prohibited except as specifically authorized by the Secretary of the Treasury. The U.S. argued Section 515.201 could apply to a non-Cuban foreign national, as well as to a U.S. national, and that its application would in each and every case offset any discriminatory treatment imposed by Sections 211(a)(2) and (b) on an original Cuban owner. The Appellate Body rejected this argument. For complete offsetting to occur, the U.S. would need to prove a key phrase in the *CACR*, "having an interest in," overlaps in coverage with the scope of the relevant criterion in Sections 211(a)(2) and (b), "used in connection with." The U.S. failed to prove the point.]

295. Finally, the United States referred to its longstanding doctrine of non-recognition of foreign confiscations. However, this policy could not possibly apply to trademarks that existed *in the United States* when a business or assets connected with a trademark composed of the same or substantially similar signs were confiscated *in Cuba*.

296. Thus, we conclude that Sections 211(a)(2) and (b) are inconsistent with the national treatment obligation of the United States under [Article 2.1 of the *TRIPS Agreement* in conjunction with Article 2(1) of] the *Paris Convention* (1967) and [Article 3.1 of] the *TRIPS Agreement* at the level of original owners. And, therefore, we reverse the Panel's findings. . . .

X. Article 4 of the *TRIPS Agreement*

297. Like the national treatment obligation, the obligation to provide most-favoured-nation treatment has long been one of the cornerstones of the world trading system. For more than fifty years, the obligation to provide most-favoured-nation treatment in Article I of the GATT 1994 has been both central and essential to assuring the success of a global rules-based system for trade in goods. Unlike the national treatment principle, there is no provision in the *Paris Convention* (1967) that establishes a most-favoured-nation obligation with respect to rights in trademarks or other industrial property. However, the framers of the *TRIPS Agreement* decided to extend the most-favoured-nation obligation to the protection of intellectual property rights covered by that *Agreement*. As a cornerstone of the world trading system, the most-favoured-nation obligation must be accorded the same significance with respect to intellectual property rights under the *TRIPS Agreement* that it has long been accorded with respect to trade in goods under the GATT. It is, in a word, fundamental.

. . . .

299. The European Communities claimed before the Panel that Sections 211(a)(2) and (b) are inconsistent with Article 4 of the *TRIPS Agreement*. [The Panel rejected the EC claims, holding that neither Section denies Cuban nationals any advantage, favour, privilege or immunity that it accords to other foreign nationals.]

. . . .

305. The allegations submitted by the European Communities on most-favoured-nation treatment of original owners are similar to those described in the previous section on national treatment. . . .

306. Like the situation posed by the European Communities earlier, the one set forth in the most-favoured-nation treatment involves two separate owners who acquired rights, either at common law or based on registration, in two separate United States trademarks, before the Cuban confiscation occurred. Each of these two United States trademarks is the same, or substantially similar to, signs or a combination of signs of which a trademark registered in Cuba is composed. That same or similar Cuban trademark was used in connection with a business or assets that were confiscated in Cuba. Neither of the two original owners of the two United States trademarks was the owner of that same or similar trademark that was registered in Cuba. Those two original owners each now seek to assert rights in the United States in their two respective United States trademarks. The situation of these two original owners of these two United States trademarks is identical in every relevant respect, but one. That one difference is this: one original owner is a national of Cuba, and the other original owner is a national of a country other than Cuba or the United States. We will refer, for the sake of convenience, to this other original owner as "a non-Cuban foreign national."

307. . . . [T]he European Communities argues that, on the face of the statute, the original owner who is a Cuban national is subject to Sections 211(a)(2) and (b), and the original owner who is a non-Cuban foreign national is not. This alone, as the European Communities sees it, is sufficient for us to find that Sections 211(a)(2) and (b) violate the most-favoured-nation obligation of the United States.

308. We agree with the European Communities that the situation it describes on appeal is within the scope of the statute *on its face*. . . . [T]he term "designated national" as defined in Section 515.305 of 31 CFR and Section 211(d)(1) includes non-Cuban foreign nationals only when they are successors-in-interest to Cuba or a Cuban national. Non-Cuban foreign nationals who are original owners are not covered by the definition of "designated national" and are thereby not subject to Sections 211(a)(2) and (b).

309. Therefore, here too, as with national treatment, the European Communities has established a *prima facie* case that Sections 211(a)(2) and (b) are discriminatory on their face, as between a Cuban national and a non-Cuban foreign national both of whom are original owners of United States trademarks composed of the same or substantially similar signs as a trademark used in connection with a business or assets that were confiscated in Cuba.

310. As it did in respect of the national treatment claim, the United States attempts to rebut the European Communities' most-favoured-nation claim with arguments intended to demonstrate that Sections 211(a)(2) and (b) do not apply to a Cuban national who is an original owner of a United States trademark. The United States arguments on this claim are the same as their arguments on national treatment. We have already addressed these arguments. And, as these United States arguments have not changed, our conclusions have not changed either. . . .

. . . .

319. We, therefore, reverse the Panel's findings . . . to the extent that they concern the treatment of original owners, and find, in this respect, that Section 211(a)(2) and Section 211(b) are inconsistent with Article 4 of the *TRIPS Agreement*.

V. SPECIAL 301 BLACK LISTING

"Special 301" is Section 182 of the *Trade Act of 1974*, as amended, 19 U.S.C. Section 2242.[10] It was added to the *1974 Act* by Section 1303 of the *Omnibus Trade and Competitiveness Act of 1988*. Special 301 requires the United States Trade Representative (USTR) annually to give Congress (specifically, the House Ways and Means and Senate Finance Committees) information on countries that lack or fail to enforce IPRs, The USTR must do so within 30 days after issuing its yearly study of foreign trade barriers under Section 301 of the *1974 Act*. The Section 301 analysis is called the *National Trade Estimate Report (NTE)*. (*See* 19 U.S.C. § 2241(b).) The 30 day rule means the USTR must put out the Special 301 Report on or before 30 April each year. The Special 301 Report must address not only conventional IPRs, *i.e.*, patents, trademarks, and copyrights, but also semiconductor mask works, textile designs, trade secrets, and plant breeder's rights. Critically, it must cover market access issues relevant to IPR holders.

What are the fundamental purposes of blacklisting under Special 301? One answer is to increase the leverage of the USTR in trade negotiations. Another answer is that public proclamation of countries with lax IPR regimes is a sanction in itself — shame. Presumably, most countries seek to avoid the reputation of being an IP brigand. A third answer is that advocates in a foreign country of strong IP protection and vigorous enforcement can use the actuality, or spectre, of being put on the Special 301 list as leverage in their domestic political environments. They can point to Special 301 to persuade recalcitrant constituencies in their country that IP reform is required. Otherwise, they can say, U.S. businesses will eschew trade and investment with their country.

In respect of all three responses, consider whether overt American pressure might be counterproductive. Is every country crestfallen when the U.S. government publicly proclaims displeasure with it? Might there be rally-around-the-flag effect in blacklisted countries against heavy-handedness by a hegemonic power? To be even-handed, however, query whether any other

---

10 *See* URUGUAY ROUND TRADE AGREEMENT, STATEMENT OF ADMINISTRATIVE ACTION, UNDERSTANDING ON RULES AND PROCEDURES GOVERNING THE SETTLEMENT OF DISPUTES, H.R. Doc. No. 316, 103d Cong., 2d Sess., at 1031-32 (27 Sept. 1994).

country has the willingness or ability to take a resolute stand on IP protection and enforcement? Is, then, Special 301 a particular instance of the broad international role in which the U.S. finds, or casts itself, in — the reluctant sheriff?

Under Special 301, the USTR must identify any country, whether a WTO Member or not, and whether a party to an FTA or not, which

- denies "adequate and effective" IPR protection, specifically, patent, trademark, copyright, or semiconductor mask work protection, or

- "fair and equitable market access" to United States persons relying on such protection.

(*See* 19 U.S.C. § 2242(a).) The USTR's annual Special 301 review process can lead to a trading partner being placed on one of three lists. In order of ascending severity, they are:

(1) "Watch List,"

(2) "Priority Watch List," and

(3) "Priority List."

The Special 301 statute does not mandate the first two lists. Rather, the USTR created them by administrative fiat, as alternatives to the severest black listing category.

As the USTR's Watch List is the least severe form of black listing, it simply names countries warranting special attention. They are of particular concern, because they engage in IP practices that pose market access barriers. The Priority Watch List is a moderately severe form of black listing. Countries on this list meet some, but not all, of the criteria for "priority foreign country" designation. The USTR carefully monitors these countries to determine whether further Special 301 action is needed, and takes active, bilateral steps to resolve deficiencies in their legal apparatus for IPR protection.

From the Priority Watch List, a country can move "up." China, India, and Thailand are among prominent countries the USTR placed (on 26 May 1989, following the USTR's first annual review) on the Priority Watch List. Failing (in the USTR's view) to make significant improvements to IP protection while on that list, they graduated (on 26 April 1991) to the Priority List. "Downward" mobility also is possible. Indonesia was on the Priority Watch List from 2001 until 6 November 2006. On that date, the USTR pronounced itself pleased with Indonesian reforms, and downgraded the country to the Watch List. What had Indonesia done to justify the lesser black listing? It took action against illegal manufacturing of pirated optical discs, namely, stronger licensing requirements on factories and additional raids on both production facilities and retail outlets. It also enacted a new customs law clarifying the authority of the government to seize infringing goods. And, it commenced public awareness campaigns.

Observe the change in Indonesia's status occurred through an out of cycle review (OCR). Accordingly, the USTR need not wed itself to annual reviews. What factors might influence the decision to conduct an OCR? To be sure, all Special 301 reviews, in contrast to Section 337 actions, can be initiated only by the USTR. But, this arrangement does not mean private parties are without a voice. To the contrary, an IPR holder can petition the USTR to initiate a Special 301 action if it feels a foreign country merits investigation. (*See* 19 U.S.C. § 2412(a).) Of course, whether it is successful may depend in part on its economic significance and its lobbying clout.

Three statutory criteria must be satisfied before the USTR affixes to a country the label "priority foreign country" and places it on the Priority List.

  i.   The country must have the "most onerous or egregious" acts, policies, or practices that deny either "adequate and effective" IPRs or "fair and equitable" market access to United States persons that rely on IP protection.

  ii. The country's IP acts, practices, or policies must have the "greatest adverse impact," whether actual or potential, on American products.

  iii. The country must not have entered into good faith negotiations, either multilateral or bilateral, to provide adequate and effective IP protection.

(*See* 19 U.S.C. § 2242(b)(1)(A)-(C).) At any point, the USTR can make or revoke this designation — but, it must give Congress a detailed explanation for its move. (*See* 19 U.S.C. § 2242(c).) In addition to these criteria, the USTR must consider the history of IP law and practice in an investigated country, whether it has been listed as a "priority foreign country" previously, and its behavior on enhanced IP protection and enforcement. Notably, the USTR may put a country on the Priority List even if it is in compliance with the *TRIPs Agreement*. That is because the *Agreement* does not cover all aspects of IP that might affect U.S. persons seeking to protect or enforce rights overseas. Is it, therefore, fair to characterize Special 301 as a unilateral tool to push for *TRIPs* Plus obligations?

Undoubtedly, Priority List designation is the most severe form of black listing. That is because of the link between Special 301 and Section 301. Within 30 days after identifying a priority foreign country, the USTR must initiate a Section 301 investigation of that country. (*See* 19 U.S.C. § 2412(b)(2)(A).) That is, within one month of being put on the Special 301 list, a country can expect to be the target of a Section 301 inquiry. Only in two circumstances is the link not automatic. First, if the USTR decides a Section 301 investigation would be detrimental to U.S. economic interests, and explains to Congress why, then it does not commence an inquiry. (*See* 19 U.S.C. § 2412(b)(2)(B)-(C).) Second, the USTR need not initiate a case if it believes retaliatory action against an allegedly violating country would be ineffective. (*See* 19 U.S.C. § 2412(c).)

Not surprisingly, a Section 301 investigation of a Priority List country focuses on alleged IPR violations in that country. The USTR must consult with the Commissioner of Patents and Trademarks and the Register of Copyrights. (*See* 19 U.S.C. § 2412(b)(2)(D).) The investigation must be completed within 6 (or, if there are complex issues or substantial progress is being made, 9) months. (*See* 19 U.S.C. § 2414(a)(3)(A)-(B).) These times are tighter than a Section 301 investigation not triggered by Special 301.

Section 301 investigations, including those triggered by Special 301, entail the threat of retaliatory action by the U.S. against another country's behavior.

If the acts, practices, or policies in question of the other country continue, then the USTR must take "appropriate and feasible" action to enforce America's trade rights and eliminate the violating behavior. (19 U.S.C. § 2411(a)(1), (b).) Retaliation is subject to the direction of the President. (*See* §§ 2411(a)-(b), 2415(a)(1).)

One of two prerequisites must be fulfilled before retaliation can occur. The first prerequisite is the USTR affirmatively determines that "the rights to which the United States is entitled under any trade agreement are being denied. . . ." (19 U.S.C. § 2414(a)(1)(A)(i).) Thus, for example, violation of a bilateral IP agreement, *NAFTA* Chapter 17, or the *TRIPs Agreement* would satisfy this prerequisite.

The other prerequisite is somewhat confusing. It has two alternative prongs: the USTR must find that an act, policy, or practice of a country under investigation either (1) "violates, . . . or otherwise denies benefits to the United States under, any trade agreement" or "is unjustifiable and burdens or restricts United States commerce" (19 U.S.C. §§ 2411(a)(1)(B), (i)-(ii), 2414 (a)(1)(A)(ii)), or (2) is "unreasonable or discriminatory and burdens or restricts United States commerce" (19 U.S.C. §§ 2411(b)(1), 2414(a)(1)(A)(ii)). The rubric for the first prong is "mandatory action," and for the second is "discretionary action." Before making a final determination (unless expeditious action is required), the USTR must give an opportunity for public comment and consult with advisory committees. It may request the views of the ITC as to the probable impact of retaliatory action on the U.S. economy. (*See* 19 U.S.C. § 2414(b).)

Retaliation may take the form of suspension of benefits of concessions otherwise due to the violating country under a trade agreement, or an increase in tariffs on, or erection of non-tariff barriers against, its imports. (*See* 19 U.S.C. §§ 2411(c)(1)(A)-(B), 2416(b).) With certain exceptions, retaliatory action must take effect within 30 days after the USTR's affirmative determination. (*See* 19 U.S.C. § 2415(a)(1)). The USTR may delay implementing retaliation for up to 180 days in conditions set forth in § 2415(a)(2).)

TABLE OF CASES

[References are to pages; principal cases appear in capital letters.]

UNITED STATES CASES

[References are to pages; principal cases appear in capital letters.]

[References are to pages; principal cases appear in capital letters.]

GATT and WTO CASES

[References are to pages; principal cases appear in capital letters.]

INDEX

[References are to pages.]

A

ADJUDICATION
Antidumping or countervailing duty case . . . 921
Free trade, foundations of . . . 141
Imperfections . . . 167
Procedural "common law"
    Burden of proof . . . 164
    Exhaustion of domestic remedies 161
    Fact-finding by panels . . . 166
    Judicial economy . . . 162
    Ripeness and mootness . . . 159
    Standing to bring complaint . . . 158
    Sufficiency of complaint . . . 162
Settlement systems (See DISPUTE SETTLEMENT)
WTO *DSU*
    Direct versus indirect effect . . . 154
    Multi-step procedure . . . 150
    "Nullification or impairment" and "adverse impact" . . . 149
    Resolving pre-Uruguay Round weaknesses . . . 148

ADJUSTMENTS
Dignity and truth . . . 974
Export price and constructed export price (See EXPORT PRICE AND CONSTRUCTED EXPORT PRICE, subhead: Adjustments)
Normal value, adjustments to
    Circumstances of sale . . . 978
    Differences in merchandise . . . 983
    Dignity and truth . . . 974
    Direct selling expenses . . . 975
    Tabular summary . . . 967
    Zero sum game . . . 965
Trade adjustment assistance (See TRADE ADJUSTMENT ASSISTANCE)
Zero sum game . . . 965

AD LAW
Dumping and protectionism
    Batting averages . . . 879
    GATT Article VI and definition of "dumping" . . . 871
    Protectionist abuse, risk of . . . 876
Early GATT cases . . . 873
Kennedy Round . . . 873
Neoclassical economic analysis
    Harmlessness . . . 881
    International price discrimination and its conditions . . . 879
    Predation . . . 884
    Repeal . . . 885

AD LAW—Cont.
Tokyo Round *Antidumping Codes* . . . 873
WTO *Antidumping Agreement*
    Generally . . . 874
    Remedies . . . 875
    Standard of review . . . 874

AFRICA
Preferential programs (See PREFERENTIAL PROGRAMS, subhead: Special help for Africa)

AGRICULTURE
Doha Round (See DOHA ROUND, subhead: Agricultural issues)
Domestic support and export subsidies (See DOMESTIC SUPPORT AND EXPERT SUBSIDIES, subhead: Agricultural export subsidies and red light export subsidies)
Farmers
    Doha Round discussions . . . 124
    Trade adjustment assistance . . . 287
Subsidies
    Generally . . . 63
    Export subsidies . . . 111

ANTIDUMPING LAW (See AD LAW)

ANTIDUMPING OR COUNTERVAILING DUTY CASE
Generally . . . 902
Appeals and WTO adjudication . . . 921
Filing petition, standing, and sufficiency . . . 906
Final determinations . . . 915
Preliminary determinations . . . 912
Remedial orders and limits . . . 916
Remedies against "unfair" trade . . . 869
Reviews . . . 918
Tokyo Round *Antidumping Codes* . . . 873
WTO *Antidumping Agreement*
    Generally . . . 874
    Remedies . . . 875
    Standard of review . . . 874

B

BALANCE OF PAYMENTS (BOP)
Exception for developing countries to GATT obligations (See SPECIAL AND DIFFERENTIAL TREATMENT, subhead: BOP exception for developing countries to GATT obligations)
Foreign exchange controls . . . 429
India
    Consultations with BOP Committee . . . 1284

I–1

C

[References are to pages.]

[References are to pages.]

[References are to pages.]

[References are to pages.]

[References are to pages.]

Z